PROFESSIONAL ASP.NET 4

PROFESSIONAL

ASP.NET 4

PROFESSIONAL

ASP.NET 4

IN C# AND VB

Bill Evjen
Scott Hanselman
Devin Rader

Wiley Publishing, Inc.

Professional ASP.NET 4: In C# and VB

Published by
Wiley Publishing, Inc.
10475 Crosspoint Boulevard
Indianapolis, IN 46256
www.wiley.com

Published simultaneously in Canada

ISBN: 978-0-470-50220-4

Manufactured in the United States of America

10 9 8 7 6 5 4 3 2 1

Library of Congress Control Number: 2009943645

To Tuija, always.

—Bill Evjen

To Momo and the boys. Toot!

—Scott Hanselman

ABOUT THE AUTHORS

BILL EVJEN is an active proponent of .NET technologies and community-based learning initiatives for .NET. He has been actively involved with .NET since the first bits were released in 2000. In the same year, Bill founded the St. Louis .NET User Group (www.stlnet.org), one of the world's first such groups. Bill is also the founder and former executive director of the International .NET Association (www.ineta.org), which represents more than 500,000 members worldwide.

Based in St. Louis, Missouri, Bill is an acclaimed author and speaker on ASP.NET and Services. He has authored or coauthored more than 20 books including *Professional C# 2010, Professional VB 2008, ASP.NET Professional Secrets, XML Web Services for ASP.NET, and Web Services Enhancements: Understanding the WSE for Enterprise Applications* (all published by Wiley). In addition to writing, Bill is a speaker at numerous conferences, including DevConnections, VSLive!, and TechEd. Along with these items, Bill works closely with Microsoft as a Microsoft Regional Director and an MVP.

Bill is the Global Head of Platform Architecture for Thomson Reuters, Lipper, the international news and financial services company (www.thomsonreuters.com). He graduated from Western Washington University in Bellingham, Washington, with a Russian language degree. When he isn't tinkering on the computer, he can usually be found at his summer house in Toivakka, Finland. You can reach Bill on Twitter at @billevjen.

SCOTT HANSELMAN works for Microsoft as a Principal Program Manager Lead in the Server and Tools Online Group, aiming to spread the good word about developing software, most often on the Microsoft stack. Before this, Scott was the Chief Architect at Corillian, an eFinance enabler, for 6+ years, and before Corillian, he was a Principal Consultant at Microsoft Gold Partner for 7 years. He was also involved in a few things like the MVP and RD programs and will speak about computers (and other passions) whenever someone will listen to him. He blogs at www.hanselman.com, podcasts at www.hanselminutes.com, and runs a team that contributes to www.asp.net, www.windowsclient.net, and www.silverlight.net. Follow Scott on Twitter @shanselman.

DEVIN RADER works at Infragistics where he focuses on delivering great experiences to developers using their controls. He's done work on all of the .NET platforms, but most recently has been focused on Web technologies ASP.NET and Silverlight. As a co-founder of the St. Louis .NET User group and a former INETA board member, and a member of the Central New Jersey .NET user group, he's an active supporter of the .NET developer community. He's also co-author or technical editor of numerous books on .NET, including Wrox's *Silverlight 3 Programmer's Reference.* Follow Devin on Twitter @devinrader.

ABOUT THE TECHNICAL EDITORS

CARLOS FIGUEROA has been developing and designing Web solutions for the last 8 years, participating in international projects for the pharmaceutical industry, banking, commercial air transportation, and the government. During these years, Carlos has been deeply involved as an early adopter of Microsoft Web development technologies, such as ASP.NET and Silverlight.

He has been awarded Microsoft Most Valuable Professional for the last 5 years and holds the MCAD certification. Carlos is a Senior Software Developer at Oshyn, Inc. (`www.oshyn.com`), a company specialized on delivering innovative business solutions for the web, mobile devices and emerging technology platforms. At Oshyn, Carlos is dedicated to help some of the most recognizable brands in the world to achieve technology success. You can reach Carlos at `cfigueroa1982@hotmail.com` or follow him on twitter `@carlosfigueroa`.

ANDREW MOORE is a graduate of Purdue University–Calumet in Hammond, Indiana, and has been developing software since 1998 for radar systems, air traffic management, discrete-event simulation, and business communications applications using C, C++, C#, and Java on the Windows, UNIX, and Linux platforms. Andrew is also a contributor to the Wrox Blox article series.

He is currently working as a Senior Software Engineer at Interactive Intelligence, Inc., in Indianapolis, Indiana, developing server-side applications for a multimedia unified business communications platform. Andrew lives in Indiana with his wife Barbara and children Sophia and Andrew.

CREDITS

ACQUISITIONS EDITOR
Paul Reese

SENIOR PROJECT EDITOR
Kevin Kent

TECHNICAL EDITORS
Carlos Figueroa
Andrew Moore

PRODUCTION EDITOR
Daniel Scribner

COPY EDITOR
Paula Lowell

EDITORIAL DIRECTOR
Robyn B. Siesky

EDITORIAL MANAGER
Mary Beth Wakefield

ASSOCIATE DIRECTOR OF MARKETING
David Mayhew

PRODUCTION MANAGER
Tim Tate

VICE PRESIDENT AND EXECUTIVE GROUP PUBLISHER
Richard Swadley

VICE PRESIDENT AND EXECUTIVE PUBLISHER
Barry Pruett

ASSOCIATE PUBLISHER
Jim Minatel

PROJECT COORDINATOR, COVER
Lynsey Stanford

PROOFREADERS
Word One

INDEXER
J & J Indexing

COVER DESIGNER
Michael E. Trent

COVER IMAGE
© Jon Feingersh Photography Inc / Blend Images / Jupiter Images

ACKNOWLEDGMENTS

THANKS TO KEVIN KENT, PAUL REESE, AND JIM MINATEL for the opportunity to work on such a great book. In addition to my co-authors, I would like to thank my family for putting up with all the writing. Thank you Tuija, Sofia, Henri, and Kalle!

—Bill Evjen

CONTENTS

INTRODUCTION

SIMPLY PUT, ASP.NET 4 IS AN AMAZING TECHNOLOGY to use to build your Web solutions! When ASP.NET 1.0 was introduced in 2000, many considered it a revolutionary leap forward in the area of Web application development. ASP.NET 2.0 was just as exciting and revolutionary, and ASP.NET 4 is continuing a forward march in providing the best framework today in building applications for the Web. ASP.NET 4 continues to build on the foundation laid by the release of ASP.NET 1.0/2.0/3.5 by focusing on the area of developer productivity.

This book covers the whole of ASP.NET. It not only introduces new topics, but it also shows you examples of these new technologies in action. So sit back, pull up that keyboard, and enjoy!

A LITTLE BIT OF HISTORY

Before organizations were even thinking about developing applications for the Internet, much of the application development focused on thick desktop applications. These thick-client applications were used for everything from home computing and gaming to office productivity and more. No end was in sight for the popularity of this application model.

During that time, Microsoft developers developed thick-client applications using mainly Visual Basic (VB).

Visual Basic was not only a programming language — it was tied to an IDE that allowed for easy thick-client application development. In the Visual Basic model, developers could drop controls onto a form, set properties for these controls, and provide code behind them to manipulate the events of the control. For example, when an end user clicked a button on one of the Visual Basic forms, the code behind the form handled the event.

Then, in the mid-1990s, the Internet arrived on the scene. Microsoft was unable to move the Visual Basic model to the development of Internet-based applications. The Internet definitely had a lot of power, and right away, the problems facing the thick-client application model were revealed. Internet-based applications created a single instance of the application that everyone could access. Having one instance of an application meant that when the application was upgraded or patched, the changes made to this single instance were immediately available to each and every user visiting the application through a browser.

To participate in the Web application world, Microsoft developed Active Server Pages (ASP). ASP was a quick and easy way to develop Web pages. ASP pages consisted of a single page that contained a mix of markup and languages. The power of ASP was that you could include VBScript or JScript code instructions in the page executed on the Web server before the page was sent to the end user's Web browser. This was an easy way to create dynamic Web pages customized based on instructions dictated by the developer.

ASP used script between brackets and percentage signs `<% %>` to control server-side behaviors. A developer could then build an ASP page by starting with a set of static HTML. Any dynamic element needed by the page was defined using a scripting language (such as VBScript or JScript). When a user requested the page from the server by using a browser, the `asp.dll` (an ISAPI application that provided a bridge between the scripting language and the Web server) would take hold of the page and define all the dynamic aspects of the page on-the-fly based on the programming logic specified in the script. After all the dynamic aspects of the page were defined, the result was an HTML page output to the browser of the requesting client.

As the Web application model developed, more and more languages mixed in with the static HTML to help manipulate the behavior and look of the output page. Over time, such a large number of languages, scripts, and plain text could be placed in a typical ASP page that developers began to refer to pages that used these features as *spaghetti code*. For example, having a page that used HTML, VBScript, JavaScript, Cascading Style Sheets, T-SQL, and more was quite possible. In certain instances, these pages became a manageability nightmare.

ASP evolved and new versions were released. ASP 2.0 and 3.0 were popular because the technology made creating Web pages relatively straightforward and easy. Their popularity was enhanced because they appeared in the late 1990s, just as the dotcom era was born. During this time, a mountain of new Web pages and portals were developed, and ASP was one of the leading technologies individuals and companies used to build them. Even today, you can still find a lot of `.asp` pages on the Internet — including some of Microsoft's own Web pages.

However, even at the time of the final release of Active Server Pages in late 1998, Microsoft employees Marc Anders and Scott Guthrie had other ideas. Their ideas generated what they called XSP (an abbreviation with no meaning) — a new way of creating Web applications in an object-oriented manner instead of in the procedural manner of ASP 3.0. They showed their idea to many different groups within Microsoft, and they were well received. In the summer of 2000, the beta of what was then called ASP+ was released at Microsoft's Professional Developers Conference. The attendees eagerly started working with it. When the technology became available (with the final release of the .NET Framework 1.0), it was renamed ASP.NET — receiving the .NET moniker that most of Microsoft's new products were receiving at that time.

Before the introduction of .NET, the model that classic ASP provided and what developed in Visual Basic were so different that few VB developers also developed Web applications, and few Web application developers also developed the thick-client applications of the VB world. There was a great divide. ASP.NET bridged this gap. ASP.NET brought a Visual Basic–style eventing model to Web application development, providing much-needed state management techniques over stateless HTTP. Its model is much like the earlier Visual Basic model in that a developer can drag and drop a control onto a design surface or form, manipulate the control's properties, and even work with the code behind these controls to act on certain events that occur during their lifecycles. What ASP.NET created is really the best of both models, as you will see throughout this book.

I know you will enjoy working with this latest release of ASP.NET 4. Nothing is better than getting your hands on a new technology and seeing what is possible. The following section discusses the goals of ASP.NET so that you can find out what to expect from this new offering!

THE GOALS OF ASP.NET

ASP.NET 4 is another major release of the product and builds on the previous releases with additional classes and capabilities. This release of the Framework and Visual Studio was code-named *Hawaii* internally at Microsoft. ASP.NET 4 continues on a path to make ASP.NET developers the most productive developers in the Web space. This book also focuses on the new additions to ASP.NET 4 and the .NET Framework 4 with the release of ASP.NET 4.

Ever since the release of ASP.NET 2.0, the Microsoft team has focused its goals on developer productivity, administration, and management, as well as performance and scalability.

Developer Productivity

Much of the focus of ASP.NET 4 is on productivity. Huge productivity gains were made with the release of ASP.NET 1.*x* and 2.0; could it be possible to expand further on those gains?

One goal the development team had for ASP.NET was to eliminate much of the tedious coding that ASP.NET originally required and to make common ASP.NET tasks easier. The developer productivity capabilities are presented throughout this book. Before venturing into these capabilities, this introduction looks at the older ASP.NET 1.0 technology to make a comparison to ASP.NET 4. Listing I-1 provides an example of using ASP.NET 1.0 to build a table in a Web page that includes the capability to perform simple paging of the data provided.

LISTING I-1: Showing data in a DataGrid server control with paging enabled (VB only)

```
<%@ Page Language="VB" AutoEventWireup="True" %>
<%@ Import Namespace="System.Data" %>
<%@ Import Namespace="System.Data.SqlClient" %>

<script runat="server">

    Private Sub Page_Load(ByVal sender As System.Object, _
      ByVal e As System.EventArgs)
        If Not Page.IsPostBack Then
            BindData()
        End If
    End Sub

    Private Sub BindData()
        Dim conn As SqlConnection = New _
           SqlConnection("server='localhost';
           trusted_connection=true; Database='Northwind'")
        Dim cmd As SqlCommand = _
           New SqlCommand("Select * From Customers", conn)
        conn.Open()

        Dim da As SqlDataAdapter = New SqlDataAdapter(cmd)
        Dim ds As New DataSet

        da.Fill(ds, "Customers")

        DataGrid1.DataSource = ds
        DataGrid1.DataBind()
    End Sub

    Private Sub DataGrid1_PageIndexChanged(ByVal source As Object, _
      ByVal e As _
       System.Web.UI.WebControls.DataGridPageChangedEventArgs)
        DataGrid1.CurrentPageIndex = e.NewPageIndex
        BindData()
    End Sub

</script>
<html>
<head>
</head>
<body>
    <form runat="server">
        <asp:DataGrid id="DataGrid1" runat="server"
         AllowPaging="True"
         OnPageIndexChanged="DataGrid1_PageIndexChanged">
        </asp:DataGrid>
    </form>
</body>
</html>
```

Although quite a bit of code is used here, this is a dramatic improvement over the amount of code required to accomplish this task using classic Active Server Pages 3.0. We will not go into the details of this older code; it just demonstrates that to add any additional common functionality (such as paging) for the data shown in a table, the developer had to create custom code.

This is one area where the developer productivity gains are most evident. ASP.NET 4 provides a control called the GridView server control. This control is much like the DataGrid server control, but the GridView server control (besides offering many additional features) contains the built-in capability to apply paging, sorting, and editing of data with relatively little work on your part. Listing I-2 shows an example of the GridView server control. This example builds a table of data from the Customers table in the Northwind database that includes paging.

LISTING I-2: Viewing a paged dataset with the GridView server control

```
<%@ Page Language="VB" %>

<script runat="server">

</script>

<html xmlns=http://www.w3.org/1999/xhtml>
<head runat="server">
    <title>GridView Demo</title>
</head>
<body>
    <form runat="server">
        <asp:GridView ID="GridView1" Runat="server"
         AllowPaging="True"
         DataSourceId="Sqldatasource1" />
        <asp:SqlDataSource ID="SqlDataSource1" Runat="server"
         SelectCommand="Select * From Customers"
         ProviderName="System.Data.OleDb"
         ConnectionString="Provider=SQLOLEDB;Server=localhost;uid=sa;
         pwd=password;database=Northwind" />
    </form>
</body>
</html>
```

That's it! You can apply paging by using a couple of server controls. You turn on this capability using a server control attribute, the `AllowPaging` attribute of the GridView control:

```
<asp:GridView ID="GridView1" Runat="server" AllowPaging="True" DataSourceId="SqlDataSource1" />
```

The other interesting event occurs in the code section of the document:

```
<script runat="server"></script>
```

These two lines of code are not actually needed to run the file. They are included here to make a point — *you don't need to write any server-side code to make this all work!* You need to include only some server controls: one control to get the data and one control to display the data. Then the controls are wired together.

Performance and Scalability

One of the goals for ASP.NET that was set by the Microsoft team was to provide the world's fastest Web application server. This book also addresses a number of performance tactics available in ASP.NET 4.

One of the most exciting performance capabilities is the caching capability aimed at exploiting Microsoft's SQL Server. ASP.NET 4 includes a feature called *SQL cache invalidation*. Before ASP.NET 2.0, caching the results that came from SQL Server and updating the cache based on a time interval was possible — for example, every 15 seconds or so. This meant that the end user might see stale data if the result set changed sometime during that 15-second period.

In some cases, this time interval result set is unacceptable. In an ideal situation, the result set stored in the cache is destroyed if any underlying change occurs in the source from which the result set is retrieved — in this case, SQL Server. With ASP.NET 4, you can make this happen with the use of SQL cache invalidation. This means that when the result set from SQL Server changes, the output cache is triggered to change, and the end user always sees the latest result set. The data presented is never stale.

ASP.NET 4 provides 64-bit support. This means that you can run your ASP.NET applications on 64-bit Intel or AMD processors.

Because ASP.NET 4 is fully backward compatible with ASP.NET 1.0, 1.1, 2.0, and 3.5, you can now take any former ASP.NET application, recompile the application on the .NET Framework 4, and run it on a 64-bit processor.

ADDITIONAL FEATURES OF ASP.NET 4

You just learned some of the main goals of the ASP.NET team that built ASP.NET. To achieve these goals, ASP.NET provides a mountain of features to make your development process easier. A few of these features are described in the following sections.

ASP.NET Developer Infrastructures

An exciting aspect of ASP.NET is that infrastructures are in place for you to use in your applications. The ASP.NET team selected some of the most common programming operations performed with Web applications to be built directly into ASP.NET. This saves you considerable time and coding.

Membership and Role Management

Prior to ASP.NET 2.0, if you were developing a portal that required users to log in to the application to gain privileged access, invariably you had to create it yourself. Creating applications with areas that are accessible only to select individuals can be tricky.

You will find that with ASP.NET 4 this capability is built in. You can validate users as shown in Listing I-3.

LISTING I-3: Validating a user in code

VB

```
If (Membership.ValidateUser (Username.Text, Password.Text)) Then
    ' Allow access code here
End If
```

C#

```
if (Membership.ValidateUser (Username.Text, Password.Text)) {
    // Allow access code here
}
```

A series of APIs, controls, and providers in ASP.NET 4 enable you to control an application's user membership and role management. Using these APIs, you can easily manage users and their complex roles — creating, deleting, and editing them. You get all this capability by using the APIs or a built-in Web tool called the Web Site Administration Tool.

As far as storing users and their roles, ASP.NET 4 uses an `.mdf` file (the file type for the SQL Server Express Edition) for storing all users and roles. You are in no way limited to just this data store, however. You can expand everything offered to you by ASP.NET and build your own providers using whatever you fancy as a data store. For example, if you want to build your user store in LDAP or within an Oracle database, you can do so quite easily.

Personalization

One advanced feature that portals love to offer their membership base is the capability to personalize their offerings so that end users can make the site look and function however they want. The capability to personalize an application and store the personalization settings is completely built into the ASP.NET Framework.

Because personalization usually revolves around a user and possibly a role that this user participates in, the personalization architecture can be closely tied to the membership and role infrastructures. You have a couple of options for storing the created personalization settings. The capability to store these settings in either Microsoft Access or in SQL Server is built into ASP.NET 4. As with the capabilities of the membership and role APIs, you can use the flexible provider model, and then either change how the built-in provider uses the available data store or build your own custom data provider to work with a completely new data store. The personalization API also supports a union of data stores, meaning that you can use more than one data store if you want.

Because creating a site for customization using these APIs is so easy, this feature is quite a value-add for any application you build.

The ASP.NET Portal Framework

During the days of ASP.NET 1.0, developers could go to the ASP.NET team's site (found at `asp.net`) and download some Web application demos such as IBuySpy. These demos are known as Developer Solution Kits and are used as the basis for many of the Web sites on the Internet today. Some were even extended into open source frameworks such as DotNetNuke.

The nice thing about some of these frameworks was that you could use the code they provided as a basis to build either a Web store or a portal. You simply took the base code as a starting point and extended it. For example, you could change the look and feel of the presentation part of the code or introduce advanced functionality into its modular architecture. Developer Solution Kits are quite popular because they make performing these types of operations so easy.

Because of the popularity of frameworks, ASP.NET 4 offers built-in capability for using Web Parts to easily build portals. The possibilities for what you can build using the Portal Framework is astounding. The power of building and using Web Parts is that it easily enables end users to completely customize the portal for their own preferences.

Site Navigation

The ASP.NET team members realize that end users want to navigate through applications with ease. The mechanics to make this work in a logical manner are sometimes hard to code. The team solved the problem in ASP.NET with a series of navigation-based server controls.

For example, you can build a site map for your application in an XML file that specific controls can inherently work from. Listing I-4 shows a sample site map file.

LISTING I-4: An example of a site map file

```
<?xml version="1.0" encoding="utf-8" ?>

<siteMap xmlns="http://schemas.microsoft.com/AspNet/SiteMap-File-1.0">
    <siteMapNode title="Home" description="Home Page"
     url="default.aspx">
       <siteMapNode title="News" description="The Latest News"
        url="News.aspx">
          <siteMapNode title="U.S." description="U.S. News"
           url="News.aspx?cat=us" />
```

```
            <siteMapNode title="World" description="World News"
             url="News.aspx?cat=world" />
            <siteMapNode title="Technology"
             description="Technology News"
             url="News.aspx?cat=tech" />
            <siteMapNode title="Sports" description="Sports News"
             url="News.aspx?cat=sport" />
         </siteMapNode>
         <siteMapNode title="Finance"
          description="The Latest Financial Information"
           url="Finance.aspx">
            <siteMapNode title="Quotes"
             description="Get the Latest Quotes"
             url="Quotes.aspx" />
            <siteMapNode title="Markets"
             description="The Latest Market Information"
             url="Markets.aspx">
               <siteMapNode title="U.S. Market Report"
                description="Looking at the U.S. Market"
                url="MarketsUS.aspx" />
               <siteMapNode title="NYSE"
                description="The New York Stock Exchange"
                url="NYSE.aspx" />
            </siteMapNode>
            <siteMapNode title="Funds" description="Mutual Funds"
             url="Funds.aspx" />
         </siteMapNode>
         <siteMapNode title="Weather" description="The Latest Weather"
          url="Weather.aspx" />
      </siteMapNode>
   </siteMap>
```

After you have a site map in place, you can use this file as the data source behind a couple of site navigation server controls, such as the TreeView and the SiteMapPath server controls. The TreeView server control enables you to place an expandable site navigation system in your application. Figure I-1 shows you an example of one of the many looks you can give the TreeView server control.

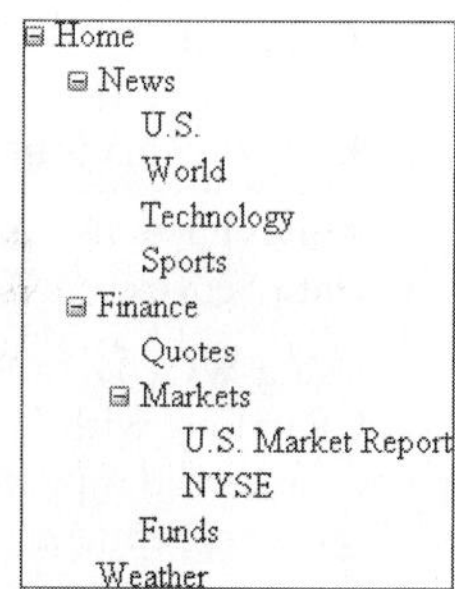

FIGURE I-1

SiteMapPath is a control that provides the capability to place what some call *breadcrumb navigation* in your application so that the end user can see the path that he has taken in the application and can easily navigate to higher levels in the tree. Figure I-2 shows you an example of the SiteMapPath server control at work.

Home > Finance > Markets > U.S. Market Report

FIGURE I-2

These site navigation capabilities provide a great way to get programmatic access to the site layout and even to take into account things like end-user roles to determine which parts of the site to show.

The ADO.NET Entity Framework

Most developers need to work with an underlying database of some kind. Whether that is a Microsoft SQL Server database or an Oracle database, your applications are usually pulling content of some kind to work with. The difficulty in working with an underlying database is that a database and your object-oriented code handle objects in such dramatically different ways.

In the database world, your data structures are represented in tables, and collections within items (such as a `Customer` object with associated `Orders`) are simply represented as two tables with a `Join` statement required between them. In contrast, in your object-oriented code, these objects are represented so that the

`Orders` item is simply a property within the `Customers` object. Bringing these two worlds together and mapping these differences have always been a bit laborious.

ASP.NET 4 includes the ability to work with the ADO.NET Entity Framework, which you will find is somewhat similar to working with LINQ to SQL. The purpose of the ADO.NET Entity Framework is to allow you to create an Entity Data Model (EDM) that will make mapping the object-oriented objects that you create along with how these objects are represented in the database easy.

One advantage of the ADO.NET Entity Framework is that it works with many different types of databases, so you will not be limited to working with a single database as you are with LINQ to SQL. Another advantage is that the ADO.NET Entity Framework is the basis of some other exciting technologies that ASP.NET 4 includes, such as ADO.NET Data Services.

ASP.NET Dynamic Data

Another great ASP.NET feature is called ASP.NET Dynamic Data. This capability enables you to easily create a reporting and data entry application from a database in just a couple of minutes.

Working with ASP.NET Dynamic Data is as simple as pointing to an Entity Data Model that you created in your application and allowing the dynamic data engine to create the Web pages for you that provide you with full create, edit, update, and delete capabilities over the database.

ASP.NET Dynamic Data requires that you have an Entity Data Model in place for it to work. The nice thing is that you are not limited to working with just the ADO.NET Entity Framework — you can also work with any LINQ to SQL models that you have created.

One great feature of the architecture of ASP.NET Dynamic Data is that it is based on working with templates in the dynamic generation of the pages for the site. As a developer working with this system, you are able to use the system "as-is" or even take pieces of it and incorporate its abilities in any of your pre-existing ASP.NET applications.

WCF Data Services

ASP.NET 4 also includes another great feature called WCF Data Services. Formally known as ADO.NET Data Services, WCF Data Services enables you to create a RESTful service interface against your database.

Using WCF Data Services, you can provide the capability to use the URL of the request as a command-driven URI along with HTTP verbs to direct the server on how you want to deal with the underlying data. You can create, read, update, or delete underlying database data using this technology, but as the implementer of the interface, you are also just as able to limit and restrict end user capability and access.

The ASP.NET Compilation System

Compilation in ASP.NET 1.0 was always a tricky scenario. With ASP.NET 1.0, you could build an application's code-behind files using ASP.NET and Visual Studio, deploy it, and then watch as the `.aspx` files were compiled page by page as each page was requested. If you made any changes to the code-behind file in ASP.NET 1.0, it was not reflected in your application until the entire application was rebuilt. That meant that the same page-by-page request had to be done again before the entire application was recompiled.

Everything about how ASP.NET 1.0 worked with classes and compilation is different from how it is in ASP.NET today. The mechanics of the compilation system actually begin with how a page is structured in ASP.NET 4. In ASP.NET 1.0, you constructed your pages either by using the code-behind model or by placing all the server code inline between `<script>` tags on your `.aspx` page. Most pages were constructed using the code-behind model because this was the default when using Visual Studio .NET 2002 or 2003. Creating your page using the inline style in these IDEs was quite difficult. If you did, you were deprived of the use of IntelliSense, which can be quite the lifesaver when working with the tremendously large collection of classes that the .NET Framework offers.

ASP.NET 4 offers a different code-behind model from the 1.0/1.1 days because the .NET Framework 4 has the capability to work with *partial classes* (also called partial types). Upon compilation, the separate files are combined into a single offering. This gives you much cleaner code-behind pages. The code that was part of the `Web Form Designer Generated` section of your classes is separated from the code-behind classes that you create yourself. Contrast this with the ASP.NET 1.0 `.aspx` file's need to derive from its own code-behind file to represent a single logical page.

ASP.NET 4 applications can include a App_Code directory where you place your class's source. Any class placed here is dynamically compiled and reflected in the application. You do not use a separate build process when you make changes as you did with ASP.NET 1.0. This is a *just save and hit* deployment model like the one in classic ASP 3.0. Visual Studio 2010 also automatically provides IntelliSense for any objects that are placed in the App_Code directory, whether you are working with the code-behind model or are coding inline.

ASP.NET 4 also provides you with tools that enable you to pre-compile your ASP.NET applications — both `.aspx` pages and code behind — so that no page within your application has latency when it is retrieved for the first time. Doing this is also a great way to discover any errors in the pages without invoking every page. Precompiling your ASP.NET 2.0 (as well as 3.5 or 4) applications is as simple as using `aspnet_compiler.exe` and employing some of the available flags. As you pre-compile your entire application, you also receive error notifications if any errors are found anywhere within it. Pre-compilation also enables you to deliver only the created assembly to the deployment server, thereby protecting your code from snooping, unwanted changes, and tampering after deployment. You will see examples of these scenarios later in this book.

Health Monitoring for Your ASP.NET Applications

The built-in health monitoring capabilities are rather significant features designed to make managing a deployed ASP.NET application easier. Health monitoring provides what the term implies — the capability to monitor the health and performance of your deployed ASP.NET applications.

Using the health monitoring system enables you to perform event logging for health monitoring events, which are called *Web events*, such as failed logins, application starts and stops, or any unhandled exceptions. The event logging can occur in more than one place; therefore, you can log to the event log or even back to a database. In addition to performing this disk-based logging, you can also use the system to e-mail health monitoring information.

Besides working with specific events in your application, you can also use the health monitoring system to take health snapshots of a running application. As you can with most systems that are built into ASP.NET 4, you can extend the health monitoring system and create your own events for recording application information.

Health monitoring is already enabled by default in the system `.config` files. The default setup for health monitoring logs all errors and failure audits to the event log. For instance, throwing an error in your application results in an error notification in the Application log.

You can change the default event logging behaviors simply by making some minor changes to your application's `web.config` file. For instance, suppose that you want to store this error event information in a SQL Express file contained within the application. You can make this change by adding a `<healthMonitoring>` node to your `web.config` file as presented in Listing I-5.

LISTING I-5: Defining health monitoring in the web.config file

```
<healthMonitoring enabled="true">
  <providers>
     <clear />
     <add name="SqlWebEventProvider"
      connectionStringName="LocalSqlServer"
      maxEventDetailsLength="1073741823" buffer="false"
      bufferMode="Notification"
      type="System.Web.Management.SqlWebEventProvider,
         System.Web,Version=4.0.0.0,Culture=neutral,
         PublicKeyToken=b03f5f7f11d50a3a"/>
  </providers>
  <rules>
     <clear />
     <add name="All Errors Default" eventName="All Errors"
      provider="SqlWebEventProvider"
      profile="Default" minInstances="1" maxLimit="Infinite"
      minInterval="00:01:00" custom="" />
     <add name="Failure Audits Default" eventName="Failure Audits"
      provider="SqlWebEventProvider" profile="Default"
      minInstances="1"
      maxLimit="Infinite" minInterval="00:01:00" custom="" />
  </rules>
</healthMonitoring>
```

After this change, events are logged in the `ASPNETDB.MDF` file that is automatically created on your behalf if it does not already exist in your project.

Opening this SQL Express file, you will find an `aspnet_WebEvent_Events` table where all this information is stored.

You will learn much more about the health monitoring capabilities provided with ASP.NET 4 in Chapter 34.

Reading and Writing Configuration Settings

Using the `WebConfigurationManager` class, you have the capability to read and write to the server or application configuration files. This means that you can write and read settings in the `machine.config` or the `web.config` files that your application uses.

The capability to read and write to configuration files is not limited to working with the local machine in which your application resides. You can also perform these operations on remote servers and applications.

Of course, a GUI-based way exists in which you can perform these read or change operations on the configuration files at your disposal. The exciting thing, however, is that the built-in GUI tools that provide this functionality (such as the ASP.NET MMC snap-in when using Windows XP or the latest IIS interface if you are using Windows 7) use the `WebConfigurationManager` class, which is also available for building custom administration tools.

Listing I-6 shows an example of reading a connection string from an application's `web.config` file.

LISTING I-6: Reading a connection string from the application's web.config file

```
Protected Sub Page_Load(ByVal sender As Object,
 ByVal e As System.EventArgs)
   Try
      Dim connectionString As String =
         ConfigurationManager.ConnectionStrings("Northwind").
            ConnectionString.ToString()
```

```
        Label1.Text = connectionString
    Catch ex As Exception
        Label1.Text = "No connection string found."
    End Try
End Sub
```

C#

```
protected void Page_Load(object sender, EventArgs e)
{
    try
    {
        string connectionString =
            ConfigurationManager.ConnectionStrings["Northwind"].
                ConnectionString.ToString();
        Label1.Text = connectionString;
    }
    catch (Exception)
    {
        Label1.Text = "No connection string found.";
    }
}
```

This little bit of code writes the Northwind connection string found in the `web.config` file to the screen using a Label control. As you can see, grabbing items from the configuration file is rather simple.

Localization

ASP.NET is making localizing applications easier than ever. In addition to using Visual Studio, you can create resource files (`.resx`) that allow you to dynamically change the pages you create based on the culture settings of the requestor.

ASP.NET 4 provides the capability to provide resources application-wide or just to particular pages in your application through the use of two application folders — App_GlobalResources and App_LocalResources.

The items defined in any `.resx` files you create are then accessible directly in the ASP.NET server controls or programmatically using expressions such as

```
<%= Resources.Resource.Question %>
```

This system is straightforward and simple to implement. Chapter 32 covers this topic in greater detail.

Expanding on the Page Framework

ASP.NET pages can be built based on visual inheritance. This was possible in the Windows Forms world, but it is also possible with ASP.NET. You also gain the capability to easily apply a consistent look and feel to the pages of your application by using themes. Many of the difficulties in working with ADO.NET are made easier through a series of data source controls that take care of accessing and retrieving data from a large collection of data stores.

Master Pages

With the capability of *master pages* in ASP.NET, you can use visual inheritance within your ASP.NET applications. Because many ASP.NET applications have a similar structure throughout their pages, building a page template once and using that same template throughout the application is logical.

In ASP.NET, you do this by creating a `.master` page, as shown in Figure I-3.

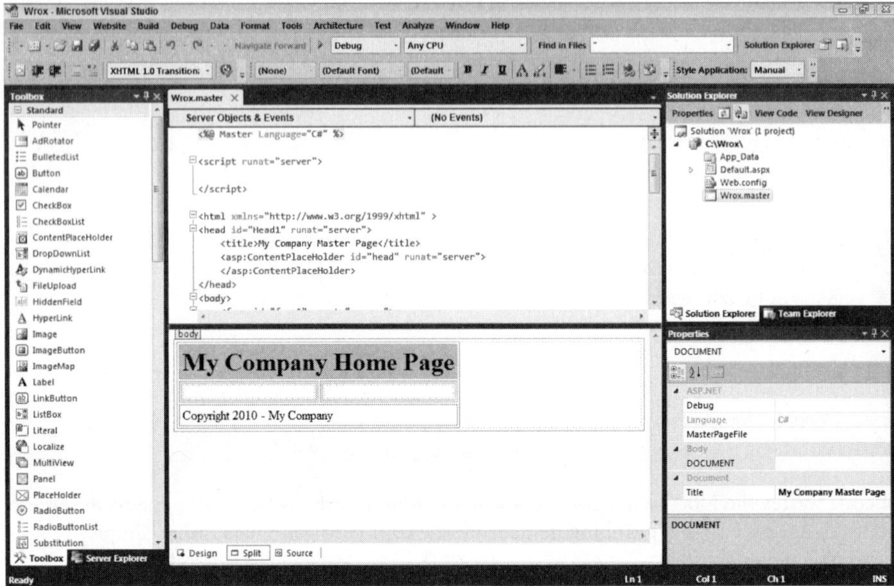

FIGURE I-3

An example master page might include a header, footer, and any other elements that all the pages can share. Besides these core elements, which you might want on every page that inherits and uses this template, you can place `<asp:ContentPlaceHolder>` server controls within the master page itself for the subpages (or content pages) to use to change specific regions of the master page template. The editing of the subpage is shown in Figure I-4.

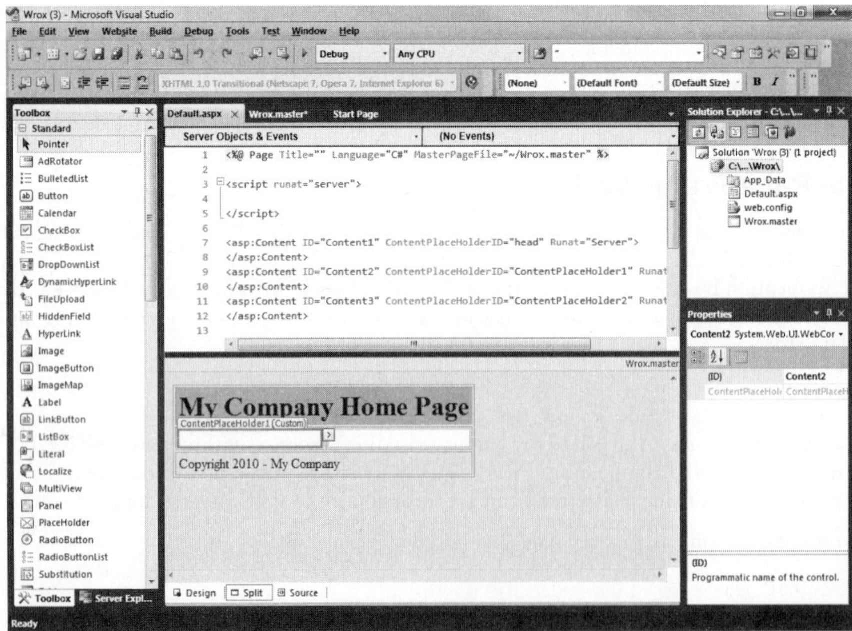

FIGURE I-4

When an end user invokes one of the subpages, she is actually looking at a single page compiled from both the subpage and the master page that the particular subpage inherited from. This also means that the server and client code from both pages are enabled on the new single page.

The nice thing about master pages is that you have a single place to make any changes that affect the entire site. This eliminates making changes to each and every page within an application.

Themes

The inclusion of themes in ASP.NET has made providing a consistent look and feel across your entire site quite simple. Themes are simple text files where you define the appearance of server controls that can be applied across the site, to a single page, or to a specific server control. You can also easily incorporate graphics and Cascading Style Sheets (CSS), in addition to server control definitions.

Themes are stored in the App_Theme directory within the application root for use within that particular application. One cool capability of themes is that you can dynamically apply them based on settings that use the personalization service provided by ASP.NET. Each unique user of your portal or application can have her own personalized look and feel that she has chosen from your offerings.

Objects for Accessing Data

One of the more code-intensive tasks in ASP.NET 1.0 was the retrieval of data. In many cases, this meant working with a number of objects. If you have been working with ASP.NET for a while, then you know that it was an involved process to display data from a Microsoft SQL Server table within a DataGrid server control. For instance, you first had to create a number of new objects. They included a `SqlConnection` object followed by a `SqlCommand` object. When those objects were in place, you then created a `SqlDataReader` to populate your DataGrid by binding the result to the DataGrid. In the end, a table appeared containing the contents of the data you were retrieving (such as the Customers table from the Northwind database).

Today, ASP.NET eliminates this intensive procedure with the introduction of a set of objects that work specifically with data access and retrieval. These data controls are so easy to use that you access and retrieve data to populate your ASP.NET server controls without writing any code. You saw an example of this in Listing I-2, where an `<asp:SqlDataSource>` server control retrieved rows of data from the Customers table in the Northwind database from SQL Server. This SqlDataSource server control was then bound to the GridView server control via the use of simple attributes within the GridView control itself. It really could not be any easier!

The great news about this functionality is that it is not limited to just Microsoft's SQL Server. In fact, several data source server controls are at your disposal. You also have the capability to create your own. In addition to the SqlDataSource server control, ASP.NET 4 includes the AccessDataSource, XmlDataSource, ObjectDataSource, SiteMapDataSource, and LinqDataSource server controls. You will use all these data controls later in this book.

WHAT YOU NEED FOR ASP.NET 4

You might find that installing Visual Studio 2010 is best to work through the examples in this book; you can, however, just use Microsoft's Notepad and the command-line compilers that come with the .NET Framework 4. To work through *every* example in this book, you need the following:

- Windows Server 2003, Windows Server 2008, Windows 2000, Windows XP, Windows Vista, or Windows 7
- Visual Studio 2010 (this will install the .NET Framework 4)
- SQL Server 2000, 2005, or 2008
- Microsoft Access or SQL Server Express Edition

The nice thing is that you are not required to have Microsoft Internet Information Services (IIS) to work with ASP.NET 4 because ASP.NET includes a built-in Web server based on the previously released Microsoft Cassini technology. Moreover, if you do not have a full-blown version of SQL Server, don't be alarmed. Many examples that use this database can be altered to work with Microsoft's SQL Server Express Edition, which you will find free on the Internet.

WHO SHOULD READ THIS BOOK?

This book was written to introduce you to the features and capabilities that ASP.NET 4 offers, as well as to give you an explanation of the foundation that ASP.NET provides. We assume you have a general understanding of Web technologies, such as previous versions of ASP.NET, Active Server Pages 2.0/3.0, or JavaServer Pages. If you understand the basics of Web programming, you should not have much trouble following along with this book's content.

If you are brand new to ASP.NET, be sure to check out *Beginning ASP.NET 4: In C# and VB* by Imar Spaanjaars (Wiley Publishing, Inc., 2010) to help you understand the basics.

In addition to working with Web technologies, we also assume that you understand basic programming constructs, such as variables, `For Each` loops, and object-oriented programming.

You may also be wondering whether this book is for the Visual Basic developer or the C# developer. We are happy to say that it is for both! When the code differs substantially, this book provides examples in both VB and C#.

WHAT THIS BOOK COVERS

This book explores the release of ASP.NET 4. It covers each major new feature included in ASP.NET 4 in detail. The following list tells you something about the content of each chapter.

- **Chapter 1, "Application and Page Frameworks."** The first chapter covers the frameworks of ASP.NET applications as well as the structure and frameworks provided for single ASP.NET pages. This chapter shows you how to build ASP.NET applications using IIS or the built-in Web server that comes with Visual Studio 2010. This chapter also shows you the folders and files that are part of ASP.NET. It discusses ways to compile code and shows you how to perform cross-page posting. This chapter ends by showing you easy ways to deal with your classes from within Visual Studio 2010.
- **Chapters 2, 3, and 4.** These three chapters are grouped together because they all deal with server controls. This batch of chapters starts by examining the idea of the server control and its pivotal role in ASP.NET development. In addition to looking at the server control framework, these chapters delve into the plethora of server controls that are at your disposal for ASP.NET development projects. Chapter 2, "ASP.NET Server Controls and Client-Side Scripts," looks at the basics of working with server controls. Chapter 3, "ASP.NET Web Server Controls," covers the controls that have been part of the ASP.NET technology since its initial release and the controls that have been added in each of the ASP.NET releases. Chapter 4, "Validation Server Controls," describes a special group of server controls: those for validation. You can use these controls to create beginning-to-advanced form validations.
- **Chapter 5, "Working with Master Pages."** Master pages are a great capability of ASP.NET. They provide a means of creating templated pages that enable you to work with the entire application, as opposed to single pages. This chapter examines the creation of these templates and how to apply them to your content pages throughout an ASP.NET application.
- **Chapter 6, "Themes and Skins."** The Cascading Style Sheet files you are allowed to use in ASP.NET 1.0/1.1 are simply not adequate in many regards, especially in the area of server controls. When using these early versions, the developer can never be sure of the HTML output these files might generate.

This chapter looks at how to deal with the styles that your applications require and shows you how to create a centrally managed look-and-feel for all the pages of your application by using themes and the skin files that are part of a theme.

- **Chapter 7, "Data Binding."** One of the more important tasks of ASP.NET is presenting data, and this chapter shows you how to do that. ASP.NET provides a number of controls to which you can attach data and present it to the end user. This chapter looks at the underlying capabilities that enable you to work with the data programmatically before issuing the data to a control.
- **Chapter 8, "Data Management with ADO.NET."** This chapter presents the ADO.NET data model provided by ASP.NET, which allows you to handle the retrieval, updating, and deleting of data quickly and logically. This data model enables you to use one or two lines of code to get at data stored in everything from SQL Server to XML files.
- **Chapter 9, "Querying with LINQ."** The .NET Framework 4 includes a nice access model language called LINQ. LINQ is a set of extensions to the .NET Framework that encompass language-integrated query, set, and transform operations. This chapter introduces you to LINQ and how to effectively use this feature in your Web applications today.
- **Chapter 10, "Working with XML and LINQ to XML."** Without a doubt, XML has become one of the leading technologies used for data representation. For this reason, the .NET Framework and ASP.NET 4 have many capabilities built into their frameworks that enable you to easily extract, create, manipulate, and store XML. This chapter takes a close look at the XML technologies built into ASP.NET and the underlying .NET Framework.
- **Chapter 11, "Introduction to the Provider Model."** A number of systems are built into ASP.NET that make the lives of developers so much easier and more productive than ever before. These systems are built on an architecture called a *provider model*, which is rather extensible. This chapter gives an overview of this provider model and how it is used throughout ASP.NET 4.
- **Chapter 12, "Extending the Provider Model."** After an introduction of the provider model, this chapter looks at some of the ways to extend the provider model found in ASP.NET 4. This chapter also reviews a couple of sample extensions to the provider model.
- **Chapter 13, "Site Navigation."** It is quite apparent that many developers do not simply develop single pages — they build applications. Therefore, they need mechanics that deal with functionality throughout the entire application, not just the pages. One of the application capabilities provided by ASP.NET 4 is the site navigation system covered in this chapter. The underlying navigation system enables you to define your application's navigation structure through an XML file, and it introduces a whole series of navigation server controls that work with the data from these XML files.
- **Chapter 14, "Personalization."** Developers are always looking for ways to store information pertinent to the end user. After it is stored, this personalization data has to be persisted for future visits or for grabbing other pages within the same application. The ASP.NET team developed a way to store this information — the ASP.NET personalization system. The great thing about this system is that you configure the entire behavior of the system from the `web.config` file.
- **Chapter 15, "Membership and Role Management."** This chapter covers the membership and role management system developed to simplify adding authentication and authorization to your ASP.NET applications. These two systems are extensive; they make some of the more complicated authentication and authorization implementations of the past a distant memory. This chapter focuses on using the `web.config` file for controlling how these systems are applied, as well as on the server controls that work with the underlying systems.
- **Chapter 16, "Portal Frameworks and Web Parts."** This chapter explains Web Parts — a way of encapsulating pages into smaller and more manageable objects. The great thing about Web Parts is that they can be made of a larger Portal Framework, which can then enable end users to completely modify how the Web Parts are constructed on the page — including their appearance and layout.

- **Chapter 17, "HTML and CSS Design with ASP.NET."** Visual Studio 2010 places a lot of focus on building a CSS-based Web. This chapter takes a close look at how you can effectively work with HTML and CSS design for your ASP.NET applications.
- **Chapter 18, "ASP.NET AJAX."** AJAX is a hot buzzword in the Web application world these days. AJAX is an acronym for *Asynchronous JavaScript and XML*. In Web application development, it signifies the capability to build applications that make use of the `XMLHttpRequest` object. Visual Studio 2010 contains the ability to build AJAX-enabled ASP.NET applications from the default install of the IDE. This chapter takes a look at this way to build your applications.
- **Chapter 19, "ASP.NET AJAX Control Toolkit."** Along with the capabilities to build ASP.NET applications that make use of the AJAX technology, a series of controls is available to make the task rather simple. This chapter takes a good look at the ASP.NET AJAX Control Toolkit and how to use this toolkit with your applications today.
- **Chapter 20, "Security."** This chapter discusses security beyond the membership and role management features provided by ASP.NET 4. This chapter provides an in-depth look at the authentication and authorization mechanics inherent in the ASP.NET technology, as well as HTTP access types and impersonations.
- **Chapter 21, "State Management."** Because ASP.NET is a request-response–based technology, state management and the performance of requests and responses take on significant importance. This chapter introduces these two separate but important areas of ASP.NET development.
- **Chapter 22, "Caching."** Because of the request-response nature of ASP.NET, caching (storing previously generated results, images, and pages) on the server becomes rather important to the performance of your ASP.NET applications. This chapter looks at some of the advanced caching capabilities provided by ASP.NET, including the SQL cache invalidation feature which is part of ASP.NET 4. This chapter also takes a look at object caching and object caching extensibility.
- **Chapter 23, "Debugging and Error Handling."** Being able to handle unanticipated errors in your ASP.NET applications is vital for any application that you build. This chapter tells you how to properly structure error handling within your applications. It also shows you how to use various debugging techniques to find errors that your applications might contain.
- **Chapter 24, "File I/O and Streams."** More often than not, you want your ASP.NET applications to work with items that are outside the base application. Examples include files and streams. This chapter takes a close look at working with various file types and streams that might come into your ASP.NET applications.
- **Chapter 25, "User and Server Controls."** Not only can you use the plethora of server controls that come with ASP.NET, but you can also use the same framework these controls use and build your own. This chapter describes building your own server controls and how to use them within your applications.
- **Chapter 26, "Modules and Handlers."** Sometimes, just creating dynamic Web pages with the latest languages and databases does not give you, the developer, enough control over an application. At times, you need to be able to dig deeper and create applications that can interact with the Web server itself. You want to be able to interact with the low-level processes, such as how the Web server processes incoming and outgoing HTTP requests. This chapter looks at two methods of manipulating the way ASP.NET processes HTTP requests: HttpModule and HttpHandler. Each method provides a unique level of access to the underlying processing of ASP.NET, and each can be a powerful tool for creating Web applications.
- **Chapter 27, "ASP.NET MVC."** ASP.NET MVC is the latest major addition to ASP.NET and has generated a lot of excitement from the development community. ASP.NET MVC supplies you with the means to create ASP.NET using the Model-View-Controller models that many developers expect. ASP.NET MVC provides developers with the testability, flexibility, and maintainability in the applications they build. It is important to remember that ASP.NET MVC is not meant to be

a replacement to the ASP.NET everyone knows and loves, but instead is simply a different way to construct your applications.

- **Chapter 28, "Using Business Objects."** Invariably, you are going to have components created with previous technologies that you do not want to rebuild but that you do want to integrate into new ASP.NET applications. If this is the case, the .NET Framework makes incorporating your previous COM components into your applications fairly simple and straightforward. This chapter also shows you how to build .NET components instead of turning to the previous COM component architecture.
- **Chapter 29, "ADO.NET Entity Framework."** Mapping objects from the database to the objects within your code is always a laborious and sometimes difficult process. The inclusion of the ADO.NET Entity Framework in ASP.NET makes this task significantly simpler. Using Visual Studio 2010, you are able to visually design your entity data models and then very easily access these models from code allowing the ADO.NET Entity Framework to handle the connections and transactions to the underlying database.
- **Chapter 30, "ASP.NET Dynamic Data."** This feature in ASP.NET 4 allows you to quickly and easily put together a reporting and data entry application from your database. You are also able to take these same capabilities and incorporate them into a pre-existing application.
- **Chapter 31, "Working with Services."** XML Web services have monopolized all the hype for the past few years, and a major aspect of the Web services model within .NET is part of ASP.NET. This chapter reveals the ease not only of building XML Web services, but consuming them in an ASP.NET application. This chapter then ventures further by describing how to build XML Web services that utilize SOAP headers and how to consume this particular type of service. Another feature in ASP.NET, WCF Data Services, allows you to create a RESTful service layer using an Entity Data Model. Using this capability, you can quickly set up a service layer that allows you to expose your content as AtomPub or JSON, which will allow the consumer to completely interact with the underlying database.
- **Chapter 32, "Building Global Applications."** Developers usually build Web applications in the English language and then, as the audience for the application expands, they realize the need to globalize the application. Of course, building the Web application to handle an international audience right from the start is ideal, but, in many cases, this may not be possible because of the extra work it requires. ASP.NET provides an outstanding way to address the internationalization of Web applications. Changes to the API, the addition of capabilities to the server controls, and even Visual Studio itself equip you to do the extra work required to more easily bring your application to an international audience. This chapter looks at some of the important items to consider when building your Web applications for the world.
- **Chapter 33, "Configuration."** Configuration in ASP.NET can be a big topic because the ASP.NET team is not into building black boxes; instead, it is building the underlying capabilities of ASP.NET in a fashion that can easily be expanded on later. This chapter teaches you to modify the capabilities and behaviors of ASP.NET using the various configuration files at your disposal.
- **Chapter 34, "Instrumentation."** ASP.NET gives you greater capability to apply instrumentation techniques to your applications. The ASP.NET Framework includes performance counters, the capability to work with the Windows Event Tracing system, possibilities for application tracing (covered in Chapter 23 of this book), and the most exciting part of this discussion — a health monitoring system that allows you to log a number of different events over an application's lifetime. This chapter takes an in-depth look at this health monitoring system.
- **Chapter 35, "Administration and Management."** Besides making it easier for the developer to be more productive in building ASP.NET applications, the ASP.NET team also put considerable effort into making the managing of applications easier. In the past, using ASP.NET 1.0/1.1, you managed ASP.NET applications by changing values in an XML configuration file. This chapter provides an overview of the GUI tools that come with ASP.NET today that enable you to manage your Web applications easily and effectively.

- **Chapter 36, "Packaging and Deploying ASP.NET Applications."** So you have built an ASP.NET application — now what? This chapter takes the building process one step further and shows you how to package your ASP.NET applications for easy deployment. Many options are available for working with the installers and compilation model to change what you are actually giving your customers.
- **Appendix A, "Migrating Older ASP.NET Projects."** In some cases, you build your ASP.NET 4 applications from scratch, starting everything new. In many instances, however, this is not an option. You need to take an ASP.NET application that was previously built on the 1.0, 1.1, 2.0, or 3.5 versions of the .NET Framework and migrate the application so that it can run on the .NET Framework 4. This appendix focuses on migrating ASP.NET 1.*x*, 2.0, or 3.5 applications to the 4 Framework.
- **Appendix B, "ASP.NET Ultimate Tools."** This appendix takes a look at the tools available to you as an ASP.NET developer. Many of the tools here will help you to expedite your development process and, in many cases, make you a better developer.
- **Appendix C, "Silverlight 3 and ASP.NET."** Silverlight is a means to build fluid applications using XAML. This technology enables developers with really rich vector-based applications.
- **Appendix D, "Dynamic Types and Languages."** As of the release of ASP.NET 4, you can now build your Web applications using IronRuby and IronPython. This appendix takes a quick look at using dynamic languages in building your Web applications.
- **Appendix E, "ASP.NET Online Resources."** This small appendix points you to some of the more valuable online resources for enhancing your understanding of ASP.NET.

CONVENTIONS

This book uses a number of different styles of text and layout to help differentiate among various types of information. Here are examples of the styles used and an explanation of what they mean:

- New words being defined are shown in *italics*.
- Keys that you press on the keyboard, such as Ctrl and Enter, are shown in initial caps and spelled as they appear on the keyboard.
- File names, file extensions, URLs, and code that appears in regular paragraph text are shown in a `monospaced` typeface.

A block of code that you can type as a program and run is shown on separate lines, like this:

```
public static void Main()
{
   AFunc(1,2,"abc");
}
```

or like this:

```
public static void Main()    {       AFunc(1,2,"abc");    }
```

Sometimes you see code in a mixture of styles, like this:

```
// If we haven't reached the end, return true, otherwise
// set the position to invalid, and return false.
pos++;
if (pos < 4)
   return true;
else {
   pos = -1;
   return false;
}
```

When mixed code is shown like this, the bold code is what you should focus on in the current example.

We demonstrate the syntactical usage of methods, properties, and so on using the following format:

```
SqlDependency="database:table"
```

Here, the italicized parts indicate *placeholder text*: object references, variables, or parameter values that you need to insert.

Most of the code examples throughout the book are presented as numbered listings that have descriptive titles, like this:

LISTING I-7: Targeting WML devices in your ASP.NET pages

Each listing is numbered (for example, *Listing 1-3*) where the first number represents the chapter number and the number following the hyphen represents a sequential number that indicates where that listing falls within the chapter. Downloadable code from the Wrox Web site (`www.wrox.com`) also uses this numbering system (for the most part) so that you can easily locate the examples you are looking for.

All code is shown in both VB and C#, when warranted. The exception is for code in which the only difference is, for example, the value given to the `Language` attribute in the `Page` directive. In such situations, we don't repeat the code for the C# version; the code is shown only once, as in the following example:

```
<%@ Page Language="VB"%>

<html xmlns="http://www.w3.org/1999/xhtml">
<head runat="server">
    <title>DataSetDataSource</title>
</head>
<body>
    <form id="form1" runat="server">
       <asp:DropDownList ID="Dropdownlist1" Runat="server" DataTextField="name"
        DataSourceID="XmlDataSource1">
       </asp:DropDownList>

       <asp:XmlDataSource ID="XmlDataSource1" Runat="server"
        DataFile="</Painters.xml">
       </asp:DataSetDataSource>
   </form>
</body>
</html>
```

SOURCE CODE

As you work through the examples in this book, you may choose either to type all the code manually or to use the source code files that accompany the book. All the source code used in this book is available for download at `www.wrox.com`. When you get to the site, simply locate the book's title (either by using the Search box or one of the topic lists) and click the Download Code link. You can then choose to download all the code from the book in one large Zip file or download just the code you need for a particular chapter.

Because many books have similar titles, you may find it easiest to search by ISBN; this book's ISBN is 978-0-470-50220-4.

After you download the code, just decompress it with your favorite compression tool. Alternatively, you can go to the main Wrox code download page at `www.wrox.com/dynamic/books/download.aspx` to see the code available for this book and all other Wrox books. Remember that you can easily find the code you are looking for by referencing the listing number of the code example from the book, such as "Listing 1-1."

We used these listing numbers when naming most of the downloadable code files. Those few listings that are not named by their listing number are accompanied by the file name so you can easily find them in the downloadable code files.

ERRATA

We make every effort to ensure that there are no errors in the text or in the code. However, no one is perfect, and mistakes do occur. If you find an error in one of our books, such as a spelling mistake or faulty piece of code, we would be very grateful if you would tell us about it. By sending in errata, you may spare another reader hours of frustration; at the same time, you are helping us provide even higher-quality information.

To find the errata page for this book, go to `www.wrox.com` and locate the title using the Search box or one of the title lists. Then, on the book details page, click the Book Errata link. On this page, you can view all errata that have been submitted for this book and posted by Wrox editors. A complete book list including links to each book's errata is also available at `www.wrox.com/misc-pages/booklist.shtml`.

If you do not spot "your" error already on the Book Errata page, go to `www.wrox.com/contact/techsupport.shtml` and complete the form there to send us the error you have found. We will check the information and, if appropriate, post a message to the book's errata page and fix the problem in subsequent editions of the book.

P2P.WROX.COM

For author and peer discussion, join the P2P forums at `p2p.wrox.com`. The forums are a Web-based system for you to post messages relating to Wrox books and technologies and to interact with other readers and technology users. The forums offer a subscription feature that enables you to receive e-mail on topics of interest when new posts are made to the forums. Wrox authors, editors, other industry experts, and your fellow readers are represented in these forums.

At `http://p2p.wrox.com` you will find a number of different forums that will help you not only as you read this book but also as you develop your own applications. To join the forums, just follow these steps:

1. Go to `p2p.wrox.com` and click the Register link.
2. Read the terms of use and click Agree.
3. Supply the information required to join, as well as any optional information you want to provide, and click Submit.

You will receive an e-mail with information describing how to verify your account and complete the joining process.

You can read messages in the forums without joining P2P, but you must join in order to post messages.

After you join, you can post new messages and respond to other users' posts. You can read messages at any time on the Web. If you want to have new messages from a particular forum e-mailed to you, click the Subscribe to this Forum icon by the forum name in the forum listing.

For more information about how the forum software works, as well as answers to many common questions specific to P2P and Wrox books, be sure to read the P2P FAQs. Simply click the FAQ link on any P2P page.

1

Application and Page Frameworks

WHAT'S IN THIS CHAPTER?

- Choosing application location and page structure options
- Working with page directives, page events, and application folders
- Choosing compilation options

The evolution of ASP.NET continues! The progression from Active Server Pages 3.0 to ASP.NET 1.0 was revolutionary, to say the least. And now the revolution continues with the latest release of ASP.NET — version 4. The original introduction of ASP.NET 1.0 fundamentally changed the Web programming model. ASP.NET 4 is just as revolutionary in the way it will increase your productivity. As of late, the primary goal of ASP.NET is to enable you to build powerful, secure, dynamic applications using the least possible amount of code. Although this book covers the new features provided by ASP.NET 4, it also covers all the offerings of ASP.NET technology.

If you are new to ASP.NET and building your first set of applications in ASP.NET 4, you may be amazed by the vast amount of wonderful server controls it provides. You may marvel at how it enables you to work with data more effectively using a series of data providers. You may be impressed at how easily you can build in security and personalization.

The outstanding capabilities of ASP.NET 4 do not end there, however. This chapter looks at many exciting options that facilitate working with ASP.NET pages and applications. One of the first steps you, the developer, should take when starting a project is to become familiar with the foundation you are building on and the options available for customizing that foundation.

APPLICATION LOCATION OPTIONS

With ASP.NET 4, you have the option — using Visual Studio 2010 — to create an application with a virtual directory mapped to IIS or a standalone application outside the confines of IIS. Whereas, the early Visual Studio .NET 2002/2003 IDEs forced developers to use IIS for all Web applications, Visual Studio 2008/2010 (and Visual Web Developer 2008/2010 Express Edition, for that matter) includes a built-in Web server that you can use for development, much like the one used in the past with the ASP.NET Web Matrix.

This built-in Web server was previously presented to developers as a code sample called Cassini. In fact, the code for this mini Web server is freely downloadable from the ASP.NET team Web site found at `www.asp.net`.

The following section shows you how to use the built-in Web server that comes with Visual Studio 2010.

Built-in Web Server

By default, Visual Studio 2010 builds applications without the use of IIS. You can see this when you select File ➪ New ➪ Web Site in the IDE. By default, the location provided for your application is in `C:\Users\BillEvjen\Documents\Visual Studio 10\WebSites` if you are using Windows 7 (shown in Figure 1-1). It is not `C:\Inetpub\wwwroot\` as it would have been in Visual Studio .NET 2002/2003. By default, any site that you build and host inside `C:\Users\BillEvjen\Documents\Visual Studio 10\WebSites` (or any other folder you create) uses the built-in Web server that is part of Visual Studio 2010. If you use the built-in Web server from Visual Studio 2010, you are not locked into the WebSites folder; you can create any folder you want in your system.

FIGURE 1-1

To change from this default, you have a handful of options. Click the Browse button in the New Web Site dialog. The Choose Location dialog opens, shown in Figure 1-2.

If you continue to use the built-in Web server that Visual Studio 2010 provides, you can choose a new location for your Web application from this dialog. To choose a new location, select a new folder and save your `.aspx` pages and any other associated files to this directory. When using Visual Studio 2010, you can run your application completely from this location. This way of working with the ASP.NET pages you create is ideal if you do not have access to a Web server because it enables you to build applications that do not reside on a machine with IIS. This means that you can even develop ASP.NET applications on operating systems such as Windows 7 Home Edition.

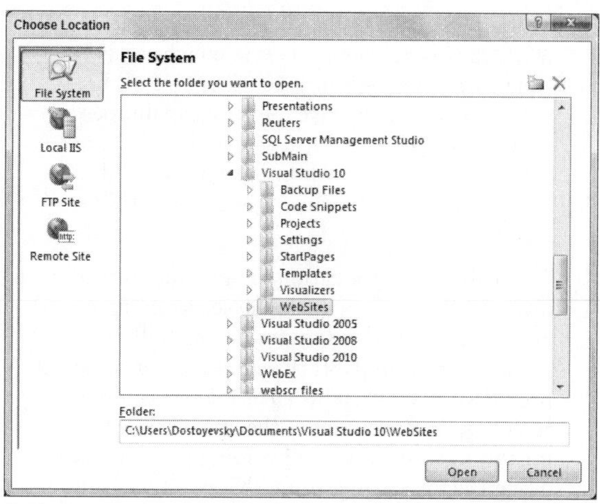

FIGURE 1-2

IIS

From the Choose Location dialog, you can also change where your application is saved and which type of Web server your application employs. To use IIS (as you probably did when you used Visual Studio .NET 2002/2003), select the Local IIS button in the dialog. This changes the results in the text area to show you a list of all the virtual application roots on your machine. You are required to run Visual Studio as an administrator user if you want to see your local IIS instance.

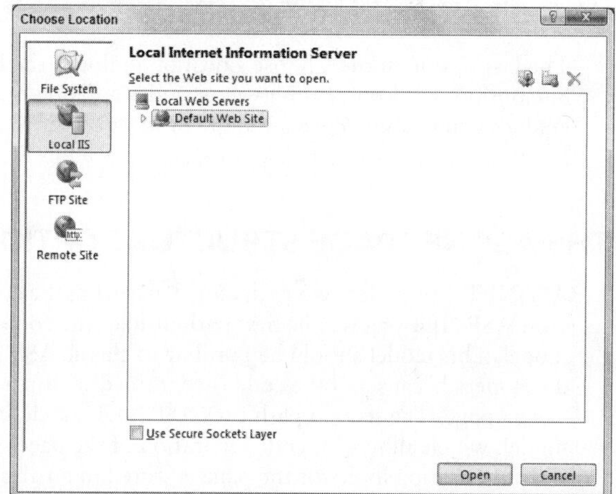

FIGURE 1-3

To create a new virtual root for your application, highlight Default Web Site. Two accessible buttons appear at the top of the dialog box (see Figure 1-3). When you look from left to right, the first button in the upper-right corner of the dialog box is for creating a new Web application — or a virtual root. This button is shown as a globe inside a box. The second button enables you to create virtual directories for any of the virtual roots you created. The third button is a Delete button, which allows you to delete any selected virtual directories or virtual roots on the server.

After you have created the virtual directory you want, click the Open button. Visual Studio 2010 then goes through the standard process to create your application. Now, however, instead of depending on the built-in Web server from ASP.NET 4, your application will use IIS. When you invoke your application, the URL now consists of something like `http://localhost/MyWeb/Default.aspx`, which means it is using IIS.

FTP

Not only can you decide on the type of Web server for your Web application when you create it using the Choose Location dialog, but you can also decide where your application is going to be located. With the previous options, you built applications that resided on your local server. The FTP option enables you to actually store and even code your applications while they reside on a server somewhere else in your enterprise — or on the other side of the planet. You can also use the FTP capabilities to work on different locations within the same server. Using this capability provides a wide range of possible options. You can see this in Figure 1-4.

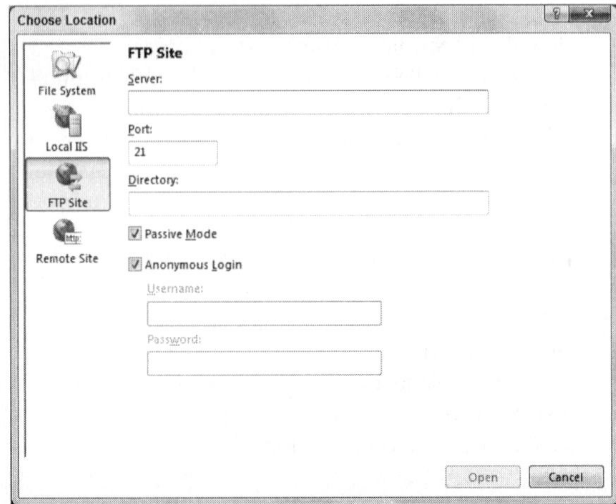

FIGURE 1-4

To create your application on a remote server using FTP, simply provide the server name, the port to use, and the directory — as well as any required credentials. If the correct information is provided, Visual Studio 2010 reaches out to the remote server and creates the appropriate files for the start of your application, just as if it were doing the job locally. From this point on, you can open your project and connect to the remote server using FTP.

Web Site Requiring FrontPage Extensions

The last option in the Choose Location dialog is the Remote Site option. Clicking this button provides a dialog that enables you to connect to a remote or local server that utilizes FrontPage Extensions. This option is displayed in Figure 1-5.

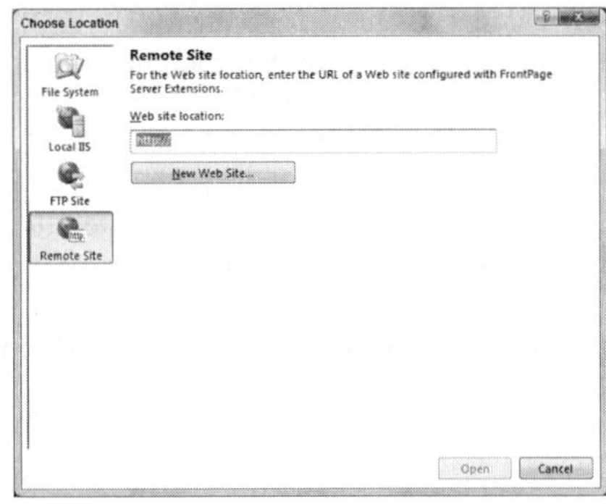

FIGURE 1-5

THE ASP.NET PAGE STRUCTURE OPTIONS

ASP.NET 4 provides two paths for structuring the code of your ASP.NET pages. The first path utilizes the code-inline model. This model should be familiar to classic ASP 2.0/3.0 developers because all the code is contained within a single `.aspx` page. The second path uses ASP.NET's code-behind model, which allows for code separation of the page's business logic from its presentation logic. In this model, the presentation logic for the page is stored in an `.aspx` page, whereas the logic piece is stored in a separate class file: `.aspx.vb` or `.aspx.cs`. Using the code-behind model is considered the best practice because it provides a clean model in separation of pure UI elements from code that manipulates these elements. It is also seen as a better means in maintaining code.

One of the major complaints about Visual Studio .NET 2002 and 2003 is that it forced you to use the code-behind model when developing your ASP.NET pages because it did not understand the code-inline model. The code-behind model in ASP.NET was introduced as a new way to separate the presentation code and business logic. Listing 1-1 shows a typical `.aspx` page generated using Visual Studio .NET 2002 or 2003.

LISTING 1-1: A typical .aspx page from ASP.NET 1.0/1.1

Available for download on Wrox.com

```
<%@ Page Language="vb" AutoEventWireup="false" Codebehind="WebForm1.aspx.vb"
    Inherits="WebApplication.WebForm1"%>
<!DOCTYPE HTML PUBLIC "-//W3C//DTD HTML 4.0 Transitional//EN">
<HTML>
 <HEAD>
    <title>WebForm1</title>
    <meta name="GENERATOR" content="Microsoft Visual Studio .NET 7.1">
    <meta name="CODE_LANGUAGE" content="Visual Basic .NET 7.1">
```

```
        <meta name="vs_defaultClientScript" content="JavaScript">
        <meta name="vs_targetSchema"
          content="http://schemas.microsoft.com/intellisense/ie5">
    </HEAD>
    <body>
        <form id="Form1" method="post" runat="server">
            <P>What is your name?<br>
            <asp:TextBox id="TextBox1" runat="server"></asp:TextBox><BR>
            <asp:Button id="Button1" runat="server" Text="Submit"></asp:Button></P>
            <P><asp:Label id="Label1" runat="server"></asp:Label></P>
        </form>
    </body>
</HTML>
```

The code-behind file created within Visual Studio .NET 2002/2003 for the `.aspx` page is shown in Listing 1-2.

Available for download on Wrox.com

LISTING 1-2: A typical .aspx.vb/.aspx.cs page from ASP.NET 1.0/1.1

```
Public Class WebForm1
    Inherits System.Web.UI.Page

#Region " Web Form Designer Generated Code "

    'This call is required by the Web Form Designer.
     <System.Diagnostics.DebuggerStepThrough()> Private Sub InitializeComponent()

    End Sub
    Protected WithEvents TextBox1 As System.Web.UI.WebControls.TextBox
    Protected WithEvents Button1 As System.Web.UI.WebControls.Button
    Protected WithEvents Label1 As System.Web.UI.WebControls.Label

   'NOTE: The following placeholder declaration is required by the Web Form
        Designer.
   'Do not delete or move it.
    Private designerPlaceholderDeclaration As System.Object

    Private Sub Page_Init(ByVal sender As System.Object, ByVal e As
      System.EventArgs) Handles MyBase.Init
        'CODEGEN: This method call is required by the Web Form Designer
        'Do not modify it using the code editor.
         InitializeComponent()
    End Sub

#End Region

    Private Sub Page_Load(ByVal sender As System.Object, ByVal e As
      System.EventArgs) Handles MyBase.Load
        'Put user code to initialize the page here
    End Sub

    Private Sub Button1_Click(ByVal sender As System.Object, ByVal e As
      System.EventArgs) Handles Button1.Click
        Label1.Text = "Hello " & TextBox1.Text
    End Sub
End Class
```

In this code-behind page from ASP.NET 1.0/1.1, you can see that a lot of the code that developers never have to deal with is hidden in the `#Region` section of the page. Because ASP.NET 4 is built on top of .NET 4, it can take advantage of the .NET Framework capability of partial classes. Partial classes enable you to separate your classes into multiple class files, which are then combined into a single class when the application is compiled. Because ASP.NET 4 combines all this page code for you behind the scenes when the application is compiled, the code-behind files you work with in ASP.NET 4 are simpler in appearance and the model is easier to use. You are presented with only the pieces of the class that you need. Next, this chapter presents a look at both the inline and code-behind models from ASP.NET 4.

Inline Coding

With the .NET Framework 1.0/1.1, developers went out of their way (and outside Visual Studio .NET) to build their ASP.NET pages inline and avoid the code-behind model that was so heavily promoted by Microsoft and others. Visual Studio 2010 (as well as Visual Web Developer 2010 Express Edition) allows you to build your pages easily using this coding style. To build an ASP.NET page inline instead of using the code-behind model, you simply select the page type from the Add New Item dialog and make sure that the Place Code in Separate File check box is not selected. You can get at this dialog (see Figure 1-6) by right-clicking the project or the solution in the Solution Explorer and selecting Add New Item.

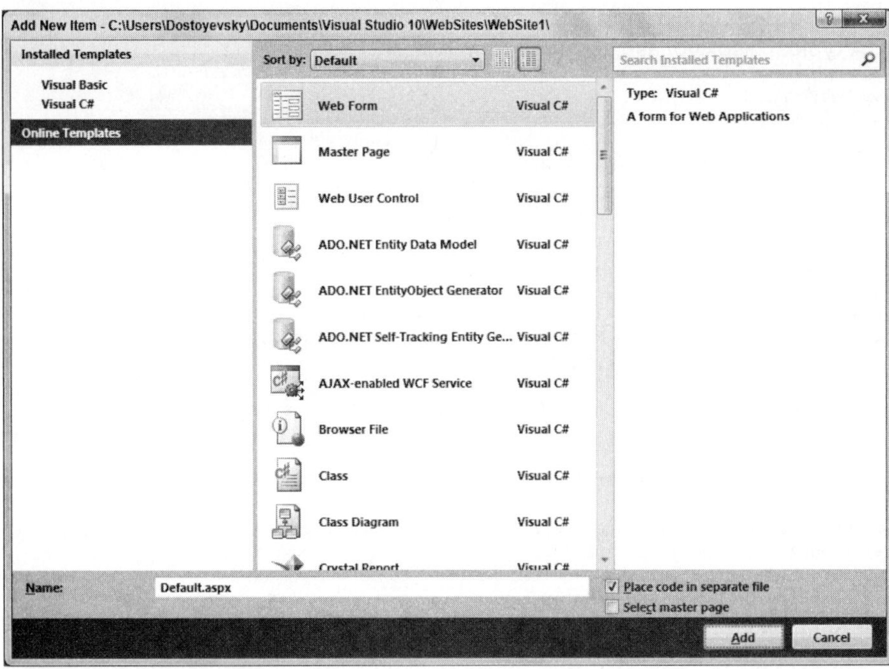

FIGURE 1-6

From here, you can see the check box you need to unselect if you want to build your ASP.NET pages inline. In fact, many page types have options for both inline and code-behind styles. Table 1-1 shows your inline options when selecting files from this dialog.

TABLE 1-1

FILE OPTIONS USING INLINE CODING	FILE CREATED
Web Form	`.aspx` file
AJAX Web Form	`.aspx` file
Master Page	`.master` file
AJAX Master Page	`.master` file
Web User Control	`.ascx` file
Web Service	`.asmx` file

By using the Web Form option with a few controls, you get a page that encapsulates not only the presentation logic, but the business logic as well. This is illustrated in Listing 1-3.

LISTING 1-3: A simple page that uses the inline coding model

Available for download on Wrox.com

```
<%@ Page Language="VB" %>

<!DOCTYPE html PUBLIC "-//W3C//DTD XHTML 1.1//EN"
 "http://www.w3.org/TR/xhtml11/DTD/xhtml11.dtd">

<script runat="server">
    Protected Sub Button1_Click(ByVal sender As Object,
       ByVal e As System.EventArgs)

        Label1.Text = "Hello " & Textbox1.Text
    End Sub
</script>

<html xmlns="http://www.w3.org/1999/xhtml" >
<head runat="server">
    <title>Simple Page</title>
</head>
<body>
    <form id="form1" runat="server">
        What is your name?<br />
        <asp:Textbox ID="Textbox1" Runat="server"></asp:Textbox><br />
        <asp:Button ID="Button1" Runat="server" Text="Submit"
         OnClick="Button1_Click" />
        <p><asp:Label ID="Label1" Runat="server"></asp:Label></p>
    </form>
</body>
</html>
```

C#

```
<%@ Page Language="C#" %>

<!DOCTYPE html PUBLIC "-//W3C//DTD XHTML 1.1//EN"
 "http://www.w3.org/TR/xhtml11/DTD/xhtml11.dtd">

<script runat="server">
    protected void Button1_Click(object sender, System.EventArgs e)
    {
        Label1.Text = "Hello " + Textbox1.Text;
    }
</script>
```

From this example, you can see that all the business logic is encapsulated in between `<script>` tags. The nice feature of the inline model is that the business logic and the presentation logic are contained within the same file. Some developers find that having everything in a single viewable instance makes working with the ASP.NET page easier. Another great thing is that Visual Studio 2010 provides IntelliSense when working with the inline coding model and ASP.NET 4. Before Visual Studio 2005, this capability did not exist. Visual Studio .NET 2002/2003 forced you to use the code-behind model and, even if you rigged it so your pages were using the inline model, you lost all IntelliSense capabilities.

Code-Behind Model

The other option for constructing your ASP.NET 4 pages is to build your files using the code-behind model.

It is important to note that the more preferred method is the code-behind model rather than the inline model. This method employs the proper segmentation between presentation and business logic in many cases. You will find that many of the examples in this book use an inline coding model because it works well in showing an example in one listing. Even though the example is using an inline coding style, it is my recommendation that you move the code to employ the code-behind model.

To create a new page in your ASP.NET solution that uses the code-behind model, select the page type you want from the New File dialog. To build a page that uses the code-behind model, you first select the page in the Add New Item dialog and make sure the Place Code in Separate File check box is selected. Table 1-2 shows you the options for pages that use the code-behind model.

TABLE 1-2

FILE OPTIONS USING CODE-BEHIND	FILE CREATED
Web Form	`.aspx` file; `.aspx.vb` or `.aspx.cs` file
AJAX Web Form	`.aspx` file; `.aspx.vb` or `.aspx.cs` file
Master Page	`.master` file; `.master.vb` or `.master.cs` file
AJAX Master Page	`.master.vb` or `.master.cs` file
Web User Control	`.ascx` file; `.ascx.vb` or `.ascx.cs` file
Web Service	`.asmx` file; `.vb` or `.cs` file

The idea of using the code-behind model is to separate the business logic and presentation logic into separate files. Doing this makes working with your pages easier, especially if you are working in a team environment where visual designers work on the UI of the page and coders work on the business logic that sits behind the presentation pieces. Earlier in Listings 1-1 and 1-2, you saw how pages using the code-behind model in ASP.NET 1.0/1.1 were constructed. To see the difference in ASP.NET 4, look at how its code-behind pages are constructed. These differences are illustrated in Listing 1-4 for the presentation piece and Listing 1-5 for the code-behind piece.

LISTING 1-4: An .aspx page that uses the ASP.NET 4 code-behind model

Available for download on Wrox.com

VB

```
<%@ Page Language="VB" AutoEventWireup="false" CodeFile="Default.aspx.vb"
    Inherits="_Default" %>

<!DOCTYPE html PUBLIC "-//W3C//DTD XHTML 1.1//EN"
 "http://www.w3.org/TR/xhtml11/DTD/xhtml11.dtd">

<html xmlns="http://www.w3.org/1999/xhtml">
<head runat="server">
    <title>Simple Page</title>
</head>
<body>
    <form id="form1" runat="server">
        What is your name?<br />
        <asp:Textbox ID="Textbox1" Runat="server"></asp:Textbox><br />
        <asp:Button ID="Button1" Runat="server" Text="Submit"
         OnClick="Button1_Click" />
        <p><asp:Label ID="Label1" Runat="server"></asp:Label></p>
    </form>
</body>
</html>
```

C#

```
<%@ Page Language="C#" CodeFile="Default.aspx.cs" Inherits="_Default" %>
```

LISTING 1-5: A code-behind page

Available for download on Wrox.com

```
Partial Class _Default
    Inherits System.Web.UI.Page

    Protected Sub Button1_Click(ByVal sender As Object, _
       ByVal e As System.EventArgs) Handles Button1.Click

        Label1.Text = "Hello " & TextBox1.Text
    End Sub
End Class
```

C#

```
using System;
using System.Collections.Generic;
using System.Linq;
using System.Web;
using System.Web.UI;
using System.Web.UI.WebControls;

public partial class _Default : System.Web.UI.Page
{
    protected void Button1_Click(object sender, EventArgs e)
    {
       Label1.Text = "Hello " + Textbox1.Text;
    }
}
```

The `.aspx` page using this ASP.NET 4 code-behind model has some attributes in the `Page` directive that you should pay attention to when working in this mode. The first is the `CodeFile` attribute. This attribute in the `Page` directive is meant to point to the code-behind page that is used with this presentation page. In this case, the value assigned is `Default.aspx.vb` or `Default.aspx.cs`. The second attribute needed is the `Inherits` attribute. This attribute was available in previous versions of ASP.NET, but was little used before ASP.NET 2.0. This attribute specifies the name of the class that is bound to the page when the page is compiled. The directives are simple enough in ASP.NET 4. Look at the code-behind page from Listing 1-5.

The code-behind page is rather simple in appearance because of the partial class capabilities that .NET 4 provides. You can see that the class created in the code-behind file uses partial classes, employing the `Partial` keyword in Visual Basic 2010 and the `partial` keyword from C# 2010. This enables you to simply place the methods that you need in your page class. In this case, you have a button-click event and nothing else.

Later in this chapter, you look at the compilation process for both of these models.

ASP.NET 4 PAGE DIRECTIVES

ASP.NET directives are something that is a part of every ASP.NET page. You can control the behavior of your ASP.NET pages by using these directives. Here is an example of the `Page` directive:

```
<%@ Page Language="VB" AutoEventWireup="false" CodeFile="Default.aspx.vb"
    Inherits="_Default" %>
```

Eleven directives are at your disposal in your ASP.NET pages or user controls. You use these directives in your applications whether the page uses the code-behind model or the inline coding model.

Basically, these directives are commands that the compiler uses when the page is compiled. Directives are simple to incorporate into your pages. A directive is written in the following format:

```
<%@ [Directive] [Attribute=Value] %>
```

From this, you can see that a directive is opened with a `<%@` and closed with a `%>`. Putting these directives at the top of your pages or controls is best because this is traditionally where developers expect to see them (although the page still compiles if the directives are located at a different place). Of course, you can also add more than a single attribute to your directive statements, as shown in the following:

```
<%@ [Directive] [Attribute=Value] [Attribute=Value] %>
```

Table 1-3 describes the directives at your disposal in ASP.NET 4.

TABLE 1-3

DIRECTIVE	DESCRIPTION
`Assembly`	Links an assembly to the page or user control for which it is associated.
`Control`	Page directive meant for use with user controls (`.ascx`).
`Implements`	Implements a specified .NET Framework interface.
`Import`	Imports specified namespaces into the page or user control.
`Master`	Enables you to specify master page–specific attributes and values to use when the page parses or compiles. This directive can be used only with master pages (`.master`).
`MasterType`	Associates a class name to a page to get at strongly typed references or members contained within the specified master page.
`OutputCache`	Controls the output caching policies of a page or user control.
`Page`	Enables you to specify page-specific attributes and values to use when the page parses or compiles. This directive can be used only with ASP.NET pages (`.aspx`).
`PreviousPageType`	Enables an ASP.NET page to work with a postback from another page in the application.
`Reference`	Links a page or user control to the current page or user control.
`Register`	Associates aliases with namespaces and class names for notation in custom server control syntax.

The following sections provide a quick review of each of these directives.

@Page

The `@Page` directive enables you to specify attributes and values for an ASP.NET page (`.aspx`) to be used when the page is parsed or compiled. This is the most frequently used directive of the bunch. Because the ASP.NET page is such an important part of ASP.NET, you have quite a few attributes at your disposal. Table 1-4 summarizes the attributes available through the `@Page` directive.

TABLE 1-4

ATTRIBUTE	DESCRIPTION
`AspCompat`	Permits the page to be executed on a single-threaded apartment thread when given a value of `True`. The default setting for this attribute is `False`.
`Async`	Specifies whether the ASP.NET page is processed synchronously or asynchronously.
`AsyncTimeout`	Specifies the amount of time in seconds to wait for the asynchronous task to complete. The default setting is 45 seconds.
`AutoEventWireup`	Specifies whether the page events are autowired when set to `True`. The default setting for this attribute is `True`.
`Buffer`	Enables HTTP response buffering when set to `True`. The default setting for this attribute is `True`.
`ClassName`	Specifies the name of the class that is bound to the page when the page is compiled.

ATTRIBUTE	DESCRIPTION
ClientIDMode	Specifies the algorithm that the page should use when generating ClientID values for server controls that are on the page. The default value is AutoID (the mode that was used for ASP.NET pages prior to ASP.NET 4). This is a new attribute of ASP.NET 4.
ClientTarget	Specifies the target user agent a control should render content for. This attribute needs to be tied to an alias defined in the `<clientTarget>` section of the `web.config` file.
CodeFile	References the code-behind file with which the page is associated.
CodeFileBaseClass	Specifies the type name of the base class to use with the code-behind class, which is used by the `CodeFile` attribute.
CodePage	Indicates the code page value for the response.
CompilationMode	Specifies whether ASP.NET should compile the page or not. The available options include `Always` (the default), `Auto`, or `Never`. A setting of `Auto` means that if possible, ASP.NET will not compile the page.
CompilerOptions	Compiler string that indicates compilation options for the page.
CompileWith	Takes a `String` value that points to the code-behind file used.
ContentType	Defines the HTTP content type of the response as a standard MIME type.
Culture	Specifies the culture setting of the page. ASP.NET 3.5 and 4 include the capability to give the `Culture` attribute a value of `Auto` to enable automatic detection of the culture required.
Debug	Compiles the page with debug symbols in place when set to `True`.
Description	Provides a text description of the page. The ASP.NET parser ignores this attribute and its assigned value.
EnableEventValidation	Specifies whether to enable validation of events in postback and callback scenarios. The default setting of `True` means that events will be validated.
EnableSessionState	Session state for the page is enabled when set to `True`. The default setting is `True`.
EnableTheming	Page is enabled to use theming when set to `True`. The default setting for this attribute is `True`.
EnableViewState	View state is maintained across the page when set to `True`. The default value is `True`.
EnableViewStateMac	Page runs a machine-authentication check on the page's view state when the page is posted back from the user when set to `True`. The default value is `False`.
ErrorPage	Specifies a URL to post to for all unhandled page exceptions.
Explicit	Visual Basic `Explicit` option is enabled when set to `True`. The default setting is `False`.
Language	Defines the language being used for any inline rendering and script blocks.
LCID	Defines the locale identifier for the Web Form's page.
LinePragmas	`Boolean` value that specifies whether line pragmas are used with the resulting assembly.
MasterPageFile	Takes a `String` value that points to the location of the master page used with the page. This attribute is used with content pages.
MaintainScrollPositionOnPostback	Takes a `Boolean` value, which indicates whether the page should be positioned exactly in the same scroll position or whether the page should be regenerated in the uppermost position for when the page is posted back to itself.

continues

TABLE 1-4 *(continued)*

ATTRIBUTE	DESCRIPTION
MetaDescription	Allows you to specify a page's description in a meta tag for SEO purposes. This is a new attribute in ASP.NET 4.
MetaKeywords	Allows you to specify a page's keywords in a meta tag for SEO purposes. This is a new attribute in ASP.NET 4.
ResponseEncoding	Specifies the response encoding of the page content.
SmartNavigation	Specifies whether to activate the ASP.NET Smart Navigation feature for richer browsers. This returns the postback to the current position on the page. The default value is False. Since ASP.NET 2.0, SmartNavigation has been deprecated. Use the SetFocus() method and the MaintainScrollPositionOnPostback property instead.
Src	Points to the source file of the class used for the code behind of the page being rendered.
Strict	Compiles the page using the Visual Basic Strict mode when set to True. The default setting is False.
StylesheetTheme	Applies the specified theme to the page using the ASP.NET themes feature. The difference between the StylesheetTheme and Theme attributes is that StylesheetTheme will not override preexisting style settings in the controls, whereas Theme will remove these settings.
Theme	Applies the specified theme to the page using the ASP.NET themes feature.
Title	Applies a page's title. This is an attribute mainly meant for content pages that must apply a page title other than what is specified in the master page.
Trace	Page tracing is enabled when set to True. The default setting is False.
TraceMode	Specifies how the trace messages are displayed when tracing is enabled. The settings for this attribute include SortByTime or SortByCategory. The default setting is SortByTime.
Transaction	Specifies whether transactions are supported on the page. The settings for this attribute are Disabled, NotSupported, Supported, Required, and RequiresNew. The default setting is Disabled.
UICulture	The value of the UICulture attribute specifies what UI Culture to use for the ASP.NET page. ASP.NET 3.5 and 4 include the capability to give the UICulture attribute a value of Auto to enable automatic detection of the UICulture.
ValidateRequest	When this attribute is set to True, the form input values are checked against a list of potentially dangerous values. This helps protect your Web application from harmful attacks such as JavaScript attacks. The default value is True.
ViewStateEncryptionMode	Specifies how the ViewState is encrypted on the page. The options include Auto, Always, and Never. The default is Auto.
WarningLevel	Specifies the compiler warning level at which to stop compilation of the page. Possible values are 0 through 4.

Here is an example of how to use the @Page directive:

```
<%@ Page Language="VB" AutoEventWireup="false" CodeFile="Default.aspx.vb"
    Inherits="_Default" %>
```

@Master

The `@Master` directive is quite similar to the `@Page` directive except that the `@Master` directive is meant for master pages (`.master`). In using the `@Master` directive, you specify properties of the templated page that you will be using in conjunction with any number of content pages on your site. Any content pages (built using the `@Page` directive) can then inherit from the master page all the master content (defined in the master page using the `@Master` directive). Although they are similar, the `@Master` directive has fewer attributes available to it than does the `@Page` directive. The available attributes for the `@Master` directive are shown in Table 1-5.

TABLE 1-5

ATTRIBUTE	DESCRIPTION
`AutoEventWireup`	Specifies whether the master page's events are autowired when set to `True`. Default setting is `True`.
`ClassName`	Specifies the name of the class that is bound to the master page when compiled.
`CodeFile`	References the code-behind file with which the page is associated.
`CompilationMode`	Specifies whether ASP.NET should compile the page. The available options include `Always` (the default), `Auto`, or `Never`. A setting of `Auto` means that if possible, ASP.NET will not compile the page.
`CompilerOptions`	Compiler string that indicates compilation options for the master page.
`CompileWith`	Takes a `String` value that points to the code-behind file used for the master page.
`Debug`	Compiles the master page with debug symbols in place when set to `True`.
`Description`	Provides a text description of the master page. The ASP.NET parser ignores this attribute and its assigned value.
`EnableTheming`	Indicates the master page is enabled to use theming when set to `True`. The default setting for this attribute is `True`.
`EnableViewState`	Maintains view state for the master page when set to `True`. The default value is `True`.
`Explicit`	Indicates that the Visual Basic `Explicit` option is enabled when set to `True`. The default setting is `False`.
`Inherits`	Specifies the `CodeBehind` class for the master page to inherit.
`Language`	Defines the language that is being used for any inline rendering and script blocks.
`LinePragmas`	`Boolean` value that specifies whether line pragmas are used with the resulting assembly.
`MasterPageFile`	Takes a `String` value that points to the location of the master page used with the master page. It is possible to have a master page use another master page, which creates a nested master page.
`Src`	Points to the source file of the class used for the code behind of the master page being rendered.
`Strict`	Compiles the master page using the Visual Basic `Strict` mode when set to `True`. The default setting is `False`.
`WarningLevel`	Specifies the compiler warning level at which you want to abort compilation of the page. Possible values are from `0` to `4`.

Here is an example of how to use the `@Master` directive:

```
<%@ Master Language="VB" CodeFile="MasterPage1.master.vb"
    AutoEventWireup="false" Inherits="MasterPage" %>
```

@Control

The @Control directive is similar to the @Page directive except that @Control is used when you build an ASP.NET user control. The @Control directive allows you to define the properties to be inherited by the user control. These values are assigned to the user control as the page is parsed and compiled. The available attributes are fewer than those of the @Page directive, but quite a few of them allow for the modifications you need when building user controls. Table 1-6 details the available attributes.

TABLE 1-6

ATTRIBUTE	DESCRIPTION
AutoEventWireup	Specifies whether the user control's events are autowired when set to True. Default setting is True.
ClassName	Specifies the name of the class that is bound to the user control when the page is compiled.
ClientIDMode	Specifies the algorithm that the page should use when generating ClientID values for server controls that are on the page. The default value is AutoID (the mode that was used for ASP.NET pages prior to ASP.NET 4). This is a new attribute of ASP.NET 4.
CodeFileBaseClass	Specifies the type name of the base class to use with the code-behind class, which is used by the CodeFile attribute.
CodeFile	References the code-behind file with which the user control is associated.
CompilerOptions	Compiler string that indicates compilation options for the user control.
CompileWith	Takes a String value that points to the code-behind file used for the user control.
Debug	Compiles the user control with debug symbols in place when set to True.
Description	Provides a text description of the user control. The ASP.NET parser ignores this attribute and its assigned value.
EnableTheming	User control is enabled to use theming when set to True. The default setting for this attribute is True.
EnableViewState	View state is maintained for the user control when set to True. The default value is True.
Explicit	Visual Basic Explicit option is enabled when set to True. The default setting is False.
Inherits	Specifies the CodeBehind class for the user control to inherit.
Language	Defines the language used for any inline rendering and script blocks.
LinePragmas	Boolean value that specifies whether line pragmas are used with the resulting assembly.
Src	Points to the source file of the class used for the code behind of the user control being rendered.
Strict	Compiles the user control using the Visual Basic Strict mode when set to True. The default setting is False.
WarningLevel	Specifies the compiler warning level at which to stop compilation of the user control. Possible values are 0 through 4.

The @Control directive is meant to be used with an ASP.NET user control. The following is an example of how to use the directive:

```
<%@ Control Language="VB" Explicit="True"
    CodeFile="WebUserControl.ascx.vb" Inherits="WebUserControl"
    Description="This is the registration user control." %>
```

@Import

The `@Import` directive allows you to specify a namespace to be imported into the ASP.NET page or user control. By importing, all the classes and interfaces of the namespace are made available to the page or user control. This directive supports only a single attribute: `Namespace`.

The `Namespace` attribute takes a `String` value that specifies the namespace to be imported. The `@Import` directive cannot contain more than one attribute/value pair. Because of this, you must place multiple namespace imports in multiple lines as shown in the following example:

```
<%@ Import Namespace="System.Data" %>
<%@ Import Namespace="System.Data.SqlClient" %>
```

Several assemblies are already being referenced by your application. You can find a list of these imported namespaces by looking in the root `web.config` file found at `C:\Windows\Microsoft.NET\Framework\v4.0.xxxxx\Config`. You can find this list of assemblies being referenced from the `<assemblies>` child element of the `<compilation>` element. The settings in the root `web.config` file are as follows:

```
<assemblies>
   <add assembly="mscorlib" />
   <add assembly="Microsoft.CSharp, Version=4.0.0.0, Culture=neutral,
    PublicKeyToken=b03f5f7f11d50a3a" />
   <add assembly="System, Version=4.0.0.0, Culture=neutral,
    PublicKeyToken=b77a5c561934e089" />
   <add assembly="System.Configuration, Version=4.0.0.0, Culture=neutral,
    PublicKeyToken=b03f5f7f11d50a3a" />
   <add assembly="System.Web, Version=4.0.0.0, Culture=neutral,
    PublicKeyToken=b03f5f7f11d50a3a" />
   <add assembly="System.Data, Version=4.0.0.0, Culture=neutral,
    PublicKeyToken=b77a5c561934e089" />
   <add assembly="System.Web.Services, Version=4.0.0.0, Culture=neutral,
    PublicKeyToken=b03f5f7f11d50a3a" />
   <add assembly="System.Xml, Version=4.0.0.0, Culture=neutral,
    PublicKeyToken=b77a5c561934e089" />
   <add assembly="System.Drawing, Version=4.0.0.0, Culture=neutral,
    PublicKeyToken=b03f5f7f11d50a3a" />
   <add assembly="System.EnterpriseServices, Version=4.0.0.0, Culture=neutral,
    PublicKeyToken=b03f5f7f11d50a3a" />
   <add assembly="System.Web.Mobile, Version=4.0.0.0, Culture=neutral,
    PublicKeyToken=b03f5f7f11d50a3a" />
   <add assembly="System.IdentityModel, Version=4.0.0.0, Culture=neutral,
    PublicKeyToken=b77a5c561934e089" />
   <add assembly="System.Runtime.Serialization, Version=4.0.0.0, Culture=neutral,
    PublicKeyToken=b77a5c561934e089" />
   <add assembly="System.Xaml, Version=4.0.0.0, Culture=neutral,
    PublicKeyToken=b77a5c561934e089" />
   <add assembly="System.ServiceModel, Version=4.0.0.0, Culture=neutral,
    PublicKeyToken=b77a5c561934e089" />
   <add assembly="System.ServiceModel.Activation, Version=4.0.0.0, Culture=neutral,
    PublicKeyToken=31bf3856ad364e35"/>
   <add assembly="System.ServiceModel.Channels, Version=4.0.0.0, Culture=neutral,
    PublicKeyToken=31bf3856ad364e35"/>
   <add assembly="System.ServiceModel.Web, Version=4.0.0.0, Culture=neutral,
    PublicKeyToken=31bf3856ad364e35"/>
   <add assembly="System.Activities, Version=4.0.0.0, Culture=neutral,
    PublicKeyToken=31bf3856ad364e35"/>
   <add assembly="System.ServiceModel.Activities, Version=4.0.0.0, Culture=neutral,
    PublicKeyToken=31bf3856ad364e35"/>
   <add assembly="System.WorkflowServices, Version=4.0.0.0, Culture=neutral,
    PublicKeyToken=31bf3856ad364e35"/>
   <add assembly="System.Xaml.Hosting, Version=4.0.0.0, Culture=neutral,
    PublicKeyToken=31bf3856ad364e35"/>
   <add assembly="System.Core, Version=4.0.0.0, Culture=neutral,
```

```
     PublicKeyToken=b77a5c561934e089" />
    <add assembly="System.Web.Extensions, Version=4.0.0.0, Culture=neutral,
     PublicKeyToken=31bf3856ad364e35" />
    <add assembly="System.Data.DataSetExtensions, Version=4.0.0.0, Culture=neutral,
     PublicKeyToken=b77a5c561934e089" />
    <add assembly="System.Xml.Linq, Version=4.0.0.0, Culture=neutral,
     PublicKeyToken=b77a5c561934e089" />
    <add assembly="System.ComponentModel.DataAnnotations, Version=4.0.0.0,
     Culture=neutral, PublicKeyToken=31bf3856ad364e35"/>
    <add assembly="System.Web.DynamicData, Version=4.0.0.0, Culture=neutral,
     PublicKeyToken=31bf3856ad364e35"/>
    <add assembly="System.Data.Entity, Version=4.0.0.0, Culture=neutral,
     PublicKeyToken=b77a5c561934e089" />
    <add assembly="System.Web.Entity, Version=4.0.0.0, Culture=neutral,
     PublicKeyToken=b77a5c561934e089"/>
    <add assembly="System.Data.Linq, Version=4.0.0.0, Culture=neutral,
     PublicKeyToken=b77a5c561934e089" />
    <add assembly="System.Data.Entity.Design, Version=4.0.0.0, Culture=neutral,
     PublicKeyToken=b77a5c561934e089" />
    <add assembly="System.Web.ApplicationServices, Version=4.0.0.0, Culture=neutral,
     PublicKeyToken=31bf3856ad364e35" />
    <add assembly="*" />
</assemblies>
```

Because of this reference in the root `web.config` file, these assemblies need not be referenced in a References folder, as you would have done in ASP.NET 1.0/1.1. You can actually add or delete assemblies that are referenced from this list. For example, if you have a custom assembly referenced continuously by each and every application on the server, you can simply add a similar reference to your custom assembly next to these others. Note that you can perform this same task through the application-specific `web.config` file of your application as well.

Even though assemblies might be referenced, you must still import the namespaces of these assemblies into your pages. The same root `web.config` file contains a list of namespaces automatically imported into each and every page of your application. This is specified through the `<namespaces>` child element of the `<pages>` element.

```
<namespaces>
   <add namespace="System" />
   <add namespace="System.Collections" />
   <add namespace="System.Collections.Generic" />
   <add namespace="System.Collections.Specialized" />
   <add namespace="System.ComponentModel" />
   <add namespace="System.ComponentModel.DataAnnotations" />
   <add namespace="System.Configuration" />
   <add namespace="System.Data.Entity.Design" />
   <add namespace="System.Data.Linq" />
   <add namespace="System.Linq" />
   <add namespace="System.Text" />
   <add namespace="System.Text.RegularExpressions" />
   <add namespace="System.Web" />
   <add namespace="System.Web.Caching" />
   <add namespace="System.DynamicData" />
   <add namespace="System.Web.SessionState" />
   <add namespace="System.Web.Security" />
   <add namespace="System.Web.Profile" />
   <add namespace="System.Web.UI" />
   <add namespace="System.Web.UI.WebControls" />
   <add namespace="System.Web.UI.WebControls.WebParts" />
   <add namespace="System.Web.UI.HtmlControls" />
   <add namespace="System.Xml.Linq" />
</namespaces>
```

From this XML list, you can see that quite a number of namespaces are imported into each and every one of your ASP.NET pages. Again, you can feel free to modify this selection in the root `web.config` file or even make a similar selection of namespaces from within your application's `web.config` file.

For instance, you can import your own namespace in the `web.config` file of your application to make the namespace available on every page where it is utilized.

```
<?xml version="1.0"?>
<configuration>
   <system.web>
      <pages>
         <namespaces>
            <add namespace="MyCompany.Utilities" />
         </namespaces>
      </pages>
   </system.web>
</configuration>
```

Remember that importing a namespace into your ASP.NET page or user control gives you the opportunity to use the classes without fully identifying the class name. For example, by importing the namespace `System.Data.OleDb` into the ASP.NET page, you can refer to classes within this namespace by using the singular class name (`OleDbConnection` instead of `System.Data.OleDb.OleDbConnection`).

@Implements

The `@Implements` directive gets the ASP.NET page to implement a specified .NET Framework interface. This directive supports only a single attribute: `Interface`.

The `Interface` attribute directly specifies the .NET Framework interface. When the ASP.NET page or user control implements an interface, it has direct access to all its events, methods, and properties.

Here is an example of the `@Implements` directive:

```
<%@ Implements Interface="System.Web.UI.IValidator" %>
```

@Register

The `@Register` directive associates aliases with namespaces and class names for notation in custom server control syntax. You can see the use of the `@Register` directive when you drag and drop a user control onto any of your `.aspx` pages. Dragging a user control onto the `.aspx` page causes Visual Studio 2010 to create a `@Register` directive at the top of the page. This registers your user control on the page so that the control can then be accessed on the `.aspx` page by a specific name.

The `@Register` directive supports five attributes, as described in Table 1-7.

TABLE 1-7

ATTRIBUTE	DESCRIPTION
`Assembly`	The assembly you are associating with the `TagPrefix`.
`Namespace`	The namespace to relate with `TagPrefix`.
`Src`	The location of the user control.
`TagName`	The alias to relate to the class name.
`TagPrefix`	The alias to relate to the namespace.

Here is an example of how to use the `@Register` directive to import a user control to an ASP.NET page:

```
<%@ Register TagPrefix="MyTag" Namespace="MyName.MyNamespace"
    Assembly="MyAssembly" %>
```

@Assembly

The @Assembly directive attaches assemblies, the building blocks of .NET applications, to an ASP.NET page or user control as it compiles, thereby making all the assembly's classes and interfaces available to the page. This directive supports two attributes: Name and Src.

- Name: Enables you to specify the name of an assembly used to attach to the page files. The name of the assembly should include the filename only, not the file's extension. For instance, if the file is MyAssembly.vb, the value of the name attribute should be MyAssembly.
- Src: Enables you to specify the source of the assembly file to use in compilation.

The following provides some examples of how to use the @Assembly directive:

```
<%@ Assembly Name="MyAssembly" %>
<%@ Assembly Src="MyAssembly.vb" %>
```

@PreviousPageType

This directive is used to specify the page from which any cross-page postings originate. Cross-page posting between ASP.NET pages is explained later in the section "Cross-Page Posting."

The @PreviousPageType directive is a directive that works with the cross-page posting capability that ASP.NET 4 provides. This simple directive contains only two possible attributes: TypeName and VirtualPath:

- TypeName: Sets the name of the derived class from which the postback will occur.
- VirtualPath: Sets the location of the posting page from which the postback will occur.

@MasterType

The @MasterType directive associates a class name to an ASP.NET page to get at strongly typed references or members contained within the specified master page. This directive supports two attributes:

- TypeName: Sets the name of the derived class from which to get strongly typed references or members.
- VirtualPath: Sets the location of the page from which these strongly typed references and members will be retrieved.

Details of how to use the @MasterType directive are shown in Chapter 5. Here is an example of its use:

```
<%@ MasterType VirtualPath="~/Wrox.master" %>
```

@OutputCache

The @OutputCache directive controls the output caching policies of an ASP.NET page or user control. This directive supports the ten attributes described in Table 1-8.

TABLE 1-8

ATTRIBUTE	DESCRIPTION
CacheProfile	Allows for a central way to manage an application's cache profile. Use the CacheProfile attribute to specify the name of the cache profile detailed in the web.config file.
Duration	The duration of time in seconds that the ASP.NET page or user control is cached.
Location	Location enumeration value. The default is Any. This is valid for .aspx pages only and does not work with user controls (.ascx). Other possible values include Client, Downstream, None, Server, and ServerAndClient.
NoStore	Specifies whether to send a no-store header with the page.
Shared	Specifies whether a user control's output can be shared across multiple pages. This attribute takes a Boolean value and the default setting is false.

ATTRIBUTE	DESCRIPTION
SqlDependency	Enables a particular page to use SQL Server cache invalidation.
VaryByControl	Semicolon-separated list of strings used to vary the output cache of a user control.
VaryByCustom	String specifying the custom output caching requirements.
VaryByHeader	Semicolon-separated list of HTTP headers used to vary the output cache.
VaryByParam	Semicolon-separated list of strings used to vary the output cache.

Here is an example of how to use the `@OutputCache` directive:

```
<%@ OutputCache Duration="180" VaryByParam="None" %>
```

Remember that the `Duration` attribute specifies the amount of time in *seconds* during which this page is to be stored in the system cache.

@Reference

The `@Reference` directive declares that another ASP.NET page or user control should be compiled along with the active page or control. This directive supports just a single attribute:

- `VirtualPath`: Sets the location of the page or user control from which the active page will be referenced.

Here is an example of how to use the `@Reference` directive:

```
<%@ Reference VirtualPath="~/MyControl.ascx" %>
```

ASP.NET PAGE EVENTS

ASP.NET developers consistently work with various events in their server-side code. Many of the events that they work with pertain to specific server controls. For instance, if you want to initiate some action when the end user clicks a button on your Web page, you create a button-click event in your server-side code, as shown in Listing 1-6.

LISTING 1-6: A sample button-click event shown in VB

```
Protected Sub Button1_Click(sender As Object, e As EventArgs) Handles Button1.Click
   Label1.Text = TextBox1.Text
End Sub
```

In addition to the server controls, developers also want to initiate actions at specific moments when the ASP.NET page is being either created or destroyed. The ASP.NET page itself has always had a number of events for these instances. The following list shows you all the page events you could use in ASP.NET 1.0/1.1:

- `AbortTransaction`
- `CommitTransaction`
- `DataBinding`
- `Disposed`
- `Error`
- `Init`
- `Load`
- `PreRender`
- `Unload`

One of the more popular page events from this list is the `Load` event, which is used in VB as shown in Listing 1-7.

LISTING 1-7: Using the Page_Load event

```
Protected Sub Page_Load(ByVal sender As Object, ByVal e As System.EventArgs)
   Handles Me.Load

   Response.Write("This is the Page_Load event")
End Sub
```

Besides the page events just shown, ASP.NET 4 has the following events:

- `InitComplete`: Indicates the initialization of the page is completed.
- `LoadComplete`: Indicates the page has been completely loaded into memory.
- `PreInit`: Indicates the moment immediately before a page is initialized.
- `PreLoad`: Indicates the moment before a page has been loaded into memory.
- `PreRenderComplete`: Indicates the moment directly before a page has been rendered in the browser.

An example of using any of these events, such as the `PreInit` event, is shown in Listing 1-8.

LISTING 1-8: Using page events

VB

```
<script runat="server" language="vb">
    Protected Sub Page_PreInit(ByVal sender As Object, ByVal e As System.EventArgs)
       Page.Theme = Request.QueryString("ThemeChange")
    End Sub
</script>
```

C#

```
<script runat="server">
    protected void Page_PreInit(object sender, System.EventArgs e)
    {
       Page.Theme = Request.QueryString["ThemeChange"];
    }
</script>
```

If you create an ASP.NET 4 page and turn on tracing, you can see the order in which the main page events are initiated. They are fired in the following order:

1. `PreInit`
2. `Init`
3. `InitComplete`
4. `PreLoad`
5. `Load`
6. `LoadComplete`
7. `PreRender`
8. `PreRenderComplete`
9. `Unload`

With the addition of these choices, you can now work with the page and the controls on the page at many different points in the page-compilation process. You see these useful page events in code examples throughout the book.

DEALING WITH POSTBACKS

When you are working with ASP.NET pages, be sure you understand the page events just listed. They are important because you place a lot of your page behavior inside these events at specific points in a page lifecycle.

In Active Server Pages 3.0, developers had their pages post to other pages within the application. ASP.NET pages typically post back to themselves to process events (such as a button-click event).

For this reason, you must differentiate between posts for the first time a page is loaded by the end user and *postbacks*. A postback is just that — a posting back to the same page. The postback contains all the form information collected on the initial page for processing if required.

Because of all the postbacks that can occur with an ASP.NET page, you want to know whether a request is the first instance for a particular page or is a postback from the same page. You can make this check by using the `IsPostBack` property of the `Page` class, as shown in the following example:

VB

```
If Page.IsPostBack = True Then
   ' Do processing
End If
```

C#

```
if (Page.IsPostBack == true) {
   // Do processing
}
```

In addition to checking against a `True` or `False` value, you can also find out whether the request is not a postback in the following manner:

VB

```
If Not Page.IsPostBack Then
   ' Do processing
End If
```

C#

```
if (!Page.IsPostBack) {
   // Do processing
}
```

CROSS-PAGE POSTING

One common feature in ASP 3.0 that is difficult to achieve in ASP.NET 1.0/1.1 is the capability to do cross-page posting. Cross-page posting enables you to submit a form (say, `Page1.aspx`) and have this form and all the control values post themselves to another page (`Page2.aspx`).

Traditionally, any page created in ASP.NET 1.0/1.1 simply posted to itself, and you handled the control values within this page instance. You could differentiate between the page's first request and any postbacks by using the `Page.IsPostBack` property, as shown here:

```
If Page.IsPostBack Then
   ' deal with control values
End If
```

Even with this capability, many developers still wanted to be able to post to another page and deal with the first page's control values on that page. This is something that is possible in ASP.NET today, and it is quite a simple process.

For an example, create a page called `Page1.aspx` that contains a simple form. Listing 1-9 shows this page.

LISTING 1-9: Page1.aspx

Available for download on Wrox.com

VB

```
<%@ Page Language="VB" %>

<!DOCTYPE html PUBLIC "-//W3C//DTD XHTML 1.1//EN"
 "http://www.w3.org/TR/xhtml11/DTD/xhtml11.dtd">

<script runat="server">
    Protected Sub Button1_Click(ByVal sender As Object,
       ByVal e As System.EventArgs)

        Label1.Text = "Hello " & TextBox1.Text & "<br />" &
```

continues

LISTING 1-9 *(continued)*

```
            "Date Selected: " & Calendar1.SelectedDate.ToShortDateString()
    End Sub
</script>

<html xmlns="http://www.w3.org/1999/xhtml">
<head runat="server">
    <title>First Page</title>
</head>
<body>
    <form id="form1" runat="server">
        Enter your name:<br />
        <asp:Textbox ID="TextBox1" Runat="server">
        </asp:Textbox>
        <p>
        When do you want to fly?<br />
        <asp:Calendar ID="Calendar1" Runat="server"></asp:Calendar></p>
        <br />
        <asp:Button ID="Button1" Runat="server" Text="Submit page to itself"
         OnClick="Button1_Click" />
        <asp:Button ID="Button2" Runat="server" Text="Submit page to Page2.aspx"
         PostBackUrl="</Page2.aspx" />
        <p>
        <asp:Label ID="Label1" Runat="server"></asp:Label></p>
    </form>
</body>
</html>
```

C#

```
<%@ Page Language="C#" %>

<script runat="server">
    protected void Button1_Click (object sender, System.EventArgs e)
    {
        Label1.Text = "Hello " + TextBox1.Text + "<br />" +
            "Date Selected: " + Calendar1.SelectedDate.ToShortDateString();
    }
</script>
```

The code from `Page1.aspx`, as shown in Listing 1-9, is quite interesting. Two buttons are shown on the page. Both buttons submit the form, but each submits the form to a different location. The first button submits the form to itself. This is the behavior that has been the default for ASP.NET 1.0/1.1. In fact, nothing is different about `Button1`. It submits to `Page1.aspx` as a postback because of the use of the `OnClick` property in the button control. A `Button1_Click` method on `Page1.aspx` handles the values that are contained within the server controls on the page.

The second button, `Button2`, works quite differently. This button does not contain an `OnClick` method as the first button did. Instead, it uses the `PostBackUrl` property. This property takes a string value that points to the location of the file to which this page should post. In this case, it is `Page2.aspx`. This means that `Page2.aspx` now receives the postback and all the values contained in the `Page1.aspx` controls. Look at the code for `Page2.aspx`, shown in Listing 1-10.

LISTING 1-10: Page2.aspx

Available for download on Wrox.com

VB

```
<%@ Page Language="VB" %>

<!DOCTYPE html PUBLIC "-//W3C//DTD XHTML 1.1//EN"
 "http://www.w3.org/TR/xhtml11/DTD/xhtml11.dtd">

<script runat="server">
    Protected Sub Page_Load(ByVal sender As Object, ByVal e As System.EventArgs)
```

```
        Dim pp_Textbox1 As TextBox
        Dim pp_Calendar1 As Calendar

        pp_Textbox1 = CType(PreviousPage.FindControl("Textbox1"), TextBox)
        pp_Calendar1 = CType(PreviousPage.FindControl("Calendar1"), Calendar)

        Label1.Text = "Hello " & pp_Textbox1.Text & "<br />" &
            "Date Selected: " & pp_Calendar1.SelectedDate.ToShortDateString()
    End Sub
</script>

<html xmlns="http://www.w3.org/1999/xhtml" >
<head runat="server">
    <title>Second Page</title>
</head>
<body>
    <form id="form1" runat="server">
        <asp:Label ID="Label1" Runat="server"></asp:Label>
    </form>
</body>
</html>
```

C#

```
<%@ Page Language="C#" %>

<!DOCTYPE html PUBLIC "-//W3C//DTD XHTML 1.1//EN"
 "http://www.w3.org/TR/xhtml11/DTD/xhtml11.dtd">

<script runat="server">
    protected void Page_Load(object sender, System.EventArgs e)
    {
        TextBox pp_Textbox1;
        Calendar pp_Calendar1;

        pp_Textbox1 = (TextBox)PreviousPage.FindControl("Textbox1");
        pp_Calendar1 = (Calendar)PreviousPage.FindControl("Calendar1");

        Label1.Text = "Hello " + pp_Textbox1.Text + "<br />" + "Date Selected: " +
           pp_Calendar1.SelectedDate.ToShortDateString();
    }
</script>
```

You have a couple of ways of getting at the values of the controls that are exposed from `Page1.aspx` from the second page. The first option is displayed in Listing 1-10. To get at a particular control's value that is carried over from the previous page, you simply create an instance of that control type and populate this instance using the `FindControl()` method from the `PreviousPage` property. The `String` value assigned to the `FindControl()` method is the `Id` value, which is used for the server control from the previous page. After this is assigned, you can work with the server control and its carried-over values just as if it had originally resided on the current page. You can see from the example that you can extract the `Text` and `SelectedDate` properties from the controls without any problem.

Another way of exposing the control values from the first page (`Page1.aspx`) is to create a `Property` for the control, as shown in Listing 1-11.

LISTING 1-11: Exposing the values of the control from a property

Available for download on Wrox.com

VB

```
<%@ Page Language="VB" %>

<!DOCTYPE html PUBLIC "-//W3C//DTD XHTML 1.1//EN"
 "http://www.w3.org/TR/xhtml11/DTD/xhtml11.dtd">

<script runat="server">
```

continues

LISTING 1-11 *(continued)*

```
    Public ReadOnly Property pp_TextBox1() As TextBox
        Get
            Return TextBox1
        End Get
    End Property

    Public ReadOnly Property pp_Calendar1() As Calendar
        Get
            Return Calendar1
        End Get
    End Property

    Protected Sub Button1_Click(ByVal sender As Object, ByVal e As System.EventArgs)
        Label1.Text = "Hello " & TextBox1.Text & "<br />" &
            "Date Selected: " & Calendar1.SelectedDate.ToShortDateString()
    End Sub
</script>
```

C#

```
<%@ Page Language="C#" %>

<!DOCTYPE html PUBLIC "-//W3C//DTD XHTML 1.1//EN"
 "http://www.w3.org/TR/xhtml11/DTD/xhtml11.dtd">

<script runat="server">
    public TextBox pp_TextBox1
    {
        get
        {
            return TextBox1;
        }
    }

    public Calendar pp_Calendar1
    {
        get
        {
            return Calendar1;
        }
    }

    protected void Button1_Click (object sender, System.EventArgs e)
    {
        Label1.Text = "Hello " + TextBox1.Text + "<br />" +
            "Date Selected: " + Calendar1.SelectedDate.ToShortDateString();
    }
</script>
```

Filename Page1b.aspx

Now that these properties are exposed on the posting page, the second page (`Page2.aspx`) can more easily work with the server control properties that are exposed from the first page. Listing 1-12 shows you how `Page2.aspx` works with these exposed properties.

LISTING 1-12: Consuming the exposed properties from the first page

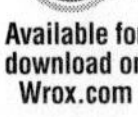

Available for download on Wrox.com

VB

```
<%@ Page Language="VB" %>
<%@ PreviousPageType VirtualPath="Page1.aspx" %>

<!DOCTYPE html PUBLIC "-//W3C//DTD XHTML 1.1//EN"
```

```
 "http://www.w3.org/TR/xhtml11/DTD/xhtml11.dtd">

<script runat="server">
    Protected Sub Page_Load(ByVal sender As Object, ByVal e As System.EventArgs)
        Label1.Text = "Hello " & PreviousPage.pp_Textbox1.Text & "<br />" &
            "Date Selected: " &
            PreviousPage.pp_Calendar1.SelectedDate.ToShortDateString()
    End Sub
</script>
```

C#

```
<%@ Page Language="C#" %>
<%@ PreviousPageType VirtualPath="Page1.aspx" %>

<!DOCTYPE html PUBLIC "-//W3C//DTD XHTML 1.1//EN"
 "http://www.w3.org/TR/xhtml11/DTD/xhtml11.dtd">

<script runat="server">
    protected void Page_Load(object sender, System.EventArgs e)
    {
        Label1.Text = "Hello " + PreviousPage.pp_TextBox1.Text + "<br />" +
           "Date Selected: " +
           PreviousPage.pp_Calendar1.SelectedDate.ToShortDateString();
    }
</script>
```

Filename Page2b.aspx

To be able to work with the properties that `Page1.aspx` exposes, you have to strongly type the `PreviousPage` property to `Page1.aspx`. To do this, you use the `PreviousPageType` directive. This directive allows you to specifically point to `Page1.aspx` with the use of the `VirtualPath` attribute. When that is in place, notice that you can see the properties that `Page1.aspx` exposes through IntelliSense from the `PreviousPage` property. This is illustrated in Figure 1-7.

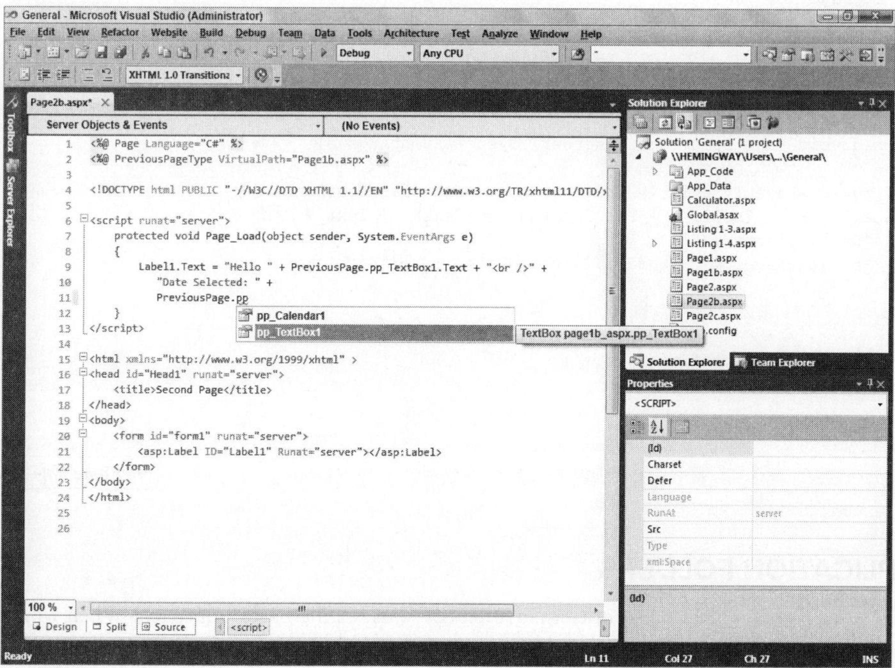

FIGURE 1-7

As you can see, working with cross-page posting is straightforward. Notice that when you are cross posting from one page to another, you are not restricted to working only with the postback on the second page. In fact, you can still create methods on `Page1.aspx` that work with the postback before moving onto `Page2.aspx`. To do this, you simply add an `OnClick` event for the button in `Page1.aspx` and a method. You also assign a value for the `PostBackUrl` property. You can then work with the postback on `Page1.aspx` and then again on `Page2.aspx`.

What happens if someone requests `Page2.aspx` before she works her way through `Page1.aspx`? Determining whether the request is coming from `Page1.aspx` or whether someone just hit `Page2.aspx` directly is actually quite easy. You can work with the request through the use of the `IsCrossPagePostBack` property that is quite similar to the `IsPostBack` property from ASP.NET 1.0/1.1. The `IsCrossPagePostBack` property enables you to check whether the request is from `Page1.aspx`. Listing 1-13 shows an example of this.

LISTING 1-13: Using the IsCrossPagePostBack property

Available for download on Wrox.com

VB

```
<%@ Page Language="VB" %>
<%@ PreviousPageType VirtualPath="Page1.aspx" %>

<!DOCTYPE html PUBLIC "-//W3C//DTD XHTML 1.1//EN"
 "http://www.w3.org/TR/xhtml11/DTD/xhtml11.dtd">

<script runat="server">
    Protected Sub Page_Load(ByVal sender As Object, ByVal e As System.EventArgs)
      If Not PreviousPage Is Nothing AndAlso PreviousPage.IsCrossPagePostBack Then
        Label1.Text = "Hello " & PreviousPage.pp_Textbox1.Text & "<br />" &
            "Date Selected: " &
            PreviousPage.pp_Calendar1.SelectedDate.ToShortDateString()
      Else
        Response.Redirect("Page1.aspx")
      End If
    End Sub
</script>
```

C#

```
<%@ Page Language="C#" %>
<%@ PreviousPageType VirtualPath="Page1.aspx" %>

<!DOCTYPE html PUBLIC "-//W3C//DTD XHTML 1.1//EN"
 "http://www.w3.org/TR/xhtml11/DTD/xhtml11.dtd">

<script runat="server">
    protected void Page_Load(object sender, System.EventArgs e)
    {
      if (PreviousPage != null && PreviousPage.IsCrossPagePostBack) {
        Label1.Text = "Hello " + PreviousPage.pp_TextBox1.Text + "<br />" +
           "Date Selected: " +
           PreviousPage.pp_Calendar1.SelectedDate.ToShortDateString();
      }
      else
      {
         Response.Redirect("Page1.aspx");
      }
    }
</script>
```

Filename Page2c.aspx

ASP.NET APPLICATION FOLDERS

When you create ASP.NET applications, notice that ASP.NET 4 uses a file-based approach. When working with ASP.NET, you can add as many files and folders as you want within your application without recompiling each and every time a new file is added to the overall solution. ASP.NET 4 includes the capability to automatically precompile your ASP.NET applications dynamically.

ASP.NET 1.0/1.1 compiled everything in your solution into a DLL. This is no longer necessary because ASP.NET applications now have a defined folder structure. By using the ASP.NET-defined folders, you can have your code automatically compiled for you, your application themes accessible throughout your application, and your globalization resources available whenever you need them. Look at each of these defined folders to see how they work. The first folder reviewed is the App_Code folder.

App_Code Folder

The App_Code folder is meant to store your classes, `.wsdl` files, and typed datasets. Any of these items stored in this folder are then automatically available to all the pages within your solution. The nice thing about the App_Code folder is that when you place something inside this folder, Visual Studio 2010 automatically detects this and compiles it if it is a class (`.vb` or `.cs`), automatically creates your XML Web service proxy class (from the `.wsdl` file), or automatically creates a typed dataset for you from your `.xsd` files. After the files are automatically compiled, these items are then instantaneously available to any of your ASP.NET pages that are in the same solution. Look at how to employ a simple class in your solution using the App_Code folder.

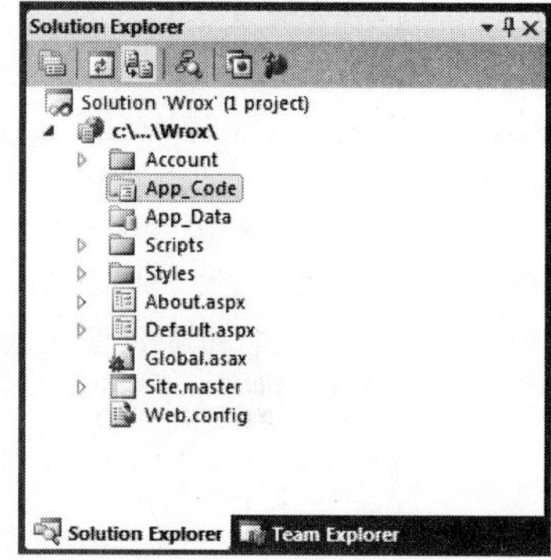

FIGURE 1-8

The first step is to create an App_Code folder. To do this, simply right-click the solution and choose Add ASP.NET Folder ⇨ App_Code. Right away, you will notice that Visual Studio 2010 treats this folder differently than the other folders in your solution. The App_Code folder is shown in a different color (gray) with a document pictured next to the folder icon. See Figure 1-8.

After the App_Code folder is in place, right-click the folder and select Add New Item. The Add New Item dialog that appears gives you a few options for the types of files that you can place within this folder. The available options include an AJAX-enabled WCF Service, a Class file, a LINQ to SQL Class, an ADO.NET Entity Data Model, an ADO.NET EntityObject Generator, a Sequence Diagram, a Text Template, a Text file, a DataSet, a Report, and a Class Diagram if you are using Visual Studio 2010. Visual Web Developer 2010 Express Edition offers only a subset of these files. For the first example, select the file of type Class and name the class `Calculator.vb` or `Calculator.cs`. Listing 1-14 shows how the `Calculator` class should appear.

LISTING 1-14: The Calculator class

Available for download on Wrox.com

VB

```
Imports Microsoft.VisualBasic

Public Class Calculator
    Public Function Add(ByVal a As Integer, ByVal b As Integer) As Integer
        Return (a + b)
    End Function
End Class
```

C#

```
using System;

public class Calculator
{
    public int Add(int a, int b)
        {
            return (a + b);
    }
}
```

Filenames Calculator.vb and Calculator.cs

What's next? Just save this file, and it is now available to use in any pages that are in your solution. To see this in action, create a simple `.aspx` page that has just a single Label server control. Listing 1-15 shows you the code to place within the `Page_Load` event to make this new class available to the page.

LISTING 1-15: An .aspx page that uses the Calculator class

Available for download on Wrox.com

```
<%@ Page Language="VB" %>

<!DOCTYPE html PUBLIC "-//W3C//DTD XHTML 1.1//EN"
 "http://www.w3.org/TR/xhtml11/DTD/xhtml11.dtd">

<script runat="server">
    Protected Sub Page_Load(ByVal sender As Object, ByVal e As System.EventArgs)
        Dim myCalc As New Calculator
        Label1.Text = myCalc.Add(12, 12)
    End Sub
</script>
```

C#

```
<%@ Page Language="C#" %>

<!DOCTYPE html PUBLIC "-//W3C//DTD XHTML 1.1//EN"
 "http://www.w3.org/TR/xhtml11/DTD/xhtml11.dtd">

<script runat="server">
    protected void Page_Load(object sender, System.EventArgs e)
    {
        Calculator myCalc = new Calculator();
        Label1.Text = myCalc.Add(12, 12).ToString();
    }
</script>
```

Filename Calculator.aspx

When you run this `.aspx` page, notice that it utilizes the `Calculator` class without any problem, with no need to compile the class before use. In fact, right after saving the `Calculator` class in your solution or moving the class to the App_Code folder, you also instantaneously receive IntelliSense capability on the methods that the class exposes (as illustrated in Figure 1-9).

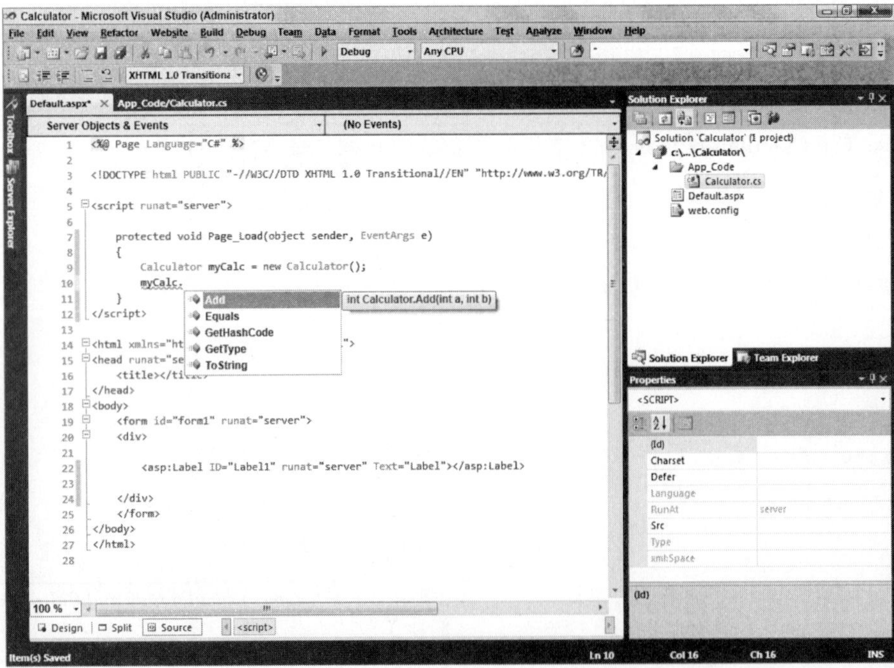

FIGURE 1-9

To see how Visual Studio 2010 works with the App_Code folder, open the `Calculator` class again in the IDE and add a `Subtract` method. Your class should now appear as shown in Listing 1-16.

LISTING 1-16: Adding a Subtract method to the Calculator class

Available for download on Wrox.com

VB

```
Imports Microsoft.VisualBasic

Public Class Calculator
    Public Function Add(ByVal a As Integer, ByVal b As Integer) As Integer
        Return (a + b)
    End Function

    Public Function Subtract(ByVal a As Integer, ByVal b As Integer) As Integer
        Return (a - b)
    End Function
End Class
```

C#

```
using System;

public class Calculator
{
    public int Add(int a, int b)
    {
            return (a + b);
    }

    public int Subtract(int a, int b)
    {
            return (a - b);
    }
}
```

Filenames Calculator.vb and Calculator.cs

After you have added the `Subtract` method to the `Calculator` class, save the file and go back to your `.aspx` page. Notice that the class has been recompiled by the IDE, and the new method is now available to your page. You see this directly in IntelliSense. Figure 1-10 shows this in action.

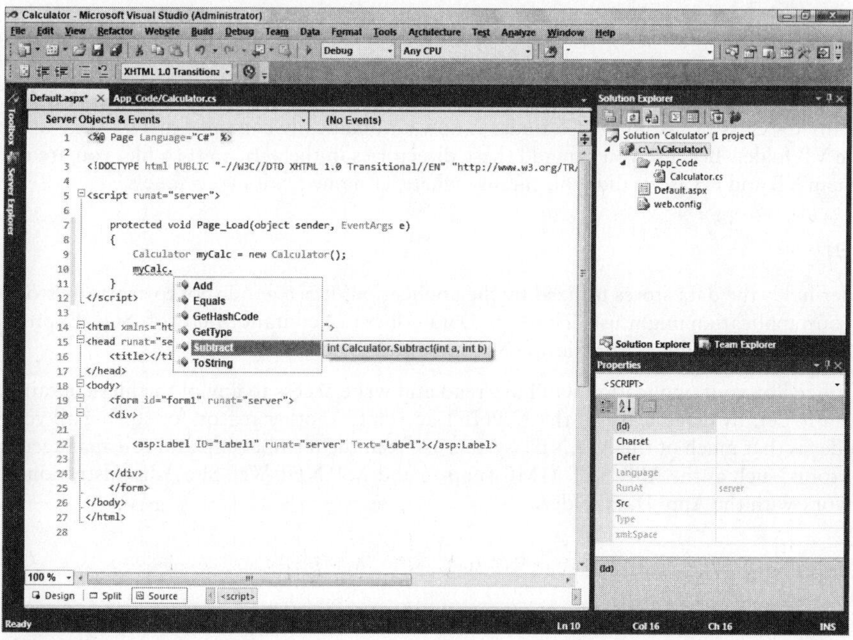

FIGURE 1-10

Everything placed in the App_Code folder is compiled into a single assembly. The class files placed within the App_Code folder are not required to use a specific language. This means that even if all the pages of the solution are written in Visual Basic 2010, the `Calculator` class in the App_Code folder of the solution can be built in C# (`Calculator.cs`).

Because all the classes contained in this folder are built into a single assembly, you *cannot* have classes of different languages sitting in the root App_Code folder, as in the following example:

```
\App_Code
   Calculator.cs
   AdvancedMath.vb
```

Having two classes made up of different languages in the App_Code folder (as shown here) causes an error to be thrown. It is impossible for the assigned compiler to work with two different languages. Therefore, to be able to work with multiple languages in your App_Code folder, you must make some changes to the folder structure and to the `web.config` file.

The first step is to add two new subfolders to the App_Code folder — a VB folder and a CS folder. This gives you the following folder structure:

```
\App_Code
   \VB
      Add.vb
   \CS
      Subtract.cs
```

This still will not correctly compile these class files into separate assemblies, at least not until you make some additions to the `web.config` file. Most likely, you do not have a `web.config` file in your solution at this moment, so add one through the Solution Explorer. After it is added, change the `<compilation>` node so that it is structured as shown in Listing 1-17.

LISTING 1-17: Structuring the web.config file so that classes in the App_Code folder can use different languages

```
<compilation>
   <codeSubDirectories>
      <add directoryName="VB"></add>
      <add directoryName="CS"></add>
   </codeSubDirectories>
</compilation>
```

Now that this is in place in your `web.config` file, you can work with each of the classes in your ASP.NET pages. In addition, any C# class placed in the CS folder is now automatically compiled just like any of the classes placed in the VB folder. Because you can add these directories in the `web.config` file, you are not required to name them VB and CS as we did; you can use whatever name tickles your fancy.

App_Data Folder

The App_Data folder holds the data stores utilized by the application. It is a good spot to centrally store all the data stores your application might use. The App_Data folder can contain Microsoft SQL Express files (`.mdf` files), Microsoft Access files (`.mdb` files), XML files, and more.

The user account utilized by your application will have read and write access to any of the files contained within the App_Data folder. By default, this is the ASPNET account. Another reason for storing all your data files in this folder is that much of the ASP.NET system — from the membership and role management systems to the GUI tools, such as the ASP.NET MMC snap-in and ASP.NET Web Site Administration Tool — is built to work with the App_Data folder.

App_Themes Folder

Themes are a way of providing a common look-and-feel to your site across every page. You implement a theme by using a `.skin` file, CSS files, and images used by the server controls of your site. All these elements can make a *theme*, which is then stored in the App_Themes folder of your solution. By storing these elements within the App_Themes folder, you ensure that all the pages within the solution can take advantage of the theme and easily apply its elements to the controls and markup of the page. Themes are discussed in great detail in Chapter 6 of this book.

App_GlobalResources Folder

Resource files are string tables that can serve as data dictionaries for your applications when these applications require changes to content based on things such as changes in culture. You can add Assembly Resource Files (`.resx`) to the App_GlobalResources folder, and they are dynamically compiled and made part of the solution for use by all your `.aspx` pages in the application. When using ASP.NET 1.0/1.1, you had to use the `resgen.exe` tool and had to compile your resource files to a `.dll` or `.exe` for use within your solution. Dealing with resource files in ASP.NET 4 is considerably easier. Simply placing your application-wide resources in this folder makes them instantly accessible. Localization is covered in detail in Chapter 32.

App_LocalResources Folder

Even if you are not interested in constructing application-wide resources using the App_GlobalResources folder, you may want resources that can be used for a single `.aspx` page. You can do this very simply by using the App_LocalResources folder.

You can add resource files that are page-specific to the App_LocalResources folder by constructing the name of the `.resx` file in the following manner:

- `Default.aspx.resx`
- `Default.aspx.fi.resx`
- `Default.aspx.ja.resx`
- `Default.aspx.en-gb.resx`

Now, the resource declarations used on the `Default.aspx` page are retrieved from the appropriate file in the App_LocalResources folder. By default, the `Default.aspx.resx` resource file is used if another match is not found. If the client is using a culture specification of `fi-FI` (Finnish), however, the `Default.aspx.fi.resx` file is used instead. Localization of local resources is covered in detail in Chapter 32.

App_WebReferences Folder

The App_WebReferences folder is a new name for the previous Web References folder that was used in versions of ASP.NET prior to ASP.NET 3.5. Now you can use the App_WebReferences folder and have automatic access to the remote Web services referenced from your application. Chapter 31 covers Web services in ASP.NET.

App_Browsers Folder

The App_Browsers folder holds `.browser` files, which are XML files used to identity the browsers making requests to the application and understanding the capabilities these browsers have. You can find a list of globally accessible `.browser` files at `C:\Windows\Microsoft.NET\Framework\v4.0.xxxxx\Config\Browsers`. In addition, if you want to change any part of these default browser definition files, just copy the appropriate `.browser` file from the Browsers folder to your application's App_Browsers folder and change the definition.

COMPILATION

You already saw how Visual Studio 2010 compiles pieces of your application as you work with them (for instance, by placing a class in the App_Code folder). The other parts of the application, such as the `.aspx` pages, can be compiled just as they were in earlier versions of ASP.NET by referencing the pages in the browser.

When an ASP.NET page is referenced in the browser for the first time, the request is passed to the ASP.NET parser that creates the class file in the language of the page. It is passed to the ASP.NET parser based on the file's extension (`.aspx`) because ASP.NET realizes that this file extension type is meant for its handling and processing. After the class file has been created, the class file is compiled into a DLL and then written to the disk of the Web server. At this point, the DLL is instantiated and processed, and an output is generated for the initial requester of the ASP.NET page. This is detailed in Figure 1-11.

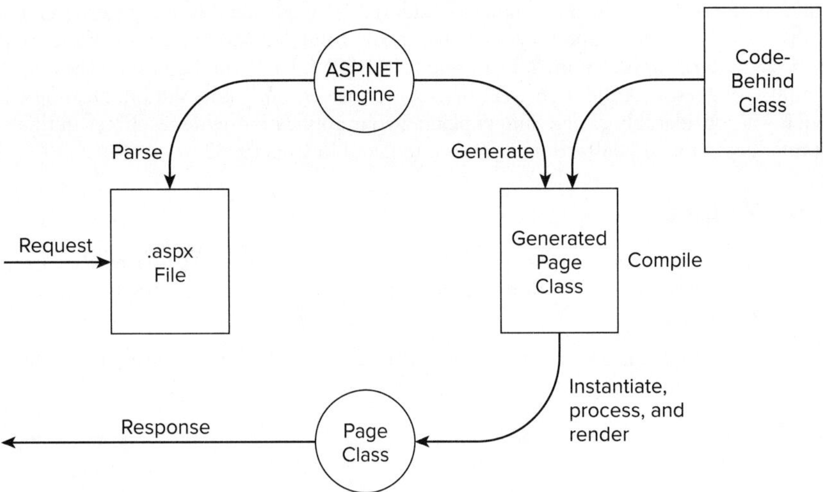

FIGURE 1-11

On the next request, great things happen. Instead of going through the entire process again for the second and respective requests, the request simply causes an instantiation of the already-created DLL, which sends out a response to the requester. This is illustrated in Figure 1-12.

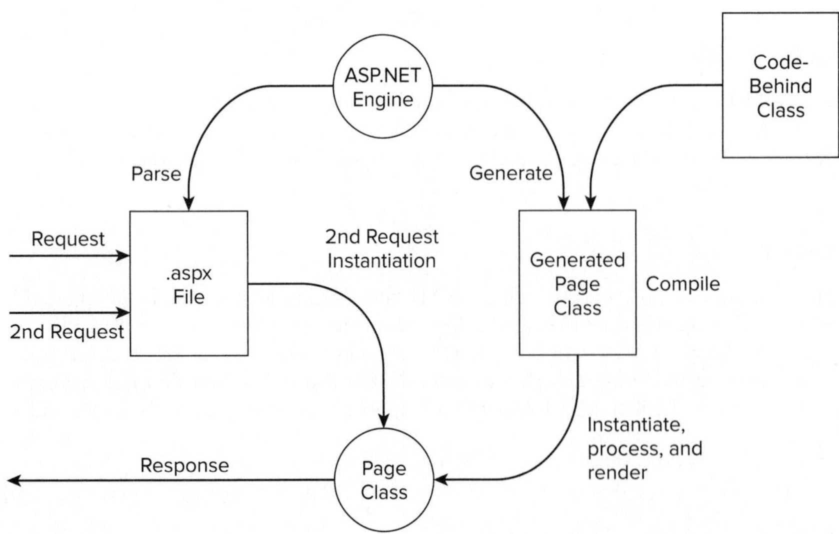

FIGURE 1-12

Because of the mechanics of this process, if you made changes to your `.aspx` code-behind pages, you found it necessary to recompile your application. This was quite a pain if you had a larger site and did not want your end users to experience the extreme lag that occurs when an `.aspx` page is referenced for the first time after compilation. Many developers, consequently, began to develop their own tools that automatically go out and hit every single page within their application to remove this first-time lag hit from the end user's browsing experience.

ASP.NET provides a few ways to precompile your entire application with a single command that you can issue through a command line. One type of compilation is referred to as *in-place precompilation*. To precompile your entire ASP.NET application, you must use the `aspnet_compiler.exe` tool that comes with ASP.NET. You navigate to the tool using the Command window. Open the Command window and navigate to `C:\Windows\Microsoft.NET\Framework\v4.0.xxxxx\`. When you are there, you can work with the `aspnet_compiler` tool. You can also get to this tool directly from the Visual Studio 2010 Command Prompt. Choose Start ➪ All Programs ➪ Microsoft Visual Studio 2010 ➪ Visual Studio Tools ➪ Visual Studio Command Prompt (2010).

After you get the command prompt, you use the `aspnet_compiler.exe` tool to perform an in-place precompilation using the following command:

```
aspnet_compiler -p "C:\Inetpub\wwwroot\WROX" -v none
```

You then get a message stating that the precompilation is successful. The other great thing about this precompilation capability is that you can also use it to find errors on any of the ASP.NET pages in your application. Because it hits each and every page, if one of the pages contains an error that won't be triggered until runtime, you get notification of the error immediately as you employ this precompilation method.

The next precompilation option is commonly referred to as *precompilation for deployment*. This outstanding capability of ASP.NET enables you to compile your application down to some DLLs, which can then be deployed to customers, partners, or elsewhere for your own use. Not only are minimal steps required to do this, but also after your application is compiled, you simply have to move around the DLL and some placeholder files for the site to work. This means that your Web site code is completely removed and placed in the DLL when deployed.

However, before you take these precompilation steps, create a folder in your root drive called, for example, Wrox. This folder is the one to which you will direct the compiler output. When it is in place, you can return to the compiler tool and give the following command:

```
aspnet_compiler -v [Application Name] -p [Physical Location] [Target]
```

Therefore, if you have an application called `ThomsonReuters` located at `C:\Websites\ThomsonReuters`, you use the following commands:

```
aspnet_compiler -v /ThomsonReuters -p C:\Websites\ThomsonReuters C:\Wrox
```

Press the Enter key, and the compiler either tells you that it has a problem with one of the command parameters or that it was successful (shown in Figure 1-13). If it was successful, you can see the output placed in the target directory.

FIGURE 1-13

In the example just shown, `-v` is a command for the virtual path of the application, which is provided by using `/ThomsonReuters`. The next command is `–p`, which is pointing to the physical path of the application.

In this case, it is `C:\Websites\ThomsonReuters`. Finally, the last bit, `C:\Wrox`, is the location of the compiler output. Table 1-9 describes some of the possible commands for the `aspnet_compiler.exe` tool.

TABLE 1-9

COMMAND	DESCRIPTION
`-m`	Specifies the full IIS metabase path of the application. If you use the `-m` command, you cannot use the `-v` or `-p` command.
`-v`	Specifies the virtual path of the application to be compiled. If you also use the `-p` command, the physical path is used to find the location of the application.
`-p`	Specifies the physical path of the application to be compiled. If this is not specified, the IIS metabase is used to find the application.
`-u`	If this command is utilized, it specifies that the application is updatable.
`-f`	Specifies to overwrite the target directory if it already exists.
`-d`	Specifies that the debug information should be excluded from the compilation process.
`[targetDir]`	Specifies the target directory where the compiled files should be placed. If this is not specified, the output files are placed in the application directory.

After compiling the application, you can go to `C:\Wrox` to see the output. Here you see all the files and the file structures that were in the original application. However, if you look at the content of one of the files, notice that the file is simply a placeholder. In the actual file, you find the following comment:

```
This is a marker file generated by the precompilation tool
and should not be deleted!
```

In fact, you find a `Code.dll` file in the bin folder where all the page code is located. Because it is in a DLL file, it provides great code obfuscation as well. From here on, all you do is move these files to another server using FTP or Windows Explorer, and you can run the entire Web application from these files. When you have an update to the application, you simply provide a new set of compiled files. Figure 1-14 shows a sample output.

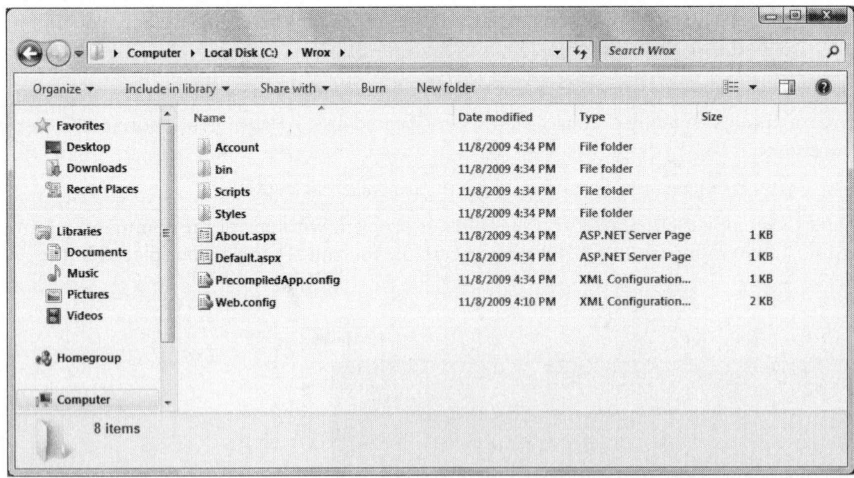

FIGURE 1-14

Note that this compilation process does not compile *every* type of Web file. In fact, it compiles only the ASP.NET-specific file types and leaves out of the compilation process the following types of files:

- HTML files
- XML files
- XSD files

- web.config files
- Text files

You cannot do much to get around this, except in the case of the HTML files and the text files. For these file types, just change the file extensions of these file types to .aspx; they are then compiled into the Code.dll like all the other ASP.NET files.

BUILD PROVIDERS

As you review the various ASP.NET folders, note that one of the more interesting folders is the App_Code folder. You can simply drop code files, XSD files, and even WSDL files directly into the folder for automatic compilation. When you drop a class file into the App_Code folder, the class can automatically be utilized by a running application. In the early days of ASP.NET, if you wanted to deploy a custom component, you had to precompile the component before being able to utilize it within your application. Now ASP.NET simply takes care of all the work that you once had to do. You do not need to perform any compilation routine.

Which file types are compiled in the App_Code folder? As with most things in ASP.NET, this is determined through settings applied in a configuration file. Listing 1-18 shows a snippet of configuration code taken from the master web.config file found in ASP.NET 4.

LISTING 1-18: Reviewing the list of build providers

```
<compilation>
   <buildProviders>
      <add extension=".aspx" type="System.Web.Compilation.PageBuildProvider" />
      <add extension=".ascx"
       type="System.Web.Compilation.UserControlBuildProvider" />
      <add extension=".master"
       type="System.Web.Compilation.MasterPageBuildProvider" />
      <add extension=".asmx"
       type="System.Web.Compilation.WebServiceBuildProvider" />
      <add extension=".ashx"
       type="System.Web.Compilation.WebHandlerBuildProvider" />
      <add extension=".soap"
       type="System.Web.Compilation.WebServiceBuildProvider" />
      <add extension=".resx" type="System.Web.Compilation.ResXBuildProvider" />
      <add extension=".resources"
       type="System.Web.Compilation.ResourcesBuildProvider" />
      <add extension=".wsdl" type="System.Web.Compilation.WsdlBuildProvider" />
      <add extension=".xsd" type="System.Web.Compilation.XsdBuildProvider" />
      <add extension=".js" type="System.Web.Compilation.ForceCopyBuildProvider" />
      <add extension=".lic"
       type="System.Web.Compilation.IgnoreFileBuildProvider" />
      <add extension=".licx"
       type="System.Web.Compilation.IgnoreFileBuildProvider" />
      <add extension=".exclude"
       type="System.Web.Compilation.IgnoreFileBuildProvider" />
      <add extension=".refresh"
       type="System.Web.Compilation.IgnoreFileBuildProvider" />
      <add extension=".edmx"
       type="System.Data.Entity.Design.AspNet.
          EntityDesignerBuildProvider" />
      <add extension=".xoml" type="System.ServiceModel.Activation.
          WorkflowServiceBuildProvider, System.WorkflowServices,
          Version=4.0.0.0, Culture=neutral,
          PublicKeyToken=31bf3856ad364e35" />
      <add extension=".svc"
       type="System.ServiceModel.Activation.ServiceBuildProvider,
          System.ServiceModel.Activation, Version=4.0.0.0,
          Culture=neutral, PublicKeyToken=31bf3856ad364e35" />
```

continues

LISTING 1-18 *(continued)*

```
        <add extension=".xamlx"
         type="System.Xaml.Hosting.XamlBuildProvider,
            System.Xaml.Hosting, Version=4.0.0.0, Culture=neutral,
            PublicKeyToken=31bf3856ad364e35" />
      </buildProviders>
   </compilation>
```

This section contains a list of build providers that can be used by two entities in your development cycle. The build provider is first used is during development when you are building your solution in Visual Studio 2010. For instance, placing a .wsdl file in the App_Code folder during development in Visual Studio causes the IDE to give you automatic access to the dynamically compiled proxy class that comes from this .wsdl file. The other entity that uses the build providers is ASP.NET itself. As stated, simply dragging and dropping a .wsdl file in the App_Code folder of a deployed application automatically gives the ASP.NET application access to the created proxy class.

A build provider is simply a class that inherits from System.Web.Compilation.BuildProvider. The <buildProviders> section in the web.config file allows you to list the build provider classes that will be utilized. The capability to dynamically compile any WSDL file is defined by the following line in the configuration file.

```
<add extension=".wsdl" type="System.Web.Compilation.WsdlBuildProvider" />
```

This means that any file utilizing the .wsdl file extension is compiled using the WsdlBuildProvider, a class that inherits from BuildProvider. Microsoft provides a set number of build providers out of the box for you to use. As you can see from the set in Listing 1-18, a number of providers are available in addition to the WsdlBuildProvider, including providers such as the XsdBuildProvider, PageBuildProvider, UserControlBuildProvider, MasterPageBuildProvider, and more. Just by looking at the names of some of these providers you can pretty much understand what they are about. The next section, however, reviews some other providers whose names might not ring a bell right away.

Using the Built-in Build Providers

Two of the providers that this section covers are the ForceCopyBuildProvider and the IgnoreFileBuildProvider, both of which are included in the default list of providers.

The ForceCopyBuildProvider is basically a provider that copies only those files for deployment that use the defined extension. (These files are not included in the compilation process.) An extension that utilizes the ForceCopyBuildProvider is shown in the predefined list in Listing 1-18. This is the .js file type (a JavaScript file extension). Any .js files are simply copied and not included in the compilation process (which makes sense for JavaScript files). You can add other file types that you want to be a part of this copy process with the command shown here:

```
<add extension=".chm" type="System.Web.Compilation.ForceCopyBuildProvider" />
```

In addition to the ForceCopyBuildProvider, you should also be aware of the IgnoreFileBuildProvider class. This provider causes the defined file type to be ignored in the deployment or compilation process. This means that any file type defined with IgnoreFileBuildProvider is simply ignored. Visual Studio will not copy, compile, or deploy any file of that type. So, if you are including Visio diagrams in your project, you can simply add the following <add> element to the web.config file to have this file type ignored. An example is presented here:

```
<add extension=".vsd" type="System.Web.Compilation.IgnoreFileBuildProvider" />
```

With this in place, all .vsd files are ignored.

Using Your Own Build Providers

In addition to using the predefined build providers out of the box, you can also take this build provider stuff one step further and construct your own custom build providers to use within your applications.

For example, suppose you wanted to construct a `Car` class dynamically based upon settings applied in a custom `.car` file that you have defined. You might do this because you are using this `.car` definition file in multiple projects or many times within the same project. Using a build provider makes defining these multiple instances of the `Car` class simpler.

Listing 1-19 presents an example of the `.car` file type.

Available for download on Wrox.com

LISTING 1-19: An example of a .car file

```
<?xml version="1.0" encoding="utf-8" ?>
<car name="EvjenCar">
  <color>Blue</color>
  <door>4</door>
  <speed>150</speed>
</car>
```

Filename Evjen.car

In the end, this XML declaration specifies the name of the class to compile as well as some values for various properties and a method. These elements make up the class. Now that you understand the structure of the `.car` file type, the next step is to construct the build provider. To accomplish this task, create a new Class Library project in the language of your choice within Visual Studio. Name the project `CarBuildProvider`. The `CarBuildProvider` contains a single class — `Car.vb` or `Car.cs`. This class inherits from the base class `BuildProvider` and overrides the `GenerateCode()` method of the `BuildProvider` class. Listing 1-20 presents this class.

Available for download on Wrox.com

LISTING 1-20: The CarBuildProvider

VB

```
Imports System.IO
Imports System.Web.Compilation
Imports System.Xml
Imports System.CodeDom

Public Class Car
    Inherits BuildProvider

    Public Overrides Sub GenerateCode(ByVal myAb As AssemblyBuilder)
        Dim carXmlDoc As XmlDocument = New XmlDocument()

        Using passedFile As Stream = Me.OpenStream()
            carXmlDoc.Load(passedFile)
        End Using

        Dim mainNode As XmlNode = carXmlDoc.SelectSingleNode("/car")
        Dim selectionMainNode As String = mainNode.Attributes("name").Value

        Dim colorNode As XmlNode = carXmlDoc.SelectSingleNode("/car/color")
        Dim selectionColorNode As String = colorNode.InnerText

        Dim doorNode As XmlNode = carXmlDoc.SelectSingleNode("/car/door")
        Dim selectionDoorNode As String = doorNode.InnerText

        Dim speedNode As XmlNode = carXmlDoc.SelectSingleNode("/car/speed")
        Dim selectionSpeedNode As String = speedNode.InnerText

        Dim ccu As CodeCompileUnit = New CodeCompileUnit()
        Dim cn As CodeNamespace = New CodeNamespace()
        Dim cmp1 As CodeMemberProperty = New CodeMemberProperty()
        Dim cmp2 As CodeMemberProperty = New CodeMemberProperty()
        Dim cmm1 As CodeMemberMethod = New CodeMemberMethod()
```

continues

LISTING 1-20 *(continued)*

```
        cn.Imports.Add(New CodeNamespaceImport("System"))

        cmp1.Name = "Color"
        cmp1.Type = New CodeTypeReference(GetType(System.String))
        cmp1.Attributes = MemberAttributes.Public
        cmp1.GetStatements.Add(New CodeSnippetExpression("return """ &
           selectionColorNode & """"))

        cmp2.Name = "Doors"
        cmp2.Type = New CodeTypeReference(GetType(System.Int32))
        cmp2.Attributes = MemberAttributes.Public
        cmp2.GetStatements.Add(New CodeSnippetExpression("return " &
           selectionDoorNode))

        cmm1.Name = "Go"
        cmm1.ReturnType = New CodeTypeReference(GetType(System.Int32))
        cmm1.Attributes = MemberAttributes.Public
        cmm1.Statements.Add(New CodeSnippetExpression("return " &
           selectionSpeedNode))

        Dim ctd As CodeTypeDeclaration = New CodeTypeDeclaration(selectionMainNode)
        ctd.Members.Add(cmp1)
        ctd.Members.Add(cmp2)
        ctd.Members.Add(cmm1)

        cn.Types.Add(ctd)
        ccu.Namespaces.Add(cn)

        myAb.AddCodeCompileUnit(Me, ccu)
    End Sub

End Class
```

C#

```
using System.IO;
using System.Web.Compilation;
using System.Xml;
using System.CodeDom;

namespace CarBuildProvider
{
    class Car : BuildProvider
    {
        public override void GenerateCode(AssemblyBuilder myAb)
        {
            XmlDocument carXmlDoc = new XmlDocument();

            using (Stream passedFile = OpenStream())
            {
                carXmlDoc.Load(passedFile);
            }
            XmlNode mainNode = carXmlDoc.SelectSingleNode("/car");
            string selectionMainNode = mainNode.Attributes["name"].Value;

            XmlNode colorNode = carXmlDoc.SelectSingleNode("/car/color");
            string selectionColorNode = colorNode.InnerText;

            XmlNode doorNode = carXmlDoc.SelectSingleNode("/car/door");
            string selectionDoorNode = doorNode.InnerText;

            XmlNode speedNode = carXmlDoc.SelectSingleNode("/car/speed");
            string selectionSpeedNode = speedNode.InnerText;
```

```
            CodeCompileUnit ccu = new CodeCompileUnit();
            CodeNamespace cn = new CodeNamespace();
            CodeMemberProperty cmp1 = new CodeMemberProperty();
            CodeMemberProperty cmp2 = new CodeMemberProperty();
            CodeMemberMethod cmm1 = new CodeMemberMethod();

            cn.Imports.Add(new CodeNamespaceImport("System"));

            cmp1.Name = "Color";
            cmp1.Type = new CodeTypeReference(typeof(string));
            cmp1.Attributes = MemberAttributes.Public;
            cmp1.GetStatements.Add(new CodeSnippetExpression("return \"" +
               selectionColorNode + "\""));

            cmp2.Name = "Doors";
            cmp2.Type = new CodeTypeReference(typeof(int));
            cmp2.Attributes = MemberAttributes.Public;
            cmp2.GetStatements.Add(new CodeSnippetExpression("return " +
               selectionDoorNode));

            cmm1.Name = "Go";
            cmm1.ReturnType = new CodeTypeReference(typeof(int));
            cmm1.Attributes = MemberAttributes.Public;
            cmm1.Statements.Add(new CodeSnippetExpression("return " +
               selectionSpeedNode));

            CodeTypeDeclaration ctd = new CodeTypeDeclaration(selectionMainNode);
            ctd.Members.Add(cmp1);
            ctd.Members.Add(cmp2);
            ctd.Members.Add(cmm1);

            cn.Types.Add(ctd);
            ccu.Namespaces.Add(cn);

            myAb.AddCodeCompileUnit(this, ccu);
        }
    }
}
```

Filenames Car.vb and Car.cs

As you look over the `GenerateCode()` method, you can see that it takes an instance of `AssemblyBuilder`. This `AssemblyBuilder` object is from the `System.Web.Compilation` namespace and, because of this, your Class Library project must have a reference to the `System.Web` assembly. With all the various objects used in this `Car` class, you also have to import in the following namespaces:

```
Imports System.IO
Imports System.Web.Compilation
Imports System.Xml
Imports System.CodeDom
```

When you have done this, one of the tasks remaining in the `GenerateCode()` method is loading the `.car` file. Because the `.car` file is using XML for its form, you are able to load the document easily using the `XmlDocument` object. From there, by using the CodeDom, you can create a class that contains two properties and a single method dynamically. The class that is generated is an abstract representation of what is defined in the provided `.car` file. On top of that, the name of the class is also dynamically driven from the value provided via the name attribute used in the main `<Car>` node of the `.car` file.

The `AssemblyBuilder` instance that is used as the input object then compiles the generated code along with everything else into an assembly.

What does it mean that your ASP.NET project has a reference to the `CarBuildProvider` assembly in its project? It means that you can create a `.car` file of your own definition and drop this file into the

App_Code folder. The second you drop the file into the App_Code folder, you have instant programmatic access to the definition specified in the file.

To see this in action, you need a reference to the build provider in either the server's `machine.config` or your application's `web.config` file. A reference is shown in Listing 1-21.

Available for download on Wrox.com

LISTING 1-21: Making a reference to the build provider in the web.config file

```
<configuration>
   <system.web>
      <compilation debug="false">
         <buildProviders>
            <add extension=".car" type="CarBuildProvider.Car"/>
         </buildProviders>
      </compilation>
   </system.web>
</configuration>
```

The `<buildProviders>` element is a child element of the `<compilation>` element. The `<buildProviders>` element takes a couple of child elements to add or remove providers. In this case, because you want to add a reference to the custom `CarBuildProvider` object, you use the `<add>` element. The `<add>` element can take two possible attributes — `extension` and `type`. You must use both of these attributes. In the `extension` attribute, you define the file extension that this build provider will be associated with. In this case, you use the `.car` file extension. This means that any file using this file extension is associated with the class defined in the `type` attribute. The `type` attribute then takes a reference to the `CarBuildProvider` class that you built — `CarBuildProvider.Car`.

With this reference in place, you can create the `.car` file that was shown earlier in Listing 1-19. Place the created `.car` file in the App_Code folder. You instantly have access to a dynamically generated class that comes from the definition provided via the file. For example, because I used `EvjenCar` as the value of the name attribute in the `<Car>` element, this will be the name of the class generated, and I will find this exact name in IntelliSense as I type in Visual Studio.

If you create an instance of the `EvjenCar` class, you also find that you have access to the properties and the method that this class exposes. This is shown in Figure 1-15.

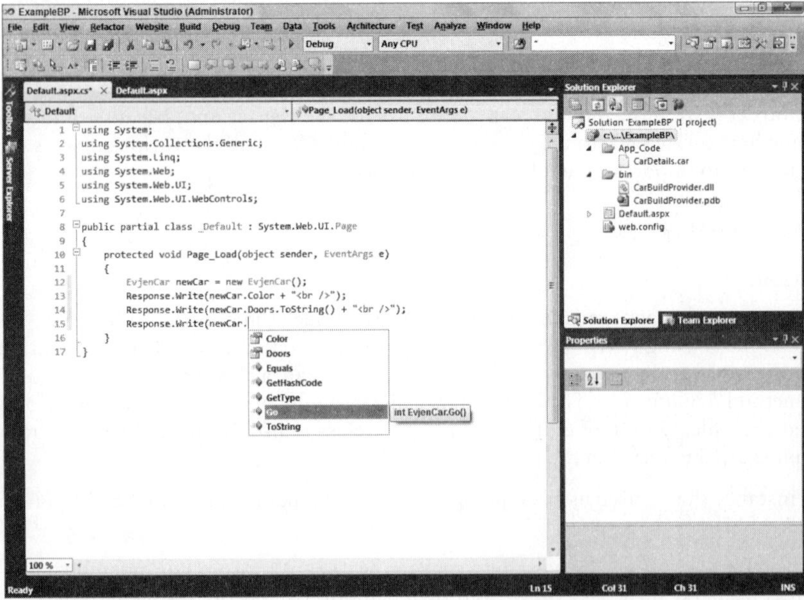

FIGURE 1-15

In addition to getting access to the properties and methods of the class, you also gain access to the values that are defined in the .car file. This is shown in Figure 1-16. The simple code example shown in Figure 1-15 is used for this browser output.

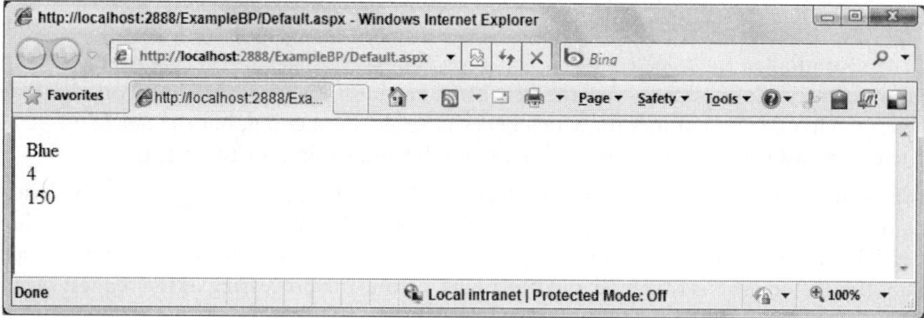

FIGURE 1-16

Although a Car class is not the most useful thing in the world, this example shows you how to take the build provider mechanics into your own hands to extend your application's capabilities.

GLOBAL.ASAX

If you add a new item to your ASP.NET application, you get the Add New Item dialog. From here, you can see that you can add a Global Application Class to your applications. This adds a Global.asax file. This file is used by the application to hold application-level events, objects, and variables — all of which are accessible application-wide. Active Server Pages developers had something similar with the Global.asa file.

Your ASP.NET applications can have only a single Global.asax file. This file supports a number of items. When it is created, you are given the following template:

```
<%@ Application Language="VB" %>

<script runat="server">

    Sub Application_Start(ByVal sender As Object, ByVal e As EventArgs)
        ' Code that runs on application startup
    End Sub

    Sub Application_End(ByVal sender As Object, ByVal e As EventArgs)
        ' Code that runs on application shutdown
    End Sub

    Sub Application_Error(ByVal sender As Object, ByVal e As EventArgs)
        ' Code that runs when an unhandled error occurs
    End Sub

    Sub Session_Start(ByVal sender As Object, ByVal e As EventArgs)
        ' Code that runs when a new session is started
    End Sub

    Sub Session_End(ByVal sender As Object, ByVal e As EventArgs)
        ' Code that runs when a session ends.
        ' Note: The Session_End event is raised only when the sessionstate mode
        ' is set to InProc in the Web.config file. If session mode is
        ' set to StateServer
        ' or SQLServer, the event is not raised.
    End Sub

</script>
```

Just as you can work with page-level events in your .aspx pages, you can work with overall application events from the Global.asax file. In addition to the events listed in this code example, the following list details some of the events you can structure inside this file:

- Application_Start: Called when the application receives its very first request. It is an ideal spot in your application to assign any application-level variables or state that must be maintained across all users.
- Session_Start: Similar to the Application_Start event except that this event is fired when an individual user accesses the application for the first time. For instance, the Application_Start event fires once when the first request comes in, which gets the application going, but the Session_Start is invoked for each end user who requests something from the application for the first time.
- Application_BeginRequest: Although it is not listed in the preceding template provided by Visual Studio 2010, the Application_BeginRequest event is triggered before each and every request that comes its way. This means that when a request comes into the server, before this request is processed, the Application_BeginRequest is triggered and dealt with before any processing of the request occurs.
- Application_AuthenticateRequest: Triggered for each request and enables you to set up custom authentications for a request.
- Application_Error: Triggered when an error is thrown anywhere in the application by any user of the application. This is an ideal spot to provide application-wide error handling or an event recording the errors to the server's event logs.
- Session_End: When running in InProc mode, this event is triggered when an end user leaves the application.
- Application_End: Triggered when the application comes to an end. This is an event that most ASP.NET developers won't use that often because ASP.NET does such a good job of closing and cleaning up any objects that are left around.

In addition to the global application events that the Global.asax file provides access to, you can also use directives in this file as you can with other ASP.NET pages. The Global.asax file allows for the following directives:

- @Application
- @Assembly
- @Import

These directives perform in the same way when they are used with other ASP.NET page types.

An example of using the Global.asax file is shown in Listing 1-22. It demonstrates how to log when the ASP.NET application domain shuts down. When the ASP.NET application domain shuts down, the ASP.NET application abruptly comes to an end. Therefore, you should place any logging code in the Application_End method of the Global.asax file.

LISTING 1-22: Using the Application_End event in the Global.asax file

Available for download on Wrox.com

VB

```
<%@ Application Language="VB" %>
<%@ Import Namespace="System.Reflection" %>
<%@ Import Namespace="System.Diagnostics" %>

<script runat="server">

    Sub Application_End(ByVal sender As Object, ByVal e As EventArgs)
        Dim MyRuntime As HttpRuntime =
           GetType(System.Web.HttpRuntime).InvokeMember("_theRuntime",
           BindingFlags.NonPublic Or BindingFlags.Static Or _
           BindingFlags.GetField,
           Nothing, Nothing, Nothing)

        If (MyRuntime Is Nothing) Then
            Return
```

```
            End If

            Dim shutDownMessage As String =
               CType(MyRuntime.GetType().InvokeMember("_shutDownMessage",
               BindingFlags.NonPublic Or BindingFlags.Instance Or
               BindingFlags.GetField,
               Nothing, MyRuntime, Nothing), System.String)

            Dim shutDownStack As String =
               CType(MyRuntime.GetType().InvokeMember("_shutDownStack",
               BindingFlags.NonPublic Or BindingFlags.Instance Or
               BindingFlags.GetField,
               Nothing, MyRuntime, Nothing), System.String)

            If (Not EventLog.SourceExists(".NET Runtime")) Then
                EventLog.CreateEventSource(".NET Runtime", "Application")
            End If

            Dim logEntry As EventLog = New EventLog()
            logEntry.Source = ".NET Runtime"
            logEntry.WriteEntry(String.Format(
               "shutDownMessage={0}\r\n\r\n_shutDownStack={1}",
               shutDownMessage, shutDownStack), EventLogEntryType.Error)
        End Sub

    </script>
```

C#

```
    <%@ Application Language="C#" %>
    <%@ Import Namespace="System.Reflection" %>
    <%@ Import Namespace="System.Diagnostics" %>

    <script runat="server">

        void Application_End(object sender, EventArgs e)
        {
            HttpRuntime runtime =

    (HttpRuntime)typeof(System.Web.HttpRuntime).InvokeMember("_theRuntime",
               BindingFlags.NonPublic | BindingFlags.Static |
    BindingFlags.GetField,
               null, null, null);

            if (runtime == null)
            {
                return;
            }

            string shutDownMessage =
               (string)runtime.GetType().InvokeMember("_shutDownMessage",
               BindingFlags.NonPublic | BindingFlags.Instance | BindingFlags.GetField,
               null, runtime, null);

            string shutDownStack =
               (string)runtime.GetType().InvokeMember("_shutDownStack",
               BindingFlags.NonPublic | BindingFlags.Instance | BindingFlags.GetField,
               null, runtime, null);

            if (!EventLog.SourceExists(".NET Runtime"))
            {
                EventLog.CreateEventSource(".NET Runtime", "Application");
            }
```

continues

LISTING 1-22 *(continued)*

```
            EventLog logEntry = new EventLog();
            logEntry.Source = ".NET Runtime";
            logEntry.WriteEntry(String.Format("\r\n\r\n_" +
               "shutDownMessage={0}\r\n\r\n_shutDownStack={1}",
               shutDownMessage, shutDownStack), EventLogEntryType.Error);
    }

</script>
```

With this code in place in your `Global.asax` file, start your ASP.NET application. Next, do something to cause the application to restart. You could, for example, make a change to the `web.config` file while the application is running. This triggers the `Application_End` event, and you see the following addition (shown in Figure 1-17) to the event log.

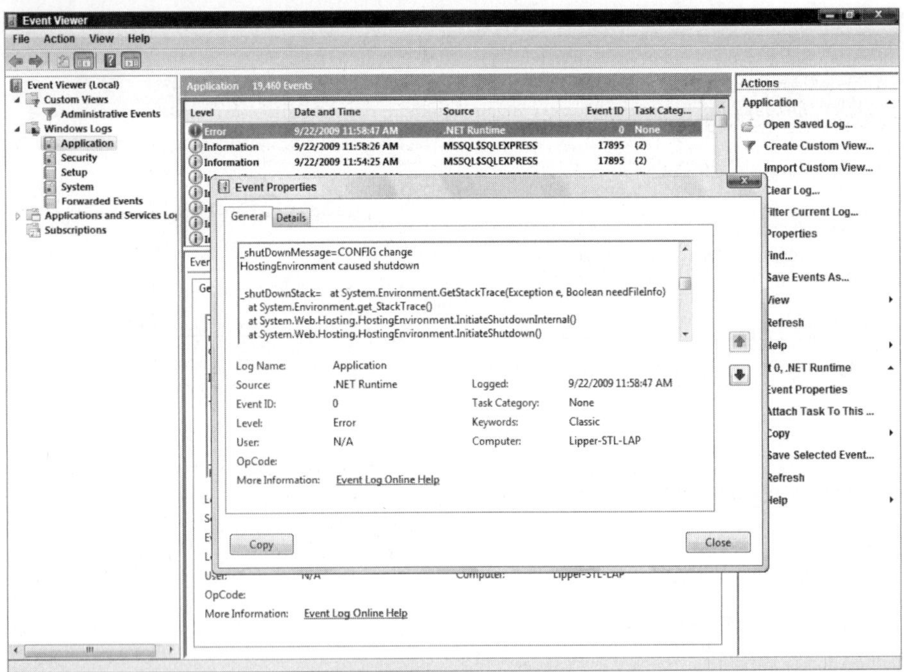

FIGURE 1-17

WORKING WITH CLASSES THROUGH VISUAL STUDIO 2010

So far, this chapter has shown you how to work with classes within your ASP.NET projects. In constructing and working with classes, you will find that Visual Studio 2010 is quite helpful. One particularly useful item is the class designer file. The class designer file has an extension of `.cd` and gives you a visual way to view your class, as well as all the available methods, properties, and other class items it contains.

To see this designer in action, create a new Class Library project in the language of your choice. This project has a single class file, `Class1.vb` or `.cs`. Delete this file and create a new class file called `Calculator.vb` or `.cs`, depending on the language you are using. From here, complete the class by creating a simple `Add()` and `Subtract()` method. Each of these methods takes in two parameters (of type `Integer`) and returns a single `Integer` with the appropriate calculation performed.

After you have the `Calculator` class in place, the easiest way to create your class designer file for this particular class is to right-click on the `Calculator.vb` file directly in the Solution Explorer and select View Class Diagram from the menu. This creates a `ClassDiagram1.cd` file in your solution.

Figure 1-18 presents the visual file, `ClassDiagram1.cd`.

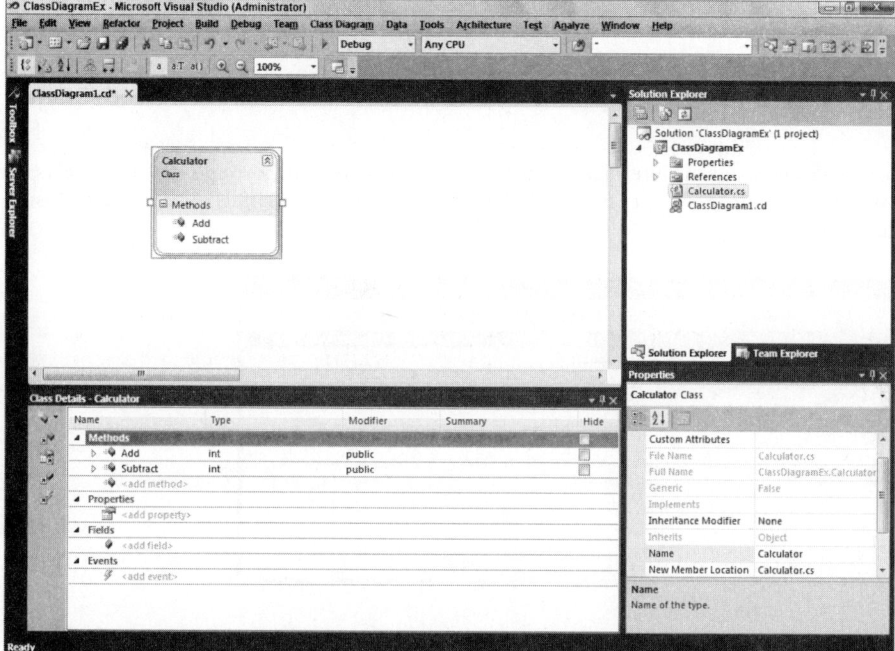

FIGURE 1-18

The new class designer file gives you a design view of your class. In the document window of Visual Studio, you see a visual representation of the `Calculator` class. The class is represented in a box and provides the name of the class, as well as two available methods that are exposed by the class. Because of the simplicity of this class, the details provided in the visual view are limited.

You can add additional classes to this diagram simply by dragging and dropping class files onto the design surface. You can then arrange the class files on the design surface as you want. A connection is in place for classes that are inherited from other class files or classes that derive from an interface or abstract class. In fact, you can extract an interface from the class you just created directly in the class designer by right-clicking on the Calculator class box and selecting Refactor ⇨ Extract Interface from the provided menu (if you are working with C#). This launches the Extract Interface dialog (shown in Figure 1-19) that enables you to customize the interface creation.

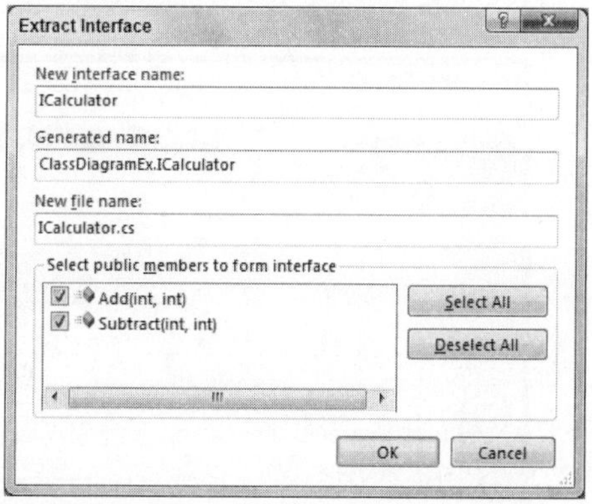

FIGURE 1-19

After you click OK, the `ICalculator` interface is created and is then visually represented in the class diagram file, as illustrated in Figure 1-20.

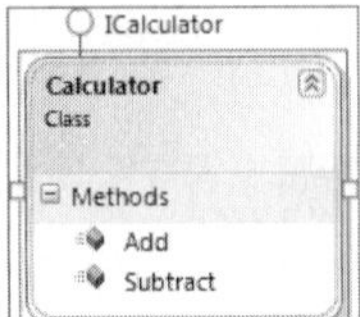

FIGURE 1-20

In addition to creating items such as interfaces on-the-fly, you can also modify your `Calculator` class by adding additional methods, properties, events, and more through the Class Details pane found in Visual Studio (see Figure 1-21).

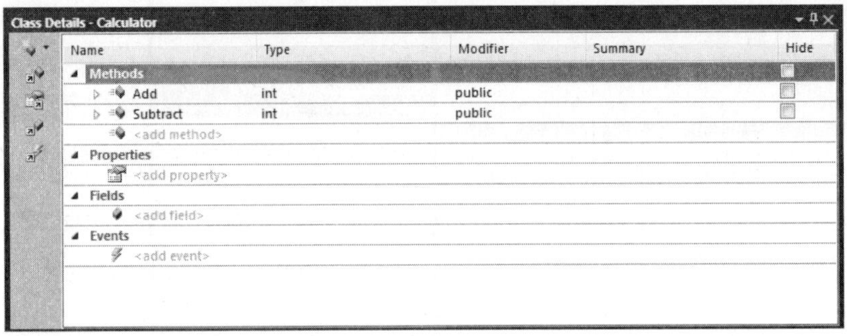

FIGURE 1-21

From this view of the class, you can directly add any additional methods, properties, fields, or events without directly typing code in your class file. When you enter these items in the Class Details view, Visual Studio generates the code for you on your behalf. For an example of this, add the additional `Multiply()` and `Divide()` methods that the `Calculator` class needs. Expanding the plus sign next to these methods shows the parameters needed in the signature. This is where you add the required `a` and `b` parameters. When you have finished, your Class Details screen should appear as shown in Figure 1-22.

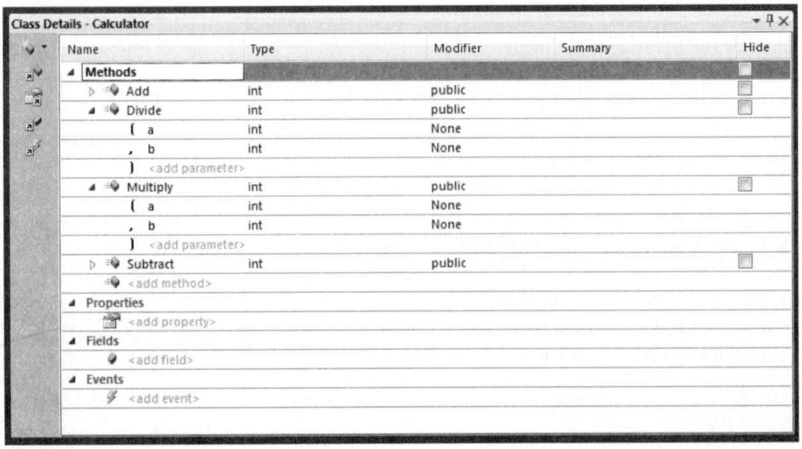

FIGURE 1-22

After you have added new `Multiply()` and `Divide()` methods and the required parameters, you see that the code in the `Calculator` class has changed to indicate these new methods are present. When the framework of the method is in place, you also see that the class has not been implemented in any fashion. The C# version of the `Multiply()` and `Divide()` methods created by Visual Studio is presented in Listing 1-23.

LISTING 1-23: The framework provided by Visual Studio's class designer

```
public int Multiply(int a, int b)
{
   throw new System.NotImplementedException();
}

public int Divide(int a, int b)
{
   throw new System.NotImplementedException();
}
```

The new class designer files give you a powerful way to view and understand your classes better — sometimes a picture really is worth a thousand words. One interesting last point on the `.cd` file is that Visual Studio is really doing all the work with this file. If you open the `ClassDesigner1.cd` file in Notepad, you see the results presented in Listing 1-24.

LISTING 1-24: The real ClassDesigner1.cd file as it appears in Notepad

```
<?xml version="1.0" encoding="utf-8"?>
<ClassDiagram MajorVersion="1" MinorVersion="1">
  <Class Name="ClassDiagramEx.Calculator">
    <Position X="1.25" Y="0.75" Width="1.5" />
    <TypeIdentifier>
      <HashCode>AAIAAAAAAQAAAAAAAAADAAAAAAAAAAAAAAAAAAAAAAA=</HashCode>
      <FileName>Calculator.cs</FileName>
    </TypeIdentifier>
    <Lollipop Position="0.2" />
  </Class>
  <Font Name="Segoe UI" Size="8.25" />
</ClassDiagram>
```

As you can see, it is a rather simple XML file that defines the locations of the class and the items connected to the class.

SUMMARY

This chapter covered a lot of ground. It discussed some of the issues concerning ASP.NET applications as a whole and the choices you have when building and deploying these new applications. With the help of Visual Studio 2010, you have options about which Web server to use when building your application and whether to work locally or remotely through the built-in FTP capabilities.

ASP.NET 4 and Visual Studio 2010 make it easy to build your pages using an inline coding model or to select a code-behind model that is simpler to use and easier to deploy than in the past. You also learned about the cross-posting capabilities and the fixed folders that ASP.NET 4 has incorporated to make your life easier. These folders make their resources available dynamically with no work on your part. You saw some of the outstanding compilation options that are at your disposal. Finally, you looked at ways in which Visual Studio 2010 makes it easy to work with the classes of your project.

As you worked through some of the examples, you may have been thinking, "WOW!" But wait . . . there's plenty more to come!

ASP.NET Server Controls and Client-Side Scripts

WHAT'S IN THIS CHAPTER?

- Building ASP.NET pages with server controls
- Working with HTML server controls
- Identifying server controls
- Modifying server controls with JavaScript

As discussed in the previous chapter, ASP.NET evolved from Microsoft's earlier Web technology called Active Server Pages (referred to as *ASP* then and *classic ASP* today). This model was completely different from today's ASP.NET. Classic ASP used interpreted languages to accomplish the construction of the final HTML document before it was sent to the browser. ASP.NET, on the other hand, uses true compiled languages to accomplish the same task. The idea of building Web pages based on objects in a compiled environment is one of the main focuses of this chapter.

This chapter looks at how to use a particular type of object in ASP.NET pages called a *server control* and how you can profit from using this control. We also introduce a particular type of server control — the HTML server control. The chapter also demonstrates how you can use JavaScript in ASP.NET pages to modify the behavior of server controls.

The rest of this chapter shows you how to use and manipulate server controls, both visually and programmatically, to help with the creation of your ASP.NET pages.

ASP.NET SERVER CONTROLS

In the past, one of the difficulties of working with classic ASP was that you were completely in charge of the entire HTML output from the browser by virtue of the server-side code you wrote. Although this might seem ideal, it created a problem because each browser interpreted the HTML given to it in a slightly different manner.

The two main browsers out there at the time were Microsoft's Internet Explorer and Netscape Navigator. This meant that not only did developers have to be cognizant of the browser type to which they were outputting HTML, but they also had to take into account which versions of those particular browsers might be making a request to their application. Some developers resolved the issue by creating two separate applications. When an end user made an initial request to the application, the code made a browser check to see what browser type was making the request. Then, the ASP page would redirect the request down one path for an IE user or down another path for a Netscape user.

Because requests came from so many different versions of the same browser, the developer often designed for the lowest possible version that might be used to visit the site. Essentially, everyone lost out by using the lowest common denominator as the target. This technique ensured that the page was rendered properly in most browsers making a request, but it also forced the developer to dumb-down his application. If applications were always built for the lowest common denominator, the developer could never take advantage of some of the more advanced features offered by newer browser versions.

ASP.NET server controls overcome these obstacles. When using the server controls provided by ASP.NET, you are not specifying the HTML to be output from your server-side code. Rather, you are specifying the functionality you want to see in the browser and letting ASP.NET decide on the output to be sent to the browser.

When a request comes in, ASP.NET examines the request to see which browser type is making the request, as well as the version of the browser, and then it produces HTML output specific to that browser. This process is accomplished by processing a User Agent header retrieved from the HTTP Request to *sniff* the browser. This means that you can now build for the best browsers out there without worrying about whether features will work in the browsers making requests to your applications. Because of the previously described capabilities, you will often hear these controls referred to as *smart controls*.

Types of Server Controls

ASP.NET provides two distinct types of server controls — HTML server controls and Web server controls. Each type of control is quite different and, as you work with ASP.NET, you will see that much of the focus is on the Web server controls. This does not mean that HTML server controls have no value. They do provide you with many capabilities — some that Web server controls do not give you.

You might be asking yourself which is the better control type to use. The answer is that it really depends on what you are trying to achieve. HTML server controls map to specific HTML elements. You can place an `HtmlTable` server control on your ASP.NET page that works dynamically with a `<table>` element. On the other hand, Web server controls map to specific functionality that you want on your ASP.NET pages. This means an `<asp:Panel>` control might use a `<table>` or another element altogether — it really depends on the capability of the browser making the request.

Table 2-1 provides a summary of information on when to use HTML server controls and when to use Web server controls.

TABLE 2-1

CONTROL TYPE	WHEN TO USE THIS CONTROL TYPE
HTML Server	When converting traditional ASP 3.0 Web pages to ASP.NET Web pages and speed of completion is a concern. It is a lot easier to change your HTML elements to HTML server controls than it is to change them to Web server controls. When you prefer a more HTML-type programming model. When you want to explicitly control the code that is generated for the browser. Though, simply using ASP.NET MVC for this (covered in Chapter 27) might be a better answer.
Web Server	When you require a richer set of functionality to perform complicated page requirements. When you are developing Web pages that will be viewed by a multitude of browser types and that require different code based upon these types. When you prefer a more Visual Basic–type programming model that is based on the use of controls and control properties.

Of course, some developers like to separate certain controls from the rest and place them in their own categories. For instance, you may see references to the following types of controls:

- **List controls:** These control types allow data to be bound to them for display purposes of some kind.
- **Rich controls:** Controls, such as the Calendar control, that display richer content and capabilities than other controls.

- **Validation controls:** Controls that interact with other form controls to validate the data that they contain.
- **User controls:** These are not really controls, but page templates that you can work with as you would a server control on your ASP.NET page.
- **Custom controls:** Controls that you build yourself and use in the same manner as the supplied ASP.NET server controls that come with the default install of ASP.NET 4.

When you are deciding between HTML server controls and Web server controls, remember that no hard and fast rules exist about which type to use. You might find yourself working with one control type more than another, but certain features are available in one control type that might not be available in the other. If you are trying to accomplish a specific task and you do not see a solution with the control type you are using, look at the other control type because it may very well hold the answer. Also, realize that you can mix and match these control types. Nothing says that you cannot use both HTML server controls and Web server controls on the same page or within the same application.

Building with Server Controls

You have a couple of ways to use server controls to construct your ASP.NET pages. You can actually use tools that are specifically designed to work with ASP.NET 4 that enable you to visually drag and drop controls onto a design surface and manipulate the behavior of the control. You can also work with server controls directly through code input.

Working with Server Controls on a Design Surface

Visual Studio 2010 enables you to visually create an ASP.NET page by dragging and dropping visual controls onto a design surface. You can get to this visual design option by clicking the Design tab at the bottom of the IDE when viewing your ASP.NET page. You can also show the Design view and the Source code view in the same document window. This is a feature available in Visual Studio 2008 and Visual Studio 2010. When the Design view is present, you can place the cursor on the page in the location where you want the control to appear and then double-click the control you want in the Toolbox window of Visual Studio. Unlike the 2002 and 2003 versions of Visual Studio, Visual Studio 2010 does a really good job of not touching your code when switching between the Design and Source tabs.

In the Design view of your page, you can highlight a control and the properties for the control appear in the Properties window. For example, Figure 2-1 shows a Button control selected in the design panel and its properties are displayed in the Properties window on the lower right.

Changing the properties in the window changes the appearance or behavior of the highlighted control. Because all controls inherit from a specific base class (`WebControl`), you can also highlight multiple controls at the same time and change the base properties of all the controls at once. You do this by holding down the Ctrl key as you make your control selections.

Coding Server Controls

You also can work from the code page directly. Because many developers prefer this, it is the default when you first create your ASP.NET page. Hand-coding your own ASP.NET pages may seem to be a slower approach than simply dragging and dropping controls onto a design surface, but it isn't as slow as you might think. You get plenty of assistance in coding your applications from Visual Studio 2010. As you start typing in Visual Studio, the IntelliSense features kick in and help you with code auto-completion. Figure 2-2, for example, shows an IntelliSense drop-down list of possible code completion statements that appeared as the code was typed.

The IntelliSense focus is on the most commonly used attribute or statement for the control or piece of code that you are working with. Using IntelliSense effectively as you work is a great way to code with great speed.

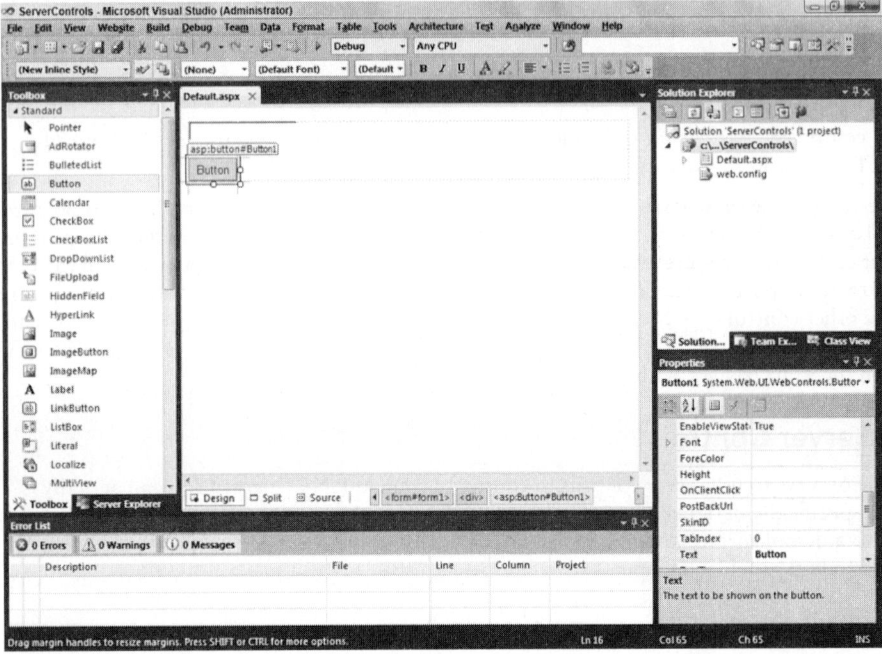

FIGURE 2-1

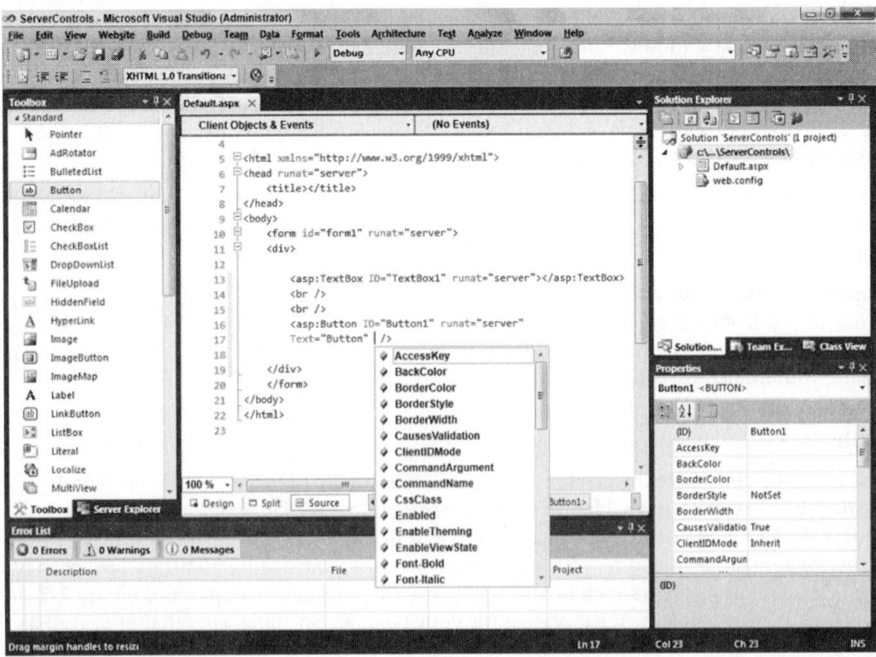

FIGURE 2-2

As with Design view, the Source view of your page lets you drag and drop controls from the Toolbox onto the code page itself. For example, dragging and dropping a TextBox control onto the code page produces the same results as dropping it on the design page:

```
<asp:TextBox ID="TextBox1" Runat="server"></asp:TextBox>
```

You can also highlight a control in Source view or simply place your cursor in the code statement of the control, and the Properties window displays the properties of the control. Now, you can apply properties directly in the Properties window of Visual Studio, and these properties are dynamically added to the code of your control.

Working with Server Control Events

As discussed in Chapter 1, ASP.NET uses more of a traditional Visual Basic event model than classic ASP. Instead of working with interpreted code, you are actually coding an event-based structure for your pages. Classic ASP used an interpreted model — when the server processed the Web page, the code of the page was interpreted line-by-line in a linear fashion where the only "event" implied was the page loading. This meant that occurrences you wanted to be initiated early in the process were placed at the top of the page.

Today, ASP.NET uses an event-driven model. Items or coding tasks are initiated only when a particular event occurs. A common event in the ASP.NET programming model is `Page_Load`, which is illustrated in Listing 2-1.

LISTING 2-1: Working with specific page events

VB

```
Protected Sub Page_Load(ByVal sender As Object, ByVal e As System.EventArgs)
   ' Code actions here
End Sub
```

C#

```
protected void Page_Load(object sender, EventArgs e)
{
   // Code actions here
}
```

Not only can you work with the overall page — as well as its properties and methods at particular moments in time through page events — but you can also work with the server controls contained on the page through particular control events. For example, one common event for a button on a form is `Button_Click`, which is illustrated in Listing 2-2.

LISTING 2-2: Working with a Button Click event

VB

```
Protected Sub Button1_Click(ByVal sender As Object, ByVal e As System.EventArgs)
   ' Code actions here
End Sub
```

C#

```
protected void Button1_Click(object sender, EventArgs e)
{
   // Code actions here
}
```

The event shown in Listing 2-2 is fired only when the end user actually clicks the button on the form that has an `OnClick` attribute value of `Button1_Click`. Therefore, not only does the event handler exist in the server-side code of the ASP.NET page, but that handler is also hooked up using the `OnClick` property of the server control in the associated ASP.NET page markup, as illustrated in the following code:

```
<asp:Button ID="Button1" Runat="server" Text="Button" OnClick="Button1_Click" />
```

How do you fire these events for server controls? You have a couple of ways to go about it. The first way is to pull up your ASP.NET page in the Design view and double-click the control for which you want to create a server-side event. For instance, double-clicking a Button server control in Design view creates the structure of the `Button1_Click` event within your server-side code, whether the code is in a code-behind file or inline. This creates a stub handler for that server control's most popular event.

With that said, be aware that a considerable number of additional events are available to the Button control that you cannot get at by double-clicking the control. To access them, from any of the views within the IDE, choose the control from the Properties dialog. Then you find a lightning bolt icon that provides you a list of all the control's events. From here, you simply can double-click the event you are interested in, and Visual Studio creates the stub of the function you need. Figure 2-3 shows the event list displayed. You might, for example, want to work with the Button control's `PreRender` event rather than its `Click` event. The handler for the event you choose is placed in your server-side code.

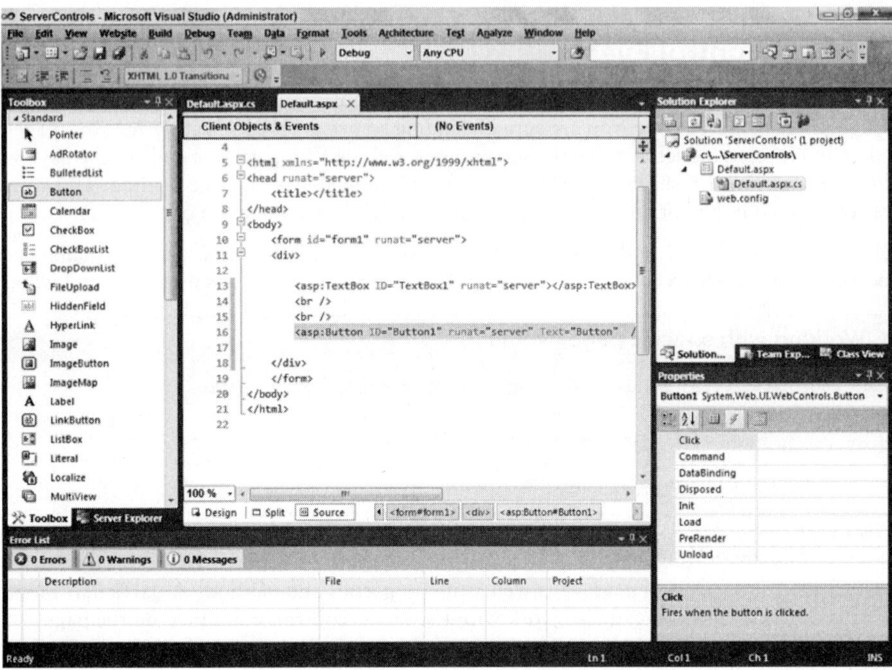

FIGURE 2-3

After you have an event structure in place, you can program specific actions that you want to occur when the event is fired.

APPLYING STYLES TO SERVER CONTROLS

More often than not, you want to change the default style (which is basically no style) to the server controls you implement in your applications. You most likely want to build your Web applications so that they reflect your own look-and-feel. One way to customize the appearance of the controls in your pages is to change the controls' properties.

As stated earlier in this chapter, to get at the properties of a particular control you simply highlight the control in the Design view of the page from Visual Studio. If you are working from the Source view, place the cursor in the code of the control. The properties presented in the Properties window allow you to control the appearance and behavior of the selected control.

Examining the Controls' Common Properties

Many of the default server controls that come with ASP.NET 4 are derived from the `WebControl` class and share similar properties that enable you to alter their appearance and behavior. Not all the derived controls use all the available properties (although many are implemented). Another important point is that not all server controls are implemented from the `WebControl` class. For instance, the Literal, PlaceHolder, Repeater, and XML server controls do not derive from the `WebControl` base class, but instead the `Control` class.

HTML server controls also do not derive from the `WebControl` base class because they are more focused on the set attributes of particular HTML elements. Table 2-2 lists the common properties the server controls share.

TABLE 2-2

PROPERTY	DESCRIPTION
`AccessKey`	Enables you to assign a character to be associated with the Alt key so that the end user can activate the control using quick-keys on the keyboard. For instance, you can assign a Button control an `AccessKey` property value of `K`. Now, instead of clicking the button on the ASP.NET page (using a pointer controlled by the mouse), the end user can simply press Alt + K.
`Attributes`	Enables you to define additional attributes for a Web server control that are not defined by a public property.
`BackColor`	Controls the color shown behind the control's layout on the ASP.NET page.
`BorderColor`	Assigns a color that is shown around the physical edge of the server control.
`BorderWidth`	Assigns a value to the width of the line that makes up the border of the control. Placing a number as the value assigns the number as a pixel-width of the border. The default border color is black if the `BorderColor` property is not used in conjunction with the `BorderWidth` property setting.
`BorderStyle`	Enables you to assign the design of the border that is placed around the server control. By default, the border is created as a straight line, but a number of different styles can be used for your borders. Other possible values for the `BorderStyle` property include `Dotted, Dashed, Solid, Double, Groove, Ridge, Inset,` and `Outset.`
`ClientIDMode`	Allows you to get or set the algorithm that is used to create the value of the `ClientID` property.
`CssClass`	Assigns a custom CSS (Cascading Style Sheet) class to the control.
`Enabled`	Enables you to turn off the functionality of the control by setting the value of this property to `False`. By default, the `Enabled` property is set to `True`.
`EnableTheming`	Enables you to turn on theming capabilities for the selected server control. The default value is `True`.
`EnableViewState`	Enables you to specify whether view state should be persisted for this control.
`Font`	Sets the font for all the text that appears anywhere in the control.
`ForeColor`	Sets the color of all the text that appears anywhere in the control.
`Height`	Sets the height of the control.
`SkinID`	Sets the skin to use when theming the control.
`Style`	Enables you to apply CSS styles to the control.
`TabIndex`	Sets the control's tab position in the ASP.NET page. This property works in conjunction with other controls on the page.
`ToolTip`	Assigns text that appears in a yellow box in the browser when a mouse pointer is held over the control for a short length of time. This can be used to add more instructions for the end user.
`Width`	Sets the width of the control.

You can see these common properties in many of the server controls you work with. Some of the properties of the `WebControl` class presented here work directly with the theming system built into ASP.NET such as the `EnableTheming` and `SkinID` properties. These properties are covered in more detail in Chapter 6. You also see additional properties that are specific to the control you are viewing. Learning about the properties from the preceding table enables you to quickly work with Web server controls and to modify them to your needs.

Next, look at some additional methods of customizing the look-and-feel of your server controls.

Changing Styles Using Cascading Style Sheets

One method of changing the look-and-feel of specific elements on your ASP.NET page is to apply a *style* to the element. The most rudimentary method of applying a defined look-and-feel to your page elements is to use various style-changing HTML elements such as `<font>`, `<b>`, and `<i>` directly.

All ASP.NET developers should have a good understanding of HTML. For more information on HTML, please read Wrox's Beginning Web Programming with HTML, XHTML, and CSS *(Wiley Publishing, Inc.; ISBN 978-0470-25931-3). You can also learn more about HTML and CSS design in ASP.NET by looking at Chapter 17 of this book.*

Using various HTML elements, you can change the appearance of many items contained on your pages. For instance, you can change a string's style as follows:

```
<font face="verdana">Pork chops and applesauce</font>
```

You can go through an entire application and change the style of page elements using any of the appropriate HTML elements. You will quickly find that this method works, but it is tough to maintain. To make any global style changes to your application, this method requires that you go through your application line-by-line to change each item individually. This can get cumbersome very fast!

Besides applying HTML elements to items to change their style, you can use another method known as *Cascading Style Sheets* (CSS). This alternative, but greatly preferred, styling technique allows you to assign formatting properties to HTML tags throughout your document in a couple of different ways. One way is to apply these styles directly to the HTML elements in your pages using *inline styles*. The other way involves placing these styles in an external stylesheet that either can be placed directly in an ASP.NET page or kept in a separate document that is simply referenced in the ASP.NET page. You explore these methods in the following sections.

Applying Styles Directly to HTML Elements

The first method of using CSS is to apply the styles directly to the tags contained in your ASP.NET pages. For instance, you apply a style to a string, as shown in Listing 2-3.

LISTING 2-3: Applying CSS styles directly to HTML elements

```
<p style="color:blue; font-weight:bold">
   Pork chops and applesauce
</p>
```

This text string is changed by the CSS included in the <p> element so that the string appears bold and blue. Using the style attribute of the <p> element, you can change everything that appears between the opening and closing <p> elements. When the page is generated, the first style change applied is to the text between the <p> elements. In this example, the text has changed to the color blue because of the `color: blue` declaration, and then the `font-weight:bold` declaration is applied. You can separate the styling declarations using semicolons, and you can apply as many styles as you want to your elements.

Applying CSS styles in this manner presents the same problem as simply applying various HTML style elements — this is a tough structure to maintain. If styles are scattered throughout your pages, making global style changes can be rather time consuming. Putting all the styles together in a stylesheet is the best approach. A couple of methods can be used to build your stylesheets.

Working with the Visual Studio Style Builder

Visual Studio 2010 includes Style Builder, a tool that makes the building of CSS styles fairly simple. It can be quite a time saver because so many possible CSS definitions are available to you. If you are new to CSS, this tool can make all the difference.

The Visual Studio Style Builder enables you to apply CSS styles to individual elements or to construct your own stylesheets. To access the New Style tool when applying a style to a single page element, highlight the page element and then while in the Design view of the IDE, select Format ➪ New Style from the VS 2010 menu. The Style Builder is shown in Figure 2-4.

You can use the Visual Studio Style Builder to change quite a bit about your selected item. After making all the changes you want and clicking OK, you see the styles you chose applied to the selected element.

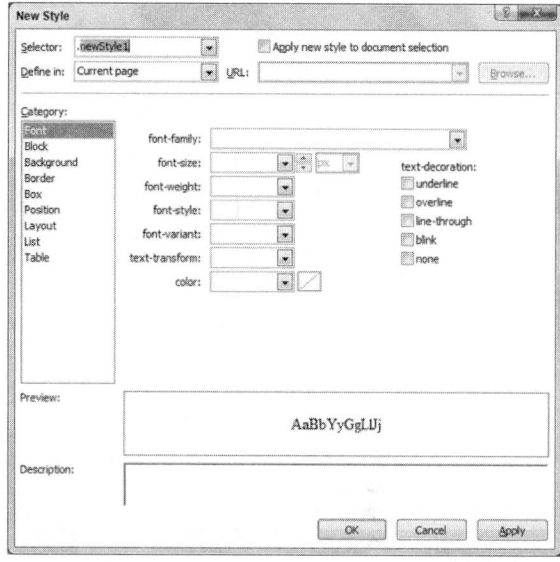

FIGURE 2-4

Creating External StyleSheets

You can use a couple of different methods to create stylesheets. The most common method is to create an *external* stylesheet — a separate stylesheet file that is referenced in the pages that employ the defined styles. To begin the creation of your external stylesheet, add a new item to your project. From the Add New Item dialog box, create a stylesheet called `StyleSheet.css`. Add the file to your project by pressing the Add button. Figure 2-5 shows the result.

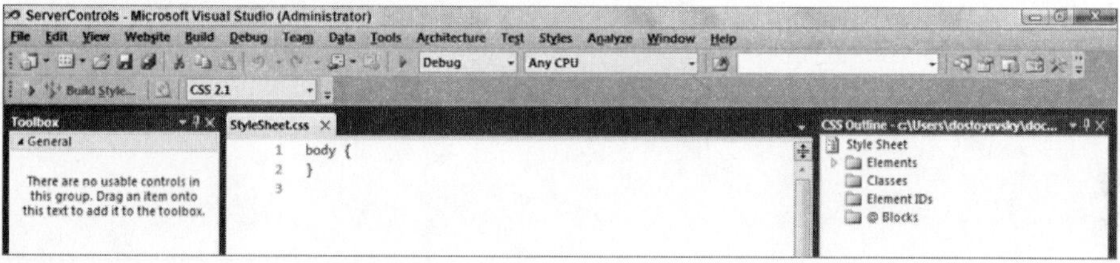

FIGURE 2-5

Using an external stylesheet within your application enables you to make global changes to the look-and-feel of your application quickly. Simply making a change at this central point cascades the change as defined by the stylesheet to your entire application.

Creating Internal Stylesheets

The second method for applying a stylesheet to a particular ASP.NET page is to bring the defined stylesheet into the actual document by creating an *internal* stylesheet. Instead of making a reference to an external stylesheet file, you bring the style definitions into the document. Note, however, that it is considered best practice to use external, rather than internal, stylesheets.

Consider using an internal stylesheet only if you are applying certain styles to a small number of pages within your application. Listing 2-4 shows the use of an internal stylesheet.

LISTING 2-4: Using an internal stylesheet

Available for download on Wrox.com

```
<%@ Page Language="VB" %>

<html xmlns="http://www.w3.org/1999/xhtml" >
<head runat="server">
```

continues

LISTING 2-4 *(continued)*

```
        <title>My ASP.NET Page</title>

        <style type="text/css">
           <!--
              body {
                 font-family: Verdana;
              }

              a:link {
                 text-decoration: none;
                 color: blue;
              }

              a:visited {
                 text-decoration: none;
                 color: blue;
              }

              a:hover {
                 text-decoration: underline;
                 color: red;
              }

           -->
        </style>

    </head>
    <body>
        <form id="form1" runat="server">
        <div>
            <a href="Default.aspx">Home</a>
        </div>
        </form>
    </body>
    </html>
```

Filename InternalStyleSheet.aspx

In this document, the internal stylesheet is set inside the opening and closing `<head>` elements. Although this is not a requirement, it is considered best practice. The stylesheet itself is placed between `<style>` tags with a type attribute defined as `text/css`.

HTML comment tags are included because not all browsers support internal stylesheets (it is generally the older browsers that do not accept them). Putting HTML comments around the style definitions hides these definitions from very old browsers. Except for the comment tags, the style definitions are handled in the same way they are done in an external stylesheet.

CSS Changes in ASP.NET 4

Prior to this release of ASP.NET, the rendered HTML from the ASP.NET server controls that you used weren't always compliant with the latest HTML standards that were out there.

An example of this is that when disabling a server control prior to ASP.NET 4, you would only need to set the `Enabled` property of the server control to `false`. This would render the control on the page but with a disabled attribute as illustrated here:

```
<span id="Label1" disabled="disabled">Hello there!</span>
```

The latest HTML standards doesn't allow for this construct. You are only allowed to use the `disabled` attribute on `<input>` elements. When working with ASP.NET 4, you will now have a property in the

<pages> element within the `web.config` file that will instruct ASP.NET what version style to use when rendering controls.

```
<pages controlRenderingCompatibilityVersion="4.0" />
```

If you have this set to `4.0`, as shown in the preceding code line, ASP.NET will now disable the control using CSS correctly as shown here:

```
<span id="Label1" class="aspNetDisabled">Hello there!</span>
```

As you can see, this time ASP.NET sets the `class` attribute rather than the `disabled` attribute. However, it is always possible to set the `controlRenderingCompatibilityVersion` value to `3.5` to revert to the old way of control rendering if you wish.

HTML SERVER CONTROLS

ASP.NET enables you to take HTML elements and, with relatively little work on your part, turn them into server-side controls. Afterward, you can use them to control the behavior and actions of elements implemented in your ASP.NET pages.

Of course, you can place any HTML you want in your pages. You have the option of using the HTML placed in the page as a server-side control. You can also find a list of HTML elements contained in the Toolbox of Visual Studio (shown in Figure 2-6).

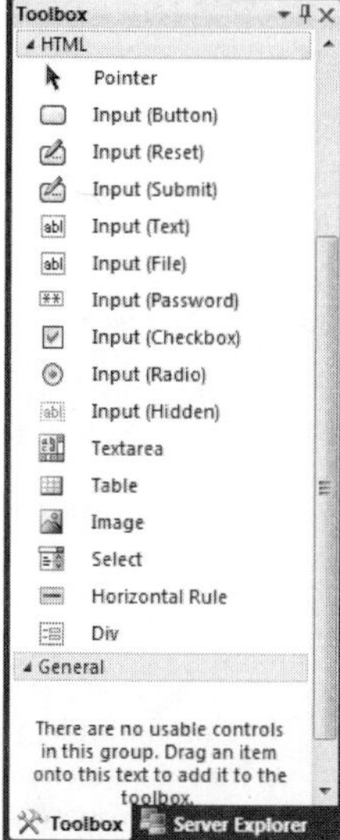

FIGURE 2-6

Dragging and dropping any of these HTML elements from the Toolbox to the Design or Source view of your ASP.NET page in the Document window simply produces the appropriate HTML element. For instance, placing an HTML Button control on your page produces the following results in your code:

```
<input id="Button1" type="button" value="button" />
```

In this state, the Button control is not a server-side control. It is simply an HTML element and nothing more. You can turn this into an HTML server control very easily. In Source view, you simply change the HTML element by adding a `runat="server"` to the control:

```
<input id="Button1" type="button" value="button" runat="server" />
```

After the element is converted to a server control (through the addition of the `runat="server"` attribute and value), you can work with the selected element on the server side as you would work with any of the Web server controls. Listing 2-5 shows an example of some HTML server controls.

Available for download on Wrox.com

LISTING 2-5: Working with HTML server controls

VB

```
<%@ Page Language="VB" %>

<script runat="server">
    Protected Sub Button1_ServerClick(ByVal sender As Object, _
       ByVal e As System.EventArgs)
        Response.Write("Hello " & Text1.Value)
    End Sub
</script>

<html xmlns="http://www.w3.org/1999/xhtml">
<head runat="server">
    <title>Using HTML Server Controls</title>
</head>
<body>
    <form id="form1" runat="server">
    <div>
        What is your name?<br />
        <input id="Text1" type="text" runat="server" />
        <input id="Button1" type="button" value="Submit" runat="server"
```

continues

LISTING 2-5 *(continued)*

```
            onserverclick="Button1_ServerClick" />
        </div>
        </form>
    </body>
    </html>
```

C#

```
<%@ Page Language="C#" %>

<script runat="server">
    protected void Button1_ServerClick(object sender, EventArgs e)
    {
        Response.Write("Hello " + Text1.Value);
    }
</script>
```

Filename HTMLServerControls.aspx

In this example, you can see two HTML server controls on the page. Both are simply typical HTML elements with the additional `runat="server"` attribute added. If you are working with HTML elements as server controls, you must include an `id` attribute so that the server control can be identified in the server-side code.

The Button control includes a reference to a server-side event using the `OnServerClick` attribute. This attribute points to the server-side event that is triggered when an end user clicks the button — in this case, `Button1_ServerClick`. Within the `Button1_ServerClick` event, the value placed in the text box is output by using the `Value` property.

Looking at the HtmlControl Base Class

All the HTML server controls use a class that is derived from the `HtmlControl` base class (fully qualified as `System.Web.UI.HtmlControls.HtmlControl`). These classes expose many properties from the control's derived class. Table 2-3 details some of the properties available from this base class. Some of these items are themselves derived from the base `Control` class.

TABLE 2-3

METHOD OR PROPERTY	DESCRIPTION
`Attributes`	Provides a collection of name/value of all the available attributes specified in the control, including custom attributes.
`Disabled`	Allows you to get or set whether the control is disabled using a Boolean value.
`EnableTheming`	Enables you, using a Boolean value, to get or set whether the control takes part in the page theming capabilities.
`EnableViewState`	Allows you to get or set a Boolean value that indicates whether the control participates in the page's view state capabilities.
`ID`	Allows you to get or set the unique identifier for the control.
`Page`	Allows you to get a reference to the `Page` object that contains the specified server control.
`Parent`	Gets a reference to the parent control in the page control hierarchy.
`Site`	Provides information about the container for which the server control belongs.
`SkinID`	When the `EnableTheming` property is set to `True`, the `SkinID` property specifies the named skin that should be used in setting a theme.
`Style`	Makes references to the CSS style collection that applies to the specified control.
`TagName`	Provides the name of the element that is generated from the specified control.
`Visible`	Specifies whether the control is visible (rendered) on the generated page.

You can find a more comprehensive list in the SDK.

Looking at the HtmlContainerControl Class

The `HtmlControl` base class is used for those HTML classes that are focused on HTML elements that can be contained within a single node. For instance, the `<img>`, `<input>`, and `<link>` elements work from classes derived from the `HtmlControl` class.

Other HTML elements such as `<a>`, `<form>`, and `<select>`, require an opening and closing set of tags. These elements use classes that are derived from the `HtmlContainerControl` class — a class specifically designed to work with HTML elements that require a closing tag.

Because the `HtmlContainerControl` class is derived from the `HtmlControl` class, you have all the `HtmlControl` class's properties and methods available to you as well as some new items that have been declared in the `HtmlContainerControl` class itself. The most important of these are the `InnerText` and `InnerHtml` properties:

- `InnerHtml`: Enables you to specify content that can include HTML elements to be placed between the opening and closing tags of the specified control.
- `InnerText`: Enables you to specify raw text to be placed between the opening and closing tags of the specified control.

Looking at All the HTML Classes

It is quite possible to work with every HTML element because a corresponding class is available for each one of them. The .NET Framework documentation shows the following classes for working with your HTML server controls:

- `HtmlAnchor` controls the `<a>` element.
- `HtmlButton` controls the `<button>` element.
- `HtmlForm` controls the `<form>` element.
- `HtmlHead` controls the `<head>` element.
- `HtmlImage` controls the `<img>` element.
- `HtmlInputButton` controls the `<input type="button">` element.
- `HtmlInputCheckBox` controls the `<input type="checkbox">` element.
- `HtmlInputFile` controls the `<input type="file">` element.
- `HtmlInputHidden` controls the `<input type="hidden">` element.
- `HtmlInputImage` controls the `<input type="image">` element.
- `HtmlInputPassword` controls the `<input type="password">` element.
- `HtmlInputRadioButton` controls the `<input type="radio">` element.
- `HtmlInputReset` controls the `<input type="reset">` element.
- `HtmlInputSubmit` controls the `<input type="submit">` element.
- `HtmlInputText` controls the `<input type="text">` element.
- `HtmlLink` controls the `<link>`element.
- `HtmlMeta` controls the `<meta>` element.
- `HtmlSelect` controls the `<select>` element.
- `HtmlTable` controls the `<table>` element.
- `HtmlTableCell` controls the `<td>` element.
- `HtmlTableRow` controls the `<tr>` element.
- `HtmlTextArea` controls the `<textarea>` element.
- `HtmlTitle` controls the `<title>` element.

You gain access to one of these classes when you convert an HTML element to an HTML server control. For example, convert the `<title>` element to a server control this way:

```
<title id="Title1" runat="Server"/>
```

That gives you access to the `HtmlTitle` class for this particular HTML element. Using this class instance, you can perform a number of tasks including providing a text value for the page title dynamically:

VB

```
Title1.Text = DateTime.Now.ToString()
```

C#

```
Title1.Text = DateTime.Now.ToString();
```

You can get most of the HTML elements you need by using these classes, but a considerable number of other HTML elements are at your disposal that are not explicitly covered by one of these HTML classes. For example, the `HtmlGenericControl` class provides server-side access to any HTML element you want.

Using the HtmlGenericControl Class

You should be aware of the importance of the `HtmlGenericControl` class; it gives you some capabilities that you do not get from any other server control offered by ASP.NET. For instance, using the `HtmlGenericControl` class, you can get server-side access to the `<meta>`, `<p>`, `<span>`, or other elements that would otherwise be unreachable.

Listing 2-6 shows you how to change the `<meta>` element in your page using the `HtmlGenericControl` class.

LISTING 2-6: Changing the <meta> element using the HtmlGenericControl class

Available for download on Wrox.com

VB

```
<%@ Page Language="VB" %>

<script runat="server">
    Protected Sub Page_Load(ByVal sender As Object, ByVal e As System.EventArgs)
        Meta1.Attributes("Name") = "description"
        Meta1.Attributes("CONTENT") = "Generated on: " & DateTime.Now.ToString()
    End Sub
</script>

<html xmlns="http://www.w3.org/1999/xhtml">
<head runat="server">
    <title>Using the HtmlGenericControl class</title>
    <meta id="Meta1" runat="server" />
</head>
<body>
    <form id="form1" runat="server">
    <div>
        The rain in Spain stays mainly in the plains.
    </div>
    </form>
</body>
</html>
```

C#

```
<%@ Page Language="C#" %>

<script runat="server">
    protected void Page_Load(object sender, EventArgs e)
    {
        Meta1.Attributes["Name"] = "description";
        Meta1.Attributes["CONTENT"] = "Generated on: " + DateTime.Now.ToString();
    }
</script>
```

Filename HTMLGenericControl.aspx

In this example, the page's `<meta>` element is turned into an HTML server control with the addition of the `id` and `runat` attributes. Because the `HtmlGenericControl` class (which inherits from `HtmlControl`) can work with a wide range of HTML elements, you cannot assign values to HTML attributes in the same manner as you do when working with the other HTML classes (such as `HtmlInputButton`). You assign values to the attributes of an HTML element using the `HtmlGenericControl` class's `Attributes` property, specifying the attribute you are working with as a string value.

The following is a partial result of running the example page:

```
<html xmlns="http://www.w3.org/1999/xhtml">
<head>
    <meta id="Meta1" Name="description"
     CONTENT="Generated on: 2/5/2010 2:42:52 PM"></meta>
    <title>Using the HtmlGenericControl class</title>
</head>
```

By using the `HtmlGenericControl` class, along with the other HTML classes, you can manipulate every element of your ASP.NET pages from your server-side code.

IDENTIFYING ASP.NET SERVER CONTROLS

When you create your ASP.NET pages with a series of controls, many of the controls are nested and many are even dynamically laid out by ASP.NET itself. For instance, when you are working with user controls, the GridView, ListView, Repeater, and more, ASP.NET is constructing a complicated control tree that is rendered to the page.

What happens when this occurs is that ASP.NET needs to provide these dynamic controls with IDs. When it does this, you end up with IDs such as `GridView1$ctl02$ctl00`. These sorts of control IDs are not a good thing because they are unpredictable and make it difficult to work with the control from client-side code.

To help this situation, ASP.NET 4 is the first release that includes the ability to control the IDs that are used for your controls. To demonstrate the issue, Listing 2-7 shows some code that results in some unpredictable client IDs for the controls. To start, first create a user control.

LISTING 2-7: A user control with some simple controls

Available for download on Wrox.com

```
<%@ Control Language="C#" AutoEventWireup="true"
    CodeFile="WebUserControl.ascx.cs" Inherits="WebUserControl" %>

<asp:TextBox ID="TextBox1" runat="server"></asp:TextBox>
<br />
<asp:Button ID="Button1" runat="server" Text="Button" />
```

Then the next step is to use this user control within one of your ASP.NET pages. This is illustrated here in Listing 2-8.

LISTING 2-8: Making use of the user control within a simple ASP.NET page

Available for download on Wrox.com

```
<%@ Page Language="C#" AutoEventWireup="true"
    CodeFile="Default.aspx.cs" Inherits="_Default" Trace="true" %>

<%@ Register src="WebUserControl.ascx" tagname="WebUserControl" tagprefix="uc1" %>

<html xmlns="http://www.w3.org/1999/xhtml">
<head runat="server">
    <title>Working with Control IDs</title>
</head>
<body>
    <form id="form1" runat="server">
```

continues

LISTING 2-8 *(continued)*

```
        <div>
            <uc1:WebUserControl ID="WebUserControl1" runat="server" />

        </div>
        </form>
    </body>
    </html>
```

So this user control on the page contains only two simple server controls that are then rendered onto the page. If you look back at Listing 2-7, you can see that they have pretty simple control IDs assigned to them. There is a TextBox server control with the ID value of TextBox1 and a Button server control with the ID value of Button1.

Looking at the page code from Listing 2-8, you can see in the @Page directive that the Trace attribute is set to true. This gives you the ability to see the ClientID that is produced in the control tree of the page. Running this page, you see the following results in the page, as shown in Figure 2-7.

Control Tree

Control UniqueID	Type
__Page	ASP.default_aspx
ctl02	System.Web.UI.LiteralControl
ctl00	System.Web.UI.HtmlControls.HtmlHead
ctl01	System.Web.UI.HtmlControls.HtmlTitle
ctl03	System.Web.UI.LiteralControl
form1	System.Web.UI.HtmlControls.HtmlForm
ctl04	System.Web.UI.LiteralControl
WebUserControl1	ASP.webusercontrol_ascx
WebUserControl1$TextBox1	System.Web.UI.WebControls.TextBox
WebUserControl1$ctl00	System.Web.UI.LiteralControl
WebUserControl1$Button1	System.Web.UI.WebControls.Button
WebUserControl1$ctl01	System.Web.UI.LiteralControl
ctl05	System.Web.UI.LiteralControl
ctl06	System.Web.UI.LiteralControl

FIGURE 2-7

If you look at the source code for the page, you see the following snippet of code:

```
<div>
   <input name="WebUserControl1$TextBox1" type="text" id="WebUserControl1_TextBox1" />
   <br />
   <input type="submit" name="WebUserControl1$Button1" value="Button"
    id="WebUserControl1_Button1" />
</div>
```

From this, you can see the ASP.NET assigned control IDs are lengthy and something you probably wouldn't choose yourself. The TextBox server control was output with a name value of WebUserControl1$TextBox1 and an id value of WebUserControl1_TextBox1. A lot of this is done to make sure that the controls end up with a unique ID.

ASP.NET 4 includes the ability to control these assignments through the use of the ClientIDMode attribute. The possible values of this attribute include AutoID, Inherit, Predictable, and Static. An example of setting this value is provided here:

```
<uc1:WebUserControl ID="WebUserControl1" runat="server" ClientIDMode="AutoID" />
```

This example uses AutoID, forcing the naming to abide by how it was done in the .NET Framework 3.5 and earlier. Using this gives you the following results:

- **name:** WebUserControl1$TextBox1
  WebUserControl1$Button1
- **id:** WebUserControl1_TextBox1
  WebUserControl1_Button1

If you use Inherit, it simply copies how it is done by the containing control, the page, or the application. Therefore, for this example, you would end up with the same values as if you used AutoID. The Inherit value is the default value for all controls.

Predictable is generally used for databound controls that have a nesting of other controls (for example, the Repeater control). When used with a ClientIDRowSuffix property value, it appends this value rather than increments with a number (for example, ctrl1, ctrl2).

A value of `Static` gives you the name of the control you have assigned. It is up to you to ensure the uniqueness of the identifiers. Setting the `ClientIDMode` to `Static` for the user control in our example gives you the following values:

- **name:** `WebUserControl1$TextBox1`
  `WebUserControl1$Button1`
- **id:** `TextBox1`
  `Button1`

You can set the `ClientID` property at the control, container control, user control, page, or even application level via the `<pages>` element in the `machine.config` or `web.config` file.

Now with this new capability, you will find that working with your server controls using technologies like JavaScript on the client is far easier than before. The next section takes a look at using JavaScript within your ASP.NET pages.

MANIPULATING PAGES AND SERVER CONTROLS WITH JAVASCRIPT

Developers generally like to include some of their own custom JavaScript functions in their ASP.NET pages. You have a couple of ways to do this. The first is to apply JavaScript directly to the controls on your ASP.NET pages. For example, look at a simple TextBox server control, shown in Listing 2-9, which displays the current date and time.

LISTING 2-9: Showing the current date and time

VB

```
Protected Sub Page_Load(ByVal sender As Object, ByVal e As System.EventArgs)
   TextBox1.Text = DateTime.Now.ToString()
End Sub
```

C#

```
protected void Page_Load(object sender, EventArgs e) {
   TextBox1.Text = DateTime.Now.ToString();
}
```

This little bit of code displays the current date and time on the page of the end user. The problem is that the date and time displayed are correct for the Web server that generated the page. If someone sits in the Pacific time zone (PST), and the Web server is in the Eastern time zone (EST), the page won't be correct for that viewer. If you want the time to be correct for anyone visiting the site, regardless of where they reside in the world, you can employ JavaScript to work with the TextBox control, as illustrated in Listing 2-10.

Available for download on Wrox.com

LISTING 2-10: Using JavaScript to show the current time for the end user

```
<%@ Page Language="VB" %>

<html xmlns="http://www.w3.org/1999/xhtml" >
<head runat="server">
    <title>Using JavaScript</title>
</head>
<body onload="javascript:document.forms[0]['TextBox1'].value=Date();">
    <form id="form1" runat="server">
    <div>
        <asp:TextBox ID="TextBox1" Runat="server" Width="300"></asp:TextBox>
    </div>
    </form>
</body>
</html>
```

Filename CurrentTimeJS.aspx

In this example, even though you are using a standard TextBox server control from the Web server control family, you can get at this control using JavaScript that is planted in the `onload` attribute of the `<body>` element. The value of the `onload` attribute actually points to the specific server control via an anonymous function by using the value of the `ID` attribute from the server control: `TextBox1`. You can get at other server controls on your page by employing the same methods. This bit of code produces the result illustrated in Figure 2-8.

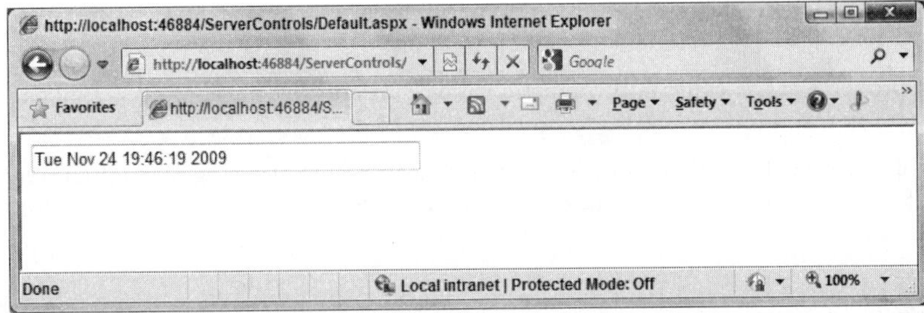

FIGURE 2-8

ASP.NET uses the `Page.ClientScript` property to register and place JavaScript functions on your ASP.NET pages. Three of these methods are reviewed here. More methods and properties than just these three are available through the `ClientScript` object (which references an instance of `System.Web.UI.ClientScriptManager`), but these are the more useful ones. You can find the rest in the SDK documentation.

The `Page.RegisterStartupScript` and the `Page.RegisterClientScriptBlock` methods from the .NET Framework 1.0/1.1 are now considered obsolete. Both of these possibilities for registering scripts required a key/script set of parameters. Because two separate methods were involved, there was an extreme possibility that some key name collisions would occur. The `Page.ClientScript` property is meant to bring all the script registrations under one umbrella, making your code less error prone.

Using Page.ClientScript.RegisterClientScriptBlock

The `RegisterClientScriptBlock` method allows you to place a JavaScript function at the top of the page. This means that the script is in place for the startup of the page in the browser. Its use is illustrated in Listing 2-11.

LISTING 2-11: Using the RegisterClientScriptBlock method

Available for download on Wrox.com

VB

```
<%@ Page Language="VB" %>

<script runat="server">
    Protected Sub Page_Load(ByVal sender As Object, ByVal e As System.EventArgs)
      Dim myScript As String = "function AlertHello() { alert('Hello ASP.NET'); }"
      Page.ClientScript.RegisterClientScriptBlock(Me.GetType(), "MyScript",
         myScript, True)
    End Sub
</script>

<html xmlns="http://www.w3.org/1999/xhtml">
<head runat="server">
    <title>Adding JavaScript</title>
</head>
```

```
<body>
    <form id="form1" runat="server">
    <div>
        <asp:Button ID="Button1" Runat="server" Text="Button"
         OnClientClick="AlertHello()" />
    </div>
    </form>
</body>
</html>
```

C#

```
<%@ Page Language="C#" %>

<script runat="server">
    protected void Page_Load(object sender, EventArgs e)
    {
      string myScript = @"function AlertHello() { alert('Hello ASP.NET'); }";
      Page.ClientScript.RegisterClientScriptBlock(this.GetType(),
         "MyScript", myScript, true);
    }
</script>
```

Filename RegisterClientScriptBlock.aspx

From this example, you can see that you create the JavaScript function `AlertHello()` as a string called `myScript`. Then using the `Page.ClientScript.RegisterClientScriptBlock` method, you program the script to be placed on the page. The two possible constructions of the `RegisterClientScriptBlock` method are the following:

- `RegisterClientScriptBlock` (*type*, *key*, *script*)
- `RegisterClientScriptBlock` (*type*, *key*, *script*, *script tag specification*)

In the example from Listing 2-11, you are specifying the type as `Me.GetType()`, the key, the script to include, and then a `Boolean` value setting of `True` so that .NET places the script on the ASP.NET page with `<script>` tags automatically. When running the page, you can view the source code for the page to see the results:

```
<html xmlns="http://www.w3.org/1999/xhtml">
<head><title>
    Adding JavaScript
</title></head>
<body>
    <form method="post" action="JavaScriptPage.aspx" id="form1">
<div>
<input type="hidden" name="__VIEWSTATE"
 value="/wEPDwUKMTY3NzE5MjIyMGRkiyYSRMg+bcXi9DiawYlbxndiTDo=" />
</div>


<script type="text/javascript">
<!--
function AlertHello() { alert('Hello ASP.NET'); }// -->
</script>

    <div>
        <input type="submit" name="Button1" value="Button" onclick="AlertHello();"
         id="Button1" />
    </div>
    </form>
</body>
</html>
```

From this, you can see that the script specified was indeed included on the ASP.NET page before the page code. Not only were the `<script>` tags included, but the proper comment tags were added around the script (so older browsers will not break).

Using Page.ClientScript.RegisterStartupScript

The `RegisterStartupScript` method is not too much different from the `RegisterClientScriptBlock` method. The big difference is that the `RegisterStartupScript` places the script at the bottom of the ASP.NET page instead of at the top. In fact, the `RegisterStartupScript` method even takes the same constructors as the `RegisterClientScriptBlock` method:

- `RegisterStartupScript` (*type*, *key*, *script*)
- `RegisterStartupScript` (type, key, script, script tag specification)

So what difference does it make where the script is registered on the page? A lot, actually!

If you have a bit of JavaScript that is working with one of the controls on your page, in most cases you want to use the `RegisterStartupScript` method instead of `RegisterClientScriptBlock`. For example, you'd use the following code to create a page that includes a simple `<asp:TextBox>` control that contains a default value of `Hello ASP.NET`.

```
<asp:TextBox ID="TextBox1" Runat="server">Hello ASP.NET</asp:TextBox>
```

Then use the `RegisterClientScriptBlock` method to place a script on the page that utilizes the value in the `TextBox1` control, as illustrated in Listing 2-12.

LISTING 2-12: Improperly using the RegisterClientScriptBlock method

VB

```
Protected Sub Page_Load(ByVal sender As Object, ByVal e As System.EventArgs)
   Dim myScript As String = "alert(document.forms[0]['TextBox1'].value);"
   Page.ClientScript.RegisterClientScriptBlock(Me.GetType(), "myKey", myScript,
      True)
End Sub
```

C#

```
protected void Page_Load(object sender, EventArgs e)
{
   string myScript = @"alert(document.forms[0]['TextBox1'].value);";
   Page.ClientScript.RegisterClientScriptBlock(this.GetType(),
      "MyScript", myScript, true);
}
```

Running this page (depending on the version of IE you are using) gives you a JavaScript error, as shown in Figure 2-9.

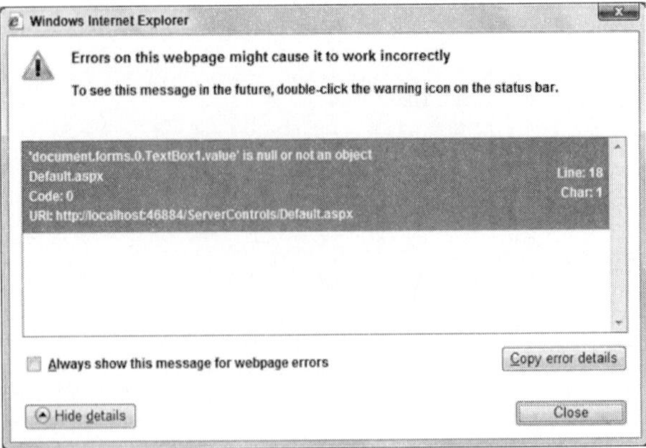

FIGURE 2-9

The reason for the error is that the JavaScript function fired before the text box was even placed on the screen. Therefore, the JavaScript function did not find `TextBox1`, and that caused an error to be thrown by the page. Now try the `RegisterStartupScript` method shown in Listing 2-13.

LISTING 2-13: Using the RegisterStartupScript method

Available for download on Wrox.com

VB

```
Protected Sub Page_Load(ByVal sender As Object, ByVal e As System.EventArgs)
   Dim myScript As String = "alert(document.forms[0]['TextBox1'].value);"
   Page.ClientScript.RegisterStartupScript(Me.GetType(), "myKey", myScript,
      True)
End Sub
```

C#

```
protected void Page_Load(object sender, EventArgs e)
{
   string myScript = @"alert(document.forms[0]['TextBox1'].value);";
   Page.ClientScript.RegisterStartupScript(this.GetType(),
      "MyScript", myScript, true);
}
```

Filename RegisterStartupScript.aspx

This approach puts the JavaScript function at the bottom of the ASP.NET page, so when the JavaScript actually starts, it finds the `TextBox1` element and works as planned. The result is shown in Figure 2-10.

FIGURE 2-10

Using Page.ClientScript.RegisterClientScriptInclude

The final method is `RegisterClientScriptInclude`. Many developers place their JavaScript inside a `.js` file, which is considered a best practice because it makes it very easy to make global JavaScript changes to the application. You can register the script files on your ASP.NET pages using the `RegisterClientScriptInclude` method illustrated in Listing 2-14.

LISTING 2-14: Using the RegisterClientScriptInclude method

VB

```
Dim myScript As String = "myJavaScriptCode.js"
Page.ClientScript.RegisterClientScriptInclude("myKey", myScript)
```

C#

```
string myScript = "myJavaScriptCode.js";
Page.ClientScript.RegisterClientScriptInclude("myKey", myScript);
```

This creates the following construction on the ASP.NET page:

```
<script src="myJavaScriptCode.js" type="text/javascript"></script>
```

CLIENT-SIDE CALLBACK

ASP.NET 4 includes a client callback feature that enables you to retrieve page values and populate them to an already-generated page without regenerating the page. This was introduced with ASP.NET 2.0. This capability makes it possible to change values on a page without going through the entire postback cycle; that means you can update your pages without completely redrawing the page. End users will not see the page flicker and reposition, and the pages will have a flow more like the flow of a thick-client application.

To work with the callback capability, you have to know a little about working with JavaScript. This book does not attempt to teach you JavaScript. If you need to get up to speed on this rather large topic, check out Wrox's *Beginning JavaScript, Fourth Edition*, by Paul Wilton and Jeremy McPeak (Wiley Publishing, Inc., ISBN: 978-0-470-52593-7).

You can also accomplish client callbacks in a different manner using ASP.NET AJAX. You will find more information on this in Chapters 18 and 19.

Comparing a Typical Postback to a Callback

Before you jump into some examples of the callback feature, first look at a comparison to the current postback feature of a typical ASP.NET page.

When a page event is triggered on an ASP.NET page that is working with a typical postback scenario, a lot is going on. The diagram in Figure 2-11 illustrates the process.

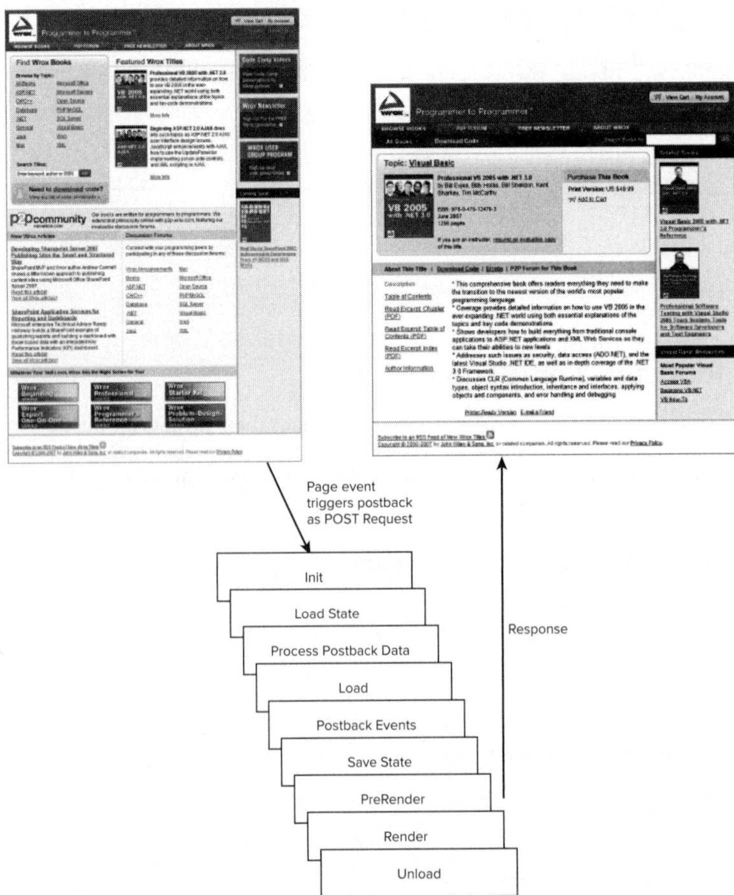

FIGURE 2-11

In a normal postback situation, an event of some kind triggers an HTTP Post request to be sent to the Web server. An example of such an event might be the end user clicking a button on the form. This sends the HTTP Post request to the Web server, which then processes the request with the `IPostbackEventHandler` and runs the request through a series of page events. These events include loading the state (as found in the view state of the page), processing data, processing postback events, and finally rendering the page to be interpreted by the consuming browser once again. The process completely reloads the page in the browser, which is what causes the flicker and the realignment to the top of the page.

On the other hand, you have the alternative of using the callback capabilities, as shown in the diagram in Figure 2-12.

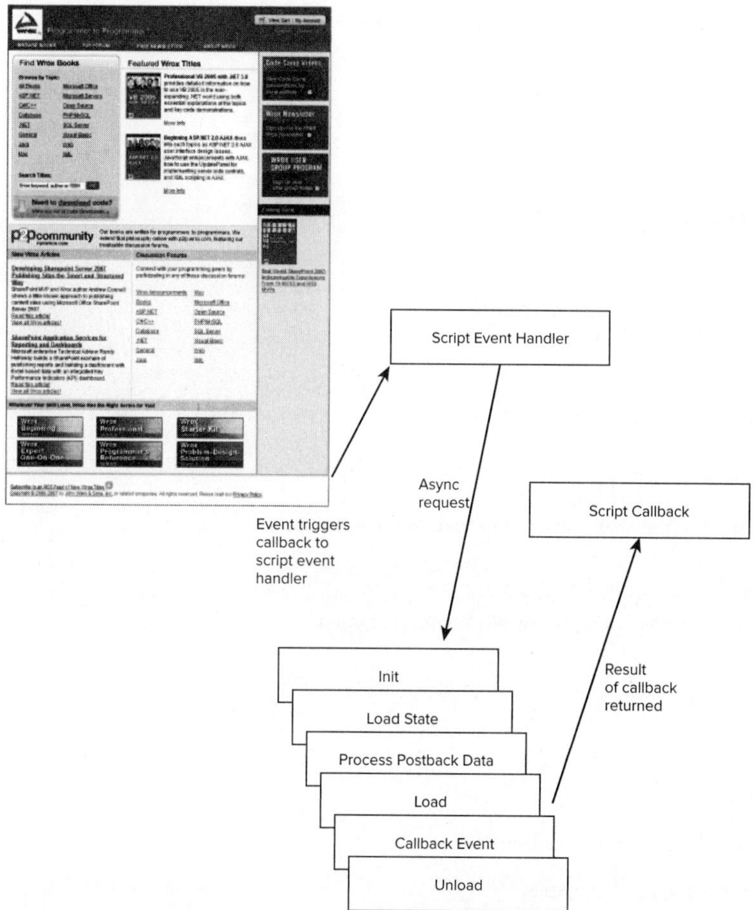

FIGURE 2-12

In this case, an event (again, such as a button click) causes the event to be posted to a script event handler (a JavaScript function) that sends off an asynchronous request to the Web server for processing. `ICallbackEventHandler` runs the request through a pipeline similar to what is used with the postback — but you notice that some of the larger steps (such as rendering the page) are excluded from the process chain. After the information is loaded, the result is returned to the script callback object. The script code then pushes this data into the Web page using JavaScript's capabilities to do this without refreshing the page. To understand how this all works, look at the simple example in the following section.

Using the Callback Feature — A Simple Approach

Begin examining the callback feature by looking at how a simple ASP.NET page uses it. For this example, you have only an HTML button control and a TextBox server control (the Web server control version). The idea is that when the end user clicks the button on the form, the callback service is initiated and a random number is populated into the text box. Listing 2-15 shows an example of this in action.

LISTING 2-15: Using the callback feature to populate a random value to a Web page

Available for download on Wrox.com

.aspx page (VB version)

```
<%@ Page Language="VB" AutoEventWireup="false" CodeFile="RandomNumber.aspx.vb"
    Inherits="RandomNumber" %>

<html xmlns="http://www.w3.org/1999/xhtml">
<head runat="server">
    <title>Callback Page</title>

    <script type="text/javascript">
        function GetNumber(){
            UseCallback();
        }

        function GetRandomNumberFromServer(TextBox1, context){
            document.forms[0].TextBox1.value = TextBox1;
        }
    </script>

</head>
<body>
    <form id="form1" runat="server">
    <div>
        <input id="Button1" type="button" value="Get Random Number"
         onclick="GetNumber()" />
        <br />
        <br />
        <asp:TextBox ID="TextBox1" Runat="server"></asp:TextBox>
    </div>
    </form>
</body>
</html>
```

VB (code-behind)

```
Partial Class RandomNumber
    Inherits System.Web.UI.Page
    Implements System.Web.UI.ICallbackEventHandler

    Dim _callbackResult As String = Nothing

    Protected Sub Page_Load(ByVal sender As Object, ByVal e As System.EventArgs) _
       Handles Me.Load

        Dim cbReference As String =
           Page.ClientScript.GetCallbackEventReference(
             Me, "arg", "GetRandomNumberFromServer", "context")
        Dim cbScript As String = "function UseCallback(arg, context)" & _
           "{" & cbReference & ";" & "}"

        Page.ClientScript.RegisterClientScriptBlock(Me.GetType(),
           "UseCallback", cbScript, True)
    End Sub
```

```
    Public Sub RaiseCallbackEvent(ByVal eventArgument As String)
       Implements System.Web.UI.ICallbackEventHandler.RaiseCallbackEvent

       _callbackResult = Rnd().ToString()
    End Sub

    Public Function GetCallbackResult() As String _
       Implements System.Web.UI.ICallbackEventHandler.GetCallbackResult

        Return _callbackResult
    End Function
End Class
```

C# (code-behind)

```
using System;
using System.Data;
using System.Configuration;
using System.Collections;
using System.Web;
using System.Web.Security;
using System.Web.UI;
using System.Web.UI.WebControls;
using System.Web.UI.WebControls.WebParts;
using System.Web.UI.HtmlControls;

public partial class RandomNumber : System.Web.UI.Page,
   System.Web.UI.ICallbackEventHandler
{
    private string _callbackResult = null;

    protected void Page_Load(object sender, EventArgs e)
    {
        string cbReference =
          Page.ClientScript.GetCallbackEventReference(this,
             "arg", "GetRandomNumberFromServer", "context");
        string cbScript = "function UseCallback(arg, context)" +
           "{" + cbReference + ";" + "}";

        Page.ClientScript.RegisterClientScriptBlock(this.GetType(),
           "UseCallback", cbScript, true);
    }

    public void RaiseCallbackEvent(string eventArg)
    {
        Random rnd = new Random();
        _callbackResult = rnd.Next().ToString();
    }

    public string GetCallbackResult()
    {
        return _callbackResult;
    }
}
```

Filenames RandomNumber.aspx, RandomNumber.aspx.vb, and RandomNumber.aspx.cs

When this page is built and run in the browser, you get the results shown in Figure 2-13.

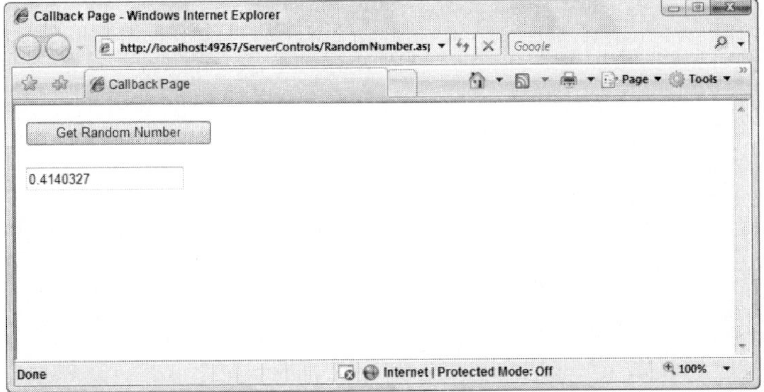

FIGURE 2-13

Clicking the button on the page invokes the client callback capabilities of the page, and the page then makes an asynchronous request to the code behind of the same page. After getting a response from this part of the page, the client script takes the retrieved value and places it inside the text box — all without doing a page refresh!

Now look at the `.aspx` page, which simply contains an HTML button control and a TextBox server control. Notice that a standard HTML button control is used because a typical `<asp:button>` control does not work here. No worries. When you work with the HTML button control, just be sure to include an `onclick` event to point to the JavaScript function that initiates this entire process:

```
<input id="Button1" type="button" value="Get Random Number"
 onclick="GetNumber()" />
```

You do not have to do anything else with the controls themselves. The final thing to include in the page is the client-side JavaScript functions to take care of the callback to the server-side functions. `GetNumber()` is the first JavaScript function that's instantiated. It starts the entire process by calling the name of the client script handler that is defined in the page's code behind. A `string` type result from `GetNumber()` is retrieved using the `GetRandomNumberFromServer()` function. `GetRandomNumberFromServer()` simply populates the `string` value retrieved and makes that the value of the Textbox control — specified by the value of the `ID` attribute of the server control (`TextBox1`):

```
<script type="text/javascript">
   function GetNumber(){
      UseCallback();
   }

   function GetRandomNumberFromServer(TextBox1, context){
      document.forms[0].TextBox1.value = TextBox1;
   }
</script>
```

Now turn your attention to the code behind.

The `Page` class of the Web page implements the `System.Web.UI.ICallbackEventHandler` interface:

```
Partial Class RandomNumber
    Inherits System.Web.UI.Page
    Implements System.Web.UI.ICallbackEventHandler

    ' Code here

End Class
```

This interface requires you to implement a couple of methods — the `RaiseCallbackEvent` and the `GetCallbackResult` methods, both of which work with the client script request. `RaiseCallback Event` enables you to do the work of retrieving the value from the page, but the value can be only of type `string`:

```
Public Sub RaiseCallbackEvent(ByVal eventArgument As String)
   Implements System.Web.UI.ICallbackEventHandler.RaiseCallbackEvent

   _callbackResult = Rnd().ToString()
End Sub
```

The `GetCallbackResult` is the method that actually grabs the returned value to be used:

```
Public Function GetCallbackResult() As String
   Implements System.Web.UI.ICallbackEventHandler.GetCallbackResult

        Return _callbackResult
End Function
```

In addition, the `Page_Load` event includes the creation and placement of the client callback script manager (the function that will manage requests and responses) on the client:

```
Dim cbReference As String = Page.ClientScript.GetCallbackEventReference(Me, "arg",
   "GetRandomNumberFromServer", "context")
Dim cbScript As String = "function UseCallback(arg, context)" &
   "{" & cbReference & ";" & "}"

Page.ClientScript.RegisterClientScriptBlock(Me.GetType(),
   "UseCallback", cbScript, True)
```

The function placed on the client for the callback capabilities is called `UseCallback()`. This `string` is then populated to the Web page itself using the `Page.ClientScript.RegisterClientScripBlock` that also puts `<script>` tags around the function on the page. Make sure that the name you use here is the same name you use in the client-side JavaScript function presented earlier.

In the end, you have a page that refreshes content without refreshing the overall page. This opens the door to a completely new area of possibilities. One caveat is that the callback capabilities described here use XmlHTTP and, therefore, the client browser needs to support XmlHTTP (Microsoft's Internet Explorer and FireFox do support this feature). Because of this, .NET Framework 2.0, 3.5, and 4 have the `SupportsCallBack` and the `SupportsXmlHttp` properties. To ensure this support, you could put a check in the page's code behind when the initial page is being generated. It might look similar to the following:

VB

```
If (Page.Request.Browser.SupportsXmlHTTP) Then

End If
```

C#

```
if (Page.Request.Browser.SupportsXmlHTTP == true) {

}
```

Using the Callback Feature with a Single Parameter

Now you will build a Web page that utilizes the callback feature but requires a parameter to retrieve a returned value. At the top of the page, place a text box that gathers input from the end user, a button, and another text box to populate the page with the result from the callback.

The page asks for a ZIP Code from the user and then uses the callback feature to instantiate an XML Web service request on the server. The Web service returns the latest weather for that particular ZIP Code in a string format. Listing 2-16 shows an example of the page.

LISTING 2-16: Using the callback feature with a Web service

Available for download on Wrox.com

.aspx page (VB version)

```
<%@ Page Language="VB" AutoEventWireup="false" CodeFile="WSCallback.aspx.vb"
    Inherits="WSCallback" %>
<html xmlns="http://www.w3.org/1999/xhtml">
<head runat="server">
    <title>Web Service Callback</title>

    <script type="text/javascript">
        function GetTemp(){
            var zipcode = document.forms[0].TextBox1.value;
            UseCallback(zipcode, "");
        }

        function GetTempFromServer(TextBox2, context){
            document.forms[0].TextBox2.value = "Zipcode: " +
            document.forms[0].TextBox1.value + " | Temp: " + TextBox2;
        }
    </script>
</head>
<body>
    <form id="form1" runat="server">
    <div>
        <asp:TextBox ID="TextBox1" Runat="server"></asp:TextBox>
        <br />
        <input id="Button1" type="button" value="Get Temp" onclick="GetTemp()" />
        <br />
        <asp:TextBox ID="TextBox2" Runat="server" Width="400px">
        </asp:TextBox>
        <br />
        <br />
    </div>
    </form>
</body>
</html>
```

VB (code-behind)

```
Partial Class WSCallback
    Inherits System.Web.UI.Page
    Implements System.Web.UI.IcallbackEventHandler

    Dim _callbackResult As String = Nothing

    Protected Sub Page_Load(ByVal sender As Object, ByVal e As System.EventArgs)
       Handles Me.Load

        Dim cbReference As String = Page.ClientScript.GetCallbackEventReference(
           Me, "arg", "GetTempFromServer", "context")
        Dim cbScript As String = "function UseCallback(arg, context)" & _
           "{" & cbReference & ";" & "}"

        Page.ClientScript.RegisterClientScriptBlock(Me.GetType(),
           "UseCallback", cbScript, True)
    End Sub

    Public Sub RaiseCallbackEvent(ByVal eventArgument As String)
       Implements System.Web.UI.ICallbackEventHandler.RaiseCallbackEvent
```

```
        Dim ws As New Weather.TemperatureService
        _callbackResult = ws.getTemp(eventArgument).ToString()
    End Sub
    Public Function GetCallbackResult() As String
       Implements System.Web.UI.ICallbackEventHandler.GetCallbackResult

        Return _callbackResult
    End Function
End Class
```

C# (code-behind)

```
using System;
using System.Data;
using System.Configuration;
using System.Collections;
using System.Web;
using System.Web.Security;
using System.Web.UI;
using System.Web.UI.WebControls;
using System.Web.UI.WebControls.WebParts;
using System.Web.UI.HtmlControls;

public partial class WSCallback : System.Web.UI.Page,
   System.Web.UI.ICallbackEventHandler
{
    private string _callbackResult = null;

    protected void Page_Load(object sender, EventArgs e)
    {
        string cbReference = Page.ClientScript.GetCallbackEventReference(this,
           "arg", "GetTempFromServer", "context");
        string cbScript = "function UseCallback(arg, context)" +
           "{" + cbReference + ";" + "}";

        Page.ClientScript.RegisterClientScriptBlock(this.GetType(),
           "UseCallback", cbScript, true);
    }

    public void RaiseCallbackEvent(string eventArg)
    {
        Weather.TemperatureService ws = new Weather.TemperatureService();
        _callbackResult = ws.getTemp(eventArg).ToString();
    }
    public string GetCallbackResult()
    {
        return _callbackResult;
    }
}
```

Filenames WSCallback.aspx, WSCallback.aspx.vb, and WSCallback.aspx.cs

What you do not see on this page from the listing is that a Web reference has been made to a theoretical remote Web service that returns the latest weather to the application based on a ZIP Code the user supplied.

For more information on working with Web services in your ASP.NET applications, check out Chapter 31.

After building and running this page, you get the results illustrated in Figure 2-14.

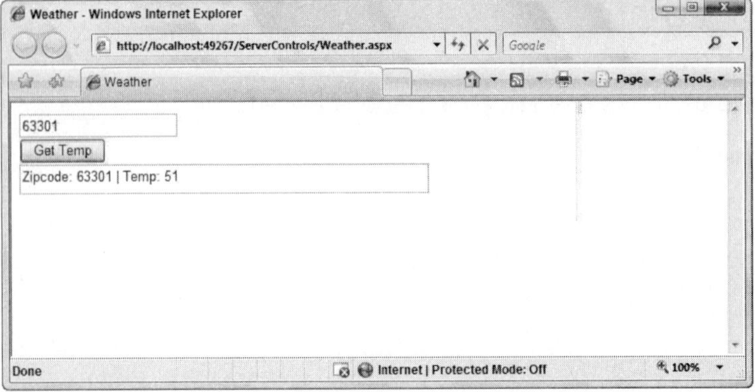

FIGURE 2-14

The big difference with the client callback feature is that this example sends in a required parameter. That is done in the `GetTemp()` JavaScript function on the `.aspx` part of the page:

```
function GetTemp(){
   var zipcode = document.forms[0].TextBox1.value;
   UseCallback(zipcode, "");
}
```

The JavaScript function shows the population that the end user input into `TextBox1` and places its value in a variable called `zipcode` that is sent as a parameter in the `UseCallback()` method.

This example, like the previous one, updates the page without doing a complete page refresh.

Using the Callback Feature — A More Complex Example

So far, you have seen an example of using the callback feature to pull back a single item as well as to pull back a string whose output is based on a single parameter that was passed to the engine. The next example takes this operation one step further and pulls back a collection of results based upon a parameter provided.

This example works with an instance of the Northwind database found in SQL Server. For this example, create a single page that includes a TextBox server control and a button. Below that, place a table that will be populated with the customer details from the customer ID provided in the text box. The `.aspx` page for this example is provided in Listing 2-17.

Available for download on Wrox.com

LISTING 2-17: An ASP.NET page to collect the CustomerID from the end user

.aspx Page

```
<%@ Page Language="VB" AutoEventWireup="false"
    CodeFile="Default.aspx.vb" Inherits="_Default" %>

<html xmlns="http://www.w3.org/1999/xhtml">
<head runat="server">
    <title>Customer Details</title>

    <script type="text/javascript">
        function GetCustomer(){
            var customerCode = document.forms[0].TextBox1.value;
            UseCallback(customerCode, "");
        }
```

```
            function GetCustDetailsFromServer(result, context){
                var i = result.split("|");
                customerID.innerHTML = i[0];
                companyName.innerHTML = i[1];
                contactName.innerHTML = i[2];
                contactTitle.innerHTML = i[3];
                address.innerHTML = i[4];
                city.innerHTML = i[5];
                region.innerHTML = i[6];
                postalCode.innerHTML = i[7];
                country.innerHTML = i[8];
                phone.innerHTML = i[9];
                fax.innerHTML = i[10];
            }
        </script>
</head>
<body>
    <form id="form1" runat="server">
    <div>
        <asp:TextBox ID="TextBox1" runat="server"></asp:TextBox> 
        <input id="Button1" type="button" value="Get Customer Details"
         onclick="GetCustomer()" /><br />
        <br />
      <table cellspacing="0" cellpadding="4" rules="all" border="1"
       id="DetailsView1"
       style="background-color:White;border-color:#3366CC;border-width:1px;
          border-style:None;height:50px;width:400px;border-collapse:collapse;">
        <tr style="color:#003399;background-color:White;">
           <td>CustomerID</td><td><span id="customerID" /></td>
        </tr><tr style="color:#003399;background-color:White;">
           <td>CompanyName</td><td><span id="companyName" /></td>
        </tr><tr style="color:#003399;background-color:White;">
           <td>ContactName</td><td><span id="contactName" /></td>
        </tr><tr style="color:#003399;background-color:White;">
           <td>ContactTitle</td><td><span id="contactTitle" /></td>
        </tr><tr style="color:#003399;background-color:White;">
           <td>Address</td><td><span id="address" /></td>
        </tr><tr style="color:#003399;background-color:White;">
           <td>City</td><td><span id="city" /></td>
        </tr><tr style="color:#003399;background-color:White;">
           <td>Region</td><td><span id="region" /></td>
        </tr><tr style="color:#003399;background-color:White;">
           <td>PostalCode</td><td><span id="postalCode" /></td>
        </tr><tr style="color:#003399;background-color:White;">
           <td>Country</td><td><span id="country" /></td>
        </tr><tr style="color:#003399;background-color:White;">
           <td>Phone</td><td><span id="phone" /></td>
        </tr><tr style="color:#003399;background-color:White;">
           <td>Fax</td><td><span id="fax" /></td>
        </tr>
      </table>
    </div>
    </form>
</body>
</html>
```

Filename CallbackNorthwind.aspx

As in the previous examples, two JavaScript functions are contained in the page. The first, `GetCustomer()`, is the function that passes in the parameter to be processed by the code-behind file on the application server. This is quite similar to what appeared in the previous example.

The second JavaScript function, however, is different. Looking over this function, you can see that it is expecting a long string of multiple values:

```
function GetCustDetailsFromServer(result, context){
   var i = result.split("|");
   customerID.innerHTML = i[0];
   companyName.innerHTML = i[1];
   contactName.innerHTML = i[2];
   contactTitle.innerHTML = i[3];
   address.innerHTML = i[4];
   city.innerHTML = i[5];
   region.innerHTML = i[6];
   postalCode.innerHTML = i[7];
   country.innerHTML = i[8];
   phone.innerHTML = i[9];
   fax.innerHTML = i[10];
}
```

The multiple results expected are constructed in a pipe-delimited string, and each of the values is placed into an array. Then each string item in the array is assigned to a particular `<span>` tag in the ASP.NET page. For instance, look at the following bit of code:

```
customerID.innerHTML = i[0];
```

The `i[0]` variable is the first item found in the pipe-delimited string, and it is assigned to the `customerID` item on the page. This `customerID` identifier comes from the following `<span>` tag found in the table:

```
<span id="customerID" />
```

Now, turn your attention to the code-behind file for this page, as shown in Listing 2-18.

LISTING 2-18: The code-behind file for the Customer Details page

Available for download on Wrox.com

VB

```
Imports System.Data
Imports System.Data.SqlClient

Partial Class CallbackNorthwind
    Inherits System.Web.UI.Page
    Implements System.Web.UI.ICallbackEventHandler

    Dim _callbackResult As String = Nothing

    Public Function GetCallbackResult() As String _
       Implements System.Web.UI.ICallbackEventHandler.GetCallbackResult
        Return _callbackResult
    End Function

    Public Sub RaiseCallbackEvent(ByVal eventArgument As String)
       Implements System.Web.UI.ICallbackEventHandler.RaiseCallbackEvent
        Dim conn As SqlConnection = New _
           SqlConnection("Data Source=.;Initial Catalog=Northwind;User ID=sa")
        Dim cmd As SqlCommand = New _
           SqlCommand("Select * From Customers Where CustomerID ='" &
           eventArgument & "'", conn)

        conn.Open()

        Dim MyReader As SqlDataReader
        MyReader = cmd.ExecuteReader(CommandBehavior.CloseConnection)
```

```
            Dim MyValues(10) As String

            While MyReader.Read()
                MyValues(0) = MyReader("CustomerID").ToString()
                MyValues(1) = MyReader("CompanyName").ToString()
                MyValues(2) = MyReader("ContactName").ToString()
                MyValues(3) = MyReader("ContactTitle").ToString()
                MyValues(4) = MyReader("Address").ToString()
                MyValues(5) = MyReader("City").ToString()
                MyValues(6) = MyReader("Region").ToString()
                MyValues(7) = MyReader("PostalCode").ToString()
                MyValues(8) = MyReader("Country").ToString()
                MyValues(9) = MyReader("Phone").ToString()
                MyValues(10) = MyReader("Fax").ToString()
            End While

            Conn.Close()

            _callbackResult = String.Join("|", MyValues)
        End Sub

        Protected Sub Page_Load(ByVal sender As Object, _
           ByVal e As System.EventArgs) Handles Me.Load
            Dim cbReference As String = _
               Page.ClientScript.GetCallbackEventReference(Me, "arg", _
                  "GetCustDetailsFromServer", "context")
            Dim cbScript As String = "function UseCallback(arg, context)" & _
               "{" & cbReference & ";" & "}"

            Page.ClientScript.RegisterClientScriptBlock(Me.GetType(), _
               "UseCallback", cbScript, True)
        End Sub
    End Class
```

C#

```
using System;
using System.Data;
using System.Configuration;
using System.Collections;
using System.Web;
using System.Web.Security;
using System.Web.UI;
using System.Web.UI.WebControls;
using System.Web.UI.WebControls.WebParts;
using System.Web.UI.HtmlControls;
using System.Data.SqlClient;

public partial class CallbackNorthwind : System.Web.UI.Page,
   System.Web.UI.ICallbackEventHandler
{
    private string _callbackResult = null;

    protected void Page_Load(object sender, EventArgs e)
    {
        string cbReference = Page.ClientScript.GetCallbackEventReference(this,
           "arg", "GetCustDetailsFromServer", "context");
        string cbScript = "function UseCallback(arg, context)" +
           "{" + cbReference + ";" + "}";

        Page.ClientScript.RegisterClientScriptBlock(this.GetType(),
           "UseCallback", cbScript, true);
    }
```

contiuues

LISTING 2-18 *(continued)*

```
        #region ICallbackEventHandler Members

        public string GetCallbackResult()
        {
            return _callbackResult;
        }

        public void RaiseCallbackEvent(string eventArgument)
        {
            SqlConnection conn = new
               SqlConnection("Data Source=.;Initial Catalog=Northwind;User ID=sa");
            SqlCommand cmd = new
               SqlCommand("Select * From Customers Where CustomerID ='" +
               eventArgument + "'", conn);

            conn.Open();

            SqlDataReader MyReader;
            MyReader = cmd.ExecuteReader(CommandBehavior.CloseConnection);

            string[] MyValues = new string[11];

            while (MyReader.Read())
            {
                MyValues[0] = MyReader["CustomerID"].ToString();
                MyValues[1] = MyReader["CompanyName"].ToString();
                MyValues[2] = MyReader["ContactName"].ToString();
                MyValues[3] = MyReader["ContactTitle"].ToString();
                MyValues[4] = MyReader["Address"].ToString();
                MyValues[5] = MyReader["City"].ToString();
                MyValues[6] = MyReader["Region"].ToString();
                MyValues[7] = MyReader["PostalCode"].ToString();
                MyValues[8] = MyReader["Country"].ToString();
                MyValues[9] = MyReader["Phone"].ToString();
                MyValues[10] = MyReader["Fax"].ToString();
            }

            _callbackResult = String.Join("|", MyValues);
        }

        #endregion
    }
```

Filenames CallbackNorthwind.aspx.vb and CallbackNorthwind.aspx.cs

Much of this document is quite similar to the document in the previous example using the callback feature. The big difference comes in the `RaiseCallbackEvent()` method. This method first performs a `SELECT` statement on the Customers database based upon the `CustomerID` passed in via the `eventArgument` variable. The result retrieved from this `SELECT` statement is then made part of a string array, which is finally concatenated using the `String.Join()` method before being passed back as the value of the `_callbackResult` object.

With this code in place, you can now populate an entire table of data using the callback feature. This means that the table is populated with no need to refresh the page. The results from this code operation are presented in Figure 2-15.

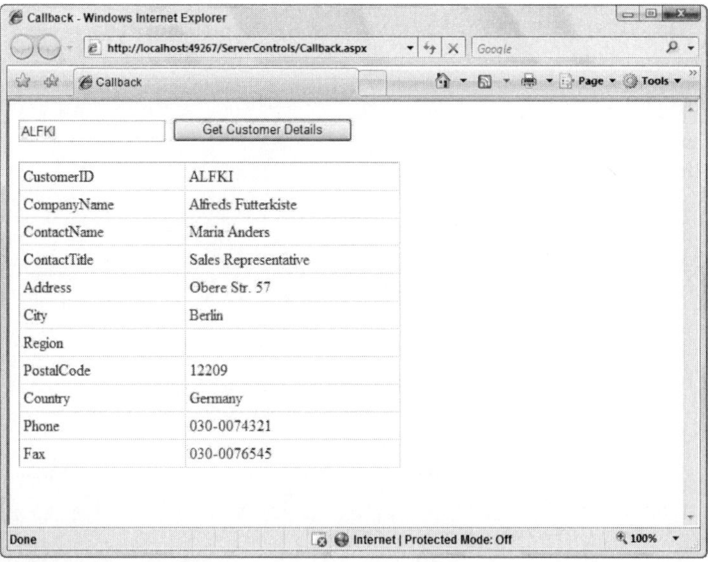

FIGURE 2-15

SUMMARY

This chapter gave you one of the core building blocks of an ASP.NET page — the server control. The server control is an object-oriented approach to page development that encapsulates page elements into modifiable and expandable components.

The chapter also introduced you to how to customize the look-and-feel of your server controls using Cascading Style Sheets (CSS). Working with CSS in ASP.NET 4 is easy and quick, especially if you have Visual Studio 2010 to assist you. Finally, this chapter looked at both using HTML server controls and adding JavaScript to your pages to modify the behaviors of your controls.

SUMMARY

3

ASP.NET Web Server Controls

WHAT'S IN THIS CHAPTER?

- Reviewing key Web server controls
- Differentiating between Web server control features
- Removing items from a collection

Of the two types of server controls, HTML server controls and Web server controls, the latter is considered the more powerful and flexible. The previous chapter looked at how to use HTML server controls in applications. HTML server controls enable you to manipulate HTML elements from your server-side code. On the other hand, Web server controls are powerful because they are not explicitly tied to specific HTML elements; rather, they are more closely aligned to the specific functionality that you want to generate. As you will see throughout this chapter, Web server controls can be very simple or rather complex depending on the control you are working with.

The purpose of the large collection of controls is to make you more productive. These controls give you advanced functionality that, in the past, you would have had to laboriously program or simply omit. In the classic ASP days, for example, few calendars were used on Internet Web sites. With the introduction of the Calendar server control in ASP.NET 1.0, calendar creation on a site became a trivial task. Building an image map on top of an image was another task that was difficult to achieve in ASP.NET 1.*x*, but this capability was introduced as a new server control in ASP.NET 2.0. As ASP.NET evolves through the releases, new controls are always added that help to make you a more productive Web developer.

This chapter introduces some of the available Web server controls. The first part of the chapter focuses on the Web server controls that were around since the first days of ASP.NET. Then the chapter explores the server controls that were introduced after the initial release of ASP.NET. This chapter does not discuss every possible control because some server controls are introduced and covered in other chapters throughout the book as they might be more related to that particular topic.

AN OVERVIEW OF WEB SERVER CONTROLS

The Web server control is ASP.NET's most-used component. Although you may have seen a lot of potential uses of the HTML server controls shown in the previous chapter, Web server controls are definitely a notch higher in capability. They allow for a higher level of functionality that becomes more apparent as you work with them.

The HTML server controls provided by ASP.NET work in that they map to specific HTML elements. You control the output by working with the HTML attributes that the HTML element provides. The attributes can be changed dynamically on the server side before they are finally output to the client. There is a lot of power in this, and you have some HTML server control capabilities that you simply do not have when you work with Web server controls.

Web server controls work differently. They do not map to specific HTML elements, but instead enable you to define functionality, capability, and appearance without the attributes that are available to you through a collection of HTML elements. When constructing a Web page that is made up of Web server controls, you are describing the functionality, the look-and-feel, and the behavior of your page elements. You then let ASP.NET decide how to output this construction. The output, of course, is based on the capabilities of the container that is making the request. This means that each requestor might see a different HTML output because each is requesting the same page with a different browser type or version. ASP.NET takes care of all the browser detection and the work associated with it on your behalf.

Unlike HTML server controls, Web server controls are not only available for working with common Web page form elements (such as text boxes and buttons), but they can also bring some advanced capabilities and functionality to your Web pages. For instance, one common feature of many Web applications is a calendar. No HTML form element places a calendar on your Web forms, but a Web server control from ASP.NET can provide your application with a full-fledged calendar, including some advanced capabilities. In the past, adding calendars to your Web pages was not a small programming task. Today, adding calendars with ASP. NET is rather simple and is achieved with a single line of code!

Remember that when you are constructing your Web server controls, you are actually constructing a control — *a set of instructions* — that is meant for the server (not the client). By default, all Web server controls provided by ASP.NET use an `asp:` at the beginning of the control declaration. The following is a typical Web server control:

```
<asp:Label ID="Label1" runat="server" Text="Hello World"></asp:Label>
```

Like HTML server controls, Web server controls require an `ID` attribute to reference the control in the server-side code, as well as a `runat="server"` attribute declaration. As you do for other XML-based elements, you need to properly open and close Web server controls using XML syntax rules. In the preceding example, you can see the `<asp:Label>` control has a closing `</asp:Label>` element associated with it. You could have also closed this element using the following syntax:

```
<asp:Label ID="Label1" Runat="server" Text="Hello World" />
```

The rest of this chapter examines some of the Web server controls available to you in ASP.NET.

THE LABEL SERVER CONTROL

The Label server control is used to display text in the browser. Because this is a server control, you can dynamically alter the text from your server-side code. As you saw from the preceding examples of using the `<asp:Label>` control, the control uses the `Text` attribute to assign the content of the control as shown here:

```
<asp:Label ID="Label1" runat="server" Text="Hello World" />
```

Instead of using the `Text` attribute, however, you can place the content to be displayed between the `<asp:Label>` elements like this:

```
<asp:Label ID="Label1" runat="server">Hello World</asp:Label>
```

You can also provide content for the control through programmatic means, as illustrated in Listing 3-1.

LISTING 3-1: Programmatically providing text to the Label control

VB

```
Label1.Text = "Hello ASP.NET"
```

C#

```
Label1.Text = "Hello ASP.NET";
```

The Label server control has always been a control that simply showed text. Ever since ASP.NET 2.0, it has a little bit of extra functionality. The big change since this release of the framework is that you can now give items in your form hot-key functionality (also known as *accelerator* keys). This causes the page to focus on a particular server control that you declaratively assign to a specific hot-key press (for example, using Alt+N to focus on the first text box on the form).

A hot key is a quick way for the end user to initiate an action on the page. For instance, if you use Microsoft Internet Explorer, you can press Ctrl+N to open a new instance of IE. Hot keys have always been quite common in thick-client applications (Windows Forms), and now you can use them in ASP.NET. Listing 3-2 shows an example of how to give hot-key functionality to two text boxes on a form.

LISTING 3-2: Using the Label server control to provide hot-key functionality

Available for download on Wrox.com

```
<%@ Page Language="VB" %>

<html xmlns="http://www.w3.org/1999/xhtml">
<head runat="server">
    <title>Label Server Control</title>
</head>
<body>
    <form id="form1" runat="server">
        <p>
            <asp:Label ID="Label1" runat="server" AccessKey="N"
             AssociatedControlID="Textbox1">User<u>n</u>ame</asp:Label>
            <asp:TextBox ID="TextBox1" runat="server"></asp:TextBox></p>
        <p>
            <asp:Label ID="Label2" runat="server" AccessKey="P"
             AssociatedControlID="Textbox2"><u>P</u>assword</asp:Label>
            <asp:TextBox ID="TextBox2" Runat="server"></asp:TextBox></p>
        <p>
            <asp:Button ID="Button1" runat="server" Text="Submit" />
        </p>
    </form>
</body>
</html>
```

Hot keys are assigned with the `AccessKey` attribute. In this case, `Label1` uses `N`, and `Label2` uses `P`. The second attribute for the Label control is the `AssociatedControlID` attribute. The `String` value placed here associates the Label control with another server control on the form. The value must be one of the other server controls on the form. If not, the page gives you an error when invoked.

With these two controls in place, when the page is called in the browser, you can press Alt+N or Alt+P to automatically focus on a particular text box in the form. In Figure 3-1, HTML-declared underlines indicate the letters to be pressed along with the Alt key to create focus on the control adjoining the text. This is not required, but we highly recommend it because it is what the end user expects when working with hot keys. In this example, the letter `n` in `Username` and the letter `P` in `Password` are underlined.

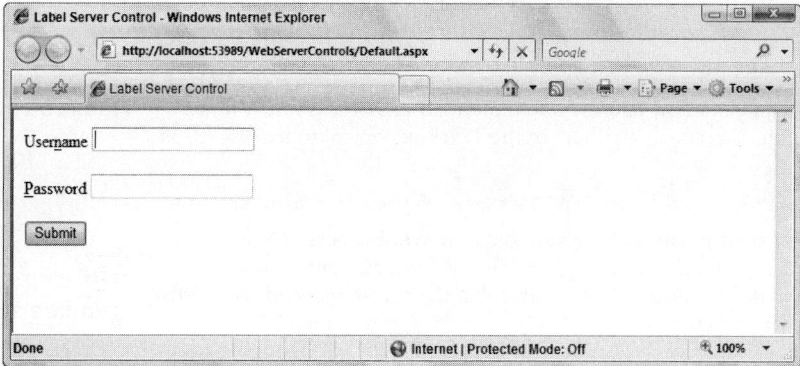

FIGURE 3-1

When working with hot keys, be aware that not all letters are available to use with the Alt key. Microsoft Internet Explorer already uses Alt+F, E, V, I, O, T, A, W, and H. If you use any of these letters, IE actions supersede any actions you place on the page.

THE LITERAL SERVER CONTROL

The Literal server control works very much like the Label server control does. This control was always used in the past for text that you wanted to push out to the browser but keep unchanged in the process (a literal state). A Label control alters the output by placing `<span>` elements around the text as shown:

```
<span id="Label1">Here is some text</span>
```

The Literal control just outputs the text without the `<span>` elements. One feature found in this server control is the attribute `Mode`. This attribute enables you to dictate how the text assigned to the control is interpreted by the ASP.NET engine.

If you place some HTML code in the string that is output (for instance, `<b>Here is some text</b>`), the Literal control outputs just that and the consuming browser shows the text as bold:

Here is some text

Try using the `Mode` attribute as illustrated here:

```
<asp:Literal ID="Literal1" runat="server" Mode="Encode"
 Text="<b>Here is some text</b>"></asp:Literal>
```

Adding `Mode="Encode"` encodes the output before it is received by the consuming application:

```
&lt;b&gt;Label&lt;/b&gt;
```

Now, instead of the text being converted to a bold font, the `<b>` elements are displayed:

```
<b>Here is some text</b>
```

This is ideal if you want to display code in your application. Other values for the `Mode` attribute include `Transform` and `PassThrough`. `Transform` looks at the consumer and includes or removes elements as needed. For instance, not all devices accept HTML elements so, if the value of the `Mode` attribute is set to `Transform`, these elements are removed from the string before it is sent to the consuming application. A value of `PassThrough` for the `Mode` property means that the text is sent to the consuming application without any changes being made to the string.

THE TEXTBOX SERVER CONTROL

One of the main features of Web pages is to offer forms that end users can use to submit their information for collection. The TextBox server control is one of the most used controls in this space. As its name suggests, the control provides a text box on the form that enables the end user to input text. You can map the TextBox control to three different HTML elements used in your forms.

First, the TextBox control can be used as a standard HTML text box, as shown in the following code snippet:

```
<asp:TextBox ID="TextBox1" runat="server"></asp:TextBox>
```

This code creates a text box on the form that looks like the one shown in Figure 3-2.

FIGURE 3-2

Second, the TextBox control can allow end users to input their passwords into a form. This is done by changing the `TextMode` attribute of the TextBox control to `Password`, as illustrated here:

```
<asp:TextBox ID="TextBox1" runat="server" TextMode="Password"></asp:TextBox>
```

When asking end users for their passwords through the browser, it is best practice to provide a text box that encodes the content placed in this form element. Using an attribute and value of `TextMode="Password"` ensures that the text is encoded with either a star (*) or a dot, as shown in Figure 3-3.

FIGURE 3-3

Third, the TextBox server control can be used as a multiline text box. The code for accomplishing this task is as follows:

```
<asp:TextBox ID="TextBox1" runat="server" TextMode="MultiLine"
 Width="300px" Height="150px"></asp:TextBox>
```

Giving the `TextMode` attribute a value of `MultiLine` creates a multilined text box in which the end user can enter a larger amount of text in the form. The `Width` and `Height` attributes set the size of the text area, but these are optional attributes — without them, the text area is produced in its smallest size. Figure 3-4 shows the use of the preceding code after adding some text.

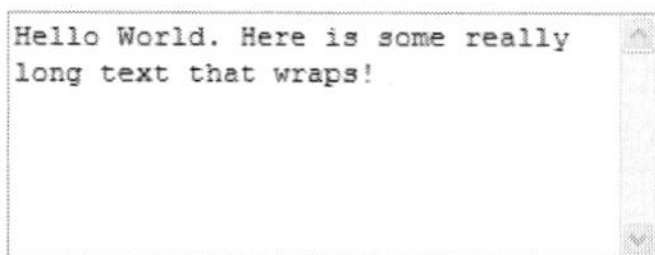

FIGURE 3-4

When working with a multilined text box, be aware of the `Wrap` attribute. When set to `True` (which is the default), the text entered into the text area wraps to the next line if needed. When set to `False`, the end user can type continuously in a single line until she presses the Enter key, which brings the cursor down to the next line.

Using the Focus() Method

Because the TextBox server control is derived from the base class of `WebControl`, one of the methods available to it is `Focus()`. The `Focus()` method enables you to dynamically place the end user's cursor in an appointed form element (not just the TextBox control, but in any of the server controls derived from the `WebControl` class). With that said, it is probably most often used with the TextBox control, as illustrated in Listing 3-3.

LISTING 3-3: Using the Focus() method with the TextBox control

VB

```
Protected Sub Page_Load(ByVal sender As Object, ByVal e As System.EventArgs)
   TextBox1.Focus()
End Sub
```

C#

```
protected void Page_Load(object sender, EventArgs e)
{
   TextBox1.Focus();
}
```

When the page using this method is loaded in the browser, the cursor is already placed inside of the text box, ready for you to start typing. There is no need to move your mouse to get the cursor in place so you can start entering information in the form. This is ideal for those folks who take a keyboard approach to working with forms.

Using AutoPostBack

ASP.NET pages work in an event-driven way. When an action on a Web page triggers an event, server-side code is initiated. One of the more common events is an end user clicking a button on the form. If you double-click the button in Design view of Visual Studio 2010, you can see the code page with the structure of the `Button1_Click` event already in place. This is because `OnClick` is the most common event of the Button control. Double-clicking the TextBox control constructs an `OnTextChanged` event. This event is triggered when the end user moves the cursor focus outside the text box, either by clicking another element on the page after entering something into a text box, or by simply tabbing out of the text box. The use of this event is shown in Listing 3-4.

LISTING 3-4: Triggering an event when a TextBox change occurs

```
<%@ Page Language="VB" %>

<script runat="server">
```

continues

LISTING 3-4 *(continued)*

```
    Protected Sub TextBox1_TextChanged(ByVal sender As Object,
       ByVal e As System.EventArgs)

        Response.Write("OnTextChanged event triggered")
    End Sub

    Protected Sub Button1_Click(ByVal sender As Object,
       ByVal e As System.EventArgs)

        Response.Write("OnClick event triggered")
    End Sub
</script>

<html xmlns="http://www.w3.org/1999/xhtml">
<head runat="server">
    <title>OnTextChanged Page</title>
</head>
<body>
    <form id="form1" runat="server">
    <div>
        <asp:TextBox ID="TextBox1" runat="server" AutoPostBack="True"
         OnTextChanged="TextBox1_TextChanged"></asp:TextBox>
        <asp:Button ID="Button1" runat="server" Text="Button"
         OnClick="Button1_Click" />
    </div>
    </form>
</body>
</html>
```

C#

```
<%@ Page Language="C#" %>

<script runat="server">
    protected void TextBox1_TextChanged(object sender, EventArgs e)
    {
        Response.Write("OnTextChanged event triggered");
    }

    protected void Button1_Click(object sender, EventArgs e)
    {
        Response.Write("OnClick event triggered");
    }
</script>
```

As you build and run this page, notice that you can type something in the text box, but once you tab out of it, the `OnTextChanged` event is triggered and the code contained in the `TextBox1_TextChanged` event runs. To make this work, you must add the `AutoPostBack` attribute to the TextBox control and set it to `True`. This causes the Web page to look for any text changes prior to an actual page postback. For the `AutoPostBack` feature to work, the browser viewing the page must support ECMAScript.

Using AutoCompleteType

You want the forms you build for your Web applications to be as simple to use as possible. You want to make them easy and quick for the end user to fill out the information and proceed. If you make a form too onerous, the people who come to your site may leave without completing it.

One of the great capabilities for any Web form is smart auto-completion. You may have seen this yourself when you visited a site for the first time. As you start to fill out information in a form, a drop-down list appears below the text box as you type, showing you a value that you have typed in a previous form. The plain text box you were working with has become a smart text box. Figure 3-5 shows an example of this feature.

FIGURE 3-5

A great aspect of the TextBox control is the `AutoCompleteType` attribute, which enables you to apply the auto-completion feature to your own forms. You have to help the text boxes on your form to recognize the type of information that they should be looking for. What does that mean? Well, first look at the possible values of the `AutoCompleteType` attribute:

```
BusinessCity             Disabled              HomeStreetAddress
BusinessCountryRegion    DisplayName           HomeZipCode
BusinessFax              Email                 JobTitle
BusinessPhone            FirstName             LastName
BusinessState            Gender                MiddleName
BusinessStateAddress     HomeCity              None
BusinessUrl              HomeCountryRegion     Notes
BusinessZipCode          HomeFax               Office
Cellular                 Homepage              Pager
Company                  HomePhone             Search
Department               HomeState
```

From this list, you can see that if your text box is asking for the end user's home street address, you want to use the following in your TextBox control:

```
<asp:TextBox ID="TextBox1" runat="server"
 AutoCompleteType="HomeStreetAddress"></asp:TextBox>
```

As you view the source of the text box you created, you can see that the following construction has occurred:

```
<input name="TextBox1" type="text" vcard_name="vCard.Home.StreetAddress"
 id="TextBox1" />
```

This feature makes your forms easier to work with. Yes, it is a simple thing but sometimes the little things keep the viewers coming back again and again to your Web site.

THE BUTTON SERVER CONTROL

Another common control for your Web forms is a button that can be constructed using the Button server control. Buttons are the usual element used to submit forms. Most of the time you are simply dealing with items contained in your forms through the Button control's `OnClick` event, as illustrated in Listing 3-5.

LISTING 3-5: The Button control's OnClick event

VB

```
Protected Sub Button1_Click(ByVal sender As Object, ByVal e As System.EventArgs)
   ' Code here
End Sub
```

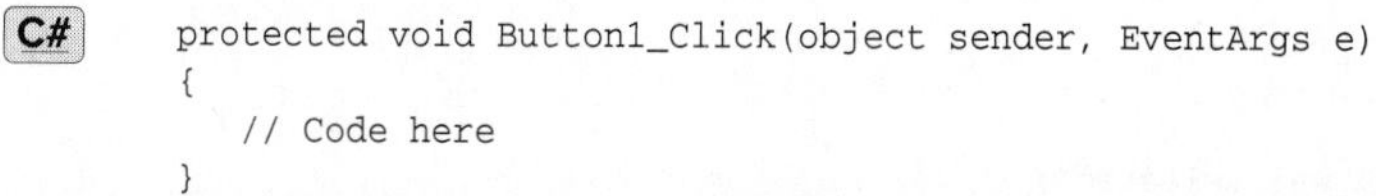

C#

```
protected void Button1_Click(object sender, EventArgs e)
{
   // Code here
}
```

The Button control is one of the easier controls to use, but there are a couple of properties of which you must be aware: `CausesValidation` and `CommandName`. They are discussed in the following sections.

The CausesValidation Property

If you have more than one button on your Web page and you are working with the validation server controls, you may not want to fire the validation for each button on the form. Setting the `CausesValidation` property to `False` is a way to use a button that will not fire the validation process. This is explained in more detail in Chapter 4.

The CommandName Property

You can have multiple buttons on your form all working from a single event. The nice thing is that you can also tag the buttons so that the code can make logical decisions based on which button on the form was clicked. You must construct your Button controls in the manner illustrated in Listing 3-6 to take advantage of this behavior.

LISTING 3-6: Constructing multiple Button controls to work from a single function

```
<asp:Button ID="Button1" runat="server" Text="Button 1"
 OnCommand="Button_Command" CommandName="DoSomething1" />
<asp:Button ID="Button2" runat="server" Text="Button 2"
 OnCommand="Button_Command" CommandName="DoSomething2" />
```

Looking at these two instances of the Button control, you should pay attention to several things. The first thing to notice is what is not present — any attribute mention of an `OnClick` event. Instead, you use the `OnCommand` event, which points to an event called `Button_Command`. You can see that both Button controls are working from the same event. How does the event differentiate between the two buttons being clicked? Through the value placed in the `CommandName` property. In this case, they are indeed separate values — `DoSomething1` and `DoSomething2`.

The next step is to create the `Button_Command` event to deal with both these buttons by simply typing one out or by selecting the `Command` event from the drop-down list of available events for the Button control from the code view of Visual Studio. In either case, you should end up with an event like the one shown in Listing 3-7.

LISTING 3-7: The Button_Command event

VB

```
Protected Sub Button_Command(ByVal sender As Object,
  ByVal e As System.Web.UI.WebControls.CommandEventArgs)

   Select Case e.CommandName
      Case "DoSomething1"
         Response.Write("Button 1 was selected")
      Case "DoSomething2"
         Response.Write("Button 2 was selected")
   End Select

End Sub
```

C#

```
protected void Button_Command(Object sender,
   System.Web.UI.WebControls.CommandEventArgs e)
{
   switch (e.CommandName)
   {
      case("DoSomething1"):
         Response.Write("Button 1 was selected");
         break;
      case("DoSomething2"):
         Response.Write("Button 2 was selected");
         break;
   }
}
```

Notice that this method uses `System.Web.UI.WebControls.CommandEventArgs` instead of the typical `System.EventArgs`. This gives you access to the member `CommandName` used in the `Select Case` (`switch`) statement as `e.CommandName`. Using this object, you can check for the value of the `CommandName` property used by the button that was clicked on the form and take a specific action based upon the value passed.

You can add some parameters to be passed in to the `Command` event beyond what is defined in the `CommandName` property. You do this by using the Button control's `CommandArgument` property. Adding values to the property enables you to define items a bit more granularly if you want. You can get at this value via server-side code using `e.CommandArgument` from the `CommandEventArgs` object.

Buttons That Work with Client-Side JavaScript

Buttons are frequently used for submitting information and causing actions to occur on a Web page. Before ASP.NET 1.0/1.1, people intermingled quite a bit of JavaScript in their pages to fire JavaScript events when a button was clicked. The process became more cumbersome in ASP.NET 1.0/1.1, but ever since ASP.NET 2.0, it has been much easier.

You can create a page that has a JavaScript event, as well as a server-side event, triggered when the button is clicked, as illustrated in Listing 3-8.

LISTING 3-8: Two types of events for the button

Available for download on Wrox.com

```
<%@ Page Language="VB" %>

<script runat="server">
    Protected Sub Button1_Click(ByVal sender As Object, _
       ByVal e As System.EventArgs)

        Response.Write("Postback!")
    End Sub
</script>

<script language="javascript">
   function AlertHello()
   {
      alert('Hello ASP.NET');
   }
</script>

<html xmlns="http://www.w3.org/1999/xhtml">
<head runat="server">
    <title>Button Server Control</title>
</head>
<body>
    <form id="form1" runat="server">
        <asp:Button ID="Button1" runat="server" Text="Button"
         OnClientClick="AlertHello()" OnClick="Button1_Click" />
    </form>
</body>

</html>
```

C#

```
<%@ Page Language="C#" %>

<script runat="server">
    protected void Button1_Click(object sender, EventArgs e)
    {
        Response.Write("Postback!");
    }
</script>
```

The first thing to notice is the attribute for the Button server control: `OnClientClick`. It points to the client-side function, unlike the `OnClick` attribute that points to the server-side event. This example uses a JavaScript function called `AlertHello()`.

One cool thing about Visual Studio 2010 is that it can work with server-side script tags that are right alongside client-side script tags. It all works together seamlessly. In the example, after the JavaScript alert dialog is issued (see Figure 3-6) and the end user clicks OK, the page posts back as the server-side event is triggered.

FIGURE 3-6

Another interesting attribute for the button controls is `PostBackUrl`. It enables you to perform cross-page posting, instead of simply posting your ASP.NET pages back to the same page, as shown in the following example:

```
<asp:Button ID="Button2" runat="server" Text="Submit page to Page2.aspx"
 PostBackUrl="Page2.aspx" />
```

Cross-page posting is covered in greater detail in Chapter 1.

THE LINKBUTTON SERVER CONTROL

The LinkButton server control is a variation of the Button control. It is the same except that the LinkButton control takes the form of a hyperlink. Nevertheless, it is not a typical hyperlink. When the end user clicks the link, it behaves like a button. This is an ideal control to use if you have a large number of buttons on your Web form.

A LinkButton server control is constructed as follows:

```
<asp:LinkButton ID="LinkButton1" Runat="server" OnClick="LinkButton1_Click">
   Submit your name to our database
</asp:LinkButton>
```

Using the LinkButton control gives you the results shown in Figure 3-7.

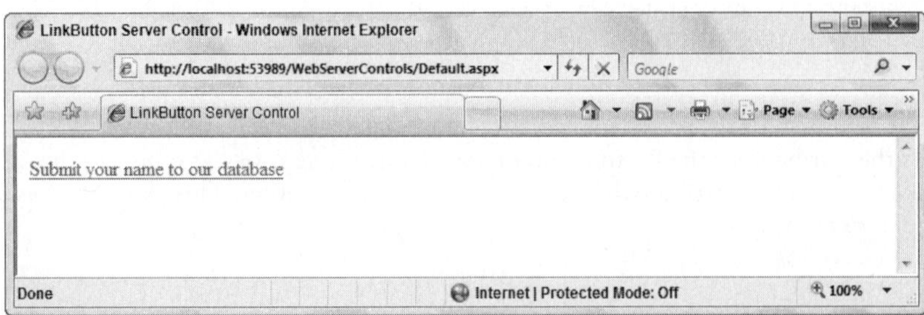

FIGURE 3-7

THE IMAGEBUTTON SERVER CONTROL

The ImageButton control is also a variation of the Button control. It is almost exactly the same as the Button control except that it enables you to use a custom image as the form's button instead of the typical buttons used on most forms. This means that you can create your own buttons as images and the end users can click the images to submit form data. A typical construction of the ImageButton is as follows:

```
<asp:ImageButton ID="ImageButton1" runat="server"
 OnClick="ImageButton1_Click" ImageUrl="MyButton.jpg" />
```

The ImageButton control specifies the location of the image used by using the `ImageUrl` property. From this example, you can see that the `ImageUrl` points to `MyButton.jpg`. The big difference between the ImageButton control and the LinkButton or Button controls is that ImageButton takes a different construction for the `OnClick` event. It is shown in Listing 3-9.

LISTING 3-9: The Click event for the ImageButton control

VB

```
Protected Sub ImageButton1_Click(ByVal sender As Object,
   ByVal e As System.Web.UI.WebControls.ImageClickEventArgs)
   ' Code here
End Sub
```

C#

```
protected void ImageButton1_Click(object sender,
   System.Web.UI.WebControls.ImageClickEventArgs e)
{
   // Code here
}
```

The construction uses the `ImageClickEventArgs` object instead of the `System.EventArgs` object usually used with the LinkButton and Button controls. You can use this object to determine where in the image the end user clicked by using both `e.X` and `e.Y` coordinates.

The Search and Play Video buttons on the page shown in Figure 3-8 are image buttons.

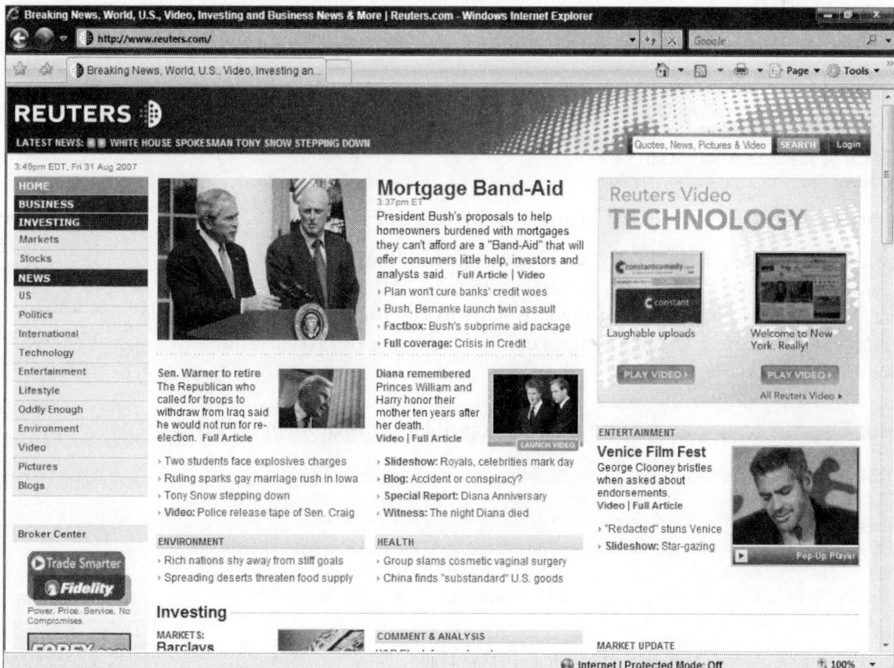

FIGURE 3-8

THE HYPERLINK SERVER CONTROL

The HyperLink server control enables you to programmatically work with any hyperlinks on your Web pages. Hyperlinks are links that allow end users to transfer from one page to another. You can set the text of a hyperlink using the control's `Text` attribute:

```
<asp:HyperLink ID="HyperLink1" runat="server" Text="Go to this page here"
 NavigateUrl="</Default2.aspx"></asp:HyperLink>
```

This server control creates a hyperlink on your page with the text `Go to this page here`. When the link is clicked, the user is redirected to the value that is placed in the `NavigateUrl` property (in this case, the `Default2.aspx` page).

The interesting thing about the HyperLink server control is that it can be used for images as well as text. Instead of using the `Text` attribute, it uses the `ImageUrl` property:

```
<asp:HyperLink ID="HyperLink1" runat="server" ImageUrl="</MyLinkImage.gif"
 NavigateUrl="</Default2.aspx"></asp:HyperLink>
```

The HyperLink control is a great way to dynamically place hyperlinks on a Web page based either upon user input in a form or on database values that are retrieved when the page is loaded.

THE DROPDOWNLIST SERVER CONTROL

The DropDownList server control enables you to place an HTML select box on your Web page and program against it. It is ideal when you have a large collection of items from which you want the end user to select a single item. It is usually used for a medium- to large-sized collection. If the collection size is relatively small, consider using the RadioButtonList server control (described later in this chapter).

The select box generated by the DropDownList control displays a single item and allows the end user to make a selection from a larger list of items. Depending on the number of choices available in the select box, the end user may have to scroll through a list of items. Note that the appearance of the scroll bar in the drop-down list is automatically created by the browser depending on the browser version and the number of items contained in the list.

Here is the code for DropDownList control:

```
<asp:DropDownList ID="DropDownList1" runat="server">
   <asp:ListItem>Car</asp:ListItem>
   <asp:ListItem>Airplane</asp:ListItem>
   <asp:ListItem>Train</asp:ListItem>
</asp:DropDownList>
```

This code generates a drop-down list in the browser, as shown in Figure 3-9.

FIGURE 3-9

The DropDownList control comes in handy when you start binding it to various data stores. The data stores can either be arrays, database values, XML file values, or values found elsewhere. For an example of binding the DropDownList control, this next example looks at dynamically generating a DropDownList control from one of three available arrays, as shown in Listing 3-10.

LISTING 3-10: Dynamically generating a DropDownList control from an array

Available for download on Wrox.com

VB

```
<%@ Page Language="VB" %>

<script runat="server">
    Protected Sub DropDownList1_SelectedIndexChanged(ByVal sender As Object,
      ByVal e As System.EventArgs)
        Dim CarArray() As String = {"Ford", "Honda", "BMW", "Dodge"}
        Dim AirplaneArray() As String = {"Boeing 777", "Boeing 747", "Boeing 737"}
        Dim TrainArray() As String = {"Bullet Train", "Amtrack", "Tram"}

        If DropDownList1.SelectedValue = "Car" Then
```

```
            DropDownList2.DataSource = CarArray
        ElseIf DropDownList1.SelectedValue = "Airplane" Then
            DropDownList2.DataSource = AirplaneArray
        ElseIf DropDownList1.SelectedValue = "Train" Then
            DropDownList2.DataSource = TrainArray
        End If

        DropDownList2.DataBind()
        DropDownList2.Visible = (DropDownList1.SelectedValue <> _
            "Select an Item")
    End Sub

    Protected Sub Button1_Click(ByVal sender As Object,
       ByVal e As System.EventArgs)

        Response.Write("You selected <b>" & _
           DropDownList1.SelectedValue.ToString() & ": " &
           DropDownList2.SelectedValue.ToString() & "</b>")
    End Sub
</script>

<html xmlns="http://www.w3.org/1999/xhtml">
<head runat="server">
    <title>DropDownList Page</title>
</head>
<body>
    <form id="form1" runat="server">
    <div>
        Select transportation type:<br />
        <asp:DropDownList ID="DropDownList1" runat="server"
         OnSelectedIndexChanged="DropDownList1_SelectedIndexChanged"
         AutoPostBack="true">
            <asp:ListItem>Select an Item</asp:ListItem>
            <asp:ListItem>Car</asp:ListItem>
            <asp:ListItem>Airplane</asp:ListItem>
            <asp:ListItem>Train</asp:ListItem>
        </asp:DropDownList> 
        <asp:DropDownList ID="DropDownList2" runat="server" Visible="false">
        </asp:DropDownList>
        <asp:Button ID="Button1" runat="server" Text="Select Options"
         OnClick="Button1_Click" />
    </div>
    </form>
</body>
</html>
```

C#

```
<%@ Page Language="C#" %>

<script runat="server">
    protected void DropDownList1_SelectedIndexChanged(object sender, EventArgs e)
    {
        string[] carArray = new[] {"Ford", "Honda", "BMW", "Dodge"};
        string[] airplaneArray = new[] {"Boeing 777", "Boeing 747",
           "Boeing 737"};
        string[] trainArray = new[] {"Bullet Train", "Amtrack", "Tram"};

        if (DropDownList1.SelectedValue == "Car") {
            DropDownList2.DataSource = carArray; }
        else if (DropDownList1.SelectedValue == "Airplane") {
            DropDownList2.DataSource = airplaneArray; }
        else if (DropDownList1.SelectedValue == "Train") {
```

continues

LISTING 3-10 *(continued)*

```
                DropDownList2.DataSource = trainArray; }

            DropDownList2.DataBind();
            DropDownList2.Visible = DropDownList1.SelectedValue != "Select an Item";
        }

        protected void Button1_Click(object sender, EventArgs e)
        {
            Response.Write("You selected <b>" +
               DropDownList1.SelectedValue.ToString() + ": " +
               DropDownList2.SelectedValue.ToString() + "</b>");
        }
    </script>
```

In this example, the second drop-down list is dynamically generated based upon the value selected from the first drop-down list. For instance, selecting `Car` from the first drop-down list dynamically creates a second drop-down list on the form that includes a list of available car selections.

This is possible because of the use of the `AutoPostBack` feature of the `DropDownList` control. When the `AutoPostBack` property is set to `True`, the method provided through the `OnSelectedIndexChanged` event is fired when a selection is made. In the example, the `DropDownList1_SelectedIndexChanged` event is fired, dynamically creating the second drop-down list.

In this method, the content of the second drop-down list is created in a string array and then bound to the second DropDownList control through the use of the `DataSource` property and the `DataBind()` method.

When built and run, this page looks like the one shown in Figure 3-10.

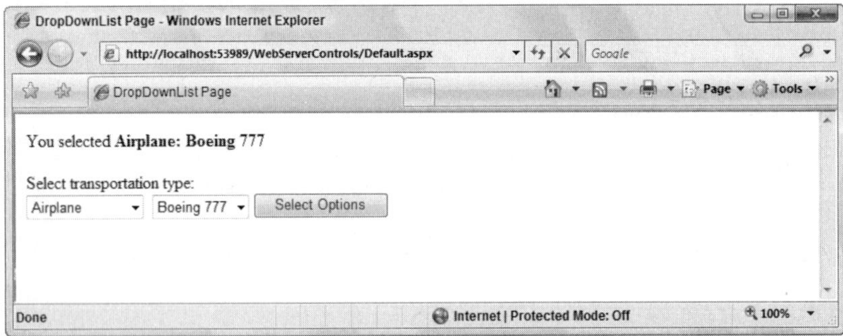

FIGURE 3-10

VISUALLY REMOVING ITEMS FROM A COLLECTION

The DropDownList, ListBox, CheckBoxList, and RadioButtonList server controls give you the capability to visually remove items from the collection displayed in the control, although you can still work with the items that are not displayed in your server-side code.

The ListBox, CheckBoxList, and RadioButtonList controls are discussed shortly in this chapter.

For a quick example of removing items, create a drop-down list with three items, including one that you will not display. On the postback, however, you can still work with the ListItem's `Value` or `Text` property, as illustrated in Listing 3-11.

LISTING 3-11: Disabling certain ListItems from a collection

Available for download on Wrox.com

```
<%@ Page Language="VB" %>

<script runat="server">
    Protected Sub DropDownList1_SelectedIndexChanged(ByVal sender As Object,
       ByVal e As System.EventArgs)
         Response.Write("You selected item number " &
           DropDownList1.SelectedValue & "<br>")
         Response.Write("You didn't select item number " &
           DropDownList1.Items(1).Value)
    End Sub
</script>

<html>
<head runat="server">
    <title>DropDownList Server Control</title>
</head>
<body>
    <form id="form1" runat="server">
        <asp:DropDownList ID="DropDownList1" Runat="server" AutoPostBack="True"
         OnSelectedIndexChanged="DropDownList1_SelectedIndexChanged">
            <asp:ListItem Value="1">First Choice</asp:ListItem>
            <asp:ListItem Value="2" Enabled="False">Second Choice</asp:ListItem>
            <asp:ListItem Value="3">Third Choice</asp:ListItem>
        </asp:DropDownList>
    </form>
</body>
</html>
```

C#

```
<%@ Page Language="C#" %>

<script runat="server">
    protected void DropDownList1_SelectedIndexChanged(object sender, EventArgs e)
    {
         Response.Write("You selected item number " +
           DropDownList1.SelectedValue + "<br>");
         Response.Write("You didn't select item number " +
           DropDownList1.Items[1].Value);
    }
</script>
```

From the code, you can see that the `<asp:ListItem>` element has an attribute: `Enabled`. The Boolean value given to this element dictates whether an item in the collection is displayed. If you use `Enabled="False"`, the item is not displayed, but you still have the capability to work with the item in the server-side code displayed in the `DropDownList1_SelectedIndexChanged` event. The result of the output from these `Response.Write` statements is shown in Figure 3-11.

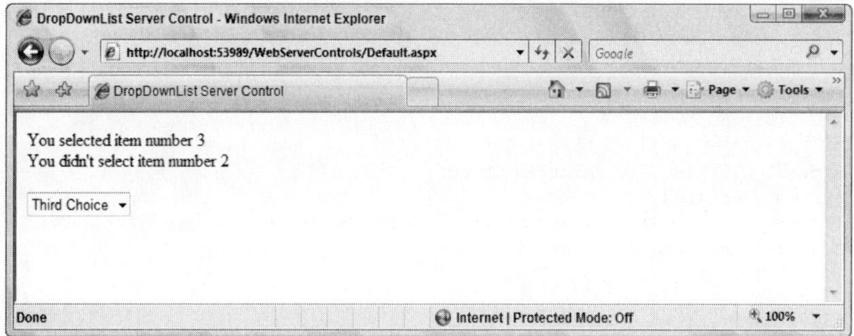

FIGURE 3-11

THE LISTBOX SERVER CONTROL

The ListBox server control has a function similar to the DropDownList control. It displays a collection of items. The ListBox control behaves differently from the DropDownList control in that it displays more of the collection to the end user, and it enables the end user to make multiple selections from the collection — something that is not possible with the DropDownList control.

A typical ListBox control appears in code as follows:

```
<asp:ListBox ID="ListBox1" runat="server">
   <asp:ListItem>Hematite</asp:ListItem>
   <asp:ListItem>Halite</asp:ListItem>
   <asp:ListItem>Limonite</asp:ListItem>
   <asp:ListItem>Magnetite</asp:ListItem>
</asp:ListBox>
```

This generates the browser display illustrated in Figure 3-12.

Hematite
Halite
Limonite
Magnetite

FIGURE 3-12

Allowing Users to Select Multiple Items

You can use the `SelectionMode` attribute to let your end users make multiple selections from what is displayed by the ListBox control. Here's an example:

```
<asp:ListBox ID="ListBox1" runat="server" SelectionMode="Multiple">
   <asp:ListItem>Hematite</asp:ListItem>
   <asp:ListItem>Halite</asp:ListItem>
   <asp:ListItem>Limonite</asp:ListItem>
   <asp:ListItem>Magnetite</asp:ListItem>
</asp:ListBox>
```

The possible values of the `SelectionMode` property include `Single` and `Multiple`. Setting the value to `Multiple` allows the end user to make multiple selections in the list box. The user must hold down either the Ctrl or Shift keys while making selections. Holding down the Ctrl key enables the user to make a single selection from the list while maintaining previous selections. Holding down the Shift key enables a range of multiple selections.

An Example of Using the ListBox Control

The ListBox control shown in Listing 3-12 allows multiple selections to be displayed in the browser when a user clicks the Submit button. The form should also have an additional text box and button at the top that enables the end user to add additional items to the ListBox.

LISTING 3-12: Using the ListBox control

```
<%@ Page Language="VB" %>

<script runat="server">
    Protected Sub Button1_Click(ByVal sender As Object,
       ByVal e As System.EventArgs)

        ListBox1.Items.Add(TextBox1.Text.ToString())
    End Sub

    Protected Sub Button2_Click(ByVal sender As Object,
       ByVal e As System.EventArgs)

        Label1.Text = "You selected from the ListBox:<br>"
        For Each li As ListItem In ListBox1.Items
            If li.Selected = True Then
                label1.Text += li.Text & "<br>"
```

```
            End If
        Next
    End Sub
</script>

<html xmlns="http://www.w3.org/1999/xhtml">
<head runat="server">
    <title>Using the ListBox</title>
</head>
<body>
    <form id="form1" runat="server">
    <div>
        <asp:TextBox ID="TextBox1" runat="server"></asp:TextBox>
        <asp:Button ID="Button1" runat="server" Text="Add an additional item"
         OnClick="Button1_Click" /><br /><br />

        <asp:ListBox ID="ListBox1" runat="server" SelectionMode="multiple">
           <asp:ListItem>Hematite</asp:ListItem>
           <asp:ListItem>Halite</asp:ListItem>
           <asp:ListItem>Limonite</asp:ListItem>
           <asp:ListItem>Magnetite</asp:ListItem>
        </asp:ListBox><br /><br />

        <asp:Button ID="Button2" runat="server" Text="Submit"
         OnClick="Button2_Click" /><br /><br />
        <asp:Label ID="Label1" runat="server"></asp:Label>
    </div>
    </form>
</body>
</html>
```

C#

```
<%@ Page Language="C#" %>

<script runat="server">
    protected void Button1_Click(object sender, EventArgs e)
    {
       ListBox1.Items.Add(TextBox1.Text.ToString());
    }

    protected void Button2_Click(object sender, EventArgs e)
    {
       Label1.Text = "You selected from the ListBox:<br>";
       foreach (ListItem li in ListBox1.Items) {
           if (li.Selected) {
               Label1.Text += li.Text + "<br>";
           }
       }
    }
</script>
```

This is an interesting example. First, some default items (four common minerals) are already placed inside the ListBox control. However, the text box and button at the top of the form allow the end user to add additional minerals to the list. Users can then make one or more selections from the ListBox, including selections from the items that they dynamically added to the collection. After a user makes his selection and clicks the button, the `Button2_Click` event iterates through the `ListItem` instances in the collection and displays only the items that have been selected.

This control works by creating an instance of a `ListItem` object and using its `Selected` property to see if a particular item in the collection has been selected. The use of the `ListItem` object is not limited to the ListBox control (although that is what is used here). You can dynamically add or remove items from a collection and get at items and their values using the `ListItem` object in the DropDownList, CheckBoxList, and RadioButtonList controls as well. It is a list-control feature. When this page is built and run, you get the results presented in Figure 3-13.

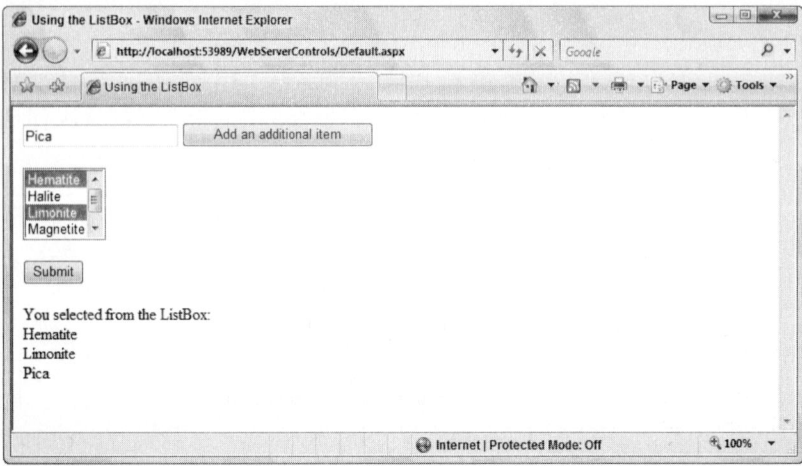

FIGURE 3-13

Adding Items to a Collection

To add items to the collection, you can use the following short syntax:

```
ListBox1.Items.Add(TextBox1.Text)
```

Look at the source code created in the browser, and you should see something similar to the following generated dynamically:

```
<select size="4" name="ListBox1" multiple="multiple" id="ListBox1">
     <option value="Hematite">Hematite</option>
     <option value="Halite">Halite</option>
     <option value="Limonite">Limonite</option>
     <option value="Magnetite">Magnetite</option>
     <option value="Olivine">Olivine</option>
</select>
```

You can see that the dynamically added value is a text item, and you can see its value. You can also add instances of the ListItem object to get different values for the item name and value:

VB
```
ListBox1.Items.Add(New ListItem("Olivine", "MG2SI04"))
```

C#
```
ListBox1.Items.Add(new ListItem("Olivine", "MG2SI04"));
```

This example adds a new instance of the `ListItem` object — adding not only the textual name of the item, but also the value of the item (its chemical formula). It produces the following results in the browser:

```
<option value="MG2SI04">Olivine</option>
```

THE CHECKBOX SERVER CONTROL

Check boxes on a Web form enable your users to either make selections from a collection of items or specify a value of an item to be yes/no, on/off, or true/false. Use either the CheckBox control or the CheckBoxList control to include check boxes in your Web forms.

The CheckBox control allows you to place single check boxes on a form; the CheckBoxList control allows you to place collections of check boxes on the form. You can use multiple CheckBox controls on your ASP.NET pages, but then you are treating each check box as its own element with its own associated events. On the other hand, the CheckBoxList control allows you to take multiple check boxes and create specific events for the entire group.

Listing 3-13 shows an example of using the CheckBox control.

LISTING 3-13: Using a single instance of the CheckBox control

Available for download on Wrox.com

```
<%@ Page Language="VB" %>
<script runat="server">
    Protected Sub CheckBox1_CheckedChanged(ByVal sender As Object,
      ByVal e As System.EventArgs)
        Response.Write("Thanks for your donation!")
    End Sub
</script>

<html xmlns="http://www.w3.org/1999/xhtml">
<head runat="server">
    <title>CheckBox control</title>
</head>
<body>
    <form id="form1" runat="server">
    <div>
        <asp:CheckBox ID="CheckBox1" runat="server" Text="Donate $10 to our cause!"
         OnCheckedChanged="CheckBox1_CheckedChanged" AutoPostBack="true" />
    </div>
    </form>
</body>
</html>
```

C#

```
<%@ Page Language="C#" %>

<script runat="server">
    protected void CheckBox1_CheckedChanged(object sender, EventArgs e)
    {
        Response.Write("Thanks for your donation!");
    }
</script>
```

This produces a page that contains a single check box asking for a monetary donation. Using the `CheckedChanged` event, `OnCheckedChanged` is used within the CheckBox control. The attribute's value points to the `CheckBox1_CheckedChanged` event, which fires when the user checks the check box. It occurs only if the `AutoPostBack` property is set to `True` (this property is set to `False` by default). Running this page produces the results shown in Figure 3-14.

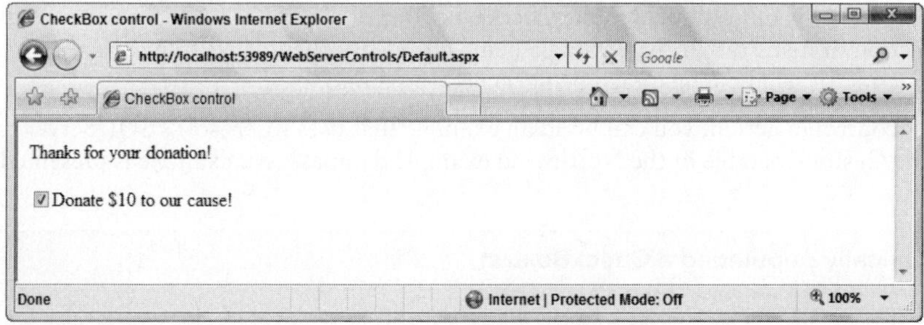

FIGURE 3-14

How to Determine Whether Check Boxes Are Checked

You might not want to use the `AutoPostBack` feature of the check box, but instead want to determine if the check box is checked after the form is posted back to the server. You can make this check through an `If Then` statement, as illustrated in the following example:

```
If (CheckBox1.Checked = True) Then
   Response.Write("CheckBox is checked!")
End If
```

```
if (CheckBox1.Checked == true) {
   Response.Write("Checkbox is checked!");
}
```

This check is done on the CheckBox value using the control's `Checked` property. The property's value is a Boolean value, so it is either `True` (checked) or `False` (not checked).

Assigning a Value to a Check Box

You can also use the `Checked` property to make sure a check box is checked based on other dynamic values:

VB

```
If (Member = True) Then
   CheckBox1.Checked = True
End If
```

C#

```
if (Member == true) {
   CheckBox1.Checked = true;
}
```

Aligning Text Around the Check Box

In the previous check box example, the text appears to the right of the actual check box, as shown in Figure 3-15.

Donate $10 to our cause!

FIGURE 3-15

Using the CheckBox control's `TextAlign` property, you can realign the text so that it appears on the other side of the check box:

```
<asp:CheckBox ID="CheckBox1" runat="server" Text="Donate $10 to our cause!"
 OnCheckedChanged="CheckBox1_CheckedChanged" AutoPostBack="true"
 TextAlign="Left" />
```

The possible values of the `TextAlign` property are either `Right` (the default setting) or `Left`. This property is also available to the CheckBoxList, RadioButton, and RadioButtonList controls. Assigning the value `Left` produces the result shown in Figure 3-16.

Donate $10 to our cause!

FIGURE 3-16

THE CHECKBOXLIST SERVER CONTROL

The CheckBoxList server control is quite similar to the CheckBox control, except that the former enables you to work with a collection of items rather than a single item. The idea is that a CheckBoxList server control instance is a collection of related items, each being a check box unto itself.

To see the CheckBoxList control in action, you can build an example that uses Microsoft's SQL Server to pull information from the Customers table of the Northwind example database. An example is presented in Listing 3-14.

LISTING 3-14: Dynamically populating a CheckBoxList

Available for download on Wrox.com

VB

```
<%@ Page Language="VB" %>

<script runat="server">
    Protected Sub Button1_Click(ByVal sender As Object,
       ByVal e As System.EventArgs)

        Label1.Text = "You selected:<br>"
        For Each li As ListItem In CheckBoxList1.Items
            If li.Selected = True Then
                Label1.Text += li.Text & "<br>"
            End If
```

```
        Next
    End Sub
</script>

<html xmlns="http://www.w3.org/1999/xhtml">
<head runat="server">
    <title>CheckBoxList control</title>
</head>
<body>
    <form id="form1" runat="server">
    <div>
        <asp:Button ID="Button1" runat="server" Text="Submit Choices"
         OnClick="Button1_Click" /><br /><br />
        <asp:Label ID="Label1" runat="server"></asp:Label>
        <br />
        <asp:CheckBoxList ID="CheckBoxList1" runat="server"
         DataSourceID="SqlDataSource1" DataTextField="CompanyName"
         RepeatColumns="3" BorderColor="Black"
         BorderStyle="Solid" BorderWidth="1px">
        </asp:CheckBoxList>
        <asp:SqlDataSource ID="SqlDataSource1" runat="server"
         SelectCommand="SELECT [CompanyName] FROM [Customers]"
            ConnectionString="<%$ ConnectionStrings:AppConnectionString1 %>">
        </asp:SqlDataSource>
    </div>
    </form>
</body>
</html>
```

C#

```
<%@ Page Language="C#" %>

<script runat="server">
    protected void Button1_Click(object sender, EventArgs e)
    {
       Label1.Text = "You selected:<br>";
       foreach (ListItem li in CheckBoxList1.Items) {
           if (li.Selected == true) {
               Label1.Text += li.Text + "<br>";
           }
       }
    }
</script>
```

This ASP.NET page has a SqlDataSource control on the page that pulls the information you need from the Northwind database. From the `SELECT` statement used in this control, you can see that you are retrieving the `CompanyName` field from each of the listings in the Customers table.

The CheckBoxList control binds itself to the SqlDataSource control using a few properties:

```
<asp:CheckBoxList ID="CheckBoxList1" runat="server"
 DataSourceID="SqlDataSource1" DataTextField="CompanyName"
 RepeatColumns="3" BorderColor="Black"
 BorderStyle="Solid" BorderWidth="1px">
</asp:CheckBoxList>
```

The `DataSourceID` property is used to associate the CheckBoxList control with the results that come back from the SqlDataSource control. Then the `DataTextField` property is used to retrieve the name of the field you want to work with from the results. In this example, it is the only one that is available: the `CompanyName`. That's it! CheckBoxList generates the results you want.

The remaining code consists of styling properties, which are pretty interesting. The `BorderColor`, `BorderStyle`, and `BorderWidth` properties enable you to put a border around the entire check box list. The most interesting property is the `RepeatColumns` property, which specifies how many columns (three in this example) can be used to display the results.

When you run the page, you get the results shown in Figure 3-17.

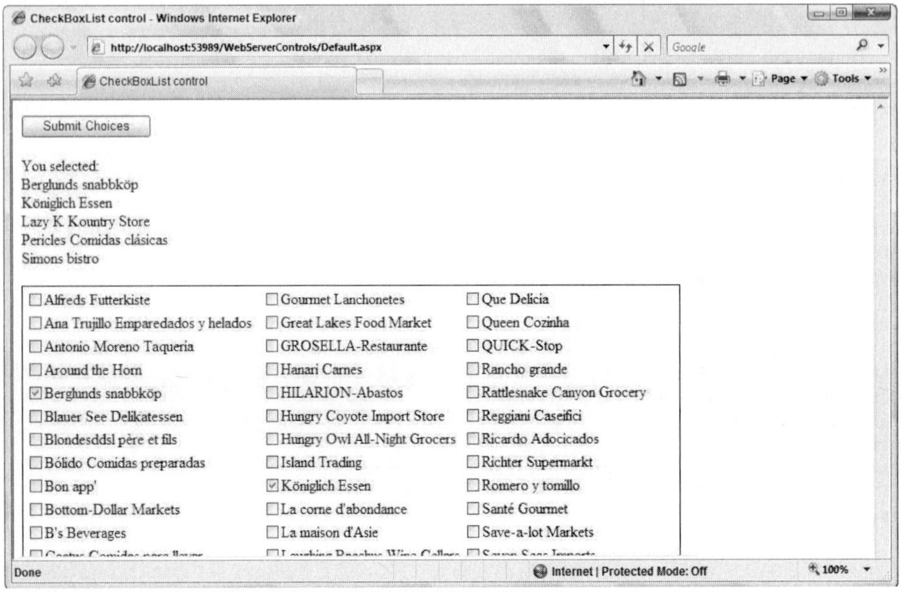

FIGURE 3-17

The `RepeatDirection` property instructs the CheckBoxList control about how to lay out the items bound to the control on the Web page. Possible values include `Vertical` and `Horizontal`. The default value is `Vertical`. Setting it to `Vertical` with a `RepeatColumn` setting of `3` gives the following results:

```
CheckBox1    CheckBox5    CheckBox9
CheckBox2    CheckBox6    CheckBox10
CheckBox3    CheckBox7    CheckBox11
CheckBox4    CheckBox8    CheckBox12
```

When the `RepeatDirection` property is set to `Horizontal`, you get the check box items laid out in a horizontal fashion:

```
CheckBox1    CheckBox2    CheckBox3
CheckBox4    CheckBox5    CheckBox6
CheckBox7    CheckBox8    CheckBox9
CheckBox10   CheckBox11   CheckBox12
```

THE RADIOBUTTON SERVER CONTROL

The RadioButton server control is quite similar to the CheckBox server control. It places a radio button on your Web page. Unlike a check box, however, a single radio button on a form does not make much sense. Radio buttons are generally form elements that require at least two options. A typical set of RadioButton controls on a page takes the following construction:

```
<asp:RadioButton ID="RadioButton1" runat="server" Text="Yes" GroupName="Set1" />
<asp:RadioButton ID="RadioButton2" runat="server" Text="No" GroupName="Set1"/>
```

Figure 3-18 shows the result.

FIGURE 3-18

When you look at the code for the RadioButton control, note the standard `Text` property that places the text next to the radio button on the Web form. The more important property here is `GroupName`, which can be set in one of the RadioButton controls to match what it is set to in the other. This enables the radio buttons on the Web form to work together for the end user. How do they work together? Well, when one of the radio buttons on the form is checked, the circle associated with the item selected appears filled in. Any other filled-in circle from the same group in the collection is removed, ensuring that only one of the radio buttons in the collection is selected.

Listing 3-15 shows an example of using the RadioButton control.

LISTING 3-15: Using the RadioButton server control

Available for download on Wrox.com

```
<%@ Page Language="VB" %>

<script runat="server">
    Protected Sub RadioButton_CheckedChanged(ByVal sender As Object,
      ByVal e As System.EventArgs)
        If RadioButton1.Checked = True Then
            Response.Write("You selected Visual Basic")
        Else
            Response.Write("You selected C#")
        End If
    End Sub
</script>

<html xmlns="http://www.w3.org/1999/xhtml">
<head runat="server">
    <title>RadioButton control</title>
</head>
<body>
    <form id="form1" runat="server">
    <div>
        <asp:RadioButton ID="RadioButton1" runat="server" Text="Visual Basic"
         GroupName="LanguageChoice" OnCheckedChanged="RadioButton_CheckedChanged"
         AutoPostBack="True" />
        <asp:RadioButton ID="RadioButton2" runat="server" Text="C#"
         GroupName="LanguageChoice" OnCheckedChanged="RadioButton_CheckedChanged"
         AutoPostBack="True" />
    </div>
    </form>
</body>
</html>
```

C#

```
<%@ Page Language="C#" %>

<script runat="server">
    protected void RadioButton_CheckedChanged(object sender, EventArgs e)
    {
        if (RadioButton1.Checked == true) {
           Response.Write("You selected Visual Basic");
        }
        else {
           Response.Write("You selected C#");
        }
    }
</script>
```

Like the CheckBox, the RadioButton control has a `CheckedChanged` event that puts an `OnCheckedChanged` attribute in the control. The attribute's value points to the server-side event that is fired when a selection is made using one of the two radio buttons on the form. Remember that the `AutoPostBack` property needs to be set to `True` for this to work correctly.

Figure 3-19 shows the results.

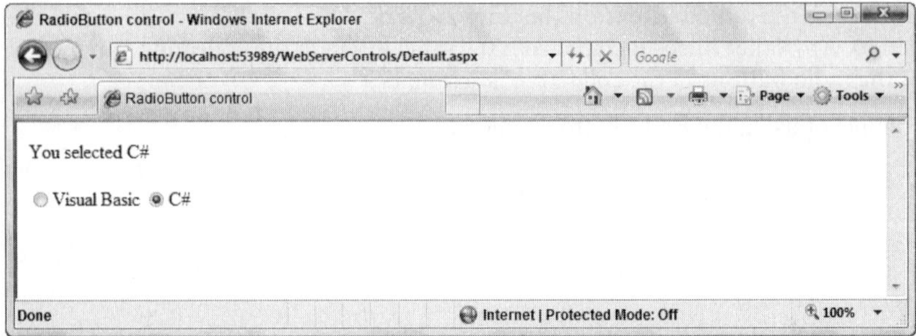

FIGURE 3-19

One advantage that the RadioButton control has over a RadioButtonList control (which is discussed next) is that it enables you to place other items (text, controls, or images) between the RadioButton controls themselves. RadioButtonList, however, is always a straight list of radio buttons on your Web page.

THE RADIOBUTTONLIST SERVER CONTROL

The RadioButtonList server control lets you display a collection of radio buttons on a Web page. The RadioButtonList control is quite similar to the CheckBoxList and other list controls in that it allows you to iterate through to see what the user selected, to make counts, or to perform other actions.

A typical RadioButtonList control is written to the page in the following manner:

```
<asp:RadioButtonList ID="RadioButtonList1" runat="server">
   <asp:ListItem Selected="True">English</asp:ListItem>
   <asp:ListItem>Russian</asp:ListItem>
   <asp:ListItem>Finnish</asp:ListItem>
   <asp:ListItem>Swedish</asp:ListItem>
</asp:RadioButtonList>
```

Like the other list controls, this one uses instances of the `ListItem` object for each of the items contained in the collection. From the example, you can see that if the `Selected` property is set to `True`, one of the `ListItem` objects is selected by default when the page is generated for the first time. This produces the results shown in Figure 3-20.

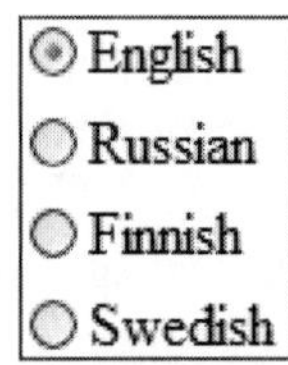

FIGURE 3-20

The `Selected` property is not required, but it is a good idea if you want the end user to make some sort of selection from this collection. Using it makes it impossible to leave the collection blank.

You can use the RadioButtonList control to check for the value selected by the end user in any of your page methods. Listing 3-16 shows a `Button1_Click` event that pushes out the value selected in the RadioButtonList collection.

LISTING 3-16: Checking the value of the item selected from a RadioButtonList control

VB

```
<%@ Page Language="VB" %>

<script runat="server">
    Protected Sub Button1_Click(ByVal sender As Object,
       ByVal e As System.EventArgs)

        Label1.Text = "You selected: " &
           RadioButtonList1.SelectedItem.ToString()
    End Sub
</script>
```

C#

```
<%@ Page Language="C#" %>

<script runat="server">
    protected void Button1_Click(object sender, EventArgs e)
    {
       Label1.Text = "You selected: " +
          RadioButtonList1.SelectedItem.ToString();
    }
</script>
```

This bit of code gets at the item selected from the RadioButtonList collection of `ListItem` objects. It is how you work with other list controls that are provided in ASP.NET. The RadioButtonList also affords you access to the `RepeatColumns` and `RepeatDirection` properties (these were explained in the CheckBoxList section). You can bind this control to items that come from any of the data source controls so that you can dynamically create radio button lists on your Web pages.

IMAGE SERVER CONTROL

The Image server control enables you to work with the images that appear on your Web page from the server-side code. It is a simple server control, but it can give you the power to determine how your images are displayed on the browser screen. A typical Image control is constructed in the following manner:

```
<asp:Image ID="Image1" runat="server" ImageUrl="~/MyImage1.gif" />
```

The important property here is `ImageUrl`. It points to the file location of the image. In this case, the location is specified as the `MyImage.gif` file.

Listing 3-17 shows an example of how to dynamically change the `ImageUrl` property.

LISTING 3-17: Changing the ImageUrl property dynamically

Available for download on Wrox.com

VB

```
<%@ Page Language="VB" %>

<script runat="server">
   Protected Sub Button1_Click(ByVal sender As Object, ByVal e As System.EventArgs)
        Image1.ImageUrl = "~/MyImage2.gif"
   End Sub
</script>

<html xmlns="http://www.w3.org/1999/xhtml">
<head runat="server">
    <title>Image control</title>
</head>
<body>
    <form id="form1" runat="server">
    <div>
        <asp:Image ID="Image1" runat="server" ImageUrl="~/MyImage1.gif" /><br />
        <br />
        <asp:Button ID="Button1" runat="server" Text="Change Image"
         OnClick="Button1_Click" />
    </div>
    </form>
</body>
</html>
```

C#

```
<%@ Page Language="C#" %>

<script runat="server">
    protected void Button1_Click(object sender, EventArgs e)
    {
       Image1.ImageUrl = "~/MyImage2.gif";
    }
</script>
```

In this example, an image (MyImage1.gif) is shown in the browser when the page is loaded for the first time. When the end user clicks the button on the page, a new image (MyImage2.gif) is loaded in the postback process.

Special circumstances can prevent end users from viewing an image that is part of your Web page. They might be physically unable to see the image, or they might be using a text-only browser. In these cases, their browsers look for the <img> element's longdesc attribute that points to a file containing a long description of the image that is displayed.

For these cases, the Image server control includes a DescriptionUrl attribute. The value assigned to it is a text file that contains a thorough description of the image with which it is associated. Here is how to use it:

```
<asp:Image ID="Image1" runat="server" DescriptionUrl="~/Image01.txt"  />
```

This code produces the following results in the browser:

```
<img id="Image1" src="INETA.jpg" longdesc="Image01.txt" alt="" />
```

Remember that the image does not support the user clicking the image. If you want to program events based on button clicks, use the ImageButton server control discussed earlier in this chapter.

TABLE SERVER CONTROL

Tables are one of the Web page's more common elements because the HTML <table> element is one possible format utilized for controlling the layout of your Web page (CSS being the other). The typical construction of the Table server control is as follows:

```
<asp:Table ID="Table1" runat="server">
   <asp:TableRow Runat="server" Font-Bold="True"
    ForeColor="Black" BackColor="Silver">
      <asp:TableHeaderCell>First Name</asp:TableHeaderCell>
      <asp:TableHeaderCell>Last Name</asp:TableHeaderCell>
   </asp:TableRow>
   <asp:TableRow>
      <asp:TableCell>Bill</asp:TableCell>
      <asp:TableCell>Evjen</asp:TableCell>
   </asp:TableRow>
  <asp:TableRow>
      <asp:TableCell>Devin</asp:TableCell>
      <asp:TableCell>Rader</asp:TableCell>
   </asp:TableRow>
</asp:Table>
```

First Name	Last Name
Bill	Evjen
Devin	Rader

FIGURE 3-21

This produces the simple three-rowed table shown in Figure 3-21.

You can do a lot with the Table server control. For example, you can dynamically add rows to the table, as illustrated in Listing 3-18.

LISTING 3-18: Dynamically adding rows to the table

Available for download on Wrox.com

VB

```
Protected Sub Page_Load(ByVal sender As Object, ByVal e As System.EventArgs)
   Dim tr As New TableRow()

   Dim fname As New TableCell()
   fname.Text = "Scott"
   tr.Cells.Add(fname)

   Dim lname As New TableCell()
   lname.Text = "Hanselman"
   tr.Cells.Add(lname)

   Table1.Rows.Add(tr)
```

```
    End Sub
```

C#

```
    protected void Page_Load(object sender, EventArgs e)
    {
       TableRow tr = new TableRow();

       TableCell fname = new TableCell();
       fname.Text = "Scott";
       tr.Cells.Add(fname);

       TableCell lname = new TableCell();
       lname.Text = "Hanselman";
       tr.Cells.Add(lname);

       Table1.Rows.Add(tr);
    }
```

To add a single row to a Table control, you have to create new instances of the `TableRow` and `TableCell` objects. You create the `TableCell` objects first and then place them within a `TableRow` object that is added to a `Table` object.

The Table server control obviously contains some extra features beyond what has been presented. One of the simpler features is the capability to add captions to the tables on Web pages. Figure 3-22 shows a table with a caption.

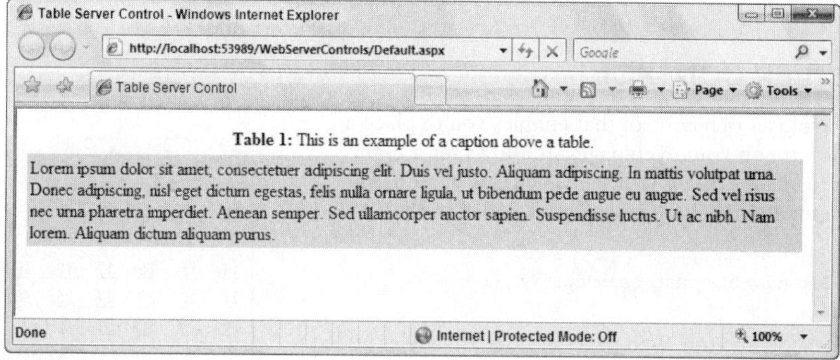

FIGURE 3-22

To give your table a caption, simply use the `Caption` attribute in the Table control, as illustrated in Listing 3-19.

LISTING 3-19: Using the Caption attribute

Available for download on Wrox.com

```
<%@ Page Language="VB" %>

<html xmlns="http://www.w3.org/1999/xhtml">
<head runat="server">
    <title>Table Server Control</title>
</head>
<body>
    <form id="form1" runat="server">
        <asp:Table ID="Table1" runat="server"
         Caption="<b>Table 1:</b> This is an example of a caption above a table."
         BackColor="Gainsboro">
            <asp:TableRow ID="Tablerow1" Runat=server>
                <asp:TableCell ID="Tablecell1" Runat="server">Lorem ipsum dolor sit
                 amet, consectetuer adipiscing elit. Duis vel justo. Aliquam
```

continues

LISTING 3-19 *(continued)*

```
                    adipiscing. In mattis volutpat urna. Donec adipiscing, nisl eget
                    dictum egestas, felis nulla ornare ligula, ut bibendum pede augue
                    eu augue. Sed vel risus nec urna pharetra imperdiet. Aenean
                    semper. Sed ullamcorper auctor sapien. Suspendisse luctus. Ut ac
                    nibh. Nam lorem. Aliquam dictum aliquam purus.</asp:TableCell>
                </asp:TableRow>
            </asp:Table>
        </form>
    </body>
    </html>
```

By default, the caption is placed at the top center of the table, but you can control where it is placed by using another attribute — `CaptionAlign`. Its possible settings include `Bottom`, `Left`, `NotSet`, `Right`, and `Top`.

In the early days of ASP.NET, an `<asp:Table>` element contained any number of `<asp:TableRow>` elements. In ASP.NET 4, you can nest some additional elements within the `<asp:Table>` element. These elements include `<asp:TableHeaderRow>` and `<asp:TableFooterRow>`. They add either a header or footer to your table, enabling you to use the Table server control to page through lots of data but still retain some text in place to indicate the type of data being handled. This is quite a powerful feature when you work with mobile applications that dictate that sometimes end users can move through only a few records at a time.

THE CALENDAR SERVER CONTROL

The Calendar server control is a rich control that enables you to place a full-featured calendar directly on your Web pages. It allows for a high degree of customization to ensure that it looks and behaves in a unique manner. The Calendar control, in its simplest form, is coded in the following manner:

```
<asp:Calendar ID="Calendar1" runat="server">
</asp:Calendar>
```

This code produces a calendar on your Web page without any styles added, as shown in Figure 3-23.

<			March 2010			>
Sun	Mon	Tue	Wed	Thu	Fri	Sat
28	1	2	3	4	5	6
7	8	9	10	11	12	13
14	15	16	17	18	19	20
21	22	23	24	25	26	27
28	29	30	31	1	2	3
4	5	6	7	8	9	10

FIGURE 3-23

Making a Date Selection from the Calendar Control

The calendar allows you to navigate through the months of the year and to select specific days in the exposed month. A simple application that enables the user to select a day of the month is shown in Listing 3-20.

LISTING 3-20: Selecting a single day in the Calendar control

Available for download on Wrox.com

```
<%@ Page Language="VB" %>

<script runat="server">
    Protected Sub Calendar1_SelectionChanged(ByVal sender As Object,
      ByVal e As System.EventArgs)
        Response.Write("You selected: " &
          Calendar1.SelectedDate.ToShortDateString())
    End Sub
</script>

<html xmlns="http://www.w3.org/1999/xhtml">
```

```
<head id="Head1" runat="server">
    <title>Using the Calendar Control</title>
</head>
<body>
    <form id="form1" runat="server">
    <div>
        <asp:Calendar ID="Calendar1" runat="server"
         OnSelectionChanged="Calendar1_SelectionChanged">
        </asp:Calendar>
    </div>
    </form>
</body>
</html>
```

C#

```
<%@ Page Language="C#" %>

<script runat="server">
    protected void Calendar1_SelectionChanged(object sender, EventArgs e)
    {
        Response.Write("You selected: " +
          Calendar1.SelectedDate.ToShortDateString());
    }
</script>
```

Running this application pulls up the calendar in the browser. The end user can then select a single date in it. After a date is selected, the `Calendar1_SelectionChanged` event is triggered and makes use of the `OnSelectionChange` attribute. This event writes the value of the selected date to the screen. The result is shown in Figure 3-24.

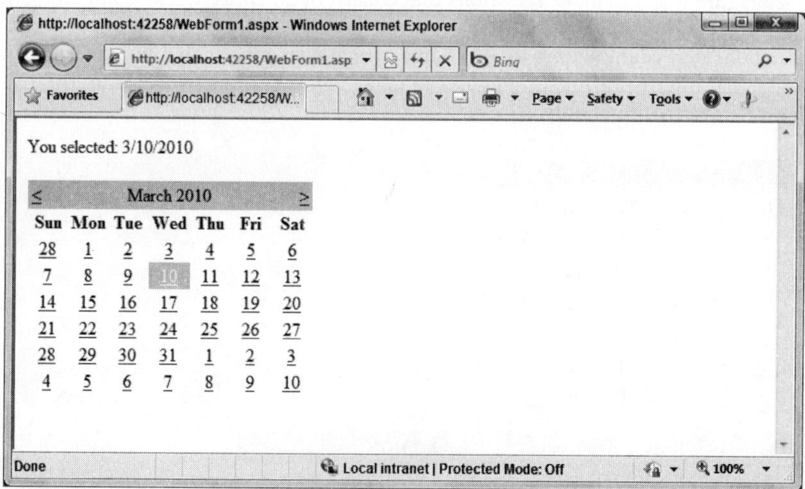

FIGURE 3-24

Choosing a Date Format to Output from the Calendar

When you use the `Calendar1_SelectionChanged` event, the selected date is written out using the `ToShortDateString()` method. The Calendar control also allows you to write out the date in a number of other formats, as detailed in the following list:

- `ToFileTime`: Converts the selection to the local operating system file time: `129094776000000000`.
- `ToFileTimeUtc`: Converts the selection to the operating system file time, but instead of using the local time zone, the UTC time is used: `129094560000000000`.

- `ToLocalTime`: Converts the current coordinated universal time (UTC) to local time: `1/31/2010 6:00:00 PM`.
- `ToLongDateString`: Converts the selection to a human-readable string in a long format: `Monday, February 01, 2010`.
- `ToLongTimeString`: Converts the selection to a time value (no date is included) of a long format: `12:00:00 AM`.
- `ToOADate`: Converts the selection to an OLE Automation date equivalent: `40210`.
- `ToShortDateString`: Converts the selection to a human-readable string in a short format: `2/1/2010`.
- `ToShortTimeString`: Converts the selection to a time value (no date is included) in a short format: `12:00 AM`.
- `ToString`: Converts the selection to the following: `2/1/2010 12:00:00 AM`.
- `ToUniversalTime`: Converts the selection to universal time (UTC): `2/1/2010 6:00:00 AM`.

Making Day, Week, or Month Selections

By default, the Calendar control enables you to make single day selections. You can use the `SelectionMode` property to change this behavior to allow your users to make week or month selections from the calendar instead. The possible values of this property include `Day`, `DayWeek`, `DayWeekMonth`, and `None`.

The `Day` setting enables you to click a specific day in the calendar to highlight it (this is the default). When you use the setting of `DayWeek`, you can still make individual day selections, but you can also click the arrow next to the week (see Figure 3-25) to make selections that consist of an entire week. Using the setting of `DayWeekMonth` lets users make individual day selections or week selections. A new arrow appears in the upper-left corner of the calendar that enables users to select an entire month (also shown in Figure 3-25). A setting of `None` means that it is impossible for the end user to make any selections, which is useful for calendars on your site that are informational only.

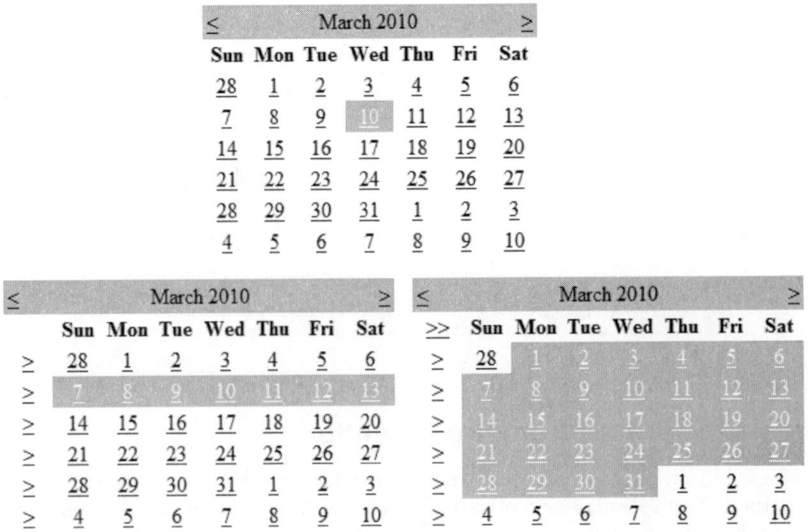

<			March 2010			>
Sun	Mon	Tue	Wed	Thu	Fri	Sat
28	1	2	3	4	5	6
7	8	9	10	11	12	13
14	15	16	17	18	19	20
21	22	23	24	25	26	27
28	29	30	31	1	2	3
4	5	6	7	8	9	10

<				March 2010			>
	Sun	Mon	Tue	Wed	Thu	Fri	Sat
>	28	1	2	3	4	5	6
>	7	8	9	10	11	12	13
>	14	15	16	17	18	19	20
>	21	22	23	24	25	26	27
>	28	29	30	31	1	2	3
>	4	5	6	7	8	9	10

<				March 2010			>
>>	Sun	Mon	Tue	Wed	Thu	Fri	Sat
>	28	1	2	3	4	5	6
>	7	8	9	10	11	12	13
>	14	15	16	17	18	19	20
>	21	22	23	24	25	26	27
>	28	29	30	31	1	2	3
>	4	5	6	7	8	9	10

FIGURE 3-25

Working with Date Ranges

Even if an end user makes a selection that encompasses an entire week or an entire month, you get back from the selection only the first date of this range. If, for example, you allow users to select an entire month and one selects July 2010, what you get back (using `ToShortDateString()`) is `7/1/2010` — the first date in the date range of the selection. That might work for you, but if you require all the dates in the selected range, Listing 3-21 shows you how to get them.

LISTING 3-21: Retrieving a range of dates from a selection

Available for download on Wrox.com

```
<%@ Page Language="VB" %>
```

```
<script runat="server">
    Protected Sub Calendar1_SelectionChanged(ByVal sender As Object,
      ByVal e As System.EventArgs)
        Label1.Text = "<b><u>You selected the following date/dates:</u></b><br>"

        For i As Integer = 0 To (Calendar1.SelectedDates.Count - 1)
            Label1.Text += Calendar1.SelectedDates.Item(i).ToShortDateString() &
              "<br>"
        Next
    End Sub
</script>

<html xmlns="http://www.w3.org/1999/xhtml">
<head id="Head1" runat="server">
    <title>Using the Calendar Control</title>
</head>
<body>
    <form id="form1" runat="server">
    <div>
        <asp:Calendar ID="Calendar1" runat="server"
         OnSelectionChanged="Calendar1_SelectionChanged"
         SelectionMode="DayWeekMonth">
        </asp:Calendar><p>
        <asp:Label ID="Label1" runat="server"></asp:Label></p>
    </div>
    </form>
</body>
</html>
```

C#

```
<%@ Page Language="C#" %>

<script runat="server">
    protected void Calendar1_SelectionChanged(object sender, EventArgs e)
    {
        Label1.Text = "<b><u>You selected the following date/dates:</u></b><br>";

        for (int i=0; i<Calendar1.SelectedDates.Count; i++) {
            Label1.Text += Calendar1.SelectedDates[i].ToShortDateString() +
              "<br>";
        }
    }
</script>
```

In this example, the Calendar control lets users make selections that can be an individual day, a week, or even a month. Using a `For Next` loop, you iterate through a selection by using the `SelectedDates.Count` property. The code produces the results shown in Figure 3-26.

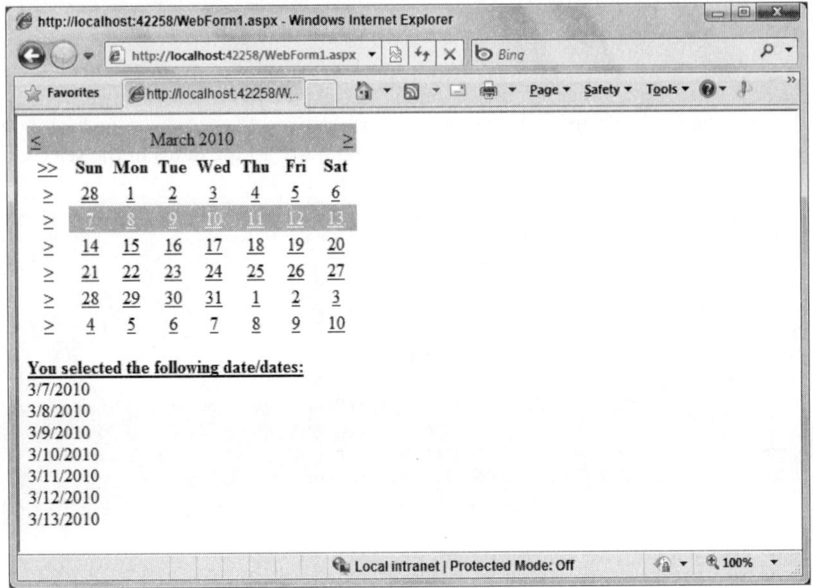

FIGURE 3-26

You can get just the first day of the selection by using the following:

VB
```
Calendar1.SelectedDates.Item(0).ToShortDateString()
```

C#
```
Calendar1.SelectedDates[0].ToShortDateString();
```

And you can get the last date in the selected range by using:

VB
```
Calendar1.SelectedDates.Item(Calendar1.SelectedDates.Count-1).ToShortDateString()
```

C#
```
Calendar1.SelectedDates[Calendar1.SelectedDates.Count-1].ToShortDateString();
```

As you can see, this is possible using the `Count` property of the `SelectedDates` object.

Modifying the Style and Behavior of Your Calendar

There is a lot to the Calendar control — definitely more than can be covered in this chapter. One nice thing about the Calendar control is the ease of extensibility that it offers. Begin exploring new ways to customize this control further by looking at one of the easiest ways to change it — applying a style to the control.

Using Visual Studio, you can give the controls a new look-and-feel from the Design view of the page you are working with. Highlight the Calendar control and open the control's smart tag to see the Auto Format link. That gives you a list of available styles that can be applied to your Calendar control.

The Calendar control is not alone in this capability. Many other rich controls offer a list of styles. You can always find this capability in the control's smart tag.

Some of the styles are shown in Figure 3-27.

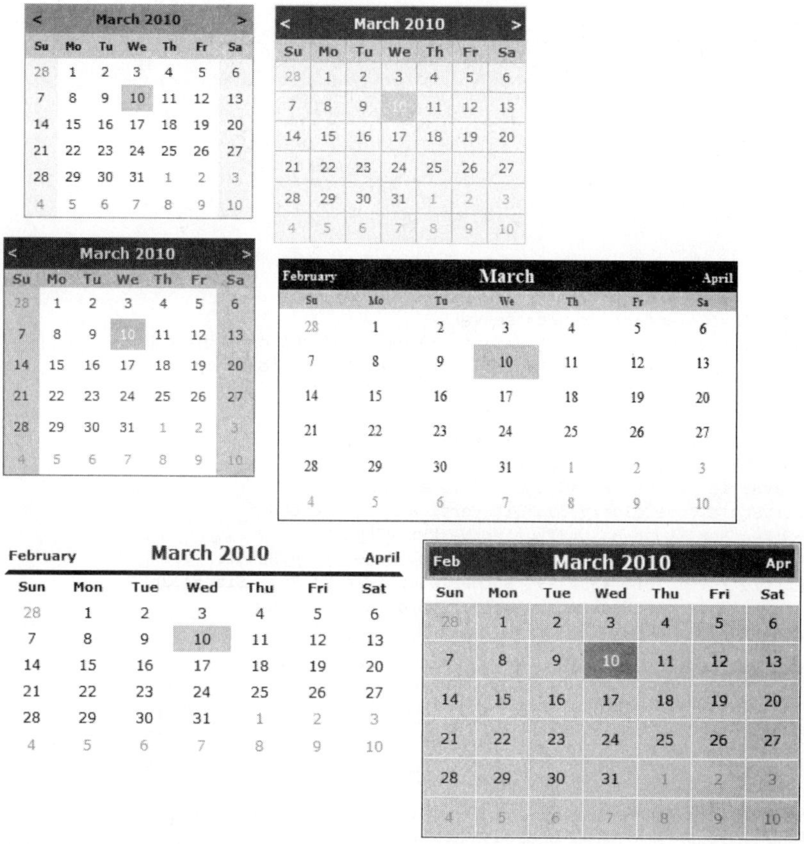

FIGURE 3-27

In addition to changing the style of the Calendar control, you can work with the control during its rendering process. The Calendar control includes an event called `DayRender` that allows you to control how a single date or all the dates in the calendar are rendered. Listing 3-22 shows an example of how to change one of the dates being rendered in the calendar.

LISTING 3-22: Controlling how a day is rendered in the Calendar

```
<%@ Page Language="VB" %>

<script runat="server">
    Protected Sub Calendar1_DayRender(ByVal sender As Object,
      ByVal e As System.Web.UI.WebControls.DayRenderEventArgs)
        e.Cell.VerticalAlign = VerticalAlign.Top

        If (e.Day.DayNumberText = "25") Then
            e.Cell.Controls.Add(New LiteralControl("<p>User Group Meeting!</p>"))
            e.Cell.BorderColor = Drawing.Color.Black
            e.Cell.BorderWidth = 1
            e.Cell.BorderStyle = BorderStyle.Solid
            e.Cell.BackColor = Drawing.Color.LightGray
        End If
```

continues

LISTING 3-22 *(continued)*

```
    End Sub
</script>

<html xmlns="http://www.w3.org/1999/xhtml">
<head id="Head1" runat="server">
    <title>Using the Calendar Control</title>
</head>
<body>
    <form id="form1" runat="server">
    <div>
        <asp:Calendar ID="Calendar1" runat="server"
         OnDayRender="Calendar1_DayRender" Height="190px" BorderColor="White"
         Width="350px" ForeColor="Black" BackColor="White" BorderWidth="1px"
         NextPrevFormat="FullMonth" Font-Names="Verdana" Font-Size="9pt">
            <SelectedDayStyle ForeColor="White"
             BackColor="#333399"></SelectedDayStyle>
            <OtherMonthDayStyle ForeColor="#999999"></OtherMonthDayStyle>
            <TodayDayStyle BackColor="#CCCCCC"></TodayDayStyle>
            <NextPrevStyle ForeColor="#333333" VerticalAlign="Bottom"
             Font-Size="8pt" Font-Bold="True"></NextPrevStyle>
            <DayHeaderStyle Font-Size="8pt" Font-Bold="True"></DayHeaderStyle>
            <TitleStyle ForeColor="#333399" BorderColor="Black" Font-Size="12pt"
                Font-Bold="True" BackColor="White" BorderWidth="4px">
            </TitleStyle>
        </asp:Calendar>
    </div>
    </form>
</body>
</html>
```

C#

```
<%@ Page Language="C#" %>

<script runat="server">
    protected void Calendar1_DayRender(object sender, DayRenderEventArgs e)
    {
        e.Cell.VerticalAlign = VerticalAlign.Top;

        if (e.Day.DayNumberText == "25")
        {
            e.Cell.Controls.Add(new LiteralControl("<p>User Group Meeting!</p>"));
            e.Cell.BorderColor = System.Drawing.Color.Black;
            e.Cell.BorderWidth = 1;
            e.Cell.BorderStyle = BorderStyle.Solid;
            e.Cell.BackColor = System.Drawing.Color.LightGray;
        }

    }
</script>
```

In this example, you use a Calendar control with a little style to it. When the page is built and run in the browser, you can see that the 25th of every month in the calendar has been changed by the code in the `Calendar1_DayRender` event. The calendar is shown in Figure 3-28.

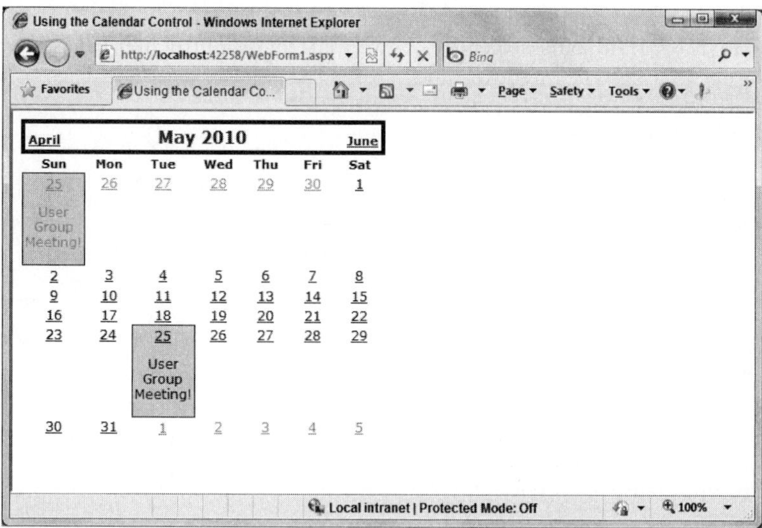

FIGURE 3-28

The Calendar control in this example adds an `OnDayRender` attribute that points to the `Calendar1_DayRender` event. The method is run for each of the days rendered in the calendar. The class constructor shows that you are not working with the typical `System.EventArgs` class, but instead with the `DayRenderEventArgs` class. It gives you access to each of the days rendered in the calendar.

The two main properties from the `DayRenderEventArgs` class are `Cell` and `Day`. The `Cell` property gives you access to the space in which the day is being rendered, and the `Day` property gives you access to the specific date being rendered in the cell.

From the actions being taken in the `Calendar1_DayRender` event, you can see that both properties are used. First, the `Cell` property sets the vertical alignment of the cell to `Top`. If it didn't, the table might look a little strange when one of the cells has content. Next, a check is made to see if the day being rendered (checked with the `Day` property) is the 25th of the month. If it is, the `If Then` statement runs using the `Cell` property to change the styling of just that cell. The styling change adds a control, as well as makes changes to the border and color of the cell.

As you can see, working with individual dates in the calendar is fairly straightforward. You can easily give them the content and appearance you want.

A nice feature of the `Day` property is that you can turn off the option to select a particular date or range of dates by setting the `Day` property's `IsSelectable` property to `False`:

VB

```
If (e.Day.Date < DateTime.Now) Then
   e.Day.IsSelectable = False
End If
```

C#

```
if (e.Day.Date < DateTime.Now) {
   e.Day.IsSelectable = false;
}
```

ADROTATOR SERVER CONTROL

Although Web users find ads rather annoying, advertising continues to be prevalent everywhere on the Web. With the AdRotator control, you can configure your application to show a series of advertisements to the end users. With this control, you can use advertisement data from sources other than the standard XML file that was used with the early versions of this control.

If you are using an XML source for the ad information, first create an XML advertisement file. The advertisement file allows you to incorporate some elements that give you a lot of control over the appearance and behavior of your ads. Listing 3-23 shows an example of an XML advertisement file.

LISTING 3-23: The XML advertisement file

```
<?xml version="1.0" encoding="utf-8" ?>
<Advertisements
 xmlns="http://schemas.microsoft.com/AspNet/AdRotator-Schedule-File">
 <Ad>
    <ImageUrl>book1.gif</ImageUrl>
    <NavigateUrl>http://www.wrox.com</NavigateUrl>
    <AlternateText>Visit Wrox Today!</AlternateText>
    <Impressions>50</Impressions>
    <Keyword>VB.NET</Keyword>
 </Ad>
 <Ad>
    <ImageUrl>book2.gif</ImageUrl>
    <NavigateUrl>http://www.wrox.com</NavigateUrl>
    <AlternateText>Visit Wrox Today!</AlternateText>
    <Impressions>50</Impressions>
    <Keyword>XML</Keyword>
 </Ad>
</Advertisements>
```

This XML file, used for storing information about the advertisements that appear in your application, has just a few elements detailed in Table 3-1. Remember that all elements are optional.

TABLE 3-1

ELEMENT	DESCRIPTION
ImageUrl	Takes a string value that indicates the location of the image to use.
NavigateUrl	Takes a string value that indicates the URL to post to when the image is clicked.
AlternateText	Takes a string value that is used for display if images are turned off in the client's browser or if the image is not found.
Impressions	Takes a numerical value that indicates the likelihood of the image being selected for display.
Keyword	Takes a string value that sets the category of the image in order to allow for the filtering of ads.

Now that the XML advertisement file is in place, you can simply use the AdRotator control to read from this file. Listing 3-24 shows an example of this in action.

LISTING 3-24: Using the AdRotator control as a banner ad

Available for download on Wrox.com

```
<%@ Page Language="VB" %>

<html xmlns="http://www.w3.org/1999/xhtml" >
<head runat="server">
    <title>AdRotator Page</title>
</head>
<body>
    <form id="form1" runat="server">
        <asp:AdRotator ID="AdRotator1" runat="server"
         AdvertisementFile="MyAds.xml" />
        <p>Lorem ipsum dolor sit
        amet, consectetuer adipiscing elit. Duis vel justo. Aliquam
        adipiscing. In mattis volutpat urna. Donec adipiscing, nisl eget
```

```
        dictum egestas, felis nulla ornare ligula, ut bibendum pede augue
        eu augue. Sed vel risus nec urna pharetra imperdiet. Aenean
        semper. Sed ullamcorper auctor sapien. Suspendisse luctus. Ut ac
        nibh. Nam lorem. Aliquam dictum aliquam purus.</p>
    </form>
</body>
</html>
```

The example shows the ad specified in the XML advertisement file as a banner ad at the top of the page.

You are not required to place all your ad information in the XML advertisement file. Instead, you can use another data source to which you bind the AdRotator. For instance, you bind the AdRotator to a `SqlDataSource` object that is retrieving the ad information from SQL Server in the following fashion:

```
<asp:AdRotator ID="AdRotator1" runat="server"
 DataSourceId="SqlDataSource1" AlternateTextField="AlternateTF"
 ImageUrlField="Image" NavigateUrlField="NavigateUrl" />
```

The `AlternateTextField`, `ImageUrlField`, and `NavigateUrlField` properties point to the column names that are used in SQL Server for those items.

THE XML SERVER CONTROL

The Xml server control provides a means of getting XML and transforming it using an XSL style sheet. The Xml control can work with your XML in a couple of different ways. The simplest method is by using the construction shown in Listing 3-25. This control is covered in more detail in Chapter 10.

LISTING 3-25: Displaying an XML document

```
<asp:Xml ID="Xml1" runat="server" DocumentSource="~/MyXMLFile.xml"
 TransformSource="MyXSLFile.xslt"></asp:Xml>
```

This method takes only a couple of attributes to make it work: `DocumentSource`, which points to the path of the XML file, and `TransformSource`, which provides the XSLT file to use in transforming the XML document.

The other way to use the Xml server control is to load the XML into an object and then pass the object to the Xml control, as illustrated in Listing 3-26.

LISTING 3-26: Loading the XML file to an object before providing it to the Xml control

VB

```
Dim MyXmlDoc as XmlDocument = New XmlDocument()
MyXmlDoc.Load(Server.MapPath("Customers.xml"))

Dim MyXslDoc As XslCompiledTransform = New XslCompiledTransform()
MyXslDoc.Load(Server.MapPath("CustomersSchema.xslt"))

Xml1.Document = MyXmlDoc
Xml1.Transform = MyXslDoc
```

C#

```
XmlDocument MyXmlDoc = new XmlDocument();
MyXmlDoc.Load(Server.MapPath("Customers.xml"));

XslCompiledTransform MyXsltDoc = new XslCompiledTransform();
MyXsltDoc.Load(Server.MapPath("CustomersSchema.xslt"));

Xml1.Document = MyXmlDoc;
Xml1.Transform = MyXslDoc;
```

To make this work, you have to ensure that the `System.Xml` and `System.Xml.Xsl` namespaces are imported into your page. The example loads both the XML and XSL files and then assigns these files as the values of the `Document` and `Transform` properties.

PANEL SERVER CONTROL

The Panel server control encapsulates a set of controls you can use to manipulate or lay out your ASP.NET pages. It is basically a wrapper for other controls, enabling you to take a group of server controls along with other elements (such as HTML and images) and turn them into a single unit.

The advantage of using the Panel control to encapsulate a set of other elements is that you can manipulate these elements as a single unit using one attribute set in the Panel control itself. For example, setting the `Font-Bold` attribute to `True` causes each item within the Panel control to adopt this attribute.

The Panel control also has the capability to scroll with scrollbars that appear automatically depending on the amount of information that Panel control holds. You can even specify how the scrollbars should appear.

For an example of using scrollbars, look at a long version of the Lorem Ipsum text (found at `www.lipsum.com`) and place that text within the Panel control, as shown in Listing 3-27.

LISTING 3-27: Using the scrollbar feature with the Panel server control

```
<%@ Page Language="VB" %>

<html>
<head runat="server">
    <title>Panel Server Control Page</title>
</head>
<body>
    <form id="form1" runat="server">
        <asp:Panel ID="Panel1" runat="server" Height="300" Width="300"
         ScrollBars="auto">
           <p>Lorem ipsum dolor sit amet…</p>
        </asp:Panel>
    </form>
</body>
</html>
```

By assigning values to the `Height` and `Width` attributes of the Panel server control and using the `ScrollBars` attribute (in this case, set to `Auto`), you can display the information it contains within the defined area using scrollbars (see Figure 3-29).

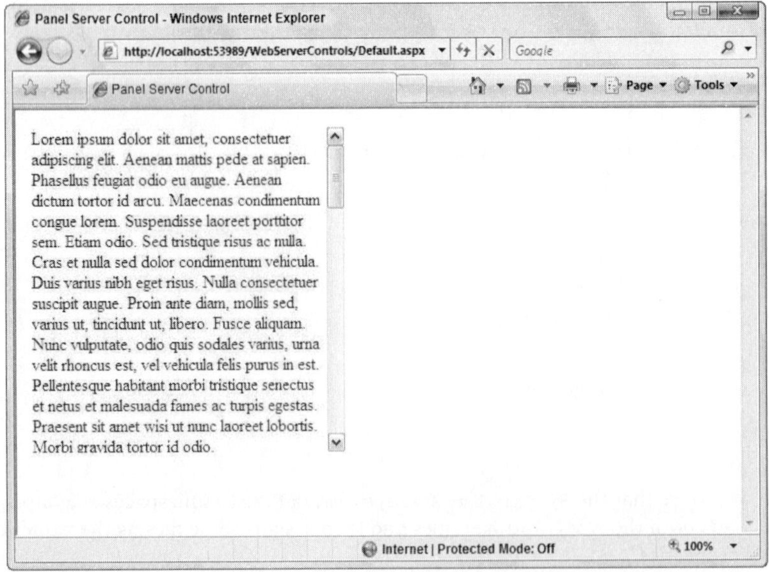

FIGURE 3-29

As you can see, a single vertical scrollbar has been added to the set area of 300 × 300 pixels. The Panel control wraps the text by default as required. To change this behavior, use the `Wrap` attribute, which takes a `Boolean` value:

```
<asp:Panel ID="Panel1" runat="server"
 Height="300" Width="300" ScrollBars="Auto"
 Wrap="False" />
```

Turning off wrapping may cause the horizontal scrollbar to turn on (depending on what is contained in the panel section).

If you do not want to let the ASP.NET engine choose which scrollbars to activate, you can actually make that decision by using the `ScrollBars` attribute. In addition to `Auto`, its values include `None`, `Horizontal`, `Vertical`, and `Both`.

Another interesting attribute that enables you to change the behavior of the Panel control is `HorizontalAlign`. It enables you to set how the content in the Panel control is horizontally aligned. The possible values of this attribute include `NotSet`, `Center`, `Justify`, `Left`, and `Right`. Figure 3-30 shows a collection of Panel controls with different horizontal alignments.

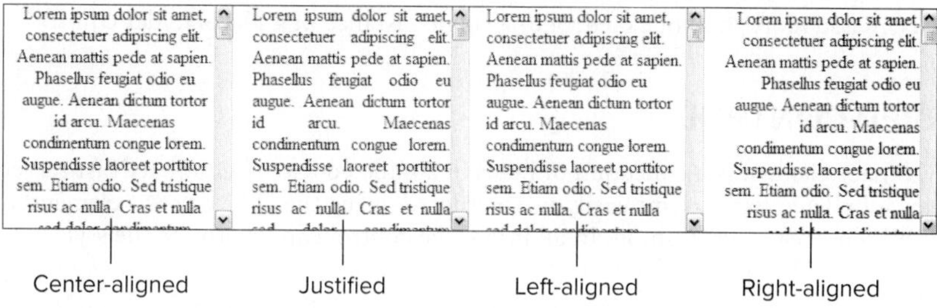

FIGURE 3-30

It is also possible to move the vertical scrollbar to the left side of the Panel control by using the `Direction` attribute. `Direction` can be set to `NotSet`, `LeftToRight`, and `RightToLeft`. A setting of `RightToLeft` is ideal when you are dealing with languages that are written from right to left (some Asian languages, for example). However, that setting also moves the scrollbar to the left side of the Panel control. If the scrollbar is moved to the left side and the `HorizontalAlign` attribute is set to `Left`, your content resembles Figure 3-31.

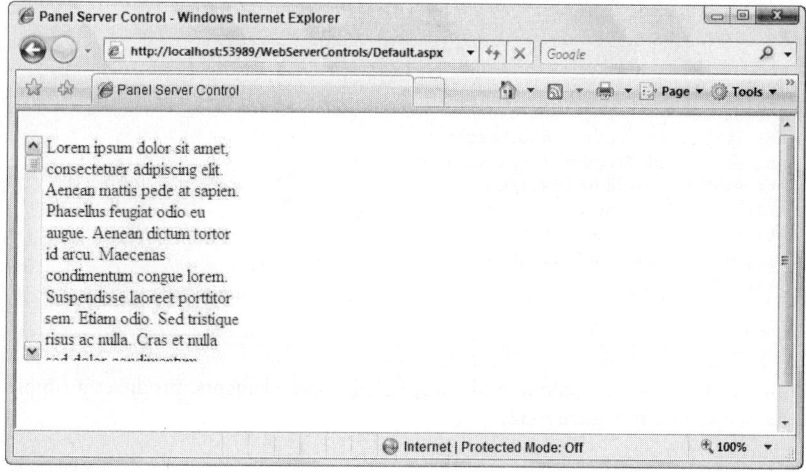

FIGURE 3-31

THE PLACEHOLDER SERVER CONTROL

The PlaceHolder server control works just as its name implies — it is a placeholder for you to interject objects dynamically into your page. Think of it as a marker with which you can add other controls. The capability to add controls to a page at a specific point also works with the Panel control.

To see how it works, insert a PlaceHolder control into your page and then add controls to it from your server-side code in the manner shown in Listing 3-28.

LISTING 3-28: Using PlaceHolder to add controls to a page dynamically

VB

```
Dim NewLabelControl As New Label()
NewLabelControl.Text = "Hello there"
PlaceHolder1.Controls.Add(NewLabelControl)
```

C#

```
Label NewLabelControl = new Label();
NewLabelControl.Text = "Hello there";
PlaceHolder1.Controls.Add(NewLabelControl);
```

This example creates a new instance of a Label control and populates it with a value before it is added to the PlaceHolder control. You can add more than one control to a single instance of a PlaceHolder control.

BULLETEDLIST SERVER CONTROL

One common HTML Web page element is a collection of items in a bulleted list. The BulletedList server control is meant to display a bulleted list of items easily in an ordered (using the HTML <ol> element) or unordered (using the HTML <ul> element) fashion. In addition, the control can determine the style used for displaying the list.

The BulletedList control can be constructed of any number of <asp:ListItem> controls or can be data-bound to a data source of some kind and populated based upon the contents retrieved. Listing 3-29 shows a bulleted list in its simplest form.

LISTING 3-29: A simple BulletedList control

Available for download on Wrox.com

```
<%@ Page Language="VB" %>

<html xmlns="http://www.w3.org/1999/xhtml">
<head runat="server">
    <title>BulletedList Server Control</title>
</head>
<body>
    <form id="form1" runat="server">
        <asp:BulletedList ID="Bulletedlist1" runat="server">
            <asp:ListItem>United States</asp:ListItem>
            <asp:ListItem>United Kingdom</asp:ListItem>
            <asp:ListItem>Finland</asp:ListItem>
            <asp:ListItem>Russia</asp:ListItem>
            <asp:ListItem>Sweden</asp:ListItem>
            <asp:ListItem>Estonia</asp:ListItem>
        </asp:BulletedList>
    </form>
</body>
</html>
```

The use of the <asp:BulletedList> element, along with <asp:ListItem> elements, produces a simple bulleted list output like the one shown in Figure 3-32.

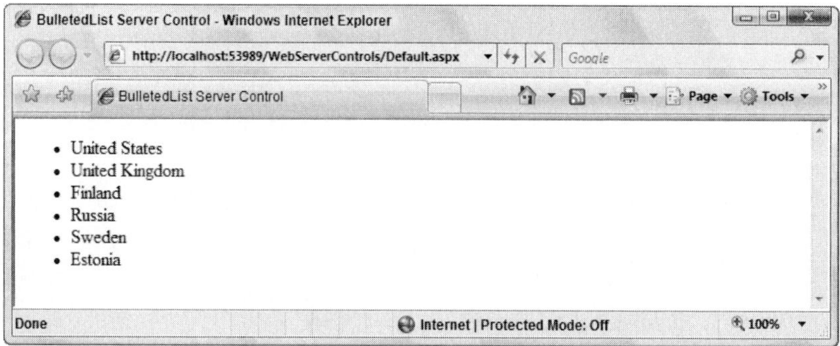

FIGURE 3-32

The BulletedList control also enables you to easily change the style of the list with just one or two attributes. The `BulletStyle` attribute changes the style of the bullet that precedes each line of the list. It has possible values of `Numbered`, `LowerAlpha`, `UpperAlpha`, `LowerRoman`, `UpperRoman`, `Disc`, `Circle`, `Square`, `NotSet`, and `CustomImage`. Figure 3-33 shows examples of these styles (minus the `CustomImage` setting that enables you to use any image of your choice).

FIGURE 3-33

You can change the starting value of the first item in any of the numbered styles (`Numbered`, `LowerAlpha`, `UpperAlpha`, `LowerRoman`, `UpperRoman`) by using the `FirstBulletNumber` attribute. If you set the attribute's value to `5` when you use the `UpperRoman` setting, for example, you get the format illustrated in Figure 3-34.

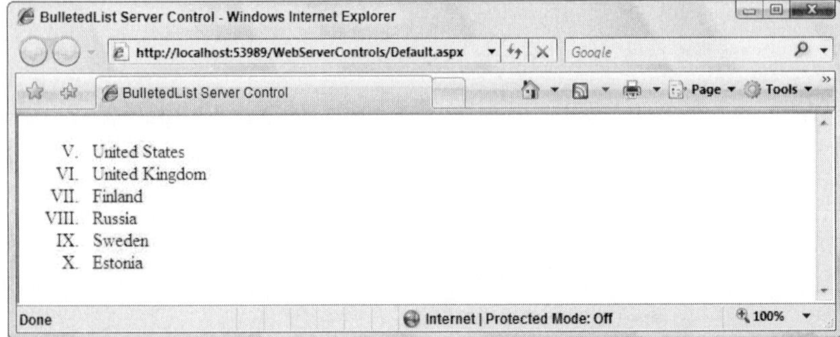

FIGURE 3-34

To employ images as bullets, use the `CustomImage` setting in the BulletedList control. You must also use the `BulletImageUrl` attribute in the following manner:

```
<asp:BulletedList ID="Bulletedlist1" runat="server"
BulletStyle="CustomImage" BulletImageUrl="~/myImage.gif">
```

Figure 3-35 shows an example of image bullets.

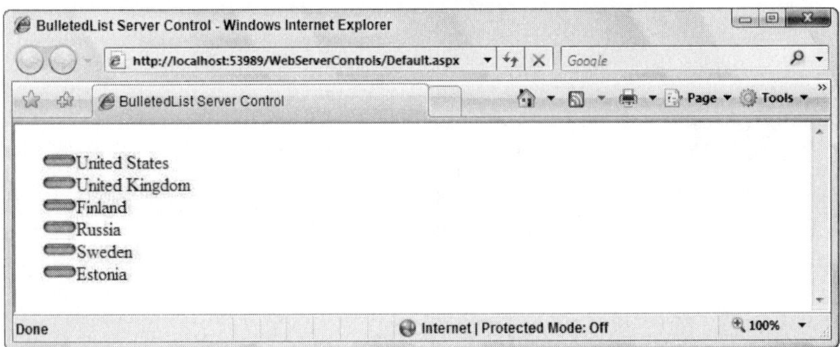

FIGURE 3-35

The BulletedList control has an attribute called `DisplayMode`, which has three possible values: `Text`, `HyperLink`, and `LinkButton`. `Text` is the default and has been used so far in the examples. Using `Text` means that the items in the bulleted list are laid out only as text. `HyperLink` means that each of the items is turned into a hyperlink — any user clicking the link is redirected to another page, which is specified by the `<asp:ListItem>` control's `Value` attribute. A value of `LinkButton` turns each bulleted list item into a hyperlink that posts back to the same page. It enables you to retrieve the selection that the end user makes, as illustrated in Listing 3-30.

LISTING 3-30: Using the LinkButton value for the DisplayMode attribute

```
<%@ Page Language="VB"%>

<script runat="server">
    Protected Sub BulletedList1_Click(ByVal sender As Object,
       ByVal e As System.Web.UI.WebControls.BulletedListEventArgs)

         Label1.Text = "The index of item you selected: " & e.Index &
            "<br>The value of the item selected: " &
            BulletedList1.Items(e.Index).Text
    End Sub
```

```
</script>

<html xmlns="http://www.w3.org/1999/xhtml" >
<head runat="server">
    <title>BulletedList Server Control</title>
</head>
<body>
    <form id="form1" runat="server">
        <asp:BulletedList ID="BulletedList1" runat="server"
         OnClick="BulletedList1_Click" DisplayMode="LinkButton">
            <asp:ListItem>United States</asp:ListItem>
            <asp:ListItem>United Kingdom</asp:ListItem>
            <asp:ListItem>Finland</asp:ListItem>
            <asp:ListItem>Russia</asp:ListItem>
            <asp:ListItem>Sweden</asp:ListItem>
            <asp:ListItem>Estonia</asp:ListItem>
        </asp:BulletedList>
        <asp:Label ID="Label1" runat="server">
        </asp:Label>
    </form>
</body>
</html>
```

C#

```
<%@ Page Language="C#"%>

<script runat="server">
    protected void BulletedList1_Click(object sender,
       System.Web.UI.WebControls.BulletedListEventArgs e)
    {
         Label1.Text = "The index of item you selected: " + e.Index +
            "<br>The value of the item selected: " +
            BulletedList1.Items[e.Index].Text;
    }
</script>
```

In this example, the `DisplayMode` attribute is set to `LinkButton`, and the `OnClick` attribute is used to point to the `BulletedList1_Click` event. `BulletedList1_Click` uses the `BulletedListEventArgs` object, which only exposes the `Index` property. Using that, you can determine the index number of the item selected.

You can directly access the `Text` value of a selected item by using the `Items` property, or you can use the same property to populate an instance of the `ListItem` object, as shown here:

```
Dim blSelectedValue As ListItem = BulletedList1.Items(e.Index)
```

```
ListItem blSelectedValue = BulletedList1.Items[e.Index];
```

Now that you have seen how to create bulleted lists with items that you declaratively place in the code, look at how to create dynamic bulleted lists from items that are stored in a data store. The following example shows how to use the BulletedList control to data-bind to results coming from a data store; in it, all information is retrieved from an XML file.

The first step is to create the XML in Listing 3-31.

LISTING 3-31: FilmChoices.xml

Available for download on Wrox.com

```
<?xml version="1.0" encoding="utf-8"?>
<FilmChoices>
   <Film
     Title="Close Encounters of the Third Kind"
     Year="1977"
     Director="Steven Spielberg" />
   <Film
     Title="Grease"
```

continues

LISTING 3-31 *(continued)*

```
      Year="1978"
      Director="Randal Kleiser" />
    <Film
      Title="Lawrence of Arabia"
      Year="1962"
      Director="David Lean" />
</FilmChoices>
```

To populate the BulletedList server control with the `Title` attribute from the `FilmChoices.xml` file, use an XmlDataSource control to access the file, as illustrated in Listing 3-32.

LISTING 3-32: Dynamically populating a BulletedList server control

Available for download on Wrox.com

```
<%@ Page Language="VB" %>

<html xmlns="http://www.w3.org/1999/xhtml" >
<head runat="server">
    <title>BulletedList Server Control</title>
</head>
<body>
    <form id="form1" runat="server">
       <asp:BulletedList ID="BulletedList1" runat="server"
         DataSourceID="XmlDataSource1" DataTextField="Title">
       </asp:BulletedList>
       <asp:XmlDataSource ID="XmlDataSource1" runat="server"
         DataFile="~/FilmChoices.xml" XPath="FilmChoices/Film">
       </asp:XmlDataSource>
    </form>
</body>
</html>
```

In this example, you use the `DataSourceID` attribute to point to the XmlDataSource control (as you would with any control that can be bound to one of the data source controls). After you are connected to the data source control, you specifically point to the `Title` attribute using the `DataTextField` attribute. After the two server controls are connected and the page is run, you get a bulleted list that is completely generated from the contents of the XML file. Figure 3-36 shows the result.

The XmlDataSource server control has some limitations in that the binding to the BulletedList server control worked in the previous example only because the `Title` *value was an XML attribute and not a subelement. The XmlDataSource control exposes XML attributes as properties only when data binding. If you are going to want to work with subelements, then you are going to have to perform an XSLT transform using the XmlDataSource control's* `TransformFile` *attribute to turn elements into attributes.*

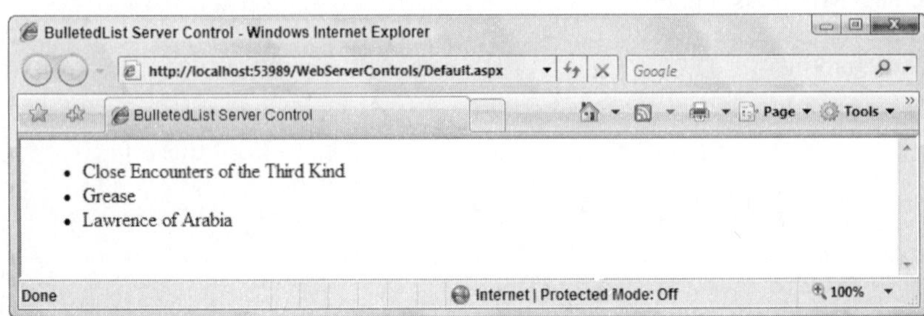

FIGURE 3-36

HIDDENFIELD SERVER CONTROL

For many years now, developers have been using hidden fields in their Web pages to work with state management. The `<input type="hidden">` element is ideal for storing items that have no security context to them. These items are simply placeholders for data points that you want to store in the page itself instead of using the `Session` object or intermingling the data with the view state of the page. View state is another great way to store information in a page, but many developers turn off this feature to avoid corruption of the view state or possible degradation of page performance.

Any time a hidden field is placed within a Web page, it is not interpreted in the browser in any fashion, although it is completely viewable by end users if they look at the source of the HTML page.

Listing 3-33 is an example of using the HiddenField server control to hold a GUID that can be used from page to page simply by carrying over its value as the end user navigates through your application.

LISTING 3-33: Working with the HiddenField server control

Available for download on Wrox.com

```
<%@ Page Language="VB" %>

<script runat="server" language="vb">
    Protected Sub Page_Load(ByVal sender As Object, ByVal e As System.EventArgs)
       HiddenField1.Value = System.Guid.NewGuid().ToString()
    End Sub
</script>

<html xmlns="http://www.w3.org/1999/xhtml" >
<head runat="server">
    <title>HiddenField Server Control</title>
</head>
<body>
    <form id="form1" runat="server">
       <asp:HiddenField ID="HiddenField1" runat="Server" />
    </form>
</body>
</html>
```

C#

```
<%@ Page Language="C#"%>

<script runat="server">
    protected void Page_Load(object sender, EventArgs e)
    {
        HiddenField1.Value = System.Guid.NewGuid().ToString();
    }
</script>
```

In this example, the `Page_Load` event populates the `HiddenField1` control with a GUID. You can see the hidden field and its value by looking at the source of the blank HTML page that is created. You should see a result similar to the following (the GUID will have a different value, of course):

```
<input type="hidden" name="HiddenField1" id="HiddenField1"
 value="a031e77c-379b-4b4a-887c-244ee69584d5" />
```

On the page postback, ASP.NET can detect whether the HiddenField server control has changed its value since the last post. This enables you to change the HiddenField value with client-side script and then work with the changes in a page event.

The HiddenField server control has an event called `ValueChanged` that you can use when the value is changed:

```
Protected Sub HiddenField1_ValueChanged(ByVal sender As Object,
   ByVal e As System.EventArgs)
   ' Handle event here
```

```
End Sub
```

```
protected void HiddenField1_ValueChanged(object sender, EventArgs e)
{
   // Handle event here
}
```

The ValueChanged event is triggered when the ASP.NET page is posted back to the server if the value of the HiddenField server control has changed since the last time the page was drawn. If the value has not changed, the method is never triggered. Therefore, the method is useful to act upon any changes to the HiddenField control — such as recording a value to the database or changing a value in the user's profile.

FILEUPLOAD SERVER CONTROL

In the very early days of ASP.NET, you could upload files using the HTML FileUpload server control. This control put an `<input type="file">` element on your Web page to enable the end user to upload files to the server. To use the file, however, you had to make a couple of modifications to the page. For example, you were required to add `enctype="multipart/form-data"` to the page's `<form>` element.

Ever since ASP.NET 2.0, you have been able to use the FileUpload server control that makes the process of uploading files to a server even simpler. When giving a page the capability to upload files, you simply include the `<asp:FileUpload>` control and ASP.NET takes care of the rest, including adding the `enctype` attribute to the page's `<form>` element.

Uploading Files Using the FileUpload Control

After the file is uploaded to the server, you can also take hold of the uploaded file's properties and either display them to the end user or use these values yourself in your page's code behind. Listing 3-34 shows an example of using the FileUpload control. The page contains a single FileUpload control, plus a Button and a Label control.

LISTING 3-34: Uploading files using the FileUpload control

Available for download on Wrox.com

```
<%@ Page Language="VB"%>

<script runat="server">
   Protected Sub Button1_Click(ByVal sender As Object, ByVal e As System.EventArgs)
        If FileUpload1.HasFile Then
            Try
                FileUpload1.SaveAs("C:\Uploads\" &
                   FileUpload1.FileName)
                Label1.Text = "File name: " &
                   FileUpload1.PostedFile.FileName & "<br>" &
                   "File Size: " & _
                   FileUpload1.PostedFile.ContentLength & " kb<br>" &
                   "Content type: " &
                   FileUpload1.PostedFile.ContentType
            Catch ex As Exception
                Label1.Text = "ERROR: " & ex.Message.ToString()
            End Try
        Else
            Label1.Text = "You have not specified a file."
        End If
   End Sub
</script>

<html xmlns="http://www.w3.org/1999/xhtml" >
<head runat="server">
    <title>FileUpload Server Control</title>
</head>
```

```
<body>
    <form id="form1" runat="server">
        <asp:FileUpload ID="FileUpload1" runat="server" />
        <p>
        <asp:Button ID="Button1" runat="server" Text="Upload"
         OnClick="Button1_Click" /></p>
        <p>
        <asp:Label ID="Label1" runat="server"></asp:Label></p>
    </form>
</body>
</html>
```

C#

```
<%@ Page Language="C#"%>

<script runat="server">
    protected void Button1_Click(object sender, EventArgs e)
    {
        if (FileUpload1.HasFile)
           try {
              FileUpload1.SaveAs("C:\\Uploads\\" + FileUpload1.FileName);
              Label1.Text = "File name: " +
                   FileUpload1.PostedFile.FileName + "<br>" +
                   FileUpload1.PostedFile.ContentLength + " kb<br>" +
                   "Content type: " +
                   FileUpload1.PostedFile.ContentType;
           }
            catch (Exception ex) {
              Label1.Text = "ERROR: " + ex.Message.ToString();
            }
        else
        {
           Label1.Text = "You have not specified a file.";
        }
    }
</script>
```

From this example, you can see that the entire process is rather simple. The single button on the page initiates the upload process. The FileUpload control itself does not initiate the uploading process. You must initiate it through another event such as `Button_Click`.

When compiling and running this page, you may notice a few things in the generated source code of the page. An example of the generated source code is presented here:

```
<html xmlns="http://www.w3.org/1999/xhtml" >
<head id="Head1"><title>
 FileUpload Server Control
</title></head>
<body>
    <form name="form1" method="post" action="FileUpload.aspx" id="form1"
     enctype="multipart/form-data">
<div>
<input type="hidden" name="__VIEWSTATE" id="__VIEWSTATE"
 value="/wEPDwUKMTI3ODM5MzQ0Mg9kFgICAw8WAh4HZW5jdHlwZQUTbXVsdGlwYXJ0L2Zvcm
 0tZGF0YWRkrSpgAFaEKed5+5/8+zKglFfVLCE=" />
</div>

        <input type="file" name="FileUpload1" id="FileUpload1" />
        <p>
        <input type="submit" name="Button1" value="Upload" id="Button1" /></p>
        <p>
```

```
            <span id="Label1"></span></p>

    <div>

    <input type="hidden" name="__EVENTVALIDATION" id="__EVENTVALIDATION"
      value="/wEWAgL1wLWICAKM54rGBqfR8MhZIDWVowox+TUvybG5Xj0y" />
    </div></form>
    </body>
    </html>
```

The first thing to notice is that because the FileUpload control is on the page, ASP.NET 4 modified the page's `<form>` element on your behalf by adding the appropriate `enctype` attribute. Also notice that the FileUpload control was converted to an HTML `<input type="file">` element.

After the file is uploaded, the first check (done in the file's `Button1_Click` event handler) examines whether a file reference was actually placed within the `<input type="file">` element. If a file was specified, an attempt is made to upload the referenced file to the server using the `SaveAs()` method of the FileUpload control. That method takes a single `String` parameter, which should include the location where you want to save the file. In the `String` parameter used in Listing 3-34, you can see that the file is being saved to a folder called Uploads, which is located in the `C:\` drive.

The `PostedFile.FileName` attribute is used to give the saved file the same name as the file it was copied from. If you want to name the file something else, simply use the `SaveAs()` method in the following manner:

```
FileUpload1.SaveAs("C:\Uploads\UploadedFile.txt")
```

You could also give the file a name that specifies the time it was uploaded:

```
FileUpload1.SaveAs("C:\Uploads\" & System.DateTime.Now.ToFileTimeUtc() & ".txt")
```

After the upload is successfully completed, the Label control on the page is populated with metadata of the uploaded file. In the example, the file's name, size, and content type are retrieved and displayed on the page for the end user. When the file is uploaded to the server, the page generated is similar to that shown in Figure 3-37.

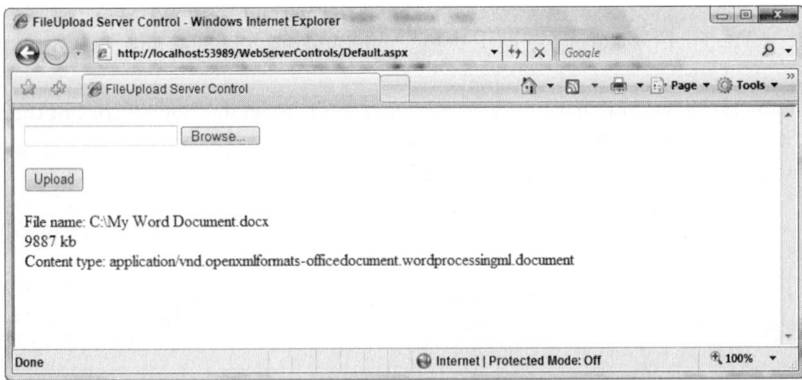

FIGURE 3-37

Uploading files to another server can be an error-prone affair. It is vital to upload files in your code using proper exception handling. That is why the file in the example is uploaded using a `Try Catch` statement.

Giving ASP.NET Proper Permissions to Upload Files

You might receive errors when your end users upload files to your Web server through the FileUpload control in your application. These might occur because the destination folder on the server is not writable for the account used by ASP.NET. If ASP.NET is not enabled to write to the folder you want, you can enable it using the folder's properties.

First, right-click on the folder where the ASP.NET files should be uploaded and select Properties from the provided menu. The Properties dialog for the selected folder opens. Click the Security tab to make sure the ASP.NET Machine Account is included in the list and has the proper permissions to write to disk. If it is enabled, you see something similar to what is presented in Figure 3-38.

If you do not see the ASP.NET Machine Account in the list of users allowed to access the folder, add ASP.NET by clicking the Add button and entering ASPNET (without the period) in the text area provided (see Figure 3-39).

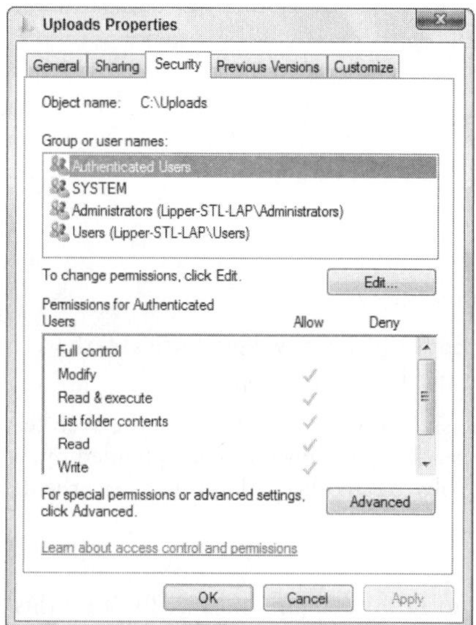

FIGURE 3-38

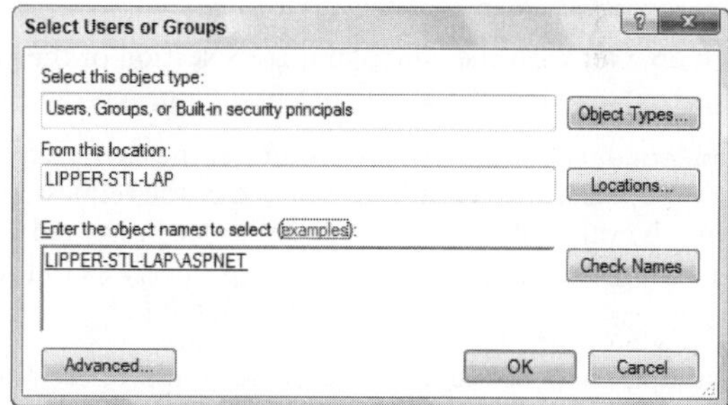

FIGURE 3-39

Click OK, and you can then click the appropriate check boxes to provide the permissions needed for your application.

Understanding File Size Limitations

Your end users might never encounter an issue with the file upload process in your application, but you should be aware that some limitations exist. When users work through the process of uploading files, a size restriction is actually sent to the server for uploading. The default size limitation is 4MB (4096KB); the transfer fails if a user tries to upload a file that is larger than 4096KB.

A size restriction protects your application. You want to prevent malicious users from uploading numerous large files to your Web server in an attempt to tie up all the available processes on the server. Such an occurrence is called a *denial of service attack*. It ties up the Web server's resources so that legitimate users are denied responses from the server.

One of the great things about .NET, however, is that it usually provides a way around limitations. You can usually change the default settings that are in place. To change the limit on the allowable upload file size, you make some changes in either the root `web.config` file (found in the ASP.NET 4 configuration folder at `C:\WINDOWS\Microsoft.NET\Framework\v4.0.xxxxx\CONFIG`) or in your application's `web.config` file.

In the `web.config` file, you can create a node called `<httpRuntime>`. In this file, you apply the settings so that the default allowable file size is dictated by the actual request size permitted to the Web server (4096KB). The `<httpRuntime>` section of the `web.config.comments` file is shown in Listing 3-35.

LISTING 3-35: Changing the file-size limitation setting in the web.config file

```
<httpRuntime
 executionTimeout="110"
 maxRequestLength="4096"
 requestLengthDiskThreshold="80"
 useFullyQualifiedRedirectUrl="false"
 minFreeThreads="8"
 minLocalRequestFreeThreads="4"
 appRequestQueueLimit="5000"
 enableKernelOutputCache="true"
 enableVersionHeader="true"
 requireRootedSaveAsPath="true"
 enable="true"
 shutdownTimeout="90"
 delayNotificationTimeout="5"
 waitChangeNotification="0"
 maxWaitChangeNotification="0"
 enableHeaderChecking="true"
 sendCacheControlHeader="true"
 apartmentThreading="false" />
```

You can do a lot with the `<httpRuntime>` section of the `web.config` file, but two properties — the `maxRequestLength` and `executionTimeout` properties — are especially interesting.

The `maxRequestLength` property is the setting that dictates the size of the request made to the Web server. When you upload files, the file is included in the request; you alter the size allowed to be uploaded by changing the value of this property. The value presented is in kilobytes. To allow files larger than the default of 4MB, change the `maxRequestLength` property as follows:

```
maxRequestLength="11000"
```

This example changes the `maxRequestLength` property's value to 11,000KB (around 10MB). With this setting in place, your end users can upload 10MB files to the server. When changing the `maxRequestLength` property, be aware of the setting provided for the `executionTimeout` property. This property sets the time (in seconds) for a request to attempt to execute to the server before ASP.NET shuts down the request (whether or not it is finished). The default setting is `90` seconds. The end user receives a timeout error notification in the browser if the time limit is exceeded. If you are going to permit larger requests, remember that they take longer to execute than smaller ones. If you increase the size of the `maxRequestLength` property, you should examine whether to increase the `executionTimeout` property as well.

If you are working with smaller files, it is advisable to reduce the size allotted for the request to the Web server by decreasing the value of the `maxRequestLength` *property. This helps safeguard your application from a denial of service attack.*

Making these changes in the `web.config` file applies this setting to all the applications that are on the server. If you want to apply this only to the application you are working with, apply the `<httpRuntime>` node to the `web.config` file of your application, overriding any setting that is in the root `web.config` file. Make sure this node resides between the `<system.web>` nodes in the configuration file.

Uploading Multiple Files from the Same Page

So far, you have seen some good examples of how to upload a file to the server without much hassle. Now, look at how to upload multiple files to the server from a single page.

No built-in capabilities in the Microsoft .NET Framework enable you to upload multiple files from a single ASP.NET page. With a little work, however, you can easily accomplish this task just as you would have in the past using .NET 1.*x*.

The trick is to import the `System.IO` class into your ASP.NET page and then to use the `HttpFileCollection` class to capture all the files that are sent in with the `Request` object. This approach enables you to upload as many files as you want from a single page.

If you wanted to, you could simply handle each and every FileUpload control on the page individually, as shown in Listing 3-36.

LISTING 3-36: Handling each FileUpload control individually

VB

```
If FileUpload1.HasFile Then
   ' Handle file
End If

If FileUpload2.HasFile Then
   ' Handle file
End If
```

C#

```
if (FileUpload1.HasFile) {
   // Handle file
}

if (FileUpload2.HasFile) {
   // Handle file
}
```

If you are working with a limited number of file upload boxes, this approach works; but at the same time you may, in certain cases, want to handle the files using the `HttpFileCollection` class. This is especially true if you are working with a dynamically generated list of server controls on your ASP.NET page.

For an example of this, you can build an ASP.NET page that has three FileUpload controls and one Submit button (using the Button control). After the user clicks the Submit button and the files are posted to the server, the code behind takes the files and saves them to a specific location on the server. After the files are saved, the file information that was posted is displayed in the ASP.NET page (see Listing 3-37).

LISTING 3-37: Uploading multiple files to the server

Available for download on Wrox.com

```
Protected Sub Button1_Click(ByVal sender As Object,
   ByVal e As System.EventArgs)

   Dim filepath As String = "C:\Uploads"
   Dim uploadedFiles As HttpFileCollection = Request.Files
   Dim i As Integer = 0

   Do Until i = uploadedFiles.Count
     Dim userPostedFile As HttpPostedFile = uploadedFiles(i)

     Try
        If (userPostedFile.ContentLength > 0) Then
           Label1.Text += "<u>File #" & (i + 1) & "</u><br>"
           Label1.Text += "File Content Type: " &
              userPostedFile.ContentType & "<br>"
           Label1.Text += "File Size: " &
              userPostedFile.ContentLength & "kb<br>"
           Label1.Text += "File Name: " &
              userPostedFile.FileName & "<br>"

           userPostedFile.SaveAs(filepath & "\" &
```

continues

LISTING 3-37 *(continued)*

```
                    System.IO.Path.GetFileName(userPostedFile.FileName))

                Label1.Text += "Location where saved: " &
                    filepath & "\" &
                    System.IO.Path.GetFileName(userPostedFile.FileName) &
                    "<p>"
            End If
        Catch ex As Exception
            Label1.Text += "Error:<br>" & ex.Message
        End Try
        i += 1
    Loop
End Sub
```

C#

```
protected void Button1_Click(object sender, EventArgs e)
{
    string filepath = "C:\\Uploads";
    HttpFileCollection uploadedFiles = Request.Files;

    for (int i = 0; i < uploadedFiles.Count; i++)
    {
        HttpPostedFile userPostedFile = uploadedFiles[i];

        try
        {
            if (userPostedFile.ContentLength > 0 )
            {
                Label1.Text += "<u>File #" + (i+1) +
                    "</u><br>";
                Label1.Text += "File Content Type: " +
                    userPostedFile.ContentType + "<br>";
                Label1.Text += "File Size: " +
                    userPostedFile.ContentLength + "kb<br>";
                Label1.Text += "File Name: " +
                    userPostedFile.FileName + "<br>";

                userPostedFile.SaveAs(filepath + "\\" +
                    System.IO.Path.GetFileName(userPostedFile.FileName));

                Label1.Text += "Location where saved: " +
                    filepath + "\\" +
                    System.IO.Path.GetFileName(userPostedFile.FileName) +
                    "<p>";
            }
        }
        catch (Exception Ex)
        {
            Label1.Text += "Error: <br>" + Ex.Message;
        }
    }
}
```

This ASP.NET page enables the end user to select up to three files and click the Upload Files button, which initializes the `Button1_Click` event. Using the `HttpFileCollection` class with the `Request.Files` property lets you gain control over all the files that are uploaded from the page. When the files are in this state, you can do whatever you want with them. In this case, the files' properties are examined and written to the screen. In the end, the files are saved to the Uploads folder in the root directory of the server. The result of this action is illustrated in Figure 3-40.

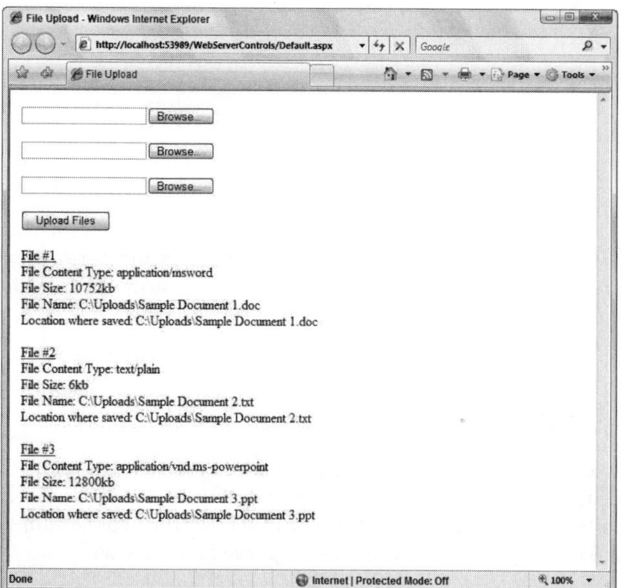

FIGURE 3-40

Placing the Uploaded File into a Stream Object

One nice feature of the FileUpload control is that it not only gives you the capability to save the file to disk, but it also lets you place the contents of the file into a `Stream` object. You do this by using the `FileContent` property, as demonstrated in Listing 3-38.

LISTING 3-38: Uploading the file contents into a Stream object

```
Dim myStream As System.IO.Stream
myStream = FileUpload1.FileContent
```

```
System.IO.Stream myStream;
myStream = FileUpload1.FileContent;
```

In this short example, an instance of the `Stream` object is created. Then, using the FileUpload control's `FileContent` property, the content of the uploaded file is placed into the object. This is possible because the `FileContent` property returns a `Stream` object.

Moving File Contents from a Stream Object to a Byte Array

Because you have the capability to move the file contents to a `Stream` object of some kind, it is also fairly simple to move the contents of the file to a `Byte` array (useful for such operations as placing files in a database of some kind). To do so, first move the file contents to a `MemoryStream` object and then convert the object to the necessary `Byte` array object. Listing 3-39 shows the process.

LISTING 3-39: Uploading the file contents into a Byte array

```
Dim myByteArray() As Byte
Dim myStream As System.IO.MemoryStream

myStream = FileUpload1.FileContent
```

continues

LISTING 3-39 *(continued)*

```
myByteArray = myStream.ToArray()
```

```
Byte myByteArray[];
System.IO.Stream myStream;

myStream = FileUpload1.FileContent;
myByteArray = myStream.ToArray();
```

In this example, instances of a `Byte` array and a `MemoryStream` object are created. First, the `MemoryStream` object is created using the FileUpload control's `FileContent` property as you did previously. Then it's fairly simple to use the `MemoryStream` object's `ToArray()` method to populate the `myByteArray()` instance. After the file is placed into a `Byte` array, you can work with the file contents as necessary.

MULTIVIEW AND VIEW SERVER CONTROLS

The MultiView and View server controls work together to give you the capability to turn on/off sections of an ASP.NET page. Turning sections on and off, which means activating or deactivating a series of View controls within a MultiView control, is similar to changing the visibility of Panel controls. For certain operations, however, you may find that the MultiView control is easier to manage and work with.

The sections, or views, do not change on the client-side; rather, they change with a postback to the server. You can put any number of elements and controls in each view, and the end user can work through the views based upon the sequence numbers that you assign to the views.

You can build these controls (like all server controls) from the source view or design view. If working with Visual Studio 2010, you can drag and drop a MultiView control onto the design surface and then drag and drop any number of View controls inside the MultiView control. Place the elements you want within the View controls. When you are finished, you have something like the view shown in Figure 3-41.

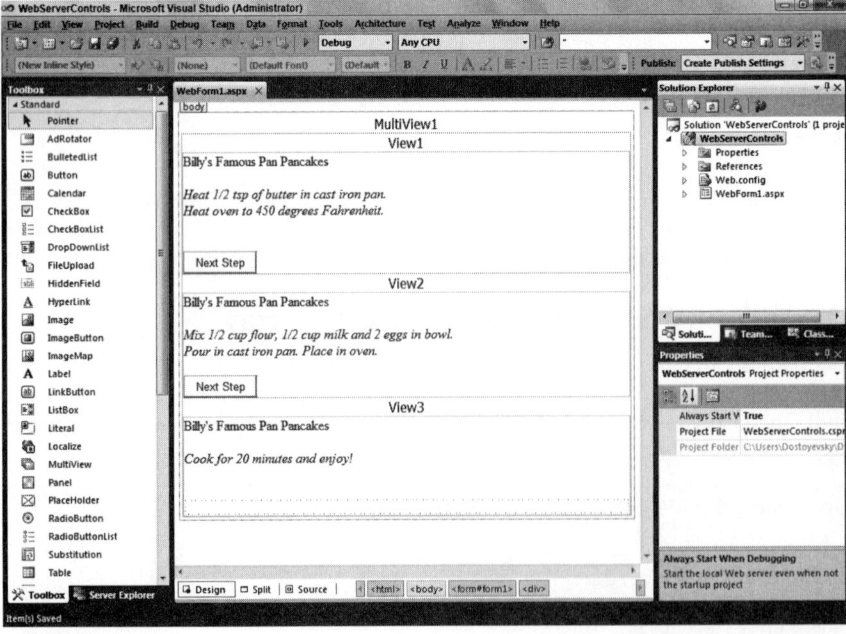

FIGURE 3-41

You also can create your controls directly in the code, as shown in Listing 3-40.

LISTING 3-40: Using the MultiView and View server controls

Available for download on Wrox.com

VB

```
<%@ Page Language="VB"%>

<script runat="server">
    Protected Sub Page_Load(ByVal sender As Object, ByVal e As System.EventArgs)
        If Not Page.IsPostBack Then
            MultiView1.ActiveViewIndex = 0
        End If
    End Sub
    Sub NextView(ByVal sender As Object, ByVal e As System.EventArgs)
        MultiView1.ActiveViewIndex += 1
    End Sub
</script>

<html xmlns="http://www.w3.org/1999/xhtml" >
<head runat="server">
    <title>MultiView Server Control</title>
</head>
<body>
    <form id="form1" runat="server">
        <asp:MultiView ID="MultiView1" runat="server">
            <asp:View ID="View1" runat="server">
                Billy's Famous Pan Pancakes<p />
                <i>Heat 1/2 tsp of butter in cast iron pan.<br />
                   Heat oven to 450 degrees Fahrenheit.<br />
                </i><p />
                <asp:Button ID="Button1" runat="server" Text="Next Step"
                 OnClick="NextView" />
            </asp:View>
            <asp:View ID="View2" runat="server">
                Billy's Famous Pan Pancakes<p />
                <i>Mix 1/2 cup flour, 1/2 cup milk and 2 eggs in bowl.<br />
                   Pour in cast iron pan. Place in oven.</i><p />
                <asp:Button ID="Button2" runat="server" Text="Next Step"
                 OnClick="NextView" />
            </asp:View>
            <asp:View ID="View3" runat="server">
                Billy's Famous Pan Pancakes<p />
                <i>Cook for 20 minutes and enjoy!<br />
                </i><p />
            </asp:View>
        </asp:MultiView>
    </form>
</body>
</html>
```

C#

```
<%@ Page Language="C#"%>

<script runat="server">
    protected void Page_Load(object sender, EventArgs e)
    {
        if (!Page.IsPostBack)
        {
            MultiView1.ActiveViewIndex = 0;
        }
    }

    void NextView(object sender, EventArgs e)
    {
        MultiView1.ActiveViewIndex += 1;
    }
</script>
```

This example shows three views expressed in the MultiView control. Each view is constructed with an `<asp:View>` server control that also needs `ID` and `Runat` attributes. A button is added to each of the first two views (`View1` and `View2`) of the MultiView control. The buttons point to a server-side event that triggers the MultiView control to progress onto the next view within the series of views.

Before either of the buttons can be clicked, the MultiView control's `ActiveViewIndex` attribute is assigned a value. By default, the `ActiveViewIndex`, which describes the view that should be showing, is set to -1. This means that no view shows when the page is generated. To start on the first view when the page is drawn, set the `ActiveViewIndex` property to `0`, which is the first view because this is a zero-based index. Therefore, the code from Listing 3-40 first checks to see if the page is in a postback situation, and if not, the `ActiveViewIndex` is assigned to the first View control.

Each of the buttons in the MultiView control triggers the `NextView` method. `NextView` simply adds one to the `ActiveViewIndex` value, thereby showing the next view in the series until the last view is shown. The view series is illustrated in Figure 3-42.

FIGURE 3-42

In addition to the Next Step button on the first and second views, you could place a button in the second and third views to enable the user to navigate backward through the views. To do this, create two buttons titled Previous Step in the last two views and point them to the following method in their `OnClick` events:

VB

```
Sub PreviousView(ByVal sender As Object, ByVal e As System.EventArgs)
    MultiView1.ActiveViewIndex -= 1
End Sub
```

C#

```
void PreviousView(object sender, EventArgs e)
{
    MultiView1.ActiveViewIndex -= 1;
}
```

Here, the `PreviousView` method subtracts one from the `ActiveViewIndex` value, thereby showing the previous view in the view series.

Another option is to spice up the MultiView control by adding a step counter that displays (to a Label control) which step in the series the end user is currently performing. In the `Page_PreRender` event, you add the following line:

VB

```
Label1.Text = "Step " & (MultiView1.ActiveViewIndex + 1).ToString() &
   " of " & MultiView1.Views.Count.ToString()
```

C#

```
Label1.Text = "Step " + (MultiView1.ActiveViewIndex + 1).ToString() +
   " of " + MultiView1.Views.Count.ToString();
```

Now when working through the MultiView control, the end user sees `Step 1 of 3` on the first view, which changes to `Step 2 of 3` on the next view, and so on.

WIZARD SERVER CONTROL

Much like the MultiView control, the Wizard server control enables you to build a sequence of steps that is displayed to the end user. Web pages are all about either displaying or gathering information and, in many cases, you don't want to display all the information at once — nor do you always want to gather everything from the end user at once. Sometimes, you want to trickle the information in from or out to the end user.

When you are constructing a step-by-step process that includes logic on the steps taken, use the Wizard control to manage the entire process. The first time you use the Wizard control, notice that it allows for a far greater degree of customization than does the MultiView control.

In its simplest form, the Wizard control can be just an `<asp:Wizard>` element with any number of `<asp:WizardStep>` elements. Listing 3-41 creates a Wizard control that works through three steps.

Available for download on Wrox.com

LISTING 3-41: A simple Wizard control

```
<%@ Page Language="VB"%>

<html xmlns="http://www.w3.org/1999/xhtml" >
<head runat="server">
    <title>Wizard server control</title>
</head>
<body>
    <form id="form1" runat="server">
        <asp:Wizard ID="Wizard1" runat="server" DisplaySideBar="True"
         ActiveStepIndex="0">
            <WizardSteps>
                <asp:WizardStep runat="server" Title="Step 1">
                    This is the first step.</asp:WizardStep>
                <asp:WizardStep runat="server" Title="Step 2">
                    This is the second step.</asp:WizardStep>
                <asp:WizardStep runat="server" Title="Step 3">
                    This is the third and final step.</asp:WizardStep>
            </WizardSteps>
        </asp:Wizard>
    </form>
</body>
</html>
```

In this example, three steps are defined with the `<asp:WizardSteps>` control. Each step contains content — simply text in this case, although you can put in anything you want, such as other Web server controls or even user controls. The order in which the `WizardSteps` are defined is based completely on the order in which they appear within the `<WizardSteps>` element.

The `<asp:Wizard>` element itself contains a couple of important attributes. The first is `DisplaySideBar`. In this example, it is set to `True` by default — meaning that a side navigation system in the displayed control enables the end user to quickly navigate to other steps in the process. The `ActiveStepIndex` attribute of the Wizard control defines the first wizard step. In this case, it is the first step — `0`.

The three steps of the example Wizard control are shown in Figure 3-43.

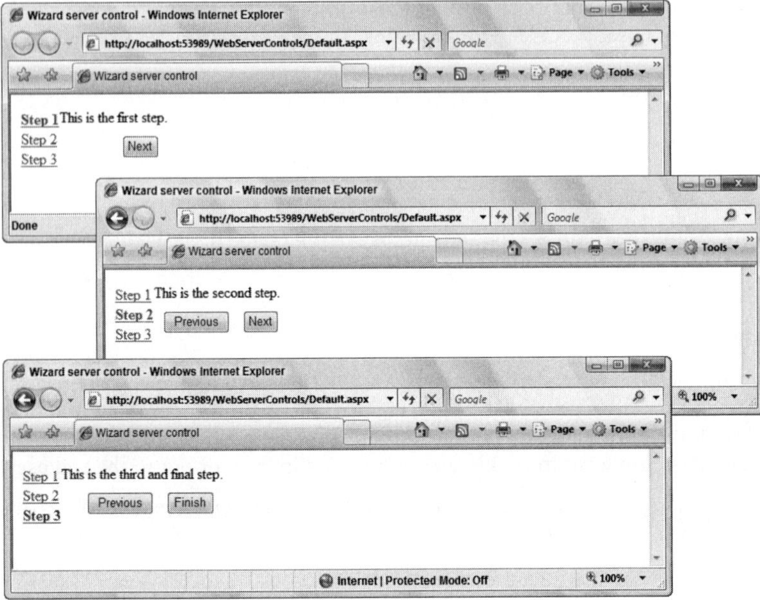

FIGURE 3-43

The side navigation allows for easy access to the defined steps. The Wizard control adds appropriate buttons to the steps in the process. The first step has simply a Next button, the middle step has Previous and Next buttons, and the final step has Previous and Finish buttons. The user can navigate through the steps using either the side navigation or the buttons on each of the steps. You can customize the Wizard control in so many ways that it tends to remind me of the other rich Web server controls from ASP.NET, such as the Calendar control. Because so much is possible, only a few of the basics are covered — the ones you are most likely to employ in some of the Wizard controls you build.

Customizing the Side Navigation

The steps in the Figure 3-43 example are defined as Step 1, Step 2, and Step 3. The links are created based on the `Title` property's value that you give to each of the `<asp:WizardStep>` elements in the Wizard control:

```
<asp:WizardStep runat="server" Title="Step 1">
 This is the first step.</asp:WizardStep>
```

By default, each wizard step created in Design view is titled `Step X` (with `X` being the number in the sequence). You can easily change the value of the `Title` attributes of each of the wizard steps to define the steps as you see fit. Figure 3-44 shows the side navigation of the Wizard control with renamed titles.

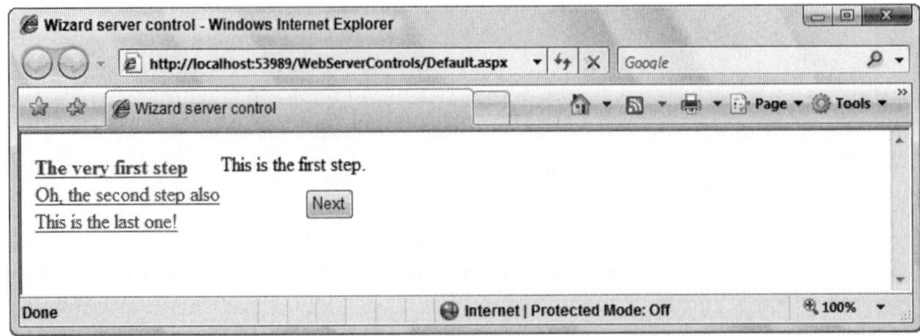

FIGURE 3-44

Examining the AllowReturn Attribute

Another interesting point of customization for the side navigation piece of the Wizard control is the `AllowReturn` attribute. By setting this attribute on one of the wizard steps to `False`, you can remove the capability for end users to go back to this step after they have viewed it. The end user cannot navigate backward to any viewed steps that contain the attribute, but he would be able to return to any steps that do not contain the attribute or that have it set to `True`:

```
<asp:WizardStep runat="server" Title="Step 1" AllowReturn="False">
 This is the first step.</asp:WizardStep>
```

Working with the StepType Attribute

Another interesting attribute in the `<asp:WizardStep>` element is `StepType`. The `StepType` attribute defines the structure of the buttons used on the steps. By default, the Wizard control places only a Next button on the first step. It understands that you do not need the Previous button there. It also knows to use a Next and Previous button on the middle step, and it uses Previous and Finish buttons on the last step. It draws the buttons in this fashion because, by default, the `StepType` attribute is set to `Auto`, meaning that the Wizard control determines the placement of buttons. You can, however, take control of the `StepType` attribute in the `<asp:WizardStep>` element to make your own determination about which buttons are used for which steps.

In addition to `Auto`, `StepType` value options include `Start`, `Step`, `Finish`, and `Complete`. `Start` means that the step defined has only a Next button. It simply allows the user to proceed to the next step in the series. A value of `Step` means that the wizard step has Next and Previous buttons. A value of `Finish` means that the step includes a Previous and a Finish button. `Complete` enables you to give some final message to the end user who is working through the steps of your Wizard control. In the Wizard control shown in Listing 3-42, for example, when the end user gets to the last step and clicks the Finish button, nothing happens and the user just stays on the last page. You can add a final step to give an ending message, as shown in Listing 3-42.

LISTING 3-42: Having a complete step in the wizard step collection

```
<WizardSteps>
   <asp:WizardStep runat="server" Title="Step 1">
    This is the first step.</asp:WizardStep>
   <asp:WizardStep runat="server" Title="Step 2">
    This is the second step.</asp:WizardStep>
   <asp:WizardStep runat="server" Title="Step 3">
    This is the third and final step.</asp:WizardStep>
   <asp:WizardStep runat="server" Title="Final Step" StepType="Complete">
    Thanks for working through the steps.</asp:WizardStep>
</WizardSteps>
```

When you run this Wizard control in a page, you still see only the first three steps in the side navigation. Because the last step has a `StepType` set to `Complete`, it does not appear in the side navigation list. When the end user clicks the Finish button in Step 3, the last step — `Final Step` — is shown and no buttons appear with it.

Adding a Header to the Wizard Control

The Wizard control enables you to place a header at the top of the control by means of the `HeaderText` attribute in the main `<asp:Wizard>` element. Listing 3-43 provides an example.

LISTING 3-43: Working with the HeaderText attribute

```
<asp:Wizard ID="Wizard1" runat="server" ActiveStepIndex="0"
 HeaderText=" Step by Step with the Wizard control "
 HeaderStyle-BackColor="DarkGray" HeaderStyle-Font-Bold="true"
 HeaderStyle-Font-Size="20">
  ...
</asp:Wizard>
```

This code creates a header that appears on each of the steps in the wizard. The result of this snippet is shown in Figure 3-45.

FIGURE 3-45

Working with the Wizard's Navigation System

As stated earlier, the Wizard control allows for a very high degree of customization — especially in the area of style. You can customize every single aspect of the process, as well as how every element appears to the end user.

Pay particular attention to the options that are available for customization of the navigation buttons. By default, the wizard steps use Next, Previous, and Finish buttons throughout the entire series of steps. From the main `<asp:Wizard>` element, you can change everything about these buttons and how they work.

First, if you look through the long list of attributes available for this element, notice that one available button is not shown by default: the Cancel button. Set the value of the `DisplayCancelButton` attribute to `True`, and a Cancel button appears within the navigation created for each and every step, including the final step in the series. Figure 3-46 shows a Cancel button in a step.

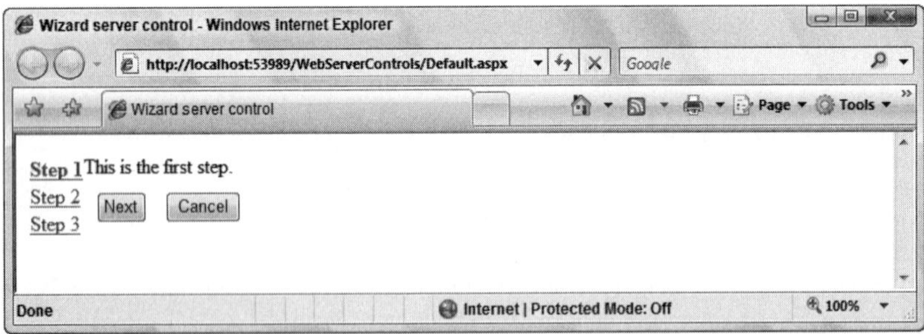

FIGURE 3-46

After you decide which buttons to use within the Wizard navigation, you can choose their style. By default, regular buttons appear; you can change the button style with the `CancelButtonType`, `FinishStepButtonType`, `FinishStepPreviousButtonType`, `NextStepButtonType`, `PreviousStepButtonType`, and `StartStepNextButtonType` attributes. If you use any of these button types and want all the buttons consistently styled, you must change each attribute to the same value. The possible values of these button-specific elements include `Button`, `Image`, and `Link`. `Button` is the default and means that the navigation system uses buttons. A value of `Image` enables you to use image buttons, and `Link` turns a selected item in the navigation system into a hyperlink.

In addition to these button-specific attributes of the `<asp:Wizard>` element, you can also specify a URL to which the user is directed when the user clicks either the Cancel or Finish buttons. To redirect the user with one of these buttons, you use the CancelDestinationPageUrl or the FinishDestinationPageUrl attributes and set the appropriate URL as the destination.

Finally, you are not required to use the default text included with the buttons in the navigation system. You can change the text of each of the buttons with the use of the CancelButtonText, FinishStepButtonText, FinishStepPreviousButtonText, NextStepButtonText, PreviousStepButtonText, and the StartStepNextButtonText attributes.

Utilizing Wizard Control Events

One of the most convenient capabilities of the Wizard control is that it enables you to divide large forms into logical pieces. The end user can then work systematically through each section of the form. The developer, dealing with the inputted values of the form, has a few options because of the various events that are available in the Wizard control.

The Wizard control exposes events for each of the possible steps that an end user might take when working with the control. Table 3-2 describes each of the available events.

TABLE 3-2

EVENT	DESCRIPTION
ActiveStepChanged	Triggers when the end user moves from one step to the next. It does not matter if the step is the middle or final step in the series. This event simply covers each step change generically.
CancelButtonClick	Triggers when the end user clicks the Cancel button in the navigation system.
FinishButtonClick	Triggers when the end user clicks the Finish button in the navigation system.
NextButtonClick	Triggers when the end user clicks the Next button in the navigation system.
PreviousButtonClick	Triggers when the end user clicks the Previous button in the navigation system.
SideBarButtonClick	Triggers when the end user clicks one of the links contained within the sidebar navigation of the Wizard control.

By working with these events, you can create a multi-step form that saves all the end user's input information when he changes from one step to the next. You can also use the FinishButtonClick event to save everything that was stored in each of the steps at the end of the process. The Wizard control remembers all the end user's input in each of the steps by means of the view state in the page, which enables you to work with all these values in the last step. It also gives the end user the capability to go back to previous steps and change values before those values are saved to a data store.

The event appears in your code behind or inline code, as shown in Listing 3-44.

LISTING 3-44: The FinishButtonClick event

VB

```
<script runat="server">
    Sub Wizard1_FinishButtonClick(ByVal sender As Object,
       ByVal e As System.Web.UI.WebControls.WizardNavigationEventArgs)

    End Sub
</script>
```

C#

```
<script runat="server">
    void Wizard1_FinishButtonClick(object sender, WizardNavigationEventArgs e)
    {

    }
</script>
```

The `OnFinishButtonClick` attribute should be added to the main `<asp:Wizard>` element to point at the `Wizard1_FinishButtonClick` event. Listing 3-45 shows how to do this.

LISTING 3-45: The <asp:Wizard> Element Changes

```
<asp:Wizard ID="Wizard1" runat="server" ActiveStepIndex="0"
 OnFinishButtonClick="Wizard1_FinishButtonClick">
```

The Wizard control is one of the great controls that enable you to break up longer workflows into more manageable pieces for your end users. By separating longer Web forms into various wizard steps, you can effectively make your forms easy to understand and less daunting to the end user.

Using the Wizard Control to Show Form Elements

So far, you have learned how to work with each of the Wizard control steps, including how to add steps to the process and how to work with the styling of the control. Now look at how you put form elements into the Wizard control to collect information from the end user in a stepped process. This is just as simple as the first examples of the Wizard control that used only text in each of the steps.

One nice thing about putting form elements in the Wizard step process is that the Wizard control remembers each input into the form elements from step to step, enabling you to save the results of the entire form at the last step. It also means that when the end user presses the Previous button, the data that he entered into the form previously is still there and can be changed.

Work through a stepped process that enters form information by building a registration process. The last step of the process saves the results to a database of your choice, although in this example, you just push the results to a Label control on the page. Listing 3-46 shows the first part of the process.

LISTING 3-46: Building the form in the Wizard control

```
<asp:Wizard ID="Wizard1" runat="Server">
   <WizardSteps>
      <asp:WizardStep ID="WizardStep1" runat="server"
       Title="Provide Personal Info">
         First name:<br />
         <asp:TextBox ID="fnameTextBox" runat="server"></asp:TextBox><br />
         Last name:<br />
         <asp:TextBox ID="lnameTextBox" runat="server"></asp:TextBox><br />
         Email:<br />
         <asp:TextBox ID="emailTextBox" runat="server"></asp:TextBox><br />
      </asp:WizardStep>
      <asp:WizardStep ID="WizardStep2" runat="server"
       Title="Membership Information">
         Are you already a member of our group?<br />
         <asp:RadioButton ID="RadioButton1" runat="server" Text="Yes"
          GroupName="Member" />
         <asp:RadioButton ID="RadioButton2" runat="server" Text="No"
          GroupName="Member" />
      </asp:WizardStep>
      <asp:WizardStep ID="WizardStep3" runat="server" Title="Provided Information"
       StepType="Complete" OnActivate="WizardStep3_Activate">
         <asp:Label ID="Label1" runat="server" />
      </asp:WizardStep>
   </WizardSteps>
</asp:Wizard>
```

This Wizard control has three steps. The first step asks for the user's personal information, and the second asks for the user's membership information. The third step contains a Label control that pushes out all the information that was input. This is done through the `Activate` event that is specific for the `WizardStep` object on the third WizardStep control. The code for the `WizardStep3_Activate` event is shown in Listing 3-47.

LISTING 3-47: Adding an Activate event to a WizardStep object

VB

```
Protected Sub WizardStep3_Activate(ByVal sender As Object,
  ByVal e As System.EventArgs)

  ' You could save the inputted data to the database here instead
   Label1.Text = "First name: " & fnameTextBox.Text.ToString() & "<br>" & _
      "Last name: " & lnameTextBox.Text.ToString() & "<br>" &
      "Email: " & emailTextBox.Text.ToString()
End Sub
```

C#

```
protected void WizardStep3_Activate(object sender, EventArgs e)
{
   Label1.Text = "First name: " + fnameTextBox.Text.ToString() + "<br>" +
      "Last name: " + lnameTextBox.Text.ToString() + "<br>" +
      "Email: " + emailTextBox.Text.ToString();
}
```

When the end user comes to the third step in the display, the `WizardStep3_Activate` method from Listing 3-47 is invoked. Using the `OnActivate` attribute in the third WizardStep control, the content provided by the end user in earlier steps is used to populate a Label control. The three steps are shown in Figure 3-47.

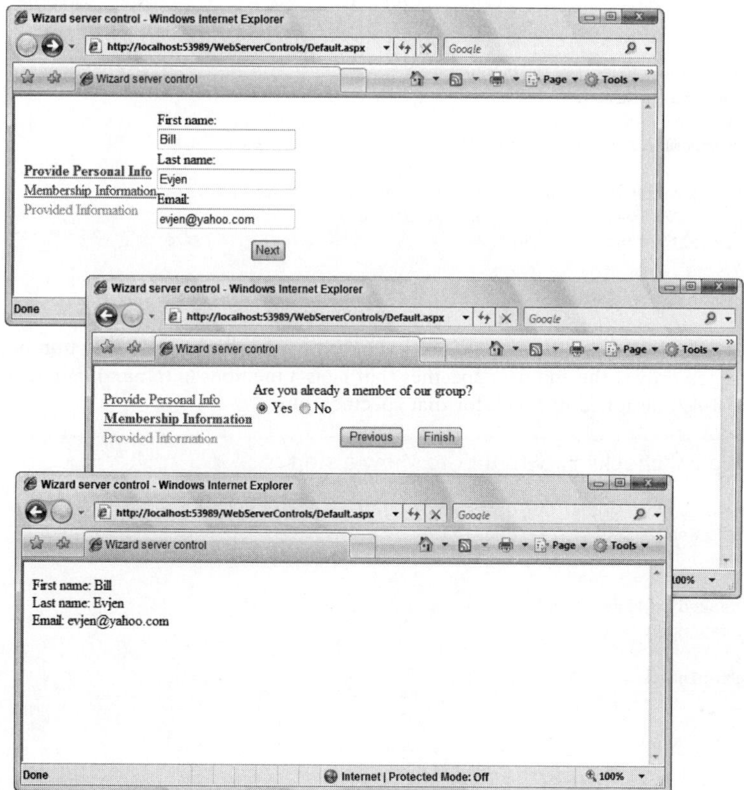

FIGURE 3-47

This example is simple and straightforward, but you can increase the complexity a little bit. Imagine you want to add another WizardStep control to the process, and you want to display it only if a user specifies that he is a member in `WizardStep2`. If he answers from the radio button selection that he is not a member, you have him skip the new step and go straight to the final step where the results are displayed in the Label control. First, add an additional `WizardStep` to the Wizard control, as shown in Listing 3-48.

LISTING 3-48: Adding an additional WizardStep

```
<asp:Wizard ID="Wizard1" runat="Server">
   <WizardSteps>
      <asp:WizardStep ID="WizardStep1" runat="server"
       Title="Provide Personal Info">
         First name:<br />
         <asp:TextBox ID="fnameTextBox" runat="server"></asp:TextBox><br />
         Last name:<br />
         <asp:TextBox ID="lnameTextBox" runat="server"></asp:TextBox><br />
         Email:<br />
         <asp:TextBox ID="emailTextBox" runat="server"></asp:TextBox><br />
      </asp:WizardStep>
      <asp:WizardStep ID="WizardStep2" runat="server"
       Title="Membership Information">
         Are you already a member of our group?<br />
         <asp:RadioButton ID="RadioButton1" runat="server" Text="Yes"
          GroupName="Member" />
         <asp:RadioButton ID="RadioButton2" runat="server" Text="No"
          GroupName="Member" />
      </asp:WizardStep>
      <asp:WizardStep ID="MemberStep" runat="server"
       Title="Provide Membership Number">
         Membership Number:<br />
         <asp:TextBox ID="mNumberTextBox" runat="server"></asp:TextBox>
      </asp:WizardStep>
      <asp:WizardStep ID="WizardStep3" runat="server" Title="Provided Information"
       StepType="Complete" OnActivate="WizardStep3_Activate">
         <asp:Label ID="Label1" runat="server" />
      </asp:WizardStep>
   </WizardSteps>
</asp:Wizard>
```

A single step was added to the workflow — one that simply asks the member for his membership number. Because you want to show this step only if the end user specifies that he is a member in `WizardStep2`, you add an event (shown in Listing 3-49) designed to check for that specification.

LISTING 3-49: Applying logical checks on whether to show a step

VB

```
Sub Wizard1_NextButtonClick(ByVal sender As Object,
  ByVal e As System.Web.UI.WebControls.WizardNavigationEventArgs)

   If e.NextStepIndex = 2 Then
      If RadioButton1.Checked = True Then
         Wizard1.ActiveStepIndex = 2
      Else
         Wizard1.ActiveStepIndex = 3
      End If
   End If
```

```
End Sub
```

C#

```
void Wizard1_NextButtonClick(object sender, WizardNavigationEventArgs e)
{
   if (e.NextStepIndex == 2) {
      if (RadioButton1.Checked == true) {
         Wizard1.ActiveStepIndex = 2; }
      else {
         Wizard1.ActiveStepIndex = 3; }
   }
}
```

To check whether you should show a specific step in the process, use the `NextButtonClick` event from the Wizard control. The event uses the `WizardNavigationEventArgs` class instead of the typical `EventArgs` class that gives you access to the `NextStepIndex` number, as well as to the `CurrentStep Index` number.

In the example from Listing 3-49, you check whether the next step to be presented in the process is `2`. Remember that this is index `2` from a zero-based index (0, 1, 2, and so on). If it is Step `2` in the index, you check which radio button is selected from the previous WizardStep. If the `RadioButton1` control is checked (meaning that the user is a member), the next step in the process is assigned as index `2`. If the `RadioButton2` control is selected, the user is not a member, and the index is then assigned as `3` (the final step), thereby bypassing the membership step in the process.

You could also take this example and alter it a bit so that you show a WizardStep only if the user is contained within a specific role (such as Admin).

Role management is covered in Chapter 15.

Showing only a WizardStep if the user is contained within a certain role is demonstrated in Listing 3-50.

LISTING 3-50: Applying logical checks on whether to show a step based upon roles

VB

```
Sub Wizard1_NextButtonClick(ByVal sender As Object,
  ByVal e As System.Web.UI.WebControls.WizardNavigationEventArgs)

   If e.NextStepIndex = 2 Then
      If (Roles.IsUserInRole("ManagerAccess") Then
         Wizard1.ActiveStepIndex = 2
      Else
         Wizard1.ActiveStepIndex = 3
      End If
   End If
End Sub
```

C#

```
void Wizard1_NextButtonClick(object sender, WizardNavigationEventArgs e)
{
   if (e.NextStepIndex == 2) {
      if (Roles.IsUserInRole("ManagerAccess")) {
         Wizard1.ActiveStepIndex = 2; }
      else {
         Wizard1.ActiveStepIndex = 3; }
      }
   }
}
```

IMAGEMAP SERVER CONTROL

The ImageMap server control enables you to turn an image into a navigation menu. In the past, many developers would break an image into multiple pieces and put it together again in a table, reassembling the pieces into one image. When the end user clicked a particular piece of the overall image, the application picked out which piece of the image was chosen and based actions upon that particular selection.

With the ImageMap control, you can take a single image and specify particular hotspots on the image using coordinates. An example is shown in Listing 3-51.

LISTING 3-51: Specifying sections of an image that are clickable

Available for download on Wrox.com

```
<%@ Page Language="VB"%>

<script runat="server">
    Protected Sub Imagemap1_Click(ByVal sender As Object,
       ByVal e As System.Web.UI.WebControls.ImageMapEventArgs)

          Response.Write("You selected: " & e.PostBackValue)
    End Sub
</script>

<html xmlns="http://www.w3.org/1999/xhtml" >
<head runat="server">
    <title>ImageMap Control</title>
</head>
<body>
    <form id="form1" runat="server">
        <asp:ImageMap ID="Imagemap1" runat="server" ImageUrl="Kids.jpg"
         Width="300" OnClick="Imagemap1_Click" HotSpotMode="PostBack">
            <asp:RectangleHotSpot Top="0" Bottom="225" Left="0" Right="150"
             AlternateText="Sofia" PostBackValue="Sofia">
            </asp:RectangleHotSpot>
            <asp:RectangleHotSpot Top="0" Bottom="225" Left="151" Right="300"
             AlternateText="Henri" PostBackValue="Henri">
            </asp:RectangleHotSpot>
        </asp:ImageMap>
    </form>
</body>
</html>
```

C#

```
<%@ page language="C#"%>

<script runat="server">
    protected void Imagemap1_Click(object sender,
       System.Web.UI.WebControls.ImageMapEventArgs e) {

          Response.Write("You selected: " + e.PostBackValue);
    }
</script>
```

This page brings up an image of my children. If you click the left side of the image, you select Sofia, and if you click the right side of the image, you select Henri. You know which child you selected through a `Response.Write` statement, as shown in Figure 3-48.

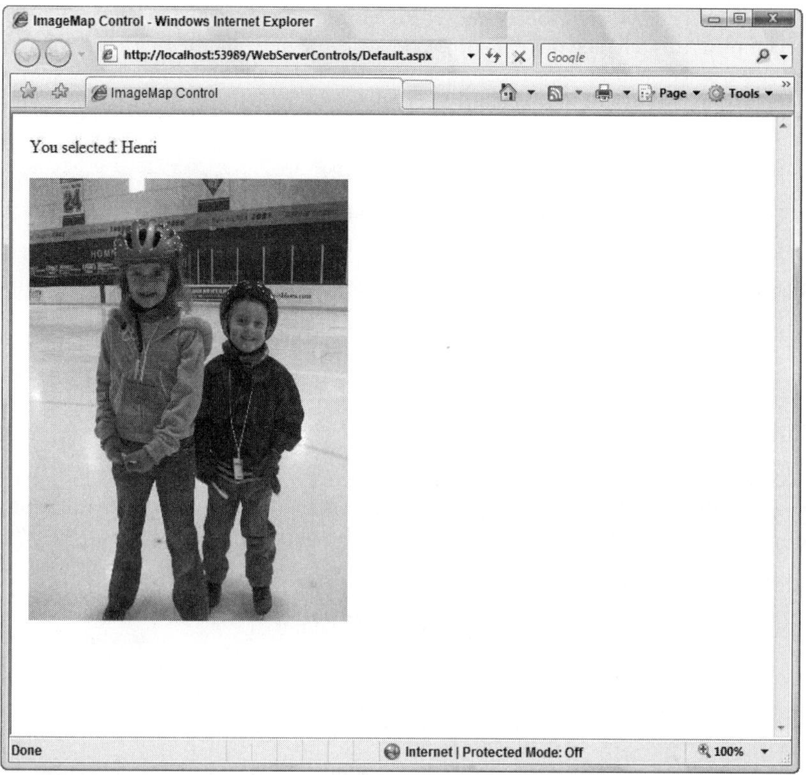

FIGURE 3-48

The ImageMap control enables you to specify hotspots in a couple of different ways. From the example in Listing 3-51, you can see that hotspots are placed in a rectangular fashion using the `<asp:RectangleHotSpot>` element. The control takes the `Top`, `Bottom`, `Left`, and `Right` coordinates of the rectangle that is to be the hotspot. Besides the `<asp:RectangleHotSpot>` control, you can also use the `<asp:CircleHotSpot>` and the `<asp:PolygonHotSpot>` controls. Each control takes coordinates appropriate to its shape.

After you define the hotspots on the image, you can respond to the end user click of the hotspot in several ways. You first specify how to deal with the hotspot clicks in the root `<asp:ImageMap>` element with the use of the `HotSpotMode` attribute.

The `HotSpotMode` attribute can take the values `PostBack`, `Navigate`, or `InActive`. In the previous example, the `HotSpotMode` value is set to `PostBack` — meaning that after the end user clicks the hotspot, you want to postback to the server and deal with the click at that point.

Because the `HotSpotMode` is set to `PostBack` and you have created several hotspots, you must determine which hotspot is selected. You make this determination by giving each hotspot (`<asp:RectangleHotSpot>`) a postback value with the `PostBackValue` attribute. The example uses `Sofia` as the value of the first hotspot and `Henri` as the value for the second.

The `PostBackValue` attribute is also the helper text that appears in the browser (in the yellow box) directly below the mouse cursor when the end user hovers the mouse over the hotspot.

After the user clicks one of the hotspots, the event procedure displays the value that was selected in a `Response.Write` statement.

Instead of posting back to the server, you can also navigate to an entirely different URL when a particular hotspot is selected. To accomplish this, change the `HotSpotMode` attribute in the main `<asp:ImageMap>` element to the value `Navigate`. Then, within the `<asp:RectangleHotSpot>` elements, simply use the `NavigateUrl` attribute and assign the location to which the end user should be directed if that particular hotspot is clicked:

```
<asp:ImageMap ID="Imagemap1" runat="server" ImageUrl="kids.jpg"
 HotSpotMode="Navigate">
   <asp:RectangleHotSpot Top="0" Bottom="225" Left="0" Right="150"
    AlternateText="Sofia" NavigateUrl="SofiaPage.aspx">
   </asp:RectangleHotSpot>
   <asp:RectangleHotSpot Top="0" Bottom="225" Left="151" Right="300"
    AlternateText="Henri" NavigateUrl="HenriPage.aspx">
   </asp:RectangleHotSpot>
</asp:ImageMap>
```

CHART SERVER CONTROL

One of the newest controls available to you now with ASP.NET 4 is the Chart server control. This control made its way into the core part of ASP.NET through a previous acquisition of the Dundas charting company and is a great control for getting you up and running with some good-looking charts.

The new Chart server control supports many chart types including:

- Point
- FastPoint
- Bubble
- Line
- Spline
- StepLine
- FastLine
- Bar
- StackedBar
- StackedBar100
- Column
- StackedColumn
- StackedColumn100
- Area
- SplineArea
- StackedArea
- StackedArea100
- Pie
- Doughnut
- Stock
- CandleStick
- Range
- SplineRange
- RangeBar
- RangeColumn
- Radar
- Polar
- ErrorBar
- BoxPlot
- Renko
- ThreeLineBreak
- Kagi
- PointAndFigure
- Funnel
- Pyramid

Those are a lot of different chart styles! You can find the Chart server control in the toolbox of Visual Studio 2010 underneath the Data tab. It is part of the `System.Web.DataVisualization` namespace.

When you drag it from the toolbox and place it on the design surface of your page, you are presented with a visual representation of the chart type that are you going to use. See Figure 3-49 for an example.

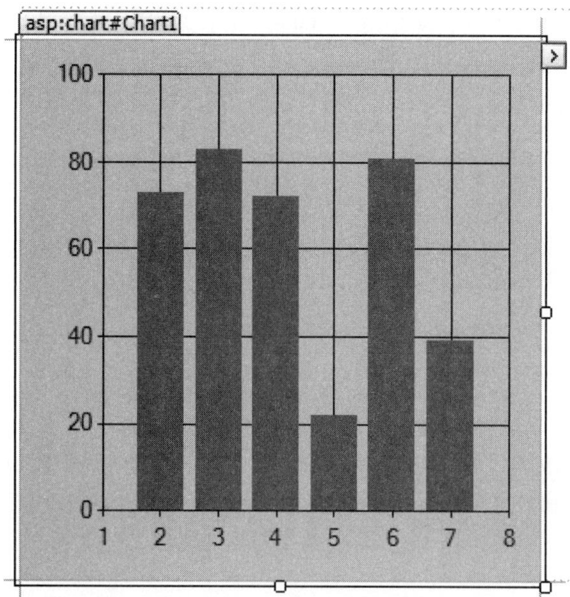

FIGURE 3-49

Open up the smart tag for the control, and you find that you can assign a data provider for the chart as well as select the chart type you are interested in using. Changing the chart type gives you a sample of what that chart looks like (even if you are not yet working with any underlying data) in the design view of the IDE. The smart tag is shown in Figure 3-50.

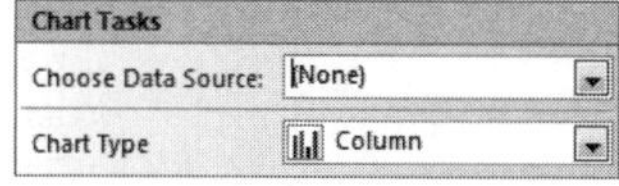

FIGURE 3-50

There is a lot to this control, probably more than all the others and this single control could almost warrant a book on its own. To get you up and running with this chart server control, follow this simple example.

Create a new web application and add the AdventureWorks database to your App_Data folder within the application. After that is accomplished, drag and drop the Chart server control onto the design surface of your page. From the smart tag of the control, select <New Data Source> from the drop-down menu when choosing your data source. Work your way through this wizard making sure that you are choosing a SQL data source as your option. As you work through the wizard, you are going to want to choose the option that allows you to choose a custom SQL statement and use the following SQL for this operation:

```
SELECT TOP (5) Production.Product.Name, Sales.SalesOrderDetail.OrderQty
FROM Sales.SalesOrderDetail INNER JOIN Production.Product
ON Sales.SalesOrderDetail.ProductID = Production.Product.
ProductID
ORDER BY Sales.SalesOrderDetail.OrderQty DESC
```

With that in place and the new chart server control bound to this data source control, you now find that you have more options in the smart tag of the chart server control. This is presented in Figure 3-51.

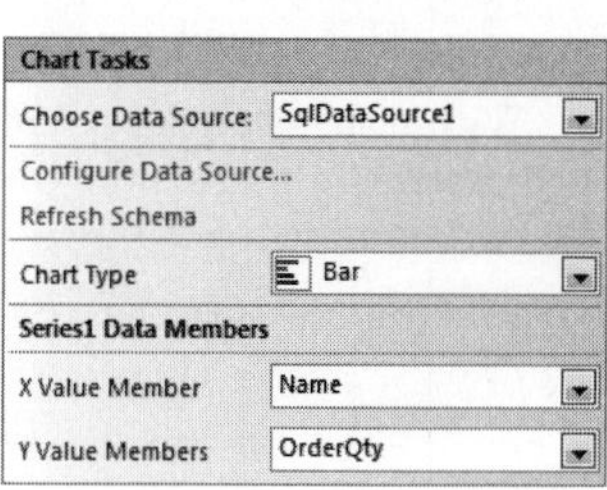

FIGURE 3-51

Now you can select the series data members and choose what is on the x-axis and what is on the y-axis. From Figure 3-51, you can see that I have assigned the Name of the product to be on the x-axis and the quantity ordered to be on the y-axis. After widening the chart's width a bit, you end up with code similar to the following as illustrated here in Listing 3-52.

LISTING 3-52: Charting with the new Chart server control

Available for download on Wrox.com

```
<%@ Page Language="C#" AutoEventWireup="true"
    CodeBehind="WebForm1.aspx.cs" Inherits="WebServerControls.WebForm1" %>
<%@ Register Assembly="System.Web.DataVisualization, Version=4.0.0.0,
      Culture=neutral, PublicKeyToken=31bf3856ad364e35"
    Namespace="System.Web.UI.DataVisualization.Charting" TagPrefix="asp" %>

<html xmlns="http://www.w3.org/1999/xhtml">
<head runat="server">
    <title>MultiView Server Control</title>
</head>
<body>
    <form id="form1" runat="server">
    <div>
        <asp:Chart ID="Chart1" runat="server"
         DataSourceID="SqlDataSource1"
         Width="500px">
            <Series>
                <asp:Series ChartType="Bar" Name="Series1"
                 XValueMember="Name"
                 YValueMembers="OrderQty" YValuesPerPoint="2">
                </asp:Series>
            </Series>
            <ChartAreas>
                <asp:ChartArea Name="ChartArea1">
                </asp:ChartArea>
            </ChartAreas>
        </asp:Chart>
        <asp:SqlDataSource ID="SqlDataSource1" runat="server"
         ConnectionString="<%$ ConnectionStrings:ConnectionString %>"
         SelectCommand="SELECT TOP (5) Production.Product.Name,
           Sales.SalesOrderDetail.OrderQty FROM Sales.SalesOrderDetail
           INNER JOIN Production.Product ON
           Sales.SalesOrderDetail.ProductID =
           Production.Product.ProductID ORDER BY
           Sales.SalesOrderDetail.OrderQty DESC">
        </asp:SqlDataSource>
    </div>
    </form>
</body>
</html>
```

From this, you can see that there isn't much code needed to wire everything up. Most notably, you can see that putting this Chart server control on your page actually added a `@Register` directive to the top of the page. This is unlike most of the ASP.NET server controls.

Within the `<Series>` element of this control, you can have as many series as you want, and this is something that is quite common when charting multiple items side by side (such as a time series of prices for two or more stocks).

Running this code, you get results similar to what is presented here in Figure 3-52.

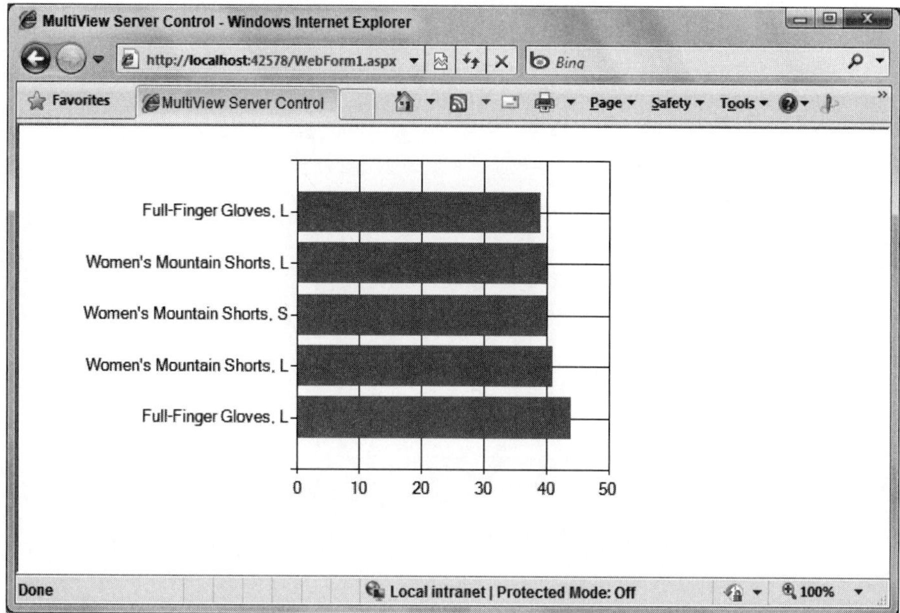

FIGURE 3-52

SUMMARY

This chapter explored numerous server controls, their capabilities, and the features they provide. With ASP.NET 4, you have more than 50 server controls at your disposal.

Because you have so many server controls at your disposal when you are creating your ASP.NET applications, you have to think carefully about which is the best control for the task. Many controls seem similar, but they offer different features. These controls guarantee that you can build the best possible applications for all browsers.

Server controls are some of the most useful tools you will find in your ASP.NET arsenal. They are quite useful and can save you a lot of time. This chapter introduced you to some of these controls and to the different ways you might incorporate them into your next projects. All these controls are wonderful options to use on any of your ASP.NET pages and make it much easier to develop the functionality that your pages require.

SUMMARY

Validation Server Controls

WHAT'S IN THIS CHAPTER?

- Understanding the provided validation server controls
- Working with both client- and server-side validations

When you look at the Toolbox window in Visual Studio 2010 — especially if you've read Chapters 2 and 3, which cover the various server controls at your disposal — you may be struck by the number of server controls that come with ASP.NET 4. This chapter takes a look at a specific type of server control you find in the Toolbox window: the *validation server control*.

Validation server controls are a series of controls that enable you to work with the information your end users input into the form elements of the applications you build. These controls work to ensure the validity of the data being placed in the form.

Before you learn how to use these controls, however, this chapter first takes a look at the process of validation.

UNDERSTANDING VALIDATION

People have been constructing Web applications for a number of years. Usually the motivation is to provide or gather information. In this chapter, you focus on the information-gathering aspect of Web applications. If you collect data with your applications, collecting *valid* data should be important to you. If the information isn't valid, there really isn't much point in collecting it.

Validation comes in degrees. Validation is a set of rules that you apply to the data you collect. These rules can be many or few and enforced either strictly or in a lax manner: it really depends on you. No perfect validation process exists because some users may find a way to cheat to some degree, no matter what rules you establish. The trick is to find the right balance of the fewest rules and the proper strictness, without compromising the usability of the application.

The data you collect for validation comes from the Web forms you provide in your applications. Web forms are made up of different types of HTML elements that are constructed using raw HTML form elements, ASP.NET HTML server controls, or ASP.NET Web Form server controls. In the end, your forms are made up of many different types of HTML elements, such as text boxes, radio buttons, check boxes, drop-down lists, and more.

As you work through this chapter, you see the different types of validation rules that you can apply to your form elements. Remember that you have no way to validate the *truthfulness* of the information you collect; instead, you apply rules that respond to such questions as:

- Is something entered in the text box?
- Is the data entered in the text box in the form of an e-mail address?

Notice from these questions that you can apply more than a single validation rule to an HTML form element (examples of this appear later in this chapter). In fact, you can apply as many rules to a single element as you want. Applying more rules to elements increases the strictness of the validation applied to the data.

Just remember that data collection on the Internet is one of the Internet's most important features, so you must make sure that the data you collect has value and meaning. You ensure this value by eliminating any chance that the information collected does not abide by the rules you outline.

CLIENT-SIDE VERSUS SERVER-SIDE VALIDATION

If you are new to Web application development, you might not be aware of the difference between client-side and server-side validation. Suppose that the end user clicks the Submit button on a form after filling out some information. What happens in ASP.NET is that this form is packaged in a *request* and sent to the server where the application resides. At this point in the request/response cycle, you can run validation checks on the information submitted. Doing this is called *server-side validation* because it occurs on the server.

On the other hand, supplying a script (usually in the form of JavaScript) in the page that is posted to the end user's browser to perform validations on the data entered in the form *before* the form is posted back to the originating server is also possible. In this case, *client-side validation* has occurred.

Both types of validation have their pros and cons. Active Server Pages 2.0/3.0 developers (from the classic ASP days) are quite aware of these pros and cons because they have probably performed all the validation chores themselves. Many developers spent a considerable amount of their classic ASP programming days coding various validation techniques for performance and security.

Client-side validation is quick and responsive for the end user. It is something end users expect of the forms that they work with. If something is wrong with the form, using client-side validation ensures that the end user knows about it as soon as possible. Client-side validation also pushes the processing power required of validation to the client, meaning that you don't need to spin CPU cycles on the server to process the same information because the client can do the work for you.

With this said, client-side validation is the more insecure form of validation. When a page is generated in an end user's browser, this end user can look at the code of the page quite easily (simply by right-clicking his mouse in the browser and selecting View Code). When he does so, in addition to seeing the HTML code for the page, he can also see all the JavaScript that is associated with the page. If you are validating your form client-side, it doesn't take much for the crafty hacker to repost a form (containing the values he wants in it) to your server as valid. Cases also exist in which clients have simply disabled the client-scripting capabilities in their browsers — thereby making your validations useless. Therefore, client-side validation should be considered a convenience and a courtesy to the end user and never a security mechanism.

The more secure form of validation is server-side validation. Server-side validation means that the validation checks are performed on the server instead of on the client. It is more secure because these checks cannot be easily bypassed. Instead, the form data values are checked using server code (C# 4 or VB) on the server. If the form isn't valid, the page is posted back to the client as invalid. Although it is more secure, server-side validation can be slow. It is sluggish simply because the page has to be posted to a remote location and checked. Your end user might not be the happiest surfer in the world if, after waiting 20 seconds for a form to post, he is told his e-mail address isn't in the correct format.

So what is the correct path? Well, actually, both! The best approach is always to perform client-side validation first and then, after the form passes and is posted to the server, to perform the validation checks again using server-side validation. This approach provides the best of both worlds. It is secure because hackers can't simply bypass the validation. They may bypass the client-side validation, but they quickly find that their form data is checked once again on the server after it is posted. This validation technique is also highly effective — giving you both the quickness and snappiness of client-side validation.

ASP.NET VALIDATION SERVER CONTROLS

Getting the forms that are present on your Web pages to deal with validation is a common task in web development. For this reason, with the initial release of ASP.NET, the ASP.NET team introduced a series of validation server controls meant to make implementing sound validation for forms a snap.

ASP.NET not only introduces form validations as server controls, but it also makes these controls rather smart. As stated earlier, one of the tasks of classic ASP developers was to determine where to perform form validation — either on the client or on the server. The ASP.NET validation server controls eliminate this dilemma because ASP.NET performs browser detection when generating the ASP.NET page and makes decisions based on the information it gleans.

This means that if the browser can support the JavaScript that ASP.NET can send its way, the validation occurs on the client-side. If the client cannot support the JavaScript meant for client-side validation, this JavaScript is omitted and the validation occurs on the server.

The best part about this scenario is that even if client-side validation is initiated on a page, ASP.NET still performs the server-side validation when it receives the submitted page, thereby ensuring security won't be compromised. This decisive nature of the validation server controls means that you can build your ASP.NET Web pages to be the best they can possibly be — rather than dumbing-down your Web applications for the lowest common denominator.

Presently, seven validation controls are available to you in ASP.NET 4. No new validation server controls have been added to ASP.NET since the initial release of the technology, but ASP.NET 2.0 introduced some new features, such as validation groups and new JavaScript capabilities. Both these features are discussed in this chapter. The available validation server controls include:

- RequiredFieldValidator
- CompareValidator
- RangeValidator
- RegularExpressionValidator
- CustomValidator
- DynamicValidator
- ValidationSummary

Working with ASP.NET validation server controls is no different from working with any other ASP.NET server control. Each of these controls allows you to drag and drop it onto a design surface or to work with it directly from the code of your ASP.NET page. You can also modify these controls so that they appear exactly as you want — ensuring the visual uniqueness that your applications might require. You see some aspects of both of these items throughout this chapter.

If the ASP.NET Validation controls don't meet your needs, you can certainly write your own custom validation controls. However, third-party controls are available such as Peter Blum's Validation and More (VAM) from `www.peterblum.com/DES`*, which includes more than 50 ASP.NET validation controls.*

Table 4-1 describes the functionality of each of the available validation server controls.

TABLE 4-1

VALIDATION SERVER CONTROL	DESCRIPTION
RequiredFieldValidator	Ensures that the user does not skip a form entry field.
CompareValidator	Allows for comparisons between the user's input and another item using a comparison operator (equals, greater than, less than, and so on).
RangeValidator	Checks the user's input based upon a lower- and upper-level range of numbers or characters.
RegularExpressionValidator	Checks that the user's entry matches a pattern defined by a regular expression. This control is good to use to check e-mail addresses and phone numbers.
CustomValidator	Checks the user's entry using custom-coded validation logic.
DynamicValidator	Works with exceptions that are thrown from entity data models and extension methods. This control is part of the ASP.NET Dynamic Data Framework. This validator is covered in Chapter 30.
ValidationSummary	Displays all the error messages from the validators in one specific spot on the page.

Validation Causes

Validation doesn't just happen; it occurs in response to an event. In most cases, it is a button click event. The Button, LinkButton, and ImageButton server controls all have the capability to cause a page's form validation to initiate. This is the default behavior. Dragging and dropping a Button server control onto your form gives you the following initial result:

```
<asp:Button ID="Button1" runat="server" Text="Button" />
```

If you look through the properties of the Button control, you can see that the `CausesValidation` property is set to `True`. As stated, this behavior is the default — all buttons on the page, no matter how many there are, cause the form validation to fire.

If you have multiple buttons on an ASP.NET page, and you don't want each and every button to initiate the form validation, you can set the `CausesValidation` property to `False` for all the buttons you want to ignore the validation process (for example, a form's Cancel button):

```
<asp:Button ID="Button1" runat="server" Text="Cancel" CausesValidation="false" />
```

The RequiredFieldValidator Server Control

The RequiredFieldValidator control simply checks to see whether *something* was entered into the HTML form element. It is a simple validation control, but it is one of the most frequently used. You must have a RequiredFieldValidator control for each form element on which you want to enforce a *value-required* rule.

Listing 4-1 shows a simple use of the RequiredFieldValidator control.

LISTING 4-1: A simple use of the RequiredFieldValidator server control

```
<%@ Page Language="VB" %>

<script runat="server">
   Protected Sub Button1_Click(ByVal sender As Object, ByVal e As System.EventArgs)
      If Page.IsValid Then
        Label1.Text = "Page is valid!"
      End If
   End Sub
</script>
```

```
<html xmlns="http://www.w3.org/1999/xhtml">
<head runat="server">
    <title>RequiredFieldValidator</title>
</head>
<body>
    <form id="form1" runat="server">
    <div>
        <asp:TextBox ID="TextBox1" runat="server"></asp:TextBox>
        <asp:RequiredFieldValidator ID="RequiredFieldValidator1"
         runat="server" Text="Required!" ControlToValidate="TextBox1">
        </asp:RequiredFieldValidator>
        <br />
        <asp:Button ID="Button1" runat="server" Text="Submit"
         OnClick="Button1_Click" />
        <br />
        <br />
        <asp:Label ID="Label1" runat="server"></asp:Label>
    </div>
    </form>
</body>
</html>
```

C#

```
<%@ Page Language="C#" %>

<script runat="server">
    protected void Button1_Click(Object sender, EventArgs e) {
      if (Page.IsValid) {
       Label1.Text = "Page is valid!";
      }
    }
</script>
```

Build and run this page. A simple text box and button appear on the page. Don't enter any value inside the text box, and click the Submit button. Figure 4-1 shows the result.

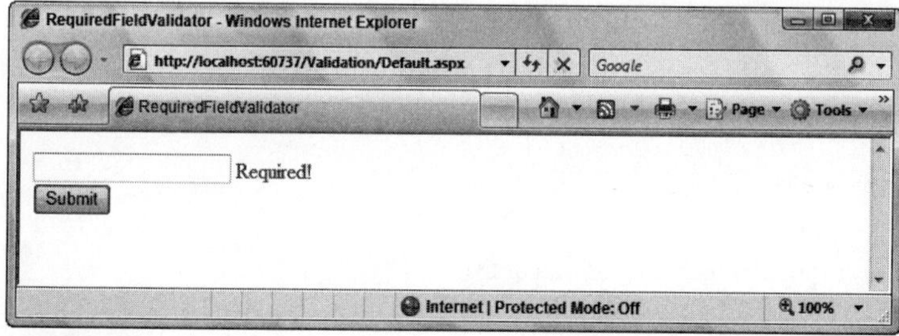

FIGURE 4-1

Now look at the code from this example. First, nothing is different about the TextBox, Button, or Label controls. They are constructed just as they would be if you were not using any type of form validation. This page does contain a simple RequiredFieldValidator control, however. Several properties of this control are especially notable because you will use them in most of the validation server controls you create.

The first property to look at is the `Text` property. This property is the value that is shown to the end user via the Web page if the validation fails. In this case, it is a simple `Required!` string. The second property to look at is the `ControlToValidate` property. This property is used to make an association between this validation server control and the ASP.NET form element that requires the validation. In this case, the value specifies the only element in the form — the text box.

As you can see from this example, the error message is constructed from an attribute within the `<asp:RequiredFieldValidator>` control. You can also accomplish this same task by using the `Text` attribute, as shown in Listing 4-2.

LISTING 4-2: Using the Text attribute

Available for download on Wrox.com

```
<asp:RequiredFieldValidator ID="RequiredFieldValidator1"
 runat="server" Text="Required!" ControlToValidate="TextBox1">
</asp:RequiredFieldValidator>
```

You can also express this error message between the <asp:RequiredFieldValidator> opening and closing nodes, as shown in Listing 4-3.

LISTING 4-3: Placing values between nodes

Available for download on Wrox.com

```
<asp:RequiredFieldValidator ID="RequiredFieldValidator1"
 runat="server" ControlToValidate="TextBox1">
 Required!
</asp:RequiredFieldValidator>
```

Looking at the Results Generated

Again, the RequiredFieldValidator control uses client-side validation if the browser allows for such an action. You can see the client-side validation for yourself (if your browser allows for it) by right-clicking on the page and selecting View Source from the menu. In the page code, you see the JavaScript shown in Listing 4-4.

LISTING 4-4: The generated JavaScript

```
… page markup removed for clarity here …

<script type="text/javascript">
//<![CDATA[
function WebForm_OnSubmit() {
if (typeof(ValidatorOnSubmit) == "function" &&
   ValidatorOnSubmit() == false) return false;
return true;
}
//]]>
</script>

… page markup removed for clarity here …

<script type="text/javascript">
//<![CDATA[
var Page_Validators =  new
  Array(document.getElementById("RequiredFieldValidator1"));
//]]>
</script>

<script type="text/javascript">
//<![CDATA[
var RequiredFieldValidator1 = document.all ?
  document.all["RequiredFieldValidator1"] :
  document.getElementById("RequiredFieldValidator1");
RequiredFieldValidator1.controltovalidate = "TextBox1";
RequiredFieldValidator1.evaluationfunction =
  "RequiredFieldValidatorEvaluateIsValid";
RequiredFieldValidator1.initialvalue = "";
//]]>
</script>

<script type="text/javascript">
//<![CDATA[
```

```
var Page_ValidationActive = false;
if (typeof(ValidatorOnLoad) == "function") {
    ValidatorOnLoad();
}

function ValidatorOnSubmit() {
    if (Page_ValidationActive) {
        return ValidatorCommonOnSubmit();
    }
    else {
        return true;
    }
}
        //]]>
</script>
```

In the page code, you may also notice some changes to the form elements (the former server controls) that deal with the submission of the form and the associated validation requirements.

Using the InitialValue Property

Another important property when working with the RequireFieldValidator control is the `InitialValue` property. Sometimes you have form elements that are populated with some default properties (for example, from a data store), and these form elements might present the end user with values that require changes before the form can be submitted to the server.

When using the `InitialValue` property, you specify to the RequiredFieldValidator control the initial text of the element. The end user is then required to change that text value before he can submit the form. Listing 4-5 shows an example of using this property.

Available for download on Wrox.com

LISTING 4-5: Working with the InitialValue property

```
<asp:TextBox ID="TextBox1" runat="server">My Initial Value</asp:TextBox>
  
<asp:RequiredFieldValidator ID="RequiredFieldValidator1"
 runat="server" Text="Please change the value of the textbox!"
 ControlToValidate="TextBox1" InitialValue="My Initial Value">
</asp:RequiredFieldValidator>
```

In this case, you can see that the `InitialValue` property contains a value of `My Initial Value`. When the page is built and run, the text box contains this value as well. The RequiredFieldValidator control requires a change in this value for the page to be considered valid.

Disallowing Blank Entries and Requiring Changes at the Same Time

In the preceding example of the use of the `InitialValue` property, an interesting problem arises. If you run the associated example, one thing the end user can do to get past the form validation is to submit the page with no value entered in this particular text box. A blank text box does not fire a validation error because the RequiredFieldValidator control is now reconstructed to force the end user only to *change* the default value of the text box (which he did when he removed the old value). When you reconstruct the RequiredFieldValidator control in this manner, nothing in the validation rule requires that *something* be entered in the text box — just that the initial value be changed. The possibility exists for the user to completely bypass the form validation process by just removing anything entered in this text box.

A way around this problem exists, however, and it goes back to the earlier discussion about how a form is made up of multiple validation rules — some of which are assigned to the same form element. To both require a change to the initial value of the text box and disallow a blank entry (thereby making the element a required element), you must put an additional RequiredFieldValidator control on the page. This second RequiredFieldValidator control is associated with the same text box as the first RequiredFieldValidator control. This method is illustrated in the example shown in Listing 4-6.

Available for download on Wrox.com

LISTING 4-6: Using two RequiredFieldValidator controls for one form element

```
<asp:TextBox ID="TextBox1" runat="server">My Initial Value</asp:TextBox> 

<asp:RequiredFieldValidator ID="RequiredFieldValidator1" runat="server"
 Text="Please change value" ControlToValidate="TextBox1"
 InitialValue="My Initial Value"></asp:RequiredFieldValidator>

<asp:RequiredFieldValidator ID="RequiredFieldValidator2" runat="server"
 Text="Do not leave empty" ControlToValidate="TextBox1">
</asp:RequiredFieldValidator>
```

In this example, you can see that the text box does indeed have two RequiredFieldValidator controls associated with it. The first, `RequiredFieldValidator1`, requires a change to the default value of the text box through the use of the `InitialValue` property. The second RequiredFieldValidator control, `RequiredFieldValidator2`, simply makes the `TextBox1` control a form element that requires a value. You get the behavior you want by applying two validation rules to a single form element.

Validating Drop-Down Lists with the RequiredFieldValidator Control

So far, you have seen a lot of examples of using the RequiredFieldValidator control with a series of text boxes, but you can just as easily use this validation control with other form elements as well.

For example, you can use the RequiredFieldValidator control with an `<asp:DropDownList>` server control. Suppose that you have a drop-down list that requires the end user to select her profession from a list of items. The first line of the drop-down list includes instructions to the end user about what to select, and you want to make this line a required form element as well. Listing 4-7 shows the code to do so.

Available for download on Wrox.com

LISTING 4-7: Drop-down list validations

```
<asp:DropDownList id="DropDownList1" runat="server">
   <asp:ListItem Selected="True">Select a profession</asp:ListItem>
   <asp:ListItem>Programmer</asp:ListItem>
   <asp:ListItem>Lawyer</asp:ListItem>
   <asp:ListItem>Doctor</asp:ListItem>
   <asp:ListItem>Artist</asp:ListItem>
</asp:DropDownList>
   
<asp:RequiredFieldValidator id="RequiredFieldValidator1"
  runat="server" Text="Please make a selection"
  ControlToValidate="DropDownList1"
  InitialValue="Select a profession">
</asp:RequiredFieldValidator>
```

Just as when you work with the text box, the RequiredFieldValidator control in this example associates itself with the DropDownList control using the `ControlToValidate` property. The drop-down list to which the validation control is bound has an initial value — `Select a profession`. You obviously don't want your end user to retain that value when she posts the form back to the server. So again, you use the `InitialValue` property of the RequiredFieldValidator control. The value of this property is assigned to the initial selected value of the drop-down list. This value forces the end user to select one of the provided professions in the drop-down list before she is able to post the form.

The CompareValidator Server Control

The CompareValidator control enables you to compare two form elements as well as to compare values contained within form elements to constants that you specify. For example, you can specify that a form element's value must be an integer and greater than a specified number. You can also state that values must be strings, dates, or other data types that are at your disposal.

Validating Against Other Controls

One of the more common ways of using the CompareValidator control is to make a comparison between two form elements. For example, suppose that you have an application that requires users to have passwords in order to access the site. You create one text box asking for the user's password and a second text box that asks the user to confirm the password. Because the text box is in password mode, the end user cannot see what she is typing — just the number of characters that she has typed. To reduce the chances of the end user mistyping her password and inputting this incorrect password into the system, you ask her to confirm the password. After the form is input into the system, you simply have to make a comparison between the two text boxes to see whether they match. If they match, it is likely that the end user typed the password correctly, and you can input the password choice into the system. If the two text boxes do not match, you want the form to be invalid. Listing 4-8, demonstrates this situation.

LISTING 4-8: Using the CompareValidator to test values against other control values

Available for download on Wrox.com

```
<%@ Page Language="VB" %>
<script runat="server">

    Protected Sub Button1_Click(sender As Object, e As EventArgs)
       If Page.IsValid Then
          Label1.Text = "Passwords match"
       End If
    End Sub

</script>

<html xmlns="http://www.w3.org/1999/xhtml">
<head runat="server">
    <title>CompareFieldValidator</title>
</head>
<body>
    <form runat="server" id="Form1">
        <p>
            Password<br />
            <asp:TextBox ID="TextBox1" runat="server"
             TextMode="Password"></asp:TextBox>
              
            <asp:CompareValidator ID="CompareValidator1"
             runat="server" Text="Passwords do not match!"
             ControlToValidate="TextBox2"
             ControlToCompare="TextBox1"></asp:CompareValidator>
        </p>
        <p>
            Confirm Password<br />
            <asp:TextBox ID="TextBox2" runat="server"
             TextMode="Password"></asp:TextBox>
        </p>
        <p>
            <asp:Button ID="Button1" OnClick="Button1_Click"
             runat="server" Text="Login"></asp:Button>
        </p>
        <p>
            <asp:Label ID="Label1" runat="server"></asp:Label>
        </p>
    </form>
</body>
</html>
```

continues

LISTING 4-8 *(continued)*

```
<%@ Page Language="C#" %>
<script runat="server">

    protected void Button1_Click(Object sender, EventArgs e) {
       if (Page.IsValid)
          Label1.Text = "Passwords match";
    }

</script>
```

Looking at the CompareValidator control on the form, you can see that it is similar to the RequiredFieldValidator control. The CompareValidator control has a property called `ControlToValidate` that associates itself with one of the form elements on the page. In this case, you need only a single CompareValidator control on the page because a single comparison is made. In this example, you are making a comparison between the value of `TextBox2` and that of `TextBox1`. Therefore, you use the `ControlToCompare` property. This specifies what value is compared to `TextBox2`. In this case, the value is `TextBox1`.

It's as simple as that. If the two text boxes do not match after the page is posted by the end user, the value of the `Text` property from the CompareValidator control appears in the browser. Figure 4-2 shows an example of this situation.

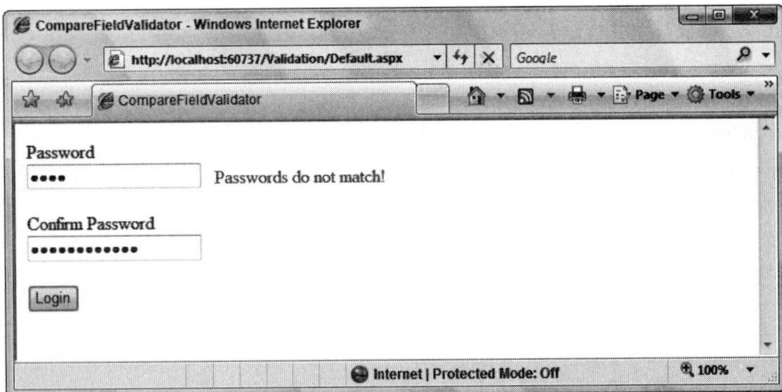

FIGURE 4-2

Validating Against Constants

Besides being able to validate values against values in other controls, you can also use the CompareValidator control to make comparisons against constants of specific data types. For example, suppose you have a text box on your registration form that asks for the age of the user. In most cases, you want to get back an actual number and not something such as `aa` or `bb` as a value. Listing 4-9 shows you how to ensure that you get back an actual number.

Available for download on Wrox.com

LISTING 4-9: Using the CompareValidator to validate against constants

```
Age:
<asp:TextBox ID="TextBox1" runat="server" MaxLength="3">
</asp:TextBox>
 
<asp:CompareValidator ID="CompareValidator1" runat="server"
  Text="You must enter a number"
  ControlToValidate="TextBox1" Type="Integer"
  Operator="DataTypeCheck"></asp:CompareValidator>
```

In this example, the end user is required to type a number into the text box. If she attempts to bypass the validation by entering a fake value that contains anything other than a number, the page is identified as invalid, and the CompareValidator control displays the value of the `Text` property.

To specify the data types that you want to use in these comparisons, you simply use the `Type` property. The `Type` property can take the following values:

- `Currency`
- `Date`
- `Double`
- `Integer`
- `String`

Not only can you make sure that what is entered is of a specific data type, but you can also make sure that what is entered is valid when compared to specific constants. For example, you can make sure what is entered in a form element is greater than, less than, equal to, greater than or equal to, or less than or equal to a specified value. Listing 4-10 shows an example of this situation.

LISTING 4-10: Making comparisons with the CompareValidator control

Available for download on Wrox.com

```
Age:
<asp:TextBox ID="TextBox1" runat="server"></asp:TextBox>
   
<asp:CompareValidator ID="CompareValidator1" runat="server"
  Operator="GreaterThan" ValueToCompare="18"
  ControlToValidate="TextBox1"
  Text="You must be older than 18 to join" Type="Integer">
</asp:CompareValidator>
```

In this case, the CompareValidator control not only associates itself with the `TextBox1` control and requires that the value must be an integer, but it also uses the `Operator` and the `ValueToCompare` properties to ensure that the number is greater than 18. Therefore, if the end user enters a value of 18 or less, the validation fails, and the page is considered invalid.

The `Operator` property can take one of the following values:

- `Equal`
- `NotEqual`
- `GreaterThan`
- `GreaterThanEqual`
- `LessThan`
- `LessThanEqual`
- `DataTypeCheck`

The `ValueToCompare` property is where you place the constant value used in the comparison. In the preceding example, it is the number `18`.

The RangeValidator Server Control

The RangeValidator control is quite similar to that of the CompareValidator control, but it makes sure that the end-user value or selection provided is within a specified range as opposed to being just greater than or less than a specified constant. For an example of this control, think back to the text-box element that asks for the age of the end user and performs a validation on the value provided. Listing 4-11 demonstrates this validation.

Available for download on Wrox.com

LISTING 4-11: Using the RangeValidator control to test an integer value

```
Age:
<asp:TextBox ID="TextBox1" runat="server"></asp:TextBox>
  
<asp:RangeValidator ID="RangeValidator1" runat="server"
 ControlToValidate="TextBox1" Type="Integer"
 Text="You must be between 30 and 40"
 MaximumValue="40" MinimumValue="30"></asp:RangeValidator>
```

In this example, this page consists of a text box asking for the age of the end user. The RangeValidator control makes an analysis of the value provided and makes sure the value is somewhere in the range of 30 to 40. You set the range using the `MaximumValue` and `MinimumValue` properties. The RangeValidator control also makes sure what is entered is an integer data type. It uses the `Type` property, which is set to `Integer`. The collection of screenshots in Figure 4-3 shows this example in action.

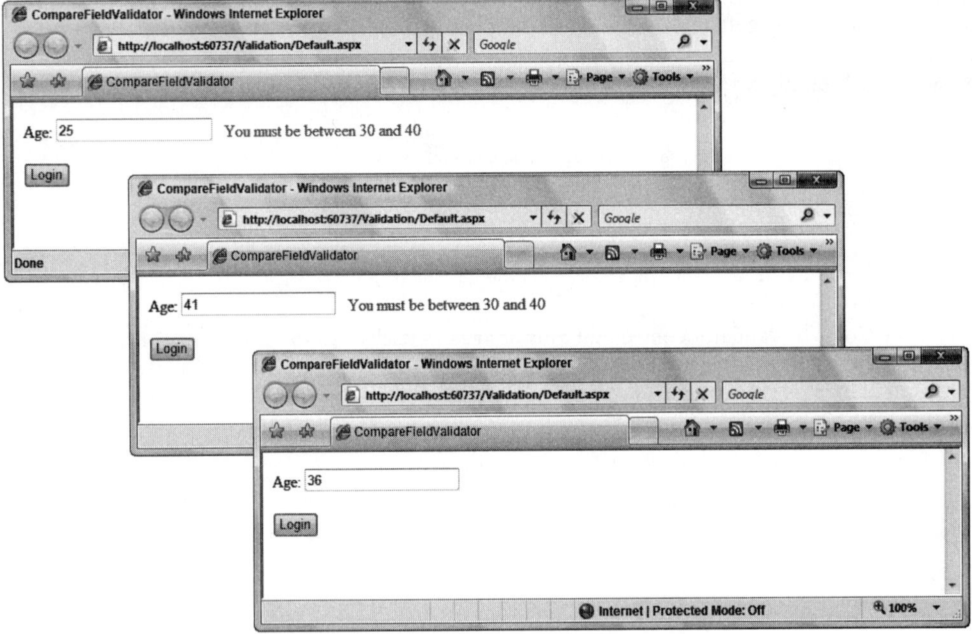

FIGURE 4-3

As you can see from the screenshots in Figure 4-3, a value of less than 30 causes the RangeValidator control to fire, as does a number greater than 40. A value that is somewhere between 30 and 40 (in this case 36) conforms to the validation rule of the control.

The RangeValidator control is not only about validating numbers (although it is most often used in this fashion). It can also be about validating a range of string characters as well as other items, including calendar dates. By default, the `Type` property of any of the validation controls is set to `String`. You can use the RangeValidator control to make sure what is entered in another server control (such as a calendar control) is within a certain range of dates.

For example, suppose that you are building a Web form that asks for a customer's arrival date, and the arrival date needs to be within two weeks of the current date. You can use the RangeValidator control to test for these scenarios quite easily.

Because the date range that you want to check is dynamically generated, you assign the `MaximumValue` and `MinimumValue` attributes programmatically in the `Page_Load` event. In the Designer, your sample page for this example should look like Figure 4-4.

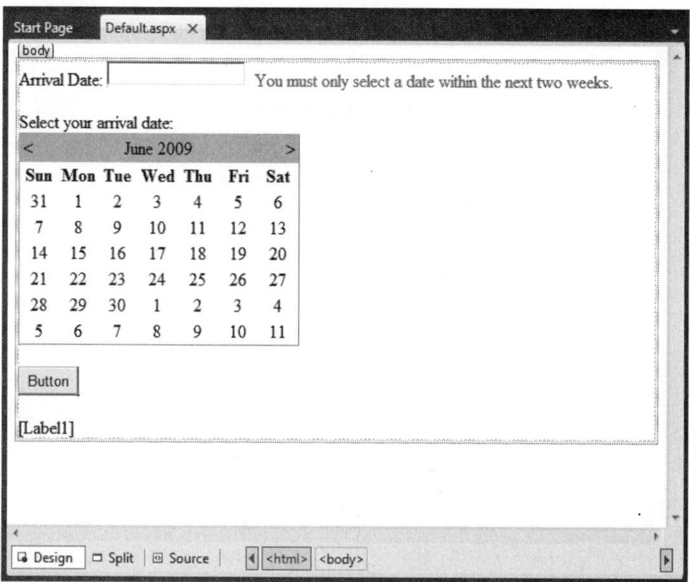

FIGURE 4-4

The idea is that the end user will select a date from the Calendar control, which will then populate the TextBox control. Then, when the end user clicks the form's button, he is notified if the date selected is invalid. If the date selected is valid, that date is presented through the Label control on the page. Listing 4-12 presents the code for this example.

LISTING 4-12: Using the RangeValidator control to test a string date value

Available for download on Wrox.com

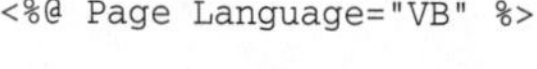

VB

```
<%@ Page Language="VB" %>

<script runat="server">
    Protected Sub Page_Load(ByVal sender As Object, ByVal e As System.EventArgs)
        RangeValidator1.MinimumValue = DateTime.Now.ToShortDateString()
        RangeValidator1.MaximumValue = DateTime.Now.AddDays(14).ToShortDateString()
    End Sub

    Protected Sub Calendar1_SelectionChanged(ByVal sender As Object, _
      ByVal e As System.EventArgs)
        TextBox1.Text = Calendar1.SelectedDate.ToShortDateString()
    End Sub

    Protected Sub Button1_Click(ByVal sender As Object, _
      ByVal e As System.EventArgs)
        If Page.IsValid Then
            Label1.Text = "You are set to arrive on: " & TextBox1.Text
        End If
    End Sub
</script>

<html xmlns="http://www.w3.org/1999/xhtml">
```

continues

LISTING 4-12 *(continued)*

```
<head runat="server">
    <title>Date Validation Check</title>
</head>
<body>
    <form id="form1" runat="server">
        Arrival Date:
        <asp:TextBox ID="TextBox1" runat="server"></asp:TextBox> 
        <asp:RangeValidator ID="RangeValidator1" runat="server"
         Text="You must only select a date within the next two weeks."
         ControlToValidate="TextBox1" Type="Date"></asp:RangeValidator><br />
        <br />
        Select your arrival date:<br />
        <asp:Calendar ID="Calendar1" runat="server"
         OnSelectionChanged="Calendar1_SelectionChanged"></asp:Calendar>
         
        <br />
        <asp:Button ID="Button1" runat="server" Text="Button"
         OnClick="Button1_Click" />
        <br />
        <br />
        <asp:Label ID="Label1" runat="server"></asp:Label>
    </form>
</body>
</html>
```

C#

```
<%@ Page Language="C#" %>

<script runat="server">
    protected void Page_Load(object sender, EventArgs e)
    {
        RangeValidator1.MinimumValue = DateTime.Now.ToShortDateString();
        RangeValidator1.MaximumValue =
           DateTime.Now.AddDays(14).ToShortDateString();
    }

    protected void Calendar1_SelectionChanged(object sender, EventArgs e)
    {
        TextBox1.Text = Calendar1.SelectedDate.ToShortDateString();
    }

    protected void Button1_Click(object sender, EventArgs e)
    {
        if (Page.IsValid)
        {
            Label1.Text = "You are set to arrive on: " + TextBox1.Text.ToString();
        }
    }
</script>
```

From this code, you can see that when the page is loaded, the `MinimumValue` and `MaximumValue` attributes are assigned a dynamic value. In this case, the `MinimumValue` gets the `DateTime.Now.ToShortDateString()` value, whereas the `MaximumValue` gets a date of 14 days later.

After the end user selects a date, the selected date is populated in the `TextBox1` control using the `Calendar1_SelectionChanged` event. After the user selects a date and clicks the button on the page, the `Button1_Click` event is fired and the page is checked for form validity using the `Page.IsValid` property. An invalid page gives you the result shown in Figure 4-5.

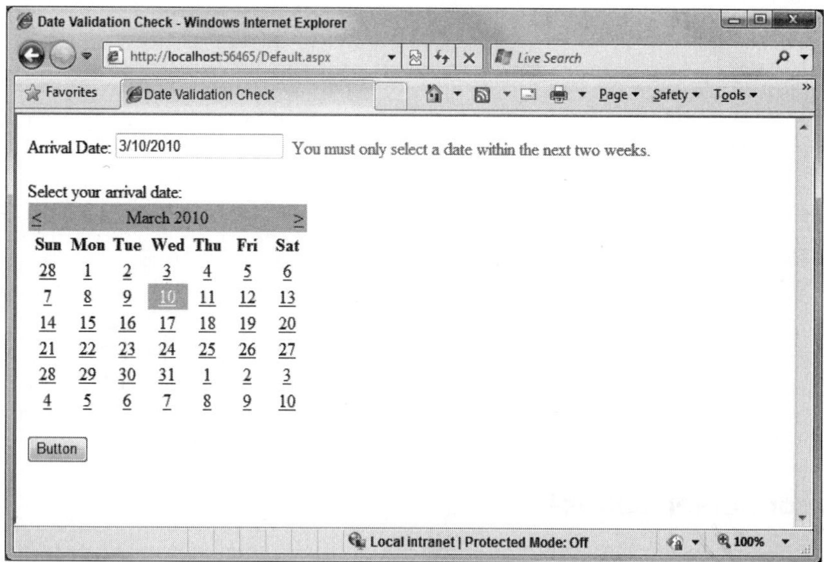

FIGURE 4-5

The RegularExpressionValidator Server Control

One exciting control that developers like to use is the RegularExpressionValidator control. This control offers a lot of flexibility when you apply validation rules to your Web forms. Using the RegularExpressionValidator control, you can check a user's input based on a pattern that you define using a regular expression.

This means that you can define a structure that a user's input will be applied against to see whether its structure matches the one that you define. For example, you can define that the structure of the user input must be in the form of an e-mail address or an Internet URL; if it doesn't match this definition, the page is considered invalid. Listing 4-13 shows you how to validate what is typed into a text box by making sure it is in the form of an e-mail address.

LISTING 4-13: Making sure the text-box value is an e-mail address

Available for download on Wrox.com

```
Email:
<asp:TextBox ID="TextBox1" runat="server"></asp:TextBox>
   
<asp:RegularExpressionValidator ID="RegularExpressionValidator1"
  runat="server" ControlToValidate="TextBox1"
  Text="You must enter an email address"
  ValidationExpression="\w+([-+.]\w+)*@\w+([-.]\w+)*\.\w+([-.]\w+)*">
</asp:RegularExpressionValidator>
```

Just like the other validation server controls, the RegularExpressionValidator control uses the `ControlToValidate` property to bind itself to the TextBox control, and it includes a `Text` property to push out the error message to the screen if the validation test fails. The unique property of this validation control is the `ValidationExpression` property. This property takes a string value, which is the regular expression you are going to apply to the input value.

Visual Studio 2010 makes using regular expressions a little easier through the use of the Regular Expression Editor. This editor provides a few commonly used regular expressions that you might want to apply to your RegularExpressionValidator. To get at this editor, you work with your page from Design view. Be sure to highlight the `RegularExpressionValidator1` server control in this Design view to see the control's properties. In the Property window of Visual Studio, click the button found next to the `ValidationExpression` property to launch the Regular Expression Editor. Figure 4-6 shows this editor.

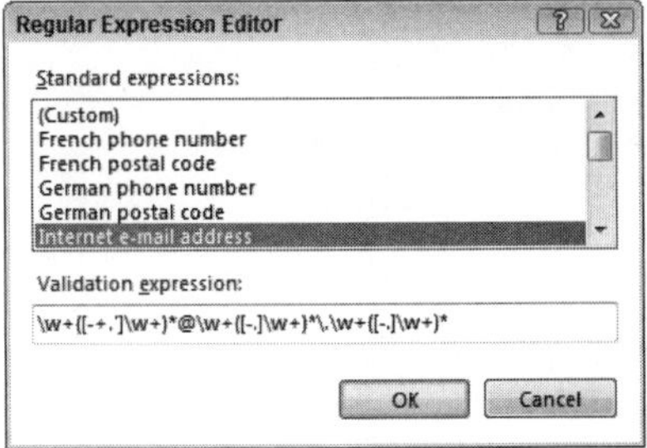

FIGURE 4-6

Using this editor, you can find regular expressions for things like e-mail addresses, Internet URLs, Zip codes, phone numbers, and social security numbers. In addition to working with the Regular Expression Editor to help you with these sometimes-complicated regular expression strings, you can also find a good-sized collection of them at an Internet site called RegExLib found at `www.regexlib.com`.

The CustomValidator Server Control

So far, you have seen a wide variety of validation controls that are at your disposal. In many cases, these validation controls address many of the validation rules that you want to apply to your Web forms. Sometimes, however, none of these controls works for you, and you have to go beyond what they offer. This is where the CustomValidator control comes into play.

The CustomValidator control enables you to build your own client-side or server-side validations that you can then easily apply to your Web forms. Doing so enables you to make validation checks against values or calculations performed in the data tier (for example, in a database), or to make sure that the user's input validates against some arithmetic validation (for example, determining whether a number is even or odd). You can do quite a bit with the CustomValidator control.

Using Client-Side Validation

One of the worthwhile functions of the CustomValidator control is its capability to easily provide custom client-side validations. Many developers have their own collections of JavaScript functions they employ in their applications, and using the CustomValidator control is one easy way of getting these functions implemented.

For example, look at a simple form that asks for a number from the end user. This form uses the CustomValidator control to perform a custom client-side validation on the user input to make sure that the number provided is divisible by 5. Listing 4-14 shows the code for this validation.

LISTING 4-14: Using the CustomValidator control to perform client-side validations

```
<%@ Page Language="VB" %>

<script runat="server">
   Protected Sub Button1_Click(ByVal sender As Object, ByVal e As System.EventArgs)
       Label1.Text = "VALID NUMBER!"
   End Sub
</script>

<html xmlns="http://www.w3.org/1999/xhtml">
<head runat="server">
    <title>CustomValidator</title>

    <script type="text/javascript">
```

```
            function validateNumber(oSrc, args) {
               args.IsValid = (args.Value % 5 == 0);
            }
        </script>

    </head>
    <body>
        <form id="form1" runat="server">
        <div>
            <p>
                Number:
                <asp:TextBox ID="TextBox1"
                 runat="server"></asp:TextBox>
                  
                <asp:CustomValidator ID="CustomValidator1"
                 runat="server" ControlToValidate="TextBox1"
                 Text="Number must be divisible by 5"
                 ClientValidationFunction="validateNumber">
                </asp:CustomValidator>
            </p>
            <p>
                <asp:Button ID="Button1" OnClick="Button1_Click"
                 runat="server" Text="Button"></asp:Button>
            </p>
            <p>
                <asp:Label ID="Label1" runat="server"></asp:Label>
            </p>
        </div>
        </form>
    </body>
    </html>
```

C#

```
    <%@ Page Language="C#" %>
    <script runat="server">

        protected void Button1_Click(Object sender, EventArgs e) {
           Label1.Text = "VALID NUMBER!";
        }

    </script>
```

Looking over this Web form, you can see a couple of things happening. It is a simple form with only a single text box requiring user input. The user clicks the button that triggers the `Button1_Click` event, which in turn populates the `Label1` control on the page. It carries out this simple operation only if all the validation checks are performed and the user input passes these tests.

One item that is different about this page is the inclusion of the second `<script>` block found within the `<head>` section. This is the custom JavaScript. Note that Visual Studio 2010 is very friendly toward these kinds of constructions, even when you are switching between the Design and Code views of the page — something Visual Studio editions prior to 2008 were rather poor at dealing with. This JavaScript function — `validateNumber` — is shown here:

```
<script type="text/javascript">
   function validateNumber(oSrc, args) {
      args.IsValid = (args.Value % 5 == 0);
   }
</script>
```

This second `<script>` section is the client-side JavaScript that you want the CustomValidator control to use when making its validation checks on the information entered into the text box. The JavaScript functions you employ are going to use the `args.IsValid` property and set this property to either `true` or `false` depending on the outcome of the validation check. In this case, the user input (`args.Value`) is checked to see whether it is divisible by 5. The Boolean value returned is then assigned to the `args.IsValid` property, which is then used by the CustomValidator control.

The CustomValidator control, like the other controls before it, uses the `ControlToValidate` property to associate itself with a particular element on the page. The property that you are interested in here is the `ClientValidationFunction` property. The string value provided to this property is the name of the client-side function that you want this validation check to employ when the CustomValidator control is triggered. In this case, it is `validateNumber`:

```
ClientValidationFunction="validateNumber"
```

If you run this page and make an invalid entry, you produce the result shown in Figure 4-7.

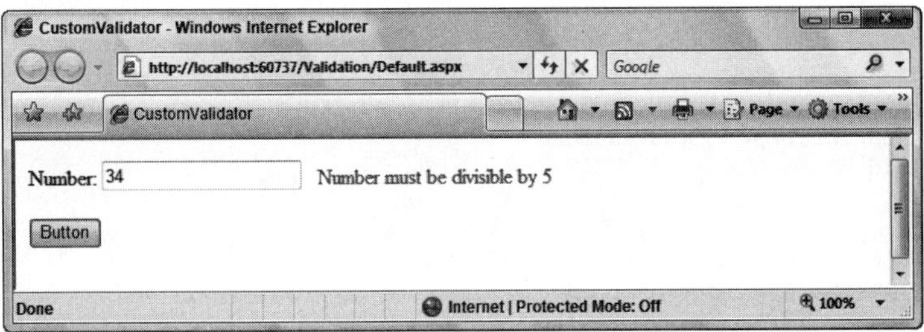

FIGURE 4-7

Using Server-Side Validation

Now let's move this same validation check from the client to the server. The CustomValidator control enables you to make custom server-side validations a reality as well. You will find that creating your server-side validations is just as easy as creating client-side validations.

If you create your own server-side validations, you can make them as complex as your applications require. For example, using the CustomValidator for server-side validations is something you do if you want to check the user's input against dynamic values coming from XML files, databases, or elsewhere.

For an example of using the CustomValidator control for some custom server-side validation, you can work with the same example as you did when creating the client-side validation. Now, create a server-side check that makes sure a user input number is divisible by 5, as shown in Listing 4-15.

LISTING 4-15: Using the CustomValidator control to perform server-side validations

```
<%@ Page Language="VB" %>

<script runat="server">
   Protected Sub Button1_Click(ByVal sender As Object, ByVal e As System.EventArgs)
       If Page.IsValid Then
          Label1.Text = "VALID ENTRY!"
       End If
   End Sub

   Sub ValidateNumber(sender As Object, args As ServerValidateEventArgs)
       Try
          Dim num As Integer = Integer.Parse(args.Value)
          args.IsValid = ((num mod 5) = 0)
       Catch ex As Exception
          args.IsValid = False
       End Try
   End Sub
</script>
```

```
<html xmlns="http://www.w3.org/1999/xhtml">
<head runat="server">
    <title>CustomValidator</title>
</head>
<body>
    <form id="form1" runat="server">
    <div>
        <p>
            Number:
            <asp:TextBox ID="TextBox1"
             runat="server"></asp:TextBox>
              
             <asp:CustomValidator ID="CustomValidator1"
             runat="server" ControlToValidate="TextBox1"
             Text="Number must be divisible by 5"
             OnServerValidate="ValidateNumber"></asp:CustomValidator>
        </p>
        <p>
            <asp:Button ID="Button1" OnClick="Button1_Click"
             runat="server" Text="Button"></asp:Button>
        </p>
        <p>
            <asp:Label ID="Label1" runat="server"></asp:Label>
        </p>
    </div>
    </form>
</body>
</html>
```

C#

```
<%@ Page Language="C#" %>

<script runat="server">

    protected void Button1_Click(Object sender, EventArgs e) {
         if (Page.IsValid) {
            Label1.Text = "VALID ENTRY!";
         }
    }

    void ValidateNumber(object source, ServerValidateEventArgs args)
    {
       try
       {
          int num = int.Parse(args.Value);
          args.IsValid = ((num%5) == 0);
       }
       catch(Exception ex)
       {
          args.IsValid = false;
       }
    }

</script>
```

Instead of a client-side JavaScript function in the code, this example includes a server-side function — `ValidateNumber`. The `ValidateNumber` function, as well as all functions that are being constructed to work with the CustomValidator control, must use the `ServerValidateEventArgs` object as one of the parameters in order to get the data passed to the function for the validation check. The `ValidateNumber` function itself is nothing fancy. It simply checks to see whether the provided number is divisible by 5.

From within your custom function, which is designed to work with the CustomValidator control, you actually get at the value coming from the form element through the `args.Value` object. Then you set the `args.IsValid` property to either `True` or `False` depending on your validation checks. From the preceding example, you can see that the `args.IsValid` is set to `False` if the number is not divisible by 5 and also that an exception is thrown (which would occur if a string value were input into the form element). After the custom function is established, the next step is to apply it to the CustomValidator control, as shown in the following example:

```
<asp:CustomValidator ID="CustomValidator1"
 runat="server" ControlToValidate="TextBox1"
 Text="Number must be divisible by 5"
 OnServerValidate="ValidateNumber"></asp:CustomValidator>
```

To make the association between a CustomValidator control and a function that you have in your server-side code, you simply use the `OnServerValidate` attribute. The value assigned to this property is the name of the function — in this case, `ValidateNumber`.

Running this example causes the postback to come back to the server and the validation check (based on the `ValidateNumber` function) to be performed. From here, the page reloads and the `Page_Load` event is called. In the example from Listing 4-15, you can see that a check is done to see whether the page is valid. This check uses the `Page.IsValid` property:

```
If Page.IsValid Then
   Label1.Text = "VALID ENTRY!"
End If
```

Using Client-Side and Server-Side Validation Together

As stated earlier in this chapter, you have to think about the security of your forms and to ensure that the data you are collecting from the forms is valid data. For this reason, when you decide to employ client-side validations (as you did in Listing 4-14), you should take steps to also reconstruct the client-side function as a server-side function. When you have done this task, you should associate the CustomValidator control to both the client-side and server-side functions. In the case of the number check validation from Listings 4-14 and 4-15, you can use both validation functions in your page and then change the CustomValidator control to point to both of these functions, as shown in Listing 4-16.

Available for download on Wrox.com

LISTING 4-16: The CustomValidator control with client- and server-side validations

```
<asp:CustomValidator ID="CustomValidator1"
    runat="server" ControlToValidate="TextBox1"
    Text="Number must be divisible by 5"
    ClientValidationFunction="validateNumber"
    OnServerValidate="ValidateNumber"></asp:CustomValidator>
```

From this example, you can see it is simply a matter of using both the `ClientValidationFunction` and the `OnServerValidate` attributes at the same time.

The ValidationSummary Server Control

The ValidationSummary control is not a control that performs validations on the content input into your Web forms. Instead, this control is the reporting control, which the other validation controls on a page use. You can use this validation control to consolidate error reporting for all the validation errors that occur on a page instead of leaving it up to each and every individual validation control.

You might want this capability for larger forms, which have a comprehensive form validation process. In this case, you may find having all the possible validation errors reported to the end user in a single and easily identifiable manner to be rather user-friendly. You can display these error messages in a list, bulleted list, or paragraph.

By default, the ValidationSummary control shows the list of validation errors as a bulleted list, as shown in Listing 4-17.

Available for download on Wrox.com

LISTING 4-17: A partial page example of the ValidationSummary control

```
<p>First name
   <asp:TextBox ID="TextBox1" runat="server"></asp:TextBox>
     
   <asp:RequiredFieldValidator ID="RequiredFieldValidator1"
    runat="server" ErrorMessage="You must enter your first name"
    ControlToValidate="TextBox1"></asp:RequiredFieldValidator>
</p>
<p>Last name
   <asp:TextBox ID="TextBox2" runat="server"></asp:TextBox>
     
   <asp:RequiredFieldValidator ID="RequiredFieldValidator2"
    runat="server" ErrorMessage="You must enter your last name"
    ControlToValidate="TextBox2"></asp:RequiredFieldValidator>
</p>
<p>
   <asp:Button ID="Button1" OnClick="Button1_Click" runat="server"
    Text="Submit"></asp:Button>
</p>
<p>
   <asp:ValidationSummary ID="ValidationSummary1" runat="server"
    HeaderText="You received the following errors:">
   </asp:ValidationSummary>
</p>
<p>
   <asp:Label ID="Label1" runat="server"></asp:Label>
</p>
```

This example asks the end user for her first and last name. Each text box in the form has an associated RequiredFieldValidator control assigned to it. When the page is built and run, the user's clicking the Submit button with no values placed in either of the text boxes causes both validation errors to fire. Figure 4-8 shows this result.

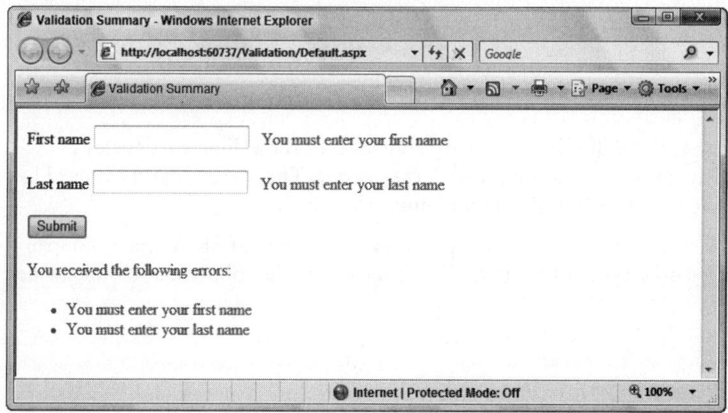

FIGURE 4-8

As in earlier examples of validation controls on the form, these validation errors appear next to each of the text boxes. You can see, however, that the ValidationSummary control also displays the validation errors as a bulleted list in red at the location of the control on the Web form. In most cases, you do not want these errors to appear twice on a page for the end user. You can change this behavior by using the `Text` property of the validation controls, in addition to the `ErrorMessage` property, as you have typically done throughout this chapter. Listing 4-18 shows this approach.

LISTING 4-18: Using the Text property of a validation control

Available for download on Wrox.com

```
<asp:RequiredFieldValidator ID="RequiredFieldValidator1"
 runat="server" ErrorMessage="You must enter your first name" Text="*"
 ControlToValidate="TextBox1"></asp:RequiredFieldValidator>
```

or

```
<asp:RequiredFieldValidator ID="RequiredFieldValidator1"
 runat="server" ErrorMessage="You must enter your first name"
 ControlToValidate="TextBox1">*</asp:RequiredFieldValidator>
```

Listing 4-18 shows two ways to accomplish the same task. The first is to use the `Text` property and the second option is to place the provided output between the tags of the `<asp:RequiredFieldValidator>` elements. Making this type of change to the validation controls produces the results shown in Figure 4-9.

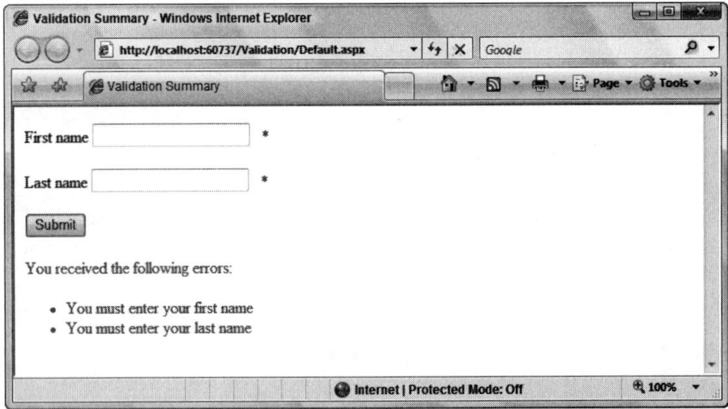

FIGURE 4-9

To get this result, just remember that the ValidationSummary control uses the validation control's `ErrorMessage` property for displaying the validation errors if they occur. The `Text` property is used by the validation control and is not utilized at all by the ValidationSummary control.

In addition to bulleted lists, you can use the `DisplayMode` property of the ValidationSummary control to change the display of the results to other types of formats. This control has the following possible values:

- `BulletList`
- `List`
- `SingleParagraph`

You can also utilize a dialog box instead of displaying the results to the Web page. Listing 4-19 shows an example of this behavior.

LISTING 4-19: Using a dialog box to report validation errors

Available for download on Wrox.com

```
<asp:ValidationSummary ID="ValidationSummary1" runat="server"
 ShowMessageBox="true" ShowSummary="false"></asp:ValidationSummary>
```

From this code example, you can see that the `ShowSummary` property is set to `False` — meaning that the bulleted list of validation errors are not shown on the actual Web page. However, because the `ShowMessageBox` property is set to `True`, you now get these errors reported in a message box, as shown in Figure 4-10.

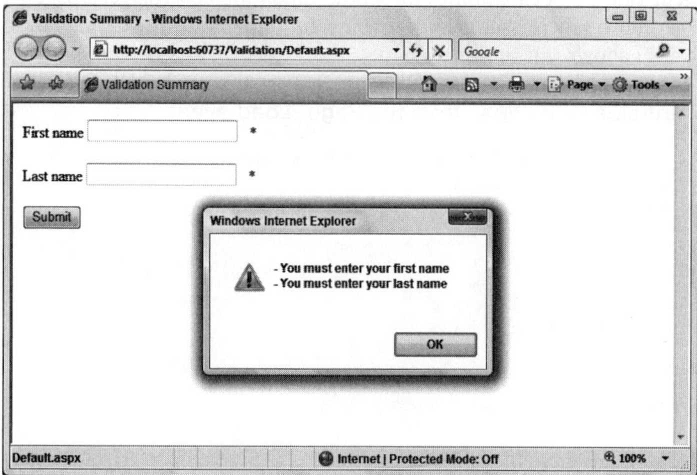

FIGURE 4-10

TURNING OFF CLIENT-SIDE VALIDATION

Because validation server controls provide clients with client-side validations automatically (if the requesting container can properly handle the JavaScript produced), you might, at times, want a way to control this behavior.

Turning off the client-side capabilities of these controls so that they don't independently send client-side capabilities to the requestors is quite possible. For example, you might want all validations done on the server, no matter what capabilities the requesting containers offer. You can take a few approaches to turning off this functionality.

The first option is at the control level. Each of the validation server controls has a property called `EnableClientScript`. This property is set to `True` by default, but setting it to `False` prevents the control from sending out a JavaScript function for validation on the client. Instead, the validation check is done on the server. Listing 4-20 shows the use of this property.

LISTING 4-20: Disabling client-side validations in a validation control

Available for download on Wrox.com

```
<asp:RequiredFieldValidator ID="RequiredFieldValidator1" runat="server"
 Text="*" ControlToValidate="TextBox1" EnableClientScript="false" />
```

You can also remove a validation control's client-side capability programmatically (shown in Listing 4-21).

LISTING 4-21: Removing the client-side capabilities programmatically

Available for download on Wrox.com

VB

```
Protected Sub Page_Load(ByVal sender As Object, ByVal e As System.EventArgs)
   RequiredFieldValidator1.EnableClientScript = False
End Sub
```

C#

```
protected void Page_Load(Object sender, EventArgs e) {
   RequiredFieldValidator1.EnableClientScript = false;
}
```

Another option is to turn off the client-side script capabilities for all the validation controls on a page from within the `Page_Load` event. This method can be rather helpful if you want to dynamically decide not to allow client-side validation. Listing 4-22 shows this option.

LISTING 4-22: Disabling all client-side validations from the Page_Load event

Available for download on Wrox.com

VB

```
Protected Sub Page_Load(ByVal sender As Object, ByVal e As System.EventArgs)
   For Each bv As BaseValidator In Page.Validators
      bv.EnableClientScript = False
   Next
End Sub
```

C#

```
<protected void Page_Load(Object sender, EventArgs e) {
   foreach(BaseValidator bv in Page.Validators)
   {
      bv.EnableClientScript = false;
   }
}
```

By looking for each instance of a `BaseValidator` object in the validators contained on an ASP.NET page, this `For Each` loop turns off client-side validation capabilities for each and every validation control the page contains.

USING IMAGES AND SOUNDS FOR ERROR NOTIFICATIONS

So far, you have been displaying simple textual messages for the error notifications that come from the validation server controls. In most instances, you are going to do just that — display some simple textual messages to inform end users that they typed something into the form that doesn't pass your validation rules.

An interesting tip regarding the validation controls is that you are not limited to just text — you can also use images and sounds for error notifications.

To use an image for the error, you use the `Text` property of any of the validation controls. You simply place some appropriate HTML as the value of this property, as shown in Listing 4-23.

LISTING 4-23: Using images for error notifications

Available for download on Wrox.com

```
<asp:RequiredFieldValidator ID="RequiredFieldValidator1"
 runat="server" Text='<img src="error.gif">'
 ControlToValidate="TextBox1"></asp:RequiredFieldValidator>
```

As you can see from this example, instead of some text being output to the Web page, the value of the `Text` property is an HTML string. This bit of HTML is used to display an image. Be sure to notice the use of the single and double quotation marks so you won't get any errors when the browser generates the page. This example produces something similar to Figure 4-11.

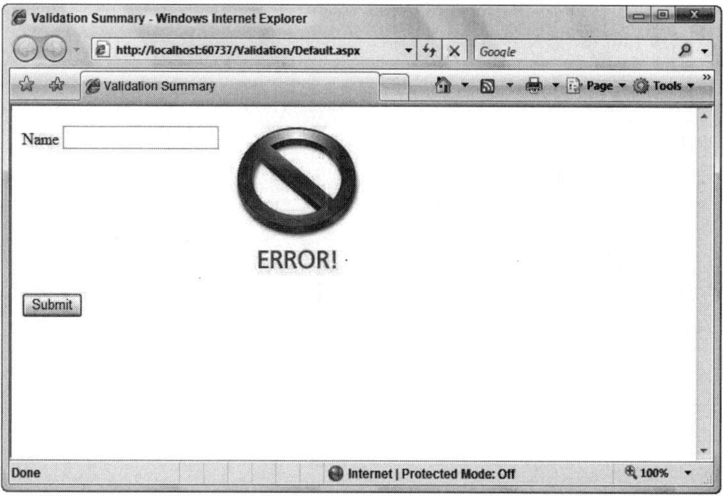

FIGURE 4-11

The other interesting twist you can create is to add a sound notification when the end user errs. You can do so the same way you display an image for error notifications. Listing 4-24 shows an example of this.

LISTING 4-24: Using sound for error notifications

Available for download on Wrox.com

```
<asp:RequiredFieldValidator ID="RequiredFieldValidator1"
 runat="server" Text='<bgsound src="C:\Windows\Media\tada.wav">'
 ControlToValidate="TextBox1" EnableClientScript="false">
</asp:RequiredFieldValidator>
```

You can find a lot of the Windows system sounds in the `C:\Windows\Media` directory. In this example, the `Text` uses the `<bgsound>` element to place a sound on the Web form (works only with Internet Explorer). The sound plays only when the end user triggers the validation control.

When working with sounds for error notifications, you have to disable the client-side script capability for that particular control because if you do not, the sound plays when the page loads in the browser, whether or not a validation error has been triggered.

WORKING WITH VALIDATION GROUPS

In many instances, developers want to place more than one form on a single page. This was always possible in ASP.NET 1.0/1.1 because different button clicks could be used to perform different server-side events. Some issues related to this type of construction were problematic, however.

One of these issues was the difficulty of having validation controls for each of the forms on the page. Different validation controls were often assigned to two distinct forms on the page. When the end user submitted one form, the validation controls in the other form were fired (because the user was not working with that form), thereby stopping the first form from being submitted.

Figure 4-12, for example, shows a basic page for the St. Louis .NET User Group that includes two forms.

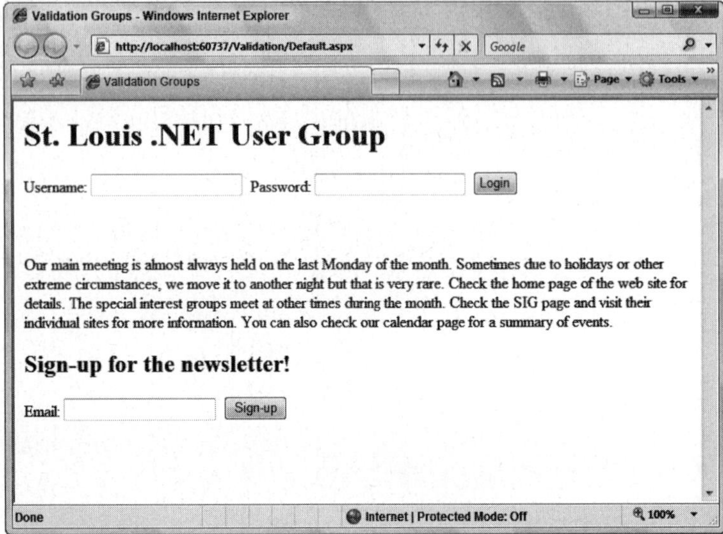

FIGURE 4-12

One of the forms is for members of the site to supply their usernames and passwords to log into the Members Only section of the site. The second form on the page is for anyone who wants to sign up for the user group's newsletter. Each form has its own button and some validation controls associated with it. The problem arises when someone submits information for one of the forms. For example, if you were a member of the group, you would supply your username and password, and click the Login button. The validation controls for the newsletter form would fire because no e-mail address was placed in that particular form. If someone interested in getting the newsletter places an e-mail address in the last text box and clicks the Sign-up button, the validation controls in the first form fire because no username and password were input in that form.

ASP.NET WebControls contains a `ValidationGroup` property that enables you to separate the validation controls into separate groups. It enables you to activate only the required validation controls when an end user clicks a button on the page. Listing 4-25 shows an example of separating the validation controls on a user group page into different buckets.

LISTING 4-25: Using the ValidationGroup property

Available for download on Wrox.com

```
<%@ Page Language="VB" %>

<html xmlns="http://www.w3.org/1999/xhtml">
<head runat="server">
    <title>Validation Groups</title>
</head>
<body>
    <form id="form1" runat="server">
    <div>
        <h1>St. Louis .NET User Group</h1>
        <p>Username:
        <asp:TextBox ID="TextBox1" runat="server"></asp:TextBox>  Password:
        <asp:TextBox ID="TextBox2" runat="server"
         TextMode="Password"></asp:TextBox> 
        <asp:Button ID="Button1" runat="server" Text="Login"
         ValidationGroup="Login" />
            <br />
            <asp:RequiredFieldValidator ID="RequiredFieldValidator1" runat="server"
```

```
            Text="* You must submit a username!"
            ControlToValidate="TextBox1" ValidationGroup="Login">
            </asp:RequiredFieldValidator>
            <br />
            <asp:RequiredFieldValidator ID="RequiredFieldValidator2" runat="server"
            Text="* You must submit a password!"
            ControlToValidate="TextBox2" ValidationGroup="Login">
            </asp:RequiredFieldValidator>
        <p>
            Our main meeting is almost always held on the last Monday of the month.
            Sometimes due to holidays or other extreme circumstances,
            we move it to another night but that is very rare. Check the home page
            of the web site for details. The special
            interest groups meet at other times during the month. Check the SIG
            page and visit their individual sites for more information.
            You can also check our calendar page for a summary of events.<br />
        </p>
        <h2>Sign-up for the newsletter!</h2>
        <p>Email:
        <asp:TextBox ID="TextBox3" runat="server"></asp:TextBox> 
        <asp:Button ID="Button2" runat="server" Text="Sign-up"
         ValidationGroup="Newsletter" /> 
            <br />
            <asp:RegularExpressionValidator ID="RegularExpressionValidator1"
             runat="server"
             Text="* You must submit a correctly formatted email address!"
             ControlToValidate="TextBox3" ValidationGroup="Newsletter"
             ValidationExpression="\w+([-+.]\w+)*@\w+([-.]\w+)*\.\w+([-.]\w+)*">
             </asp:RegularExpressionValidator>
             <br />
             <asp:RequiredFieldValidator ID="RequiredFieldValidator3" runat="server"
             Text="* You forgot your email address!"
             ControlToValidate="TextBox3" ValidationGroup="Newsletter">
             </asp:RequiredFieldValidator>
      </p>
    </div>
    </form>
</body>
</html>
```

The `ValidationGroup` property on this page is shown in bold. You can see that this property takes a `String` value. Also note that not only validation controls have this property. The core server controls also have the `ValidationGroup` property because things like button clicks must be associated with specific validation groups.

In this example, each of the buttons has a distinct validation group assignment. The first button on the form uses `Login` as a value, and the second button on the form uses `Newsletter` as a value. Then each of the validation controls is associated with one of these validation groups. Because of these associations, when the end user clicks the Login button on the page, ASP.NET recognizes that it should work only with the validation server controls that have the same validation group name. ASP.NET ignores the validation controls assigned to other validation groups.

Using this enhancement, you can now have multiple sets of validation rules that fire only when you want them to fire (see Figure 4-13).

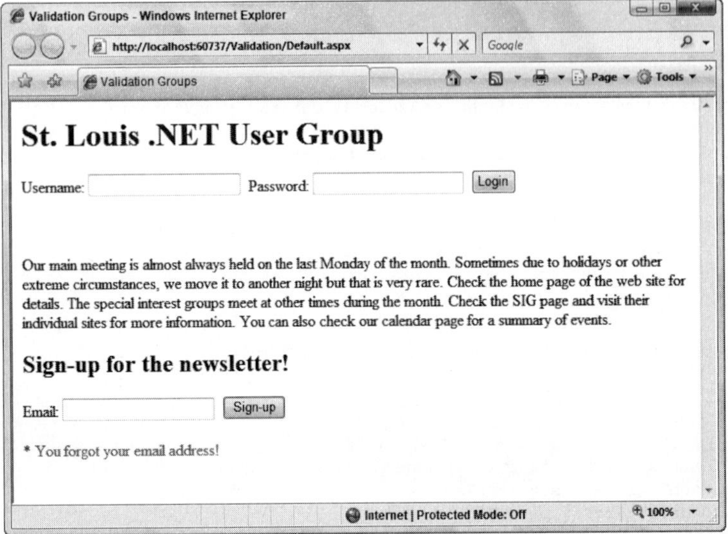

FIGURE 4-13

Another great feature with the validation controls is a property called `SetFocusOnError`. This property takes a `Boolean` value and, if a validation error is thrown when the form is submitted, the property places the page focus on the form element that receives the error. The `SetFocusOnError` property is used in the following example:

```
<asp:RequiredFieldValidator ID="RequiredFieldValidator1" runat="server"
 Text="* You must submit a username!"
 ControlToValidate="TextBox1" ValidationGroup="Login" SetFocusOnError="true">
</asp:RequiredFieldValidator>
```

If `RequiredFieldValidator1` throws an error because the end user didn't place a value in `TextBox1`, the page is redrawn with the focus on `TextBox1`, as shown in Figure 4-14.

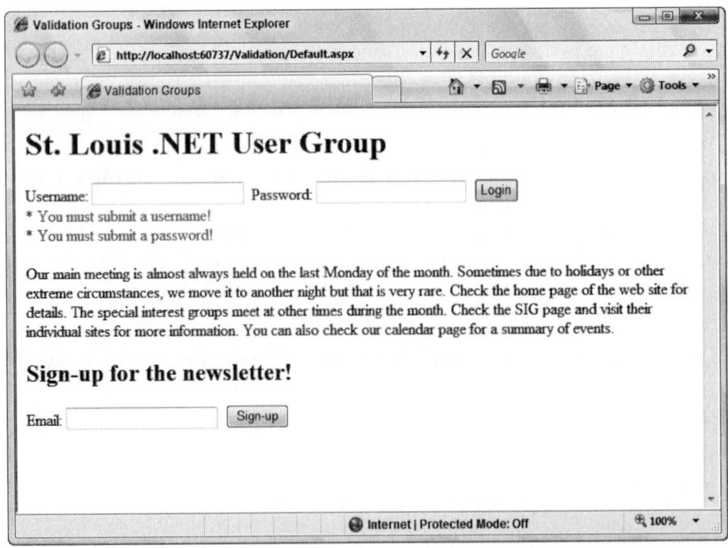

FIGURE 4-14

Note that if you have multiple validation controls on your page with the `SetFocusOnError` property set to `True`, and more than one validation error occurs, the uppermost form element that has a validation error gets the focus. In the previous example, if both the username text box (`TextBox1`) and the password text box (`TextBox2`) have validation errors associated with them, the page focus is assigned to the username text box because it is the first control on the form with an error.

SUMMARY

Validation controls are a powerful tool at your disposal when you are working with forms. They bring a lot of functionality in a simple-to-use package and, like most things in the .NET world, you can easily get them to look and behave exactly as you want them to.

Remember that the purpose of having forms in your applications is to collect data, but this data collection has no meaning if the data is not valid. This means that you must establish validation rules that can be implemented in your forms through a series of different controls — the validation server controls.

This chapter covered various validation controls in detail, including:

- RequiredFieldValidator
- CompareValidator
- RangeValidator
- RegularExpressionValidator
- CustomValidator
- DynamicValidator
- ValidationSummary

In addition to looking at the base validation controls, this chapter also discussed how to apply client-side and server-side validations.

5

Working with Master Pages

WHAT'S IN THIS CHAPTER?

- Coding master pages and content pages
- Using master pages to specify default content
- Assigning master pages programmatically
- Nesting master pages
- Master pages for different browsers
- Using master pages with ASP.NET AJAX

Visual inheritance is a great feature you can use to build your Web pages provided in ASP.NET. This feature was first introduced to ASP.NET in version 2.0. In effect, you can create a single template page that can be used as a foundation for any number of ASP.NET content pages in your application. These templates, called *master pages*, increase your productivity by making your applications easier to build and easier to manage after they are built. Visual Studio 2010 includes full designer support for master pages, making the developer experience richer than ever before. This chapter takes a close look at how to utilize master pages to the fullest extent in your applications and begins by explaining the advantages of master pages.

WHY DO YOU NEED MASTER PAGES?

Most Web sites today have common elements used throughout the entire application or on a majority of the pages within the application. For example, if you look at the main page of the Reuters News Web site (found at `www.reuters.com`), you see common elements that are used throughout the entire Web site. These common areas are labeled in Figure 5-1.

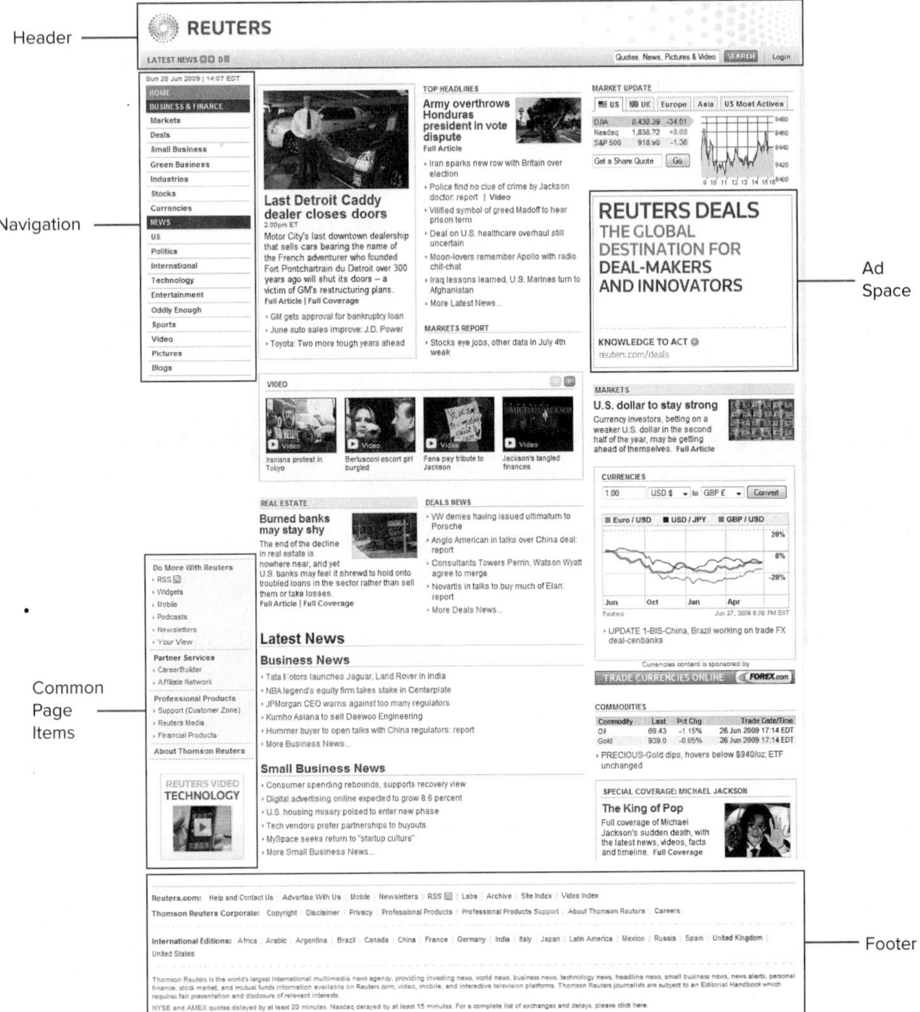

FIGURE 5-1

In this screen shot, notice the header section, the navigation section, and the footer section on the page. In fact, nearly every page within the entire application uses these same elements. Even before master pages, you had ways to put these elements into every page through a variety of means; but in most cases, doing so posed difficulties.

Some developers simply copy and paste the code for these common sections to each and every page that requires them. This works, but it's rather labor intensive. However, if you use the copy-and-paste method, whenever a change is required to one of these common sections of the application, you have to go into each and every page and duplicate the change. That's not much fun and an ineffective use of your time!

In the days of Classic Active Server Pages, one popular option was to put all the common sections into what was called an *include file*. You could then place this file within your page like this:

```
<!-- #include virtual="/myIncludes/header.asp" -->
```

The problem with using `include` files was that you had to take into account the newly opened HTML tags in the header `include` file. These tags had to be closed in the main document or in the footer `include` file. Keeping all the HTML tags in order was usually difficult, especially if multiple people worked on a project. Web pages sometimes displayed strange results because of inappropriate or nonexistent tag closings or openings. Working with `include` files in a visual designer was also difficult. Using `include` files didn't allow the developer to see the entire page as it would appear in a browser. The developer ended up developing the page in sections and *hoping* that the pieces would come together as planned. Many hours were wasted "chasing tables" opened in an `include` file and possibly closed later!

With the introduction of ASP.NET 1.0 in 2000, developers started using *user controls* to encapsulate common sections of their Web pages. For example, you could build a Web page that included header, navigation, and footer sections by simply dragging and dropping these sections of code onto each page that required them.

This technique worked, but it also raised some issues. Before Visual Studio 2005 and ASP.NET 2.0, user controls caused problems similar to those related to `include` files. When you worked in the Design view of your Web page, the common areas of the page displayed only as gray boxes in Visual Studio .NET 2002 and 2003. This made building a page harder: you could not visualize what the page you were building actually looked like until you compiled and ran the completed page in a browser. User controls also suffered from the same problem as `include` files — you had to match up the opening and closing of your HTML tags in two separate files. Personally, we prefer user controls over `include` files, but user controls aren't perfect template pieces for use throughout an application. You will find that Visual Studio corrects some of the problems by rendering user-control content in the Design view. User controls are ideal if you are including only small sections on a Web page; they are still rather cumbersome, however, when working with larger page templates.

In light of the issues with `include` files and user controls, the ASP.NET team developed the idea of *master pages* — an outstanding way of applying templates to your applications. They *inverted* the way the developer attacks the problem. Master pages live *outside* the pages you develop, whereas user controls live within your pages and are doomed to duplication. These master pages draw a more distinct line between the common areas that you carry over from page to page and the content areas that are unique on each page. You will find that working with master pages is easy and fun. The next section of this chapter looks at some of the basics of master pages in ASP.NET.

THE BASICS OF MASTER PAGES

Master pages are an easy way to provide a template that can be used by any number of ASP.NET pages in your application. In working with master pages, you create a master file that is the template referenced by a *subpage* or *content page*. Master pages use a `.master` file extension, whereas content pages use the `.aspx` file extension you're used to; but content pages are declared as such within the file's `Page` directive.

You can place anything you want to be included as part of the template in the `.master` file. This can include the header, navigation, and footer sections used across the Web application. The content page then contains all the page content except for the master page's elements. At runtime, the ASP.NET engine combines these elements into a single page for the end user. Figure 5-2 shows a diagram of how this process works.

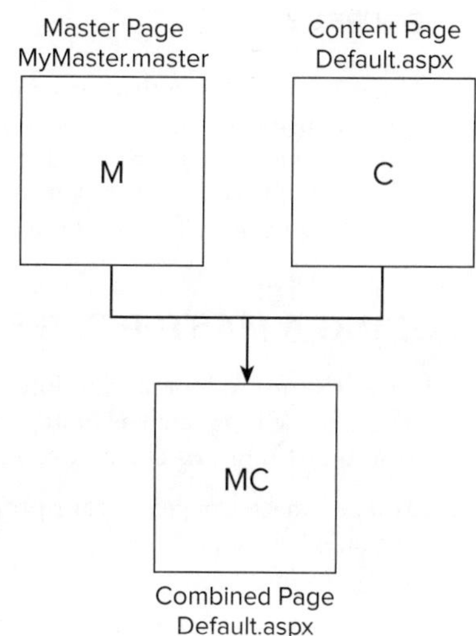

FIGURE 5-2

One of the nice things about working with master pages is that you can see the template in the IDE when you are creating the content pages. Because you can see the entire page while you are working on it, developing content pages that use a template is much easier. While you are working on the content page, all the templated items are shaded gray and are not editable. The only items that are alterable are clearly shown in the template. These workable areas, called *content areas*, originally are defined in the master page itself. Within the master page, you specify the areas of the page that the content pages can use. You can have more than one content area in your master page if you want. Figure 5-3 shows the master page with a couple of content areas shown.

If you look at the screenshot from Figure 5-3, you can sort of see two defined areas on the page — these are content areas. The content area is represented in the Design view of the page by a light dotted box that represents the ContentPlaceHolder control. Also, if you hover your mouse over the content area, you will see the name of the control appear above the control (although lightly). This hovering is also shown in action in Figure 5-3.

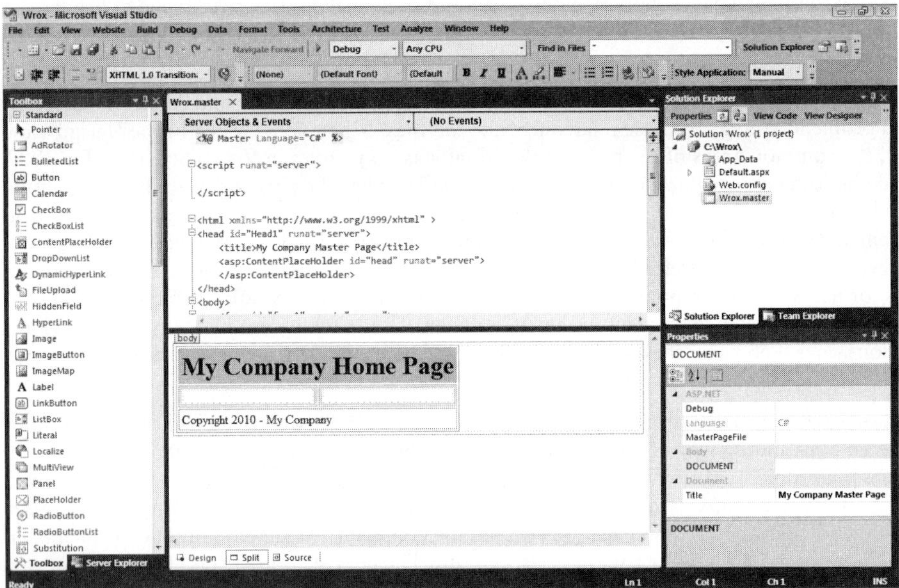

FIGURE 5-3

Companies and organizations will find using master pages ideal, as the technology closely models their typical business requirements. Many companies have a common look and feel that they apply across their intranet. They can now provide the divisions of their company with a `.master` file to use when creating a department's section of the intranet. This process makes keeping a consistent look and feel across its entire intranet quite easy for the company.

CODING A MASTER PAGE

Now it's time to look at building the master page shown previously in Figure 5-3. You can create one in any text-based editor, such as Notepad or Visual Web Developer Express Edition, or you can use the new Visual Studio 2010. In this chapter, you see how it is done with Visual Studio 2010.

You add master pages to your projects in the same way as regular `.aspx` pages — choose the Master Page option when you add a new file to your application, as shown in Figure 5-4.

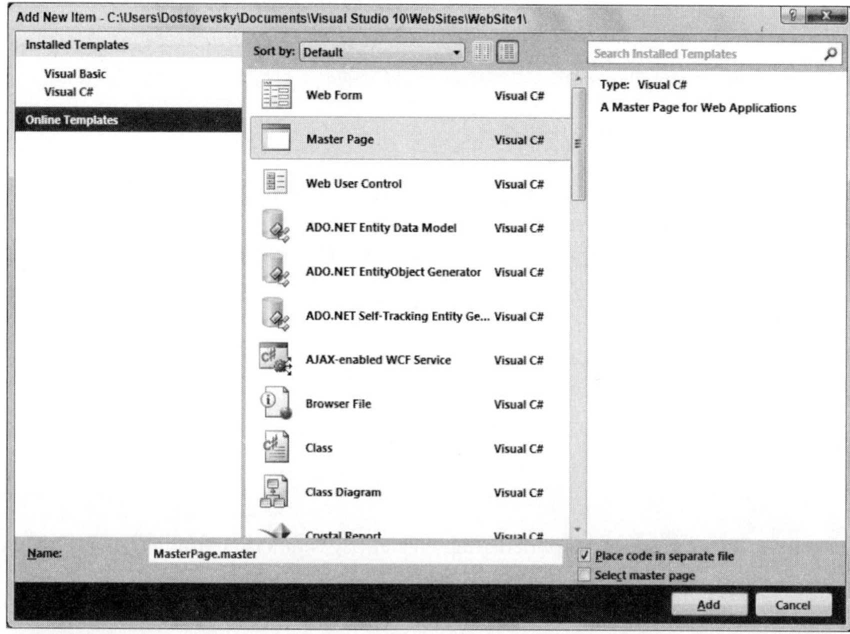

FIGURE 5-4

Because it's quite similar to any other `.aspx` page, the Add New Item dialog enables you to choose from a master page using the inline coding model or a master page that places its code in a separate file. Not placing your server code in a separate file means that you use the inline code model for the page you are creating. This option creates a single `.master` page. Choosing the option to place your code in a separate file means that you use the new code-behind model with the page you are creating. Selecting the "Place code in separate file" check box creates a single `.master` page, along with an associated `.master.vb` or `.master.cs` file. You also have the option of nesting your master page within another master page by selecting the Select master page option, but this is covered later in this chapter.

A sample master page that uses the inline-coding model is shown in Listing 5-1.

Available for download on Wrox.com

LISTING 5-1: A sample master page

```
<%@ Master Language="VB" %>

<script runat="server">

</script>
<html xmlns="http://www.w3.org/1999/xhtml" >
<head runat="server">
    <title>My Company Master Page</title>
    <asp:ContentPlaceHolder id="head" runat="server">
    </asp:ContentPlaceHolder>
</head>
<body>
    <form id="form1" runat="server">
        <table cellpadding="3" border="1">
            <tr style="background:silver">
                <td colspan="2">
                    <h1>My Company Home Page</h1>
                </td>
            </tr>
            <tr>
                <td>
```

continues

LISTING 5-1 *(continued)*

```
                    <asp:ContentPlaceHolder ID="ContentPlaceHolder1"
                     runat="server">
                    </asp:ContentPlaceHolder>
                </td>
                <td>
                    <asp:ContentPlaceHolder ID="ContentPlaceHolder2"
                     runat="server">
                    </asp:ContentPlaceHolder>
                </td>
            </tr>
            <tr>
                <td colspan="2">
                    Copyright 2010 - My Company
                </td>
            </tr>
        </table>
    </form>
</body>
</html>
```

This is a simple master page. The great thing about creating master pages in Visual Studio 2010 is that you can work with the master page in Code view, but you can also switch over to Design view to create your master pages just as you would any other ASP.NET page.

Start by reviewing the code for the master page. The first line is the directive:

```
<%@ Master Language="VB" %>
```

Instead of using the `Page` directive, as you would with a typical `.aspx` page, you use the `Master` directive for a master page. This master page uses only a single attribute, `Language`. The `Language` attribute's value here is `VB`, but of course, you can also use `C#` if you are building a C# master page.

You code the rest of the master page just as you would any other `.aspx` page. You can use server controls, raw HTML and text, images, events, or anything else you normally would use for any `.aspx` page. This means that your master page can have a `Page_Load` event as well or any other event that you deem appropriate.

In the code shown in Listing 5-1, notice the use of the server control — the `<asp:ContentPlaceHolder>` control. This control defines the areas of the template where the content page can place its content:

```
<tr>
   <td>
      <asp:ContentPlaceHolder ID="ContentPlaceHolder1"
       runat="server">
      </asp:ContentPlaceHolder>
   </td>
   <td>
      <asp:ContentPlaceHolder ID="ContentPlaceHolder2"
       runat="server">
      </asp:ContentPlaceHolder>
   </td>
</tr>
```

In the case of this master page, two defined areas exist where the content page can place content. Our master page contains a header and a footer area. It also defines two areas in the page where any inheriting content page can place its own content. Look at how a content page uses this master page.

CODING A CONTENT PAGE

Now that you have a master page in place in your application, you can use this new template for any content pages in your application. Right-click the application in the Solution Explorer and choose Add New Item to create a new content page within your application.

To create a content page or a page that uses this master page as its template, you select a typical Web form from the list of options in the Add New Item dialog (see Figure 5-5). Instead of creating a typical Web form, however, you select the Select master page check box. This gives you the option of associating this Web form later to some master page.

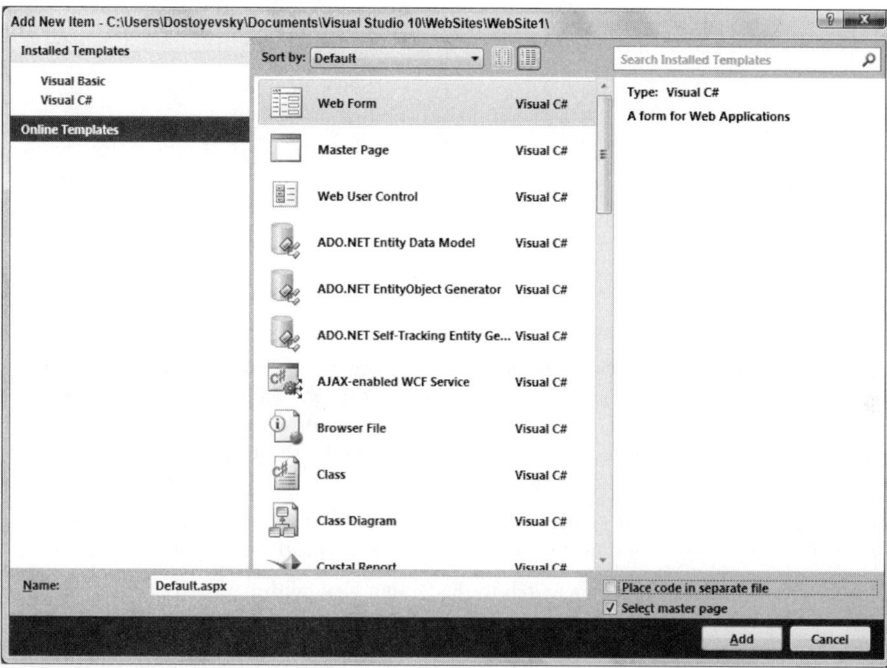

FIGURE 5-5

After you name your content page and click the Add button in the Add New Item dialog, the Select a Master Page dialog appears, as shown in Figure 5-6.

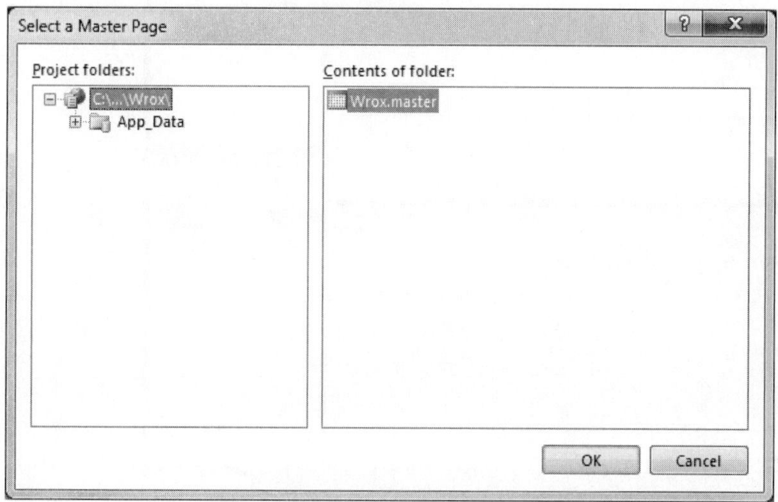

FIGURE 5-6

This dialog enables you to choose the master page from which you want to build your content page. You choose from the available master pages that are contained within your application. For this example, select the new master page that you created in Listing 5-1 and click OK. This creates the content page. The created page is a simple `.aspx` page with only a couple of lines of code contained in the file, as shown in Listing 5-2.

LISTING 5-2: The created content page

Available for download on Wrox.com

VB

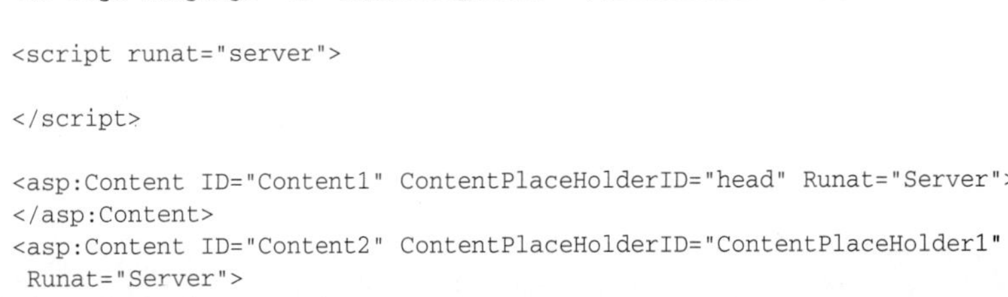

```
<%@ Page Language="VB" MasterPageFile="~/Wrox.master" Title="" %>

<script runat="server">

</script>

<asp:Content ID="Content1" ContentPlaceHolderID="head" Runat="Server">
</asp:Content>
<asp:Content ID="Content2" ContentPlaceHolderID="ContentPlaceHolder1"
 Runat="Server">
</asp:Content>
```

This content page is not much different from the typical `.aspx` page you have coded in the past. The big difference is the inclusion of the `MasterPageFile` attribute within the `Page` directive. The use of this attribute indicates that this particular `.aspx` page constructs its controls based on another page. The location of the master page within the application is specified as the value of the `MasterPageFile` attribute.

The other big difference is that it contains neither the `<form id="form1" runat="server">` tag nor any opening or closing HTML tags that would normally be included in a typical `.aspx` page.

This content page may seem simple, but if you switch to the Design view within Visual Studio 2010, you see the power of using content pages. Figure 5-7 shows what you get with visual inheritance.

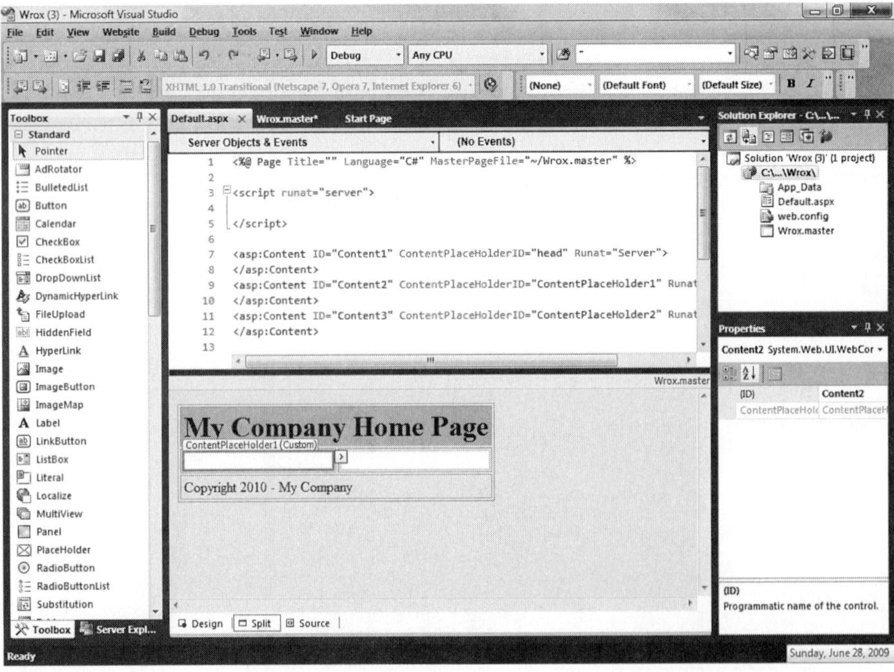

FIGURE 5-7

In this screenshot, you can see that just by using the `MasterPageFile` attribute in the `Page` directive, you are able to visually inherit everything that the `Wrox.master` file exposes. From the Design view within Visual Studio, you can also see what master page you are working with because the name of the referenced master page appears in the upper-right corner of the Design view page. If you try to click into the gray area that represents what is inherited from the master page, your cursor changes to show you are not allowed, as illustrated in Figure 5-8 (the cursor is on the word Page in the title).

My Company Home Page
ContentPlaceHolder1 (Custom)
Copyright 2010 - My Company

FIGURE 5-8

All the common areas defined in the master page are shown in gray, whereas the content areas that you specified in the master page using the `<asp:ContentPlaceHolder>` server control are shown clearly and available for additional content in the content page. You can add any content to these defined content areas as if you were working with a regular `.aspx` page. Listing 5-3 shows an example of using this `.master` page for a content page.

LISTING 5-3: The content page that uses Wrox.master

VB

```
<%@ Page Language="VB" MasterPageFile="~/Wrox.master" %>

<script runat="server">
    Protected Sub Button1_Click(ByVal sender As Object,
       ByVal e As System.EventArgs)

       Label1.Text = "Hello " & TextBox1.Text & "!"
   End Sub
</script>

<asp:Content ID="Content1" ContentPlaceHolderId="ContentPlaceHolder1"
 runat="server">
    <b>Enter your name:</b><br />
    <asp:Textbox ID="TextBox1" runat="server" />
    <br />
    <br />
    <asp:Button ID="Button1" runat="server" Text="Submit"
     OnClick="Button1_Click" /><br />
    <br />
    <asp:Label ID="Label1" runat="server" Font-Bold="True" />
</asp:Content>

<asp:Content ID="Content2" ContentPlaceHolderId="ContentPlaceHolder2"
 runat="server">
        <asp:Image ID="Image1" runat="server" ImageUrl="wrox.gif" />
</asp:Content>
```

C#

```
<%@ Page Language="C#" MasterPageFile="~/Wrox.master" %>

<script runat="server">
    protected void Button1_Click(object sender, System.EventArgs e)
    {
        Label1.Text = "Hello " + TextBox1.Text + "!";
    }
</script>
```

Right away you see some differences. As stated before, this page has no `<form id="form1" runat="server">` tag nor any opening or closing `<html>` tags. These tags are not included because they are located in the master page. Also notice the server control — the `<asp:Content>` server control.

```
<asp:Content ID="Content1" ContentPlaceHolderId="ContentPlaceHolder1"
 runat="server">
   ...
</asp:Content>
```

The `<asp:Content>` server control is a defined content area that maps to a specific `<asp:ContentPlaceHolder>` server control on the master page. In this example, you can see that the `<asp:Content>` server control maps itself to the `<asp:ContentPlaceHolder>` server control in the master page that has the `ID` of `ContentPlaceHolder1`. Within the content page, you don't have to worry about specifying the location of the content because it is already defined within the master page. Therefore, your only concern is to place the appropriate content within the provided content sections, allowing the master page to do most of the work for you.

Just as when you work with any typical `.aspx` page, you can create any event handlers for your content page. In this case, you are using just a single event handler — the button click when the end user submits the form. The created `.aspx` page that includes the master page and content page material is shown in Figure 5-9.

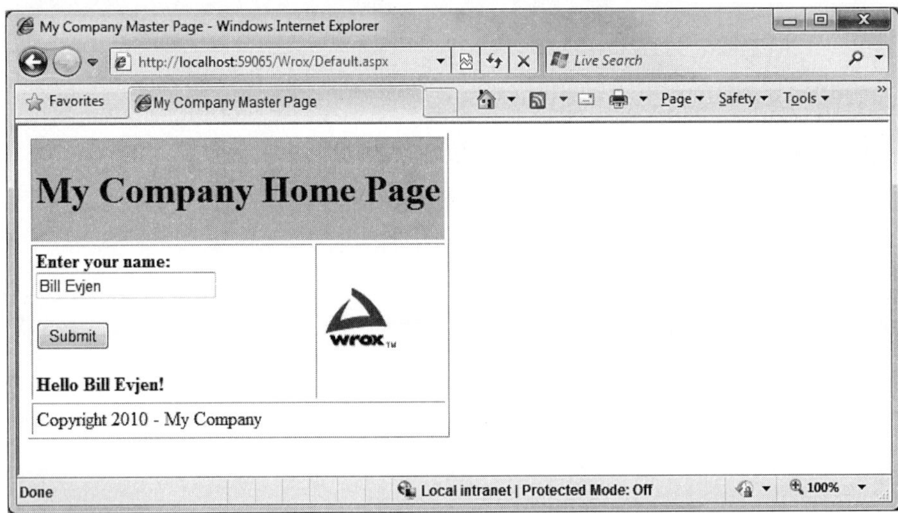

FIGURE 5-9

Mixing Page Types and Languages

One interesting point: When you use master pages, you are not tying yourself to a specific coding model (inline or code-behind), nor are you tying yourself to the use of a specific language. You can feel free to mix these elements within your application because they all work well.

You could use the master page created earlier, knowing that it was created using the inline-coding model, and then build your content pages using the code-behind model. Listing 5-4 shows a content page created using a Web form that uses the code-behind option.

LISTING 5-4: A content page that uses the code-behind model

Available for download on Wrox.com

.aspx (VB)

```
<%@ Page Language="VB" MasterPageFile="~/Wrox.master" AutoEventWireup="false"
    CodeFile="MyContentPage.aspx.vb" Inherits="MyContentPage" %>

<asp:Content ID="Content1" ContentPlaceHolderID="head" Runat="Server">
</asp:Content>
```

```
<asp:Content ID="Content2" ContentPlaceHolderId="ContentPlaceHolder1"
 runat="server">
    <b>Enter your name:</b><br />
    <asp:Textbox ID="TextBox1" runat="server" />
    <br />
    <br />
    <asp:Button ID="Button1" runat="server" Text="Submit" /><br />
    <br />
    <asp:Label ID="Label1" runat="server" Font-Bold="True" />
</asp:Content>

<asp:Content ID="Content3" ContentPlaceHolderId="ContentPlaceHolder2"
 runat="server">
        <asp:Image ID="Image1" runat="server" ImageUrl="wrox.gif" />
</asp:Content>
```

VB Code-Behind

```
Partial Class MyContentPage
   Inherits System.Web.UI.Page

   Protected Sub Button1_Click(ByVal sender As Object, _
     ByVal e As System.EventArgs) Handles Button1.Click

      Label1.Text = "Hello " & TextBox1.Text & "!"
   End Sub

End Class
```

C# Code-Behind

```
public partial class MyContentPage : System.Web.UI.Page
{
    protected void Button1_Click (object sender, System.EventArgs e)
    {
        Label1.Text = "Hello " + TextBox1.Text + "!";
    }
}
```

Even though the master page is using the inline-coding model, you can easily create content pages (such as the page shown in Listing 5-4) that use the code-behind model. The pages will still work perfectly.

Not only can you mix the coding models when using master pages, you can also mix the programming languages you use for the master or content pages. Just because you build a master page in C# doesn't mean that you are required to use C# for all the content pages that use this master page. You can also build content pages in Visual Basic. For a good example, create a master page in C# that uses the `Page_Load` event handler and then create a content page in Visual Basic. When it is complete, run the page. It works perfectly well. This means that even though you might have a master page in one of the available .NET languages, the programming teams that build applications from the master page can use whatever .NET language they want. You have to love the openness that the .NET Framework offers!

Specifying Which Master Page to Use

You just observed that specifying at page level which master page to use is quite easy. In the `Page` directive of the content page, you simply use the `MasterPageFile` attribute:

```
<%@ Page Language="VB" MasterPageFile="~/Wrox.master" %>
```

Besides specifying the master page that you want to use at the page level, you have a second way to specify which master page you want to use in the `web.config` file of the application, as shown in Listing 5-5.

LISTING 5-5: Specifying the master page in the web.config file

```
<configuration>
   <system.web>
      <pages masterPageFile="~/Wrox.master" />
   </system.web>
</configuration>
```

Specifying the master page in the `web.config` file causes every single content page you create in the application to inherit from the specified master page. If you declare your master page in the `web.config` file, you can create any number of content pages that use this master page. Once specified in this manner, the content page's `Page` directive can then be constructed in the following manner:

```
<%@ Page Language="VB" %>
```

You can easily override the application-wide master page specification by simply declaring a different master page within your content page:

```
<%@ Page Language="VB" MasterPageFile="~/MyOtherCompany.master" %>
```

By specifying the master page in the `web.config` file, you are not really saying that you want *all* the `.aspx` pages to use this master page. If you create a normal Web form and run it, ASP.NET will know that the page is not a content page and will run the page as a normal `.aspx` page.

If you want to apply the master page template to only a specific subset of pages (such as pages contained within a specific folder of your application), you can use the `<location>` element within the `web.config` file, as shown in Listing 5-6.

LISTING 5-6: Specifying the master page for a specific folder in the web.config file

```
<configuration>

    <location path="AdministrationArea">
        <system.web>
           <pages masterPageFile="~/WroxAdmin.master" />
        </system.web>
    </location>

</configuration>
```

With the addition of this `<location>` section in the `web.config` file, you have now specified that a specific folder (`AdministrationArea`) will use a different master file template. You do so using the path attribute of the `<location>` element. The value of the `path` attribute can be a folder name as shown, or it can even be a specific page — such as `AdminPage.aspx`.

Working with the Page Title

When you create content pages in your application, by default all the content pages automatically use the title that is declared in the master page. For example, you have primarily been using a master page with the title `My Company Master Page`. Every content page that is created using this particular master page also uses the same `My Company Master Page` title. You can avoid this by specifying the page's title using the `Title` attribute in the `@Page` directive in the content page. You can also work with the page title programmatically in your content pages. To accomplish this, in the code of the content page, you use the `Master` object. The `Master` object conveniently has a property called `Title`. The value of this property is the page title that is used for the content page. You code it as shown in Listing 5-7.

LISTING 5-7: Coding a custom page title for the content page

Available for download on Wrox.com

VB

```
<%@ Page Language="VB" MasterPageFile="~/Wrox.master" %>

<script runat="server">
    Protected Sub Page_LoadComplete(ByVal sender As Object, _
       ByVal e As System.EventArgs)

        Master.Page.Title = "This page was generated on: " & _
           DateTime.Now.ToString()
    End Sub
</script>
```

C#

```
<%@ Page Language="C#" MasterPageFile="~/Wrox.master" %>

<script runat="server">
    protected void Page_LoadComplete(object sender, EventArgs e)
    {
        Master.Page.Title = "This page was generated on: " +
           DateTime.Now.ToString();
    }
</script>
```

Working with Controls and Properties from the Master Page

When working with master pages from a content page, you actually have good access to the controls and the properties that the master page exposes. The master page, when referenced by the content page, exposes a property called `Master`. You use this property to get at control values or custom properties that are contained in the master page itself.

To see an example of this control you have, create a GUID (unique identifier) in the master page that you can retrieve on the content page that is using the master. For this example, use the master page that was created in Listing 5-1, but add a Label server control and the `Page_Load` event (see Listing 5-8).

LISTING 5-8: A master page that creates a GUID on the first request

Available for download on Wrox.com

VB

```
<%@ Master Language="VB" %>

<script runat="server">
    Protected Sub Page_Load(ByVal sender As Object, ByVal e As System.EventArgs)
        If Not Page.IsPostBack Then
            Label1.Text = System.Guid.NewGuid().ToString()
        End If
    End Sub
</script>

<html xmlns="http://www.w3.org/1999/xhtml" >
<head runat="server">
    <title>My Company Master Page</title>
    <asp:ContentPlaceHolder id="head" runat="server">
    </asp:ContentPlaceHolder>
</head>
<body>
    <form id="form1" runat="server">
        <table cellpadding="3" border="1">
            <tr bgcolor="silver">
                <td colspan="2">
                    <h1>My Company Home Page</h1>
                    <b>User's GUID:  
                        <asp:Label ID="Label1" runat="server" /></b>
                </td>
```

continues

LISTING 5-8 *(continued)*

```
            </tr>
            <tr>
                <td>
                    <asp:ContentPlaceHolder ID="ContentPlaceHolder1"
                     runat="server">
                    </asp:ContentPlaceHolder>
                </td>
                <td>
                    <asp:ContentPlaceHolder ID="ContentPlaceHolder2"
                     runat="server">
                    </asp:ContentPlaceHolder>
                </td>
            </tr>
            <tr>
                <td colspan="2">
                    Copyright 2010 - My Company
                </td>
            </tr>
        </table>
    </form>
</body>
</html>
```

C#

```
    protected void Page_Load(object sender, EventArgs e)
    {
        if (!Page.IsPostBack)
        {
            Label1.Text = System.Guid.NewGuid().ToString();
        }
    }
```

Now you have a Label control on the master page that you can access from the content page. You have a couple of ways to accomplish this task. The first is to use the `FindControl()` method that the master page exposes. Listing 5-9 shows this approach.

LISTING 5-9: Getting at the Label's Text value in the content page

Available for download on Wrox.com

VB

```
<%@ Page Language="VB" MasterPageFile="~/Wrox.master" %>

<script runat="server" language="vb">
    Protected Sub Page_LoadComplete(ByVal sender As Object, _
       ByVal e As System.EventArgs)

        Label1.Text = CType(Master.FindControl("Label1"), Label).Text
    End Sub

    Protected Sub Button1_Click(ByVal sender As Object, _
       ByVal e As System.EventArgs)

        Label2.Text = "Hello " & TextBox1.Text & "!"
    End Sub
</script>

<asp:Content ID="Content1" ContentPlaceHolderID="head" Runat="Server">
</asp:Content>

<asp:Content ID="Content2" ContentPlaceHolderId="ContentPlaceHolder1"
 runat="server">
    <b>Your GUID number from the master page is:<br />
    <asp:Label ID="Label1" runat="server" /></b><p>
```

```
        <b>Enter your name:</b><br />
        <asp:Textbox ID="TextBox1" runat="server" />
        <br />
        <br />
        <asp:Button ID="Button1" runat="server" Text="Submit"
         OnClick="Button1_Click" /><br />
        <br />
        <asp:Label ID="Label2" runat="server" Font-Bold="True" /></p>
</asp:Content>

<asp:Content ID="Content3" ContentPlaceHolderId="ContentPlaceHolder2"
 runat="server">
        <asp:Image ID="Image1" runat="server" ImageUrl="Wrox.gif" />
</asp:Content>
```

C#

```
<%@ Page Language="C#" MasterPageFile="~/Wrox.master" %>

<script runat="server">

    protected void Page_LoadComplete(object sender, EventArgs e)
    {
        Label1.Text = (Master.FindControl("Label1") as Label).Text;
    }

    protected void Button1_Click(object sender, EventArgs e)
    {
        Label2.Text = "<b>Hello " + TextBox1.Text + "!</b>";
    }
</script>
```

In this example, the master page in Listing 5-8 creates a GUID that it stores as a text value in a Label server control on the master page itself. The `ID` of this Label control is `Label1`. The master page generates this GUID only on the first request for this particular content page. From here, you then populate one of the content page's controls with this value.

The interesting thing about the content page is that you put code in the `Page_LoadComplete` event handler so that you can get at the GUID value that is on the master page. This event in ASP.NET fires immediately after the `Page_Load` event fires. Event ordering is covered later in this chapter, but the `Page_Load` event in the content page always fires before the `Page_Load` event in the master page. In order to get at the newly created GUID (if it is created in the master page's `Page_Load` event), you have to get the GUID in an event that comes after the `Page_Load` event — and that is where the `Page_LoadComplete` comes into play. Therefore, within the content page's `Page_LoadComplete` event, you populate a Label server control within the content page itself. Note that the Label control in the content page has the same `ID` as the Label control in the master page, but this doesn't make a difference. You can differentiate between them with the use of the `Master` property.

Not only can you get at the server controls that are in the master page in this way, you can get at any custom properties that the master page might expose as well. Look at the master page shown in Listing 5-10; it uses a custom property for the `<h1>` section of the page.

LISTING 5-10: A master page that exposes a custom property

Available for download on Wrox.com

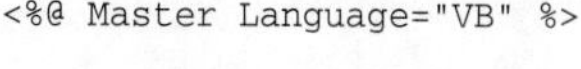

VB

```
<%@ Master Language="VB" %>

<script runat="server">
    Protected Sub Page_Load(ByVal sender As Object, ByVal e As System.EventArgs)
        If Not Page.IsPostBack Then
            Label1.Text = Guid.NewGuid().ToString()
        End If
    End Sub
```

continues

LISTING 5-10 *(continued)*

```
    Dim m_PageHeadingTitle As String = "My Company"

    Public Property PageHeadingTitle() As String
        Get
            Return m_PageHeadingTitle
        End Get
        Set(ByVal Value As String)
            m_PageHeadingTitle = Value
        End Set
    End Property
</script>

<html xmlns="http://www.w3.org/1999/xhtml" >
<head id="Head1" runat="server">
    <title>My Company Master Page</title>
    <asp:ContentPlaceHolder id="head" runat="server">
    </asp:ContentPlaceHolder>
</head>
<body>
    <form id="Form1" runat="server">
        <table cellpadding="3" border="1">
            <tr bgcolor="silver">
                <td colspan="2">
                    <h1><%= PageHeadingTitle %></h1>
                    <b>User's GUID:  
                        <asp:Label ID="Label1" runat="server" /></b>
                </td>
            </tr>
            <tr>
                <td>
                    <asp:ContentPlaceHolder ID="ContentPlaceHolder1"
                     runat="server">
                    </asp:ContentPlaceHolder>
                </td>
                <td>
                    <asp:ContentPlaceHolder ID="ContentPlaceHolder2"
                     runat="server">
                    </asp:ContentPlaceHolder>
                </td>
            </tr>
            <tr>
                <td colspan="2">
                    Copyright 2010 - My Company
                </td>
            </tr>
        </table>
    </form>
</body>
</html>
```

C#

```
<%@ Master Language="C#" %>

<script runat="server">
    protected void Page_Load(object sender, EventArgs e)
    {
        if (!Page.IsPostBack)
        {
```

```
                Label1.Text = System.Guid.NewGuid().ToString();
            }
        }

        string m_PageHeadingTitle = "My Company";

        public string PageHeadingTitle
        {
            get
            {
                return m_PageHeadingTitle;
            }
            set
            {
                m_PageHeadingTitle = value;
            }
        }
    </script>
```

In this master page example, the master page is exposing the property you created called `PageHeadingTitle`. A default value of `"My Company"` is assigned to this property. You then place it within the HTML of the master page file between some `<h1>` elements, which makes the default value become the heading used on the page within the master page template. Although the master page already has a value it uses for the heading, any content page that is using this master page can override the `<h1>` title heading. Listing 5-11 shows the process.

LISTING 5-11: A content page that overrides the property from the master page

Available for download on Wrox.com

```
<%@ Page Language="VB" MasterPageFile="~/Wrox.master" %>
<%@ MasterType VirtualPath="~/Wrox.master" %>

<script runat="server">
    Protected Sub Page_Load(ByVal sender As Object, ByVal e As System.EventArgs)
        Master.PageHeadingTitle = "My Company-Division X"
    End Sub
</script>
```

```
<%@ Page Language="C#" MasterPageFile="~/Wrox.master" %>
<%@ MasterType VirtualPath="~/Wrox.master" %>

<script runat="server">
    protected void Page_Load(object sender, EventArgs e)
    {
        Master.PageHeadingTitle = "My Company-Division X";
    }
</script>
```

From the content page, you can assign a value to the property that is exposed from the master page by the use of the `Master` property. As you can see, this is quite simple to do. Remember that not only can you get at any public properties that the master page might expose, but you can also retrieve any methods that the master page contains as well.

The item that makes this all possible is the use of the `MasterType` page directive. The `MasterType` directive allows you to make a strongly typed reference to the master page and allows you to access the master page's properties via the `Master` object.

Earlier, you saw how to get at the server controls that are on the master page by using the `FindControl()` method. The `FindControl()` method works fine, but it is a late-bound approach, and as such, the method call may fail if the control were removed from markup. Use defensive coding practices and always check for null when returning objects from `FindControl()`. Using the mechanics just illustrated (with the use of public properties shown in Listing 5-10), you can use another approach to expose any server controls on the master page. You may find this approach to be more effective.

To take this different approach, you simply expose the server control as a public property, as shown in Listing 5-12.

Available for download on Wrox.com

LISTING 5-12: Exposing a server control from a master page as a public property

VB

```
<%@ Master Language="VB" %>

<script runat="server">
    Public Property MasterPageLabel1() As Label
        Get
            Return Label1
        End Get
        Set(ByVal Value As Label)
            Label1 = Value
        End Set
    End Property
</script>
```

C#

```
<%@ Master Language="C#" %>

<script runat="server">
    public Label MasterPageLabel1
    {
        get
        {
            return Label1;
        }
        set
        {
            Label1 = value;
        }
    }
</script>
```

In this case, a public property called `MasterPageLabel1` provides access to the Label control that uses the `ID` of `Label1`. You can now create an instance of the `MasterPageLabel1` property on the content page and override any of the attributes of the Label server control. So if you want to increase the size of the GUID that the master page creates and displays in the `Label1` server control, you can simply override the `Font.Size` attribute of the Label control, as shown in Listing 5-13.

Available for download on Wrox.com

LISTING 5-13: Overriding an attribute from the Label control that is on the master page

```
<%@ Page Language"VB" MasterPageFile"~/Wrox.master" %>
<%@ MasterType VirtualPath"~/Wrox.master" %>

<script runat"server">
    Protected Sub Page_Load(ByVal sender As Object, ByVal e As System.EventArgs)
        Master.MasterPageLabel1.Font.Size = 25
    End Sub
</script>
```

```
<%@ Page Language"C#" MasterPageFile"~/Wrox.master" %>
<%@ MasterType VirtualPath"~/Wrox.master" %>
```

```
<script runat"server">
    protected void Page_Load(object sender, EventArgs e)
    {
        Master.MasterPageLabel1.Font.Size = 25;
    }
</script>
```

This approach may be the most effective way to get at any server controls that the master page exposes to the content pages.

SPECIFYING DEFAULT CONTENT IN THE MASTER PAGE

As you have seen, the master page enables you to specify content areas that the content page can use. Master pages can consist of just one content area, or they can be made up of multiple content areas. The nice thing about content areas is that when you create a master page, you can specify default content for the content area. You can leave this default content in place to be utilized by the content page if you choose not to override it. Listing 5-14 shows a master page that specifies some default content within a content area.

LISTING 5-14: Specifying default content in the master page

Available for download on Wrox.com

```
<%@ Master Language="VB" %>

<html xmlns="http://www.w3.org/1999/xhtml" >
<head runat="server">
    <title>My Company</title>
    <asp:ContentPlaceHolder id="head" runat="server">
    </asp:ContentPlaceHolder>
</head>
<body>
    <form id="form1" runat="server">
        <asp:ContentPlaceHolder ID="ContentPlaceHolder1" runat="server">
        Here is some default content.
        </asp:ContentPlaceHolder><p>
        <asp:ContentPlaceHolder ID="ContentPlaceHolder2" runat="server">
        Here is some more default content.
        </asp:ContentPlaceHolder></p>
    </form>
</body>
</html>
```

To place default content within one of the content areas of the master page, you simply put it in the `ContentPlaceHolder` server control on the master page itself. Any content page that inherits this master page also inherits the default content. Listing 5-15 shows a content page that overrides just one of the content areas from this master page.

LISTING 5-15: Overriding some default content in the content page

Available for download on Wrox.com

```
<%@ Page Language="VB" MasterPageFile="~/MasterPage.master" %>

<asp:Content ID="Content3" ContentPlaceHolderId="ContentPlaceHolder2"
 runat="server">
   Here is some new content.
</asp:Content>
```

This code creates a page with one content area that shows content coming from the master page itself in addition to other content that comes from the content page (see Figure 5-10).

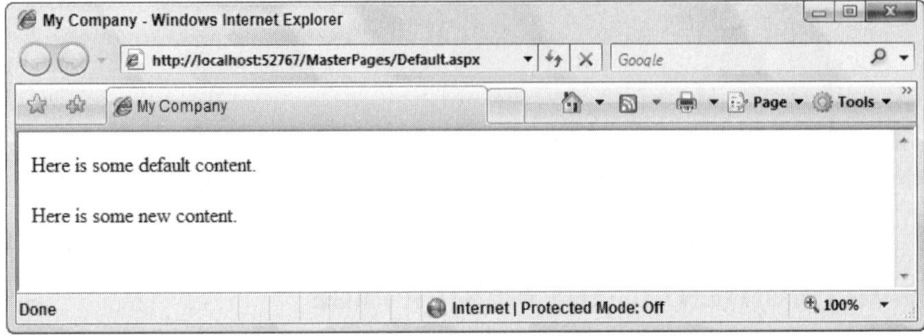

FIGURE 5-10

The other interesting point when you work with content areas in the Design mode of Visual Studio 2010 is that the smart tag enables you to work easily with the default content.

When you first start working with the content page, you will notice that all the default content is at first populated in all the Content server controls. You can change the content by clicking on the control's smart tag and selecting the Create Custom Content option from the provided menu. This option enables you to override the master page content and insert your own defined content. After you have placed some custom content inside the content area, the smart tag shows a different option — Default to Master's Content. This option enables you to return the default content that the master page exposes to the content area and to erase whatever content you have already placed in the content area — thereby simply returning to the default content. If you choose this option, you will be warned that you are about to delete any custom content you placed within the Content server control (see Figure 5-11).

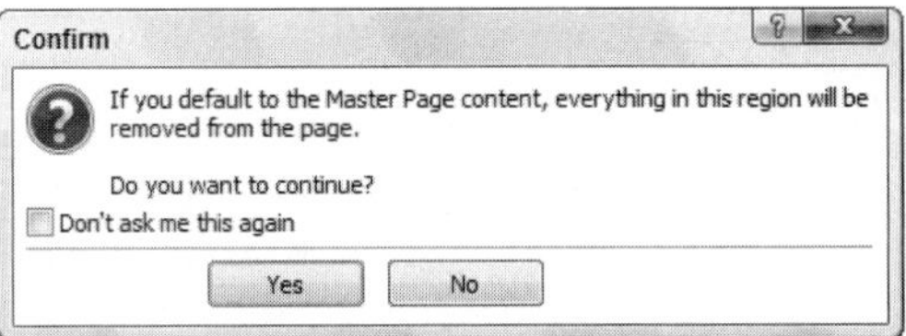

FIGURE 5-11

After changing one of the Content control's default content, you might see something like Figure 5-12.

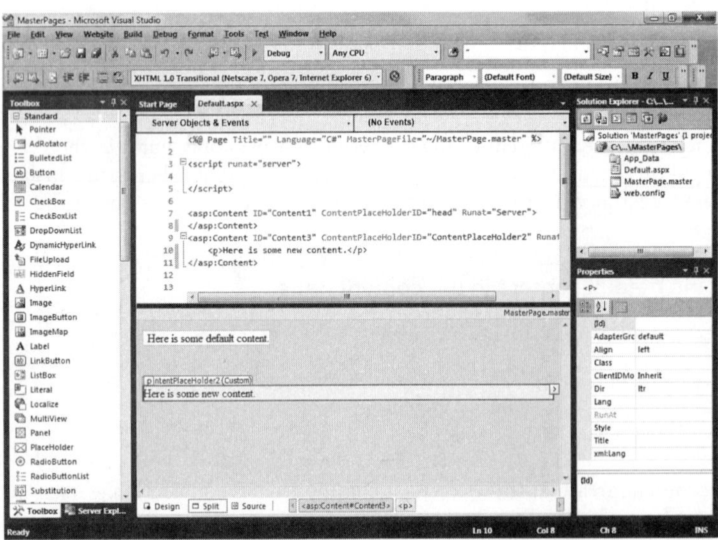

FIGURE 5-12

PROGRAMMATICALLY ASSIGNING THE MASTER PAGE

From any content page, you can easily assign a master page programmatically. You assign the master page to the content page using the `Page.MasterPageFile` property. You can use this property regardless of whether another master page is already assigned in the `@Page` directive.

To assign a master page with the `Page.MasterPageFile` property you use the `PreInit` event. The `PreInit` event is the earliest point in which you can access the Page lifecycle. For this reason, this event is where you need to assign any master page that is used by any content pages. The `PreInit` is an important event to make note of when you are working with master pages, because it is the only point where you can affect both the master and content page before they are combined into a single instance. Listing 5-16 shows how to assign the master page programmatically from the content page.

LISTING 5-16: Using Page_PreInit to assign the master page programmatically

Available for download on Wrox.com

```
<%@ Page Language="VB" %>

<script runat="server">
    Protected Sub Page_PreInit(ByVal sender As Object, ByVal e As System.EventArgs)
        Page.MasterPageFile = "~/MyMasterPage.master"
    End Sub
</script>
```

```
<%@ Page Language="C#" %>

<script runat="server">
    protected void Page_PreInit(object sender, EventArgs e)
    {
        Page.MasterPageFile = "~/MyMasterPage.master";
    }
</script>
```

In this case, when the page is dynamically being generated, the master page is assigned to the content page in the beginning of the page construction process. Note that the content page must have the expected Content controls; otherwise, an error is thrown.

NESTING MASTER PAGES

I hope you see the power that master pages provide to help you create templated Web applications. So far, you have been creating a single master page that the content page can use. Most companies and organizations, however, are not just two layers. Many divisions and groups exist within the organization that might want to use variations of the master by, in effect, having a master page within a master page. With ASP.NET, this type of page is quite possible.

For example, imagine that Reuters is creating a master page to be used throughout the entire company intranet. Not only does the Reuters enterprise want to implement this master page companywide, but various divisions within Reuters also want to provide templates for the subsections of the intranet directly under their control. For example, Reuters Europe and Reuters America each want their own unique master page, as illustrated in Figure 5-13.

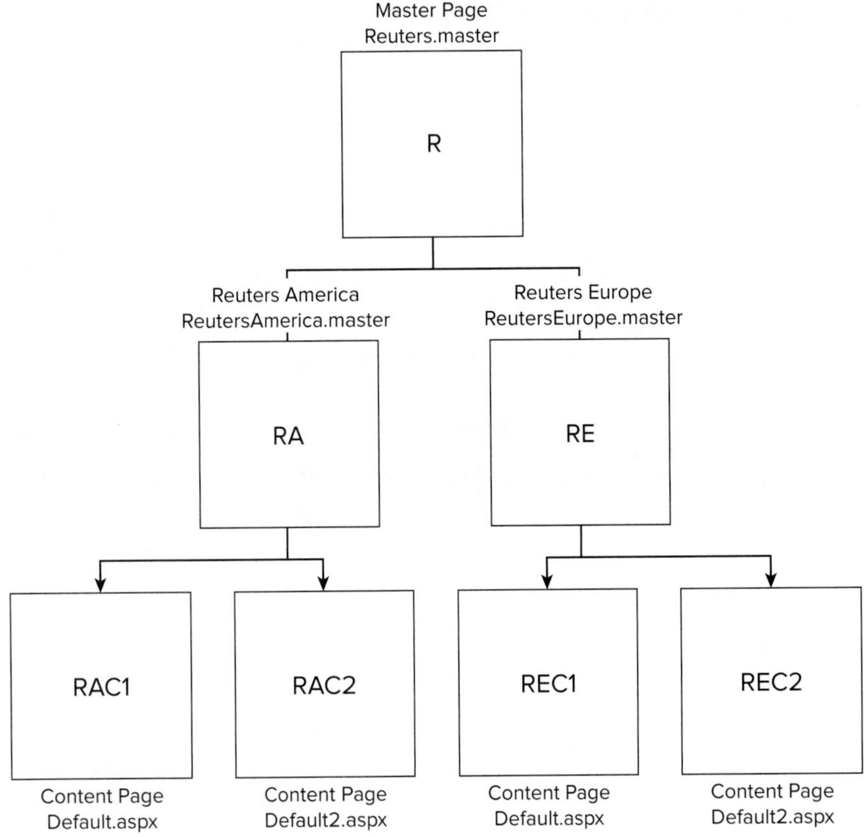

FIGURE 5-13

To get these unique pages, the creators of the Reuters Europe and Reuters America master pages simply create a master page that inherits from the global master page, as shown in Listing 5-17.

LISTING 5-17: The main master page

Available for download on Wrox.com

```
<%@ Master Language="VB" %>

<html xmlns="http://www.w3.org/1999/xhtml" >
<head runat="server">
    <title>Reuters</title>
    <asp:ContentPlaceHolder id="head" runat="server">
    </asp:ContentPlaceHolder>
</head>
<body>
    <form id="form1" runat="server">
        <p><asp:Label ID="Label1" runat="server" BackColor="LightGray"
            BorderColor="Black" BorderWidth="1px" BorderStyle="Solid"
            Font-Size="XX-Large"> Reuters Main Master Page </asp:Label></p>
        <asp:ContentPlaceHolder ID="ContentPlaceHolder1" runat="server">
        </asp:ContentPlaceHolder>
    </form>
</body>
</html>
```

Filename ReutersMain.master

This master page is simple, but excellent for showing you how this nesting capability works. The main master page is the master page used globally in the company. It has the ContentPlaceHolder server control with the `ID` of `ContentPlaceHolder1`.

You create a submaster or nested master page in the same manner as you would when building any other master page. From the Add New Item dialog, select the Master Page option and make sure you have the Select master page option selected, as illustrated in Figure 5-14. Again, the Select a Master Page dialog appears, in which you make a master page selection.

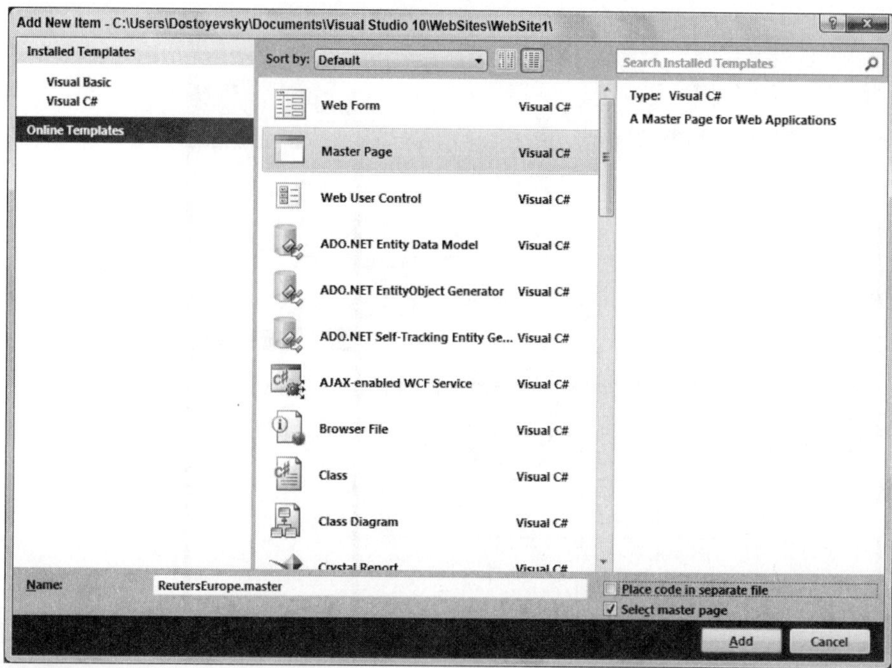

FIGURE 5-14

Listing 5-18 shows how you can work with this main master from a submaster file.

Available for download on Wrox.com

LISTING 5-18: The submaster page

```
<%@ Master Language="VB" MasterPageFile="~/ReutersMain.master" %>

<asp:Content ID="Content1" ContentPlaceHolderID="head" Runat="Server">
</asp:Content>

<asp:Content ID="Content2" ContentPlaceHolderId="ContentPlaceHolder1"
 runat="server">
    <asp:Label ID="Label1" runat="server" BackColor="#E0E0E0" BorderColor="Black"
     BorderStyle="Dotted" BorderWidth="2px" Font-Size="Large">
     Reuters Europe </asp:Label><br /><hr />

        <asp:ContentPlaceHolder ID="ContentPlaceHolder1" runat="server">
        </asp:ContentPlaceHolder>
</asp:Content>
```

Filename ReutersEurope.master

Looking this page over, you can see that it isn't much different than a typical `.aspx` page that makes use of a master page. The `MasterPageFile` attribute is used just the same, but instead of using the `@Page` directive, it uses the `@Master` page directive. Then the `Content2` control also uses the `ContentPlaceHolderId` attribute of the Content control. This attribute ties this content area to the content area `ContentPlaceHolder1`, which is defined in the main master page.

One feature of ASP.NET is the ability to view nested master pages directly in the Design view of Visual Studio 2010. Prior to Visual Studio 2008, trying to present a nested master page would actually throw an error. Figure 5-15 shows a nested master page in the Design view of Visual Studio 2010.

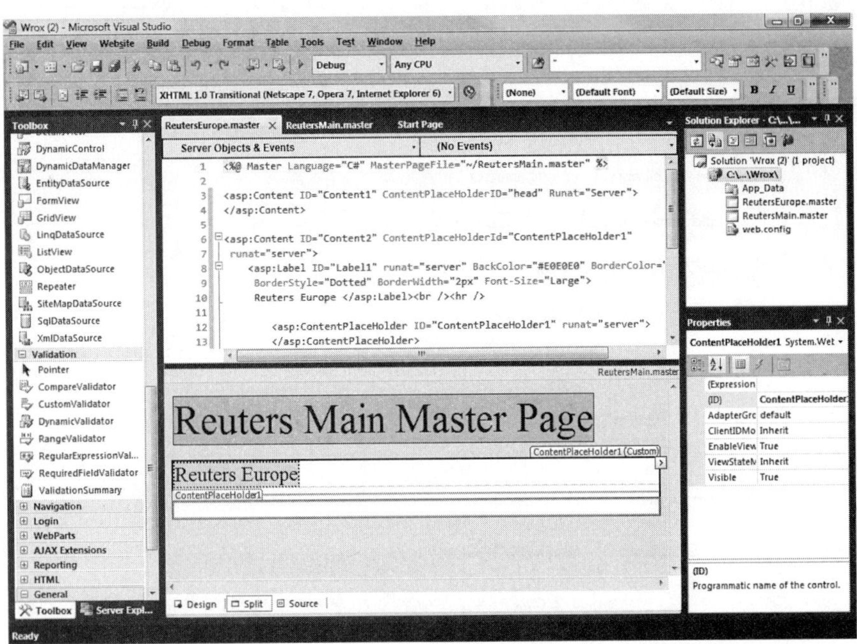

FIGURE 5-15

Within the submaster page presented in Listing 5-18, you can also now use as many ContentPlaceHolder server controls as you want. Any content page that uses this master can use these controls. Listing 5-19 shows a content page that uses the submaster page `ReutersEurope.master`.

LISTING 5-19: The content page

Available for download on Wrox.com

Default.aspx

```
<%@ Page Language="VB" MasterPageFile="~/ReutersEurope.master" %>

<asp:Content ID="Content1" ContentPlaceHolderId="ContentPlaceHolder1"
 runat="server">
    Hello World
</asp:Content>
```

As you can see, in this content page the value of the `MasterPageFile` attribute in the `@Page` directive is the submaster page that you created. Inheriting the `ReutersEurope` master page actually combines both master pages (`ReutersMain.master` and `ReutersEurope.master`) into a single master page. The Content control in this content page points to the content area defined in the submaster page as well. You can see this in the code with the use of the `ContentPlaceHolderId` attribute. In the end, you get a very non-artistic page, as shown in Figure 5-16.

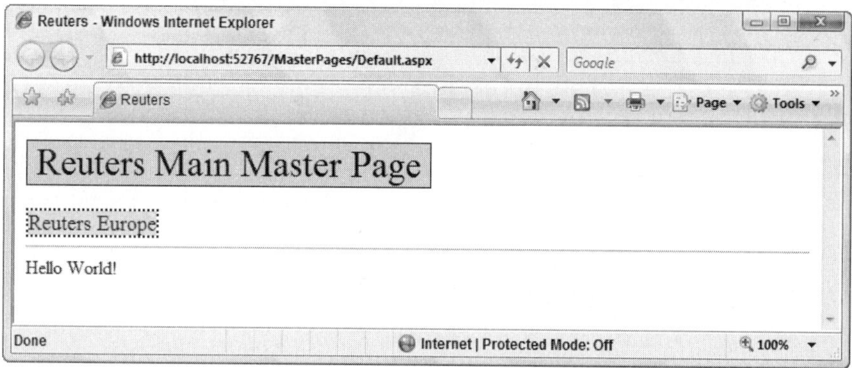

FIGURE 5-16

As you can see, creating a content page that uses a submaster page works quite well.

CONTAINER-SPECIFIC MASTER PAGES

In many cases, developers are building applications that will be viewed in a multitude of different containers. Some viewers may view the application in Microsoft Internet Explorer and some might view it using Firefox or Google Chrome. And still other viewers may call up the application on a Pocket PC or Nokia cell phone.

For this reason, ASP.NET allows you to use multiple master pages within your content page. Depending on the viewing container used by the end user, the ASP.NET engine pulls the appropriate master file. Therefore, you want to build container-specific master pages to provide your end users with the best possible viewing experience by taking advantage of the features that a specific container provides. Listing 5-20 demonstrates the capability to use multiple master pages.

Available for download on Wrox.com

LISTING 5-20: A content page that can work with more than one master page

```
<%@ Page Language="VB" MasterPageFile="~/Wrox.master"
       Mozilla:MasterPageFile="~/WroxMozilla.master"
       Opera:MasterPageFile="~/WroxOpera.master" %>

<asp:Content ID="Content1" ContentPlaceHolderID="head" Runat="Server">
</asp:Content>

<asp:Content ID="Content2" ContentPlaceHolderId="ContentPlaceHolder1"
 runat="server">
    Hello World
</asp:Content>
```

As you can see from this example content page, it can work with three different master page files. The first one uses the attribute `MasterPageFile`. It is the default setting used for any page that doesn't fit the criteria for any of the other options. This means that if the requestor is not a Mozilla or Opera browser, the default master page, `Wrox.master`, is used. However, if the requestor is an Opera browser, `WroxOpera.master` is used instead, as illustrated in Figure 5-17.

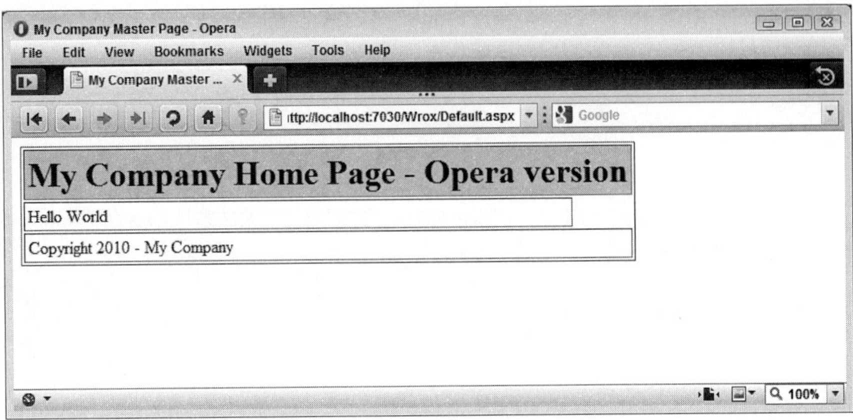

FIGURE 5-17

You can find a list of available browsers on the production server where the application will be hosted at `C:\Windows\Microsoft.NET\Framework\v4.0.xxxxx\CONFIG\Browsers`. Some of the available options include the following:

- avantgo
- cassio
- Default
- docomo
- ericsson
- EZWap
- gateway
- generic
- goAmerica
- ie
- Jataayu
- jphone
- legend
- MME
- mozilla
- netscape
- nokia
- openwave
- opera
- palm
- panasonic
- pie
- webtv
- winwap
- xiino

Of course, you can also add any additional `.browser` files that you deem necessary.

EVENT ORDERING

When you work with master pages and content pages, both can use the same events (such as the `Load` event). Be sure you know which events come before others. You are bringing two classes together to create a single page class, and a specific order is required. When an end user requests a content page in the browser, the event ordering is as follows:

1. **Master page child controls initialization:** All server controls contained within the master page are first initialized.
2. **Content page child controls initialization:** All server controls contained in the content page are initialized.
3. **Master page initialization:** The master page itself is initialized.

4. **Content page initialization:** The content page is initialized.
5. **Content page load:** The content page is loaded (this is the `Page_Load` event followed by the `Page_LoadComplete` event).
6. **Master page load:** The master page is loaded (this is also the `Page_Load` event followed by the `Page_LoadComplete` event).
7. **Master page child controls load:** The server controls on the master page are loaded onto the page.
8. **Content page child controls load:** The server controls on the content page are loaded onto the page.

Pay attention to this event ordering when building your applications. If you want to use server control values that are contained on the master page within a specific content page, for example, you can't retrieve the values of these server controls from within the content page's `Page_Load` event. This is because this event is triggered before the master page's `Page_Load` event. This problem prompted the creation of the `Page_LoadComplete` event in the .NET Framework 2.0. The content page's `Page_LoadComplete` event follows the master page's `Page_Load` event. You can, therefore, use this ordering to get at values from the master page even though it isn't populated when the content page's `Page_Load` event is triggered.

CACHING WITH MASTER PAGES

When working with typical `.aspx` pages, you can apply output caching to the page by using the following construct (or variation thereof):

```
<%@ OutputCache Duration="10" Varybyparam="None" %>
```

This line caches the page in the server's memory for 10 seconds. Many developers use output caching to increase the performance of their ASP.NET pages. Using it on pages with data that doesn't become stale too quickly also makes a lot of sense.

How do you go about applying output caching to ASP.NET pages when working with master pages? You cannot apply caching to just the master page. You cannot put the `OutputCache` directive on the master page itself. If you do so, on the page's second retrieval, you get an error because the application cannot find the cached page.

To work with output caching when using a master page, stick the `OutputCache` directive in the content page. Doing so caches both the contents of the content page and the contents of the master page (remember, it is just a single page at this point). The `OutputCache` directive placed in the master page does not cause the master page to produce an error, but it will not be cached. This directive works in the content page only.

Another new and interesting feature of ASP.NET 4 in regards to working with any caching capabilities is that ASP.NET now enables you to control view state at the control level. Although you might immediately think of being able to control view state in this manner with controls such as the GridView or something that generally has a lot of view state, you can also use this new capability with the ContentPlaceHolder control.

For example, you can construct something such as the following:

```
<asp:ContentPlaceHolder ID="ContentPlaceHolder1" runat="server"
 ViewStateMode="Disabled">

</asp:ContentPlaceHolder>
```

In this case, `ContentPlaceHolder1` will not use view state even if the rest of the page is using it. The available options for the `ViewStateMode` property include `Disabled`, `Enabled`, and `Inherit`. `Disabled` turns off view state for the control, `Enabled` turns it on, and `Inherit` takes the value that is assigned in the `@Page` directive. Removing view state improves the performance of your pages.

ASP.NET AJAX AND MASTER PAGES

Many of the larger ASP.NET applications today make use of master pages and the power this technology provides in the ability of building templated Web sites. ASP.NET 4 includes ASP.NET AJAX as part of the default install, and you will find that master pages and Ajax go together quite well.

Chapter 18 covers ASP.NET AJAX.

Every page that is going to make use of AJAX capabilities must have the ScriptManager control on the page. If the page that you want to use AJAX with is a content page making use of a master page, then you must place the ScriptManager control on the master page itself.

Note that you can have only one ScriptManager on a page.

It isn't too difficult to set up your master page so that it is Ajax-enabled. In order to do this, you will simply need to add a ScriptManager server control to the master page itself. Listing 5-21 shows an example of this in action.

LISTING 5-21: The AJAX master page

Available for download on Wrox.com

```
<%@ Master Language="VB" %>

<script runat="server">

</script>

<html xmlns="http://www.w3.org/1999/xhtml">
<head runat="server">
    <title></title>
    <asp:ContentPlaceHolder id="head" runat="server">
    </asp:ContentPlaceHolder>
</head>
<body>
    <form id="form1" runat="server">
    <div>
        <asp:ScriptManager ID="ScriptManager1" runat="server" />
        <asp:ContentPlaceHolder id="ContentPlaceHolder1" runat="server">

        </asp:ContentPlaceHolder>
    </div>
    </form>
</body>
</html>
```

YOU CAN DOWNLOAD THE CODE FOUND IN THIS BOOK. VISIT WROX.COM AND SEARCH FOR ISBN 9780470502204

As you can see from Listing 5-21, the only real difference between this AJAX master page and the standard master page is the inclusion of the ScriptManager server control. You want to use this technique if your master page includes any AJAX capabilities whatsoever, even if the content page makes no use of AJAX at all.

The ScriptManager control on the master page also is beneficial if you have common JavaScript items to place on all the pages of your Web application. For example, Listing 5-22 shows how you could easily include JavaScript on each page through the master page.

LISTING 5-22: Including scripts through your master page

Available for download on Wrox.com

```
<%@ Master Language="VB" %>

<html xmlns"http://www.w3.org/1999/xhtml">
<head runat="server">
    <title></title>
    <asp:ContentPlaceHolder id="head" runat="server">
    </asp:ContentPlaceHolder>
</head>
<body>
    <form id="form1" runat="server">
    <div>
        <asp:ScriptManager ID="ScriptManager1" runat="server">
             <Scripts>
                <asp:ScriptReference Path="myScript.js" />
            </Scripts>
        </asp:ScriptManager>
        <asp:ContentPlaceHolder id="ContentPlaceHolder1" runat="server">

        </asp:ContentPlaceHolder>
    </div>
    </form>
</body>
</html>
```

In this example, the `myScript.js` file will now be included on every content page that makes use of this AJAX master page. If your content page also needs to make use of AJAX capabilities, then you simply cannot add another ScriptManager control to the page. Instead, the content page will need to make use of the ScriptManager control that is already present on the master page.

That said, if your content page needs to add additional items to the ScriptManager control, it is able to access this control on the master page using the ScriptManagerProxy server control. Using the ScriptManagerProxy control gives you the ability to add any items to the ScriptManager that are completely specific to the instance of the content page that makes the inclusions.

For example, Listing 5-23 shows how a content page would add additional scripts to the page through the ScriptManagerProxy control.

LISTING 5-23: Adding additional items using the ScriptManagerProxy control

Available for download on Wrox.com

```
<%@ Page Language="VB" MasterPageFile="~/AjaxMaster.master" %>

<asp:Content ID="Content1" ContentPlaceHolderID="head" runat="Server">
</asp:Content>
<asp:Content ID="Content2" ContentPlaceHolderID="ContentPlaceHolder1"
 runat="Server">

 <asp:ScriptManagerProxy ID="ScriptManagerProxy1" runat="server">
     <Scripts>
         <asp:ScriptReference Path="myOtherScript.js" />
     </Scripts>
 </asp:ScriptManagerProxy>
</asp:Content>
```

In this case, this content page uses the ScriptManagerProxy control to add an additional script to the page. This ScriptManagerProxy control works exactly the same as the main ScriptManager control except that it is meant for content pages making use of a master page. The ScriptManagerProxy control will then interact with the page's ScriptManager control to perform the actions necessary.

SUMMARY

When you create applications that use a common header, footer, or navigation section on nearly every page of the application, master pages are a great solution. Master pages are easy to implement and enable you to make changes to each and every page of your application by changing a single file. Imagine how much easier this method makes managing large applications that contain thousands of pages.

This chapter described master pages in ASP.NET and explained how you build and use master pages within your Web applications. In addition to the basics, the chapter covered master page event ordering, caching, and specific master pages for specific containers. In the end, when you are working with templated applications, master pages should be your first option — the power of this approach is immense.

Themes and Skins

WHAT'S IN THIS CHAPTER?

- Applying and removing themes
- Making your own themes
- Working with themes programmatically and in conjunction with custom controls

When you build a Web application, it usually has a similar look-and-feel across all its pages. Not too many applications are designed with each page dramatically different from the next. Generally, for your applications, you use similar fonts, colors, and server control styles across all the pages.

You can apply these common styles individually to each and every server control or object on each page, or you can use a capability provided by ASP.NET 4 to centrally specify these styles. All pages or parts of pages in the application can then access them.

Themes are the text-based style definitions in ASP.NET 4 that are the focus of this chapter.

USING ASP.NET THEMES

Themes are similar to Cascading Style Sheets (CSS) in that they enable you to define visual styles for your Web pages. Themes go further than CSS, however, in that they enable you to apply styles, graphics, and even CSS files themselves to the pages of your applications. You can apply ASP.NET themes at the application, page, or server control level. Themes then are larger and more encompassing than CSS as they can also include CSS as a major part of how they work.

Applying a Theme to a Single ASP.NET Page

In order to see how to use one of these themes, create a basic page, which includes some text, a text box, a button, and a calendar, as shown in Listing 6-1.

LISTING 6-1: An ASP.NET page that does not use themes

Available for download on Wrox.com

```
<%@ Page Language="VB" %>
<html xmlns="http://www.w3.org/1999/xhtml">
<head runat="server">
    <title>STLNET</title>
</head>
<body>
    <form id="form1" runat="server">
        <h1>St. Louis .NET User Group</h1><br />
        <asp:Textbox ID="TextBox1" runat="server" /><br />
        <br />
        <asp:Calendar ID="Calendar1" runat="server" /><br />
        <asp:Button ID="Button1" runat="server" Text="Button" />
    </form>
</body>
</html>
```

This simple page shows some default server controls that appear just as you would expect, but that you can change with an ASP.NET theme. When this theme-less page is called in the browser, it should look like Figure 6-1.

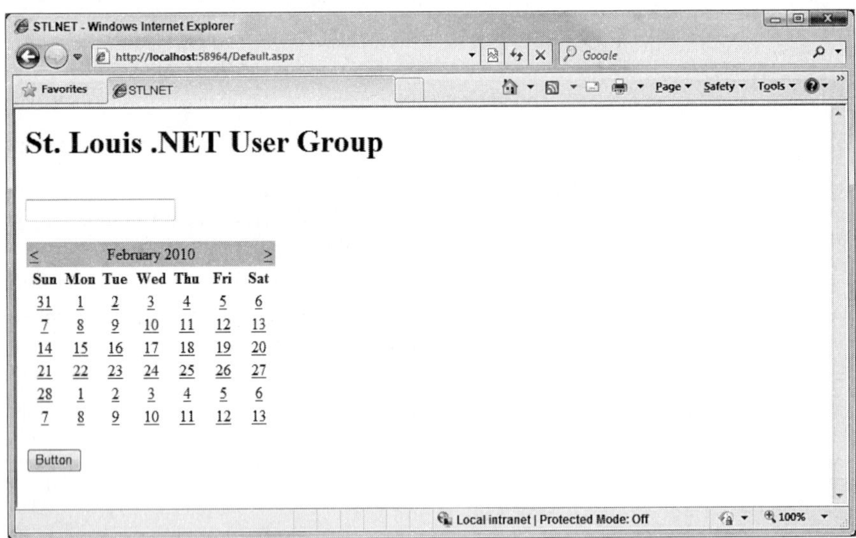

FIGURE 6-1

You can instantly change the appearance of this page without changing the style of each server control on the page. From within the `Page` directive, you simply apply an ASP.NET theme that you have either built (shown later in this chapter) or downloaded from the Internet:

```
<%@ Page Language="VB" Theme="SmokeAndGlass" %>
```

Adding the `Theme` attribute to the `Page` directive changes the appearance of everything on the page that is defined in an example `SmokeAndGlass` theme file. Using this theme, when we invoked the page in the browser, we got the result shown in Figure 6-2.

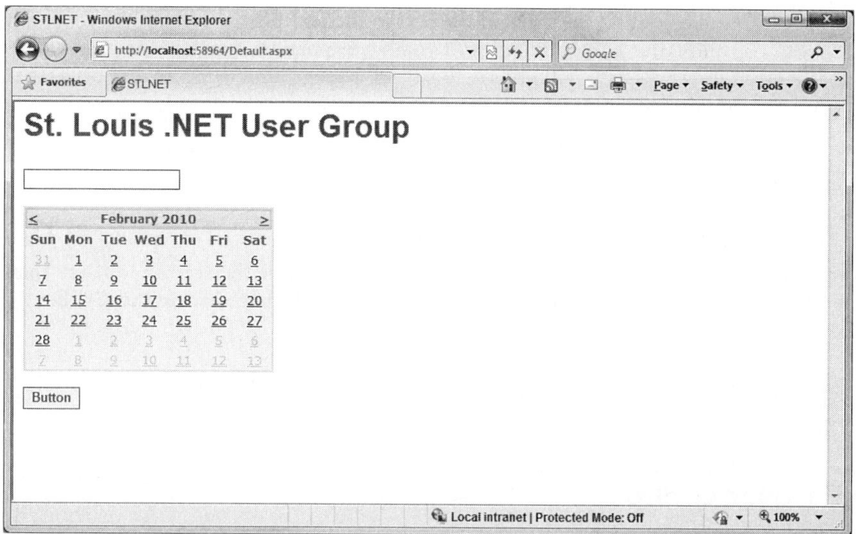

FIGURE 6-2

From here, you can see that everything — including the font, font color, text box, button, and more — has changed appearance. If you have multiple pages, you may find that not having to think about applying styles to everything you do as you build because the styles are already centrally defined for you is nice.

Applying a Theme to an Entire Application

In addition to applying an ASP.NET theme to your ASP.NET pages using the `Theme` attribute within the `Page` directive, you can also apply it at an application level from the `web.config` file, as shown in Listing 6-2.

LISTING 6-2: Applying a theme application-wide from the web.config file

Available for download on Wrox.com

```
<?xml version="1.0"?>

<configuration>
   <system.web>
      <pages theme="SmokeAndGlass" />
   </system.web>
</configuration>
```

If you specify the theme in the `web.config` file, you do not need to define the theme again in the `Page` directive of your ASP.NET pages. This theme is applied automatically to each and every page within your application. If you wanted to apply the theme to only a specific part of the application in this fashion, then you can do the same, but in addition, can make use of the `<location/>` element to specify the areas of the applications for which the theme should be applied.

Removing Themes from Server Controls

Whether themes are set at the application level or on a page, at times you want an alternative to the theme that has been defined. For example, change the text box server control that you have been working with (from Listing 6-1) by making its background black and using white text:

```
<asp:Textbox ID="TextBox1" runat="server"
 BackColor="#000000" ForeColor="#ffffff" />
```

You specify the black background color and the color of the text in the text box directly in the control itself with the use of the `BackColor` and `ForeColor` attributes. If you have applied a theme to the page where this text box control is located, however, you will not see this black background or white text because these changes are overridden by the theme itself.

To apply a theme to your ASP.NET page but not to this text box control, you simply use the `EnableTheming` property of the text box server control:

```
<asp:Textbox ID="TextBox1" runat="server"
 BackColor="#000000" ForeColor="#ffffff" EnableTheming="false" />
```

If you apply this property to the text box server control from Listing 6-1 while the `SmokeAndGlass` theme is still applied to the entire page, the theme is applied to every control on the page *except* the text box. Figure 6-3 shows this result.

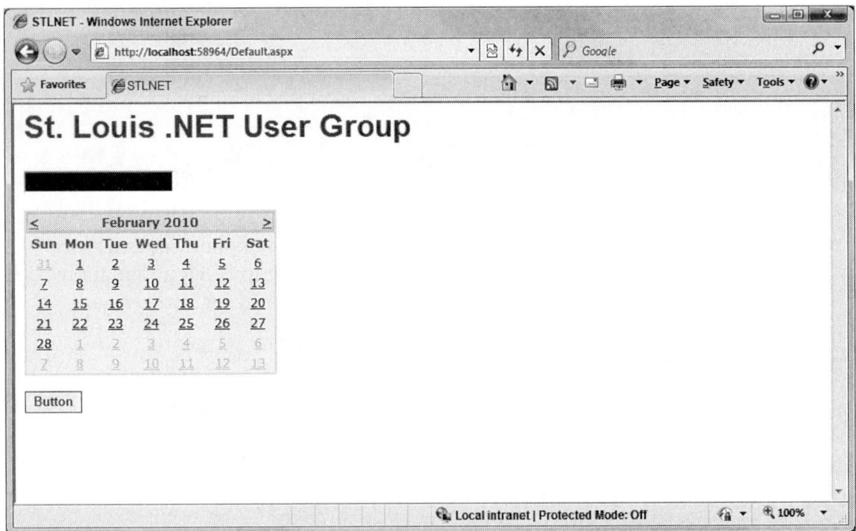

FIGURE 6-3

If you want to turn off theming for multiple controls within a page, consider using the Panel control (or any container control) to encapsulate a collection of controls and then set the `EnableTheming` attribute of the Panel control to `False`. This setting disables theming for each control contained within the Panel control.

Removing Themes from Web Pages

Now what if, when you set the theme for an entire application in the `web.config` file, you want to exclude a single ASP.NET page? Removing a theme setting at the page level is quite possible, just as it is at the server control level.

The `Page` directive includes an `EnableTheming` attribute that you can use to remove theming from your ASP.NET pages. To remove the theme that would be applied by the theme setting in the `web.config` file, you simply construct your `Page` directive in the following manner:

```
<%@ Page Language="VB" EnableTheming="False" %>
```

This construct sets the theme to nothing — thereby removing any settings that were specified in the `web.config` file. When this directive is set to `False` at the page or control level, the `Theme` directory is not searched, and no `.skin` files are applied (`.skin` files are used to define styles for ASP.NET server controls). When it is set to `True` at the page or control level, the `Theme` directory is searched and `.skin` files are applied.

If themes are disabled because the `EnableTheming` attribute is set to `False` at the page level, you can still enable theming for specific controls on this page by setting the `EnableTheming` property for the control to `True` and applying a specific theme at the same time, as shown here:

```
<asp:Textbox ID="TextBox1" runat="server"
 BackColor="#000000" ForeColor="#ffffff" EnableTheming="true" SkinID="mySkin"
/>
```

Understanding Themes When Using Master Pages

When working with ASP.NET applications that make use of master pages, notice that both the `Page` and `Master` page directives include an `EnableTheming` attribute.

Chapter 5 covers master pages.

If both the `Page` and `Master` page directives include the `EnableTheming` attribute, what behavior results if both are used? Suppose you have defined your theme in the `web.config` file of your ASP.NET application and you specify in the master page that theming is disabled using the `EnableTheming` attribute as shown here:

```
<%@ Master Language="VB" EnableTheming="false" %>
```

In this case, what is the behavior for any content pages using this master page? If the content page that is using this master page does not make any specification on theming (it does not use the `EnableTheming` attribute), what is specified in the master page naturally takes precedence and no theme is utilized as required by the `false` setting. Even if you have set the `EnableTheming` value in the content page, any value that is specified in the master page takes precedence. This means that if theming is set to `false` in the master page and set to `true` in the content page, the page is constructed with the value provided from the master page — in this case, `false`. Even if the value is set to `false` in the master page, however, you can override this setting at the control level rather than doing it in the `Page` directive of the content page.

Understanding the StyleSheetTheme Attribute

The `Page` directive also includes the attribute `StyleSheetTheme` that you can use to apply themes to a page. So, the big question is: If you have a `Theme` attribute and a `StyleSheetTheme` attribute for the `Page` directive, what is the difference between the two?

```
<%@ Page Language="VB" StyleSheetTheme="Summer" %>
```

The `StyleSheetTheme` attribute works the same as the `Theme` attribute in that you can use it to apply a theme to a page. The difference is that when the attributes are set locally on the page within a particular control, the attributes are overridden by the theme if you use the `Theme` attribute. They are kept in place, however, if you apply the page's theme using the `StyleSheetTheme` attribute. Suppose you have a text box control such as the following:

```
<asp:Textbox ID="TextBox1" runat="server"
 BackColor="#000000" ForeColor="#ffffff" />
```

In this example, the `BackColor` and `ForeColor` settings are overridden by the theme if you have applied it using the `Theme` attribute in the `Page` directive. If, instead, you applied the theme using the `StyleSheetTheme` attribute in the `Page` directive, the `BackColor` and `ForeColor` settings remain in place, even if they are explicitly defined in the theme.

CREATING YOUR OWN THEMES

You will find that creating themes in ASP.NET is a rather simple process — although sometimes it does require some artistic capabilities. You can apply the themes you create at the application, page, or server control level. Themes are a great way to easily apply a consistent look-and-feel across your entire application.

Creating the Proper Folder Structure

In order to create your own themes for an application, you first need to create the proper folder structure in your application. To do so, right-click your project and add a new folder. Name the folder App_Themes. You can also create this folder by right-clicking on your project in Visual Studio and selecting Add ASP.NET Folder ➪ Theme. Notice when you do this that the theme folder within the App_Themes folder does not have the typical folder icon next to it, but instead has a folder icon that includes a paintbrush, as shown in Figure 6-4.

FIGURE 6-4

Within the App_Themes folder, you can create an additional theme folder for each and every theme that you might use in your application. For example, if you are going to have four themes — *Summer*, *Fall*, *Winter*, and *Spring* — then you create four folders that are named appropriately.

You might use more than one theme in your application for many reasons — season changes, day/night changes, different business units, category of user, or even user preferences.

Each theme folder must contain the elements of the theme, which can include the following:

- A single skin file
- CSS files
- Images

Creating a Skin

A *skin* is a definition of styles applied to the server controls in your ASP.NET page. Skins can work in conjunction with CSS files or images. To create a theme to use in your ASP.NET applications, you use just a single skin file in the theme folder. The skin file can have any name, but it must have a `.skin` file extension.

Even though you have four theme folders in your application, concentrate on the creation of the Summer theme for the purposes of this chapter. Right-click the Summer folder, select Add New Item, and select Skin File from the listed options. Name the file **Summer.skin**. Then complete the skin file as shown in Listing 6-3.

Available for download on Wrox.com

LISTING 6-3 The Summer.skin file

```
<asp:Label runat="server" ForeColor="#004000" Font-Names="Verdana"
           Font-Size="X-Small" />

<asp:Textbox runat="server" ForeColor="#004000" Font-Names="Verdana"
           Font-Size="X-Small" BorderStyle="Solid" BorderWidth="1px"
           BorderColor="#004000" Font-Bold="True" />
```

```
<asp:Button runat="server" ForeColor="#004000" Font-Names="Verdana"
            Font-Size="X-Small" BorderStyle="Solid" BorderWidth="1px"
            BorderColor="#004000" Font-Bold="True" BackColor="#FFE0C0" />
```

Filename Summer.skin

This code is just a sampling of what the `Summer.skin` file should contain. To use it in a real application, you should actually make a definition for each and every server control option. In this case, you have a definition in place for three different types of server controls: Label, TextBox, and Button. After you save the `Summer.skin` file in the Summer folder, your file structure should look like Figure 6-5 from the Solution Explorer of Visual Studio 2010.

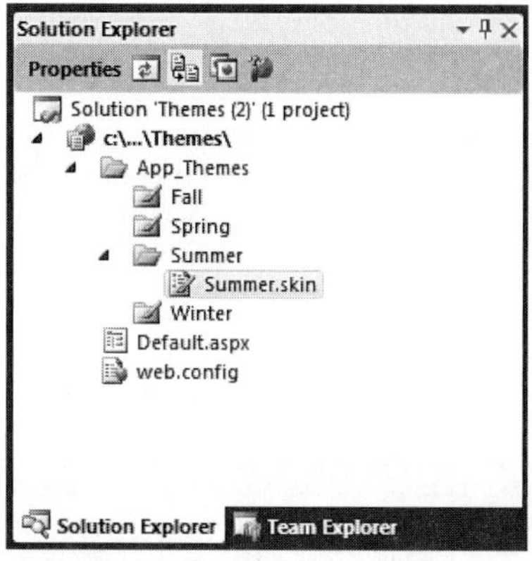

FIGURE 6-5

As with the regular server control definitions that you put on a typical `.aspx` page, these control definitions must contain the `runat="server"` attribute. If you specify this attribute in the skinned version of the control, you also include it in the server control you put on an `.aspx` page that uses this theme. Also notice that no `ID` attribute is specified in the skinned version of the control. If you specify an `ID` attribute here, you get an error when a page tries to use this theme.

As you can see, you can supply a lot of different visual definitions to these three controls, and these definitions should give the page a *summery* look and feel. An ASP.NET page in this project can then simply use this custom theme, as was shown earlier in this chapter (see also Listing 6-4).

LISTING 6-4: Using the Summer theme in an ASP.NET page

Available for download on Wrox.com

```
<%@ Page Language="VB" Theme="Summer" %>

<script runat="server">
   Protected Sub Button1_Click(ByVal sender As Object, ByVal e As System.EventArgs)
      Label1.Text = "Hello " & TextBox1.Text
   End Sub
</script>

<html xmlns="http://www.w3.org/1999/xhtml">
<head runat="server">
    <title>St. Louis .NET User Group</title>
</head>
<body>
    <form id="form1" runat="server">
        <asp:Textbox ID="TextBox1" runat="server">
        </asp:Textbox>
        <br />
        <br />
        <asp:Button ID="Button1" runat="server" Text="Submit Your Name"
         OnClick="Button1_Click" />
        <br />
        <br />
        <asp:Label ID="Label1" runat="server" />
    </form>
</body>
</html>
```

continues

LISTING 6-4 *(continued)*

C#

```
<%@ Page Language="C#" Theme="Summer" %>

<script runat="server">
    protected void Button1_Click(object sender, System.EventArgs e)
    {
        Label1.Text = "Hello " + TextBox1.Text.ToString();
    }
</script>
```

Looking at the server controls on this .aspx page, you can see that no styles are associated with them. They are just the default server controls that you drag and drop onto the design surface of Visual Studio 2010. There is, however, the style that you defined in the Summer.skin file, as shown in Figure 6-6.

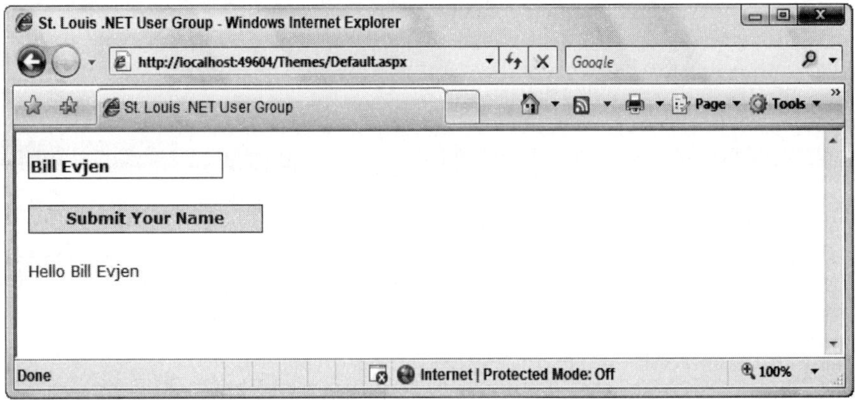

FIGURE 6-6

Including CSS Files in Your Themes

In addition to the server control definitions that you create from within a .skin file, you can make further definitions using Cascading Style Sheets (CSS). You might have noticed, when using a .skin file, that you could define only the styles associated with server controls and nothing else. However, developers usually use quite a bit more than server controls in their ASP.NET pages. For example, ASP.NET pages are routinely made up of HTML server controls, raw HTML, or even raw text. At present, the *Summer* theme has only a Summer.skin file associated with it. Any other items have no style whatsoever applied to them.

For a theme that goes beyond the server controls, you must further define the theme style so that HTML server controls, HTML, and raw text are all changed according to the theme. You achieve this task with a CSS file within your theme folder.

Creating CSS files for your themes when using Visual Studio 2010 is rather easy. Right-click the Summer theme folder and select Add New Item. In the list of options, select the option Style Sheet and name it Summer.css. The Summer.css file should be sitting right next to your Summer.skin file. This action creates an empty .css file for your theme. I will not go into the details of how to make a CSS file using Visual Studio 2010 and the CSS creation tool because Chapter 2 of this book covers these items. The process is also the same as in previous versions of Visual Studio. Just remember that the dialog that comes with Visual Studio 2010 enables you to completely define your CSS page with no need to actually code anything. A sample dialog is shown in Figure 6-7.

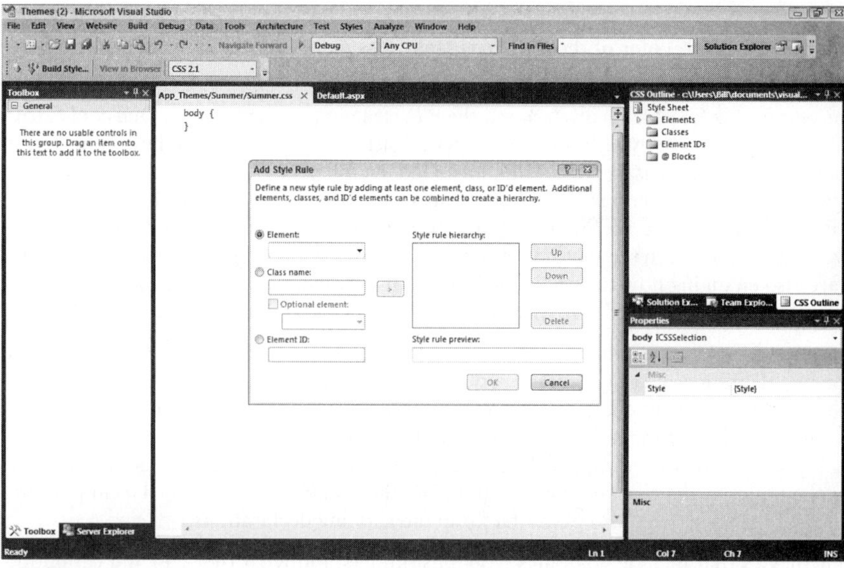

FIGURE 6-7

To create a comprehensive theme with this dialog, you define each HTML element that might appear in the ASP.NET page or you make use of class names or element IDs. This process can be a lot of work, but it is worth it in the end. For now, create a small CSS file that changes some of the non-server control items on your ASP.NET page. Listing 6-5 shows this CSS file.

LISTING 6-5: A CSS file with some definitions

Available for download on Wrox.com

```
body
{
 font-size: x-small;
 font-family: Verdana;
 color: #004000;
}

a:link {
 color: Blue;
 text-decoration: none;
}

a:visited
{
 color: Blue;
 text-decoration: none;
}

a:hover {
 color: Red;
 text-decoration: underline overline;
}
```

Filename Summer.css

In this CSS file, four things are defined. First, you define text that is found within the `<body>` tag of the page (basically all the text). Generally, plenty of text can appear in a typical ASP.NET page that is not placed inside an `<asp:Label>` or `<asp:Literal>` tag. Therefore, you can define how your text should appear in the CSS file; otherwise, your Web page may appear quite odd at times. In this case, a definition is in place for the size, the font family, and the color of the text. You make this definition the same as the one for the `<asp:Label>` server control in the `Summer.skin` file.

The next three definitions in this CSS file revolve around the `<a>` element (for hyperlinks). One cool feature that many Web pages use is responsive hyperlinks — or hyperlinks that change when you hover a mouse over them. The `A:link` definition defines what a typical link looks like on the page. The `A:visited` definition defines the look of the link if the end user has clicked on the link previously (without this definition, it is typically purple in IE). Then the `A:hover` definition defines the appearance of the hyperlink when the end user hovers the mouse over the link. You can see that not only are these three definitions changing the color of the hyperlink, but they are also changing how the underline is used. In fact, when the end user hovers the mouse over a hyperlink on a page using this CSS file, an underline and an overline appear on the link itself.

In CSS files, the order in which the style definitions appear in the `.css` file is important. A CSS file is an interpreted file — the first definition in the CSS file is applied first to the page, next the second definition is applied, and so forth. Some styles might change previous styles, so make sure your style definitions are in the proper order. For example, if you put the `A:hover` style definition first, you would never see it. The `A:link` and `A:visited` definitions would supersede it because they are defined after it. In addition to order, other factors such as the target media type, importance (whether the declaration is specified as important or normal), and the origin of the style sheet also play a factor in interpreting declarations.

In working with your themes that include `.css` files, you must understand what they can and cannot do for you. For example, examine an `.aspx` file that contains two text boxes — one text box created using a server control and another text box created using a typical `<input>` HTML element:

```
<asp:Textbox ID="TextBox1" runat="server" /> 
<input type="text" />
```

Suppose you have a definition for the TextBox server control in the `.skin` file:

```
<asp:Textbox runat="server" ForeColor="#004000" Font-Names="Verdana"
 BackColor="#ffffff" Font-Size="X-Small" BorderStyle="Solid" BorderWidth="1px"
 BorderColor="#004000" Font-Bold="True" />
```

However, what if you also have a definition in your `.css` file for each `<input>` element in the ASP.NET page as shown in the following?

```
INPUT
{
  background-color: black;
}
```

When you run the `.aspx` page with these kinds of style conflicts, the `.skin` file takes precedence over styles applied to every HTML element that is created using ASP.NET server controls regardless of what the `.css` file says. In fact, this sort of scenario gives you a page in which the `<input>` element that is created from the server control is white, as defined in the `.skin` file, and the second text box is black, as defined in the `.css` file (see Figure 6-8).

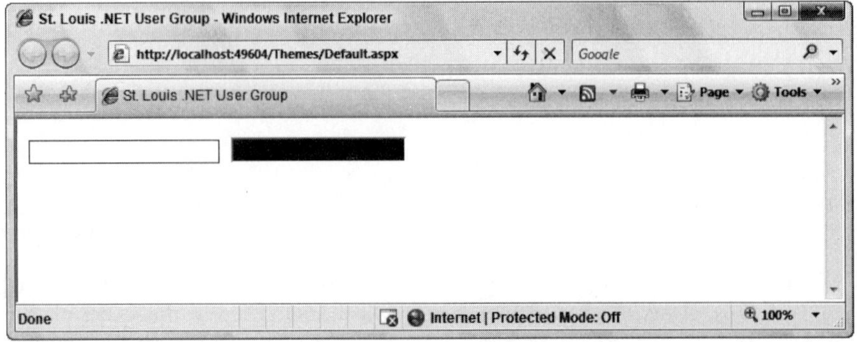

FIGURE 6-8

Again, other factors besides the order in which the items are defined can alter the appearance of your page. In addition to order, other factors such as the target media type, importance (whether the declaration is specified as important or normal), and the origin of the style sheet also play a factor in interpreting declarations.

Having Your Themes Include Images

Probably one of the coolest reasons why themes, rather than CSS, are the better approach for applying a consistent style to your Web page is that themes enable you to incorporate actual images into the style definitions.

Many controls use images to create a better visual appearance. The first step in incorporating images into your server controls that consistently use themes is to create an Images folder within the theme folder itself, as shown in Figure 6-9.

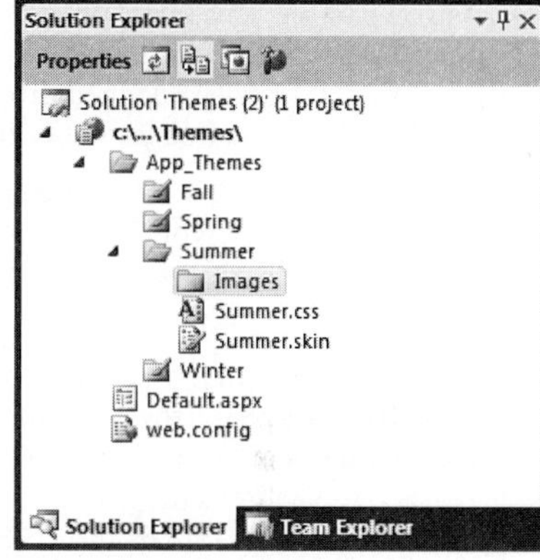

FIGURE 6-9

You have a couple of easy ways to use the images that you might place in this folder. The first is to incorporate the images directly from the `.skin` file itself. You can do so with the TreeView server control. The TreeView control can contain images used to open and close nodes for navigation purposes. You can place images in your theme for each and every TreeView control in your application. If you do so, you can then define the TreeView server control in the `.skin` file, as shown in Listing 6-6.

LISTING 6-6: Using images from the theme folder in a TreeView server control

Available for download on Wrox.com

```
<asp:TreeView runat="server" BorderColor="#FFFFFF" BackColor="#FFFFFF"
   ForeColor="#585880" Font-Size=".9em" Font-Names="Verdana"
   LeafNodeStyle-ImageUrl="images\summer_iconlevel.gif"
   RootNodeStyle-ImageUrl="images\summer_iconmain.gif"
   ParentNodeStyle-ImageUrl="images\summer_iconmain.gif" NodeIndent="30"
   CollapseImageUrl="images\summer_minus.gif"
   ExpandImageUrl="images\summer_plus.gif">
  ...
</asp:TreeView>
```

When you run a page containing a TreeView server control, it is populated with the images held in the Images folder of the theme.

Incorporating images into the TreeView control is easy. The control even specifically asks for an image location as an attribute. WebPart controls are used to build portals. Listing 6-7 is an example of a WebPart definition from a `.skin` file that incorporates images from the Images folder of the theme.

LISTING 6-7: Using images from the theme folder in a WebPartZone server control

Available for download on Wrox.com

```
<asp:WebPartZone ID="WebPartZone1" runat="server"
 DragHighlightColor="#6464FE" BorderStyle="double"
 BorderColor="#E7E5DB" BorderWidth="2pt" BackColor="#F8F8FC"
 cssclass="theme_fadeblue" Font-Size=".9em" Font-Names="Verdana">
    <FooterStyle ForeColor="#585880" BackColor="#CCCCCC"></FooterStyle>
    <HelpVerb ImageURL="images/SmokeAndGlass_help.gif"
     checked="False" enabled="True" visible="True"></HelpVerb>
    <CloseVerb ImageURL="images/SmokeAndGlass_close.gif"
     checked="False" enabled="True" visible="True"></CloseVerb>
    <RestoreVerb ImageURL="images/SmokeAndGlass_restore.gif"
     checked="False" enabled="True" visible="True"></RestoreVerb>
```

continues

LISTING 6-7 *(continued)*

```
    <MinimizeVerb ImageURL="images/SmokeAndGlass_minimize.gif"
     checked="False" enabled="True" visible="True"></MinimizeVerb>
    <EditVerb ImageURL="images/SmokeAndGlass_edit.gif"
     checked="False" enabled="True" visible="True"></EditVerb>
</asp:WebPartZone>
```

As you can see, this series of toolbar buttons, which is contained in a WebPartZone control, now uses images that come from the aforementioned `SmokeAndGlass` theme. When this WebPartZone is then generated, the style is defined directly from the `.skin` file, but the images specified in the `.skin` file are retrieved from the Images folder in the theme itself.

Not all server controls enable you to work with images directly from the Themes folder by giving you an `image` attribute to work with. If you don't have this capability, you must work with the `.skin` file and the CSS file together. If you do, you can place your theme-based images in any element you want. Next is a good example of how to do this.

Place the image that you want to use in the Images folder just as you normally would. Then define the use of the images in the `.css` file. The continued `SmokeAndGlass` example in Listing 6-8 demonstrates this technique.

LISTING 6-8: Part of the CSS file from SmokeAndGlass.css

Available for download on Wrox.com

```
.theme_header {
 background-image :url( images/smokeandglass_brownfadetop.gif);
}

.theme_highlighted {
 background-image :url( images/smokeandglass_blueandwhitef.gif);
}

.theme_fadeblue {
 background-image :url( images/smokeandglass_fadeblue.gif);
}
```

These styles are not for a specific HTML element; instead, they are CSS classes that you can put into any HTML element that you want. In this case, each CSS class mentioned here is defining a specific background image to use for the element.

After it is defined in the CSS file, you can utilize this CSS class in the `.skin` file when defining your server controls. Listing 6-9 shows you how.

LISTING 6-9: Using the CSS class in one of the server controls defined in the .skin file

Available for download on Wrox.com

```
<asp:Calendar runat="server" BorderStyle="double" BorderColor="#E7E5DB"
 BorderWidth="2" BackColor="#F8F7F4" Font-Size=".9em" Font-Names="Verdana">
    <TodayDayStyle BackColor="#F8F7F4" BorderWidth="1" BorderColor="#585880"
     ForeColor="#585880" />
    <OtherMonthDayStyle BackColor="transparent" ForeColor="#CCCCCC" />
    <SelectedDayStyle ForeColor="#6464FE" BackColor="transparent"
      CssClass="theme_highlighted" />
    <TitleStyle Font-Bold="True" BackColor="#CCCCCC" ForeColor="#585880"
      BorderColor="#CCCCCC" BorderWidth="1pt" CssClass="theme_header" />
    <NextPrevStyle Font-Bold="True" ForeColor="#585880"
     BorderColor="transparent" BackColor="transparent" />
    <DayStyle ForeColor="#000000"
     BorderColor="transparent" BackColor="transparent" />
    <SelectorStyle Font-Bold="True" ForeColor="#696969" BackColor="#F8F7F4" />
    <WeekendDayStyle Font-Bold="False" ForeColor="#000000"
     BackColor="transparent" />
```

```
        <DayHeaderStyle Font-Bold="True" ForeColor="#585880"
         BackColor="Transparent" />
    </asp:Calendar>
```

This Calendar server control definition from a `.skin` file uses one of the earlier CSS classes in its definition. It actually uses an image that is specified in the CSS file in two different spots within the control (shown in bold). It is first specified in the `<SelectedDayStyle>` element. Here you see the attribute and value `CssClass="theme_highlighted"`. The other spot is within the `<TitleStyle>` element. In this case, it is using `theme_header`. When the control is rendered, these CSS classes are referenced and finally point to the images that are defined in the CSS file.

FIGURE 6-10

Interestingly, the images used here for the header of the Calendar control don't really have much to them. The `smokeandglass_brownfadetop.gif` image used for this example is simply a thin, gray sliver, as shown in Figure 6-10.

This very small image (in this case, very thin) is actually repeated as often as necessary to make it equal the length of the header in the Calendar control. The image is lighter at the top and darkens toward the bottom. Repeating the image horizontally gives a three-dimensional effect to the control. Try it out, and you can get the result shown in Figure 6-11.

FIGURE 6-11

DEFINING MULTIPLE SKIN OPTIONS

Using the themes technology in ASP.NET, you can have a single theme; but also, within the theme's `.skin` file, you can have specific controls that are defined in multiple ways. You can frequently take advantage of this feature within your themes. For example, you might have text box elements scattered throughout your application, but you might not want each and every text box to have the same visual appearance. In this case, you can create multiple versions of the `<asp:Textbox>` server control within your `.skin` file. In Listing 6-10 you see how to create multiple versions of the `<asp:Textbox>` control in the `.skin` file from Listing 6-3.

Available for download on Wrox.com

LISTING 6-10: The Summer.skin file, which contains multiple versions of the <asp:Textbox> server control

```
<asp:Label runat="server" ForeColor="#004000" Font-Names="Verdana"
           Font-Size="X-Small" />

<asp:Textbox runat="server" ForeColor="#004000" Font-Names="Verdana"
           Font-Size="X-Small" BorderStyle="Solid" BorderWidth="1px"
           BorderColor="#004000" Font-Bold="True" />

<asp:Textbox runat="server" ForeColor="#000000" Font-Names="Verdana"
           Font-Size="X-Small" BorderStyle="Dotted" BorderWidth="5px"
           BorderColor="#000000" Font-Bold="False" SkinID="TextboxDotted" />

<asp:Textbox runat="server" ForeColor="#000000" Font-Names="Arial"
           Font-Size="X-Large" BorderStyle="Dashed" BorderWidth="3px"
           BorderColor="#000000" Font-Bold="False" SkinID="TextboxDashed" />

<asp:Button runat="server" ForeColor="#004000" Font-Names="Verdana"
           Font-Size="X-Small" BorderStyle="Solid" BorderWidth="1px"
           BorderColor="#004000" Font-Bold="True" BackColor="#FFE0C0" />
```

In this .skin file, you can see three definitions in place for the TextBox server control. The first one is the same as before. Although the second and third definitions have a different style, they also contain a new attribute in the definition — SkinID. To create multiple definitions of a single element, you use the SkinID attribute to differentiate among the definitions. The value used in the SkinID can be anything you want. In this case, it is TextboxDotted and TextboxDashed.

Note that no SkinID attribute is used for the first <asp:Textbox> definition. By not using one, you are saying that this is the default style definition to use for each <asp:Textbox> control on an ASP.NET page that uses this theme but has no pointer to a particular SkinID.

Take a look at a sample .aspx page that uses this .skin file in Listing 6-11.

Available for download on Wrox.com

LISTING 6-11: A sample .aspx page that uses the Summer.skin file with multiple text box style definitions

```
<%@ Page Language="VB" Theme="Summer" %>

<html xmlns="http://www.w3.org/1999/xhtml">
<head runat="server">
    <title>Different SkinIDs</title>
</head>
<body>
    <form id="form1" runat="server">
    <p>
        <asp:Textbox ID="TextBox1" runat="server">Textbox1</asp:Textbox>
    </p><p>
        <asp:Textbox ID="TextBox2" runat="server"
         SkinId="TextboxDotted">Textbox2</asp:Textbox>
    </p><p>

        <asp:Textbox ID="TextBox3" runat="server"
         SkinId="TextboxDashed">Textbox3</asp:Textbox>
    </p>
    </form>
</body>
</html>
```

This small .aspx page shows three text boxes, each of a different style. When you run this page, you get the results shown in Figure 6-12.

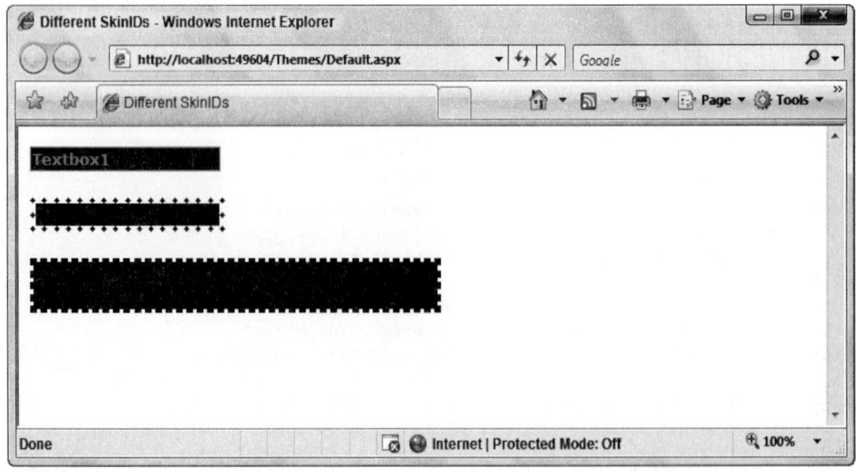

FIGURE 6-12

The first text box does not point to any particular SkinID in the .skin file. Therefore, the default skin is used. As stated before, the default skin is the one in the .skin file that does not have a SkinID attribute in it. The second text box then contains SkinID="TextboxDotted" and, therefore, inherits the style definition defined in the TextboxDotted skin in the Summer.skin file. The third text box takes the SkinID TextboxDashed and is also changed appropriately.

As you can see, defining multiple versions of a control that you can use throughout your entire application is quite simple.

PROGRAMMATICALLY WORKING WITH THEMES

So far, you have seen examples of working with ASP.NET themes in a declarative fashion, but you can also work with themes programmatically.

Assigning the Page's Theme Programmatically

To programmatically assign the theme to the page, use the construct shown in Listing 6-12.

LISTING 6-12: Assigning the theme of the page programmatically

Available for download on Wrox.com

```
<script runat="server">
    Protected Sub Page_PreInit(ByVal sender As Object, ByVal e As System.EventArgs)
        Page.Theme = Request.QueryString("ThemeChange")
    End Sub
</script>
```

C#

```
<script runat="server">
    protected void Page_PreInit(object sender, System.EventArgs e)
    {
        Page.Theme = Request.QueryString["ThemeChange"];
    }
</script>
```

You must set the Theme of the Page property in or before the Page_PreInit event for any static controls that are on the page. If you are working with dynamic controls, set the Theme property before adding it to the Controls collection.

Assigning a Control's SkinID Programmatically

Another option is to assign a specific server control's SkinID property programmatically (see Listing 6-13).

LISTING 6-13: Assigning the server control's SkinID property programmatically

Available for download on Wrox.com

```
<script runat="server">
    Protected Sub Page_PreInit(ByVal sender As Object, ByVal e As System.EventArgs)
        TextBox1.SkinID = "TextboxDashed"
    End Sub
</script>
```

C#

```
<script runat="server">
    protected void Page_PreInit(object sender, System.EventArgs e)
    {
        TextBox1.SkinID = "TextboxDashed";
    }
</script>
```

Again, you assign this property before or in the Page_PreInit event in your code.

THEMES, SKINS, AND CUSTOM CONTROLS

If you are building custom controls in an ASP.NET world, understand that end users can also apply themes to the controls that they use in their pages. By default, your custom controls are theme-enabled whether your custom control inherits from `Control` or `WebControl`.

To disable theming for your control, you can simply use the `Themeable` attribute on your class, as shown in Listing 6-14.

LISTING 6-14: Disabling theming for your custom controls

Available for download on Wrox.com

VB

```
Imports System
Imports System.Collections.Generic
Imports System.ComponentModel
Imports System.Text
Imports System.Web
Imports System.Web.UI
Imports System.Web.UI.WebControls

<DefaultProperty("HeaderText"), _
 ToolboxData("<{0}:WebCustomControl1 runat=server></{0}:WebCustomControl1>"), _
   Themeable(False)> _
Public Class WebCustomControl1
    Inherits WebControl

    <Bindable(True), Category("Appearance"), DefaultValue("Enter Value"), _
     Localizable(True)> Property HeaderText() As String
        Get
            Dim s As String = CStr(ViewState("HeaderText"))
            If s Is Nothing Then
                Return String.Empty
            Else
                Return s
            End If
        End Get

        Set(ByVal Value As String)
            ViewState("HeaderText") = Value
        End Set
    End Property


    Protected Overrides Sub RenderContents(ByVal output As HtmlTextWriter)
        output.Write("<h1>" & HeaderText & "<h1>")
    End Sub

End Class
```

C#

```
using System;
using System.Collections.Generic;
using System.ComponentModel;
using System.Text;
using System.Web;
using System.Web.UI;
using System.Web.UI.WebControls;

namespace ControlForThemes

{
    [DefaultProperty("HeaderText")]
    [ToolboxData("<{0}:WebCustomControl1 runat=server></{0}:WebCustomControl1>")]
```

```
        [Themeable(false)]
        public class WebCustomControl1 : WebControl
        {
            [Bindable(true)]
            [Category("Appearance")]
            [DefaultValue("Enter Value")]
            [Localizable(true)]
            public string HeaderText
            {
                get
                {
                    String s = (String)ViewState["HeaderText"];
                    return ((s == null) ? String.Empty : s);
                }

                set
                {
                    ViewState["HeaderText"] = value;
                }
            }

            protected override void RenderContents(HtmlTextWriter output)
            {
                output.Write("<h1>" + HeaderText + "<h1>");
            }
        }
    }
```

Looking over the code from the preceding example, you can see that theming was disabled by applying the `Themeable` attribute to the class and setting it to `False`.

You can use a similar approach to disable theming for the individual properties that might be in your custom controls, as shown in Listing 6-15.

LISTING 6-15: Disabling theming for properties in your custom controls

Available for download on Wrox.com

VB

```
<Bindable(True), Category("Appearance"), DefaultValue("Enter Value"), _
  Localizable(True), Themeable(False)> Property HeaderText() As String
    Get
        Dim s As String = CStr(ViewState("HeaderText"))
        If s Is Nothing Then
            Return String.Empty
        Else
            Return s
        End If
    End Get

    Set(ByVal Value As String)
        ViewState("HeaderText") = Value
    End Set
End Property
```

```
    [Bindable(true)]
    [Category("Appearance")]
    [DefaultValue("Enter Value")]
    [Localizable(true)]
    [Themeable(false)]
    public string HeaderText
    {
        get
        {
            String s = (String)ViewState["HeaderText"];
```

continues

LISTING 6-15 *(continued)*

```
                return ((s == null) ? String.Empty : s);
            }

            set
            {
                ViewState["HeaderText"] = value;
            }
        }
```

In this case, you set the `Themeable` attribute at the property level to `False` in the same manner as you did at the class level.

If you have enabled themes for these items, how would you go about applying a theme definition to a custom control? For this example, use the custom server control shown in Listing 6-14, but set the `Themeable` attributes to `True`. Next, create a `.skin` file in a theme and add the control to the theme as you would any other ASP.NET server control, as shown in Listing 6-16.

LISTING 6-16: Changing properties in a custom control in the .skin file

Available for download on Wrox.com

```
<%@ Register Assembly="ControlForThemes" Namespace="ControlForThemes"
    TagPrefix="cc1" %>
<cc1:webcustomcontrol1 runat="server" HeaderText="FROM THE SKIN FILE" />
```

When defining custom server controls in your themes, you use the same approach as you would when placing a custom server control inside of a standard ASP.NET `.aspx` page. In Listing 6-16, you can see that the custom server control is registered in the `.skin` file using the `@Register` page directive. This directive gives the custom control a `TagPrefix` value of `cc1`. Note that the `TagPrefix` values presented in this page can be different from those presented in any other `.aspx` page that uses the same custom control. The only things that have to be the same are the `Assembly` and `Namespace` attributes that point to the specific control being defined in the file. Also note the control definition in the skin file, as with other standard controls, does not require that you specify an `ID` attribute, but only the `runat` attribute along with any other property that you want to override.

Next, create a standard `.aspx` page that uses your custom server control. Before running the page, be sure to apply the defined theme on the page using the `Theme` attribute in the `@Page` directive. With everything in place, running the page produces the following results in the browser:

```
FROM THE SKIN FILE
```

This value, which was specified in the skin file, is displayed no matter what you apply as the `HeaderText` value in the server control.

In addition to changing values of custom properties that are contained in server control, you can also change the inherited properties that come from `WebControl`. For example, you can change settings in your skin file as shown in Listing 6-17.

LISTING 6-17: Changing inherited properties in the custom control

Available for download on Wrox.com

```
<%@ Register Assembly="ControlForThemes" Namespace="ControlForThemes"
    TagPrefix="cc1" %>
<cc1:webcustomcontrol1 runat="server" BackColor="Gray" />
```

With this code in place, you have changed one of the inherited properties from the skin file. This setting changes the background color of the server control to gray (even if it is set to something else in the control itself). Figure 6-13 shows the result.

You can find more information on building your own custom server controls in Chapter 25.

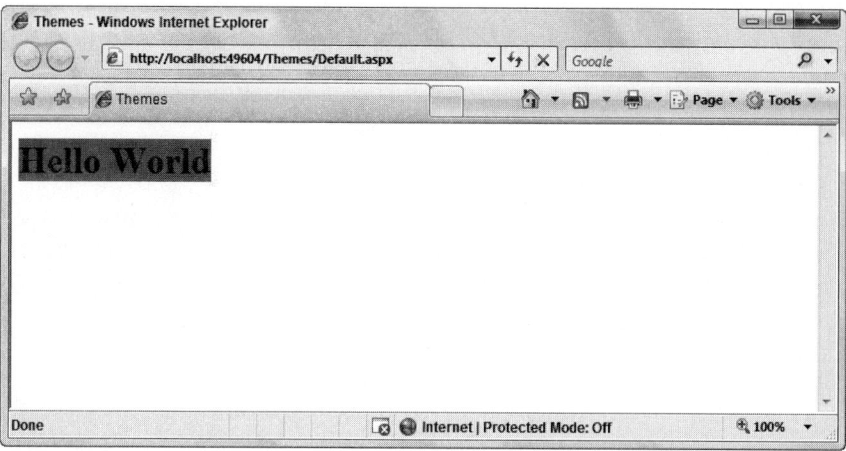

FIGURE 6-13

SUMMARY

With the availability of themes and skins in ASP.NET 4, applying a consistent look and feel across your entire application is quite easy. Remember that themes can contain only simple server control definitions in a `.skin` file or elaborate style definitions, which include not only `.skin` files, but also CSS style definitions and even images!

As you will see later in the book, you can use themes in conjunction with the personalization features that ASP.NET provides. This personalization enables your end users to customize their experiences by selecting their own themes. Your application can present a theme just for them, and it can remember their choices through the APIs that ASP.NET 4 offers.

Data Binding

WHAT'S IN THIS CHAPTER?

- Working with data source controls
- Using inline data-binding syntax
- Data-binding expressions

When it was originally released, one of the most exciting features of ASP.NET was its ability to bind entire collections of data to controls at runtime without requiring you to write large amounts of code. The controls understood they were data-bound and would render the appropriate HTML for each item in the data collection. Additionally, you could bind the controls to any type of data sources, from simple arrays to complex Oracle database query results. This was a huge step forward from ASP, in which each developer was responsible for writing all the data access code, looping through a recordset, and manually rendering the appropriate HTML code for each record of data.

In later versions of ASP.NET Microsoft took the concept of server-side data binding and expanded it to make it even easier to understand and use by introducing a new layer of data abstraction called data source controls, simplifying how you add data to your application. It also brought into the toolbox a series of new and powerful databound controls such as the GridView, DetailsView, ListView, and FormView.

This chapter explores these server-side data source controls, and describes other data-binding features in ASP.NET. It shows how you can use the data source controls to easily and quickly bind data to data-bound controls. It also focuses on the power of the data-bound list controls included in ASP.NET. Finally, you take a look at changes in the inline data binding syntax and inline XML data binding.

ASP.NET also includes the ability to perform data binding on the client side using its AJAX library. The client-side binding capabilities of ASP.NET are discussed in Chapter 18.

DATA SOURCE CONTROLS

In ASP.NET 1.0/1.1, you typically performed a data-binding operation by writing some data access code to retrieve a `DataReader` or a `DataSet` object; then you bound that data object to a server control such as a DataGrid, DropDownList, or ListBox. If you wanted to update or delete the bound data, you were then responsible for writing the data access code to do that. Listing 7-1 shows a typical example of a data-binding operation in ASP.NET 1.0/1.1.

LISTING 7-1: Typical data-binding operation in ASP.NET 1.0/1.1

VB

```
Dim conn As New SqlConnection()
Dim cmd As New SqlCommand("SELECT * FROM Customers", conn)

Dim da As New SqlDataAdapter(cmd)

Dim ds As New DataSet()
da.Fill(ds)

DataGrid1.DataSource = ds
DataGrid1.DataBind()
```

C#

```
SqlConnection conn = new SqlConnection();
SqlCommand cmd = new SqlCommand("SELECT * FROM Customers", conn);

SqlDataAdapter da = new SqlDataAdapter(cmd);

DataSet ds = new DataSet();
da.Fill(ds);

DataGrid1.DataSource = ds;
DataGrid1.DataBind();
```

Since ASP.NET 1.0/1.1, ASP.NET has introduced an additional layer of abstraction through the use of data source controls. As shown in Figure 7-1, these controls abstract the use of an underlying data provider, such as the SQL Data Provider or the OLE DB Data Provider. This means you no longer need to concern yourself with the hows and whys of using the data providers, instead letting the data source controls do the heavy lifting for you. You need to know only where your data is and, if necessary, how to construct a query for performing CRUD (Create, Retrieve, Update, and Delete) operations.

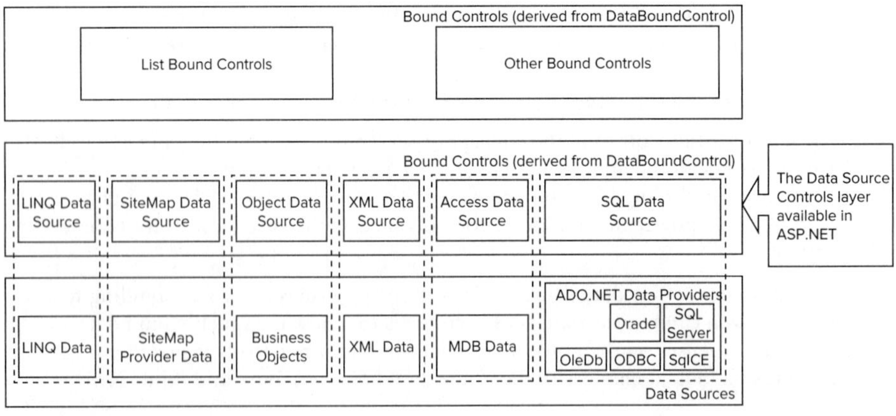

FIGURE 7-1

Additionally, because the data source controls all derive from the `Control` class, you can use them much as you would any other Web Server control. For instance, you can define and control the behavior of the data source control either declaratively in declarative markup or programmatically. This means you can perform all manner of data access and manipulation without ever having to write one line of code. In fact, although you certainly can control the data source controls from code, most of the samples in this chapter show you how to perform powerful database queries using nothing more than the Visual Studio 2010 wizards and declarative syntax.

ASP.NET has seven built-in data source controls, each used for a specific type of data access. Table 7-1 lists and describes each data source control.

TABLE 7-1

CONTROL NAME	DESCRIPTION
SqlDataSource control	Provides access to any data source that has an ADO.NET Data Provider available; by default, the control has access to the ODBC, OLE DB, SQL Server, Oracle, and SQL Server CE providers.
LinqDataSource control	Provides access to different types of data objects using LINQ queries.
ObjectDataSource control	Provides specialized data access to business objects or other classes that return data.
XmlDataSource control	Provides specialized data access to XML documents, either physically or in memory.
SiteMapDataSource control	Provides specialized access to site map data for a Web site that is stored by the site map provider.
AccessDataSource control	Provides specialized access to Access databases.
EntityDataSource	Provides specialized access to an Entity Data Model (EDM).

All the data source controls are derived from either the `DataSourceControl` class or the `HierachicalDataSourceControl` class, both of which are derived from `Control` and implement the `IDataSource` and `IListSource` interfaces. This means that although each control is designed for use with a specific source of data, they all share a basic set of core functionality. It also means that should you need to, you can easily create your own custom data source controls based on the structure of your specific data sources.

SqlDataSource Control

The SqlDataSource control is the data source control to use if your data is stored in a SQL Server, SQL Server Express, Oracle Server, ODBC data source, OLE DB data source, or Windows SQL CE Database. The control provides an easy-to-use wizard that walks you through the configuration process, or you can modify the control manually by changing the control attributes directly in Source view. In this section you see by using the control's wizard how you can create and configure a SqlDataSource control, as well as how you can add filters to the queries executed by the control. After you complete the configuration, you can examine the source code it generates. In later sections of this book, you see how in conjunction with other data controls like GridView, you can allow users to update and delete data through the SqlDataSource control.

Begin using the control by opening an ASP.NET Web page inside a Visual Studio Web site project and dragging the SqlDataSource control from the toolbox onto the form. You find all the data-related controls located under the Data section in the Visual Studio toolbox.

Configuring a Data Connection

After the control has been dropped onto the Web page, you need to tell it what database connection it should use. The easiest way to do this is by using the Configure Data Source Wizard, shown in Figure 7-2. Launch this wizard by selecting the Configure Data Source option from the data source control's smart tag menu.

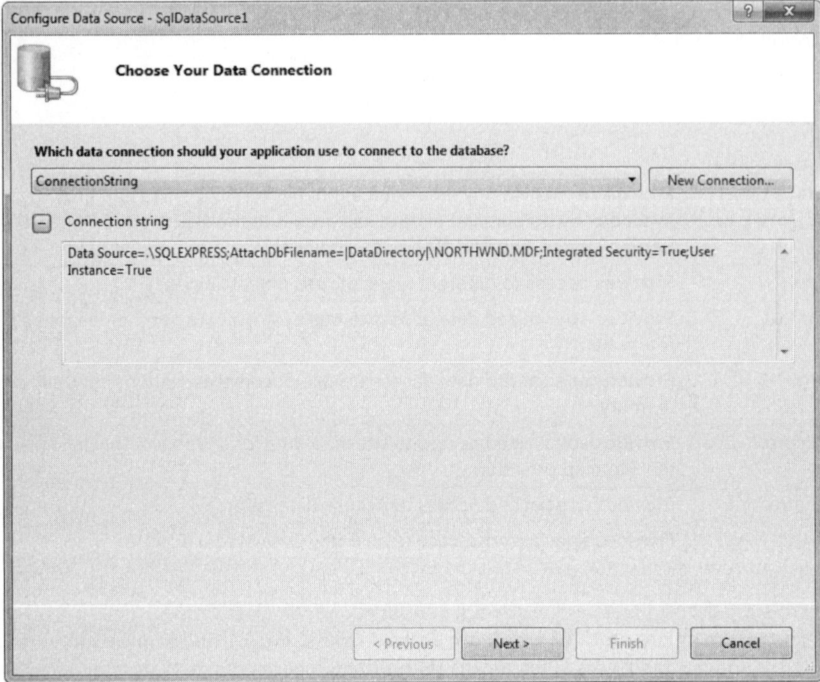

FIGURE 7-2

After the wizard opens, you can select an existing database connection from the drop-down list or create a new connection. Most of the samples shown in this chapter use the Northwind database as their data source, so if it does not already exist, you can create a new connection to the Northwind database.

Beginning with Microsoft SQL Server 2005, Microsoft no longer includes the Northwind sample database as part of the standard installation. You can still download the installation scripts for the sample database from the following location:

`www.microsoft.com/downloads/details.aspx?FamilyId=06616212-0356-46A0-8DA2-EEBC53A68034&displaylang=en`

To create a new connection, click the New Connection button to open the Choose Data Source dialog. This dialog allows you to select the specific data source for this connection and the data provider to use for the data source.

The list of providers is generated from the data contained in the `DbProviderFactory` *node of the* `machine.config` *file. If you have additional providers to display in the wizard you can modify your* `machine.config` *file to include specific providers' information.*

After you've selected the source and provider, click the Continue button to open the Add Connection dialog. This dialog allows you to set all the properties of the new database connection. Figure 7-3 shows the dialog for configuring a SQL Server database connection.

Simply fill in the appropriate information for your database connection, click the Test Connection button to verify that your connection information is correct, and then click OK to return to the Configure Data Source wizard.

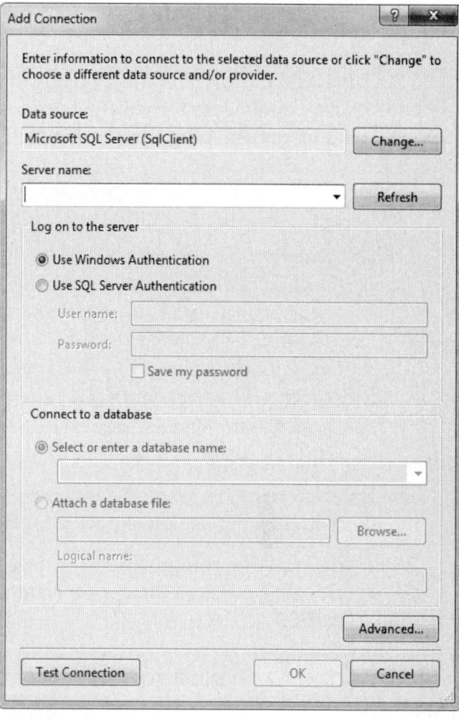

FIGURE 7-3

After you have returned to the Configure Data Source Wizard, notice that the connection you created is listed in the available connections drop-down list. When you select a connection from the drop-down the connection information shows in the Data Connection info area. This allows you to easily review the connection information for the Connection selected in the drop-down list.

Click the Next button to continue to the wizard's next step, which allows you to save your database connection information to your `web.config` file. Storing the connection here can make maintenance and deployment of your application easier. This screen allows you to specify the key under which the connection information should be stored in the configuration file. Should you choose not to store your connection information in the `web.config` file, it is stored in the actual `.aspx` page as a property of the `SqlDataSource` control named `ConnectionString`. If the provider chosen was not the SQL Data Provider, a property named `ProviderName` will be used to store that setting.

The next step in the wizard allows you to select the data to retrieve from the database. As you can see in Figure 7-4, a drop-down list of all the tables and views available in the database is shown. You can select a table or view, and the specific columns you want to include in the query. Select all columns available using an asterisk (*), or choose specific columns by selecting the check box located next to each column name.

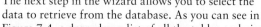

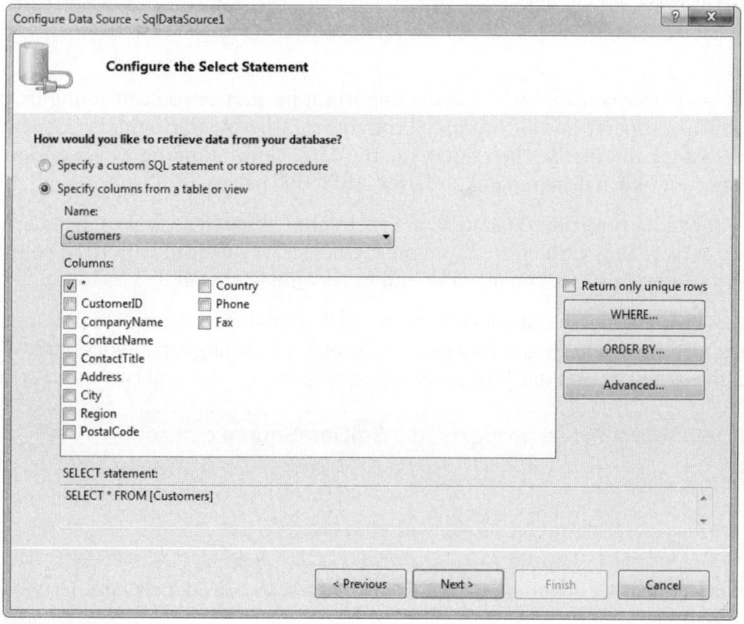

FIGURE 7-4

The WHERE and ORDER BY buttons allow you to specify `WHERE` and `ORDER BY` clauses for filtering and sorting the results of the query. For now, do not enter any additional `WHERE` or `ORDER BY` settings.

The Advanced button contains two advanced options. You can have the wizard generate `INSERT`, `UPDATE`, and `DELETE` statements for your data, based on the `SELECT` statement you created. You can also configure the data source control to use Optimistic Concurrency to prevent data concurrency issues.

Optimistic Concurrency is a database technique that can help you prevent the accidental overwriting of data. When Optimistic Concurrency is enabled, the Update and Delete SQL statements used by the SqlDataSource control are modified so that they include both the original and updated values. When the queries are executed, the data in the targeted record is compared to the SqlDataSource controls' original values and if a difference is found, which indicates that the data has changed since it was originally retrieved by the SqlDataSource control, the Update or Delete will not occur.

The final screen of the wizard allows you to preview the data selected by your data source control to verify the query is working as you expect it to. Simply click the Finish button to complete the wizard.

When you are done configuring your data connection, change to Source view in Visual Studio to see how the wizard has generated the appropriate attributes for your control. It should look something like the code in Listing 7-2.

LISTING 7-2: Typical sqldatasource control generated by visual studio

Available for download on Wrox.com

```
<asp:SqlDataSource ID="SqlDataSource1" Runat="server"
    SelectCommand="SELECT * FROM [Customers]"
    ConnectionString="<%$ ConnectionStrings:ConnectionString %>" />
```

You can see that the control uses a declarative syntax to configure which connection it should use by creating a `ConnectionString` attribute, and what query to execute by creating a `SelectCommand` attribute. A little later in this chapter, you look at how to configure the `SqlDataSource` control to execute `INSERT`, `UPDATE`, and `DELETE` commands as this data changes.

Data Source Mode Property

After you've set up a basic SqlDataSource control, one of many important properties you can configure is the `DataSourceMode` property. This property allows you to tell the control whether it should use a `DataSet` (the default selection) or a `DataReader` internally when retrieving the data. Understanding which option is right for your application is important when designing data-driven ASP.NET pages.

If you choose to use a `DataReader`, data is retrieved using what is commonly known as *firehose mode*, or using a forward-only, read-only cursor. This is the fastest and most efficient way to read data from your data source because a `DataReader` does not have the memory and processing overhead of a `DataSet`.

Choosing to use a `DataSet` makes the data source control more powerful by enabling the control to perform other operations such as filtering, sorting, and paging. It also enables the built-in caching capabilities of the control. The code in Listing 7-3 shows how to add the `DataSourceMode` property to your SqlDataSource control.

LISTING 7-3: Adding the DataSourceMode property to a SqlDataSource control

Available for download on Wrox.com

```
<asp:SqlDataSource ID="SqlDataSource1" Runat="server"
    SelectCommand="SELECT * FROM [Customers]"
    ConnectionString="<%$ ConnectionStrings:ConnectionString %>"
    DataSourceMode="DataSet" />
```

Each `DataSourceMode` option offers distinct advantages and disadvantages, so consider this property carefully when designing your Web site.

Filtering Data Using SelectParameters

Of course, when selecting data from your data source, you may not want to get every single row of data from a view or table. You want to be able to specify parameters in your query to limit the data that is returned. You saw that by using the Configure Data Source Wizard you can add WHERE clauses to your query. "Under the hood" the wizard is actually using the SqlDataSource's SelectParameters collection to create parameters that it uses at runtime to filter the data returned from the query.

The SelectParameters collection consists of types that derive from the Parameters class. You can combine any number of parameters in the collection. The data source control then uses these to create a dynamic SQL query. Table 7-2 lists and describes the available parameter types.

TABLE 7-2

PARAMETER	DESCRIPTION
ControlParameter	Uses the value of a property of the specified control
CookieParameter	Uses the key value of a cookie
FormParameter	Uses the key value from the Forms collection
QueryStringParameter	Uses a key value from the QueryString collection
ProfileParameter	Uses a key value from the user's profile
SessionParameter	Uses a key value from the current user's session

Because all the parameter controls derive from the Parameter class, they all contain several useful common properties. Some of these properties are shown in Table 7-3.

TABLE 7-3

PROPERTY	DESCRIPTION
Type	Allows you to strongly type the value of the parameter
ConvertEmptyStringToNull	Indicates the control should convert the value assigned to it to Null if it is equal to System.String.Empty
DefaultValue	Allows you to specify a default value for the parameter if it is evaluated as Null

The code in Listing 7-4 shows an example of adding a QueryStringParameter to the SelectParameters collection of the SqlDataSource control. As you can see, the SelectCommand query has been modified to include a WHERE clause. When you run this code, the value of the query string field ID is bound to the @CustomerID placeholder in your SelectCommand, allowing you to select only those customers whose CustomerID field matches the value of the query string field.

Available for download on Wrox.com

LISTING 7-4: Filtering select data using SelectParameter controls

```
<asp:SqlDataSource ID="SqlDataSource1" Runat="server"
    SelectCommand="SELECT * FROM [Customers]
                   WHERE ([CustomerID] = @CustomerID)"
    ConnectionString="<%$ ConnectionStrings:ConnectionString %>"
    DataSourceMode="DataSet">
    <SelectParameters>
        <asp:QueryStringParameter Name="CustomerID"
            QueryStringField="ID" Type="String">
        </asp:QueryStringParameter>
    </SelectParameters>
</asp:SqlDataSource>
```

In addition to using the Configure Data Source Wizard to create the `SelectParameters` collection, you can manually define them in markup, or create parameters using the Command and Parameter Editor dialog, which you access by modifying the `SelectQuery` property of the SqlDataSource control while you are viewing the Web page in design mode. Figure 7-5 shows the Command and Parameter Editor dialog.

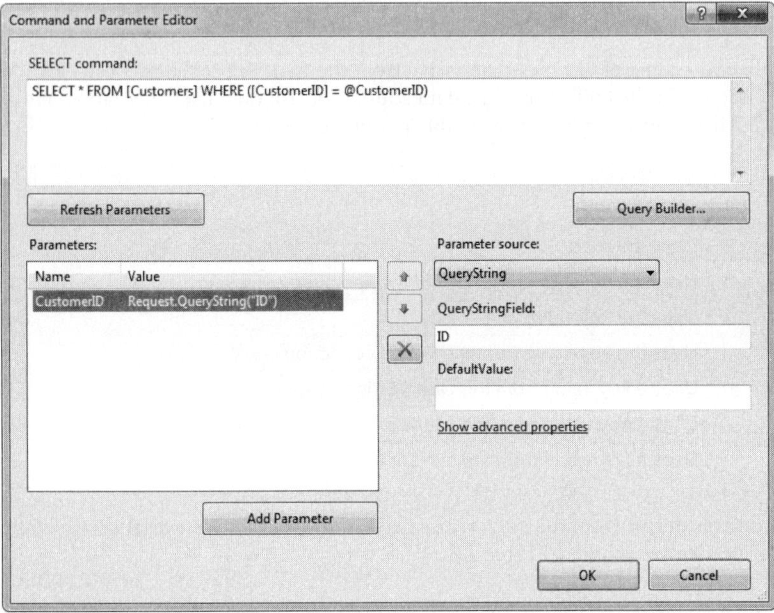

FIGURE 7-5

This dialog gives you another fast and friendly way to create `SelectParameters` for your query. Simply select the Parameter source from the drop-down list and enter the required parameter data. Figure 7-5 demonstrates how to add the `QueryStringParameter` based on the value of the `querystring` field ID to your SqlDataSource control.

The SqlDataSource control includes an additional way to filter results called the `FilterParameters`. `FilterParameters` provide the same basic filtering capabilities as `SelectParameters`, but using a different technique. The specific differences between `SelectParameters` and `FilterParameters` are discussed later in this chapter.

ConflictDetection Property

The `ConflictDetection` property allows you to tell the SqlDataSource control to enable the detection of data conflicts, also called data concurrency, before updating or deleting data. Conflict detection allows you to prevent users from accidentally overwriting each other's updates when more than one user is updating the same database data. When the property is set to `OverwriteChanges`, the control uses a *Last in Wins* style of updating data. In this style, the control updates the database data regardless of any changes that may have been made to it between the time it was retrieved by the control and the time the update is made.

If the value is set to `CompareAllValues`, the data source control first compares the data originally retrieved by it to the data currently in the database. If the control detects differences between the original data and what is currently in the database, it does not allow the update to continue. Otherwise it updates the data.

Listing 7-5 shows how to add the `ConflictDetection` property to the SqlDataSource control.

LISTING 7-5: Adding the ConflictDetection property to a SqlDataSource control

Available for download on Wrox.com

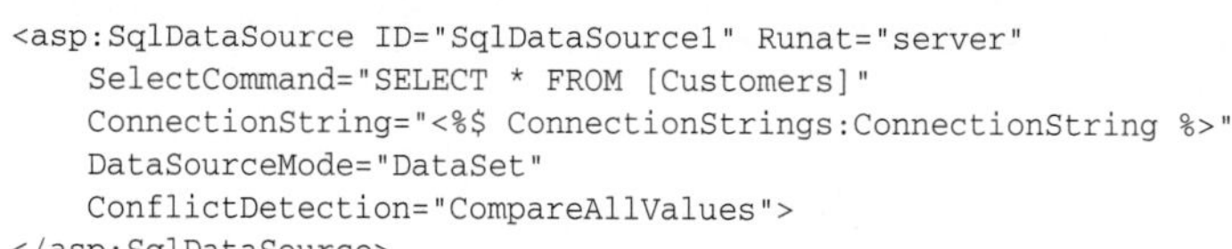

```
<asp:SqlDataSource ID="SqlDataSource1" Runat="server"
    SelectCommand="SELECT * FROM [Customers]"
    ConnectionString="<%$ ConnectionStrings:ConnectionString %>"
    DataSourceMode="DataSet"
    ConflictDetection="CompareAllValues">
</asp:SqlDataSource>
```

As described earlier, you can use the Configure Data Source Wizard to enable Conflict Detection in the control. Doing this automatically adds the `ConflictDetection` attribute to the control and sets it to `CompareAllValues`. The wizard modifies the `Update` and `Delete` parameter collections to include parameters for the original data values as well. It also modifies the SQL statement of the control so that it compares the original data values to the new values. You can recognize the newly added parameters because the wizard simply prepends the prefix `original` to each data column name. Listing 7-6 shows you what the modified `UpdateParameters` looks like.

LISTING 7-6: Adding original value parameters to the UpdateParameters collection

Available for download on Wrox.com

```
<UpdateParameters>
    <asp:Parameter Name="CompanyName" Type="String" />
    <asp:Parameter Name="ContactName" Type="String" />
    <asp:Parameter Name="ContactTitle" Type="String" />
    <asp:Parameter Name="Address" Type="String" />
    <asp:Parameter Name="City" Type="String" />
    <asp:Parameter Name="Region" Type="String" />
    <asp:Parameter Name="PostalCode" Type="String" />
    <asp:Parameter Name="Country" Type="String" />
    <asp:Parameter Name="Phone" Type="String" />
    <asp:Parameter Name="Fax" Type="String" />
    <asp:Parameter Name="original_CustomerID" Type="String" />
    <asp:Parameter Name="original_CompanyName" Type="String" />
    <asp:Parameter Name="original_ContactName" Type="String" />
    <asp:Parameter Name="original_ContactTitle" Type="String" />
    <asp:Parameter Name="original_Address" Type="String" />
    <asp:Parameter Name="original_City" Type="String" />
    <asp:Parameter Name="original_Region" Type="String" />
    <asp:Parameter Name="original_PostalCode" Type="String" />
    <asp:Parameter Name="original_Country" Type="String" />
    <asp:Parameter Name="original_Phone" Type="String" />
    <asp:Parameter Name="original_Fax" Type="String" />
</UpdateParameters>
```

Finally, the SqlDataSource Wizard sets an additional property called `OldValueParameterFormatString`. This attribute determines the prefix for the original data values. By default, the value is `{0}`, but you have complete control over this.

One way to determine whether your update has encountered a concurrency error is by testing the `AffectedRows` property in the SqlDataSource's `Updated` event. Listing 7-7 shows one way to do this.

LISTING 7-7: Detecting concurrency errors after updating data

Available for download on Wrox.com

VB

```
Protected Sub SqlDataSource1_Updated(ByVal sender as Object,
    ByVal e As System.Web.UI.WebControls.SqlDataSourceStatusEventArgs)

    If (e.AffectedRows > 0) Then
            Me.lblMessage.Text = "The record has been updated"
    Else
            Me.lblMessage.Text = "Possible concurrency violation"
    End If
End Sub
```

continues

LISTING 7-7 *(continued)*

```
protected void SqlDataSource1_Updated(object sender,
    SqlDataSourceStatusEventArgs e)
{
    if (e.AffectedRows > 0)
        this.lblMessage.Text = "The record has been updated";
    else
        this.lblMessage.Text = "Possible concurrency violation";
}
```

SqlDataSource Events

The SqlDataSource control provides a number of events that you can hook into to affect the behavior of the SqlDataSource control or to react to events that occur while the SqlDataSource control is executing. The control provides events that are raised before and after the `SELECT`, `INSERT`, `UPDATE`, and `DELETE` commands are executed. You can use these events to alter the SQL command being sent to the data source by the control. You can cancel the operation or determine whether an error has occurred while executing the SQL command.

Handling Database Errors

The data source control events are very useful for trapping and handling errors that occur while you are attempting to execute a SQL command against the database. For instance, Listing 7-8 demonstrates how you can use the SqlDataSource control's `Updated` event to handle a database error that has bubbled back to the application as an exception.

LISTING 7-8: Using the SqlDataSource control's Updated event to handle database errors

Available for download on Wrox.com

VB

```
Protected Sub SqlDataSource1_Updated(ByVal sender As Object,
    ByVal e As System.Web.UI.WebControls.SqlDataSourceStatusEventArgs)

    If (e.Exception IsNot Nothing) Then
        Me.lblMessage.Text = e.Exception.Message
        e.ExceptionHandled = True
    End If
End Sub
```

```
protected void SqlDataSource1_Updated(object sender,
    System.Web.UI.WebControls.SqlDataSourceStatusEventArgs e)
{
    if (e.Exception != null)
    {
        this.lblMessage.Text = e.Exception.Message;
        e.ExceptionHandled = true;
    }
}
```

Notice that the sample tests to see whether the `Exception` property is `null`; if it is not, this indicates an exception has occurred and the application can handle the exception.

An extremely important part of this sample is the code that sets the `ExceptionHandled` property. By default, this property returns `False`. Therefore, even if you detect the `Exception` property is not null and you attempt to handle the error, the exception still bubbles out of the application. Setting the `ExceptionHandled` property to `True` tells .NET that you have successfully handled the exception and that it is safe to continue executing. Note that the `AccessDataSource` and `ObjectDataSource` controls, which are discussed later in this chapter, also function in this manner.

Although the SqlDataSource control is powerful, a number of other data source controls might suit your specific data access scenario better.

Using the SqlDataSource with Oracle

Although the queries the SqlDataSource control generates are fairly database generic, scenarios exist where it generates queries that are optimized for SQL Server. This is obviously not desirable if you are using Oracle as your database. In previous versions of .NET you could use the SqlDataSource control with the OracleClient APIs to connect to an Oracle database. However starting with .NET 4 Microsoft has deprecated its OracleClient APIs, instead recommending developers use the Oracle Data Provider for .NET (ODP.NET). To find more information about the Oracle Data Provider for .NET and using it in ASP.NET applications go to `www.oracle.com/technology/tech/windows/odpnet/index.html`.

AccessDataSource Control

Although you can use the SqlDataSource to connect to Access databases, ASP.NET also provides a special `AccessDataSource` control. This control gives you specialized access to Access databases using the Jet Data provider, but it still uses SQL commands to perform data retrieval because it is derived from the SqlDataSource.

Despite its relative similarity to the SqlDataSource control, the AccessDataSource control has some specialized parts. For example, the control does not require you to set a `ConnectionString` property. Instead, the control uses a `DataFile` property to allow you to directly specify the Access `.mdb` file you want to use for data access.

A side effect of not having the `ConnectionString` *property is that the* `AccessDataSource` *cannot connect to password-protected databases. If you need to access a password-protected Access database, you can use the SqlDataSource control, which allows you to provide the username and password as part of the connection string.*

Additionally, because the `AccessDataSource` uses the `System.Data.OleDb` to perform actual data access, the order of parameters matters. You need to verify that the order of the parameters in any `SELECT`, `INSERT`, `UPDATE`, or `DELETE` parameters collection matches the order of the parameters in the SQL statement.

LinqDataSource Control

Much like the SqlDataSource control, which generates queries for SQL databases by converting its property settings into SQL queries, the LinqDataSource generates queries for data objects in your application by converting its property settings into LINQ queries.

This chapter focuses primarily on how to use the LinqDataSource control and its design-time configuration options. If you want to learn more about LINQ, its syntax, and how it works with different object types, refer to Chapter 9 in this book.

When you drag the control onto the Visual Studio design surface, you can use the smart tag to configure the control. Figure 7-6 shows the initial screen of the configuration wizard.

From this screen you can choose the context object you want to use as the source of your data. The context object is the base object that contains the data you want to query. By default, the wizard shows only objects that are derived from the `System.Data.Linq.DataContext` base class, which are normally data context classes created by LINQ to SQL. The wizard does give you the option of seeing all objects in your application (even those included as references in your project) and allows you to select one of those as your context object.

Configure Data Source - LinqDataSource1
Choose a Context Object
Select a context object that can be used to retrieve or update data.
Show only DataContext objects
Choose your context object:
CS.LINQ2SQL.NorthwindCSDataContext
< Previous
Next >
Finish
Cancel

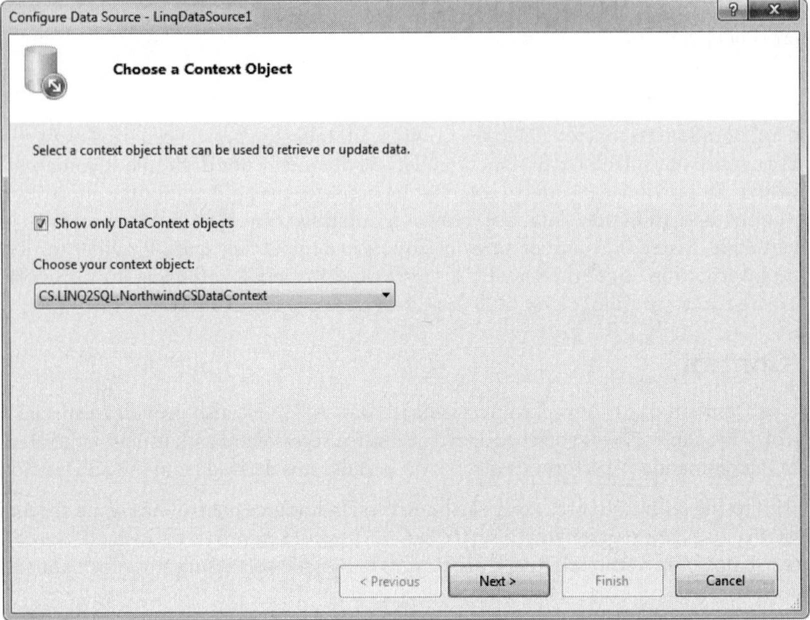

FIGURE 7-6

After you have selected your context object, you can select the specific data in the context object you want to bind to, as shown in Figure 7-7. If you are binding to a class derived from `DataContext`, the table drop-down list shows all the data tables contained in the context object. If you are binding to a standard class, then the drop-down allows you to select any enumerable property exposed by the context object.

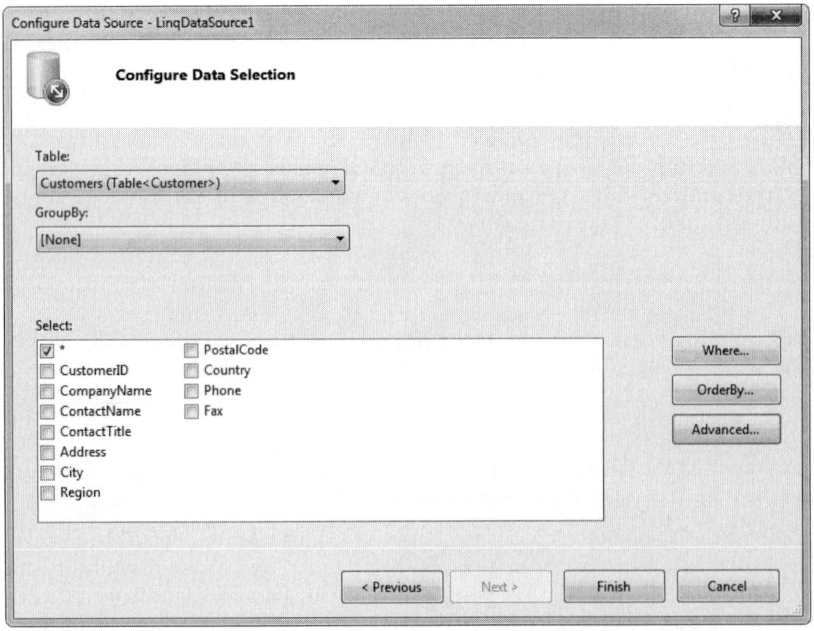

Configure Data Source - LinqDataSource1
Configure Data Selection
Table:
Customers (Table<Customer>)
GroupBy:
[None]
Select:
*
CustomerID
CompanyName
ContactName
ContactTitle
Address
City
Region
PostalCode
Country
Phone
Fax
Where...
OrderBy...
Advanced...
< Previous
Next >
Finish
Cancel

FIGURE 7-7

After you have selected your data, you can click the Finish button and complete the wizard. Listing 7-9 shows the markup that is generated by the wizard after it has been configured to use the `NorthwindDataContext` object created by LINQ to SQL as its context object and the Customers table as its data.

LISTING 7-9: The basic LinqDataSource control markup

Available for download on Wrox.com

```
<asp:LinqDataSource ID="LinqDataSource1" runat="server"
    ContextTypeName="NorthwindDataContext" TableName="Customers"
    EnableInsert="True" EnableUpdate="True" EnableDelete="True"
    EntityTypeName="">
```

The LinqDataSource is now ready to be bound to a data control such as a GridView or ListView.

Notice that the markup generated by the control includes three properties: `EnableInsert`, `EnableUpdate`, and `EnableDelete`. Using these properties you can configure the control to allow `INSERT`, `UPDATE`, and `DELETE` actions if the underlying data source supports them. Because the data source control knows that it is connected to a LINQ to SQL data context object, which by default supports these actions, it has automatically enabled them.

The LinqDataSource also includes a number of other basic configuration options you can use to control the selection of data from the context object. As shown in Figure 7-7, the configuration wizard also allows you to select specific fields from the data source to include.

Although using the LinqDataSource control can be a convenient way to control which fields are displayed in a bound control such as the GridView, it also causes the underlying LINQ query to return an anonymous type, which does not support inserting, updating, or deletion of data. If you simply want to limit the data shown by the bound list control, you may want to consider defining the fields to display in the bound list control rather than in the data source control.

If you choose to select specific fields for the LinqDataSource control to return, the wizard adds the `Select` attribute to the LINQ query it generates. This is shown in Listing 7-10, where the control has been modified to return only the CustomerID, ContactName, ContactTitle, and Region fields.

LISTING 7-10: Specifying LinqDataSource control data fields

Available for download on Wrox.com

```
<asp:LinqDataSource ID="LinqDataSource1" runat="server"
    ContextTypeName="NorthwindDataContext" TableName="Customers"
    Select="new (CustomerID, ContactName, ContactTitle, Region)">
</asp:LinqDataSource>
```

To see the results of the query, you can bind the control to a GridView control. After you do this, you see that only these four specified fields are displayed. If no `Select` property is specified, the LinqDataSource control simply returns all public properties exposed by the data object.

Query Parameters

The LinqDataSource control also allows you to specify different query parameters such as `Where` and `OrderBy`. Configuration of either option is available by clicking the Where or OrderBy buttons in the Controls Configuration Wizard.

Filtering Queries Using Where

The Where parameters are created using the same basic Parameters syntax used by other data source controls, which means that you can provide values from a variety of runtime sources such as Form fields, Querystring values, or even Session values. Listing 7-11 demonstrates the use of Where parameters.

Available for download on Wrox.com

LISTING 7-11: Specifying Where clause parameters

```
<asp:LinqDataSource ID="LinqDataSource1" runat="server"
    ContextTypeName="NorthwindDataContext" TableName="Customers"
    Select="new (CustomerID, ContactName, ContactTitle, Region)"
    Where="CustomerID == @CustomerID">
    <WhereParameters>
        <asp:querystringparameter DefaultValue="0" Name="CustomerID"
            QueryStringField="ID" Type="String" />
    </WhereParameters>
</asp:LinqDataSource>
```

You can add multiple Where parameters that the control will automatically concatenate in its Where property using the AND operator. You can manually change the default value of the Where property if you want to have multiple WhereParameters defined, but only use a subset, or if you want to change which parameters are used dynamically at runtime. This is shown in Listing 7-12, where the LinqDataSource control has several Where parameters defined, but by default is using only one.

Available for download on Wrox.com

LISTING 7-12: Using one of multiple defined WhereParameters

```
<asp:LinqDataSource ID="LinqDataSource1" runat="server"
     ContextTypeName="NorthwindDataContext" TableName="Customers"
     Select="new (CustomerID, ContactName, ContactTitle, Region)"
     Where="Country == @Country"
     OrderBy="Region, ContactTitle, ContactName">
    <WhereParameters>
        <asp:querystringparameter DefaultValue="0" Name="CustomerID"
            QueryStringField="ID" Type="String" />
        <asp:querystringparameter DefaultValue="USA" Name="Country"
            QueryStringField="country" Type="String" />
        <asp:FormParameter DefaultValue="AZ" Name="Region"
            FormField="region" Type="String" />
     </WhereParameters>
</asp:LinqDataSource>
```

In this case, although three WhereParameters are defined, the Where property uses only the Country parameter. Changing the Where property's value at runtime to use any of the defined parameters, based perhaps on a configuration setting set by the end user, would be simple.

The LinqDataSource control also includes a property called AutoGenerateWhereClause, which can simplify the markup created by the control. When set to True, the control ignores the value of the Where property and automatically uses each parameter specified in the Where parameters collection in the query's Where clause.

Sorting Queries Using OrderBy

When defining an OrderBy clause, the wizard creates a comma-delimited list of fields as the value for the control's OrderBy property. The value of the OrderBy property is then appended to the control's LINQ query when it is executed.

The control also exposes an OrderByParameters collection, which you can also use to specify OrderBy values. However, in most cases using the simple OrderBy property will be sufficient. You would need to use the OrderBy parameters collection only if you need to determine the value of a variable at runtime, and then order the query results based on that value.

Grouping Query Data Using GroupBy

The LinqDataSource control also makes specifying a grouping for the data returned by the query easy. In the configuration wizard, you can select the GroupBy field for the query. After a field is selected, the wizard then creates a new anonymous type based on the GroupBy field. The type includes two fields by default. The first is `key`, which represents the group objects specified in the `GroupBy` property, and the second is `it`, which represents the grouped objects. You can also add your own properties to the type and execute functions against the grouped data such as `Average`, `Min`, `Max`, and `Count`. Listing 7-13 demonstrates a very simple grouping using the LinqDataSource control.

LISTING 7-13: Simple data grouping

Available for download on Wrox.com

```
<asp:LinqDataSource ID="LinqDataSource1" runat="server"
    ContextTypeName="NorthwindDataContext" TableName="Products"
    Select="new (key as Category, it as Products,
            Average(UnitPrice) as Average_UnitPrice)"
    GroupBy="Category">
</asp:LinqDataSource>
```

You can see in this sample that the Products table has been grouped by its `Category` property. The LinqDataSource control created a new anonymous type containing the `key` (aliased as `Category`) and `it` (aliased as `Products`) fields. Additionally, the custom property `average_unitprice` has been added, which calculates the average unit price of the products in each category. When you execute this query and bind the results to a GridView, a simple view of the calculated average unit price is displayed. The Category and Products are not displayed because they are complex object types, and the GridView is not capable of displaying them directly.

You can access the data in either key by using the standard ASP.NET `Eval()` function. In a GridView you would do this by creating a `TemplateField`, and using `ItemTemplate` to insert the `Eval` statement as shown here:

```
<asp:TemplateField>
    <ItemTemplate>
       <%# Eval("Category.CategoryName") %>
    </ItemTemplate>
</asp:TemplateField>
```

In this case, `TemplateField` displays the `CategoryName` for each grouped category in the data.

Accessing the grouped items is just as easy. If, for example, you wanted to include a bullet list of each product in an individual group, you would simply add another `TemplateField`, insert a BulletList control, and bind it to the Products field returned by the query, as shown next:

```
 <asp:TemplateField>
    <ItemTemplate>
         <asp:BulletedList DataSource='<%# Eval("Products") %>'
            DataTextField="ProductName" runat="server" ID="BulletedList" />
    </ItemTemplate>
</asp:TemplateField>
```

Using the QueryExtender for Complex Filters

Although the LinqDataSource control includes built-in capabilities for filtering data, these capabilities do not expose the full power that LINQ provides to create queries that include filters. This is where the QueryExtender comes into play, by allowing you to define complex searches, data range filters, complex multi-column `OrderBy` clauses, and even completely custom expressions. Table 7-4 shows the available filter expression types.

TABLE 7-4

EXPRESSION TYPE	DESCRIPTION
SearchExpression	Searches a field or fields for string values and compares them to a specified string. The expression can perform "StartsWith", "EndsWith", or "Contains" searches.
RangeExpression	Like the SearchExpression, but uses a pair of values to define a minimum and maximum range.
PropertyExpression	Compares a property value of a column to a specified value.
OrderByExpression	Enables you to sort data by a specified column and sort direction.
CustomExpression	Enables you to provide a custom LINQ expression.
MethodExpression	Enables you to invoke a method containing a custom LINQ query.
OfTypeExpression	Enables you to filter elements in the data source by type.

The QueryExtender works with any data source control that implements the `IQueryableDataSource` interface. By default this includes the LinqDataSource control and the EntityDataSource control, which is discussed in the next section.

To see how you can use the QueryExtender, you can modify Listing 7-9 to filter the data returned by the LinqDataSource. Start by dragging a QueryExtender control onto the design surface from the toolbox. In the page markup, connect the QueryExtender to the LinqDataSource by specifying the ID of the LinqDataSource control as the QueryExtender's `TargetControlID` property value. Now all you have to do is define the filter expressions you want to use within the QueryExtender. Listing 7-14 demonstrates using a SearchExpression.

Available for download on Wrox.com

LISTING 7-14: Using the QueryExtender control to filter query results

```
<asp:LinqDataSource ID="LinqDataSource1" runat="server"
    ContextTypeName="VB.NorthwindVBDataContext" TableName="Customers"
    EnableInsert="True" EnableUpdate="True" EnableDelete="True"
    EntityTypeName="" />
<asp:QueryExtender ID="QueryExtender2"
    runat="server" TargetControlID="LinqDataSource1">
    <asp:SearchExpression SearchType="StartsWith"
        DataFields="CustomerID">
        <asp:QueryStringParameter DefaultValue="A"
            QueryStringField="s" />
    </asp:SearchExpression>
</asp:QueryExtender>
```

As you can see, using a `QueryStringParameter`, the expression filters the query results to only `CustomerIDs` that start with the value specified by the querystring field "`search`".

Data Concurrency

Like the SqlDataSource control, the LinqDataSource control allows for data concurrency checks when updating or deleting data. As its name implies, the `StoreOriginalValuesInViewState` property indicates whether the data source control should store the original data values in ViewState. Doing this when using LINQ to SQL as the underlying data object allows LINQ to SQL to perform data concurrency checking before submitting updates or deleting data.

Storing the original data in ViewState, however, can cause the size of your Web page to grow significantly, affecting the performance of your Web site, so you may want to disable the storing of data in ViewState. If you do, recognize that you are now responsible for any data concurrency checking that your application requires.

LinqDataSource Events

The LinqDataSource control also includes a number of useful events that you can use to react to actions taken by the control at runtime. Standard before and after events for `SELECT`, `INSERT`, `UPDATE`, and `DELETE` actions are all exposed and allow you to add, remove, or modify parameters from the control's various parameter collections, or even cancel the event entirely.

Additionally, the post action events allow you to determine whether an exception has occurred while attempting to execute an `INSERT`, `UPDATE`, or `DELETE`. If an exception has occurred, these events allow you to react to those exceptions, and either mark the exception as handled, or allow it to continue to bubble up through the application.

EntityDataSource Control

The EntityDataSource is a specialized data source control designed for applications that make use of the ADO.NET Entity Framework.

For an in-depth discussion of the Entity Framework, see Chapter 29.

The EntityDataSource control handles selecting, updating, inserting, and deleting data for data controls on a Web page as well as automatically enabling sorting and paging of data, allowing you to easily bind to and navigate data from an Entity Data Model (EDM). Like all other data source controls, you get started using the EntityDataSource control by dragging it from the Visual Studio toolbox onto the design surface and then selecting the Configure option from the control's smart tag to load the control's Configuration Wizard. After the wizard opens, select or supply a connection string for the control, then select the Default Container Name and click Next. An example of selecting a connection to a data model of the Northwind database is shown in Figure 7-8.

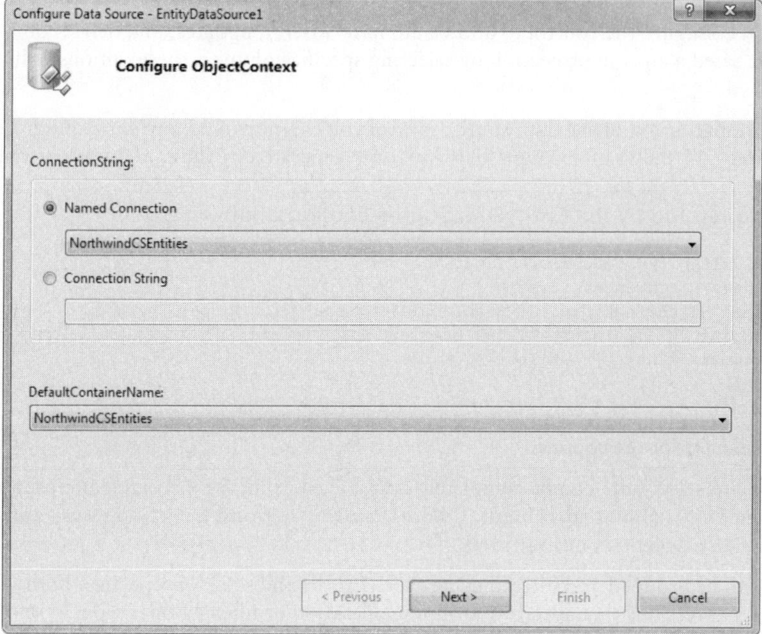

FIGURE 7-8

The next screen allows you to select the specific EntitySetName you want to expose through the data source control. If you want to ensure that only a specific type is returned from the query, then you can also specify an EntityTypeFilter. After an EntitySetName is selected, you can create custom projections of properties by selecting them from the list. Figure 7-9 demonstrates selecting the Customers EntitySetName from the Northwind data model.

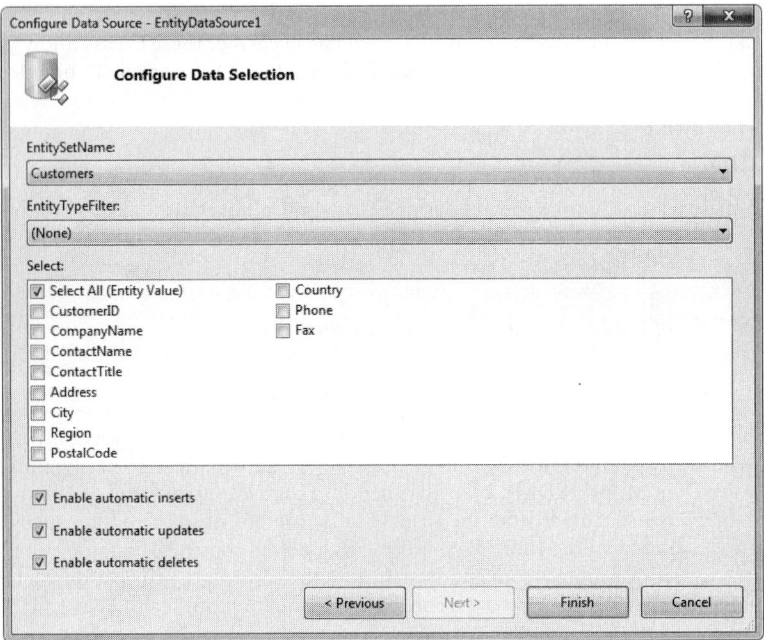

FIGURE 7-9

Finally on this screen you can configure the control to allow automatic inserts, updates, and deletes of data. Note that if you have created a custom projection by selecting specific columns, these options will be disabled.

After you've completed the configuration of the data source control you can now bind any databound control to it as normal. Listing 7-15 shows an example of the markup generated by the configuration wizard.

Available for download on Wrox.com

LISTING 7-15: Markup generated by the EntityDataSource configuration wizard

```
<asp:EntityDataSource ID="EntityDataSource1" runat="server"
    ConnectionString="name=NorthwindEntities"
    DefaultContainerName="NorthwindEntities" EnableDelete="True"
    EnableFlattening="False" EnableInsert="True" EnableUpdate="True"
    EntitySetName="Customers" EntityTypeFilter="Customer">
</asp:EntityDataSource>
```

The EntityDataSource control includes a variety of other properties and events that you can use to customize even further the behavior of the control.

The query used by the control to select data can be completely customized using the `CommandText` property. This property accepts an Entity SQL command as input. If both `CommandText` and `EntitySetName` are set, the control throws an `InvalidOperationException`.

The control also allows data to be grouped and filtered using the `GroupBy` and `Where` properties. Both properties accept Entity SQL expressions that specify a grouping operation or filtering operation, respectively.

Using the `CommandText` or `GroupBy` properties results in the data source control generating a custom projection, which as discussed earlier means that inserts, updates, and deletes are ignored, even if explicitly enabled.

You can specify parameters that can be used in any of the control's queries as you can in any data source control. The control includes `WhereParameter`, `SelectParameter`, `InsertParameter`, and a variety of other parameter collections, where you can define any of the standard parameters such as `ControlParameter` or `QueryStringParameter`.

XmlDataSource Control

The `XmlDataSource` control provides you with a simple way of binding XML documents, either in-memory or located on a physical drive. The control provides you with a number of properties that make specifying an XML file containing data and an XSLT transform file for converting the source XML into a more suitable format easy. You can also provide an XPath query to select only a certain subset of data.

You can use the XmlDataSource control's Configure Data Source Wizard, shown in Figure 7-10, to configure the control.

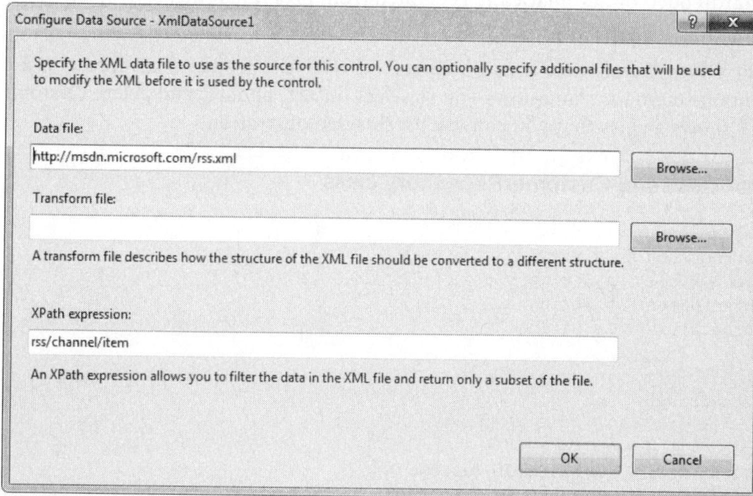

FIGURE 7-10

Listing 7-16 shows how you might consume an RSS feed from the MSDN Web site, selecting all the item nodes within it for binding to a bound list control such as the GridView.

LISTING 7-16: Using the XmlDataSource control to consume an RSS feed

Available for download on Wrox.com

```
<asp:XmlDataSource ID="XmlDataSource1" Runat="server"
    DataFile="http://msdn.microsoft.com/rss.xml"
    XPath="rss/channel/item" />
```

In addition to the declarative attributes you can use with the XmlDataSource, a number of other helpful properties and events are available.

Many times your XML is not stored in a physical file, but rather is simply a string stored in your application memory or possibly in a database. The control provides the `Data` property, which accepts a simple string of XML to which the control can bind. Note that if both the `Data` and `DataFile` properties are set, the `DataFile` property takes precedence over the `Data` property.

Additionally, in certain scenarios, you may want to export the bound XML out of the XmlDataSource control to other objects or even save any changes that have been made to the underlying XML if it has been bound to a control such as a GridView. The XmlDataSource control provides two methods to accommodate this. One method is the `GetXmlDocument` method, which allows you to export the XML by returning a basic `System.Xml.XmlDocument` object that contains the XML loaded in the data source control.

The other way is by using the control's `Save` method to persist changes made to the XmlDataSource control's loaded XML back to disk. Executing this method assumes you have provided a file path in the `DataFile` property.

The XmlDataSource control also provides you with a number of specialized events. The `Transforming` event that is raised before the XSLT transform specified in the `Transform` or `TransformFile` properties is applied and allows you to supply custom arguments to the transform.

ObjectDataSource Control

The `ObjectDataSource` control gives you the power to bind data controls directly to middle-layer business objects that can be hard-coded or automatically generated from programs such as Object Relational (O/R) mappers.

To demonstrate how to use the ObjectDataSource control, create a class in the project that represents a Customer and a class that contains methods that allows you to select, insert, update, and delete Customers from a collection. Listing 7-17 shows a class that you can use for this demonstration.

LISTING 7-17: A Customer class and CustomerRepository class

Available for download on Wrox.com

VB

```
Public Class Customer
    Public Property CustomerID() As String
    Public Property CompanyName() As String
    Public Property ContactName() As String
    Public Property ContactTitle() As String
End Class

Public Class CustomerRepository

    Public Function [Select](
        ByVal customerID As String) As List(Of Customer)
        ' Implement logic here to retrieve the Customer
        '  data based on the methods customerID parameter
        Dim _customers As New List(Of Customer)
        _customers.Add(New Customer() With {
                    .CompanyName = "Acme", .ContactName = "Wiley Cyote",
                    .ContactTitle = "President", .CustomerID = "ACMEC"})
        Return _customers
    End Function

    Public Sub Insert(ByVal c As Customer)
        ' Implement Insert logic
    End Sub

    Public Sub Update(ByVal c As Customer)
        ' Implement Update logic
    End Sub

    Public Sub Delete(ByVal c As Customer)
        ' Implement Delete logic
    End Sub
```

```
End Class
```

C#

```
public class Customer
{
    public string CustomerID { get; set; }
    public string CompanyName { get; set; }
    public string ContactName { get; set; }
    public string ContactTitle { get; set; }
}

public class CustomerRepository
{
    public CustomerRepository()
    {
    }

    public List<Customer> Select(string customerId)
    {
        // Implement logic here to retrieve the Customer
        // data based on the methods customerId parameter
        List<Customer> _customers = new List<Customer>();
        _customers.Add(new Customer() {
            CompanyName = "Acme", ContactName = "Wiley Cyote",
            ContactTitle = "President", CustomerID = "ACMEC" });
        return _customers;
    }

    public void Insert(Customer c)
    {
        // Implement Insert logic
    }

    public void Update(Customer c)
    {
        // Implement Update logic
    }

    public void Delete(Customer c)
    {
        // Implement Delete logic
    }

}
```

To start using the ObjectDataSource, drag the control onto the design surface and open the Configuration Wizard from the control's smart tag. When the wizard opens, select the business object you want to use as your data source from the drop-down list. The list shows all the classes located in the App_Code folder of your Web site that can be successfully compiled. In this case, you want to use the `CustomerRepository` class shown in Listing 7-17.

Click the Next button, and the wizard asks you to specify which methods it should use for the CRUD operations it can perform: SELECT, INSERT, UPDATE, and DELETE. Each tab lets you select a specific method located in your business class to perform the specific action. Figure 7-11 shows that you want the control to use a method called `Select()` to retrieve data.

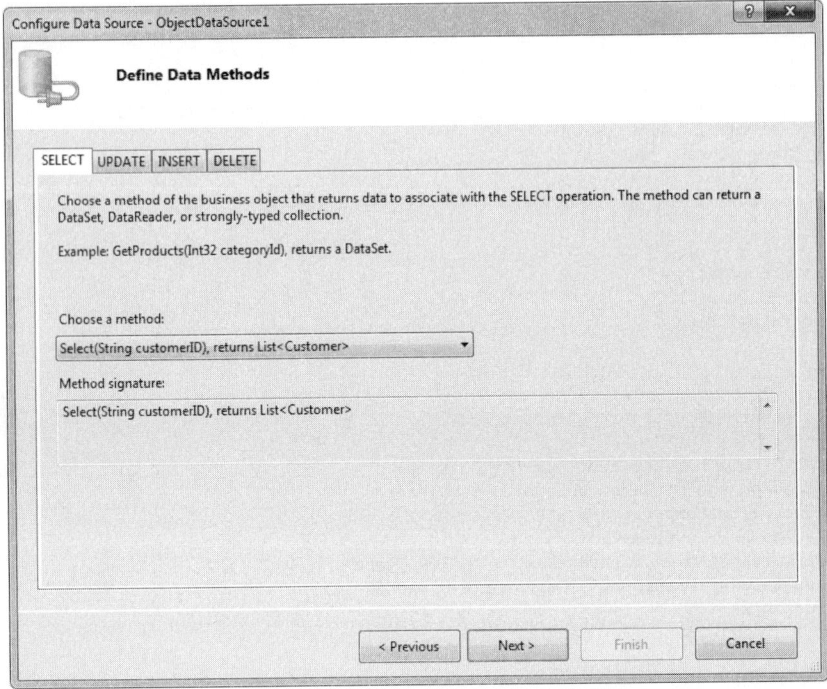

FIGURE 7-11

The methods the ObjectDataSource uses to perform CRUD operations must follow certain rules in order for the control to understand. For example, the control's `SELECT` method must return a `DataSet`, `DataReader`, or a strongly typed collection. Each of the control's operation tabs explains what the control expects of the method you specify for it to use. Additionally, if a method does not conform to the rules that specific operation expects, it is not listed in the drop-down list on that tab.

Finally, if your `SELECT` method contains parameters, the wizard lets you create `SelectParameters` you can use to provide the method parameter data.

When you have completed configuring the ObjectDataSource, you should have code in your page source like that shown in Listing 7-18.

LISTING 7-18: The ObjectDataSource code generated by the configuration wizard

Available for download on Wrox.com

```
<asp:ObjectDataSource ID="ObjectDataSource1" runat="server"
    DeleteMethod="Delete" InsertMethod="Insert"
    SelectMethod="Select" TypeName="CustomerRepository"
    UpdateMethod="Update" DataObjectTypeName="Customer">
    <SelectParameters>
        <asp:QueryStringParameter Name="customerId"
            QueryStringField="ID" Type="string" />
    </SelectParameters>
</asp:ObjectDataSource>
```

As you can see, the wizard has generated the attributes for the `SELECT`, `UPDATE`, `INSERT`, and `DELETE` methods you specified in the wizard. Also notice that it has added the `Select` parameter. Depending on your application, you could change this to any of the `Parameter` objects discussed earlier, such as a `ControlParameter` or `QueryStringParameter` object.

The ObjectDataSource control exposes several useful events that you can hook into. It includes events that are raised before and after the control performs any of the CRUD actions, such as selecting or deleting events.

It also includes pre- and post-events that are raised when the object that is serving as the data source is created or disposed of, as well as when an event that is raised before a filter is applied to the data. All these events give you great power when you must react to the different ways the ObjectDataSource control behaves.

SiteMapDataSource Control

The `SiteMapDataSource` enables you to work with data stored in your Web site's SiteMap configuration file if you have one. This can be useful if you are changing your site map data at runtime, perhaps based on user rights or status.

Note two items regarding the SiteMapDataSource control. One is that it does not support any of the data caching options that exist in the other data source controls provided (covered in the next section), so you cannot automatically cache your sitemap data. Another is that the SiteMapDataSource control does not have any configuration wizards like the other data source controls. This is because the SiteMap control can be bound only to the SiteMap configuration data file of your Web site, so no other configuration is possible.

Listing 7-19 shows an example of using the SiteMap control.

LISTING 7-19: Using the SiteMapDataSource control

Available for download on Wrox.com

```
<asp:SiteMapDataSource ID="SiteMapDataSource1" Runat="server" />
```

Using the SiteMapDataSource control is discussed in greater detail in Chapter 13.

DATA SOURCE CONTROL CACHING

ASP.NET includes a great caching infrastructure that allows you to cache on the server arbitrary objects for set periods of time. You can learn more about ASP.NET caching in Chapter 22.

The data source controls leverage this built-in caching infrastructure to allow you to easily cache their query results. Each control uses the same basic syntax for configuring caching, allowing you to create simple caching policies including a cache direction, expiration policies, and key dependencies.

The SqlDataSource control's caching features are available only if you have set the `DataSourceMode` *property to* `DataSet`*. If it is set to* `DataReader`*, the control will throw a* `NotSupportedException`*.*

The cache duration can be set to a specific number of seconds, or you can set it to `Infinite` to force the cached data to never expire. Listing 7-20 shows how you can easily add caching features to a data source control.

LISTING 7-20: Enabling caching on a SqlDataSource control

Available for download on Wrox.com

```
<asp:SqlDataSource ID="SqlDataSource1" Runat="server"
    SelectCommand="SELECT * FROM [Customers]"
    ConnectionString="<%$ ConnectionStrings:ConnectionString %>"
    DataSourceMode="DataSet" ConflictDetection="CompareAllValues"
    EnableCaching="True" CacheKeyDependency="SomeKey"
    CacheDuration="Infinite" />
```

Some controls also extend the core set of caching features with additional caching functionality specific to their data sources. For example, if you are using the SqlDataSource control you can use that control's `SqlCacheDependency` property to create SQL dependencies.

STORING CONNECTION INFORMATION

In ASP.NET applications, the `web.config` file is a great way of storing application configuration data in a readable and portable format. Many people use the file to store things like the database connection information their applications use. It is easy to access from within the application, creates a single central location for the configuration data, and is a cinch to change just by editing the XML.

If you've tried using the SqlDataSource control, you likely already have added a new `<connectionStrings>` section containing a connection string to your `web.config` file. If not, Listing 7-21 shows how ASP.NET stores a connection string.

LISTING 7-21: A typical connection string saved in the web.config file

Available for download on Wrox.com

```
<connectionStrings>
    <add name="AppConnectionString1"
         connectionString="Server=localhost;
             User ID=sa;Password=password;Database=Northwind;
             Persist Security Info=True"
         providerName="System.Data.SqlClient" />
</connectionStrings>
```

Storing connection strings in this special configuration section allows ASP.NET to expose the `ConnectionString` section to you at runtime using the `ConnectionStringSettings` class. This class contains a collection of all the connection strings entries in your `web.config` file and allows you to add, modify, or remove connection strings at runtime, as shown in Listing 7-22.

LISTING 7-22: Modifying connection string properties at runtime

Available for download on Wrox.com

VB

```
Dim conn As New ConnectionStringSettings()
conn.ConnectionString = _
    "Server=localhost;User ID=sa;Password=password" & _
    "Database=Northwind;Persist Security Info=True"
conn.Name = "AppConnectionString1"
conn.ProviderName = "System.Data.SqlClient"

' Add the new connection string to the web.config
Dim config As Configuration =
    System.Web.Configuration.
    WebConfigurationManager.OpenWebConfiguration(
        Request.ApplicationPath)
config.ConnectionStrings.ConnectionStrings.Add(conn)
config.Save(ConfigurationSaveMode.Minimal)
```

C#

```
ConnectionStringSettings conn = new ConnectionStringSettings();
conn.ConnectionString =
    "Server=localhost;User ID=sa;Password=password; " +
    "Database=Northwind;Persist Security Info=True";
conn.Name = "NewConnectionString1";
conn.ProviderName = "System.Data.SqlClient";

// Add the new connection string to the web.config
Configuration config =
    System.Web.Configuration.
    WebConfigurationManager.OpenWebConfiguration(
        Request.ApplicationPath);
config.ConnectionStrings.ConnectionStrings.Add(conn);
config.Save(ConfigurationSaveMode.Minimal);
```

As you can see, the `Configuration` class returned from the `WebConfigurationManager`'s `OpenWebConfiguration` method has a `ConnectionStrings` collection that contains all the connection strings for your application.

Additionally, the `SqlConnectionStringBuilder` class allows you to build connection strings using strongly typed properties and then add them to your `ConnectionStringSettings` collection. Listing 7-23 shows how you can use the `ConnectionStringBuilder` class to dynamically assemble connection strings at runtime and save them to your `web.config` file.

LISTING 7-23: Building connection strings using ConnectionStringBuilder

Available for download on Wrox.com

VB

```
Dim config As Configuration =
    System.Web.Configuration.
        WebConfigurationManager.OpenWebConfiguration(
            Request.ApplicationPath)

Dim conn As ConnectionStringSettings =
    config.ConnectionStrings.
        ConnectionStrings("NewVBConnectionString1")

Dim builder As New
    System.Data.SqlClient.SqlConnectionStringBuilder(
        conn.ConnectionString)

' Change the connection string properties
builder.DataSource = "localhost"
builder.InitialCatalog = "Northwind1"
builder.UserID = "sa"
builder.Password = "password"
builder.PersistSecurityInfo = True

conn.ConnectionString = builder.ConnectionString

config.ConnectionStrings.ConnectionStrings.Add(conn)
config.Save(ConfigurationSaveMode.Minimal)
```

C#

```
Configuration config = System.Web.Configuration.
    WebConfigurationManager.OpenWebConfiguration(
      Request.ApplicationPath);
ConnectionStringSettings conn = config.ConnectionStrings.
    ConnectionStrings["NewCSConnectionString1"];

System.Data.SqlClient.SqlConnectionStringBuilder builder =
    new System.Data.SqlClient.SqlConnectionStringBuilder(
            conn.ConnectionString
        );

// Change the connection string properties
builder.DataSource = "localhost";
builder.InitialCatalog = "Northwind1";
builder.UserID = "sa";
builder.Password = "password";
builder.PersistSecurityInfo = true;

conn.ConnectionString = builder.ConnectionString;

config.ConnectionStrings.ConnectionStrings.Add(conn);
config.Save(ConfigurationSaveMode.Minimal);
```

USING BOUND LIST CONTROLS WITH DATA SOURCE CONTROLS

Although the data source controls in ASP.NET are useful, in the end all they provide you with is a collection of data. You still need to take this data and display it in your application. Thankfully ASP.NET also includes a set of great data display controls that are easily connected to a data source control, again using declarative syntax, allowing you to display the data in your application without the need to write a line of code.

Although the declarative model in ASP.NET is fantastic, sometimes you will want to use code to connect a data source with a data display control. Each control includes a `DataBind()` *method you can use to bind data to a control. The method includes a Boolean overload that allows you to turn the display control's data-binding events on or off to help you improve the performance of your application when you do not need those events.*

GridView

The GridView control is a powerful data grid control that allows you to display an entire collection of data, add sorting and paging, and perform inline editing.

Start using the GridView by dragging the control onto the design surface of an ASP.NET Web page. When you do this, you will be prompted to select a data source control to bind to the grid. You can use the SqlDataSource control created earlier in the chapter.

Listing 7-24 shows a simple use of the GridView with a SqlDataSource control. In this example the explicit field definitions have been removed to allow the control to automatically generate columns based on the structure of the data source.

LISTING 7-24: Using the GridView control in an ASP.NET Web page

Available for download on Wrox.com

```
<html>
<head runat="server">
    <title>Using the GridView Control</title>
</head>
<body>
    <form id="form1" runat="server">
    <div>
        <asp:GridView ID="GridView1" runat="server"
            DataSourceID="SqlDataSource1">
        </asp:GridView>

        <asp:SqlDataSource ID="SqlDataSource1" Runat="server"
            SelectCommand="SELECT * FROM [Customers]"
            ConnectionString=
                "<%$ ConnectionStrings:ConnectionString %>"
            DataSourceMode="DataSet"
            ConflictDetection="CompareAllValues" EnableCaching="True"
            CacheKeyDependency="MyKey" CacheDuration="Infinite">
        </asp:SqlDataSource>
    </div>
    </form>
</body>
</html>
```

When you run the page, ASP.NET executes the database query using the SqlDataSource control and then binds the results to the GridView control. The GridView control generates a table layout containing all the data returned from the query. Figure 7-12 shows what your Web page looks like when you execute the code in the browser.

CustomerID	CompanyName	ContactName	ContactTitle	Address	City	Region	PostalCode	Country	Phone	Fax
ALFKI	Alfreds Futterkiste	Maria Anders	Sales Representative	Obere Str. 57	Berlin		12209	Germany	030-0074321	030-0076545
ANATR	Ana Trujillo Emparedados y helados	Ana Trujillo	Owner	Avda. de la Constitución 2222	México D.F.		05021	Mexico	(5) 555-4729	(5) 555-3745
ANTON	Antonio Moreno Taqueria	Antonio Moreno	Owner	Mataderos 2312	México D.F.		05023	Mexico	(5) 555-3932	
AROUT	Around the Horn	Thomas Hardy	Sales Representative	120 Hanover Sq.	London		WA1 1DP	UK	(171) 555-7788	(171) 555-6750
BERGS	Berglunds snabbköp	Christina Berglund	Order Administrator	Berguvsvägen 8	Luleå		S-958 22	Sweden	0921-12 34 65	0921-12 34 67
BLAUS	Blauer See Delikatessen	Hanna Moos	Sales Representative	Forsterstr. 57	Mannheim		68306	Germany	0621-08460	0621-08924
BLONP	Blondesddsl père et fils	Frédérique Citeaux	Marketing Manager	24, place Kléber	Strasbourg		67000	France	88.60.15.31	88.60.15.32
BOLID	Bólido Comidas preparadas	Martin Sommer	Owner	C/ Araquil, 67	Madrid		28023	Spain	(91) 555 22 82	(91) 555 91 99
BONAP	Bon app'	Laurence Lebihan	Owner	12, rue des Bouchers	Marseille		13008	France	91.24.45.40	91.24.45.41
BOTTM	Bottom-Dollar Markets	Elizabeth Lincoln	Accounting Manager	23 Tsawassen Blvd.	Tsawassen	BC	T2F 8M4	Canada	(604) 555-4729	(604) 555-3745
BSBEV	B's Beverages	Victoria Ashworth	Sales Representative	Fauntleroy Circus	London		EC2 5NT	UK	(171) 555-1212	

FIGURE 7-12

After you assign the GridView a data source, normally the grid updates itself to match the data source schema, setting its `AutoGenerateFields` property to false and generating a field in the GridView's Columns collection for each public property or database table column exposed by the data source. Listing 7-25 shows the collection of explicit column definitions.

LISTING 7-25: Explicitly defined GridView columns

Available for download on Wrox.com

```
<asp:GridView ID="GridView1" runat="server" DataSourceID="SqlDataSource1"
    AutoGenerateColumns="False" DataKeyNames="CustomerID">
    <Columns>
        <asp:BoundField DataField="CustomerID"
            HeaderText="CustomerID" ReadOnly="True"
            SortExpression="CustomerID" />
        <asp:BoundField DataField="CompanyName"
            HeaderText="CompanyName" SortExpression="CompanyName" />
        <asp:BoundField DataField="ContactName"
            HeaderText="ContactName" SortExpression="ContactName" />
        <asp:BoundField DataField="ContactTitle"
            HeaderText="ContactTitle" SortExpression="ContactTitle" />
        <asp:BoundField DataField="Address" HeaderText="Address"
            SortExpression="Address" />
        <asp:BoundField DataField="City" HeaderText="City"
            SortExpression="City" />
        <asp:BoundField DataField="Region" HeaderText="Region"
            SortExpression="Region" />
        <asp:BoundField DataField="PostalCode" HeaderText="PostalCode"
```

continues

LISTING 7-25 *(continued)*

```
                SortExpression="PostalCode" />
            <asp:BoundField DataField="Country" HeaderText="Country"
                SortExpression="Country" />
            <asp:BoundField DataField="Phone" HeaderText="Phone"
                SortExpression="Phone" />
            <asp:BoundField DataField="Fax" HeaderText="Fax"
                SortExpression="Fax" />
        </Columns>
    </asp:GridView>
```

Notice that when creating the column definitions, the control by default uses the `BoundField` type for each column. Each `BoundField` has the `DataField` property, which connects the field to a property of the data source, and the `SortExpression` defined. The control also detects read-only properties in the data source and sets the field's `ReadOnly` property.

You can use the Refresh Schema option in the control's smart tag if the data source schema changes. Also, later in the chapter you look at using different fields in the GridView. Finally, the control's smart tag also includes options for formatting, paging, sorting, and selection, which you use later in this chapter.

When the GridView is rendering, it raises a number of events that you can use to alter the control's output or add additional custom logic to your application. These are described in Table 7-5.

TABLE 7-5

EVENT NAME	DESCRIPTION
`DataBinding`	Raised as the GridView's data-binding expressions are about to be evaluated.
`RowCreated`	Raised each time a new row is created in the grid. Before the grid can be rendered, a `GridViewRow` object must be created for each row in the control. The `RowCreated` event allows you to insert custom content into the row as it is being created.
`RowDataBound`	Raised as each `GridViewRow` is bound to the corresponding data in the data source. This event allows you to evaluate the data being bound to the current row and to affect the output if you need to.
`DataBound`	Raised after the binding is completed and the GridView is ready to be rendered.

The `RowDataBound` event is especially useful, enabling you to inject logic into the binding process for each data source item being bound to the GridView. Listing 7-26 shows how you can use this event to examine the data being bound to the current grid row and to insert special logic, in this example checking to see whether the items Region value is `null`. If a null value is found, logic changes the `ForeColor` and `BackColor` properties of the GridView's row.

LISTING 7-26: Using the RowDataBound to insert custom rendering logic

Available for download on Wrox.com

```
<script runat="server">
    Protected Sub GridView1_RowDataBound(ByVal sender As Object,
        ByVal e As System.Web.UI.WebControls.GridViewRowEventArgs)

        If (e.Row.DataItem IsNot Nothing) Then
            Dim drv As System.Data.DataRowView =
                CType(e.Row.DataItem, System.Data.DataRowView)

            If (drv("Region") Is System.DBNull.Value) Then
                e.Row.BackColor = System.Drawing.Color.Red
```

```
                e.Row.ForeColor = System.Drawing.Color.White
            End If
        End If
    End Sub
</script>
```

C#

```
<script runat="server">
    protected void GridView1_RowDataBound(object sender,
                                          GridViewRowEventArgs e)
    {
        if (e.Row.DataItem != null)
        {
            System.Data.DataRowView drv =
                (System.Data.DataRowView)e.Row.DataItem;

            if (drv["Region"] == System.DBNull.Value)
            {
                e.Row.BackColor = System.Drawing.Color.Red;
                e.Row.ForeColor = System.Drawing.Color.White;
            }
        }
    }
</script>
```

The GridView also includes events that correspond to selecting, inserting, updating, and deleting data. You will learn more about these events later in the chapter.

Handling Null and Empty Data Conditions

In some cases, the data source bound to the GridView may not contain any data for the control to bind to. In these cases you may want to provide the end user with some feedback informing them of this situation. The GridView includes two mechanisms to do this.

One option is to use the `EmptyDataText` property. This property allows you to specify a string of text that is displayed to the user when no data is present for the GridView to bind to. When the ASP.NET page loads and the GridView determines no data is available in its bound data source, it creates a special DataRow containing the `EmptyDataText` value and displays that to the user. Listing 7-27 shows how you can add this property to the GridView.

LISTING 7-27: Adding EmptyDataText to the GridView

Available for download on Wrox.com

```
<asp:GridView ID="GridView1" Runat="server"
    DataSourceID="SqlDataSource1" DataKeyNames="CustomerID"
    AutoGenerateColumns="True"
    EmptyDataText="No data was found using your query"></asp:GridView>
```

The other option is to use the EmptyDataTemplate control template to completely customize the special row the user sees when no data exists for the control to bind to.

A control template is simply a container that gives you the capability to add other content such as text, HTML controls, or even ASP.NET controls. The GridView control provides you with a variety of templates for various situations, including the EmptyDataTemplate template. This chapter examines these templates throughout the rest of this section.

You can access the template from the Visual Studio design surface in two ways. One option is to right-click the GridView control, expand the Edit Template option in the context menu, and select the EmptyDataTemplate item from the menu. This procedure is shown in Figure 7-13.

The other option is to select the Edit Templates option from the GridView's smart tag. Selecting this option puts the GridView into template editing mode and presents you with a dialog from which you can choose the specific template you want to edit. Simply select EmptyDataTemplate from the drop-down list, as shown in Figure 7-14.

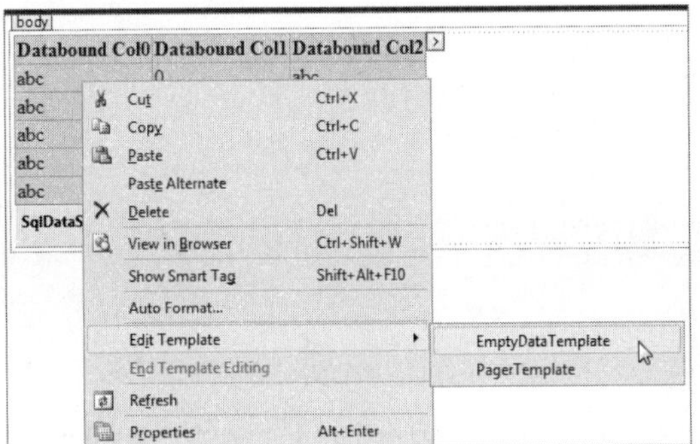

FIGURE 7-13

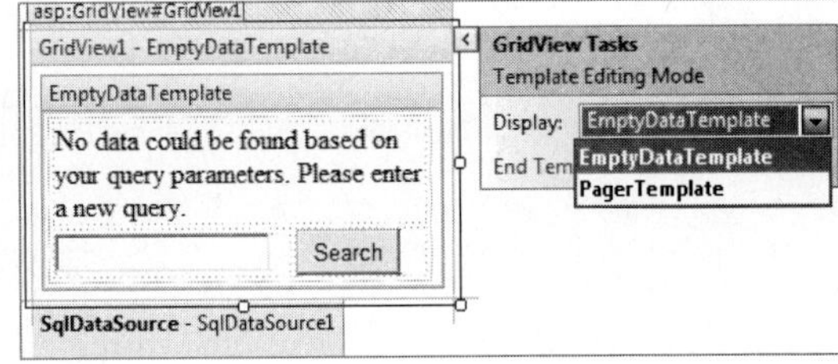

FIGURE 7-14

After you have entered template editing mode, you can add custom text and/or controls to the template editor on the design surface. When you have finished editing the template, right-click, or open the GridView's smart tag and select the End Template Editing option.

Switching to Source view, you see that an `<EmptyDataTemplate>` element has been added to the GridView control. The element contains all the content you added while editing the template. Listing 7-28 shows an example of an `EmptyDataTemplate`.

LISTING 7-28: Using EmptyDataTemplate

```
<EmptyDataTemplate>
    <table style="width: 225px">
        <tr>
            <td colspan="2">
                No data could be found based on your query parameters.
                Please enter a new query.</td>
        </tr>
        <tr>
            <td style="width: 162px">
                <asp:TextBox ID="TextBox1"
                     runat="server"></asp:TextBox></td>
            <td style="width: 102px">
                <asp:Button ID="Button1"
                     runat="server" Text="Search" /></td>
        </tr>
    </table>
</EmptyDataTemplate>
```

You could, of course, have also added the template and its contents while in Source view.

The GridView also allows you to configure a value to display if the GridView encounters a `Null` value when binding to a data source. For an example of this, add a column using a `<asp:BoundField>` control, as shown in Listing 7-29.

LISTING 7-29: Using the Null value

Available for download on Wrox.com

```
<asp:BoundField DataField="Region" HeaderText="Region"
      NullDisplayText="N/A" SortExpression="Region" />
```

The `<asp:BoundField>` is configured to display the Region column from the Customers table. As you look through the data in the Region column, notice that not every row has a value in it. If you don't want to display just a blank cell, you can use the `NullDisplayText` property to configure the GridView to display text in place of the empty items in the column. Figure 7-15 shows the results of setting a value for this property.

Using the GridView server control - Windows Internet Explorer

http://localhost:1934/Chapter%2007/VB/Listing7-2!

Favorites | Suggested Sites ▾ | Web Slice Gallery ▾

Using the GridView server control | Page ▾ Safety ▾ Tools ▾

CustomerID	CompanyName	ContactName	ContactTitle	Address	City	Region	PostalCode	Country	Phone	Fax
ALFKI	Alfreds Futterkiste	Maria Anders	Sales Representative	Obere Str. 57	Berlin	N/A	12209	Germany	030-0074321	030-0076545
ANATR	Ana Trujillo Emparedados y helados	Ana Trujillo	Owner	Avda. de la Constitución 2222	México D.F.	N/A	05021	Mexico	(5) 555-4729	(5) 555-3745
ANTON	Antonio Moreno Taqueria	Antonio Moreno	Owner	Mataderos 2312	México D.F.	N/A	05023	Mexico	(5) 555-3932	
AROUT	Around the Horn	Thomas Hardy	Sales Representative	120 Hanover Sq.	London	N/A	WA1 1DP	UK	(171) 555-7788	(171) 555-6750
BERGS	Berglunds snabbköp	Christina Berglund	Order Administrator	Berguvsvägen 8	Luleå	N/A	S-958 22	Sweden	0921-12 34 65	0921-12 34 67
BLAUS	Blauer See Delikatessen	Hanna Moos	Sales Representative	Forsterstr. 57	Mannheim	N/A	68306	Germany	0621-08460	0621-08924
BLONP	Blondesddsl père et fils	Frédérique Citeaux	Marketing Manager	24, place Kléber	Strasbourg	N/A	67000	France	88.60.15.31	88.60.15.32
BOLID	Bólido Comidas preparadas	Martin Sommer	Owner	C/ Araquil, 67	Madrid	N/A	28023	Spain	(91) 555 22 82	(91) 555 91 99
BONAP	Bon app'	Laurence Lebihan	Owner	12, rue des Bouchers	Marseille	N/A	13008	France	91.24.45.40	91.24.45.41
BOTTM	Bottom-Dollar Markets	Elizabeth Lincoln	Accounting Manager	23 Tsawassen Blvd.	Tsawassen	BC	T2F 8M4	Canada	(604) 555-4729	(604) 555-3745
BSBEV	B's Beverages	Victoria	Sales	Fauntleroy	London	N/A	EC2 5NT	UK	(171) 555-	

Done | Local intranet | Protected Mode: Off | 75%

FIGURE 7-15

Column Sorting

The capability to sort data is one of the most basic tools users have to navigate through data. To enable sorting in the GridView control just set the `AllowSorting` attribute to `True`. The control takes care of all the sorting logic for you internally. Listing 7-30 shows how to add this attribute to your grid.

LISTING 7-30: Adding sorting to the GridView control

Available for download on Wrox.com

```
<asp:GridView ID="GridView1" Runat="server"
    DataSourceID="SqlDataSource1" DataKeyNames="CustomerID"
    AutoGenerateColumns="True" AllowSorting="True"></asp:GridView>
```

After enabling sorting, you will see that all the grid's column headers have now become hyperlinks. Clicking a header sorts the data in that column. Figure 7-16 shows your grid after the data has been sorted by country.

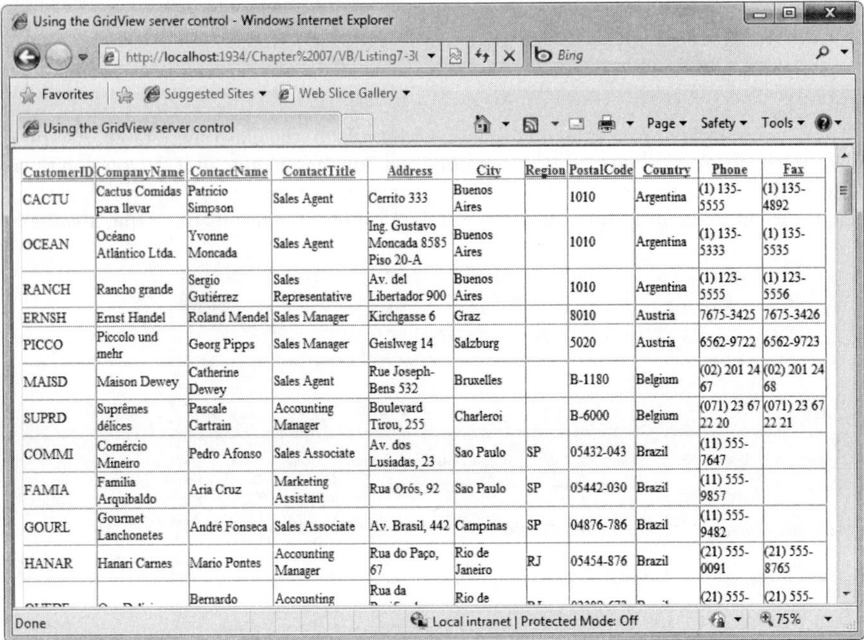

FIGURE 7-16

The GridView sorting can handle both ascending and descending sorting. Repeatedly click on a column header to cause the sort order to switch back and forth between ascending and descending. The GridView also includes a `Sort` method that can accept multiple `SortExpressions` to enable multicolumn sorting. Listing 7-31 shows how you can use the GridView's Sorting event to implement multicolumn sorting.

LISTING 7-31: Adding multicolumn sorting to the GridView

Available for download on Wrox.com

VB

```
<script runat="server">
    Protected Sub GridView1_Sorting(ByVal sender As Object,
                                    ByVal e As GridViewSortEventArgs)

        Dim oldExpression As String = GridView1.SortExpression
        Dim newExpression As String = e.SortExpression

        If (oldExpression.IndexOf(newExpression) < 0) Then
            If (oldExpression.Length > 0) Then
                e.SortExpression = newExpression & "," & oldExpression
            Else
                e.SortExpression = newExpression
            End If
        Else
            e.SortExpression = oldExpression
        End If
    End Sub
</script>
```

C#

```
<script runat="server">
    protected void GridView1_Sorting(object sender,
                                     GridViewSortEventArgs e)
    {
        string oldExpression = GridView1.SortExpression;
        string newExpression = e.SortExpression;
```

```
            if (oldExpression.IndexOf(newExpression) < 0)
            {
                if (oldExpression.Length > 0)
                    e.SortExpression = newExpression + "," + oldExpression;
                else
                    e.SortExpression = newExpression;
            }
            else
            {
                e.SortExpression = oldExpression;
            }
        }
</script>
```

The listing uses the `Sorting` event to manipulate the value of the control's `SortExpression` property. The event's parameters enable you to examine the current sort expression, direction of the sort, or even cancel the sort action altogether. The GridView also offers a `Sorted` event, which is raised after the sort has completed.

Paging GridView Data

The GridView also allows you to easily add another common grid feature — paging. To enable paging, set the `AllowPaging` property to `True` or select the Enable Paging check box in the GridView's smart tag. The control defaults to a page size of 10 records and adds the pager to the bottom of the grid. Listing 7-32 shows an example of modifying your grid to enable sorting and paging.

Available for download on Wrox.com

LISTING 7-32: Enabling sorting and paging on the GridView control

```
<asp:GridView ID="GridView1" Runat="server"
    DataSourceID="SqlDataSource1" DataKeyNames="CustomerID"
    AutoGenerateColumns="True" AllowSorting="True"
    AllowPaging="True"></asp:GridView>
```

After enabling sorting and paging in your GridView, you should have a page that looks similar to Figure 7-17.

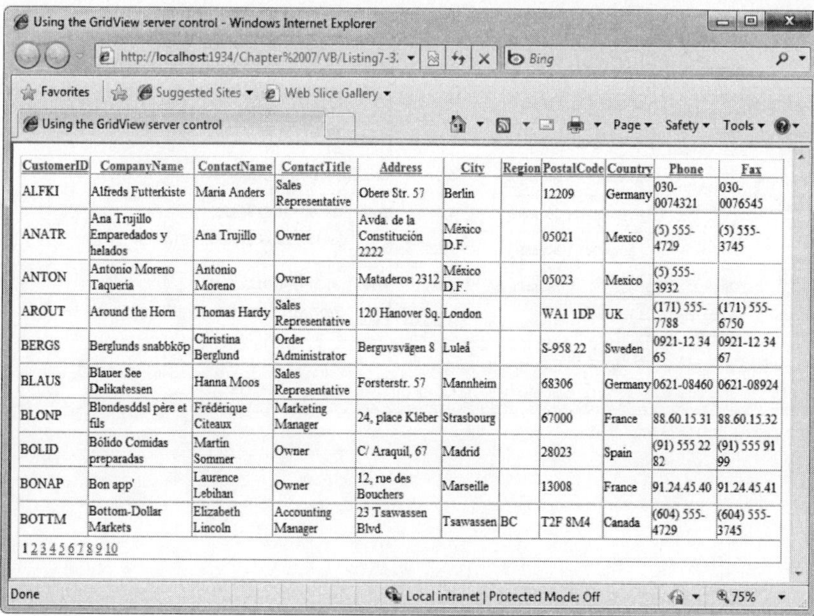

CustomerID	CompanyName	ContactName	ContactTitle	Address	City	Region	PostalCode	Country	Phone	Fax
ALFKI	Alfreds Futterkiste	Maria Anders	Sales Representative	Obere Str. 57	Berlin		12209	Germany	030-0074321	030-0076545
ANATR	Ana Trujillo Emparedados y helados	Ana Trujillo	Owner	Avda. de la Constitución 2222	México D.F.		05021	Mexico	(5) 555-4729	(5) 555-3745
ANTON	Antonio Moreno Taquería	Antonio Moreno	Owner	Mataderos 2312	México D.F.		05023	Mexico	(5) 555-3932	
AROUT	Around the Horn	Thomas Hardy	Sales Representative	120 Hanover Sq.	London		WA1 1DP	UK	(171) 555-7788	(171) 555-6750
BERGS	Berglunds snabbköp	Christina Berglund	Order Administrator	Berguvsvägen 8	Luleå		S-958 22	Sweden	0921-12 34 65	0921-12 34 67
BLAUS	Blauer See Delikatessen	Hanna Moos	Sales Representative	Forsterstr. 57	Mannheim		68306	Germany	0621-08460	0621-08924
BLONP	Blondesddsl père et fils	Frédérique Citeaux	Marketing Manager	24, place Kléber	Strasbourg		67000	France	88.60.15.31	88.60.15.32
BOLID	Bólido Comidas preparadas	Martín Sommer	Owner	C/ Araquil, 67	Madrid		28023	Spain	(91) 555 22 82	(91) 555 91 99
BONAP	Bon app'	Laurence Lebihan	Owner	12, rue des Bouchers	Marseille		13008	France	91.24.45.40	91.24.45.41
BOTTM	Bottom-Dollar Markets	Elizabeth Lincoln	Accounting Manager	23 Tsawassen Blvd.	Tsawassen	BC	T2F 8M4	Canada	(604) 555-4729	(604) 555-3745

1 2 3 4 5 6 7 8 9 10

FIGURE 7-17

The GridView includes a variety of properties that allow you to customize paging. For instance, you can control the number of records displayed on the page using the GridView's `PageSize` attribute. The `PagersSettings Mode` attribute allows you to dictate how the grid's pager is displayed using the various pager modes including `NextPrevious`, `NextPreviousFirstLast`, `Numeric` (the default value), or `NumericFirstLast`. Additionally, specifying the `PagerStyle` element in the GridView, you can customize how the grid displays the pager text, including font color, size, and type, as well as text alignment and a variety of other style options. Listing 7-33 shows how you can customize your GridView control to use the `NextPrevious` mode and style the pager text using the `PagerStyle` element.

LISTING 7-33: Using the PagerStyle and PagerSettings properties in the GridView control

Available for download on Wrox.com

```
<asp:GridView ID="GridView1" Runat="server" DataSourceID="SqlDataSource1"
     DataKeyNames="CustomerID" AutoGenerateColumns="True"
     AllowSorting="True" AllowPaging="True" PageSize="10">
     <PagerStyle HorizontalAlign="Center" />
     <PagerSettings Position="TopAndBottom"
          FirstPageText="Go to the first page"
          LastPageText="Go to the last page"
          Mode="NextPreviousFirstLast">
     </PagerSettings>
</asp:GridView>
```

Figure 7-18 shows the grid after changing the pager style options and setting the `PagerSettings Mode` property to `NextPreviousFirstLast`.

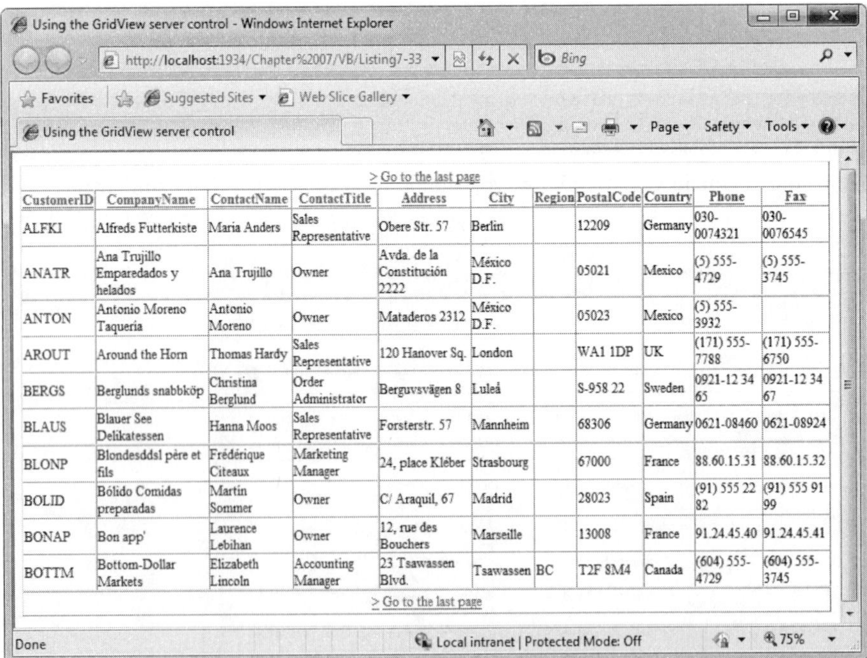

CustomerID	CompanyName	ContactName	ContactTitle	Address	City	Region	PostalCode	Country	Phone	Fax
ALFKI	Alfreds Futterkiste	Maria Anders	Sales Representative	Obere Str. 57	Berlin		12209	Germany	030-0074321	030-0076545
ANATR	Ana Trujillo Emparedados y helados	Ana Trujillo	Owner	Avda. de la Constitución 2222	México D.F.		05021	Mexico	(5) 555-4729	(5) 555-3745
ANTON	Antonio Moreno Taqueria	Antonio Moreno	Owner	Mataderos 2312	México D.F.		05023	Mexico	(5) 555-3932	
AROUT	Around the Horn	Thomas Hardy	Sales Representative	120 Hanover Sq.	London		WA1 1DP	UK	(171) 555-7788	(171) 555-6750
BERGS	Berglunds snabbköp	Christina Berglund	Order Administrator	Berguvsvägen 8	Luleå		S-958 22	Sweden	0921-12 34 65	0921-12 34 67
BLAUS	Blauer See Delikatessen	Hanna Moos	Sales Representative	Forsterstr. 57	Mannheim		68306	Germany	0621-08460	0621-08924
BLONP	Blondesddsl père et fils	Frédérique Citeaux	Marketing Manager	24, place Kléber	Strasbourg		67000	France	88.60.15.31	88.60.15.32
BOLID	Bólido Comidas preparadas	Martin Sommer	Owner	C/ Araquil, 67	Madrid		28023	Spain	(91) 555 22 82	(91) 555 91 99
BONAP	Bon app'	Laurence Lebihan	Owner	12, rue des Bouchers	Marseille		13008	France	91.24.45.40	91.24.45.41
BOTTM	Bottom-Dollar Markets	Elizabeth Lincoln	Accounting Manager	23 Tsawassen Blvd.	Tsawassen	BC	T2F 8M4	Canada	(604) 555-4729	(604) 555-3745

FIGURE 7-18

Because the list of `PagerSetting` and `PagerStyle` properties is so long, all options are not listed here, but you can find a full list of the options in the Visual Studio Help documents.

The GridView control also offers two events you can use to customize the standard paging behavior of the grid. The `PageIndexChanging` and `PageIndexChanged` events are raised before and after the GridView's current page index changes. The page index changes when the user clicks the pager links in the grid. The `PageIndexChanging` event parameters allow you to examine the value of the new page index before it actually changes or even cancel the paging event altogether.

The GridView also includes the `EnableSortingAndPagingCallbacks` property that allows you to indicate whether the control should use client callbacks to perform sorting and paging. Enabling this property changes the GridView's paging and sorting behaviors to use client-side AJAX callbacks to retrieve data, rather than a full-page postback.

If you are interested in learning more about other ways you can integrate AJAX into your ASP.NET applications, Chapters 18 and 19 introduce you to the ASP.NET AJAX Framework and how you can leverage its capabilities in your applications.

Customizing Columns in the GridView

Frequently the data you need to display in your grid is not simply text data, but data that you want to display using other types of controls or perhaps don't want to display at all.

If you have your grid configured to automatically generate columns based on the bound data source, the grid creates fields for each public property exposed by the data source. Additionally for all of these properties, except those that return a Boolean type, the grid defaults to using its standard BoundField type, which treats all types as strings. For Boolean types the grid will use the CheckBoxField by default.

These default behaviors might not be optimal in your application. For example, the samples shown thus far have been retrieving the CustomerID as part of the `SELECT` query. Because by default the GridView control displays all columns returned as part of a query, this property is also shown. However, showing IDs is usually not very useful to end users, so you may find that hiding this data from the end user is better.

Or perhaps you are storing the Web site address for all of your customers and want the CustomerName column to be displayed as a hyperlink, allowing your end users to link directly to a Customer's Web site. The GridView includes a number of specialized Field types that make displaying things like hyperlinks, check boxes, or buttons in grid columns easy.

You have two ways to configure columns in the GridView: through options in the GridView's smart tag or by editing the column markup directly in Source view.

Clicking the Edit Columns link in the GridView's smart tag opens the Fields dialog window, shown in Figure 7-19. From here you can change any existing column's visibility, header text, the usual style options, and many other properties of the column.

Selecting the Add New Column link from the GridView control's smart tag displays the Add Field dialog, shown in Figure 7-20. This dialog includes options that allow you to add completely new columns to your grid. Depending on which column field type you select from the drop-down list, the dialog presents you with the appropriate options for that column type.

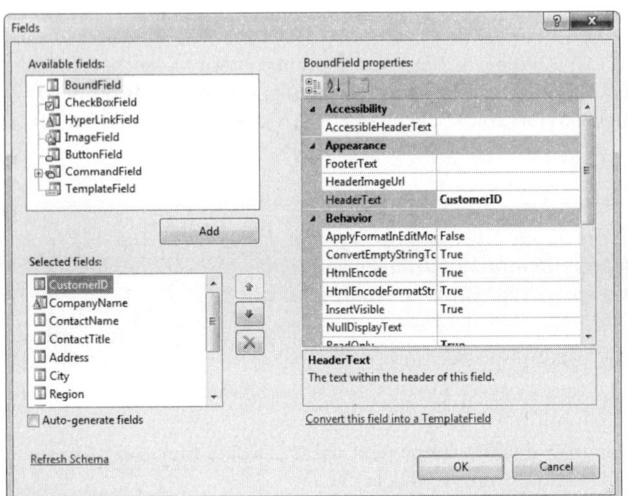

FIGURE 7-19

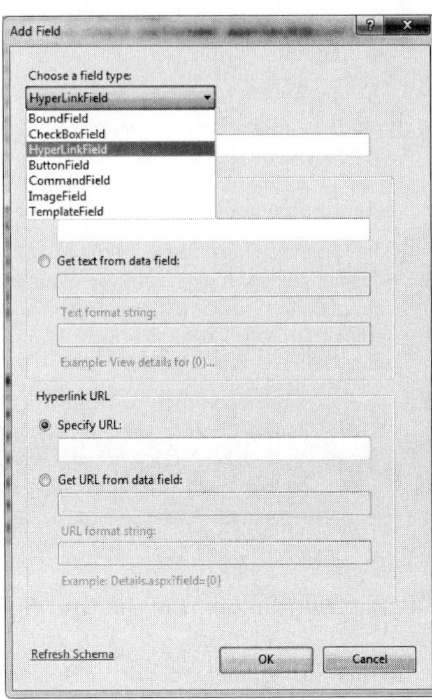

FIGURE 7-20

The Add Field dialog lets you select one of the field types described in Table 7-6.

TABLE 7-6

FIELD CONTROL	DESCRIPTION
BoundField	Displays the value of a field in a data source. This is the default column type of the GridView control.
CheckBoxField	Displays a check box for each item in the GridView control. This column field type is commonly used to display fields with a Boolean value.
HyperLinkField	Displays the value of a field in a data source as a hyperlink. This column field type allows you to bind a second field to the hyperlink's URL.
ButtonField	Displays a command button for each item in the GridView control. This allows you to create a column of custom button controls, such as an Add or Remove button.
CommandField	Represents a field that displays command buttons to perform select, edit, insert, or delete operations in a data-bound control.
ImageField	Automatically displays an image when the data in the field represents an image.
TemplateField	Displays user-defined content for each item in the GridView control according to a specified template. This column field type allows you to create a customized column field.

In the example described earlier where you want to allow end users to link to a Customer's Web site, you want to select the HyperLinkField from the drop-down list. The Add Field dialog changes and lets you enter in the hyperlink information, including the URL, the data field, and a format string for the column.

You can also modify the grid's columns in the Source view, manually adding or editing any of the field types listed in the previous table. Listing 7-34 shows how you can add the appropriate markup in Source view to create a HyperLinkField.

LISTING 7-34: Adding a HyperLinkField control to the GridView

Available for download on Wrox.com

```
<asp:HyperLinkField DataTextField="CompanyName"
    HeaderText="CompanyName" DataNavigateUrlFields="CustomerID,Country"
    SortExpression="CompanyName"
    DataNavigateUrlFormatString=
        http://www.example.com/Customer.aspx?id={0}&country={1} />
```

When you add a Field in Source view you need to make sure you specify a property name from your data source on the field. Each field type exposes a different property (or set of properties) that allow you to define this connection between the field and data source. In the previous example you can see that the `HyperLinkField`'s `DataNavigateUrlFields` property actually allows you to provide a comma-delimited list of data source property names. This allows you to specify multiple data source values to bind to this column. You can then use these fields in your format string to pass two query string parameters.

Using the TemplateField Column

A key column type available in the GridView control is the TemplateField column. This column type allows you to completely customize the contents of column cells by defining templates.

The TemplateField provides you with six different templates that enable you to customize different areas or states of the column, such as edit state. Table 7-7 describes the available templates.

TABLE 7-7

TEMPLATE NAME	DESCRIPTION
ItemTemplate	Template used for displaying an item in the TemplateField of the data-bound control
AlternatingItemTemplate	Template used for displaying the alternating items of the TemplateField
EditItemTemplate	Template used for displaying a TemplateField item in edit state
InsertItemTemplate	Template used for displaying a TemplateField item in insert state
HeaderTemplate	Template used for displaying the header section of the TemplateField
FooterTemplate	Template used for displaying the footer section of the TemplateField

To use the TemplateField in a GridView, add the column type to a grid using the Add Field dialog as described in the previous section. The `<asp:TemplateField>` tag serves as a container for the various templates the column can contain. To add content to the templates you can use the template editing features of the Visual Studio 2010 design surface or manually add content directly to the TemplateField element in Source view.

You have two ways to access the template editing features from the Visual Studio design surface. The first option is to right-click the GridView and choose the Column[*nn*] (where *nn* is your specific column index) option from the Edit Template option in the context menu. When you use this method, each available template for the column is displayed on the Visual Studio 2010 design surface, as shown in Figure 7-21.

The second option is to open the GridView control's smart tag and select the Edit Template command. This opens a menu, shown in Figure 7-22, that allows you to select the column template you want to edit.

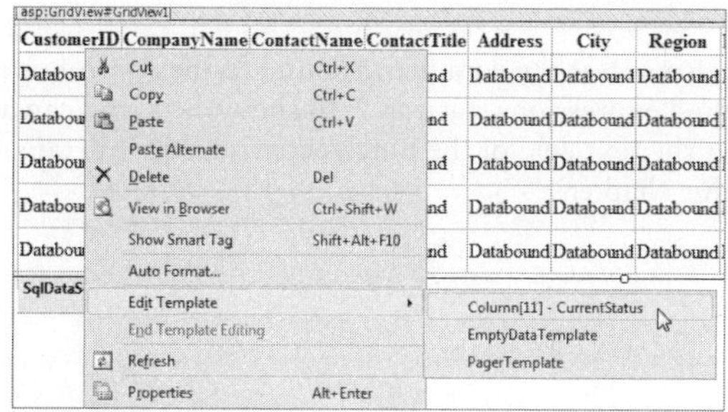

FIGURE 7-21

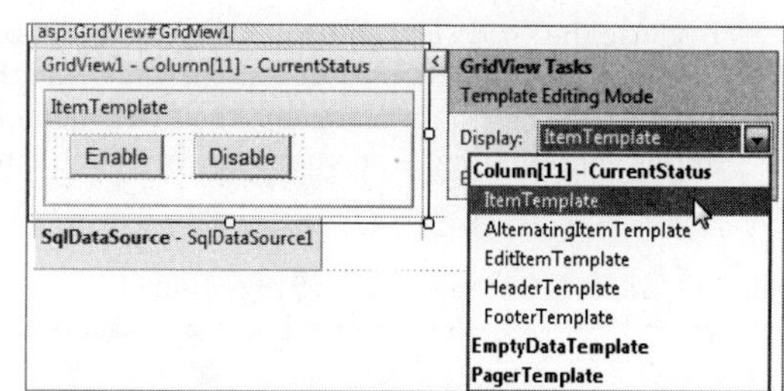

FIGURE 7-22

The ItemTemplate controls the default contents of each cell of the column. Listing 7-35 demonstrates how you can use the ItemTemplate to customize the contents of the column.

LISTING 7-35: Using ItemTemplate

```
<asp:TemplateField HeaderText="CurrentStatus">
    <ItemTemplate>
        <table>
            <tr>
                <td align="center" style="width: 78px">
                    <asp:Button ID="Button2"
                         runat="server" Text="Enable" /></td>
                <td align="center" style="width: 76px">
                    <asp:Button ID="Button3"
                         runat="server" Text="Disable" /></td>
            </tr>
        </table>
    </ItemTemplate>
</asp:TemplateField>
```

In the sample the ItemTemplate contains a combination of an HTML table and ASP.NET Button controls. Figure 7-23 shows what the sample looks like when it is displayed in the browser.

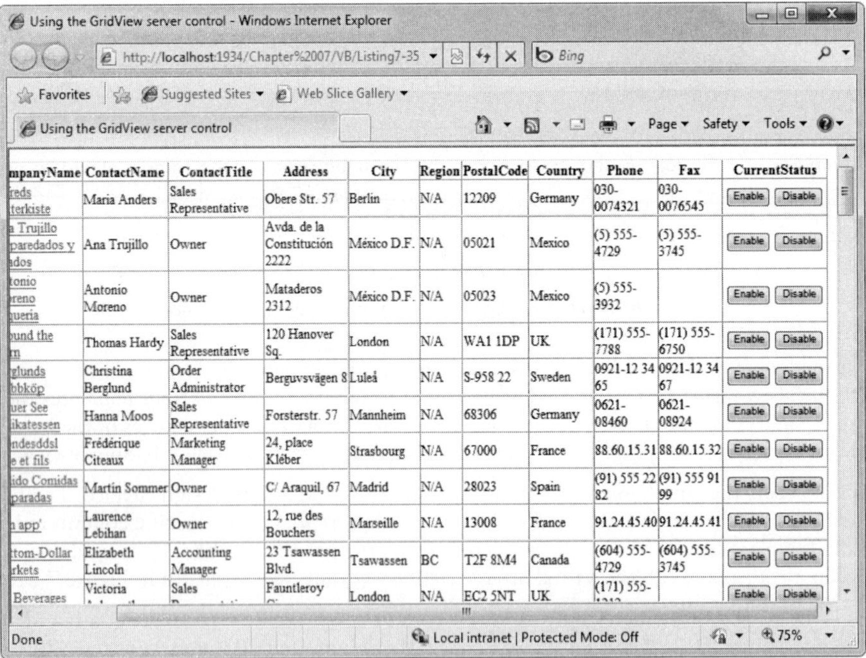

FIGURE 7-23

Because the GridView control is data-bound, you can also access the data being bound to the control using data-binding expressions such as the Eval, XPath, or Bind expressions. Listing 7-36 shows how you can add a data-binding expression using the `Eval` method to set the text field of the Button control. More details about data-binding expressions can be found later in this chapter.

Available for download on Wrox.com

LISTING 7-36: Adding a data-binding expression

```
<asp:TemplateField HeaderText="CurrentStatus">
    <ItemTemplate>
        <table>
            <tr>
                <td align="center" style="width: 78px">
                    <asp:Button ID="Button2" runat="server"
                       Text='<%# "Enable " + Eval("CustomerID") %>' />
                </td>
                <td align="center" style="width: 76px">
                    <asp:Button ID="Button3" runat="server"
                       Text='<%# "Disable " + Eval("CustomerID") %>' />
                </td>
            </tr>
        </table>
    </ItemTemplate>
</asp:TemplateField>
```

Other common templates available in the TemplateField are the InsertTemplate and EditTemplate. These templates are used by the grid when a row enters insert or edit mode. Inserting and editing data in the GridView control, including using the InsertItemTemplate and EditItemTemplate, are reviewed in the next section.

Editing GridView Row Data

Users not only want to view the data in their browser, but they also want to be able to edit the data and save changes back to the data source. When combined with data source controls, the GridView control makes editing data bound to the grid easy. To demonstrate just how easy enabling editing is, you can modify the SqlDataSource and GridView controls used in the previous samples to allow users to edit the Customers data.

Note that although in this chapter you focus on updating data in a GridView bound to a SqlDataSource control, you can also update data when connecting the GridView to other data source controls. The configuration needed to enable end users to place grid rows into edit mode and insert or delete data via the GridView is identical regardless of the bound data source control. The configuration needed to enable the data source control to persist these changes to the underlying data store is specific to each data source control. If you are using a data source control other than the SqlDataSource, you can refer to the section in this chapter that discusses the details of persisting inserts, updates, and deletes of data for that control.

Configuring the SqlDataSource for Updates

To get started, first modify the SqlDataSource control by adding an `UpdateCommand` either by using the Configure Data Source wizard or by manually adding the markup in source view. This property tells the data source control what SQL command it should execute when an update needs to be performed. Listing 7-37 shows the markup needed to add the `UpdateCommand` property.

Available for download on Wrox.com

LISTING 7-37: Adding an UpdateCommand to a SqlDataSource control

```
<asp:SqlDataSource ID="SqlDataSource1" Runat="server"
    SelectCommand="SELECT * FROM [Customers]"
    ConnectionString="<%$ ConnectionStrings:ConnectionString %>"
    DataSourceMode="DataSet"
    UpdateCommand="UPDATE [Customers] SET [CompanyName] = @CompanyName,
        [ContactName] = @ContactName, [ContactTitle] = @ContactTitle,
        [Address] = @Address, [City] = @City, [Region] = @Region,
        [PostalCode] = @PostalCode, [Country] = @Country,
        [Phone] = @Phone,[Fax] = @Fax
        WHERE [CustomerID] = @original_CustomerID">
</asp:SqlDataSource>
```

Notice that the `UpdateCommand` includes a number of placeholders such as `@CompanyName`, `@Country`, `@Region`, and `@CustomerID`. These placeholders represent the information that will come from the GridView when a row is updated. Each placeholder corresponds to a `Parameter` element defined in the SqlDataSource control's `UpdateParameters` collection. The `UpdateParameters` collection, shown in Listing 7-38, works much like the `SelectParameters` element discussed earlier in the chapter.

LISTING 7-38: Adding UpdateParameters to the SqlDataSource control

Available for download on Wrox.com

```
<UpdateParameters>
    <asp:Parameter Type="String" Name="CompanyName"></asp:Parameter>
    <asp:Parameter Type="String" Name="ContactName"></asp:Parameter>
    <asp:Parameter Type="String" Name="ContactTitle"></asp:Parameter>
    <asp:Parameter Type="String" Name="Address"></asp:Parameter>
    <asp:Parameter Type="String" Name="City"></asp:Parameter>
    <asp:Parameter Type="String" Name="Region"></asp:Parameter>
    <asp:Parameter Type="String" Name="PostalCode"></asp:Parameter>
    <asp:Parameter Type="String" Name="Country"></asp:Parameter>
    <asp:Parameter Type="String" Name="Phone"></asp:Parameter>
    <asp:Parameter Type="String" Name="Fax"></asp:Parameter>
    <asp:Parameter Type="String" Name="CustomerID"></asp:Parameter>
</UpdateParameters>
```

Each `Parameter` uses two properties to create a connection to the underlying data source, `Name`, which is the database column name, and `Type`, which is the database column's data type. In this case, all the parameters are of type `String`.

Remember that you can also use any of the parameter types mentioned earlier in the chapter, such as the `ControlParameter` or `QueryStringParameter` in the `UpdateParameters` element.

Configuring GridView for Updates

Now that you have configured the SqlDataSource for updates, you need to create a way to place a row in the GridView into edit mode and a way to tell the GridView what the database table's primary key is.

The GridView includes two built-in ways to place a row into edit mode: the `AutoGenerateEditButton` property and the `CommandField`.

When the `AutoGenerateEditButton` property is set to `True`, this tells the grid to add a `ButtonField` column with an edit button for each row. Clicking one of the buttons places the associated row into edit mode. Listing 7-39 shows how to add the `AutoGenerateEditButton` attribute to the GridView control.

LISTING 7-39: Adding the AutoGenerateEditButton property to a GridView

Available for download on Wrox.com

```
<asp:GridView ID="GridView1" Runat="server"
    DataSourceID="SqlDataSource1" DataKeyNames="CustomerID"
    AutoGenerateColumns="True" AllowSorting="True" AllowPaging="True"
    AutoGenerateEditButton="true" />
```

The GridView control also includes `AutoGenerateSelectButton` and `AutoGenerateDeleteButton` properties, which allow you to easily add row selection and row deletion capabilities to the grid.

The `CommandField` column is a special field type that allows you to enable end users to execute different commands on rows in the GridView. Listing 7-40 shows how to configure the `CommandField` to allow the end user to place a row into edit mode.

LISTING 7-40: Adding edit functionality using a CommandField

Available for download on Wrox.com

```
<asp:CommandField ShowHeader="True" HeaderText="Command"
    ShowEditButton="True" />
```

The `CommandField` includes a `ShowEditButton` property that when set to `True`, displays the Edit command in this column. You can control how the command is displayed in the grid using the `ButtonType` property, which allows you to display the command as a link, a button, or even an image. Figure 7-24 shows what the grid looks like after adding the `CommandField` with the `edit` command displayed.

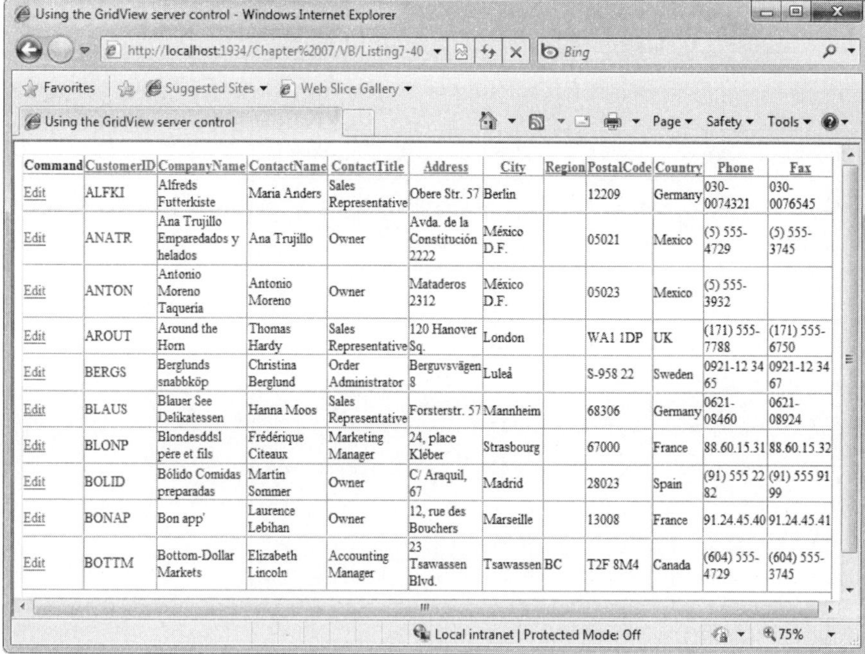

Command	CustomerID	CompanyName	ContactName	ContactTitle	Address	City	Region	PostalCode	Country	Phone	Fax
Edit	ALFKI	Alfreds Futterkiste	Maria Anders	Sales Representative	Obere Str. 57	Berlin		12209	Germany	030-0074321	030-0076545
Edit	ANATR	Ana Trujillo Emparedados y helados	Ana Trujillo	Owner	Avda. de la Constitución 2222	México D.F.		05021	Mexico	(5) 555-4729	(5) 555-3745
Edit	ANTON	Antonio Moreno Taqueria	Antonio Moreno	Owner	Mataderos 2312	México D.F.		05023	Mexico	(5) 555-3932	
Edit	AROUT	Around the Horn	Thomas Hardy	Sales Representative	120 Hanover Sq.	London		WA1 1DP	UK	(171) 555-7788	(171) 555-6750
Edit	BERGS	Berglunds snabbköp	Christina Berglund	Order Administrator	Berguvsvägen 8	Luleå		S-958 22	Sweden	0921-12 34 65	0921-12 34 67
Edit	BLAUS	Blauer See Delikatessen	Hanna Moos	Sales Representative	Forsterstr. 57	Mannheim		68306	Germany	0621-08460	0621-08924
Edit	BLONP	Blondesddsl père et fils	Frédérique Citeaux	Marketing Manager	24, place Kléber	Strasbourg		67000	France	88.60.15.31	88.60.15.32
Edit	BOLID	Bólido Comidas preparadas	Martin Sommer	Owner	C/ Araquil, 67	Madrid		28023	Spain	(91) 555 22 82	(91) 555 91 99
Edit	BONAP	Bon app'	Laurence Lebihan	Owner	12, rue des Bouchers	Marseille		13008	France	91.24.45.40	91.24.45.41
Edit	BOTTM	Bottom-Dollar Markets	Elizabeth Lincoln	Accounting Manager	23 Tsawassen Blvd.	Tsawassen	BC	T2F 8M4	Canada	(604) 555-4729	(604) 555-3745

FIGURE 7-24

Now if you browse to your Web page, you see that a new edit column has been added. Clicking the Edit link allows the user to edit the contents of that particular data row.

The `CommandField` element also has attributes that allow you to control exactly what is shown in the column. You can dictate whether the column displays commands such as Cancel, Delete, Edit, Insert, or Select.

To complete configuring the grid to allow editing, you need to ensure the grid knows which database table columns are configured as its primary key. You can specify this using the GridView's `DataKeyNames` property, which is shown in Listing 7-41.

LISTING 7-41: Adding the DataKeyNames to the GridView control

Available for download on Wrox.com

```
<asp:GridView ID="GridView1" Runat="server"
    DataSourceID="SqlDataSource1" DataKeyNames="CustomerID"
    AutoGenerateColumns="False" AllowSorting="True" AllowPaging="True">
```

If the primary key of the table is more than one column, you can specify more than one column name setting using a comma-delimited list.

You can control which columns the grid allows to be edited by adding the `ReadOnly` property to the columns that you do not want users to edit. Listing 7-42 shows how you can add the `ReadOnly` property to the ID column.

LISTING 7-42: Adding the ReadOnly property to a BoundField

Available for download on Wrox.com

```
<asp:BoundField DataField="CustomerID" HeaderText="CustomerID"
    SortExpression="CustomerID" ReadOnly="True" />
```

Now if you browse to the Web page again and click the Edit button, you should see that the ID column is not editable. This is shown in Figure 7-25.

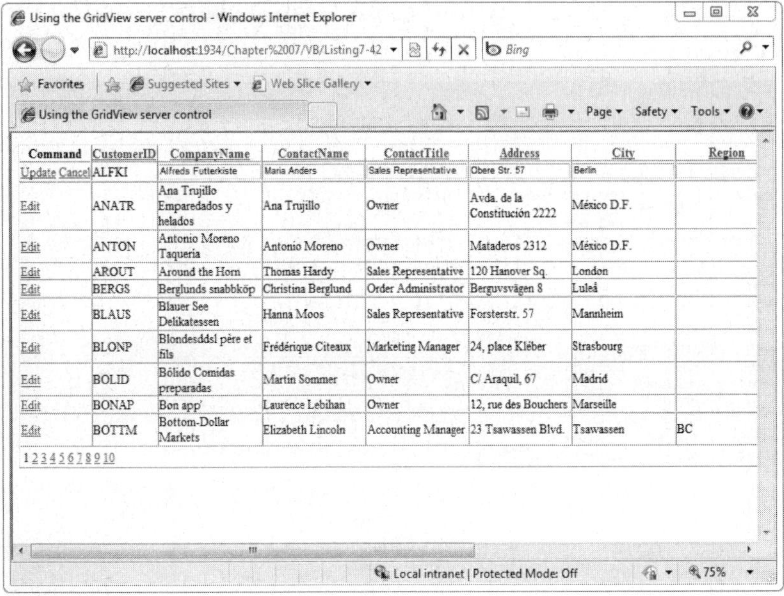

FIGURE 7-25

Handling Errors When Updating Data

As much as you try to prevent them, errors may happen when you try to save data. If you allow your users to update data in your GridView control, you should implement error handling to make sure unhandled errors do not bubble up to the user.

You can check for errors when updating data through the GridView, using the `RowUpdated` event. Listing 7-43 shows how to check for errors after an attempt to update data.

LISTING 7-43: Checking for Update errors using the RowUpdated event

Available for download on Wrox.com

VB

```
<script runat="server">
    Protected Sub GridView1_RowUpdated(ByVal sender As Object,
       ByVal e As System.Web.UI.WebControls.GridViewUpdatedEventArgs)

        If e.Exception IsNot Nothing Then
            Me.lblErrorMessage.Text = e.Exception.Message
        End If
    End Sub
</script>
```

C#

```
<script runat="server">
    protected void GridView1_RowUpdated(object sender,
                                    GridViewUpdatedEventArgs e)
    {
        if (e.Exception != null)
        {
            this.lblErrorMessage.Text = e.Exception.Message;
        }
    }
</script>
```

The `RowUpdated` event arguments include an `Exception` property. The listing checks to see whether this property is null. If not, that indicates an error has occurred, and a message is shown to the end user.

Using the TemplateField's EditItemTemplate

Earlier in the chapter, you were introduced to the TemplateField and some of the templates it includes. One of those templates is the EditItemTemplate, which the grid uses when a TemplateField column for a row enters edit mode. Using the EditItemTemplate allows you to completely customize the data editing experience of the user. For instance, a better editing experience for the Region column would be to present the possible values as a DropDownList rather than as a simple text box, which is the default editing experience for the BoundField.

To do this, you simply change the Region column from a BoundField to a TemplateField and add an ItemTemplate and an EditItemTemplate. In the EditItemTemplate, you can add a DropDownList control and provide the proper data-binding information so that the control is bound to a unique list of Regions. Listing 7-44 shows how you can add the ItemTemplate and EditItemTemplate to the GridView.

LISTING 7-44: Adding the ItemTemplate and EditItemTemplate to the GridView

Available for download on Wrox.com

```
<asp:TemplateField HeaderText="Country">
    <ItemTemplate><%# Eval("Country") %></ItemTemplate>
    <EditItemTemplate>
        <asp:DropDownList ID="DropDownList1" runat="server"
            DataSourceID="SqlDataSource2"
            DataTextField="Country" DataValueField="Country">
        </asp:DropDownList>
        <asp:SqlDataSource ID="SqlDataSource2" runat="server"
            ConnectionString=
                "<%$ ConnectionStrings:ConnectionString %>"
            SelectCommand="SELECT DISTINCT [Country] FROM [Customers]">
        </asp:SqlDataSource>
    </EditItemTemplate>
</asp:TemplateField>
```

A simple `Eval` data-binding expression is used in the ItemTemplate to display the value of the column in the row's default display mode. In the EditItemTemplate, a DropDownList control bound to a SqlDataSource control is included.

To show the currently selected Country in the DropDownList control, you use the `RowDataBound` event. Listing 7-45 shows how this is done.

LISTING 7-45: Using RowDataBound event to select a DropDownList item

Available for download on Wrox.com

VB

```
<script runat="server">
    Protected Sub GridView1_RowDataBound(ByVal sender As Object,
        ByVal e As System.Web.UI.WebControls.GridViewRowEventArgs)

        'Check for a row in edit mode.
        If ((e.Row.RowState = DataControlRowState.Edit) Or
            (e.Row.RowState = (DataControlRowState.Alternate Or
            DataControlRowState.Edit))) Then

            Dim drv As System.Data.DataRowView =
                CType(e.Row.DataItem, System.Data.DataRowView)

            Dim ddl As DropDownList =
                CType(e.Row.Cells(8).
                    FindControl("DropDownList1"), DropDownList)
            Dim li As ListItem = ddl.Items.
                FindByValue(drv("Country").ToString())
```

continues

LISTING 7-45 *(continued)*

```
            li.Selected = True
        End If
    End Sub
</script>
```

C#

```
<script runat="server">
    protected void GridView1_RowDataBound(object sender,
                                          GridViewRowEventArgs e)
    {
        // Check for a row in edit mode.
        if ( (e.Row.RowState == DataControlRowState.Edit) ||
             (e.Row.RowState == (DataControlRowState.Alternate |
                                 DataControlRowState.Edit)) )
        {
            System.Data.DataRowView drv =
                (System.Data.DataRowView)e.Row.DataItem;

            DropDownList ddl =
                (DropDownList)e.Row.Cells[8].
                    FindControl("DropDownList1");
            ListItem li =
                 ddl.Items.FindByValue(drv["Country"].ToString());
            li.Selected = true;
        }
    }
</script>
```

To set the DropDownList value, first check that the currently bound GridViewRow is in edit mode by using the `RowState` property. The `RowState` property is a bitwise combination of DataControlRowState values. Table 7-8 shows you the possible states for a GridViewRow.

TABLE 7-8

ROWSTATE	DESCRIPTION
Alternate	Indicates that this row is an alternate row.
Edit	Indicates the row is currently in edit mode.
Insert	Indicates the row is a new row, and is currently in insert mode.
Normal	Indicates the row is currently in a normal state.
Selected	Indicates the row is currently the selected row in the GridView.

To determine the current RowState correctly, you may need to make multiple comparisons against the `RowState` property. The RowState can be in multiple states at once — for example, alternate and edit; therefore, you need to use a bitwise comparison to properly determine whether the GridViewRow is in an edit state.

After the row is determined to be in an edit state, locate the DropDownList control in the proper cell by using the `FindControl` method. This method allows you to locate a server control by name. After you find the DropDownList control, locate the appropriate DropDownList ListItem and set its `Selected` property to `True`.

You also need to use a GridView event to add the value of the DropDownList control back into the GridView after the user updates the row. For this, you can use the `RowUpdating` event as shown in Listing 7-46.

LISTING 7-46: Using RowUpdating

Available for download on Wrox.com

```
<script runat="server">
    Protected Sub GridView1_RowUpdating(ByVal sender As Object,
        ByVal e As System.Web.UI.WebControls.GridViewUpdateEventArgs)

        Dim gvr As GridViewRow =
            Me.GridView1.Rows(Me.GridView1.EditIndex)
        Dim ddl As DropDownList =
            CType(gvr.Cells(8).
                FindControl("DropDownList1"), DropDownList)
        e.NewValues("Country") = ddl.SelectedValue
    End Sub
</script>
```

C#

```
<script runat="server">
    protected void GridView1_RowUpdating(object sender,
                                         GridViewUpdateEventArgs e)
    {
        GridViewRow gvr =
            this.GridView1.Rows[this.GridView1.EditIndex];
        DropDownList ddl =
            (DropDownList)gvr.Cells[8].FindControl("DropDownList1");
        e.NewValues["Country"] = ddl.SelectedValue;
    }
</script>
```

In this event, you determine the GridViewRow that is currently being edited using the `EditIndex`. This property contains the index of the GridViewRow that is currently in an edit state. After you find the row, locate the DropDownList control in the proper row cell using the `FindControl` method, as in the previous listing. After you find the DropDownList control, simply add the `SelectedValue` of that control to the GridView controls `NewValues` collection.

Deleting GridView Data

Deleting data from the table produced by the GridView is even easier than editing data. Just a few additions to the SqlDataSource and GridView enable you to delete an entire row of data from the table.

Like the Edit buttons, you can add a Delete button to the grid by setting the `AutoGenerateDeleteButton` property to `True` or by using the `CommandField`. Using the `AutoGenerateDeleteButton` property is shown in Listing 7-47.

LISTING 7-47: Adding a delete link to the GridView

Available for download on Wrox.com

```
<asp:GridView ID="GridView2" Runat="server"
     DataSourceID="SqlDataSource1" DataKeyNames="CustomerID"
     AutoGenerateColumns="True" AllowSorting="True" AllowPaging="True"
     AutoGenerateEditButton="true" AutoGenerateDeleteButton="true"/>
```

The SqlDataSource control changes are also trivial and can be made using the Configure Data Source wizard or manually in markup. Listing 7-48 shows how you can add the `DeleteCommand` to the control.

LISTING 7-48: Adding delete functionality to the SqlDataSource Control

Available for download on Wrox.com

```
<asp:SqlDataSource ID="SqlDataSource1" Runat="server"
     SelectCommand="SELECT * FROM [Customers]"
     ConnectionString="<%$ ConnectionStrings:ConnectionString %>"
     DataSourceMode="DataSet"
     DeleteCommand="DELETE From Customers
                    WHERE (CustomerID = @CustomerID)"
```

continues

LISTING 7-48 *(continued)*

```
        UpdateCommand="UPDATE [Customers]
             SET [CompanyName] = @CompanyName,
             [ContactName] = @ContactName, [ContactTitle] = @ContactTitle,
             [Address] = @Address, [City] = @City, [Region] = @Region,
             [PostalCode] = @PostalCode, [Country] = @Country,
             [Phone] = @Phone, [Fax] = @Fax
             WHERE [CustomerID] = @original_CustomerID">
       <%-- Update parameters removed for clarity --%>
   </asp:SqlDataSource>
```

Just like the `UpdateCommand` property, the `DeleteCommand` property makes use of named parameters to determine which row should be deleted. Because of this, you define this parameter from within the SqlDataSource control. To do this, add a `<DeleteParameters>` section to the SqlDataSource control. This is shown in Listing 7-49.

LISTING 7-49: Adding a <DeleteParameters> section to the SqlDataSource control

Available for download on Wrox.com

```
<DeleteParameters>
   <asp:Parameter Name="CustomerID" Type="String">
   </asp:Parameter>
</DeleteParameters>
```

This is the only parameter needed for the `<DeleteParameters>` collection because the SQL command for this deletion requires only the CustomerID from the row to delete the entire row. Running the sample displays a Delete link in the grid, which when clicked deletes the selected row.

Remember that just like when you update data, when you delete data checking for database errors is a good idea. Listing 7-50 shows how you can use the GridView's `RowDeleted` event and the SqlDataSources `Deleted` event to check for errors that might have occurred during the deletion.

LISTING 7-50: Using the RowDeleted event to catch SQL errors

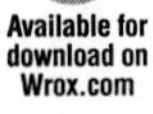

Available for download on Wrox.com

VB

```
<script runat="server">
    Protected Sub GridView1_RowDeleted(ByVal sender As Object,
       ByVal e As GridViewDeletedEventArgs)

        If (Not IsDBNull (e.Exception)) Then
            Me.lblErrorMessage.Text = e.Exception.Message
            e.ExceptionHandled = True
        End If
    End Sub

    Protected Sub SqlDataSource1_Deleted(ByVal sender As Object,
    ByVal e As System.Web.UI.WebControls.SqlDataSourceStatusEventArgs)

        If (e.Exception IsNot Nothing) Then
            Me.lblErrorMessage.Text = e.Exception.Message
            e.ExceptionHandled = True
        End If
    End Sub
</script>
```

C#

```
<script runat="server">
    protected void GridView1_RowDeleted(object sender,
                                        GridViewDeletedEventArgs e)
    {
        if (e.Exception != null)
        {
            this.lblErrorMessage.Text = e.Exception.Message;
```

```
            e.ExceptionHandled = true;
        }
    }

    protected void SqlDataSource1_Deleted(object sender,
                                    SqlDataSourceStatusEventArgs e)
    {
        if (e.Exception != null)
        {
            this.lblErrorMessage.Text = e.Exception.Message;
            e.ExceptionHandled = true;
        }
    }
</script>
```

Notice that both events provide `Exception` properties as part of their event arguments. If these properties are not empty, then an exception has occurred that you can handle. If you do choose to handle the exception, then you should set the `ExceptionHandled` property to `True`; otherwise, the exception will continue to bubble up to the end user.

Other GridView Formatting Features

The GridView control includes numerous other properties that let you adjust the look and feel of the control in fine detail. The `Caption` property allows you to set a caption at the top of the grid. The `ShowHeader` and `ShowFooter` properties enable you to control whether the column headers or footers are shown. The control also includes eight different *style properties* that give you control over the look and feel of different parts of the grid. Table 7-9 describes the style properties.

TABLE 7-9

STYLE PROPERTY	DESCRIPTION
`AlternatingRowStyle`	Style applied to alternating GridView rows
`EditRowStyle`	Style applied to a GridView row in edit mode
`EmptyDataRowStyle`	Style applied to the EmptyDataRow when datarows are available for the grid to bind to
`FooterStyle`	Style applied to the footer of the GridView
`HeaderStyle`	Style applied to the header of the GridView
`PagerStyle`	Style applied to the GridView pager
`RowStyle`	Style applied to the default GridView row
`SelectedRowStyle`	Style applied to the currently selected GridView row

These style properties let you set the font, forecolor, backcolor, alignment, and many other style-related properties for these individual areas of the grid.

The GridView smart tag also includes an AutoFormat option that enables you to select from a list of predefined styles to apply to the control.

DetailsView

The DetailsView control is a data-bound control that enables you to view a single data record at a time. Although the GridView control is an excellent control for viewing a collection of data, there are many scenarios where you want to show a single record rather than an entire collection. The DetailsView control allows you to do this and provides many of the same data manipulation and display capabilities as the GridView, including features such as paging, updating, inserting, and deleting data.

To start using the DetailsView, drag the control onto the design surface. Like the GridView, you can use the DetailsView's smart tag to create and set the data source for the control. The samples in this section will use the same SqlDataSource control that was used for the GridView samples in the previous section. Set the SqlDataSource as the DetailsView's data source and run the page. Listing 7-51 shows the markup for a DetailsView bound to a SqlDataSource control.

Available for download on Wrox.com

LISTING 7-51: A DetailsView control bound to a SqlDataSource

```
<html xmlns="http://www.w3.org/1999/xhtml">
<head id="Head1" runat="server">
    <title></title>
</head>
<body>
    <form id="form1" runat="server">
    <div>
        <asp:DetailsView ID="DetailsView1" Runat="server"
             DataSourceID="SqlDataSource1" DataKeyNames="CustomerID"
             AutoGenerateRows="True"></asp:DetailsView>

        <asp:SqlDataSource ID="SqlDataSource1" Runat="server"
            SelectCommand="SELECT * FROM [Customers]"
            ConnectionString=
                "<%$ ConnectionStrings:ConnectionString %>"
            DataSourceMode="DataSet">
        </asp:SqlDataSource>
    </div>
    </form>
</body>
</html>
```

As shown in Figure 7-26, the control displays a single record, the first record returned by the SqlData Source query.

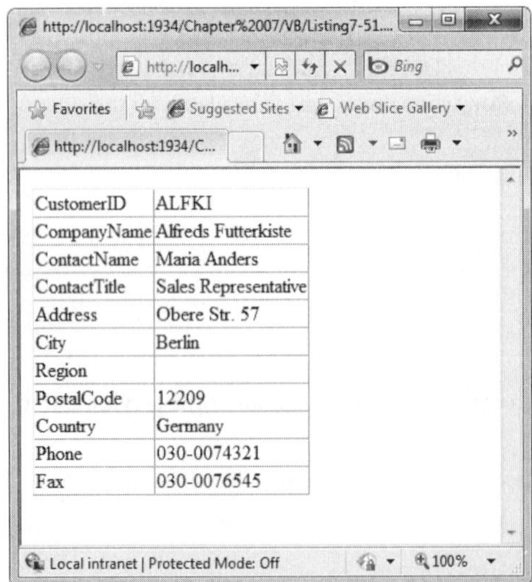

FIGURE 7-26

If you simply want to display a single record, you would probably want to change the SqlDataSource control's `SelectCommand` so that it returns only one Customer, rather than returning all Customers as the query does. However, if you are returning more than a single object from the database, you can allow your end users to page through the data by setting the DetailsView's `AllowPaging` property to `True`, as shown in Listing 7-52.

LISTING 7-52: Enabling paging on the DetailsView control

Available for download on Wrox.com

```
<asp:DetailsView ID="DetailsView1" Runat="server"
     DataSourceID="SqlDataSource1" DataKeyNames="CustomerID"
     AutoGenerateRows="True" AllowPaging="true"></asp:DetailsView>
```

You can either select the Enable Paging check box in the DetailsView smart tag or add the property to the control in Source view. Also, like the GridView, the DetailsView control enables you to customize the control's pager using the `PagerSettings-Mode`, as well as the `Pager` style.

Customizing the DetailsView Display

You can customize the appearance of the DetailsView control by picking and choosing which fields the control displays. By default, the control displays each public property from its bound data source. However, using the same basic syntax used for the GridView control you can specify that only certain properties be displayed. This is illustrated in Listing 7-53.

LISTING 7-53: Customizing the display of the DetailsView control

Available for download on Wrox.com

```
<asp:DetailsView ID="DetailsView1" Runat="server"
     DataSourceID="SqlDataSource1" DataKeyNames="CustomerID"
     AutoGenerateRows="False">
     <Fields>
          <asp:BoundField ReadOnly="True" HeaderText="CustomerID"
               DataField="CustomerID" SortExpression="CustomerID"
               Visible="False" />
          <asp:BoundField ReadOnly="True" HeaderText="CompanyName"
               DataField="CompanyName" SortExpression="CompanyName" />
          <asp:BoundField HeaderText="ContactName"
               DataField="ContactName" SortExpression="ContactName" />
          <asp:BoundField HeaderText="ContactTitle"
               DataField="ContactTitle"
               SortExpression="ContactTitle" />
      </Fields>
</asp:DetailsView>
```

In this example, only four fields from the Customers table are defined using `BoundField` objects in the DetailsView's `Fields` collection.

Using the DetailsView and GridView Together

Next, this section looks at a common master/detail display scenario, which uses both the GridView and the DetailsView. In this example, you use the GridView to display a master view of the data and the DetailsView to show the details of the selected GridView row. The Customers table is the data source. Listing 7-54 shows the code needed for this.

LISTING 7-54: Using the GridView and DetailsView together

Available for download on Wrox.com

```
<html>
<head id="Head1" runat="server">
    <title>GridView & DetailsView Controls</title>
</head>
<body>
    <form id="form1" runat="server">
        <p>
            <asp:GridView ID="GridView1" runat="server"
                 DataSourceId="SqlDataSource1"
                 DataKeyNames="CustomerID"
                 AutoGenerateSelectButton="True" AllowPaging="True"
                 AutoGenerateColumns="True" PageSize="5">
```

continues

LISTING 7-54 *(continued)*

```
                <SelectedRowStyle ForeColor="White" BackColor="#738A9C"
                     Font-Bold="True" />
            </asp:GridView>
        </p>
        <p><b>Customer Details:</b></p>
        <asp:DetailsView ID="DetailsView1" runat="server"
             DataSourceId="SqlDataSource2"
             AutoGenerateRows="True" DataKeyNames="CustomerID">
        </asp:DetailsView>

        <asp:SqlDataSource ID="SqlDataSource1" runat="server"
             SelectCommand="SELECT * FROM [Customers]"
             ConnectionString=
                 "<%$ ConnectionStrings:ConnectionString %>" />

        <asp:SqlDataSource ID="SqlDataSource2" runat="server"
             SelectCommand="SELECT * FROM [Customers]"
             FilterExpression="CustomerID='{0}'"
             ConnectionString=
                 "<%$ ConnectionStrings:ConnectionString %>">
             <FilterParameters>
                 <asp:ControlParameter Name="CustomerID"
                      ControlId="GridView1"
                      PropertyName="SelectedValue" />
             </FilterParameters>
        </asp:SqlDataSource>
    </form>
</body>
</html>
```

Running this sample in your browser, you get the results shown in Figure 7-27.

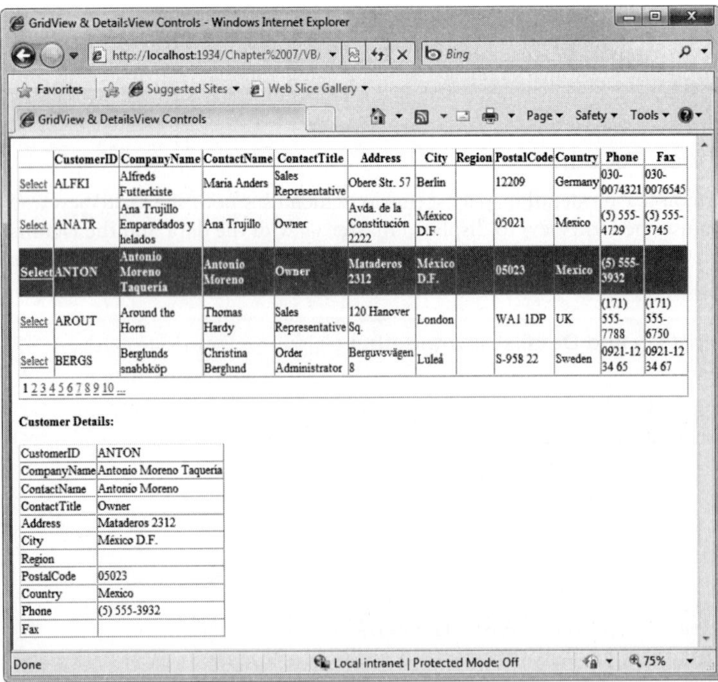

FIGURE 7-27

As shown in the figure, the row highlighted in gray indicates a row in the GridView has been selected. The details of this selected row are shown in the DetailsView control directly below the GridView control.

To see how this works, look at the changes that were made to the second SqlDataSource control, named SqlDataSource2. A `FilterExpression` used to filter the data retrieved by the `SelectCommand` has been added. In this case, the value of the `FilterExpression` is set to `CustomerID='{0}'` indicating that the control should filter the data it returns by the CustomerID value given to it.

The parameter specified in the `FilterExpression`, `CustomerID`, is defined in the SqlDataSource control's `<FilterParameters>` collection. The sample uses an `<asp:ControlParameter>` to specify the GridView control's `SelectedValue` property to populate the parameter's value.

SelectParameters versus FilterParameters

You might have noticed in the previous example that the `FilterParameters` seem to provide the same functionality as the `SelectParameters`, which were discussed in the "SqlDataSource Control" section of this chapter. Although both produce essentially the same result, they use very different methods. As you saw in the previous section, using the `SelectParameters` allows the developer to inject values into a `WHERE` clause specified in the `SelectCommand`. This limits the rows that are returned from the SQL Server and held in memory by the data source control. The advantage is that by limiting the amount of data returned from SQL, you can make your application faster and reduce the amount of memory it consumes. The disadvantage is that you are confined to working with the limited subset of data returned by the SQL query.

`FilterParameters`, on the other hand, do not use a `WHERE`, instead requiring all the data to be returned from the server and then applying a filter to the data source control's in-memory data. The disadvantage of the filter method is that more data has to be returned from the data store. However, in some cases such as when you are performing many filters of one large chunk of data (for instance, to enable paging in the DetailView) this is an advantage as you do not have to call out to your data store each time you need the next record. All the data is stored in cache memory by the data source control.

Inserting, Updating, and Deleting Data Using DetailsView

Inserting data using the DetailsView is similar to inserting data through the GridView control. To insert data using the DetailsView, simply add the `AutoGenerateInsertButton` property to the DetailsView control as shown in Listing 7-55.

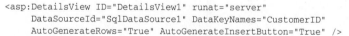

LISTING 7-55: Adding an AutoGenerateInsertButton property to the DetailsView

Available for download on Wrox.com

```
<asp:DetailsView ID="DetailsView1" runat="server"
     DataSourceId="SqlDataSource1" DataKeyNames="CustomerID"
     AutoGenerateRows="True" AutoGenerateInsertButton="True" />
```

Then add the `InsertCommand` and corresponding `InsertParameter` elements to the SqlDataSource control, as shown in Listing 7-56.

LISTING 7-56: Adding an InsertCommand to the SqlDataSource control

Available for download on Wrox.com

```
<asp:SqlDataSource ID="SqlDataSource1" runat="server"
    SelectCommand="SELECT * FROM [Customers]"
    InsertCommand="INSERT INTO [Customers] ([CustomerID],
        [CompanyName], [ContactName], [ContactTitle], [Address],
        [City], [Region], [PostalCode], [Country], [Phone], [Fax])
        VALUES (@CustomerID, @CompanyName, @ContactName, @ContactTitle,
        @Address, @City, @Region, @PostalCode,@Country, @Phone, @Fax)"
```

continues

LISTING 7-56 *(continued)*

```
    DeleteCommand="DELETE FROM [Customers]
                   WHERE [CustomerID] = @original_CustomerID"
    ConnectionString="<%$ ConnectionStrings:ConnectionString %>">
    <InsertParameters>
        <asp:Parameter Type="String" Name="CustomerID"></asp:Parameter>
        <asp:Parameter Type="String"
                       Name="CompanyName"></asp:Parameter>
        <asp:Parameter Type="String"
                       Name="ContactName"></asp:Parameter>
        <asp:Parameter Type="String"
                       Name="ContactTitle"></asp:Parameter>
        <asp:Parameter Type="String" Name="Address"></asp:Parameter>
        <asp:Parameter Type="String" Name="City"></asp:Parameter>
        <asp:Parameter Type="String" Name="Region"></asp:Parameter>
        <asp:Parameter Type="String" Name="PostalCode"></asp:Parameter>
        <asp:Parameter Type="String" Name="Country"></asp:Parameter>
        <asp:Parameter Type="String" Name="Phone"></asp:Parameter>
        <asp:Parameter Type="String" Name="Fax"></asp:Parameter>
    </InsertParameters>
</asp:SqlDataSource>
```

Figure 7-28 shows the DetailsView control page loaded in the browser in insert mode, ready to add a new record.

Figure 7-29 shows the DetailsView control after a new record has been inserted.

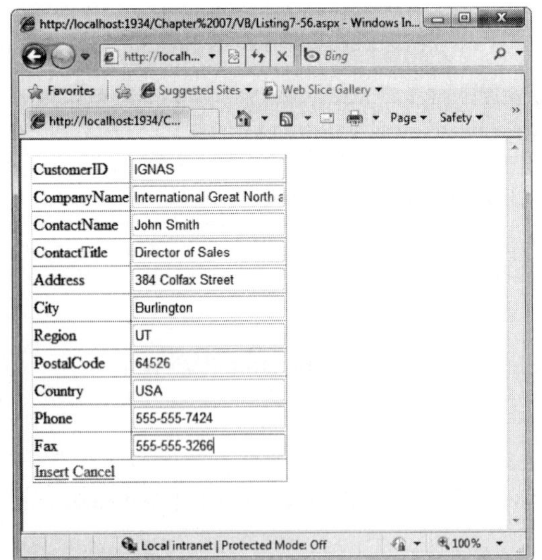

FIGURE 7-28

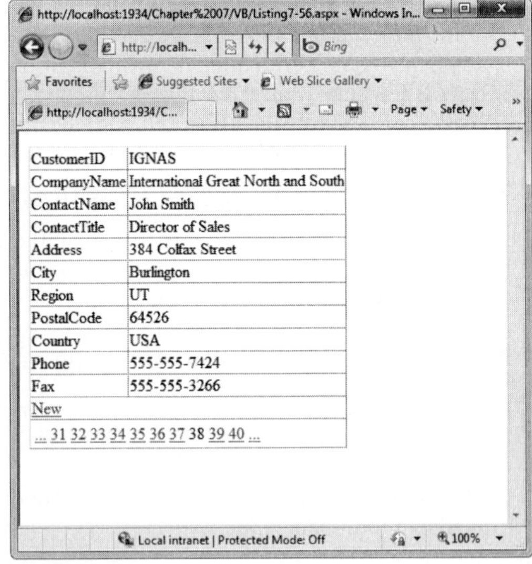

FIGURE 7-29

Updating and deleting data using the DetailsView control are similar to updating and deleting data from the GridView. Simply specify the `UpdateCommand` or `DeleteCommand` attributes in the DetailView control; then provide the proper `UpdateParameters` and `DeleteParameters` elements.

ListView

ASP.NET includes another list-style control that bridges the gap between the highly structured GridView control, and the anything goes, unstructured controls like DataList and Repeater.

In the past, many developers who wanted a grid-style data control chose the GridView because it was easy to use and offered powerful features such as data editing, paging, and sorting. Unfortunately, the more developers dug into the control, the more they found that controlling the way it rendered its HTML output was exceedingly difficult. This was problematic if you wanted to lighten the amount of markup generated by the control, or use CSS exclusively to control the control's layout and style.

On the other side of the coin, many developers were drawn to the DataList or Repeater because of the enhanced control they got over rendering. These controls contained little to no notion of layout and allowed developers total freedom in laying out their data. Unfortunately, these controls lacked some of the basic features of the GridView, such as paging and sorting, or in the case of the Repeater, any notion of data editing.

This is where the ListView can be useful. The control itself emits no runtime generated HTML markup; instead it relies on a series of 11 different control templates that represent the different areas of the control and the possible states of those areas. Within these templates you can place markup auto-generated by the control at design-time, or markup created by the developer, but in either case the developer retains complete control over not only the markup for individual data items in the control, but of the markup for the layout of the entire control. Additionally, because the control readily understands and handles data editing and paging, you can let the control do much of the data management work, allowing you to focus primarily on the display of your data.

Getting Started with the ListView

To get started using the ListView, simply drop the control on the design surface and assign a data source to it just as you would any other data-bound list control. After you assign the data source, however, you will see that no design-time layout preview is available as you might expect. This is because, by default, the ListView has no layout defined and it is completely up to you to define the control's layout. In fact, the design-time rendering of the control even tells you that you need to define at least an ItemTemplate and LayoutTemplate to use the control. The LayoutTemplate serves as the root template for the control, and the ItemTemplate serves as the template for each individual data item in the control.

You have two options for defining the templates needed by the ListView. You can either edit the templates directly by changing the Current View option in the ListView smart tag, or you can select a predefined layout from the control's smart tag. Changing Current View allows you to see a runtime view of each of the available templates, and edit the contents of those templates directly just as you would normally edit any other control template. Figure 7-30 shows the Current View drop-down in the ListView's smart tag.

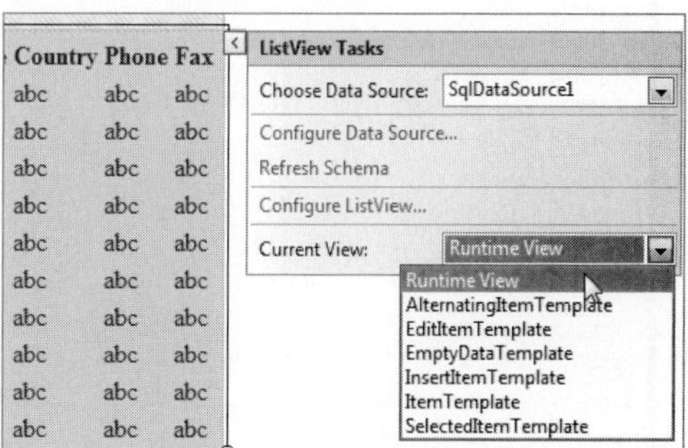

FIGURE 7-30

The second option, and probably the easier to start with, is to choose a predefined layout template from the Configure ListView dialog. To open this dialog, simply click the ConfigureListView option from the smart tag. Once open, you are presented with a dialog that lets you select between several different pre-defined layouts, select different style options, and even configure basic behavior options such as editing and paging. This dialog is shown in Figure 7-31.

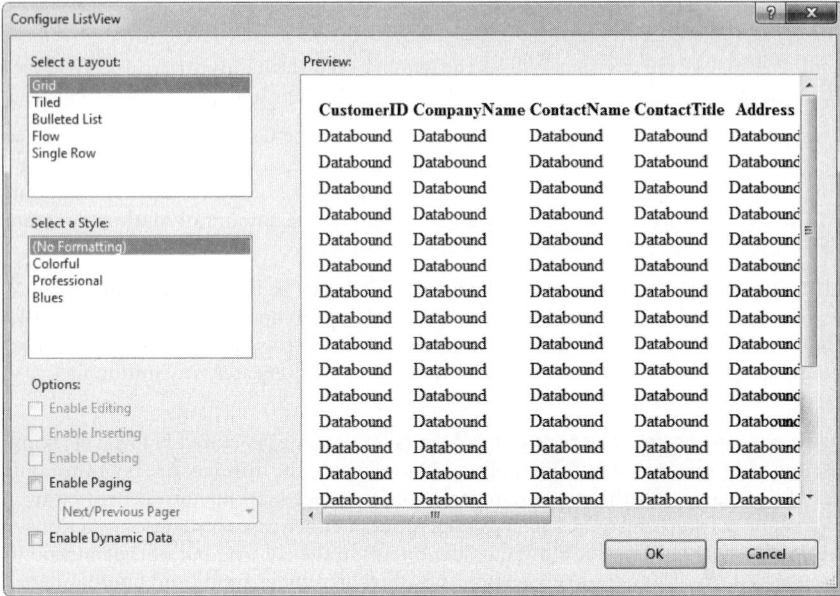

FIGURE 7-31

The control includes five different layout types: Grid, Tiled, Bulleted List, Flow, and Single Row and four different style options. A preview of each type is presented in the dialog, and as you change the currently selected layout and style, the preview is updated.

To see exactly how the control defines each layout option, select the Grid layout with the Colorful style and enable Inserting, Editing, Deleting, and Paging. Click OK to apply your choices and close the dialog box. When the dialog box closes, you should now see that you get a design-time preview of your layout and running the page results in the ListView generating a grid layout, as shown in Figure 7-32.

```
<asp:SqlDataSource ID="SqlDataSource1" runat="server"
```

100 %

div

CustomerID	CompanyName	ContactName	ContactTitle	Address	City	Region	PostalCode	Country	Phone	Fax
abc	abc	abc	abc	abc	abc	abc	abc	abc	abc	abc
abc	abc	abc	abc	abc	abc	abc	abc	abc	abc	abc
abc	abc	abc	abc	abc	abc	abc	abc	abc	abc	abc
abc	abc	abc	abc	abc	abc	abc	abc	abc	abc	abc
abc	abc	abc	abc	abc	abc	abc	abc	abc	abc	abc
abc	abc	abc	abc	abc	abc	abc	abc	abc	abc	abc
abc	abc	abc	abc	abc	abc	abc	abc	abc	abc	abc
abc	abc	abc	abc	abc	abc	abc	abc	abc	abc	abc
abc	abc	abc	abc	abc	abc	abc	abc	abc	abc	abc
abc	abc	abc	abc	abc	abc	abc	abc	abc	abc	abc
abc	abc	abc	abc	abc	abc	abc	abc	abc	abc	abc
abc	abc	abc	abc	abc	abc	abc	abc	abc	abc	abc
abc	abc	abc	abc	abc	abc	abc	abc	abc	abc	abc
abc	abc	abc	abc	abc	abc	abc	abc	abc	abc	abc

FIGURE 7-32

ListView Templates

After you have applied a layout template to the ListView, if you look at the Source window in Visual Studio, you can see that to provide the layout the control actually generated a significant chunk of markup. This markup is generated based on the layout that you chose in the Configure ListView dialog.

If you closely examine the markup that has been generated for the Grid layout used in the previous section, you will see that, by default, the control creates markup for seven different control templates: the ItemTemplate, AlternatingItemTemplate, SelectedItemTemplate, InsertItemTemplate, EditItemTemplate, EmptyDataTemplate, and LayoutTemplate. These are just some of the 11 different templates that the control exposes, and that you can use to provide markup for the different states of the control. Choosing a different predefined layout option results in the control generating a different collection of templates. Of course, you can also always manually add or remove any of the templates yourself. All 11 templates are listed in the Table 7-10.

TABLE 7-10

TEMPLATE NAME	DESCRIPTION
ItemTemplate	Provides a user Interface for each data item in the control
AlternatingItemTemplate	Provides a unique UI for alternating data items in the control
SelectedItemTemplate	Provides a unique UI for the currently selected data item
InsertItemTemplate	Provides a UI for inserting a new data item into the control
EditItemTemplate	Provides a UI for editing an existing data item in the control
EmptyItemTemplate	Provides a unique UI for rows created when there is no more data to display in the last group of the current page
EmptyDataTemplate	The template shown when the bound data object contains no data items
LayoutTemplate	The template that serves as the root container for the ListView control and is used to control the overall layout of the data items
GroupSeparatorTemplate	Used to provide a separator UI between groups
GroupTemplate	Used to provide a unique UI for grouped content
ItemSeparatorTemplate	Used to provide a separator UI between each data item

The use of templates allows the ListView control to retain a very basic level of information about the markup sections and states which can comprise the ListView, while still being able to give you almost total control over the UI of the ListView.

ListView Data Item Rendering

Although the ListView is generally very flexible, allowing you almost complete control over the way it displays its bound data, it does have some basic structure that defines how the templates described in the previous section are related to one another. As described previously, at a minimum, the control requires you to define two templates, the LayoutTemplate and ItemTemplate. The LayoutTemplate is the root control template and therefore where you should define the overall layout for the collection of data items in the ListView.

For example, if you examine the template markup generated by the Grid layout, you can see the LayoutTemplate includes a `<table>` element definition, a single table row (`<tr>`) definition, and a `<td.>` element defined for each column header.

The ItemTemplate, on the other hand, is where you define the layout for an individual data item. If you again look at the markup generated for the Grid layout, its ItemTemplate is a single table row (`<tr>`) element followed by a series of table cell (`<td>`) elements that contain the actual data.

When the ListView renders itself, it knows that the ItemTemplate should be rendered within the LayoutTemplate, but what is needed is a mechanism to tell the control exactly where within the LayoutTemplate to place the ItemTemplate. The ListView control does this by looking within the LayoutTemplate for an Item Container. The Item Container is an HTML container element with the `runat = "server"` attribute set and an `id` attribute whose value is `itemContainer`. The element can be any valid HTML container element, although if you examine the default Grid LayoutTemplate you will see that it uses the `<tbody>` element.

```
<tbody id="itemContainer">
</tbody>
```

Adding to the overall flexibility of the control, even the specific Item Container element `id` that ListView looks for can be configured. Although by default the control will attempt to locate an element whose `id` attribute is set to `itemContainer`, you can change the `id` value the control will look for by changing the control's `ItemContainerID` property.

If the control fails to locate an appropriate HTML element designated as the Item Container, it will throw an exception.

The ListView uses the element identified as the `itemContainer` to position not only the ItemTemplate, but any item-level template, such as the AlternativeItemTemplate, EditItemTemplate, EmptyItemTemplate, InsertItemTemplate, ItemSeparatorTemplate, and SelectedItemTemplate. During rendering, it simply places the appropriate item template into the Item Container, depending on the state of the data item (selected, editing, or alternate) for each data item it is bound to.

ListView Group Rendering

In addition to the Item Container, the ListView also supports another container type, the Group Container. The Group Container works in conjunction with the GroupTemplate to allow you to divide a large group of data items into smaller sets. The number of items in each group is set by the control's `GroupItemCount` property. This is useful is when you want to output some additional HTML after some number of item templates have been rendered. When using the GroupTemplate, the same problem exists as was discussed in the prior section. In this case, however, rather than having two templates to relate, introducing the GroupTemplate means you have three templates to relate: the ItemTemplate to the GroupTemplate, and the GroupTemplate to the LayoutTemplate.

When the ListView renders itself, it looks to see whether a GroupTemplate has been defined. If the control finds a GroupTemplate, then it checks to see whether a Group Container is provided in the LayoutTemplate. If you have defined the GroupTemplate, then the control requires that you define a Group Container; otherwise it throws an exception. The Group Container works the same way as the Item Container described in the previous section, except that the container element's `id` value should be `groupContainer`, rather than `itemContainer`. As with Item Container, the specific `id` value the control looks for can be changed by altering the `GroupContainerID` property of the control.

You can see an example of the Group Container being used by looking at the markup generated by the ListViews Tiled layout. The LayoutTemplate of this layout shows a table serving as the Group Container, shown here:

```
<table id="groupContainer" runat="server" border="0" style="">
</table>
```

After a GroupContainer is defined, you need to define an Item Container, but rather than doing this in the LayoutTemplate, you need to do it in the GroupTemplate. Again, looking at the Tiled layout, you can see that within its GroupTemplate, it defined a table row that serves as the Item Container.

```
<tr id="itemContainer" runat="server">
</tr>
```

When rendering, the ListView will output its LayoutTemplate first, and then output the GroupTemplate. The ItemTemplate is then output the number of times defined by the `GroupItemCount` property. When the group item count has been reached, the ListView outputs the GroupTemplate, then ItemTemplate again, repeating this process for each data item it is bound to.

Using the EmptyItemTemplate

When using the GroupTemplate, it is also important to keep in mind that the number of data items bound to the ListView control may not be perfectly divisible by the GroupItemCount value. This is especially important to keep in mind if you have created a ListView layout that is dependent on HTML tables for its data item arrangement because there is a chance that the last row may end up defining fewer table cells than previous table rows, making the HTML output by the control invalid, and possibly causing rendering problems. To solve this, the ListView control includes the EmptyItemTemplate. This template is rendered if you are using the GroupTemplate, and there are not enough data items remaining to reach the `GroupItemCount` value. Figure 7-33 shows an example of when the EmptyItemTemplate would be used.

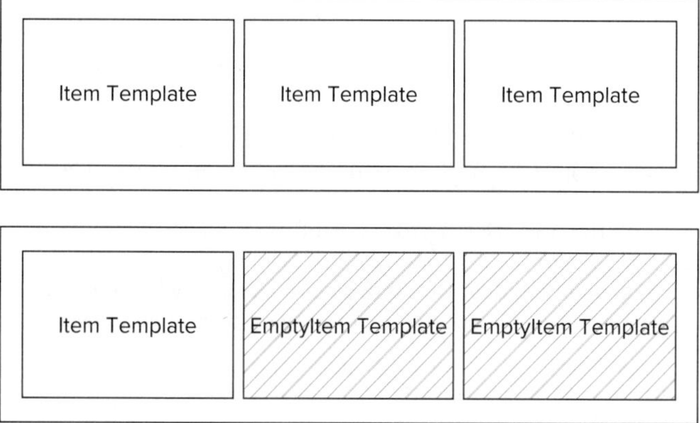

FIGURE 7-33

In this scenario, the data source bound to the ListView control contains four data items, but the `GroupItemCount` for the control is set to `3`, meaning there will be three ItemTemplates rendered in each group. You can see that this means for the second group rendered, there will only be a single data item remaining to render; therefore, the control will use the EmptyItemTemplate, if defined, to fill the remaining items.

You can also see another example of the use of the EmptyItemTemplate in the ListView's Tiled layout.

ListView Data Binding and Commands

Because the ListView does not generate any layout markup at runtime and does not include any of the auto field generation logic as you may be used to in the GridView, each template uses the standard ASP.NET inline data-binding syntax to position the values of each data item in the defined layout. The inline data-binding syntax is covered in detail later in this chapter.

You can see an example of inline binding by examining the ItemTemplate of the default Grid layout created by the control. In this template, each column of the bound data source is displayed using an ASP.NET label whose text property is set to a data-binding evaluation expression:

```
<asp:Label ID="ProductNameLabel" runat="server"
    Text='<%# Eval("ProductName") %>' />
```

Because the control uses this flexible model to display the bound data, you can leverage it to place the data wherever you want within the template, and even use the features of ASP.NET data binding to manipulate the bound data before it is displayed.

Every ListView template that displays bound data uses the same ASP.NET binding syntax, and simply provides a different template around it. For example, if you enable editing in the Grid layout you will see that the EditItemTemplate simply replaces the ASP.NET Label used by the ItemTemplate with a TextBox or CheckBox depending on the underlying data type.

```
<asp:TextBox ID="ProductNameTextBox" runat="server"
    Text='<%# Bind("ProductName") %>' />
```

Again, this flexibility allows you to choose exactly how you want to allow your end user to edit the data (if you want it to be editable). Instead of a standard ASP.NET TextBox, you could easily replace this with a DropDownList, or even a third-party editing control.

To get the ListView to show the EditItemTemplate for a data item, the control uses the same commands concept found in the GridView control. The ItemTemplate provides three commands (see Table 7-11) you can use to change the state of a data item.

TABLE 7-11

COMMAND NAME	DESCRIPTION
`Edit`	Places the specific data item into edit mode and shows the EditTemplate for the data item
`Delete`	Deletes the specific data item from the underlying data source
`Select`	Sets the ListView controls Selected index to the index of the specific data item

These commands are used in conjunction with the ASP.NET Button control's `CommandName` property. You can see these commands used in ItemTemplate of the ListViews default Grid layout by enabling editing and deleting using the ListView configuration dialog. Doing this generates a new column with an Edit and Delete button, each of which specified the `CommandName` property set to Edit and Delete, respectively.

```
<asp:Button ID="DeleteButton" runat="server"
    CommandName="Delete" Text="Delete" />
<asp:Button ID="EditButton" runat="server"
    CommandName="Edit" Text="Edit" />
```

Other templates in the ListView offer other commands, as shown in Table 7-12.

TABLE 7-12

TEMPLATE	COMMAND NAME	DESCRIPTION
EditItemTemplate	Update	Updates the data in the ListView's data source and returns the data item to the ItemTemplate display
EditItemTemplate	Cancel	Cancels the edit and returns the data item to the ItemTemplate
InsertItemTemplate	Insert	Inserts the data into the ListView's data source
InsertItemTemplate	Cancel	Cancels the insert and resets the InsertTemplate controls binding values

ListView Paging and the Pager Control

ASP.NET includes another control called the DataPager control that the ListView uses to provide paging capabilities. The DataPager control is designed to display the navigation for paging to the end user and to coordinate data paging with any databound control that implements the `IPagableItemContainer` interface, which in ASP.NET is the ListView control. In fact, you will notice that if you enable paging on the ListView control by checking the Paging check box in the ListView configuration dialog, the control simply inserts a new DataPager control into its LayoutTemplate. The default paging markup generated by the ListView for the Grid layout is shown here:

```
<asp:datapager ID="DataPager1" runat="server">
    <Fields>
        <asp:nextpreviouspagerfield ButtonType="Button" FirstPageText="First"
            LastPageText="Last" NextPageText="Next" PreviousPageText="Previous"
            ShowFirstPageButton="True" ShowLastPageButton="True" />
    </Fields>
</asp:datapager>
```

The markup for the control shows that within the DataPager, a `Fields` collection has been created, which contains a `NextPreviousPagerField` object. As its name implies, using the `NextPreviousPager` object results in the DataPager rendering Next and Previous buttons as its user interface. The DataPager control includes three types of `Field` objects: the `NextPreviousPagerField`; the `NumericPagerField` object, which generates a simple numeric page list; and the `TemplatePagerField`, which allows you to specify your own custom paging user interface. Each of these different `Field` types includes a variety of properties that you can use to control exactly how the DataPager displays the user interface. Additionally, because the DataPager exposes a `Fields` collection rather than a simple `Field` property, you can actually display several different `Field` objects within a single DataPager control.

The `TemplatePagerField` is a unique type of `Field` object that contains no user interface itself, but simply exposes a template that you can use to completely customize the pager's user interface. Listing 7-57 demonstrates the use of the `TemplatePagerField`.

Available for download on Wrox.com

LISTING 7-57: Creating a custom DataPager user interface

```
<asp:DataPager ID="DataPager1" runat="server">
    <Fields>
        <asp:TemplatePagerField>
            <PagerTemplate>
                Page
                <asp:Label ID="Label1" runat="server"
                    Text=
                    "<%# (Container.StartRowIndex/Container.PageSize)+1%>" />
                of
                <asp:Label ID="Label2" runat="server"
                    Text=
                    "<%# Container.TotalRowCount/Container.PageSize%>" />
            </PagerTemplate>
        </asp:TemplatePagerField>
    </Fields>
</asp:DataPager>
```

Notice that the sample uses ASP.NET data binding to provide the total page count, page size and the row that the page should start on; these are values exposed by the DataPager control.

If you want to use custom navigation controls in the PagerTemplate, such as a Button control to change the currently displayed page, you would create a standard Click event handler for the Button. Within that event handler you can access the DataPager's `StartRowIndex`, `TotalRowCount`, and `PageSize` properties to calculate the new `StartRowIndex` the ListView should use when it renders.

Unlike the paging provided by the GridView, the DataPager control, because it is a separate control, gives you total freedom over where to place it on your Web page. The samples you have seen so far have all looked at the DataPager control when it is placed directly in a ListView, but the control can be placed anywhere on the Web form. In Listing 7-58, the only significant change you should notice is the use of the `PagedControlID` property.

Available for download on Wrox.com

LISTING 7-58: Placing the DataPager control outside of the ListView

```
<asp:DataPager ID="DataPager1" runat="server"
     PagedControlID="ListView1">
    <Fields>
        <asp:NumericPagerField />
    </Fields>
</asp:DataPager>
```

The PageControlID property allows you to specify explicitly which control this pager should work with.

FormView

The FormView control functions like the DetailsView control in that it displays a single data item from a bound data source control and allows adding, editing, and deleting data. What makes it unique is that it displays the data in custom templates, which gives you much greater control over how the data is displayed and edited. Figure 7-34 shows a FormView control ItemTemplate being edited in Visual Studio. You can see that you have complete control over how your data is displayed. The FormView control also contains an EditItemTemplate and InsertItemTemplate that allows you to determine how the control displays when entering edit or insert mode.

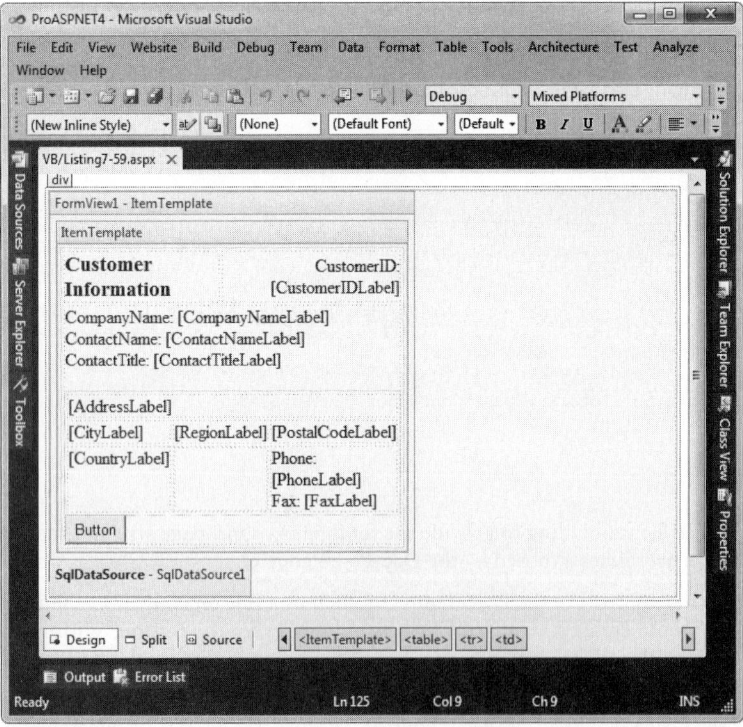

FIGURE 7-34

While Figure 7-34 shows the FormView control in action in Visual Studio, Figure 7-35 shows the control displaying its ItemTemplate, reflecting the custom layout that was designed in Visual Studio.

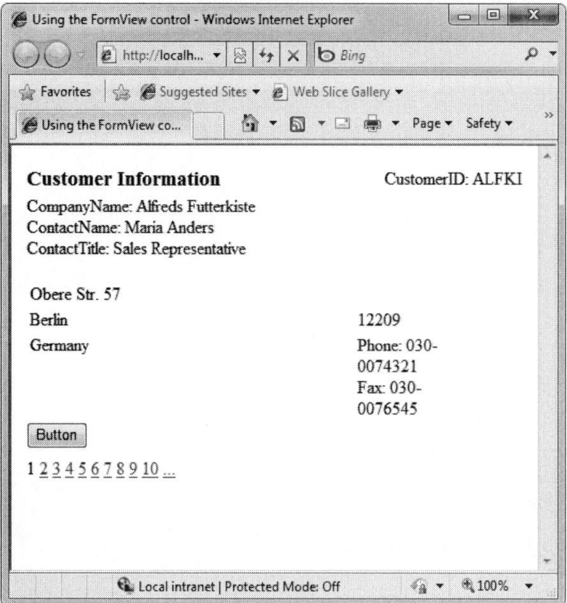

FIGURE 7-35

In Figure 7-36, you see the control in edit mode, showing the standard EditItemTemplate layout.

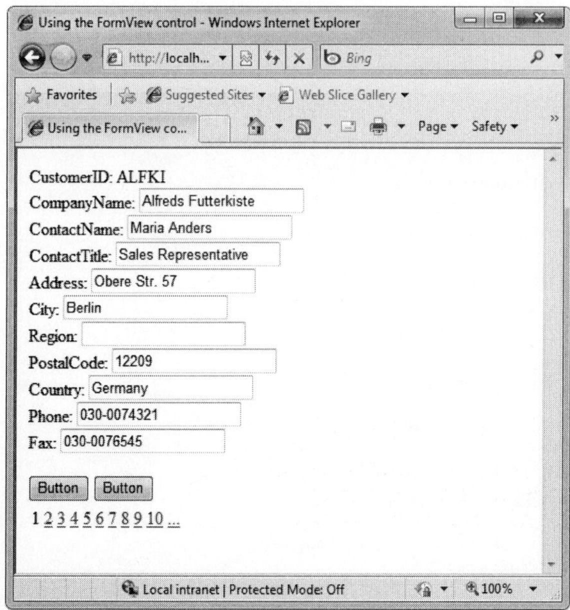

FIGURE 7-36

Listing 7-59 shows the code that Visual Studio generates when designing the FormView control's customized ItemTemplate.

LISTING 7-59: Using a FormView control to display and edit data

Available for download on Wrox.com

```
<html xmlns="http://www.w3.org/1999/xhtml" >
<head runat="server">
    <title>Using the FormView control</title>
</head>
<body>
    <form id="form1" runat="server">
    <div>
        <asp:FormView ID="FormView1" Runat="server"
             DataSourceID="SqlDataSource1"
             DataKeyNames="CustomerID" AllowPaging="True">
            <EditItemTemplate>
                CustomerID:
                <asp:Label Text='<%# Eval("CustomerID") %>'
                     Runat="server" ID="CustomerIDLabel1">
                </asp:Label><br />
                CompanyName:
                <asp:TextBox Text='<%# Bind("CompanyName") %>'
                     Runat="server"
                     ID="CompanyNameTextBox"></asp:TextBox><br />
                ContactName:
                <asp:TextBox Text='<%# Bind("ContactName") %>'
                     Runat="server"
                     ID="ContactNameTextBox"></asp:TextBox><br />
                ContactTitle:
                <asp:TextBox Text='<%# Bind("ContactTitle") %>'
                    Runat="server"
                    ID="ContactTitleTextBox"></asp:TextBox><br />
                Address:
                <asp:TextBox Text='<%# Bind("Address") %>'
                     Runat="server"
                     ID="AddressTextBox"></asp:TextBox><br />
                City:
                <asp:TextBox Text='<%# Bind("City") %>' Runat="server"
                     ID="CityTextBox"></asp:TextBox><br />
                Region:
                <asp:TextBox Text='<%# Bind("Region") %>'
                     Runat="server"
                     ID="RegionTextBox"></asp:TextBox><br />
                PostalCode:
                <asp:TextBox Text='<%# Bind("PostalCode") %>'
                     Runat="server"
                     ID="PostalCodeTextBox"></asp:TextBox><br />
                Country:
                <asp:TextBox Text='<%# Bind("Country") %>'
                     Runat="server"
                     ID="CountryTextBox"></asp:TextBox><br />
                Phone:
                <asp:TextBox Text='<%# Bind("Phone") %>' Runat="server"
                     ID="PhoneTextBox"></asp:TextBox><br />
                Fax:
                <asp:TextBox Text='<%# Bind("Fax") %>' Runat="server"
                     ID="FaxTextBox"></asp:TextBox><br />
                <br />
                <asp:Button ID="Button2" Runat="server" Text="Button"
                     CommandName="update" />
                <asp:Button ID="Button3" Runat="server" Text="Button"
                     CommandName="cancel" />
            </EditItemTemplate>
            <ItemTemplate>
                <table width="100%">
                    <tr>
```

```
            <td style="width: 439px">
            <b>
            <span style="font-size: 14pt">
                Customer Information</span>
            </b>
            </td>
            <td style="width: 439px" align="right">
                CustomerID:
                <asp:Label ID="CustomerIDLabel"
                     Runat="server"
                     Text='<%# Bind("CustomerID") %>'>
                     </asp:Label></td>
        </tr>
        <tr>
            <td colspan="2">
                CompanyName:
                <asp:Label ID="CompanyNameLabel"
                     Runat="server"
                     Text='<%# Bind("CompanyName") %>'>
                     </asp:Label><br />
                ContactName:
                <asp:Label ID="ContactNameLabel"
                     Runat="server"
                     Text='<%# Bind("ContactName") %>'>
                     </asp:Label><br />
                ContactTitle:
                <asp:Label ID="ContactTitleLabel"
                     Runat="server"
                     Text='<%# Bind("ContactTitle") %>'>
                     </asp:Label><br />
                <br />
                <table width="100%"><tr>
                    <td colspan="3">
                        <asp:Label ID="AddressLabel"
                             Runat="server"
                             Text='<%# Bind("Address") %>'>
                                 </asp:Label></td>
                    </tr>
                    <tr>
                    <td style="width: 100px">
                        <asp:Label ID="CityLabel"
                             Runat="server"
                             Text='<%# Bind("City") %>'>
                                 </asp:Label></td>
                    <td style="width: 100px">
                        <asp:Label ID="RegionLabel"
                             Runat="server"
                             Text='<%# Bind("Region") %>'>
                                 </asp:Label></td>
                    <td style="width: 100px">
                        <asp:Label ID="PostalCodeLabel"
                             Runat="server"
                           Text='<%# Bind("PostalCode") %>'>
                                </asp:Label>
                        </td>
                    </tr>
                    <tr>
                    <td style="width: 100px" valign="top">
                        <asp:Label ID="CountryLabel"
                             Runat="server"
                             Text='<%# Bind("Country") %>'>
                                 </asp:Label></td>
```

continues

LISTING 7-59 *(continued)*

```
                                    <td style="width: 100px"></td>
                                    <td style="width: 100px">Phone:
                                        <asp:Label ID="PhoneLabel"
                                              Runat="server"
                                              Text='<%# Bind("Phone") %>'>
                                                       </asp:Label><br />
                                            Fax:
                                        <asp:Label ID="FaxLabel"
                                              Runat="server"
                                              Text='<%# Bind("Fax") %>'>
                                                 </asp:Label><br />
                                        </td>
                                    </tr></table>
                                <asp:Button ID="Button1" Runat="server"
                                     Text="Button" CommandName="edit" />
                            </td>
                        </tr></table>
                </ItemTemplate>
            </asp:FormView>
            <asp:SqlDataSource ID="SqlDataSource1" Runat="server"
                 SelectCommand="SELECT * FROM [Customers]"
                 ConnectionString=
                      "<%$ ConnectionStrings:ConnectionString %>">

            </asp:SqlDataSource>

        </div>
        </form>
    </body>
    </html>
```

OTHER DATABOUND CONTROLS

ASP.NET contains a variety of other simple controls that can be bound to data sources. This section looks at some of these other controls and how you can connect them to data in your Web application.

TreeView

The TreeView displays hierarchically structured data. Because of this, it can be bound only to the XmlDataSource and the SiteMapDataSource controls that are designed to bind to hierarchically structured data sources like a SiteMap file. Listing 7-60 shows a sample SiteMap file you can use for your SiteMapDataSource control.

Available for download on Wrox.com

LISTING 7-60: A SiteMap file for your samples

```
<siteMap>
    <siteMapNode url="page3.aspx" title="Home" description="" roles="">
        <siteMapNode url="page2.aspx"
                     title="Content" description="" roles="" />
        <siteMapNode url="page4.aspx"
                     title="Links" description="" roles="" />
        <siteMapNode url="page1.aspx"
                     title="Comments" description="" roles="" />
    </siteMapNode>
</siteMap>
```

Listing 7-61 shows how you can bind a TreeView control to a SiteMapDataSource control to generate navigation for your Web site.

LISTING 7-61: Using the TreeView with a SiteMapDataSource control

Available for download on Wrox.com

```
<html xmlns="http://www.w3.org/1999/xhtml" >
<head runat="server">
    <title>Using the TreeView control</title>
</head>
<body>
    <form id="form1" runat="server">
    <div>
        <asp:TreeView ID="TreeView1" Runat="server"
             DataSourceID="SiteMapDataSource1" />
        <asp:SiteMapDataSource ID="SiteMapDataSource1"
             Runat="server" />
    </div>
    </form>
</body>
</html>
```

AdRotator

The familiar AdRotator control is a great control for displaying rotating data, like ads, in your application. It can be bound to either a SqlDataSource or XmlDataSource control. Listing 7-62 shows an example of binding the AdRotator to a SqlDataSource control.

LISTING 7-62: Using the AdRotator with a SqlDataSource control

Available for download on Wrox.com

```
<asp:AdRotator ID="AdRotator1" runat="server"
     DataSourceId="SqlDataSource1" AlternateTextField="AlternateTF"
     ImageUrlField="Image" NavigateUrlField="NavigateUrl" />
```

For an in-depth discussion of the AdRotator control, see Chapter 3.

Menu

The last control in this section is the Menu control. Like the TreeView control, it is capable of displaying hierarchical data in a vertical *pop-out style* menu. Also like the TreeView control, it can be bound only to the XmlDataSource and the SiteMapDataSource controls. Listing 7-63 shows how you can use the same SiteMap data used earlier in the TreeView control sample, and modify it to display using the new Menu control.

LISTING 7-63: Using the Menu control with a SiteMapDataSource control

Available for download on Wrox.com

```
<html xmlns="http://www.w3.org/1999/xhtml" >
<head runat="server">
    <title>Using the Menu control</title>
</head>
<body>
    <form id="form1" runat="server">
    <div>
        <asp:Menu ID="Menu1" Runat="server"
             DataSourceID="SiteMapDataSource1" />
        <asp:SiteMapDataSource ID="SiteMapDataSource1"
             Runat="server" />
    </div>
    </form>
</body>
</html>
```

For more information about the Menu control, see Chapter 13.

INLINE DATA-BINDING SYNTAX

Another feature of data binding in ASP.NET is inline data-binding syntax. Inline syntax in ASP.NET 1.0/1.1 was primarily relegated to templated controls such as the DataList or the Repeater controls, and even then it was sometimes difficult and confusing to make it work as you wanted it to. In ASP.NET 1.0/1.1, if you needed to use inline data binding, you might have created something like the procedure shown in Listing 7-64.

LISTING 7-64: Using DataBinders in ASP.NET 1.0

Available for download on Wrox.com

```
<asp:Repeater ID="Repeater1" runat="server"
     DataSourceID="SqlDataSource1">
    <HeaderTemplate>
        <table>
    </HeaderTemplate>
    <ItemTemplate>
       <tr>
          <td>
              <%# Container.DataItem("ProductID")%><BR/>
              <%# Container.DataItem("ProductName")%><BR/>
              <%# DataBinder.Eval(
                      Container.DataItem, "UnitPrice", "{0:c}")%><br/>
           </td>
        </tr>
    </ItemTemplate>
    <FooterTemplate>
        </table>
    </FooterTemplate>
</asp:Repeater>
```

As you can see in this sample, you are using a Repeater control to display a series of employees. Because the Repeater control is a templated control, you use data binding to output the employee-specific data in the proper location of the template. Using the `Eval` method also allows you to provide formatting information such as Date or Currency formatting at render-time.

In later versions of ASP.NET, the concept of inline data binding remains basically the same, but you are given a simpler syntax and several powerful binding tools to use.

Data-Binding Syntax

ASP.NET contains three different ways to perform data binding. One way is that you can continue to use the existing method of binding, using the `Container.DataItem` syntax:

```
<%# Container.DataItem("Name") %>
```

This is good because it means you won't have to change your existing Web pages if you are migrating from prior versions of ASP.NET. But if you are creating new Web pages, you should probably use the simplest form of binding, using the `Eval` method directly:

```
<%# Eval("Name") %>
```

You can also continue to format data using the formatter overload of the `Eval` method:

```
<%# Eval("HireDate", "{0:mm dd yyyy}" ) %>
```

In addition to these changes, ASP.NET includes a form of data binding called *two-way data binding*. Two-way data binding allows you to support both read and write operations for bound data. This is done using the `Bind` method, which, other than using a different method name, works just like the `Eval` method:

```
<%# Bind("Name") %>
```

The `Bind` method should be used in new controls such as the GridView, DetailsView, or FormView, where auto-updates to the data source are implemented.

When working with the data binding statements, remember that anything between the `<%# %>` delimiters is treated as an expression. This is important because it gives you additional functionality when data binding. For example, you could append additional data:

```
<%# "Foo " + Eval("Name") %>
```

Or you can even pass the evaluated value to a method:

```
<%# DoSomeProcess( Eval("Name") )%>
```

XML Data Binding

Because XML is becoming ever more prevalent in applications, ASP.NET also includes several ways to bind specifically to XML data sources. These data-binding expressions give you powerful ways of working with the hierarchical format of XML. Additionally, except for the different method names, these binding methods work exactly the same as the `Eval` and `Bind` methods discussed earlier. These binders should be used when you are using the XmlDataSource control. The first binding format that uses the `XPathBinder` class is shown in the following code:

```
<% XPathBinder.Eval(Container.DataItem, "employees/employee/Name") %>
```

Notice that rather than specifying a column name as in the `Eval` method, the `XPathBinder` binds the result of an XPath query. Like the standard `Eval` expression, the XPath data binding expression also has a shorthand format:

```
<% XPath("employees/employee/Name") %>
```

Also, like the `Eval` method, the XPath data binding expression supports applying formatting to the data:

```
<% XPath("employees/employee/HireDate", "{0:mm dd yyyy}") %>
```

The `XPathBinder` returns a single node using the XPath query provided. Should you want to return multiple nodes from the XmlDataSource Control, you can use the class's `Select` method. This method returns a list of nodes that match the supplied XPath query:

```
<% XPathBinder.Select(Container.DataItem,"employees/employee") %>
```

Or use the shorthand syntax:

```
<% XpathSelect("employees/employee") %>
```

EXPRESSIONS AND EXPRESSION BUILDERS

Finally, ASP.NET introduces the concept of expressions and expression builders. Expressions are statements that are parsed by ASP.NET at runtime to return a data value. ASP.NET automatically uses expressions to do things like retrieve the database connection string when it parses the SqlDataSource control, so you may have already seen these statements in your pages. An example of the `ConnectionString` expression is shown in Listing 7-65.

LISTING 7-65: A ConnectionString expression

Available for download on Wrox.com

```
<asp:SqlDataSource ID="SqlDataSource1" Runat="server"
    SelectCommand="SELECT * FROM [Customers]"
    ConnectionString="<%$ ConnectionStrings:ConnectionString %>" />
```

When ASP.NET is attempting to parse an ASP.NET Web page, it looks for expressions contained in the `<%$ %>` delimiters. This indicates to ASP.NET that this is an expression to be parsed. As shown in the previous listing, it attempts to locate the `NorthwindConnectionString` value from the `web.config` file. ASP.NET knows to do this because of the `ConnectionStrings` expression prefix, which tells ASP.NET to use the `ConnectionStringsExpressionBuilder` class to parse the expression.

ASP.NET includes several expression builders, including one for retrieving values from the `AppSettings` section of `web.config` file: one for retrieving `ConnectionStrings` as shown in Listing 7-65, and one for retrieving localized resource file values. Listings 7-66 and 7-67 demonstrate using the AppSettingsExpressionBuilder and the ResourceExpressionBuilder.

LISTING 7-66: Using AppSettingsExpressionBuilder

Available for download on Wrox.com

```
<asp:Label runat="server" ID="Label1"
    Text="<%$ AppSettings: LabelText %>" />
```

LISTING 7-67: Using ResourceExpressionBuilder

Available for download on Wrox.com

```
<asp:Label runat="server" ID="Label1"
    Text="<%$ Resources: MyAppResources,Label1Text %>" />
```

In addition to using the expression builder classes, you can also create your own expressions by deriving a class from the System.Web.Compilation.ExpressionBuilder base class. This base class provides you with several methods you must override if you want ASP.NET to parse your expression properly. Listing 7-68 shows a simple custom expression builder.

LISTING 7-68: Using a simple custom expression builder

Available for download on Wrox.com

VB

```
<ExpressionPrefix("MyCustomExpression")>
<ExpressionEditor("MyCustomExpressionEditor")>
Public Class MyFirstCustomExpression
    Inherits ExpressionBuilder

    Public Overrides Function GetCodeExpression(
        ByVal entry As BoundPropertyEntry,
        ByVal parsedData As Object,
        ByVal context As ExpressionBuilderContext) _
        As System.CodeDom.CodeExpression

        Return New CodeCastExpression("Int64",
            New CodePrimitiveExpression(1000))
    End Function
End Class
```

C#

```
[ExpressionPrefix("MyFirstCustomExpression")]
[ExpressionEditor("MyFirstCustomExpressionEditor")]
public class MyFirstCustomExpression : ExpressionBuilder
{
    public override System.CodeDom.CodeExpression
        GetCodeExpression(BoundPropertyEntry entry, object parsedData,
            ExpressionBuilderContext context)
    {
        return new CodeCastExpression("Int64",
            new CodePrimitiveExpression(1000));
    }
}
```

In examining this sample, notice several items. First, you have derived the MyCustomExpression class from ExpressionBuilder as discussed earlier. Second, you have overridden the GetCodeExpression method. This method supplies you with several parameters that can be helpful in executing this method, and it returns a CodeExpression object to ASP.NET that it can execute at runtime to retrieve the data value.

The CodeExpression *class is a base class in .NET's CodeDom infrastructure. Classes that are derived from the* CodeExpression *class provide abstracted ways of generating .NET code, whether VB or C#. This CodeDom infrastructure is what helps you create and run code dynamically at runtime.*

The BoundPropertyEntry parameter entry tells you exactly which property the expression is bound to. For example, in Listings 7-66 and 7-67, the Label's Text property is bound to the AppSettings and Resources expressions. The object parameter parsedData contains any data that was parsed and returned by the ParseExpression method that you see later on in the chapter. Finally, the ExpressionBuilderContext parameter context allows you to reference the virtual path or templated control associated with the expression.

In the body of the GetCodeExpression method, you are creating a new CodeCastExpression object, which is a class derived from the CodeExpression base class. The CodeCastExpression tells .NET to generate the appropriate code to execute a cast from one data type to another. In this case, you are casting the value 1000 to an Int64 datatype. When .NET executes the CodeCastExpression, it is (in a sense) writing the C# code ((long)(1000)), or (if your application was written in VB) CType(1000,Long). Note that a wide variety of classes derive from the CodeExpression class that you can use to generate your final code expression.

The final lines to note are the two attributes that have been added to the class. The ExpressionPrefix and ExpressionEditor attributes help .NET figure out that this class should be used as an expression, and they also help .NET locate the proper expression builder class when it comes time to parse the expression.

After you have created your expression builder class, you let .NET know about it. You do this by adding an expressionBuilders node to the compilation node in your web.config file. Notice that the value of the ExpressionPrefix is added to the expressionBuilder to help ASP.NET locate the appropriate expression builder class at runtime.

```
<compilation debug="true" strict="false" explicit="true">
    <expressionBuilders>
        <add expressionPrefix="MyCustomExpression" type="MyCustomExpression"/>
    </expressionBuilders>
</compilation>
```

The GetCodeExpression method is not the only member available for overriding in the ExpressionBuilder class. Several other useful members include the ParseExpression, SupportsEvaluate, and EvaluateExpression methods.

The ParseExpression method lets you pass parsed expression data into the GetCodeExpression method. For example, in Listing 7-68, the CodeCastExpression value 1000 was hard-coded. If, however, you want to allow a developer to pass that value in as part of the expression, you simply use the ParseExpression method as shown in Listing 7-69.

LISTING 7-69: Using ParseExpression

Available for download on Wrox.com

VB

```
<ExpressionPrefix("MyCustomExpression")>
<ExpressionEditor("MyCustomExpressionEditor")>
Public Class MySecondCustomExpression
    Inherits ExpressionBuilder

    Public Overrides Function GetCodeExpression(
        ByVal entry As BoundPropertyEntry,
        ByVal parsedData As Object,
        ByVal context As ExpressionBuilderContext) _
        As System.CodeDom.CodeExpression

        Return New CodeCastExpression("Int64",
            New CodePrimitiveExpression(parsedData))
    End Function

    Public Overrides Function ParseExpression(
        ByVal expression As String,
        ByVal propertyType As Type,
```

continues

LISTING 7-69 *(continued)*

```
        ByVal context As ExpressionBuilderContext) As Object

        Return expression
    End Function
End Class
```

C#

```
[ExpressionPrefix("MySecondCustomExpression")]
[ExpressionEditor("MySecondCustomExpressionEditor")]
public class MySecondCustomExpression : ExpressionBuilder
{
    public override System.CodeDom.CodeExpression
        GetCodeExpression(BoundPropertyEntry entry, object parsedData,
            ExpressionBuilderContext context)
    {
        return new CodeCastExpression("Int64",
            new CodePrimitiveExpression(parsedData));
    }
    public override object ParseExpression
        (string expression, Type propertyType,
         ExpressionBuilderContext context)
    {
        return expression;
    }
}
```

The last two `ExpressionBuilder` overrides to examine are the `SupportsEvaluate` and `EvaluateExpression` members. You need to override these methods if you are running your Web site in a no-compile scenario (you have specified `compilationMode = "never"` in your `@Page` directive). The `SupportEvaluate` property returns a Boolean indicating to ASP.NET whether this expression can be evaluated while a page is executing in no-compile mode. If `True` is returned and the page is executing in no-compile mode, the `EvaluateExpression` method is used to return the data value rather than the `GetCodeExpression` method. The `EvaluateExpression` returns an object representing the data value. See Listing 7-70.

LISTING 7-70: Overriding SupportsEvaluate and EvaluateExpression

Available for download on Wrox.com

VB

```
<ExpressionPrefix("MyCustomExpression")>
<ExpressionEditor("MyCustomExpressionEditor")>
Public Class MyThirdCustomExpression
    Inherits ExpressionBuilder

    Public Overrides Function GetCodeExpression(
        ByVal entry As BoundPropertyEntry,
        ByVal parsedData As Object,
        ByVal context As ExpressionBuilderContext) _
        As System.CodeDom.CodeExpression

        Return New CodeCastExpression("Int64",
            New CodePrimitiveExpression(parsedData))
    End Function

    Public Overrides Function ParseExpression(
        ByVal expression As String,
        ByVal propertyType As Type,
        ByVal context As ExpressionBuilderContext) As Object

        Return expression
    End Function
```

```
    Public Overrides ReadOnly Property SupportsEvaluate As Boolean
        Get
            Return True
        End Get
    End Property

    Public Overrides Function EvaluateExpression(
        ByVal target As Object,
        ByVal Entry As BoundPropertyEntry,
        ByVal parsedData As Object,
        ByVal context As ExpressionBuilderContext) As Object

        Return parsedData
    End Function

End Class
```

C#

```
[ExpressionPrefix("MyThirdCustomExpression")]
[ExpressionEditor("MyThirdCustomExpressionEditor")]
public class MyThirdCustomExpression : ExpressionBuilder
{
    public override System.CodeDom.CodeExpression
        GetCodeExpression(BoundPropertyEntry entry, object parsedData,
            ExpressionBuilderContext context)
    {
        return new CodeCastExpression("Int64",
            new CodePrimitiveExpression(parsedData));
    }

    public override object ParseExpression
        (string expression, Type propertyType,
         ExpressionBuilderContext context)
    {
        return expression;
    }

    public override bool SupportsEvaluate
    {
        get
        {
            return true;
        }
    }

    public override object EvaluateExpression(object target,
        BoundPropertyEntry entry, object parsedData,
        ExpressionBuilderContext context)
    {
        return parsedData;
    }
}
```

As shown in Listing 7-70, you can simply return `True` from the `SupportsEvaluate` property if you want to override the `EvaluateExpression` method. Then all you do is return an object from the `EvaluateExpression` method.

SUMMARY

In this chapter, you examined data binding in ASP.NET. Data source controls such as the LinqDataSource control, SqlDataSource control, or XmlDataSource control make querying and displaying data from any number of data sources an almost trivial task. Using the data source controls' own wizards, you learned how easy it is to generate powerful data access functionality with almost no code required.

You examined how even a beginning developer can easily combine the data source controls with the GridView, ListView, and DetailsView controls to create powerful data manipulation applications with a minimal amount of coding.

You saw how ASP.NET includes a multitude of controls that can be data-bound, examining the features of the controls that are included in the ASP.NET toolbox, such as the GridView, TreeView, ListView, FormView, and Menu controls.

Finally, you looked at how the inline data-binding syntax has been improved and strengthened with the addition of the XML-specific data-binding expressions.

Data Management with ADO.NET

WHAT'S IN THIS CHAPTER?

- Working with key ADO.NET features
- Common ADO.NET operations
- Working with SQL Server and Oracle
- Getting to know the DataList and ListView Server controls
- Working with asynchronous commands

This chapter provides information on programming with the data management features that are part of ADO.NET, a key component of the .NET Framework and of your ASP.NET development. The discussion begins with the basics of ADO.NET and later dives into the ways you can use various features that make up ADO.NET to manage data contained in a relational database.

ADO.NET, first introduced in version 1.0 of the .NET Framework, provided an extensive array of features to handle live data in a connected mode or data that is disconnected from its underlying data store. ADO.NET 1.0 was primarily developed to address two specific problems in getting at data. The first had to do with the user's need to access data once and to iterate through a collection of data in a single instance. This need often arose in Web application development.

ADO.NET addresses a couple of the most common data-access strategies that are used for applications today. When classic ADO was developed, many applications could be connected to the data store almost indefinitely. With the explosion of the Internet as the means of data communication, a data technology is required to make data accessible and updateable in a disconnected architecture.

The first of these common data-access scenarios is one in which a user must locate a collection of data and iterate through this data a single time. This is a popular scenario for Web pages. When a request for data from a Web page that you have created is received, you can simply fill a table with data from a data store. In this case, you go to the data store, grab the data that you want, send the data across the wire, and then populate the table. In this scenario, the goal is to get the data in place as fast as possible.

The second way to work with data in this disconnected architecture is to grab a collection of data and use this data separately from the data store itself. This could be on the server or even on the client.

Although the data is disconnected, you want the ability to keep the data (with all of its tables and relations in place) on the client side. Classic ADO data was represented by a single table that you could iterate through. ADO.NET, however, can be a reflection of the data store itself, with tables, columns, rows, and relations all in place. When you are done with the client-side copy of the data, you can persist the changes that you made in the local copy of data directly back into the data store. The technology that gives you this capability is the `DataSet`, which will be covered shortly.

Although classic ADO was geared for a two-tiered environment (client-server), ADO.NET addresses a multi-tiered environment. ADO.NET is easy to work with because it has a unified programming model. This unified programming model makes working with data on the server the same as working with data on the client. Because the models are the same, you find yourself more productive when working with ADO.NET.

ADO.NET offers many advanced features and many different ways to retrieve your data and manipulate it before presenting it to the end user. This chapter focuses on the core of ADO.NET; other chapters, such as Chapter 29, look at other means to get at your underlying data.

BASIC ADO.NET FEATURES

This chapter begins with a quick look at the basics of ADO.NET and then provides an overview of basic ADO.NET capabilities, namespaces, and classes. It also reviews how to work with the `Connection`, `Command`, `DataAdapter`, `DataSet`, and `DataReader` objects.

Common ADO.NET Tasks

Before jumping into the depths of ADO.NET, step back and make sure that you understand some of the common tasks you might perform programmatically within ADO.NET. This next section looks at the process of selecting, inserting, updating, and deleting data.

The following example makes use of the `Northwind.mdf` *SQL Server Express Database file. You can find this sample database at* `www.microsoft.com/downloads/details.aspx?familyid=06616212-0356-46a0-8da2-eebc53a68034&displaylang=en`. *After you install it, you will find the* `Northwind.mdf` *file in the* `C:\SQL Server 2000 Sample Databases` *directory. To add this database to your ASP.NET application, create an App_Data folder within your project (if it isn't already there), right-click on the folder, and select Add Existing Item. From the provided dialog box, you can then browse to the location of the* `Northwind.mdf` *file that you just installed. If you are having trouble getting the permissions to work with the database, make a data connection to the file from the Visual Studio Server Explorer by right-clicking on the Data Connections node and selecting Add New Connection from the provided menu. Visual Studio asks you to be made the appropriate user for the database. Then Visual Studio will make the appropriate changes on your behalf for this to occur.*

Selecting Data

After the connection to the data source is open and ready to use, you probably want to read the data from the data source. If you do not want to manipulate the data, but simply to read it or transfer it from one spot to another, you use the `DataReader` class.

In the following example (Listing 8-1), you use the `GetCompanyNameData()` function to provide a list of company names from the SQL Northwind database.

LISTING 8-1: Reading the data from a SQL database using the DataReader class

Available for download on Wrox.com

```
Imports Microsoft.VisualBasic
Imports System.Collections.Generic
Imports System.Data
Imports System.Data.SqlClient

Public Class SelectingData
    Public Function GetCompanyNameData() As List(Of String)
        Dim conn As SqlConnection
        Dim cmd As SqlCommand
        Dim cmdString As String = "Select CompanyName from Customers"
        conn = New SqlConnection("Data Source=.\SQLEXPRESS;AttachDbFilename=
           |DataDirectory|\NORTHWND.MDF;Integrated Security=True;
           User Instance=True")' Put this string on one line in your code
        cmd = New SqlCommand(cmdString, conn)
        conn.Open()

        Dim myReader As SqlDataReader
        Dim returnData As List(Of String) = New List(Of String)
        myReader = cmd.ExecuteReader(CommandBehavior.CloseConnection)

        While myReader.Read()
            returnData.Add(myReader("CompanyName").ToString())
        End While

        Return returnData
    End Function
End Class
```

C#

```
using System.Data;
using System.Data.SqlClient;
using System.Collections.Generic;

public class SelectingData
{
    public List<string> GetCompanyNameData()
    {
        SqlConnection conn;
        SqlCommand cmd;
        string cmdString = "Select CompanyName from Customers";
        conn = new
            SqlConnection(@"Data Source=.\SQLEXPRESS;AttachDbFilename=
                |DataDirectory|\NORTHWND.MDF;Integrated Security=True;
                User Instance=True");  // Put this string on one line in your code
        cmd = new SqlCommand(cmdString, conn);
        conn.Open();

        SqlDataReader myReader;
        List<string> returnData = new List<string>();

        myReader = cmd.ExecuteReader(CommandBehavior.CloseConnection);

        while (myReader.Read())
        {
            returnData.Add(myReader["CompanyName"].ToString());

        }

        return returnData;
    }
}
```

In this example, you create an instance of both the SqlConnection and the SqlCommand classes. Then, before you open the connection, you simply pass the SqlCommand class a SQL command selecting specific data from the Northwind database. After your connection is opened (based upon the commands passed in), you create a DataReader. To read the data from the database, you iterate through the data with the DataReader by using the myReader.Read() method. After the List(Of String) object is built, the connection is closed, and the object is returned from the function.

Inserting Data

When working with data, you often insert the data into the data source. Listing 8-2 shows you how to do this. This data might have been passed to you by the end user through the XML Web Service, or it might be data that you generated within the logic of your class.

LISTING 8-2: Inserting data into SQL Server

Available for download on Wrox.com

VB

```
Public Sub InsertData()
    Dim conn As SqlConnection
    Dim cmd As SqlCommand
    Dim cmdString As String = "Insert Customers (CustomerID,
       CompanyName, ContactName) Values ('BILLE', 'XYZ Company', 'Bill Evjen')"
    conn = New SqlConnection("Data Source=.\SQLEXPRESS;AttachDbFilename=
           |DataDirectory|\NORTHWND.MDF;Integrated Security=True;
           User Instance=True")' Put this string on one line in your code
    cmd = New SqlCommand(cmdString, conn)
    conn.Open()

    cmd.ExecuteNonQuery()
    conn.Close()
End Sub
```

C#

```
public void InsertData()
{
    SqlConnection conn;
    SqlCommand cmd;
    string cmdString = @"Insert Customers (CustomerID, CompanyName,
       ContactName) Values ('BILLE', 'XYZ Company', 'Bill Evjen')";
    conn = new
           SqlConnection(@"Data Source=.\SQLEXPRESS;AttachDbFilename=
               |DataDirectory|\NORTHWND.MDF;Integrated Security=True;
               User Instance=True");  // Put this string on one line in your code
    cmd = new SqlCommand(cmdString, conn);
    conn.Open();

    cmd.ExecuteNonQuery();
    conn.Close();
}
```

Inserting data into SQL is straightforward and simple. Using the SQL command string, you insert specific values for specific columns. The actual insertion is initiated using the cmd.ExecuteNonQuery() command. It executes a command on the data when you don't want anything in return.

Updating Data

In addition to inserting new records into a database, you frequently update existing rows of data in a table. Imagine a table in which you can update multiple records at once. In the example in Listing 8-3, you want to update an employee table by putting a particular value in the emp_bonus column if the employee has been at the company for five years or longer.

LISTING 8-3: Updating data in SQL Server

Available for download on Wrox.com

```
Public Function UpdateEmployeeBonus() As Integer
    Dim conn As SqlConnection
    Dim cmd As SqlCommand
    Dim RecordsAffected as Integer
    Dim cmdString As String = "UPDATE Employees SET emp_bonus=1000 WHERE " & _
       "yrs_duty>=5"
    conn = New SqlConnection("Data Source=.\SQLEXPRESS;AttachDbFilename=
           |DataDirectory|\NORTHWND.MDF;Integrated Security=True;
           User Instance=True")' Put this string on one line in your code
    cmd = New SqlCommand(cmdString, conn)
    conn.Open()

    RecordsAffected = cmd.ExecuteNonQuery()
    conn.Close()

    Return RecordsAffected
End Function
```

C#

```
public int UpdateEmployeeBonus()
{
    SqlConnection conn;
    SqlCommand cmd;
    int RecordsAffected;
    string cmdString = @"UPDATE Employees SET emp_bonus=1000 WHERE yrs_duty>=5";
    conn = new
        SqlConnection(@"Data Source=.\SQLEXPRESS;AttachDbFilename=
            |DataDirectory|\NORTHWND.MDF;Integrated Security=True;
            User Instance=True");  // Put this string on one line in your code

    cmd = new SqlCommand(cmdString, conn);
    conn.Open();

    RecordsAffected = cmd.ExecuteNonQuery();
    conn.Close();

    return RecordsAffected;
}
```

This update function iterates through all the employees in the table and changes the value of the `emp_bonus` field to `1000` if an employee has been with the company for more than five years. This is done with the SQL command string. The great thing about these update capabilities is that you can capture the number of records that were updated by assigning the `ExecuteNonQuery()` command to the `RecordsAffected` variable. The total number of affected records is then returned by the function.

Deleting Data

Along with reading, inserting, and updating data, you sometimes need to delete data from the data source. Deleting data is a simple process of using the SQL command string and then the `ExecuteNonQuery()` command as you did in the update example. See Listing 8-4 for an illustration of this process.

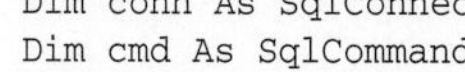

LISTING 8-4: Deleting data from SQL Server

Available for download on Wrox.com

```
Public Function DeleteEmployee() As Integer
    Dim conn As SqlConnection
    Dim cmd As SqlCommand
    Dim RecordsAffected as Integer
    Dim cmdString As String = "DELETE Employees WHERE LastName='Evjen'"
```

continues

LISTING 8-4 *(continued)*

```
    conn = New SqlConnection("Data Source=.\SQLEXPRESS;AttachDbFilename=
           |DataDirectory|\NORTHWND.MDF;Integrated Security=True;
           User Instance=True")' Put this string on one line in your code
    cmd = New SqlCommand(cmdString, conn)
    conn.Open()

    RecordsAffected = cmd.ExecuteNonQuery()
    conn.Close()

    Return RecordsAffected
End Function
```

C#

```
public int DeleteEmployee()
{
    SqlConnection conn;
    SqlCommand cmd;
    int RecordsAffected;
    string cmdString = @"DELETE Employees WHERE LastName='Evjen'";
    conn = new
        SqlConnection(@"Data Source=.\SQLEXPRESS;AttachDbFilename=
            |DataDirectory|\NORTHWND.MDF;Integrated Security=True;
            User Instance=True");  // Put this string on one line in your code
    cmd = new SqlCommand(cmdString, conn);
    conn.Open();

    RecordsAffected = cmd.ExecuteNonQuery();
    conn.Close();

    return RecordsAffected;
}
```

You can assign the `ExecuteNonQuery()` command to an `Integer` variable (just as you did for the update function) to return the number of records deleted.

Basic ADO.NET Namespaces and Classes

Table 8-1 shows the six core ADO.NET namespaces. In addition to these namespaces, each new data provider can have its own namespace. As an example, the SQL Server–focused .NET data provider adds a namespace of `System.Data.SqlClient`.

TABLE 8-1

NAMESPACE	DESCRIPTION
`System.Data`	This namespace is the core of ADO.NET. It contains classes used by all data providers. It contains classes to represent tables, columns, rows, and the `DataSet` class. It also contains several useful interfaces, such as `IDbCommand`, `IDbConnection`, and `IDbDataAdapter`. These interfaces are used by all managed providers, enabling them to plug into the core of ADO.NET.
`System.Data.Common`	This namespace defines common classes that are used as base classes for data providers. All data providers share these classes. A few examples are `DbConnection` and `DbDataAdapter`.
`System.Data.OleDb`	This namespace defines classes that work with OLE-DB data sources using the .NET OleDb data provider. It contains classes such as `OleDbConnection` and `OleDbCommand`.

NAMESPACE	DESCRIPTION
`System.Data.Odbc`	This namespace defines classes that work with the ODBC data sources using the .NET ODBC data provider. It contains classes such as `OdbcConnection` and `OdbcCommand`.
`System.Data.SqlClient`	This namespace defines a data provider for the SQL Server 7.0 or higher database. It contains classes such as `SqlConnection` and `SqlCommand`.
`System.Data.SqlTypes`	This namespace defines a few classes that represent specific data types for the SQL Server database.

ADO.NET has three distinct types of classes commonly referred to as `Disconnected`, `Shared`, and `Data Providers`. The `Disconnected` classes provide the basic structure for the ADO.NET Framework. A good example of this type of class is the `DataTable` class. The objects of this class are capable of storing data without any dependency on a specific data provider. The `Shared` classes form the base classes for data providers and are shared among all data providers. The `Data Provider` classes are meant to work with different kinds of data sources. They are used to perform all data-management operations on specific databases. The `SqlClient` data provider, for example, works only with the SQL Server database.

A data provider contains `Connection`, `Command`, `DataAdapter`, and `DataReader` objects. Typically, in programming ADO.NET, you first create the `Connection` object and provide it with the necessary information, such as the connection string. You then create a `Command` object and provide it with the details of the SQL command that is to be executed. This command can be an inline SQL text command, a stored procedure, or direct table access. You can also provide parameters to these commands if needed. After you create the `Connection` and the `Command` objects, you must decide whether the command returns a result set. If the command doesn't return a result set, you can simply execute the command by calling one of its several `Execute` methods. On the other hand, if the command returns a result set, you must make a decision about whether you want to retain the result set for future uses without maintaining the connection to the database. If you want to retain the result set, you must create a `DataAdapter` object and use it to fill a `DataSet` or a `DataTable` object. These objects are capable of maintaining their information in a disconnected mode. However, if you don't want to retain the result set, but rather to simply process the command in a swift fashion, you can use the `Command` object to create a `DataReader` object. The `DataReader` object needs a live connection to the database, and it works as a forward-only, read-only cursor.

Using the Connection Object

The `Connection` object creates a link (or connection) to a specified data source. This object must contain the necessary information to discover the specified data source and to log in to it properly using a defined username and password combination. This information is provided via a single string called a *connection string*. You can also store this connection string in the `web.config` file of your application.

Every type of data provider has a connection object of some kind. The data provider for working with a SQL data store includes a `SqlConnection` class that performs this type of operation. The `SqlConnection` object is a class that is specific to the `SqlClient` provider. As discussed earlier in this chapter, the `SqlClient` provider is built for working with the SQL Server 7.0 and higher databases. Table 8-2 shows the properties for the `SqlConnection` class.

TABLE 8-2

PROPERTY	DESCRIPTION
`ConnectionString`	This property allows you to read or provide the connection string that the `SqlConnection` object should use.
`Database`	This read-only property returns the name of the database to use after the connection is opened.
`Datasource`	This read-only property returns the name of the instance of the SQL Server database used by the `SqlConnection` object.
`State`	This read-only property returns the current state of the connection. The possible values are `Broken`, `Closed`, `Connecting`, `Executing`, `Fetching`, and `Open`.

Connecting to a data source is probably the most common task when you are working with data. This example and the ones that follow assume that you have a SQL Server database. To connect to your SQL Server database, you use the `SqlConnection` class, as shown in Listing 8-5.

LISTING 8-5: Connecting to a SQL database

Available for download on Wrox.com

```
Dim conn as SqlConnection
conn = New SqlConnection("Data Source=.\SQLEXPRESS;AttachDbFilename=
          |DataDirectory|\NORTHWND.MDF;Integrated Security=True;
          User Instance=True")' Put this string on one line in your code
conn.Open()
```

C#

```
SqlConnection conn;
conn = new
        SqlConnection(@"Data Source=.\SQLEXPRESS;AttachDbFilename=
          |DataDirectory|\NORTHWND.MDF;Integrated Security=True;
          User Instance=True");  // Put this string on one line in your code

conn.Open();
```

To make this connection work, be sure that the proper namespaces are imported before you start using any of the classes that work with SQL. The first means in making a connection is to create an instance of the `SqlConnection` class and assign it to the `conn` instance. This `SqlConnection` class is initialized after you pass in the connection string as a parameter to the class. In this case, you are connecting to the Northwind database that resides on your local machine using the system administrator's login credentials.

Another means of making a connection is to put the connection string within the application's `web.config` file and then to make a reference to the `web.config` file. With ASP.NET 4, you will find that there is an easy way to manage the storage of your connection strings using the `web.config` file. This is actually a better way to store your connection strings rather than hard-coding them within the code of the application itself. In addition to having a single point in the application where the credentials for database access can be managed, storing credentials in the `web.config` file also gives you the ability to encrypt the credentials.

To define your connection string within the `web.config` file, you are going to make use of the `<connectionStrings>` section. Within this section, you can place an `<add>` element to define your connection. An example of this is illustrated in Listing 8-6.

LISTING 8-6: Providing your connection string within the web.config file

Available for download on Wrox.com

```
<connectionStrings>
  <add name="DSN_Northwind" connectionString="Data
   Source=.\SQLEXPRESS;AttachDbFilename=|DataDirectory|\NORTHWND.MDF;Integrated
   Security=True;User Instance=True"
```

```
  providerName="System.Data.SqlClient" />
</connectionStrings>
```

In many places of this chapter, you will see that the actual connection string is broken up on multiple lines. This connection string needs to be on a single line within your code or broken up with string concatenation.

Now that you have a connection string within the `web.config` file, you can then make use of that connection string directly in your code by using the `ConnectionManager` object, as illustrated in Listing 8-7.

LISTING 8-7: Using the connection string found in the web.config file

VB

```
conn = New _
   SqlConnection( _
   ConfigurationManager.ConnectionStrings("DSN_Northwind").ConnectionString)
```

C#

```
conn = new
   SqlConnection(
   ConfigurationManager.ConnectionStrings["DSN_Northwind"].ConnectionString);
```

For this line of code to work, you must make a reference to the `System.Configuration` namespace.

When you complete your connection to the data source, be sure that you close the connection by using `conn.Close()`. The .NET Framework does not implicitly release the connections when they fall out of scope.

Using the Command Object

The `Command` object uses the `Connection` object to execute SQL queries. These queries can be in the form of inline text, stored procedures, or direct table access. If the SQL query uses a `SELECT` clause, the result set it returns is usually stored in either a `DataSet` or a `DataReader` object. The `Command` object provides a number of *Execute* methods that you can use to perform various types of SQL queries.

Next, look at some of the more useful properties of the `SqlCommand` class, as shown in Table 8-3.

TABLE 8-3

PROPERTY	DESCRIPTION
`CommandText`	This read/write property allows you to set or retrieve either the T-SQL statement or the name of the stored procedure.
`CommandTimeout`	This read/write property gets or sets the number of seconds to wait while attempting to execute a particular command. The command is aborted after it times out and an exception is thrown. The default time allotted for this operation is 30 seconds.
`CommandType`	This read/write property indicates the way the `CommandText` property should be interpreted. The possible values are `StoredProcedure`, `TableDirect`, and `Text`. The value of `Text` means that your SQL statement is inline or contained within the code itself.
`Connection`	This read/write property gets or sets the `SqlConnection` object that should be used by this `Command` object.

Next, take a look at the various Execute methods (Table 8-4) that can be called from a `Command` object.

TABLE 8-4

PROPERTY	DESCRIPTION
`ExecuteNonQuery`	This method executes the command specified and returns the number of rows affected.
`ExecuteReader`	This method executes the command specified and returns an instance of the `SqlDataReader` class. The DataReader object is a read-only and forward-only cursor.
`ExecuteRow`	This method executes the command and returns an instance of the `SqlRecord` class. This object contains only a single returned row.
`ExecuteScalar`	This method executes the command specified and returns the first column of the first row in the form of a generic object. The remaining rows and columns are ignored.
`ExecuteXmlReader`	This method executes the command specified and returns an instance of the `XmlReader` class. This method enables you to use a command that returns the results set in the form of an XML document.

Using the DataReader Object

The `DataReader` object is a simple forward-only and read-only cursor. It requires a live connection with the data source and provides a very efficient way of looping and consuming all or part of the result set. This object cannot be directly instantiated. Instead, you must call the `ExecuteReader` method of the `Command` object to obtain a valid `DataReader` object.

When using a `DataReader` object, be sure to close the connection when you are done using the data reader. If not, then the connection stays alive. The connection utilized stays alive until it is explicitly closed using the `Close()` method or until you have enabled your `Command` object to close the connection. You can close the connection after using the data reader in one of two ways. One way is to provide the `CommandBehavior.CloseConnection` enumeration while calling the `ExecuteMethod` of the `Command` object. This approach works only if you loop through the data reader until you reach the end of the result set, at which point the reader object automatically closes the connection for you. However, if you don't want to keep reading the data reader until the end of the result set, you can call the `Close()` method of the `Connection` object yourself.

Listing 8-8 shows the `Connection`, `Command`, and `DataReader` objects in action. It shows how to connect to the Northwind database (an example database for Microsoft SQL Server), read the Customers table within this database, and display the results in a GridView server control.

LISTING 8-8: The SqlConnection, SqlCommand, and SqlDataReader objects in action

Available for download on Wrox.com

VB

```
<%@ Page Language="VB" %>
<%@ Import Namespace="System.Data" %>
<%@ Import Namespace="System.Data.SqlClient" %>
<%@ Import Namespace="System.Configuration" %>

<script runat="server">
    Protected Sub Page_Load(ByVal sender As Object,
            ByVal e As System.EventArgs)

        If Not Page.IsPostBack Then
            Dim MyReader As SqlDataReader

            Dim MyConnection As SqlConnection = New SqlConnection()

            MyConnection.ConnectionString =
              ConfigurationManager.ConnectionStrings("DSN_Northwind").ConnectionString
```

```
            Dim MyCommand As SqlCommand = New SqlCommand()
            MyCommand.CommandText = "SELECT TOP 3 * FROM CUSTOMERS"
            MyCommand.CommandType = CommandType.Text
            MyCommand.Connection = MyConnection

            MyCommand.Connection.Open()
            MyReader = MyCommand.ExecuteReader(CommandBehavior.CloseConnection)

            gvCustomers.DataSource = MyReader
            gvCustomers.DataBind()

            MyCommand.Dispose()
            MyConnection.Dispose()
        End If
    End Sub
</script>

<html>
<body>
    <form id="form1" runat="server">
    <div>
        <asp:GridView ID="gvCustomers" runat="server">
        </asp:GridView>
    </div>
    </form>
</body>
</html>
```

C#

```
<%@ Page Language="C#" %>
<%@ Import Namespace="System.Data" %>
<%@ Import Namespace="System.Data.SqlClient" %>
<%@ Import Namespace="System.Configuration" %>

<script runat="server">
    protected void Page_Load(object sender, EventArgs e)
    {
        if (!Page.IsPostBack)
        {
            SqlDataReader MyReader;
            SqlConnection MyConnection = new SqlConnection();
            MyConnection.ConnectionString =
              ConfigurationManager.ConnectionStrings["DSN_Northwind"].ConnectionString;

            SqlCommand MyCommand = new SqlCommand();
            MyCommand.CommandText = "SELECT TOP 3 * FROM CUSTOMERS";
            MyCommand.CommandType = CommandType.Text;
            MyCommand.Connection = MyConnection;

            MyCommand.Connection.Open();
            MyReader = MyCommand.ExecuteReader(CommandBehavior.CloseConnection);

            gvCustomers.DataSource = MyReader;
            gvCustomers.DataBind();

            MyCommand.Dispose();
            MyConnection.Dispose();
        }
    }
</script>
```

The code shown in Listing 8-8 uses the `SqlConnection` class to create a connection with the Northwind database using the connection string stored in the `web.config` file. This connection string is then retrieved using the `ConfigurationManager` class. Storing your connection strings inside the `web.config` file and referencing them in this manner is always best. If you have a single place to work with your connection strings, any task is a lot more manageable than if you place all your connection strings in the actual code of your application.

After working with the connection string, this bit of code from Listing 8-8 creates a `Command` object using the `SqlCommand` class because you are interested in working with a SQL database. Next, the code provides the command text, command type, and connection properties. After the command and the connection are created, the code opens the connection and executes the command by calling the `ExecuteReader` method of the `MyCommand` object. After receiving the data reader from the `Command` object, you simply bind the retrieved results to an instance of the GridView control. Figure 8-1 shows the results.

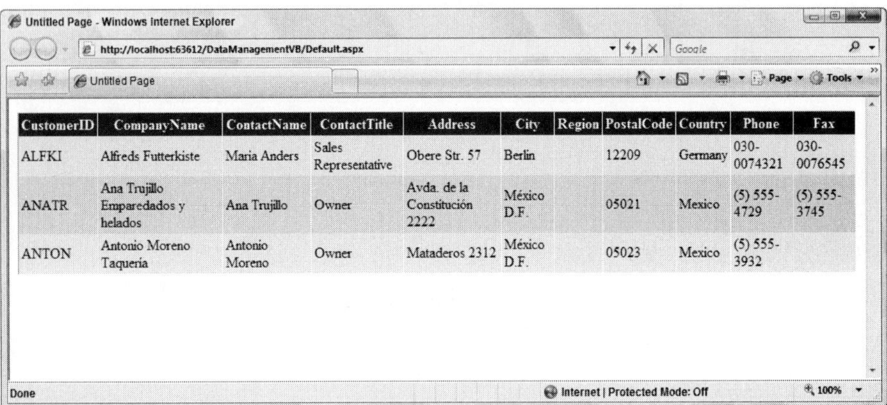

FIGURE 8-1

Using DataAdapter

The `SqlDataAdapter` is a special class whose purpose is to bridge the gap between the disconnected `DataTable` objects and the physical data source. The `SqlDataAdapter` provides a two-way data transfer mechanism. It is capable of executing a `SELECT` statement on a data source and transferring the result set into a `DataTable` object. It is also capable of executing the standard `INSERT`, `UPDATE`, and `DELETE` statements and extracting the input data from a `DataTable` object.

The commonly used properties offered by the `SqlDataAdapter` class are shown in the Table 8-5.

TABLE 8-5

PROPERTY	DESCRIPTION
`SelectCommand`	This read/write property sets or gets an object of type `SqlCommand`. This command is automatically executed to fill a `DataTable` with the result set.
`InsertCommand`	This read/write property sets or gets an object of type `SqlCommand`. This command is automatically executed to insert a new record to the SQL Server database.
`UpdateCommand`	This read/write property sets or gets an object of type `SqlCommand`. This command is automatically executed to update an existing record on the SQL Server database.
`DeleteCommand`	This read/write property sets or gets an object of type `SqlCommand`. This command is automatically executed to delete an existing record on the SQL Server database.

The `SqlDataAdapter` class also provides a method called `Fill()`. Calling the `Fill()` method automatically executes the command provided by the `SelectCommand` property, receives the result set, and copies it to a `DataTable` object.

The code example in Listing 8-9 illustrates how to use an object of `SqlDataAdapter` class to fill a `DataTable` object.

LISTING 8-9: Using an object of SqlDataAdapter to fill a DataTable

Available for download on Wrox.com

VB

```
<%@ Page Language="VB" %>
<%@ Import Namespace="System.Data" %>
<%@ Import Namespace="System.Data.SqlClient" %>
<%@ Import Namespace="System.Configuration" %>

<script runat="server">
    Protected Sub Page_Load(ByVal sender As Object,
           ByVal e As System.EventArgs)

        If Not Page.IsPostBack Then
           Dim MyTable As DataTable = New DataTable()
           Dim MyConnection As SqlConnection = New SqlConnection()
           MyConnection.ConnectionString =
           ConfigurationManager.ConnectionStrings("DSN_Northwind").ConnectionString

           Dim MyCommand As SqlCommand = New SqlCommand()
           MyCommand.CommandText = "SELECT TOP 5 * FROM CUSTOMERS"
           MyCommand.CommandType = CommandType.Text
           MyCommand.Connection = MyConnection
           Dim MyAdapter As SqlDataAdapter = New SqlDataAdapter()
           MyAdapter.SelectCommand = MyCommand
           MyAdapter.Fill(MyTable)

           gvCustomers.DataSource = MyTable.DefaultView
           gvCustomers.DataBind()

           MyAdapter.Dispose()
           MyCommand.Dispose()
           MyConnection.Dispose()
        End If

    End Sub
</script>
```

C#

```
<%@ Page Language="C#" %>
<%@ Import Namespace="System.Data" %>
<%@ Import Namespace="System.Data.SqlClient" %>
<%@ Import Namespace="System.Configuration" %>

<script runat="server">
    protected void Page_Load(object sender, EventArgs e)
    {
        if (!Page.IsPostBack)
        {

            DataTable MyTable = new DataTable();

            SqlConnection MyConnection = new SqlConnection();
            MyConnection.ConnectionString =
                ConfigurationManager.
                ConnectionStrings["DSN_Northwind"].ConnectionString;

            SqlCommand MyCommand = new SqlCommand();
            MyCommand.CommandText = "SELECT TOP 5 * FROM CUSTOMERS";
            MyCommand.CommandType = CommandType.Text;
            MyCommand.Connection = MyConnection;
            SqlDataAdapter MyAdapter = new SqlDataAdapter();
            MyAdapter.SelectCommand = MyCommand;
```

continues

LISTING 8-9 *(continued)*

```
                MyAdapter.Fill(MyTable);

                gvCustomers.DataSource = MyTable.DefaultView;
                gvCustomers.DataBind();

                MyAdapter.Dispose();
                MyCommand.Dispose();
                MyConnection.Dispose();          }
        }
    </script>
```

The code shown in Listing 8-9 creates a `Connection` and `Command` object and then proceeds to create an instance of the `SqlDataAdapter` class. It then sets the `SelectCommand` property of the `DataAdapter` object to the `Command` object it had previously created. After the `DataAdapter` object is ready for executing, the code executes the `Fill()` method, passing it an instance of the `DataTable` class. The `Fill()` method populates the `DataTable` object. Figure 8-2 shows the result of executing this code.

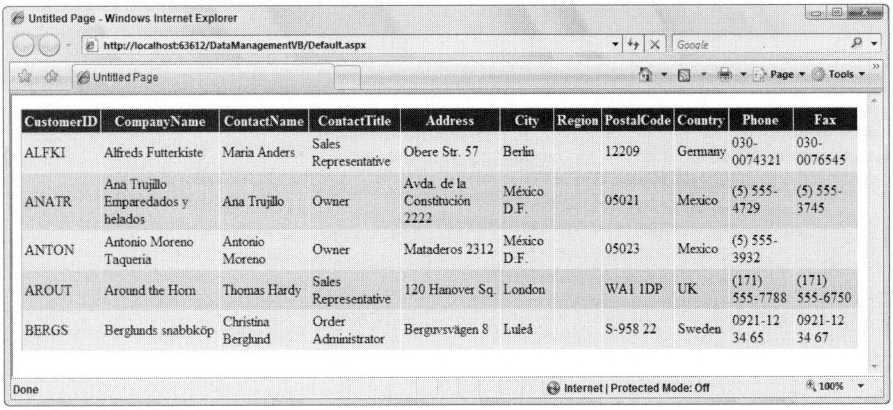

CustomerID	CompanyName	ContactName	ContactTitle	Address	City	Region	PostalCode	Country	Phone	Fax
ALFKI	Alfreds Futterkiste	Maria Anders	Sales Representative	Obere Str. 57	Berlin		12209	Germany	030-0074321	030-0076545
ANATR	Ana Trujillo Emparedados y helados	Ana Trujillo	Owner	Avda. de la Constitución 2222	México D.F.		05021	Mexico	(5) 555-4729	(5) 555-3745
ANTON	Antonio Moreno Taquería	Antonio Moreno	Owner	Mataderos 2312	México D.F.		05023	Mexico	(5) 555-3932	
AROUT	Around the Horn	Thomas Hardy	Sales Representative	120 Hanover Sq.	London		WA1 1DP	UK	(171) 555-7788	(171) 555-6750
BERGS	Berglunds snabbköp	Christina Berglund	Order Administrator	Berguvsvägen 8	Luleå		S-958 22	Sweden	0921-12 34 65	0921-12 34 67

FIGURE 8-2

Using Parameters

Most serious database programming, regardless of how simple it might be, requires you to configure SQL statements using parameters. Using parameters helps guard against possible SQL injection attacks. Obviously, a discussion on the basics of ADO.NET programming is not complete without covering the use of parameterized SQL statements.

Creating a parameter is as simple as declaring an instance of the `SqlParameter` class and providing it the necessary information, such as parameter name, value, type, size, direction, and so on. Table 8-6 shows the properties of the `SqlParameter` class.

TABLE 8-6

PROPERTY	DESCRIPTION
`ParameterName`	This read/write property gets or sets the name of the parameter.
`SqlDbType`	This read/write property gets or sets the SQL Server database type of the parameter value.
`Size`	This read/write property sets or gets the size of the parameter value.
`Direction`	This read/write property sets or gets the direction of the parameter, such as `Input`, `Output`, or `InputOutput`.

PROPERTY	DESCRIPTION
`SourceColumn`	This read/write property maps a column from a `DataTable` to the parameter. It enables you to execute multiple commands using the `SqlDataAdapter` object and pick the correct parameter value from a `DataTable` column during the command execution.
`Value`	This read/write property sets or gets the value provided to the parameter object. This value is passed to the parameter defined in the command during runtime.

Listing 8-10 modifies the code shown in Listing 8-5 to use two parameters while retrieving the list of customers from the database.

LISTING 8-10: The use of a parameterized SQL statement

Available for download on Wrox.com

```
<%@ Page Language="VB" %>
<%@ Import Namespace="System.Data" %>
<%@ Import Namespace="System.Data.SqlClient" %>
<%@ Import Namespace="System.Configuration" %>

<script runat="server">
    Protected Sub Page_Load(ByVal sender As Object,
            ByVal e As System.EventArgs)
        If Not Page.IsPostBack Then
            Dim MyReader As SqlDataReader

            Dim CityParam As SqlParameter
                   Dim ContactParam As SqlParameter

            Dim MyConnection As SqlConnection = New SqlConnection()
            MyConnection.ConnectionString =
              ConfigurationManager.ConnectionStrings("DSN_Northwind").ConnectionString
            Dim MyCommand As SqlCommand = New SqlCommand()
            MyCommand.CommandText =
              "SELECT * FROM CUSTOMERS WHERE CITY = @CITY AND CONTACTNAME = @CONTACT"
            MyCommand.CommandType = CommandType.Text
            MyCommand.Connection = MyConnection
            CityParam = New SqlParameter()
            CityParam.ParameterName = "@CITY"
            CityParam.SqlDbType = SqlDbType.VarChar
            CityParam.Size = 15
            CityParam.Direction = ParameterDirection.Input
            CityParam.Value = "Berlin"

            ContactParam = New SqlParameter()
            ContactParam.ParameterName = "@CONTACT"
            ContactParam.SqlDbType = SqlDbType.VarChar
            ContactParam.Size = 15
            ContactParam.Direction = ParameterDirection.Input
            ContactParam.Value = "Maria Anders"

            MyCommand.Parameters.Add(CityParam)
            MyCommand.Parameters.Add(ContactParam)

            MyCommand.Connection.Open()
            MyReader = MyCommand.ExecuteReader(CommandBehavior.CloseConnection)

            gvCustomers.DataSource = MyReader
            gvCustomers.DataBind()
```

continues

LISTING 8-10 *(continued)*

```
            MyCommand.Dispose()
            MyConnection.Dispose()
        End If

    End Sub
</script>
```

C#

```
<%@ Page Language="C#" %>
<%@ Import Namespace="System.Data" %>
<%@ Import Namespace="System.Data.SqlClient" %>
<%@ Import Namespace="System.Configuration" %>

<script runat="server">
    protected void Page_Load(object sender, EventArgs e)
    {
       if (!Page.IsPostBack)
       {
            SqlDataReader MyReader;
            SqlParameter CityParam;
            SqlParameter ContactParam;

            SqlConnection MyConnection = new SqlConnection();
            MyConnection.ConnectionString =
              ConfigurationManager.ConnectionStrings["DSN_Northwind"].ConnectionString;

            SqlCommand MyCommand = new SqlCommand();
            MyCommand.CommandText =
              "SELECT * FROM CUSTOMERS WHERE CITY = @CITY AND CONTACTNAME = @CONTACT";
            MyCommand.CommandType = CommandType.Text;
            MyCommand.Connection = MyConnection;

            CityParam = new SqlParameter();
            CityParam.ParameterName = "@CITY";
            CityParam.SqlDbType = SqlDbType.VarChar;
            CityParam.Size = 15;
            CityParam.Direction = ParameterDirection.Input;
            CityParam.Value = "Berlin";

            ContactParam = new SqlParameter();
            ContactParam.ParameterName = "@CONTACT";
            ContactParam.SqlDbType = SqlDbType.VarChar;
            ContactParam.Size = 15;
            ContactParam.Direction = ParameterDirection.Input;
            ContactParam.Value = "Maria Anders";

            MyCommand.Parameters.Add(CityParam);
            MyCommand.Parameters.Add(ContactParam);

            MyCommand.Connection.Open();
            MyReader = MyCommand.ExecuteReader(CommandBehavior.CloseConnection);

            gvCustomers.DataSource = MyReader;
            gvCustomers.DataBind();

            MyCommand.Dispose();

            MyConnection.Dispose();
       }
    }
</script>
```

The code shown in Listing 8-8 uses a parameterized SQL statement that receives the name of the city and the contact person to narrow the result set. These parameters are provided by instantiating a couple of instances of the `SqlParameter` class and filling in the appropriate name, type, size, direction, and value properties for each object of `SqlParameter` class. From there, you add the populated parameters to the `Command` object by invoking the `Add()` method of the `Parameters` collection. Figure 8-3 shows the result of executing this code.

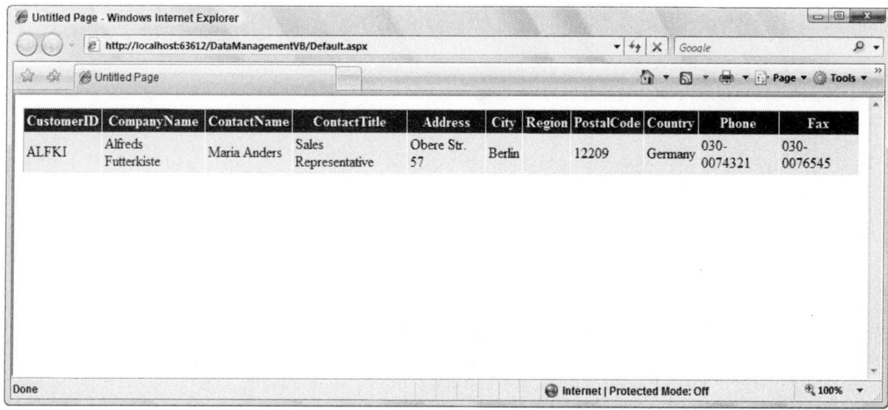

FIGURE 8-3

Understanding DataSet and DataTable

Most programmers agree that the `DataSet` class is the most commonly used part of ADO.NET in real-world, database-driven applications. This class provides mechanisms for managing data when it is disconnected from the data source. This capability to handle data in a disconnected state was first introduced in .NET during the 1.0 version of ADO.NET. When the .NET Framework version 3.5 of ADO.NET was released, it retained all the features of its predecessors and provided a few newer, much-needed features. You will also find these in the .NET Framework 4.

An object created from the `DataSet` class works as a container for other objects that are created from the `DataTable` class. The `DataTable` object represents a logical table in memory. It contains rows, columns, primary keys, constraints, and relations with other `DataTable` objects. Therefore, you could have a `DataSet` that is made up of two distinct tables such as a Customers and an Orders table. Then you could use the `DataSet`, just as you would any other relational data source, to make a relation between the two tables in order to show all the orders for a particular customer.

Most of the disconnected data-driven programming is actually done using one or more `DataTable` objects within the `DataSet`. However, the previous versions of ADO.NET didn't allow you to work directly with the `DataTable` object for some very important tasks, such as reading and writing data to and from an XML file. It didn't even allow you to serialize the `DataTable` object independently of the larger and encompassing `DataSet` object. This limitation required you to always use the `DataSet` object to perform any operation on a `DataTable`. The current version of ADO.NET removes this limitation and enables you to work directly with the `DataTable` for all your needs. In fact, we recommend that you don't use the `DataSet` object unless you need to work with multiple `DataTable` objects and need a container object to manage them. If you end up working with only a single table of information, then working with an instance of the `DataTable` object rather than a `DataSet` that contains only a single `DataTable` is best.

The current version of ADO.NET provides the capability to load a `DataTable` in memory by consuming a data source using a `DataReader`. In the past, you were sometimes restricted to creating multiple overloads of the same method just to work with both the `DataReader` and the `DataTable` objects. Now you have the flexibility to write the data access code one time and reuse the DataReader — either directly or to fill a DataTable, as shown in Listing 8-11.

LISTING 8-11: How to load a DataTable from a DataReader

Available for download on Wrox.com

VB

```
<%@ Page Language="VB" %>
<%@ Import Namespace="System.Data" %>
<%@ Import Namespace="System.Data.SqlClient" %>
<%@ Import Namespace="System.Configuration" %>

<script runat="server">
    Protected Sub Page_Load(ByVal sender As Object,
            ByVal e As System.EventArgs)

        If Not Page.IsPostBack Then
            Dim MyDataTable As DataTable
            Dim MyReader As SqlDataReader
            Dim CityParam As SqlParameter

            Dim MyConnection As SqlConnection = New SqlConnection()
            MyConnection.ConnectionString =
              ConfigurationManager.ConnectionStrings("DSN_Northwind").ConnectionString

            Dim MyCommand As SqlCommand = New SqlCommand()
            MyCommand.CommandText =
                    "SELECT * FROM CUSTOMERS WHERE CITY = @CITY"
            MyCommand.CommandType = CommandType.Text
            MyCommand.Connection = MyConnection

            CityParam = New SqlParameter()
            CityParam.ParameterName = "@CITY"
            CityParam.SqlDbType = SqlDbType.VarChar
            CityParam.Size = 15
            CityParam.Direction = ParameterDirection.Input
            CityParam.Value = "London"

            MyCommand.Parameters.Add(CityParam)

            MyCommand.Connection.Open()
            MyReader = MyCommand.ExecuteReader(CommandBehavior.CloseConnection)
            MyDataTable = New DataTable()

            ' Loading DataTable using a DataReader
            MyDataTable.Load(MyReader)

            gvCustomers.DataSource = MyDataTable
            gvCustomers.DataBind()

            MyDataTable.Dispose()
            MyCommand.Dispose()
            MyConnection.Dispose()
        End If

    End Sub

</script>
```

C#

```
<%@ Page Language="C#" %>
<%@ Import Namespace="System.Data" %>
<%@ Import Namespace="System.Data.SqlClient" %>
<%@ Import Namespace="System.Configuration" %>
```

```
<script runat="server">
    protected void Page_Load(object sender, EventArgs e)
    {
        if (!Page.IsPostBack )
        {
            DataTable MyDataTable;
            SqlDataReader MyReader;
            SqlParameter CityParam;

            SqlConnection MyConnection = new SqlConnection();
            MyConnection.ConnectionString =
              ConfigurationManager.ConnectionStrings["DSN_Northwind"].ConnectionString;

            SqlCommand MyCommand = new SqlCommand();
            MyCommand.CommandText =
               "SELECT * FROM CUSTOMERS WHERE CITY = @CITY";
            MyCommand.CommandType = CommandType.Text;
            MyCommand.Connection = MyConnection;

            CityParam = new SqlParameter();
            CityParam.ParameterName = "@CITY";
            CityParam.SqlDbType = SqlDbType.VarChar;
            CityParam.Size = 15;
            CityParam.Direction = ParameterDirection.Input;
            CityParam.Value = "London";

            MyCommand.Parameters.Add(CityParam);
            MyCommand.Connection.Open();
            MyReader = MyCommand.ExecuteReader(CommandBehavior.CloseConnection);

            MyDataTable = new DataTable();

            // Loading DataTable using a DataReader
            MyDataTable.Load(MyReader);

            gvCustomers.DataSource = MyDataTable;
            gvCustomers.DataBind();

            MyDataTable.Dispose();
            MyCommand.Dispose();
            MyConnection.Dispose();
        }
    }
</script>
```

Not only can you load a `DataTable` object from a `DataReader` object, you can also retrieve a `DataTableReader` from an existing `DataTable` object. You accomplish this by calling the `CreateDataReader` method of the `DataTable` class. This method returns an instance of the `DataTableReader` object that can be passed to any method that expects to receive a `DataReader`.

Deciding When to Use a DataSet

As revolutionary as a `DataSet` might be, it is not the best choice in every situation. Often, using a `DataSet` might not be appropriate; instead, using a `DataReader` might be better.

With ADO 2.6, performing a command upon a data store and getting back a single collection of data made up of any number of rows was possible. You could then iterate through this collection of data and use it in some fashion. Now ADO.NET can use the `DataSet` to return a collection of data that actually keeps its structure when removed from the data store. In some situations, you benefit greatly from keeping this copy in its original format. By doing so, you can keep the data disconnected in an in-memory cache in its separate tables and work with the tables individually or apply relationships between the tables. You can work with the tables in much the same manner as you do with other relational data sources — using a parent/child relationship. If working with certain data with all its relationships in place is to your advantage (to enforce a parent/child relationship upon the data), then in this case, of course, using a DataSet as opposed to a DataReader is better.

Because the DataSet is a disconnected copy of the data, you can work with the same records repeatedly without having to go back to the data store. This capability can greatly increase performance and lessen the load upon the server. Having a copy of the data separate from the data store also enables you to continuously handle and shape the data locally. For instance, you might need to repeatedly filter or sort through a collection of data. In this case, working with a DataSet rather than going back and forth to the data store itself would be of great advantage.

Probably one of the greatest uses of the DataSet is to work with multiple data stores and come away with a single collection of data. So for instance, if you have your Customers table within SQL and the orders information for those particular customers within an Oracle database, you can very easily query each data store and create a single DataSet with a Customers and an Orders table in place that you can use in any fashion you choose. The DataSet is just a means of storage for data and doesn't concern itself with where the data came from. Therefore, if you are working with data that is coming from multiple data stores, then using the DataSet is to your benefit.

Because the DataSet is based upon XML and XML Schemas, moving the DataSet around — whether you are transporting it across tiers, processes, or between disparate systems or applications — is quite easy. If the application or system to which you are transferring the DataSet doesn't understand DataSets, the DataSet represents itself as an XML file. So basically, any system or application that can interpret and understand XML can work with the DataSet. This makes it a very popular transport vehicle, and you see an example of it when you transport the DataSet from an XML Web service.

Last but not least, the DataSet enables you to program data with ease. It is much simpler than anything that has been provided before the .NET Framework came onto the scene. Putting the data within a class object allows you to programmatically access the DataSet, and the code example in Listing 8-12 shows you just how easy it can be.

LISTING 8-12: An example of working with the DataSet object

Available for download on Wrox.com

VB

```
Dim conn As SqlConnection = New SqlConnection
   (ConfigurationManager.ConnectionStrings("DSN_Northwind").ConnectionString)
conn.Open()
Dim da As SqlDataAdapter = New SqlDataAdapter("Select * from Customers", conn)
Dim ds As DataSet = New DataSet()
da.Fill(ds, "CustomersTable")
```

C#

```
SqlConnection conn = new SqlConnection
   (ConfigurationManager.ConnectionStrings["DSN_Northwind"].ConnectionString);
conn.Open();
SqlDataAdapter da = new SqlDataAdapter("Select * from Customers", conn);
DataSet ds = new DataSet();
da.Fill(ds, "CustomersTable");
```

Basically, when you work with data, you have to weigh when to use the DataSet. In some cases, you get extreme benefits from using this piece of technology that is provided with ADO.NET. Sometimes, however, you may find that using the DataSet is not in your best interests. Instead, using the DataReader is best.

The DataSet can be used whenever you choose, but sometimes you would rather use the DataReader and work directly against the data store. By using the command objects, such as the SqlCommand and the OleDbCommand objects, you have a little more direct control over what is executed and what you get back as a result set. In situations where this control is vital, not using the DataSet is to your advantage.

When you don't use the DataSet, you don't incur the cost of extra overhead because you are reading and writing directly to the data source. Performing operations in this manner means you don't have to instantiate any additional objects — avoiding unnecessary steps.

This is especially true in a situation when you work with Web Forms in ASP.NET. If you are dealing with Web Forms, the Web pages are re-created each and every time. When this happens, not only is the page re-created by the call to the data source, the `DataSet` is also re-created unless you are caching the `DataSet` in some fashion. This can be an expensive process; so, in situations such as this, you might find it to your benefit to work directly off the data source using the `DataReader`. In most situations when you are working with Web Forms, you want to work with the `DataReader` instead of creating a `DataSet`.

The Typed DataSet

As powerful as the `DataSet` is, it still has some limitations. The `DataSet` is created at runtime. It accesses particular pieces of data by making certain assumptions. Look at how you normally access a specific field in a `DataSet` that is not strongly typed (Listing 8-13).

LISTING 8-13: Accessing a field in a DataSet

VB

```
ds.Tables("Customers").Rows(0).Columns("CompanyName") = "XYZ Company"
```

C#

```
ds.Tables["Customers"].Rows[0].Columns["CompanyName"] = "XYZ Company";
```

The preceding code looks at the Customers table, the first row (remember, everything is zero-based) in the column `CompanyName`, and assigns the value of `XYZ Company` to the field. This is simple and straightforward, but it is based upon certain assumptions and is generated at runtime. The `"Customers"` and `"CompanyName"` words are string literals in this line of code. If they are spelled wrong or if these items aren't in the table, an error occurs at runtime.

Listing 8-14 shows you how to assign the same value to the same field by using a typed `DataSet`.

LISTING 8-14: Accessing a field in a typed DataSet

VB

```
ds.Customers(0).CompanyName = "XYZ Company"
```

C#

```
ds.Customers[0].CompanyName = "XYZ Company";
```

Now the table name and the field to be accessed are not treated as string literals but, instead, are encased in an XML Schema and a class that is generated from the `DataSet` class. When you create a typed `DataSet`, you are creating a class that implements the tables and fields based upon the schema used to generate the class. Basically, the schema is coded into the class.

As you compare the two examples, you see that a typed `DataSet` is easier to read and understand. It is less error-prone, and errors are realized at compile time as opposed to runtime.

In the end, typed `DataSets` are optional, and you are free to use either style as you code.

Using Oracle as Your Database with ASP.NET

If you work in the enterprise space, in many cases you must work with an Oracle backend database. ADO.NET used to have a built-in capability to work with Oracle using the `System.Data.OracleClient` namespace. You will still find this namespace present, but you will notice that it has now been deprecated. In fact, your upgraded applications that use this namespace will continue to work on the .NET Framework 4 and you will not continue to get compiler warnings or errors when using it. Microsoft will also continue to support it from a security standpoint, but it is highly recommended (and we agree) that you instead use a third-party Oracle client. The recommendation is for you to use Oracle's ODP.NET found at `http://www.oracle.com/technology/tech/windows/odpnet/index.html`.

To connect ASP.NET to your Oracle database, you must install the Oracle 11g Client on your Web server. You can get this piece of software from the Oracle Web site found at `oracle.com`. If you are able to connect to your Oracle database from your Web server using SQL*Plus (an Oracle IDE for working with an Oracle database), you can use the Oracle-built Oracle data provider, `Oracle.DataAccess.Client`.

If you are still having trouble connecting to your Oracle database, you also might try to make sure that the database connection is properly defined in your server's `.ora` *file found at* `C:\Oracle\product\11.x.x\Client_1\NETWORK\ADMIN`. *Note that the version number might be different.*

After you know you can connect to your Oracle database, you can make use of this Oracle data provider. To utilize these capabilities to connect to Oracle, your ASP.NET application must add the appropriate references to your code, as demonstrated in Listing 8-15.

LISTING 8-15: Referencing the Oracle.DataAccess.Client namespace

VB

```
Imports System.Data
Imports Oracle.DataAccess.Client
```

C#

```
using System.Data;
using Oracle.DataAccess.Client;
```

With all the references in place, you are able to work with an Oracle backend in much the same manner as you work with a SQL Server backend. Listing 8-16 shows you just how similar it is.

LISTING 8-16: Using the OracleClient object to connect to an Oracle database

Available for download on Wrox.com

VB

```
Dim conn As OracleConnection
Dim cmd As OracleCommand

Dim cmdString As String = "Select CompanyName from Customers"
conn = New
   OracleConnection("User Id=bevjen;Password=bevjen01;Data Source=myOracleDB")
cmd = New OracleCommand(cmdString, conn)
cmd.CommandType = CommandType.Text

conn.Open()
```

C#

```
OracleConnection conn;
OracleCommand cmd;

string cmdString = "Select CompanyName from Customers";
conn = new
   OracleConnection("User Id=bevjen;Password=bevjen01;Data Source=myOracleDB");
cmd = new OracleCommand(cmdString, conn);
cmd.CommandType = CommandType.Text;

conn.Open();
```

After you are connected and performing the PL-SQL commands you want, you can use the `OracleDataReader` object just as you would use the `SqlDataReader` object.

THE DATALIST SERVER CONTROL

The DataList control has been around since the beginning of ASP.NET. It is part of a series of controls that enable you to display your data (especially repeated types of data) using templates. Templates enable you to create more sophisticated layouts for your data and perform functions that controls such as the GridView server control cannot.

Template-based controls like the DataList control require more work on your part. For example, you have to build common tasks for yourself. You cannot rely on other data controls, which you might be used to, such as paging.

Looking at the Available Templates

The idea, when using template-based controls such as the DataList control, is that you put together specific templates to create your desired detailed layout. The DataList control has a number of templates that you can use to build your display. The available templates are defined here in Table 8-7.

TABLE 8-7

TEMPLATE	DESCRIPTION
`AlternatingItemTemplate`	Works in conjunction with the `ItemTemplate` to provide a layout for all the odd rows within the layout. This is commonly used if you want to have a grid or layout where each row is distinguished in some way (such as having a different background color).
`EditItemTemplate`	Allows for a row or item to be defined on how it looks and behaves when editing.
`FooterTemplate`	Allows the last item in the template to be defined. If this is not defined, then no footer will be used.
`HeaderTemplate`	Allows the first item in the template to be defined. If this is not defined, then no header will be used.
`ItemTemplate`	The core template that is used to define a row or layout for each item in the display.
`SelectedItemTemplate`	Allows for a row or item to be defined on how it looks and behaves when selected.
`SeparatorTemplate`	The layout of any separator that is used between the items in the display.

Working with ItemTemplate

Although seven templates are available for use with the DataList control, at a minimum, you are going to need the ItemTemplate. The example in Listing 8-17 shows the company names from the Northwind database.

Available for download on Wrox.com

LISTING 8-17: Showing the company names from the Northwind database using DataList

```
<%@ Page Language="VB" AutoEventWireup="false"
CodeFile="DataListControl.aspx.vb"
    Inherits="DataListControl" %>

<html xmlns="http://www.w3.org/1999/xhtml">
<head runat="server">
    <title>DataList Control</title>
</head>
<body>
    <form id="form1" runat="server">
    <div>
        <asp:DataList ID="DataList1" runat="server" DataSourceID="SqlDataSource1">
            <ItemTemplate>
                Company Name:
                <asp:Label ID="CompanyNameLabel" runat="server"
                    Text='<%# Eval("CompanyName") %>' />
```

continues

LISTING 8-17 *(continued)*

```
                <br />
                <br />
            </ItemTemplate>
        </asp:DataList>
        <asp:SqlDataSource ID="SqlDataSource1" runat="server"
            ConnectionString="<%$ ConnectionStrings:DSN_Northwind %>"
            SelectCommand="SELECT [CompanyName] FROM [Customers]">
        </asp:SqlDataSource>
    </div>
    </form>
</body>
</html>
```

As stated, the DataList control requires, at a minimum, an `ItemTemplate` element where you define the page layout for each item that is encountered from the data source. In this case, all the data is pulled from the Northwind database sample using the SqlDataSource control. The SqlDataSource control pulls only the CompanyName column from the Customers table. From there, the ItemTemplate section of the DataList control defines two items within it. The first item is a static item, "Company Name:", followed by a single ASP.NET server control, the Label server control. Second, the item is then followed by a couple of standard HTML elements. The `Text` property of the Label control uses inline data binding (as shown in the previous chapter of this book) to bind the values that are coming out of the SqlDataSource control. If more than one data point were coming out of the SqlDataSource control, you could still specifically grab the data point that you are interested in using by specifying the item in the `Eval` statement:

```
<asp:Label ID="CompanyNameLabel" runat="server"
 Text='<%# Eval("CompanyName") %>' />
```

Using the code from Listing 8-17 gives you the results illustrated in Figure 8-4.

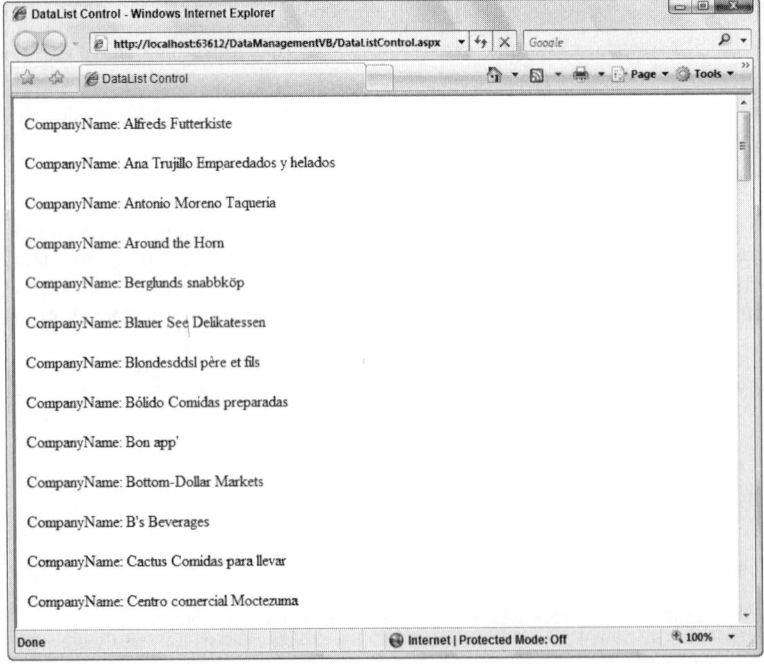

FIGURE 8-4

If you then look at the source of the page, you can see that the DataList control uses tables by default to lay out the elements.

```
<table id="DataList1" cellspacing="0" border="0" style="border-collapse:collapse;">
   <tr>
      <td>
         CompanyName:
         <span id="DataList1_ctl00_CompanyNameLabel">Alfreds Futterkiste</span>
         <br />
         <br />
      </td>
   </tr><tr>
      <td>
         CompanyName:
         <span id="DataList1_ctl01_CompanyNameLabel">
          Ana Trujillo Emparedados y helados</span>
         <br />
         <br />
      </td>
   </tr>

   <!-- Code removed for clarity -->

</table>
```

Although this table layout is the default, you can change this so that the DataList control outputs <span> tags instead. You do this through the use of the `RepeatLayout` property of the DataList control. You will need to rework your DataList, as shown in Listing 8-18.

LISTING 8-18: Changing the output style using RepeatLayout

```
<asp:DataList ID="DataList1" runat="server" DataSourceID="SqlDataSource1"
 RepeatLayout="Flow">
   <ItemTemplate>
    Company Name:
    <asp:Label ID="CompanyNameLabel" runat="server"
     Text='<%# Eval("CompanyName") %>' />
    <br />
    <br />
   </ItemTemplate>
</asp:DataList>
```

The possible options for the `RepeatLayout` property are either `Table` or `Flow`. `Table`, which is the default setting. Here is the output you will get when looking at the source of the page when using the `Flow` setting:

```
<span id="DataList1">
   <span>
      CompanyName:
      <span id="DataList1_ctl00_CompanyNameLabel">Alfreds Futterkiste</span>
         <br />
         <br />
      </span><br />
   <span>
       CompanyName:
       <span id="DataList1_ctl01_CompanyNameLabel">
        Ana Trujillo Emparedados y helados</span>
       <br />
       <br />
   </span>
```

```
    <!-- Code removed for clarity -->

</span>
```

Working with Other Layout Templates

You will find that the other templates are just as easy to work with as the ItemTemplate. Listing 8-19 shows you how to add the AlternatingItemTemplate and the SeparatorTemplate to the company name display.

LISTING 8-19: Using both the AlternatingItemTemplate and the SeparatorTemplate

Available for download on Wrox.com

```
<%@ Page Language="VB" AutoEventWireup="false"
    CodeFile="DataListControl.aspx.vb"
    Inherits="DataListControl" %>

<html xmlns="http://www.w3.org/1999/xhtml">
<head runat="server">
    <title>DataList Control</title>
</head>
<body>
    <form id="form1" runat="server">
    <div>
        <asp:DataList ID="DataList1" runat="server" DataSourceID="SqlDataSource1">
            <ItemTemplate>
                Company Name:
                <asp:Label ID="CompanyNameLabel" runat="server"
                    Text='<%# Eval("CompanyName") %>' />
                <br />
                <br />
            </ItemTemplate>
            <AlternatingItemTemplate>
                CompanyName:
                <asp:Label ID="CompanyNameLabel" runat="server"
                 BackColor="LightGray"
                 Text='<%# Eval("CompanyName") %>' />
                <br />
                <br />
            </AlternatingItemTemplate>
            <SeparatorTemplate>
                <hr />
            </SeparatorTemplate>
        </asp:DataList>
        <asp:SqlDataSource ID="SqlDataSource1" runat="server"
            ConnectionString="<%$ ConnectionStrings:DSN_Northwind %>"
            SelectCommand="SELECT [CompanyName] FROM [Customers]">
        </asp:SqlDataSource>
    </div>
    </form>
</body>
</html>
```

In this case, the AlternatingItemTemplate is a repeat of the ItemTemplate, but the addition of the `BackColor` property to the Label control is contained within the item. The SeparatorTemplate is used between each item, whether the ItemTemplate or the AlternatingItemTemplate is being rendered. In this case, a simple `<hr />` element is used to draw a line between each item. Figure 8-5 shows the output of this code.

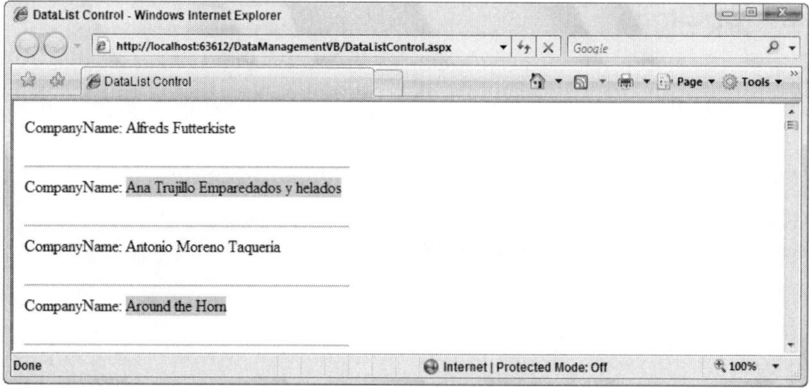

FIGURE 8-5

This process allows you to change how items are defined within the alternating rows and to put a separator between the elements. If you wanted just alternating row colors or an alternating style, using the `<AlternatingItemTemplate>` element might not always be the best approach, but you will find that using the `<AlternatingItemStyle>` element is better instead. Listing 8-20 presents using this approach.

LISTING 8-20: Using template styles

Available for download on Wrox.com

```
<asp:DataList ID="DataList1" runat="server" DataSourceID="SqlDataSource1"
 BackColor="White" BorderColor="#999999" BorderStyle="Solid" BorderWidth="1px"
 CellPadding="3" ForeColor="Black" GridLines="Vertical">
   <FooterStyle BackColor="#CCCCCC" />
   <AlternatingItemStyle BackColor="#CCCCCC" />
   <SelectedItemStyle BackColor="#000099" Font-Bold="True" ForeColor="White" />
   <HeaderStyle BackColor="Black" Font-Bold="True" ForeColor="White" />
   <ItemTemplate>
      CompanyName:
      <asp:Label ID="CompanyNameLabel" runat="server"
       Text='<%# Eval("CompanyName") %>' />
      <br />
      <br />
   </ItemTemplate>
</asp:DataList>
```

You will notice that each of the available templates also has an associated style element. Figure 8-6 shows the use of these styles.

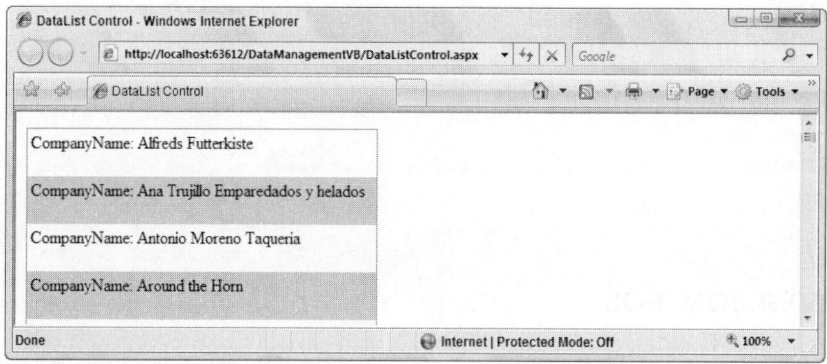

FIGURE 8-6

Working with Multiple Columns

Template-based controls are better at displaying items in multiple columns than other controls, such as the GridView control. The `RepeatColumns` property takes care of this sort of display. Listing 8-21 shows the code for making use of this property.

Available for download on Wrox.com

LISTING 8-21: Creating multiple columns using the RepeatColumns property

```
<asp:DataList ID="DataList1" runat="server" DataSourceID="SqlDataSource1"
 CellPadding="2" RepeatColumns="3" RepeatDirection="Horizontal">
   <ItemTemplate>
    Company Name:
    <asp:Label ID="CompanyNameLabel" runat="server"
     Text='<%# Eval("CompanyName") %>' />
    <br />
    <br />
   </ItemTemplate>
</asp:DataList>
```

Running this bit of code in your page produces the results shown in Figure 8-7.

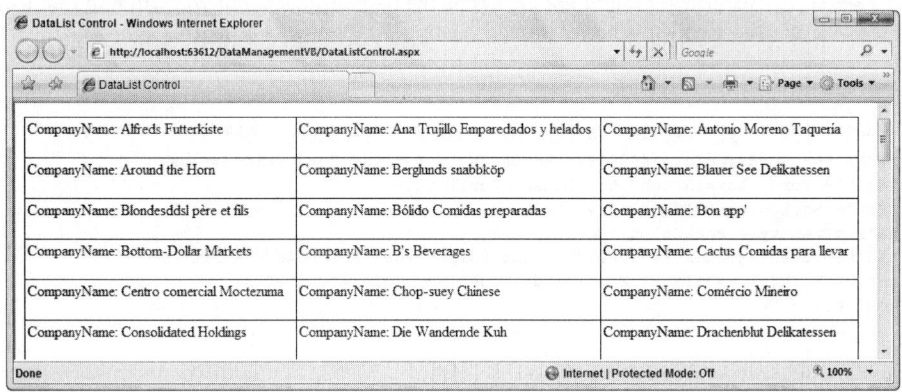

FIGURE 8-7

The `RepeatDirection` property instructs the DataList control about how to lay out the items bound to the control on the Web page. Possible values include `Vertical` and `Horizontal`. The default value is `Vertical`. Setting it to `Vertical` with a `RepeatColumn` setting of `3` gives the following results:

```
Item1    Item5    Item9
Item2    Item6    Item10
Item3    Item7    Item11
Item4    Item8    Item12
```

When the `RepeatDirection` property is set to `Horizontal`, you get the items laid out in a horizontal fashion:

```
Item1    Item2    Item3
Item4    Item5    Item6
Item7    Item8    Item9
Item10   Item11   Item12
```

THE LISTVIEW SERVER CONTROL

One of the newest template-based controls is the ListView control. This control became available in the 3.5 version of the .NET Framework. This control is considered a better alternative to the DataList control. You will find that this control gives you more control over the layout and works quite nicely in Visual Studio because it provides a set of wizards to easily set up your layout with the most common options.

As with the DataList control, the ListView control has a series of templates at your disposal. Each one of these templates controls a specific aspect of the layout. Table 8-8 defines the layout options available to the ListView control.

TABLE 8-8

TEMPLATE	DESCRIPTION
`LayoutTemplate`	The core template that allows you to define the structure of the entire layout. Using this layout, you can use tables, spans, or anything else you want to lay out your data elements.
`ItemTemplate`	Defines the layout for each individual item in the data collection.
`ItemSeparatorTemplate`	Defines the layout of any separator that is used between items.
`GroupTemplate`	A group container element that can contain any number of data items.
`GroupSeparatorTemplate`	Defines the layout of any separator that is used between groups.
`EmptyItemTemplate`	Defines the layout of the empty items that might be contained within a group. For example, if you group by ten items and the last page contains only seven items, then the last three items will use this template.
`EmptyDataTemplate`	Defines the layout for items that do not contain data.
`SelectedItemTemplate`	Allows for a row or item to be defined on how it looks and behaves when selected.
`AlternatingItemTemplate`	Works in conjunction with the `ItemTemplate` to provide a layout for all the odd rows within the layout. This is commonly used if you want to have a grid or layout where each row is distinguished in some way (such as having a different background color).
`EditItemTemplate`	Allows for a row or item to be defined on how it looks and behaves when editing.
`InsertItemTemplate`	Allows for a row or item to be defined on how it looks and behaves when performing an insert.

Next, the following sections look at using some of these templates in your ASP.NET page.

Connecting the ListView to a Database

When you are creating a page that makes use of the ListView control, build a basic page with a ListView control on it, as illustrated in Listing 8-22.

Available for download on Wrox.com

LISTING 8-22: Creating the base page

```
<%@ Page Language="VB" AutoEventWireup="false"
    CodeFile="ListViewControl.aspx.vb"
    Inherits="ListViewControl" %>

<html xmlns="http://www.w3.org/1999/xhtml">
<head runat="server">
    <title>ListView Control</title>
</head>
<body>
    <form id="form1" runat="server">
    <div>

        <asp:ListView ID="ListView1" runat="server" DataKeyNames="CustomerID"
            DataSourceID="SqlDataSource1">
        </asp:ListView>
```

continues

LISTING 8-22 *(continued)*

```
        <asp:SqlDataSource ID="SqlDataSource1" runat="server"
            ConnectionString="<%$ ConnectionStrings:DSN_Northwind %>"
            SelectCommand="SELECT * FROM [Customers] ORDER BY [CompanyName]"
            InsertCommand="INSERT INTO [Customers] ([CustomerID], [CompanyName],
               [ContactName], [ContactTitle], [Address], [City], [Region],
               [PostalCode], [Country], [Phone], [Fax]) VALUES (@CustomerID,
               @CompanyName, @ContactName, @ContactTitle, @Address, @City, @Region,
               @PostalCode, @Country, @Phone, @Fax)"
            UpdateCommand="UPDATE [Customers] SET [CompanyName] = @CompanyName,
               [ContactName] = @ContactName, [ContactTitle] = @ContactTitle,
               [Address] = @Address, [City] = @City, [Region] = @Region,
               [PostalCode] = @PostalCode, [Country] = @Country, [Phone] = @Phone,
               [Fax] = @Fax WHERE [CustomerID] = @CustomerID">
            <UpdateParameters>
                <asp:Parameter Name="CompanyName" Type="String" />
                <asp:Parameter Name="ContactName" Type="String" />
                <asp:Parameter Name="ContactTitle" Type="String" />
                <asp:Parameter Name="Address" Type="String" />
                <asp:Parameter Name="City" Type="String" />
                <asp:Parameter Name="Region" Type="String" />
                <asp:Parameter Name="PostalCode" Type="String" />
                <asp:Parameter Name="Country" Type="String" />
                <asp:Parameter Name="Phone" Type="String" />
                <asp:Parameter Name="Fax" Type="String" />
                <asp:Parameter Name="CustomerID" Type="String" />
            </UpdateParameters>
            <InsertParameters>
                <asp:Parameter Name="CustomerID" Type="String" />
                <asp:Parameter Name="CompanyName" Type="String" />
                <asp:Parameter Name="ContactName" Type="String" />
                <asp:Parameter Name="ContactTitle" Type="String" />
                <asp:Parameter Name="Address" Type="String" />
                <asp:Parameter Name="City" Type="String" />
                <asp:Parameter Name="Region" Type="String" />
                <asp:Parameter Name="PostalCode" Type="String" />
                <asp:Parameter Name="Country" Type="String" />
                <asp:Parameter Name="Phone" Type="String" />
                <asp:Parameter Name="Fax" Type="String" />
            </InsertParameters>
        </asp:SqlDataSource>
    </div>
    </form>
</body>
</html>
```

In this case, you have a base ListView control and a SqlDataSource control that has been wired up to the Northwind sample database, and you have provided Select, Update, and Insert methods. The ListView control itself is then bound to the SqlDataSource control. It provides the primary key of the table for working with the various queries using the `DataKeyNames` property.

Creating the Layout Template

Now that you have the base page created, the next step is to create the layout of the overall control using the `LayoutTemplate`. Listing 8-23 illustrates the use of this template.

Available for download on Wrox.com

LISTING 8-23: Using the LayoutTemplate element

```
<LayoutTemplate>
   <table runat="server">
      <tr runat="server">
```

```
            <td runat="server">
               <table ID="itemPlaceholderContainer" runat="server" border="1"
                style="background-color: #FFFFFF;border-collapse: collapse;
                       border-color: #999999;border-style:none;border-width:1px;
                       font-family: Verdana, Arial, Helvetica, sans-serif;">
                 <tr runat="server" style="background-color:#DCDCDC;color: #000000;">
                    <th runat="server"></th>
                    <th runat="server">Customer ID</th>
                    <th runat="server">Company Name</th>
                    <th runat="server">Contact Name</th>
                 </tr>
                 <tr ID="itemPlaceholder" runat="server"></tr>
               </table>
            </td>
         </tr>
         <tr runat="server">
            <td runat="server" style="text-align: center;background-color: #CCCCCC;
             font-family: Verdana, Arial, Helvetica, sans-serif;color: #000000;">
               <asp:DataPager ID="DataPager1" runat="server">
                  <Fields>
                     <asp:NextPreviousPagerField ButtonType="Button"
                      ShowFirstPageButton="True" ShowNextPageButton="False"
                      ShowPreviousPageButton="False" />
                     <asp:NumericPagerField />
                     <asp:NextPreviousPagerField ButtonType="Button"
                      ShowLastPageButton="True" ShowNextPageButton="False"
                      ShowPreviousPageButton="False" />
                  </Fields>
               </asp:DataPager>
            </td>
         </tr>
      </table>
   </LayoutTemplate>
```

This layout template constructs the layout as a grid using tables to lay out the items. A styled table is defined with a header in place. The most important part of laying out the template is that the container itself is defined using a control with the `ID` value of `itemPlaceholderContainer`. You also must make the element a server control by adding the `runat` property:

```
<table ID="itemPlaceholderContainer" runat="server" border="1"
 style="background-color: #FFFFFF;border-collapse: collapse;
 border-color: #999999;border-style:none;border-width:1px;
 font-family: Verdana, Arial, Helvetica, sans-serif;">

</table>
```

The placeholder for each data item must take the same form, but the `ID` of the server control you make must have a value of `itemPlaceholder`.

```
<table ID="itemPlaceholderContainer" runat="server" border="1"
 style="background-color: #FFFFFF;border-collapse: collapse;
 border-color: #999999;border-style:none;border-width:1px;
 font-family: Verdana, Arial, Helvetica, sans-serif;">
   <tr runat="server" style="background-color:#DCDCDC;color: #000000;">
      <th runat="server"></th>
      <th runat="server">Customer ID</th>
      <th runat="server">Company Name</th>
      <th runat="server">Contact Name</th>
   </tr>

<tr ID="itemPlaceholder" runat="server"></tr>

</table>
```

Keeping the `itemPlaceholder` element within the itemPlaceholderContainer control, within the layout template, is important. It cannot sit outside of the container.

The final part of this layout is the DataPager server control. This server control became part of ASP.NET with version 3.5.

```
<asp:DataPager ID="DataPager1" runat="server">
   <Fields>
      <asp:NextPreviousPagerField ButtonType="Button"
       ShowFirstPageButton="True" ShowNextPageButton="False"
       ShowPreviousPageButton="False" />
      <asp:NumericPagerField />
      <asp:NextPreviousPagerField ButtonType="Button"
       ShowLastPageButton="True" ShowNextPageButton="False"
       ShowPreviousPageButton="False" />
   </Fields>
</asp:DataPager>
```

The DataPager works with template-based data in allowing you to control how end users move across the pages of the data collection.

If you are showing something a bit more simple, such as a list, prior to ASP.NET 4, you were required to have a `<LayoutTemplate>` as shown in Listing 8-24.

LISTING 8-24: An ASP.NET 3.5 required LayoutTemplate

Available for download on Wrox.com

```
<LayoutTemplate>
  <asp:PlaceHolder ID="ItemPlaceHolder" runat="server"></asp:PlaceHolder>
</LayoutTemplate>
```

With the release of ASP.NET 4, you do not have to include the `<LayoutTemplate>` section, and the definition in your `<ItemTemplate>` (discussed next) will still work just fine.

Now that the LayoutTemplate is in place, you next create the ItemTemplate.

Creating the ItemTemplate

The ItemTemplate that you create is quite similar to the ItemTemplate that is part of the DataList control that was discussed earlier. In this case, however, the ItemTemplate is placed in the specific spot within the layout of the page where you defined the `itemPlaceholder` control to be. Listing 8-25 shows the ItemTemplate for this example.

LISTING 8-25: Building the ItemTemplate

Available for download on Wrox.com

```
<ItemTemplate>
   <tr style="background-color:#DCDCDC;color: #000000;">
      <td>
         <asp:Button ID="EditButton" runat="server"
          CommandName="Edit" Text="Edit" />
      </td>
      <td>
         <asp:Label ID="CustomerIDLabel" runat="server"
          Text='<%# Eval("CustomerID") %>' />
      </td>
      <td>
         <asp:Label ID="CompanyNameLabel" runat="server"
          Text='<%# Eval("CompanyName") %>' />
      </td>
      <td>
         <asp:Label ID="ContactNameLabel" runat="server"
          Text='<%# Eval("ContactName") %>' />
```

```
        </td>
    </tr>
</ItemTemplate>
```

Creating the EditItemTemplate

The EditItemTemplate is the area that shows up when you decide to edit the data item (in this case, a row of data). Listing 8-26 shows the EditItemTemplate in use.

Available for download on Wrox.com

LISTING 8-26: Building the EditItemTemplate

```
<EditItemTemplate>
    <tr style="background-color:#008A8C;color: #FFFFFF;">
        <td>
            <asp:Button ID="UpdateButton" runat="server"
             CommandName="Update" Text="Update" />
            <asp:Button ID="CancelButton" runat="server"
             CommandName="Cancel" Text="Cancel" />
        </td>
        <td>
            <asp:Label ID="CustomerIDLabel1" runat="server"
             Text='<%# Eval("CustomerID") %>' />
        </td>
        <td>
            <asp:TextBox ID="CompanyNameTextBox" runat="server"
             Text='<%# Bind("CompanyName") %>' />
        </td>
        <td>
            <asp:TextBox ID="ContactNameTextBox" runat="server"
             Text='<%# Bind("ContactName") %>' />
        </td>
    </tr>
</EditItemTemplate>
```

In this case, the EditItemTemplate, when shown, displays Update and Cancel buttons to manipulate the editing options. When you're editing, you place the values within text boxes and the values are then updated into the database through the `Update` command.

Creating the EmptyItemTemplate

If no values are in the database, then you should prepare to gracefully show something in your layout. The `EmptyItemTemplate` is used in Listing 8-27 to perform that operation.

Available for download on Wrox.com

LISTING 8-27: Building the EmptyItemTemplate

```
<EmptyDataTemplate>
    <table runat="server"
     style="background-color: #FFFFFF;border-collapse: collapse;
         border-color: #999999;border-style:none;border-width:1px;">
        <tr>
            <td>No data was returned.</td>
        </tr>
    </table>
</EmptyDataTemplate>
```

Creating the InsertItemTemplate

The last template looked at here is the `InsertItemTemplate`. This template allows you to define how a form should be laid out for inserting data, similar to that used in the `ItemTemplate`, into the data store.

Listing 8-28 shows an example of using the `InsertItemTemplate`.

LISTING 8-28: Building the InsertItemTemplate

Available for download on Wrox.com

```
<InsertItemTemplate>
   <tr style="">
      <td>
         <asp:Button ID="InsertButton" runat="server" CommandName="Insert"
          Text="Insert" />
         <asp:Button ID="CancelButton" runat="server" CommandName="Cancel"
          Text="Clear" />
      </td>
      <td>
         <asp:TextBox ID="CustomerIDTextBox" runat="server"
          Text='<%# Bind("CustomerID") %>' />
      </td>
      <td>
         <asp:TextBox ID="CompanyNameTextBox" runat="server"
          Text='<%# Bind("CompanyName") %>' />
      </td>
      <td>
         <asp:TextBox ID="ContactNameTextBox" runat="server"
          Text='<%# Bind("ContactName") %>' />
      </td>
   </tr>
</InsertItemTemplate>
```

Viewing the Results

After you have created an additional AlternatingItemTemplate that is the same as the ItemTemplate (but styled differently), you can then run the page. Then you will be presented with your own custom grid. Figure 8-8 presents an example.

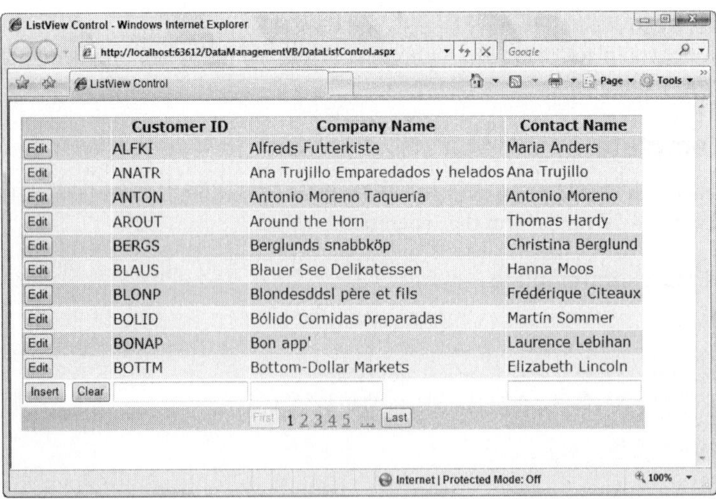

FIGURE 8-8

From this figure, you can see that all your defined elements are in place. The header is defined using the LayoutTemplate. The items in the grid are defined using the ItemTemplate. The AlternatingItemTemplate, the insert form, is defined using the InsertTemplate. The page navigation is defined by the DataPager server control. Again, the DataPager control is defined within the LayoutTemplate itself.

Editing items in this template is as simple as clicking on the Edit button. Clicking it changes the view to the EditTemplate for the selected item, as illustrated in Figure 8-9.

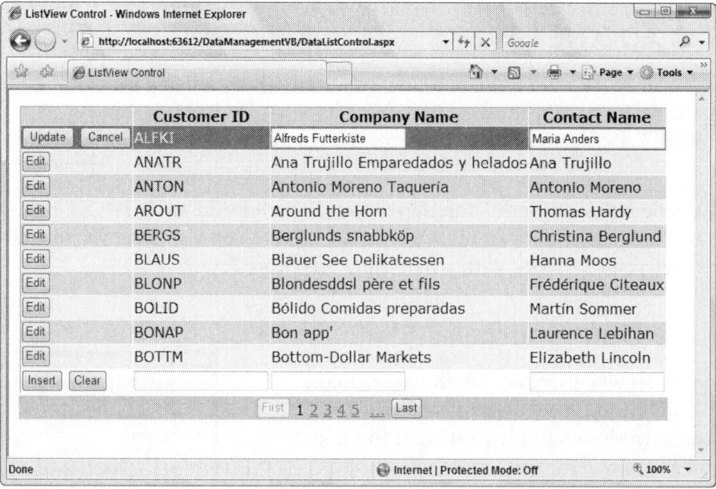

FIGURE 8-9

After you enter the edit mode, you can change any of the values within the text boxes and then click the Update button to update the data to the new values. You can also cancel out of the operation by clicking the Cancel button.

Inserting data is as simple as filling out the form and clicking on the Insert button, shown in Figure 8-10.

FIGURE 8-10

Although this example shows a grid as the output of the ListView control, you can also structure it so that your data items are presented in any fashion you want (such as bulleted lists).

USING VISUAL STUDIO FOR ADO.NET TASKS

Earlier, this chapter covered how to construct a `DataSet` and how to fill it with data using the `DataAdapter`. Although you can always build this construction yourself, you also have the option of building data access into your ASP.NET applications using some of the wizards available from Visual Studio 2010.

The following example, which is a little bit of a lengthy one, shows you how to build an ASP.NET page that displays the results from a `DataSet` that gets its data from two separate tables. You will discover several different wizards in Visual Studio that you can work with when using ADO.NET.

Creating a Connection to the Data Source

As in code, one of the first things you do when working with data is make a connection to the data source. Visual Studio provides a visual way to make connections to your data stores. In this example, you want to make a connection to the Northwind database in SQL Server.

When you open the Server Explorer, notice the section for data connections (see Figure 8-11).

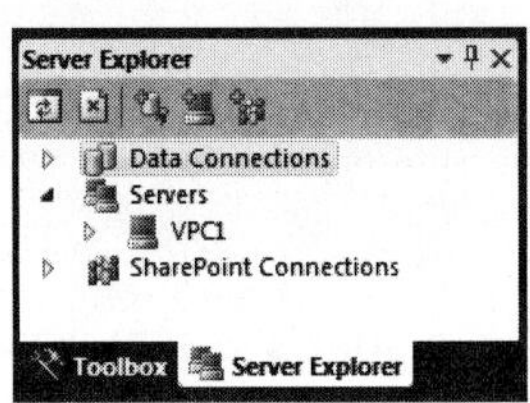

FIGURE 8-11

The steps to create a data connection to the Northwind database in SQL Server are straightforward. Right-click on Data Connections and choose Add Connection. The Data Link Properties dialog box appears. This dialog box, by default, asks for a connection to SQL Server. If you are going to connect to a different source, such as Microsoft Access, simply click on the Provider tab and change the provider.

Figure 8-12 shows the Add Connection dialog box and the settings that you need to connect to your local SQL Server Express Edition.

If you are connecting to a SQL Server that resides on your local host, you want to put a period (.) in the box that asks you to select or enter a server name. If you are working from a local SQL Server Express Edition file in your project (such as what is shown in Figure 8-12), then you want to use your server name with `\SQLEXPRESS`. Put in your login credentials for SQL Server and then use the drop-down list to select the database that you want to make the connection to. The other option, if you are using a SQL Server Express Edition file, is to select the physical database file by using the Attach a Database File option.

From this dialog box, you can also test the connection to ensure that everything works properly. If everything is in place, you get a confirmation stating such. Clicking OK then causes a connection to appear in the Solution Explorer.

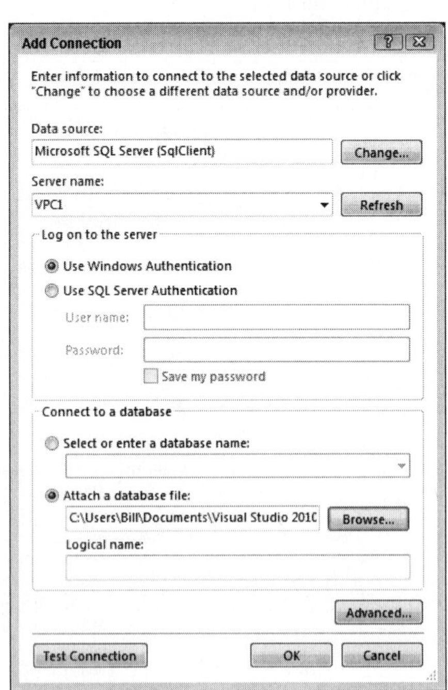

FIGURE 8-12

Expanding this connection, you find a way to access the data source just as you would by using the SQL Server Enterprise Manager (see Figure 8-13).

From this pane, you can work with the database and view information about all the tables and fields that are contained within the database. More specifically, you can view and work with Database Diagrams, Tables, Views, Stored Procedures, and Functions.

After you have run through this wizard, you have a connection to the Northwind database that can be used by any components that you place on any component designer that you might be working with in your application.

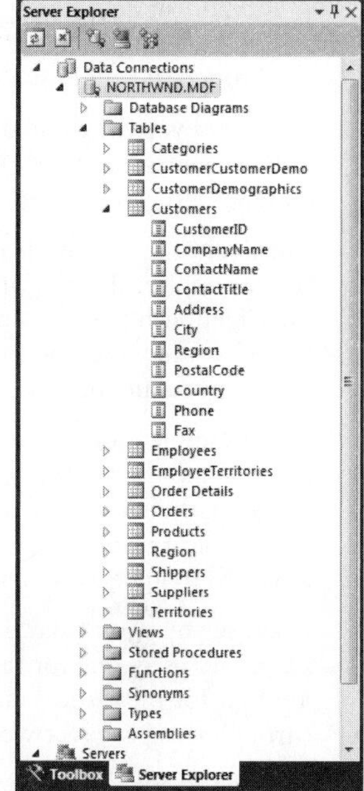

FIGURE 8-13

Working with a Dataset Designer

With the database connection now in place, the next step is to create a typed `DataSet` object in your project that pulls its data from the Northwind database. First, make sure that your application has an App_Code folder within the solution. Right-clicking on the folder will allow you to add a new item to the folder. From the provided dialog box, add a `DataSet` called `CustomerOrders.xsd`. The message shown in Figure 8-14 then appears.

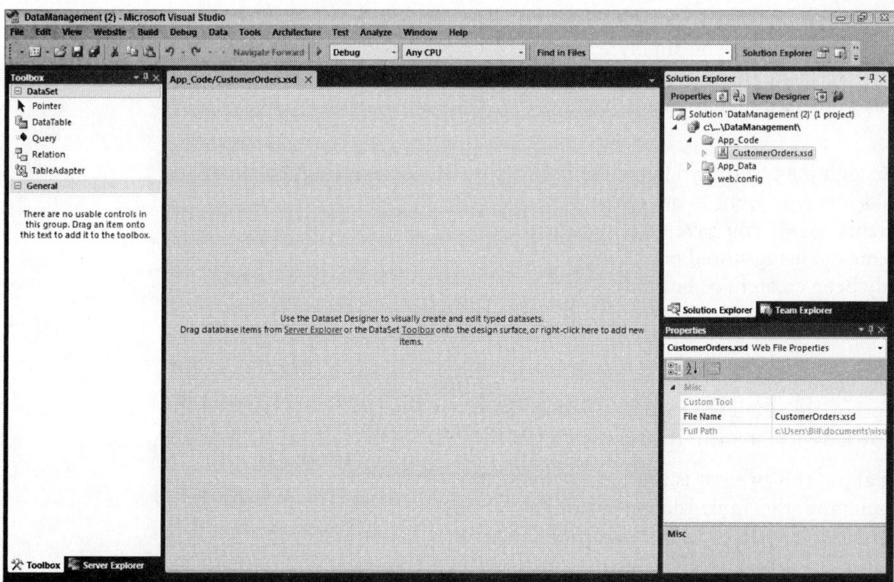

FIGURE 8-14

This page is referred to as the Dataset Designer. This is the design surface for any non-visual components that you incorporate within your `DataSet` object. Just as you can drag and drop controls onto a design surface for any Windows Forms or Web Forms application, the Dataset Designer enables you to drag and drop components onto this surface.

A component does not appear visually in your applications, but a visual representation of the component sits on the design surface. Highlighting the component allows you to modify its settings and properties in the Properties window.

What can you drag and drop onto this surface? In the following examples, you see how to work with `TableAdapter` and `DataTable` objects on this design surface. If you open the Toolbox window and click the DataSet tab, you see some additional components that you can use on this design surface.

The goal of this example is to return a `DataSet` to the end user through an XML Web service. To accomplish this, you must incorporate a `Data Adapter` to extract the data from the data source and to populate the `DataSet` before passing it on.

This example uses the Northwind database, so drag and drop a `TableAdapter` onto the `DataSet` design surface. Dragging and dropping a `TableAdapter` onto your design surface causes a wizard to appear, as shown in Figure 8-15.

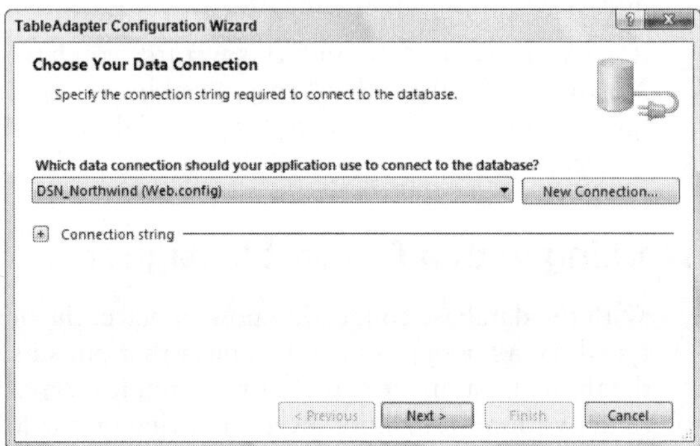

FIGURE 8-15

Because you want this `DataSet` to contain two `DataTables` — one for the Customers table and another for the Orders table — you must go through this process twice.

It is important to note that the job of the `TableAdapter` object is to make the connection to the specified table as well as to perform all the select, update, insert, and delete commands that are required. For this example, you simply want the `TableAdapter` to make the select call and then later to update any changes that are made back to the SQL Server.

As you work through the wizard, you come to a screen that asks how you want to query the database (see Figure 8-16). You have three options: using SQL statements, using stored procedures that have already been created, or building brand-new stored procedures directly from this wizard.

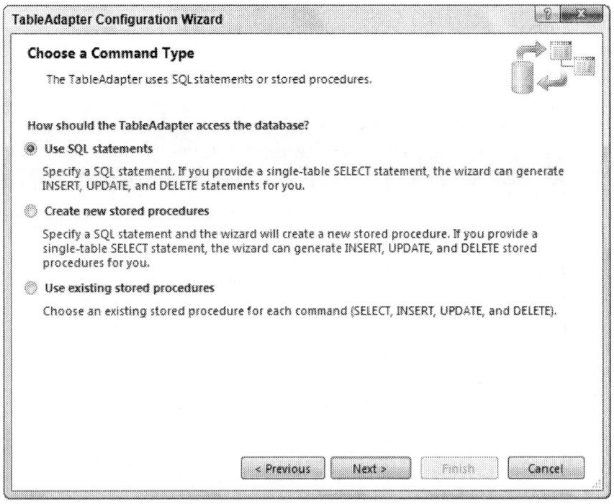

FIGURE 8-16

For this example, choose Use SQL statements. Selecting this option opens a text box where you can write your own SQL statement if you want.

The great thing about this process is that, after you create a SQL `select` command, the TableAdapter wizard also creates the associated `insert`, `update`, and `delete` commands for you. You also have the option of building your queries using the Query Builder. This enables you to graphically design the query yourself. If this option is selected, you can choose from a list of tables in the Northwind database. For the first `TableAdapter`, choose Customers. For the second `TableAdapter`, choose Orders. You make your selection by clicking the Add button and then closing the dialog box (see Figure 8-17).

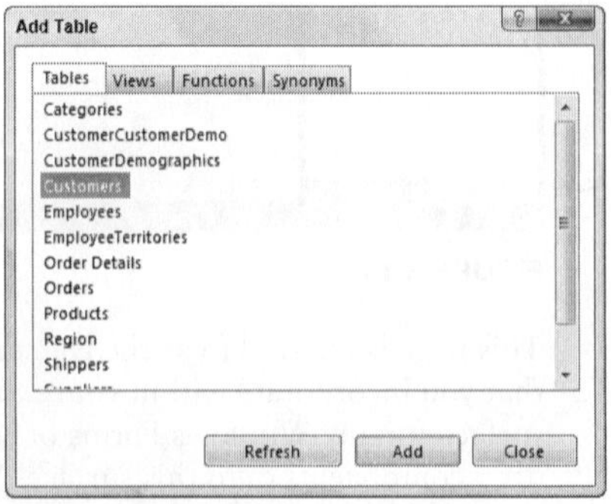

FIGURE 8-17

After you close the Add Table dialog box, you see a visual representation of the table that you selected in the Query Builder dialog box (see Figure 8-18). You can then select some or all of the fields to be returned from the query. For this example, you want everything returned from both the Customers and the Orders table, so select the first check box with the asterisk (`*`). Notice that the query listed in this dialog box now says `SELECT * FROM Customers`. After the word "Customers," add text to the query so that it looks like the following:

```
SELECT Customers.* FROM Customers WHERE (CustomerID LIKE @Customer)
```

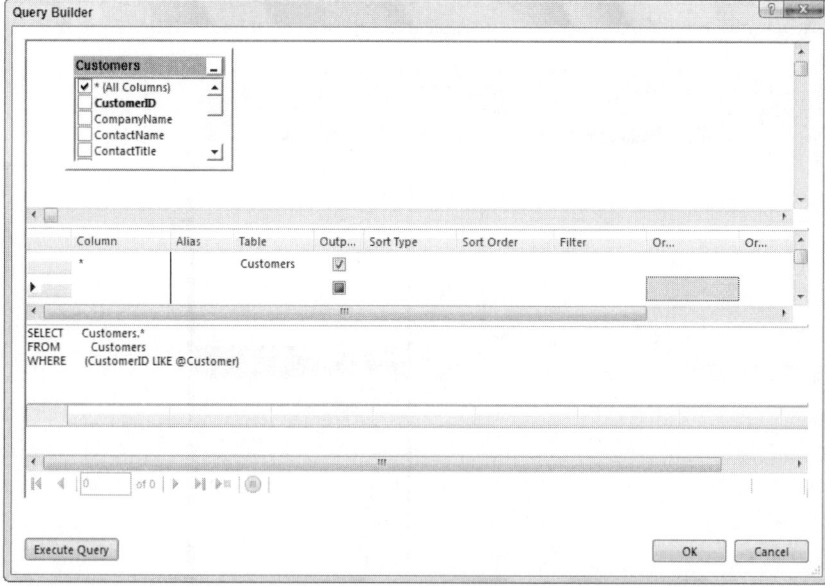

FIGURE 8-18

With this query, you specify that you want to return the customer information when the `CustomerID` fits the parameter that you pass into the query from your code (using `@Customer`).

After your query is in place, simply click OK and then click the Next button to have not only the `select` query, but also the `insert`, `update`, and `delete` queries generated for you.

Figure 8-19 shows you the final page after all the queries have been generated.

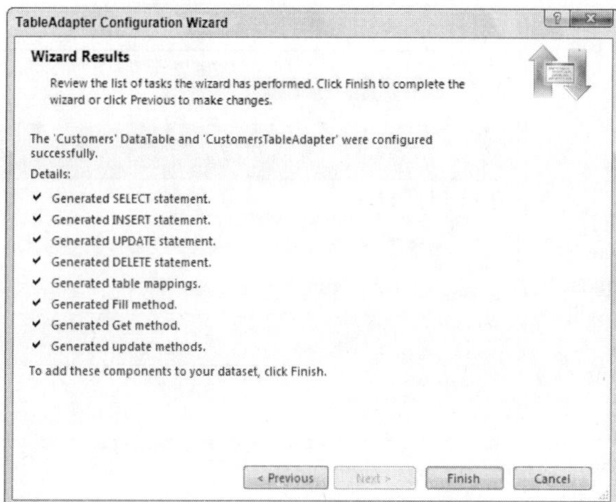

FIGURE 8-19

After you reach this point, you can either click the Previous button to return to one of the prior steps to change a setting or the query itself, or you can click the Finish button to apply everything to your `TableAdapter`. After you are finished using the wizard, notice there is a visual representation of the `CustomersTableAdapter` that you just created (see Figure 8-20). Along with it is a `DataTable` object for the Customers table. The `TableAdapter` and the `DataTable` objects that are shown on the design surface are also labeled with their IDs. Therefore, in your code, you can address the `TableAdapter` that you just built by referring to it as `CustomerOrdersTableAdapters.CustomersTableAdapter`. The second `TableAdapter` that queries the Orders table is then shown and referred to as `CustomerOrdersTableAdapters.OrdersTableAdapter`.

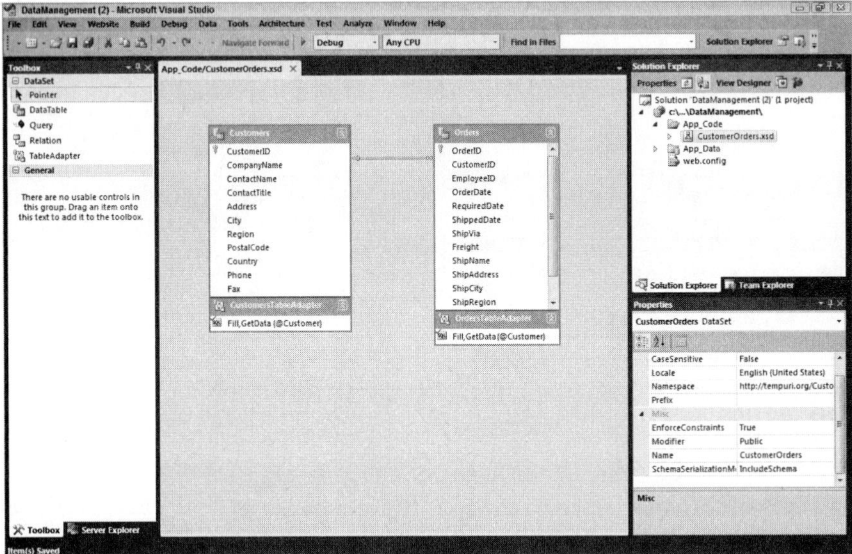

FIGURE 8-20

After you have the two DataAdapters in place, you will also notice that there is an automatic relation put into place for you. This is represented by the line between the two items on the page. Right-clicking on the relation, you can edit the relation with the Relation dialog box (see Figure 8-21).

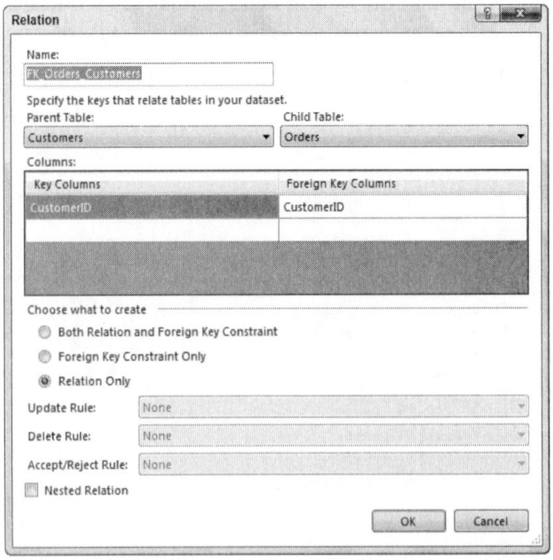

In the end, Visual Studio has taken care of a lot for you. Again, this is not the only way to complete all these tasks.

FIGURE 8-21

Using the CustomerOrders DataSet

Now comes the fun part — building the ASP.NET page that will use all the items that were just created! The goal is to allow the end user to send in a request that contains just the CustomerID. In return, he will get back a complete `DataSet` containing not only the customer information, but also all the relevant order information. Listing 8-29 shows you the code to build all this functionality. You need only a single method in addition to the `Page_Load`: the `GetCustomerOrders()` method. The page should be laid out as shown in Figure 8-22.

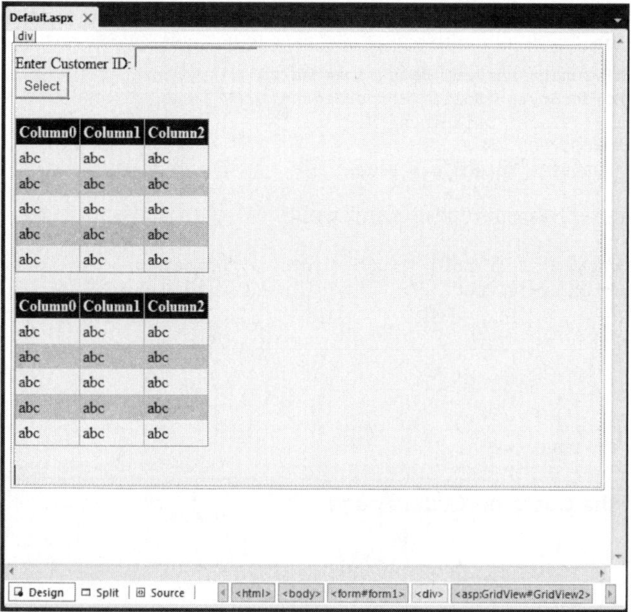

FIGURE 8-22

The page that you create should contain a single TextBox control, a Button control, and two GridView controls (GridView1 and GridView2). Listing 8-29 shows the code for the page.

Available for download on Wrox.com

LISTING 8-29: The .aspx page

```
<%@ Page Language="VB" AutoEventWireup="false" CodeFile="Default.aspx.vb"
    Inherits="_Default" %>

<html xmlns="http://www.w3.org/1999/xhtml">
<head runat="server">
    <title>CustomerOrders</title>
</head>
<body>
    <form id="form1" runat="server">
    <div>
        Enter Customer ID:
        <asp:TextBox ID="TextBox1" runat="server"></asp:TextBox>
        <br />
        <asp:Button ID="Button1" runat="server" Text="Select" />
        <br />
        <br />
        <asp:GridView ID="GridView1" runat="server" BackColor="White"
            BorderColor="#999999" BorderStyle="Solid" BorderWidth="1px"
            CellPadding="3" ForeColor="Black" GridLines="Vertical">
            <FooterStyle BackColor="#CCCCCC" />
            <PagerStyle BackColor="#999999" ForeColor="Black"
             HorizontalAlign="Center" />
            <SelectedRowStyle BackColor="#000099" Font-Bold="True"
             ForeColor="White" />
            <HeaderStyle BackColor="Black" Font-Bold="True" ForeColor="White" />
            <AlternatingRowStyle BackColor="#CCCCCC" />
        </asp:GridView>
        <br />
```

continues

LISTING 8-29 *(continued)*

```
        <asp:GridView ID="GridView2" runat="server" BackColor="White"
            BorderColor="#999999" BorderStyle="Solid" BorderWidth="1px"
            CellPadding="3" ForeColor="Black" GridLines="Vertical">
            <FooterStyle BackColor="#CCCCCC" />
            <PagerStyle BackColor="#999999" ForeColor="Black"
             HorizontalAlign="Center" />
            <SelectedRowStyle BackColor="#000099" Font-Bold="True"
             ForeColor="White" />
            <HeaderStyle BackColor="Black" Font-Bold="True" ForeColor="White" />
            <AlternatingRowStyle BackColor="#CCCCCC" />
        </asp:GridView>
    </div>
    </form>
</body>
</html>
```

Listing 8-30 presents the code-behind for the page.

LISTING 8-30: The code-behind for the CustomerOrders page

Available for download on Wrox.com

VB

```
Imports System

Partial Class _Default
    Inherits System.Web.UI.Page

    Protected Sub Page_Load(ByVal sender As Object, ByVal e As System.EventArgs) _
     Handles Me.Load
        If Page.IsPostBack Then
            GetCustomerOrders(TextBox1.Text)
        End If
    End Sub

    Protected Sub GetCustomerOrders(ByVal custId As String)
        Dim myDataSet As New CustomerOrders
        Dim custDA As New CustomerOrdersTableAdapters.CustomersTableAdapter
        Dim ordersDA As New CustomerOrdersTableAdapters.OrdersTableAdapter

        custDA.Fill(myDataSet.Customers, custId)
        ordersDA.Fill(myDataSet.Orders, custId)

        myDataSet.Customers(0).Phone = "NOT AVAILABLE"
        myDataSet.Customers(0).Fax = "NOT AVAILABLE"

        GridView1.DataSource = myDataSet.Tables("Customers")
        GridView1.DataBind()

        GridView2.DataSource = myDataSet.Tables("Orders")
        GridView2.DataBind()
    End Sub
End Class
```

C#

```
using System;
using CustomerOrdersTableAdapters;

public partial class _Default : System.Web.UI.Page
{
    protected void Page_Load(object sender, EventArgs e)
    {
        if (Page.IsPostBack)
        {
            GetCustomerOrders(TextBox1.Text);
        }
    }
```

```
    protected void GetCustomerOrders(string custId)
    {
        CustomerOrders myDataSet = new CustomerOrders();
        CustomersTableAdapter custDA = new CustomersTableAdapter();
        OrdersTableAdapter ordersDA = new OrdersTableAdapter();

        custDA.Fill(myDataSet.Customers, custId);
        ordersDA.Fill(myDataSet.Orders, custId);

        myDataSet.Customers[0].Phone = "NOT AVAILABLE";
        myDataSet.Customers[0].Fax = "NOT AVAILABLE";

        GridView1.DataSource = myDataSet.Tables["Customers"];
        GridView1.DataBind();

        GridView2.DataSource = myDataSet.Tables["Orders"];
        GridView2.DataBind();
    }
}
```

Now there is not much code here. One of the first things done in the method is to create an instance of the typed `DataSet`. In the next two lines of code, the `custDA` and the `ordersDA` objects are used. In this case, the only accepted parameter, `custId`, is being set for both the DataAdapters. After this parameter is passed to the `TableAdapter`, this `TableAdapter` queries the database based upon the `select` query that you programmed into it earlier using the TableAdapter wizard.

After the query, the `TableAdapter` is instructed to fill the instance of the `DataSet`. Before the `DataSet` is returned to the consumer, you can change how the result is output to the client. If you are passing customer information, you might want to exclude some of the information. Because the `DataSet` is a typed `DataSet`, you have programmatic access to the tables. In this example, the code specifies that in the `DataSet`, in the Customers table, in the first row (remember it is zero-based), make the value of the Phone and Fax fields equal to `NOT AVAILABLE`.

By compiling and running the ASP.NET page, you can test it from the test page using the CustomerID of ALFKI (the first record of the Customers table in the Northwind database). The results are returned to you in the browser (see Figure 8-23).

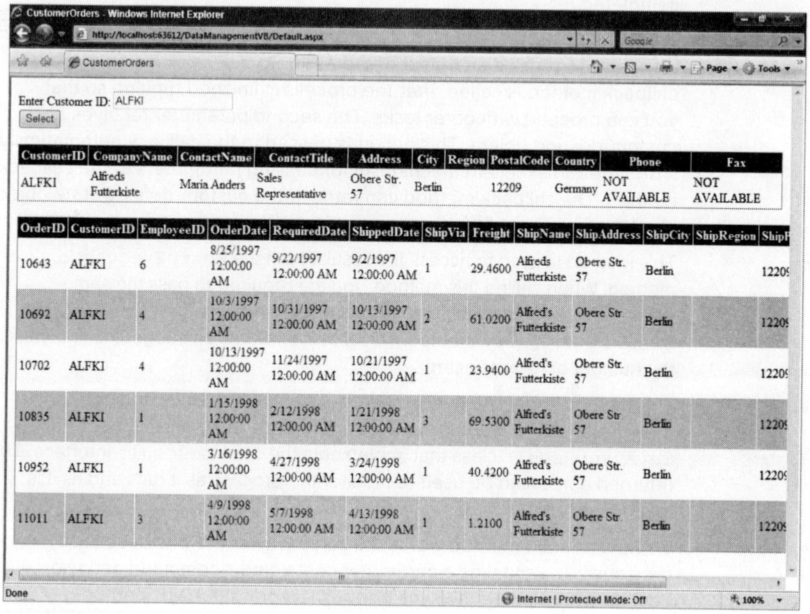

CustomerOrders - Windows Internet Explorer

Enter Customer ID: ALFKI

Select

CustomerID	CompanyName	ContactName	ContactTitle	Address	City	Region	PostalCode	Country	Phone	Fax
ALFKI	Alfreds Futterkiste	Maria Anders	Sales Representative	Obere Str. 57	Berlin		12209	Germany	NOT AVAILABLE	NOT AVAILABLE

OrderID	CustomerID	EmployeeID	OrderDate	RequiredDate	ShippedDate	ShipVia	Freight	ShipName	ShipAddress	ShipCity	ShipRegion	ShipF
10643	ALFKI	6	8/25/1997 12:00:00 AM	9/22/1997 12:00:00 AM	9/2/1997 12:00:00 AM	1	29.4600	Alfreds Futterkiste	Obere Str. 57	Berlin		1220
10692	ALFKI	4	10/3/1997 12:00:00 AM	10/31/1997 12:00:00 AM	10/13/1997 12:00:00 AM	2	61.0200	Alfred's Futterkiste	Obere Str. 57	Berlin		1220
10702	ALFKI	4	10/13/1997 12:00:00 AM	11/24/1997 12:00:00 AM	10/21/1997 12:00:00 AM	1	23.9400	Alfred's Futterkiste	Obere Str. 57	Berlin		1220
10835	ALFKI	1	1/15/1998 12:00:00 AM	2/12/1998 12:00:00 AM	1/21/1998 12:00:00 AM	3	69.5300	Alfred's Futterkiste	Obere Str. 57	Berlin		1220
10952	ALFKI	1	3/16/1998 12:00:00 AM	4/27/1998 12:00:00 AM	3/24/1998 12:00:00 AM	1	40.4200	Alfred's Futterkiste	Obere Str. 57	Berlin		1220
11011	ALFKI	3	4/9/1998 12:00:00 AM	5/7/1998 12:00:00 AM	4/13/1998 12:00:00 AM	1	1.2100	Alfred's Futterkiste	Obere Str. 57	Berlin		1220

Done   Internet | Protected Mode: Off   100%

FIGURE 8-23

ASYNCHRONOUS COMMAND EXECUTION

When you process data using ADO or previous versions of ADO.NET, each command is executed sequentially. The code waits for each command to complete before the next one is processed. When you use a single database, the sequential processing enables you to reuse the same connection object for all commands. However, with the introduction of MARS, you can now use a single connection for multiple, concurrent database access. Since the introduction of ADO.NET 2.0, ADO.NET has enabled users to process database commands asynchronously. This enables you to not only use the same connection, but also to use it in a parallel manner. The real advantage of asynchronous processing becomes apparent when you are accessing multiple data sources — especially when the data access queries across these databases aren't dependent on each other. You can now open a connection to the database in an asynchronous manner. When you are working with multiple databases, you can now open connections to them in a parallel fashion as well.

In order to open your connections asynchronously, be sure to add `Asynchronous Processing = true;` *to your connection string.*

Asynchronous Methods of the SqlCommand Class

The `SqlCommand` class provides a few additional methods that facilitate executing commands asynchronously. Table 8-9 summarizes these methods.

TABLE 8-9

METHOD	DESCRIPTION
`BeginExecuteNonQuery()`	This method expects a query that doesn't return any results and starts it asynchronously. The return value is a reference to an object of the `SqlAsyncResult` class that implements the `IAsyncResult` interface. The returned object can be used to monitor the process as it runs and when it is completed.
`BeginExecuteNonQuery (callback, stateObject)`	This overloaded method also starts the process asynchronously, and it expects to receive an object of the `AsynchCallback` instance. The callback method is called after the process is finished running so that you can proceed with other tasks. The second parameter receives any custom-defined object. This object is passed to the callback automatically. It provides an excellent mechanism for passing parameters to the callback method. The callback method can retrieve the custom-defined state object by using the `AsyncState` property of the `IAsyncResult` interface.
`EndExecuteNonQuery (asyncResult)`	This method is used to access the results from the `BeginExecuteNonQuery` method. When calling this method, you are required to pass the same `SqlAsyncResult` object that you received when you called the `Begin Execute NonQuery` method. This method returns an integer value containing the number of rows affected.
`BeginExecuteReader`	This method expects a query that returns a result set and starts it asynchronously. The return value is a reference to an object of `SqlAsyncResult` class that implements the `IAsyncResult` interface. The returned object can be used to monitor the process as it runs and as it is completed.
`BeginExecuteReader (commandBehavior)`	This overloaded method works the same way as the one described previously. It also takes a parameter containing a command behavior enumeration just like the synchronous `ExecuteReader` method.

METHOD	DESCRIPTION
BeginExecuteReader (callback, stateObject)	This overloaded method starts the asynchronous process and it expects to receive an object of the AsyncCallback instance. The callback method is called after the process finishes running so that you can proceed with other tasks. The second parameter receives any custom-defined object. This object is passed to the callback automatically. It provides an excellent mechanism for passing parameters to the callback method. The callback method can retrieve the custom-defined state object by using the AsyncState property of the IAsyncResult interface.
BeginExecuteReader (callback, stateObject, commandBehavior)	This overloaded method takes an instance of the AsyncCallback class and uses it to fire a callback method when the process has finished running. The second parameter receives a custom object to be passed to the callback method, and the third parameter uses the command behavior enumeration in the same way as the synchronous ExecuteReader method.
EndExecuteReader	This method is used to access the results from the BeginExecuteReader method. When calling this method, you are required to pass the same SqlAsyncResult object that you received when you called the BeginExecuteReader method. This method returns a SqlDataReader object containing the result of the SQL query.
BeginExecuteXmlReader	This method expects a query that returns the result set as XML. The return value is a reference to an object of SqlAsyncResult class that implements the IAsyncResult interface. The returned object can be used to monitor the process as it runs and as it is completed.
BeginExecuteXmlReader (callback, stateObject)	This overloaded method starts the asynchronous process, and it expects to receive an object of the AsyncCallback instance. The callback method is called after the process has finished running so that you can proceed with other tasks. The second parameter receives any custom-defined object. This object is passed to the callback automatically. It provides an excellent mechanism for passing parameters to the callback method. The callback method can retrieve the custom-defined state object by using the AsyncState property of the IAsyncResult interface.
EndExecuteXmlReader	This method is used to access the results from the BeginExecuteXmlReader method. When calling this method, you are required to pass the same SqlAsyncResult object that you received when you called the BeginExecuteXmlReader method. This method returns an XML Reader object containing the result of the SQL query.

IAsyncResult Interface

All the asynchronous methods for the SqlCommand class return a reference to an object that exposes the IAsyncResult interface. Table 8-10 shows the properties of this interface.

TABLE 8-10

PROPERTY	DESCRIPTION
AsyncState	This read-only property returns an object that describes the state of the process.
AsyncWaitHandle	This read-only property returns an instance of WaitHandle that can be used to set the time out, test whether the process has completed, and force the code to wait for completion.
CompletedSynchronously	This read-only property returns a Boolean value that indicates whether the process was executed synchronously.
IsCompleted	This read-only property returns a Boolean value indicating whether the process has completed.

AsyncCallback

Some of the asynchronous methods of the `SqlCommand` class receive an instance of the `AsyncCallback` class. This class is not specific to ADO.NET and is used by many objects in the .NET Framework. It is used to specify those methods that you want to execute after the asynchronous process has finished running. This class uses its constructor to receive the address of the method that you want to use for callback purposes.

WaitHandle Class

This class is an abstract class used for multiple purposes such as causing the execution to wait for any or all asynchronous processes to finish. To process more than one database command asynchronously, you can simply create an array containing wait handles for each asynchronous process. Using the static methods of the `WaitHandle` class, you can cause the execution to wait for either any or all wait handles in the array to finish processing.

The `WaitHandle` class exposes a few methods, as shown in Table 8-11.

TABLE 8-11

METHOD	DESCRIPTION
`WaitOne`	This method waits for a single asynchronous process to complete or time out. It returns a Boolean value containing `True` if the process completed successfully and `False` if it timed out.
`WaitOne (milliseconds, exitContext)`	This overloaded method receives an integer value as the first parameter. This value represents the time out in milliseconds. The second parameter receives a Boolean value specifying whether the method requires asynchronous context and should be set to `False` for asynchronous processing.
`WaitOne (timeSpan, exitContext)`	This overloaded method receives a `TimeSpan` object to represent the time-out value. The second parameter receives a Boolean value specifying whether the method requires asynchronous context and should be set to `False` for Asynchronous processing.
`WaitAny (waitHandles)`	This is a static method used if you are managing more than one `WaitHandle` in the form of an array. Using this method causes the execution to wait for any of the asynchronous processes that have been started and whose wait handles are in the array being passed to it. The `WaitAny` method must be called repeatedly — once for each `WaitHandle` you want to process.
`WaitAny (waitHandles, milliseconds, exitContext)`	This overloaded method receives the time-out value in the form of milliseconds and a Boolean value specifying whether the method requires asynchronous context. It should be set to `False` for asynchronous processing.
`WaitAny (waitHandles, timeSpan, exitContext)`	This overloaded method receives the time-out value in the form of a `TimeSpan` object. The second parameter receives a Boolean value specifying whether the method requires asynchronous context. It should be set to `False` for asynchronous processing.
`WaitAll (waitHandles)`	This static method is used to wait for all asynchronous processes to finish running.
`WaitAll (waitHandles, milliseconds, exitContext)`	This overloaded method receives the time-out value in the form of milliseconds and a Boolean value specifying whether the method requires asynchronous context. It should be set to `False` for asynchronous processing.

METHOD	DESCRIPTION
`WaitAll (waitHandles, timeSpan, exitContext)`	This overloaded method receives the time-out value in the form of a `TimeSpan` object. The second parameter receives a Boolean value specifying whether the method requires asynchronous context. It should be set to `False` for asynchronous processing.
`Close ( )`	This method releases all wait handles and reclaims their resources.

Now that you understand asynchronous methods added to the `SqlCommand` and how to properly interact with them, you can write some code to see the asynchronous processing in action.

Approaches of Asynchronous Processing in ADO.NET

You can process asynchronous commands in three distinct ways.

- One approach, the poll approach, starts the asynchronous process and starts polling the `IAsyncResult` object to see when the process has finished.
- The second and most elegant method, the wait approach, associates a wait handle with the asynchronous process. Using this approach, you can start all the asynchronous processing you want and then wait for all or any of them to finish so that you can process them accordingly.
- The third approach (callback) is to provide a callback method while starting the asynchronous process. This approach enables you to perform other tasks in parallel. When the asynchronous process finishes, it fires the callback method that cleans up after the process and notifies other parts of the program that the asynchronous process has finished.

The Poll Approach

The code shown in Listing 8-31 creates an inline SQL statement to retrieve the top five records from the Orders table from the Northwind database. It starts the asynchronous process by calling the `BeginExecuteReader`. After the asynchronous process has started, it uses a `while` loop to wait for the process to finish. While waiting, the main thread sleeps for 10 milliseconds after checking the status of the asynchronous process. After the process has finished, it retrieves the result using the `EndExecuteReader` method. This approach allows you to poll for the results. As noted earlier in the chapter, remember that you need to add `Asynchronous Processing = true;` to your connection string for this to work.

LISTING 8-31: The poll approach to working with asynchronous commands

Available for download on Wrox.com

```
<%@ Page Language="VB" %>
<%@ Import Namespace="System.Data" %>
<%@ Import Namespace="System.Data.SqlClient" %>
<%@ Import Namespace="System.Configuration" %>

<script runat="server">
    Protected Sub Page_Load(ByVal sender As Object, ByVal e As System.EventArgs)
        Dim DBCon As SqlConnection
        Dim Command As SqlCommand = New SqlCommand()
        Dim OrdersReader As SqlDataReader
        Dim ASyncResult As IAsyncResult

        DBCon = New SqlConnection()
        DBCon.ConnectionString =
           ConfigurationManager.ConnectionStrings(-DSN_NorthWind").ConnectionString

        Command.CommandText =
                "SELECT TOP 5 Customers.CompanyName, Customers.ContactName, " &
```

continues

LISTING 8-31 *(continued)*

```
                "Orders.OrderID, Orders.OrderDate, " &
                "Orders.RequiredDate, Orders.ShippedDate " &
                "FROM Orders, Customers " &
                "WHERE Orders.CustomerID = Customers.CustomerID " &
                "ORDER BY Customers.CompanyName, Customers.ContactName"
        Command.CommandType = CommandType.Text
        Command.Connection = DBCon

        DBCon.Open()

        ' Starting the asynchronous processing
        ASyncResult = Command.BeginExecuteReader()

        ' This loop with keep the main thread waiting until the
        ' asynchronous process is finished
        While Not ASyncResult.IsCompleted
            ' Sleeping current thread for 10 milliseconds
            System.Threading.Thread.Sleep(10)
        End While

        ' Retrieving result from the asynchronous process
        OrdersReader = Command.EndExecuteReader(ASyncResult)

        ' Displaying result on the screen
        gvOrders.DataSource = OrdersReader
        gvOrders.DataBind()

        ' Closing connection
        DBCon.Close()
    End Sub
</script>

<html xmlns="http://www.w3.org/1999/xhtml" >
<head id="Head1" runat="server">
    <title>The Poll Approach</title>
</head>
<body>
    <form id="form1" runat="server">
    <div>
    <asp:GridView ID="gvOrders" runat="server"
     AutoGenerateColumns="False" Width="100%">
        <Columns>
            <asp:BoundField HeaderText="Company Name"
             DataField="CompanyName"></asp:BoundField>
            <asp:BoundField HeaderText="Contact Name"
             DataField="ContactName"></asp:BoundField>
            <asp:BoundField HeaderText="Order Date"
             DataField="orderdate" DataFormatString="{0:d}"></asp:BoundField>
            <asp:BoundField HeaderText="Required Date" DataField="requireddate"
             DataFormatString="{0:d}"></asp:BoundField>
            <asp:BoundField HeaderText="Shipped Date" DataField="shippeddate"
             DataFormatString="{0:d}"></asp:BoundField>
        </Columns>
    </asp:GridView>
    </div>
    </form>
</body>
</html>
```

C#

```
<%@ Page Language="C#" %>
<%@ Import Namespace="System.Data" %>
<%@ Import Namespace="System.Data.SqlClient" %>
<%@ Import Namespace="System.Configuration" %>

<script runat="server">
    protected void Page_Load(object sender, EventArgs e)
    {
        SqlConnection DBCon;
        SqlCommand Command = new SqlCommand();
        SqlDataReader OrdersReader;
        IAsyncResult ASyncResult;

        DBCon = new SqlConnection();
        DBCon.ConnectionString =
           ConfigurationManager.ConnectionStrings["DSN_NorthWind"].ConnectionString;

        Command.CommandText =
                "SELECT TOP 5 Customers.CompanyName, Customers.ContactName, " +
                "Orders.OrderID, Orders.OrderDate, " +
                "Orders.RequiredDate, Orders.ShippedDate " +
                "FROM Orders, Customers " +
                "WHERE Orders.CustomerID = Customers.CustomerID " +
                "ORDER BY Customers.CompanyName, Customers.ContactName";

        Command.CommandType = CommandType.Text;
        Command.Connection = DBCon;

        DBCon.Open();

        // Starting the asynchronous processing
        ASyncResult = Command.BeginExecuteReader();

        // This loop with keep the main thread waiting until the
        // asynchronous process is finished
        while (!ASyncResult.IsCompleted)
        {
            // Sleeping current thread for 10 milliseconds
            System.Threading.Thread.Sleep(10);
        }

        // Retrieving result from the asynchronous process
        OrdersReader = Command.EndExecuteReader(ASyncResult);

        // Displaying result on the screen
        gvOrders.DataSource = OrdersReader;
        gvOrders.DataBind();

        // Closing connection
        DBCon.Close();
    }
</script>
```

Setting a break point at the `while` loop enables you to see that the code execution continues after calling the `BeginExecuteReader` method. The code then continues to loop until the asynchronous execution has finished.

The Wait Approach

The most elegant of the three approaches is neither the poll approach, which we just discussed, nor the callback approach, which we discuss shortly. The approach that provides the highest level of flexibility, efficiency, and (admittedly) a bit more complexity is the wait approach. Using this approach, you can write code that starts multiple asynchronous processes and waits for any or all of the processes to finish running. This approach allows you to wait for only those processes that are dependent on each other and to proceed with the ones that don't. This approach, by its design, requires you to think about asynchronous processes in great detail. You must pick a good candidate for running in parallel and, most importantly, determine how different processes depend on each other. The complexity of this approach requires you to understand its details and design the code accordingly. The end result is, typically, a very elegant code design that makes the best use of synchronous and asynchronous processing models.

The code shown in Listing 8-32 uses the `WaitOne` method of the `WaitHandle` class. This method causes the program execution to wait until the asynchronous process has finished running.

LISTING 8-32: The wait approach to handling a single asynchronous process

Available for download on Wrox.com

VB

```
<%@ Page Language="VB" %>
<%@ Import Namespace="System.Data" %>
<%@ Import Namespace="System.Data.SqlClient" %>
<%@ Import Namespace="System.Configuration" %>

<script runat="server">
    Protected Sub Page_Load(ByVal sender As Object, ByVal e As System.EventArgs)
        Dim DBCon As SqlConnection
        Dim Command As SqlCommand = New SqlCommand()
        Dim OrdersReader As SqlDataReader
        Dim ASyncResult As IAsyncResult
        Dim WHandle As Threading.WaitHandle

        DBCon = New SqlConnection()
        DBCon.ConnectionString =
           ConfigurationManager.ConnectionStrings("DSN_NorthWind").ConnectionString


        Command.CommandText =
                "SELECT TOP 5 Customers.CompanyName, Customers.ContactName, " &
                "Orders.OrderID, Orders.OrderDate, " &
                "Orders.RequiredDate, Orders.ShippedDate " &
                "FROM Orders, Customers " &
                "WHERE Orders.CustomerID = Customers.CustomerID " &
                "ORDER BY Customers.CompanyName, Customers.ContactName"

        Command.CommandType = CommandType.Text
        Command.Connection = DBCon

        DBCon.Open()

        ' Starting the asynchronous processing
        ASyncResult = Command.BeginExecuteReader()


        WHandle = ASyncResult.AsyncWaitHandle

        If WHandle.WaitOne = True Then
            ' Retrieving result from the asynchronous process
            OrdersReader = Command.EndExecuteReader(ASyncResult)

            ' Displaying result on the screen
            gvOrders.DataSource = OrdersReader
            gvOrders.DataBind()

            ' Closing connection
            DBCon.Close()
        Else
```

```
            ' Asynchronous process has timed out. Handle this
            ' situation here.
        End If
    End Sub
</script>

<html xmlns="http://www.w3.org/1999/xhtml" >
<head id="Head1" runat="server">
    <title>The Wait Approach</title>
</head>
<body>
    <form id="form1" runat="server">
    <div>
    <asp:GridView ID="gvOrders" runat="server"
     AutoGenerateColumns="False" Width="100%">
       <Columns>
          <asp:BoundField HeaderText="Company Name"
           DataField="CompanyName"></asp:BoundField>
          <asp:BoundField HeaderText="Contact Name"
           DataField="ContactName"></asp:BoundField>
          <asp:BoundField HeaderText="Order Date"
           DataField="orderdate" DataFormatString="{0:d}"></asp:BoundField>
          <asp:BoundField HeaderText="Required Date" DataField="requireddate"
           DataFormatString="{0:d}"></asp:BoundField>
          <asp:BoundField HeaderText="Shipped Date" DataField="shippeddate"
           DataFormatString="{0:d}"></asp:BoundField>
       </Columns>
    </asp:GridView>
    </div>
    </form>
</body>
</html>
```

C#

```
<%@ Page Language="C#" %>
<%@ Import Namespace="System.Data" %>
<%@ Import Namespace="System.Data.SqlClient" %>
<%@ Import Namespace="System.Configuration" %>
<script runat="server">
    protected void Page_Load(object sender, EventArgs e)
    {
        SqlConnection DBCon;
        SqlCommand Command = new SqlCommand();
        SqlDataReader OrdersReader;
        IAsyncResult ASyncResult;
        System.Threading.WaitHandle WHandle;

        DBCon = new SqlConnection();
        DBCon.ConnectionString =
           ConfigurationManager.ConnectionStrings("DSN_NorthWind").ConnectionString

        Command.CommandText =
                "SELECT TOP 5 Customers.CompanyName, Customers.ContactName, " +
                "Orders.OrderID, Orders.OrderDate, " +
                "Orders.RequiredDate, Orders.ShippedDate " +
                "FROM Orders, Customers " +
                "WHERE Orders.CustomerID = Customers.CustomerID " +
                "ORDER BY Customers.CompanyName, Customers.ContactName";

        Command.CommandType = CommandType.Text;
        Command.Connection = DBCon;

        DBCon.Open();
```

continues

LISTING 8-32 *(continued)*

```
            // Starting the asynchronous processing
            ASyncResult = Command.BeginExecuteReader();

            WHandle = ASyncResult.AsyncWaitHandle;

            if (WHandle.WaitOne() == true)
            {
                // Retrieving result from the asynchronous process
                OrdersReader = Command.EndExecuteReader(ASyncResult);

                // Displaying result on the screen
                gvOrders.DataSource = OrdersReader;
                gvOrders.DataBind();

                // Closing connection
                DBCon.Close();
            }
            else
            {
                // Asynchronous process has timed out. Handle this
                // situation here.
            }
        }
    </script>
```

If you set a break point and step through this code, you will notice that the program execution stops at the `WHandle.WaitOne` method call. The program automatically resumes when the asynchronous commands finishes its execution.

Using Multiple Wait Handles

The real power of the wait approach doesn't become apparent until you start multiple asynchronous processes. The code shown in Listing 8-33 starts two asynchronous processes. One process queries a database to get information about a specific customer and runs another query to retrieve all orders submitted by that the same customer. The code example shown in this listing creates two separate `Command` objects, DataReader objects, and wait handles. However, it uses the same connection object for both queries to demonstrate how well Multiple Active Result Set (MARS) supports work in conjunction with the asynchronous processing. For this to work, you must add `MultipleActiveResultSets=True` to your connection string.

LISTING 8-33: Use of multiple wait handles in conjunction with MARS

Available for download on Wrox.com

VB

```
<%@ Page Language="VB" %>
<%@ Import Namespace="System.Data" %>
<%@ Import Namespace="System.Data.SqlClient" %>
<%@ Import Namespace="System.Configuration" %>

<script runat="server">
    Protected Sub Page_Load(ByVal sender As Object, ByVal e As System.EventArgs)
        Dim DBCon As SqlConnection
        Dim OrdersCommand As SqlCommand = New SqlCommand()
        Dim CustCommand As SqlCommand = New SqlCommand()
        Dim OrdersReader As SqlDataReader
        Dim CustReader As SqlDataReader
        Dim OrdersASyncResult As IAsyncResult
        Dim CustAsyncResult As IAsyncResult

        Dim WHandles(1) As System.Threading.WaitHandle
        Dim OrdersWHandle As System.Threading.WaitHandle
        Dim CustWHandle As System.Threading.WaitHandle

        DBCon = New SqlConnection()
```

```
        DBCon.ConnectionString = _
           ConfigurationManager.ConnectionStrings("DSN_NorthWind").ConnectionString

        CustCommand.CommandText =
           "SELECT * FROM Customers WHERE CompanyName = 'Alfreds Futterkiste'"

        CustCommand.CommandType = CommandType.Text
        CustCommand.Connection = DBCon

        ' Selecting all orders for a specific customer
        OrdersCommand.CommandText =
                "SELECT Customers.CompanyName, Customers.ContactName, " &
                "Orders.OrderID, Orders.OrderDate, " &
                "Orders.RequiredDate, Orders.ShippedDate " &
                "FROM Orders, Customers " &
                "WHERE Orders.CustomerID = Customers.CustomerID " &
                "AND Customers.CompanyName = 'Alfreds Futterkiste' " &
                "ORDER BY Customers.CompanyName, Customers.ContactName"

        OrdersCommand.CommandType = CommandType.Text
        OrdersCommand.Connection = DBCon

        DBCon.Open()

        ' Retrieving customer information asynchronously
        CustAsyncResult = CustCommand.BeginExecuteReader()

        ' Retrieving orders list asynchronously
        OrdersASyncResult = OrdersCommand.BeginExecuteReader()

        CustWHandle = CustAsyncResult.AsyncWaitHandle
        OrdersWHandle = OrdersASyncResult.AsyncWaitHandle

        ' Filling Wait Handles array with the two wait handles we
        ' are going to use in this code
        WHandles(0) = CustWHandle
        WHandles(1) = OrdersWHandle

        System.Threading.WaitHandle.WaitAll(WHandles)

        CustReader = CustCommand.EndExecuteReader(CustAsyncResult)

        OrdersReader = OrdersCommand.EndExecuteReader(OrdersASyncResult)

        gvCustomers.DataSource = CustReader
        gvCustomers.DataBind()

        gvOrders.DataSource = OrdersReader
        gvOrders.DataBind()

        DBCon.Close()
    End Sub
</script>

<html xmlns="http://www.w3.org/1999/xhtml" >
<head id="Head1" runat="server">
    <title>Wait All Approach</title>
</head>
<body>
    <form id="form1" runat="server">
    <div>
    <asp:GridView ID="gvCustomers" Width="100%" runat="server"></asp:GridView>
```

continues

LISTING 8-33 *(continued)*

```
    <br /><br />
    <asp:GridView ID="gvOrders" Width="100%" AutoGenerateColumns="False"
     runat="server">
       <Columns>
          <asp:BoundField HeaderText="Company Name"
           DataField="CompanyName"></asp:BoundField>
          <asp:BoundField HeaderText="Contact Name"
           DataField="ContactName"></asp:BoundField>
          <asp:BoundField HeaderText="Order Date" DataField="orderdate"
           DataFormatString="{0:d}"></asp:BoundField>
          <asp:BoundField HeaderText="Required Date" DataField="requireddate"
           DataFormatString="{0:d}"></asp:BoundField>
          <asp:BoundField HeaderText="Shipped Date" DataField="shippeddate"
           DataFormatString="{0:d}"></asp:BoundField>
       </Columns>
    </asp:GridView>
    </div>
    </form>
</body>
</html>
```

C#

```
<%@ Page Language="C#" %>
<%@ Import Namespace="System.Data" %>
<%@ Import Namespace="System.Data.SqlClient" %>
<%@ Import Namespace="System.Configuration" %>

<script runat="server">

    protected void Page_Load(object sender, EventArgs e)
    {
        SqlConnection DBCon;
        SqlCommand OrdersCommand = new SqlCommand();
        SqlCommand CustCommand = new SqlCommand();
        SqlDataReader OrdersReader;
        SqlDataReader CustReader;
        IAsyncResult OrdersASyncResult;
        IAsyncResult CustAsyncResult;

        System.Threading.WaitHandle[] WHandles = new
           System.Threading.WaitHandle[2];
        System.Threading.WaitHandle OrdersWHandle;
        System.Threading.WaitHandle CustWHandle;

        DBCon = new SqlConnection();
        DBCon.ConnectionString =
           ConfigurationManager.ConnectionStrings["DSN_NorthWind"].ConnectionString;

        CustCommand.CommandText =
           "SELECT * FROM Customers WHERE CompanyName = 'Alfreds Futterkiste'";

        CustCommand.CommandType = CommandType.Text;
        CustCommand.Connection = DBCon;

        // Selecting all orders for a specific customer
        OrdersCommand.CommandText =
                "SELECT Customers.CompanyName, Customers.ContactName, " +
                "Orders.OrderID, Orders.OrderDate, " +
                "Orders.RequiredDate, Orders.ShippedDate " +
                "FROM Orders, Customers " +
                "WHERE Orders.CustomerID = Customers.CustomerID " +
                "AND Customers.CompanyName = 'Alfreds Futterkiste' " +
                "ORDER BY Customers.CompanyName, Customers.ContactName";
```

```
            OrdersCommand.CommandType = CommandType.Text;
            OrdersCommand.Connection = DBCon;

            DBCon.Open();

            // Retrieving customer information asynchronously
            CustAsyncResult = CustCommand.BeginExecuteReader();

            // Retrieving orders list asynchronously
            OrdersASyncResult = OrdersCommand.BeginExecuteReader();

            CustWHandle = CustAsyncResult.AsyncWaitHandle;
            OrdersWHandle = OrdersASyncResult.AsyncWaitHandle;

            // Filling Wait Handles array with the two wait handles we
            // are going to use in this code
            WHandles[0] = CustWHandle;
            WHandles[1] = OrdersWHandle;

            System.Threading.WaitHandle.WaitAll(WHandles);

            CustReader = CustCommand.EndExecuteReader(CustAsyncResult);

            OrdersReader = OrdersCommand.EndExecuteReader(OrdersASyncResult);

            gvCustomers.DataSource = CustReader;
            gvCustomers.DataBind();

            gvOrders.DataSource = OrdersReader;
            gvOrders.DataBind();

            DBCon.Close();
        }
    </script>
```

When you compile and execute the code shown in Listing 8-33, you see the result on the screen, as shown in Figure 8-24. This figure clearly shows two GridView controls that were used in the code example. The GridView control on the top shows the result of executing a query that retrieved all information related to a specific customer. The GridView control on the bottom shows the results of executing the second query that retrieved a list of all orders submitted by a specific customer.

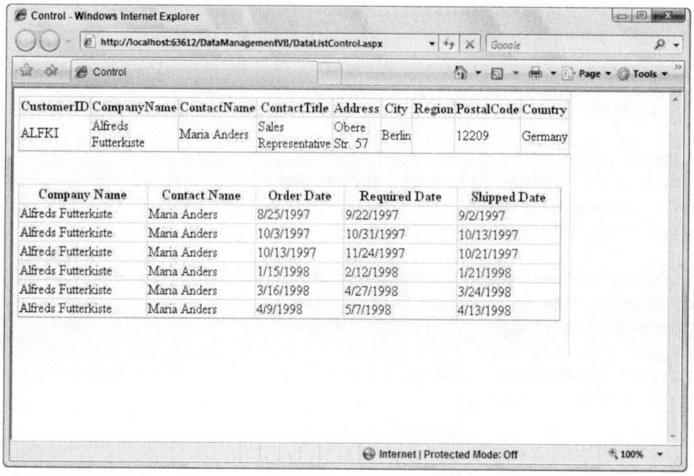

FIGURE 8-24

The code shown in Listing 8-33 reveals some of the elegance of using the wait approach. However, it is still not the most efficient code you can write with ADO.NET. The code should allow for a wait until both asynchronous processes finish running before the data binds the result sets to the respective GridView controls.

You can change the code shown in Listing 8-33 just a little to gain even more efficiency. Replace the `WaitAll` method with the `WaitAny` method. The `WaitAny` method enables you to handle the results of each of the asynchronous processes as soon as each is completed without waiting for other processing to finish. To use the `WaitAny` method and still manage the execution of all asynchronous processes, you can also add a loop that enables you to make sure that all asynchronous processes are handled after they are completed.

The `WaitAny` method returns an Integer value that indicates an array index of the wait handle that has finished running. Using this return value, you can easily find the correct wait handle and process the result set retrieved from the query that was executed in that particular process, as shown in Listing 8-34.

LISTING 8-34: Use of the WaitAny method to process multiple asynchronous processes

Available for download on Wrox.com

VB

```
<%@ Page Language="VB" %>
<%@ Import Namespace="System.Data" %>
<%@ Import Namespace="System.Data.SqlClient" %>
<%@ Import Namespace="System.Configuration" %>

<script runat="server">
    Protected Sub Page_Load(ByVal sender As Object, ByVal e As System.EventArgs)
        Dim DBCon As SqlConnection
        Dim OrdersCommand As SqlCommand = New SqlCommand()
        Dim CustCommand As SqlCommand = New SqlCommand()
        Dim OrdersReader As SqlDataReader
        Dim CustReader As SqlDataReader
        Dim OrdersASyncResult As IAsyncResult
        Dim CustAsyncResult As IAsyncResult

        Dim WHIndex As Integer
        Dim WHandles(1) As Threading.WaitHandle
        Dim OrdersWHandle As Threading.WaitHandle
        Dim CustWHandle As Threading.WaitHandle

        DBCon = New SqlConnection()
        DBCon.ConnectionString =
           ConfigurationManager.ConnectionStrings("DSN_NorthWind").ConnectionString

        CustCommand.CommandText =
           "SELECT * FROM Customers WHERE CompanyName = 'Alfreds Futterkiste'"

        CustCommand.CommandType = CommandType.Text
        CustCommand.Connection = DBCon

        OrdersCommand.CommandText =
                "SELECT Customers.CompanyName, Customers.ContactName, " &
                "Orders.OrderID, Orders.OrderDate, " &
                "Orders.RequiredDate, Orders.ShippedDate " &
                "FROM Orders, Customers " &
                "WHERE Orders.CustomerID = Customers.CustomerID " &
                "AND Customers.CompanyName = 'Alfreds Futterkiste' " &
                "ORDER BY Customers.CompanyName, Customers.ContactName"

        OrdersCommand.CommandType = CommandType.Text
        OrdersCommand.Connection = DBCon

        ' Opening the database connection
        DBCon.Open ()
```

```
        ' Retrieving customer information asynchronously
        CustAsyncResult = CustCommand.BeginExecuteReader()

        ' Retrieving orders list asynchronously
        OrdersASyncResult = OrdersCommand.BeginExecuteReader()

        CustWHandle = CustAsyncResult.AsyncWaitHandle
        OrdersWHandle = OrdersASyncResult.AsyncWaitHandle

        ' Filling Wait Handles array with the two wait handles we
        ' are going to use in this code
        WHandles(0) = CustWHandle
        WHandles(1) = OrdersWHandle

        ' Looping 2 times because there are 2 wait handles
        ' in the array
        For Index As Integer = 0 To 1
            ' We are only waiting for any of the two
            ' asynchronous process to finish running
            WHIndex = Threading.WaitHandle.WaitAny(WHandles)

            ' The return value from the WaitAny method is
            ' the array index of the Wait Handle that just
            ' finished running
            Select Case WHIndex
                Case 0
                    CustReader = CustCommand.EndExecuteReader(CustAsyncResult)

                    gvCustomers.DataSource = CustReader
                    gvCustomers.DataBind()
                Case 1
                    OrdersReader =
                       OrdersCommand.EndExecuteReader(OrdersASyncResult)

                    gvOrders.DataSource = OrdersReader
                    gvOrders.DataBind()

            End Select
        Next

        ' Closing connection
        DBCon.Close()
    End Sub
</script>

<html xmlns="http://www.w3.org/1999/xhtml" >
<head id="Head1" runat="server">

    <title>The Wait Any Approach</title>
</head>
<body>
    <form id="form1" runat="server">
    <div>
    <asp:GridView ID="gvCustomers" Width="100%" runat="server"></asp:GridView>
    <br /><br />
    <asp:GridView ID="gvOrders" Width="100%" AutoGenerateColumns="False"
     runat="server">
       <Columns>
          <asp:BoundField HeaderText="Company Name"
           DataField="CompanyName"></asp:BoundField>
```

continues

LISTING 8-34 *(continued)*

```
            <asp:BoundField HeaderText="Contact Name"
             DataField="ContactName"></asp:BoundField>
            <asp:BoundField HeaderText="Order Date" DataField="orderdate"
             DataFormatString="{0:d}"></asp:BoundField>
            <asp:BoundField HeaderText="Required Date" DataField="requireddate"
             DataFormatString="{0:d}"></asp:BoundField>
            <asp:BoundField HeaderText="Shipped Date" DataField="shippeddate"
             DataFormatString="{0:d}"></asp:BoundField>
         </Columns>
      </asp:GridView>
      </div>
      </form>
</body>
</html>
```

C#

```
<%@ Page Language="C#" %>
<%@ Import Namespace="System.Data" %>
<%@ Import Namespace="System.Data.SqlClient" %>
<%@ Import Namespace="System.Configuration" %>

<script runat="server">
    protected void Page_Load(object sender, EventArgs e)
    {
        SqlConnection DBCon;
        SqlCommand OrdersCommand = new SqlCommand();
        SqlCommand CustCommand = new SqlCommand();
        SqlDataReader OrdersReader;
        SqlDataReader CustReader;
        IAsyncResult OrdersASyncResult;
        IAsyncResult CustAsyncResult;

        int WHIndex;
        System.Threading.WaitHandle[] WHandles =
           new System.Threading.WaitHandle[2];
        System.Threading.WaitHandle OrdersWHandle;
        System.Threading.WaitHandle CustWHandle;

        DBCon = new SqlConnection();
        DBCon.ConnectionString =
           ConfigurationManager.ConnectionStrings["DSN_NorthWind"].ConnectionString;

        CustCommand.CommandText =
           "SELECT * FROM Customers WHERE CompanyName = 'Alfreds Futterkiste'";

        CustCommand.CommandType = CommandType.Text;
        CustCommand.Connection = DBCon;

        OrdersCommand.CommandText =
              "SELECT Customers.CompanyName, Customers.ContactName, " +
              "Orders.OrderID, Orders.OrderDate, " +
              "Orders.RequiredDate, Orders.ShippedDate " +
              "FROM Orders, Customers " +
              "WHERE Orders.CustomerID = Customers.CustomerID " +
              "AND Customers.CompanyName = 'Alfreds Futterkiste' " +
              "ORDER BY Customers.CompanyName, Customers.ContactName";

        OrdersCommand.CommandType = CommandType.Text;
        OrdersCommand.Connection = DBCon;

        // Opening the database connection
        DBCon.Open();
```

```
            // Retrieving customer information asynchronously
            CustAsyncResult = CustCommand.BeginExecuteReader();

            // Retrieving orders list asynchronously
            OrdersASyncResult = OrdersCommand.BeginExecuteReader();

            CustWHandle = CustAsyncResult.AsyncWaitHandle;
            OrdersWHandle = OrdersASyncResult.AsyncWaitHandle;

            // Filling Wait Handles array with the two wait handles we
            // are going to use in this code
            WHandles[0] = CustWHandle;
            WHandles[1] = OrdersWHandle;

            // Looping 2 times because there are 2 wait handles
            // in the array
            for (int Index = 0; Index < 2; Index++ )
            {
                // We are only waiting for any of the two
                // asynchronous process to finish running
                WHIndex = System.Threading.WaitHandle.WaitAny(WHandles);

                // The return value from the WaitAny method is
                // the array index of the Wait Handle that just
                // finished running
                switch (WHIndex)
                {
                    case 0:
                        CustReader = CustCommand.EndExecuteReader(CustAsyncResult);

                        gvCustomers.DataSource = CustReader;
                        gvCustomers.DataBind();

                        break;
                    case 1:
                        OrdersReader =
                           OrdersCommand.EndExecuteReader(OrdersASyncResult);

                        gvOrders.DataSource = OrdersReader;
                        gvOrders.DataBind();
                        break;
                }
            }
            // Closing connection
            DBCon.Close();
        }
    </script>
```

Next, look at the callback approach. Using this approach, you assign a callback method to the asynchronous process and use it to display the result returned by executing the SQL query.

The Callback Approach

Listing 8-35 creates an inline SQL statement that retrieves the top five records from the database. It starts the asynchronous process by calling the `BeginExecuteReader` method and passing it to the callback delegate. No further processing is needed, and the method ends after the asynchronous process has started. After the callback method is fired, it retrieves the result and displays it on the screen.

LISTING 8-35: Asynchronous command processing using the callback approach

Available for download on Wrox.com

VB

```
<%@ Page Language="VB" %>
<%@ Import Namespace="System.Data" %>
<%@ Import Namespace="System.Data.SqlClient" %>
<%@ Import Namespace="System.Configuration" %>

<script runat="server">
    Private Sub Page_Load(ByVal sender As Object, ByVal e As System.EventArgs)
        Dim DBCon As SqlConnection
        Dim Command As SqlCommand = New SqlCommand()
        Dim ASyncResult As IAsyncResult

        DBCon = New SqlConnection()
        Command = New SqlCommand()
        DBCon.ConnectionString =
           ConfigurationManager.ConnectionStrings("DSN_NorthWind").ConnectionString

        ' Selecting top 5 records from the Orders table
        Command.CommandText =
                "SELECT TOP 5 Customers.CompanyName, Customers.ContactName, " &
                "Orders.OrderID, Orders.OrderDate, " &
                "Orders.RequiredDate, Orders.ShippedDate " &
                "FROM Orders, Customers " &
                "WHERE Orders.CustomerID = Customers.CustomerID " &
                "ORDER BY Customers.CompanyName, Customers.ContactName"

        Command.CommandType = CommandType.Text
        Command.Connection = DBCon

        DBCon.Open()

        ' Starting the asynchronous processing
        AsyncResult = Command.BeginExecuteReader(New AsyncCallback(AddressOf CBMethod),
           CommandBehavior.CloseConnection)
    End Sub

    Public Sub CBMethod(ByVal ar As SQLAsyncResult)
        Dim OrdersReader As SqlDataReader

        ' Retrieving result from the asynchronous process
        OrdersReader = ar.EndExecuteReader(ar)

        ' Displaying result on the screen
        gvOrders.DataSource = OrdersReader
        gvOrders.DataBind()
    End Sub
</script>

<html xmlns="http://www.w3.org/1999/xhtml" >
<head id="Head1" runat="server">
    <title>The Call Back Approach</title>
</head>
<body>
    <form id="form1" runat="server">
    <div>
    <asp:GridView ID="gvOrders" Width="100%" AutoGenerateColumns="False"
     runat="server">
       <Columns>
          <asp:BoundField HeaderText="Company Name"
           DataField="CompanyName"></asp:BoundField>
```

```
            <asp:BoundField HeaderText="Contact Name"
             DataField="ContactName"></asp:BoundField>
            <asp:BoundField HeaderText="Order Date" DataField="orderdate"
             DataFormatString="{0:d}"></asp:BoundField>
            <asp:BoundField HeaderText="Required Date" DataField="requireddate"
             DataFormatString="{0:d}"></asp:BoundField>
            <asp:BoundField HeaderText="Shipped Date" DataField="shippeddate"
             DataFormatString="{0:d}"></asp:BoundField>
         </Columns>
      </asp:GridView>
      </div>
      </form>
</body>
</html>
```

C#

```
<%@ Page Language="C#" %>
<%@ Import Namespace="System.Data" %>
<%@ Import Namespace="System.Data.SqlClient" %>
<%@ Import Namespace="System.Configuration" %>

<script runat="server">
    protected void Page_Load(object sender, EventArgs e)
    {
        SqlConnection DBCon;
        SqlCommand Command = new SqlCommand();
        IAsyncResult ASyncResult;
        DBCon = new SqlConnection();
        Command = new SqlCommand();
        DBCon.ConnectionString =
           ConfigurationManager.ConnectionStrings["DSN_NorthWind"].ConnectionString;

        // Selecting top 5 records from the Orders table
        Command.CommandText =
                "SELECT TOP 5 Customers.CompanyName, Customers.ContactName, " +
                "Orders.OrderID, Orders.OrderDate, " +
                "Orders.RequiredDate, Orders.ShippedDate " +
                "FROM Orders, Customers " +
                "WHERE Orders.CustomerID = Customers.CustomerID " +
                "ORDER BY Customers.CompanyName, Customers.ContactName";

        Command.CommandType = CommandType.Text;
        Command.Connection = DBCon;

        DBCon.Open();

        // Starting the asynchronous processing
        AsyncResult = Command.BeginExecuteReader(new AsyncCallback(CBMethod),
           CommandBehavior.CloseConnection);
    }

    public void CBMethod(SQLAsyncResult ar)
    {
        SqlDataReader OrdersReader;

        // Retrieving result from the asynchronous process
        OrdersReader = ar.EndExecuteReader(ar);

        // Displaying result on the screen
        gvOrders.DataSource = OrdersReader;
        gvOrders.DataBind();
    }
</script>
```

The callback approach enables you to handle the result of a command execution at a different part of your code. This feature is useful in cases where the command execution takes longer than usual and you want to respond to the user without waiting for the command execution to finish.

Canceling Asynchronous Processing

The asynchronous process often takes longer than expected. To alleviate this problem, you can provide an option to the user to cancel the process without waiting for the result. Canceling an asynchronous process is as easy as calling the `Cancel` method on the appropriate `Command` object. This method doesn't return any value. To roll back the work that was already completed by the `Command` object, you must provide a custom transaction to the `Command` object before executing the query. You can also handle the rollback or the commit process yourself.

Asynchronous Connections

Now that you understand how to execute multiple database queries asynchronously using the `Command` object, take a quick look at how you can open database connections asynchronously, as well. The principles of working with asynchronous connections are the same as when you work with asynchronous commands. You can still use any of the three approaches you learned previously.

In ADO.NET, the `SqlConnection` class exposes a couple of properties needed when working asynchronously. Table 8-12 shows these properties.

TABLE 8-12

PROPERTY	DESCRIPTION
`Asynchronous`	This read-only property returns a Boolean value indicating whether the connection has been opened asynchronously.

`State`	This property returns a value from `System.Data.ConnectionState` enumeration indicating the state of the connection. The possible values are as follows:
	`Broken`
	`Closed`
	`Connecting`
	`Executing`
	`Fetching`
	`Open`

SUMMARY

In summary, ADO.NET is a powerful tool to incorporate within your ASP.NET applications. ADO.NET has a number of technologies that provide you with data solutions that you could only dream of in the past.

Visual Studio also makes ADO.NET programming quick and easy when you use the wizards that are available. In this chapter, you saw a number of the wizards. You do not have to use these wizards to work with ADO.NET. On the contrary, you can use some of the wizards and create the rest of the code yourself, or you can use none of the wizards. In any case, you have complete and full access to everything that ADO.NET provides.

This chapter covered a range of advanced features of ADO.NET as well. These features are designed to give you the flexibility to handle database processing in a manner never before possible with either of the previous versions of ADO.NET or ADO.

This chapter also covered the features of Multiple Active Result Sets (MARS), which enable you to reuse a single open connection for multiple accesses to the database, even if the connection is currently processing a result set. This feature becomes even more powerful when it is used in conjunction with the asynchronous command processing.

Querying with LINQ

WHAT'S IN THIS CHAPTER?

- Exploring the different types of LINQ queries
- Understanding the limitations of traditional query methods
- Simplifying query operations with LINQ

.NET 3.5 introduced a new technology called Language Integrated Query, or LINQ (pronounced "link"). LINQ is designed to fill the gap that exists between traditional .NET languages, which offer strong typing and full object-oriented development, and query languages such as SQL, with syntax specifically designed for query operations. With the introduction of LINQ into .NET, the query becomes a first-class concept in .NET, whether you are talking about object, XML, or data queries.

LINQ includes three basic types of queries: LINQ to Objects; LINQ to XML (or XLINQ); and LINQ used in the context of databases, like LINQ to SQL or LINQ to Entities. Each type of query offers specific capabilities and is designed to query a specific source.

This chapter offers a look at all three flavors of LINQ, and how each enables you to simplify query operations. It also covers some language features of the .NET CLR that you use to create LINQ queries, as well as the tooling support in Visual Studio to support using LINQ.

LINQ TO OBJECTS

The first and most basic flavor of LINQ is LINQ to Objects. LINQ to Objects enables you to perform complex query operations against any enumerable object (any object that implements the IEnumerable interface). Although the notion of creating enumerable objects that can be queried or sorted is not new to .NET, doing this in versions prior to version 3.5 usually required a significant amount of code. Often that code would end up being so complex that it would be hard for other developers to read and understand, making it difficult to maintain.

Understanding Traditional Query Methods

In order to really understand how LINQ improves your ability to query collections, you really need to understand how querying is done without it. To do this, take a look at how you might create a simple query that includes a group and sort without using LINQ. Listing 9-1 shows a simple Movie class you can use as the basis of these examples.

LISTING 9-1: A basic Movie class

Available for download on Wrox.com

VB

```
Imports Microsoft.VisualBasic

    Public Class Movie
        Public Property Title() As String
        Public Property Director() As String
        Public Property Genre() As Integer
        Public Property Runtime() As Integer
        Public Property ReleaseDate() As DateTime
    End Class
```

C#

```
using System;

public class Movie
{
    public string Title { get; set; }
    public string Director { get; set; }
    public int Genre { get; set; }
    public int RunTime { get; set; }
    public DateTime ReleaseDate { get; set; }
}
```

This basic class is used throughout this section and the following LINQ to Object section.

Now that you have a basic class to work with, it's time to look at how you would normally use the class. Listing 9-2 demonstrates how to create a simple generic list of the Movie objects in an ASP.NET page and then bind that list to a GridView control. The GridView displays the values of all public properties exposed by the Movie class. Please change the formatting of the dates to what works for the locale of your development machine for this example to work.

LISTING 9-2: Generating a list of Movie objects and binding to a GridView

Available for download on Wrox.com

VB

```
<%@ Page Language="VB" %>
<%@ Import Namespace="System.Collections.Generic" %>

<script runat="server">
    Protected Sub Page_Load(ByVal sender As Object, ByVal e As System.EventArgs)
        Dim movies = GetMovies()

        Me.GridView1.DataSource = movies
        Me.GridView1.DataBind()
    End Sub

    Public Function GetMovies() As List(Of Movie)
      Dim movies As New List(Of Movie) From { _
          New Movie With {.Title = "Shrek", .Director = "Andrew Adamson", _
                .Genre = 0, .ReleaseDate = DateTime.Parse("5/16/2001"), _
                .Runtime = 89}, _
          New Movie With {.Title = "Fletch", .Director = "Michael Ritchie", _
               .Genre = 0, .ReleaseDate = DateTime.Parse("5/31/1985"), _
               .Runtime = 96}, _
          New Movie With {.Title = "Casablanca", .Director = "Michael Curtiz", _
                .Genre = 1, .ReleaseDate = DateTime.Parse("1/1/1942"), _
                .Runtime = 102}, _
          New Movie With {.Title = "Batman", .Director = "Tim Burton", _
                .Genre = 1, .ReleaseDate = DateTime.Parse("6/23/1989"), _
                .Runtime = 126}, _
          New Movie With {.Title = "Dances with Wolves", _
               .Director = "Kevin Costner", .Genre = 1, _
               .ReleaseDate = DateTime.Parse("11/21/1990"), .Runtime = 180}, _
```

```
New Movie With {.Title = "Dirty Dancing", .Director = "Emile Ardolino", _
      .Genre = 1, .ReleaseDate = DateTime.Parse("8/21/1987"), _
      .Runtime = 100}, _
New Movie With {.Title = "The Parent Trap", .Director = "Nancy Meyers", _
      .Genre = 0, .ReleaseDate = DateTime.Parse("7/29/1998"), _
      .Runtime = 127}, _
New Movie With {.Title = "Ransom", .Director = "Ron Howard", _
      .Genre = 1, .ReleaseDate = DateTime.Parse("11/8/1996"), _
      .Runtime = 121}, _
New Movie With {.Title = "Ocean's Eleven", _
      .Director = "Steven Soderbergh", .Genre = 1, _
      .ReleaseDate = DateTime.Parse("12/7/2001"), .Runtime = 116}, _
New Movie With {.Title = "Steel Magnolias", .Director = "Herbert Ross", _
      .Genre = 1, .ReleaseDate = DateTime.Parse("11/15/1989"), _
      .Runtime = 117}, _
New Movie With {.Title = "Mystic Pizza", .Director = "Donald Petrie", _
      .Genre = 1, .ReleaseDate = DateTime.Parse("10/21/1988"), _
      .Runtime = 104}, _
New Movie With {.Title = "Pretty Woman", .Director = "Garry Marshall", _
      .Genre = 1, .ReleaseDate = DateTime.Parse("3/23/1990"), _
      .Runtime = 119}, _
New Movie With {.Title = "Interview with the Vampire", _
      .Director = "Neil Jordan", .Genre = 1, _
      .ReleaseDate = DateTime.Parse("11/11/1994"), .Runtime = 123}, _
New Movie With {.Title = "Top Gun", .Director = "Tony Scott", _
      .Genre = 2, .ReleaseDate = DateTime.Parse("5/16/1986"), _
      .Runtime = 110}, _
New Movie With {.Title = "Mission Impossible", _
      .Director = "Brian De Palma", .Genre = 2, _
      .ReleaseDate = DateTime.Parse("5/22/1996"), .Runtime = 110}, _
New Movie With {.Title = "The Godfather", _
      .Director = "Francis Ford Coppola", .Genre = 1, _
      .ReleaseDate = DateTime.Parse("3/24/1972"), .Runtime = 175}, _
New Movie With {.Title = "Carlito's Way", .Director = "Brian De Palma", _
      .Genre = 1, .ReleaseDate = DateTime.Parse("11/10/1993"), _
      .Runtime = 144}, _
New Movie With {.Title = "Robin Hood: Prince of Thieves", _
      .Director = "Kevin Reynolds", .Genre = 1, _
      .ReleaseDate = DateTime.Parse("6/14/1991"), .Runtime = 143}, _
New Movie With {.Title = "The Haunted", .Director = "Robert Mandel", _
      .Genre = 1, .ReleaseDate = DateTime.Parse("5/6/1991"), _
      .Runtime = 100}, _
New Movie With {.Title = "Old School", .Director = "Todd Phillips", _
      .Genre = 0, .ReleaseDate = DateTime.Parse("2/21/2003"), _
      .Runtime = 91}, _
New Movie With {.Title = "Anchorman: The Legend of Ron Burgundy", _
      .Director = "Adam McKay", .Genre = 0, _
      .ReleaseDate = DateTime.Parse("7/9/2004"), .Runtime = 94}, _
New Movie With {.Title = "Bruce Almighty", .Director = "Tom Shadyac", _
      .Genre = 0, .ReleaseDate = DateTime.Parse("5/23/2003"), _
      .Runtime = 101}, _
New Movie With {.Title = "Ace Ventura: Pet Detective", _
      .Director = "Tom Shadyac", .Genre = 0, _
      .ReleaseDate = DateTime.Parse("2/4/1994"), .Runtime = 86}, _
New Movie With {.Title = "Goonies", .Director = "Richard Donner", _
      .Genre = 0, .ReleaseDate = DateTime.Parse("6/7/1985"), _
      .Runtime = 114}, _
New Movie With {.Title = "Sixteen Candles", .Director = "John Hughes", _
      .Genre = 1, .ReleaseDate = DateTime.Parse("5/4/1984"), _
      .Runtime = 93}, _
New Movie With {.Title = "The Breakfast Club", _
      .Director = "John Hughes", .Genre = 1, _
      .ReleaseDate = DateTime.Parse("2/15/1985"), .Runtime = 97}, _
```

continues

LISTING 9-2 *(continued)*

```
            New Movie With {.Title = "Pretty in Pink", .Director = "Howard Deutch", _
                .Genre = 1, .ReleaseDate = DateTime.Parse("2/28/1986"), _
                .Runtime = 96}, _
            New Movie With {.Title = "Weird Science", .Director = "John Hughes", _
                .Genre = 0, .ReleaseDate = DateTime.Parse("8/2/1985"), _
                .Runtime = 94}, _
            New Movie With {.Title = "Breakfast at Tiffany's", _
                .Director = "Blake Edwards", .Genre = 1, _
                .ReleaseDate = DateTime.Parse("10/5/1961"), .Runtime = 115}, _
            New Movie With {.Title = "The Graduate", .Director = "Mike Nichols", _
                .Genre = 1, .ReleaseDate = DateTime.Parse("4/2/1968"), _
                .Runtime = 105}, _
            New Movie With {.Title = "Dazed and Confused", _
                .Director = "Richard Linklater", .Genre = 0, _
                .ReleaseDate = DateTime.Parse("9/24/1993"), .Runtime = 103}, _
            New Movie With {.Title = "Arthur", .Director = "Steve Gordon", _
                .Genre = 1, .ReleaseDate = DateTime.Parse("9/25/1981"), _
                .Runtime = 97}, _
            New Movie With {.Title = "Monty Python and the Holy Grail", _
                .Director = "Terry Gilliam", .Genre = 0, _
                .ReleaseDate = DateTime.Parse("5/10/1975"), .Runtime = 91}, _
              New Movie With {.Title = "Dirty Harry", .Director = "Don Siegel", _
                .Genre = 2, .ReleaseDate = DateTime.Parse("12/23/1971"), _
                .Runtime = 102} _
              }

          Return movies

      End Function
  </script>

  <html xmlns="http://www.w3.org/1999/xhtml">
  <head runat="server">
      <title>My Favorite Movies</title>
  </head>
  <body>
      <form id="form1" runat="server">
      <div>
          <asp:GridView ID="GridView1" runat="server">
          </asp:GridView>
      </div>
      </form>
  </body>

  </html>
```

C#

```
  <script runat="server">

      protected void Page_Load(object sender, EventArgs e)
      {
          var movies = GetMovies();

          this.GridView1.DataSource = movies;
          this.GridView1.DataBind();
      }

      public List<Movie> GetMovies()
      {
          return new List<Movie> {
              new Movie { Title="Shrek", Director="Andrew Adamson", Genre=0,
                 ReleaseDate=DateTime.Parse("5/16/2001"), RunTime=89 },
```

```
new Movie { Title="Fletch", Director="Michael Ritchie", Genre=0,
   ReleaseDate=DateTime.Parse("5/31/1985"), RunTime=96 },
new Movie { Title="Casablanca", Director="Michael Curtiz", Genre=1,
   ReleaseDate=DateTime.Parse("1/1/1942"), RunTime=102 },
new Movie { Title="Batman", Director="Tim Burton", Genre=1,
   ReleaseDate=DateTime.Parse("6/23/1989"), RunTime=126 },
new Movie { Title="Dances with Wolves",
   Director="Kevin Costner", Genre=1,
   ReleaseDate=DateTime.Parse("11/21/1990"), RunTime=180 },
new Movie { Title="Dirty Dancing", Director="Emile Ardolino", Genre=1,
   ReleaseDate=DateTime.Parse("8/21/1987"), RunTime=100 },
new Movie { Title="The Parent Trap", Director="Nancy Meyers", Genre=0,
   ReleaseDate=DateTime.Parse("7/29/1998"), RunTime=127 },
new Movie { Title="Ransom", Director="Ron Howard", Genre=1,
   ReleaseDate=DateTime.Parse("11/8/1996"), RunTime=121 },
new Movie { Title="Ocean's Eleven",
   Director="Steven Soderbergh", Genre=1,
   ReleaseDate=DateTime.Parse("12/7/2001"), RunTime=116 },
new Movie { Title="Steel Magnolias", Director="Herbert Ross", Genre=1,
   ReleaseDate=DateTime.Parse("11/15/1989"), RunTime=117 },
new Movie { Title="Mystic Pizza", Director="Donald Petrie", Genre=1,
   ReleaseDate=DateTime.Parse("10/21/1988"), RunTime=104 },
new Movie { Title="Pretty Woman", Director="Garry Marshall", Genre=1,
   ReleaseDate=DateTime.Parse("3/23/1990"), RunTime=119 },
new Movie { Title="Interview with the Vampire",
   Director="Neil Jordan", Genre=1,
   ReleaseDate=DateTime.Parse("11/11/1994"), RunTime=123 },
new Movie { Title="Top Gun", Director="Tony Scott", Genre=2,
   ReleaseDate=DateTime.Parse("5/16/1986"), RunTime=110 },
new Movie { Title="Mission Impossible",
   Director="Brian De Palma", Genre=2,
   ReleaseDate=DateTime.Parse("5/22/1996"), RunTime=110 },
new Movie { Title="The Godfather", Director="Francis Ford Coppola",
   Genre=1, ReleaseDate=DateTime.Parse("3/24/1972"), RunTime=175 },
new Movie { Title="Carlito's Way", Director="Brian De Palma",
   Genre=1, ReleaseDate=DateTime.Parse("11/10/1993"), RunTime=144 },
new Movie { Title="Robin Hood: Prince of Thieves",
   Director="Kevin Reynolds",
   Genre=1, ReleaseDate=DateTime.Parse("6/14/1991"), RunTime=143 },
new Movie { Title="The Haunted", Director="Robert Mandel",
   Genre=1, ReleaseDate=DateTime.Parse("5/6/1991"), RunTime=100 },
new Movie { Title="Old School", Director="Todd Phillips",
   Genre=0, ReleaseDate=DateTime.Parse("2/21/2003"), RunTime=91 },
new Movie { Title="Anchorman: The Legend of Ron Burgundy",
   Director="Adam McKay", Genre=0,
   ReleaseDate=DateTime.Parse("7/9/2004"), RunTime=94 },
new Movie { Title="Bruce Almighty", Director="Tom Shadyac",
   Genre=0, ReleaseDate=DateTime.Parse("5/23/2003"), RunTime=101 },
new Movie { Title="Ace Ventura: Pet Detective", Director="Tom Shadyac",
   Genre=0, ReleaseDate=DateTime.Parse("2/4/1994"), RunTime=86 },
new Movie { Title="Goonies", Director="Richard Donner",
   Genre=0, ReleaseDate=DateTime.Parse("6/7/1985"), RunTime=114 },
new Movie { Title="Sixteen Candles", Director="John Hughes",
   Genre=1, ReleaseDate=DateTime.Parse("5/4/1984"), RunTime=93 },
new Movie { Title="The Breakfast Club", Director="John Hughes",
   Genre=1, ReleaseDate=DateTime.Parse("2/15/1985"), RunTime=97 },
new Movie { Title="Pretty in Pink", Director="Howard Deutch",
   Genre=1, ReleaseDate=DateTime.Parse("2/28/1986"), RunTime=96 },
new Movie { Title="Weird Science", Director="John Hughes",
   Genre=0, ReleaseDate=DateTime.Parse("8/2/1985"), RunTime=94 },
new Movie { Title="Breakfast at Tiffany's", Director="Blake Edwards",
   Genre=1, ReleaseDate=DateTime.Parse("10/5/1961"), RunTime=115 },
```

continues

LISTING 9-2 *(continued)*

```
            new Movie { Title="The Graduate", Director="Mike Nichols",
               Genre=1, ReleaseDate=DateTime.Parse("4/2/1968"), RunTime=105 },
            new Movie { Title="Dazed and Confused", Director="Richard Linklater",
               Genre=0, ReleaseDate=DateTime.Parse("9/24/1993"), RunTime=103 },
            new Movie { Title="Arthur", Director="Steve Gordon",
               Genre=1, ReleaseDate=DateTime.Parse("9/25/1981"), RunTime=97 },
            new Movie { Title="Monty Python and the Holy Grail",
               Director="Terry Gilliam",
               Genre=0, ReleaseDate=DateTime.Parse("5/10/1975"), RunTime=91 },
            new Movie { Title="Dirty Harry", Director="Don Siegel",
               Genre=2, ReleaseDate=DateTime.Parse("12/23/1971"), RunTime=102 }
        };
    }
</script>
```

Running the sample generates a typical ASP.NET Web page that includes a simple grid showing all the Movie data on it.

Now, what happens when you want to start performing queries on the list of movies? For example, you might want to filter this data to show only a specific genre of movie. Listing 9-3 shows a typical way you might perform this filtering.

LISTING 9-3: Filtering the list of Movie objects

Available for download on Wrox.com

VB

```
Protected Sub Page_Load(ByVal sender As Object, ByVal e As System.EventArgs)
    Dim movies = GetMovies()

    Dim query As New List(Of Movie)()
    For Each m In movies
        If (m.Genre = 0) Then
            query.Add(m)
        End If
    Next

    Me.GridView1.DataSource = query
    Me.GridView1.DataBind()
End Sub
```

C#

```
protected void Page_Load(object sender, EventArgs e)
{
    var movies = GetMovies();

    var query = new List<Movie>();
    foreach (var m in movies)
    {
        if (m.Genre == 0) query.Add(m);
    }

    this.GridView1.DataSource = query;
    this.GridView1.DataBind();
}
```

As this sample shows, to filter the data so that the page displays Movies in a specific genre only requires the creation of a new temporary collection and the use of a `foreach` loop to iterate through the data.

Although this technique seems easy enough, it still requires that you define what you want done (find all movies in the genre) and also that you explicitly define how it should be done (use a temporary collection and a `foreach` loop). Additionally, what happens when you need to perform more complex queries, involving grouping or sorting? Now the complexity of the code dramatically increases, as shown in Listing 9-4.

LISTING 9-4: Grouping and sorting the list of Movie objects

Available for download on Wrox.com

```
Public Class Grouping
    Public Property Genre() As Integer
    Public Property MovieCount() As Integer
End Class

Protected Sub Page_Load(ByVal sender As Object, ByVal e As System.EventArgs)
    Dim movies = GetMovies()

    Dim groups As New Dictionary(Of String, Grouping)

    For Each m In movies

        If (Not groups.ContainsKey(m.Genre)) Then
            groups(m.Genre) = _
                New Grouping With {.Genre = m.Genre, .MovieCount = 0}
        End If

        groups(m.Genre).MovieCount = groups(m.Genre).MovieCount + 1
    Next

    Dim results As New List(Of Grouping)(groups.Values)
    results.Sort(AddressOf MovieSort)

    Me.GridView1.DataSource = results
    Me.GridView1.DataBind()
End Sub

Private Function MovieSort(ByVal x As Grouping, ByVal y As Grouping) As Integer
    Return IIf(x.MovieCount > y.MovieCount, -1, _
        IIf(x.MovieCount < y.MovieCount, 1, 0))
End Function
```

C#

```
public class Grouping
{
    public int Genre { get; set; }
    public int MovieCount { get; set; }
}

protected void Page_Load(object sender, EventArgs e)
{
    var movies = GetMovies();

    Dictionary<int, Grouping> groups = new Dictionary<int, Grouping>();
    foreach (Movie m in movies)
    {
        if (!groups.ContainsKey(m.Genre))
        {
            groups[m.Genre] = new Grouping { Genre = m.Genre, MovieCount = 0 };
        }
        groups[m.Genre].MovieCount++;
    }

    List<Grouping> results = new List<Grouping>(groups.Values);
    results.Sort(delegate(Grouping x, Grouping y)
    {
        return
            x.MovieCount > y.MovieCount ? -1 :
            x.MovieCount < y.MovieCount ? 1 :
            0;
    });
```

continues

LISTING 9-4 *(continued)*

```
        this.GridView1.DataSource = results;
        this.GridView1.DataBind();
    }
```

To group the Movie data into genres and count how many movies are in each genre requires the addition of a new class, the creation of a Dictionary, and the implementation of a delegate, all fairly complex requirements for such a seemingly simple task. And again, not only do you have to define very specifically what you want done, but also very explicitly how it should be done.

Additionally, because the complexity of the code increases so much, actually determining what this code is doing becomes quite difficult. Consider this: what if you were asked to modify this code in an existing application that you were unfamiliar with? How long would it take you to figure out what it was doing?

Replacing Traditional Queries with LINQ

LINQ was created to address many of the shortcomings of querying collections of data that were discussed in the previous section. Rather than requiring you to very specifically define exactly how you want a query to execute, LINQ gives you the power to stay at a more abstract level. By simply defining what you want the query to return, you leave it up to .NET and its compilers to determine the specifics of exactly how the query will be run.

In the preceding section, you looked at the current state of object querying with today's .NET languages. In this section, you take a look at LINQ and see how using it can greatly simplify these queries, as well as other types of queries. The samples in this section start out by simply modifying the samples from the previous section to show you how easy LINQ makes the same tasks.

Before you get started, understand that LINQ is an extension to .NET and, therefore, is isolated in its own set of assemblies. The base LINQ functionality is located in the `System.Core.dll` assembly. This assembly does not replace any existing framework functionality, but simply augments it. Additionally, by default, projects in Visual Studio include a reference to this assembly so when starting a new ASP.NET Web project, LINQ should be readily available to you.

Basic LINQ Queries and Projections

In order to start modifying the prior section's samples to using LINQ queries, you first must add the LINQ namespace to the Web page, as shown in Listing 9-5.

LISTING 9-5: Adding the LINQ namespace

```
<%@ Import Namespace="System.Linq" %>
```

Adding this namespace gives the page access to all the basic LINQ functionality. If you are using the code-behind development model, then the LINQ namespace should already be included in your code-behind class.

Note that the default web.config file included with a Visual Basic Web site already includes the System.Linq namespace declaration in it, so if you are using this type of project you do not need to manually add the namespace.

Next, you can start modifying code from Listing 9-2. If you remember, this basic sample simply generates a generic list of movies and binds the list to a GridView control. Listing 9-6 shows how the code can be modified to use LINQ to query the movies list and bind the resultset to the GridView.

LISTING 9-6: Creating a query with LINQ

Available for download on Wrox.com

```
Protected Sub Page_Load(ByVal sender As Object, ByVal e As System.EventArgs)
    Dim movies = GetMovies()

    Dim query = From m In movies _
                Select m

    Me.GridView1.DataSource = query
    Me.GridView1.DataBind()
End Sub
```

C#

```
protected void Page_Load(object sender, EventArgs e)
{
    var movies = GetMovies();

    var query = from m in movies
                select m;

    this.GridView1.DataSource = query;
    this.GridView1.DataBind();
}
```

If you deconstruct the code sample, you can see three basic actions happening. First, the code uses the `GetMovies()` method to obtain the generic `List<Movie>` collection.

Next, the code uses a very simple LINQ query to select all the Movie objects from the generic movies collection. Notice that this specific LINQ query utilizes language keywords like `from` and `select` in the query statement. These syntax additions are first-class members of the .NET languages; therefore, Visual Studio can offer you development assistance, such as strong type checking and IntelliSense, which makes finding and fixing problems in your code easier.

The query also defines a new variable `m`. This variable is used in two ways in the query. First, by defining it in the `from` statement from `m`, you are telling LINQ to make `m` represent the individual collection item, which in this case is a `Movie` object. Telling LINQ this enables it to understand the structure of the objects you are querying and, as you will see later, also gives you IntelliSense to help create the query.

The second use of `m` in the query is in the `select` statement. Using `m` in the `select` statement tells LINQ to output a projection that matches the structure of `m`. In this case, that means LINQ creates a projection that matches the `Movie` object structure.

You could just as easily have created your own custom projection by explicitly defining the fields you wanted returned from the query using the new keyword along with the `select` operator, as shown in Listing 9-7.

LISTING 9-7: Creating a custom projection with LINQ

Available for download on Wrox.com

```
Protected Sub Page_Load(ByVal sender As Object, ByVal e As System.EventArgs)
    Dim movies = GetMovies()

    Dim query = From m In movies _
                Select New With {m.Title, m.Genre}
    Me.GridView1.DataSource = query
    Me.GridView1.DataBind()
End Sub
```

```
protected void Page_Load(object sender, EventArgs e)
{
    var movies = GetMovies();

    var query = from m in movies
```

continues

LISTING 9-7 *(continued)*

```
                  select new { m.Title, m.Genre };

        this.GridView1.DataSource = query;
        this.GridView1.DataBind();
    }
```

Notice that rather than simply selecting m, here you have defined a new projection containing only the Title and Genre values.

You can even go so far as to explicitly define the field names that the objects in the resultset will expose. For example, you may want to more explicitly name the Title and Genre fields to more fully describe their contents. Using LINQ, this naming task is easy, as shown in Listing 9-8.

Available for download on Wrox.com

LISTING 9-8: Creating custom projection field names

VB

```
Protected Sub Page_Load(ByVal sender As Object, ByVal e As System.EventArgs)
    Dim movies = GetMovies()

    Dim query = From m In movies _
                Select New With {.MovieTitle = m.Title, .MovieGenre = m.Genre}

    Me.GridView1.DataSource = query
    Me.GridView1.DataBind()
End Sub
```

C#

```
protected void Page_Load(object sender, EventArgs e)
{
    var movies = GetMovies();

    var query = from m in movies
                select new { MovieTitle = m.Title, MovieGenre = m. Genre };

    this.GridView1.DataSource = query;
    this.GridView1.DataBind();
}
```

This sample explicitly defined the fields that will be exposed by the resultset as `MovieTitle` and `MovieGenre`. You can see in Figure 9-1 that because of this change, the column headers in the GridView have changed to match.

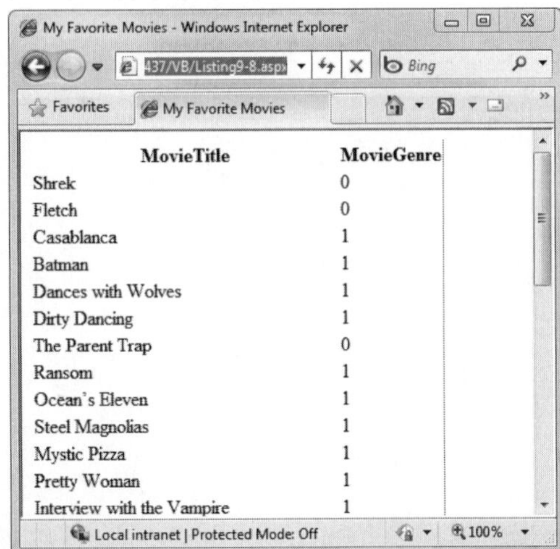

FIGURE 9-1

Finally, the code binds the GridView control to the enumerable list of Movie objects returned by the LINQ query.

As shown in Figure 9-2, running the code from Listing 9-6 results in the same vanilla Web page as the one generated by Listing 9-2.

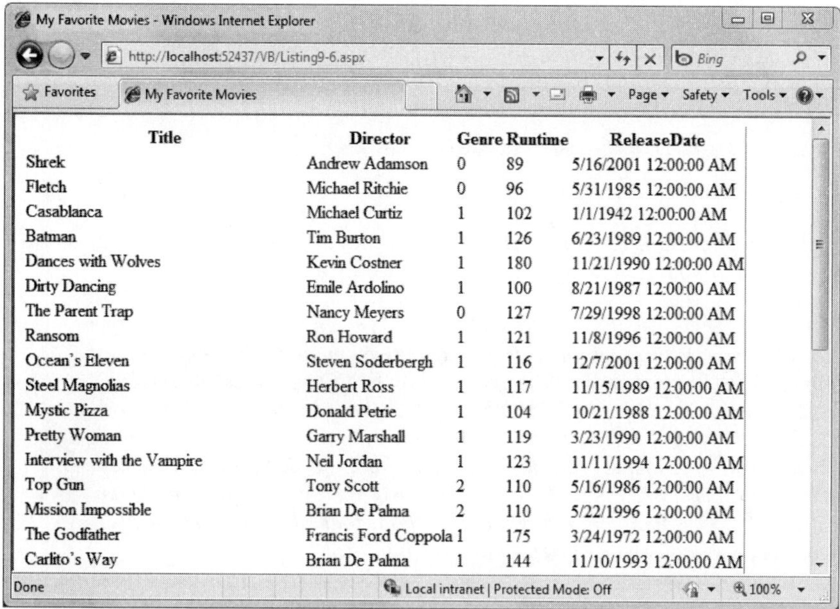

Title	Director	Genre	Runtime	ReleaseDate
Shrek	Andrew Adamson	0	89	5/16/2001 12:00:00 AM
Fletch	Michael Ritchie	0	96	5/31/1985 12:00:00 AM
Casablanca	Michael Curtiz	1	102	1/1/1942 12:00:00 AM
Batman	Tim Burton	1	126	6/23/1989 12:00:00 AM
Dances with Wolves	Kevin Costner	1	180	11/21/1990 12:00:00 AM
Dirty Dancing	Emile Ardolino	1	100	8/21/1987 12:00:00 AM
The Parent Trap	Nancy Meyers	0	127	7/29/1998 12:00:00 AM
Ransom	Ron Howard	1	121	11/8/1996 12:00:00 AM
Ocean's Eleven	Steven Soderbergh	1	116	12/7/2001 12:00:00 AM
Steel Magnolias	Herbert Ross	1	117	11/15/1989 12:00:00 AM
Mystic Pizza	Donald Petrie	1	104	10/21/1988 12:00:00 AM
Pretty Woman	Garry Marshall	1	119	3/23/1990 12:00:00 AM
Interview with the Vampire	Neil Jordan	1	123	11/11/1994 12:00:00 AM
Top Gun	Tony Scott	2	110	5/16/1986 12:00:00 AM
Mission Impossible	Brian De Palma	2	110	5/22/1996 12:00:00 AM
The Godfather	Francis Ford Coppola	1	175	3/24/1972 12:00:00 AM
Carlito's Way	Brian De Palma	1	144	11/10/1993 12:00:00 AM

FIGURE 9-2

LINQ also includes the ability to order the results using the `order by` statement. As with SQL, you can choose to order the results in either ascending or descending order, as shown in Listing 9-9.

LISTING 9-9: Controlling data ordering using LINQ

Available for download on Wrox.com

VB

```
Protected Sub Page_Load(ByVal sender As Object, ByVal e As System.EventArgs)
    Dim movies = GetMovies()

    Dim query = From m In movies _
                Order By m.Title Descending _
                Select New With {.MovieTitle = m.Title, .MovieGenre = m.Genre}

    Me.GridView1.DataSource = query
    Me.GridView1.DataBind()
End Sub
```

C#

```
protected void Page_Load(object sender, EventArgs e)
{
    var movies = GetMovies();

    var query = from m in movies
                orderby m.Title descending
                select new { MovieTitle = m.Title, MovieGenre = m. Genre };

    this.GridView1.DataSource = query;
    this.GridView1.DataBind();
}
```

Another great feature of the LINQ syntax is the dramatic improvement in readability and understandability that it makes in your code. LINQ enables you to simply express the intention of your query, indicating to the compiler what you want your code to do, but leaving it up to the compiler to best determine how it should be done.

Although these keywords are what enable you to construct LINQ queries using a simple and clear SQL-like syntax, rest assured no magic is occurring. These keywords actually map to extension methods on the Movies collection. You could actually write the same LINQ query directly using these extension methods, as follows:

VB
```
Dim query = movies.Select( Function(m as Movie) m )
```

C#
```
var query = movies.Select(m => m);
```

This is what the compiler translates the keyword syntax into during its compilation process. You may be wondering how the `Select` *method got added to the generic* `List<Movies>` *collection, because if you look at the object structure of* `List<T>`*, there is no* `Select` *method. LINQ adds the* `Select` *method and many other methods it uses to the base Enumerable class, using extension methods. Therefore, any class that implements IEnumerable will be extended by LINQ with these methods. You can see all the methods added by LINQ by right-clicking on the* `Select` *method in Visual Studio and choosing the View Definition option from the context menu. Doing this causes Visual Studio to display the class metadata for LINQ's Enumerable class. If you scroll through this class, you will see not only* `Select`*, but also other methods such as* `Where`*,* `Count`*,* `Min`*,* `Max`*, and many other methods that LINQ automatically adds to any object that implements the IEnumerable interface.*

Delayed Execution

An interesting feature of LINQ is its delayed execution behavior. This means that even though you may execute the query statements at a specific point in your code, LINQ is smart enough to delay the actual execution of the query until it is accessed. For example, in the previous samples, although the LINQ query was written before the binding of the GridView controls, LINQ will not actually execute the query you have defined until the GridView control begins to enumerate through the query results.

Query Filters

LINQ also supports adding query filters using a familiar SQL-like `where` syntax. You can modify the LINQ query from Listing 9-3 to add filtering capabilities by adding a `where` clause to the query, as shown in Listing 9-10.

LISTING 9-10: Adding a filter to a LINQ query

Available for download on Wrox.com

VB
```
Protected Sub Page_Load(ByVal sender As Object, ByVal e As System.EventArgs)
    Dim movies = GetMovies()

    Dim query = From m In movies _
                Where m.Genre = 0 _
                Select m

    Me.GridView1.DataSource = query
    Me.GridView1.DataBind()
End Sub
```

C#
```
protected void Page_Load(object sender, EventArgs e)
{
    var movies = GetMovies();
```

```
        var query = from m in movies
                    where m.Genre==0
                    select m;

        this.GridView1.DataSource = query;
        this.GridView1.DataBind();
    }
```

By adding this simple `where` clause to the LINQ query, the results returned by the query are filtered to show movies from the 0 genre only, as shown in Figure 9-3.

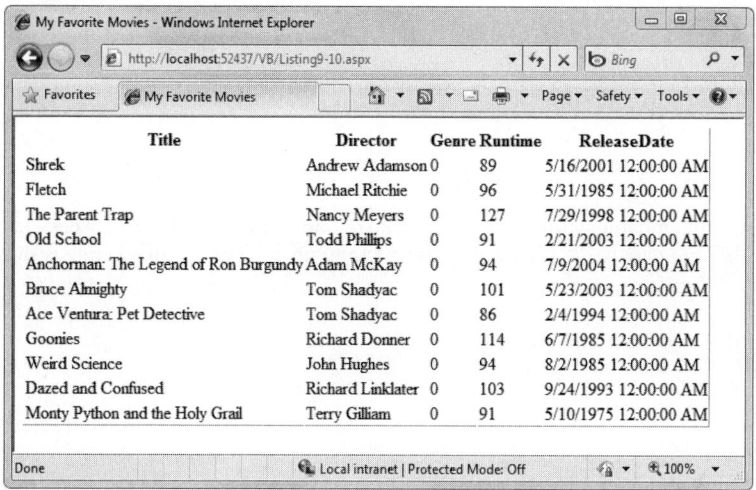

FIGURE 9-3

Also, notice that, because LINQ is a first-class member of .NET, Visual Studio is able to provide an excellent coding experience as you are constructing your LINQ queries. In this sample, as you enter the `where` clause, Visual Studio gives you IntelliSense for the possible parameters of `m` (the Movie object), as shown in Figure 9-4.

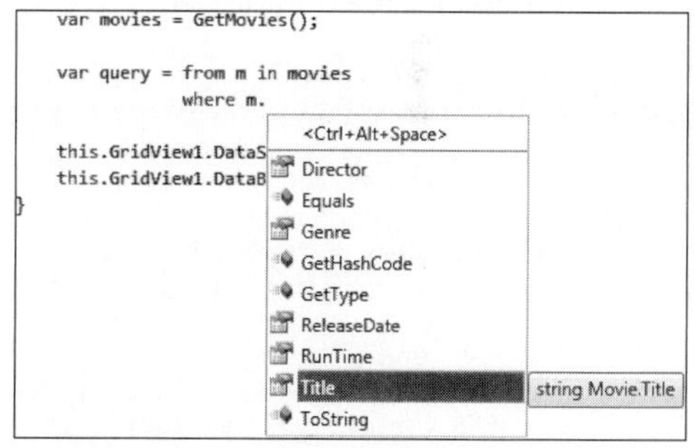

FIGURE 9-4

The `where` clause in LINQ behaves similarly to the SQL `where` clause, enabling you to include subqueries and multiple `where` clauses, as shown in Listing 9-11.

LISTING 9-11: Adding a Where clause to a LINQ query

```
Protected Sub Page_Load(ByVal sender As Object, ByVal e As System.EventArgs)
    Dim movies = GetMovies()

    Dim query = From m In movies _
                Where m.Genre = 0 And m.Runtime > 92 _
                Select m

    Me.GridView1.DataSource = query
    Me.GridView1.DataBind()
End Sub
```

continues

LISTING 9-11 *(continued)*

```
protected void Page_Load(object sender, EventArgs e)
{
    var movies = GetMovies();

    var query = from m in movies
                where m.Genre == 0 && m.RunTime > 92
                select m;

    this.GridView1.DataSource = query;
    this.GridView1.DataBind();
}
```

In this sample, the `where` clause includes two parameters, one restricting the movie genre, the other restricting the movie's runtime.

Data Grouping

LINQ also greatly simplifies grouping data, again using a SQL-like `group` syntax. To show how easy LINQ makes grouping, you can modify the original Listing 9-4 to use a LINQ query. The modified code is shown in Listing 9-12.

LISTING 9-12: Grouping data using a LINQ query

Available for download on Wrox.com

```
Protected Sub Page_Load(ByVal sender As Object, ByVal e As System.EventArgs)
    Dim movies = GetMovies()

    Dim query = From m In movies _
                Group By m.Genre Into g = Group, Count()

    Me.GridView1.DataSource = query
    Me.GridView1.DataBind()
End Sub
```

```
protected void Page_Load(object sender, EventArgs e)
{
    var movies = GetMovies();

    var query = from m in movies
                group m by m.Genre into g
                select new { Genre = g.Key, Count = g.Count() };

    this.GridView1.DataSource = query;
    this.GridView1.DataBind();
}
```

This LINQ query uses the `group` keyword to group the movie data by genre. Additionally, because a group action does not naturally result in any output, the query creates a custom query projection using the techniques discussed earlier. Figure 9-5 shows the results of this query.

Using LINQ to do this grouping enables you to significantly reduce the lines of code required. If you compare the amount of code required to perform the grouping action in Listing 9-4 with that in the previous listing using LINQ, you can see that the number of lines of code has dropped from 18 to 3, and the readability and clarity of the code has improved.

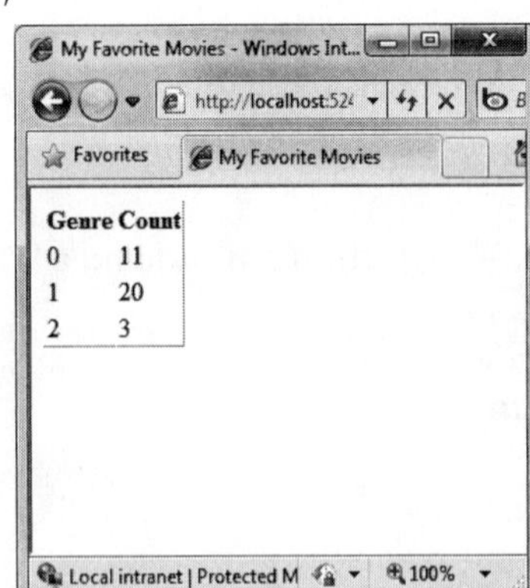

FIGURE 9-5

Using Other LINQ Operators

Besides basic selection, filtering, and grouping, LINQ also includes many operators you can execute on enumerable objects. Most of these operators are available for you to use and are similar to operators you find in SQL, such as `Count`, `Min`, `Max`, `Average`, and `Sum`, as shown in Listing 9-13.

LISTING 9-13: Using LINQ query operators

Available for download on Wrox.com

VB

```
Protected Sub Page_Load(ByVal sender As Object, ByVal e As System.EventArgs)
    Dim movies = GetMovies()

    Me.TotalMovies.Text = movies.Count.ToString()
    Me.LongestRuntime.Text = movies.Max(Function(m) m.Runtime).ToString()
    Me.ShortestRuntime.Text = movies.Min(Function(m) m.Runtime).ToString()
    Me.AverageRuntime.Text = movies.Average(Function(m) m.Runtime).ToString()

End Sub
```

C#

```
protected void Page_Load(object sender, EventArgs e)
{
    var movies = GetMovies();

    this.TotalMovies.Text = movies.Count.ToString();
    this.LongestRuntime.Text = movies.Max(m => m.RunTime).ToString();
    this.ShortestRuntime.Text = movies.Min(m => m.RunTime).ToString();
    this.AverageRuntime.Text = movies.Average(m => m.RunTime).ToString();
}
```

This listing demonstrates the use of the `Count`, `Max`, `Min`, and `Average` operators with the `movies` collection. Notice that for all but the `Count` operator, you must provide the method with the specific field you want to execute the operation on. You do this using a Lambda expression.

Making LINQ Joins

LINQ also supports the unioning of data from different collections using a familiar SQL-like join syntax. For example, in the sample data thus far, you have only been able to display the genre as a numeric ID. Displaying the name of each genre instead would actually be preferable. To do this, you simply create a Genre class, which defines the properties of the genre, as shown in Listing 9-14.

LISTING 9-14: A simple Genre class

Available for download on Wrox.com

VB

```
Public Class Genre

    Public Property ID() As Integer

    Public Property Name() As String
End Class
```

C#

```
public class Genre
{
    public int ID { get; set; }
    public string Name { get; set; }
}
```

Next you can add a `GetGenres` method to your Web page that returns a list of Genre objects, as shown in Listing 9-15.

LISTING 9-15: Populating a collection of Genres

Available for download on Wrox.com

VB

```
Public Function GetGenres() As List(Of Genre)
    Dim genres As Genre() = { _
        New Genre With {.ID = 0, .Name = "Comedy"}, _
        New Genre With {.ID = 1, .Name = "Drama"}, _
        New Genre With {.ID = 2, .Name = "Action"} _
    }

    Return New List(Of Genre)(genres)
End Function
```

C#

```
public List<Genre> GetGenres()
{
    return new List<Genre> {
                new Genre { ID=0, Name="Comedy" } ,
                new Genre { ID=1, Name="Drama" } ,
                new Genre { ID=2, Name="Action" }
            };
}
```

Finally, you can modify the Page Load event, including the LINQ query, to retrieve the Genres list and, using LINQ, join that to the Movies list, as shown in Listing 9-16.

LISTING 9-16: Joining Genre data with Movie data using a LINQ query

Available for download on Wrox.com

VB

```
Protected Sub Page_Load(ByVal sender As Object, ByVal e As System.EventArgs)
    Dim movies = GetMovies()
    Dim genres = GetGenres()

    Dim query = From m In movies Join g In genres _
                On m.Genre Equals g.ID _
                Select New With {.Title = m.Title, .Genre = g.Name}

    GridView1.DataSource = query
    GridView1.DataBind()
End Sub
```

C#

```
protected void Page_Load(object sender, EventArgs e)
{
    var movies = GetMovies();
    var genres = GetGenres();

    var query = from m in movies
                join g in genres on m.Genre equals g.ID
                select new { m.Title, Genre = g.Name } ;

    this.GridView1.DataSource = query;
    this.GridView1.DataBind();
}
```

As you can see in this sample, the join syntax is relatively simple. You tell LINQ to include the genres object and then tell LINQ which fields it should associate.

Paging Using LINQ

LINQ also makes including paging logic in your Web application much easier by exposing the `Skip` and `Take` methods. The `Skip` method enables you to skip a defined number of records in the resultset. The `Take` method enables you to specify the number of records to return from the resultset. By calling `Skip` and then `Take`, you can return a specific number of records from a specific location of the resultset, as shown in Listing 9-17.

LISTING 9-17: Simple paging using LINQ methods

Available for download on Wrox.com

VB

```
Protected Sub Page_Load(ByVal sender As Object, ByVal e As System.EventArgs)
    Dim movies = GetMovies()
    Dim genres = GetGenres()

    Dim query = (From m In movies _
                 Join g In genres On m.Genre Equals g.ID _
                 Select New With {m.Title, .Genre = g.Name}).Skip(10).Take(10)

    Me.GridView1.DataSource = query
    Me.GridView1.DataBind()
    End Sub
```

C#

```
protected void Page_Load(object sender, EventArgs e)
{
    var movies = GetMovies();
    var genres = GetGenres();

    var query = (from m in movies
                join g in genres on m.Genre equals g.ID
                select new { m.Title, g.Name }).Skip(10).Take(10);

    this.GridView1.DataSource = query;
    this.GridView1.DataBind();
}
```

When running this code, you will see that the results start with the tenth record in the list, and only ten records are displayed.

LINQ TO XML

The second flavor of LINQ is called LINQ to XML (or XLINQ). As the name implies, LINQ to XML enables you to use the same basic LINQ syntax to query XML documents. As with the basic LINQ features, the LINQ to XML features of .NET are included as an extension to the basic .NET Framework and do not change any existing functionality. Also, as with the core LINQ features, the LINQ to XML features are contained in their own separate assembly, the System.Xml.Linq assembly.

This section shows how you can use LINQ to query XML, using the same basic Movie data as in the previous section, but converted to XML. Listing 9-18 shows a portion of the Movie data converted to a simple XML document. You can find the XML file containing the complete set of converted data in the downloadable code for this chapter.

LISTING 9-18: Sample movies XML data file

Available for download on Wrox.com

```
<?xml version="1.0" encoding="utf-8" ?>
<Movies>
  <Movie>
    <Title>Shrek</Title>
    <Director>Andrew Adamson</Director>
    <Genre>0</Genre>
    <ReleaseDate>5/16/2001</ReleaseDate>
    <RunTime>89</RunTime>
  </Movie>
  <Movie>
    <Title>Fletch</Title>
    <Director>Michael Ritchie</Director>
    <Genre>0</Genre>
    <ReleaseDate>5/31/1985</ReleaseDate>
```

continues

LISTING 9-18 *(continued)*

```
      <RunTime>96</RunTime>
    </Movie>
    <Movie>
      <Title>Casablanca</Title>
      <Director>Michael Curtiz</Director>
      <Genre>1</Genre>
      <ReleaseDate>1/1/1942</ReleaseDate>
      <RunTime>102</RunTime>
    </Movie>
  </Movies>
```

So you can see how to use LINQ to XML to query XML documents, this section walks you through some of the same basic queries you started with in the previous section. Listing 9-19 demonstrates a simple selection query using LINQ to XML.

LISTING 9-19: Querying the XML data file using LINQ

Available for download on Wrox.com

VB

```
<%@ Page Language="VB" %>

<script runat="server">
    Protected Sub Page_Load(ByVal sender As Object, ByVal e As System.EventArgs)
        Dim query = From m In _
                    XElement.Load(MapPath("Movies.xml")).Elements("Movie") _
                    Select m

        Me.GridView1.DataSource = query
        Me.GridView1.DataBind()
    End Sub
</script>

<html xmlns="http://www.w3.org/1999/xhtml">
<head runat="server">
    <title>My Favorite Movies</title>
</head>
<body>
    <form id="form1" runat="server">
    <div>
        <asp:GridView ID="GridView1" runat="server">
        </asp:GridView>
    </div>
    </form>
</body>
</html>
```

C#

```
<%@ Page Language="C#" %>
<%@ Import Namespace="System.Linq" %>
<%@ Import Namespace="System.Xml.Linq" %>
<script runat="server">
    protected void Page_Load(object sender, EventArgs e)
    {
        var query = from m in
                        XElement.Load(MapPath("Movies.xml")).Elements("Movie")
                    select m;

        this.GridView1.DataSource = query;
        this.GridView1.DataBind();
    }
</script>
```

Notice that in this query, you tell LINQ directly where to load the XML data from, and from which elements in that document it should retrieve the data, which in this case are all the Movie elements. Other than that minor change, the LINQ query is identical to queries you have seen previously.

When you execute this code, you get a page that looks like Figure 9-6.

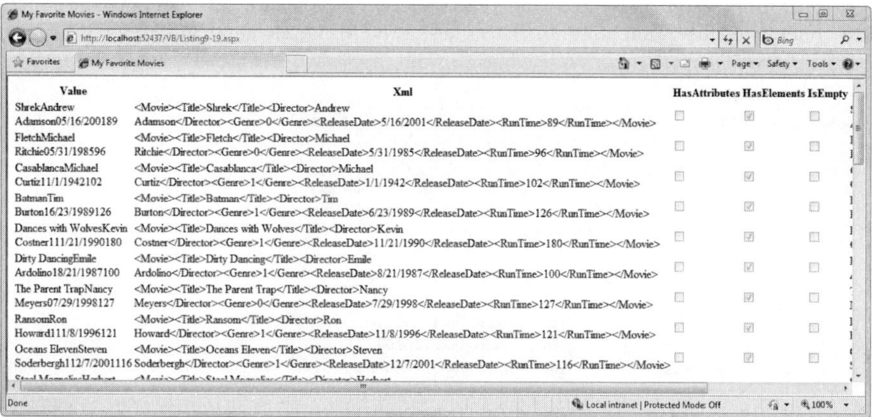

FIGURE 9-6

Notice that the fields included in the resultset of the query don't really show the node data as you might have expected, with each child node as a separate Field in the GridView. This is because the query used in the Listing returns a collection of generic XElement objects, not Movie objects as you might have expected. This is because by itself LINQ has no way of identifying what object type each node should be mapped to. Thankfully, you can add a bit of mapping logic to the query to tell it to map each node to a Movie object and how the nodes' sub-elements should map to the properties of the Movie object, as shown in Listing 9-20.

LISTING 9-20: Mapping XML elements using LINQ

Available for download on Wrox.com

VB

```
Protected Sub Page_Load(ByVal sender As Object, ByVal e As System.EventArgs)
    Dim query = From m In XElement.Load(MapPath("Movies.xml")).Elements("Movie") _
                Select New Movie With { _
                                .Title = CStr(m.Element("Title")), _
                                .Director = CStr(m.Element("Director")), _
                                .Genre = CInt(m.Element("Genre")), _
                                .ReleaseDate = CDate(m.Element("ReleaseDate")), _
                                .Runtime = CInt(m.Element("Runtime")) _
                            }

    Me.GridView1.DataSource = query
    Me.GridView1.DataBind()
End Sub
```

C#

```
protected void Page_Load(object sender, EventArgs e)
{
    var query = from m in XElement.Load(MapPath("Movies.xml")).Elements("Movie")
                select new Movie {
                            Title = (string)m.Element("Title"),
                            Director = (string)m.Element("Director"),
                            Genre = (int)m.Element("Genre"),
                            ReleaseDate = (DateTime)m.Element("ReleaseDate"),
                            RunTime = (int)m.Element("RunTime")
                        };
```

continues

LISTING 9-20 *(continued)*

```
        this.GridView1.DataSource = query;
        this.GridView1.DataBind();
    }
```

As you can see, we have modified the query to include mapping logic so that LINQ knows what our actual intentions are — to create a resultset that contains the values of the Movie elements' inner nodes. Running this code now results in a GridView that contains what we want, as shown in Figure 9-7.

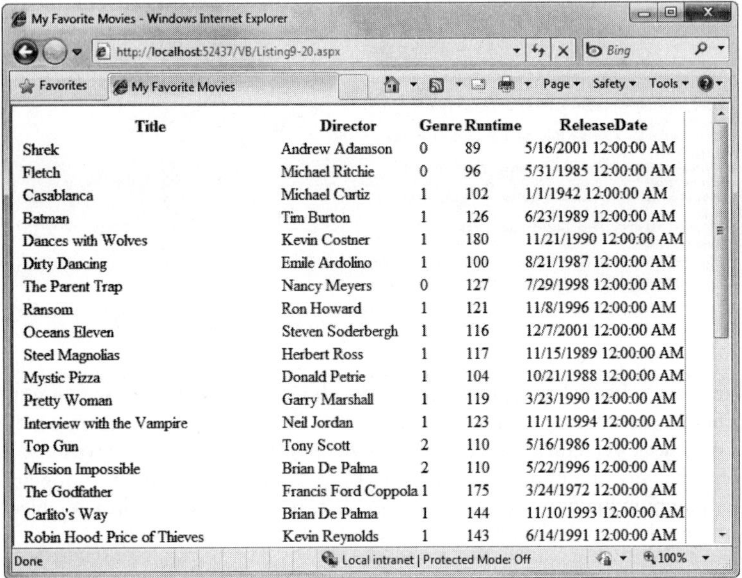

Title	Director	Genre	Runtime	ReleaseDate
Shrek	Andrew Adamson	0	89	5/16/2001 12:00:00 AM
Fletch	Michael Ritchie	0	96	5/31/1985 12:00:00 AM
Casablanca	Michael Curtiz	1	102	1/1/1942 12:00:00 AM
Batman	Tim Burton	1	126	6/23/1989 12:00:00 AM
Dances with Wolves	Kevin Costner	1	180	11/21/1990 12:00:00 AM
Dirty Dancing	Emile Ardolino	1	100	8/21/1987 12:00:00 AM
The Parent Trap	Nancy Meyers	0	127	7/29/1998 12:00:00 AM
Ransom	Ron Howard	1	121	11/8/1996 12:00:00 AM
Oceans Eleven	Steven Soderbergh	1	116	12/7/2001 12:00:00 AM
Steel Magnolias	Herbert Ross	1	117	11/15/1989 12:00:00 AM
Mystic Pizza	Donald Petrie	1	104	10/21/1988 12:00:00 AM
Pretty Woman	Garry Marshall	1	119	3/23/1990 12:00:00 AM
Interview with the Vampire	Neil Jordan	1	123	11/11/1994 12:00:00 AM
Top Gun	Tony Scott	2	110	5/16/1986 12:00:00 AM
Mission Impossible	Brian De Palma	2	110	5/22/1996 12:00:00 AM
The Godfather	Francis Ford Coppola	1	175	3/24/1972 12:00:00 AM
Carlito's Way	Brian De Palma	1	144	11/10/1993 12:00:00 AM
Robin Hood: Price of Thieves	Kevin Reynolds	1	143	6/14/1991 12:00:00 AM

FIGURE 9-7

Note that the XElement's `Load` method attempts to load the entire XML document; therefore, trying to load very large XML files using this method is not a good idea.

Joining XML Data

LINQ to XML supports all the same query filtering and grouping operations as LINQ to Objects. It also supports joining data and can actually union together data from two different XML documents — a task that previously would have been quite difficult. Take a look at the same basic join scenario as was presented in the "LINQ to Objects" section. Again, the basic XML data includes only an ID value for the Genre. Showing the actual Genre name with the resultset would, however, be better.

In the case of the XML data, rather than being kept in a separate List, the Genre data is actually stored in a completely separate XML file, shown in Listing 9-21.

LISTING 9-21: Genres XML data

Available for download on Wrox.com

```
<?xml version="1.0" encoding="utf-8" ?>
<Genres>
    <Genre>
        <ID>0</ID>
        <Name>Comedy</Name>
    </Genre>
```

```
        <Genre>
            <ID>1</ID>
            <Name>Drama</Name>
        </Genre>
        <Genre>
            <ID>2</ID>
            <Name>Action</Name>
        </Genre>
    </Genres>
```

To join the data together, you can use a very similar join query to that used in Listing 9-16. It is shown in Listing 9-22.

LISTING 9-22: Joining XML data using LINQ

Available for download on Wrox.com

VB

```
Protected Sub Page_Load(ByVal sender As Object, ByVal e As System.EventArgs)

    Dim query = From m In _
                XElement.Load(MapPath("Listing9-18.xml")).Elements("Movie") _
                Join g In _
                XElement.Load(MapPath("Listing9-21.xml")).Elements("Genre") _
                    On CInt(m.Element("Genre")) Equals CInt(g.Element("ID")) _
                Select New With { _
                     .Title = CStr(m.Element("Title")), _
                     .Director = CStr(m.Element("Director")), _
                     .Genre = CStr(g.Element("Name")), _
                     .ReleaseDate = CDate(m.Element("ReleaseDate")), _
                     .Runtime = CInt(m.Element("RunTime")) _
                }

    Me.GridView1.DataSource = query
    Me.GridView1.DataBind()
End Sub
```

C#

```
protected void Page_Load(object sender, EventArgs e)
{
    var query = from m in XElement.Load(MapPath("Movies.xml")).Elements("Movie")
                join g in XElement.Load(MapPath("Genres.xml")).Elements("Genre")
                    on (int)m.Element("Genre") equals (int)g.Element("ID")
                select new {
                           Title = (string)m.Element("Title"),
                           Director = (string)m.Element("Director"),
                           Genre = (string)g.Element("Name"),
                           ReleaseDate = (DateTime)m.Element("ReleaseDate"),
                           RunTime = (int)m.Element("RunTime")
                       };

    this.GridView1.DataSource = query;
    this.GridView1.DataBind();
}
```

In this sample, you can see that using the `XElement.Load` method as part of the LINQ join statement tells LINQ where to load the Genre data from. After the data is joined, you can access the elements of the Genre data as you can the elements of the Movie data.

LINQ TO SQL

LINQ to SQL is the last form of LINQ in this release of .NET. LINQ to SQL, as the name implies, enables you to quickly and easily query SQL-based data sources, such as SQL Server 2005 and above. As with the prior flavors of LINQ, LINQ to SQL is an extension of .NET. Its features are located in the System.Data .Linq assembly.

In addition to the normal IntelliSense and strong type checking that every flavor of LINQ gives you, LINQ to SQL also includes a basic Object Relation (O/R) mapper directly in Visual Studio. The O/R mapper enables you to quickly map SQL-based data sources to CLR objects that you can then use LINQ to query. It is the easiest way to get started using LINQ to SQL.

You use the O/R mapper by adding the new LINQ to SQL Classes file to your Web site project. The LINQ to SQL File document type allows you to easily and visually create data contexts that you can then access and query with LINQ queries. Figure 9-8 shows the LINQ to SQL Classes file type in the Add New Item dialog.

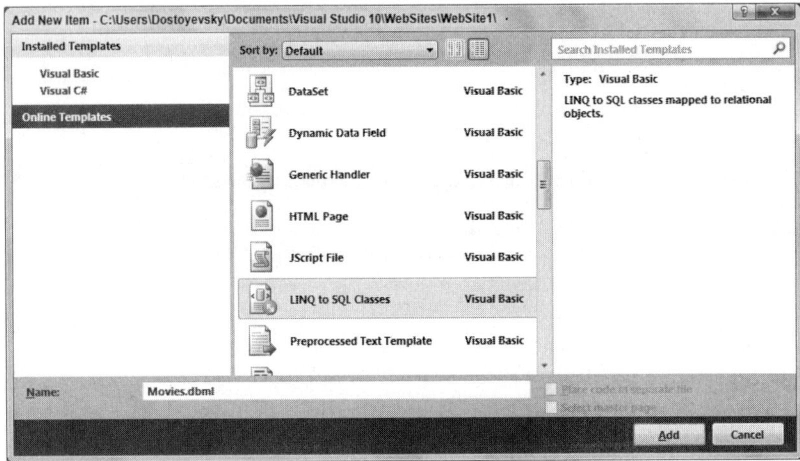

FIGURE 9-8

After you click the Add New Items dialog's OK button to add the file to your project, Visual Studio notifies you that it wants to add the LINQ to SQL File to your Web site's App_Code directory. Because the file is located there, the data context created by the LINQ to SQL Classes file will be accessible from anywhere in your Web site.

After the file has been added, Visual Studio automatically opens it in the LINQ to SQL design surface. This simple Object Relation mapper design tool enables you to add, create, remove, and relate data objects. As you modify objects to the design surface, LINQ to SQL generates object classes that mirror the structure of each of those objects. Later, when you are ready to begin writing LINQ queries against the data objects, these classes allow Visual Studio to provide you with design-time IntelliSense support, strong typing, and compile-time type checking. Because the O/R mapper is primarily designed to be used with LINQ to SQL, creating CLR object representations of SQL objects, such as tables, views, and stored procedures, is easy.

The demonstration for using LINQ to SQL uses the same sample Movie data used in previous sections of this chapter. For this section, the data is stored in a SQL Server Express database.

A copy of this database named Movies.mdf is included in the downloadable code from the Wrox Web site (`www.wrox.com`*).*

After the design surface is open and ready, open the Visual Studio Server Explorer tool, locate the Movies database, and expand the database's Tables folder. Drag the Movies table from the Server Explorer onto the design surface. Notice that as soon as you drop the database table onto the design surface, it is automatically interrogated to identify its structure. A corresponding entity class is created by the designer and shown on the design surface.

When you drop table objects onto the LINQ to SQL design surface, Visual Studio examines the entities' names and will, if necessary, attempt to automatically "pluralize" the class names it generated. It does this in order to help you more closely follow the .NET Framework class naming standards. For example, if you drop a table called Products from a database onto the design surface, it would automatically choose the singular name Product as the name of the generated class.

Unfortunately, although the designer generally does a good job at figuring out the correct pluralization for the class names, it's not 100% accurate. Case in point, simply look at how it incorrectly pluralizes the Movies table to Movy when you drop it onto the design surface. Thankfully, the designer also allows you to change the name of entities on the design surface. You can do so simply by selecting the entity on the design surface and clicking on the entity's name in the designer.

After you have added the Movie entity, drag the Genres table onto the design surface. Again, Visual Studio creates a class representation of this table (and notice it gives it the singular name Genre). Additionally, it detects an existing foreign key relationship between the Movie and Genre. Because it detects this relationship, a dashed line is added between the two tables. The line's arrow indicates the direction of the foreign key relationship that exists between the two tables. Figure 9-9 shows the LINQ to SQL design surface with Movies and Genres tables added.

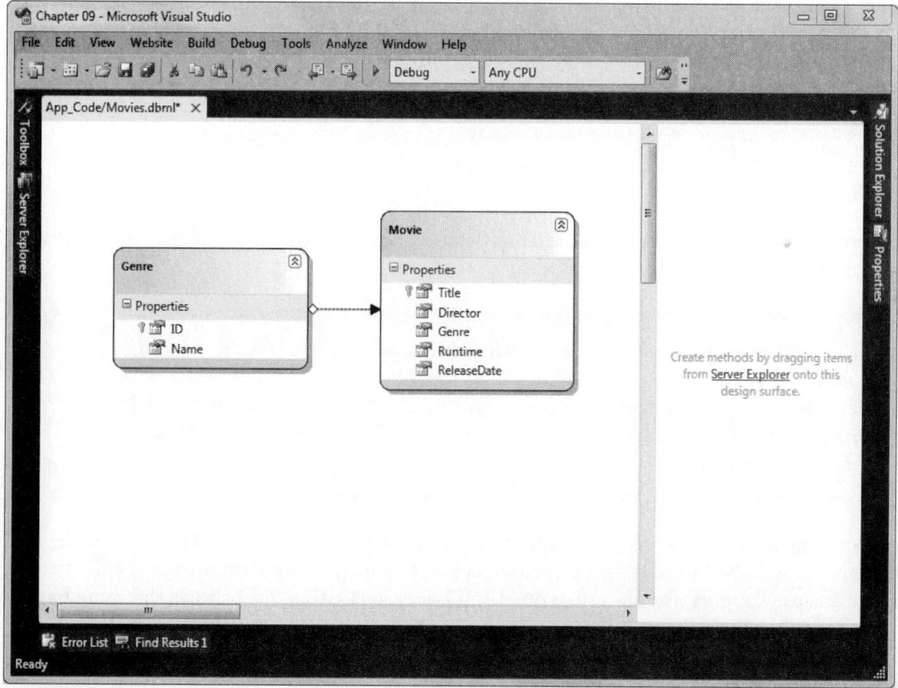

FIGURE 9-9

Now that you have set up your LINQ to SQL file, accessing its data context and querying its data is simple. To start, you create an instance of the data context in the Web page where you will be accessing the data, as shown in Listing 9-23.

LISTING 9-23: Creating a new data context

Available for download on Wrox.com

```
<%@ Page Language="VB" %>

<script runat="server">
    Protected Sub Page_Load(ByVal sender As Object, ByVal e As System.EventArgs)
        Dim dc As New MoviesDataContext()
    End Sub
</script>

<html xmlns="http://www.w3.org/1999/xhtml">
<head runat="server">
    <title> My Favorite Movies </title>
</head>
<body>
    <form id="form1" runat="server">
    <div>
        <asp:GridView ID="GridView1" runat="server">
        </asp:GridView>

    </div>
    </form>
</body>
</html>
```

C#

```
<script runat="server">
    protected void Page_Load(object sender, EventArgs e)
    {
        MoviesDataContext dc = new MoviesDataContext();

    }
</script>
```

In this case, you created an instance of the MoviesDataContext, which is the name of the data context class generated by the LINQ to SQL file you added earlier.

Because the data context class is automatically generated by the LINQ to SQL file, its name will change each time you create a new LINQ to SQL file. The name of this class is determined by appending the name of your LINQ to SQL Class file with the DataContext suffix, so had you named your LINQ to SQL file AdventureWorks.dbml, the data context class would have been AdventureWorksDataContext.

After you have added the data context to your page, you can begin writing LINQ queries against it. As mentioned earlier, because LINQ to SQL–generated object classes mirror the structure of the database tables, you get IntelliSense support as you write your LINQ queries. Listing 9-24 shows the same basic Movie listing query that has been shown in prior sections.

LISTING 9-24: Querying movie data from LINQ to SQL

Available for download on Wrox.com

```
Protected Sub Page_Load(ByVal sender As Object, ByVal e As System.EventArgs)
    Dim dc As New MoviesDataContext()

    Dim query = From m In dc.Movies _
                Select m
```

```
        Me.GridView1.DataSource = query
        Me.GridView1.DataBind()
    End Sub
```

C#

```
    protected void Page_Load(object sender, EventArgs e)
    {
        MoviesDataContext dc = new MoviesDataContext();

        var query = from m in dc.Movies
                    select m;

        this.GridView1.DataSource = query;
        this.GridView1.DataBind();
    }
```

As is shown in Figure 9-10, running the code generates a raw list of the Movies in the database.

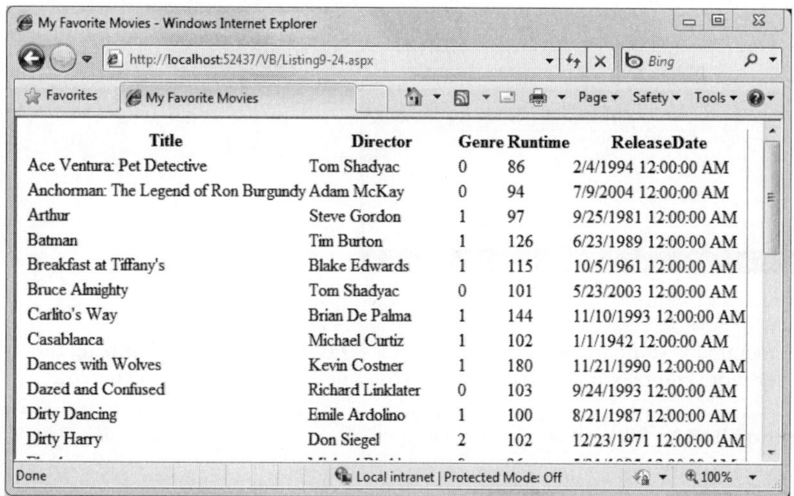

FIGURE 9-10

Note that we did not have to write any of the database access code that would typically have been required to create this page. LINQ has taken care of that for us, even generating the SQL query based on our LINQ syntax. You can see the SQL that LINQ generated for the query by writing the query to the Visual Studio output window, as shown in Listing 9-25.

LISTING 9-25: Writing the LINQ to SQL query to the output window

Available for download on Wrox.com

VB

```
    Protected Sub Page_Load(ByVal sender As Object, ByVal e As System.EventArgs)
        Dim dc As New MoviesDataContext()

        Dim query = From m In dc.Movies _
                    Select m

        System.Diagnostics.Debug.WriteLine(query)

        Me.GridView1.DataSource = query
        Me.GridView1.DataBind()
    End Sub
```

continues

LISTING 9-25 *(continued)*

C#

```
protected void Page_Load(object sender, EventArgs e)
{
    MoviesDataContext dc = new MoviesDataContext();

    var query = from m in dc.Movies
                select m;

    System.Diagnostics.Debug.WriteLine(query);

    this.GridView1.DataSource = query;
    this.GridView1.DataBind();
}
```

Now, when you debug the Web site using Visual Studio, you can see the SQL query, as shown in Figure 9-11.

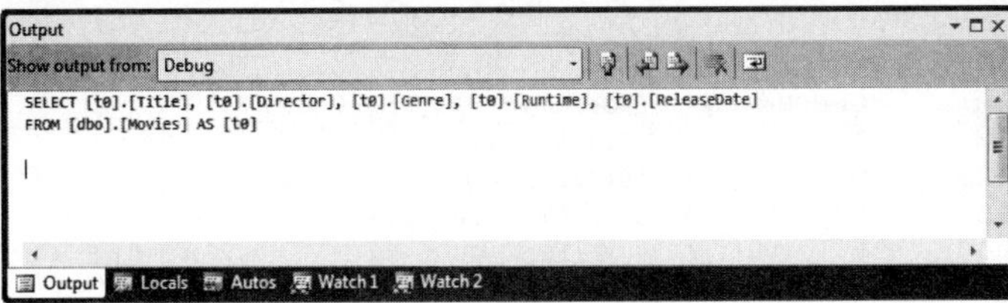

FIGURE 9-11

As you can see, the SQL generated is standard SQL syntax, and LINQ is quite good at optimizing the queries it generates, even for more complex queries such as the grouping query shown in Listing 9-26.

LISTING 9-26: Grouping LINQ to SQL data

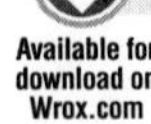

Available for download on Wrox.com

VB

```
Protected Sub Page_Load(ByVal sender As Object, ByVal e As System.EventArgs)
    Dim dc As New MoviesDataContext()

    Dim query = From m In dc.Movies _
                Group By m.Genre Into g = Group, Count()

    System.Diagnostics.Debug.WriteLine(query)

    Me.GridView1.DataSource = query
    Me.GridView1.DataBind()

End Sub
```

C#

```
protected void Page_Load(object sender, EventArgs e)
{
    MoviesDataContext dc = new MoviesDataContext();

    var query = from m in dc.Movies
                group m by m.Genre into g
                select new { Genre  = g.Key, Count = g.Count() };

    System.Diagnostics.Debug.WriteLine(query);
```

```
        this.GridView1.DataSource = query;
        this.GridView1.DataBind();
    }
```

Figure 9-12 shows the generated SQL for this query.

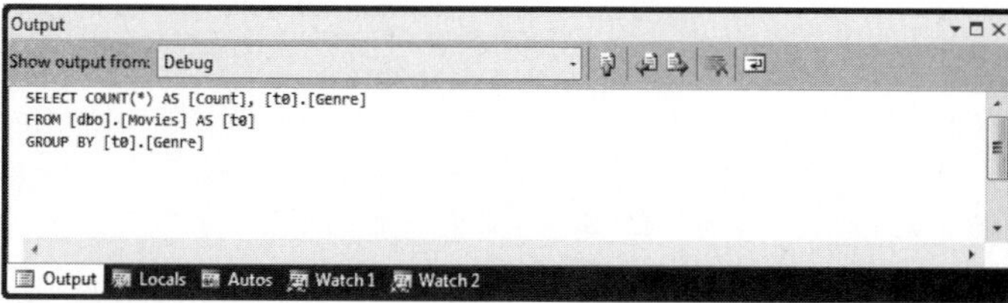

FIGURE 9-12

Note that SQL to LINQ generates SQL that is optimized for the version of SQL Server you're using.

LINQ also includes a logging option you can enable by setting the Log property of the data context.

Although LINQ to SQL does an excellent job generating the SQL query syntax, there may be times where using other SQL query methods, such as stored procedures or views, is more appropriate. LINQ supports using the predefined queries as well.

To use a SQL view with LINQ to SQL, you simply drag the view onto the LINQ to SQL design surface, just as you would a standard SQL table. Views appear on the design surface, just as the tables we added earlier did. After the view is on the design surface, you can execute queries against it, just as you did the SQL tables, as shown in Listing 9-27.

LISTING 9-27: Querying LINQ to SQL data using a view

Available for download on Wrox.com

VB

```
Protected Sub Page_Load(ByVal sender As Object, ByVal e As System.EventArgs)
    Dim dc As New MoviesDataContext()

    Dim query = From m In dc.AllMovies _
                Select m

    System.Diagnostics.Debug.WriteLine(query)

    Me.GridView1.DataSource = query
    Me.GridView1.DataBind()
End Sub
```

C#

```
protected void Page_Load(object sender, EventArgs e)
{
    MoviesDataContext dc = new MoviesDataContext();

    var query = from m in dc.AllMovies
                select m;

    System.Diagnostics.Debug.WriteLine(query);

    this.GridView1.DataSource = query;
    this.GridView1.DataBind();
}
```

Unlike tables or views, which LINQ to SQL exposes as properties, stored procedures can require parameters. Therefore, LINQ to SQL exposes them from the data context object as method calls, allowing you to provide method parameter values, which are translated by LINQ into stored procedure parameters. Listing 9-28 shows a simple stored procedure you can use to retrieve a specific genre from the database.

LISTING 9-28: Simple SQL stored procedure

```
CREATE PROCEDURE dbo.GetGenre
    (
    @id int
    )

AS
    SELECT * FROM Genre WHERE ID = @id
```

You can add a stored procedure to your LINQ to SQL designer just as you did the tables and views, by dragging them from the Server Explorer onto the LINQ to SQL Classes design surface. If you expect your stored procedure to return a collection of data from a table in your database, you should drop the stored procedure onto the LINQ class that represents the types returned by the query. The stored procedure shown in Listing 9-28 will return all the Genre records that match the provided ID. Therefore, you should drop the GetGenres stored procedure onto the Genres table in the Visual Studio designer. This tells the designer to generate a method that returns a generic collection of Genre objects. When you drop the stored procedure onto the design surface, unlike the tables and views, the stored procedure appears in a list on the right side of the design surface. Figure 9-13 shows the GetGenre stored procedure after its being added.

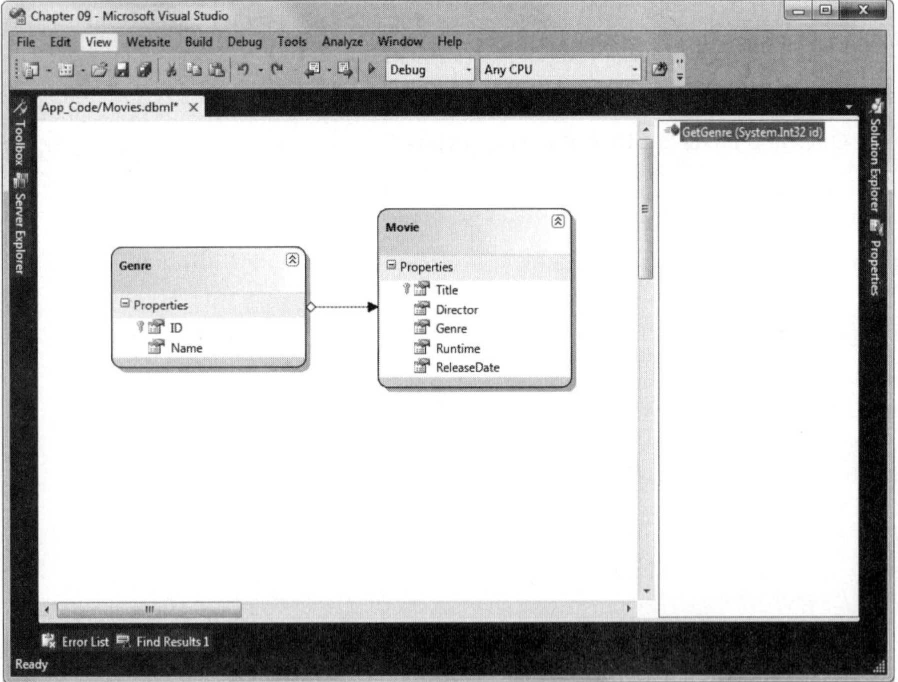

FIGURE 9-13

After you have added the stored procedures, you can access them through the data context, just as you did the table and views you accessed. As stated earlier, however, LINQ to SQL exposes them as method calls. Therefore, they may require you to provide method parameters, as shown in Listing 9-29.

LISTING 9-29: Selecting data from a stored procedure

Available for download on Wrox.com

VB

```
Protected Sub Page_Load(ByVal sender As Object, ByVal e As System.EventArgs)
    Dim dc As New MoviesDataContext()

    Me.GridView1.DataSource = dc.GetGenre(1)
    Me.GridView1.DataBind()
End Sub
```

C#

```
protected void Page_Load(object sender, EventArgs e)
{
    MoviesDataContext dc = new MoviesDataContext();

    this.GridView1.DataSource = dc.GetGenre(1);
    this.GridView1.DataBind();
}
```

Making Insert, Update, and Delete Queries through LINQ

Not only can you use LINQ to SQL to create powerful queries that select data from a data source, but you can also use it to manage insert, update, and delete operations. By default, LINQ to SQL does these operations in much the same manner as when selecting data. LINQ to SQL uses the object class representations of the SQL structures and dynamically generates SQL Insert, Update, and Delete commands. As with selection, you can also use stored procedures to perform the insert, update, or delete.

Inserting Data Using LINQ

Inserting data using LINQ to SQL is as easy as creating a new instance of the object you want to insert, and adding that to the object collection. The LINQ classes provide two methods, `InsertOnSubmit` and `InsertAllOnSubmit`, that make creating and adding any object to a LINQ collection simple. The `InsertOnSubmit` method accepts a single entity as its method parameter, allowing you to insert a single entity, whereas the `InsertAllOnSubmit` method accepts a collection as its method parameter, allowing you to insert an entire collection of data in a single method call.

After you have added your objects, LINQ to SQL does require the extra step of calling the Data Context objects `SubmitChanges` method. Calling this method tells LINQ to initiate the Insert action. Listing 9-30 shows an example of creating a new Movies object, and then adding it to the Movies collection and calling `SubmitChanges` to persist the change back to the SQL database.

LISTING 9-30: Inserting data using LINQ to SQL

Available for download on Wrox.com

VB

```
Protected Sub Page_Load(ByVal sender As Object, ByVal e As System.EventArgs)
    Dim dc As New MoviesDataContext()

    Dim m As New Movie With {.Title = "The Princess Bride", _
        .Director = "Rob Reiner", .Genre = 0, _
        .ReleaseDate = DateTime.Parse("9/25/1987"), .Runtime = 98}

    dc.Movies.InsertOnSubmit(m)
    dc.SubmitChanges()

End Sub
```

C#

```
protected void Page_Load(object sender, EventArgs e)
{
    MoviesDataContext dc = new MoviesDataContext();
```

continues

LISTING 9-30 *(continued)*

```
        Movie m = new Movie { Title="The Princess Bride",
            Director="Rob Reiner", Genre=0,
            ReleaseDate=DateTime.Parse("9/25/1987"), Runtime=98 };

        dc.Movies.InsertOnSubmit(m);
        dc.SubmitChanges();
    }
```

Using Stored Procedures to Insert Data

Of course, you might already have a complex stored procedure written to handle the insertion of data into your database table. LINQ makes it simple to use an existing stored procedure to insert data into a table. To do this, on the LINQ to SQL design surface, select the entity you want to insert data into, which in this case is the Movies entity. After selecting the entity, open its properties window and locate the Default Methods section, as shown in Figure 9-14.

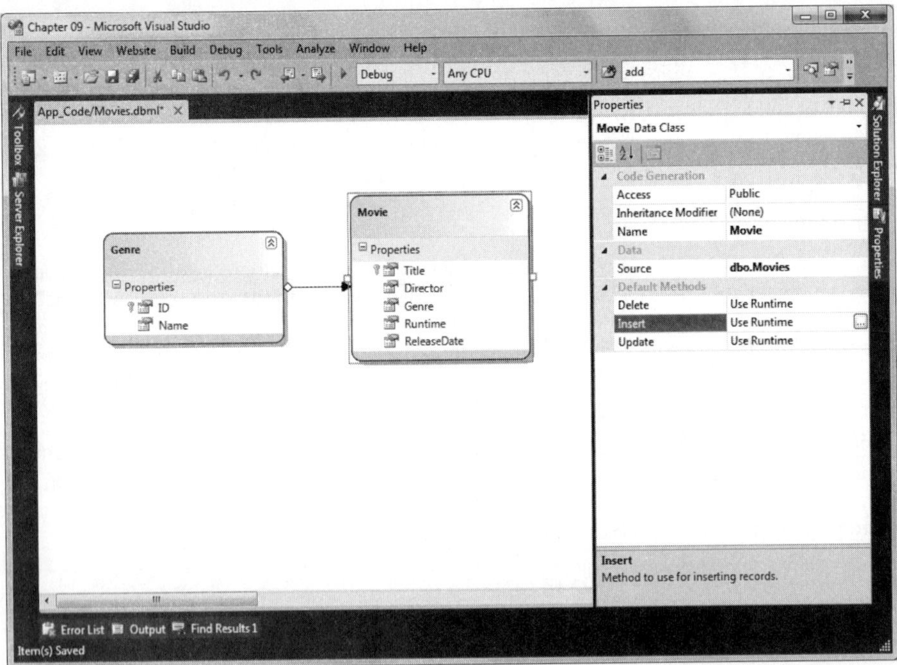

FIGURE 9-14

The Default Methods section contains three properties, Delete, Insert, and Update, which define the behavior LINQ should use when executing these actions on the Movies table. By default, each property is set to the value `UseRuntime`, which tells LINQ to dynamically generate SQL statements at runtime. Because you want to insert data into the table using a stored procedure, open the Insert properties Configure Behavior dialog.

In the dialog, change the Behavior radio button selection from Use Runtime to Customize. Next, select the appropriate stored procedure from the drop-down list below the radio buttons. When you select the stored procedure, LINQ automatically tries to match the table columns to the stored procedure input parameters. However, you can change these manually, if needed.

The final Configure Behavior dialog is shown in Figure 9-15.

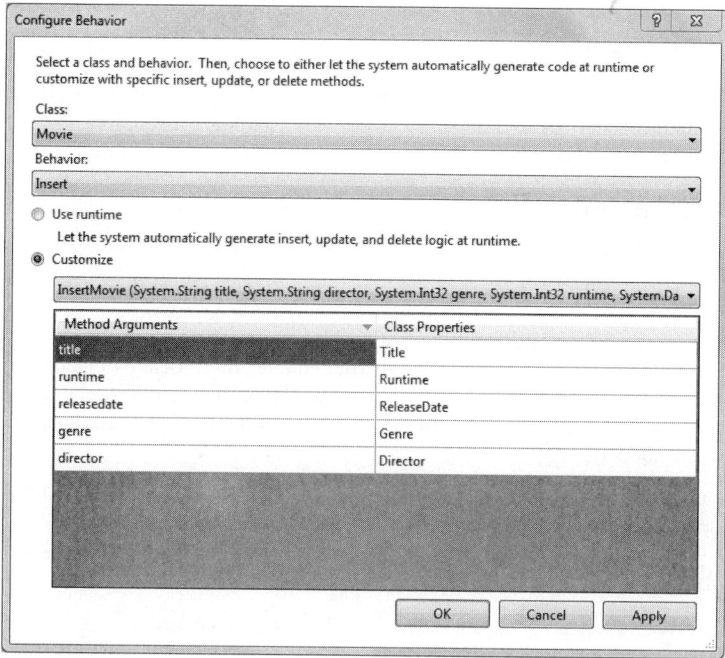

FIGURE 9-15

Now, when you run the code from Listing 9-30, LINQ will use the stored procedure you configured instead of dynamically generating a SQL Insert statement.

Updating Data Using LINQ

Updating data with LINQ is very similar to inserting data. The first step is to get the specific object you want to update. You can do this by using the `Single` method of the collection you want to change. The scalar `Single` method returns a single object from the collection based on its input parameter. If more than one record matches the parameters, the `Single` method simply returns the first match.

After you have the record you want to update, you simply change the object's property values and then call the data context's `SubmitChanges` method. Listing 9-31 shows the code required to update a specific movie.

Available for download on Wrox.com

LISTING 9-31: Updating data using LINQ to SQL

VB

```
Protected Sub Page_Load(ByVal sender As Object, ByVal e As System.EventArgs)
    Dim dc As New MoviesDataContext()

    Dim movie = dc.Movies.Single(Function(m) m.Title = "Fletch")
    movie.Genre = 1

    dc.SubmitChanges()
End Sub
```

C#

```
protected void Page_Load(object sender, EventArgs e)
{
    MoviesDataContext dc = new MoviesDataContext();

    var movie = dc.Movies.Single(m => m.Title == "Fletch");
    movie.Genre = 1;

    dc.SubmitChanges();
}
```

> **HANDLING DATA CONCURRENCY**
>
> LINQ to SQL also includes and uses by default optimistic concurrency. That means that if two users retrieve the same record from the database and both try to update it, the first user to submit his or her update to the server wins. If the second user attempts to update the record after the first, LINQ to SQL will detect that the original record has changed and will raise a ChangeConflictException.

Deleting Data Using LINQ

Finally, LINQ to SQL also enables you to delete data from your SQL data source. Each data class object generated by the LINQ to SQL designer also includes two methods that enable you to delete objects from the collection, the `DeleteOnSubmit` and `DeleteAllOnSubmit` methods. As the names imply, the `DeleteOnSubmit` method removes a single object from the collection, whereas the `DeleteAllOnSubmit` method removes all records from the collection.

Listing 9-32 shows how you can use LINQ and the `DeleteOnSubmit` and `DeleteAllOnSubmit` methods to delete data from your data source.

LISTING 9-32: Deleting data using LINQ to SQL

Available for download on Wrox.com

VB

```
Protected Sub Page_Load(ByVal sender As Object, ByVal e As System.EventArgs)
    Dim dc As New MoviesDataContext()

    'Select and remove all Action movies
    Dim query = From m In dc.Movies _
                Where (m.Genre = 2) _
                Select m

    dc.Movies.DeleteAllOnSubmit(query)

    'Select a single movie and remove it
    Dim movie = dc.Movies.Single(Function(m) m.Title = "Fletch")
    dc.Movies.DeleteOnSubmit(movie)

    dc.SubmitChanges()
End Sub
```

C#

```
protected void Page_Load(object sender, EventArgs e)
{
    MoviesDataContext dc = new MoviesDataContext();

    //Select and remove all Action movies
    var query = from m in dc.Movies
                where m.Genre == 2
                select m;

    dc.Movies.DeleteAllOnSubmit(query);

    //Select a single movie and remove it
    var movie = dc.Movies.Single(m => m.Title == "Fletch");
    dc.Movies.DeleteOnSubmit(movie);

    dc.SubmitChanges();
}
```

As with the other SQL commands, you must remember to call the data context's `SubmitChanges` method in order to commit the changes back to the SQL data source.

Extending LINQ

This chapter focuses primarily on the LINQ capabilities included in the .NET Framework, but LINQ is highly extensible and can be used to create query frameworks over just about any data source. Although showing you how to implement your own LINQ provider is beyond the scope of this chapter, lots of implementations of LINQ query a wide variety of data stores such as LDAP, Sharepoint, and even Amazon.com.

Roger Jennings from Oakleaf Systems maintains a list of third-party LINQ providers on his blog at `http://oakleafblog.blogspot.com/2007/03/third-party-linq-providers.html`.

SUMMARY

This chapter introduced you to the Language Integrated Query, or LINQ, features of .NET 4, which greatly simplify the querying of data in .NET. LINQ makes the query a first-class concept, embedded directly in .NET.

This review of LINQ presented the current methods for performing object queries, including basic data filtering, grouping, and sorting. You discovered the shortcomings of traditional object query techniques, including the requirement for developers to define not only what the query should do, but also exactly how it should do it. Additionally, you saw how even simple operations can result in highly complex code that can be difficult to read and maintain.

LINQ has three basic types: LINQ to Objects, LINQ to XML, and LINQ to SQL. Each flavor of LINQ uses the same basic query syntax to dramatically simplify the querying of objects, XML, or SQL. You can use the basic SQL-like query syntax for selection, filtering, and grouping. This query syntax is clean and easily readable, and also includes many of the same operator features as SQL.

The basic O/R mapper that is included with LINQ to SQL makes creating CLR objects that represent SQL structures, such as tables, views, and stored procedures, easy. After the CLR objects are created, you can use LINQ to query the objects.

Using LINQ to SQL, you can easily change the data in your database, using generated SQL statements or using custom stored procedures.

10

Working with XML and LINQ to XML

WHAT'S IN THIS CHAPTER?

- The Basics of XML
- XmlReader and XmlWriter
- XmlDocument and XPathDocument
- Creating XML with LINQ for XML
- XSLT
- Databases and XML

This is not a book about XML, the eXtensible Markup Language, but XML has become such a part of an ASP.NET programmer's life that the topic deserves its own chapter. Although most of the XML functionality in the .NET Framework appears to be in the `System.Xml` namespace, you can find XML's influence throughout the entire framework, including `System.Data` and `System.Web`.

XML is oft maligned and misunderstood. To some, XML is simply a text-based markup language; to others, it is an object serialization format or a document-encoding standard. In fact, XML has become the de facto standard manner in which data passes around the Internet. XML, however, is not really a technology as much as it is a set of standards or guiding principles. It provides a structure within which data can be stored, but the XML specification doesn't dictate how XML processors, parsers, formatters, and data access methods should be written or implemented. `System.Xml`, `System.Xml.Linq`, and other namespaces contain the .NET Framework view on how programmers should manipulate XML. Some of its techniques, such as XSLT and XML Schema, are standards-based. Others, like `XmlReader` and `XmlWriter`, started in the world of the .NET Framework, and now Java has similar classes. The .NET Framework 3.5 and above brings LINQ and LINQ to XML as a Language-Integrated Query over XML to the table.

This is an ASP.NET book, aimed at the professional Web developer, so it can't be a book all about LINQ. However, a single chapter can't do LINQ justice. Rather than making this a chapter that focuses exclusively on just `System.Xml` or `System.Xml.Linq`, this chapter presents the LINQ model and syntax as a juxtaposition to the way you're used to manipulating XML. The examples include both the traditional and the new LINQ way of doing things. We recognize that you won't go and rewrite all your `System.Xml` code to use LINQ just because it's cool, but seeing the new syntax alongside what you are used to is an excellent way to learn the syntax, and it also assists you in making decisions on which technology to use going forward.

In this chapter some listings include a "q" in the numbering scheme. These listings demonstrate how you can use LINQ to XML to accomplish the same task shown in the previous related listing. For example, Listing 10-5q shows the way you would accomplish the task from Listing 10-5 using LINQ to XML.

You learned about LINQ and its flexibility in Chapter 9. For the purposes of this chapter, know that `System.Xml.Linq` introduces a series of objects such as XDocument and XElement that in some ways complement the existing APIs, but in many ways eclipse them. You'll also see how these classes have provided "bridges" back and forth between `System.Xml` and `System.Xml.Linq` that will enable you to use many new techniques for clearer, simpler code, while still utilizing the very useful, powerful, and well-tested features of the `System.Xml` classes you're used to.

Ultimately, however, remember that although the .NET Framework has its own unique style of API around the uses of XML, the XML consumed and produced by these techniques is standards-based and can be used by other languages that consume XML. This chapter covers all the major techniques for manipulating XML provided by the .NET Framework. `XmlReader` and `XmlWriter` offer incredible speed but may require a bit more thought. The XmlDocument, or DOM, is the most commonly used method for manipulating XML, but you'll pay dearly in performance penalties without careful use. ADO.NET DataSets have always provided XML support, and their deep support continues with .NET 4. XML Stylesheet Tree Transformations (XSLT) gained debugging capabilities in Visual Studio 2005, and improved with new features in Visual Studio 2008 and beyond, such as XSLT Data Breakpoints and better support in the editor for loading large documents. Visual Studio 2010 includes an amazing new XSD visual editor (which you can see pictured later in the chapter in Figure 10-3) that really enables a "big-picture view" of complex schemas. Additionally, XSLT stylesheets can be compiled into assemblies even more easily with the command-line stylesheet compiler. ASP.NET continues to make development easier with some simple yet powerful server controls to manipulate XML.

Its flexibility and room for innovation make XML very powerful and a joy to work with.

Note that when the acronym XML appears by itself, the whole acronym is capitalized, but when it appears in a function name or namespace, only the X is capitalized, as in `System.Xml` *or* `XmlTextReader`*. Microsoft's API Design Guidelines dictate that if an abbreviation of three or more characters appears in a variable name, class name, or namespace, the first character is capitalized.*

THE BASICS OF XML

Listing 10-1, a `Books.xml` document that represents a bookstore's inventory database, is one of the sample documents used in this chapter. This sample document has been used in various MSDN examples for many years.

LISTING 10-1: The Books.xml XML document

Available for download on Wrox.com

```
<?xml version='1.0'?>
<!-- This file is a part of a book store inventory database -->
<bookstore xmlns="http://example.books.com">
    <book genre="autobiography" publicationdate="1981" ISBN="1-861003-11-0">
        <title>The Autobiography of Benjamin Franklin</title>
```

```
        <author>
            <first-name>Benjamin</first-name>
            <last-name>Franklin</last-name>
        </author>
        <price>8.99</price>
    </book>
    <book genre="novel" publicationdate="1967" ISBN="0-201-63361-2">
        <title>The Confidence Man</title>
        <author>
            <first-name>Herman</first-name>
            <last-name>Melville</last-name>
        </author>
        <price>11.99</price>
    </book>
    <book genre="philosophy" publicationdate="1991" ISBN="1-861001-57-6">
        <title>The Gorgias</title>
        <author>
            <first-name>Sidas</first-name>
            <last-name>Plato</last-name>
        </author>
        <price>9.99</price>
    </book>
</bookstore>
```

The first line of Listing 10-1, starting with `<?xml version='1.0'?>`, is an XML declaration. This line should always appear before the first element in the XML document and indicates the version of XML with which this document is compliant.

The second line is an XML comment and uses the same syntax as an HTML comment. This isn't a coincidence; remember that XML and HTML are both descendants of SGML, the Standard Generalized Markup Language. Comments are always optional in XML documents.

The third line, `<bookstore>`, is the opening tag of the root element or document entity of the XML document. An XML document can have only one root element. The last line in the document is the closing tag `</bookstore>` of the root element. No elements of the document can appear after the final closing tag `</bookstore>`. The `<bookstore>` element contains an `xmlns` attribute such as `xmlns="http://example.books.com"`. Namespaces in XML are similar to namespaces in the .NET Framework because they provide *qualification of elements and attributes*. It's very likely that someone else in the world has created a bookstore XML document before, and it's also likely he or she chose an element such as `<book>` or `<bookstore/>`. A namespace is defined to make your `<book>` element different from any others and to deal with the chance that other `<book>` elements might appear with yours in the same document — it's possible with XML.

This namespace is often a URL (Uniform/Universal Resource Locator), but it actually can be a URI (Uniform/Universal Resource Identifier). A namespace can be a GUID or a nonsense string such as `www-computerzen-com:schema` as long as it is unique. Recently, the convention has been to use a URL because URLs are ostensibly unique, thus making the document's associated schema unique. You'll find out more about schemas and namespaces in the next section.

The fourth line is a little different because the `<book>` element contains some additional attributes such as `genre`, `publicationdate`, and `ISBN`. The order of the elements matters in an XML document, but the order of the attributes does not. These attributes are said to be *on* or *contained within* the book element. Consider the following line of code:

```
<book genre="autobiography" publicationdate="1981" ISBN="1-861003-11-0">
```

Notice that every element following this line has a matching end tag, similar to the example that follows:

```
<example>This is a test</example>
```

If no matching end tag is used, the XML is not well formed; technically it isn't even XML! These next two example XML fragments are not well formed because the elements don't match up:

```
<example>This is a test

<example>This is a test</anothertag>
```

If the `<example>` element is empty, it might appear like this:

```
<example></example>
```

Alternatively, it could appear as a shortcut like this:

```
<example/>
```

The syntax is different, but the semantics are the same. The difference between the syntax and the semantics of an XML document is crucial for understanding what XML is trying to accomplish. XML documents are text files by their nature, but the information — the information set — is representable using text that isn't exact. The set of information is the same, but the actual bytes are not.

Note that attributes appear only within start tags or empty elements such as `<book genre="scifi"></book>` *or* `<book genre = "scifi" />`*. Visit the World Wide Web Consortium's (W3C) XML site at* `www.w3.org/XML/` *for more detailed information on XML.*

The XML InfoSet

The XML InfoSet is a W3C concept that describes what is and isn't significant in an XML document. The InfoSet isn't a class, a function, a namespace, or a language — the InfoSet is a concept.

Listing 10-2 describes two XML documents that are syntactically different but semantically the same.

LISTING 10-2: XML syntax versus semantics

Available for download on Wrox.com

XML document

```
<?xml version='1.0'?>
<bookstore>
    <book genre="autobiography" publicationdate="1981" ISBN="1-861003-11-0">
        <title>The Autobiography of Benjamin Franklin</title>
        <author>
            <first-name>Benjamin</first-name>
            <last-name>Franklin</last-name>
        </author>
        <price></price>
    </book>
</bookstore>
```

XML document that differs in syntax, but not in semantics

```
<?xml version='1.0'?><bookstore><book genre="autobiography"
publicationdate="1981" ISBN="1-861003-11-0"><title>The Autobiography of
Benjamin Franklin</title><author><first-name>Benjamin</first-name>
<last-name>Franklin</last-name></author><price/></book></bookstore>
```

Certainly, the first document in Listing 10-2 is easier for a human to read, but the second document is just as easy for a computer to read. The second document has insignificant whitespace removed.

Notice also that the empty `<price/>` element is different in the two documents. The first uses the verbose form, whereas the second element uses the shortcut form to express an empty element. However, *both are empty elements.*

You can manipulate XML as elements and attributes. You can visualize XML as a tree of nodes. You rarely, if ever, have to worry about angle brackets or parse text yourself. A text-based differences (diff) tool would report that these two documents are different because their character representations are different. An XML-based differences tool would report (correctly) that they are the same document. Each document contains the same InfoSet.

You can run a free XML Diff Tool online at `www.deltaxml.com/free/compare/`.

XSD–XML Schema Definition

XML documents must be well formed at the very least. However, just because a document is well formed doesn't ensure that its elements are in the right order, have the right name, or are the correct data types. After creating a well-formed XML document, you should ensure that your document is also *valid*. A *valid* XML document is well formed and also has an associated XML Schema Definition (XSD) that describes what elements, simple types, and complex types are allowed in the document.

The schema for the `Books.xml` file is a glossary or vocabulary for the bookstore described in an XML Schema definition. In programming terms, an XML Schema is a type definition, whereas an XML document is an instance of that type. Listing 10-3 describes one possible XML Schema called `Books.xsd` that validates against the `Books.xml` file.

Available for download on Wrox.com

LISTING 10-3: The Books.xsd XML Schema

```
<?xml version="1.0" encoding="utf-8" ?>
<xsd:schema xmlns:xsd="http://www.w3.org/2001/XMLSchema"
xmlns:tns="http://example.books.com"
xmlns="http://example.books.com"
targetNamespace="http://example.books.com"
elementFormDefault="qualified">

    <xsd:element name="bookstore" type="bookstoreType"/>

    <xsd:complexType name="bookstoreType">
        <xsd:sequence maxOccurs="unbounded">
            <xsd:element name="book" type="bookType"/>
        </xsd:sequence>
    </xsd:complexType>

    <xsd:complexType name="bookType">
        <xsd:sequence>
            <xsd:element name="title" type="xsd:string"/>
            <xsd:element name="author" type="authorName"/>
            <xsd:element name="price" type="xsd:decimal"/>
        </xsd:sequence>
        <xsd:attribute name="genre" type="xsd:string"/>
        <xsd:attribute name="publicationdate" type="xsd:string"/>
        <xsd:attribute name="ISBN" type="xsd:string"/>
    </xsd:complexType>

    <xsd:complexType name="authorName">
        <xsd:sequence>
            <xsd:element name="first-name" type="xsd:string"/>
            <xsd:element name="last-name" type="xsd:string"/>
        </xsd:sequence>
    </xsd:complexType>
</xsd:schema>
```

The XML Schema in Listing 10-3 starts by including a series of namespace prefixes used in the schema document as attributes on the root element. The prefix `xsd:` is declared on the root element (`xmlns:xsd="http://www.w3.org/2001/XMLSchema"`) and then used on all other elements of that schema. The default namespace assumed for any elements without prefixes is described by the `xmlns` attribute like this:

```
xmlns="http://example.books.com"
```

A namespace-qualified element has a prefix such as `<xsd:element>`. The target namespace for all elements in this schema is declared with the `targetNamespace` attribute.

XML Schema can be daunting at first; but if you read each line to yourself as a *declaration*, it makes more sense. For example, the line

```
<xsd:element name="bookstore" type="bookstoreType"/>
```

declares that an element named `bookstore` has the type `bookstoreType`. Because the `targetNamespace` for the schema is `http://example.books.com`, that is the namespace of each declared type in the `Books.xsd` schema. If you refer to Listing 10-1, you see that the namespace of the `Books.xml` document is also `http://example.books.com`.

For more detailed information on XML Schema, visit the W3C's XML Schema site at `www.w3.org/XML/Schema`.

Editing XML and XML Schema in Visual Studio 2010

If you start up Visual Studio 2010 and open the `Books.xml` file into the editor, you notice immediately that the Visual Studio editor provides syntax highlighting and formats the XML document as a nicely indented tree. If you start writing a new XML element anywhere, you don't have access to IntelliSense. Even though the `http://example.books.com` namespace is the default namespace, Visual Studio 2010 has no way to find the `Books.xsd` file; it could be located anywhere. Remember that the namespace is *not* a URL. It's a URI — an identifier. Even if it were a URL, going out on the Web looking for a schema wouldn't be appropriate for the editor, or any program you write. You have to be explicit when associating XML Schema with instance documents.

Classes and methods are used to validate XML documents when you are working programmatically, but the Visual Studio editor needs a hint to find the `Book.xsd` schema. Assuming the `Books.xsd` file is in the same directory as `Books.xml`, you have three ways to inform the editor:

- Open the `Books.xsd` schema in Visual Studio in another window while the `Books.xml` file is also open.
- Include a `schemaLocation` attribute in the `Books.xml` file.

  If you open at least one XML file with the `schemaLocation` attribute set, Visual Studio uses that schema for any other open XML files that don't include the attribute.
- Add the `Books.xsd` schema to the list of schemas that Visual Studio knows about internally by adding it to the `Schemas` property in the document properties window of the `Books.xml` file. When schemas are added in this way, Visual Studio checks the document's namespace and determines whether it already knows of a schema that matches.

The `schemaLocation` attribute is in a different namespace, so include the `xmlns` namespace attribute and your chosen prefix for the schema's location, as shown in Listing 10-4.

Available for download on Wrox.com

LISTING 10-4: Updating the Books.xml file with a schemaLocation attribute

```
<?xml version='1.0'?>
<!-- This file is a part of a book store inventory database -->
<bookstore xmlns="http://example.books.com"
```

```
xmlns:xsi="http://www.w3.org/2001/XMLSchema-instance"
xsi:schemaLocation="http://example.books.com Books.xsd">
    <book genre="autobiography" publicationdate="1981" ISBN="1-861003-11-0">
        <title>The Autobiography of Benjamin Franklin</title>
        ...Rest of the XML document omitted for brevity...
```

The format for the `schemaLocation` attribute consists of pairs of strings separated by spaces, where the first string in each pair is a namespace URI and the second string is the location of the schema. The location can be relative, as shown in Listing 10-4, or it can be an `http://` URL or `file://` location.

When the `Books.xsd` schema can be located for the `Books.xml` document, Visual Studio 2010's XML Editor becomes considerably more useful. Not only does the editor underline incorrect elements with blue squiggles, it also includes tooltips and IntelliSense for the entire document, as shown in Figure 10-1.

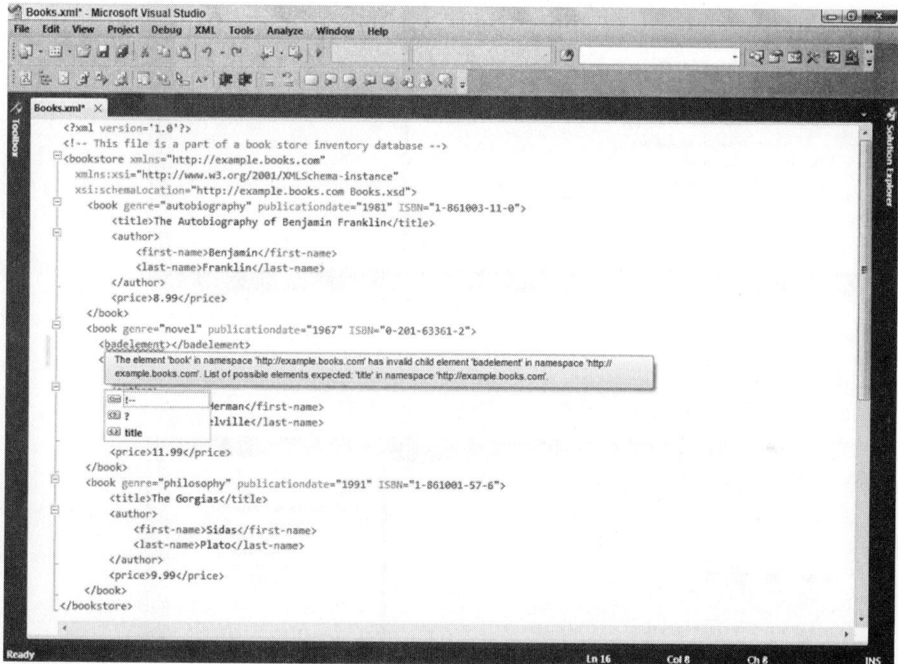

FIGURE 10-1

When the XML Schema file from Listing 10-3 is loaded into the Visual Studio Editor, the default view in Visual Studio 2010 for standard XSDs is the dramatic new XSD Editor, shown in Figure 10-2, rather than the DataSet Designer as in Visual Studio 2005. This new XSD Editor is included in Visual Studio 2010 Standard Edition and above. More and more people who work with XSDs have to work with dozens of them, and managing a large number of data types becomes difficult. The new XSD Editor introduces a number views, including Graph View and Workspace View. You can see Workspace View in Figure 10-3. Note that the complete schema set is visible in the XML Schema Explorer toolbox, and the developer can bring a subset of elements and complex types into the Workspace View for visualization.

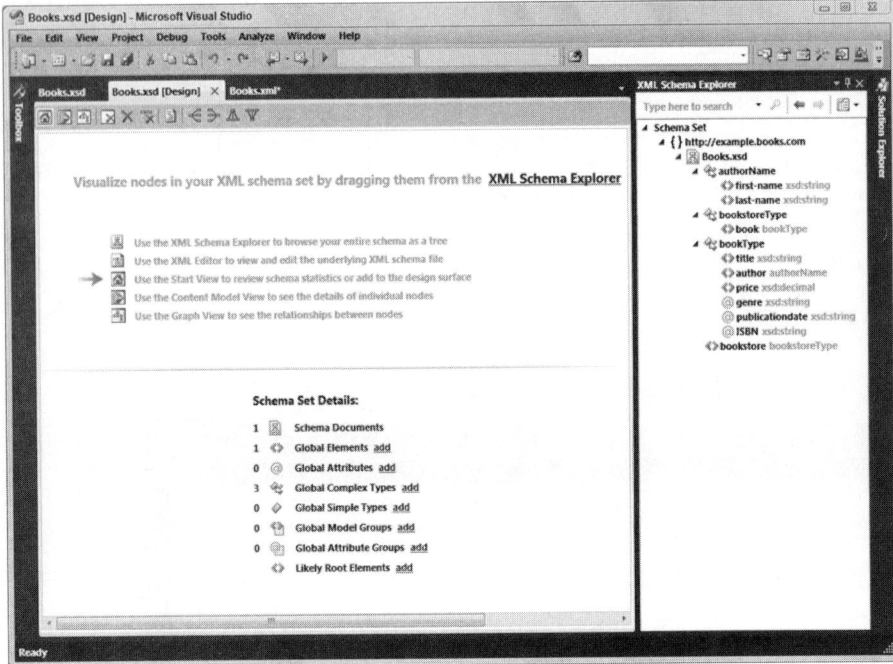

FIGURE 10-2

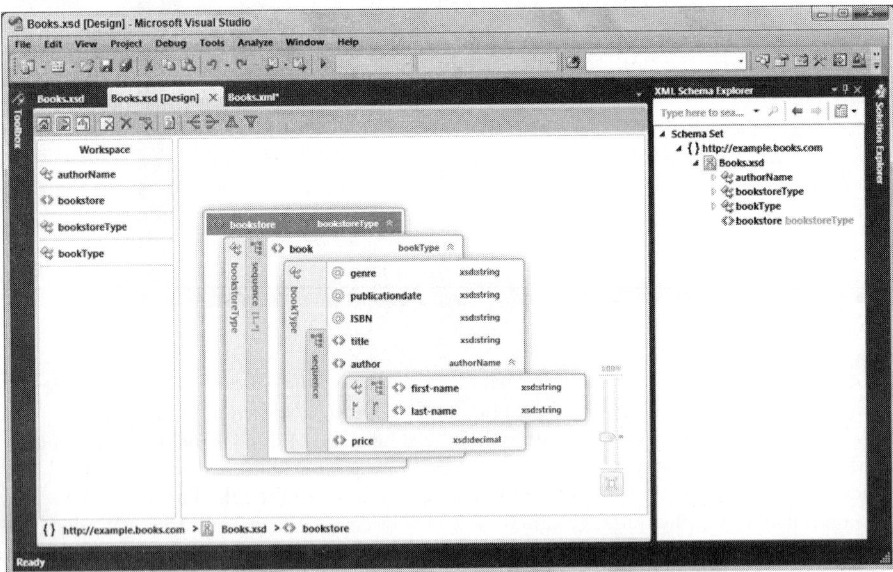

FIGURE 10-3

The Schema Explorer toolbox window presents a comprehensive tree-view of complex schemas in a much more scalable and appropriate way than can a more traditional ER-Diagram. The visualizer has been a long time coming (nearly three years) and it really is a joy to use for a large schema sets. You can connect to the team and learn more about the process of building it at `http://blogs.msdn.com/xmlteam/`.

After you have created an XML Schema that correctly describes an XML document, you're ready to start programmatically manipulating XML. The `System.Xml` and `System.Xml.Linq` namespaces provide a number of ways to create, access, and query XML. XML Schemas provide valuable typing information for all XML consumers who are type-aware.

XMLREADER AND XMLWRITER

`XmlReader` offers a *pull-style* API over an XML document that is unique to the .NET Framework. It provides fast, forward-only, read-only access to XML documents. These documents may contain elements in multiple namespaces. `XmlReader` is actually an abstract class that other classes derive from to provide specific concrete instances like `XmlTextReader` and `XmlNodeReader`.

Things changed slightly with `XmlReader` between .NET Framework 1.1 and 2.0, although nothing significant changed in the `XmlReader` and `XmlWriter` classes in .NET 3.5 and .NET 4 because most of the new functionality was around LINQ. Since .NET 1.1, several convenient new methods have been added, and the way you create `XmlReader` has changed for the better. `XmlReader` has become a factory. The primary way for you to create an instance of an `XmlReader` is by using the Static/Shared `Create` method. Rather than creating concrete implementations of the `XmlReader` class, you create an instance of the `XmlReaderSettings` class and pass it to the `Create` method. You specify the features you want for your `XmlReader` object with the `XmlReaderSettings` class. For example, you might want a specialized `XmlReader` that checks the validity of an XML document with the `IgnoreWhiteSpace` and `IgnoreComments` properties pre-set. The `Create` method of the `XmlReader` class provides you with an instance of an `XmlReader` without requiring you to decide which implementation to use. You can also add features to existing `XmlReaders` by chaining instances of the `XmlReader` class with each other because the `Create` method of `XmlReader` takes another `XmlReader` as a parameter.

If you are accustomed to using the `XmlDocument` or DOM to write an entire XML fragment or document into memory, you will find using `XmlReader` to be a very different process. A good analogy is that `XmlReader` is to `XmlDocument` what the ADO ForwardOnly recordset is to the ADO Static recordset. Remember that the ADO Static recordset loads the entire results set into memory and holds it there. Certainly, you wouldn't use a Static recordset if you want to retrieve only a few values. The same basic rules apply to the `XmlReader` class. If you're going to run through the document only once, you don't want to hold it in memory; you want the access to be as fast as possible. `XmlReader` is the right decision in this case.

Listing 10-5 creates an `XmlReader` class instance and iterates forward through it, counting the number of books in the `Books.xml` document from Listing 10-1. The `XmlReaderSettings` object specifies the features that are required, rather than the actual kind of `XmlReader` to create. In this example, `IgnoreWhitespace` and `IgnoreComments` are set to `True`. The `XmlReaderSettings` object is created with these property settings and then passed to the `Create` method of `XmlReader`.

LISTING 10-5: Processing XML with an XmlReader

Available for download on Wrox.com

VB

```
Imports System.IO
Imports System.Xml

Partial Class _Default
    Inherits System.Web.UI.Page

    Protected Sub Page_Load(ByVal sender As Object, ByVal e As System.EventArgs) _
           Handles Me.Load
        Dim bookcount As Integer = 0
        Dim settings As New XmlReaderSettings()

        settings.IgnoreWhitespace = True
        settings.IgnoreComments = True
```

continues

LISTING 10-5 *(continued)*

```
        Dim booksFile As String = Server.MapPath("books.xml")
        Using reader As XmlReader = XmlReader.Create(booksFile, settings)
            While (reader.Read())
                If (reader.NodeType = XmlNodeType.Element _
                        And "book" = reader.LocalName) Then
                    bookcount += 1
                End If
            End While
        End Using
        Response.Write(String.Format("Found {0} books!", bookcount))
    End Sub
End Class
```

C#

```
using System;
using System.IO;
using System.Xml;

public partial class _Default : System.Web.UI.Page
{
    protected void Page_Load(object sender, EventArgs e)
    {
        int bookcount = 0;
        XmlReaderSettings settings = new XmlReaderSettings();

        settings.IgnoreWhitespace = true;
        settings.IgnoreComments = true;

        string booksFile = Server.MapPath("books.xml");
        using (XmlReader reader = XmlReader.Create(booksFile, settings))
        {
            while (reader.Read())
            {
                if (reader.NodeType == XmlNodeType.Element &&
                        "book" == reader.LocalName)
                {
                    bookcount++;
                }
            }
        }
        Response.Write(String.Format("Found {0} books!", bookcount));
    }
}
```

Notice the use of the `XmlReader.Create` method in Listing 10-5. You may be used to creating concrete implementations of an `XmlReader`, but if you try this technique, you should find it much more flexible because you can reuse the `XmlReaderSettings` objects in the creation of other instances of `XmlReader`. `XmlReader` implements `IDisposable`, so the `Using` keyword is correct in both VB and C#.

In Listing 10-5, the `Books.xml` file is in the same directory as this ASPX page, so a call to `Server.MapPath` gets the complete path to the XML file. The filename with full path is then passed into `XmlReader.Create`, along with the `XmlReaderSettings` instance from a few lines earlier.

The `Read` method continues to return `true` if the node was read successfully. It will return `false` when no more nodes are left to read. From the point of view of an `XmlReader`, everything is a node, including whitespace, comments, attributes, elements, and end elements. If Listing 10-5 had simply spun through the `while` loop incrementing the `bookcount` variable each time `reader.LocalName` equaled `book`, the final value for `bookcount` would have been six. You would have counted both the beginning `book` tag and the ending `book` tag. Consequently, you have to be more explicit, and ensure that the `if` statement is modified to check not only the `LocalName` but also the `NodeType`.

The `Reader.LocalName` *property contains the non–namespace qualified name of that node. The* `Reader.Name` *property is different and contains the fully qualified name of that node, including namespace. The* `Reader.LocalName` *property is used in the example in Listing 10-5 for simplicity and ease. You find out more about namespaces a little later in the chapter.*

Using XDocument Rather Than XmlReader

The `System.Xml.Linq` namespace introduces an `XDocument` class that presents a much friendlier face than `XmlDocument` while still allowing for interoperability with `XmlReaders` and `XmlWriters`. Listing 10-5q accomplishes the same thing as Listing 10-5, but uses `XDocument` instead. The `XDocument` is loaded just like an `XmlDocument`, but the syntax for retrieving the desired elements is significantly different.

The syntax for this query is very clean, but slightly reversed from what you may be used to if you've used T-SQL. Rather than using `select . . . from`, this syntax uses the standard LINQ `from . . . select` syntax. It asks the `booksXML XDocument` for all of its `book` descendants, and they are selected into the `book` range variable. The value of all the book `title` elements is then selected into the `books` variable.

VB takes the opportunity in Visual Studio 2008 and beyond to distinguish itself considerably from C# by including a number of bits of "syntactic sugar," which makes the experience of working with Visual Basic and XML more integrated. Notice the use of the `Imports` keyword to declare an XML namespace, as well as the use of ". . . <>" to indicate the method call to `Descendants` and ".<>" to call `Elements`. This extraordinary level of XML integration with the compiler really makes working with XML in VB a joy — and this is a C# lover speaking.

LISTING 10-5q: Processing XML with an XDocument

Available for download on Wrox.com

```
Imports System.IO
Imports System.Xml
Imports System.Linq
Imports System.Xml.Linq
Imports <xmlns:b="http://example.books.com">

Partial Class _Default
    Inherits System.Web.UI.Page

    Protected Sub Page_Load(ByVal sender As Object, ByVal e As System.EventArgs) _
           Handles Me.Load

        Dim booksXML = XDocument.Load(Server.MapPath("books.xml"))
        Dim books = From book In booksXML...<b:book> Select book.<b:title>.Value

        Response.Write(String.Format("Found {0} books!", books.Count()))
    End Sub
End Class
```

```
using System;
using System.IO;
using System.Linq;
using System.Xml.Linq;

public partial class _Default : System.Web.UI.Page
{
    protected void Page_Load(object sender, EventArgs e)
    {
        XDocument booksXML = XDocument.Load(Server.MapPath("books.xml"));
```

continues

LISTING 10-5q *(continued)*

```
            var books = from book in
                        booksXML.Descendants("{http://example.books.com}book")
                        select book.Element("{http://example.books.com}title").Value;
            Response.Write(String.Format("Found {0} books!", books.Count()));
        }
    }
```

In both the C# and VB examples, advantage is taken of the implicit typing by not indicating the return type in the call to `XDocument.Descendents`. In VB, `Dim books` is used, and in C#, `var books` is used. Because this example uses the `from ... select` syntax to select the books from the `booksXml` object, the type of the variable `books` is `System.Linq.Enumerable.SelectIterator`, which is ultimately `IEnumerable`. The `count` method is added by LINQ as an extension method, allowing the retrieval of the number of books.

Notice also that the `Books.xml` document has a namespace of `http://examples.books.com`, so elements with this namespace are included in the query using the LINQ for XML format of `namespaceelement`. Later examples show the use of the `XNamespace` object to make the C# syntax slightly cleaner.

Using Schema with XmlTextReader

The code in Listing 10-5 reads any XML document regardless of its schema, and if the document contains an element named `book`, the code counts it. If this code is meant to count books of a particular schema type only, specifically the books from the `Books.xml` file, it should be validated against the `Books.xsd` schema.

Now modify the creation of the `XmlReader` class from Listing 10-5 to validate the `XmlDocument` against the XML Schema used earlier in the chapter. Note that the `XmlValidatingReader` class is now considered obsolete because all reader creation is done using the `Create` method of the `XmlReader` class.

Listing 10-6 shows a concrete example of how easy it is to add schema validation to code using `XmlReaderSettings` and the `XmlReader Create` method.

LISTING 10-6: Validating XML with an XmlReader against an XML Schema

Available for download on Wrox.com

VB

```
Imports System.Xml.Schema
Protected Sub Page_Load(ByVal sender As Object, ByVal e As System.EventArgs) _
        Handles Me.Load
    Dim bookcount As Integer = 0
    Dim settings As New XmlReaderSettings()
    Dim booksSchemaFile As String = Server.MapPath("books.xsd")
    settings.Schemas.Add(Nothing, XmlReader.Create(booksSchemaFile))
    settings.ValidationType = ValidationType.Schema
    settings.ValidationFlags = _
        XmlSchemaValidationFlags.ReportValidationWarnings
    AddHandler settings.ValidationEventHandler, _
    AddressOf settings_ValidationEventHandler
    settings.IgnoreWhitespace = True
    settings.IgnoreComments = True

    Dim booksFile As String = Server.MapPath("books.xml")
    Using reader As XmlReader = XmlReader.Create(booksFile, settings)
        While (reader.Read())
            If (reader.NodeType = XmlNodeType.Element _
                    And "book" = reader.LocalName) Then
                bookcount += 1
            End If
        End While
    End Using
    Response.Write(String.Format("Found {0} books!", bookcount))
End Sub
```

```
Sub settings_ValidationEventHandler(ByVal sender As Object, _
        ByVal e As System.Xml.Schema.ValidationEventArgs)
    Response.Write(e.Message)
End Sub
```

C#

```
using System.Xml.Schema;
protected void Page_Load(object sender, EventArgs e)
{
    int bookcount = 0;
    XmlReaderSettings settings = new XmlReaderSettings();
    string booksSchemaFile = Server.MapPath("books.xsd");
    settings.Schemas.Add(null, XmlReader.Create(booksSchemaFile));
    settings.ValidationType = ValidationType.Schema;
    settings.ValidationFlags =
    XmlSchemaValidationFlags.ReportValidationWarnings;
    settings.ValidationEventHandler +=
           new ValidationEventHandler(settings_ValidationEventHandler);
    settings.IgnoreWhitespace = true;
    settings.IgnoreComments = true;

    string booksFile = Server.MapPath( "books.xml");
    using (XmlReader reader = XmlReader.Create(booksFile, settings))
    {
        while (reader.Read())
        {
            if (reader.NodeType == XmlNodeType.Element &&
                    "book" == reader.LocalName)
            {
                bookcount++;
            }
        }
    }
    Response.Write(String.Format("Found {0} books!", bookcount));
}
void settings_ValidationEventHandler(object sender,
        System.Xml.Schema.ValidationEventArgs e)
{
    Response.Write(e.Message);
}
```

When validating XML, the validator uses the `schemaLocation` hint found in the XML instance document. If an XML instance document does not contain enough information to find an XML Schema, the instance document expects an `XmlSchemaSet` object on the `XmlReaderSettings` object. In the interest of being explicit, Listing 10-6 shows this technique. The `XmlReaderSettings` object has a `Schemas` collection available as a property and many overloads for the `Add` method. This listing passes `null` into the `Add` method as the first parameter, indicating that the `targetNamespace` is specified in the schema. Optionally, XML documents can also contain their schemas inline.

The validator needs a way to let you know when validation problems occur. The `XmlReaderSettings` object has a validation event handler that notifies you as validation events occur. Also, a handler is included for the validation event that writes the message to the browser.

Validating Against a Schema Using an XDocument

Much of `System.Xml.Linq` is "bridged" to `System.Xml` by using extension methods. For example, the `XDocument` class has an extension `Validate` method that takes a standard `System.Xml.Schema.XmlSchemaSet` as a parameter, allowing you to validate an `XDocument` against an XML Schema.

In Listing 10-6q, the `XmlSchemaSet` is loaded in the standard way, and then passed into the `XDocument`'s validate method.

LISTING 10-6q: Validating XML with a LINQ XDocument against an XML Schema

Available for download on Wrox.com

```
Imports System
Imports System.Xml
Imports System.Linq
Imports System.Xml.Linq
Imports System.Xml.Schema

Imports <xmlns:b="http://example.books.com">

Partial Class _Default
    Inherits System.Web.UI.Page

    Protected Sub Page_Load(ByVal sender As Object, ByVal e As System.EventArgs) _
           Handles Me.Load
        Dim schemas = New XmlSchemaSet()
        schemas.Add(Nothing, XmlReader.Create(Server.MapPath("books.xsd")))
        Dim booksXML = XDocument.Load(Server.MapPath("books.xml"))
        booksXML.Validate(schemas, AddressOf ValidationEventHandler, True)

        Dim books = From book In booksXML...<b:book> _
                    Select book.<b:title>.Value

        Response.Write(String.Format("Found {0} books!", books.Count()))
    End Sub

    Sub ValidationEventHandler(ByVal sender As Object, _
            ByVal e As System.Xml.Schema.ValidationEventArgs)
        Response.Write(e.Message)
    End Sub
End Class
```

C#

```
using System;
using System.Xml;
using System.Xml.Linq;
using System.Linq;
using System.Xml.Schema;

public partial class _Default : System.Web.UI.Page
{
    protected void Page_Load(object sender, EventArgs e)
    {
        string booksSchemaFile = Server.MapPath("books.xsd");
        string booksFile = Server.MapPath("books.xml");

        XmlSchemaSet schemas = new XmlSchemaSet();
        schemas.Add(null, XmlReader.Create(booksSchemaFile));
        XDocument booksXML = XDocument.Load(booksFile);
        booksXML.Validate(schemas, (senderParam, eParam) =>
                                   {
                                     Response.Write(eParam.Message);
                                   }, true);
        XNamespace ns = "http://example.books.com";
        var books = from book in booksXML.Descendants(ns + "book")
                    select book.Element(ns + "title").Value;
        Response.Write(String.Format("Found {0} books!", books.Count()));
    }
}
```

Notice the unique syntax for an anonymous event handler in the C# example in Listing 10-6q. Rather than creating a separate method and passing it into the call to `Validate`, C# 3.0 programmers can pass the method body anonymously in as a parameter to the `Validate` method. The `(param1, param2) => { method }` syntax can be a bit jarring initially, as you might not be used to seeing an equals-greater-than, but it makes for much tidier code.

Including NameTable Optimization

`XmlReader` internally uses a `NameTable` that lists all the known elements and attributes with namespaces that are used in that document. This process is called *atomization* — literally meaning that the XML document is broken up into its atomic parts. There's no need to store the string `book` more than once in the internal structure if you can make `book` an object reference that is held in a table with the names of other elements.

Although this is an internal implementation detail, it is a supported and valid way that you can measurably speed up your use of XML classes, such as `XmlReader` and `XmlDocument`. You add name elements to the `NameTable` that you know will be in the document. Listings 10-5 and 10-6 use string comparisons to compare a string literal with `reader.LocalName`. These comparisons can also be optimized by turning them into object reference comparisons that are many, many times faster. Additionally, an XML `NameTable` can be shared across multiple instances of `System.Xml` classes and even between `XmlReaders` and `XmlDocuments`. This topic is covered shortly.

Because you are counting `book` elements, create a `NameTable` including this element (`book`), and instead of comparing string against string, compare object reference against object reference, as shown in Listing 10-7.

LISTING 10-7: Optimizing XmlReader with a NameTable

Available for download on Wrox.com

VB

```
Protected Sub Page_Load(ByVal sender As Object, ByVal e As System.EventArgs) _
        Handles Me.Load
    Dim bookcount As Integer = 0
    Dim settings As New XmlReaderSettings()
    Dim nt As New NameTable()
    Dim book As Object = nt.Add("book")

    settings.NameTable = nt
    Dim booksSchemaFile As String = _
        Path.Combine(Request.PhysicalApplicationPath, "books.xsd")
    settings.Schemas.Add(Nothing, XmlReader.Create(booksSchemaFile))
    settings.ValidationType = ValidationType.Schema
    settings.ValidationFlags = _
    XmlSchemaValidationFlags.ReportValidationWarnings

    AddHandler settings.ValidationEventHandler, _

        AddressOf settings_ValidationEventHandler
    settings.IgnoreWhitespace = True
    settings.IgnoreComments = True

    Dim booksFile As String = _
    Path.Combine(Request.PhysicalApplicationPath, "books.xml")
    Using reader As XmlReader = XmlReader.Create(booksFile, settings)
        While (reader.Read())
If (reader.NodeType = XmlNodeType.Element _
      And book.Equals(reader.LocalName)) Then
     'A subtle, but significant change!
                bookcount += 1
            End If
        End While
    End Using
    Response.Write(String.Format("Found {0} books!", bookcount))
End Sub
```

continues

LISTING 10-7 *(continued)*

```
protected void Page_Load(object sender, EventArgs e)
{
    int bookcount = 0;
    XmlReaderSettings settings = new XmlReaderSettings();
     NameTable nt = new NameTable();
    object book = nt.Add("book");

    settings.NameTable = nt;
    string booksSchemaFile = Path.Combine(Request.PhysicalApplicationPath,
        "books.xsd");

    settings.Schemas.Add(null, XmlReader.Create(booksSchemaFile));
    settings.ValidationType = ValidationType.Schema;
    settings.ValidationFlags =
        XmlSchemaValidationFlags.ReportValidationWarnings;

    settings.ValidationEventHandler +=
        new ValidationEventHandler(settings_ValidationEventHandler);

    settings.IgnoreWhitespace = true;
    settings.IgnoreComments = true;

    string booksFile = Path.Combine(Request.PhysicalApplicationPath, "books.xml");
    using (XmlReader reader = XmlReader.Create(booksFile, settings))
    {
        while (reader.Read())
        {
if (reader.NodeType == XmlNodeType.Element &&
            book.Equals(reader.LocalName)) //A subtle, but significant change!
            {
                bookcount++;
            }
        }
    }
    Response.Write(String.Format("Found {0} books!", bookcount));
}
```

The `NameTable` is added to the `XmlSettings` object, and the `Add` method of the `NameTable` returns an object reference to the just-added atom that is stored, in this case, in an object reference named `book`. The `book` reference is then used later to make a comparison to the `reader.LocalName` property. We specifically chose to use the `Equals` method that is present on all objects within that .NET Framework to emphasize that this is specifically an object identity check for equality. These two objects are either the same identical atoms or they are not. The `book` object that is returned from the `Add` method on the `NameTable` is the identical object that the reader uses when parsing the `book` element from the `Books.xml` XML document.

In the example in Listing 10-7, in which you count a very small number of books, you probably won't have a measurable performance gain. However, for larger XML documents that approach sizes of 1MB, you may see performance gains of as much as 10 to 15 percent — especially for the involved calculations and manipulations of `XmlReader`. Additionally, because the `NameTable` is cached within the `XmlReaderSettings` object, that `NameTable` is reused when the `XmlReaderSettings` object is reused for other `System.Xml` objects. This creates additional potential performance gains.

Retrieving .NET CLR Types from XML

Retrieving CLR types from an `XmlReader` is considerably simpler than it was in the old days in the 1.*x* Framework. If you've used SQL Server data reader objects before, retrieving data types from `XmlReader` should feel very familiar. Previously, the framework used a helper class called `XmlConvert`. When combined with the `ReadElementString` method on `XmlReader`, this helper class retrieved a strong, simple type, as shown in the following code:

```
//Retrieving a double from an XmlReader in the .NET Framework 1.1
Double price = XmlConvert.ToDouble(reader.ReadElementString());
//Has been replaced by and improved in the .NET Framework 2.0
Double price = reader.ReadElementContentAsDouble();
```

You can see the removal of the unnecessary double method call results in much cleaner and easier-to-read code. Listing 10-8 not only adds the counting of books, but also prints the total price of all books using `ReadElementContentAs` when your `XmlReader` is currently on an element, or `ReadContentAs` if on text content. If schema information is available to the reader, `ReadElementContentAsObject` returns the value directly as, in this case, a decimal. If the reader does not have any schema information, it attempts to convert the string to a decimal. A whole series of `ReadElementContentAs` and `ReadContentAs` methods, including `ReadElementContentAsBoolean` and `ReadElementContentAsInt`, is available. Note that the code specific to `XmlSchema` has been removed from Listing 10-8 in the interest of brevity.

LISTING 10-8: Using XmlReader.ReadElementContentAs

Available for download on Wrox.com

VB

```
Dim bookcount As Integer = 0
Dim booktotal As Decimal = 0
Dim settings As New XmlReaderSettings()
Dim nt As New NameTable()
Dim book As Object = nt.Add("book")
Dim price As Object = nt.Add("price")
settings.NameTable = nt

Dim booksFile As String = _
Path.Combine(Request.PhysicalApplicationPath, "books.xml")
Using reader As XmlReader = XmlReader.Create(booksFile, settings)
    While (reader.Read())
        If (reader.NodeType = XmlNodeType.Element _
            And book.Equals(reader.LocalName)) Then
            bookcount += 1
        End If
        If (reader.NodeType = XmlNodeType.Element _
           And price.Equals(reader.LocalName)) Then
           booktotal += reader.ReadElementContentAsDecimal()
        End If
    End While
End Using
Response.Write(String.Format("Found {0} books that total {1:C}!", _
    bookcount, booktotal))
```

C#

```
int bookcount = 0;
decimal booktotal = 0;
XmlReaderSettings settings = new XmlReaderSettings();
string booksSchemaFile = Path.Combine(Request.PhysicalApplicationPath,
                         "books.xsd");
NameTable nt = new NameTable();
object book = nt.Add("book");
object price = nt.Add("price");
settings.NameTable = nt;

string booksFile = Path.Combine(Request.PhysicalApplicationPath, "books.xml");

using (XmlReader reader = XmlReader.Create(booksFile, settings))
{
    while (reader.Read())
    {
        if (reader.NodeType == XmlNodeType.Element &&
            book.Equals(reader.LocalName))//A subtle, but significant change!
        {
            bookcount++;
        }
```

continues

LISTING 10-8 *(continued)*

```
if (reader.NodeType == XmlNodeType.Element &&
        price.Equals(reader.LocalName))
        {
            booktotal +=
                reader.ReadElementContentAsDecimal ();
        }
    }
}

Response.Write(String.Format("Found {0} books that total {1:C}!",
    bookcount, booktotal));
```

The booktotal variable from Listing 10-8 is strongly typed as a decimal so that, in the String.Format call, it can be formatted as currency using the formatting string { 1:C }. This results in output from the browser similar to the following:

```
Found 3 books that total $30.97!
```

ReadSubtree and XmlSerialization

Not only does XmlReader help you retrieve simple types from XML, it can also help you retrieve more complicated types using XML serialization and ReadSubtree.

XML serialization allows you to add attributes to an existing class that give hints to the XML serialization on how to represent an object as XML. XML serialization serializes only the public properties of an object, not the private ones.

When you create an XmlSerializer, a Type object is passed into the constructor, and the XmlSerializer uses reflection to examine whether the object can create a temporary assembly that knows how to read and write this particular object as XML. The XmlSerializer uses a concrete implementation of XmlReader internally to serialize these objects.

Instead of retrieving the author's first name and last name using XmlReader.ReadAsString, Listing 10-10 uses ReadSubtree and a new strongly typed Author class that has been marked up with XML serialization attributes, as shown in Listing 10-9. ReadSubtree "breaks off" a new XmlReader at the current location, that XmlReader is passed to an XmlSerializer, and a complex type is created. The Author class includes XmlElement attributes that indicate, for example, that although there is a property called FirstName, it should be serialized and deserialized as "first-name."

LISTING 10-9: An Author class with XML serialization attributes matching Books.xsd

Available for download on Wrox.com

VB

```
Imports System.Xml.Serialization
<XmlRoot(ElementName:="author", _
Namespace:="http://example.books.com")> Public Class Author
    <XmlElement(ElementName:="first-name")> Public FirstName As String
    <XmlElement(ElementName:="last-name")> Public LastName As String
End Class
```

C#

```
using System.Xml.Serialization;
[XmlRoot(ElementName = "author", Namespace = "http://example.books.com")]
public class Author
{
    [XmlElement(ElementName = "first-name")]
    public string FirstName;

    [XmlElement(ElementName = "last-name")]
    public string LastName;
}
```

Next, this Author class is used along with XmlReader.ReadSubtree and XmlSerializer to output the names of each book's author. Listing 10-10 shows just the additional statements added to the While loop.

LISTING 10-10: Reading author instances from an XmlReader using XmlSerialization

Available for download on Wrox.com

```
'Create factory early
Dim factory As New XmlSerializerFactory
Using reader As XmlReader = XmlReader.Create(booksFile, settings)
    While (reader.Read())
        If (reader.NodeType = XmlNodeType.Element _
           And author.Equals(reader.LocalName)) Then

           'Then use the factory to create and cache serializers
           Dim xs As XmlSerializer = factory.CreateSerializer(GetType(Author))
           Dim a As Author = CType(xs.Deserialize(reader.ReadSubtree), Author)
           Response.Write(String.Format("Author: {1}, {0}<BR/>", _
              a.FirstName, a.LastName))
        End If
    End While
End Using
```

C#

```
//Create factory early
XmlSerializerFactory factory = new XmlSerializerFactory();

using (XmlReader reader = XmlReader.Create(booksFile, settings))
{
    while (reader.Read())
    {
        if (reader.NodeType == XmlNodeType.Element &&
              author.Equals(reader.LocalName))
        {
            //Then use the factory to create and cache serializers
            XmlSerializer xs = factory.CreateSerializer(typeof(Author));
            Author a = (Author)xs.Deserialize(reader.ReadSubtree());
            Response.Write(String.Format("Author: {1}, {0}<BR/>",
                a.FirstName, a.LastName));
        }
    }
}
```

The only other addition to the code, as you can guess, is the author object atom (used only in the Equals statement) that is added to the NameTable just as the book and price were, via Dim author As Object = nt.Add("author").

When you create an XmlSerializer instance for a specific type, the framework uses reflection to create a temporary type-specific assembly to handle serialization and deserialization. The .NET Framework 2.0 introduced a new XmlSerializerFactory that automatically handles caching of these temporary assemblies. This small factory provides an important layer of abstraction that allows you to structure your code in a way that is convenient without worrying about creating XmlSerializer instances ahead of time.

Creating CLR Objects from XML with LINQ to XML

Although a direct bridge doesn't exist between the XmlSerializer and System.Xml.Linq, a very clean way does exist for creating CLR objects within the LINQ to XML syntax. This syntax can also be a little more flexible and more forgiving than the traditional XmlSerializer, as shown in Listing 10-10q.

LISTING 10-10q: Reading author instances via LINQ to XML

Available for download on Wrox.com

```
Dim booksXML = XDocument.Load(Server.MapPath("books.xml"))

Dim authors = From book In booksXML...<books:book> Select New Author _
    With {.FirstName = book.<books:author>.<books:first-name>.Value, _
          .LastName = book.<books:author>.<books:last-name>.Value}

    For Each a As Author In authors
    Response.Write(String.Format("Author: {1}, {0}<BR/>", a.FirstName, a.LastName))
Next
```

C#

```
XDocument booksXML = XDocument.Load(Server.MapPath("books.xml"));
XNamespace ns = "http://example.books.com";

var authors = from book in booksXML.Descendants(ns + "author")
              select new Author
              {
                  FirstName = book.Element(ns + "first-name").Value,
                  LastName = book.Element(ns + "last-name").Value
              };
foreach (Author a in authors)
{
    Response.Write(String.Format("Author: {1}, {0}<BR/>",
                   a.FirstName, a.LastName));
}
```

Again, note the unique syntax in the VB example, where "..." is used rather than "descendants." On the C# side, notice how cleanly a new `Author` object is created with the `select new` syntax, and within the curly braces that the new `Author` object has its property values copied over from the XML elements. The VB example assumes the same namespace `Imports` statement as shown earlier in the chapter in Listing 10-6q.

Creating XML with XmlWriter

`XmlWriter` works exactly like `XmlReader` except in reverse. Using string concatenation to quickly create XML documents or fragments of XML is very tempting, but you should resist the urge! Remember that the whole point of XML is the representation of the InfoSet, not the angle brackets. If you concatenate string literals together with `StringBuilder` to create XML, you are dropping below the level of the InfoSet to the implementation details of the format. Tell yourself that XML documents are not strings!

Most people find it helpful (as a visualization tool) to indent the method calls to the `XmlWriter` with the same structure as the resulting XML document. However, VB in Visual Studio is much more aggressive than C# in keeping the code indented a specific way. It does not allow this kind of artificial indentation unless Smart Indenting is changed to either Block or None by using Tools ➪ Options ➪ Text Editor ➪ Basic ➪ Tabs.

`XmlWriter` also has a settings class called, obviously, `XmlWriterSettings`. This class has options for indentation, new lines, encoding, and XML conformance level. Listing 10-11 uses `XmlWriter` to create a `bookstore` XML document and output it directly to the ASP.NET `Response.OutputStream`. All the HTML tags in the ASPX page must be removed for the XML document to be output correctly. Another way to output XML easily is with an ASHX `HttpHandler`.

The unusual indenting in Listing 10-11 is significant and very common when using `XmlWriter`. It helps the programmer visualize the hierarchical structure of an XML document.

LISTING 10-11: Writing out a bookstore with XmlWriter

Available for download on Wrox.com

Default.aspx—C#

```
<%@ Page Language="C#" codefile="Default.aspx.cs" Inherits="Default_aspx" %>
```

Default.aspx—VB

```
<%@ Page Language="VB" codefile="Default.aspx.vb" Inherits="Default_aspx" %>
```

VB

```
Protected Sub Page_Load(ByVal sender As Object, ByVal e As System.EventArgs) _
Handles Me.Load

Dim price As Double = 49.99
Dim publicationdate As New DateTime(2005, 1, 1)
Dim isbn As String = "1-057-610-0"
Dim a As New Author()
a.FirstName = "Scott"
a.LastName = "Hanselman"

Dim settings As New XmlWriterSettings()
settings.Indent = True
settings.NewLineOnAttributes = True

Response.ContentType = "text/xml"

Dim factory As New XmlSerializerFactory()

Using writer As XmlWriter = XmlWriter.Create(Response.OutputStream, settings)

    'Note the artificial, but useful, indenting
    writer.WriteStartDocument()
        writer.WriteStartElement("bookstore")
            writer.WriteStartElement("book")
                writer.WriteStartAttribute("publicationdate")
                    writer.WriteValue(publicationdate)
                writer.WriteEndAttribute()
                writer.WriteStartAttribute("ISBN")
                    writer.WriteValue(isbn)
                writer.WriteEndAttribute()
                writer.WriteElementString("title", "ASP.NET 2.0")
                writer.WriteStartElement("price")
                    writer.WriteValue(price)
                writer.WriteEndElement() 'price
                Dim xs As XmlSerializer = _
                    factory.CreateSerializer(GetType(Author))
                xs.Serialize(writer, a)
            writer.WriteEndElement() 'book
        writer.WriteEndElement() 'bookstore
    writer.WriteEndDocument()
End Using

End Sub
```

```
protected void Page_Load(object sender, EventArgs e)
{
Double price = 49.99;
DateTime publicationdate = new DateTime(2005, 1, 1);
String isbn = "1-057-610-0";
```

continues

LISTING 10-11 *(continued)*

```
Author a = new Author();
a.FirstName = "Scott";
a.LastName = "Hanselman";

XmlWriterSettings settings = new XmlWriterSettings();
settings.Indent = true;
settings.NewLineOnAttributes = true;

Response.ContentType = "text/xml";

XmlSerializerFactory factory = new XmlSerializerFactory();

using (XmlWriter writer =
        XmlWriter.Create(Response.OutputStream, settings))
{
    //Note the artificial, but useful, indenting
    writer.WriteStartDocument();
        writer.WriteStartElement("bookstore");
            writer.WriteStartElement("book");
                writer.WriteStartAttribute("publicationdate");
                    writer.WriteValue(publicationdate);
                writer.WriteEndAttribute();
                writer.WriteStartAttribute("ISBN");
                    writer.WriteValue(isbn);
                writer.WriteEndAttribute();
                writer.WriteElementString("title", "ASP.NET 2.0");
                writer.WriteStartElement("price");
                    writer.WriteValue(price);
                writer.WriteEndElement(); //price
                XmlSerializer xs = factory.CreateSerializer(typeof(Author));
                xs.Serialize(writer, a);
            writer.WriteEndElement(); //book
        writer.WriteEndElement(); //bookstore
    writer.WriteEndDocument();
}

}
```

The `Response.ContentType` in Listing 10-11 is set to `"text/xml"` to indicate to Internet Explorer that the result is XML. An `XmlSerializer` is created in the middle of the process and serialized directly to `XmlWriter`. The `XmlWriterSettings.Indent` property includes indentation that makes the resulting XML document more palatable for human consumption. Setting both this property and `NewLineOnAttributes` to `false` results in a smaller, more compact document.

Creating XML with LINQ for XML

Listing 10-11q accomplishes the same thing as Listing 10-11 but with LINQ for XML. It won't be as lightening fast as `XmlWriter`, but it will still be extremely fast and it is very easy to read.

Notice the dramatic difference between the VB and C# examples. The VB example uses a VB9 compiler feature called Xml Literals. The XML structure is typed directly in the code without any quotes. It's not a string. The compiler will turn the XML literal into a tree of XElements similar to the syntax used in the C# example. The underlying LINQ to XML technology is the same — only the syntax differs. One syntax thing to note in the VB example is the exclusion of double quotes around the attributes for `publicationdate` and `ISBN`. The quotes are considered part of the serialization format of the attribute value and they will be added automatically for you when the final XML is created.

LISTING 10-11q: Writing out a bookstore with XElement trees

Available for download on Wrox.com

VB

```
Imports System.Xml
Imports System.Xml.Linq

Partial Class _Default
    Inherits System.Web.UI.Page

    Protected Sub Page_Load(ByVal sender As Object, ByVal e As System.EventArgs)
      Handles Me.Load
        Dim price As Double = 49.99
        Dim publicationdate As New DateTime(2005, 1, 1)
        Dim isbn As String = "1-057-610-0"
        Dim a As New Author()
        a.FirstName = "Scott"
        a.LastName = "Hanselman"

        Response.ContentType = "text/xml"

        Dim books = <bookstore xmlns="http://examples.books.com">
                     <book publicationdate=<%= publicationdate %> ISBN=<%= isbn %>>
                            <title>ASP.NET 2.0</title>
                            <price><%= price %></price>
                            <author>
                                <first-name><%= a.FirstName %></first-name>
                                <last-name><%= a.LastName %></last-name>
                            </author>
                     </book>
                 </bookstore>

        Response.Write(books)
    End Sub
End Class
```

C#

```
using System;
using System.Xml.Linq;

public partial class _Default : System.Web.UI.Page
{
    protected void Page_Load(object sender, EventArgs e)
    {
        Double price = 49.99;
        DateTime publicationdate = new DateTime(2005, 1, 1);
        String isbn = "1-057-610-0";
        Author a = new Author();
        a.FirstName = "Scott";
        a.LastName = "Hanselman";

        Response.ContentType = "text/xml";
        XNamespace ns = "http://example.books.com";
        XDocument books = new XDocument(
            new XElement(ns + "bookstore",
                new XElement(ns + "book",
                    new XAttribute("publicationdate", publicationdate),
                    new XAttribute("ISBN", isbn),
                    new XElement(ns + "title", "ASP.NET 2.0 Book"),
                    new XElement(ns + "price", price),
                    new XElement(ns + "author",
```

continues

LISTING 10-11q *(continued)*

```
                        new XElement(ns + "first-name", a.FirstName),
                        new XElement(ns + "last-name", a.LastName)
                        )
                    )
                )
            );
        Response.Write(books);
    }
}
```

Even though the C# example appears on multiple lines, it could be all on one line because it is one single expression. The constructors for `XElement` and `XDocument` take an array of parameters that is arbitrarily long, allowing you to create an XML Document structure more declaratively. If you compare this listing to Listing 10-11, you'll notice that the indentation in the `XmlWriter` example makes the sample more readable, but doesn't affect document structure. However, with `XDocument/XElement` declarations, the document structure is expressed by how the objects are nested as they are passed into each other's constructors.

There was a "Paste XML as XLinq" feature that didn't make it into the released product but was shipped as a Sample. This add-in adds a menu item to your Visual Studio Edit Menu that will take XML from the clipboard and paste it into the editor as an XElement expression. You can find it from within Visual Studio via the Help ➪ Samples ➪ Visual C# Samples folder. The sample is called `PasteXmlAsLinq` *and can be compiled and copied to any Visual Studio AddIns folder.*

Bridging XmlSerializer and LINQ to XML

There isn't a direct bridge between `XmlSerialization` and the LINQ classes; both `XDocument` and `XElement` include a `CreateWriter` method that returns an `XmlWriter`. When that returned `XmlWriter` has its `Close` method called, all the generated XML is turned into `XElements` and added to the parent `XDocument` or `XElement`. This allows you to mix `XElements` and `XmlSerialization` techniques within a single expression. Although this could be considered an unusual use case, `XmlSerialization` happens often, and it's useful to realize how well the new and the old work together. The BCL expands with each new .NET Framework version, but the new things from .NET 4 still work great with the classes you know and love from .NET 2.0.

This C# example is the same as Listing 10-11 except it creates an Extension Class to extend `XmlSerializer` with a `SerializeAsXElement` method that returns an `XElement` containing the result of the serialization. First, the extension:

```
static class XmlSerializerExtension
{
    public static XElement SerializeAsXElement(this XmlSerializer xs, object o)
    {
        XDocument d = new XDocument();
        using (XmlWriter w = d.CreateWriter())
        {
            xs.Serialize(w, o);
        }
        XElement e = d.Root;
        e.Remove();
        return e;
    }
}
```

Notice that the class and method are `static`, and the `this` keyword refers to the class being extended, in this case `XmlSerializer`. An `XDocument` is created and an `XmlWriter` is returned. The `XmlSerializer` then serializes the object to this `XmlWriter`. Then there is a little nuance as the root element is removed from the document. This avoids cloning of the returned element during any subsequent uses within a functional construction.

Now, the extension method on the `XmlSerializer` can be called within the middle of the `XElement` functional construction, as shown here:

```
XmlSerializer xs = new XmlSerializer(typeof(Author));
XDocument books = new XDocument(
    new XElement(ns + "bookstore",
        new XElement(ns + "book",
            new XAttribute("publicationdate", publicationdate),
            new XAttribute("ISBN", isbn),
            new XElement(ns + "title", "ASP.NET 2.0 Book"),
            new XElement(ns + "price", price),
            xs.SerializeAsXElement(a)
            )
        )
    );
```

The resulting XML is identical to the output of Listing 10-11. Now you have three different ways to create XML: with a Writer, with LINQ to XML, and as a hybrid of `XmlSerialization` and LINQ. You can come up other combinations as well that maximize existing code reuse and ease of development.

Improvements for XmlReader and XmlWriter

A few helper methods and changes make using `XmlReader` and `XmlWriter` even simpler starting with .NET Framework 2.0 and continuing with .NET 4:

- `ReadSubtree`: This method reads the current node of an `XmlReader` and returns a new `XmlReader` that traverses the current node and all of its descendants. It allows you to chop off a portion of the XML InfoSet and process it separately.
- `ReadToDescendant` and `ReadToNextSibling`: These two methods provide convenient ways to advance the `XmlReader` to specific elements that appear later in the document.
- `Dispose`: `XmlReader` and `XmlWriter` both implement `IDisposable`, which means that they support the `Using` keyword. `Using`, in turn, calls `Dispose`, which calls the `Close` method. These methods are now less problematic because you no longer have to remember to call `Close` to release any resources. This simple but powerful technique has been used in the listings in this chapter.

XMLDOCUMENT AND XPATHDOCUMENT

In the .NET Framework 1.1, the `XmlDocument` was one of the most common ways to manipulate XML. It is similar to using a static ADO recordset because it parses and loads the entire `XmlDocument` into memory. Often the `XmlDocument` is the first class a programmer learns to use, and consequently, as a solution it becomes the hammer in his toolkit. Unfortunately, not every kind of XML problem is a nail. `XmlDocuments` have been known to use many times their file size in memory. Often an `XmlDocument` is referred to as the DOM or Document Object Model. The `XmlDocument` is compliant with the W3C DOM implementation and should be familiar to anyone who has used a DOM implementation.

Problems with the DOM

A number of potential problems exist with the `XmlDocument` class in the .NET Framework. The data model of the `XmlDocument` is very different from other XML query languages such as XSLT and XPath. The `XmlDocument` is editable and provides a familiar API for those who used MSXML in Visual Basic 6. Often, however, people use the XmlDocument to search for data within a larger document, but the XmlDocument isn't designed for searching large amounts of information. The XPathDocument is read-only and optimized for XPath queries or XPath-heavy technologies such as XSLT. The XPathDocument is much, much faster than the XmlDocument for loading and querying XML.

The XPathDocument is very focused around the InfoSet because it has a much-optimized internal structure. Be aware, however, that it does throw away insignificant whitespaces and CDATA sections, so it is not appropriate if you want the XPathDocument to maintain the identical number of bytes that you originally created. However, if you're focused more on the set of information that is contained within your document, you can be assured that the XPathDocument contains everything that your source document contains.

A general rule for querying data is that you should use the XPathDocument instead of the XmlDocument — except in situations where you must maintain compatibility with previous versions of the .NET Framework. The XPathDocument supports all the type information from any associated XML Schema and supports the schema validation via the Validate method. The XPathDocument lets you load XML documents to URLs, files, or streams. The XPathDocument is also the preferred class to use for the XSLT transformations covered later in this chapter.

XPath, the XPathDocument, and XmlDocument

The XPathDocument is so named because it is the most efficient way to use XPath expressions over an in-memory data structure. The XPathDocument implements the IXPathNavigable interface, allowing you to iterate over the underlying XML by providing an XPathNavigator. The XPathNavigator class differs from the XmlReader because rather than forward-only, it provides random access over your XML, similar to a read-only ADO Keyset recordset versus a forward-only recordset.

You typically want to use an XPathDocument to move around freely, forward and backward, within a document. XPathDocument is read-only, while XmlDocument allows read-write access.

The XmlDocument includes in-memory validation. Using the XmlReader, the only way to validate the XML is from a stream or file. The XmlDocument allows in-memory validation without the file or stream access using Validate(). XmlDocument also has capability to subscribe to events like NodeChanged, NodeInserting, and the like.

XPath is a query language best learned by example. You must know it to make good use of the XPathDocument. Here are some valid XPath queries that you can use with the Books.xml file. XPath is a rich language in its own right, with many dozens of functions. As such, fully exploring XPath is beyond the scope of this book, but Table 10-1 should give you a taste of what's possible.

TABLE 10-1

XPATH FUNCTION	RESULT
//book[@genre = "novel"]/title	Recursively from the root node, gets the titles of all books whose genre attribute is equal to novel
/bookstore/book[author/last-name = "Melville"]	Gets all books that are children of bookstore whose author's last name is Melville
/bookstore/book/author[last-name = "Melville"]	Gets all authors that are children of book whose last name is Melville
//book[title = "The Gorgias" or title = "The Confidence Man"]	Recursively from the root node, gets all books whose title is either The Gorgias or The Confidence Man
//title[contains(., "The")]	Gets all titles that contain the string The
//book[not(price[.>10.00])]	Gets all books whose prices are not greater than 10.00

Listing 10-12 queries an `XPathDocument` for books whose prices are less than $10.00 and outputs the price. To illustrate using built-in XPath functions, this example uses a greater-than instead of using a less-than. It then inverts the result using the built-in `not()` method. XPath includes a number of functions for string concatenation, arithmetic, and many other uses. The `XPathDocument` returns an `XPathNavigator` as a result of calling `CreateNavigator`. The `XPathNavigator` is queried using an XPath passed to the `Select` method and returns an `XPathNodeIterator`. That `XPathNodeIterator` is `foreach` enabled via `IEnumerable`. As Listing 10-12 uses a read-only `XPathDocument`, it will not update the data in memory.

LISTING 10-12: Querying XML with XPathDocument and XPathNodeIterator

Available for download on Wrox.com

VB

```
'Load document
Dim booksFile As String = Server.MapPath("books.xml")
Dim document As New XPathDocument(booksFile)
Dim nav As XPathNavigator = document.CreateNavigator()

'Add a namespace prefix that can be used in the XPath expression
Dim namespaceMgr As New XmlNamespaceManager(nav.NameTable)
namespaceMgr.AddNamespace("b", "http://example.books.com")

'All books whose price is not greater than 10.00
For Each node As XPathNavigator In nav.Select( _
        "//b:book[not(b:price[. > 10.00])]/b:price", namespaceMgr)
    Dim price As Decimal = _
        CType(node.ValueAs(GetType(Decimal)), Decimal)
    Response.Write(String.Format("Price is {0}<BR/>", _
        price))
Next
```

C#

```
//Load document
string booksFile = Server.MapPath("books.xml");

XPathDocument document = new XPathDocument(booksFile);
XPathNavigator nav = document.CreateNavigator();

//Add a namespace prefix that can be used in the XPath expression
XmlNamespaceManager namespaceMgr = new XmlNamespaceManager(nav.NameTable);
namespaceMgr.AddNamespace("b", "http://example.books.com");

//All books whose price is not greater than 10.00
foreach(XPathNavigator node in
    nav.Select("//b:book[not(b:price[. > 10.00])]/b:price",
    namespaceMgr))
{
    Decimal price = (decimal)node.ValueAs(typeof(decimal));
    Response.Write(String.Format("Price is {0}<BR/>",
        price));
}
```

If you then want to modify the underlying XML nodes, in the form of an `XPathNavigator`, you would use an `XmlDocument` instead of an `XPathDocument`. Your XPath expression evaluation may slow you down, but you will gain the capability to edit. Beware of this trade-off in performance. Most often, you will want to use the read-only `XPathDocument` whenever possible. Listing 10-13 illustrates this change with the new or changed portions appearing in bold. Additionally, now that the document is editable, the price is increased 20 percent.

LISTING 10-13: Querying and editing XML with XmlDocument and XPathNodeIterator

Available for download on Wrox.com

```
'Load document
Dim booksFile As String = Server.MapPath("books.xml")
Dim document As New XmlDocument()
document.Load(booksFile)
Dim nav As XPathNavigator = document.CreateNavigator()

'Add a namespace prefix that can be used in the XPath expression
Dim namespaceMgr As New XmlNamespaceManager(nav.NameTable)
namespaceMgr.AddNamespace("b", "http://example.books.com")
'All books whose price is not greater than 10.00
For Each node As XPathNavigator In nav.Select( _
        "//b:book[not(b:price[. > 10.00])]/b:price", namespaceMgr)
    Dim price As Decimal = CType(node.ValueAs(GetType(Decimal)), Decimal)

    node.SetTypedValue(price * CDec(1.2))
    Response.Write(String.Format("Price raised from {0} to {1}<BR/>", _
        price, _
        CType(node.ValueAs(GetType(Decimal)), Decimal)))
Next
```

C#

```
//Load document
string booksFile = Server.MapPath("books.xml");
XmlDocument document = new XmlDocument();
document.Load(booksFile);
XPathNavigator nav = document.CreateNavigator();

//Add a namespace prefix that can be used in the XPath expression
XmlNamespaceManager namespaceMgr = new XmlNamespaceManager(nav.NameTable);
namespaceMgr.AddNamespace("b", "http://example.books.com");

//All books whose price is not greater than 10.00
foreach(XPathNavigator node in
    nav.Select("//b:book[not(b:price[. > 10.00])]/b:price",
    namespaceMgr))
{
    Decimal price = (decimal)node.ValueAs(typeof(decimal));
    node.SetTypedValue(price * 1.2M);
    Response.Write(String.Format("Price inflated raised from {0} to {1}<BR/>",
        price,
        node.ValueAs(typeof(decimal))));
}
```

Listing 10-13 changes the `XPathDocument` to an `XmlDocument`, and adds a call to `XPathNavigator.SetTypedValue` to update the price of the document in memory. The resulting document could then be persisted to storage as needed. If `SetTypedValue` was instead called on the `XPathNavigator` that was returned by `XPathDocument`, a `NotSupportedException` would be thrown because the `XPathDocument` is read-only.

The `Books.xml` document loaded from disk uses `http://example.books.com` as its default namespace. Because the `Books.xsd` XML Schema is associated with the `Books.xml` document, and it assigns the default namespace to be `http://example.books.com`, the XPath must know how to resolve that namespace. Otherwise, you cannot determine whether an XPath expression with the word `book` in it refers to a book from this namespace or another book entirely. An `XmlNamespaceManager` is created, and `b` is arbitrarily used as the namespace prefix for the XPath expression.

Namespace resolution can be very confusing because it is easy to assume that your XML file is all alone in the world and that specifying a node named `book` is specific enough to enable the system to find it. However, remember that your XML documents should be thought of as living among all the XML in the world — this makes providing a qualified namespace all the more important. The `XmlNamespaceManager` in

Listings 10-12 and 10-13 is passed into the call to `Select` to associate the prefix with the appropriate namespace. Remember, the namespace is unique, not the prefix; the prefix is simply a convenience acting as an alias to the longer namespace. If you find that you're having trouble getting an XPath expression to work and no nodes are being returned, find out whether your source XML has a namespace specified and whether it matches up with a namespace in your XPath.

Using XPath with XDocuments in LINQ for XML

You can use XPath against an `XDocument` object by adding a reference to the `System.Xml.XPath` namespace via a `Using` or `Imports` statement. Adding this namespace reference to your code file's scope adds new extension methods to the `XDocument`. You'll get useful additions like `CreateNavigator` that gets you an `XPathNavigator`. You'll also get the very useful `XPathSelectElements` that is similar to the `SelectNodes` and `SelectSingleNode` methods of `System.Xml.XmlDocument`. These extension methods are part of the "bridge classes" that provide smooth integration between `System.Xml` and `System.Xml.Linq`. Consider Listing 10-12q.

LISTING 10-12q: Querying XDocuments with XPath Expressions

Available for download on Wrox.com

```
Dim booksFile As String = Server.MapPath("books.xml")
Dim document As XDocument = XDocument.Load(booksFile)

'Add a namespace prefix that can be used in the XPath expression
Dim namespaceMgr As New XmlNamespaceManager(New NameTable())
namespaceMgr.AddNamespace("b", "http://example.books.com")

'All books whose price is not greater than 10.00
Dim nodes = document.XPathSelectElements(
    "//b:book[not(b:price[. > 10.00])]/b:price", namespaceMgr)

For Each node In nodes
    Response.Write(node.Value + "<BR/>")
Next
```

```
//Load document
string booksFile = Server.MapPath("books.xml");
XDocument document = XDocument.Load(booksFile);

//Add a namespace prefix that can be used in the XPath expression.
// Note the need for a NameTable. It could be new or come from elsewhere.
XmlNamespaceManager namespaceMgr = new XmlNamespaceManager(new NameTable());
namespaceMgr.AddNamespace("b", "http://example.books.com");

var nodes = document.XPathSelectElements(
    "//b:book[not(b:price[. > 10.00])]/b:price",namespaceMgr);

//All books whose price is not greater than 10.00
foreach (var node in nodes)
{
    Response.Write(node.Value + "<BR/>");
}
```

Notice that the added method in Listing 10-12q, `XPathSelectElements`, still requires an `IXmlNamespaceResolver`, so you create a new `NameTable` and map the namespaces and prefixes explicitly via `XmlNamespaceManager`. When using XElements and simple queries, you're better off using LINQ to XML and the XElement-specific methods such as `Elements()` and `Descendants()` rather than XPath.

DATASETS

The `System.Data` namespace and `System.Xml` namespace have started mingling their functionality for some time. DataSets are a good example of how relational data and XML data meet in a hybrid class library. During the COM and XML heyday, the ADO 2.5 recordset sported the capability to persist as XML. The dramatic inclusion of XML functionality in a class library focused entirely on manipulation of relational data was a boon for developer productivity. XML could be pulled out of SQL Server and manipulated.

Persisting DataSets to XML

Classes within `System.Data` use `XmlWriter` and `XmlReader` in a number of places. Now that you're more familiar with `System.Xml` concepts, be sure to take note of the method overloads provided by the classes within `System.Data`. For example, the `DataSet.WriteXml` method has four overloads, one of which takes in `XmlWriter`. Most of the methods with `System.Data` are very pluggable with the classes from `System.Xml`. Listing 10-14 shows another way to retrieve the XML from relational data by loading a DataSet from a SQL command and writing it directly to the browser with the `Response` object's `OutputStream` property using `DataSet.WriteXml`.

LISTING 10-14: Extracting XML from a SQL Server with System.Data.DataSet

Available for download on Wrox.com

VB

```
Dim connStr As String = "Data Source=.\\SQLEXPRESS;
                         Initial Catalog=Northwind;
                         Integrated Security=SSPI;
                         "

Using conn As New SqlConnection(connStr)
    Dim command As New SqlCommand("select * from customers", conn)
    conn.Open()
    Dim ds As New DataSet()
    ds.DataSetName = "Customers"
    ds.Load(command.ExecuteReader(), LoadOption.OverwriteChanges, "Customer")
    Response.ContentType = "text/xml"
    ds.WriteXml(Response.OutputStream)
End Using
```

C#

```
string connStr = "Data Source=.\\SQLEXPRESS;
                  Initial Catalog=Northwind;
                  Integrated Security=SSPI;
                  ";

using (SqlConnection conn = new SqlConnection(connStr))
{
    SqlCommand command = new SqlCommand("select * from customers", conn);
    conn.Open();
    DataSet ds = new DataSet();
    ds.DataSetName = "Customers";
    ds.Load(command.ExecuteReader(), LoadOption.OverwriteChanges, "Customer");
    Response.ContentType = "text/xml";
    ds.WriteXml(Response.OutputStream);
}
```

DataSets have a fairly fixed format, as illustrated in this example. The root node of the document is `Customers`, which corresponds to the `DataSetName` property. DataSets contain one or more named `DataTable` objects, and the names of these `DataTables` define the wrapper element — in this case, `Customer`. The name of the `DataTable` is passed into the `load` method of the DataSet. The correlation between the DataSet's name, `DataTable`'s name, and the resulting XML is not obvious when using DataSets. The resulting XML is shown in the browser in Figure 10-4.

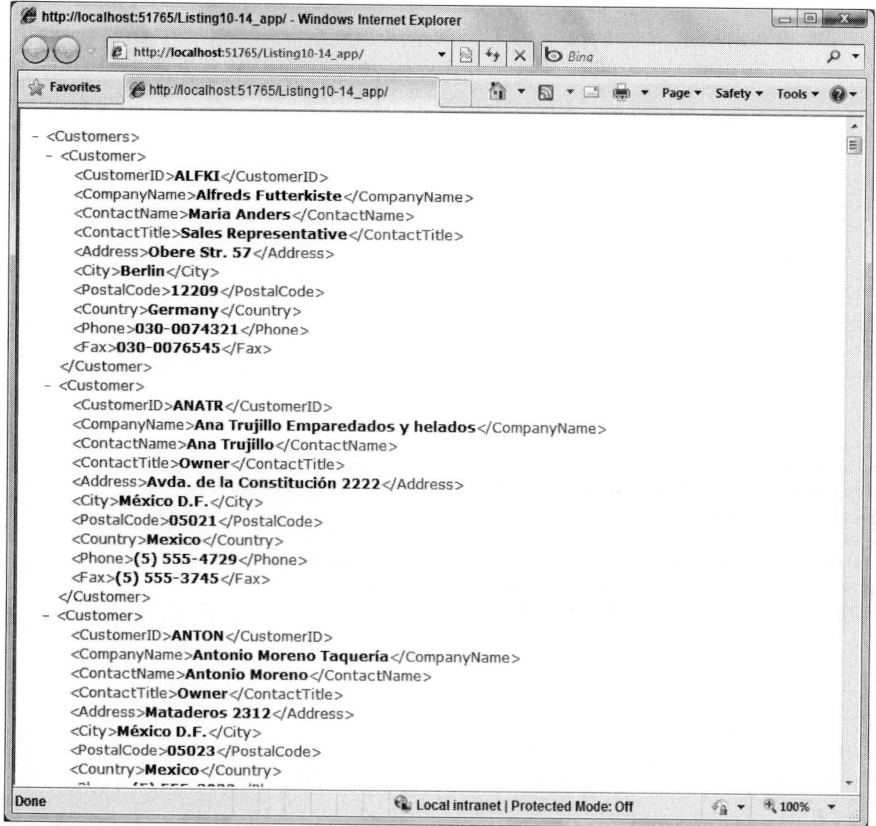

FIGURE 10-4

DataSets present a data model that is very different from the XML way of thinking about data. Much of the XML-style of thinking revolves around the InfoSet or the DOM, whereas DataSets are row- and column-based. The `XmlDataDocument` is an attempt to present these two ways of thinking in one relatively unified model.

XmlDataDocument

Although DataSets have their own relatively inflexible format for using XML, the `XmlDocument` class does not. To bridge this gap, an unusual hybrid object, the `XmlDataDocument`, is introduced. This object maintains the full fidelity of all the XML structure and allows you to access XML via the `XmlDocument` API without losing the flexibility of a relational API. An `XmlDataDocument` contains a DataSet of its own and can be called DataSet-aware. Its internal DataSet offers a relational view of the XML data. Any data contained within the XML data document that does not map into the relational view is not lost, but becomes available to the DataSet's APIs.

The `XmlDataDocument` is a constructor that takes a DataSet as a parameter. Any changes made to the `XmlDataDocument` are reflected in the DataSet and vice versa.

Now take the DataSet loaded in Listing 10-14 and manipulate the data with the `XmlDataDocument` and DOM APIs you're familiar with. Next, jump back into the world of `System.Data` and see that the DataSets underlying DataRows have been updated with the new data, as shown in Listing 10-15.

LISTING 10-15: Changing DataSets using the DOM APIs from XmlDataDocument

Available for download on Wrox.com

```
connStr As String = "Data Source=.\\SQLEXPRESS;
                         Initial Catalog=Northwind;
                         Integrated Security=SSPI;
                         "

Using conn As New SqlConnection(connStr)
    Dim command As New SqlCommand("select * from customers", conn)
    conn.Open()
    Dim ds As New DataSet()
    ds.DataSetName = "Customers"
    ds.Load(command.ExecuteReader(), LoadOption.OverwriteChanges, "Customer")
    'Response.ContentType = "text/xml"
    'ds.WriteXml(Response.OutputStream)
    'Added in Listing 10-15
    Dim doc As New XmlDataDocument(ds)
    doc.DataSet.EnforceConstraints = False
    Dim node As XmlNode = _
    doc.SelectSingleNode("//Customer[CustomerID = 'ANATR']/ContactTitle")
    node.InnerText = "Boss"
    doc.DataSet.EnforceConstraints = True
    Dim dr As DataRow = doc.GetRowFromElement(CType(node.ParentNode, XmlElement))
    Response.Write(dr("ContactName").ToString() & " is the ")
    Response.Write(dr("ContactTitle").ToString())
End Using
```

C#

```
string connStr = "Data Source=.\\SQLEXPRESS;
                  Initial Catalog=Northwind;
                  Integrated Security=SSPI;
                  ";

using (SqlConnection conn = new SqlConnection(connStr))
{
    SqlCommand command = new SqlCommand("select * from customers", conn);
    conn.Open();
    DataSet ds = new DataSet();
    ds.DataSetName = "Customers";
    ds.Load(command.ExecuteReader(), LoadOption.OverwriteChanges,"Customer");
    //Response.ContentType = "text/xml";
    //ds.WriteXml(Response.OutputStream);
    //Added in Listing 10-15
    XmlDataDocument doc = new XmlDataDocument(ds);
    doc.DataSet.EnforceConstraints = false;
    XmlNode node = doc.SelectSingleNode(@"//Customer[CustomerID
        = 'ANATR']/ContactTitle");
    node.InnerText = "Boss";
    doc.DataSet.EnforceConstraints = true;
    DataRow dr = doc.GetRowFromElement((XmlElement)node.ParentNode);
    Response.Write(dr["ContactName"].ToString() + " is the ");
    Response.Write(dr["ContactTitle"].ToString());
}
```

Listing 10-15 extends Listing 10-14 by first commenting out changing the HTTP `ContentType` and the call to `DataSet.WriteXml`. After the DataSet is loaded from the database, it is passed to the `XmlDataDocument` constructor. At this point, the `XmlDataDocument` and the DataSet refer to the same set of information. The `EnforceConstraints` property of the DataSet is set to `false` to allow changes to the DataSet. When `EnforceConstraints` is later set to `true`, if any constraint rules were broken, an exception is thrown. An `XPath` expression is passed to the DOM method `SelectSingleNode`, selecting the `ContactTitle` node of a particular customer, and its text is changed to `Boss`. Then by calling `GetRowFromElement` on the `XmlDataDocument`, the context jumps from the world of the `XmlDocument` back to the world of the DataSet. Column names are passed into the `indexing` property of the returned `DataRow`, and the output is shown in this line:

```
Ana Trujillo is the Boss
```

The data is loaded from the SQL server and then manipulated and edited with `XmlDocument`-style methods; a string is then built using a `DataRow` from the underlying DataSet.

XML is clearly more than just angle brackets. XML data can come from files, from databases, from information sets like the DataSet object, and certainly from the Web. Today, however, a considerable amount of data is stored in XML format, so a specific data source control was added to ASP.NET just for retrieving and working with XML data.

THE XMLDATASOURCE CONTROL

The `XmlDataSource` control enables you to connect to your XML data and to use this data with any of the ASP.NET data-bound controls. Just like the `SqlDataSource` and the `AccessDataSource` controls, the `XmlDataSource` control also enables you not only to retrieve data, but also to insert, delete, and update data items.

One unfortunate caveat of the `XmlDataSource` *is that its* `XPath` *attribute does not support documents that use namespace qualification. Examples in this chapter use the* `Books.xml` *file with a default namespace of* `http://examples.books.com`. *It is very common for XML files to use multiple namespaces, including a default namespace. As you learned when you created an* `XPathDocument` *and queried it with XPath, the namespace in which an element exists is very important. The regrettable reality is there is no way to use a namespace qualified XPath expression or to make the* `XmlDataSource` *control aware of a list of prefix/namespace pairs via the* `XmlNamespaceManager` *class. However, the* `XPath` *function used in the* `ItemTemplate` *of the templated* `DataList` *control can take an* `XmlNamespaceManager` *as its second parameter and query XML returned from the* `XmlDataSource` *— as long as the control does not include an* `XPath` *attribute with namespace qualification, or you can just omit it all together. That said, for these examples to work, you must remove the namespaces from your source XML and use XPath queries that include no namespace qualification, as shown in Listing 10-16.*

You can use a `DataList` control or any DataBinding-aware control and connect to an `<asp:XmlDataSource>` control. The technique for binding a control directly to the `Books.xml` file is illustrated in Listing 10-16.

Available for download on Wrox.com

LISTING 10-16: Using a DataList control to display XML content

```
<%@ Page Language="VB" AutoEventWireup="false"
CodeFile="Default.aspx.vb" Inherits="Default_aspx" %>
<html xmlns="http://www.w3.org/1999/xhtml" >
    <head id="Head1" runat="server">
        <title>XmlDataSource</title>
    </head>
```

continues

LISTING 10-16 *(continued)*

```
    <body>
    <form id="form1" runat="server">
        <asp:datalist id="DataList1" DataSourceID="XmlDataSource1" runat="server">
            <ItemTemplate>
                <p><b><%# XPath("author/first-name") %>
                    <%# XPath("author/last-name")%></b>
                    wrote <%# XPath("title") %></p>
            </ItemTemplate>
        </asp:datalist>
        <asp:xmldatasource id="XmlDataSource1" runat="server"
            datafile="~/Books.xml"
            xpath="//bookstore/book"/>
    </form>
    </body>
</html>
```

This example is simple, but it shows you the ease of using the `XmlDataSource` control. You should focus on two attributes in this example. The first is the `DataFile` attribute. This attribute points to the location of the XML file. Because the file resides in the root directory of the application, it is simply `~/Books.xml`. The next attribute included in the `XmlDataSource` control is the `XPath` attribute. The `XmlDataSource` control uses the `XPath` attribute for the filtering of XML data. In this case, the `XmlDataSource` control is taking everything within the `<book>` set of elements. The value `//bookstore/book` means that the `XmlDataSource` control navigates to the `<bookstore>` element and then to the `<book>` element within the specified XML file and returns a list of all books.

The `DataList` control then must specify its `DataSourceID` as the `XmlDataSource` control. In the `<ItemTemplate>` section of the `DataList` control, you can retrieve specific values from the XML file by using XPath commands within the template. The XPath commands filter the data from the XML file. The first value retrieved is an element attribute (`author/first-name`) that is contained in the `<book>` element. If you are retrieving an attribute of an element, you preface the name of the attribute with an *at* (`@`) symbol. The next two XPath commands get the last name and the title of the book. Remember to separate nodes with a forward slash (`/`). When run in the browser, this code produces the results illustrated in the following list:

```
Benjamin Franklin wrote The Autobiography of Benjamin Franklin

Herman Melville wrote The Confidence Man

Sidas Plato wrote The Gorgias
```

Note that if you wrote the actual code, this entire exercise would be done entirely in the ASPX page itself!

Besides working from static XML files such as the `Books.xml` file shown earlier, the `XmlDataSource` control has the capability to work from dynamic, URL-accessible XML files. One popular XML format that is pervasive on the Internet today is the *weblog*. These *blogs*, or personal diaries, can be viewed either in the browser, through an RSS-aggregator, or as pure XML.

In Figure 10-5, you can see the XML from my blog's RSS feed. I've saved the XML to a local file and removed a stylesheet so I can see what the XML looks like when viewed directly in the browser. (You can find a lot of blogs to play with for this example at `weblogs.asp.net`.)

FIGURE 10-5

Now that you know the location of the XML from the blog, you can use this XML with the `XmlDataSource` control and display some of the results in a `DataList` control. Listing 10-17 shows the code for this example.

LISTING 10-17: Displaying an XML RSS blog feed

Available for download on Wrox.com

```
<%@ Page Language="VB"%>
<html xmlns="http://www.w3.org/1999/xhtml" >
    <head runat="server">
        <title>XmlDataSource</title>
    </head>
    <body>
    <form id="form1" runat="server">
        <asp:DataList ID="DataList1" Runat="server" DataSourceID="XmlDataSource1">
            <HeaderTemplate>
                <table border="1" cellpadding="3">
            </HeaderTemplate>
            <ItemTemplate>
                <tr><td><b><%# XPath("title") %></b><br />
                <i><%# XPath("pubDate") %></i><br />
                <%# XPath("description") %></td></tr>
```

continues

LISTING 10-17 *(continued)*

```
                </ItemTemplate>
                <AlternatingItemTemplate>
                    <tr bgcolor="LightGrey"><td><b><%# XPath("title") %></b><br />
                    <i><%# XPath("pubDate") %></i><br />
                    <%# XPath("description") %></td></tr>
                </AlternatingItemTemplate>
                <FooterTemplate>
                    </table>
                </FooterTemplate>
            </asp:DataList>
            <asp:XmlDataSource ID="XmlDataSource1" Runat="server"
            DataFile="http://www.hanselman.com/blog/feed"
            XPath="rss/channel/item">
            </asp:XmlDataSource>
        </form>
        </body>
    </html>
```

Looking at the code in Listing 10-17, you can see that the `DataFile` points to a URL where the XML is retrieved. The `XPath` property filters and returns all the `<item>` elements from the RSS feed. The `DataList` control creates an HTML table and pulls out specific data elements from the RSS feed, such as the `<title>`, `<pubDate>`, and `<description>` elements.

Running this page in the browser, you get something similar to the results shown in Figure 10-6.

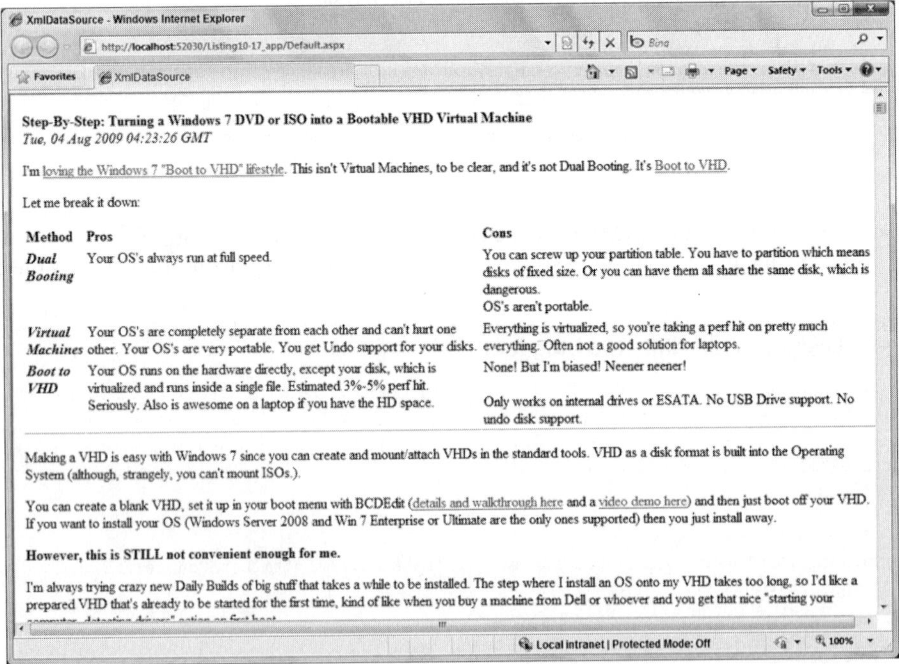

FIGURE 10-6

This approach also works with XML Web services, even ones for which you can pass in parameters using HTTP-GET. You just set up the `DataFile` property value in the following manner:

```
DataFile="http://www.someserver.com/GetWeather.asmx/ZipWeather?zipcode=63301"
```

There is no end to the number of places you can find and use XML: files, databases, Web sites, and services. Sometimes you will want to manipulate the XML via queries or programmatically, and sometimes you will want to take the XML "tree" and transform it into a tree of a different form.

XSLT

XSLT is a tree transformation language also written in XML syntax. It's a strange hybrid of a declarative and a programmatic language, and some programmers would argue that it's not a language at all. Others, who use a number of XSLT scripting extensions, would argue that it is a very powerful language. Regardless of the controversy, XSLT transformations are very useful for changing the structure of XML files quickly and easily, often using a very declarative syntax.

The best way to familiarize yourself with XSLT is to look at an example. Remember that the `Books.xml` file used in this chapter is a list of books and their authors. The XSLT in Listing 10-18 takes that document and transforms it into a document that is a list of authors.

Available for download on Wrox.com

LISTING 10-18: Books.xslt

XSLT

```
<?xml version="1.0" encoding="utf-8" ?>
<xsl:stylesheet xmlns:xsl="http://www.w3.org/1999/XSL/Transform" version="1.0">
    <xsl:template match="/">
        <xsl:element name="Authors">
            <xsl:apply-templates select="//book"/>
        </xsl:element>
    </xsl:template>
    <xsl:template match="book">
        <xsl:element name="Author">
            <xsl:value-of select="author/first-name"/>
            <xsl:text> </xsl:text>
            <xsl:value-of select="author/last-name"/>
        </xsl:element>
    </xsl:template>
</xsl:stylesheet>
```

Remember that XSLT is XML vocabulary in its own right, so it makes sense that it has its own namespace and namespace prefix. XSLT is typically structured with a series of templates that match elements in the source document. The XSLT document doesn't describe what the result looks like as much as it declares what steps must occur for the transformation to succeed. Remembering that your goal is an XML file with a list of authors, you match on the root node of `Books.xml` and output a root element for the resulting document named `<Authors>`. Then `<xsl:apply-templates select = "//book"/>` indicates to the processor that it should continue looking for templates that, in this case, match the XPath expression `//book`. Below the first template is a second template that handles all book matches. It outputs a new element named `<Author>`.

XSLT is very focused on context, so imagining a cursor that is on a particular element of the source document is often helpful. Immediately after outputting the `<Author>` element, the processor is in the middle of the template match on the `book` element. All XPath expressions in this example are relative to the `book` element. So the `<xsl:value-of select = "author/first-name">` directive searches for the author's first name relative to the `book` element. The `<xsl:text> </xsl:text>` directive is interesting to note because it is explicit and a reminder that a difference exists between significant whitespace and insignificant whitespace. It is important, for example, that a space is put between the author's first and last names, so it must be called out explicitly.

The resulting document is shown in Figure 10-7.

This example only scratches the surface of XSLT's power. Although a full exploration of XSLT is beyond the scope of this book, other books by Wrox Press cover the topic more fully. Remember that the .NET Framework implements the 1.0 implementation of XSLT. As of January 2007, XSLT 2.0 and XPath 2.0 are W3C Recommendations. However, XSLT 1.0 is still much more widely used, and the .NET Framework has decided so far to not support XSLT 2.0 in favor of other ways to query and manipulate XML.

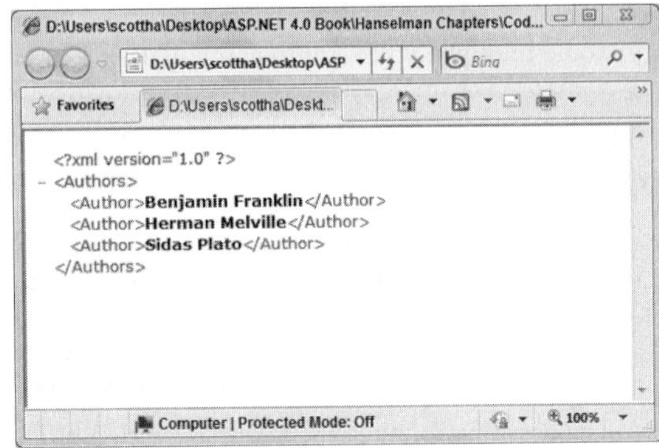

FIGURE 10-7

Figure 10-7 shows the resulting XML as the `Books.xslt` transformation is applied to `Books.xml`. You can apply XSLT transformations in a number of ways, both declarative and programmatic. These are described in the following sections.

XslCompiledTransform

The `XslTransform` class was used in the .NET Framework 1.*x* for XSLT transformation. In the .NET Framework 2.0 and beyond, the `XslCompiledTransform` class is the primary XSLT processor. It is such an improvement that `XslTransform` is deprecated and marked with the `Obsolete` attribute. The compiler will now advise you to use `XslCompiledTransform`. The system generates MSIL code on the call to `Compile()` and the XSLT executes many times faster than previous techniques. This compilation technique also includes full debugging support from within Visual Studio, which is covered a little later in this chapter.

The `XPathDocument` *is absolutely optimized for XSLT transformations and should be used instead of the* `XmlDocument` *if you would like a 15 to 30 percent performance gain in your transformations. Remember that XSLT contains XPath, and when you use XPath, use an* `XPathDocument`. *According to the team's numbers, XSLT is 400 percent faster in .NET Framework 2.0 and beyond.*

`XslCompiledTransform` has only two methods: `Load` and `Transform`. The compilation happens without any effort on your part. Listing 10-19 loads the `Books.xml` file into an `XPathDocument` and transforms it using `Books.xslt` and an `XslCompiledTransform`. Even though there are only two methods, there are *14* overrides for `Transform` and 6 for `Load`. That may seem a little daunting at first, but there is a simple explanation.

The `Load` method can handle loading a stylesheet from a string, an `XmlReader`, or any class that implements `IXPathNavigable`. An `XsltSettings` object can be passed in optionally with any of the previous three overloads, giving you six to choose from. `XsltSettings` includes options to enable the `document()` XSLT–specific function via the `XsltSettings.EnableDocumentFunction` property or enable embedded script blocks within XSLT via `XsltSettings.EnableScript`. These advanced options are disabled by default for security reasons. Alternatively, you can retrieve a pre-populated `XslSettings` object via the static property `XsltSettings.TrustedXslt`, which has enabled both these settings.

If you think it is odd that the class that does the work is called the `XslCompiledTransform` *and not the* `XsltCompiledTransform`, *but* `XsltSettings` *includes the* t, *remember that the* t *in XSLT means* transformation.

Note in Listing 10-19 that the `Response.Output` property eliminates an unnecessary string allocation. In the example, `Response.Output` is a `TextWriter` wrapped in an `XmlTextWriter` and passed directly to the `Execute` method.

LISTING 10-19: Executing an XslCompiledTransform

Available for download on Wrox.com

```
Response.ContentType = "text/xml"

Dim xsltFile As String = Server.MapPath("books.xslt")
Dim xmlFile As String = Server.MapPath("books.xml")

Dim xslt As New XslCompiledTransform()
xslt.Load(xsltFile)

Dim doc As New XPathDocument(xmlFile)
xslt.Transform(doc, New XmlTextWriter(Response.Output))
```

C#

```
Response.ContentType = "text/xml";

string xsltFile = Server.MapPath("books.xslt");
string xmlFile = Server.MapPath("books.xml");

XslCompiledTransform xslt = new XslCompiledTransform();
xslt.Load(xsltFile);

XPathDocument doc = new XPathDocument(xmlFile);
xslt.Transform(doc, new XmlTextWriter(Response.Output));
```

Named arguments may be passed into an `XslTransform` or `XslCompiledTransform` if the stylesheet takes parameters. The following code snippet illustrates the use of `XslArgumentList`:

```
XslTransform transformer = new XslTransform();
transformer.Load("foo.xslt");

XslArgumentList args = new XslArgumentList();
args.Add("ID", "SOMEVALUE");

transformer.Transform("foo.xml", args, Response.OutputStream);
```

The XML resulting from an XSLT transformation can be manipulated with any of the `system.XML` APIs that have been discussed in this chapter. One common use of XSLT is to flatten hierarchical and, sometimes, relational XML documents into a format that is more conducive to output as HTML. The results of these transformations to HTML can be placed inline within an existing ASPX document.

The XSLTC.exe Command-Line Compiler

Compiled stylesheets are very useful, but there is a slight performance hit as the stylesheets are compiled at runtime. Therefore, starting with the .NET Framework 3.5, you have `XSLTC.exe`, a command-line XSLT compiler.

Usage is simple — you simply pass in as many source XSLT files as you like and specify the assembly output file. From a Visual Studio 2010 command prompt, use the following:

```
Xsltc /c:Wrox.Book.CompiledStylesheet books.xslt /out:Books.dll
```

Now, add a reference to the newly created `Books.dll` in your project from Listing 10-19, and change one line:

```
XslCompiledTransform xslt = new XslCompiledTransform();
xslt.Load(typeof(Wrox.Book.MyCompiledStyleSheet));
```

Rather than loading the XSLT from a file, it's now loaded pre-compiled directly from the generated assembly. Using the XSLT Compiler makes deployment much easier as you can put many XSLTs in a single assembly, but most important, you eliminate code-generation time.

If your XSLT uses `msxsl:script` elements, that code will be compiled into separate assemblies, one per language used. You can merge these resulting assemblies with ILMerge, located at `http://research.microsoft.com/~mbarnett/ILMerge.aspx`, as a post-build step.XML Web Server Control.

XSLT transformations can also be a very quick way to get information out to the browser as HTML. Consider this technique as yet another tool in your toolbox. HTML is a tree, and HTML is a cousin of XML, so an XML tree can be transformed into an HTML tree. A benefit of using XSLT transformations to create large amounts of static text, like HTML tables, is that the XSLT file can be kept external to the application. You can make quick changes to its formatting without a recompile. A problem when using XSLT transformations is that they can become large and very unruly when someone attempts to use them to generate the entire user interface experience. The practice was in vogue in the mid-nineties to use XSLT transformations to generate entire Web sites, but the usefulness of this technique breaks down when complex user interactions are introduced. That said, XSLT has a place, not only for transforming data from one format to another, but also for creating reasonable chunks of your user interface — as long as you don't go overboard.

In the next example, the output of the XSLT is HTML rather than XML. Note the use of the `<xsl:output method = "html">` directive. When this directive is omitted, the default output of an XSLT transformation is XML. This template begins with a match on the root node. It is creating an HTML fragment rather than an entire HTML document. Its first output is the `<h3>` tag with some static text. Next comes a table tag and the header row, and then the `<xsl:apply-template>` element selects all books within the source XML document. For every `book` element in the source document, the second template is invoked with the responsibility of outputting one table row per book. Calls to `<xsl:value-of>` select each of the book's subnodes and output them within the `<td>` tags (see Listing 10-20).

Available for download on Wrox.com

LISTING 10-20: BookstoHTML.xslt used with the XML Web Server Control

XSLT

```
<?xml version="1.0" encoding="utf-8" ?>
<xsl:stylesheet xmlns:xsl="http://www.w3.org/1999/XSL/Transform"
        xmlns:b="http://example.books.com" version="1.0">
    <xsl:output method="html"/>
    <xsl:template match="/">
        <h3>List of Authors</h3>
        <table border="1">
            <tr>
                <th>First</th><th>Last</th>
            </tr>
            <xsl:apply-templates select="//b:book"/>
        </table>
    </xsl:template>
    <xsl:template match="b:book">
        <tr>
            <td><xsl:value-of select="b:author/b:first-name"/></td>
            <td><xsl:value-of select="b:author/b:last-name"/></td>
        </tr>
    </xsl:template>
</xsl:stylesheet>
```

ASPX

```
<%@ Page Language="VB" %>
<html xmlns="http://www.w3.org/1999/xhtml" >
```

```
        <head runat="server"><title>HTML/XSLT Transformation</title></head>
        <body>
            <form id="form1" runat="server">
                <div>
                    <asp:Xml ID="Xml1" Runat="server"
                        DocumentSource="~/Books.xml"
                        TransformSource="~/bookstoHTML.xslt"/>
                </div>
            </form>
        </body>
    </html>
```

Notice the use of namespace prefixes in Listing 10-20. The source namespace is declared with the prefix `b` as in `xmlns:b="http://example.books.com,"` and the `b` prefix is subsequently used in XPath expressions like `//b:book`. The XSLT in Listing 10-20 can use the `XSLTCommand` to perform this transformation on the server-side because the entire operation is declarative and requires just two inputs — the XML document and the XSLT document. The XML Web server control makes the transformation easy to perform from the ASPX page and does not require any language-specific features. The `DocumentSource` property of the control holds the path to the `Books.xml` file, whereas the `TransformSource` property holds the path to the `BookstoHTML.xslt` file:

```
<h3>List of Authors</h3>
<table border="1">
    <tr>
        <th>First</th>
        <th>Last</th>
    </tr>
    <tr>
        <td>Benjamin</td>
        <td>Franklin</td>
    </tr>
    <tr>
        <td>Herman</td>
        <td>Melville</td>
    </tr>
    <tr>
        <td>Sidas</td>
        <td>Plato</td>
    </tr>
</table>
```

The results of this transformation are output inline to this HTML document and appear between the two `<div>` tags. You see the results of this HTML fragment in the previous code and in the browser's output shown in Figure 10-8.

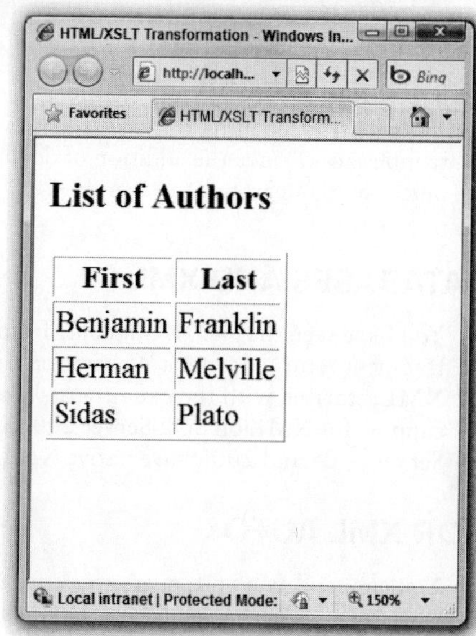

FIGURE 10-8

XSLT Debugging

One of the exciting new additions to ASP.NET 2.0 and Visual Studio was XSLT debugging. Visual Studio 2005 enabled breakpoints on XSLT documents, and Visual Studio 2008 and 2010 include XSLT Debugger Data Breakpoints — the ability to break on nodes within the source XML document. However, be aware that XSLT debugging is available only in the Professional and Team System versions of Visual Studio and only when using the `XslCompiledTransform` class.

By passing the Boolean value `true` into the constructor of `XslCompiledTransform`, you can step into and debug your XSLT transformations within the Microsoft Development Environment.

```
Dim xslt As New XslCompiledTransform(True)
```

In Listing 10-19, change the call to the constructor of `XslCompiledTransform` to include the value `true` and set a breakpoint on the `Transform` method. When you reach that breakpoint, press F11 to step into the transformation. Figure 10-9 shows a debugging session of the `Books.xslt/Books.xml` transformation in process.

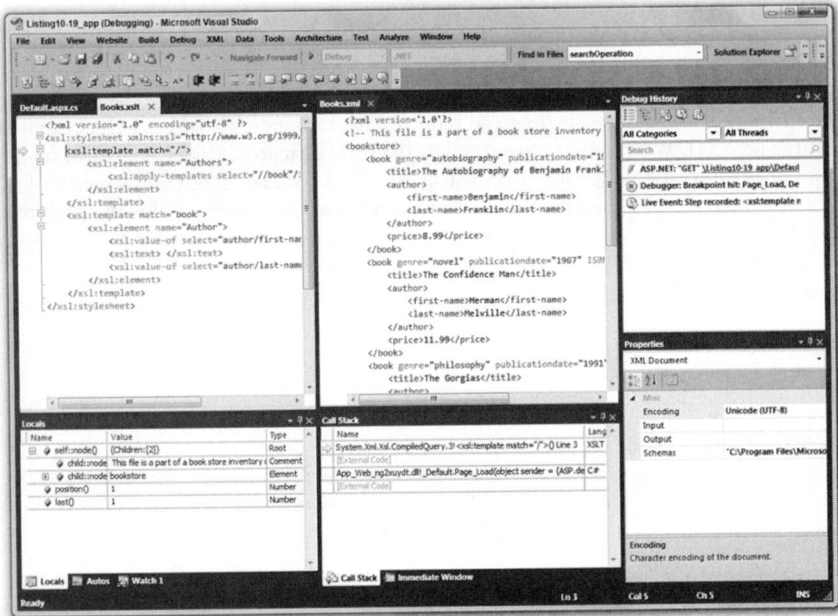

FIGURE 10-9

In the past, debugging XSLT was largely an opaque process that required a third-party application to troubleshoot. Since the addition of debugging XSLT to Visual Studio, your XML experience is just that much more integrated and seamless.

DATABASES AND XML

You have seen that XML can come from any source whether it be a Web service, a file on disk, an XML fragment returned from a Web server, or a database. SQL Server and ADO have rich support for XML, starting with the `ExecuteXmlReader` method of the `System.Data.SqlCommand` class. Additional support for XML on SQL Server 2000 is included with SQLXML 3.0 and its XML extensions, and SQL Server 2005 and 2008 have native XML data type support built right in.

FOR XML AUTO

You can modify a SQL query to return XML with the `FOR XML AUTO` clause. If you take a simple query such as `select * from customers`, you just change the statement like so:

```
select * from customers FOR XML AUTO
```

XML AUTO returns XML fragments rather than a full XML document with a document element. Each row in the database becomes one element; each column in the database becomes one attribute on the element. Notice that each element in the following result set is named Customers because the select clause is from customers:

```
<Customers CustomerID="ALFKI" CompanyName="Alfreds Futterkiste"
ContactName="Maria Anders" ContactTitle="Sales Representative"
Address="Obere Str. 57" City="Berlin" PostalCode="12209"
Country="Germany" Phone="030-0074321" Fax="030-0076545" />
<Customers CustomerID="ANATR" CompanyName="Ana Trujillo Emparedados y
helados" ContactName="Ana Trujillo" ContactTitle="Owner" Address="Avda.
de la Constitucion 2222" City="Mexico D.F." PostalCode="05021"
Country="Mexico" Phone="(5) 555-4729" Fax="(5) 555-3745" />
```

If you add ELEMENTS to the query like so

```
select * from customers FOR XML AUTO, ELEMENTS
```

you get an XML fragment like this:

```
<Customers>
    <CustomerID>ALFKI</CustomerID>
    <CompanyName>Alfreds Futterkiste</CompanyName>
    <ContactName>Maria Anders</ContactName>
    <ContactTitle>Sales Representative</ContactTitle>
    <Address>Obere Str. 57</Address>
    <City>Berlin</City>
    <PostalCode>12209</PostalCode>
    <Country>Germany</Country>
    <Phone>030-0074321</Phone>
    <Fax>030-0076545</Fax>
</Customers>
<Customers>
    <CustomerID>ANATR</CustomerID>
    <CompanyName>Ana Trujillo Emparedados y helados</CompanyName>
    <ContactName>Ana Trujillo</ContactName>
    <ContactTitle>Owner</ContactTitle>
    <Address>Avda. de la Constitucion 2222</Address>
    <City>Mexico D.F.</City>
    <PostalCode>05021</PostalCode>
    <Country>Mexico</Country>
    <Phone>(5) 555-4729</Phone>
    <Fax>(5) 555-3745</Fax>
</Customers>
```

The previous example is just a fragment with no document element. To perform an XSLT transformation, you need a document element (sometimes incorrectly referred to as the "root node"), and you probably want to change the <Customers> elements to <Customer>. By using an alias like as Customer in the select statement, you can affect the name of each row's element. The query select * from Customers as Customer for XML AUTO, ELEMENTS changes the name of the element to <Customer>.

Now, put together all the things you've learned from this chapter and create an XmlDocument, edit and manipulate it, retrieve data from SQL Server as an XmlReader, and style that information with XSLT into an HTML table all in just a few lines of code.

First, add a document element to the document retrieved by the SQL query select * from Customers as Customer for XML AUTO, ELEMENTS, as shown in Listing 10-21.

LISTING 10-21: Retrieving XML from SQL Server 2000 using FOR XML AUTO

Available for download on Wrox.com

```
Dim connStr As String = "Data Source=.\\SQLEXPRESS;
                         Initial Catalog=Northwind;
                         Integrated Security=SSPI;"
Dim x As New XmlDocument()
Dim xpathnav As XPathNavigator = x.CreateNavigator()
Using conn As New SqlConnection(connStr)
    conn.Open()
    Dim command As New SqlCommand("select * from Customers as Customer " & _
        "for XML AUTO, ELEMENTS", conn)
    Using xw As XmlWriter = xpathnav.PrependChild()
        xw.WriteStartElement("Customers")
        Using xr As XmlReader = command.ExecuteXmlReader()
            xw.WriteNode(xr, True)
        End Using
        xw.WriteEndElement()
    End Using
End Using
Response.ContentType = "text/xml"
x.Save(Response.Output)
```

C#

```
string connStr = "Data Source=.\\SQLEXPRESS;
                  Initial Catalog=Northwind;
                  Integrated Security=SSPI;";
XmlDocument x = new XmlDocument();
XPathNavigator xpathnav = x.CreateNavigator();
using (SqlConnection conn = new SqlConnection(connStr))
{
    conn.Open();
    SqlCommand command = new SqlCommand(
        "select * from Customers as Customer for XML AUTO, ELEMENTS", conn);
    using (XmlWriter xw = xpathnav.PrependChild())
    {
        xw.WriteStartElement("Customers");
        using (XmlReader xr = command.ExecuteXmlReader())
        {
            xw.WriteNode(xr, true);
        }
        xw.WriteEndElement();
    }
}
Response.ContentType = "text/xml";
x.Save(Response.Output);
```

This code creates an `XmlDocument` called `Customers`. Then it executes the SQL command and retrieves the XML data into an `XmlReader`. An `XPathNavigator` is created from the `XmlDocument`, and a child node is prepended to the document. A single call to the `WriteNode` method of the `XmlWriter` retrieved from the `XPathDocument` moves the entire XML fragment into the well-formed `XmlDocument`. Because the SQL statement contained `from Customers as Customer` as a table alias, each XML element is named `<Customer>`. Then, for this example, the resulting XML document is output directly to the `Response` object. You see the resulting XML in the browser shown in Figure 10-10.

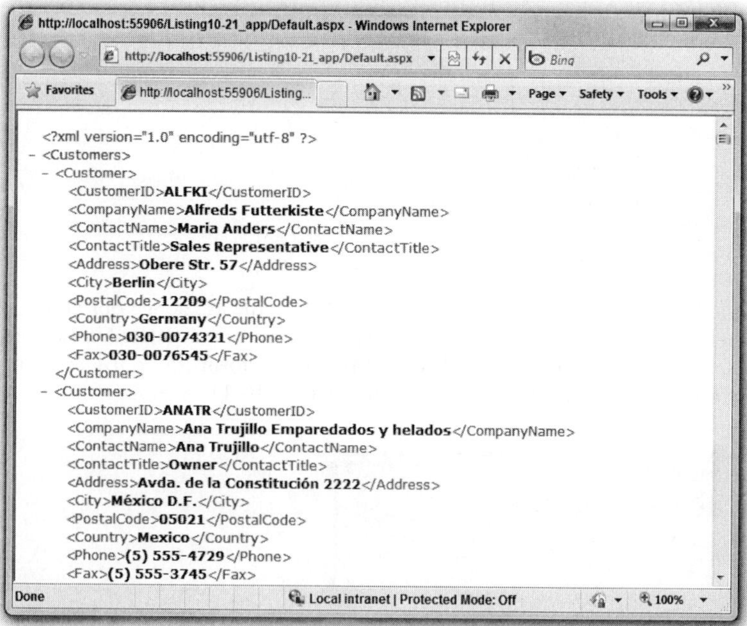

FIGURE 10-10

Of course, seeing the resulting XML is nice, but styling that information with XSLT is far more useful. The XML Web Server control mentioned earlier is perfect for this task. However, in Listing 10-22, rather than setting both the `TransformSource` and `DocumentSource` properties as in Listing 10-20, you set only the `TransformSource` property at design time, and the `XmlDocument` is the one created in the code-behind of Listing 10-21.

Available for download on Wrox.com

LISTING 10-22: The ASPX page and XSLT to style the XML from SQL Server

ASPX

```
<%@ Page Language="C#" CodeFile="Default.aspx.cs" Inherits="Default_aspx" %>
<asp:xml id="Xml1" runat="server" transformsource="</customersToHtml.xslt"/>
```

XSLT

```
<?xml version="1.0" encoding="utf-8" ?>
<xsl:stylesheet xmlns:xsl="http://www.w3.org/1999/XSL/Transform" version="1.0">
    <xsl:output method="html"/>
    <xsl:template match="/">
        <h3>List of Customers</h3>
        <table border="1">
            <tr>
                <th>Company Name</th><th>Contact Name</th><th>Contact Title</th>
            </tr>
            <xsl:apply-templates select="//Customer"/>
        </table>
    </xsl:template>
    <xsl:template match="Customer">
        <tr>
            <td><xsl:value-of select="CompanyName"/></td>
            <td><xsl:value-of select="ContactName"/></td>
            <td><xsl:value-of select="ContactTitle"/></td>
        </tr>
```

continues

LISTING 10-22 *(continued)*

```
    </xsl:template>
</xsl:stylesheet>
```

VB

```
'Response.ContentType = "text/xml"
'x.Save(Response.Output)
Xml1.XPathNavigator = xpathnav
```

C#

```
//Response.ContentType = "text/xml";
//x.Save(Response.Output);
Xml1.XPathNavigator = xpathnav;
```

In the code-behind file, the lines that set `ContentType` and write the XML to the `Response` object are commented out, and instead the `XPathNavigator` from the `XmlDocument` that is manipulated in Listing 10-21 is set as a property of the XML Web Server control. The control then performs the XSLT `Stylesheet` transformation, and the results are output to the browser, as shown in Figure 10-11.

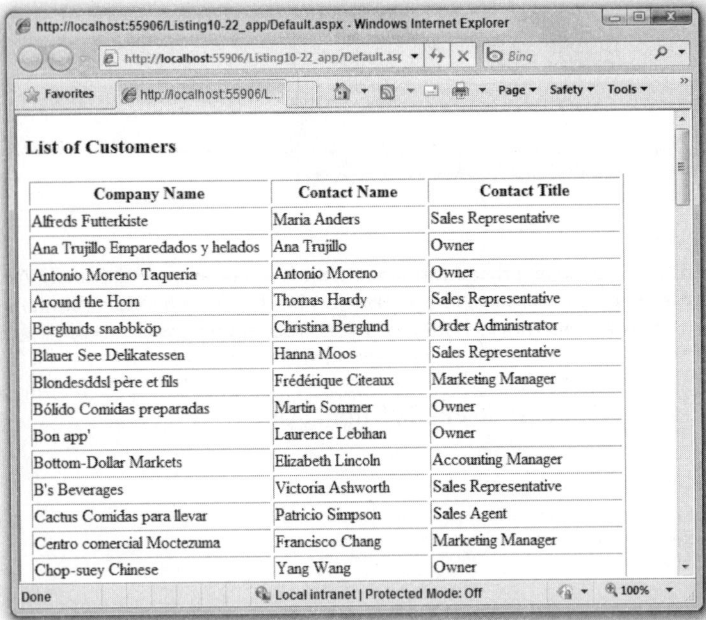

Company Name	Contact Name	Contact Title
Alfreds Futterkiste	Maria Anders	Sales Representative
Ana Trujillo Emparedados y helados	Ana Trujillo	Owner
Antonio Moreno Taqueria	Antonio Moreno	Owner
Around the Horn	Thomas Hardy	Sales Representative
Berglunds snabbköp	Christina Berglund	Order Administrator
Blauer See Delikatessen	Hanna Moos	Sales Representative
Blondesddsl père et fils	Frédérique Citeaux	Marketing Manager
Bólido Comidas preparadas	Martín Sommer	Owner
Bon app'	Laurence Lebihan	Owner
Bottom-Dollar Markets	Elizabeth Lincoln	Accounting Manager
B's Beverages	Victoria Ashworth	Sales Representative
Cactus Comidas para llevar	Patricio Simpson	Sales Agent
Centro comercial Moctezuma	Francisco Chang	Marketing Manager
Chop-suey Chinese	Yang Wang	Owner

FIGURE 10-11

You have an infinite amount of flexibility within the `System.Xml`, `System.Xml.Linq`, and `System.Data` namespaces. Microsoft has put together a fantastic series of APIs that interoperate beautifully. When you're creating your own APIs that expose or consume XML, compare them to the APIs that Microsoft has provided — if you expose your data over an `XmlReader` or `IXPathNavigable` interface, you are sure to make your users much happier. Passing XML around with these more flexible APIs (rather than as simple and opaque strings) provides a much more comfortable and intuitive expression of the XML information set.

Remember that the `XmlReader` that is returned from `SqlCommand.ExecuteXmlReader()` is holding its SQL connection open, so you must call `Close()` when you're done using the `XmlReader`. The easiest way to ensure that this is done is the `using` statement. An `XmlReader` implements `IDisposable` and calls `Close()` for you as the variable leaves the scope of the `using` statement.

SQL Server and the XML Data Type

You've seen that retrieving data from SQL Server 2000 is straightforward, if a little limited. SQL Server 2005, originally codenamed Yukon, and SQL Server 2008 include a number of very powerful XML-based features. Dare Obasanjo, a former XML Program Manager at Microsoft has said, "The rise of the ROX [Relational-Object-XML] database has begun." SQL Server 2005 and 2008 are definitely leading the way.

One of the things that is particularly tricky about mapping XML and the XML information set to the relational structure that SQL Server shares with most databases is that most XML data has a hierarchical structure. Relational databases structure hierarchical data with foreign key relationships. Relational data often has no order, but the order of the elements within `XmlDocument` is very important. SQL Server 2005 introduced a new data type called, appropriately, `XML`. Previously, data was stored in an `nvarchar` or other string-based data type. In SQL Server 2005 and 2008, you can have a table with a column of type `XML`, and each XML data type can have associated XML Schema.

The `FOR XML` syntax is improved to include the `TYPE` directive, so a query that includes `FOR XML TYPE` returns the results as a single XML-typed value. This XML data is returned with a new class called `System.Data.SqlXml`. It exposes its data as an `XmlReader` retrieved by calling `SqlXml.CreateReader`, so you'll find it to be very easy to use because it works like all the other examples you've seen in this chapter.

In a DataSet returned from SQL Server 2005 or 2008, XML data defaults to being a string unless `DataAdapter.ReturnProviderSpecificTypes = true` *is set or a schema is loaded ahead of time to specify the column type.*

The `XML` data type stores data as a new internal binary format that is more efficient to query. The programmer doesn't have to worry about the details of how the XML is stored if it continues to be available on the XQuery or in `XmlReader`. You can mix column types in a way that was not possible in SQL Server 2000. If you're used to returning data as either a DataSet or an `XmlReader`, with SQL Server 2005 or 2008, you can return a DataSet where some columns contain XML and some contain traditional SQL Server data types.

Generating Custom XML from SQL 2008

You've seen a number of ways to programmatically generate custom XML from a database. Before reading this book, you've probably used `FOR XML AUTO` to generate fairly basic XML and then modified the XML in post-processing to meet your needs. This was formerly a very common pattern. `FOR XML AUTO` was fantastically easy; and `FOR XML EXPLICIT`, a more explicit way to generate XML, was very nearly impossible to use.

SQL Server 2005 added and SQL Server 2008 contains the `PATH` method to `FOR XML`, which makes arbitrary XML creation available to mere mortals. SQL 2008's XML support features very intuitive syntax and very clean namespace handling.

Listing 10-23 is an example of a query that returns custom XML. The `WITH XMLNAMESPACES` commands at the start of the query set the stage by defining a default namespace and using column-style name aliasing to associate namespaces with namespace prefixes. In this example, `addr:` is the prefix for `urn:hanselman.com/northwind/address`.

LISTING 10-23: Returning custom XML from SQL Server

```
use Northwind;
WITH XMLNAMESPACES (
 DEFAULT 'urn:hanselman.com/northwind'
 , 'urn:hanselman.com/northwind/address' as "addr"
)
```

continues

LISTING 10-23 *(continued)*

```
SELECT CustomerID as "@ID",
           CompanyName,
           Address as "addr:Address/addr:Street",
           City as "addr:Address/addr:City",
           Region as "addr:Address/addr:Region",
           PostalCode as "addr:Address/addr:Zip",
           Country as "addr:Address/addr:Country",
           ContactName as "Contact/Name",
           ContactTitle as "Contact/Title",
           Phone as "Contact/Phone",
           Fax as "Contact/Fax"
FROM Customers
FOR XML PATH('Customer'), ROOT('Customers'), ELEMENTS XSINIL
```

The aliases using the `AS` keyword declaratively describe the elements and their nesting relationships, whereas the `PATH` keyword defines an element for the Customers table. The `ROOT` keyword defines the root node of the document.

The `ELEMENTS` keyword, along with `XSINIL`, describes how you handle null. Without these keywords, no XML element is created for a row's column that contains null; this absence of data in the database causes the omission of data in the resulting XML document. When the `ELMENTS XSINIL` combination is present, an element outputs using an explicit `xsi:nil` syntax such as `<addr:Region xsi:nil="true" />`.

When you run the example, SQL 2008 outputs an XML document like the one that follows. Note that the namespaces and prefixes are just as you defined them.

```
<Customers xmlns:xsi="http://www.w3.org/2001/XMLSchema-instance"
xmlns:addr="urn:hanselman.com/northwind/address"
xmlns="urn:hanselman.com/northwind">
  <Customer ID="ALFKI">
    <CompanyName>Alfreds Futterkiste</CompanyName>
    <addr:Address>
      <addr:Street>Obere Str. 57</addr:Street>
      <addr:City>Berlin</addr:City>
      <addr:Region xsi:nil="true" />
      <addr:Zip>12209</addr:Zip>
      <addr:Country>Germany</addr:Country>
    </addr:Address>
    <Contact>
      <Name>Maria Anders</Name>
      <Title>Sales Representative</Title>
      <Phone>030-0074321</Phone>
      <Fax>030-0076545</Fax>
    </Contact>
  </Customer>
...the rest of the document removed for brevity...
```

The resulting XML can now be manipulated using an `XmlReader` or any of the techniques discussed in this chapter.

Adding a Column of Untyped XML

SQL Server can produce XML from a query, and it can now also store XML in a single column. Because XML is a first-class data type within SQL Server 2008, adding a new column to the Customers table of the Northwind Database is straightforward. You can use any SQL Server management tool you like. I use the SQL Server Management Studio Express, a free download that can be used with any SQL SKU (including the free SQL Express 2008). Bring up your Query Analyzer or Management Studio Express and, with the Northwind database selected, execute the following query:

```
use Northwind;
BEGIN TRANSACTION
```

```
GO
ALTER TABLE dbo.Customers ADD
 Notes xml NULL
GO
COMMIT
```

Note the `xml` type keyword after `Notes` in the preceding example. If an XML Schema were already added to the database, you could add this new column and associate it with a named Schema Collection all at once using this syntax.

```
use Northwind;
BEGIN TRANSACTION
GO
ALTER TABLE dbo.Customers ADD
 Notes xml(DOCUMENT dbo.NorthwindCollection)
 GO
COMMIT
```

Here, the word `DOCUMENT` indicates that the column will contain a complete XML document. Use `CONTENT` to store fragments of XML that don't contain a root node. You haven't added a schema yet, so that's the next step. So far, you've added a `Notes` column to the Customers table that can be populated with prose. For example, a customer service representative could use it to describe interactions she's had with the customer, entering text into a theoretical management system.

Adding an XML Schema

Although the user could store untyped XML data in the Notes field, you should really include some constraints on what's allowed. XML data can be stored typed or untyped, as a fragment with no root node or as a document. Because you want to store Customer interaction data entered and viewed from a Web site, ostensibly containing prose, XHTML is a good choice.

XML data is validated by XML Schemas, as discussed earlier in the chapter. However, SQL Server 2008 is a database, not a file system. It needs to store the schemas you want to reference in a location it can get to. You add a schema or schemas to SQL Server 2008 using queries formed like this:

```
CREATE XML SCHEMA COLLECTION YourCollection AS 'your complete xml schema here'
```

You'll be using the XHTML 1.0 Strict schema located on the W3C Web site shown at `http://w3.org/TR/xhtml1-schema/#xhtml1-strict`. Copy the entire schema to a file, or download the schema directly from `http://w3.org/2002/08/xhtml/xhtml1-strict.xsd`. Note that you want to download this file directly, not necessarily view it in your browser.

When executing your query, you include the entire XSD inline in your schema. However, you should watch for few things. First, escape any single quotes so that ' becomes `''` — that is, two single quotes, ***not*** one double — using a search and replace. Second, because SQL Server uses the MSXML6 XML parser to parse its XML, take into consideration a limitation in that parser. MSXML6 already has the `xml:` namespace prefix and associated namespace hard-coded internally, so you should remove the line from your schema that contains that namespace. This little oddity is documented, but buried within MSDN at `http://msdn2.microsoft.com/ms177489(en-US,SQL.90).aspx` and applies only to a few predefined schemas like this one that uses the `xml:` prefix and/or the `http://www.w3.org/XML/1998/namespace` namespace. In the fragment that follows, I've bolded the line you need to remove.

```
Use Northwind;
CREATE XML SCHEMA COLLECTION NorthwindCollection AS
'<?xml version="1.0" encoding="UTF-8"?>
<xs:schema version="1.0" xml:lang="en"
    xmlns:xs="http://www.w3.org/2001/XMLSchema"
    targetNamespace="http://www.w3.org/1999/xhtml"
    xmlns="http://www.w3.org/1999/xhtml"
    xmlns:xml="http://www.w3.org/XML/1998/namespace"
    elementFormDefault="qualified">
...the rest of the schema has been omitted for brevity...
</xs:schema>';
```

Instead, you want to execute a query like this, noting the single quote and semicolon at the very end.

```
Use Northwind;
CREATE XML SCHEMA COLLECTION NorthwindCollection AS
'<?xml version="1.0" encoding="UTF-8"?>
<xs:schema version="1.0" xml:lang="en"
    xmlns:xs="http://www.w3.org/2001/XMLSchema"
    targetNamespace="http://www.w3.org/1999/xhtml"
    xmlns="http://www.w3.org/1999/xhtml"
    elementFormDefault="qualified">
...the rest of the schema has been omitted for brevity...
</xs:schema>';
```

You may get a few schema validation warnings when you execute this query because of the complexity of the XHTML schema, but you can ignore them. Figure 10-12 shows the new NorthwindCollection schemas added to the Northwind database.

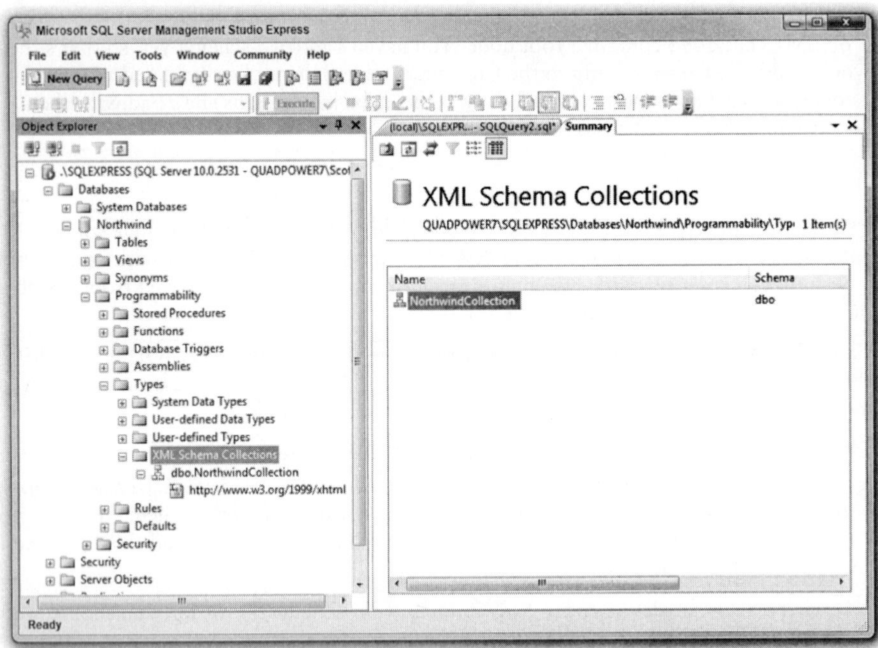

FIGURE 10-12

Although Figure 10-12 shows the NorthwindCollection within the Object Explorer, you can also confirm that your schema has been added correctly using SQL, as shown in the example that follows:

```
Use Northwind;
SELECT XSN.name
FROM    sys.xml_schema_collections XSC
    JOIN sys.xml_schema_namespaces XSN ON
        (XSC.xml_collection_id = XSN.xml_collection_id)
```

The output of the query is something like the following. You can see that the XHTML namespace appears at the end along with the schemas that already existed in the system.

```
http://www.w3.org/2001/XMLSchema
http://schemas.microsoft.com/sqlserver/2004/sqltypes
http://www.w3.org/XML/1998/namespace
http://www.w3.org/1999/xhtml
```

Next you should associate the new column with the new schema collection. Using the Management Studio, you create one composite script that automates this process. In this case, however, you can continue to take it step by step so you see what's happening underneath.

Associating an XML Typed Column with a Schema

You can use the Microsoft SQL Server Management Studio Express to associate the NorthwindCollection with the new Notes column. Open the Customers table of the Northwind Database and, within its Column collection, right-click and select Modify. Select the Notes column, as shown in Figure 10-13. Within the Notes column's property page, open the XML Type Specification property and select the NorthwindCollection from the Schema Collection dropdown. Also, set the `Is XML Document` property to `Yes`.

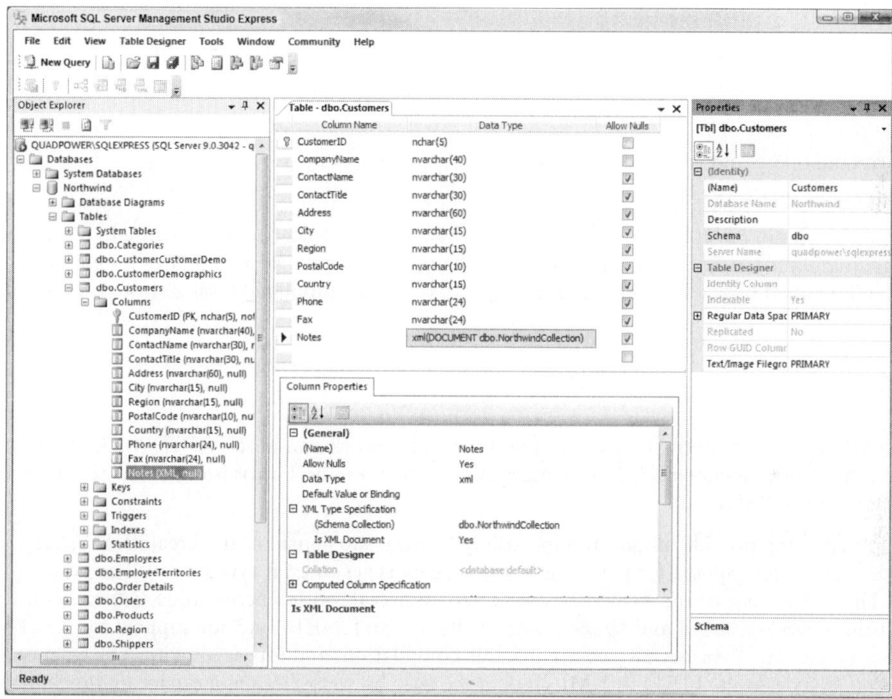

FIGURE 10-13

At this point, you can save your table and a change script is generated and executed. If you want to see and save the change script after making a modification but before saving the changes, right-click in the grid and select Generate Change Script. Click the Save toolbar button or Ctrl+S to commit your changes to the Customers table.

Now that you've added a new Notes column and associated it with an XHTML schema, you're ready to add some data to an existing row.

Inserting XML Data into an XML Column

You start by adding some data to a row within the Northwind database's Customer table. Add some notes to the famous first row, the customer named Alfreds Futterkiste, specifically CustomerID ALFKI. You add or update data to a column with the XML type just as you add to any data type. For example, you can try an UPDATE query.

```
Use Northwind;
UPDATE Customers SET Notes = N'<HTML></HTML>' WHERE CustomerID = 'ALFKI';
```

Upon executing this query, you get this result:

```
Msg 6913, Level 16, State 1, Line 1
XML Validation: Declaration not found for element 'HTML'. Location: /*:HTML[1]
```

What's this? Oh, yes, you associated a schema with the XML column, so the included document must conform, in this case, to the XHTML specification. Now, try again with a valid XHTML document that includes a correct namespace.

```
Use Northwind;
UPDATE Customers SET Notes = N'
<html xmlns="http://www.w3.org/1999/xhtml" xml:lang="en">
 <head>
  <title>Notes about Alfreds</title>
 </head>
 <body>
  <p>He is a nice enough fellow.</p>
 </body>
</html>'
WHERE CustomerID = 'ALFKI';
```

Execute this corrected query and you see a success message.

```
(1 row(s) affected)
```

After you've typed a column as XML and associated an XML Schema, SQL Server 2005/8 will allow only XML documents that validate. The data can be retrieved from SQL Server using standard System.Data techniques. It can be pulled out of a `DataReader` or a `DataSet` and manipulated with `XmlReaders` or as an `XmlDocument`.

SUMMARY

XML and the XML InfoSet are both pervasive in the .NET Framework and in ASP.NET. All ASP.NET configuration files include associated XML Schema, and the Visual Studio Editor is even smarter about XML documents that use XSDs.

`XmlReader` and `XmlWriter` provide unique and incredibly fast ways to consume and create XML; they now also include even better support for mapping XML Schema types to CLR types, as well as other improvements. The `XmlDocument` and `XPathDocument` remain useful tools, whereas the `XmlDataDocument` straddles the world of `System.Data` and `System.Xml`. ASP.NET and .NET 4 include support for XSLT via not only `XslCompiledTransform` but also command-line compilation, and tops it all with XSLT debugging support for compiled stylesheets. LINQ to XML lives in the `System.Xml.Linq` namespace and includes supporting classes for a tightly integrated IntelliSense-supported coding experience. VB9 and beyond took XML support to the next level with XML literals and XML namespace imports. The bridge classes and extension methods make the transition between `System.Xml` and `System.Xml.Linq` clean and intuitive.

All these ways to manipulate XML via the Base Class Library are married with XML support in SQL Server 2000, 2005, and 2008. SQL Server 2005 and beyond also include the XML data type for storing XML in a first-class column type validated by XML Schemas stored in the database.

11

Introduction to the Provider Model

WHAT'S IN THIS CHAPTER?

- What providers are
- What the provider model comprises for ASP.NET 4
- Configuring providers

The ASP.NET provider model is an important framework to understand as you build your applications. The ASP.NET provider model was a major change introduced back with the release of ASP.NET 2.0, so you probably already know that ASP.NET is a way to build applications for the Internet. *For the Internet* means that an application's display code travels over HTTP, which is a stateless protocol. ASP.NET works with a disconnected architecture. The simple nature of this model means that requests come in and then responses are sent back. On top of that, ASP.NET does not differentiate one request from another. The server containing an ASP.NET application is simply reacting to any request thrown at it.

This means that a developer building a Web application has to put some thought into how users can remain in context between their requests to the server as they work through the application. Keeping a user in context means recording state, the state of the user, to some type of data store. This can be done in multiple ways, and no one way is the *perfect* way. Rather, you must choose one of the available methods.

You can read about maintaining state in an ASP.NET application in Chapter 21.

State can be stored via multiple methods, some of which include

- Application state
- Session state
- The Cache object

You use all these methods on the server, but you can also employ your own custom methods — such as simply storing state in a database using your own custom schema. Writing state back to the clients, either directly on their computers or by placing state in the HTML output in the response, is also possible. Some of these methods include

- Cookies
- Querystrings
- Hidden Fields
- ViewState

Whether it is one of the built-in providers that comes with ASP.NET or a custom one you've put together yourself, you will find that using a provider is a nice model for managing your state. Next, let's take a look at what is a provider and how you can use it.

UNDERSTANDING THE PROVIDER

These previous state mechanisms work rather well; but most of them are rudimentary and have short life spans. ASP.NET 4 includes a handful of systems (such as a membership and role management system) that handle state for users between multiple requests/response transactions. In fact, these systems require state management capabilities that go well beyond the limited time frames that are possible in the previously mentioned state management methods. Therefore, many of these systems must record state in more advanced modes — something that is easy to do in ASP.NET. Recording state to data stores in more advanced modes is accomplished through the use of *providers*.

> A provider *is an object that allows for programmatic access to data stores, processes, and more.*

In the past, when working with ASP.NET 1.*x*, you might have encountered a rudimentary provider model that was present in the system. This provider model was an object that sat between the `Session` object and the actual place in which the sessions were stored. By default, sessions in ASP.NET are stored `InProc`, meaning in the same process where ASP.NET is running. In ASP.NET 1.*x* (and in ASP.NET 4 for that matter), you can simply change the provider used for the `Session` object; this will, in turn, change where the session is stored. The available providers for storing session information include

- `InProc`
- `StateServer`
- `SQLServer`

Besides `InProc`, you can use `StateServer` that enables you to store sessions in a process that is entirely separate from the one in which ASP.NET runs. This protects your sessions if the ASP.NET process shuts down. You can also store your sessions to disk (in a database for example) using the `SQLServer` option. This method enables you to store your sessions directly in Microsoft's SQL Server. How do you go about changing the provider that is used for sessions? You can do this in a couple of ways.

One option to change the provider used for sessions is through the Internet Information Services (IIS) Manager, as shown in Figure 11-1.

The other option is to go directly to a system-wide configuration file (such as the `machine.config` file) or to an application configuration file (such as the `web.config`). In the file, change the name of the session state provider that is to be used within the `<sessionState>` section of the configuration document.

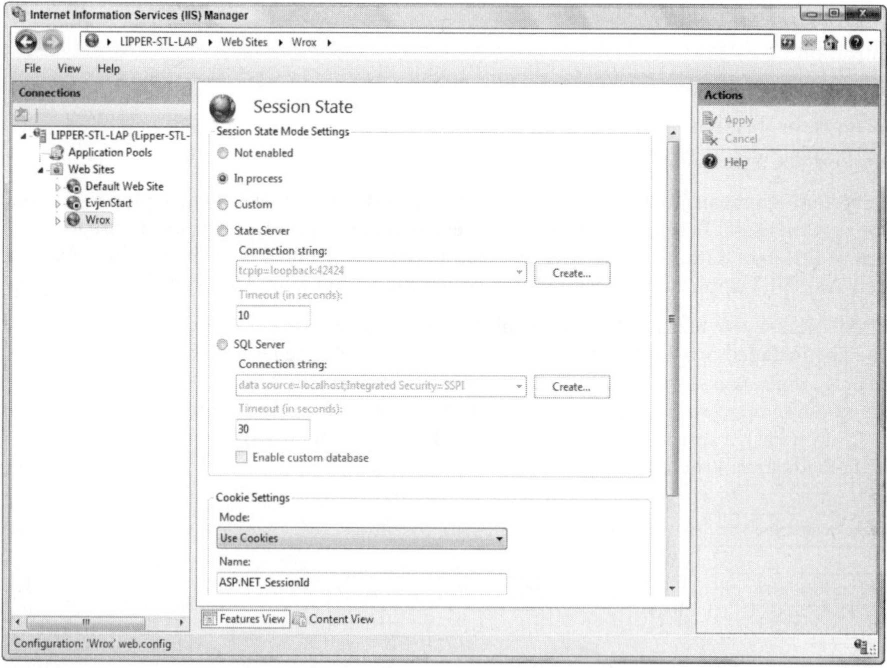

FIGURE 11-1

Since ASP.NET 2.0, you have been able to take this provider model one step further than you ever could before. You will discover this next.

THE PROVIDER MODEL IN ASP.NET 4

Back when ASP.NET 2.0 was being developed, plenty of requests came into the ASP.NET team. Users wanted to be able to store sessions by means other than the three methods — `InProc`, `StateServer`, and `SQLServer`. For example, one such request was for a provider that could store sessions in an Oracle database. This might seem as if it's a logical thing to add to ASP.NET in the days of ASP.NET 1.1. But if the team added a provider for Oracle, they would soon get requests to add even more providers for other databases and data storage methods. For this reason, instead of building providers for each and every possible scenario, the developers designed a provider model that enabled them to add any providers they wanted. Thus, the new provider model found in ASP.NET was born.

Today, ASP.NET 4 includes a lot of systems that require state storage of some kind. Also, instead of recording state in a fragile mode (the way sessions are stored by default), many of these systems require that their state be stored in more concrete data stores such as databases or XML files. This also allows a longer-lived state for the users visiting an application — something else that is required by these systems.

The systems based upon the provider model found in ASP.NET 4 that require advanced state management include the following:

- Membership
- Role management

- Site navigation
- Personalization
- Health monitoring Web events
- Web Parts personalization
- Configuration file protection

The membership system is a means to allow ASP.NET to work from a user store of some kind to create, delete, or edit application users. Because it is rather apparent that developers want to work with an unlimited amount of different data stores for their user store, they need a means to change the underlying user store for their ASP.NET applications easily. The provider model found in ASP.NET 4 is the answer.

Out of the box, ASP.NET 4 provides a couple of membership providers that enable you to store user information. The included providers are the SQL Server and the Active Directory membership providers (found at `System.Web.Security.SqlMembershipProvider` and `System.Web.Security.ActiveDirectoryMembershipProvider`, respectively). In fact, for each of the systems (as well as for some of the ASP.NET 1.*x* systems), a series of providers is available to alter the way the state of that system is recorded. Figure 11-2 illustrates these providers.

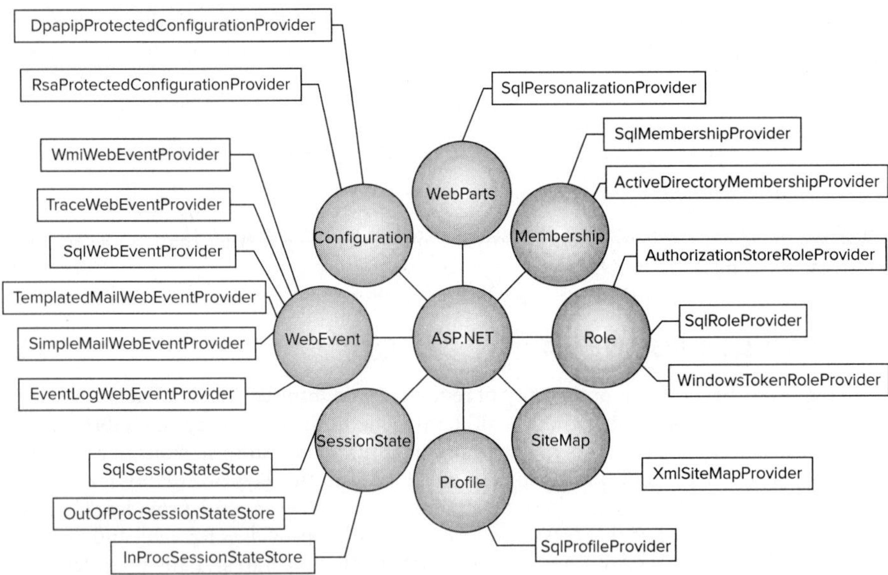

FIGURE 11-2

As you can see from the diagram, ASP.NET provides a large number of providers out of the box. Some systems have only a single provider (such as the profile system that includes only a provider to connect to SQL Server), whereas other systems include multiple providers (such as the WebEvents provider that includes six separate providers). Next, this chapter reviews how to set up SQL Server to work with a number of the providers presented in this chapter. You can use SQL Server 7.0, 2000, 2005, or 2008 for the backend data store for many of the providers presented (although not all of them). After this explanation, you review each of the available providers built into ASP.NET 4.

Setting Up Your Provider to Work with Microsoft SQL Server 7.0, 2000, 2005, or 2008

Quite a number of providers work with SQL Server. For example, the membership, role management, personalization, and other systems work with SQL Server right out of the box. However, all these systems work with the Microsoft SQL Server Express Edition file (`.mdf`) by default instead of with one of the full-blown versions of SQL Server such as SQL Server 7.0, SQL Server 2000, SQL Server 2005, or SQL Server 2008.

To work with any of these databases, you must set up the database using the `aspnet_regsql.exe` tool. Working with `aspnet_regsql.exe` creates the necessary tables, roles, stored procedures, and other items needed by the providers. To get at this tool, open up the Visual Studio 2010 Command Prompt by selecting Start ➪ All Programs ➪ Microsoft Visual Studio 2010 ➪ Visual Studio Tools ➪ Visual Studio 2010 Command Prompt. This gives you access to the ASP.NET SQL Server Setup Wizard. The ASP.NET SQL Server Setup Wizard is an easy-to-use tool that facilitates setup of the SQL Server to work with many of the systems that are built into ASP.NET 4, such as the membership, role management, and personalization systems. The Setup Wizard provides two ways for you to set up the database: using a command-line tool or using a GUI tool. First, look at the command-line version of the tool.

The ASP.NET SQL Server Setup Wizard Command-Line Tool

The command-line version of the Setup Wizard gives the developer optimal control over how the database is created. Working from the command line to use this tool is not difficult, so don't be intimidated by it.

You can get at the actual tool, `aspnet_regsql.exe`, from the Visual Studio Command Prompt if you have Visual Studio 2010. At the command prompt, type `aspnet_regsql.exe -?` to get a list of all the command-line options at your disposal for working this tool.

Table 11-1 describes some of the available options for setting up your SQL Server instance to work with the personalization framework.

TABLE 11-1

COMMAND OPTION	DESCRIPTION
`-?`	Displays a list of available option commands.
`-W`	Uses the Wizard mode. This uses the default installation if no other parameters are used.
`-S <server>`	Specifies the SQL Server instance to work with.
`-U <login>`	Specifies the username to log in to SQL Server. If you use this, you also use the `-P` command.
`-P <password>`	Specifies the password to use for logging in to SQL Server. If you use this, you also use the `-U` command.
`-E`	Provides instructions to use the current Windows credentials for authentication.
`-C`	Specifies the connection string for connecting to SQL Server. If you use this, you can avoid using the `-U` and `-P` commands because they are specified in the connection string itself.
`-A all`	Adds support for all the available SQL Server operations provided by ASP.NET including membership, role management, profiles, site counters, and page/control personalization.

continues

TABLE 11-1 *(continued)*

COMMAND OPTION	DESCRIPTION
`-A p`	Adds support for working with profiles.
`-R all`	Removes support for all the available SQL Server operations that have been previously installed. These include membership, role management, profiles, site counters, and page/control personalization.
`-R p`	Removes support for the profile capability from SQL Server.
`-d <database>`	Specifies the database name to use with the application services. If you don't specify a name of a database, aspnetdb is used.
`-sqlexportonly <filename>`	Instead of modifying an instance of a SQL Server database, use this command in conjunction with the other commands to generate a SQL script that adds or removes the features specified. This command creates the scripts in a file that has the name specified in the command.

To modify SQL Server to work with the personalization provider using this command-line tool, you enter a command such as the following:

```
aspnet_regsql.exe -A all -E
```

After you enter the preceding command, the command-line tool creates the features required by all the available ASP.NET 4 systems. The results are shown in the tool itself, as you see in Figure 11-3.

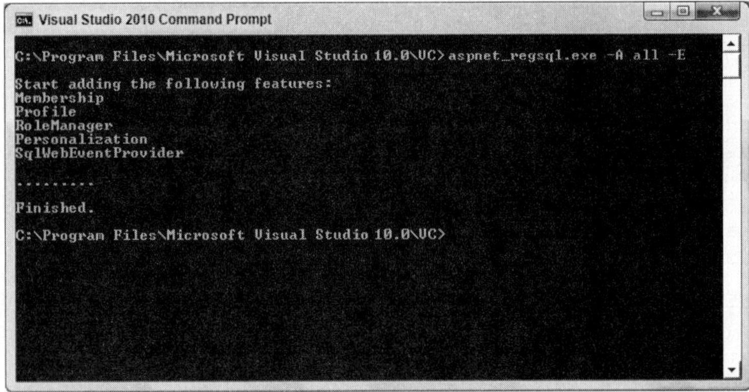

FIGURE 11-3

When this action is completed, you can see that a new database, `aspnetdb`, has been created in the Microsoft SQL Server Management Studio, which is part of Microsoft SQL Server 2008 (the database used for this example). You now have the appropriate tables for working with all the ASP.NET systems that are able to work with SQL Server (see Figure 11-4).

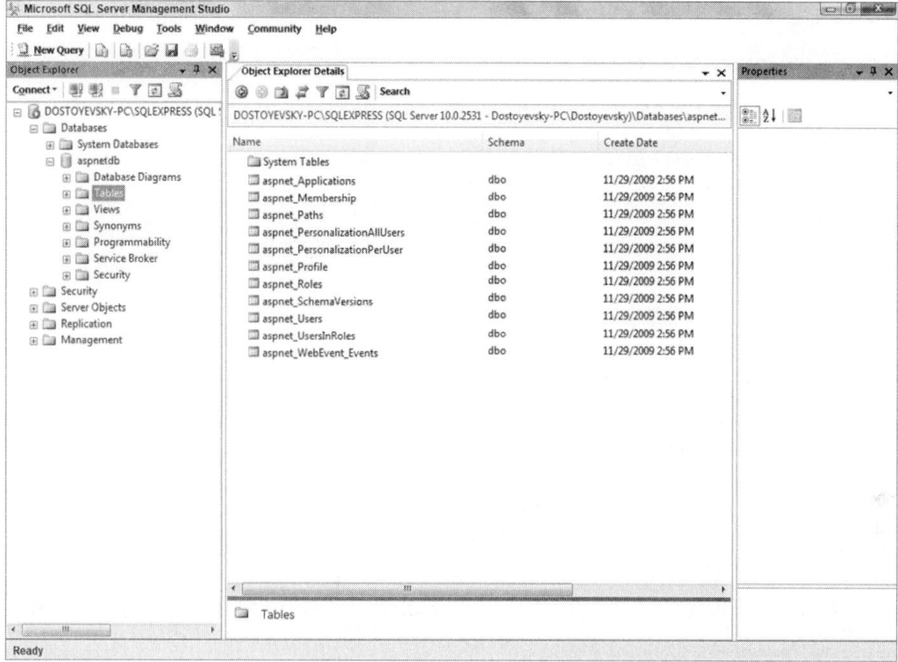

FIGURE 11-4

One advantage of using the command-line tool rather than the GUI-based version of the ASP.NET SQL Server Setup Wizard is that you can install in the database just the features that you are interested in working with instead of installing everything (as the GUI-based version does). For example, if you are going to have only the membership system interact with SQL Server 2008 — not any of the other systems (such as role management and personalization) — then you can configure the setup so that only the tables, roles, stored procedures, and other items required by the membership system are established in the database. To set up the database for the membership system only, you use the following command on the command line.

```
aspnet_regsql.exe -A m -E
```

The ASP.NET SQL Server Setup Wizard GUI Tool

Instead of working with the tool through the command line, you can also work with a GUI version of the same wizard. To get at the GUI version, type the following at the Visual Studio command prompt:

```
aspnet_regsql.exe
```

At this point, the ASP.NET SQL Server Setup Wizard welcome screen appears, as shown in Figure 11-5.

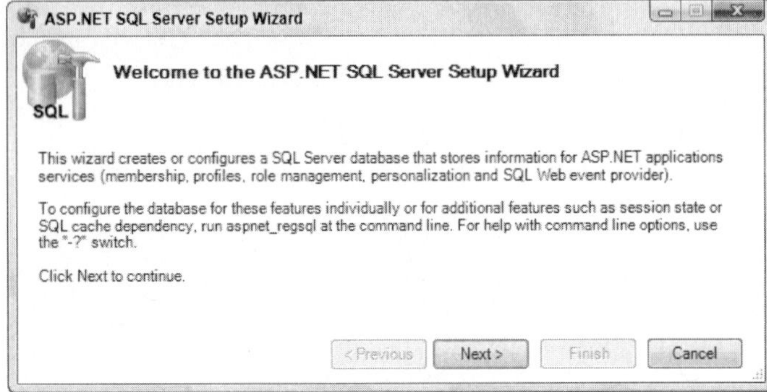

FIGURE 11-5

Clicking Next gives you a new screen that offers two options: one to install management features into SQL Server and the other to remove them (see Figure 11-6).

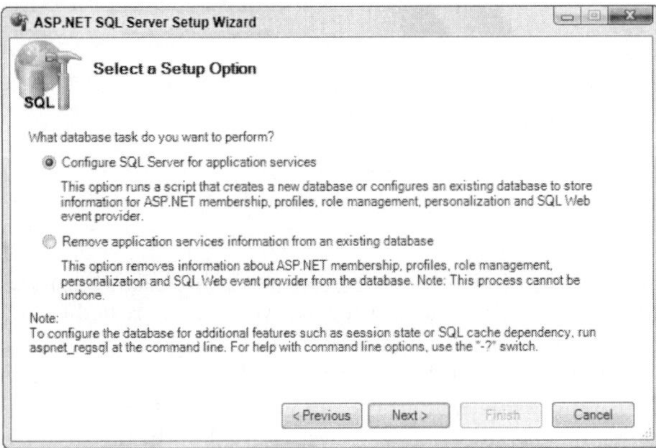

FIGURE 11-6

From here, choose the Configure SQL Server for application services and click the Next button. The third screen (see Figure 11-7) asks for the login credentials to SQL Server and the name of the database to perform the operations. The Database option is `<default>` — meaning that the wizard creates a database called `aspnetdb`. If you want to choose a different folder, such as the application's database, choose the appropriate option.

ASP.NET SQL Server Setup Wizard
Select the Server and Database
SQL
Specify the SQL Server name, database name to create or remove, and the credentials to use when connecting to the database.
Note: The credentials must identify a user account that has permissions to create or remove a database.
Server: EVJEN01
Windows authentication
SQL Server authentication
User name:
Password:
Database: <default>
< Previous
Next >
Finish
Cancel

FIGURE 11-7

After you have made your server and database selections, click Next. The screen shown in Figure 11-8 asks you to confirm your settings. If everything looks correct, click Next — otherwise, click Previous and correct your settings.

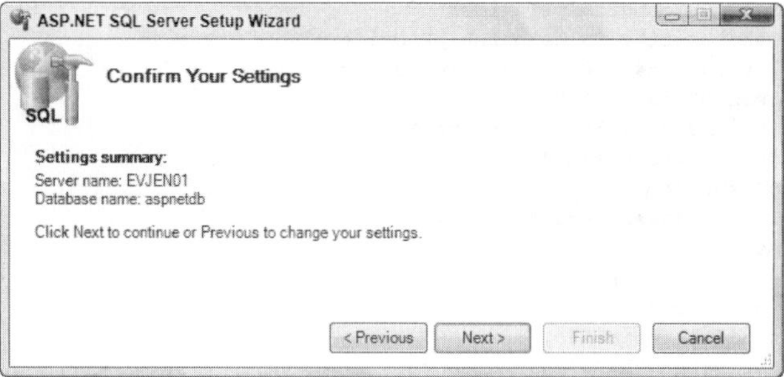

FIGURE 11-8

When this is complete, a screen appears, notifying you that everything was set up correctly.

Connecting Your Default Provider to a New SQL Server Instance

After you set up the full-blown Microsoft SQL Server to work with the various systems provided by ASP. NET, you create a connection string to the database in your `machine.config` or `web.config` file, as shown in Listing 11-1.

Available for download on Wrox.com

LISTING 11-1: Changing the connection string in the machine.config.comments or your web.config file to work with SQL Server 2008

```
<configuration>

     <connectionStrings>
        <add name="LocalSqlServer"
         connectionString="Data Source=127.0.0.1;Integrated Security=SSPI" />
     </connectionStrings>

</configuration>
```

You may want to change the values provided if you are working with a remote instance of SQL Server rather than an instance that resides on the same server as the application. Changing this value in the `machine.config` file changes how each and every ASP.NET application uses this provider. Applying this setting in the `web.config` file causes only the local application to work with this instance.

After the connection string is set up, look further in the `<providers>` section of the section you are going to work with. For example, if you are using the membership provider, you want to work with the `<membership>` element in the configuration file. The settings to change the SQL Server are shown in Listing 11-2.

Available for download on Wrox.com

LISTING 11-2: Altering the SQL Server used via configuration

```
<configuration>

  <connectionStrings>
     <add name="LocalSql2008Server"
      connectionString="Data Source=127.0.0.1;Integrated Security=SSPI";
        Initial Catalog=aspnetdb;" />
  </connectionStrings>

  <system.web>
```

continues

LISTING 11-2 *(continued)*

```
            <membership defaultProvider="AspNetSql2008MembershipProvider">
                <providers>
                    <add name="AspNetSql2008MembershipProvider"
                        type="System.Web.Security.SqlMembershipProvider,
                           System.Web, Version=4.0.0.0, Culture=neutral,
                           PublicKeyToken=b03f5f7f11d50a3a"
                        connectionStringName="LocalSql2008Server"
                        enablePasswordRetrieval="false"
                        enablePasswordReset="true"
                        requiresQuestionAndAnswer="true"
                        applicationName="/"
                        requiresUniqueEmail="false"
                        passwordFormat="Hashed"
                        maxInvalidPasswordAttempts="5"
                        minRequiredPasswordLength="7"
                        minRequiredNonalphanumericCharacters="1"
                        passwordAttemptWindow="10"
                        passwordStrengthRegularExpression="" />
                </providers>
            </membership>
        </system.web>

    </configuration>
```

With these changes in place, the SQL Server 2008 instance is now one of the providers available for use with your applications. The name of this provider instance is `AspNetSql2008MembershipProvider`. You can see that this instance also uses the connection string of `LocalSql2008Server`, which was defined in Listing 11-1.

Pay attention to some important attribute declarations from Listing 11-2. The first is that the provider used by the membership system is defined via the `defaultProvider` attribute found in the main `<membership>` node. Using this attribute, you can specify whether the provider is one of the built-in providers or whether it is a custom provider that you have built yourself or received from a third party. With the code from Listing 11-2 in place, the membership provider now works with Microsoft SQL Server 2008 (as shown in this example) instead of the Microsoft SQL Server Express Edition files.

Next, you look at the providers that come built into the ASP.NET 4 install — starting with the membership system providers.

Membership Providers

The membership system enables you to easily manage users in your ASP.NET applications. As with most of the systems provided in ASP.NET, it features a series of server controls that interact with a defined provider to either retrieve or record information to and from the data store defined by the provider. Because a provider exists between the server controls and the data stores where the data is retrieved and recorded, having the controls work from an entirely different backend is fairly trivial. You just change the underlying provider of the overall system (in this case, the membership system) by making a simple configuration change in the ASP.NET application. It really makes no difference to the server controls.

As previously stated, ASP.NET 4 provides two membership providers out of the box:

- `System.Web.Security.SqlMembershipProvider`: Provides you with the capability to use the membership system to connect to Microsoft's SQL Server 2000/2005/2008 as well as with Microsoft SQL Server Express Edition.
- `System.Web.Security.ActiveDirectoryMembershipProvider`: Provides you with the capability to use the membership system to connect to Microsoft's Active Directory.

Both of these membership provider classes inherit from the `MembershipProvider` base class, as illustrated in Figure 11-9.

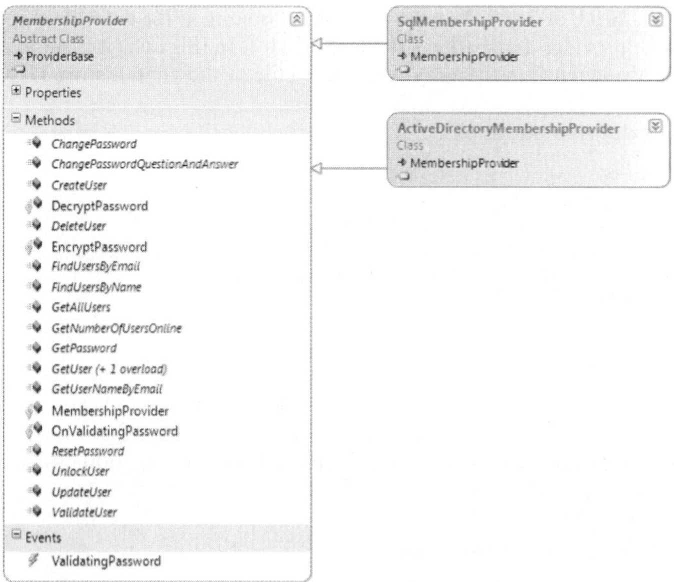

FIGURE 11-9

Next, you review each of these providers.

System.Web.Security.SqlMembershipProvider

The default provider is the `SqlMembershipProvider` instance. You find this default declaration for every ASP.NET application that resides on the application server in the `machine.config` file. You find this file in `C:\WINDOWS\Microsoft.NET\Framework\v4.0.21006\CONFIG`. Listing 11-3 shows the definition of this provider, which is located in the `machine.config` file.

Available for download on Wrox.com

LISTING 11-3: A SqlMembershipProvider instance declaration

```
<configuration>
   <system.web>
        <membership>
            <providers>
               <add name="AspNetSqlMembershipProvider"
                type="System.Web.Security.SqlMembershipProvider,
                   System.Web, Version=4.0.0.0, Culture=neutral,
                   PublicKeyToken=b03f5f7f11d50a3a"
                connectionStringName="LocalSqlServer"
                enablePasswordRetrieval="false" enablePasswordReset="true"
                requiresQuestionAndAnswer="true" applicationName="/"
                requiresUniqueEmail="false" passwordFormat="Hashed"
                maxInvalidPasswordAttempts="5" minRequiredPasswordLength="7"
                minRequiredNonalphanumericCharacters="1" passwordAttemptWindow="10"
                passwordStrengthRegularExpression=""/>
            </providers>
        </membership>
   </system.web>
</configuration>
```

From this listing, you can see that a single instance of the `SqlMembershipProvider` object is defined in the `machine.config` file. This single instance is named `AspNetSqlMembershipProvider`. This is also where you find the default behavior settings for your membership system. By default, this provider is also configured to work with a SQL Server Express Edition instance rather than a full-blown version of SQL Server such as SQL Server 2000, 2005, or 2008. You can see this by looking at the defined `connectionStringName` property in the provider declaration from Listing 11-3. In this case, it is set to `LocalSqlServer`. `LocalSqlServer` is also defined in the `machine.config` file as shown in Listing 11-4.

LISTING 11-4: The LocalSqlServer defined instance

Available for download on Wrox.com

```
<configuration>
  <connectionStrings>
    <clear />
    <add name="LocalSqlServer"
     connectionString="data source=.\SQLEXPRESS;Integrated Security=SSPI;
        AttachDBFilename=|DataDirectory|aspnetdb.mdf;User Instance=true"
     providerName="System.Data.SqlClient" />
  </connectionStrings>
</configuration>
```

You can see this connection string information is set for a local SQL Server Express Edition file (an `.mdf` file). Of course, you are not required to work with only these file types for the `SqlMembershipProvider` capabilities. Instead, you can also set it up to work with either Microsoft's SQL Server 7.0, 2000, 2005, or 2008 (as was previously shown).

System.Web.Security.ActiveDirectoryMembershipProvider

It is also possible for the membership system provided from ASP.NET 4 to connect this system to a Microsoft Active Directory instance or even Active Directory Application Mode (ADAM), which is a standalone directory product. Because the default membership provider is defined in the `machine.config` files at the `SqlMembershipProvider`, you must override these settings in your application's `web.config` file.

Before creating a defined instance of the `ActiveDirectoryMembershipProvider` in your `web.config` file, you must define the connection string to the Active Directory store, as shown in Listing 11-5.

LISTING 11-5: Defining the connection string to the Active Directory store

Available for download on Wrox.com

```
<configuration>
   <connectionStrings>
      <add name="ADConnectionString"
       connectionString=
       "LDAP://domain.myAdServer.com/CN=Users,DC=domain,DC=testing,DC=com" />
   </connectionStrings>
</configuration>
```

With the connection in place, you can create an instance of the `ActiveDirecotryMembershipProvider` in your `web.config` file that associates itself to this connection string, as illustrated in Listing 11-6.

LISTING 11-6: Defining the ActiveDirectoryMembershipProvider instance

Available for download on Wrox.com

```
<configuration>

   <connectionStrings>
      <add name="ADConnectionString"
       connectionString=
       "LDAP://domain.myAdServer.com/CN=Users,DC=domain,DC=testing,DC=com" />
   </connectionStrings>

   <system.web>
     <membership
      defaultProvider="AspNetActiveDirectoryMembershipProvider">
      <providers>
        <add name="AspNetActiveDirectoryMembershipProvider"
          type="System.Web.Security.ActiveDirectoryMembershipProvider,
```

```
              System.Web, Version=4.0.0.0, Culture=neutral,
              PublicKeyToken=b03f5f7f11d50a3a"
            connectionStringName="ADConnectionString"
            connectionUserName="UserWithAppropriateRights"
            connectionPassword="PasswordForUser"
            connectionProtection="Secure"
            enablePasswordReset="true"
            enableSearchMethods="true"
            requiresQuestionAndAnswer="true"
            applicationName="/"
            description="Default AD connection"
            requiresUniqueEmail="false"
            clientSearchTimeout="30"
            serverSearchTimeout="30"
            attributeMapPasswordQuestion="department"
            attributeMapPasswordAnswer="division"
            attributeMapFailedPasswordAnswerCount="singleIntAttribute"
            attributeMapFailedPasswordAnswerTime="singleLargeIntAttribute"
            attributeMapFailedPassswordAnswerLockoutTime="singleLargeIntAttribute"
            maxInvalidPasswordAttemps = "5"
            passwordAttemptWindow = "10"
            passwordAnswerAttemptLockoutDuration = "30"
            minRequiredPasswordLength="7"
            minRequiredNonalphanumericCharacters="1"
            passwordStrengthRegularExpression=
              "@\"(?=.{6,})(?=(.*\d){1,})(?=(.*\W){1,})" />
        />
      </providers>
    </membership>
  </system.web>

</configuration>
```

Although not all these attributes are required, this list provides you with the available attributes of the `ActiveDirectoryMembershipProvider`. In fact, you can easily declare the instance in its simplest form, as shown here:

```
<membership defaultProvider="AspNetActiveDirectoryMembershipProvider">
  <providers>
    <add name="AspNetActiveDirectoryMembershipProvider"
      type="System.Web.Security.ActiveDirectoryMembershipProvider,
        System.Web, Version=4.0.0.0, Culture=neutral,
        PublicKeyToken=b03f5f7f11d50a3a"
      connectionStringName="ADConnectionString" />
  </providers>
</membership>
```

Again, with either the `SqlMembershipProvider` or the `ActiveDirectoryMembershipProvider` in place, the membership system server controls (such as the Login server control) as well as the membership API, once configured, will record and retrieve their information via the provider you have established. That is the power of the provider model that the ASP.NET team has established. You continue to see this power as you learn about the rest of the providers detailed in this chapter.

Role Providers

After a user is logged into the system (possibly using the ASP.NET membership system), the ASP.NET role management system enables you to work with the role of that user to authorize him for a particular access to the overall application. The role management system in ASP.NET 4, as with the other systems, has a set of providers to store and retrieve role information in an easy manner. This, of course, doesn't mean that you are bound to one of the three available providers in the role management system. Instead, you can extend one of the established providers or even create your own custom provider.

By default, ASP.NET 4 offers three providers for the role management system. These providers are defined in the following list:

- `System.Web.Security.SqlRoleProvider`: Provides you with the capability to use the ASP.NET role management system to connect to Microsoft's SQL Server 2000/2005/2008 as well as to Microsoft SQL Server Express Edition.
- `System.Web.Security.WindowsTokenRoleProvider`: Provides you with the capability to connect the ASP.NET role management system to the built-in Windows security group system.
- `System.Web.Security.AuthorizationStoreRoleProvider`: Provides you with the capability to connect the ASP.NET role management system to either an XML file, Active Directory, or in an Active Directory Application Mode (ADAM) store.

These three classes for role management inherit from the `RoleProvider` base class, as illustrated in Figure 11-10.

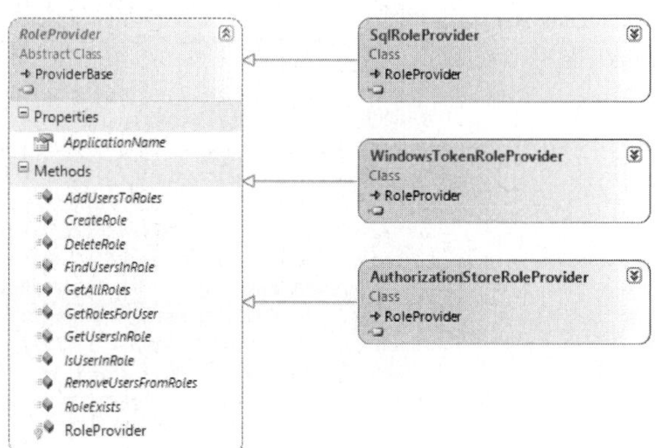

FIGURE 11-10

System.Web.Security.SqlRoleProvider

The role management system in ASP.NET uses SQL Server Express Edition files by default (just as the membership system does). The connection to the SQL Server Express file uses `SqlRoleProvider`, but you can just as easily configure your SQL Server 7.0, 2000, 2005, or 2008 server to work with the role management system through `SqlRoleProvider`. The procedure for setting up your full-blown SQL Server is described in the beginning of this chapter.

Looking at the `SqlRoleProvider` instance in the `machine.config.comments` file, you will notice the syntax as defined in Listing 11-7. The `machine.config.comments` file provides documentation on the `machine.config` and shows you the details of the default settings that are baked into the ASP.NET Framework.

Available for download on Wrox.com

LISTING 11-7: A SqlRoleProvider instance declaration

```
<configuration>
  <system.web>
     <roleManager enabled="false" cacheRolesInCookie="false"
      cookieName=".ASPXROLES" cookieTimeout="30" cookiePath="/"
      cookieRequireSSL="false" cookieSlidingExpiration="true"
      cookieProtection="All" defaultProvider="AspNetSqlRoleProvider"
      createPersistentCookie="false" maxCachedResults="25">
        <providers>
           <add name="AspNetSqlRoleProvider"
            connectionStringName="LocalSqlServer" applicationName="/"
            type="System.Web.Security.SqlRoleProvider,
            System.Web, Version=4.0.0.0, Culture=neutral,
            PublicKeyToken=b03f5f7f11d50a3a" />
        </providers>
     </roleManager>
  </system.web>
</configuration>
```

As stated, this is part of the default `<roleManager>` declaration that is baked into the overall ASP.NET Framework (note again that you can change any of these defaults by making a new declaration in your web.config file). As you can see, role management is disabled by default through the enabled attribute found in the <roleManager> node (it is set to false by default). Also, pay attention to the defaultProvider attribute in the <roleManager> element. In this case, it is set to AspNetSqlRoleProvider. This provider is defined in the same code example. To connect to the Microsoft SQL Server 2008 instance that was defined earlier (in the membership system examples), you can use the syntax shown in Listing 11-8.

Available for download on Wrox.com

LISTING 11-8: Connecting the role management system to SQL Server 2008

```
<configuration>

  <connectionStrings>
     <add name="LocalSql2008Server"
      connectionString="Data Source=127.0.0.1;Integrated Security=SSPI" />
  </connectionStrings>
  <system.web>
        <roleManager enabled="true" cacheRolesInCookie="true"
         cookieName=".ASPXROLES" cookieTimeout="30" cookiePath="/"
         cookieRequireSSL="false" cookieSlidingExpiration="true"
         cookieProtection="All" defaultProvider="AspNetSqlRoleProvider"
         createPersistentCookie="false" maxCachedResults="25">
            <providers>
                <clear />
                <add connectionStringName="LocalSql2008Server" applicationName="/"
                 name="AspNetSqlRoleProvider"
                 type="System.Web.Security.SqlRoleProvider, System.Web,
                   Version=4.0.0.0, Culture=neutral,
                   PublicKeyToken=b03f5f7f11d50a3a" />
            </providers>
        </roleManager>
  </system.web>
</configuration>
```

With this in place, you can now connect to SQL Server 2008. Next is a review of the second provider available to the role management system.

System.Web.Security.WindowsTokenRoleProvider

The Windows operating system has a role system built into it. This Windows security group system is an ideal system to use when you are working with intranet-based applications where you might have all users already in defined roles. This, of course, works best if you have anonymous authentication turned off for your ASP.NET application, and you have configured your application to use Windows Authentication.

Chapter 20 discusses Windows Authentication for ASP.NET applications.

Some limitations exist when you are using WindowsTokenRoleProvider. This is a read-only provider because ASP.NET is not allowed to modify the settings applied in the Windows security group system. This means that not all the methods provided via the RoleProvider abstract class are usable when working with this provider. From the WindowsTokenRoleProvider class, the only methods you have at your disposal are IsUserInRole and GetUsersInRole.

To configure your WindowsTokenRoleProvider instance, you use the syntax defined in Listing 11-9.

LISTING 11-9: A WindowsTokenRoleProvider instance

Available for download on Wrox.com

```
<configuration>
   <system.web>

      <authentication mode="Windows" />

      <roleManager defaultProvider="WindowsProvider"
       enabled="true"
       cacheRolesInCookie="false">
         <providers>
            <add
             name="WindowsProvider"
             type="System.Web.Security.WindowsTokenRoleProvider" />
         </providers>
      </roleManager>

   </system.web>
</configuration>
```

Remember that you have to declare the default provider using the `defaultProvider` attribute in the `<roleManager>` element to change the assigned provider from the `SqlRoleProvider` association.

System.Web.Security.AuthorizationStoreRoleProvider

The final role provider available to you from a default install of ASP.NET is `AuthorizationStoreRoleProvider`. This role provider class allows you to store roles inside of an Authorization Manager policy store. These types of stores are also referred to as AzMan stores. As with `WindowsTokenRoleProvider`, `AuthorizationStoreRoleProvider` is a bit limited because it is unable to support any AzMan business rules.

To use `AuthorizationStoreRoleProvider`, you must first make a connection in your `web.config` file to the XML data store used by AzMan, as shown in Listing 11-10.

LISTING 11-10: Making a connection to the AzMan policy store

Available for download on Wrox.com

```
<configuration>
  <connectionStrings>
    <add name="LocalPolicyStore"
         connectionString="msxml://<\App_Data\datafilename.xml" />
  </connectionStrings>
</configuration>
```

Note that when you work with these XML-based policy files, storing them in the App_Data folder is best. Files stored in the App_Data folder cannot be pulled up in the browser.

After the connection string is in place, the next step is to configure your `AuthorizationStoreRoleProvider` instance. This takes the syntax defined in Listing 11-11.

LISTING 11-11: Defining the AuthorizationStoreRoleProvider instance

Available for download on Wrox.com

```
<configuration>

  <connectionStrings>
    <add name="MyLocalPolicyStore"
         connectionString="msxml://<\App_Data\datafilename.xml" />
  </connectionStrings>

  <system.web>
```

```
    <authentication mode="Windows" />
    <identity impersonate="true" />

    <roleManager defaultProvider="AuthorizationStoreRoleProvider"
      enabled="true"
      cacheRolesInCookie="true"
      cookieName=".ASPROLES"
      cookieTimeout="30"
      cookiePath="/"
      cookieRequireSSL="false"
      cookieSlidingExpiration="true"
      cookieProtection="All" >
      <providers>
        <clear />
          <add
            name="AuthorizationStoreRoleProvider"
            type="System.Web.Security.AuthorizationStoreRoleProvider"
            connectionStringName="MyLocalPolicyStore"
            applicationName="SampleApplication"
            cacheRefreshInterval="60"
            scopeName="" />
      </providers>
    </roleManager>

  </system.web>

</configuration>
```

Next, this chapter reviews the single personalization provider available in ASP.NET.

The Personalization Provider

As with the membership system found in ASP.NET, the personalization system (also referred to as the profile system) is another system that is based on the provider model. This system makes associations between the end user viewing the application and any data points stored centrally that are specific to that user. As stated, these personalization properties are stored and maintained on a per-user basis. ASP.NET provides a single provider for data storage.

This provider is detailed here:

- `System.Web.Profile.SqlProfileProvider`: Provides you with the capability to use the ASP.NET personalization system to connect to Microsoft's SQL Server 2000/2005/2008 as well as to Microsoft SQL Server Express Edition.

This single class for the personalization system inherits from the `ProfileProvider` base class, as shown in Figure 11-11.

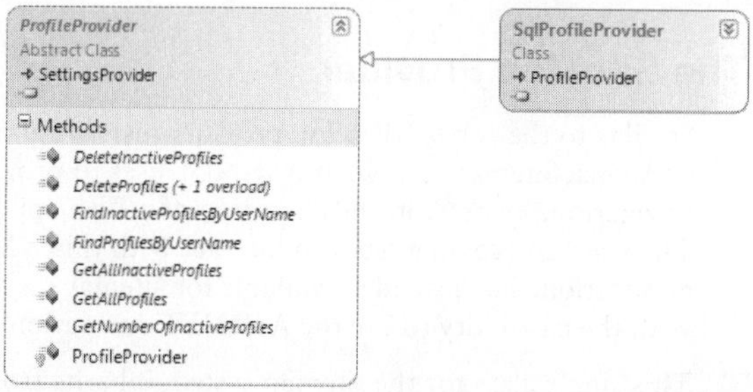

FIGURE 11-11

As with the other providers covered so far, `SqlProfileProvider` connects to a Microsoft SQL Server Express Edition file by default. Although this is the default, you can change the connection to work with SQL Server 7.0, 2000, 2005, or 2008. For example, if you are connecting to a SQL Server 2008 database, you define your connection in the `web.config` file and then associate your `SqlProfileProvider` declaration to this connection string. Listing 11-12 presents this scenario.

LISTING 11-12: Connecting the SqlProfileProvider to SQL Server 2008

```
<configuration>

     <connectionStrings>
        <add name="LocalSql2008Server"
         connectionString="Data Source=127.0.0.1;Integrated Security=SSPI" />
     </connectionStrings>

     <system.web>

     <profile>
        <providers>
           <clear />
           <add name="AspNetSql2008ProfileProvider"
            connectionStringName="LocalSql2008Server" applicationName="/"
            type="System.Web.Profile.SqlProfileProvider, System.Web,
              Version=4.0.0.0, Culture=neutral,
              PublicKeyToken=b03f5f7f11d50a3a" />
        </providers>

         <properties>
           <add name="FirstName" />
           <add name="LastName" />
           <add name="LastVisited" />
           <add name="Age" />
           <add name="Member" />
         </properties>
     </profile>

    </system.web>

</configuration>
```

Remember that to store profile information in your SQL Server database, you have to configure this database so the proper tables, stored procedures, and other items are created. This task was discussed earlier in the chapter.

The SiteMap Provider

Similar to the personalization provider just discussed, ASP.NET 4 provides a single provider to work with sitemaps. Sitemaps are what ASP.NET uses to provide you with a centralized way of maintaining site navigation. By default, the definition of a Web application's navigation is located in a structured XML file. The sitemap provider lets you interact with this XML file, the `.sitemap` file, which you create for your application. The provider available for sitemaps is `System.Web.XmlSiteMapProvider`, which provides you with the capability to use the ASP.NET navigation system to connect to an XML-based file.

This single class for the sitemap system inherits from the `StaticSiteMapProvider` base class, which is a partial implementation of the `SiteMapProvider` base class, as shown in Figure 11-12.

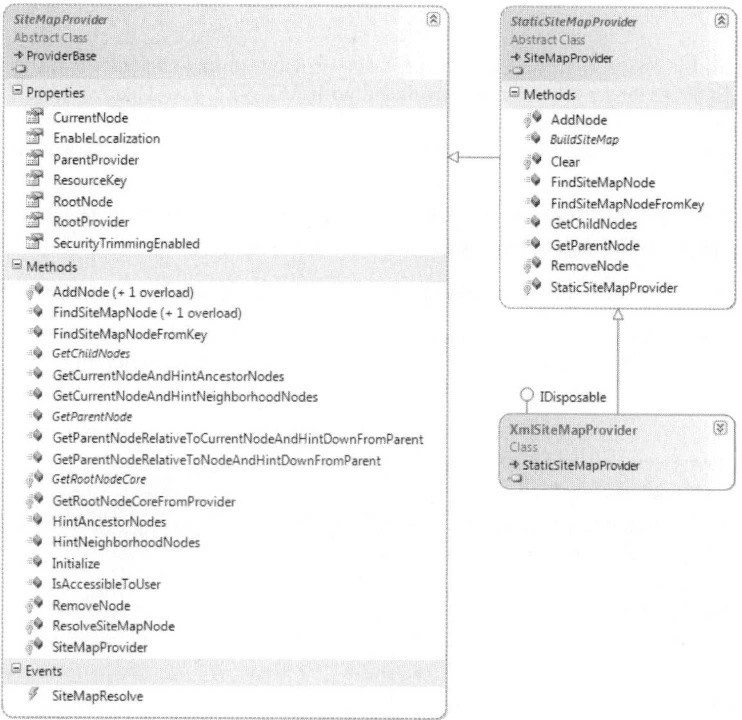

FIGURE 11-12

This is the first provider introduced so far that does not connect to a SQL Server database by default. Instead, this provider is designed to work with a static XML file. This XML file uses a particular schema and is covered in considerable detail in Chapter 13.

Listing 11-13 shows the code required to configure `XmlSiteMapProvider`.

Available for download on Wrox.com

LISTING 11-13: Defining an XmlSiteMapProvider instance in the web.config file

```
<configuration>
   <system.web>

      <siteMap defaultProvider="MyXmlSiteMapProvider" enabled="true">
         <providers>
            <add name="MyXmlSiteMapProvider"
             description="SiteMap provider that reads in .sitemap files."
             type="System.Web.XmlSiteMapProvider, System.Web, Version=4.0.0.0,
               Culture=neutral, PublicKeyToken=b03f5f7f11d50a3a"
             siteMapFile="AnotherWeb.sitemap" />
         </providers>
      </siteMap>

   </system.web>
</configuration>
```

The `XmlSiteMapProvider` allows only a single root element in the strictly designed `web.sitemap` file. The default filename of the XML file it is looking for is `web.sitemap`, although you can change this default setting (as you can see in Listing 11-13) by using the `siteMapFile` attribute within the provider declaration in the `web.config` file.

SessionState Providers

As mentioned in the beginning of the chapter, an original concept of a provider model existed when the idea of managing session state in different ways was first introduced with ASP.NET 1.*x*. The available modes of storing session state for your users include `InProc`, `StateServer`, `SQLServer`, or even `Custom`. Each mode has definite pros and cons associated with it, and you should examine each option thoroughly when deciding which session state mode to use.

You can find more information on these session state modes in Chapter 21.

This provider model is a bit different from the others discussed so far in this chapter. The `SessionStateModule` class is a handler provided to load one of the available session state modes. Each of these modes is defined here:

- `System.Web.SessionState.InProcSessionStateStore`: Provides you with the capability to store sessions in the same process as the ASP.NET worker process. This is by far the best-performing method of session state management.
- `System.Web.SessionState.OutOfProcSessionStateStore`: Provides you with the capability to store sessions in a process separate from the ASP.NET worker process. This mode is a little more secure, but a little worse in performance than the InProc mode.
- `System.Web.SessionState.SqlSessionStateStore`: Provides you with the capability to store sessions in SQL Server. This is by far the most secure method of storing sessions, but it is the worst performing mode of the three available methods.

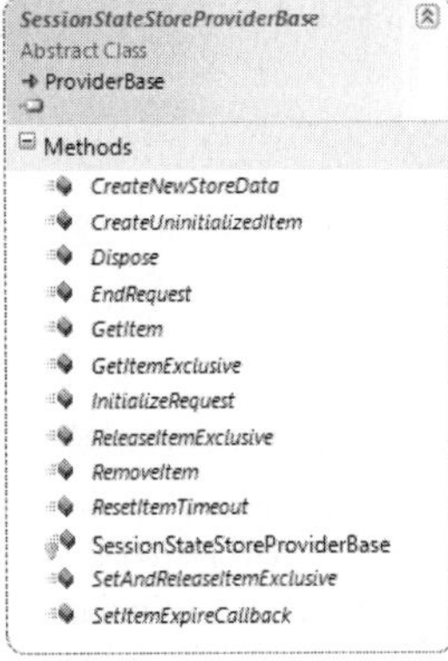

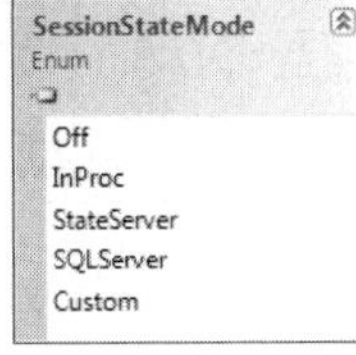

FIGURE 11-13

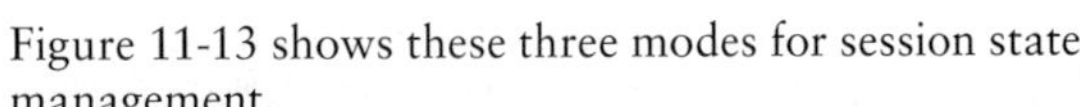

Figure 11-13 shows these three modes for session state management.

Next, this chapter reviews each of the three modes that you can use out of the box in your ASP.NET 4 applications.

System.Web.SessionState.InProcSessionStateStore

The `InProcSessionStateStore` mode is the default mode for ASP.NET 1.*x* and for ASP.NET 2.0, 3.5, and 4. In this mode, the sessions generated are held in the same process as that being used by the ASP.NET worker process (`aspnet_wp.exe` or `w3wp.exe`). This mode is the best performing, but some problems exist with this mode as well. Because the sessions are stored in the same process, whenever the worker process is recycled, all the sessions are destroyed. Worker processes can be recycled for many reasons (such as a change to the `web.config` file, the `Global.asax` file, or a setting in IIS that requires the process to be recycled after a set time period).

Listing 11-14 shows an example of the configuration in the `web.config` file for working in the InProc mode.

LISTING 11-14: Defining the InProc mode for session state management in the web.config file

Available for download on Wrox.com

```
<configuration>
   <system.web>

      <sessionState mode="InProc">
```

```
      </sessionState>

   </system.web>
</configuration>
```

As you can see, this mode is rather simple. The next method reviewed is the out-of-process mode — also referred to as the StateServer mode.

System.Web.SessionState.OutOfProcSessionStateStore

In addition to the InProc mode, the StateServer mode is an out-of-process method of storing session state. This method does not perform as well as one that stores the sessions in the same process as the ASP.NET worker process. This makes sense because the method must jump process boundaries to work with the sessions you are employing. Although the performance is poorer than it is in the InProc mode, the `OutOfProcSessionStateStore` method is more reliable than running the sessions using `InProcSessionStateStore`. If your application's worker process recycles, the sessions that this application is working with are still maintained. This capability is vital for those applications that are critically dependent upon sessions.

Listing 11-15 shows an example of using `OutOfProcSessionStateStore`.

Available for download on Wrox.com

LISTING 11-15: Running sessions out of process using OutOfProcSessionStateStore

```
<configuration>
   <system.web>

      <sessionState mode="StateServer"
       stateConnectionString="tcpip=127.0.0.1:42424">
      </sessionState>

   </system.web>
</configuration>
```

When using the StateServer mode, you also must define where the sessions are stored using the `stateConnectionString` attribute. In this case, the local server is used, meaning that the sessions are stored on the same machine, but in an entirely separate process. You could have just as easily stored the sessions on a different server by providing the appropriate IP address as a value for this attribute. In addition to the IP address, note that port 42424 is used. This port is required when using the StateServer mode for sessions. Chapter 21 covers changing the port for the StateServer.

System.Web.SessionState.SqlSessionStateStore

The final provider for session state management available to you in ASP.NET is the `SqlSessionStateStore`. This method is definitely the most resilient of the three available modes. With that said, however, it is also the worst performing of the three modes. Setting up your database appropriately is important if you use this method of session state storage. Again, Chapter 21 shows you how to set up your database.

To configure your application to work with `SqlSessionStateStore`, you must configure the `web.config` file as detailed in Listing 11-16.

Available for download on Wrox.com

LISTING 11-16: Defining SqlSessionStateStore in the web.config file

```
<configuration>
   <system.web>

      <sessionState mode="SQLServer"
       allowCustomSqlDatabase="true"
       sqlConnectionString="Data Source=127.0.0.1;
         database=MyCustomASPStateDatabase;Integrated Security=SSPI">
      </sessionState>

   </system.web>
</configuration>
```

Next, you review the providers available for the Web events architecture.

Web Event Providers

Among all the available systems provided in ASP.NET 4, more providers are available for the health monitoring system than for any other system. The health monitoring system enables ASP.NET application administrators to evaluate the health of a running ASP.NET application and to capture events (errors and other possible triggers) that can then be stored via one of the available providers. These events are referred to as *Web events*. A large list of events can be monitored via the health monitoring system, and this means that you can start recording items such as authentication failures/successes, all errors generated, ASP.NET worker process information, request data, response data, and more. Recording items means using one of the providers available to record to a data store of some kind.

Chapter 34 covers health monitoring in ASP.NET 4.

By default, ASP.NET 4 offers seven possible providers for the health monitoring system. This is more than for any of the other ASP.NET systems. These providers are defined in the following list:

- `System.Web.Management.EventLogWebEventProvider`: Provides you with the capability to use the ASP.NET health monitoring system to record security operation errors and all other errors into the Windows event log.
- `System.Web.Management.SimpleMailWebEventProvider`: Provides you with the capability to use the ASP.NET health monitoring system to send error information in an e-mail.
- `System.Web.Management.TemplatedMailWebEventProvider`: Similar to the `SimpleMailWebEventProvider`, the `TemplatedMailWebEventProvider` class provides you with the capability to send error information in a templated e-mail. Templates are defined using a standard `.aspx` page.
- `System.Web.Management.SqlWebEventProvider`: Provides you with the capability to use the ASP.NET health monitoring system to store error information in SQL Server. As with the other SQL providers for the other systems in ASP.NET, the `SqlWebEventProvider` stores error information in SQL Server Express Edition by default.
- `System.Web.Management.TraceWebEventProvider`: Provides you with the capability to use the ASP.NET health monitoring system to send error information to the ASP.NET page tracing system.
- `System.Web.Management.IisTraceWebEventProvider`: Provides you with the capability to use the ASP.NET health monitoring system to send error information to the IIS tracing system.
- `System.Web.Management.WmiWebEventProvider`: Provides you with the capability to connect the ASP.NET health monitoring system, the Windows Management Instrumentation (WMI) event provider.

These seven providers for the ASP.NET health monitoring system inherit from either the `WebEventProvider` base class, or the `BufferedWebEventProvider` (which, in turn, inherits from `WebEventProvider`), as shown in Figure 11-14.

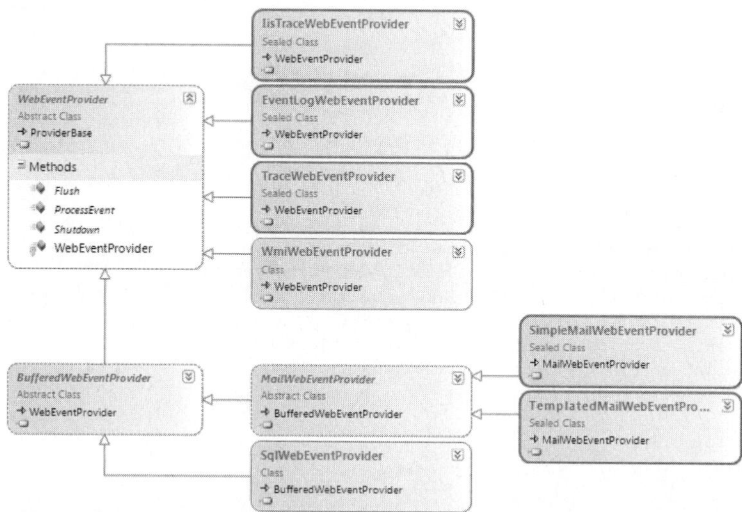

FIGURE 11-14

What is the difference between the `WebEventProvider` class and the `BufferedWebEventProvider`? The big difference is that the `WebEventProvider` writes events as they happen, whereas the `BufferedWebEventProvider` holds Web events until a collection of them is made. The collection is then written to the database or sent in an e-mail in a batch. If you use the `SqlWebEventProvider` class, you actually want this batch processing to occur rather than having the provider make a connection to the database and write to it for each Web event that occurs.

Next, this chapter looks at each of the seven available providers for the health monitoring system.

System.Web.Management.EventLogWebEventProvider

Traditionally, administrators and developers are used to reviewing system and application errors in the built-in Windows event log. The items in the event log can be viewed via the Event Viewer. You find this GUI-based tool for viewing events by selecting Administration Tools in the Control Panel and then selecting Event Viewer.

By default, the health monitoring system uses the Windows event log to record the items that are already specified in the server's configuration files or items you have specified in the `web.config` file of your application. If you look in the `web.config.comments` file in the CONFIG folder of the Microsoft .NET Framework installed on your server, you see that the `EventLogWebEventProvider` is detailed in this location. Listing 11-17 presents the code.

Available for download on Wrox.com

LISTING 11-17: The EventLogWebEventProvider declared in the web.config.comments file

```
<configuration>
   <system.web>

      <healthMonitoring heartbeatInterval="0" enabled="true">
         <bufferModes>
            <!-- Removed for clarity -->
         </bufferModes>
         <providers>
            <clear />
            <add name="EventLogProvider"
             type="System.Web.Management.EventLogWebEventProvider,
               System.Web,Version=4.0.0.0,Culture=neutral,
```

continues

LISTING 11-17 *(continued)*

```
              PublicKeyToken=b03f5f7f11d50a3a" />
           <!-- Removed for clarity -->
        </providers>
        <profiles>
           <!-- Removed for clarity -->
        </profiles>
        <rules>
           <add name="All Errors Default" eventName="All Errors"
            provider="EventLogProvider" profile="Default" minInstances="1"
            maxLimit="Infinite" minInterval="00:01:00" custom="" />
           <add name="Failure Audits Default" eventName="Failure Audits"
            provider="EventLogProvider" profile="Default" minInstances="1"
            maxLimit="Infinite" minInterval="00:01:00" custom="" />
        </rules>
        <eventMappings>
           <!-- Removed for clarity -->
        </eventMappings>
     </healthMonitoring>

  </system.web>
</configuration>
```

As you can see from Listing 11-17, a lot of possible settings can be applied in the health monitoring system. Depending on the rules and event mappings you have defined, these items are logged into the event log of the server that is hosting the application. Looking closely at the `<rules>` section of the listing, you can see that specific error types are assigned to be monitored. In this section, two types of errors are trapped in the health monitoring system — `All Errors Default` and `Failure Audits Default`.

When one of the errors defined in the `<rules>` section is triggered and captured by the health monitoring system, it is recorded. Where it is recorded depends upon the specified provider. The provider attribute used in the `<add>` element of the `<rules>` section determines this. In both cases in the example in Listing 11-17, you can see that the `EventLogProvider` is the assigned provider. This means that the Windows error log is used for recording the errors of both types.

As you work through the rest of the providers, note that the health monitoring system behaves differently when working with providers than the other systems that have been introduced in this chapter. Using the health monitoring system in ASP.NET 4, you are able to assign more than one provider at a time. This means that you are able to specify in the `web.config` *file that errors are logged not only into the Windows event log, but also into any other data store using any other provider you designate. Even for the same Web event type, you can assign the Web event to be recorded to the Windows event log and SQL Server at the same time, for example.*

System.Web.Management.SimpleMailWebEventProvider

Sometimes when errors occur in your applications, you as an administrator or a concerned developer want e-mail notification of the problem. In addition to recording events to disk using something such as the `EventLogWebEventProvider`, you can also have the error notification e-mailed to you using the `SimpleMailWebEventProvider`. As it states in the provider name, the e-mail is a simply constructed one. Listing 11-18 shows you how you would go about adding e-mail notification in addition to writing the errors to the Windows event log.

Available for download on Wrox.com

LISTING 11-18: The SimpleMailWebEventProvider definition

```
<configuration>
   <system.web>

      <healthMonitoring heartbeatInterval="0" enabled="true">
         <bufferModes>
            <add name="Website Error Notification"
             maxBufferSize="100"
             maxFlushSize="20"
             urgentFlushThreshold="1"
             regularFlushInterval="Infinite"
             urgentFlushInterval="00:01:00"
             maxBufferThreads="1" />
         </bufferModes>
         <providers>
            <clear />
            <add name="EventLogProvider"
             type="System.Web.Management.EventLogWebEventProvider,
               System.Web,Version=4.0.0.0,Culture=neutral,
               PublicKeyToken=b03f5f7f11d50a3a" />
            <add name="SimpleMailProvider"
             type="System.Web.Management.SimpleMailWebEventProvider,
              System.Web, Version=4.0.0.0, Culture=neutral,
              PublicKeyToken=b03f5f7f11d50a3a"
             from="website@company.com"
             to="admin@company.com"
             cc="adminLevel2@company.com
             bcc="director@company.com"
             bodyHeader="Warning!"
             bodyFooter="Please investigate ASAP."
             subjectPrefix="Action required."
             buffer="true"
             bufferMode="Website Error Notification"
             maxEventLength="4096"
             maxMessagesPerNotification="1" />
         </providers>
         <profiles>
            <!-- Removed for clarity -->
         </profiles>
         <rules>
            <add name="All Errors Default" eventName="All Errors"
             provider="EventLogProvider" profile="Default" minInstances="1"
             maxLimit="Infinite" minInterval="00:01:00" custom="" />
            <add name="Failure Audits Default" eventName="Failure Audits"
             provider="EventLogProvider" profile="Default" minInstances="1"
             maxLimit="Infinite" minInterval="00:01:00" custom="" />
            <add name="All Errors Simple Mail" eventName="All Errors"
             provider="SimpleMailProvider" profile="Default" />
            <add name="Failure Audits Default" eventName="Failure Audits"
             provider="SimpleMailProvider" profile="Default" />
         </rules>
         <eventMappings>
            <!-- Removed for clarity -->
         </eventMappings>
      </healthMonitoring>

   </system.web>
</configuration>
```

In this example, the errors that occur are captured and not only written to the event log, but are also e-mailed to the end users specified in the provider definition. One very interesting point of the `SimpleMailWebEventProvider` is that this class inherits from the `BufferedWebEventProvider` instead of from the `WebEventProvider` as the `EventLogWebEventProvider` does. Inheriting from the `BufferedWebEventProvider` means that you can have the health monitoring system build a collection of error notifications before sending them on. The `<bufferModes>` section defines how the buffering works.

System.Web.Management.TemplatedMailWebEventProvider

The aforementioned `SimpleMailWebEventProvider` does exactly what its name states — it sends out a simple, text-based e-mail. To send out a more artistically crafted e-mail that contains even more information, you can use the `TemplatedMailWebEventProvider`. Just like the `SimpleMailWebEventProvider`, you simply define the provider appropriately in the `<healthMonitoring>` section. Listing 11-19 presents the model for this definition.

LISTING 11-19: The TemplatedMailWebEventProvider definition

Available for download on Wrox.com

```
<providers>
   <clear />
   <add name="EventLogProvider"
    type="System.Web.Management.EventLogWebEventProvider,
      System.Web,Version=4.0.0.0,Culture=neutral,
      PublicKeyToken=b03f5f7f11d50a3a" />
   <add name="TemplatedMailProvider"
    type="System.Web.Management.TemplatedMailWebEventProvider,
      System.Web, Version=4.0.0.0, Culture=neutral,
      PublicKeyToken=b03f5f7f11d50a3a"
    template="../mailtemplates/errornotification.aspx"
    from="website@company.com"
    to="admin@company.com"
    cc="adminLevel2@company.com
    bcc="director@company.com"
    bodyHeader="Warning!"
    bodyFooter="Please investigate ASAP."
    subjectPrefix="Action required."
    buffer="true"
    bufferMode="Website Error Notification"
    maxEventLength="4096"
    maxMessagesPerNotification="1" />
</providers>
```

The big difference between this provider declaration and the `SimpleMailWebEventProvider` appears in bold in Listing 11-19. The `TemplatedMailWebEventProvider` has a `template` attribute that specifies the location of the template to use for the e-mail that is created and sent from the health monitoring system.

Again, Chapter 34 provides details on using the templated e-mail notification in the health monitoring system.

System.Web.Management.SqlWebEventProvider

In many instances, you may want to write to disk when you are trapping and recording the Web events that occur in your application. The `EventLogWebEventProvider` is an excellent provider because it writes these Web events to the Windows event log on your behalf. However, in some instances, you may want to write these Web events to disk elsewhere. In this case, a good alternative is writing these Web events to SQL Server instead (or even in addition to the writing to an event log).

Writing to SQL Server gives you some benefits over writing to the Windows event log. When your application is running in a Web farm, you might want all the errors that occur across the farm to be written to a single location. In this case, writing all Web events that are trapped via the health monitoring system to a SQL Server instance to which all the servers in the Web farm can connect makes sense.

By default, the `SqlWebEventProvider` (like the other SQL Server-based providers covered so far in this chapter) uses SQL Server Express Edition as its underlying database. To connect to the full-blown version of SQL Server instead, you need a defined connection as shown in Listing 11-20.

LISTING 11-20: The LocalSql2008Server defined instance

Available for download on Wrox.com

```
<configuration>

     <connectionStrings>
        <add name="LocalSql2008Server"
         connectionString="Data Source=127.0.0.1;Integrated Security=SSPI" />
     </connectionStrings>

</configuration>
```

With this connection in place, the next step is to use this connection in your `SqlWebEventProvider` declaration in the `web.config` file, as illustrated in Listing 11-21.

LISTING 11-21: Writing Web events to SQL Server 2008 using the SqlWebEventProvider

Available for download on Wrox.com

```
<configuration>
   <system.web>

      <healthMonitoring>

         <!-- Other nodes removed for clarity -->

         <providers>
            <clear />
            <add name="SqlWebEventProvider"
             type="System.Web.Management.SqlWebEventProvider,System.Web"
             connectionStringName="LocalSql2008Server"
             maxEventDetailsLength="1073741823"
             buffer="true"
             bufferMode="SQL Analysis" />
         </providers>
      </healthMonitoring>

   </system.web>
</configuration>
```

Events are now recorded in SQL Server 2008 on your behalf. The nice thing about the `SqlWebEventProvider` is that, as with the `SimpleMailWebEventProvider` and the `TemplatedMailWebEventProvider`, the `SqlWebEventProvider` inherits from the `BufferedWebEventProvider`. This means that the Web events can be written in batches as opposed to one by one. You trigger these batches by using the `buffer` and `bufferMode` attributes in the provider declaration. It works in conjunction with the settings applied in the `<bufferModes>` section of the `<healthMonitoring>` declarations.

System.Web.Management.TraceWebEventProvider

One method of debugging an ASP.NET application is to use the tracing capability built into the system. Tracing enables you to view details on the request, application state, cookies, the control tree, the form collection, and more. You output Web events to the trace output via the `TraceWebEventProvider` object. Setting the `TraceWebEventProvider` instance in a configuration file is shown in Listing 11-22.

LISTING 11-22: Writing Web events to the trace output using TraceWebEventProvider

Available for download on Wrox.com

```
<configuration>
   <system.web>

      <healthMonitoring>

         <!-- Other nodes removed for clarity -->

         <providers>
            <clear />
            <add name="TraceWebEventProvider"
             type="System.Web.Management.TraceWebEventProvider,System.Web"
             maxEventLength="4096"
             maxMessagesPerNotification="1" />
         </providers>

      </healthMonitoring>

   </system.web>
</configuration>
```

Remember, even with the provider in place, you must assign the provider to the particular errors you want to trap. You do so through the `<rules>` section of the health monitoring system.

The `IIsTraceWebEventProvider` is the same except that the tracing information is sent to IIS rather than to the ASP.NET tracing system.

System.Web.Management.WmiWebEventProvider

The last provider built into the health monitoring system is the `WmiWebEventProvider`. This provider enables you to map any Web events that come from the health monitoring system to Windows Management Instrumentation (WMI) events. When passed to the WMI subsystem, you can represent the events as objects. You accomplish this mapping to WMI events through the `aspnet.mof` file found at `C:\WINDOWS\Microsoft.NET\Framework\v4.0.21006`.

By default, the `WmiWebEventProvider` is already set up for you, and you simply need to map the Web events you are interested in to the already declared `WmiWebEventProvider` in the `<rules>` section of the health monitoring declaration. This declaration is documented in `web.config.comments` file in the CONFIG folder of the Microsoft .NET Framework install on your server and is shown in Listing 11-23 (the `WmiWebEventProvider` appears in bold).

LISTING 11-23: The WmiWebEventProvider definition in the web.config.comments file

Available for download on Wrox.com

```
<configuration>
   <system.web>

      <healthMonitoring>

         <!-- Other nodes removed for clarity -->

         <providers>
            <clear />
            <add name="EventLogProvider"
             type="System.Web.Management.EventLogWebEventProvider,
               System.Web,Version=4.0.0.0,Culture=neutral,
               PublicKeyToken=b03f5f7f11d50a3a" />
            <add connectionStringName="LocalSqlServer"
             maxEventDetailsLength="1073741823" buffer="false"
             bufferMode="Notification" name="SqlWebEventProvider"
             type="System.Web.Management.SqlWebEventProvider,
```

```
              System.Web,Version=4.0.0.0,Culture=neutral,
              PublicKeyToken=b03f5f7f11d50a3a" />
           <add name="WmiWebEventProvider"
            type="System.Web.Management.WmiWebEventProvider,
              System.Web,Version=4.0.0.0,Culture=neutral,
              PublicKeyToken=b03f5f7f11d50a3a" />
        </providers>

     </healthMonitoring>

  </system.web>
</configuration>
```

Remember, the wonderful thing about how the health monitoring system uses the provider model is that it permits more than a single provider for the Web events that the system traps.

Configuration Providers

A wonderful feature of ASP.NET 4 is that it enables you to actually encrypt sections of your configuration files. You are able to encrypt defined ASP.NET sections of the `web.config` file as well as custom sections that you have placed in the file yourself. This is an ideal way of keeping sensitive configuration information away from the eyes of everyone who peruses the file repository of your application.

By default, ASP.NET 4 provides two possible configuration providers out of the box. These providers are defined as follows:

- `System.Configuration.DpapiProtectedConfigurationProvider`: Provides you with the capability to encrypt and decrypt configuration sections using the Data Protection API (DPAPI) that is built into the Windows operating system.
- `System.Configuration.RsaProtectedConfigurationProvider`: Provides you with the capability to encrypt and decrypt configuration sections using an RSA public-key encryption algorithm.

These two providers used for encryption and decryption of the configuration sections inherit from the `ProtectedConfigurationProvider` base class as illustrated in Figure 11-15.

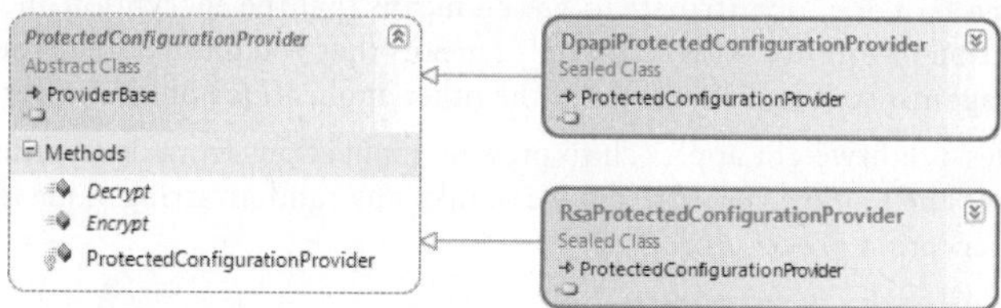

FIGURE 11-15

You can find information on how to use these providers to encrypt and decrypt configuration sections in Chapter 33.

Next, this chapter will take you through each of these providers.

System.Configuration.DpapiProtectedConfigurationProvider

The `DpapiProtectedConfigurationProvider` class enables you to encrypt and decrypt configuration sections using the Windows Data Protection API (DPAPI). This provider enables you to perform these encryption and decryption tasks on a per-machine basis. This provider is not good to use on a Web farm. If you are using protected configuration on your configuration files in a Web farm, you might want to turn your attention to the `RsaProtectedConfigurationProvider`.

If you look in the machine.config on your server, you see a definition in place for both the DpapiProtectedConfigurationProvider and the RsaProtectedConfigurationProvider. The RsaProtectedConfigurationProvider is set as the default configuration provider. To establish the DpapiProtectedConfigurationProvider as the default provider, you might use the web.config file of your application, or you might change the defaultProvider attribute in the machine.config file for the <configProtectedData> node. Changing it in the web.config file is shown in Listing 11-24.

LISTING 11-24: Using the DpapiProtectedConfigurationProvider in the web.config file

```
<configuration>

  <configProtectedData defaultProvider="DataProtectionConfigurationProvider">
    <providers>
      <clear />
      <add name="DataProtectionConfigurationProvider"
       type="System.Configuration.DpapiProtectedConfigurationProvider,
         System.Configuration, Version=4.0.0.0,
         Culture=neutral, PublicKeyToken=b03f5f7f11d50a3a"
       description="Uses CryptProtectData and CryptUnProtectData Windows
         APIs to encrypt and decrypt"
       useMachineProtection="true"
       keyEntropy="RandomStringValue" />
    </providers>
  </configProtectedData>

</configuration>
```

The provider is defined within the <configProtectedData> section of the configuration file. Note that this configuration section sits *outside* the <system.web> section.

The two main attributes of this provider definition are as follows:

- The useMachineProtection attribute by default is set to true, meaning that all applications in the server share the same means of encrypting and decrypting configuration sections. This also means that applications residing on the same machine can perform encryption and decryption against each other. Setting the useMachineProtection attribute to false means that the encryption and decryption are done on an application basis only. This setting also means that you must change the account that the application runs against so it is different from the other applications on the server.
- The keyEntropy attribute provides a lightweight approach to prevent applications from decrypting each other's configuration sections. The keyEntropy attribute can take any random string value to take part in the encryption and decryption processes.

System.Configuration.RsaProtectedConfigurationProvider

The default provider for encrypting and decrypting configuration sections is the RsaProtectedConfigurationProvider. You can see this setting in the machine.config file on your application server. Listing 11-25 presents code from the machine.config file.

LISTING 11-25: The RsaProtectedConfigurationProvider declaration in the machine.config file

```
<configuration>

  <configProtectedData defaultProvider="RsaProtectedConfigurationProvider">
    <providers>
      <add name="RsaProtectedConfigurationProvider"
       type="System.Configuration.RsaProtectedConfigurationProvider,
         System.Configuration, Version=4.0.0.0, Culture=neutral,
         PublicKeyToken=b03f5f7f11d50a3a"
```

```
        description="Uses RsaCryptoServiceProvider to encrypt and decrypt"
        keyContainerName="NetFrameworkConfigurationKey" cspProviderName=""
        useMachineContainer="true" useOAEP="false" />
      <add name="DataProtectionConfigurationProvider"
        type="System.Configuration.DpapiProtectedConfigurationProvider,
          System.Configuration, Version=4.0.0.0, Culture=neutral,
          PublicKeyToken=b03f5f7f11d50a3a"
        description="Uses CryptProtectData and CryptUnProtectData
          Windows APIs to encrypt and decrypt"
        useMachineProtection="true" keyEntropy="" />
    </providers>
  </configProtectedData>

</configuration>
```

The `RsaProtectedConfigurationProvider` uses Triple-DES encryption to encrypt the specified sections of the configuration file. This provider only has a few attributes available to it.

The `keyContainerName` attribute is the defined key container that is used for the encryption/decryption process. By default, this provider uses the default key container built into the .NET Framework, but you can easily switch an application to another key container via this attribute.

The `cspProviderName` attribute is only used if you have specified a custom cryptographic service provider (CSP) to use with the Windows Cryptographic API (CAPI). If so, you specify the name of the CSP as the value of the `cspProviderName` attribute.

The `useMachineContainer` attribute enables you to specify that you want either a machine-wide or user-specific key container. This attribute is quite similar to the `useMachineProtection` attribute found in the `DpapiProtectedConfigurationProvider`.

The `useOAEP` attribute specifies whether to turn on the Optional Asymmetric Encryption and Padding (OAEP) capability when performing the encryption/decryption process. This is set to `false` by default only because Windows 2000 does not support this capability. If your application is being hosted on Windows Server 2008 or Windows Server 2003, you can change the value of the `useOAEP` attribute to `true`.

The Web Parts Provider

Another feature of ASP.NET 4 is the capability to build your applications utilizing the Web Parts portal framework. This portal framework provides an outstanding way to build a modular Web site that can be customized with dynamically reapplied settings on a per-user basis. Web Parts are objects in the portal framework that the end user can open, close, minimize, maximize, or move from one part of the page to another.

Web Parts and this portal framework are covered in Chapter 16.

The state of these modular components, the Web Parts, must be stored somewhere so they can be reissued on the next visit for the assigned end user. The single provider available for remembering the state of the Web Parts is `System.Web.UI.WebControls.WebParts.SqlPersonalizationProvider`, which provides you with the capability to connect the ASP.NET 4 portal framework to Microsoft's SQL Server 2000, 2005, 2008 as well as to Microsoft SQL Server Express Edition.

This single class for the portal framework inherits from the `PersonalizationProvider` base class, as illustrated in Figure 11-16.

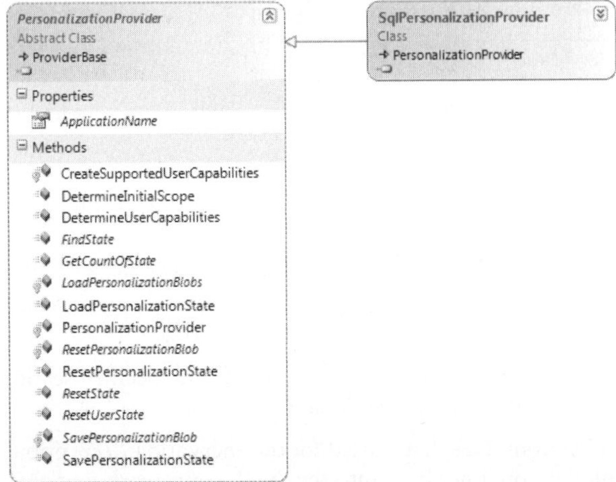

FIGURE 11-16

You will find the defined `SqlPersonalizationProvider` in the `web.config` file found in the .NET Framework's configuration folder (`C:\WINDOWS\Microsoft.NET\Framework\v4.0.21006\CONFIG`). Listing 11-26 presents this definition.

Available for download on Wrox.com

LISTING 11-26: The SqlPersonalizationProvider definition in the web.config file

```
<configuration>

    <system.web>

        <webParts>
            <personalization>
                <providers>
                  <add connectionStringName="LocalSqlServer"
                  name="AspNetSqlPersonalizationProvider"
                  type="System.Web.UI.WebControls.WebParts.
                    SqlPersonalizationProvider, System.Web,
                    Version=4.0.0.0, Culture=neutral,
                    PublicKeyToken=b03f5f7f11d50a3a" />
                </providers>
                <authorization>
                    <deny users="*" verbs="enterSharedScope" />
                    <allow users="*" verbs="modifyState" />
                </authorization>
            </personalization>

            <transformers>
                <add name="RowToFieldTransformer"
                type="System.Web.UI.WebControls.WebParts.RowToFieldTransformer" />
                <add name="RowToParametersTransformer"
                type="System.Web.UI.WebControls.WebParts.
                  RowToParametersTransformer" />
            </transformers>
        </webParts>

    </system.web>

</configuration>
```

As you can see, the provider declaration is shown in bold in Listing 11-26. As with the other SQL Server-based providers presented in this chapter, this provider works with SQL Server Express Edition by default. To change it to work with SQL Server 2000, 2005, or 2008, you must make a connection to your database within the `<connectionStrings>` section and make an association to this new connection string in the `SqlPersonalizationProvider` declaration using the `connectionStringName` attribute.

CONFIGURING PROVIDERS

As you have seen in this chapter, you can easily associate these systems in ASP.NET 4 to a large base of available providers. From there, you can also configure the behavior of the associated providers through the attributes exposed from the providers. You can easily do this configuring through either the system-wide configuration files (such as the `machine.config` file) or through more application-specific configuration files (such as the `web.config` file).

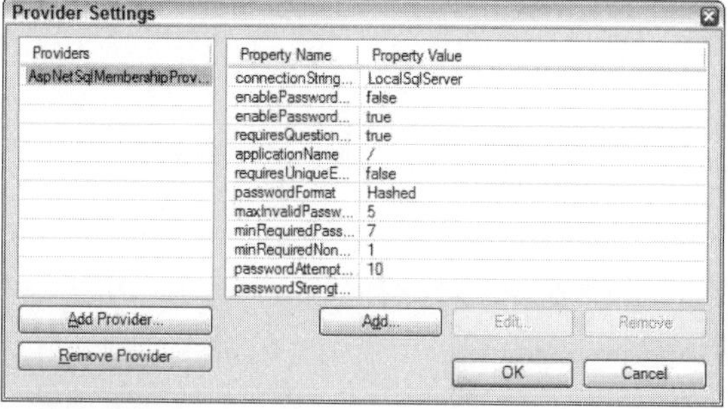

FIGURE 11-17

You can also just as easily configure providers through the GUI-based configuration systems such as the ASP.NET Web Site Administration Tool or through the ASP.NET MMC snap-in. Chapter 35 covers both of these items in detail. Figure 11-17 shows an example of using the ASP.NET MMC snap-in with the older Windows XP to visually configure a provider.

From this figure, you can see that you can add and remove providers in the membership system of your application. You can also change the values assigned to individual attributes directly in the GUI.

SUMMARY

This chapter covered the basics of the provider model and what providers are available to you as you start working with the various ASP.NET systems at your disposal. Understanding the built-in providers available for each of these systems and how you can fine-tune the behaviors of each provider is important.

This provider model allows for an additional level of abstraction and permits you to decide for yourself on the underlying data stores to be used for the various systems. For example, you have the power to decide whether to store the membership and role management information in SQL Server or in Oracle without making any changes to business or presentation logic!

The next chapter shows how to take the provider model to the next level.

12

Extending the Provider Model

WHAT'S IN THIS CHAPTER?

- Modifying and extending providers
- Building your own providers

The last chapter introduced the provider model found in ASP.NET 4 and explained how it is used with the membership and role management systems.

As discussed in the previous chapter, these systems in ASP.NET 4 require that some type of user state be maintained for long periods of time. Their time-interval and security requirements for state storage are greater than those for earlier systems that simply used the `Session` object. Out of the box, ASP .NET 4 gives you a series of providers to use as the underlying connectors for any data storage needs that arise from state management for these systems.

The providers that come with the default install of the .NET Framework 4 include the most common means of state management data storage needed to work with any of the systems. But like most things in .NET, you can customize and extend the providers that are supplied.

This chapter looks at some of the ways to extend the provider model found in ASP.NET 4. This chapter also reviews a couple of sample extensions to the provider model. First, however, you look at some of the simpler ways to modify and extend the providers already present in the default install of .NET 4.

PROVIDERS ARE ONE TIER IN A LARGER ARCHITECTURE

Remember from the previous chapter that providers allow you to define the data-access tier for many of the systems in ASP.NET 4. They also enable you to define your core business logic implementation on how the data is manipulated or handled. They enable you to use the various controls and APIs that compose these systems in a uniform manner regardless of the underlying data storage method of the provider. The provider model also allows you to easily swap one provider for another without affecting the underlying controls and API that are interacting with the provider. Figure 12-1 presents this model.

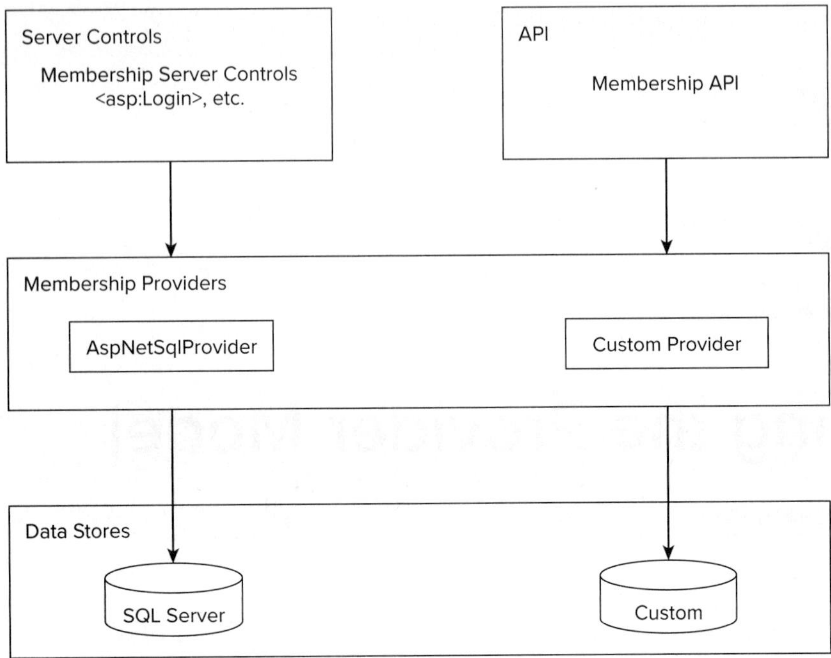

FIGURE 12-1

From this diagram, you can see that both the controls utilized in the membership system, as well as the Membership API, use the defined provider. Changing the underlying provider does not change the controls or the API, but you can definitely modify how these items behave (as you will see shortly). You can also simply change the location where the state management required by these items is stored. Changing the underlying provider, in this case, does not produce any change whatsoever in the controls or the API; instead, their state management data points are simply rerouted to another data store type.

MODIFYING THROUGH ATTRIBUTE-BASED PROGRAMMING

Probably the easiest way to modify the behaviors of the providers built into the .NET Framework 4 is through attribute-based programming. In ASP.NET 4, you can apply quite advanced behavior modification through attribute usage. You can apply both the server controls and the settings in the various application configuration files. Using the definitions of the providers found in either the `machine.config` files or within the root `web.config` file, you can really change provider behavior. This chapter gives you an example of how to modify the `SqlMembershipProvider`.

Simpler Password Structures Through the SqlMembershipProvider

When you create users with the `SqlMembershipProvider` instance, whether you are using SQL Server Express or Microsoft's SQL Server 2000/2005/2008, notice that the password required to create a user is a semi-strong password. This is evident when you create a user through the ASP.NET Web Site Administration Tool, as illustrated in Figure 12-2.

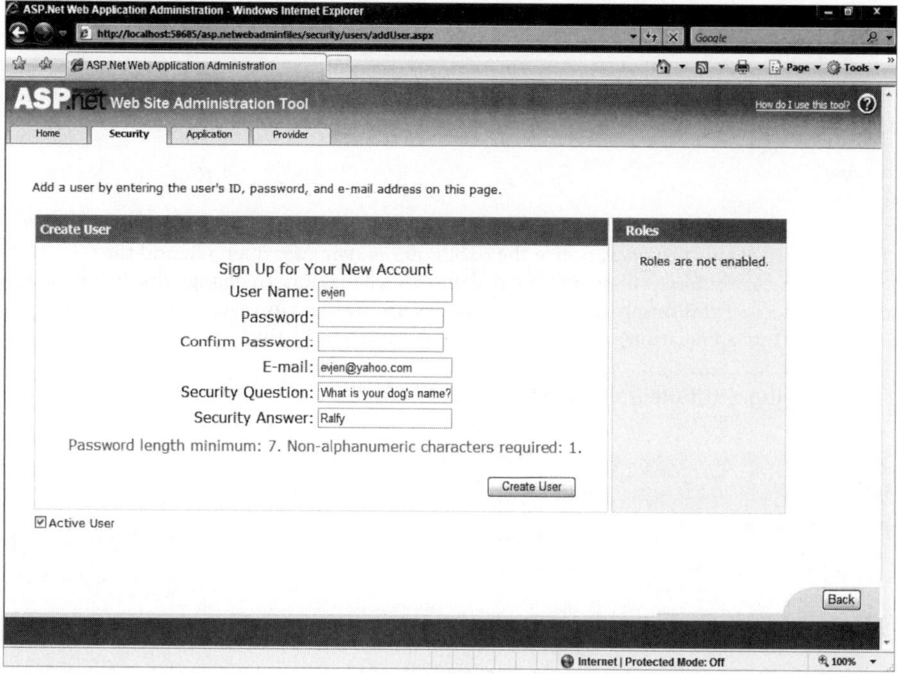

FIGURE 12-2

On this screen, I attempted to enter a password and was notified that the password did not meet the application's requirements. Instead, I was warned that the minimum password length is seven characters and that at least one non-alphanumeric character is required. This means that a password such as *Bubbles!* is what is required. This kind of behavior is specified by the membership provider and not by the controls or the API used in the membership system. You find the definition of the requirements in the `machine.config.comments` file located at `C:\WINDOWS\Microsoft.NEt\Framework\v4.0.xxxxx\CONFIG`. Listing 12-1 presents this definition.

Available for download on Wrox.com

LISTING 12-1: The SqlMembershipProvider instance declaration

```
<configuration>
   <system.web>
        <membership defaultProvider="AspNetSqlMembershipProvider"
         userIsOnlineTimeWindow="15" hashAlgorithmType="">
            <providers>
                <clear />
                <add connectionStringName="LocalSqlServer"
                 enablePasswordRetrieval="false"
                 enablePasswordReset="true"
                 requiresQuestionAndAnswer="true"
                 applicationName="/"
                 requiresUniqueEmail="false"
                 passwordFormat="Hashed"
                 maxInvalidPasswordAttempts="5"
                 minRequiredPasswordLength="7"
                 minRequiredNonalphanumericCharacters="1"
                 passwordAttemptWindow="10"
                 passwordStrengthRegularExpression=""
                 name="AspNetSqlMembershipProvider"
```

continues

LISTING 12-1 *(continued)*

```
                type="System.Web.Security.SqlMembershipProvider,
                  System.Web, Version=4.0.0.0, Culture=neutral,
                  PublicKeyToken=b03f5f7f11d50a3a" />
            </providers>
        </membership>
    </system.web>
</configuration>
```

Looking over the attributes of this provider, notice the minRequiredPasswordLength and the minRequiredNonalphanumericCharacters attributes define this behavior. To change this behavior across every application on the server, you simply change these values in this file. However, we suggest simply changing these values in your application's web.config file, as shown in Listing 12-2.

Available for download on Wrox.com

LISTING 12-2: Changing attribute values in the web.config file

```
<configuration>

   <system.web>

        <authentication mode="Forms" />
        <membership>
          <providers>
            <clear />
            <add name="AspNetSqlMembershipProvider"
             type="System.Web.Security.SqlMembershipProvider,
               System.Web, Version=4.0.0.0, Culture=neutral,
               PublicKeyToken=b03f5f7f11d50a3a"
             connectionStringName="LocalSqlServer"
             enablePasswordRetrieval="false"
             enablePasswordReset="true"
             requiresQuestionAndAnswer="true"
             requiresUniqueEmail="false"
             passwordFormat="Hashed"
             maxInvalidPasswordAttempts="5"
             minRequiredPasswordLength="4"
             minRequiredNonalphanumericCharacters="0"
             passwordAttemptWindow="10" />
          </providers>
        </membership>

   </system.web>

</configuration>
```

In this example, the password requirements are changed through the minRequiredPasswordLength and minRequiredNonalphanumericCharacters attributes. In this case, the minimum length allowed for a password is four characters, and none of those characters is required to be non-alphanumeric (for example, a special character such as !, $, or #).

Redefining a provider in the application's web.config file is a fairly simple process. In the example in Listing 12-2, you can see that the <membership> element is quite similar to the same element presented in the machine.config file.

You have a couple of options when defining your own instance of the SqlMembershipProvider. One approach, as presented in Listing 12-2, is to redefine the named instance of the SqlMembershipProvider that is defined in the machine.config file (AspNetSqlMembershipProvider, the value from the name attribute in the provider declaration). If you take this approach, you must *clear* the previous defined instance of AspNetSqlMembershipProvider. You must redefine the AspNetSqlMembershipProvider using the <clear /> node within the <providers> section. Failure to do so causes an error to be thrown stating that this provider name is already defined.

After you have cleared the previous instance of `AspNetSqlMembershipProvider`, you redefine this provider using the <add> element. In the case of Listing 12-2, you can see that the password requirements are redefined with the use of new values for the `minRequiredPasswordLength` and the `minRequiredNonalphanumericCharacters` attributes (shown in bold).

The other approach to defining your own instance of the `SqlMembershipProvider` is to give the provider defined in the <add> element a unique value for the `name` attribute. If you take this approach, you must specify this new named instance as the default provider of the membership system using the `defaultProvider` attribute. Listing 12-3 presents this approach.

LISTING 12-3: Defining your own named instance of the SqlMembershipProvider

Available for download on Wrox.com

```
<membership defaultProvider="MyVeryOwnAspNetSqlMembershipProvider">
   <providers>
      <add name="MyVeryOwnAspNetSqlMembershipProvider"
       type="System.Web.Security.SqlMembershipProvider,
         System.Web, Version=4.0.0.0, Culture=neutral,
         PublicKeyToken=b03f5f7f11d50a3a"
       connectionStringName="LocalSqlServer"
       enablePasswordRetrieval="false"
       enablePasswordReset="true"
       requiresQuestionAndAnswer="true"
       requiresUniqueEmail="false"
       passwordFormat="Hashed"
       maxInvalidPasswordAttempts="5"
       minRequiredPasswordLength="4"
       minRequiredNonalphanumericCharacters="0"
       passwordAttemptWindow="10" />
   </providers>
</membership>
```

In this case, the `SqlMembershipProvider` instance in the `machine.config` file (defined under the `AspNetSqlMembershipProvider` name) is not even redefined. Instead, a completely new named instance (`MyVeryOwnAspNetSqlMembershipProvider`) is defined here in the `web.config` file.

Stronger Password Structures Through the SqlMembershipProvider

Next, this chapter shows you how to actually make the password structures a little more complicated. You can, of course, accomplish this task in a couple of ways. One approach is to use the same `minRequiredPasswordLength` and `minRequiredNonalphanumericCharacters` attributes (as shown earlier) to make the password meet a required length (longer passwords usually mean more secure passwords) and to make the password contain a certain number of non-alphanumeric characters (which also makes for a more secure password).

Another option is to use the `passwordStrengthRegularExpression` attribute. If the `minRequiredPasswordLength` and the `minRequiredNonalphanumericCharacters` attributes cannot give you the password structure you are searching for, then using the `passwordStrengthRegularExpression` attribute is your next best alternative.

For an example of using this attribute, suppose you require that the user's password is his or her U.S. Social Security number. You can then define your provider as shown in Listing 12-4.

LISTING 12-4: A provider instance in the web.config file to change the password structure

Available for download on Wrox.com

```
<configuration>

   <system.web>

      <authentication mode="Forms" />

      <membership>
        <providers>
```

continues

LISTING 12-4 *(continued)*

```
            <clear />
            <add name="AspNetSqlMembershipProvider"
             type="System.Web.Security.SqlMembershipProvider,
               System.Web, Version=4.0.0.0, Culture=neutral,
               PublicKeyToken=b03f5f7f11d50a3a"
             connectionStringName="LocalSqlServer"
             enablePasswordRetrieval="false"
             enablePasswordReset="true"
             requiresQuestionAndAnswer="true"
             requiresUniqueEmail="false"
             passwordFormat="Hashed"
             maxInvalidPasswordAttempts="5"
             passwordAttemptWindow="10"
             passwordStrengthRegularExpression="\d{3}-\d{2}-\d{4}" />
         </providers>
       </membership>

    </system.web>
 </configuration>
```

Instead of using the `minRequiredPasswordLength` and the `minRequiredNonalphanumericCharacters` attributes, the `passwordStrengthRegularExpression` attribute is used and given a value of `\d{3}-\d{2}-\d{4}`. This regular expression means that the password should have three digits followed by a dash or hyphen, followed by two digits and another dash or hyphen, finally followed by four digits.

The lesson here is that you have many ways to modify the behaviors of the providers already available in the .NET Framework 4 install. You can adapt a number of providers built into the framework to suit your needs by using attribute-based programming. The `SqlMembershipProvider` example demonstrated this technique, and you can just as easily make similar types of modifications to any of the other providers.

EXAMINING PROVIDERBASE

All the providers derive in some fashion from the `ProviderBase` class, found in the `System.Configuration.Provider` namespace. `ProviderBase` is an abstract class used to define a base template for inheriting providers. Looking at `ProviderBase`, note that there isn't much to this abstract class, as illustrated in Figure 12-3.

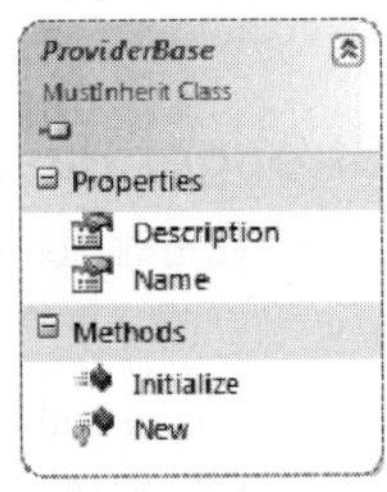

FIGURE 12-3

As stated, there is not much to this class. It is really just a root class for a provider that exists to allow providers to initialize themselves.

The `Name` property is used to provide a friendly name, such as AspNetSqlRoleProvider. The `Description` property is used to enable a textual description of the provider, which can then be used later by any administration tools. The main item in the `ProviderBase` class is the `Initialize()` method. Here is the constructor for `Initialize()`:

```
public virtual void Initialize(string name,
   System.Collections.Specialized.NameValueCollection config);
```

Note the two parameters to the `Initialize()` method. The first is the `name` parameter, which is simply the value assigned to the `name` attribute in the provider declaration in the configuration file. The `config` parameter is of type `NameValueCollection`, which is a collection of name/value pairs. These name/value pairs are the items that are also defined in the provider declaration in the configuration file as all the various attributes and their associated values.

When looking over the providers that are included in the default install of ASP.NET 4, note that each of the providers has defined a class you can derive from that implements the `ProviderBase` abstract class. For example, looking at the model in place for the membership system, you can see a base `MembershipProvider` instance that is inherited in the final `SqlMembershipProvider` declaration. The `MembershipProvider`, however, implements `ProviderBase` itself. Figure 12-4 presents this model.

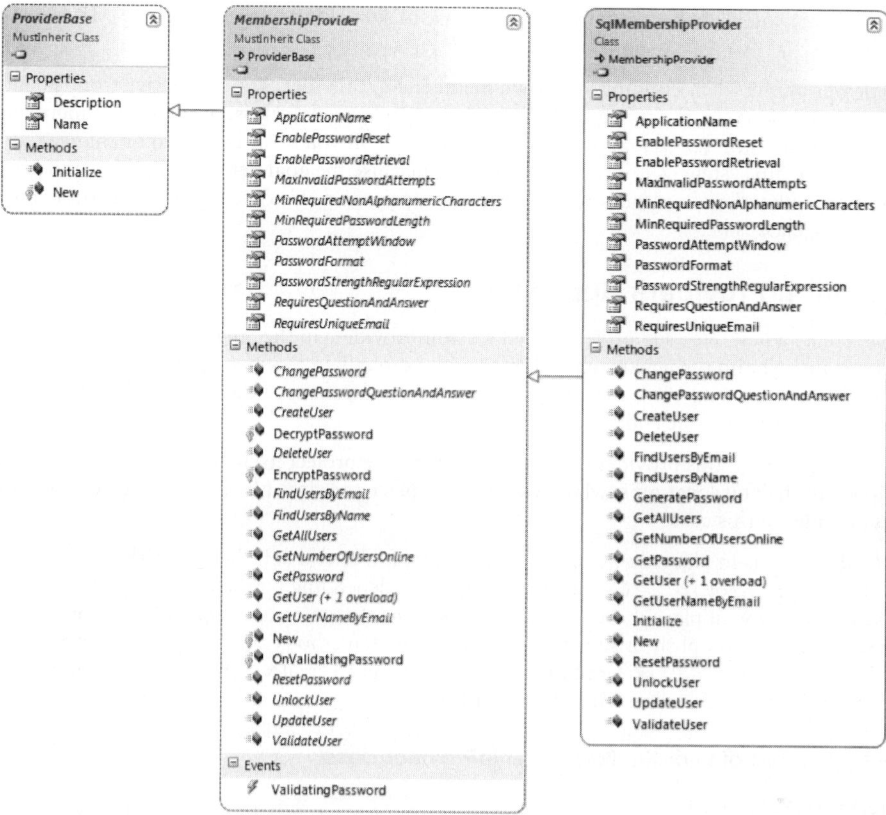

FIGURE 12-4

Notice that each of the various systems has a specific base provider implementation for you to work with. There really cannot be a single provider that addresses the needs of all the available systems. Looking at Figure 12-4, you can see that the `MembershipProvider` instance exposes some very specific functionality required by the ASP.NET membership system. The methods exposed are definitely not needed by the role management system or the Web Parts capability.

With these various base implementations in place, when you are creating your own customizations for working with the ASP.NET membership system, you have a couple of options available to you. First, you can simply create your own provider directly implementing the `ProviderBase` class and working from the ground up. We do not recommend this approach, however, because abstract classes are already in place for you to use with the various systems. Therefore, as we mentioned, you can just implement the `MembershipProvider` instance (a better approach) and work from the model it provides. Finally, if you are working with SQL Server in some capacity and simply want to change the underlying behaviors of this provider, you can inherit from `SqlMembershipProvider` and modify the behavior of the class from this inheritance. Next, this chapter covers the various means of extending the provider model through examples.

BUILDING YOUR OWN PROVIDERS

You now examine the process of building your own provider to use within your ASP.NET application. Actually, providers are not that difficult to put together (as you will see shortly) and can even be created directly in any of your ASP.NET 4 projects. The example demonstrates building a membership provider that works from an XML file. For a smaller Web site, this scenario might be common. For larger Web sites and

Web-based applications, you probably want to use a database of some kind, rather than an XML file, for managing users.

You have a couple of options when building your own membership provider. You can derive from a couple of classes, the `SqlMembershipProvider` class or the `MembershipProvider` class, to build the functionality you need. You derive from the `SqlMembershipProvider` class only if you want to extend or change the behavior of the membership system as it interacts with SQL. Because the goal here is to build a read-only XML membership provider, deriving from this class is inappropriate. In this case, basing everything on the `MembershipProvider` class is best.

Creating the CustomProviders Application

For this example, create a new Web site project called CustomProviders in the language of your choice. For this example, you want to build the new membership provider directly in the Web application itself. Another option is to build the provider in a Class Library project and then to reference the generated DLL in your Web project. Either way is fine in the end.

Because you are going to build this provider directly in the Web site project itself, you create the App_Code folder in your application. This location is where you want to place the class file that you create. The class file is the actual provider in this case.

After the App_Code folder is in place, create a new class in this folder and call the class either `XmlMembershipProvider.vb` or `XmlMembershipProvider.cs`, depending on the language you are using. With this class now in place, have your new `XmlMembershipProvider` class derive from `MembershipProvider`. To accomplish this task and to know which methods and properties to override, you can use Visual Studio 2010 to build a skeleton of the class you want to create. You can step through this process starting with the code demonstrated in Listing 12-5.

LISTING 12-5: The start of your XmlMembershipProvider class

Available for download on Wrox.com

VB

```
Imports Microsoft.VisualBasic

Public Class XmlMembershipProvider
    Inherits MembershipProvider

End Class
```

C#

```
using System;
using System.Collections.Generic;
using System.Linq;
using System.Web;
using System.Web.Security;

/// <summary>
/// Summary description for XmlMembershipProvider
/// </summary>
public class XmlMembershipProvider: MembershipProvider
{
 public XmlMembershipProvider()
 {
         //
         // TODO: Add constructor logic here
         //
 }
}
```

You make only a few changes to the basic class, `XmlMembershipProvider`. You can see that some extra namespaces are imported into the file. This is done so you can later take advantage of .NET's XML capabilities, generics, and more. Notice also that this new class, the `XmlMembershipProvider` class, inherits from `MembershipProvider`.

Constructing the Class Skeleton Required

In order to get Visual Studio 2010 to build your class with the appropriate methods and properties, take the following steps (depending on the language you are using). If you are using Visual Basic, all you have to do is press the Enter key. In C#, all you have to do is right-click on the `MembershipProvider` statement in your code and simply select Implement Abstract Class from the available options. Another option is to place the cursor on the `MembershipProvider` statement in the document window and then select Edit ⇨ IntelliSense ⇨ Implement Abstract Class from the Visual Studio menu. After you perform one of these operations, you see the full skeleton of the class in the document window of Visual Studio. Listing 12-6 shows the code that is generated if you are creating a Visual Basic `XmlMembershipProvider` class.

LISTING 12-6: Code generated for the XmlMembershipProvider class by Visual Studio

VB (only)

```
Imports Microsoft.VisualBasic

Public Class XmlMembershipProvider
    Inherits MembershipProvider

    Public Overrides Property ApplicationName() As String
        Get

        End Get
        Set(ByVal value As String)
        End Set
    End Property

    Public Overrides Function ChangePassword(ByVal username As String, _
      ByVal oldPassword As String, ByVal newPassword As String) As Boolean

    End Function

    Public Overrides Function ChangePasswordQuestionAndAnswer(ByVal username _
      As String, ByVal password As String, ByVal newPasswordQuestion As String, _
      ByVal newPasswordAnswer As String) As Boolean

    End Function

    Public Overrides Function CreateUser(ByVal username As String, _
      ByVal password As String, ByVal email As String, _
      ByVal passwordQuestion As String, ByVal passwordAnswer As String, _
      ByVal isApproved As Boolean, ByVal providerUserKey As Object, _
      ByRef status As System.Web.Security.MembershipCreateStatus) As _
      System.Web.Security.MembershipUser

    End Function

    Public Overrides Function DeleteUser(ByVal username As String, _
      ByVal deleteAllRelatedData As Boolean) As Boolean

    End Function

    Public Overrides ReadOnly Property EnablePasswordReset() As Boolean
        Get

        End Get
    End Property

    Public Overrides ReadOnly Property EnablePasswordRetrieval() As Boolean
        Get
```

continues

LISTING 12-6 *(continued)*

```
        End Get
    End Property
    Public Overrides Function FindUsersByEmail(ByVal emailToMatch As String, _
      ByVal pageIndex As Integer, ByVal pageSize As Integer, _
      ByRef totalRecords As Integer) As _
      System.Web.Security.MembershipUserCollection

    End Function

    Public Overrides Function FindUsersByName(ByVal usernameToMatch As String, _
      ByVal pageIndex As Integer, ByVal pageSize As Integer, _
      ByRef totalRecords As Integer) As _
      System.Web.Security.MembershipUserCollection

    End Function


    Public Overrides Function GetAllUsers(ByVal pageIndex As Integer, _
      ByVal pageSize As Integer, ByRef totalRecords As Integer) As _
      System.Web.Security.MembershipUserCollection

    End Function

    Public Overrides Function GetNumberOfUsersOnline() As Integer

    End Function

    Public Overrides Function GetPassword(ByVal username As String, _
      ByVal answer As String) As String

    End Function

    Public Overloads Overrides Function GetUser(ByVal providerUserKey As Object, _
      ByVal userIsOnline As Boolean) As System.Web.Security.MembershipUser

    End Function

    Public Overloads Overrides Function GetUser(ByVal username As String, _
      ByVal userIsOnline As Boolean) As System.Web.Security.MembershipUser

    End Function

    Public Overrides Function GetUserNameByEmail(ByVal email As String) As String

    End Function

    Public Overrides ReadOnly Property MaxInvalidPasswordAttempts() As Integer
        Get

        End Get
    End Property

    Public Overrides ReadOnly Property MinRequiredNonAlphanumericCharacters() _
      As Integer
        Get

        End Get
    End Property
```

```
        Public Overrides ReadOnly Property MinRequiredPasswordLength() As Integer
            Get

            End Get
        End Property

        Public Overrides ReadOnly Property PasswordAttemptWindow() As Integer
            Get

            End Get
        End Property

        Public Overrides ReadOnly Property PasswordFormat() As _

          System.Web.Security.MembershipPasswordFormat
            Get

            End Get
        End Property

        Public Overrides ReadOnly Property PasswordStrengthRegularExpression() As _
          String
            Get

            End Get
        End Property

        Public Overrides ReadOnly Property RequiresQuestionAndAnswer() As Boolean
            Get

            End Get
        End Property

        Public Overrides ReadOnly Property RequiresUniqueEmail() As Boolean
            Get

            End Get
        End Property

        Public Overrides Function ResetPassword(ByVal username As String, _
          ByVal answer As String) As String

        End Function

        Public Overrides Function UnlockUser(ByVal userName As String) As Boolean

        End Function

        Public Overrides Sub UpdateUser(ByVal user As _
          System.Web.Security.MembershipUser)

        End Sub

        Public Overrides Function ValidateUser(ByVal username As String, _
          ByVal password As String) As Boolean

        End Function
    End Class
```

Wow, that's a lot of code! Although the skeleton is in place, the next step is to build some of the items that will be utilized by the provider that Visual Studio laid out for you — starting with the XML file that holds all the users allowed to access the application.

Creating the XML User Data Store

Because this provider is an XML membership provider, the intent is to read the user information from an XML file rather than from a database such as SQL Server. For this reason, you must define the XML file structure that the provider can make use of. Listing 12-7 shows the structure used for this example.

LISTING 12-7: The XML file used to store usernames and passwords

Available for download on Wrox.com

```
<?xml version="1.0" encoding="utf-8" ?>
<Users>
  <User>
    <Username>BillEvjen</Username>
    <Password>Bubbles</Password>
    <Email>evjen@yahoo.com</Email>
    <DateCreated>11/10/2009</DateCreated>
  </User>
  <User>
    <Username>ScottHanselman</Username>
    <Password>YabbaDabbaDo</Password>
    <Email>123@msn.com</Email>
    <DateCreated>10/20/2009</DateCreated>
  </User>
  <User>
    <Username>DevinRader</Username>
    <Password>BamBam</Password>
    <Email>456@msn.com</Email>
    <DateCreated>9/23/2009</DateCreated>
  </User>
</Users>
```

This XML file holds only three user instances, all of which include the username, password, e-mail address, and the date on which the user is created. Because it is a data file, you should place this file in the App_Data folder of your ASP.NET application. You can name the file anything you want; but in this case, we have named the file `UserDatabase.xml`.

Later, this chapter reviews how to grab these values from the XML file when validating users.

Defining the Provider Instance in the web.config File

As you saw in the last chapter on providers, you define a provider and its behavior in a configuration file (such as the `machine.config` or the `web.config` file). Because this provider is being built for a single application instance, this example defines the provider in the `web.config` file of the application.

The default provider is the `SqlMembershipProvider`, and this is defined in the `machine.config` file on the server. For this example, you must override this setting and establish a new default provider. The XML membership provider declaration in the `web.config` should appear as shown in Listing 12-8.

LISTING 12-8: Defining the XmlMembershipProvider in the web.config file

Available for download on Wrox.com

```
<configuration>
   <system.web>

      <authentication mode="Forms"/>

      <membership defaultProvider="XmlFileProvider">
         <providers>
            <add name="XmlFileProvider" type="XmlMembershipProvider"
             xmlUserDatabaseFile="</App_Data/UserDatabase.xml"/>
         </providers>
      </membership>

   </system.web>
</configuration>
```

In this listing, you can see that the default provider is defined as the `XmlFileProvider`. Because this provider name will not be found in any of the parent configuration files, you must define `XmlFileProvider` in the `web.config` file.

Using the `defaultProvider` attribute, you can define the name of the provider you want to use for the membership system. In this case, it is `XmlFileProvider`. Then you define the `XmlFileProvider` instance using the `<add>` element within the `<providers>` section. The `<add>` element gives a name for the provider — `XmlFileProvider`. It also points to the class (or type) of the provider. In this case, it is the skeleton class you just created — `XmlMembershipProvider`.

Beyond the attributes already used so far, you can create any attribute in your provider declaration that you want. Whatever type of provider you create, however, you must address the attributes in your provider and act upon the values that are provided with the attributes. In the case of the simple `XmlMembershipProvider`, only a single custom attribute exists — `xmlUserDatabaseFile`. This attribute points to the location of the user database XML file. For this provider, it is an optional attribute. If you do not provide a value for `xmlUserDatabaseFile`, you have a default value. In Listing 12-8, however, you can see that a value is indeed provided for the XML file to use. Note that the `xmlUserDatabaseFile` is simply the filename and nothing more.

One attribute is not shown in the example, but is an allowable attribute because it is addressed in the `XmlMemberhipProvider` class. This attribute, the `applicationName` attribute, points to the application that the `XmlMembershipProvider` instance should address. Here is the default value, which you can also place in this provider declaration within the configuration file:

```
applicationName="/"
```

Not Implementing Methods and Properties of the MembershipProvider Class

Now, turn your attention to the `XmlMembershipProvider` class. The next step is to implement any methods or properties needed by the provider. You are not required to make any *real* use of the methods contained in this skeleton; instead, you can simply build-out only the methods you are interested in working with. For example, if you do not allow for programmatic access to change passwords (and, in turn, the controls that use this programmatic access), you either want to not initiate an action or to throw an exception if someone tries to implement this method, as shown in Listing 12-9.

LISTING 12-9: Not implementing one of the available methods by throwing an exception

VB

```
Public Overrides Function ChangePassword(ByVal username As String, _
  ByVal oldPassword As String, ByVal newPassword As String) As Boolean
        Throw New NotSupportedException()
End Function
```

C#

```
public override bool ChangePassword(string username,
  string oldPassword, string newPassword)
{
   throw new NotSupportedException();
}
```

In this case, a `NotSupportedException` is thrown if the `ChangePassword()` method is invoked. If you do not want to throw an actual exception, you can simply return a `false` value and not take any other action, as shown in Listing 12-10 (although not throwing anything back might annoy a developer who is trying to implement this provider and does not understand the underlying logic of the method).

LISTING 12-10: Not implementing one of the available methods by returning a false value

Available for download on Wrox.com

VB

```
Public Overrides Function ChangePassword(ByVal username As String, _
  ByVal oldPassword As String, ByVal newPassword As String) As Boolean
        Return False
End Function
```

continues

LISTING 12-10 *(continued)*

```
public override bool ChangePassword(string username,
  string oldPassword, string newPassword)
{
   return false;
}
```

This chapter does not address every possible action you can take with `XmlMembershipProvider`, and therefore, you may want to work through the available methods and properties of the derived `MembershipProvider` instance and make the necessary changes to any items that you won't be using.

Implementing Methods and Properties of the MembershipProvider Class

Now it is time to implement some of the methods and properties available from the `MembershipProvider` class in order to get the `XmlMembershipProvider` class to work. The first items are some private variables that multiple methods can utilize throughout the class. Listing 12-11 presents these variable declarations.

LISTING 12-11: Declaring some private variables in the XmlMembershipProvider class

Available for download on Wrox.com

VB

```
Public Class XmlMembershipProvider
    Inherits MembershipProvider

    Private _AppName As String
    Private _MyUsers As Dictionary(Of String, MembershipUser)
    Private _FileName As String
   ' Code removed for clarity
End Class
```

```
public class XmlMembershipProvider : MembershipProvider
{
    private string _AppName;
    private Dictionary<string, MembershipUser> _MyUsers;
    private string _FileName;

  ' Code removed for clarity

}
```

The variables being declared are items needed by multiple methods in the class. The `_AppName` variable defines the application using the XML membership provider. In all cases, it is the local application. You also want to place all the members found in the XML file into a collection of some type. This example uses a dictionary generic type named `_MyUsers`. Finally, this example points to the file to use with the `_FileName` variable.

Defining the ApplicationName Property

After the private variables are in place, the next step is to define the `ApplicationName` property. You now make use of the first private variable — `AppName`. Listing 12-12 presents the property definition of `ApplicationName`.

LISTING 12-12: Defining the ApplicationName property

Available for download on Wrox.com

```
Public Overrides Property ApplicationName() As String
   Get
      Return _AppName
   End Get
   Set(ByVal value As String)
      _AppName = value
   End Set
End Property
```

C#

```
public override string ApplicationName
{
   get
   {
      return _AppName;
   }
   set
   {
      _AppName = value;
   }
}
```

Now that the `ApplicationName` property is defined and in place, you next retrieve the values defined in the `web.config` file's provider declaration (`XmlFileProvider`).

Extending the Initialize() Method

You now extend the `Initialize()` method so that it reads in the custom attribute and its associated values as defined in the provider declaration in the `web.config` file. Look through the class skeleton of your `XmlMembershipProvider` class, and note that no `Initialize()` method is included in the list of available items.

The `Initialize()` method is invoked when the provider is first initialized. Overriding this method is not a requirement, and therefore, you won't see it in the declaration of the class skeleton. To put the `Initialize()` method in place within the `XmlMembershipProvider` class, simply type `Public Overrides` (for Visual Basic) or `public override` (for C#) in the class. IntelliSense then presents you with the `Initialize()` method, as shown in Figure 12-5.

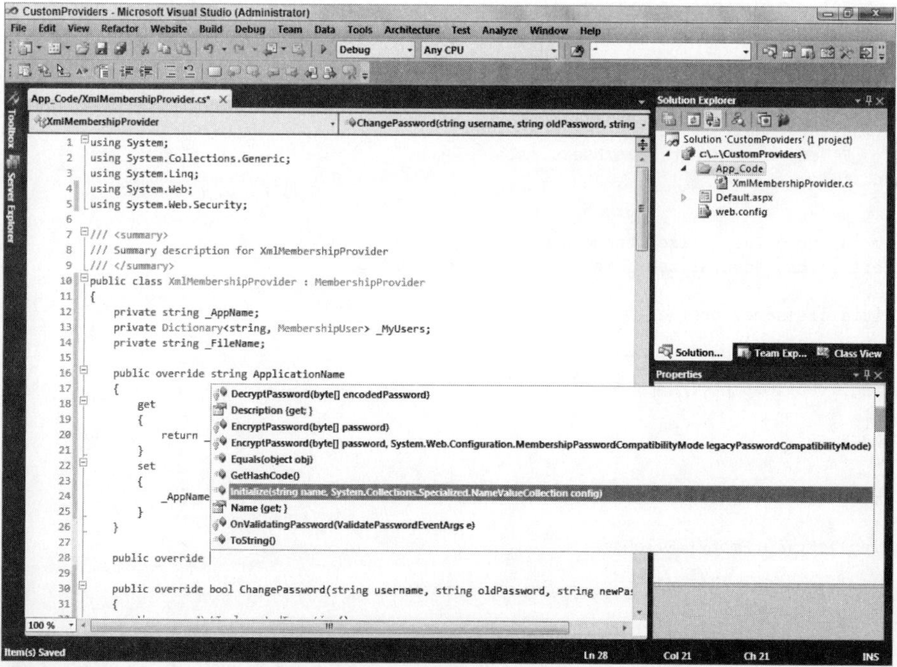

FIGURE 12-5

Placing the `Initialize()` method in your class in this manner is quite easy. Select the `Initialize()` method from the list in IntelliSense and press the Enter key. This method gives you a base construction of the method in your code, as shown in Listing 12-13.

LISTING 12-13: The beginnings of the Initialize() method

Available for download on Wrox.com

VB

```
Public Overrides Sub Initialize(ByVal name As String, _
   ByVal config As System.Collections.Specialized.NameValueCollection)
        MyBase.Initialize(name, config)
End Sub
```

C#

```
public override void Initialize(string name,
  System.Collections.Specialized.NameValueCollection config)
{
   base.Initialize(name, config);
}
```

The `Initialize()` method takes two parameters. The first parameter is the name of the parameter. The second is the name/value collection from the provider declaration in the `web.config` file. This collection includes all the attributes and their values, such as the `xmlUserDatabaseFile` attribute and the value of the name of the XML file that holds the user information. Using `config`, you can gain access to these defined values.

For the `XmlFileProvider` instance, you address the `applicationName` attribute and the `xmlUserDatabaseFile` attribute as shown in Listing 12-14.

LISTING 12-14: Extending the Initialize() method

Available for download on Wrox.com

VB

```
Public Overrides Sub Initialize(ByVal name As String, _
  ByVal config As System.Collections.Specialized.NameValueCollection)
        MyBase.Initialize(name, config)

        _AppName = config("applicationName")

        If (String.IsNullOrEmpty(_AppName)) Then
            _AppName = "/"
        End If

        _FileName = config("xmlUserDatabaseFile")

        If (String.IsNullOrEmpty(_FileName)) Then
            _FileName = "</App_Data/Users.xml"
        End If
End Sub
```

C#

```
public override void Initialize(string name,
  System.Collections.Specialized.NameValueCollection config)
{
   base.Initialize(name, config);

   _AppName = config["applicationName"];

   if (String.IsNullOrEmpty(_AppName))
   {
      _AppName = "/";
   }

   _FileName = config["xmlUserDatabaseFile"];

   if (String.IsNullOrEmpty(_FileName))
   {
      _FileName = "</App_Data/Users.xml";
   }
}
```

Besides performing the initialization using `MyBase.Initialize()`, you retrieve both the `applicationName` and `xmlUserDatabaseFile` attributes' values using `config`. In all cases, you should first check whether the value is either null or empty. You use the `String.IsNullOrEmpty()` method to assign default values if the attribute is missing for the provider declaration in the `web.config` file. In the case of the `XmlFileProvider` instance, this is, in fact, the case. The `applicationName` attribute in the `XmlFileProvider` declaration is actually not declared and, for this reason, the default value of / is actually assigned as the value.

In the case of the `xmlUserDatabaseFile` attribute, a value is provided. If no value is provided in the `web.config` file, the provider looks for an XML file named `Users.xml` found in the App_Data folder.

Validating Users

One of the more important features of the membership provider is that it validates users (it authenticates them). The validation of users is accomplished through the ASP.NET Login server control. This control, in turn, makes use of the `Membership.ValidateUser()` method that ends up using the `ValidateUser()` method in the `XmlMembershipProvider` class.

Now that the `Initialize()` method and private variables are in place, you can start giving the provider some functionality. Listing 12-15 presents the implementation of the `ValidateUser()` method.

LISTING 12-15: Implementing the ValidateUser() method

Available for download on Wrox.com

VB

```
Public Overrides Function ValidateUser(ByVal username As String, _
  ByVal password As String) As Boolean
   If (String.IsNullOrEmpty(username) Or String.IsNullOrEmpty(password)) Then
      Return False
   End If

   Try
      ReadUserFile()

      Dim mu As MembershipUser

      If (_MyUsers.TryGetValue(username.ToLower(), mu)) Then
         If (mu.Comment = password) Then
            Return True
         End If
      End If

      Return False
   Catch ex As Exception
      Throw New Exception(ex.Message.ToString())
   End Try
End Function
```

C#

```
public override bool ValidateUser(string username, string password)
{
   if (String.IsNullOrEmpty(username) || String.IsNullOrEmpty(password))
   {
      return false;
   }

   try
   {
      ReadUserFile();

      MembershipUser mu;

      if (_MyUsers.TryGetValue(username.ToLower(), out mu))
      {
         if (mu.Comment == password)
         {
            return true;
         }
      }

      return false;
   }
   catch (Exception ex)
   {
      throw new Exception(ex.Message.ToString());
   }
}
```

Looking over the `ValidateUser()` method, you can see that it takes two parameters: the username and the password of the user (both of type `String`). The value returned from `ValidateUser()` is a `Boolean` — just a `True` or `False` value to inform of the success for failure of the validation process.

One of the first operations performed in the `ValidateUser()` method is a check to determine whether either the username or the password is missing from the invocation. If one of these items is missing in the request, a `False` value is returned.

From there, a `Try Catch` is done to check whether the user and the user's password are included in the XML file. The process of getting the user information out of the XML file and into the `MyUsers` variable is done by the `ReadUserFile()` method. This method is described shortly, but the important concept is that the `_MyUsers` variable is an instance of the `Dictionary` generic class. The key is a lowercase string value of the username, whereas the value is of type `MembershipUser`, a type provided via the membership system.

After the `_MyUsers` object is populated with all users in the XML file, a `MembershipUser` instance is created. This object is the output of a `TryGetValue` operation. The `MembershipUser` does not contain the password of the user, and for this reason, the `ReadUserFile()` method makes the user's password the value of the `Comment` property of the `MembershipUser` class. If the username is found in the dictionary collection, then the password of that particular `MembershipUser` instance is compared to the value in the `Comment` property. The return value from the `ValidateUser()` method is `True` if they are found to be the same.

As you can see, this method really is dependent upon the results that come from the `ReadUserFile()` method, which is covered next.

Building the ReadUserFile() Method

The `ReadUserFile()` method reads the contents of the XML file that contains all the users for the application. This method is a custom method, and its work is done outside of the `ValidateUser()` method. This means you can reuse it in other methods you might want to implement (such as the `GetAllUsers()` method). The only job of the `ReadUserFile()` method is to read the contents of the XML file and place all the users in the `_MyUsers` variable, as shown in Listing 12-16.

LISTING 12-16: The ReadUserFile() method to get all the users of the application

Available for download on Wrox.com

```
Private Sub ReadUserFile()
    If (_MyUsers Is Nothing) Then
        SyncLock (Me)
            _MyUsers = New Dictionary(Of String, MembershipUser)()
            Dim xd As XmlDocument = New XmlDocument()
            xd.Load(HostingEnvironment.MapPath(_FileName))
            Dim xnl As XmlNodeList = xd.GetElementsByTagName("User")

            For Each node As XmlNode In xnl
                Dim mu As MembershipUser = New MembershipUser(Name, _
                    node("Username").InnerText, _
                    Nothing, _
                    node("Email").InnerText, _
                    String.Empty, _
                    node("Password").InnerText, _
                    True, _
                    False, _
                    DateTime.Parse(node("DateCreated").InnerText), _
                    DateTime.Now, _
                    DateTime.Now, _
                    DateTime.Now, _
                    DateTime.Now)

                _MyUsers.Add(mu.UserName.ToLower(), mu)
            Next
```

```
        End SyncLock
    End If
End Sub
```

C#

```
private void ReadUserFile()
{
      if (_MyUsers == null)
      {
        lock (this)
        {
         _MyUsers = new Dictionary<string, MembershipUser>();
         XmlDocument xd = new XmlDocument();
         xd.Load(HostingEnvironment.MapPath(_FileName));
         XmlNodeList xnl = xd.GetElementsByTagName("User");

         foreach (XmlNode node in xnl)
         {
            MembershipUser mu = new MembershipUser(Name,
               node["Username"].InnerText,
               null,
               node["Email"].InnerText,
               String.Empty,
               node["Password"].InnerText,
               true,
               false,
               DateTime.Parse(node["DateCreated"].InnerText),
               DateTime.Now,
               DateTime.Now,
               DateTime.Now,
               DateTime.Now);

               _MyUsers.Add(mu.UserName.ToLower(), mu);
         }
      }
   }
}
```

You are going to need to import the `System.Xml` *and* `System.Web.Hosting` *namespaces for this code to work.*

The first action of the `ReadUserFile()` method is to place a lock on the action that is going to occur in the thread being run. This is a unique feature in ASP.NET. When you are writing your own providers, be sure you use thread-safe code. For most items that you write in ASP.NET, such as an HttpModule or an HttpHandler (covered in Chapter 26), you don't need to make them thread-safe. These items may have multiple requests running on multiple threads, and each thread making a request to either the HttpModule or the HttpHandler sees a unique instance of these items.

Unlike an HttpHandler, only one instance of a provider is created and utilized by your ASP.NET application. If multiple requests are being made to your application, all these threads are trying to gain access to the single provider instance contained in the application. Because more than one request might be coming into the provider instance at the same time, you should create the provider in a thread-safe manner. You can do so by using a lock operation when performing tasks such as file I/O operations. To lock the access, use the `SyncLock` (for Visual Basic) and the `lock` (for C#) statements in the `ReadUserFile()` method.

The advantage of this code construction, however, is that a single instance of the provider is running in your application. After the `_MyUsers` object is populated with the contents of the XML file, you have no need to repopulate the object. The provider instance doesn't just disappear after a response is issued to the requestor. Instead, the provider instance is contained in memory and utilized for multiple requests, which is the reason for checking whether `_MyUsers` contains any values before reading the XML file.

If you find that _MyUsers is null, use the XmlDocument object to get at every <User> element in the document. For each <User> element in the document, the values are assigned to a MembershipUser instance. The MembershipUser object takes the following arguments:

```
MembershipUser(
  providerName As String, _
  name As String, _
  providerUserKey As Object, _
  email As String, _
  passwordQuestion As String, _
  comment As String, _
  isApproved As Boolean, _
  isLockedOut As Boolean, _
  creationDate As DateTime, _
  lastLoginDate As DateTime, _
  lastActivityDate As DateTime, _
  lastPasswordChangedDate As DateTime, _
  lastLockoutDate As DateTime)
```

Although you do not provide a value for each and every item in this construction, the values that are really needed are pulled from the XML file using the XmlNode object. Then, after the MembershipUser object is populated with everything you want, the next job is to add these items to the _MyUsers object using the following:

```
_MyUsers.Add(mu.UserName.ToLower(), mu)
```

With the ReadUserFile() method in place, as stated, you can now use it in more than the ValidateUser() method. Remember that after the _MyUsers collection is populated, you don't need to repopulate the collection again. Instead, it remains in place for the other methods to make use of. Next, this chapter looks at using what has been demonstrated so far in your ASP.NET application.

Using the XmlMembershipProvider for User Login

If you have made it this far in the example, you do not need to do much more to make use of the XmlMembershipProvider class. At this point, you should have the XML data file in place that is a representation of all the users of your application (this XML file appears earlier in Listing 12-7) and the XmlFileProvider declaration in the web.config file of your application (the changes to the web.config file appear in Listing 12-8). Of course, another necessary item is either the XmlMembershipProvider.vb or .cs class in the App_Code folder of your application. However, if you built the provider as a class library, you want to just make sure the DLL created is referenced correctly in your ASP.NET application (which means the DLL is in the Bin folder). After you have these items in place, getting started with using the provider is simple.

For a quick example, simply create a Default.aspx page that has only the text: You are authenticated!

Next, you create a Login.aspx page, and place a single Login server control on the page. You won't need to make any other changes to the Login.aspx page besides placing the control. Users can now log in to the application.

For information on the membership system, which includes detailed explanations of the various server controls it offers, visit Chapter 15.

When you have those two files in place within your mini-ASP.NET application, the next step is to make some minor changes to the web.config file to allow for Forms authentication and to deny all anonymous users to view any of the pages. Listing 12-17 presents this bit of code.

LISTING 12-17: Denying anonymous users to view the application in the web.config file

Available for download on Wrox.com

```
<configuration>
   <system.web>

      <authentication mode="Forms"/>
      <authorization>
         <deny users="?"/>
      </authorization>

      <!-- Other settings removed for clarity -->

   </system.web>
</configuration>
```

Now, run the `Default.aspx` page, and you are immediately directed to the `Login.aspx` page (you should have this file created in your application and it should contain only a single Login server control) where you apply one of the username and password combinations that are present in the XML file. It is as simple as that!

The nice thing with the provider-based model found in ASP.NET 4 is that the controls that are working with the providers don't know the difference when these large changes to the underlying provider are made. In this example, you have removed the default `SqlMembershipProvider` and replaced it with a read-only XML provider, and the Login server control is really none the wiser. When the end user clicks the Log In button within the Login server control, the control is still simply making use of the `Membership.ValidateUser()` method, which is working with the `XmlMembershipProvider` that was just created. As you should see by now, this model is powerful.

EXTENDING PRE-EXISTING PROVIDERS

In addition to building your own providers from one of the base abstract classes such as `MembershipProvider`, another option is to simply extend one of the pre-existing providers that come with ASP.NET.

For example, you might be interested in using the membership and role management systems with SQL Server but want to change how the default providers (`SqlMembershipProvider` or `SqlRoleProvider`) work under the covers. If you are going to work with an underlying data store that is already utilized by one of the providers available out of the box, then actually changing the behavior of the available provider makes a lot more sense than building a brand-new provider from the ground up.

The other advantage of working from a pre-existing provider is that no need exists to override everything the provider exposes. Instead, if you are interested in changing only a particular behavior of a built-in provider, you might only need to override a couple of the exposed methods and nothing more, making this approach rather simple and quick to achieve in your application.

Next, this chapter looks at extending one of the built-in providers to change the underlying functionality of the provider.

Limiting Role Capabilities with a New LimitedSqlRoleProvider Provider

Suppose you want to utilize the role management system in your ASP.NET application and have every intention of using a SQL Server backend for the system. Suppose you also want to limit what roles developers can create in their applications, and you want to remove their capability to add users to a particular role in the system.

Instead of building a role provider from scratch from the `RoleProvider` abstract class, deriving your provider from `SqlRoleProvider` and simply changing the behavior of a few methods that deal with the creation of roles and adding users to roles makes more sense.

For this example, create the provider in your application within the App_Code folder as before. In reality, however, you probably want to create a Class Library project if you want to use this provider across your company so that your development teams can use a DLL rather than a modifiable class file.

Within the App_Code folder, create a class file called `LimitedSqlRoleProvider.vb` or `.cs`. You want this class to inherit from `SqlRoleProvider`, and this gives you the structure shown in Listing 12-18.

LISTING 12-18: The beginnings of the LimitedSqlRoleProvider class

Available for download on Wrox.com

VB

```
Imports Microsoft.VisualBasic
Imports System.Configuration.Provider

Public Class LimitedSqlRoleProvider
    Inherits SqlRoleProvider

End Class
```

C#

```
using System;
using System.Collections.Generic;
using System.Linq;
using System.Web;
using System.Web.Security;

public class LimitedSqlRoleProvider : SqlRoleProvider
{

}
```

Creating this class is similar to creating the `XmlMembershipProvider` class. When you did that, however, you were able to use Visual Studio to build the entire class skeleton of all the methods and properties you had to override to get the new class up and running. In this case, if you try to do the same thing in Visual Studio, you get an error (if using C#) or, perhaps, no result at all (if using Visual Basic) because you are not working with an abstract class. You do not need to override an enormous number of methods and properties. Instead, because you are deriving from a class that already inherits from one of these abstract classes, you can get by with overriding only the methods and properties that you must work with and nothing more.

To get at this list of methods and properties within Visual Studio, you simply type `Public Overrides` (when using Visual Basic) or `public override` (when using C#). IntelliSense then provides you with a large drop-down list of available methods and properties to work with, as shown in Figure 12-6.

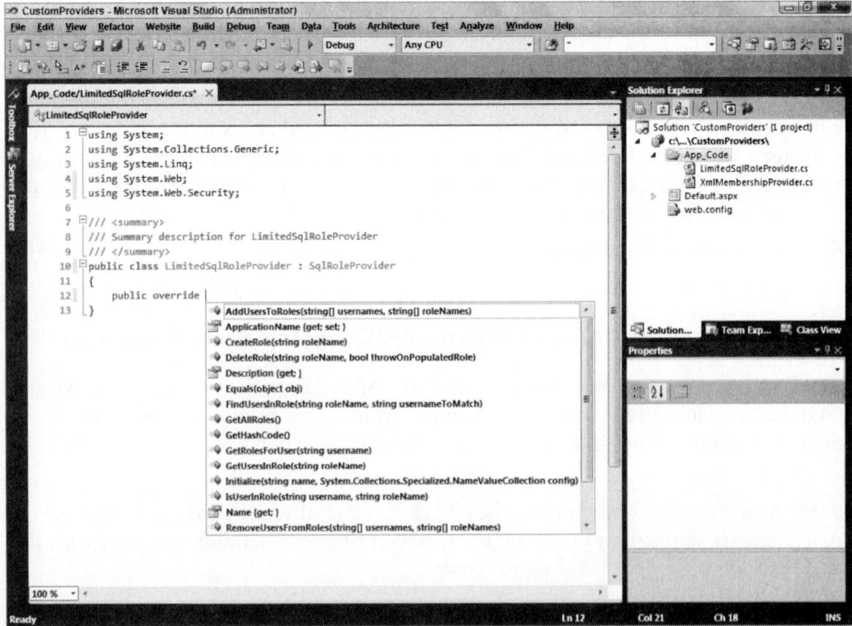

FIGURE 12-6

For this example, you only override the `CreateRole()`, `AddUsersToRoles()`, and `DeleteRole()` methods. They are described next.

The CreateRole() Method

The `CreateRole()` method in the `SqlRoleProvider` class allows developers to add any role to the system. The only parameter required for this method is a string value that is the name of the role. For this example, instead of letting developers create any role they want, this provider limits the role creation to only the *Administrator* and *Manager* roles. To accomplish this in the `CreateRole()` method, you code the method as presented in Listing 12-19.

LISTING 12-19: Allowing only the Administrator or Manager role in the CreateRole() method

Available for download on Wrox.com

VB

```
Public Overrides Sub CreateRole(ByVal roleName As String)
   If (roleName = "Administrator" Or roleName = "Manager") Then
     MyBase.CreateRole(roleName)
   Else
     Throw New _
      ProviderException("Role creation limited to only Administrator and Manager")
   End If
End Sub
```

C#

```
public override void CreateRole(string roleName)
{
   if (roleName == "Administrator" || roleName == "Manager")
   {
      base.CreateRole(roleName);
   }
   else
   {
     throw new
      ProviderException("Role creation limited to only Administrator and Manager");
   }
}
```

You are going to need to import the `System.Configuration.Provider` *namespace for this code to work.*

In this method, you can see that a check is first done to determine whether the role being created is either Administrator or Manager. If the role being created is not one of these defined roles, a `ProviderException` is thrown informing the developer of which roles he or she is allowed to create.

If Administrator or Manager is one of the roles, then the base class (`SqlRoleProvider`) `CreateRole()` method is invoked.

The DeleteRole() Method

If you allow developers using this provider to create only specific roles, you might not want them to delete any role after it is created. If this is the case, you want to override the `DeleteRole()` method of the `SqlRoleProvider` class, as shown in Listing 12-20.

LISTING 12-20: Disallowing the DeleteRole() method

Available for download on Wrox.com

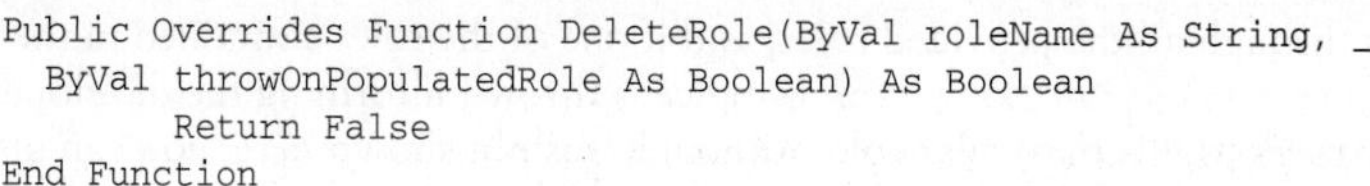

VB

```
Public Overrides Function DeleteRole(ByVal roleName As String, _
  ByVal throwOnPopulatedRole As Boolean) As Boolean
        Return False
End Function
```

continues

LISTING 12-20 *(continued)*

```
public override bool DeleteRole(string roleName, bool throwOnPopulatedRole)
{
   return false;
}
```

Looking at the `DeleteRole()` method, you can see that deleting any role is completely disallowed. Instead of raising the base class's `DeleteRole()` and returning the following:

```
Return MyBase.DeleteRole(roleName, throwOnPopulatedRole)
```

a `False` value is returned and no action is taken. Another approach is to throw a `NotSupportedException`, as shown here:

```
Throw New NotSupportedException()
```

The AddUsersToRoles() Method

As you look over the methods that can be overridden, notice that only one single method allows you to add any number of users to any number of roles. Multiple methods in the `Roles` class actually map to this method. If you look at the `Roles` class, notice the `AddUserToRole()`, `AddUserToRoles()`, `AddUsersToRole()`, and `AddUsersToRoles()` methods at your disposal. All these actually map to the `AddUsersToRoles()` method that is available in the `RoleProvider` base class.

For example, suppose you want to enable developers to add users only to the Manager role but not to add any users to the Administrator role. You could accomplish something like this by constructing a method, as shown in Listing 12-21.

LISTING 12-21: Disallowing users to be added to a particular role

Available for download on Wrox.com

VB

```
Public Overrides Sub AddUsersToRoles(ByVal usernames() As String, _
  ByVal roleNames() As String)

   For Each roleItem As String In roleNames
      If roleItem = "Administrator" Then
         Throw New _
            ProviderException("You are not authorized to add any users" & _
               " to the Administrator role")
      End If
   Next

   MyBase.AddUsersToRoles(usernames, roleNames)
End Sub
```

C#

```
public override void AddUsersToRoles(string[] usernames, string[] roleNames)
{
   foreach (string roleItem in roleNames)
   {
      if (roleItem == "Administrator")
      {
         throw new ProviderException("You are not authorized to add any users" +
           " to the Administrator role");
      }
   }

   base.AddUsersToRoles(usernames, roleNames);
}
```

This overridden method iterates through all the provided roles, and if one of the roles contained in the string array is the role Administrator, then a `ProviderException` instance is thrown informing the developer that he or she is not allowed to add any users to this particular role. Although it is not shown here, you can also take the same approach with the `RemoveUsersFromRoles()` method exposed from the `RoleProvider` base class.

Using the New LimitedSqlRoleProvider Provider

After you have the provider in place and ready to use, you have to make some modifications to the `web.config` file in order to use this provider in your ASP.NET application. You learn how you add what you need to the `web.config` file for this provider in Listing 12-22.

LISTING 12-22: Making the appropriate changes to the web.config file for the provider

Available for download on Wrox.com

```
<configuration>
   <system.web>

     <roleManager defaultProvider="LimitedProvider" enabled="true">
       <providers>
         <add connectionStringName="LocalSqlServer" applicationName="/"
          name="LimitedProvider"
          type="LimitedSqlRoleProvider" />
       </providers>
     </roleManager>
   </system.web>
</configuration>
```

Remember that you have to define the provider to use in your application by providing a value for the `defaultProvider` attribute and defining that provider further in the `<providers>` section. You also have to enable the provider by setting the `enabled` attribute to `true`. By default, the role management system is disabled.

Using the `<add>` element, you can add a provider instance that makes use of the `LimitedSqlRoleProvider` class. Because this provider derives from the `SqlRoleProvider` class, you must use some of the same attributes that this provider requires, such as the `connectionStringName` attribute that points to the connection string to use to connect to the specified SQL instance.

After you have the new `LimitedSqlRoleProvider` instance in place and defined in the `web.config` file, you can use the `Roles` class in your application just as you normally would, but notice the behavior of this class is rather different from the normal `SqlRoleProvider`.

To see it in action, construct a simple ASP.NET page that includes a TextBox, Button, and Label server control. The page should appear as shown in Listing 12-23.

LISTING 12-23: Using Roles.CreateRole()

Available for download on Wrox.com

```
<%@ Page Language="VB" %>
<script runat="server">
    Protected Sub Button1_Click(ByVal sender As Object, _
      ByVal e As System.EventArgs)

        Try
            Roles.CreateRole(TextBox1.Text)
            Label1.Text = "Role successfully created."
        Catch ex As Exception
            Label1.Text = ex.Message.ToString()
        End Try
    End Sub
</script>

<html xmlns="http://www.w3.org/1999/xhtml" >
<head runat="server">
    <title>Main Page</title>
</head>
<body>
    <form id="form1" runat="server">
    <div>
        Role Name:<br />
```

continues

LISTING 12-23 *(continued)*

```
            <asp:TextBox ID="TextBox1" runat="server"></asp:TextBox><br />
            <br />
            <asp:Button ID="Button1" runat="server" Text="Create Role"
             OnClick="Button1_Click" /><br />
            <br />
            <asp:Label ID="Label1" runat="server"></asp:Label></div>
        </form>
    </body>
    </html>
```

C#

```
<%@ Page Language="C#" %>

<script runat="server">
    protected void Button1_Click(object sender, EventArgs e)
    {
        try
        {
            Roles.CreateRole(TextBox1.Text);
            Label1.Text = "Role successfully created.";
        }
        catch (Exception ex)
        {
            Label1.Text = ex.Message.ToString();
        }
    }
</script>
```

This simple ASP.NET page enables you to type in a string value in the text box and to attempt to create a new role using this value. Note that anything other than the role Administrator and Manager results in an error. So, when the `Roles.CreateRole()` is called, an error is produced if the rules defined by the provider are not followed. In fact, running this page and typing in a role other than the Administrator or Manager role gives you the results presented in Figure 12-7.

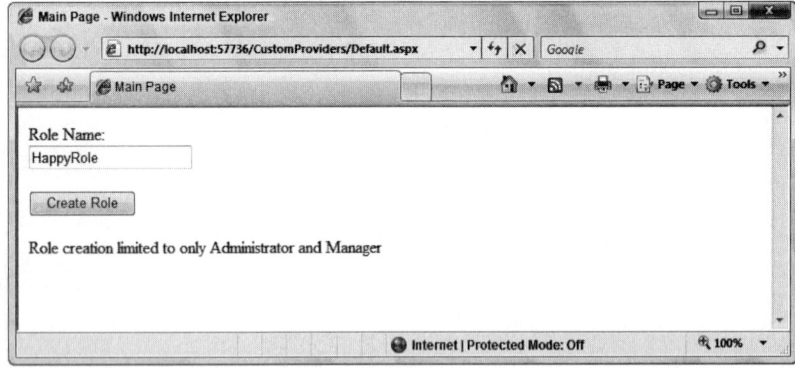

FIGURE 12-7

To show this provider in action, create another ASP.NET page that allows you to add users to a particular role. As stated, you can do so with a number of available methods, but in this case, this example uses the `Roles.AddUserToRole()` method, shown in Listing 12-24.

Available for download on Wrox.com

LISTING 12-24: Attempting to add users to a role through the new role provider

```
<%@ Page Language="VB" %>

<script runat="server">
    Protected Sub Button1_Click(ByVal sender As Object, _
      ByVal e As System.EventArgs)

        Try
            Roles.AddUserToRole(TextBox1.Text, TextBox2.Text)
            Label1.Text = "User successfully added to role"
        Catch ex As Exception
            Label1.Text = ex.Message.ToString()
        End Try
    End Sub
</script>

<html xmlns="http://www.w3.org/1999/xhtml" >
<head runat="server">
    <title>Main Page</title>
</head>
<body>
    <form id="form1" runat="server">
    <div>
        Add the following user:<br />
        <asp:TextBox ID="TextBox1" runat="server"></asp:TextBox><br />
        <br />
        To role:<br />
        <asp:TextBox ID="TextBox2" runat="server"></asp:TextBox><br />
        <br />
        <asp:Button ID="Button1" runat="server" Text="Add User to Role"
         OnClick="Button1_Click" /><br />
        <br />
        <asp:Label ID="Label1" runat="server"></asp:Label></div>
    </form>
</body>
</html>
```

C#

```
<%@ Page Language="C#" %>

<script runat="server">
    protected void Button1_Click(object sender, EventArgs e)
    {
        try
        {
            Roles.AddUserToRole(TextBox1.Text, TextBox2.Text);
            Label1.Text = "User successfully added to role";
        }
        catch (Exception ex)
        {
            Label1.Text = ex.Message.ToString();
        }
    }
</script>
```

In this example, two text boxes are provided. The first asks for the username and the second asks for the role to add the user to. The code for the button click event uses the `Roles.AddUserToRole()` method. Because you built the provider, you know that an error is thrown if there is an attempt to add a user to the Administrator role. This attempt is illustrated in Figure 12-8.

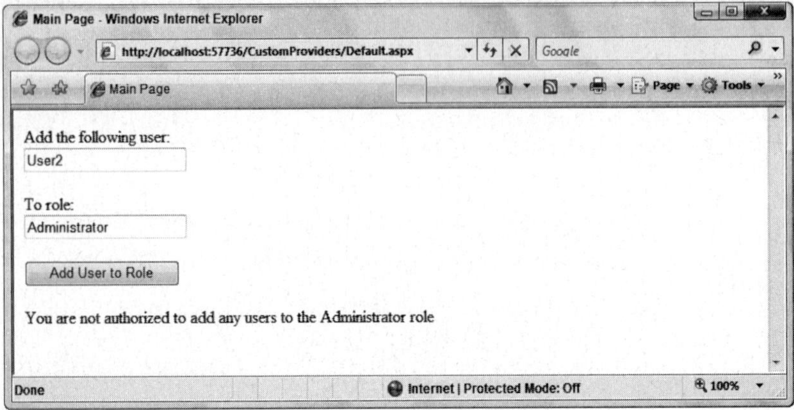

FIGURE 12-8

In this case, an attempt was made to add User2 to the Administrator role. This, of course, throws an error and returns the error message that is defined in the provider.

SUMMARY

From this chapter and the last chapter, you got a good taste of the provider model and what it means to the ASP.NET 4 applications you build today. Although a lot of providers are available to you out of the box to use for interacting with one of the many systems provided in ASP.NET, you are not limited to just these providers. You definitely can either build your own providers or even extend the functionality of the providers already present in the system.

This chapter looked at both of these scenarios. First, you built your own provider to use the membership system with an XML data store for the user data, and then you worked through an example of extending the `SqlRoleProvider` class (something already present in ASP.NET) to change the underlying behavior of this provider.

13

Site Navigation

WHAT'S IN THIS CHAPTER?

- Using `.sitemap` files and the SiteMapPath server control
- Using the TreeView and Menu server controls
- Taking advantage of URL mapping
- Localizing your `Web.sitemap` files and filtering the results of the site navigation contents

The Web applications that you develop generally have more than a single page to them. Usually, you create a number of Web pages that are interconnected in some fashion. If you also build the navigation around your collection of pages, you make it easy for the end user to successfully work through your application in a straightforward manner.

Currently, you must choose from among a number of different ways to expose the paths through your application to the end user. The difficult task of site navigation is compounded when you continue to add pages to the overall application.

The present method for building navigation within Web applications is to sprinkle pages with hyperlinks. Hyperlinks are generally added to Web pages by using include files or user controls. They can also be directly hard-coded onto a page so that they appear in the header or the sidebar of the page being viewed. The difficulties in working with navigation become worse when you move pages around or change page names. Sometimes, developers are forced to go to each and every page in the application just to change some aspect of the navigation.

ASP.NET 4 tackles this problem by providing a navigation system that makes managing how end users work through the applications you create quite trivial. This capability in ASP.NET is complex; but the great thing is that it can be as simple as you need it to be, or you can actually get in deep and control every aspect of how it works.

The site navigation system includes the capability to define your entire site in an XML file that is called a *sitemap*. After you define a sitemap, you can work with it programmatically using the `SiteMap` class. Another aspect of the sitemap capability available in ASP.NET is a data provider that is specifically developed to work with sitemap files and to bind them to a series of navigation-based server controls. This chapter looks at all these components in the ASP.NET 4 navigation system. The following section introduces sitemaps.

XML-BASED SITEMAPS

Although a sitemap is not a required element (as you see later), one of the common first steps you take in working with the ASP.NET 4 navigation system is building a sitemap for your application. A sitemap is an XML description of your site's structure.

You use this sitemap to define the navigational structure of all the pages in your application and how they relate to one another. If you do this according to the ASP.NET sitemap standard, you can then interact with this navigation information using either the `SiteMap` class or the SiteMapDataSource control. By using the SiteMapDataSource control, you can then bind the information in the sitemap file to a variety of data-binding controls, including the navigation server controls provided by ASP.NET.

To create a sitemap file for your application, add a sitemap or an XML file to your application. When asked, you name the XML file `Web.sitemap`; this file is already in place if you select the Sitemap option. The file is named `Web` and has the file extension of `.sitemap`. Take a look at an example of a `.sitemap` file, shown here in Listing 13-1.

Available for download on Wrox.com

LISTING 13-1: An example of a Web.sitemap file

```
<?xml version="1.0" encoding="utf-8" ?>

<siteMap xmlns="http://schemas.microsoft.com/AspNet/SiteMap-File-1.0" >
   <siteMapNode title="Home" description="Home Page" url="Default.aspx">
      <siteMapNode title="News" description="The Latest News" url="News.aspx">
         <siteMapNode title="U.S." description="U.S. News"
          url="News.aspx?cat=us" />
         <siteMapNode title="World" description="World News"
          url="News.aspx?cat=world" />
         <siteMapNode title="Technology" description="Technology News"
          url="News.aspx?cat=tech" />
         <siteMapNode title="Sports" description="Sports News"
          url="News.aspx?cat=sport" />
      </siteMapNode>
      <siteMapNode title="Finance" description="The Latest Financial Information"
        url="Finance.aspx">
         <siteMapNode title="Quotes" description="Get the Latest Quotes"
          url="Quotes.aspx" />
         <siteMapNode title="Markets" description="The Latest Market Information"
          url="Markets.aspx">
            <siteMapNode title="U.S. Market Report"
             description="Looking at the U.S. Market" url="MarketsUS.aspx" />
            <siteMapNode title="NYSE"
             description="The New York Stock Exchange" url="NYSE.aspx" />
         </siteMapNode>
         <siteMapNode title="Funds" description="Mutual Funds"
          url="Funds.aspx" />
      </siteMapNode>
      <siteMapNode title="Weather" description="The Latest Weather"
       url="Weather.aspx" />
   </siteMapNode>
</siteMap>
```

Filename Web.sitemap

So what does this file give you? Well, it gives you a logical structure that ASP.NET can now use in the rest of the navigation system it provides. Next, this chapter examines how this file is constructed.

The root node of this XML file is a `<siteMap>` element. Only one `<siteMap>` element can exist in the file. Within the `<siteMap>` element is a single root `<siteMapNode>` element. This is generally the start page of the application. In the case of the file in Listing 13-1, the root `<siteMapNode>` points to the `Default.aspx` page, the start page:

```
<siteMapNode title="Home" description="Home Page" url="Default.aspx">
```

Table 13-1 describes the most common attributes in the `<siteMapNode>` element.

TABLE 13-1

ATTRIBUTE	DESCRIPTION
`Title`	The `title` attribute provides a textual description of the link. The `String` value used here is the text used for the link.
`description`	The `description` attribute not only reminds you what the link is for, but also is used for the `ToolTip` attribute on the link. The `ToolTip` attribute is the yellow box that shows up next to the link when the end user hovers the cursor over the link for a couple of seconds.
`url`	The `url` attribute describes where the file is located in the solution. If the file is in the root directory, simply use the filename, such as `"Default.aspx"`. If the file is located in a subfolder, be sure to include the folders in the String value used in this attribute. For example, "`MySubFolder/Markets.aspx`".

After you have the first `<siteMapNode>` in place, you can then nest as many additional `<siteMapNode>` elements as you need within the root `<siteMapNode>` element. You can also create additional link-levels by creating child `<siteMapNode>` elements for any parent `<siteMapNode>` in the structure.

The example in Listing 13-1 gives the application the following navigational structure:

```
Home
   News
      U.S.
      World
      Technology
      Sports
   Finance
      Quotes
      Markets
         U.S. Market Report
         NYSE
      Funds
   Weather
```

You can see that this structure goes down three levels in some places. One of the easiest places to use this file is with the SiteMapPath server control that comes with ASP.NET. The SiteMapPath server control in ASP.NET is built to work specifically with the `.sitemap` files.

SITEMAPPATH SERVER CONTROL

Using the `.sitemap` file you just created with the SiteMapPath server control provided with ASP.NET is quite easy. You can find this control in the Navigation section of the Visual Studio 2010 IDE.

The SiteMapPath control creates navigation functionality that you once might either have created yourself or have seen elsewhere in Web pages on the Internet. The SiteMapPath control creates what some refer to as *breadcrumb navigation*. This linear path defines where the end user is in the navigation structure. The `Reuters.com` Web site, shown in Figure 13-1, uses this type of navigation. A black box shows the breadcrumb navigation used on the page.

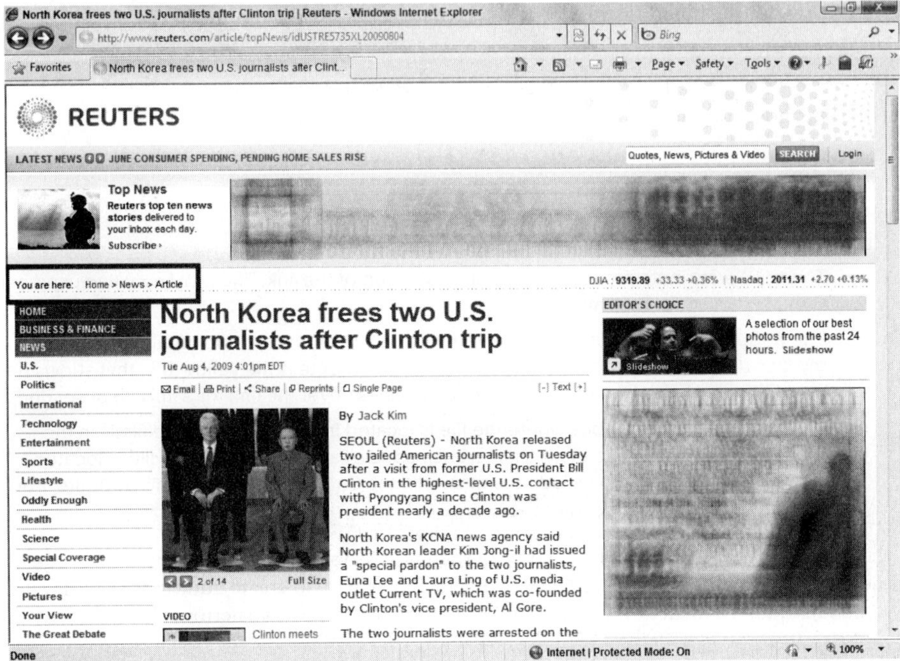

FIGURE 13-1

The purpose of this type of navigation is to show end users where they are in relation to the rest of the site. Traditionally, coding this kind of navigation has been tricky, to say the least; but with the SiteMapPath server control, you should find coding for this type of navigation a breeze.

You should first create an application that has the `Web.sitemap` file created in Listing 13-1. From there, create a WebForm called `MarketsUS.aspx`. This file is defined in the `Web.sitemap` file as being on the lowest tier of files in the application.

The SiteMapPath control is so easy to work with that it doesn't even require a data source control to hook it up to the `Web.sitemap` file where it infers all its information. All you do is drag and drop a SiteMapPath control onto your `MarketsUS.aspx` page. In the end, you should have a page similar to the one shown in Listing 13-2.

LISTING 13-2: Using the Web.sitemap file with a SiteMapPath server control

Available for download on Wrox.com

```
<%@ Page Language="VB" %>

<html xmlns="http://www.w3.org/1999/xhtml">
<head runat="server">
    <title>Using the SiteMapPath Server Control</title>
</head>
<body>
    <form id="form1" runat="server">
        <asp:SiteMapPath ID="Sitemappath1" runat="server">
        </asp:SiteMapPath>
    </form>
</body>
</html>
```

Not much to it, is there? It really is that easy. Run this page and you see the results shown in Figure 13-2.

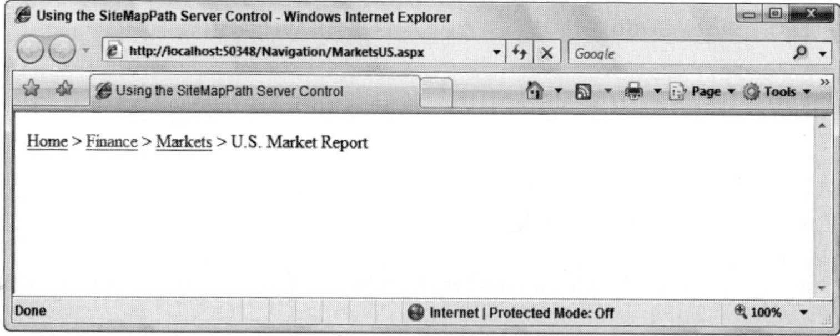

FIGURE 13-2

This screenshot shows that you are on the U.S. Market Report page at `MarketsUS.aspx`. As an end user, you can see that this page is part of the Markets section of the site; Markets, in turn, is part of the Finance section of the site. With breadcrumb navigation, end users who understand the structure of the site and their place in it can quickly select the links to navigate to any location in the site.

If you hover your mouse over the Finance link, you see a tooltip appear after a couple of seconds, as shown in Figure 13-3.

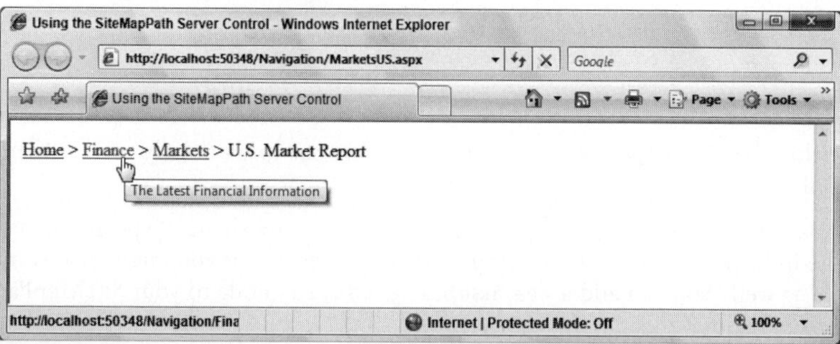

FIGURE 13-3

This tooltip, which reads `The Latest Financial Information`, comes from the description attribute of the `<siteMapNode>` element in the `Web.sitemap` file.

```
<siteMapNode title="Finance" description="The Latest Financial Information"
 url="Finance.aspx">
```

The SiteMapPath control works automatically, requiring very little work on your part. You just add the basic control to your page, and the control automatically creates the breadcrumb navigation you have just seen. However, you can use the properties discussed in the following sections to modify the appearance and behavior of the control.

The PathSeparator Property

One important style property for the SiteMapPath control is the `PathSeparator` property. By default, the SiteMapPath control uses a greater-than sign (>) to separate the link elements. You can change it by reassigning a new value to the `PathSeparator` property. Listing 13-3 illustrates the use of this property.

LISTING 13-3: Changing the PathSeparator value

Available for download on Wrox.com

```
<asp:SiteMapPath ID="Sitemappath1" runat="server" PathSeparator=" | ">
</asp:SiteMapPath>
```

Or

```
<asp:SiteMapPath ID="Sitemappath1" runat="server">
   <PathSeparatorTemplate> | </PathSeparatorTemplate>
</asp:SiteMapPath>
```

The SiteMapPath control in this example uses the pipe character (|), which is found above the Enter key. When it is rendered, you get the results shown in Figure 13-4.

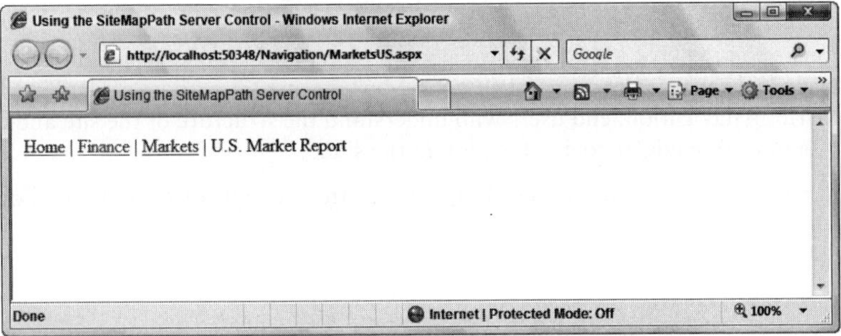

FIGURE 13-4

As you can see, you can use either the `PathSeparator` attribute or the `<PathSeparatorTemplate>` element within the SiteMapPath control.

With the use of the `PathSeparator` attribute or the `<PathSeparatorTemplate>` element, specifying what you want to use to separate the links in the breadcrumb navigation is quite easy, but you might also want to give this pipe some visual style as well. You can add a `<PathSeparatorStyle>` node to your SiteMapPath control. Listing 13-4 shows an example of this.

LISTING 13-4: Adding style to the PathSeparator property

Available for download on Wrox.com

```
<asp:SiteMapPath ID="Sitemappath1" runat="server" PathSeparator=" | ">
   <PathSeparatorStyle Font-Bold="true" Font-Names="Verdana" ForeColor="#663333"
    BackColor="#cccc66"></PathSeparatorStyle>
</asp:SiteMapPath>
```

Okay, it may not be pretty, but by using the `<PathSeparatorStyle>` element with the `SiteMapPath` control, you can change the visual appearance of the separator elements. Figure 13-5 shows the results.

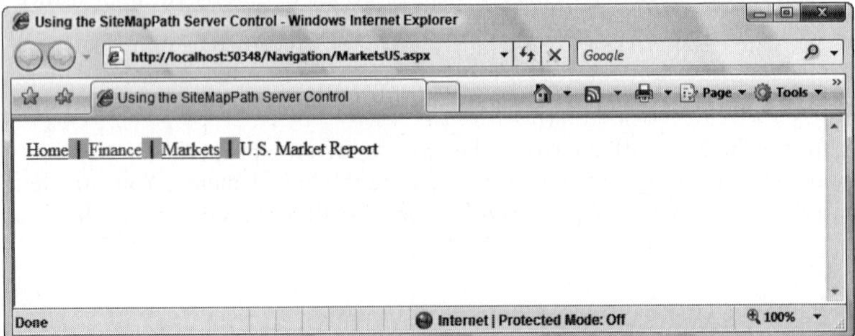

FIGURE 13-5

Using these constructs, you can also add an image as the separator, as shown in Listing 13-5.

Available for download on Wrox.com

LISTING 13-5: Using an image as the separator

```
<%@ Page Language="VB" %>

<html xmlns="http://www.w3.org/1999/xhtml">
<head runat="server">
    <title>Using the SiteMapPath Server Control</title>
</head>
<body>
    <form id="form1" runat="server">
        <asp:SiteMapPath ID="SiteMapPath1" runat="server">
            <PathSeparatorTemplate>
                <asp:Image ID="Image1" runat="server" ImageUrl="divider.gif" />
            </PathSeparatorTemplate>
        </asp:SiteMapPath>
   </form>
</body>
</html>
```

To utilize an image as the separator between the links, you use the `<PathSeparatorTemplate>` element and place an Image control within it. In fact, you can place any type of control between the navigation links that the SiteMapPath control produces.

The PathDirection Property

Another interesting property to use with the SiteMapPath control is `PathDirection`. This property changes the direction of the links generated in the output. Only two settings are possible for this property: `RootToCurrent` and `CurrentToRoot`.

The Root link is the first link in the display and is usually the Home page. The Current link is the link for the page currently being displayed. By default, this property is set to `RootToCurrent`. Changing the example to `CurrentToRoot` produces the results shown in Figure 13-6.

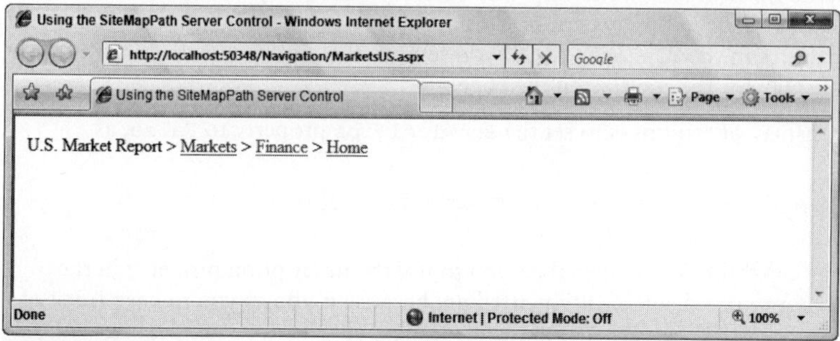

FIGURE 13-6

The ParentLevelsDisplayed Property

In some cases, your navigation may go quite deep. You can see on the sitemap shown in Listing 13-1 that you go three pages deep, which isn't a big deal. Some of you, however, might be dealing with sites that go quite a number of pages deeper. In these cases, using the SiteMapPath control might be a bit silly. Doing so would display a huge list of pages.

In a case like this, you can turn to the `ParentLevelsDisplayed` property that is part of the SiteMapPath control. When set, this property displays pages only as deep as specified. Therefore, if you are using the SiteMapPath control with the `Web.sitemap`, as shown in Listing 13-1, and you give the `ParentLevelsDisplayed` property a value of `3`, you don't notice any change to your page. It already displays the path three pages deep. If you change this value to 2, however, the SiteMapPath control is constructed as follows:

```
<asp:SiteMapPath ID="Sitemappath1" runat="server" ParentLevelsDisplayed="2">
</asp:SiteMapPath>
```

Notice the result of this change in Figure 13-7. The SiteMapPath control shows links only two pages deep and doesn't show the Home page link.

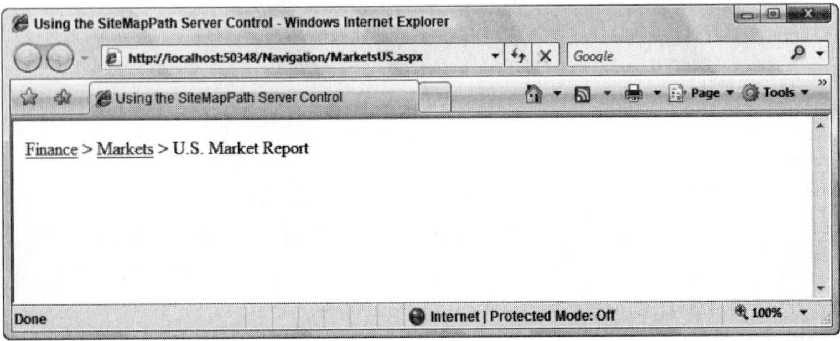

FIGURE 13-7

By default, no limit is set on the number of links shown, so the SiteMapPath control just generates the specified number of links based on what is labeled in the sitemap file.

The ShowToolTips Property

By default, the SiteMapPath control generates tooltips for each link if a description property is used within the `Web.sitemap` file. Remember, a tooltip is the text that appears onscreen when an end user hovers the mouse over one of the links in the SiteMapPath control. This capability was shown earlier in this chapter.

There may be times when you do not want your SiteMapPath control to show any tooltips for the links that it generates. For these situations, you can actually turn off this capability in a couple of ways. The first way is to omit any description attributes in the `.sitemap` file. If you remove these attributes from the file, the SiteMapPath has nothing to display for the tooltips on the page.

The other way to turn off the display of tooltips is to set the `ShowToolTips` property to `False`, as shown here:

```
<asp:SiteMapPath ID="Sitemappath1" runat="server" ShowToolTips="false">
</asp:SiteMapPath>
```

This code turns off the tooltips capability but still enables you to use the description property in the `.sitemap` file. You may still want to use the description attribute because it allows you to keep track of what the links in your file are used for. This feature is quite advantageous when you are dealing with hundreds or even thousands of links in your application.

The SiteMapPath Control's Child Elements

You already saw the use of the `<PathSeparatorStyle>` and the `<PathSeparatorTemplate>` child elements for the SiteMapPath control, but additional child elements exist. Table 13-2 covers each of the available child elements.

TABLE 13-2

CHILD ELEMENT	DESCRIPTION
`CurrentNodeStyle`	Applies styles to the link in the SiteMapPath navigation for the currently displayed page.
`CurrentNodeTemplate`	Applies a template construction to the link in the SiteMapPath navigation for the currently displayed page.
`NodeStyle`	Applies styles to all links in the SiteMapPath navigation. The settings applied in the `CurrentNodeStyle` or `RootNodeStyle` elements supersede any settings placed here.
`NodeTemplate`	Applies a template construction to all links in the SiteMapPath navigation. The settings applied in the `CurrentNodeTemplate` or `RootNodeTemplate` elements supersede any settings placed here.
`PathSeparatorStyle`	Applies styles to the link dividers in the SiteMapPath navigation.
`PathSeparatorTemplate`	Applies a template construction to the link dividers in the SiteMapPath navigation.
`RootNodeStyle`	Applies styles to the first link (the root link) in the SiteMapPath navigation.
`RootNodeTemplate`	Applies a template construction to the first link in the SiteMapPath navigation.

TREEVIEW SERVER CONTROL

The TreeView server control is a rich server control for rendering a hierarchy of data, so it is quite ideal for displaying what is contained in your `.sitemap` file. Figure 13-8 shows you how it displays the contents of the sitemap (again from Listing 13-1) that you have been working with thus far in this chapter. This figure first shows a completely collapsed TreeView control at the top of the screen; the second TreeView control has been completely expanded.

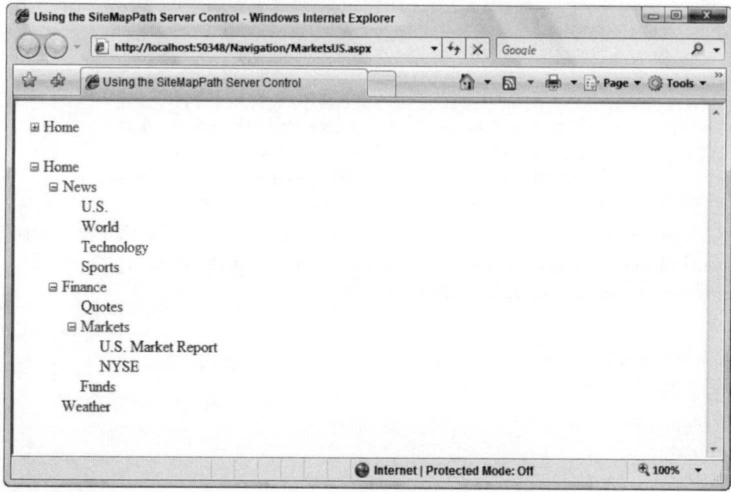

FIGURE 13-8

This control can dynamically load the nodes to be displayed as they are selected by the expandable and collapsible framework of the control. If the control can render the TreeView output along with some client-side script, the control can make a call back to the server if someone expands one of the nodes in the control to get the subnodes of the selected item. This feature is ideal if your site navigation system is large. In this case, loading nodes of the TreeView control dynamically greatly helps performance. One of the great features of this postback capability is that it is done under the covers and does not require the ASP.NET page to be completely refreshed. Of course, this capability is there only if the browser accepts the client-side code that goes along with the TreeView control. If the browser does not, the control knows this and renders only what is appropriate (pulling all the information that is required of the entire TreeView control). It only performs these JavaScript-based postbacks for those clients who can work with this client-side script.

You can definitely see this scenario in action if you run the TreeView control on a page that is being monitored by an HTTP sniffer of some kind to monitor the traffic moving across the wire.

A good sniffer we recommend is Fiddler by Eric Lawrence of Microsoft; it is freely downloadable on the Internet at `fiddlertool.com`.

If your browser allows client-side script and you expand one of the expandable nodes of the TreeView control, your HTTP request will be similar to the following:

```
POST /Navigation/Default.aspx HTTP/1.1
Accept: */*
Accept-Language: en-us
Referrer: http://localhost:1882/Navigation/Default.aspx
Content-Type: application/x-www-form-urlencoded
Accept-Encoding: gzip, deflate
User-Agent: Mozilla/4.0 (compatible; MSIE 7.0; Windows NT 6.0; SLCC1;
.NET CLR 2.0.50727; Media Center PC 5.0; .NET CLR 3.0.04506;
.NET CLR 3.5.20404; .NET CLR 1.1.4322; .NET CLR 4.0.21006)
Host: localhost:1882
Content-Length: 904
Proxy-Connection: Keep-Alive
Pragma: no-cache

__EVENTTARGET=&__EVENTARGUMENT=&TreeView1_ExpandState=c&TreeView1_SelectedNode=Tree
View1t0&TreeView1_PopulateLog=&__VIEWSTATE=%2FwEPDwUKLTY0ODk0OTE2Mg9kFgICBA9kFgICAw
88KwAJAgAPFggeDU5ldmVyRXhwYW5kZWRkHgtfIURhdGFCb3VuZGceDFNlbGVjdGVkTm9kZQULVHJlZVZpZ
XcxdDAeCUxhc3RJbmRleAIBZAgUKwACBQMwOjAUKwACFhAeBFRleHQFBEhvbWUeBVZhbHVlBQRIb21lHgtO
YXZpZ2F0ZVVybAUYL05hdmlnYXRpb24vRGVmYXVsdC5hc3B4HgdUb29sVGlwBQlIb21lIFBhZ2UeCERhdGF
QYXRoBRgvbmF2aWdhdGlvbi9kZWZhdWx0LmFzcHgeCURhdGFCb3VuZGceCFNlbGVjdGVkZx4QUG9wdWxhdG
VPbkRlbWFuZGdkZBgBBR5fX0NvbnRyb2xzUmVxdWlyZVBvc3RCYWNrS2V5X18WAwURTG9naW4xJFJlbWVtY
mVyTWUFF0xvZ2luMSRMb2dpbkltYWdlQnV0dG9uBQlUcmVlVmlldzFtwszVpUMxFTDtpERnNjgEIkWWbg%3
D%3D&Login1$UserName=&Login1$Password=&__CALLBACKID=TreeView1&__CALLBACKPARAM=0%7C1
%7Ctft%7C4%7CHome24%7C%2Fnavigation%2Fdefault.aspxHome&__EVENTVALIDATION=%2FwEWBgKg
8Yn8DwKUvNa1DwL666vYDAKC0q%2BkBgKnz4ybCAKn5fLxBaSy6WQwPagNZsHisWRoJfuiopOe
```

The response from your ASP.NET application will *not* be the entire page that holds the TreeView control, but instead, it is a small portion of HTML that is used by a JavaScript method on the page and is loaded into the TreeView control dynamically. Here is a sample response:

```
HTTP/1.1 200 OK
Server: ASP.NET Development Server/8.0.0.0
Date: Sat, 11 Feb 2010 17:55:02 GMT
X-AspNet-Version: 4.0.21006
Cache-Control: private, no-store
Content-Type: text/html; charset=utf-8
Content-Length: 1756
Connection: Close

112|/wEWCgKg8Yn8DwKUvNa1DwL666vYDAKC0q+kBgKnz4ybCAKn5fLxBQKAgtPaBALEmcbhCgK8nZDfCAL
M/ZK8AR/nFcl4nlPgp6HcFlU6YiFBfoNM14|nn|<div id="TreeView1n6Nodes"
style="display:none;">
```

```
<table cellpadding="0" cellspacing="0" style="border-width:0;">
        <tr>
                <td><div style="width:20px;height:1px"></div></td><td><div
                 style="width:20px;height:1px"><img
                 src="/Navigation/WebResource.axd?d=GOWKLfnbFU9fYyy
                 PCMT8DIfngU4PXeMiAHxJNuXB-tU1&amp;t=632662834831594592" alt="" />
                </div></td><td><div style="width:20px;height:1px"><img
                 src="/Navigation/WebResource.axd?d=GOWKLfnbFU9fYyyPCMT8DIfngU
                 4PXeMiAHxJNuXB-tU1&amp;t=632662834831594592" alt="" />
                </div></td><td><img
                 src="/Navigation/WebResource.axd?d=GOWKLfnbFU9fYyy
                 PCMT8DCXmyNCWX5x-n_pSXFIW2qE1&amp;t=632662834831594592"
                 alt="" /></td><td style="white-space:nowrap;">
                <a href="/Navigation/MarketsUSasdf.aspx"
                 title="Looking at the U.S. Market" id="TreeView1t12"
                 style="text-decoration:none;">U.S. Market Report</a></td>
        </tr>
</table><table cellpadding="0" cellspacing="0" style="border-width:0;">
        <tr>
                 <td><div style="width:20px;height:1px"></div></td><td><div
                 style="width:20px;height:1px"><img
                 src="/Navigation/WebResource.axd?d=GOWKLfnbFU9fYyyPCMT8DI
                 fngU4PXeMiAHxJNuXB-tU1&amp;t=632662834831594592" alt="" />
                </div></td><td><div style="width:20px;height:1px"><img
                 src="/Navigation/WebResource.axd?d=GOWKLfnbFU9fYyyPCMT8DI
                 fngU4PXeMiAHxJNuXB-tU1&amp;t=632662834831594592" alt="" />
                </div></td><td><img
                 src="/Navigation/WebResource.axd?d=GOWKLfnbFU9fY
                 yyPCMT8DGyYai5iS-79vjeYzdeJoiI1&amp;t=632662834831594592"
                 alt="" />
                </td><td style="white-space:nowrap;">
                <a href="/Navigation/NYSE.aspx" title="The New York Stock Exchange"
                 id="TreeView1t13" style="text-decoration:none;">NYSE</a></td>
       </tr>
</table>
</div>
```

This postback capability is rather powerful, but if you want to disable it (even for browsers that can handle it), you just set the `PopulateNodesFromClient` attribute to `false` in the TreeView control (the default value is `true`).

The TreeView control is quite customizable; but first, take a look at how to create a default version of the control using the `.sitemap` file from Listing 13-1. For this example, continue to use the `MarketsUS.aspx` page you created earlier.

The first step is to create a SiteMapDataSource control on the page. When working with the TreeView control that displays the contents of your `.sitemap` file, you must apply one of these data source controls. The TreeView control doesn't just bind to your sitemap file automatically as the SiteMapPath control does.

After a basic SiteMapDataSource control is in place, position a TreeView control on the page and set the `DataSourceId` property to `SiteMapDataSource1`. When you have finished, your code should look like Listing 13-6.

Available for download on Wrox.com

LISTING 13-6: A basic TreeView control

```
<%@ Page Language="VB" %>

<html xmlns="http://www.w3.org/1999/xhtml">
<head runat="server">
    <title>Using the TreeView Server Control</title>
</head>
<body>
```

continues

LISTING 13-6 *(continued)*

```
    <form id="form1" runat="server">
        <asp:SiteMapPath ID="SiteMapPath1" runat="server">
        </asp:SiteMapPath>
        <br /><p>
        <asp:TreeView ID="TreeView1" runat="server"
         DataSourceID="SiteMapDataSource1">
        </asp:TreeView>
        <asp:SiteMapDataSource ID="SiteMapDataSource1" runat="server" /></p>
    </form>
</body>
</html>
```

After you run the page and expand the TreeView control, the results appear as shown in Figure 13-9.

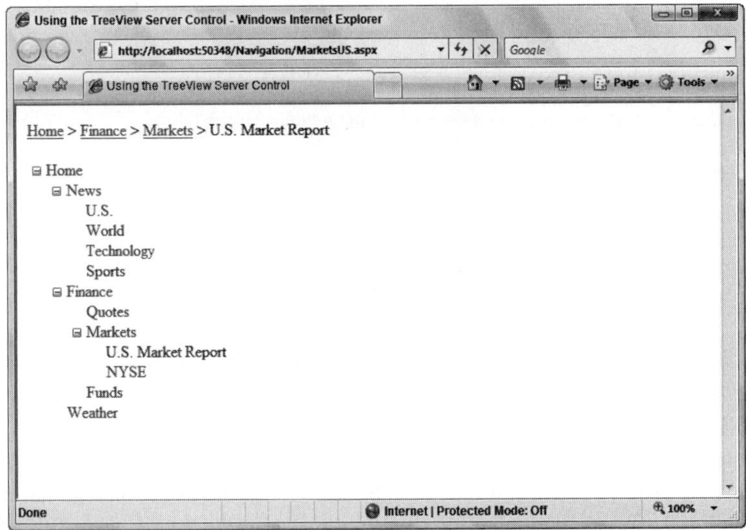

FIGURE 13-9

This TreeView control is very basic. The great thing about this control is that it allows for a high degree of customization and even gives you the capability to use some predefined styles that come prepackaged with ASP.NET 4.

Identifying the TreeView Control's Built-In Styles

As stated, the TreeView control does come with a number of pre-built styles right out of the box. The best way to utilize these predefined styles is to do so from the Design view of your page. Click on the arrow located in the upper-right section of the server control in the Design view in Visual Studio 2010 to find the Auto Format option. Click this option and a number of styles become available to you. Selecting one of these styles changes the code of your TreeView control to adapt to that chosen style. For example, if you choose `MSDN` from the list of options, the simple one-line TreeView control you created is converted to what is shown in Listing 13-7.

Available for download on Wrox.com

LISTING 13-7: A TreeView control with the MSDN style applied to it

```
<asp:TreeView ID="TreeView1" runat="server" DataSourceID="SiteMapDataSource1"
 ImageSet="Msdn" NodeIndent="10">
   <ParentNodeStyle Font-Bold="False" />
```

```
    <HoverNodeStyle BackColor="#CCCCCC" BorderColor="#888888" BorderStyle="Solid"
     Font-Underline="True" />
    <SelectedNodeStyle BackColor="White" BorderColor="#888888" BorderStyle="Solid"
     BorderWidth="1px" Font-Underline="False" HorizontalPadding="3px"
     VerticalPadding="1px" />
    <NodeStyle Font-Names="Verdana" Font-Size="8pt" ForeColor="Black"
     HorizontalPadding="5px" NodeSpacing="1px" VerticalPadding="2px" />
</asp:TreeView>
```

As you can see, if you use these built-in styles, then completely changing the look and feel of the TreeView control is not too difficult. When you run this bit of code, you get the results shown in Figure 13-10.

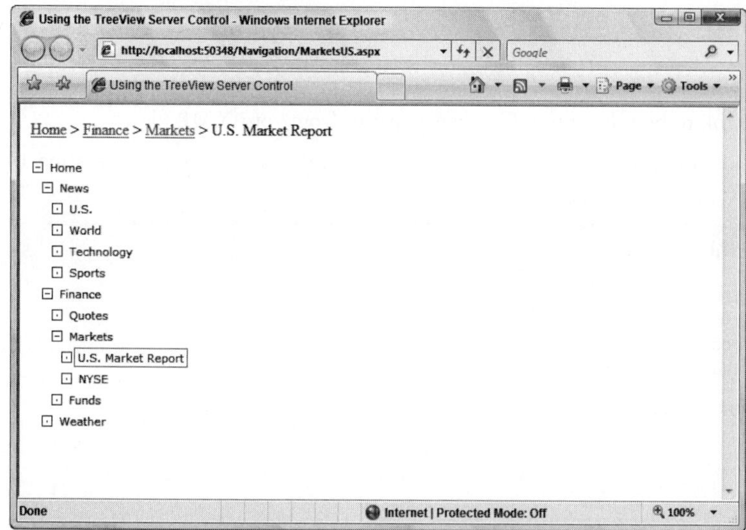

FIGURE 13-10

Examining the Parts of the TreeView Control

To master working with the TreeView control, you must understand the terminology used for each part of the hierarchical tree that is created by the control.

Every element or entry in the TreeView control is called a *node*. The uppermost node in the hierarchy of nodes is the *root node*. A TreeView control can have multiple root nodes. Any node, including the root node, is also considered a *parent node* if it has any nodes that are directly under it in the hierarchy of nodes. The nodes directly under this parent node are referred to as *child nodes*. Each parent node can have one or more child nodes. A node that contains no child nodes is called a *leaf node*.

The following is based on the sitemap shown earlier and details the use of this terminology:

```
Home - Root node, parent node
  News - Parent node, child node
     U.S. - Child node, leaf node
     World - Child node, leaf node
     Technology - Child node, leaf node
     Sports - Child node, leaf node
  Finance - Parent node, child node
     Quotes - Child node, leaf node
     Markets - Parent node, child node
        U.S. Market Report - Child node, leaf node
        NYSE - Child node, leaf node
     Funds - Child node, leaf node
  Weather - Child node, leaf node
```

From this listing, you can see what each node is and how it is referred to in the hierarchy of nodes. For example, the `U.S. Market Report` node is a leaf node—meaning that it doesn't have any child nodes associated with it. However, it is also a child node to the `Markets` node, which is a parent node to the `U.S. Market Report` node. If you are working with the `Markets` node directly, it is also a child node to the `Finance` node, which is its parent node. The main point to take away from all this is that each node in the sitemap hierarchy has a relationship to the other nodes in the hierarchy. You must understand these relationships because you can programmatically work with these nodes (as is demonstrated later in this chapter), and the methods used for working with them include terms such as `RootNode`, `CurrentNode`, and `ParentNode`.

Binding the TreeView Control to an XML File

You are not limited to working with just a `.sitemap` file in order to populate the nodes of your TreeView controls. You have many ways to get this done. One cool way is to use the XmlDataSource control (instead of the SiteMapDataSource control) to populate your TreeView controls from your XML files.

For an example of this, create a hierarchical list of items in an XML file called `Hardware.xml`. Listing 13-8 shows an example of this file.

Available for download on Wrox.com

LISTING 13-8: Hardware.xml

```
<?xml version="1.0" encoding="utf-8"?>
<Hardware>
    <Item Category="Motherboards">
        <Option Choice="Asus" />
        <Option Choice="Abit" />
    </Item>
    <Item Category="Memory">
        <Option Choice="128mb" />
        <Option Choice="256mb" />
        <Option Choice="512mb" />
    </Item>
    <Item Category="HardDrives">
        <Option Choice="40GB" />
        <Option Choice="80GB" />
        <Option Choice="100GB" />
    </Item>
    <Item Category="Drives">
        <Option Choice="CD" />
        <Option Choice="DVD" />
        <Option Choice="DVD Burner" />
    </Item>
</Hardware>
```

Filename Hardware.xml

As you can see, this list is not meant to be used for site navigation purposes, but instead for allowing the end user to make a selection from a hierarchical list of options. This XML file is divided into four categories of available options: `Motherboards`, `Memory`, `HardDrives`, and `Drives`. To bind your TreeView control to this XML file, use an XmlDataSource control that specifies the location of the XML file you are going to use. Then, within the TreeView control itself, use the `<asp:TreeNodeBinding>` element to specify which elements to bind in the XML file to populate the nodes of the TreeView control, as shown in Listing 13-9.

Available for download on Wrox.com

LISTING 13-9: Binding a TreeView control to the Hardware.xml file

```
<%@ Page Language="VB" %>

<html xmlns="http://www.w3.org/1999/xhtml">
<head runat="server">
```

```
        <title>Latest Hardware</title>
    </head>
    <body>
        <form id="form1" runat="server">
            <asp:TreeView ID="TreeView1" runat="server" DataSourceID="XmlDataSource1">
                <DataBindings>
                    <asp:TreeNodeBinding DataMember="Hardware"
                     Text="Computer Hardware" />
                    <asp:TreeNodeBinding DataMember="Item" TextField="Category" />
                    <asp:TreeNodeBinding DataMember="Option" TextField="Choice" />
                </DataBindings>
            </asp:TreeView>
            <asp:XmlDataSource ID="XmlDataSource1" runat="server"
             DataFile="Hardware.xml">
            </asp:XmlDataSource>
        </form>
    </body>
    </html>
```

The first item to look at is the `<asp:XmlDataSource>` control. It is just as simple as the previous `<asp:SiteMapDataSource>` control, but it points at the `Hardware.xml` file using the `DataFile` property.

The next step is to create a TreeView control that binds to this particular XML file. You can bind a default TreeView control directly to the XmlDataSource control as follows:

```
<asp:TreeView ID="TreeView1" runat="server" DataSourceId="XmlDataSource1" />
```

When you do this, you get the *incorrect* result shown in Figure 13-11.

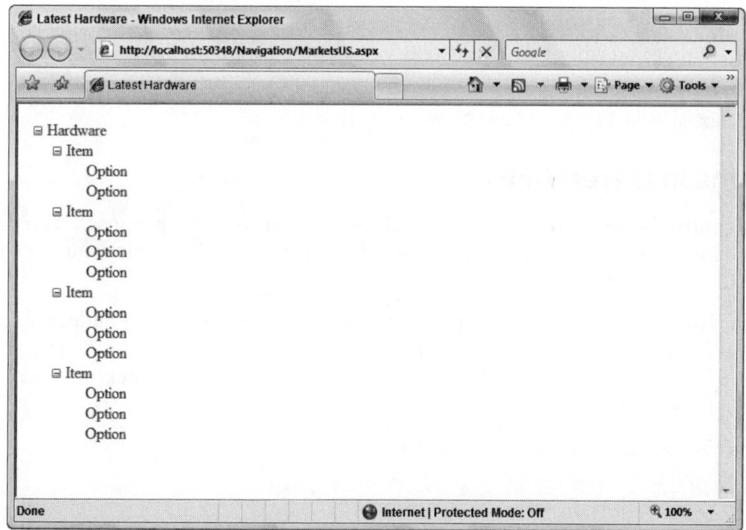

FIGURE 13-11

As you can see, the TreeView control binds just fine to the `Hardware.xml` file, but looking at the nodes within the TreeView control, you can see that it is simply displaying the names of the actual XML elements from the file itself. Because this isn't what you want, you specify how to bind to the XML file with the use of the `<DataBindings>` element within the TreeView control.

The `<DataBindings>` element encapsulates one or more `TreeNodeBinding` objects. Two of the more important available properties of a `TreeNodeBinding` object are the `DataMember` and `TextField` properties. The `DataMember` property points to the name of the XML element that the TreeView control should look for. The `TextField` property specifies the XML attribute that the TreeView should look for in that particular XML element. If you use the `<DataBindings>` element correctly, using the `<DataBindings>` construct, you get the result shown in Figure 13-12.

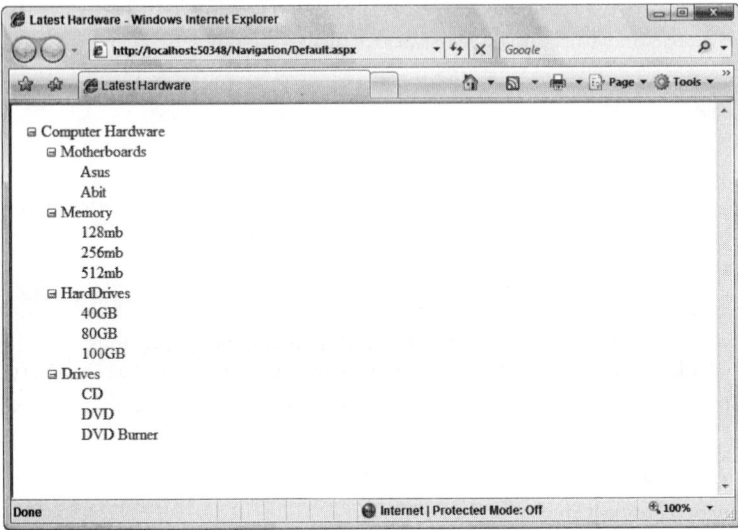

FIGURE 13-12

You can also see from Listing 13-9 that you can override the text value of the root node from the XML file, `<Hardware>`, and have it appear as `Computer Hardware` in the TreeView control, as follows:

```
<asp:TreeNodeBinding DataMember="Hardware" Text="Computer Hardware" />
```

Selecting Multiple Options in a TreeView

As stated earlier, the TreeView control is not meant to be used exclusively for navigation purposes. You can use it for all sorts of things. In many cases, you can present a hierarchical list from which you want the end user to select one or more items.

One great built-in feature of the TreeView control is the capability to put check boxes next to nodes within the hierarchical items in the list. These boxes enable end users to make multiple selections. The TreeView control contains a property called `ShowCheckBoxes` that you can use to create check boxes next to many different types of nodes within a list of items.

Table 13-3 lists the available values for the `ShowCheckBoxes` property.

TABLE 13-3

VALUE	DESCRIPTION
`All`	Applies check boxes to each and every node within the TreeView control.
`Leaf`	Applies check boxes to only the nodes that have no additional child elements.
`None`	Applies no check boxes to any node within the TreeView control.
`Parent`	Applies check boxes to only the nodes considered parent nodes within the TreeView control. A parent node has at least one child node associated with it.
`Root`	Applies a check box to any root node contained within the TreeView control.

When working with the ShowCheckBoxes property, you can set it declaratively in the control itself, as follows:

```
<asp:TreeView ID="Treeview1" runat="server" Font-Underline="false"
 DataSourceID="XmlDataSource1" ShowCheckBoxes="Leaf">
   ...
</asp:TreeViewTreeView>
```

Or you can set it programmatically by using the following code:

VB

```
TreeView1.ShowCheckBoxes = TreeNodeTypes.Leaf
```

C#

```
TreeView1.ShowCheckBoxes = TreeNodeTypes.Leaf;
```

For an example of using check boxes with the TreeView control, let's continue to expand on the computer hardware example from Listing 13-9. Create a hierarchical list that enables people to select multiple items from the list in order to receive additional information about them. Listing 13-10 shows an example of this list.

Available for download on Wrox.com

LISTING 13-10: Applying check boxes next to the leaf nodes within the hierarchical list of nodes

VB

```
<%@ Page Language="VB" %>
<script runat="server">
   Protected Sub Button1_Click(ByVal sender As Object, ByVal e As System.EventArgs)
        If TreeView1.CheckedNodes.Count > 0 Then
            Label1.Text = "We are sending you information on:<p>"

            For Each node As TreeNode In TreeView1.CheckedNodes
                Label1.Text += node.Text & " " & node.Parent.Text & "<br>"
            Next
        Else
            Label1.Text = "You didn't select anything. Sorry!"
        End If
   End Sub
</script>
<html xmlns="http://www.w3.org/1999/xhtml">
<head runat="server">
    <title>Latest Hardware</title>
</head>
<body>
    <form runat="server">
        Please select the items you are interested in:
        <p>
        <asp:TreeView ID="TreeView1" runat="server" Font-Underline="False"
         DataSourceID="XmlDataSource1" ShowCheckBoxes="Leaf">
            <DataBindings>
                <asp:TreeNodeBinding DataMember="Hardware"
                 Text="Computer Hardware" />
                <asp:TreeNodeBinding DataMember="Item" TextField="Category" />
                <asp:TreeNodeBinding DataMember="Option" TextField="Choice" />
            </DataBindings>
        </asp:TreeView>
        <p>
        <asp:Button ID="Button1" runat="server" Text="Submit Choices"
         OnClick="Button1_Click" />
        </p>
        <asp:XmlDataSource ID="XmlDataSource1" runat="server"
```

continues

LISTING 13-10 *(continued)*

```
                DataFile="Hardware.xml">
            </asp:XmlDataSource>
            </p>
            <asp:Label ID="Label1" runat="Server" />
        </form>
    </body>
    </html>
```

C#

```
<%@ Page Language="C#" %>
<script runat="server">
    protected void Button1_Click(object sender, System.EventArgs e)
    {
        if (TreeView1.CheckedNodes.Count > 0)
        {
            Label1.Text = "We are sending you information on:<p>";
            foreach (TreeNode node in TreeView1.CheckedNodes)
            {
                Label1.Text += node.Text + " " + node.Parent.Text + "<br>";
            }
        }
        else
        {
            Label1.Text = "You didn't select anything. Sorry!";
        }
    }
</script>
```

In this example, you first set the `ShowTextBoxes` property to `Leaf`, meaning that you are interested in having check boxes appear only next to items in the TreeView control that do not contain any child nodes. The items with check boxes next to them should be the last items that can be expanded in the hierarchical list.

After setting this property, you then work with the items that are selected by the end user in the `Button1_Click` event. The first thing you should check is whether any selection at all was made:

```
If TreeView1.CheckedNodes.Count > 0 Then
   ...
End If
```

In this case, the number of checked nodes on the postback needs to be greater than zero, meaning that at least one was selected. If so, you can execute the code within the `If` statement. The `If` statement then proceeds to populate the Label control that is on the page. To populate the Label control with data from the selected nodes, you use a `For Each` statement, as shown here:

```
For Each node As TreeNode In TreeView1.CheckedNodes
   ...
Next
```

This works with an instance of a `TreeNode` object and checks each `TreeNode` object within the `TreeView1` collection of checked nodes.

For each node that is checked, you grab the node's `Text` value and the `Text` value of this node's parent node to further populate the Label control, as follows:

```
Label1.Text += node.Text & " " & node.Parent.Text & "<br>"
```

In the end, you get a page that produces the results shown in Figure 13-13.

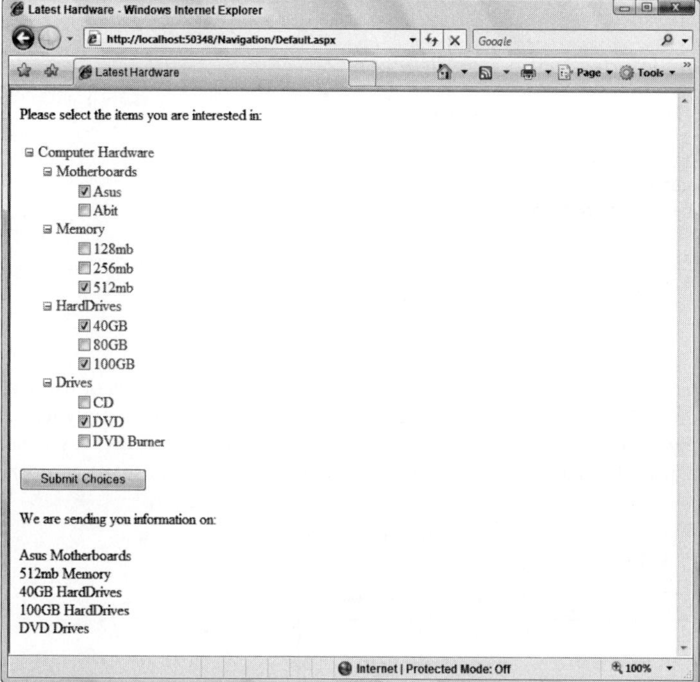

FIGURE 13-13

Specifying Custom Icons in the TreeView Control

The TreeView control allows for a high degree of customization. You saw earlier in the chapter that you can customize the look and feel of the TreeView control by specifying one of the built-in styles. Applying one of these styles dramatically changes the appearance of the control. One of the most noticeable changes concerns the icons used for the nodes within the TreeView control. Although it is not as easy as just selecting one of the styles built into the TreeView control, you can apply your own icons to be used for the nodes within the hierarchical list of nodes.

The TreeView control contains the properties discussed in Table 13-4. These properties enable you to specify your own images to use for the nodes of the control.

TABLE 13-4

PROPERTY	DESCRIPTION
`CollapseImageUrl`	Applies a custom image next to nodes that have been expanded to show any of their child nodes and have the capability of being collapsed.
`ExpandImageUrl`	Applies a custom image next to nodes that have the capability of being expanded to display their child nodes.
`LeafNodeStyle-ImageUrl`	Applies a custom image next to a node that has no child nodes and is last in the hierarchical chain of nodes.
`NoExpandImageUrl`	Applies a custom image to nodes that, for programmatic reasons, cannot be expanded or to nodes that are leaf nodes. This property is primarily used for spacing purposes to align leaf nodes with their parent nodes.
`ParentNodeStyle-ImageUrl`	Applies a custom image only to the parent nodes within the TreeView control.
`RootNodeStyle-ImageUrl`	Applies a custom image next to only the root nodes within the TreeView control.

Listing 13-11 shows an example of these properties in use.

LISTING 13-11: Applying custom images to the TreeView control

Available for download on Wrox.com

```
<asp:TreeView ID="TreeView1" runat="server" Font-Underline="False"
 DataSourceId="XmlDataSource1"
 CollapseImageUrl="Images/CollapseImage.gif"
 ExpandImageUrl="Images/ExpandImage.gif"
 LeafNodeStyle-ImageUrl="Images/LeafImage.gif">
   <DataBindings>
      <asp:TreeNodeBinding DataMember="Hardware" Text="Computer Hardware" />
      <asp:TreeNodeBinding DataMember="Item" TextField="Category" />
      <asp:TreeNodeBinding DataMember="Option" TextField="Choice" />
   </DataBindings>
</asp:TreeView>
```

Specifying these three images to precede the nodes in your control overrides the default values of using a plus (+) sign and a minus (–) sign for the expandable and collapsible nodes. It also overrides simply using an image for any leaf nodes when, by default, nothing is used. Using the code from Listing 13-11, you get something similar to the results illustrated in Figure 13-14 (depending on the images you use, of course).

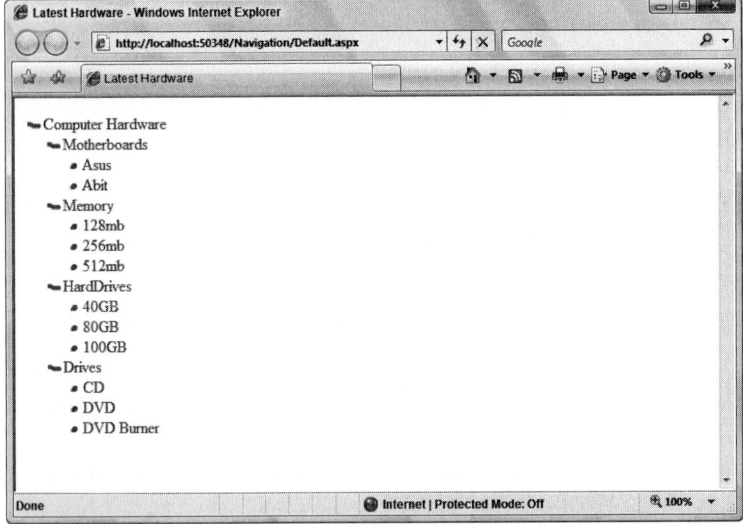

FIGURE 13-14

Specifying Lines Used to Connect Nodes

Because the TreeView control shows a hierarchical list of items to the end user, you sometimes want to show the relationship between these hierarchical items more explicitly than is shown by default with the TreeView control. One possibility is to show line connections between parent and child nodes within the display. Simply set the `ShowLines` property of the TreeView control to `True` (by default, this property is set to `False`):

```
<asp:TreeView ID="TreeView1" runat="server" Font-Underline="False"
 DataSourceId="XmlDataSource1" ShowCheckBoxes="Leaf" ShowLines="True">
   ...
</asp:TreeViewTreeView>
```

This code gives the result shown in Figure 13-15.

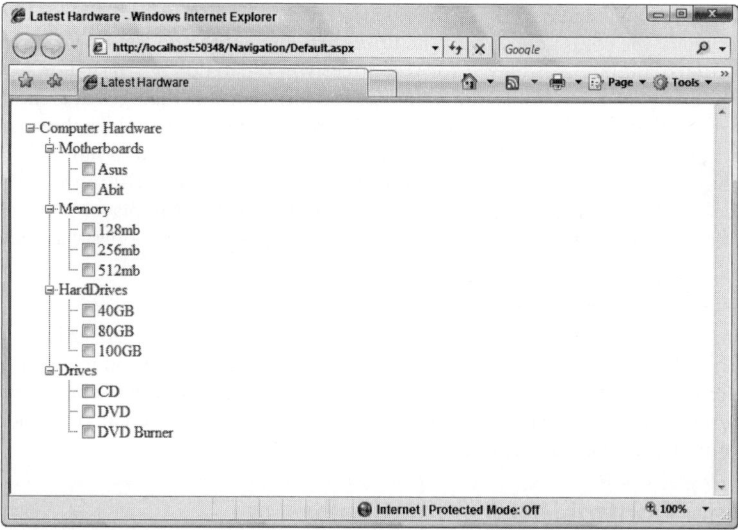

FIGURE 13-15

If the `ShowLines` property is set to `True`, you can also define your own lines and images within the TreeView control. Doing so is quite easy because Visual Studio 2010 provides you with an ASP.NET TreeView Line Image Generator tool. This tool enables you to visually design how you want the lines and corresponding expanding and collapsing images to appear. After you have it set up as you want, the tool then creates all the necessary files for any of your TreeView controls to use.

To get at the tool, move to the Design view of your file and click the smart tag for the TreeView control that is on your page. Here, you find the option Customize Line Images. You will not see this option unless the Show Lines check box is selected. Click it and the ASP.NET TreeView Line Generator dialog appears (shown in Figure 13-16).

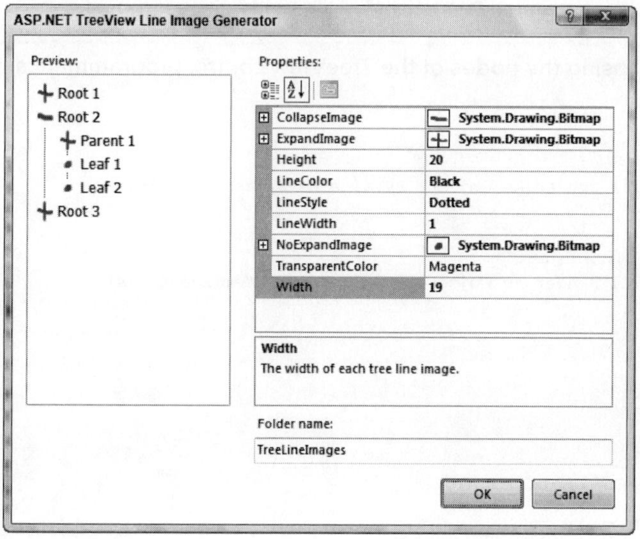

FIGURE 13-16

From within this dialog, you can select the images used for the nodes that require an Expand, Collapse, or NoCollapse icon. You can also specify the color and style of the lines that connect the nodes. As you create your styles, a sample TreeView control output is displayed for you directly in the dialog box based on how your styles are to be applied. The final step is to choose the output of the files that this dialog will create. When you have completed this step, click OK. This generates a long list of new files to the folder that you specified in the dialog. By default, the ASP.NET TreeView Line Image Generator wants you to name the output folder TreeLineImages, but feel free to name it as you want. If the folder does not exist in the project, you are prompted to allow Visual Studio to create the folder for you. After this folder is in place, the TreeView control can use your new images and styles if you set the `LineImagesFolder` property as follows:

```
<asp:TreeView ID="TreeView1" runat="server" ShowLines="True"
 DataSourceId="SiteMapDataSource1" LineImagesFolder="TreeViewLineImages">
```

The important properties are shown in bold. You must set the `ShowLines` property to `True`. After it is set, the property uses the default settings displayed earlier, unless you have specified a location where it can retrieve custom images and styles using the `LineImagesFolder` property. As you can see, this simply points to the new folder, TreeViewLineImages, which contains all the new images and styles you created. Look in the folder — seeing what is output by the tool is interesting.

Working with the TreeView Control Programmatically

So far, with the TreeView control, you have learned how to work with the control declaratively. The great thing about ASP.NET is that you are not simply required to work with its components declaratively, but you can also manipulate these controls programmatically.

The TreeView control has an associated `TreeView` class that enables you to completely manage the TreeView control and how it functions from within your code. The next section looks at how to use some of the more common ways to control the `TreeView` programmatically.

Expanding and Collapsing Nodes Programmatically

One thing you can do with your TreeView control is to expand or collapse the nodes within the hierarchy programmatically. You can do so by using either the `ExpandAll` or `CollapseAll` methods from the `TreeView` class. Listing 13-12 shows you one of the earlier TreeView controls that you used in Listing 13-6, but with a couple of buttons above it that you can now use to initiate the expanding and collapsing of the nodes.

LISTING 13-12: Expanding and collapsing the nodes of the TreeView control programmatically

Available for download on Wrox.com

```
<%@ Page Language="VB" %>

<script runat="server">
   Protected Sub Button1_Click(ByVal sender As Object, ByVal e As System.EventArgs)
        TreeView1.ExpandAll()
   End Sub

   Protected Sub Button2_Click(ByVal sender As Object, ByVal e As System.EventArgs)
        TreeView1.CollapseAll()
   End Sub
</script>

<html xmlns="http://www.w3.org/1999/xhtml">
<head runat="server">
    <title>TreeView Control</title>
</head>
<body>
    <form id="Form1" runat="server">
        <p>
            <asp:Button ID="Button1" runat="server" Text="Expand Nodes"
             OnClick="Button1_Click" />
```

```
                <asp:Button ID="Button2" runat="server" Text="Collapse Nodes"
                 OnClick="Button2_Click" />
                <br />
                <br />
            <asp:TreeView ID="TreeView1" runat="server"
             DataSourceId="SiteMapDataSource1">
            </asp:TreeView>
            <asp:SiteMapDataSource ID="SiteMapDataSource1" runat="server" /></p>
        </form>
    </body>
    </html>
```

C#

```
<%@ Page Language="C#" %>

<script runat="server">
    protected void Button1_Click(object sender, System.EventArgs e)
    {
        TreeView1.ExpandAll();
    }

    protected void Button2_Click(object sender, System.EventArgs e)
    {
        TreeView1.CollapseAll();
    }
</script>
```

Running this page gives you two buttons above your TreeView control. Clicking the first button invokes the `ExpandAll()` method and completely expands the entire list of nodes. Clicking the second button invokes the `CollapseAll()` method and completely collapses the list of nodes (see Figure 13-17).

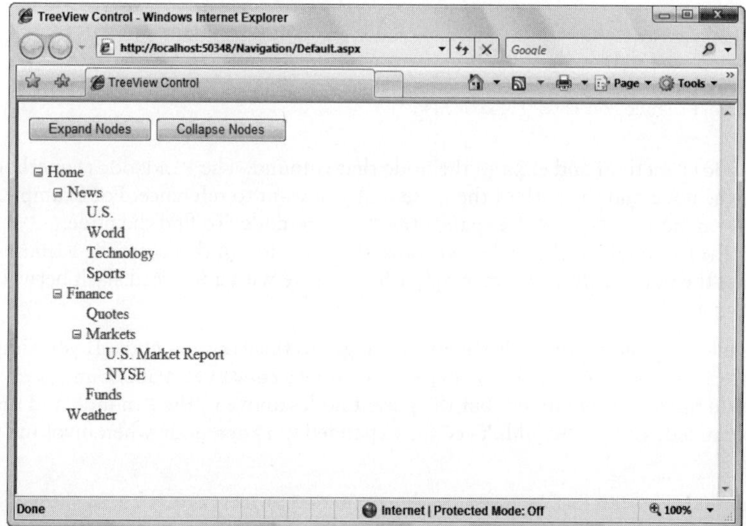

FIGURE 13-17

The example shown in Listing 13-12 is nice, but it expands and collapses the nodes only on end-user actions (when the end user clicks the button). Being able to initiate this action programmatically would be even nicer.

You might want to simply place the `TreeView1.CollapseAll()` command within the `Page_Load` event, but if you try this technique, you'll see that it doesn't work. Instead, you use the `OnDataBound` attribute within the TreeView control:

```
<asp:TreeView ID="TreeView1" runat="server"
 DataSourceId="SiteMapDataSource1" OnDataBound="TreeView1_DataBound">
</asp:TreeView>
```

The value of this attribute points to a method in your code, as shown here:

VB

```
Protected Sub TreeView1_DataBound(ByVal sender As Object, _
  ByVal e As System.EventArgs)
   TreeView1.CollapseAll()
End Sub
```

C#

```
protected void TreeView1_DataBound(object sender, System.EventArgs e)
{
   TreeView1.CollapseAll();
}
```

Now when you run the page, notice that the TreeView control is completely collapsed when the page is first loaded in the browser.

You can also expand or collapse specific nodes within the tree instead of just working the entire list. For this example, use the `TreeView1_DataBound()` method you just created. Using the sitemap from Listing 13-1, change the `TreeView1_DataBound()` method so that it appears as shown in Listing 13-13.

LISTING 13-13: Expanding specific nodes programmatically

Available for download on Wrox.com

VB

```
Protected Sub TreeView1_DataBound(ByVal sender As Object,
  ByVal e As System.EventArgs)
   TreeView1.CollapseAll()
   TreeView1.FindNode("Home").Expand()
   TreeView1.FindNode("Home/Finance").Expand()
   TreeView1.FindNode("Home/Finance/Markets").Expand()
End Sub
```

C#

```
protected void TreeView1_DataBound(object sender, System.EventArgs e)
{
   TreeView1.CollapseAll();
   TreeView1.FindNode("Home").Expand();
   TreeView1.FindNode("Home/Finance").Expand();
   TreeView1.FindNode("Home/Finance/Markets").Expand();
}
```

In this case, you use the `FindNode()` method and expand the node that is found. The `FindNode()` method takes a `String` value, which is the node and the path of the node that you want to reference. For example, `TreeView1.FindNode("Home/Finance").Expand()` expands the `Finance` node. To find the node, specifying the entire path from the root node to the node you want to work with (in this case, the `Finance` node) is important. You separate the nodes within the sitemap path structure with a forward slash between each of the nodes in the sitemap path.

Note that you had to expand each of the nodes individually until you got to the `Finance` node. If you simply used `TreeView1.FindNode("Home/Finance/Markets").Expand()` in the `TreeView1_DataBound()` method, the `Markets` node would indeed be expanded, but the parent nodes above it (the `Finance` and `Home` nodes) would not have been expanded, and you wouldn't see the expanded `Markets` node when invoking the page. (Try it; it's interesting.)

Instead of using the `Expand` method, you can just as easily set the `Expanded` property to `True`, as shown in Listing 13-14.

LISTING 13-14: Expanding nodes programmatically using the Expanded property

Available for download on Wrox.com

VB

```
Protected Sub TreeView1_DataBound(ByVal sender As Object,
  ByVal e As System.EventArgs)
   TreeView1.CollapseAll()
   TreeView1.FindNode("Home").Expanded = True
   TreeView1.FindNode("Home/Finance").Expanded = True
   TreeView1.FindNode("Home/Finance/Markets").Expanded = True
End Sub
```

```
protected void TreeView1_DataBound(object sender, System.EventArgs e)
{
   TreeView1.CollapseAll();
   TreeView1.FindNode("Home").Expanded = true;
   TreeView1.FindNode("Home/Finance").Expanded = true;
   TreeView1.FindNode("Home/Finance/Markets").Expanded = true;
}
```

Although you focus on the `Expand` method and the `Expanded` property here, you can just as easily programmatically collapse nodes using the `Collapse()` method. No `Collapsed` property really exists. Instead, you simply set the `Expanded` property to `False`.

Adding Nodes

Another interesting thing you can do with the TreeView control is to add nodes to the overall hierarchy programmatically. The TreeView control is made up of a collection of `TreeNode` objects. Therefore, as you see in previous examples, the `Finance` node is actually a `TreeNode` object that you can work with programmatically. It includes the capability to add other `TreeNode` objects.

A `TreeNode` object typically stores a `Text` and `Value` property. The `Text` property is what is displayed in the TreeView control for the end user. The `Value` property is an additional data item that you can use to associate with this particular `TreeNode` object. Another property that you can use (if your TreeView control is a list of navigational links) is the `NavigateUrl` property. Listing 13-15 demonstrates how to add nodes programmatically to the same sitemap from Listing 13-1 that you have been using.

LISTING 13-15: Adding nodes programmatically to the TreeView control

Available for download on Wrox.com

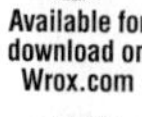

```
<%@ Page Language="VB" %>

<script runat="server">
   Protected Sub Button1_Click(ByVal sender As Object, ByVal e As System.EventArgs)
        TreeView1.ExpandAll()
   End Sub

   Protected Sub Button2_Click(ByVal sender As Object, ByVal e As System.EventArgs)
        TreeView1.CollapseAll()
   End Sub

   Protected Sub Button3_Click(ByVal sender As Object, ByVal e As System.EventArgs)
        Dim myNode As New TreeNode
        myNode.Text = TextBox1.Text
        myNode.NavigateUrl = TextBox2.Text
        TreeView1.FindNode("Home/Finance/Markets").ChildNodes.Add(myNode)
   End Sub
</script>

<html xmlns="http://www.w3.org/1999/xhtml">
<head runat="server">
    <title>TreeView Control</title>
</head>
<body>
    <form id="Form1" runat="server">
        <p>
            <asp:Button ID="Button1" runat="server" Text="Expand Nodes"
             OnClick="Button1_Click" />
            <asp:Button ID="Button2" runat="server" Text="Collapse Nodes"
             OnClick="Button2_Click" /></p>
        <p>
            <strong>Text of new node:</strong>
            <asp:TextBox ID="TextBox1" runat="server">
            </asp:TextBox>
        </p>
```

continues

LISTING 13-15 *(continued)*

```
        <p>
            <strong>Destination URL of new node:</strong>
            <asp:TextBox ID="TextBox2" runat="server">
            </asp:TextBox>
            <br />
            <br />
            <asp:Button ID="Button3" runat="server" Text="Add New Node"
             OnClick="Button3_Click" />
        </p>
        <p>
        <asp:TreeView ID="TreeView1" runat="server"
         DataSourceId="SiteMapDataSource1">
        </asp:TreeView></p>
        <p>
        <asp:SiteMapDataSource ID="SiteMapDataSource1" runat="server" /></p>
    </form>
</body>
</html>
```

C#

```
protected void Button3_Click(object sender, System.EventArgs e)
{
   TreeNode myNode = new TreeNode();
   myNode.Text = TextBox1.Text;
   myNode.NavigateUrl = TextBox2.Text;
   TreeView1.FindNode("Home/Finance/Markets").ChildNodes.Add(myNode);
}
```

This page contains two text boxes and a new Button control. The first text box is used to populate the `Text` property of the new node that is created. The second text box is used to populate the `NavigateUrl` property of the new node.

If you run the page, you can expand the entire hierarchy by clicking the `Expand Nodes` button. Then you can add additional child nodes to the `Markets` node. To add a new node programmatically, use the `FindNode` method as you did before to find the `Markets` node. When you find it, you can add additional child nodes by using the `ChildNodes.Add()` method and pass in a `TreeNode` object instance. Submitting `NASDAQ` in the first text box and `Nasdaq.aspx` in the second text box changes your TreeView control, as illustrated in Figure 13-18.

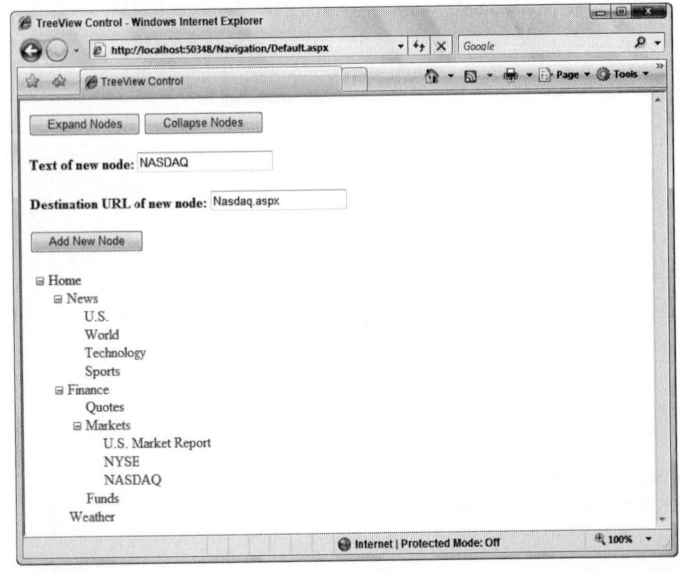

FIGURE 13-18

After it is added, the node stays added even after the hierarchy tree is collapsed and reopened. You can also add as many child nodes as you want to the `Markets` node. Note that, although you are changing nodes programmatically, this in no way alters the contents of the data source (the XML file, or the `.sitemap` file). These sources remain unchanged throughout the entire process.

MENU SERVER CONTROL

One of the cooler navigation controls found in ASP.NET 4 is the Menu server control. This control is ideal for allowing the end user to navigate a larger hierarchy of options while utilizing very little browser real estate in the process. Figure 13-19 shows you what the menu control looks like when it is either completely collapsed or completely extended down one of the branches of the hierarchy.

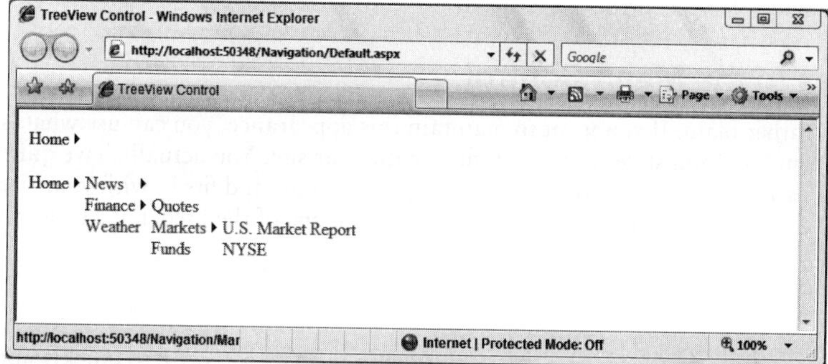

FIGURE 13-19

From here, you can see that the first Menu control displayed simply shows the Home link with a small arrow to the right of the display. The arrow means that more options are available that relate to this upmost link in the hierarchy. The second Menu control displayed shows what the default control looks like when the end user works down one of the branches provided by the sitemap.

The Menu control is an ideal control to use when you have lots of options—whether these options are selections the end user can make or navigation points provided by the application in which they are working. The Menu control can provide a multitude of options and consumes little space in the process.

Using the Menu control in your ASP.NET applications is rather simple. The Menu control works with a SiteMapDataSource control. You can drag and drop the SiteMapDataSource control and the Menu control onto the Visual Studio 2010 design surface and connect the two by using the Menu control's `DataSourceId` property. Alternatively, you can create and connect them directly in code. Listing 13-16 shows an example of the Menu control in its simplest form.

Available for download on Wrox.com

LISTING 13-16: A simple use of the Menu control

```
<%@ Page Language="VB" %>

<html xmlns="http://www.w3.org/1999/xhtml" >
<head runat="server">
    <title>Menu Server Control</title>
</head>
<body>
    <form id="form1" runat="server">
        <asp:SiteMapDataSource ID="SiteMapDataSource1" runat="server" />
```

continues

LISTING 13-16 *(continued)*

```
        <asp:Menu ID="Menu1" runat="server" DataSourceID="SiteMapDataSource1">
        </asp:Menu>
    </form>
</body>
</html>
```

From this example, you can see that we are using a SiteMapDataSource control that automatically works with the application's `Web.sitemap` file. The only other item included is the Menu control, which uses the typical `ID` and `runat` attributes and the `DataSourceID` attribute to connect it with what is retrieved from the SiteMapDataSource control.

Although the default Menu control is rather simple, you can highly customize how it looks and works by redefining its properties. The following sections look at some examples of how you can modify the appearance and change the behavior of this control.

Applying Different Styles to the Menu Control

By default, the Menu control is rather plain. If you want to maintain this appearance, you can use what is provided or simply change the font sizes and styles to make it fit in with your site. You actually have quite a number of ways in which you can modify this control so that it appears unique and fits in with your site. Either you can customize this control's appearance yourself, or you can use one of the predefined styles that come with the control.

Using a Predefined Style

Visual Studio 2010 includes some predefined styles that you can use with the Menu control to quickly apply a look-and-feel to the displayed menu of items. Some of the provided styles include `Classic`, `Professional`, and more. To apply one of these predefined styles, you work with the Menu control from the Design view of your page. Within the Design view, highlight the Menu control and expand the control's smart tag. From here, you see a list of options for working with this control. To change the look-and-feel of the control, click the Auto Format link and select one of the styles.

Performing this operation changes the code of your control by applying a set of style properties. For example, if you select the `Classic` option, you get the results shown in Listing 13-17.

LISTING 13-17: Code changes when you apply a style to the Menu control

Available for download on Wrox.com

```
<asp:Menu ID="Menu1" runat="server" DataSourceID="SiteMapDataSource1"
 BackColor="#B5C7DE" ForeColor="#284E98"
 Font-Names="Verdana" Font-Size="0.8em" StaticSubMenuIndent="10px"
 DynamicHorizontalOffset="2">
   <StaticSelectedStyle BackColor="#507CD1"></StaticSelectedStyle>
   <StaticMenuItemStyle HorizontalPadding="5"
    VerticalPadding="2"></StaticMenuItemStyle>
   <DynamicMenuStyle BackColor="#B5C7DE"></DynamicMenuStyle>
   <DynamicSelectedStyle BackColor="#507CD1"></DynamicSelectedStyle>
   <DynamicMenuItemStyle HorizontalPadding="5"
    VerticalPadding="2"></DynamicMenuItemStyle>
   <DynamicHoverStyle ForeColor="White" Font-Bold="True"
    BackColor="#284E98"></DynamicHoverStyle>
   <StaticHoverStyle ForeColor="White" Font-Bold="True"
    BackColor="#284E98"></StaticHoverStyle>
</asp:Menu>
```

You can see a lot of added styles that change the menu items that appear in the control. Figure 13-20 shows how this style selection appears in the browser.

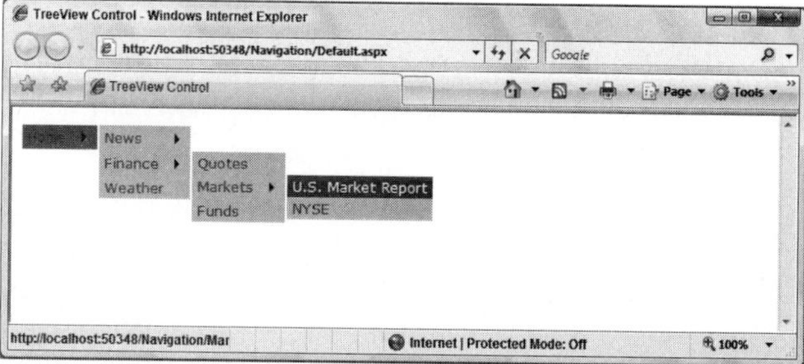

FIGURE 13-20

Changing the Style for Static Items

The Menu control considers items in the hierarchy to be either *static* or *dynamic*. Static items from this example would be the `Home` link that appears when the page is generated. Dynamic links are the items that appear dynamically when the user hovers the mouse over the `Home` link in the menu. Changing the styles for both these types of nodes in the menu is possible.

To apply a specific style to the static links that appear, you must add a static style element to the Menu control. The Menu control includes the following static style elements:

- `<StaticHoverStyle>`
- `<StaticItemTemplate>`
- `<StaticMenuItemStyle>`
- `<StaticMenuStyle>`
- `<StaticSelectedStyle>`

The important options from this list include the `<StaticHoverStyle>` and the `<StaticMenuItemStyle>` elements. The `<StaticHoverStyle>` is what you use to define the style of the static item in the menu when the end user hovers the mouse over the option. The `<StaticMenuItemStyle>` is what you use for the style of the static item when the end user is not hovering the mouse over the option.

Listing 13-18 shows adding a style that is applied when the end user hovers the mouse over static items.

Available for download on Wrox.com

LISTING 13-18: Adding a hover style to static items in the menu control

```
<asp:Menu ID="Menu1" runat="server" DataSourceID="SiteMapDataSource1">
    <StaticHoverStyle BackColor="DarkGray" BorderColor="Black" BorderStyle="Solid"
     BorderWidth="1"></StaticHoverStyle>
</asp:Menu>
```

This little example adds a background color and border to the static items in the menu when the end user hovers the mouse over the item. Figure 13-21 shows the result.

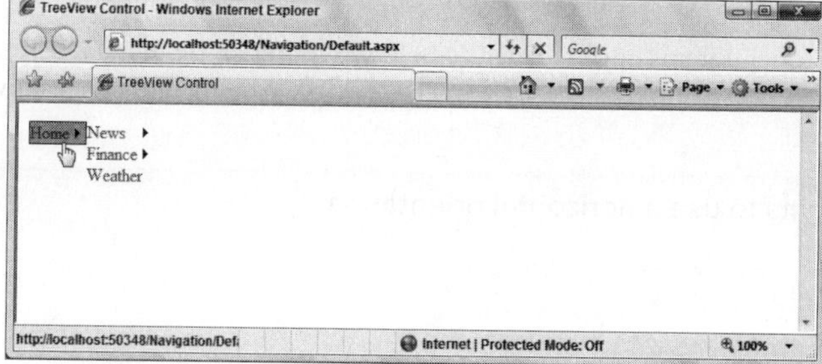

FIGURE 13-21

Adding Styles to Dynamic Items

Adding styles to the dynamic items of the menu control is just as easy as adding them to static items. The Menu control has a number of different elements for modifying the appearance of dynamic items, including the following:

- <DynamicHoverStyle>
- <DynamicItemTemplate>
- <DynamicMenuItemStyle>
- <DynamicMenuStyle>
- <DynamicSelectedStyle>

These elements change menu items the same way as the static versions of these elements, but they change only the items that dynamically pop out from the static items. Listing 13-19 shows an example of applying the hover style to dynamic items.

LISTING 13-19: Adding a hover style to dynamic items in the menu control

Available for download on Wrox.com

```
<asp:Menu ID="Menu1" runat="server" DataSourceID="Sitemapdatasource1">
   <StaticHoverStyle BackColor="DarkGray" BorderColor="Black" BorderStyle="Solid"
    BorderWidth="1"></StaticHoverStyle>
   <DynamicHoverStyle BackColor="DarkGray" BorderColor="Black" BorderStyle="Solid"
    BorderWidth="1"></DynamicHoverStyle>
</asp:Menu>
```

This code produces the results shown in Figure 13-22.

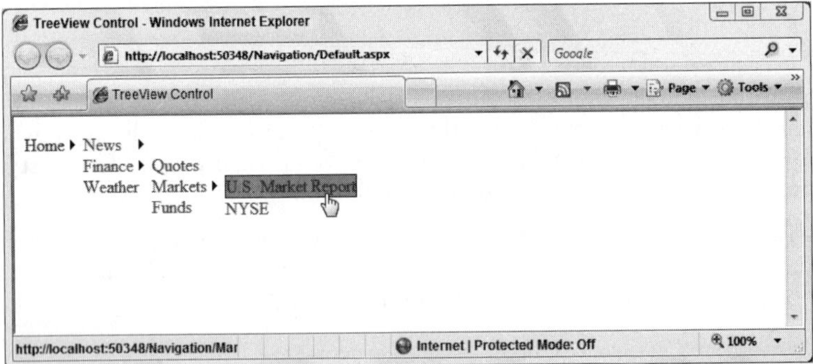

FIGURE 13-22

Changing the Layout of the Menu Items

By default, the dynamic menu items are displayed from left to right. This means that, as the items in the menu expand, they are continually displayed in a vertical fashion. You can actually control this behavior, but another option is available to you.

The other option is to have the first level of menu items appear directly below the first static item (horizontally). You change this behavior by using the `Orientation` attribute of the Menu control, as shown in Listing 13-20.

LISTING 13-20: Forcing the menu items to use a horizontal orientation

Available for download on Wrox.com

```
<asp:Menu ID="Menu1" runat="server" DataSourceID="SiteMapDataSource1"
 Orientation="Horizontal">
</asp:Menu>
```

This code produces the results shown in Figure 13-23.

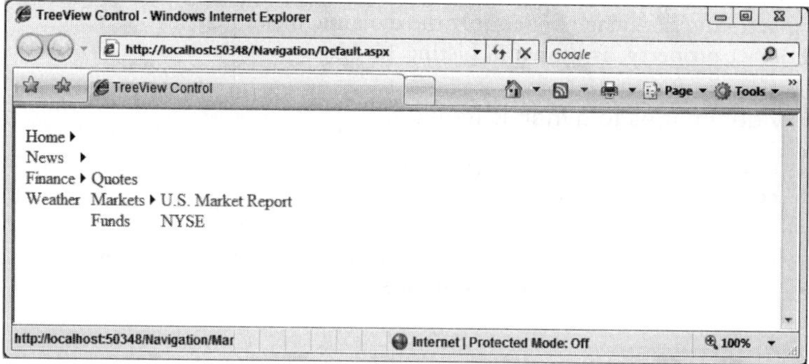

FIGURE 13-23

The `Orientation` attribute can take a value of `Horizontal` or `Vertical` only. The default value is `Vertical`.

Changing the Pop-Out Symbol

As the default, an arrow is used as the pop-out symbol for the menu items generated, whether they are static or dynamic, as shown in Figure 13-24.

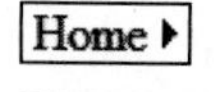

FIGURE 13-24

You are not forced to use this arrow symbol; in fact, you can change it to an image with relatively little work. Listing 13-21 shows how to accomplish this task.

LISTING 13-21: Using custom images

Available for download on Wrox.com

```
<asp:Menu ID="Menu1" runat="server" DataSourceID="SiteMapDataSource1"
 Orientation="Horizontal" DynamicPopOutImageUrl="myArrow.gif"
 StaticPopOutImageUrl="myArrow.gif">
</asp:Menu>
```

To change the pop-out symbol to an image of your choice, you use the `DynamicPopOutImageUrl` or `StaticPopOutImageUrl` properties. The `String` value these attributes take is simply the path of the image you want to use. Depending on the image used, it produces something similar to what you see in Figure 13-25.

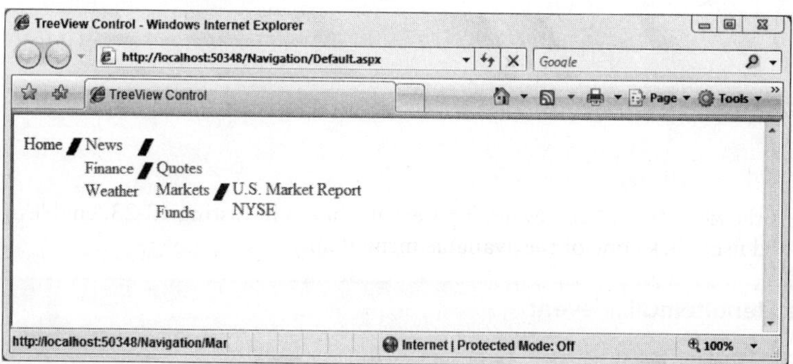

FIGURE 13-25

Separating Menu Items with Images

Another nice styling option of the Menu control is the capability to add a divider image to the menu items. You use the `StaticBottomSeparatorImageUrl`, `StaticTopSeparatorImageUrl`,

DynamicBottomSeparatorImageUrl, and DynamicTopSeparatorImageUrl properties, depending on where you want to place the separator image.

For example, if you wanted to place a divider image under only the dynamic menu items, you use the DynamicBottomSeparatorImageUrl property, as shown in Listing 13-22.

Available for download on Wrox.com

LISTING 13-22: Applying divider images to dynamic items

```
<asp:Menu ID="Menu1" runat="server" DataSourceID="SiteMapDataSource1"
 DynamicBottomSeparatorImageUrl="myDivider.gif">
</asp:Menu>
```

All the properties of the Menu control that define the image to use for the dividers take a String value that points to the location of the image. Figure 13-26 shows the result of Listing 13-22.

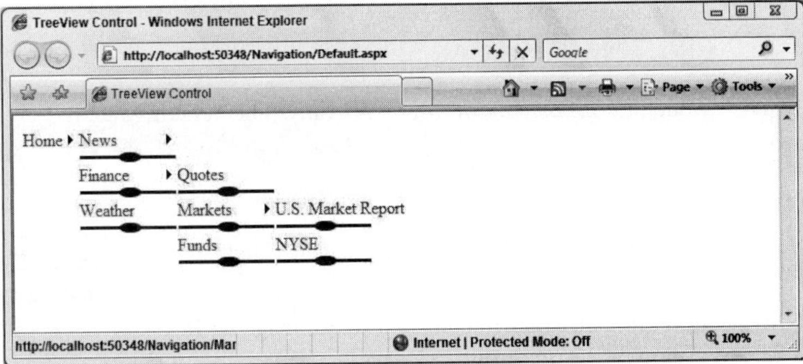

FIGURE 13-26

Using Menu Events

The Menu control exposes events such as the following:

- DataBinding
- DataBound
- Disposed
- Init
- Load
- MenuItemClick
- MenuItemDataBound
- PreRender
- Unload

One nice event to be aware of is the MenuItemClick event. This event, shown in Listing 13-23, enables you to take some action when the end user clicks one of the available menu items.

LISTING 13-23: Using the MenuItemClick event

```
Protected Sub Menu1_MenuItemClick(ByVal sender As Object,
   ByVal e As System.Web.UI.WebControls.MenuEventArgs)

  ' Code for event here

End Sub
```

C#

```
protected void Menu1_MenuItemClick(object sender, MenuEventArgs e)
{

   // Code for event here

}
```

This delegate uses the MenuEventArgs data class and provides you access to the text and value of the item selected from the menu.

Binding the Menu Control to an XML File

Just as with the TreeView control, binding the Menu control to items that come from other data source controls provided with ASP.NET 4 is possible. Although most developers are likely to use the Menu control to enable end users to navigate to URL destinations, you can also use the Menu control to enable users to make selections.

As an example, take the previous XML file, Hardware.xml, which was used with the TreeView control from Listing 13-8 earlier in the chapter. For this example, the Menu control works with an XmlDataSource control. When the end user makes a selection from the menu, you populate a Listbox on the page with the items selected. Listing 13-24 shows the code for this control.

LISTING 13-24: Using the Menu control with an XML file

Available for download on Wrox.com

VB

```
<%@ Page Language="VB" %>

<script runat="server">
    Protected Sub Menu1_MenuItemClick(ByVal sender As Object,
       ByVal e As System.Web.UI.WebControls.MenuEventArgs)

        Listbox1.Items.Add(e.Item.Parent.Value & " : " & e.Item.Value)
    End Sub
</script>

<html xmlns="http://www.w3.org/1999/xhtml">
<head runat="server">
    <title>Menu Server Control</title>
</head>
<body>
    <form id="form1" runat="server">
        <asp:Menu ID="Menu1" runat="server" DataSourceID="XmlDataSource1"
         OnMenuItemClick="Menu1_MenuItemClick">
            <DataBindings>
                <asp:MenuItemBinding DataMember="Item"
                 TextField="Category"></asp:MenuItemBinding>
                <asp:MenuItemBinding DataMember="Option"
                 TextField="Choice"></asp:MenuItemBinding>
            </DataBindings>
        </asp:Menu>
        <p>
        <asp:ListBox ID="Listbox1" runat="server">
        </asp:ListBox></p>
        <asp:xmldatasource ID="XmlDataSource1" runat="server"
         datafile="Hardware.xml" />
    </form>
</body>
</html>
```

C#

```
<%@ Page Language="C#" %>

<script runat="server">
   protected void Menu1_MenuItemClick(object sender, MenuEventArgs e)
   {
      Listbox1.Items.Add(e.Item.Parent.Value + " : " + e.Item.Value);
   }
</script>
```

From this example, you can see that instead of using the `<asp:TreeNodeBinding>` elements, as you did with the TreeView control, the Menu control uses the `<asp:MenuItemBinding>` elements to make connections to items listed in the XML file, `Hardware.xml`. In addition, the root element of the Menu control, the `<asp:Menu>` element, now includes the `OnMenuItemClick` attribute, which points to the event delegate `Menu1_MenuItemClick`.

The `Menu1_MenuItemClick` delegate includes the data class `MenuEventArgs`, which enables you to get at both the values of the child and parent elements selected. For this example, both are used and then populated into the Listbox control, as illustrated in Figure 13-27.

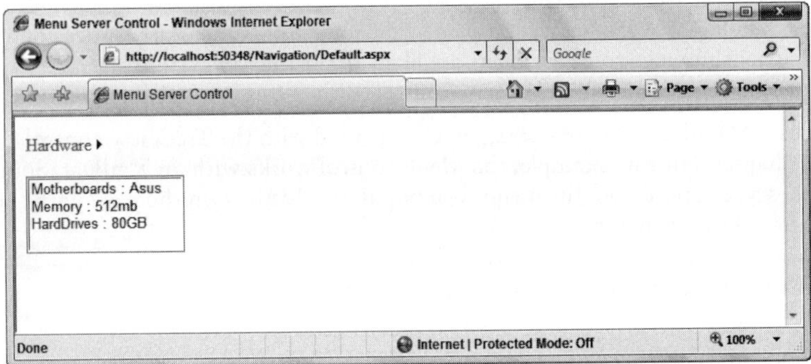

FIGURE 13-27

SITEMAP DATA PROVIDER

A series of data providers in the form of DataSource controls is available in ASP.NET 4. One of these DataSource controls now at your disposal, which you looked at earlier in the chapter, is the SiteMapDataSource control. This DataSource control was developed to work with sitemaps and the controls that can bind to them.

Some controls do not need a SiteMapDataSource control in order to bind to the application's sitemap (which is typically stored in the `Web.sitemap` file). Earlier in the chapter, you saw this in action when using the SiteMapPath control. This control was able to work with the `Web.sitemap` file directly — without the need for this data provider.

Certain navigation controls, however, such as the TreeView control and the DropDownList control, require an intermediary SiteMapDataSource control to retrieve the site navigation information.

The SiteMapDataSource control is simple to use as demonstrated throughout this chapter. The SiteMapDataSource control in its simplest form is illustrated here:

```
<asp:SiteMapDataSource ID="SiteMapDataSource1" runat="server" />
```

In this form, the SiteMapDataSource control simply grabs the info as a tree hierarchy (as consistently demonstrated so far). Be aware that a number of properties do change how the data is displayed in any control that binds to the data output.

ShowStartingNode

The `ShowStartingNode` property determines whether the root node of the `.sitemap` file is retrieved with the retrieved collection of node objects. This property takes a `Boolean` value and is set to `True` by default. If you are working with the `Web.sitemap` file shown in Listing 13-1, you construct your SiteMapDataSource control as shown in Listing 13-25 to remove the root node from the collection.

LISTING 13-25: Removing the root node from the retrieved node collection

Available for download on Wrox.com

```
<%@ Page Language="VB" %>

<html xmlns="http://www.w3.org/1999/xhtml">
<head runat="server">
    <title>Menu Server Control</title>
</head>
<body>
    <form id="form1" runat="server">
        <asp:SiteMapDataSource ID="SiteMapDataSource1" runat="server"
           ShowStartingNode="False" />
        <asp:Menu ID="Menu1" runat="server" DataSourceID="SiteMapDataSource1">
        </asp:Menu>
    </form>
</body>
</html>
```

This code produces a menu like the one shown in Figure 13-28.

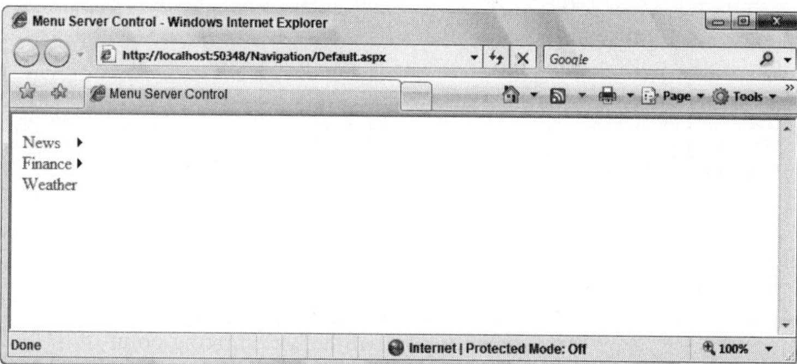

FIGURE 13-28

From this screenshot, you can see that, indeed, the root node has been removed, and the menu shown starts by using all the child nodes of the root node.

StartFromCurrentNode

The `StartFromCurrentNode` property causes the SiteMapDataProvider to retrieve only a node collection that starts from the current node of the page being viewed. By default, this property is set to `False`, meaning that the SiteMapDataProvider always retrieves all the available nodes (from the root node to the current node).

For an example of this property, use the `.sitemap` file from Listing 13-1 and create a page called `Markets.aspx`. This page in the hierarchy of the node collection is a child node of the Finance node, as well as having two child nodes itself: U.S. Market Report and NYSE. Listing 13-26 shows an example of setting the `StartFromCurrentNode` property to `True`.

LISTING 13-26: The Markets.aspx page using the StartFromCurrentNode property

Available for download on Wrox.com

```
<%@ Page Language="VB" %>

<html xmlns="http://www.w3.org/1999/xhtml">
<head runat="server">
    <title>Menu Server Control</title>
</head>
```

continues

LISTING 13-26 *(continued)*

```
<body>
    <form id="form1" runat="server">
        <asp:SiteMapDataSource ID="SiteMapDataSource1" runat="server"
           StartFromCurrentNode="True" />
        <asp:Menu ID="Menu1" runat="server" DataSourceID="SiteMapDataSource1">
        </asp:Menu>
    </form>
</body>
</html>
```

This simple property addition produces the result shown in Figure 13-29.

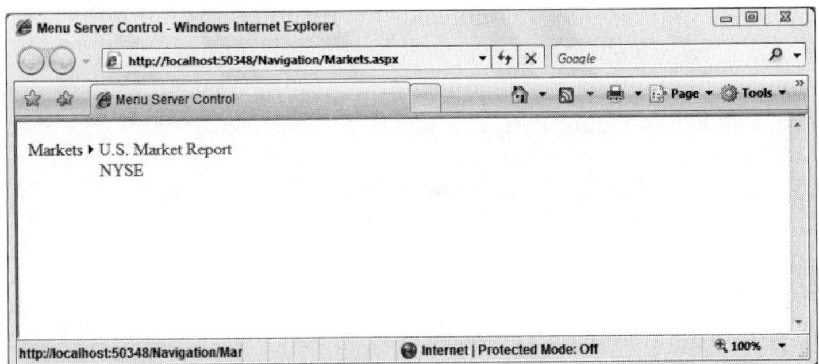

FIGURE 13-29

StartingNodeOffset

The `StartingNodeOffset` property takes an `Integer` value that determines the starting point of the hierarchy collection. By default, this property is set to `0`, meaning that the node collection retrieved by the SiteMapDataSource control starts at the root node. Any other value provides the offset from the root node and, in turn, makes this the new starting point. From the example provided in Listing 13-1, you know that the collection starts with the Home page found at `Default.aspx`, a page that you have seen in numerous examples in this chapter.

If you set this property's value to `1`, the starting point of the collection is one space off the default starting point (the Home page starting at `Default.aspx`). For example, if the page using the SiteMapDataSource control is the `MarketsUS.aspx` page, the node collection starts with the Finance page (`Finance.aspx`).

```
Home   Offset 0
  News   Offset 1
     U.S.   Offset 2
     World   Offset 2
     Technology   Offset 2
     Sports   Offset 2
  Finance   Offset 1
     Quotes   Offset 2
     Markets   Offset 2
        U.S. Market Report   Offset 3
        NYSE   Offset 3
     Funds   Offset 2
  Weather   Offset 1
```

From this hierarchy, you can see how much each node is offset from the root node. Therefore, if you set the `StartingNodeOffset` property to `1` and you are browsing on the U.S. Market Report page, you can see that the node collection starts with the Finance page (`Finance.aspx`), and the other child nodes of the root node (News and Weather) are not represented in the node collection because the `Finance.aspx` page is on the direct hierarchical path of the requested page.

StartingNodeUrl

The `StartingNodeUrl` property enables you to specify the page found in the `.sitemap` file from which the node collection should start. By default, the value of this property is empty; but when set to something such as `Finance.aspx`, the collection starts with the Finance page as the root node of the node collection. Listing 13-27 shows an example of using the `StartingNodeUrl` property.

LISTING 13-27: Using the StartingNodeUrl property

Available for download on Wrox.com

```
<%@ Page Language="VB" %>

<html xmlns="http://www.w3.org/1999/xhtml">
<head runat="server">
    <title>Menu Server Control</title>
</head>
<body>
    <form id="form1" runat="server">
        <asp:SiteMapDataSource ID="SiteMapDataSource1" runat="server"
           StartingNodeUrl="Finance.aspx" />
        <asp:Menu ID="Menu1" runat="server" DataSourceID="SiteMapDataSource1">
        </asp:Menu>
    </form>
</body>
</html>
```

When the `StartingNodeUrl` property value is encountered, the value is compared against the `url` attributes in the `Web.sitemap` file. When a match is found, the matched page is the one used as the root node in the node collection retrieved by the SiteMapDataSource control.

SITEMAP API

The `SiteMap` class is an in-memory representation of the site's navigation structure. This class is great for programmatically working around the hierarchical structure of your site. The `SiteMap` class comes with a couple of objects that make working with the navigation structure easy. Table 13-5 describes these objects (or public properties).

TABLE 13-5

PROPERTIES	DESCRIPTION
`CurrentNode`	Retrieves a `SiteMapNode` object for the current page
`RootNode`	Retrieves a `SiteMapNode` object that starts from the root node and the rest of the site's navigation structure
`Provider`	Retrieves the default `SiteMapProvider` for the current sitemap
`Providers`	Retrieves a collection of available, named `SiteMapProvider` objects

Listing 13-28 shows an example of working with some `SiteMap` objects by demonstrating how to use the `CurrentNode` object from the `Markets.aspx` page.

LISTING 13-28: Working with the CurrentNode object

Available for download on Wrox.com

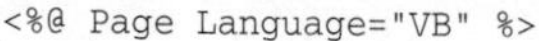

```
<%@ Page Language="VB" %>
```

VB

```
<script runat="server" language="vb">
    Protected Sub Page_Load(ByVal sender As Object, ByVal e As System.EventArgs)
        Label1.Text = SiteMap.CurrentNode.Description & "<br>" &
            SiteMap.CurrentNode.HasChildNodes & "<br>" &
```

continues

LISTING 13-28 *(continued)*

```
                SiteMap.CurrentNode.NextSibling.ToString() & "<br>" &
                SiteMap.CurrentNode.ParentNode.ToString() & "<br>" &
                SiteMap.CurrentNode.PreviousSibling.ToString() & "<br>" &
                SiteMap.CurrentNode.RootNode.ToString() & "<br>" &
                SiteMap.CurrentNode.Title & "<br>" &
                SiteMap.CurrentNode.Url
    End Sub
</script>

<html xmlns="http://www.w3.org/1999/xhtml">
<head runat="server">
    <title>SiteMapDataSource</title>
</head>
<body>
    <form id="form1" runat="server">
        <asp:Label ID="Label1" runat="server"></asp:Label>
    </form>
</body>
</html>
```

C#

```
<%@ Page Language="C#" %>

<script runat="server">
    protected void Page_Load(object sender, System.EventArgs e)
    {
        Label1.Text = SiteMap.CurrentNode.Description + "<br>" +
            SiteMap.CurrentNode.HasChildNodes + "<br>" +
            SiteMap.CurrentNode.NextSibling.ToString() + "<br>" +
            SiteMap.CurrentNode.ParentNode.ToString() + "<br>" +
            SiteMap.CurrentNode.PreviousSibling.ToString() + "<br>" +
            SiteMap.CurrentNode.RootNode.ToString() + "<br>" +
            SiteMap.CurrentNode.Title + "<br>" +
            SiteMap.CurrentNode.Url;
    }
</script>
```

As you can see from this little bit of code, by using the `SiteMap` class and the `CurrentNode` object, you can work with a plethora of information regarding the current page. Running this page, you get the following results printed to the screen:

```
The Latest Market Information
True
Funds
Finance
Quotes
Home
Markets
/SiteNavigation/Markets.aspx
```

Using the `CurrentNode` property, you can actually create your own style of the SiteMapPath control, as shown in Listing 13-29.

LISTING 13-29: Creating a custom navigation display using the CurrentNode property

Available for download on Wrox.com

VB

```
<%@ Page Language="VB" %>

<script runat="server" language="vb">
    Protected Sub Page_Load(ByVal sender As Object, ByVal e As System.EventArgs)
        Hyperlink1.Text = SiteMap.CurrentNode.ParentNode.ToString()
```

```
        Hyperlink1.NavigateUrl = SiteMap.CurrentNode.ParentNode.Url

        Hyperlink2.Text = SiteMap.CurrentNode.PreviousSibling.ToString()
        Hyperlink2.NavigateUrl = SiteMap.CurrentNode.PreviousSibling.Url

        Hyperlink3.Text = SiteMap.CurrentNode.NextSibling.ToString()
        Hyperlink3.NavigateUrl = SiteMap.CurrentNode.NextSibling.Url
    End Sub
</script>

<html xmlns="http://www.w3.org/1999/xhtml" >
<head runat="server">
    <title>SiteMapDataSource</title>
</head>
<body>
    <form id="form1" runat="server">
        Move Up:
        <asp:Hyperlink ID="Hyperlink1" runat="server"></asp:Hyperlink><br />
        <-- <asp:Hyperlink ID="Hyperlink2" runat="server"></asp:Hyperlink> |
        <asp:Hyperlink ID="Hyperlink3" runat="server"></asp:Hyperlink> -->
    </form>
</body>
</html>
```

C#

```
<%@ Page Language="C#" %>

<script runat="server">
    protected void Page_Load(object sender, System.EventArgs e)
    {
        Hyperlink1.Text = SiteMap.CurrentNode.ParentNode.ToString();
        Hyperlink1.NavigateUrl = SiteMap.CurrentNode.ParentNode.Url;

        Hyperlink2.Text = SiteMap.CurrentNode.PreviousSibling.ToString();
        Hyperlink2.NavigateUrl = SiteMap.CurrentNode.PreviousSibling.Url;

        Hyperlink3.Text = SiteMap.CurrentNode.NextSibling.ToString();
        Hyperlink3.NavigateUrl = SiteMap.CurrentNode.NextSibling.Url;
    }
</script>
```

When run, this page gives you your own custom navigation structure, as shown in Figure 13-30.

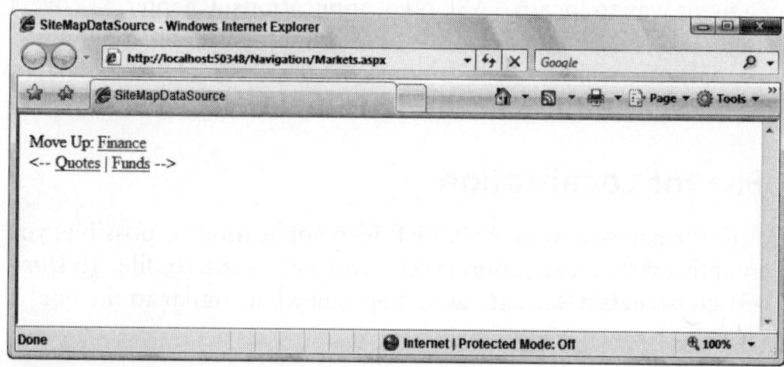

FIGURE 13-30

URL MAPPING

The URLs used by Web pages can sometimes get rather complex as your application grows and grows. Sometimes, you could be presenting Web pages that change their content based on query strings that are provided via the URL, such as

```
http://www.asp.net/forums/view.aspx?forumid=12&categoryid=6
```

In other cases, your Web page might be so deep within a hierarchy of folders that the URL has become rather cumbersome for an end user to type or remember when they want to pull up the page later in their browser. There are also moments when you want a collection of pages to look like they are the same page or a single destination.

In cases such as these, you can take advantage of an ASP.NET feature called *URL mapping*. URL mapping enables you to map complex URLs to simpler ones. You accomplish this mapping through settings you apply in the `web.config` file using the `<urlMappings>` element (see Listing 13-30).

LISTING 13-30: Mapping URLs using the <urlMappings> element

Available for download on Wrox.com

```
<configuration>

   <system.web>

      <urlMappings>
         <add url="~/Content.aspx" mappedUrl="~/SystemNews.aspx?categoryid=5" />
      </urlMappings>

   </system.web>

</configuration>
```

This example uses a fake URL — `Content.aspx` — that is mapped to a more complicated URL: `SystemNews.aspx?categoryid=5`. With this construction in place, when the end user types the URL, `Content.aspx`, the application knows to invoke the more complicated URL `SystemNews.aspx?categoryid=5` page. This takes place without the URL even being changed in the browser. Even after the page has completely loaded, the browser will still show the `Content.aspx` page as the destination — thereby tricking the end user, in a sense.

It is important to note that in this situation, the end user is routed to `SystemNews.aspx?categoryid=5` *no matter what — even if a* `Content.aspx` *page exists! Therefore, mapping to pages that are not actually contained within your application is important.*

SITEMAP LOCALIZATION

The improved resource files (`.resx`) are a great way to localize ASP.NET applications. Chapter 32 covers this localization of Web applications using ASP.NET. However, this introduction focused on applying localization features to the pages of your applications, but didn't demonstrate how to take this localization capability further by applying it to items such as the `Web.sitemap` file.

Structuring the Web.sitemap File for Localization

Just as applying localization instructions to the pages of your ASP.NET Web applications is possible, you can also use the same framework to accomplish your localization tasks in the `Web.sitemap` file. To show you this technique in action, Listing 13-31 constructs a `Web.sitemap` file somewhat similar to the one presented in Listing 13-1, but much simpler.

LISTING 13-31: Creating a basic .sitemap file for localization

Available for download on Wrox.com

```
<?xml version="1.0" encoding="utf-8" ?>

<siteMap xmlns="http://schemas.microsoft.com/AspNet/SiteMap-File-1.0"
 enableLocalization="true">
 <siteMapNode url="Default.aspx" resourceKey="Home">
        <siteMapNode url="News.aspx" resourceKey="News">
```

```
                    <siteMapNode url="News.aspx?cat=us" resourceKey="NewsUS" />
                    <siteMapNode url="News.aspx?cat=world" resourceKey="NewsWorld" />
                    <siteMapNode url="News.aspx?cat=tech" resourceKey="NewsTech" />
                    <siteMapNode url="News.aspx?cat=sport" resourceKey="NewsSport" />
            </siteMapNode>
    </siteMapNode>
</siteMap>
```

Listing 13-31 shows a rather simple `Web.sitemap` file. To enable the localization capability from the `Web.sitemap` file, you have to turn on this capability by using the `enableLocalization` attribute in the `<siteMap>` element and setting it to `true`. After it is enabled, you can then define each of the navigation nodes as you would normally, using the `<siteMapNode>` element. In this case, however, because you are going to define the contents of these navigation pieces (most notably, the `title` and `description` attributes) in various `.resx` files, you do not need to repeatedly define these items in this file. That means you need to define only the `url` attribute for this example. It is important to note, however, that you could also define this attribute through your `.resx` files, thereby forwarding end users to different pages depending on their defined culture settings.

The next attribute to note is the `resourceKey` attribute used in the `<siteMapNode>` elements. This key is used and defined in the various `.resx` files you will implement. Take the following `<siteMapNode>` element as an example:

```
<siteMapNode url="News.aspx" resourceKey="News">
   ...
</siteMapNode>
```

In this case, the value of the `resourceKey` (and the key that will be used in the `.resx` file) is `News`. This means that you can define the values of the `title` and `description` attributes in the `.resx` file using the following syntax:

```
News.Title
News.Description
```

Now that the `Web.sitemap` is in place, the next step is to make some minor modifications to the `Web.config` file, as shown next.

Making Modifications to the Web.config File

Now that the `Web.sitemap` file is in place and ready, the next step is to provide some minor additions to the `Web.config` file. In order for your Web application to make an automatic detection of the culture of the users visiting the various pages you are providing, you must set the `Culture` and `UICulture` settings in the `@Page` directive, or set these attributes for automatic detection in the `<globalization>` element of the `Web.config` file.

When you are working with navigation and the `Web.sitemap` file, as in this example, making this change in the `Web.config` file is actually best so that it automatically takes effect on each and every page in your application. Adding it to the `Web.config` file makes it much simpler because you won't have to make these additions yourself to each and every page.

To make these changes, open your `Web.config` file and add a `<globalization>` element, as shown in Listing 13-32.

Available for download on Wrox.com

LISTING 13-32: Adding culture detection to the Web.config file

```
<configuration>
   <system.web>

      <globalization culture="auto" uiCulture="auto" />

   </system.web>
</configuration>
```

For the auto-detection capabilities to occur, you simply set the `culture` and `uiCulture` attributes to `auto`. You also could have defined the values as `auto:en-US`, which means that the automatic culture detection capabilities should occur, but if the culture defined is not found in the various resource files, then use `en-US` (American English) as the default culture. However, because you are going to define a default `Web.sitemap` set of values, there really is no need for you to bring forward this construction.

Next, you create the assembly resource files that define the values used by the `Web.sitemap` file.

Creating Assembly Resource (.resx) Files

To create a set of assembly resource files that you will use with the `Web.sitemap` file, create a folder in your project called App_GlobalResources. If you are using Visual Studio 2010 or Visual Web Developer, you can add this folder by right-clicking on the project and selecting Add ASP.NET Folder ➪ App_GlobalResources.

After the folder is in place, add two assembly resource files to this folder. Name the first file `Web.sitemap.resx` and the second one `Web.sitemap.fi.resx`. Your goal with these two files is to have a default set of values for the `Web.sitemap` file that will be defined in the `Web.sitemap.resx` file, and a version of these values that has been translated to the Finnish language and is contained in the `Web.sitemap.fi.resx` file.

The `fi` value used in the name will be the file used by individuals who have their preferred language set to `fi-FI`. Table 13-6 describes other variations of these constructions.

TABLE 13-6

.RESX FILE	CULTURE SERVED
`Web.sitemap.resx`	The default values used when the end user's culture cannot be identified through another `.resx` file
`Web.sitemap.en.resx`	The resource file used for all `en` (English) users
`Web.sitemap.en-gb.resx`	The resource file used for the English speakers of Great Britain
`Web.sitemap.fr-ca.resx`	The resource file used for the French speakers of Canada
`Web.sitemap.ru.resx`	The resource file used for Russian speakers

Now that the `Web.sitemap.resx` and `Web.sitemap.fi.resx` files are in place, the next step is to fill these files with values. To accomplish this task, you use the keys defined earlier directly in the `Web.sitemap` file. Figure 13-31 shows the result of this exercise.

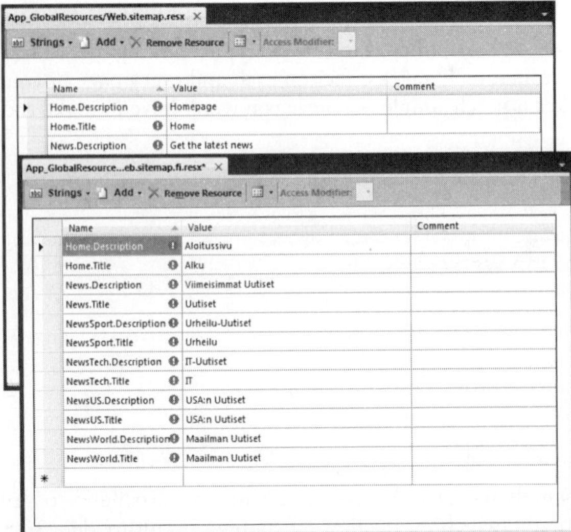

FIGURE 13-31

Although the IDE states that these are not valid identifiers, the application still works with this model. After you have the files in place, you can test how this localization endeavor works, as shown in the following section.

Testing the Results

Create a page in your application and place a TreeView server control on the page. In addition to the TreeView control, you must also include a SiteMapDataSource control to work with the `Web.sitemap` file you created. Be sure to tie the two controls together by giving the TreeView control the attribute `DataSourceID="SiteMapDataSource1"`, as demonstrated earlier in this chapter.

⊟ Home
⊟ News
U.S. News
World
Technology
Sports

FIGURE 13-32

If you have your language preference in Microsoft's Internet Explorer set to `en-us` (American English), you will see the results shown in Figure 13-32.

When you pull up the page in the browser, the culture of the request is checked. Because the only finely grained preference defined in the example is for users using the culture of `fi` (Finnish), the default `Web.sitemap.resx` is used instead. Because of this, the `Web.sitemap.resx` file is used to populate the values of the TreeView control, as shown in Figure 13-32. If the requestor has a culture setting of `fi`, however, he gets an entirely different set of results.

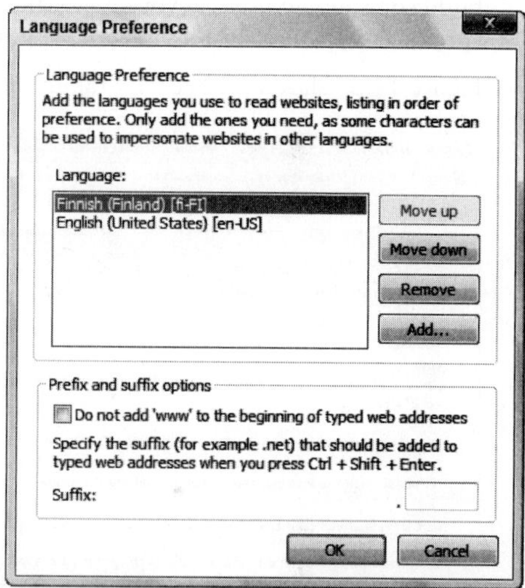

FIGURE 13-33

To test this out, change the preferred language used in IE by selecting Tools ➪ Internet Options in IE. On the first tab (General), click the Languages button at the bottom of the dialog. The Language Preferences dialog appears. Click the Add button and add the Finnish language setting to the list of options. The final step is to use the Move Up button to move the Finnish choice to the top of the list. In the end, you should see something similar to what is shown in Figure 13-33.

With this setting in place, running the page with the TreeView control gives you the result shown in Figure 13-34.

Now, when the page is requested, the culture is set to `fi` and correlates to the `Web.sitemap.fi.resx` file instead of to the default `Web.sitemap.resx` file.

⊟ Alku
⊟ Uutiset
USA:n uutiset
Maailman Uutiset
IT
Urheilu

FIGURE 13-34

SECURITY TRIMMING

If you have been following the examples so far in this chapter, you might notice that one of the attributes available to a `<siteMapNode>` tag hasn't yet been discussed. The `roles` attribute is a powerful one that allows you to provide an authorization model to the items contained in the navigation system. This really means that you have the capability to display *only* the navigational items that a user is entitled to see and nothing more. The term commonly used for this behavior is *security trimming*. This section looks at how to apply security trimming to the application you are building in ASP.NET 4.

This capability is a good example of two ASP.NET 4 systems interacting with one another in the site navigation system. Security trimming works only when you have enabled the ASP.NET 4 role management system. Chapter 15 covers this system in more detail. Be sure to check out this chapter because this section does not go into much detail about this system.

As an example of security trimming in your ASP.NET applications, this section shows you how to limit access to the navigation of your application's administration system to only those users who are contained within a specific application role.

Setting Up Role Management for Administrators

The first step in applying security trimming is to set up your application to handle roles. This process is actually rather simple. One easy way to accomplish this task is to open the ASP.NET Web Site Administration Tool for your application and enable role management directly in this Web-based tool. You can get to this administration tool by clicking the ASP.NET Configuration button in the menu of the Solution Explorer in Visual Studio. This button has the logo of a hammer and a globe.

After launching the ASP.NET Web Site Administration Tool, select the Security tab; a new page then appears where you can administer the membership and role management systems for your application.

First, you enable and build up the role management system, and then, you also enable the membership system. Chapter 15 covers the membership system in detail. After you turn on the membership system, you build some actual users in your application. You want a user to log in to your application and be assigned a specific role. This role assignment changes the site navigation system display.

Figure 13-35 shows the Security tab in the ASP.NET Web Site Administration Tool.

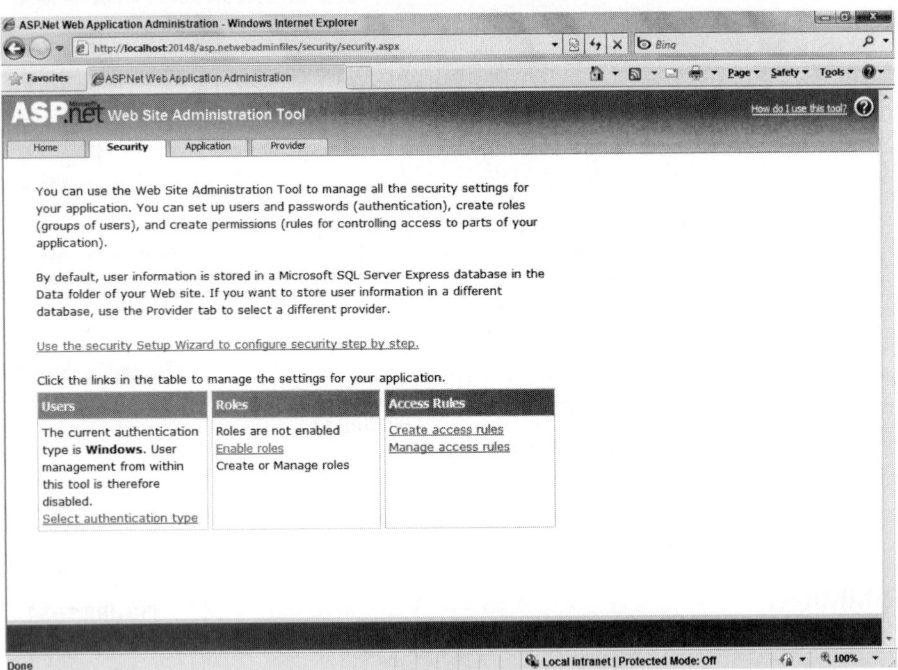

FIGURE 13-35

On this page, you can easily enable the role management system by selecting the Enable roles link. After you have done this, you are informed that no roles exist in the system. To create the role that you need for the site navigation system, select the Create or Manage roles link. A new page then appears where you can create the administrator role. For this example, I named the role Admin.

After adding the Admin role, click the Back button and then select the authentication type that is utilized for the application. You want to make sure that you have selected the "From the internet" option. This enables you to create a user in the system. By default, these users are stored in the Microsoft SQL Server Express Edition file that ASP.NET creates in your application. After you have selected the authentication type, you can then create the new user and place the user in the Admin role by making sure the role is selected (using a check box) on the screen where you are creating the user.

After you are satisfied that a user has been created and placed in the Admin role, you can check whether the settings are appropriately set in the `web.config` file, as presented in Listing 13-33.

LISTING 13-33: The role management system enabled in the web.config file

Available for download on Wrox.com

```
<configuration>
   <system.web>

      <authentication mode="Forms" />
      <roleManager enabled="true" />

   </system.web>
</configuration>
```

Setting Up the Administrators' Section

The next step is to set up a page for administrators only. For this example, I named the page `AdminOnly.aspx`, and it contains only a simple string value welcoming administrators to the page. This page is locked down only for users who are contained in the Admin role. This lockdown is done by making the appropriate settings in the `web.config` file, as shown in Listing 13-34.

LISTING 13-34: Locking down the AdminOnly.aspx page in the web.config

Available for download on Wrox.com

```
<configuration>
  <location path="AdminOnly.aspx">
    <system.web>
      <authorization>
        <allow roles="Admin" />
        <deny users="*" />
      </authorization>
    </system.web>
  </location>
</configuration>
```

Now, because the `AdminOnly.aspx` page is accessible only to the users who are in the Admin role, the next step is to allow users to log in to the application. The application demo accomplishes this task by creating a `Default.aspx` page that contains a Login server control as well as a TreeView control bound to a SiteMapDataSource control. Listing 13-35 presents this simple ASP.NET page.

LISTING 13-35: The Default.aspx page

Available for download on Wrox.com

```
<%@ Page Language="VB" %>

<html xmlns="http://www.w3.org/1999/xhtml">
<head runat="server">
    <title>Main Page</title>
</head>
<body>
    <form id="form1" runat="server">
    <div>
        <asp:Login ID="Login1" runat="server">
        </asp:Login>
        <br />
        <asp:TreeView ID="TreeView1" runat="server"
         DataSourceID="SiteMapDataSource1" ShowLines="True">
        </asp:TreeView>
        <br />
        <asp:SiteMapDataSource ID="SiteMapDataSource1" runat="server" />
```

continues

LISTING 13-35 *(continued)*

```
        </div>
        </form>
    </body>
    </html>
```

With the `Default.aspx` page in place, you make another change to the `Web.sitemap` file that was originally presented in Listing 13-1. For this example, you add a `<siteMapNode>` element that works with the new `AdminOnly.aspx` page. This node is presented here:

```
<siteMapNode title="Administration" description="The Administrators page"
 url="AdminOnly.aspx" roles="Admin" />
```

After all items are in place in your application, the next step is to enable security trimming for the site navigation system.

Enabling Security Trimming

By default, security trimming is disabled. Even if you start applying values to the `roles` attribute for any `<siteMapNode>` element in your `web.config` file, it does not work. To enable security trimming, you must fine-tune the provider declaration for the site navigation system.

To make the necessary changes to the XmlSiteMapProvider, you must make these changes high up in the configuration chain, such as to the `machine.config` file or the default `web.config` file, or you can make the change lower down, such as in your application's `web.config` file. This example makes the change in the `web.config` file.

To alter the XmlSiteMapProvider in the `web.config` file, you first clear out the already declared instance. After it is cleared, you then redeclare a new instance of the XmlSiteMapProvider, but this time, you enable security trimming, as shown in Listing 13-36.

Available for download on Wrox.com

LISTING 13-36: Enabling security trimming in the provider

```
<configuration>
   <system.web>

      <siteMap>
        <providers>
          <clear />
          <add siteMapFile="web.sitemap" name="AspNetXmlSiteMapProvider"
              type="System.Web.XmlSiteMapProvider, System.Web, Version=4.0.0.0,
                 Culture=neutral, PublicKeyToken=b03f5f7f11d50a3a"
                 securityTrimmingEnabled="true" />
        </providers>
      </siteMap>

   </system.web>
</configuration>
```

From this example, you can see that a new XmlSiteMapProvider is defined, and the `securityTrimmingEnabled` attribute is then set to `true` (shown in bold). With security trimming enabled, the `roles` attribute in the `<siteMapNode>` element is utilized in the site navigation system.

To test it out for yourself, run the `Default.aspx` page. A page appears that does not include the link to the administration portion of the page, as illustrated in Figure 13-36.

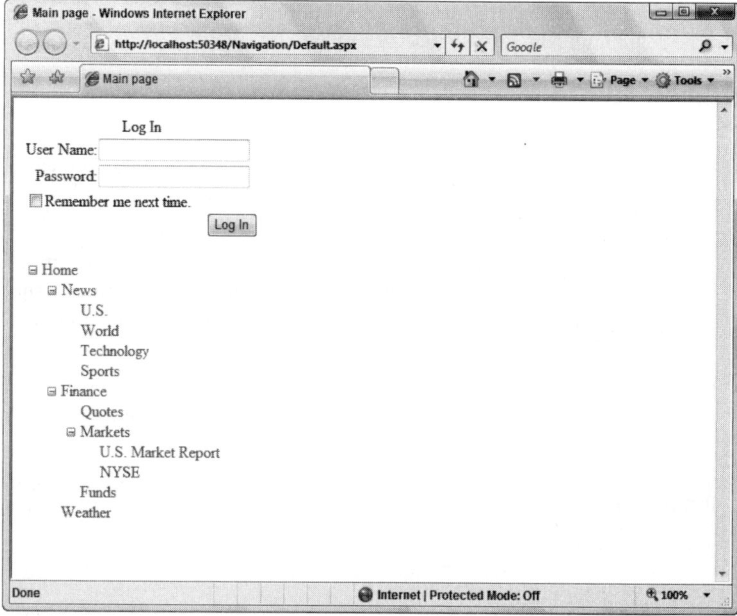

FIGURE 13-36

From this figure, you can see that the Administration link is not present in the TreeView control. Now, however, log in to the application as a user contained in the Admin role. You then see that, indeed, the site navigation has changed to reflect the role of the user, as presented in Figure 13-37.

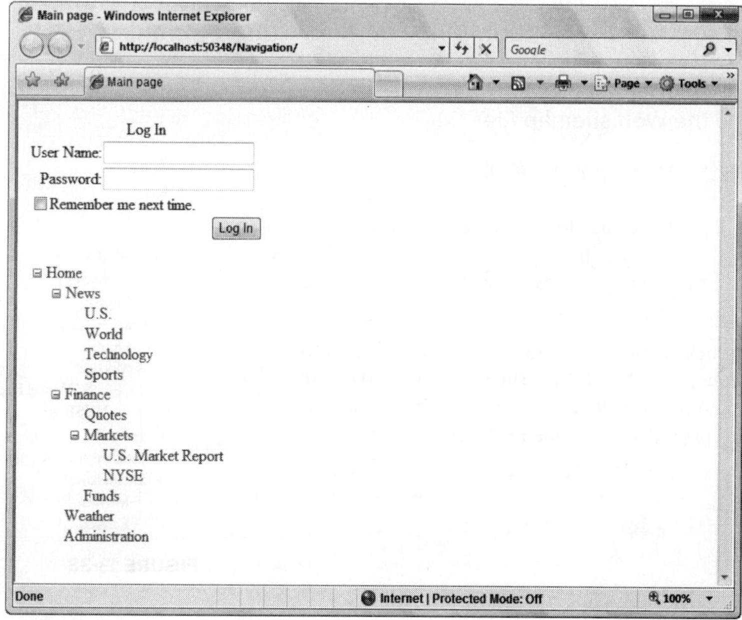

FIGURE 13-37

Security trimming is an ideal way of automatically altering the site navigation that is presented to users based upon the roles they have in the role management system.

NESTING SITEMAP FILES

You are not required to place all your site navigation within a single `Web.sitemap` file. In fact, you can spread it out into multiple `.sitemap` files if you want and then bring them all together into a single `.sitemap` file — also known as *nesting* `.sitemap` files.

For example, suppose you are using the sitemap file from Listing 13-1 and you have a rather large amount of site navigation to add under the area of *Entertainment*. You could put all this new information in the current `Web.sitemap` file, or you could keep all the Entertainment links in another sitemap file and just reference that in the main sitemap file.

In the simplest case, nesting sitemap files is easily achievable. To see it in action, create a new `.sitemap` file (called `Entertainment.sitemap`) and place this file in your application. Listing 13-37 presents an example `Entertainment.sitemap` file.

Available for download on Wrox.com

LISTING 13-37: The Entertainment.sitemap

```
<?xml version="1.0" encoding="utf-8" ?>
<siteMap xmlns="http://schemas.microsoft.com/AspNet/SiteMap-File-1.0" >
    <siteMapNode url="Entertainment.aspx" title="Entertainment"
     description="The Entertainment Page">
        <siteMapNode url="Movies.aspx" title="Movies"
         description="The Latest in Movies" />
        <siteMapNode url="Fashion.aspx" title="Fashion"
         description="The Latest in Fashion" />
    </siteMapNode>
</siteMap>
```

You can place the `Entertainment.sitemap` in the root directory where you also have the main `Web.sitemap` file. Now, working from the sitemap file from the earlier Listing 13-1, you make the following addition to the bottom of the list, as presented in Listing 13-38.

LISTING 13-38: Additions to the Web.sitemap file

```
<siteMapNode siteMapFile="Entertainment.sitemap" />
```

Instead of using the standard `url`, `title`, and `description` attributes, you just point to the other sitemap file to be included in this main sitemap file using the `siteMapFile` attribute. Running this page gives you results similar to those presented in Figure 13-38.

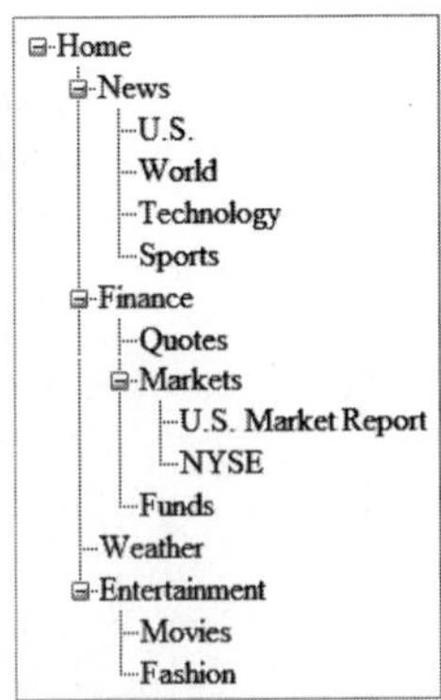

FIGURE 13-38

Another approach to nesting sitemap files is to build a second provider in the sitemap provider model definitions, and then to use the `provider` attribute within the `<siteMapNode>` element to reference this declaration. To accomplish this task, you add a new sitemap provider reference in the `web.config` file, as is illustrated in Listing 13-39.

Available for download on Wrox.com

LISTING 13-39: Using another provider in the same Web.sitemap file

```
<configuration>
   <system.web>

      <siteMap>
        <providers>
          <add siteMapFile="Entertainment.sitemap" name="AspNetXmlSiteMapProvider2"
              type="System.Web.XmlSiteMapProvider, System.Web, Version=4.0.0.0,
                 Culture=neutral, PublicKeyToken=b03f5f7f11d50a3a" />
        </providers>
      </siteMap>

   </system.web>
</configuration>
```

From this bit of code, you can see that a second provider is defined. Defining a second sitemap provider does not mean that you have to use the `<clear />` element in the `<provider>` section, but instead, you simply define a new provider that has a new name. In this case, the name of the provider is `AspNetXmlSiteMapProvider2`. Also, within this provider definition, the `siteMapFile` attribute is used to point to the name of the sitemap file that should be utilized.

With this in place, you can then reference this declaration by using the `provider` attribute within the `<siteMapNode>` element of the `Web.sitemap` file. To add the `Entertainment.sitemap` file in this manner, your `<siteMapNode>` element should take the form presented in Listing 13-40.

LISTING 13-40: Using a second provider in the Web.sitemap file

```
<siteMapNode provider="AspNetXmlSiteMapProvider2" />
```

This code gives you the same results as those shown in Figure 13-38. Besides providing another way of nesting sitemap files, you gain a lot of power using the `provider` attribute. If you build a new sitemap provider that pulls sitemap navigation information from another source (rather than from an XML file), you can mix those results in the main `Web.sitemap` file. The end result could have items that come from two or more completely different data sources.

SUMMARY

This chapter introduced the navigation mechanics that ASP.NET 4 provides. At the core of the navigation capabilities is the power to detail the navigation structure in an XML file, which various navigation controls — such as the new TreeView and SiteMapPath controls — can then utilize.

The powerful functionality that the navigation capabilities provide saves you a tremendous amount of coding time.

In addition to showing you the core infrastructure for navigation in ASP.NET 4, this chapter also described both the TreeView and SiteMapPath controls and how to use them throughout your applications. The great thing about these controls is that, right out of the box, they can richly display your navigation hierarchy and enable the end user to work through the site easily. In addition, these controls are easily changeable so that you can go beyond the standard appearance and functionality that they provide.

Along with the TreeView server control, this chapter also looked at the Menu server control. You will find a lot of similarities between these two controls as they both provide a means to look at hierarchical data.

Finally, this chapter looked at how to achieve URL mapping, as well as how to localize your `Web.sitemap` files and filter the results of the site navigation contents based upon a user's role in the role management system.

14

Personalization

WHAT'S IN THIS CHAPTER?

- Exploring ASP.NET's personalization capabilities
- Working with personalization properties
- Storing data using personalization providers
- Working with anonymous users

Many Web applications must be customized with information that is specific to the end user who is presently viewing the page. In the past, the developer usually provided storage of personalization properties for end users viewing the page by means of cookies, the `Session` object, or the `Application` object. Cookies enabled storage of persistent items so that when the end user returned to a Web page, any settings related to him were retrieved in order to be utilized again by the application. Cookies are not the best way to approach persistent user data storage, however, mainly because they are not accepted by all computers and also because a crafty end user can easily alter them.

As you will see in Chapter 15, ASP.NET membership and role management capabilities are ways that ASP.NET can conveniently store information about the user. How can you, as the developer, use the same mechanics to store custom information?

ASP.NET 4 provides you with an outstanding feature — *personalization*. The ASP.NET personalization engine provided with this latest release can make an automatic association between the end user viewing the page and any data points stored for that user. The personalization properties that are maintained on a per-user basis are stored on the server and not on the client. These items are conveniently placed in a data store of your choice (such as Microsoft's SQL Server) and, therefore, the end user can then access these personalization properties on later site visits.

This feature is an ideal way to start creating highly customizable and user-specific sites without building any of the plumbing beforehand. In this case, the plumbing has been built for you! This chapter shows you how the personalization feature is yet another way that the ASP.NET team is making developers more productive and their jobs easier.

THE PERSONALIZATION MODEL

The personalization model provided with ASP.NET 4 is simple and, as with most items that come with ASP.NET, is an extensible model as well. Figure 14-1 shows a simple diagram that outlines the personalization model.

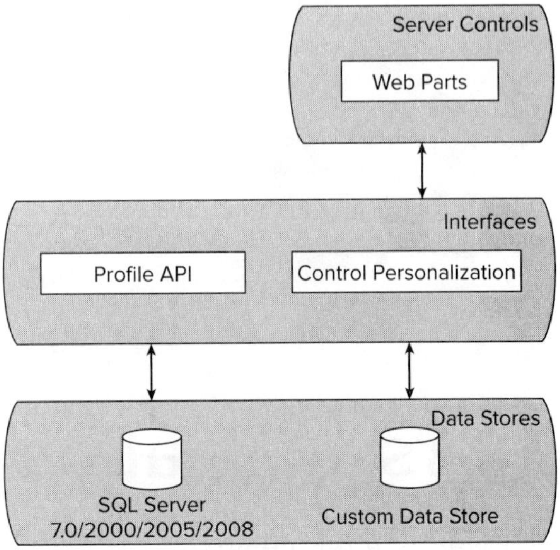

From this diagram, you can see the three layers in this model. Look at the middle layer of the personalization model — the Personalization Services layer. This layer contains the Profile API. This Profile API layer enables you to program your end user's data points into one of the lower-layer data stores. Also included in this layer are the server control personalization capabilities, which are important for the Portal Framework and the use of Web Parts. Chapter 16 discusses the Portal Framework and Web Parts.

FIGURE 14-1

Although certain controls built into ASP.NET can utilize the personalization capabilities for storing information about the page settings, you can also use this engine to store your own data points. As with Web Parts, you can use these points within your ASP.NET pages.

Below the Personalization Services layer, you'll find the default personalization data provider for working with Microsoft's SQL Server 2008, 2005, or 2000, as well as Microsoft's SQL Server Express Edition. You are not limited to just this one data store when applying the personalization features of ASP.NET 4; you can also extend the model and create a custom data provider for the personalization engine.

You can read about how to create your own providers in Chapter 12.

Now that you have looked briefly at the personalization model, you can begin using it by creating some stored personalization properties that you can use later within your applications.

CREATING PERSONALIZATION PROPERTIES

The nice thing about creating custom personalization properties is that you can do it so easily. After these properties are created, you gain the capability to have strongly typed access to them. Creating personalization properties that are used only by authenticated users, and also some that anonymous users can utilize, is also possible. These data points are powerful — mainly because you can start using them immediately in your application without building any underlying infrastructures to support them. As an example of working with the ASP.NET personalization system, this chapter starts with creating some simple personalization properties. Later, you learn how to use these personalization properties within your application.

Adding a Simple Personalization Property

When adding a personalization property, you must decide what data items from the user you are going to store. For this example, create a few items about the user that you can use within your application; assume that you want to store the following information about the user:

- First name
- Last name
- Last visited
- Age
- Membership status

ASP.NET has a heavy dependency on storing configurations inside XML files, and the ASP.NET 4 personalization engine is no different. All these customization points concerning the end user are defined and stored within the web.config file of the application, as shown in Listing 14-1.

LISTING 14-1: Creating personalization properties in the web.config file

Available for download on Wrox.com

```
<configuration>
  <system.web>

     <profile>

        <properties>

           <add name="FirstName" />
           <add name="LastName" />
           <add name="LastVisited" />
           <add name="Age" />
           <add name="Member" />

        </properties>

      </profile>

      <authentication mode="Windows" />

  </system.web>
</configuration>
```

Filename Web.config

Within the web.config file and nested within the <system.web> section of the file, you create a <profile> section in order to work with the ASP.NET 4 personalization engine. Within this <profile> section of the web.config file, you create a <properties> section. In this section, you can define all the properties you want the personalization engine to store.

From this code example, you can see that defining simple properties using the <add> element is rather easy. This element simply takes the name attribute, which takes the name of the property you want to persist.

You start out with the assumption that accessing the page you will build with these properties is already authenticated using Windows authentication (you can read more on authentication and authorization in the next chapter). Later in this chapter, you look at how to apply personalization properties to anonymous users as well. The capability to apply personalization properties to anonymous users is disabled by default (for good reasons).

After you have defined these personalization properties, using them is just as easy as it is to define them. The next section looks at how to use these definitions in an application.

Using Personalization Properties

Now that you have defined the personalization properties in the web.config file, you can use these items in code. For example, you can create a simple form that asks for some of this information from the end user. On the Button_Click event, the data is stored in the personalization engine. Listing 14-2 shows an example of this.

LISTING 14-2: Using the defined personalization properties

Available for download on Wrox.com

```
<%@ Page Language="VB" %>

<script runat="server">
  Protected Sub Button1_Click(ByVal sender As Object, ByVal e As System.EventArgs)
    If Page.User.Identity.IsAuthenticated Then
       Profile.FirstName = TextBox1.Text
       Profile.LastName = TextBox2.Text
       Profile.Age = TextBox3.Text
       Profile.Member = Radiobuttonlist1.SelectedItem.Text
       Profile.LastVisited = DateTime.Now().ToString()

       Label1.Text = "Stored information includes:<p>" &
          "First name: " & Profile.FirstName &
          "<br>Last name: " & Profile.LastName &
          "<br>Age: " & Profile.Age &
          "<br>Member: " & Profile.Member &
          "<br>Last visited: " & Profile.LastVisited
    Else
       Label1.Text = "You must be authenticated!"
    End If
  End Sub
</script>

<html xmlns="http://www.w3.org/1999/xhtml">
<head runat="server">
    <title>Storing Personalization</title>
</head>
<body>
   <form id="form1" runat="server">
       <p>First Name:
       <asp:TextBox ID="TextBox1" Runat="server"></asp:TextBox></p>
       <p>Last Name:
       <asp:TextBox ID="TextBox2" Runat="server"></asp:TextBox></p>
       <p>Age:
       <asp:TextBox ID="TextBox3" Runat="server" Width="50px"
        MaxLength="3"></asp:TextBox></p>
       <p>Are you a member?
       <asp:RadioButtonList ID="Radiobuttonlist1" Runat="server">
           <asp:ListItem Value="1">Yes</asp:ListItem>
           <asp:ListItem Value="0" Selected="True">No</asp:ListItem>
       </asp:RadioButtonList></p>
       <p><asp:Button ID="Button1" Runat="server" Text="Submit"
           OnClick="Button1_Click" />
       </p>
       <hr /><p>
       <asp:Label ID="Label1" Runat="server"></asp:Label></p>
   </form>
</body>
</html>
```

C#

```
<%@ Page Language="C#" %>

<script runat="server">
    protected void Button1_Click(object sender, EventArgs e)
    {
      if (Page.User.Identity.IsAuthenticated)
      {
        Profile.FirstName = TextBox1.Text;
        Profile.LastName = TextBox2.Text;
        Profile.Age = TextBox3.Text;
        Profile.Member = Radiobuttonlist1.SelectedItem.Text;
```

```
            Profile.LastVisited = DateTime.Now.ToString();

            Label1.Text = "Stored information includes:<p>" +
                "First name: " + Profile.FirstName +
                "<br>Last name: " + Profile.LastName +
                "<br>Age: " + Profile.Age +
                "<br>Member: " + Profile.Member +
                "<br>Last visited: " + Profile.LastVisited;
        }
        else
        {
            Label1.Text = "You must be authenticated!";
        }
    }
</script>
```

Working with personalization properties is similar to the way you worked with the `Session` object in the past, but note that the personalization properties you are storing and retrieving are not key based. Therefore, when working with them you do not need to remember key names.

All items stored by the personalization system are type cast to a particular .NET data type. By default, these items are stored as type `String`, and you have early-bound access to the items stored. To store an item, you simply populate the personalization property directly using the `Profile` object:

```
Profile.FirstName = TextBox1.Text
```

To retrieve the same information, you simply grab the appropriate property of the `Profile` class as shown here:

```
Label1.Text = Profile.FirstName
```

The great thing about using the `Profile` class and all the personalization properties defined in the Code view is that this method provides IntelliSense as you build your pages. When you are working with the `Profile` class in this view, all the items you define are listed as available options through the IntelliSense feature, as illustrated in Figure 14-2.

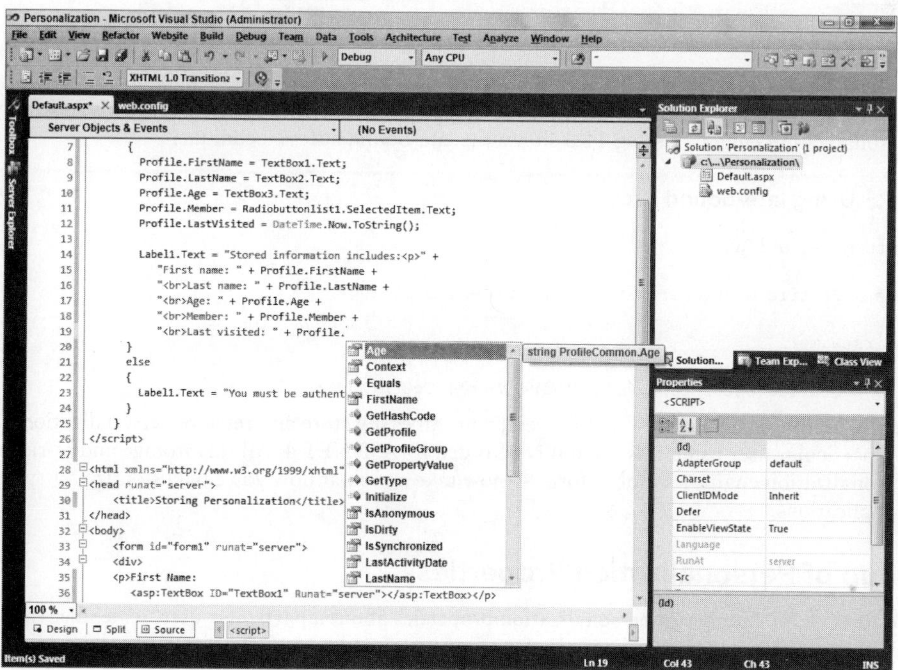

FIGURE 14-2

All these properties are accessible in IntelliSense because the `Profile` class is hidden and dynamically compiled behind the scenes whenever you save the personalization changes made to the `web.config` file. After these items are saved in the `web.config` file, these properties are available to you throughout your application in a strongly typed manner.

When run, the page from Listing 14-2 produces the results shown in Figure 14-3.

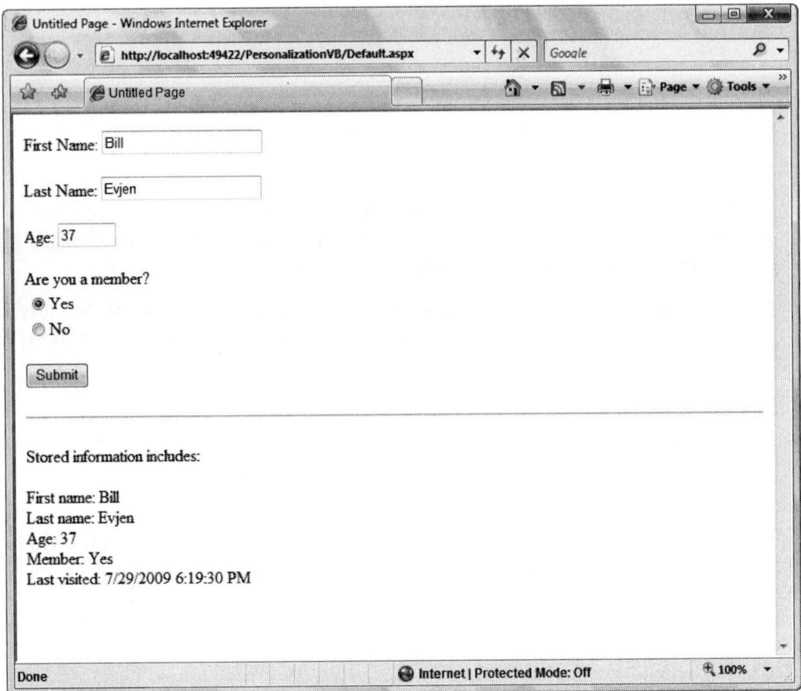

FIGURE 14-3

In addition to using early-bound access techniques, you can also use late-bound access for the items that you store in the personalization engine. Listing 14-3 shows the late-bound access technique.

LISTING 14-3: Using late-bound access

VB

```
Dim myFirstName As String

myFirstName = Profile.GetPropertyValue("FirstName").ToString()
```

C#

```
string myFirstName;

myFirstName = Profile.GetPropertyValue("FirstName").ToString();
```

Whether it is early-bound access or late-bound access, you can easily store and retrieve personalization properties for a particular user using this capability afforded by ASP.NET 4. All this storage and retrieval is done in the personalization engine's simplest form — now take a look at how you can customize for specific needs in your applications.

Adding a Group of Personalization Properties

If you want to store a large number of personalization properties about a particular user, remember that you are not just storing personalization properties for a particular page, but for the *entire* application.

This means that items you have stored about a particular end user somewhere in the beginning of the application can be retrieved later for use on any other page within the application. Because different sections of your Web applications store different personalization properties, you sometimes end up with a large collection of items to be stored and then made accessible.

To make it easier not only to store the items, but also to retrieve them, the personalization engine enables you to store your personalization properties in groups, as shown in Listing 14-4.

Available for download on Wrox.com

LISTING 14-4: Creating personalization groups in the web.config file

```
<configuration>
  <system.web>

     <profile>

        <properties>

           <add name="FirstName" />
           <add name="LastName" />
           <add name="LastVisited" />
           <add name="Age" />

           <group name="MemberDetails">
              <add name="Member" />
              <add name="DateJoined" />
              <add name="PaidDuesStatus" />
              <add name="Location" />
           </group>

           <group name="FamilyDetails">
              <add name="MarriedStatus" />
              <add name="DateMarried" />
              <add name="NumberChildren" />
              <add name="Location" />
           </group>

        </properties>

     </profile>

     <authentication mode="Windows" />

  </system.web>
</configuration>
```

From the code in Listing 14-4, which is placed within the `web.config` file, you can see that two groups are listed. The first group is the `MemberDetails` group, which has four specific items defined; the second group — `FamilyDetails` — has three other related items defined. Personalization groups are defined using the `<group>` element within the `<properties>` definition. The name of the group is specified using the `name` attribute, just as you specify the `<add>` element. You can have as many groups defined as you deem necessary or as have been recommended as good practice to employ.

Using Grouped Personalization Properties

From Listing 14-4, you can also see that some items are not defined in any particular group. Mixing properties defined from within a group with those that are not is possible. The items not defined in a group in Listing 14-4 can still be accessed in the manner illustrated previously:

```
Label1.Text = Profile.FirstName
```

Now, concerning working with personalization groups, you can access your defined items in a logical manner using nested namespaces:

```
Label1.Text = Profile.MemberDetails.DateJoined

Label2.Text = Profile.FamilyDetails.MarriedStatus
```

From this example, you can see that two separate items from each of the defined personalization groups were accessed in a logical manner. When you study the defined properties in the `web.config` file of your application, you can see that each of the groups in the example has a property with the same name — `Location`. This is possible because they are defined using personalization groups. With this structure, getting at each of the `Location` properties by specifying the appropriate group is now possible:

```
Label1.Text = Profile.MemberDetails.Location

Label2.Text = Profile.FamilyDetails.Location
```

Defining Types for Personalization Properties

By default, when you store personalization properties, these properties are created as type `System.String`. Changing the type to another type altogether through configuration settings within the `web.config` file is quite easy, however. To define the name of the personalization property along with its appropriate type, you use the `type` attribute of the `<add>` element contained within the `<properties>` section, as shown in Listing 14-5.

LISTING 14-5: Defining types for personalization properties

Available for download on Wrox.com

```
<properties>

   <add name="FirstName" type="System.String" />
   <add name="LastName" type="System.String" />
   <add name="LastVisited" type="System.DateTime" />
   <add name="Age" type="System.Int32" />
   <add name="Member" type="System.Boolean" />

</properties>
```

The first two properties, `FirstName` and `LastName`, are cast as type `System.String`. This is not actually required. Even if you omitted this step, they would still be cast as type `String` because that is the default type of any property defined in the personalization system (if no other type is defined). The next personalization property is the `LastVisited` property, which is defined as type `System.DateTime` and used to store the date and time of the end user's last visit to the page. Beyond that, you can see the rest of the personalization properties are defined using a specific .NET data type.

This approach is preferred because it gives you type-checking capabilities as you code your application and use the personalization properties you have defined.

Using Custom Types

As you can see from the earlier examples that show you how to define types for the personalization properties, defining and type casting properties to particular data types that are available in the .NET Framework is quite simple. Items such as `System.Integer`, `System.String`, `System.DateTime`, `System.Byte`, and `System.Boolean` are easily defined within the `web.config` file. But how do you go about defining complex types?

Personalization properties that utilize custom types are just as easy to define as personalization properties that use simple types. Custom types give you the capability to store complex items such as shopping cart information or other status information from one use of the application to the next. Listing 14-6 first shows a class, `ShoppingCart`, which you use later in one of the personalization property definitions.

LISTING 14-6: Creating a class to use as a personalization type

Available for download on Wrox.com

```
<Serializable()> _
Public Class ShoppingCart
    Private PID As String
    Private CompanyProductName As String
    Private Number As Integer
    Private Price As Decimal
    Private DateAdded As DateTime

    Public Property ProductID() As String
        Get
            Return PID
        End Get
        Set(ByVal value As String)
            PID = value
        End Set
    End Property

    Public Property ProductName() As String
        Get
            Return CompanyProductName
        End Get
        Set(ByVal value As String)
            CompanyProductName = value
        End Set
    End Property

    Public Property NumberSelected() As Integer
        Get
            Return Number
        End Get
        Set(ByVal value As Integer)
            Number = value
        End Set
    End Property

    Public Property ItemPrice() As Decimal
        Get
            Return Price
        End Get
        Set(ByVal value As Decimal)
            Price = value
        End Set
    End Property

    Public Property DateItemAdded() As DateTime
        Get
            Return DateAdded
        End Get
        Set(ByVal value As DateTime)
            DateAdded = value
        End Set
    End Property
End Class
```

```
using System;

[Serializable]
public class ShoppingCart
{
    private string PID;
    private string CompanyProductName;
```

continues

LISTING 14-6 *(continued)*

```
        private int Number;
        private decimal Price;
        private DateTime DateAdded;

        public ShoppingCart() {}

        public string ProductID
        {
            get {return PID;}
            set {PID = value;}
        }

        public string ProductName
        {
            get { return CompanyProductName; }
            set { CompanyProductName = value; }
        }

        public int NumberSelected
        {
            get { return Number; }
            set { Number = value; }
        }

        public decimal ItemPrice
        {
            get { return Price; }
            set { Price = value; }
        }

        public DateTime DateItemAdded
        {
            get { return DateAdded; }
            set { DateAdded = value; }
        }
    }
```

Filenames ShoppingCart.vb and ShoppingCart.cs

This simple shopping cart construction can now store the end user's shopping cart basket as the user moves around on an e-commerce site. The basket can even be persisted when the end user returns to the site at another time. Be sure to note that the class requires a `Serializable` attribute preceding the class declaration to ensure proper transformation to XML or binary.

Listing 14-7 shows how you would specify from within the `web.config` file that a personalization property is this complex type, such as a `ShoppingCart` type.

LISTING 14-7: Using complex types for personalization properties

```
<properties>

    <add name="FirstName" type="System.String" />
    <add name="LastName" type="System.String" />
    <add name="LastVisited" type="System.DateTime" />
    <add name="Age" type="System.Int32" />
    <add name="Member" type="System.Boolean" />
    <add name="Cart" type="ShoppingCart" serializeAs="Binary" />
</properties>
```

Just as the basic data types are stored in the personalization data stores, this construction allows you to easily store custom types and to have them serialized into the end data store in the format you choose.

In this case, the `ShoppingCart` object is serialized as a binary object into the data store. The `serializeAs` attribute can take the values defined in the following list:

- `Binary`: Serializes and stores the object as binary data within the chosen data store.
- `ProviderSpecific`: Stores the object based upon the direction of the provider. This simply means that instead of the personalization engine determining the serialization of the object, the serialization is simply left up to the personalization provider specified.
- `String`: The default setting. Stores the personalization properties as a string inside the chosen data store.
- `XML`: Takes the object and serializes it into an XML format before storing it in the chosen data store.

Providing Default Values

In addition to defining the data types of the personalization properties, you can also define their default values directly in the `web.config` file. By default, the personalization properties you create do not have a value, but you can easily change this using the `defaultValue` attribute of the `<add>` element. Listing 14-8 shows how to define default.

Available for download on Wrox.com

LISTING 14-8: Defining default values for personalization properties

```
<properties>

    <add name="FirstName" type="System.String" />
    <add name="LastName" type="System.String" />
    <add name="LastVisited" type="System.DateTime" />
    <add name="Age" type="System.Int32" />
    <add name="Member" type="System.Boolean" defaultValue="false" />
</properties>
```

From this example, you can see that only one of the personalization properties is provided with a default value. The last personalization property, `Member` in this example, is given a default value of `false`. This means that when you add a new end user to the personalization property database, `Member` is defined instead of remaining a blank value within the system.

Making Personalization Properties Read-Only

Making personalization properties read-only is also possible. To do it, you simply add the `readOnly` attribute to the `<add>` element:

```
<add name="StartDate" type="System.DateTime" readOnly="true" />
```

To make the personalization property a read-only property, you give the `readOnly` attribute a value of `true`. By default, this property is set to `false`.

ANONYMOUS PERSONALIZATION

A great feature in ASP.NET enables anonymous end users to utilize the personalization features it provides. This is important if a site requires registration of some kind. In these cases, end users do not always register for access to the greater application until they have first taken advantage of some of the basic services. For example, many e-commerce sites allow anonymous end users to shop a site and use the site's shopping cart before the shoppers register with the site.

Enabling Anonymous Identification of the End User

By default, anonymous personalization is turned off because it consumes database resources on popular sites. Therefore, one of the first steps in allowing anonymous personalization is to turn on this feature using the appropriate setting in the web.config file. You must also make some changes regarding how the properties are actually defined in the web.config file and to determine whether you are going to allow anonymous personalization for your application.

As shown in Listing 14-9, you can turn on anonymous identification to enable the personalization engine to identify the unknown end users using the <anonymousIdentification> element.

Available for download on Wrox.com

LISTING 14-9: Allowing anonymous identification

```
<configuration>
  <system.web>

       <anonymousIdentification enabled="true" />

  </system.web>
</configuration>
```

To enable anonymous identification of the end users who might visit your applications, you add an <anonymousIdentification> element to the web.config file within the <system.web> nodes. Then within the <anonymousIdentification> element, you use the enabled attribute and set its value to true. Remember that by default, this value is set to false.

When anonymous identification is turned on, ASP.NET uses a unique identifier for each anonymous user who comes to the application. This identifier is sent with each and every request, although after the end user becomes authenticated by ASP.NET, the identifier is removed from the process.

For an anonymous user, information is stored by default as a cookie on the end user's machine. Additional information (the personalization properties that you enable for anonymous users) is stored in the specified data store on the server.

To see the use of anonymous identification in action, turn off the Windows Authentication for your example application and, instead, use Forms Authentication. Listing 14-10 demonstrates this change.

Available for download on Wrox.com

LISTING 14-10: Turning off windows authentication and using forms authentication

```
<configuration>
  <system.web>

       <anonymousIdentification enabled="true" />

       <authentication mode="Forms" />

  </system.web>
</configuration>
```

With this code in place, if you run the page from the earlier example in Listing 14-2, you see the header presented in Listing 14-11.

LISTING 14-11: Setting an anonymous cookie in the HTTP header

```
HTTP/1.1 200 OK
Server: ASP.NET Development Server/10.0.0.0
Date: Sat, 11 Feb 2010 19:23:37 GMT
X-AspNet-Version: 4.0.21006
Set-Cookie:
.ASPXANONYMOUS=UH5CftJlxgEkAAAAZTJkN2I3YjUtZDhkOS00NDE2LWFlYjEtOTVjMjVmMzMxZWRmHoBU
As9A055rziDrMQ1Hu_fC_hM1; expires=Sat, 22-Apr-2010 06:03:36 GMT; path=/; HttpOnly
Cache-Control: private
Content-Type: text/html; charset=utf-8
Content-Length: 1419
Connection: Close
```

From this HTTP header, you can see that a cookie — .ASPXANONYMOUS — is set to a hashed value for later retrieval by the ASP.NET personalization system.

Changing the Name of the Cookie for Anonymous Identification

Cookies are used by default under the cookie name .ASPXANONYMOUS. You can change the name of this cookie from the <anonymousIdentification> element in the web.config file by using the cookieName attribute, as shown in Listing 14-12.

Available for download on Wrox.com

LISTING 14-12: Changing the name of the cookie

```
<configuration>
  <system.web>

       <anonymousIdentification
           enabled="true"
           cookieName=".ASPXEvjenWebApplication" />
  </system.web>
</configuration>
```

Changing the Length of Time the Cookie Is Stored

Also, by default, the cookie stored on the end user's machine is stored for 100,000 minutes (which is almost 70 days). If you want to change this value, you do it within this <anonymousIdentification> element using the cookieTimeout attribute, as shown in Listing 14-13.

Available for download on Wrox.com

LISTING 14-13: Changing the length of time the cookie is stored

```
<configuration>
  <system.web>

       <anonymousIdentification
           enabled="true"
           cookieTimeout="1440" />
  </system.web>
</configuration>
```

In this case, the cookieTimeout value was changed to 1440 — meaning 1,440 minutes (or one day). This setting would be ideal for something like a shopping cart where you do not want to persist the identification of the end user too long.

Changing How the Identifiers Are Stored

Although anonymous identifiers are stored through the use of cookies, you can also easily change this method. Cookies are, by far, the preferred way to achieve identification, but you can also do it without the use of cookies. Other options include using the URI or device profiles. Listing 14-14 shows an example of using the URI to place the identifiers.

Available for download on Wrox.com

LISTING 14-14: Specifying how cookies are stored

```
<configuration>
  <system.web>

       <anonymousIdentification
           enabled="true"
           cookieless="UseUri" />
  </system.web>
</configuration>
```

Besides UseUri, other options include UseCookies, AutoDetect, and UseDeviceProfile. The following list reviews each of the options:

- `UseCookies`: This setting is the default. If you set no value, ASP.NET assumes this is the value. `UseCookies` means that a cookie is placed on the end user's machine for identification.
- `UseUri`: This value means that a cookie *will not* be stored on the end user's machine, but instead the unique identifier will be munged within the URL of the page. This approach is the same one used for cookieless sessions in ASP.NET 1.0/1.1. Although this setting is great if developers want to avoid sticking a cookie on an end user's machine, it does create strange-looking URLs and can be an issue when an end user bookmarks pages for later retrieval.
- `AutoDetect`: Using this value means that you are letting the ASP.NET engine decide whether to use cookies or use the URL approach for the anonymous identification. This decision is made on a per-user basis and performs a little worse than the other two options. ASP.NET must check the end user before deciding which approach to use. My suggestion is to use `AutoDetect` instead of `UseUri` if you absolutely must allow for end users who have cookies turned off (which is rare these days).
- `UseDeviceProfile`: Configures the identifier for the device or browser that is making the request.

Looking at the Anonymous Identifiers Stored

In order to make the anonymous identifiers unique, a globally unique GUID is used. You can also now grab hold of this unique identifier for your own use. In order to retrieve the GUID, the `Request` object has been enhanced with an `AnonymousID` property. The `AnonymousID` property returns a value of type `String`, which you can use in your code, as shown here:

```
Label1.Text = Request.AnonymousID
```

Working with Anonymous Identification

In working with the creation of anonymous users, be aware of an important event that you can use from your `Global.asax` file for managing the process:

- `AnonymousIdentification_Creating`

By using the `AnonymousIdentification_Creating` event, you can work with the identification of the end user as it occurs. For example, if you do not want to use GUIDs for uniquely identifying the end user, you can change the identifying value from this event instead.

To do so, create the event using the event delegate of type `AnonymousIdentificationEventArgs`, as shown in Listing 14-15.

LISTING 14-15: Changing the unique identifier of the anonymous user

Available for download on Wrox.com

VB

```
Public Sub AnonymousIdentification_Creating(ByVal sender As Object, _
   ByVal e As AnonymousIDentificationEventArgs)

        e.AnonymousID = "Bubbles " & DateTime.Now()

End Sub
```

C#

```
public void AnonymousIdentification_Creating(object sender,
   AnonymousIDentificationEventArgs e)
{
       e.AnonymousID = "Bubbles " + DateTime.Now;
}
```

The `AnonymousIdentificationEventArgs` event delegate exposes an `AnonymousID` property that assigns the value used to uniquely identify the anonymous user. Now, instead of a GUID to uniquely identify the anonymous user as

```
d13fafec-244a-4d21-9137-b213236ebedb
```

the `AnonymousID` property is changed within the `AnonymousIdentification_Creating` event to

```
Bubbles 2/10/2010 2:07:33 PM
```

Anonymous Options for Personalization Properties

If you have tried to get the anonymous capability working, you might have received the error shown in Figure 14-4.

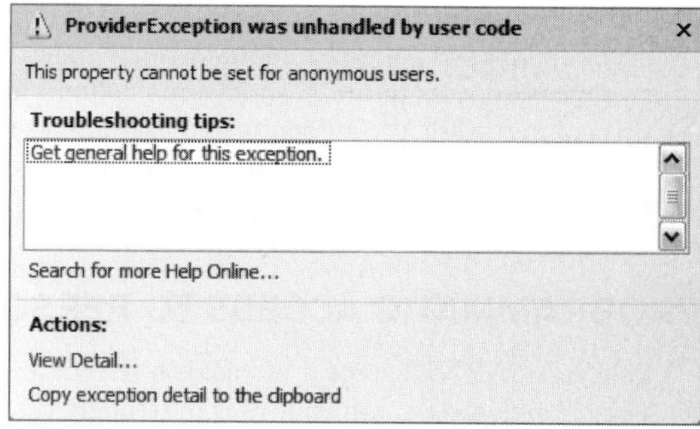

FIGURE 14-4

To get your application to work with anonymous users, you must specify which personalization properties you want to enable for the anonymous users visiting your pages. You can also do this through the `web.config` file by adding the `allowAnonymous` attribute to the `<add>` element of the properties you have defined within the `<properties>` section (see Listing 14-16).

LISTING 14-16: Turning on anonymous capabilities personalization properties

Available for download on Wrox.com

```
<properties>

   <add name="FirstName" type="System.String" />
   <add name="LastName" type="System.String" />
   <add name="LastVisited" type="System.DateTime" allowAnonymous="true" />
   <add name="Age" type="System.Integer" />
   <add name="Member" type="System.Boolean" />

</properties>
```

In this example, the `LastVisited` property is set to allow anonymous users by setting the `allowAnonymous` attribute to `true`. Because this property is the only one that works with anonymous users, the rest of the defined properties do not store information for these types of users. If you are still checking if the user is authenticated in your code, be sure to comment that out for these examples to work.

Warnings about Anonymous User Profile Storage

Taking into account everything said so far about anonymous users, you should be very careful about how you approach anonymous user profile storage. Storing profile information about anonymous users can dramatically populate the data store you are using. For example, in my examples, I used Microsoft's SQL Server Express Edition, and I stored profile information for one authenticated user and then for a single anonymous user. This puts information for both these users in the aspnet_Profile and the aspnet_Users table.

Figure 14-5 shows the two users listed in the aspnet_Users table.

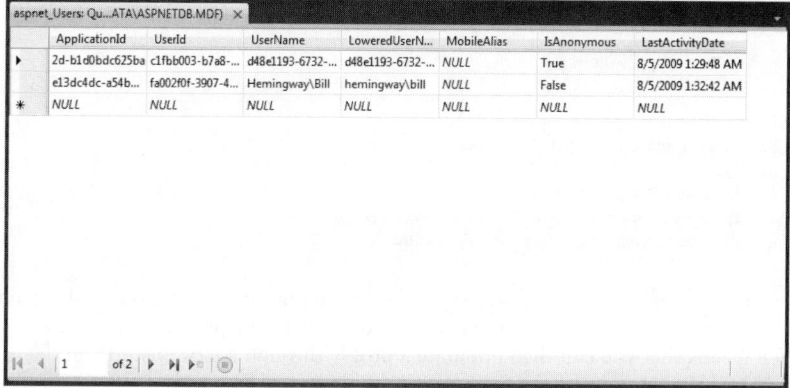

aspnet_Users: Qu...ATA\ASPNETDB.MDF)

	ApplicationId	UserId	UserName	LoweredUserN...	MobileAlias	IsAnonymous	LastActivityDate
▸	2d-b1d0bdc625ba	c1fbb003-b7a8-...	d48e1193-6732-...	d48e1193-6732-...	NULL	True	8/5/2009 1:29:48 AM
	e13dc4dc-a54b...	fa002f0f-3907-4...	Hemingway\Bill	hemingway\bill	NULL	False	8/5/2009 1:32:42 AM
*	NULL	NULL	NULL	NULL	NULL	NULL	NULL

1 of 2

FIGURE 14-5

In this figure, the anonymous user is the first line in the table, and you can see that this user has a rather cryptic name, which is the `Request.AnonymousID` presented earlier. The other big difference between the two users appears in the `IsAnonymous` column in the table. The anonymous user has a setting of `true` for this column while the authenticated user has a setting of `false`. Because your database can fill up quickly with anonymous user information, you should weigh which information you really must store on these types of users.

PROGRAMMATIC ACCESS TO PERSONALIZATION

When an ASP.NET page is invoked, ASP.NET creates a class (`ProfileCommon`) by inheriting from the `ProfileBase` class, which it uses to strongly type the profile properties that were defined in the `web.config` file. This created class, meant to deal with the user's profile store, gets and sets profile properties through the use of the `GetPropertyValue` and `SetPropertyValue` methods from the `ProfileBase` class.

As you would expect, ASP.NET provides you with the hooks necessary to get at specific `Profile` events using the `ProfileModule` class. The `ProfileModule` class is what ASP.NET itself uses to create and store profile information in the page's `Profile` object.

The `ProfileModule` class exposes three events that you can use to handle your user's profile situations. These events, `MigrateAnonymous`, `Personalize`, and `ProfileAutoSaving`, are focused around the area of authentication. Because you just saw how to work with anonymous users in your applications, this section now looks at how to migrate these users from anonymous users to authenticated users — because you are most likely going to want to move their profile properties as well as change their status.

Migrating Anonymous Users

When working with anonymous users, you must be able to migrate anonymous users to registered users. For example, after an end user fills a shopping cart, he can register on the site to purchase the items. At that moment, the end user switches from being an anonymous user to a registered user.

For this reason, ASP.NET provides a `Profile_MigrateAnonymous` event handler enabling you to migrate anonymous users to registered users. The `Profile_MigrateAnonymous` event requires a data class of type `ProfileMigrateEventArgs`. You place it either in the page that deals with the migration or within the `Global.asax` file (if it can be used from anywhere within the application). Listing 14-17 shows the use of this event.

LISTING 14-17: Migrating anonymous users for particular personalization properties

Available for download on Wrox.com

VB

```
Public Sub Profile_MigrateAnonymous(ByVal sender As Object, _
   ByVal e As ProfileMigrateEventArgs)

      Dim anonymousProfile As ProfileCommon = Profile.GetProfile(e.AnonymousID)
      Profile.LastVisited = anonymousProfile.LastVisited

End Sub
```

C#

```
public void Profile_MigrateAnonymous(object sender,
   ProfileMigrateEventArgs e)
{
      ProfileCommon anonymousProfile = Profile.GetProfile(e.AnonymousID);
      Profile.LastVisited = anonymousProfile.LastVisited
}
```

In this example, you create an instance of the `ProfileCommon` object and populate it with the profile from the visiting anonymous user. From there, you can use the instance to get at all the profile properties of that anonymous user, which means that you can then populate a profile through a movement from the anonymous user's profile information to the authenticated user's profile system.

Listing 14-17 shows how to migrate a single personalization property from an anonymous user to the new registered user. In addition to migrating single properties, you can also migrate properties that come from personalization groups, as shown in Listing 14-18.

LISTING 14-18: Migrating anonymous users for items in personalization groups

Available for download on Wrox.com

```
Public Sub Profile_MigrateAnonymous(ByVal sender As Object, _
   ByVal e As ProfileMigrateEventArgs)

      Dim au As ProfileCommon = Profile.GetProfile(e.AnonymousID)

      If au.MemberDetails.DateJoined <> "" Then
         Profile.MemberDetails.DateJoined = DateTime.Now().ToString()
         Profile.FamilyDetails.MarriedStatus = au.FamilyDetails.MarriedStatus
      End If

      AnonymousIdentificationModule.ClearAnonymousIdentifier()
End Sub
```

C#

```
public void Profile_MigrateAnonymous(object sender,
   ProfileMigrateEventArgs e)
{
      ProfileCommon au = Profile.GetProfile(e.AnonymousID);

      if (au.MemberDetails.DateJoined != String.Empty) {
         Profile.MemberDetails.DateJoined = DateTime.Now.ToString();
         Profile.FamilyDetails.MarriedStatus = au.FamilyDetails.MarriedStatus;
      }

      AnonymousIdentificationModule.ClearAnonymousIdentifier();
}
```

Using this event in the `Global.asax` file enables you to logically migrate anonymous users as they register themselves with your applications. The migration process also enables you to pick and choose which items you migrate and to change the values as you want.

Personalizing Profiles

Besides working with anonymous users from the `Global.asax` file, you can also programmatically personalize the profiles retrieved from the personalization store. You do so through the use of the `Profile_Personalize` event. Listing 14-19 demonstrates an example use of this event.

LISTING 14-19: Personalizing a retrieved profile

Available for download on Wrox.com

```
Public Sub Profile_Personalize(sender As Object, args As ProfileEventArgs)
  Dim checkedProfile As ProfileCommon

  If User Is Nothing Then Return

  checkedProfile = CType(ProfileBase.Create(User.Identity.Name), ProfileCommon)

  If (Date.Now.IsDaylightSavingTime()) Then
    checkedProfile = checkedProfile.GetProfile("TimeDifferenceUser")
  Else
    checkedProfile = checkedProfile.GetProfile("TimeUser")
  End If

  If Not checkedProfile Is Nothing Then
    args.Profile = checkedProfile
  End If
End Sub
```

C#

```
public void Profile_Personalize(object sender, ProfileEventArgs args)
```

continues

LISTING 14-19 *(continued)*

```
{
  ProfileCommon checkedProfile;

  if (User == null) { return; }

  checkedProfile = (ProfileCommon)ProfileBase.Create(User.Identity.Name);

  if (DateTime.Now.IsDaylightSavingTime()) {
    checkedProfile = checkedProfile.GetProfile("TimeDifferenceUser");
  }
  else {
    checkedProfile = checkedProfile.GetProfile("TimeUser");
  }

  if (checkedProfile != null) {
    args.Profile = checkedProfile;
  }
}
```

In this case, based on a specific parameter (whether it is Daylight Savings Time or something else), you are able to assign a specific profile to the user. You do this by using the `ProfileModule.Personalize` event, which you would usually stick inside the `Global.asax` page.

Determining Whether to Continue with Automatic Saves

When you are working with the profile capabilities provided by ASP.NET, the page automatically saves the profile values to the specified data store at the end of the page's execution. This capability, which is turned on (set to `true`) by default, can be set to `false` through the use of the `automaticSaveEnabled` attribute in the `<profile>` node in the `web.config` file, as shown in Listing 14-20.

LISTING 14-20: Working with the automaticSaveEnabled attribute

Available for download on Wrox.com

```
<profile automaticSaveEnabled="false">

  <properties>

     <add name="FirstName" />
     <add name="LastName" />
     <add name="LastVisited" />
     <add name="Age" />
     <add name="Member" />

  </properties>

</profile>
```

If you have set the `automaticSaveEnabled` attribute value to `false`, you will have to invoke the `ProfileBase.Save()` method yourself. In most cases though, you are going to leave this setting on `true`. After a page request has been made and finalized, the `ProfileModule.ProfileAutoSaving` event is raised. You can also work with this event, as shown in Listing 14-21. You would place this event in the `Global.asax` file.

LISTING 14-21: Using the profileautosaving event to turn off the auto-saving feature

Available for download on Wrox.com

VB

```
Public Sub Profile_ProfileAutoSaving(sender As Object,
 args As ProfileAutoSaveEventArgs)

  If Profile.PaidDueStatus.HasChanged Then
    args.ContinueWithProfileAutoSave = True
```

```
    Else
      args.ContinueWithProfileAutoSave = False
    End If
  End Sub
```

C#

```
public void Profile_ProfileAutoSaving(object sender, ProfileAutoSaveEventArgs args)
{
  if (Profile.PaidDueStatus.HasChanged)
    args.ContinueWithProfileAutoSave = true;
  else
    args.ContinueWithProfileAutoSave = false;
}
```

In this case, when the `Profile_ProfileAutoSaving` event is triggered, you can then work within this event and change some behaviors. Listing 14-21 looks to see whether the `Profile.PaidDueStatus` property has changed. If it has changed, the auto-saving feature of the profile system is continued; if the `Profile.PaidDueStatus` has not changed, the auto-saving feature is turned off.

PERSONALIZATION PROVIDERS

As shown in Figure 14-1 earlier in the chapter, the middle tier of the personalization model, the personalization API layer, communicates with a series of default data providers. By default, the personalization model uses Microsoft SQL Server Express Edition files for storing the personalization properties you define. You are not limited to just this type of data store, however. You can also use the Microsoft SQL Server data provider to allow you to work with Microsoft SQL Server 7.0, 2000, 2005, and SQL Server 2008. Besides the Microsoft SQL Server data provider, the architecture also allows you to create your own data providers if one of these data stores does not fit your requirements.

Working with SQL Server Express Edition

The Microsoft SQL Server data provider does allow you to work with your SQL Server Express Edition files. The SQL Server data provider is the default provider used by the personalization system provided by ASP.NET. When used with Visual Studio 2010, the IDE places the `ASPNETDB.MDF` file within your application's App_Data folder.

As you look through the `machine.config` file, notice the sections that deal with how the personalization engine works with this database. In the first reference to the `LocalSqlServer` file, you find a connection string to this file (shown in Listing 14-22) within the `<connectionStrings>` section of the file.

Available for download on Wrox.com

LISTING 14-22: Adding a connection string to the SQL Server Express file

```
<configuration>

    <connectionStrings>
        <clear />
        <add name="LocalSqlServer"
         connectionString="data source=.\SQLEXPRESS;Integrated Security=SSPI;
         AttachDBFilename=|DataDirectory|aspnetdb.mdf;User Instance=true"
         providerName="System.Data.SqlClient" />
    </connectionStrings>

</configuration>
```

In this example, you see that a connection string with the name `LocalSqlServer` has been defined. The location of the file, specified by the `connectionString` attribute, points to the relative path of the file. This means that in every application you build that utilizes the personalization capabilities, the default SQL Server provider should be located in the application's App_Data folder and have the name of `ASPNETDB.MDF`.

The SQL Server Express file's connection string is specified through the `LocalSqlServer` declaration within this `<connectionStrings>` section. You can see the personalization engine's reference to this in the

<profile> section within the machine.config file. The <profile> section includes a subsection listing all the providers available to the personalization engine, as shown in Listing 14-23.

Available for download on Wrox.com

LISTING 14-23: Adding a new SQL Server data provider

```
<configuration>
  <system.web>

        <profile>
            <providers>
                <add name="AspNetSqlProfileProvider"
                 connectionStringName="LocalSqlServer" applicationName="/"
                 type="System.Web.Profile.SqlProfileProvider, System.Web,
                   Version=4.0.0.0, Culture=neutral,
                   PublicKeyToken=b03f5f7f11d50a3a" />
            </providers>
        </profile>

  </system.web>
</configuration>
```

From this, you can see that you add a provider by using the <add> element. Within this element, the connectionStringName attribute points to what was declared in the <connectionString> attribute from Listing 14-22.

You can specify an entirely different Microsoft SQL Server Express Edition file other than the one specified in the machine.config file. Create a connection string that points to a new SQL Server Express file that is a templated version of the ASPNETDB.mdb file. At this point, you can use <connectionString> to point to this new file. If you change these values in the machine.config file, all the ASP.NET applications that reside on the server will then use this specified file. If you make the changes only to the web.config file, however, only the application using this particular web.config file uses this new data store. Other applications on the server remain unchanged.

Working with Microsoft's SQL Server 7.0/2000/2005/2008

You will likely find working with the personalization framework using the SQL Server Express files quite easy. But when you work with larger applications that require the factors of performance and reliability, you should use the SQL Server personalization provider along with SQL Server 7.0, 2000, 2005, or 2008. If this data store is available, you should always try to use this option instead of the default SQL Server Express Edition files.

If you worked with the SQL Server personalization provider using SQL Server Express files as explained earlier, you probably found it easy to use. The personalization provider works right out of the box — without any setup or configuration on your part. Using the SQL Server personalization provider with a full-blown version of SQL Server, however, is a bit of a different story. Although working with it is not difficult, you must set up and configure your SQL Server before using it.

ASP.NET 4 provides a couple of ways to set up and configure SQL Server for the personalization framework. One way is through the ASP.NET SQL Server Setup Wizard, and the other is by running some of the SQL Server scripts provided with the .NET Framework 4.

Chapter 11 covers using the ASP.NET SQL Server Setup Wizard in detail.

To use the ASP.NET SQL Server Setup Wizard to set up your SQL Server for the ASP.NET 4 personalization features, open the aspnet_regsql.exe tool by invoking it from the Visual Studio 2010 Command Prompt. You open this command prompt by selecting Start ➪ All Programs ➪ Visual Studio 2010 ➪ Visual Studio

Tools ➪ Visual Studio 2010 Command Prompt. At the prompt, type in **aspnet_regsql.exe** to open the GUI of the ASP.NET SQL Server Setup Wizard. If you step through the wizard, you can set up your SQL Server instance for many of the ASP.NET systems, such as the personalization system.

Using SQL Scripts to Install Personalization Features

Another option for setting up and configuring SQL Server for the personalization framework is to use the same SQL scripts that these tools and wizards use. If you look at `C:\WINDOWS\Microsoft.NET\Framework\v4.0.xxxxx\`, from this location, you can see the install and remove scripts — `InstallPersonalization.sql` and `UninstallPersonalization.sql`. Running these scripts provides your database with the tables needed to run the personalization framework. Be forewarned that you must run the `InstallCommon.sql` script before running the personalization script (or any of the new other ASP.NET system scripts).

Configuring the Provider for SQL Server 2008

After you have set up your SQL Server database for the personalization system, the next step is to redefine the personalization provider so that it works with this instance (instead of with the default Microsoft SQL Server Express Edition files).

You accomplish this step in the `web.config` file of your application. Here, you want to configure the provider and then define this provider instance as the provider to use. Listing 14-24 shows these additions plus the enlarged `<profile>` section of the `web.config` file.

LISTING 14-24: Connecting the SqlProfileProvider to SQL Server 2008

Available for download on Wrox.com

```
<configuration>

     <connectionStrings>
        <add name="LocalSql2008Server"
         connectionString="data source=127.0.0.1;Integrated Security=SSPI" />
     </connectionStrings>

     <profile defaultProvider="AspNetSql2008ProfileProvider">
        <providers>
           <clear />
           <add name="AspNetSql2008ProfileProvider"
            connectionStringName="LocalSql2008Server" applicationName="/"
            type="System.Web.Profile.SqlProfileProvider, System.Web,
              Version=4.0.0.0, Culture=neutral,
              PublicKeyToken=b03f5f7f11d50a3a" />
        </providers>

        <properties>
           <add name="FirstName" />
           <add name="LastName" />
           <add name="LastVisited" />
           <add name="Age" />
           <add name="Member" />
        </properties>
     </profile>

</configuration>
```

The big change you make to this profile definition is to use the `defaultProvider` attribute with a value that is the name of the provider you want to use — in this case the newly created SQL Server provider `AspNetSql2008ProfileProvider`. You can also make this change to the `machine.config` file by changing the `<profile>` element, as shown in Listing 14-25.

LISTING 14-25: Using SQL Server as the provider in the machine.config file

Available for download on Wrox.com

```
<configuration>
  <system.web>

     ...

     <profile enabled="true" defaultProvider="AspNetSql2008ProfileProvider">

     ...

     </profile>

     ...

  </system.web>
</configuration>
```

This change forces each and every application that resides on this server to use this new SQL Server provider instead of the default SQL Server provider (unless this command is overridden in the application's `web.config` file).

Using Multiple Providers

You are not limited to using a single data store or provider. Instead, you can use any number of providers. You can even specify the personalization provider for each property defined. This means that you can use the default provider for most properties, as well as allowing a few of them to use an entirely different provider (see Listing 14-26).

LISTING 14-26: Using different providers

Available for download on Wrox.com

```
<configuration>
  <system.web>

     <profile
     defaultProvider="AspNetSqlProvider">
              <properties>

                  <add name="FirstName" />
                  <add name="LastName" />
                  <add name="LastVisited" />
                  <add name="Age" />
                  <add name="Member" provider="AspNetSql2008ProfileProvider" />
              </properties>

       </profile>

  </system.web>
</configuration>
```

From this example, you can see that a default provider is specified — `AspNetSqlProvider`. Unless another provider is specified, this provider is used. The only property that changes this setting is the property `Member`. The `Member` property uses an entirely different personalization provider. In this case, it employs the Access provider (`AspNetSql2008ProfileProvider`) through the use of the `provider` attribute of the `<add>` element. With this attribute, you can define a specific provider for each and every property that is defined.

MANAGING APPLICATION PROFILES

When you put into production an ASP.NET application that uses profile information, you quickly realize that you need a way to manage all the profile information collected over the lifecycle of the application. As you look at the ASP.NET MMC snap-in or the ASP.NET Web Site Administration Tool, note that neither of these tools gives you a way to delete a specific user's profile information or even to cleanse a database of profile information for users who haven't been active in a while.

ASP.NET 4 gives you the means to manage the profile information that your application stores, through the use of the `ProfileManager` class available in .NET.

Through the use of the `ProfileManager` class, you can build in the administration capabilities to completely manage the profile information that is stored by your application. In addition to being able to access property values, such as the name of the provider being used by the personalization system or the name of the application in question, you also have a large number of methods available in the `ProfileManager` class to retrieve all sorts of other information concerning your user's profile. Through the `ProfileManager` class, you also have the capability to perform actions on this stored profile information including cleansing the database of old profile information.

Properties of the ProfileManager Class

Table 14-1 details the properties of the `ProfileManager` class.

TABLE 14-1

PROPERTIES	DESCRIPTION
`ApplicationName`	Gets or sets the name of the application to work with
`AutomaticSaveEnabled`	Gets or sets a Boolean value indicating whether the profile information is stored at the end of the page execution
`Enabled`	Gets or sets a Boolean value indicating whether the application is able to use the personalization system
`Provider`	Gets the name of the provider being used for the personalization system
`Providers`	Gets a collection of all the providers available for the ASP.NET application

You can see that these properties include a bit of information about the personalization system and the providers available to it that you can integrate into any management system you build. Next, this chapter looks at the methods available for the `ProfileManager` class.

Methods of the ProfileManager Class

A good number of methods are available to the `ProfileManager` class that help you manage the profiles of the users of your application. Table 14-2 briefly describes these methods.

TABLE 14-2

METHODS	DESCRIPTION
`DeleteInactiveProfiles`	Provides you with the capability to delete any profiles that haven't seen any activity for a specified time period
`DeleteProfile`	Provides you with the capability to delete a specific profile
`DeleteProfiles`	Provides you with the capability to delete a collection of profiles
`FindInactiveProfilesBy UserName`	Provides you with all the inactive profiles under a specific username according to a specified date
`FindProfilesByUserName`	Provides you with all the profiles from a specific username
`GetAllInactiveProfiles`	Provides you with all the profiles that have been inactive since a specified date
`GetAllProfiles`	Provides you with a collection of all the profiles
`GetNumberOf InactiveProfiles`	Provides you with the number of inactive profiles from a specified date
`GetNumberOfProfiles`	Provides you with the number of total profiles in the system

As you can see from this list of methods, you can do plenty to manage the profile information that is stored in your database.

Next, this chapter looks at building a profile manager administration page for your ASP.NET application. This example builds it as an ASP.NET page, but you can just as easily build it as a console application.

Building the ProfileManager.aspx Page

To create a simple profile manager for your application, create a single ASP.NET page in your application called `ProfileManager.aspx`. You use this page to manage the profiles that are stored in the database for this particular application.

This page includes a number of controls, but the most important is a DropDownList control that holds all the usernames of entities that have profile information in the database. You might see the same username a couple of times depending on what you are doing with your application. Remember that a single user can have multiple profiles in the database.

Using the DropDownList control, you can select a user and see information about his profile stored in your data store. From this page, you can also delete his profile information. You can actually perform many operations with the `ProfileManager` class, but this is a good example of some basic ones.

Listing 14-27 presents the code for the `ProfileManager.aspx`.

LISTING 14-27: The ProfileManager.aspx page

Available for download on Wrox.com

VB

```
<%@ Page Language="VB" %>

<script runat="server">
    Protected Sub Page_Load(ByVal sender As Object, ByVal e As System.EventArgs)
        If (DropDownList1.Items.Count = 0) Then
            WriteDropdownList()
            WriteUserOutput()
        End If
    End Sub

    Protected Sub DeleteButton_Click(ByVal sender As Object,
      ByVal e As System.EventArgs)
        ProfileManager.DeleteProfile(DropDownList1.Text.ToString())
        DropDownList1.Items.Clear()
        WriteDropdownList()
        WriteUserOutput()
    End Sub

    Protected Sub SelectButton_Click(ByVal sender As Object,
      ByVal e As System.EventArgs)
        WriteUserOutput()
    End Sub

    Protected Sub WriteUserOutput()
        Dim outputInt As Integer
        Dim pic As ProfileInfoCollection = New ProfileInfoCollection()
        pic = ProfileManager.
          FindProfilesByUserName(ProfileAuthenticationOption.All,
          DropDownList1.Text.ToString(), 0, 1, outputInt)

        DetailsView1.DataSource = pic
        DetailsView1.DataBind()
    End Sub

    Protected Sub WriteDropdownList()
        Dim outputInt As Integer
        Dim pic As ProfileInfoCollection = New ProfileInfoCollection()
```

```
        pic = ProfileManager.Provider.
           GetAllProfiles(ProfileAuthenticationOption.All, 0, 10000, outputInt)

        For Each proInfo As ProfileInfo In pic
            Dim li As ListItem = New ListItem()
            li.Text = proInfo.UserName.ToString()

            DropDownList1.Items.Add(li)
        Next

        Label1.Text = outputInt.ToString()
    End Sub
</script>

<html xmlns="http://www.w3.org/1999/xhtml" >
<head id="Head1" runat="server">
    <title>ProfileAdmin Page</title>
</head>
<body>
    <form id="form1" runat="server">
    <div>
        <b>Profile Manager<br />
        </b>
        <br />
        Total number of users in system:
        <asp:Label ID="Label1" runat="server"></asp:Label><br />
         <br />
        <asp:DropDownList ID="DropDownList1" runat="server">
        </asp:DropDownList> 
        <asp:Button ID="SelectButton" runat="server"
         OnClick="SelectButton_Click"
            Text="Get User Profile Information" /><br />
        <br />
        <asp:DetailsView ID="DetailsView1" runat="server" CellPadding="4"
         ForeColor="#333333" GridLines="None"
            Height="50px">
            <FooterStyle BackColor="#1C5E55" Font-Bold="True" ForeColor="White" />
            <EditRowStyle BackColor="#7C6F57" />
            <PagerStyle BackColor="#666666" ForeColor="White"
             HorizontalAlign="Center" />
            <HeaderStyle BackColor="#1C5E55" Font-Bold="True" ForeColor="White" />
            <AlternatingRowStyle BackColor="White" />
            <CommandRowStyle BackColor="#C5BBAF" Font-Bold="True" />
            <RowStyle BackColor="#E3EAEB" />
            <FieldHeaderStyle BackColor="#D0D0D0" Font-Bold="True" />
        </asp:DetailsView>
        <br />
        <asp:Button ID="DeleteButton" runat="server"
         Text="Delete Selected User's Profile Information"
         OnClick="DeleteButton_Click" />
    </div>
    </form>
</body>
</html>
```

C#

```
<%@ Page Language="C#" %>

<script runat="server">

    protected void Page_Load(object sender, EventArgs e)
    {
        if (DropDownList1.Items.Count == 0)
```

continues

LISTING 14-27 *(continued)*

```
        {
            WriteDropdownList();
            WriteUserOutput();
        }
    }

    protected void DeleteButton_Click(object sender, EventArgs e)
    {
        ProfileManager.DeleteProfile(DropDownList1.Text.ToString());
        DropDownList1.Items.Clear();
        WriteDropdownList();
        WriteUserOutput();
    }

    protected void SelectButton_Click(object sender, EventArgs e)
    {
        WriteUserOutput();
    }

    protected void WriteUserOutput()
    {
        int outputInt;
        ProfileInfoCollection pic = new ProfileInfoCollection();
        pic = ProfileManager.FindProfilesByUserName
           (ProfileAuthenticationOption.All,
            DropDownList1.Text.ToString(), 0, 1, out outputInt);

        DetailsView1.DataSource = pic;
        DetailsView1.DataBind();
    }

    protected void WriteDropdownList()
    {
        int outputInt;
        ProfileInfoCollection pic = ProfileManager.Provider.GetAllProfiles
           (ProfileAuthenticationOption.All, 0, 10000, out outputInt);

        foreach (ProfileInfo proInfo in pic)
        {
            ListItem li = new ListItem();
            li.Text = proInfo.UserName.ToString();

            DropDownList1.Items.Add(li);
        }

        Label1.Text = outputInt.ToString();
    }
</script>
```

Examining the ProfileManager.aspx Page's Code

As you look over the code of the `ProfileManager.aspx` page, note that the `ProfileManager` class is used to perform a couple of different operations.

The `ProfileManager` class's `GetAllProfiles()` method is used to populate the DropDownList control that is on the page. Here is the constructor of this method:

```
GetAllProfiles(
   authenticationOption,
   pageIndex,
   pageSize,
   totalRecords)
```

The `GetAllProfiles()` method takes a number of parameters, the first of which allows you to define whether you are using this method for *all* profiles in the system, or just the anonymous or authenticated user's profiles contained in the system. In this example, all the profiles are retrieved with this method. This is accomplished using the `ProfileAuthenticationOption` enumeration. Then, the other parameters of the `GetAllProfiles()` method require you to specify a page index and the number of records to retrieve from the database. There is not a *get all* option (because of the potential size of the data that might be retrieved); so instead, in this example, you specify the first page of data (using `0`) and that this page contains the first 10,000 records (which is basically a *get all* for this application). The last parameter of the `GetAllProfiles()` method enables you to retrieve the count of the records if you want to use that anywhere within your application or if you want to use that number to iterate through the records. The `ProfileManager.aspx` page uses this number to display within the `Label1` server control.

In return from the `GetAllProfiles()` method, you get a `ProfileInfoCollection` object, which is a collection of `ProfileInfo` objects. Iterating through all the `ProfileInfo` objects in the `ProfileInfoCollection`, you are able to pull out some of the main properties for a particular user's profile information. In this example, just the `UserName` property of the `ProfileInfo` object is used to populate the DropDownList control on the page.

When the end user selects one of the users from the drop-down list, the `FindProfilesByUserName()` method is used to display the profile of the selected user. Again, a `ProfileInfoCollection` object is returned from this method as well.

To delete the profile of the user selected in the DropDownList control, simply use the `DeleteProfile()` method and pass in the name of the selected user like so:

```
ProfileManager.DeleteProfile(DropDownList1.Text.ToString())
DropDownList1.Items.Clear()
WriteDropdownList()
WriteUserOutput()
```

After you delete the profile from the system, that name will not appear in the drop-down list anymore (because the DropDownList control has been redrawn). If you look in the database, particularly at the aspnet_Profile table, you see that the profile of the selected user is, in fact, deleted. However, also notice that the user (even if the user is anonymous) is still stored in the aspnet_Users table.

If you want to delete not only the profile information of the user but also delete the user from the aspnet_Users table, you invoke the `DeleteUser()` method from the `Membership` class:

```
ProfileManager.DeleteProfile(DropDownList1.Text.ToString())
Membership.DeleteUser(DropDownList1.Text.ToString())
DropDownList1.Items.Clear()
WriteDropdownList()
WriteUserOutput()
```

This use of the `DeleteUser()` method also deletes the selected user from the aspnet_Users table. You could have also achieved the same thing by using the other constructor of the `DeleteUser()` method:

```
Membership.DeleteUser(DropDownList1.Text.ToString(), True)
DropDownList1.Items.Clear()
WriteDropdownList()
WriteUserOutput()
```

The second parameter used in this operation of the `DeleteUser()` method deletes all data related to that user across *all* the tables held in the `ASPNETDB.mdf` database.

Running the ProfileManager.aspx Page

When you compile and run the ProfileManager.aspx page, you see results similar to those shown in Figure 14-6.

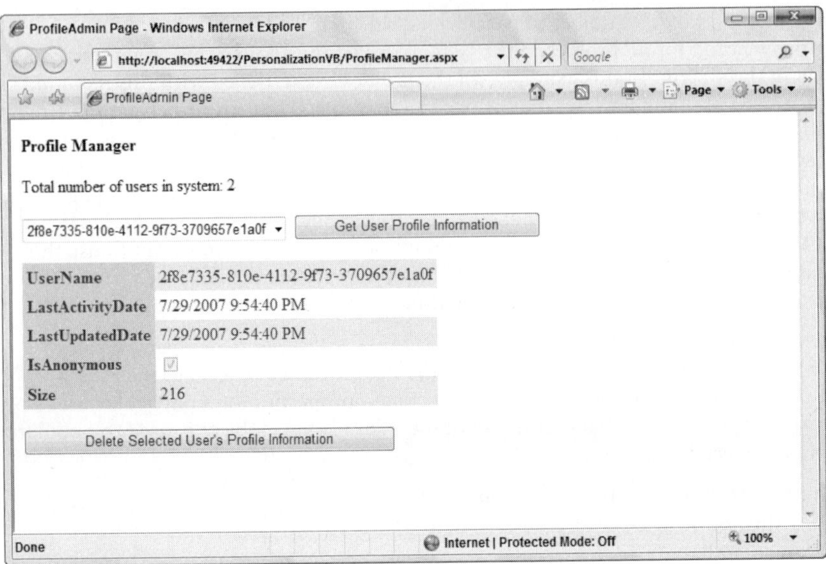

FIGURE 14-6

From this screen, you can see that this page is dealing with an anonymous user (based upon the GUID for the username). You can also see that the `IsAnonymous` column is indeed checked. From this page, you can then delete this user's profile information by selecting the appropriate button on the page.

SUMMARY

The personalization capabilities provided by ASP.NET 4 make it incredibly easy to make your Web applications unique for all end users, whether they are authenticated or anonymous. This system enables you to store everything from basic data types provided by the .NET Framework to custom types that you create. This system is more versatile and extensible than using the `Session` or `Application` objects. The data is stored via a couple of built-in personalization providers that ship with ASP.NET. These providers include ones that connect with either Microsoft's SQL Server Express Edition files or Microsoft SQL Server 2008, 2005, 2000, or 7.0.

You can also use the `ProfileManager` class to manage your system's profile information. This includes the capability to monitor and delete profiles as you deem necessary.

15

Membership and Role Management

WHAT'S IN THIS CHAPTER?

- Managing ASP.NET 4 authentication and authorization
- Adding and managing roles
- Working with ASP.NET Login server controls
- Creating a customized registration process
- Reviewing the Membership and Roles APIs and the controls that utilize them

The authentication and authorization of users are important functions in many Web sites and browser-based applications. Traditionally, when working with Microsoft's Windows Forms applications (thick-client), you depended on Windows Integrated Authentication; when working with browser-based applications (thin-client), you used forms authentication.

Forms authentication enabled you to take requests that were not yet authenticated and redirect them to an HTML form using HTTP client-side redirection. The user provided his login information and submitted the form. After the application authenticated the request, the user received an HTTP cookie, which was then used on any subsequent requests. This kind of authentication was fine in many ways, but it required developers to build every element and even manage the back-end mechanics of the overall system. This task was daunting for many developers and, in most cases, it was rather time-consuming.

ASP.NET 4 includes an authentication and authorization management service that takes care of the login, authentication, authorization, and management of users who require access to your Web pages or applications. This outstanding *membership and role management service* is an easy-to-implement framework that works out of the box using Microsoft SQL Server as the backend data store. This framework also includes an API that allows for programmatic access to the capabilities of both the membership and role management services. In addition, a number of membership and role management–focused server controls make it easy to create Web applications that incorporate everything these services have to offer.

Before you look at the membership and role management features of ASP.NET 4, understanding the basic principles of authentication and authorization is vital. The following provides a quick review:

- **Authentication** is a process that determines the identity of a user. After a user has been authenticated, a developer can determine whether the identified user has *authorization* to proceed. Giving an entity authorization if no authentication process has been applied is impossible. Authentication is provided in ASP.NET 4 using the membership service.
- **Authorization** is the process of determining whether an authenticated user is allowed access to any part of an application, access to specific points of an application, or access only to specific datasets that the application provides. When you authenticate and authorize users or groups, you can customize a site based on user types or preferences. Authorization is provided in ASP.NET 4 using a role management service.

ASP.NET 4 AUTHENTICATION

ASP.NET 4 provides the membership management service to deal with authenticating users to access a page or an entire site. The ASP.NET management service not only provides an API suite for managing users, but it also gives you some server controls, which in turn work with this API. These server controls work with the end user through the process of authentication. You look at the functionality of these controls shortly.

Setting Up Your Web Site for Membership

Before you can use the security controls that are provided with ASP.NET 4, you first have to set up your application to work with the membership service. How you do this depends on how you approach the security framework provided.

By default, ASP.NET 4 uses the built-in `SqlMembershipProvider` instance for storing details about the registered users of your application. For the initial demonstrations, the examples in this chapter work with forms-based authentication. You can assume for these examples that the application is on the public Internet and, therefore, is open to the public for registration and viewing. If it were an intranet-based application (meaning that all the users are on a private network), you could use Windows Integrated Authentication for authenticating users.

ASP.NET 4, as you know, offers a data provider model that handles the detailed management required to interact with multiple types of underlying data stores. Figure 15-1 shows a diagram of the ASP.NET 4 membership service.

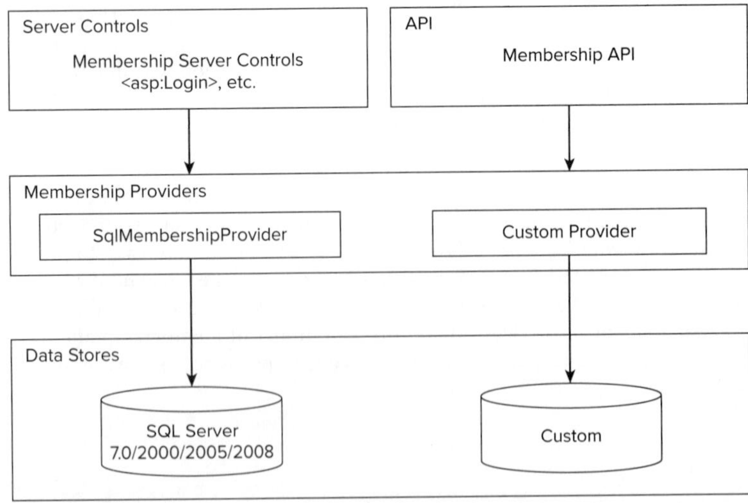

FIGURE 15-1

From the diagram, you can see that, like the rest of the ASP.NET provider models, the membership providers can access a wide variety of underlying data stores. In this diagram, you can see the built-in Microsoft SQL Server data store. You can also build your own membership providers to get at any other custom data stores that work with user credentials. Above the membership providers in the diagram, you can see a collection of security-focused server controls that utilize the access granted by the underlying membership providers to work with the users in the authentication process.

Adding an <authentication> Element to the web.config File

To have the forms authentication element in your Web application work with the membership service, the first step is to turn on forms authentication within the `web.config` file. To do so, create a `web.config` file (if you do not already have one in your application). Next, add the section shown in Listing 15-1 to this file.

Available for download on Wrox.com

LISTING 15-1: Adding forms authentication to the web.config file

```
<?xml version="1.0" encoding="utf-8"?>
<configuration>
    <system.web>
        <authentication mode="Forms" />
    </system.web>
</configuration>
```

The simple addition of the `<authentication>` element to the `web.config` file turns on everything that you need to start using the membership service provided by ASP.NET 4. To turn on the forms authentication using this element, you simply give the value `Forms` to the `mode` attribute. This is a forms authentication example, but other possible values of the `mode` attribute include `Windows`, `Passport`, or `None`.

IIS authentication schemes include basic, digest, and Integrated Windows Authentication. Passport authentication points to a centralized service provided by Microsoft that offers a single login and core profile service for any member sites. It costs money to use Passport, which has also been deprecated by Microsoft.

Because the `mode` attribute in our example is set to `Forms`, you can move on to the next step of adding users to the data store. You can also change the behavior of the forms authentication system at this point by making some modifications to the `web.config` file. These possibilities are reviewed next.

Adding a <forms> Element to the web.config File

Using forms authentication, you can provide users with access to a site or materials based upon credentials they input into a Web-based form. When an end user attempts to access a Web site, he is entering the site using anonymous authentication, which is the default authentication mode. If he is found to be anonymous, he can be redirected (by ASP.NET) to a specified login page. After the end user inputs the appropriate login information and passes the authentication process, he is provided with an HTTP cookie, which can be used in any subsequent requests.

You can modify the behavior of the forms-based authentication by defining that behavior within a `<forms>` section in the `web.config` file. You can see the possibilities of the forms authentication setting in Listing 15-2, which shows possible changes to the `<forms>` section in the `web.config` file.

Available for download on Wrox.com

LISTING 15-2: Modifying the form's authentication behavior

```
<?xml version="1.0" encoding="utf-8"?>
<configuration>
    <system.web>
        <authentication mode="Forms">
            <forms name=".ASPXAUTH"
                   loginUrl="Login.aspx"
                   protection="All"
```

continues

LISTING 15-2 *(continued)*

```
                    timeout="30"
                    path="/"
                    requireSSL="false"
                    slidingExpiration="true"
                    cookieless="UseDeviceProfile" />
        </authentication>
    </system.web>
</configuration>
```

You can set these as you want, and you have plenty of options for values other than the ones that are displayed. Also, as stated earlier, these values are not required. You can use the membership service right away with only the configuration setting that is shown in Listing 15-1.

You can find some interesting settings in Listing 15-2, however. You can really change the behavior of the forms authentication system by adding this `<forms>` element to the `web.config` file. If you do this, however, make sure that you have the `<forms>` element nested within the `<authentication>` elements. The following list describes the possible attributes of the `<forms>` element:

- `name`: Defines the name used for the cookie sent to end users after they have been authenticated. By default, this cookie is named `.ASPXAUTH`.
- `loginUrl`: Specifies the page location to which the HTTP request is redirected for logging in the user if no valid authentication cookie (`.ASPXAUTH` or otherwise) is found. By default, it is set to `Login.aspx`.
- `protection`: Specifies the amount of protection that you want to apply to the cookie that is stored on the end user's machine after he has been authenticated. The possible settings include `All`, `None`, `Encryption`, and `Validation`. You should always attempt to use `All`.
- `timeout`: Defines the amount of time (in minutes) after which the cookie expires. The default value is 30 minutes.
- `path`: Specifies the path for cookies issued by the application.
- `requireSSL`: Defines whether you require that credentials be sent over an encrypted wire (SSL) instead of clear text.
- `slidingExpiration`: Specifies whether the timeout of the cookie is on a sliding scale. The default value is `true`. This means that the end user's cookie does not expire until 30 minutes (or the time specified in the `timeout` attribute) after the last request to the application has been made. If the value of the `slidingExpiration` attribute is set to `false`, the cookie expires 30 minutes from the first request.
- `cookieless`: Specifies how the cookies are handled by ASP.NET. The possible values include `UseDeviceProfile`, `UseCookies`, `AutoDetect`, and `UseUri`. The default value is `UseDeviceProfile`. This value detects whether to use cookies based on the user agent of the device. `UseCookies` requires that all requests have the credentials stored in a cookie. `AutoDetect` auto-determines whether the details are stored in a cookie on the client or within the URI (this is done by sending a test cookie first). Finally, `UseUri` forces ASP.NET to store the details within the URI on all instances.

Now that forms authentication is turned on, the next step is adding users to the Microsoft SQL Server Express Edition data store, `ASPNETDB.mdf`.

Adding Users

To add users to the membership service, you can register users into the Microsoft SQL Server Express Edition data store. The first question you might ask is, "Where is this data store?"

Of course, you can use a number of editions of Microsoft's SQL Server to work through the examples in this book. With that said, this chapter uses the default database the membership system uses in creating users.

The Microsoft SQL Server provider for the membership system can use a SQL Server Express Edition file that is structured specifically for the membership service (and other ASP.NET systems, such as the role management system). ASP.NET is set to automatically create this particular file for you if the appropriate file does not exist already. To create the `ASPNETDB.mdf` file, you work with the ASP.NET server controls that utilize an aspect of the membership service. When the application requires the `ASPNETDB.mdf` file, ASP.NET creates this file on your behalf in the App_Data folder.

After the data store is in place, it is time to start adding users to the data store.

Using the CreateUserWizard Server Control

The CreateUserWizard server control is one that can be used in conjunction with the membership service. You can find this and the other controls mentioned in this chapter under the Login section in the Visual Studio 2010 Toolbox. The CreateUserWizard control enables you to plug registered users into your data store for later retrieval. If a page in your application allows end users to register for your site, you want, at a minimum, to retrieve a login and password from the user and place these values in the data store. This enables the end user to access these items later to log in to the application using the membership system.

To make your life as simple as possible, the CreateUserWizard control takes complete control of registration on your behalf. Listing 15-3 shows a simple use of the control.

LISTING 15-3: Allowing end users to register with the site

Available for download on Wrox.com

```
<%@ Page Language="VB" %>

<html xmlns="http://www.w3.org/1999/xhtml">
<head runat="server">
    <title>Creating Users</title>
</head>
<body>
    <form id="form1" runat="server">
        <asp:CreateUserWizard ID="CreateUserWizard1" Runat="server"
         BorderWidth="1px" BorderColor="#FFDFAD" BorderStyle="Solid"
         BackColor="#FFFBD6" Font-Names="Verdana">
            <TitleTextStyle Font-Bold="True" BackColor="#990000"
             ForeColor="White"></TitleTextStyle>
        </asp:CreateUserWizard>
    </form>
</body>
</html>
```

This page simply uses the CreateUserWizard control and nothing more. This one control enables you to register end users for your Web application. This particular CreateUserWizard control has a little style applied to it, but this control can be as simple as

```
<asp:CreateUserWizard ID="CreateUserWizard1" Runat="server">
</asp:CreateUserWizard>
```

When this code is run, an end user is presented with the form shown in Figure 15-2.

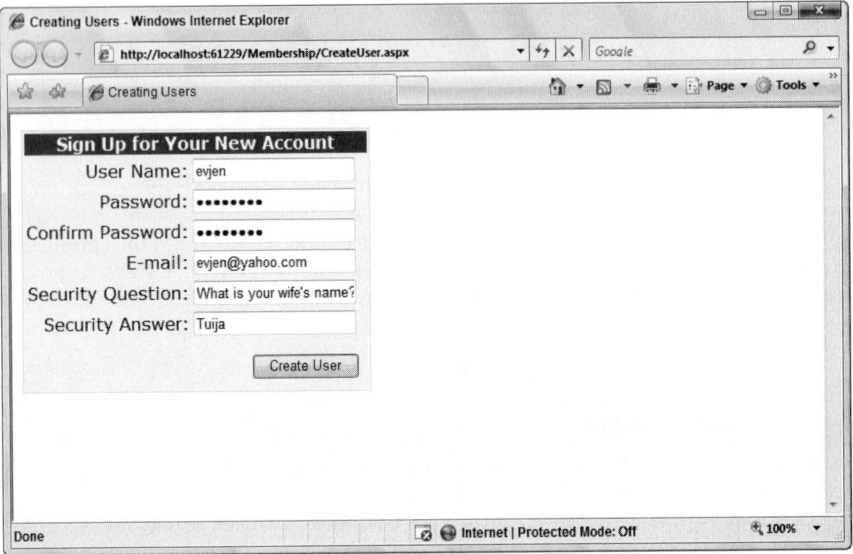

FIGURE 15-2

This screenshot shows the form as it would appear when filled out by the end user and includes information such as the username, password, e-mail address, as well as a security question-and-answer section. Clicking the Create User button places this defined user information into the data store.

The username and password provided via this control enable the end user to log in to the application later through the Login server control. A Confirm Password text box is also included in the form of the CreateUser server control to ensure that the password provided is spelled correctly. An e-mail address text box is included (in case end users forget their login credentials and want the credentials e-mailed to them at some later point in time). Finally, the security question and answer are used to verify the identity of the end user before any credentials or user information is changed or later provided via the browser.

After the end user clicks the Create User button on this form, a confirmation of the information being stored appears (see Figure 15-3).

FIGURE 15-3

Seeing Where Users Are Stored

Now that you have used the CreateUserWizard control to add a user to the membership service, look at where this information is stored. If you used Visual Studio to create the Microsoft SQL Server Express Edition file in which you want to store the user information, the file is created when the previous example is run and you complete the form process as shown in the preceding figures. When the example is run and completed, you can click the Refresh button in the Solution Explorer to find the `ASPNETDB.mdf` file, which is located in the App_Data folder of your project. Many different tables are included in this file, but you are interested in the `aspnet_Membership` table only.

When you open the `aspnet_Membership` table (by right-clicking the table in the Server Explorer and selecting Show Table Data), the users you entered are in the system, as illustrated in Figure 15-4.

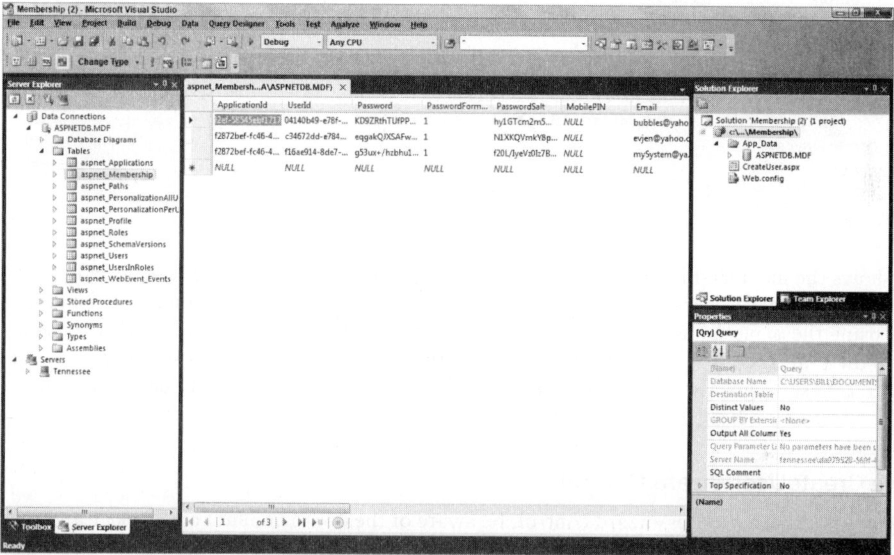

FIGURE 15-4

The user password in this table is not stored as clear text; instead, it is hashed, which is a one-way form of encryption that cannot be reversed easily. When a user logs in to an application that is using the ASP.NET 4 membership service, his or her password is immediately hashed and then compared to the hashed password stored in the database. If the two hashed strings do not compare, the passwords are not considered a match. Storing clear text passwords is considered a security risk, so you should never do so without weighing the risk involved.

A note regarding the passwords used in ASP.NET 4: If you are having difficulty entering users because of a password error, it might be because ASP.NET requires strong passwords by default. All passwords input into the system must be at least seven characters and contain at least one non-alphanumeric character (such as `[`, `]`, `!`, `@`, `#`, or `$`). Whew! An example password of this combination is

```
Bevjen7777$
```

Although this type of password is a heck of a lot more secure, a password like this is sometimes difficult to remember. You can actually change the behavior of the membership provider so that it doesn't require such difficult passwords by reworking the membership provider in the `web.config` file, as shown in Listing 15-4.

Available for download on Wrox.com

LISTING 15-4: Modifying the membership provider in web.config

```
<configuration>
   <system.web>

      <membership>
         <providers>
            <clear />
            <add name="AspNetSqlMembershipProvider"
             type="System.Web.Security.SqlMembershipProvider, System.Web,
               Version=4.0.0.0, Culture=neutral, PublicKeyToken=b03f5f7f11d50a3a"
             connectionStringName="ApplicationServices"
             enablePasswordRetrieval="false"
             enablePasswordReset="true"
             requiresQuestionAndAnswer="false"
             requiresUniqueEmail="true"
             passwordFormat="Hashed"
             minRequiredNonalphanumericCharacters="0"
             minRequiredPasswordLength="3" />
         </providers>
      </membership>

   </system.web>
</configuration>
```

This example shows the membership provider reworked for SQL Server so that it does not actually require any non-alphanumeric characters and allows passwords as small as three characters in length. You do this by using the `minRequiredNonalphanumericCharacters` and `minRequiredPasswordLength` attributes. With these in place, you can now create users with these password rules as set forth in these configuration settings. Modifying the membership provider is covered in more detail later in this chapter.

Working with the CreateUserWizard Control

When you work with the CreateUserWizard control, be aware of the `ContinueButtonClick()` and the `CreatedUser()` events. The `ContinueButtonClick()` event is triggered when the Continue button on the second page is clicked after the user has been successfully created (see Listing 15-5).

LISTING 15-5: The ContinueButtonClick event

VB

```
Protected Sub CreateUserWizard1_ContinueButtonClick(ByVal sender As Object,
   ByVal e As System.EventArgs)

      Response.Redirect("Default.aspx")
End Sub
```

C#

```
protected void CreateUserWizard1_ContinueButtonClick(object sender, EventArgs e)
{
   Response.Redirect("Default.aspx");
}
```

In this example, after the user has been added to the membership service through the form provided by the CreateUserWizard control, he or she can click the Continue button to be redirected to another page in the application. This is done with a simple `Response.Redirect` statement. Remember when you use this event, you must add an `OnContinueButtonClick = "CreateUserWizard1_ContinueButtonClick"` to the `<asp:CreateUserWizard>` control.

The `CreatedUser()` event is triggered when a user is successfully created in the data store. Listing 15-6 shows the use of this event.

LISTING 15-6: The CreatedUser() event

VB

```
Protected Sub CreateUserWizard1_CreatedUser(ByVal sender As Object,
   ByVal e As System.EventArgs)

      ' Code here
End Sub
```

C#

```
protected void CreateUserWizard1_CreatedUser(object sender, EventArgs e)
{
   // Code here
}
```

Use this event if you want to take any additional actions when a user is registered to the service.

Incorporating Personalization Properties in the Registration Process

As you saw in the previous chapter on personalization, using the personalization management system that comes with ASP.NET 4 and storing user-specific details is fairly simple. The registration process provided by the CreateUserWizard control is an ideal spot to retrieve this information from the user to store directly in the personalization system. The retrieval is not too difficult to incorporate into your code.

The first step, as you learned in the previous chapter on personalization, is to have some personalization points defined in the application's `web.config` file, as shown in Listing 15-7.

Available for download on Wrox.com

LISTING 15-7: Creating personalization properties in the web.config file

```
<configuration>
  <system.web>

     <profile>

        <properties>

           <add name="FirstName" />
           <add name="LastName" />
           <add name="LastVisited" />
           <add name="Age" />
           <add name="Member" />

        </properties>

     </profile>

  </system.web>
</configuration>
```

Now that these properties are defined in the `web.config` file, you can use them when you create users in the ASP.NET membership system. Again, using the CreateUserWizard control, you can create a process that requires the user to enter his or her preferred username and password in the first step, and then the second step asks for these custom-defined personalization points. Listing 15-8 shows a CreateUserWizard control that incorporates this idea.

LISTING 15-8: Using personalization properties with the CreateUserWizard control

Available for download on Wrox.com

```
<%@ Page Language="VB" %>

<script runat="server">
    Protected Sub CreateUserWizard1_CreatedUser(ByVal sender As Object, _
       ByVal e As System.EventArgs)

        Dim pc As ProfileCommon = New ProfileCommon()
        pc.Initialize(CreateUserWizard1.UserName.ToString(), True)

        pc.FirstName = Firstname.Text
        pc.LastName = Lastname.Text
        pc.Age = Age.Text

        pc.Save()
    End Sub
</script>

<html xmlns="http://www.w3.org/1999/xhtml">
<head id="Head1" runat="server">
    <title>Creating Users with Personalization</title>
</head>
<body>
    <form id="form1" runat="server">
        <asp:CreateUserWizard ID="CreateUserWizard1" Runat="server"
         BorderWidth="1px" BorderColor="#FFDFAD" BorderStyle="Solid"
         BackColor="#FFFBD6" Font-Names="Verdana"
         LoginCreatedUser="true" OnCreatedUser="CreateUserWizard1_CreatedUser" >
            <WizardSteps>
                <asp:WizardStep ID="WizardStep1" Runat="server"
                 Title="Additional Information" StepType="Start">
                    <table width="100%"><tr><td>
                    Firstname: </td><td>
                    <asp:TextBox ID="Firstname" Runat="server"></asp:TextBox>
                    </td></tr><tr><td>
                    Lastname: </td><td>
                    <asp:TextBox ID="Lastname" Runat="server"></asp:TextBox>
                    </td></tr><tr><td>
                    Age: </td><td>
                    <asp:TextBox ID="Age" Runat="server"></asp:TextBox>
                    </td></tr></table>
                </asp:WizardStep>
                <asp:CreateUserWizardStep Runat="server"
                 Title="Sign Up for Your New Account">
                </asp:CreateUserWizardStep>
                <asp:CompleteWizardStep Runat="server" Title="Complete">
                </asp:CompleteWizardStep>
            </WizardSteps>
            <StepStyle BorderColor="#FFDFAD" Font-Names="Verdana"
             BackColor="#FFFBD6" BorderStyle="Solid"
             BorderWidth="1px"></StepStyle>
            <TitleTextStyle Font-Bold="True" BackColor="#990000"
             ForeColor="White"></TitleTextStyle>
        </asp:CreateUserWizard>
    </form>
</body>
</html>
```

C#

```
<%@ Page Language="C#" %>

<script runat="server">
    protected void CreateUserWizard1_CreatedUser(object sender, EventArgs e)
    {
        ProfileCommon pc = new ProfileCommon();
        pc.Initialize(CreateUserWizard1.UserName.ToString(), true);

        pc.FirstName = Firstname.Text;
        pc.LastName = Lastname.Text;
        pc.Age = Age.Text;

        pc.Save();
    }
</script>
```

With this change to the standard registration process as is defined by a default instance of the CreateUserWizard control, your registration system now includes the request for properties stored and retrieved using the `ProfileCommon` object. Then, using the `ProfileCommon.Initialize()` method, you initialize the property values for the current user. Next, you set the property values using the strongly typed access to the profile properties available via the `ProfileCommon` object. After all the values have been set, you use the `Save()` method to finalize the process.

You can define a custom step within the CreateUserWizard control by using the `<WizardSteps>` element. Within this element, you can construct a series of registration steps in whatever fashion you choose. From the `<WizardSteps>` section, shown in Listing 15-8, you can see that three steps are defined. The first is the custom step in which the end user's personalization properties are requested with the `<asp:WizardStep>` control. Within the `<asp:WizardStep>` control, a table is laid out and a custom form is created.

Two additional steps are defined within Listing 15-8: a step to create the user (using the `<asp:CreateUserWizardStep>` control) and a step to confirm the creation of a new user (using the `<asp:CompleteWizardStep>` control). The order in which these steps appear is the order in which they are presented to the end user.

After the steps are created the way you want, you can then store the custom properties using the CreateUserWizard control's `CreatedUser()` event:

```
Protected Sub CreateUserWizard1_CreatedUser(ByVal sender As Object,
  ByVal e As System.EventArgs)

    Dim pc As ProfileCommon = New ProfileCommon()
    pc.Initialize(CreateUserWizard1.UserName.ToString(), True)

    pc.FirstName = Firstname.Text
    pc.LastName = Lastname.Text
    pc.Age = Age.Text

    pc.Save()
End Sub
```

You are not limited to having a separate step in which you ask for personal bits of information; you can incorporate these items directly into the `<asp:CreateUserWizardStep>` step itself. An easy way to do this is to switch to the Design view of your page and pull up the smart tag for the CreateUserWizard control. Then click the Customize Create User Step link (shown in Figure 15-5).

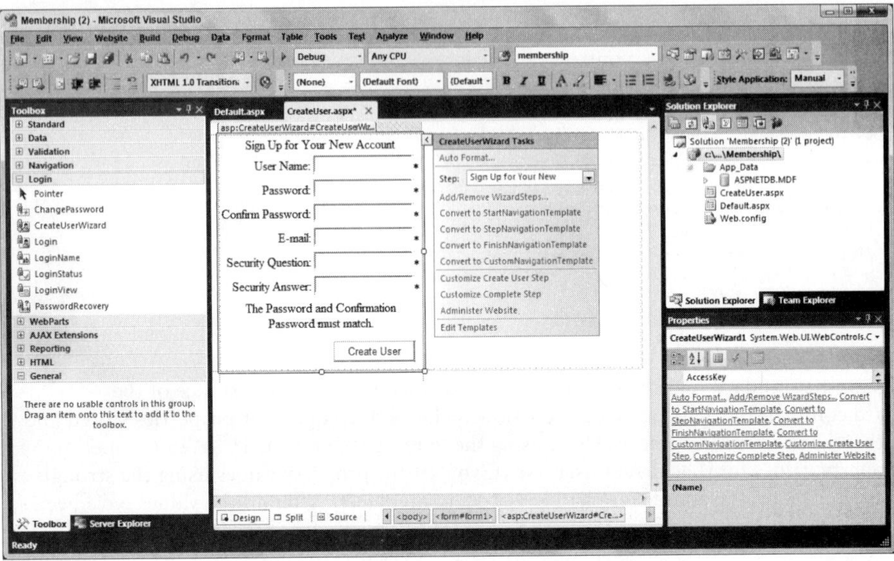

FIGURE 15-5

Clicking on the Customize Create User Step details the contents of this particular step within a new `<ContentTemplate>` section that is now contained within the `<asp:CreateUserWizardStep>` control. Within the `<ContentTemplate>` element, you can see the complete default form used for creating a new user. At this point, you are free to change the form by adding your own sections that request the end user's personal information. From this detailed form, you can also remove items. For example, if you are not interested in asking for the security question and answer, you can remove these two items from the form (remember that you must disable the question-and-answer requirement in the membership provider definition). By changing this default form, you can completely customize the registration process for your end users (see Figure 15-6).

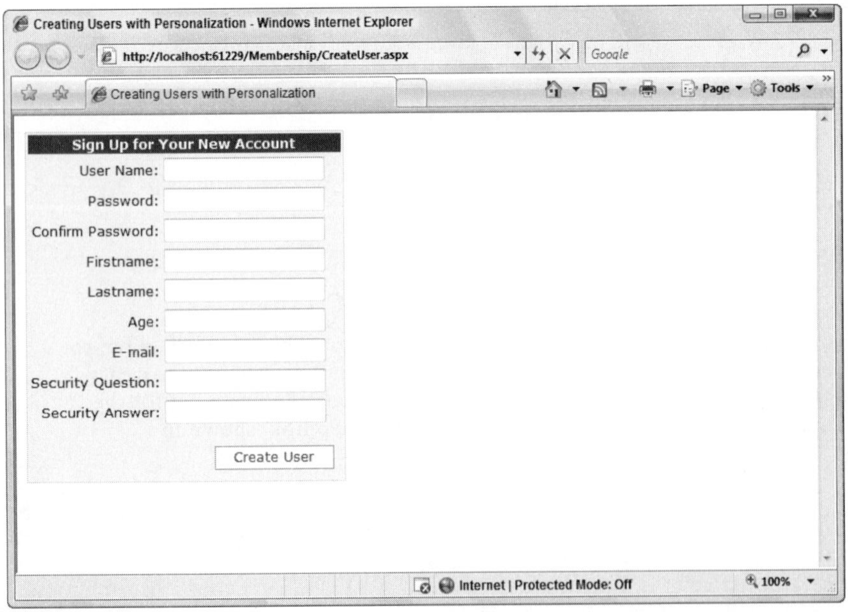

FIGURE 15-6

Adding Users Programmatically

You are not limited to using only server controls to register or add new users to the membership service. ASP.NET 4 provides a Membership API for performing this task programmatically. This feature is ideal for creating your own mechanics for adding users to the service — or if you are modifying a Web application that was created using ASP.NET 1.0/1.1.

The Membership API includes the `CreateUser()` method for adding users to the service. The `CreateUser()` method includes four possible signatures:

```
Membership.CreateUser(username As String, password As String)

Membership.CreateUser(username As String, password As String,
email As String)

Membership.CreateUser(username As String, password As String,
email As String, passwordQuestion As String,
passwordAnswer As String, isApproved As Boolean,
   ByRef status As System.Web.Security.MembershipCreateStatus)

Membership.CreateUser(username As String, password As String,
email As String, passwordQuestion As String,
passwordAnswer As String, isApproved As Boolean, providerUserKey As Object
   ByRef status As System.Web.Security.MembershipCreateStatus)
```

You can use this method to create users. The nice thing about this method is that you are not required to create an instance of the `Membership` class; you use it directly. Listing 15-9 shows a simple use of the `CreateUser()` method.

LISTING 15-9: Creating users programmatically

Available for download on Wrox.com

VB

```
<%@ Page Language="VB" %>

<script runat="server">
Protected Sub Button1_Click(ByVal sender As Object, ByVal e As System.EventArgs)
   Try
      Membership.CreateUser(TextBox1.Text, TextBox2.Text)
      Label1.Text = "Successfully created user " & TextBox1.Text
   Catch ex As MembershipCreateUserException
      Label1.Text = "Error: " & ex.ToString()
   End Try
End Sub
</script>

<html xmlns="http://www.w3.org/1999/xhtml">
<head runat="server">
    <title>Creating a User</title>
</head>
<body>
    <form id="form1" runat="server">
        <h1>Create User</h1>
        <p>Username<br />
            <asp:TextBox ID="TextBox1" Runat="server"></asp:TextBox>
        </p>
        <p>Password<br />
            <asp:TextBox ID="TextBox2" Runat="server"
             TextMode="Password"></asp:TextBox>
        </p>
        <p>
            <asp:Button ID="Button1" Runat="server" Text="Create User"
             OnClick="Button1_Click" />
        </p>
```

continues

LISTING 15-9 *(continued)*

```
        <p>
            <asp:Label ID="Label1" Runat="server"></asp:Label>
        </p>
    </form>
</body>
</html>
```

C#

```
<%@ Page Language="C#" %>

<script runat="server">
    protected void Button1_Click(object sender, EventArgs e)
    {
        try
        {
            Membership.CreateUser(TextBox1.Text.ToString(),
               TextBox2.Text.ToString());
            Label1.Text = "Successfully created user " + TextBox1.Text;
        }
        catch (MembershipCreateUserException ex)
        {
            Label1.Text = "Error: " + ex.ToString();
        }
    }
</script>
```

So, use either the CreateUserWizard control or the `CreateUser()` method found in the Membership API to create users for your Web applications with relative ease. This functionality was possible in the past with ASP.NET 1.0/1.1, but it was a labor-intensive task. Ever since ASP.NET 2.0, you can create users either with a single control or with a single line of code.

From this bit of code, you can see that if a problem occurs when creating the user with the `CreateUser()` method, a `MembershipCreateUserException` is thrown. In this example, the exception is written to the screen within a Label server control. Here is an example of an exception written to the screen:

```
Error: System.Web.Security.MembershipCreateUserException: The password-answer
supplied is invalid. at System.Web.Security.Membership.CreateUser(String username,
String password, String email) at System.Web.Security.Membership.CreateUser(String
username, String password) at ASP.default_aspx.Button1_Click(Object sender,
EventArgs e) in c:\Documents and Settings\BillEvjen\My Documents\Visual Studio
10\WebSites\Membership\Default.aspx:line 10
```

You might not want such details sent to the end user. You might prefer to return a simpler message to the end user with something like the following construct:

```
Label1.Text = "Error: " & ex.Message.ToString();
```

This gives you results as simple as the following:

```
Error: The password-answer supplied is invalid.
```

You can also capture the specific error using the `MembershipCreateUserException` and return something that might be a little more appropriate. Listing 15-10 presents an example of this usage.

LISTING 15-10: Capturing the specific MembershipCreateUserException value

Available for download on Wrox.com

VB

```
<%@ Page Language="VB" %>

<script runat="server">

    Protected Sub Button1_Click(ByVal sender As Object,
      ByVal e As System.EventArgs)
        Try
            Membership.CreateUser(TextBox1.Text, TextBox2.Text)
```

```
                Label1.Text = "Successfully created user " & TextBox1.Text
            Catch ex As MembershipCreateUserException
                Select Case ex.StatusCode
                    Case MembershipCreateStatus.DuplicateEmail
                        Label1.Text = "You have supplied a duplicate email address."
                    Case MembershipCreateStatus.DuplicateUserName
                        Label1.Text = "You have supplied a duplicate username."
                    Case MembershipCreateStatus.InvalidEmail
                        Label1.Text = "You have not supplied a proper email address."
                    Case Else
                        Label1.Text = "ERROR: " & ex.Message.ToString()
                End Select
            End Try
        End Sub
</script>

<html xmlns="http://www.w3.org/1999/xhtml">
<head id="Head1" runat="server">
    <title>Creating a User</title>
</head>
<body>
    <form id="form1" runat="server">
        <h1>Create User</h1>
        <p>Username<br />
            <asp:TextBox ID="TextBox1" Runat="server"></asp:TextBox>
        </p>
        <p>Password<br />
            <asp:TextBox ID="TextBox2" Runat="server"
             TextMode="Password"></asp:TextBox>
        </p>
        <p>
            <asp:Button ID="Button1" Runat="server" Text="Create User"
             OnClick="Button1_Click" />
        </p>
        <p>
            <asp:Label ID="Label1" Runat="server"></asp:Label>
        </p>
    </form>
</body>
</html>
```

C#

```
<%@ Page Language="C#" %>

<script runat="server">
    protected void Button1_Click(object sender, EventArgs e)
    {
        try
        {
            Membership.CreateUser(TextBox1.Text, TextBox2.Text);
            Label1.Text = "Successfully created user " + TextBox1.Text;
        }
        catch (MembershipCreateUserException ex)
        {
            switch(ex.StatusCode)
            {
                case MembershipCreateStatus.DuplicateEmail:
                    Label1.Text = "You have supplied a duplicate email address.";
                    break;
                case MembershipCreateStatus.DuplicateUserName:
                    Label1.Text = "You have supplied a duplicate username.";
                    break;
                case MembershipCreateStatus.InvalidEmail:
                    Label1.Text = "You have not supplied a proper email address.";
                    break;
```

continues

LISTING 15-10 *(continued)*

```
                default:
                    Label1.Text = "ERROR: " + ex.Message.ToString();
                    break;
            }
        }
    }
</script>
```

In this case, you are able to look for the specific error that occurred in the `CreateUser` process. Here, this code is looking for only three specific items, but the list of available error codes includes the following:

- `MembershipCreateStatus.DuplicateEmail`
- `MembershipCreateStatus.DuplicateProviderUserKey`
- `MembershipCreateStatus.DuplicateUserName`
- `MembershipCreateStatus.InvalidAnswer`
- `MembershipCreateStatus.InvalidEmail`
- `MembershipCreateStatus.InvalidPassword`
- `MembershipCreateStatus.InvalidProviderUserKey`
- `MembershipCreateStatus.InvalidQuestion`
- `MembershipCreateStatus.InvalidUserName`
- `MembershipCreateStatus.ProviderError`
- `MembershipCreateStatus.Success`
- `MembershipCreateStatus.UserRejected`

In addition to giving better error reports to your users by defining what is going on, you can use these events to take any actions that might be required.

Changing How Users Register with Your Application

You determine how users register with your applications and what is required of them by the membership provider you choose. You will find a default membership provider and its applied settings are established within the `machine.config` file. If you dig down in the `machine.config` file on your server, you find the code shown in Listing 15-11.

LISTING 15-11: Membership provider settings in the machine.config file

Available for download on Wrox.com

```
<membership>
  <providers>
    <add name="AspNetSqlMembershipProvider"
     type="System.Web.Security.SqlMembershipProvider, System.Web,
        Version=4.0.0.0, Culture=neutral, PublicKeyToken=b03f5f7f11d50a3a"
     connectionStringName="LocalSqlServer"
     enablePasswordRetrieval="false"
     enablePasswordReset="true"
     requiresQuestionAndAnswer="true"
     applicationName="/"
     requiresUniqueEmail="false"
     passwordFormat="Hashed"
     maxInvalidPasswordAttempts="5"
     minRequiredPasswordLength="7"
     minRequiredNonalphanumericCharacters="1"
     passwordAttemptWindow="10"
     passwordStrengthRegularExpression="" />
  </providers>
</membership>
```

This section of the `machine.config` file shows the default membership provider that comes with ASP .NET 4 — named `AspNetSqlProvider`. If you are adding membership providers for server-wide use, add them to this `<membership>` section of the `machine.config` file; if you intend to use them for only a specific application instance, you can add them to your application's `web.config` file.

The important attributes of the SqlMembershipProvider definition include the `enablePasswordRetrieval`, `enablePasswordReset`, `requiresQuestionAndAnswer`, `requiresUniqueEmail`, and `PasswordFormat` attributes. Table 15-1 defines these attributes.

TABLE 15-1

ATTRIBUTE	DESCRIPTION
`enablePasswordRetrieval`	Defines whether the provider supports password retrievals. This attribute takes a `Boolean` value. The default value is `False`. When it is set to `False`, passwords cannot be retrieved although they can be changed with a new random password.
`enablePasswordReset`	Defines whether the provider supports password resets. This attribute takes a `Boolean` value. The default value is `True`.
`requiresQuestionAndAnswer`	Specifies whether the provider should require a question-and-answer combination when a user is created. This attribute takes a `Boolean` value, and the default value is `False`.
`requiresUniqueEmail`	Defines whether the provider should require a unique e-mail to be specified when the user is created. This attribute takes a `Boolean` value, and the default value is `False`. When set to `True`, only unique e-mail addresses can be entered into the data store.
`passwordFormat`	Defines the format in which the password is stored in the data store. The possible values include `Hashed`, `Clear`, and `Encrypted`. The default value is `Hashed`. Hashed passwords use SHA1, whereas encrypted passwords use Triple-DES encryption.

In addition to having these items defined in the `machine.config` file, you can also redefine them again (thus overriding the settings in the `machine.config`) in the `web.config` file.

Asking for Credentials

After you have users who can access your Web application using the membership service provided by ASP. NET, you can then give these users the means to log in to the site. This requires little work on your part. Before you learn about the controls that enable users to access your applications, you should make a few more modifications to the `web.config` file.

Turning Off Access with the <authorization> Element

After you make the changes to the `web.config` file by adding the `<authentication>` and `<forms>` elements (Listings 15-1 and 15-2), your Web application is accessible to each and every user that browses to any page your application contains. To prevent open access, you have to deny unauthenticated users access to the pages of your site.

Listing 15-12 shows the code for denying unauthenticated users access to your site.

Available for download on Wrox.com

LISTING 15-12: Denying unauthenticated users

```
<?xml version="1.0" encoding="utf-8"?>
<configuration>
```

continues

LISTING 15-12 *(continued)*

```
    <system.web>
        <authentication mode="Forms" />
        <authorization>
           <deny users="?" />
        </authorization>
    </system.web>
</configuration>
```

Using the <authorization> and <deny> elements, you can deny specific users access to your Web application — or (as in this case) simply deny every unauthenticated user (this is what the question mark signifies).

Now that everyone but authenticated users has been denied access to the site, you want to make it easy for viewers of your application to become authenticated users. To do so, use the Login server control.

Using the Login Server Control

The Login server control enables you to turn unauthenticated users into authenticated users by allowing them to provide login credentials that can be verified in a data store of some kind. In the examples so far, you have used Microsoft SQL Server Express Edition as the data store, but you can just as easily use the full-blown version of Microsoft's SQL Server (such as Microsoft's SQL Server 7.0, 2000, 2005, or 2008).

The first step in using the Login control is to create a new Web page titled `Login.aspx`. This is the default page to which unauthenticated users are redirected to obtain their credentials. Remember that you can change this behavior by changing the value of the <forms> element's `loginUrl` attribute in the `web.config` file.

The `Login.aspx` page simply needs an <asp:Login> control to give the end user everything he or she needs to become authenticated, as shown in Listing 15-13.

Available for download on Wrox.com

LISTING 15-13: Providing a login for the end user using the Login control

```
<%@ Page Language="VB" %>

<html xmlns="http://www.w3.org/1999/xhtml">
<head runat="server">
    <title>Login Page</title>
</head>
<body>
    <form id="form1" runat="server">
        <asp:Login ID="Login1" Runat="server">
        </asp:Login>
    </form>
</body>
</html>
```

In the situation established here, if the unauthenticated user hits a different page in the application, he or she is redirected to the `Login.aspx` page. You can see how ASP.NET tracks the location in the URL from the address bar in the browser:

```
http://localhost:18436/Membership/Login.aspx?ReturnUrl=%2fMembership%2fDefault.aspx
```

The login page, using the Login control, is shown in Figure 15-7.

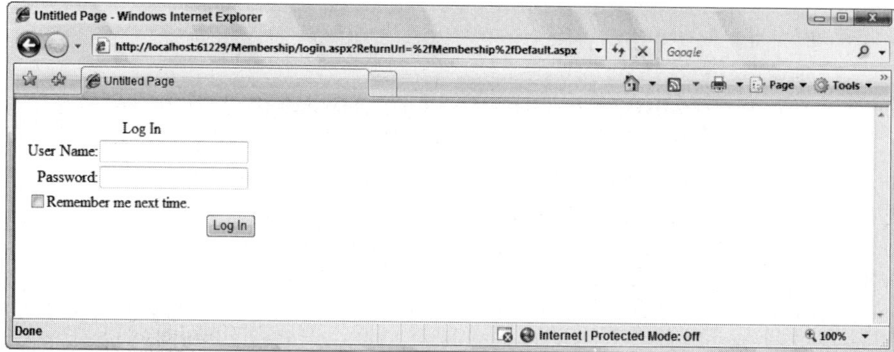

FIGURE 15-7

From this figure, you can see that the Login control asks the user for a username and password. A check box allows a cookie to be stored on the client machine. This cookie enables the end user to bypass future logins. You can remove the check box and related text created to remember the user by setting the Login control's `DisplayRememberMe` property to `False`.

In addition to the `DisplayRememberMe` property, you can work with this aspect of the Login control by using the `RememberMeText` and the `RememberMeSet` properties. The `RememberMeText` property is rather self-explanatory because its value simply defines the text set next to the check box. The `RememberMeSet` property, however, is fairly interesting. The `RememberMeSet` property takes a `Boolean` value (by default, it is set to `False`) that specifies whether to set a persistent cookie on the client's machine after a user has logged in using the Login control. If set to `True` when the `DisplayRememberMe` property is also set to `True`, the check box is simply checked by default when the Login control is generated in the browser. If the `DisplayRememberMe` property is set to `False` (meaning the end user does not see the check box or cannot select the option of persisting the login cookie) and the `RememberMeSet` is set to `True`, a cookie is set on the user's machine automatically without the user's knowledge or choice in the matter. You should think carefully about taking this approach because end users sometimes use public computers, and this method would mean you are setting authorization cookies on public machines.

This cookie remains on the client's machine until the user logs out of the application (if this option is provided). With the persisted cookie, and assuming the end user has not logged out of the application, the user never needs to log in again when he returns to the application because his credentials are provided by the contents found in the cookie. After the end user has logged in to the application, he is returned to the page he originally intended to access.

You can also modify the look-and-feel of the Login control just as you can for the other controls. One way to do this is by clicking the Auto Format link in the control's smart tag. There you find a list of options for modifying the look-and-feel of the control (see Figure 15-8).

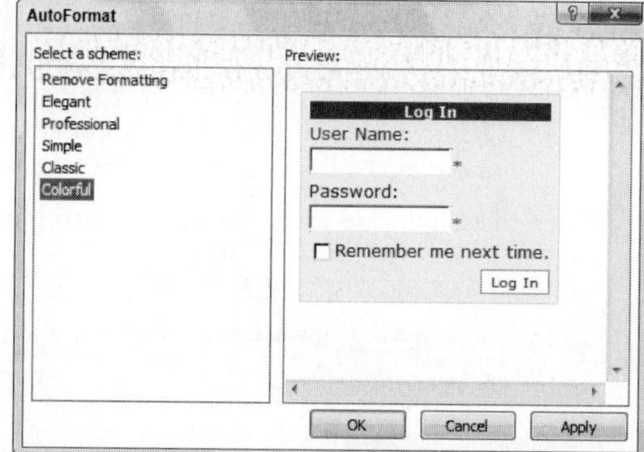

FIGURE 15-8

Select the Colorful option, for example, and the code is modified. Listing 15-14 shows the code generated for this selection.

LISTING 15-14: A formatted Login control

```
<asp:Login ID="Login1" Runat="server" BackColor="#FFFBD6"
 BorderColor="#FFDFAD" BorderPadding="4" BorderStyle="Solid"
 BorderWidth="1px" Font-Names="Verdana" Font-Size="0.8em"
```

continues

LISTING 15-14 *(continued)*

```
ForeColor="#333333" TextLayout="TextOnTop">
   <TextBoxStyle Font-Size="0.8em" />
   <LoginButtonStyle BackColor="White" BorderColor="#CC9966"
    BorderStyle="Solid" BorderWidth="1px" Font-Names="Verdana"
    Font-Size="0.8em" ForeColor="#990000" />
   <InstructionTextStyle Font-Italic="True" ForeColor="Black" />
   <TitleTextStyle BackColor="#990000" Font-Bold="True" Font-Size="0.9em"
    ForeColor="White" />
</asp:Login>
```

From this listing, you can see that a number of sub-elements are used to modify particular items displayed by the control. The available styling elements for the Login control include the following:

- `<CheckboxStyle>`
- `<FailureTextStyle>`
- `<HyperLinkStyle>`
- `<InstructionTextStyle>`
- `<LabelStyle>`
- `<LoginButtonStyle>`
- `<TextBoxStyle>`
- `<TitleTextStyle>`
- `<ValidatorTextStyle>`

The Login control has numerous properties that allow you to alter how the control appears and behaves. An interesting change you can make is to add some links at the bottom of the control to provide access to additional resources. With these links, you can give users the capability to get help or register for the application so that they can be provided with any login credentials.

You can provide links to do the following:

- Redirect users to a help page using the `HelpPageText`, `HelpPageUrl`, and `HelpPageIconUrl` properties.
- Redirect users to a registration page using the `CreateUserText`, `CreateUserUrl`, and `CreateUserIconUrl` properties.
- Redirect users to a page that allows them to recover their forgotten passwords using the `PasswordRecoveryText`, `PasswordRecoveryUrl`, and `PasswordRecoveryIconUrl` properties.

When these links are used, the Login control looks like what is shown in Figure 15-9.

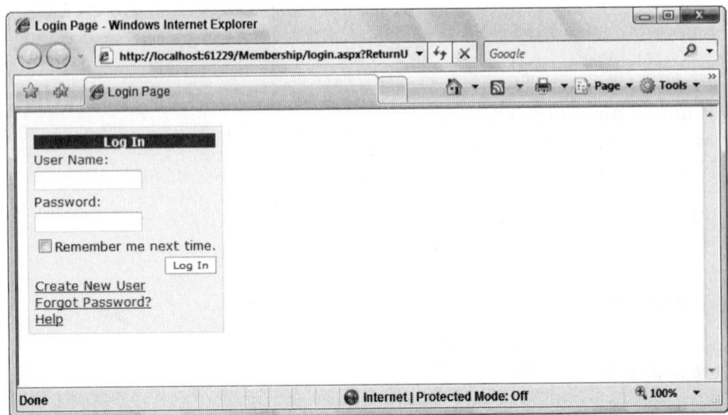

FIGURE 15-9

Logging In Users Programmatically

Besides using the pre-built mechanics of the Login control, you can also perform this task programmatically using the Membership class. To validate credentials that you receive, you use the `ValidateUser()` method of this class. The `ValidateUser()` method takes a single signature:

```
Membership.ValidateUser(username As String, password As String)
```

Listing 15-15 presents this method.

LISTING 15-15: Validating a user's credentials programmatically

Available for download on Wrox.com

VB

```
If Membership.ValidateUser(TextBox1.Text, TextBox2.Text) Then
   FormsAuthentication.RedirectFromLoginPage(TextBox1.Text, False)
Else
   Label1.Text = "You are not registered with the site."
End If
```

C#

```
if (Membership.ValidateUser(TextBox1.Text, TextBox2.Text) {
   FormsAuthentication.RedirectFromLoginPage(TextBox1.Text.ToString(), false);
}
else {
   Label1.Text = "You are not registered with the site.";
}
```

The `ValidateUser()` method returns a `Boolean` value of `True` if the user credentials pass the test and `False` if they do not. From the code snippet in Listing 15-15, you can see that end users whose credentials are verified as correct are redirected from the login page using the `RedirectFromLoginPage()` method. This method takes the username and a `Boolean` value that specifies whether the credentials are persisted through a cookie setting.

Locking Out Users Who Provide Bad Passwords

When providing a user login form in any application you build, always guard against repeated bogus password attempts. If you have a malicious end user who knows a username, he may try to access the application by repeatedly trying different passwords. You want to guard against this kind of activity. You don't want to allow this person to try hundreds of possible passwords with this username.

ASP.NET has built-in protection against this type of activity. If you look in the aspnet_Membership table, you see two columns focused on protecting against this activity. These columns are `FailedPasswordAttemptCount` and `FailedPasswordAttemptWindowStart`.

By default, a username can be used with an incorrect password in a login attempt only five times within a 10-minute window. On the fifth failed attempt, the account is locked down. You do this in ASP.NET by setting the `IsLockedOut` column to `True`.

You can actually control the number of password attempts that are allowed and the length of the attempt window for your application. These two items are defined in the SqlMembershipProvider declaration in the `machine.config` file. You can change the values either in the server-wide configuration files or in your application's `web.config` file. Listing 15-16 presents code for changing these values in your `web.config` file.

LISTING 15-16: Changing the values for password attempts in the provider declaration

Available for download on Wrox.com

```
<configuration>
   <system.web>

      <membership defaultProvider="AspNetSqlMembershipProvider">
        <providers>
          <clear />
          <add connectionStringName="ApplicationServices"
           applicationName="/"
           maxInvalidPasswordAttempts="3"
           passwordAttemptWindow="15"
           name="AspNetSqlMembershipProvider"
```

continues

LISTING 15-16 *(continued)*

```
            type="System.Web.Security.SqlMembershipProvider, System.Web,
              Version=4.0.0.0, Culture=neutral, PublicKeyToken=b03f5f7f11d50a3a" />
          </providers>
        </membership>

      </system.web>
    </configuration>
```

To determine the number of password attempts that are allowed, use `maxInvalidPasswordAttempts`. This example changes the value to `3`, meaning that users are allowed to enter an incorrect password three times before being locked out (within the time window defined). The default value of the `maxInvalidPasswordAttempts` attribute is `5`. You can set the time allowed for bad password attempts to `15` minutes using the `passwordAttemptWindow` attribute. The default value of this attribute is `10`, so an extra five minutes is added.

Now that these items are in place, the next step is to test it. Listing 15-17 provides you with an example of the test. It assumes you have an application established with a user already in place.

LISTING 15-17: A sample page to test password attempts

Available for download on Wrox.com

VB

```
<%@ Page Language="VB" %>

<script runat="server">
    Protected Sub Button1_Click(ByVal sender As Object,
      ByVal e As System.EventArgs)

        If CheckBox1.Checked = True Then
            Dim user As MembershipUser = Membership.GetUser(TextBox1.Text)
            user.UnlockUser()
        End If

        If Membership.ValidateUser(TextBox1.Text, TextBox2.Text) Then
            Label1.Text = "You are logged on!"
        Else
            Dim user As MembershipUser = Membership.GetUser(TextBox1.Text)
            Label1.Text = "Locked out value: " & user.IsLockedOut.ToString()
        End If
    End Sub
</script>

<html xmlns="http://www.w3.org/1999/xhtml">
<head runat="server">
    <title>Login Page</title>
</head>
<body>
    <form id="form1" runat="server">
    <div>
        <h1>Login User</h1>
        <p>
            <asp:CheckBox ID="CheckBox1" runat="server" Text="Unlock User" />
        </p>
        <p>
            Username<br />
            <asp:TextBox ID="TextBox1" Runat="server"></asp:TextBox>
        </p>
        <p>Password<br />
            <asp:TextBox ID="TextBox2" Runat="server"
             TextMode="Password"></asp:TextBox>
        </p>
```

```
            <p>
                <asp:Button ID="Button1" Runat="server" Text="Login"
                 OnClick="Button1_Click" />
            </p>
            <p>
                <asp:Label ID="Label1" Runat="server"></asp:Label>
            </p>
        </div>
        </form>
    </body>
    </html>
```

C#

```
<%@ Page Language="C#" %>

<script runat="server">
    protected void Button1_Click(object sender, EventArgs e)
    {
        if (CheckBox1.Checked == true)
        {
            MembershipUser user = Membership.GetUser(TextBox1.Text);
            user.UnlockUser();
        }

        if (Membership.ValidateUser(TextBox1.Text, TextBox2.Text))
        {
            Label1.Text = "You are logged on!";
        }
        else
        {
            MembershipUser user = Membership.GetUser(TextBox1.Text);
            Label1.Text = "Locked out value: " + user.IsLockedOut.ToString();
        }
    }
</script>
```

This page contains two text boxes: one for the username and another for the password. Above these, however, is a check box that you can use to unlock a user after you have locked down the account because of bad password attempts.

If you run this page and enter three consecutive bad passwords for your user, you get the results presented in Figure 15-10.

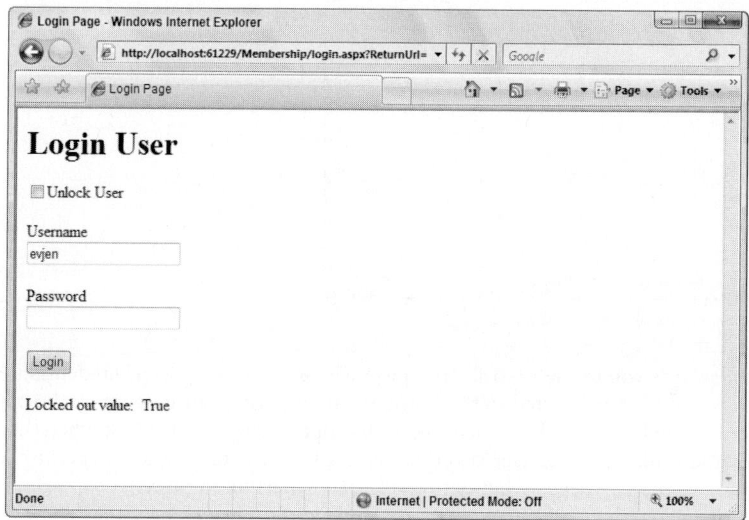

FIGURE 15-10

The `IsLockedOut` property is read through an instantiation of the `MembershipUser` object. This object allows you programmatic access to the user data points contained in the aspnet_Membership table. In this case, the `IsLockedOut` property is retrieved and displayed to the screen. The `MembershipUser` object also exposes a lot of available methods — one of which is the `UnlockUser()` method. This method is invoked if the check box is selected in the button-click event.

Working with Authenticated Users

After users are authenticated, ASP.NET 4 provides a number of different server controls and methods that you can use to work with the user details. Included in this collection of tools are the LoginStatus and the LoginName controls.

The LoginStatus Server Control

The LoginStatus server control enables users to click a link to log in or log out of a site. For a good example of this control, remove the <deny> element from the `web.config` file so that the pages of your site are accessible to unauthenticated users. Then code your `Default.aspx` page so that it is similar to the code shown in Listing 15-18.

LISTING 15-18: Login and logout features of the LoginStatus control

Available for download on Wrox.com

```
<%@ Page Language="VB" %>

<html xmlns="http://www.w3.org/1999/xhtml">
<head runat="server">
    <title>Login or Logout</title>
</head>
<body>
    <form id="form1" runat="server">
        <asp:LoginStatus ID="LoginStatus1" Runat="server" />
    </form>
</body>
</html>
```

Running this gives you a simple page that contains only a hyperlink titled `Login`, as shown in Figure 15-11.

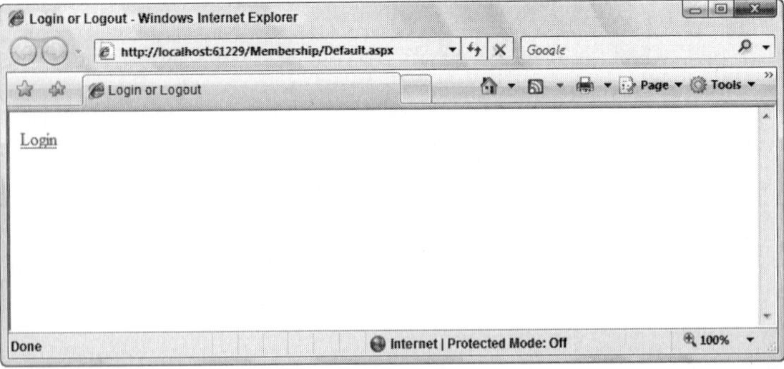

FIGURE 15-11

Clicking the `Login` hyperlink forwards you to the `Login.aspx` page where you provide your credentials. After the credentials are provided, you are redirected to the `Default.aspx` page — although now the page includes a hyperlink titled `Logout` (see Figure 15-12). The LinkStatus control displays one link when the user is unauthenticated and another link when the user is authenticated. Clicking the `Logout` hyperlink logs out the user and redraws the `Default.aspx` page — but with the `Login` hyperlink in place.

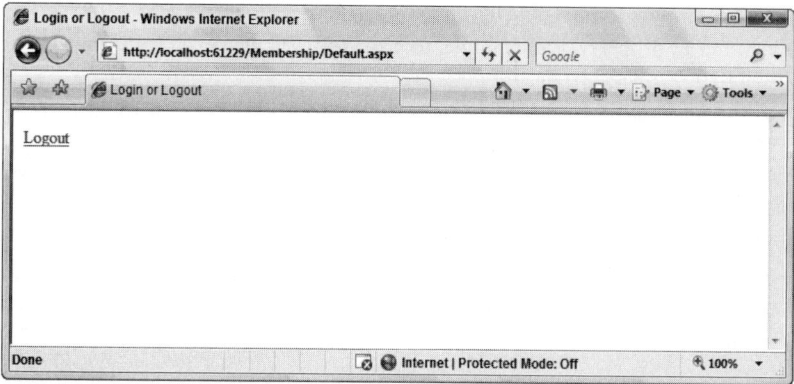

FIGURE 15-12

The LoginName Server Control

The LoginName server control enables you to display the username of the authenticated user. This practice is common today. For an example of it, change the `Default.aspx` page so that it now includes the authenticated user's login name when that user is logged in, as illustrated in Listing 15-19.

LISTING 15-19: Displaying the username of the authenticated user

Available for download on Wrox.com

```
<%@ Page Language="VB" %>

<html xmlns="http://www.w3.org/1999/xhtml">
<head runat="server">
    <title>Login or Logout</title>
</head>
<body>
    <form id="form1" runat="server">
        <asp:LoginStatus ID="LoginStatus1" Runat="server" />
        <p><asp:LoginName ID="LoginName1" Runat="server"
            Font-Bold="True" Font-Size="XX-Large" /></p>
    </form>
</body>
</html>
```

When the user logs in to the application and is returned to the `Default.aspx` page, he sees his username displayed, as well as the hyperlink generated by the LoginStatus control (see Figure 15-13).

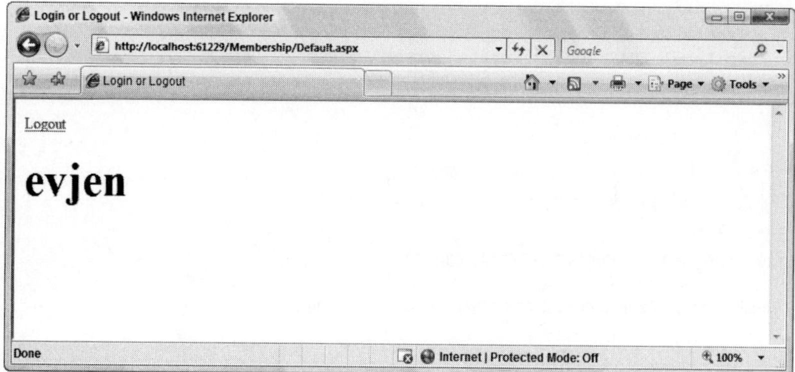

FIGURE 15-13

In addition to just showing the username of the logged in user, you can also add text by using the LoginName control's `FormatString` property. For example, to provide a welcome message along with the username, you construct the LoginName control as follows:

```
<asp:LoginName ID="LoginName1" Runat="Server"
 FormatString="Welcome to our Website {0}!" />
```

You can also simply use the following construction in one of the page events. (This is shown in VB; if you are using C#, add a semicolon at the end of the line.)

```
LoginName1.FormatString = "Welcome to the site {0}!"
```

When the page is generated, ASP.NET replaces the `{0}` part of the string with the username of the logged-in user. This provides you with a result similar to the following:

```
Welcome to the site evjen!
```

If you do not want to show the username when using the LoginName control, simply omit the `{0}` aspect of the string. The control then places the `FormatString` property's value on the page.

Showing the Number of Users Online

One cool feature of the membership service is that you can display how many users are online at a given moment. This option is an especially popular one for a portal or a forum that wants to impress visitors to the site with its popularity.

To show the number of users online, you use the `GetNumberOfUsersOnline` method provided by the `Membership` class. You can add to the `Default.aspx` page shown in Figure 15-11 with the code provided in Listing 15-20.

LISTING 15-20: Displaying the number of users online

Available for download on Wrox.com

VB

```
<%@ Page Language="VB" %>
<script runat="server">
    Protected Sub Page_Load(ByVal sender As Object, ByVal e As System.EventArgs)
        Label1.Text = Membership.GetNumberOfUsersOnline().ToString()
    End Sub
</script>
<html xmlns="http://www.w3.org/1999/xhtml">
<head runat="server">
    <title>Login or Logout</title>
</head>
<body>
    <form id="form1" runat="server">
        <asp:LoginStatus ID="LoginStatus1" Runat="server" />
        <p><asp:LoginName ID="LoginName1" Runat="server"
            Font-Bold="True" Font-Size="XX-Large" /></p>
        <p>There are <asp:Label ID="Label1" Runat="server" Text="0" />
         users online.</p>
    </form>
</body>
</html>
```

C#

```
<%@ Page Language="C#" %>

<script runat="server">
   protected void Page_Load(object sender, EventArgs e)
   {
      Label1.Text = Membership.GetNumberOfUsersOnline().ToString();
   }
</script>
```

When the page is generated, it displays the number of users who have logged on in the last 15 minutes. Figure 15-14 shows an example of what is generated.

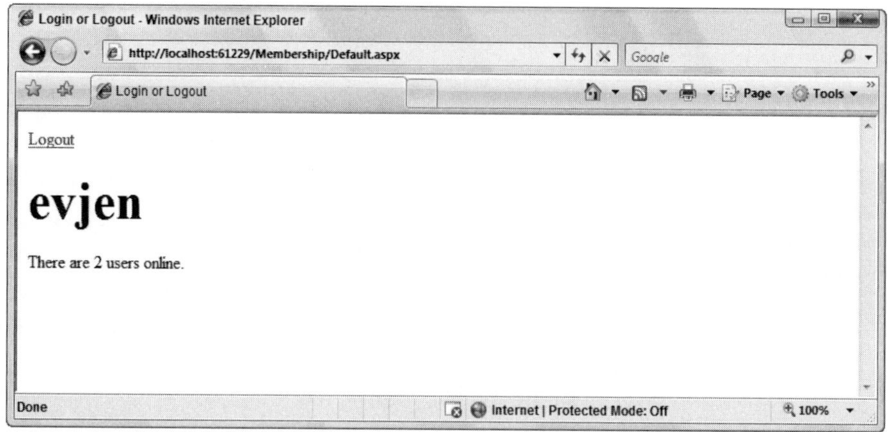

FIGURE 15-14

You can see that two users have logged on in the last 15 minutes. This 15-minute period is determined in the `machine.config` file from within the `<membership>` element:

```
<membership userIsOnlineTimeWindow="15" >
</membership>
```

By default, the `userIsOnlineTimeWindow` is set to `15`. The number is specified here in minutes. To increase the time window, you simply increase this number. In addition to specifying this number from within the `machine.config` file, you can also set this number in the `web.config` file.

Dealing with Passwords

Many of us seem to spend our lives online and have username/password combinations for many different Web sites on the Internet. For this reason, end users forget passwords or want to change them every so often. ASP.NET provides a couple of server controls that work with the membership service so that end users can either change their passwords or retrieve forgotten passwords.

The ChangePassword Server Control

The ChangePassword server control enables end users to change their passwords directly in the browser. Listing 15-21 shows a use of the ChangePassword control.

Available for download on Wrox.com

LISTING 15-21: Allowing users to change passwords

```
<%@ Page Language="VB" %>

<html xmlns="http://www.w3.org/1999/xhtml">
<head runat="server">
    <title>Change Your Password</title>
</head>
<body>
    <form id="form1" runat="server">
        <asp:LoginStatus ID="LoginStatus1" Runat="server" />
        <p><asp:ChangePassword ID="ChangePassword1" Runat="server">
           </asp:ChangePassword><p>
    </form>
</body>
</html>
```

This example is a rather simple use of the `<asp:ChangePassword>` control. Running this page produces the results shown in Figure 15-15.

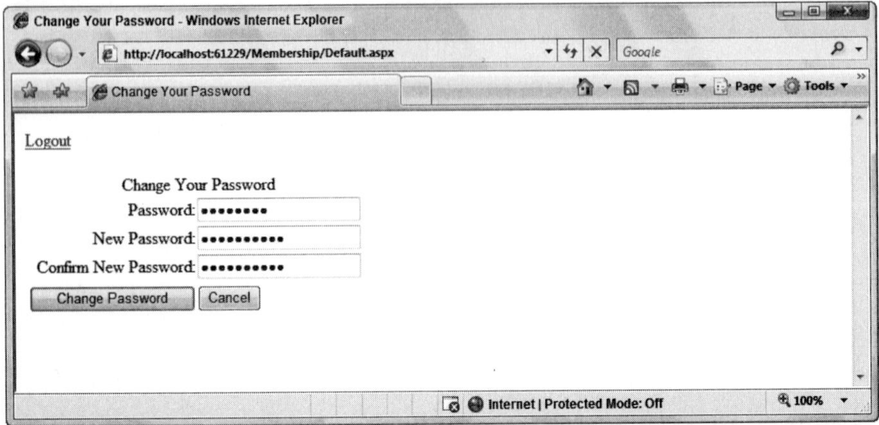

FIGURE 15-15

The ChangePassword control produces a form that asks for the previous password. It also requires the end user to type the new password twice. Clicking the Change Password button launches an attempt to change the password if the user is logged in. If the end user is not logged in to the application yet, he or she is redirected to the login page. Only a logged-in user can change a password. After the password is changed, the end user is notified (see Figure 15-16).

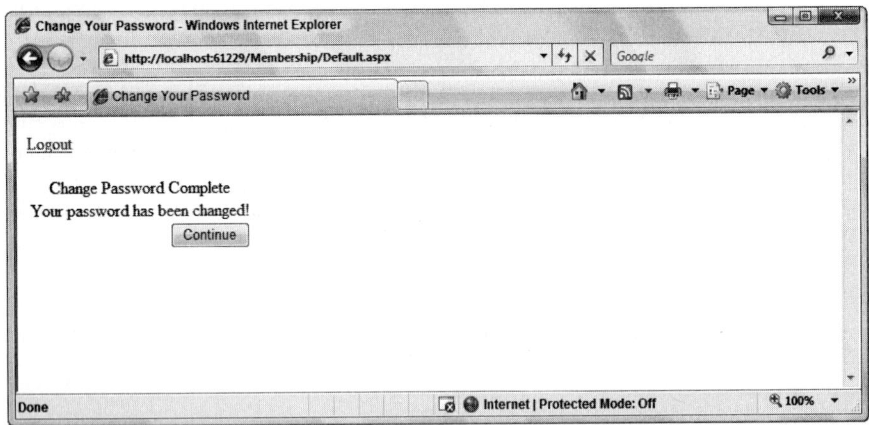

FIGURE 15-16

Remember that end users are allowed to change their passwords because the `enablePasswordReset` attribute of the membership provider is set to `true`. To deny this capability, set the `enablePasswordReset` attribute to `false`.

You can also specify rules on how the passwords must be constructed when an end user attempts to change her password. For instance, you might want to require that the password contain more than a certain number of characters or that it use numbers and/or special characters in addition to alphabetic characters. Using the `NewPasswordRegularExpression` attribute, you can specify the construction required for the new password, as shown here:

```
NewPasswordRegularExpression='@\"(?=.{6,})(?=(.*\d){1,})(?=(.*\W){1,})'
```

Any new passwords created by the end user are checked against this regular expression. If there isn't a match, you can use the `NewPasswordRegularExpressionErrorMessage` attribute (one of the lengthier names for an attribute in ASP.NET) to cause an error message to appear within the control output.

The PasswordRecovery Server Control

People simply forget their passwords. For this reason, you should provide the means to retrieve passwords from your data store. The PasswordRecovery server control provides an easy way to accomplish this task.

Password recovery usually means sending the end user's password to that user in an e-mail. Therefore, you need to set up an SMTP server (it might be the same as the application server). You configure for SMTP in the `web.config` file, as illustrated in Listing 15-22.

Available for download on Wrox.com

LISTING 15-22: Configuring passwords to be sent via e-mail in the web.config file

```
<configuration>
   <system.web>
      <!-- Removed for clarity -->
   </system.web>

   <system.net>

      <mailSettings>
         <smtp from="someuser@email.com">
            <network host="localhost" port="25"
             defaultCredentials="true" />
         </smtp>
      </mailSettings>

   </system.net>
</configuration>
```

After you have the `<mailSettings>` element set up correctly, you can start to use the PasswordRecovery control. Listing 15-23 shows a simple use of the PasswordRecovery control.

Available for download on Wrox.com

LISTING 15-23: Using the PasswordRecovery control

```
<%@ Page Language="VB" %>

<html xmlns="http://www.w3.org/1999/xhtml">
<head runat="server">
    <title>Getting Your Password</title>
</head>
<body>
    <form id="form1" runat="server">
        <asp:PasswordRecovery ID="PasswordRecovery1" Runat="server">
            <MailDefinition From="someuser@email.com">
            </MailDefinition>
        </asp:PasswordRecovery>
    </form>
</body>
</html>
```

The `<asp:PasswordRecovery>` element needs a `<MailDefinition>` sub-element. The `<MailDefinition>` element contains details about the e-mail to be sent to the end user. The minimum requirement is that the `From` attribute is used, which provides the e-mail address for the From part of the e-mail. The `String` value of this attribute should be an e-mail address. Other attributes for the `<MailDefinition>` element include the following:

- `BodyFileName`
- `CC`
- `From`
- `IsBodyHtml`
- `Priority`
- `Subject`

When you run this page, the PasswordRecovery control asks for the user's username, as shown in Figure 15-17.

FIGURE 15-17

When it has the username, the membership service retrieves the question and answer that was earlier entered by the end user and generates the view shown in Figure 15-18.

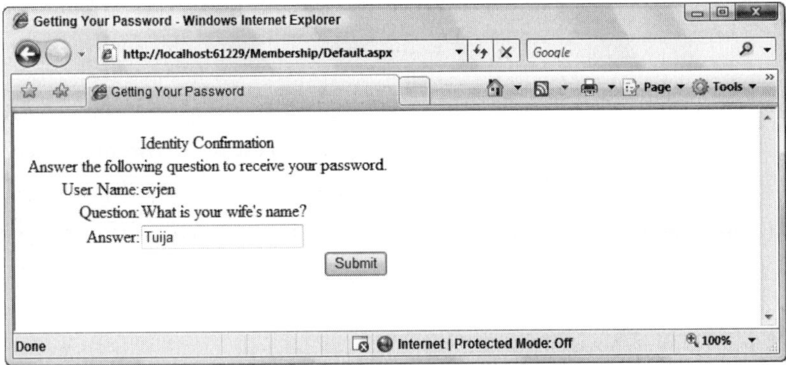

FIGURE 15-18

If the question is answered correctly (notice that the answer is case sensitive), an e-mail containing the password is generated and mailed to the end user. If the question is answered incorrectly, an error message is displayed. Of course, a question will not be used if you have the Question/Answer feature of the membership system disabled.

Changing some of your membership service settings is important for this entire process to work. At present, it will not work because of the way in which a user's password is hashed. The membership service data store is not storing the actual password — just a hashed version of it. Of course, receiving a hashed password is useless for an end user.

For you to be able to send back an actual password to the user, you must change how the passwords are stored in the membership service data store. You do this (as stated earlier in the chapter) by changing the `PasswordFormat` attribute of your membership data provider. The other possible values (besides `Hashed`) are `Clear` and `Encrypted`. Changing the value to either `Clear` or `Encrypted` makes it possible for the passwords to be sent back to the end user in a readable format.

Generating Random Passwords

Certain applications must generate a random password when creating a user. In the days of ASP.NET 1.0/1.1, this was something you had to code yourself. ASP.NET 2.0 and above, on the other hand, include a helper method that enables you to retrieve random passwords. Listing 15-24 shows an example of creating a helper method to pull a random password.

LISTING 15-24: Generating a random password

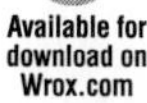

Available for download on Wrox.com

VB

```
Protected Function GeneratePassword() As String
   Dim returnPassword As String
   returnPassword = Membership.GeneratePassword(10, 3)

   Return returnPassword
End Function
```

C#

```
protected string GeneratePassword()
{
   string returnPassword;
   returnPassword = Membership.GeneratePassword(10, 3);

   return returnPassword;
}
```

To generate a password randomly in ASP.NET, you can use the `GeneratePassword()` helper method. This method allows you to generate a random password of a specified length, and you can specify how many non-alphanumeric characters the password should contain (at minimum). This example utilizes this method five times to produce the results shown here (of course, your results will be different):

- `D](KQg6s2[`
- `$X.M9]*x2-`
- `Q+lIy2#zD%`
- `%kWZL@zy&f`
- `o]&IhL#iU1`

With your helper method in place, you can create users with random passwords, as shown in Listing 15-25.

LISTING 15-25: Creating users with a random password

VB

```
Membership.CreateUser(TextBox1.Text, GeneratePassword().ToString())
```

C#

```
<Membership.CreateUser(TextBox1.Text, GeneratePassword().ToString());
```

ASP.NET 4 AUTHORIZATION

Now that you can deal with the registration and authentication of users who want to access your Web applications, the next step is authorization. What are they allowed to see and what roles do they take? These questions are important for any Web application. The following section explains how to show only certain items to authenticated users while you show different items to unauthenticated users.

Using the LoginView Server Control

The LoginView server control enables you to control who views what information on a particular part of a page. Using the LoginView control, you can dictate which parts of the pages are for authenticated users and which parts of the pages are for unauthenticated users. Listing 15-26 shows an example of this control.

LISTING 15-26: Controlling information viewed via the LoginView control

Available for download on Wrox.com

```
<%@ Page Language="VB" %>

<html xmlns="http://www.w3.org/1999/xhtml">
<head runat="server">
    <title>Changing the View</title>
</head>
```

continues

LISTING 15-26 *(continued)*

```
<body>
    <form id="form1" runat="server">
        <asp:LoginStatus ID="LoginStatus1" Runat="server" />
        <p>
        <asp:LoginView ID="LoginView1" Runat="server">
            <LoggedInTemplate>
                Here is some REALLY important information that you should know
                about all those people that are not authenticated!
            </LoggedInTemplate>
            <AnonymousTemplate>
                Here is some basic information for you.
            </AnonymousTemplate>
        </asp:LoginView><p>
    </form>
</body>
</html>
```

The `<asp:LoginView>` control is a templated control that takes two possible sub-elements — the `<LoggedInTemplate>` and `<AnonymousTemplate>` elements. In this case, the information defined in the `<AnonymousTemplate>` section (see Figure 15-19) is for unauthenticated users.

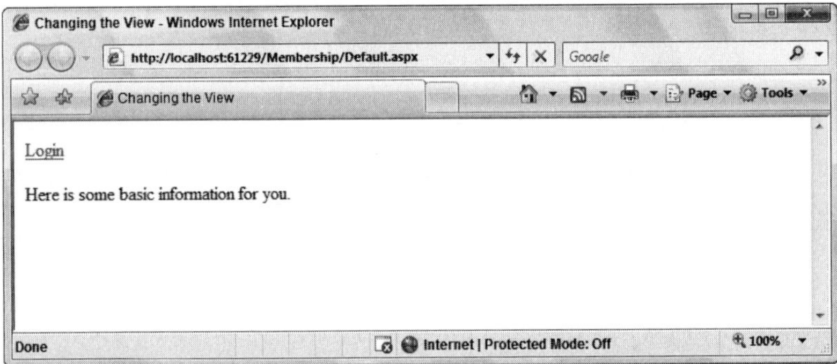

FIGURE 15-19

It is quite different from what authenticated users see defined in the `<LoggedInTemplate>` section (see Figure 15-20).

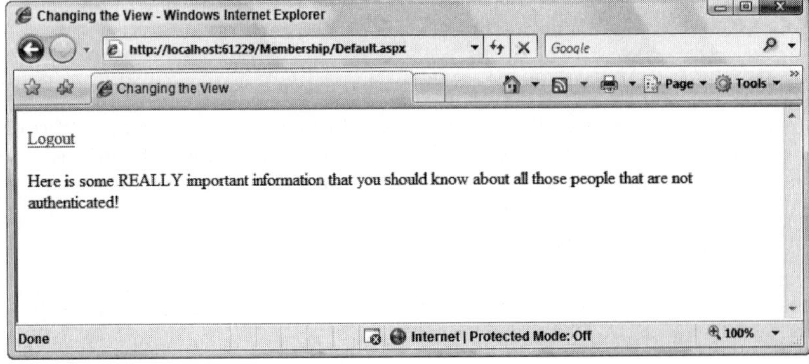

FIGURE 15-20

Only simple ASCII text is placed inside both of these templates, but you can actually place anything else within the template including additional server controls. This means that you can show entire sections of pages, including forms, from within the templated sections.

Besides using just the `<LoggedInTemplate>` and the `<AnonymousTemplate>` of the LoginView control, you can also enable sections of a page or specific content for entities that are part of a particular role — such as someone who is part of the `Admin` group. You can accomplish this by using the `<RoleGroups>` section of the LoginView control, as shown in Listing 15-27

Available for download on Wrox.com

LISTING 15-27: Providing a view for a particular group

```
<%@ Page Language="VB" %>

<html xmlns="http://www.w3.org/1999/xhtml">
<head runat="server">
    <title>Changing the View</title>
</head>
<body>
    <form id="form1" runat="server">
        <asp:LoginStatus ID="LoginStatus1" Runat="server" />
        <p>
        <asp:LoginView ID="LoginView1" Runat="server">
            <LoggedInTemplate>
                Here is some REALLY important information that you should know
                about all those people that are not authenticated!
            </LoggedInTemplate>
            <AnonymousTemplate>
                Here is some basic information for you.
            </AnonymousTemplate>
             <RoleGroups>
                <asp:RoleGroup Roles="Admins">
                    <ContentTemplate>
                       You are an Admin!
                    </ContentTemplate>
                </asp:RoleGroup>
                <asp:RoleGroup Roles="CoolPeople">
                    <ContentTemplate>
                       You are cool!
                    </ContentTemplate>
                </asp:RoleGroup>
            </RoleGroups>
        </asp:LoginView><p>
    </form>
</body>
</html>
```

To show content for a particular group of users, you add a `<RoleGroups>` element to the LoginView control. The `<RoleGroups>` section can take one or more RoleGroup controls (you will not find this control in Visual Studio's Toolbox). To provide content to display using the RoleGroup control, you provide a `<ContentTemplate>` element, which enables you to define the content to be displayed for an entity that belongs to the specified role. What is placed in the `<ContentTemplate>` section completely depends on you. You can place raw text (as shown in the example) or even other ASP.NET controls.

Be cautious of the order in which you place the defined roles in the `<RoleGroups>` section. When users log in to a site, they are first checked to see whether they match one of the defined roles. The first (uppermost) role matched is the view used for the LoginView control — even if they match more than one role. You can also place more than one role in the `Roles` attribute of the `<asp:RoleGroups>` control, like this:

```
<asp:RoleGroup Roles="CoolPeople, HappyPeople">
   <ContentTemplate>
      You are cool or happy (or both)!
   </ContentTemplate>
</asp:RoleGroup>
```

Setting Up Your Web Site for Role Management

In addition to the membership service just reviewed, ASP.NET provides you with the other side of the end-user management service — the ASP.NET role management service. The membership service covers all the details of authentication for your applications, whereas the role management service covers authorization. Just as the membership service can use any of the data providers listed earlier, the role management service can also use a provider that is focused on SQL Server (SqlRoleProvider) or any custom providers. In fact, this service is comparable to the membership service in many ways. Figure 15-21 shows you a simple diagram that details some particulars of the role management service.

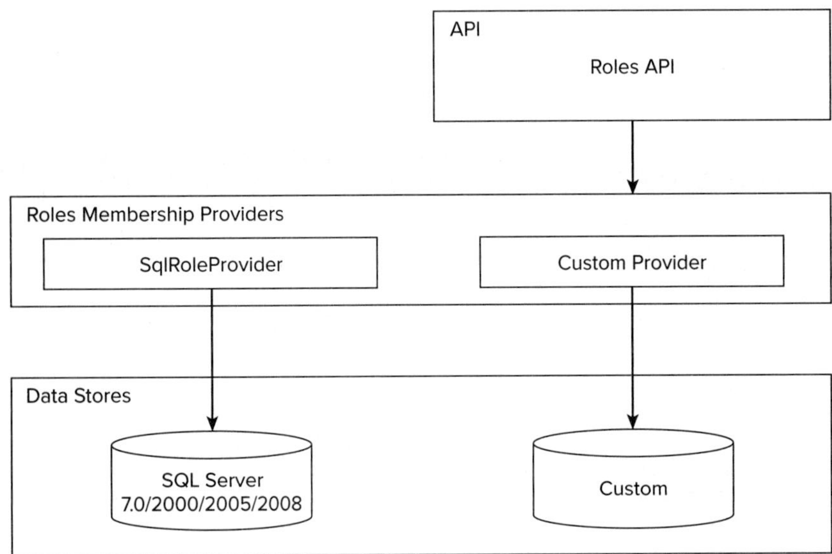

FIGURE 15-21

Making Changes to the <roleManager> Section

The first step in working with the role management service is to change any of the role management provider's behaviors either in the `machine.config` or from the `web.config` files. If you look in the `machine.config.comments` file, you will see an entire section that deals with the role management service (see Listing 15-28).

LISTING 15-28: Role management provider settings in the machine.config.comments file

Available for download on Wrox.com

```
<roleManager
 enabled="false"
 cacheRolesInCookie="false"
 cookieName=".ASPXROLES"
 cookieTimeout="30"
 cookiePath="/"
 cookieRequireSSL="false"
 cookieSlidingExpiration="true"
 cookieProtection="All"
 defaultProvider="AspNetSqlRoleProvider"
 createPersistentCookie="false"
 maxCachedResults="25">
   <providers>
      <clear />
      <add connectionStringName="LocalSqlServer" applicationName="/"
       name="AspNetSqlRoleProvider" type="System.Web.Security.SqlRoleProvider,
```

```
            System.Web, Version=4.0.0.0, Culture=neutral,
            PublicKeyToken=b03f5f7f11d50a3a" />
        <add applicationName="/" name="AspNetWindowsTokenRoleProvider"
            type="System.Web.Security.WindowsTokenRoleProvider, System.Web,
            Version=4.0.0.0, Culture=neutral, PublicKeyToken=b03f5f7f11d50a3a" />
    </providers>
</roleManager>
```

The role management service documents its settings from within the `machine.config.comments` file, as shown in the previous code listing. You can make changes to these settings either directly in the `machine.config` file or by overriding any of the higher level settings you might have by making changes in the `web.config` file itself (thereby making changes only to the application at hand).

The main settings are defined in the `<roleManager>` element. Table 15-2 defines some of the attributes of the `<roleManager>` element.

TABLE 15-2

ATTRIBUTE	DESCRIPTION
`enabled`	Defines whether the role management service is enabled for the application. This attribute takes a `Boolean` value and is set to `False` by default. This means that the role management service is disabled by default. This is done to avoid breaking changes that would occur for users migrating from ASP.NET 1.0/1.1 to ASP.NET 2.0, 3.5, or 4. Therefore, you must first change this value to `True` in either the `machine.config` or the `web.config` file.
`cacheRolesInCookie`	Defines whether the roles of the user can be stored within a cookie on the client machine. This attribute takes a `Boolean` value and is set to `True` by default. This situation is ideal because retrieving the roles from the cookie prevents ASP.NET from looking up the roles of the user via the role management provider. Set it to `False` if you want the roles to be retrieved via the provider for all instances.
`cookieName`	Defines the name used for the cookie sent to the end user for role management information storage. By default, this cookie is named `.ASPXROLES`, and you probably will not change this.
`cookieTimeout`	Defines the amount of time (in minutes) after which the cookie expires. The default value is `30` minutes.
`cookieRequireSSL`	Defines whether you require that the role management information be sent over an encrypted wire (SSL) instead of being sent as clear text. The default value is `False`.
`cookieSlidingExpiration`	Specifies whether the timeout of the cookie is on a sliding scale. The default value is `True`. This means that the end user's cookie does not expire until 30 minutes (or the time specified in the `cookieTimeout` attribute) after the last request to the application has been made. If the value of the `cookieSlidingExpiration` attribute is set to `False`, the cookie expires 30 minutes from the first request.
`createPersistentCookie`	Specifies whether a cookie expires or whether it remains alive indefinitely. The default setting is `False` because a persistent cookie is not always advisable for security reasons.
`cookieProtection`	Specifies the amount of protection you want to apply to the cookie stored on the end user's machine for management information. The possible settings include `All`, `None`, `Encryption`, and `Validation`. You should always attempt to use `All`.
`defaultProvider`	Defines the provider used for the role management service. By default, it is set to `AspNetSqlRoleProvider`.

Making Changes to the web.config File

The next step is to configure your web.config file so that it can work with the role management service. Certain pages or subsections of your application may be accessible only to people with specific roles. To manage this access, you define the access rights in the web.config file. Listing 15-29 shows the necessary changes.

LISTING 15-29: Changing the web.config file

Available for download on Wrox.com

```
<?xml version="1.0" encoding="utf-8"?>
<configuration>

    <system.web>
        <compilation targetFramework="4.0">
        <roleManager enabled="true"/>
        <authentication mode="Forms" />
        <authorization>
           <deny users="?" />
        </authorization>
    </system.web>

    <location path="AdminPage.aspx">
        <system.web>
           <authorization>
              <allow roles="AdminPageRights" />
              <deny users="*" />
           </authorization>
        </system.web>
    </location>

</configuration>
```

This web.config file is doing a couple of things. First, the function of the first <system.web> section is no different from that of the membership service shown earlier in the chapter. The <deny> element is denying all unauthenticated users across the board.

The second section of this web.config file is rather interesting. The <location> element is used to define the access rights of a particular page in the application (AdminPage.aspx). In this case, only users contained in the AdminPageRights role are allowed to view the page, but all other users — regardless of whether they are authenticated — are not allowed to view the page. When using the asterisk (*) as a value of the users attribute of the <deny> element, you are saying that all users (regardless of whether they are authenticated) are not allowed to access the resource being defined. This overriding denial of access, however, is broken open a bit via the use of the <allow> element, which allows users contained within a specific role.

Adding and Retrieving Application Roles

Now that the machine.config or the web.config file is in place, you can add roles to the role management service. The role management service, just like the membership service, uses data stores to store information about the users. These examples focus primarily on using Microsoft SQL Server Express Edition as the provider because it is the default provider.

One big difference between the role management service and the membership service is that no server controls are used for the role management service. You manage the application's roles and the user's role details through a Roles API or through the Web Site Administration Tool provided with ASP.NET 4. Listing 15-30 shows how to use some of the new methods to add roles to the service.

LISTING 15-30: Adding roles to the application

Available for download on Wrox.com

VB

```
<%@ Page Language="VB" %>

<script runat="server">
```

```
    Protected Sub Page_Load(ByVal sender As Object, ByVal e As System.EventArgs)
        If Not Page.IsPostBack Then
           ListBoxDataBind()
        End If
    End Sub

    Protected Sub Button1_Click(ByVal sender As Object, ByVal e As System.EventArgs)
        Roles.CreateRole(TextBox1.Text)
        ListBoxDataBind()
    End Sub

    Protected Sub ListBoxDataBind()
        ListBox1.DataSource = Roles.GetAllRoles()
        ListBox1.DataBind()
    End Sub
</script>

<html xmlns="http://www.w3.org/1999/xhtml">
<head runat="server">
    <title>Role Manager</title>
</head>
<body>
    <form id="form1" runat="server">
        <h1>Role Manager</h1>
        Add Role:<br />
        <asp:TextBox ID="TextBox1" Runat="server"></asp:TextBox>
        <p><asp:Button ID="Button1" Runat="server" Text="Add Role to Application"
            OnClick="Button1_Click" /></p>
        Roles Defined:<br />
        <asp:ListBox ID="ListBox1" Runat="server">
        </asp:ListBox>
    </form>
</body>
</html>
```

C#

```
<%@ Page Language="C#" %>

<script runat="server">
   protected void Page_Load(object sender, EventArgs e)
   {
      if (!Page.IsPostBack)
      {
         ListBoxDataBind();
      }
   }

   protected void Button1_Click(object sender, EventArgs e)
   {
      Roles.CreateRole(TextBox1.Text.ToString());
      ListBoxDataBind();
   }

   protected void ListBoxDataBind()
   {
      ListBox1.DataSource = Roles.GetAllRoles();
      ListBox1.DataBind();
   }
</script>
```

This example enables you to enter roles into the text box and then to submit them to the role management service. The roles contained in the role management service then appear in the list box, as illustrated in Figure 15-22.

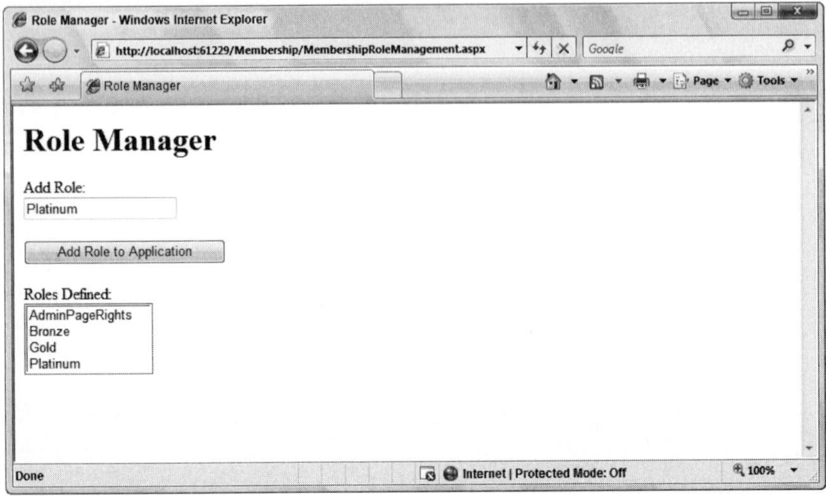

FIGURE 15-22

To enter the roles into the management service, you simply use the `CreateRole()` method of the `Roles` class. As with the `Membership` class, you do not instantiate the `Roles` class. To add roles to the role management service, use the `CreateRole()` method that takes only a single parameter — the name of the role as a `String` value:

```
Roles.CreateRole(rolename As String)
```

With this method, you can create as many roles as you want, but each role must be unique — otherwise an exception is thrown.

To retrieve the roles that are in the application's role management service (such as the list of roles displayed in the list box from the earlier example), you use the `GetAllRoles()` method of the `Roles` class. This method returns a `String` collection of all the available roles in the service:

```
Roles.GetAllRoles()
```

Deleting Roles

It would be just great to sit and add roles to the service all day long. Every now and then, however, you might want to delete roles from the service as well. Deleting roles is just as easy as adding roles to the role management service. To delete a role, you use one of the `DeleteRole()` method signatures. The first option of the `DeleteRole()` method takes a single parameter — the name of the role as a `String` value. The second option takes the name of the role plus a `Boolean` value that determines whether to throw an exception when one or more members are contained within that particular role (so that you don't accidentally delete a role with users in it when you don't mean to):

```
Roles.DeleteRole(rolename As String)

Roles.DeleteRole(rolename As String, throwOnPopulatedRole As Boolean)
```

Listing 15-31 is a partial code example that builds on Listing 15-30. For this example, you add an additional button that initiates a second button-click event that deletes the role from the service.

LISTING 15-31: Deleting roles from the application

Available for download on Wrox.com

VB

```
Protected Sub DeleteButton_Click(ByVal sender As Object,
   ByVal e As System.EventArgs)

   For Each li As ListItem In ListBox1.Items
      If li.Selected = True Then
```

```
            Roles.DeleteRole(li.ToString())
        End If
    Next

    ListBoxDataBind()
End Sub
```

C#

```
protected void DeleteButton_Click(object sender, EventArgs e)
{
    foreach (ListItem li in ListBox1.Items) {
        if (li.Selected == true) {
            Roles.DeleteRole(li.ToString());
        }
    }

    ListBoxDataBind();
}
```

This example deletes the selected items from the ListBox control. If more than one selection is made (meaning that you have placed the attribute `SelectionMode = "Multiple"` in the ListBox control), each of the roles is deleted from the service, in turn, in the `For Each` loop. Although `Roles.DeleteRole(li.ToString())` is used to delete the role, `Roles.DeleteRole(li.ToString(), True)` could also be used to make sure that no roles are deleted if that role contains any members.

Adding Users to Roles

Now that the roles are in place and it is possible to delete these roles if required, the next step is adding users to the roles created. A role does not do much good if no users are associated with it. To add a single user to a single role, you use the following construct:

```
Roles.AddUserToRole(username As String, rolename As String)
```

To add a single user to multiple roles at the same time, you use this construct:

```
Roles.AddUserToRoles(username As String, rolenames() As String)
```

To add multiple users to a single role, you use the following construct:

```
Roles.AddUsersToRole(usernames() As String, rolename As String)
```

Finally, to add multiple users to multiple roles, you use the following construct:

```
Roles.AddUsersToRoles(usernames() As String, rolenames() As String)
```

The parameters that can take collections, whether they are `usernames()` or `rolenames()`, are presented to the method as `String` arrays.

Getting All the Users of a Particular Role

Looking up information is easy in the role management service, whether you are determining which users are contained within a particular role or whether you want to know the roles that a particular user belongs to.

Methods are available for either of these scenarios. First, look at how to determine all the users contained in a particular role, as illustrated in Listing 15-32.

LISTING 15-32: Looking up users in a particular role

Available for download on Wrox.com

```
<%@ Page Language="VB" %>

<script runat="server">
    Protected Sub Page_Load(ByVal sender As Object, ByVal e As System.EventArgs)
        If Not Page.IsPostBack Then
            DropDownDataBind()
        End If
```

continues

LISTING 15-32 *(continued)*

```
    End Sub

    Protected Sub Button1_Click(ByVal sender As Object, ByVal e As System.EventArgs)
        GridView1.DataSource = Roles.GetUsersInRole(DropDownList1.SelectedValue)
        GridView1.DataBind()
        DropDownDataBind()
    End Sub

    Protected Sub DropDownDataBind()
       DropDownList1.DataSource = Roles.GetAllRoles()
       DropDownList1.DataBind()
    End Sub

</script>

<html xmlns="http://www.w3.org/1999/xhtml">
<head runat="server">
    <title>Role Manager</title>
</head>
<body>
    <form id="form1" runat="server">
        Roles:
        <asp:DropDownList ID="DropDownList1" Runat="server">
        </asp:DropDownList>
        <asp:Button ID="Button1" Runat="server" Text="Get Users In Role"
         OnClick="Button1_Click" />
        <br />
        <br />
        <asp:GridView ID="GridView1" Runat="server">
        </asp:GridView>
    </form>
</body>
</html>
```

C#

```
<%@ Page Language="C#" %>

<script runat="server">
   protected void Page_Load(object sender, EventArgs e)
   {
      if (!Page.IsPostBack)
      {
         DropDownDataBind();
      }
   }

   protected void Button1_Click(object sender, EventArgs e)
   {
      GridView1.DataSource = Roles.GetUsersInRole(DropDownList1.SelectedValue);
      GridView1.DataBind();
      DropDownDataBind();
   }

   protected void DropDownDataBind()
   {
      DropDownList1.DataSource = Roles.GetAllRoles();
      DropDownList1.DataBind();
   }
</script>
```

This page creates a drop-down list that contains all the roles for the application. Clicking the button displays all the users for the selected role. Users of a particular role are determined using the `GetUsersInRole()` method. This method takes a single parameter — a `String` value representing the name of the role:

```
Roles.GetUsersInRole(rolename As String)
```

When run, the page looks similar to the page shown in Figure 15-23.

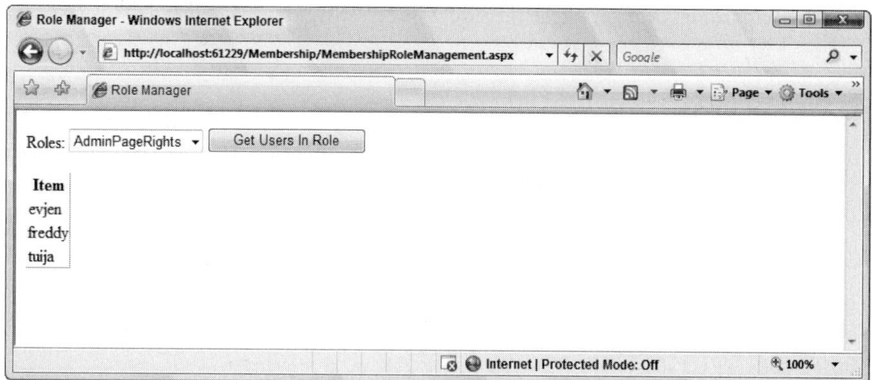

FIGURE 15-23

Getting All the Roles of a Particular User

To determine all the roles for a particular user, create a page with a single text box and a button. In the text box, you type the name of the user; a button click initiates the retrieval and populates a GridView control. Listing 15-33 presents the button click event (where all the action is).

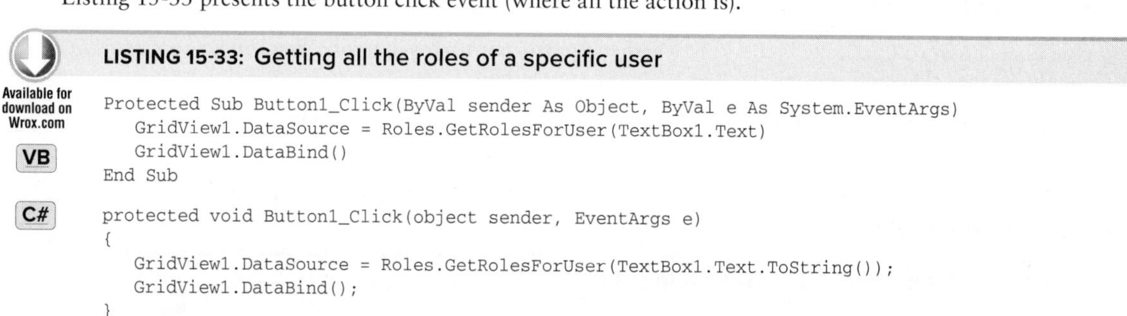

LISTING 15-33: Getting all the roles of a specific user

Available for download on Wrox.com

VB

```
Protected Sub Button1_Click(ByVal sender As Object, ByVal e As System.EventArgs)
   GridView1.DataSource = Roles.GetRolesForUser(TextBox1.Text)
   GridView1.DataBind()
End Sub
```

C#

```
protected void Button1_Click(object sender, EventArgs e)
{
   GridView1.DataSource = Roles.GetRolesForUser(TextBox1.Text.ToString());
   GridView1.DataBind();
}
```

The preceding code produces something similar to what is shown in Figure 15-24.

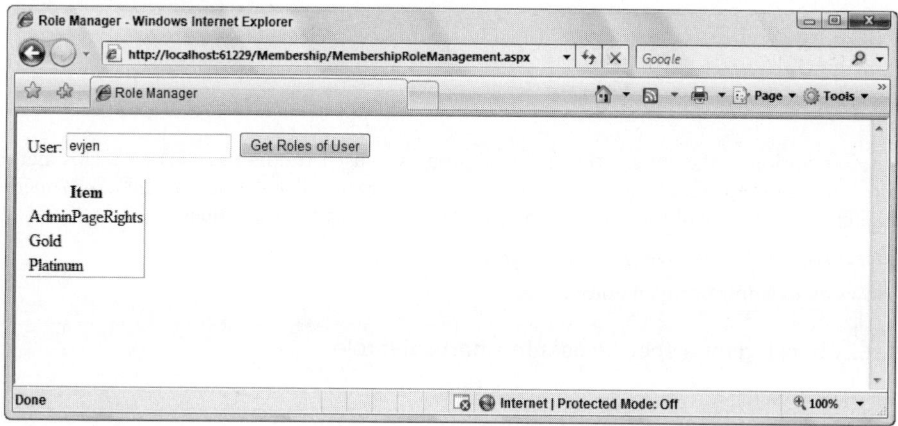

FIGURE 15-24

To get the roles of a particular user, you simply use the `GetRolesForUser()` method. This method has two possible signatures. The first is shown in the preceding example — a `String` value that represents the name of the user. The other option is an invocation of the method without any parameters listed. This returns the roles of the user who has logged in to the membership service.

Removing Users from Roles

In addition to adding users to roles, you can also easily remove users from roles. To delete or remove a single user from a single role, you use the following construct:

```
Roles.RemoveUserFromRole(username As String, rolename As String)
```

To remove a single user from multiple roles at the same time, you use this construct:

```
Roles.RemoveUserFromRoles(username As String, rolenames() As String)
```

To remove multiple users from a single role, you use the following construct:

```
Roles.RemoveUsersFromRole(usernames() As String, rolename As String)
```

Finally, to remove multiple users from multiple roles, you use the following construct:

```
Roles.RemoveUsersFromRoles(usernames() As String, rolenames() As String)
```

The parameters shown as collections, whether they are `usernames()` or `rolenames()`, are presented to the method as `String` arrays.

Checking Users in Roles

One final action you can take is checking whether a particular user is in a role. You can go about this in a couple of ways. The first is using the `IsUserInRole()` method.

The `IsUserInRole()` method takes two parameters — the username and the name of the role:

```
Roles.IsUserInRole(username As String, rolename As String)
```

This method returns a `Boolean` value on the status of the user, and you can use it as shown in Listing 15-34.

LISTING 15-34: Checking a user's role status

VB

```
If (Roles.IsUserInRole(TextBox1.Text, "AdminPageRights")) Then
  ' perform action here
End If
```

C#

```
if (Roles.IsUserInRole(TextBox1.Text.ToString(), "AdminPageRights"))
{
   // perform action here
}
```

The other option, in addition to the `IsUserInRole()` method, is to use `FindUsersInRole()`. This method enables you make a name search against all the users in a particular role. The `FindUsersInRole()` method takes two parameters — the name of the role and the username, both as `String` values:

```
Roles.FindUsersInRole(rolename As String, username As String)
```

Listing 15-35 shows an example of this method.

LISTING 15-35: Checking for a specific user in a particular role

Available for download on Wrox.com

VB

```
<%@ Page Language="VB" %>

<script runat="server">
   Protected Sub Button1_Click(ByVal sender As Object, ByVal e As System.EventArgs)
       GridView1.DataSource =
          Roles.FindUsersInRole("AdminPageRights", TextBox1.Text)
```

```
        GridView1.DataBind()
    End Sub
</script>

<html xmlns="http://www.w3.org/1999/xhtml" >
<head runat="server">
    <title>Role Manager</title>
</head>
<body>
    <form id="form1" runat="server">
        <asp:TextBox ID="TextBox1" Runat="server"></asp:TextBox>
        <asp:Button ID="Button1" Runat="server" Text="Button"
         OnClick="Button1_Click" />
        <p><asp:GridView ID="GridView1" Runat="server">
        </asp:GridView></p>
    </form>
</body>
</html>
```

C#

```
<%@ Page Language="C#" %>

<script runat="server">
   protected void Button1_Click(object sender, EventArgs e)
   {
        GridView1.DataSource =
           Roles.FindUsersInRole("AdminPageRights", TextBox1.Text.ToString());
        GridView1.DataBind();
   }
</script>
```

Understanding How Roles Are Cached

By default, after you retrieve a user's roles from the data store underlying the role management service, you can store these roles as a cookie on the client machine. This is done so you do not have to access the data store each and every time the application needs a user's role status. A bit of risk always exists when working with cookies because the end user can manipulate the cookie and thereby gain access to information or parts of an application that normally would be forbidden to that particular user.

Although roles are cached in a cookie, the default is that they are cached for only 30 minutes at a time. You can deal with this role cookie in several ways — some of which might help to protect your application better.

One protection for your application is to delete this role cookie, using the `DeleteCookie()` method of the Roles API, when the end user logs on to the site, as illustrated in Listing 15-36.

LISTING 15-36: Deleting the end user's role cookie upon authentication

Available for download on Wrox.com

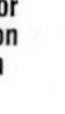

VB

```
If Membership.ValidateUser(TextBox1.Text, TextBox2.Text) Then
   Roles.DeleteCookie()
   FormsAuthentication.RedirectFromLoginPage(TextBox1.Text, False)
Else
   Label1.Text = "You are not registered with the site."
End If
```

C#

```
if (Membership.ValidateUser(TextBox1.Text.ToString(), TextBox2.Text.ToString())
{
   Roles.DeleteCookie();
   FormsAuthentication.RedirectFromLoginPage(TextBox1.Text.ToString(), false);
}
else {
   Label1.Text = "You are not registered with the site.";
}
```

Using `Roles.DeleteCookie()` does exactly what you would think — it deletes from the client machine any cookie that is used to define the user's roles. If the end user is re-logging into the site, no problem should arise with re-authenticating his exact roles within the application. There is no need to rely on the contents of the cookie. This step provides a little more protection for your site.

USING THE WEB SITE ADMINISTRATION TOOL

You can also perform many of the actions shown in this chapter through the Web Site Administration Tool shown in Figure 15-25. You can get at the ASP.NET Web Site Administration Tool by selecting Website ➪ ASP.NET Configuration from the Visual Studio 2010 menu.

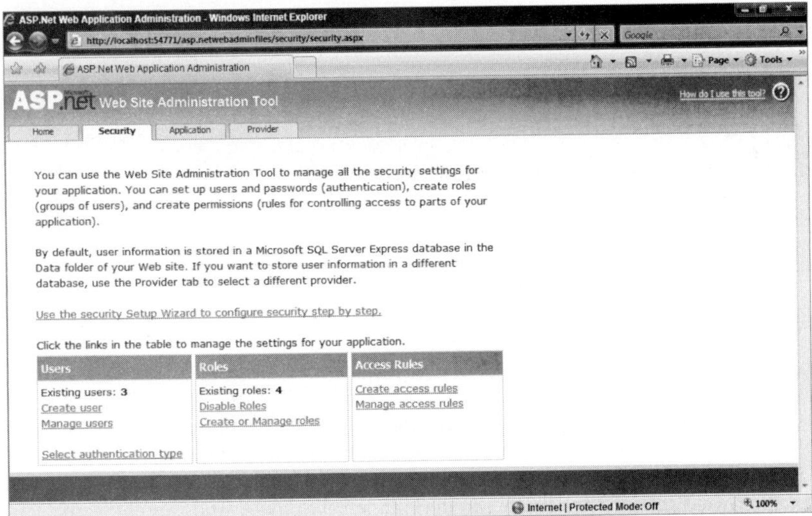

FIGURE 15-25

Although you can easily use this tool to perform all the actions for you, often you perform these actions through your own applications as well. Knowing all the possibilities when programming an ASP.NET application is important.

Chapter 35 provides details on the Web Site Administration Tool.

PUBLIC METHODS OF THE MEMBERSHIP API

Table 15-3 presents the public methods of the Membership API. You would use this API when working with the authentication process of your application.

TABLE 15-3

MEMBERSHIP METHODS	DESCRIPTION
`CreateUser`	Adds a new user to the appointed data store.
`DeleteUser`	Deletes a specified user from the data store.
`FindUsersByEmail`	Returns a collection of users who have an e-mail address to match the one provided.
`FindUsersByName`	Returns a collection of users who have a username to match the one provided.

MEMBERSHIP METHODS	DESCRIPTION
`GeneratePassword`	Generates a random password of a length that you specify.
`GetAllUsers`	Returns a collection of all the users contained in the data store.
`GetNumberOfUsersOnline`	Returns an Integer that specifies the number of users who have logged in to the application. The time window during which users are counted is specified in the `machine.config` or the `web.config` files.
`GetUser`	Returns information about a particular user from the data store.
`GetUserNameByEmail`	Retrieves a username of a specific record from the data store based on an e-mail address search.
`UpdateUser`	Updates a particular user's information in the data store.
`ValidateUser`	Returns a Boolean value indicating whether a specified set of credentials is valid.

PUBLIC METHODS OF THE ROLES API

Table 15-4 provides the public methods of the Roles API. You would use this API when working with the authorization process of your application.

TABLE 15-4

ROLES METHODS	DESCRIPTION
`AddUsersToRole`	Adds a collection of users to a specific role.
`AddUsersToRoles`	Adds a collection of users to a collection of roles.
`AddUserToRole`	Adds a specific user to a specific role.
`AddUserToRoles`	Adds a specific user to a collection of roles.
`CreateRole`	Adds a new role to the appointed data store.
`DeleteCookie`	Deletes the cookie on the client used to store the roles to which the user belongs.
`DeleteRole`	Deletes a specific role in the data store. Using the proper parameters for this method, you can also control whether roles are deleted or kept intact whether or not that particular role contains users.
`FindUsersInRole`	Returns a collection of users who have a username to match the one provided.
`GetAllRoles`	Returns a collection of all the roles stored in the data store.
`GetRolesForUser`	Returns a collection of roles for a specific user.
`IsUserInRole`	Returns a Boolean value that specifies whether a user is contained in a particular role.
`RemoveUserFromRole`	Removes a specific user from a specific role.
`RemoveUserFromRoles`	Removes a specific user from a collection of roles.
`RemoveUsersFromRole`	Removes a collection of users from a specific role.
`RemoveUsersFromRoles`	Removes a collection of users from a collection of roles.
`RoleExists`	Returns a Boolean value indicating whether a role exists in the data store.

SUMMARY

This chapter covered two outstanding features available to ASP.NET 4. The membership and role management services that are a part of ASP.NET make managing users and their roles almost trivial.

This chapter reviewed both the Membership and Roles APIs and the controls that also utilize these APIs. These controls and APIs follow the same data provider models as the rest of ASP.NET. The examples were presented using Microsoft SQL Server Express Edition for the backend storage, but you can easily configure these systems to work with another type of data store.

16

Portal Frameworks and Web Parts

WHAT'S IN THIS CHAPTER?

- Working with the Portal Framework
- Using the WebPartManager, WebPartZone, and WebPart controls to create dynamic Web sites
- Creating custom Web Part controls

Internet and intranet applications have changed considerably since their introduction in the 1990s. Today's applications do not simply display the same canned information to every viewer; they do much more. Because of the wealth of information being exposed to end users, Internet and intranet applications must integrate large amounts of customization and personalization into their offerings.

Web sites that provide a plethora of offerings give end users the option to choose which parts of the site they want to view and which parts they want to hide. Ideally, end users can personalize the pages, deciding for themselves the order in which the content appears on the page. They should be able to move items around on the page as if it were a design surface.

In this situation, after pages are customized and established, end users need the capability to export their final page settings for storage. You certainly would not want an end user who has highly customized a page or a series of pages in your portal to be forced to reapply the settings each time he visits the site. Instead, you want to retain these setting points by moving them to a data store for later exposure.

Adding this kind of functionality is *expensive* — expensive in the sense that it can take a considerable amount of work on the part of the developer. Prior to ASP.NET 2.0, the developer had to build a personalization framework to be used by each page requiring the functionality. This type of work is error prone and difficult to achieve, which is why in most cases it was not done.

But wait . . .

INTRODUCING WEB PARTS

To make retaining the page customization settings that your end users apply to your page easier, Microsoft has included Web Parts as part of ASP.NET ever since version 2.0. Web Parts, part of the larger Portal Framework, provide an outstanding way to build a modular Web site that can be customized with dynamically reapplied settings on a per-user basis. *Web Parts* are objects in the *Portal Framework* which the end user can open, close, minimize, maximize, or move from one part of the page to another.

The Portal Framework enables you to build pages that contain multiple Web Parts — which are part of the ASP.NET server control framework and are used like any other ASP.NET server controls. This means that you can also extend Web Parts if necessary.

The components of the Portal Framework provide the means to build a truly dynamic Web site, whether that site is a traditional Internet site, an intranet site, a browser-based application, or any other typical portal.

When you first look at Web Parts in ASP.NET 4, they may remind you of Microsoft's SharePoint offering. Be forewarned, however, that these two technologies are not the same. Web Parts and the resulting Portal Framework, besides being offered in ASP.NET, are also used by the Windows SharePoint Services (WSS). Microsoft, as it often does, is simply creating singular technologies that can be used by other Microsoft offerings. In this process, Microsoft is trying to reach the Holy Grail of computing — *code reuse!*

The modular and customizable sites that you can build with the Portal Framework enable you to place the Web page in view into several possible modes for the end user. The following list describes each of these available modes and what each means to the end user viewing the page:

- **Normal Mode:** Puts the page in a normal state, which means that the end user cannot edit or move sections of the page. This is the mode used for standard page viewing.
- **Edit Mode:** Enables end users to select particular sections on the page for editing. The selected section allows all types of editing capabilities from changing the part's title, the part's color, or even setting custom properties — such as allowing the end user to specify his or her zip code to pull up a customized weather report.
- **Design Mode:** Enables end users to rearrange the order of the page's modular components. The end user can bring items higher or lower within a zone, delete items from a zone, or move items from one page zone to another.
- **Catalog Mode:** Displays a list of available sections (Web Parts) that can be placed in the page. Catalog mode also allows the end user to select in which zone on the page the items should appear.

Figure 16-1 shows a screenshot of a sample portal utilizing the Portal Framework with the Edit mode enabled.

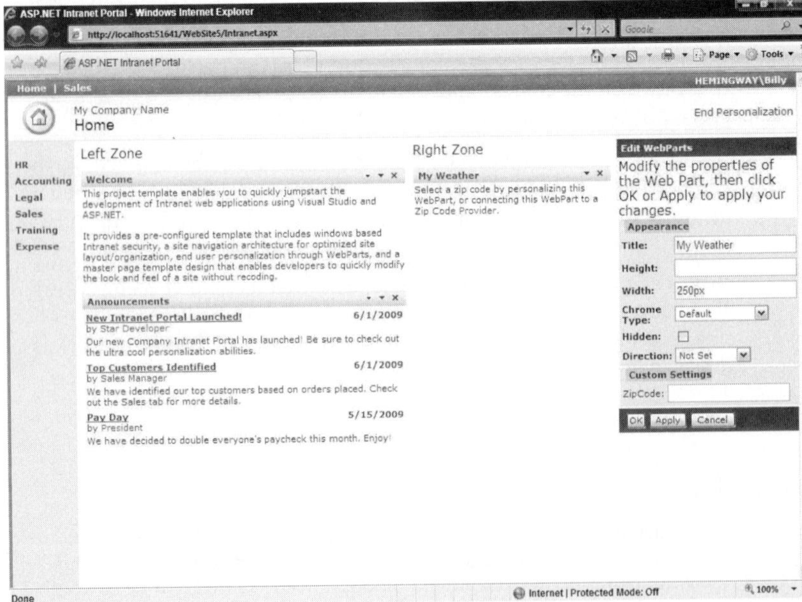

FIGURE 16-1

The Portal Framework is a comprehensive and well-thought-out framework that enables you to incorporate everything you would normally include in your ASP.NET applications. You can apply security using either Windows Authentication or Forms Authentication just as you can with a standard ASP.NET page. This framework also enables you to leverage the other aspects of ASP.NET, such as applying role management, personalization, and membership features to any portal that you build.

To help you understand how to build your own application on top of the Portal Framework, this chapter begins with the creation of a simple page that makes use of this framework's utilities.

BUILDING DYNAMIC AND MODULAR WEB SITES

As you begin using the Portal Framework to build Web sites, note that the framework defines everything in *zones*. There are zones for laying out as well as for editing content. The zones that a page might incorporate are managed by a Portal Framework manager. The Portal Framework manager performs the management on your behalf, meaning that you do not have to manage them yourself in any fashion. This feature makes working with the Portal Framework a breeze.

This framework contains a lot of moving parts, and these multiple pieces are heavily dependent upon each other. For this reason, this section starts at the beginning by examining the Portal Framework manager control: WebPartManager.

Introducing the WebPartManager Control

The WebPartManager control is an ASP.NET server control that completely manages the state of the zones and the content placed in these zones on a per-user basis. This control, which has no visual aspect, can add and delete items contained within each zone of the page. The WebPartManager control can also manage the communications sometimes required between different elements contained in the zones. For example, you can pass a specific name/value pair from one item to another item within the same zone, or between items contained in entirely separate zones. The WebPartManager control provides the capabilities to make this communication happen.

The WebPartManager control must be in place on every page in your application that works with the Portal Framework. A single WebPartManager control does not manage an entire application; instead, it manages on a per-page basis.

You can also place a WebPartManager server control on the master page (if you are using one) to avoid having to place one on each and every content page.

Listing 16-1 shows a WebPartManager control added to an ASP.NET page.

LISTING 16-1: Adding a WebPartManager control to an ASP.NET page

Available for download on Wrox.com

```
<%@ Page Language="VB" %>

<html xmlns="http://www.w3.org/1999/xhtml">
<head runat="server">
    <title>Web Parts Example</title>
</head>
<body>
    <form id="form1" runat="server">
        <asp:WebPartManager ID="Webpartmanager1" runat="server">
```

continues

LISTING 16-1 *(continued)*

```
            </asp:WebPartManager>
        </form>
    </body>
    </html>
```

If you want to work from the design surface of Visual Studio 2010, you can drag and drop the WebPartManager control from the Toolbox to the design surface — but remember, it does not have a visual aspect and appears only as a gray box. You can find the WebPartManager control (and the other server controls that are part of the Portal Framework) in the WebParts section of the Toolbox, as shown in Figure 16-2.

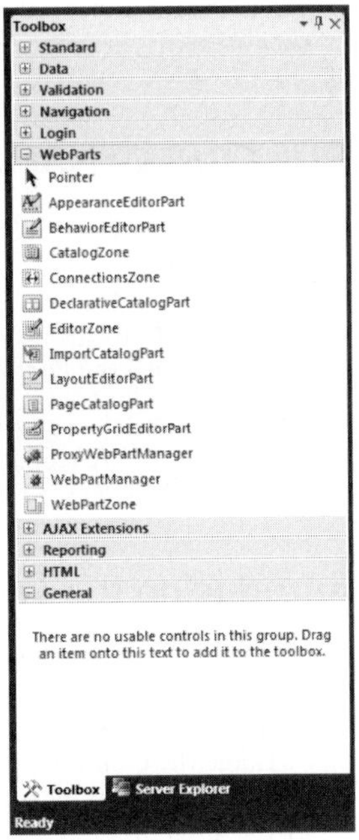

FIGURE 16-2

Working with Zone Layouts

After you place the WebPartManager control on the page, the next step is to create zones from which you can utilize the Portal Framework. You should give this step some thought because it contributes directly to the usability of the page you are creating. Web pages are constructed in a linear fashion — either horizontally or vertically. Web pages are managed in square boxes — usually using tables that organize the columns and rows in which items appear on the page.

Web zones define specific rows or columns as individual content areas managed by the WebPartManager. For an example of a Web page that uses these zones create a table similar to the one shown in Figure 16-3.

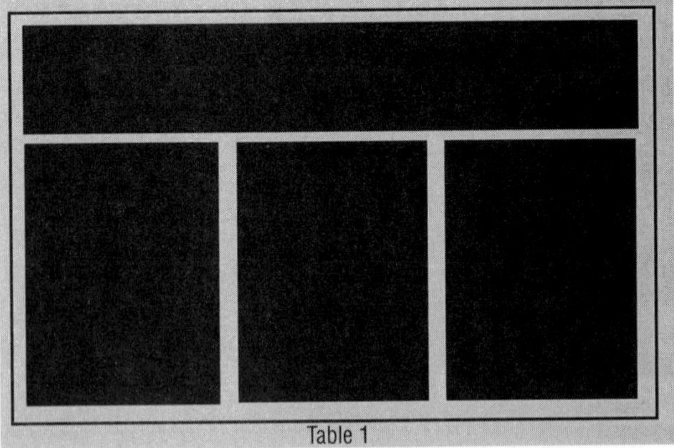

FIGURE 16-3

The black sections in Figure 16-3 represent Web zones. Listing 16-2 presents the code used to produce the table with some basic controls in each of the zones.

LISTING 16-2: Creating multiple Web zones

Available for download on Wrox.com

```
<%@ Page Language="VB"%>
<%@ Register Src="DailyLinks.ascx" TagName="DailyLinks" TagPrefix="uc1" %>

<html xmlns="http://www.w3.org/1999/xhtml">
<head runat="server">
    <title>Web Parts Example</title>
</head>
```

```
<body>
    <form id="form1" runat="server">
        <asp:WebPartManager ID="Webpartmanager1" runat="server">
        </asp:WebPartManager>
        <table cellpadding="5" border="1">
            <tr>
                <td colspan="3">
                    <h1>Bill Evjen's Web Page</h1>
                    <asp:WebPartZone ID="WebPartZone1" runat="server"
                     LayoutOrientation="Horizontal">
                        <ZoneTemplate>
                            <asp:Label ID="Label1" runat="server" Text="Label"
                             Title="Welcome to my web page!">
                             Welcome to the page!
                            </asp:Label>
                        </ZoneTemplate>
                    </asp:WebPartZone>
                </td>
            </tr>
            <tr valign="top">
                <td>
                    <asp:WebPartZone ID="WebPartZone2" runat="server">
                        <ZoneTemplate>
                            <asp:Image ID="Image1" runat="server"
                             ImageUrl="~/Images/Tuija.jpg" Width="150px"
                             Title="Tuija at the Museum">
                            </asp:Image>
                            <uc1:DailyLinks ID="DailyLinks1" runat="server"
                             Title="Daily Links">
                            </uc1:DailyLinks>
                        </ZoneTemplate>
                    </asp:WebPartZone>
                </td>
                <td>
                    <asp:WebPartZone ID="WebPartZone3" runat="server">
                        <ZoneTemplate>
                            <asp:Calendar ID="Calendar1" runat="server"
                             Title="Calendar">
                            </asp:Calendar>
                        </ZoneTemplate>
                    </asp:WebPartZone>
                </td>
                <td><!-- Blank for now -->
                </td>
            </tr>
        </table>
    </form>
</body>
</html>
```

This page now has sections like the ones shown in Figure 16-3: a header section that runs horizontally and three vertical sections underneath the header. Running this page provides the result shown in Figure 16-4.

This page includes the `<asp:WebPartManager>` control that manages the items contained in the three zones on this page. Within the table, the `<asp:WebPartZone>` server control specifies three Web zones. You can

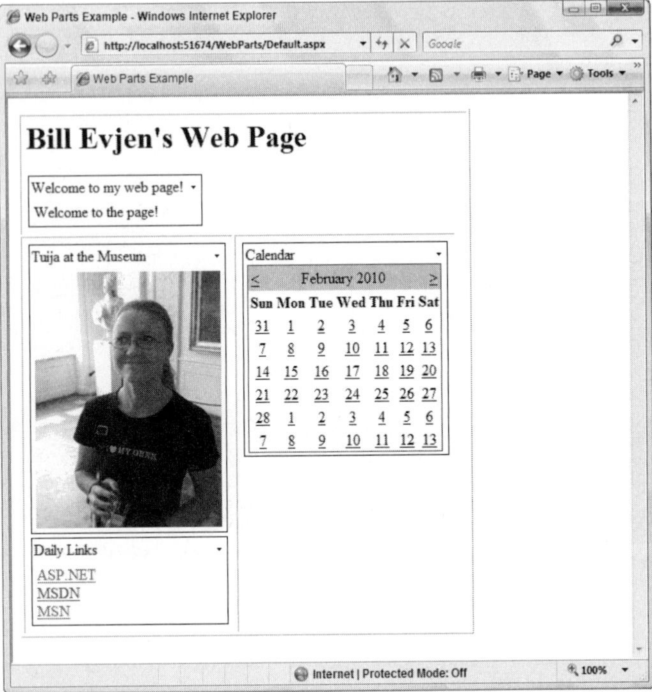

FIGURE 16-4

declare each Web zone in one of two ways. You can use the `<asp:WebPartZone>` element directly in the code, or you can create the zones within the table by dragging and dropping WebPartZone controls onto the design surface at appropriate places within the table. In Figure 16-4, the table border width is intentionally turned on and set to `1` in order to show the location of the Web zones in greater detail. Figure 16-5 shows what the sample from Listing 16-2 looks like in the Design view of Visual Studio 2010.

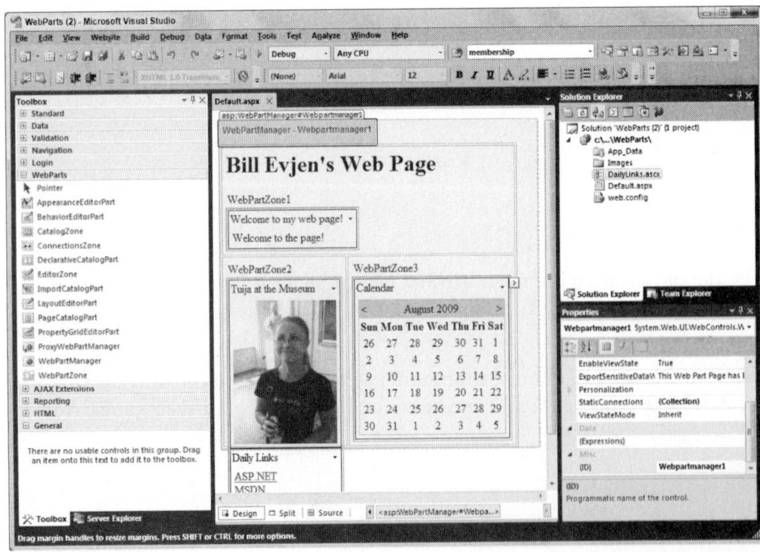

FIGURE 16-5

When using Visual Studio 2010, note that by default this IDE creates a Microsoft SQL Server Express Edition file called `ASPNETDB.MDF` and stores it in the App_Data folder of your Web Project. This database file is where the Portal Framework stores all the customization points.

Note that if you want this Portal Framework to run from SQL Server 7.0, 2000, 2005, or 2008, you should follow the set-up instructions that are defined in Chapter 11.

Now that you have seen the use of WebPartZone controls, which are managed by the WebPartManager control, the next section takes a closer look at the WebPartZone server control itself.

Understanding the WebPartZone Control

The WebPartZone control defines an area of items, or Web Parts, that can be moved, minimized, maximized, deleted, or added based on programmatic code or user preferences. When you drag and drop WebPartZone controls onto the design surface using Visual Studio 2010, the WebPartZone control is drawn at the top of the zone, along with a visual representation of any of the items contained within the zone.

You can place almost anything in one of the Web zones. For example, you can include the following:

- HTML elements
- HTML server controls (when putting a `runat = "server"` on the element)
- Web server controls
- User controls
- Custom controls

WebPartZone controls are declared like this:

```
<asp:WebPartZone ID="WebPartZone1" runat="server"></asp:WebPartZone>
```

The LayoutOrientation Attribute

You can display the Web Parts declared within a WebPartZone control either horizontally or vertically. By default, all the items are displayed vertically, but to display the items horizontally, you simply add the `LayoutOrientation` attribute to the `<asp:WebPartZone>` element:

```
<asp:WebPartZone ID="WebPartZone1" runat="server"
 LayoutOrientation="Horizontal"></asp:WebPartZone>
```

The first row in the table from Listing 16-2 uses horizontal orientation, whereas the other two zones use the default vertical orientation.

The ZoneTemplate Element

In order to include items within the templated WebPartZone control, you must include a `<ZoneTemplate>` element.

The `ZoneTemplate` element encapsulates all the items contained within a particular zone. The order in which they are listed in the `ZoneTemplate` section is the order in which they appear in the browser until changed by the end user or by programmatic code. The sample `<ZoneTemplate>` section used earlier is illustrated here:

```
<asp:WebPartZone ID="WebPartZone2" runat="server">
   <ZoneTemplate>
      <asp:Image ID="Image1" runat="server"
       ImageUrl="~/Images/Tuija.jpg" Width="150" Title="Tuija at the Museum">
      </asp:Image>
      <uc1:DailyLinks ID="DailyLinks1" runat="server" Title="Daily Links">
```

```
            </uc1:DailyLinks>
        </ZoneTemplate>
    </asp:WebPartZone>
```

This zone contains two items — an Image server control and a user control consisting of a collection of links that come from an XML file.

Default Web Part Control Elements

By default, when you generate a page using the code from Listing 16-2, you discover that you can exert only minimal control over the Web Parts themselves. In the default view, which is not the most artistic in this case, you are able only to minimize or close a Web Part. You can see these options when you click on the down arrow that appears next to the name of the Web Part.

Figure 16-6 shows what the Web Part that contains the Calendar control looks like after you minimize it. Notice also that if you opt to close one of the Web Parts, the item completely disappears. There seems to be no way to make it come back — even if you shut down the page and restart it. This is by design — so don't worry. I will show you how to get it back!

FIGURE 16-6

A few of the items included in the zones have new titles. By default, the title that appears at the top of the Web Part is the name of the control. For example, you can see that the Calendar control is simply titled Calendar. If you add a Button control or any other control to the zone, at first it is simply titled Untitled. To give better and more meaningful names to the Web Parts that appear in a zone, you simply add a `Title` attribute to the control — just as was done with the Image control and the User control, which both appear on the page. In the preceding code example, the Image control is renamed to `Tuija at the Museum`, and the user control is given the `Title` value `Daily Links`.

Besides this little bit of default functionality, you can do considerably more with the Web Parts contained within this page, but you have to make some other additions. These are reviewed next.

Allowing the User to Change the Mode of the Page

Working with the `WebPartManager` class either directly or through the use of the WebPartManager server control, you can have the mode of the page changed. Changing the mode of the page being viewed allows the user to add, move, or change the pages they are working with. The nice thing about the Web Part capabilities of ASP.NET is that these changes are then recorded to the `ASPNETDB.MDF` database file and are, therefore, re-created the next time the user visits the page.

Using the `WebPartManager` object, you can enable the user to do the following, as defined in this list:

- **Add new Web Parts to the page:** Includes Web Parts not displayed on the page by default and Web Parts that the end user has previously deleted. This aspect of the control works with the catalog capabilities of the Portal Framework, which is discussed shortly.
- **Enter the Design mode for the page:** Enables the end user to drag and drop elements around the page. The end user can use this capability to change the order in which items appear in a zone or to move items from one zone to another.
- **Modify the Web Parts settings:** Enables the end user to customize aspects of the Web Parts, such as their appearance and behavior. It also allows the end user to modify any custom settings that developers apply to the Web Part.
- **Connect Web Parts on the page:** Enables the end user to make a connection between one or more Web Parts on the page. For example, when an end user working in a financial services application enters a stock symbol into an example Web Part, he or she can use a connection to another Web Part to see a stock chart change or news appear based on that particular stock symbol. All of this is based on the variable defined in the first Web Part.

Building on Listing 16-2, Listing 16-3 adds a DropDownList control to the table's header. This drop-down list provides a list of available modes the user can employ to change how the page is displayed. Again, the mode of the page determines the actions the user can initiate directly on the page (this is demonstrated later in this chapter).

LISTING 16-3: Adding a list of modes to the page

Available for download on Wrox.com

VB

```
<%@ Page Language="VB"%>
<%@ Register Src="DailyLinks.ascx" TagName="DailyLinks" TagPrefix="uc1" %>
<script runat="server">
    Protected Sub DropDownList1_SelectedIndexChanged(ByVal sender As Object,
       ByVal e As System.EventArgs)

     Dim wpDisplayMode As WebParts.WebPartDisplayMode =
     Webpartmanager1.SupportedDisplayModes(DropDownList1.SelectedValue.ToString())
      Webpartmanager1.DisplayMode = wpDisplayMode
    End Sub

    Protected Sub Page_Init(ByVal sender As Object, ByVal e As System.EventArgs)
      For Each wpMode As WebPartDisplayMode In _
         Webpartmanager1.SupportedDisplayModes

            Dim modeName As String = wpMode.Name
            Dim dd_ListItem As ListItem = New ListItem(modeName, modeName)
            DropDownList1.Items.Add(dd_ListItem)
      Next
    End Sub
</script>
<html xmlns="http://www.w3.org/1999/xhtml">
<head id="Head1" runat="server">
    <title>Web Parts Example</title>
</head>
<body>
```

continues

LISTING 16-3 *(continued)*

```
    <form id="form1" runat="server">
        <asp:WebPartManager ID="Webpartmanager1" runat="server">
        </asp:WebPartManager>
        <table cellpadding="5" border="1">
            <tr>
                <td colspan="2">
                    <h1>Bill Evjen's Web Page</h1>
                    <asp:WebPartZone ID="WebPartZone1" runat="server"
                     LayoutOrientation="Horizontal">
                        <ZoneTemplate>
                            <asp:Label ID="Label1" runat="server" Text="Label"
                             Title="Welcome to my web page!">
                             Welcome to the page!
                            </asp:Label>
                        </ZoneTemplate>
                    </asp:WebPartZone>
                </td>
                <td valign="top">
                    Select mode:
                    <asp:DropDownList ID="DropDownList1" runat="server"
                     AutoPostBack="True"
                     OnSelectedIndexChanged="DropDownList1_SelectedIndexChanged">
                    </asp:DropDownList>
                </td>
            </tr>
            <tr valign="top">
                <td>
                    <asp:WebPartZone ID="WebPartZone2" runat="server">
                        <ZoneTemplate>
                            <asp:Image ID="Image1" runat="server"
                             ImageUrl="</Images/Tuija.jpg" Width="150px"
                             Title="Tuija at the Museum">
                            </asp:Image>
                            <uc1:DailyLinks ID="DailyLinks1" runat="server"
                             Title="Daily Links">
                            </uc1:DailyLinks>
                        </ZoneTemplate>
                    </asp:WebPartZone>
                </td>
                <td>
                    <asp:WebPartZone ID="WebPartZone3" runat="server">
                        <ZoneTemplate>
                            <asp:Calendar ID="Calendar1" runat="server"
                             Title="Calendar">
                            </asp:Calendar>
                        </ZoneTemplate>
                    </asp:WebPartZone>
                </td>
                <td><!-- Blank for now -->
                </td>
            </tr>
        </table>
    </form>
</body>
</html>
```

C#

```
<%@ Page Language="C#"%>
<%@ Register Src="DailyLinks.ascx" TagName="DailyLinks" TagPrefix="uc1" %>
<script runat="server">
    protected void DropDownList1_SelectedIndexChanged(object sender, EventArgs e)
    {
      WebParts.WebPartDisplayMode wpDisplayMode =
```

```
Webpartmanager1.SupportedDisplayModes[DropDownList1.SelectedValue.ToString()];
        Webpartmanager1.DisplayMode = wpDisplayMode;
    }

    protected void Page_Init(object sender, EventArgs e)
    {
        foreach (WebPartDisplayMode wpMode in
           Webpartmanager1.SupportedDisplayModes)
        {
            string modeName = wpMode.Name;
            ListItem dd_ListItem = new ListItem(modeName, modeName);
            DropDownList1.Items.Add(dd_ListItem);
        }
    }
</script>
```

This code adds a drop-down list to the top of the table, as shown in Figure 16-7. This drop-down list allows the end user to switch between the Browse and Design modes.

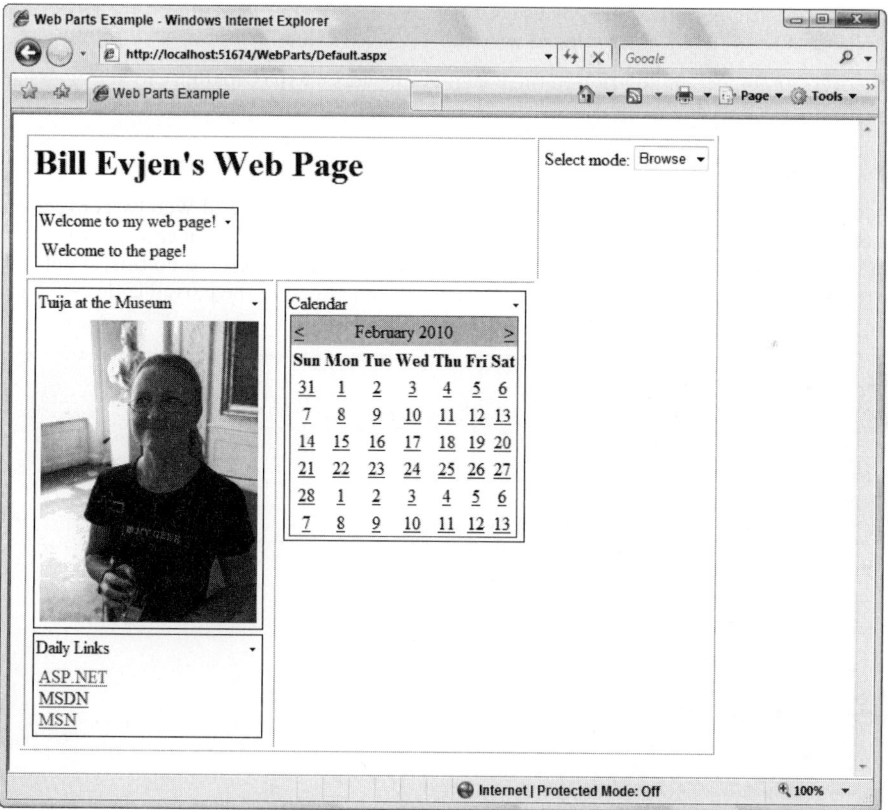

FIGURE 16-7

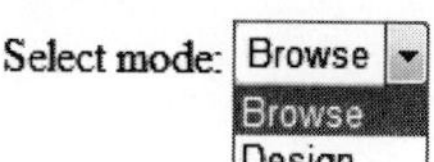

FIGURE 16-8

When the end user clicks the link, a drop-down window of options appears, as shown in Figure 16-8.

Using the `Page_Init` event, you can populate the drop-down list with the available page modes that are accessible at this particular time. In this case, it is Browse and Design. The Browse mode is the default mode used when the page is first created. The Design mode causes the ASP.NET page to show the WebPartZone sections. In this mode, the user can drag and drop controls from one section to another with relative ease. Again, the positioning of the elements contained in the page is remembered from one application visit to the next.

It is important to note that the Design mode works only in Internet Explorer browsers.

The DropDownList control is populated by iterating through a list of available `WebPartDisplayMode` objects contained in the `SupportedDisplayModes` property (which is of type `WebPartDisplayMode Collection`). These modes are available through the `Webpartmanager1` control, which was placed on the page and is in charge of managing the modes and changing the modes of the page. These `WebPartDisplayMode` objects are then used to populate the DropDownList control.

When the end user selects one of the available modes displayed in the DropDownList control, by the use of the `AutoPostBack` feature of the control, the page then changes to the selected mode. This is done in the code first by creating an instance of a `WebPartDisplayMode` object and populating it with the value of the mode selected from the drop-down list. Then, by use of this `WebPartDisplayMode` object, the `DisplayMode` property of the `WebPartManager` object is assigned with this retrieved value.

The next section covers an important addition to the Portal Framework — the capability to add Web Parts dynamically to a page.

Adding Web Parts to a Page

The next step is to rework the example so that the end user has a built-in way to add Web Parts to the page through the use of the Portal Framework. The ASP.NET Portal Framework enables an end user to add Web Parts, but you must also provide the end user with a list of items he or she can add. To do this, simply add a Catalog Zone to the last table cell in the bottom of the table, as illustrated in the partial code example in Listing 16-4.

Available for download on Wrox.com

LISTING 16-4: Adding a Catalog Zone

```
<tr valign="top">
   <td>
      <asp:WebPartZone ID="WebPartZone2" runat="server">
         <ZoneTemplate>
            <asp:Image ID="Image1" runat="server"
             ImageUrl="</Images/Tuija.jpg" Width="150px"
             Title="Tuija at the Museum">
            </asp:Image>
            <uc1:DailyLinks ID="DailyLinks1" runat="server"
             Title="Daily Links">
            </uc1:DailyLinks>
         </ZoneTemplate>
      </asp:WebPartZone>
   </td>
   <td>
      <asp:WebPartZone ID="WebPartZone3" runat="server">
         <ZoneTemplate>
            <asp:Calendar ID="Calendar1" runat="server"
             Title="Calendar">
            </asp:Calendar>
         </ZoneTemplate>
      </asp:WebPartZone>
   </td>
   <td>
      <asp:CatalogZone ID="Catalogzone1" runat="server">
         <ZoneTemplate>
```

```
                <asp:PageCatalogPart ID="Pagecatalogpart1" runat="server"/>
            </ZoneTemplate>
        </asp:CatalogZone>
    </td>
</tr>
```

After a Catalog Zone section is present on the page, the page is enabled for the Catalog mode. You need to create a Catalog Zone section by using the `<asp:CatalogZone>` control. This process is similar to creating a Web Part Zone, but the Catalog Zone is specifically designed to allow for categorization of the items that can be placed on the page. Notice that Catalog mode does not appear as an option in the drop-down list of available modes until a CatalogZone control is placed on the page. If no CatalogZone control is present on the page, this option is not displayed.

After the Catalog Zone is in place, the next step is to create a `<ZoneTemplate>` section within the Catalog Zone because this is also a templated control. Inside the `<ZoneTemplate>` element is a single control — the PageCatalogPart control. If you run the page after adding the PageCatalogPart control and change the mode to Catalog, you will see the results shown in Figure 16-9.

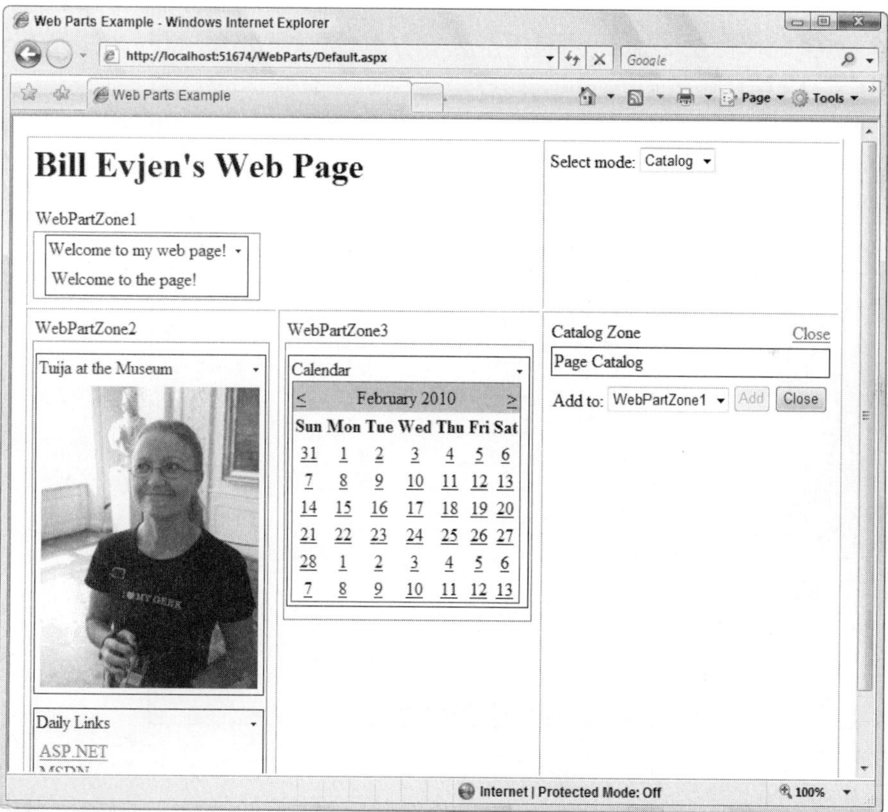

FIGURE 16-9

To get some items to appear in the list (because none do at present), delete one or more items (any items contained on the page when viewing the page in the browser) from the page's default view and enter the Catalog mode by selecting Catalog from the drop-down list of modes.

At this point, you can see the deleted Web Parts in the Catalog Zone. The PageCatalogPart control contains a title and check box list of items that can be selected. The PageCatalogPart control also includes a drop-down list of all the available Web Part Zones on the page. From here, you can place the selected Web Parts into one of the Web Part Zones available from this list. After you select the Web Parts and the appropriate zone in which you want to place the item, you click the Add button and the items appear in the specified locations.

Moving Web Parts

Not only can the end user change the order in which Web Parts appear in a zone, but he or she can also move Web Parts from one zone to another. By adding the capability to enter the Design mode through the drop-down list that you created earlier, you have already provided the end user with this capability. He or she simply enters the Design mode, which allows for this type of movement.

The Design option in the drop-down list changes the page so that the user can see the zones defined on the page, as illustrated in Figure 16-10.

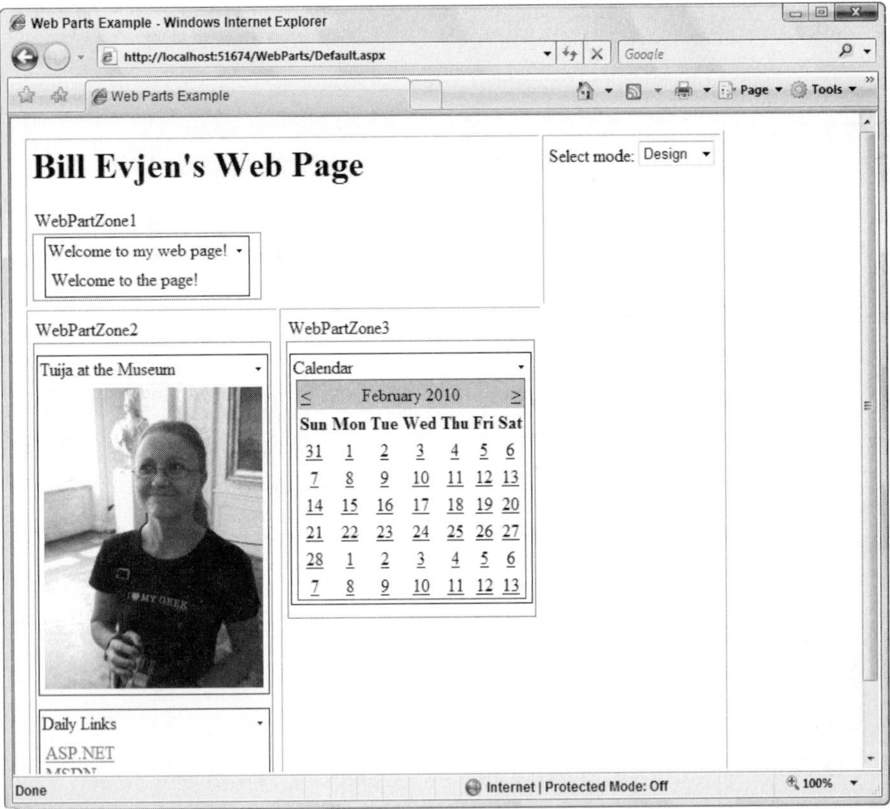

FIGURE 16-10

From this figure, you can see the three zones (`WebPartZone1`, `WebPartZone2`, and `WebPartZone3`). At this point, the end user can select one of the Web Parts contained in one of these zones and either change its order in the zone or move it to an entirely different zone on the page. To grab one of the Web Parts, the user simply clicks and holds the left mouse button on the title of the Web Part. When done correctly, the crosshair, which appears when the end user hovers over the Web Part's title, turns into an arrow. This means that the user has grabbed hold of the Web Part and can drag it to another part of the page. While the user drags the Web Part around the page, a visual representation of the item appears (see Figure 16-11). In this state, the Web Part is a bit transparent and its location in the state of the page is defined with a blue line (the darker line shown at the top of `WebPartZone3`). Releasing the left mouse button drops the Web Part at the blue line's location.

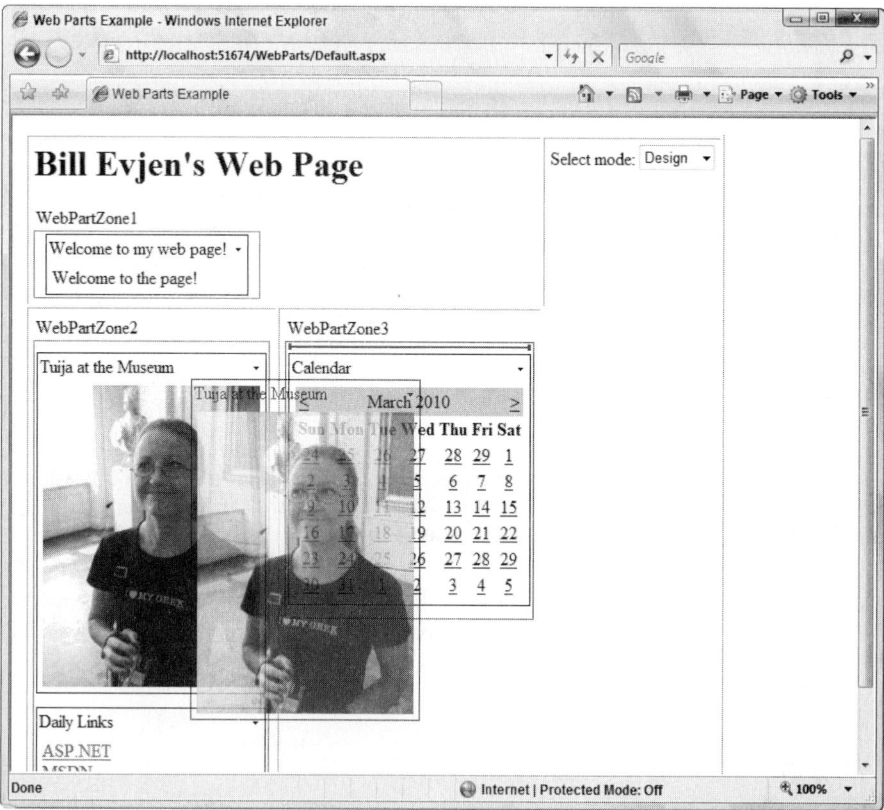

FIGURE 16-11

After the end user places all the items where he or she wants them, the locations of the items on the page are saved for later use.

When that user reopens the browser, everything is then drawn in the last state in which he or she left the page. This is done on a per-user basis, so any other users browsing to the same page see either their own modified results or the default view if it is a first visit to the page.

The user can then leave the Design view by opening the list of options from the drop-down list of modes and selecting Browse.

Another way to move Web Parts is to enter the Catalog mode of the page (which is now one of the options in the drop-down list due to the addition of the Catalog Zone section). The Catalog mode enables you to add deleted items to the page, but it also allows you to modify the location of the items on the page by providing the same drag-and-drop capability as the Design mode.

Modifying the Web Part Settings

Another option in the list of modes that you can add to the drop-down list is to allow your end users to edit the actual Web Parts themselves to a degree. This is done through the available Edit mode, and it enables the end user to modify settings determining appearance, behavior, and layout for a particular Web Part on the page.

To make this functionality work, you must add an Editor Zone to the page just as you add the Catalog Zone, as shown in Listing 16-5. You place this bit of new code within the same table directly below the Catalog Zone declaration.

LISTING 16-5: Adding an Editor Zone to the page

Available for download on Wrox.com

```
<td>
   <asp:CatalogZone ID="Catalogzone1" runat="server">
      <ZoneTemplate>
         <asp:PageCatalogPart ID="Pagecatalogpart1" runat="server"/>
      </ZoneTemplate>
   </asp:CatalogZone>
   <asp:EditorZone ID="Editorzone1" runat="server">
      <ZoneTemplate>
         <asp:AppearanceEditorPart ID="Appearanceeditorpart1" runat="server" />
         <asp:BehaviorEditorPart ID="Behavioreditorpart1" runat="server" />
         <asp:LayoutEditorPart ID="Layouteditorpart1" runat="server" />
         <asp:PropertyGridEditorPart ID="PropertyGridEditorPart1" runat="server" />
      </ZoneTemplate>
   </asp:EditorZone>
</td>
```

Just like the `<asp:CatalogZone>`, the `<asp:EditorZone>` control is a templated control that requires a `<ZoneTemplate>` section. Within this section, you can place controls that allow for the modification of the appearance, behavior, and layout of the selected Web Part. These controls include `<asp:AppearanceEditorPart>`, `<asp:BehaviorEditorPart>`, `<asp:LayoutEditorPart>`, and `<asp:PropertyGridEditorPart>`.

When you run this new section of code and select Edit from the drop-down list of modes, the arrow that is next to the Web Part title from each of the Web Parts on the page will show an Edit option, as illustrated in Figure 16-12.

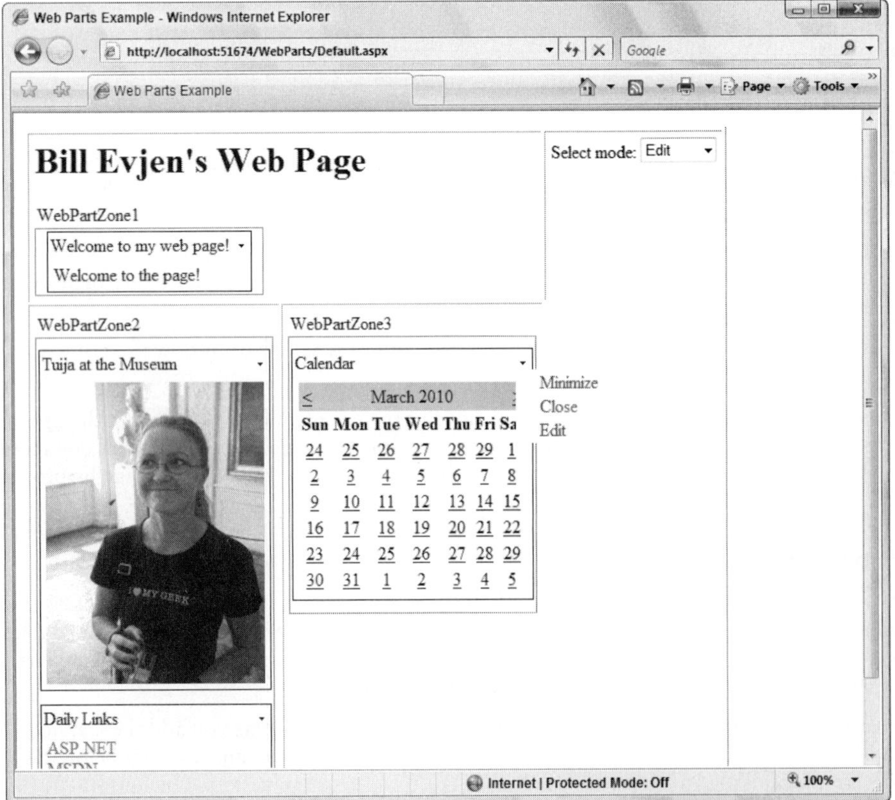

FIGURE 16-12

After you select the Edit option from this list of three options, the right column of the table shows the various editing sections for this particular Web Part.

The Appearance section enables the end user to change the Web Part's details, including the title, how the title appears, and other appearance-related items such as the item's height and width. Figure 16-13 shows the Appearance section.

FIGURE 16-13

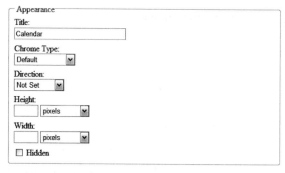

The Behavior section (shown in Figure 16-14) enables the end user to select whether the Web Part can be closed, minimized, or exported. This section allows you to change behavior items for either yourself only (a single user) or for everyone in the system (a shared view of the Web Part). Using the shared view, the Behavior section is generally used to allow site editors (or admins) to change the dynamics of how end users can modify Web Parts. General viewers of the page most likely will not see this section.

FIGURE 16-14

To get the Behavior section to appear, you first must make the changes to the `Web.config` file presented in Listing 16-6.

LISTING 16-6: Getting the Behavior section to appear through settings in the Web.config

Available for download on Wrox.com

```
<configuration>
   <system.web>
      <webParts>
         <personalization>
```

continues

LISTING 16-6 *(continued)*

```
            <authorization>
               <allow users="*" verbs="enterSharedScope" />
            </authorization>
         </personalization>
      </webParts>
   </system.web>
</configuration>
```

After the `Web.config` file is in place, the next step is to add a bit of code to your `Page_Load` event, as shown in Listing 16-7.

Available for download on Wrox.com

LISTING 16-7: Adding some code to allow the Behavior section to appear

```
If Webpartmanager1.Personalization.Scope = PersonalizationScope.User _
   AndAlso Webpartmanager1.Personalization.CanEnterSharedScope Then

      Webpartmanager1.Personalization.ToggleScope()
End If
```

C#

```
if (Webpartmanager1.Personalization.Scope == PersonalizationScope.User
   && Webpartmanager1.Personalization.CanEnterSharedScope)
{
     Webpartmanager1.Personalization.ToggleScope();
}
```

The Layout section (shown in Figure 16-15) enables the end user to change the order in which Web Parts appear in a zone or move Web Parts from one zone to another. This feature is quite similar to the drag-and-drop capabilities illustrated previously, but this section allows for the same capabilities through the manipulation of simple form elements.

Layout
Chrome State:
Normal
Zone:
WebPartZone3
Zone Index:
0

FIGURE 16-15

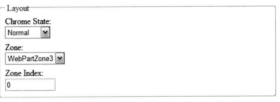

The PropertyGridEditorPart, although not demonstrated yet, allows end users to modify properties that are defined in your own custom server controls. At the end of this chapter, you look at building a custom Web Part and using the PropertyGridEditorPart to allow end users to modify one of the publicly exposed properties contained in the control.

After you are satisfied with the appearance and layout of the Web Parts and have made the necessary changes to the control's properties in one of the editor parts, simply click OK or Apply.

Making Connections

You have the ability to make a connection between two Web Parts using the `<asp:ConnectionsZone>` control. This control enables you to make property connections between two Web Parts on the same page. For example, within the Weather Web Part built into one of ASP.NET's pre-built applications, you can have a separate Web Part that is simply a text box and a button that allows the end user to input a zip code. This, in turn, modifies the contents in the original Weather Web Part.

Modifying Zones

One aspect of the Portal Framework that merits special attention is the capability to modify zones on the page. These zones allow for a high degree of modification — not only in the look-and-feel of the items placed in the zone, but also in terms of the behaviors of zones and the items contained in the zones as well. Following are some examples of what you can do to modify zones.

Turning Off the Capability for Modifications in a Zone

As you have seen, giving end users the capability to move Web Parts around the page is quite easy, whether within a zone or among entirely different zones. When working with the Portal Framework and multiple zones on a page, you do not always want to allow the end user to freely change the items that appear in every zone. You want the items placed in some zones to be left alone. Listing 16-8 shows an example of this scenario.

LISTING 16-8: Turning off the zone modification capability

Available for download on Wrox.com

```
<asp:WebPartZone ID="WebPartZone1" runat="server"
 LayoutOrientation="Horizontal" AllowLayoutChange="false">
   <ZoneTemplate>
      <asp:Label ID="Label1" runat="server" Text="Label"
       Title="Welcome to my web page!">
       Welcome to the page!
      </asp:Label>
   </ZoneTemplate>
</asp:WebPartZone>
```

In this example, the first Web Part Zone, `WebPartZone1`, uses the `AllowLayoutChange` attribute with a value of `False`, which turns off the end user's capability to modify this particular Web Part Zone. When you run this page and go to the design mode, notice that you cannot drag and drop any of the Web Parts from the other zones into `WebPartZone1`. Neither can you grab hold of the Label Web Part contained in `WebPartZone1`. No capability exists to minimize and close the Web Parts contained in this zone. It allows absolutely no modifications to the zone's layout.

You may notice another interesting change when you are working in the page catalog mode with the `AllowLayoutChange` attribute set to `False`. After you select items to add to the page through the page catalog, `WebPartZone1` does not appear in the drop-down list of places where you can publish the Web Parts (see Figure 16-16). From this figure, you can see that only `WebPartZone2` and `WebPartZone3` appear and allow modifications.

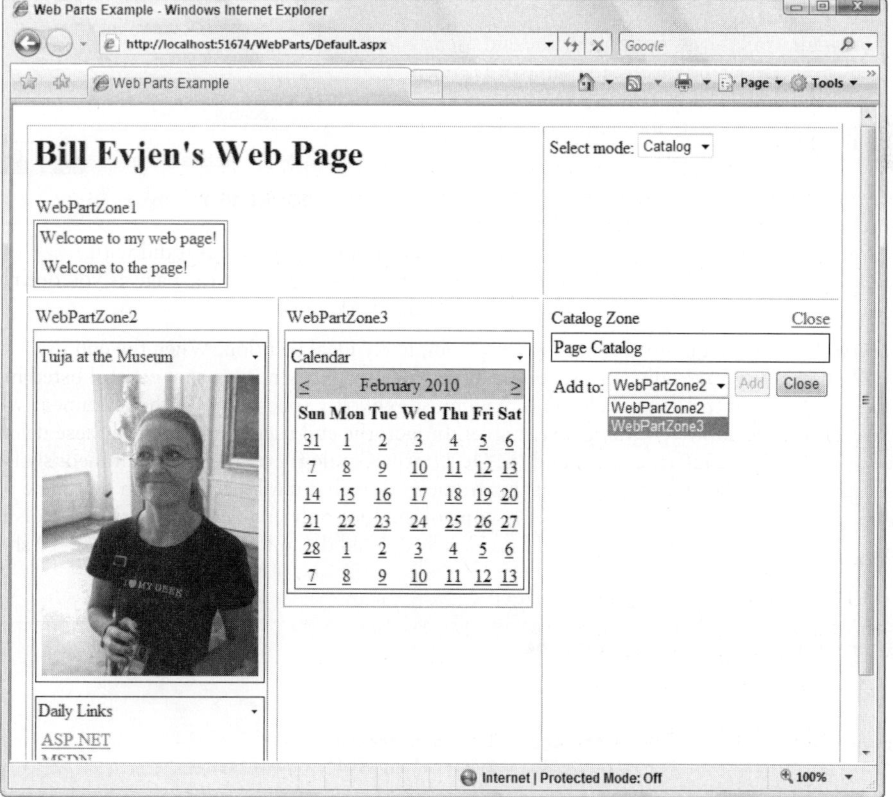

FIGURE 16-16

Adding Controls through Other Means

Earlier in this chapter, you examined how to use the <asp:PageCatalogPart> control to restore controls to a page after they had been deleted. Although the <asp:PageCatalogPart> is ideal for this task, you might also want to allow the end user to add Web Parts that are not on the page by default. You may want to enable the end user to add more than one of any particular Web Part to a page. For these situations, you work with the <asp:DeclarativeCatalogPart> control.

Listing 16-9 shows an example of using this type of catalog system in place of the <asp:PageCatalogPart> control.

LISTING 16-9: Using the DeclarativeCatalogPart control

Available for download on Wrox.com

```
<asp:CatalogZone ID="Catalogzone1" runat="server">
   <ZoneTemplate>
      <asp:DeclarativeCatalogPart ID="Declarativecatalogpart1" runat="server">
         <WebPartsTemplate>
            <uc1:CompanyContactInfo ID="CompanyContact" runat="Server"
             Title="Company Contact Info" />
            <uc1:PhotoAlbum ID="PhotoAlbum" runat="Server" Title="Photo Album" />
            <uc1:Customers ID="Customers" runat="Server" Title="Customers" />
            <uc1:Locations ID="Locations" runat="Server" Title="Locations" />
         </WebPartsTemplate>
      </asp:DeclarativeCatalogPart>
   </ZoneTemplate>
</asp:CatalogZone>
```

Instead of using the <asp:PageCatalogPart> control, this catalog uses the <asp:DeclarativeCatalog Part> control. This templated control needs a <WebPartsTemplate> section where you can place all the controls you want available as options for the end user. The controls appear in the check box list in the same order in which you declare them in the <WebPartsTemplate> section. Figure 16-17 shows how the catalog looks in the Design view in Visual Studio 2010.

FIGURE 16-17

This catalog lets you select items from the list of Web Parts and assign the location of the zone in which they will be placed. After they are placed, notice that the option to add these Web Parts has not disappeared as it did with the earlier PageCatalogPart control. In fact, you can add as many of these items to the page as you deem necessary — even if it is to the same zone within the Portal Framework.

Using the DeclarativeCatalogPart control is not always a completely ideal solution. When the end user closes one of the Web Parts that initially appears on the page, he or she may not see that control listed in the DeclarativeCatalogPart control's list of elements. You must explicitly specify that it should appear when you write the code for the DeclarativeCatalogPart control. In fact, the end user cannot re-add these deleted items. Using both the PageCatalogPart control and the DeclarativeCatalogPart control simultaneously is sometimes the best solution. The great thing about this framework is that it allows you to do that. The Portal Framework melds both controls into a cohesive control that not only enables you to add controls that are not on the page by default, but also lets you add previously deleted default controls. Listing 16-10 shows an example of this.

LISTING 16-10: Combining both catalog types

Available for download on Wrox.com

```
<asp:CatalogZone ID="Catalogzone1" runat="server">
   <ZoneTemplate>
      <asp:PageCatalogPart ID="Pagecatalogpart1" runat="server" />
      <asp:DeclarativeCatalogPart ID="Declarativecatalogpart1" runat="server">
         <WebPartsTemplate>
```

```
            <uc1:CompanyContactInfo ID="CompanyContact" runat="Server"
             Title="Company Contact Info" />
            <uc1:PhotoAlbum ID="PhotoAlbum" runat="Server" Title="Photo Album" />
            <uc1:Customers ID="Customers" runat="Server" Title="Customers" />
            <uc1:Locations ID="Locations" runat="Server" Title="Locations" />
          </WebPartsTemplate>
        </asp:DeclarativeCatalogPart>
    </ZoneTemplate>
</asp:CatalogZone>
```

In this example, both the PageCatalogPart control and the DeclarativeCatalogPart control are contained within the `<ZoneTemplate>` section. When you run this page, you see the results shown in Figure 16-18.

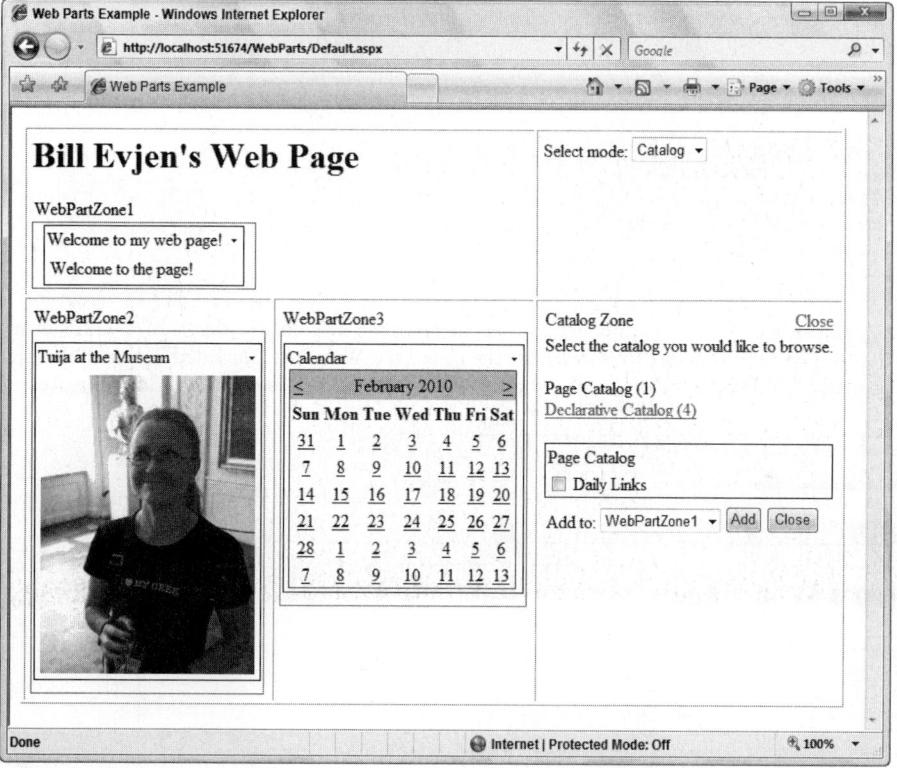

FIGURE 16-18

You can see that each catalog is defined within the Catalog Zone. Figure 16-18 shows the PageCatalogPart control's collection of Web Parts (defined as Page Catalog). Also, note that a link to the Declarative Catalog is provided for that particular list of items. Note that the order in which the catalogs appear in the `<ZoneTemplate>` section is the order in which the links appear in the Catalog Zone.

Web Part Verbs

Web Part verbs declare the actions of the items (such as Minimize and Close) that appear in the title. These verbs are basically links that initiate an action for a particular Web Part. The available list of Web Part verbs includes the following:

- `<CloseVerb>`
- `<ConnectVerb>`

- <DeleteVerb>
- <EditVerb>
- <ExportVerb>
- <HelpVerb>
- <MinimizeVerb>
- <RestoreVerb>

The `<asp:WebPartZone>` control allows you to control these verbs by nesting the appropriate verb elements within the `<asp:WebPartZone>` element itself. After these are in place, you can manipulate how these items appear in all the Web Parts that appear in the chosen Web Part Zone.

For example, look at graying out the default Close link included with a Web Part. Listing 16-11 shows how to gray out this link.

LISTING 16-11: Graying out the Close link in a Web Part

Available for download on Wrox.com

```
<asp:WebPartZone ID="WebPartZone3" runat="server">
        <CloseVerb Enabled="False" />
        <ZoneTemplate>
            <asp:Calendar ID="Calendar1" runat="server">
            </asp:Calendar>
        </ZoneTemplate>
</asp:WebPartZone>
```

In this example, you can see that you simply need to set the `Enabled` attribute of the `<CloseVerb>` element to `False` in order to gray out the Close link in any of the generated Web Parts included in this Web Part Zone. If you construct the Web Part Zone in this manner, you achieve the results shown in Figure 16-19.

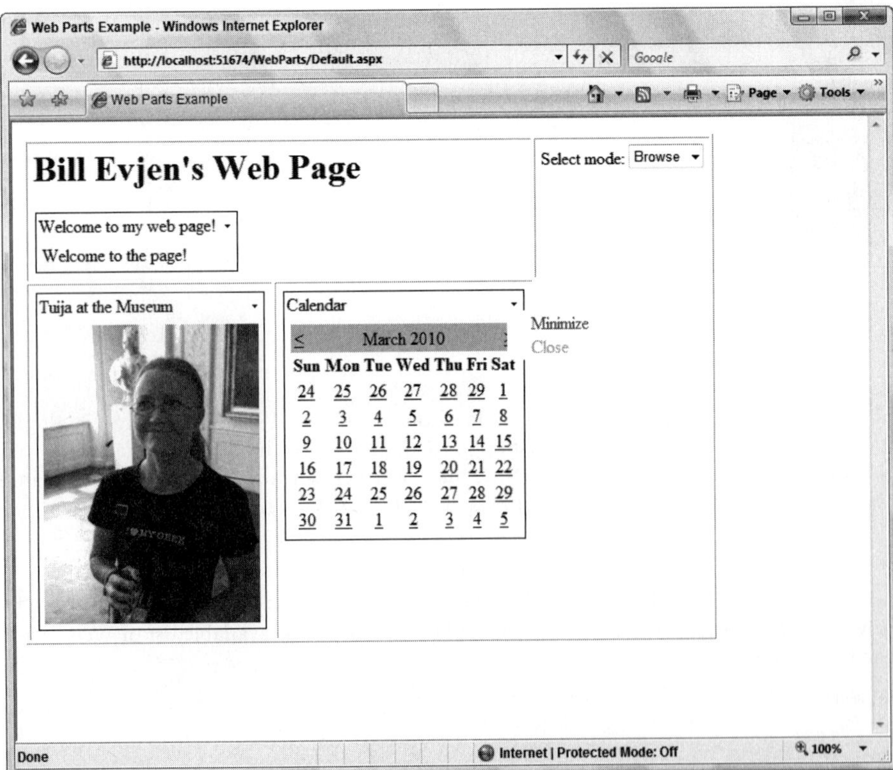

FIGURE 16-19

If you do not want to gray out the Close link (or any other verb link contained within the Web Part), you must instead use the `Visible` attribute of the appropriate verb (see Listing 16-12).

Available for download on Wrox.com

LISTING 16-12: Removing the Close link in a Web Part

```
<asp:WebPartZone ID="WebPartZone3" runat="server">
      <CloseVerb Visible="False" />
      <ZoneTemplate>
         <asp:Calendar ID="Calendar1" runat="server">
         </asp:Calendar>
      </ZoneTemplate>
</asp:WebPartZone>
```

Using the `Visible` attribute produces the screen shown in Figure 16-20.

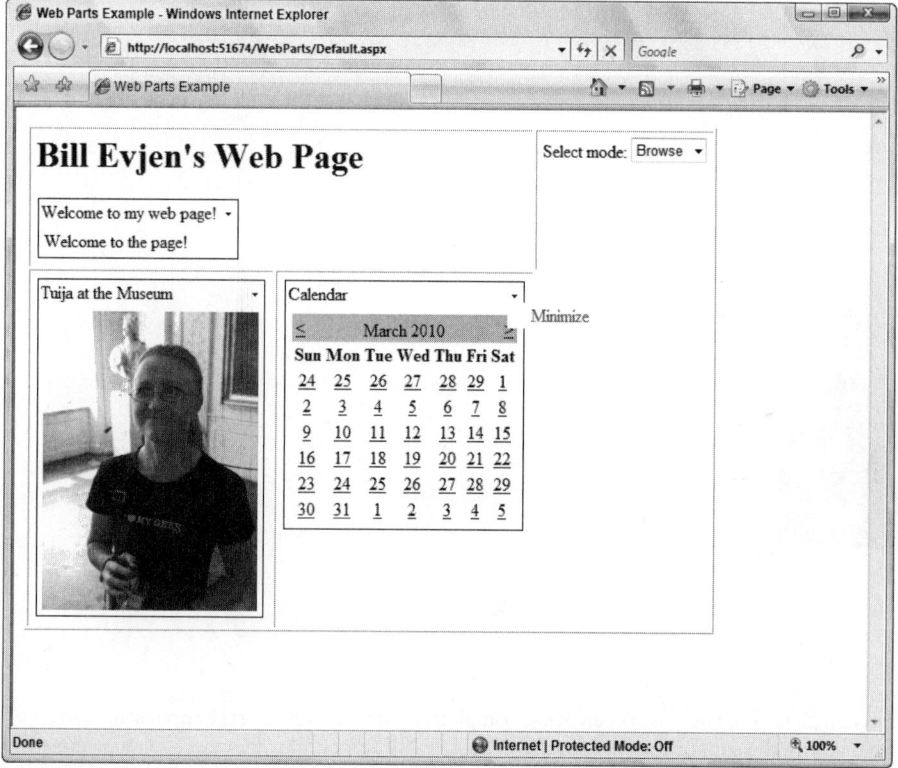

FIGURE 16-20

Verb elements provide another exciting feature: they give you the capability to use images that would appear next to the text of an item. Using images with the text makes the Web Parts appear more like the overall Windows environment. For instance, you can change the contents of `WebPartZone3` again so that it now uses images with the text for the Close and Minimize links, as illustrated in Listing 16-13.

Available for download on Wrox.com

LISTING 16-13: Using images for the Web Part verbs

```
<asp:WebPartZone ID="WebPartZone3" runat="server">
      <CloseVerb ImageUrl="Images/CloseVerb.gif" />
```

continues

LISTING 16-13 *(continued)*

```
        <MinimizeVerb ImageUrl="Images/MinimizeVerb.gif" />
        <ZoneTemplate>
            <asp:Calendar ID="Calendar1" runat="server">
            </asp:Calendar>
        </ZoneTemplate>
    </asp:WebPartZone>
```

To point to an image for the verb, use the `ImageUrl` attribute. This produces something similar to Figure 16-21, depending on the images you use.

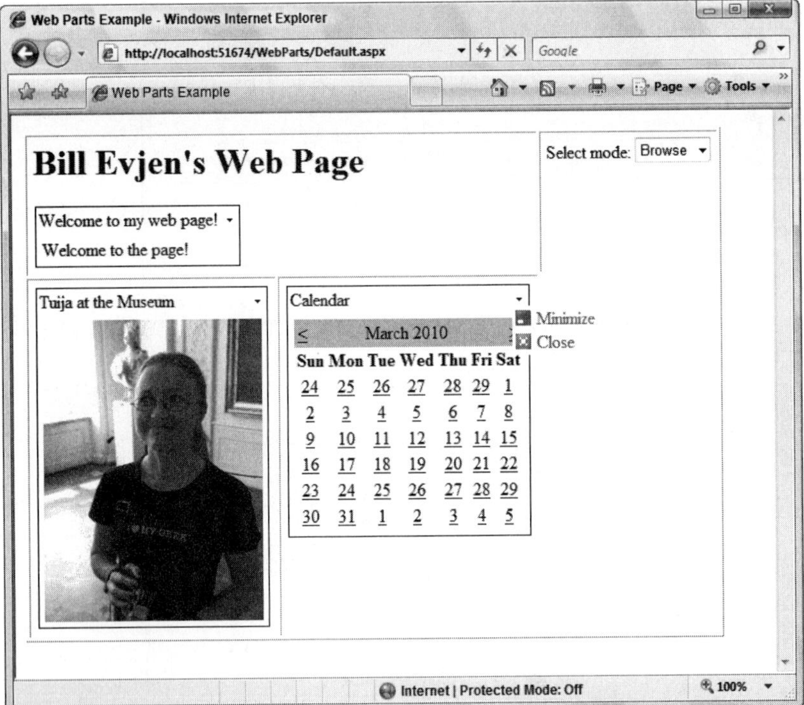

FIGURE 16-21

This chapter, thus far, has concentrated on creating completely customizable portal applications in a declarative manner using the capabilities provided by the ASP.NET Portal Framework. As with most aspects of ASP.NET, however, not only can you work with appearance and functionality in a declarative fashion, but you can also create the same constructs through server-side code.

WORKING WITH CLASSES IN THE PORTAL FRAMEWORK

The Portal Framework provides three main classes for dealing with the underlying framework presented in this chapter: `WebPartManager`, `WebPartZone`, and `WebPart`.

The `WebPartManager` class allows you to perform multiple operations in your server-side code. Table 16-1 shows a partial listing of some of the properties that this class provides.

TABLE 16-1

WEBPARTMANAGER CLASS PROPERTIES	DESCRIPTION
`Connections`	Provides a collection of all the connections between Web Parts contained on the page.
`DisplayMode`	Allows you to change the page's display mode. Possible choices include `CatalogDisplayMode`, `ConnectDisplayMode`, `DesignDisplayMode`, `EditDisplayMode`, and `BrowseDisplayMode`.
`SelectedWebPart`	Allows you to perform multiple operations on the selected Web Part.
`WebParts`	Provides a collection of all the Web Parts contained on the page.
`Zones`	Provides a collection of all the Web Part Zones contained on the page.

Beyond the properties of the `WebPartManager` class, you also have an extensive list of available methods at your disposal. Table 16-2 outlines some of the available methods of the `WebPartManager` class.

TABLE 16-2

WEBPARTMANAGER CLASS METHODS	DESCRIPTION
`AddWebPart`	Allows you to dynamically add new Web Parts to a particular zone on the page.
`ConnectWebParts`	Allows you to connect two Web Parts together via a common property or value.
`DeleteWebPart`	Allows you to dynamically delete new Web Parts from a particular zone on the page.
`DisconnectWebParts`	Allows you to delete a connection between two Web Parts.
`MoveWebPart`	Allows you to move a Web Part from one zone to another, or allows you to change the index order in which Web Parts appear in a particular zone.

Whereas the `WebPartManager` class allows you to manipulate the location, addition, and deletion of Web Parts that appear in the page as a whole, the `WebPartZone` class allows you to modify a single Web Part Zone on the page. Table 16-3 provides a list of some properties available to the `WebPartZone` class.

TABLE 16-3

WEBPARTZONE CLASS PROPERTIES	DESCRIPTION
`AllowLayoutChange`	Takes a `Boolean` value and either enables or disables the Web Part Zone's capability to accept or allow any changes in the Web Parts it contains.
`BackColor, BackImageUrl, BorderColor, BorderStyle, BorderWidth`	Enable you to modify the Web Part Zone's general appearance.
`CloseVerb`	References the Close verb for a particular Web Part Zone from which you can then manipulate the verb's `Description`, `Enabled`, `ImageUrl`, `Text`, and `Visible` properties.
`ConnectVerb`	References a Web Part Zone's Connect verb from which you can then manipulate the verb's `Description`, `Enabled`, `ImageUrl`, `Text`, and `Visible` properties.

continues

TABLE 16-3 *(continued)*

WEBPARTZONE CLASS PROPERTIES	DESCRIPTION
`DragHighlightColor`	Takes a `System.Color` value that sets the color of the Web Part Zone's border if focused when the moving of Web Parts is in operation. This also changes the color of the line that appears in the Web Part Zone specifying where to drop the Web Part.
`EditVerb`	References a Web Part Zone's Edit verb from which you can then manipulate the verb's `Description`, `Enabled`, `ImageUrl`, `Text`, and `Visible` properties.
`EmptyZoneText`	Sets the text that is shown in the zone if a Web Part is not set in the zone.
`HeaderText`	Sets header text.
`Height`	Sets the height of the Web Part Zone.
`HelpVerb`	References a Web Part Zone's Help verb from which you can then manipulate the verb's `Description`, `Enabled`, `ImageUrl`, `Text`, and `Visible` properties.
`MenuLabelStyle, MenuLabelText`	Enable you to modify the drop-down menu that appears when end users edit a Web Part. These properties let you apply an image, alter the text, or change the style of the menu.
`MinimizeVerb`	References a Web Part Zone's Minimize verb from which you can then manipulate the verb's `Description`, `Enabled`, `ImageUrl`, `Text`, and `Visible` properties.
`LayoutOrientation`	Enables you to change the Web Part Zone's orientation from horizontal to vertical or vice versa.
`RestoreVerb`	References a Web Part Zone's Restore verb, from which you can then manipulate the verb's `Description`, `Enabled`, `ImageUrl`, `Text`, and `Visible` properties.
`VerbButtonType`	Enables you to change the button style. Choices include `ButtonType.Button`, `ButtonType.Image`, or `ButtonType.Link`.
`WebParts`	Provides a collection of all the Web Parts contained within the zone.
`Width`	Sets the width of the Web Part Zone.

You have a plethora of options to manipulate the look-and-feel of the Web Part Zone and the items contained therein.

The final class is the `WebPart` class. This class enables you to manipulate specific Web Parts located on the page. Table 16-4 details some of the properties available in the `WebPart` class.

TABLE 16-4

WEBPART CLASS PROPERTIES	DESCRIPTION
`AllowClose`	Takes a `Boolean` value that specifies whether the Web Part can be closed and removed from the page.
`AllowEdit`	Takes a `Boolean` value that specifies whether the end user can edit the Web Part.
`AllowHide`	Takes a `Boolean` value that specifies whether the end user can hide the Web Part within the Web Part Zone. If the control is hidden, it is still in the zone, but invisible.

WEBPART CLASS PROPERTIES	DESCRIPTION
AllowMinimize	Takes a Boolean value that specifies whether the end user can collapse the Web Part.
AllowZoneChange	Takes a Boolean value that specifies whether the end user can move the Web Part from one zone to another.
BackColor, BackImageUrl, BorderColor, BorderStyle, BorderWidth	Enable you to modify the Web Part's general appearance.
ChromeState	Specifies whether the Web Part chrome is in a normal state or is minimized.
ChromeType	Specifies the chrome type that the Web Part uses. Available options include BorderOnly, Default, None, TitleAndBorder, and TitleOnly.
Direction	Specifies the direction of the text or items placed within the Web Part. Available options include LeftToRight, NotSet, and RightToLeft. This property is ideal for dealing with Web Parts that contain Asian text that is read from right to left.
HelpMode	Specifies how the help items display when the end user clicks the Help verb. Available options include Modal, Modeless, and Navigate. Modal displays the help items within a modal window if the end user's browser supports modal windows. If not, a pop-up window appears. Modeless means that a pop-up window appears for every user. Navigate redirects the user to the appropriate help page (specified by the HelpUrl property) when he clicks on the Help verb.
HelpUrl	Used when the HelpMode is set to Navigate. Takes a String value that specifies the location of the page the end user is redirected to when he clicks on the Help verb.
ScrollBars	Applies scroll bars to the Web Part. Available values include Auto, Both, Horizontal, None, and Vertical.
Title	Specifies the text for the Web Part's title. Text appears in the title bar section.
TitleIconImageUrl	Enables you to apply an icon to appear next to the title by specifying to the icon image's location as a String value of the property.
TitleUrl	Specifies the location to direct the end user when the Web Part's title Web Part is clicked. When set, the title is converted to a link; when not set, the title appears as regular text.
Zone	Allows you to refer to the zone in which the Web Part is located.

CREATING CUSTOM WEB PARTS

When adding items to a page that utilizes the Portal Framework, you add the pre-existing ASP.NET Web server controls, user controls, or custom controls. In addition to these items, you can also build and incorporate custom Web Parts. Using the WebParts class, you can create your own custom Web Parts. Although similar to ASP.NET custom server control development, the creation of custom Web Parts adds some additional capabilities. Creating a class that inherits from the WebPart class instead of the Control class enables your control to use the personalization features and to work with the larger Portal Framework, thereby allowing for the control to be closed, maximized, minimized, and more.

To create a custom Web Part control, the first step is to create a project in Visual Studio 2010. From Visual Studio, choose File ➪ New Project. The New Project dialog opens. From this dialog, select ASP.NET Server Control. Name the project MyStateListBox and click OK to create the project. You are presented with a class that contains the basic framework for a typical ASP.NET server control. Ignore this framework; you are going to change it so that your class creates a custom Web Parts control instead of an ASP.NET custom server control. Listing 16-14 details the creation of a custom Web Part control.

LISTING 16-14: Creating a custom Web Part control

Available for download on Wrox.com

```
Imports System
Imports System.Web
Imports System.Web.UI.WebControls
Imports System.Web.UI.WebControls.WebParts

Namespace Wrox

    Public Class StateListBox
        Inherits WebPart

        Private _LabelStartText As String = " Enter State Name: "
        Dim StateInput As New TextBox
        Dim StateContents As New ListBox

        Public Sub New()
            Me.AllowClose = False
        End Sub

        <Personalizable(), WebBrowsable()>
        Public Property LabelStartText() As String
            Get
                Return _LabelStartText
            End Get
            Set(ByVal value As String)
                _LabelStartText = value
            End Set
        End Property

        Protected Overrides Sub CreateChildControls()
            Controls.Clear()

            Dim InstructionText As New Label
            InstructionText.BackColor = Drawing.Color.LightGray
            InstructionText.Font.Name = "Verdana"
            InstructionText.Font.Size = 10
            InstructionText.Font.Bold = True
            InstructionText.Text = LabelStartText
            Me.Controls.Add(InstructionText)

            Dim LineBreak As New Literal
            LineBreak.Text = "<br />"
            Me.Controls.Add(LineBreak)

            Me.Controls.Add(StateInput)

            Dim InputButton As New Button
            InputButton.Text = "Input State"
            AddHandler InputButton.Click, AddressOf Me.Button1_Click
            Me.Controls.Add(InputButton)

            Dim Spacer As New Literal
            Spacer.Text = "<p>"
            Me.Controls.Add(Spacer)

            Me.Controls.Add(StateContents)

            ChildControlsCreated = True
```

```
        End Sub

        Public Sub Button1_Click(ByVal sender As Object, ByVal e As EventArgs)
            StateContents.Items.Add(StateInput.Text)
            StateInput.Text = String.Empty
            StateInput.Focus()
        End Sub

    End Class

End Namespace
```

C#

```
using System;
using System.Web.UI.WebControls;
using System.Web.UI.WebControls.WebParts;

namespace Wrox
{
    public class StateListBox : WebPart
    {
        private String _LabelStartText = " Enter State Name: ";
        readonly TextBox StateInput = new TextBox();
        readonly ListBox StateContents = new ListBox();

        public StateListBox()
        {
            AllowClose = false;
        }

        [Personalizable, WebBrowsable]
        public String LabelStartText
        {
            get { return _LabelStartText; }
            set { _LabelStartText = value; }
        }

        protected override void CreateChildControls()
        {
            Controls.Clear();

            Label InstructionText = new Label();
            InstructionText.BackColor = System.Drawing.Color.LightGray;
            InstructionText.Font.Name = "Verdana";
            InstructionText.Font.Size = 10;
            InstructionText.Font.Bold = true;
            InstructionText.Text = LabelStartText;
            Controls.Add(InstructionText);

            Literal LineBreak = new Literal();
            LineBreak.Text = "<br />";
            Controls.Add(LineBreak);

            Controls.Add(StateInput);

            Button InputButton = new Button();
            InputButton.Text = "Input State";
            InputButton.Click += this.Button1_Click;
            Controls.Add(InputButton);

            Literal Spacer = new Literal();
            Spacer.Text = "<p>";
            Controls.Add(Spacer);
```

continues

LISTING 16-14 *(continued)*

```
                Controls.Add(StateContents);

                ChildControlsCreated = true;
            }

            private void Button1_Click(object sender, EventArgs e)
            {
                StateContents.Items.Add(StateInput.Text);
                StateInput.Text = String.Empty;
                StateInput.Focus();
            }
        }
    }
```

To review, you first import the `System.Web.UI.WebControls.WebParts` namespace. The important step in the creation of this custom control is to make sure that it inherits from the `WebPart` class instead of the customary `Control` class. As stated earlier, this gives the control access to the advanced functionality of the Portal Framework that a typical custom control would not have.

VB

```
Public Class StateListBox
   Inherits WebPart

End Class
```

C#

```
public class StateListBox : WebPart
{

}
```

After the class structure is in place, you will need to define a few properties as well as a constructor. The constructor directly uses some of the capabilities that the `WebPart` class provides. These capabilities would not be available if this custom control has the `Control` class as its base class and is making use of the `WebPart.AllowClose` property.

VB

```
Public Sub New()
   Me.AllowClose = False
End Sub
```

C#

```
public StateListBox()
{
   AllowClose = false;
}
```

This constructor creates a control that explicitly sets the control's `AllowClose` property to `False` — meaning that the Web Part will not have a Close link associated with it when generated in the page. Because of the use of the `WebPart` class instead of the `Control` class, you will find, in addition to the `AllowClose` property, other `WebPart` class properties such as `AllowEdit`, `AllowHide`, `AllowMinimize`, `AllowZoneChange`, and more.

In the example shown in Listing 16-14, you see a custom-defined property: `LabelStartText`. This property allows the developer to change the instruction text displayed at the top of the control. The big difference with this custom property is that it is preceded by the `Personalizable` and the `WebBrowsable` attributes.

The `Personalizable` attribute enables the property for personalization, whereas the `WebBrowsable` attribute specifies whether the property should be displayed in the Properties window in Visual Studio. You can define the `Personalizable` attribute further using a `PersonalizationScope` enumeration. The only two possible enumerations — `Shared` and `User` — can be defined in the following ways:

VB

```
<Personalizable(PersonalizationScope.Shared), WebBrowsable()>
Public Property LabelStartText() As String
   Get
      Return _LabelStartText
   End Get
   Set(ByVal value As String)
      _LabelStartText = value
   End Set
End Property
```

C#

```
[Personalizable(PersonalizationScope.Shared), WebBrowsable]
public String LabelStartText
{
   get { return _LabelStartText; }
   set { _LabelStartText = value; }
}
```

A `PersonalizationScope` of `User` means that any modifications are done on a per-user basis. This is the default setting and means that if a user makes modifications to the property, the changes are seen only by that particular user and not by the other users who browse the page. If the `PersonalizationScope` is set to `Shared`, changes made by one user can be viewed by others requesting the page.

After you have any properties in place, the next step is to define what gets rendered to the page by overriding the `CreateChildControls` method. From the example in Listing 16-14, the `CreateChildControls` method renders Label, Literal, TextBox, Button, and ListBox controls. In addition to defining the properties of some of these controls, a single event is associated with the Button control (`Button1_Click`) that is also defined in this class.

Now that the custom Web Part control is in place, build the project so that a DLL is created. Open up the ASP.NET Web project where you want to utilize this new control and, from the Visual Studio Toolbox, add the new control. You can quickly accomplish this task by right-clicking in the Toolbox on the tab where you want the new control to be placed. After right-clicking the appropriate tab, select Choose Items. Click the Browse button and point to the new `MyStateListBox.dll` that you just created. After this is done, the StateListBox control is highlighted and checked in the Choose Toolbox Items dialog, as illustrated in Figure 16-22.

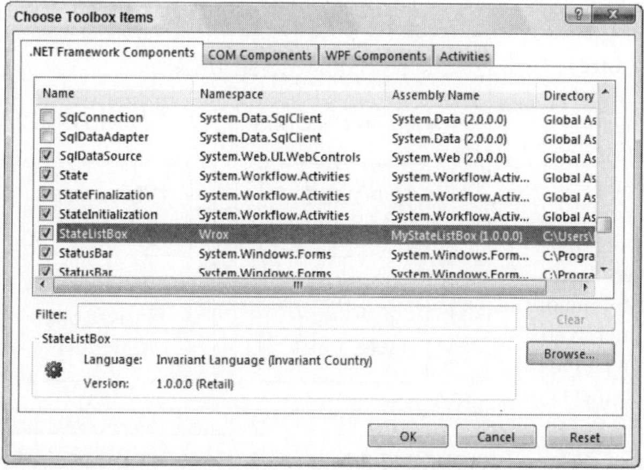

FIGURE 16-22

Clicking OK adds the control to your Toolbox. Now you are ready to use this new control as a Web Part control. To do this, simply drag and drop the control into one of your Web Part Zone areas. This does a couple of things, one of which is that it registers the control on the page using the Register directive:

```
<%@ Register TagPrefix="cc1" Namespace="MyStateListBox.Wrox"
    Assembly="MyStateListBox" %>
```

Once registered, the control can be used on the page. If dragged and dropped onto the page's design surface, you get a control in the following construct:

```
<cc1:StateListBox runat="server" ID="StateListBox1"
 LabelStartText=" Enter State Name: " AllowClose="False" />
```

The two important things to notice with this construct is that the custom property, `LabelStartText`, is present and has the default value in place, and the `AllowClose` attribute is included. The `AllowClose` attribute is present only because earlier you made the control's inherited class `WebPart` and not `Control`. Because `WebPart` was made the inherited class, you have access to these Web Part–specific properties. When the StateListBox control is drawn on the page, you can see that, indeed, it is part of the larger Portal Framework and allows for things such as minimization and editing. End users can use this custom Web Part control as if it were any other type of Web Part control. As you can see, you have a lot of power when you create your own Web Part controls.

And because `LabelStartText` uses the `WebBrowsable` attribute, you can use the PropertyGridEditor Part control to allow end users to edit this directly in the browser. With this in place, as was demonstrated earlier in Listing 16-5, an end user will see the following editing capabilities after switching to Edit mode (see Figure 16-23).

Property Grid
LabelStartText:
Enter State Name:

FIGURE 16-23

CONNECTING WEB PARTS

In working with Web Parts, you sometimes need to connect them in some fashion. *Connecting* them means that you must pass a piece of information (an object) from one Web Part to another Web Part on the page.

For instance, you might want to transfer the text value (such as a zip code or a name) that someone enters in a text box to other Web Parts in the page. Another example is a DropDownList control that specifies all the available currencies in the system. An end user's selection from the drop-down list drives changes in all the other Web Parts on that page that deal with this currency value selection. When you need to build constructions in this manner, you can use the Web Part connection capabilities defined here, or you might be able to work with other ASP.NET systems available (such as the personalization capabilities provided through the profile system).

When connecting Web Parts, you should be aware of the specific rules on how these Web Parts interact with one another. If you want to make a connection from one Web Part to another, one of the Web Parts must be the *provider*. This provider Web Part is the component that supplies the piece of information required by any other Web Parts. The Web Parts that require this information are the *consumer* Web Parts. A Web Part provider can supply information to one or more consumer Web Parts; however, a consumer Web Part can only connect with a single provider Web Part. You cannot have a consumer Web Part that connects to more than one provider Web Part.

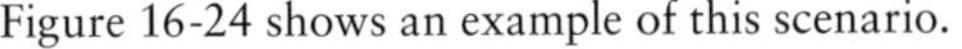

Figure 16-24 shows an example of this scenario.

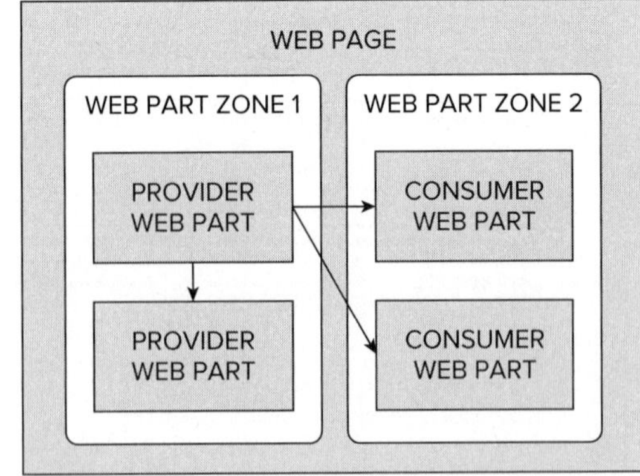

FIGURE 16-24

From this diagram, you can see that using a single provider Web Part with multiple consumer Web Parts is possible regardless of the Web Part Zone area in which the consumer Web Part resides.

When working with provider and consumer Web Parts, be aware that no matter how simple or complicated the Web Part is, you must wrap the Web Part by making it a custom Web Part. You do this to expose the correct item or property from the provider Web Part or to utilize the passed value in the correct manner for the consumer Web Part. This chapter reviews a simple example of connecting Web Parts. Although many steps are required to accomplish this task, you definitely get a lot of value from it as well.

Building the Provider Web Part

In order to build a provider Web Part that can be utilized by any consumer Web Part residing on the page, you first create an interface exposing the item you want to pass from one Web Part to another.

For this example, suppose you want to provide a text box as a Web Part that allows the end user to input a value. This value is then utilized by a calendar control contained within a Web Part in an entirely different Web Part Zone on the page using the Calendar control's `Caption` property.

Listing 16-15 demonstrates this interface.

LISTING 16-15: Building an interface to expose the property used to pass to a Web Part

```
Namespace Wrox.ConnectionManagement
    Public Interface IStringForCalendar
        Property CalendarString() As String
    End Interface
End Namespace
```

```
namespace Wrox.ConnectionManagement
{
    public interface IStringForCalendar
    {
        string CalendarString { get; set;}
    }
}
```

From this bit of code, you can see that the interface, `IStringForCalendar`, is quite simple. It exposes only a single String property — `CalendarString`. This interface is then utilized by the custom provider Web Part shown next.

You build the custom provider Web Part like any other custom Web Part in the manner demonstrated earlier in this chapter. The only difference is that you also provide some extra details so ASP.NET knows what item you are exposing from the Web Part and how this value is retrieved. Listing 16-16 presents this custom provider Web Part.

LISTING 16-16: Building a custom provider Web Part

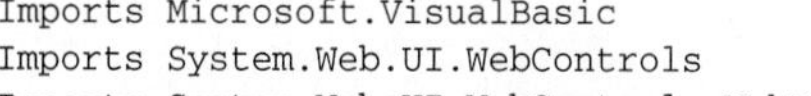

```
Imports Microsoft.VisualBasic
Imports System.Web.UI.WebControls
Imports System.Web.UI.WebControls.WebParts

Namespace Wrox.ConnectionManagement
    Public Class TextBoxChanger
        Inherits WebPart
        Implements IStringForCalendar

        Private myTextBox As TextBox
        Private _calendarString As String = String.Empty

        <Personalizable()> _
        Public Property CalendarString() As String Implements
          Wrox.ConnectionManagement.IStringForCalendar.CalendarString

            Get
                Return _calendarString
            End Get
            Set(ByVal value As String)
```

continues

LISTING 16-16 *(continued)*

```
                _calendarString = value
            End Set

        End Property

        <ConnectionProvider("Provider for String From TextBox",
            "TextBoxStringProvider")>
        Public Function TextBoxStringProvider() As IStringForCalendar
            Return Me
        End Function

        Protected Overrides Sub CreateChildControls()
            Controls.Clear()
            myTextBox = New TextBox()
            Me.Controls.Add(myTextBox)
            Dim myButton As Button = New Button()
            myButton.Text = "Change Calendar Caption"
            AddHandler myButton.Click, AddressOf Me.myButton_Click
            Me.Controls.Add(myButton)
        End Sub

        Private Sub myButton_Click(ByVal sender As Object, ByVal e As EventArgs)
            If myTextBox.Text <> String.Empty Then
                CalendarString = myTextBox.Text
                myTextBox.Text = String.Empty
            End If
        End Sub
    End Class
End Namespace
```

C#

```
using System;
using System.Web.UI.WebControls;
using System.Web.UI.WebControls.WebParts;

namespace Wrox.ConnectionManagement
{
    public class TextBoxChanger : WebPart, IStringForCalendar
    {
        private TextBox myTextBox;
        private string _calendarString = String.Empty;

        [Personalizable]
        public string CalendarString
        {
            get { return _calendarString; }
            set { _calendarString = value; }
        }

        [ConnectionProvider("Provider for String From TextBox",
            "TextBoxStringProvider")]
        public IStringForCalendar TextBoxStringProvider()
        {
            return this;
        }

        protected override void CreateChildControls()
        {
            Controls.Clear();
            myTextBox = new TextBox();
            Controls.Add(myTextBox);
            Button myButton = new Button();
```

```
            myButton.Text = "Change Calendar Caption";
            myButton.Click += this.myButton_Click;
            Controls.Add(myButton);
        }

        private void myButton_Click(object sender, EventArgs e)
        {
            if (myTextBox.Text != String.Empty)
            {
                CalendarString = myTextBox.Text;
                myTextBox.Text = String.Empty;
            }
        }
    }
}
```

Not only does this Web Part inherit the `WebPart` class, this provider Web Part implements the interface, `IStringForCalendar`, which was created earlier in Listing 16-15. From `IStringForCalendar`, the single `String` property is utilized and given the `Personalizable()` attribute. The important bit from the code presented in Listing 16-16 is the `TextBoxStringProvider()` method. This method returns a type of `IStringForCalendar` and is defined even further using the `ConnectionProvider` attribute. This attribute enables you to give a friendly name to the provider as well a programmatic name that can be used within the consumer custom Web Part that you will build shortly.

Using the `CreateChildControls()` method, you lay out the design of the Web Part. In this case, a text box and button are the only controls that make up this Web Part. In addition to simply laying out the controls on the design surface, you use this method to assign any specific control events — such as a button-click event — by assigning handlers to the controls that require them.

Finally, from within the button-click event of this Web Part (`myButton_Click`), the exposed property of `IStringForCalendar` is assigned a value. Everything is now in place for a consumer Web Part. The construction of this second Web Part is demonstrated next.

Building the Consumer Web Part

After you have a provider Web Part in place on your page, you can utilize the object it supplies for any number of consumer Web Parts on the same page. In this example, however, you are interested in using the `String` value coming from the TextBox control in the provider Web Part. The consumer Web Part takes this `String` and assigns it as the value of the Calendar control's `Caption` property. Listing 16-17 presents the construction of the consumer Web Part.

LISTING 16-17: The consumer Web Part

Available for download on Wrox.com

```
Imports Microsoft.VisualBasic
Imports System.Web.UI.WebControls
Imports System.Web.UI.WebControls.WebParts

Namespace Wrox.ConnectionManagement
    Public Class ModifyableCalendar
        Inherits WebPart

        Private _myProvider As IStringForCalendar
        Private _stringTitle As String
        Private myCalendar As Calendar = New Calendar()

        <ConnectionConsumer("Calendar Title Consumer", "CalendarTitleConsumer")>
        Public Sub RetrieveTitle(ByVal Provider As IStringForCalendar)
            _myProvider = Provider
        End Sub
```

continues

LISTING 16-17 *(continued)*

```
        Protected Overrides Sub OnPreRender(ByVal e As EventArgs)
            EnsureChildControls()

            If Not (Me._myProvider Is Nothing) Then
                _stringTitle = _myProvider.CalendarString.Trim()
                myCalendar.Caption = _stringTitle
            End If
        End Sub

        Protected Overrides Sub CreateChildControls()
            Controls.Clear()
            Me.Controls.Add(myCalendar)
        End Sub
    End Class
End Namespace
```

C#

```
using System;
using System.Web.UI.WebControls;
using System.Web.UI.WebControls.WebParts;

namespace Wrox.ConnectionManagement
{
    public class ModifyableCalendar : WebPart
    {
        private IStringForCalendar _myProvider;
        string _stringTitle;
        Calendar myCalendar;

        [ConnectionConsumer("Calendar Title Consumer", "CalendarTitleConsumer")]
        public void RetrieveTitle(IStringForCalendar Provider)
        {
            _myProvider = Provider;
        }

        protected override void OnPreRender(EventArgs e)
        {
            EnsureChildControls();

            if (_myProvider != null)
            {
                _stringTitle = _myProvider.CalendarString.Trim();
                myCalendar.Caption = _stringTitle;
            }
        }

        protected override void CreateChildControls()
        {
            Controls.Clear();
            myCalendar = new Calendar();
            Controls.Add(myCalendar);
        }
    }
}
```

This new custom Web Part, `ModifyableCalendar`, is simply a class that inherits from `WebPart` and nothing more. It requires a reference to the interface `IStringForCalendar`. Because `IStringForCalendar` is part of the same namespace, you can provide a simple reference to this interface.

Your consumer Web Part requires a method that is the connection point for a provider Web Part on the same page. In this case, the `RetrieveTitle()` method is constructed using the `ConnectionConsumer` attribute before the method declaration. Like the `ConnectionProvider` attribute that was utilized in the provider Web Part, the `ConnectionConsumer` Web Part enables you to give your Web Part a friendly name and a reference name to use programmatically.

Then, the value retrieved from the provider Web Part is grabbed from within the `PreRender()` method of the Web Part and assigned to the Calendar control before the actual Calendar control is placed on the page from within the `CreateChildControls()` method.

Now that both a provider and a consumer Web Part are available to you, the next step is to get them both on an ASP.NET page and build the mechanics to tie the two Web Parts together, as demonstrated next.

Connecting Web Parts on an ASP.NET Page

When in the process of connecting Web Parts, remember that you need a provider Web Part and a consumer Web Part. These items are detailed in Listings 16-16 and 16-17, respectively. When working with the process of connecting Web Parts, it is not simply a matter of placing both of these items on the page to get the connections to take place. In addition to this step, you have to wire the Web Parts together.

You do this wiring of Web Part connections through the WebPartManager control that is discussed at the beginning part of this chapter. Listing 16-18 details the ASP.NET page used for this example.

LISTING 16-18: The ASP.NET page that connects two Web Part controls

Available for download on Wrox.com

```
<%@ Page Language="VB" %>
<%@ Register Namespace="Wrox.ConnectionManagement"
    TagPrefix="connectionControls" %>

<html xmlns="http://www.w3.org/1999/xhtml">
<head runat="server">
    <title>Connecting Web Parts</title>
</head>
<body>
    <form id="form1" runat="server">
    <div>
        <asp:WebPartManager ID="WebPartManager1" runat="server">
            <StaticConnections>
                <asp:WebPartConnection ID="WebPartConnection1"
                 ConsumerID="ModifyableCalendar1"
                 ConsumerConnectionPointID="CalendarTitleConsumer"
                 ProviderID="TextBoxChanger1"
                 ProviderConnectionPointID="TextBoxStringProvider">
                </asp:WebPartConnection>
            </StaticConnections>
        </asp:WebPartManager>
        <table cellpadding="3">
            <tr valign="top">
                <td style="width: 100px">
                    <asp:WebPartZone ID="WebPartZone1" runat="server">
                        <ZoneTemplate>
                            <connectionControls:TextBoxChanger
                             ID="TextBoxChanger1"
                             runat="server" Title="Provider Web Part" />
                        </ZoneTemplate>
                    </asp:WebPartZone>
                </td>
                <td style="width: 100px">
                    <asp:WebPartZone ID="WebPartZone2" runat="server">
                        <ZoneTemplate>
                            <connectionControls:ModifyableCalendar
                             ID="ModifyableCalendar1" runat="server"
                             Title="Consumer Web Part" />
                        </ZoneTemplate>
```

continues

LISTING 16-18 *(continued)*

```
                    </asp:WebPartZone>
                </td>
            </tr>
        </table>
    </div>
    </form>
</body>
</html>
```

This ASP.NET page that utilizes Web Parts contains a single two-cell table. Each cell in the table contains a single WebPartZone control — `WebPartZone1` and `WebPartZone2`.

Before connecting the Web Parts, the new custom Web Part controls are registered in the ASP.NET page using the `@Register` page directive. This directive simply points to the namespace `Wrox.ConnectionManagement`. This is the namespace used by the interface and the two custom Web Part controls.

Each of the custom Web Parts is placed within its own WebPartZone control. The two Web Part controls are tied together using the WebPartManager control.

```
<asp:WebPartManager ID="WebPartManager1" runat="server">
   <StaticConnections>
      <asp:WebPartConnection ID="WebPartConnection1"
       ConsumerID="ModifyableCalendar1"
       ConsumerConnectionPointID="CalendarTitleConsumer"
       ProviderID="TextBoxChanger1"
       ProviderConnectionPointID="TextBoxStringProvider">
      </asp:WebPartConnection>
   </StaticConnections>
</asp:WebPartManager>
```

The WebPartManager server control nests the defined connection inside of the `<StaticConnections>` section of the declaration. The definition is actually accomplished using the WebPartConnection server control. This control takes four important attributes required in order to make the necessary connections. The first set of two attributes deals with definitions of the consumer settings. Of these, the `ConsumerID` attribute references the name of the control on the ASP.NET page (through its ID attribute) and the `ConsumerConnectionPointID` references the ID of the object working as the connection point for the consumer. Looking back, you find this is the `RetrieveTitle()` method shown in the following code snippet:

```
<ConnectionConsumer("Calendar Title Consumer", "CalendarTitleConsumer")>
 Public Sub RetrieveTitle(ByVal Provider As IStringForCalendar)
    _myProvider = Provider
 End Sub
```

The second set of attributes required by the WebPartConnection deals with the provider Web Part. The first attribute of this set is the `ProviderID` attribute that makes reference to the name of the control on the ASP.NET page, which is considered the provider. The second attribute, `ProviderConnectionPointID` is quite similar to the `ConsumerConnectionPointID` attribute, but the `ProviderConnectionPointID` attribute references the ID of the object working as the provider in the connection process.

```
<ConnectionProvider("Provider for String From TextBox", "TextBoxStringProvider")>
 Public Function TextBoxStringProvider() As IStringForCalendar
    Return Me
 End Function
```

Running this page gives you the results illustrated in Figure 16-25.

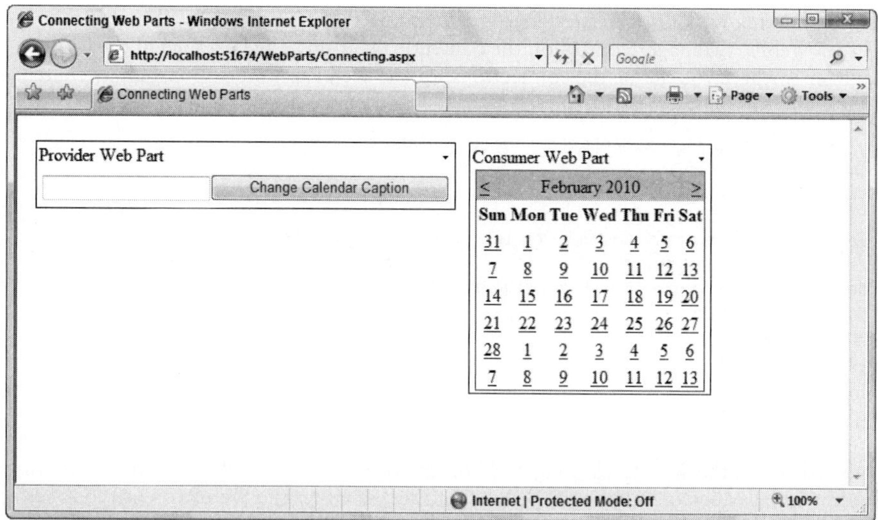

FIGURE 16-25

If you type any text string in the text box in the provider Web Part on the page and click the button within this control, the Calendar control uses this `String` value as its value for the `Caption` property, as demonstrated in Figure 16-26.

As you can see from this example, you take a lot of steps to make this happen, but the steps aren't too difficult. In this example, a simple `String` object was passed from one Web Part to another. You could, however, use the exact same process to pass more complex objects (even custom objects) or larger items such as a `DataSet` object.

FIGURE 16-26

Understanding the Difficulties in Dealing with Master Pages When Connecting Web Parts

You should note one final consideration about dealing with connecting Web Parts on your ASP.NET pages. You might have already realized that this process gets rather difficult when you are working with ASP.NET pages that make use of the master page capability provided by ASP.NET.

You are allowed only a single WebPartManager control on an ASP.NET page. Many times, when you are working with master pages, putting this control in the master page itself rather than in the content pages that make use of the master page makes a lot of sense. If you are taking this approach, it does not make much sense to start using WebPartConnection controls within the master page. You can easily have controls with the same ID on multiple content pages. If you do so, the references made within the WebPartConnection control might not be meant for these other controls. For this reason, you need to make use of the ProxyWebPartManager control.

Suppose you have a master page with a WebPartManager control. In this case, the WebPartManager control can be rather simple, as shown here:

```
<asp:WebPartManager ID="WebPartManager1" runat="server">
</asp:WebPartManager>
```

With this WebPartManager control on your `.master` page, you ensure this single instance manages the Web Parts contained in each and every content page making use of this particular master page.

Next, if a content page making use of this master page is attempting to connect some Web Parts, you must place a ProxyWebPartManager control on the content page itself. This instance of the ProxyWebPartManager is where you define the connections for the Web Parts on this particular content page. This is illustrated in the following code snippet:

```
<asp:ProxyWebPartManager ID="ProxyWebPartManager1" runat="server">
   <StaticConnections>
      <asp:WebPartConnection ID="WebPartConnection1"
       ConsumerID="ModifyableCalendar1"
       ConsumerConnectionPointID="CalendarTitleConsumer"
       ProviderID="TextBoxChanger1"
       ProviderConnectionPointID="TextBoxStringProvider">
      </asp:WebPartConnection>
   </StaticConnections>
</asp:ProxyWebPartManager>
```

SUMMARY

This chapter introduced you to the WebPartManager, WebPartZone, and the WebPart controls. Not only do these controls allow for easy customization of the look-and-feel of either the Web Parts or the zones in which they are located, but you can also use the framework provided to completely modify the behavior of these items.

This chapter also showed you how to create your own custom Web Part controls. Creating your own controls was always one of the benefits provided by ASP.NET, and this benefit has been taken one step further with the capability to create Web Part controls. Web Part controls enable you to take advantage of some of the more complex features that you do not get with custom ASP.NET server controls.

You may find the Portal Framework to be one of the more exciting features of ASP.NET; you may like the idea of creating completely modular and customizable Web pages. End users like this feature, and it is quite easy for developers to implement. Just remember that you do not have to implement every feature explained in this chapter; with the framework provided, however, you can choose the functionality that you want.

17

HTML and CSS Design with ASP.NET

WHAT'S IN THIS CHAPTER?

- Understanding the basics of CSS
- Using CSS in Visual Studio
- Using CSS with the ASP.NET server controls

When HTML was first introduced by Tim Berners-Lee, it was intended to be a simple way for researchers using the Internet to format and cross-link their research documents. At the time, the Web was still primarily text-based; therefore, the formatting requirements for these documents were fairly basic. HTML needed only a small handful of basic layout concepts such as a title, paragraph, headers, and lists. As the Web was opened up to the general public, graphical browsers were introduced, and as requirements for formatting Web pages continued to expand, newer versions of HTML were introduced. These newer versions expanded the original capabilities of HTML to accommodate the new, rich graphical browser environment, allowing table layouts, richer font styling, images, and frames.

Although all of these improvements to HTML were helpful, HTML still proved to be inadequate for allowing developers to create complex, highly stylized Web pages. Therefore, in 1994 a new technology called Cascading Style Sheets (CSS) was introduced. CSS served as a complementary technology to HTML, giving developers of Web pages the power they needed to finely control the style of their Web pages.

As the Web has matured, CSS has gained popularity as developers realized that it has significant advantages over standard HTML styling capabilities. Unlike HTML, which was originally conceived as primarily a layout mechanism, CSS was conceived from the beginning to provide rich styling capabilities to Web pages. The cascading nature of CSS makes it easy to apply styles with a broad stroke to an entire application, and only where necessary override those styles. CSS makes externally defining Web site style information easy, allowing for a clear separation of Web page style and structure. CSS also allows developers to greatly reduce the file size of a Web page, which translates into faster page load times and reduced bandwidth consumption.

Although the point of this chapter is not to convince you that CSS is the best solution for styling your Web site, it will help you understand how you can leverage these technologies in your ASP.NET-based Web applications. The chapter starts with a brief overview of CSS and how it works with HTML, and then moves into creating Web sites in Visual Studio using HTML and CSS. Finally, you look at how you can use ASP.NET and CSS together.

CAVEATS

Although this chapter includes a lot of great information about HTML and CSS, and how you can use them in conjunction with ASP.NET and Visual Studio, you should be aware of several caveats.

First, because there is no way that a single chapter can begin to cover the entire breadth of HTML and CSS, if you are looking for an in-depth discussion of these topics, you can check out the Wrox title *Beginning CSS: Cascading Style Sheets for Web Design, 2nd Edition*, by Richard York (Wiley, 2007).

Second, because CSS is simply a specification, actually interpreting and implementing that specification is up to each browser vendor. As is so often the case in Web development, each browser has its own quirks in how it implements (or sometimes does not implement) different CSS features. Even though the samples in this chapter were tested on Internet Explorer 8, be sure to thoroughly test your Web sites in multiple browsers on multiple platforms to ensure that your CSS is rendering appropriately in each browser you are targeting.

Finally, the DOCTYPE you use in your Web pages can influence how the browser applies the CSS styles included in your Web page. You should understand how different DOCTYPES influence the browser's rendering process in your Web page.

HTML AND CSS OVERVIEW

From the beginning of the Web, continuing to today, HTML serves as the primary mechanism for defining the content blocks of your Web page, and is the easiest way to define the layout of your Web page. HTML includes a variety of layout tags you can use, including table, list, and grouping elements. You can combine these elements to create highly complex layouts in your Web page. Figure 17-1 illustrates a single Web page that defines a basic layout using a variety of HTML elements.

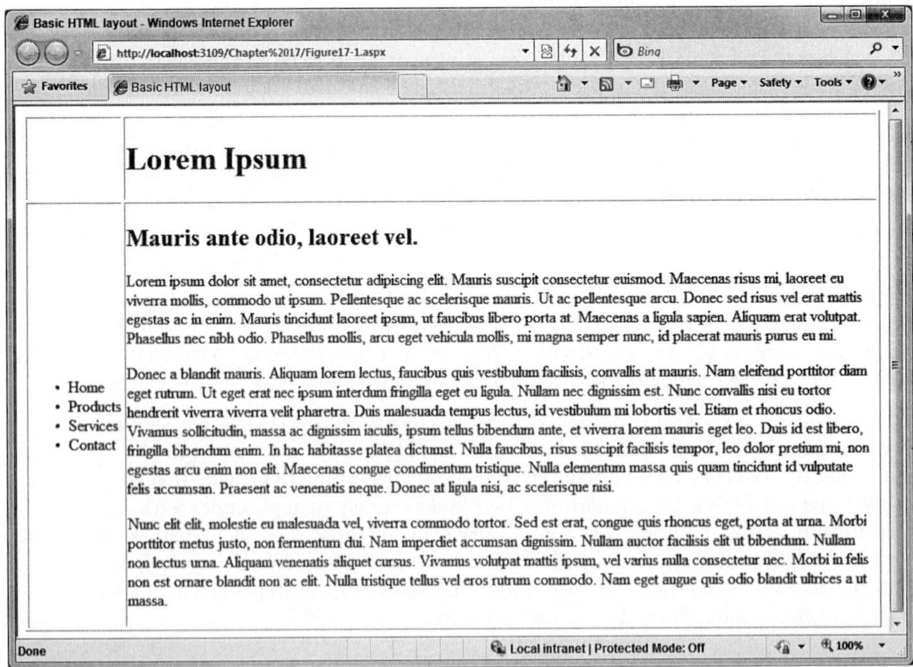

FIGURE 17-1

Although this layout is interesting, it lacks all but the most basic styling. To solve this problem, many developers would be tempted to add HTML-based formatting tags. For example, if I wanted to change the font and color of the text in the first paragraph, I might change its HTML to something like this:

```
<font face="Arial" Color="Maroon">
```

In fact, in the early days of Web design tools, this code is what most of them generated when the user added styling to their Web pages, and for a while, using `font` tags looked like a great solution to the problem of styling your Web pages.

Web developers and designers quickly learned, however, that using the `font` tag quickly leads to a mess of spaghetti HTML, with `font` tags being splattered throughout the HTML. Imagine that if, in the previous example, you not only wanted to set the control and color, but some of the work also needed to be bold, others needed to be a different color or font face, some a different font size, some underlined, and some displayed as superscript. Imagine how many font tags you would need then and how it would increase the weight of the Web page and decrease its maintainability. Using `font` tags (and other style-related tags) meant that a clear and clean separation no longer existed between the structure and content of the Web page, but instead both were mashed together into a single complex document.

The introduction of CSS to the Web development and design world brought it back to a clean and elegant solution for styling Web pages. CSS meant a style could be defined in a single location for the entire Web site, and simply referenced on the elements requiring the style. Using CSS brought back the logic separation between Web page content and the styles used to display it.

Creating Style Sheets

Like HTML, CSS is an interpreted language. When a Web page request is processed by a Web server, the server's response can include style sheets, which are simply collections of CSS instructions. The style sheets can be included in the server's response in three different ways: through external style sheet files, through internal style sheets embedded directly in the Web page, or through inline style sheets.

External Sheets

External style sheets are collections of CSS styles stored outside of the Web pages that will use them — generally files using the .css extension. Visual Studio makes adding external style sheet files to your application simple by including a Style Sheet file template in the Add New Item dialog box, as shown in Figure 17-2.

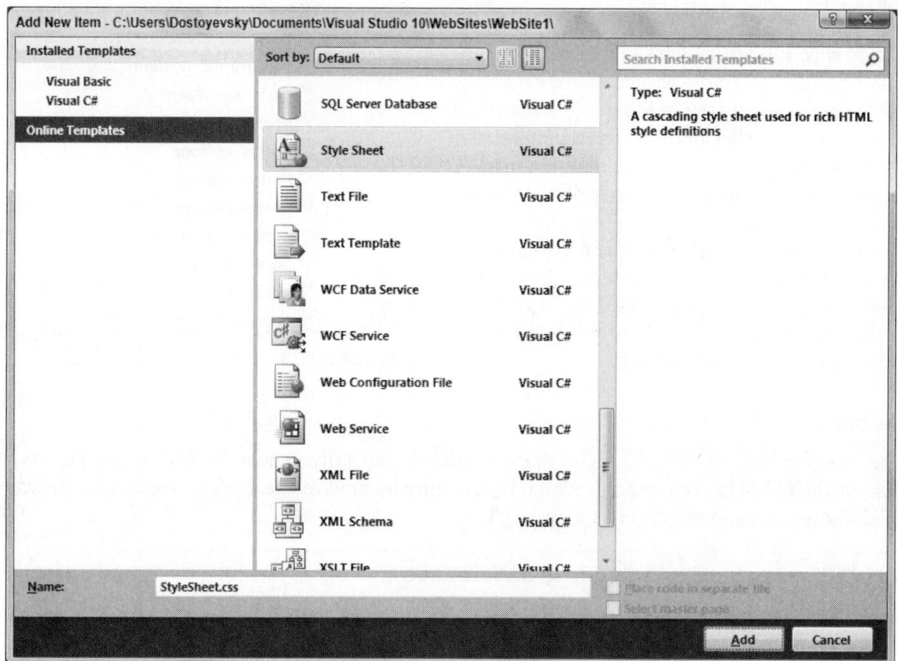

FIGURE 17-2

After the Style Sheet is created by Visual Studio, inserting new styles is easy. Visual Studio even gives you CSS IntelliSense when working with styles in the document, as shown in Figure 17-3.

You link external style sheets into Web pages by using the HTML <link> tag. A single Web page can contain multiple style sheet references, as shown in Listing 17-1.

LISTING 17-1: Using external style sheets in a Web page

Available for download on Wrox.com

```
<!DOCTYPE html PUBLIC "-//W3C//DTD XHTML 1.0 Transitional//EN"
"http://www.w3.org/TR/xhtml1/DTD/xhtml1-transitional.dtd">

<html xmlns="http://www.w3.org/1999/xhtml">
<head runat="server">
    <title>External CSS Sample</title>
    <link href="SampleStyles.css" rel="stylesheet" type="text/css" />
</head>
<body>
    <form id="form1" runat="server">
       <div>Lorum Ipsum</div>
    </form>
</body>
</html>
```

You can add multiple link tags to a single Web page to link several different style sheets into the page. You can also use the CSS import statement directly in your style sheet to actually link multiple style sheets together:

```
@import url("layout.css");
```

Using the import statement has the advantage that you can alter the style sheets linked together without having to modify every Web page in your site. Instead, you can simply link each page to a master external style sheet, which in turn will use the import statement to link in other external style sheets. Note that older browsers may not understand this syntax and will simply ignore the command.

Using external style sheets in your Web site offers several advantages. First, because external style sheets are kept outside of the Web pages in your site, adding a link tag to all of your Web pages is easier rather than trying to manage the styles directly in each page. This also makes maintenance easier because if you decide to update the style of your Web site in the future, you have a single location in which styles are kept. Finally, using external style sheets can also help the performance of your Web site by allowing the browser to take advantage of its caching capabilities. Like other files downloaded by the browser, the style sheets will be cached on the client after they have been downloaded.

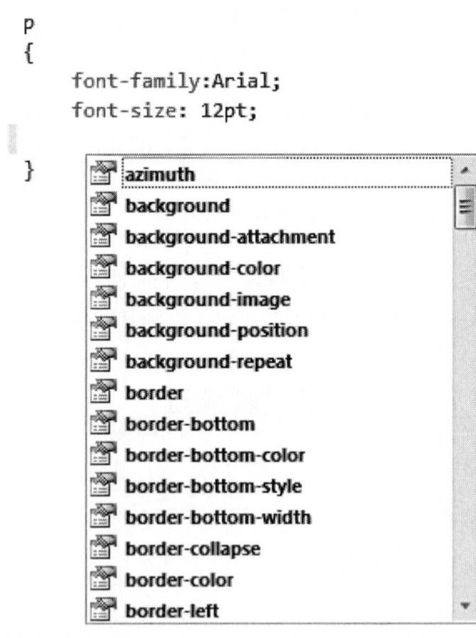

FIGURE 17-3

Internal Style Sheets

Internal style sheets are collections of CSS styles that are stored internally in a single Web page. The styles are located inside of the HTML <style> tag, which is generally located in the <head> section of the Web page. Listing 17-2 shows an example of internal style sheets.

LISTING 17-2: Using internal style sheets in a Web page

Available for download on Wrox.com

```
<!DOCTYPE html PUBLIC "-//W3C//DTD XHTML 1.0 Transitional//EN"
"http://www.w3.org/TR/xhtml1/DTD/xhtml1-transitional.dtd">
```

```
<html xmlns="http://www.w3.org/1999/xhtml">
<head runat="server">
    <title> Internal CSS Sample</title>
    <style type="text/css">
        div
        {
             font-family:Arial;
        }
    </style>
</head>
<body>
    <form id="form1" runat="server">
       <div>Lorum Ipsum</div>
    </form>
</body>
</html>
```

It is important when you create internal style sheets that when you create style blocks, you make sure to include the `type` attribute with the style tag so the browser knows how to properly interpret the block. Additionally, as with external style sheets, Visual Studio also gives you IntelliSense support to make adding properties easy for you.

Inline Styles

Inline styles are CSS styles that are applied directly to an individual HTML element using the element's `Style` attribute, which is available on most HTML elements. Listing 17-3 shows an example of inline styles.

LISTING 17-3: Using inline styles in a Web page

Available for download on Wrox.com

```
<!DOCTYPE html PUBLIC "-//W3C//DTD XHTML 1.0 Transitional//EN"
"http://www.w3.org/TR/xhtml1/DTD/xhtml1-transitional.dtd">

<html xmlns="http://www.w3.org/1999/xhtml">
<head runat="server">
     <title>Inline CSS Sample</title>
</head>
<body>
    <form id="form1" runat="server">
       <div style="font-family:Arial;">Lorum Ipsum</div>
    </form>
</body>
</html>
```

CSS Rules

Regardless of how they are stored, after CSS styles are sent from the server to the client, the browser is responsible for parsing the styles and applying them to the appropriate HTML elements in the Web page. If a style is stored in either an external or internal style sheet, the styles will be defined as a CSS rule. Rules are what the browser uses to determine what styling to apply to which HTML elements.

Inline styles do not need to be defined as a rule because they are automatically applied to the element they are included with. Therefore, the browser does not need to select the elements to apply it to.

A rule is made up of two parts: the selector and its properties. Figure 17-4 shows an example of a CSS rule.


```
p
{
    font-family: Arial;
    font-size: 12pt;
    color: Maroon;
    padding: 5px;
    letter-spacing: 3pt;
    text-decoration: underline;
    font-weight: bold;
    line-height: 1px;
    text-align: center;
}
```

FIGURE 17-4

Selectors

The *selector* is the portion of the rule that dictates exactly how the Web browser should select the elements to apply the style to. CSS includes a variety of types of selectors, each of which defines a different element selection technique.

Universal Selectors

The Universal selector indicates that the style should apply to any element in the Web page. The sample that follows shows a Universal selector, which would change the font of any element that supports the `font-family` property to Arial.

```
*
{
    font-family:Arial;
}
```

Type Selectors

The Type selector allows you to create a style that applies to a specific type of HTML element. The style will then be applied to all elements of that type in the Web page. The following sample shows a Type selector configured for the HTML paragraph tag, which will change the font family of all `<p>` tags in the Web page to Arial.

```
p
{
    font-family:Arial;
}
```

Descendant Selectors

Descendant selectors allow you to create styles that target HTML elements that are descendants of a specific type of element. The following sample demonstrates a style that will be applied to any `<span>` tag that is a descendant of a `<div>`.

```
div span
{
    font-family:Arial;
}
```

Child Selectors

The Child selector is similar to the Descendant selector except unlike the Descendant selector, which searches the entire descendant hierarchy of an element, the Child selector restricts its element search to only those elements that are direct children of the parent element. The following code shows a modification of the Descendant selector, making it a Child selector:

```
div > span
{
    font-family:Arial;
}
```

Attribute Selectors

Attribute selectors enable you to define a style that is applied to elements based on the existence of element attributes rather than the actual element name. For example, the following sample creates a style that is applied to any element in the Web page that has the `href` attribute set:

```
*[href]
{
    font-family:Arial;
}
```

Note that Attribute selectors are not supported by Internet Explorer 6.

Adjacent Selectors

Adjacent selectors enable you to select HTML elements that are immediately adjacent to another element type. For example, in an unordered list, you might want to highlight the first list item and then have all the following items use a different style. You can use an Adjacent selector to do this, as shown in the following sample:

```
li
{
    font-size:xx-large;
}

li+li
{
    font-size:medium;
}
```

In this sample, a default Type selector has been created for the list item element (`<li>`), which will change the font size of the text in the element to extra, extra large. However, a second Adjacent selector has been created, which will override the Type selector for all list items after the first, changing the font size back to normal.

Class Selectors

Class selectors are a special type of CSS selector that allows you to apply a style to any element with a specific class name. The class name is defined in HTML using the `class` attribute, which is present on almost every element. Class selectors are distinguished from other selector types by prefixing them with a single period (.).

```
.title
{
    font-size:larger;
    font-weight:bold;
}
```

This CSS rule would then be applied to any element whose class attribute value matched the rule name, an example of which is shown here:

```
<div class="title">Lorum Ipsum</div>
```

When creating Class selectors, note that the class name may not begin with a numeric character. Also, CSS class names can contain alphanumeric characters. Spaces, symbols, and even underscores are not allowed. Finally, make sure that you match the casing of your class name when using it in the HTML. Although CSS itself is not case sensitive, some HTML DocTypes dictate that the `class` and `id` attributes be treated as case sensitive.

ID Selectors

ID selectors are another special type of CSS selector that allows you to create styles that target elements with specific ID values. ID selectors are distinguished from other selector types by prefixing them with a hash mark (#).

```
#title
{
    font-size:larger;
    font-weight:bold;
}
```

This CSS rule would be applied to any element whose `id` attribute value matched the rule name, an example of which is shown here:

```
<div id="title">Lorum Ipsum</div>
```

Pseudo Classes

CSS also includes a series of pseudo class selectors that give you additional options in creating style rules. You can add pseudo classes to other selectors to allow you to create more complex rules.

First-Child Pseudo Class

The first-child pseudo class allows you to indicate that the rule should select the first child element *M* of an element *N*. The following is an example of using the first-child pseudo class:

```
#title p:first-child
{
    font-size:xx-small;
}
```

The previously defined rule states that the style should be applied to the first paragraph tag found within any element with an `id` attribute value of `title`. In the following HTML, that means that the text `First Child` would have the style applied to it:

```
<div id="title">Lorum <p>First Child</p><p>Second Child</p> Ipsum</div>Link Pseudo Classes
```

CSS includes a number of pseudo classes specifically related to anchor tags. These special pseudo classes allow you to define styles for the different states of an anchor tag:

```
a:link
{
    color:Maroon;
}
a:visited
{
    color:Silver;
}
```

In this sample, two rules have been created, the first of which applies a style to the unvisited links in a page, whereas the second applies a different style to the visited links.

Dynamic Pseudo Classes

The dynamic pseudo classes are special CSS classes that are applied by the browser based on actions performed by the end user such as hovering over an element, activating an element, or giving an element focus.

```
a:hover
{
    color:Maroon;
}
a:active
{
    color:Silver;
}
a:focus
{
    color:Olive;
}
```

Although the sample demonstrates the use of the dynamic pseudo classes with the anchor tag, you can use them with any HTML element. Note, however, that support for the dynamic pseudo classes in different browsers varies.

Language Pseudo Class

The language pseudo class allows you to define specific rules based on the end user's language settings.

```
:lang(de)
{
    quotes: '<<' '>>' '\2039' '\203A'
}
```

In this sample, the `lang` pseudo class is used to set the quotes for a Web page that is German. IE 7 does not support the `lang` pseudo class.

Pseudo Elements

CSS also includes several pseudo elements that allow you to make selections of items in the Web page that are not true elements.

The pseudo elements available are first-line, first-letter, before, and after. The following samples demonstrate the use of these elements:

```
p:first-line
{
    font-style:italic;
}
p:first-letter
{
    font-size:xx-large;
}
```

The pseudo first-line and first-letter elements allow you to apply special styling to the first line and first letter of a content block.

```
p:before
{
    content: url(images/quote.gif);
}
p:after
{
    content: '<<end>>';
}
```

The pseudo `before` and `after` elements allow you to insert content before or after the targeted element, in this case a paragraph element. The content you insert can be a URL, string, quote character, counter, or the value of an attribute of the element.

Selector Grouping

When creating CSS rules, CSS allows you group several selectors together into a single rule. The following sample demonstrates a single rule that combines three Type selectors:

```
h1, h2, h3
{
    color:Maroon;
}
```

This rule then results in the forecolor of the text content of any h1, h2, or h3 tag being maroon.

Selector Combinations

CSS also allows you to combine multiple selector types (Listing 17-4). For example, you can create Class selectors that target specific HTML elements in addition to matching the `class` attribute value.

LISTING 17-4: Combining multiple selector types in a single CSS rule

Available for download on Wrox.com

```
<!DOCTYPE html PUBLIC "-//W3C//DTD XHTML 1.0 Transitional//EN"
"http://www.w3.org/TR/xhtml1/DTD/xhtml1-transitional.dtd">

<html xmlns="http://www.w3.org/1999/xhtml">
<head id="Head1" runat="server">
    <title>Combining Selector Types</title>
    <style type="text/css">
        .title
        {
            font-family:Courier New;
        }

        div.title
        {
            font-family:Arial;
        }
    </style>
</head>
<body>
    <form id="form1" runat="server">
        <p class="title">Lorum Ipsum</p>
        <div class="title">Lorum Ipsum</div>
    </form>
</body>
</html>
```

Merged Styles

CSS also merges styles when several style rules are defined that apply to a given HTML element. For example, in the sample code that follows in Listing 17-5, a Class selector and a Type selector are defined. Both of these selectors apply to the paragraph element in the HTML. When the browser interprets the styles, it merges both onto the element.

LISTING 17-5: Merging styles from multiple rules onto a single element

Available for download on Wrox.com

```
<html xmlns="http://www.w3.org/1999/xhtml">
<head id="Head1" runat="server">
    <title>Merging Styles</title>
    <style type="text/css">
        .title
        {
            text-decoration:underline;
        }

        p
        {
            font-family:Courier New;
        }
    </style>
</head>
<body>
    <form id="form1" runat="server">
        <p class="title">Lorum Ipsum</p>
    </form>
</body>
</html>
```

As you can see in Figure 17-5, both the font and the text decoration of the single paragraph element have been styled, even though two separate style rules defined the style.

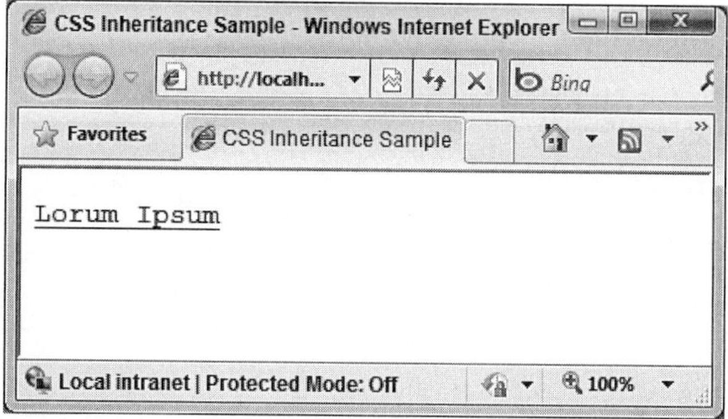

FIGURE 17-5

You can also merge multiple styles by defining multiple rules using different selector types. If a single HTML element matches all the rules, the styles from each rule will be merged together. Listing 17-6 shows an example where a single element matches multiple rules.

Available for download on Wrox.com

LISTING 17-6: Multiple selector matches on a single element

```
<!DOCTYPE html PUBLIC "-//W3C//DTD XHTML 1.0 Transitional//EN"
"http://www.w3.org/TR/xhtml1/DTD/xhtml1-transitional.dtd">

<html xmlns="http://www.w3.org/1999/xhtml">
<head runat="server">
    <title>Multiple Selector matches</title>
    <style type="text/css">
        p
        {
            font-family:Arial;
            color:Blue;
        }

        p#book
        {
            font-size:xx-large;
        }

        p.title
        {
            font-family: Courier New;
        }
    </style>
</head><body>
    <form id="form1" runat="server">
      <p id="book" class="title"
          style="letter-spacing:5pt;">Lorum Ipsum</p>
    </form>
</body>
</html>
```

In this case, because the paragraph tag defines the `id`, `class`, and `style` attributes, each of the Style rules match; therefore, each of their styles get merged onto the element.

Finally, you can use the class attribute itself to merge multiple styles onto the same element, as shown in Listing 17-7. The class attribute allows you to specify multiple class names in a space-delimited string.

LISTING 17-7: Assigning multiple Class selectors to a single element

Available for download on Wrox.com

```
<!DOCTYPE html PUBLIC "-//W3C//DTD XHTML 1.0 Transitional//EN"
"http://www.w3.org/TR/xhtml1/DTD/xhtml1-transitional.dtd">

<html xmlns="http://www.w3.org/1999/xhtml">
<head runat="server">
    <title>Multiple Class Selectors</title>
    <style type="text/css">
        p.title
        {
            font-family: Courier New;
            letter-spacing:5pt;
        }

        p.summer
        {
            color:Blue;
        }

        p.newproduct
        {
            font-weight:bold;
            color:Red;
        }
    </style>
</head>
<body>
    <form id="form1" runat="server">
       <p class="title newproduct summer">Lorum Ipsum</p>
    </form>
</body>
</html>
```

In this case, the three classes — `title`, `summer`, and `newproduct` — have all been defined in the `class` attribute. This means that these three styles will be merged onto the paragraph element.

Note that, in this case, the order in which the CSS classes are defined in the internal style sheet also influences how the styles are merged onto the paragraph tag. Even though the summer class is last in the list of classes defined in the `class` attribute, the `newproduct` rule overrides the `summer` rule's color property because the `newproduct` rule is defined after the `summer` rule in the internal style sheet.

CSS Inheritance

CSS includes the concept of style inheritance, and it works because the browser views the different locations that a style can be defined in (external, internal, or inline) as a hierarchical structure. Figure 17-6 shows this inheritance by demonstrating how the `font-family` property of a paragraph Type selector rule, defined in three different locations, could be overridden by other style rules.

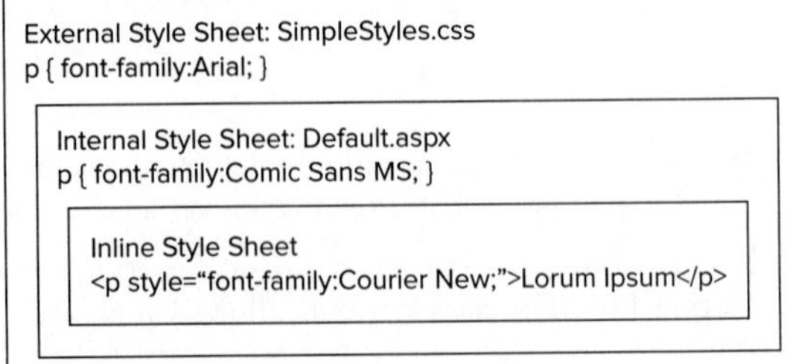

External Style Sheet: SimpleStyles.css
p { font-family:Arial; }
Internal Style Sheet: Default.aspx
p { font-family:Comic Sans MS; }
Inline Style Sheet
<p style="font-family:Courier New;">Lorum Ipsum</p>

FIGURE 17-6

As you can see from the figure, the general rule is that the closer the style definition is to the element it applies to, the more precedence it will take. In this case, the paragraph text would ultimately be displayed using the Courier New font family because that is defined in the inline style.

Inheritance not only applies to styles kept in separate file locations, but also to styles within the same location, which means that sometimes you also must think about the order in which you define your styles. For example, Listing 17-8 shows a style sheet that contains two Type selectors, both targeting the paragraph element, both setting the `font-family` style property. Obviously, both of these cannot be applied to the same element, so CSS simply chooses the selector that is closest to the paragraph tags.

Available for download on Wrox.com

LISTING 17-8: Using style overriding within the same internal style sheet

```
<!DOCTYPE html PUBLIC "-//W3C//DTD XHTML 1.0 Transitional//EN"
"http://www.w3.org/TR/xhtml1/DTD/xhtml1-transitional.dtd">

<html xmlns="http://www.w3.org/1999/xhtml">
<head runat="server">
    <title>Styling Overriding</title>
    <style type="text/css">
        p
        {
            font-family:Arial
        }

        p
        {
            font-family: Courier New;
        }
    </style>
</head>
<body>
    <form id="form1" runat="server">
       <p>Lorum Ipsum</p>
    </form>
</body>
</html>
```

Running this sample, you will see that the font applied is the Courier New font.

Note that you should be careful when combining styles from external style sheets and internal style sheets. Remember that the browser will ultimately choose the style that is defined closest to the specific elements. This means that as the browser begins to parse the Web page, internal styles defined before external styles are considered further away from the HTML elements. Thus, the browser will use the styles located in the external style sheet. If you plan on storing style rules in both internal and external style sheets, remember to include the external style sheets `<link>` tags before the internal style sheets `<style>` block in your Web page.

Element Layout and Positioning

CSS is useful not only for styling elements in a page, but also for positioning elements. CSS actually gives you a much more flexible system for positioning elements than HTML itself. CSS bases the positioning of elements in a Web page on the *box model*. After an element's box behavior has been determined, you can position it using several different techniques.

The CSS Box Model

A core element of positioning in CSS is the box model. The box model defines how every element in HTML is treated by the browser as a rectangular box. The box is comprised of different parts, including margins, padding, borders, and content. Figure 17-7 shows how all of these elements are combined to form the box.

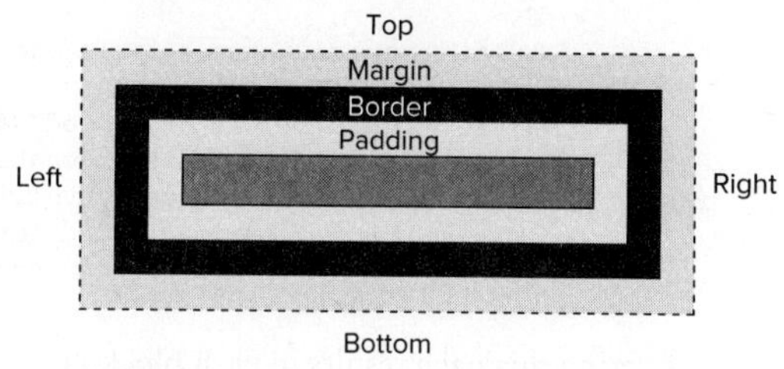

FIGURE 17-7

All the separate elements that make up the box can influence its position within the Web page, and unless otherwise specified, each is given a default value of zero. The height and width of the element is equal to the height and width of the outer edge of the margin, which, as you can see in the previous image, is not necessarily the height and width of the content.

HTML provides you with two different types of boxes: the block box and the inline box. Block boxes are typically represented by tags such as `<p>`, `<div>`, or `<table>`. For block boxes, the containing block is used to determine the position of its child blocks. Additionally, block boxes can contain only inline or block boxes, but not both.

Listing 17-9 shows an example of a page containing a single parent block and two child block elements.

LISTING 17-9: Creating block box elements

Available for download on Wrox.com

```
<div>
    Lorem ipsum dolor sit amet, consectetuer adipiscing elit.
    <div>
        Donec et velit a risus convallis porttitor.
        Vestibulum nisi metus, imperdiet sed, mollis
        condimentum, nonummy eu, magna.
    </div>
    <div>
         Duis lobortis felis in est. Nulla eu velit ut nisi
         consequat vulputate.
    </div>
    Vestibulum vel metus. Integer ut quam. Ut dignissim, sapien
    sit amet malesuada aliquam, quam quam vulputate nibh, ut
    pulvinar velit lorem at eros. Sed semper lacinia diam. In
    faucibus nonummy arcu. Duis venenatis interdum quam. Aliquam
    ut dolor id leo scelerisque convallis. Suspendisse non velit.
    Quisque nec metus. Lorum ipsum dolor sit amet, consectetuer
    adipiscing elit. Praesent pellentesque interdum magna.
</div>
```

The second box type is the inline box. Inline boxes are typically represented by tags such as `B`, `I`, and `SPAN` as well as actual text and content. Listing 17-10 shows how you can modify the previous listing to include inline boxes.

LISTING 17-10: Creating inline box elements

Available for download on Wrox.com

```
<div>
    Lorem <b>ipsum</b> dolor sit amet, consectetuer adipiscing elit.
    <div>
        Donec et velit a risus <b>convallis</b> porttitor.
        Vestibulum nisi mets, imperdiet sed, mollis
        condimentum, nonummy eu, magna.
    </div>
    <div>Duis lobortis felis in est.
        <span>Nulla eu velit ut nisi consequat vulputate.</span>
    </div>
    <i>Vestibulum vel metus.</i> Integer ut quam. Ut dignissim, sapien
    sit amet malesuada aliquam, quam quam vulputate nibh, ut
    pulvinar velit lorem at eros. Sed semper lacinia diam. In
    faucibus nonummy arcu. Duis venenatis interdum quam. Aliquam
    ut dolor id leo scelerisque convallis. Suspendisse non velit.
    Quisque nec metus. Lorem ipsum dolor sit amet, consectetuer
    adipiscing elit. Praesent pellentesque interdum magna
</div>
```

Rendering this page results in each block beginning a new line. Figure 17-8 shows the markup rendered in the browser.

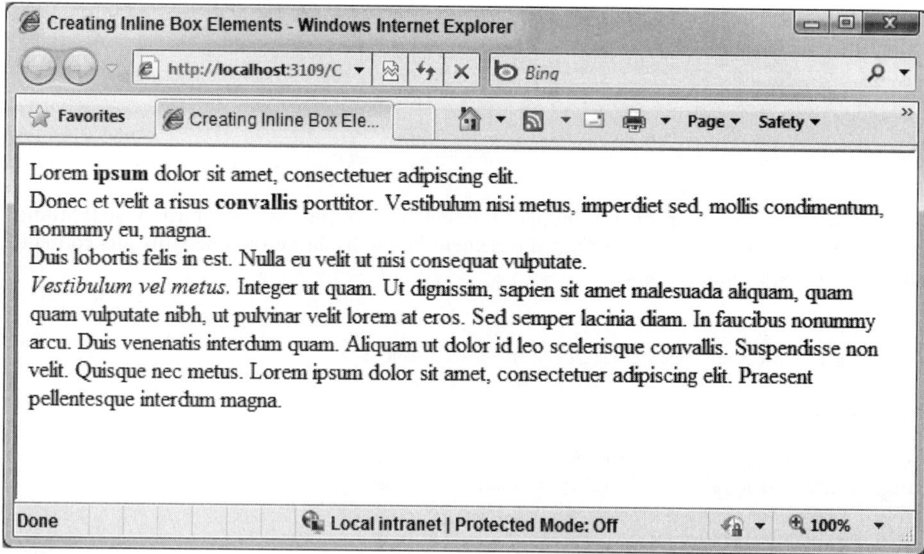

FIGURE 17-8

The Visual Studio design surface can help you get a clear picture of the layout of a `div` as well. When you select an individual `div` element, the design surface highlights the selected element, as shown in Figure 17-9.

div Lorem **ipsum** dolor sit amet, consectetuer adipiscing elit.
Donec et velit a risus **convallis** porttitor. Vestibulum nisi metus, imperdiet sed, mollis condimentum, nonummy eu, magna.
Duis lobortis felis in est. Nulla eu velit ut nisi consequat vulputate.
Vestibulum vel metus. Integer ut quam. Ut dignissim, sapien sit amet malesuada aliquam, quam quam vulputate nibh, ut pulvinar velit lorem at eros. Sed semper lacinia diam. In faucibus nonummy arcu. Duis venenatis interdum quam. Aliquam ut dolor id leo scelerisque convallis. Suspendisse non velit. Quisque nec metus. Lorem ipsum dolor sit amet, consectetuer adipiscing elit. Praesent pellentesque interdum magna.

FIGURE 17-9

At the beginning of this section, I stated that a block will always contain either inline or block boxes, but it's interesting to note that in this case, because the first line of text contains an inline box, and the next contains a block box, it looks like the parent `div` is violating that rule. However, what is actually happening is that the browser automatically adds an anonymous block box around the first line of text when the page is rendered. Figure 17-10 highlights the block boxes as the browser sees them.

```
<div>
    Lorem <b>ipsum</b> dolor sit amet, consectetuer adipiscing elit.
    <div>Donec et velit a risus <b>convallis</b> porttitor.
    Vestibulum nisi metus, imperdiet sed, mollis condimentum,
    nonummy eu, magna.</div>
    <div>Duis lobortis felis in est. <span>Nulla eu velit ut nisi
    consequat vulputate.</span>
    </div>
    <i>Vestibulum vel metus.</i> Integer ut quam. Ut dignissim,
    sapien sit amet malesuada aliquam, quam quam vulputate nibh,
    ut pulvinar velit lorem at eros. Sed semper lacinia diam. In
    faucibus nonummy arcu. Duis venenatis interdum quam. Aliquam ut
    dolor id leo scelerisque convallis. Suspendisse non velit.
    Quisque nec metus. Lorem ipsum dolor sit amet, consectetuer
    adipiscing elit. Praesent pellentesque interdum magna.
</div>
```

FIGURE 17-10

You can explicitly set which box behavior an element will exhibit by using the `position` attribute. For example, setting the `position` property on the second `div`, as shown here, results in the layout of the content changing.

```
<div style="display:inline;">
    Donec et velit a risus <b>convallis</b> porttitor.  Vestibulum nisi
    metus,imperdiet sed, mollis condimentum, nonummy eu, magna.
</div>
```

Figure 17-11 shows how adding this property changes the rendering of the markup on the Visual Studio design surface. You can see that now, rather than the element being displayed on a new line, its content is simply continued from the previous block.

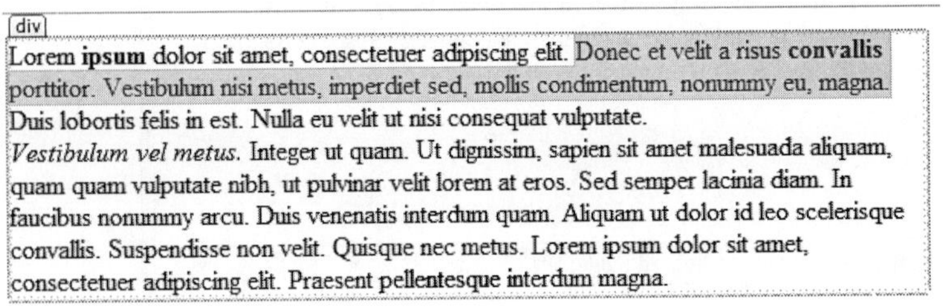

div

Lorem **ipsum** dolor sit amet, consectetuer adipiscing elit. Donec et velit a risus **convallis** porttitor. Vestibulum nisi metus, imperdiet sed, mollis condimentum, nonummy eu, magna. Duis lobortis felis in est. Nulla eu velit ut nisi consequat vulputate.
Vestibulum vel metus. Integer ut quam. Ut dignissim, sapien sit amet malesuada aliquam, quam quam vulputate nibh, ut pulvinar velit lorem at eros. Sed semper lacinia diam. In faucibus nonummy arcu. Duis venenatis interdum quam. Aliquam ut dolor id leo scelerisque convallis. Suspendisse non velit. Quisque nec metus. Lorem ipsum dolor sit amet, consectetuer adipiscing elit. Praesent pellentesque interdum magna.

FIGURE 17-11

You can also set the `display` property to `none` to completely remove the element from the Web page layout. If you have elements whose `display` property is set to `none`, or an element whose `visibility` property is set to `hidden`, Visual Studio gives you the option of showing or hiding these elements on its design surface.

As shown in Figure 17-12, two options on the View menu allow you to toggle the design surface visibility of elements with these properties set.

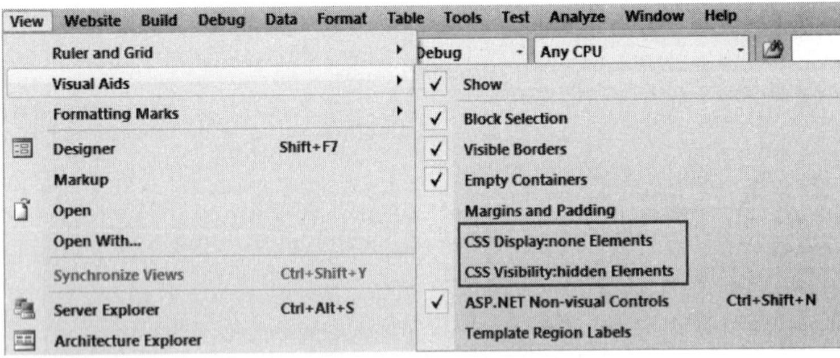

FIGURE 17-12

Positioning CSS Elements

CSS provides you with three primary positioning mechanisms: normal, absolute, and relative. Each type offers a different behavior you can use to lay out the elements in your page. To specify the type of layout behavior you want an element to use, you can set the CSS `position` property. Each element can have its own `position` property set, allowing you to use multiple positioning schemes within the same Web page.

Normal Positioning

Using normal positioning, block items flow vertically, and inline items flow horizontally, left to right. This behavior is the default, and is used when no other value is provided for the `position` property. Figure 17-13 demonstrates the layout of four separate blocks using normal positioning.

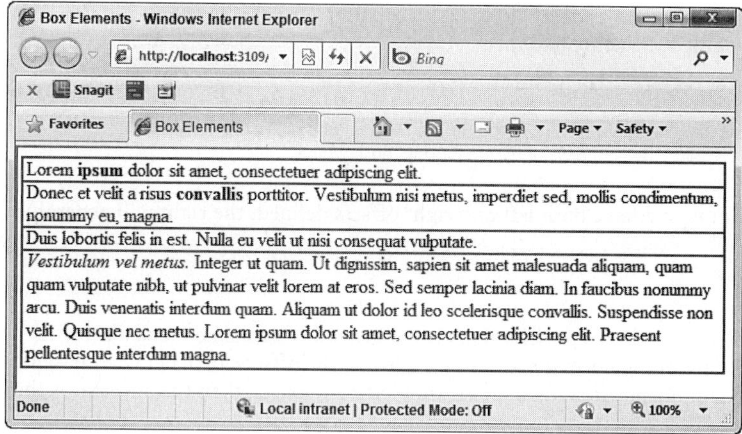

FIGURE 17-13

As you can see, each block item flows vertically as expected.

Relative Positioning

Using relative positioning, elements are initially positioned using normal layout. The surrounding boxes are positioned and then the box is moved based on its offset properties: `top`, `bottom`, `left`, and `right`. Figure 17-14 shows the same content as in the prior section, but now the third block box has been styled to use relative positioning. Visual Studio is helping you out by providing positioning lines for the block, showing you that its top offset is being calculated based on the normal top position of the block, and the left offset from the normal left position. Visual Studio even lets you visually position the block by grabbing the element's tag label and dragging it over the design surface.

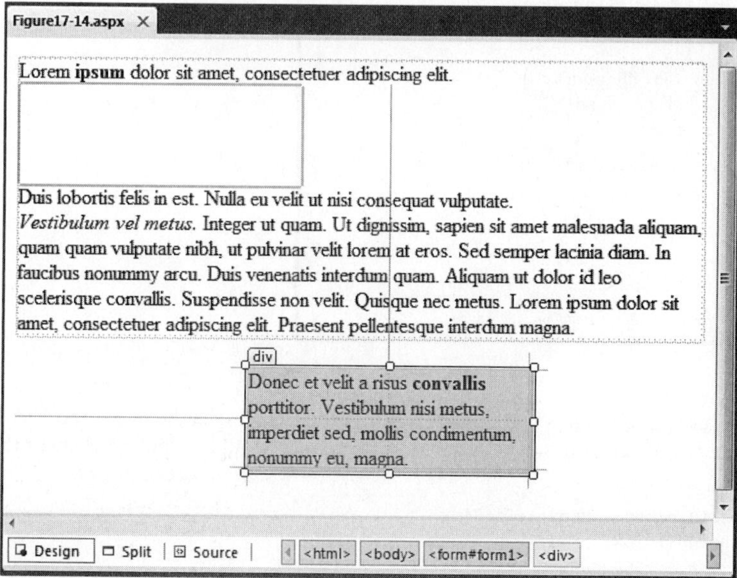

FIGURE 17-14

As you position the element on the design surface, the element's top and left values are being updated. You will end up with an element looking something like this:

```
<div style="position: relative;top: 214px;left: 62px;
          width: 239px;height: 81px">
    Donec et velit a risus <b>convallis</b> porttitor. Vestibulum nisi
    metus, imperdiet sed, mollis condimentum, nonummy eu, magna.
</div>
```

If you are using relative positioning and have both left and right offsets defined, the right will generally be ignored.

Absolute Positioning

Absolute positioning works much like relative positioning, except instead of an element calculating its offset position based on its position in the normal positioning scheme, the offsets are calculated based on the position of its closest absolutely positioned ancestor. If no element exists, then the ancestor is the browser window itself.

Figure 17-15 shows how blocks using absolute positioning are displayed on the Visual Studio design surface. As you can see, unlike the display of the relative positioned element shown in the previous section, this time the positioning lines extend all the way to the edge of the design surface. This is because the block is using the browser window to calculate its offset.

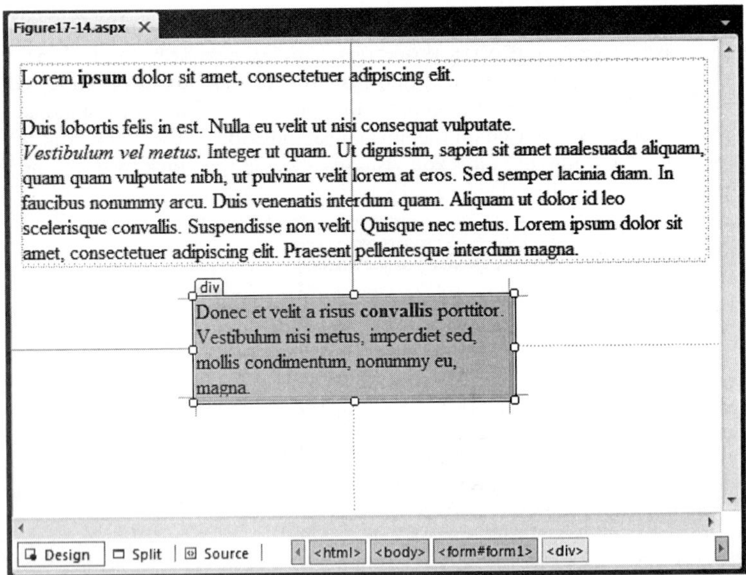

FIGURE 17-15

As with relative blocks, you can use the element's tag label to position the element on the page, and Visual Studio will automatically update the offset values. The block in Figure 17-15 would output an element that looks something like this:

```
<div style="position: absolute;top: 180px;left:94px;
          width:239px;height:81px;">
    Donec et velit a risus <b>convallis</b> porttitor. Vestibulum nisi
    metus, imperdiet sed, mollis condimentum, nonummy eu, magna.
</div>
```

Floating Elements

Another option for controlling the position of elements using CSS is the `float` property. The `float` property allows you to float an element to the left or right side of a block. The floating block is positioned vertically as it would normally be in normal position, but horizontally shifted as far left or right as possible. Listing 17-11 demonstrates floating the same block used in previous samples in this section.

Available for download on Wrox.com

LISTING 17-11: Floating a block element to the right

```
<!DOCTYPE html PUBLIC "-//W3C//DTD XHTML 1.0 Transitional//EN"
"http://www.w3.org/TR/xhtml1/DTD/xhtml1-transitional.dtd">

<html xmlns="http://www.w3.org/1999/xhtml">
<head id="Head1" runat="server">
</head><body>
    <form id="form1" runat="server">
    <div id="asdas" class="werwer">
        Lorem ipsum dolor sit amet, consectetuer adipiscing elit.
    </div>
    <div style="float:right;width: 236px;">
        Donec et velit a risus <b>convallis</b> porttitor.
        Vestibulum nisi metus, imperdiet sed, mollis
        condimentum, nonummy eu, magna.
    </div>
    <div>
         Duis lobortis felis in est. Nulla eu velit ut nisi
         consequat vulputate.
    </div>
    <div>
         Vestibulum vel metus. Integer ut quam. Ut dignissim, sapien
         sit amet malesuada aliquam, quam quam vulputate nibh, ut
         pulvinar velit lorem at eros. Sed semper lacinia diam. In
         faucibus nonummy arcu. Duis venenatis interdum quam. Aliquam
         ut dolor id leo scelerisque convallis. Suspendisse non velit.
         Quisque nec metus. Lorem ipsum dolor sit amet, consectetuer
         adipiscing elit. Praesent pellentesque interdum magna.
    </div>
    </form>
</body>
</html>
```

The block has been modified to include the `float` property in its style. When this is done, Visual Studio correctly positions the element to the far right side of the page, as shown in Figure 17-16.

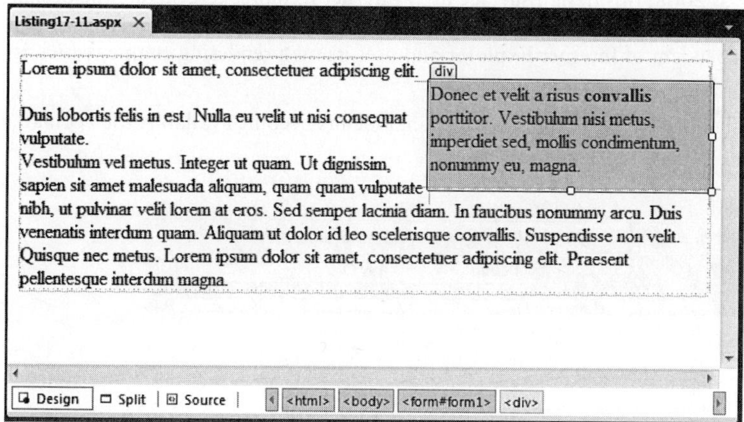

FIGURE 17-16

The !important Attribute

As you saw earlier in this chapter, the browser will choose to apply the closest style to the element, which can mean that properties of other applied styles might be overridden. As with many other rules in CSS this, too, is not absolute. CSS provides a mechanism to circumvent this rule called the `!important` attribute. Properties that have this attribute applied can prevent other CSS rules from overriding its value. Listing 17-8 showed how the `font-family` property can be overridden. You can see how the `!important` attribute works by modifying this sample to use the attribute. This is shown in Listing 17-12.

Available for download on Wrox.com

LISTING 17-12: Using the !important attribute to control style overriding

```
<html xmlns="http://www.w3.org/1999/xhtml">
<head id="Head1" runat="server">

    <style type="text/css">
        p
        {
            font-family:Arial !important;
        }

        p
        {
            font-family: Courier New;
        }
    </style>
</head>
<body>
    <form id="form1" runat="server">
       <p>Lorum Ipsum</p>
    </form>
</body>
</html>
```

In this case, rather than the paragraph being shown in Courier New, it will use the Arial font because it has been marked with the `!important` attribute.

WORKING WITH HTML AND CSS IN VISUAL STUDIO

Working with HTML and CSS to create compelling Web site designs can be quite daunting. Thankfully, Visual Studio provides you with a variety of tools that help simplify page layout and CSS management.

As you are probably already familiar with, Visual Studio includes a great WYSIWYG design surface. In versions of Visual Studio prior to 2008, this design surface used Internet Explorer to generate the design view, but starting in Visual Studio 2008 and continuing in Visual Studio 2010, the design surface is written to be completely independent of Internet Explorer and uses its own rendering engine, which is CSS 2.1– compliant.

In Visual Studio, when the Design View has focus, two additional menus become available: the Format menu and the Table menu, as shown in Figure 17-17.

FIGURE 17-17

The Table menu, as you might guess, includes a set of tools that allow you to Insert, Delete, Select, and Modify the HTML tables in your Web page. Selecting the Insert Table option from the Table menu opens the Insert Table dialog box shown in Figure 17-18, which allows you to easily specify properties of your table. You can define the number of table rows and columns, the cell padding and spacing, and border attributes, and when you click OK, Visual Studio automatically generates the appropriate table HTML in your Web page.

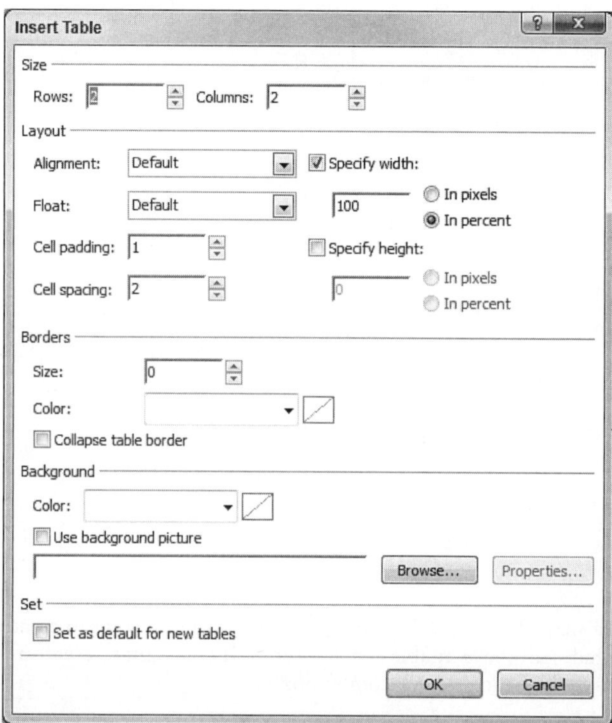

FIGURE 17-18

When you select an existing table in your Web page, the Table menu lets you insert and delete table rows, columns, and cells. The Modify menu option also allows you to split an existing cell into two separate cells, merge two cells into a single cell, and configure row and column sizing.

The Format menu includes basic element formatting options such as accessing the elements CSS class; setting fore- and background colors, font, and position; and converting content to different types of lists.

Working with CSS in Visual Studio

Visual Studio offers a variety of tools specifically designed to make working with CSS a great experience. To create a new style for your Web page, simply select the New Style option from the Format menu. The New Style dialog box opens, as shown in Figure 17-19.

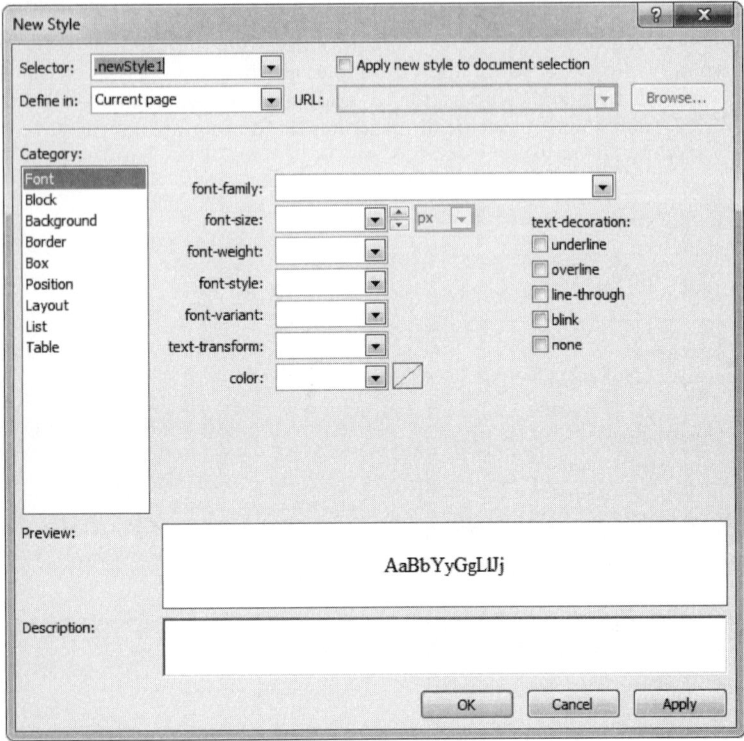

FIGURE 17-19

This dialog box makes creating a new style a snap. To start, select the type of selector you want to create from the Selector drop-down list, which includes all the available element types. If you want to create a Class or ID selector, simply type the Style name into the Selector combo box.

Next, you select where you want to create the style from the Define In combo box. You can select Current Page to create an internal style sheet, New Style Sheet to create a new external style sheet file, or Existing Style Sheet to insert the style into an existing style sheet file. If you select either New Style Sheet or Existing Style Sheet, you must provide a value for the URL combo box.

Finally, to have this style apply to the element (or elements) currently selected in the design surface, select the "Apply new style to document" check box.

After you have entered the selector you want to use and chosen a location to define the style, you can set the style's properties. Simply select the property category from the Category list box and set the property values. The Preview area gives you a real-time preview of your new style. Additionally, the Description area shows you the actual property syntax created by Visual Studio. Click OK to close the dialog box.

After you begin to create styles for your application, you need to be able to manage and apply those styles to elements in your application. Visual Studio includes three tool windows you can use to manage style sheets, apply styles to elements, and easily inspect the style properties applied to an element.

Manage Styles Tool Window

The first tool to explore is the Manage Styles tool window, which you can open by selecting Manage Styles from the CSS Styles submenu of the View menu. This tool window, shown in Figure 17-20, gives you the bird's-eye view of all the styles available to the current Web page open in Visual Studio.

If you examine the contents of this tool, you see that the top portion includes two important links: New Style, which opens the New Style dialog box and allows you to create new CSS styles as described earlier in this section; and the Attach Style Sheet link, which allows you to import new style sheets into a Web page. Using this option to attach style sheets to the Web page causes Visual Studio to insert `<link>` tags into your Web page for you.

Remember that you must be careful about the order of your link tags and style blocks to make sure that your styles are applied correctly.

The next portion of the tool window displays all the styles available to the page. Styles are color coded according to their selector type using colored bullets: blue for Type selectors, green for Class selectors, and red for ID selectors. Styles used within the page are shown with a gray circle surrounding the colored bullet. Should your Web page contain multiple linked style sheets, or inline style sheets, these styles would be grouped together making it easy to determine where a style is defined.

Also, as you can see in Figure 17-20, the tool window lets you view style sheets attached to the Web page via the CSS Imports statement. By expanding the `layout.css` node shown in the figure, you can see a listing of all the styles included in that style sheet.

Finally, the bottom of the tool window includes a preview area, allowing you to see a real-time preview of each style.

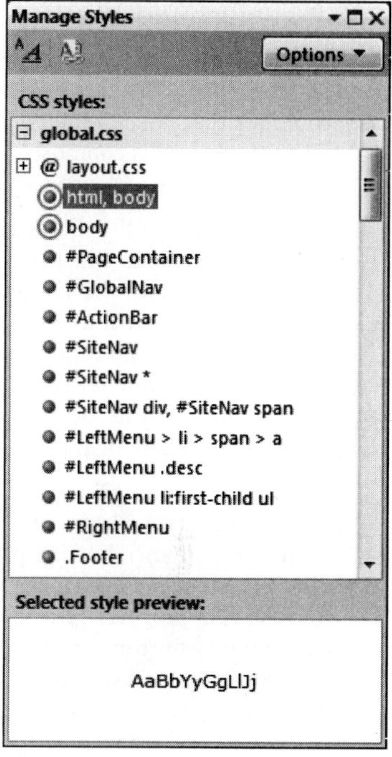

FIGURE 17-20

Apply Styles Tool Window

The second tool to help you use CSS in Visual Studio is the Apply Styles tool window. As with the Manage Styles tool window, the Apply Styles tool window gives you an easy way to view the CSS Styles available in your application and apply them to elements in a Web page. From the tool window, you can attach CSS files to the Web page, making external CSS Styles available; select page styles to apply or remove from an element; and modify styles. As with the other CSS tool windows, the Apply Styles tool window displays the available styles based on the CSS inheritance order, with external styles being shown first, then the page styles section, and finally the inline styles shown last. The Apply Styles window also is contextually sensitive to the currently selected element and will show only those styles in your application that can be applied to the element type. Styles are also grouped according to the CSS selector style, with a different visual indicator for each selector type.

The tool window shown in Figure 17-21 shows the styles available for an anchor tag `<a>`. The tool first shows all styles in the attached `global.css` file, then the styles in the current page, and finally, if applied, the element's inline styles. You can click on styles in any of these sections to apply them to the element.

The Apply Styles tool also includes the intelligence to properly apply multiple Class selectors (hold down the Ctrl key while you click Class selectors in the list), but prevent you from selecting multiple ID selectors because that would result in invalid CSS. The tool will also not let you deselect Type selectors or inline styles.

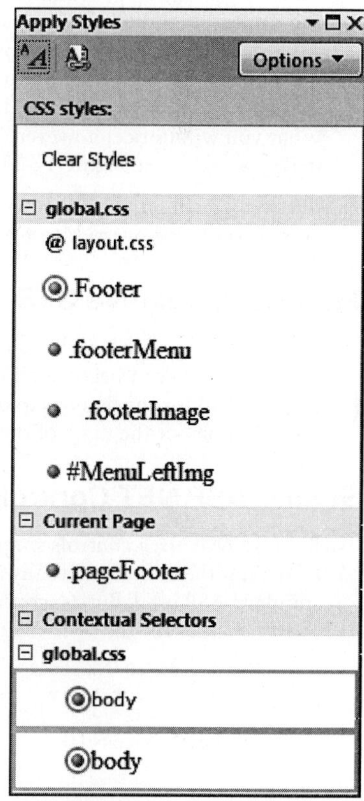

FIGURE 17-21

CSS Properties Tool Window

The final tool is the CSS Properties tool window shown in Figure 17-22. This handy tool window shows you all the CSS properties that have been applied to the currently selected element. The tool window is composed of two separate parts: the Applied Rules list and the CSS properties grid.

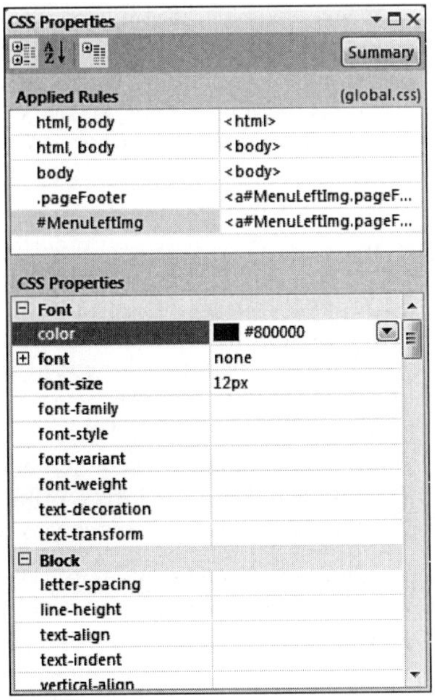

The Applied Rules list shows all the CSS rules that are applied to the selected element. The list is automatically sorted to show you the inheritance chain of the applied rules with the outermost rules at the top, moving down to the innermost rules. That means that rules contained in external CSS files are automatically sorted to the top of the list, and inline styles are sorted to the bottom. You can click on each rule in the list and alter the properties that are shown in the CSS Properties grid displayed below.

The CSS Properties grid works in a similar fashion to the standard .NET properties grid, showing you all the CSS properties available for the element and showing properties that have values set in bold. Additionally, you can set property values for a CSS rule directly from the CSS property grid. Also in the CSS Properties tool window is a Summary button that allows you to change the display of the CSS Properties grid to show only properties that have values set. This feature can be very useful because HTML elements can have a large number of CSS properties.

FIGURE 17-22

Because CSS also includes the concept of property inheritance, which is generally not available in a standard .NET object, the CSS Rules list and CSS Properties grid have been designed to help you fully understand where a specific property value applied to an element is being defined. As you click on each rule in the CSS Rules list, the CSS Properties grid updates to reflect that rule's properties. What you will notice, however, is that certain properties have a red strikethrough. (See Figure 17-23.)

The strikethrough of a property indicates that the value of that property is being overridden by a rule closer to the element.

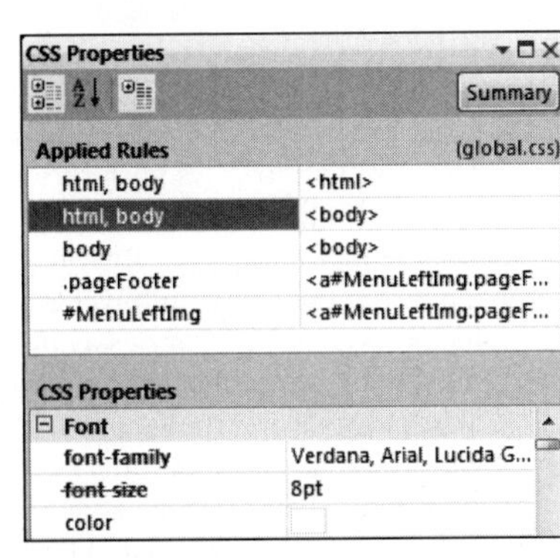

FIGURE 17-23

Managing Relative CSS Links in Master Pages

When working with CSS links in a master page, managing the link to the CSS can become difficult because the `Link` tag will not resolve a relative URL properly. A workaround for this issue is to define the tag as normal, but give it an ID. Then at runtime, in the Page Load event, simply set the `Href` of the link tag to the proper relative URL.

Styling ASP.NET Controls

Because ASP.NET controls simply render HTML markup, using CSS to style them is fairly easy. In fact, by default the controls actually already use inline CSS styles. You can see this in action by looking at the standard ASP.NET Button control. The standard method for styling ASP.NET controls like the Button is to provide values for the style-related properties exposed by the control, which is shown here:

```
<asp:Button ID="Button1" runat="server" BackColor="#3333FF"
    BorderColor="Silver" BorderStyle="Double" BorderWidth="3px"
    Font-Bold="True" Font-Size="Large" ForeColor="White"
    Text="Button" />
```

When ASP.NET processes the Web page containing this control, it converts a button into a standard HTML Input tag, and it also converts the style properties you have set into CSS styles and applies them to the `input` tag. The HTML and CSS rendered by the button is shown here:

```
<input type="submit" name="Button1" value="Button" id="Button1"
    style="color:White;background-color:#3333FF;border-color:Silver;
border-width:3px;
            border-style:Double;font-size:Large;font-weight:bold;" />
```

Setting style properties directly on the ASP.NET controls is a fast and simple way to style the ASP.NET controls in your application. Additionally, because these are standard properties on the controls, you can also set them at runtime using code.

```
protected void Page_Load(object sender, EventArgs e)
{
    this.Button1.BackColor =
        System.Drawing.ColorTranslator.FromHtml("#3333FF");
    this.Button1.BorderColor = System.Drawing.Color.Silver;
    this.Button1.BorderStyle= BorderStyle.Double;
    this.Button1.BorderWidth = Unit.Pixel(3);
    this.Button1.Font.Bold=true;
    this.Button1.Font.Size=FontUnit.Large;
    this.Button1.ForeColor=System.Drawing.Color.White;
}
```

Although using properties to set style info is easy and convenient, it does have some drawbacks, especially when you use the same technique with larger repeating controls. One drawback is that using inline styles makes controlling the styling of your Web site at a higher, more abstract level difficult. If you want every button in your Web site to have a specific style, generally you would have to manually set that style on every Button control in your entire site. Themes can help solve this problem but are not always useful, especially when you are mixing ASP.NET controls with standard HTML controls.

Another drawback is that for controls that generate a large amount of repetitive HTML, such as the GridView, having inline styles on every element of each iteration of HTML adds a lot of extra weight to your Web page.

Thankfully, every ASP.NET server control exposes a `CssClass` property. This property allows you to provide one or more Class selector rules to the control. Although this technique is helpful, and usually better than letting the control render inline styles, it still requires you to be familiar with the HTML that the control will render at runtime. Listing 17-13 shows how you can use the `CssClass` attribute to style the ASP.NET Button control.

LISTING 17-13: Styling a standard ASP.NET Button control using CSS

Available for download on Wrox.com

```
<!DOCTYPE html PUBLIC "-//W3C//DTD XHTML 1.0 Transitional//EN"
"http://www.w3.org/TR/xhtml1/DTD/xhtml1-transitional.dtd">

<html xmlns="http://www.w3.org/1999/xhtml">
<head id="Head1" runat="server">

    <link href="SpringStyles.css" rel="stylesheet" type="text/css" />
    <style>
        .search
        {
            color:White;
            font-weight:bolder;
            background-color:Green;
        }
    </style>
</head>
<body>
```

continues

LISTING 17-13 *(continued)*

```
        <form id="form1" runat="server">
            <asp:Button ID="Button1"
                CssClass="search" runat="server" Text="Button" />
        </form>
    </body>
    </html>
```

In this case, the Button will have the search class applied to it.

SUMMARY

CSS is a great way to add style to your Web site. It's a powerful and convenient mechanism that allows you to create complex styles and layouts for your Web site. A full discussion of CSS would require much more time and space than available here, so this chapter focused on showing you some of the basic concepts of CSS, the tools Visual Studio provides you to work more easily with CSS, and how you can use CSS with ASP.NET server controls. If you are interested in learning more about the details of CSS, we recommend that you pick up the Wrox title *Beginning CSS: Cascading Style Sheets for Web Design, 2nd Edition,* by Richard York (Wiley, 2007).

This chapter provided an overview of CSS, introducing you to external, internal, and inline style sheets. You learned about the various selector types that CSS offers and about basic layout and positioning of CSS elements, including how the box model works to influence element positions in your Web page.

Next you reviewed the tools available in Visual Studio, including the Style Manager and CSS Properties tool windows, that make working with CSS easy.

Finally, you looked at how to use CSS with the ASP.NET server controls.

18

ASP.NET AJAX

WHAT'S IN THIS CHAPTER?

- Developing applications with ASP.NET AJAX
- Using ASP.NET AJAX's server-side controls

AJAX continues to be one of the hot buzzwords in the Web application world at the moment. AJAX is an acronym for *Asynchronous JavaScript and XML*, and, in Web application development, it signifies the capability to build applications that make use of the `XMLHttpRequest` object.

The creation and the inclusion of the `XMLHttpRequest` object in JavaScript and the fact that most upper-level browsers support it led to the creation of the AJAX model. AJAX applications, although they have been around for a few years, gained popularity after Google released a number of notable, AJAX-enabled applications such as Google Maps and Google Suggest from its R&D labs. These applications demonstrated the value of AJAX and were noticed by the world at large.

Shortly thereafter, Microsoft released a beta for a new toolkit that enabled developers to incorporate AJAX features in their Web applications. This toolkit, code-named *Atlas* and later renamed ASP.NET AJAX, makes using AJAX features in your applications extremely simple.

The ASP.NET AJAX Toolkit was *not* part of the default .NET Framework 2.0 install. If you are using the .NET Framework 2.0, then it is an extra component that you must download from the Internet. If you are using ASP.NET 3.5 or 4, then you don't have to worry about installing the ASP.NET AJAX Toolkit because everything you need is already in place for you.

UNDERSTANDING THE NEED FOR AJAX

Today, when building an application, you have the option of creating a thick-client or a thin-client application. A *thick-client* application is typically a compiled executable that end users can run in the confines of their own environment — usually without any dependencies elsewhere (such as an upstream server). Generally, the technology to build this type of application is written in the Windows Forms technology, or MFC in the C++ world. A *thin-client* application is typically one that has its processing and rendering controlled at a single point (the upstream server), and the results of the view are sent down as HTML to a browser to be viewed by a client. To work, this type of technology generally requires that the end user be connected to the Internet or an intranet of some kind.

Each type of application has its pros and cons. The thick-client style of application is touted as more fluid and more responsive to an end user's actions. In a Web-based application, the complaint has been for many years that every action by an end user takes numerous seconds and results in a jerky page refresh. In turn, the problem with a thick-client style of application has always been that the application sits on the end user's machine, and any patches or updates to the application require you to somehow upgrade each and every machine on which the application sits. In contrast, the thin-client application, or the Web application architecture, includes only one instance of the application. The application, in this case, is installed on a Web server, and any updates that need to occur happen only to this instance. End users who are calling the application through their browsers always get the latest and greatest version of the application. That model has a lot of power to it.

With this said, it is important to understand that Microsoft is making huge inroads into solving this thick- or thin-client problem, and you now have options that completely change this model. For instance, the Windows Presentation Foundation technology offered by Microsoft and the Silverlight technology blurs the lines between the two traditional application styles.

Even with the existing Windows Forms and ASP.NET technologies to build the respective thick- or thin-client applications, these technologies are advancing to a point where they are blurring the lines even further. ASP.NET AJAX, in particular, is further removing any of the negatives that would have stopped you from building an application on the Web.

ASP.NET AJAX makes your Web applications seem more fluid than ever before. AJAX-enabled applications are responsive and give the end user immediate feedback and direction through the workflows that you provide. The power of this alone makes the study of this technology and its incorporation into your projects of the utmost importance.

Before AJAX

So, what is AJAX doing to your Web application? Take a look at what a Web page does when it does *not* use AJAX. Figure 18-1 shows a typical request-and-response activity for a Web application.

In this figure, an end user makes a request from his browser to the application that is stored on your Web server. The server processes the request and ASP.NET renders a page, which is then sent to the requestor as a response. The response, when received by the end user, is displayed within the end user's browser.

From here, many events that take place within the application instance as it sits within the end user's browser cause the complete request-and-response process to reoccur. For instance, the end user might click a radio button, a check box, a button, a calendar, or anything else, and this action causes the entire Web page to be refreshed or a new page to be provided.

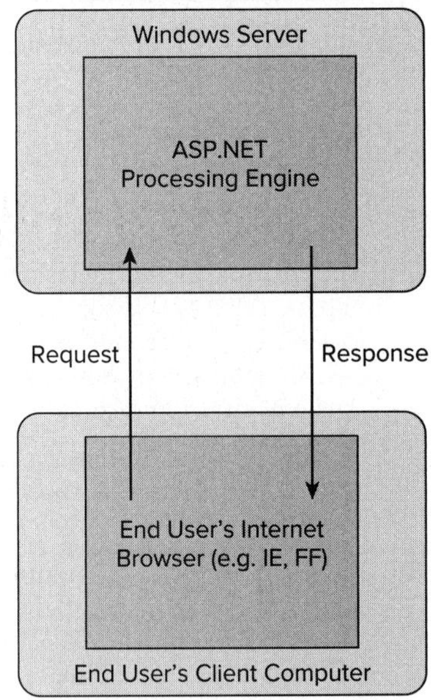

FIGURE 18-1

AJAX Changes the Story

In contrast, an AJAX-enabled Web page includes a JavaScript library on the client that takes care of issuing the calls to the Web server. It does this when it is possible to send a request and get a response for just part of the page and when using script; the client library updates that part of the page without updating the entire page. An entire page is a lot of code to send down to the browser to process each and every time. By processing just part of the page, the end user experiences what some people term "fluidity" in the page, which makes the page seem more responsive. The amount of code required to update just a portion of a page is less and produces the responsiveness the end user expects. Figure 18-2 shows a diagram of how this works.

Figure 18-2 demonstrates that the first thing that happens is that the entire page is delivered in the initial request and response. From there, any partial updates required by the page are done using the client script library. This library can make asynchronous page requests and update just the portion of the page that needs updating. One major advantage to this is that a minimal amount of data is transferred for the updates to occur. Updating a partial page is better than recalling the entire page for what is just a small change to the page.

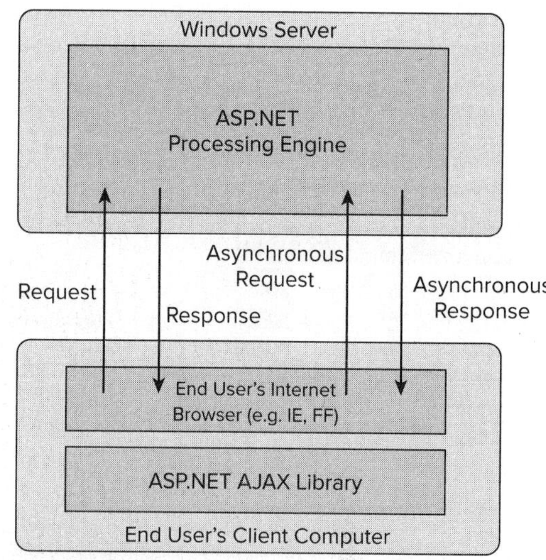

FIGURE 18-2

AJAX is dependent on a few technologies for it to work. The first is the `XMLHttpRequest` object. This object allows the browser to communicate to a back-end server and has been available in the Microsoft world since Internet Explorer 5 through the MSXML ActiveX component. Of course, the other major component is JavaScript. This technology provides the client-side initiation to communication with the back-end services and takes care of packaging a message to send to any server-side services. Another aspect of AJAX is support for DHTML and the Document Object Model (DOM). These pieces change the page when the asynchronous response is received from the server. Finally, the last piece is the data that is being transferred from the client to the server. This transfer is done in XML, or more important JavaScript Object Notation (JSON).

Support for the `XMLHttpRequest` object gives JavaScript functions within the client script library the capability to call server-side events. As stated, HTTP requests are typically issued by a browser. The browser also takes care of processing the response that comes from the server and then usually regenerates the entire Web page in the browser after a response is issued. Figure 18-3 details this process.

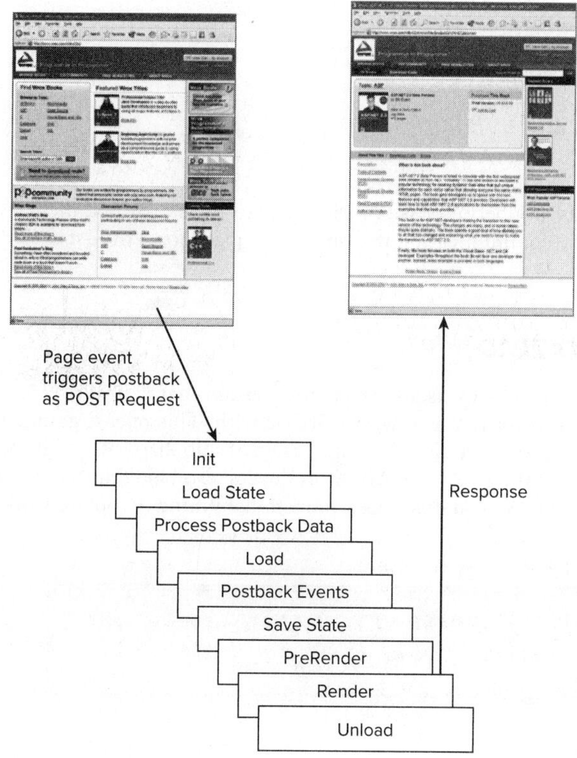

FIGURE 18-3

If you use the `XMLHttpRequest` object from your JavaScript library, then you do not actually issue full-page requests from the browser. Instead, you use a client-side script engine (which is basically a JavaScript function) to initiate the request and also to receive the response. Because you are also not issuing a request and response to deal with the entire Web page, you can skip a lot of the page processing because it is not needed. This is the essence of an AJAX Web request. It is illustrated in Figure 18-4.

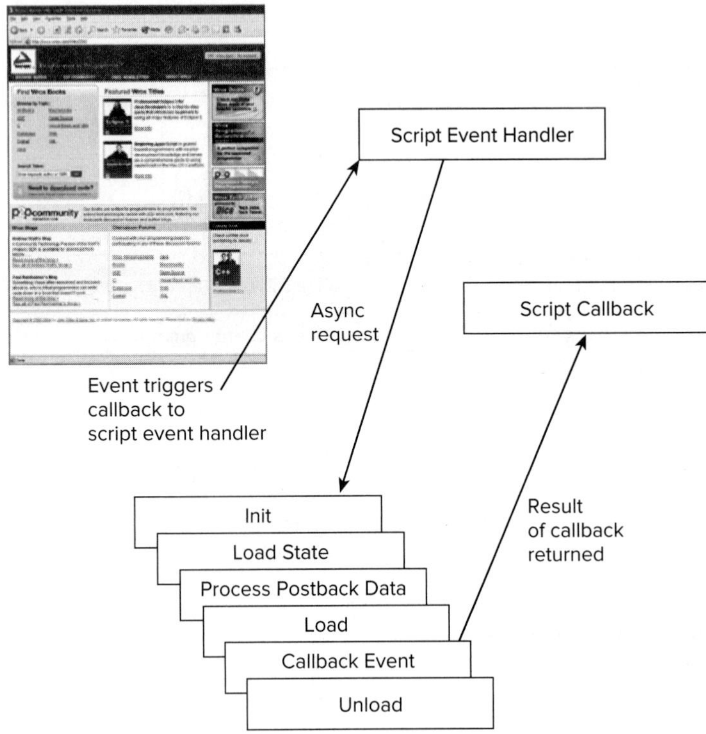

FIGURE 18-4

As stated, AJAX opens the door to a tremendous number of possibilities. Microsoft has provided the necessary script engines to automate much of the communication that must take place for AJAX-style functionality to occur.

ASP.NET AJAX AND VISUAL STUDIO 2010

Prior to Visual Studio 2008, the ASP.NET AJAX product was a separate installation that you were required to install on your machine and the Web server that you were working with. This release gained in popularity quite rapidly and is now a part of the Visual Studio 2008 and Visual Studio 2010 offerings. Not only is it a part of the Visual Studio 2010 IDE, but the ASP.NET AJAX product is also baked into the .NET Framework 4. This means that to use ASP.NET AJAX, you don't need to install anything if you are working with ASP.NET 4.

If you are using an ASP.NET version prior to the ASP.NET 3.5 release, then you need to visit `www.asp.net/AJAX` *to get the components required to work with AJAX.*

Because ASP.NET AJAX is just part of the ASP.NET Framework, when you create a new Web application, you do not need to create a separate type of ASP.NET application. Instead, all ASP.NET applications that you create are now AJAX-enabled.

Overall, Microsoft has fully integrated the entire ASP.NET AJAX experience so you can easily use Visual Studio and its visual designers to work with your AJAX-enabled pages and even have the full debugging story that you would want to have with your applications. Using Visual Studio 2010, you can also debug the JavaScript that you are using in the pages.

In addition, it is important to note that Microsoft focused a lot of attention on cross-platform compatibility with ASP.NET AJAX. You will find that the AJAX-enabled applications that you build on the .NET Framework 4 can work within all the major up-level browsers out there (such as Firefox and Opera).

Client-Side Technologies

The ASP.NET AJAX story really has two parts. The first is a client-side framework and a set of services that are completely on the client-side. The other part of the story is a server-side framework. Remember that the client-side of ASP.NET AJAX is all about the client communicating asynchronous requests to the server-side of the offering.

For this reason, Microsoft offers a Client Script Library, which is a JavaScript library that takes care of the required communications. Figure 18-5 shows the Client Script Library.

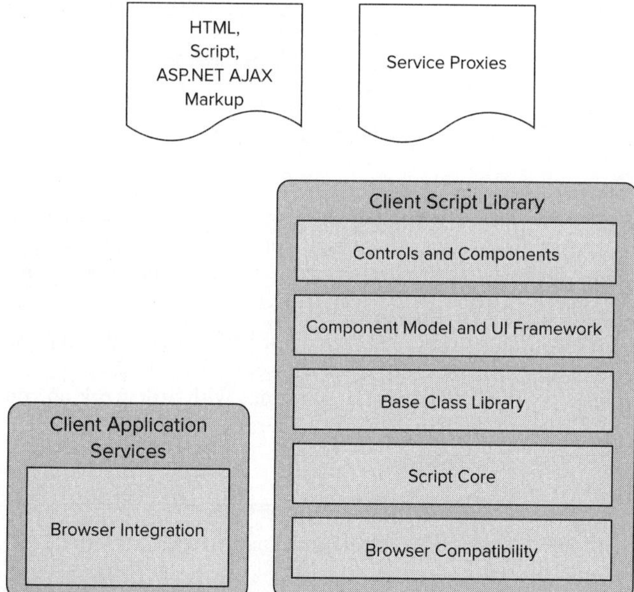

FIGURE 18-5

The Client Script Library provides a JavaScript, object-oriented interface that is reasonably consistent with aspects of the .NET Framework. Because browser compatibility components are built in, any work that you build in this layer or (in most cases) work that you let ASP.NET AJAX perform for you here will function with a multitude of different browsers. Also, several components support a rich UI infrastructure that produces many things that would take some serious time to build yourself.

The interesting thing about the client-side technologies that are provided by ASP.NET AJAX is that they are completely independent of ASP.NET. In fact, any developer can freely download the Microsoft AJAX

Library (again from `asp.net/AJAX`) and use it with other Web technologies such as PHP (`php.net`) and Java Server Pages (JSP). With that said, the entire Web story is a lot more complete with the server-side technologies that are provided with ASP.NET AJAX.

Server-Side Technologies

As an ASP.NET developer, you will likely spend most of your time on the server-side aspect of ASP.NET AJAX. Remember that ASP.NET AJAX is all about the client-side technologies talking back to the server-side technologies. You can actually perform quite a bit on the server-side of ASP.NET AJAX.

The server-side framework knows how to deal with client requests (such as putting responses in the correct format). The server-side framework also takes care of the marshalling of objects back and forth between JavaScript objects and the .NET objects that you are using in your server-side code. Figure 18-6 illustrates the server-side framework provided by ASP.NET AJAX.

When you have the .NET Framework 4, you will have the ASP.NET AJAX Server Extensions on top of the core ASP.NET Framework, the Windows Communication Foundation, as well as ASP.NET-based Web services (`.asmx`).

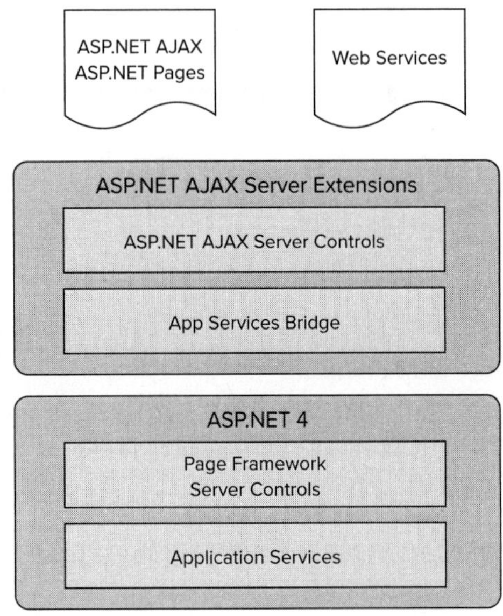

FIGURE 18-6

Developing with ASP.NET AJAX

A couple of types of Web developers exist out there. There are the Web developers who are accustomed to working with ASP.NET and who have experience working with server-side controls and manipulating these controls on the server-side. Then there are developers who concentrate on the client-side and work with DHTML and JavaScript to manipulate and control the page and its behaviors.

With that said, it is important to realize that ASP.NET AJAX was designed for both types of developers. If you want to work more on the server-side of ASP.NET AJAX, then you can use the ScriptManager control and the UpdatePanel control to AJAX-enable your current ASP.NET applications with little work on your part. You can do all this work using the same programming models that you are quite familiar with in ASP.NET.

You find out more about both the ScriptManager and the UpdatePanel controls later in this chapter.

In turn, you can also use the Client Script Library directly and gain greater control over what is happening on the client's machine. Next, this chapter looks at building a simple Web application that makes use of AJAX.

BUILDING ASP.NET AJAX APPLICATIONS

Now that you understand the reasons for AJAX, the next step is to build a basic sample using this framework. Create a new Empty ASP.NET Web Site application using the New Web Site dialog. Name the project `AJAXWebSite`. Notice (as shown in Figure 18-7) that there is not a separate type of ASP.NET project for building an ASP.NET AJAX application because every ASP.NET application that you now build is AJAX-enabled.

FIGURE 18-7

After you create the application, you are presented with what is now a standard Web Site project. If you were building this application with ASP.NET 3.5, you would have noticed some additional settings in the `web.config` file. In this case, at the top of the `web.config` file, you would find some configuration sections that are registered that deal with AJAX in particular. In the case of ASP.NET 4, this same section of configuration previously found in the `web.config` file is now found back in the `machine.config` file. Listing 18-1 presents this section from the `machine.config`.

LISTING 18-1: The <configSections> element found in the machine.config

```
<?xml version=""1.0"?>

<configuration>
  <configSections>
     <sectionGroup name="system.web.extensions"
      type="System.Web.Configuration.SystemWebExtensionsSectionGroup,
      System.Web.Extensions, Version=4.0.0.0, Culture=neutral,
      PublicKeyToken=31bf3856ad364e35">
     <sectionGroup name="scripting"
      type="System.Web.Configuration.ScriptingSectionGroup,
        System.Web.Extensions, Version=4.0.0.0, Culture=neutral,
        PublicKeyToken=31bf3856ad364e35">
     <section name="scriptResourceHandler"
      type="System.Web.Configuration.
        ScriptingScriptResourceHandlerSection, System.Web.Extensions,
        Version=4.0.0.0, Culture=neutral,
        PublicKeyToken=31bf3856ad364e35" requirePermission="false"
```

continues

LISTING 18-1 *(continued)*

```
        allowDefinition="MachineToApplication"/>
      <sectionGroup name="webServices"
       type="System.Web.Configuration.ScriptingWebServicesSectionGroup,
         System.Web.Extensions, Version=4.0.0.0, Culture=neutral,
         PublicKeyToken=31bf3856ad364e35">
      <section name="jsonSerialization"
       type="System.Web.Configuration.ScriptingJsonSerializationSection,
         System.Web.Extensions, Version=4.0.0.0, Culture=neutral,
         PublicKeyToken=31bf3856ad364e35" requirePermission="false"
       allowDefinition="Everywhere"/>
      <section name="profileService"
       type="System.Web.Configuration.ScriptingProfileServiceSection,
         System.Web.Extensions, Version=4.0.0.0, Culture=neutral,
         PublicKeyToken=31bf3856ad364e35" requirePermission="false"
       allowDefinition="MachineToApplication"/>
      <section name="authenticationService"
       type="System.Web.Configuration.
         ScriptingAuthenticationServiceSection, System.Web.Extensions,
         Version=4.0.0.0, Culture=neutral,
         PublicKeyToken=31bf3856ad364e35" requirePermission="false"
       allowDefinition="MachineToApplication"/>
      <section name="roleService"
       type="System.Web.Configuration.ScriptingRoleServiceSection,
         System.Web.Extensions, Version=4.0.0.0, Culture=neutral,
         PublicKeyToken=31bf3856ad364e35" requirePermission="false"
       allowDefinition="MachineToApplication"/>
      </sectionGroup>
      </sectionGroup>
    </sectionGroup>
  </configSections>

<!-- Configuration removed for clarity -->

</configuration>
```

The placement of this code within the `machine.config` file is one of the reasons why the ASP.NET 4 `web.config` file is so clean. Next, you build a simple ASP.NET page that does not yet make use of AJAX.

Building a Simple ASP.NET Page without AJAX

To build a simple page that does not yet make use of the AJAX capabilities offered by ASP.NET 4, your page needs only a Label control and Button server control. Listing 18-2 presents the code for the page.

LISTING 18-2: A simple ASP.NET 4 page that does not use AJAX

Available for download on Wrox.com

VB

```
<%@ Page Language="VB" %>

<script runat="server">
    Protected Sub Button1_Click(ByVal sender As Object, _
       ByVal e As System.EventArgs)

        Label1.Text = DateTime.Now.ToString()
    End Sub</script>

<html xmlns="http://www.w3.org/1999/xhtml">
<head runat="server">
    <title>My Normal ASP.NET Page</title>
</head>
<body>
```

```
    <form id="form1" runat="server">
    <div>
        <asp:Label ID="Label1" runat="server"></asp:Label>
        <br />
        <br />
        <asp:Button ID="Button1" runat="server" Text="Click to get machine time"
            onclick="Button1_Click" />
    </div>
    </form>
</body>
</html>
```

C#

```
<%@ Page Language="C#" %>

<script runat="server">
    protected void Button1_Click(object sender, EventArgs e)
    {
        Label1.Text = DateTime.Now.ToString();
    }
</script>
```

When you open this page in the browser, it contains only a single button. When the button is clicked, the Label control that is on the page is populated with the time from the server machine. Before the button is clicked, the page's code is similar to the code presented in Listing 18-3.

LISTING 18-3: The page output for a page that is not using AJAX

```
<!DOCTYPE html PUBLIC "-//W3C//DTD XHTML 1.0 Transitional//EN"
 "http://www.w3.org/TR/xhtml1/DTD/xhtml1-transitional.dtd">

<html xmlns="http://www.w3.org/1999/xhtml">
<head><title>
    My Normal ASP.NET Page
</title></head>
<body>
    <form method="post" action="Default.aspx" id="form1">
      <div class="aspNetHidden">
         <input type="hidden" name="__VIEWSTATE" id="__VIEWSTATE"
          value="/wEPDwULLTE4OTg4OTc0MjVkZMWQqs
                 XZabSMPF1F9N7eG+niQuNjUX/leoJ4tMKUONqz" />
      </div>
      <div class="aspNetHidden">
         <input type="hidden" name="__EVENTVALIDATION"
          id="__EVENTVALIDATION"
          value="/wEWAgK0purjBwKM54rGBuxRc38kEm6T4P4
                 ioDTduLs1C0GyKDT+ClTR9HlZdAdH" />
      </div>
      <div>
         <span id="Label1"></span>
         <br />
         <br />
         <input type="submit" name="Button1"
          value="Click to get machine time" id="Button1" />
      </div>
    </form>
</body>
</html>
```

There is not much in this code. There is a little ViewState and a typical form that will be posted back to the `Default.aspx` page. When the end user clicks the button on the page, a full Postback to the server occurs, and the entire page is reprocessed and returned to the client's browser. Really, the only change made to the page is that the `<span id="Lable1"></span>` element is populated with a value, but in this case, the entire page is returned.

Building a Simple ASP.NET Page with AJAX

The next step is to build on the page from Listing 18-2 and add AJAX capabilities to it. In this example, you add some additional controls. Two of the controls are typical ASP.NET server controls — another Label and Button server control. In addition to these controls, you must add some ASP.NET AJAX controls.

FIGURE 18-8

In the Visual Studio 2010 Toolbox is a section titled AJAX Extensions. This section is shown in Figure 18-8.

From AJAX Extensions, add a ScriptManager server control to the top of the page and include the second Label and Button control inside the UpdatePanel control. The UpdatePanel control is a template server control and allows you to include any number of items within it (just as other templated ASP.NET server controls). When you have your page set up, it should look something like Figure 18-9.

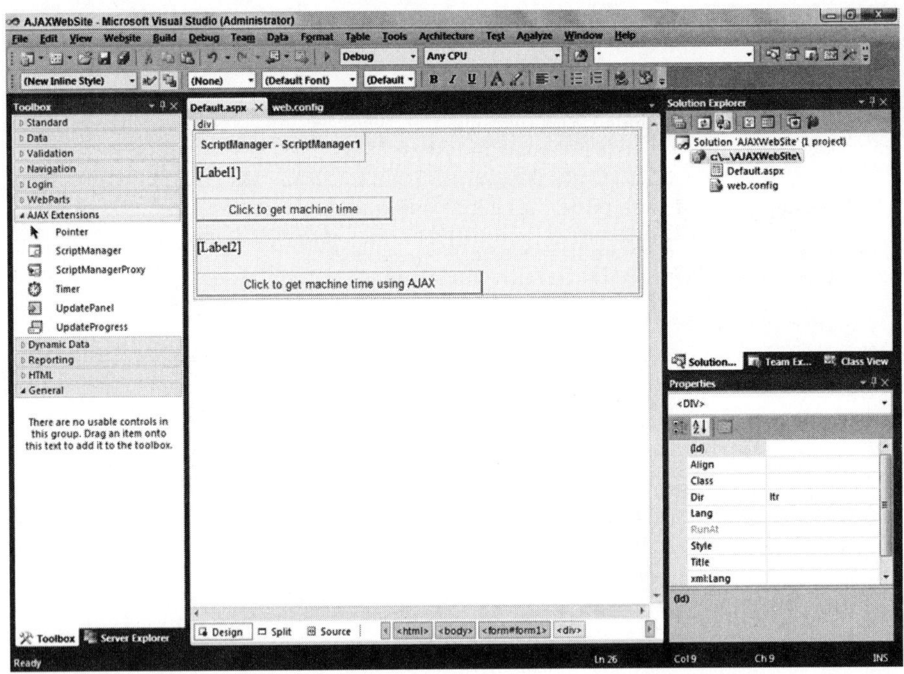

FIGURE 18-9

Listing 18-4 shows the code for this page.

LISTING 18-4: A simple ASP.NET AJAX page

```
<%@ Page Language="VB" %>

<script runat="server">
    Protected Sub Button1_Click(ByVal sender As Object, _
       ByVal e As System.EventArgs)
        Label1.Text = DateTime.Now.ToString()
```

```
    End Sub

    Protected Sub Button2_Click(ByVal sender As Object, _
       ByVal e As System.EventArgs)
        Label2.Text = DateTime.Now.ToString()
    End Sub
</script>
<html xmlns="http://www.w3.org/1999/xhtml">
<head runat="server">
    <title>My ASP.NET AJAX Page</title>
</head>
<body>
    <form id="form1" runat="server">
    <div>
        <asp:ScriptManager ID="ScriptManager1" runat="server">
        </asp:ScriptManager>
        <asp:Label ID="Label1" runat="server"></asp:Label>
        <br />
        <br />
        <asp:Button ID="Button1" runat="server"
            Text="Click to get machine time"
            onclick="Button1_Click" />
        <br />
        <br />
        <asp:UpdatePanel ID="UpdatePanel1" runat="server">
            <ContentTemplate>
                <asp:Label ID="Label2" runat="server"
                 Text=""></asp:Label>
                <br />
                <br />
                <asp:Button ID="Button2" runat="server"
                 Text="Click to get machine time using AJAX"
                 onclick="Button2_Click" />
            </ContentTemplate>
        </asp:UpdatePanel>
    </div>
    </form>
</body>
</html>
```

C#

```
<%@ Page Language="C#" %>

<script runat="server">
    protected void Button1_Click(object sender, EventArgs e)
    {
        Label1.Text = DateTime.Now.ToString();
    }

    protected void Button2_Click(object sender, EventArgs e)
    {
        Label2.Text = DateTime.Now.ToString();
    }
</script>
```

When you open this page in the browser, it has two buttons. The first button causes a complete page Postback and updates the current time in the Label1 server control. Clicking on the second button causes an AJAX asynchronous Postback. Clicking this second button updates the current server time in the Label2 server control. When you click the AJAX button, the time in Label1 will not change at all, as it is outside of the UpdatePanel. Figure 18-10 presents a screenshot of the final result.

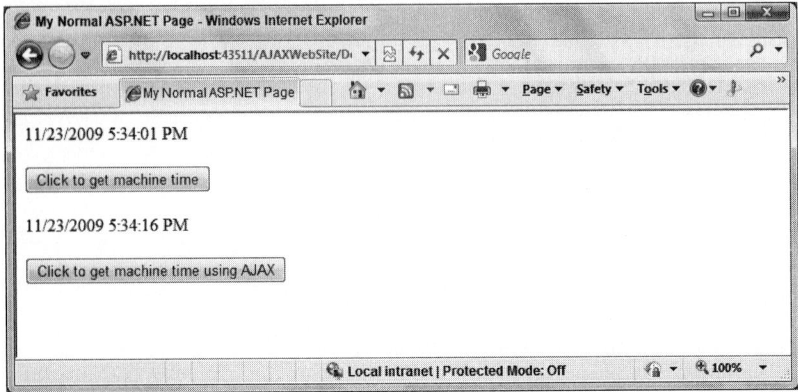

FIGURE 18-10

When you first open the page from Listing 18-4, the code of the page is quite different from the page that you built without using AJAX. Listing 18-5 shows the page results that you will see.

LISTING 18-5: The page output for a page that is using AJAX

```
<html xmlns="http://www.w3.org/1999/xhtml">
<head><title>
   My ASP.NET AJAX Page
</title></head>
<body>
    <form method="post" action="Default.aspx" id="form1">
<div class="aspNetHidden">
<input type="hidden" name="__EVENTTARGET" id="__EVENTTARGET"
 value="" />
<input type="hidden" name="__EVENTARGUMENT" id="__EVENTARGUMENT"
 value="" />
<input type="hidden" name="__VIEWSTATE" id="__VIEWSTATE"
 value="/wEPDwULLTE4NzE5NTc5MzRkZDRIzHpPZg4GaO9Hox9A/RnOflkm" />
</div>

<script type="text/javascript">
//<![CDATA[
var theForm = document.forms['form1'];
if (!theForm) {
    theForm = document.form1;
}
function __doPostBack(eventTarget, eventArgument) {
    if (!theForm.onsubmit || (theForm.onsubmit() != false)) {
        theForm.__EVENTTARGET.value = eventTarget;
        theForm.__EVENTARGUMENT.value = eventArgument;
        theForm.submit();
    }
}
//]]>
</script>

<script src="/AJAXWebSite/WebResource.axd?d=o84znEj-
 n4cYi0Wg0pFXCg2&amp;t=633285028458684000"
 type="text/javascript"></script>

<script src="/AJAXWebSite/ScriptResource.axd?
 d=FETsh5584DXpx8XqIhEM50YSKyR2GkoMoAqraYEDU5_
```

```
gi1SUmL2Gt7rQTRBAw561SojJRQe0OjVI8SiYDjmpYmFP0
CO8wBFGhtKKJwm2MeE1&amp;t=633285035850304000"
type="text/javascript"></script>
<script type="text/javascript">
//<![CDATA[
if (typeof(Sys) === 'undefined') throw new Error('ASP.NET AJAX
  client-side
  framework failed to load.');
//]]>
</script>

<script src="/AJAXWebSite/ScriptResource.axd?
 d=FETsh5584DXpx8XqIhEM50YSKyR2GkoMoAqraYEDU5_
 gi1SUmL2Gt7rQTRBAw5617AYfmRViCoO21Z3XwZ33TGiC
 t92e_UOqfrP30mdEYnJYs09ulU1xBLj8TjXOLR1k0&amp;t=633285035850304000"
 type="text/javascript"></script>
    <div>
        <script type="text/javascript">
//<![CDATA[
Sys.WebForms.PageRequestManager._initialize('ScriptManager1', 'form1',
    'UpdatePanel1'], [], [], 90);
//]]>
</script>
        <span id="Label1"></span>
        <br />
        <br />
        <input type="submit" name="Button1"
         value="Click to get machine time"
         id="Button1" />
        <br />
        <br />
        <div id="UpdatePanel1">

                <span id="Label2"></span>
                <br />
                <br />
                <input type="submit" name="Button2"
                 value="Click to get machine
                 time using AJAX" id="Button2" />
        </div>
    </div>
</form>
</body>
</html>
```

From there, if you click Button1 and perform the full-page Postback, you get this entire bit of code back in a response — even though you are interested in updating only a small portion of the page! However, if you click Button2 — the AJAX button — you send the request shown in Listing 18-6.

LISTING 18-6: The asynchronous request from the ASP.NET AJAX page

```
POST /AJAXWebSite/Default.aspx HTTP/1.1
Accept: */*
Accept-Language: en-US
Referer: http://localhost:62203/AJAXWebSite/Default.aspx
x-microsoftAJAX: Delta=true
Content-Type: application/x-www-form-urlencoded; charset=utf-8
Cache-Control: no-cache
Accept-Encoding: gzip, deflate
User-Agent: Mozilla/4.0 (compatible; MSIE 8.0; Windows NT 6.1; SLCC2;
.NET CLR 2.0.50727; .NET CLR 3.5.30729; .NET CLR 3.0.30729;
```

continues

LISTING 18-6 *(continued)*

```
Media Center PC 6.0; .NET4.0C; .NET4.0E; .NET CLR 1.1.4322)
Host: localhost:62203
Content-Length: 334
Proxy-Connection: Keep-Alive
Pragma: no-cache

ScriptManager1=UpdatePanel1%7CButton2&__EVENTTARGET=&__EVENTARGUMENT=&_
_VIEWSTATE=%2FwEPDwULLTE4NzE5NTc5MzQPZBYCAgQPZBYCAgMPDxYCHgRUZXh0BRQxMS
8zLzIwMDcgMjoxNzo1NSBQTWRkZHZxUyYQG0M25t8U7vLbHRJuKlcS&__EVENTVALIDATIO
N=%2FwEWAwKCxdk9AoznisYGArursYYI1844hk7V466AsW31G5yIZ73%2Bc6o%3D&Button
2=Click%20to%20get%20machine%20time%20using%20Ajax
```

Listing 18-7 shows the response for this asynchronous request.

LISTING 18-7: The asynchronous response from the ASP.NET AJAX page

```
HTTP/1.1 200 OK
Server: ASP.NET Development Server/10.0.0.0
Date: Tue, 24 Nov 2009 19:17:58 GMT
X-AspNet-Version: 4.0.21006
Cache-Control: private
Content-Type: text/plain; charset=utf-8
Content-Length: 796
Connection: Close

1|#||4|240|updatePanel|UpdatePanel1|
                <span id="Label2">11/23/2009 6:07:02 PM</span>
                <br />
                <br />
                <input type="submit" name="Button2"
         value="Click to get machine time using AJAX" id="Button2" />

|144|hiddenField|__VIEWSTATE|/wEPDwULLTE4NzE5NTc5MzQPZBYCAgQPZBYCAgcPZBYCZg9kFgICAQ8PFgIe
BFRleHQFFTExLzIzLzIwMDkgNjowNzowMiBQTWRkZL3F5GzbqchgQqa45tPLrEZ9EM7SVuNusJkCULh5BjCN|72|
hiddenField|__EVENTVALIDATION|/wEWAwLe9aL7CgK7q7GGCAKM54rGBiRNYsdbOVLVpTJOAwfCON/
Wi2w+bTGzq7rqlIRqqTRd|0|asyncPostBackControlIDs|||0|postBackControlIDs|||26|
updatePanelIDs||tUpdatePanel1,UpdatePanel1|0|childUpdatePanelIDs|||25|panelsToRefreshIDs
||UpdatePanel1,
UpdatePanel1|2|asyncPostBackTimeout||90|12|formAction||Default.aspx|22|pageTitle||
My ASP.NET AJAX Page|
|
```

From Listing 18-7, you can see that the response is much smaller than an entire Web page! In fact, the main part of the response is only the code that is contained within the UpdatePanel server control and nothing more. The items at the bottom of the output deal with the ViewState of the page (as it has now changed) and some other small page changes.

ASP.NET AJAX'S SERVER-SIDE CONTROLS

When you look at the AJAX Extensions section in the Visual Studio 2010 Toolbox, you will notice that not many controls are at your disposal. The controls there are focus on allowing you to AJAX-enable your ASP.NET applications. They are enabling controls. If you are looking for more specific server controls that take advantage of the AJAX model, then look at the ASP.NET AJAX Control Toolkit — a separate download that is covered in Chapter 19.

Table 18-1 describes the ASP.NET AJAX server controls that come with ASP.NET 4.

TABLE 18-1

ASP.NET AJAX SERVER CONTROL	DESCRIPTION
ScriptManager	A component control that manages the marshalling of messages to the AJAX-enabled server for the parts of the page requiring partial updates. Every ASP.NET page will require a ScriptManager control in order to work. Note that you can have only a single ScriptManager control on a page.
ScriptManagerProxy	A component control that acts as a ScriptManager control for a content page. The ScriptManagerProxy control, which sits on the content page (or sub-page), works in conjunction with a required ScriptManager control that resides on the master page.
Timer	The Timer control executes client-side events at specific intervals and allows specific parts of your page to update or refresh at these moments.
UpdatePanel	A container control that allows you to define specific areas of the page that are enabled to work with the ScriptManager. These areas can then, in turn, make the partial page Postbacks and update themselves outside the normal ASP.NET page Postback process.
UpdateProgress	A control that allows you to display a visual element to the end user to show that a partial-page Postback is occurring to the part of the page making the update. This control is ideal to use when you have long-running AJAX updates.

The next few sections of this chapter look at these controls and how to use them within your ASP.NET pages.

The ScriptManager Control

Probably the most important control in your ASP.NET AJAX arsenal is the ScriptManager server control, which works with the page to allow for partial page rendering. You use a single ScriptManager control on each page for which you want to use the AJAX capabilities provided by ASP.NET 4. When placed in conjunction with the UpdatePanel server control, AJAX-enabling your ASP.NET applications can be as simple as adding two server controls to the page, and then you are ready to go!

The ScriptManager control takes care of managing the JavaScript libraries that are used on your page as well as marshalling the messages back and forth between the server and the client for the partial page rendering process. The marshalling of the messages can be done using either SOAP or JSON through the ScriptManager control.

If you place only a single ScriptManager control on your ASP.NET page, it takes care of loading the JavaScript libraries needed by ASP.NET AJAX. Listing 18-8 presents the page for this task.

LISTING 18-8: An ASP.NET page that includes only the ScriptManager control

Available for download on Wrox.com

```
<%@ Page Language="VB" %>

<html xmlns="http://www.w3.org/1999/xhtml">
<head runat="server">
    <title>The ScriptManager Control</title>
</head>
<body>
    <form id="form1" runat="server">
    <div>
        <asp:ScriptManager ID="ScriptManager1" runat="server">
        </asp:ScriptManager>
    </div>
    </form>
</body>
</html>
```

From Listing 18-8, you can see that this control is like all other ASP.NET controls and needs only an `ID` and a `runat` attribute to do its work. Listing 18-9 shows the page output from this bit of ASP.NET code.

LISTING 18-9: The page output from the ScriptManager control

```
<html xmlns="http://www.w3.org/1999/xhtml">
<head><title>
 The ScriptManager Control
</title></head>
<body>
    <form method="post" action="Default.aspx" id="form1">
<div class="aspNetHidden">
<input type="hidden" name="__EVENTTARGET" id="__EVENTTARGET"
 value="" />
<input type="hidden" name="__EVENTARGUMENT" id="__EVENTARGUMENT"
 value="" />
<input type="hidden" name="__VIEWSTATE" id="__VIEWSTATE"
 value="/wEPDwULLTEzNjQ0OTQ1MDdkZO9dCw2QaeC4D8AwACTbOkD1OX4h" />
</div>

<script type="text/javascript">
//<![CDATA[
var theForm = document.forms['form1'];
if (!theForm) {
    theForm = document.form1;
}
function __doPostBack(eventTarget, eventArgument) {
    if (!theForm.onsubmit || (theForm.onsubmit() != false)) {
        theForm.__EVENTTARGET.value = eventTarget;
        theForm.__EVENTARGUMENT.value = eventArgument;
        theForm.submit();
    }
}
//]]>
</script>

<script src="/AJAXWebSite/WebResource.axd?d=o84znEj-
 n4cYi0Wg0pFXCg2&amp;t=633285028458684000"
 type="text/javascript"></script>

<script src="/AJAXWebSite/ScriptResource.axd?d=
 FETsh5584DXpx8XqIhEM50YSKyR2GkoMoAqraYEDU5_gi1SUmL2Gt7rQTRBAw561SojJR
 Qe0OjVI8SiYDjmpYmFP0CO8wBFGhtKKJwm2MeE1&amp;t=633285035850304000"
 type="text/javascript"></script>
<script type="text/javascript">
//<![CDATA[
if (typeof(Sys) === 'undefined') throw new Error('ASP.NET AJAX client-side
 framework failed to load.');
//]]>
</script>

<script
src="/AJAXWebSite/ScriptResource.axd?d=
 FETsh5584DXpx8XqIhEM50YSKyR2GkoMoAqraYEDU5_gi1SUmL2Gt7rQTRBAw5617A
 YfmRViCoO21Z3XwZ33TGiCt92e_UOqfrP30mdEYnJYs09ulU1xBLj
 8TjXOLR1k0&amp;t=633285035850304000"
 type="text/javascript"></script>
    <div>
        <script type="text/javascript">
//<![CDATA[
Sys.WebForms.PageRequestManager._initialize('ScriptManager1',
    'form1', [], [], [], 90);
//]]>
```

```
</script>
    </div>
</form>
</body>
</html>
```

The page output shows that a number of JavaScript libraries load with the page. Also notice that the scripts' sources are dynamically registered and available through the HTTP handler provided through the `ScriptResource.axd` handler.

If you are interested in seeing the contents of the JavaScript libraries, you can use the `src` *attribute's URL in the address bar of your browser, and you will be prompted to download the JavaScript file that is referenced. You will be prompted to save the* `ScriptResource.axd` *file, but you can rename it to use a* `.txt` *or* `.js` *extension if you want.*

An interesting point about the ScriptManager is that it deals with the scripts that are sent to the client by taking the extra step to compress them.

The ScriptManagerProxy Control

The ScriptManagerProxy control was actually introduced in Chapter 5, as this control deals specifically with master pages. As with the ScriptManager control covered in the previous section, you need a single ScriptManager control on each page that is going to be working with ASP.NET AJAX. However, with that said, the big question is what do you do when you are using master pages? Do you need to put the ScriptManager control on the master page, and how does this work with the content pages that use the master page?

When you create a new master page from the Add New Item dialog, you simply just select the typical Master Page option and just change the code a bit in order to deal with Ajax. This is demonstrated here in Listing 18-10.

LISTING 18-10: The AJAX Master Page

Available for download on Wrox.com

```
<%@ Master Language="VB" %>

<script runat="server">

</script>

<html xmlns="http://www.w3.org/1999/xhtml">
<head runat="server">
    <title>Untitled Page</title>
    <asp:ContentPlaceHolder id="head" runat="server">
    </asp:ContentPlaceHolder>
</head>
<body>
    <form id="form1" runat="server">
    <div>
        <asp:ScriptManager ID="ScriptManager1" runat="server" />
        <asp:ContentPlaceHolder id="ContentPlaceHolder1"
         runat="server">

        </asp:ContentPlaceHolder>
    </div>
    </form>
</body>
</html>
```

This code shows that, indeed, a ScriptManager control is on the page and that this page will be added to each and every content page that uses this master page. You do not need to do anything special to a content page to use the ASP.NET AJAX capabilities provided by the master page. Instead, you can create a content page that is no different from any other content page that you might be used to creating.

However, if you want to modify the ScriptManager control that is on the master page in any way, then you must add a ScriptManagerProxy control to the content page, as shown in Listing 18-11.

LISTING 18-11: Adding to the ScriptManager control from the content page

Available for download on Wrox.com

```
<%@ Page Language="VB" MasterPageFile="~/AJAXMaster.master" %>

<asp:Content ID="Content1" ContentPlaceHolderID="head"
 Runat="Server">
</asp:Content>
<asp:Content ID="Content2"
 ContentPlaceHolderID="ContentPlaceHolder1"
 Runat="Server">
 <asp:ScriptManagerProxy ID="ScriptManagerProxy1" runat="server">
     <Scripts>
         <asp:ScriptReference Path="myOtherScript.js" />
     </Scripts>
 </asp:ScriptManagerProxy>
</asp:Content>
```

In this case, the content page adds to the ScriptManager control that is on the master page by interjecting a script reference from the content page. If you use a ScriptManagerProxy control on a content page and a ScriptManager control does not happen to be on the master page, then you will get an error.

The Timer Control

One common task when working with asynchronous Postbacks from your ASP.NET pages is that you might want these asynchronous Postbacks to occur at specific intervals in time. To accomplish this, you use the Timer control available from the AJAX Extensions part of the toolbox. A simple example to demonstrate how this control works involves putting some timestamps on your page and setting Postbacks to occur at specific timed intervals, as illustrated in Listing 18-12.

LISTING 18-12: Using the Timer control

Available for download on Wrox.com

```
<%@ Page Language="VB" %>

<script runat="server">
    Protected Sub Page_Load(ByVal sender As Object,
     ByVal e As System.EventArgs)
        If Not Page.IsPostBack
           Label1.Text = DateTime.Now.ToString()
        End If
    End Sub

    Protected Sub Timer1_Tick(ByVal sender As Object,
     ByVal e As System.EventArgs)
        Label1.Text = DateTime.Now.ToString()
    End Sub
</script>
<html xmlns="http://www.w3.org/1999/xhtml">
<head runat="server">
    <title>Timer Example</title>
</head>
<body>
    <form id="form1" runat="server">
```

```
        <div>
            <asp:ScriptManager ID="ScriptManager1" runat="server" />
            <asp:UpdatePanel ID="UpdatePanel1" runat="server">
                <ContentTemplate>
                    <asp:Label ID="Label1" runat="server"
                     Text="Label"></asp:Label>
                    <asp:Timer ID="Timer1" runat="server"
                     OnTick="Timer1_Tick"
                     Interval="10000">
                    </asp:Timer>
                </ContentTemplate>
            </asp:UpdatePanel>
        </div>
        </form>
    </body>
    </html>
```

C#

```
    <%@ Page Language="C#" %>

    <script runat="server">
        protected void Page_Load(object sender, EventArgs e)
        {
            if (!Page.IsPostBack) {
               Label1.Text = DateTime.Now.ToString();
            }
        }

        protected void Timer1_Tick(object sender, EventArgs e)
        {
            Label1.Text = DateTime.Now.ToString();
        }
    </script>
```

In this case, only three controls are on the page. The first is the ScriptManager control, followed by a Label and the Timer control. When this page loads for the first time, the Label control is populated with the `DateTime` value through the invocation of the `Page_Load` event handler. After this initial load of the `DateTime` value to the Label control, the Timer control takes care of changing this value.

The `OnTick` attribute from the Timer control enables you to accomplish this task. It points to the function triggered when the time span specified in the `Interval` attribute is reached.

The `Interval` attribute is set to `10000`, which is 10,000 milliseconds (remember that there are 1,000 milliseconds to every second). This means that every 10 seconds an asynchronous Postback is performed and the `Timer1_Tick()` function is called.

When you run this page, you see the time change on the page every 10 seconds.

The UpdatePanel Control

The UpdatePanel server control is an AJAX-specific control that is part of ASP.NET 4. The UpdatePanel control is the control that you are likely to use the most when dealing with AJAX. This control preserves the Postback model and allows you to perform a partial page render.

The UpdatePanel control is a container control, which means that it does not actually have UI-specific items associated with it. It is a way to trigger a partial page Postback and update only the portion of the page that the UpdatePanel specifies.

The <ContentTemplate> Element

You have a couple of ways to deal with the controls on the page that initiate the asynchronous page Postbacks. The first is by far the simplest and is shown in Listing 18-13.

LISTING 18-13: Putting the triggers inside of the UpdatePanel control

Available for download on Wrox.com

```
<%@ Page Language="VB" %>

<script runat="server">
    Protected Sub Button1_Click(ByVal sender As Object,
       ByVal e As System.EventArgs)

       Label1.Text = "This button was clicked on " & _
           DateTime.Now.ToString()
    End Sub
</script>

<html xmlns="http://www.w3.org/1999/xhtml">
<head runat="server">
    <title>UpdatePanel Control</title>
</head>
<body>
    <form id="form1" runat="server">
    <div>
        <asp:ScriptManager ID="ScriptManager1" runat="server">
        </asp:ScriptManager>
        <asp:UpdatePanel ID="UpdatePanel1" runat="server">
            <ContentTemplate>
                <asp:Label ID="Label1" runat="server"></asp:Label>
                <br />
                <br />
                <asp:Button ID="Button1" runat="server"
                 Text="Click to initiate async request"
                 OnClick="Button1_Click" />
            </ContentTemplate>
        </asp:UpdatePanel>
    </div>
    </form>
</body>
</html>
```

C#

```
<%@ Page Language="C#" %>

<script runat="server">
    protected void Button1_Click(object sender, EventArgs e)
    {
        Label1.Text = "This button was clicked on " +
          DateTime.Now.ToString();
    }
</script>
```

In this case, the Label and Button server controls are contained within the UpdatePanel server control. The `<asp:UpdatePanel>` element has two possible sub-elements: `<ContentTemplate>` and `<Triggers>`. Any content that needs to be changed with the asynchronous page Postbacks should be contained within the `<ContentTemplate>` section of the UpdatePanel control.

By default, any type of control trigger (something that would normally trigger a page Postback) that is contained within the `<ContentTemplate>` section instead causes the asynchronous page Postback. That means, in the case of Listing 18-13, the button on the page will trigger an asynchronous page Postback instead of a full-page Postback. Each click on the button changes the time displayed in the Label control.

The <Triggers> Element

Listing 18-13 demonstrates one of the big issues with this model: When the asynchronous Postback occurs, you are not only sending the date/time value for the Label control, but also sending back the entire code for the button that is on the page, as presented here:

```
265|updatePanel|UpdatePanel1|
    <span id="Label1">This button was clicked on 11/23/2009 11:45:21 AM</span>
    <br />
    <br />
    <input type="submit" name="Button1" value="Click to initiate async request"
     id="Button1" />
|164|hiddenField|__VIEWSTATE|/wEPDwUKLTU2NzQ4MzIwMw9kFgICBA9kFgICAw9kFgJmD2QWAgIBDw
8WAh4EVGV4dAUxVGhpcyBidXR0b24gd2FzIGNsaWNrZWQgb24gMTEvMTgvMjAwNyAxMTo0NToyMSBBTWRkZ
KJIG4WwhyQvUwPCX4PxI5FEUFtC|48|hiddenField|__EVENTVALIDATION|/wEWAgL43YXdBwKM54rGBl
I52OYVl/McOV61BYd/3wSj+RkD|0|asyncPostBackControlIDs|||0|postBackControlIDs|||13|
updatePanelIDs||tUpdatePanel1|0|childUpdatePanelIDs|||12|panelsToRefreshIDs||
UpdatePanel1|2|asyncPostBackTimeout||90|22|formAction||SimpleUpdatePanel.aspx|11|
pageTitle||UpdatePanel|
```

This bit of code that is sent back to the client via the asynchronous Postback shows that the entire section contained within the UpdatePanel control is reissued. You can slim down your pages by including only the portions of the page that are actually updating. If you take the button outside of the `<ContentTemplate>` section of the UpdatePanel control, then you must include a `<Triggers>` section within the control.

The reason for this is that although the content that you want to change with the asynchronous Postback is all contained within the `<ContentTemplate>` section, you need to tie up a page event to cause the Postback to occur. This is how the `<Triggers>` section of the UpdatePanel control is used. You use this section of the control to specify the various triggers that initiate an asynchronous page Postback. Using the `<Triggers>` element within the UpdatePanel control, you can rewrite Listing 18-13, as shown in Listing 18-14.

LISTING 18-14: Using a trigger to cause the asynchronous page Postback

Available for download on Wrox.com

VB

```
<%@ Page Language="VB" %>

<script runat="server">
    Protected Sub Button1_Click(ByVal sender As Object,
       ByVal e As System.EventArgs)

       Label1.Text = "This button was clicked on " & _
         DateTime.Now.ToString()
    End Sub
</script>

<html xmlns="http://www.w3.org/1999/xhtml">
<head runat="server">
    <title>UpdatePanel</title>
</head>
<body>
    <form id="form1" runat="server">
    <div>
        <asp:ScriptManager ID="ScriptManager1" runat="server">
        </asp:ScriptManager>
        <asp:UpdatePanel ID="UpdatePanel1" runat="server">
            <ContentTemplate>
                <asp:Label ID="Label1" runat="server"></asp:Label>
            </ContentTemplate>
            <Triggers>
                <asp:AsyncPostBackTrigger ControlID="Button1"
                 EventName="Click" />
            </Triggers>
        </asp:UpdatePanel>
        <br />
        <br />
        <asp:Button ID="Button1" runat="server"
         Text="Click to initiate async request"
         OnClick="Button1_Click" />
```

continues

LISTING 18-14 *(continued)*

```
        </div>
        </form>
</body>
</html>
```

C#

```
<%@ Page Language="C#" %>

<script runat="server">

    protected void Button1_Click(object sender, EventArgs e)
    {
        Label1.Text = "This button was clicked on " +
          DateTime.Now.ToString();
    }
</script>
```

In this case, the Button control and the HTML elements are outside of the `<ContentTemplate>` section of the UpdatePanel control and, therefore, will not be sent back to the client for each asynchronous page Postback. The only item contained in the `<ContentTemplate>` section is the only item on the page that needs to change with the Postbacks — the Label control. Tying this all together is the `<Triggers>` section.

The `<Triggers>` section can contain two possible controls: AsyncPostBackTrigger and PostBackTrigger. In this case, the AsyncPostBackTrigger is used. The PostBackTrigger control will cause a full-page Postback, whereas the AsyncPostBackTrigger control will cause only an asynchronous page Postback (obviously, as described by the names of the controls).

As you can see from the example in Listing 18-14, which uses the AsyncPostBackTrigger element, only two attributes are used to tie the Button control to the trigger for the asynchronous Postback: the `ControlID` and the `EventName` attributes. The control you want to act as the initiator of the asynchronous page Postback is put here (the control's name as specified by the control's `ID` attribute). The `EventName` attribute's value is the name of the event for the control that is specified in the `ControlID` that you want to be called in the asynchronous request from the client. In this case, the Button control's `Click()` event is called, and this is the event that changes the value of the control that resides within the `<ContentTemplate>` section of the UpdatePanel control.

Running this page and clicking on the button gives you a smaller asynchronous response back to the client:

```
 108|updatePanel|UpdatePanel1|
   <span id="Label1">This button was clicked on 11/18/2007 11:58:56 AM</span>
|164|hiddenField|__VIEWSTATE|/wEPDwUKMjA2NjQ2MDYzNw9kFgICBA9kFgICAw9kFgJmD2QWAgIBDw
8WAh4EVGV4dAUxVGhpcyBidXR0b24gd2FzIGNsaWNrZWQgb24gMTEvMTgvMjAwNyAxMTo1ODo1NiBBTWRkZ
PJA9uj9wwRaasgTrZo85rVvLnoi|48|hiddenField|__EVENTVALIDATION|/wEWAgKK3YDTDAKM54rGBq
rbjV4/u4ks3aKsn7Xz8xNFE8G/|7|asyncPostBackControlIDs||Button1|0|postBackControlIDs|
||13|updatePanelIDs||tUpdatePanel1|0|childUpdatePanelIDs|||12|panelsToRefreshIDs||
UpdatePanel1|2|asyncPostBackTimeout||90|22|formAction||SimpleUpdatePanel.aspx|11|
pageTitle||UpdatePanel|
```

Although not considerably smaller than the previous example, it is, in fact, just a bit smaller — the size similarity is really due to the size of the page used in this example (pages that are more voluminous would show more dramatic improvements). Pages with heavy content associated with them can show some dramatic size reductions, depending on how you structure your pages with the UpdatePanel control.

Building Triggers Using Visual Studio 2010

If you like to work on the design surface of Visual Studio when building your ASP.NET pages, then you will find that there is good support for building your ASP.NET AJAX pages, including the creation of triggers in the UpdatePanel control. To see this in action, place a single UpdatePanel server control on your page and view the control in the Properties dialog within Visual Studio. The Triggers item in the list has a button next to it that allows you to modify the items associated with it, as illustrated in Figure 18-11.

Clicking on this button in the Properties dialog launches the UpdatePanelTrigger Collection Editor, as shown in Figure 18-12. This editor allows you to add any number of triggers and to associate them to a control and a control event very easily.

FIGURE 18-11

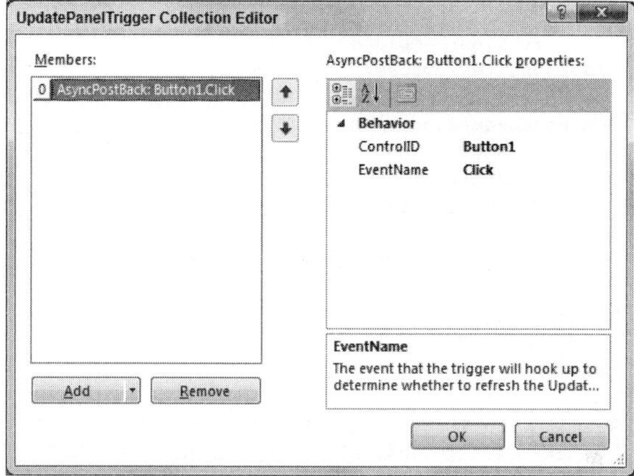

FIGURE 18-12

Clicking OK adds the trigger to the `<Triggers>` section of your UpdatePanel control.

The UpdateProgress Control

The final server control in the AJAX Extensions section of Visual Studio 2010 is the UpdateProgress control. Some asynchronous Postbacks take some time to execute because of the size of the response or because of the computing time required to get a result together to send back to the client. The UpdateProgress control allows you to provide a visual signifier to the clients to show that, indeed, work is being done and that they will get results soon (and that the browser didn't just lock up).

Listing 18-15 shows a textual implementation of the UpdateProgress control.

LISTING 18-15: Using the UpdateProgress control to show a text message to the client

```
<%@ Page Language="VB" %>

<script runat="server">
    Protected Sub Button1_Click(ByVal sender As Object,
       ByVal e As System.EventArgs)
       System.Threading.Thread.Sleep(10000)
       Label1.Text = "This button was clicked on" & _
         DateTime.Now.ToString()
    End Sub
</script>

<html xmlns="http://www.w3.org/1999/xhtml">
<head runat="server">
    <title>UpdatePanel</title>
</head>
<body>
    <form id="form1" runat="server">
    <div>
        <asp:ScriptManager ID="ScriptManager1" runat="server">
        </asp:ScriptManager>
```

continues

LISTING 18-15 *(continued)*

```
            <asp:UpdateProgress ID="UpdateProgress1" runat="server">
                <ProgressTemplate>
                    An update is occurring…
                </ProgressTemplate>
            </asp:UpdateProgress>
            <asp:UpdatePanel ID="UpdatePanel1" runat="server"
             UpdateMode="Conditional">
                <ContentTemplate>
                    <asp:Label ID="Label1" runat="server"></asp:Label>
                </ContentTemplate>
                <Triggers>
                    <asp:AsyncPostBackTrigger ControlID="Button1"
                     EventName="Click" />
                </Triggers>
            </asp:UpdatePanel>
            <br />
            <br />
            <asp:Button ID="Button1" runat="server"
             Text="Click to initiate async request"
             OnClick="Button1_Click" />
        </div>
        </form>
    </body>
    </html>
```

C#

```
    <%@ Page Language="C#" %>
    <script runat="server">

        protected void Button1_Click(object sender, EventArgs e)
        {

            System.Threading.Thread.Sleep(10000);
            Label1.Text = "This button was clicked on" +
              DateTime.Now.ToString();
        }
    </script>
```

To add some delay to the response (to simulate a long-running computer process), the `Thread.Sleep()` method is called. From here, you add an UpdateProgress control to the part of the page where you want the update message to be presented. In this case, the UpdateProgress control was added above the UpdatePanel server control. This control does not go inside the UpdatePanel control; instead, it sits outside of the control. However, like the UpdatePanel control, the UpdateProgress control is a template control.

The UpdateProgress control has only a single sub-element: the `<ProgressTemplate>` element. Whatever you place in this section of the control will appear when the UpdateProgress control is triggered. In this case, the only item present in this section of the control is some text. When you run this page, the update shown in Figure 18-13 appears.

FIGURE 18-13

The text appears immediately in this case and will not disappear until the asynchronous Postback has finished. The code you put in the `<ProgressTemplate>` section is actually contained in the page, but its display is turned off through CSS.

```
<div id="UpdateProgress1" style="display:none;">
   An update is occurring…
</div>
```

Controlling When the Message Appears

Right now, the UpdateProgress appears as soon as the button is clicked. However, some of your processes might not take that long, and you might not always want a progress notification going out to the client. The UpdateProgress control includes a `DisplayAfter` attribute, which allows you to control when the progress update message appears. Listing 18-16 shows the use of the `DisplayAfter` attribute.

LISTING 18-16: Using the DisplayAfter attribute

```
<asp:UpdateProgress ID="UpdateProgress1" runat="server" DisplayAfter="5000">
   <ProgressTemplate>
      An update is occurring...
   </ProgressTemplate>
</asp:UpdateProgress>
```

The value of the `DisplayAfter` property is a number that represents the number of milliseconds that the UpdateProgress control will wait until it displays what is contained within the `<ProgressTemplate>` section. The code in Listing 18-16 specifies that the text found in the `<ProgressTemplate>` section will not be displayed for 5,000 milliseconds (5 seconds).

Adding an Image to the <ProcessTemplate>

The previous examples, which use the UpdateProgress control, use this control with text, but you can put anything you want within this template control. For instance, you can put a spinning wheel image that will show the end user that the request is being processed. Listing 18-17 shows the use of the image.

LISTING 18-17: Using an image in the <ProcessTemplate> section

```
<asp:UpdateProgress ID="UpdateProgress1" runat="server"
 DisplayAfter="5000">
   <ProgressTemplate>
      <asp:Image ID="Image1" runat="server"
       ImageUrl="</spinningwheel.gif" />
   </ProgressTemplate>
</asp:UpdateProgress>
```

Just as in the text approach, the code for the image is already placed on the client's page instance and is just turned off via CSS.

```
<div id="UpdateProgress1" style="display:none;">
   <img id="Image1" src="spinningwheel.gif" style="border-width:0px;" />
</div>
```

USING MULTIPLE UPDATEPANEL CONTROLS

So far, this chapter has showed you how to work with a single UpdatePanel control, but it is important to realize that you can have multiple UpdatePanel controls on a single page. This, in the end, gives you the ability to control the output to specific regions of the page when you want.

Listing 18-18 presents an example of using more than a single UpdatePanel control.

LISTING 18-18: Using more than one UpdatePanel control

Available for download on Wrox.com

```
<%@ Page Language="VB" %>

<script runat="server">
    Protected Sub Button1_Click(ByVal sender As Object,
       ByVal e As System.EventArgs)

       Label1.Text = "Label1 was populated on " & _
         DateTime.Now.ToString()
       Label2.Text = "Label2 was populated on " & _
         DateTime.Now.ToString()
    End Sub
</script>

<html xmlns="http://www.w3.org/1999/xhtml">
<head runat="server">
    <title>Multiple UpdatePanel Controls</title>
</head>
<body>
    <form id="form1" runat="server">
    <div>
        <asp:ScriptManager ID="ScriptManager1" runat="server">
        </asp:ScriptManager>
        <asp:UpdatePanel ID="UpdatePanel1" runat="server">
            <ContentTemplate>
                <asp:Label ID="Label1" runat="server"></asp:Label>
            </ContentTemplate>
            <Triggers>
                <asp:AsyncPostBackTrigger ControlID="Button1"
                 EventName="Click" />
            </Triggers>
        </asp:UpdatePanel>
        <asp:UpdatePanel ID="UpdatePanel2" runat="server">
            <ContentTemplate>
                <asp:Label ID="Label2" runat="server"></asp:Label>
            </ContentTemplate>
        </asp:UpdatePanel>
        <br />
        <br />
        <asp:Button ID="Button1" runat="server"
         Text="Click to initiate async request"
         OnClick="Button1_Click" />
    </div>
    </form>
</body>
</html>
```

C#

```
<%@ Page Language="C#" %>

<script runat="server">
    protected void Button1_Click(object sender, EventArgs e)
    {
        Label1.Text = "Label1 was populated on " + DateTime.Now;
        Label2.Text = "Label2 was populated on " + DateTime.Now;
    }
</script>
```

This page is interesting. It has two UpdatePanel controls: `UpdatePanel1` and `UpdatePanel2`. Both of these controls contain a single Label control that at one point can take a date/time value from a server response.

The `UpdatePanel1` control has an associated trigger: the Button control on the page. When this button is clicked, the `Button1_Click()` event triggers and does its job. If you run this page, both of the UpdatePanel controls are updated according to the `Button1_Click()` event, as illustrated in Figure 18-14.

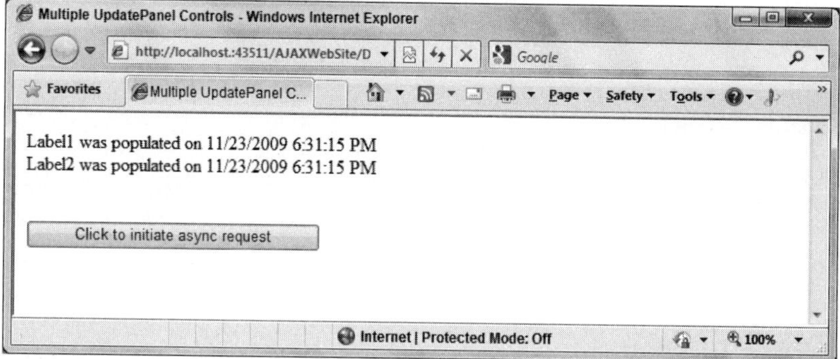

FIGURE 18-14

Both UpdatePanel sections were updated with the `button-click` event because, by default, all UpdatePanel controls on a single page update with *each* asynchronous Postback that occurs. This means that the Postback that occurred with the `Button1` button control also causes a Postback to occur with the `UpdatePanel2` control.

You can actually control this behavior through the UpdatePanel's `UpdateMode` property. The `UpdateMode` property can take two possible enumerations — `Always` and `Conditional`. If you do not set this property, then it uses the value of `Always`, meaning that each UpdatePanel control always updates with each asynchronous request.

The other option is to set the property to `Conditional`. This means that the UpdatePanel updates only if one of the trigger conditions is met. For an example of this, change the UpdatePanel controls on the page so that they are now using an `UpdateMode` of `Conditional`, as shown in Listing 18-19.

LISTING 18-19: Using more than one UpdatePanel control

Available for download on Wrox.com

```
<%@ Page Language="VB" %>

<script runat="server">
    Protected Sub Button1_Click(ByVal sender As Object, _
       ByVal e As System.EventArgs)

       Label1.Text = "Label1 was populated on " & _
         DateTime.Now.ToString()
       Label2.Text = "Label2 was populated on " & _
         DateTime.Now.ToString()
    End Sub
</script>

<html xmlns="http://www.w3.org/1999/xhtml">
<head runat="server">
    <title>Multiple UpdatePanel Controls</title>
</head>
<body>
    <form id="form1" runat="server">
    <div>
        <asp:ScriptManager ID="ScriptManager1" runat="server">
        </asp:ScriptManager>
```

continues

LISTING 18-19 *(continued)*

```
        <asp:UpdatePanel ID="UpdatePanel1" runat="server"
         UpdateMode="Conditional">
            <ContentTemplate>
                <asp:Label ID="Label1" runat="server"></asp:Label>
            </ContentTemplate>
            <Triggers>
                <asp:AsyncPostBackTrigger ControlID="Button1"
                 EventName="Click" />
            </Triggers>
        </asp:UpdatePanel>
        <asp:UpdatePanel ID="UpdatePanel2" runat="server"
         UpdateMode="Conditional">
            <ContentTemplate>
                <asp:Label ID="Label2" runat="server"></asp:Label>
            </ContentTemplate>
        </asp:UpdatePanel>
        <br />
        <br />
        <asp:Button ID="Button1" runat="server"
         Text="Click to initiate async request"
         OnClick="Button1_Click" />
    </div>
    </form>
</body>
</html>
```

C#

```
<%@ Page Language="C#" %>

<script runat="server">
    protected void Button1_Click(object sender, EventArgs e)
    {
        Label1.Text = "Label1 was populated on " + DateTime.Now;
        Label2.Text = "Label2 was populated on " + DateTime.Now;
    }
</script>
```

Now that both of the UpdatePanel controls are set to have an `UpdateMode` of `Conditional`, when running this page, you will see the results presented in Figure 18-15.

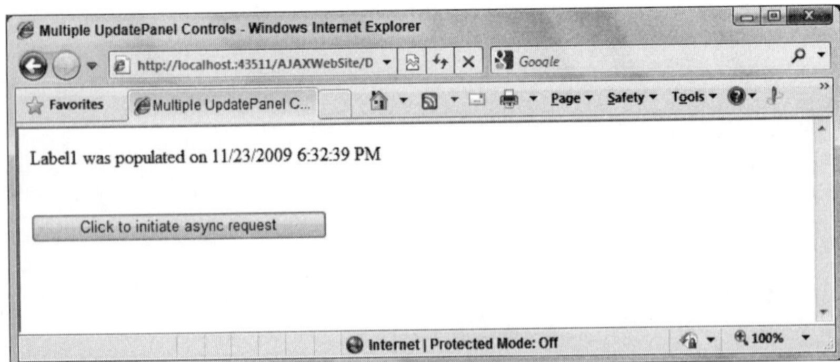

FIGURE 18-15

In this case, only the right Label control, `Label1`, was updated with the asynchronous request even though the `Button1_Click()` event tries to change the values of both `Label1` and `Label2`. The reason for this is that the `UpdatePanel2` control had no trigger that was met.

WORKING WITH PAGE HISTORY

One issue when working with any AJAX page is that when the end user clicks the browser's Back button, it destroys the asynchronous requests that are occurring between the current page and the server and any kind of state that you might be managing between these requests.

Prior to ASP.NET 3.5 SP1, if you had a process of working with AJAX in the page and you clicked the Back button within the browser, you would go to the page that was just prior to the AJAX-enabled page, regardless of the asynchronous page requests that occurred prior to this action.

Also, if your first page in navigation is a series of asynchronous page requests, as an end user, you will never see the option to click on the Back button of the page, even if you work your way quite far into the navigation that the page provides.

Ever since the release of ASP.NET 3.5 SP1, you have the capability to work with the back history of your application. It isn't as simple as just activating something; it will take a little bit of coding to accomplish what you want. You will need to work through a process of telling the ASP.NET page what state you are going to keep track of as you allow end users to navigate with the Back and Forward buttons on the browser.

To see this scenario in action, create a simple page that uses AJAX. This page is presented in Listing 18-20.

LISTING 18-20: Building a basic ASP.NET AJAX page

Available for download on Wrox.com

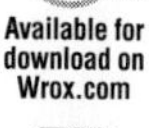

VB

```
<%@ Page Language="VB" %>

<script runat="server">
    Protected Sub Button1_Click(ByVal sender As Object,
       ByVal e As System.EventArgs)

       PopulateFields(TextBox1.Text)

    End Sub

    Private Sub PopulateFields(ByVal InputName As String)
       If InputName Is Nothing Then
          Label1.Text = "Hello there. What is your name?"
       Else
          Label1.Text = "Hello there " & InputName
       End If
    End Sub
</script>

<html xmlns="http://www.w3.org/1999/xhtml">
<head runat="server">
    <title>Ajax Page</title>
</head>
<body>
    <form id="form1" runat="server">
    <div>
        <asp:ScriptManager ID="ScriptManager1" runat="server">
        </asp:ScriptManager>
        <asp:UpdatePanel ID="UpdatePanel1" runat="server">
            <ContentTemplate>
                <asp:Label ID="Label1" runat="server"
                 Text="Hello there. What is your name?">
                </asp:Label><br />
                <br />
                <asp:TextBox ID="TextBox1"
                 runat="server"></asp:TextBox><br />
                <asp:Button ID="Button1" runat="server"
```

continues

LISTING 18-20 *(continued)*

```
                    Text="Submit Name"
                    OnClick="Button1_Click" />
                </ContentTemplate>
            </asp:UpdatePanel>
        </div>
        </form>
</body>
</html>
```

C#

```
<%@ Page Language="C#" %>

<script runat="server">

    protected void Button1_Click(object sender, EventArgs e)
    {
        PopulateFields(TextBox1.Text);
    }

    private void PopulateFields(string InputName)
    {
        if(InputName == null)
        {
            Label1.Text = "Hello there. What is your name?";
        }
        else
        {
            Label1.Text = "Hello there " + InputName;
        }
    }

</script>
```

This is a standard ASP.NET AJAX page, and nothing tricky is going on here. In this case, you use AJAX to enter your name into the text box, and then this name is put into the Label control that is on the page. However, if you enter more than one name, you will find that it *seems* as if you are working through multiple pages, but the browser's navigation buttons (the Back and Forward buttons) are not enabled, and you do not have the option to work back to the previous items you entered into the text box.

Unfortunately, end users expect this type of behavior, so the new capability adds the back history to these types of pages.

If you are using ASP.NET 3.5 SP1 or ASP.NET 4 and you look at the ScriptManager control that is on the page, you will notice a property called `EnableHistory`. It is set to `False` by default, but for this example, you want to set this property to `True`.

The changes made to the `EnableHistory` property are not the only change you must put into place when working with the back history on ASP.NET AJAX pages. You need to instruct ASP.NET on how to remember the previous page and what to do when a user navigates to a previous page (or even a later page if the user has clicked the Back button a few times).

You can specify easily the history points to remember and the indexes to use when you are on the page. Listing 18-21 shows a complete instance of a page that remembers the state for users working with the Back and Forward buttons on the browser.

LISTING 18-21: Adding history capabilities

```
<%@ Page Language="VB" %>

<script runat="server">

    Protected Sub Button1_Click(ByVal sender As Object,
      ByVal e As EventArgs)
```

```
        PopulateFields(TextBox1.Text)
    End Sub

    Private Sub PopulateFields(ByVal InputName As String)
        If InputName Is Nothing Then
            Label1.Text = "Hello there. What is your name?"
        Else
            Label1.Text = "Hello there " & InputName
        End If

        If ScriptManager1.IsInAsyncPostBack AndAlso
          (Not ScriptManager1.IsNavigating) Then
            ScriptManager1.AddHistoryPoint("myIndexPoint",
              InputName,
              String.Format("Entering name: {0}", InputName))
        Else
            TextBox1.Text = InputName
            Page.Title = String.Format("Entering name: {0}",
            InputName)
        End If
    End Sub

    Protected Sub ScriptManager1_Navigate(ByVal sender As Object,
      ByVal e As HistoryEventArgs)
        PopulateFields(e.State("myIndexPoint"))
    End Sub

</script>

<html xmlns="http://www.w3.org/1999/xhtml">
<head runat="server">
    <title>Ajax Page</title>
</head>
<body>
    <form id="form1" runat="server">
    <div>
        <asp:ScriptManager ID="ScriptManager1" runat="server"
         EnableHistory="True"
         OnNavigate="ScriptManager1_Navigate">
        </asp:ScriptManager>
        <asp:UpdatePanel ID="UpdatePanel1" runat="server">
            <ContentTemplate>
                <asp:Label ID="Label1" runat="server"
                 Text="Hello there. What is your name?">
                </asp:Label><br />
                <br />
                <asp:TextBox ID="TextBox1"
                 runat="server"></asp:TextBox><br />
                <asp:Button ID="Button1" runat="server"
                 Text="Submit Name"
                 OnClick="Button1_Click" />
            </ContentTemplate>
        </asp:UpdatePanel>
    </div>
    </form>
</body>
</html>
```

C#

```
<%@ Page Language="C#" %>

<script runat="server">

    protected void Button1_Click(object sender, EventArgs e)
    {
```

continues

LISTING 18-21 *(continued)*

```
            PopulateFields(TextBox1.Text);
        }

        private void PopulateFields(string InputName)
        {
            if(InputName == null)
            {
                Label1.Text = "Hello there. What is your name?";
            }
            else
            {
                Label1.Text = "Hello there " + InputName;
            }

            if (ScriptManager1.IsInAsyncPostBack &&
                !ScriptManager1.IsNavigating)
            {
                ScriptManager1.AddHistoryPoint("myIndexPoint", InputName,
                  string.Format("Entering name: {0}", InputName));
            }
            else
            {
                TextBox1.Text = InputName;
                Page.Title = string.Format("Entering name: {0}",
                  InputName);
            }
        }

        protected void ScriptManager1_Navigate(object sender,
           HistoryEventArgs e)
        {
            PopulateFields(e.State["myIndexPoint"]);
        }

    </script>
```

Now, looking at the event that occurs when the button on the page is clicked, you can see there are some changes to it to deal with the registration of the history point:

```
If ScriptManager1.IsInAsyncPostBack AndAlso
  (Not ScriptManager1.IsNavigating) Then
    ScriptManager1.AddHistoryPoint("myIndexPoint", InputName,
      String.Format("Entering name: {0}", InputName))
Else
    TextBox1.Text = InputName
    Page.Title = String.Format("Entering name: {0}", InputName)
End If
```

A check occurs to see whether the ScriptManager control on the page is performing an asynchronous Postback or is not navigating. If either of these is the case, then a history point is registered using the `AddHistoryPoint()` event. The idea of the `AddHistoryPoint()` call is that you are able to add a key/value pair to define the state of the index that you want the page to remember. In this case, the key is the string `myIndexPoint` and the value is what was provided from the Textbox server control that is on the page. The last option in the list of input parameters is the title to use for the page. This page title will appear in the browser on the page tab (if you have page tabs) as well as in the list of navigation items in the list of option items for the Back and Forward buttons.

In addition to calling `AddHistoryPoint()` with a single key/value pair, you can also pass in an entire set of them using the `NameValueCollection` object.

So, in the case of this example, the key `myIndexPoint` is used along with the value of what was placed in the `TextBox1` server control, and this name is also used in the page title.

After you have this code in place, you must also create a `Navigate()` method off the ScriptManager control that instructs what should be done when one of the buttons is used. You use this method to provide the index of the item that you are working with:

```
Protected Sub ScriptManager1_Navigate(ByVal sender As Object,
  ByVal e As HistoryEventArgs)
    PopulateFields(e.State("myIndexPoint"))
End Sub
```

Here, you can see that `HistoryEventArgs` provides you with the access to the items that you have registered.

Running this page now, sequentially entering in names, and clicking on the page's button control provides you with a history of items in the Back button list of options. You are able also to navigate back to this item (or forward, if that's what is needed), and you will be returned to the page that you were working with. This list from the Back button is illustrated in Figure 18-16.

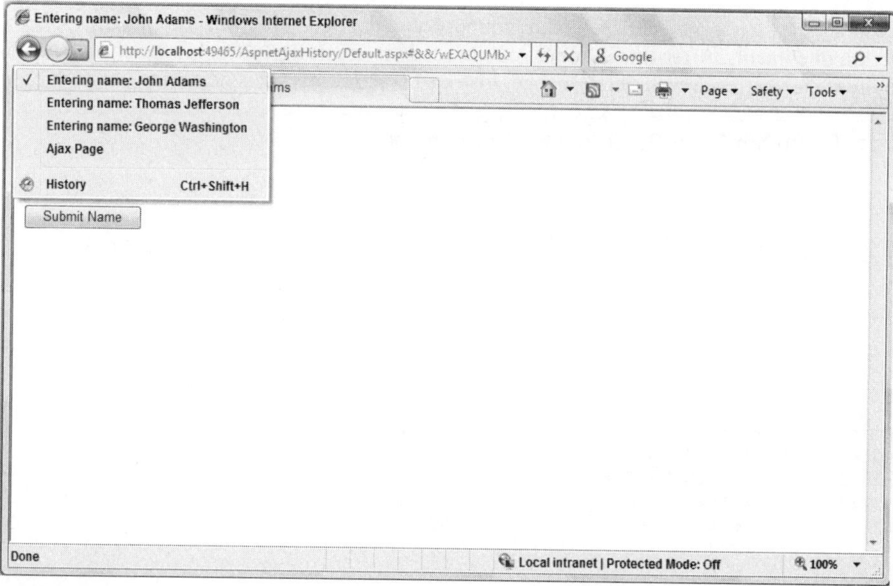

FIGURE 18-16

From the URL on the page, you are able to see how the state is stored. In this case, you end up with something similar to the following:

```
http://localhost:4465/AjaxBackHisory/Default.aspx#&&/
  wEXAQUMbXlJbmRleFBvaW50BQpCaWxsIEV2amVuOW812mPjenfD0898ad+mhcy6EIw=
```

Notice that the index point is encrypted in the URL. This is the default behavior, although, as with most things in ASP.NET, you can change this behavior. To change it, from the ScriptManager control, you set the `EnableSecureHistoryState` property to `False`.

```
<asp:ScriptManager ID="ScriptManager1" runat="server" EnableHistory="True"
  OnNavigate="ScriptManager1_Navigate" EnableSecureHistoryState="False">
```

With this code in place, you get a URL something like the following:

```
http://localhost:4465/AjaxBackHisory/Default.aspx#&&myIndexPoint=Bill+Evjen
```

SCRIPT COMBINING

By default, ASP.NET AJAX pages sometimes download a number of different scripts for the page that is being viewed. When they are being downloaded separately, the performance is worse overall for the page.

The reason for this is that the browser must make a separate request for each of the scripts on the page. This means that the time to get all the scripts is longer than if it were done in one larger batch. Also, calling the scripts separately means that the overall load to the page that is being delivered is larger than otherwise.

ASP.NET 4 includes the capability to combine the scripts into a single request and response. This is termed *script combining*.

You are able to specify to ASP.NET the scripts that you want combined via the ScriptManager server control on your page. The trick is figuring out what scripts need to be combined, as it isn't always that apparent.

For this reason, there is a CodePlex project on the Internet that provides you a server control that you can place on the page to help you figure this out. The server control, ScriptReferenceProfiler, provides you with a list of the scripts that are required for the page. You can find this control at the following address:

```
http://www.codeplex.com/aspnet/Release/ProjectReleases.aspx?ReleaseId=13356
```

This project is a simple `.dll` file. Simply right-click within the toolbox of Visual Studio and select Choose Items from the provided menu. A dialog of new controls that you can add to the toolbox then appears. Click the Browse button and navigate to the `.dll` file that you just downloaded. After selecting it, click OK to add it to your collection of controls. After this is done, you are ready to create an example page that will be used to combine the scripts for better overall performance. Listing 18-22 presents this new page.

LISTING 18-22: Using the ScriptReferenceProfiler control

Available for download on Wrox.com

```
<%@ Page Language="vb" %>

<%@ Register Assembly="ScriptReferenceProfiler"
      Namespace="ScriptReferenceProfiler"
      TagPrefix="cc1" %>
<%@ Register assembly="AjaxControlToolkit"
      Namespace="AjaxControlToolkit" TagPrefix="asp" %>

<script runat="server">

    Protected Sub Button1_Click(ByVal sender As Object, _
      ByVal e As EventArgs)
        Label1.Text = "Hello " & TextBox1.Text & ".<br />" & _
          "Today is " & TextBox2.Text
    End Sub

</script>

<html xmlns="http://www.w3.org/1999/xhtml">
<head runat="server">
    <title>Script Combining</title>
</head>
<body>
    <form id="form1" runat="server">
    <div>
        <asp:ScriptManager ID="ScriptManager1" runat="server">
        </asp:ScriptManager>
        <asp:UpdatePanel ID="UpdatePanel1" runat="server">
            <ContentTemplate>
                What is your name?<br />
                <asp:TextBox ID="TextBox1"
                 runat="server"></asp:TextBox>
                <br /><br />
                What is today&#39;s date?<br />
                <asp:TextBox ID="TextBox2"
                 runat="server"></asp:TextBox>
                <asp:CalendarExtender ID="TextBox2_CalendarExtender"
                    runat="server"
```

```
                    Enabled="True" TargetControlID="TextBox2">
                </asp:CalendarExtender>
                <br /><br />
                <asp:Button ID="Button1" runat="server"
                 Text="Submit"
                 OnClick="Button1_Click" />
                <br /><br />
                <asp:Label ID="Label1" runat="server"></asp:Label>
            </ContentTemplate>
        </asp:UpdatePanel>
        <cc1:ScriptReferenceProfiler ID="ScriptReferenceProfiler1"
         runat="server" />
    </div>
    </form>
</body>
</html>
```

C#

```
<%@ Page Language="C#" %>

<%@ Register Assembly="ScriptReferenceProfiler"
      Namespace="ScriptReferenceProfiler"
      TagPrefix="cc1" %>
<%@ Register assembly="AjaxControlToolkit"
      Namespace="AjaxControlToolkit" TagPrefix="asp" %>

<script runat="server">
    protected void Button1_Click(object sender, EventArgs e)
    {
        Label1.Text = "Hello " + TextBox1.Text + ".<br />"
            + "Today is " + TextBox2.Text;
    }

</script>
```

This simple page uses AJAX to update a Label server control on the page based on some end user input into your page. The two text box controls that are on the page ask for the end user's name and the current date. Adding the ScriptReferenceProfiler control will add a couple of `@Register` page directives at the top of the page.

Running the page, you see the following results, as illustrated in Figure 18-17.

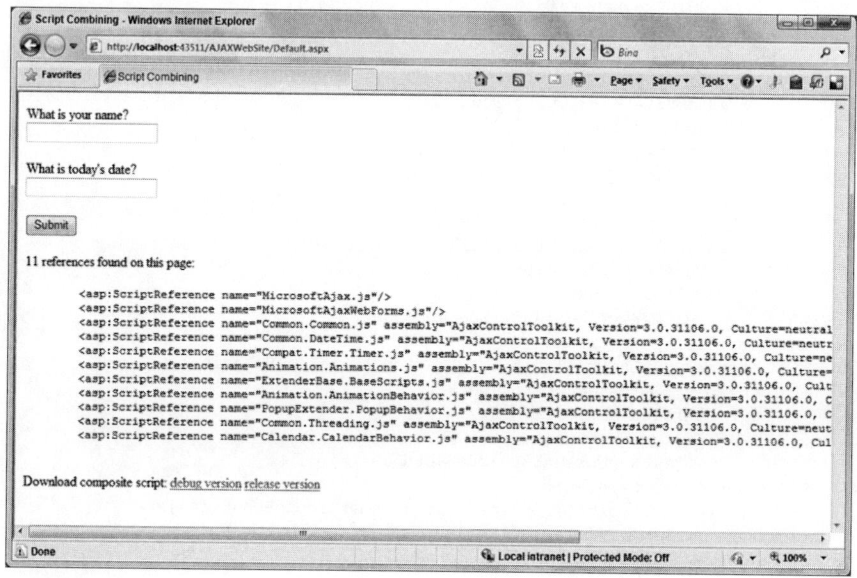

FIGURE 18-17

This page provides you with a list of scripts that are being called for on the page. You are now able to use the ScriptManager control on the page and specify that these are scripts that you are interested in loading with the script-combining feature of ASP.NET.

To accomplish this task, copy the provided configuration script from the page in the browser and paste this text into your ScriptManager control within the <CompositeScript> section (see Listing 18-23).

LISTING 18-23: Combining scripts using the ScriptManager server control

Available for download on Wrox.com

```
<html xmlns="http://www.w3.org/1999/xhtml">
<head runat="server">
    <title>Script Combining</title>
</head>
<body>
    <form id="form1" runat="server">
    <div>
        <asp:ScriptManager ID="ScriptManager1" runat="server">
            <CompositeScript>
                <Scripts>
                    <asp:ScriptReference name="MicrosoftAjax.js"/>
                      <asp:ScriptReference
                       name="MicrosoftAjaxWebForms.js"/>
                      <asp:ScriptReference
                       name="AjaxControlToolkit.Common.Common.js"
                         assembly="AjaxControlToolkit,
                           Version=3.0.311106.0,
                           Culture=neutral,
                           PublicKeyToken=28f01b0e84b6d53e"/>
                      <asp:ScriptReference
                       name="AjaxControlToolkit.Common.DateTime.js"
                         assembly="AjaxControlToolkit,
                           Version=3.0.311106.0,
                           Culture=neutral,
                           PublicKeyToken=28f01b0e84b6d53e"/>
                      <asp:ScriptReference
                       name="AjaxControlToolkit.Compat.Timer.Timer.js"
                         assembly="AjaxControlToolkit,
                           Version=3.0.311106.0,
                           Culture=neutral,
                           PublicKeyToken=28f01b0e84b6d53e"/>
                      <asp:ScriptReference
                       name="AjaxControlToolkit.Animation.Animations.js"
                         assembly="AjaxControlToolkit,
                           Version=3.0.311106.0,
                           Culture=neutral,
                           PublicKeyToken=28f01b0e84b6d53e"/>
                      <asp:ScriptReference
                       name="AjaxControlToolkit.ExtenderBase.BaseScripts.js"
                         assembly="AjaxControlToolkit,
                           Version=3.0.311106.0,
                           Culture=neutral,
                           PublicKeyToken=28f01b0e84b6d53e"/>
                      <asp:ScriptReference
                       name="AjaxControlToolkit.Animation.AnimationBehavior.js"
                         assembly="AjaxControlToolkit,
                           Version=3.0.311106.0,
                           Culture=neutral,
                           PublicKeyToken=28f01b0e84b6d53e"/>
                      <asp:ScriptReference
                       name="AjaxControlToolkit.PopupExtender.PopupBehavior.js"
                         assembly="AjaxControlToolkit,
```

```
                                Version=3.0.311106.0,
                                Culture=neutral,
                                PublicKeyToken=28f01b0e84b6d53e"/>
                        <asp:ScriptReference
                         name="AjaxControlToolkit.Common.Threading.js"
                           assembly="AjaxControlToolkit,
                             Version=3.0.311106.0,
                             Culture=neutral,
                             PublicKeyToken=28f01b0e84b6d53e"/>
                        <asp:ScriptReference
                         name="AjaxControlToolkit.Calendar.CalendarBehavior.js"
                           assembly="AjaxControlToolkit,
                             Version=3.0.311106.0,
                             Culture=neutral,
                             PublicKeyToken=28f01b0e84b6d53e"/>
                </Scripts>
            </CompositeScript>
        </asp:ScriptManager>
        <asp:UpdatePanel ID="UpdatePanel1" runat="server">
            <ContentTemplate>
                What is your name?<br />
                <asp:TextBox ID="TextBox1"
                 runat="server"></asp:TextBox>
                <br /><br />
                What is today&#39;s date?<br />
                <asp:TextBox ID="TextBox2"
                 runat="server"></asp:TextBox>
                <cc2:CalendarExtender ID="TextBox2_CalendarExtender"
                 runat="server"
                    Enabled="True" TargetControlID="TextBox2">
                </cc2:CalendarExtender>
                <br /><br />
                <asp:Button ID="Button1" runat="server"
                 Text="Submit"
                 OnClick="Button1_Click" />
                <br /><br />
                <asp:Label ID="Label1" runat="server"></asp:Label>
            </ContentTemplate>
        </asp:UpdatePanel>
    </div>
    </form>
</body>
</html>
```

Having all of these defined scripts in the `<CompositeScript>` section will now signify that all these scripts are to be combined and sent to the page collectively, thereby improving the overall performance of your ASP.NET application.

SUMMARY

ASP.NET AJAX, although only a few years old, is an outstanding technology and will fundamentally change the way Web application development is approached. No longer do you need to completely tear down a page and rebuild it for each and every request. Instead, you are able to rebuild the pages slowly in sections as the end user requests them. The line between the thin-client world and the thick-client world just got a lot more blurred.

This chapter explored the core foundation of ASP.NET AJAX that is available with the default install of Visual Studio 2010. Beyond that, AJAX offers much more, including the ASP.NET AJAX Control Toolkit, the focus of the next chapter.

19

ASP.NET AJAX Control Toolkit

WHAT'S IN THIS CHAPTER?

- Installing the ASP.NET AJAX Control Toolkit
- Adding interactivity and animation to your Web pages

ASP.NET AJAX applications were introduced in the previous chapter. With the install of the .NET Framework 4 and through using Visual Studio 2010, you will find a few controls available that allow you to build ASP.NET applications with server-side AJAX capabilities. This is the framework to take your applications to the next level because you can accomplish so much with it, including adding specific AJAX capabilities to your user and custom server controls. Every AJAX enhancement added to your application will make your application seem more fluid and responsive to the end user.

You might be wondering where the big AJAX-enabled server controls are for this edition of Visual Studio 2010 if this is indeed a new world for building Web applications. The reason you do not see a new section of AJAX server controls is that Microsoft has treated them as an open source project instead of just blending them into Visual Studio 2010.

Developers at Microsoft and in the community have been working on a series of AJAX-capable server controls that you can use in your ASP.NET applications. These controls are collectively called the ASP.NET AJAX Control Toolkit. Recently, Microsoft has made the ASP.NET AJAX Control Toolkit a part of the Microsoft AJAX Library found at `www.asp.net/ajaxlibrary`. Downloading the library, you will find that it now also includes the complete AJAX Control Toolkit. Figure 19-1 shows the download page for the AJAX Library.

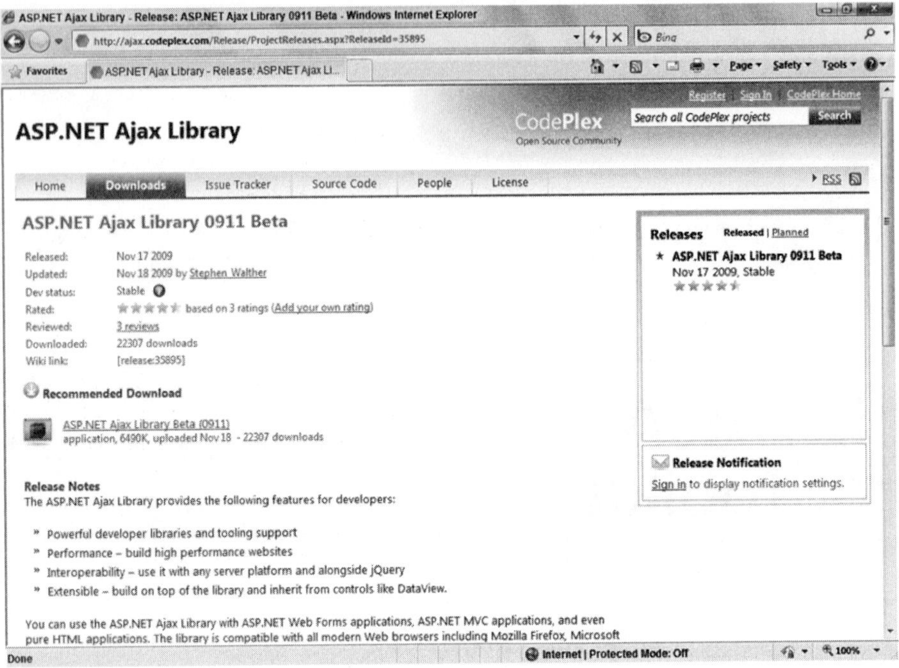

FIGURE 19-1

As you may remember from the last chapter, ASP.NET AJAX is the foundation on which to build richer Web applications that leverage the browser more fully, but it does not have the rich UI elements that really blur the distinction between Web and desktop applications. With the Microsoft AJAX Library, you can apply familiar object-oriented design concepts and use the scripts across a variety of modern browsers. ASP.NET AJAX includes several powerful ASP.NET controls that make adding AJAX functionality to an existing application or building better user experiences into a new application easy. The AJAX Toolkit, however, was developed to provide rich ASP.NET AJAX controls that you can use to make your Web applications really come to life. The Toolkit makes pushing the user interface of an application beyond what users expect from a Web application easy.

The Toolkit is a shared source project with code contributions from developers from Microsoft and elsewhere. Most developers who work with ASP.NET AJAX should also download the Toolkit for the additional set of controls it contains. The AJAX Library download mentioned earlier allows you to download a compiled DLL with the controls and extenders, or you can download the source code and project files and compile it yourself. Either way, make sure you add the DLL to your Toolbox in Visual Studio, as described shortly.

The Toolkit contains some controls that have AJAX functionality and many control extenders. The control extenders attach to another control to enhance or "extend" the control's functionality. When you install the Toolkit, it creates a sample Web application that has some examples of using the controls. Because the controls cover such a wide variety of application-development areas, they are presented in this chapter in categories: page layout controls and user interface effects. Within each category, the controls are listed alphabetically and the control names are self-explanatory to make locating the information you need when using this chapter for later reference easy.

Also, note that the Toolkit project is ongoing and will continue to evolve as developers contribute to it. This chapter is up-to-date as of the time of this writing, but the expectation is that more will be added to the Toolkit regularly. Most interesting is that even though this is an open source project, now that the AJAX Control Toolkit is included with the AJAX Library from Microsoft, it is also a supported product from Microsoft.

DOWNLOADING AND INSTALLING THE AJAX CONTROL TOOLKIT

Because the ASP.NET AJAX Control Toolkit is not part of the default install of Visual Studio 2010, you must set up the controls yourself. Again, the control toolkit's site on Microsoft's AJAX site offers a couple of options.

One option is the control toolkit that is specifically targeted at Visual Studio 2008 or greater. This chapter focuses on using the control toolkit with Visual Studio 2010. Another option is you can download the ASP.NET AJAX Control Toolkit as either source code or a compiled DLL, depending on your needs.

The source code option enables you to take the code for the controls and ASP.NET AJAX extenders and change the behavior of the controls or extenders yourself. The DLL option is a single Visual Studio installer file and a sample application.

There are a couple of parts to this install. One part provides a series of controls that were built with AJAX capabilities in mind. Another part is a series of control extenders (extensions for pre-existing controls).

To get set up, download the `.zip` file from the aforementioned site at `www.asp.net/ajaxlibrary` and unzip it where you want on your machine. Then follow these steps:

1. Install the controls into Visual Studio. Adding the controls to your Visual Studio 2010 Toolbox is very easy. Right-click in the Toolbox and select Add Tab from the provided menu. Name the tab as you want — for this example, the tab is called AJAX Controls.
2. With the new tab in your Toolbox, right-click the tab and select Choose Items from the provided menu, as illustrated in Figure 19-2. The Choose Toolbox Items dialog appears.

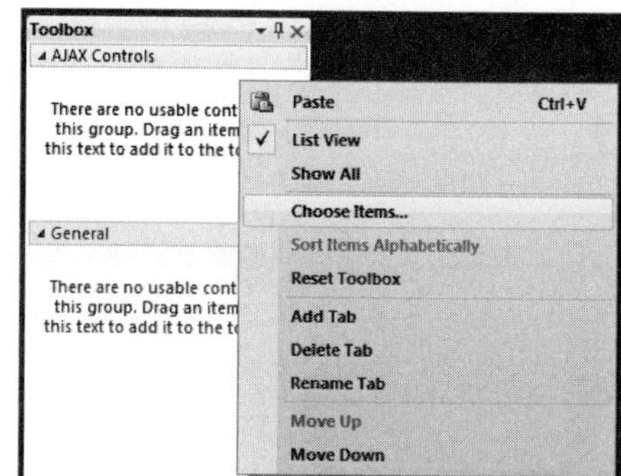

FIGURE 19-2

3. Select the `AjaxControlToolkit.dll` from the download. When you find the DLL and click Open, the Choose Toolbox Items dialog changes to include the controls that are contained within this DLL. The controls are highlighted in the dialog and are already selected for you (as shown in Figure 19-3).

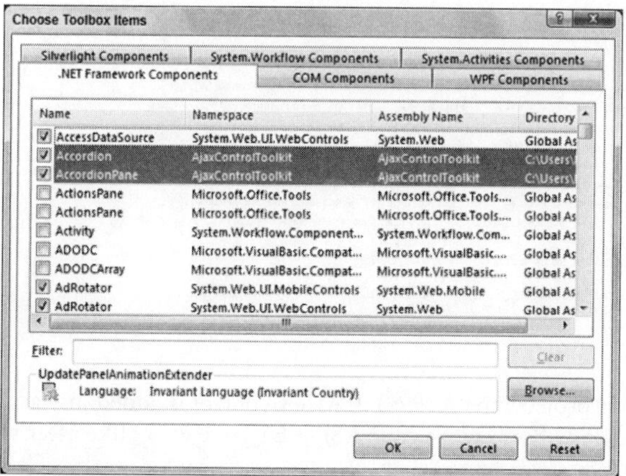

FIGURE 19-3

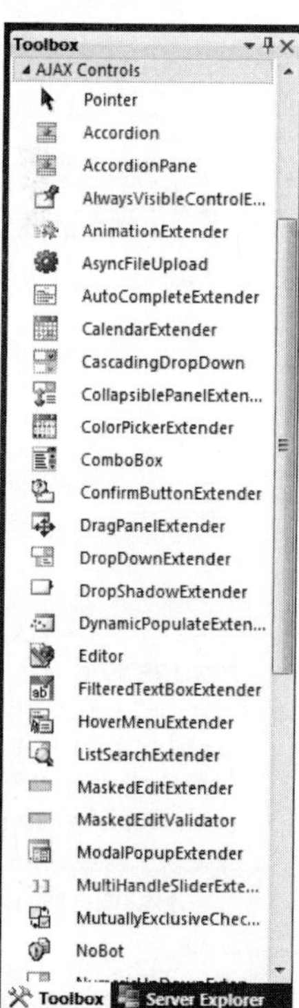

FIGURE 19-4

4. Click OK, and the ASP.NET AJAX Control Toolkit's controls will be added to your Visual Studio Toolbox. Figure 19-4 presents the end result.

More than 40 controls and extenders have been added to the Toolbox for use in your ASP.NET applications.

THE ASP.NET AJAX CONTROLS

The number of controls and extenders available from the Control Toolkit is large. As stated, more than 40 controls and extenders are at your disposal. This section looks at these items and how you can use them in your ASP.NET applications.

When you add an ASP.NET AJAX server control to your page, you may notice that a number of DLLs focused on localization into a number of languages have been added to the Bin folder of your solution. All the resource files have been organized into language folders within the folder. Figure 19-5 presents an example of what you will find.

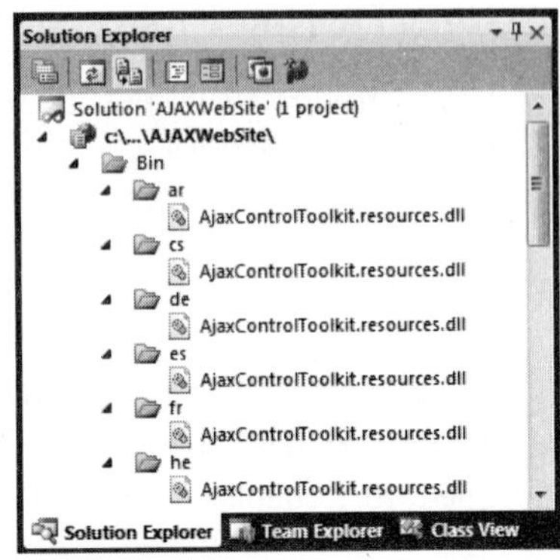

FIGURE 19-5

Looking at one of the DLLs with Lutz Roeder's .NET Reflector tool (`www.red-gate.com/products/reflector`), notice that it is focused on the client-side localization required by many applications. As an example, the `AjaxControlToolkit.resources.dll` for the Russian language within Reflector is shown in Figure 19-6.

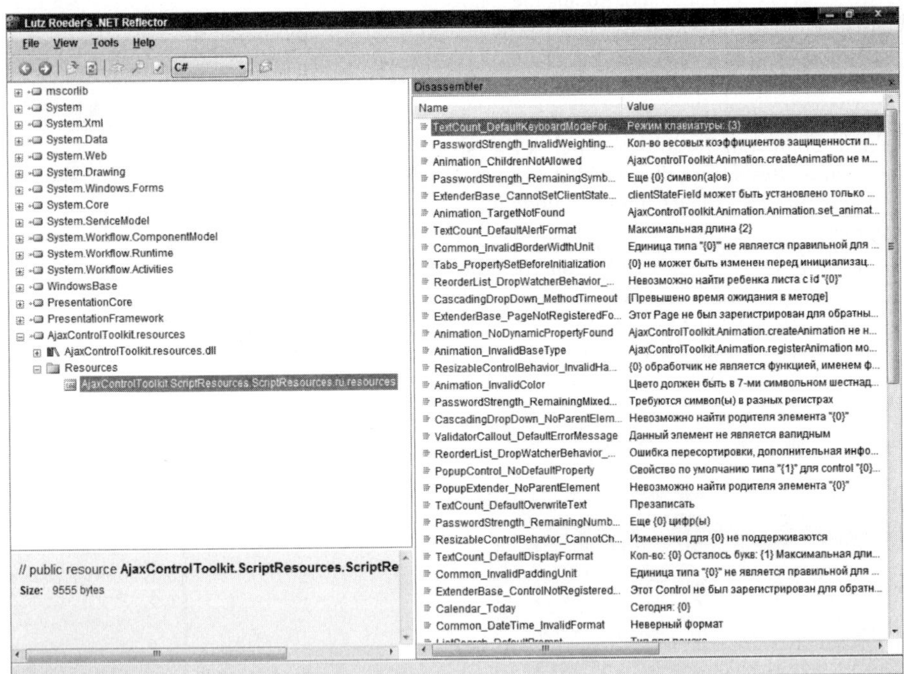

FIGURE 19-6

In addition to the localization DLLs added to your project, the ASP.NET AJAX control is added just as any other custom server control in ASP.NET. Listing 19-1 shows what your ASP.NET page looks like after the addition of a single ASP.NET AJAX control to it.

LISTING 19-1: Changes to the ASP.NET page after adding an ASP.NET AJAX control

Available for download on Wrox.com

```
<%@ Page Language=""C#"" AutoEventWireup=""true""
    CodeFile="Default.aspx.cs" Inherits="_Default" %>

<%@ Register Assembly="AjaxControlToolkit"
```

```
    Namespace="AjaxControlToolkit" TagPrefix="asp" %>

<!DOCTYPE html PUBLIC "-//W3C//DTD XHTML 1.0 Transitional//EN"
 "http://www.w3.org/TR/xhtml1/DTD/xhtml1-transitional.dtd">

<html xmlns="http://www.w3.org/1999/xhtml">
<head runat="server">
    <title>First Page</title>
</head>
<body>
    <form id="form1" runat="server">
    <div>
       <asp:ToolkitScriptManager ID="ToolkitScriptManager1" runat="server" />

        <asp:AlwaysVisibleControlExtender
         ID="AlwaysVisibleControlExtender1" runat="server"
         TargetControlID="TextBox1">
        </asp:AlwaysVisibleControlExtender>

        <asp:TextBox ID="TextBox1" runat="server"></asp:TextBox>
    </div>
    </form>
</body>
</html>
```

In this example, you can see that the ASP.NET AJAX control is registered on the page using the `@Register` directive. This directive points to the `AJAXControlToolkit` assembly and gives all controls that use this assembly reference a tag prefix of `asp`.

Another interesting aspect to the controls that are provided through the AJAX Control Toolkit is the ToolkitScriptManager control. This control derives from the base ScriptManager control and extends it to handle script combining for you by default, thus making your pages more expedient than before. The examples provided in this chapter make use of this newer version of the ScriptManager control.

ASP.NET AJAX Control Toolkit Extenders

The first set of items you look at includes the extenders that are part of the ASP.NET AJAX Control Toolkit. Extenders are basically controls that reach out and extend other controls. For example, you can think of the ASP.NET Validation Controls (covered in Chapter 4 of this book) as extender controls themselves. For instance, you can add a RequiredFieldValidator server control to a page and associate it to a TextBox control. This extends the TextBox control and changes its behavior. Normally it would just accept text. Now, if nothing is entered into the control, then the control will trigger an event back to the RequiredFieldValidator control whose client-side behavior is controlled by JavaScript.

The ASP.NET AJAX Control Toolkit's extenders accomplish the same thing. The controls extend the behavior of the ASP.NET server controls with additional JavaScript on the client as well as some server-side communications.

The ASP.NET AJAX extender controls are built using the ASP.NET AJAX extensions framework. The next few pages focus on using these extenders within your ASP.NET applications.

AlwaysVisibleControlExtender

When presenting information in the browser, you may want to keep a piece of information fixed in the user's view. Screen space is a limited commodity, and sometimes a screen element should always be available without the user ever having to scroll. The AlwaysVisibleControlExtender lets you designate any ASP.NET control as having this distinction. You specify a position for the control using the AlwaysVisibleControlExtender, and while the user scrolls the page to view other information, the control you designate is always kept in view. It seems to move around as the user scrolls the screen or resizes the window, so that it stays in the same relative position in the viewable portion of the browser window.

The AlwaysVisibleControlExtender has only six properties. Listing 19-2 presents an example of using this control.

LISTING 19-2: Using the AlwaysVisibleControlExtender

Available for download on Wrox.com

VB

```
<%@ Page Language="VB" %>

<%@ Register Assembly="AjaxControlToolkit"
    Namespace="AjaxControlToolkit" TagPrefix="asp" %>

<script runat="server">
    Protected Sub Button1_Click(ByVal sender As Object,
       ByVal e As System.EventArgs)

        Response.Write("The page has been submitted!")
    End Sub
</script>

<html xmlns="http://www.w3.org/1999/xhtml">
<head runat="server">
    <title>AlwaysVisibleControlExtender</title>
</head>
<body>
    <form id="form1" runat="server">
    <div>
        <asp:ToolkitScriptManager ID="ToolkitScriptManager1" runat="server" />
        <asp:AlwaysVisibleControlExtender
         ID="AlwaysVisibleControlExtender1"
            runat="server" TargetControlID="Panel1"
            HorizontalOffset="10"
            HorizontalSide="Right" VerticalOffset="10">
        </asp:AlwaysVisibleControlExtender>
        Form Element :
        <asp:TextBox ID="TextBox1" runat="server"></asp:TextBox>
        <br />
        Form Element :
        <asp:TextBox ID="TextBox2" runat="server"></asp:TextBox>
        <br />

        <!-- Excessive code removed for clarity -->

        Form Element :
        <asp:TextBox ID="TextBox29" runat="server"></asp:TextBox>
        <br />
        Form Element :
        <asp:TextBox ID="TextBox30" runat="server"></asp:TextBox>
        <br />
        <br />
        <asp:Panel ID="Panel1" runat="server">
            <asp:Button ID="Button1" runat="server" Text="Submit"
             OnClick="Button1_Click" />
            <asp:Button ID="Button2" runat="server" Text="Clear" />
        </asp:Panel>
    </div>
    </form>
</body>
</html>
```

C#

```
<%@ Page Language="C#" %>

<%@ Register Assembly="AjaxControlToolkit"
```

```
    Namespace="AjaxControlToolkit" TagPrefix="asp" %>

<script runat="server">
    protected void Button1_Click(object sender, EventArgs e)
    {
        Response.Write("The page has been submitted!");
    }
</script>
```

This code presents a very long form that requires end users to scroll the page in their browser. The AlwaysVisibleControlExtender control is present, and its presence requires that you also have a ScriptManager control on the page (this is the same requirement for all ASP.NET AJAX controls).

The `AlwaysVisibleControlExtender1` control extends the `Panel1` control through the use of the `TargetControlID` attribute. In this case, the value of the `TargetControlID` attribute points to the `Panel1` control. The `Panel1` control contains the form's Submit button. The result of the code from Listing 19-2 is shown in Figure 19-7.

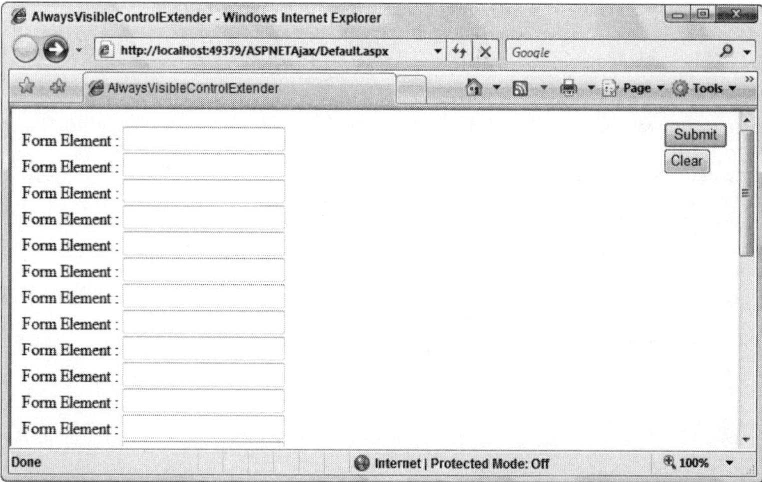

FIGURE 19-7

The location of the Submit and Clear buttons on the page is controlled via a combination of several control attributes. The location on the page is determined by the `HorizontalSide` (possible values include `Center`, `Left`, and `Right`) and `VerticalSide` properties (possible values include `Bottom`, `Middle`, and `Top`). A padding is also placed around the control using the `HorizontalOffset` and `VerticalOffset` properties, both of which are set to `10` pixels in this example.

AnimationExtender

The AnimationExtender server control provides a tremendous amount of capabilities. It allows you to program fluid animations to the controls that you put on the page. You can do a lot with this control — much more than can be shown in this chapter.

This control allows you to program elements that can move around the page based on specific end user triggers (such as a button click). Specific events are available for you to program your animations against. These events are as follows:

- `OnClick`
- `OnHoverOver`

- `OnHoverOut`
- `OnLoad`
- `OnMouseOver`
- `OnMouseOut`

Creating animations is not as straightforward as many would like because it has little Visual Studio support, such as wizards or even IntelliSense. For an example of creating your first animation, Listing 19-3 shows how you can fade an element in and out of the page based on an end user action.

LISTING 19-3: Using the AnimationExtender to fade a background color

Available for download on Wrox.com

```
<%@ Page Language="C#" %>

<%@ Register Assembly="AjaxControlToolkit"
    Namespace="AjaxControlToolkit" TagPrefix="asp" %>

<html xmlns="http://www.w3.org/1999/xhtml">
<head runat="server">
    <title>AnimationExtender</title>
</head>
<body>
    <form id="form1" runat="server">
    <div>
        <asp:ToolkitScriptManager ID="ToolkitScriptManager1" runat="server" />
        <asp:AnimationExtender ID="AnimationExtender1" runat="server"
            TargetControlID="Panel1">
            <Animations>
                <OnClick>
                    <Sequence>
                        <Color PropertyKey="background"
                         StartValue="#999966"
                         EndValue="#FFFFFF" Duration="5.0" />
                    </Sequence>
                </OnClick>
            </Animations>
        </asp:AnimationExtender>
        <asp:Panel ID="Panel1" runat="server" BorderColor="Black"
            BorderWidth="3px" Font-Bold="True" Width="600px">
            Lorem ipsum dolor sit amet, consectetuer adipiscing elit.
            Donec accumsan lorem. Ut consectetuer tempus metus.
            Aenean tincidunt venenatis tellus. Suspendisse molestie
            cursus ipsum. Curabitur ut lectus. Nulla ac dolor nec elit
            convallis vulputate. Nullam pharetra pulvinar nunc. Duis
            orci. Phasellus a tortor at nunc mattis congue.
            Vestibulum porta tellus eu orci. Suspendisse quis massa.
            Maecenas varius, erat non ullamcorper nonummy, mauris erat
            eleifend odio, ut gravida nisl neque a ipsum. Vivamus
            facilisis. Cras viverra. Curabitur ut augue eget dolor
            semper posuere. Aenean at magna eu eros tempor
            pharetra. Aenean mauris.
        </asp:Panel>
    </div>
    </form>
</body>
</html>
```

In this case, when you open the page from Listing 19-3, you will see that it uses a single AnimationExtender control that is working off the Panel1 control. This connection is made using the `TargetControlID` property.

As stated, IntelliSense is not enabled when you are typing the code that is contained within the AnimationExtender control, so you need to look in the documentation for the animations that you want to create. In the case of the previous example, the `<OnClick>` element is utilized to define a sequence of events that need to occur when the control is clicked. For this example, only one animation is defined within the `<Sequence>` element — a color change to the background of the element. Here, the `<Color>` element states that the background CSS property will need to start at the color `#999966` and change completely to color `#FFFFFF` within `5` seconds (defined using the `Duration` property).

When you open this page and click on the Panel element, you will see the color change in a 5-second duration from the described start color to the end color.

AutoCompleteExtender

The AutoCompleteExtender control enables you to help end users find what they might be looking for when they need to type in search terms within a text box. This feature, used on a lot of search sites today, helps in that when you start typing characters in the text box, you get results from a datastore that match what you have typed so far as a drop-down list directly below the textbox you are working with in the search.

To establish something similar for yourself, create a new page that contains only a ScriptManager control, an AutoCompleteExtender control, and a TextBox control. The ASP.NET portion of the page should appear as presented in Listing 19-4.

LISTING 19-4: The ASP.NET page

Available for download on Wrox.com

```
<%@ Page Language="C#" AutoEventWireup="true"
    CodeFile="AutoComplete.aspx.cs" Inherits="AutoComplete" %>

<%@ Register Assembly="AjaxControlToolkit"
    Namespace="AjaxControlToolkit" TagPrefix="asp" %>

<html xmlns="http://www.w3.org/1999/xhtml">
<head runat="server">
    <title>AutoComplete</title>
</head>
<body>
    <form id="form1" runat="server">
    <div>
        <asp:ToolkitScriptManager ID="ToolkitScriptManager1" runat="server">
        </asp:ToolkitScriptManager>
        <asp:AutoCompleteExtender ID="AutoCompleteExtender1"
         runat="server" TargetControlID="TextBox1"
         ServiceMethod="GetCompletionList" UseContextKey="True">
        </asp:AutoCompleteExtender>
        <asp:TextBox ID="TextBox1" runat="server"></asp:TextBox>
    </div>
    </form>
</body>
</html>
```

Filename AutoCompleteExtender.aspx

Again, like the other ASP.NET AJAX controls, you extend the TextBox control using the `TargetControlID` property. When you first add these controls to the page, you will not have the `ServiceMethod` property defined in the AutoCompleteExtender control. Using Visual Studio 2010, you can make the framework for a service method and tie the extender control to this method all from the design surface. After expanding the TextBox control's smart tag, select the Add AutoComplete page method option from the provided menu, shown in Figure 19-8.

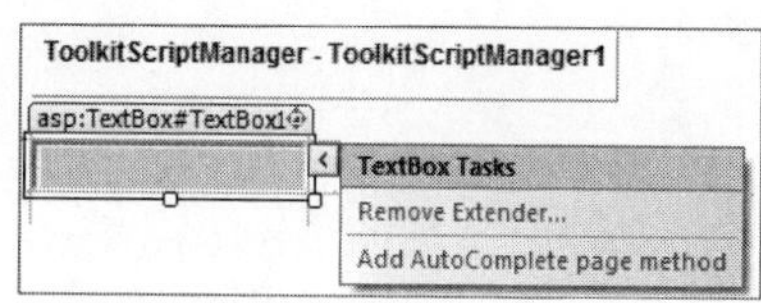

FIGURE 19-8

This action creates a service method in the code-behind for your page. Listing 19-5 shows the steps necessary to complete this method to call the company names from the Northwind database.

Chapter 8 has instructions on downloading and using the Northwind database.

LISTING 19-5: The code-behind that sets up the service method for auto-complete

Available for download on Wrox.com

VB

```
Imports System.Data
Imports System.Data.SqlClient

Partial Class AutoComplete
    Inherits System.Web.UI.Page

    <System.Web.Services.WebMethodAttribute(),
     System.Web.Script.Services.ScriptMethodAttribute()>
    Public Shared Function GetCompletionList(ByVal _
      prefixText As String, ByVal count As Integer) As String()
        Dim conn As SqlConnection
        Dim cmd As SqlCommand
        Dim cmdString As String =
      "Select CompanyName from Customers WHERE CompanyName LIKE'" &
           prefixText & "%'"
        conn = New SqlConnection("Data Source=.\SQLEXPRESS;
           AttachDbFilename=|DataDirectory|\NORTHWND.MDF;
           Integrated Security=True;User Instance=True")
        ' Put this string on one line in your code
        cmd = New SqlCommand(cmdString, conn)
        conn.Open()

        Dim myReader As SqlDataReader
        Dim returnData As List(Of String) = New List(Of String)
        myReader = cmd.ExecuteReader(CommandBehavior.CloseConnection)

        While myReader.Read()
            returnData.Add(myReader("CompanyName").ToString())
        End While

        Return returnData.ToArray()
    End Function
End Class
```

C#

```
using System.Collections.Generic;
using System.Data;
using System.Data.SqlClient;
public partial class AutoComplete : System.Web.UI.Page
{
    [System.Web.Services.WebMethodAttribute(),
     System.Web.Script.Services.ScriptMethodAttribute()]
    public static string[] GetCompletionList(string prefixText,
       int count, string contextKey)
    {
        SqlConnection conn;
        SqlCommand cmd;
        string cmdString =
         "Select CompanyName from Customers WHERE CompanyName LIKE'" +
           prefixText + "%'";
        conn = new
            SqlConnection(@"Data Source=.\SQLEXPRESS;
```

```
            AttachDbFilename=|DataDirectory|\NORTHWND.MDF;
            Integrated Security=True;User Instance=True");
        // Put this string on one line in your code
        cmd = new SqlCommand(cmdString, conn);
        conn.Open();

        SqlDataReader myReader;
        List<string> returnData = new List<string>();

        myReader = cmd.ExecuteReader(CommandBehavior.CloseConnection);

        while (myReader.Read())
        {
            returnData.Add(myReader["CompanyName"].ToString());
        }

        return returnData.ToArray();
    }
}
```

Filenames AutoCompleteExtender.aspx.vb and AutoCompleteExtender.aspx.cs

When you run this page and type the characters **alf** into the text box, the `GetCompletionList()` method is called, passing in these characters. These characters are retrievable through the `prefixText` parameter (you can also use the `count` parameter, which is defaulted at `10`). The Northwind database is called using the `prefixText` value and this is what is returned back to the TextBox1 control. In the end, you get a drop-down list of the items that match the first three characters that were entered into the text box. This is illustrated in Figure 19-9.

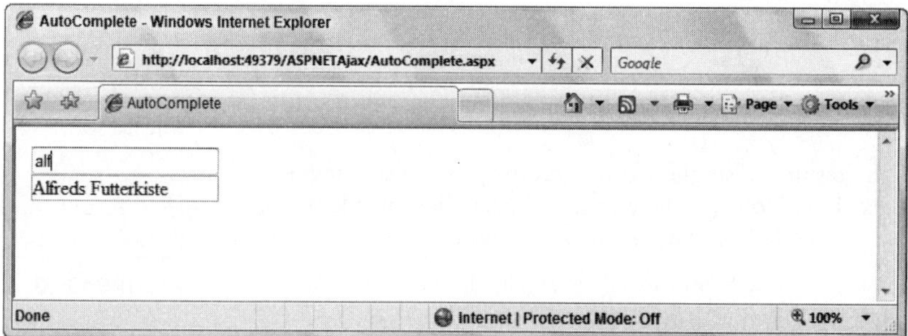

FIGURE 19-9

It is good to know that the results, once called the first time, are cached. This caching is controlled via the `EnableCaching` property (it is defaulted to `true`). You can also change the style of the drop-down auto-complete list, configure how many elements appear, and much more with this feature. One more point that is important is that you are not required to call out a method that is exposed on the same page as the control as the example in this book demonstrates, but you can also call out another server-side method on another page, or a Web method.

CalendarExtender

Selecting a date is a common requirement of many applications. It is also one of the most common points in a form that can hinder form submission. End users are often slowed down by trying to figure out the format of the date that the form requires. The CalendarExtender control enables you to make it simple for your end users to select a date within a form. The CalendarExtender attaches to a text box and pops up a calendar for selecting a date. By default, the calendar is shown when the text box gets focus, but if you set the PopupButtonID to the ID of another control, then the calendar will become visible when that control is clicked.

The best way to set up fast date selection in a form is to provide a calendar that can be navigated and allow a date to quickly be selected, which will then be translated to a textual date format in the text box. The CalendarExtender is very easy to use with just a few key properties. The TargetControlID points to the text box that receives the selected date. The Format property specifies the string format for the date input of the text box. The CalendarExtender control gives you all the client-side code required for this kind of action. Listing 19-6 shows you an example of providing a calendar control off your text box controls.

LISTING 19-6: Using a calendar control from a TextBox control

Available for download on Wrox.com

```
<%@ Page Language="VB" %>

<%@ Register Assembly="AjaxControlToolkit"
    Namespace="AjaxControlToolkit" TagPrefix="asp" %>

<html xmlns="http://www.w3.org/1999/xhtml">
<head runat="server">
    <title>CalendarExtender</title>
</head>
<body>
    <form id="form1" runat="server">
    <div>
        <asp:ToolkitScriptManager ID="ToolkitScriptManager1" runat="server">
        </asp:ToolkitScriptManager>
        <asp:CalendarExtender ID="CalendarExtender1" runat="server"
         TargetControlID="TextBox1">
        </asp:CalendarExtender>
        <asp:TextBox ID="TextBox1" runat="server"></asp:TextBox>
    </div>
    </form>
</body>
</html>
```

FIGURE 19-10

3/10/2010

FIGURE 19-11

When you run this page, the result is a single text box on the page, appearing no different from any other text box. However, when the end user clicks inside of the text box, a calendar appears directly below it, as shown in Figure 19-10.

Then, when the end user selects a date from the calendar, the date is placed as text within the text box as illustrated in Figure 19-11.

Some of the properties exposed from this control are FirstDayOfWeek and PopupPosition (which has the options BottomLeft, BottomRight, TopLeft, and TopRight). You can also change how the calendar is initiated on the client. Some sites offer a calendar button next to the text box and only pop up the calendar option when the end user clicks the button. If this is something that you want to do on your pages, then use the PopupButtonID property, which you must point to the ID of the image or button that you are using.

CollapsiblePanelExtender

The CollapsiblePanelExtender server control allows you to collapse one control into another. When working with two Panel server controls, you can provide a nice way to control any real estate issues that you might be experiencing on your ASP.NET page.

The CollapsiblePanelExtender is similar to the Accordion control (presented later in this chapter), but it does not target multiple content areas. An ASP.NET panel control is shown or hidden from view based on the user's interaction with a given control. This allows you to hide something the user does not always need to see. The TargetControlID is shown when the ExpandControlID is clicked or hidden when the

`CollapseControlID` is clicked. Alternatively, it can be shown or hidden based on a mouse hover if the `AutoCollapse` and `AutoExpand` properties are set to `True`.

Listing 19-7 demonstrates the use of a CollapsiblePanelExtender to set the panel size to `0` when it is collapsed and to `300` pixels when it is expanded. Another panel is used as the selector for expanding and collapsing the panel. In addition, a label is included that is designated as the `TextLabelID`. The value of the Label control is changed between the `ExpandedText` and `CollapsedText` values based on the current state.

Available for download on Wrox.com

LISTING 19-7: Using CollapsiblePanelExtender with two Panel controls

```
<%@ Page Language="C#" %>

<%@ Register Assembly="AjaxControlToolkit"
    Namespace="AjaxControlToolkit" TagPrefix="asp" %>

<html xmlns="http://www.w3.org/1999/xhtml">
<head id="Head1" runat="server">
    <title>CollapsiblePanelExtender</title>
</head>
<body>
    <form id="form1" runat="server">
    <div>
        <asp:ToolkitScriptManager ID="ToolkitScriptManager1" runat="server">
        </asp:ToolkitScriptManager>
        <asp:Panel ID="Panel1" runat="server" BackColor="#000066"
         ForeColor="White">
            <asp:Label ID="Label2" runat="server"
             Text="This is my title"></asp:Label>
            <asp:Label ID="Label1" runat="server"></asp:Label>
        </asp:Panel>
        <asp:Panel ID="Panel2" runat="server" Style="overflow: hidden;"
         Height="0">
            Lorem ipsum dolor sit amet, consectetuer adipiscing elit.
            Donec accumsan lorem. Ut consectetuer tempus metus.
            Aenean tincidunt venenatis tellus. Suspendisse molestie
            cursus ipsum. Curabitur ut lectus. Nulla ac dolor nec elit
            convallis vulputate. Nullam pharetra pulvinar nunc. Duis
            orci. Phasellus a tortor at nunc mattis congue. Vestibulum
            porta tellus eu orci. Suspendisse quis massa.
            Maecenas varius, erat non ullamcorper nonummy, mauris erat
            eleifend odio, ut gravida nisl neque a ipsum. Vivamus
            facilisis. Cras viverra. Curabitur ut augue eget dolor
            semper posuere. Aenean at magna eu eros tempor pharetra.
            Aenean mauris.
        </asp:Panel>
        <asp:CollapsiblePanelExtender ID="CollapsiblePanelExtender1"
         runat="server"
         TargetControlID="Panel2" Collapsed="true"
         ExpandControlID="Panel1"
         CollapseControlID="Panel1"
         CollapsedSize="1"
         ExpandedSize="300" CollapsedText="[Click to expand]"
         ExpandedText="[Click to collapse]" TextLabelID="Label1"
         SuppressPostBack="true">
        </asp:CollapsiblePanelExtender>
    </div>
    </form>
</body>

</html>
```

In this case, when the page opens for the first time you will see only the contents of `Panel1` — the title panel. By default, you would usually see both controls, but because the `Collapsed` property is set to `True` in the control, you will see only `Panel1`. Clicking the Panel control will then expose the contents of `Panel2`. In fact, the contents will slide out from the `Panel1` control. Tying these two controls together to perform this action is accomplished through the use of the CollapsiblePanelExtender control. This control's `TargetControlID` is assigned to the second Panel control — `Panel2`, as this is the control that needs to expand onto the page. The `ExpandControlID` property is the control that initiates the expansion.

Once expanded, it is when the end user clicks on `Panel2` that the contents will disappear by sliding back into `Panel1`. This is accomplished through the use of the `CollapseControlID` property being assigned to Panel2.

The CollapsiblePanelExtender control has a number of properties that allow you to fine-tune how the expanding and collapsing occur. For instance, you could have also set the `Label1` control to be the initiator of this process and even change the text of the Label control depending on the whether `Panel2` is collapsed or expanded. This use is illustrated in Listing 19-8.

LISTING 19-8: Using a Label control to expand or collapse the Panel control

Available for download on Wrox.com

```
<asp:CollapsiblePanelExtender ID="CollapsiblePanelExtender1"
 runat="server"
 TargetControlID="Panel2" Collapsed="True" ExpandControlID="Label1"
 CollapseControlID="Label1"
 CollapsedText="[Click to expand]"
 ExpandedText="[Click to collapse]"
 TextLabelID="Label1">
</asp:CollapsiblePanelExtender>
```

In this case, when the end user clicks on the `Label1` control, not only will `Panel2` expand and collapse, but also the text within the `Label1` control will change accordingly.

ColorPickerExtender

One of the difficult data points to retrieve from an end user is color. This particular data point is tough to define if you are using just text. If you have an open selection of colors, how does the end user define a darker shade of blue? For this reason, you have the ColorPickerExtender to quickly and easily extend something like a TextBox control to a tool that makes this selection process a breeze. Listing 19-9 shows a quick and easy way to do this task.

LISTING 19-9: Using the ColorPickerExtender control to allow for color selection

Available for download on Wrox.com

```
<%@ Page Language="C#" %>

<%@ Register Assembly="AjaxControlToolkit"
    Namespace="AjaxControlToolkit" TagPrefix="asp" %>

<html xmlns="http://www.w3.org/1999/xhtml">
<head runat="server">
    <title>ColorPickerExtender</title>
</head>
<body>
    <form id="form1" runat="server">
    <div>
        <asp:ToolkitScriptManager ID="ToolkitScriptManager1" runat="server">
        </asp:ToolkitScriptManager>
        <br />
        Pick your favorite color:<br />
        <asp:TextBox ID="TextBox1" runat="server"></asp:TextBox>
        <asp:ColorPickerExtender ID="ColorPickerExtender1"
         runat="server" TargetControlID="TextBox1">
```

```
            </asp:ColorPickerExtender>
        </div>
        </form>
    </body>
    </html>
```

When this page opens, you simply have a single TextBox server control on the page. Applying focus to this TextBox control pops up the color selector, as illustrated here in black and white in Figure 19-12.

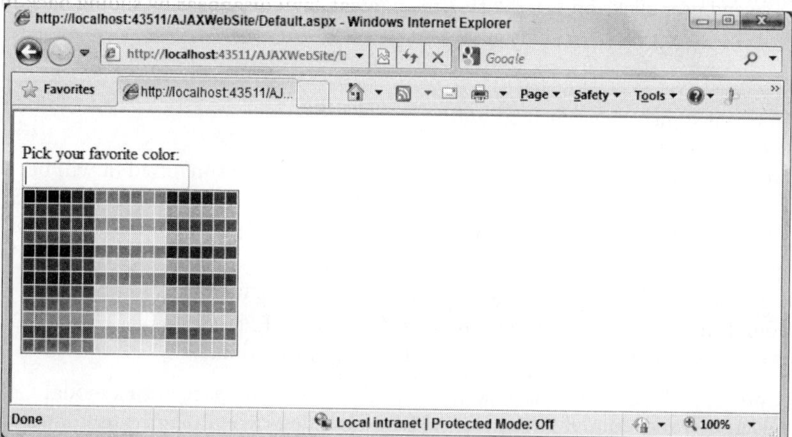

FIGURE 19-12

The end user then can scroll across the color options and after the user selects one of these colors, the pop-up disappears and the hexadecimal color code is shown in the TextBox. This end result is presented here in Figure 19-13.

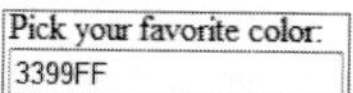

FIGURE 19-13

ConfirmButtonExtender and ModalPopupExtender

Usually before allowing your end users to make deletions of data via a browser application, you want to confirm such actions with the end user. ConfirmButtonExtender allows you to question the end user's action and reconfirm that he wants the action to occur. Listing 19-10 shows how to use this control.

LISTING 19-10: Using the ConfirmButtonExtender control to reconfirm a user action

Available for download on Wrox.com

```
<%@ Page Language="C#" %>

<%@ Register Assembly="AjaxControlToolkit"
    Namespace="AjaxControlToolkit" TagPrefix="asp" %>

<html xmlns="http://www.w3.org/1999/xhtml">
<head runat="server">
    <title>ConfirmButtonExtender</title>
</head>
<body>
    <form id="form1" runat="server">
    <div>
        <asp:ToolkitScriptManager ID="ToolkitScriptManager1" runat="server">
        </asp:ToolkitScriptManager>
        <asp:ConfirmButtonExtender ID="ConfirmButtonExtender1"
         runat="server" TargetControlID="Button1"
         ConfirmText="Are you sure you wanted to click this button?">
        </asp:ConfirmButtonExtender>
```

continues

LISTING 19-10 *(continued)*

```
            <asp:Button ID="Button1" runat="server" Text="Button" />
        </div>
        </form>
    </body>
    </html>
```

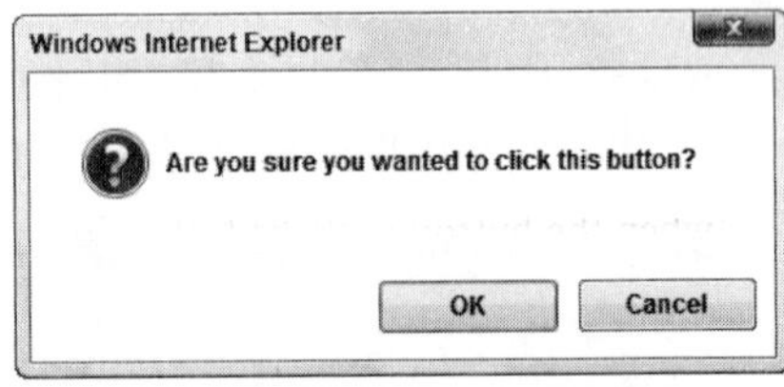

FIGURE 19-14

In this case, the ConfirmButtonExtender extends the Button1 server control and adds a confirmation dialog using the text defined with the `ConfirmText` property. Figure 19-14 shows this page.

If the end user clicks OK in this instance, then the page will function normally as if the dialog never occurred. However, if Cancel is clicked, the dialog will, by default, disappear and the form will not be submitted (it will be as if the button were not clicked at all). In this case, you can also capture the Cancel button being clicked and perform a client-side operation by using the `OnClientClick` event and giving it a value of a client-side JavaScript function.

Instead of using the browser's modal dialogs, you can even go as far as creating your own to use as the confirmation form. To accomplish this task, you need to use the ModalPopupExtender server control. The ModalPopupExtender control points to another control to use for the confirmation.

The ModalPopupExtender prevents the user from interacting with the underlying page until a modal dialog has been addressed by the user. It is very similar to the HoverMenuExtender, except that the user must work with the control designated by the `PopupControlID` before he can proceed. It has properties for specifying the `OkControlID` and the `CancelControlID`, along with `OnOkScript` and `OnCancelScript` properties that will run based on the user's selection. Listing 19-11 shows how to use this control.

Available for download on Wrox.com

LISTING 19-11: Using the ModalPopupExtender control to create your own confirmation form

```
<%@ Page Language="C#" %>

<%@ Register Assembly="AjaxControlToolkit"
    Namespace="AjaxControlToolkit" TagPrefix="asp" %>

<html xmlns="http://www.w3.org/1999/xhtml">
<head runat="server">
    <title>ConfirmButtonExtender</title>
</head>
<body>
    <form id="form1" runat="server">
    <div>
        <asp:ToolkitScriptManager ID="ToolkitScriptManager1" runat="server">
        </asp:ToolkitScriptManager>
        <asp:ConfirmButtonExtender ID="ConfirmButtonExtender1"
         runat="server" TargetControlID="Button1"
         DisplayModalPopupID="ModalPopupExtender1">
        </asp:ConfirmButtonExtender>
        <asp:ModalPopupExtender ID="ModalPopupExtender1" runat="server"
            CancelControlID="ButtonNo" OkControlID="ButtonYes"
            PopupControlID="Panel1"
            TargetControlID="Button1">
        </asp:ModalPopupExtender>
        <asp:Button ID="Button1" runat="server" Text="Button" />
        <asp:Panel ID="Panel1" runat="server"
         style="display:none; background-color:White; width:200;
         border-width:2px; border-color:Black; border-style:solid;
         padding:20px;">
         Are you sure you wanted to click this button?<br />
```

```
            <asp:Button ID="ButtonYes" runat="server" Text="Yes" />
            <asp:Button ID="ButtonNo" runat="server" Text="No" />
        </asp:Panel>
    </div>
    </form>
</body>
</html>
```

In this example, the ConfirmButtonExtender still points to the Button1 control on the page, meaning that when the button is clicked, the ConfirmButtonExtender will take action. Instead of using the `ConfirmText` property, the `DisplayModalPopupID` property is used. In this case, it points to the ModalPopupExtender1 control — another extender control.

The ModalPopupExtender control, in turn, references the Panel1 control on the page through the use of the `PopupControlID` property. The contents of this Panel control are used for the confirmation on the button click. For this to work, the ModalPopupExtender control must have a value for the `OkControlID` and the `CancelControlID` properties. In this case, these two properties point to the two Button controls that are contained within the Panel control. When you run this page, you get the results shown in Figure 19-15.

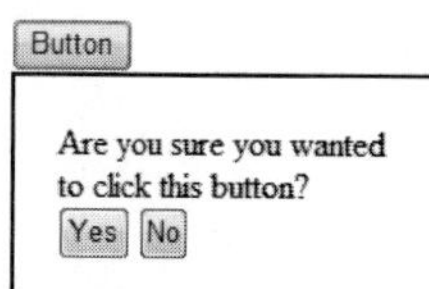

FIGURE 19-15

DragPanelExtender

The DragPanelExtender enables you to define areas where end users can move elements around the page as they want. The end user actually has the ability to drag and drop the element anywhere on the browser page.

To enable this feature, you must do a few things. The first suggestion is to create a `<div>` area on the page that is large enough to drag the item around in. From here, you need to specify what will be used as the drag handle and another control that will follow the drag handle around. In the example in Listing 19-12, the Label control is used as the drag handle, and the `Panel2` control is the content that is dragged around the screen.

Available for download on Wrox.com

LISTING 19-12: Dragging a Panel control around the page

```
<%@ Page Language="C#" %>

<%@ Register Assembly="AjaxControlToolkit"
    Namespace="AjaxControlToolkit" TagPrefix="asp" %>

<html xmlns="http://www.w3.org/1999/xhtml">
<head runat="server">
    <title>DragPanel control</title>
</head>
<body>
    <form id="form1" runat="server">
    <div>
        <asp:ToolkitScriptManager ID="ToolkitScriptManager1" runat="server">
        </asp:ToolkitScriptManager>
        <div style="height: 600px;">
            <asp:DragPanelExtender ID="DragPanelExtender1"
             runat="server"
             DragHandleID="Label1" TargetControlID="Panel1">
            </asp:DragPanelExtender>
            <asp:Panel ID="Panel1" runat="server" Width="450px">
                <asp:Label ID="Label1" runat="server"
                 Text="Drag this Label control to move the control"
                 BackColor="DarkBlue" ForeColor="White"></asp:Label>
                <asp:Panel ID="Panel2" runat="server" Width="450px">
            Lorem ipsum dolor sit amet, consectetuer adipiscing elit.
            Donec accumsan lorem. Ut consectetuer tempus metus.
            Aenean tincidunt venenatis tellus. Suspendisse molestie
```

continues

LISTING 19-12 *(continued)*

```
                cursus ipsum. Curabitur ut lectus. Nulla ac dolor nec elit
                convallis vulputate. Nullam pharetra pulvinar nunc. Duis
                orci. Phasellus a tortor at nunc mattis congue.
                Vestibulum porta tellus eu orci. Suspendisse quis massa.
                Maecenas varius, erat non ullamcorper nonummy, mauris erat
                eleifend odio, ut gravida nisl neque a ipsum. Vivamus
                facilisis. Cras viverra. Curabitur
                ut augue eget dolor semper posuere. Aenean at magna eu eros
                tempor pharetra. Aenean mauris.
                    </asp:Panel>
                </asp:Panel>
            </div>
        </div>
        </form>
    </body>
    </html>
```

This example creates a `<div>` element that has a height of `600` pixels. Within this defined area, the example uses a DragPanelExtender control and targets the `Panel1` control through the use of the `TargetControlID` property being assigned to this control.

Within the `Panel1` control are two other server controls — a Label and another Panel control. The Label control is assigned to be the drag handle using the `DragHandleID` property of the DragPanelExtender control. With this little bit of code in place, you are now able to drag the Panel1 control around on your browser window. Figure 19-16 shows the Label control being used as a handle to drag around the Panel control.

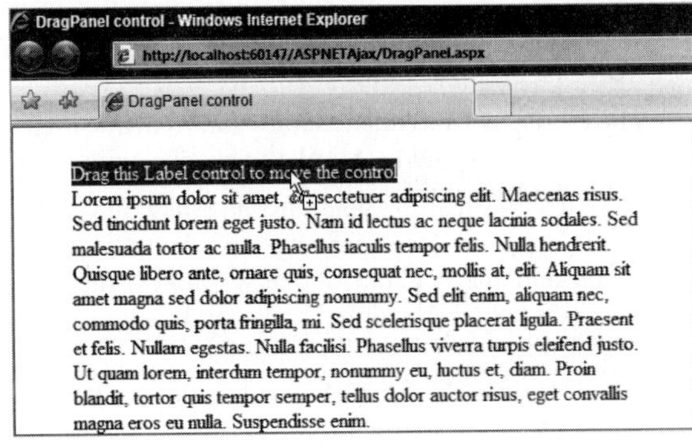

FIGURE 19-16

DropDownExtender

The DropDownExtender control allows you to take any control and provide a drop-down list of options below it for selection. It provides a different framework from a typical drop-down list control as it allows for an extreme level of customization. Listing 19-13 shows how you can even use an image as the initiator of a drop-down list of options.

LISTING 19-13: Using an Image control as an initiator of a drop-down list

Available for download on Wrox.com

VB

```
<%@ Page Language="VB" %>

<%@ Register Assembly="AjaxControlToolkit"
    Namespace="AjaxControlToolkit" TagPrefix="asp" %>

<script runat="server">
    Protected Sub Page_Load(ByVal sender As Object,
      ByVal e As System.EventArgs)
        Image1.ImageUrl = "Images/Creek.jpg"
    End Sub

    Protected Sub Option_Click(ByVal sender As Object,
      ByVal e As System.EventArgs)
        Image1.ImageUrl = "Images/" & DirectCast(sender,
```

```
        LinkButton).Text & ".jpg"
    End Sub
</script>

<html xmlns="http://www.w3.org/1999/xhtml">
<head runat="server">
    <title>DropDownExtender Control</title>
</head>
<body>
    <form id="form1" runat="server">
    <div>
        <asp:ToolkitScriptManager ID="ToolkitScriptManager1" runat="server">
        </asp:ToolkitScriptManager>
        <asp:UpdatePanel ID="UpdatePanel1" runat="server">
            <ContentTemplate>
                <asp:DropDownExtender ID="DropDownExtender1"
                 runat="server"
                 DropDownControlID="Panel1" TargetControlID="Image1">
                </asp:DropDownExtender>
                <asp:Image ID="Image1" runat="server">
                </asp:Image>
            <asp:Panel ID="Panel1" runat="server" Height="50px"
             Width="125px">
                <asp:LinkButton ID="Option1" runat="server"
                 OnClick="Option_Click">Creek</asp:LinkButton>
                <asp:LinkButton ID="Option2" runat="server"
                 OnClick="Option_Click">Dock</asp:LinkButton>
                <asp:LinkButton ID="Option3" runat="server"
                 OnClick="Option_Click">Garden</asp:LinkButton>
            </asp:Panel>
            </ContentTemplate>
        </asp:UpdatePanel>
    </div>
    </form>
</body>
</html>
```

C#

```
<%@ Page Language="C#" %>

<%@ Register Assembly="AjaxControlToolkit"
    Namespace="AjaxControlToolkit" TagPrefix="asp" %>

<script runat="server">
    protected void Page_Load(object sender, EventArgs e)
    {
        Image1.ImageUrl = "Images/Creek.jpg";
    }

    protected void Option_Click(object sender, EventArgs e)
    {
        Image1.ImageUrl = "Images/" + ((LinkButton)sender).Text
          + ".jpg";
    }
</script>
```

In this case, a DropDownExtender control is tied to an Image control that displays a specific image on the `Page_Load()` event. The DropDownExtender control has two specific properties that need to be filled. The first is the `TargetControlID` property that defines the control that becomes the initiator of the drop-down list. The second property is the `DropDownControlID` property, which defines the element on the page that will be used for the drop-down items that appear below the control. In this case, it is a Panel control with three LinkButton controls.

Each of the LinkButton controls designates a specific image that should appear on the page. Selecting one of the options changes the image to the choice through the `Option_Click()` method. Running this page gives you the results illustrated in Figure 19-17.

FIGURE 19-17

DropShadowExtender

The DropShadowExtender allows you to add a DropShadow effect to an ASP.NET panel or image on the page. You set the `TargetControlID`, and you can then control the `Width` and `Opacity`, and whether the corners should be `Rounded`. If the panel can be moved or resized, you can also set the `TrackPosition` property to `True` to indicate that JavaScript should run to track the panel and update the DropShadow as needed.

Your first thought for where to use this might be an image (as shown in Listing 19-14), but you can use it for any control that you want.

LISTING 19-14: Using DropShadowExtender with an Image control

Available for download on Wrox.com

```
<%@ Page Language="C#" %>

<%@ Register Assembly="AjaxControlToolkit"
    Namespace="AjaxControlToolkit" TagPrefix="asp" %>

<html xmlns="http://www.w3.org/1999/xhtml">
<head runat="server">
    <title>DropShadowExtender Control</title>
</head>
<body>
    <form id="form1" runat="server"> <div>
        <asp:ToolkitScriptManager ID="ToolkitScriptManager1" runat="server">
        </asp:ToolkitScriptManager>
        <asp:DropShadowExtender ID="DropShadowExtender1" runat="server"
         TargetControlID="Image1">
        </asp:DropShadowExtender>
        <asp:Image ID="Image1" runat="server"
         ImageUrl="Images/Garden.jpg" />
    </div>
    </form>
</body>
</html>
```

In this example, accomplishing this is as simple as using the DropShadowExtender control with a `TargetControlID` of `Image1`. With this in place, the image will appear in the browser, as shown in Figure 19-18.

FIGURE 19-18

As stated, in addition to images, you can use DropShadowExtender for almost anything. Listing 19-15 shows how to use it with a Panel control.

Available for download on Wrox.com

LISTING 19-15: Using the DropShadowExtender with a Panel control

```
<%@ Page Language="C#" %>

<%@ Register Assembly="AjaxControlToolkit"
    Namespace="AjaxControlToolkit" TagPrefix="asp" %>

<html xmlns="http://www.w3.org/1999/xhtml">
<head runat="server">
    <title>DropShadowExtender Control</title>
</head>
<body>
    <form id="form1" runat="server"> <div>
        <asp:ToolkitScriptManager ID="ToolkitScriptManager1" runat="server">
        </asp:ToolkitScriptManager>
        <asp:DropShadowExtender ID="DropShadowExtender1" runat="server"
         TargetControlID="Panel1" Rounded="True">
        </asp:DropShadowExtender>
        <asp:Panel ID="Panel1" runat="server" BackColor="Orange"
         Width="300" HorizontalAlign="Center">
            <asp:Login ID="Login1" runat="server">
            </asp:Login>
        </asp:Panel>
    </div>
    </form>
</body>
</html>
```

In this case, a Panel control with a Login control is extended with the DropShadowExtender control. The result is quite similar to that of the Image control's result. However, one addition to the DropShadowExtender control here is that the `Rounded` property is set to `True` (by default, it is set to `False`). This produces the look shown in Figure 19-19.

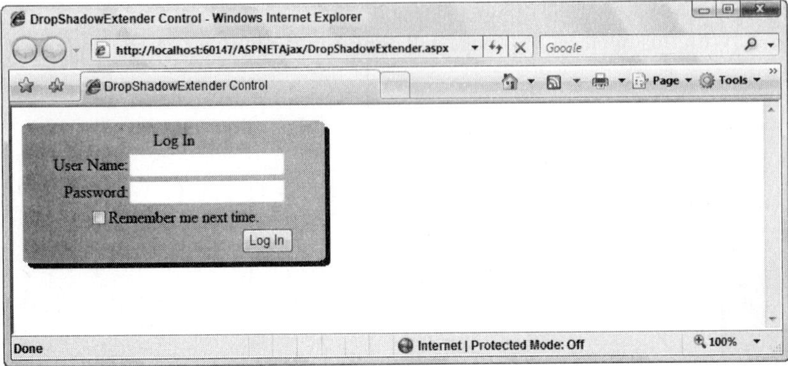

FIGURE 19-19

As you can see from Figure 19-19, not only are the edges of the drop shadow rounded, but also the entire Panel control has rounded edges. Other style properties that you can work with include the `Opacity` property, which controls the opacity of the drop shadow only, and the `Radius` property, which controls the radius used in rounding the edges and obviously works only if the `Rounded` property is set to `True`. By default, the `Opacity` setting is set at `1`, which means 100% visible. To set it at, say, 50% opacity, you need to set the `Opacity` value to `.5`.

DynamicPopulateExtender

The DynamicPopulateExtender control allows you to send dynamic HTML output to a Panel control. For this to work, you need one control or event that triggers a call back to the server to get the HTML that in turn gets pushed into the Panel control, thereby making a dynamic change on the client.

As with the AutoCompleteExtender control, you need a server-side event that returns something to the client asynchronously. Listing 19-16 shows the code required to use this control on the `.aspx` page.

Available for download on Wrox.com

LISTING 19-16: Using the DynamicPopulateExtender control to populate a Panel control

.ASPX

```
<%@ Page Language="VB" AutoEventWireup="true"
    CodeFile="DynamicPopulateExtender.aspx.vb"
    Inherits="DynamicPopulateExtender" %>

<%@ Register Assembly="AjaxControlToolkit"
    Namespace="AjaxControlToolkit" TagPrefix="asp" %>

<html xmlns="http://www.w3.org/1999/xhtml">
<head runat="server">
    <title>DynamicPopulateExtender Control</title>
    <script type="text/javascript">
      function updateGrid(value) {
        var behavior = $find('DynamicPopulateExtender1');
        if (behavior) {
            behavior.populate(value);
        }
      }
    </script>
</head>
<body>
    <form id="form1" runat="server">
    <div>
        <asp:ToolkitScriptManager ID="ToolkitScriptManager1" runat="server" />
```

```
        <asp:DynamicPopulateExtender ID="DynamicPopulateExtender1"
         runat="server"
         TargetControlID="Panel1" ServiceMethod="GetDynamicContent">
        </asp:DynamicPopulateExtender>
        <div onclick="updateGrid(this.value);" value='0'>
        <asp:LinkButton ID="LinkButton1" runat="server"
         OnClientClick="return false;">Customers</asp:LinkButton></div>
        <div onclick="updateGrid(this.value);" value='1'>
        <asp:LinkButton ID="LinkButton2" runat="server"
         OnClientClick="return false;">Employees</asp:LinkButton></div>
        <div onclick="updateGrid(this.value);" value='2'>
        <asp:LinkButton ID="LinkButton3" runat="server"
         OnClientClick="return false;">Products</asp:LinkButton></div>
        <asp:Panel ID="Panel1" runat="server">
        </asp:Panel>
    </div>
    </form>
</body>
</html>
```

Filename DynamicPopulateExtender.aspx

This .aspx page is doing a lot, one thing being that a client-side JavaScript function called `updateGrid()` calls the DynamicPopulateExtender control that is on the page. You will also find three LinkButton server controls, each of which is encased within a `<div>` element that calls the `updateGrid()` function and provides a value that is passed into the function. Because you want the `<div>` element's `onclick` event to be triggered with a click and not the LinkButton control's click event, each LinkButton contains an `OnClientClick` attribute that simply does nothing. This is accomplished using `return false;`.

The DynamicPopulateExtender control on the page targets the `Panel1` control as the container that will take the HTML that comes from the server on an asynchronous request. The DynamicPopulateExtender control knows where to go get the HTML using the `ServiceMethod` attribute. The value of this attribute calls the `GetDynamicContent()` method, which is in the page's code-behind file.

After the .aspx page is in place, the next step is to create the code-behind page. This page will contain the server-side method that is called by the DynamicPopulateExtender control. This is presented in Listing 19-17.

LISTING 19-17: The code-behind page of the DynamicPopulateExtender.aspx page

Available for download on Wrox.com

VB

```
Imports System.Data
Imports System.Data.SqlClient
Imports System.IO

Partial Class DynamicPopulateExtender
    Inherits System.Web.UI.Page

    <System.Web.Services.WebMethodAttribute()>
    <System.Web.Script.Services.ScriptMethodAttribute()>
    Public Shared Function GetDynamicContent(ByVal contextKey As _
      System.String) As System.String
        Dim conn As SqlConnection
        Dim cmd As SqlCommand
        Dim cmdString As String = "Select * from Customers"

        Select Case contextKey
            Case "1"
                cmdString = "Select * from Employees"
            Case "2"
                cmdString = "Select * from Products"
```

continues

LISTING 19-17 *(continued)*

```
        End Select

        conn = New SqlConnection("Data Source=.\SQLEXPRESS;
            AttachDbFilename=|DataDirectory|\NORTHWND.MDF;
            Integrated Security=True;User Instance=True")
            ' Put this string on one line in your code
        cmd = New SqlCommand(cmdString, conn)
        conn.Open()

        Dim myReader As SqlDataReader
        myReader = cmd.ExecuteReader(CommandBehavior.CloseConnection)

        Dim dt As New DataTable
        dt.Load(myReader)
        myReader.Close()

        Dim myGrid As New GridView
        myGrid.ID = "GridView1"
        myGrid.DataSource = dt
        myGrid.DataBind()

        Dim sw As New StringWriter
        Dim htw As HtmlTextWriter = New HtmlTextWriter(sw)

        myGrid.RenderControl(htw)
        htw.Close()

        Return sw.ToString()
    End Function
End Class
```

C#

```
using System.Data;
using System.Data.SqlClient;
using System.IO;
using System.Web.UI;
using System.Web.UI.WebControls;

public partial class DynamicPopulateExtender : System.Web.UI.Page
{
    [System.Web.Services.WebMethodAttribute(),
     System.Web.Script.Services.ScriptMethodAttribute()]
    public static string GetDynamicContent(string contextKey)
    {
        SqlConnection conn;
        SqlCommand cmd;
        string cmdString = "Select * from Customers";

        switch (contextKey)
        {
            case ("1"):
                cmdString = "Select * from Employees";
                break;
            case ("2"):
                cmdString = "Select * from Products";
                break;
        }

        conn = new
            SqlConnection(@"Data Source=.\SQLEXPRESS;
               AttachDbFilename=|DataDirectory|\NORTHWND.MDF;
```

```
                Integrated Security=True;User Instance=True");
                // Put this string on one line in your code
            cmd = new SqlCommand(cmdString, conn);
            conn.Open();

            SqlDataReader myReader;
            myReader = cmd.ExecuteReader(CommandBehavior.CloseConnection);

            DataTable dt = new DataTable();
            dt.Load(myReader);
            myReader.Close();

            GridView myGrid = new GridView();
            myGrid.ID = "GridView1";
            myGrid.DataSource = dt;
            myGrid.DataBind();

            StringWriter sw = new StringWriter();
            HtmlTextWriter htw = new HtmlTextWriter(sw);

            myGrid.RenderControl(htw);
            htw.Close();

            return sw.ToString();
        }
    }
```

Filenames DynamicPopulateExtender.aspx.vb and DynamicPopulateExtender.aspx.cs

This code is the code-behind page for the `DynamicPopulateExtender.aspx` page and contains a single method that is callable asynchronously. The `GetDynamicContent()` method takes a single parameter, `contextKey`, a string value that can be used to determine what link the end user clicked.

Based on the selection, a specific command string is used to populate a `DataTable` object. From here, the `DataTable` object is used as the data source for a programmatic GridView control that is rendered and returned as a string to the client. The client will take the large string and use the text to populate the `Panel1` control that is on the page. Figure 19-20 shows the result of clicking one of the links.

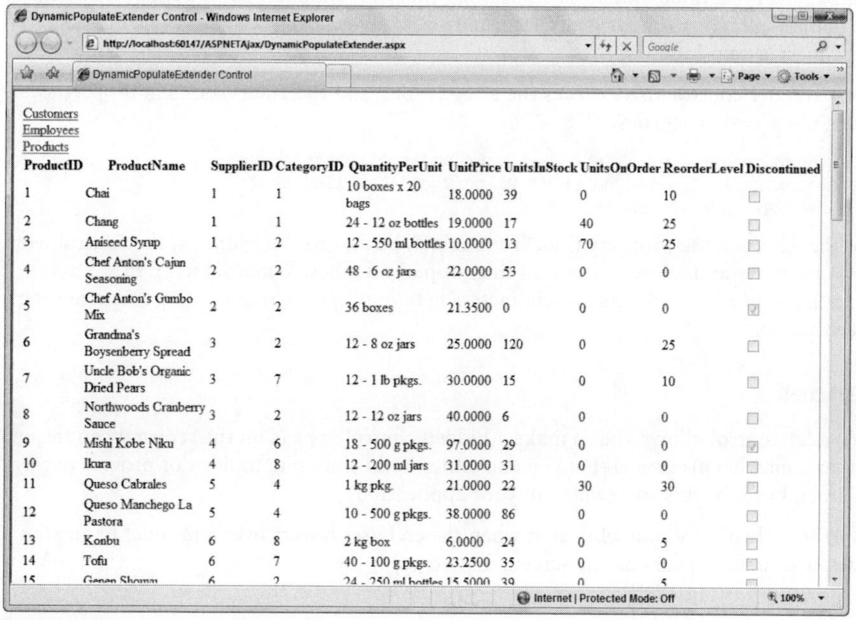

FIGURE 19-20

FilteredTextBoxExtender

The FilteredTextBoxExtender control works off a TextBox control to specify the types of characters the end user can input into the control. For instance, if you want the end user to be able to enter only numbers into the text box, then you can associate a FilteredTextBoxExtender to the TextBox control and specify such behavior. Listing 19-18 presents an example of this.

Available for download on Wrox.com

LISTING 19-18: Filtering a text box to use only numbers

```
<%@ Page Language="C#" %>

<%@ Register Assembly="AjaxControlToolkit"
    Namespace="AjaxControlToolkit" TagPrefix="asp" %>

<html xmlns="http://www.w3.org/1999/xhtml">
<head runat="server">
    <title>FilteredTextBoxExtender Control</title>
</head>
<body>
    <form id="form1" runat="server">
    <div>
        <asp:ToolkitScriptManager ID="ToolkitScriptManager1" runat="server">
        </asp:ToolkitScriptManager>
        <asp:FilteredTextBoxExtender ID="FilteredTextBoxExtender1"
         runat="server"
         TargetControlID="TextBox1" FilterType="Numbers">
        </asp:FilteredTextBoxExtender>
        <asp:TextBox ID="TextBox1" runat="server"></asp:TextBox>
    </div>
    </form>
</body>
</html>
```

In this case, a FilteredTextBoxExtender control is attached to the TextBox1 control through the use of the `TargetControlID` property. The FilteredTextBoxExtender control has a property called `FilterType` that has the possible values of `Custom`, `LowercaseLetters`, `Numbers`, and `UppercaseLetters`.

This example uses a `FilterType` value of `Numbers`, meaning that only numbers can be entered into the text box. If the end user tries to enter any other type of information, then nothing happens — it will seem to the end user as if the key doesn't even function.

The FilteredTextBoxExtender control also exposes the `FilterMode` and the `InvalidChars` properties. Here is an example of using these two properties:

```
<asp:FilteredTextBoxExtender ID="FilteredTextBoxExtender1" runat="server"
 TargetControlID="TextBox1" InvalidChars="*" FilterMode="InvalidChars">
</asp:FilteredTextBoxExtender>
```

The default value of the `FilterMode` property is `ValidChars`. When set to `ValidChars`, the control works from the `FilterType` property and allows only what this property defines. When set to `InvalidChars`, you then use the `InvalidChars` property and put the characters here (multiple characters all go together with no space or item between them).

HoverMenuExtender

The HoverMenuExtender control allows you to make a hidden control appear on the screen when the end user hovers on another control. This means that you can either build elaborate tooltips or provide extra functionality when an end user hovers somewhere in your application.

One example is to change a ListView control so that when the end user hovers over a product name, the Edit button for that row of data appears on the screen. The code for the `<ItemTemplate>` in the ListView control is partially shown in Listing 19-19.

LISTING 19-19: Adding a hover button to the ListView control's ItemTemplate

```
<ItemTemplate>
   <tr style="background-color:#DCDCDC;color:#000000;">
      <td>
         <asp:HoverMenuExtender ID="HoverMenuExtender1" runat="server"
          TargetControlID="ProductNameLabel" PopupControlID="Panel1"
          PopDelay="25" OffsetX="-50">
         </asp:HoverMenuExtender>
         <asp:Panel ID="Panel1" runat="server" Height="50px"
          Width="125px">
            <asp:Button ID="EditButton" runat="server"
             CommandName="Edit" Text="Edit" />
         </asp:Panel>
      </td>
      <td>
         <asp:Label ID="ProductIDLabel" runat="server"
          Text='<%# Eval("ProductID") %>' />
      </td>
      <td>
         <asp:Label ID="ProductNameLabel" runat="server"
          Text='<%# Eval("ProductName") %>' />
      </td>

      <!-- Code removed for clarity -->

   </tr>
</ItemTemplate>
```

Here, a HoverMenuExtender control is attached to the Label control with the `ID` of `ProductNameLabel`, which appears in each row of the ListView control. This is done using the `TargetControlID` property, whereas the `PopupControlID` property is used to assign the control that appears dynamically when a user hovers the mouse over the targeted control.

The HoverMenuExtender control exposes several properties that control the style and behaviors of the pop-up. The `PopDelay` property is used in this example and provides a means to delay the pop-up from occurring (in milliseconds). The `OffsetX` and `OffsetY` properties specify the location of the pop-up based on the targeted control. In this case, the offset is set to `-50` (pixels). Figure 19-21 shows the results of the operation.

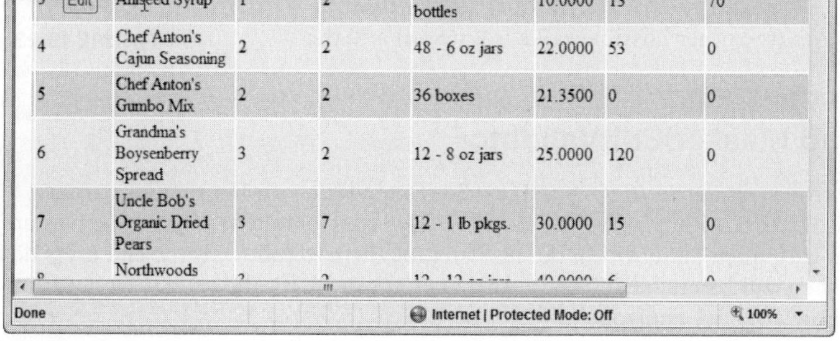

FIGURE 19-21

ListSearchExtender

The ListSearchExtender control extends either a ListBox or a DropDownList control, although not always with the best results in browsers such as Opera and Safari. This extender allows you to provide search capabilities through large collections that are located in either of these controls. This alleviates the need for the end users to search through the collection to find the item they are looking for.

When utilized, the extender adds a search text that shows the characters the end user types for their search area above the control. Listing 19-20 shows the use of this extender.

Available for download on Wrox.com

LISTING 19-20: Extending a ListBox control with the ListSearchExtender control

```
<%@ Page Language="C#" %>

<%@ Register Assembly="AjaxControlToolkit"
    Namespace="AjaxControlToolkit" TagPrefix="asp" %>

<html xmlns="http://www.w3.org/1999/xhtml">
<head runat="server">
    <title>ListSearchExtender Control</title>
</head>
<body>
    <form id="form1" runat="server">
    <div>
        <asp:ToolkitScriptManager ID="ToolkitScriptManager1" runat="server">
        </asp:ToolkitScriptManager>
        <asp:ListSearchExtender ID="ListSearchExtender1" runat="server"
         TargetControlID="ListBox1">
        </asp:ListSearchExtender>
        <asp:ListBox ID="ListBox1" runat="server" Width="150">
            <asp:ListItem>Aardvark</asp:ListItem>
            <asp:ListItem>Bee</asp:ListItem>
            <asp:ListItem>Camel</asp:ListItem>
            <asp:ListItem>Dog</asp:ListItem>
            <asp:ListItem>Elephant</asp:ListItem>
        </asp:ListBox>
    </div>
    </form>
</body>
</html>
```

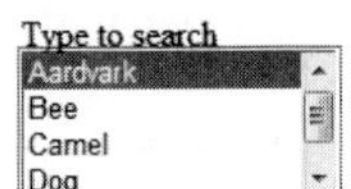

FIGURE 19-22

In this case, the only property used in the ListSearchExtender control is the `TargetControlID` property to associate which control it extends. Running this page produces the results shown in Figure 19-22.

Then, as an end user, when you start typing, you will see what you are typing in the text above the control (as shown in Figure 19-23).

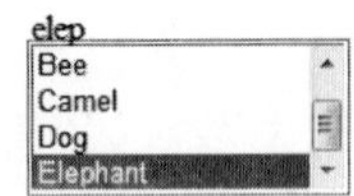

FIGURE 19-23

You can customize the text that appears at the top of the control with the `PromptCssClass`, `PromptPosition`, and `PromptText` properties. By default, the `PromptPosition` is set to `Top` (the other possible value is `Bottom`) and the `PromptText` value is `Type to search`.

MaskedEditExtender and MaskedEditValidator

The MaskedEditExtender control is similar to the FilteredTextBoxExtender control in that it restricts the end user from entering specific text within a TextBox control. This control takes the process one step further by providing end users with a template within the text box for them to follow. If the end users do not follow the template, then they will be unable to proceed and might receive a validation warning from the control using the MaskedEditValidator control.

Listing 19-21 provides an example of using both of these controls.

LISTING 19-21: Using both the MaskedEditExtender and the MaskedEditValidator controls

Available for download on Wrox.com

```
<%@ Page Language="C#" %>

<%@ Register Assembly="AjaxControlToolkit"
    Namespace="AjaxControlToolkit" TagPrefix="asp" %>

<html xmlns="http://www.w3.org/1999/xhtml">
<head runat="server">
    <title>MaskedEditExtender Control</title>
</head>
<body>
    <form id="form1" runat="server">
    <div>
        <asp:ToolkitScriptManager ID="ToolkitScriptManager1" runat="server">
        </asp:ToolkitScriptManager>
        <asp:MaskedEditExtender ID="MaskedEditExtender1" runat="server"
         TargetControlID="TextBox1" MaskType="Number" Mask="999">
        </asp:MaskedEditExtender>
        <asp:TextBox ID="TextBox1" runat="server"></asp:TextBox>
        <asp:MaskedEditValidator ID="MaskedEditValidator1"
         runat="server" ControlExtender="MaskedEditExtender1"
         ControlToValidate="TextBox1" IsValidEmpty="False"
         EmptyValueMessage="A three digit number is required!"
         Display="Dynamic"></asp:MaskedEditValidator>
    </div>
    </form>
</body>
</html>
```

In this case, the MaskedEditExtender control uses the `TargetControlID` to associate itself with the TextBox1 control. The `MaskType` property supplies the type of mask or filter to place on the text box. The possible values include:

- `None`: No validation will be performed.
- `Date`: Date validation will occur.
- `DateTime`: Date and time validation will occur.
- `Number`: A number validation will occur.
- `Time`: A time validation will occur

Listing 19-21 uses `Number` and then specifies the mask or template the numbers need to take. This is done through the use of the `Mask` property. In this case, the `Mask` property is set to `999`. This means that all numbers can be only three digits in length.

Using `999` as a value to the `Mask` property means that when an end user enters a value in the text box, he will be presented with three underscores inside the text box. Figure 19-24 shows the template for entering items.

FIGURE 19-24

If the `Mask` property is changed to `99,999.99` as follows:

```
<asp:MaskedEditExtender ID="MaskedEditExtender1" runat="server"
 TargetControlID="TextBox1" MaskType="Number" Mask="99,999.99">
</asp:MaskedEditExtender>
```

then the text box template appears, as illustrated in Figure 19-25.

FIGURE 19-25

From Figure 19-25, you can see that the comma and the period are present in the template. As the end users type, they do not need to retype these values. The cursor will simply move to the next section of numbers required.

As you can see from the `Mask` property value, numbers are represented by the number `9`. When working with other `MaskType` values, you also need to be aware of the other mask characters:

- `9` — Only a numeric character
- `L` — Only a letter
- `$` — Only a letter or a space
- `C` — Only a custom character (case sensitive)
- `A` — Only a letter or a custom character
- `N` — Only a numeric or custom character
- `?` — Any character

In addition to the character specifications, the template uses delimiters, which are detailed in the following list:

- `/` is a date separator.
- `:` is a time separator.
- `.` is a decimal separator.
- `,` is a thousand separator.
- `\` is the escape character.
- `{` is the initial delimiter for repetition of masks.
- `}` is the final delimiter for repetition of masks.

Using some of these items, you can easily change MaskedEditExtender to deal with a `DateTime` value:

```
<asp:MaskedEditExtender ID="MaskedEditExtender1" runat="server"
 TargetControlID="TextBox1" MaskType="DateTime" Mask="99/99/9999 99:99:99">
</asp:MaskedEditExtender>
```

The template created in the text box for this is shown in Figure 19-26.

FIGURE 19-26

The MaskedEditExtender control has many properties that are exposed to control and manipulate the behavior and style of the text box. The MaskedEditExtender control can work in conjunction with the MaskedEditValidator control, which provides validation against the text box controls.

In the earlier example, the validation was accomplished through an instance of the MaskedEditValidator control.

```
<asp:MaskedEditValidator ID="MaskedEditValidator1" runat="server"
 ControlExtender="MaskedEditExtender1" ControlToValidate="TextBox1"
 IsValidEmpty="False" EmptyValueMessage="A three digit number is required!"
 Display="Dynamic"></asp:MaskedEditValidator>
```

This control uses the `ControlExtender` property to associate itself with the MaskedEditExtender control and uses the `ControlToValidate` property to watch a specific control on the form. By default, the `IsValidEmpty` property is set to `True`. Changing it to `False` means that the end user will be required to enter some value in the text box in order to pass validation and not receive the error message that is presented in the `EmptyValueMessage` property.

Triggering the MaskedEditValidator control gives you something like the message shown in Figure 19-27. It is important to remember that you can style the control in many ways to produce the validation message appearance that you are looking for.

A three digit number is required!

FIGURE 19-27

MutuallyExclusiveCheckBoxExtender

Often, you want to offer a list of check boxes that behave as if they are radio buttons. That is, when you have a collection of check boxes, you want the end user to make only a single selection from the provided list of items.

Using the MutuallyExclusiveCheckBoxExtender control, you can perform such an action. Listing 19-22 shows you how to accomplish this task.

LISTING 19-22: Using the MutuallyExclusiveCheckBoxExtender control with check boxes

Available for download on Wrox.com

```
<%@ Page Language="C#" %>

<%@ Register Assembly="AjaxControlToolkit"
    Namespace="AjaxControlToolkit" TagPrefix="asp" %>

<html xmlns="http://www.w3.org/1999/xhtml">
<head runat="server">
    <title>MutuallyExclusiveCheckBoxExtender Control</title>
</head>
<body>
    <form id="form1" runat="server">
    <div>
        <asp:ToolkitScriptManager ID="ToolkitScriptManager1" runat="server">
        </asp:ToolkitScriptManager>
        <asp:MutuallyExclusiveCheckBoxExtender
         ID="MutuallyExclusiveCheckBoxExtender1" runat="server"
         TargetControlID="CheckBox1" Key="MyCheckboxes" />
        <asp:CheckBox ID="CheckBox1" runat="server" Text="Blue" />
        <br />
        <asp:MutuallyExclusiveCheckBoxExtender
         ID="MutuallyExclusiveCheckBoxExtender2" runat="server"
         TargetControlID="CheckBox2" Key="MyCheckboxes" />
        <asp:CheckBox ID="CheckBox2" runat="server" Text="Brown" />
        <br />
        <asp:MutuallyExclusiveCheckBoxExtender
         ID="MutuallyExclusiveCheckBoxExtender3" runat="server"
         TargetControlID="CheckBox3" Key="MyCheckboxes" />
        <asp:CheckBox ID="CheckBox3" runat="server" Text="Green" />
        <br />
        <asp:MutuallyExclusiveCheckBoxExtender
         ID="MutuallyExclusiveCheckBoxExtender4" runat="server"
         TargetControlID="CheckBox4" Key="MyCheckboxes" />
        <asp:CheckBox ID="CheckBox4" runat="server" Text="Orange" />
        <br />
    </div>
    </form>
</body>
</html>
```

Associating a MutuallyExclusiveCheckBoxExtender control with a CheckBoxList control is impossible; therefore, each of the check boxes needs to be laid out with CheckBox controls as the previous code demonstrates. You need to have one MutuallyExclusiveCheckBoxExtender control for each CheckBox control on the page.

You form a group of CheckBox controls by using the `Key` property. All the check boxes that you want in one group need to have the same `Key` value. In the example in Listing 19-22, all the check boxes share a `Key` value of `MyCheckboxes`.

Running this page results in a list of four check boxes. When you select one of the check boxes, a check mark appears. Then, when you select another check box, the first check box you selected gets deselected. The best part is that you can even deselect what you have selected in the group, thereby selecting nothing in the check box group.

NumericUpDownExtender

The NumericUpDownExtender control allows you to put some up/down indicators next to a TextBox control that enable the end user to more easily control a selection.

A simple example of this is illustrated in Listing 19-23.

Available for download on Wrox.com

LISTING 19-23: Using the NumericUpDownExtender control

```
<%@ Page Language="C#" %>

<%@ Register Assembly="AjaxControlToolkit"
    Namespace="AjaxControlToolkit" TagPrefix="asp" %>

<html xmlns="http://www.w3.org/1999/xhtml">
<head runat="server">
    <title>NumericUpDownExtender Control</title>
</head>
<body>
    <form id="form1" runat="server">
    <div>
        <asp:ToolkitScriptManager ID="ToolkitScriptManager1" runat="server">
        </asp:ToolkitScriptManager>
        <asp:NumericUpDownExtender ID="NumericUpDownExtender1"
         runat="server" TargetControlID="TextBox1" Width="150"
         Maximum="10" Minimum="1">
        </asp:NumericUpDownExtender>
        <asp:TextBox ID="TextBox1" runat="server"></asp:TextBox>
    </div>
    </form>
</body>
</html>
```

The NumericUpDownExtender control here extends the TextBox control on the page. When using the NumericUpDownExtender control, you must specify the width of the control with the `Width` property. Otherwise, you will see only the up and down arrow keys and not the text box area. In this case, the `Width` property is set to `150` (pixels). The `Maximum` and `Minimum` properties provide the range used by the up and down indicators.

With a `Maximum` value setting of `10` and a `Minimum` value of `1`, the only range in the control will be 1 through 10. Running this page produces the results shown in Figure 19-28.

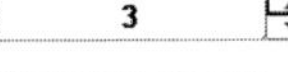

FIGURE 19-28

In addition to numbers, as shown in Listing 19-23, you can use text, as illustrated in Listing 19-24.

Available for download on Wrox.com

LISTING 19-24: Using characters instead of numbers with NumericUpDownExtender

```
<asp:NumericUpDownExtender ID="NumericUpDownExtender1" runat="server"
 TargetControlID="TextBox1" Width="150"
 RefValues="Blue;Brown;Green;Orange;Black;White">
</asp:NumericUpDownExtender>
```

In this case, the words are defined within the `RefValues` property (all separated with a semicolon). This gives you the results presented in Figure 19-29.

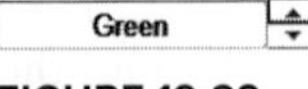

FIGURE 19-29

PagingBulletedListExtender

The PagingBulletedListExtender control allows you to take long bulleted lists and easily apply alphabetic paging to the list. For an example of this, Listing 19-25 works off the Customers table within the Northwind database.

LISTING 19-25: Paging a bulleted list from the Northwind database

Available for download on Wrox.com

```
<%@ Page Language="C#" %>

<%@ Register Assembly="AjaxControlToolkit"
    Namespace="AjaxControlToolkit" TagPrefix="asp" %>

<html xmlns="http://www.w3.org/1999/xhtml">
<head runat="server">
    <title>PagingBulletedListExtender Control</title>
</head>
<body>
    <form id="form1" runat="server">
    <div>
        <asp:ToolkitScriptManager ID="ToolkitScriptManager1" runat="server">
        </asp:ToolkitScriptManager>
        <asp:PagingBulletedListExtender
         ID="PagingBulletedListExtender1"
         runat="server" TargetControlID="BulletedList1">
        </asp:PagingBulletedListExtender>
        <asp:SqlDataSource ID="SqlDataSource1" runat="server"
            ConnectionString="Data Source=.\SQLEXPRESS;
               AttachDbFilename=|DataDirectory|\NORTHWND.MDF;
               Integrated Security=True;User Instance=True"
            ProviderName="System.Data.SqlClient"
            SelectCommand="SELECT [CompanyName] FROM [Customers]">
        </asp:SqlDataSource>
        <asp:BulletedList ID="BulletedList1" runat="server"
            DataSourceID="SqlDataSource1" DataTextField="CompanyName"
            DataValueField="CompanyName">
        </asp:BulletedList>
    </div>
    </form>
</body>
</html>
```

This code pulls all the `CompanyName` values from the Customers table of the Northwind database and binds those values to the BulletList control on the page. Running this page gives you the results illustrated in Figure 19-30.

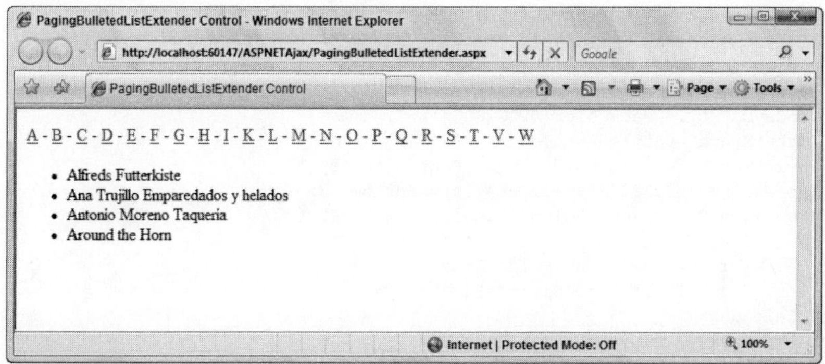

FIGURE 19-30

From this figure, you can see that the paging is organized alphabetically on the client side. Only the letters for which there are values appear in the linked list of letters. Clicking any of the letters gives you the items from the bulleted list that start with that character.

PopupControlExtender

The PopupControlExtender control allows you to create a pop-up for any control on your page. For instance, you can completely mimic the CalendarExtender control that was presented earlier by creating a pop-up containing a Calendar control off a TextBox control. Listing 19-26 mimics this behavior.

LISTING 19-26: Creating a CalendarExtender control with PopupControlExtender

Available for download on Wrox.com

```
<%@ Page Language="VB" %>

<%@ Register Assembly="AjaxControlToolkit"
    Namespace="AjaxControlToolkit" TagPrefix="asp" %>

<script runat="server">
    Protected Sub Calendar1_SelectionChanged(ByVal sender As Object,
      ByVal e As System.EventArgs)
        PopupControlExtender1.Commit(
           Calendar1.SelectedDate.ToShortDateString())
    End Sub
</script>

<html xmlns="http://www.w3.org/1999/xhtml"><head runat="server">
    <title>PopupControlExtender Control</title>
</head>
<body>
    <form id="form1" runat="server">
    <div>
        <asp:ToolkitScriptManager ID="ToolkitScriptManager1" runat="server">
        </asp:ToolkitScriptManager>
        <asp:PopupControlExtender ID="PopupControlExtender1"
         runat="server" TargetControlID="TextBox1"
         PopupControlID="UpdatePanel1" OffsetY="25">
        </asp:PopupControlExtender>
        <asp:TextBox ID="TextBox1" runat="server"></asp:TextBox>
        <asp:UpdatePanel ID="UpdatePanel1" runat="server">
            <ContentTemplate>
                <asp:Calendar ID="Calendar1" runat="server"
                 BackColor="White" BorderColor="White"
                 BorderWidth="1px" Font-Names="Verdana"
                 Font-Size="9pt" ForeColor="Black" Height="190px"
                 NextPrevFormat="FullMonth" Width="350px"
                 OnSelectionChanged="Calendar1_SelectionChanged">
                    <SelectedDayStyle BackColor="#333399"
                     ForeColor="White" />
                    <TodayDayStyle BackColor="#CCCCCC" />
                    <OtherMonthDayStyle ForeColor="#999999" />
                    <NextPrevStyle Font-Bold="True" Font-Size="8pt"
                     ForeColor="#333333" VerticalAlign="Bottom" />
                    <DayHeaderStyle Font-Bold="True" Font-Size="8pt" />
                    <TitleStyle BackColor="White" BorderColor="Black"
                     BorderWidth="4px" Font-Bold="True"
                     Font-Size="12pt" ForeColor="#333399" />
                </asp:Calendar>
            </ContentTemplate>
        </asp:UpdatePanel>
    </div>
    </form>
</body>
</html>
```

C#

```
<%@ Page Language="C#" %>

<%@ Register Assembly="AjaxControlToolkit"
Namespace="AjaxControlToolkit"
    TagPrefix="asp" %>

<script runat="server">
    protected void Calendar1_SelectionChanged(object sender,
       EventArgs e)
    {
        PopupControlExtender1.Commit(
           Calendar1.SelectedDate.ToShortDateString());
    }
</script>
```

When running this page, you get a single text box on the page. Click within the text box and a pop-up calendar appears so you can select a date that will be populated back into the text box (as illustrated in Figure 19-31).

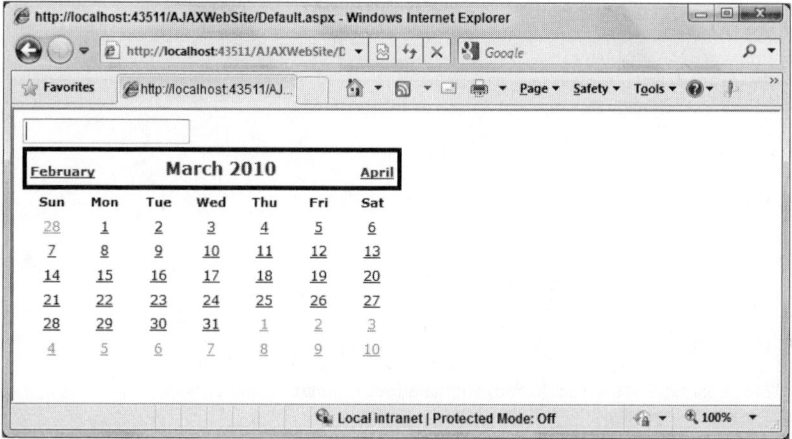

FIGURE 19-31

You will want to place your pop-up control within an ASP.NET AJAX UpdatePanel control and to pass the value from the pop-up control back to the target control (the TextBox1 control), so you use the `Commit()` method:

```
PopupControlExtender1.Commit(Calendar1.SelectedDate.ToShortDateString())
```

ResizableControlExtender

In many situations, you may want to limit the size of an element when it is initially displayed but allow users to grow or shrink the element as they see fit. The ResizableControlExtender makes this easy. Place the ResizableControl on the page and point it to an ASP.NET Panel control using the `TargetControlID` property.

The ResizableControlExtender control allows you to take a Panel control and give end users the ability to grab a handle and change the size of the element. Anything you put inside the Panel control will then change in size depending on how the end user extends the item. For this to work, you also need to create a handle for the end user to work from in pulling or contracting the item.

Use the `HandleCssClass` property to specify the style information about the appearance of the handle the user selects to begin resizing the panel. The `ResizableCssClass` property refers to style information shown while the panel is being altered.

The control also exposes events that are raised that you can attach code to in order to react to the panel being resized: `OnClientResizeBegin`, `OnClientResizing`, and finally `OnClientResize`. These are very useful for actions such as altering text size or retrieving additional data if the panel is enlarged or hiding elements if the panel is shrunk. Listing 19-27 is an example of using the ResizableControlExtender with the CSS information inline in the page. The example shows you how to use the ResizableControlExtender with an image.

LISTING 19-27: Using the ResizableControlExtender control with an image

Available for download on Wrox.com

```
<%@ Page Language="C#" %>

<%@ Register Assembly="AjaxControlToolkit"
    Namespace="AjaxControlToolkit" TagPrefix="asp" %>

<html xmlns="http://www.w3.org/1999/xhtml">
<head runat="server">
    <title>ResizableControlExtender Control</title>
    <style type="text/css">
        .handle
        {
            width:10px;
            height:10px;
            background-color:Black;
        }
        .resizable
        {
            border-style:solid;
            border-width:2px;
            border-color:Black;
        }
    </style>
</head>
<body>
    <form id="form1" runat="server">
    <div>
        <asp:ToolkitScriptManager ID="ToolkitScriptManager1" runat="server">
        </asp:ToolkitScriptManager>
        <asp:ResizableControlExtender ID="ResizableControlExtender1"
         runat="server"
         TargetControlID="Panel1" HandleCssClass="handle"
         ResizableCssClass="resizable">
        </asp:ResizableControlExtender>
        <asp:Panel ID="Panel1" runat="server" Width="300" Height="225">
            <asp:Image ID="Image1" runat="server"
             ImageUrl="Images/Garden.jpg"
             style="width:100%; height:100%"/>
        </asp:Panel>
    </div>
    </form>
</body>
</html>
```

In this example, the ResizableControlExtender control depends on CSS to create the handle for the end user to grab to resize the Panel control. The `TargetControlID` property points to the control to be resized.

Two CSS references are in the ResizableControlExtender control. One deals with the control as it sits on the screen with no end user interaction. This is really to show the end user that there is an ability to resize the element. This is done through the `HandleCssClass` property. The value of this property points to the CSS class `handle` contained within the same file. The second CSS reference deals with the control as it is clicked and held (when the end user does not let up with the mouse click performed). This one is done with the `ResizableCssClass` property. The value of this property points to the CSS class `resizable`.

When compiled and run, the code should generate the same page presented in Figure 19-32.

FIGURE 19-32

You can see in the top screenshot how the image looks when there is no end user interaction. In this case, there is a black square (as defined by the CSS) in the lower-right corner of the image. The screenshot on the bottom shows what happens when the end user grabs the handle and starts changing the shape of the image.

RoundedCornersExtender

The RoundedCornersExtender control allows you to put rounded corners on the elements on your page. As with the ResizableControlExtender control, you put the element you are interested in working with inside of a Panel control. Listing 19-28 shows this done with a Login server control.

LISTING 19-28: Rounding the corners of the Panel control containing a Login server control

Available for download on Wrox.com

```
<%@ Page Language="C#" %>

<%@ Register Assembly="AjaxControlToolkit" Namespace="AjaxControlToolkit" TagPrefix="asp" %>

<html xmlns="http://www.w3.org/1999/xhtml">
<head runat="server">
    <title>RoundedCornersExtender Control</title>
</head>
<body>
    <form id="form1" runat="server">
    <div>
        <asp:ToolkitScriptManager ID="ToolkitScriptManager1" runat="server">
```

continues

LISTING 19-28 *(continued)*

```
            </asp:ToolkitScriptManager>
            <asp:RoundedCornersExtender ID="RoundedCornersExtender1"
             runat="server" TargetControlID="Panel1">
            </asp:RoundedCornersExtender>
            <asp:Panel ID="Panel1" runat="server" Width="250px"
             HorizontalAlign="Center" BackColor="Orange">
                <asp:Login ID="Login1" runat="server">
                </asp:Login>
            </asp:Panel>
        </div>
        </form>
    </body>
    </html>
```

Here, the RoundedCornersExtender control simply points to the Panel control with the `TargetControlID` property. This Panel control has a background color of orange to show that the corners are indeed rounded. The result of this bit of code is illustrated in Figure 19-33.

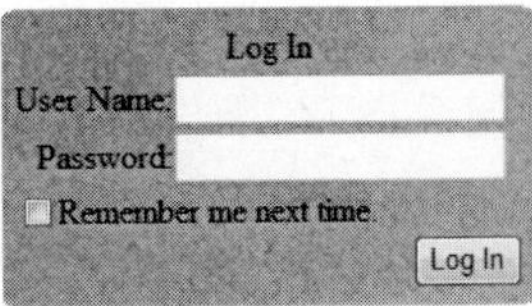

FIGURE 19-33

You can control the degree of the rounded corners using the `Radius` property of the RoundedCornersExtender control. By default, this property is set to a value of `5`. You can even choose the corners that you want to round using the `Corners` property. The possible values of the `Corners` property include `All`, `Bottom`, `BottomLeft`, `BottomRight`, `Left`, `None`, `Right`, `Top`, `TopLeft`, and `TopRight`.

SliderExtender and MultiHandleSliderExtender

The SliderExtender control actually extends a TextBox control to make it look like nothing it normally does. This ASP.NET AJAX control gives you the ability to create a true slider control that allows the end user to select a range of numbers using a mouse instead of typing in the number. Listing 19-29 shows a simple example of using the slider.

Available for download on Wrox.com

LISTING 19-29: Using the SliderExtender control

```
<%@ Page Language="C#" %>

<%@ Register Assembly="AjaxControlToolkit"
    Namespace="AjaxControlToolkit" TagPrefix="asp" %>

<html xmlns="http://www.w3.org/1999/xhtml">
<head runat="server">
    <title>SliderExtender Control</title>
</head>
<body>
    <form id="form1" runat="server">
    <div>
        <asp:ToolkitScriptManager ID="ToolkitScriptManager1" runat="server">
        </asp:ToolkitScriptManager>
        <asp:SliderExtender ID="SliderExtender1" runat="server"
         TargetControlID="TextBox1">
        </asp:SliderExtender>
        <asp:TextBox ID="TextBox1" runat="server"></asp:TextBox>
    </div>
    </form>
</body>
</html>
```

This little bit of code to tie a SliderExtender control to a typical TextBox control is simple and produces the result presented in Figure 19-34.

FIGURE 19-34

This is fine, but it is hard for the end users to tell what number they are selecting. Therefore, you might find it better to give a signifier to the end user. Adding a Label control to the page (called Label1) and changing the SliderExtender control to include a `BoundControlID` property gives you the signifier that you are looking for. Here is the code for this change:

```
<asp:SliderExtender ID="SliderExtender1" runat="server" TargetControlID="TextBox1"
 BoundControlID="Label1">
</asp:SliderExtender>
```

This small change produces the result (with the appropriate Label control on the page) shown in Figure 19-35.

50

FIGURE 19-35

Now when the end users slide the handle on the slider, they see the number that they are working with quite easily. Some of the following properties are available to the SliderExtender control:

- `Decimal`: Allows you to specify the number of decimals the result should take. The more decimals you have, the more unlikely the end user will be able to pick an exact number.
- `HandleCssClass`: The CSS class that you are using to design the handle.
- `HandleImageUrl`: The image file you are using to represent the handle.
- `Length`: The length of the slider in pixels. The default value is `150`.
- `Maximum`: The maximum number represented in the slider. The default value is `100`.
- `Minimum`: The minimum number represented in the slider. The default value is `0`.
- `Orientation`: The orientation of the slider. The possible values include `Horizontal` and `Vertical`. The default value is `Horizontal`.
- `RailCssClass`: The CSS class that you are using to design the rail of the slider.
- `ToolTipText`: The tooltip when the end user hovers over the slider. Using `0` within the text allows you to show the end user the position the slider is currently in.

The MultiHandleSliderExtender is basically the same thing, but this particular extender allows you to have more than one handle for the end user to work with. This works great if you need a slider that needs to do things like allow the end user to select a range or a minimum/maximum value.

SlideShowExtender

The SlideShowExtender control allows you to put an image slideshow in the browser. The slideshow controls enable the end user to move to the next or previous images as well as to simply play the images as a slideshow with a defined wait between each image. Listing 19-30 shows an example of creating a slideshow.

Available for download on Wrox.com

LISTING 19-30: Creating a slideshow with three images

.ASPX

```
<%@ Page Language="VB" AutoEventWireup="true"
    CodeFile="SlideShowExtender.aspx.vb"
    Inherits="SlideShowExtender" %>

<%@ Register Assembly="AjaxControlToolkit"
    Namespace="AjaxControlToolkit" TagPrefix="asp" %>

<html xmlns="http://www.w3.org/1999/xhtml">
<head runat="server">
    <title>SlideShowExtender Control</title>
```

continues

LISTING 19-30 *(continued)*

```
</head>
<body>
    <form id="form1" runat="server">
    <div>
        <asp:ToolkitScriptManager ID="ToolkitScriptManager1" runat="server">
        </asp:ToolkitScriptManager>
        <asp:Panel ID="Panel1" runat="server" Width="300px"
         HorizontalAlign="Center">
            <asp:SlideShowExtender ID="SlideShowExtender1"
                runat="server"
                ImageTitleLabelID="LabelTitle" TargetControlID="Image1"
                UseContextKey="True" NextButtonID="ButtonNext"
                PlayButtonID="ButtonPlay"
                PreviousButtonID="ButtonPrevious"
                SlideShowServiceMethod="GetSlides"
                ImageDescriptionLabelID="LabelDescription">
            </asp:SlideShowExtender>
            <asp:Label ID="LabelTitle" runat="server" Text="Label"
             Font-Bold="True"></asp:Label><br /><br />
            <asp:Image ID="Image1" runat="server"
             ImageUrl="Images/Garden.jpg" /><br />
            <asp:Label ID="LabelDescription" runat="server"
             Text="Label"></asp:Label><br /><br />
            <asp:Button ID="ButtonPrevious" runat="server"
             Text="Previous" />
            <asp:Button ID="ButtonNext" runat="server" Text="Next" />
            <asp:Button ID="ButtonPlay" runat="server" />
        </asp:Panel>
    </div>
    </form>
</body>
</html>
```

Filename SlideShowExtender.aspx

The SlideShowExtender control has a lot of properties available. You can specify the location where you are defining the image title and description using the `ImageTitleLabelID` and the `ImageDescriptionLabelID` properties. In addition, this page contains three Button controls: one to act as the Previous button, another for the Next button, and the final one as the Play button. However, it is important to note that when the Play button is clicked (to start the slideshow), it turns into the Stop button.

The `SlideShowServiceMethod` property is important because it points to the server-side method that returns the images that are part of the slide show. In this case, it is referring to a method called `GetSlides`, which is represented in Listing 19-31.

LISTING 19-31: The GetSlides method implementation

Available for download on Wrox.com

VB

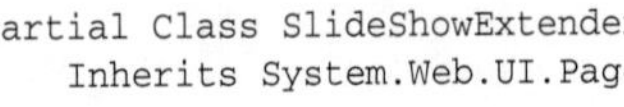

```
Partial Class SlideShowExtender
    Inherits System.Web.UI.Page

    <System.Web.Services.WebMethodAttribute()>
    <System.Web.Script.Services.ScriptMethodAttribute()>
    Public Shared Function GetSlides(ByVal _
     contextKey As System.String) As AjaxControlToolkit.Slide()

               Return New AjaxControlToolkit.Slide() {
                  New AjaxControlToolkit.Slide("Images/Creek.jpg",
                     "The Creek", "This is a picture of a creek."),
                  New AjaxControlToolkit.Slide("Images/Dock.jpg",
```

```
                    "The Dock", "This is a picture of a dock."),
                New AjaxControlToolkit.Slide("Images/Garden.jpg",
                    "The Garden", "This is a picture of a garden.") }
    End Function
End Class
```

C#

```
public partial class SlideShowExtender : System.Web.UI.Page
{
    [System.Web.Services.WebMethodAttribute(),
     System.Web.Script.Services.ScriptMethodAttribute()]
    public static AjaxControlToolkit.Slide[]
      GetSlides(string contextKey)
    {
        return new AjaxControlToolkit.Slide[] {
            new AjaxControlToolkit.Slide("Images/Creek.jpg",
              "The Creek", "This is a picture of a creek."),
            new AjaxControlToolkit.Slide("Images/Dock.jpg",
              "The Dock", "This is a picture of a dock."),
            new AjaxControlToolkit.Slide("Images/Garden.jpg",
              "The Garden", "This is a picture of a garden.") };
    }
}
```

Filenames SlideShowExtender.aspx.vb and SlideShowExtender.aspx.cs

With the code-behind in place, the SlideShowExtender has a server-side method to call for the photos. This method, called `GetSlides()`, returns an array of `Slide` objects that require the location of the object (the path), the title, and the description. When running this page, you get something similar to the results shown in Figure 19-36.

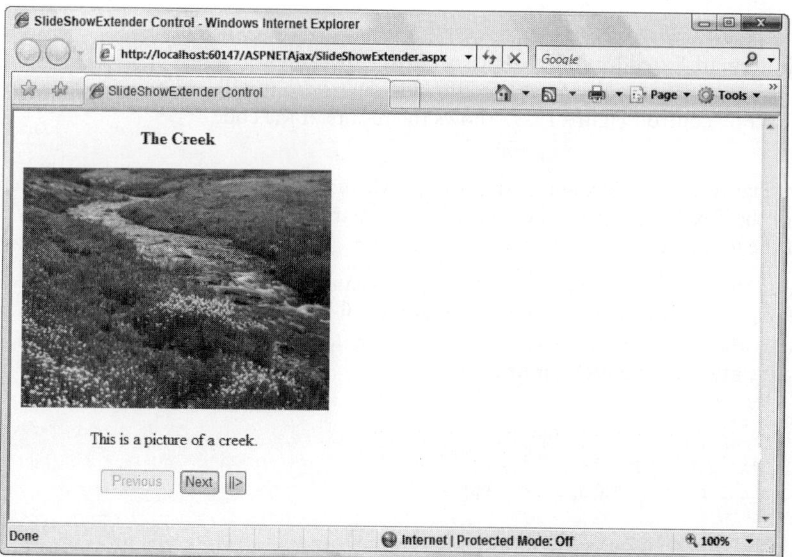

FIGURE 19-36

Clicking the Play button on the page rotates the images until they are done. They will not repeat in a loop unless you have the SlideShowExtender control's `Loop` property set to `True`. (It is set to `False` by default.)

The other important property to pay attention to is the `PlayInterval` property. The value of this property is an integer that represents the number of milliseconds that the browser will take to change to the next photo in the series of images. By default, this is set to `3000` milliseconds.

TextBoxWatermarkExtender

The TextBoxWatermarkExtender control allows you to put instructions within controls for the end users, which gives them a better understanding of what to use the control for. This can be text or even images (when using CSS). Listing 19-32 shows an example of using this control with a TextBox server control.

LISTING 19-32: Using the TextBoxWatermarkExtender control with a TextBox control

Available for download on Wrox.com

```
<%@ Page Language="C#" %>

<%@ Register Assembly="AjaxControlToolkit"
    Namespace="AjaxControlToolkit" TagPrefix="asp" %>

<html xmlns="http://www.w3.org/1999/xhtml">
<head runat="server">
    <title>TextBoxWatermarkExtender Control</title>
</head>
<body>
    <form id="form1" runat="server">
    <div>
        <asp:ToolkitScriptManager ID="ToolkitScriptManager1" runat="server">
        </asp:ToolkitScriptManager>
        <asp:TextBoxWatermarkExtender ID="TextBoxWatermarkExtender1"
         runat="server" WatermarkText="Enter in something here!"
         TargetControlID="TextBox1">
        </asp:TextBoxWatermarkExtender>
        <asp:TextBox ID="TextBox1" runat="server"></asp:TextBox>
    </div>
    </form>
</body>
</html>
```

In this case, the TextBoxWatermarkExtender control is associated with a simple TextBox control and uses the `WatermarkText` property to provide the text that will appear inside the actual TextBox control. Figure 19-37 shows the results of the code from this listing.

Enter in something here!

FIGURE 19-37

The text in the image from Figure 19-37 is straight text with no style inside of the TextBox control. When the end user clicks inside of the TextBox control, the text will disappear and the cursor will be properly placed at the beginning of the text box.

To apply some style to the content that you use as a watermark, you can use the `WatermarkCssClass` property. You can change the code to include a bit of style, as shown in Listing 19-33.

LISTING 19-33: Applying style to the watermark

Available for download on Wrox.com

```
<%@ Page Language="C#" %>

<%@ Register Assembly="AjaxControlToolkit"
    Namespace="AjaxControlToolkit" TagPrefix="asp" %>

<html xmlns="http://www.w3.org/1999/xhtml">
<head runat="server">
    <title>TextBoxWatermarkExtender Control</title>
    <style type="text/css">
        .watermark
        {
         width:150px;
         font:Verdana;
         font-style:italic;
```

```
            color:GrayText;
        }

    </style>
</head>
<body>
    <form id="form1" runat="server">
    <div>
        <asp:ToolkitScriptManager ID="ToolkitScriptManager1" runat="server">
        </asp:ToolkitScriptManager>
        <asp:TextBoxWatermarkExtender ID="TextBoxWatermarkExtender1"
         runat="server" WatermarkText="Enter in something here!"
         TargetControlID="TextBox1"
         WatermarkCssClass="watermark">
        </asp:TextBoxWatermarkExtender>
        <asp:TextBox ID="TextBox1" runat="server"></asp:TextBox>
    </div>
    </form>
</body>
</html>
```

This time, the `WatermarkCssClass` property is used and points to the inline CSS class, `watermark`, which is on the page. Running this page, you will see the style applied as shown in Figure 19-38.

Enter in something here!

FIGURE 19-38

ToggleButtonExtender

The ToggleButtonExtender control works with CheckBox controls and allows you to use an image of your own instead of the standard check box images that the CheckBox controls typically use. Using the ToggleButtonExtender control, you are able to specify images for checked, unchecked, and disabled statuses. Listing 19-34 shows an example of using this control.

LISTING 19-34: Using the ToggleButtonExtender control

Available for download on Wrox.com

```
<%@ Page Language="C#" %>

<%@ Register Assembly="AjaxControlToolkit"
    Namespace="AjaxControlToolkit" TagPrefix="asp" %>

<html xmlns="http://www.w3.org/1999/xhtml">
<head runat="server">
    <title>ToggleButtonExtender Control</title>
</head>
<body>
    <form id="form1" runat="server">
    <div>
        <asp:ToolkitScriptManager ID="ToolkitScriptManager1" runat="server">
        </asp:ToolkitScriptManager>
        <asp:MutuallyExclusiveCheckBoxExtender
         ID="MutuallyExclusiveCheckBoxExtender1" runat="server"
         Key="MyCheckBoxes" TargetControlID="CheckBox1">
        </asp:MutuallyExclusiveCheckBoxExtender>
        <asp:MutuallyExclusiveCheckBoxExtender
         ID="MutuallyExclusiveCheckBoxExtender2" runat="server"
         Key="MyCheckBoxes" TargetControlID="CheckBox2">
        </asp:MutuallyExclusiveCheckBoxExtender>
        <asp:ToggleButtonExtender ID="ToggleButtonExtender1"
         runat="server" TargetControlID="CheckBox1"
         UncheckedImageUrl="Images/Unchecked.gif"
         CheckedImageUrl="Images/Checked.gif"
         CheckedImageAlternateText="Checked"
```

continues

LISTING 19-34 *(continued)*

```
        UncheckedImageAlternateText="Not Checked" ImageWidth="25"
        ImageHeight="25">
       </asp:ToggleButtonExtender>
       <asp:CheckBox ID="CheckBox1" runat="server"
        Text=" Option One" />
       <asp:ToggleButtonExtender ID="ToggleButtonExtender2"
        runat="server" TargetControlID="CheckBox2"
        UncheckedImageUrl="Images/Unchecked.gif"
        CheckedImageUrl="Images/Checked.gif"
        CheckedImageAlternateText="Checked"
        UncheckedImageAlternateText="Not Checked" ImageWidth="25"
        ImageHeight="25">
       </asp:ToggleButtonExtender>
       <asp:CheckBox ID="CheckBox2" runat="server"
        Text=" Option Two" />
    </div>
    </form>
</body>
</html>
```

This page has two CheckBox controls. Each check box has an associated ToggleButtonExtender control along with a MutuallyExclusiveCheckBoxExtender control to tie the two check boxes together. The ToggleButtonExtender control uses the `CheckedImageUrl` and the `UncheckedImageUrl` properties to specify the appropriate images to use. Then, if images are disabled by the end user's browser instance, the text that is provided in the `CheckedImageAlternateText` and `UncheckedImageAlternateText` properties is used instead. You will also need to specify values for the `ImageWidth` and `ImageHeight` properties for the page to run.

Running this page, you get results similar to those presented in Figure 19-39.

Option One
Option Two

FIGURE 19-39

UpdatePanelAnimationExtender

Animating an UpdatePanel as its content is being refreshed is a common scenario. The UpdatePanelAnimationExtender allows you to use the broad set of animations available in the Toolkit and will automatically coordinate playing them when the specified UpdatePanel is being updated or when the update has completed.

The UpdatePanelAnimationExtender control allows you to apply an animation to a Panel control for two specific events. The first is the `OnUpdating` event and the second is the `OnUpdated` event. You can then use the animation framework provided by ASP.NET AJAX to change the page's style based on these two events. Listing 19-35 shows an example of using the `OnUpdated` event when the end user clicks a specific date within a Calendar control contained within the UpdatePanel control on the page.

LISTING 19-35: Using animations on the OnUpdated event

Available for download on Wrox.com

```
<%@ Page Language="VB" %>

<%@ Register Assembly="AjaxControlToolkit"
    Namespace="AjaxControlToolkit" TagPrefix="asp" %>

<script runat="server">
    Protected  Sub Calendar1_SelectionChanged(ByVal sender As Object, _
      ByVal e As EventArgs)
        Label1.Text = "The date selected is " &
           Calendar1.SelectedDate.ToLongDateString()
    End Sub
```

```
</script>

<html xmlns="http://www.w3.org/1999/xhtml">
<head runat="server">
    <title>UpdatePanelAnimationExtender Control</title>
</head>
<body>
    <form id="form1" runat="server">
    <div>
        <asp:ToolkitScriptManager ID="ToolkitScriptManager1" runat="server">
        </asp:ToolkitScriptManager>
        <asp:UpdatePanelAnimationExtender
         ID="UpdatePanelAnimationExtender1"
         runat="server" TargetControlID="UpdatePanel1">
            <Animations>
                <OnUpdated>
                    <Sequence>
                        <Color PropertyKey="background"
                         StartValue="#999966"
                         EndValue="#FFFFFF" Duration="5.0" />
                    </Sequence>
                </OnUpdated>
            </Animations>
        </asp:UpdatePanelAnimationExtender>
        <asp:UpdatePanel ID="UpdatePanel1" runat="server">
            <ContentTemplate>
                <asp:Label ID="Label1" runat="server"></asp:Label>
                <br />
                <asp:Calendar ID="Calendar1" runat="server"
                    onselectionchanged="Calendar1_SelectionChanged">
                </asp:Calendar>
            </ContentTemplate>
        </asp:UpdatePanel>
    </div>
    </form>
</body>
</html>
```

C#

```
<%@ Page Language="C#" %>

<%@ Register Assembly="AjaxControlToolkit"
Namespace="AjaxControlToolkit"
    TagPrefix="asp" %>

<script runat="server">
    protected void Calendar1_SelectionChanged(object sender,
      EventArgs e)
    {
        Label1.Text = "The date selected is " +
           Calendar1.SelectedDate.ToLongDateString();
    }
</script>
```

With this bit of code, when you click a date within the Calendar control, the entire background of the UpdatePanel holding the calendar changes from one color to another for a 5-second duration as specified in the animation you built. The animations you define can get complex, and building deluxe animations is beyond the scope of this chapter.

ValidatorCalloutExtender

The last extender control covered is the ValidatorCalloutExtender control. This control allows you to add a more noticeable validation message to end users working with a form. You associate this control not with the control that is being validated, but instead with the validation control itself. An example of associating the ValidatorCalloutExtender control with a RegularExpressionValidator control is presented in Listing 19-36.

LISTING 19-36: Creating validation callouts with the ValidatorCalloutExtender

Available for download on Wrox.com

```
<%@ Page Language="C#" %>

<%@ Register Assembly="AjaxControlToolkit"
    Namespace="AjaxControlToolkit" TagPrefix="asp" %>

<html xmlns="http://www.w3.org/1999/xhtml">
<head runat="server">
    <title>ValidatorCalloutExtender Control</title>
</head>
<body>
    <form id="form1" runat="server">
    <div>
        <asp:ToolkitScriptManager ID="ToolkitScriptManager1" runat="server">
        </asp:ToolkitScriptManager>
        <asp:ValidatorCalloutExtender ID="ValidatorCalloutExtender1"
         runat="server" TargetControlID="RegularExpressionValidator1">
        </asp:ValidatorCalloutExtender>
        Email Address: 
        <asp:TextBox ID="TextBox1" runat="server"></asp:TextBox>
        <asp:RegularExpressionValidator
         ID="RegularExpressionValidator1" runat="server"
         ErrorMessage="You must enter an email address" Display="None"
         ControlToValidate="TextBox1"
         ValidationExpression=
           "\w+([-+.']\w+)*@\w+([-.]\w+)*\.\w+([-.]\w+)*">
        </asp:RegularExpressionValidator><br />
        <asp:Button ID="Button1" runat="server" Text="Submit" />
    </div>
    </form>
</body>
</html>
```

This page has a single text box for the form, a Submit button, and a RegularExpressionValidator control. You build the RegularExpressionValidator control as you would normally, except you make use of the `Display` property and set it to `None`. You do not want the normal ASP.NET validation control to also display its message, as it will collide with the one displayed with the ValidatorCalloutExtender control. Although the `Display` property is set to `None`, you still use the `ErrorMessage` property to provide the error message. Running this page produces the results presented in Figure 19-40.

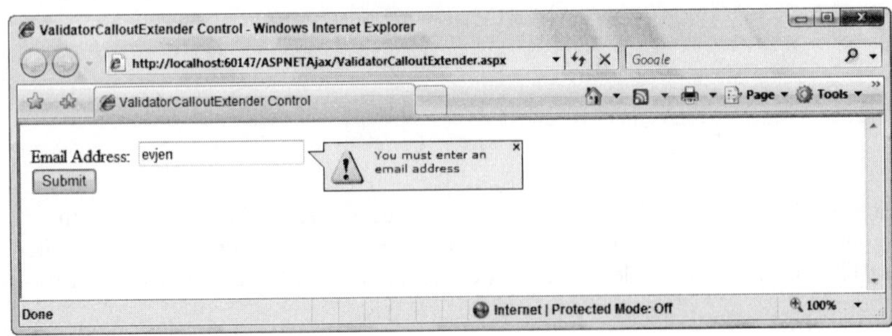

FIGURE 19-40

ASP.NET AJAX CONTROL TOOLKIT SERVER CONTROLS

The following ASP.NET AJAX controls actually do not always extend other ASP.NET controls, but instead, are controls themselves. The following sections detail some of these controls.

Accordion Control

The Accordion control is used to specify a set of panes, similar to the famous navigation menu in Microsoft Outlook. Each pane is made up of a header template and a content template. The header templates of all panes are always visible, whereas only one content template is visible. The user selects which pane to view by clicking on the header. The content from the previously active pane is hidden from view, and the content of the newly selected pane is displayed instead.

The Accordion control can provide a fade transition when switching among active panes. Set the `FadeTransitions` property to `True` and then you can set the `TransitionDuration` and `FramesPerSecond` values. The default values are `250` milliseconds and `40` frames per second, respectively.

The `SelectedIndex` property lets you declaratively and programmatically control which pane to show. Other important properties are the `AutoSize` and `Height` properties. The `AutoSize` property is `None` by default, meaning that the size of the Accordion control changes based on the active pane. Other content on the screen may be shifted to accommodate the changing size. However, when the `AutoSize` property is set to `Limit`, the size is restricted to the `Height` value. The active pane will display scrollbars if the content is larger than the space available. The other possible value is `Fill`, which will result in expanding a pane if the content is not large enough to satisfy the `Height` value provided. Listing 19-37 shows the Accordion control in action. The Accordion control is used with two panes.

Available for download on Wrox.com

LISTING 19-37: An Accordion control with two AccordionPane controls

```
<%@ Page Language="C#" %>

<%@ Register Assembly="AjaxControlToolkit"
    Namespace="AjaxControlToolkit" TagPrefix="asp" %>

<html xmlns="http://www.w3.org/1999/xhtml">
<head runat="server">
    <title>Accordion Control</title>
    <style type="text/css">
        .titlebar
        {
            background-color:Blue;
            color:White;
            font-size:large;
            font-family:Verdana;
            border:solid 3px Black;
        }
    </style>
</head>
<body>
    <form id="form1" runat="server">
    <div>
        <asp:ToolkitScriptManager ID="ToolkitScriptManager1" runat="server">
        </asp:ToolkitScriptManager>
        <asp:Accordion ID="Accordion1" runat="server" HeaderCssClass="titlebar"
         HeaderSelectedCssClass="titlebar"
         FadeTransitions="true"
         TransitionDuration="333"
```

continues

LISTING 19-37 *(continued)*

```
            FramesPerSecond="30">
               <Panes>
               <asp:AccordionPane runat="server">
                   <Header>
                       This is the first pane
                   </Header>
                   <Content>
               Lorem ipsum dolor sit amet, consectetuer adipiscing elit.
               Donec accumsan lorem. Ut consectetuer tempus metus.
               Aenean tincidunt venenatis tellus. Suspendisse molestie
               cursus ipsum. Curabitur ut lectus. Nulla ac dolor nec elit
               convallis vulputate. Nullam pharetra pulvinar nunc. Duis
               orci. Phasellus a tortor at nunc mattis congue.
               Vestibulum porta tellus eu orci. Suspendisse quis massa.
               Maecenas varius, erat non ullamcorper nonummy, mauris erat
               eleifend odio, ut gravida nisl neque a ipsum. Vivamus
               facilisis. Cras viverra. Curabitur
               ut augue eget dolor semper posuere. Aenean at magna eu eros
               tempor pharetra. Aenean mauris.
                   </Content>
               </asp:AccordionPane>
               <asp:AccordionPane runat="server">
                   <Header>
                       This is the second pane
                   </Header>
                   <Content>
               Lorem ipsum dolor sit amet, consectetuer adipiscing elit.
               Donec accumsan lorem. Ut consectetuer tempus metus.
               Aenean tincidunt venenatis tellus. Suspendisse molestie
               cursus ipsum. Curabitur ut lectus. Nulla ac dolor nec elit
               convallis vulputate. Nullam pharetra pulvinar nunc. Duis
               orci. Phasellus a tortor at nunc mattis congue.
               Vestibulum porta tellus eu orci. Suspendisse quis massa.
               Maecenas varius, erat non ullamcorper nonummy, mauris erat
               eleifend odio, ut gravida nisl neque a ipsum. Vivamus
               facilisis. Cras viverra. Curabitur
               ut augue eget dolor semper posuere. Aenean at magna eu eros
               tempor pharetra. Aenean mauris.
                   </Content>
               </asp:AccordionPane>
               </Panes>
            </asp:Accordion>
        </div>
        </form>
    </body>
    </html>
```

A single CSS class is defined in the document and this class, `titlebar`, is used as the value of the `HeaderCssClass` and the `HeaderSelectedCssClass` properties. The Accordion control here contains two AccordionPane controls. The sub-elements of the AccordionPane control are the `<Header>` and the `<Content>` elements. The items placed in the `<Header>` section will be in the clickable pane title, whereas the items contained within the `<Content>` section will slide out and appear when the associated header is selected.

You will notice that there is also a transition effect in place when the panes are switched. Running this page produces the results illustrated in Figure 19-41.

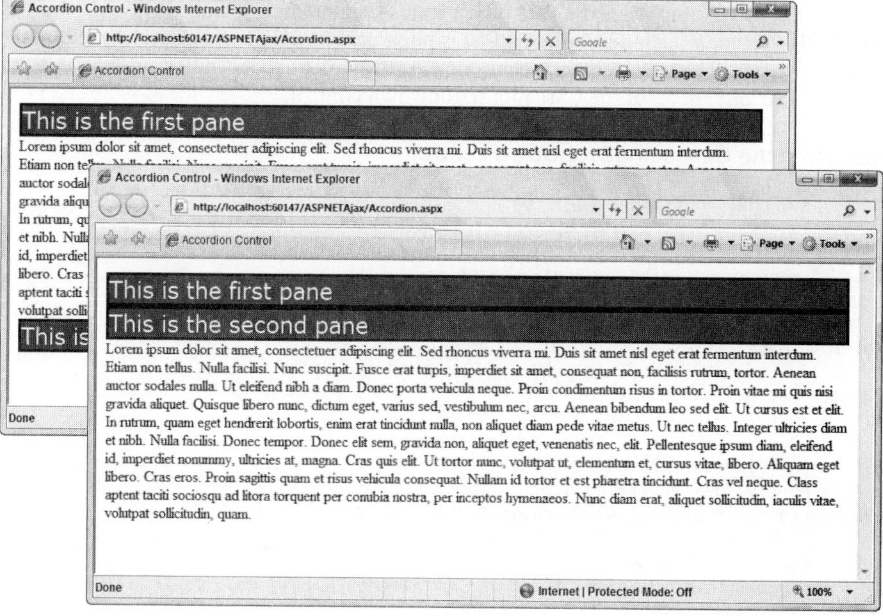

FIGURE 19-41

This figure shows a screenshot of each of the panes selected. Some of the more important properties are described in the following list:

- `AutoSize`: Defines how the control deals with its size expansion and shrinkage. The possible values include `None`, `Fill`, and `Limit`. The default is `None` and when used, items below the control may move to make room for the control expansion. A value of `Fill` works with the `Height` property and the control will fill to the required `Height`. This means that some of the panes may need to grow to accommodate the space whereas other panes might need to shrink and include a scrollbar to handle the limited space from the height restriction. A value of `Limit` also works with the `Height` property and will never grow larger than this value. It is possible that the pane might be smaller than the specified height.
- `TransitionDuration`: The number of milliseconds it takes to transition to another pane.
- `FramesPerSecond`: The number of frames per second to use to transition to another pane.
- `RequireOpenedPane`: Specifies that at least one pane is required to be open at all times. The default setting of this property is `True`. A value of `False` means that all panes can be collapsed.

Finally, the properties of `DataSource`, `DataSourceID`, and `DataMember` allow you to bind to this control from your code.

CascadingDropDown

The available options for one DropDownList can be a function of the selection made in another DropDownList. The CascadingDropDown control makes enabling this in your application easy. You set the `TargetControlID` to the DropDownList that should be populated by a call back to the server. You also assign a category to classify the DropDownList.

Before the DropDownList is populated, the value of the `PromptText` property is presented. Moreover, while the call to the server is underway, the value of the `LoadingText` property is displayed. You can set the `ServicePath` property to call a `ServiceMethod` on a separate Web service, or you can just set the `ServiceMethod` name to a static `ScriptMethod` located directly in the page, as illustrated in Listing 19-38.

The first DropDownList in this example lets the user pick a state. This example includes only Missouri and Oregon. When a state is selected, a second DropDownList is populated based on the value selected by the user in the first DropDownList. The way to specify that one DropDownList is dependent on the value of another is to set the `ParentControlID` of the CascadingDropDown control.

Available for download on Wrox.com

LISTING 19-38: Using the CascadingDropDown control

VB

```
<%@ Import Namespace="System.Web.Services" %>
<%@ Import Namespace="AjaxControlToolkit" %>
<%@ Register Assembly="AjaxControlToolkit"
    Namespace="AjaxControlToolkit" TagPrefix="asp" %>

<html xmlns="http://www.w3.org/1999/xhtml">
<head id="Head1" runat="server">

   <script runat="server" language="vb">

      <WebMethod, System.Web.Script.Services.ScriptMethod> _
       Public Shared Function GetStates(ByVal _
         knownCategoryValues As String, _
         ByVal category As String) As CascadingDropDownNameValue()

          Return New Object() { New _
            CascadingDropDownNameValue("Missouri", "Missouri"), _
            New CascadingDropDownNameValue("Oregon", "Oregon") }
       End Function

      <WebMethod, System.Web.Script.Services.ScriptMethod> _
       Public Shared Function GetCounties(ByVal _
         knownCategoryValues As String, _
         ByVal category As String) As CascadingDropDownNameValue()

          If knownCategoryValues.Contains("Missouri") Then
             Return New Object() { New _
               CascadingDropDownNameValue("St. Charles", _
                "St. Charles"), _
               New CascadingDropDownNameValue("St. Louis", _
                "St. Louis"), _
               New CascadingDropDownNameValue("Jefferson", _
                "Jefferson"), _
               New CascadingDropDownNameValue("Warren", "Warren"), _
               New CascadingDropDownNameValue("Franklin", "Franklin") }
          End If


          If knownCategoryValues.Contains("Oregon") Then
            Return New Object() { New _
              CascadingDropDownNameValue("Baker", "Baker"), _
              New CascadingDropDownNameValue("Benton", "Benton"), _
              New CascadingDropDownNameValue("Clackamas", "Clackamas"),
              New CascadingDropDownNameValue("Clatsop", "Clatsop"), _
              New CascadingDropDownNameValue("Columbia", "Columbia") }
          End If

          Return Nothing
       End Function

   </script>

    <title>CascadingDropDown</title>
```

```
</head>
<body>
    <form id="form1" runat="server">
    <asp:ToolkitScriptManager runat="server" ID="scriptManager" />
    <div>
        <asp:DropDownList runat="server" ID="ddl1" Width="200" />
        <br />
        <asp:DropDownList runat="server" ID="ddl2" Width="200" />
        <br />
        <asp:CascadingDropDown runat="server" ID="cdd1"
            TargetControlID="ddl1"
            PromptText="Select a State"
            Category="state" LoadingText="[Loading States]"
            ServiceMethod="GetStates" />
        <asp:CascadingDropDown runat="server" ID="cdd2"
            TargetControlID="ddl2"
            ParentControlID="ddl1"
            PromptText="Select County" Category="county"
            LoadingText="[Loading Counties]"
            ServiceMethod="GetCounties" />
    </div>
    </form>
</body>
</html>
```

C#

```
<%@ Import Namespace="System.Web.Services" %>
<%@ Import Namespace="AjaxControlToolkit" %>
<%@ Register Assembly="AjaxControlToolkit"
    Namespace="AjaxControlToolkit" TagPrefix="asp" %>

<html xmlns="http://www.w3.org/1999/xhtml">
<head id="Head1" runat="server">

    <script runat="server" language="C#">

        [WebMethod]
        [System.Web.Script.Services.ScriptMethod]
        public static CascadingDropDownNameValue[]
               GetStates(string knownCategoryValues, string category)
        {
            return new[] {
        new CascadingDropDownNameValue("Missouri", "Missouri"),
        new CascadingDropDownNameValue("Oregon", "Oregon") };
        }

        [WebMethod]
        [System.Web.Script.Services.ScriptMethod]
        public static CascadingDropDownNameValue[]
               GetCounties(string knownCategoryValues, string category)
        {
            if (knownCategoryValues.Contains("Missouri"))
            {
                return new[] {
                    new CascadingDropDownNameValue("St. Charles",
                      "St. Charles"),
                    new CascadingDropDownNameValue("St. Louis",
                      "St. Louis"),
                    new CascadingDropDownNameValue("Jefferson",
                      "Jefferson"),
                    new CascadingDropDownNameValue("Warren", "Warren"),
```

continues

LISTING 19-38 *(continued)*

```
                    new CascadingDropDownNameValue("Franklin",
                      "Franklin") };
            }
            if (knownCategoryValues.Contains("Oregon"))
            {
                return new[] {
                    new CascadingDropDownNameValue("Baker", "Baker"),
                    new CascadingDropDownNameValue("Benton", "Benton"),
                    new CascadingDropDownNameValue("Clackamas",
                      "Clackamas"),
                    new CascadingDropDownNameValue("Clatsop",
                      "Clatsop"),
                    new CascadingDropDownNameValue("Columbia",
                      "Columbia") };
            }
            return null;
        }

    </script>
```

NoBot Control

The NoBot control works to determine how entities interact with your forms. It helps you ensure that actual humans are working with your forms and some automated code isn't working through your application.

The NoBot control is illustrated in Listing 19-39.

Available for download on Wrox.com

LISTING 19-39: Using the NoBot control to limit a login form

.ASPX

```
<%@ Page Language="VB" AutoEventWireup="true" CodeFile="NoBot.aspx.vb"
    Inherits="NoBot" %>
<%@ Register Assembly="AjaxControlToolkit"
    Namespace="AjaxControlToolkit" TagPrefix="asp" %>

<html xmlns="http://www.w3.org/1999/xhtml">
<head runat="server">
    <title>NoBot Control</title>
</head>
<body>
    <form id="form1" runat="server">
    <div>
        <asp:ToolkitScriptManager ID="ToolkitScriptManager1" runat="server">
        </asp:ToolkitScriptManager>
        <asp:NoBot ID="NoBot1" runat="server"
            CutoffMaximumInstances="3"
            CutoffWindowSeconds="15" ResponseMinimumDelaySeconds="10"
            OnGenerateChallengeAndResponse=
              "NoBot1_GenerateChallengeAndResponse" />
        <asp:Login ID="Login1" runat="server">
        </asp:Login>
        <asp:Label ID="Label1" runat="server"></asp:Label>
    </div>
    </form>
</body>
</html>
```

Filename NoBot.aspx

The NoBot control has three important properties to be aware of when controlling how your forms are submitted. These properties include `CutoffMaximumInstances`, `CutoffWindowSeconds`, and `ResponseMinimumDelaySeconds`.

`CutoffMaximumInstances` is the number of times the end user is allowed to try to submit the form within the number of seconds specified by the `CutoffWindowSeconds` property. The `ResponseMinimumDelaySeconds` property defines the minimum number of seconds the end user has to submit the form. If you know the form you are working with will take some time, then setting this property to a value (even if it is `5` seconds) will help stop submissions that are not made by humans.

The `OnGenerateChallengeAndResponse` property allows you to define the server-side method that works with the challenge and allows you to provide a response based on the challenge. This property is used in Listing 19-39 and posts back to the user the status of the form submission.

The code-behind for this page is represented in Listing 19-40.

LISTING 19-40: The code-behind for the NoBot control's OnGenerateChallengeAndResponse

Available for download on Wrox.com

VB

```
Imports System
Imports AjaxControlToolkit

Public partial Class NoBot
 Inherits System.Web.UI.Page
    Protected Sub NoBot1_GenerateChallengeAndResponse(ByVal _
      sender As Object,
      ByVal void As AjaxControlToolkit.NoBotEventArgs)
      Handles NoBot1.GenerateChallengeAndResponse

        Dim state As NoBotState
        NoBot1.IsValid(state)

        Label1.Text = state.ToString()
    End Sub
End Class
```

C#

```
using System;
using AjaxControlToolkit;

public partial class NoBot : System.Web.UI.Page
{
    protected void NoBot1_GenerateChallengeAndResponse(object sender,
        AjaxControlToolkit.NoBotEventArgs e)
    {
        NoBotState state;
        NoBot1.IsValid(out state);

        Label1.Text = state.ToString();
    }
}
```

Filenames NoBot.aspx.vb and NoBot.aspx.cs

Running this page and trying to submit the form before the ten-second minimum time results in an invalid submission. In addition, trying to submit the form more than three times within 15 seconds results in an invalid submission.

PasswordStrength Control

The PasswordStrength control allows you to check the contents of a password in a TextBox control and validate its strength. It will also then give a message to the end user about whether the strength is reasonable. Listing 19-41 presents a simple example of the PasswordStrength control.

LISTING 19-41: Using the PasswordStrength control with a TextBox control

Available for download on Wrox.com

```
<%@ Page Language="C#" %>

<%@ Register Assembly="AjaxControlToolkit"
    Namespace="AjaxControlToolkit" TagPrefix="asp" %>

<html xmlns="http://www.w3.org/1999/xhtml">
<head runat="server">
    <title>Password Strength Control</title>
</head>
<body>
    <form id="form1" runat="server">
    <div>
        <asp:ToolkitScriptManager ID="ToolkitScriptManager1" runat="server">
        </asp:ToolkitScriptManager>
        <asp:PasswordStrength ID="PasswordStrength1" runat="server"
         TargetControlID="TextBox1">
        </asp:PasswordStrength>
        <asp:TextBox ID="TextBox1" runat="server"></asp:TextBox>
    </div>
    </form>
</body>
</html>
```

This simple page produces a single text box, and when end users start typing in the text box, they will be notified on the strength of the submission as they type. This is illustrated in Figure 19-42.

FIGURE 19-42

Some of the important properties to work with here include `MinimumLowerCaseCharacters`, `MinimumNumericCharacters`, `MinimumSymbolCharacters`, `MinimumUpperCaseCharacters`, and `PreferredPasswordLength`.

Rating Control

The Rating control gives your end users the ability to view and set ratings (such as star ratings). You have control over the number of ratings, the look of the filled ratings, the look of the empty ratings, and more. Listing 19-42 shows you a page that shows a five-star rating system that gives end users the ability to set the rating themselves.

LISTING 19-42: A rating control that the end user can manipulate

Available for download on Wrox.com

```
<%@ Page Language="C#" %>

<%@ Register Assembly="AjaxControlToolkit"
    Namespace="AjaxControlToolkit" TagPrefix="asp" %>

<html xmlns="http://www.w3.org/1999/xhtml">
<head runat="server">
    <title>Rating Control</title>
    <style type="text/css">
        .ratingStar {
            font-size: 0pt;
            width: 13px;
            height: 12px;
            margin: 0px;
            padding: 0px;
            cursor: pointer;
            display: block;
```

```
            background-repeat: no-repeat;
        }

        .filledRatingStar {
            background-image: url(Images/FilledStar.png);
        }

        .emptyRatingStar {
            background-image: url(Images/EmptyStar.png);
        }

        .savedRatingStar {
            background-image: url(Images/SavedStar.png);
        }
    </style>
</head>
<body>
    <form id="form1" runat="server">
    <div>
        <asp:ToolkitScriptManager ID="ToolkitScriptManager1" runat="server">
        </asp:ToolkitScriptManager>
        <asp:Rating ID="Rating1" runat="server"
         StarCssClass="ratingStar"
         WaitingStarCssClass="savedRatingStar"
         FilledStarCssClass="filledRatingStar"
         EmptyStarCssClass="emptyRatingStar">
        </asp:Rating>
    </div>
    </form>
</body>
</html>
```

Here, the Rating control uses a number of CSS classes to define its look and feel in various states. In addition to the CSS class properties (`StarCssClass`, `WaitingStarCssClass`, `FilledStarCssClass`, and `EmptyCssClass`), you can also specify rating alignments, the number of rating items (the default is `5`), the width, the current rating, and more. The code presented in Listing 19-42 produces the results shown in Figure 19-43.

FIGURE 19-43

TabContainer Control

The TabContainer and TabPanel controls make presenting the familiar tabbed UI easy. The user is presented with a set of tabs across the top of a single pane of content displayed for the active tab. When the user selects a different tab, the content is changed. Tabs are a great way to control a page that has a lot of content to present. The TabContainer control can contain one or more TabPanel controls that provide you with a set of tabs that show content one tab at a time.

The TabContainer allows you to attach a server event called the `ActiveTabChanged` event, which is fired during a Postback if the active tab has changed. You can also use the `OnClientActiveTabChanged` event to have your JavaScript event triggered in the browser when the user selects a different tab. The `ScrollBars` property lets you designate whether scrollbars should be `Horizontal`, `Vertical`, `Both`, `None`, or set to `Auto`, in which case the control makes the determination.

The TabPanel control has a `<HeaderTemplate>` for the tab and a `<ContentTemplate>` for the body. You can forego using the `<HeaderTemplate>` and specify the `HeaderText` property instead. It also has an event that will be triggered when the tab is selected called `OnClientClick`. One particularly interesting feature of the Tabs feature is the ability to disable tabs programmatically in JavaScript in the browser by setting the `Enabled` property to `False`.

Listing 19-43 shows an example of a TabContainer control with three TabPanel controls.

LISTING 19-43: Showing three tabs in a TabContainer control

Available for download on Wrox.com

```
<%@ Page Language="C#" %>

<%@ Register Assembly="AjaxControlToolkit"
    Namespace="AjaxControlToolkit" TagPrefix="asp" %>

<html xmlns="http://www.w3.org/1999/xhtml">
<head runat="server">
    <title>TabContainer Control</title>
</head>
<body>
    <form id="form1" runat="server">
    <div>
        <asp:ToolkitScriptManager ID="ToolkitScriptManager1" runat="server">
        </asp:ToolkitScriptManager>
        <asp:TabContainer ID="TabContainer1" runat="server"
         Height="300px">
            <asp:TabPanel runat="server">
                <HeaderTemplate>Tab 1</HeaderTemplate>
                <ContentTemplate>
                 Here is some tab one content.
                </ContentTemplate>
            </asp:TabPanel>
            <asp:TabPanel runat="server">
                <HeaderTemplate>Tab 2</HeaderTemplate>
                <ContentTemplate>
                 Here is some tab two content.
                </ContentTemplate>
            </asp:TabPanel>
            <asp:TabPanel runat="server">
                <HeaderTemplate>Tab 3</HeaderTemplate>
                <ContentTemplate>
                 Here is some tab three content.
                </ContentTemplate>
            </asp:TabPanel>
        </asp:TabContainer>
    </div>
    </form>
</body>
</html>
```

Figure 19-44 presents the result of this simple page.

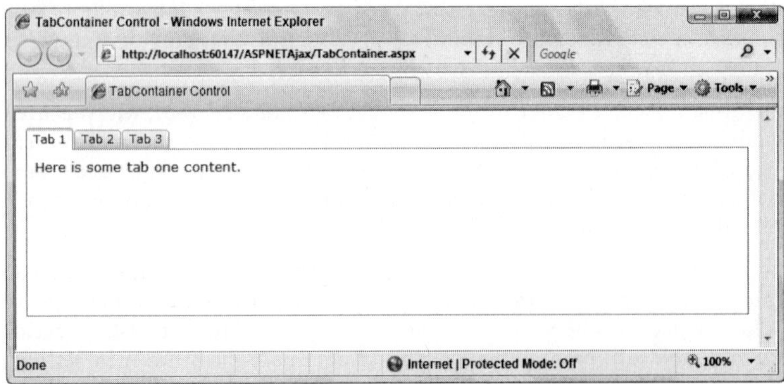

FIGURE 19-44

SUMMARY

The ASP.NET AJAX Control Toolkit makes adding rich animations and interactivity to a Web application easy. In addition to being able to use the UpdatePanel control to enable asynchronous updates of page content, you can use the UpdatePanelAnimation to show the user that background processing is occurring. The Toolkit helps blur the distinction between desktop applications and Web applications. Modal dialogs and pop-up dialogs start to push the Web application beyond what the user expects from working in the browser.

As you can see, a myriad of these controls are at your disposal. The best thing about this is that this is a community effort along with Microsoft and the list of available ASP.NET AJAX controls is only going to grow over time.

This chapter explored a lot of the ASP.NET AJAX controls and how to use them in your ASP.NET applications. Remember to visit the Microsoft AJAX page for these controls often and take advantage of the newest offerings out there.

20

Security

WHAT'S IN THIS CHAPTER?

- Using Windows-based and forms-based authentication
- Managing programmatic authorization
- Securing through IIS

Not every page that you build with ASP.NET is meant to be open and accessible to everyone on the Internet. Sometimes, you want to build pages or sections of an application that are accessible to only a select group of your choosing. For this reason, you need the security measures explained in this chapter. They can help protect the data behind your applications and the applications themselves from fraudulent use.

Security is a very wide-reaching term. During every step of the application-building process, you must, without a doubt, be aware of how mischievous end users might attempt to bypass your lockout measures. You must take steps to ensure that no one can take over the application or gain access to its resources. Whether it involves working with basic server controls or accessing databases, you should be thinking through the level of security you want to employ to protect yourself.

How security is applied to your applications is truly a measured process. For instance, a single ASP.NET page on the Internet, open to public access, has different security requirements than does an ASP.NET application that is available only to selected individuals because it deals with confidential information such as credit card numbers or medical information.

The first step is to apply the appropriate level of security for the task at hand. Because you can take so many different actions to protect your applications and the resources, you have to decide for yourself which of these measures to employ. This chapter looks at some of the possibilities for protecting your applications.

Notice that security is discussed throughout this book. In addition, a couple chapters focus on specific security frameworks provided by ASP.NET that are not discussed in this chapter. Chapters 14 and 15 discuss ASP.NET's membership and role management frameworks, as well as the personalization features in this version. These topics are aspects of security that can make building safe applications even easier for you. Although these security frameworks are provided with this latest release of ASP.NET, you can still build your own measures as you did in the previous versions of ASP.NET. This chapter discusses how to do so.

An important aspect of security is how you handle the authentication and authorization for accessing resources in your applications. Before you begin working through some of the authentication/authorization possibilities in ASP.NET, which is what this chapter covers, you should know exactly what we mean by those two terms:

- As discussed in Chapter 15, *authentication* is the process that determines the identity of a user. After a user has been authenticated, a developer can determine whether the identified user has authorization to proceed. Giving an entity authorization is impossible if no authentication process has been applied.
- *Authorization* is the process of determining whether an authenticated user is permitted access to any part of an application, access to specific points of an application, or access only to specified datasets that the application provides. Authenticating and authorizing users and groups enable you to customize a site based on user types or preferences.

APPLYING AUTHENTICATION MEASURES

ASP.NET provides many different types of authentication measures to use within your applications, including basic authentication, digest authentication, forms authentication, and Integrated Windows authentication. You also can develop your own authentication methods. You should never authorize access to resources you mean to be secure if you have not applied an authentication process to the requests for the resources.

The different authentication modes are established through settings that can be applied to the application's `web.config` file or in conjunction with the application server's Internet Information Services (IIS) instance.

ASP.NET is configured through a series of `.config` files on the application server. These XML-based files enable you to easily change how ASP.NET behaves. Having these settings sit within an XML-based file is an ideal way to work with the configuration settings you require. ASP.NET configuration files are applied in a hierarchical manner. The .NET Framework provides a server-level configuration file called the `machine.config` file, which you can find at `C:\Windows\Microsoft.NET\Framework\v4.0.`*`xxxxx`*`\CONFIG`. The folder contains the `machine.config` file. This file provides ASP.NET application settings at a server-level, meaning that the settings are applied to each and every ASP.NET application that resides on the particular server.

A `web.config` file is another XML-based configuration file that resides in the root directory of the Web application. The settings applied in the `web.config` file override the same settings applied in the higher-level `machine.config` file.

You can even nest the `web.config` files so that the main application `web.config` file is located in the root directory of your application, but additional `web.config` files reside in some of the application's subdirectories (see Figure 20-1). The `web.config` files contained in any of the subdirectories supersede the root directory's `web.config` file. Therefore, any settings applied through a subdirectory's `web.config` file change whatever was set in the application's main `web.config` file.

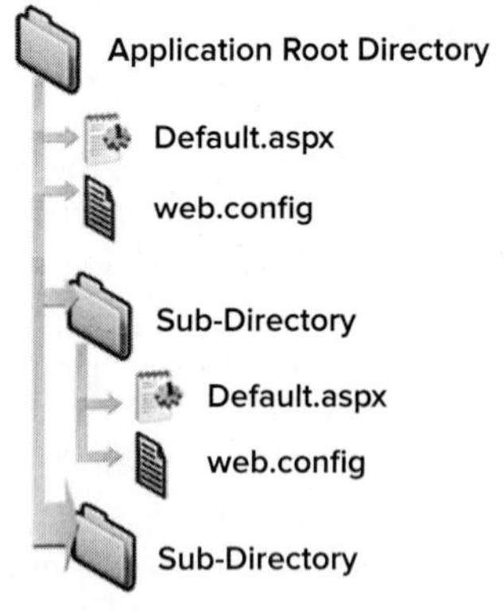

FIGURE 20-1

In many of the examples in this chapter, you use the `web.config` file to apply the authentication and authorization mechanics you want in your applications. You also can work with IIS to apply settings directly to your applications.

IIS is the Web server that handles all the incoming HTTP requests that come into the server. You must modify IIS to perform as you want. IIS hands a request to the ASP.NET engine only if the page has a specific file extension (for example, `.aspx`). In this chapter, you will work with IIS 7.0, as well.

The <authentication> Node

You use the `<authentication>` node in the application's `web.config` file to set the type of authentication your ASP.NET application requires:

```
<system.web>
   <authentication mode="Windows|Forms|Passport|None">

   </authentication>
</system.web>
```

The `<authentication>` node uses the `mode` attribute to set the form of authentication that is to be used. Options include `Windows`, `Forms`, `Passport`, and `None`. Each option is explained in Table 20-1.

TABLE 20-1

PROVIDER	DESCRIPTION
`Windows`	Windows authentication is used together with IIS authentication. Authentication is performed by IIS in the following ways: basic, digest, or Integrated Windows Authentication. When IIS authentication is complete, ASP.NET uses the authenticated identity to authorize access. This is the default setting.
`Forms`	Requests that are not authenticated are redirected to an HTML form using HTTP client-side redirection. The user provides his login information and submits the form. If the application authenticates the request, the system issues a form that contains the credentials or a key for reacquiring the identity.
`Passport`	A centralized authentication service provided by Microsoft that offers single login and core profile services for member sites. This mode of authentication was de-emphasized by Microsoft at the end of 2005.
`None`	No authentication mode is in place with this setting.

As you can see, a couple of methods are at your disposal for building an authentication/authorization model for your ASP.NET applications. The next section examines the Windows mode of authentication.

Windows-Based Authentication

Windows-based authentication is handled between the Windows server where the ASP.NET application resides and the client machine. In a Windows-based authentication model, the requests go directly to IIS to provide the authentication process. This type of authentication is quite useful in an intranet environment, where you can let the server deal completely with the authentication process — especially in environments where users are already logged on to a network. In this scenario, you simply grab and utilize the credentials that are already in place for the authorization process.

IIS first takes the user's credentials from the domain login. If this process fails, IIS displays a pop-up dialog box so the user can enter or re-enter his login information. To set up your ASP.NET application to work with Windows-based authentication, begin by creating some users and groups.

Creating Users

You use aspects of Windows-based authentication to allow specific users who have provided a domain login to access your application or parts of your application. Because it can use this type of authentication, ASP.NET makes working with applications that are deployed in an intranet environment quite easy. If a user has logged on to a local computer as a domain user, he will not need to be authenticated again when accessing a network computer in that domain.

The following steps show you how to create a user. It is important to note that you must have sufficient rights to be authorized to create users on a server. If you are authorized, the steps to create users are as follows:

1. Within your Windows XP or Windows Server 2003 server, choose Start ➪ Control Panel ➪ Administrative Tools ➪ Computer Management. If you are using Windows 7, choose Start ➪ Control Panel ➪ System and Security ➪ Administrative Tools ➪ Computer Management. Either one opens the Computer Management utility. It manages and controls resources on the local Web server. You can accomplish many things using this utility, but the focus here is on the creation of users.

2. Expand the System Tools node.
3. Expand the Local Users and Groups node.
4. Select the Users folder. You see something similar to the results shown in Figure 20-2.

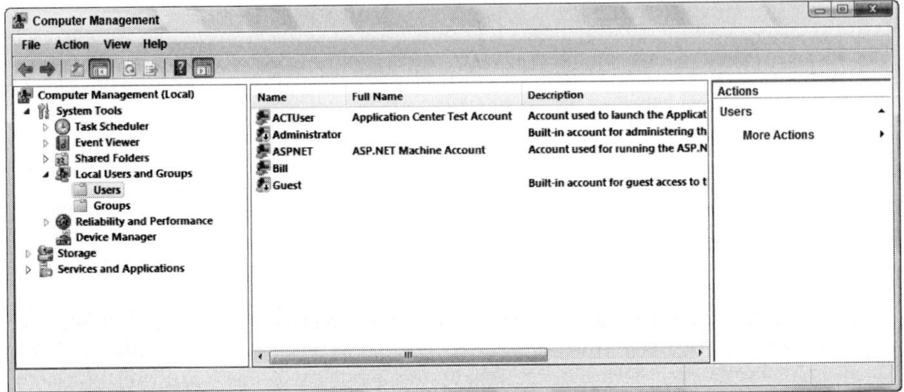

FIGURE 20-2

5. Right-click the Users folder and select New User. The New User dialog appears, as shown in Figure 20-3.
6. Give the user a name, password, and description stating that this is a test user. In this example, the user is called **Bubbles**.
7. Clear the check box that requires the user to change his password at the next login.
8. Click the Create button. Your test user is created and presented in the Users folder of the Computer Management utility, as shown in Figure 20-4.

FIGURE 20-3

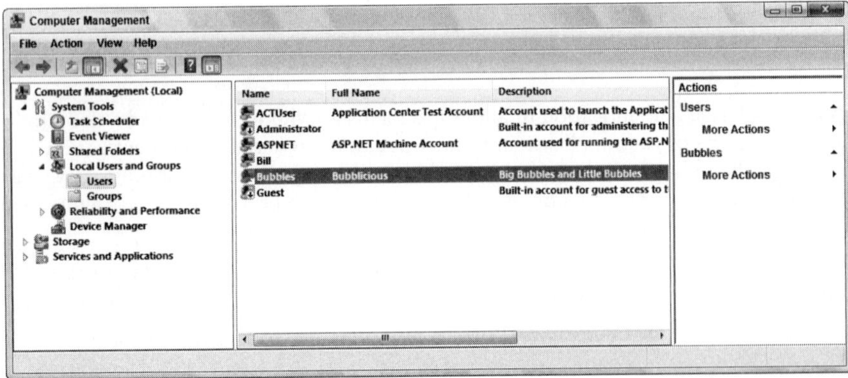

FIGURE 20-4

Now create a page to work with this user.

Authenticating and Authorizing a User

Now create an application that enables the user to enter it. You work with the application's `web.config` file to control which users are allowed to access the site and which users are not allowed.

Add the section presented in Listing 20-1 to your `web.config` file.

LISTING 20-1: Denying all users through the web.config file

```
<system.web>
   <authentication mode="Windows" />
   <authorization>
      <deny users="*" />
   </authorization>
</system.web>
```

In this example, the `web.config` file is configuring the application to employ Windows-based authentication using the `<authentication>` element's mode attribute. In addition, the `<authorization>` element is used to define specifics about the users or groups who are permitted access to the application. In this case, the `<deny>` element specifies that all users (even if they are authenticated) are denied access to the application. Not permitting specific users with the `<allow>` element does not make much sense, but for this example, leave it as it is. Figure 20-5 shows the results.

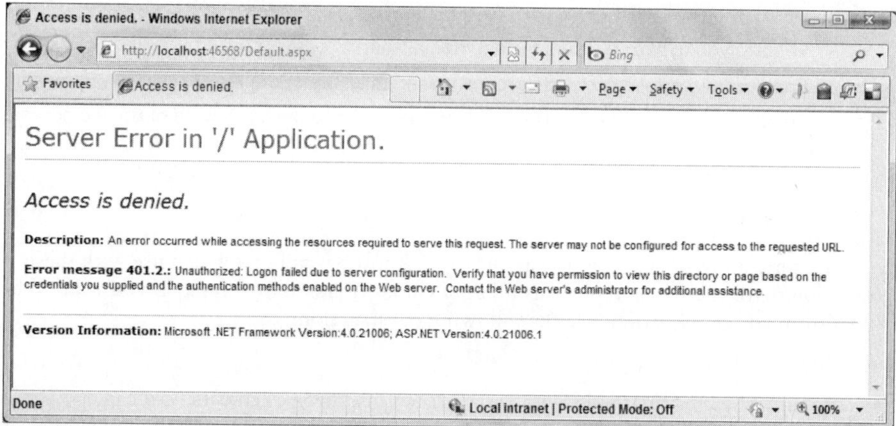

FIGURE 20-5

Any end user — authenticated or not — who tries to access the site sees a large "Access is denied" statement in his or her browser window, which is just what you want for those not allowed to access your application!

In most instances, however, you want to allow at least some users to access your application. Use the `<allow>` element in the `web.config` file to allow a specific user. Here is the syntax:

```
<allow users="Domain\Username" />
```

Listing 20-2 shows how the user is permitted access.

LISTING 20-2: Allowing a single user through the web.config file

```
<system.web>
   <authentication mode="Windows" />
```

continues

LISTING 20-2 *(continued)*

```
    <authorization>
       <allow users="REUTERS-EVJEN\Bubbles"/>
       <deny users="*"/>
    </authorization>
 </system.web>
```

Even though all users (even authenticated ones) are denied access through the use of the <deny> element, the definitions defined in the <allow> element take precedence. In this example, a single user — Bubbles — is allowed.

Now, if you are logged on to the client machine as the user Bubbles and run the page in the browser, you get access to the application.

Looking Closely at the <allow> and <deny> Nodes

The <allow> and <deny> nodes enable you to work not only with specific users, but also with groups. The elements support the attributes defined in Table 20-2.

TABLE 20-2

ATTRIBUTE	DESCRIPTION
Users	Enables you to specify users by their domain and/or name.
Roles	Enables you to specify access groups that are allowed or denied access.
Verbs	Enables you to specify the HTTP transmission method that is allowed or denied access.

When using any of these attributes, you can specify all users with the use of the asterisk (*):

```
<allow roles="*" />
```

In this example, all roles are allowed access to the application. Another symbol you can use with these attributes is the question mark (?), which represents all anonymous users. For example, if you want to block all anonymous users from your application, use the following construction:

```
<deny users="?" />
```

When using users, roles, or verbs attributes with the <allow> or <deny> elements, you can specify multiple entries by separating the values with a comma. If you are going to allow more than one user, you can either separate these users into different elements, as shown here:

```
<allow users="MyDomain\User1" />
<allow users="MyDomain\User2" />
```

or you can use the following:

```
<allow users="MyDomain\User1, MyDomain\User2" />
```

Use the same construction when defining multiple roles and verbs.

Authenticating and Authorizing a Group

You can define groups of individuals allowed or denied access to your application or the application's resources. Your server can contain a number of different groups, each of which can have any number of users belonging to it. The possibility also exists for a single user to belong to multiple groups. Pull up the Computer Management utility to access the list of the groups defined on the server you are working with. Simply click the Groups folder in the Computer Management utility, and the list of groups appears, as illustrated in Figure 20-6.

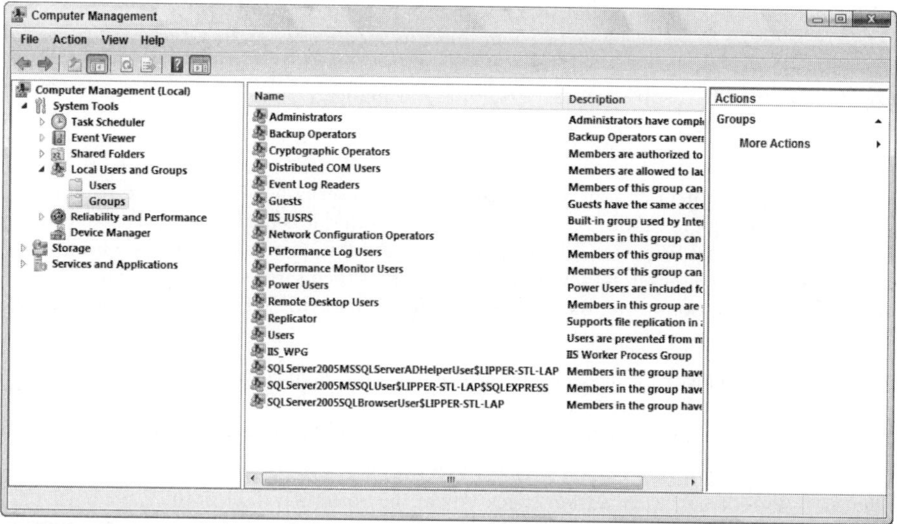

FIGURE 20-6

Right-click the Groups folder to select New Group. The New Group dialog appears (see Figure 20-7).

To create a group, give it a name and description; then click the Add button and select the users whom you want to be a part of the group. After a group is created, you can allow it access to your application like this:

```
<allow roles="MyGroup" />
```

You can use the `roles` attribute in either the `<allow>` or `<deny>` element to work with a group that you have created or with a specific group that already exists.

FIGURE 20-7

Authenticating and Authorizing an HTTP Transmission Method

In addition to authenticating and authorizing specific users or groups of users, you can also authorize or deny requests that come via a specific HTTP transmission protocol. You do so using the `verbs` attribute in the `<allow>` and `<deny>` elements.

```
<deny verbs="GET, DEBUG" />
```

In this example, requests that come in using the HTTP GET or HTTP DEBUG protocols are denied access to the site. Possible values for the `verbs` attribute include `POST`, `GET`, `HEAD`, and `DEBUG`.

Integrated Windows Authentication

So far, you have been using the default Integrated Windows authentication mode for the authentication/authorization process. This is fine if you are working with an intranet application and each of the clients is using Windows, the only system that the authentication method supports. This system of authentication also requires the client to be using Microsoft's Internet Explorer for straight-through processing (if you don't want your end users to be challenged), which might not always be possible.

Integrated Windows authentication was previously known as NTLM or Windows NT Challenge/Response authentication. This authentication model has the client prove its identity by sending a hash of its credentials to the server that is hosting the ASP.NET application. Along with Microsoft's Active Directory, a client can also use Kerberos if it is using Microsoft's Internet Explorer 5 or higher.

Basic Authentication

Another option is to use Basic authentication, which also requires a username and password from the client for authentication. The big plus about Basic authentication is that it is part of the HTTP specification and therefore is supported by most browsers. The negative aspect of Basic authentication is that it passes the username and password to the server as clear text, meaning that the username and password are quite visible to prying eyes. For this reason, using Basic authentication along with SSL (*Secure Sockets Layer*) is important.

If you are using IIS 5 or 6, to implement Basic authentication for your application, you must pull up IIS and open the Properties dialog for the Web site you are working with. Select the Directory Security tab and click the Edit button in the Anonymous Access and Authentication Control box. The Authentication Methods dialog box opens.

Uncheck the Integrated Windows Authentication check box at the bottom and select the Basic Authentication check box above it (see Figure 20-8). When you do, you are warned that this method transmits usernames and passwords as clear text.

End by clicking OK in the dialog. Now your application uses Basic authentication instead of Integrated Windows authentication.

If you are using Windows 7, finding the option to enable Basic authentication is not easy. Instead, you first have to enable IIS 7 to use Basic authentication by choosing Start ➪ Control Panel ➪ Programs ➪ Programs and Features ➪ Turn Windows features on or off. From the provided dialog box, navigate to the Internet Information Services section and expand until you arrive at World Wide Web Services ➪ Security. From here, select the Basic Authentication option and click OK to install. Figure 20-9 shows this option.

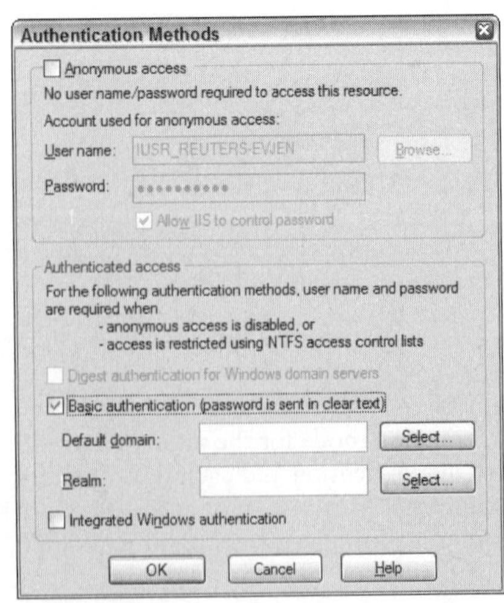

FIGURE 20-8

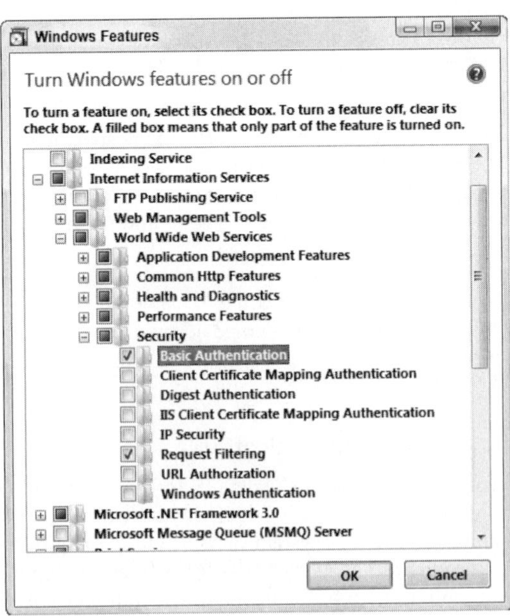

FIGURE 20-9

After this option is installed, you can then return to the Internet Information Services (IIS) Manager and select the Authentication option in the IIS section for the virtual directory you are focusing on. From there, highlight the Basic Authentication option and select Enable from the Actions pane, as illustrated in Figure 20-10 after enabling this feature.

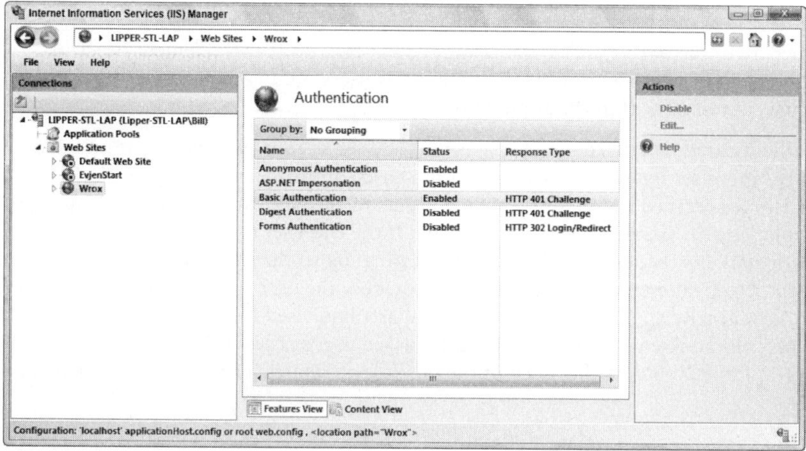

FIGURE 20-10

Digest Authentication

Digest authentication is the final mode you are going to explore in this chapter. This model alleviates the Basic authentication problem of passing the client's credentials as clear text. Instead, Digest authentication uses an algorithm to encrypt the client's credentials before they are sent to the application server.

To use Digest authentication, you are required to have a Windows domain controller. One of the main issues that arises with Digest authentication is that it is not supported on all platforms and requires browsers that conform to the HTTP 1.1 specification. Digest authentication, however, not only works well with firewalls, but is also compatible with proxy servers.

You can select Digest authentication as the choice for your application in the same Authentication Methods dialog — simply select the Digest Authentication check box from the properties dialog if you are using IIS 5 or 6. If you are using IIS 7, you need to install Digest Authentication just as you installed Basic Authentication. After you install it, you can find this option and are able to enable it from the Authentication section within the IIS Manager.

Forms-Based Authentication

Forms-based authentication is a popular mode of authenticating users to access an entire application or specific resources within an application. Using it enables you to put the login form directly in the application so that the end user simply enters his username and password into an HTML form contained within the browser itself. One negative aspect of forms-based authentication is that the usernames and passwords are sent as clear text unless you are using SSL.

Implementing forms-based authentication in your Web application is easy and relatively straightforward. To begin, you make some modifications to your application's `web.config` file, as illustrated in Listing 20-3.

LISTING 20-3: Modifying the web.config file for forms-based authentication

Available for download on Wrox.com

```
<system.web>
   <authentication mode="Forms">
      <forms name="Wrox" loginUrl="Login.aspx" path="/" />
   </authentication>
```

continues

LISTING 20-3 *(continued)*

```
    <authorization>
      <deny users="?" />
    </authorization>
  </system.web>
```

You must apply this structure to the `web.config` file. Using the `<authorization>` element described earlier, you are denying access to the application to all anonymous users. Only authenticated users are allowed to access any page contained within the application.

If the requestor is not authenticated, what is defined in the `<authentication>` element is put into action. The value of the `mode` attribute is set to `Forms` to employ forms-based authentication for your Web application. The next attribute specified is `loginUrl`, which points to the page that contains the application's login form. In this example, `Login.aspx` is specified as a value. If the end user trying to access the application is not authenticated, his request is redirected to `Login.aspx` so that the user can be authenticated and authorized to proceed. After valid credentials have been provided, the user is returned to the location in the application where he originally made the request. The final attribute used here is `path`. It simply specifies the location in which to save the cookie used to persist the authorized user's access token. In most cases, you want to leave the value as `/`. Table 20-3 describes each of the possible attributes for the `<forms>` element.

TABLE 20-3

ATTRIBUTE	DESCRIPTION
`name`	This name is assigned to the cookie saved in order to remember the user from request to request. The default value is `.ASPXAUTH`.
`loginUrl`	Specifies the URL to which the request is redirected for login if no valid authentication cookie is found. The default value is `Login.aspx`.
`protection`	Specifies the amount of protection you want to apply to the authentication cookie. The four available settings are: `All`: The application uses both data validation and encryption to protect the cookie. This is the default setting. `None`: Applies no encryption to the cookie. `Encryption`: The cookie is encrypted but data validation is not performed on it. Cookies used in this manner might be subject to plain text attacks. `Validation`: The opposite of the `Encryption` setting. Data validation is performed, but the cookie is not encrypted.
`path`	Specifies the path for cookies issued by the application. In most cases, you want to use `/`, which is the default setting.
`timeout`	Specifies the amount of time, in minutes, after which the cookie expires. The default value is `30`.
`cookieless`	Specifies whether the forms-based authentication process should use cookies when working with the authentication/authorization process.
`defaultUrl`	Specifies the default URL.
`domain`	Specifies the domain name to be sent with forms authentication cookies.
`slidingExpiration`	Specifies whether to apply a sliding expiration to the cookie. If set to `True`, the expiration of the cookie is reset with each request made to the server. The default value is `False`.
`enableCrossAppsRedirect`	Specifies whether to allow for cross-application redirection.
`requireSSL`	Specifies whether a Secure Sockets Layer (SSL) connection is required when transmitting authentication information.

After the `web.config` file is in place, the next step is to create a typical page for your application that people can access. Listing 20-4 presents a simple page.

Available for download on Wrox.com

LISTING 20-4: A simple page — Default.aspx

```
<%@ Page Language="VB" %>

<html xmlns="http://www.w3.org/1999/xhtml">
<head runat="server">
    <title>The Application</title>
</head>
<body>
    <form id="form1" runat="server">
    <div>
       Hello World
    </div>
    </form>
</body>
</html>
```

As you can see, this page simply writes `Hello World` to the browser. The real power of forms authentication is shown in the `Login.aspx` page presented in Listing 20-5.

Available for download on Wrox.com

LISTING 20-5: The Login.aspx page

VB

```
<%@ Page Language="VB" %>

<script runat="server">
    Protected Sub Button1_Click(ByVal sender As Object,
      ByVal e As System.EventArgs)

        If (TextBox1.Text = "BillEvjen" And TextBox2.Text = "Bubbles") Then
            FormsAuthentication.RedirectFromLoginPage(TextBox1.Text, True)
        Else
            Response.Write("Invalid credentials")
        End If
    End Sub
</script>

<html xmlns="http://www.w3.org/1999/xhtml">
<head runat="server">
    <title>Login Page</title>
</head>
<body>
    <form id="form1" runat="server">
    <div>
        Username<br />
        <asp:TextBox ID="TextBox1" runat="server"></asp:TextBox><br />
        <br />
        Password<br />
        <asp:TextBox ID="TextBox2" runat="server"
         TextMode="Password"></asp:TextBox><br />
        <br />
        <asp:Button ID="Button1" OnClick="Button1_Click" runat="server"
         Text="Submit" />
    </div>
    </form>
</body>
</html>
```

continues

LISTING 20-5 *(continued)*

Available for download on Wrox.com

```
<%@ Page Language="C#"%>

<script runat="server">
   protected void Button1_Click(object sender, EventArgs e)
    {
        if (TextBox1.Text == "BillEvjen" && TextBox2.Text == "Bubbles") {
            FormsAuthentication.RedirectFromLoginPage(TextBox1.Text, true);
        }
        else {
            Response.Write("Invalid credentials");
        }
    }
</script>
```

Filename Login.aspx

`Login.aspx` has two simple TextBox controls and a Button control that asks the user to submit his username and password. The `Button1_Click` event uses the `RedirectFromLoginPage` method of the `FormsAuthentication` class. This method does exactly what its name implies — it redirects the request from `Login.aspx` to the original requested resource.

`RedirectFromLoginPage` takes two arguments. The first is the name of the user, used for cookie authentication purposes. This argument does not actually map to an account name and is used by ASP.NET's URL authorization capabilities. The second argument specifies whether a durable cookie should be issued. If this is set to `True`, the end user does not need to log in again to the application from one browser session to the next.

Using the three pages you have constructed, each request for the `Default.aspx` page from Listing 20-4 causes ASP.NET to check that the proper authentication token is in place. If the proper token is not found, the request is directed to the specified login page (in this example, `Login.aspx`). Looking at the URL in the browser, you can see that ASP.NET is using a querystring value to remember where to return the user after he has been authorized to proceed:

```
http://localhost:35089/Security/Login.aspx?ReturnUrl=%2fSecurity%2fDefault.aspx
```

Here, the querystring `ReturnUrl` is used with a value of the folder and page that was the initial request.

Look more closely at the `Login.aspx` page from Listing 20-5, and note that the values placed in the two text boxes are checked to make sure they abide by a specific username and password. If they do, the `RedirectFromLoginPage` method is invoked; otherwise, the `Response.Write()` statement is used. In most cases, you do not want to hardcode a username and password in your code. Many other options exist for checking whether usernames and passwords come from authorized users. Some of the other options follow.

Authenticating Against Values Contained in the web.config File

The previous example is not the best approach for dealing with usernames and passwords offered for authentication. Hardcoding these things directly into your applications is never a good idea. Take a quick look at storing these values in the `web.config` file itself.

The `<forms>` element in the `web.config` file that you worked with in Listing 20-3 can also take a sub-element. The sub-element, `<credentials>`, allows you to specify username and password combinations directly in the `web.config` file. You can choose from a couple of ways to add these values. Listing 20-6 shows the simplest method.

Available for download on Wrox.com

LISTING 20-6: Modifying the web.config file to add username/password values

```
<system.web>
   <authentication mode="Forms">
      <forms name="Wrox" loginUrl="Login.aspx" path="/">
         <credentials passwordFormat="Clear">
            <user name="BillEvjen" password="Bubbles" />
```

```
            </credentials>
         </forms>
      </authentication>

      <authorization>
         <deny users="?" />
      </authorization>
   </system.web>
```

The <credentials> element has been included to add users and their passwords to the configuration file. <credentials> takes a single attribute — passwordFormat. The possible values of passwordFormat are Clear, MD5, and SHA1. The following list describes each of these options:

- Clear: Passwords are stored in clear text. The user password is compared directly to this value without further transformation.
- MD5: Passwords are stored using a Message Digest 5 (MD5) hash digest. When credentials are validated, the user password is hashed using the MD5 algorithm and compared for equality with this value. The clear-text password is never stored or compared. This algorithm produces better performance than SHA1.
- SHA1: Passwords are stored using the SHA1 hash digest. When credentials are validated, the user password is hashed using the SHA1 algorithm and compared for equality with this value. The clear-text password is never stored or compared. Use this algorithm for best security.

In the example from Listing 20-6, you use a setting of Clear. This method is not the most secure, but it is used for demonstration purposes. A sub-element of <credentials> is <user>; that is where you define the username and password for the authorized user with the attributes name and password.

The next step is to change the Button1_Click event on the Login.aspx page shown earlier, as illustrated in Listing 20-7.

LISTING 20-7: Changing the Login.aspx page to work with the web.config file

Available for download on Wrox.com

VB

```
<%@ Page Language="VB" %>

<script runat="server">
    Protected Sub Button1_Click(ByVal sender As Object,
      ByVal e As System.EventArgs)

        If FormsAuthentication.Authenticate(TextBox1.Text, TextBox2.Text) Then
            FormsAuthentication.RedirectFromLoginPage(TextBox1.Text, True)
        Else
            Response.Write("Invalid credentials")
        End If
    End Sub
</script>
```

C#

```
<%@ Page Language="C#"%>

<script runat="server">
    protected void Button1_Click(object sender, EventArgs e)
    {

        if (FormsAuthentication.Authenticate(TextBox1.Text, TextBox2.Text)) {
            FormsAuthentication.RedirectFromLoginPage(TextBox1.Text, true);
        }
        else {
            Response.Write("Invalid credentials");
        }
    }
</script>
```

In this example, you simply use the `Authenticate()` method to get your ASP.NET page to look at the credentials stored in the `web.config` file for verification. The `Authenticate()` method takes two parameters — the username and the password that you are passing in to be checked. If the credential lookup is successful, the `RedirectFromLoginPage` method is invoked.

It is best not to store your users' passwords in the `web.config` file as clear text, as the preceding example did. Instead, use one of the available hashing capabilities so you can keep the end user's password out of sight of prying eyes. To do this, simply store the hashed password in the configuration file, as shown in Listing 20-8.

LISTING 20-8: Using encrypted passwords

Available for download on Wrox.com

```
<forms name="Wrox" loginUrl="Login.aspx" path="/">
  <credentials passwordFormat="SHA1">
     <user name="BillEvjen" password="58356FB4CAC0B801F011B397F9DFF45ADB863892" />
  </credentials>
</forms>
```

Using this kind of construct makes it impossible for even the developer to discover a password, because the clear-text password is never used. The `Authenticate()` method in the `Login.aspx` page hashes the password using SHA1 (because it is the method specified in the `web.config` file's `<credentials>` node) and compares the two hashes for a match. If a match is found, the user is authorized to proceed.

When using SHA1 or MD5, the only changes you make are in the `web.config` file and nowhere else. You do not have to make any changes to the login page or to any other page in the application. To store hashed passwords, however, you use the `FormsAuthentication.HashPasswordForStoringInConfigFile()` method (one of the longer method names in the .NET Framework). You use this method in the following manner:

```
FormsAuthentication.HashPasswordForStoringInConfigFile(TextBox2.Text, "SHA1")
```

Authenticating Against Values in a Database

Another common way to retrieve username/password combinations is by getting them directly from a datastore of some kind. This enables you, for example, to check the credentials input by a user against values stored in Microsoft's SQL Server. Listing 20-9 presents the code for this credentials check.

LISTING 20-9: Checking credentials in SQL Server (Login.aspx)

Available for download on Wrox.com

VB

```
<%@ Page Language="VB" %>
<%@ Import Namespace="System.Data" %>
<%@ Import Namespace="System.Data.SqlClient" %>

<script runat="server">
    Protected Sub Button1_Click(ByVal sender As Object,
      ByVal e As System.EventArgs)

        Dim conn As SqlConnection
        Dim cmd As SqlCommand
        Dim cmdString As String = "SELECT [Password] FROM [AccessTable] WHERE" &
           " (([Username] = @Username) AND ([Password] = @Password))"

        conn = New SqlConnection("Data Source=localhost;Initial " &
           "Catalog=Northwind;Persist Security Info=True;User ID=sa")
        cmd = New SqlCommand(cmdString, conn)

        cmd.Parameters.Add("@Username", SqlDbType.VarChar, 50)
        cmd.Parameters("@Username").Value = TextBox1.Text
        cmd.Parameters.Add("@Password", SqlDbType.VarChar, 50)
        cmd.Parameters("@Password").Value = TextBox2.Text
```

```
            conn.Open()

            Dim myReader As SqlDataReader

            myReader = cmd.ExecuteReader(CommandBehavior.CloseConnection)

            If myReader.Read() Then
               FormsAuthentication.RedirectFromLoginPage(TextBox1.Text, False)
            Else
               Response.Write("Invalid credentials")
            End If

            myReader.Close()
        End Sub
    </script>
```

C#

```
    <%@ Page Language="C#"%>
    <%@ Import Namespace="System.Data" %>
    <%@ Import Namespace="System.Data.SqlClient" %>

    <script runat="server">
        protected void Button1_Click(object sender, EventArgs e)
        {

            SqlConnection conn;
            SqlCommand cmd;
            string cmdString = "SELECT [Password] FROM [AccessTable] WHERE" +
               " (([Username] = @Username) AND ([Password] = @Password))";

            conn = new SqlConnection("Data Source=localhost;Initial " +
               "Catalog=Northwind;Persist Security Info=True;User ID=sa");
            cmd = new SqlCommand(cmdString, conn);

            cmd.Parameters.Add("@Username", SqlDbType.VarChar, 50);
            cmd.Parameters["@Username"].Value = TextBox1.Text;
            cmd.Parameters.Add("@Password", SqlDbType.VarChar, 50);
            cmd.Parameters["@Password"].Value = TextBox2.Text;
            conn.Open();

            SqlDataReader myReader;

            myReader = cmd.ExecuteReader(CommandBehavior.CloseConnection);

            if (myReader.Read()) {
               FormsAuthentication.RedirectFromLoginPage(TextBox1.Text, false);
            }
            else {
               Response.Write("Invalid credentials");
            }
            myReader.Close();

        }
    </script>
```

Leave everything else from the previous examples the same, except for the `Login.aspx` page. You can now authenticate usernames and passwords against data stored in SQL Server. In the `Button1_Click` event, a connection is made to SQL Server. (For security reasons, you should store your connection string in the `web.config` file.) Two parameters are passed in — the inputs from `TextBox1` and `TextBox2`. If a result is returned, the `RedirectFromLoginPage()` method is invoked.

Using the Login Control with Forms Authentication

You have seen how to use ASP.NET forms authentication with standard ASP.NET server controls, such as simple TextBox and Button controls. You can also use the ASP.NET server controls — such as the Login server control — with your custom-developed forms-authentication framework instead of using other controls. This really shows the power of ASP.NET — you can combine so many pieces to construct the solution you want.

Listing 20-10 shows a modified `Login.aspx` page using the new Login server control.

LISTING 20-10: Using the Login server control on the Login.aspx page

Available for download on Wrox.com

```
<%@ Page Language="VB" %>

<script runat="server">
    Protected Sub Login1_Authenticate(ByVal sender As Object,
      ByVal e As System.Web.UI.WebControls.AuthenticateEventArgs)

        If (Login1.UserName = "BillEvjen" And Login1.Password = "Bubbles") Then
            FormsAuthentication.RedirectFromLoginPage(Login1.UserName,
               Login1.RememberMeSet)
        Else
            Response.Write("Invalid credentials")
        End If
    End Sub
</script>

<html xmlns="http://www.w3.org/1999/xhtml" >
<head runat="server">
    <title>Login Page</title>
</head>
<body>
    <form id="form1" runat="server">
    <div>
        <asp:Login ID="Login1" runat="server" OnAuthenticate="Login1_Authenticate">
        </asp:Login>
    </div>
    </form>
</body>
</html>
```

C#

```
<%@ Page Language="C#" %>

<script runat="server">
    protected void Login1_Authenticate(object sender, AuthenticateEventArgs e)
    {
        if (Login1.UserName == "BillEvjen" && Login1.Password == "Bubbles") {
            FormsAuthentication.RedirectFromLoginPage(Login1.UserName,
               Login1.RememberMeSet);
        }
        else {
            Response.Write("Invalid credentials");
        }
    }
</script>
```

Because no Button server control is on the page, you use the Login control's `OnAuthenticate` attribute to point to the authentication server-side event — `Login1_Authenticate()`. The event takes care of the authorization lookup (although the values are hardcoded in this example). The username text box of the Login control can be accessed via the `Login1.UserName` declaration, and the password can be accessed using `Login1.Password`. You use the `Login1.RememberMeSet` property to specify whether to persist the authentication cookie for the user so that he is remembered on his next visit.

This example is a bit simpler than creating your own login form using TextBox and Button controls. You can give the Login control a predefined look-and-feel that is provided for you. You can also get at the subcontrol properties of the Login control a bit more easily. In the end, what methods you employ in your ASP.NET applications are really up to you.

Looking Closely at the FormsAuthentication Class

As you can tell from the various examples in the forms authentication part of this chapter, a lot of what goes on depends on the `FormsAuthentication` class itself. For this reason, you should learn what that class is all about.

`FormsAuthentication` provides a number of methods and properties that enable you to read and control the authentication cookie as well as other information (such as the return URL of the request). Table 20-4 details some of the methods and properties available in the `FormsAuthentictation` class.

TABLE 20-4

METHOD/PROPERTY	DESCRIPTION
`Authenticate`	This method is used to authenticate credentials that are stored in a configuration file (such as the `web.config` file).
`Decrypt`	Returns an instance of a valid, encrypted authentication ticket retrieved from an HTTP cookie as an instance of a `FormsAuthenticationTicket` class.
`Encrypt`	Creates a string that contains a valid encrypted authentication ticket that can be used in an HTTP cookie.
`FormsCookieName`	Returns the name of the cookie for the current application.
`FormsCookiePath`	Returns the cookie path (the location of the cookie) for the current application.
`GetAuthCookie`	Provides an authentication cookie for a specified user.
`GetRedirectUrl`	Returns the URL to which the user is redirected after being authorized by the login page.
`HashPasswordFor Storing InConfigFile`	Creates a hash of a provided string password. This method takes two parameters — one is the password and the other is the type of hash to perform on the string. Possible hash values include `SHA1` and `MD5`.
`Initialize`	Performs an initialization of the `FormsAuthentication` class by reading the configuration settings in the `web.config` file, as well as getting the cookies and encryption keys used in the given instance of the application.
`RedirectFromLogin Page`	Performs a redirection of the HTTP request back to the original requested page. This should be performed only after the user has been authorized to proceed.
`RenewTicketIfOld`	Conditionally updates the sliding expiration on a `FormsAuthenticationTicket` instance.
`RequireSSL`	Specifies whether the cookie should be transported via SSL only (HTTPS).
`SetAuthCookie`	Creates an authentication ticket and attaches it to a cookie that is contained in the outgoing response.
`SignOut`	Removes the authentication ticket.
`SlidingExpiration`	Provides a Boolean value indicating whether sliding expiration is enabled.

Passport Authentication

Though an option, Microsoft's Passport technologies are used by very few Internet sites and applications. In fact, Microsoft completely de-emphasized Passport in 2005, and most companies interested in global authentication/authorization standards are turning toward the Liberty Alliance Project endeavors for a solution (`www.projectliberty.org`).

AUTHENTICATING SPECIFIC FILES AND FOLDERS

You may not want to require credentials for each and every page or resource in your application. For example, you might have a public Internet site with pages anyone can access without credentials, although you might have an administration section as part of your application that might require authentication/authorization measures.

URL authorization enables you to use the web.config file to apply the settings you need. Using URL authorization, you can apply any of the authentication measures to only specific files or folders. Listing 20-11 shows an example of locking down a single file.

LISTING 20-11: Applying authorization requirements to a single file

Available for download on Wrox.com

```
<configuration>
   <system.web>
      <authentication mode="None" />

      <!-- The rest of your web.config file settings go here -->

   </system.web>

   <location path="AdminPage.aspx">
      <system.web>
         <authentication mode="Windows" />

         <authorization>
            <allow users="ReutersServer\EvjenB" />
            <deny users="*" />
         </authorization>
      </system.web>
   </location>
</configuration>
```

This web.config file construction keeps the Web application open to the general public while, at the same time, it locks down a single file contained within the application — the AdminPage.aspx page. You accomplish this lockdown through the <location> element. <location> takes a single attribute (path) to specify the resource defined within the <system.web> section of the web.config file.

In the example, the <authentication> and <authorization> elements are used to provide the authentication and authorization details for the AdminPage.aspx page. For this page, Windows authentication is applied, and the only user allowed access is EvjenB in the ReutersServer domain. You can have as many <location> sections in your web.config file as you want.

PROGRAMMATIC AUTHORIZATION

So far, you have seen a lot of authentication examples that simply provide a general authorization to a specific page or folder within the application. Yet, you may want to provide more granular authorization measures for certain items on a page. For example, you might provide a link to a specific document only for users who have an explicit Windows role. Other users may see something else. You also might want additional commentary or information for specified users, while other users see a condensed version of the information. Whatever your reason, this role-based authorization practice is possible in ASP.NET by working with certain objects.

You can use the Page object's User property, which provides an instance of the IPrincipal object. The User property provides a single method and a single property:

- Identity: This property provides an instance of the System.Security.Principal.IIdentity object for you to get at specific properties of the authenticated user.
- IsInRole: This method takes a single parameter, a string representation of the system role. It returns a Boolean value that indicates whether the user is in the role specified.

Working with User.Identity

The `User.Identity` property enables you to work with some specific contextual information about the authorized user. Using the property within your ASP.NET applications enables you to make resource-access decisions based on the information the object provides.

With `User.Identity`, you can gain access to the user's name, his or her authentication type, and whether he or she is authenticated. Table 20-5 details the properties provided through `User.Identity`.

TABLE 20-5

ATTRIBUTE	DESCRIPTION
`AuthenticationType`	Provides the authentication type of the current user. Example values include `Basic`, `NTLM`, `Forms`, and `Passport`.
`IsAuthenticated`	Returns a Boolean value specifying whether the user has been authenticated.
`Name`	Provides the username of the user as well as the domain of the user (only if he logged on with a Windows account).

For some examples of working with the `User` object, take a look at checking the user's login name. To do this, you use code similar to that shown in Listing 20-12.

LISTING 20-12: Getting the username of the logged-in user

VB

```
Dim UserName As String
UserName = User.Identity.Name
```

C#

```
string userName;
userName = User.Identity.Name;
```

Another task you can accomplish with the `User.Identity` object is checking whether the user has been authenticated through your application's authentication methods, as illustrated in Listing 20-13.

LISTING 20-13: Checking whether the user is authenticated

VB

```
Dim AuthUser As Boolean
AuthUser = User.Identity.IsAuthenticated
```

C#

```
bool authUser;
authUser = User.Identity.IsAuthenticated;
```

This example provides you with a Boolean value indicating whether the user has been authenticated. You can also use the `IsAuthenticated` method in an `If/Then` statement, as shown in Listing 20-14.

LISTING 20-14: Using an If/Then statement that checks authentication

VB

```
If (User.Identity.IsAuthenticated) Then
   ' Do some actions here for authenticated users
Else
   ' Do other actions here for unauthenticated users
End If
```

C#

```
if (User.Identity.IsAuthenticated) {
   // Do some actions here for authenticated users
}
else {
   // Do other actions here for unauthenticated users
}
```

You can also use the `User` object to check the authentication type of the user. You do so with the `AuthenticationType` property, illustrated in Listing 20-15.

LISTING 20-15: Using the AuthenticationType property

VB

```
Dim AuthType As String
AuthType = User.Identity.AuthenticationType
```

C#

```
string authType;
authType = User.Identity.AuthenticationType;
```

Again, the result is `Basic`, `NTLM`, `Forms`, or `Passport`.

Working with User.IsInRole()

If you are using Windows-based authentication, you can check to make sure that an authenticated user is in a specific Windows role. For example, you might want to show specific information only for users in the `Subscribers` group in the Computer Management Utility. To accomplish that, you can use the `User` object's `IsInRole` method, as shown in Listing 20-16.

LISTING 20-16: Checking whether the user is part of a specific role

VB

```
If (User.IsInRole("ReutersServer\Subscribers")) Then
   ' Private information for subscribers
Else
   ' Public information
End If
```

C#

```
if (User.IsInRole("ReutersServer\\Subscribers")) {
    // Private information for subscribers
}
else {
    // Public information
}
```

The `IsInRole` method's parameter provides a string value that represents the domain and the group (Windows role). In this case, you specify that any user in the `Subscribers` Windows role from the `ReutersServer` domain is permitted to see some information not available to users who don't belong to that specific role.

Another possibility is to specify some of the built-in groups available to you. Ever since Windows 2000, Windows has included a series of built-in accounts such as Administrator, Guest, PrintOperator, and User. You can access these built-in accounts in a couple of ways. One is to specify the built-in account with the domain directly:

```
User.IsInRole("ReutersServer\Administrator")
```

The other possibility is to use the `BUILTIN` keyword:

```
User.IsInRole("BUILTIN\Administrator")
```

Pulling More Information with WindowsIdentity

So far, in working with the user's identity information, you have used the standard `Identity` object that is part of ASP.NET by default. If you are working with Windows-based authentication, you also have the option of using the `WindowsIdentity` object and other objects. To gain access to these richer objects, create a reference to the `System.Security.Principal` object in your application.

Used in combination with the `Identity` object from the preceding examples, these additional objects make certain tasks even easier. For example, if you are working with roles, `System.Security.Principal` provides access to the `WindowsBuiltInRole` enumeration.

Listing 20-17 is an example of using the `WindowsBuiltInRole` enumeration.

LISTING 20-17: Using the WindowsBuiltInRole enumeration

VB

```
Dim AdminUser As Boolean
AdminUser = User.IsInRole(WindowsBuiltInRole.Administrator.ToString())
```

C#

```
bool adminUser;
adminUser = User.IsInRole(WindowsBuiltInRole.Administrator.ToString());
```

Instead of specifying a string value of the domain and the role, you can use the `WindowsBuiltInRole` enumeration to easily access specific roles on the application server. When working with this and other enumerations, you also have IntelliSense (see Figure 20-11) to help you make your selections easily.

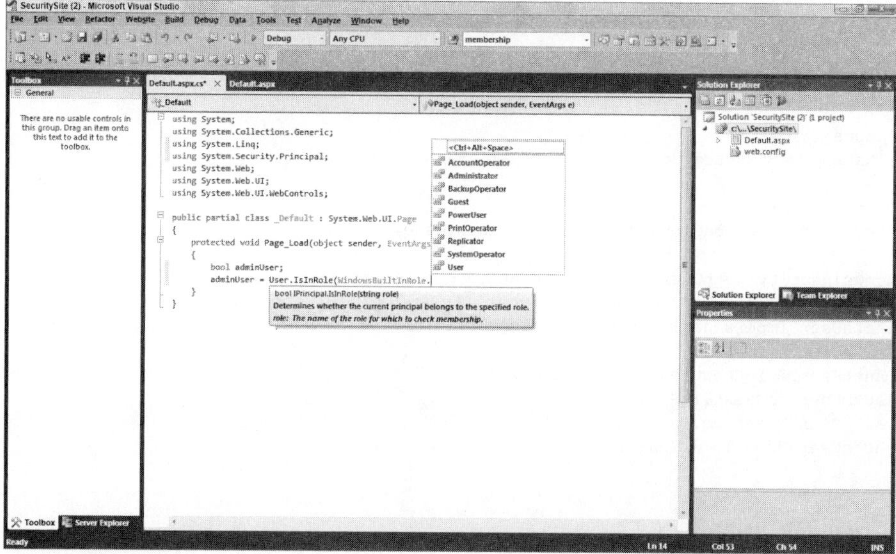

FIGURE 20-11

The roles in the `WindowsBuiltInRole` enumeration include the following:

- AccountOperator
- Administrator
- BackupOperator
- Guest
- PowerUser
- PrintOperator
- Replicator
- SystemOperator
- User

Using `System.Security.Principal`, you have access to the `WindowsIdentity` object, which is much richer than working with the default `Identity` object. Listing 20-18 lists some of the additional information you can get through the `WindowsIdentity` object.

LISTING 20-18: Using the WindowsIdentity object

Available for download on Wrox.com

VB

```
<%@ Page Language="VB" %>
<%@ Import Namespace="System.Security.Principal" %>

<script runat="server">
    Protected Sub Page_Load(ByVal sender As Object,
      ByVal e As System.EventArgs)

       Dim AuthUser As WindowsIdentity = WindowsIdentity.GetCurrent()
       Response.Write(AuthUser.AuthenticationType.ToString() & "<br>" &
          AuthUser.ImpersonationLevel.ToString() & "<br>" &
          AuthUser.IsAnonymous.ToString() & "<br>" &
          AuthUser.IsAuthenticated.ToString() & "<br>" &
          AuthUser.IsGuest.ToString() & "<br>" &
          AuthUser.IsSystem.ToString() & "<br>" &
          AuthUser.Name.ToString())
    End Sub
</script>
```

C#

```
<%@ Page Language="C#" %>
<%@ Import Namespace="System.Security.Principal" %>

<script runat="server">
    protected void Page_Load(object sender, EventArgs e)
    {
       WindowsIdentity AuthUser = WindowsIdentity.GetCurrent();
       Response.Write(AuthUser.AuthenticationType.ToString() + "<br>" +
          AuthUser.ImpersonationLevel.ToString() + "<br>" +
          AuthUser.IsAnonymous.ToString() + "<br>" +
          AuthUser.IsAuthenticated.ToString() + "<br>" +
          AuthUser.IsGuest.ToString() + "<br>" +
          AuthUser.IsSystem.ToString() + "<br>" +
          AuthUser.Name.ToString());
    }
</script>
```

In this example, an instance of the `WindowsIdentity` object is created and populated with the current identity of the user accessing the application. Then you have access to a number of properties that are written to the browser using a `Response.Write()` statement. The displayed listing shows information about the current user's credentials, such as whether the user is authenticated, anonymous, or running under a guest account or a system account. It also gives you the user's authentication type and login name. Figure 20-12 shows a result.

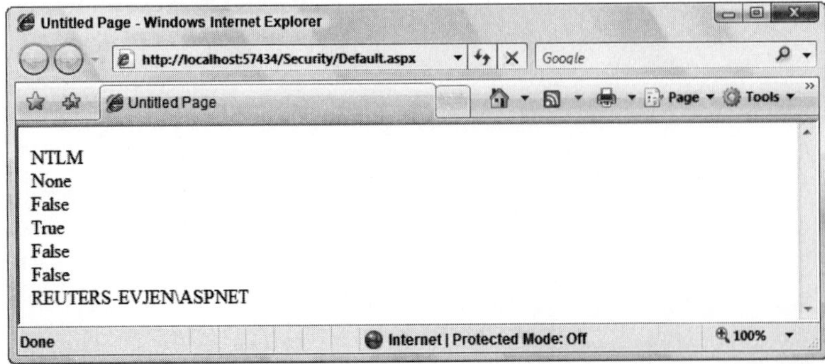

FIGURE 20-12

IDENTITY AND IMPERSONATION

By default, ASP.NET runs under an account that has limited privileges. For example, you might find that although the account can gain access to a network, it cannot be authenticated to any other computer on the network.

The account setting is provided in the `machine.config` file:

```
<processModel
 enable="true"
 userName="machine"
 password="AutoGenerate" />
```

These settings force ASP.NET to run under the system account (ASPNET or Network Service). This is really specified through the `userName` attribute that contains a value of `machine`. The other possible value you can have for this attribute is `system`. Here's what each entails:

- `machine`: The most secure setting. You should have good reasons to change this value. It's the ideal choice mainly because it forces the ASP.NET account to run under the fewest number of privileges possible.
- `system`: Forces ASP.NET to run under the local SYSTEM account, which has considerably more privileges to access networking and files.

Specifying an account of your choosing using the `<processModel>` element in either the `machine.config` or `web.config` files is also possible:

```
<processModel
 enable="true"
 userName="MySpecifiedUser"
 password="MyPassword" />
```

In this example, ASP.NET is run under a specified administrator or user account instead of the default ASPNET or Network Service account. It inherits all the privileges this account offers. You should consider encrypting this section of the file. Chapter 33 covers encrypting sections of a configuration file.

You can also change how ASP.NET behaves in whatever account it is specified to run under through the `<identity>` element in the `web.config` file. The `<identity>` element in the `web.config` file allows you to turn on *impersonation*. Impersonation provides ASP.NET with the capability to run as a process using the privileges of another user for a specific session. In more detail, impersonation allows ASP.NET to run under the account of the entity making the request to the application. To turn on this impersonation capability, you use the `impersonate` attribute in the `<identity>` element, as shown here:

```
<configuration>
   <system.web>

      <identity impersonate="true" />

   </system.web>
</configuration>
```

By default, the `impersonate` attribute is set to `false`. Setting this property to `true` ensures that ASP.NET runs under the account of the person making the request to the application. If the requestor is an anonymous user, ASP.NET runs under the IUSR_MachineName account. To see this in action, run the example shown in Listing 20-18, but this time with impersonation turned on (`true`). Instead of getting a username of `REUTERS-EVJEN\ASPNET` as the user, you get the name of the user who is requesting the page — REUTERS-EVJEN\Administrator in this example — as shown in Figure 20-13.

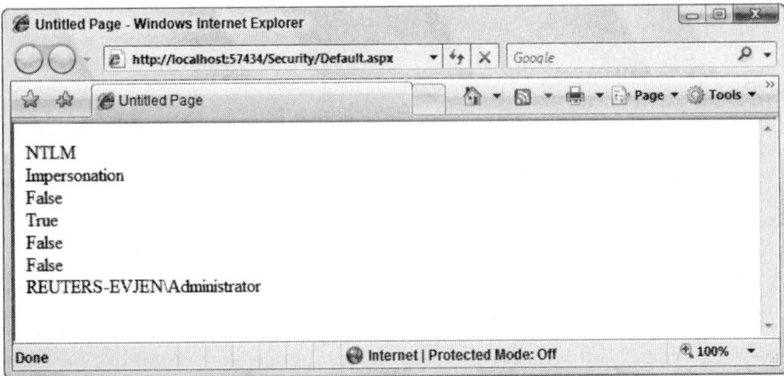

FIGURE 20-13

You also have the option of running ASP.NET under a specified account that you declare using the <identity> element in the web.config file:

```
<identity impersonate="true" userName="MySpecifiedUser" password="MyPassword" />
```

As shown, you can run the ASP.NET process under an account that you specify through the userName and password attributes. These values are stored as clear text in the web.config file.

Look at the root web.config file, and you can see that ASP.NET runs under full trust, meaning that it has some rather high-level capabilities to run and access resources. Here is the setting:

```
<system.web>

    <location allowOverride="true">
        <system.web>
            <securityPolicy>
                <trustLevel name="Full" policyFile="internal"/>
                <trustLevel name="High" policyFile="web_hightrust.config"/>
                <trustLevel name="Medium" policyFile="web_mediumtrust.config"/>
                <trustLevel name="Low" policyFile="web_lowtrust.config"/>
                <trustLevel name="Minimal" policyFile="web_minimaltrust.config"/>
            </securityPolicy>
            <trust level="Full" originUrl=""/>
            <fullTrustAssemblies />
            <partialTrustVisibleAssemblies />
        </system.web>
    </location>

</system.web>
```

Five possible settings exist for the level of trust that you give ASP.NET — Full, High, Medium, Low, and Minimal. You specify the level of trust applied through the <trust> element's level attribute. By default, it is set to Full. Each one points to a specific configuration file for the policy in which the level can find its trust level settings. The Full setting does not include a policy file because it simply skips all the code access security checks.

SECURING THROUGH IIS

ASP.NET works in conjunction with IIS; not only can you apply security settings directly in ASP.NET (through code or configuration files), but you can also apply additional security measures in IIS itself. IIS enables you to apply access methods you want by working with users and groups (which were discussed earlier in the chapter), working with restricting IP addresses, file extensions, and more. Security through IIS is deserving of a chapter in itself, but the major topics are explored here.

IP Address and Domain Name Restrictions

You can work with the restriction of IP addresses and domain names in Windows Server 2008, Windows Server 2003, Windows 2000 Server, or Windows NT. Through IIS 6.0, you can apply specific restrictions based on a single computer's IP address, a group of computers, or even a specific domain name.

To access this capability, pull up the Internet Information Services (IIS) Manager and right-click on either the Web site you are interested in working with or on the Default Web Site node to simply apply the settings to every Web application on the server. From the menu, choose Properties and select the Directory Security tab.

Click the Edit button in the IP Address and domain name restrictions box, and a dialog appears. The resulting dialog enables you to grant or restrict access based on an IP address or domain name. These dialogs are shown in Figure 20-14.

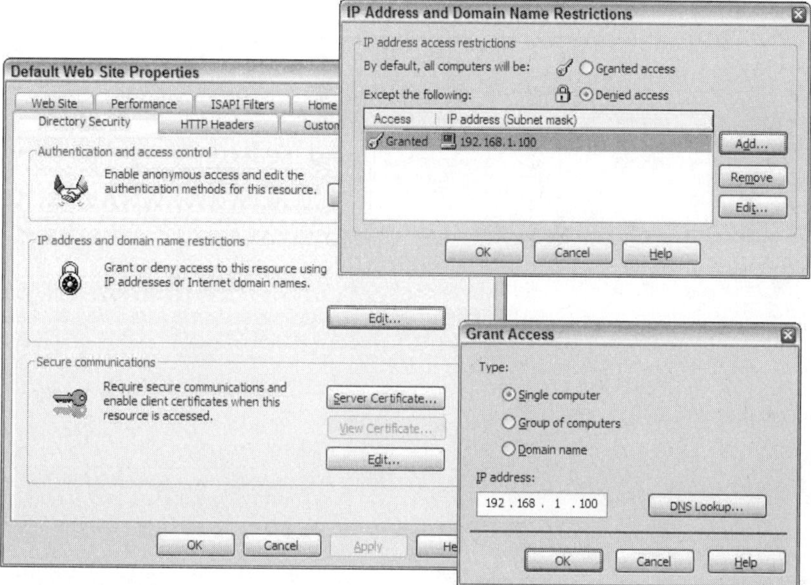

FIGURE 20-14

Think twice about restricting based on a domain name. It can hinder performance when the reverse DNS lookup is performed on each request to check the domain.

You not only can restrict specific IP addresses and domain names, but you can also restrict everyone and just allow specified entities based on the same items. Although Figure 20-14 shows restricting a specific IP address, you can restrict or grant access to an entire subnet, as well. Figure 20-15 shows how to grant access just to the servers on the 192.168.1.0 subnet (defined by a Linksys router).

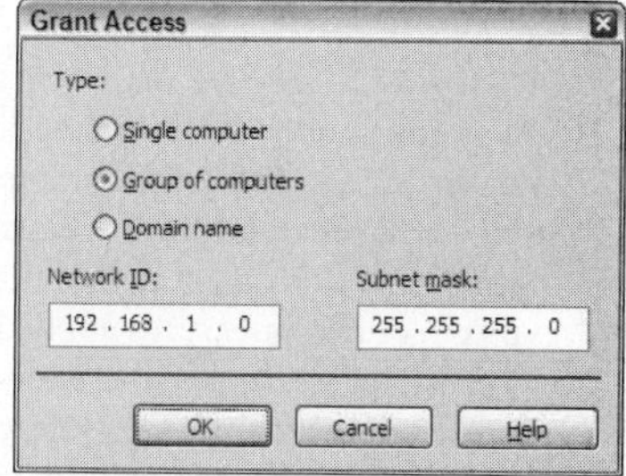

FIGURE 20-15

Working with File Extensions

You can work with many types of files in ASP.NET. These files are defined by their extensions. For example, you know that `.aspx` is a typical ASP.NET page, and `.asmx` is an ASP.NET Web service file extension. These files are actually mapped by IIS to the ASP.NET DLL, `aspnet_isapi.dll`.

To access the dialog in IIS 6.0 that maps the file extensions, pull up the Properties dialog of your Web application in IIS or pull up the Default Web Site Properties. In a specific Web application, you must work from the Directory tab; but if you are working with the Default Web Site Properties dialog, you can instead use the Home Directory tab. From these tabs, click the Configuration button in the Application Settings box. The Application Configuration dialog includes a Mapping tab, where the mappings are configured. Highlight `.aspx` in the list of mappings and click the Edit button. Figure 20-16 shows the result.

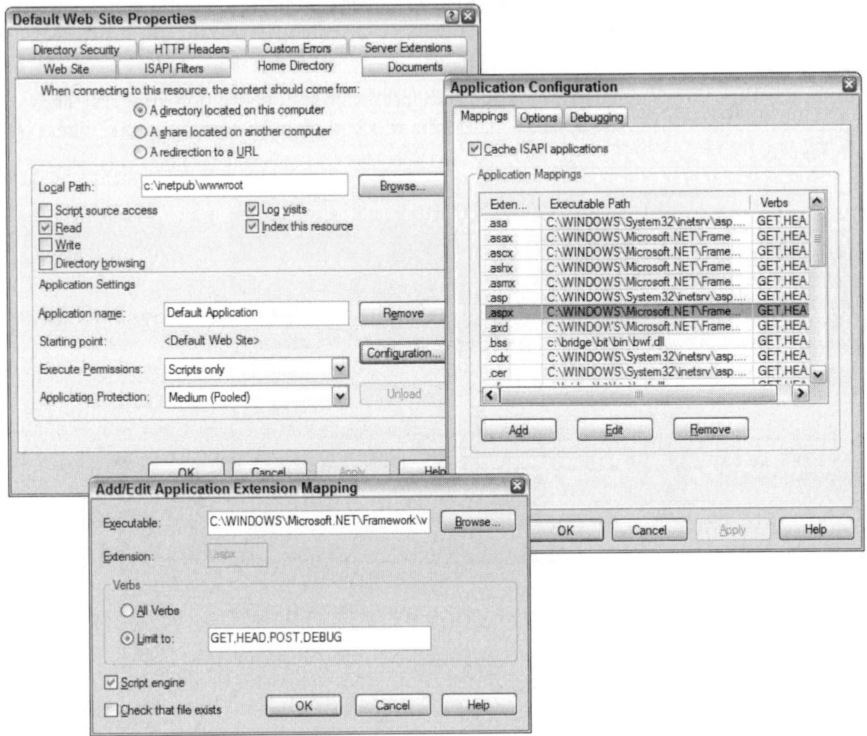

FIGURE 20-16

In the Executable text box, you can see that all `.aspx` pages map to the `aspnet_isapi.dll` from ASP.NET, and that you can also specify which types of requests are allowed in the application. You can either allow all verbs (for example, `GET` or `POST`) or specify which verbs are allowed access to the application.

One important point regarding these mappings is that you do not see `.html`, `.htm`, `.jpg`, or other file extensions such as `.txt` in the list. Your application will not be passing requests for these files to ASP.NET. That might not be a big deal, but in working through the various security examples in this chapter, you might want to have the same type of security measures applied to these files as to `.aspx` pages. If, for example, you want all `.html` pages to be included in the forms authentication model that you require for your ASP.NET application, you must add `.html` (or whatever file extension you want) to the list. To do so, click the Add button in the Application Configuration dialog.

In the next dialog, you can add the ASP.NET DLL to the Executable text box, and the appropriate file extension and verbs to the list, before adding the mapping to your application's mapping table. Figure 20-17 illustrates this example.

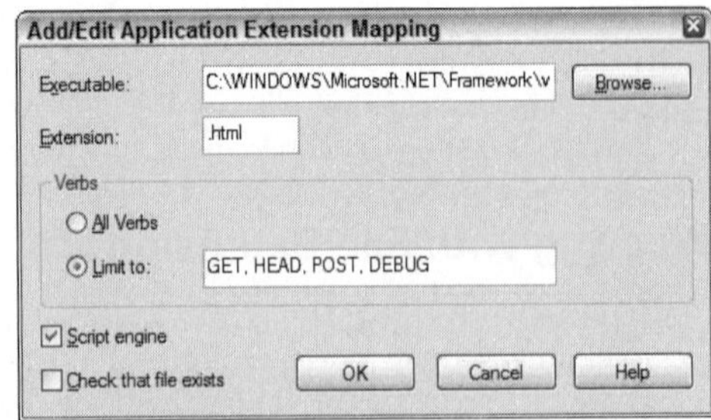

FIGURE 20-17

When dealing with the security of your site, you have to remember all the files that might not be included in the default mapping list and add the ones you think should fall under the same security structure.

If you are working with Windows 7, you can get to the same functionality through the IIS Manager. In this tool, select Handler Mappings in the IIS section. You will find a large list of mappings that have already been provided, as illustrated in Figure 20-18.

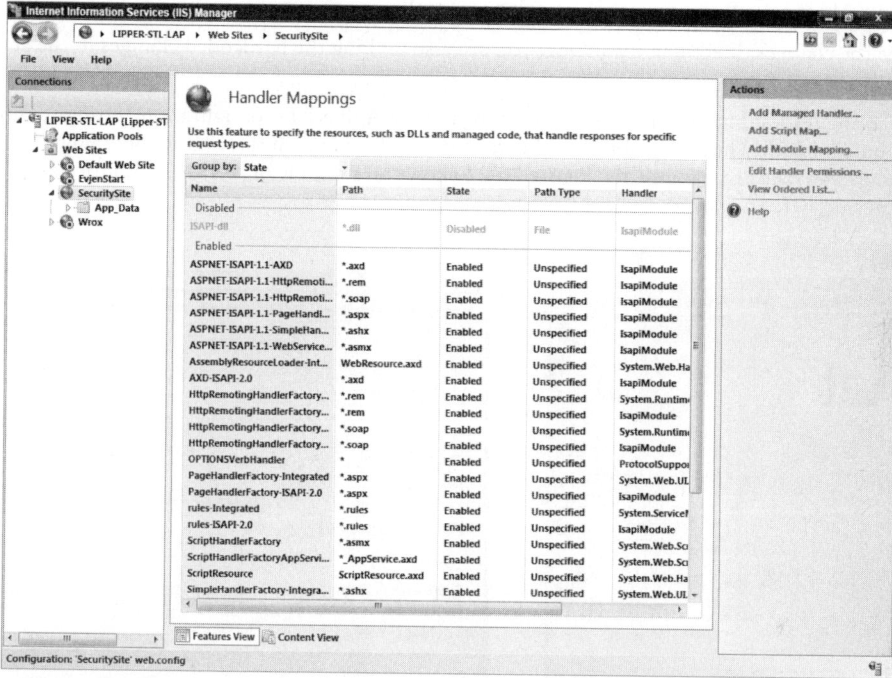

FIGURE 20-18

By highlighting the `*.aspx` option and clicking the Edit button, you see that this extension is mapped to the handler `System.Web.UI.PageHandlerFactory`, as shown in Figure 20-19.

Clicking the Request Restrictions button provides a dialog that enables you to select the verbs allowed (as shown in Figure 20-20).

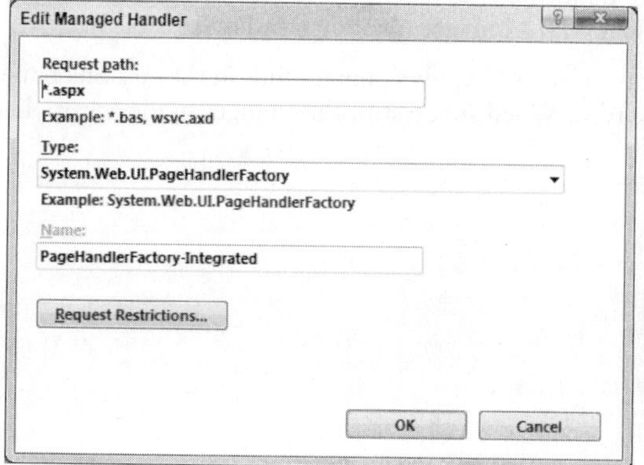

FIGURE 20-19

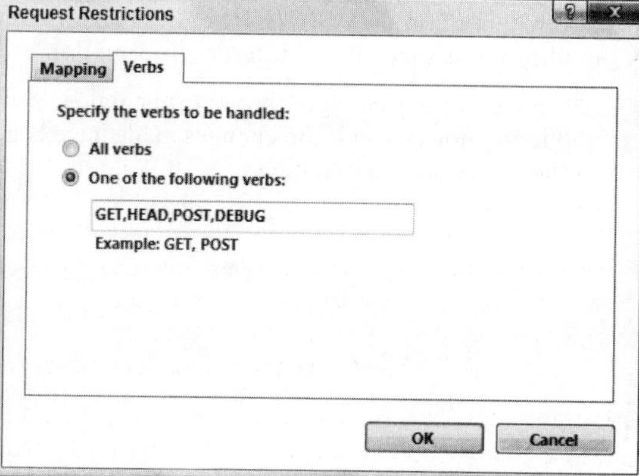

FIGURE 20-20

Using the ASP.NET MMC Snap-In

The ASP.NET MMC console enables you to edit the `web.config` and `machine.config` files using an easy-to-use GUI instead of having to dig through the text of those files yourself to make the necessary changes. This option is only available in either Windows Server 2003 or Windows XP. You can also modify and change most of the items examined in this book using this dialog. The plug-in is available on the ASP.NET tab (see Figure 20-21) of your Web application running under IIS.

When you make the changes directly in the dialog, you are also making the hardcoded changes to the actual configuration files.

Click the Edit Configuration button on the ASP.NET tab, and the ASP.NET Configuration Settings dialog opens. There, you can modify how your forms authentication model works in the GUI without going to the application's `web.config` file directly. Figure 20-22 shows an example of working with forms authentication in the GUI.

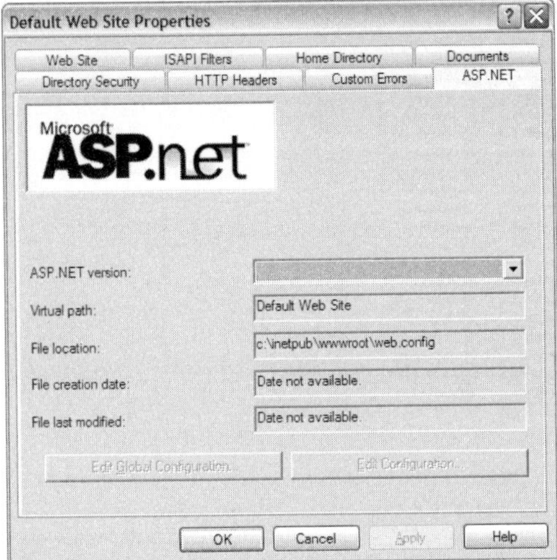

FIGURE 20-21

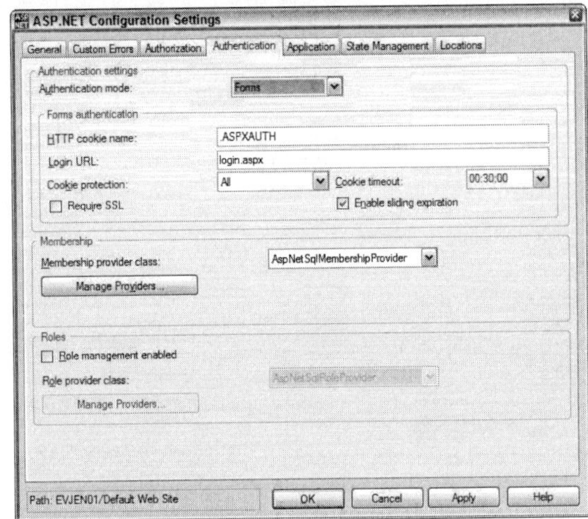

FIGURE 20-22

Using the IIS 7.0 Manager

You will not find the ASP.NET MMC Snap-In within Windows 7. Instead, you can make all the same site modifications through the Internet Information Services (IIS) Manager (as shown in Figure 20-23).

After making any changes through this dialog, you can select the Apply Changes link in the Actions pane, and it will notify you if the changes made have been saved. When successful, the changes made are applied to the site's `web.config` file.

FIGURE 20-23

SUMMARY

This chapter covered some of the foundation items of ASP.NET security and showed you how to apply both authentication and authorization to your Web applications. It reviewed some of the various authentication and authorization models at your disposal, such as Basic, Digest, and Windows Integrated Authentication. Other topics included forms-based authentication and how to construct your own forms-based authentication models outside of the ones provided via ASP.NET 4 by using the membership and role management capabilities it provides. The chapter also discussed how to use authentication properties within your applications and how to authorize users and groups based on those properties. This chapter also took a look at securing your applications through IIS.

21

State Management

WHAT'S IN THIS CHAPTER?

- Using the Session object
- Other options for controlling state

Why is state management such a difficult problem that it requires an entire chapter in a book on programming? In the old days (about 18 years ago), using standard client-server architecture meant using a fat client and a fat server. Perhaps your Visual Basic 6 application could talk to a database. The state was held either on the client-side or in the server-side database. Typically, you could count on a client having a little bit of memory and a hard drive of its own to manage state. The most important aspect of traditional client/server design, however, was that the client was *always* connected to the server. It's easy to forget, but HTTP is a stateless protocol. For the most part, a connection is built up and torn down each time a call is made to a remote server. Yes, HTTP 1.1 includes a keep-alive technique that provides optimizations at the TCP level. Even with these optimizations, the server has no way to determine that subsequent connections came from the same client.

Although the Web has the richness of DHTML and Ajax, JavaScript, and HTML 4.0 on the client side, the average high-powered Intel Core Duo with a few gigabytes of RAM is still being used only to render HTML. The fact that such powerful computers on the client side are still so vastly underutilized when it comes to storing state is quite ironic. Additionally, although many individuals have broadband, it is not universally used. Developers must still respect and pay attention to the dial-up users of the world. When was the last time that your project manager told you that bandwidth was not an issue for your Web application?

The ASP.NET concept of a session that is maintained over the statelessness of HTTP is not a new one, and it existed before ASP.NET and even before classic ASP. It is a very effective and elegant way to maintain state. However, a number of different choices are available to you, of which the ASP.NET session is just one. A few subtle changes between ASP.NET 1.*x* and 2.0/3.5/4 have occurred that are covered in this chapter. The `Session` object remains as before, but the option to plug in your own session state provider is now available.

YOUR SESSION STATE CHOICES

Given a relatively weak client, a stateless protocol such as HTTP, and ASP.NET on the server side, how do you manage state on the Web? Figure 21-1 is a generalized diagram that identifies the primary means available for managing state. The problem is huge, and the solution range is even larger. This chapter assumes that you are not using Java applets or ActiveX controls to manage state. Although these options are certainly valid (though complex) solutions to the state problem, they are beyond the scope of this book.

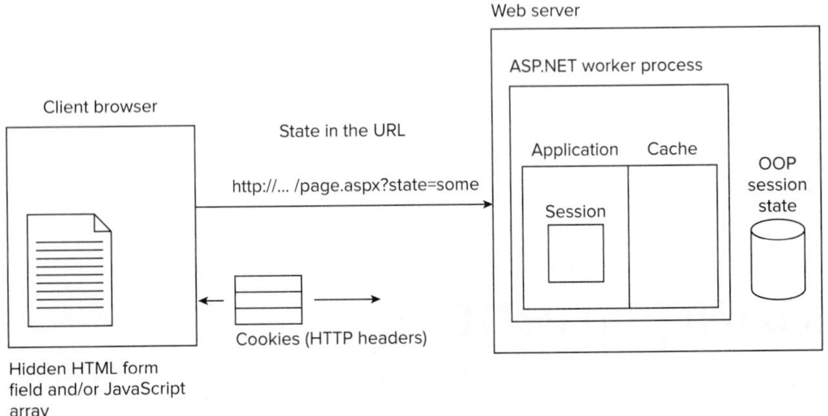

FIGURE 21-1

If you remember one thing about state management, remember this: There is no right answer. Some answers are more right than others, certainly; but many, many ways exist for managing state. Think about your last project. How many days were spent trying to decide where you should manage state? The trick is to truly understand the pros and cons of each method.

To make an educated decision about a method, you should understand the lifecycle of a request and the opportunities for state management at each point in the process:

1. A Web browser makes an `HTTP GET` request for a page on your server, `http://myserver/myapp/mypage.aspx`. This client Web browser has *never* visited your site before.
2. IIS and your ASP.NET application respond by returning HTML rendered by `mypage.aspx`. Additionally, `mypage.aspx` returns a cookie with a unique ID to track this Web browser. Remember that a cookie is actually a slightly abstract concept. The cookie is set by returning a Set-Cookie HTTP Header to the client. The client then promises to return the values of the cookie in every subsequent HTTP call in the HTTP header. The *state* in this example is actually an agreement between the client and server to bounce the cookie back and forth on every request in response.
3. The HTML that is returned may contain hidden text boxes such as `<input type="hidden" value="somestate"/>`. These text boxes are similar to cookies because they are passed back to the server if the form on this page is submitted. Cookies are set per domain; hidden form fields are set per page.
4. Upon the next request, the previously set cookies are returned to the server. If this request was the submission of the form as an `HTTP POST`, all fields in the form are returned — hidden or otherwise.
5. The unique identifier that was set earlier as a cookie can now be used as a key into any kind of server-side state mechanism. That state might be as simple as an in-memory hashtable, or as complicated as a SQL database.

One of the repeating themes you might notice is the agreement between the client and the server to pass information back and forth. That information can be in the URL, in HTTP headers, or even in the submitted form as an input field.

On the server side, you have a few options. You will want to weigh the options based on the amount of memory you have available, the amount of data you want to store, and how often you will require access to the data.

Tables 21-1 and 21-2 express each of the server-side and client-side options and list a few pros and cons for each.

TABLE 21-1

SERVER-SIDE OPTION	PROS	CONS
Application State	Fast. Shared among all users.	State is stored once per server in multiple server configurations.
Cache Object (Application Scope)	Like the Application State but includes expiration via dependencies (see Chapter 22 on caching).	State is stored once per server in multiple server configurations.
Session State	Three choices: in process, out of process, DB-backed. Can be configured as cookieless.	Can be abused. You pay a serialization cost when objects leave the process. In process requires Web server affinity. Cookieless configuration makes hijacking easier.
Database	State can be accessed by any server in a Web farm.	Pay a serialization and persistence cost when objects leave the process. Requires a SQL Server license.

On the client side, every available option costs you in bandwidth. Each option involves passing data back and forth from client to server. Every byte of data you store will be paid for twice: once when it is passed to the server and once when it is passed back.

TABLE 21-2

CLIENT-SIDE OPTION	PROS	CONS
Cookie	Simple	Can be rejected by browser. Not appropriate for large amounts of data. Inappropriate for sensitive data. Size cost is paid on *every* HTTP request and response.
Hidden Field	Simple for page-scoped data	Not appropriate for large amounts of data. Inappropriate for sensitive data.
ViewState	Simple for page-scoped data	Encoding of serialized object as binary Base64-encoded data adds approximately 30 percent overhead. Small serialization cost. Has a negative reputation, particularly with DataGrids.
ControlState	Simple for page-scoped control-specific data	Like ViewState, but used for controls that require ViewState even if the developer has turned it off.
QueryString (URL)	Incredibly simple and often convenient if you want your URLs to be modified directly by the end user	Comparatively complex. Can't hold a lot of information. Inappropriate for sensitive data. Easily modified by the end user.

These tables provide you with some of the server-side and client-side options. Chapter 22 covers the improvements to caching in ASP.NET 4.

UNDERSTANDING THE SESSION OBJECT IN ASP.NET

In classic ASP, the `Session` object was held in-process (as was everything) to the IIS process. The user received a cookie with a unique key in the form of a GUID. The Session key was an index into a dictionary where object references could be stored.

In all versions of ASP.NET the `Session` object offers an in-process option, but also includes an out-of-process and a database-backed option. Additionally, the developer has the option to enable a *cookieless* session state where the Session key appears in the URL rather than being sent as a cookie.

Sessions and the Event Model

The `HttpApplication` object raises a series of events during the life of the HTTP protocol request:

- `BeginRequest`: This event fires at the beginning of every request.
- `AuthenticateRequest`: This event is used by the security module and indicates that a request is about to be authenticated. This is where the security module, or you, determines who the user is.
- `AuthorizeRequest`: This event is used by the security module and indicates that a request is about to be authorized. This is where the security module, or you, determines what the user is allowed to do.
- `ResolveRequestCache`: This event is used by the caching module to determine whether this now-authorized request can bypass any additional processing.
- `AcquireRequestState`: This event indicates that all session state associated with this HTTP request is about to be acquired.

Session state is available to you, the developer, after *the* `AcquireRequestState` *event fires. The session state key that is unique to each user is retrieved either from a cookie or from the URL.*

- `PreRequestHandlerExecute`: This is the last event you get before the `HttpHandler` class for this request is called.

Your application code, usually in the form of a `Page`*, executes at this point in the process.*

- `PostRequestHandlerExecute`: This event fires just after the `HttpHandler` is called.
- `ReleaseRequestState`: Indicates that the session state should be stored. Session state is persisted at this point, using whatever session-state module is configured in `web.config`.
- `UpdateRequestCache`: All work is complete, and the resulting output is ready to be added to the cache.
- `EndRequest`: This is the last event called during a request.

You can see from the preceding list that `AcquireRequestState` and `ReleaseRequestState` are two significant events in the life of the `Session` object.

By the time your application code executes, the `Session` object has been populated using the session key that was present in the cookie or, as you see later, from the URL. If you want to handle some processing at the time the session begins, rather than handling it in `AcquireRequestState`, you can define an event handler for the `Start` event of a session state HttpModule.

```
Sub Session_OnStart()
    'this fires after session state has been acquired by the SessionStateModule.
End Sub
```

The `Session` *object includes both* `Start` *and* `End` *events that you can hook event handlers to for your own needs. However, the* `Session_OnEnd` *event is supported only in the in-process session state mode. This event will not be raised if you use out-of-process State Server or SQL Server modes. The session ends, but your handlers will never hear about it.*

Pre- and post-events occur at almost every point within the life of an HTTP request. Session state can be manipulated at any point after `AcquireRequestState`, including in the `Global.asax` within the `Session_OnStart` event.

The `HttpSessionState` object can be used within any event in a subclass of the `Page` object. The pages you create in ASP.NET derive from `System.Web.UI.Page`, and you can access session state as a collection because `System.Web.SessionState.HttpSessionState` implements `ICollection`.

The `Page` has a public property aptly named `Session` that automatically retrieves the `Session` from the current `HttpContext`. Even though it seems as if the `Session` object lives inside the page, it actually lives in the `HttpContext`, and the page's public `Session` property actually retrieves the reference to the session state. This convenience not only makes it more comfortable for the classic ASP programmer, but saves you a little typing as well.

The `Session` object can be referred to within a page in this way:

```
Session["SomeSessionState"] = "Here is some data";
```

or

```
HttpContext.Current.Session["SomeSessionState"] = "Here is some data";
```

The fact that the `Session` object actually lives in the current HTTP context is more than just a piece of trivia. This knowledge enables you to access the `Session` object in contexts other than the page (such as in your own `HttpHandler`).

Configuring Session State Management

All the code within a page refers to the `Session` object using the dictionary-style syntax seen previously, but the `HttpSessionState` object uses a provider pattern to extract possible choices for session state storage. You can choose between the included providers by changing the `sessionState` element in the `web.config` file. ASP.NET ships with the following three storage providers:

- **In-Process Session State Store:** Stores sessions in the ASP.NET in-memory cache.
- **Out-Of-Process Session State Store:** Stores sessions in the ASP.NET State Server service `aspnet_state.exe`.
- **Sql Session State Store:** Stores sessions in Microsoft SQL Server database and is configured with `aspnet_regsql.exe`.

The format of the `web.config` file's `sessionState` element is shown in the following code:

```
<configuration>
   <system.web>
      <sessionState mode="Off|InProc|StateServer|SQLServer|Custom" ../>
   </system.web>
...
```

Begin configuring session state by setting the `mode="InProc"` attribute of the `sessionState` element in the `web.config` file of a new Web site. This is the most common configuration for session state within ASP.NET and is also the fastest, as you see next.

In-Process Session State

When the configuration is set to `InProc`, session data is stored in the `HttpRuntime`'s internal cache in an implementation of `ISessionStateItemCollection` that implements `ICollection`. The session state key is a 120-bit value string that indexes this global dictionary of object references. When session state is in process, objects are stored as live references. This mechanism is incredibly fast because no serialization occurs, nor do objects leave the process space. Certainly, your objects are not garbage-collected if they exist in the `In-Process Session` object because a reference is still being held.

Additionally, because the objects are stored (held) in memory, they use up memory until that session times out. If a user visits your site and hits one page, he might cause you to store a 40MB `XmlDocument` object in an in-process session. If that user never comes back, you are left sitting on that large chunk of memory for the next 20 minutes or so (a configurable value) until the session ends.

InProc Gotchas

Although the InProc session model is the fastest, the default, and the most common, it does have a significant limitation. If the worker process or application domain recycles, all session state data is lost. In addition, the ASP.NET application may restart for a number of reasons, such as the following:

- You have changed the `web.config` or `Global.asax` file or "touched" it by changing its modified date.
- You have modified files in the `\bin` or `\App_Code` directory.
- The `processModel` element has been set in the `web.config` or `machine.config` file indicating when the application should restart. Conditions that could generate a restart might be a memory limit or request-queue limit.
- Antivirus software modifies any of the previously mentioned files. This is particularly common with antivirus software that *inoculates* files.

This said, in-process session state works great for smaller applications that require only a single Web server, or in situations where IP load balancing is returning each user to the server where his original session was created.

If a user already has a session key, but is returned to a different machine than the one on which his session was created, a new session is created on that new machine using the session ID supplied by the user. Of course, that new session is empty and unexpected results may occur. However, if `regenerateExpiredSessionId` is set to `True` in the `web.config` file, a new session ID is created and assigned to the user.

Web Gardening

Web gardening is a technique for multiprocessor systems wherein multiple instances of the ASP.NET worker process are started up and assigned with processor affinity. On a larger Web server with as many as four CPUs, you could have anywhere from one to four worker processes hosting ASP.NET. *Processor affinity* means literally that an ASP.NET worker process has an affinity for a particular CPU. It's "pinned" to that CPU. This technique is usually enabled only in very large Web farms.

Do not forget that in-process session state is just that — in-process. Even if your Web application consists of only a single Web server and all IP traffic is routed to that single server, you have no guarantee that each subsequent request will be served on the same processor. A Web garden must follow many of the same rules that a Web farm follows.

If you are using Web gardening on a multiprocessor system, you must not use in-process session state or you lose sessions. In-process session state is appropriate only where there is a 1:1 ratio of applications to application domains.

Storing Data in the Session Object

In the following simple example, in a `Button_Click` event, the content of the text box is added to the `Session` object with a specific key. The user then clicks to go to another page within the same application, and the data from the `Session` object is retrieved and presented in the browser.

Note the use of the `<asp:HyperLink>` control. Certainly, that markup could have been hard-coded as HTML, but this small distinction will serve us well later. Additionally, the URL is relative to this site, not absolute. Watch for it to help you later in this chapter.

Listing 21-1 illustrates how simple using the `Session` object is. It behaves like any other `IDictionary` collection and allows you to store keys of type `String` associated with any kind of object. The `Retrieve.aspx` file referenced will be added in Listing 21-2.

Available for download on Wrox.com

LISTING 21-1: Setting values in session state

ASP.NET

```
<%@ Page Language="C#" CodeFile="Default.aspx.cs" Inherits="_Default" %>

<html xmlns="http://www.w3.org/1999/xhtml" >
<head runat="server">
    <title>Session State</title>
</head>
<body>
    <form id="form1" runat="server">
    <div>
        <asp:TextBox ID="TextBox1" Runat="server"></asp:TextBox>
        <asp:Button ID="Button1" Runat="server" Text="Store in Session"
        OnClick="Button1_Click" />
        <br />
        <asp:HyperLink ID="HyperLink1" Runat="server"
         NavigateUrl="Retrieve.aspx">Next Page</asp:HyperLink>
    </div>
    </form>
</body>
</html>
```

VB

```
Partial Class _Default
   Inherits System.Web.UI.Page

    Protected Sub Button1_Click(ByVal sender As Object, _
            ByVal e As System.EventArgs)
        Session("mykey") = TextBox1.Text
    End Sub

End Class
```

C#

```
public partial class _Default : System.Web.UI.Page
{
    protected void Button1_Click(object sender, EventArgs e)
    {
        Session["mykey"] = TextBox1.Text;
    }
}
```

The page from Listing 21-1 renders in the browser as shown in Figure 21-2. The `Session` object is accessed as any dictionary indexed by a string key.

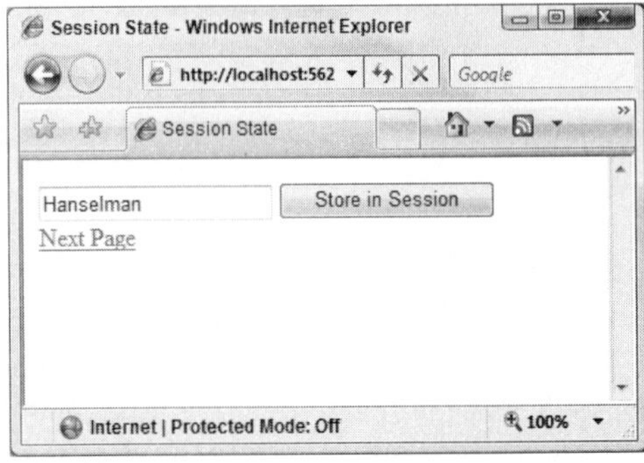

FIGURE 21-2

More details about the page and the `Session` object can be displayed to the developer if page tracing is enabled. You add this element to your application's `web.config` file inside the `<system.web>` element, as follows:

```
<trace enabled="true" pageOutput="true"/>
```

Now tracing is enabled, and the tracing output is sent directly to the page. More details on tracing and debugging are given in Chapter 23. For now, make this change and refresh your browser.

In Figure 21-3, the screenshot is split to show both the top and roughly the middle of the large amount of trace information that is returned when trace is enabled. Session state is very much baked into the fabric of ASP.NET. You can see in the Request Details section of the trace that not only was this page the result of an `HTTP POST` but the session ID was as well — elevated to the status of first-class citizen. However, the ASP.NET session ID lives as a cookie by default, as you can see in the `Cookies` collection at the bottom of the figure.

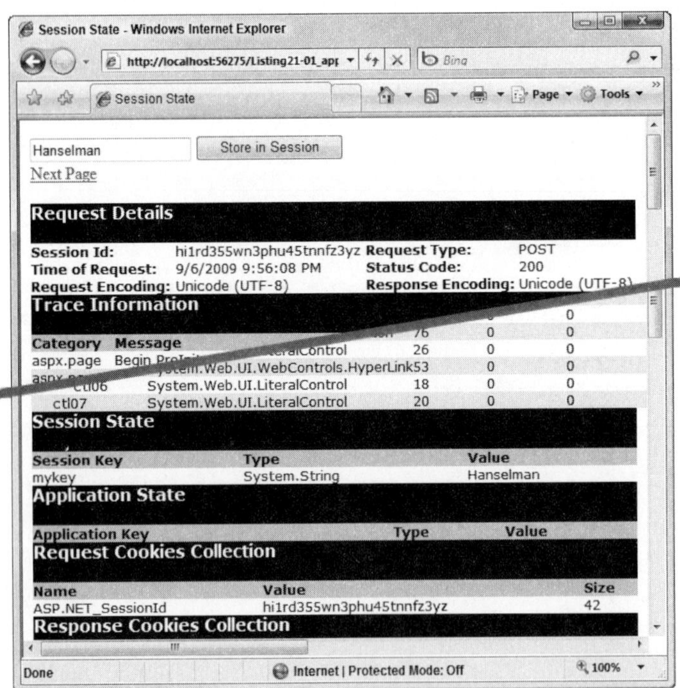

FIGURE 21-3

The default name for that cookie is `ASP.NET_SessionId`, but its name can be configured via the `cookieName` attribute of the `<sessionState>` element in the `web.config` file. Some large enterprises allow only certain named cookies past their proxies, so you might need to change this value when working on an extranet or a network with a gateway server; but this would be a very rare occurrence. The `cookieName` is changed to use the name "Foo" in the following example:

```
<sessionState cookieName="Foo" mode="InProc"></sessionState>
```

The trace output shown in Figure 21-3 includes a section listing the contents of the `Session State` collection. In the figure, you can see that the name `mykey` and the value `Hanselman` are currently stored. Additionally, you see the CLR data type of the stored value; in this case, it's `System.String`.

The Value column of the trace output comes from a call to the contained object's `ToString()` method. If you store your own objects in the session, you can override `ToString()` to provide a text-friendly representation of your object that might make the trace results more useful.

Now add the next page, `retrieve.aspx`, which pulls this value out of the session. Leave the `retrieve.aspx` page as the IDE creates it and add a `Page_Load` event handler, as shown in Listing 21-2.

LISTING 21-2: Retrieving values from the session

Available for download on Wrox.com

VB

```
Partial Class Retrieve
   Inherits System.Web.UI.Page

   Protected Sub Page_Load(ByVal sender As Object, ByVal e As System.EventArgs) _
       Handles Me.Load

        Dim myValue As String = CType(Session("mykey"), String)
        Response.Write(myValue)
    End Sub
End Class
```

C#

```
public partial class Retrieve : System.Web.UI.Page
{
    protected void Page_Load(object sender, EventArgs e)
    {
        string myValue = (string)Session["mykey"];
        Response.Write(myValue);
    }
}
```

Because the session contains object references, the resulting object is converted to a string by way of a cast in C# or the `CType` or `CStr` function in VB.

Making Sessions Transparent

It is unfortunate that a cast is usually required to retrieve data from the `Session` object. Combined with the string key used as an index, it makes for a fairly weak contract between the page and the `Session` object. You can create a session helper that is specific to your application to hide these details, or you can add properties to a base `Page` class that presents these objects to your pages in a friendlier way. Because the generic `Session` object is available as a property on `System.Web.UI.Page`, add a new class derived from `Page` that exposes a new property named `MyKey`.

Start by right-clicking your project and selecting Add New Item from the context menu to create a new class. Name it `SmartSessionPage` and click OK. The IDE may tell you that it would like to put this new class in the App_Code folder to make it available to the whole application. Click Yes.

Your new base page is very simple. Via derivation, it does everything that `System.Web.UI.Page` does, plus it has a new property, as shown in Listing 21-3.

LISTING 21-3: A more session-aware base page

Available for download on Wrox.com

VB

```
Imports Microsoft.VisualBasic
Imports System
Imports System.Web
```

continues

LISTING 21-3 *(continued)*

```
Public Class SmartSessionPage
    Inherits System.Web.UI.Page

    Private Const MYSESSIONKEY As String = "mykey"
    Public Property MyKey() As String
        Get
            Return CType(Session(MYSESSIONKEY), String)
        End Get
        Set(ByVal value As String)
            Session(MYSESSIONKEY) = value
        End Set
    End Property
End Class
```

C#

```
using System;
using System.Web;

public class SmartSessionPage : System.Web.UI.Page
{
    private const string MYKEY = "mykey";
    public string MyKey
    {
        get
        {
            return (string)Session[MYKEY];
        }
        set
        {
            Session[MYKEY] = value;
        }
    }
}
```

Now, return to your code from Listing 21-1 and derive your pages from this new base class. To do this, change the base class in the code-beside files to inherit from `SmartSessionPage`. Listing 21-4 shows how the class in the code-behind file derives from the `SmartSessionPage`, which in turn derives from `System.Web.UI.Page`. Listing 21-4 outlines the changes to make to Listing 21-1.

LISTING 21-4: Deriving from the new base page

Available for download on Wrox.com

Default.aspx.vb code

VB

```
Partial Class _Default
    Inherits SmartSessionPage

   Protected Sub Button1_Click(ByVal sender As Object, ByVal e As System.EventArgs)

      ' Session("mykey") = TextBox1.Text
        MyKey = TextBox1.Text
   End Sub
End Class
```

C#

Default.aspx.cs Code

```
public partial class _Default : SmartSessionPage
{
    protected void Button1_Click(object sender, EventArgs e)
```

```
        {
            //Session["mykey"] = TextBox1.Text;
            MyKey = TextBox1.Text;
        }
    }
```

In this code, you change the access to the `Session` object so it uses the new public property. After the changes in Listing 21-3, all derived pages have a public property called `MyKey`. This property can be used without any concern about casting or session key indexes. Additional specific properties can be added as other objects are included in the session.

Here is an interesting language note: In Listing 21-3 the name of the private string value collides with the public property in VB because they differ only in case. In C#, a private variable named `MYKEY` and a public property named `MyKey` are both acceptable. Be aware of things like this when creating APIs that will be used with multiple languages. Aim for CLS compliance.

Advanced Techniques for Optimizing Session Performance

By default, all pages have write access to the `Session`. Because it's possible that more than one page from the same browser client might be requested at the same time (using frames, more than one browser window on the same machine, and so on), a page holds a reader/writer lock on the same `Session` for the duration of the page request. If a page has a writer lock on the same `Session`, all other pages requested in the same `Session` must wait until the first request finishes. To be clear, the `Session` is locked only for that session ID. These locks do not affect other users with different `Sessions`.

In order to get the best performance out of your pages that use `Session`, ASP.NET allows you to declare exactly what your page requires of the `Session` object via the `EnableSessionState @Page` attribute. The options are `True`, `False`, or `ReadOnly`:

- `EnableSessionState="True"`: The page requires read and write access to the `Session`. The `Session` with that session ID will be locked during each request.
- `EnableSessionState="False"`: The page does not require access to the `Session`. If the code uses the `Session` object anyway, an `HttpException` is thrown, stopping page execution.
- `EnableSessionState="ReadOnly"`: The page requires read-only access to the `Session`. A reader lock is held on the `Session` for each request, but concurrent reads from other pages can occur. The order in which locks are requested is essential. As soon as a writer lock is requested, even before a thread is granted access, all subsequent reader lock requests are blocked, regardless of whether a reader lock is currently held or not. Although ASP.NET can obviously handle multiple requests, only one request at a time gets write access to a session.

By modifying the `@Page` direction in `Default.aspx` and `Retrieve.aspx` to reflect each page's actual need, you affect performance when the site is under load. Add the `EnableSessionState` attribute to the pages, as shown in the following code:

VB

Default.aspx

```
<%@ Page Language="VB" EnableSessionState="True" AutoEventWireup="false"
    CodeFile="Default.aspx.vb" Inherits="_Default" %>
```

Retrieve.aspx

```
<%@ Page Language="VB" EnableSessionState="ReadOnly" AutoEventWireup="false"
    CodeFile="Retrieve.aspx.vb" Inherits="Retrieve" %>
```

C#

Default.aspx

```
<%@ Page Language="C#" EnableSessionState="True"
    CodeFile="Default.aspx.cs" Inherits="_Default"%>
```

Retrieve.aspx

```
<%@ Page Language="C#" EnableSessionState="ReadOnly"
    CodeFile="Retrieve.aspx.cs" Inherits="Retrieve" %>
```

Under the covers, ASP.NET is using marker interfaces from the `System.Web.SessionState` namespace to keep track of each page's needs. When the partial class for `Default.aspx` is generated, it implements the `IRequiresSessionState` interface, whereas `Retrieve.aspx` implements `IReadOnlySessionState`. All `HttpRequests` are handled by objects that implement `IHttpHandler`. Pages are handled by a `PageHandlerFactory`. You can find more on `HttpHandlers` in Chapter 26. Internally, the `SessionStateModule` is executing code similar to the pseudocode that follows:

```
If TypeOf HttpContext.Current.Handler Is IReadOnlySessionState Then
    Return SessionStateStore.GetItem(itemKey)
Else'If TypeOf HttpContext.Current.Handler Is IRequiresSessionState
    Return SessionStateStore.GetItemExclusive(itemKey)
End If
```

As the programmer, you know things about the intent of your pages at compile time that ASP.NET cannot figure out at runtime. By including the `EnableSessionState` attribute in your pages, you allow ASP.NET to operate more efficiently. Remember, ASP.NET always makes the most conservative decision unless you give it more information to act upon.

Performance Tip: *If you are coding a page that doesn't require anything of the session, by all means, set* `EnableSessionState="False"`. *This causes ASP.NET to schedule that page ahead of pages that require* `Session` *and helps with the overall scalability of your app. Additionally, if your application doesn't use* `Session` *at all, set* `Mode="Off"` *in your* `web.config` *file to reduce overhead for the entire application.*

Out-of-Process Session State

Out-of-process session state is held in a process called `aspnet_state.exe` that runs as a Windows Service. You can start the ASP.NET state service by using the Services MMC snap-in or by running the following `net` command from an administrative command line:

```
net start aspnet_state
```

By default, the State Service listens on TCP port 42424, but this port can be changed at the registry key for the service, as shown in the following code. The State Service is not started by default.

```
HKEY_LOCAL_MACHINE\SYSTEM\CurrentControlSet\Services\
aspnet_state\Parameters\Port
```

Change the `web.config` file's settings from `InProc` to `StateServer`, as shown in the following code. Additionally, you must include the `stateConnectionString` attribute with the IP address and port on which the session state service is running. In a Web farm (a group of more than one Web server), you could run the state service on any single server or on a separate machine entirely. In this example, the State Server is running on the local machine, so the IP address is the localhost IP 127.0.0.1. If you run the State Server on another machine, make sure the appropriate port is open — in this case, TCP port 42424.

```
<configuration>
   <system.web>
```

```
        <sessionState mode="StateServer"
            stateConnectionString="tcpip=127.0.0.1:42424"/>
    </system.web>
</configuration>
```

The State Service used is always the most recent one installed with ASP.NET. That means that if you are running ASP.NET 2.0/3.5/or 4 and 1.1 on the same machine, all the states stored in `Session` objects for any and all versions of ASP.NET are kept together in a single instance of the ASP.NET State Service.

Because your application's code runs in the ASP.NET Worker Process (`aspnet_wp.exe`, or `w3wp.exe`) and the State Service runs in the separate `aspnet_state.exe` process, objects stored in the session cannot be stored as references. Your objects must physically leave the worker process via binary serialization.

For a world-class, highly available, and scalable Web site, consider using a session model other than InProc. Even if you can guarantee via your load-balancing appliance that your sessions will be sticky, *you still have application-recycling issues to contend with. The out-of-process State Service's data is persisted across application pool recycles but not computer reboots. However, if your state is stored on a different machine entirely, it will survive Web server recycles and reboots.*

Only classes that have been marked with the `[Serializable]` attribute may be serialized. In the context of the `Session` object, think of the `[Serializable]` attribute as a permission slip for instances of your class to leave the worker process.

Update the `SmartSessionPage` file in your `\App_Code` directory to include a new class called `Person`, as shown in Listing 21-5. Be sure to mark it as `Serializable` or you will see the error shown in Figure 21-4.

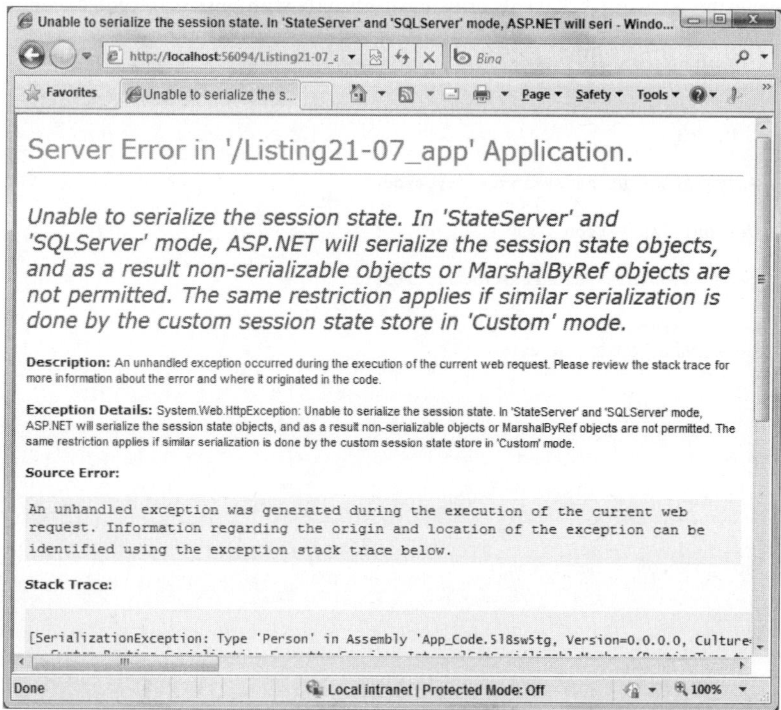

FIGURE 21-4

As long as you have marked your objects as `[Serializable]`, they will be allowed out of the ASP.NET process. Notice that the objects in Listing 21-5 are marked `[Serializable]`.

LISTING 21-5: A serializable object that can be used in the out-of-process session

Available for download on Wrox.com

VB

```
<Serializable()> _
Public Class Person
    Public firstName As String
    Public lastName As String

    Public Overrides Function ToString() As String
        Return String.Format("Person Object: {0} {1}", firstName, lastName)
    End Function
End Class
```

C#

```
[Serializable]
public class Person
{
   public string firstName;
   public string lastName;

   public override string ToString()
   {
      return String.Format("Person Object: {0} {1}", firstName, lastName);
   }
}
```

Because you put an instance of the `Person` class from Listing 21-5 into the `Session` object that is currently configured as `StateServer`, you should add a strongly typed property to the base `Page` class from Listing 21-3. In Listing 21-6 you see the strongly typed property added. Note the cast on the property `Get`, and the strongly typed return value indicating that this property deals only with objects of type `Person`.

LISTING 21-6: Adding a strongly typed property to SmartSessionPage

Available for download on Wrox.com

VB

```
Public Class SmartSessionPage
    Inherits System.Web.UI.Page

    Private Const MYSESSIONPERSONKEY As String = "myperson"

    Public Property MyPerson() As Person
        Get
            Return CType(Session(MYSESSIONPERSONKEY), Person)
        End Get
        Set(ByVal value As Person)
            Session(MYSESSIONPERSONKEY) = value
        End Set
    End Property

End Class
```

C#

```
public class SmartSessionPage : System.Web.UI.Page
{

    private const string MYPERSON = "myperson";

    public Person MyPerson
    {
        Get
        {
            return (Person)Session[MYPERSON];
        }
```

```
            Set
            {
            Session[MYPERSON] = value;
            }
        }
    }
```

Now, add code to create a new `Person`, populate its fields from the text box, and put the instance into the now out-of-process session State Service. Then, retrieve the `Person` and write its values out to the browser using the overloaded `ToString()` method from Listing 21-5.

Certain classes in the Framework Class Library are not marked as serializable. If you use objects of this type within your own objects, these objects are not *serializable at all. For example, if you include a DataRow field in a class and add your object to the State Service, you receive a message telling you it "... is not marked as serializable" because the DataRow includes objects that are not serializable.*

In Listing 21-7, the value of the `TextBox` is split into a string array and the first two strings are put into a `Person` instance. For example, if you entered `"Scott Hanselman"` as a value, `"Scott"` is put into `Person.firstName` and `"Hanselman"` is put into `Person.lastName`. The values you enter should appear when they are retrieved later in `Retrieve.aspx` and written out to the browser with the overloaded `ToString()` method.

LISTING 21-7: Setting and retrieving objects from the session using State Service and a base page

Available for download on Wrox.com

Default.aspx.vb

VB

```
Partial Class _Default
    Inherits SmartSessionPage

   Protected Sub Button1_Click(ByVal sender As Object, ByVal e As System.EventArgs)
        Dim names As String()
        names = TextBox1.Text.Split(" "c)' " "c creates a char
        Dim p As New Person()
        p.firstName = names(0)
        p.lastName = names(1)
        Session("myperson") = p
   End Sub
End Class
```

Retrieve.aspx.vb

```
Partial Class Retrieve
        Inherits SmartSessionPage

    Protected Sub Page_Load(ByVal sender As Object, ByVal e As System.EventArgs) _
            Handles Me.Load
        Dim p As Person = MyPerson
        Response.Write(p)' ToString will be called!
    End Sub
End Class
```

C#

Default.aspx.cs

```
public partial class _Default : SmartSessionPage
{
    protected void Button1_Click(object sender, EventArgs e)
    {
```

continues

LISTING 21-7 *(continued)*

```
            string[] names = TextBox1.Text.Split(' ');
            Person p = new Person();
            p.firstName = names[0];
            p.lastName = names[1];
            Session["myperson"] = p;
        }
    }
```

Retrieve.aspx.cs

```
public partial class Retrieve : SmartSessionPage
{
    protected void Page_Load(object sender, EventArgs e)
    {
        Person p = MyPerson;
        Response.Write(p); //ToString will be called!
    }
}
```

Now, launch the browser, enter your name (or `"Scott Hanselman"` if you like), click the button to store it in the `Session`, and then visit `Retrieve.aspx` via the hyperlink. You see the result of the `ToString()` method via `Response.Write`, as shown in Figure 21-5.

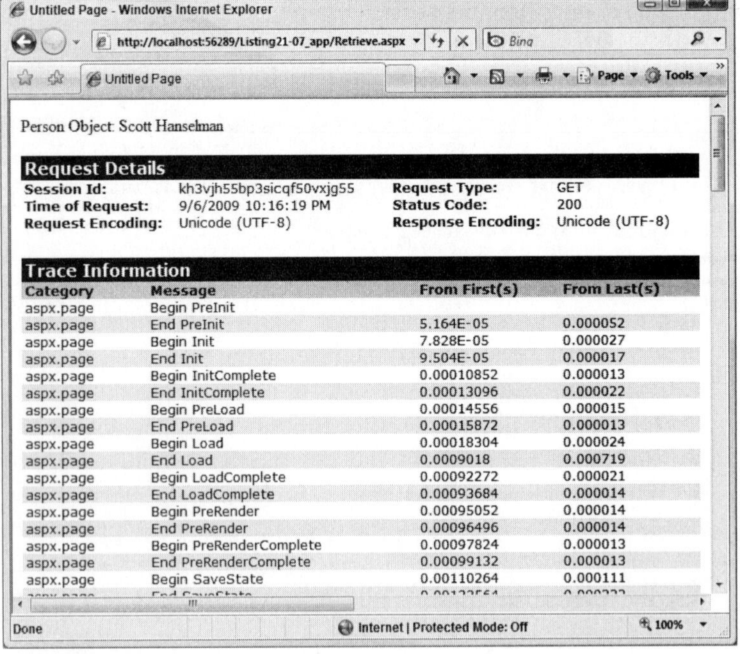

FIGURE 21-5

The completed code and techniques shown in Listing 21-7 illustrate a number of best practices for session management:

- Mark your objects as `Serializable` if you might ever use non-In-Proc session state.
- Even better, do all your development with a local session state server. This forces you to discover non-serializable objects early, gives you a sense of the performance and memory usages of `aspnet_state.exe`, and allows you to choose from any of the session options at deployment time.

- Use a base Page class or helper object with strongly typed properties to simplify your code. It enables you to hide the casts made to session keys otherwise referenced throughout your code.

These best practices apply to all state storage methods, including SQL session state (covered shortly). When using out-of-process session state, whether as described previously or using the SQL-backed session state, the objects that are stored within this state are serialized and deserialized back and forth in order for your applications to work with this type of state. Some of the objects that you are moving to be serialized into memory can be quite large.

ASP.NET 4 includes a new capability to compress the objects that are stored in out-of-process state. This is illustrated in the following snippet of code:

```
<sessionState
  mode="SqlServer"
  sqlConnectionString="data source=dbserver;Initial Catalog=aspnetstate"
  allowCustomSqlDatabase="true"
  compressionEnabled="true"
/>
```

When compression is enabled through the use of the compressionEnabled attribute, the System.IO.Compression.GZipStream class is used. By default, the compressionEnabled attribute is set to false. By doing this compression, you will notice a significant difference in the amount of memory used to store your state.

SQL-Backed Session State

ASP.NET sessions can also be stored in a SQL Server database. InProc offers speed, State Server offers a resilience/speed balance, and storing sessions in SQL Server offers resilience that can serve sessions to a large Web farm that persists across IIS restarts, if necessary.

SQL-backed session state is configured with aspnet_regsql.exe. This tool adds and removes support for a number of ASP.NET features such as cache dependency (see Chapter 22) and personalization/membership (see Chapters 14 and 15), as well as session support. When you run aspnet_regsql.exe from the command line without any options, surprisingly, it pops up a GUI as shown in Figure 21-6. This utility is located in the .NET Framework's installed directory, usually C:\Windows\Microsoft.NET\Framework\v4.0.

FIGURE 21-6

The text of the dialog shown in Figure 21-6 contains instructions to run aspnet_regsql from the command line with a "-?" switch. You have a huge number of options, so you will want to pipe it through in a form like aspnet_regsql -? | more. Here are the session state–specific options:

```
                  -- SESSION STATE OPTIONS --

-ssadd                   Add support for SQLServer mode session state.

-ssremove                Remove support for SQLServer mode session state.

-sstype t|p|c            Type of session state support:

                         t: temporary. Session state data is stored in the
                         "tempdb" database. Stored procedures for managing
```

```
                          session are installed in the "ASPState" database.
                          Data is not persisted if you restart SQL. (Default)

                          p: persisted. Both session state data and the stored
                          procedures are stored in the "ASPState" database.

                          c: custom. Both session state data and the stored
                          procedures are stored in a custom database. The
                          database name must be specified.

-d <database>             The name of the custom database to use if -sstype is
                          "c".
```

Three options exist for session state support: t, p, and c. The most significant difference is that the -sstype t option does not persist session state data across SQL Server restarts, whereas the -sstype p option does. Alternatively, you can specify a custom database with the -c option and give the database name with -d database.

The following command-line example configures your system for SQL session support with the SQL Server on localhost with an sa password of *wrox* and a persistent store in the ASPState database. (Certainly, you know not to deploy your system using sa and a weak password, but this simplifies the example. Ideally, you would use Windows Integration Authentication and give the Worker Process identity access to the ASPState database.) If you are using SQL Express, replace "localhost" with ".\SQLEXPRESS". If you are not using Windows Authentication, you may need to explicitly enable the sa account from the Management Studio, run this tool, and then disable the sa account for security reasons.

```
C:\ >aspnet_regsql -S localhost -U sa -P wrox -ssadd -sstype p
Start adding session state.
...........
Finished.
```

Next, open up Enterprise Manager and look at the newly created database. Two tables are created — ASPStateTempApplications and ASPStateTempSessions — as well as a series of stored procedures to support moving the session back and forth from SQL to memory.

If your SQL Server has its security locked down tight, you might get an Error 15501 after executing aspnet_regsql.exe that says, "An error occurred during the execution of the SQL file 'InstallSqlState.sql'." The SQL error number is 15501 and the SqlException message is

```
This module has been marked OFF. Turn on 'Agent XPs' in order to be able to access
the module. If the job does not exist, an error from msdb.dbo.sp_delete_job
is expected.
```

This message is rather obscure, but aspnet_regsql.exe is trying to tell you that the extended stored procedures it needs to enable session state are not enabled for security reasons. You will need to allow them explicitly. To do so, execute the following commands within the SQL Server 2008 Query Analyzer or the SQL Server 2008 Express Manager:

```
USE master
EXECUTE sp_configure 'show advanced options', 1
RECONFIGURE WITH OVERRIDE
GO
EXECUTE sp_configure 'Agent XPs', 1
RECONFIGURE WITH OVERRIDE
GO
EXECUTE sp_configure 'show advanced options', 0
RECONFIGURE WITH OVERRIDE
GO
```

Now, change the web.config <sessionState> element to use SQL Server, as well as the new connection string:

```
<sessionState mode="SQLServer" sqlConnectionString="data source=127.0.0.1;user
id=sa;password=Wrox"/>
```

The session code shown in Listing 21-7 continues to work as before. However, if you open up the ASPStateTempSessions table, you see the serialized objects. Notice in Figure 21-7 that the session ID from the trace appears as a primary key in a row in the ASPStateTempSessions table.

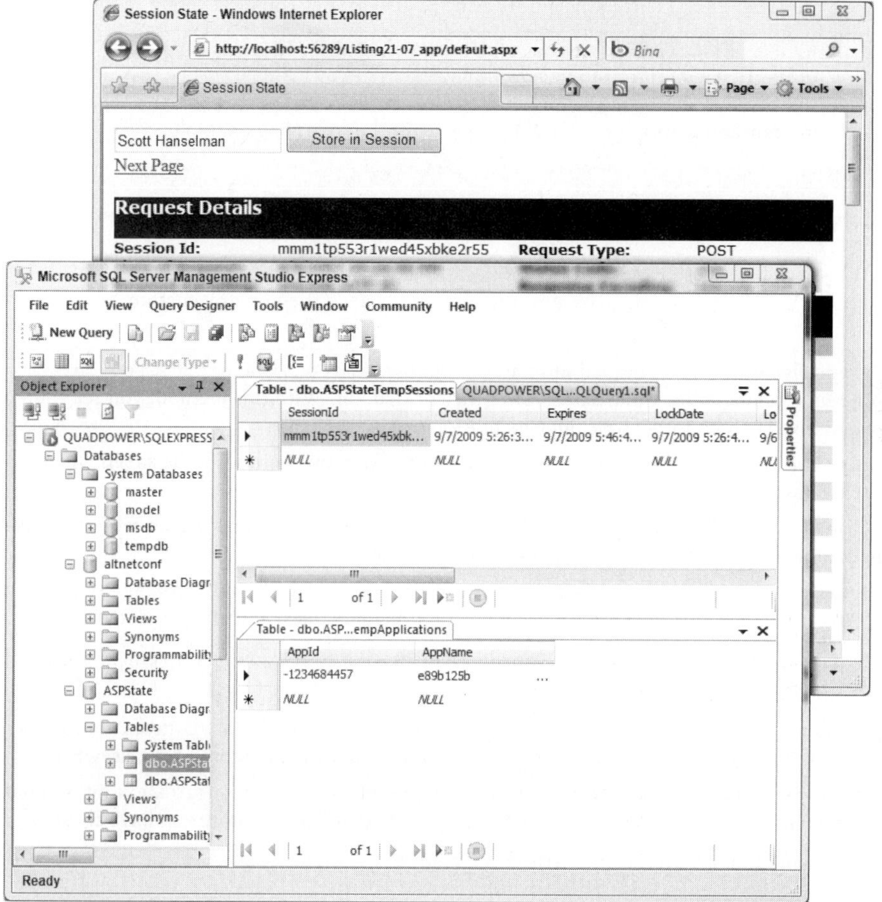

FIGURE 21-7

Figure 21-7 shows the SessionId as seen in the Request Details of ASP.NET tracing. That SessionId appears in the SessionId column of the ASPStateTempSessions table in the ASPState database just created. Notice also the ASPStateTempApplications table that keeps track of each IIS application that may be using the same database to manage sessions.

If you want to use your own database to store session state, you specify the database name with the -d <database> switch of aspnet_regsql.exe and include the allowCustomSqlDatabase="true" attribute and the name of the database in the connection string:

```
<sessionState allowCustomSqlDatabase="true" mode="SQLServer"
sqlConnectionString="data source=127.0.0.1; database=MyCustomASPStateDatabase;"/>
```

The user ID and password can be included in the connection string; or Windows Integrated Security can be used if the ASP.NET Worker Process's identity is configured with access in SQL Server.

Extending Session State with Other Providers

ASP.NET session state is built on a new, extensible, provider-based storage model. You can implement custom providers that store session data in other storage mechanisms simply by deriving from `SessionStateStoreProviderBase`. This extensibility feature also allows you to generate session IDs via your own algorithms by implementing `ISessionIDManager`.

You start by creating a class that inherits from `SessionStateStoreProviderBase`. The session module will call methods on any session provider as long as it derives from `SessionStateStoreProviderBase`. Register your custom provider in your application's `web.config` file, as in the following example:

```
<sessionState mode ="Custom" customProvider ="WroxProvider">
    <providers >
        <add name ="WroxProvider" type ="Wrox.WroxStore, WroxSessionSupplier"/>
    </providers>
</sessionState>
```

ASP.NET initializes the `SessionStateModule`, and these methods are called on any custom implementation:

- `Initialize`: This method is inherited ultimately from `System.Configuration.Provider.ProviderBase` and is called immediately after the constructor. With this method, you set your provider name and call up to the base implementation of `Initialize`.
- `SetItemExpireCallback`: With this method, you can register any methods to be called when a session item expires.
- `InitializeRequest`: This method is called by the `SessionStateModule` for each request. This is an early opportunity to get ready for any requests for data that are coming.
- `CreateNewStoreData`: With this method, you create a new instance of `SessionStateStoreData`, the data structure that holds session items, the session timeout values, and any static items.

When a session item is requested, ASP.NET calls your implementation to retrieve it. Implement the following methods to retrieve items:

- `GetItemExclusive`: This method enables you to get `SessionStateStoreData` from your chosen store. You may have created an Oracle provider, stored data in XML, or stored data elsewhere.
- `GetItem`: This is your opportunity to retrieve it as you did in `GetItemExclusive`, except without exclusive locking. You may or may not care, depending on what backing store you have chosen.

When it's time to store an item, the following method is called:

- `SetAndReleaseItemExculsive`: Here you should save the `SessionStateStoreData` object to your custom store.

A number of third-party session state providers are available — both open source and for sale.

ScaleOut Software released the first third-party ASP.NET State Provider in the form of their StateServer product. It fills a niche between the ASP.NET included singleton StateServer and the SQL Server Database State Provider. ScaleOut Software's StateServer is an out-of-process service that runs on each machine in the Web farm and ensures that session state is stored in a transparent and distributed manner among machines in the farm. You can learn more about StateServer and its ASP.NET Session Provider at `www.scaleoutsoftware.com`.

The derivation-based provider module for things such as session state will no doubt continue to create a rich ecosystem of enthusiasts who will help push the functionality to new places Microsoft did not expect.

Cookieless Session State

In the previous example, the ASP.NET session state ID was stored in a cookie. Some devices do not support cookies, or a user may have turned off cookie support in his browser. Cookies are convenient because the values are passed back and forth with every request and response. That means every `HttpRequest` contains cookie values, and every `HttpResponse` contains cookie values. What is the only other thing that is passed back and forth with every `Request` and `Response`? The answer is the URL.

If you include the `cookieless="UseUri"` attribute in the `web.config` file, ASP.NET does not send the ASP.NET session ID back as a cookie. Instead, it modifies every URL to include the session ID just before the requested page:

```
<sessionState mode="SQLServer" cookieless="UseUri" sqlConnectionString="data
 source=127.0.0.1;user id=sa;password=Wrox"></sessionState>
```

Notice that the session ID appears in the URL as if it were a directory of its own situated between the actual Web site virtual directory and the page. With this change, server-side user controls such as the `HyperLink` control, used in Listing 21-1, have their properties automatically modified. The link in Listing 21-1 could have been hard-coded as HTML directly in the Designer, but then ASP.NET could not modify the target URL shown in Figure 21-8.

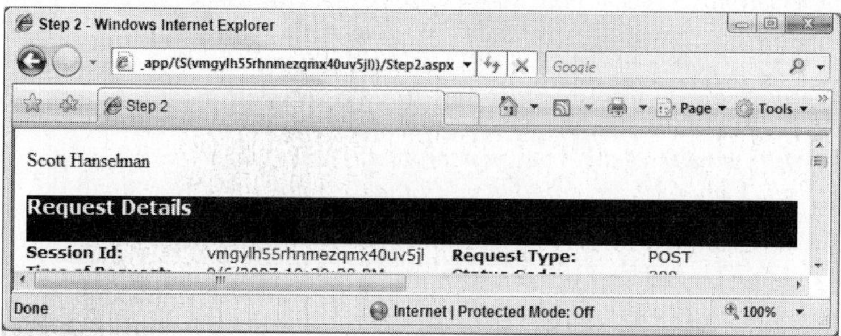

FIGURE 21-8

The session ID is a string that contains only the ASCII characters allowed in a URL. That makes sense when you realize that moving from a cookie-based session state system to a cookieless system requires putting that session state value in the URL.

Notice in Figure 21-8 that the request URL contains a session ID within parentheses. One disadvantage to cookieless sessions is how easily they can be tampered with. Certainly, cookies can be tampered with using HTTP sniffers, but URLs can be edited by anyone. The only way session state is maintained is if *every* URL includes the session ID in this way.

Additionally, all URLs *must* be relative. Remember that the session ID appears as if it were a directory. The session is lost if an absolute URL such as `/myapp/retrieve.aspx` is invoked. If you are generating URLs on the server side, use `HttpResponse.ApplyAppPathModifier()`. It changes a URL when the session ID is embedded, as shown here:

```
Response.Write(Response.ApplyAppPathModifier("foo/bar.aspx"));
```

The previous line generates a URL similar to the following:

```
/myapp/ (S(avkbnbml4n1n5mi5dmfqnu45))/foo/bar.aspx
```

Notice that not only was session information added to the URL, but it was also converted from a relative URL to an absolute URL, including the application's virtual directory. This method can be useful when you need to use `Response.Redirect` or build a URL manually to redirect from an HTTP page to an HTTPS page while still maintaining cookieless session state.

Choosing the Correct Way to Maintain State

Now that you are familiar with the variety of options available for maintaining state in ASP.NET, here's some real-world advice from production systems. The in-process (InProc) session provider is the fastest method, of course, because everything held in memory is a live object reference. This provider is held in the `HttpApplication`'s cache and, as such, it is susceptible to application recycles. If you use Windows 2000 Server or Windows XP, the `aspnet_wp.exe` process manages the ASP.NET HTTP pipeline. If you are running Windows Server 2003, Windows Server 2008, or Windows 7, `w3wp.exe` is the default process that hosts the runtime.

You must find a balance between the robustness of the out-of-process state service and the speed of the in-process provider. In the authors' experience, the out-of-process state service is usually about 15 percent slower than the in-process provider because of the serialization overhead and the marshaling that needs to occur. SQL session state is about 25 percent slower than InProc. Of course, your mileage will likely vary. Do not let these numbers concern you too much. Be sure to do scalability testing on your applications before you panic and make inappropriate decisions.

It is worth saying again: We recommend that all developers use out-of-process session state during development, even if this is not the way your application will be deployed. Forcing yourself to use the out-of-process provider enables you to catch any potential problems with custom objects that do not carry the `Serializable` *attribute. If you design your entire site using the in-process provider and then discover, late in the project, that requirements force you to switch to the SQL or out-of-process providers, you have no guarantee that your site will work as you wrote it. Developing with the out-of-process provider gives you the best of both worlds and does not affect your final deployment method. Think of it as an insurance policy that costs you nothing upfront.*

THE APPLICATION OBJECT

The `Application` object is the equivalent of a bag of global variables for your ASP.NET application. Global variables have been considered harmful for many years in other programming environments, and ASP.NET is no different. You should give some thought to what you want to put in the `Application` object and why. Often, the more flexible `Cache` object that helps you control an object's lifetime is the more useful. Caching is discussed in depth in Chapter 22.

The `Application` object is not global to the machine; it is global to the `HttpApplication`. If you are running in the context of a Web farm, each ASP.NET application on each Web server has its own `Application` object. Because ASP.NET applications are multithreaded and are receiving requests that are being handled by your code on multiple threads, access to the `Application` object should be managed using the `Application.Lock` and `Application.Unlock` methods. If your code does not call Unlock directly (which it should, shame on you) the lock is removed implicitly at the end of the `HttpRequest` that called Lock originally.

This small example shows you how to lock the `Application` object just before inserting an object. Other threads that might be attempting to write to the `Application` will wait until it is unlocked. This example assumes there is an integer already stored in `Application` under the key `GlobalCount`.

VB

```
Application.Lock()
Application("GlobalCount") = CType(Application("GlobalCount"), Integer) + 1
Application.UnLock()
```

C#

```
Application.Lock();
Application["GlobalCount"] = (int)Application["GlobalCount"] + 1;
Application.UnLock();
```

Object references can be stored in the `Application`, as in the `Session`, but they must be cast back to their known types when retrieved (as shown in the preceding sample code).

QUERYSTRINGS

The URL, or QueryString, is the ideal place for navigation-specific — not user-specific — data. The QueryString is the most hackable element on a Web site, and that fact can work for you or against you. For example, if your navigation scheme uses your own page IDs at the end of a query string (such as `/localhost/mypage.aspx?id=54`) be prepared for a user to play with that URL in his browser, and try every value for `id` under the sun. Do not blindly cast `id` to an `int`, and if you do, have a plan if it fails. A good idea is to return `Response.StatusCode=404` when someone changes a URL to an unreasonable value. Another fine idea that Amazon.com implemented was the *Smart 404*. Perhaps you have seen these: They say "Sorry you didn't find what you're looking for. Did you mean ________?"

Remember, your URLs are the first thing your users may see, even before they see your HTML. *Hackable* URLs — hackable even by my mom — make your site more accessible. Which of these URLs is friendlier and more hackable (for the *right* reason)?

```
http://reviews.cnet.com/Philips_42PF9996/4505-6482_7-31081946.html?tag=cnetfd.sd
```

or

```
http://www.hanselman.com/blog/CategoryView.aspx?category=Movies
```

COOKIES

Do you remember the great cookie scare of 1997? Most users were not quite sure just what a cookie was, but they were all convinced that cookies were evil and were storing their personal information. Back then, it *was* likely that personal information was stored in the cookie! Never, ever store sensitive information, such as a user ID or password, in a cookie. Cookies should be used to store only non-sensitive information, or information that can be retrieved from an authoritative source. Cookies should not be trusted, and their contents should be able to be validated. For example, if a Forms Authentication cookie has been tampered with, the user is logged out and an exception is thrown. If an invalid session ID cookie is passed in for an expired session, a new cookie can be assigned.

When you store information in cookies, remember that it is quite different from storing data in the `Session` object:

- Cookies are passed back and forth on *every* request. That means you are paying for the size of your cookie during *every* `HTTP GET` and `HTTP POST`. If you have ten 1-pixel spacer GIFs on your page used for table layouts, the user's browser is sending the same cookie *eleven* times: once for the page itself, and once for each spacer GIF, even if the GIF is already cached.
- Cookies can be stolen, sniffed, and faked. If your code counts on a cookie's value, have a plan in your code for the inevitability that the cookie will be corrupted or tampered with.
- What is the expected behavior of your application if a cookie does not show? What if it is 4096 bytes? Be prepared. You should design your application around the "principle of least surprise." Your application should attempt to heal itself if cookies are found missing or if they are larger than expected.
- Think twice before Base64 encoding anything large and placing it in a cookie. If your design depends on this kind of technique, rethink using either the session or another backing-store.

POSTBACKS AND CROSS-PAGE POSTBACKS

In classic ASP, in order to detect logical events such as a button being clicked, developers had to inspect the `Form` collection of the `Request` object. Yes, a button was clicked in the user's browser, but no object model was built on top of stateless HTTP and HTML. ASP.NET 1.*x* introduced the concept of the postback, wherein a server-side event was raised to alert the developer of a client-side action. If a button is clicked on the browser, the Form collection is POSTed back to the server, but now ASP.NET allows the developer to write code in events such as `Button1_Click()` and `TextBox1_Changed()`.

However, this technique of posting *back* to the same page is counterintuitive, especially when you are designing user interfaces that aim to create wizards to give the user the sense of forward motion.

This chapter is about all aspects of state management. Postbacks and cross-page postbacks, however, are covered extensively in Chapter 1, so this chapter touches on them only in the context of state management. Postbacks were introduced in ASP.NET 1.*x* to provide an eventing subsystem for Web development. Having only single-page postbacks in 1.*x* was inconvenient, however, and that caused many developers to store small objects in the `Session` on a postback and then redirect to the next page to pick up the stored data. With cross-page postbacks, data can be posted "forward" to a different page, often obviating the need for storing small bits of data that could otherwise be passed directly.

ASP.NET 2.0 and above includes the notion of a `PostBackUrl` to all the Button controls including LinkButton and ImageButton. The `PostBackUrl` property is both part of the markup when a control is presented as part of the ASPX page, as shown in the following code snippet, and is a property on the server-side component that is available in the code-behind:

```
<asp:Button PostBackUrl="url" ..>
```

When a button control with the `PostBackUrl` property set is clicked, the page does not post back to itself; instead, the page is posted to the URL assigned to the button control's `PostBackUrl` property. When a cross-page request occurs, the `PreviousPage` property of the current `Page` class holds a reference to the page that caused the postback. To get a control reference from the `PreviousPage`, use the `Controls` property or use the `FindControl()` method.

Create a fresh site with a `Default.aspx` (as shown in Listing 21-8). Put a `TextBox` and a `Button` on it, and set the `Button PostBackUrl` property to `Step2.aspx`. Then create a `Step2.aspx` page with a single `Label` and add a `Page_Load` handler by double-clicking the HTML Designer.

Available for download on Wrox.com

LISTING 21-8: Cross-page postbacks

Default.aspx

```
<html xmlns="http://www.w3.org/1999/xhtml" >
<head runat="server">
    <title>Cross-page PostBacks</title>
</head>
<body>
    <form id="form1" runat="server">
    <div>
        <asp:TextBox ID="TextBox1" Runat="server"></asp:TextBox>
        <asp:Button ID="Button1" Runat="server" Text="Button"
             PostBackUrl="</Step2.aspx" />
    </div>
    </form>
</body>
</html>
```

Step2.aspx

```
<html xmlns="http://www.w3.org/1999/xhtml" >
<head runat="server">
    <title>Step 2</title>
</head>
```

```
<body>
    <form id="form1" runat="server">
    <div>
        <asp:Label ID="Label1" runat="server" Text="Label"></asp:Label>
    </div>
    </form>
</body>
</html>
```

VB **Step2.aspx.vb**

```
Partial Class Step2
    Inherits System.Web.UI.Page

    Protected Sub Page_Load(ByVal sender As Object, ByVal e As System.EventArgs) _
             Handles Me.Load

        If PreviousPage IsNot Nothing AndAlso PreviousPage.IsCrossPagePostBack Then
            Dim text As TextBox =
                    CType(PreviousPage.FindControl("TextBox1"), TextBox)
            If text IsNot Nothing Then
                Label1.Text = text.Text
            End If
        End If

    End Sub

End Class
```

C# **Step2.aspx.cs**

```
using System;
using System.Web.UI.WebControls;

public partial class Step2 : System.Web.UI.Page
{
    protected void Page_Load(object sender, EventArgs e)
    {
        if (PreviousPage != null && PreviousPage.IsCrossPagePostBack)
        {
            TextBox text = PreviousPage.FindControl("TextBox1") as TextBox;
            if (text != null)
            {
                Label1.Text = text.Text;
            }
        }
    }

}
```

In Listing 21-8, `Default.aspx` posts *forward* to `Step2.aspx`, which can then access the `Page.PreviousPage` property and retrieve a populated instance of the `Page` that caused the postback. A call to `FindControl` and a cast retrieves the `TextBox` from the previous page and copies its value into the Label of `Step2.aspx`.

HIDDEN FIELDS, VIEWSTATE, AND CONTROLSTATE

Hidden input fields such as `<input type="hidden" name="foo">` are sent back as name/value pairs in a Form `POST` exactly like any other control, except that they are not rendered. Think of them as hidden text boxes. Figure 21-9 shows a HiddenField control on the Visual Studio Designer with its available properties. Hidden fields are available in all versions of ASP.NET.

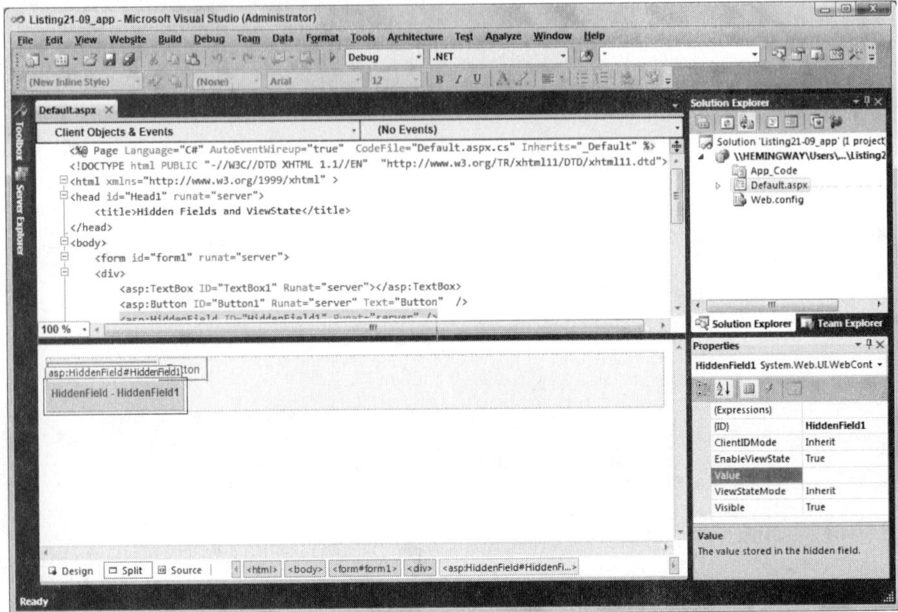

FIGURE 21-9

ViewState, on the other hand, exposes itself as a collection of key/value pairs like the `Session` object, but renders itself as a hidden field with the name `"__VIEWSTATE"` like this:

```
<input type="hidden" name="__VIEWSTATE" value="/AAASSDAS...Y/lOI=" />
```

Any objects put into the ViewState must be marked `Serializable`. ViewState serializes the objects with a special binary formatter called the LosFormatter. LOS stands for *limited object serialization*. It serializes any kind of object, but it is optimized to contain strings, arrays, and hashtables.

To see this at work, create a new page and drag a `TextBox`, `Button`, and `HiddenField` onto it. Double-click in the Designer to create a `Page_Load` and include the code from Listing 21-9. This example adds a string to `HiddenField.Value`, but adds an instance of a `Person` to the `ViewState` collection. This listing illustrates that while ViewState is persisted in a single HTML `TextBox` on the client, it can contain both simple types such as strings, and complex types such as `Person`. This technique has been around since ASP .NET 1.*x* and continues to be a powerful and simple way to persist small pieces of data without utilizing server resources.

LISTING 21-9: Hidden fields and ViewState

Available for download on Wrox.com

ASPX

```
<html xmlns="http://www.w3.org/1999/xhtml" >
<head runat="server">
    <title>Hidden Fields and ViewState</title>
</head>
<body>
    <form id="form1" runat="server">
    <div>
        <asp:TextBox ID="TextBox1" Runat="server"></asp:TextBox>
        <asp:Button ID="Button1" Runat="server" Text="Button"  />
        <asp:HiddenField ID="HiddenField1" Runat="server" />
```

```
        </div>
    </form>
</body>
</html>
```

VB

```
<Serializable> _
Public Class Person
    Public firstName As String
    Public lastName As String
End Class

Partial Class _Default
    Inherits System.Web.UI.Page

    Protected Sub Page_Load(ByVal sender As Object, ByVal e As System.EventArgs) _
            Handles Me.Load

        If Not Page.IsPostBack Then
            HiddenField1.Value = "foo"
            ViewState("AnotherHiddenValue") = "bar"

            Dim p As New Person
            p.firstName = "Scott"
            p.lastName = "Hanselman"
            ViewState("HiddenPerson") = p
        End If

    End Sub

End Class
```

C#

```
using System;
using System.Web.UI.WebControls;
using System.Web.UI.HtmlControls;

[Serializable]
public class Person
{
    public string firstName;
    public string lastName;
}

public partial class _Default : System.Web.UI.Page
{

    protected void Page_Load(object sender, EventArgs e)
    {
        if (!Page.IsPostBack)
        {
            HiddenField1.Value = "foo";
            ViewState["AnotherHiddenValue"] = "bar";

            Person p = new Person();
            p.firstName = "Scott";
            p.lastName = "Hanselman";
            ViewState["HiddenPerson"] = p;
        }
    }
}
```

In Listing 21-9, a string is added to a `HiddenField` and to the `ViewState` collection. Then, a `Person` instance is added to the `ViewState` collection with another key. A fragment of the rendered HTML is shown in the following code:

```
<form method="post" action="Default.aspx" id="form1">
<div>
<input type="hidden" name="__VIEWSTATE"
value="/wEPDwULLTIxMjQ3OTEzODcPFgQeEkFub3RoZXJIaWRkZW5WYWx1ZQUDYmFyHgxIaWRkZW5QZXJz
b24ypwEAAQAAAP////8BAAAAAAAAAAwCAAAAP3ZkcTVqYzdxLCBWZXJzaW9uPTAuMC4wLjAsIEN1bHR1cmU
9bmV1dHJhbCwgUHVibGljS2V5VG9rZW49bnVsbAUBAAAAE0RlZmF1bHRfYXNweCtQZXJzb24CAAAACWZpcn
N0TmFtZQhsYXN0TmFtZQEBAgAAAAYDAAAABVNjb3R0BgQAAAAJSGFuc2VsbWFuC2RkI/CLauUviFo58BF8v
pSNsjY/lOI=" />
</div>
    <div>
        <input name="TextBox1" type="text" id="TextBox1" />
        <input type="submit" name="Button1" value="Button" id="Button1" />
        <input type="hidden" name="HiddenField1" id="HiddenField1" value="foo" />
    </div>
</form>
```

Notice that the `ViewState` value uses only valid ASCII characters to represent all its contents. Do not let the sheer mass of it fool you. It is big and it appears to be opaque. However, it is just a hidden text box and is automatically `POST`ed back to the server. The entire `ViewState` collection is available to you in the `Page_Load`. The value of the `HiddenField` is stored as plain text.

Neither ViewState nor Hidden Fields are acceptable for any kind of sensitive data.

People often complain about the size of ViewState and turn it off completely without realizing its benefits. The release of ASP.NET 2.0 cut the size of serialized ViewState nearly in half. You can find a number of tips on using ViewState on my blog by Googling for "Hanselman ViewState." Fritz Onion's free ViewStateDecoder tool from `www.pluralsight.com` *is a great way to gain insight into what is stored in your pages' ViewState. Note also Nikhil Kotari's detailed blog post on ViewState improvements at* `www.nikhilk.net/ViewStateImprovements.aspx`.

By default, the ViewState field is sent to the client with a *salted hash* to prevent tampering. Salting means that the ViewState's data has a unique value appended to it before it is encoded. As Keith Brown says, "Salt is just one ingredient to a good stew." The technique used is called HMAC, or hashed message authentication code. As shown in the following code, you can use the `<machineKey>` element of the `web.config` file to specify the `validationKey`, as well as the algorithm used to protect ViewState. This section of the file and the `decryptionKey` attribute also affect how Forms Authentication cookies are encrypted (see Chapter 20 for more on forms authentication).

```
<machineKey validationKey="AutoGenerate,IsolateApps"
 decryptionKey="AutoGenerate,IsolateApps" validation="SHA1" />
```

If you are running your application in a Web farm, `<validationKey>` and `<decryptionKey>` have to be manually set to the same value. Otherwise, ViewState generated from one machine could be `POST`ed back to a machine in the farm with a different key! The keys should be 128 characters long (the maximum) and generated totally by random means. If you add `IsolateApps` to these values, ASP.NET generates a unique encrypted key for each application using each application's application ID.

I like to use security guru Keith Brown's GenerateMachineKey tool, which you can find at `www.pluralsight.com/tools.aspx`, *to generate these keys randomly.*

The validation attribute can be set to SHA1 or MD5 to provide tamper-proofing, but you can include added protection by encrypting ViewState as well. In ASP.NET 1.1, you can encrypt ViewState only by using the value 3DES in the validation attribute, and ASP.NET 1.1 will use the key in the decryptionKey attribute for encryption. However, since the release of ASP.NET 2.0, there is now a decryption attribute that is used exclusively for specifying the encryption and decryption mechanisms for forms authentication tickets, and the validation attribute is used exclusively for ViewState, which can now be encrypted using 3DES or AES and the key stored in the validationKey attribute.

With ASP.NET 4, you can also add the ViewStateEncryptionMode attribute to the <pages> configuration element with two possible values, Auto or Always. Setting the attribute to Always will force encryption of ViewState, whereas setting it to Auto will encrypt ViewState only if a control requested encryption using the new Page.RegisterRequiresViewStateEncryption method.

Added protection can be applied to ViewState by setting Page.ViewStateUserKey in the Page_Init to a unique value such as the user's ID. This must be set in Page_Init because the key should be provided to ASP.NET before ViewState is loaded or generated. For example:

```
protected void Page_Init (Object sender, EventArgs e)
{
    if (User.Identity.IsAuthenticated)
        ViewStateUserKey = User.Identity.Name;
}
```

When optimizing their pages, ASP.NET programmers often disable ViewState for many controls when that extra bit of state is not absolutely necessary. However, in ASP.NET 1.*x*, disabling ViewState was a good way to break many third-party controls, as well as the included DataGrid's sorting functionality. ASP.NET now includes a second, parallel ViewState-like collection called ControlState. This dictionary can be used for round-tripping crucial information of limited size that should not be disabled even when ViewState is. You should only store data in the ControlState collection that is absolutely critical to the functioning of the control.

Recognize that ViewState, and also ControlState, though not secure, is a good place to store small bits of a data and state that don't quite belong in a cookie or in the Session object. If the data that must be stored is relatively small and local to that specific instance of your page, ViewState is a much better solution than littering the Session object with lots of transient data.

USING HTTPCONTEXT.CURRENT.ITEMS FOR VERY SHORT-TERM STORAGE

The Items collection of HttpContext is one of ASP.NET's best-kept secrets. It is an IDictionary key/value collection of objects that's shared across the life of a single HttpRequest. That's a *single* HttpRequest. Why would you want to store state for such a short period of time? Consider these reasons:

- **When you share content between IHttpModules and IHttpHandlers:** If you write a custom IHttpModule, you can store context about the user for use later in a page.
- **When you communicate between two instances of the same UserControl on the same page:** Imagine you are writing a UserControl that serves banner ads. Two instances of the same control could select their ads from HttpContext.Items to prevent showing duplicates on the same page.
- **When you store the results of expensive calls that might otherwise happen twice or more on a page:** If you have multiple UserControls that each show a piece of data from a large, more expensive database retrieval, those UserControls can retrieve the necessary data from HttpContext.Items. The database is hit only once.
- **When individual units within a single HttpRequest need to act on the same or similar data:** If the lifetime of your data is just one request, consider using HttpContext.Items as a short-term cache.

The Items collection holds objects, just like many of the collections that have been used in this chapter. You need to cast those objects back to their specific type when they are retrieved.

Within a Web-aware database access layer, per-request caching can be quickly implemented with the simple coding pattern shown here. Note that this sample code is a design pattern, and there is no `MyData` class; it is for illustration.

VB

```
Public Shared Function GetExpensiveData(ID As Integer) As MyData
  Dim key as string = "data" & ID.ToString()
  Dim d as MyData = _
      CType(HttpContext.Current.Items(key), MyData)
  If d Is Nothing Then
    d = New Data()
   'Go to the Database, do whatever...
    HttpContext.Current.Items(key) = d
  End If
  Return d
End Function
```

VB

```
public static MyData GetExpensiveData(int ID)
{
  string key = "data" + ID.ToString();
  MyData d = (MyData) HttpContext.Current.Items[key];
  if (d == null)
  {
    d = new Data();
    //Go to the Database, do whatever...
    HttpContext.Current.Items[key] = d;
  }
  return d;
}
```

This code checks the `Items` collection of the current `HttpContext` to see whether the data is already there. If it's not, the data is retrieved from the appropriate backing store and then stored in the `Items` collection. Subsequent calls to this function within the same `HttpRequest` receive the already-cached object.

As with all optimizations and caching, premature optimization is the root of all evil. Measure your need for caching and measure your improvements. Do not cache just because it *feels right*; cache because it makes sense.

SUMMARY

This chapter explored the many ways to manage state within your ASP.NET application. The `Session` object and its providers offer many choices. Each has its own pros and cons for managing state in the form of object references and serialized objects in a way that can be made largely transparent to the application. Server-side session state data can have its unique identifying key stored in a cookie, or the key can be carried along in the URL. Cookies can also be used independently to store small amounts of data and persist it between visits, albeit in much smaller amounts and with simpler types. Hidden fields, ViewState, ControlState, postbacks, and cross-page postbacks offer possibilities for managing small bits of state within a multi-page user experience. `HttpContext.Current.Items` offers a perfect place to hold transient state, living the life of only a single `HttpRequest`. QueryStrings are an old standby for holding non-private state that is appropriate for navigation.

Subsequent versions of ASP.NET have improved on ASP.NET 1.*x*'s state management options with a flexible Session State Provider module, the addition of ControlState for user controls, and cross-page postbacks for a more mature programming model.

22

Caching

WHAT'S IN THIS CHAPTER?

- Dealing with caching in ASP.NET
- Using SQL cache invalidation
- Working with caching programmatically

Performance is a key requirement for any application or piece of code that you develop. The browser helps with client-side caching of text and images, whereas the server-side caching you choose to implement is vital for creating the best possible performance. *Caching* is the process of storing frequently used data on the server to fulfill subsequent requests. You will discover that grabbing objects from memory is much faster than re-creating the Web pages or items contained in them from scratch each time they are requested. Caching increases your application's performance, scalability, and availability. The more you fine-tune your application's caching approach, the better it performs.

This chapter focuses on caching, including the SQL cache invalidation capabilities that ASP.NET provides. This chapter takes a close look at this unique aspect of caching. When you are using SQL cache invalidation, if the result set from SQL Server changes, the output cache can be triggered to change automatically. This ensures that the end user always sees the latest result set, and the data presented is never stale. After introducing SQL cache invalidation, this chapter also covers other performance enhancements. It discusses the Post-Cache Substitution feature, which caches entire pages while dynamically replacing specified bits of content. Lastly, this chapter covers a capability that enables a developer to create custom dependencies.

CACHING

You have several ways to deal with caching in ASP.NET, one of which being that you can cache an entire HTTP response (the entire Web page) using a mechanism called output caching. Two other methods are partial page caching and data caching. The following sections describe these methods.

Output Caching

Output caching is a way to keep the dynamically generated page content in the server's memory or disk for later retrieval. This type of cache saves post-rendered content so it will not have to be regenerated again the next time it is requested. After a page is cached, it can be served up again when any subsequent requests are made to the server. You apply output caching by inserting an `OutputCache` page directive at the top of an `.aspx` page, as follows:

```
<%@ OutputCache Duration="60" VaryByParam="None" %>
```

The `Duration` attribute defines the number of seconds a page is stored in the cache. The `VaryByParam` attribute determines which versions of the page output are actually cached. You can generate different responses based on whether an HTTP-POST or HTTP-GET response is required. Other than the attributes for the `OutputCache` directive, ASP.NET includes the `VaryByHeader`, `VaryByCustom`, `VaryByControl`, and `Location` attributes. Additionally, the `Shared` attribute can affect UserControls, as you will see later.

Caching in ASP.NET is implemented as an `HttpModule` that listens to all `HttpRequests` that come through the ASP.NET worker process. The `OutputCacheModule` listens to the application's `ResolveRequestCache` and `UpdateRequestCache` events, handles cache hits and misses, and returns the cached HTML, bypassing the Page Handler if need be.

VaryByParam

The `VaryByParam` attribute can specify which `QueryString` parameters cause a new version of the page to be cached:

```
<%@ OutputCache Duration="90" VaryByParam="pageId;subPageId" %>
```

For example, if you have a page called `navigation.aspx` that includes navigation information in the `QueryString`, such as `pageId` and `subPageId`, the `OutputCache` directive shown here caches the page for every different value of `pageId` and `subPageId`. In this example, the number of pages is best expressed with an equation:

```
cacheItems = (num of pageIds) * (num of subPageIds)
```

where `cacheItems` is the number of rendered HTML pages that would be stored in the cache. Pages are cached only after they are requested and pass through the `OutputCacheModule`. The maximum amount of cache memory in this case is used only after every possible combination is visited at least once. Although these are just *potential* maximums, creating an equation that represents your system's potential maximum is an important exercise.

If you want to cache a new version of the page based on any differences in the `QueryString` parameters, use `VaryByParam="*"`, as in the following code:

```
<%@ OutputCache Duration="90" VaryByParam="*" %>
```

"Doing the math" when using the VaryBy attributes is important. For example, you could add `VaryByHeader` and cache a different version of the page based on the browser's reported `User-Agent` HTTP header.

```
<%@ OutputCache Duration="90" VaryByParam="*" VaryByHeader="User-Agent"%>
```

The `User-Agent` identifies the user's browser type. ASP.NET can automatically generate different renderings of a given page that are customized to specific browsers, so in many cases saving these various renderings in the cache makes sense. A Firefox user might have slightly different HTML than an IE user, so you do not want to send all users the exact same post-rendered HTML. Literally dozens, if not hundreds, of `User-Agent` strings exist in the wild because they identify more than just the browser type; this `OutputCache` directive could multiply into thousands of different versions of this page being cached, depending on server load. In this case, you should measure the cost of the caching against the cost of re-creating the page dynamically.

Always cache what will give you the biggest performance gain, and prove that assumption with testing. Don't "cache by coincidence" using attributes like `VaryByParam="*"`. *A common general rule is to cache the least possible amount of data at first and add more caching later if you determine a need for it. Remember that the server memory is a limited resource so you may want configure the use of disk caching in some cases. Be sure to balance your limited resources with security as a primary concern; do not put sensitive data on the disk.*

VaryByControl

`VaryByControl` can be a very easy way to get some serious performance gains from complicated UserControls that render a lot of HTML that does not change often. For example, imagine a UserControl that renders a ComboBox showing the names of all the countries in the world. Perhaps those names are retrieved from a database and rendered in the combo box as follows:

```
<%@ OutputCache Duration="2592000" VaryByControl="comboBoxOfCountries" %>
```

Certainly, the names of the world's countries do not change that often, so the `Duration` might be set to a month (in seconds). The rendered output of the UserControl is cached, allowing a page using that control to reap performance benefits of caching the control while the page itself remains dynamic.

VaryByCustom

Although the `VaryBy` attributes offer a great deal of power, sometimes you need more flexibility. If you want to take the `OutputCache` directive from the previous navigation example and cache by a value stored in a cookie, you can add `VaryByCustom`. The value of `VaryByCustom` is passed into the `GetVaryByCustomString` method that can be added to the `Global.asax.cs`. This method is called every time the page is requested, and it is the function's responsibility to return a value.

A different version of the page is cached for each unique value returned. For example, suppose your users have a cookie called `Language` that has three potential values: en, es, and fr. You want to allow users to specify their preferred language, regardless of their language reported by their browser. `Language` also has a fourth potential value — it may not exist! Therefore, the `OutputCache` directive in the following example caches many versions of the page, as described in this equation:

```
cacheItems = (num of pageIds) * (num of subPageIds) * (4 possible Language values)
```

To summarize, suppose there were ten potential values for `pageId`, five potential `subPageId` values for each `pageId`, and four possible values for `Language`. That adds up to 200 different potential cached versions of this single navigation page. This math is not meant to scare you away from caching, but you should realize that with great (caching) power comes great responsibility.

The following `OutputCache` directive includes `pageId` and `subPageId` as values for `VaryByParam`, and `VaryByCustom` passes in the value of `"prefs"` to the `GetVaryByCustomString` callback function in Listing 22-1:

```
<%@ OutputCache Duration="90" VaryByParam="pageId;subPageId" VaryByCustom="prefs"%>
```

Caching in ASP.NET involves a tradeoff between CPU and memory: how hard is it to make this page, versus whether you can afford to hold 200 versions of it. If it is only 5KB of HTML, a potential megabyte of memory could pay off handsomely versus thousands and thousands of database accesses. Because most pages will hit the database at least once during a page cycle, every page request served from the cache saves you a trip to the database. Efficient use of caching can translate into cost savings if fewer database servers and licenses are needed.

The code in Listing 22-1 returns the value stored in the `Language` cookie. The `arg` parameter to the `GetVaryByCustomString` method contains the string `"prefs"`, as specified in `VaryByCustom`.

LISTING 22-1: GetVaryByCustomString callback method in the HttpApplication

Available for download on Wrox.com

VB

```
Overrides Function GetVaryByCustomString(ByVal context As HttpContext,
        ByVal arg As String) As String
    If arg.ToLower() = "prefs" Then
        Dim cookie As HttpCookie = context.Request.Cookies("Language")
        If cookie IsNot Nothing Then
            Return cookie.Value
        End If
    End If
    Return MyBase.GetVaryByCustomString(context, arg)
End Function
```

continues

LISTING 22-1 *(continued)*

C#

```
public override string GetVaryByCustomString(HttpContext context, string arg)
{
    if(arg.ToLower() == "prefs")
    {
      HttpCookie cookie = context.Request.Cookies["Language"];
      if(cookie != null)
      {
          return cookie.Value;
      }
    }
    return base.GetVaryByCustomString(context, arg);
}
```

The `GetVaryByCustomString` method in Listing 22-1 is used by the `HttpApplication` in `Global.asax.cs` and will be called for every page that uses the `VaryByCustom OutputCache` directive. If your application has many pages that use `VaryByCustom`, you can create a switch statement and a series of helper functions to retrieve whatever information you want from the user's HttpContext and to generate unique values for cache keys.

Extending <outputCache>

With the release of ASP.NET 4, you are now able to extend how the `OutputCache` directive works and have it instead work off your own custom means to caching. This means that you can wire the `OutputCache` directive to any type of caching means including distributed caches, cloud caches, disc, XML, or anything else you can dream up.

To accomplish this, you are required to create a custom output-cache provider as a class and this class will need to inherit from the new `System.Web.Caching.OutputCacheProvider` class. To inherit from `OutputCacheProvider`, you must override the `Add()`, `Get()`, `Remove()`, and `Set()` methods to implement your custom version of output caching.

After you have your custom implementation in place, the next step is to configure this in a configuration file: the `machine.config` or the `web.config` file. Some changes have been made to the `<outputCache>` element in the configuration file to allow you to apply your custom cache extensions.

The `<outputCache>` element is found within the `<caching>` section of the configuration file and it now includes a new `<providers>` subelement.

```
<caching>
   <outputCache>
      <providers>
      </providers>
   </outputCache>
</caching>
```

Within the new `<providers>` element, you can nest an `<add>` element to make the appropriate references to your new output cache capability you built by deriving from the `OutputCacheProvider` class.

```
<caching>
   <outputCache defaultProvider="AspNetInternalProvider">
      <providers>
         <add name="myDistributedCacheExtension"
          type="Wrox.OutputCacheExtension.DistributedCacheProvider,
                   DistributedCacheProvider" />
      </providers>
   </outputCache>
</caching>
```

With this new `<add>` element in place, your new extended output cache is available to use. One new addition here to also pay attention to is the new `defaultProvider` attribute within the `<outputCache>` element. In this case, it is set to `AspNetInternalProvider`, which is the default setting in the configuration file. This means that by default the output cache works as it always has done and stores its cache in the memory of the computer that the program is running.

With your own output cache provider in place, you can now point to this provider through the `OutputCache` directive on the page as defined here:

```
<%@ OutputCache Duration="90" VaryByParam="*"
    providerName="myDistributedCacheExtension" %>
```

If the provider name isn't defined, then the provider that is defined in the configuration's `defaultProvider` attribute is utilized.

Partial Page (UserControl) Caching

Similar to output caching, *partial page caching* enables you to cache only specific blocks of a Web page. You can, for example, cache only the center of the page the user sees. Partial page caching is achieved with the caching of user controls so you can build your ASP.NET pages to utilize numerous user controls and then apply output caching to the selected user controls. This, in essence, caches only the parts of the page that you want, leaving other parts of the page outside the reach of caching. This feature is nice and, if done correctly, can lead to pages that perform better. This requires a modular design to be planned up front so you can partition the components of the page into logical units composed of user controls.

Typically, UserControls are designed to be placed on multiple pages to maximize reuse of common functionality. However, when these UserControls (`.ascx` files) are cached with the `@OutputCache` directive's default attributes, they are cached on a per-page basis. That means that even if a UserControl outputs the identical HTML when placed on `pageA.aspx` as it does when placed on `pageB.aspx`, its output is cached twice. By enabling the `Shared="true"` attribute, the UserControl's output can be shared among multiple pages and on sites that make heavy use of shared UserControls:

```
<%@ OutputCache Duration="300" VaryByParam="*" Shared="true" %>
```

The resulting memory savings can be surprisingly large because you only cache one copy of the post-rendered user control instead of caching a copy for each page. As with all optimizations, you need to test both for correctness of output as well as memory usage.

If you have an ASCX UserControl using the `OutputCache` *directive, remember that the UserControl* exists only for the first request. *If a UserControl has its HTML retrieved from the* `OutputCache`*, the control does not really exist on the ASPX page. Instead, a PartialCachingControl is created that acts as a proxy or* ghost *of that control.*

Any code in the ASPX page that requires a UserControl to be constantly available will fail if that control is reconstituted from the `OutputCache`. So be sure to always check for this type of caching before using any control. The following code fragment illustrates the kind of logic required when accessing a potentially cached UserControl:

VB

```
Protected Sub Page_Load()
    If Not PossiblyCachedUserControl is Nothing Then
       ' Place code manipulating PossiblyCachedUserControl here.
    End If
End Sub
```

C#

```
protected void Page_Load()
{
    if (PossiblyCachedUserControl != null)
    {
       // Place code manipulating PossiblyCachedUserControl here.
    }
}
```

Post-Cache Substitution

Output caching has typically been an all-or-nothing proposition. The output of the entire page is cached for later use. However, often you want the benefits of output caching, but you also want to keep a small bit of dynamic content on the page. It would be a shame to cache a page but be unable to output a dynamic "Welcome, Scott!"

Ever since ASP.NET 2.0, a means has existed of using a post-cache substitution as an opportunity to affect the about-to-be-rendered page. A control is added to the page that acts as a placeholder. It calls a method that you specify after the cached content has been returned. The method returns any string output you like, but you should be careful not to abuse the feature. If your post-cache substitution code calls an expensive stored procedure, you could easily lose any performance benefits you might have expected.

Post-cache substitution is an easy feature to use. It gives you two ways to control the substitution:

- Call the `Response.WriteSubstitution` method, passing it a reference to the desired substitution method callback.
- Add an `<asp:Substitution>` control to the page at the desired location, and set its `methodName` attribute to the name of the callback method.

To try this feature, create a new Web site with a `Default.aspx` page. Drag a label control and a substitution control to the design surface. The code in Listing 22-2 updates the label to display the current time, but the page is cached immediately and future requests return that cached value. Set the `methodName` property in the substitution control to `GetUpdatedTime`, meaning the name of the static method that is called after the page is retrieved from the cache.

The callback function must be static because the page that is rendered does not really exist at this point (an instance of it does not). Because you do not have a page instance to work with, this method is limited in its scope. However, the current `HttpContext` is passed into the method, so you have access to the `Session`, `Request`, and `Response`. The string returned from this method is injected into the `Response` in place of the substitution control.

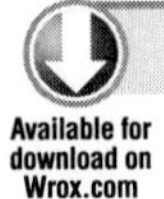

Available for download on Wrox.com

LISTING 22-2: Using the substitution control

ASPX

```
<%@ Page Language="C#" CodeFile="Default.aspx.cs" Inherits="_Default" %>
<%@ OutputCache Duration="30" VaryByParam="None" %>

<html xmlns="http://www.w3.org/1999/xhtml" >
<head >
    <title>Substitution Control</title>
</head>
<body>
    <form id="form1" runat="server">
    <div>
        <asp:Label ID="Label1" Runat="server" Text="Label"></asp:Label>
        <br />
        <asp:Substitution ID="Substitution1" Runat="server"
             methodName="GetUpdatedTime" />
        <br />
    </div>
    </form>
</body>
</html>
```

VB

```
Partial Class _Default
        Inherits System.Web.UI.Page
    Public Shared Function GetUpdatedTime(ByVal context As HttpContext) As String
```

```
        Return DateTime.Now.ToLongTimeString() + " by " +
                context.User.Identity.Name
    End Function

    Protected Sub Page_Load(ByVal sender As Object, ByVal e As System.EventArgs) _
            Handles Me.Load
        Label1.Text = DateTime.Now.ToLongTimeString()
    End Sub
End Class
```

C#

```
public partial class _Default : System.Web.UI.Page
{
    public static string GetUpdatedTime(HttpContext context)
    {
        return DateTime.Now.ToLongTimeString() + " by " +
                context.User.Identity.Name;
    }
    protected void Page_Load(object sender, EventArgs e)
    {
        Label1.Text = DateTime.Now.ToLongTimeString();
    }
}
```

The ASPX page in Listing 22-2 has a label and a Post-Cache Substitution control. The control acts as a placeholder in the spot where you want fresh content injected after the page is returned from the cache. The very first time the page is visited only the label is updated because no cached content is returned. The second time the page is visited, however, the entire page is retrieved from the cache — the page handler is not called and, consequently, none of the page-level events fire. However, the `GetUpdatedTime` method is called after the cache module completes its work. Figure 22-1 shows the result if the first line is cached and the second line is created dynamically.

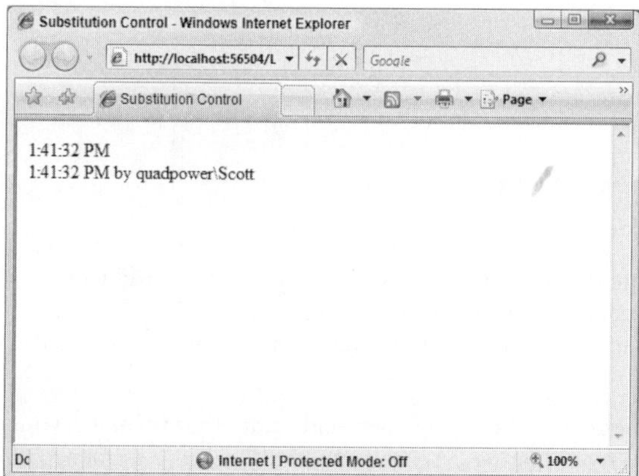

FIGURE 22-1

HttpCachePolicy and Client-Side Caching

Caching is more than just holding data in memory on the server-side. A good caching strategy should also include the browser and its client-side caches, controlled by the Cache-Control HTTP header. HTTP headers are hints and directives to the browser on how to handle a request.

Some people recommend using HTML `<META>` tags to control caching behavior. Be aware that neither the browsers nor routers along the way are obligated to pay attention to these directives. You might have more success using HTTP headers to control caching.

Because HTTP headers travel outside the body of the HTTP message, you have several options for viewing them. You can enable tracing (see Chapter 23) and view the headers from the tracing output. Figure 22-2 shows the free TcpTrace redirector from `PocketSoap.com`.

> *For background information on HTTP headers and controlling caching, see the document RFC 2616: Hypertext Transfer Protocol - HTTP/1.1, available on the World Wide Web Consortium's site at* `www.w3c.org`. *You might also check out Fiddler at* `www.fiddlertool.com/fiddler` *and FireBug for Firefox at* `www.getfirebug.com`. *Commercial tools such as HttpWatch from* `www.httpwatch.com` *add more features.*

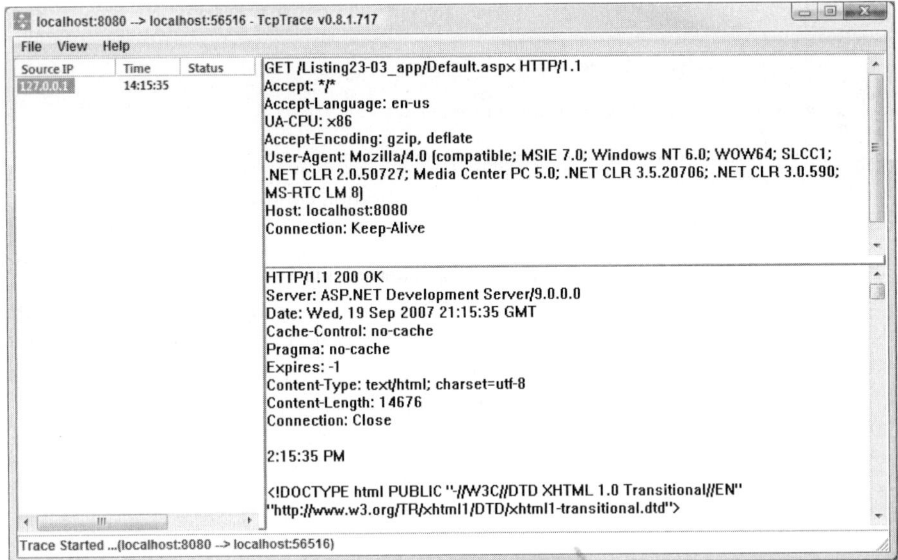

FIGURE 22-2

Create a `Default.aspx` that writes the current time in its `Load` event. Now, view the default HTTP headers used by ASP.NET, as in Figure 22-2 with page-level tracing turned on. Note that one header, `Cache-Control: private`, indicates to routers and other intermediates that this response is intended only for you (private).

The `HttpCachePolicy` class gives you an object model for managing client-side state that insulates you from adding HTTP headers yourself. Add the lines from Listing 22-3 to your `Page_Load` to influence the response's headers and the caching behavior of the browser. This listing tells the browser not to cache this response in memory nor store it on disk. It also directs the response to expire immediately.

LISTING 22-3: Using HTTP headers to force the browser not to cache on the client side

Available for download on Wrox.com

```
Protected Sub Page_Load(ByVal sender As Object,
  ByVal e As System.EventArgs) Handles Me.Load

    Response.Cache.SetCacheability(HttpCacheability.NoCache)
    Response.Cache.SetNoStore()
    Response.Cache.SetExpires(DateTime.MinValue)

    Response.Write(DateTime.Now.ToLongTimeString())
```

```
End Sub
```

```
protected void Page_Load(object sender, EventArgs e)
{
    Response.Cache.SetCacheability(HttpCacheability.NoCache);
    Response.Cache.SetNoStore();
    Response.Cache.SetExpires(DateTime.MinValue);

    Response.Write(DateTime.Now.ToLongTimeString());
}
```

Compare the results of running Listing 22-3 in the *before* Figure 22-2 and then in the *after* Figure 22-3. Two new HTTP headers have been injected directing the client's browser and the `Cache-Control` header has changed to `no-cache, no-store`. The Output Caching `HttpModule` will respect these HTTP headers, so sending `no-cache, no-store` to the browser also advises the `HttpModule` to record the response as a cache miss.

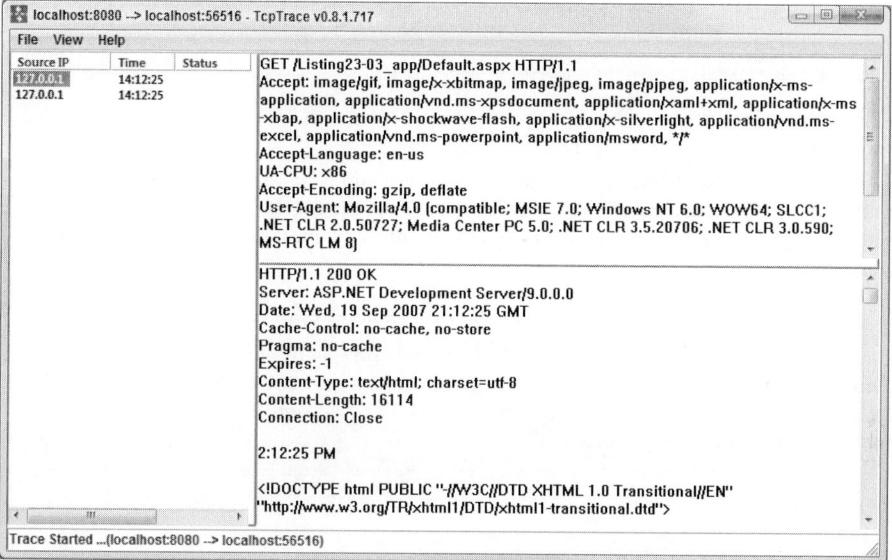

FIGURE 22-3

If your ASP.NET application contains a considerable number of relatively static or non–time-sensitive pages, consider what your client-side caching strategy is. Taking advantage of the disk space and the memory of your users' powerful client machines is better than burdening your server's limited resources.

CACHING PROGRAMMATICALLY

Output Caching is a very declarative business. UserControls and pages can be marked up with `OutputCache` directives and dramatically change the behavior of your site. Declarative caching controls the lifecycle of HTML markup, but ASP.NET also includes deep imperative programmatic support for caching objects.

Data Caching Using the Cache Object

Another method of caching is to use the `System.Web.Caching.Cache` object to start caching specific data items for later use on a particular page or group of pages. The `Cache` object enables you to store everything from simple name/value pairs to more complex objects such as datasets and entire `.aspx` pages.

Although it is quite similar to session state, the `Cache` *object is shared by all users of the particular Web server's app domain that is hosting this application. Therefore, if you put a particular item in the cache, all users will be able to see that object. This may not work as expected in a server farm scenario because you cannot be assured of which server the user will hit next, and even if there is only one server involved, more than one app domain may be running this application. In addition, the server is free to invalidate any cached item at any time if it needs to reclaim some of the memory.*

You use the `Cache` object in the following fashion:

VB
```
Cache("WhatINeedToStore") = myDataSet
```

C#
```
Cache["WhatINeedToStore"] = myDataSet;
```

After an item is in the cache, you can retrieve it later as shown here:

VB
```
Dim ds As New DataSet
ds = CType(Cache("WhatINeedToStore"), DataSet)
```

C#
```
DataSet ds = new DataSet();
ds = (DataSet)Cache["WhatINeedToStore"];
```

Using the `Cache` object is an outstanding way to cache your pages and is, in fact, what the `OutputCache` directive uses under the covers. This small fragment shows the simplest use of the `Cache` object. Simply put an object reference in it. However, the real power of the `Cache` object comes with its capability to invalidate itself. That is where cache dependencies come in.

You must always follow the pattern of testing to see whether an item is in the cache, and if not, you need to do whatever processing is necessary to re-create the object. After it's re-created, you can insert it back into the cache to become available for the next request.

Controlling the ASP.NET Cache

Ordinarily the default parameters set by ASP.NET for the caching subsystem are appropriate for general use. They are configurable, however, within the `machine.config` or `web.config` files. These options let you make changes like preventing cached items from expiring when the system is under memory pressure, or turning off item expiration completely. You can set the maximize size of the application's private bytes before the cache begins to flush items.

```
<system.web>
  <cache disableMemoryCollection="false"
  disableExpiration="false" privateBytesLimit="0"
  percentagePhysicalMemoryUsedLimit="90"
  privateBytesPollTime="00:02:00" />
...snip...
```

I encourage you to leave the default values as they are unless you have done formal profiling of your application and understand how it utilizes the cache. You can find more detail on this section on MSDN at `http://msdn.microsoft.com/en-us/library/ms228248.aspx`.

Cache Dependencies

Using the `Cache` object, you can store and invalidate items in the cache based on several different dependencies. Way back in ASP.NET 1.0/1.1, the only possible dependencies were the following:

- File-based dependencies
- Key-based dependencies
- Time-based dependencies

When inserting items into the cache using the `Cache` object, you set the dependencies with the `Insert` method, as shown in the following example:

```
Cache.Insert("DSN", connectionString,
   New CacheDependency(Server.MapPath("myconfig.xml")))
```

By using a *dependency* when the item being referenced changes, you remove the cache for that item from memory.

Cache dependencies have been improved ever since ASP.NET 2.0 with the addition of the `AggregateCacheDependency` class, the extendable `CacheDependency` class, and the capability to create your own custom `CacheDependency` classes. These three things are discussed in the following sections.

The AggregateCacheDependency Class

The `AggregateCacheDependency` class is like the `CacheDependency` class but it enables you to create an association connecting an item in the cache with many disparate dependencies of *different types*. For example, if you have a cached data item that is built from XML from a file and you have information from a SQL database table, you can create an `AggregateCacheDependency` with inserted `CacheDependency` objects for each subdependency. To do this, you call `Cache.Insert()` and add the `AggregateCacheDependency` instance. For example:

```
Dim agg as new AggregateCacheDependency()
agg.Insert(New CacheDependency(Server.MapPath("myconfig.xml")))
agg.Insert(New SqlCacheDependency("Northwind", "Customers"))
Cache.Insert("DSN", connectionString, agg)
```

Note that `AggregateCacheDependency` is meant to be used with *different* kinds of `CacheDependency` classes. If you simply want to associate one cached item with multiple files, use an overload of `CacheDependency`, as in this example:

VB

```
Cache.Insert("DSN", yourObject,
    New System.Web.Caching.CacheDependency(
        New String()
        {
          Server.MapPath("foo.xml"),
          Server.MapPath("bar.xml")
        }
    )
)
```

C#

```
Cache.Insert("DSN", yourObject,
    new System.Web.Caching.CacheDependency(
        new string[]
        {
             Server.MapPath("foo.xml"),
             Server.MapPath("bar.xml")
        }
    )
);
```

The `AggregateCacheDependency` class is made possible by the support for extending the previously sealed `CacheDependency` class. You can use this innovation to create your own custom `CacheDependency`.

The Unsealed CacheDependency Class

A big change in caching ever since ASP.NET 2.0 was released was that the `CacheDependency` class had been refactored and unsealed (or made overrideable). This allowed us to create classes that inherit from the `CacheDependency` class and create more elaborate dependencies that are not limited to the `Time`, `Key`, or `File` dependencies.

When you create your own cache dependencies, you have the option to add procedures for such things as Web services data, only-at-midnight dependencies, or textual string changes within a file. The dependencies you create are limited only by your imagination. The unsealing of the `CacheDependency` class puts you in the driver's seat to let you decide when items in the cache need to be invalidated.

Along with the unsealing of the `CacheDependency` class, the ASP.NET team also built a SQL Server cache dependency — `SqlCacheDependency`. When a cache becomes invalid because a table changes within the underlying SQL Server, you now know it immediately in your ASP.NET application.

Because `CacheDependency` is unsealed, you can derive your own custom cache dependencies; that's what you do in the next section.

Creating Custom Cache Dependencies

ASP.NET has time-based, file-based, and SQL-based `CacheDependency` support. You might ask yourself why you would write your own `CacheDependency`. Here are a few ideas:

- Invalidate the cache from the results of an Active Directory lookup query
- Invalidate the cache upon arrival of an MSMQ or MQSeries message
- Create an Oracle-specific `CacheDependency`
- Invalidate the cache using data reported from an XML Web service
- Update the cache with new data from a Stock Price service

The `CacheDependency` class exposes three members and a constructor overload that developers can use to do this work:

- `GetUniqueID`: When overridden, enables you to return a unique identifier for a custom cache dependency to the caller.
- `DependencyDispose`: Used for disposing of resources used by the custom cache dependency class. When you create a custom cache dependency, you are required to implement this method.
- `NotifyDependencyChanged`: Called to cause expiration of the cache item dependent on the custom cache dependency instance.
- The `CacheDependency` public constructor.

Listing 22-4 creates a new `RssCacheDependency` that invalidates a cache key if an RSS (Rich Site Summary) XML document has changed.

LISTING 22-4: Creating an RssCacheDependency class

Available for download on Wrox.com

```
Imports System
Imports System.Web
Imports System.Threading
Imports System.Web.Caching
Imports System.Xml

Public Class RssCacheDependency
        Inherits CacheDependency

    Dim backgroundThread As Timer
    Dim howOften As Integer = 900
    Dim RSS As XmlDocument
```

```
    Dim RSSUrl As String

    Public Sub New(ByVal URL As String, ByVal polling As Integer)
        howOften = polling
        RSSUrl = URL
        RSS = RetrieveRSS(RSSUrl)

        If backgroundThread Is Nothing Then
            backgroundThread = New Timer(
                New TimerCallback(AddressOf CheckDependencyCallback),
                Me, (howOften * 1000), (howOften * 1000))
        End If
    End Sub

    Function RetrieveRSS(ByVal URL As String) As XmlDocument
        Dim retVal As New XmlDocument
        retVal.Load(URL)
        Return retVal
    End Function

    Public Sub CheckDependencyCallback(ByVal Sender As Object)
        Dim CacheDepends As RssCacheDependency =
            CType(Sender, RssCacheDependency)
        Dim NewRSS As XmlDocument = RetrieveRSS(RSSUrl)
        If Not NewRSS.OuterXml = RSS.OuterXml Then
            CacheDepends.NotifyDependencyChanged(CacheDepends, EventArgs.Empty)
        End If
        End Sub

    Protected Overrides Sub DependencyDispose()
        backgroundThread = Nothing
        MyBase.DependencyDispose()
    End Sub

    Public ReadOnly Property Document() As XmlDocument
        Get
            Return RSS
        End Get
    End Property
End Class
```

C#

```
using System;
using System.Web;
using System.Threading;
using System.Web.Caching;
using System.Xml;

public class RssCacheDependency : CacheDependency
{
    Timer backgroundThread;
    int howOften = 900;
    XmlDocument RSS;
    string RSSUrl;

    public RssCacheDependency(string URL, int polling)
    {
        howOften = polling;
        RSSUrl = URL;
        RSS = RetrieveRSS(RSSUrl);

        if (backgroundThread == null)
        {
```

continues

LISTING 22-4 *(continued)*

```
                backgroundThread = new Timer(
                        new TimerCallback(CheckDependencyCallback),
                        this, (howOften * 1000), (howOften * 1000));
            }
        }

        public XmlDocument RetrieveRSS(string URL)
        {
            XmlDocument retVal = new XmlDocument();
            retVal.Load(URL);
            return retVal;
        }

        public void CheckDependencyCallback(object sender)
        {
            RssCacheDependency CacheDepends = sender as RssCacheDependency;
            XmlDocument NewRSS = RetrieveRSS(RSSUrl);
            if (NewRSS.OuterXml != RSS.OuterXml)
            {
                CacheDepends.NotifyDependencyChanged(CacheDepends, EventArgs.Empty);
            }
        }

        override protected void DependencyDispose()
        {
            backgroundThread = null;
            base.DependencyDispose();
        }

        public XmlDocument Document
        {
            get
            {
                return RSS;
            }
        }
    }
```

Create a new Web site and put the `RssCacheDependency` class in the Code folder. Create a `Default.aspx` and drag two text boxes, a label, and a button onto the HTML Design view. Execute the Web site and enter an RSS URL for a blog (like mine at `http://feeds.feedburner.com/ScottHanselman`), and click the button. The program checks the `Cache` object using the URL itself as a key. If the `XmlDocument` containing RSS does not exist in the cache, a new `RssCacheDependency` is created with a 10-minute (600-second) timeout. The `XmlDocument` is then cached, and all future requests within the next 10 minutes to this page retrieve the RSS `XmlDocument` from the cache.

Next, your new `RssCacheDependency` class from Listing 22-4 is illustrated in the following fragment. The `RssCacheDependency` is created and passed into the call to `Cache.Insert()`. The `Cache` object handles the lifetime and calling of the methods of the `RssCacheDependency` instance:

VB

```
<%@ Page Language="VB" ValidateRequest="false" %>

<html>
<head runat="server">
    <title>Custom Cache Dependency Example</title>
</head>
<body>
    <form runat="server"> RSS URL:
        <asp:TextBox ID="TextBox1" Runat="server"/>
        <asp:Button ID="Button1" onclick="Button1_Click" Runat="server"
```

```
            Text="Get RSS" />
            Cached:<asp:Label ID="Label2" Runat="server"></asp:Label><br />
            RSS:<br />
            <asp:TextBox ID="TextBox2" Runat="server" TextMode="MultiLine"
             Width="800px" Height="300px"></asp:TextBox>
        </form>
    </body>
    </html>

    <script runat="server">
        Sub Button1_Click(ByVal sender As Object, ByVal e As System.EventArgs)
            Dim RSSUrl As String = TextBox1.Text
            Label2.Text = "Loaded From Cache"
            If Cache(TextBox1.Text) Is Nothing Then
                Label2.Text = "Loaded Fresh"
                Dim itDepends As New RssCacheDependency(RSSUrl, 600)
                Cache.Insert(RSSUrl, itDepends.Document, itDepends)
            End If
            TextBox2.Text = CType(Cache(TextBox1.Text),
                System.Xml.XmlDocument).OuterXml
        End Sub
    </script>
```

C#

```
    <%@ Page Language="C#" ValidateRequest="false" %>
    <script runat="server">
        void Button1_Click(object sender, System.EventArgs e)
        {
            string RSSUrl = TextBox1.Text;
            Label2.Text = "Loaded From Cache";
            if (Cache[TextBox1.Text] == null)
            {
                Label2.Text = "Loaded Fresh";
                RssCacheDependency itDepends = new RssCacheDependency(RSSUrl, 600);
                Cache.Insert(RSSUrl, itDepends.Document, itDepends);
            }
            TextBox2.Text = ((System.Xml.XmlDocument)Cache[TextBox1.Text]).OuterXml;
        }
    </script>
```

The `RssCacheDependency` class creates a `Timer` background thread to poll for changes in the RSS feed. If it detects changes, the `RssCacheDependency` notifies the caching subsystem with the `NotifyDependencyChanged` event. The cached value with that key clears, and the next page view forces a reload of the requested RSS from the specified feed.

.NET 4's New Object Caching Option

From what you have seen so far with the `System.Web.Caching.Cache` object, you can see that it is quite powerful and allows for you to even create a custom cache. This extensibility and power has changed under the hood of the `Cache` object, though.

Driving this is the `System.Runtime.Caching.dll`, as what was in the `System.Web` version has been refactored out and everything was rebuilt into the new namespace of `System.Runtime.Caching`.

The reason for this change wasn't so much for the ASP.NET developer, but instead for other application types such as Windows Forms, Windows Presentation Foundation apps, and more. The reason for this is that the `System.Web.Caching.Cache` object was so useful that other application developers were bringing over the `System.Web` namespace into their projects to make use of this object. So, to get away from a Windows Forms developer needing to bring the `System.Web.dll` into their project just to use the `Cache` object it provided, this was all extracted out and extended with the `System.Runtime.Caching` namespace.

As an ASP.NET developer, you can still make use of the `System.Web.Caching.Cache` object just as you did in all the prior versions of ASP.NET. It isn't going away. However, it is important to note that as the .NET Framework evolves, the .NET team will be making its investments into the `System.Runtime.Caching` namespace rather than `System.Web.Caching`. This means that over time, you will most likely see additional enhancements in the `System.Runtime.Caching` version that don't appear in the `System.Web.Caching` namespace as you might expect. With that said, it doesn't also mean that you need to move everything over to the new `System.Runtime.Caching` namespace to make sure you are following the strategic path of Microsoft, because the two caches are managed together under the covers.

This section runs through an example of using the cache from the `System.Runtime.Caching` namespace. For this example, the ASP.NET page simply uses a Label control that shows the name of a user that is stored in an XML file. The first step is to create an XML file and name the file `Username.xml`. This simple file is presented here in Listing 22-5.

Available for download on Wrox.com

LISTING 22-5: The contents of the Username.xml file

```
<?xml version="1.0" encoding="utf-8" ?>
<usernames>
  <user>Bill Evjen</user>
</usernames>
```

With this XML file sitting in the root of your drive, now turn your attention to the `Default.aspx` code behind page to use the name in the file and present it into a single Label control on the page. The code behind for the Default.aspx page is presented here in Listing 22-6.

Available for download on Wrox.com

LISTING 22-6: Using the System.Runtime.Caching namespace

VB

```
Imports System
Imports System.Collections.Generic
Imports System.Linq
Imports System.Runtime.Caching
Imports System.Xml.Linq

Partial Public Class _Default
    Inherits System.Web.UI.Page

    Protected Sub Page_Load(ByVal sender As Object,
      ByVal e As EventArgs) Handles Me.Load

        Dim cache As ObjectCache = MemoryCache.Default

        Dim usernameFromXml As String =
          TryCast(cache("userFromXml"), String)

        If usernameFromXml Is Nothing Then
            Dim userFilePath As New List(Of String)()
            userFilePath.Add("C:\Username.xml")

            Dim policy As New CacheItemPolicy()
            policy.ChangeMonitors.Add(New
              HostFileChangeMonitor(userFilePath))

            Dim xdoc As XDocument =
              XDocument.Load("C:\Username.xml")
            Dim query = From u In xdoc.Elements("usernames")
                Select u.Value

            usernameFromXml = query.First().ToString()

            cache.Set("userFromXml", usernameFromXml, policy)
```

```
        End If

        Label1.Text = usernameFromXml
    End Sub
End Class
```

C#

```
using System;
using System.Collections.Generic;
using System.Linq;
using System.Runtime.Caching;
using System.Xml.Linq;

namespace RuntimeCaching
{
    public partial class Default : System.Web.UI.Page
    {
        protected void Page_Load(object sender, EventArgs e)
        {
            ObjectCache cache = MemoryCache.Default;

            string usernameFromXml = cache["userFromXml"] as string;

            if (usernameFromXml == null)
            {
                List<string> userFilePath = new List<string>();
                userFilePath.Add(@"C:\Username.xml");

                CacheItemPolicy policy = new CacheItemPolicy();
                policy.ChangeMonitors.Add(new
                   HostFileChangeMonitor(userFilePath));

                XDocument xdoc = XDocument.Load(@"C:\Username.xml");
                var query = from u in xdoc.Elements("usernames")
                            select u.Value;

                usernameFromXml = query.First().ToString();

                cache.Set("userFromXml", usernameFromXml, policy);
            }

            Label1.Text = usernameFromXml;
        }
    }
}
```

This example from Listing 22-6 makes use of the new cache at `System.Runtime.Caching`. You need to reference this namespace in your ASP.NET project for this to work.

To start, you create a default instance of the cache object.

```
ObjectCache cache = MemoryCache.Default;
```

You then can work with this cache as you would with the traditional ASP.NET cache object.

```
string usernameFromXml = cache["userFromXml"] as string;
```

To get the cache started, you need to create an object that defines what type of cache you are dealing with. You can build a custom implementation, or you can use one of the default implementations provided with .NET 4.

```
CacheItemPolicy policy = new CacheItemPolicy();
policy.ChangeMonitors.Add(new HostFileChangeMonitor(userFilePath));
```

The `HostFileChangeMonitor` is a means to look at directories and file paths and monitor for change. So, for instance, when the XML file changes, that triggers an invalidation of the cache. Other implementations of the `ChangeMonitor` object include the `FileChangeMonitor` and the `SqlChangeMonitor`.

Running this example, notice that the text *Bill Evjen* is loaded into the cache on the first run, and this text appears in the Label1 control. Keep your application running and then you can go back to the XML file and change the value, and you will then notice that this causes the cache to be invalidated on the page's refresh.

USING THE SQL SERVER CACHE DEPENDENCY

To utilize the SQL Server Cache Dependency feature in ASP.NET, you must perform a one-time setup of your SQL Server database. To set up your SQL Server, use the `aspnet_regsql.exe` tool found at `C:\Windows\MicroSoft.NET\Framework\v4.0.xxxxx\`. This tool makes the necessary modifications to SQL Server so that you can start working with the SQL cache invalidation features.

Follow these steps when using the SQL Server Cache Dependency features:

1. Enable your database for SQL Cache Dependency support.
2. Enable a table or tables for SQL Cache Dependency support.
3. Include SQL connection string details in the ASP.NET application's `web.config` file.
4. Utilize the SQL Cache Dependency features in one of the following ways:
    - Programmatically create a `SqlCacheDependency` object in code.
    - Add a `SqlDependency` attribute to an `OutputCache` directive.
    - Add a `SqlCacheDependency` instance to the `Response` object via `Response.AddCacheDependency`.

This section explains all the steps required and the operations available to you.

To start, you need to get at the `aspnet_regsql.exe` tool. Open the Visual Studio Command Prompt by choosing Start ➪ All Programs ➪ Microsoft Visual Studio 2010 ➪ Visual Studio Tools ➪ Visual Studio Command Prompt (2010) from the Windows Start menu. After the prompt launches, type this command:

```
aspnet_regsql.exe -?
```

This code outputs the help command list for this command-line tool, as shown in the following:

```
                        -- SQL CACHE DEPENDENCY OPTIONS --

-d <database>           Database name for use with SQL cache dependency. The
                         database can optionally be specified using the
                         connection string with the -c option instead.
                         (Required)

-ed                     Enable a database for SQL cache dependency.

-dd                     Disable a database for SQL cache dependency.

-et                     Enable a table for SQL cache dependency. Requires -t
                        option.

-dt                     Disable a table for SQL cache dependency. Requires -t
                        option.

-t <table>              Name of the table to enable or disable for SQL cache
                        dependency. Requires -et or -dt option.

-lt                     List all tables enabled for SQL cache dependency.
```

The following sections show you how to use some of these commands.

Enabling Databases for SQL Server Cache Invalidation

To use SQL Server cache invalidation with a SQL Server database, begin with two steps. The first step enables the appropriate database. In the second step, you enable the tables that you want to work with. You must perform both steps for this process to work. If you want to enable your databases for SQL cache invalidation and you are working on the computer where the SQL Server instance is located, you can use the following construct. If your SQL instance is on another computer, change `localhost` in this example to the name of the remote machine.

```
aspnet_regsql.exe -S localhost -U sa -P password -d Northwind-ed
```

This produces something similar to the following output:

```
Enabling the database for SQL cache dependency.
..
Finished.
```

From this command prompt, you can see that you simply enabled the Northwind database (a sample database for SQL Server) for SQL cache invalidation. The name of the SQL machine was passed in with `-S`, the username with `-U`, the database with `-d`, and most importantly, the command to enable SQL cache invalidation was `-ed`.

Please refer to Chapter 8 on how to download the sample Northwind database.

Now that you have enabled the database for SQL cache invalidation, you can enable one or more tables contained within the Northwind database.

Enabling Tables for SQL Server Cache Invalidation

You enable more tables by using the following command:

```
aspnet_regsql.exe -S localhost -U sa -P password -d Northwind -t Customers-et

aspnet_regsql.exe -S localhost -U sa -P password -d Northwind -t Products-et
```

You can see that this command is not much different from the one for enabling the database, except for the extra `-t Customers` entry and the use of `-et` to enable the table rather than `-ed` to enable a database. `Customers` is the name of the table that is enabled in this case.

Go ahead and enable both the Customers and Product tables. You run the command once per table. After a table is successfully enabled, you receive the following response:

```
Enabling the table for SQL cache dependency.
.
Finished.
```

After the table is enabled, you can begin using the SQL cache invalidation features. However, before you do, the following section shows you what happens to SQL Server 2000 when you enable these features. This is followed by a section that looks at SQL cache invalidation in SQL Server 2005 and 2008.

Looking at SQL Server 2000

Now that the Northwind database and the Customers and Products tables have all been enabled for SQL cache invalidation, look at what has happened in SQL Server. If you open the SQL Server Enterprise Manager, you see a new table contained within the Northwind database — `AspNet_SqlCacheTablesForChangeNotification` (whew, that's a long one!). Your screen should look like Figure 22-4. Note that SQL Server 2000 is not supported on Windows 7, so this screenshot is of a *remote* SQL 2000 machine viewed from the SQL Management Studio running on Windows 7.

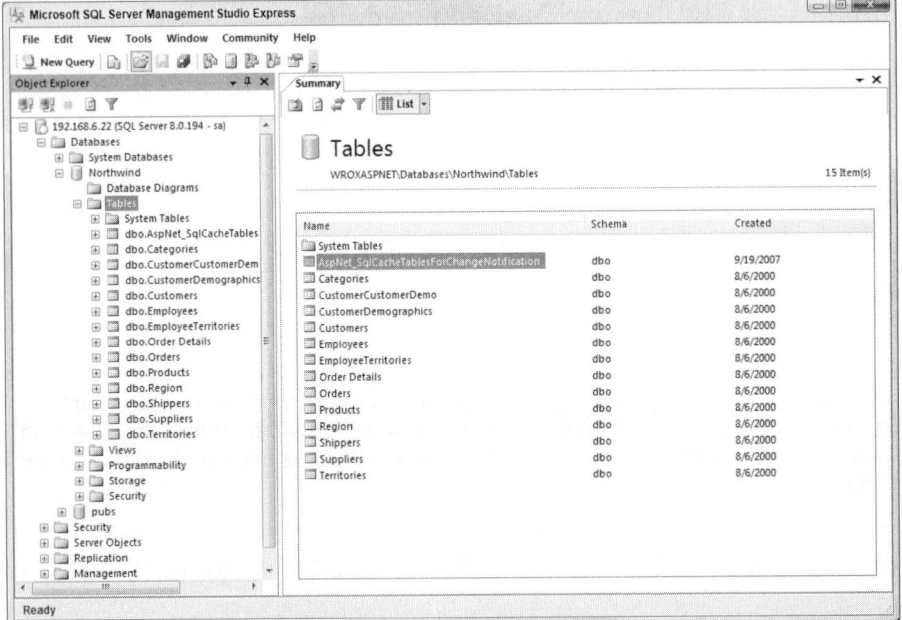

FIGURE 22-4

At the top of the list of tables in the right pane, you see the `AspNet_SqlCacheTablesForChangeNotification` table. ASP.NET uses this table to learn which tables are being monitored for change notification and also to make note of any changes to the tables being monitored. The table is actually quite simple when you look at the details, as illustrated in Figure 22-5.

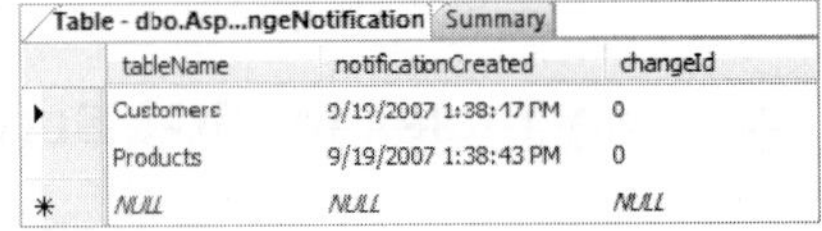

Table - dbo.Asp...ngeNotification | Summary

	tableName	notificationCreated	changeId
▸	Customers	9/19/2007 1:38:17 PM	0
	Products	9/19/2007 1:38:43 PM	0
*	NULL	NULL	NULL

FIGURE 22-5

In this figure, you can see three columns in this new table. The first is the `tableName` column. This column simply shows a `String` reference to the names of the tables contained in the same database. Any table named here is enabled for SQL cache invalidation.

The second column, `notificationCreated`, shows the date and time when the table was enabled for SQL cache invalidation. The final column, `changeId`, is used to communicate to ASP.NET any changes to the included tables. ASP.NET monitors this column for changes and, depending on the value, either uses what is stored in memory or makes a new database query.

Looking at the Tables That Are Enabled

Using the `aspnet_regsql.exe` tool, you can see (by using a simple command) which tables are enabled in a particular database. If you are working through the preceding examples, you see that so far you have enabled the Customers and Products tables of the Northwind database. To get a list of the tables that are enabled, use something similar to the following command:

```
aspnet_regsql.exe -S localhost -U sa -P password -d Northwind -lt
```

The `-lt` command produces a simple list of tables enabled for SQL cache invalidation. Inputting this command produces the following results:

```
Listing all tables enabled for SQL cache dependency:
Customers
Products
```

Disabling a Table for SQL Server Cache Invalidation

Now that you know how to enable your SQL Server database for SQL Server cache invalidation, look at how you remove the capability for a specific table to be monitored for this process. To remove a table from the SQL Server cache invalidation process, you use the `-dt` command.

In the preceding example, using the `-lt` command showed that you have both the Customers and Products tables enabled. Next, you remove the Products table from the process using the following command:

```
aspnet_regsql.exe -S localhost -U sa -P password -d Northwind -t Products-dt
```

You can see that all you do is specify the name of the table using the `-t` command followed by a `-dt` command (disable table). The command line for disabling table caching will again list the tables that are enabled for SQL Server cache invalidation; this time, the Products table is not listed — instead, Customers, the only enabled table, is listed.

Disabling a Database for SQL Server Cache Invalidation

Not only can you pick and choose the tables that you want to remove from the process, but you can also disable the entire database for SQL Server cache invalidation. To disable an entire database, you use the `-dd` command (disable database).

Note that disabling an entire database for SQL Server cache invalidation also means that every single table contained within this database is also disabled.

This example shows the Northwind database being disabled on my computer:

```
C:\>aspnet_regsql -S localhost -U sa -P wrox -d Northwind -dd
Disabling the database for SQL cache dependency.
..
Finished.
```

To ensure that the table is no longer enabled for SQL Server cache invalidation, I attempted to list the tables that were enabled for cache invalidation using the `-lt` command. I received the following error:

```
C:\ >aspnet_regsql -S localhost -U sa -P wrox -d Northwind -lt
An error has happened. Details of the exception:
The database is not enabled for SQL cache notification. To enable a database for
SQL cache notification, please use SQLCacheDependencyAdmin.EnableNotifications
method, or the command line tool aspnet_regsql.exe.
```

If you now open the Northwind database in the SQL Server Enterprise Manager, you can see that the `AspNet_SqlCacheTablesForChangeNotification` table has been removed for the database.

SQL Server 2005 and 2008 Cache Invalidation

As you have seen, standard SQL Server 2000 cache invalidation uses a table-level mechanism using a polling model every few seconds to monitor what tables have changed. SQL Server 2000's technique not only requires preparation of the database, its polling is rather expensive, and its caching is quite coarse.

SQL Server 2005 and 2008 support a different, more granular series of notification that doesn't require polling. Direct notification of changes is a built-in feature of these versions of SQL Server and is presented via the ADO.NET `SqlCommand`. For example:

```
Protected Sub Page_Load(ByVal sender as Object, ByVal e as System.EventArgs)

    Response.Write("Page created: " + DateTime.Now.ToLongTimeString())
```

```
    Dim connStr As String =
      ConfigurationManager.ConnectionStrings("AppConnectionString1").ConnectionString
    SqlDependency.Start(connStr)
    Dim connection As New SqlConnection(connStr)
    Dim command as New SqlCommand("Select * FROM Customers", connection)

    Dim depends as New SqlCacheDependency(command)

    Connection.Open
    GridView1.DataSource = command.ExecuteReader()
    GridView1.DataBind()

    Connection.Close

     "Now, do what you want with the sqlDependency object like:
    Response.AddCacheDependency(depends)

End Sub
```

SQL Server 2005 and 2008 supports both programmatic and declarative techniques when caching. Use the string "CommandNotification" in the OutputCache directive to enable notification-based caching for a page as in this example. You can specify SQL caching options either programmatically or declaratively, but not both. Note that you must first call System.Data.SqlClient.SqlDependency.Start, passing in the connection string, to start the SQL notification engine.

```
<%@ OutputCache Duration="3600" VaryByParam="none"
    SqlDependency="CommandNotification"%>
```

Alternatively, if you're using a SqlDataSource control from within your ASP.NET page, you would do the following:

```
<asp:SqlDataSource EnableCaching="true" SqlCacheDependency="CommandNotification"
    CacheDuration="2600" />
```

As data changes within SQL Server 2005 and 2008, SQL and ADO.NET automatically invalidate data cached on the Web server.

CONFIGURING YOUR ASP.NET APPLICATION

After you enable a database for SQL Server cache invalidation and enable a couple of tables within this database, the next step is to configure your application for SQL Server cache invalidation.

To configure your application to work with SQL Server cache invalidation, the first step is to make some changes to the web.config file. In the web.config file, specify that you want to work with the Northwind database, and you want ASP.NET connected to it.

Listing 22-7 shows an example of how you should change your web.config file to work with SQL Server cache invalidation. The pollTime attribute is not needed if you are using SQL Server 2005 or 2008 notification because it uses database events instead of the polling needed for earlier versions.

LISTING 22-7: Configuring the web.config file

Available for download on Wrox.com

```
<configuration xmlns="http://schemas.microsoft.com/.NetConfiguration/v2.0">

   <connectionStrings>
      <add name="AppConnectionString1" connectionString="Data Source=localhost;
        User ID=sa;Password=wrox;Database=Northwind;Persist Security Info=False"
        providerName="System.Data.SqlClient" />
```

```
    </connectionStrings>

    <system.web>

      <caching>
        <sqlCacheDependency enabled="true">
          <databases>
            <add name="Northwind" connectionStringName="AppConnectionString1"
             pollTime="500" />
          </databases>
        </sqlCacheDependency>
      </caching>

    </system.web>
  </configuration>
```

From this listing, you can see that the first thing established is the connection string to the Northwind database using the `<connectionStrings>` element in the `web.config` file. Note the name of the connection string because it is utilized later in the configuration settings for SQL Server cache invalidation.

The SQL Server cache invalidation is configured using the `<caching>` element. This element must be nested within the `<system.web>` elements. Because you are working with a SQL Server cache dependency, you must use a `<sqlCacheDependency>` child node. You enable the entire process by using the `enabled="true"` attribute. After this attribute is enabled, you work with the `<databases>` section. You use the `<add>` element, nested within the `<databases>` nodes, to reference the Northwind database. Table 22-1 explains all the attributes of the `<add>` element.

TABLE 22-1

ATTRIBUTE	DESCRIPTION
`name`	The `name` attribute provides an identifier to the SQL Server database.
`connectionStringName`	The `connectionStringName` attribute specifies the name of the connection. Because the connection string in the preceding example is called `AppConnectionString1`, you use this value for the `connectionStringName` attribute as well.
`pollTime`	The `pollTime` attribute specifies the time interval from one SQL Server poll to the next. The default is .5 seconds or 500 milliseconds (as shown in the example). This is not needed for SQL Server 2005 and 2008 notification.

Now that the `web.config` file is set up correctly, you can start using SQL Server cache invalidation on your pages. ASP.NET makes a separate SQL Server request on a completely different thread to the `AspNet_SqlCacheTablesForChangeNotification` table to see whether the `changeId` number has been incremented. If the number is changed, ASP.NET knows that an underlying change has been made to the SQL Server table and that a new result set should be retrieved. When it checks to see whether it should make a SQL Server call, the request to the small `AspNet_SqlCacheTablesForChangeNotification` table has a single result. With SQL Server cache invalidation enabled, this is done so quickly that you really notice the difference.

TESTING SQL SERVER CACHE INVALIDATION

Now that the `web.config` file is set up and ready to go, the next step is to actually apply these capabilities to a page. Listing 22-8 is an example of a page using the SQL Server cache invalidation process.

LISTING 22-8: An ASP.NET page utilizing SQL Server cache invalidation

Available for download on Wrox.com

VB

```
<%@ Page Language="VB" %>
<%@ OutputCache Duration="3600" VaryByParam="none"
    SqlDependency="Northwind:Customers"%>

<script runat="server">
    Protected Sub Page_Load(ByVal sender As Object, ByVal e As System.EventArgs)
        Label1.Text = "Page created at " & DateTime.Now.ToShortTimeString ()
    End Sub
</script>

<html xmlns="http://www.w3.org/1999/xhtml" >
<head runat="server">
    <title>Sql Cache Invalidation</title>
</head>
<body>
    <form id="form1" runat="server">
        <asp:Label ID="Label1" Runat="server"></asp:Label><br />
        <br />
        <asp:GridView ID="GridView1" Runat="server" DataSourceID="SqlDataSource1">
        </asp:GridView>
        <asp:SqlDataSource ID="SqlDataSource1" Runat="server"
         SelectCommand="Select * From Customers"
         ConnectionString="<%$ ConnectionStrings:AppConnectionString1 %>"
         ProviderName="<%$ ConnectionStrings:AppConnectionString1.providername %>">
        </asp:SqlDataSource>
    </form>
</body>
</html>
```

C#

```
<%@ Page Language="C#" %>
<%@ OutputCache Duration="3600" VaryByParam="none"
    SqlDependency="Northwind:Customers"%>

<script runat="server">
    protected void Page_Load(object sender, System.EventArgs e)
    {
        Label1.Text = "Page created at " + DateTime.Now.ToShortTimeString();
    }
</script>
```

The first and most important part of this page is the `OutputCache` page directive that is specified at the top of the file. Typically, the `OutputCache` directive specifies how long the page output is held in the cache using the `Duration` attribute. Next is the `VaryByParam` attribute. An addition here is the `SqlDependency` attribute. This enables a particular page to use SQL Server cache invalidation. The following line shows the format of the value for the `SqlDependency` attribute:

```
SqlDependency="database:table"
```

The value of `Northwind:Customers` specifies that you want the SQL Server cache invalidation enabled for the Customers table within the Northwind database. The `Duration` attribute of the `OutputCache` directive shows you that, typically, the output of this page is stored in the cache for a long time — but this cache is invalidated immediately if the Customers table has any underlying changes made to the data that it contains.

A change to any of the cells in the Customers table of the Northwind database invalidates the cache, and a new cache is generated from the result, which now contains a new SQL Server database request. Figure 22-6 shows an example of the page generated the first time it is run.

Untitled Page - Windows Internet Explorer

http://localhost:58292/Listing22-08_app/Default.aspx

Page created: 2:22:43 PM

CustomerID	CompanyName	ContactName	ContactTitle	Address	City	Region	PostalC
ALFKI	Alfreds Futterkiste	Maria Anders	Sales Representative	Obere Str. 57	Berlin		12209
ANATR	Ana Trujillo Emparedados y helados	Ana Trujillo	Owner	Avda. de la Constitución 2222	México D.F.		05021
ANTON	Antonio Moreno Taqueria	Antonio Moreno	Owner	Mataderos 2312	México D.F.		05023
AROUT	Around the Horn	Thomas Hardy	Sales Representative	120 Hanover Sq.	London		WA1 1D
BERGS	Berglunds snabbköp	Christina Berglund	Order Administrator	Berguvsvägen 8	Luleå		S-958 22

Internet | Protected Mode: Off 100%

FIGURE 22-6

From this figure, you can see the contents of the customer with the `CustomerID` of `ALFKI`. For this entry, go to SQL Server and change the value of the `ContactName` from `Maria Anders` to `Mary Anders`. If you were not using SQL Server cache invalidation, this change would have done nothing to the output cache. The original page output in the cache would still be present and the end user would still see the `Maria Anders` entry for the duration specified in the page's `OutputCache` directive. However, because you are using SQL Server cache invalidation, after the underlying information in the table is changed, the output cache is invalidated, a new result set is retrieved, and the new result set is cached. When a change has been made, you see the results as shown in Figure 22-7.

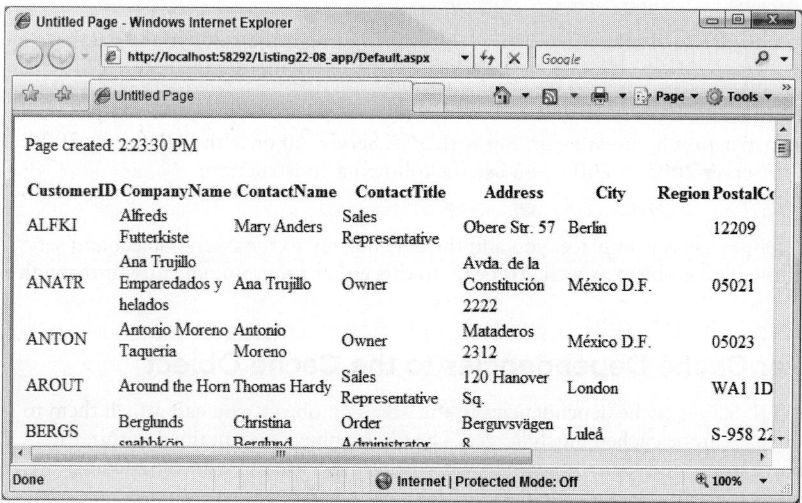

Untitled Page - Windows Internet Explorer

http://localhost:58292/Listing22-08_app/Default.aspx

Page created: 2:23:30 PM

CustomerID	CompanyName	ContactName	ContactTitle	Address	City	Region	PostalC
ALFKI	Alfreds Futterkiste	Mary Anders	Sales Representative	Obere Str. 57	Berlin		12209
ANATR	Ana Trujillo Emparedados y helados	Ana Trujillo	Owner	Avda. de la Constitución 2222	México D.F.		05021
ANTON	Antonio Moreno Taqueria	Antonio Moreno	Owner	Mataderos 2312	México D.F.		05023
AROUT	Around the Horn	Thomas Hardy	Sales Representative	120 Hanover Sq.	London		WA1 1D
BERGS	Berglunds snabbköp	Christina Berglund	Order Administrator	Berguvsvägen 8	Luleå		S-958 22

Done Internet | Protected Mode: Off 100%

FIGURE 22-7

Notice also that the text "Page created at" includes an updated time indicating when this page was rendered.

Adding More Than One Table to a Page

The preceding example shows how to use SQL Server cache invalidation for a single table on the ASP.NET page. What do you do if your page is working with two or more tables?

To add more than one table, you use the `OutputCache` directive shown here:

```
SqlDependency="database:table;database:table"
```

From this example, you can see that the value of the `SqlDependency` attribute separates the databases and tables with a semicolon. If you want to work with both the Customers table and the Products table of the Northwind database, you construct the value of the `SqlDependency` attribute as follows:

```
SqlDependency="Northwind:Customers;Northwind:Products"
```

Attaching SQL Server Cache Dependencies to the Request Object

In addition to changing settings in the `OutputCache` directive to activate SQL Server cache invalidation, you can also set the SQL Server cache invalidation programmatically. To do so, use the `SqlCacheDependency` class, which is illustrated in Listing 22-9.

LISTING 22-9: Working with SQL Server cache invalidation programmatically

Available for download on Wrox.com

VB

```
Dim myDependency As SqlCacheDependency =
   New SqlCacheDependency("Northwind", "Customers")
Response.AddCacheDependency(myDependency)
Response.Cache.SetValidUntilExpires(true)
Response.Cache.SetExpires(DateTime.Now.AddMinutes(60))
Response.Cache.SetCacheability(HttpCacheability.Public)
```

C#

```
SqlCacheDependency myDependency = new SqlCacheDependency("Northwind", "Customers");
Response.AddCacheDependency(myDependency);
Response.Cache.SetValidUntilExpires(true);
Response.Cache.SetExpires(DateTime.Now.AddMinutes(60));
Response.Cache.SetCacheability(HttpCacheability.Public);
```

You first create an instance of the `SqlCacheDependency` object, assigning it the value of the database and the table at the same time. The `SqlCacheDependency` class takes the following parameters:

```
SqlCacheDependency(databaseEntryName As String, tablename As String)
```

You use this parameter construction if you are working with SQL Server 7.0 or with SQL Server 2000. If you are working with SQL Server 2005 or 2008, you use the following construction:

```
SqlCacheDependency(sqlCmd As System.Data.SqlClient.SqlCommand)
```

After the `SqlCacheDependency` class is in place, you add the dependency to the `Cache` object and set some of the properties of the `Cache` object as well. You can do this either programmatically or through the `OutputCache` directive.

Attaching SQL Server Cache Dependencies to the Cache Object

In addition to attaching SQL Server cache dependencies to the `Request` object, you can attach them to the `Cache` object for data that can be cached much longer. The `Cache` object is contained within the `System.Web.Caching` namespace, and it enables you to work programmatically with the caching of any type of objects. Listing 22-10 shows a page that utilizes the `Cache` object with the `SqlDependency` object.

LISTING 22-10: Using the Cache object with the SqlDependency object

Available for download on Wrox.com

VB

```
<%@ Page Language="VB" %>
<%@ Import Namespace="System.Data"%>
<%@ Import Namespace="System.Data.SqlClient"%>

<script runat="server">
    Protected Sub Page_Load(ByVal sender As Object, ByVal e As System.EventArgs)
        Dim myCustomers As DataSet
        myCustomers = CType(Cache("firmCustomers"), DataSet)

        If myCustomers Is Nothing Then
           Dim conn As SqlConnection =
            New SqlConnection(
 ConfigurationManager.ConnectionStrings("AppConnectionString1").ConnectionString)
           Dim da As SqlDataAdapter =
            New SqlDataAdapter("Select * From Customers", conn)

           myCustomers = New DataSet
           da.Fill(myCustomers)

           Dim myDependency As SqlCacheDependency =
              New SqlCacheDependency("Northwind", "Customers")
           Cache.Insert("firmCustomers", myCustomers, myDependency)

           Label1.Text = "Produced from database."
        Else
           Label1.Text = "Produced from Cache object."
        End If

        GridView1.DataSource = myCustomers
        GridView1.DataBind()
    End Sub
</script>

<html xmlns="http://www.w3.org/1999/xhtml" >
<head runat="server">
    <title>Sql Cache Invalidation</title>
</head>
<body>
    <form id="form1" runat="server">
        <asp:Label ID="Label1" Runat="server"></asp:Label><br />
        <br />
        <asp:GridView ID="GridView1" Runat="server"></asp:GridView>
    </form>
</body>
</html>
```

C#

```
<%@ Page Language="C#" %>
<%@ Import Namespace="System.Data" %>
<%@ Import Namespace="System.Data.SqlClient" %>

<script runat="server">
    protected void Page_Load(object sender, System.EventArgs e)
    {
       DataSet myCustomers;
       myCustomers = (DataSet)Cache["firmCustomers"];

       if (myCustomers == null)
       {
```

continues

LISTING 22-10 *(continued)*

```
            SqlConnection conn = new
             SqlConnection(
   ConfigurationManager.ConnectionStrings["AppConnectionString1"].ConnectionString);
            SqlDataAdapter da = new
               SqlDataAdapter("Select * from Customers", conn);

            myCustomers = new DataSet();
            da.Fill(myCustomers);

            SqlCacheDependency myDependency = new
               SqlCacheDependency("Northwind", "Customers");
            Cache.Insert("firmCustomers", myCustomers, myDependency);

            Label1.Text = "Produced from database.";
          }
          else
          {
            Label1.Text = "Produced from Cache object.";
          }

          GridView1.DataSource = myCustomers;
          GridView1.DataBind();
    }
    </script>
```

In this example, the `SqlCacheDependency` class associated itself to the Customers table in the Northwind database as before. This time, however, you use the `Cache` object to insert the retrieved dataset along with a reference to the `SqlCacheDependency` object. The `Insert()` method of the `Cache` class is constructed as follows:

```
Cache.Insert(key As String, value As Object,
dependencies As System.Web.Caching.CacheDependency)
```

You can also insert more information about the dependency using the following construct:

```
Cache.Insert(key As String, value As Object,
dependencies As System.Web.Caching.CacheDependency
absoluteExpiration As Date, slidingExpiration As System.TimeSpan)
```

And finally:

```
Cache.Insert(key As String, value As Object,
dependencies As System.Web.Caching.CacheDependency
absoluteExpiration As Date, slidingExpiration As System.TimeSpan)
priority As System.Web.Caching.CacheItemPriority,
onRemoveCallback As System.Web.Caching.CacheItemRemovedCallback)
```

The SQL Server cache dependency created comes into action and does the same polling as it would have done otherwise. If any of the data in the Customers table has changed, the `SqlCacheDependency` class invalidates what is stored in the cache. When the next request is made, the `Cache("firmCustomers")` is found to be empty and a new request is made to SQL Server. The `Cache` object again repopulates the cache with the new results generated.

Figure 22-8 shows the results generated when the ASP.NET page from Listing 22-8 is called for the first time.

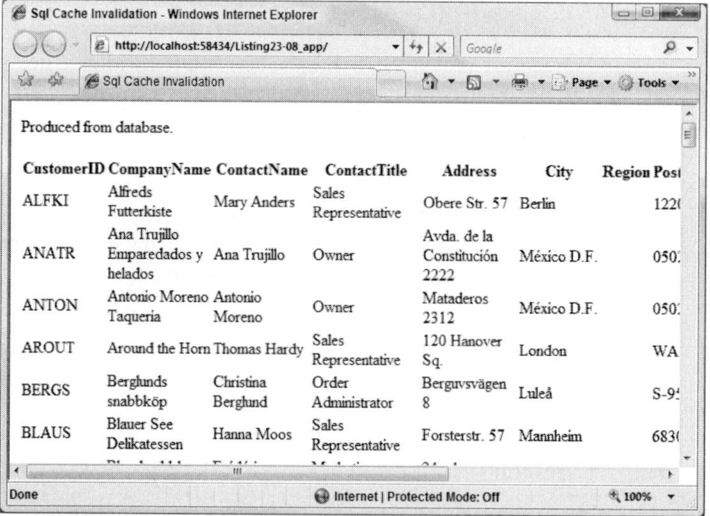

FIGURE 22-8

Because this is the first time that the page is generated, nothing is in the cache. The `Cache` object is then placed in the result set along with the association to the SQL Server cache dependency. Figure 22-9 shows the result for the second request. Notice that the HTML table is identical because it was generated from the identical `DataSet`, but the first line of the page has changed to indicate that this output was produced from cache.

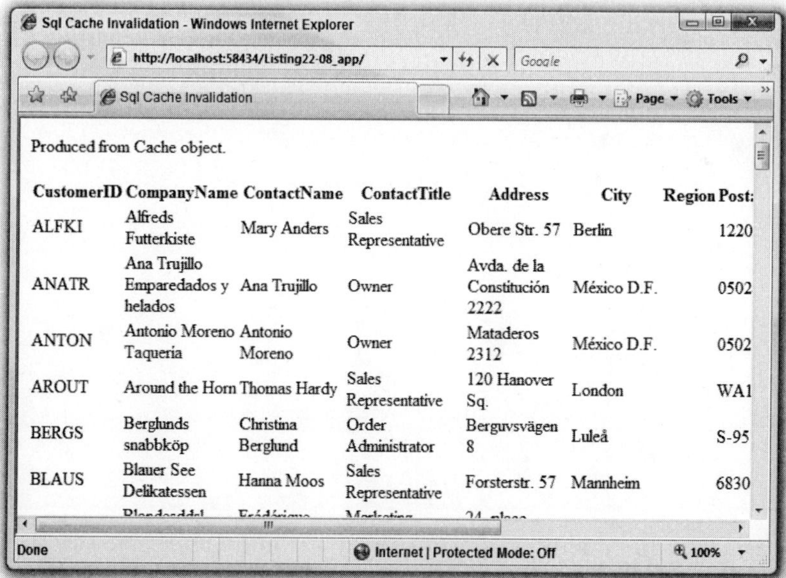

FIGURE 22-9

On the second request, the dataset is already contained within the cache; therefore, it is retrievable. You are not required to hit SQL Server to get the full results again. If any of the information has changed within SQL Server itself, however, the `Cache` object returns nothing; a new result set is retrieved.

SUMMARY

SQL Server cache invalidation is an outstanding feature of ASP.NET that enables you to invalidate items stored in the cache when underlying changes occur to the data in the tables being monitored. Post-Cache Substitution fills in an important gap in ASP.NET's technology, enabling you to have both the best highly dynamic content and a high-performance Web site with caching.

When you are monitoring changes to the database, you can configure these procedures easily in the `web.config` file, or you can work programmatically with cache invalidation directly in your code. These changes are possible because the `CacheDependency` object has been unsealed. You can now inherit from this object and create your own cache dependencies. The SQL Server cache invalidation process is the first example of this capability.

23

Debugging and Error Handling

WHAT'S IN THIS CHAPTER?

- Tracing your ASP.NET applications
- Exploring ASP.NET debugging options
- Handling exceptions and errors efficiently

Your code always runs exactly as you wrote it, and you will *never* get it right the first time. So, expect to spend about 30 percent of your time debugging, and to be a successful debugger, learn to use the available tools effectively. Visual Studio has upped the ante, giving you a host of features that greatly improve your debugging experience. Having so many features, however, can be overwhelming at first. This chapter breaks down all the techniques available to you, one at a time, while presenting a holistic view of Visual Studio, the Common Language Runtime (CLR), and the Base Class Library (BCL).

> *Everyone knows that debugging is twice as hard as writing a program in the first place. So if you're as clever as you can be when you write it, how will you ever debug it?*
>
> — Brian Kernigham

Additionally, because debugging is more than stepping through code, this chapter discusses efficient error and exception handling, tracing and logging, and cross-language (C#, Visual Basic, client-side JavaScript, XSLT, and SQL Stored Procedure) debugging.

DESIGN-TIME SUPPORT

Visual Studio has always done a good job of warning you of potential errors at design time. *Syntax notifications* or *squiggles* underline code that won't compile or that might cause an error before you have compiled the project. A *new error notification* pops up when an exception occurs during a debugging session and recommends a course of action that prevents the exception. At every step, Visual Studio tries to be smarter, anticipating your needs and catching common mistakes.

Rico Mariani, the Chief Architect of Visual Studio, has used the term "The Pit of Success" to describe the experience Microsoft wants you to have with Visual Studio. When Microsoft designed these features, it wanted the customer to simply fall into winning practices. The company tried to achieve this by making it more difficult for you to write buggy code or make common mistakes. Microsoft's developers put a great deal of thought into building APIs that point you in the right direction.

Syntax Notifications

Both the Visual Basic and C# editors show squiggles and tooltips for many syntax errors well before compilation, as illustrated in Figure 23-1.

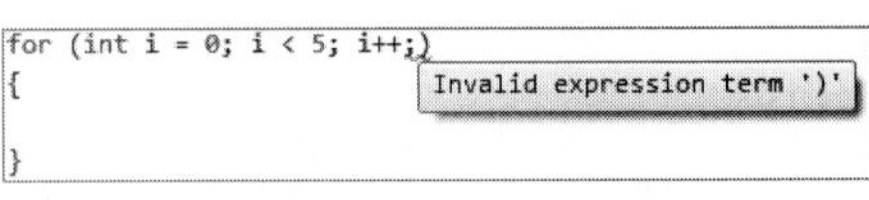
for (int i = 0; i < 5; i++;)
{
Invalid expression term ')'
}

FIGURE 23-1

Syntax notifications aren't just for CLR programming languages; Visual Studio works just as well through the XML Editor and includes capabilities like the following:

- Full XML 1.0 syntax checking
- Support for XSD and DTD validation and IntelliSense
- Support for XSLT 1.0 syntax checking

Figure 23-2 shows a detailed tooltip indicating that the element `<junk>` does not have any business being in the `web.config` file. The editor knows this because of a combination of the XSD validation support in the XML Editor and the addition of schemas for configuration files such as `web.config`. This change is welcome for anyone who, when manually editing a `web.config` file, has wondered whether he guessed the right elements. See Chapter 10 for more details on these XML-related features.

```
Web.config* ×
<?xml version="1.0"?>

<!--
  For more information on how to configure your ASP.NET application, please visit
  http://go.microsoft.com/fwlink/?LinkId=152368
  -->

<configuration>
  <connectionStrings>
    <junk></junk>
    < The element 'connectionStrings' has invalid child element 'junk'. List of possible
      elements expected: 'add, remove, clear'.                                     DataD
      providerName="System.Data.SqlClient" />
  </connectionStrings>
```

FIGURE 23-2

The ASPX/HTML Editor benefits from these capabilities as well; for example, Figure 23-3 shows a warning that the `<badElement/>` element is not available in the active schema. Code that appears in `<script runat="Server"/>` blocks in ASP.NET pages is also parsed and marked with squiggles. This makes including code in your pages considerably easier. Notice also that the ASP.NET page in Figure 23-3 has an XHTML DOCTYPE declaration on the first line, and the HTML element has a default XHTML namespace. This HTML page is treated as XML because XHTML has been targeted.

XHTML is the HTML vocabulary of markup expressed with all the syntax rules of XML. For example, in HTML you could create a `<br>` tag and never close it. In XHTML you use the closing tag `<br />`. XHTML documents look exactly like HTML documents because they are, in fact, expressing the same semantics. Because XHTML documents are XML, they require a namespace on their root element and should have a DOCTYPE as well.

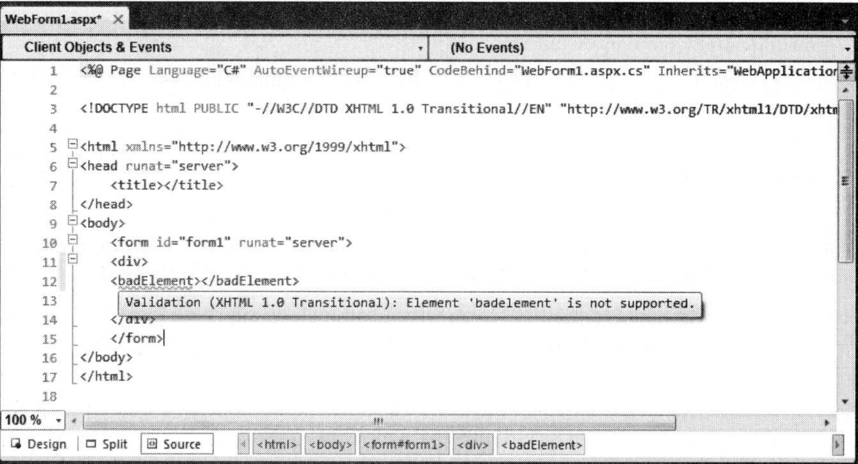

FIGURE 23-3

To add a `<badElement>` element, you must put it in its own namespace and add a namespace declaration in the root HTML element.

The Visual Basic Editor takes assistance to the next level with a *smart tag* like the pulldown/button that appears when you hover your mouse cursor over a squiggle. A very nicely rendered modeless window appears with your code in a box along with some suggested changes to make your code compile. Figure 23-4 shows a recommendation to insert a missing `End If`; making the correction is simple — just click `Insert the missing 'End If'`.

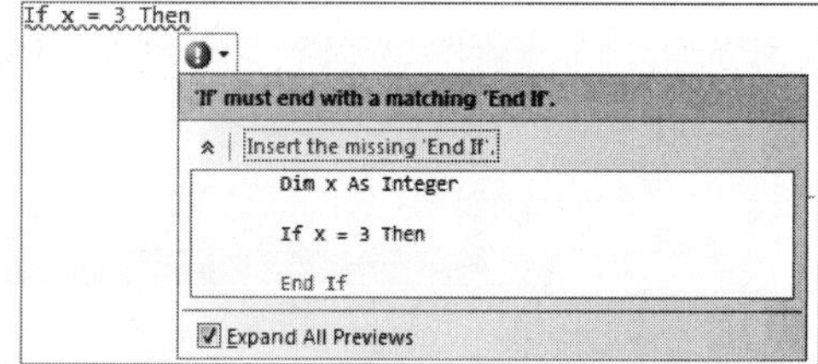

FIGURE 23-4

All these design-time features exist to help you ensure better code while it's being written, before it's been compiled and run. Two related features help you run arbitrary code within the development environment as well as organize the tasks still to be performed.

Immediate and Command Window

The Immediate window lets you run arbitrary bits of code in design mode without compiling your application. You can evaluate code at design time or while you are debugging. It can be a great way to test a line of code or a static method quickly. The Immediate mode of this window is used primarily for debugging.

Access the Immediate window from Debug ➪ Windows ➪ Immediate. To evaluate a variable or run a method, simply click in the Immediate window and type a question mark (?) followed by the expression, variable, or method you want to evaluate.

The Immediate window can also be switched into the Command window by prefacing commands with a greater-than sign (>). When you enter a greater-than sign in the Immediate or Command window, an IntelliSense drop-down appears exposing the complete Visual Studio object model as well as any macros that you may have recorded. Command mode of this window is used for executing Visual Studio commands without using the menus. You can also execute commands that may not have a menu item.

If you type `>alias` into the Command window, you receive a complete list of all current aliases and their definitions. Some useful command aliases include the following:

- `>Log filename /overwrite /on|off`: The `Log` command starts logging all output from the command window to a file. If no filename is included for logging, go to `cmdline.log`. This is one of the more useful and least-used features of the debugger, and reason enough to learn a few things about the Immediate and Command windows.

- `>Shell args /command /output /dir:folder`: The `Shell` command allows you to launch executable programs from within the Visual Studio Command window such as utilities, command shells, batch files, and so on.

Task List

The Task list in Visual Studio is more useful than you might think. People who have not given it much attention are missing out on a great feature. The Task list supports two views: User Tasks and Comments.

The User Tasks view enables you to add and modify tasks, which can include anything from "Remember to Test" to "Buy Milk." These tasks are stored in the `.suo` (solution user options) that is a parallel partner to the `.sln` files.

The Comments view shows text from the comments in your code where those lines are prefixed with a specific token. Visual Studio comes configured to look for the `TODO:` token, but you can add your own in Tools ➪ Options ➪ Environment ➪ Task List.

In Figure 23-5, the comment token `HACK` has been added in the Options dialog box. A comment appears in the source with `HACK:` preceding it, so that comment line automatically appears in the Task List in the docked window at the bottom of Visual Studio. The three circles in Figure 23-5 illustrate the connection between the word `HACK` added to the Options dialog box and its subsequent appearance in the source code and Task List. You and your team can add as many of these tokens as you want.

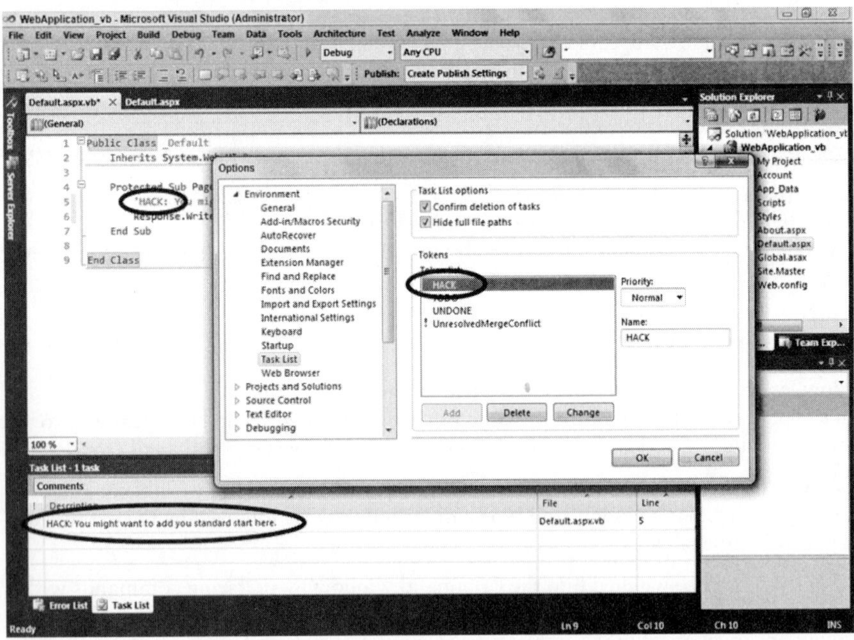

FIGURE 23-5

TRACING

Tracing is a way to monitor the execution of your ASP.NET application. You can record exception details and program flow in a way that does not affect the program's output. In classic ASP, tracing and debugging facilities were nearly nonexistent, forcing developers to use "got here" debugging in the form of many

Response.Write statements that litter the resulting HTML with informal trace statements announcing to the programmer that the program "got here" and "got there" with each new line executed. This kind of intrusive tracing was very inconvenient to clean up and many programmers ended up creating their own informal trace libraries to get around these classic ASP limitations.

In ASP.NET, there is rich support for tracing. The destination for trace output can be configured with TraceListeners such as the EventLogTraceListener. Configuration of TraceListeners is covered later in this section. ASP.NET allows for trace forwarding between the ASP.NET page-specific Trace class and the standard Base Class Library's (BCL) System.Diagnostics.Trace used by non-Web developers. Additionally, the resolution of the timing output by ASP.NET tracing has a precision of 18 digits for highly accurate profiling.

System.Diagnostics.Trace and ASP.NET's Page.Trace

Multiple things are named *Trace* in the whole of the .NET Framework, so it may appear that tracing isn't unified between Web and non-Web applications. Don't be confused because there is a class called System.Diagnostics.Trace and there is also a public property on System.Web.UI.Page called Trace. The Trace property on the Page class gives you access to the System.Web.TraceContext and the ASP.NET-specific tracing mechanism. The TraceContext class collects all the details and timing of a Web request. It contains a number of methods, but the one you will use the most is Write. It also includes Warn, which simply calls Write(), and also ensures that the output generated by Warn is colored red.

If you're writing an ASP.NET application that has no supporting components or other assemblies that may be used in a non-Web context, you can usually get a great deal of utility using only the ASP.NET TraceContext. However, ASP.NET support tracing is different from the rest of the base class library's tracing. You will explore ASP.NET's tracing facilities first, and then learn how to bridge the gap and see some features that make debugging even easier.

Page-Level Tracing

ASP.NET tracing can be enabled on a page-by-page basis by adding Trace="true" to the Page directive in any ASP.NET page:

```
<%@ Page Language="C#" Inherits="System.Web.UI.Page" Trace="true" %>
```

Additionally, you can add the TraceMode attribute that sets SortByCategory or the default, SortByTime. You might include a number of categories, one per subsystem, and use SortByCategory to group them, or you might use SortByTime to see the methods that take up the most CPU time for your application. You can enable tracing programmatically as well, using the Trace.IsEnabled property. The capability to enable tracing programmatically means you can enable tracing via a querystring, cookie, or IP address; it's up to you.

Application Tracing

Alternatively, you can enable tracing for the entire application by adding tracing settings in the web.config file. In the following example, pageOutput="false" and requestLimit="20" are used, so trace information is stored for 20 requests, but not displayed on the page:

```
<configuration>
   <system.web>
       <trace enabled="true" pageOutput="false" requestLimit="20"
           traceMode="SortByTime" localOnly="true" />
   </system.web>
</configuration>
```

The page-level settings take precedence over settings in the web.config file, so if enabled="false" is set in the web.config file but trace="true" is set on the page, tracing occurs.

Viewing Trace Data

Tracing can be viewed for multiple page requests at the application level by requesting a special page (of sorts) called `trace.axd`. Note that `trace.axd` doesn't actually exist; it is actually provided by `System.Web.Handlers.TraceHandler`, a special `IHttpHandler` to which `trace.axd` is bound. When ASP.NET detects an HTTP request for `trace.axd`, that request is handled by the `TraceHandler` rather than by a page.

Create a Web site and a page, and in the `Page_Load` event, call `Trace.Write()`. Enable tracing in the `web.config` file as shown in Listing 23-1.

LISTING 23-1: Tracing using Page.Trace

Available for download on Wrox.com

Web.config

```
<configuration>
   <system.web>
       <trace enabled="true" pageOutput="true" />
   </system.web>
</configuration>
```

VB

```
Protected Sub Page_Load(ByVal sender As Object,
  ByVal e As System.EventArgs)
   Handles Me.Load'All on one line!
       Trace.Write("This message is from the START OF the Page_Load method!")
End Sub
```

C#

```
protected void Page_Load(object sender, EventArgs e)
{
   Trace.Write("This message is from the START of the Page_Load method!");
}
```

Open the page in the browser a few times and notice that, although this page doesn't create any HTML to speak of, a great deal of trace information is presented in the browser, as shown in Figure 23-6, because the setting is `pageOutput="true"`.

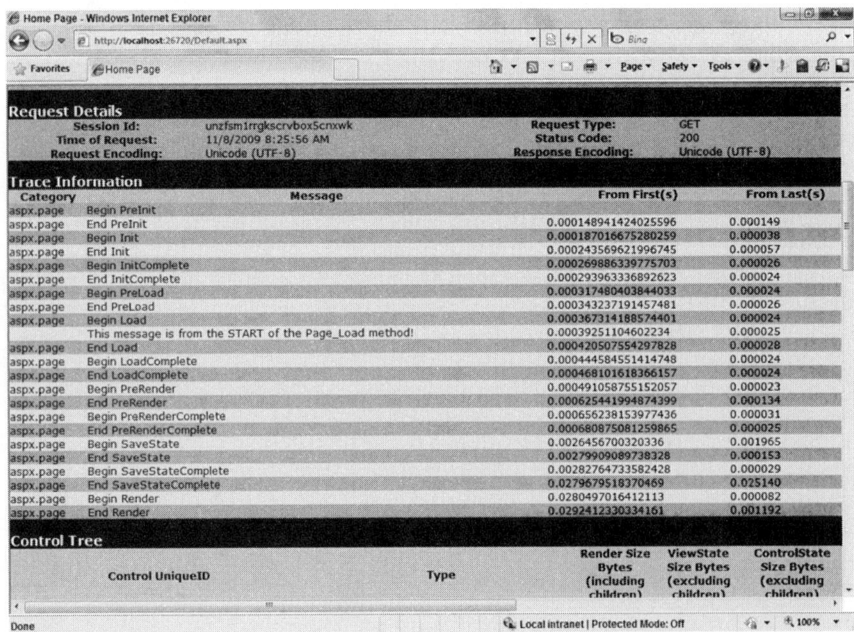

FIGURE 23-6

The message from `Trace.Write` appears after `Begin Load` and before `End Load` — it's right in the middle of the `Page_Load` method where you put it. The page was automatically JIT-compiled as you ran it, and that initial performance hit is over. Now that it's been compiled into native code, a subsequent run of this same page, performed by clicking Refresh in the browser, took only 0.000167 seconds on my laptop because the page had already compiled. Collecting this kind of very valuable performance timing data between trace statements is very easy and extremely useful.

Incidentally, this simple page is more than 100 times faster than when the first edition of this book was written in 2004. Both computers and the Just-In-Time compilation process (JITter) continue to improve!

Eleven different sections of tracing information provide a great deal of detail and specific insight into the ASP.NET page-rendering process, as described in Table 23-1.

TABLE 23-1

SECTION	DESCRIPTION
Request Details	Includes the ASP.NET session ID, the character encoding of the request and response, and the HTTP conversation's returned status code. Be aware of the request and response encoding, especially if you are using any non-Latin character sets. If you are returning languages other than English, you'll want your encoding to be UTF-8. Fortunately, that is the default.
Trace Information	Includes all the `Trace.Write` methods called during the lifetime of the HTTP request and a great deal of information about timing. This is probably the most useful section for debugging. The timing information located here is valuable when profiling and searching for methods in your application that take too long to execute.
Control Tree	Presents an HTML representation of the ASP.NET Control Tree. Shows each control's unique ID, runtime type, the number of bytes it took to be rendered, and the bytes it requires in ViewState and ControlState. Do not undervalue the usefulness of these two sections, particularly of the three columns showing the weight of each control. The weight of the control indicates the number of bytes occupied in ViewState and/or ControlState by that particular control. Be aware of the number of bytes that each of your controls uses, especially if you write your own custom controls, as you want your controls to return as few bytes as possible to keep overall page weight down.
Session State	Lists all the keys for a particular user's session, their types, and their values. Shows only the current user's session state.
Application State	Lists all the keys in the current application's `Application` object and their types and values.
Request Cookies	Lists all the cookies passed in during the page's request.
Response Cookies	Lists all the cookies that were passed back during the page's response.
Headers Collection	Shows all the headers that might be passed in during the request from the browser, including `Accept-Encoding`, indicating whether the browser supports compressed HTTP responses; `Accept-Languages`, a list of ISO language codes that indicate the order of the user's language preferences; and `User-Agent`, the identifying string for the user's browser. The string also contains information about the user's operating system and the version or versions of the .NET Framework he is running (on IE).
Form Collection	Displays a complete dump of the Form collection and all its keys and values.
Querystring Collection	Displays a dump of the Querystring collection and all its contained keys and values.
Server Variables	A complete dump of name-value pairs of everything that the Web server knows about the application and the requesting browser.

Page output of tracing shows only the data collected for the current page request. However, when visiting `http://localhost/yoursite/trace.axd` you will see detailed data collected for all requests to the site thus far. If you're using the built-in ASP.NET Development Server, remove the current page from the URL and replace it with `trace.axd`. Do not change the automatically selected port or path.

Again, `trace.axd` is an internal handler, not a real page. When it's requested from a local browser, as shown in Figure 23-7, it displays all tracing information for all requests up to a preset limit.

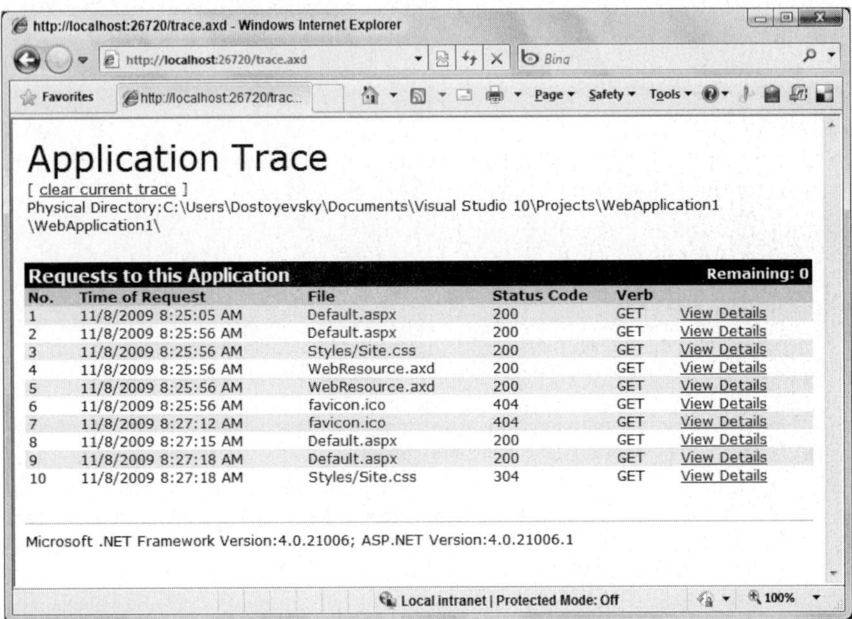

FIGURE 23-7

Figure 23-7 shows that ten requests have been made to this application and the right side of the header indicates "Remaining: 0". That means that there is one more request remaining before tracing stops for this application. After that final request, tracing data is not saved until an application recycle or until you click "Clear current trace" from the `trace.axd` page. The request limit can be raised in the `web.config` file at the expense of memory:

```
<trace requestLimit="100" pageOutput="true" enabled="true"/>
```

The maximum request limit value is 10000. If you try to use any greater value, ASP.NET uses 10000 anyway and gives you no error. However, you can add a property called `mostRecent` to the trace section in ASP.NET. When set to `true`, it shows the most recent requests that are stored in the trace log up to the request limit — instead of showing tracing in the order it occurs (the default) — without using up a lot of memory. Setting `mostRecent` to true causes memory to be used only for the trace information it stores and automatically throws away tracing information over the `requestLimit`.

Clicking View Details from `Trace.axd` on any of these requests takes you to a request-specific page with the same details shown in Figure 23-6.

Tracing from Components

The tracing facilities of ASP.NET are very powerful and can stand alone. However, you saw a previous mention of `System.Diagnostics.Trace`, the tracing framework in the Base Class Library that is not Web-specific and that receives consistent and complete tracing information when an ASP.NET application calls a non–Web-aware component. This can be confusing. Which should you use?

System.Diagnostics.Trace is the core .NET Framework tracing library. Along with System.Diagnostics.Debug, this class provides flexible, non-invasive tracing and debug output for any application. However, as mentioned earlier, rich tracing is built into the System.Web namespace. As a Web developer, you will find yourself using ASP.NET's tracing facilities. You may need to have ASP.NET-specific tracing forwarded to the base framework's System.Diagnostics.Trace, or more likely, you will want to have your non–Web-aware components output their trace calls to ASP.NET so you can take advantage of trace.axd and other ASP.NET-specific features.

Additionally, some confusion surrounds Trace.Write and Debug.Write functions. Look at the source code for Debug.Write, and you see something like this:

```
[Conditional("DEBUG")]
public static void Write(string message)
{
     TraceInternal.Write(message);
}
```

Notice that Debug.Write calls a function named TraceInternal.Write, which has a conditional attribute indicating that Debug.Write is compiled only if the debug preprocessor directive was set. In other words, you can put as many calls to Debug.Write as you want in your application without affecting your performance when you compile in Release mode. This enables you to be as verbose as you want during the debugging phase of development.

TraceInternal cycles through all attached trace listeners, meaning all classes that derive from the TraceListener base class and are configured in that application's configuration file. The default TraceListener lives in the aptly named DefaultTraceListener class and calls the Win32 API OutputDebugString. OutputDebugString sends your string into the abyss and, if a debugger is listening, it is displayed. If no debugger is listening, OutputDebugString does nothing. Everyone knows the debugger listens for output from OutputDebugString, so this can be a very effective way to listen in on debug versions of your application.

For quick-and-dirty no-touch debugging, try using DebugView from SysInternals at http://technet.microsoft.com/en-us/sysinternals/bb896647.aspx. *DebugView requires no installation, works great with all your calls to* Debug.Writer, *and has many cool features such as highlighting and logging to a file.*

Now, if you look at the source code for Trace.Write (that's TRACE not DEBUG), you see something like this:

```
[Conditional("TRACE")]
public static void Write(string message)
{
     TraceInternal.Write(message);
}
```

The only difference between Debug.Write and Trace.Write given these two source snippets is the conditional attribute indicating the preprocessor directive TRACE. You can conditionally compile your assemblies to include tracing statements, debug statements, both, or neither. Most people keep TRACE defined even for release builds and use the configuration file to turn tracing on and off. More than likely, the benefits you gain from making tracing available to your users far outweigh any performance issues that might arise.

Because Trace.Write calls the DefaultTraceListener just like Debug.Write, you can use any debugger to tap into tracing information. So, what's the difference?

When designing your application, think about your deployment model. Are you going to ship debug builds or release builds? Do you want a way for end users or systems engineers to debug your application using log files or the event viewer? Are there things you want only the developer to see?

Typically, you want to use tracing and Trace.Write for any formal information that could be useful in debugging your application in a production environment. Trace.Write gives you everything that Debug.Write does, except it uses the TRACE preprocessor directive and is not affected by debug or release builds.

This means you have four possibilities for builds: Debug On, Trace On, Both On, or Neither On. You choose what is right for you. Typically, use Both On for debug builds and Trace On for production builds. You can specify these conditional attributes in the property pages or the command line of the compiler, as well as with the C# #define keyword or #CONST keyword for Visual Basic.

Trace Forwarding

You often find existing ASP.NET applications that have been highly instrumented and make extensive use of the ASP.NET TraceContext class. ASP.NET includes an attribute to the web.config <trace> element that allows you to route messages emitted by ASP.NET tracing to System.Diagnostics.Trace: writeToDiagnosticsTrace.

```
<trace writeToDiagnosticsTrace="true" pageOutput="true" enabled="true"/>
```

When you set writeToDiagnosticsTrace to true, all calls to System.Web.UI.Page.Trace.Write (the ASP.NET TraceContext) also go to System.Diagnostics.Trace.Write, enabling you to use all the standard TraceListeners and tracing options that are covered later in this chapter. The simple writeToDiagnoticsTrace setting connects the ASP.NET tracing functionality with the rest of the base class library. I use this feature when I am deep in debugging my pages, and it is easily turned off using this configuration switch. I believe that more information is better than less, but you may find the exact page event information too verbose. Try it and form your own opinion.

TraceListeners

Output from System.Diagnostics.Trace methods is routable by a TraceListener to a text file, to ASP.NET, to an external monitoring system, even to a database. This powerful facility is a woefully underused tool in many ASP.NET developers' toolbelts. In the early days of ASP.NET, some component developers who knew their components were being used within ASP.NET would introduce a direct reference to System.Web and call HttpContext.Current.Trace. They did this so that their tracing information would appear in the developer-friendly ASP.NET format. All components called within the context of an HttpRequest automatically receive access to that request's current context, enabling the components to talk directly to the request and retrieve cookies or collect information about the user.

However, assuming an HttpContext will always be available is dangerous for a number of reasons. First, you are making a big assumption when you declare that your component can be used only within the context of an HttpRequest. Notice that this is said within the context of *a request*, not within the context of *an application*. If you access HttpContext.Current even from within the Application_Start, you will be surprised to find that HttpContext.Current is null. Second, marrying your component's functionality to HttpContext makes using your application in any non-Web context tricky if not impossible, and unit testing becomes particularly difficult.

If you have a component that is being used by a Web page, but it also needs to be unit tested outside of Web context or must be called from any other context, do not call HttpContext.Current.Trace. Instead, use the standard System.Diagnostics.Trace and redirect output to the ASP.NET tracing facilities using the WebPageTraceListener described in the next section. Using the standard trace mechanism means your component can be used in any context, Web or otherwise. You will still be able to view the component's trace output with a TraceListener.

The framework comes with a number of very useful TraceListeners; you can add them programmatically or via a .config file. For example, you can programmatically add a TraceListener log to a file, as shown in Listing 23-2. These snippets required the System.Diagnostics and System.IO namespaces.

LISTING 23-2: Configuring TraceListeners

VB

```
Dim myTextListener As New
  TextWriterTraceListener(File.Create("c:\myListener.log"))
Trace.Listeners.Add(myTextListener)
```

C#

```
TextWriterTraceListener myTextListener = new
  TextWriterTraceListener(File.Create(@"c:\myListener.log"));
Trace.Listeners.Add(myTextListener);
```

You can do the same thing declaratively in the `web.config` file via an `add` element that passes in the type of `TraceListener` to use, along with any initializing data it might need. `TraceListeners` already configured in `machine.config` or a parent `web.config` file can also be removed using the `remove` tag, along with their name:

```
<configuration>
 <system.diagnostics>
     <trace autoflush="false" indentsize="4">
         <listeners>
            <add name="myListener"
                type="System.Diagnostics.TextWriterTraceListener"
                initializeData="c:\myListener.log" />
            <remove name="Default" />
         </listeners>
     </trace>
 </system.diagnostics>
</configuration>
```

`TraceListeners`, such as `TextWriterTraceListener`, that access a resource (such as a file, event log, or database) require that the ASP.NET worker process be run as a user who has sufficient access. To write to `c:\foo\example.log`, for example, the ASP.NET worker process requires explicit write access in the Access Control List (ACL) of that file.

Notice the preceding example also optionally removes the default `TraceListener`. If you write your own `TraceListener`, you must provide a fully qualified assembly name in the `type` attribute.

Using the ASP.NET WebPageTraceListener

The ASP.NET `WebPageTraceListener` derives from `System.Diagnostics.TraceListener` and automatically forwards tracing information from any component calls to `System.Diagnostics.Trace.Write`. This enables you to write your components using the most generic trace provider and to see its tracing output in the context of your ASP.NET application.

The `WebPageTraceListener` is added to the `web.config` file as shown in the following example. Note that we use the fully qualified assembly name for `System.Web`:

```
<configuration>
 <system.diagnostics>
     <trace autoflush="false" indentsize="4">
         <listeners>
             <add name="webListener"
                type="System.Web.WebPageTraceListener, System.Web, Version=4.0.0.0,
                      Culture=neutral, PublicKeyToken=b03f5f7f11d50a3a"/>
         </listeners>
     </trace>
 </system.diagnostics>
 <system.web>
       <trace enabled="true" pageOutput="false" localOnly="true" />
 </system.web>
</configuration>
```

Figure 23-8 shows output from a call to `System.Diagnostics.Trace.Write` from a referenced library. It appears within ASP.NET's page tracing. The line generated from the referenced library is circled in this figure.

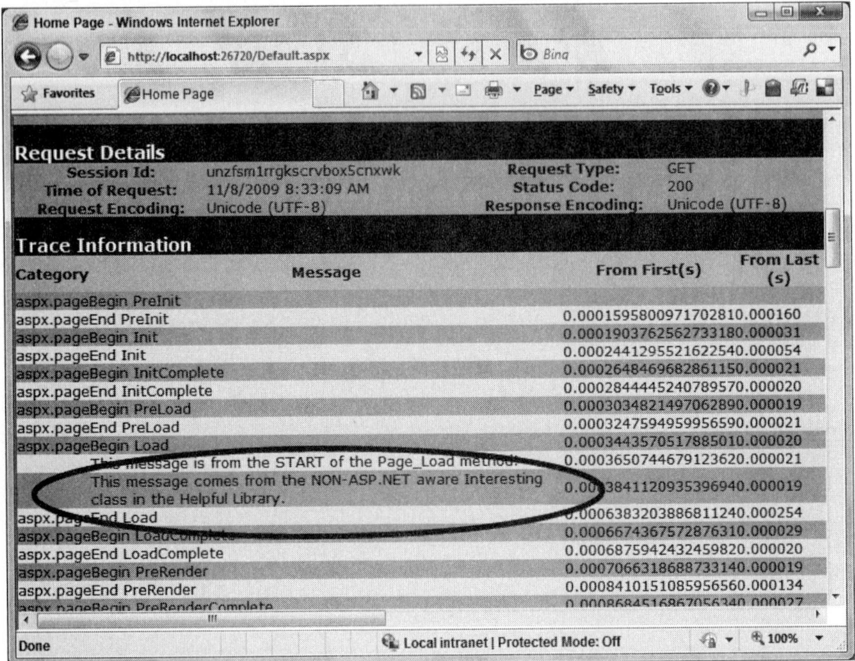

FIGURE 23-8

EventLogTraceListener

Tracing information can also be sent to the event log using the `EventLogTraceListener`. Doing this can be a little tricky because ASP.NET requires explicit write access to the event log:

```
<configuration>
 <system.diagnostics>
     <trace autoflush="false" indentsize="4">
         <listeners>
             <add name="EventLogTraceListener"
                 type="System.Diagnostics.EventLogTraceListener"
                 initializeData="Wrox"/>
         </listeners>
     </trace>
 </system.diagnostics>
</configuration>
```

Notice that `"Wrox"` is passed in as a string to the `initializeData` attribute as the `TraceListener` is added. The string `"Wrox"` appears as the application or *source* for this event. This works fine when debugging your application; most likely, the debugging user has the appropriate access. However, when your application is deployed, it will probably run under a less privileged account, so you must give explicit write access to a registry key such as `HKLM\System\CurrentControlSet\Services\EventLog\Application\Wrox`, where `"Wrox"` is the same string passed in to `initializeData`. Remember that registry keys have ACLs (Access Control Lists) just as files do. Use `RegEdit.exe` to change the permissions on a registry key by right-clicking the key and selecting Properties, and setting the ACL just like you would for a file.

Be careful when using the `EventLogTraceListener` because your event log can fill up fairly quickly if you have a particularly chatty application. Figure 23-9 shows the same tracing output used in Figure 23-8, this time in the event log. The Event Viewer has changed since Windows Vista, and you will need to create a simple Custom View that shows only “Wrox” events.

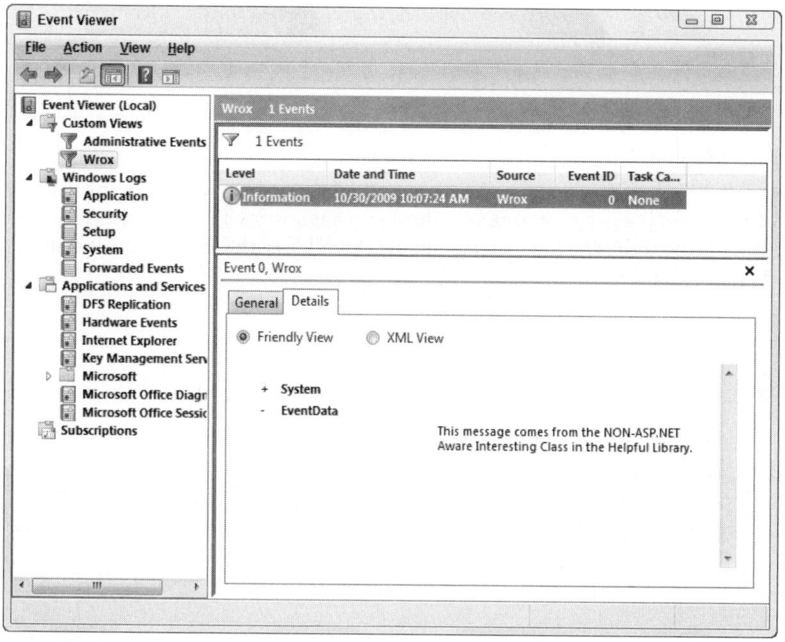

FIGURE 23-9

Other Useful Listeners

The .NET Framework 4 includes two additional `TraceListeners` in addition to the `WebPageTraceListener`:

- `XmlWriterTraceListener`: Derives from `TextWriterTraceListener` and writes out a strongly typed XML file.
- `DelimitedListTraceListener`: Also derives from `TextWriterTraceListener`; writes out comma-separated values (CSV) files.

One of the interesting things to note about the XML created by the `XmlWriterTraceListener` — it is not well-formed XML! Specifically, it doesn't have a root node; it's just a collection of peer nodes, as shown in the following code. This may seem like it goes against many of the ideas you have been told about XML, but think of each event as a document. Each stands alone and can be consumed alone. They just happen to be next to each other in one file. Certainly, the absence of an ultimate closing tag cleverly dodges the issue of well-formedness and allows easy appending to a file.

```
<E2ETraceEvent xmlns=\"http://schemas.microsoft.com/2004/06/E2ETraceEvent\">
    <System xmlns=\"http://schemas.microsoft.com/2004/06/windows/eventlog/system\">
        <EventID>0</EventID>
        <Type>3</Type>
        <SubType Name="Information">0</SubType>
        <Level>8</Level>
        <TimeCreated SystemTime="2009-11-05T12:43:44.4234234Z">
        <Source Name="WroxChapter23.exe"/>
        <Correlation ActivityID="{00000000-0000-0000-0000-000000000000>
        <Execution ProcessName="WroxChapter23.exe" ProcessID="4234" ThreadID="1"/>
        <Channel/>
        <Computer>SCOTTPC</Computer>
    </System>
    <ApplicationData>Your Text Here</ApplicationData>
</E2ETraceEvent>
<E2ETraceEvent xmlns=\"http://schemas.microsoft.com/2004/06/E2ETraceEvent\">
```

```
    <System xmlns=\"http://schemas.microsoft.com/2004/06/windows/eventlog/system\">
        <EventID>0</EventID>
        <Type>3</Type>
... the XML continues ...
```

The "E2E" in `E2ETraceEvent` stands for end-to-end. Notice that it includes information such as your computer name and a "correlation id."

Ever since the .NET Framework 3.5, there has been one additional `TraceListener` added to the list, the `IisTraceListener`. Much like the `WebPageTraceListener` bridges Diagnostics Tracing with ASP.NET tracing, the `IisTraceListener` bridges the tracing mechanism of ASP.NET with IIS 7.0. This listener lets us raise events to the IIS 7.0 infrastructure.

Diagnostic Switches

Recompiling your application just because you want to change tracing characteristics is often not convenient. Sometimes you may want to change your configuration file to add and remove `TraceListeners`. At other times, you may want to change a configuration parameter or "flip a switch" to adjust the amount of detail the tracing produces. That is where `Switch` comes in. `Switch` is an abstract base class that supports a series of diagnostic switches that you can control by using the application's configuration file.

BooleanSwitch

To use a `BooleanSwitch`, create an instance and pass in the switch name that appears in the application's `config` file (see Listing 23-3).

Available for download on Wrox.com

LISTING 23-3: Using diagnostic switches

```
<configuration>
 <system.diagnostics>
  <switches>
   <add name="ImportantSwitch" value="1" /> <!-- This is for the BooleanSwitch -->
   <add name="LevelSwitch" value="3" />     <!-- This is for the TraceSwitch -->
   <add name="SourceSwitch" value="4" />    <!-- This is for the SourceSwitch -->
  </switches>
 </system.diagnostics>
</configuration>
```

Switches can be used in an `if` statement for any purpose, but they are most useful in the context of tracing along with `System.Diagnostics.Trace.WriteIf`:

VB

```
Dim aSwitch As New BooleanSwitch("ImportantSwitch", "Show errors")
System.Diagnostics.Trace.WriteIf(aSwitch.Enabled, "The Switch is enabled!")
```

C#

```
BooleanSwitch aSwitch = new BooleanSwitch("ImportantSwitch", "Show errors");
System.Diagnostics.Trace.WriteIf(aSwitch.Enabled, "The Switch is enabled!");
```

If `ImportantSwitch` is set to `1`, or a non-zero value, in the `config` file, the call to `WriteIf` sends a string to trace output.

TraceSwitch

`TraceSwitch` offers five levels of tracing from 0 to 4, implying an increasing order: Off, Error, Warning, Info, and Verbose. You construct a `TraceSwitch` exactly as you create a `BooleanSwitch`:

VB

```
Dim tSwitch As New TraceSwitch("LevelSwitch", "Trace Levels")
System.Diagnostics.Trace.WriteIf(tSwitch.TraceInfo, "The Switch is 3 or more!")
```

C#

```
TraceSwitch tSwitch = new TraceSwitch("LevelSwitch", "Trace Levels");
System.Diagnostics.Trace.WriteIf(tSwitch.TraceInfo, "The Switch is 3 or more!");
```

A number of properties on the `TraceSwitch` class return `true` if the switch is at the same level or at a higher level than the property's value. For example, the `TraceInfo` property will return `true` if the switch's value is set to 3 or more.

SourceSwitch

Since the release of the .NET Framework 2.0, you have been able to use `SourceSwitch`, which is similar to `TraceSwitch` but provides a greater level of granularity. You call `SourceSwitch.ShouldTrace` with an `EventType` as the parameter:

VB

```
Dim sSwitch As New SourceSwitch("SourceSwitch", "Even More Levels")
System.Diagnostics.Trace.WriteIf(sSwitch.ShouldTrace(TraceEventType.Warning),
                                 "The Switch is 3 or more!")
```

C#

```
SourceSwitch sSwitch = new SourceSwitch("SourceSwitch", " Even More Levels");
System.Diagnostics.Trace.WriteIf(sSwitch.ShouldTrace(TraceEventType.Warning),
                                 "The Switch is 4 or more!");
```

Web Events

It does not exactly qualify as debugging, but you will find a series of application-monitoring and health-monitoring tools within the system has been added in ASP.NET's `System.Web.Management` namespace in ASP.NET. These tools can be as valuable as tracing information in helping you monitor, maintain, and diagnose the health of your application. The system has an event model and event engine that can update your application with runtime details. It has a number of built-in events, including application lifetime events such as start and stop and a heartbeat event. You can take these base classes and events and build on them to create events of your own. For example, you might want to create an event that tells you when a user downloads a particularly large file or when a new user is created in your personalization database. You can have your application send an e-mail to you once a day with statistics.

For instance, you can create your own event by deriving from `System.Web.Management.WebBaseEvent`, as shown in Listing 23-4.

LISTING 23-4: Web events

Available for download on Wrox.com

VB

```
Imports System
Imports System.Web.Management

Namespace Wrox
    Public Class WroxEvent
       Inherits WebBaseEvent

        Public Const WroxEventCode As Integer = WebEventCodes.WebExtendedBase + 1
        Public Sub New(ByVal message As String, ByVal eventSource As Object)
            MyBase.New(message, eventSource, WroxEventCode)
        End Sub
    End Class
End Namespace
```

C#

```
namespace Wrox
{
    using System;
    using System.Web.Management;

    public class WroxEvent: WebBaseEvent
    {
        public const int WroxEventCode = WebEventCodes.WebExtendedBase + 1;
        public WroxEvent(string message, object eventSource) :
             base(message, eventSource, WroxEventCode){}
     }
}
```

Later, in a sample `Page_Load`, you raise this event to the management subsystem:

VB

```
Protected Sub Page_Load(sender As Object, e As EventArgs)
    ' Raise a custom event
    Dim anEvent As Wrox.WroxEvent = New Wrox.WroxEvent("Someone visited here", Me)
    anEvent.Raise()
End Sub
```

C#

```
protected void Page_Load(Object sender, EventArgs e)
{
    // Raise a custom event
    Wrox.WroxEvent anEvent = new Wrox.WroxEvent("Someone visited here!", this);
    anEvent.Raise();
}
```

The event is caught by the management subsystem and can be dispatched to different providers based on a number of rules. This is a much more formal kind of tracing than a call to `Trace.WriteLine`, so you create a strongly typed event class for events specific to your application:

Web.config

```
<?xml version="1.0"?>
<configuration>
    <system.web>
        <healthMonitoring enabled="true">
            <providers>
                <add name="WroxDatabaseLoggingProvider"
                    type="System.Web.Management.SqlWebEventProvider"
                    connectionStringName="QuickStartSqlServer"
                    maxEventDetailsLength="1073741823"
                    buffer="false"/>
            </providers>
            <rules>
                <add
                    name="Application Lifetime Events Rule"
                    eventName="All Events"
                    provider="WroxDatabaseLoggingProvider"
                    profile="Critical" />
            </rules>
        </healthMonitoring>
    </system.web>
</configuration>
```

DEBUGGING

Visual Studio includes two configurations by default: *debug* and *release*. The debug configuration automatically defines the debug and trace constants, enabling your application to provide context to a troubleshooter. The option to generate debugging information is turned on by default, causing a program database (or debug) file (PDB) to be generated for each assembly and your solution. They appear in the same bin folder as your assemblies. Remember, however, that the actual compilation to native code does not occur in Visual Studio, but rather at runtime using Just-In-Time compilation (JIT). The JIT will automatically optimize your code for speed. Optimized code, however, is considerably harder to debug because the operations that are generated may not correspond directly to lines in your source code. For debug purposes, this option is set to `false`.

What's Required

The PDBs are created when either the C# compiler (`csc.exe`) or Visual Basic compiler (`vbc.exe`) is invoked with the `/debug:full` command lines switch. As an option, if you use `/debug:pdbonly`, you will generate PDBs but still direct the compiler to produce release-mode code.

Debug versus Release

The debug and release configurations that come with Visual Studio are generally sufficient for your needs. However, these configurations control only the compilation options of the code-behind files. Remember that, depending on how you have chosen to design your ASP.NET application, the ASP.NET `.aspx` files may be compiled the first time they are hit, or the entire application may compile the first time a page is hit. You can control these compilation settings via the compilation elements within the `<system.web>` section of your application's `web.config` file. Set `<compilation debug="true">` to produce binaries as you do when using the `/debug:full` switches. PDBs are also produced.

The average developer is most concerned with the existence of PDB files. When these files exist in your ASP.NET applications bin folder, the runtime provides you with line numbers. Of course, line numbers greatly assist in debugging. You cannot step through source code during an interactive debugging session without these files.

An interesting CLR Internals trick: Call `System.Diagnostics.Debugger.Launch` *within your assembly, even if the assembly was compiled via* `/debug:pdbonly`*, and the debugger pops up. The JIT compiler compiles code on the first call to a method, and the code that it generates is debuggable because JIT knows that a debugger is attached.*

Debugging and the JIT Dialog

When an unhandled error occurs in an ASP.NET application, the default error handler for the ASP.NET worker process catches it and tries to output some HTML that expresses what happened. However, when you are debugging components outside of ASP.NET, perhaps within the context of unit testing, the debug dialog box appears when the .NET application throws an unhandled exception.

If something has gone horribly wrong with an ASP.NET application, it is conceivable that you may find a Web server with the dialog box popped up waiting for your input. This can be especially inconvenient if the machine has no keyboard or monitor hooked up. The day may come when you want to turn off the debug dialog box that appears, and you have two options to do this:

- You can disable JIT Debugging from the registry. The proper registry key is `HKLM\Software\Microsoft\.NETFramework\DbgJITDebugLaunchSetting`. The option has three possible values:
  - `0`: Prompts the user by means of a message box. The choices presented include Continue, which results in a stack dump and process termination, and Attach a Debugger, which means the runtime spawns the debugger listed in the DbgManagedDebugger registry key. If no key exists, the debugger releases control and the process is terminated.
  - `1`: Does not display a dialog box. This results in a stack dump and then process termination.
  - `2`: Launches the debugger listed in the DbgManagedDebugger registry key.

For this option, the registry entry must be set to `0` *for the dialog box to show up.*

- To disable the JIT debug dialog box and still present an error dialog box, within Visual Studio.NET, choose Tools ➪ Options ➪ Debugging ➪ Just-In-Time and deselect the provided options. Instead of the Select a Debugger dialog box, an OK/Cancel dialog box will appear during an unhandled exception.

IIS versus ASP.NET Development Server

ASP.NET greatly simplifies your Web developing experience by enabling you to develop applications without IIS (Internet Information Server — the Web server) on your developer machine. Rather than the traditional style of creating a virtual directory and mapping it to a physical directory, a directory can be opened as a Web site simply by telling Visual Studio that it is a Web site. When you open a Web site from the File menu, the first option on the list of places to open from is the file system. Visual Studio considers any folder that you open to be the root of a Web site. Other options, of course, are opening Web sites from your local IIS instance, FTP, or source control.

Using the IIS option works much as it does in previous versions of Visual Studio with a few convenient changes such as the capability to create a Web site or map a virtual directory directly from the Open Web Site dialog. However, stuff that is more interesting happens after you open a Web site from the file system.

By default, Web sites that exist only on the file system have a "just-in-time" Web server instantiated called the ASP.NET Development Server. The small Web server hosts the exact same ASP.NET page rendering at runtime that is hosted within IIS on a deployed production site. The page-rendering behavior should be identical under the small server as it is under IIS. You should be aware of a few important differences and specific caveats to ensure a smooth transition from development to production.

Create a new Web site by selecting File ⇨ New ⇨ Web Site and immediately pressing F5 to begin a debugging session. You are greeted with a Debugging Not Enabled dialog box. The first option automatically adds a new `web.config` file with debugging enabled. (Earlier versions of Visual Studio required a tedious manual process.) Click OK and balloon help appears in the system tray announcing that the ASP.NET Development Server has started up. It also shows what random high-number port the Web server has selected on the local host. When you close your browser and stop your debugging session, the tiny Web server shuts down.

The ASP.NET Development Server is an application, not a service. It is not a replacement for IIS, nor does it try to be. It is really just a broker that sits between the developer and the ASP.NET page renderer, and it contains very few, if any, of the security benefits that IIS includes. It is loosely based on a .NET 1.*x* project, code-named Cassini, which is downloadable from `www.asp.net/downloads/archived/cassini/`. This sample project was meant to illustrate how to use the `System.Web.Hosting` namespace. The Cassini project was the grandparent, and now the ASP.NET Development Server is a first-class member of the Visual Studio product family. Including this tiny Web server with the Development Environment also allows Visual Studio to be used on lower grade Windows systems that are unable to run IIS.

The small Web server runs under the same user context that runs Visual Studio. If your application requires a specific security context, such as an anonymous user or specific domain user, consider using IIS as your development Web server. Additionally, because the Web server starts up on a port other than port 80, be sure to use best practices while developing your site's navigation scheme. Often, developers assume their site's URL will not include a port number (it will default to port 80), that their site may appear within a specific subdomain (`bar.foo.com`), or that their site will appear within a subdirectory (`www.foo.com/bar`). Consider making your navigation relative to the virtual root of your application so your application is resilient enough to be run in many contexts.

Starting a Debugging Session

You have a number of ways to enter an interactive debugging session with ASP.NET. Visual Studio can fire up the ASP.NET worker process, load your newly compiled Web site, and attach the debugging to the worker process automatically. Alternatively, you can attach a debugger to a site that is already running. Visual Studio also includes a new simpler remote debugging tool for cross-machine debugging.

F5 Debugging

When you start debugging an ASP.NET application, Visual Studio takes into consideration all the Start options within your project properties. Just as ASP.NET 1.*x* Visual Studio can be set to launch the browser on a specific page, the new version allows you to start debugging using the currently selected page. The specific page has been selected so that the Visual Studio debugger can automatically attach the correct process, which might be the Visual Studio Web Server, the ASP.NET worker process, or a remote debug monitor.

Attaching to a Process

Jumping into an interactive debugging session of a Web site that is already running, and at known state, is often more convenient than starting an application from scratch each time you debug. To begin debugging a site that is already running, from Visual Studio's Debug menu, select Attach to Process. The dialog has been improved from previous versions of Visual Studio and includes a Refresh button and simplifies most common debugging use cases by showing only those processes that belong to the user and that are in the currently running session.

Also included is a transport drop-down with the default transport selected. The default allows you to select processes on your computer or on a remote computer that's running the Remote Debugging Monitor. Other options are there for smart client or unmanaged debugging.

The only difference between starting a Debug session via F5 and attaching to a process manually is that when you debug via F5, Visual Studio automatically starts up a browser or external application for you. Remember that if you use Attach to Process, it is assumed that you have already done the work of starting up the process. The ASP.NET worker processes under IIS will start up when the site has been hit with an `HttpRequest` *at least once. The debugger can now attach to the running worker process.*

Sometimes you want to debug an ASP.NET application that is already running on your computer. If that application was not started by Visual Studio and you want to attach to it, select Attach to Process from the Debug menu and choose either `ASPNET_WP.exe` (if you are running Windows XP) or `W3WP.exe` (if you are running Windows 2003/2008 server or Windows 7). Be careful that you are not trying to debug an application that is actively servicing other users or you may ruin their experience.

Simpler Remote Debugging

Remote debugging got simpler since Visual Studio 2005. However, in the interest of security, you must have the appropriate credentials to perform remote debugging. You will find a Remote Debugger folder in `C:\Program Files\Microsoft Visual Studio 10.0\Common7\IDE`. In Figure 23-10, Explorer is shown open and the Remote Debugger folder is selected and has been configured as a shared directory for access over the local network.

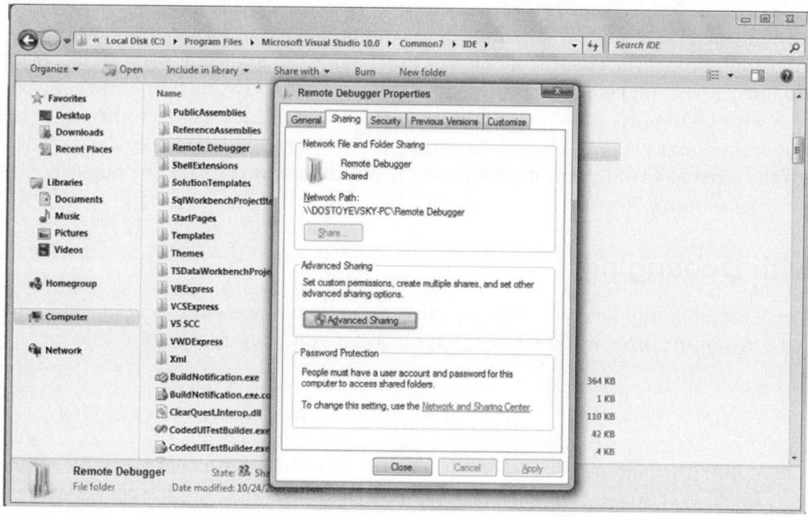

FIGURE 23-10

To begin, you must set up remote debugging on the machine that contains the application you want to debug. Rather than performing a complicated installation, you can now use the Remote Debug Monitor, and an application that can simply be run off a file share. The easiest scenario has you sharing these components directly from your Visual Studio machine and then running `msvsmon.exe` off the share.

Simply running the Remote Debug Monitor executable off the file share can make remote ASP.NET debugging of an already-deployed application much simpler, although you still need to manually attach to the ASP.NET worker process because automatic attaching is not supported. Do note that two versions of the debugger now exist, one for x86 processes and one for x64 processes, so make sure you are using the right debugger for your process.

You are allowed to debug a process that is running under your account and password without any special permissions. If you need to debug a process running under another account name, such as an ASP.NET worker process running as a user who is not you, you must be an administrator on the machine running the process.

The most important thing to remember when debugging remotely is this: You need to get the user account that is running as Visual Studio to map somehow to a legitimate user account on the machine running the Remote Debug Monitor (`msvsmon.exe`) machine and vice versa. The easiest way to do this is to create a local user account on both computers with the same username and password. To run `msvsmon` as a user other than Visual Studio, you must create two user accounts on each computer.

If one of the machines is located on a domain, be aware that domain accounts can be mapped to a local account. You create a local user account on both computers. However, if you pick the same username and password as your domain account, Visual Studio can be run as a domain account.

For Windows XP machines on a workgroup, the security option entitled Network Security: Shared and Security Model for Local Accounts affects your use of the Remote Debug Monitor. If this option is set to Guest Only — Local Users Authenticate As Guest, then remote debugging fails and shows you a dialog box. Configure this via the Local Security Policy MMC-based administrative tool. The warning does not affect Windows 2000 or Windows Server 2003, Windows XP, or Windows 7 computers that are joined to a domain.

Debugging Running Windows XP Service Pack 2

Make sure that TCP port 80 is set to allow ASP.NET and IIS to communicate with the remote machine. Try to keep the scope limited, using options such as Local Subnet Only, and avoid exposing your Web server to the Internet during development. Also include TCP port 135, which allows DCOM to communicate with remote machines as well as with UDP ports 4500 and 500 for IPSec-based security. Last, confirm that the Remote Debug Monitor (`msvsmon.exe`) is in the list of exceptions to the firewall. Again, avoid exposing your debugging session to the outside world. Remote debugging is usually a last resort if the bug is not reproducible for whatever reason on the developer workstation.

Tools to Help You with Debugging

The debugging experience in Visual Studio has improved arguably more than any other aspect of the environment. A number of tools, some obvious, some more subtle, assist you in every step of the debug session.

Debugger DataTips

Previous versions of Visual Studio gave you tooltips when the user hovered the mouse over variables of simple types. Visual Studio offers *DataTips*, allowing complex types to be explored using a modeless tree-style view that acts like a tooltip and provides much more information. After you traverse the tree to the node that you are interested in, that simple type can be viewed using a visualizer by clicking the small magnifying glass icon, as shown in Figure 23-11.

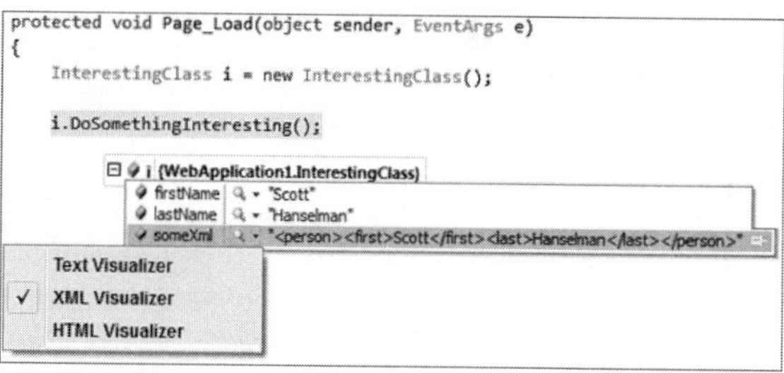

FIGURE 23-11

Visual Studio 2010 adds some extended capabilities to DataTips. One of the nice new features is the ability to pin the DataTips to stay open on your page. You do this by clicking on the pin on the right side of the DataTip. Once pinned, this DataTip will stay put exactly where you pinned it, and that means that when you scroll your code, the DataTip will scroll with the code and remain in place as expected.

Floating the DataTips is also possible by clicking once again on the pin of an already pinned DataTip. Doing so enables you to move the DataTip anywhere you want on the screen. Now if you scroll your code, the DataTip remains in place on the screen regardless of what you are doing in Visual Studio. The nice thing with floating your DataTips is that you can move them outside of the code window, and you can even move them to a second monitor if you want.

In a pinned DataTips toolbar, notice a button that allows you to put a comment in the DataTip that stays with it as you move it around. Figure 23-12 shows a DataTip with a comment.

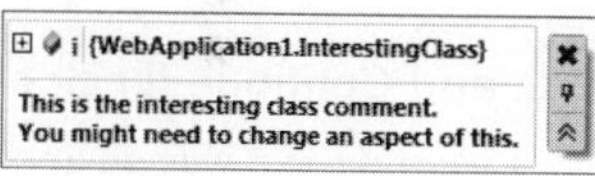

FIGURE 23-12

Finally, another new feature in Visual Studio 2010 allows you to export these DataTips by choosing Debug ➪ Export DataTips. Exporting saves all your DataTips as an XML file and allows you to provide the file to other people who can import them into their own instance of the project. The import process puts the DataTips in the places you have pinned them and includes the comments that you used.

Data Visualizers

As you see in Figure 23-11, a simple type can be viewed using any number of data visualizers. For example, if a simple variable such as a string contains a fragment of XML, you might want to visualize that data in a style that is more appropriate for the data's native format, as shown in Figure 23-13.

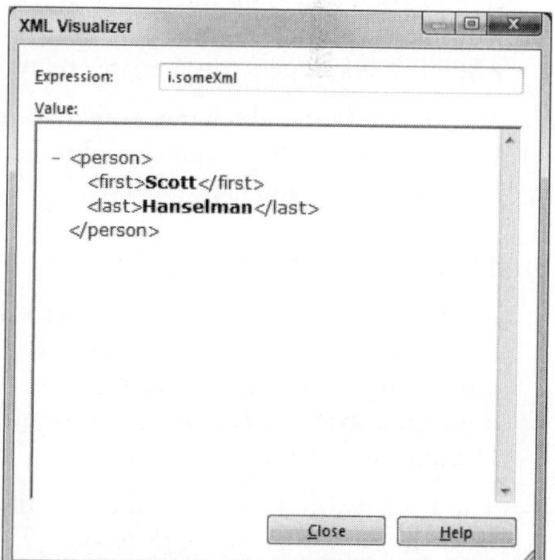

FIGURE 23-13

The visualizers are straightforward to write and, although Visual Studio ships with default visualizers for text, HTML, XML, and DataSets, look out on the Internet for additional visualizers that might include support for images, collection classes, and more. The result is a rich, unparalleled debugging experience.

Error Notifications

During an interactive debugging session, Visual Studio now strives to assist you with informative error notifications. These notifications not only report on events such as unhandled exceptions, but also offer context-sensitive troubleshooting tips and next steps for dealing with the situation. Figure 23-14 shows an unhandled `NullReferenceException` along with the good advice that you might try using the "new" keyword to create an object instance before using it. Oops!

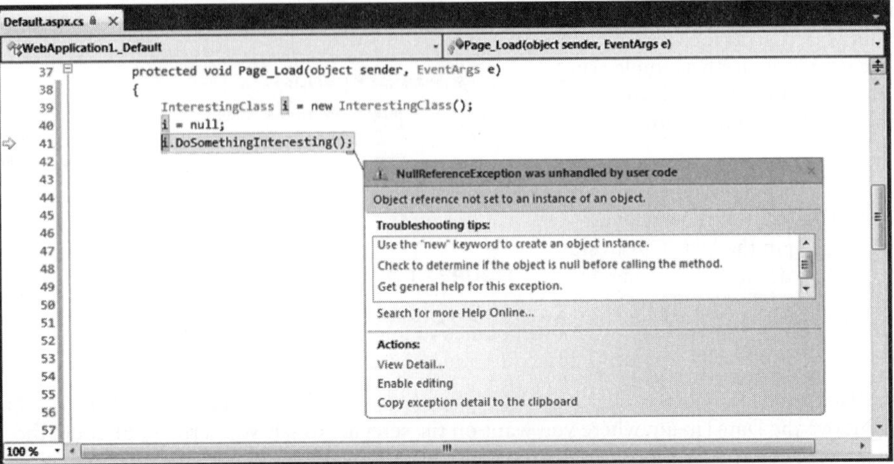

FIGURE 23-14

Edit and Continue (Lack of) Support, or Edit and Refresh

Visual Basic 6 was all about developing things quickly, and its most powerful feature was the Edit and Continue feature, which gave you capability to change code during a debugging session without restarting the session. In break mode, you could modify code fix bugs and move on. Ever since the release of the .NET Framework 2.0, you will notice that this feature has been restored for both C# and Visual Basic. Although this has a large number of developers cheering, unfortunately this feature is not available to ASP.NET developers.

In ASP.NET, your assembly is compiled not by Visual Studio, but by the ASP.NET runtime using the same technique it does during a normal Web page request by a browser. To cooperate with the debugger and support Edit and Continue within ASP.NET, a number of fantastically complex modifications to ASP.NET runtime would have been required by the development team. Rather than including support for this feature, ASP.NET developers can use *page recycling*.

This means that code changes are made during a debugging session, and then the whole page is refreshed via F5, automatically recompiled, and re-executed. Basically, ASP.NET includes support for Edit and Refresh, but not for Edit and Continue.

Just My Code Debugging

Another concept in the .NET Framework is called *Just My Code* debugging. Any method in code can be explicitly marked with the attribute `[DebuggerNonUserCode]`. Using this explicit technique and a number of other heuristic methods internal to the CLR, the debugger silently skips over code that is not important to the code at hand. You can find the preference Enable Just My Code in Tools ➪ Options ➪ Debugging.

The `[DebuggerHidden]` attribute is still available in .NET and hides methods from the debugger, regardless of the user's Just My Code preference. The .NET Framework 1.1 attribute `[DebuggerStepThrough]` tells the debugger to step through, rather than into, any method to which it is applied; the `[DebuggerNonUserCode]` attribute is a much more pervasive and complete implementation that works at runtime on delegates, virtual functions, and any arbitrarily complex code.

Be aware that these attributes and this user option exist to help you debug code effectively and not be fooled by any confusing call stacks. Although these can be very useful, be sure not to use them on your components until you are sure you will not accidentally hide the very error you are trying to debug. Typically, these attributes are used for components such as proxies or thin shim layers.

Tracepoints

Breakpoints by themselves are useful for stopping execution either conditionally or unconditionally. Standard breakpoints break always. Conditional breakpoints cause you to enter an interactive debugging session based on a condition. Tracing is useful to output the value of a variable or assertion to the debugger or to another location. If you combine all these features, what do you get? Tracepoints, a powerful Visual Studio feature. Tracepoints can save you from hitting breakpoints dozens of times just to catch an edge case variable value. They can save you from covering your code with breakpoints to catch a strange case.

To insert a tracepoint, right-click in the code editor and select Breakpoint ➪ Insert Tracepoint. You get the dialog shown in Figure 23-15. The icon that indicates a breakpoint is a red circle, and the icon for a tracepoint is a red diamond. Arbitrary strings can be created from the dialog using pseudo-variables in the form of keywords such as `$CALLSTACK` or `$FUNCTION`, as well as the values of variables in scope placed in curly braces. In Figure 23-15, the value of `i.FirstName` (placed in curly braces) is shown in the complete string with the Debug output of Visual Studio.

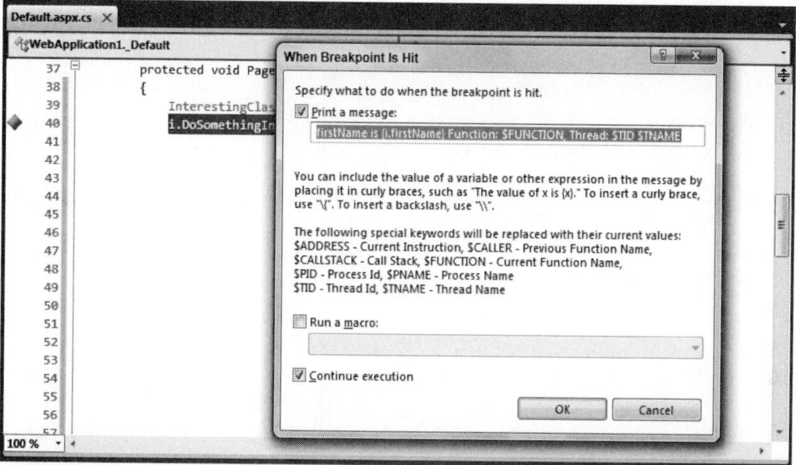

FIGURE 23-15

Breakpoint Options

Right-click on a breakpoint in your code — you access a number of options that allow you to manage some of the identifiers and behaviors of your breakpoints.

One option is to set a condition for your breakpoint. To get to the Breakpoint Condition dialog, right-click on the breakpoint and select Condition from the provided menu. Here you are presented with a textbox that allows you to create conditions that trigger the breakpoint.

A new option in Visual Studio 2010 is the ability to put labels on your breakpoints. You do so by selecting Edit labels from the breakpoint menu. This makes identifying your breakpoints from the breakpoint dialog that allows grouping and searching of these values easy.

Just as you could with DataTips, Visual Studio 2010 allows you to export your breakpoints. To export all the breakpoints, right-click on any breakpoint and select Export from the provided menu. This export allows you to save all the breakpoints in an XML file that then can be loaded by someone else. It is a convenient way to distribute these items.

Historical Debugging with IntelliTrace

One of the more exciting features of Visual Studio 2010 is a new feature called IntelliTrace. IntelliTrace provides you a historical debugger that allows you to look back in the history of your application running and allows you to jump at previous points in time to see what was occurring.

This feature only works with Visual Studio 2010 Ultimate Edition and is not available in the other editions of the IDE. As of today, it also does not work on 64-bit machines. Therefore, you need to be working with a 32-bit computer to work with the historical debugging feature.

When stopping at a breakpoint within your application, you will now be able to see this history in the IntelliTrace dialog directly as illustrated in Figure 23-16.

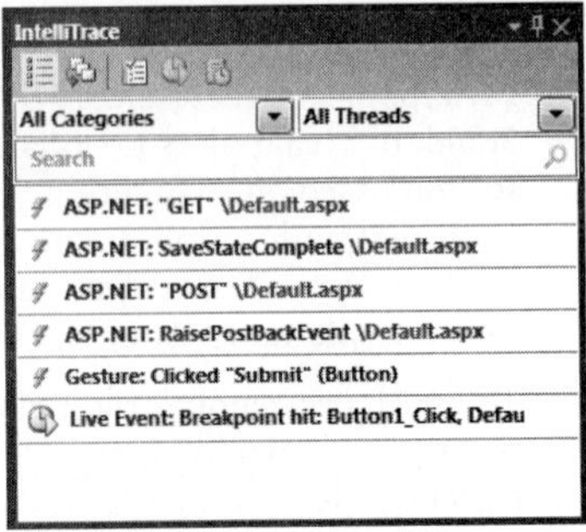

FIGURE 23-16

From here, you can jump to any point in the past and view the Locals dialog values and the Call Stack dialog values for that moment in time. The IntelliTrace capability is configurable as well. You can get to these settings by either clicking on the Open IntelliTrace Settings from the IntelliTrace toolbar or by selecting Tools ➪ Options and selecting IntelliTrace from the items in the left side of the dialog. On the General tab of the IntelliTrace section (shown here in Figure 23-17), you can enable or disable the IntelliTrace option and, if it is enabled, choose whether to record just the events or to enable even more and record events and call information.

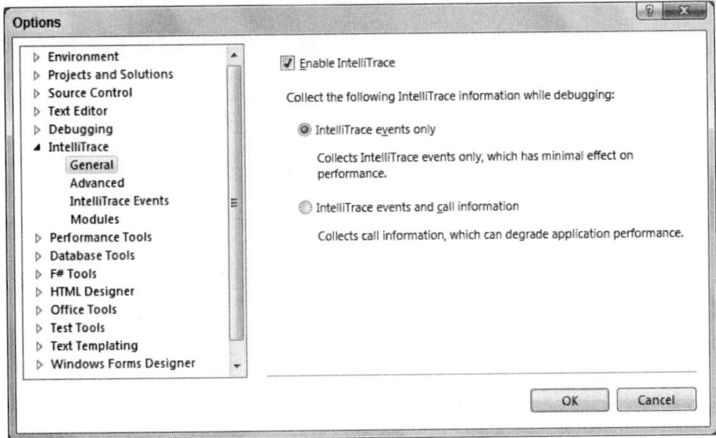

FIGURE 23-17

On the Advanced tab (shown in Figure 23-18), you can set the amount of disk space to use for recording what is going on in the application. Here you can see that the amount of space reserved is 100MB.

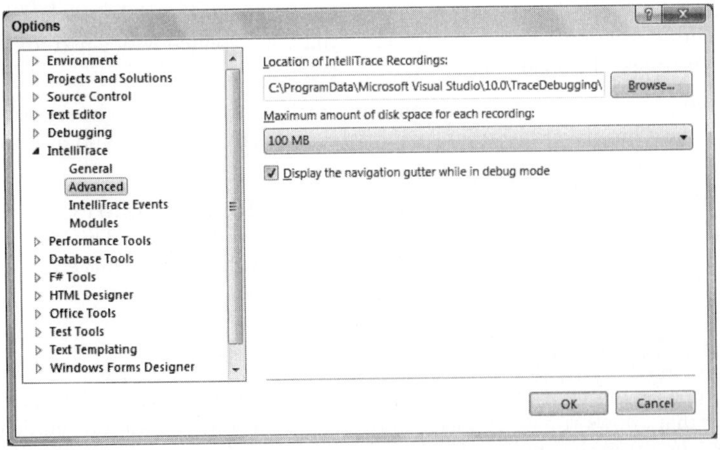

FIGURE 23-18

From the IntelliTrace Events tab, you can select the events that you want to work with. You can choose from a large series of technologies and situations by making the appropriate selections.

Finally, the Modules tab allows you to specify particular modules that IntelliTrace should work with.

Debugging Multiple Threads

Visual Studio 2010 includes a dialog that allows you to see what is going on in each of the threads your application is using. This is done through the Threads dialog shown in Figure 23-19.

Threads

Search: | Search Call Stack | Group by: Process Name | Columns

WebDev.WebServer40.EXE (id = 4356) : C:\Program Files\Common Files\microsoft shared\DevServer\10.0\WebDev.WebServer40.EXE

ID	Managed ID	Category	Name	Location	Priority
1404	1	Main Thread	Main Thread	[Managed to Native Transition]	Normal
5224	2	Worker Thread	<No Name>	<not available>	Highest
4984	3	Worker Thread	Worker Thread	[Managed to Native Transition]	Normal
4176	5	Worker Thread	<No Name>	<not available>	Normal
3572	0	Worker Thread	<No Name>	<not available>	Normal
5736	7	Worker Thread	<No Name>	<not available>	Normal
3124	96	Worker Thread	<No Name>	<not available>	Normal
5748	27	Worker Thread	<No Name>	<not available>	Normal
908	98	Worker Thread	Worker Thread	[Managed to Native Transition]	Normal
1152	95	Worker Thread	Worker Thread	WebApplication1._Default.Page_Load	Normal

Error List | Output | Locals | Autos | Threads

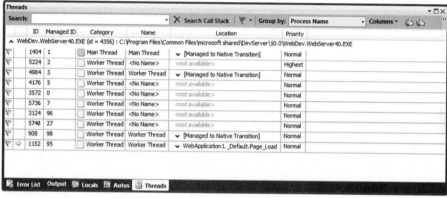

FIGURE 23-19

You can double-click on a thread and go to where that thread is in the code when debugging. You can also get a visual family tree view of the threads at work by opening up the Parallel Stacks dialog. Figure 23-20 shows this dialog.

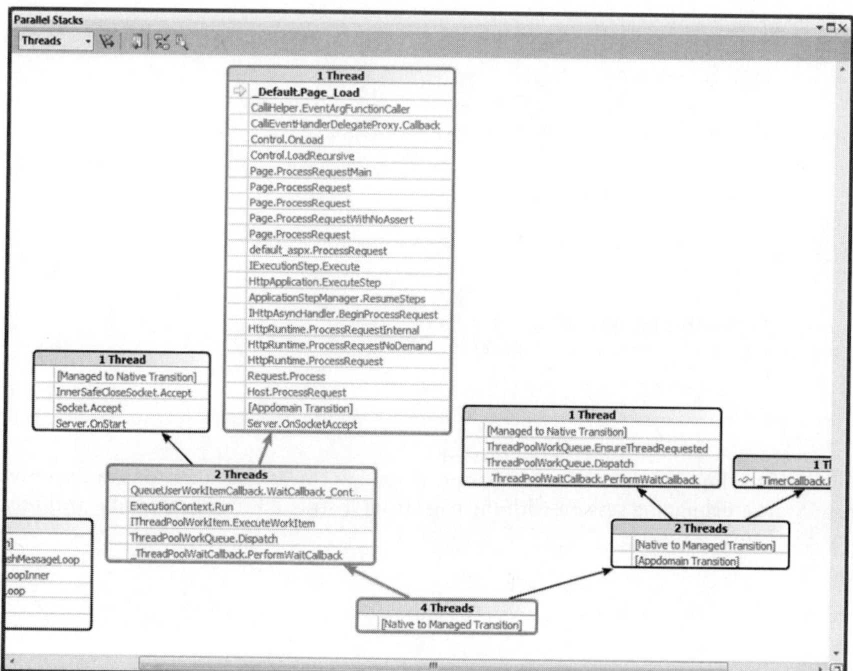

FIGURE 23-20

Client-side JavaScript Debugging

Excellent client-side JavaScript Debugging is available in Visual Studio 2010. If you run an ASP.NET application in a debugging session in Internet Explorer, you will need to enable script debugging. If you do not, you will receive a dialog similar to the one in Figure 23-21.

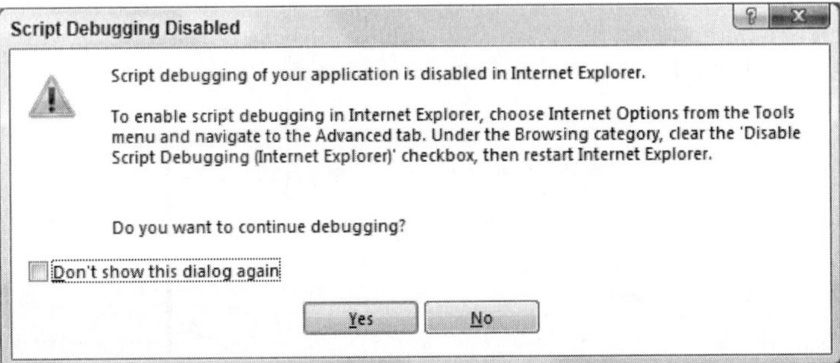

FIGURE 23-21

After you have turned on script debugging, try a simple ASP.NET page with some JavaScript that changes the text in a textbox to UPPERCASE when the button is clicked (Listing 23-5).

LISTING 23-5: Simple JavaScript debugging test

Available for download on Wrox.com

ASPX

```
<!DOCTYPE html PUBLIC "-//W3C//DTD XHTML 1.0 Transitional//EN"
"http://www.w3.org/TR/xhtml1/DTD/xhtml1-transitional.dtd">
<html xmlns="http://www.w3.org/1999/xhtml" >
<head runat="server">
   <script type="text/javascript">
       function MakeItUpper()
       {
           newText = document.getElementById("TextBox1").value.toUpperCase();
           document.getElementById("TextBox1").value = newText;
       }
   </script>
</head>
<body>
   <form id="form1" runat="server">
       <div>
           <input type="button" id="Button1" value="Upper"
               onclick="javascript:MakeItUpper()" />
           <input type="text" id="TextBox1" runat="server"/>
       </div>
   </form>
</body>
</html>
```

Put a breakpoint on one of the lines of *client-side* JavaScript. Note that this is code that runs in the browser, not on the Web server. Start a debugging session with the page from Listing 23-5. Visual Studio will break at that point, as shown in Figure 23-22.

FIGURE 23-22

The JavaScript debugger in Visual Studio supports variable tooltips, visualizers, call stacks, locals, watches, and all the features you're used to when debugging .NET-based languages.

Notice in the figure that `Default.aspx` has the word [dynamic] listed on the tab, indicating that this isn't the same `default.aspx` that was edited earlier; you can see that `default.aspx` listed on the final tab. Rather, this is the dynamically generated `default.aspx` that was delivered to the browser, including ViewState and other generated elements. Dynamically generated documents and scripts appear during the debug session in the Solution Explorer.

This rich debugging support on the client side makes creating today's JavaScript-heavy AJAX applications much easier.

SQL Stored Proc Debugging

Database projects are file-based projects that let you manage and execute database queries. You can add your existing SQL scripts to the project or create new ones and edit them within Visual Studio. Database projects and SQL debugging are not available in the Express or Standard versions of Visual Studio. They are available only in the Professional or Team Edition Visual Studio SKUs/versions.

When debugging database applications, you cannot use Step Into (F11) to step between code in the application tier into the code in SQL Server 2008 (be it T-SQL or CLR SQL). However, you can set a breakpoint in the stored procedure code and use Continue (F5) to execute code to that set breakpoint.

When debugging SQL on SQL Server 2008, be aware of any software or hardware firewalls you may be running. Sometimes your software firewall will warn you what you are trying to do. Be sure to select "unblock" in any warning dialogs to ensure that SQL Server 2008 and Visual Studio can communicate.

If you are using a SQL account to connect to the SQL Server, make sure the Windows User Account you run Visual Studio under is also an administrator on the SQL Server machine. You can add accounts to SQL Server's `sysadmin` privilege using the SQL command `sp_addsrvrolemember 'Domain\Name', 'sysadmin'`. Of course, never do this in production; and better yet, do your debugging on a machine with everything installed locally.

If you are using the NT Authentication model on the SQL Server 2008, make sure that account has permissions to run the `sp_enable_sql_debug` stored procedure. You can give account access to this stored procedure by using the SQL commands `CREATE USER UserName FOR LOGIN 'Domain\Name'` followed by `GRANT EXECUTE ON sp_enable_sql_debug TO UserName`. This creates a SQL user who is associated directly with a specific Windows User and then explicitly grants permissions to debug TSQL to that user. On SQL Server 2000, the user must have access to the extended stored procedure `sp_sdidebug`.

For slightly older installations such as Windows 2000 and Windows NT 4, or if you are using SQL 2000, be sure to visit MSDN for the latest details and tools in this space. The MSDN URL for debugging SQL Server is `http://msdn2.microsoft.com/library/zefbf0t6`.

EXCEPTION AND ERROR HANDLING

When an exception occurs in your ASP.NET application code, you can handle it in a number of ways, but the best approach is a multi-pronged one:

- Catch what you expect:
  - Use a `try/catch` around error-prone code. This can always catch specific exceptions that you can deal with, such as `System.IO.FileNotFoundException`.
  - Rather than catching exceptions around specific chunks of code at the page level, consider using the page-level error handler to catch specific exceptions that might happen anywhere on the page.
- But prepare for unhandled exceptions:
  - Set the `Page.Error` property if a specific page should show a specific error page for any unhandled exception. This can also be done using the `<%@Page>` directive or the code behind the property.
  - Have default error pages for 400 and 500 errors set in your `web.config` file.
  - Have a boilerplate `Application_OnError` handler that takes into consideration both specific exceptions that you can do something about, as well as all unhandled exceptions that you may want logged to the event log, a text file, or other instrumentation mechanism.

The phrase *unhandled exception* may be alarming, but remember that you don't do anyone any good catching an exception that you can't recover from. Unhandled exceptions are okay if they are just that — exceptional. For these situations, rely on global exception handlers for logging and friendly error pages that you can present to the user.

Why try to catch an exception by adding code everywhere if you can catch and log exceptions all in one place? A common mistake is creating a `try/catch` *block around some arbitrary code and catching the least specific exception type —* `System.Exception`*. A general rule is to not catch any exception that you cannot do anything about. Just because an exception can be thrown by a particular method doesn't mean you have to catch it. It is* exceptional, *remember? In addition, exception handlers are at both the page and the application level. Catch exceptions in these two centralized locations rather than all over.*

Handling Exceptions on a Page

To handle exceptions at a page level, override the `OnError` method that `System.Web.UI.Page` inherits from the `TemplateControl` class (see Listing 23-6). Calling `Server.GetLastError` gives you access to the exception that just occurred. Be aware that a chain of exceptions may have occurred, and you can use the `ExceptionGetBaseException` method to return the root exception.

LISTING 23-6: Page-level error handling

Available for download on Wrox.com

VB

```
Protected Overrides Sub OnError(ByVal e As System.EventArgs)
    Dim AnError As System.Exception = Server.GetLastError()
    If (TypeOf AnError.GetBaseException() Is SomeSpecificException) Then
        Response.Write("Something bad happened!")
        Response.StatusCode = 200
        Server.ClearError()
        Response.End()
    End If
End Sub
```

C#

```
protected override void OnError(EventArgs e)
{
    System.Exception anError = Server.GetLastError();
    if (anError.GetBaseException() is SomeSpecificException)
    {
        Response.Write("Something bad happened!");
        Response.StatusCode = 200;
        Server.ClearError();
        Response.End();
    }
}
```

Handling Application Exceptions

The technique of catching exceptions in a centralized location can be applied to error handling at the application level in `Global.asax`, as shown in Listing 23-7. If an exception is not caught on the page, the `web.config` file is checked for an alternate error page; if there is not one, the exception bubbles up to the application and your user sees a complete call stack.

LISTING 23-7: Application-level error handling

Available for download on Wrox.com

VB

```
Protected Sub Application_Error(sender as Object, ByVal e As System.EventArgs)
    Dim bigError As System.Exception = Server.GetLastError()
    'Example checking for HttpRequestValidationException
    If (TypeOf bigError.GetBaseException() Is HttpRequestValidationException) Then
        System.Diagnostics.Trace.WriteLine(bigError.ToString)
        Server.ClearError()
    End If
End Sub
```

C#

```
protected void Application_Error(Object sender, EventArgs e)
{
   System.Exception bigError = Server.GetLastError();
   //Example checking for HttpRequestValidationException
   if(bigError.GetBaseException() is HttpRequestValidationException )
   {
     System.Diagnostics.Trace.WriteLine(bigError.ToString());
    Server.ClearError();
   }
}
```

Unhandled application errors turn into HTTP Status Code 500 and display errors in the browser. These errors, including the complete call stack and other technical details, may be useful during development, but are hardly useful at production time. Most often, you want to create an error handler (as shown previously) to log your error and to give the user a friendlier page to view.

If you ever find yourself trying to catch exceptions of type `System.Exception`, *look at the code to see whether you can avoid it. There is almost never a reason to catch such a non-specific exception, and you are more likely to swallow exceptions that can provide valuable debugging. Check the API documentation for the framework method you are calling — a section specifically lists what exceptions an API call might throw. Never rely on an exception occurring to get a standard code path to work.*

Http Status Codes

Every `HttpRequest` results in an `HttpResponse`, and every `HttpResponse` includes a status code. Table 23-2 describes 11 particularly interesting HTTP status codes.

TABLE 23-2

STATUS CODE	EXPLANATION
200 OK	Everything went well.
301 Moved Permanently	Reminds the caller to use a new, permanent URL rather than the one he used to get here.
302 Found	Returned during a `Response.Redirect`. This is the way to say "No, no, look over here right now."
304 Not Modified	Returned as the result of a conditional `GET` when a requested document has not been modified. It is the basis of all browser-based caching. An HTTP message-body must not be returned when using a 304.
307 Temporary Redirect	Redirects calls to ASMX Web services to alternate URLs. Rarely used with ASP.NET.
400 Bad Request	Request was malformed.
401 Unauthorized	Request requires authentication from the user.
403 Forbidden	Authentication has failed, indicating that the server understood the requests but cannot fulfill it.
404 Not Found	The server has not found an appropriate file or handler to handle this request. The implication is that this may be a temporary state. This happens in ASP.NET not only because a file cannot be found, but also because it may be inappropriately mapped to an `IHttpHandler` that was not available to service the request.
410 Gone	The equivalent of a permanent 404 indicating to the client that it should delete any references to this link if possible. 404s usually indicate that the server does not know whether the condition is permanent.
500 Internal Server Error	The official text for this error is "The server encountered an unexpected condition which prevented it from fulfilling the request," but this error can occur when any unhandled exception bubbles all the way up to the user from ASP.NET.

Any status code greater than or equal to 400 is considered an error and, unless you configure otherwise, the user will likely see an unfriendly message in his browser. If you have not already handled these errors inside of the ASP.NET runtime by checking their exception types, or if the error occurred outside of ASP.NET and you want to show the user a friendly message, you can assign pages to any status code within the `web.config` file, as the following example shows:

```
<customErrors mode ="On" >
    <error statusCode ="500" redirect ="FriendlyMassiveError.aspx" />
</customErrors>
```

After making a change to the customer errors section of your `web.config` file, make sure a page is available to be shown to the user. A classic mistake in error redirection is redirecting the user to a page that will cause an error, thereby getting him stuck in a loop. Use a great deal of care if you have complicated headers or footers in your application that might cause an error if they appear on an error page. Avoid hitting the database or performing any other backend operation that requires either user authorization or that the user's session be in any specific state. In other words, make sure that the error page is a reliable standalone.

Any status code greater than or equal to 400 increments the ASP.NET Requests Failed performance counter. 401 increments Requests Failed and Requests Not Authorized. 404 and 414 increment both Requests Failed and Requests Not Found. Requests that result in a 500 status code increment Requests Failed and Requests Timed Out. If you are going to return status codes, you must realize their effects and their implications.

SUMMARY

This chapter examined the debugging tools available to you for creating robust ASP.NET applications. A successful debugging experience includes not only interactive debugging with features such as datatips, data visualizers, and error notifications, but also powerful options around configurable tracing and logging of information.

Remote debugging is easier than ever with ASP.NET, and the capability to write and debug ASP.NET pages without installing IIS removes yet another layer of complexity from the development process.

Visual Studio and its extensible debugging mechanisms continue to be expanded by intrepid bloggers and enthusiasts, which makes debugging even less tedious than it has been in the past.

24

File I/O and Streams

WHAT'S IN THIS CHAPTER?

- Managing drives, directories, and files
- Reading and writing data to various data locations
- Communicating across a network

Although most of this book concentrates on learning and using the features of ASP.NET, the .NET Framework provides an enormous amount of functionality in other areas of the Base Class Library (BCL). This chapter examines a few of the common base classes that you can use to enhance your ASP.NET applications. First, you look at using the frameworks `System.IO` namespace to manage files on the local file system. Next, you explore how to use the various `Stream` classes within the framework to read from and write different data formats to memory and the local file system. Finally, you learn how to use the .NET Framework to communicate with other computers across the Internet using common protocols such as HTTP and FTP.

A WORD ABOUT I/O SECURITY

Although this chapter is not specifically about ASP.NET security, you need to understand the impact of local system security on what the ASP.NET Worker Process is allowed to do inside of the IO namespace. Remember that generally, when your code is executed by IIS, it executes under the context of the ASP.NET Worker Process user account (ASPNET) and, therefore, your application may be restricted by that account's security rights. For example, by default, the ASP.NET Worker Process does not have rights to write to the local disk. The two main areas that you should look at to get a very basic understanding of the impact of security on an application are impersonation and user account ACLs. Chapter 20 covers ASP.NET security thoroughly.

Additionally, this chapter demonstrates how to use classes in the BCL to delete files and directories and to modify the permissions of directories and files. Recognize that permanently deleting important data from your hard drive or changing the permissions of a resource is entirely possible, and would result in your losing the ability to access the resource. *Be very careful* when using these classes against the file system.

WORKING WITH DRIVES, DIRECTORIES, AND FILES

Many times in ASP.NET applications, you need to interact with the local file system, reading directory structures, reading and writing to files, or performing other file I/O tasks. The `System.IO` namespace within the .NET Framework makes working with the file system easy. While working with the classes in the `System.IO` namespace, keep in mind that because your ASP.NET applications are executing on the server, the file system you are accessing is the one your Web application is running on. You cannot use the classes in the .NET Framework to create an ASP.NET application that can access the end user's file system.

The DriveInfo Class

You can start working with the file system by using the `DriveInfo` class. This class supplements the `GetLogicalDrives()` method of the `Directory` class and provides you with extended information on any drive registered with the server's local file system such as the name, type, size, and status of each drive. Listing 24-1 shows how to create a `DriveInfo` object for a specific drive and display local drive information on a Web page.

LISTING 24-1: Displaying local drive information

Available for download on Wrox.com

```
<script runat="server">
    Protected Sub Page_Load(ByVal sender As Object,
                            ByVal e As System.EventArgs)
        Dim drive As New System.IO.DriveInfo("C:\")
        lblDriveName.Text = drive.Name
        lblDriveType.Text = drive.DriveType.ToString()
        lblAvailableFreeSpace.Text =
            drive.AvailableFreeSpace.ToString()
        lblDriveFormat.Text = drive.DriveFormat
        lblTotalFreeSpace.Text = drive.TotalFreeSpace.ToString()
        lblTotalSize.Text = drive.TotalSize.ToString()
        lblVolumeLabel.Text = drive.VolumeLabel
    End Sub
</script>

<html xmlns="http://www.w3.org/1999/xhtml" >
<head runat="server">
    <title>Displaying Drive Information</title>
</head>
<body>
    <form id="form1" runat="server">
    <div>
        <table>
            <tr><td>Drive Name:</td><td>
                <asp:Label ID="lblDriveName"
                     runat="server" Text="Label" />
            </td></tr>
            <tr><td>Drive Type:</td><td>
                <asp:Label ID="lblDriveType"
                     runat="server" Text="Label"/>
            </td></tr>
            <tr><td>Available Free Space:</td><td>
               <asp:Label ID="lblAvailableFreeSpace"
                    runat="server" Text="Label" />
            </td></tr>
            <tr><td>Drive Format:</td><td>
                <asp:Label ID="lblDriveFormat"
                     runat="server" Text="Label" />
            </td></tr>
            <tr><td>Total Free Space:</td><td>
                <asp:Label ID="lblTotalFreeSpace"
```

```
                runat="server" Text="Label" />
        </td></tr>
        <tr><td>Total Size:</td><td>
            <asp:Label ID="lblTotalSize"
                runat="server" Text="Label" />
        </td></tr>
        <tr><td>Volume Label</td><td>
            <asp:Label ID="lblVolumeLabel"
                runat="server" Text="Label" />
        </td></tr>
    </table>
</div>
</form>
</body>
</html>
```

C#

```
<script runat="server">
    protected void Page_Load(object sender, EventArgs e)
    {
        System.IO.DriveInfo drive = new System.IO.DriveInfo(@"C:\");
        lblDriveName.Text = drive.Name;
        lblDriveType.Text = drive.DriveType.ToString();
        lblAvailableFreeSpace.Text =
            drive.AvailableFreeSpace.ToString();
        lblDriveFormat.Text = drive.DriveFormat;
        lblTotalFreeSpace.Text = drive.TotalFreeSpace.ToString();
        lblTotalSize.Text = drive.TotalSize.ToString();
        lblVolumeLabel.Text = drive.VolumeLabel;
    }
</script>
```

One of the more interesting properties in the sample is the `DriveType` enumeration. This read-only enumeration tells you what the drive type is, for example CD-ROM, Fixed, Ram, or Removable. Figure 24-1 shows you what the page looks like when you view it in a browser.

You can also enumerate through all the drives on the local file system by using the `DriveInfo`'s static `GetDrives()` method, which will provide you an array of `DriveInfo` objects. Listing 24-2 shows an example of enumerating through the local file system drives and adding each drive as a root node to a TreeView control.

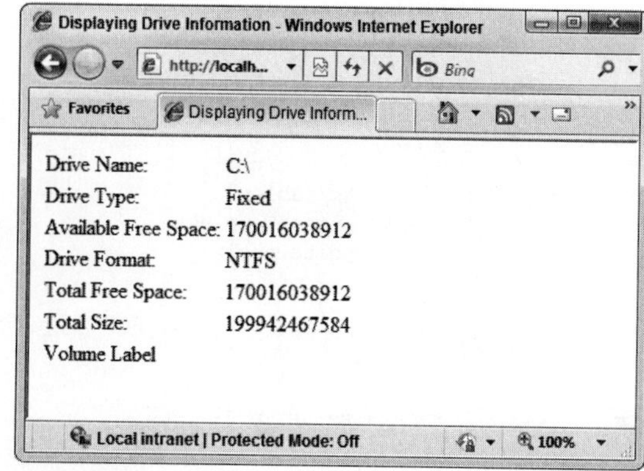

FIGURE 24-1

LISTING 24-2: Enumerating through local file system drives

Available for download on Wrox.com

VB

```
<script runat="server">
    Protected Sub Page_Load(ByVal sender As Object,
                            ByVal e As System.EventArgs)
        If (Not Page.IsPostBack) Then

            For Each drive As System.IO.DriveInfo In
                            System.IO.DriveInfo.GetDrives()
                Dim node As TreeNode = New TreeNode()
                node.Value = drive.Name

                If (drive.IsReady) Then
                    node.Text =
```

continues

LISTING 24-2 *(continued)*

```
                        String.Format("{0} - (free space: {1})",
                                 drive.Name, drive.AvailableFreeSpace)
                Else
                    node.Text =
                        String.Format("{0} - (not ready)", drive.Name)
                End If

                Me.TreeView1.Nodes.Add(node)
            Next

        End If
    End Sub
</script>

<html xmlns="http://www.w3.org/1999/xhtml" >
<head id="Head1" runat="server">
    <title>Enumerate Local System Drives</title>
</head>
<body>
    <form id="form1" runat="server">
    <asp:ScriptManager ID="ScriptManager1" runat="server">
    </asp:ScriptManager>
    <div>
        <asp:UpdatePanel runat="server" ID="UpdatePanel1">
            <ContentTemplate>
                <table>
                    <tr>
                        <td style="width: 100px" valign="top">
                            <asp:TreeView ID="TreeView1"
                                runat="server"></asp:TreeView>
                        </td>
                    </tr>
                </table>
            </ContentTemplate>
        </asp:UpdatePanel>
    </div>
    </form>
</body>
</html>
```

C#

```
<script runat="server">
    protected void Page_Load(object sender, EventArgs e)
    {
        if (!Page.IsPostBack)
        {

            foreach (System.IO.DriveInfo drive in
                     System.IO.DriveInfo.GetDrives())
            {
                TreeNode node = new TreeNode();
                node.Value = drive.Name;

                if (drive.IsReady)
                    node.Text =
                        String.Format("{0} - (free space: {1})",
                                drive.Name, drive.AvailableFreeSpace);
                else
                    node.Text =
                        String.Format("{0} - (not ready)", drive.Name);
```

```
                this.TreeView1.Nodes.Add(node);
            }
        }
    }
</script>
```

Notice that, in this sample, the drive object's read-only `IsReady` property is used to test whether the drive is accessible. If you are enumerating drives, testing for this before attempting to access any of the other drive properties is always a good idea because removable drives and network drives may not always be available when your code is executed. Figure 24-2 shows what the page looks like when viewed in the browser.

The Directory and DirectoryInfo Classes

You can build on the previous section's examples and add the ability to browse through the system's directory structure by using the `System.IO` namespace `Directory` and `DirectoryInfo` classes. .NET provides these classes for working with file system directories. The `Directory` class exposes static methods you can use to create, move, and delete any directory while the `DirectoryInfo` class represents a specific directory. The `DirectoryInfo` class allows you to perform the same actions as the `Directory` class and adds methods that allow you to enumerate the directories, child directories, and files.

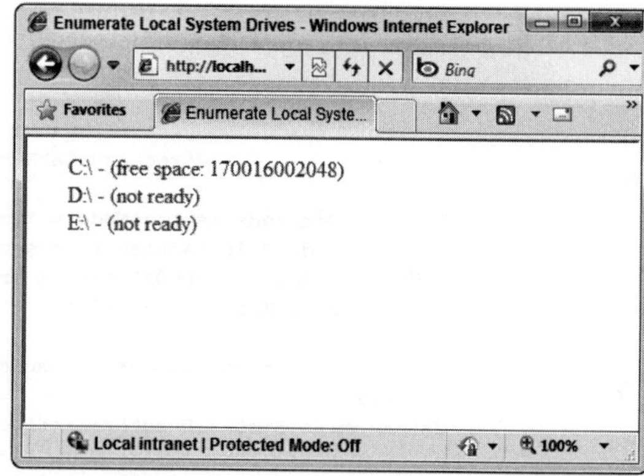

FIGURE 24-2

Continuing the sample from Listing 24-2, Listing 24-3 shows you how to use the `GetDirectories()` method of the `DirectoryInfo` class to create a method that enumerates a directory's children and adds them to a TreeView control to create a small directory browser.

LISTING 24-3: Enumerating file system directories

Available for download on Wrox.com

```
<script runat="server">

    Protected Sub Page_Load(ByVal sender As Object,
                            ByVal e As System.EventArgs)

        If (Not Page.IsPostBack) Then

            For Each drive As System.IO.DriveInfo In
                              System.IO.DriveInfo.GetDrives()

                Dim node As TreeNode = New TreeNode()
                    node.SelectAction = TreeNodeSelectAction.SelectExpand
                    node.PopulateOnDemand = True
                    node.Expanded = False
                node.Value = drive.Name

                If (drive.IsReady) Then
                    node.Text =
                        String.Format("{0} - (free space: {1})",
                                 drive.Name, drive.AvailableFreeSpace)
                Else
                    node.Text =
                        String.Format("{0} - (not ready)", drive.Name)
                End If
```

continues

LISTING 24-3 *(continued)*

```
                Me.TreeView1.Nodes.Add(node)
            Next

        End If

    End Sub

    Private Sub LoadDirectories(ByVal parent As TreeNode,
                                ByVal path As String)

        Dim directory As System.IO.DirectoryInfo =
            New System.IO.DirectoryInfo(path)

        Try
            For Each d As System.IO.DirectoryInfo In
                          directory.GetDirectories()

                Dim node As TreeNode = New TreeNode(d.Name, d.FullName)
                node.SelectAction = TreeNodeSelectAction.SelectExpand
                node.PopulateOnDemand = True
                node.Expanded = False

                parent.ChildNodes.Add(node)
            Next
        Catch ex As System.UnauthorizedAccessException
            parent.Text += " (Access Denied)"
        Catch ex As System.IO.IOException
            parent.Text +=
                String.Format(" (Unknown Error: {0})", ex.Message)
        End Try
    End Sub

    Protected Sub TreeView1_TreeNodePopulate(ByVal sender As Object,
             ByVal e As System.Web.UI.WebControls.TreeNodeEventArgs)
        LoadDirectories(e.Node, e.Node.Value)
    End Sub
</script>


<html xmlns="http://www.w3.org/1999/xhtml" >
<head id="Head1" runat="server">
    <title>Enumerate a Directory</title>
</head>
<body>
    <form id="form1" runat="server">
    <asp:ScriptManager ID="ScriptManager1" runat="server">
    </asp:ScriptManager>
    <div>
        <asp:UpdatePanel runat="server" ID="UpdatePanel1">
            <ContentTemplate>
                <table>
                    <tr>
                        <td style="width: 100px" valign="top">
                            <asp:TreeView ID="TreeView1" runat="server"
                        OnTreeNodePopulate="TreeView1_TreeNodePopulate">
                            </asp:TreeView>
                        </td>
                    </tr>
                </table>
```

```
            </ContentTemplate>
        </asp:UpdatePanel>
    </div>
    </form>
</body>
</html>
```

C#

```
<script runat="server">
    protected void Page_Load(object sender, EventArgs e)
    {
        if (!Page.IsPostBack)
        {
            foreach (System.IO.DriveInfo drive in
                     System.IO.DriveInfo.GetDrives())
            {
                TreeNode node = new TreeNode();
                node.SelectAction = TreeNodeSelectAction.SelectExpand;
                node.PopulateOnDemand = true;
                node.Expanded = false;
                node.Value = drive.Name;

                if (drive.IsReady)
                    node.Text =
                         String.Format("{0} - (free space: {1})",
                                 drive.Name, drive.AvailableFreeSpace);
                else
                    node.Text =
                        String.Format("{0} - (not ready)", drive.Name);

                this.TreeView1.Nodes.Add(node);
            }
        }
    }

    private void LoadDirectories(TreeNode parent, string path)
    {
        System.IO.DirectoryInfo directory =
            new System.IO.DirectoryInfo(path);

        try
        {
            foreach (System.IO.DirectoryInfo d in
               directory.GetDirectories())
            {
                TreeNode node = new TreeNode(d.Name, d.FullName);
                node.SelectAction = TreeNodeSelectAction.SelectExpand;
                node.PopulateOnDemand = true;
                node.Expanded = false;

                parent.ChildNodes.Add(node);
            }
        }
        catch (System.UnauthorizedAccessException ex)
        {
            parent.Text += " (Access Denied)";
        }
        catch (System.IO.IOException ex)
        {
            parent.Text +=
               string.Format(" (Unknown Error: {0})", ex.Message);
        }
    }
```

continues

LISTING 24-3 *(continued)*

```
    protected void TreeView1_TreeNodePopulate(object sender,
        TreeNodeEventArgs e)
    {
        LoadDirectories(e.Node, e.Node.Value);
    }
</script>
```

Figure 24-3 shows what the page should look like in the browser. You should now be able to browse the directory tree, much as you do in Windows Explorer, by opening and closing the TreeView nodes.

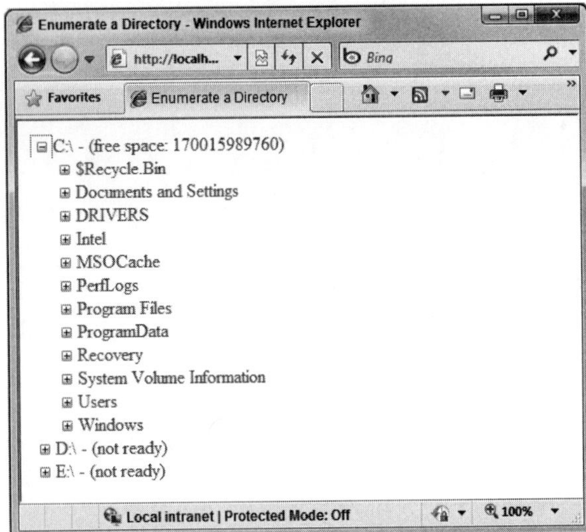

FIGURE 24-3

Notice that the example continuously creates new instances of the `DirectoryInfo` class each time the method executes in order to continue to enumerate the directory tree. You could also extend this example by displaying some additional properties as part of the `Node` text, such as the `CreationTime` or `Attributes`.

One important item to note when using the `GetDirectories()` method is that using it can come with some performance costs. This is because each time the `GetDirectories()` method is called it automatically allocates an array structure large enough to accommodate all the child directories of the parent directory and populates that array with `DirectoryInfo` objects. The method will not return until this work has completed. If you execute this method on a directory with a large number of children, or are accessing directories exposed by a network share, this allocation and population can be slow, effectively locking your application while the work is performed.

In those scenarios you can instead choose to use the `EnumerateDirectories()` method. This method returns an `IEnumerable<DirectoryInfo>` rather than an array, and therefore does not have the performance costs of the array allocation or population. To use the `EnumerateDirectories()` method, simply substitute it in Listing 24-3 for the `()` method call:

VB

```
For Each d As System.IO.DirectoryInfo In
            directory.EnumerateDirectories()
```

C#

```
foreach (System.IO.DirectoryInfo d in directory.EnumerateDirectories())
```

To perform a specific action such as creating, reading properties from, or deleting a directory, you don't have to create an instance of the `DirectoryInfo` class. You can instead use the static methods exposed by the `Directory` class. Rather than creating an object instance that represents a specific path, the static methods exposed by the `Directory` class generally require you to pass the path as a method parameter. Listing 24-4 shows how you can use the static methods exposed by the `Directory` class to create, read properties from, and delete a directory.

Remember to be very careful when deleting a folder from your hard drive. Permanently deleting important data from your system or changing the permissions of a resource is possible, and would result in your losing the ability to access the resource.

LISTING 24-4: Working with the static methods of the Directory class

Available for download on Wrox.com

VB

```
<script runat="server">

    Protected Sub Page_Load(ByVal sender As Object,
                            ByVal e As System.EventArgs)

        System.IO.Directory.CreateDirectory(MapPath("Wrox"))

        If System.IO.Directory.Exists(MapPath("Wrox")) Then

            Me.Label1.Text =
                   System.IO.Directory.GetCreationTime(
                       MapPath("Wrox")).ToString()
            Me.Label2.Text =
                   System.IO.Directory.GetLastAccessTime(
                       MapPath("Wrox")).ToString()
            Me.Label3.Text =
                    System.IO.Directory.GetLastWriteTime(
                       MapPath("Wrox")).ToString()

            System.IO.Directory.Delete(MapPath("Wrox"))
        End If
    End Sub
</script>

<html xmlns="http://www.w3.org/1999/xhtml" >
<head id="Head1" runat="server">
    <title>Using Static Methods</title>
</head>
<body>
    <form id="form1" runat="server">
    <div>
        Creation Time:
              <asp:Label ID="Label1" runat="server"
                   Text="Label"></asp:Label><br />
        Last Access Time:
              <asp:Label ID="Label2" runat="server"
                   Text="Label"></asp:Label><br />
        Last Write Time:
              <asp:Label ID="Label3" runat="server"
                   Text="Label"></asp:Label>
    </div>
    </form>
</body>
</html>
```

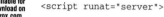

continues

LISTING 24-4 *(continued)*

```
<script runat="server">
    protected void Page_Load(object sender, EventArgs e)
    {
        System.IO.Directory.CreateDirectory(MapPath("Wrox"));

        if (System.IO.Directory.Exists(MapPath("Wrox")))
        {
            this.Label1.Text =
                      System.IO.Directory.GetCreationTime(
                          MapPath("Wrox")).ToString();
            this.Label2.Text =
                      System.IO.Directory.GetLastAccessTime(
                          MapPath("Wrox")).ToString();
            this.Label3.Text =
                      System.IO.Directory.GetLastWriteTime(
                          MapPath("Wrox")).ToString();

            System.IO.Directory.Delete(MapPath("Wrox"));
        }
    }
</script>
```

Running this sample creates a new directory called "Wrox" within the Web site. The sample then accesses and displays the new directory's Creation Time, Last Access Time, and Last Write Time properties. Finally, the "Wrox" directory is deleted.

Using Relative Paths and Setting and Getting the Current Directory

When an ASP.NET page is executed, the thread used to execute the code that generates the page by default has a current working directory. It uses this directory as its base directory if you have specified relative paths in your application. If you pass a relative filename into any `System.IO` class, the file is assumed to be located relative to the current working directory.

The default working directory for the ASP.NET Development Server is a directory under your Visual Studio install root. If you installed Visual Studio in `C:\Program Files`, your ASP.NET Development Server working directory would be `C:\Program Files\Common Files\Microsoft Shared\DevServer\10.0`.

You can find the location of your working directory by using the `Directory` class's `GetCurrentDirectory()` method. In addition, you can change the current working directory using the `Directory` class's `SetCurrentDirectory()` method.

Listing 24-5 shows you how to set and then display your working directory.

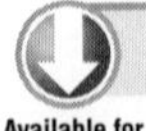

LISTING 24-5: Setting and displaying the application's working directory

Available for download on Wrox.com

```
<script runat="server">
    Protected Sub Page_Load(ByVal sender As Object,
                            ByVal e As System.EventArgs)
        Me.Label1.Text = System.IO.Directory.GetCurrentDirectory()
        System.IO.Directory.SetCurrentDirectory(MapPath(""))
        Me.Label2.Text = System.IO.Directory.GetCurrentDirectory()
    End Sub
</script>

<html xmlns="http://www.w3.org/1999/xhtml" >
<head runat="server">
    <title>Set and Display the Working Directory</title>
</head>
<body>
```

```
        <form id="form1" runat="server">
        <div>
            Old Working Directory:
                <asp:Label ID="Label1" runat="server" Text="Label" /><br />
            New Working Directory:
                <asp:Label ID="Label2" runat="server" Text="Label" />
        </div>
        </form>
    </body>
    </html>
```

C#

```
    <script runat="server">
        protected void Page_Load(object sender, EventArgs e)
        {
            this.Label1.Text = System.IO.Directory.GetCurrentDirectory();
            System.IO.Directory.SetCurrentDirectory(MapPath(""));
            this.Label2.Text = System.IO.Directory.GetCurrentDirectory();
        }
    </script>
```

Note that the directory parameter you specify in the `SetCurrentDirectory()` method must already exist; otherwise, ASP.NET will throw an exception. Knowing this, you should use the `Exists()` method of the `Directory` class to ensure the directory you are specifying does, in fact, already exist before you try to change the working directory.

When you execute the code in Listing 24-5, you should see that it displays the original working directory, and then displays the new working directory after you change it. Figure 24-4 shows what the page looks like when executed.

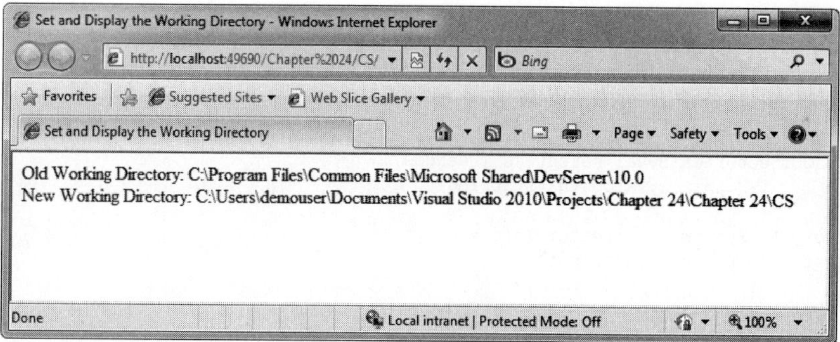

FIGURE 24-4

File and FileInfo

Now that you can display and browse a directory tree, you can expand the previous example even further by adding the files located in the currently selected directory to the display.

The simplest way to display the directories files is to bind an array of `FileInfo` objects to a GridView. You can use the `GetFiles()` method of the `DirectoryInfo` class to obtain such an array.

The `FileInfo` object, like the `DirectoryInfo` object, represents a single element in the file system (in this case a file) and allows you to perform actions on that file and access properties of the file. If you want to display only the filenames, you could use the `Directory` class's `GetFiles()` method, which returns a simple string array of filenames.

Listing 24-6 shows how to use the TreeView control's `SelectedNodeChanged` event to bind your GridView with the file information.

LISTING 24-6: Binding a GridView to directory files

Available for download on Wrox.com

VB

```
<script runat="server">

    Protected Sub Page_Load(ByVal sender As Object,
                            ByVal e As System.EventArgs)

        If (Not Page.IsPostBack) Then

            For Each drive As System.IO.DriveInfo In
                              System.IO.DriveInfo.GetDrives()

                Dim node As TreeNode = New TreeNode()
                node.SelectAction = TreeNodeSelectAction.SelectExpand
                node.PopulateOnDemand = True
                node.Expanded = False
                node.Value = drive.Name

                If (drive.IsReady) Then
                    node.Text =
                        String.Format("{0} - (free space: {1})",
                                  drive.Name, drive.AvailableFreeSpace)
                Else
                    node.Text =
                        String.Format("{0} - (not ready)", drive.Name)
                End If

                Me.TreeView1.Nodes.Add(node)
            Next

        End If

    End Sub

    Private Sub LoadDirectories(ByVal parent As TreeNode,
                                ByVal path As String)

        Dim directory As System.IO.DirectoryInfo =
            New System.IO.DirectoryInfo(path)

        Try
            For Each d As System.IO.DirectoryInfo In
                          directory.GetDirectories()

                Dim node As TreeNode = New TreeNode(d.Name, d.FullName)
                node.SelectAction = TreeNodeSelectAction.SelectExpand
                node.PopulateOnDemand = True
                node.Expanded = False

                parent.ChildNodes.Add(node)
            Next
        Catch ex As System.UnauthorizedAccessException
            parent.Text += " (Access Denied)"
        Catch ex As System.IO.IOException
            parent.Text +=
                String.Format(" (Unknown Error: {0})", ex.Message)
        End Try
    End Sub

    Protected Sub TreeView1_TreeNodePopulate(ByVal sender As Object,
              ByVal e As System.Web.UI.WebControls.TreeNodeEventArgs)
        LoadDirectories(e.Node, e.Node.Value)
    End Sub
```

```
    Protected Sub TreeView1_SelectedNodeChanged _
        (ByVal sender As Object, ByVal e As System.EventArgs)

        Dim directory As System.IO.DirectoryInfo =
           New System.IO.DirectoryInfo(Me.TreeView1.SelectedNode.Value)

        Me.GridView1.DataSource = directory.GetFiles()
        Me.GridView1.DataBind()
    End Sub
</script>

<html xmlns="http://www.w3.org/1999/xhtml" >
<head id="Head1" runat="server">
    <title>Binding a Gridview </title>
</head>
<body>
    <form id="form1" runat="server">
    <asp:ScriptManager ID="ScriptManager1" runat="server">
    </asp:ScriptManager>
    <div>
        <asp:UpdatePanel runat="server" ID="UpdatePanel1">
            <ContentTemplate>
                <table>
                    <tr>
                      <td style="width: 100px" valign="top">

            <asp:TreeView ID="TreeView1" runat="server"
                OnTreeNodePopulate="TreeView1_TreeNodePopulate"
                OnSelectedNodeChanged="TreeView1_SelectedNodeChanged"/>

                      </td>
                      <td valign="top">
                          <asp:GridView ID="GridView1" runat="server"
                                AutoGenerateColumns="False"
                                GridLines="None" CellPadding="3">
                                <Columns>
                                    <asp:BoundField DataField="Name"
                                       HeaderText="Name"
                                       HeaderStyle-HorizontalAlign=Left
                                       HeaderStyle-Font-Bold=true />
                                    <asp:BoundField DataField="Length"
                                       HeaderText="Size"
                                       ItemStyle-HorizontalAlign=Right
                                       HeaderStyle-HorizontalAlign=Right
                                       HeaderStyle-Font-Bold=true />
                                    <asp:BoundField
                                       DataField="LastWriteTime"
                                       HeaderText="Date Modified"
                                       HeaderStyle-HorizontalAlign=Left
                                       HeaderStyle-Font-Bold=true />
                                 </Columns>
                             </asp:GridView>
                         </td>
                     </tr>
                 </table>
             </ContentTemplate>
         </asp:UpdatePanel>
    </div>
    </form>
</body>
</html>
```

continues

LISTING 24-6 *(continued)*

C#

```
<script runat="server">
    protected void Page_Load(object sender, EventArgs e)
    {
        if (!Page.IsPostBack)
        {
            foreach (System.IO.DriveInfo drive in
                     System.IO.DriveInfo.GetDrives())
            {
                TreeNode node = new TreeNode();
                node.SelectAction = TreeNodeSelectAction.SelectExpand;
                node.PopulateOnDemand = true;
                node.Expanded = false;
                node.Value = drive.Name;

                if (drive.IsReady)
                    node.Text =
                        String.Format("{0} - (free space: {1})",
                                drive.Name, drive.AvailableFreeSpace);
                else
                    node.Text =
                        String.Format("{0} - (not ready)", drive.Name);

                this.TreeView1.Nodes.Add(node);
            }
        }
    }

    private void LoadDirectories(TreeNode parent, string path)
    {
        System.IO.DirectoryInfo directory =
            new System.IO.DirectoryInfo(path);

        try
        {
            foreach (System.IO.DirectoryInfo d in
                     directory.GetDirectories())
            {
                TreeNode node = new TreeNode(d.Name, d.FullName);
                node.SelectAction = TreeNodeSelectAction.SelectExpand;
                node.Expanded = false;
                node.PopulateOnDemand = true;

                parent.ChildNodes.Add(node);
            }
        }
        catch (System.UnauthorizedAccessException ex)
        {
            parent.Text += " (Access Denied)";
        }
        catch (System.IO.IOException ex)
        {
            parent.Text +=
                string.Format(" (Unknown Error: {0})", ex.Message);
        }
    }

    protected void TreeView1_TreeNodePopulate(object sender,
        TreeNodeEventArgs e)
    {
        LoadDirectories(e.Node, e.Node.Value);
```

```
    }

    protected void TreeView1_SelectedNodeChanged(object sender,
        EventArgs e)
    {
        try
        {
            System.IO.DirectoryInfo directory =
                new System.IO.DirectoryInfo(
                    this.TreeView1.SelectedNode.Value);

            this.GridView1.DataSource = directory.GetFiles();
            this.GridView1.DataBind();
        }
        catch (System.UnauthorizedAccessException ex)
        {
            TreeView1.SelectedNode.Text += " (Access Denied)";
        }
        catch (System.IO.IOException ex)
        {
            TreeView1.SelectedNode.Text +=
                string.Format(" (Unknown Error: {0})", ex.Message);
        }

    }
</script>
```

Figure 24-5 shows what your Web page looks like after you have selected a directory and the grid has been bound to the `FileInfo` array.

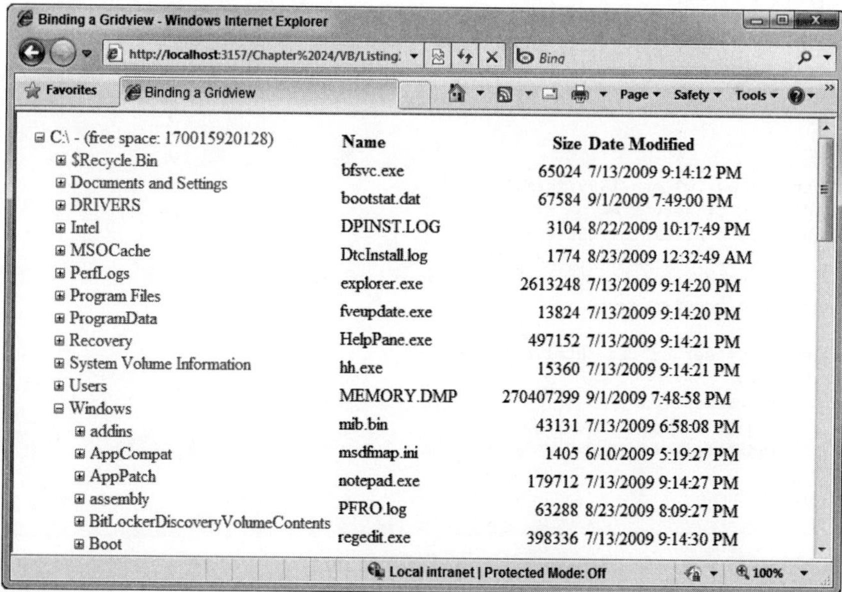

FIGURE 24-5

The `GetFiles()` method, like the `GetDirectories()` method described earlier in this section, can come with some performance costs which you should be aware of. Like the `GetDirectories()` method, the `GetFiles()` method automatically allocates an array structure large enough to accommodate all the child files of the parent directory and populates that array with `FileInfo` objects. The method will not return until this work has completed. If you execute this method on a directory with a large number of children, or are accessing directories exposed by a network share, this allocation and population can be slow, effectively locking your application while the work is performed.

In those scenarios you can instead choose to use the `EnumerateFiles()` method. This method returns an `IEnumerable<FileInfo>` rather than an array, and therefore does not have the performance costs of the array allocation or population. To use the `EnumerateFiles()` method simply substitute it in Listing 24-6 for the `GetFiles()` method call.

Although data binding to the GridView requires little work, you can also enumerate through the `FileInfo` array to display the information. Listing 24-7 shows you how to enumerate through the `FileInfo` array and display the properties to the page.

LISTING 24-7: Manually enumerating directory files

Available for download on Wrox.com

VB

```
<script runat="server">
    Protected Sub Page_Load(ByVal sender As Object,
                            ByVal e As System.EventArgs)
        Dim dir As New System.IO.DirectoryInfo(MapPath(""))

        For Each file As System.IO.FileInfo In dir.GetFiles("*.*")
            Dim row As HtmlTableRow = New HtmlTableRow()
            row.Cells.Add(
                New HtmlTableCell() With _
                    {.InnerHtml = file.Name})
            row.Cells.Add(
                New HtmlTableCell() With _
                    {.InnerHtml = file.LastWriteTime.ToString()})
            row.Cells.Add(
                New HtmlTableCell() With _
                    {.InnerHtml = file.Attributes.ToString()})
            Me.HtmlTable1.Rows.Add(row)
        Next
    End Sub
</script>

<html xmlns="http://www.w3.org/1999/xhtml" >
<head id="Head1" runat="server">
    <title>Enumerate a FileInfo</title>
</head>
<body>
    <form id="form1" runat="server">
    <div>
        <table runat="server" id="HtmlTable1">
            <tr>
                <td>Name</td>
                <td>Last Write Time</td>
                <td>Attributes</td>
            </tr>
        </table>
    </div>
    </form>
</body>
</html>
```

C#

```
<script runat="server">
    protected void Page_Load(object sender, EventArgs e)
    {
        System.IO.DirectoryInfo dir =
            new System.IO.DirectoryInfo(MapPath(""));
        foreach (System.IO.FileInfo file in dir.GetFiles("*.*"))
        {
```

```
            HtmlTableRow row = new HtmlTableRow();
            row.Cells.Add(
                new HtmlTableCell()
                    { InnerHtml = file.Name });
            row.Cells.Add(
                new HtmlTableCell()
                    { InnerHtml = file.LastWriteTime.ToString() });
            row.Cells.Add(
                new HtmlTableCell()
                    { InnerHtml = file.Attributes.ToString() });
            this.HtmlTable1.Rows.Add(row);
        }
    }
</script>
```

Listing 24-7 also shows that you can provide a file filter to the `GetFiles()` method. This allows you to limit the results from the method to specific file extensions or to files matching a specific filename portion.

Working with Paths

Although working with files and directories has been rather easy, even going all the way back to good old ASP, one of the most problematic areas has always been working with paths. Many lines of code have been written by developers to deal with concatenating partial paths together, making sure files have extensions, evaluating those extensions, stripping filenames off paths, and even more.

Thankfully, the .NET Framework provides you with a class just for dealing with paths. The `System.IO.Path` class exposes a handful of static methods that make dealing with paths a snap. Table 24-1 lists the static methods exposed by the `Path` class.

TABLE 24-1

METHOD	DESCRIPTION
`ChangeExtension`	Changes the extension of the provided path string to the provided new extension.
`Combine`	Returns a single combined path from two partial path strings.
`GetDirectoryName`	Returns the directory or directories of the provided path.
`GetExtension`	Returns the extension of the provided path.
`GetFileName`	Returns the filename of the provided path.
`GetFileNameWithoutExtension`	Returns the filename without its extension of the provided path.
`GetFullPath`	Given a non-rooted path, returns a rooted pathname based on the current working directory. For example, if the path passed in is "temp" and the current working directory is `C:\MyWebsite`, the method returns `C:\MyWebsite\temp`.
`GetInvalidFileNameChars`	Returns an array of characters that are not allowed in filenames for the current system.
`GetInvalidPathChars`	Returns an array of characters that are not allowed in pathnames for the current system.
`GetPathRoot`	Returns the root path.
`GetTempFileName`	Returns a temporary filename, located in the temporary directory returned by GetTempPath.
`GetTempPath`	Returns the temporary directory name.
`HasExtension`	Returns a Boolean value indicating whether a path has an extension.
`IsPathRooted`	Returns a Boolean value indicating whether a path is rooted.

As an example of using the `Path` class, the application shown in Figure 24-6 lets you enter a path and then displays the component parts of the path such as the root path (logical drive), the directory, filename, and extension.

The `GetInvalidPathChars` and `GetInvalidFileNameChars` methods return an array of characters that are not allowed in path and filenames, respectively. Although the specific invalid characters are dependent on the platform the application is running on, the arrays returned by these methods will most likely contain elements such as non-printable characters, special Unicode characters, or characters from non-Latin–based character sets. The characters that your browser is capable of rendering will depend on your specific platform setup.

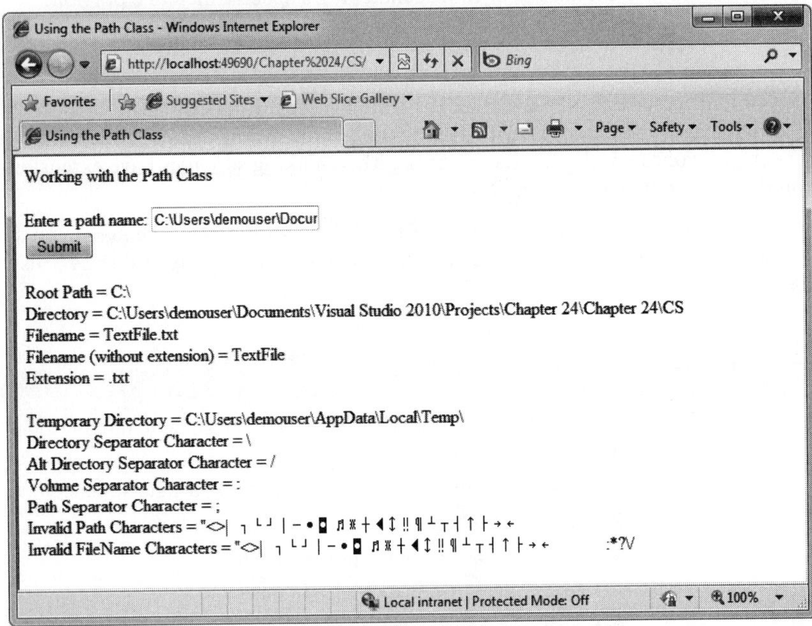

FIGURE 24-6

The code in Listing 24-8 shows how the various methods and constant properties of the `Path` class have been used to create the application shown in Figure 24-6.

LISTING 24-8: Using the Path class

Available for download on Wrox.com

```
<script runat="server">
    Protected Sub Page_Load(ByVal sender As Object,
                            ByVal e As System.EventArgs)
        If Page.IsPostBack Then
            Me.lblRootPath.Text =
                System.IO.Path.GetPathRoot(Me.txtPathName.Text)
            Me.lblDirectoryName.Text =
                System.IO.Path.GetDirectoryName(Me.txtPathName.Text)
            Me.lblFileName.Text =
                System.IO.Path.GetFileName(Me.txtPathName.Text)
```

```
            Me.lblFileNameWithoutExtension.Text =
                System.IO.Path.GetFileNameWithoutExtension(
                    Me.txtPathName.Text)
            Me.lblExtension.Text =
                System.IO.Path.GetExtension(Me.txtPathName.Text)

            Me.lblTemporaryPath.Text = System.IO.Path.GetTempPath()
            Me.lblDirectorySeparatorChar.Text =
                System.IO.Path.DirectorySeparatorChar.ToString()
            Me.lblAltDirectorySeparatorChar.Text =
                System.IO.Path.AltDirectorySeparatorChar.ToString()
            Me.lblVolumeSeparatorChar.Text =
                System.IO.Path.VolumeSeparatorChar.ToString()
            Me.lblPathSeparator.Text =
                System.IO.Path.PathSeparator.ToString()

            Me.lblInvalidChars.Text =
                 HttpUtility.HtmlEncode(
                     New String(System.IO.Path.GetInvalidPathChars()))
            Me.lblInvalidFileNameChars.Text =
                 HttpUtility.HtmlEncode(
                  New String(System.IO.Path.GetInvalidFileNameChars()))
        End If
    End Sub
</script>

<html xmlns="http://www.w3.org/1999/xhtml" >
<head runat="server">
    <title>Using the Path Class</title>
</head>
<body>
    <form id="form1" runat="server">
    <div>
        Working with the Path Class<br />
        <br />
        Enter a path name:
        <asp:TextBox ID="txtPathName" runat="server" /><br />
        <asp:Button ID="Button1" runat="server" Text="Button" /><br />
        <br />
        Root Path =
        <asp:Label ID="lblRootPath" runat="server" Text="Label" />
        <br />
        Directory =
        <asp:Label ID="lblDirectoryName" runat="server" Text="Label" />
        <br />
        Filename =
        <asp:Label ID="lblFileName" runat="server" Text="Label" />
        <br />
        Filename (without extension) =
        <asp:Label ID="lblFileNameWithoutExtension"
             runat="server" Text="Label" />
        <br />
        Extension =
        <asp:Label ID="lblExtension" runat="server" Text="Label" />
        <br />
        <br />
        Temporary Directory =
        <asp:Label ID="lblTemporaryPath" runat="server" Text="Label" />
        <br />
        Directory Separator Character =
        <asp:Label ID="lblDirectorySeparatorChar"
             runat="server" Text="Label" />
```

continues

LISTING 24-8 *(continued)*

```
            <br />
            Alt Directory Separator Character =
            <asp:Label ID="lblAltDirectorySeparatorChar"
                 runat="server" Text="Label" />
            <br />
            Volume Separator Character =
            <asp:Label ID="lblVolumeSeparatorChar"
                 runat="server" Text="Label" />
            <br />
            Path Separator Character =
            <asp:Label ID="lblPathSeparator" runat="server" Text="Label" />
            <br />
            Invalid Path Characters =
            <asp:Label ID="lblInvalidChars" runat="server" Text="Label" />
            <br />
            Invalid FileName Characters =
            <asp:Label ID="lblInvalidFileNameChars"
                 runat="server" Text="Label" />

        </div>
        </form>
    </body>
    </html>
```

C#

```
<%@ Import Namespace="System.IO" %>

<script runat="server">

    protected void Page_Load(object sender, EventArgs e)
    {
        if (Page.IsPostBack)
        {
            this.lblRootPath.Text =
                 Path.GetPathRoot(this.txtPathName.Text);
            this.lblDirectoryName.Text =
                 Path.GetDirectoryName(this.txtPathName.Text);
            this.lblFileName.Text =
                 Path.GetFileName(this.txtPathName.Text);
            this.lblFileNameWithoutExtension.Text =
                 Path.GetFileNameWithoutExtension(
                     this.txtPathName.Text);
            this.lblExtension.Text =
                           Path.GetExtension(this.txtPathName.Text);
            this.lblTemporaryPath.Text = Path.GetTempPath();
            this.lblDirectorySeparatorChar.Text =
                           Path.DirectorySeparatorChar.ToString();
            this.lblAltDirectorySeparatorChar.Text =
                           Path.AltDirectorySeparatorChar.ToString();
            this.lblVolumeSeparatorChar.Text =
                 Path.VolumeSeparatorChar.ToString();
            this.lblPathSeparator.Text = Path.PathSeparator.ToString();
            this.lblInvalidChars.Text =
               HttpUtility.HtmlEncode(
                   new String(Path.GetInvalidPathChars() ) );
            this.lblInvalidFileNameChars.Text =
               HttpUtility.HtmlEncode(
                   new String(Path.GetInvalidFileNameChars()));
        }
    }
</script>
```

File and Directory Properties, Attributes, and Access Control Lists

Finally, this section explains how you can access and modify file and directory properties, attributes, and Access Control Lists.

Samples in this section use a simple text file called `TextFile.txt` *to demonstrate the concepts. You can either create this file or substitute your own file in the sample code. A sample of this file is also included in the downloadable source code for this chapter. The samples assume the file has been added to the Web site and use the* `Server.MapPath` *method to determine the full filepath.*

Properties and Attributes

Files and directories share certain properties that you can use to determine the age of a file or directory, when it was last modified, and what attributes have been applied. You can view these properties by opening the file's Properties dialog. You open this dialog from Windows Explorer by either right-clicking on the file and selecting Properties from the context menu, or selecting Properties from the File menu. Figure 24-7 shows the file's Properties window for the text document.

Both the `DirectoryInfo` and the `FileInfo` classes let you access these properties and modify them. Listing 24-9 shows you an example of displaying the file properties.

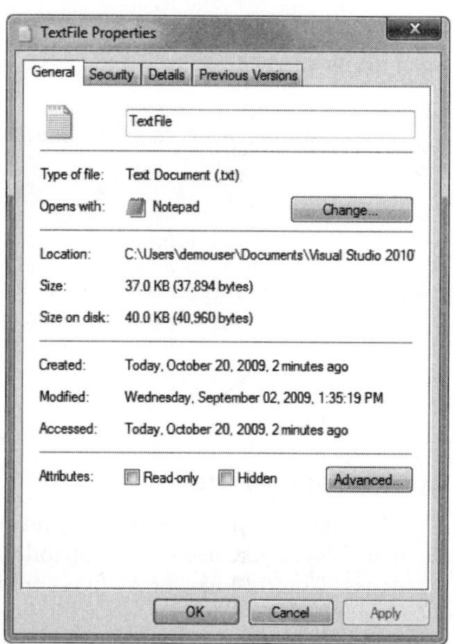

FIGURE 24-7

LISTING 24-9: Displaying and modifying the file properties

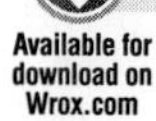

Available for download on Wrox.com

VB

```
<script runat="server">
    Protected Sub Page_Load(ByVal sender As Object,
                            ByVal e As System.EventArgs)
        Dim file As
            New System.IO.FileInfo(Server.MapPath("TextFile.txt"))
        Me.lblLocation.Text = file.FullName
        Me.lblSize.Text = file.Length.ToString()
        Me.lblCreated.Text = file.CreationTime.ToString()
        Me.lblModified.Text = file.LastWriteTime.ToString()
        Me.lblAccessed.Text = file.LastAccessTime.ToString()
        Me.lblAttributes.Text = file.Attributes.ToString()
    End Sub
</script>

<html xmlns="http://www.w3.org/1999/xhtml" >
<head id="Head1" runat="server">
```

continues

LISTING 24-9 *(continued)*

```
    <title>Using the Path Class</title>
</head>
<body>
    <form id="form1" runat="server">
    <div>
      Location: <asp:Label ID="lblLocation" runat="server" /><br />
      Size: <asp:Label ID="lblSize" runat="server" /><br />
      Created: <asp:Label ID="lblCreated" runat="server" /><br />
      Modified: <asp:Label ID="lblModified" runat="server" /><br />
      Accessed: <asp:Label ID="lblAccessed" runat="server" /><br />
      Attributes: <asp:Label ID="lblAttributes" runat="server" /><br />
    </div>
    </form>
</body>
</html>
```

C#

```
<script runat="server">
    protected void Page_Load(object sender, EventArgs e)
    {
        System.IO.FileInfo file =
            new System.IO.FileInfo(Server.MapPath("TextFile.txt"));
        this.lblLocation.Text = file.FullName;
        this.lblSize.Text = file.Length.ToString();
        this.lblCreated.Text = file.CreationTime.ToString();
        this.lblModified.Text = file.LastWriteTime.ToString();
        this.lblAccessed.Text = file.LastAccessTime.ToString();
        this.lblAttributes.Text = file.Attributes.ToString();
    }
</script>
```

Access Control Lists

Although getting the properties and attributes is useful, what many developers need is the capability to actually change the Access Control Lists, or ACLs — pronounced *Ackels* — on directories and files. ACLs are the way resources such as directories and files are secured in the NTFS file system, which is the file system used by most recent versions of Windows. You can view a file's ACLs by selecting the Security tab from the file's Properties dialog. Figure 24-8 shows the ACLs set for the `TextFile.txt` file you created.

Using the `System.AccessControl` namespace in the .NET Framework, you can query the file system for the ACL information and display it in a Web page. Listing 24-10 demonstrates how to use the Access Control classes to retrieve the ACLs for the `TextFile.txt` file included in the project.

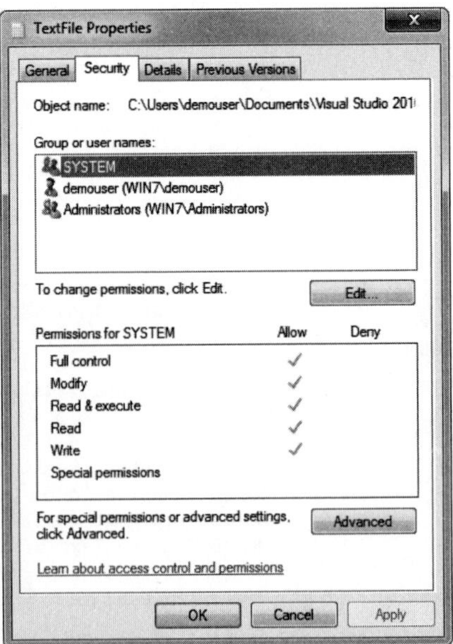

FIGURE 24-8

LISTING 24-10: Access Control List information

Available for download on Wrox.com

```
<script runat="server">
    Protected Sub Page_Load(ByVal sender As Object,
                            ByVal e As System.EventArgs)

        Dim sec As System.Security.AccessControl.FileSecurity
        sec = System.IO.File.GetAccessControl(
            Server.MapPath("TextFile.txt"))

        Me.Label1.Text =
            sec.GetOwner(
                GetType(System.Security.Principal.NTAccount)).Value

        Dim auth As _
            System.Security.AccessControl.AuthorizationRuleCollection =
                          sec.GetAccessRules(True, True,
                          GetType(System.Security.Principal.NTAccount))

        For Each r As _
             System.Security.AccessControl.FileSystemAccessRule In auth
            Dim tr As New TableRow()
            tr.Cells.Add(New TableCell() With _
                             {.Text = r.AccessControlType.ToString()})
            tr.Cells.Add(New TableCell() With _
                             {.Text = r.IdentityReference.Value})
            tr.Cells.Add(New TableCell() With _
                             {.Text = r.InheritanceFlags.ToString()})
            tr.Cells.Add(New TableCell() With _
                             {.Text = r.IsInherited.ToString()})
            tr.Cells.Add(New TableCell() With _
                             {.Text = r.PropagationFlags.ToString()})
            tr.Cells.Add(New TableCell() With _
                             {.Text = r.FileSystemRights.ToString()})
            tr.Cells.Add(New TableCell() With _
                             {.Text = r.IdentityReference.Value})
            Table1.Rows.Add(tr)
        Next
    End Sub
</script>

<html xmlns="http://www.w3.org/1999/xhtml" >
<head id="Head1" runat="server">
    <title>Displaying ACL Information</title>
</head>
<body>
    <form id="form1" runat="server">
    <div>
        <p><b>File Owner:</b>
              <asp:Label ID="Label1" runat="server" Text="Label" /></p>
        <p>
        Access Rules:<br />
        <asp:Table ID="Table1" runat="server"
          CellPadding="2" GridLines="Both">
          <asp:TableRow>
          <asp:TableHeaderCell>Control Type</asp:TableHeaderCell>
          <asp:TableHeaderCell>Identity</asp:TableHeaderCell>
          <asp:TableHeaderCell>Inheritance Flags</asp:TableHeaderCell>
```

continues

LISTING 24-10 *(continued)*

```
            <asp:TableHeaderCell>Is Inherited</asp:TableHeaderCell>
            <asp:TableHeaderCell>Propagation Flags</asp:TableHeaderCell>
            <asp:TableHeaderCell>File System Rights</asp:TableHeaderCell>
            </asp:TableRow>
          </asp:Table>
          </p>
        </div>
        </form>
    </body>
    </html>
```

C#

```
    <script runat="server">
        protected void Page_Load(object sender, EventArgs e)
        {
            System.Security.AccessControl.FileSecurity sec =
                System.IO.File.GetAccessControl(
                    Server.MapPath("TextFile.txt"));

            this.Label1.Text =
                    sec.GetOwner(
                        typeof(System.Security.Principal.NTAccount)).Value;

           System.Security.AccessControl.AuthorizationRuleCollection auth =
                            sec.GetAccessRules(true, true,
                            typeof(System.Security.Principal.NTAccount));

            foreach
             (System.Security.AccessControl.FileSystemAccessRule r in auth)
            {
                TableRow tr = new TableRow();
                tr.Cells.Add(new TableCell()
                                 { Text=r.AccessControlType.ToString() });
                tr.Cells.Add(new TableCell()
                                 { Text=r.IdentityReference.Value });
                tr.Cells.Add(new TableCell()
                                 { Text=r.InheritanceFlags.ToString() });
                tr.Cells.Add(new TableCell()
                                 { Text=r.IsInherited.ToString() });
                tr.Cells.Add(new TableCell()
                                 { Text=r.PropagationFlags.ToString() });
                tr.Cells.Add(new TableCell()
                                 { Text=r.FileSystemRights.ToString() });
                Table1.Rows.Add(tr);
            }
        }
    </script>
```

Figure 24-9 shows what the page looks like when it is executed. Note that the Identity column might be different depending on who you are logged in as when you run the page and what security mode the application is running under (Integrated Windows Authentication, Basic, or Anonymous).

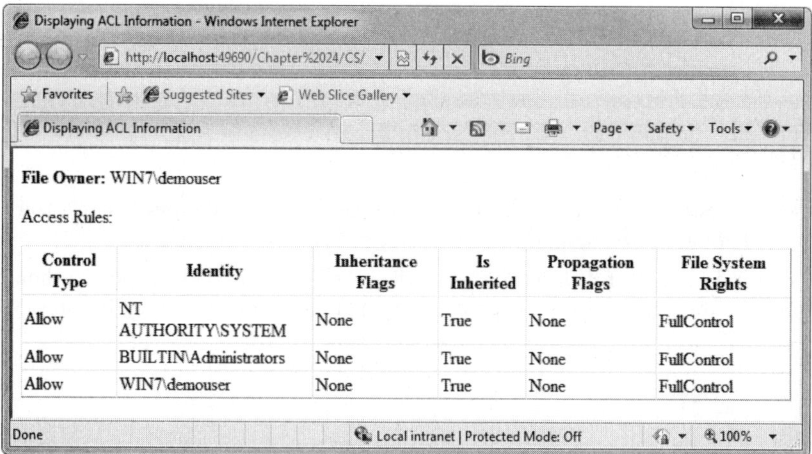

File Owner: WIN7\demouser

Access Rules:

Control Type	Identity	Inheritance Flags	Is Inherited	Propagation Flags	File System Rights
Allow	NT AUTHORITY\SYSTEM	None	True	None	FullControl
Allow	BUILTIN\Administrators	None	True	None	FullControl
Allow	WIN7\demouser	None	True	None	FullControl

FIGURE 24-9

Now it's time to take a look at actually modifying the ACL lists. In this example, you give a specific user explicit Full Control rights over the `TextFile.txt` file. You can use either an existing user or create a new test User account in Windows to run this sample. Listing 24-11 shows how to add an access rule to the `TextFile.txt` file.

LISTING 24-11: Adding a rule to the Access Control List

Available for download on Wrox.com

VB

```
Dim sec As System.Security.AccessControl.FileSecurity =
        System.IO.File.GetAccessControl(
            Server.MapPath("TextFile.txt"))

sec.AddAccessRule(
    New System.Security.AccessControl.FileSystemAccessRule(
            "WIN7\TestUser",
            System.Security.AccessControl.FileSystemRights.FullControl,
            System.Security.AccessControl.AccessControlType.Allow
            )
        )

System.IO.File.SetAccessControl(Server.MapPath("TextFile.txt"),sec)
```

C#

```
System.Security.AccessControl.FileSecurity sec =
        System.IO.File.GetAccessControl(
            Server.MapPath("TextFile.txt"));

sec.AddAccessRule(
    new System.Security.AccessControl.FileSystemAccessRule(
            @"WIN7\TestUser",
            System.Security.AccessControl.FileSystemRights.FullControl,
            System.Security.AccessControl.AccessControlType.Allow
            )
        );

System.IO.File.SetAccessControl(Server.MapPath("TextFile.txt"),sec);
```

The sample starts by getting the collection of existing security settings for the file. Next, using the `AddAccessRule` method, a new `FileSystemAccessRule` is created and added to the files collection of security settings. Creating a new `FileSystemAccessRule` requires you to provide three constructor parameters, the user you want to assign this rule to (provided in DOMAIN\USERNAME format), the rights you want to assign to this rule, and the `AccessControlType` you want to give this rule.

You can specify multiple rights to assign to the rule by using a bitwise `Or` operator, as shown in the following:

```
new System.Security.AccessControl.FileSystemAccessRule(
    "DEMO7\TestUser",
System.Security.AccessControl.FileSystemRights.Read |
        System.Security.AccessControl.FileSystemRights.Write,
    System.Security.AccessControl.AccessControlType.Allow
)
```

The preceding rule allows the TestUser account to read or write to the associated file system asset. You can also deny a specific user these rights by changing the `AccessControlType` value to `Deny`.

After running Listing 24-11, take a look at the Security tab in the file's Properties dialog, and you should see that the user has been added to the Access Control List and allowed Full Control. Figure 24-10 shows what the dialog should look like.

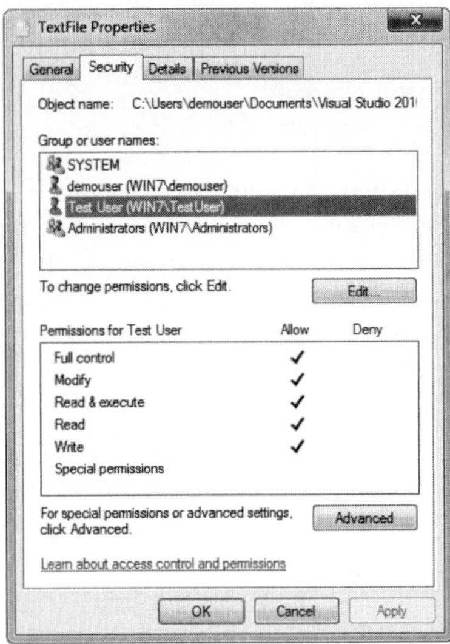

FIGURE 24-10

To remove the ACL you just added you run essentially the same code, but use the `RemoveAccessRule` method rather than the `AddAccessRule` method. Listing 24-12 shows this code.

LISTING 24-12: Removing the rule from the Access Control List

Available for download on Wrox.com

VB

```
Dim sec As System.Security.AccessControl.FileSecurity =
        System.IO.File.GetAccessControl(
            Server.MapPath("TextFile.txt"))

sec.RemoveAccessRule(
    new System.Security.AccessControl.FileSystemAccessRule(
            "WIN7\TestUser",
            System.Security.AccessControl.FileSystemRights.FullControl,
            System.Security.AccessControl.AccessControlType.Allow
            )
        )

System.IO.File.SetAccessControl(Server.MapPath("TextFile.txt"),sec)
```

```
System.Security.AccessControl.FileSecurity sec =
        System.IO.File.GetAccessControl(
            Server.MapPath("TextFile.txt"));

sec.RemoveAccessRule(
```

```
        new System.Security.AccessControl.FileSystemAccessRule(
                @"WIN7\TestUser",
                System.Security.AccessControl.FileSystemRights.FullControl,
                System.Security.AccessControl.AccessControlType.Allow
                )
        );

    System.IO.File.SetAccessControl(Server.MapPath("TextFile.txt"),sec);
```

If you open the file Properties dialog again, you see that the user has been removed from the Access Control List.

READING AND WRITING FILES

Now that you have learned how to manage the files on the local system, this section shows you how to use the .NET Framework to perform input/output (I/O) operations, such as reading and writing, on those files. The .NET Framework makes performing I/O very easy because it uses a common model of reading or writing I/O data; so regardless of the source, virtually the same code can be used. The model is based on two basic concepts: stream classes and reader/writer classes. Figure 24-11 shows the basic I/O model .NET uses and how streams, readers, and writers work together to make it possible to transfer data to and from any number of sources in any number of formats. Note that the diagram shows only some of the streams and reader/writer pairs in the .NET Framework.

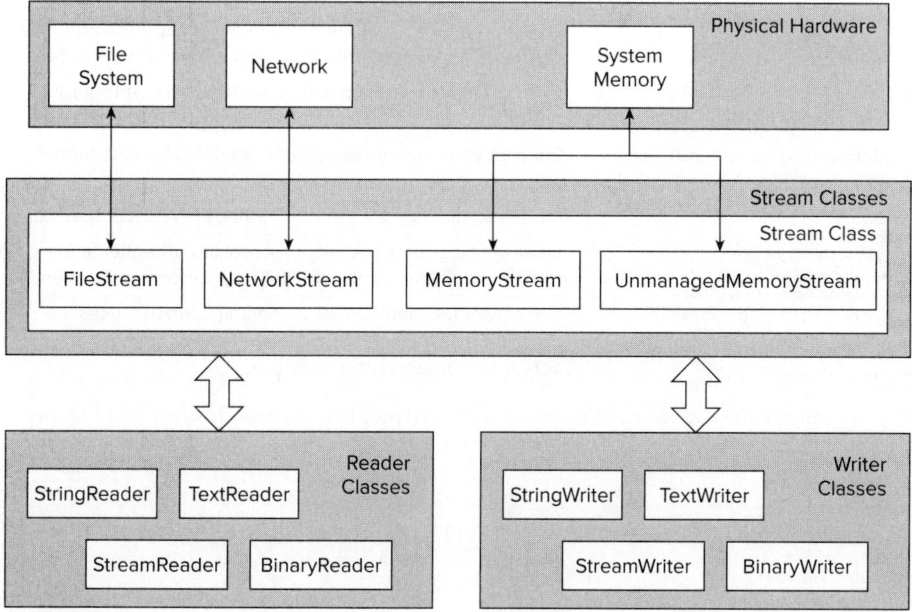

FIGURE 24-11

In this section, you dive deeper into learning how streams, readers, and writers work and how .NET makes it easy to use them to transfer data.

Streams

Regardless of the type of I/O operation you are performing in .NET, if you want to read or write data you eventually use a stream of some type. Streams are the basic mechanism .NET uses to transfer data to and from its underlying source, be it a file, communication pipe, or TCP/IP socket. The `Stream` class provides the basic functionality to read and write I/O data, but because the `Stream` class is marked as abstract, you most likely need to use one of the several classes derived from `Stream`. Each `Stream` derivation is specialized to make transferring data from a specific source easy. Table 24-2 lists some of the classes derived from the `Stream` class.

TABLE 24-2

CLASS	DESCRIPTION
`System.IO.FileStream`	Reads and writes files on a file system, as well as other file-related operating system handles (including pipes, standard input, standard output, and so on).
`System.IO.MemoryStream`	Creates streams that have memory as a backing store instead of a disk or a network connection. This can be useful in eliminating the need to write temporary files to disk or to store binary blob information in a database.
`System.IO.UnmanagedMemoryStream`	Supports access to unmanaged memory using the existing stream-based model and does not require that the contents in the unmanaged memory be copied to the heap.
`System.IO.BufferedStream`	Extends the Stream class by adding a buffering layer to read and write operations on another stream. The stream performs reads and writes in blocks (4096 bytes by default), which can result in improved efficiency.
`System.Net.Sockets.NetworkStream`	Implements the standard .NET Framework stream to send and receive data through network sockets. It supports both synchronous and asynchronous access to the network data stream.
`System.Security.Cryptography.CryptoStream`	Enables you to read and write data through cryptographic transformations.
`System.IO.Compression.GZipStream`	Enables you to compress data using the GZip data format.
`System.IO.Compression.DeflateStream`	Enables you to compress data using the Deflate algorithm. For more information, see the RFC 1951: DEFLATE 1.3 Specification.
`System.Net.Security.NegotiateStream`	Uses the Negotiate security protocol to authenticate the client, and optionally the server, in client-server communication.
`System.Net.Security.SslStream`	Necessary for client-server communication that uses the Secure Socket Layer (SSL) security protocol to authenticate the server and optionally the client.

As an example, you can use the `FileStream` to read a local system file from disk. Listing 24-13 shows how you can use the `FileStream` to read the contents of the `TextFile.txt` file used in previous sections of this chapter.

LISTING 24-13: Using a FileStream to read a system file

Available for download on Wrox.com

VB

```
<script runat="server">
    Protected Sub Page_Load(ByVal sender As Object,
                            ByVal e As System.EventArgs)
        Dim fs As New System.IO.FileStream(
            Server.MapPath("TextFile.txt"), System.IO.FileMode.Open)
        Dim data(fs.Length) As Byte
        fs.Read(data, 0, fs.Length)
        fs.Close()

        Me.lblResult.Text = ASCIIEncoding.Default.GetString(data)
    End Sub
</script>

<html xmlns="http://www.w3.org/1999/xhtml" >
<head id="Head1" runat="server">
```

```
        <title>Reading a Text File</title>
    </head>
    <body>
        <form id="form1" runat="server">
        <div>
            <asp:Label runat="server" ID="lblResult" />
        </div>
        </form>
    </body>
    </html>
```

```
    <script runat="server">
        protected void Page_Load(object sender, EventArgs e)
        {
            System.IO.FileStream fs =
                new System.IO.FileStream(
                    Server.MapPath("TextFile.txt"),
                    System.IO.FileMode.Open);
            byte[] data = new byte[fs.Length];
            fs.Read(data, 0, (int)fs.Length);
            fs.Close();

            this.lblResult.Text = ASCIIEncoding.Default.GetString(data);
        }
    </script>
```

Several items of note appear in this code. First, notice that you are creating a byte array the length of the stream, using the `Length` property to properly size the array, and then passing it to the `Read` method. The `Read` method fills the byte array with the stream data, in this case reading the entire stream into the byte array. If you want to read only a chunk of the stream or to start at a specific point in the stream simply change the value of the parameters you pass to the `Read` method.

> *Streams use byte arrays as the basic means of transporting data to and from the underlying data source. You use a byte array to read data in this sample and, later in the chapter, you learn how to create a byte array that contains data you can write to a stream.*

Second, note that you are explicitly closing the `FileStream` using the `Close` method. Streams must always be explicitly closed in order to release the resources they are using, which in this case is the file. Failing to explicitly close the stream can cause memory leaks, and it may also deny other users and applications access to the resource.

A good way to ensure that your streams will always be closed after you are done using them is to wrap them in a `Using` statement. `Using` automatically calls the stream object's `Dispose` method when the `Using` statement is closed. For the stream object, calling the `Dispose` method also automatically calls the stream's `Close` method. Utilizing the `Using` statement with stream objects is a good way to ensure that even if you do forget to explicitly add a call to close the stream, the object will be closed and the underlying resources released before the object is disposed. Listing 24-14 demonstrates how to modify the code from Listing 24-13 to use a `Using` statement.

LISTING 24-14: Using a Using statement when reading a file

Available for download on Wrox.com

```
Protected Sub Page_Load(ByVal sender As Object,
                        ByVal e As System.EventArgs)
    Using fs As New System.IO.FileStream(
        Server.MapPath("TextFile.txt"),
        System.IO.FileMode.Open)

        Dim data(fs.Length) As Byte
```

continues

LISTING 24-14 *(continued)*

```
            fs.Read(data, 0, fs.Length)

            Me.lblResult.Text = ASCIIEncoding.Default.GetString(data)
        End Using
    End Sub
```

C#

```
    protected void Page_Load(object sender, EventArgs e)
    {
        using (System.IO.FileStream fs =
            new System.IO.FileStream(
                Server.MapPath("TextFile.txt"),
                System.IO.FileMode.Open))
        {
            byte[] data = new byte[fs.Length];
            fs.Read(data, 0, (int)fs.Length);

            this.lblResult.Text = ASCIIEncoding.Default.GetString(data);
        }
    }
```

When using the `FileStream` to read files, you must pass two parameters to the `FileStream` constructor: the path to the file you want to read and a value from the `FileMode` enumeration indicating the type of access you want to use when opening the file. The `FileMode` enumeration lets you specify how the stream should be opened — for reading, writing, or both reading and writing.

Thinking about *how* you will use the opened file can become very important when designing file access in your application. Here are some access issues you might want to consider when working with files using `FileStream`:

- Will you be reading, writing, or both?
- Are you creating a new file, or appending or truncating an existing file?
- Should other programs be allowed to access the file while you are using it?
- How are you going to read or write the data in the file? Are you looking for a specific location in the file, or simply reading the entire file from beginning to end?

The `FileStream` constructor includes a number of additional overloads that let you explicitly specify how you want to use the file. These overloads let you provide values from four enumerations found in the `System.IO` namespace that can help you set fine-grain control for how the `FileStream` accesses your file:

- **FileMode:** The `FileMode` enumeration lets you control whether the file is appended, truncated, created, or opened.
- **FileAccess:** The `FileAccess` enumeration controls whether the file is opened for reading, writing, or both.
- **FileOptions:** The `FileOptions` enumeration controls several other miscellaneous options, such as random or sequential access, file encryption, or asynchronous file writing.
- **FileShare:** The `FileShare` enumeration controls the access that other users and programs have to the file while your application is using it.

Listing 24-15 shows how you can use these enumerations in the `FileStream` constructor to configure the stream to allow you to append additional data to the text file you created earlier. Providing the `Append` value from the `FileMode` enumeration and the `Write` value from the `FileAccess` enumeration tells the stream exactly what access to allow.

LISTING 24-15: Using I/O enumerations to control file behavior when writing a file

Available for download on Wrox.com

```
Protected Sub Page_Load(ByVal sender As Object,
                        ByVal e As System.EventArgs)
    Dim fs As New System.IO.FileStream(Server.MapPath("TextFile.txt"),
        System.IO.FileMode.Append, System.IO.FileAccess.Write,
        System.IO.FileShare.Read, 8, System.IO.FileOptions.None)
    Dim data() As Byte =
            System.Text.Encoding.ASCII.GetBytes(
               "This is an additional string")
    fs.Write(data, 0, data.Length)
    fs.Flush()
    fs.Close()

    Me.lblResult.Text = ASCIIEncoding.Default.GetString(data)
End Sub
```

C#

```
protected void Page_Load(object sender, EventArgs e)
{
    System.IO.FileStream fs =
        new System.IO.FileStream(Server.MapPath("TextFile.txt"),
            System.IO.FileMode.Append, System.IO.FileAccess.Write,
            System.IO.FileShare.Read, 8, System.IO.FileOptions.None);
    byte[] data =
            System.Text.Encoding.ASCII.GetBytes(
               "This is an additional string");
    fs.Write(data, 0, data.Length);
    fs.Flush();
    fs.Close();

    this.lblResult.Text = ASCIIEncoding.Default.GetString(data);
}
```

You can write to the stream by encoding a string containing the information you want to write to a byte array and then using the stream's `Write` method to write the byte array to the `FileStreams` buffer. After the write is complete, you can use the `Flush` method to instruct the `FileStream` to clear its buffer, causing the buffered data to be committed to the underlying data store (in this case the text file). Finally, as described earlier, you must close the `FileStream`, releasing any resources it is using. If you open the `TextFile.txt` file in Notepad, you should see your string has been appended to the existing text in the file.

Using the `Flush` method in this scenario is optional because the `Close` method also calls `Flush` internally to commit the data to the data store. However, because the `Flush` method does not release the `FileStream` resources as `Close` does, it can be very useful if you are going to perform multiple write operations and do not want to release and then reacquire the resources for each write operation.

As you can see, reading and writing to files using the .NET Framework is really quite easy. The good thing is that, as mentioned earlier, because .NET uses the same basic `Stream` model for a variety of data stores, you can use these same techniques for reading and writing to any of the `Stream`-derived classes shown earlier in this section. Listing 24-16 shows how you can use the same basic code to write to a `MemoryStream`, and Listing 24-17 demonstrates communicating with an NNTP server using the `NetworkStream`.

LISTING 24-16: Writing to a MemoryStream

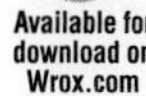

VB

```
Dim data() As Byte =
    System.Text.Encoding.ASCII.GetBytes("This is a string")
Dim ms As New System.IO.MemoryStream()
ms.Write(data, 0, data.Length)
ms.Close()
```

```
byte[] data = System.Text.Encoding.ASCII.GetBytes("This is a string");
```

continues

LISTING 24-16 *(continued)*

```
System.IO.MemoryStream ms = new System.IO.MemoryStream();
ms.Write(data, 0, data.Length);
ms.Close();
```

LISTING 24-17: Reading from a NetworkStream

Available for download on Wrox.com

VB

```
<script runat="server">
    Protected Sub Page_Load(ByVal sender As Object,
                            ByVal e As System.EventArgs)

        Dim bufferlength As Integer = 1024
        Dim response, chunk As String
        Dim downbytes(bufferlength) As Byte
        Dim sendbytes(bufferlength) As Byte
        Dim size As Integer

        Dim client As System.Net.Sockets.TcpClient =
             New System.Net.Sockets.TcpClient(
                 "msnews.microsoft.com", 119)
        Dim ns As System.Net.Sockets.NetworkStream = client.GetStream()

        size = ns.Read(downbytes, 0, bufferlength)
        response =
            System.Text.Encoding.ASCII.GetString(downbytes, 0, size)

        If response.Substring(0, 3) = "200" Then

            sendbytes =
                ASCIIEncoding.Default.GetBytes("LIST" +
                                               Environment.NewLine)
            ns.Write(sendbytes, 0, sendbytes.Length)

            response = ""
            size = ns.Read(downbytes, 0, downbytes.Length)

            While (size > 0)
                chunk = Encoding.ASCII.GetString(downbytes, 0, size)
                response += chunk

                If chunk.Substring(chunk.Length - 5, 5) =
                   Environment.NewLine & "." & Environment.NewLine Then
                    response =
                        response.Substring(0, response.Length - 3)
                    Exit While
                End If

                size = ns.Read(downbytes, 0, downbytes.Length)
            End While
        End If

        Me.lblResult.Text = response

        ns.Close()
    End Sub
</script>

<html xmlns="http://www.w3.org/1999/xhtml" >
<head id="Head1" runat="server">
    <title>Writing a Text File</title>
</head>
```

```
<body>
    <form id="form1" runat="server">
    <div>
        <asp:Literal runat="server" ID="lblResult" />
    </div>
    </form>
</body>
</html>
```

C#

```
<script runat="server">
    protected void Page_Load(object sender, EventArgs e)
    {
        int bufferlength = 1024;
        string response, chunk;
        byte[] downbytes = new byte[bufferlength];
        byte[] sendbytes = new byte[bufferlength];
        int size;

        System.Net.Sockets.TcpClient client =
            new System.Net.Sockets.TcpClient(
                "msnews.microsoft.com", 119);
        System.Net.Sockets.NetworkStream ns = client.GetStream();

        size = ns.Read(downbytes, 0, bufferlength);
        response =
            System.Text.Encoding.ASCII.GetString(downbytes, 0, size);

        if (response.Substring(0, 3) == "200")
        {
            sendbytes =
                ASCIIEncoding.Default.GetBytes("LIST" +
                                               Environment.NewLine);
            ns.Write(sendbytes, 0, sendbytes.Length);

            response = "";

            while ((size = ns.Read(downbytes,0,downbytes.Length))>0)
            {
                chunk = Encoding.ASCII.GetString(downbytes, 0, size);
                response += chunk;

                if (chunk.Substring(chunk.Length - 5, 5) ==
                    "\r\n.\r\n")
                {
                    response =
                        response.Substring(0, response.Length - 3);
                    break;
                }
            }
        }

        this.lblResult.Text = response;

        ns.Close();
    }
</script>
```

Notice that the concept in both examples is virtually identical. In Listing 24-16, you create a byte array containing the data, create a `MemoryStream` object, and then use the `Write` method to write the data to the stream. Listing 24-17 performs the same basic actions, writing the "`LIST`" command to the `NetworkStream`, but adds a loop to read the results returned from the NNTP server in 1024-byte chunks.

Readers and Writers

Other main parts of I/O in the .NET Framework are `Reader` and `Writer` classes. These classes help abstract away the reading and writing of individual bytes to and from `Streams` as you were doing in the previous section, instead enabling you to focus more on the actual data you are working with, letting the framework transform the individual bytes into the appropriate data types.

The .NET Framework provides a wide variety of reader and writer classes, each designed for reading or writing according to a specific set of rules. Table 24-3 shows a partial list of the readers available in the .NET Framework and the corresponding writer classes.

TABLE 24-3

CLASS	DESCRIPTION
`System.IO.TextReader`	Abstract class that enables the reading of a sequential series of characters.
`System.IO.StreamReader`	Reads characters from a byte stream. Derived from TextReader.
`System.IO.StringReader`	Reads textual information as a stream of in-memory characters. Derived from TextReader.
`System.IO.BinaryReader`	Reads primitive data types as binary values from a stream.
`System.Xml.XmlTextReader`	Provides fast, non-cached, forward-only access to XML.
`System.IO.TextWriter`	Abstract class that enables the writing of a sequential series of characters.
`System.IO.StreamWriter`	Writes characters to a stream. Derived from TextWriter.
`System.IO.StringWriter`	Writes textual information as a stream of in-memory characters. Derived from TextWriter.
`System.IO.BinaryWriter`	Writes primitive data types in binary to a stream.
`System.Xml.XmlTextWriter`	Provides a fast, non-cached, forward-only way of generating XML streams or files.

To see a simple example of how the readers and writers abstract reading and writing data, Listing 24-18 shows you how to use the `StreamReader` and `StreamWriter` classes to write a string to a text file and then read the contents of that text file.

LISTING 24-18: Reading and writing a text file with a StreamReader

Available for download on Wrox.com

VB

```
Dim streamwriter As New System.IO.StreamWriter(
    System.IO.File.Open(MapPath("TextFile.txt"),
    System.IO.FileMode.Open))
streamwriter.Write("This is a string")
streamwriter.Close()

Dim reader As New System.IO.StreamReader(
    System.IO.File.Open(MapPath("TextFile.txt"),
    System.IO.FileMode.Open))
Dim tmp As String = reader.ReadToEnd()
reader.Close()
```

C#

```
System.IO.StreamWriter streamwriter =
             new System.IO.StreamWriter(
                 System.IO.File.Open(MapPath("TextFile.txt"),
                 System.IO.FileMode.Open));
streamwriter.Write("This is a string");
streamwriter.Close();
```

```
System.IO.StreamReader reader =
            new System.IO.StreamReader(
                System.IO.File.Open(MapPath("TextFile.txt"),
                System.IO.FileMode.Open));
string tmp = reader.ReadToEnd();
reader.Close();
```

Notice that when you create a `StreamReader`, you must pass an existing stream instance as a constructor parameter. The reader uses this stream as its underlying data source. In this sample, you use the `File` class's static `Open` method to open a writable `FileStream` for your `StreamWriter`.

Also notice that you no longer have to deal with byte arrays. The `StreamReader` takes care of converting the data to a type that's more user-friendly than a byte array. In this case, you are using the `ReadToEnd` method to read the entire stream and convert it to a string. The `StreamReader` provides a number of different methods for reading data that you can use depending on exactly how you want to read the data, from reading a single character using the `Read` method, to reading the entire file using the `ReadToEnd` method.

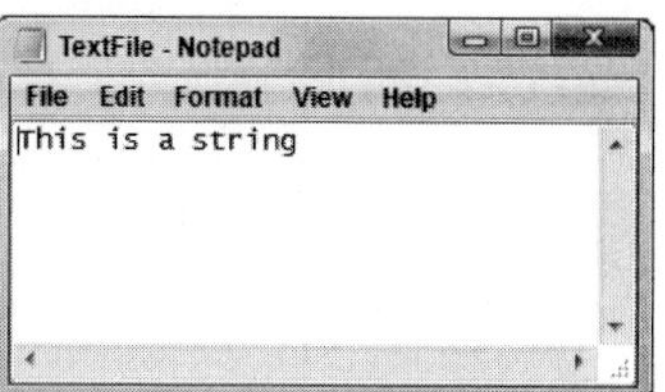

FIGURE 24-12

Figure 24-12 shows the results of your writing when you open the file in Notepad.

Now use the `BinaryReader` and `BinaryWriter` classes to read and write primitive types to a file. The `BinaryWriter` writes primitive objects in their native format, so in order to read them using the `BinaryReader`, you must select the appropriate `Read` method. Listing 24-19 shows you how to do that; in this case, you are writing a value from a number of different primitive types to the text file and then reading the same value.

LISTING 24-19: Reading and writing binary data

Available for download on Wrox.com

VB

```
Dim binarywriter As New System.IO.BinaryWriter(
        System.IO.File.Create(MapPath("binary.dat")))

binarywriter.Write("a string")
binarywriter.Write(&H12346789ABCDEF)
binarywriter.Write(&H12345678)
binarywriter.Write("c"c)
binarywriter.Write(1.5F)
binarywriter.Write(100.2D)
binarywriter.Close()

Dim binaryreader As New System.IO.BinaryReader(
    System.IO.File.Open(MapPath("binary.dat"), System.IO.FileMode.Open))

Dim a As String = binaryreader.ReadString()
Dim l As Long = binaryreader.ReadInt64()
Dim i As Integer = binaryreader.ReadInt32()
Dim c As Char = binaryreader.ReadChar()
Dim f As Double = binaryreader.ReadSingle()
Dim d As Decimal = binaryreader.ReadDecimal()
binaryreader.Close()
```

C#

```
System.IO.BinaryWriter binarywriter =
                     new System.IO.BinaryWriter(
                         System.IO.File.Create(MapPath("binary.dat")));
binarywriter.Write("a string");
binarywriter.Write(0x12346789abcdef);
binarywriter.Write(0x12345678);
```

continues

LISTING 24-19 *(continued)*

```
binarywriter.Write('c');
binarywriter.Write(1.5f);
binarywriter.Write(100.2m);
binarywriter.Close();
System.IO.BinaryReader binaryreader =
                     new System.IO.BinaryReader(
                         System.IO.File.Open(MapPath("binary.dat"),
                         System.IO.FileMode.Open));

string a = binaryreader.ReadString();
long l = binaryreader.ReadInt64();
int i = binaryreader.ReadInt32();
char c = binaryreader.ReadChar();
float f = binaryreader.ReadSingle();
decimal d = binaryreader.ReadDecimal();
binaryreader.Close();
```

If you open this file in Notepad, you will see that the `BinaryWriter` has written the nonreadable binary data to the file. Figure 24-13 shows what the content of the file looks like. The `BinaryReader` provides a number of different methods for reading various kinds of primitive types from the stream. In this sample, you use a different `Read` method for each primitive type that you write to the file.

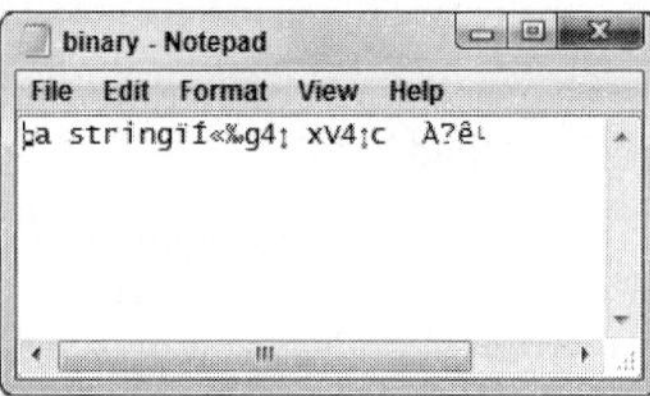

FIGURE 24-13

Finally, notice that the basic usage of both the `StreamReader`/`StreamWriter` and `BinaryReader`/`BinaryWriter` classes is virtually identical. You can apply the same basic ideas to use any of the reader or writer classes.

Encodings

The `StreamReader` by default attempts to determine the encoding format of the file. If one of the supported encodings such as UTF-8 or UNICODE is detected, it is used. If the encoding is not recognized, the default encoding of UTF-8 is used. Depending on the constructor you call, you can change the default encoding used and optionally turn off encoding detection. The following example shows how you can control the encoding that the `StreamReader` uses.

```
StreamReader reader =
           new StreamReader(MapPath(TextFile.txt"),
                                  System.Text.Encoding.Unicode);
```

The default encoding for the `StreamWriter` is also UTF-8, and you can override it in the same manner as with the `StreamReader` class.

I/O Shortcuts

Although knowing how to create and use streams is always very useful and worth studying, the .NET Framework provides you with numerous shortcuts for common tasks like reading and writing to files. For instance, if you want to read the entire file, you can simply use one of the static Read All methods of the `File` class. Using these methods, you cause .NET to handle the process of creating the `Stream` and `StreamReader` for you, and simply return the resulting string of data. This is just one example of the shortcuts that the .NET Framework provides. Listing 24-20 shows some of the others, with explanatory comments.

LISTING 24-20: Using the static methods of the File and Directory classes

Available for download on Wrox.com

```
' Opens a file and returns a FileStream
Using stream1 As System.IO.FileStream =
                System.IO.File.Open(MapPath("TextFile.txt"),
                                   System.IO.FileMode.Open)
```

```
End Using

' Opens a file and returns a StreamReader for reading the data
Using stream2 As System.IO.StreamReader =
                System.IO.File.OpenText(MapPath("TextFile.txt"))
End Using

' Opens a filestream for reading
Using stream3 As System.IO.FileStream =
                System.IO.File.OpenRead(MapPath("TextFile.txt"))
End Using

' Opens a filestream for writing
Using stream4 As System.IO.FileStream =
                System.IO.File.OpenWrite(MapPath("TextFile.txt"))
End Using

' Reads the entire file and returns a string of data
Dim data As String = System.IO.File.ReadAllText(MapPath("TextFile.txt"))

' Using a LINQ query to locate specific lines within the Textfile
Dim lines1 = From line In
    System.IO.File.ReadLines(MapPath("TextFile.txt"))
    Where line.Contains("laoreet")
    Select line

' Using a LINQ query to locate specific lines within the Textfile
Dim lines2 = From line In
    System.IO.File.ReadLines(MapPath("TextFile.txt"))
    Where line.Contains("laoreet")
    Select line

' Appends the text data to a new text file
System.IO.File.AppendAllText(MapPath("TextFile1.txt"), data)

' Appends the IEnumerable of strings to a new text file
System.IO.File.AppendAllLines(MapPath("TextFile1.txt"), lines1)

' Writes the string of data to a new file
System.IO.File.WriteAllText(MapPath("TextFile2.txt"), data)

' Writes an IEnumerable of strings to a new text file
System.IO.File.WriteAllLines(MapPath("TextFile2.txt"), lines2)
```

C#

```
// Opens a file and returns a FileStream
using (System.IO.FileStream stream1 =
       System.IO.File.Open(MapPath("TextFile.txt"),
                           System.IO.FileMode.Open)) {}

// Opens a file and returns a StreamReader for reading the data
using (System.IO.StreamReader stream2 =
       System.IO.File.OpenText(MapPath("TextFile.txt"))) {}

// Opens a filestream for reading
using (System.IO.FileStream stream3 =
       System.IO.File.OpenRead(MapPath("TextFile.txt"))) {}

// Opens a filestream for writing
using (System.IO.FileStream stream4 =
       System.IO.File.OpenWrite(MapPath("TextFile.txt"))) { }

// Reads the entire file and returns a string of data
string data = System.IO.File.ReadAllText(MapPath("TextFile.txt"));

// Using a LINQ query to locate specific lines within the Textfile
```

continues

LISTING 24-20 *(continued)*

```
var lines1 = from line in
            System.IO.File.ReadLines(MapPath("TextFile.txt"))
            where line.Contains("laoreet")
            select line;

// Using a LINQ query to locate specific lines within the Textfile
var lines2 = from line in
            System.IO.File.ReadLines(MapPath("TextFile.txt"))
            where line.Contains("laoreet")
            select line;

// Appends the text data to a new text file
System.IO.File.AppendAllText(MapPath("TextFile1.txt"), data);

//Appends the IEnumerable of strings to a new text file
System.IO.File.AppendAllLines(MapPath("TextFile1.txt"), lines1);

// Writes the string of data to a new file
System.IO.File.WriteAllText(MapPath("TextFile2.txt"), data);

// Writes an IEnumerable of strings to a new text file
System.IO.File.WriteAllLines(MapPath("TextFile2.txt"), lines2);
```

An interesting portion of Listing 24-20 to call out is the use of the LINQ queries with the `ReadLines` method. Using the LINQ queries allows you to query the lines of the text file for specific values; however, note that when using LINQ in this manner you are executing queries against objects that implement `IDisposable`. This means that when you perform an action that causes the query results to be enumerated, the underlying TextReader used to read the file contents will be closed and attempts to access it further will result in an exception being thrown.

Compressing Streams

Introduced in the .NET 2.0 Framework, the `System.IO.Compression` namespace includes classes for compressing and decompressing data using either the gzip or Deflate formats. Both compression formats use the Deflate compression algorithm and are exposed through classes derived from the `Stream` class. Using the classes is similar to using the other `Stream` classes shown in this chapter.

DeflateStream

The `DeflateStream` class creates and extracts archives compressed using the Deflate algorithm, a lossless data compression algorithm that uses a combination of LZ77 algorithm and Huffman coding. Listing 24-21 shows an example of compressing your text file using the `DeflateStream` class.

LISTING 24-21: Compressing a file using DeflateStream

Available for download on Wrox.com

VB

```
Dim filename As String = Server.MapPath("TextFile.txt")

If System.IO.File.Exists(filename) Then

    Using infile As System.IO.FileStream =
                System.IO.File.Open(filename,
                                    System.IO.FileMode.Open),
        outfile As System.IO.FileStream =
                System.IO.File.Create(
                   System.IO.Path.ChangeExtension(filename, "zip"))

        Using cstream As System.IO.Compression.DeflateStream =
```

```
                        New System.IO.Compression.DeflateStream(outfile,
                           System.IO.Compression.CompressionMode.Compress)

            Dim data(infile.Length) As Byte
            Dim counter As Integer = 0

            counter = infile.Read(data, 0, data.Length)

            While (counter <> 0)
                cstream.Write(data, 0, counter)
                counter = infile.Read(data, 0, data.Length)
            End While
        End Using
    End Using
End If
```

C#

```
string filename = Server.MapPath("TextFile.txt");

if (System.IO.File.Exists(filename))
{
    using (System.IO.FileStream infile =
           System.IO.File.Open(filename, System.IO.FileMode.Open),
        outfile =
           System.IO.File.Create(
                      System.IO.Path.ChangeExtension(filename, "zip")))
    {
        using (System.IO.Compression.DeflateStream cstream =
               new System.IO.Compression.DeflateStream(outfile,
                   System.IO.Compression.CompressionMode.Compress))
        {
            byte[] data = new byte[infile.Length];
            int counter = 0;

            while ((counter = infile.Read(data, 0, data.Length)) != 0)
            {
                cstream.Write(data, 0, counter);
            }
        }
    }
}
```

The `DeflateStream` constructor requires two parameters: the stream to write the compressed data to and the `CompressionMode` enumeration, which tells the class whether you want to compress or decompress data. After the code runs, be sure there is a file called `TextFile.zip` in your Web site directory.

GZipStream

The `GZipStream` class creates and extracts archives compressed using the Deflate algorithm. It also adds a cyclic redundancy check (CRC) value for detecting data corruption. Listing 24-22 shows an example of decompressing a file using the `GZipStream` method.

LISTING 24-22: Decompressing a file using GZipStream

Available for download on Wrox.com

VB

```
Dim filename As String = Server.MapPath("TextFile.zip")

If System.IO.File.Exists(filename) Then

    Using infile As System.IO.FileStream =
                System.IO.File.Open(filename,
                                  System.IO.FileMode.Open),
```

continues

LISTING 24-22 *(continued)*

```
        outfile As System.IO.FileStream =
                System.IO.File.Create(
                    System.IO.Path.ChangeExtension(filename, "txt"))

        Using cstream As System.IO.Compression.GZipStream =
            New System.IO.Compression.GZipStream(outfile,
                System.IO.Compression.CompressionMode.Decompress)

            Dim data(infile.Length) As Byte
            Dim counter As Integer = 0

            counter = cstream.Read(data, 0, data.Length)

            While (counter <> 0)
                outfile.Write(data, 0, counter)
                counter = cstream.Read(data, 0, data.Length)
            End While
        End Using
    End Using
End If
```

C#

```
string filename = Server.MapPath("TextFile.zip");

if (System.IO.File.Exists(filename))
{
    using (System.IO.FileStream infile =
           System.IO.File.Open(filename, System.IO.FileMode.Open),
            outfile = System.IO.File.Create(
                      System.IO.Path.ChangeExtension(filename, "txt")))
    {
        using (System.IO.Compression.GZipStream cstream =
            new System.IO.Compression.GZipStream(infile,
                System.IO.Compression.CompressionMode.Decompress))
        {
            byte[] data = new byte[infile.Length];
            int counter;

            while ((counter = cstream.Read(data, 0, data.Length)) != 0)
            {
                outfile.Write(data, 0, counter);
            }
        }
    }
}
```

Running this sample should result in a file called `TextFile.txt` being created in the Web site directory.

MEMORY-MAPPED FILES

In this chapter you have looked at how you can use stream objects to read and write files, but using streams for this does have a couple problems that you might encounter in certain scenarios.

- First, when you open a file using a stream, reading the file contents is done sequentially. This can be a problem if you are searching for a specific section of a very large file because you have to read the entire file from the beginning in order to locate the content.
- Second, opening a file using a stream can lock the file, preventing other applications or threads from reading or writing to the file.

The .NET Framework includes the `System.IO.MemoryMappedFiles` namespace, which includes a number of classes that allow you to create memory-mapped files. Memory-mapped files can be useful when you encounter the limitations of the stream objects just described.

Memory-mapped files allow you to create views that start in a random location over very large files, rather than reading the file sequentially from the beginning. Memory-mapped files also allow multiple processes to map to the same portion of a file without locking the file.

Listing 24-23 shows how you can use the classes of the `MemoryMappedFile` namespace to create a view of a file.

LISTING 24-23: Reading contents of a MemoryMappedFile

Available for download on Wrox.com

VB

```
<script runat="server">
    Protected Sub Page_Load(ByVal sender As Object,
                            ByVal e As System.EventArgs)
        Dim bytes(100) As Byte

        Using mmf As System.IO.MemoryMappedFiles.MemoryMappedFile =
           System.IO.MemoryMappedFiles.MemoryMappedFile.CreateFromFile(
                                MapPath("TextFile1.txt"),
                                System.IO.FileMode.Open, "MyTextFile")
            Using accessor As
               System.IO.MemoryMappedFiles.MemoryMappedViewAccessor =
                mmf.CreateViewAccessor(100, 100)
                accessor.ReadArray(0, bytes, 0, bytes.Length)
            End Using
        End Using

        Me.lblResult.Text = ASCIIEncoding.Default.GetString(bytes)
    End Sub
</script>

<html xmlns="http://www.w3.org/1999/xhtml">
<head runat="server">
    <title></title>
</head>
<body>
    <form id="form1" runat="server">
    <div>
        <asp:Label runat="server" ID="lblResult" />
    </div>
    </form>
</body>
</html>
```

C#

```
<script runat="server">
    protected void Page_Load(object sender, EventArgs e)
    {
        byte[] bytes = new byte[100];

        using (System.IO.MemoryMappedFiles.MemoryMappedFile mmf =
           System.IO.MemoryMappedFiles.MemoryMappedFile.CreateFromFile(
                                MapPath("TextFile1.txt"),
                                System.IO.FileMode.Open, "MyTextFile"))
           {
           using (System.IO.MemoryMappedFiles.MemoryMappedViewAccessor
                     accessor = mmf.CreateViewAccessor(100, 100))
               {
                  accessor.ReadArray(0, bytes, 0, bytes.Length);
               }
```

continues

LISTING 24-23 *(continued)*

```
        }

        this.lblResult.Text = ASCIIEncoding.Default.GetString(bytes);
    }
</script>
```

This sample loads the `TextFile.txt` file into a `MemoryMappedFile` class using the static `CreateFromFile` method, which creates a named memory-mapped file. It then creates a `MemoryMappedViewAccessor` over the file using the `MemoryMappedFiles CreateViewAccessor` method. This method's parameters allow you to specify an offset where the view accessor should start, the length of the view, and the access rights the view will have to the file.

The `MemoryMappedFile` class also allows you to create memory-mapped files that are not associated with a physical file on disk, but are rather simply a named portion of memory. You can do this using the class's static `CreateNew` method, which accepts a name and a length parameter.

After an application has created a named memory-mapped file, that file is available for other parts of the application, or even completely separate applications, to access. You can do this using the `MemoryMappedFiles OpenExisting` method.

Finally, if you prefer working with a stream style API, the `MemoryMappedFiles` namespace does include a `MemoryMappedViewStream` object, which allows you to create views on top of the memory-mapped file, and access the view using the same core stream syntax you have seen before.

WORKING WITH SERIAL PORTS

The framework provides a number of APIs located in the `System.IO.Ports` namespace (which was introduced in .NET 2.0) that allow your application to read and write to a local serial port. This feature can be useful for communicating with legacy hardware that remains commonplace in industrial automation systems, scientific analysis systems, and other industrial settings.

Listing 24-24 demonstrates how to write to one port and read from another.

LISTING 24-24: Reading and writing text with the serial port

Available for download on Wrox.com

VB

```
<script runat="server">
    Dim SerialPort1 As System.IO.Ports.SerialPort =
        New System.IO.Ports.SerialPort("COM5")
    Dim SerialPort2 As System.IO.Ports.SerialPort =
        New System.IO.Ports.SerialPort("COM6")

    Protected Sub Page_Load(ByVal sender As Object,
                            ByVal e As System.EventArgs)
        Me.SerialPort1.Open()
        Me.SerialPort2.Open()

        Me.SerialPort1.Write("Hello World")
        Me.SerialPort1.Close()
    End Sub

    Protected Sub SerialPort2_DataReceived(ByVal sender As Object,
            ByVal e As System.IO.Ports.SerialDataReceivedEventArgs) _
                                Handles SerialPort2.DataReceived
        Dim data As String = Me.SerialPort2.ReadExisting()
        Me.SerialPort2.Close()

        Me.lblResult.Text = data
    End Sub
```

```
</script>

<html xmlns="http://www.w3.org/1999/xhtml" >
<head id="Head1" runat="server">
    <title>Untitled Page</title>
</head>
<body>
    <form id="form1" runat="server">
    <div>
        <asp:Label runat="server" ID="lblResult" />
    </div>
    </form>
</body>
</html>
```

C#

```
<script runat="server">
    System.IO.Ports.SerialPort SerialPort1 =
        new System.IO.Ports.SerialPort("COM5");
    System.IO.Ports.SerialPort SerialPort2 =
        new System.IO.Ports.SerialPort("COM6");

    protected void Page_Load(object sender, EventArgs e)
    {
        this.SerialPort2.DataReceived +=
            new System.IO.Ports.SerialDataReceivedEventHandler(
                                    SerialPort2_DataReceived);

        this.SerialPort1.Open();
        this.SerialPort2.Open();

        this.SerialPort1.Write("Hello World");
        this.SerialPort1.Close();
    }

    void SerialPort2_DataReceived(object sender,
        System.IO.Ports.SerialDataReceivedEventArgs e)
    {
        string data = this.SerialPort2.ReadExisting();
        this.SerialPort2.Close();

        this.lblResult.Text = data;
    }
</script>
```

The `SerialPort` class gives you control over most aspects of the serial port, including baud rate, parity, and stop bits. The code in Listing 24-24 attempts to open the serial port COM5 and write a string of text to it. It also opens a second connection to COM6 to read data.

If your application needs to use the `SerialPort` *classes, using a Serial Port emulator can be useful to test your application without having the actual device connected. In writing applications using the serial port, I have found the Virtual Serial Port Driver from Eltima Software to be a great tool. It allows you to define virtual serial port pairs connected via loopback and the properties of the serial ports.*

IPC USING PIPES

The applications you write are often not isolated islands. They need to send and receive messages from other processes running both locally and on remote machines, known as *interprocess communication* (IPC). Pipes are a great way to allow this communication, and the `System.IO.Pipes` namespace includes classes that allow you to create both anonymous and named pipes.

Listing 24-25 demonstrates sending a string message to another process using the `NamedPipeClientStream` class.

LISTING 24-25: Sending messages using named pipes

Available for download on Wrox.com

```
Using pipeClient As System.IO.Pipes.NamedPipeClientStream =
    New System.IO.Pipes.NamedPipeClientStream(".", "testpipe",
                                    System.IO.Pipes.PipeDirection.Out)
    pipeClient.Connect(10000)

    Try
        Dim bytes() As Byte =
             ASCIIEncoding.Default.GetBytes("Hello World")
        pipeClient.Write(bytes, 0, bytes.Length)
    Catch ex As System.IO.IOException
        Console.WriteLine("ERROR: {0}", ex.Message)
    End Try

End Using
```

C#

```
using (System.IO.Pipes.NamedPipeClientStream pipeClient =
    new System.IO.Pipes.NamedPipeClientStream(".", "testpipe",
                                   System.IO.Pipes.PipeDirection.Out))
{
    pipeClient.Connect(10000);

    try
    {
        byte[] bytes = ASCIIEncoding.Default.GetBytes("Hello World");
        pipeClient.Write(bytes, 0, bytes.Length);
    }
    catch (System.IO.IOException ex)
    {
        Console.WriteLine("ERROR: {0}", ex.Message);
    }
}
```

In this sample an existing named pipe is connected to using the `NamedPipeClientStream` class. Three parameters are provided in the class constructor to configure the server's name, the pipe name, and the direction of communication in the pipe. After the stream is created, you simply use standard stream techniques to write a series of bytes to it.

NETWORK COMMUNICATIONS

Finally, this chapter takes you beyond your own systems and talks about how you can use the .NET Framework to communicate with other systems. The .NET Framework contains a rich set of classes in the `System.Net` namespace that allow you to communicate over a network using a variety of protocols and communications layers. You can perform all types of actions, from DNS resolution to programmatic HTTP posts to sending e-mail through SMTP.

WebRequest and WebResponse

The first series of classes to discuss are the `WebRequest` and `WebResponse` classes. You can use these two classes to develop applications that can make a request to a Uniform Resource Identifier (URI) and receive a response from that resource. The .NET Framework provides three derivatives of the `WebRequest` and `WebResponse` classes, each designed to communicate to a specific type of endpoint via HTTP, FTP, and file:// protocols.

HttpWebRequest and HttpWebResponse

The first pair of classes are the `HttpWebRequest` and `HttpWebResponse` classes. As you can probably guess based on their names, these two classes are designed to communicate using the HTTP protocol. Perhaps the most famous use of the `HttpWebRequest` and `HttpWebResponse` classes is to write applications that can make requests to other Web pages via HTTP and parse the resulting text to extract data. This is known as *screen scraping*.

For an example of using the `HttpWebRequest` and `HttpWebResponse` classes to screen scrape, you can use the following code to build a Web page that will serve as a simple Web browser. You also learn how to display another Web page inside of yours using an `HttpWebRequest`. In this example, you scrape the Wrox.com home page and display it in a panel on your Web page. Listing 24-26 shows the code.

LISTING 24-26: Using an HttpWebRequest to retrieve a Web page

Available for download on Wrox.com

VB

```
<script runat="server">
    Protected Sub Page_Load(ByVal sender As Object,
                            ByVal e As System.EventArgs)
        Dim url As New Uri("http://www.wrox.com/")
        If (url.Scheme = uri.UriSchemeHttp) Then
            Dim request As System.Net.HttpWebRequest =
                System.Net.HttpWebRequest.Create(url)
            request.Method = System.Net.WebRequestMethods.Http.Get
            Dim response As System.Net.HttpWebResponse =
                request.GetResponse()
            Dim reader As
                New System.IO.StreamReader(
                     response.GetResponseStream())
            Dim tmp As String = reader.ReadToEnd()
            response.Close()

            Me.Panel1.GroupingText = tmp
        End If
    End Sub
</script>

<html xmlns="http://www.w3.org/1999/xhtml" >
<head id="Head1" runat="server">
    <title>Untitled Page</title>
</head>
<body>
    <form id="form1" runat="server">
    <div>
        <p>This is the wrox.com website:</p>
        <asp:Panel ID="Panel1" runat="server"
            Height="355px" Width="480px" ScrollBars=Auto>
        </asp:Panel>
    </div>
    </form>
</body>
</html>
```

continues

LISTING 24-26 *(continued)*

C#

```
<script runat="server">
    protected void Page_Load(object sender, EventArgs e)
    {
        Uri url = new Uri("http://www.wrox.com/");
        if (url.Scheme == Uri.UriSchemeHttp)
        {
            HttpWebRequest request =
                (HttpWebRequest)HttpWebRequest.Create(url);
            request.Method = WebRequestMethods.Http.Get;
            HttpWebResponse response =
                (HttpWebResponse)request.GetResponse();
            StreamReader reader =
                new StreamReader(response.GetResponseStream());
            string tmp = reader.ReadToEnd();
            response.Close();

            this.Panel1.GroupingText = tmp;
        }
    }
</script>
```

Figure 24-14 shows what the Web page looks like when you execute the code in Listing 24-26. The `HttpWebRequest` to the Wrox.com home page returns a string containing the scraped HTML. The sample assigns the value of this string to the `GroupingText` property of the Panel control. When the final page is rendered, the browser renders the HTML that was scraped as literal content on the page.

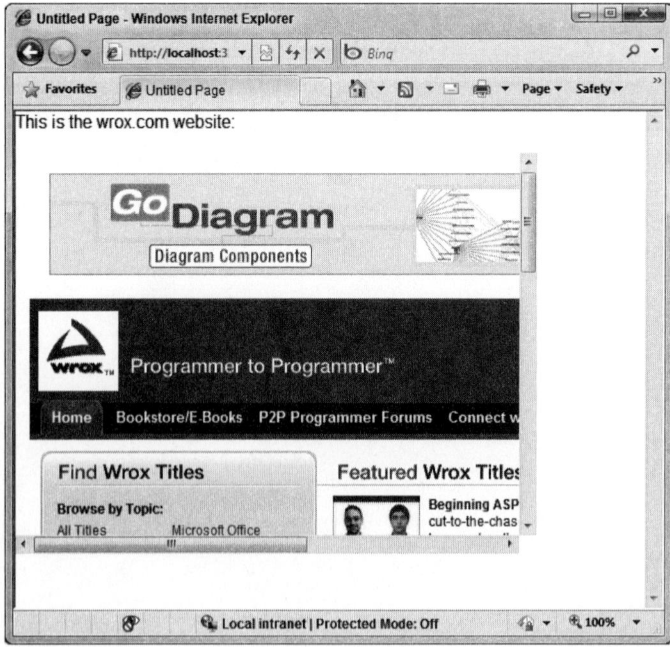

FIGURE 24-14

One other use of the HttpWebRequest and HttpWebResponse classes is to programmatically post data to another Web page, as shown in Listing 24-27.

LISTING 24-27: Using an HttpWebRequest to post data to a remote Web page

Available for download on Wrox.com

```
<script runat="server">
    Protected Sub Page_Load(ByVal sender As Object,
                            ByVal e As System.EventArgs)
        Dim url As Uri = New Uri("http://api.technorati.com/tag")

        Dim tag As String = "tag=ASP.NET"
        Dim key As String = "key=[developerkey]"
        Dim data As String = String.Format("{0}&{1}", key, tag)

        If url.Scheme = Uri.UriSchemeHttp Then

            Dim request As HttpWebRequest =
                System.Net.HttpWebRequest.Create(url)
            request.Method = System.Net.WebRequestMethods.Http.Post
            request.ContentLength = data.Length
            request.ContentType = "application/x-www-form-urlencoded"

            Dim writer As System.IO.StreamWriter =
                 New System.IO.StreamWriter(request.GetRequestStream())
            writer.Write(data)
            writer.Close()

            Dim response As System.Net.HttpWebResponse =
                request.GetResponse()
            Dim reader As System.IO.StreamReader =
                New System.IO.StreamReader(
                    response.GetResponseStream())
            Dim result As String = reader.ReadToEnd()
            response.Close()

            Me.XmlDataSource1.Data = result
        End If
    End Sub
</script>

<html xmlns="http://www.w3.org/1999/xhtml" >
<head id="Head1" runat="server">
    <title>Untitled Page</title>
</head>
<body>
    <form id="form1" runat="server">
    <div>
        <asp:XmlDataSource runat="server" ID="XmlDataSource1" />
        <asp:TreeView ID="TreeView1"
             runat="server" DataSourceID="XmlDataSource1" />
    </div>
    </form>
</body>
</html>
```

```
<script runat="server">
    protected void Page_Load(object sender, EventArgs e)
```

continues

LISTING 24-27 *(continued)*

```
    {
        Uri url = new Uri("http://api.technorati.com/tag");

        string tag = "tag=ASP.NET";
        string key = "key=[developerkey]";
        string data = string.Format("{0}&{1}", key, tag);

        if (url.Scheme == Uri.UriSchemeHttp)
        {
            System.Net.HttpWebRequest request =
               (System.Net.HttpWebRequest)
                    System.Net.HttpWebRequest.Create(url);
            request.Method = System.Net.WebRequestMethods.Http.Post;
            request.ContentLength = data.Length;
            request.ContentType = "application/x-www-form-urlencoded";

           System.IO.StreamWriter writer =
               new System.IO.StreamWriter(request.GetRequestStream());
            writer.Write( data );
            writer.Close();

            System.Net.HttpWebResponse response =
                (System.Net.HttpWebResponse)request.GetResponse();
            System.IO.StreamReader reader =
                new System.IO.StreamReader(
                    response.GetResponseStream());
            string result = reader.ReadToEnd();
            response.Close();

            this.XmlDataSource1.Data = result;
        }
    }
</script>
```

You can see that the preceding code posts a search query to the Technorati REST API and receives a chunk of XML as the response. As in the example shown earlier in Listing 24-25, you can use the XmlDataSource and the TreeView to display the XML response.

FtpWebRequest and FtpWebResponse

The classes discussed are the `FtpWebRequest` and `FtpWebResponse` classes. These two classes were new additions to the .NET 2.0 Framework, and they make executing File Transfer Protocol (FTP) commands from your Web page easy. Using these classes, implementing an entire FTP client right from your Web application is now possible. Listing 24-28 shows an example of downloading a text file from the public Microsoft.com FTP site. (See Figure 24-15.)

LISTING 24-28: Using an FtpWebRequest to download a file from an FTP site

Available for download on Wrox.com

```
<script runat="server">

    protected void Page_Load(object sender, EventArgs e)
    {
        Uri url =
            new Uri("ftp://ftp.microsoft.com/SoftLib/ReadMe.txt ");
        if (url.Scheme == Uri.UriSchemeFtp)
```

```
        {
            System.Net.FtpWebRequest request =
               (System.Net.FtpWebRequest)
                    System.Net.FtpWebRequest.Create(url);
            request.Method =
                System.Net.WebRequestMethods.Ftp.DownloadFile;
            System.Net.FtpWebResponse response =
                (System.Net.FtpWebResponse)request.GetResponse();
            System.IO.StreamReader reader =
                 new System.IO.StreamReader(
                     response.GetResponseStream());
            string tmp = reader.ReadToEnd();
            response.Close();

            this.ftpContent.InnerText = tmp;
        }
    }
</script>

<html xmlns="http://www.w3.org/1999/xhtml" >
<head id="Head1" runat="server">
    <title>Using FTP from an ASP.NET webpage</title>
</head>
<body>
    <form id="form1" runat="server">
    <div>
        <div runat="server" id="ftpContent"
            style="overflow:scroll; height: 260px; width: 450px;">
        </div>
    </div>
    </form>
</body>
</html>
```

C#

```
<script runat="server">
    Protected Sub Page_Load(ByVal sender As Object,
                            ByVal e As System.EventArgs)
        Dim url As New Uri("ftp://ftp.microsoft.com/SoftLib/ReadMe.txt")
        If (url.Scheme = Uri.UriSchemeFtp) Then
            Dim request As System.Net.FtpWebRequest =
                System.Net.FtpWebRequest.Create(url)
            request.Method =
                System.Net.WebRequestMethods.Ftp.DownloadFile
            Dim response As System.Net.FtpWebResponse =
                request.GetResponse()
            Dim reader As
                New System.IO.StreamReader(
                    response.GetResponseStream())
            Dim tmp As String = reader.ReadToEnd()
            response.Close()

            Me.ftpContent.InnerText = tmp
        End If
    End Sub
</script>
```

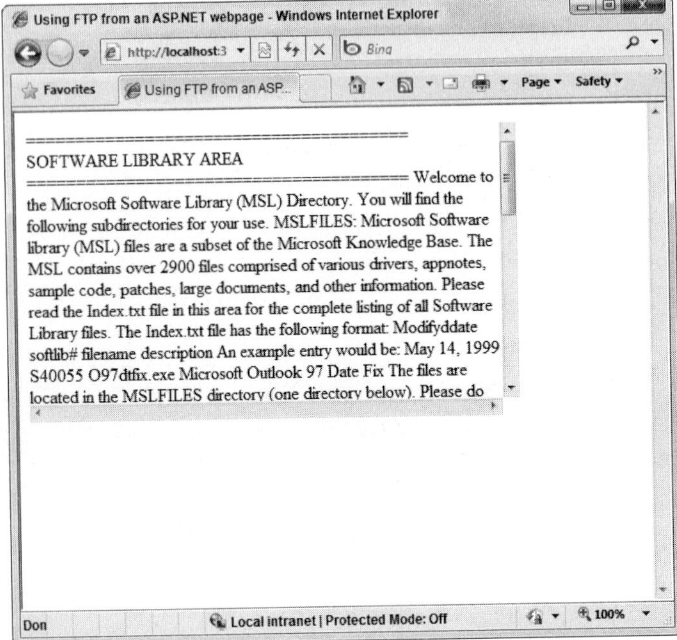

FIGURE 24-15

FileWebRequest and FileWebResponse

Next, look at the `FileWebRequest` and `FileWebResponse` classes. These classes provide a file system implementation of the `WebRequest` and `WebResponse` classes and are designed to make transferring files using the file:// protocol easy, as shown in Listing 24-29.

LISTING 24-29: Using the FileWebRequest to write to a remote file

Available for download on Wrox.com

VB

```
Dim uri As New Uri("file://DEMO7/Documents/lorum.txt")
If (uri.Scheme = uri.UriSchemeFile) Then
    Dim request As System.Net.FileWebRequest = _
        System.Net.FileWebRequest.Create(uri)
    Dim response As System.Net.FileWebResponse = request.GetResponse()
    Dim reader As
        New System.IO.StreamReader(response.GetResponseStream())
    Dim tmp As String = reader.ReadToEnd()
    response.Close()
End If
```

C#

```
Uri uri = new Uri("file://DEMO7/Documents/lorum.txt ");
if (uri.Scheme == Uri.UriSchemeFile)
{
    System.Net.FileWebRequest request =
       (System.Net.FileWebRequest)
           System.Net.FileWebRequest.Create(uri);
    System.Net.FileWebResponse response =
        (System.Net.FileWebResponse)request.GetResponse();
    System.IO.StreamReader reader =
        new System.IO.StreamReader(response.GetResponseStream());
    string tmp = reader.ReadToEnd();
    response.Close();
}
```

This listing shows a request for the `lorum.txt` file that exists in the Documents folder on the DEMO7 machine on the local network.

Sending Mail

Finally, consider a feature common to many Web applications — the capability to send e-mail from a Web page. The capability to send mail was part of the 1.0 Framework and located in the `System.Web.Mail` namespace. In the 2.0 Framework, this functionality was enhanced and moved to the `System.Net.Mail` namespace. Listing 24-30 shows an example of sending an e-mail.

LISTING 24-30: Sending mail from a Web page

Available for download on Wrox.com

```
Dim message As System.Net.Mail.MailMessage =
    New System.Net.Mail.MailMessage(
        "webmaster@example.com", "webmaster@example.com")
message.Subject = "Sending Mail with ASP.NET"
message.Body =
    "This sample email demonstrates sending email using ASP.NET"
Dim smtp As System.Net.Mail.SmtpClient =
    New System.Net.Mail.SmtpClient("localhost")
smtp.Send(message)
```

```
System.Net.Mail.MailMessage message =
    new System.Net.Mail.MailMessage(
        "webmaster@example.com", "webmaster@example.com");
message.Subject = "Sending Mail with ASP.NET";
message.Body =
    "This sample email demonstrates sending email using ASP.NET";
System.Net.Mail.SmtpClient smtp =
   new System.Net.Mail.SmtpClient("localhost");
smtp.Send(message);
```

In this sample, you first create a `MailMessage` object, which is the class that contains the actual message you want to send. The `MailMessage` class requires the To and From address be provided to its constructor, and you can either provide the parameters as strings, or you can use the `MailAddressCollection` class to provide multiple recipients' e-mail addresses.

After you create the `Message`, you use the `SmtpClient` class to actually send the message to your local SMTP server. The `SmtpClient` class allows you to specify the SMTP server from which you want to relay your e-mail.

SUMMARY

In this chapter, you looked at some of the other classes in the .NET Framework. You looked at managing the local file system by using classes in the `System.IO` namespace such as `DirectoryInfo` and the `FileInfo`, and you learned how to enumerate the local file system and manipulate both directory and file properties and directory and file Access Control Lists. Additionally, the chapter discussed the rich functionality .NET provides for working with paths.

The chapter also covered how the .NET Framework enables you to read and write data to a multitude of data locations, including the local file system, network file system, and even system memory through a common `Stream` architecture. The framework provides you with specialized classes to deal with each kind of data location. Additionally, the framework makes working with streams even easier by providing `Reader` and `Writer` classes. These classes hide much of the complexity of reading from and writing to underlying streams. Here, too, the framework provides you with a number of different `Reader` and `Writer` classes that give you the power to control exactly how your data is read or written, be it character, binary, string, or XML.

You were also introduced to the features of .NET Framework that allow you to create memory-mapped files and communicate with serial ports and with other processes through named pipes.

Finally, you learned about the variety of network communication options the .NET Framework provides. From making and sending Web requests over HTTP, FTP, and File, to sending mail, the .NET Framework offers you a full plate of network communication services.

25

User and Server Controls

WHAT'S IN THIS CHAPTER?

- Creating, interacting with, and loading user controls
- Working with server controls
- Optimizing your server controls for developers

In an object-oriented environment like .NET, the encapsulation of code into small, single-purpose, reusable objects is one of the keys to developing a robust system. For example, if your application deals with customers, you might want to consider creating a Customer object to represent a single instance of a Customer. This object would encapsulate all the properties and behaviors a Customer can perform in the system. The advantage of creating this object is that you create a single point with which other objects can interact, and a single point of code to create, debug, deploy, and maintain. Objects like a Customer object are typically known as a business objects because they encapsulate all the business logic needed for a specific entity in the system.

.NET, being an object-oriented framework, includes many other types of reusable objects. The focus of this chapter is discussing and demonstrating how you can use the .NET Framework to create two different types of reusable visual components for an ASP.NET application: user controls and server controls.

- A *user control* encapsulates existing ASP.NET controls into a single container control, which you can then easily reuse throughout your Web project.
- A *server control* encapsulates the raw HTML and client and server logic into a single object. You can program against the server control, and its contents are ultimately rendered to the client to allow the user to interact with on the Web page.

Because the topics of user controls and server controls are so large, and because discussing the intricacies of each could easily fill an entire book by itself, this chapter can't possibly investigate every option available to you. Instead, it attempts to give you a brief overview of building and using user controls and server controls and demonstrates some common scenarios for each type of control.

By the end of this chapter, you should have learned enough that you can get started building basic controls of each type and be able to continue to learn on your own.

USER CONTROLS

User controls represent the most basic form of ASP.NET visual encapsulation. Because they are the most basic, they are also the easiest to create and use. Essentially a *user control* is the grouping of existing server controls into a single-container control. This enables you to create powerful objects that you can easily use throughout an entire Web project.

Creating User Controls

Creating user controls is very simple in Visual Studio. To create a new user control, you first add a new User Control file to your Web site. From the Website menu, select the Add New Item option. After the Add New File dialog appears, select the Web User Control File template from the list and click Add. Notice that after the file is added to the project, the file has an `.ascx` extension. This extension signals to ASP.NET that this file is a user control. If you attempt to load the user control directly into your browser, ASP.NET returns an error telling you that this type of file cannot be served to the client.

If you look at the HTML source shown in Listing 25-1, you see several interesting differences from a standard ASP.NET Web page.

Available for download on Wrox.com

LISTING 25-1: A Web user control file template

```
<%@ Control Language="VB" ClassName="WebUserControl" %>

<script runat="server">

</script>
```

Notice that the source uses the `@Control` directive rather than the `@Page` directive, which a standard Web page would use. Also notice that unlike a standard ASP.NET Web page, no other HTML tags besides the `<script>` tags exist in the control. The Web page containing the user control provides the basic HTML, such as the `<body>` and `<form>` tags. In fact, if you try to add a server-side form tag to the user control, ASP.NET returns an error when the page is served to the client. The error message tells you that only one server-side form tag is allowed in your Web page.

To add controls to the form, simply drag them from the Toolbox onto your user control. Listing 25-2 shows the user control after a label and a button have been added.

Available for download on Wrox.com

LISTING 25-2: Adding controls to the Web user control

```
<%@ Control Language="VB" ClassName="WebUserControl" %>

<script runat="server">

</script>

<asp:Label ID="Label1" runat="server" Text="Label"></asp:Label>
<asp:Button ID="Button1" runat="server" Text="Button" />
```

After you add the controls to the user control, you put the user control onto a standard ASP.NET Web page. To do this, drag the file from the Solution Explorer onto your Web page.

Figure 25-1 shows the user control after it has been dropped onto a host Web page.

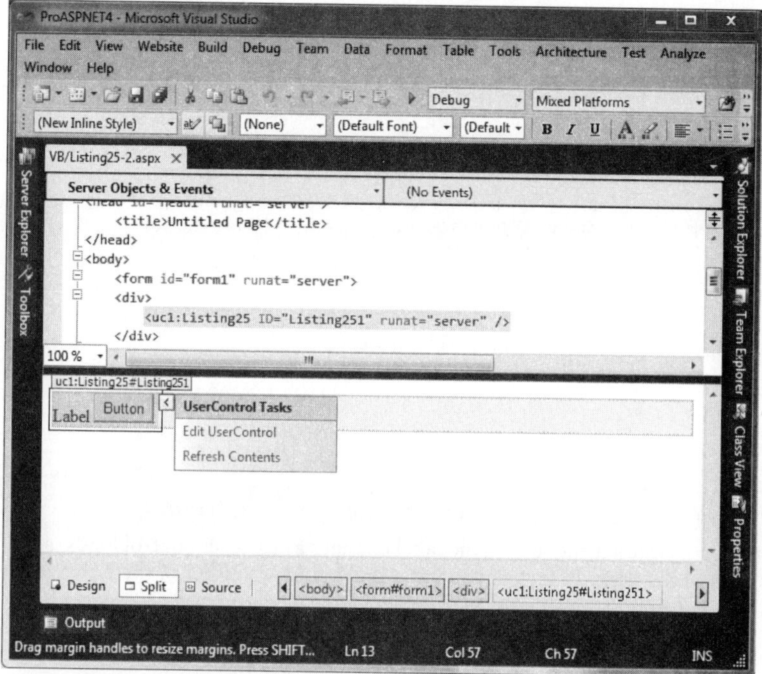

FIGURE 25-1

After you have placed the user control onto a Web page, open the page in a browser to see the fully rendered Web page.

User controls fully participate in the page-rendering life cycle, and controls contained within a user control behave just as they would if placed onto a standard ASP.NET Web page. This means that the user control has its own page events (such as Init, Load, and Prerender) that execute as the page is processed and that controls within the user control will also fire events as they normally would. Listing 25-3 shows how to use the user controls `Page_Load` event to populate the label and to handle a button's `Click` event.

LISTING 25-3: Creating control events in a user control

Available for download on Wrox.com

VB

```
<%@ Control Language="VB" ClassName="WebUserControl1" %>

<script runat="server">
    Protected Sub Page_Load(ByVal sender As Object,
                            ByVal e As System.EventArgs)
        Me.Label1.Text = "The quick brown fox jumped over the lazy dog"
    End Sub

    Protected Sub Button1_Click(ByVal sender As Object,
                                ByVal e As System.EventArgs)
        Me.Label1.Text =
                "The quick brown fox clicked the button on the page"
    End Sub
</script>

<asp:Label ID="Label1" runat="server" Text="Label"></asp:Label>
```

continues

LISTING 25-3 *(continued)*

```
<asp:Button ID="Button1" runat="server" Text="Button" OnClick="Button1_Click" />
```

C#

```
<%@ Control Language="C#" ClassName="WebUserControl1" %>

<script runat="server">

    protected void Page_Load(object sender, EventArgs e)
    {
        this.Label1.Text = "The quick brown fox jumped over the lazy dog";
    }

    protected void Button1_Click(object sender, EventArgs e)
    {
        this.Label1.Text = "The quick brown fox clicked the button on the page";
    }
</script>

<asp:Label ID="Label1" runat="server" Text="Label"></asp:Label>
<asp:Button ID="Button1" runat="server" Text="Button" OnClick="Button1_Click" />
```

When you render the Web page, you see that the text of the label changes as the user control loads, and again when you click the bottom of the page. In fact, if you put a breakpoint on either of these two events, you can see that ASP.NET does indeed break inside the user control code when the page is executed.

Interacting with User Controls

So far, you have learned how you can create user controls and add them to a Web page. You have also learned how user controls can execute their own code and fire events. Most user controls, however, are not isolated islands within their parent page. Often the host Web page will need to interact with user controls that have been placed on it. For instance, you may decide that the text you want to load in the label must be given to the user control by the host page. To do this, you simply add a public property to the user control, and then assign text using the property. Listing 25-4 shows the modified user control.

LISTING 25-4: Exposing user control properties

Available for download on Wrox.com

VB

```
<%@ Control Language="VB" ClassName="WebUserControl" %>

<script runat="server">
    Public Property Text() As String

    Protected Sub Page_Load(ByVal sender As Object,
                            ByVal e As System.EventArgs)
        Me.Label1.Text = Me.Text
    End Sub

    Protected Sub Button1_Click(ByVal sender As Object,
                                ByVal e As System.EventArgs)
        Me.Label1.Text =
                "The quick brown fox clicked the button on the page"
    End Sub
</script>

<asp:Label ID="Label1" runat="server" Text="Label"></asp:Label>
<asp:Button ID="Button1" runat="server" Text="Button" OnClick="Button1_Click" />
```

C#

```
<%@ Control Language="C#" ClassName="WebUserControl" %>

<script runat="server">
```

```
    public string Text {get;set;}

    protected void Page_Load(object sender, EventArgs e)
    {
        this.Label1.Text = this.Text;
    }

    protected void Button1_Click(object sender, EventArgs e)
    {
        this.Label1.Text =
             "The quick brown fox clicked the button on the page";
    }
</script>

<asp:Label ID="Label1" runat="server" Text="Label"></asp:Label>
<asp:Button ID="Button1" runat="server" Text="Button" OnClick="Button1_Click" />
```

After you modify the user control, you simply populate the property from the host Web page. Listing 25-5 shows how to set the `Text` property in code.

LISTING 25-5: Populating user control properties from the host Web page

Available for download on Wrox.com

VB

```
Protected Sub Page_Load(ByVal sender As Object,
                        ByVal e As System.EventArgs)
    Me.WebUserControl1.Text =
                       "The quick brown fox jumped over the lazy dog"
End Sub
```

C#

```
protected void Page_Load(object sender, EventArgs e)
{
    this. WebUserControl1.Text =
                 "The quick brown fox jumped over the lazy dog";
}
```

Note that public properties exposed by user controls will also be exposed by the Property Browser, so you can also set user control's properties using it.

User controls are simple ways of creating powerful, reusable components in ASP.NET. They are easy to create using the built-in templates. Because they participate fully in the page life cycle, you can create controls that can interact with their host page and even other controls on the host page.

Loading User Controls Dynamically

User controls can also be created and added to the Web form dynamically at runtime. The ASP.NET `Page` object includes the `LoadControl` method, which allows you to load user controls at runtime by providing the method with a virtual path to the user control you want to load. The method returns a generic `Control` object that you can then add to the page's `Controls` collection. Listing 25-6 demonstrates how you can use the `LoadControl` method to dynamically add a user control to a Web page.

LISTING 25-6: Dynamically adding a user control

Available for download on Wrox.com

VB

```
<%@ Page Language="VB" %>

<script runat="server">
    Protected Sub Page_Load(ByVal sender As Object,
                            ByVal e As System.EventArgs)
        Dim myForm As Control = Page.FindControl("Form1")
        Dim c1 As Control = LoadControl("WebUserControl.ascx")
        myForm.Controls.Add(c1)
    End Sub
```

continues

LISTING 25-6 *(continued)*

```
</script>

<html xmlns="http://www.w3.org/1999/xhtml" >
<head id="Head1" runat="server">
    <title>Untitled Page</title>
</head>
<body>
    <form id="form1" runat="server">
    <div>
    </div>
    </form>
</body>
</html>
```

C#

```
void Page_Load(object sender, EventArgs e)
{
    Control myForm = Page.FindControl("Form1");
    Control c1 = LoadControl("WebUserControl.ascx");
    myForm.Controls.Add(c1);
}
```

The first step in adding a user control to the page is to locate the page's Form control using the `FindControl` method. Should the user control contain ASP.NET controls that render form elements such as a button or text box, the user control must be added to the form element's `Controls` collection.

Adding user controls containing certain ASP.NET elements such as a Label, HyperLink, or Image directly to the `Page` *object's* `Controls` *collection is possible; however, it is generally safer to be consistent and add them to the Form. Adding a control that must be contained within the Form, such as a Button control, to the* `Pages Controls` *collection results in a runtime parser error.*

After the form has been found, the sample uses the Page's `LoadControl()` method to load an instance of the user control. The method accepts a virtual path to the user control you want to load and returns the loaded user control as a generic `Control` object.

Finally, you add the control to the `Form` object's `Controls` collection. You can also add the user control to other container controls that may be present on the Web page, such as a Panel or Placeholder control.

Remember that you need to re-add your control to the ASP.NET page each time the page performs a postback.

After you have the user control loaded, you can also work with its object model, just as you can with any other control. To access properties and methods that the user control exposes, you need to cast the control from the generic Control type to its actual type. To do that, you also need to add the `@Reference` directive to the page. This tells ASP.NET to compile the user control and link it to the ASP.NET page so that the page knows where to find the user control type. Listing 25-7 demonstrates how you can access a custom property of your user control by casting the control after loading it. The sample loads a modified user control that hosts an ASP.NET TextBox control and exposes a public property that allows you to access the TextBox control's `Text` property.

LISTING 25-7: Casting a user control to its native type

Available for download on Wrox.com

VB

```
Protected Sub Page_Load(ByVal sender As Object,
                        ByVal e As System.EventArgs)
    Dim myForm As Control = Page.FindControl("Form1")
    Dim c1 As  WebUserControl =
        CType(LoadControl("WebUserControl.ascx"),  WebUserControl)
    myForm.Controls.Add(c1)

    c1.ID = "WebUserControl1"
    c1.Text = "My users controls text"
End Sub
```

C#

```
void Page_Load(object sender, EventArgs e)
{
    Control myForm = Page.FindControl("Form1");
     WebUserControl c1 =
        (WebUserControl)LoadControl("WebUserControl.ascx");
    myForm.Controls.Add(c1);

    c1.ID = "WebUserControl1";
    c1.Text = "My users controls text";
}
```

Notice that the sample adds the control to the Form's `Controls` collection and then sets the `Text` property. The ordering of this is important as after a page postback occurs the control's ViewState is not calculated until the control is added to the `Controls` collection. Therefore, if you set the `Text` value (or any other property of the user control) before the control's ViewState is calculated, the value is not persisted in the ViewState.

One additional twist to dynamically adding user controls occurs when you are using output caching to cache the user controls. In this case, after the control has been cached, the `LoadControl` method does not return a new instance of the control. Instead, it returns the cached copy of the control. This presents problems when you try to cast the control to its native type because, after the control is cached, the `LoadControl` method returns it as a `PartialCachingControl` object rather than as its native type. Therefore, the cast in the previous sample results in an exception being thrown.

To solve this problem, you simply test the object type before attempting the cast. This is shown in Listing 25-8.

LISTING 25-8: Detecting cached user controls

Available for download on Wrox.com

VB

```
Protected Sub Page_Load(ByVal sender As Object,
                        ByVal e As System.EventArgs)
    Dim myForm As Control = Page.FindControl("Form1")
    Dim c1 As Control = LoadControl("WebUserControl.ascx")
    myForm.Controls.Add(c1)

    If c1.GetType() Is GetType(WebUserControl) Then
        'This control is not participating in OutputCache
        CType(c1, WebUserControl).ID = "myListing258"
        CType(c1, WebUserControl).Text = "My users controls text"
    ElseIf c1.GetType() Is GetType(PartialCachingControl) And
        Not (IsNothing(CType(c1, PartialCachingControl).CachedControl)) Then

        'The control is participating in output cache, but has expired
        Dim webUserControl1 As WebUserControl =
                CType(CType(c1, PartialCachingControl).CachedControl,
                      WebUserControl)
        webUserControl1.ID = "WebUserControl1"
```

continues

LISTING 25-8 *(continued)*

```
            webUserControl1.Text = "My users controls text"
        End If
    End Sub
```

C#

```
    void Page_Load(object sender, EventArgs e)
    {
        Control myForm = Page.FindControl("Form1");
        Control c1 = LoadControl("WebUserControl.ascx");
        myForm.Controls.Add(c1);

        if (c1 is  WebUserControl)
        {
            //This control is not participating in OutputCache
            ((WebUserControl)c1).ID = "WebUserControl1";
            ((WebUserControl)c1).Text = "My users controls text";
        }
        else if ((c1 is PartialCachingControl) &&
            ((PartialCachingControl)c1).CachedControl != null)
        {
            //The control is participating in output cache, but has expired
             WebUserControl webUserControl1 =
               ((WebUserControl)((PartialCachingControl)c1).CachedControl);
             webUserControl1.ID = "WebUserControl1";
             webUserControl1.Text = "My users controls text";
        }
    }
```

The sample demonstrates how you can test to see what type the `LoadControl` returns and set properties based on the type. For more information on caching, check out Chapter 22.

Finally, in the previous samples user controls have been added dynamically during the `Page_Load` event. But there may be times when you want to add the control in a different event, such as a Button's `Click` event or the `SelectedIndexChanged` event of a DropDownList control. Using these events to add user controls dynamically presents new challenges. Because these events may not be raised each time a page postback occurs, you need to create a way to track when a user control has been added so that it can be re-added to the Web page as additional postbacks occur.

A simple way to do this is to use the ASP.NET session to track when the user control is added to the Web page. Listing 25-9 demonstrates this.

LISTING 25-9: Tracking added user controls across postbacks

Available for download on Wrox.com

VB

```
<%@ Page Language="VB" %>

<script runat="server">
    Protected Sub Page_Load(ByVal sender As Object,
                            ByVal e As System.EventArgs)
        'Make sure the control has not already been added to the page
        If IsNothing(Session("WebUserControlAdded")) Or
            Not (CBool(Session("WebUserControlAdded"))) Then

            Dim myForm As Control = Page.FindControl("Form1")
            Dim c1 As Control = LoadControl("WebUserControl.ascx")
            myForm.Controls.Add(c1)

            Session("WebUserControlAdded") = True
        End If
```

```
    End Sub

    Protected Sub Button1_Click(ByVal sender As Object,
                                ByVal e As System.EventArgs)
        'Check to see if the control should be added to the page
        If Not IsNothing(Session("WebUserControlAdded")) And
            (CBool(Session("WebUserControlAdded"))) Then

            Dim myForm As Control = Page.FindControl("Form1")
            Dim c1 As Control = LoadControl("WebUserControl.ascx")
            myForm.Controls.Add(c1)
        End If
    End Sub
</script>

<html xmlns="http://www.w3.org/1999/xhtml" >
<head id="Head1" runat="server">
    <title>Untitled Page</title>
</head>
<body>
    <form id="form1" runat="server">
    <div>
        <asp:Button ID="Button1" runat="server"
             Text="Load Control" OnClick="Button1_Click" />
    </div>
    </form>
</body>
</html>
```

C#

```
<%@ Page Language="C#" %>

protected void Button1_Click(object sender, EventArgs e)
{
    //Make sure the control has not already been added to the page
    if ((Session["WebUserControlAdded"] == null) ||
        (!(bool)Session["WebUserControlAdded"]))
    {
        Control myForm = Page.FindControl("Form1");
        Control c1 = LoadControl("WebUserControl.ascx");
        myForm.Controls.Add(c1);

        Session["WebUserControlAdded"] = true;
    }
}

protected void Page_Load(object sender, EventArgs e)
{
    //Check to see if the control should be added to the page
    if ((Session["WebUserControlAdded"] != null) &&
        ((bool)Session["WebUserControlAdded"]))
    {
        Control myForm = Page.FindControl("Form1");
        Control c1 = LoadControl("WebUserControl.ascx");
        myForm.Controls.Add(c1);
    }
}
```

This sample used a simple `Session` variable to track whether the user control has been added to the page. When the Button1 `Click` event fires, the session variable is set to `True`, indicating that the user control has been added. Then, each time the page performs a postback, the `Page_Load` event checks to see whether the session variable is set to `True`, and if so, it re-adds the control to the page.

SERVER CONTROLS

The power to create server controls in ASP.NET is one of the greatest tools you can have as an ASP.NET developer. Creating your own custom server controls and extending existing controls are actually both quite easy. In ASP.NET, all controls are derived from two basic classes: `System.Web.UI.WebControls.WebControl` or `System.Web.UI.ScriptControl`. Classes derived from the `WebControl` class have the basic functionality required to participate in the Page framework. These classes include most of the common functionality needed to create controls that render a visual HTML representation and provide support for many of the basic styling elements such as Font, Height, and Width. Because the `WebControl` class derives from the `Control` class, the controls derived from it have the basic functionality to be a designable control, meaning they can be added to the Visual Studio Toolbox, dragged onto the page designer, and have their properties and events displayed in the Property Browser.

Controls derived from the `ScriptControl` class build on the functionality that the `WebControl` class provides by including additional features designed to make working with client-side script libraries easier. The class tests to ensure that a ScriptManager control is present in the hosting page during the control's PreRender stage, and also ensures that derived controls call the proper ScriptManager methods during the Render event.

Server Control Projects

To make creating a custom server control easy, Visual Studio provides two different project templates that set up a basic project structure including the files needed to get started creating a server control. Figure 25-2 shows the ASP.NET Server Control and ASP.NET AJAX Server Control projects in Visual Studios New Project dialog.

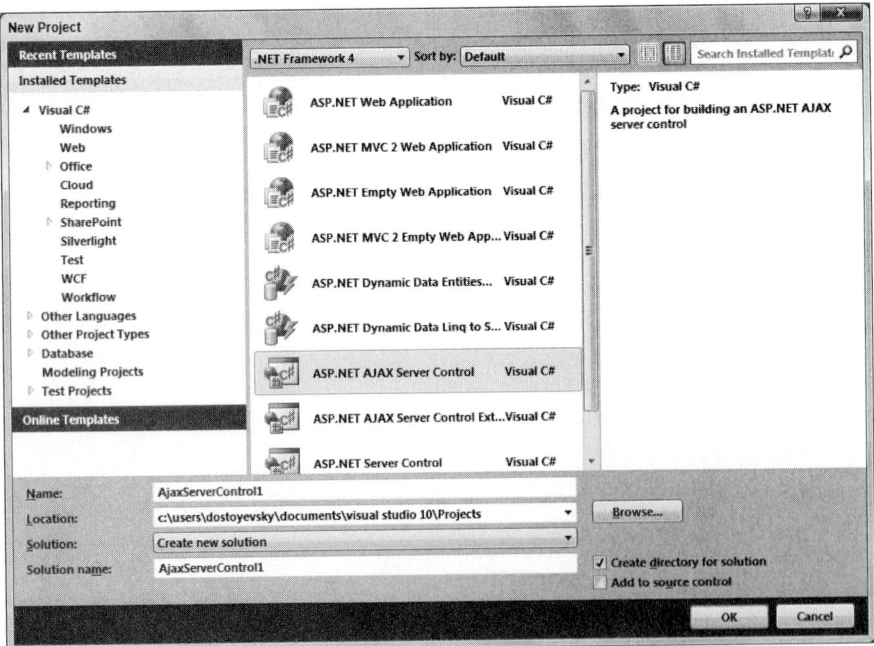

FIGURE 25-2

The ASP.NET Server Control project creates a basic class library project with a single server control class deriving from WebControl included by default. The ASP.NET AJAX Server Control project also creates a basic class library project, but includes a single server control class derived from ScriptControl and a Resource file and a JavaScript file. Creating either of these project types results in a runnable, though essentially functionless, server control.

You can add additional server control classes to the project by selecting the ASP.NET Server Control file template from the Add New Item dialog. Note that this template differs slightly from the default template included in the server control projects. It uses a different filename scheme and includes slightly different code in the default control template.

After you've created a new project, you can test the control by adding a new Web Project to the existing solution, rebuilding the entire solution, and opening the default Web page. Visual Studio automatically adds the server control to the toolbox as shown in Figure 25-3.

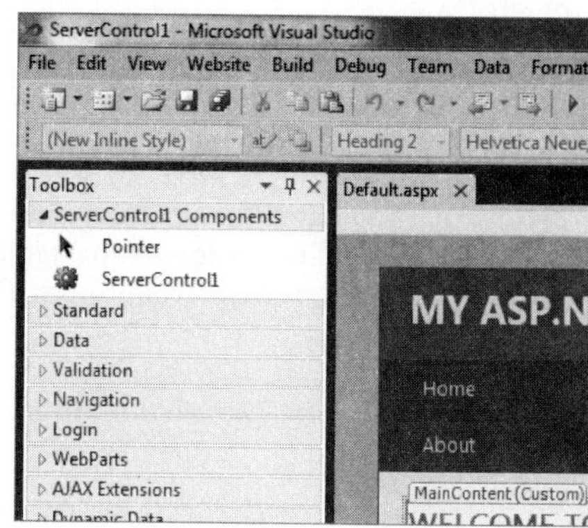

FIGURE 25-3

Visual Studio will do this for any controls contained in projects in the currently open solution.

Now simply drag the control onto the Web Form. A reference to the control is added to the project and the control is added to the Web page. Listing 25-10 shows you what the Web page source code looks like after you have added the control.

LISTING 25-10: Adding a Web Control Library to a Web page

```
<%@ Register Assembly="ServerControl1"
    Namespace="ServerControl1" TagPrefix="cc1" %>

<html xmlns="http://www.w3.org/1999/xhtml" >
<head id="Head1" runat="server">
    <title>Adding a Custom Web Control</title>
</head>
<body>
    <form id="form1" runat="server">
    <div>
        <cc1:ServerControl1 runat="server">
        </cc1:ServerControl1>
    </div>
    </form>
</body>
</html>
```

After you drag the control onto the Web form, take a look at its properties in the Properties window. Figure 25-4 shows the properties of your custom control.

Notice that the control has all the basic properties of a visual control, including various styling and behavior properties. The properties are exposed because the control was derived from the `WebControl` class. The control also inherits the base events exposed by `WebControl`.

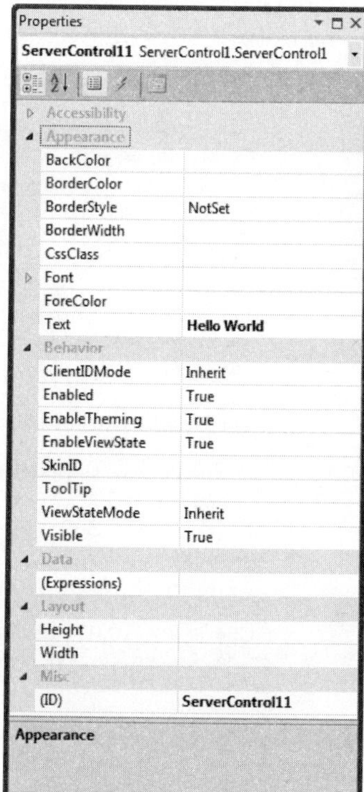

FIGURE 25-4

Make sure the control is working by entering a value for the `Text` property and viewing the page in a browser. Figure 25-5 shows what the page looks like if you set the `Text` property to `"Hello World!"`.

As expected, the control has rendered the value of the `Text` property to the Web page.

Now that you have a basic server control project up and running, you can go back and take a look at the template class created for you by the ASP.NET Server Control project. The default template is shown in Listing 25-11.

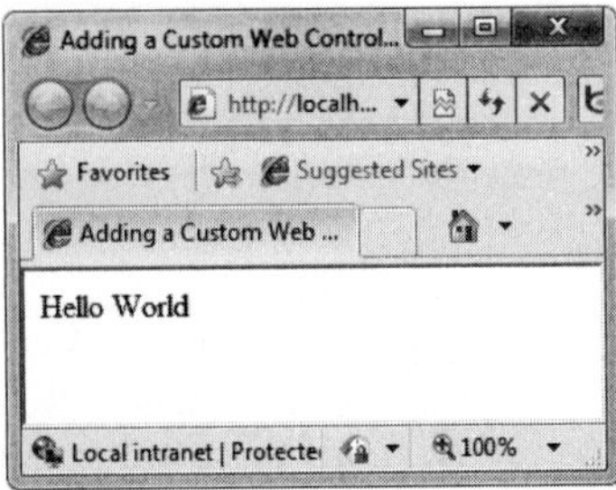

FIGURE 25-5

LISTING 25-11: The Visual Studio ASP.NET Server Control class template

Available for download on Wrox.com

VB

```
Imports System
Imports System.Collections.Generic
Imports System.ComponentModel
Imports System.Text
Imports System.Web
Imports System.Web.UI
Imports System.Web.UI.WebControls

<DefaultProperty("Text"),
 ToolboxData("<{0}:ServerControl1 runat=server></{0}:ServerControl1>")>
Public Class ServerControl1
    Inherits WebControl

    <Bindable(True), Category("Appearance"),
        DefaultValue(""), Localizable(True)>
    Property Text() As String
        Get
            Dim s As String = CStr(ViewState("Text"))
            If s Is Nothing Then
                Return "[" & Me.ID & "]"
            Else
                Return s
            End If
        End Get

        Set(ByVal Value As String)
            ViewState("Text") = Value
        End Set
    End Property

    Protected Overrides Sub RenderContents(
                            ByVal output As HtmlTextWriter)
        output.Write(Text)
    End Sub

End Class
```

C#

```
using System;
using System.Collections.Generic;
using System.ComponentModel;
using System.Linq;
using System.Text;
using System.Web;
```

```
using System.Web.UI;
using System.Web.UI.WebControls;

namespace ServerControl1
{
    [DefaultProperty("Text")]
    [ToolboxData("<{0}:ServerControl1 runat=server>" +
                 "</{0}:ServerControl1>")]
    public class ServerControl1 : WebControl
    {
        [Bindable(true)]
        [Category("Appearance")]
        [DefaultValue("")]
        [Localizable(true)]
        public string Text
        {
            get
            {
                String s = (String)ViewState["Text"];
                return ((s == null) ? "[" + this.ID + "]" : s);
            }

            set
            {
                ViewState["Text"] = value;
            }
        }

        protected override void RenderContents(HtmlTextWriter output)
        {
            output.Write(Text);
        }
    }
}
```

There are a number of interesting things to note about the default server control template generated by the project. First, notice that both the class declaration and the `Text` property are decorated by attributes. ASP.NET server controls make heavy use of attributes to indicate different types of runtime and design-time behaviors. You will learn more about the attributes you can apply to server control classes and properties later in this chapter.

Second, by default the template includes a single property called `Text` and a simple overridden method `RenderContents` that renders the value of that property to the screen. The `RenderContents` method of the control is the primary method used to output content from the server control.

If you view the HTML source of the previous sample, you will see that not only has ASP.NET added the value of the `Text` property to the HTML markup, but it has surrounded the text with a `<SPAN>` block. If you look at the code for the `WebControl` class's render method, you can see that in addition to calling the `RenderContents` method, calls to render a begin and end tag are included, inserting the `Span` tag around the control's content.

```
protected internal override void Render(HtmlTextWriter writer)
{
    this.RenderBeginTag(writer);
    this.RenderContents(writer);
    this.RenderEndTag(writer);
}
```

If you have provided an `ID` value for your control, then the `Span` tag will also, by default, render an `ID` attribute. Having the `Span` tags can sometimes be problematic, so if you want to prevent ASP.NET from automatically adding the Span tags you can override the Render method in your control and call the RenderContents method directly.

VB
```
Protected Overrides Sub Render(ByVal writer As System.Web.UI.HtmlTextWriter)
    Me.RenderContents(writer)
End Sub
```

C#
```
protected override void Render(HtmlTextWriter writer)
{
    this.RenderContents(writer);
}
```

The default server control template does a good job demonstrating how easy creating a simple server control is, but of course, this control does not have much functionality and lacks many of the features you might find in a typical server control. The rest of this chapter focuses on how you can use different features of the .NET Framework to add additional runtime and design time features to a server control.

Control Attributes

Much of the design-time experience a server control offers developers is configured by adding attributes to the server control class and properties. For example, when you look at the default control template from the previous section (Listing 25-11), notice that attributes have been applied to both the class and to the Text property. This section describes the attributes that can be applied to server controls and how they affect the behavior of the control.

Class Attributes

Class attributes for server controls can be divided into three general categories: global control runtime behaviors, how the control looks in the Visual Studio Toolbox, and how it behaves when placed on the design surface. Table 25-1 describes some of these attributes.

TABLE 25-1

ATTRIBUTE	DESCRIPTION
Designer	Indicates the designer class this control should use to render a design-time view of the control on the Visual Studio design surface
TypeConverter	Specifies what type to use as a converter for the object
DefaultEvent	Indicates the default event created when the user double-clicks the control on the Visual Studio design surface
DefaultProperty	Indicates the default property for the control
ControlBuilder	Specifies a ControlBuilder class for building a custom control in the ASP.NET control parser
ParseChildren	Indicates whether XML elements nested within the server controls tags will be treated as properties or as child controls
TagPrefix	Indicates the text the control is prefixed within the Web page HTML

Property/Event Attributes

Property attributes are used to control a number of different aspects of server controls including how your properties and events behave in the Visual Studio Property Browser and how properties and events are serialized at design time. Table 25-2 describes some of the property and event attributes you can use.

TABLE 25-2

ATTRIBUTE	DESCRIPTION
`Bindable`	Indicates that the property can be bound to a data source
`Browsable`	Indicates whether the property should be displayed at design time in the Property Browser
`Category`	Indicates the category this property should be displayed under in the Property Browser
`Description`	Displays a text string at the bottom of the Property Browser that describes the purpose of the property
`EditorBrowsable`	Indicates whether the property should be editable when shown in the Property Browser
`DefaultValue`	Indicates the default value of the property shown in the Property Browser
`DesignerSerializationVisibility`	Specifies the visibility a property has to the design-time serializer
`NotifyParentProperty`	Indicates that the parent property is notified when the value of the property is modified
`PersistChildren`	Indicates whether, at design time, the child controls of a server control should be persisted as nested inner controls
`PersistanceMode`	Specifies how a property or an event is persisted to the ASP.NET page
`TemplateContainer`	Specifies the type of `INamingContainer` that will contain the template after it is created
`Editor`	Indicates the UI Type Editor class this control should use to edit its value
`Localizable`	Indicates that the property contains text that can be localized
`Themable`	Indicates whether this property can have a theme applied to it

Obviously, the class and property/event attribute tables present a lot of information upfront. You already saw a demonstration of some of these attributes in Listing 25-11 and as you go through the rest of this chapter, samples will leverage other attributes listed in the tables.

Control Rendering

So far in this chapter you have seen how easy getting up and running with a very basic server control using the Visual Studio project templates is and how you can apply attributes in the server control to influence some basic control behaviors. The rest of the chapter focuses on how you can use features of ASP.NET to add more advanced control capabilities to your server controls.

The Page Event Life Cycle

Before digging deeper into server controls, spending a moment to look at the general ASP.NET page life cycle that server controls operate within is helpful. As the control developer, you are responsible for overriding methods that execute during the life cycle and implementing your own custom rendering logic.

Remember that when a Web browser makes a request to the server, it is using HTTP, a stateless protocol. ASP.NET provides a page-execution framework that helps create the illusion of state in a Web application. This framework is basically a series of methods and events that execute every time an ASP.NET page is processed. Figure 25-6 shows the events and methods called during the control's life cycle.

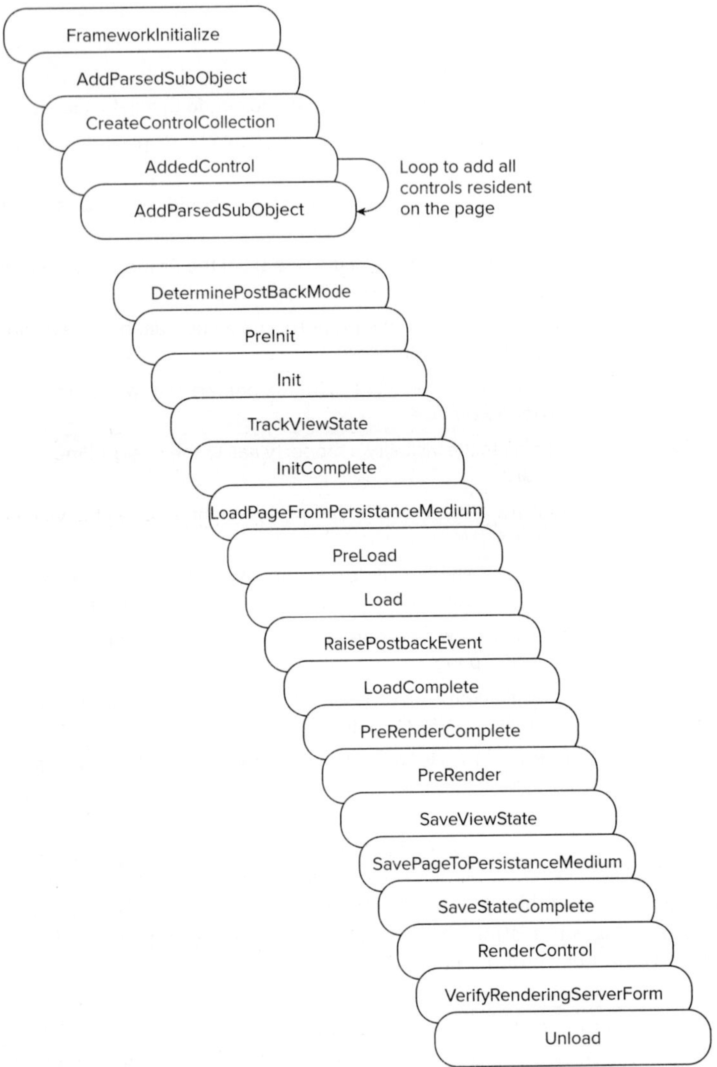

FIGURE 25-6

As you read through the rest of this chapter, you will see that a server control uses many of these events and methods. Understanding them and the order in which they execute is helpful so that as you are adding features to your server control, you can structure your logic to follow the page life cycle.

Rendering HTML Tags

The main job of a server control is to render some type of markup language to the HTTP output stream, which is returned to and displayed by the client. If your client is a standard browser, the control should emit HTML; if the client is something like a mobile device, the control may need to emit a different type of markup, such as WAP, or WML. As I stated earlier, your responsibility as the control developer is to tell the server control what markup to render. The overridden `RenderContents` method, called during the control's life cycle, is the primary location where you tell the control what you want to emit to the client. In

Listing 25-12, notice that the `RenderContents` method is used to tell the control to print the value of the `Text` property.

LISTING 25-12: Overriding the Render method

Available for download on Wrox.com

VB

```
Protected Overrides Sub RenderContents(ByVal output As HtmlTextWriter)
    output.Write(Text)
End Sub
```

C#

```
protected override void RenderContents(HtmlTextWriter output)
{
    output.Write(Text);
}
```

Also notice that the `RenderContents` method has one method parameter called `output`. This parameter is an `HtmlTextWriter` class, which is what the control uses to render HTML to the client. This special writer class is specifically designed to emit HTML 4.0–compliant HTML to the browser. The `HtmlTextwriter` class has a number of methods you can use to emit your HTML, including `RenderBeginTag` and `WriteBeginTag`. Listing 25-13 shows how you can modify the control's `Render` method to emit an HTML `<input>` tag.

LISTING 25-13: Using the HtmlTextWriter to render an HTML tag

Available for download on Wrox.com

VB

```
Protected Overrides Sub RenderContents(ByVal output As HtmlTextWriter)
    output.RenderBeginTag(HtmlTextWriterTag.Input)
    output.RenderEndTag()
End Sub
```

C#

```
protected override void RenderContents(HtmlTextWriter output)
{
    output.RenderBeginTag(HtmlTextWriterTag.Input);
    output.RenderEndTag();
}
```

First, notice that the `RenderBeginTag` method is used to emit the HTML. The advantage of using this method to emit HTML is that it requires you to select a tag from the `HtmlTextWriterTag` enumeration. Using the `RenderBeginTag` method and the `HtmlTextWriterTag` enumeration enables you to have your control automatically support down-level browsers that cannot understand HTML 4.0 syntax. If a down-level browser is detected by ASP.NET, the control automatically emits HTML 3.2 syntax instead of HTML 4.0.

Second, notice that the `RenderEndTag` method is also used. As the name suggests, this method renders the closing tag. Notice, however, that you do not have to specify in this method which tag you want to close. The `RenderEndTag` automatically closes the last begin tag rendered by the `RenderBeginTag` method, which in this case is the `<input>` tag. If you want to emit multiple HTML tags, make sure you order your `Begin` and `End` render methods properly. In Listing 25-14, for example, you add a `<div>` tag to the control. The `<div>` tag surrounds the `<input>` tag when rendered to the page.

LISTING 25-14: Using the HtmlTextWriter to render multiple HTML tags

Available for download on Wrox.com

VB

```
Protected Overrides Sub RenderContents(ByVal output As HtmlTextWriter)
    output.RenderBeginTag(HtmlTextWriterTag.Div)
    output.RenderBeginTag(HtmlTextWriterTag.Input)
    output.RenderEndTag()
    output.RenderEndTag()
End Sub
```

C#

```
protected override void RenderContents(HtmlTextWriter output)
{
```

continues

LISTING 25-14 *(continued)*

```
        output.RenderBeginTag(HtmlTextWriterTag.Div);
        output.RenderBeginTag(HtmlTextWriterTag.Input);
        output.RenderEndTag();
        output.RenderEndTag();
    }
```

Now that you have a basic understanding of how to emit simple HTML, look at the output of your control. Figure 25-7 shows the source for the page.

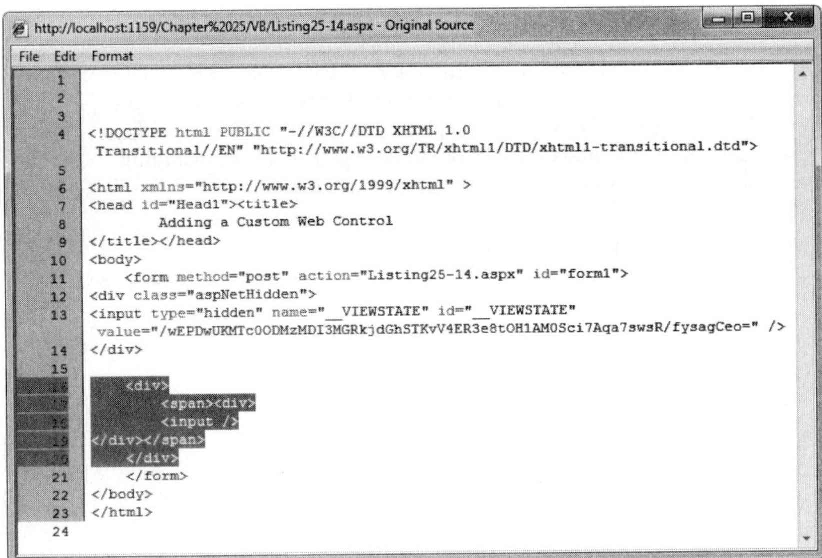

FIGURE 25-7

You can see that the control emitted some simple HTML markup. Also notice that the control was smart enough to realize that the input control did not contain any child controls and, therefore, the control did not need to render a full closing tag. Instead, it automatically rendered the shorthand `/>`, rather than `</input>`.

Adding Tag Attributes

Emitting HTML tags is a good start to building the control, but perhaps this is a bit simplistic. Normally, when rendering HTML you would emit some tag attributes (such as `ID` or `Name`) to the client in addition to the tag. Listing 25-15 shows how you can easily add tag attributes.

LISTING 25-15: Rendering HTML tag attributes

Available for download on Wrox.com

VB

```
Protected Overrides Sub RenderContents(ByVal output As HtmlTextWriter)
    output.RenderBeginTag(HtmlTextWriterTag.Div)
    output.AddAttribute(HtmlTextWriterAttribute.Type, "text")
    output.AddAttribute(HtmlTextWriterAttribute.Id, Me.ClientID & "_i")
    output.AddAttribute(HtmlTextWriterAttribute.Name,
                        Me.ClientID & "_i")
    output.AddAttribute(HtmlTextWriterAttribute.Value, Me.Text)
    output.RenderBeginTag(HtmlTextWriterTag.Input)
```

```
        output.RenderEndTag()
        output.RenderEndTag()
    End Sub
```

C#

```
    protected override void RenderContents(HtmlTextWriter output)
    {
        output.RenderBeginTag(HtmlTextWriterTag.Div);
        output.AddAttribute(HtmlTextWriterAttribute.Type, "text");
        output.AddAttribute(HtmlTextWriterAttribute.Id,
                            this.ClientID + "_i");
        output.AddAttribute(HtmlTextWriterAttribute.Name,
                            this.ClientID + "_i");
        output.AddAttribute(HtmlTextWriterAttribute.Value, this.Text);
        output.RenderBeginTag(HtmlTextWriterTag.Input);
        output.RenderEndTag();
        output.RenderEndTag();
    }
```

You can see that by using the `AddAttribute` method, you have added three attributes to the `<input>` tag. Also notice that, once again, you are using an enumeration, `HtmlTextWriterAttribute`, to select the attribute you want to add to the tag. This serves the same purpose as using the `HtmlTextWriterTag` enumeration, allowing the control to degrade its output to down-level browsers.

As with the `Render` methods, the order in which you place the `AddAttributes` methods is important. You place the `AddAttributes` methods directly before the `RenderBeginTag` method in the code. The `AddAttributes` method associates the attributes with the next HTML tag that is rendered by the `RenderBeginTag` method — in this case the `<input>` tag.

Now browse to the test page and check out the HTML source with the added tag attributes. Figure 25-8 shows the HTML source rendered by the control.

http://localhost:1159/Chapter%2025/VB/Listing25-15.aspx - Original Source

File Edit Format

```



<!DOCTYPE html PUBLIC "-//W3C//DTD XHTML 1.0
 Transitional//EN" "http://www.w3.org/TR/xhtml1/DTD/xhtml1-transitional.dtd">

<html xmlns="http://www.w3.org/1999/xhtml" >
<head id="Head1"><title>
        Adding a Custom Web Control
</title></head>
<body>
    <form method="post" action="Listing25-15.aspx" id="form1">
<div class="aspNetHidden">
<input type="hidden" name="__VIEWSTATE" id="__VIEWSTATE"
 value="/wEPDwUKMjA3OTU3MDIzNGRktNBtD3WFQ9PFYpmwDZPdDJYBTZCSEzCf8ZLzM+s/1m0=" />
</div>

    <div>
        <span id="ServerControl15"><div>
        <input type="text" id="ServerControl15_i" name="ServerControl15_i"
 value="Hello World" />
</div></span>
    </div>
    </form>
</body>
</html>

```

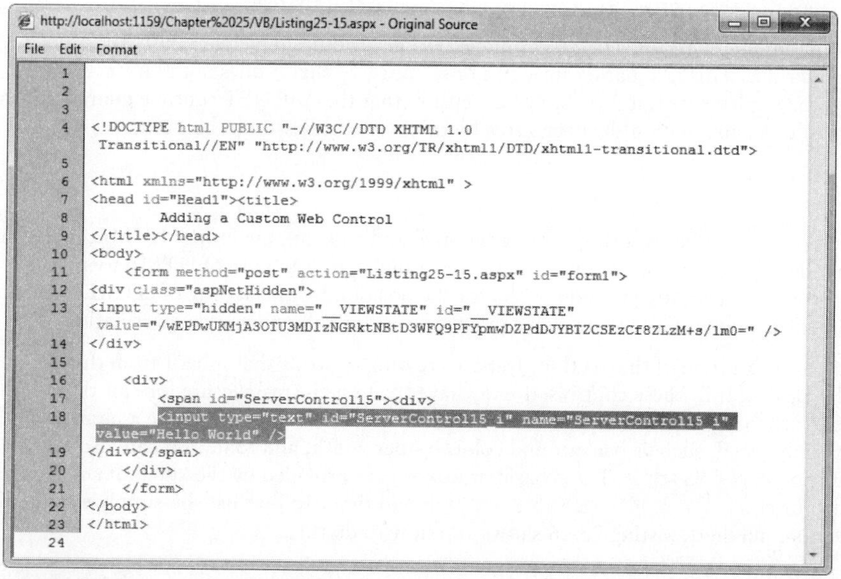

FIGURE 25-8

You can see that the tag attributes you added in the server control are now included as part of the HTML tag rendered by the control.

A Word about Control IDs

Notice that in Listing 25-15, using the control's `ClientID` property as the value of both the `Id` and `Name` attributes is important. Controls that derive from the `WebControl` class automatically expose three different types of ID properties: `ID`, `UniqueID`, and `ClientID`. Each of these properties exposes a slightly altered version of the control's ID for use in a specific scenario.

The `ID` property is the most obvious. Developers use it to get and set the control's ID. It must be unique to the page at design time.

The `UniqueID` property is a read-only property generated at runtime that returns an ID that has been prepended with the containing control's ID. This is essential so that ASP.NET can uniquely identify each control in the page's control tree, even if the control is used multiple times by a container control such as a Repeater or GridView. For example, if you add this custom control to a Repeater, the `UniqueID` for each custom control rendered by the Repeater is modified to include the Repeater's ID when the page executed:

```
MyRepeater:Ctrl0:MyCustomControl
```

Beginning with ASP.NET 4.0, the `ClientID` property can be generated differently depending on the value of the `ClientIDMode` property. The `ClientIDMode` property allows you to select one of four mechanisms that ASP.NET will use to generate the `ClientID`:

- **AutoID:** Equivalent to the behavior used in earlier versions of ASP.NET.
- **Static:** Specifies that the `ClientID` value will be the same as the ID, without concatenating the IDs of parent containers.
- **Predictable:** Primarily for use in data controls, it concatenates the IDs of a control's naming containers, but generated client ID values do not contain strings like '`ctlxxx`'. Instead you can set the `ClientIDRowSuffix` property to provide a unique value for each control generated.
- **Inherit:** Specifies that the control's ID generation is the same as its parent.

Additionally, to ensure that controls can generate a unique ID, they should implement the `INamingContainer` interface. This is a marker interface only, meaning that it does not require any additional methods to be implemented; it does, however, ensure that the ASP.NET runtime guarantees the control always has a unique name within the page's tree hierarchy, regardless of its container.

Styling HTML

So far, you have seen how easy building a simple server control and emitting the proper HTML, including attributes, are, but modern Web development techniques generally restrict the use of HTML to a basic content description mechanism, relying instead on CSS for the positioning and styling of HTML elements in a Web page. In this section, you will learn how you can have your control render style information.

As mentioned at the very beginning of this section, you are creating controls that inherit from the `WebControl` class. Because of this, these controls already have the basic infrastructure for emitting most of the standard CSS-style attributes. In the Property Browser for this control, you should see a number of style properties already listed, such as background color, border width, and font. You can also launch the style builder to create complex CSS styles. These basic properties are provided by the `WebControl` class, but it is up to you to tell your control to render the values set at design time. To do this, you simply execute the `AddAttributesToRender` method. Listing 25-16 shows you how to do this.

LISTING 25-16: Rendering style properties

Available for download on Wrox.com

VB

```
Protected Overrides Sub RenderContents(ByVal output As HtmlTextWriter)
    output.RenderBeginTag(HtmlTextWriterTag.Div)

     output.AddAttribute(HtmlTextWriterAttribute.Type, "text")
```

```
        output.AddAttribute(HtmlTextWriterAttribute.Id, Me.ClientID & "_i")
        output.AddAttribute(HtmlTextWriterAttribute.Name,
                            Me.ClientID & "_i")
        output.AddAttribute(HtmlTextWriterAttribute.Value, Me.Text)
        Me.AddAttributesToRender(output)

        output.RenderBeginTag(HtmlTextWriterTag.Input)
        output.RenderEndTag()
        output.RenderEndTag()
    End Sub
```

C#

```
    protected override void RenderContents(HtmlTextWriter output)
    {
        output.RenderBeginTag(HtmlTextWriterTag.Div);

        output.AddAttribute(HtmlTextWriterAttribute.Type, "text");
        output.AddAttribute(HtmlTextWriterAttribute.Id,
                            this.ClientID + "_i");
        output.AddAttribute(HtmlTextWriterAttribute.Name,
                            this.ClientID + "_i");
        output.AddAttribute(HtmlTextWriterAttribute.Value, this.Text);
        this.AddAttributesToRender(output);

        output.RenderBeginTag(HtmlTextWriterTag.Input);
        output.RenderEndTag();
        output.RenderEndTag();
    }
```

Executing this method tells the control to render any style information that has been set.

Note that executing this method not only causes the style-related properties to be rendered, but also several other attributes, including `ID`, `tabindex`, and `tooltip`. If you are manually rendering these attributes earlier in your control, then you may end up with duplicate attributes being rendered.

Additionally, being careful about where you execute the `AddAttributesToRender` method is important. In Listing 25-16, it is executed immediately before the `Input` tag is rendered, which means that the attributes will be rendered both on the `Input` element and on the `Span` element surrounding the `Input` element. Placing the method call before the beginning `Div` tag is rendered will ensure that the attributes are now applied to the `Div` and its surrounding span. Placing the method call after the end `Div` means only the span has the attribute applied.

Using the Property Browser, you can set the background color of the control to `Red` and the font to `Bold`. When you set these properties, they are automatically added to the control tag in the ASP.NET page. After you have added the styles, the control tag looks like this:

```
<cc1:ServerControl1 BackColor="Red" Font-Bold=true
 ID="ServerControl11" runat="server" />
```

The style changes have been persisted to the control as attributes. When you execute this page in the browser, the style information should be rendered to the HTML, making the background of the text box red and its font bold. Figure 25-9 shows the page in the browser.

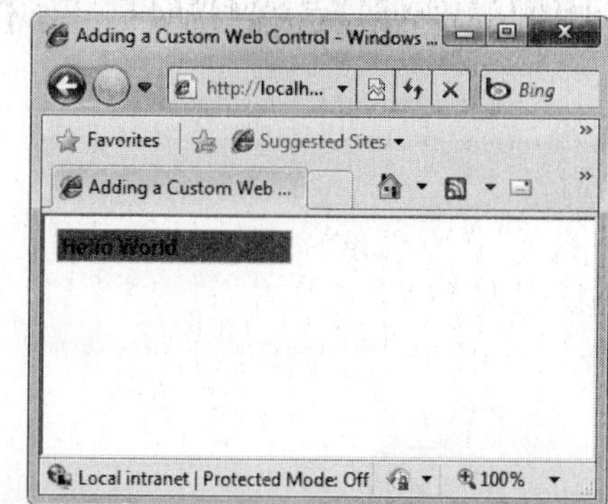

FIGURE 25-9

Once again, look at the source for this page. The style information has been rendered to the HTML as a style tag. Figure 25-10 shows the HTML emitted by the control.

```
http://localhost:1159/Chapter%2025/VB/Listing25-16.aspx - Original Source
File  Edit  Format

<!DOCTYPE html PUBLIC "-//W3C//DTD XHTML 1.0
 Transitional//EN" "http://www.w3.org/TR/xhtml1/DTD/xhtml1-transitional.dtd">

<html xmlns="http://www.w3.org/1999/xhtml" >
<head id="Head1"><title>
        Adding a Custom Web Control
</title></head>
<body>
    <form method="post" action="Listing25-16.aspx" id="form1">
<div class="aspNetHidden">
<input type="hidden" name="__VIEWSTATE" id="__VIEWSTATE"
 value="/wEPDwUKMjEyOTg4NDEwNGRkl5OXNVQpfSLiGdE11yzGWfFMdZEWpRuXaVqm7MEKfUw=" />
</div>

    <div>
        <span id="ServerControl16" style="background-color:Red;font-
weight:bold;"><div>
        <input type="text" id="ServerControl16_i" name="ServerControl16_i"
 value="Hello World" id="ServerControl16" style="background-color:Red;font-
weight:bold;" />
</div></span>
    </div>
    </form>
</body>
</html>
```

FIGURE 25-10

If you want more control over the rendering of styles in your control you can use the `HtmlTextWriters` `AddStyleAttribute` method. Similar to the `AddAttribute` method, the `AddStyleAttribute` method enables you to specify CSS attributes to add to a control using the `HtmlTextWriterStyle` enumeration. However, unlike the `AddAttribute` method, attributes added using `AddStyleAttribute` are defined inside of a style attribute on the control. Listing 25-17 demonstrates the use of the `AddStyleAttribute` method.

LISTING 25-17: Adding control styles using AddStyleAttribute

Available for download on Wrox.com

VB

```
Protected Overrides Sub RenderContents(ByVal output As HtmlTextWriter)
    output.RenderBeginTag(HtmlTextWriterTag.Div)

    output.AddAttribute(HtmlTextWriterAttribute.Type, "text")
    output.AddAttribute(HtmlTextWriterAttribute.Id, Me.ClientID & "_i")
    output.AddAttribute(HtmlTextWriterAttribute.Name,
                        Me.ClientID & "_i")
    output.AddAttribute(HtmlTextWriterAttribute.Value, Me.Text)

    output.AddStyleAttribute(
           HtmlTextWriterStyle.BackgroundColor, "Red")

    output.RenderBeginTag(HtmlTextWriterTag.Input)
    output.RenderEndTag()
    output.RenderEndTag()
End Sub
```

C#

```
protected override void RenderContents(HtmlTextWriter output)
{
    output.RenderBeginTag(HtmlTextWriterTag.Div);

    output.AddAttribute(HtmlTextWriterAttribute.Type, "text");
    output.AddAttribute(HtmlTextWriterAttribute.Id,
                        this.ClientID + "_i");
    output.AddAttribute(HtmlTextWriterAttribute.Name,
                        this.ClientID + "_i");
```

```
        output.AddAttribute(HtmlTextWriterAttribute.Value, this.Text);

        output.AddStyleAttribute(
               HtmlTextWriterStyle.BackgroundColor, "Red");

        output.RenderBeginTag(HtmlTextWriterTag.Input);
        output.RenderEndTag();
        output.RenderEndTag();
    }
```

Running this sample results in the same red background color being applied to the control.

Themes and Skins

A great feature of ASP.NET that allows you to create visual styles for your Web applications and was introduced to you in Chapter 6 is themes and skins. This section describes how you can allow your custom server controls to leverage themes and skins.

As you saw in Chapter 6, skins are essentially a way to set default values for the UI elements of controls in your Web application. You simply define the control and its properties in a `.skin` file and the values are applied to the control at runtime. Listing 25-18 shows a sample skin.

LISTING 25-18: Sample ASP.NET skin

Available for download on Wrox.com

```
<%@ Register Assembly="WebControlLibrary1"
    Namespace="WebControlLibrary1"
    TagPrefix="cc1" %>

<cc1:webcustomcontrol1 BackColor="Green" runat="server" />
```

By default, ASP.NET allows all control properties to be defined in the skin file, but obviously this is not always appropriate. Most exposed properties are non-UI related; therefore, you do not apply a theme to them. By setting the `Themeable` attribute to `False` on each of these properties, you prevent the application of a theme. Listing 25-19 shows how to do this in your control by disabling themes on the `Text` property.

LISTING 25-19: Disabling theme support on a control property

Available for download on Wrox.com

VB

```
<Bindable(True), Category("Appearance"), DefaultValue(""),
Localizable(True), Themeable(False)>
Property Text() As String
    Get
        Dim s As String = CStr(ViewState("Text"))
        If s Is Nothing Then
            Return "[" + Me.ID + "]"
        Else
            Return s
        End If
    End Get

    Set(ByVal Value As String)
        ViewState("Text") = Value
    End Set
End Property
```

C#

```
[Bindable(true)]
[Category("Appearance")]
[DefaultValue("")]
[Localizable(true)]
[Themeable(false)]
public string Text
```

continues

LISTING 25-19 *(continued)*

```
{
    get
    {
        String s = (String)ViewState["Text"];
        return ((s == null) ? "["+ this.ID + "]": s);
    }
    set
    {
        ViewState["Text"] = value;
    }
}
```

Now, if a developer attempts to define this property in his skin file, he receives a compiler error when the page is executed.

Adding Client-Side Features

Although the capability to render and style HTML is quite powerful by itself, other resources can be sent to the client, such as client-side scripts, images, and resource strings. ASP.NET provides you with some powerful tools for using client-side scripts in your server controls and retrieving other resources to the client along with the HTML your control emits. Additionally, ASP.NET includes an entire model that allows you to make asynchronous callbacks from your Web page to the server.

Emitting Client-Side Script

Having your control emit client-side script like JavaScript enables you to add powerful client-side functionality to your control. Client-side scripting languages take advantage of the client's browser to create more flexible and easy-to-use controls. ASP.NET provides a wide variety of methods for emitting client-side script that you can use to control where and how your script is rendered.

Most of the properties and methods needed to render client script are available from the `ClientScriptManager` class, which you can access using `Page.ClientScript`. Listing 25-20 demonstrates how you can use the `RegisterStartupScript` method to render JavaScript to the client. This listing adds the code into the `OnPreRender` method, rather than into the `Render` method used in previous samples. This method allows every control to inform the page about the client-side script it needs to render. After the `Render` method is called, the page is able to render all the client-side script it collected during the `OnPreRender` method. If you call the client-side script registration methods in the `Render` method, the page has already completed a portion of its rendering before your client-side script can render itself.

LISTING 25-20: Rendering a client-side script to the browser

Available for download on Wrox.com

```
Protected Overrides Sub OnPreRender(ByVal e As System.EventArgs)
    Page.ClientScript.RegisterStartupScript(GetType(Page),
       "ControlFocus", "document.getElementById('" &
       Me.ClientID & "_i" & "').focus();",
       True)
End Sub
```

```
protected override void OnPreRender(EventArgs e)
{
    Page.ClientScript.RegisterStartupScript(typeof(Page),
        "ControlFocus", "document.getElementById('" +
        this.ClientID + "_i" + "').focus();",
        true);
}
```

In this listing, the code emits client-side script to automatically move the control focus to the TextBox control when the Web page loads. When you use the `RegisterStartupScript` method, notice that it now includes an overload that lets you specify whether the method should render surrounding script tags. This can be handy if you are rendering more than one script to the page.

Also notice that the method requires a key parameter. This parameter is used to uniquely identify the script block; if you are registering more than one script block in the Web page, make sure that each block is supplied a unique key. You can use the `IsStartupScriptRegistered` method and the key to determine whether a particular script block has been previously registered on the client using the `RegisterStatupScript` method.

When you execute the page in the browser, notice that the focus is automatically placed into a text box. If you look at the source code for the Web page, you should see that the JavaScript was written to the bottom of the page, as shown in Figure 25-11.

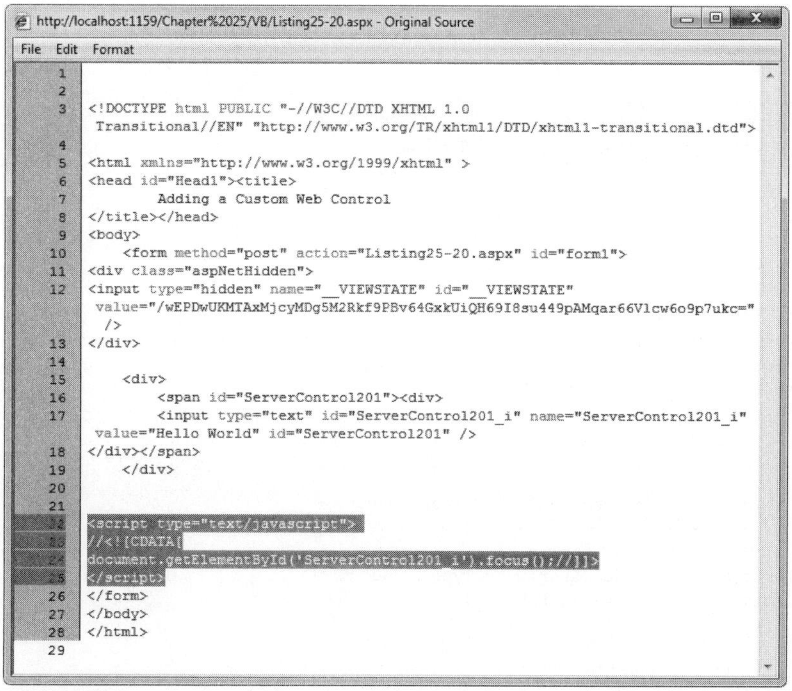

http://localhost:1159/Chapter%2025/VB/Listing25-20.aspx - Original Source

File Edit Format

```
<!DOCTYPE html PUBLIC "-//W3C//DTD XHTML 1.0
 Transitional//EN" "http://www.w3.org/TR/xhtml1/DTD/xhtml1-transitional.dtd">

<html xmlns="http://www.w3.org/1999/xhtml" >
<head id="Head1"><title>
        Adding a Custom Web Control
</title></head>
<body>
    <form method="post" action="Listing25-20.aspx" id="form1">
<div class="aspNetHidden">
<input type="hidden" name="__VIEWSTATE" id="__VIEWSTATE"
 value="/wEPDwUKMTAxMjcyMDg5M2Rkf9PBv64GxkUiQH69I8su449pAMqar66V1cw6o9p7ukc="
 />
</div>


    <div>
        <span id="ServerControl201"><div>
        <input type="text" id="ServerControl201_i" name="ServerControl201_i"
 value="Hello World" id="ServerControl201" />
</div></span>
    </div>



<script type="text/javascript">
//<![CDATA[
document.getElementById('ServerControl201_i').focus();//]]>
</script>
</form>
</body>
</html>
```

FIGURE 25-11

If you want the script to be rendered to the top of the page, you use the `RegisterClientScriptBlock` method that emits the script block immediately after the opening `<form>` element.

Keep in mind that the browser parses the Web page from top to bottom, so if you emit client-side script at the top of the page that is not contained in a function, any references in that code to HTML elements further down the page will fail. The browser has not parsed that portion of the page yet.

Being able to render script that automatically executes when the page loads is nice, but it is more likely that you will want the code to execute based on an event fired from an HTML element on your page, such as the `Click`, `Focus`, or `Blur` events. To do this, you add an attribute to the HTML element you want the event to fire from. Listing 25-21 shows you how you can modify your control's `Render` and `PreRender` methods to add this attribute.

LISTING 25-21: Using client-side script and event attributes to validate data

Available for download on Wrox.com

```
Protected Overrides Sub RenderContents(ByVal output As HtmlTextWriter)
    output.RenderBeginTag(HtmlTextWriterTag.Div)

    output.AddAttribute(HtmlTextWriterAttribute.Type, "text")
    output.AddAttribute(HtmlTextWriterAttribute.Id, Me.ClientID & "_i")
    output.AddAttribute(HtmlTextWriterAttribute.Name,
                        Me.ClientID & "_i")
    output.AddAttribute(HtmlTextWriterAttribute.Value, Me.Text)

    output.AddAttribute("OnBlur", "ValidateText(this)")

    output.RenderBeginTag(HtmlTextWriterTag.Input)
    output.RenderEndTag()

    output.RenderEndTag()

End Sub

Protected Overrides Sub OnPreRender(ByVal e As System.EventArgs)
    Page.ClientScript.RegisterStartupScript(GetType(Page),
       "ControlFocus", "document.getElementById('" & Me.ClientID &
            "_i" & "').focus();",
       True)

    Page.ClientScript.RegisterClientScriptBlock(
        GetType(Page),
        "ValidateControl",
        "function ValidateText() {" &
            "if (ctl.value=='') {" &
                "alert('Please enter a value.');ctl.focus(); }" &
        "}",
        True)
End Sub
```

C#

```
protected override void RenderContents(HtmlTextWriter output)
{
    output.RenderBeginTag(HtmlTextWriterTag.Div);
    output.AddAttribute(HtmlTextWriterAttribute.Type, "text");
    output.AddAttribute(HtmlTextWriterAttribute.Id,
                        this.ClientID + "_i");
    output.AddAttribute(HtmlTextWriterAttribute.Name,
                        this.ClientID + "_i");
    output.AddAttribute(HtmlTextWriterAttribute.Value, this.Text);

    output.AddAttribute("OnBlur", "ValidateText(this)");

    output.RenderBeginTag(HtmlTextWriterTag.Input);
    output.RenderEndTag();
    output.RenderEndTag();
}

protected override void OnPreRender(EventArgs e)
{
    Page.ClientScript.RegisterStartupScript(
        typeof(Page),
        "ControlFocus", "document.getElementById('" +
        this.ClientID + "_i" + "').focus();",
```

```
            true);

        Page.ClientScript.RegisterClientScriptBlock(
            typeof(Page),
            "ValidateControl",
            "function ValidateText(ctl) {" +
                "if (ctl.value=='') {" +
                    "alert('Please enter a value.'); ctl.focus(); }" +
            "}",
            true);
    }
```

As you can see, the TextBox control is modified to check for an empty string. An attribute that adds the JavaScript `OnBlur` event to the text box is also included. The `OnBlur` event fires when the control loses focus. When this happens, the client-side `ValidateText` method is executed, which is rendered to the client using `RegisterClientScriptBlock`.

The rendered HTML is shown in Figure 25-12.

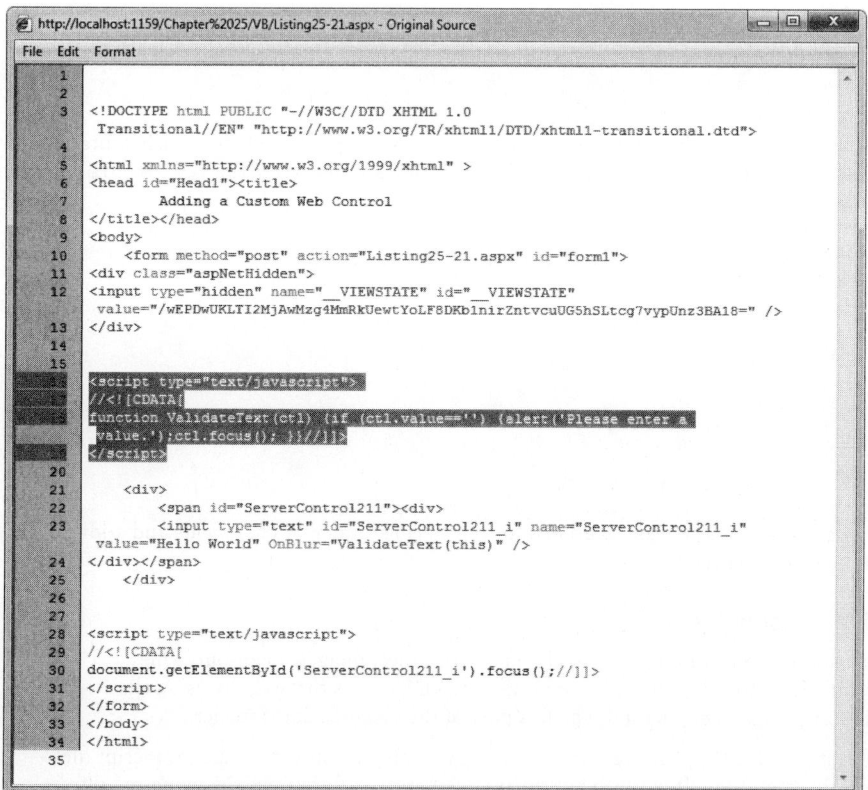

FIGURE 25-12

Embedding JavaScript in the page is powerful, but if you are writing large amounts of client-side code, you might want to consider storing the JavaScript in an external file. You can include this file in your HTML by using the `RegisterClientScriptInclude` method. This method renders a script tag using the URL you provide to it as the value of its `src` element.

```
<script src="[url]" type="text/javascript"></script>
```

Listing 25-22 shows how you can modify the validation added to the input element in Listing 25-20 to store the JavaScript validation function in an external file.

LISTING 25-22: Adding client-side script include files to a Web page

Available for download on Wrox.com

```
Protected Overrides Sub OnPreRender(ByVal e As System.EventArgs)
    Page.ClientScript.RegisterClientScriptInclude(
       "UtilityFunctions", "Listing25-23.js")

    Page.ClientScript.RegisterStartupScript(GetType(Page),
       "ControlFocus", "document.getElementById('" &
       Me.ClientID & "_i" & "').focus();",
       True)
End Sub
```

C#

```
protected override void OnPreRender(EventArgs e)
{
    Page.ClientScript.RegisterClientScriptInclude(
        "UtilityFunctions", "Listing25-23.js");

    Page.ClientScript.RegisterStartupScript(
        typeof(Page),
        "ControlFocus", "document.getElementById('" +
        this.ClientID + "_i" + "').focus();",
        true);
}
```

You have modified the `OnPreRender` event to register a client-side script file include, which contains the `ValidateText` function. You need to add a JScript file to the project and create the `ValidateText` function, as shown in Listing 25-23.

LISTING 25-23: The validation JavaScript contained in the Jscript file

Available for download on Wrox.com

```
// JScript File

function ValidateText(ctl)
{
   if (ctl.value=='') {
        alert('Please enter a value.');
        ctl.focus();
    }
}
```

The `ClientScriptManager` also provides methods for registering hidden HTML fields and adding script functions to the `OnSubmit` event.

Accessing Embedded Resources

A great way to distribute application resources like JavaScript files, images, or resource files is to embed them directly into the compiled assembly. ASP.NET makes this easy by using the `RegisterClientScriptResource` method which is part of the ClientScriptManager.

This method makes it possible for your Web pages to retrieve stored resources — like JavaScript files — from the compiled assembly at runtime. It works by using an `HttpHandler` to retrieve the requested resource from the assembly and return it to the client. The `RegisterClientScriptResource` method emits a `<script>` block whose `src` value points to this `HttpHandler`:

```
<script
     language="javascript"
     src="WebResource.axd?a=s&r=WebUIValidation.js&t=631944362841472848"
     type="text/javascript">
</script>
```

As you can see, the `WebResource.axd` handler is used to return the resource — in this case, the JavaScript file. You can use this method to retrieve any resource stored in the assembly, such as images or localized content strings from resource files.

Asynchronous Callbacks

Finally, ASP.NET also includes a convenient mechanism for enabling basic AJAX behavior, or client-side callbacks, in a server control. Client-side callbacks enable you to take advantage of the XmlHttp components found in most modern browsers to communicate with the server without actually performing a complete postback. Figure 25-13 shows how client-side callbacks work in the ASP.NET Framework.

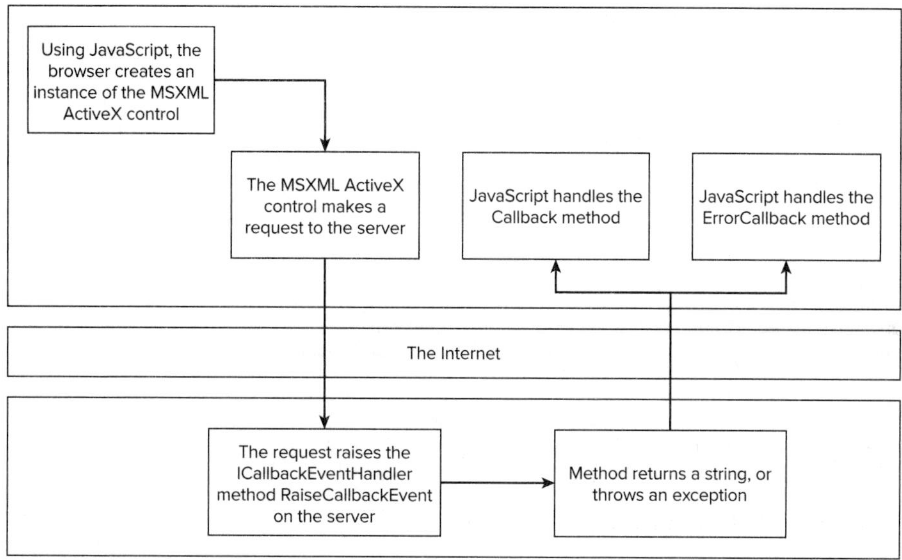

FIGURE 25-13

To enable callbacks in your server control, you implement the `System.Web.UI.ICallBackEventHander` interface. This interface requires you to implement two methods, the `RaiseCallbackEvent` method and the `GetCallbackResult method`. These server-side events fire when the client executes the callback. After you implement the interface, you want to tie your client-side events back to the server. You do this by using the `Page.ClientScript.GetCallbackEventReference` method. This method allows you to specify the two client-side functions: one to serve as the callback handler and one to serve as an error handler. Listing 25-24 demonstrates how you can modify the TextBox control's `Render` methods and add the `RaiseCallBackEvent` method to use callbacks to perform validation.

LISTING 25-24: Adding an asynchronous callback to validate data

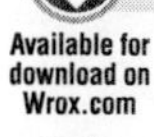
Available for download on Wrox.com

VB

```
Protected Overrides Sub RenderContents(ByVal output As HtmlTextWriter)
    output.RenderBeginTag(HtmlTextWriterTag.Div)
    output.AddAttribute(HtmlTextWriterAttribute.Type, "text")
    output.AddAttribute(HtmlTextWriterAttribute.Id, Me.ClientID & "_i")
    output.AddAttribute(HtmlTextWriterAttribute.Name,
                        Me.ClientID & "_i")
    output.AddAttribute(HtmlTextWriterAttribute.Value, Me.Text)
    output.AddAttribute("OnBlur", "ClientCallback();")
    output.RenderBeginTag(HtmlTextWriterTag.Input)
    output.RenderEndTag()
    output.RenderEndTag()

End Sub

Protected Overrides Sub OnPreRender(ByVal e As System.EventArgs)
    Page.ClientScript.RegisterClientScriptInclude(
```

continues

LISTING 25-24 *(continued)*

```
        "UtilityFunctions", "ServerControl1.js")

    Page.ClientScript.RegisterStartupScript(GetType(Page),
       "ControlFocus", "document.getElementById('" &
       Me.ClientID & "_i" & "').focus();",
       True)

    Page.ClientScript.RegisterStartupScript(
        GetType(Page), "ClientCallback",
        "function ClientCallback() {" &
            "args=document.getElementById('" &
            Me.ClientID & "_i" & "').value;" &
            Page.ClientScript.GetCallbackEventReference(Me, "args",
                "CallbackHandler", Nothing, "ErrorHandler", True) &
            "}",
        True)
End Sub

Public Sub RaiseCallbackEvent(ByVal eventArgument As String) _
    Implements System.Web.UI.ICallbackEventHandler.RaiseCallbackEvent

    Dim result As Int32
    If (Not Int32.TryParse(eventArgument, result)) Then
        Throw New Exception(
                  "The method or operation is not implemented.")
    End If
End Sub

Public Function GetCallbackResult() As String _
    Implements System.Web.UI.ICallbackEventHandler.GetCallbackResult

    Return "Valid Data"
End Function
```

C#

```
protected override void RenderContents(HtmlTextWriter output)
{
    output.RenderBeginTag(HtmlTextWriterTag.Div);

    output.AddAttribute(HtmlTextWriterAttribute.Type, "text");
    output.AddAttribute(HtmlTextWriterAttribute.Id,
                        this.ClientID + "_i");
    output.AddAttribute(HtmlTextWriterAttribute.Name,
                        this.ClientID + "_i");
    output.AddAttribute(HtmlTextWriterAttribute.Value, this.Text);
    output.AddAttribute("OnBlur", "ClientCallback();");
    output.RenderBeginTag(HtmlTextWriterTag.Input);
    output.RenderEndTag();
    output.RenderEndTag();
}
protected override void OnPreRender(EventArgs e)
{
    Page.ClientScript.RegisterClientScriptInclude(
        "UtilityFunctions", "Listing25-25.js");

    Page.ClientScript.RegisterStartupScript(
        typeof(Page),
        "ControlFocus", "document.getElementById('" +
                        this.ClientID + "_i" + "').focus();",
        true);

    Page.ClientScript.RegisterStartupScript(
```

```
            typeof(Page), "ClientCallback",
            "function ClientCallback() {" +
                "args=document.getElementById('" +
                    this.ClientID + "_i" + "').value;" +
                Page.ClientScript.GetCallbackEventReference(this, "args",
                    "CallbackHandler", null, "ErrorHandler", true) + "}",
            true);
    }

    #region ICallbackEventHandler Members

    public void RaiseCallbackEvent(string eventArgument)
    {
        int result;
        if (!Int32.TryParse(eventArgument, out result))
            throw new Exception("The method or operation is not implemented.");
    }

    public string GetCallbackResult()
    {
        return "Valid Data";
    }

    #endregion
```

As you can see, the `OnBlur` attribute has again been modified, this time by simply calling the `ClientCallback` method. This method is created and rendered during the `PreRender` event. The main purpose of this event is to populate the client-side `args` variable and call the client-side callback method.

You are using the `GetCallbackEventReference` method to generate the client-side script that actually initiates the callback. The parameters passed to the method indicate which control is initiating the callback, the names of the client-side callback method, and the name of the callback method parameters. Table 25-3 provides more details on the `GetCallbackEventReference` arguments.

TABLE 25-3

PARAMETER	DESCRIPTION
`Control`	Server control that initiates the callback.
`Argument`	Client-side variable used to pass arguments to the server-side event handler.
`ClientCallback`	Client-side function serving as the `Callback` method. This method fires when the server-side processing has completed successfully.
`Context`	Client-side variable that gets passed directly to the receiving client-side function. The context does not get passed to the server.
`ClientErrorCallback`	Client-side function serving as the `Callback` error-handler method. This method fires when the server-side processing encounters an error.

In the code, two client-side methods are called: `CallbackHandler` and `ErrorHandler`, respectively. The two method parameters are `args` and `ctx`.

In addition to the server control code changes, the two client-side callback methods have been added to the JavaScript file. Listing 25-25 shows these new functions.

Available for download on Wrox.com

LISTING 25-25: The client-side callback JavaScript functions

```
// JScript File
var args;
var ctx;

function ValidateText(ctl)
```

continues

LISTING 25-25 *(continued)*

```
{
    if (ctl.value=='') {
        alert('Please enter a value.');
        ctl.focus();
     }
}

function CallbackHandler(args,ctx)
{
    alert("The data is valid");
}

function ErrorHandler(args,ctx)
{
    alert("Please enter a number");
}
```

Now, when you view your Web page in the browser, as soon as the text box loses focus, you perform a client-side callback to validate the data. The callback raises the `RaiseCallbackEvent` method on the server, which validates the value of the text box that was passed to it in the `eventArguments`. If the value is valid, you return a string and the client-side `CallbackHandler` function fires. If the value is invalid, you throw an exception, which causes the client-side `ErrorHandler` function to execute.

Browser Capabilities

So far this chapter has described many powerful features, such as styling and emitting client-side scripts that you can utilize when writing your own custom control. But if you are taking advantage of these features, you must also consider how you can handle certain browsers, often called down-level browsers, that might not understand these advanced features or might not have them enabled. Being able to detect and react to down-level browsers is an important consideration when creating your control. ASP.NET includes some powerful tools you can use to detect the type and version of the browser making the page request, as well as what capabilities the browser supports.

.browser Files

ASP.NET uses a highly flexible method for configuring, storing, and discovering browser capabilities. All browser identification and capability information is stored in `.browser` files. ASP.NET stores these files in the `C:\Windows\Microsoft.NET\Framework\v4.0.xxxxx\CONFIG\Browsers` directory. If you open this folder, you see that ASP.NET provides you with a variety of `.browser` files that describe the capabilities of most of today's common desktop browsers, as well as information on browsers in devices such as PDAs and cellular phones. Open one of the browser files, and you see that the file contains all the identification and capability information for the browser. Listing 25-26 shows you the contents of the iPhone capabilities file.

LISTING 25-26: A sample browser capabilities file

```
<browsers>
    <!-- Mozilla/5.0 (iPhone; U; CPU like Mac OS X; en) AppleWebKit/420+ (KHTML, like Gecko)
    Version/3.0 Mobile/1A543a Safari/419.3  -->
    <gateway id="IPhone" parentID="Safari">
        <identification>
            <userAgent match="iPhone" />
        </identification>

        <capabilities>
            <capability name="mobileDeviceModel"               value="IPhone" />
            <capability name="mobileDeviceManufacturer"        value="Apple" />
            <capability name="isMobileDevice"                  value="true" />
            <capability name="canInitiateVoiceCall"            value="true" />
```

```
        </capabilities>
    </gateway>

    <!-- Mozilla/5.0 (iPod; U; CPU like Mac OS X; en) AppleWebKit/420.1 (KHTML, like Gecko)
    Version/3.0 Mobile/4A93 Safari/419.3  -->
    <gateway id="IPod" parentID="Safari">
        <identification>
            <userAgent match="iPod" />
        </identification>

        <capabilities>
            <capability name="mobileDeviceModel"              value="IPod" />
            <capability name="mobileDeviceManufacturer"       value="Apple" />
            <capability name="isMobileDevice"                 value="true" />
        </capabilities>
    </gateway>
</browsers>
```

The advantage of this method for storing browser capability information is that as new browsers are created or new versions are released, developers simply create or update a `.browser` file to describe the capabilities of that browser.

Accessing Browser Capability Information

Now that you have seen how ASP.NET stores browser capability information, you need to know how you can access this information at runtime and program your control to change what it renders based on the browser. To access capability information about the requesting browser, you can use the `Page.Request.Browser` property. This property gives you access to the `System.Web.HttpBrowserCapabilities` class, which provides information about the capabilities of the browser making the current request. The class provides you with a myriad of attributes and properties that describe what the browser can support and render and what it requires. Lists use this information to add capabilities to the TextBox control. Listing 25-27 shows how you can detect browser capabilities to make sure a browser supports JavaScript.

LISTING 25-27: Detecting browser capabilities in server-side code

```
Protected Overrides Sub OnPreRender(ByVal e As System.EventArgs)
    If (Page.Request.Browser.EcmaScriptVersion.Major > 0) Then

        Page.ClientScript.RegisterClientScriptInclude(
            "UtilityFunctions", "Listing25-25.js")

        Page.ClientScript.RegisterStartupScript(
            GetType(Page), "ClientCallback",
            "function ClientCallback() {" &
                "args=document.getElementById('" &
                Me.ClientID & "_i" & "').value;" &
                Page.ClientScript.GetCallbackEventReference(Me, "args",
                    "CallbackHandler", Nothing, "ErrorHandler", True) +
                    "}",
            True)

        Page.ClientScript.RegisterStartupScript(GetType(Page),
            "ControlFocus", "document.getElementById('" &
            Me.ClientID & "_i" & "').focus();",
            True)
    End If
End Sub
```

```
protected override void OnPreRender(EventArgs e)
{
    if (Page.Request.Browser.EcmaScriptVersion.Major > 0)
```

continues

LISTING 25-27 *(continued)*

```
        {
            Page.ClientScript.RegisterClientScriptInclude(
                "UtilityFunctions", "Listing25-25.js");

            Page.ClientScript.RegisterStartupScript(
                typeof(Page),
                "ControlFocus", "document.getElementById('" +
                    this.ClientID + "_i" + "').focus();",
                true);

            Page.ClientScript.RegisterStartupScript(
                typeof(Page), "ClientCallback",
                "function ClientCallback() {" +
                    "args=document.getElementById('" +
                    this.ClientID + "_i" + "').value;" +
                    Page.ClientScript.GetCallbackEventReference(this,
                        "args",
                        "CallbackHandler", null, "ErrorHandler", true) +
                        "}",
                true);
        }
    }
```

This is a very simple sample, but it gives you an idea of what is possible using the `HttpBrowserCapabilities` class.

Using ViewState

When developing Web applications, remember that they are built on the stateless HTTP protocol. ASP.NET gives you a number of ways to give users the illusion that they are using a stateful application, but perhaps the most ubiquitous is called ViewState. ViewState enables you to maintain the state of the objects and controls that are part of the Web page through the page's life cycle by storing the state of the controls in a hidden form field that is rendered as part of the HTML. The state contained in the form field can then be used by the application to reconstitute the page's state when a postback occurs. Figure 25-14 shows how ASP.NET stores ViewState information in a hidden form field.

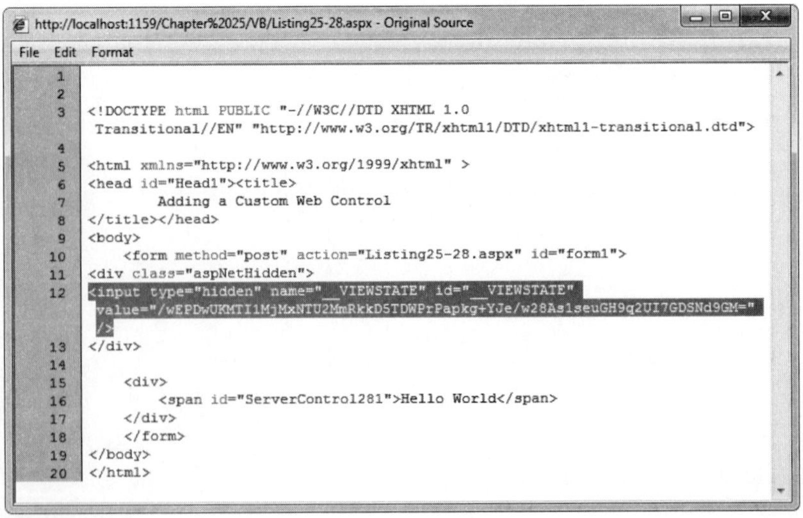

```
http://localhost:1159/Chapter%2025/VB/Listing25-28.aspx - Original Source
File Edit Format


<!DOCTYPE html PUBLIC "-//W3C//DTD XHTML 1.0
 Transitional//EN" "http://www.w3.org/TR/xhtml1/DTD/xhtml1-transitional.dtd">

<html xmlns="http://www.w3.org/1999/xhtml" >
<head id="Head1"><title>
        Adding a Custom Web Control
</title></head>
<body>
    <form method="post" action="Listing25-28.aspx" id="form1">
<div class="aspNetHidden">
<input type="hidden" name="__VIEWSTATE" id="__VIEWSTATE"
 value="/wEPDwUKMTI1MjMxNTU2MmRkkD5TDWPrPapkg+YJe/w28As1seuGH9q2UI7GDSNd9GM="
 />
</div>

    <div>
        <span id="ServerControl281">Hello World</span>
    </div>
    </form>
</body>
</html>
```

FIGURE 25-14

Notice that the page contains a hidden form field named `_ViewState`. The value of this form field is the ViewState for your Web page. By default, ViewState is enabled in all in-box server controls shipped with ASP.NET. If you write customer server controls, however, you are responsible for ensuring that a control is participating in the use of ViewState by the page.

The ASP.NET ViewState is basically a storage format that enables you to save and retrieve objects as key/value pairs. As you see in Figure 25-14, these objects are then serialized by ASP.NET and persisted as an encrypted string, which is pushed to the client as a hidden HTML form field. When the page posts back to the server, ASP.NET can use this hidden form field to reconstitute the StateBag, which you can then access as the page is processed on the server.

Because the ViewState can sometimes grow to be very large and can therefore affect the overall page size, you might consider an alternate method of storing the ViewState information. You can create your own persistence mechanism by deriving a class from the `System.Web.UI.PageStatePersister` *class and overriding its* `Load` *and* `Save` *methods.*

As shown in Listing 25-28, by default, the `Text` property included with the ASP.NET Server Control template is set up to store its value in ViewState.

LISTING 25-28: The Text property's use of ViewState

Available for download on Wrox.com

VB

```
Property Text() As String
    Get
        Dim s As String = CStr(ViewState("Text"))
        If s Is Nothing Then
            Return "[" + Me.ID + "]"
        Else
            Return s
        End If
    End Get

    Set(ByVal Value As String)
        ViewState("Text") = Value
    End Set
End Property
```

C#

```
public string Text
{
    get
    {
        String s = (String)ViewState["Text"];
        return ((s == null) ? "[" + this.ID + "]": s);
    }
    set
    {
        ViewState["Text"] = value;
    }
}
```

When creating new properties in an ASP.NET server control, you should remember to use this same technique to ensure that the values set by the end user in your control will be persisted across page postbacks.

Note that the loading of ViewState happens after the `OnInit` *event has been raised by the page. If your control makes changes to itself or another server control before the event has been raised, the changes are not saved to the ViewState.*

Types and ViewState

As mentioned in the preceding section, the ViewState is basically a generic collection of objects, but not all objects can be added to the ViewState. Only types that can be safely persisted can be used in the ViewState, so objects such as database connections or file handles should not be added to the ViewState.

Additionally, certain data types are optimized for use in the ViewState. When adding data to the ViewState, try to package the data into these types:

- Primitive Types (Int32, Boolean, and so on).
- Arrays of Primitive Types.
- ArrayList, HashTable.
- Pair, Triplet.
- Color, DataTime.
- String, IndexedString.
- HybridDictionary of these types.
- Objects that have a TypeConverter available. Be aware, however, that there is a reduction in performance if you use these types.
- Objects that are serializable (marked with the `Serializable` attribute).

Control State

At times, your control must store small amounts of critical, usually private, information across postbacks. To allow for the storage of this type of information, even if a developer disables ViewState, ASP.NET includes a separate type of ViewState called ControlState. ControlState is essentially a private ViewState for your control only, and it is not affected when ViewState is turned off.

Two methods, `SaveViewState` and `LoadViewState`, provide access to ControlState; however, the implementation of these methods is left up to you. Listing 25-29 shows how you can use the `LoadControlState` and `SaveViewState` methods.

LISTING 25-29: Using ControlState in a server control

Available for download on Wrox.com

VB

```
<DefaultProperty("Text")>
<ToolboxData("<{0}:ServerControl1 runat=server></{0}:ServerControl1>")>
Public Class ServerControl1
        Inherits WebControl

    Dim state As String
    Protected Overrides Sub OnInit(ByVal e As System.EventArgs)
        Page.RegisterRequiresControlState(Me)
        MyBase.OnInit(e)
    End Sub

    Protected Overrides Sub LoadControlState(ByVal savedState As Object)
        state = CStr(savedState)
    End Sub

    Protected Overrides Function SaveControlState() As Object
```

```
            Return CType("ControlSpecificData", Object)
        End Function

        Protected Overrides Sub Render(ByVal output As System.Web.UI.HtmlTextWriter)
            output.Write("Control State: " & state)
        End Sub

    End Class
```

C#

```
    [DefaultProperty("Text")]
    [ToolboxData("<{0}:ServerControl1 runat=server></{0}:ServerControl1>")]
    public class ServerControl1 : WebControl
    {
        string state;
        protected override void OnInit(EventArgs e)
        {
            Page.RegisterRequiresControlState(this);

            base.OnInit(e);
        }

        protected override void LoadControlState(object savedState)
        {
            state = (string)savedState;
        }

        protected override object SaveControlState()
        {
            return (object)"ControlSpecificData";
        }

        protected override void RenderContents(HtmlTextWriter output)
        {
            output.Write("Control State: " + state);
        }
    }
```

Controls intending to use ControlState must call the `Page.RegisterRequiresControlState` method before attempting to save control state data. Additionally, the `RegisterRequiresControlState` method must be called for each page load because the value is not retained through page postbacks.

Raising Postback Events

As you have seen in this chapter, ASP.NET provides a very powerful set of tools you can use to develop server controls and emit them to a client browser. But this is still one-way communication because the server only pushes data to the client. It would be useful if the server control could send data back to the server. The process of sending data back to the server is generally known as a *page postback*. You experience a page postback any time you click a form button or link that causes the page to make a new request to the Web server.

ASP.NET provides a rich framework for handling postbacks from ASP.NET Web pages. A development model that mimics the standard Windows Forms event model is provided that enables you to use controls that, even though they are rendered in the client browser, can raise events in server-side code. It also provides an easy mechanism for plugging a server control into that framework, allowing you to create controls that can initiate a page postback. Figure 25-15 shows the ASP.NET postback framework.

Init

Load State

Process Postback Data

IPostbackDataHandler
IPostbackEventHandler

Load

Postback Events

Save State

PreRender

Render

Unload

FIGURE 25-15

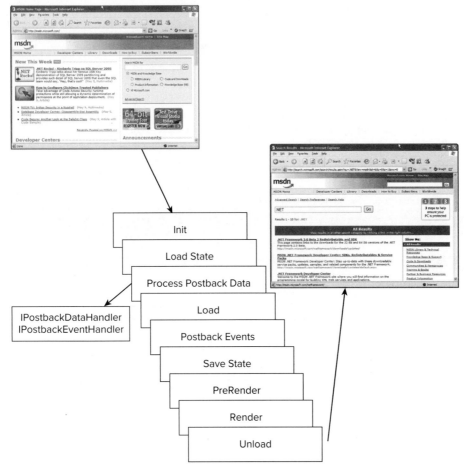

To initiate a page postback, by default ASP.NET uses client-side scripting. If you want your control to be able to initiate a postback, you must attach the postback initiation script to a HTML element event using the `GetPostBackEventReference` method during the controls render method. Listing 25-30 shows how you can attach the postback client script to the `onClick` event of a standard HTML Button element.

LISTING 25-30: Adding postback capabilities to a server control

Available for download on Wrox.com

VB

```
Protected Overrides Sub RenderContents(ByVal output As HtmlTextWriter)
    Dim p As New PostBackOptions(Me)

    output.AddAttribute(HtmlTextWriterAttribute.Onclick,
        Page.ClientScript.GetPostBackEventReference(p))

    output.AddAttribute(HtmlTextWriterAttribute.Value, "My Button")
    output.AddAttribute(HtmlTextWriterAttribute.Id,
                        Me.ClientID & "_i")
    output.AddAttribute(HtmlTextWriterAttribute.Name,
                        Me.ClientID & "_i")
    output.RenderBeginTag(HtmlTextWriterTag.Button)
    output.Write("My Button")
    output.RenderEndTag()
```

```
    End Sub
```

```
    protected override void RenderContents(HtmlTextWriter output)
    {
        PostBackOptions p = new PostBackOptions(this);

        output.AddAttribute(HtmlTextWriterAttribute.Onclick,
            Page.ClientScript.GetPostBackEventReference(p));
        output.AddAttribute(HtmlTextWriterAttribute.Id,
                            this.ClientID + "_i");
        output.AddAttribute(HtmlTextWriterAttribute.Name,
                            this.ClientID + "_i");
        output.RenderBeginTag(HtmlTextWriterTag.Button);
        output.Write("My Button");
        output.RenderEndTag();
    }
```

When the `GetPostBackEventReference` method is called, it requires a `PostBackOptions` object be passed to it. The `PostBackOptions` object allows you to specify a number of configuration options that influence how ASP.NET will initiate the postback.

You can add the postback JavaScript to any client-side event, or even add the code to a client-side function if you want to include some additional pre-postback logic for your control.

Now that the control can initiate a postback, you may want to add events to your control that execute during the pages postback. To raise server-side events from a client-side object, you implement the `System.Web.IPostBackEventHandler` interface. Listing 25-31 shows how to do this for the Button in the previous listing.

LISTING 25-31: Handling postback events in a server control

Available for download on Wrox.com

```
<DefaultProperty("Text"),
ToolboxData("<{0}:ServerControl1 runat=server></{0}:ServerControl1>")>
Public Class ServerControl1
    Inherits WebControl
    Implements IPostBackEventHandler

    Protected Overrides Sub RenderContents(
                            ByVal output As HtmlTextWriter)
        Dim p As New PostBackOptions(Me)

        output.AddAttribute(HtmlTextWriterAttribute.Onclick,
            Page.ClientScript.GetPostBackEventReference(p))

        output.AddAttribute(HtmlTextWriterAttribute.Value, "My Button")
        output.AddAttribute(HtmlTextWriterAttribute.Id,
                            Me.ClientID & "_i")
        output.AddAttribute(HtmlTextWriterAttribute.Name,
                            Me.ClientID & "_i")
        output.RenderBeginTag(HtmlTextWriterTag.Button)
        output.Write("My Button")
        output.RenderEndTag()
    End Sub

    Public Event Click()
    Public Sub OnClick(ByVal args As EventArgs)
        RaiseEvent Click()
    End Sub

    Public Sub RaisePostBackEvent(ByVal eventArgument As String) _
      Implements System.Web.UI.IPostBackEventHandler.RaisePostBackEvent
        OnClick(EventArgs.Empty)
```

continues

LISTING 25-31 *(continued)*

```
    End Sub
End Class
```

C#

```
[DefaultProperty("Text")]
[ToolboxData("<{0}:ServerControl1 runat=server></{0}:ServerControl1>")]
public class ServerControl1 : WebControl, IPostBackEventHandler
{
    protected override void RenderContents(HtmlTextWriter output)
    {
        PostBackOptions p = new PostBackOptions(this);

        output.AddAttribute(HtmlTextWriterAttribute.Onclick,
            Page.ClientScript.GetPostBackEventReference(p));
        output.AddAttribute(HtmlTextWriterAttribute.Id, this.ClientID);
        output.AddAttribute(HtmlTextWriterAttribute.Name,
                        this.ClientID);
        output.RenderBeginTag(HtmlTextWriterTag.Button);
        output.Write("My Button");
        output.RenderEndTag();
    }

    #region IPostBackEventHandler Members
    public event EventHandler Click;

    public virtual void OnClick(EventArgs e)
    {
        if (Click != null)
        {
            Click(this, e);
        }
    }

    public void RaisePostBackEvent(string eventArgument)
    {
        OnClick(EventArgs.Empty);
    }

    #endregion
}
```

When the user clicks the Button, a page postback occurs, and ASP.NET calls the `RaisePostBackEvent` method in the control, which lets you raise a server-side event. If several different client events in your control can initiate a postback, you can change the behavior of your control by using the `RaisePostBackEvent` method's `eventArgument` parameter to determine which element caused the postback. The `eventArgument` parameter is set using the `PostBackOptions` object mentioned previously.

Handling Postback Data

Now that you have learned how to store control data in ViewState and add postback capabilities to a control you can enable the control to handle data a user has entered into form fields on the page. When an ASP.NET control initiates a postback, all the form data from the page is posted to the server. A server control can access and interact with that data, storing the information in ViewState and completing the illusion of a stateful application.

To access postback data, your control must implement the `System.Web.IPostBackDataHandler` interface. This interface allows ASP.NET to hand to your control the form data that is passed back to the server during the postback.

The IPostBackDataHandler interface requires two methods to be implemented, the LoadPostData and RaisePostBackDataChangedEvent methods. Listing 25-32 shows how you implement the IPostBackDataHandler interface method in a simple text input control.

LISTING 25-32: Accessing postback data in a server control

Available for download on Wrox.com

```
<DefaultProperty("Text"),
ToolboxData("<{0}:ServerControl1 runat=server></{0}:ServerControl1>")>
Public Class ServerControl1
    Inherits WebControl
    Implements IPostBackEventHandler, IPostBackDataHandler

    <Bindable(True), Category("Appearance"),
    DefaultValue(""), Localizable(True)>
    Property Text() As String
        Get
            Dim s As String = CStr(ViewState("Text"))
            If s Is Nothing Then
                Return String.Empty
            Else
                Return s
            End If
        End Get

        Set(ByVal Value As String)
            ViewState("Text") = Value
        End Set
    End Property

    Protected Overrides Sub RenderContents(
                        ByVal output As HtmlTextWriter)
        Dim p As New PostBackOptions(Me)

        output.AddAttribute(HtmlTextWriterAttribute.Id, Me.ClientID)
        output.AddAttribute(HtmlTextWriterAttribute.Name, Me.ClientID)
        output.AddAttribute(HtmlTextWriterAttribute.Value, Me.Text)
        output.RenderBeginTag(HtmlTextWriterTag.Input)
        output.RenderEndTag()
    End Sub

    Public Function LoadPostData(ByVal postDataKey As String,
        ByVal postCollection As  _
            System.Collections.Specialized.NameValueCollection) _
        As Boolean Implements _
            System.Web.UI.IPostBackDataHandler.LoadPostData

        Me.Text = postCollection(postDataKey)
        Return False
    End Function

    Public Sub RaisePostDataChangedEvent() _
        Implements _
          System.Web.UI.IPostBackDataHandler.RaisePostDataChangedEvent

    End Sub

    Public Event Click()
    Public Sub OnClick(ByVal args As EventArgs)
        RaiseEvent Click()
```

continues

LISTING 25-32 *(continued)*

```
    End Sub

    Public Sub RaisePostBackEvent(ByVal eventArgument As String) _
      Implements System.Web.UI.IPostBackEventHandler.RaisePostBackEvent
        OnClick(EventArgs.Empty)
    End Sub
End Class
```

C#

```
[DefaultProperty("Text")]
[ToolboxData("<{0}:ServerControl1 runat=server></{0}:ServerControl1>")]
public class ServerControl1 : WebControl, IPostBackEventHandler, IPostBackDataHandler
{
    [Bindable(true)]
    [Category("Appearance")]
    [DefaultValue("")]
    [Localizable(true)]
    public string Text
    {
        get
        {
            String s = (String)ViewState["Text"];
            return ((s == null) ? "[" + this.ID + "]" : s);
        }
        set
        {
            ViewState["Text"] = value;
        }
    }

    protected override void RenderContents(HtmlTextWriter output)
    {
        PostBackOptions p = new PostBackOptions(this);

        output.AddAttribute(HtmlTextWriterAttribute.Id, this.ClientID);
        output.AddAttribute(HtmlTextWriterAttribute.Name,
                            this.ClientID);
        output.AddAttribute(HtmlTextWriterAttribute.Value, this.Text);
        output.RenderBeginTag(HtmlTextWriterTag.Input);
        output.RenderEndTag();
    }

    #region IPostBackDataHandler Members
    public bool LoadPostData(string postDataKey,
    System.Collections.Specialized.NameValueCollection postCollection)
    {
        this.Text = postCollection[postDataKey];
        return false;
    }

    public void RaisePostDataChangedEvent()
    {
    }
    #endregion

    #region IPostBackEventHandler Members
    public event EventHandler Click;

    public virtual void OnClick(EventArgs e)
```

```
        {
            if (Click != null)
            {
                Click(this, e);
            }
        }

        public void RaisePostBackEvent(string eventArgument)
        {
            OnClick(EventArgs.Empty);
        }

        #endregion
    }
```

During a postback, ASP.NET will call the `LoadPostData` method for this control, passing to it as a `NameValueCollection` any data submitted with the form. The `postDataKey` method parameter allows the control to access the postback data specific to it from the `NameValueCollection`.

Using the method parameters you can save the input element's text to the server control's `Text` property. If you remember the earlier ViewState example, the `Text` property will save the value to ViewState, allowing the control to automatically repopulate the input element's value when another page postback occurs.

The `LoadPostData` method requires you to return a Boolean value from the method. This value indicates whether ASP.NET should call the `RaisePostBackDataChangedEvent` method after the `LoadPostData` method returns. For example, if you created a `TextChanged` event in the control to notify you the controls text has changed, you would want to return `True` from this method so that you could subsequently raise that event in the `RaisePostDataChangedEvent` method.

Composite Controls

So far, in looking at Server controls, you have concentrated on emitting a single HTML element; but this can be fairly limiting. Creating extremely powerful controls often requires that you combine several HTML elements together. Although you can always use the `RenderContents` method to emit multiple HTML elements, ASP.NET also allows you to emit existing ASP.NET controls from within a custom server control. These types of controls are called *composite controls.*

To demonstrate how easy creating a composite control can be, try changing the control shown in Listing 25-32 into a composite control. Listing 25-33 shows how you can do this.

LISTING 25-33: Creating a composite control

Available for download on Wrox.com

```
<DefaultProperty("Text"),
 ToolboxData("<{0}:ServerControl1 runat=server></{0}:ServerControl1>")>
Public Class ServerControl1
    Inherits System.Web.UI.WebControls.CompositeControl

    Protected textbox As TextBox = New TextBox()

    Protected Overrides Sub CreateChildControls()
        Me.Controls.Add(textbox)
    End Sub

End Class
```

```
using System;
[DefaultProperty("Text")]
[ToolboxData("<{0}:ServerControl1 runat=server></{0}:ServerControl1>")]
public class ServerControl1 : CompositeControl
```

continues

LISTING 25-33 *(continued)*

```
{
    protected TextBox textbox = new TextBox();

    protected override void CreateChildControls()
    {
        this.Controls.Add(textbox);
    }
}
```

A number of things in this listing are important. First, notice that the control class is now inheriting from `CompositeControl`, rather than `WebControl`. Deriving from `CompositeControl` gives you a few extra features specific to this type of control.

Second, notice that no `Render` method appears in this code. Instead, you simply create an instance of another type of server control and add that to the `Controls` collection in the `CreateChildControls` method. When you run this sample, you see that it renders a text box just like the last control did. In fact, the HTML that it renders is almost identical.

When you drop a composite control (such as the control from the previous sample) onto the design surface, notice that even though you are leveraging a powerful ASP.NET TextBox control within the control, none of that control's properties are exposed to you in the Properties Explorer. To expose child control properties through the parent container, you must create corresponding properties in the parent control. For example, if you want to expose the ASP.NET text box `Text` property through the parent control, you create a `Text` property. Listing 25-34 shows how to do this.

LISTING 25-34: Exposing control properties in a composite control

Available for download on Wrox.com

VB

```
<DefaultProperty("Text"),
ToolboxData("<{0}:ServerControl1 runat=server></{0}:ServerControl1>")>
Public Class ServerControl1
    Inherits System.Web.UI.WebControls.CompositeControl

    Protected textbox As TextBox = New TextBox()

    Public Property Text() As String
        Get
            EnsureChildControls()
            Return textbox.Text
        End Get
        Set(ByVal value As String)
            EnsureChildControls()
            textbox.Text = value
        End Set
    End Property

    Protected Overrides Sub CreateChildControls()
        Me.Controls.Add(textbox)
        Me.ChildControlsCreated = True
    End Sub

End Class
```

```
[DefaultProperty("Text")]
[ToolboxData("<{0}:ServerControl1 runat=server></{0}:ServerControl1>")]
public class ServerControl1 : CompositeControl
{
    protected TextBox textbox = new TextBox();

    public string Text
```

```
        {
            get
            {
                EnsureChildControls();
                return textbox.Text;
            }
            set
            {
                EnsureChildControls();
                textbox.Text = value;
            }
        }

        protected override void CreateChildControls()
        {
            this.Controls.Add(textbox);
            this.ChildControlsCreated = true;
        }
    }
```

Notice that you use this property simply to populate the underlying control's properties. Also notice that before you access the underlying control's properties, you always call the `EnsureChildControls` method. This method ensures that children of the container control have actually been initialized before you attempt to access them.

Templated Controls

In addition to composite controls, you can also create templated controls. *Templated controls* allow the developer to specify a portion of the HTML that is used to render the control, and to nest other controls inside of a container control. You might be familiar with the Repeater or DataList control. These are both templated controls that let you specify how you want the bound data to be displayed when the page renders.

To demonstrate a templated control, the following code gives you a simple example of displaying a simple text message on a Web page. Because the control is a templated control, the developer has complete control over how the message is displayed.

To get started, create the Message server control that will be used as the template inside of a container control. Listing 25-35 shows the class that simply extends the existing Panel control by adding two additional properties, Name and Text, and a new constructor.

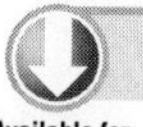

LISTING 25-35: Creating the templated control's inner control class

Available for download on Wrox.com

VB

```
Public Class Message
    Inherits System.Web.UI.WebControls.Panel
    Implements System.Web.UI.INamingContainer

    Public Property Name() As String
    Public Property Text() As String

End Class
```

C#

```
public class Message : Panel, INamingContainer
{
    public string Name { get; internal set; }
    public string Text { get; internal set; }
}
```

As you will see in a moment, you can access the public properties exposed by the `Message` class to insert dynamic content into the template. You will also see how you can display the values of the `Name` and `Text` properties as part of the rendered template control.

Next, as shown in Listing 25-36, create a new server control that will be the container for the `Message` control. This server control is responsible for rendering any template controls nested in it.

LISTING 25-36: Creating the template control container class

Available for download on Wrox.com

VB

```
<DefaultProperty("Text")>
<ToolboxData("<{0}:TemplatedControl runat=server>" &
             "</{0}:TemplatedControl>")>
Public Class TemplatedControl
    Inherits System.Web.UI.WebControls.WebControl

    <Browsable(False)> Public Property TemplateMessage() As Message

    <PersistenceMode(PersistenceMode.InnerProperty),
        TemplateContainer(GetType(Message))>
    Public Property MessageTemplate() As ITemplate

    <Bindable(True), DefaultValue("")>
    Public Property Name() As String

    <Bindable(True), DefaultValue("")>
    Public Property Text() As String

    Public Overrides Sub DataBind()
        EnsureChildControls()
        ChildControlsCreated = True

        MyBase.DataBind()
    End Sub

    Protected Overrides Sub CreateChildControls()
        Me.Controls.Clear()
        Me.TemplateMessage =
           New Message() With {.Name = Name, .Text = Text}

        If Me.MessageTemplate Is Nothing Then
            Me.MessageTemplate = New DefaultMessageTemplate()
        End If

        Me.MessageTemplate.InstantiateIn(Me.TemplateMessage)
        Controls.Add(Me.TemplateMessage)
    End Sub

    Protected Overrides Sub RenderContents(
        ByVal writer As System.Web.UI.HtmlTextWriter)

        EnsureChildControls()
        ChildControlsCreated = True

        MyBase.RenderContents(writer)
    End Sub
End Class
```

C#

```
[DefaultProperty("Text")]
[ToolboxData("<{0}:TemplatedControl runat=server>" +
             "</{0}:TemplatedControl>")]
public class TemplatedControl : WebControl
{
    [Browsable(false)]
    public Message TemplateMessage {get;internal set;}

    [PersistenceMode(PersistenceMode.InnerProperty)]
```

```
        [TemplateContainer(typeof(Message))]
        public virtual ITemplate MessageTemplate {get;set;}

        [Bindable(true)]
        [DefaultValue("")]
        public string Name {get;set;}

        [Bindable(true)]
        [DefaultValue("")]
        public string Text { get; set; }

        public override void DataBind()
        {
            EnsureChildControls();
            ChildControlsCreated = true;

            base.DataBind();
        }

        protected override void CreateChildControls()
        {
            this.Controls.Clear();
            this.TemplateMessage = new Message() { Name=Name, Text=Text};

            if (this.MessageTemplate == null)
            {
                this.MessageTemplate = new DefaultMessageTemplate();
            }

            this.MessageTemplate.InstantiateIn(this.TemplateMessage);
            Controls.Add(this.TemplateMessage);
        }

        protected override void RenderContents(HtmlTextWriter writer)
        {
            EnsureChildControls();
            ChildControlsCreated = true;

            base.RenderContents(writer);
        }
    }
```

To start to dissect this sample, first notice the `MessageTemplate` property. This property allows Visual Studio to understand that the control will contain a template and allows it to display the IntelliSense for that template. The property has been marked with the `PersistanceMode` attribute indicating that the template control should be persisted as an inner property within the control's tag in the ASPX page. Additionally, the property is marked with the `TemplateContainer` attribute, which helps ASP.NET figure out what type of template control this property represents. In this case, it's the Message template control you created earlier.

The container control exposes two public properties, Name and Text. These properties are used to populate the `Name` and `Text` properties of the Message control because that class does not allow developers to set the properties directly.

Finally, the `CreateChildControls` method, called by the `DataBind` method, does most of the heavy lifting in this control. It creates a new `Message` object, passing the values of `Name` and `Text` as constructor values. After the `CreateChildControls` method completes, the base DataBind operation continues to execute. This is important because that is where the evaluation of the Name and Text properties occurs, which allows you to insert these properties values into the template control.

After the control and template are created, you can drop them onto a test Web page. Listing 25-37 shows how the control can be used to customize the display of the data.

LISTING 25-37: Adding a templated control to a Web page

Available for download on Wrox.com

```
<%@ Page Language="VB" %>

<%@ Register Assembly="ServerControl1"
    Namespace="ServerControl1" TagPrefix="cc1" %>

<script runat="server">
    Protected Sub Page_Load(ByVal sender As Object,
                            ByVal e As System.EventArgs)
        Me.TemplatedControl1.DataBind()
    End Sub
</script>


<html xmlns="http://www.w3.org/1999/xhtml" >
<head id="Head1" runat="server">
    <title>Templated Web Controls</title>
</head>
<body>
    <form id="form1" runat="server">
    <div>
        <cc1:TemplatedControl Name="John Doe" Text="Hello World!"
            ID="TemplatedControl1" runat="server"
            Height="33px" Width="377px">
            <MessageTemplate>The user '<%# Container.Name %>'
                has a message for you: <br />"<%#Container.Text%>"
            </MessageTemplate>

        </cc1:TemplatedControl>
    </div>
    </form>
</body>
</html>
```

C#

```
<script runat="server">
    protected void Page_Load(object sender, EventArgs e)
    {
        this.TemplatedControl1.DataBind();
    }
</script>
```

As you can see in the listing, the `<cc1:TemplatedControl>` control contains a `MessageTemplate` within it, which has been customized to display the `Name` and `Text` values. Figure 25-16 shows this page after it has been rendered in the browser.

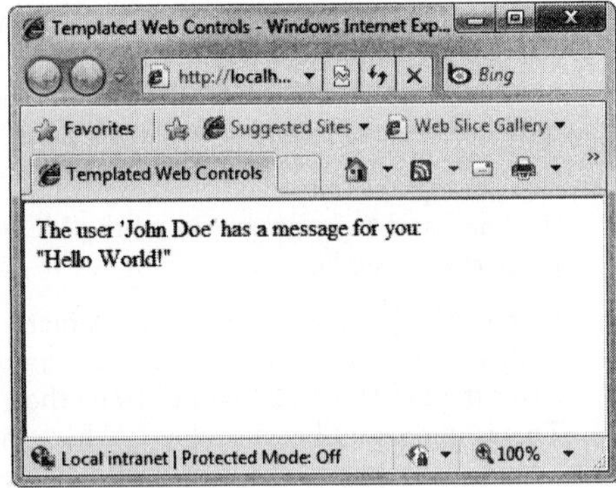

FIGURE 25-16

One additional thing to consider when creating templated controls is what should happen if the developer does not specify a template for the control. In the previous example, if you removed the `MessageTemplate` from the TemplateContainer, a `NullReferenceException` would occur when you tried to run your Web page because the container control's `MessageTemplate` property would return a null value. To prevent this, you can include a default template class as part of the container control. An example of a default template is shown in Listing 25-38.

LISTING 25-38: Creating the templated control's default template class

Available for download on Wrox.com

```
Friend Class DefaultMessageTemplate
    Implements ITemplate

    Public Sub InstantiateIn(ByVal container As System.Web.UI.Control) _
            Implements System.Web.UI.ITemplate.InstantiateIn

        Dim l As New Literal()
        l.Text = "No MessageTemplate was included."
        container.Controls.Add(l)
    End Sub
End Class
```

C#

```
internal sealed class DefaultMessageTemplate : ITemplate
{
    public void InstantiateIn(Control container)
    {
        Literal l = new Literal();
        l.Text = "No MessageTemplate was included.";
        container.Controls.Add(l);
    }
}
```

Notice that the `DefaultMessageTemplate` implements the `ITemplate` interface. This interface requires that the `InstantiateIn` method be implemented, which you use to provide the default template content.

To include the default template, simply add the class to the `TemplatedControl` class. You also need to modify the `CreateChildControls` method to detect the null `MessageTemplate` and instead create an instance of and use the default template.

VB

```
If template = Nothing Then
    template = New DefaultMessageTemplate()
End If
```

C#

```
if (template == null)
{
    template = new DefaultMessageTemplate();
}
```

Design-Time Experiences

So far in this chapter, you concentrated primarily on what gets rendered to the client's browser, but the browser is not the only consumer of server controls. Visual Studio and the developer using a server control are also consumers, and you need to consider their experiences when using your control.

ASP.NET offers numerous ways to give developers using your control a great design-time experience. Some of these require no additional coding, such as the WYSIWYG rendering of user controls and basic server controls. For more complex scenarios, ASP.NET includes a variety of options that allow you to give the developer an outstanding design-time experience when using your control.

When you write server controls, a priority should be to give the developer a design-time experience that closely replicates the runtime experience. This means altering the appearance of the control on the design surface in response to changes in control properties and the introduction of other server controls onto the design surface. Three main components are involved in creating the design-time behaviors of a server control:

- Type converters
- Designers
- UI type editors

Because a chapter can be written for each one of these topics, this section gives you just an overview of each, how they tie into a control's design-time behavior, and some simple examples of their use.

Type Converters

TypeConverter is a class that allows you to perform conversions between one type and another. Visual Studio uses type converters at design time to convert object property values to String types so that they can be displayed on the Property Browser, and it returns them to their original types when the developer changes the property.

ASP.NET includes a wide variety of type converters you can use when creating your control's design-time behavior. These range from converters that allow you to convert most numeric types, to converters that let you convert Fonts, Colors, DataTimes, and Guids. The easiest way to see what type converters are available to you in the .NET Framework is to search for types in the framework that derive from the TypeConverter class using the MSDN Library help.

After you have found a type converter that you want to use on a control property, mark the property with a TypeConverter attribute, as shown in Listing 25-39.

LISTING 25-39: Applying the TypeConverter attribute to a property

Available for download on Wrox.com

VB

```
<Bindable(True)> _
<Category("Appearance")> _
<DefaultValue("")> _
<TypeConverter(GetType(GuidConverter))> _
Property BookId() As System.Guid
        Get
            Return _bookid
        End Get

        Set(ByVal Value As System.Guid)
            _bookid = Value
        End Set
End Property
```

```
[Bindable(true)]
[Category("Appearance")]
[DefaultValue("")]
[TypeConverter(typeof(GuidConverter))]
public Guid BookId
{
    get
    {
        return _bookid;
    }

    set
    {
        _bookid = value;
    }
}
```

In this example, a property is exposed that accepts and returns an object of type Guid. The Property Browser cannot natively display a Guid object, so you convert the value to a string so that it can be displayed properly in the property browser. Marking the property with the TypeConverter attribute and, in this case, specifying the GuidConverter as the type converter you want to use, allows complex objects like a Guid to display properly in the Property Browser.

Custom Type Converters

Creating your own custom type converters if none of the in-box converters fit into your scenario is also possible. Type converters derive from the System.ComponentModel.TypeConverter class. Listing 25-40 shows a custom type converter that converts a custom object called Name to and from a string.

LISTING 25-40: Creating a custom type converter

Available for download on Wrox.com

```
Imports System
Imports System.ComponentModel
Imports System.Globalization

Public Class Name

    Private _first As String
    Private _last As String

    Public Sub New(ByVal first As String, ByVal last As String)
        _first = first
        _last = last
    End Sub

    Public Property First() As String
        Get
            Return _first
        End Get
        Set(ByVal value As String)
            _first = value
        End Set
    End Property

    Public Property Last() As String
        Get
            Return _last
        End Get
        Set(ByVal value As String)
            _last = value
        End Set
    End Property
End Class

Public Class NameConverter
    Inherits TypeConverter

    Public Overrides Function CanConvertFrom(ByVal context As _
       ITypeDescriptorContext, ByVal sourceType As Type) As Boolean

        If (sourceType Is GetType(String)) Then
            Return True
        End If

        Return MyBase.CanConvertFrom(context, sourceType)
    End Function

    Public Overrides Function ConvertFrom( _
            ByVal context As ITypeDescriptorContext, _
            ByVal culture As CultureInfo, ByVal value As Object) As Object
        If (value Is GetType(String)) Then
            Dim v As String() = (CStr(value).Split(New [Char]() {" "c}))
            Return New Name(v(0), v(1))
        End If
        Return MyBase.ConvertFrom(context, culture, value)
    End Function

    Public Overrides Function ConvertTo( _
            ByVal context As ITypeDescriptorContext, _
            ByVal culture As CultureInfo, ByVal value As Object, _
            ByVal destinationType As Type) As Object
```

continues

LISTING 25-40 *(continued)*

```
        If (destinationType Is GetType(String)) Then
            Return (CType(value, Name).First + " " + (CType(value, Name).Last))
        End If
        Return MyBase.ConvertTo(context, culture, value, destinationType)
    End Function
End Class
```

C#

```
using System;
using System.ComponentModel;
using System.Globalization;

public class Name
{
    private string _first;
    private string _last;

    public Name(string first, string last)
    {
        _first=first;
        _last=last;
    }

    public string First
    {
        get{ return _first;}
        set { _first = value;}
    }
    public string Last
    {
        get { return _last;}
        set { _last = value;}
    }
}

public class NameConverter : TypeConverter
{

   public override bool CanConvertFrom(ITypeDescriptorContext context,
      Type sourceType) {

      if (sourceType == typeof(string)) {
         return true;
      }
      return base.CanConvertFrom(context, sourceType);
   }

   public override object ConvertFrom(ITypeDescriptorContext context,
      CultureInfo culture, object value) {
      if (value is string) {
         string[] v = ((string)value).Split(new char[] {' '});
         return new Name(v[0],v[1]);
      }
      return base.ConvertFrom(context, culture, value);
   }

   public override object ConvertTo(ITypeDescriptorContext context,
      CultureInfo culture, object value, Type destinationType) {

      if (destinationType == typeof(string)) {
         return ((Name)value).First + " " + ((Name)value).Last;
```

```
        }
        return base.ConvertTo(context, culture, value, destinationType);
    }
}
```

The NameConverter class overrides three methods, CanConvertFrom, ConvertFrom, and ConvertTo. The CanConvertFrom method allows you to control what types the converter can convert from. The ConvertFrom method converts the string representation back into a Name object, and ConvertTo converts the Name object into a string representation.

After you have built your type converter, you can use it to mark properties in your control with the TypeConverter attribute, as you saw in Listing 25-39.

Control Designers

Controls that live on the Visual Studio design surface depend on *control designers* to create the design-time experience for the end user. Control designers, for both WinForms and ASP.NET, are classes that derive from the System.ComponentModel.Design.ComponentDesigner class. .NET provides an abstracted base class specifically for creating ASP.NET control designers called the System.Web.UI.Design.ControlDesigner. To access these classes you need to add a reference to the System.Design.dll assembly to your project.

.NET includes a number of in-box control designer classes that you can use when creating a custom control; but as you develop server controls, you see that .NET automatically applies a default designer. The designer it applies is based on the type of control you are creating. For instance, when you created your first TextBox control, Visual Studio used the ControlDesigner class to achieve the WYSIWYG design-time rendering of the text box. If you develop a server control derived from the ControlContainer class, .NET automatically use the ControlContainerDesigner class as the designer.

You can also explicitly specify the designer you want to use to render your control at design time using the Designer attribute on your control's class, as shown in Listing 25-41.

LISTING 25-41: Adding a Designer attribute to a control class

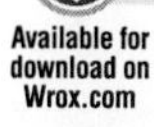

Available for download on Wrox.com

VB

```
<DefaultProperty("Text")> _
<ToolboxData("<{0}:WebCustomControl1 runat=server></{0}:WebCustomControl1>")> _
<Designer(GetType(System.Web.UI.Design.ControlDesigner))> _
Public Class WebCustomControl1
    Inherits System.Web.UI.WebControls.WebControl
```

C#

```
[DefaultProperty("Text")]
[ToolboxData("<{0}:WebCustomControl1 runat=server></{0}:WebCustomControl1>")]
[Designer(typeof(System.Web.UI.Design.ControlDesigner))]
public class WebCustomControl1 : WebControl
```

Notice that the Designer attribute has been added to the WebCustomControl1 class. You have specified that the control should use the ControlDesigner class as its designer. Other in-box designers you could have specified are:

- CompositeControlDesigner
- TemplatedControlDesigner
- DataSourceDesigner

Each designer provides a specific design-time behavior for the control, and you can select one that is appropriate for the type of control you are creating.

Design-Time Regions

As you saw earlier, ASP.NET allows you to create server controls that consist of other server controls and text. ASP.NET allows you to create server controls that have design-time editable portions using a technique called *designer regions*. Designer regions enable you to create multiple, independent regions defined within a single control and respond to events raised by a design region. This might be the designer drawing a control on the design surface or the user clicking an area of the control or entering or exiting a template edit mode.

To show how you can use designer regions, create a container control to which you can apply a custom control designer, as shown in Listing 25-42.

Available for download on Wrox.com

LISTING 25-42: Creating a composite control with designer regions

VB

```
<Designer(GetType(MultiRegionControlDesigner))> _
<ToolboxData("<{0}:MultiRegionControl runat=server width=100%>" & _
      "</{0}:MultiRegionControl>")> _
Public Class MultiRegionControl
    Inherits CompositeControl

    ' Define the templates that represent 2 views on the control
    Private _view1 As ITemplate
    Private _view2 As ITemplate

    ' These properties are inner properties
    <PersistenceMode(PersistenceMode.InnerProperty), DefaultValue("")> _
    Public Overridable Property View1() As ITemplate
        Get
            Return _view1
        End Get
        Set(ByVal value As ITemplate)
            _view1 = value
        End Set
    End Property

    <PersistenceMode(PersistenceMode.InnerProperty), DefaultValue("")> _
    Public Overridable Property View2() As ITemplate
        Get
            Return _view2
        End Get
        Set(ByVal value As ITemplate)
            _view2 = value
        End Set
    End Property

    ' The current view on the control; 0= view1, 1=view2, 2=all views
    Private _currentView As Int32 = 0
    Public Property CurrentView() As Int32
        Get
            Return _currentView
        End Get
        Set(ByVal value As Int32)
            _currentView = value
        End Set
    End Property

    Protected Overrides Sub CreateChildControls()
        MyBase.CreateChildControls()

        Controls.Clear()

        Dim template As ITemplate = View1
        If (_currentView = 1) Then
            template = View2
        End If

        Dim p As New Panel()
```

```
            Controls.Add(p)

            If (Not template Is Nothing) Then
                template.InstantiateIn(p)
            End If

        End Sub

    End Class
```

C#

```
    [Designer(typeof(MultiRegionControlDesigner))]
    [ToolboxData("<{0}:MultiRegionControl runat=\"server\" width=\"100%\">" +
        "</{0}:MultiRegionControl>")]
    public class MultiRegionControl : CompositeControl {

        // Define the templates that represent 2 views on the control
        private ITemplate _view1;
        private ITemplate _view2;

        // These properties are inner properties
        [PersistenceMode(PersistenceMode.InnerProperty), DefaultValue(null)]
        public virtual ITemplate View1 {
            get { return _view1;}
            set { _view1 = value;}
        }

        [PersistenceMode(PersistenceMode.InnerProperty), DefaultValue(null)]
        public virtual ITemplate View2 {
            get { return _view2;}
            set { _view2 = value;}
        }

        // The current view on the control; 0= view1, 1=view2, 2=all views
        private int _currentView = 0;
        public int CurrentView {
            get { return _currentView;}
            set { _currentView = value;}
        }

        protected override void CreateChildControls()
        {
            Controls.Clear();

            ITemplate template = View1;
            if (_currentView == 1)
                template = View2;

            Panel p = new Panel();
            Controls.Add(p);

            if (template != null)
                template.InstantiateIn(p);
        }
    }
```

The container control creates two `ITemplate` objects, which serve as the controls to display. The `ITemplate` objects are the control containers for this server control, allowing you to drop other server controls or text into this control. The control also uses the `Designer` attribute to indicate to Visual Studio that it should use the `MultiRegionControlDesigner` class when displaying this control on the designer surface.

Now you create the control designer that defines the regions for the control. Listing 25-43 shows the designer class.

LISTING 25-43: A custom designer class used to define designer regions

Available for download on Wrox.com

VB

```
Public Class MultiRegionControlDesigner
    Inherits System.Web.UI.Design.WebControls.CompositeControlDesigner

    Protected _currentView As Int32 = 0
    Private myControl As MultiRegionControl

    Public Overrides Sub Initialize(ByVal component As IComponent)
        MyBase.Initialize(component)
        myControl = CType(component, MultiRegionControl)
    End Sub

    Public Overrides ReadOnly Property AllowResize() As Boolean
        Get
            Return True
        End Get
    End Property

    Protected Overrides Sub OnClick(ByVal e As DesignerRegionMouseEventArgs)

        If (e.Region Is Nothing) Then
            Return
        End If

        If ((e.Region.Name = "Header0") And (Not _currentView = 0)) Then
            _currentView = 0
            UpdateDesignTimeHtml()
        End If

        If ((e.Region.Name = "Header1") And (Not _currentView = 1)) Then

            _currentView = 1
            UpdateDesignTimeHtml()
        End If
    End Sub

    Public Overrides Function GetDesignTimeHtml( _
            ByVal regions As DesignerRegionCollection) As String
        BuildRegions(regions)
        Return BuildDesignTimeHtml()
    End Function

    Protected Overridable Sub BuildRegions( _
            ByVal regions As DesignerRegionCollection)

        regions.Add(New DesignerRegion(Me, "Header0"))
        regions.Add(New DesignerRegion(Me, "Header1"))

        ' If the current view is for all, we need another editable region
        Dim edr0 As New EditableDesignerRegion(Me, "Content" & _currentView, False)
        edr0.Description = "Add stuff in here if you dare:"
        regions.Add(edr0)

        ' Set the highlight, depending upon the selected region
        If ((_currentView = 0) Or (_currentView = 1)) Then
            regions(_currentView).Highlight = True
        End If
    End Sub

    Protected Overridable Function BuildDesignTimeHtml() As String

        Dim sb As New StringBuilder()
```

```
        sb.Append(BuildBeginDesignTimeHtml())
        sb.Append(BuildContentDesignTimeHtml())
        sb.Append(BuildEndDesignTimeHtml())

        Return sb.ToString()
    End Function

    Protected Overridable Function BuildBeginDesignTimeHtml() As String
        ' Create the table layout
        Dim sb As New StringBuilder()
        sb.Append("<table ")

        ' Styles that we'll use to render for the design-surface
        sb.Append("height='" & myControl.Height.ToString() & "' width='" & _
            myControl.Width.ToString() & "'>")

        ' Generate the title or caption bar
        sb.Append("<tr height='25px' align='center' " & _
            "style='font-family:tahoma;font-size:10pt;font-weight:bold;'>" & _
            "<td style='width:50%' " & _
            DesignerRegion.DesignerRegionAttributeName & "='0'>")
        sb.Append("Page-View 1</td>")
        sb.Append("<td style='width:50%' " & _
            DesignerRegion.DesignerRegionAttributeName & "='1'>")
        sb.Append("Page-View 2</td></tr>")

        Return sb.ToString()
    End Function

    Protected Overridable Function BuildEndDesignTimeHtml() As String
        Return ("</table>")
    End Function

    Protected Overridable Function BuildContentDesignTimeHtml() As String

        Dim sb As New StringBuilder()
        sb.Append("<td colspan='2' style='")
        sb.Append("background-color:" & _
            myControl.BackColor.Name.ToString() & ";' ")

        sb.Append(DesignerRegion.DesignerRegionAttributeName & "='2'>")

        Return sb.ToString()
    End Function

    Public Overrides Function GetEditableDesignerRegionContent( _
            ByVal region As EditableDesignerRegion) As String

        Dim host As IDesignerHost = _
            CType(Component.Site.GetService(GetType(IDesignerHost)), IDesignerHost)

        If (Not host Is Nothing) Then
            Dim template As ITemplate = myControl.View1

            If (region.Name = "Content1") Then
                template = myControl.View2
            End If

            If (Not template Is Nothing) Then
                Return ControlPersister.PersistTemplate(template, host)
```

continues

LISTING 25-43 *(continued)*

```
            End If

        End If

        Return String.Empty
    End Function

    Public Overrides Sub SetEditableDesignerRegionContent( _
            ByVal region As EditableDesignerRegion, ByVal content As String)

        Dim regionIndex As Int32 = Int32.Parse(region.Name.Substring(7))

        If (content Is Nothing) Then

            If (regionIndex = 0) Then
                myControl.View1 = Nothing
            ElseIf (regionIndex = 1) Then
                myControl.View2 = Nothing
                Return
            End If

            Dim host As IDesignerHost = _
                CType(Component.Site.GetService(GetType(IDesignerHost)),
                    IDesignerHost)

            If (Not host Is Nothing) Then
                Dim template = ControlParser.ParseTemplate(host, content)

                If (Not template Is Nothing) Then
                    If (regionIndex = 0) Then
                        myControl.View1 = template
                    ElseIf (regionIndex = 1) Then
                        myControl.View2 = template
                    End If
                End If
            End If
        End If
    End Sub
End Class
```

C#

```
public class MultiRegionControlDesigner :
    System.Web.UI.Design.WebControls.CompositeControlDesigner {

    protected int _currentView = 0;

    private MultiRegionControl myControl;
    public override void Initialize(IComponent component)
    {
        base.Initialize(component);
        myControl = (MultiRegionControl)component;
    }

    public override bool AllowResize { get { return true;}}

    protected override void OnClick(DesignerRegionMouseEventArgs e)
    {
        if (e.Region == null)
            return;

        if (e.Region.Name == "Header0" && _currentView != 0) {
            _currentView = 0;
```

```
            UpdateDesignTimeHtml();
        }

        if (e.Region.Name == "Header1" && _currentView != 1) {
            _currentView = 1;
            UpdateDesignTimeHtml();
        }
    }

    public override String GetDesignTimeHtml(DesignerRegionCollection regions)
    {
        BuildRegions(regions);
        return BuildDesignTimeHtml();
    }

    protected virtual void BuildRegions(DesignerRegionCollection regions)
    {
        regions.Add(new DesignerRegion(this, "Header0"));
        regions.Add(new DesignerRegion(this, "Header1"));

        // If the current view is for all, we need another editable region
        EditableDesignerRegion edr0 = new
            EditableDesignerRegion(this, "Content" + _currentView, false);
        edr0.Description = "Add stuff in here if you dare:";
        regions.Add(edr0);

        // Set the highlight, depending upon the selected region
        if (_currentView ==0 || _currentView==1)
            regions[_currentView].Highlight = true;
    }

    protected virtual string BuildDesignTimeHtml()
    {
        StringBuilder sb = new StringBuilder();
        sb.Append(BuildBeginDesignTimeHtml());
        sb.Append(BuildContentDesignTimeHtml());
        sb.Append(BuildEndDesignTimeHtml());

        return sb.ToString();
    }

    protected virtual String BuildBeginDesignTimeHtml()
    {
        // Create the table layout
        StringBuilder sb = new StringBuilder();
        sb.Append("<table ");

        // Styles that we'll use to render for the design-surface
        sb.Append("height='" + myControl.Height.ToString() + "' width='" +
            myControl.Width.ToString() +  "'>");

        // Generate the title or caption bar
        sb.Append("<tr height='25px' align='center' " +
            "style='font-family:tahoma;font-size:10pt;font-weight:bold;'>" +
            "<td style='width:50%' " + DesignerRegion.DesignerRegionAttributeName +
            "='0'>");
        sb.Append("Page-View 1</td>");
        sb.Append("<td style='width:50%' " +
            DesignerRegion.DesignerRegionAttributeName + "='1'>");
        sb.Append("Page-View 2</td></tr>");

        return sb.ToString();
```

continues

LISTING 25-43 *(continued)*

```
    }

    protected virtual String BuildEndDesignTimeHtml()
    {
        return ("</table>");
    }

    protected virtual String BuildContentDesignTimeHtml()
    {
        StringBuilder sb = new StringBuilder();
        sb.Append("<td colspan='2' style='");
        sb.Append("background-color:" + myControl.BackColor.Name.ToString() +
            ";' ");

        sb.Append(DesignerRegion.DesignerRegionAttributeName + "='2'>");

        return sb.ToString();
    }

    public override string GetEditableDesignerRegionContent
        (EditableDesignerRegion region)
    {
        IDesignerHost host =
            (IDesignerHost)Component.Site.GetService(typeof(IDesignerHost));

        if (host != null) {
            ITemplate template = myControl.View1;

            if (region.Name == "Content1")
                template = myControl.View2;

            if (template != null)
                return ControlPersister.PersistTemplate(template, host);
        }

        return String.Empty;
    }

    public override void SetEditableDesignerRegionContent
        (EditableDesignerRegion region, string content)
    {
        int regionIndex = Int32.Parse(region.Name.Substring(7));

        if (content == null)
        {
            if (regionIndex == 0)
                myControl.View1 = null;
            else if (regionIndex == 1)
                myControl.View2 = null;
            return;
        }

        IDesignerHost host =
            (IDesignerHost)Component.Site.GetService(typeof(IDesignerHost));

        if (host != null)
        {
            ITemplate template = ControlParser.ParseTemplate(host, content);

            if (template != null)
            {
```

```
                    if (regionIndex == 0)
                        myControl.View1 = template;
                    else if (regionIndex == 1)
                        myControl.View2 = template;
                }
            }
        }
    }
```

The designer overrides the `GetDesignTimeHtml` method, calling the `BuildRegions` and `BuildDesignTimeHtml` methods to alter the HTML that the control renders to the Visual Studio design surface.

The `BuildRegions` method creates three design regions in the control, two header regions and an editable content region. The regions are added to the `DesignerRegionCollection`. The `BuildDesignTimeHtml` method calls three methods to generate the actual HTML that will be generated by the control at design time.

The designer class also contains two overridden methods for getting and setting the editable designer region content: `GetEditableDesignerRegionContent` and `SetEditableDesignerRegionContent`. These methods get or set the appropriate content HTML, based on the designer region template that is currently active.

Finally, the class contains an `OnClick` method that it uses to respond to click events fired by the control at design time. This control uses the `OnClick` event to switch the current region being displayed by the control at design time.

When you add the control to a Web form, you see that you can toggle between the two editable regions, and each region maintains its own content. Figure 25-17 shows what the control looks like on the Visual Studio design surface.

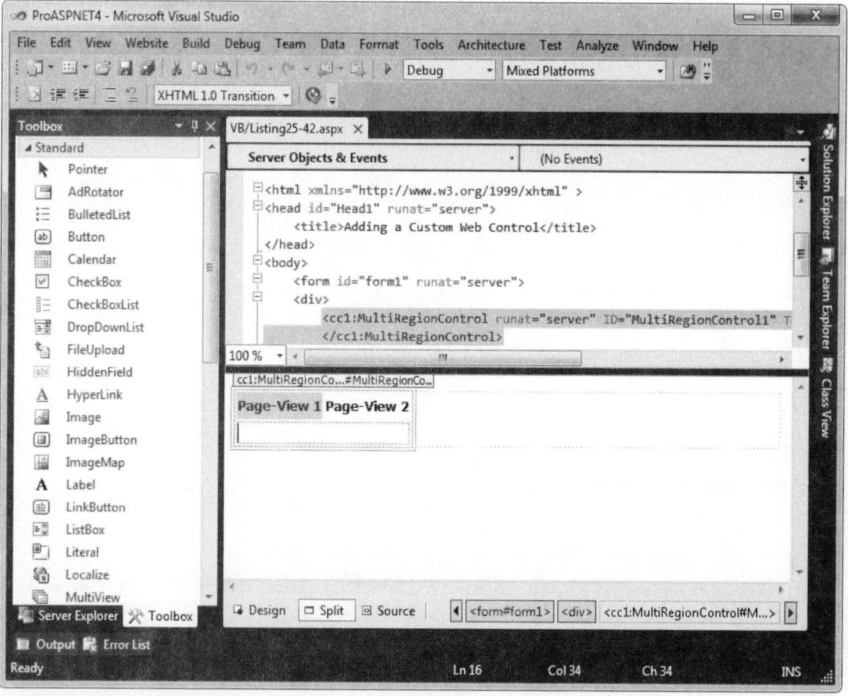

FIGURE 25-17

As you can see in Figure 25-17, the control contains three separate design regions. When you click design regions 1 or 2, the `OnClick` method in the designer fires and redraws the control on the design surface, changing the template area located in design region 3.

Designer Actions

Another great feature of ASP.NET design-time support is control smart tags. Smart tags give developers using a control quick access to common control properties. To add menu items to a server control's smart tag, you create a new class that inherits from the `DesignerActionList` class. The `DesignerActionList` contains the list of designer action items that are displayed by a server control. Classes that derive from the `DesignerActionList` class can override the `GetSortedActionItems` method, creating their own `DesignerActionItemsCollection` object to which you can add designer action items.

You can add several different types of `DesignerActionItems` types to the collection:

- `DesignerActionTextItem`
- `DesignerActionHeaderItem`
- `DesignerActionMethodItem`
- `DesignerActionPropertyItem`

Listing 25-44 shows a control designer class that contains a private class deriving from `DesignerActionList`.

LISTING 25-44: Adding designer actions to a control designer

Available for download on Wrox.com

VB

```
Public Class ServerControl44Designer
    Inherits ControlDesigner

    Private _actionLists As DesignerActionListCollection

    Public Overrides ReadOnly Property ActionLists() _
            As DesignerActionListCollection
        Get
            If IsNothing(_actionLists) Then
                _actionLists = New DesignerActionListCollection()
                _actionLists.AddRange(MyBase.ActionLists)
                _actionLists.Add(New ServerControl44ControlList(Me))
            End If
            Return _actionLists
        End Get
    End Property

    Private NotInheritable Class ServerControl44ControlList
        Inherits DesignerActionList

        Public Sub New(ByVal c As ServerControl44Designer)
            MyBase.New(c.Component)
        End Sub

        Public Overrides Function GetSortedActionItems() _
                As DesignerActionItemCollection

            Dim c As New DesignerActionItemCollection()
            c.Add(New DesignerActionTextItem("Text Action Item",
                                             "Custom Category"))
            Return c
        End Function
    End Class
End Class
```

```
public class ServerControl44Designer : ControlDesigner
{
    private DesignerActionListCollection _actionLists = null;

    public override DesignerActionListCollection ActionLists
```

```
        {
            get
            {
                if (_actionLists == null)
                {
                    _actionLists = new DesignerActionListCollection();
                    _actionLists.AddRange(base.ActionLists);
                    _actionLists.Add(new ServerControl44ControlList(this));
                }
                return _actionLists;
            }
        }

        private sealed class ServerControl44ControlList :
                             DesignerActionList
        {
            public ServerControl44ControlList(ControlDesigner c)
                : base(c.Component)
            {
            }

            public override DesignerActionItemCollection
                GetSortedActionItems()
            {
                DesignerActionItemCollection c =
                    new DesignerActionItemCollection();
                c.Add(new DesignerActionTextItem("Text Action Item",
                                                 "Custom Category"));
                return c;
            }
        }
    }
```

The control designer class overrides the `ActionsLists` property. The property creates an instance of the `TextControlList` class, which derives from `DesignerActionList` and overrides the `GetSortedActionItems` method. The method creates a new `DesignerActionListCollection`, and a `DesignerActionTextItem` is added to the collection (see Figure 25-18). The `DesignerActionTextItem` class allows you to add text menu items to the smart tag.

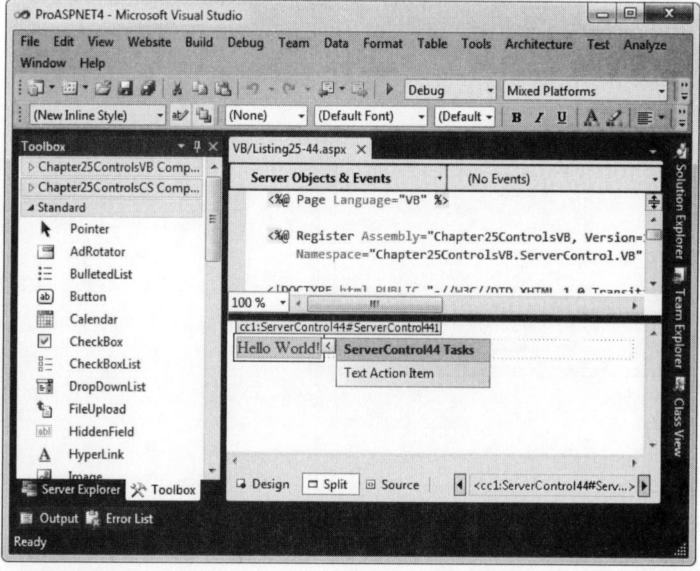

FIGURE 25-18

As shown in Figure 25-18, when you add the control to a Web page, the control now has a smart tag with the `DesignerActionTextItem` class as content.

UI Type Editors

A UI type editor is a way to provide users of your controls with a custom interface for editing properties directly from the Property Browser. One type of UI type editor you might already be familiar with is the Color Picker you see when you want to change the `ForeColor` attribute that exists on most ASP.NET controls. ASP.NET provides a wide variety of in-box UI type editors that make editing more complex property types easy. The easiest way to find what UI type editors are available in the .NET Framework is to search for types derived from the `UITypeEditor` class in the MSDN Library help.

After you find the type editor you want to use on your control property, you simply apply the UI type editor to the property using the `Editor` attribute. Listing 25-45 shows how to do this.

LISTING 25-45: Adding a UI type editor to a control property

Available for download on Wrox.com

VB

```
<Bindable(True), Category("Appearance"), DefaultValue(""),
Editor(
        GetType(System.Web.UI.Design.UrlEditor),
        GetType(System.Drawing.Design.UITypeEditor))>
Public Property Url() As String
```

C#

```
[Bindable(true)]
[Category("Appearance")]
[DefaultValue("")]
[Editor(typeof(System.Web.UI.Design.UrlEditor),
    typeof(System.Drawing.Design.UITypeEditor))]
public string Url { get; set; }
```

In this sample, you have created a `Url` property for a control. Because you know this property will be a URL, you want to give the control user a positive design-time experience. You can use the `UrlEditor` type editor to make it easier for users to select a URL. Figure 25-19 shows the URL Editor that appears when the user edits the control property.

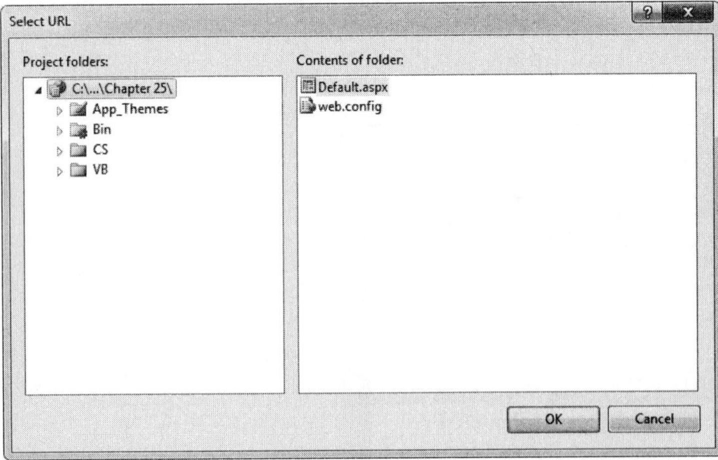

FIGURE 25-19

SUMMARY

In this chapter, you learned a number of ways you can create reusable, encapsulated chunks of code. You first looked at user controls, the simplest form of control creation. You learned how to create user controls and how you can make them interact with their host Web pages. Creating user controls is quite easy, but they lack the portability of other control-creation options.

Then, you saw how you can create your own custom server controls. You looked at many of the tools you can create by writing custom server controls. These range from tools for emitting HTML and creating CSS styles and JavaScript to those applying themes. The chapter also discussed the type of server controls you can create, ranging from server controls that simply inherit from the `WebControl` class to templated controls that give users of the control the power to define the display of the server control.

Finally, you looked at ways you can give the users of your server control a great design-time experience by providing them with type convertors, design surface interactions, and custom property editors in your server control.

26

Modules and Handlers

WHAT'S IN THIS CHAPTER?

- Interacting with the ASP.NET request processing pipeline
- Working with HttpModules and HttpHandlers

Sometimes, just creating dynamic Web pages with the latest languages and databases does not give you, the developer, enough control over an application. At times, you need to be able to dig deeper and create applications that can interact with the Web server itself. You want to be able to interact with the low-level processes, such as how the Web server processes incoming and outgoing HTTP requests.

Before ASP.NET, to get this level of control using IIS, you were forced to create ISAPI extensions or filters. This task was quite daunting and painful for many developers because creating ISAPI extensions and filters required knowledge of C/C++ and knowledge of how to create native Win32 DLLs. Thankfully, in the .NET world, creating these types of low-level applications is really no more difficult than most other applications you might build. This chapter looks at two methods of manipulating how ASP.NET processes HTTP requests, the HttpModule and the HttpHandler. Each method provides a unique level of access to the underlying processing of ASP.NET and can be a powerful tool for creating Web applications.

PROCESSING HTTP REQUESTS

Before starting to write handlers or modules, knowing how IIS and ASP.NET normally process incoming HTTP requests and what options you have for plugging custom logic into those requests is helpful. IIS is the basic endpoint for incoming HTTP requests. At a very high level, its job is to listen for and validate incoming HTTP requests. Then it routes them to the appropriate module for processing and returns any results to the original requestor. ASP.NET is one of the modules that IIS may pass requests to for processing. However, exactly how that processing happens and how you can integrate your own logic into the pipeline differs based on the version of IIS you are using.

IIS 6 and ASP.NET

If you are using IIS 6, the HTTP request processing pipeline is fairly black box to a managed code developer. IIS basically treats ASP.NET as one of the modules that it can pass requests to for processing rather than as an integrated part of the IIS request processing pipeline. Figure 26-1 shows the basic request processing pipeline of IIS 6 and ASP.NET.

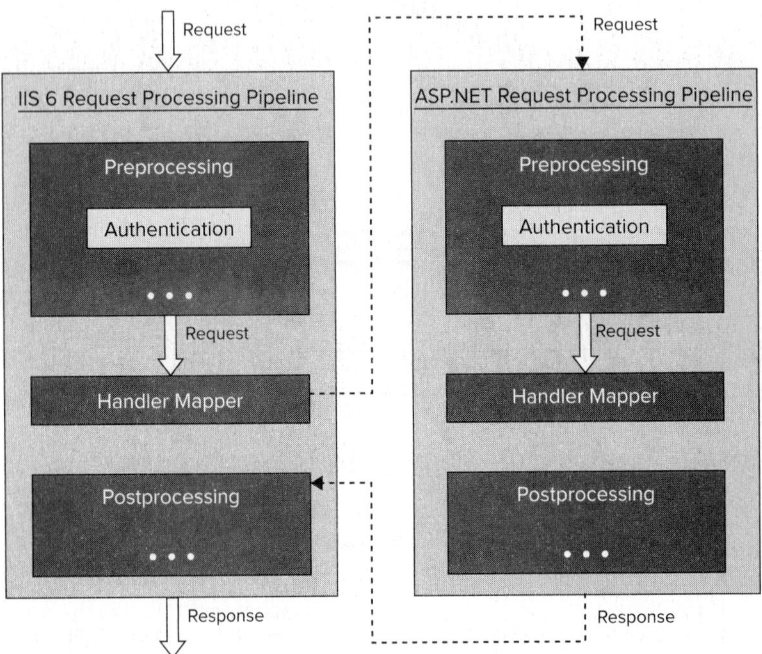

FIGURE 26-1

As you can see, the IIS and ASP.NET request pipelines are very similar and several tasks, such as authentication, are even duplicated between the two pipelines. Furthermore, although you can write handlers and modules using managed code, they are still processed in the isolated context of the ASP.NET process. If you wanted to integrate deeper into the IIS pipeline you are forced to create modules using native code.

IIS 7 and ASP.NET

Starting with IIS 7, the request processing pipeline in IIS was completely re-architected using an open and highly extensible module-based system. Instead of IIS seeing ASP.NET as a separate entity, ASP.NET was deeply integrated into the IIS request processing pipeline. As shown in Figure 26-2, the request processing pipeline was streamlined to eliminate duplicate processes and to allow you to integrate managed modules in the pipeline.

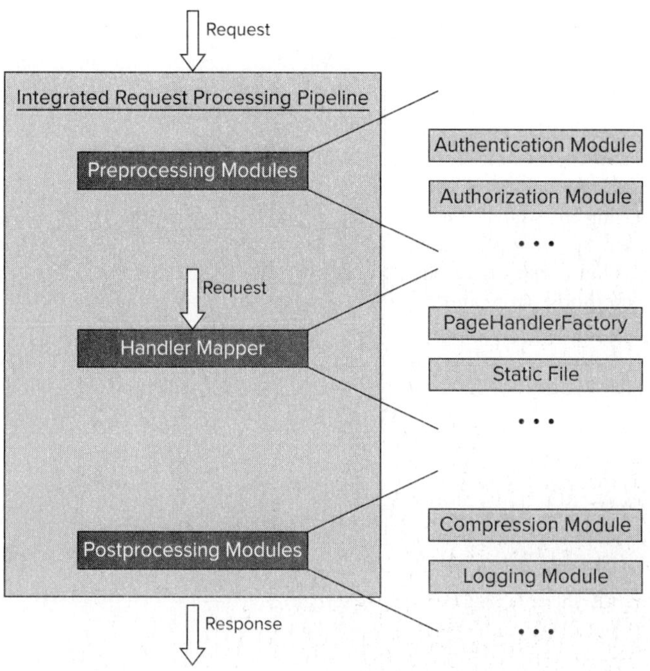

FIGURE 26-2

Because ASP.NET modules are first-class citizens, you can place them at any point in the pipeline, or even completely replace existing modules with your own custom functionality. Features that previously required you to write custom ISAPI modules in unmanaged code can simply be replaced by managed code modules containing your logic. If you are interested in learning more about the integration of ASP.NET and IIS 7, check out the Wrox title *Professional IIS 7 and ASP.NET Integrated Programming* by Shahram Khosravi (Wiley Publishing, Inc., 2007).

ASP.NET Request Processing

Regardless of the IIS version, the basic HTTP request pipeline model has two core mechanisms for handling requests: HttpModules and HttpHandlers. ASP.NET uses those two mechanisms to process incoming ASP.NET requests, generate a response, and return that response to the client. In fact, you are probably already familiar with HttpModules and HttpHandlers — although you might not know it. If you have ever used the Inbox caching or the authentication features of ASP.NET, you have used several different HttpModules. Additionally, if you have ever served up an ASP.NET application, even something as simple as a *Hello World* Web page and viewed it in a browser, you have used an HttpHandler. ASP.NET uses handlers to process and render ASPX pages and other file extensions. Modules and handlers allow you to plug into the request-processing pipeline at different points and interact with the actual requests being processed by IIS.

As you can see in both Figures 26-1 and 26-2, ASP.NET passes each incoming request through a layer of preprocessing HttpModules in the pipeline. ASP.NET allows multiple modules to exist in the pipeline for each request. After the incoming request has passed through each module, it is passed to the HttpHandler, which serves the request. Notice that although a single request may pass through many different modules, it can be processed by one handler only. The handler is generally responsible for creating a response to the incoming HTTP request. After the handler has completed execution and generated a response, the response is passed back through a series of post-processing modules, before it is returned to the client.

You should now have a basic understanding of the IIS and ASP.NET request pipeline — and how you can use HttpModules and HttpHandlers to interact with the pipeline. The following sections take an in-depth look at each of these.

HTTPMODULES

HttpModules are simple classes that can plug themselves into the request-processing pipeline. They do this by hooking into a handful of events thrown by the application as it processes the HTTP request. To create an HttpModule, you simply create a class that derives from the `System.Web.IHttpModule` interface. This interface requires you to implement two methods: `Init` and `Dispose`. Listing 26-1 shows the class stub created after you implement the `IHttpModule` interface.

LISTING 26-1: Implementing the IHttpModule interface

Available for download on Wrox.com

```
Imports Microsoft.VisualBasic

Namespace Chapter26.VB

    Public Class SimpleModule
        Implements IHttpModule

        Public Overridable Sub Init(ByVal context As HttpApplication) _
                Implements IHttpModule.Init

        End Sub

        Public Overridable Sub Dispose() Implements IHttpModule.Dispose

        End Sub

    End Class

End Namespace
```

C#

```
using System;
using System.Collections.Generic;
using System.Text;
using System.Web;

namespace Chapter26.CS
{
    class SimpleModule : IHttpModule
    {
        #region IHttpModule Members

        public void Dispose()
        {
            throw new Exception(
                    "The method or operation is not implemented.");
        }

        public void Init(HttpApplication context)
        {
            throw new Exception(
                    "The method or operation is not implemented.");
        }

        #endregion
    }
}
```

The `Init` method is the primary method you use to implement HttpModule functionality. Notice that it has a single method parameter — an `HttpApplication` object named `context`. This parameter gives you access to the current `HttpApplication` context, and it is what you use to wire up the different events that fire during the request processing. Table 26-1 shows the events that you can register in the `Init` method.

TABLE 26-1

EVENT NAME	DESCRIPTION
`AcquireRequestState`	Raised when ASP.NET runtime is ready to acquire the session state of the current HTTP request.
`AuthenticateRequest`	Raised when ASP.NET runtime is ready to authenticate the identity of the user.
`AuthorizeRequest`	Raised when ASP.NET runtime is ready to authorize the user for the resources user is trying to access.
`BeginRequest`	Raised when ASP.NET runtime receives a new HTTP request.
`Disposed`	Raised when ASP.NET completes the processing of an HTTP request.
`EndRequest`	Raised just before sending the response content to the client.
`Error`	Raised when an unhandled exception occurs during the processing of the HTTP request.
`PostRequestHandlerExecute`	Raised just after the HTTP handler finishes execution.
`PreRequestHandlerExecute`	Raised just before ASP.NET begins executing a handler for the HTTP request. After this event, ASP.NET forwards the request to the appropriate HTTP handler.
`PreSendRequestContent`	Raised just before ASP.NET sends the response contents to the client. This event allows you to change the contents before it gets delivered to the client. You can use this event to add the contents, which are common in all pages, to the page output — for example, a common menu, header, or footer.
`PreSendRequestHeaders`	Raised just before ASP.NET sends the HTTP response headers to the client. This event allows you to change the headers before they get delivered to the client. You can use this event to add cookies and custom data into headers.

To see how you can create and use an HttpModule, you can use a simple example involving modifying the HTTP output stream before it is sent to the client. This can be a simple and useful tool if you want to add text to each page served from your Web site, such as a date/time stamp or the server that processed the request, but do not want to modify each individual page in your application. To get started creating this HttpModule, create a Web project in Visual Studio and add a class file to the App_Code directory. Listing 26-2 shows the code for the HttpModule.

LISTING 26-2: Altering the output of an ASP.NET web page

Available for download on Wrox.com

VB

```
Imports Microsoft.VisualBasic

Namespace Chapter26.VB

    Public Class AppendMessage
        Implements IHttpModule

        Dim WithEvents _application As HttpApplication = Nothing

        Public Overridable Sub Init(ByVal context As HttpApplication) _
                Implements IHttpModule.Init
            _application = context
        End Sub
```

continues

LISTING 26-2 *(continued)*

```
        Public Overridable Sub Dispose() Implements IHttpModule.Dispose

        End Sub
        Public Sub context_EndRequest(
                ByVal sender As Object,
                ByVal e As EventArgs) _
            Handles _application.EndRequest

            Dim message As String =
                String.Format("processed on {0}",
                              System.DateTime.Now.ToString())

            _application.Context.Response.Output.Write(message)
        End Sub

    End Class

End Namespace
```

C#

```
using System;
using System.Collections.Generic;
using System.Text;
using System.Web;

namespace Chapter26.CS
{
    public class AppendMessage : IHttpModule
    {
        private HttpApplication _application = null;

        #region IHttpModule Members

        public void Dispose()
        {

        }

        public void Init(System.Web.HttpApplication context)
        {
            _application = context;

            context.EndRequest += new EventHandler(context_EndRequest);
        }

        void context_EndRequest(object sender, EventArgs e)
        {
            string message =
                string.Format("processed on {0}",
                    System.DateTime.Now.ToString());

            _application.Context.Response.Write(message);
        }

        #endregion
    }
}
```

You can see that the class stub from Listing 26-1 has been expanded by registering the `PreSendRequestContent` event in the `Init` method. This event fires right before the content created by the HttpHandler is sent to the client, and gives you one final opportunity to modify it.

To modify the content of the request, in the `PreSendRequestContent` handler method you simply write your modification to the HttpResponse object's output stream, which appends the content to the end of the existing content. This sample gets the current date and time and writes it to the output stream. The HTTP request is then sent back to the client.

To use this module, you must let ASP.NET know that you want to include the module in the request-processing pipeline. You do this by modifying the `web.config` file to contain a reference to the module. Listing 26-3 shows how you can add an `<httpModules>` section to your `web.config` file.

Available for download on Wrox.com

LISTING 26-3: Adding the httpModules configuration to web.config

```
<configuration>
    <system.web>
      <httpModules>
        <add name="AppendMessage"
             type="Chapter26.VB.AppendMessage, App_code" />
      </httpModules>
    </system.web>
</configuration>
```

The generic format of the `<httpModules>` section is

```
<httpModules>
    <add name="[modulename]" type="[namespace.classname, assemblyname]" />
</httpModules>
```

If you are deploying your application to an IIS 7 server, you must also add the module configuration to the `<system.webServer>` configuration section.

```
<modules>
    <add name="AppendMessage" type="Chapter26.VB.AppendMessage, App_code"/>
</modules>
```

If you have created your HttpModule in the `App_Code` directory of an ASP.NET Web site, you might wonder how you know what the `assemblyname` value should be, considering ASP.NET now dynamically compiles this code at runtime. The solution is to use the text "`App_Code`" as the assembly name, which tells ASP.NET that your module is located in the dynamically created assembly.

You can also create HttpModules as a separate class library, in which case you simply use the assembly name of the library.

After you have added this section to your `web.config` file, simply view one of the Web pages from your project in the browser. When you view the page in the browser you should not notice any difference, but, if you view the source of the page notice the timestamp you added at the bottom of the HTML.

Figure 26-3 shows what you should see when you view the page source.

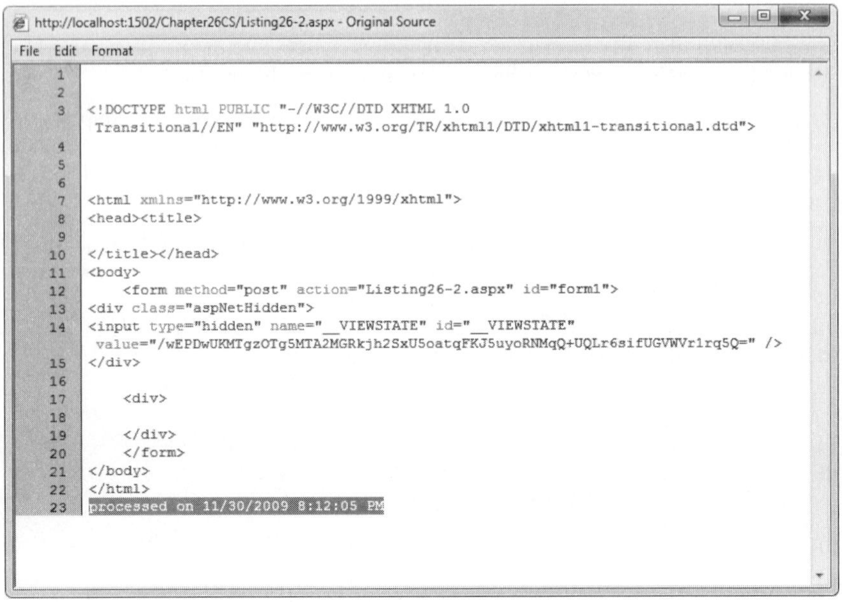

http://localhost:1502/Chapter26CS/Listing26-2.aspx - Original Source

File Edit Format

```
<!DOCTYPE html PUBLIC "-//W3C//DTD XHTML 1.0
 Transitional//EN" "http://www.w3.org/TR/xhtml1/DTD/xhtml1-transitional.dtd">



<html xmlns="http://www.w3.org/1999/xhtml">
<head><title>

</title></head>
<body>
    <form method="post" action="Listing26-2.aspx" id="form1">
<div class="aspNetHidden">
<input type="hidden" name="__VIEWSTATE" id="__VIEWSTATE"
 value="/wEPDwUKMTgzOTg5MTA2MGRkjh2SxU5oatqFKJ5uyoRNMqQ+UQLr6sifUGVWVr1rq5Q=" />
</div>

    <div>

    </div>
    </form>
</body>
</html>
processed on 11/30/2009 8:12:05 PM
```

FIGURE 26-3

HTTPHANDLERS

HttpHandlers differ from HttpModules, not only because of their positions in the request-processing pipeline (refer to Figures 26-1 and 26-2), but also because they must be mapped to a specific file extension. Handlers are the last stop for incoming HTTP requests and are ultimately the point in the request-processing pipeline that is responsible for serving up the requested content, be it an ASPX page, HTML, plain text, or an image.

Using HttpHandlers to serve up content you might normally serve using a standard ASP.NET page (such as a dynamic file download request) can be a good idea in your application because it allows you to write a specialized handler that eliminates some of the overhead of a standard ASP.NET handler.

This section demonstrates two different ways to create a simple HttpHandler that you can use to serve up images based on dynamic querystring data:

- First, you look at creating an HttpHandler using an `.ashx` file extension that allows you to get started quickly and requires no server configuration.
- Next, you learn how to create even more customized handlers by mapping your HttpHandler to a custom file extension using IIS.

Generic Handlers

In early versions of Visual Studio, HttpHandlers were somewhat hard to understand and create because little documentation was included to help developers understand handlers. In addition, Visual Studio did not provide any friendly methods for creating them.

Since Visual Studio 2005, however, this has changed, with Visual Studio providing a standard template for HttpHandlers to help you get started. To add an HttpHandler to your project, you simply select the Generic Handler file type from the Add New Item dialog. Figure 26-4 shows this dialog box with the file type selected.

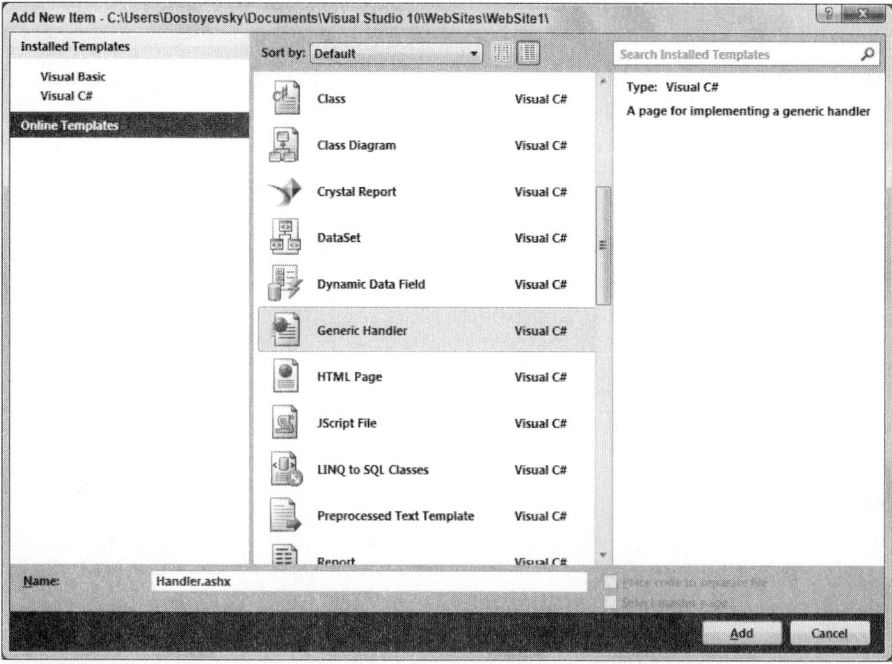

FIGURE 26-4

You can see that when you add the Generic Handler file to your project, it adds a file with an `.ashx` extension. The `.ashx` file extension is the default HttpHandler file extension set up by ASP.NET. Remember that HttpHandlers must be mapped to a unique file extension, so by default ASP.NET uses the `.ashx` extension. This feature is convenient because, otherwise, you would be responsible for adding the file extension yourself. This task is obviously not always possible, nor is it practical. Using the Custom Handler file type helps you avoid any extra configuration.

Notice the class stub that the file type automatically creates for you. Listing 26-4 shows the class.

Available for download on Wrox.com

LISTING 26-4: The HttpHandler page template

```
<%@ WebHandler Language="VB" Class="Handler4" %>

Imports System
Imports System.Web

Public Class Handler4
    Implements IHttpHandler

    Public Sub ProcessRequest(ByVal context As HttpContext) _
        Implements IHttpHandler.ProcessRequest
        context.Response.ContentType = "text/plain"
        context.Response.Write("Hello World")
    End Sub

    Public ReadOnly Property IsReusable() As Boolean _
        Implements IHttpHandler.IsReusable
        Get
            Return False
        End Get
```

continues

LISTING 26-4 *(continued)*

```
    End Property

End Class
```

C#

```
<%@ WebHandler Language="C#" Class="Handler4" %>

using System;
using System.Web;

public class Handler4 : IHttpHandler {

    public void ProcessRequest (HttpContext context) {
        context.Response.ContentType = "text/plain";
        context.Response.Write("Hello World");
    }

    public bool IsReusable {
        get {
            return false;
        }
    }

}
```

Notice that the stub implements the `IHttpHandler` interface, which requires you to implement the `ProcessRequest` method and `IsReusable` property.

- The `ProcessRequest` method is the method you use to actually process the incoming HTTP request. By default, the class stub changes the content type to plain and then writes the `"Hello World"` string to the output stream.
- The `IsReusable` property simply lets ASP.NET know whether incoming HTTP requests can reuse the sample instance of this HttpHandler.

The handler generated in the template is ready to run right away. Try executing the handler in your browser and see what happens. The interesting thing to note about this handler is that because it changes the content to text/plain, browsers handle the responses from this handler in potentially very different ways depending on a number of factors:

- Browser type and version
- Applications loaded on the system that may map to the MIME type
- Operating system and service pack level

Based on these factors, you might see the text returned in the browser, you might see Notepad open and display the text, or you might receive the Open/Save/Cancel prompt from IE. Make sure you understand the potential consequences of changing the `ContentType` header.

You can continue the example by modifying it to return an actual file. In this case, you use the handler to return an image. To do this, you simply modify the code in the `ProcessRequest` method, as shown in Listing 26-5.

LISTING 26-5: Outputting an image from an HttpHandler

```
<%@ WebHandler Language="VB" Class="Handler5" %>

Imports System
Imports System.Web

Public Class Handler5
    Implements IHttpHandler

    Public Sub ProcessRequest(ByVal context As HttpContext) _
```

```
        Implements IHttpHandler.ProcessRequest
        'Logic to retrieve the image file
        context.Response.ContentType = "image/jpeg"
        context.Response.WriteFile("Garden.jpg")
    End Sub

    Public ReadOnly Property IsReusable() As Boolean _
        Implements IHttpHandler.IsReusable
        Get
            Return False
        End Get
    End Property

End Class
```

C#

```
<%@ WebHandler Language="C#" Class="Handler5" %>

using System;
using System.Web;

public class Handler5 : IHttpHandler {

    public void ProcessRequest(HttpContext context)
    {
        //Logic to retrieve the image file
        context.Response.ContentType = "image/jpeg";
        context.Response.WriteFile("Garden.jpg");
    }

    public bool IsReusable {
        get {
            return false;
        }
    }

}
```

As you can see, you simply change the `ContentType` to `image/jpeg` to indicate that you are returning a JPEG image; then you use the `WriteFile()` method to write an image file to the output stream. Load the handler into a browser, and you see that the handler displays the image. Figure 26-5 shows the resulting Web page.

FIGURE 26-5

Now, you create a simple Web page to display the image handler. Listing 26-6 shows code for the Web page.

LISTING 26-6: A sample Web page using the HttpHandler for the image source

Available for download on Wrox.com

```
<html xmlns="http://www.w3.org/1999/xhtml" >
<head runat="server">
    <title>HttpHandler Serving an Image</title>
</head>
<body>
    <form id="form1" runat="server">
    <div>
        <img src="Listing26-5.ashx" alt="Dynamic Image" />
    </div>
    </form>
</body>
</html>
```

Although this sample is simple, you can enhance it by passing querystring parameters to your handler and using them to perform additional logic in the handler:

```
<img src="Listing26-5.ashx?imageid=123" />
```

Using the querystring data you could, for example, dynamically retrieve an image from a SQL database and return it to the client or perform some type of authentication to ensure the requestor is allowed to access this image.

Mapping a File Extension in IIS

Although using the `.ashx` file extension is convenient, you might want to create an HTTP handler for a custom file extension or even for a commonly used extension. You can use the code from the image handler to demonstrate this method.

Create a new class in the `App_Code` directory of your Web project. You can simply copy the code from the existing image handler control into this class, as shown in Listing 26-7. Notice that you remove the `WebHandler` directive because this is only a class and not a generic handler control. Other than that, the code is the same.

LISTING 26-7: The class-based image HttpHandler

Available for download on Wrox.com

```
Imports Microsoft.VisualBasic

Namespace Chapter26.VB
    Public Class MappedHandler : Implements IHttpHandler

        Public Sub ProcessRequest(ByVal context As HttpContext) _
                Implements IHttpHandler.ProcessRequest
            context.Response.ContentType = "image/jpeg"
            context.Response.WriteFile("Garden.jpg")
        End Sub

        Public ReadOnly Property IsReusable() As Boolean _
                Implements IHttpHandler.IsReusable
            Get
                Return False
            End Get
        End Property

    End Class
End Namespace
```

C#

```
using System.Web;

namespace Chapter26.CS
{
    public class MappedHandler : IHttpHandler
    {
        public void ProcessRequest(HttpContext context)
        {
            context.Response.ContentType = "image/jpeg";
            context.Response.WriteFile("Garden.jpg");
        }

        public bool IsReusable
        {
            get
            {
                return false;
            }
        }
    }
}
```

After adding your class, configure the application to show which file extension this handler serves. You do this by adding an <httpHandlers> section to the web.config file. Listing 26-8 shows the section to add for the image handler.

Available for download on Wrox.com

LISTING 26-8: Adding the httpHandlers configuration information to web.config file

```
<httpHandlers>
     <add verb="*" path="ImageHandler.img"
          type="MappedHandler, App_Code" />
</httpHandlers>
```

In the configuration section, you direct the application to use the MappedHandler class to process incoming requests for ImageHandler.img. You can also specify wildcards for the path. Specifying *.img for the path indicates that you want the application to use the MappedHandler class to process any request with the .img file extension. Specifying * indicates that you want all requests to the application to be processed using the handler.

As with HttpModules, if you are running your Web application using IIS 7, then you also must add the <httpHandler> configuration section to the <system.webServer> configuration section of your application's config file. When adding the handler configuration in this section, you must also include the name attribute.

```
<add name="ImageHandler" verb="*"
     path="ImageHandler.img"
     type="Chapter26.VB.MappedHandler, App_Code" />
```

Load the ImageHandler.img file into a browser and, again, you should see that it serves up the image. Figure 26-6 shows the results. Notice the path in the browser's address bar leads directly to the ImageHandler.img file.

FIGURE 26-6

SUMMARY

This chapter presented a number of ways you can create modules that allow you to interact with the ASP. NET request processing pipeline. You worked with HttpModules, which give you the power to plug yourself directly into the ASP.NET page-processing pipeline. The events provided to an HttpModule give you great power and flexibility to customize your applications.

You also looked at HttpHandlers. Handlers allow you to skip the ASP.NET page-processing pipeline completely and have 100 percent control over how the framework serves up requested data. You learned how to create your own image handler and then map the handler to any file or file extension you want. Using these features of ASP.NET can help you create features in your application that exercise great control over the standard page processing that ASP.NET uses.

27

ASP.NET MVC

WHAT'S IN THIS CHAPTER?

- Understanding MVC and ASP.NET
- Working with routes and URLs
- Understanding Controllers and Views

Model-View-Controller (MVC) has been an important architectural pattern in computer science for many years. Originally named Thing-Model-View-Editor in 1979, it was later simplified to Model-View-Controller. It is a powerful and elegant means of separating concerns within an application and applies itself extremely well to Web applications. Its explicit separation of concerns does add a small amount of extra complexity to an application's design, but the extraordinary benefits outweigh the extra effort. It's been used in dozens of frameworks since its introduction. You can find MVC in Java and C++, on Mac and on Windows, and inside literally dozens of frameworks.

Understanding the core concepts of MVC is critical to using it effectively. This chapter discusses the history of the MVC pattern, as well as how it is used in Web programming today.

ASP.NET MVC 1.0 shipped as a downloadable add-on to Visual Studio 2008. Now in Visual Studio 2010, ASP.NET MVC 2 ships built-in. This chapter also covers some of the limitations of ASP.NET Web forms and how ASP.NET MVC attempts to release the developer from those limitations.

The content of this chapter is adapted from Professional ASP.NET MVC 1.0 *by Rob Conery, Scott Hanselman, Phil Haack, and Scott Guthrie (Wiley, 2009). For more in-depth coverage of this topic, we recommend you check out that book.*

DEFINING MODEL-VIEW-CONTROLLER

Model-View-Controller (MVC) is an architectural pattern used to separate an application into three main aspects:

- **The Model:** A set of classes that describes the data you're working with as well as the business rules for how the data can be changed and manipulated
- **The View:** The application's user interface (UI)

- **The Controller:** A set of classes that handles communication from the user, overall application flow, and application-specific logic

This pattern is used frequently in Web programming. With ASP.NET MVC, it's translated roughly to the following:

- The Models are the classes that represent the domain in which you are interested. These domain objects often encapsulate data stored in a database as well as code used to manipulate the data and enforce domain-specific business logic. With ASP.NET MVC, this is most likely a data access layer of some kind using a tool like LINQ to SQL, Entity Framework, or NHibernate, combined with custom code containing domain-specific logic.
- The View is a dynamically generated page. In ASP.NET MVC, you implement it via the `System.Web.Mvc.ViewPage` class, which inherits from `System.Web.UI.Page`.
- The Controller is a special class that manages the relationship between the View and Model. It talks to the Model, and it decides which View to render (if any). In ASP.NET MVC, this class is conventionally denoted by the suffix "`Controller`."

MVC ON THE WEB TODAY

For many, the Web didn't really become prominent until the first graphical browsers began to flood the market, starting with Mosaic in 1993. Shortly after, dynamic Web pages began showing up using languages such as Perl and enabled by technologies like the Common Gateway Interface (CGI). The technology available in the early stages of the Web was focused more around the concept of scripting HTML to do light content-driven work, as opposed to deep application logic, which just wasn't needed back then.

As the Web grew and HTML standards began to allow for richer interactions, the notion of the Web as an application platform began to take off. In the Microsoft realm, the focus was on quick and simple (in line with the simplicity of VB), and Active Server Pages (ASP) was born in 1996.

ASP used VBScript, a very simple, lightweight language that gave developers a lot of "un-prescribed freedom" in terms of the applications they could create. A request for an ASP page would be handled by a file with the `.asp` extension, which consisted of a server-side script intermixed with HTML markup. Written in a procedural language, many ASP pages often devolved into "spaghetti code" in which the markup was intertwined with code in difficult-to-manage ways. Although writing clean ASP code was possible, it took a lot of work, and the language and tools were not sufficiently helpful. Even so, ASP did provide full control over the markup produced, it just took a lot of work.

In January of 2002, Microsoft released version 1.0 of the .NET platform, which included the original version of ASP.NET, and thus Web forms was born. Its birth provided access to advanced tools and object-oriented languages for building a Web site.

ASP.NET has grown tremendously over the last 8 years (almost a decade!) and has made developing Web pages very productive and simple by abstracting the repetitive tasks of Web development into simple drag-and-drop controls. This abstraction can be a tremendous help, but some developers have found that they want more control over the generated HTML and browser scripting, and they also want to be able to easily test their Web page logic.

As languages matured and Web server software grew in capability, MVC soon found its way into Web application architectures. But MVC didn't hit its mainstream stride until July of 2004, when a 24-year old developer at 37Signals in Chicago, Illinois, named David Heinemeier Hansson, introduced the world to his fresh way of thinking about MVC.

David, or DHH as he's known in the community, created Ruby on Rails, a Web development framework that used the Ruby language and the MVC pattern to create something special.

Now let's further delve into the new kid on the block, ASP.NET MVC, and answer the question, "Why not Web forms?"

In February of 2007, Scott Guthrie of Microsoft sketched out the core of ASP.NET MVC while flying on a plane to a conference on the east coast of the United States. It was a simple application, containing a few hundred lines of code, but the promise and potential it offered for parts of the Microsoft Web developer audience was huge.

PRODUCT TEAM ASIDE

ScottGu, or "The Gu," is legendary for prototyping cool stuff, and if he sees you in the hallway and he has his laptop, you won't be able to escape as he says, "Dude! Check this out!" His enthusiasm is infectious.

As the legend goes, at the Austin ALT.NET conference in October of 2007 in Redmond, Washington, ScottGu showed a group of developers "this cool thing he wrote on a plane" and asked whether they saw the need and what they thought of it. It was a hit. In fact, a number of people were involved with the original prototype, codenamed "Scalene." Eilon Lipton e-mailed the first prototype to the team in September of 2007, and he and ScottGu bounced prototypes, code, and ideas back and forth via e-mail, and still do!

MODEL-VIEW-CONTROLLER AND ASP.NET

ASP.NET MVC relies on many of the same core strategies that the other MVC platforms use, plus it offers the benefits of compiled and managed code and exploits new language features in .NET 3.5 and above within VB9 and C#3 such as lambdas and anonymous types. Each of the MVC frameworks used on the web usually share in some fundamental tenets:

- Convention over Configuration
- Don't repeat yourself (also known as the DRY principle)
- Plugability whenever possible
- Try to be helpful, but if necessary, get out of the developer's way

Serving Methods, Not Files

Web servers initially served up HTML stored in static files on disk. As dynamic Web pages gained prominence, Web servers served HTML generated on the fly from dynamic scripts that were also located on disk. With MVC, serving up HTML is a little different. The URL tells the routing mechanism which Controller to instantiate and which action method to call and supplies the required arguments to that method. The Controller's method then decides which View to use, and that View then does the rendering.

Rather than having a direct relationship between the URL and a file living on the Web server's hard drive, a relationship exists between the URL and a method on a controller object. ASP.NET MVC implements the "front controller" variant of the MVC pattern, and the Controller sits in front of everything except the routing subsystem.

A good way to conceive of the way that MVC works in a Web scenario is that MVC serves up the results of method calls, not dynamically generated (also known as scripted) pages. In fact, we heard a speaker once call this "RPC for the Web," which is particularly apt, although quite a bit narrower in scope.

Is This Web Forms 4.0?

One of the major concerns that we've heard when talking to people about ASP.NET MVC is that its release means the death of Web forms. This just isn't true. ASP.NET MVC is not ASP.NET Web forms 4.0. It's an alternative to Web forms, and it's a fully supported part of the framework. While Web forms continues to march on with new innovations and new developments, ASP.NET MVC will continue as a parallel alternative that's totally supported by Microsoft.

One interesting way to look at this is to refer to the namespaces these technologies live in. If you could point to a namespace and say, "That's where ASP.NET lives," it would be the `System.Web` namespace. ASP.NET MVC lives in the `System.Web.Mvc` namespace. It's not `System.Mvc`, and it's not `System.Web2`.

Although ASP.NET MVC is a separately downloadable Web component today for users of Visual Studio 2008 (often referred to by the ASP.NET team as an out-of-band [OOB] release), it has been folded into .NET Framework 4 and it's built into Visual Studio 2010 out of the box. This cements ASP.NET MVC's place as a fundamental part of ASP.NET itself.

Why Not Web Forms?

In ASP.NET Web forms, you create an instance of `System.Web.UI.Page` and put "server controls" on it (for example, a calendar and some buttons) so that the user can enter or view information. You then wire these controls to events on the `System.Web.UI.Page` to allow for interactivity. This page is then compiled, and when it's called by the ASP.NET runtime, a server-side control tree is created, each control in the tree goes through an event lifecycle, it renders itself, and the result is served back as HTML. As a result, a new Web aesthetic started to emerge — Web forms layers eventing and state management on top of HTTP — a truly stateless protocol.

Why was this abstraction necessary? Remember that Web forms was introduced to a Microsoft development community that was very accustomed to Visual Basic 6. Developers using VB6 would drag buttons onto the design surface, double-click the button, and a `Button_Click` event handler method was instantly created for them. This was an incredibly powerful way to create business applications and had everyone excited about Rapid Application Development (RAD) tools. When developers started using classic ASP, it was quite a step backward from the rich environment they were used to in Visual Basic. For better or worse, Web forms brought that Rapid Application Development experience to the Web.

However, as the Web matured and more and more people came to terms with their own understanding of HTML as well as the introduction of CSS (Cascading Style Sheets) and XHTML, a new Web aesthetic started to emerge. Web forms is still incredibly productive for developers, enabling them to create a Web-based line of business applications very quickly. However, the HTML it generates looks, well, generated and can sometimes offend the sensibilities of those who handcraft their XHTML and CSS sites. Web forms concepts like ViewState and the Postback event model have their place, but many developers want a lower-level alternative that embraces not only HTML but also HTTP itself.

Additionally, the architecture of Web forms also makes testing via the current unit testing tools such as NUnit, MbUnit, and xUnit.NET difficult. ASP.NET Web forms wasn't designed with unit testing in mind, and although a number of hacks can be found on the Web, it's fair to say that Web forms does not lend itself well to test-driven development. ASP.NET MVC offers absolute control over HTML, doesn't deny the existence of HTTP, and was designed from the ground up with an eye towards testability.

ASP.NET MVC Is Totally Different!

Yes, ASP.NET MVC is totally different. That's the whole point. It's built on top of a system of values and architectural principles that is very different from those in Web forms. ASP.NET MVC values extensibility, testability, and flexibility. It's very lightweight and doesn't make a lot of assumptions on how you will use it — aside from the fact that it assumes you appreciate the Model-View-Controller pattern.

Different developers and different projects have different needs. If ASP.NET MVC meets your needs, use it. If it doesn't, don't use it. Either way, don't be afraid.

Why "(ASP.NET > ASP.NET MVC) == True"

Creating your first MVC application is fairly straightforward. You can use any version of Visual Studio 2010 to create the basic application, including Express, Standard, Professional, or Team Edition.

If you're NOT using Visual Studio 2010, the first order of business is to install the MVC Framework on your 2008 development box. Start at `www.asp.net/mvc` by downloading the latest release. If you like living on the edge, you can often get ASP.NET MVC future releases at `www.codeplex.com/aspnet`.

What you're downloading is a set of Visual Studio project templates that will create your ASP.NET MVC Web application for you. You've used these before — every new ASP.NET Web site and ASP.NET Web application is based on a set of templates. The templates will be installed in Visual Studio, and the reference assemblies will be installed in `C:\Program Files\Microsoft ASP.NET`.

After you've installed ASP.NET MVC, you're ready to create an ASP.NET MVC application using Visual Studio 2008. Though, if you are using Visual Studio 10, then you are going to want to follow these steps:

1. Open Visual Studio 2010 by selecting File ➪ New Project.
2. From the New Project dialog box, shown in Figure 27-1, select ASP.NET MVC 2 Web Application.

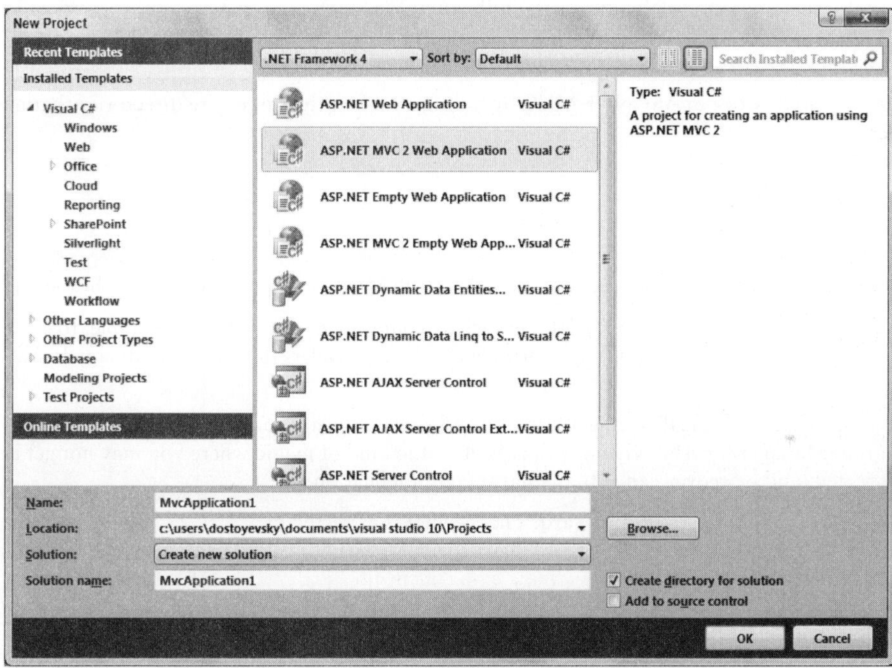

FIGURE 27-1

3. Pick your project name and where it's going to live on disk, and click OK. The Create Unit Test Project dialog appears, as shown in Figure 27-2.
4. By default the Test Framework drop-down list includes Visual Studio Unit Test as an option. Select Yes to create a solution that includes both a basic ASP.NET MVC project but also an additional MSTest Unit Test project. If you've installed a third-party unit-testing framework like MbUnit or NUnit, additional options appear in this dialog.

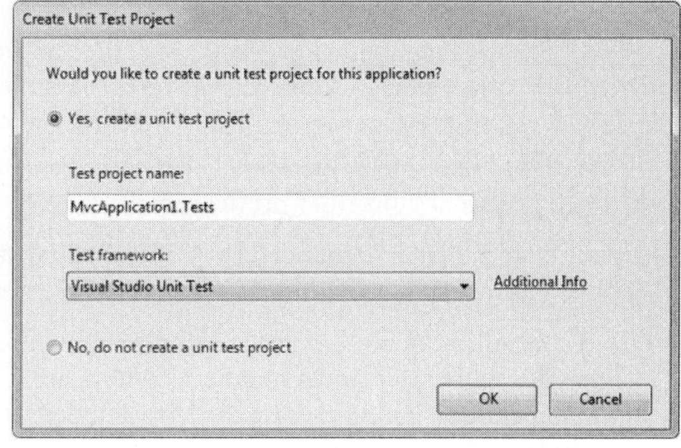

FIGURE 27-2

5. Click OK, and a solution with projects that look like that shown in Figure 27-3 appears. Note that, although this is an ASP.NET application, along with a standard class library, it has some additional folders you haven't seen before.

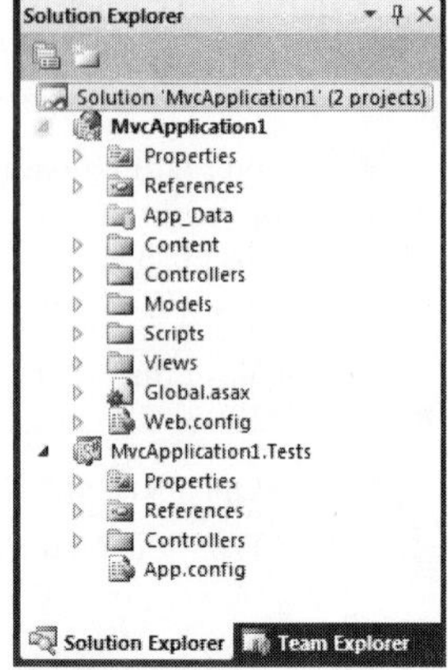

FIGURE 27-3

In fact, the application has quite a few more directories than you might be used to; this is by design. ASP.NET MVC, like other MVC frameworks, relies heavily on the idea that you can reduce effort and code by relying on some basic structural rules in your application. Ruby on Rails expresses this powerful idea very succinctly: *Convention over Configuration*.

Convention over Configuration

The concept of "Convention over Configuration" was made popular by Ruby on Rails a few years back, and essentially means the following: We know, by now, how to build a Web application. Let's roll that experience into the framework so we don't have to configure absolutely everything again.

You can see this concept at work in ASP.NET MVC by taking a look at the three core directories that make the application work:

- Controllers
- Models
- Views

You don't have to set these folder names in the `web.config` file — they are just expected to be there by convention.

This saves you the work of having to edit an XML file such as your `web.config` file, for example, to explicitly tell the MVC engine "you can find my controllers in the Controllers directory." It already knows. It's *convention*.

This feature isn't meant to be magical. Well actually it is; it's just not meant to be "black magic," as Phil Haack, the Program Manager for ASP.NET MVC, calls it — the kind of magic where you may not get the outcome you expected (and moreover can actually harm your application).

ASP.NET MVC's conventions are straightforward. This is what is expected of your application's structure:

- It has a single Controllers directory that holds your Controller classes.
- Each Controller's class name ends with "`Controller`" — `ProductController`, `HomeController`, and so on — and exists in the Controllers directory.
- It has a single Views directory for all the Views of your application.
- Views that Controllers use are located in a subdirectory of the Views main directory, and are named according to the Controller name (minus "`Controller`"). For example, the views for the `ProductController` discussed earlier would be in `/Views/Product`.
- All reusable UI elements live in a similar structure above, but in a "shared" directory off the root.

If you take a deeper, expanded look at the initial structure of the sample application, shown in Figure 27-4, you can see these conventions at work.

Two controllers, `HomeController` and `AccountController`, are in the Controllers directory, and a number of Views are in the Views directory. The following discussion focuses on the Views under `/Views/Home` named About and Index.

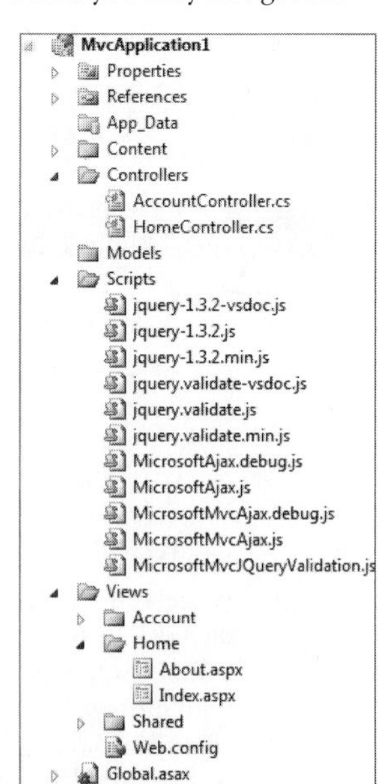

FIGURE 27-4

Although no convention is expected of you with respect to what you name your Views, you can lean on the ASP.NET MVC convention that you give your View the same name as your action. Using this convention also makes reviewing and understanding your application easier for other developers.

You can see this convention in action in the way that the template creates the Index and About views. These are also the names of the Controller actions that are called, and the code to render these views is simply:

```
return View();
```

That can be a little confusing. You can see a clear example by changing the application a little and then digging in:

1. Open `HomeController.cs`, copy and paste the `About` method, and create a duplication called `Foo`, as shown here:

   ```
   public ActionResult Foo()
   {
       ViewData["Title"] = "Foo Page";
       return View();
   }
   ```

2. Having made this one small addition, start your application. You will be prompted to modify your `web.config` file to enable debugging. Click OK to have Visual Studio automatically make the change for you. The ASP.NET Development Web Server automatically selects a high port number and your browser launches. Your browser ends up navigating to an address like `http://localhost:1074`, as shown in Figure 27-5.

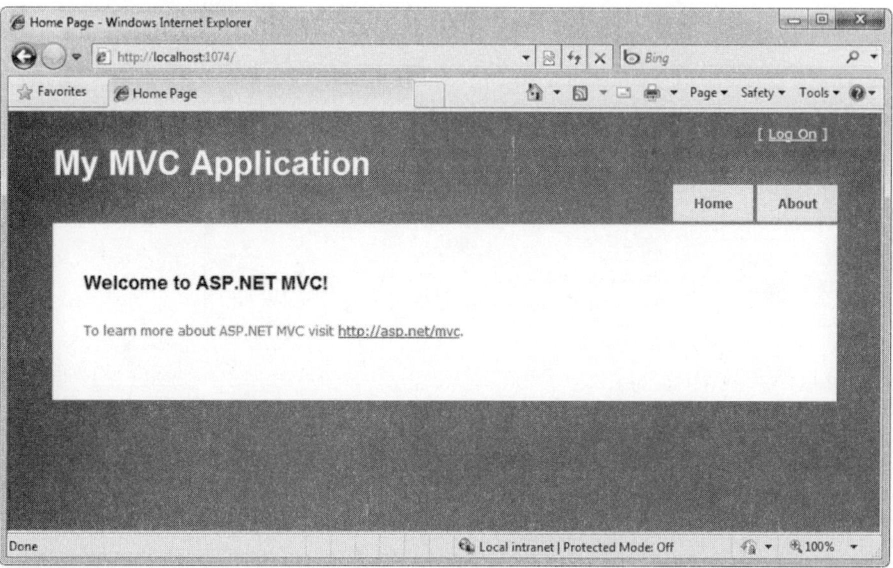

FIGURE 27-5

3. See how there's no `.aspx` extension? ASP.NET MVC puts you in full control. Now, change the relative URL in your browser's address bar from `/` to `/Home/Foo`. Things get interesting, as shown in Figure 27-6. Remember that you're just returning the result of the call to `View` in your `Foo` method. As you're in the `Foo` method of `HomeController`, the system is looking for a View called `Foo` in a number of locations. ASP.NET MVC is smart enough to give you an error message that you can actually do something useful with. It's really quite refreshing!

   ```
   System.InvalidOperationException: The view 'Foo' could not be located at these paths:
   ~/Views/Home/Foo.aspx, ~/Views/Home/Foo.ascx, ~/Views/Shared/Foo.aspx,
   ~/Views/Shared/Foo.ascx
   ```

The error message lists (see Figure 27-6) the locations where the system looked for Views, in the order searched. It gives you enough information to infer the naming convention for Views.

First, it looks in a directory under `/Views` with the name of the current Controller, in this case `Home`, then it looks in `/Views/Shared`. The `WebFormsViewEngine` that ASP.NET MVC uses by default looks for `.aspx` pages, then `.ascx` files.

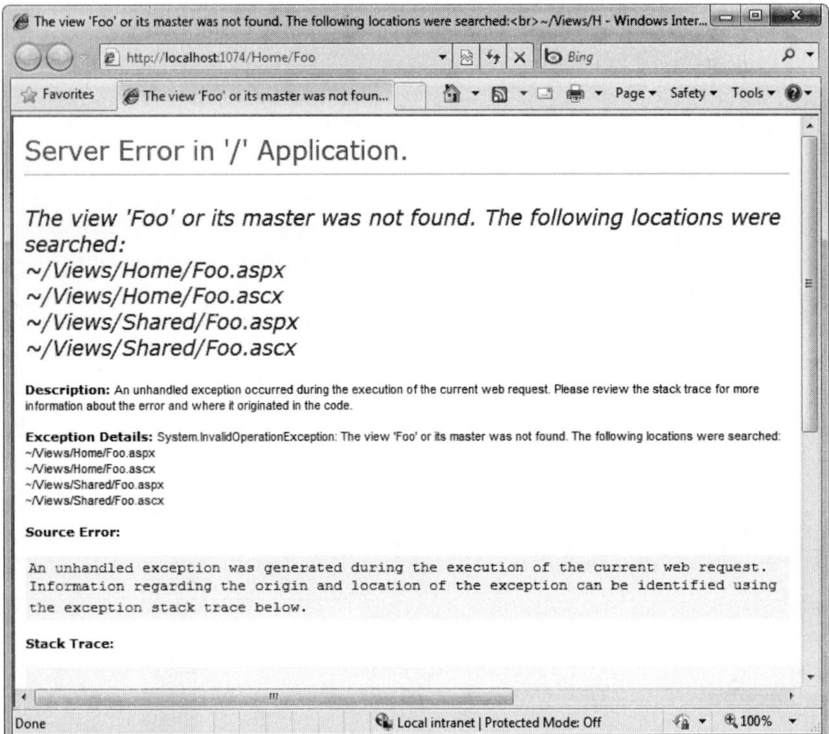

FIGURE 27-6

4. Go back into `HomeController.cs` and change the call to `View` in the `Foo` method to include the name of a View as a parameter.

```
public ActionResult Foo()
{
    ViewData["Title"] = "Foo Page";
    return View("Index");
}
```

5. Start your application again, and visit `/Home/Foo` again. The Index View is rendered, and the `Title` string appears in the browser's title.

6. Switch back over to Visual Studio and set a breakpoint on the line that returns the result of `View`. Refresh your browser, confirming that you're still at `/Home/Foo`, and get ready to dig in.

The Third Request Is the Charm

Take a moment and think about what's happening here. What's the state of affairs within your application? Your instance of Visual Studio should look more or less like Figure 27-7.

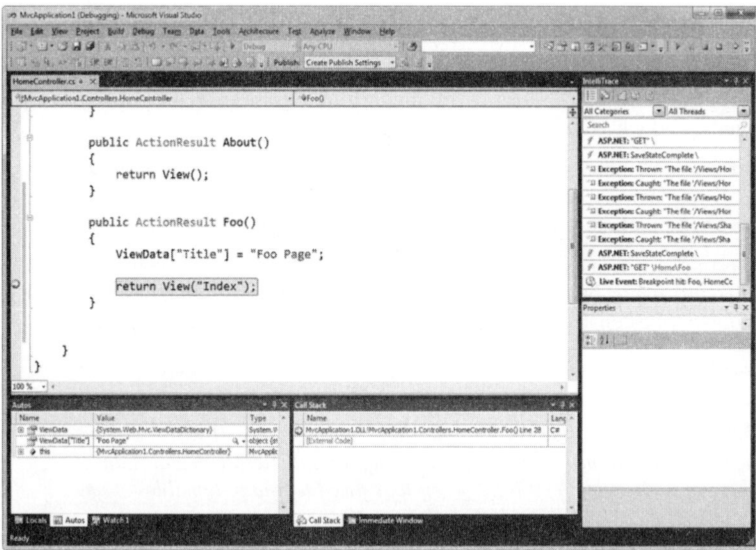

FIGURE 27-7

Spend a moment looking at Visual Studio (or the figure, if you like) and try to determine what it is telling you. How did you get here? Where are you?

You visited `/Home/Foo` in the browser, and now you're magically sitting on a breakpoint inside of the `Foo` action method. The Call Stack tool window confirms this, but doesn't tell you enough. How *did* you get here? Right-click the whitespace of the call stack, and select Show External Code. You might also drag the Call Stack tool window and "tear it off" Visual Studio to better analyze the crush of information that's going to be revealed. If you have multiple monitors, remember that Visual Studio 2010 supports that, so you can fill one whole monitor with the Call Stack tool window if you like.

The Call Stack tool window contains so much information, in fact, that the authors have taken it upon themselves to highlight some important bits of it, as shown in Figure 27-8. Remember that call stacks are read from bottom to top, where the bottom is where you started and the top is the line you are currently debugging. In this call stack, some parts are more significant than others.

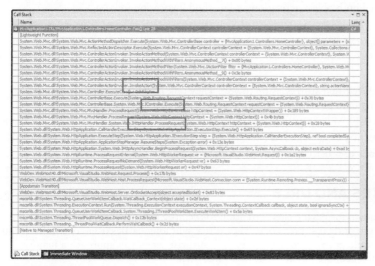

FIGURE 27-8

Starting at the bottom, you can see that the execution thread is chosen and the `HttpWorkerRequest` is being dispatched and handled by ASP.NET — specifically by `System.Web.HttpRuntime`. This is the "beginning" of ASP.NET. Note that this is `System.Web`, and you're inside `System.Web.dll` — nothing MVC specific has happened yet. If you're already familiar with Web forms, you might find it useful to remember what ASP.NET proper is, where it ends, and where ASP.NET MVC starts.

The first significant thing happens (remember, you're reading from bottom to top) in the bottom callout shown in Figure 27-8. What can you learn from this single stack frame? ASP.NET MVC is built on ASP.NET with `HttpHandlers` and `HttpModules`. That's where MVC gets its hooks in.

The fact that ASP.NET MVC is implemented as an `HttpHandler` is comforting because you know that the team "played by the rules" when writing it. No internal knowledge or secrets exist in the design of ASP.NET MVC. It's written using the same public constructs and APIs that are available to all developers.

We find great comfort in the discovery that ASP.NET MVC has no secrets in its design. Less magic in ASP.NET MVC means we can understand it more easily. If ASP.NET MVC is an `HttpHandler`, *and you've written lots of those, then it's less magical than you thought! It's also nice to see that ASP.NET itself was flexible and extensible enough to allow something like ASP.NET MVC to be created.*

Another thing you can glean from these discoveries is that because ASP.NET MVC uses `HttpHandlers` (and `HttpModules`) to do its work, MVC is built on ASP.NET. This might seem like an obvious statement to some, but a very common question is "Is ASP.NET MVC a whole new ASP.NET?" You can see from Figure 27-8 that it's not. It's built on the same infrastructure, the same "core" ASP.NET, that you've used for years.

Glance back at Figure 27-8 and look at that call stack. Remember that you're currently sitting on a breakpoint in the `Foo` method inside `HomeController`. Who created `HomeController`? Someone had to "new it up." Who called `Foo` for you? Look to the call stack, my friends.

Inside the `MvcHandler`'s `ProcessRequest` method an instance of a Controller is created by the `DefaultControllerFactory`. ASP.NET MVC creates an instance of the `HomeController` and then calls the `Execute` method on the Controller. This method in turn relies on the Controller's action invoker (by default a `ControllerActionInvoker`) to actually call the method.

Remember that you opened a browser and requested `/Home/Foo`. The ASP.NET MVC application routed the request to an `MvcHandler`. That `Handler` created an instance of the `HomeController` and called the `Foo` method. ASP.NET MVC handled both object activation and method invocation for you.

The `/Home/Foo` URL was intercepted by the `UrlRoutingModule`. That module is responsible for making sure the right URLs go to the right Controllers by parsing the URLs and creating some routing data. The MVC pipeline uses a `ControllerFactory` and a `ControllerActionInvoker` to create your controller and call its method, respectively.

Controllers exist to "do stuff." What that stuff is, is up to you. They talk to a Model, do calculations, whatever. However, they don't render HTML, and they don't talk to databases. That's separation of concerns. Controllers are concerned with controlling.

The Controller passes `ViewData` to a View, which is concerned with rendering HTML (or whatever you want). That HTML contains links to other URLs, and the cycle continues.

UNDERSTANDING ROUTES AND URLS

Software developers are well known for paying close attention to the little details, especially when it comes to the quality and structure of their source code. They often fight long battles over code indentation styles and where curly braces should go. So it comes as a bit of a surprise when you approach a majority of sites built using ASP.NET and encounter a URL that looks like this:

```
http://example.com/products/list.aspx?id=17313&catid=33723&page=3
```

For all the attention developers pay to code, why not pay the same amount of attention to the URL? It may not seem all that important, but the URL is a legitimate and widely used Web user interface.

Usability expert Jakob Nielsen (`www.useit.com`) urges developers to pay attention to URLs and provides the following guidelines for high-quality URLs:

- A domain name that is easy to remember and easy to spell
- Short URLs
- Easy-to-type URLs
- URLs that reflect the site structure
- URLs that are "hackable" to allow users to move to higher levels of the information architecture by hacking off the end of the URL
- Persistent URLs, which don't change

Traditionally, in many Web frameworks such as classic ASP, JSP, PHP, ASP.NET, and the like, the URL represents a physical file on disk. For example, when you see a request for

```
http://example.com/products/list.aspx
```

you could bet your kid's tuition that the Web site has a directory structure that contains a Products folder and a `List.aspx` file within that folder. In this case, a direct relationship exists between the URL and what physically exists on disk. When such a request is received by the Web server, the Web framework executes code associated with this file to respond to the request. In many cases, this code contains or is associated with a template that intermixes server-side declarations with HTML markup to generate the resulting markup sent back to the browser via the response.

Routing within the ASP.NET MVC Framework serves two main purposes:

- It matches incoming requests and maps them to a Controller action.
- It constructs outgoing URLs that correspond to Controller actions.

Now that you understand something of URLs and routing, it's time to take a closer look at routing and how it's different from URL rewriting.

Routing Compared to URL Rewriting

To better understand routing, many developers compare it to URL rewriting. After all, both approaches are useful in creating a separation between the URL and the code that handles the URL, which can help create "pretty" URLs for search engine optimization (SEO) purposes. One key difference, though, is that URL rewriting represents a "page-centric" view of URLs. Most rewriting schemes with ASP.NET rewrite a URL for one page to be handled by another. For example, you might see

```
/product/bolts.aspx
```

rewritten as

```
/product/display.aspx?productid=111
```

Routing, on the other hand, takes a "resource-centric" view of URLs. In this case, the URL represents a resource (not necessarily a page) on the Web. With ASP.NET routing, this resource is a piece of code that executes when the incoming request matches the route. The route determines how the request is dispatched based on the characteristics of the URL — it doesn't rewrite the URL.

Another key difference is that routing also helps generate URLs using the same mapping rules that it uses to match incoming URLs. Another way to look at it is that ASP.NET routing is more like *bidirectional* URL rewriting. Where this comparison falls short is that ASP.NET routing never actually rewrites your URL. The request URL that the user makes in the browser is the same URL your application sees throughout the entire request lifecycle.

Defining Routes

Every ASP.NET MVC application needs at least one *route* to define how the application should handle requests, but usually ends up with at least a handful. Conceivably, a very complex application could have dozens of routes or more.

In this section, you look at how to define routes. Route definitions start with the URL, which specifies a pattern that the route will match. Along with the route URL, routes can also specify default values and constraints for the various parts of the URL, providing tight control over how the route matches incoming request URLs.

In this next part of the chapter, you start with an extremely simple route and build up from there.

Setting Route URLs

After you create a new ASP.NET MVC Web application project, take a quick look at the code in `Global.asax.cs`. You'll notice that the `Application_Start` method contains a call to a method named `RegisterRoutes` method. This method is where all routes for the application are registered.

Clear out the routes in there for now and replace them with this very simple route:

```
routes.MapRoute("simple", "{first}/{second}/{third}");
```

The simplest form of the `MapRoute` method takes in a name for the route and the URL pattern for the route. The name is discussed a bit later in this section. For now, focus on the URL pattern.

Notice that the route URL consists of several URL segments (a segment is everything between slashes but not including the slashes), each of which contains a placeholder delimited using curly braces. These placeholders are referred to as URL parameters.

This structure is a pattern-matching rule used to determine whether this route applies to an incoming request. In this example, this rule will match any URL with three segments because a URL parameter, by default, matches *any* nonempty value. When it matches a URL with three segments, the text in the first segment of that URL corresponds to the `{first}` URL parameter, the value in the second segment of that URL corresponds to the `{second}` URL parameter, and the value in the third segment corresponds to the `{third}` parameter.

You can name these parameters anything you want, as in this case. When a request comes in, routing parses the request URL into a dictionary (specifically a `RouteValueDictionary` accessible via the `RequestContext`), using the URL parameter names as the keys and subsections of the URL in the corresponding position as the values. When using routes in the context of an MVC application, certain parameter names carry a special purpose. Table 27-1 displays how the route just defined converts certain URLs into a `RouteValueDictionary`.

TABLE 27-1

URL	URL PARAMETER VALUES
/products/display/123	{first} = products {second} = display {third} = 123
/foo/bar/baz	{first} = foo {second} = bar {third} = baz
/a.b/c-d/e-f	{first} = "a.b" {second} = "c-d" {third} = "e-f"

If you actually make a request to the URLs listed in the preceding table, you may notice that your ASP.NET MVC application appears to be broken. Although you can define a route with any parameter names you want, certain special parameter names are required by ASP.NET MVC for the route to function correctly — `{controller}` and `{action}`.

The value of the `{controller}` parameter is used to instantiate a controller class to handle the request. By convention, MVC appends the suffix "`Controller`" to the `{controller}` value and attempts to locate a type of that name (case insensitively) that also inherits from the `System.Web.Mvc.IController` interface.

Going back to the simple route example, change it from

```
routes.MapRoute("simple", "{first}/{second}/{third}");
```

to

```
routes.MapRoute("simple", "{controller}/{action}/{id}");
```

so that it contains the special URL parameter names.

Now looking again at the first example in Table 27-1, you see that the request for `/products/display/123` is a request for a `{controller}` named `"Products"`. ASP.NET MVC takes that value and appends the "`Controller`" suffix to get a type name, `ProductsController`. If a type of that name that implements the `IController` interface exists, it is instantiated and used to handle the request.

The `{action}` parameter value is used to indicate which method of the controller to call to handle the current request. Note that this method invocation only applies to controller classes that inherit from the `System.Web.Mvc.Controller` base class. Continuing with the example of `/products/display/123`, the method of `ProductsController` that MVC will invoke is `Display`.

Note that the third URL in Table 27-1, although it is a valid route URL, will probably not match any real Controller and action, because it would attempt to instantiate a Controller named `a.bController` and call the method named `c-d`, which is not a valid method name.

Any route parameters other than `{controller}` and `{action}` are passed as parameters to the action method, if they exist. For example, assuming the following Controller:

```
public class ProductsController : Controller
{
  public ActionResult Display(int id)
  {
    //Do something
    return View();
  }
}
```

a request for `/products/display/123` would cause MVC to instantiate this class and call the `Display` method, passing in 123 for the `id`.

In the previous example with the route URL `{controller}/{action}/{id}`, each segment contains a URL parameter that takes up the entire segment. This doesn't have to be the case. Route URLs do allow for literal values within the segments. For example, if you are integrating MVC into an existing site and want all your MVC requests to be prefaced with the word *site*, you could do it as follows:

```
site/{controller}/{action}/{id}
```

This indicates that the first segment of a URL must start with *site* to match this request. Thus, `/site/products/display/123` matches this route, but `/products/display/123` does not match.

Having URL segments that intermix literals with parameters is even possible. The only restriction is that two consecutive URL parameters are not allowed. Thus

```
{language}-{country}/{controller}/{action}
{controller}.{action}.{id}
```

are valid route URLs, but

```
{controller}{action}/{id}
```

is not a valid route. No way exists for the route to know when the controller part of the incoming request URL ends and when the action part should begin.

Looking at some other samples (shown in Table 27-2) can help you see how the URL pattern corresponds to matching URLs.

TABLE 27-2

ROUTE URL PATTERN	EXAMPLES OF URLS THAT MATCH
`{controller}/{action}/{category}`	`/products/list/beverages` `/blog/posts/123`
`service/{action}-{format}`	`/service/display-xml`
`{reporttype}/{year}/{month}/{date}`	`/sales/2008/1/23`

Under the Hood: How Routes Tie Your URL to an Action

In the last section, you walked through how routes map to Controller actions within the MVC Framework. In this section, you take a look under the hood to get a better look at how this happens and get a better picture of where the dividing line is between routing and MVC.

One common misconception is that routing is just a feature of ASP.NET MVC. During the early stages of ASP.NET MVC implementation, this was true, but after a while, it became apparent that this was a more generally useful feature. The ASP.NET Dynamic Data team in particular was also interested in using routing inside Dynamic Data itself . At that point, routing became a more general-purpose feature that has neither internal knowledge of nor dependency on MVC.

One very outward bit of proof that routing is separate is not just that it's a separate assembly but that it lives in the `System.Web.Routing` namespace, and not a theoretical `System.Web.Mvc.Routing`. You can glean a lot of information from reading into namespaces.

The discussion here focuses on routing for IIS 7 integrated mode. Some slight differences exist when using routing with IIS 7 classic mode or IIS 6. When you are using the Visual Studio built-in Web server, the behavior is very similar to the IIS 7 Integrated mode.

The High-Level Request Routing Pipeline

All this talk about routing might be a lot of information for you to process. However, it's important to understand as routing really is your most powerful tool to control your application's URLs.

Broken down into its component parts, the routing pipeline consists of the following five high-level steps:

1. `UrlRoutingModule` attempts to match the current request with the routes registered in the `RouteTable`.
2. If a route matches, then the routing module grabs the `IRouteHandler` from that route.
3. The routing module calls `GetHandler` from the `IRouteHandler`, which returns an `IHttpHandler`. Recall that a typical ASP.NET Page (also known as `System.Web.UI.Page`) is nothing more than an `IHttpHandler`.
4. `ProcessRequest` is called on the `HttpHandler`, thus handing off the request to be handled.
5. In the case of MVC, the `IRouteHandler` is by default an instance of `MvcRouteHandler`, which in turn returns an `MvcHandler` (implement `IHttpHandler`). The `MvcHandler` is responsible for instantiating the correct Controller and calling the action method on that Controller.

Route Matching

At its core, routing is simply matching requests and extracting route data from that request and passing it to an `IRouteHandler`. The algorithm for route matching is very simple from a high-level perspective.

When a request comes in, the `UrlRoutingModule` iterates through each route in the `RouteCollection` accessed via `RouteTable.Routes` in order. It then asks each route, "Can you handle this request?" If the route answers "Yes I can!", then the route lookup is done and that route gets to handle the request.

The question of whether a route can handle a request is asked by calling the method `GetRouteData`. The method returns null if the current request is not a match for the route (in other words, no real conversation is going on between the module and routes).

RouteData

Recall that when you call `GetRouteData`, it returns an instance of `RouteData`. What exactly is `RouteData`? `RouteData` contains information about the route that matched a particular request, including context information for the specific request that matched.

Recall in the previous section that we showed a route with the following URL: `{foo}/{bar}/{baz}`. When a request for `/products/display/123` comes in, the route attempts to match the request. If it does match, it then creates a dictionary that contains information parsed from the URL. Specifically, it adds a key to the dictionary for each `url` parameter in the route URL.

So in the case of `{foo}/{bar}/{baz}`, you would expect the dictionary to contain at least three keys, `"foo"`, `"bar"`, `"baz"`. In the case of `/products/display/123`, the URL is used to supply values for these dictionary keys. In this case, `foo = products`, `bar = list`, and `baz = 123`.

CONTROLLERS

You might want to remember a quick definition: Controllers within the MVC pattern are responsible for responding to user input, often making changes to the Model in response to user input.

In this way, Controllers in the MVC pattern are concerned with the flow of the application, working with data coming in, and providing data going out to the relevant View.

Defining the Controller: The IController Interface

Among the core focuses of ASP.NET MVC are extensibility and flexibility. When building software with these goals in mind, leveraging abstraction as much as possible by using interfaces is important.

For a class to be a Controller in ASP.NET MVC, it must at minimum implement the `IController` interface, and by convention the name of the class must end with the suffix "`Controller`." The naming convention is actually quite important — and you'll find that many of these small rules are in play with ASP.NET MVC, which will make your life just a little bit easier by not making you define configuration settings and attributes. Ironically, the `IController` interface is quite simple given the power it is abstracting:

```
public interface IController
{
  void Execute(RequestContext requestContext);
}
```

Creating an IController is a simple process really: When a request comes in, the routing system identifies a Controller, and it calls the `Execute` method.

The `ControllerBase` class is an abstract base class that layers a bit more API surface on top of the `IController` interface. It provides the `TempData` and `ViewData` properties, and the `Execute` method of `ControllerBase` is responsible for creating the `ControllerContext`, which provides the MVC-specific context for the current request much the same way that an instance of `HttpContext` provides the context for ASP.NET in general (providing request and response, URL, and server information, among other elements).

This base class is still very lightweight and allows developers to provide extremely customized implementations for their own Controllers, while benefiting from the action filter infrastructure in ASP.NET MVC. What it doesn't provide is the ability to convert actions into method calls. That's where the `Controller` class comes in.

The Controller Class and Actions

In theory, you could build an entire site with classes that simply implement `ControllerBase` or `IController`, and it would work. Routing would look for an `IController` by name and then call `Execute`, and you would have yourself a very, very basic Web site.

This approach, however, is akin to working with ASP.NET using raw `HttpHandlers` — it would work, but you're left to reinvent the wheel and plumb the core framework logic yourself. Interestingly, ASP.NET MVC itself is layered on top of HTTP handlers, and overall there was no need to make internal plumbing changes to ASP.NET to implement MVC. Instead, the ASP.NET MVC team simply layered this new framework on top of existing ASP.NET extensibility points. The standard approach to writing a Controller is to have it inherit from the `System.Web.Mvc.Controller` abstract base class, which implements the `ControllerBase` base class. The `Controller` class is intended to serve as the base class for all Controllers, as it provides a lot of nice behaviors to Controllers that derive from it.

Now walk through another simple Controller example, but this time add a public method. To get started with this example, open the previous example and create a new Controller by right-clicking the Controllers folder and selecting Add ➪ Controller, then name it Simple2Controller. Next, add the following code:

```
using System;
using System.Web;
using System.Web.Mvc;
public class Simple2Controller : Controller
{
    public void Hello()
    {
    Response.Write("<h1>Hello World Again!</h1>");
    }
}
```

Press Ctrl+F5 (or Debug ➪ Run) and navigate to `/Simple2/Hello` in the browser. As before, this is not exactly breathtaking, but it is a bit more interesting. Notice that the URL in the address bar directly correlates to the action method of your Controller. If you recall from earlier, the default route for MVC breaks URLs into three main components: `/{controller}/{action}/{id}`.

Take a look at how that applies to this example. The `Simple2` portion of the URL corresponds to the Controller name. The MVC Framework appends the "`Controller`" suffix to the Controller name and locates your Controller class, `Simple2Controller`.

```
/Simple2/Hello
```

The last portion of the URL corresponds to the action. The framework locates a public method with this name and attempts to call the method.

Working with Parameters

You can add any number of public methods (which are called actions from here on out to keep with convention) to a Controller class, which will all be callable via this pattern. Actions may also contain parameters. Going back to the previous example, add a new action method that takes in a parameter:

```
public class Simple2Controller : Controller
{
    public void Goodbye(string name)
    {
    Response.Write("Goodbye " + HttpUtility.HtmlEncode(name));
    }
}
```

This method is callable via the URL:

```
/Simple2/Goodbye?name=World
```

Notice that you can pass in parameters to an action method by name via the query string. You can also pass in parameters via the URL segments, discoverable by position as defined in your routes. For example, the following URL is more aesthetically pleasing to many developers and Internet users:

```
/Simple2/Goodbye/World
```

Working with parameters passed by URL segment requires you to define how routing will identify these parameters in the URL. Fortunately, the default route (created for you when you click File ➪ New) is already set up for you and contains a common URL pattern:

```
{controller}/{action}/{id}.
```

Changing the action method signature a little bit (by renaming the parameter "`name`" to "`id`") like so:

```
public class Simple2Controller : Controller
{
    public void Goodbye(string id)
    {
    Response.Write("Goodbye " + HttpUtility.HtmlEncode(id));
    }
}
```

allows you to call that method using the "cleaner" URL, and routing will pass the parameter by structured URL instead of a query string parameter:

```
/Simple2/Goodbye/World
```

Working with Multiple Parameters

What if you have a method with more than one parameter? This scenario is very common and rest assured that you can still use query strings, but if you want to pass both parameters via the URL segments, you must define a new route specifically for this situation.

For example, suppose that you have an action method that calculates the distance between two points:

```
public void Distance(int x1, int y1, int x2, int y2)
{
    double xSquared = Math.Pow(x2 - x1, 2);
    double ySquared = Math.Pow(y2 - y1, 2);
    Response.Write(Math.Sqrt(xSquared + ySquared));
}
```

Using only the default route, the request would need to look like this:

```
/Simple2/Distance?x2=1&y2=2&x1=0&y1=0
```

You can improve on this situation a bit by defining a route that allows you to specify the parameters in a cleaner format. This code goes inside the `RegisterRoutes` methods within the `Global.asax.cs` file, and uses the `MapRoute` method to define a new route:

```
routes.MapRoute("distance",
    "Simple2/Distance/{x1},{y1}/{x2},{y2}",
    new { Controller = "Simple2", action = "Distance" }
);
```

Notice that you are using the comma character to separate x and y coordinates. Now this action method is callable via the URL:

```
/Simple2/Distance/0,0/1,2
```

The presence of commas in a URL might look strange, but routing is quite powerful!

So far you've used `Response.Write` in these little example methods, but this violates the principle of separation of concerns. It's really not the business of a controller to be managing the "views" of your data. That's something better handled by the "V" in MVC; that is, Views.

VIEWS

The View is responsible for providing the user interface (UI) to the user. It is given a reference to the Model, and it transforms that Model into a format ready to be presented to the user. In ASP.NET MVC, this consists of examining the `ViewDataDictionary` handed off to it by the Controller (accessed via the `ViewData` property) and transforming that to HTML.

In the strongly typed View case, which is covered in more depth in the section on "Strongly Typed Views" later in the chapter, the `ViewDataDictionary` has a strongly typed Model object that the View renders. This Model might represent the actual domain object, such as a `Product` instance, or it might be a presentation Model object specific to the View, such as a `ProductEditViewData` instance.

Take a quick look at an example of a View. The following code sample shows the Index View within the default ASP.NET MVC project template reformatted to fit the format of this book:

```
<%@ Page Language="C#" MasterPageFile="~/Views/Shared/Site.Master"
Inherits="System.Web.Mvc.ViewPage" %>
    <asp:Content ID="indexTitle" ContentPlaceHolderID="TitleContent" runat="server">
    Home Page
    </asp:Content>
    <asp:Content ID="indexContent" ContentPlaceHolderID="MainContent" runat="server">
    <h2><%= Html.Encode(ViewData["Message"]) %></h2>
    <p>
    To learn more about ASP.NET MVC visit <a href="http://asp.net/mvc"
    title="ASP.NET MVC Website">http://asp.net/mvc</a>.
    </p>
</asp:Content>
```

This is an extremely simple example of a View, but it's useful for pointing out some of the key details of Views in ASP.NET MVC. One of the first things you'll notice is that on the surface, it looks just like a Web form. ASP.NET MVC allows you to swap out different View engines, but the default View engine is a `WebFormViewEngine`.

Technically, this is not a Web form because it doesn't include the `<form runat="server">` tag; it's really just an ASP.NET page. Views in ASP.NET MVC derive from a common base class, `System.Web.Mvc.ViewPage`, which itself derives from `System.Web.UI.Page`. Strongly typed Views derive from the generic `ViewPage<T>`.

In following with the principle of separation of concerns, Views should not contain application and business logic. In fact, they should contain as little code as possible. Although it's perfectly acceptable for a View to contain View logic, Views are generally the most difficult part of the application to test in an automated fashion, and they therefore benefit from having very little code.

Specifying a View

So far, this chapter has discussed what a View does and doesn't do, but it hasn't addressed how to specify the View that should render the output for a specific action. It turns out that this task is very easy when you follow the conventions implicit in the framework.

When you create a new project template, notice that the project contains a "Views" directory structured in a very specific manner (see Figure 27-9).

By convention, the Views directory contains a folder per Controller, with the same name as the Controller, sans the "`Controller`" suffix. Within each Controller folder, there's a View file for each action method, named the same as the action method. This provides the basis for how Views are associated to an action method.

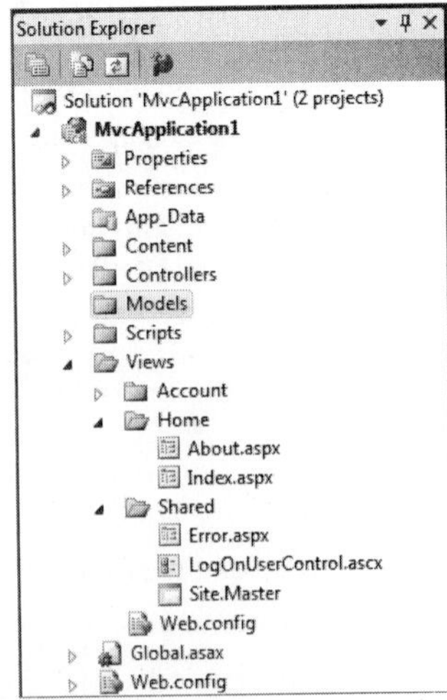

FIGURE 27-9

For example, an action method can return a `ViewResult` via the `View` method like so:

```
public class HomeController : Controller
{
    public ActionResult Index()
    {
        ViewData["Title"] = "Home Page";
        ViewData["Message"] = "Welcome to ASP.NET MVC!";
        return View();
    }
}
```

This method ought to look familiar; it's the `Index` action method of `HomeController` in the default project template. Because the View name was not specified, the `ViewResult` returned by this method looks for a View named the same as the action name in the */Views/ControllerName* directory. The View selected in this case would be `/Views/Home/Index.aspx`.

As with most things in ASP.NET MVC, this convention can be overridden. Suppose that you want the Index action to render a different View. You could supply a different View name like so:

```
public ActionResult Index()
{
    ViewData["Title"] = "Home Page";
    ViewData["Message"] = "Welcome to ASP.NET MVC!";
    return View("NotIndex");
}
```

In this case, it will still look in the `/Views/Home` directory, but choose `NotIndex.aspx` as the View. In some situations, you might even want to specify a View in a completely different directory structure.

You can use the tilde syntax to provide the full path to the View like so:

```
public ActionResult Index()
{
    ViewData["Title"] = "Home Page";
    ViewData["Message"] = "Welcome to ASP.NET MVC!";
    return View("~/Some/Other/View.aspx");
}
```

When using the tilde syntax, you must supply the file extension of the View because this bypasses the View engine's internal lookup mechanism for finding Views.

Strongly Typed Views

Suppose that you have a list of Product instances you want to display in a View. One means of doing this is to simply add the products to the View data dictionary and iterate them over the View.

For example, the code in your Controller action might look like this:

```
public ActionResult List()
{
    var products = new List<Product>();
        for(int i = 0; i < 10; i++)
        {
            products.Add(new Product {ProductName = "Product " + i});
        }
    ViewData["Products"] = products;
    return View();
}
```

In your View, you can then iterate and display the products like so:

```
<ul>
    <% foreach(Product p in (ViewData["Products"] as IEnumerable<Product>)) {%>
        <li><%= Html.Encode(p.ProductName) %></li>
    <% } %>
</ul>
```

Because the `ViewData` indexer returns an object, casting `ViewData["Products"]` to an `IEnumerable<Product>` before enumerating it is necessary. The code would be cleaner if you could provide the View with the type for the Model being sent in. This is where strongly typed Views come in.

In the Controller method, you can specify the Model via an overload of the `View` method whereby you pass in the Model:

```
public ActionResult List()
{
    var products = new List<Product>();
    for(int i = 0; i < 10; i++)
        {
            products.Add(new Product {ProductName = "Product " + i});
        }
    return View(products);
}
```

Behind the scenes, this sets the value of the `ViewData.Model` property to the value passed into the `View` method. The next step is to change the type of the View to inherit from `ViewPage<T>`. The View really has no business having a code-behind file in the MVC Model. In fact, by default, no code-behind files exist for Views in ASP.NET MVC. If you want strongly typed Views, just add the type to derive from in the `@Page` directive like this:

```
<%@ Page Language="C#" MasterPageFile="~/Views/Shared/Site.Master"
Inherits="System.Web.Mvc.ViewPage<IEnumerable<Product>>" %>
```

This is the preferred way to have strongly typed Views. Now within the markup for the View, you can access the strongly typed `ViewData.Model` property, with full IntelliSense support.

```
<ul>
    <% foreach(Product p in Model) {%>
        <li><%= Html.Encode(p.ProductName) %></li>
    <% } %>
</ul>
```

Using HTML Helper Methods

One of the traits of the ASP.NET MVC Framework often touted is that it puts you in full control of your application, including the HTML markup. Many announce this as a benefit of the framework. After all, full control is good, right? But it's really a characteristic of the framework that's only good or bad depending on the circumstance.

There are times when you don't want to have control over the markup. You would rather drop a control and have it figure out the markup because you don't care how it looks. Other times, you want to have absolute control over the markup. Being in control is great, but it also means more responsibility. You are now responsible for outputting markup that would have otherwise been handled by a server control in the Web forms world.

HTML helpers provide a middle ground. These are methods included with the framework that help with rendering markup for very common cases. In most cases, they handle common mistakes such as forgetting to encode attribute values and so on.

HtmlHelper Class and Extension Methods

The `ViewPage` class has an `HtmlHelper` property named `Html`. When you look at the methods of `HtmlHelper`, you'll notice they are rather sparse. This property is really an anchor point for attaching extension methods. When you import the `System.Web.Mvc.Html` namespace (imported by default in the default template), the `Html` property suddenly lights up with a bunch of helper methods.

In the screenshot in Figure 27-10, the extension methods are denoted by the blue down arrow (gray in the dialog shown here).

One benefit of the HtmlHelper-style approach is that, as they are just regular extension methods, if you don't like the helper methods included with the framework, you can remove this namespace and attach your own HTML helper extension methods. Likewise, it provides a convenient conventional place to add your own helper methods by simply writing extension methods of the HtmlHelper class.

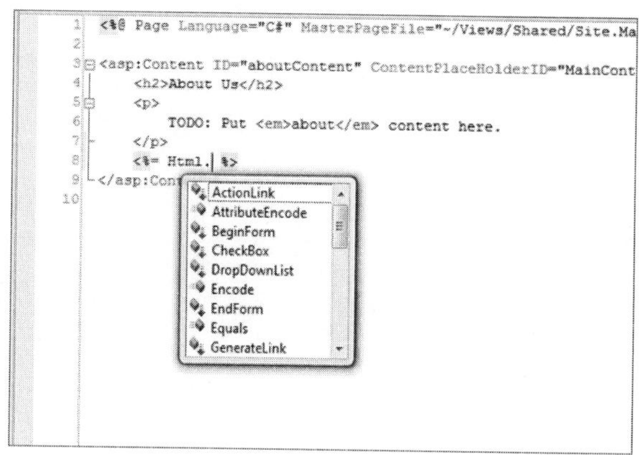

FIGURE 27-10

All helpers share a few common patterns that are worth calling out now:

- All helper's attributes encode attribute values.
- All helper's HTML encode values they display, such as link text.
- Helpers that accept a RouteValueDictionary have a corresponding overload that allows you to specify an anonymous object as the dictionary.
- Likewise, helpers that accept an IDictionary<string, object> used to specify HTML attributes, have a corresponding overload that allows you to specify an anonymous object as the dictionary.
- Helpers used to render form fields will automatically look up their current value in the ModelState dictionary. The name argument to the helper is used as the key to the dictionary.
- If the ModelState contains an error, the form helper associated with that error will render a CSS class of "input-validation-error" in addition to any explicitly specified CSS classes. The default stylesheet, style.css, included in the project template contains styling for this class.

Views and their ViewEngines have a very specific, constrained purpose. They exist to take data passed to them from the Controller, and they generate formatted output, usually HTML. Other than those simple responsibilities, or "concerns," as the developer, you are empowered to achieve the goals of your View in any way that makes you happy.

SUMMARY

The ASP.NET Web forms developer will need to get used to many differences when working with ASP.NET MVC versus Web forms. In many ways, working with ASP.NET MVC will feel like "taking a step back 10 years" to classic ASP — especially when working with the UI and Views.

For some, this is a welcome change and a breath of fresh air; for others, it just doesn't work. It does take some getting used to, but in the end, the core ASP.NET functionality and the .NET Framework in general are there to support you.

Ultimately, the most important thing to remember is that ASP.NET Web forms and ASP.NET MVC sit on top of ASP.NET proper. Think of it as ASP.NET > Web forms and ASP.NET > ASP.NET MVC. There's so much underneath both techniques that you can use either or both without fear. Many people find a hybrid model works for them, or they use a hybrid as they move from one model to the other. Pick the model that makes you feel most productive and run with it.

Be sure to download the free 200-page PDF tutorial that shows you how to create a complete ASP.NET MVC application at http://tinyurl.com/aspnetmvc. Again, for more in-depth coverage of ASP.NET MVC, check out *Professional ASP.NET MVC 1.0* from Wiley (2009). There are hundreds of resources, videos, starter kits and very active forums at http://www.asp.net/mvc to help you get started.

28

Using Business Objects

WHAT'S IN THIS CHAPTER?

- .NET interoperability
- Working with managed and unmanaged objects
- COM and ASP.NET

One of the best practices in programming is to separate your application into workable and separate components — also known as *business objects*. This makes your applications far easier to manage and enables you to achieve the goal of code reuse because you can share these components among different parts of the same application or between entirely separate applications.

Using business components enables you to build your ASP.NET applications using a true three-tier model where the business tier is in the middle between the presentation and data tiers. In addition, using business objects enables you to use multiple languages within your ASP.NET applications. Business objects can be developed in one programming language while the code used for the presentation logic is developed in another.

If you are moving any legacy applications or aspects of these applications to an ASP.NET environment, you might find that you need to utilize various COM components. This chapter shows you how to use both .NET and COM components in your ASP.NET pages and code.

This chapter also explains how you can mingle old ActiveX (COM) DLLs with new .NET components. So when all is said and done, you should feel somewhat relieved. You will see that you have not wasted all the effort you put into building componentized applications using the "latest" ActiveX technologies.

USING BUSINESS OBJECTS IN ASP.NET 4

Chapter 1 of this book provides an introduction to using .NET business objects within your ASP.NET 4 applications. ASP.NET includes a folder, App_Code, which you can place within your ASP.NET applications to hold all your .NET business objects. The nice thing about the App_Code folder is that you can simply place your uncompiled .NET objects (such as `Calculator.vb` or `Calculator.cs`) into this folder and ASP.NET takes care of compiling the objects into usable .NET business objects.

Chapter 1 also shows how you can place within the App_Code folder multiple custom folders that enable you to use business objects written in different programming languages. Using this method enables ASP.NET to compile each business object into the appropriate DLLs to be used by your ASP.NET applications.

Creating Precompiled .NET Business Objects

Even though the App_Code folder is there for your use, you might choose instead to precompile your business objects into DLLs to be used by your ASP.NET applications. This method was utilized prior to ASP.NET 2.0 and is still a method that is available today. You also might not have a choice if you are receiving your .NET business objects only as DLLs.

For now, look at how to create a simple .NET business object using Visual Studio 2010. The first step is not to create an ASP.NET project but to choose File ➪ New ➪ Project from the Visual Studio menu. This launches the New Project dialog. From this dialog, select Class Library as the project type and name the project `Calculator` (see Figure 28-1).

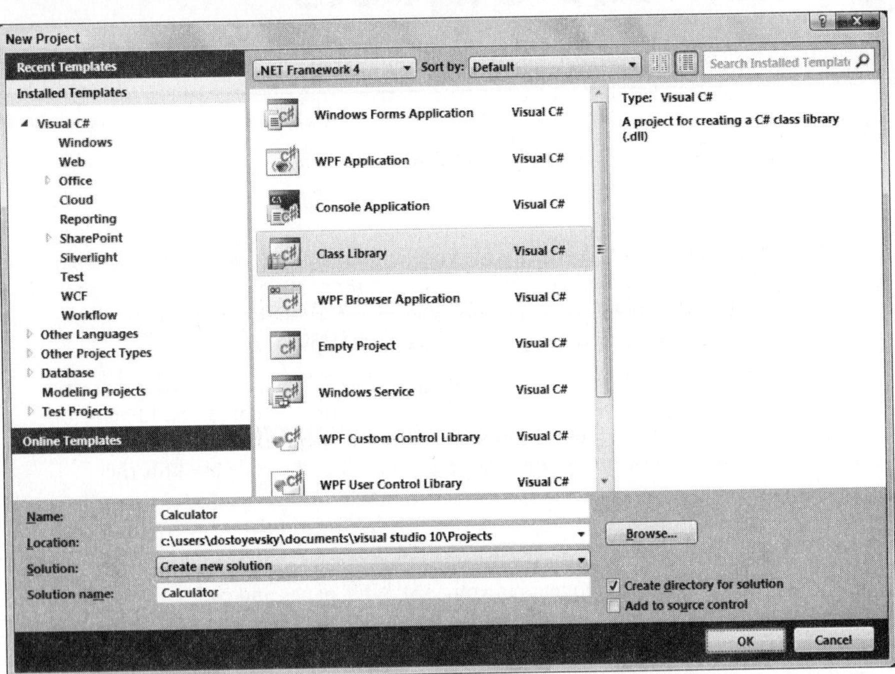

FIGURE 28-1

Using the `Class1.vb` or `Class1.cs` file that is created in the project for you, modify the class to be a simple calculator with `Add`, `Subtract`, `Multiply`, and `Divide` functions. This is illustrated using C# in Figure 28-2.

One point to pay attention to when you build your .NET components is the assembly's metadata that is stored along with the assembly. Looking at the project's properties, click the Application tab (the first tab available). Note that you can get to the project's properties by right-clicking on the project title in the Solution Explorer. On this tab's page is a button labeled Assembly Information. Clicking this button gives you a dialog where you can put in the entire business object's metadata, including the assembly's versioning information (see Figure 28-3).

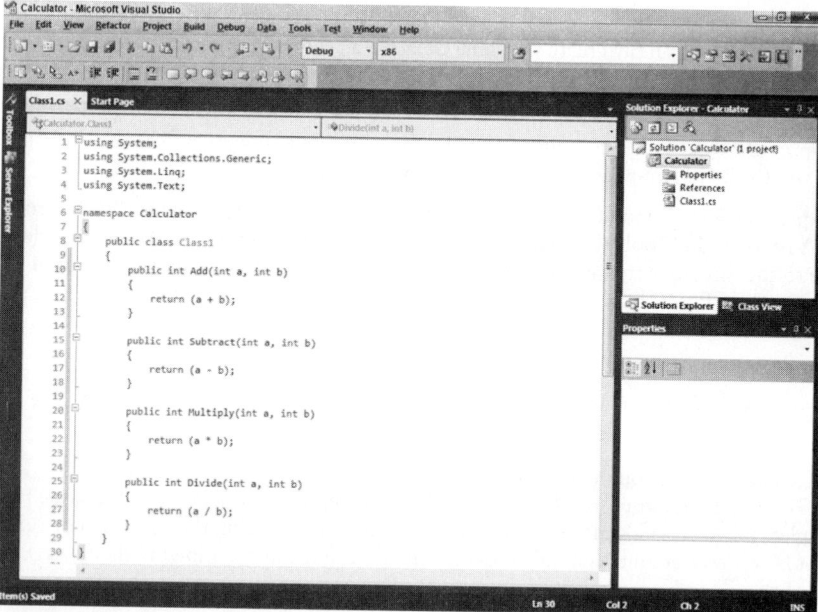

FIGURE 28-2

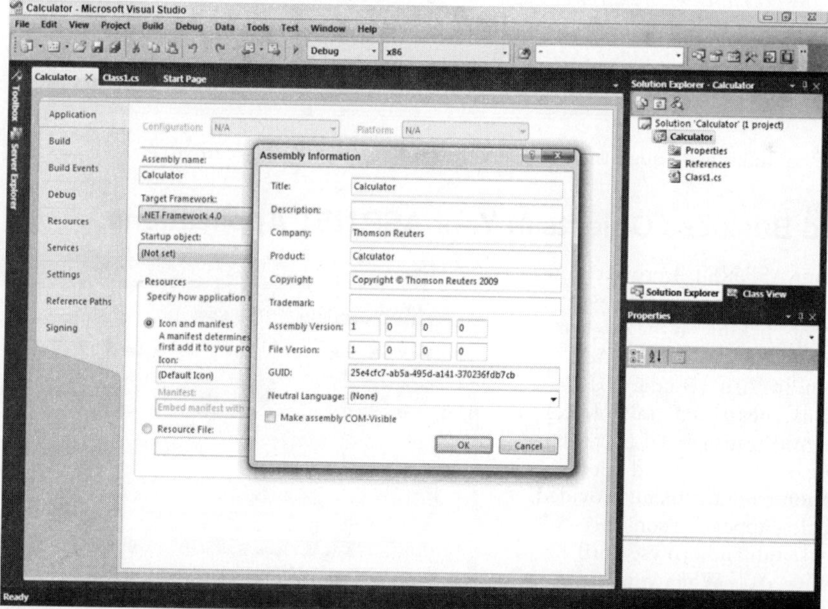

FIGURE 28-3

You are now ready to compile the business object into a usable object by choosing Build ➪ Build Calculator from the Visual Studio menu. This process compiles everything contained in this solution down to a `Calculator.dll` file. You can find this DLL in your project's `bin\debug` folder, which by default, is `C:\Users\[user]\Documents\Visual Studio 10\Projects\Calculator\Calculator\bin\Debug\Calculator.dll`, when using Windows 7.

Besides using Visual Studio 2010 to build and compile your business objects into DLLs, you can do it yourself manually. In Notepad, you simply create the same class file as shown in Figure 28-2 and save the file as `Calculator.vb` or `Calculator.cs` depending on the language you are using. After saving the file, you must compile the class into an assembly (a DLL).

The .NET framework provides you with a compiler for each of the targeted languages. This book focuses on the Visual Basic 2010 and C# 2010 compilers that come with the framework.

To compile this class, open the Visual Studio 2010 Command Prompt found at All Programs ➪ Microsoft Visual Studio 2010 ➪ Visual Studio Tools ➪ Visual Studio 2010 Command Prompt. From the provided DOS prompt, navigate to the directory that is holding your `Calculator` class (an example navigation command is `cd c:\My Files`). From the DOS prompt, type the following command if you are using the Visual Basic compiler:

```
vbc /t: library Calculator.vb
```

If your class is in C#, you use the following command:

```
csc /t:library Calculator.cs
```

As stated, each language uses its own compiler. Visual Basic uses the `vbc.exe` compiler found at `C:\Windows\Microsoft.NET\Framework\v4.0.xxxxx\`. The C# compiler, `csc.exe`, is in the same folder. In the preceding examples, `/t:library` states that you are interested in compiling the `Calculator.vb` (or `.cs`) class file into a DLL and not an executable (`.exe`), which is the default. Following the `t:/library` command is the name of the file to be compiled.

You can give the compiler many different commands — even more than Visual Studio 2010 offers. For example, if you want to make references to specific DLLs in your assembly, you must add commands such as `/r:system.data.dll`. To get a full list of all the compiler options, check out the MSDN documentation.

After you have run the commands through the compiler, the DLL is created and ready to go.

Using Precompiled Business Objects in Your ASP.NET Applications

To use any DLLs in your ASP.NET 4 project, you must create a Bin folder in the root directory of your application by right-clicking on the project within the Solution Explorer and selecting Add ASP.NET Folder ➪ Bin. In Visual Studio 2010, the `Bin` directory's icon appears as a gray folder with a gear next to it. Add your new DLL to this folder by right-clicking on the folder and selecting the Add Reference option from the menu provided. The Add Reference dialog appears. From this dialog, select the Browse tab and browse until you find the `Calculator.dll`. When you find it, highlight the DLL and click OK to add it to the Bin folder of your project. Figure 28-4 shows the Add Reference dialog.

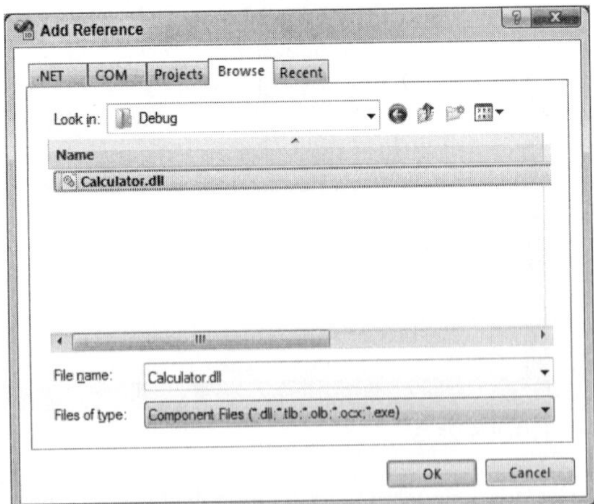

FIGURE 28-4

`Calculator.dll` is added to your project and is now accessible by the entire project. This means that you now have access to all the functions exposed through this interface. Figure 28-5 shows an example of how IntelliSense makes exploring this .NET component easier than ever.

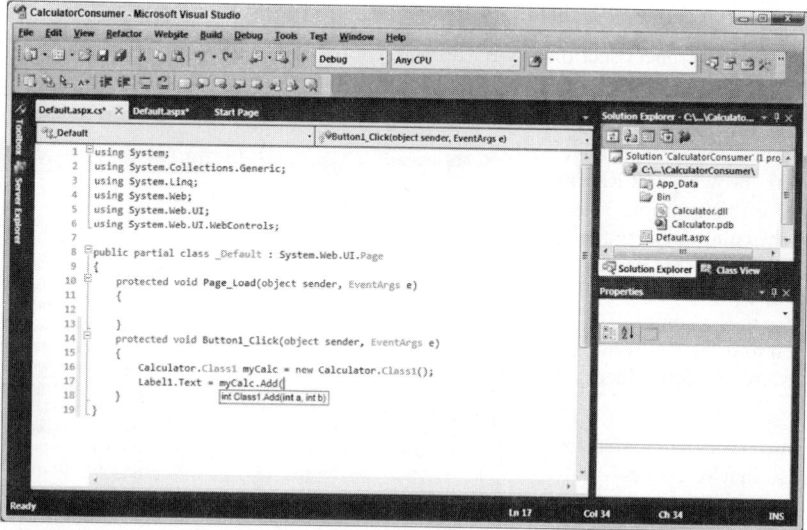

FIGURE 28-5

As you can see, creating .NET components and using them in your ASP.NET applications is rather simple. Next, it's time to take a look at using COM components.

COM INTEROP: USING COM WITHIN .NET

Microsoft knows that every one of its legions of developers out there would be quite disappointed if they couldn't use the thousands of COM controls that it has built, maintained, and improved over the years. Microsoft knows that nobody would get up and walk away from these controls to a purely .NET world.

To this end, Microsoft has provided us with COM Interoperability. COM Interop (for short) is a technology that enables .NET to wrap the functionality of a COM object with the interface of a .NET component so that your .NET code can communicate with the COM object without having to use COM techniques and interfaces in your code.

Figure 28-6 illustrates the Runtime Callable Wrapper, the middle component that directs traffic between the .NET code and the COM component.

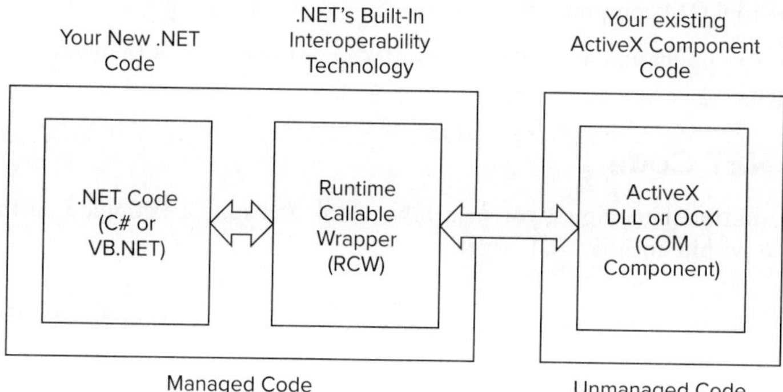

FIGURE 28-6

The Runtime Callable Wrapper

The Runtime Callable Wrapper, or RCW, is the magic piece of code that enables interaction to occur between .NET and COM. One RCW is created for each COM component in your project. To create an RCW for a COM component, you can use Visual Studio 2010.

To add an ActiveX DLL to the References section of your project, choose Website ➪ Add Reference or choose the Add Reference menu item that appears when you right-click the root node of your project in the Solution Explorer.

The Add Reference dialog box appears with five tabs: .NET, COM, Projects, Browse, and Recent, as shown in Figure 28-7. For this example, select the COM tab and locate the component that you want to add to your .NET project. After you have located the component, highlight the item and click OK to add a reference to the component to your project. You can then find the newly added component inside a newly created Bin folder in your project.

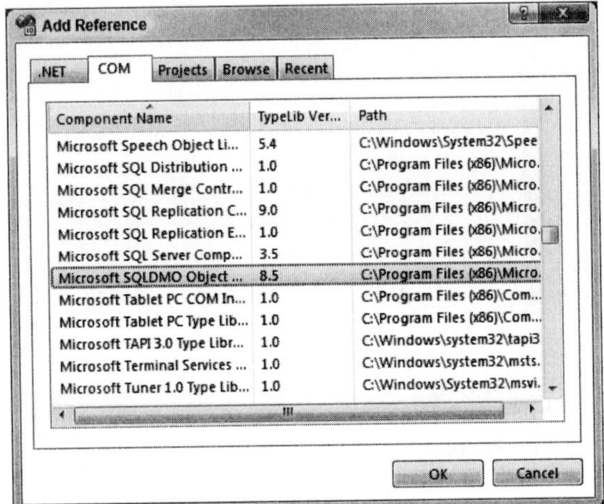

FIGURE 28-7

Your Interop library is automatically created for you from the ActiveX DLL that you told Visual Studio 2010 to use. This Interop library is the RCW component customized for your ActiveX control, as shown previously in Figure 28-6. The name of the Interop file is simply `Interop.OriginalName.DLL`.

You can also create the RCW files manually instead of doing it through Visual Studio 2010. In the .NET framework, you will find a method to create RCW Interop files for controls manually through a command-line tool called the Type Library Importer. You invoke the Type Library Importer by using the `tlbimp.exe` executable.

For example, to create the Interop library for the SQLDMO object used earlier, start up a Visual Studio 2010 Command Prompt from the Microsoft Visual Studio 2010 ➪ Visual Studio Tools group within your Start menu. From the comment prompt, type

```
tlbimp sqldmo.dll /out:sqldmoex.dll
```

In this example, the `/out:` parameter specifies the name of the RCW Interop library to be created. If you omit this parameter, you get the same name that Visual Studio would generate for you.

The Type Library Importer is useful when you are not using Visual Studio 2010 as your development environment, if you want to have more control over the assemblies that get created for you, or if you are automating the process of connecting to COM components.

The Type Library Importer is a wrapper application around the `TypeLibConvertor` class of the `System.Runtime.InteropServices` namespace.

Using COM Objects in ASP.NET Code

To continue working through some additional examples, you next take a look at a simple example of using a COM object written in Visual Basic 6 within an ASP.NET page.

In the first step, you create an ActiveX DLL that you can use for the upcoming examples. Add the Visual Basic 6 code shown in Listing 28-1 to a class called `NameFunctionsClass` and compile it as an ActiveX DLL called `NameComponent.dll`.

Available for download on Wrox.com

LISTING 28-1: VB6 code for ActiveX DLL, NameComponent.DLL

```
Option Explicit

Private m_sFirstName As String
Private m_sLastName As String

Public Property Let FirstName(Value As String)
  m_sFirstName = Value
End Property

Public Property Get FirstName() As String
  FirstName = m_sFirstName
End Property

Public Property Let LastName(Value As String)
  m_sLastName = Value
End Property

Public Property Get LastName() As String
  LastName = m_sLastName
End Property

Public Property Let FullName(Value As String)
  m_sFirstName = Split(Value, " ")(0)
  If (InStr(Value, " ") > 0) Then
    m_sLastName = Split(Value, " ")(1)
  Else
    m_sLastName = ""
  End If
End Property

Public Property Get FullName() As String
  FullName = m_sFirstName + " " + m_sLastName
End Property

Public Property Get FullNameLength() As Long
  FullNameLength = Len(Me.FullName)
End Property
```

Now that you have created an ActiveX DLL to use in your ASP.NET pages, the next step is to create a new ASP.NET project using Visual Studio 2010. Replace the HTML code in the `Default.aspx` file with the HTML code shown in Listing 28-2. This code adds a number of text boxes and labels to the HTML page, as well as the Visual Basic or C# code for the functionality.

Available for download on Wrox.com

LISTING 28-2: Using NameComponent.dll

```
<%@ Page Language="VB" %>

<script runat="server">
  Protected Sub AnalyzeName_Click(ByVal sender As Object,
     ByVal e As System.EventArgs)

    Dim Name As New NameComponent.NameFunctionsClass()
```

continues

LISTING 28-2 *(continued)*

```
    If (FirstName.Text.Length > 0) Then
      Name.FirstName = FirstName.Text
    End If

    If (LastName.Text.Length > 0) Then
      Name.LastName = LastName.Text
    End If

    If (FullName.Text.Length > 0) Then
      Name.FullName = FullName.Text
    End If

    FirstName.Text = Name.FirstName
    LastName.Text = Name.LastName
    FullName.Text = Name.FullName
    FullNameLength.Text = Name.FullNameLength.ToString

  End Sub
</script>

<html xmlns="http://www.w3.org/1999/xhtml" >
  <head runat="server">
     <title>Using COM Components</title>
  </head>
  <body>
    <form id="form1" runat="server">
      <p>
        <asp:Label ID="Label1" runat="server">First Name:</asp:Label>
         
        <asp:TextBox ID="FirstName" runat="server"></asp:TextBox>
      </p>
      <p>
        <asp:Label ID="Label2" runat="server">Last Name:</asp:Label>
         
        <asp:TextBox ID="LastName" runat="server"></asp:TextBox>
      </p>
      <p>
        <asp:Label ID="Label3" runat="server">Full Name:</asp:Label>
         
        <asp:TextBox ID="FullName" runat="server"></asp:TextBox>
      </p>
      <p>
        <asp:Label ID="Label4" runat="server">Full Name Length:</asp:Label>
         
        <asp:Label ID="FullNameLength" runat="server"
         Font-Bold="True">0</asp:Label>
      </p>
      <p>
        <asp:Button ID="AnalyzeName" runat="server"
         OnClick="AnalyzeName_Click" Text="Analyze Name"></asp:Button>
      </p>
    </form>
  </body>
</html>
```

C#

```
<%@ Page Language="C#" %>

<script runat="server">
  protected void AnalyzeName_Click(object sender, System.EventArgs e)
```

```
  {
    NameComponent.NameFunctionsClass Name =
        new NameComponent.NameFunctionsClass();

    if (FirstName.Text.Length > 0)
    {
      string firstName = FirstName.Text.ToString();
      Name.set_FirstName(ref firstName);
    }

    if (LastName.Text.Length > 0)
    {
      string lastName = LastName.Text.ToString();
      Name.set_LastName(ref lastName);
    }

    if (FullName.Text.Length > 0)
    {
      string fullName = FullName.Text.ToString();
      Name.set_FullName(ref fullName);
    }

    FirstName.Text = Name.get_FirstName();
    LastName.Text = Name.get_LastName();
    FullName.Text = Name.get_FullName();
    FullNameLength.Text = Name.FullNameLength.ToString();
  }
</script>
```

Now you must add the reference to the ActiveX DLL that you created in the previous step. To do so, follow these steps:

1. Right-click your project in the Solution Explorer dialog.
2. Select the Add Reference menu item.
3. In the Add Reference dialog box, select the Browse tab.
4. Locate the `NameComponent.dll` object by browsing to its location.
5. Click OK to add `NameComponent.dll` to the list of selected components and close the dialog box.

If you are not using Visual Studio 2010 or code-behind pages, you can still add a reference to your COM control by creating the RCW manually using the Type Library Converter and then placing an `Imports` *statement (VB) or* `using` *statement (C#) in the page.*

After you have selected your component using the Add Reference dialog, an RCW file is created for the component and added to your application.

That's all there is to it! Simply run the application to see the COM interoperability layer in action.

Figure 28-8 shows the ASP.NET page that you created. When the Analyze Name button is clicked, the fields in the First Name, Last Name, and Full Name text boxes are sent to the RCW to be passed to the `NameComponent.DLL` ActiveX component. Data is retrieved in the same manner to repopulate the text boxes and to indicate the length of the full name.

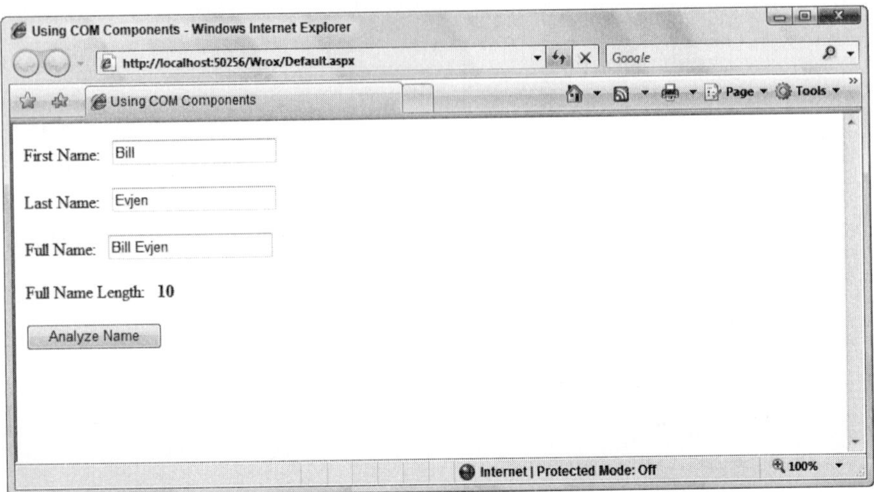

FIGURE 28-8

Accessing Tricky COM Members in C#

Sometimes, some members of COM objects do not expose themselves properly to C#. In the preceding examples, the `String` properties did not expose themselves, but the `Long` property (`FullNameLength`) did.

You know when there is a problem because, although you can see the property, you cannot compile the application. For example, instead of the code shown in Listing 28-2 for C#, use the following piece of code to set the `FirstName` property of the `NameComponent.dll` ActiveX component:

```
if (FirstName.Text.Length > 0)
  Name.FirstName = FirstName.Text.ToString();
```

When you try to compile this code, you get the following error:

```
c:\inetpub\wwwroot\wrox\Default.aspx.cs(67): Property, indexer, or event
'FirstName' is not supported by the language; try directly calling accessor methods
'NameComponent.NameFunctionsClass.get_FirstName()' or
'NameComponent.NameFunctionsClass.set_FirstName(ref string)'
```

The `FirstName` property seems to be fine. It shows up in IntelliSense, but you can't use it. Instead, you must use `set_FirstName` (and `get_FirstName` to read). These methods do not show up in IntelliSense, but rest assured, they exist.

Furthermore, these methods expect a `ref string` parameter rather than a `String`. In the example from Listing 28-2, two steps are used to do this properly. First, `String` is assigned to a local variable, and then the variable is passed to the method using `ref`.

Releasing COM Objects Manually

One of the great things about .NET is that it has its own garbage collection — it can clean up after itself. This is not always the case when using COM interoperability, however. .NET has no way of knowing when to release a COM object from memory because it does not have the built-in garbage collection mechanism that .NET relies on.

Because of this limitation, you should release COM objects from memory as soon as possible using the `ReleaseComObject` class of the `System.Runtime.InteropServices.Marshal` class:

C#

```
System.Runtime.InteropServices.Marshal.ReleaseComObject(Object);
```

Note that if you attempt to use this object again before it goes out of scope, you would raise an exception.

Error Handling

Error handling in .NET uses exceptions instead of the HRESULT values used by Visual Basic 6 applications. Luckily, the RCW does most of the work to convert between the two.

Take, for example, the code shown in Listing 28-3. In this example, a user-defined error is raised if the numerator or the denominator is greater than 1000. Also notice that we are not capturing a divide-by-zero error. Notice what happens when the ActiveX component raises the error on its own.

Begin this example by compiling the code listed in Listing 28-3 into a class named `DivideClass` within an ActiveX component called `DivideComponent.dll`.

LISTING 28-3: Raising errors in VB6

Available for download on Wrox.com

```
Public Function DivideNumber(Numerator As Double, _
                             Denominator As Double) As Double

  If ((Numerator > 1000) Or (Denominator > 1000)) Then
      Err.Raise vbObjectError + 1, _
                "DivideComponent:Divide.DivideNumber", _
                "Numerator and denominator both have to " + _
                "be less than or equal to 1000."

  End If

  DivideNumber = Numerator / Denominator

End Function
```

Next, create a new ASP.NET project; add a reference to the `DivideComponent.dll` (invoking Visual Studio 2010 to create its own copy of the RCW). Remember, you can also do this manually by using the `tlbimp` executable.

Now add the code shown in Listing 28-4 to an ASP.NET page.

LISTING 28-4: Error handling in .NET

Available for download on Wrox.com

VB

```
<%@ Page Language="VB" %>

<script runat="server">
  Protected Sub Calculate_Click(ByVal sender As Object,
     ByVal e As System.EventArgs)

    Dim Divide As New DivideComponent.DivideClass()

    Try
       Answer.Text = Divide.DivideNumber(Numerator.Text, Denominator.Text)
    Catch ex As Exception
       Answer.Text = ex.Message.ToString()
    End Try

    System.Runtime.InteropServices.Marshal.ReleaseComObject(Divide)

  End Sub
</script>

<html xmlns="http://www.w3.org/1999/xhtml">
  <head runat="server">
     <title>Using COM Components</title>
  </head>
```

continues

LISTING 28-4 *(continued)*

```
<body>
  <form id="form1" runat="server">
    <p>
      <asp:Label ID="Label1" runat="server">Numerator:</asp:Label>
       
      <asp:TextBox ID="Numerator" runat="server"></asp:TextBox>
    </p>
    <p>
      <asp:Label ID="Label2" runat="server">Denominator:</asp:Label>
       
      <asp:TextBox ID="Denominator" runat="server"></asp:TextBox>
    </p>
    <p>
      <asp:Label ID="Label3" runat="server">
       Numerator divided by Denominator:</asp:Label>
       
      <asp:Label ID="Answer" runat="server" Font-Bold="True">0</asp:Label>
    </p>
    <p>
      <asp:Button ID="Calculate"
       runat="server"
       OnClick="Calculate_Click"
       Text="Calculate">
      </asp:Button>
    </p>
  </form>
</body>
</html>
```

C#

```
<%@ Page Language="C#" %>

<script runat="server">
  protected void Calculate_Click(object sender, System.EventArgs e)
  {

    DivideComponent.DivideClass myDivide = new DivideComponent.DivideClass();

    try
    {
      double numerator = double.Parse(Numerator.Text);
      double denominator = double.Parse(Denominator.Text);
      Answer.Text = myDivide.DivideNumber(ref numerator,
         ref denominator).ToString();
    }

    catch (Exception ex)
    {
      Answer.Text = ex.Message.ToString();
    }

    System.Runtime.InteropServices.Marshal.ReleaseComObject(myDivide);

  }
</script>
```

The code in Listing 28-4 passes the user-entered values for the `Numerator` and `Denominator` to the `DivideComponent.dll` ActiveX component for it to divide. Running the application with invalid data gives the result shown in Figure 28-9.

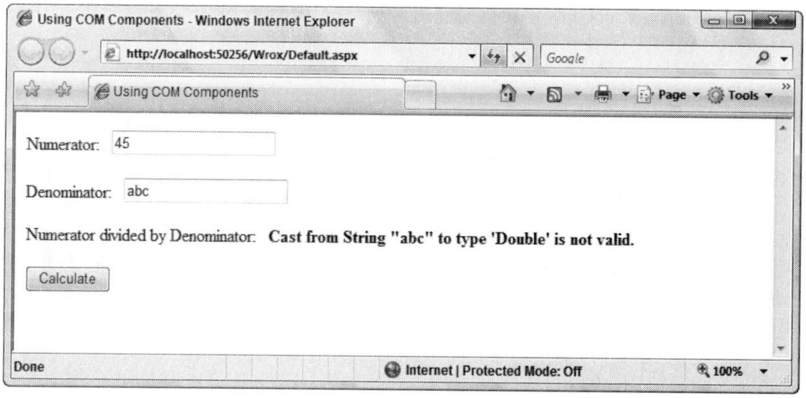

FIGURE 28-9

Depending on the language that you are using to run the ASP.NET application, you will see different values for different sets of data. For valid inputs, you will always see the correct result, of course, and for any input that is over 1000, you see the Visual Basic 6 appointed error description of `Numerator and denominator both have to be less than or equal to 1000.`

However, for invalid strings, Visual Basic 2010 reports `Cast from string "abc" to type 'Double' is not valid.` whereas C# reports `Input string was not in a correct format.` For a divide by zero, they both report `Divide by Zero` because the error is coming directly from the Visual Basic 6 runtime.

Deploying COM Components with .NET Applications

Deploying COM components with your .NET applications is very easy, especially when compared to just deploying ActiveX controls. Two scenarios are possible when deploying .NET applications with COM components:

- Using private assemblies
- Using shared or public assemblies

Private Assemblies

Installing all or parts of the ActiveX component local to the .NET application is considered installing private assemblies. In this scenario, each installation of your .NET application on the same machine has, at least, its own copy of the Interop library for the ActiveX component you are referencing, as shown in Figure 28-10.

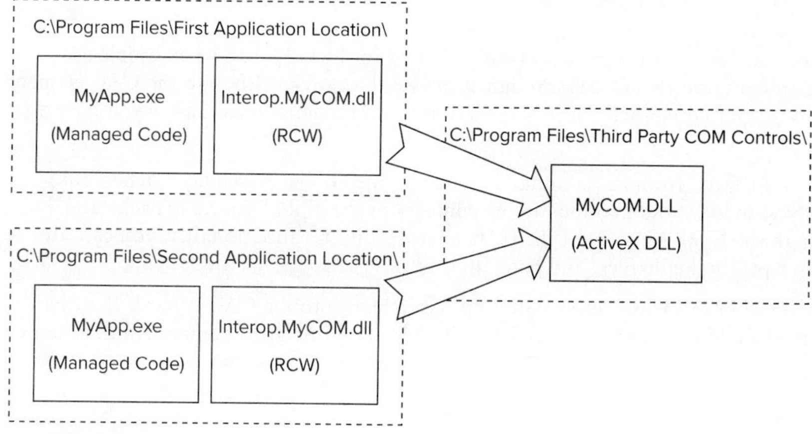

FIGURE 28-10

Whether you decide to install the ActiveX component as local to the application or in a shared directory for all calling applications is up to you.

It was once considered proper practice to separate ActiveX components into their own directory so that if these components were referenced again by other applications, you did not have to register or install the file for a second time. Using this method meant that when you upgraded a component, you automatically upgraded all the utilizing applications. However, this practice didn't work out so well. In fact, it became a very big contributor to DLL hell and the main reason why Microsoft began promoting the practice of installing private .NET component assemblies.

After you have your components physically in place, the only remaining task is to register the ActiveX component using regsvr32, just as you would when deploying an ActiveX-enabled application.

Public Assemblies

The opposite of a private assembly is a public assembly. Public assemblies share the RCW Interop DLL for other applications. In order to create a public assembly, you must put the RCW file into the *Global Assembly Cache (GAC)*, as shown in Figure 28-11.

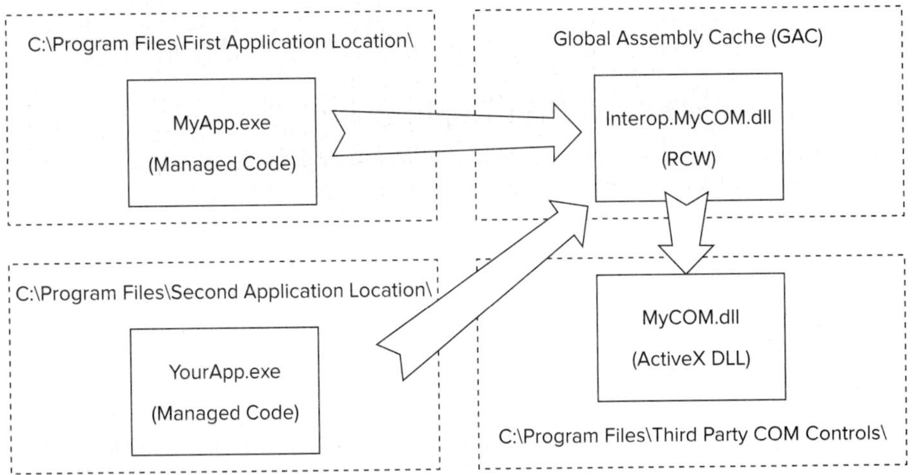

FIGURE 28-11

You can find the GAC at `C:\Windows\assembly`. Installing items in the GAC can be as simple as dragging-and-dropping an item into this folder through Windows Explorer. Although the GAC is open to everyone, blindly installing your components into this section is not recommended unless you have a very good reason to do so.

You can also add items to the GAC from the command line using the Global Assembly Cache Tool (Gacutil.exe). It enables you to view and manipulate the contents of the global assembly cache and download cache. Although the Explorer view of the GAC provides similar functionality, you can use Gacutil.exe from build scripts, makefile files, and batch files.

Finding a very good reason to install your ActiveX Interop Assemblies into the GAC is hard. If we had to pick a time to do this, it would be if and when we had a highly shared ActiveX component that many

.NET applications would be utilizing on the same machine. In a corporate environment, this might occur when you are upgrading existing business logic from ActiveX to .NET enablement on a server that many applications use. In a commercial setting, we avoid using the GAC.

USING .NET FROM UNMANAGED CODE

.NET provides the opposite of COM interoperability by enabling you to use your newly created .NET components within unmanaged code. This section discusses using .NET components with Visual Basic 6 executables. The techniques shown in this section are identical when you are using ActiveX OCXs or DLLs instead of executables.

The COM-Callable Wrapper (CCW) is the piece of the .NET framework that enables unmanaged code to communicate with your .NET component. The CCW, unlike the RCW, is not a separate DLL that you distribute with your application. Instead, the CCW is part of the .NET framework that gets instantiated once for each .NET component that you are using.

Figure 28-12 shows how the CCW marshals the communication between the unmanaged code and the .NET component in much the same way that the RCW marshals the code between managed code and COM code.

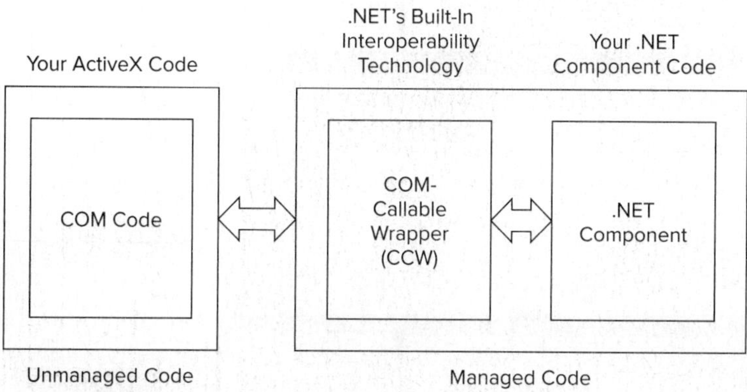

FIGURE 28-12

The COM-Callable Wrapper

The COM-Callable Wrapper or CCW, as previously stated, is not a separate DLL like the RCW. Instead, the CCW uses a specially created type library based on the .NET component. This type library is called an Interop Type Library. The Interop Type Library is statically linked with the unmanaged code so that this code can communicate with the CCW about the .NET component included in your application.

In order for a .NET component to generate an Interop Type Library, you tell Visual Studio 2010 to generate it when the component is built. Both Visual Basic and C# projects have a setting in the Compile properties section of the Class Library project's Property Pages dialog.

Right-click the project in the Solution Explorer and choose Properties to see the project's properties. Figure 28-13 shows the project's properties for a Visual Basic 2010 Class Library application. This is shown directly in the Visual Studio document window.

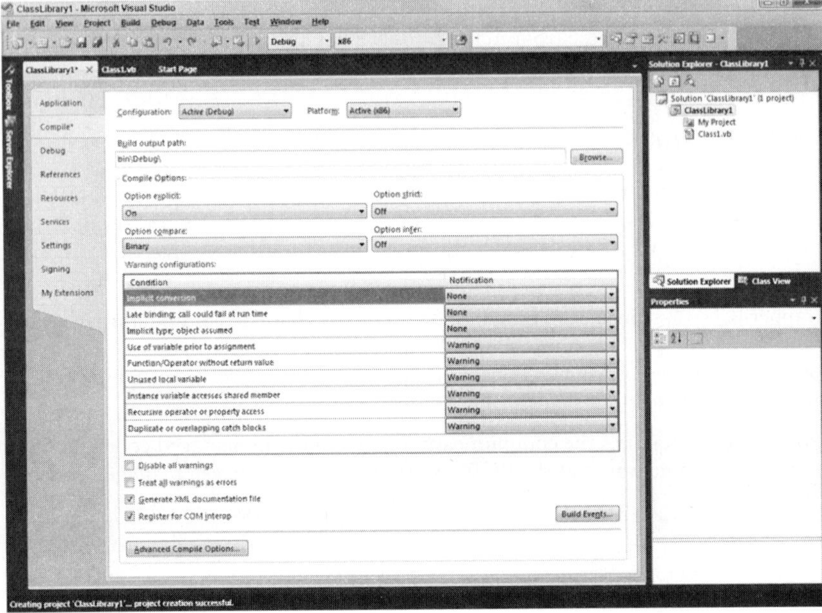

FIGURE 28-13

C# has a slightly different dialog, as shown in Figure 28-14. In both dialogs, the property is called Register for COM Interop. In Visual Basic, you can find this property on the Compile page; in C#, you can find it on the Build tab of the properties pages.

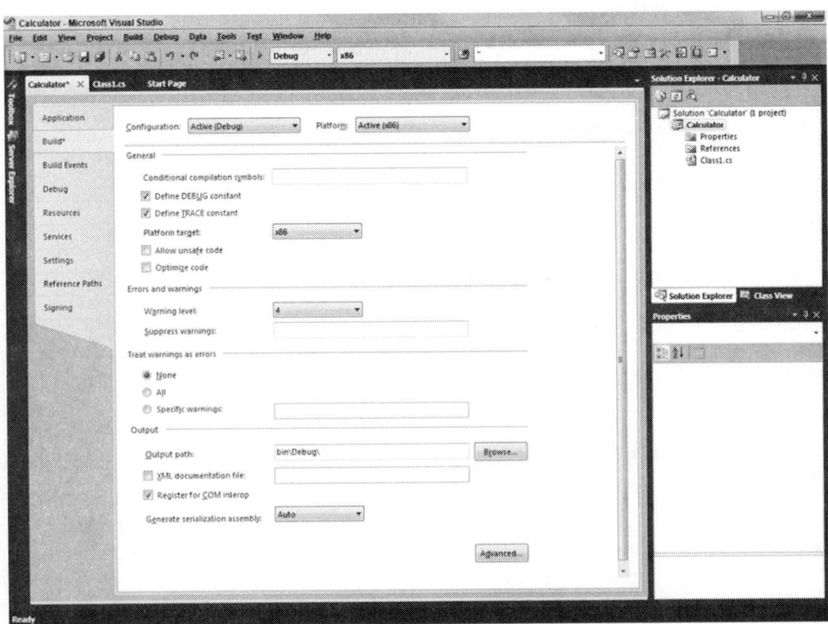

FIGURE 28-14

After you set the Register for COM Interop option by checking the check box, when you build the project, a separate type library file (.tlb) is generated for the DLL that you are building. This .tlb file is your key to including .NET components in COM applications.

Normally in Visual Basic, when you add a reference to a DLL, you navigate from the References section of the Visual Basic project to find the ActiveX DLL that you want to add. If you use .NET components, they cannot be properly referenced in this manner because they are not ActiveX. Instead, you reference the Interop Type Library, which makes the functionality of the corresponding .NET component available to your application.

The .NET framework also gives you a method to create Interop Type Library files manually for .NET components. You do this through a command-line tool called the Type Library Exporter (as compared to the Type Library Importer used for COM Interoperability). The Type Library Exporter is invoked using the tlbexp.exe executable.

For example, to create the Interop Type Library for the NameComponent.dll in the next example, you use the following command:

```
tlbexp NameComponent.dll /out:NameComponentEx.tlb
```

The /out: parameter specifies the name of the Interop Type Library that is to be created. If you omit this parameter, you get a file with the same name as the ActiveX component, but with a .tlb extension.

The Type Library Exporter is useful when you are not using Visual Studio 2010 as your development environment, if you want to have more control over the assemblies that get created for you, or if you are automating the process of connecting to .NET components.

Using .NET Components Within COM Objects

The next example illustrates how you can utilize .NET components within COM code. To begin, create and compile the .NET code found in Listing 28-5 in either Visual Basic or C#.

After you have typed your code into your Class Library project, build the component and call it NameComponent. Remember to choose to include the Register for the COM Interop setting of True (by checking the appropriate check box) from the project properties pages, as shown in Figure 28-13 for Visual Basic code and Figure 28-14 for C# code. If you aren't using Visual Studio 2010, you can use tblexp.exe to generate the Interop Type Library manually as described previously.

LISTING 28-5: The .NET component

```
Public Class NameFunctions

  Private m_FirstName As String
  Private m_LastName As String

  Public Property FirstName() As String
    Get
      Return m_FirstName
    End Get

    Set(ByVal Value As String)
      m_FirstName = Value
    End Set
  End Property

  Public Property LastName() As String
    Get
      Return m_LastName
    End Get
```

continues

LISTING 28-5 *(continued)*

```
    Set(ByVal Value As String)
      m_LastName = Value
    End Set
  End Property

  Public Property FullName() As String
    Get
      Return m_FirstName + " " + m_LastName
    End Get

    Set(ByVal Value As String)
      m_FirstName = Split(Value, " ")(0)
      m_LastName = Split(Value, " ")(1)
    End Set
  End Property

  Public ReadOnly Property FullNameLength() As Long
    Get
      FullNameLength = Len(Me.FullName)
    End Get
  End Property

End Class
```

C#

```
using System;
using System.Runtime.InteropServices;

namespace NameComponent
{
  [ComVisible(true)]
  public class NameFunctions
  {

    private string m_FirstName;
    private string m_LastName;

    public string FirstName
    {
      get
      {
        return m_FirstName;
      }
      set
      {
        m_FirstName=value;
      }
    }

    public string LastName
    {
      get
      {
        return m_LastName;
      }
      set
      {
        m_LastName=value;
      }
    }
```

```
        public string FullName
        {
          get
          {
            return m_FirstName + " " + m_LastName;
          }
          set
          {
            m_FirstName=value.Split(' ')[0];
            m_LastName=value.Split(' ')[1];
          }
        }

        public long FullNameLength
        {
          get
          {
            return this.FullName.Length;
          }
        }

      }
    }
```

Filenames NameFunctions.vb and NameFunctions.cs

After you have created the .NET component, you can then create the consuming Visual Basic 6 code shown in Listing 28-6.

LISTING 28-6: VB6 code using the .NET component

Available for download on Wrox.com

```
Option Explicit

Public Sub Main()

  Dim o As NameComponent.NameFunctions

  Set o = New NameComponent.NameFunctions

  o.FirstName = "Bill"
  o.LastName = "Evjen"

  MsgBox "Full Name is: " + o.FullName

  MsgBox "Length of Full Name is: " + CStr(o.FullNameLength)

  o.FullName = "Scott Hanselman"

  MsgBox "First Name is: " + o.FirstName

  MsgBox "Last Name is: " + o.LastName

  o.LastName = "Evjen"

  MsgBox "Full Name is: " + o.FullName

  Set o = Nothing

End Sub
```

Remember to add a reference to the .NET component. You choose Project ➪ References and select the .NET component that was created either by Visual Studio or by manually using `tlbexp.exe`.

When you run the code in Listing 28-6, you see that Visual Basic 6 does not miss a beat when communicating with the .NET component.

Registering the assemblies yourself is also possible. Earlier you learned how to manually create Interop Type Libraries with the Type Library Exporter. This tool does not register the assemblies created but instead generates only the type library.

To register the assemblies yourself, you use the Assembly Registration Tool (`regasm.exe`). This tool is similar to the `regsvr32.exe` for .NET components.

To use `regasm.exe`, use a command syntax similar to the following example:

```
regasm NameComponent.dll /tlb:NameComponentEx.tlb /regfile:NameComponent.reg
```

The `/tlb:` option specifies the name of the type library, and the `/regfile:` option specifies the name of a registry file to be created that you can use later in an installation and deployment application.

Early versus Late Binding

The preceding example illustrates the use of early binding, the technique most Visual Basic 6 developers are used to. However, in some cases, using late binding is desirable. Performing late binding with .NET components is similar to performing late binding with ActiveX components, as shown in Listing 28-7.

LISTING 28-7: Late binding with VB6

Available for download on Wrox.com

```
Option Explicit

Public Sub Main()

  Dim o As Object

  Set o = CreateObject("NameComponent.NameFunctions")

  o.FirstName = "Bill"
  o.LastName = "Evjen"

  MsgBox "Full Name is: " + o.FullName

  MsgBox "Length of Full Name is: " + CStr(o.FullNameLength)

  o.FullName = "Scott Hanselman"

  MsgBox "First Name is: " + o.FirstName

  MsgBox "Last Name is: " + o.LastName

  o.LastName = "Evjen"

  MsgBox "Full Name is: " + o.FullName

  Set o = Nothing

End Sub
```

Error Handling

Handling errors that are raised from .NET components in Visual Basic 6 is easily accomplished via the Interop functionality. Listing 28-8 shows code for both Visual Basic and C# to throw exceptions for a custom error. When the `Numerator` or the `Denominator` parameters are greater than 1000 in the `Divide` function, a custom exception is thrown up to the calling code, which is Visual Basic 6 in this example.

Notice how the divide-by-zero error possibility is not handled in this example. This is done intentionally to demonstrate how interoperability handles unhandled errors.

LISTING 28-8: Raising errors

Available for download on Wrox.com

```
Public Class CustomException
  Inherits Exception

  Sub New(ByVal Message As String)
    MyBase.New(Message)
  End Sub
End Class

Public Class DivideFunction

  Public Function Divide(ByVal Numerator As Double, _
                         ByVal Denominator As Double) As Double

    If ((Numerator > 1000) Or (Denominator > 1000)) Then
      Throw New CustomException("Numerator and denominator both " & _
                    "have to be less than or equal to 1000.")
    End If

    Divide = Numerator / Denominator

  End Function

End Class
```

C#

```
using System;

namespace DivideComponent
{
    public class CustomException:Exception
    {
      public CustomException(string message):base(message)
      {
      }
    }

  public class DivideFunction
  {
    public double Divide(double Numerator, double Denominator)
    {
      if ((Numerator > 1000) || (Denominator > 1000))
        throw new CustomException("Numerator and denominator " +
                  "both have to be less than or equal to 1000.");

      return Numerator / Denominator;
    }
  }
}
```

Now that you have the code for the .NET component, compile it with the Register for COM Interop flag set to True in the project's Property Pages dialog and call the component `DivideComponent`.

Listing 28-9 shows the consuming Visual Basic 6 code. Remember to add a reference to the Interop Type Library of the `DivideComponent` generated by Visual Studio.

LISTING 28-9: VB6 experiencing .NET errors

Available for download on Wrox.com

```
Option Explicit

Public Sub Main()

  Dim o As DivideComponent.DivideFunction

  Set o = New DivideComponent.DivideFunction

  MsgBox "1 divided by 3: " + CStr(o.divide(1, 3))

  MsgBox "1 divided by 0: " + CStr(o.divide(1, 0))

  MsgBox "2000 divided by 3000: " + CStr(o.divide(2000, 3000))

  Set o = Nothing

End Sub
```

The Visual Basic 6 code example in Listing 28-9 does not handle the errors thrown by the .NET component, but it can easily do so using `On Error`, Visual Basic 6's method for trapping raised errors.

Instead of trapping the errors, make sure that the Error Trapping setting in the Options dialog of Visual Basic 6 is set to Break in Class Module.

When the application is run, the first example of 1 divided by 3 works fine; you see the output properly. The second example, which you would expect to end in a divide-by-zero error, does not. Instead, an invalid property value is returned to Visual Basic 6. The final example, which does not pass the custom error handling in the .NET component, raises a Visual Basic error, as you would expect.

Deploying .NET Components with COM Applications

Deploying .NET components with COM applications is similar to deploying COM components with .NET applications. Two scenarios exist in this deployment scheme:

- Using private assemblies
- Using shared or public assemblies

The following sections discuss these two scenarios.

Private Assemblies

Private assemblies mean the deployment of the .NET component is installed in each individual directory where the application is installed, within the same machine. The only needed component is the .NET DLL and the calling application. The Interop Type Library that you created earlier with Visual Studio 2010 or `tlbexp.exe` is statically linked with the component or application that references the .NET component.

The only additional task you must complete is to properly register the .NET assembly using `regasm.exe`. This extra step is not needed in 100 percent of .NET applications; it is required only for the interoperability for the unmanaged code to reference the managed code. Figure 28-15 illustrates using private assemblies.

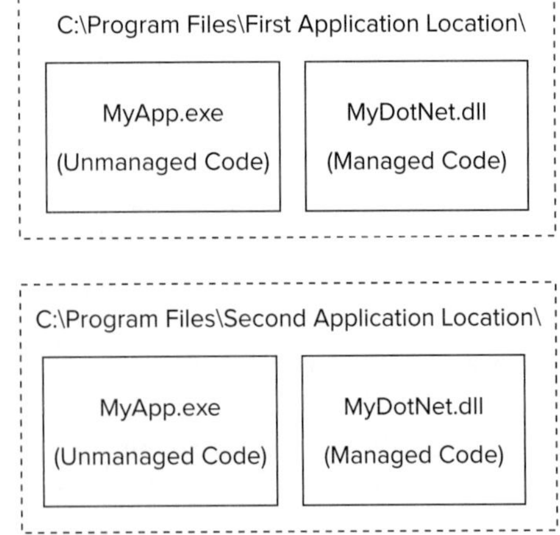

FIGURE 28-15

Public Assemblies

Figure 28-16 illustrates the use of a public assembly. This scenario involves installing the .NET component into the Global Assembly Cache (GAC).

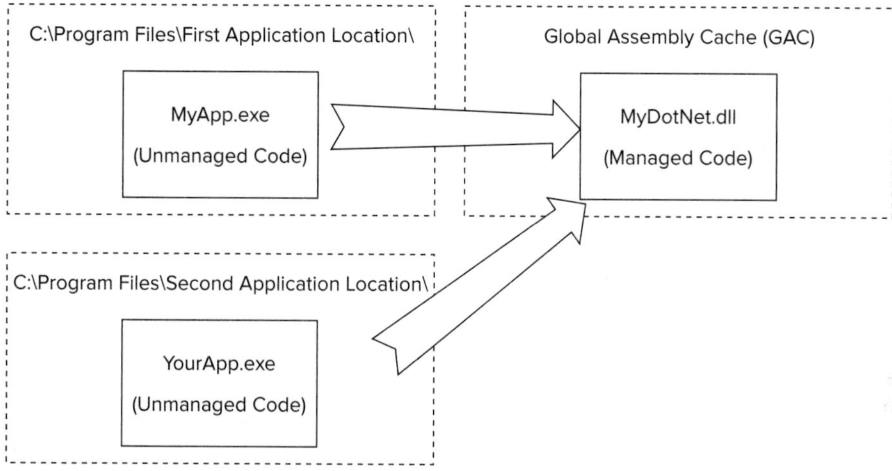

FIGURE 28-16

As with private assemblies, deployment requires only the .NET component and the consuming unmanaged code — besides the need to register the interop assembly using `regasm.exe`.

SUMMARY

When .NET was introduced, some initial concern arose about existing ActiveX controls and their place in Microsoft's vision for the future of component development. Immediately, Microsoft stepped up to the bat and offered the robust and solid .NET Interop functionality to provide a means to communicate not only from .NET managed code to COM unmanaged code, but also from COM unmanaged code to .NET managed code. The latter was an unexpected, but welcome, feature for many Visual Basic 6 developers and future .NET component builders.

This layer of interoperability has given Microsoft the position to push .NET component development as a solution for not only newly created applications, but also applications that are currently in development and ones that have already been rolled out and are now in the maintenance phase.

Interoperability has given .NET developers a means to gradually update applications without rewriting them entirely, and it has given them a way to start new .NET projects without having to wait for all the supporting components to be developed in .NET.

29

ADO.NET Entity Framework

WHAT'S IN THIS CHAPTER?

- Understanding mapping and relationships
- Creating an Entity Data Model
- Using stored procedures and the EntityDataSource control in an EDM

Nowadays, accessing data is one of the main things almost every application must do. Nearly all applications deal with data in some manner, whether that data comes from memory (in-memory data), databases, XML files, text files, or something else. Many developers find moving from the strongly typed object-oriented world of C# or Visual Basic to the data tier where objects are second-class citizens very difficult. Before the ADO.NET Entity Framework, the transition from the one world to the next was kludgy at best and was full of error-prone actions. Data access can complicate your application development for a number of reasons, including the fact that the database space and the application space are two different worlds entirely.

Microsoft consistently attempts to simplify a programmer's common tasks that are laborious and complicated by abstracting the difficulties of these tasks through a combination of new interfaces and IDE assistance. With the earlier release of the ADO.NET Entity Framework, you will find that navigating the world between the database and your application is easier than ever.

With one of the available .NET programming languages, using objects in your code really means a wonderful ability to work with strongly typed objects in your code. As a programmer, you can navigate very easily through namespaces, work with a debugger in the Visual Studio IDE, and more. However, when it comes to accessing data, things are dramatically different. You end up in a world that is not strongly typed, where debugging is painful or even non-existent, and you spend most of the time sending strings to the database as commands. As a developer, you also must be aware of the underlying data and how it is structured or how all the data points relate to one another.

Using something like the ADO.NET Entity Framework (along with LINQ), you now have a lightweight façade that provides a strongly typed interface to the underlying datastores that you are working with. Using these technologies, you can stay within the coding environment you are used to, and you have the ability to access the underlying data as objects that work with the IDE, IntelliSense, and even debugging.

This chapter provides an overview of the ADO.NET Entity Framework and how you can use this framework within your ASP.NET applications. Note that the ADO.NET Entity Framework is available only as part of the .NET Framework 3.5 SP1 or the .NET Framework 4. This means that you must have one of these versions installed in addition to Visual Studio 2008 SP1, or you must be using Visual Studio 2010.

CAN WE SPEAK THE SAME LANGUAGE?

As discussed earlier, building applications that communicate with databases should be an easier task than it is. The difficulty is that objects in code and objects in the database are inherently different beasts. Communicating objects from the database tier to other tiers of your application stack is the primary reason for the added complexity.

The ADO.NET Entity Framework provides the capability to map your application objects to your relational database schemas. For example, when you have an `Orders` table that is full of references to `Customer` objects and `StoreItem` objects, and you are working with a relational database schema, these entities are created using `JOIN` statements between various tables. However, if you are working with this construction from your C# or VB code, then you are creating an `Order` object that includes a property reference to a `Customer` object and a `StoreItem` object. Mapping these representations together for themselves has usually been the job of developers.

In the past, an effort was made to address this issue of mapping with the introduction of the `DataSet` object. This object was an in-memory table representation that included with it multiple tables, with the table joins and constraints in place. However, with the pure object-oriented code that people really wanted to develop, the `DataSet` approach was often not recommended.

When you represent your data within the database, you are representing it as a *logical model* through the database's relational schema. However, coding your application is accomplished using a *conceptual model*. Having both logical and conceptual layers forced the creation of a mapping layer. The mapping layer allows you to transfer objects from the .NET classes that you are working with in your code to the relational database schemas that you are working with within the database, as represented in Figure 29-1.

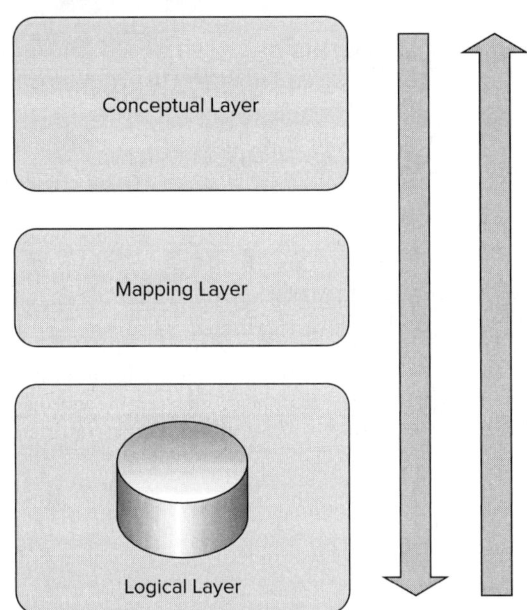

FIGURE 29-1

This mapping layer is sometimes thought of as a data access layer. Microsoft has provided a number of data access technologies over the past few years, and many third-party companies have formed around the concept of making this mapping as simple as possible. Some of the third parties even came on board to provide mapping or data access transformation to specialized databases.

Microsoft has moved forward to make the mapping of entities from the application code to the database schemas as simple as possible. The ADO.NET Entity Framework is in place so that you can write less code to get your applications out the door.

Note that you are going to need both the objects in your application code and the entities that you build within the relational schema of the database for some time to come.

So in the end, the Entity Framework consists of the following:

- A model of your database that is represented in the code of your application
- A definition of the datastore that you are working with (for example, your data representation within a SQL Server database)
- A mapping between the two elements

The Conceptual and Logical Layers

The Entity Data Model (EDM) is an abstract conceptual model of data as you want to represent it in your code. It is usually construed as .NET classes that you can manipulate as you would any other object within your code. You create this layer using the Conceptual Schema Definition Language (CSDL), which is an XML definition of your objects. What's nice about Visual Studio 2010 is that you have a visual designer to create the EDM on your behalf and under your direction.

Note that these XML files are not compiled with your application, as you will see later in this chapter.

The logical layer is defined using the Store Schema Definition Language (SSDL), which details the relational schema that you are storing within your database. This includes a definition of the tables, their relations, and their constraints.

Mapping Between Layers

The last piece of the Entity Data Model is the mapping layer. This layer maps the CSDL and the SSDL instances using the Mapping Specification Language (MSL).

It is possible for the combination of these three layers to work together for a few reasons. One is that there is a common type system within the Entity Data Model that all three layers can share. This system enables you to specify types that the code of your application will understand and then these same types will be understood by the database that you are working with. The EDM also provides the ability to work with the concept of inheritance as well as complex objects and to make the appropriate mappings between the layers.

The ADO.NET Entity Framework is the first offering from Microsoft for the .NET Framework that provides an implementation of the Entity Data Model and its constructs. In addition to the core pieces of the Entity Framework, Microsoft has also provided an O/R (*object relational*) designer in working with the creation of your entities. These items are demonstrated next.

CREATING YOUR FIRST ENTITY DATA MODEL

For an example of working with the ADO.NET Entity Framework, the first task is to work through all the steps that are required to read some data from a database and present it in your ASP.NET application.

For this example, you must have Visual Studio 2008 SP1 or Visual Studio 2010. From this IDE, create a new ASP.NET Web application called `AspnetEntityFx`, a standard ASP.NET application.

Next, you must get a database in place to work with. You can download the AdventureWorks sample database from `www.codeplex.com/MSFTDBProdSamples/Release/ProjectReleases.aspx?ReleaseId=4004`. You will find a file called `AdventureWorksDB.msi` on this page. To add this database, right-click on the App_Data folder from the Solution Explorer and select the option to add an existing item.

After you have added the database file to your project, you are ready to create your Entity Data Model. Right-click on your project within the Solution Explorer from Visual Studio and select Add ➪ New Item. The Add New Item dialog appears. From this dialog, select the Data option for the language you are working with (found in the left pane of the dialog). The available items you can add from the Data option include an ADO.NET Entity Data Model item, as shown in Figure 29-2.

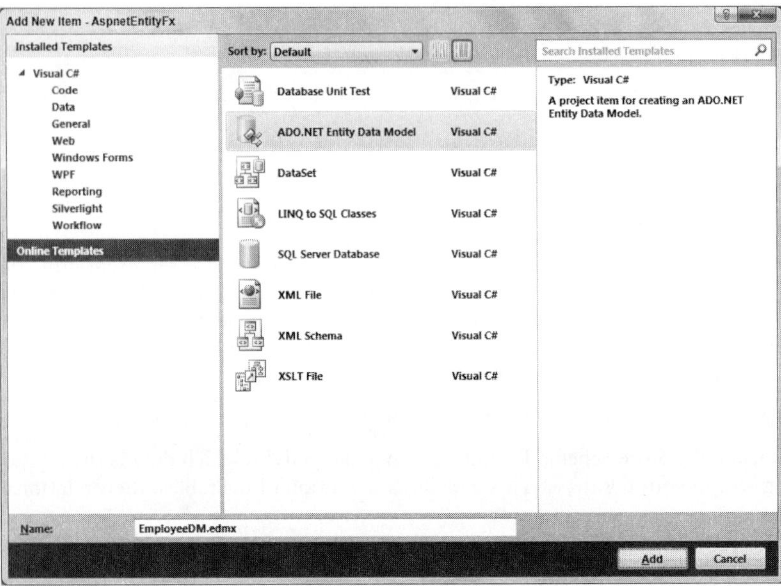

FIGURE 29-2

For this example, name your Entity Data Model `EmployeeDM.edmx` (refer to Figure 29-2).

Working Through the EDM Wizard

Adding this file when clicking the Add button does actually not insert a file right away, but instead starts a wizard. You can create an Entity Data Model in two ways. The first option is to create an Entity Data Model based on a pre-existing database. The second option is to create the Entity Data Model from a blank slate. The .NET Framework 4 now really makes the second option something you can work with easily. When you choose this second option, you can create your Entity Data Model and then use a wizard to create the database representation of that model.

The first screen in the wizard presents these options, as Figure 29-3 illustrates.

For this example, select the Generate from Database option. After you click Next in the wizard, the next step is to establish an entity connection string to the database, as shown in Figure 29-4.

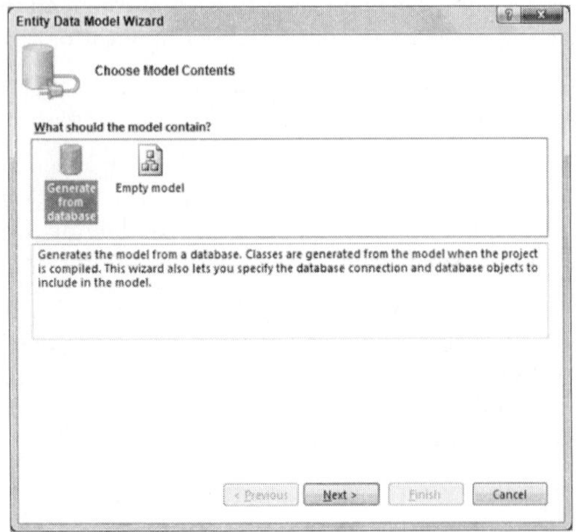

FIGURE 29-3

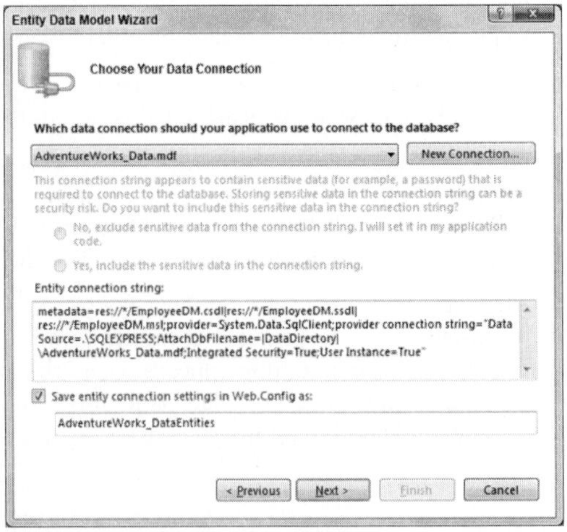

FIGURE 29-4

This wizard enables you to select the database that you want to work with from the first drop-down. The `AdventureWorks_Data.mdf` file appears as an option in this drop-down if you have added it to the project as previously instructed.

When selecting this database option in the drop-down, you will be presented with the entity connection string. It is much like a normal connection string:

```
metadata=res://*/EmployeeDM.csdl|res://*/EmployeeDM.ssdl|res://*/EmployeeDM.msl;
provider=System.Data.SqlClient;
provider connection string="Data Source=.\SQLEXPRESS;
AttachDbFilename=|DataDirectory|\AdventureWorks_Data.mdf;
Integrated Security=True;User Instance=True"
```

Notice that in addition to the normal connection string information that you might have, such as properties for the provider and the provider connection string, you also have the entity definition for what to use for the logical model and the conceptual model, as well as the mapping. The `EmployeeDM.csdl` file is for the conceptual model, `EmployeeDM.ssdl` is for the logical model, and `EmployeeDM.msl` is for the mapping required.

The final option in this dialog is like most providers' configurations that you have worked with in the past with ASP.NET; it allows you to save the connection string in the `web.config` file of your project.

When you are done with this page of the wizard, click Next to choose the tables, views, and stored procedures that you are going to require for your Entity Data Model.

For this example, expand the Table option in the treeview and select the Employee (Human Resources) table by selecting the check box next to the option (see Figure 29-5).

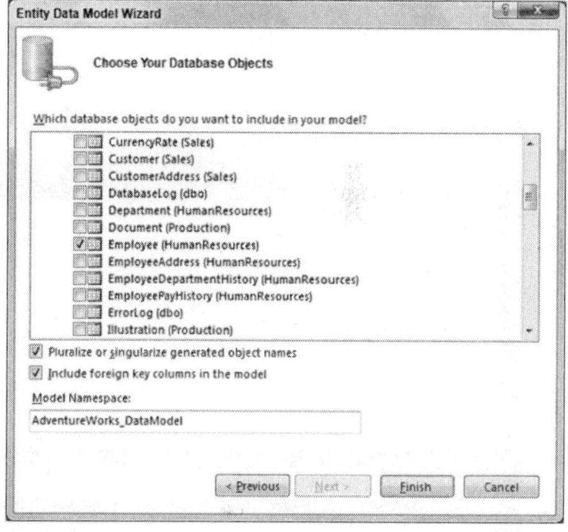

FIGURE 29-5

Notice that this part of the wizard enables you to define the namespace that you would use in accessing it from code. This example uses the default option of `AdventureWorks_DataModel`. At this point in the wizard, you will notice that the .NET Framework 4 provides some additional capabilities that the .NET Framework 3.5 SP1 didn't provide. You now have the option to pluralize or singularize the generated object names as well as to use the foreign key columns in your model. To take advantage of these features, you use the option to generate a database from the model that appears when you right-click on the design surface of the model.

This step is the last part of the wizard. When you are done selecting the options, click the Finish button. A designer surface for your Entity Data Model then appears.

Using the ADO.NET Entity Designer

The O/R designer built into Visual Studio 2010 for working with the Entity Framework is powerful because it allows you to visually configure your conceptual layer and how it maps to the logical layer.

If you worked through the wizard as defined earlier, then you will have a single `Employee` object represented on the page, as demonstrated in Figure 29-6.

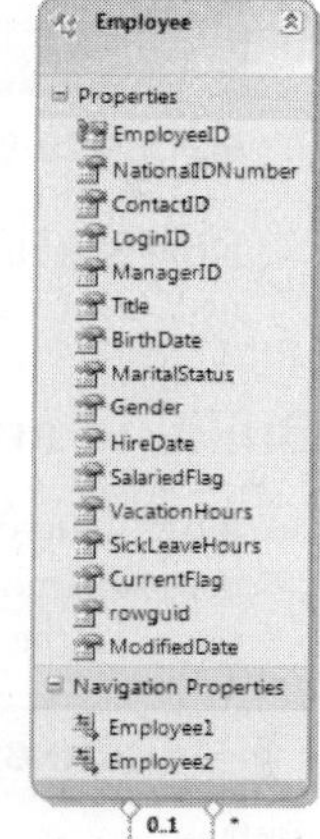

FIGURE 29-6

When you highlight the `Employee` object in the designer, some basic properties will appear in the Properties pane within Visual Studio, as illustrated in Figure 29-7.

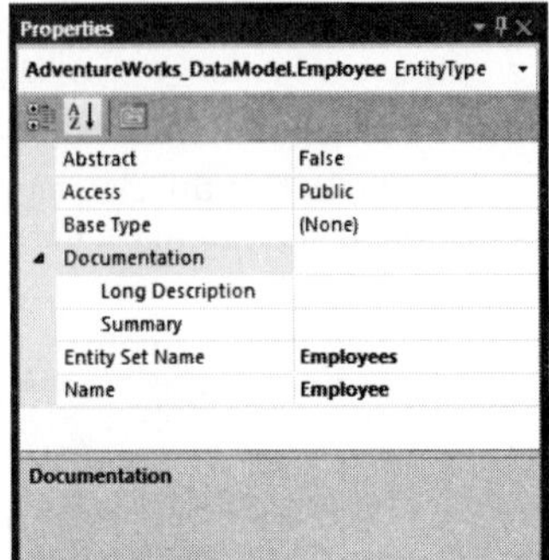

FIGURE 29-7

Here you can change the access modifier of the object and provide some basic documentation for the object. Visual Studio 2010 also provides you with some views to work with the Entity Framework. After you have created your `.edmx` file, a view is opened on your behalf — the Model Browser.

Another important view is the Entity Data Model Mapping Details window. You can get to this view in a couple of ways. You can select View ➪ Other Windows ➪ Entity Data Model Mapping Details from the Visual Studio menu, or you can right-click on the Employee object in the designer and select Table Mapping from the provided menu. Figure 29-8 presents both the Entity Data Model Browser and the Entity Data Model Mapping Details windows.

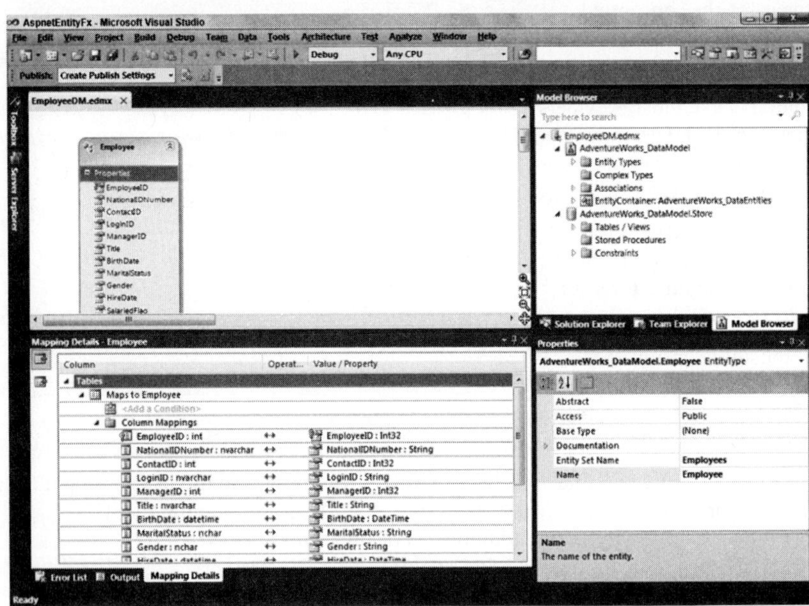

FIGURE 29-8

Now that this simple object is in place and your `.edmx` file is ready to go, the next step is to build a small ASP.NET page that will use this construct.

Building an ASP.NET Page Using Your EDM

Now that you have your Entity Data Model in place, this section shows you how to build a simple page that uses this model. The first step is to open your `BasicGrid.aspx` page and add a GridView control on the page. In the end, the code of your ASP.NET page will look like the code presented in Listing 29-1.

LISTING 29-1: A basic ASP.NET page that uses your EDM

Available for download on Wrox.com

```
<%@ Page Language="C#" AutoEventWireup="true"
    CodeBehind="BasicGrid.aspx.cs" Inherits="AspnetEntityFx._Default" %>

<html xmlns="http://www.w3.org/1999/xhtml" >
```

```
<head runat="server">
    <title>My EDM</title>
</head>
<body>
    <form id="form1" runat="server">
    <div>
        <asp:GridView ID="GridView1" runat="server">
        </asp:GridView>
    </div>
    </form>
</body>
</html>
```

Filename BasicGrid.aspx

This is the C# version of the page. Notice that only a GridView control is on the page. You will use this control to populate the results that come out of the Entity Data Model that you created.

To use the Entity Data Model, Listing 29-2 shows you the code-behind pages of the ASP.NET page that is presented in Listing 29-1.

LISTING 29-2: The code-behind page for the ASP.NET page

Available for download on Wrox.com

VB

```
Partial Public Class BasicGrid
    Inherits System.Web.UI.Page

    Protected Sub Page_Load(ByVal sender As Object,
      ByVal e As System.EventArgs) Handles Me.Load

        Dim adventureWorks_DataEntities As New
           AdventureWorks_DataEntities()

        Dim query =
         From emp In adventureWorks_DataEntities.Employees
         Select emp

        GridView1.DataSource = query
        GridView1.DataBind()
    End Sub

End Class
```

C#

```
using System;
using System.Linq;

namespace AspnetEntityFx
{
    public partial class BasicGrid : System.Web.UI.Page
    {
        protected void Page_Load(object sender, EventArgs e)
        {
            AdventureWorks_DataEntities adventureWorks_DataEntities =
               new AdventureWorks_DataEntities();

            var query = from emp in
                        adventureWorks_DataEntities.Employees
                        select emp;
```

continues

LISTING 29-2 *(continued)*

```
                GridView1.DataSource = query;
                GridView1.DataBind();
            }
        }
    }
```

Filenames BasicGrid.aspx.vb and BasicGrid.aspx.cs

As you can see, there isn't much code to this page. Running the page produces the results shown in Figure 29-9.

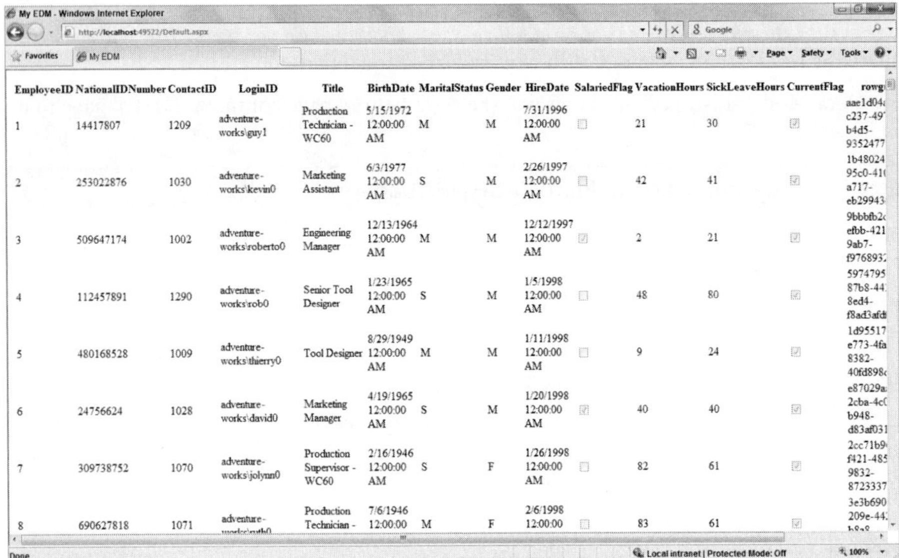

FIGURE 29-9

To work with your new Entity Data Model, an instance of the model is created:

```
Dim adventureWorks_DataEntities As New AdventureWorks_DataEntities()
```

This instance manages your connection to the database and takes care of feeding in the queries that you might perform over the datastore. The next line is a LINQ statement:

```
Dim query = _
   From emp In adventureWorks_DataEntities.Employees _
   Select emp
```

Here you are using an implicitly typed variable, `query`. The value assigned to the `query` object is the value of the `Employees` property, which is of type `IQueryable<Employee>`. This LINQ query simply pulls the entire contents from the Employee table and places the result in the `query` object for use within your code.

After the LINQ operation is complete, the `query` object is assigned and bound as a source to the GridView1 control.

```
GridView1.DataSource = query
GridView1.DataBind()
```

This simple example was of a one-to-one mapping. The next example looks at how to work with a many-to-many relationship.

UNDERSTANDING RELATIONSHIPS

The previous example was a good showing of a one-to-one mapping — an `Employee` object that mapped to the Employee table. In this section you take look at one-to-one and one-to-many relationships and many-to-one and many-to-many relationships.

One-to-One and One-to-Many Relationships

A one-to-one relationship is a construct in which one table maps to one type within your Entity Data Model. This is also called a Table per Type model (TPT).

To show this relationship in better detail, you will work with the Employee table from the previous example.

If you look through the details of the `AdventureWorld_Data.mdf` database file, you will see that there are a lot of different tables. In terms of the Employee section of the database that this example uses, you can find the database relationships illustrated in Figure 29-10.

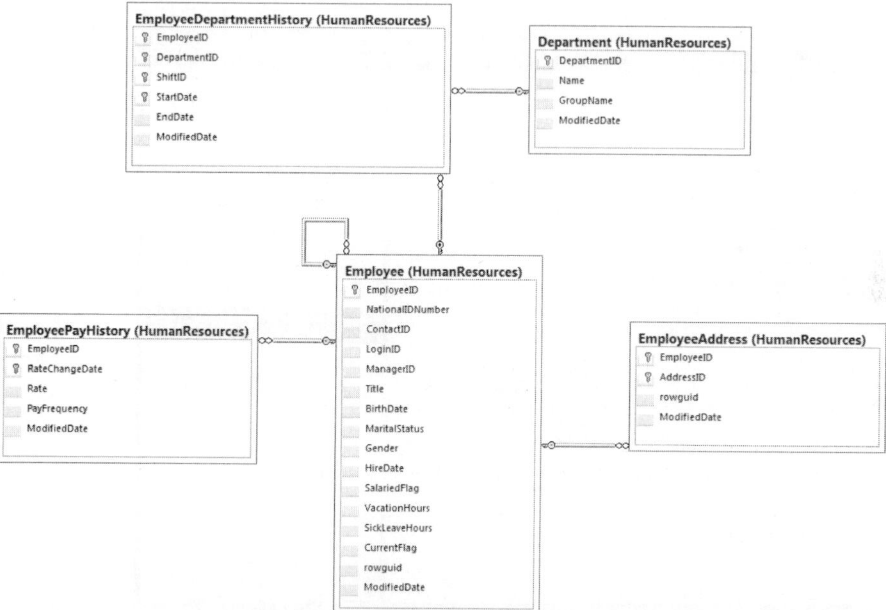

FIGURE 29-10

As you can see, in addition to the Employee table that you worked with earlier, you will find other tables such as the EmployeeDepartmentHistory, Department, EmployeeAddress, and EmployeePayHistory tables with a specific mapping.

You can see from the figure that many of these tables are related through the `EmployeeID` foreign key.

In contrast to this mapping, you can pull up the `EmployeeDM.edmx` file that you created earlier in this chapter. From the design surface of this file, right-click and select Update Model from Database from the provided menu.

An Update Wizard appears, as shown in Figure 29-11.

Now add the references to the missing tables — EmployeeDepartmentHistory, Department, EmployeeAddress, and EmployeePayHistory. From this figure, you can see that you can see that a one-to-many relationship exists with the other types of employee data.

With this construction in place, you will also find through IntelliSense that now one type (or object) maps to each of the specified tables, as illustrated in Figure 29-12.

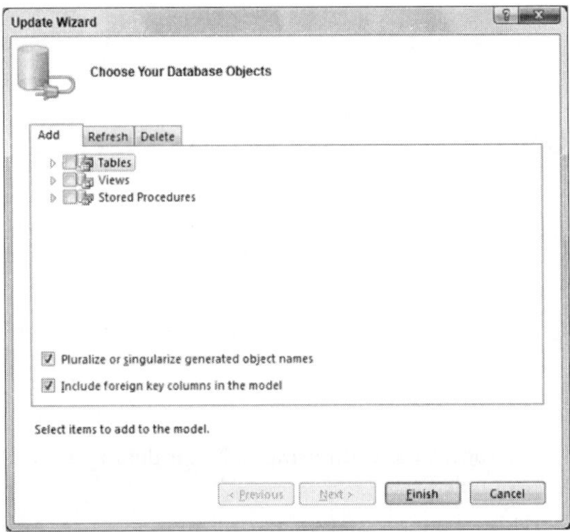

FIGURE 29-11

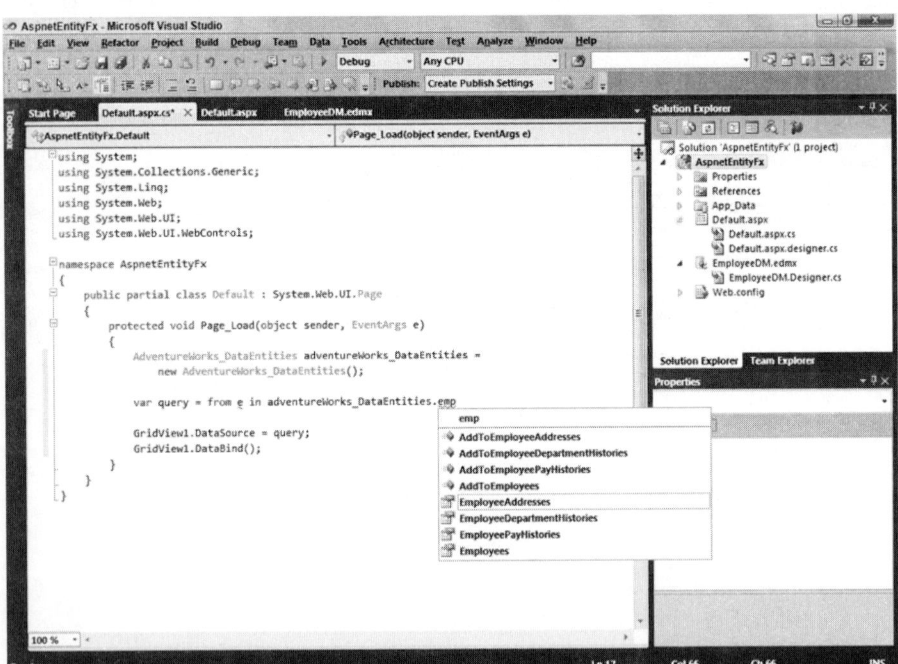

FIGURE 29-12

With these tables in place, you can work with all the objects as demonstrated here. For this page, create a simple ASP.NET page that includes only a single BulletedList control. Then from the code-behind of the page, use the code from Listing 29-3.

LISTING 29-3: Working with one-to-many mappings

Available for download on Wrox.com

VB

```
Protected Sub Page_Load(ByVal sender As Object, ByVal e As EventArgs)

   Dim adventureWorks_DataEntities As
      New AdventureWorks_DataEntities()

   For Each employee In adventureWorks_DataEntities.Employees
      Dim li As New ListItem()
      li.Text = employee.EmployeeID & " "

      If (Not employee.EmployeePayHistories.IsLoaded) Then
         employee.EmployeePayHistories.Load()
      End If

      For Each pay In employee.EmployeePayHistories
         li.Text &= "Pay Rate: " & pay.Rate & " "
      Next pay

      BulletedList1.Items.Add(li)
   Next employee
End Sub
```

C#

```
using System;
using System.Web.UI.WebControls;

namespace AspnetEntityFx
{
    public partial class _Default : System.Web.UI.Page
    {
        protected void Page_Load(object sender, EventArgs e)
        {
            AdventureWorks_DataEntities adventureWorks_DataEntities =
               new AdventureWorks_DataEntities();

            foreach (var employee in
               adventureWorks_DataEntities.Employees)
            {
                ListItem li = new ListItem();

                li.Text = employee.EmployeeID + " ";

                if (!employee.EmployeePayHistories.IsLoaded)
                {
                    employee.EmployeePayHistories.Load();
                }

                foreach (var pay in employee.EmployeePayHistories)
                {
                    li.Text += "Pay Rate: " + pay.Rate + " ";
                }

                BulletedList1.Items.Add(li);
            }
        }
    }
}
```

Filenames OneToMany.aspx.vb and OneToMany.aspx.cs

At first, the `Employees` objects are accessed and none of the other objects are actually loaded. This is why there is a check first to see if the `EmployeePaymentHistory` object is loaded using the `IsLoaded()` function. If the content is not loaded, then the `Load()` function is called.

If you run this bit of code, you get the results shown in Figure 29-13.

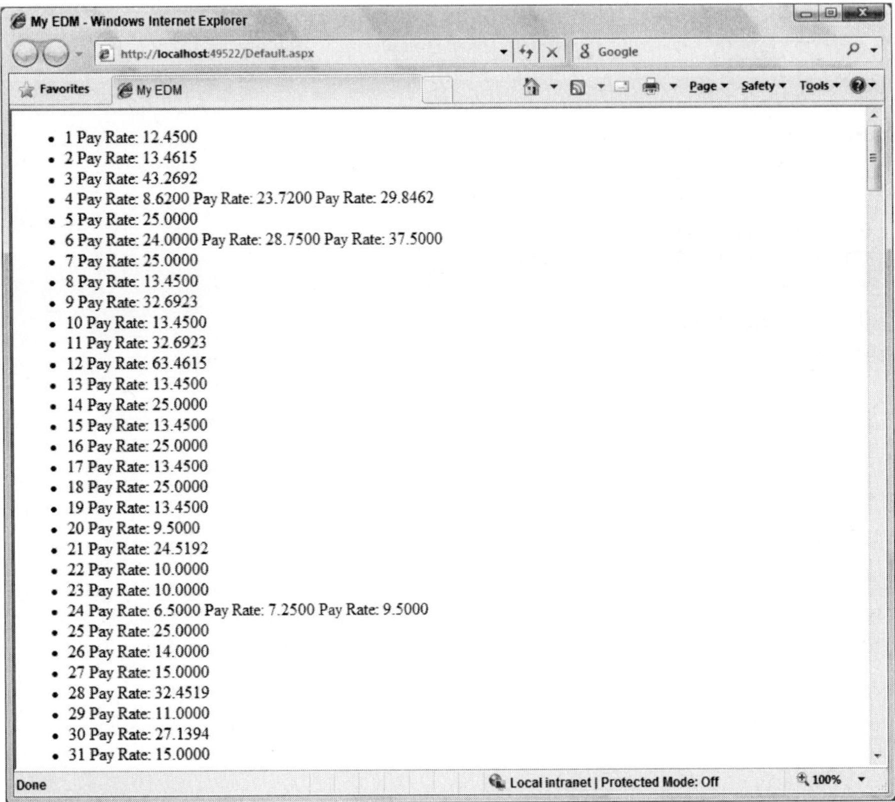

FIGURE 29-13

Many-to-One and Many-to-Many Relationships

In addition to the one-to-one and the one-to-many relationships, the Entity Framework supports many-to-one and many-to-many relationships. In these relationships, the Entity Framework will perform the appropriate table joins for you when you query the database.

Create a new Entity Data Model (`Sales.edmx` file) that includes the Customer, SalesTerritory, SalesOrderHeader, and the SalesOrderDetail tables.

You end up with a model that looks like Figure 29-14.

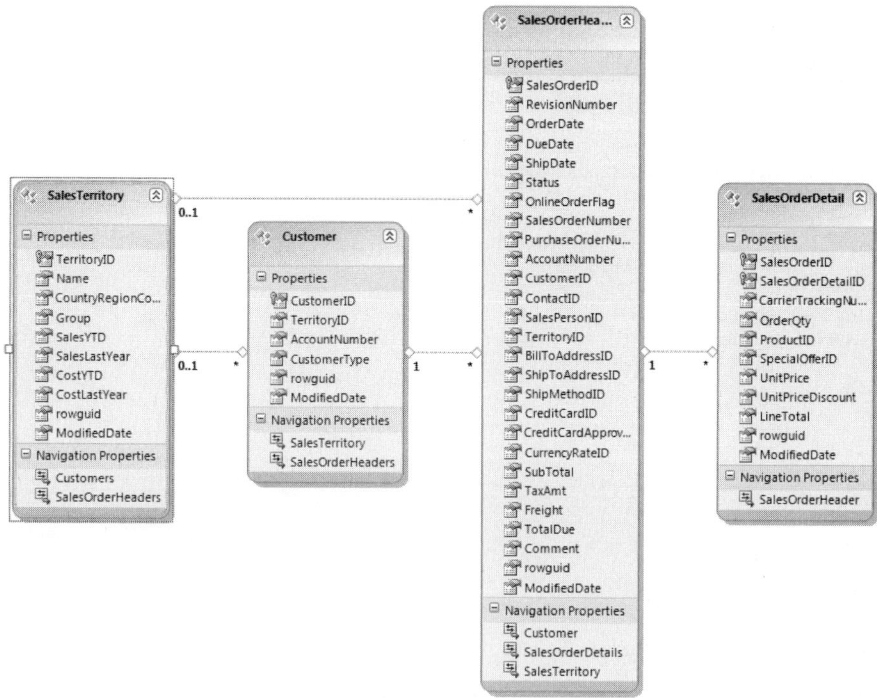

FIGURE 29-14

You can see the relationships by looking at the line that connects the visual objects on the designer. An asterisk on one end of the line indicates *many*. The number 1 appearing on the other side of the connection, as the line that is between the `SalesOrderHeader` and the `Customer` objects, indicates a many-to-one relationship. You can also view details about the relationship in the Properties window of Visual Studio upon highlighting the relationship line itself in the designer, as presented through the two `End` property values in the view.

Now look at a page that will perform some joins on your behalf across the tables. This operation is illustrated in Listing 29-4. For this example, just keep the simple page that contains only a GridView control and use the code-behind that is presented here.

LISTING 29-4: Having the Entity Framework perform joins between tables

Available for download on Wrox.com

VB

```
Imports System
Imports System.Linq

Namespace AspnetEntityFx
   Partial Public Class _Default
      Inherits System.Web.UI.Page

    Protected Sub Page_Load(ByVal sender As Object,
       ByVal e As EventArgs)

          Dim adventureWorks_DataEntities As
```

continues

LISTING 29-4 *(continued)*

```
                New AdventureWorks_DataEntities1()

            Dim query = _
                From o In adventureWorks_DataEntities.SalesOrderHeaders
                Where o.SalesOrderDetails.Any(Function(Quantity)
                    Quantity.OrderQty > 5)
                Select New With {Key o.PurchaseOrderNumber,
                         Key o.Customer.CustomerID,
                         Key o.SalesPersonID}

            GridView1.DataSource = query
            GridView1.DataBind()

        End Sub
    End Class
End Namespace
```

C#

```
using System;
using System.Linq;

namespace AspnetEntityFx
{
    public partial class _Default : System.Web.UI.Page
    {
        protected void Page_Load(object sender, EventArgs e)
        {
            AdventureWorks_DataEntities1 adventureWorks_DataEntities =
                new AdventureWorks_DataEntities1();

            var query = from o in
                 adventureWorks_DataEntities.SalesOrderHeaders
                 where o.SalesOrderDetails.Any(Quantity =>
                    Quantity.OrderQty > 5)
                 select new {o.PurchaseOrderNumber,
                    o.Customer.CustomerID, o.SalesPersonID};

            GridView1.DataSource = query;
            GridView1.DataBind();
        }
    }
}
```

Filenames ManyToMany.aspx.vb and ManyToMany.aspx.cs

This query pulls content and works from three different tables, and the Entity Framework does all the work of making the appropriate joins for you against the tables.

In this case, you are working with all the items in the SalesOrderHeader table where the quantity of the order is more than five. From the items selected, the fields are pulled for the dynamic object from across a couple of tables. Finally, the result is again bound to a standard GridView control. Figure 29-15 presents the final result.

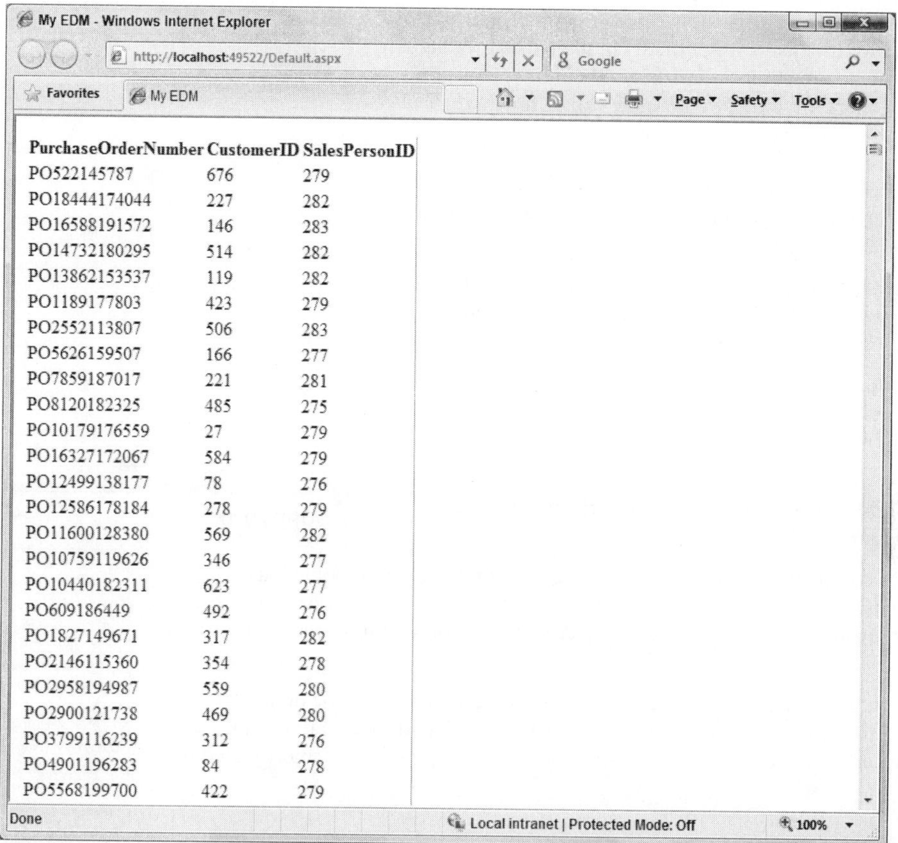

FIGURE 29-15

PERFORMING INHERITANCE WITHIN THE EDM

You can perform inheritance when constructing your Entity Data Model just as easily as you can when dealing with your objects within the CLR.

Inheritance gives you the capability to work with and look for specialized objects that you determine. For an example of this feature, in this section you modify the `Customer` object so that you can build a query that will look for a specific type of customer by object reference rather than through value interpretation.

Going back to the `Sales.edmx` file, you are going to modify the `Customer` object within this model. If you do not yet have this model, simply create a new one that contains only the Customer table. When you open the table definition of the Customer table within Visual Studio, you will see something like Figure 29-16.

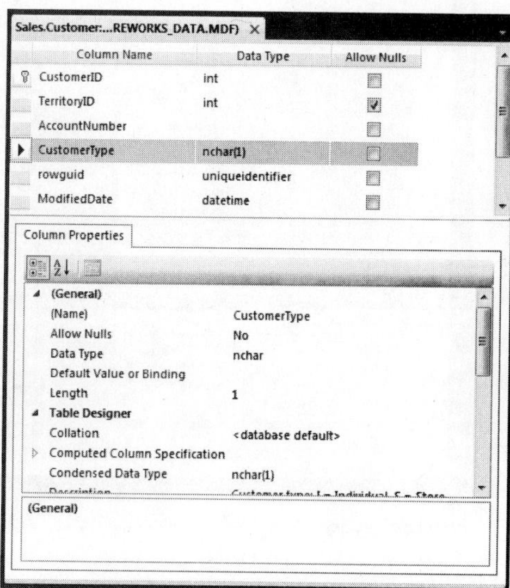

FIGURE 29-16

As you can see from this figure, the `CustomerType` property is of type `nchar(1)`, which means it is a one-character string value. If you look at the documentation for this table online, you will realize that there are only two possible values for this table: `I` and `S`. A value of `I` means that the customer is an individual, whereas a value of `S` means that the customer is a store. For this example, you will build a specialized type that is a reference to an individual customer and not a store so that you can differentiate between the two types.

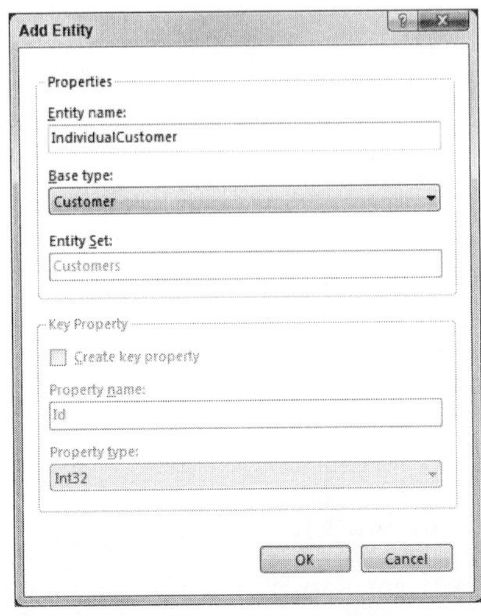

FIGURE 29-17

When your Customer table is in place, right-click on the designer surface and choose Add ➪ Entity from the provided menu. The Add Entity dialog then appears.

From this dialog, provide an entity name of `IndividualCustomer` and have it inherit from a base type of `Customer`. In the end, your Add Entity dialog should appear as shown in Figure 29-17.

This step will add a visual representation to the mapping, as illustrated in Figure 29-18.

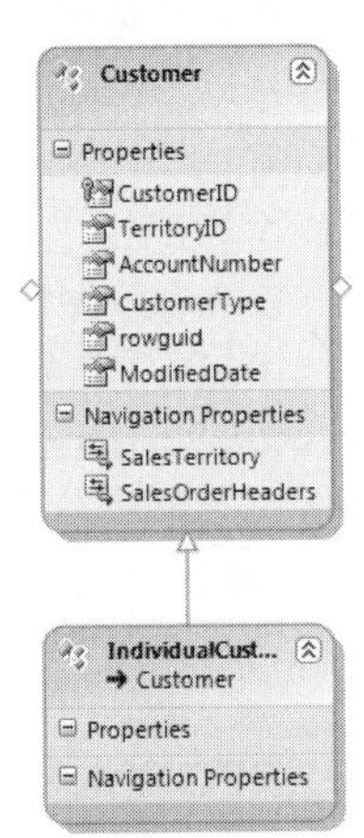

FIGURE 29-18

The next step is to further tie the two objects together and to provide some logic on their relationship. To accomplish this task you first delete the `CustomerType` scalar property from the `Customer` entity object, because you will not need it in the example.

You then highlight the `Customer` object within the designer and view the details of the mapping of this object within the Mapping Details view within Visual Studio. From this view, add a condition of `CustomerType` being equal to `S`, as demonstrated in Figure 29-19.

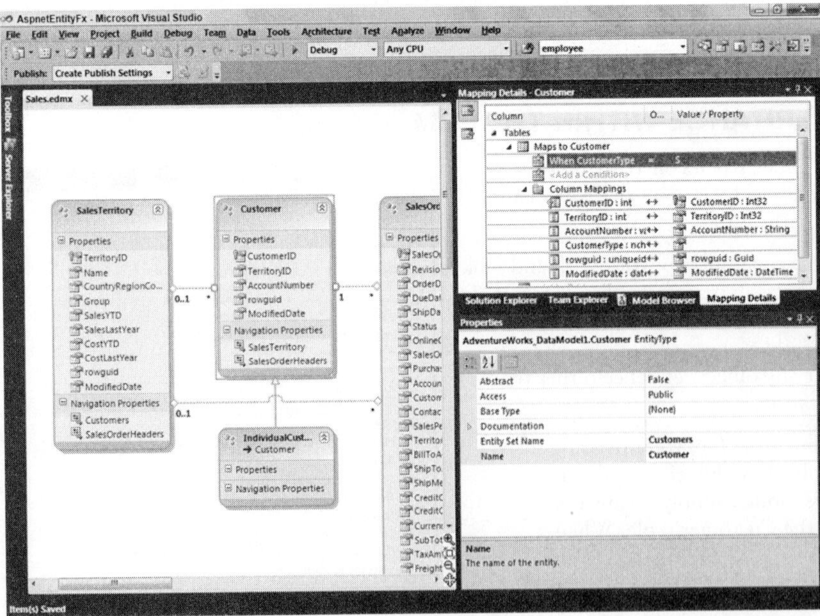

FIGURE 29-19

This setting really means that if the `CustomerType` has a value of `S`, then the object will be of type `Customer`. Now you set up the `IndividualCustomer` object. Looking at this object within the Mapping Detail view, you first must add the Customer table in the Mapping Details view. From there, create a condition where the `CustomerType` is equal to the character `I`, as illustrated in Figure 29-20.

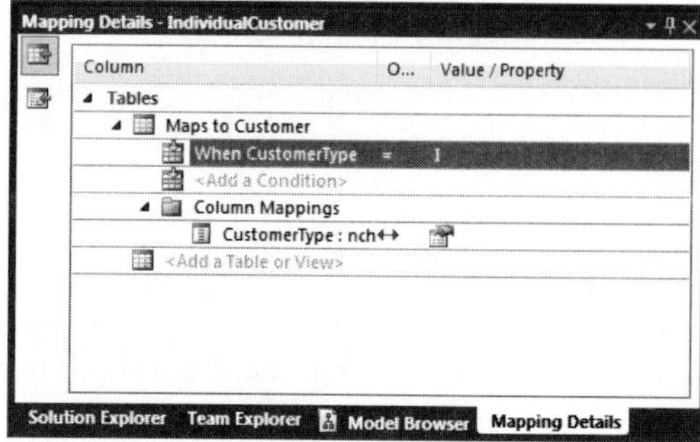

FIGURE 29-20

Now with these conditions all in place, you are really saying that if the `CustomerType` value has a value of `S`, then it is of type `Customer` in your Entity Data Model. However, if the `CustomerType` has a value of `I`, then the object type is of `IndividualCustomer`. You can work with this in your code, as illustrated in Listing 29-5.

Available for download on Wrox.com

LISTING 29-5: Using inheritance with your Entity Data Model

VB

```
Imports System
Imports System.Linq

Namespace AspnetEntityFx
    Partial Public Class Inheritance
        Inherits System.Web.UI.Page

        Protected Sub Page_Load(ByVal sender As Object,
          ByVal e As EventArgs)

            Dim adventureWorks_DataEntities As New
               AdventureWorks_DataEntities3()

            Dim query =
                From c In adventureWorks_DataEntities.Customers
                Where TypeOf c Is IndividualCustomer
                Select c

            GridView1.DataSource = query
            GridView1.DataBind()
        End Sub

    End Class
End Namespace
```

C#

```
using System;
using System.Linq;

namespace AspnetEntityFx
{
    public partial class Inheritance : System.Web.UI.Page
    {
        protected void Page_Load(object sender, EventArgs e)
        {
            AdventureWorks_DataEntities3 adventureWorks_DataEntities =
                new AdventureWorks_DataEntities3();

            var query = from c in adventureWorks_DataEntities.Customers
                        where c is IndividualCustomer
                        select c;
```

continues

LISTING 29-5 *(continued)*

```
                GridView1.DataSource = query;
                GridView1.DataBind();
            }
        }
    }
```

Filenames Inheritance.aspx.vb and Inheritance.aspx.cs

You can now put in a specific `where` clause that looks for objects of type `IndividualCustomer`:

```
Where TypeOf c Is IndividualCustomer
```

USING STORED PROCEDURES

One of the first things that you might think of when working with the Entity Framework is stored procedures. Is this new technology asking you to abandon the scores of stored procedures that you have built and have ready to use for your applications? Well, the answer is no, because you are able to work with stored procedures just as easily as everything that was previously shown in this chapter.

There are issues, however, with using stored procedures rather than entities, as discussed earlier in this chapter. In the next example, you will see the limitations as you work with stored procedures from the Northwind sample database.

Please refer to Chapter 8 on how to download the Northwind sample database.

For this example, open the previous ASP.NET Web Application project from Visual Studio and add the `NORTHWND.MDF` database file to your App_Data folder. This project should contain a single `.aspx` page that has only a GridView server control on the page. Again, your page will look something like Listing 29-6, which shows the C# version of the page.

Available for download on Wrox.com

LISTING 29-6: Your ASP.NET page for working with stored procedures

```
<%@ Page Language="C#" AutoEventWireup="true"
    CodeBehind="StoredProc.aspx.cs" Inherits="AspnetEntityFx2.StoredProc" %>

<html xmlns="http://www.w3.org/1999/xhtml" >
<head runat="server">
    <title>Working with Stored Procedures</title>
</head>
<body>
    <form id="form1" runat="server">
    <div>
        <asp:GridView ID="GridView1" runat="server">
        </asp:GridView>
    </div>
    </form>
</body>
</html>
```

Filename StoredProc.aspx

Now that the page is in place, the next step is to create your entity file, `Northwind.edmx`. Again, when creating this file, you will work through the wizard that Visual Studio provides, as discussed earlier in this chapter. When you work through the wizard, your primary concern is the screen that asks you to choose your data objects. In the previous examples in this chapter, you worked directly with the tables that the database provided, but in this case, you are not going to work with the Tables part of the tree found in this wizard. Instead, you are going to expand the Stored Procedures element in the provided tree, and you will find a list of the available stored procedures that the Northwind database provides, as illustrated in Figure 29-21.

As shown in the figure, you want to select the Ten Most Expensive Products stored procedure by selecting the check box next to the item. After selecting it, you can click the Finish button in the dialog. Now, instead of defining this entity visually on the EDM design surface, you will not find your stored procedures available in this view. Instead, you will find them in the Model Browser view within Visual Studio, as presented in Figure 29-22. Basically this view is only a reference to the stored procedure as it exists in the datastore. You are not provided an Entity Data Model to work with in this case.

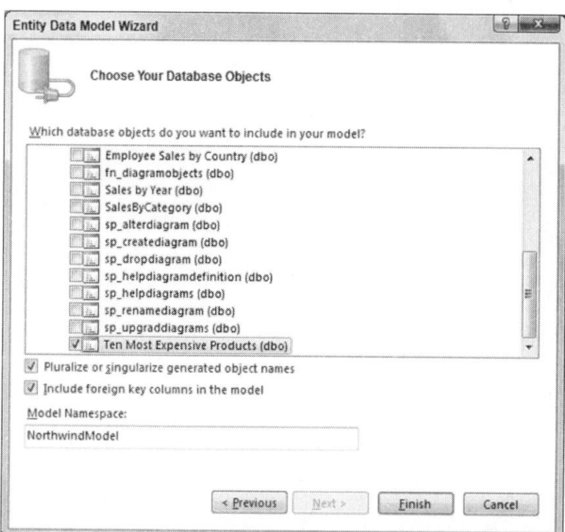

FIGURE 29-21

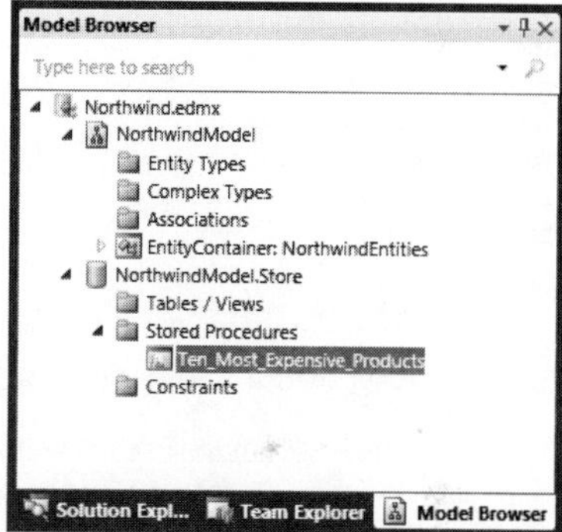

FIGURE 29-22

The reason for this is that when you are working with stored procedures, you are working with entities that cannot be altered. This situation is what it is. After the stored procedure is in place, you can then programmatically work with it, as illustrated in Listing 29-7.

LISTING 29-7: Working with stored procedures

Available for download on Wrox.com

VB

```
Imports System
Imports System.Data
Imports System.Data.Common
Imports System.Data.EntityClient

Namespace AspnetEntityFx
    Partial Public Class StoredProc
        Inherits System.Web.UI.Page
        Protected Sub Page_Load(ByVal sender As Object, _
          ByVal e As EventArgs)
            Dim northwndEntities As New NorthwindEntities()
            Dim entityConnection As EntityConnection = _
              CType(northwndEntities.Connection, EntityConnection)

            Dim storeConnection As DbConnection = _
```

continues

LISTING 29-7 *(continued)*

```
                entityConnection.StoreConnection
            Dim command As DbCommand = storeConnection.CreateCommand()
            command.CommandText = "Ten Most Expensive Products"
            command.CommandType = CommandType.StoredProcedure

            Dim openConnection As Boolean = _
               command.Connection.State = ConnectionState.Closed

            If openConnection Then
                command.Connection.Open()
            End If

            Dim result = command.ExecuteReader()

            GridView1.DataSource = result
            GridView1.DataBind()
        End Sub
    End Class
End Namespace
```

C#

```
using System;
using System.Data;
using System.Data.Common;
using System.Data.EntityClient;

namespace AspnetEntityFx
{
    public partial class StoredProc : System.Web.UI.Page
    {
        protected void Page_Load(object sender, EventArgs e)
        {
            NorthwindEntities northwndEntities =
               new NorthwindEntities();
            EntityConnection entityConnection =
               (EntityConnection)northwndEntities.Connection;

            DbConnection storeConnection =
               entityConnection.StoreConnection;
            DbCommand command = storeConnection.CreateCommand();
            command.CommandText = "Ten Most Expensive Products";
            command.CommandType = CommandType.StoredProcedure;

            bool openConnection = command.Connection.State ==
               ConnectionState.Closed;

            if (openConnection)
            {
                command.Connection.Open();
            }

            var result = command.ExecuteReader();

            GridView1.DataSource = result;
            GridView1.DataBind();
        }
    }
}
```

Filenames StoredProc.aspx.vb and StoredProc.aspx.cs

Obviously, there is a lot to this process, and there isn't much time to be saved in working with the database directly otherwise. If you are going to be working only with stored procedures, and you are not going to be using the EDM concepts, then there is questionable value in why you are using Entity Data Models at all.

With that said, you can incorporate stored procedures into your entities in some additional ways. For example, if you have a `Product` entity (from the Northwind database), you will notice, when looking at the entity in the Mapping Details section, that you are able to map insert, update, and delete procedures to the entity. You can get to this view by clicking on the Map Entity to Functions button in the leftmost panel in the Mapping Details dialog.

Still, using stored procedures is a narrow entry point into your database and disallows composable queries, which the Entity Framework powers itself on.

USING THE ENTITYDATASOURCE CONTROL

A new control that was made available to ASP.NET 3.5 SP1 and is also present in ASP.NET 4 is the EntityDataSource control. This control makes working with your Entity Data Model from your ASP.NET applications easy. As with the LinqDataSource control, you are able to allow the control itself to do the LINQ work necessary to bind to any of your controls.

Creating the Base Page

For an example of using the EntityDataSource control, first create an Entity Data Model that is the complete Northwind database. When working through the wizard in creating `Northwind.edmx`, add all the tables as shown in Figure 29-23.

Next create an ASP.NET page to work with this model. Create the page in your ASP.NET Web Application project and use the code presented in Listing 29-8.

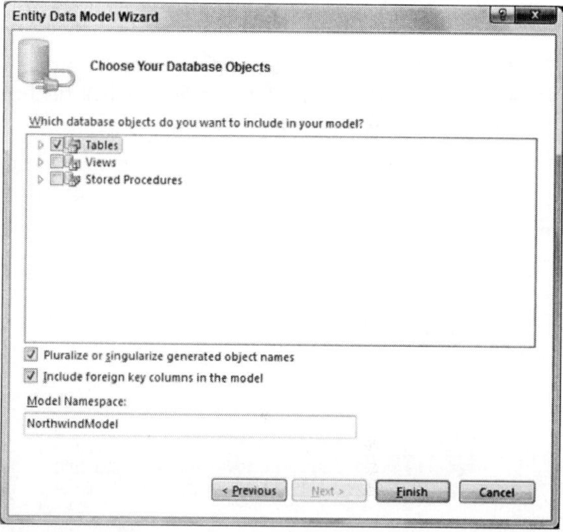

FIGURE 29-23

Available for download on Wrox.com

LISTING 29-8: Using the EntityDataSource server control

```
<%@ Page Language="C#" AutoEventWireup="true"
    CodeBehind="EntityDataSource.aspx.cs" Inherits="AspnetEntityFx. EntityDataSource" %>

<html xmlns="http://www.w3.org/1999/xhtml" >
<head runat="server">
    <title>Using the EntityDataSource Control</title>
</head>
<body>
    <form id="form1" runat="server">
    <asp:GridView ID="GridView1" runat="server">
    </asp:GridView>
    <br />
    <asp:EntityDataSource ID="EntityDataSource1" runat="server">
    </asp:EntityDataSource>
    </form>
</body>
</html>
```

Filename EntityDataSource.aspx

This page appears as a view in the designer portion of Visual Studio, as shown in Figure 29-24.

With this page in place, however, the EntityDataSource controls on the page are not configured to work with the Entity Data Model that you created, and the GridView control is not bound to this data source control.

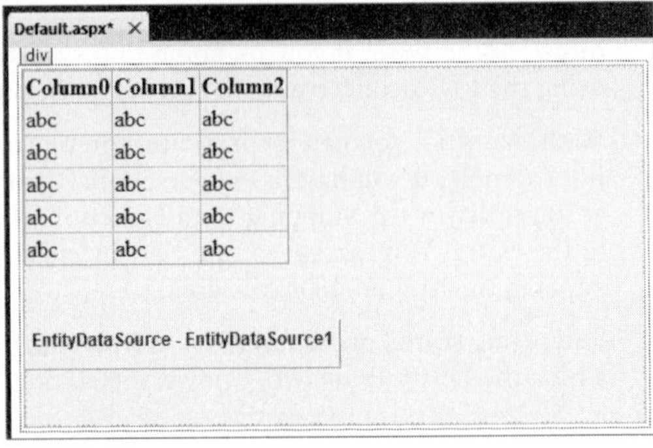

FIGURE 29-24

Configuring the Data Source Control

Now you configure the data source control on your page so that it will work from your Entity Data Model that you created earlier. To do this, you can either code the EntityDataSource control directly in the code of your ASP.NET page or work through the data source configuration wizard. For this example, you will work through the wizard.

Highlight the data source control on the design surface of your page, and you will find the Configure Data Source link from the available options. Click the link, and the first screen (see Figure 29-25) appears, asking you to configure the ObjectContext.

For this example, you work with the `NorthwindEntities` object that you created earlier. Click the Next button to configure your data selection process. In this case, as presented in Figure 29-26, you can select the Customers table.

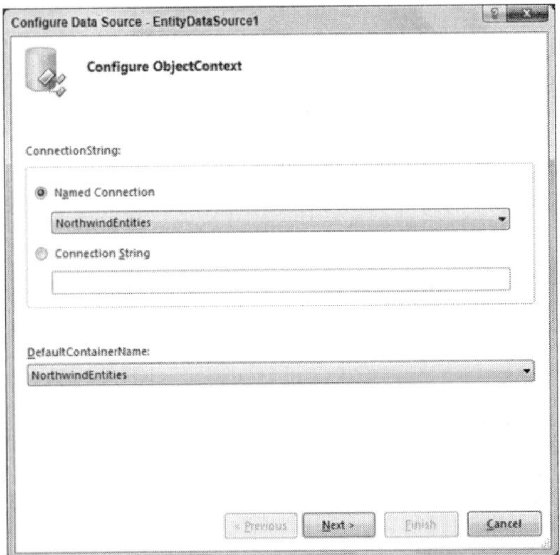

FIGURE 29-25

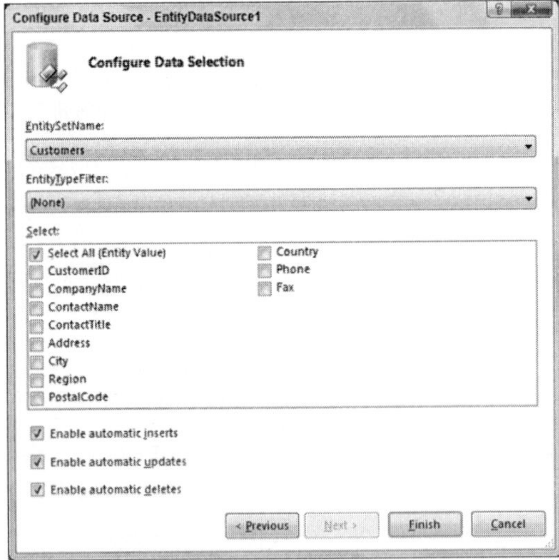

FIGURE 29-26

Notice that you can also very easily enable the insert, update, and delete functions by just selecting the appropriate check boxes in the wizard. Enabling these functions allows the EntityDataSource control to perform the appropriate LINQ operations over your Entity Data Model on your behalf.

After you have accomplished this and clicked Finish, the code shown in Listing 29-9 appears (as a C# page). Note that you should also tie the `GridView1` control to the `EntityDataSource1` control by assigning the `DataSourceID` property to this control.

Available for download on Wrox.com

LISTING 29-9: Pulling the Customer table using the EntityDataSource control

```
<%@ Page Language="C#" AutoEventWireup="true"
    CodeBehind="EntityDataSource.aspx.cs" Inherits="AspnetEntityFx. EntityDataSource" %>

<html xmlns="http://www.w3.org/1999/xhtml" >
<head runat="server">
    <title>Using the EntityDataSource Control</title>
</head>
<body>
    <form id="form1" runat="server">
    <asp:GridView ID="GridView1" runat="server" AllowPaging="True"
        AllowSorting="True" AutoGenerateColumns="False" CellPadding="4"
        DataKeyNames="CustomerID" DataSourceID="EntityDataSource1"
        ForeColor="#333333"
        GridLines="None">
        <RowStyle BackColor="#E3EAEB" />
        <Columns>
            <asp:BoundField DataField="Address" HeaderText="Address"
                SortExpression="Address" />
            <asp:BoundField DataField="City" HeaderText="City"
                SortExpression="City" />
            <asp:BoundField DataField="CompanyName"
                HeaderText="CompanyName"
                SortExpression="CompanyName" />
            <asp:BoundField DataField="ContactName"
                HeaderText="ContactName"
                SortExpression="ContactName" />
            <asp:BoundField DataField="ContactTitle"
                HeaderText="ContactTitle"
                SortExpression="ContactTitle" />
            <asp:BoundField DataField="Country" HeaderText="Country"
                SortExpression="Country" />
            <asp:BoundField DataField="CustomerID"
                HeaderText="CustomerID" ReadOnly="True"
                SortExpression="CustomerID" />
            <asp:BoundField DataField="Fax" HeaderText="Fax"
                SortExpression="Fax" />
            <asp:BoundField DataField="Phone" HeaderText="Phone"
                SortExpression="Phone" />
            <asp:BoundField DataField="PostalCode"
                HeaderText="PostalCode"
                SortExpression="PostalCode" />
            <asp:BoundField DataField="Region" HeaderText="Region"
                SortExpression="Region" />
        </Columns>
        <FooterStyle BackColor="#1C5E55" Font-Bold="True"
         ForeColor="White" />
        <PagerStyle BackColor="#666666" ForeColor="White"
         HorizontalAlign="Center" />
        <SelectedRowStyle BackColor="#C5BBAF" Font-Bold="True"
         ForeColor="#333333" />
        <HeaderStyle BackColor="#1C5E55" Font-Bold="True"
         ForeColor="White" />
        <EditRowStyle BackColor="#7C6F57" />
        <AlternatingRowStyle BackColor="White" />
    </asp:GridView>
    <asp:EntityDataSource ID="EntityDataSource1" runat="server"
        ConnectionString="name=NorthwindEntities"
```

continues

LISTING 29-9 *(continued)*

```
        DefaultContainerName="NorthwindEntities" EnableDelete="True"
        EnableInsert="True"
        EnableUpdate="True" EntitySetName="Customers">
    </asp:EntityDataSource>
    </form>
</body>
</html>
```

Filename EntityDataSource.aspx

Running this page produces the results shown in Figure 29-27 for viewing, editing, and selecting the items from your Entity Data Model.

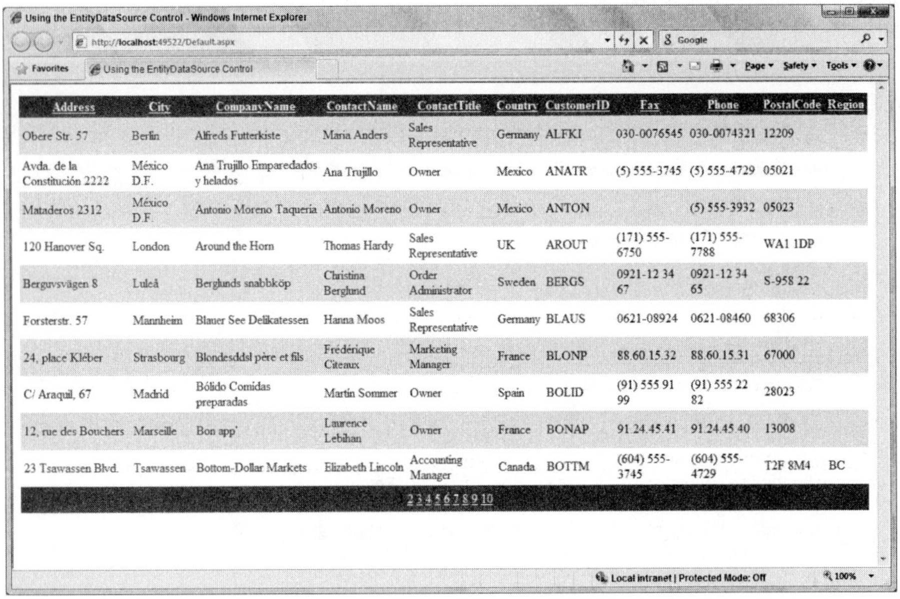

Using the EntityDataSource Control - Windows Internet Explorer
Address City CompanyName ContactName ContactTitle Country CustomerID Fax Phone PostalCode Region
Obere Str. 57 Berlin Alfreds Futterkiste Maria Anders Sales Representative Germany ALFKI 030-0076545 030-0074321 12209
Avda. de la Constitución 2222 México D.F. Ana Trujillo Emparedados y helados Ana Trujillo Owner Mexico ANATR (5) 555-3745 (5) 555-4729 05021
Mataderos 2312 México D.F. Antonio Moreno Taquería Antonio Moreno Owner Mexico ANTON (5) 555-3932 05023
120 Hanover Sq. London Around the Horn Thomas Hardy Sales Representative UK AROUT (171) 555-6750 (171) 555-7788 WA1 1DP
Berguvsvägen 8 Luleå Berglunds snabbköp Christina Berglund Order Administrator Sweden BERGS 0921-12 34 67 0921-12 34 65 S-958 22
Forsterstr. 57 Mannheim Blauer See Delikatessen Hanna Moos Sales Representative Germany BLAUS 0621-08924 0621-08460 68306
24, place Kléber Strasbourg Blondesddsl père et fils Frédérique Citeaux Marketing Manager France BLONP 88.60.15.32 88.60.15.31 67000
C/ Araquil, 67 Madrid Bólido Comidas preparadas Martín Sommer Owner Spain BOLID (91) 555 91 99 (91) 555 22 82 28023
12, rue des Bouchers Marseille Bon app' Laurence Lebihan Owner France BONAP 91.24.45.41 91.24.45.40 13008
23 Tsawassen Blvd. Tsawassen Bottom-Dollar Markets Elizabeth Lincoln Accounting Manager Canada BOTTM (604) 555-3745 (604) 555-4729 T2F 8M4 BC
1 2 3 4 5 6 7 8 9 10
Local intranet | Protected Mode: Off
100%

FIGURE 29-27

SUMMARY

This chapter reviewed some of the core principles of the ADO.NET Entity Framework. These capabilities have been available to .NET developers ever since the release of the .NET Framework 3.5 SP1 and Visual Studio 2008 SP1.

ASP.NET also includes a control that works with the Entity Framework: the EntityDataSource control.

The Entity Framework provides the ability to work with a multitude of different data sources and allows you to build a mapping layer between your object-oriented API layer and the schema-driven database layer.

30

ASP.NET Dynamic Data

WHAT'S IN THIS CHAPTER?

- Building an ASP.NET Dynamic Data application
- Using dynamic data routes
- Handling your application's display

ASP.NET offers a feature that enables you to dynamically create data-driven Web applications. ASP.NET Dynamic Data is more than purely a code generator, and although it can provide a base application, it is completely modifiable by you. This feature allows you to quickly and easily create data entry or applications that allow your end users to work with and view the backend database.

The data-driven applications require a few components in order to work: the template system, a database from which to drive the application, and the ability to work from an object model such as LINQ to SQL or LINQ to Entities.

This chapter illustrates how to build and customize an ASP.NET Dynamic Data application.

CREATING YOUR BASE APPLICATION WITH VISUAL STUDIO 2010

ASP.NET Dynamic Data's capabilities were first introduced with the .NET Framework 3.5 SP1 and have been enhanced with the release of the .NET Framework 4 and Visual Studio 2010. Figure 30-1 shows the two projects that are available in this area from Visual Studio 2010: Dynamic Data Linq to SQL Web Site and Dynamic Data Entities Web Site.

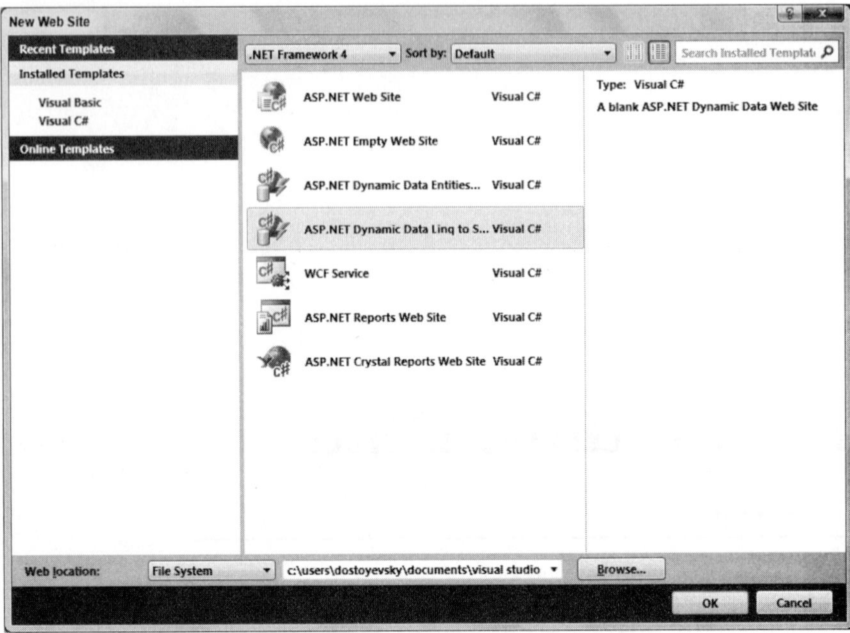

FIGURE 30-1

Which of the two application types you choose depends on how you plan to approach the object model. If you want to work with LINQ to SQL as your object model, then you will choose the Dynamic Data Linq to SQL Web Site option. If you want to work with LINQ to Entities (as discussed in the previous chapter), then you will choose the Dynamic Data Entities Web Site project. Note that if you were to reverse the choices, then you would experience various expected errors in working with your data-driven application.

For an example of working through the creation of your first data-driven application, select the Dynamic Data Linq to SQL Web Site option, as this example will work with LINQ to SQL. Name your project `MyNorthwind`.

Visual Studio 2010 will create a base application that is not connected to any database or object model from the start. It will be your job to make these connections. Before doing this, however, take a look at what Visual Studio has created for you.

Looking at the Core Files Created in the Default Application

Before you even assign the pre-generated dynamic data application to a database, much of the core application is created for you through the Visual Studio process just mentioned.

When you create the application, you will find a lot of new pieces to your ASP.NET application in the Visual Studio Solution Explorer. Figure 30-2 presents these extra items.

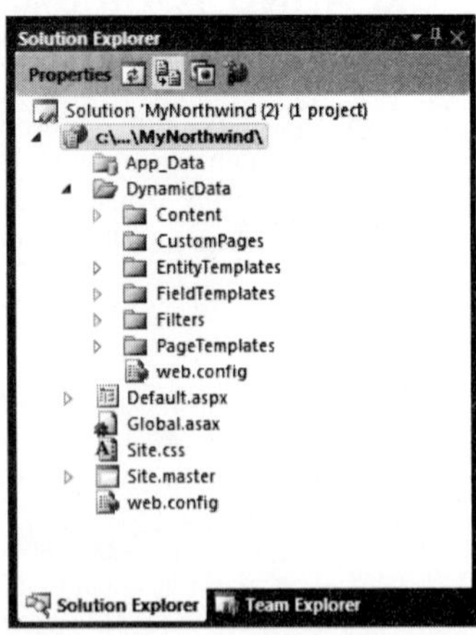

FIGURE 30-2

The items that are generated for you and what is presented here in the Visual Studio Solution Explorer are generally referred to as *scaffolding*. Even though a lot of code seems to be generated for you, do not be alarmed thinking that you are locked into a specific data-driven application. What is generated is termed "scaffolding" because it is a framework that can be taken holistically or modified and extended for any purpose. This framework is the presentation and database layer support that you will need for the auto-generation of your application. You are in no way locked into a specific set of models, looks and feels, or even an approach that you are unable to modify to suit your specific needs.

Even though you will find a lot of pre-generated code in your Solution Explorer, you are not even required to use this code to work with ASP.NET Dynamic Data. In fact, you can even add ASP.NET Dynamic Data to a pre-existing application.

Next, this chapter looks at the pre-generated application that enables you to work with your backend database.

The Dynamic Data Application

One of the biggest additions to this application operation that is dramatically different from the standard ASP.NET application is a folder called DynamicData. This folder contains the pre-generated ASP.NET application that enables you to work with your database through a browser.

The goal of this application is to enable you to work with your database through the entire CRUD process (Create, Read, Update, and Delete). Again, you can limit the amount of interactivity you provide from your application.

To view how this application works against a database, you must dig further into the controls and pages that make up the application. Expanding the DynamicData folder, you find the following folders:

- Content
- CustomPages
- EntityTemplates
- FieldTemplates
- Filters
- PageTemplates

In addition to these folders, you will find a `web.config` file that is specific to this application.

The Content folder in this part of the application includes a user control that is used in the page templates, as well as the underlying images that are used by the style sheet of the application.

The CustomPages folder is a separate folder that allows you to put any custom pages that you might include in the data-driven Web application. When you create an application from scratch, you will not find any file in this folder. It is intentionally blank.

The EntityTemplates folder is a new folder provided in ASP.NET 4 that makes getting the layout you want quite easy, thereby not requiring you to build a custom page. Initially, there is a `Default.ascx` (user control), and the edit and insert versions of this control are found in the folder.

The FieldTemplates folder is interesting because it has some of the more granular aspects of the application. The entire application is designed to work off a database, but it really does not have any idea what type of database it is going to be working from. The FieldTemplates folder is a way that the application can present any of the underlying data types that are coming from the database. Figure 30-3 shows the data types as presented in the Visual Studio Solution Explorer.

In this case, you will find data types for date/time values, integers, text, foreign keys, and more. They are represented as ASP.NET user controls, or `.ascx` files, which makes them easy for you to modify.

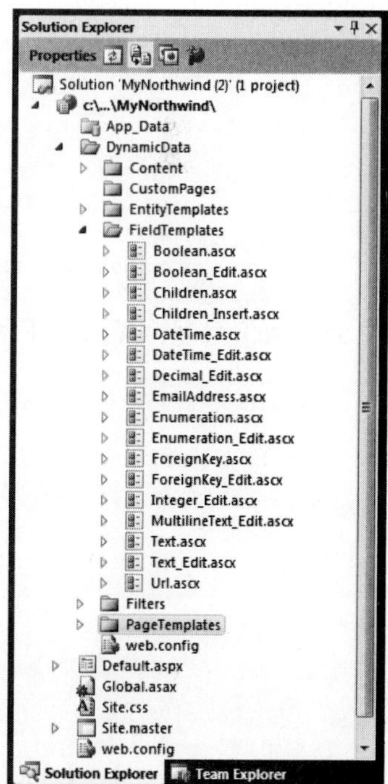

FIGURE 30-3

As an example, open the `DateTime.ascx` file, and you will get the bit of code presented in Listing 30-1.

LISTING 30-1: The DateTime.ascx file

Available for download on Wrox.com

VB

```
<%@ Control Language="VB" CodeBehind="DateTime.ascx.vb"
    Inherits="DateTimeField" %>

<asp:Literal runat="server" ID="Literal1"
 Text="<%# FieldValueString %>" />
```

C#

```
<%@ Control Language="C#" CodeBehind="DateTime.ascx.cs"
    Inherits="DateTimeField" %>

<asp:Literal runat="server" ID="Literal1"
 Text="<%# FieldValueString %>" />
```

You can see that there isn't much to the code shown in Listing 30-1. There is a simple Literal server control and nothing more. The `Text` property of the control gets populated with the variable `FieldValueString` from the code-behind file. Listing 30-2 presents this file.

LISTING 30-2: The code-behind file for DateTime.ascx

Available for download on Wrox.com

VB

```
Imports System.ComponentModel.DataAnnotations
Imports System.Web.DynamicData
Imports System.Web

Class DateTimeField
    Inherits FieldTemplateUserControl


    Public Overrides ReadOnly Property DataControl As Control
        Get
            Return Literal1
        End Get
    End Property


End Class
```

C#

```
using System;
using System.Collections.Specialized;
using System.ComponentModel.DataAnnotations;
using System.Web.DynamicData;
using System.Web;
using System.Web.UI;
using System.Web.UI.WebControls;

public partial class DateTimeField :
   System.Web.DynamicData.FieldTemplateUserControl
 {
     public override Control DataControl
     {
         get
         {
             return Literal1;
         }
     }
}
```

The data field templates inherit from `System.Web.DynamicData.FieldTemplateUserControl`, as you can see from Listing 30-2. This user control provides a read version of the data field for your application.

In addition to the data field .ascx files, there is an *edit* version of the control that is represented as a user control in addition to the *read* version of the data field. The edit versions have a filename ending in _Edit, as in the DateTime_Edit.ascx file.

Listing 30-3 presents the contents of the DateTime_Edit.ascx control.

LISTING 30-3: The DateTime_Edit.ascx file

Available for download on Wrox.com

```
<%@ Control Language="VB" CodeBehind="DateTime_Edit.ascx.vb"
    Inherits="DateTime_EditField" %>

<asp:TextBox ID="TextBox1" runat="server" CssClass="DDTextBox"
 Text='<%# FieldValueEditString %>' Columns="20"></asp:TextBox>

<asp:RequiredFieldValidator runat="server" ID="RequiredFieldValidator1"
 CssClass="DDControl DDValidator" ControlToValidate="TextBox1"
 Display="Dynamic" Enabled="false" />
<asp:RegularExpressionValidator runat="server"
 ID="RegularExpressionValidator1" CssClass="DDControl DDValidator"
 ControlToValidate="TextBox1" Display="Dynamic" Enabled="false" />
<asp:DynamicValidator runat="server" ID="DynamicValidator1"
 CssClass="DDControl DDValidator" ControlToValidate="TextBox1"
 Display="Dynamic" />
<asp:CustomValidator runat="server" ID="DateValidator"
 CssClass="DDControl DDValidator" ControlToValidate="TextBox1"
 Display="Dynamic" EnableClientScript="false" Enabled="false"
 OnServerValidate="DateValidator_ServerValidate" />
```

```
<%@ Control Language="C#" CodeBehind="DateTime_Edit.ascx.cs"
    Inherits="DateTime_EditField" %>

<asp:TextBox ID="TextBox1" runat="server" CssClass="DDTextBox"
 Text='<%# FieldValueEditString %>' Columns="20"></asp:TextBox>

<asp:RequiredFieldValidator runat="server" ID="RequiredFieldValidator1"
 CssClass="DDControl DDValidator" ControlToValidate="TextBox1"
 Display="Dynamic" Enabled="false" />
<asp:RegularExpressionValidator runat="server"
 ID="RegularExpressionValidator1" CssClass="DDControl DDValidator"
 ControlToValidate="TextBox1" Display="Dynamic" Enabled="false" />
<asp:DynamicValidator runat="server" ID="DynamicValidator1"
 CssClass="DDControl DDValidator" ControlToValidate="TextBox1"
 Display="Dynamic" />
<asp:CustomValidator runat="server" ID="DateValidator"
 CssClass="DDControl DDValidator" ControlToValidate="TextBox1"
 Display="Dynamic" EnableClientScript="false" Enabled="false"
 OnServerValidate="DateValidator_ServerValidate" />
```

As you can see, the date will be populated into a TextBox server control. In addition to this representation, a series of validation server controls validate the input before applying an edit to the database.

Listing 30-4 shows the code-behind of these pages.

LISTING 30-4: The code-behind pages from the DateTime_Edit.ascx file

Available for download on Wrox.com

```
Imports System.ComponentModel.DataAnnotations
Imports System.Web.DynamicData
Imports System.Web
```

continues

LISTING 30-4 *(continued)*

```
Class DateTime_EditField
    Inherits FieldTemplateUserControl

    Private Shared DefaultDateAttribute As DataTypeAttribute =
       New DataTypeAttribute(DataType.DateTime)

    Public Overrides ReadOnly Property DataControl As Control
        Get
            Return TextBox1
        End Get
    End Property

    Protected Sub Page_Load(ByVal sender As Object,
     ByVal e As EventArgs)
        TextBox1.ToolTip = Column.Description
        SetUpValidator(RequiredFieldValidator1)
        SetUpValidator(RegularExpressionValidator1)
        SetUpValidator(DynamicValidator1)
        SetUpCustomValidator(DateValidator)
    End Sub

    Private Sub SetUpCustomValidator(ByVal validator As CustomValidator)
        If Column.DataTypeAttribute IsNot Nothing Then
            Select Case (Column.DataTypeAttribute.DataType)
                Case DataType.Date,
                     DataType.DateTime,
                     DataType.Time

                    validator.Enabled = True
                    DateValidator.ErrorMessage =
                     HttpUtility.HtmlEncode(
      Column.DataTypeAttribute.FormatErrorMessage(Column.DisplayName))
            End Select
        ElseIf Column.ColumnType.Equals(GetType(DateTime)) Then
            validator.Enabled = True
            DateValidator.ErrorMessage = HttpUtility.HtmlEncode(
              DefaultDateAttribute.FormatErrorMessage(Column.DisplayName))
        End If
    End Sub

    Protected Sub DateValidator_ServerValidate(ByVal source As Object,
      ByVal args As ServerValidateEventArgs)
        Dim dummyResult As DateTime
        args.IsValid = DateTime.TryParse(args.Value, dummyResult)
    End Sub

    Protected Overrides Sub ExtractValues(ByVal dictionary As
     IOrderedDictionary)
        dictionary(Column.Name) = ConvertEditedValue(TextBox1.Text)
    End Sub

End Class
```

C#

```
<%@ Control Language="C#" CodeFile="DateTime_Edit.ascx.cs"
    Inherits="DateTime_EditField" %>

using System;
using System.Collections.Specialized;
using System.ComponentModel.DataAnnotations;
```

```
using System.Web.DynamicData;
using System.Web;
using System.Web.UI;
using System.Web.UI.WebControls;

public partial class DateTime_EditField :
   System.Web.DynamicData.FieldTemplateUserControl {
    private static DataTypeAttribute DefaultDateAttribute =
        new DataTypeAttribute(DataType.DateTime);
    protected void Page_Load(object sender, EventArgs e) {
        TextBox1.ToolTip = Column.Description;

        SetUpValidator(RequiredFieldValidator1);
        SetUpValidator(RegularExpressionValidator1);
        SetUpValidator(DynamicValidator1);
        SetUpCustomValidator(DateValidator);
    }

    private void SetUpCustomValidator(CustomValidator validator) {
        if (Column.DataTypeAttribute != null) {
            switch (Column.DataTypeAttribute.DataType) {
                case DataType.Date:
                case DataType.DateTime:
                case DataType.Time:
                    validator.Enabled = true;
                    DateValidator.ErrorMessage =
                      HttpUtility.HtmlEncode(
     Column.DataTypeAttribute.FormatErrorMessage(Column.DisplayName));
                    break;
            }
        }
        else if (Column.ColumnType.Equals(typeof(DateTime))) {
            validator.Enabled = true;
            DateValidator.ErrorMessage = HttpUtility.HtmlEncode(
          DefaultDateAttribute.FormatErrorMessage(Column.DisplayName));
        }
    }

    protected void DateValidator_ServerValidate(object source,
      ServerValidateEventArgs args) {
        DateTime dummyResult;
        args.IsValid = DateTime.TryParse(args.Value, out dummyResult);
    }

    protected override void ExtractValues(IOrderedDictionary
      dictionary) {
        dictionary[Column.Name] = ConvertEditedValue(TextBox1.Text);
    }

    public override Control DataControl {
        get {
            return TextBox1;
        }
    }

}
```

You can see that every time you edit something in the database that includes a `DateTime` data type, it will also appear in a textbox HTML element for that purpose. In the code-behind of the file, you assign a tooltip to the textbox element, and assign four separate validation server controls to the control.

Again, these user controls are the most granular example of how you can modify the output of the application. Another option, which you will review shortly, is to work with the page templates where these granular user controls are used.

The Filters folder is used to create drop-down menus for Booleans (true/false values), foreign keys, and enumerations. These menus enable the end user to filter tables based upon keys within the database. This folder is new for ASP.NET 4.

The PageTemplates folder contains the core pages that you use to bring the application together. Notice that pages exist for many of the core constructs that you will use in representing your tables in the application. The PageTemplates folder includes the following pages:

- `Details.aspx`
- `Edit.aspx`
- `Insert.aspx`
- `List.aspx`
- `ListDetails.aspx`

You use the `List.aspx` page for the tables in your connected database. You use the `Details.aspx` pages when you are examining a single row from the table, and you use the `ListDetails.aspx` page for examining master details views of the table and row relationships. You use the `Edit.aspx` and `Insert.aspx` pages, in turn, for the types of operations that they describe. Listing 30-5 shows a partial listing of the `List.aspx` page, specifically how it represents a table.

Available for download on Wrox.com

LISTING 30-5: A partial code example from the List.aspx page

```
<%@ Page Language="C#" MasterPageFile="~/Site.master"
    CodeBehind="List.aspx.cs" Inherits="List" %>

<%@ Register src="~/DynamicData/Content/GridViewPager.ascx"
      tagname="GridViewPager" tagprefix="asp" %>

<asp:Content ID="Content1" ContentPlaceHolderID="ContentPlaceHolder1"
 Runat="Server">
    <asp:DynamicDataManager ID="DynamicDataManager1" runat="server"
     AutoLoadForeignKeys="true">
        <DataControls>
            <asp:DataControlReference ControlID="GridView1" />
        </DataControls>
    </asp:DynamicDataManager>

    <h2 class="DDSubHeader"><%= table.DisplayName%></h2>

    <asp:UpdatePanel ID="UpdatePanel1" runat="server">
        <ContentTemplate>

            <!-- Code removed for clarity -->

        </ContentTemplate>
    </asp:UpdatePanel>
</asp:Content>
```

Again, these controls and templates do not have any built-in thoughts of what the table is going to be like. These pages are built oblivious to the underlying tables to which this application will connect. This is evident through the use of the code `<%= table.DisplayName%>`. The next step is to actually tie this application to a database.

Incorporating the Database

The next step required to build your first ASP.NET Dynamic Data application is to incorporate a database that you are able to work with. For this example, you need to include the Northwind database. The previous chapter explained how to get a copy of it or the AdventureWorks database, both of which are SQL Server Express Edition databases. Include the `Northwind.mdf` database file in the App_Data folder of your solution for this example.

After the database is in place, the next step is to establish a defined entity data model layer that will work with the underlying database. Because this example is working with the LINQ to SQL approach rather than the LINQ to Entities approach, you must add a LINQ to SQL class to your application.

To accomplish this task, right-click on your project within the Visual Studio Solution Explorer and select Add ➪ New Item from the provided menu. Then add a LINQ to SQL class by selecting that option from the middle section of the Add New Item dialog, as illustrated in Figure 30-4.

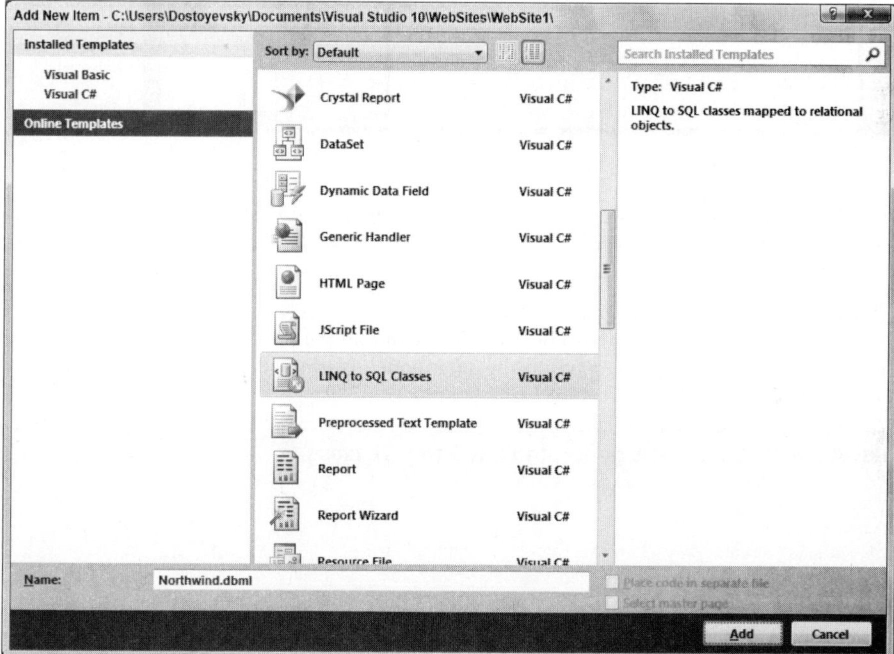

FIGURE 30-4

Name your `.dbml` file `Northwind.dbml`, as shown in Figure 30-4. The O/R (*object relational*) Designer for working with your LINQ to SQL classes then appears. It is a visual representation of the `Northwind.dbml` file (which currently does not contain any references to the database tables).

The O/R Designer has two parts. The first part is for data classes, which can be tables, classes, associations, and inheritances. Dragging such items onto the design surface gives you a visual representation of the object that you can work with. The second part (on the right side of the dialog) is for methods, which map to stored procedures within a database.

Working with the Northwind database is quite simple — it's really a matter of opening the database in the Visual Studio Server Explorer and dragging and dropping all the tables onto the design surface of the O/R Designer. Figure 30-5 shows the results.

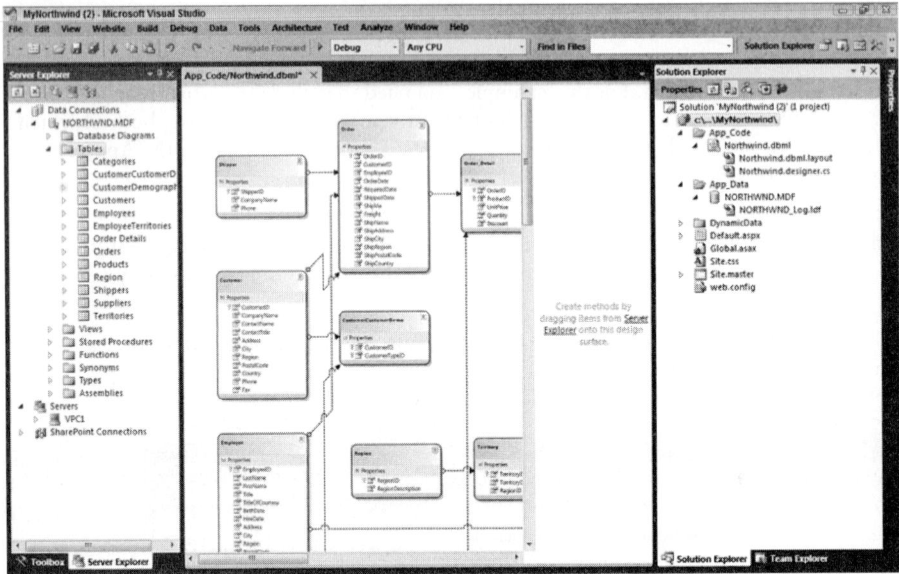

FIGURE 30-5

With this action, a bunch of code is added to the designer files of the `Northwind.dbml` file on your behalf. These classes will now give you strongly typed access to the tables of the database, and more importantly, they will be able to tie themselves to the data-driven application that has been the focus of this chapter.

You will find the code that Visual Studio generated by opening the `Northwind.designer.vb` or `Northwind.designer.cs` file within Visual Studio. Here you can find the programmatic representation of the database and the tables that you chose to add to the data model. Listing 30-6 shows a partial view of the generated code of this class.

LISTING 30-6: A partial look at the generated LINQ to SQL class

Available for download on Wrox.com

```
Option Strict On
Option Explicit On

Imports System
Imports System.Collections.Generic
Imports System.ComponentModel
Imports System.Data
Imports System.Data.Linq
Imports System.Data.Linq.Mapping
Imports System.Linq
Imports System.Linq.Expressions
Imports System.Reflection

<Global.System.Data.Linq.Mapping.DatabaseAttribute(Name:="NORTHWND")>  _
Partial Public Class NorthwindDataContext
   Inherits System.Data.Linq.DataContext

   ' Code removed for clarity

End Class
```

```
using System;
using System.Collections.Generic;
using System.ComponentModel;
```

```
using System.Data;
using System.Data.Linq;
using System.Data.Linq.Mapping;
using System.Linq;
using System.Linq.Expressions;
using System.Reflection;

[global::System.Data.Linq.Mapping.DatabaseAttribute(Name="NORTHWND")]
public partial class NorthwindDataContext : System.Data.Linq.DataContext
      {

      // Code removed for clarity

}
```

Filenames Northwind.designer.vb and Northwind.designer.cs

This code creates an implementation of the `DataContext` object called `NorthwindDataContext`, which manages the transactions that occur with the database when you are working with LINQ to SQL. The `DataContext`, in addition to managing the transactions with the database, also contains the connection string, takes care of any logging, and manages the output of the data.

There is a lot to this file. For example, you will find the tables represented as classes within the generated code. Listing 30-7 shows the class that represents the Customers table from the database.

Available for download on Wrox.com

LISTING 30-7: The code representation of the Customers table

```
<Global.System.Data.Linq.Mapping.TableAttribute(Name:="dbo.Customers")> _
Partial Public Class Customer
   Implements System.ComponentModel.INotifyPropertyChanging,
     System.ComponentModel.INotifyPropertyChanged

   ' Code removed for clarity

End Class
```

```
[global::System.Data.Linq.Mapping.TableAttribute(Name="dbo.Customers")]
public partial class Customer : INotifyPropertyChanging,
   INotifyPropertyChanged
{

   // Code removed for clarity

}
```

Filenames Northwind.designer.vb and Northwind.designer.cs

Now that the database is residing within the application and is ready to use, the next step is to wire the database to the overall application.

Registering the Data Model Within the Global.asax File

The next step is to register the `NorthwindDataContext` object within the overall solution. The `NorthwindDataContext` is the data model that was built using the LINQ to SQL class that you just created.

One of the files that was included when you built the ASP.NET Dynamic Data application from the start was a `Global.asax` file. This file is normally not included with your standard ASP.NET application by Visual Studio. When looking at this file, you will notice that there is a lot more to this file than the normal `Global.asax` file you might be used to (if you ever included one). Listing 30-8 shows the `Global.asax` file that is provided to you (minus some of the comments).

LISTING 30-8: The Global.asax file

Available for download on Wrox.com

```
<%@ Application Language="VB" %>
<%@ Import Namespace="System.ComponentModel.DataAnnotations" %>
<%@ Import Namespace="System.Web.Routing" %>
<%@ Import Namespace="System.Web.DynamicData" %>

<script RunAt="server">
Private Shared s_defaultModel As New MetaModel
Public Shared ReadOnly Property DefaultModel() As MetaModel
    Get
        Return s_defaultModel
    End Get
End Property

Public Shared Sub RegisterRoutes(ByVal routes As RouteCollection)

   ' DefaultModel.RegisterContext(GetType(YourDataContextType),
   '    New ContextConfiguration() With {.ScaffoldAllTables = False})

    routes.Add(New DynamicDataRoute("{table}/{action}.aspx") With {
        .Constraints = New RouteValueDictionary(New With {.Action =
        "List|Details|Edit|Insert"}),
        .Model = DefaultModel})
End Sub

Private Sub Application_Start(ByVal sender As Object,
   ByVal e As EventArgs)
    RegisterRoutes(RouteTable.Routes)
End Sub

</script>
```

C#

```
<%@ Application Language="C#" %>
<%@ Import Namespace="System.ComponentModel.DataAnnotations" %>
<%@ Import Namespace="System.Web.Routing" %>
<%@ Import Namespace="System.Web.DynamicData" %>

<script RunAt="server">
    private static MetaModel s_defaultModel = new MetaModel();
    public static MetaModel DefaultModel {
        get {
            return s_defaultModel;
        }
    }

    public static void RegisterRoutes(RouteCollection routes)
    {
        //DefaultModel.RegisterContext(typeof(YourDataContextType),
        //      new ContextConfiguration()
        //      { ScaffoldAllTables = false });

        routes.Add(new DynamicDataRoute("{table}/{action}.aspx")
        {
            Constraints = new RouteValueDictionary(new
               { action = "List|Details|Edit|Insert" }),
            Model = DefaultModel
        });
    }

    void Application_Start(object sender, EventArgs e)
    {
        RegisterRoutes(RouteTable.Routes);
    }

</script>
```

If you are familiar with the standard `Global.asax` file, then you will recognize the standard `Application_Start()` method that is part of the file. This method fires whenever the ASP.NET application starts up for the first time or is recycled in some manner. The `Application_Start()` method here calls a method named `RegisterRoutes()`, which does the wiring between the generated application and the data model that you created earlier.

You must register the data model that you created, the instance of the `DataContext` object. In this example, you must wire up the `NorthwindDataContext` object. Looking over the code from Listing 30-8, you can see that one of the lines of code is commented out. This is the `RegisterContext()` method call. Uncomment this line of code, and instead of having a reference to an object of type `YourDataContextType`, change it to `NorthwindDataContext`. In the end, your line of code will be as shown in Listing 30-9.

LISTING 30-9: Wiring the NorthwindDataContext object

VB

```
model.RegisterContext(GetType(NorthwindDataContext), _
   New ContextConfiguration() With {.ScaffoldAllTables = True})
```

C#

```
model.RegisterContext(typeof(NorthwindDataContext),
   new ContextConfiguration() { ScaffoldAllTables = true });
```

So, here the model is registered as a `DataContext` object of type `NorthwindDataContext`, and the `ScaffoldAllTables` property is set to `True` (the default is set to `False`), signifying that you want all the table representations in the model to be included in the generated application.

Styles and Layout

With the data model wired to the application, you are actually ready to run the application and see what it produces. However, before this operation, you must be aware of two more pieces of this application.

When you created the application, a master page and a stylesheet were also included. The master page, `Site.master`, is rather simple but does include the overall page framework that allows you to navigate the tables. There is also a simple stylesheet called `Site.css` that provides the overall style of the page.

Results of the Application

As you run the application, notice that the first page allows you to see all the tables that you made a part of your data model, as illustrated in Figure 30-6.

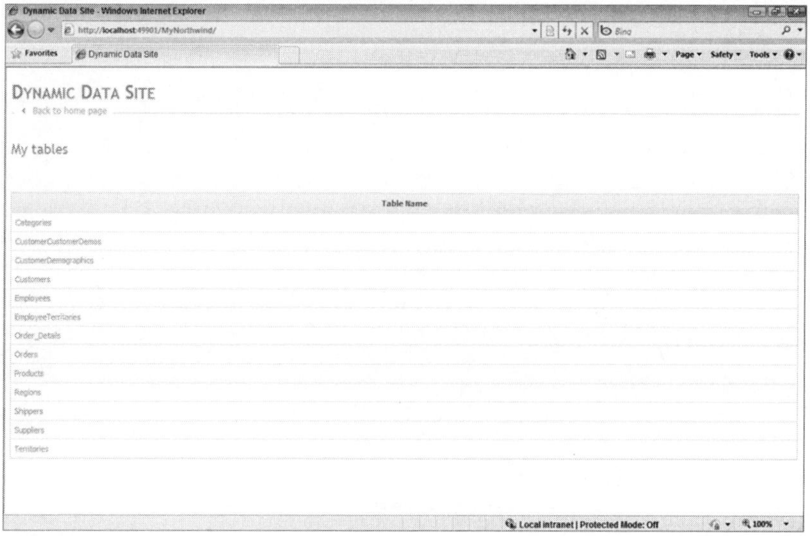

FIGURE 30-6

As an application that reads the contents of your database, it works quite simply. Clicking on a table name (which is a hyperlink in the application) provides the contents of the table. Figure 30-7 shows this view.

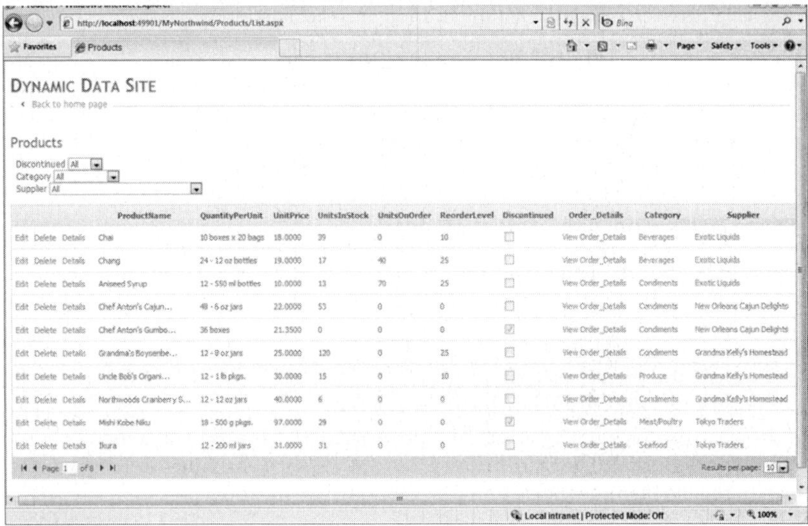

FIGURE 30-7

The table view is nicely styled and includes the ability to edit, delete, or view the details of each row in the database. In cases where a one-to-many relationship exists, you can drill down deeper into it. Another interesting part of the page is the navigation through the table. Pagination appears through the table, as shown at the bottom of the table in Figure 30-7.

In addition to being able to use the edit, delete, or detail view of the row of information in the table, you can insert new rows into the database by clicking on the Insert New Item link below the table. A view similar to that shown in Figure 30-8 appears.

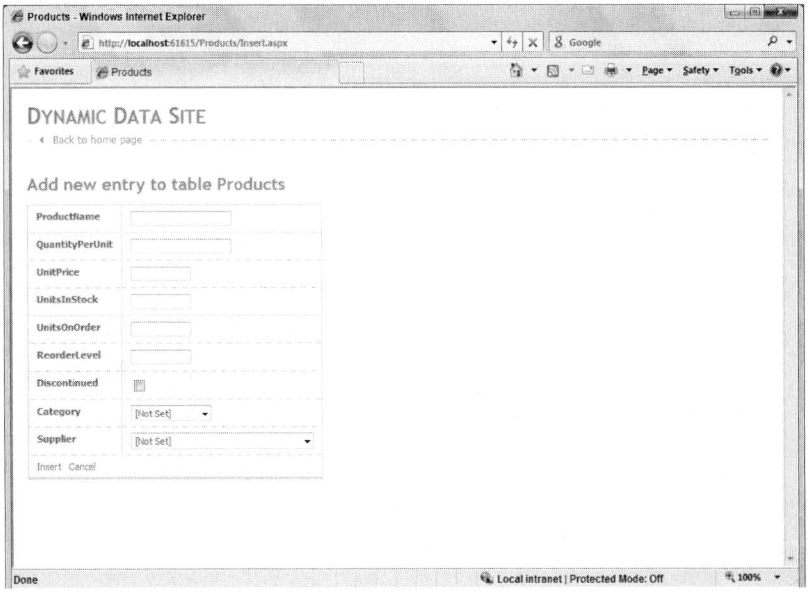

FIGURE 30-8

Editing a row makes the same type of page appear, as shown in Figure 30-9. This page resulted from clicking the Edit link next to one of the rows in the Products table.

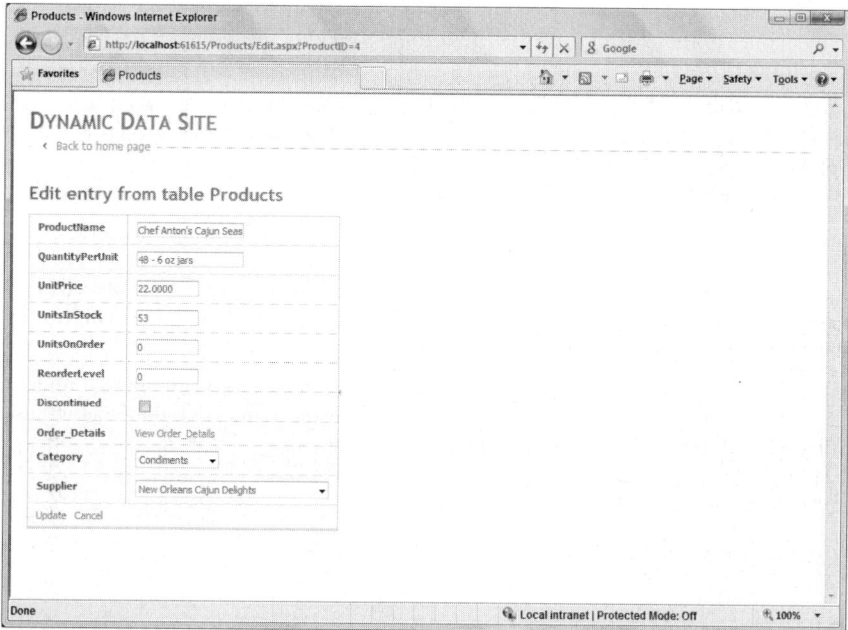

FIGURE 30-9

Another interesting aspect of this application is how it works with the one-to-many relationships of the elements in the data model. For example, clicking the Orders table link produces the view shown in Figure 30-10.

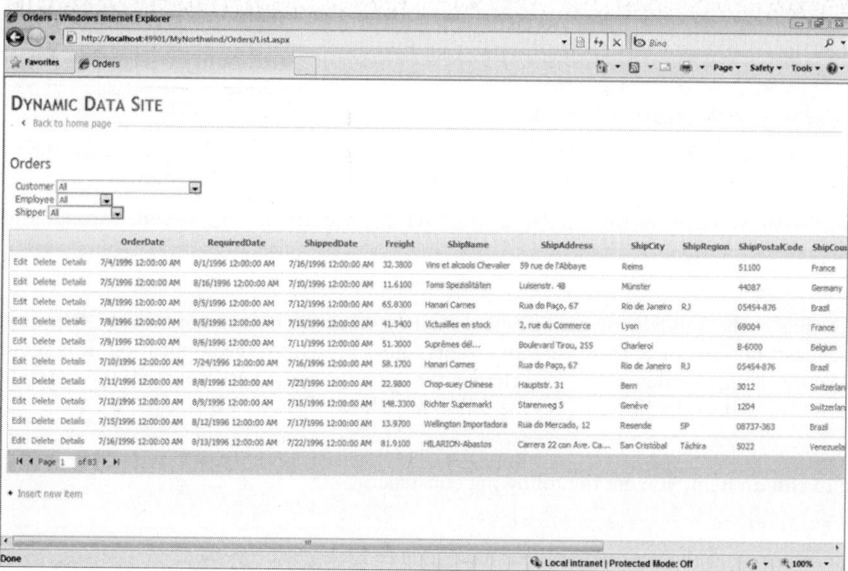

FIGURE 30-10

Here, in addition to the table and its contents, you are presented with a filtering capability via the various drop-down menus at the top of the page. In this case, you can filter the orders by customer, employee, or shipper. You can even use a combination of these elements to filter items. The other aspect to notice in Figure 30-10 about the contents of the table is that instead of a `CustomerID`, an `EmployeeID`, or a `ShipperID`, you see the names of these items, and the application is making the reference to the identifier for these items when drilling further into the views.

The final aspect to understand about this application is that because it is an ASP.NET 4 application, it makes proper use of AJAX. For example, when filtering items in the table, notice that the page makes partial refreshes without refreshing the entire page.

WORKING WITH DYNAMIC DATA ROUTES

As you can see, the application created was quite easy to implement and took only a couple of steps to accomplish. An interesting aspect of this page is how easily configurable it is overall. In particular, you can configure how the URLs are generated and what pages the routing uses.

Going back to the `Global.asax` page that you set up in the previous example, you will find that underneath the `RegisterContext()` call is a method call that sets up the page construct and URL that you will use for the application. Listing 30-10 presents what is established as the default.

LISTING 30-10: Viewing the default routing URL

VB

```
routes.Add(New DynamicDataRoute("{table}/{action}.aspx") With {
        .Constraints = New RouteValueDictionary(New With {.Action =
        "List|Details|Edit|Insert"}),
        .Model = DefaultModel})
```

C#

```
routes.Add(new DynamicDataRoute("{table}/{action}.aspx")
{
   Constraints = new RouteValueDictionary(new { action =
      "List|Details|Edit|Insert" }),
      Model = DefaultModel
});
```

If you go back to the URL that was used in something like an Edit mode operation, you will find a URL like the following:

```
http://localhost:2116/Orders/Edit.aspx?OrderID=10249
```

After the default application, you will find `Orders/Edit.aspx?OrderID=10249`. Here, `Orders` is the name of the table, `Edit` is the operation, and the `OrderID` is the filter on the order that is being worked on.

Returning to Listing 30-10, you can see this model for the URL defined directly in the code through the use of the string:

```
{table}/{action}.aspx
```

Now, if you want to change this model, you can! These are all dynamic URLs and not actual URLs as you know them from the past. For instance, there isn't an Orders folder present in the application. It is simply there as a dynamic route. This is evident when you change the dynamic route path yourself; for example, change the `routes.Add()` call so that it now says the following (shown here in VB as a partial code sample):

```
Routes.Add(New DynamicDataRoute("{action}/{table}.aspx") ...
```

Now, when you go to edit an item, you get the following construct:

```
http://localhost:2116/Edit/Orders.aspx?OrderID=10249
```

From this view, you can see that the action and the table reference have been reversed.

Looking deeper in the `Global.asax` file, you can see that two more pre-established models are at your disposal. Listing 30-11 presents both of them.

LISTING 30-11: The other two routing models

Available for download on Wrox.com

```
'routes.Add(New DynamicDataRoute("{table}/ListDetails.aspx") With { _
' .Action = PageAction.List, _
' .ViewName = "ListDetails", _
' .Model = DefaultModel})

'routes.Add(New DynamicDataRoute("{table}/ListDetails.aspx") With { _
' .Action = PageAction.Details, _
' .ViewName = "ListDetails", _
' .Model = DefaultModel})
```

C#

```
//routes.Add(new DynamicDataRoute("{table}/ListDetails.aspx") {
//    Action = PageAction.List,
//    ViewName = "ListDetails",
//    Model = DefaultModel
//});

//routes.Add(new DynamicDataRoute("{table}/ListDetails.aspx") {
//    Action = PageAction.Details,
//    ViewName = "ListDetails",
//    Model = DefaultModel
//});
```

The example previously presented in this chapter showed each of the operations (for inserting, editing, and so on) on its own separate page. Commenting this previous `routes.Add()` method out of the `Global.asax` file and uncommenting out the second and third options from this file changes the page that is output, and a master/details view now appears on the same page. Figure 30-11 shows one such view of the tables using this new routing.

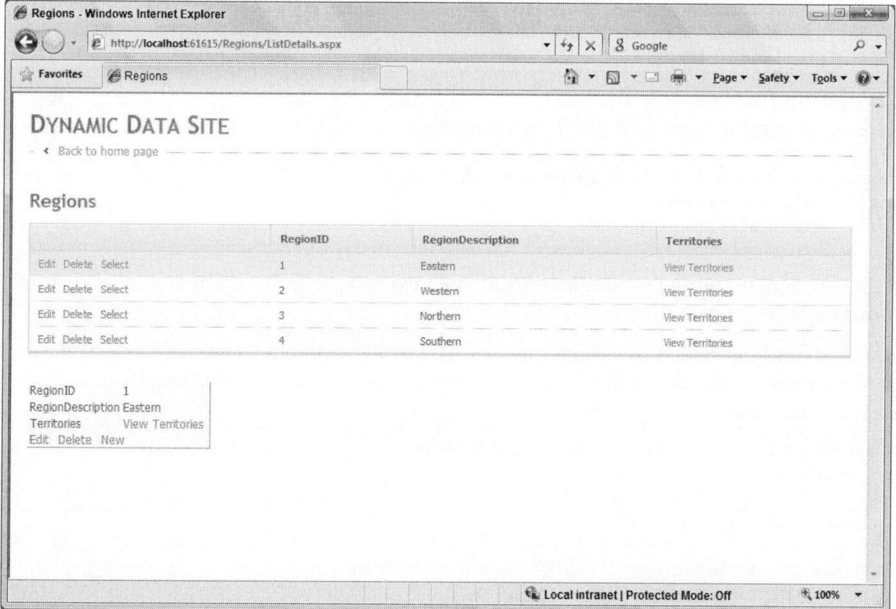

FIGURE 30-11

Now when you select an item, the details of that item also appear on the same page. Also, you are now working on a single page, so when you click the Edit link in the table, you are not sent to another page, but instead, you can now edit the contents of the row directly in the table, as shown in Figure 30-12.

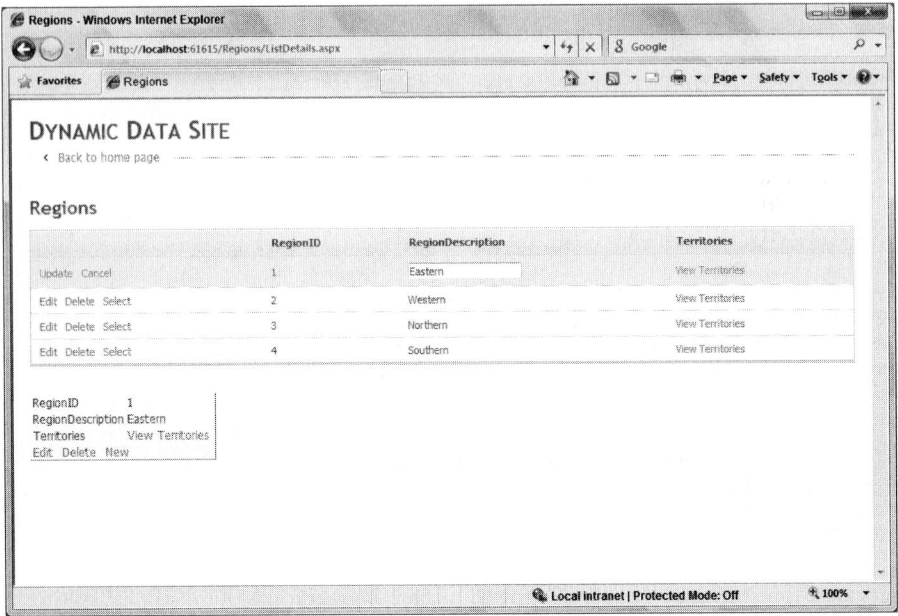

FIGURE 30-12

You need to pay attention to a couple of things when you make these routing changes. If you return to the original routing definition, you can then include the following:

VB

```
routes.Add(New DynamicDataRoute("{table}/{action}.aspx") With { _
          .Constraints = New RouteValueDictionary(New With {.Action = _
          "List|Details|Edit|Insert"}), _
          .Model = DefaultModel})
```

C#

```
routes.Add(new DynamicDataRoute("{table}/{action}.aspx")
{
   Constraints = new RouteValueDictionary(new { action =
      "List|Details|Edit|Insert" }),
      Model = DefaultModel
});
```

From this code, it is true that the route is declared using the table/action options, but just as important, notice that actions are also defined.

This code example basically identifies this route for the List, Details, Edit, and Insert actions. You could have also pointed to other options for each of the action types. The second and third entries in the `Global.asax` file do just that:

VB

```
'routes.Add(New DynamicDataRoute("{table}/ListDetails.aspx") With { _
' .Action = PageAction.List, _
' .ViewName = "ListDetails", _
' .Model = DefaultModel})
```

C#

```
//routes.Add(new DynamicDataRoute("{table}/ListDetails.aspx") {
//    Action = PageAction.List,
//    ViewName = "ListDetails",
//    Model = DefaultModel
//});
```

In this partial code example, you can see that this dynamic data route is defined only for the List operations and does not include the Edit, Insert, or Details operations. In addition, instead of going to `List.aspx` or `Details.aspx`, this operation will go to a specific page — `ListDetails.aspx`. The `ListDetails.aspx` page provides you the ability to perform everything from a single page, which is why you don't need to define the Edit, Insert, and Details operations in this case.

In addition to everything this chapter has presented thus far, another interesting task you can perform is table-specific routing.

Suppose you want to use the `ListDetails.aspx` page for all the tables *except* the Customers table. For this example, assume that you want to return to the base `List.aspx`, `Details.aspx`, and `Edit.aspx` just when the end user is working with the contents of the Customers table. In this case, you need to establish your routing as illustrated in Listing 30-12.

LISTING 30-12: Routing for specific tables

VB

```
routes.Add(New DynamicDataRoute("Customers/{action}.aspx") With { _
   .Constraints = New RouteValueDictionary(New With {.Action = _
     "List|Details|Edit|Insert"}), _
   .Model = DefaultModel, _
   .Table = "Customers"})

routes.Add(New DynamicDataRoute("{table}/ListDetails.aspx") With { _
   .Action = PageAction.List, _
   .ViewName = "ListDetails", _
   .Model = DefaultModel})

routes.Add(New DynamicDataRoute("{table}/ListDetails.aspx") With { _
   .Action = PageAction.Details, _
   .ViewName = "ListDetails", _
   .Model = DefaultModel})
```

C#

```
routes.Add(new DynamicDataRoute("Customers/{action}.aspx")
{
      Constraints = new RouteValueDictionary(new { action =
        "List|Details|Edit|Insert" }),
      Model = DefaultModel,
      Table = "Customers"
});

routes.Add(new DynamicDataRoute("{table}/ListDetails.aspx")
{
      Action = PageAction.List,
      ViewName = "ListDetails",
      Model = DefaultModel
});

routes.Add(new DynamicDataRoute("{table}/ListDetails.aspx")
{
      Action = PageAction.Details,
      ViewName = "ListDetails",
      Model = DefaultModel
});
```

In this case, a dynamic data route of `Customers/{action}.aspx` is provided and will be used when the `Table` reference is equal to the Customers table through the `Table = "Customers"` declaration in the code.

With these three routing statements, the Customers table will use the `List.aspx`, `Details.aspx`, `Edit.aspx`, and `Insert.aspx` pages, whereas all the other tables will use the `ListDetails.aspx` page.

CONTROLLING DISPLAY ASPECTS

ASP.NET Dynamic Data has a wealth of features — more than a single chapter can possibly cover. One final aspect to note is how easy removing tables and columns from the overall application is.

As shown in this chapter, you provided a data model that ended up controlling which parts of the database the data-driven application would work with. In this way, you can create new data models or even use pre-existing data models that might be present in your application.

Even though something is defined within your data model, you might not want that item present in the application. For this reason, you can use a couple of attributes to control whether a table or a column is present and can be worked with by the end user of the application.

For example, suppose you did not want the Employees table to appear in the data-driven application even though this table is present in the data model that you created. In this case, you should use the `ScaffoldTable` attribute on the class that defines the table and set it to `False`. For this method to work, open the `Northwind.designer.vb` or `Northwind.designer.cs` file and make the addition illustrated in Listing 30-13.

LISTING 30-13: Removing the Employees table from view

VB

```
<ScaffoldTable(False)> _
<Global.System.Data.Linq.Mapping.TableAttribute(Name:="dbo.Employees")> _
Partial Public Class Employee
    Implements System.ComponentModel.INotifyPropertyChanging,
       System.ComponentModel.INotifyPropertyChanged

   ' Code removed for clarity

End Class
```

C#

```
[System.ComponentModel.DataAnnotations.ScaffoldTable(false)]
[global::System.Data.Linq.Mapping.TableAttribute(Name="dbo.Employees")]
public partial class Employee : INotifyPropertyChanging,
   INotifyPropertyChanged
{

   // Code removed for clarity

}
```

To use the `ScaffoldTable` attribute, reference the `System.ComponentModel.DataAnnotations` namespace. With this reference in place, running the page will now show a list of tables that excludes the Employees table (see Figure 30-13).

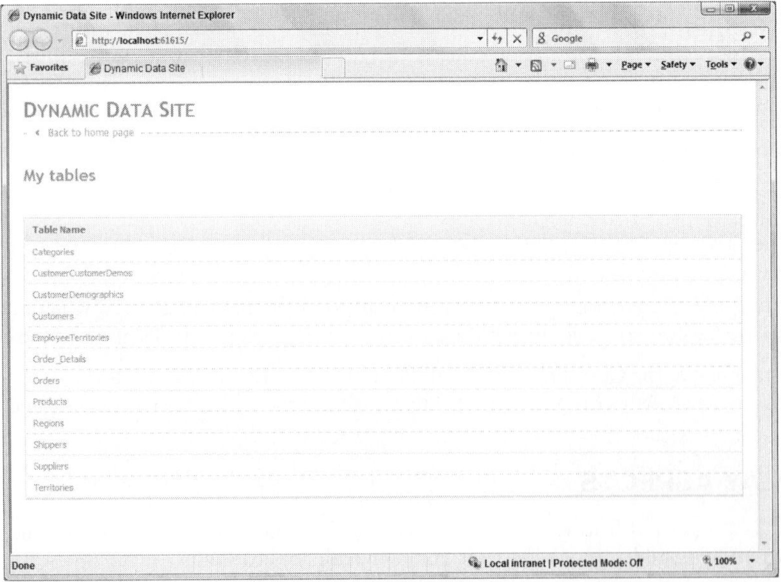

FIGURE 30-13

Similar to the `ScaffoldTable` attribute, the `ScaffoldColumn` attribute is at your disposal (along with many other attributes). When this attribute is applied to a column, that column will be removed from view in the data-driven application.

For example, suppose that you want the Employees table to be viewable, but you do not want users to be able to see employees' home telephone numbers. In this case, you can remove that column by using the `ScaffoldColumn` attribute to set the column's visibility to `False`, as illustrated in Listing 30-14.

LISTING 30-14: Setting the visibility of a column to False

VB

```
<ScaffoldColumn(False)> _
<Global.System.Data.Linq.Mapping.ColumnAttribute(Storage:="_HomePhone",
   DbType:="NVarChar(24)")> _
Public Property HomePhone() As String
      Get
         Return Me._HomePhone
      End Get
      Set(ByVal value As String)
         If (String.Equals(Me._HomePhone, value) = False) Then
            Me.OnHomePhoneChanging(value)
            Me.SendPropertyChanging()
            Me._HomePhone = value
            Me.SendPropertyChanged("HomePhone")
            Me.OnHomePhoneChanged()
         End If
      End Set
End Property
```

C#

```
[System.ComponentModel.DataAnnotations.ScaffoldColumn(false)]
[global::System.Data.Linq.Mapping.ColumnAttribute(Storage="_HomePhone",
   DbType="NVarChar(24)")]
public string HomePhone
{
   get
   {
      return this._HomePhone;
   }
   set
   {
      if ((this._HomePhone != value))
      {
         this.OnHomePhoneChanging(value);
         this.SendPropertyChanging();
         this._HomePhone = value;
         this.SendPropertyChanged("HomePhone");
         this.OnHomePhoneChanged();
      }
   }
}
```

With this code in place, users would see the table and all the columns of the table, except for the `HomePhone` column.

ADDING DYNAMIC DATA TO EXISTING PAGES

When ASP.NET Dynamic Data was first introduced with the .NET Framework 3.5 SP1, it took a bit of setup in order to get dynamic aspects on your pages. With the release of the .NET Framework 4, you will find that it is a lot easier to add dynamic portions to your Web pages.

This is now possible by using the new DynamicDataManager server control. For an example of this in action, take a look at Listing 30-15:

Available for download on Wrox.com

LISTING 30-15: Using the DynamicDataManager server control with an existing GridView control

```
<%@ Page Language="C#" %>

<html xmlns="http://www.w3.org/1999/xhtml">
<head runat="server">
    <title>DynamicDataManager Example</title>
</head>
<body>
    <form id="form1" runat="server">
    <div>

        <asp:GridView ID="GridView1" runat="server" AllowPaging="True"
            AutoGenerateColumns="True" DataKeyNames="CustomerID"
            DataSourceID="LinqDataSource1">
        </asp:GridView>
        <asp:LinqDataSource ID="LinqDataSource1" runat="server"
            ContextTypeName="NorthwindDataContext" EntityTypeName=""
            OrderBy="CompanyName"
            TableName="Customers">
        </asp:LinqDataSource>
        <asp:DynamicDataManager ID="DynamicDataManager1"
         runat="server">
            <DataControls>
                <asp:DataControlReference ControlID="GridView1" />
            </DataControls>
        </asp:DynamicDataManager>

    </div>
    </form>
</body>
</html>
```

Filename DynamicDataManager.aspx

Using the same Northwind data context from the previous examples, you will find a basic LinqDataSource control has been added to the page to work with the `GridView1` server control. The LinqDataSource has also been assigned to work off the Customers table in this example. What you want is a grid that shows a list of the customers.

The next step in building this example is to add a DynamicDataManager control to the page and to have it work with the `GridView1` control as well. This is done by adding a `<DataControls>` section and making a control reference using the `ControlID` attribute of the DataControlReference control.

Running this page will produce the following results as demonstrated here in Figure 30-14:

DynamicDataManager Example - Windows Internet Explorer

http://localhost:35043/MyNorthwind/DynamicDataManager.aspx

CustomerID	CompanyName	ContactName	ContactTitle	Address	City	Region	PostalCode	Country	Phone	Fax	CustomerCustomerDemos	Orders
ALFKI	Alfreds Futterkiste	Maria Anders	Sales Representative	Obere Str. 57	Berlin		12209	Germany	030-0074321	030-0076545	View CustomerCustomerDemos	View Orders
ANATR	Ana Trujillo Emparedad...	Ana Trujillo	Owner	Avda. de la Constituci...	México D.F.		05021	Mexico	(5) 555-4729	(5) 555-3745	View CustomerCustomerDemos	View Orders
ANTON	Antonio Moreno Taquer&...	Antonio Moreno	Owner	Mataderos 2312	México D.F.		05023	Mexico	(5) 555-3932		View CustomerCustomerDemos	View Orders
AROUT	Around the Horn	Thomas Hardy	Sales Representative	120 Hanover Sq.	London		WA1 1DP	UK	(171) 555-7788	(171) 555-6750	View CustomerCustomerDemos	View Orders
BERGS	Berglunds snabbköp	Christina Berglund	Order Administrator	Berguvsvägen 8	Luleå		S-958 22	Sweden	0921-12 34 65	0921-12 34 67	View CustomerCustomerDemos	View Orders
BLAUS	Blauer See Delikatessen	Hanna Moos	Sales Representative	Forsterstr. 57	Mannheim		68306	Germany	0621-08460	0621-08924	View CustomerCustomerDemos	View Orders
BLONP	Blondesddsl père ...	Frédérique C...	Marketing Manager	24, place Kléber	Strasbourg		67000	France	88.60.15.31	88.60.15.32	View CustomerCustomerDemos	View Orders
BOLID	Bólido Comidas pr...	Martin Sommer	Owner	C/ Araquil, 67	Madrid		28023	Spain	(91) 555 22 82	(91) 555 91 99	View CustomerCustomerDemos	View Orders
BONAP	Bon app'	Laurence Lebihan	Owner	12, rue des Bouchers	Marseille		13008	France	91.24.45.40	91.24.45.41	View CustomerCustomerDemos	View Orders
BOTTM	Bottom-Dollar Markets	Elizabeth Lincoln	Accounting Manager	23 Tsawassen Blvd.	Tsawassen BC		T2F 8M4	Canada	(604) 555-4729	(604) 555-3745	View CustomerCustomerDemos	View Orders

12345678910

Local intranet | Protected Mode: Off

FIGURE 30-14

From this example, you can see that the hierarchical content associated with the customers is interpreted and displayed as links in the table. All of this is dynamic.

Another control to be aware of is the DynamicControl server control. This is utilized when you have a templated control and want ASP.NET to make the smart decision on how to render the appropriate HTML for this control. For an example of this, redo the previous example from Listing 30-15 and change the GridView server control to a ListView server control. You will also need to change the reference in the DynamicDataManager control for this example to work.

Dragging and dropping the ListView server control onto the design surface of Visual Studio, you will notice that it now has the ability to enable the control for Dynamic Data, as is shown when configuring the ListView control in Figure 30-15.

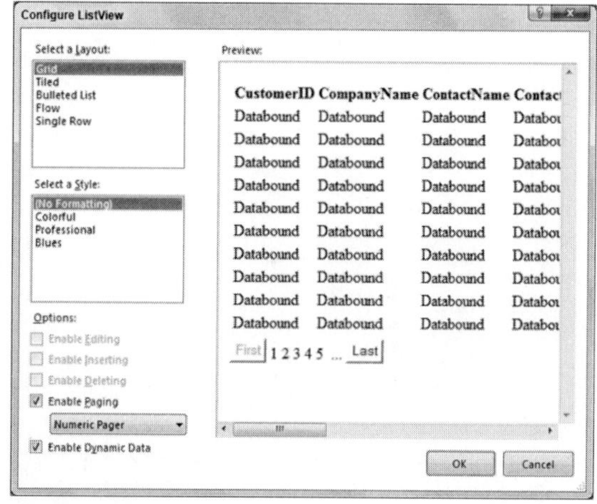

FIGURE 30-15

Checking the Enable Dynamic Data checkbox in this dialog will generate a lot of controls for all the different views provided by the template. With the code generated by Visual Studio, you will see a lot of use of the DynamicControl control. An example of one of the control instances generated (in an edit mode) is presented here:

```
<asp:DynamicControl runat="server" DataField="CompanyName" Mode="Edit" />
```

With the combination of these new controls, you can now quickly and easily add Dynamic Data to any of your ASP.NET pages.

SUMMARY

This chapter explored the capabilities in ASP.NET for building Dynamic Data-driven applications quickly and easily. These capabilities, in conjunction with Visual Studio, enable you to build a reporting application that provides full CRUD capabilities in less than five minutes.

At the same time, you can delve deep into the application and modify how the application presents the contents of your database.

31

Working with Services

WHAT'S IN THIS CHAPTER?

- Building and consuming Web services
- Understanding the Windows Communication Foundation
- Working with WCF Data Services

When the .NET Framework 1.0 was first introduced, much of the hype around its release was focused on XML Web services. In fact, Microsoft advertised that the main purpose of the newly released .NET Framework 1.0 was to enable developers to build and consume XML Web services with ease. Unfortunately, the new Web services model was slow to be accepted by the development community because it was so radically different from messaging frameworks that came before (even though it was outright better). At the time, decision makers in the development community regarded this new Web services model with a cautious eye.

Since then, Microsoft has stopped trumpeting that .NET is all about Web services and, instead, has really expanded the power of .NET and its relation to applications built within the enterprise. Still, the members of the IT community continued to look long and hard at the Web services model (Microsoft is no longer alone in hyping this technology), examining how it could help them with their current issues and problems.

This chapter looks at building XML Web services and how you can consume XML Web service interfaces and integrate them into your ASP.NET applications. It begins with the foundations of XML Web services in the .NET world by examining some of the underlying technologies such as SOAP, WSDL, and more. The middle part of this chapter focuses on the latest Microsoft messaging framework — Windows Communication Foundation, also known as WCF. Finally, the last part of this chapter shows you how to create RESTful-type services using WCF Data Services. This relatively new framework is something that you can use to quickly and easily expose your data.

COMMUNICATION BETWEEN DISPARATE SYSTEMS

It is a diverse world. In a major enterprise, very rarely do you find that the entire organization and its data repositories reside on a single vendor's platform. In most instances, organizations are made up of a patchwork of systems — some based on UNIX, some on Microsoft, and some on other systems. There probably will not be a day when everything resides on a single platform where all the data moves seamlessly from one server to another. For that reason, these various systems must be able to talk to one another. If disparate systems can communicate easily, moving unique datasets around the enterprise becomes a simple process — alleviating the need for replication systems and data stores.

When XML (eXtensible Markup Language) was introduced, it became clear that the markup language would be the structure to bring the necessary integration into the enterprise. XML's power comes from the fact that it can be used regardless of the platform, language, or data store of the system using it to expose DataSets.

XML has its roots in the Standard Generalized Markup Language (SGML), which was created in 1986. Because SGML was so complex, something a bit simpler was needed — thus, the birth of XML.

XML is considered ideal for data representation purposes because it enables developers to structure XML documents as they see fit. For this reason, it is also a bit chaotic. Sending self-structured XML documents between dissimilar systems does not make a lot of sense — you would have to custom build the exposure and consumption models for each communication pair.

Vendors and the industry as a whole soon realized that XML needed a specific structure that put some rules in place to clarify communication. The rules defining XML structure make the communication between the disparate systems just that much easier. Tool vendors can now automate the communication process, as well as provide for the automation of the possible creation of all the components of applications using the communication protocol.

The industry settled on using SOAP (Simple Object Access Protocol) to make the standard XML structure work. Previous attempts to solve the communication problem that arose included component technologies such as Distributed Component Object Model (DCOM), Remote Method Invocation (RMI), Common Object Request Broker Architecture (CORBA), and Internet Inter-ORB Protocol (IIOP). These first efforts failed because each of these technologies was either driven by a single vendor or (worse yet) very vendor-specific. Implementing them across the entire industry was, therefore, impossible.

SOAP enables you to expose and consume complex data structures, which can include items such as DataSets, or just tables of data that have all their relations in place. SOAP is relatively simple and easy to understand. Like ASP.NET, XML Web services are also primarily engineered to work over HTTP. The DataSets you send or consume can flow over the same Internet wires (HTTP), thereby bypassing many firewalls (as they move through port 80).

So what is actually going across the wire? ASP.NET Web services generally use SOAP over HTTP using the HTTP Post protocol. An example SOAP request (from the client to the Web service residing on a Web server) takes the structure shown in Listing 31-1.

LISTING 31-1: A SOAP request

```
POST /MyWebService/Service.asmx HTTP/1.1
Host: www.wrox.com
Content-Type: text/xml; charset=utf-8
Content-Length: 19
SOAPAction: "http://tempuri.org/HelloWorld"

<?xml version="1.0" encoding="utf-8"?>
<soap:Envelope xmlns:xsi="http://www.w3.org/2001/XMLSchema-instance"
 xmlns:xsd="http://www.w3.org/2001/XMLSchema"
 xmlns:soap="http://schemas.xmlsoap.org/soap/envelope/">
  <soap:Body>
    <HelloWorld xmlns="http://tempuri.org/" />
  </soap:Body>
</soap:Envelope>
```

The request is sent to the Web service to invoke the `HelloWorld` WebMethod (WebMethods are discussed later in this chapter). Listing 31-2 shows the SOAP response from the Web service.

LISTING 31-2: A SOAP response

```
HTTP/1.1 200 OK
Content-Type: text/xml; charset=utf-8
Content-Length: 14

<?xml version="1.0" encoding="utf-8"?>
<soap:Envelope xmlns:xsi="http://www.w3.org/2001/XMLSchema-instance"
 xmlns:xsd="http://www.w3.org/2001/XMLSchema"
 xmlns:soap="http://schemas.xmlsoap.org/soap/envelope/">
  <soap:Body>
    <HelloWorldResponse xmlns="http://tempuri.org/">
      <HelloWorldResult>Hello World</HelloWorldResult>
    </HelloWorldResponse>
  </soap:Body>
</soap:Envelope>
```

In the examples from Listings 31-1 and 31-2, you can see that what is contained in this message is an XML file. In addition to the normal XML declaration of the `<xml>` node, you see a structure of XML that is the SOAP message. A SOAP message uses a root node of `<soap:Envelope>` that contains the `<soap:Body>` or the body of the SOAP message. Other elements that can be contained in the SOAP message include a SOAP header, `<soap:Header>`, and a SOAP fault, `<soap:Fault>`.

For more information about the structure of a SOAP message, be sure to check out the SOAP specifications. You can find them at the W3C Web site, `www.w3.org/tr/soap`.

BUILDING A SIMPLE XML WEB SERVICE

Building an XML Web service means that you are interested in exposing some information or logic to another entity either within your organization, to a partner, or to your customers. In a more granular sense, building a Web service means that you, as a developer, simply make one or more methods from a class you create that is enabled for SOAP communication.

You can use Visual Studio 2010 to build an XML Web service. The first step is to actually create a new Web site by selecting File ➪ New ➪ Web Site from the IDE menu. The New Web Site dialog opens. Select ASP.NET Empty Web Site, as shown in Figure 31-1.

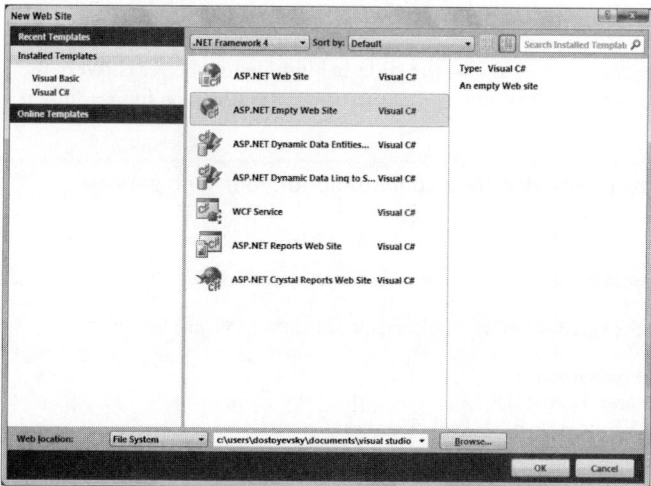

FIGURE 31-1

Once the project is created, right click to add a new file to the project. Select Web Service (WebService.asmx) from the list of options. This will create a single XML Web service named `WebService.asmx`. You will find it's code-behind file, `WebService.vb` or `WebService.cs`, in the App_Code folder (See Figure 31-2).

Check out the `WebService.asmx` file. All ASP.NET Web service files use the `.asmx` file extension instead of the `.aspx` extension used by typical ASP.NET pages.

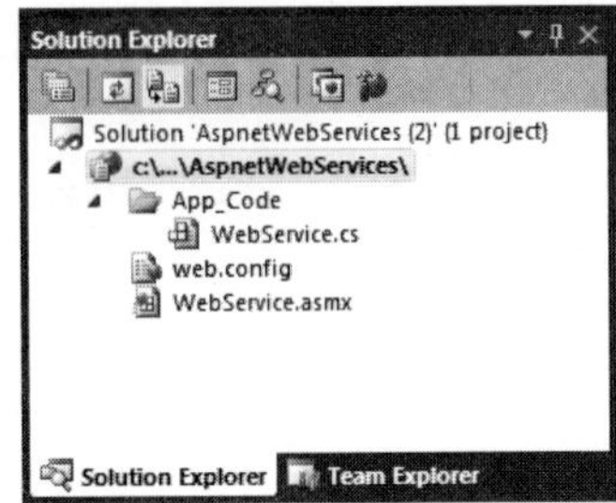

FIGURE 31-2

The WebService Page Directive

Open the `WebService.asmx` file in Visual Studio, and you see that the file contains only the `WebService` page directive, as illustrated in Listing 31-3.

LISTING 31-3: Contents of the Service.asmx file

```
<%@ WebService Language="VB" CodeBehind="~/App_Code/WebService.vb"
    Class="WebService" %>
```

You use the `@WebService` directive instead of the `@Page` directive.

The simple `@WebService` directive has only four possible attributes. The following list explains these attributes:

- `Class`: Required. It specifies the class used to define the methods and data types visible to the XML Web service clients.
- `CodeBehind`: Required only when you are working with an XML Web service file using the code-behind model. It enables you to work with Web services in two separate and more manageable pieces instead of a single file. The `CodeBehind` attribute takes a string value that represents the physical location of the second piece of the Web service — the class file containing all the Web service logic. In ASP.NET, placing the code-behind files in the App_Code folder is best, starting with the default Web service created by Visual Studio when you initially opened the Web service project.
- `Debug`: Optional. It takes a setting of either `True` or `False`. If the `Debug` attribute is set to `True`, the XML Web service is compiled with debug symbols in place; setting the value to `False` ensures that the Web service is compiled without the debug symbols in place.
- `Language`: Required. It specifies the language that is used for the Web service.

Looking at the Base Web Service Class File

Now look at the `WebService.vb` or `WebService.cs` file — the code-behind file for the XML Web. By default, a structure of code is already in place in the `WebService.vb` or `WebService.cs` file, as shown in Listing 31-4.

LISTING 31-4: Default code structure provided by Visual Studio for your Web service

Available for download on Wrox.com

VB

```
Imports System.Web
Imports System.Web.Services
Imports System.Web.Services.Protocols

' To allow this Web Service to be called from script, using ASP.NET AJAX,uncomment
' the following line.
' <System.Web.Script.Services.ScriptService()> _
<WebService(Namespace:="http://tempuri.org/")> _
<WebServiceBinding(ConformsTo:=WsiProfiles.BasicProfile1_1)> _
```

```
<Global.Microsoft.VisualBasic.CompilerServices.DesignerGenerated()> _
Public Class Service
     Inherits System.Web.Services.WebService

    <WebMethod()> _
    Public Function HelloWorld() As String
        Return "Hello World"
    End Function

End Class
```

C#

```
using System;
using System.Collections.Generic;
using System.Linq;
using System.Web;
using System.Web.Services;

[WebService(Namespace = "http://tempuri.org/")]
[WebServiceBinding(ConformsTo = WsiProfiles.BasicProfile1_1)]
// To allow this Web Service to be called from script, using ASP.NET AJAX,
// uncomment the following line.
// [System.Web.Script.Services.ScriptService]
public class Service : System.Web.Services.WebService
{
    public Service () {

        //Uncomment the following line if using designed components
        //InitializeComponent();
    }

    [WebMethod]
    public string HelloWorld() {
        return "Hello World";
    }

}
```

Some minor changes to the structure have been made since the release of the .NET Framework 3.5. You will notice that the `System.Linq` namespace is now included in the C# solution. In addition, the other change in this version is the inclusion of the commented `System.Web.Script.Services.ScriptService` object to work with ASP.NET AJAX scripts. To make use of this attribute, you simply uncomment the item.

Since the .NET 1.0/1.1 days, there also have been some big changes. One is that the `System.Web.Services.Protocols` namespace is included by default in the VB version. Therefore, in working with SOAP headers and other capabilities provided via this namespace, you do not need to worry about including it.

The other addition is the `<WebServiceBinding>` attribute. It builds the XML Web service responses that conform to the WS-I Basic Profile 1.0 release (found at `www.ws-i.org/Profiles/BasicProfile-1.0-2004-04-16.html`).

Besides these changes, very little has changed in this basic *Hello World* structure.

Exposing Custom Datasets as SOAP

To build your own Web service example, delete the `Service.asmx` file and create a new file called `Customers.asmx`. This Web service will expose the Customers table from SQL Server. Then jump into the code shown in Listing 31-5.

LISTING 31-5: An XML Web service that exposes the Customers table from Northwind

Available for download on Wrox.com

```
Imports System.Web
Imports System.Web.Services
Imports System.Web.Services.Protocols
Imports System.Data
Imports System.Data.SqlClient

<WebService(Namespace := "http://www.wrox.com/customers")> _
<WebServiceBinding(ConformsTo:=WsiProfiles.BasicProfile1_1)> _
Public Class Customers
     Inherits System.Web.Services.WebService

    <WebMethod()> _
    Public Function GetCustomers() As DataSet
        Dim conn As SqlConnection
        Dim myDataAdapter As SqlDataAdapter
        Dim myDataSet As DataSet
        Dim cmdString As String = "Select * From Customers"

        conn = New SqlConnection("Server=localhost;uid=sa;pwd=;database=Northwind")
        myDataAdapter = New SqlDataAdapter(cmdString, conn)

        myDataSet = New DataSet()
        myDataAdapter.Fill(myDataSet, "Customers")

        Return myDataSet
    End Function

End Class
```

C#

```
using System;
using System.Web;
using System.Web.Services;
using System.Web.Services.Protocols;
using System.Data;
using System.Data.SqlClient;

[WebService(Namespace = "http://www.wrox.com/customers")]
[WebServiceBinding(ConformsTo = WsiProfiles.BasicProfile1_1)]
public class Customers : System.Web.Services.WebService
{

    [WebMethod]
    public DataSet GetCustomers() {
       SqlConnection conn;
       SqlDataAdapter myDataAdapter;
       DataSet myDataSet;
       string cmdString = "Select * From Customers";

       conn = new SqlConnection("Server=localhost;uid=sa;pwd=;database=Northwind");
       myDataAdapter = new SqlDataAdapter(cmdString, conn);

       myDataSet = new DataSet();
       myDataAdapter.Fill(myDataSet, "Customers");

       return myDataSet;
    }

}
```

The WebService Attribute

All Web services are encapsulated within a class. The class is defined as a Web service by the `WebService` attribute placed before the class declaration. Here is an example:

```
<WebService(Namespace := "http://www.wrox.com/customers")> _
```

The `WebService` attribute can take a few properties. By default, the `WebService` attribute is used in your Web service along with the `Namespace` property, which has an initial value of `http://tempuri.org/`. This is meant to be a temporary namespace, and you should replace it with a more meaningful and original name, such as the URL where you are hosting the XML Web service. In the example, the `Namespace` value was changed to `www.wrox.com/customers`. Remember that the value does not have to be an actual URL; it can be any string value you want. The idea is that it should be unique. Using a URL is common practice because a URL is always unique.

Notice that the two languages define their properties within the `WebService` attribute differently. Visual Basic 2010 uses a colon and an equal sign to set the property:

```
Namespace:="http://www.wrox.com/customers"
```

C# uses just an equal sign to assign the properties within the `WebService` attribute values:

```
Namespace="http://www.wrox.com/customers"
```

Other possible `WebService` properties include `Name` and `Description`. `Name` enables you to change how the name of the Web service is presented to the developer via the ASP.NET test page (the test page is discussed a little later in the chapter). `Description` allows you to provide a textual description of the Web service. The description is also presented on the ASP.NET Web service test page. If your `WebService` attribute contains more than a single property, separate the properties using a comma. Here's an example:

```
<WebService(Namespace:="http://www.wrox.com/customers", Name:="GetCustomers")> _
```

The WebMethod Attribute

In Listing 31-5, the class called `Customers` has only a single `WebMethod`. A `WebService` class can contain any number of `WebMethods`, or a mixture of standard methods along with methods that are enabled to be `WebMethods` via the use of the attribute preceding the method declaration. The only methods that are accessible across the HTTP wire are the ones to which you have applied the `WebMethod` attribute.

As with the `WebService` attribute, `WebMethod` can also contain some properties, which are described in the following list:

- `BufferResponse`: When `BufferResponse` is set to `True`, the response from the XML Web service is held in memory and sent as a complete package. If it is set to `False`, the default setting, the response is sent to the client as it is constructed on the server.
- `CacheDuration`: Specifies the number of seconds that the response should be held in the system's cache. The default setting is `0`, which means that caching is disabled. Putting an XML Web service's response in the cache increases the Web service's performance.
- `Description`: Applies a text description to the `WebMethod` that appears on the `.aspx` test page of the XML Web service.
- `EnableSession`: Setting `EnableSession` to `True` enables session state for a particular `WebMethod`. The default setting is `False`.

- `MessageName`: Applies a unique name to the `WebMethod`. This step is required if you are working with overloaded `WebMethods` (discussed later in the chapter).
- `TransactionOption`: Specifies the transactional support for the `WebMethod`. The default setting is `Disabled`. If the `WebMethod` is the root object that initiated the transaction, the Web service can participate in a transaction with another `WebMethod` that requires a transaction. Other possible values include `NotSupported`, `Supported`, `Required`, and `RequiresNew`.

The XML Web Service Interface

The Customers Web service from Listing 31-5 has only a single `WebMethod` that returns a DataSet containing the complete Customers table from the SQL Server Northwind database.

Running `Customers.asmx` in the browser pulls up the ASP.NET Web service test page. This visual interface to your Web service is really meant either for testing purposes or as a reference page for developers interested in consuming the Web services you expose. Figure 31-3 shows the page generated for the Customers Web service.

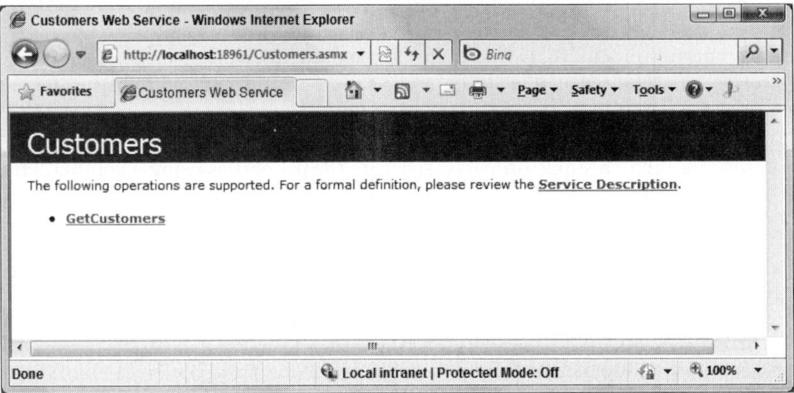

FIGURE 31-3

The interface shows the name of the Web service in the blue bar (the dark bar in this black-and-white image) at the top of the page. By default, the name of the class is used unless you changed the value through the `Description` property of the `WebService` attribute, as defined earlier. A bulleted list of links to the entire Web service's `WebMethods` is displayed. This example has only one `WebMethod`: `GetCustomers()`.

A link to the Web service's Web Services Description Language (WSDL) document is also available (the link is titled "Service Description" in the figure). The WSDL file is the actual interface with the Customers Web service. The XML document (shown in Figure 31-4) is not really meant for human consumption; it is designed to work with tools such as Visual Studio, informing the tool what the Web service requires to be consumed. Each Web service requires a request that must have parameters of a specific type. When the request is made, the Web service response comes back with a specific set of data defined using specific data types. Everything you need for the request and a listing of exactly what you are getting back in a response (if you are the consumer) is described in the WSDL document.

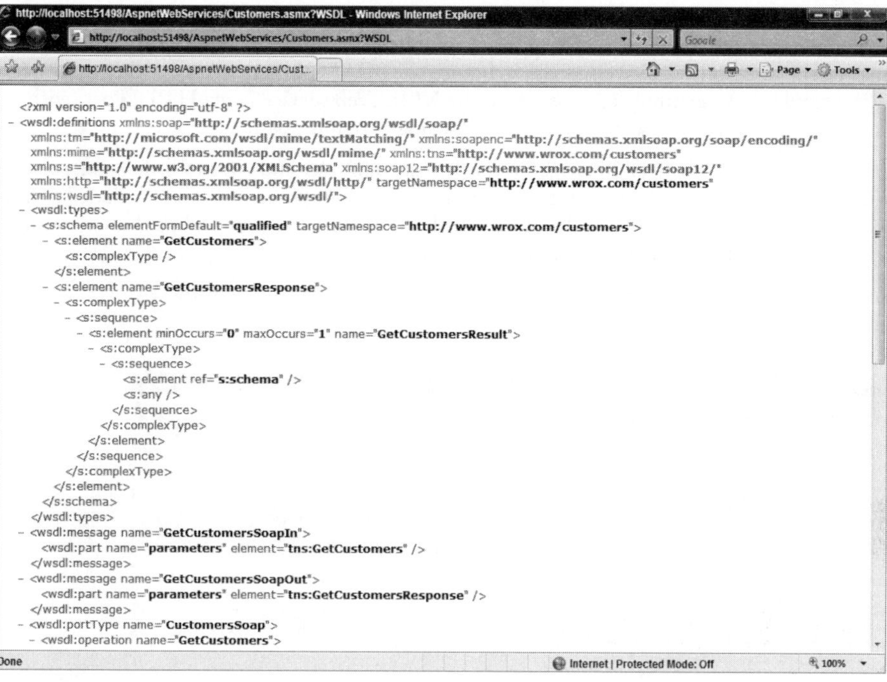

FIGURE 31-4

Clicking the `GetCustomers` link gives you a new page, shown in Figure 31-5, that not only describes the `WebMethod` in more detail, but also allows you to test the `WebMethod` directly in the browser.

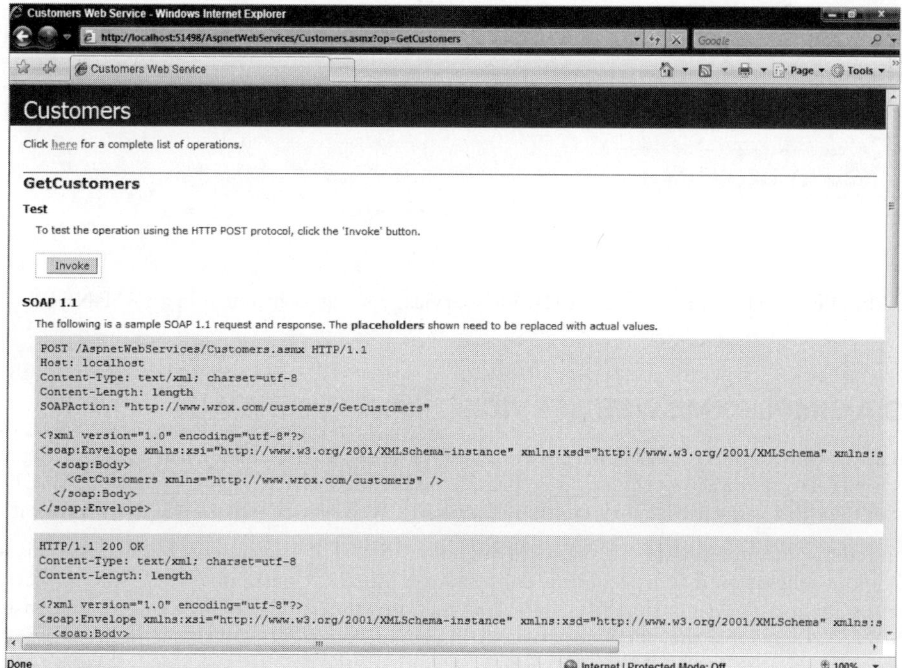

FIGURE 31-5

At the top of the page is the name of the XML Web service (`Customers`); below that is the name of this particular `WebMethod` (`GetCustomers`). The page shows you the structure of the SOAP messages that are required to consume the `WebMethod`, as well as the structure the SOAP message takes for the response. Below the SOAP examples is an example of consuming the XML Web service using HTTP Post (with name/value pairs). Using this method of consumption instead of using SOAP is possible.

You can test the `WebMethod` directly from the page. In the Test section, you find a form. If the `WebMethod` you are calling requires an input of some parameters to get a response, you see some text boxes included so you can provide the parameters before clicking the Invoke button. If the `WebMethod` you are calling does not require any parameters, you see only the Invoke button and nothing more.

Clicking Invoke actually sends a SOAP request to the Web service, causing a new browser instance with the result to appear, as illustrated in Figure 31-6.

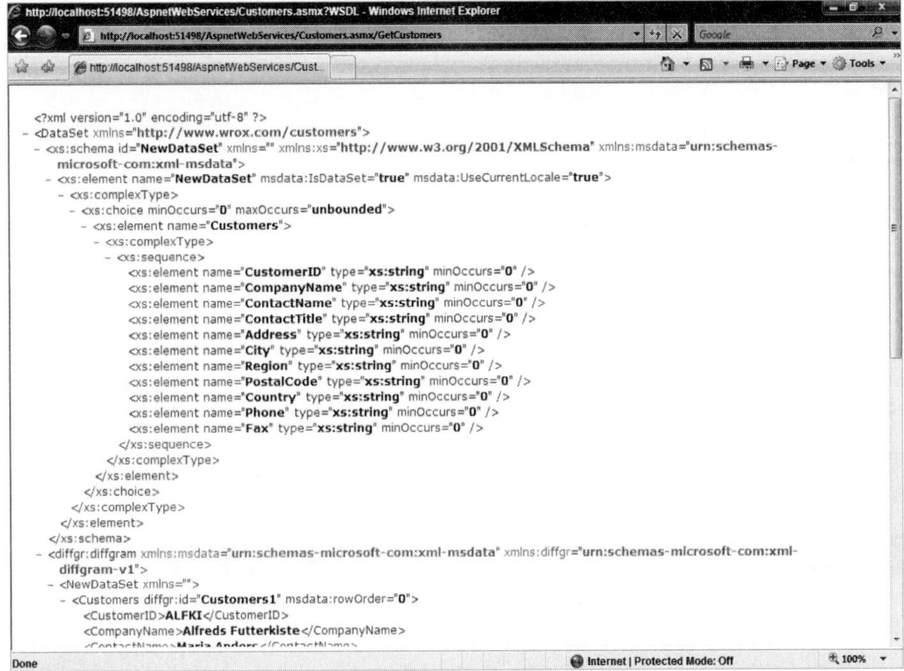

FIGURE 31-6

Now that everything is in place to expose the XML Web service, you can consume it in an ASP.NET application.

CONSUMING A SIMPLE XML WEB SERVICE

So far, you have seen only half of the XML Web service story. Exposing data and logic as SOAP to disparate systems across the enterprise or across the world is a simple task using .NET, and particularly ASP.NET. The other half of the story is the actual consumption of an XML Web service into an ASP.NET application.

You are not limited to consuming XML Web services only into ASP.NET applications; but because this is an ASP.NET book, it focuses on that aspect of the consumption process. Consuming XML Web services into other types of applications is not that difficult and, in fact, is rather similar to how you would consume them using ASP.NET. Remember that the Web services you come across can be consumed in Windows

Forms, mobile applications, databases, and more. You can even consume XML Web services with other Web services, so you can have a single Web service made up of what is basically an aggregate of other Web services.

Adding a Web Reference

To consume the Customers Web service that you created earlier in this chapter, create a new ASP.NET Web site called `CustomerConsumer`. The first step in consuming an XML Web service in an ASP.NET application is to make a reference to the remote object — the Web service. You do so by right-clicking on the root node of your project from within the Visual Studio Solution Explorer and selecting Add Web Reference. The Add Web Reference dialog box appears, shown in Figure 31-7.

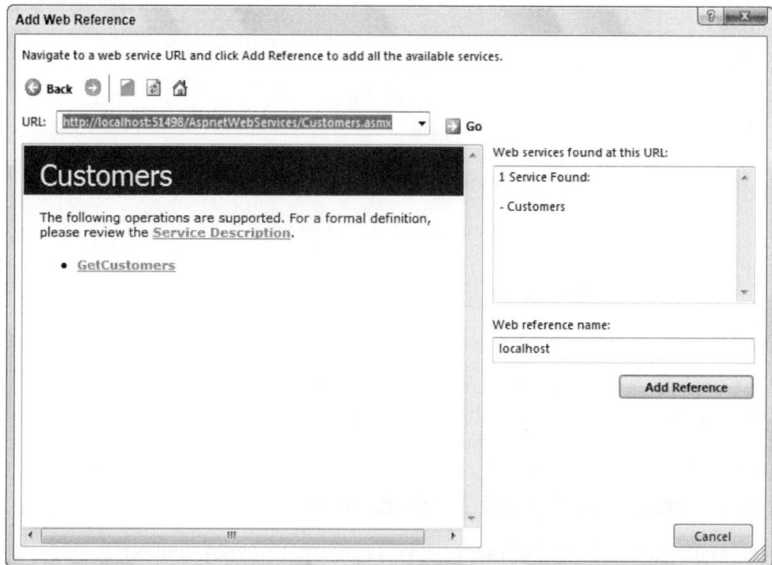

FIGURE 31-7

The Add Web Reference dialog box enables you to point to a particular `.asmx` file to make a reference to it. Understand that the Add Web Reference dialog box is really looking for WSDL files. Microsoft's XML Web services automatically generate WSDL files based on the `.asmx` files themselves. To pull up the WSDL file in the browser, simply type in the URL of your Web service's `.asmx` file and add a `?WSDL` at the end of the string. For example, you might have the following construction (this is not an actual Web service, but simply an example):

```
http://www.wrox.com/MyWebService/Customers.asmx?WSDL
```

Because the Add Web Reference dialog box automatically finds where the WSDL file is for any Microsoft-based XML Web service, you should simply type in the URL of the actual WSDL file for any non–Microsoft-based XML Web service.

If you are using Microsoft's Visual Studio and its built-in Web server instead of IIS, you will be required to also interject the port number the Web server is using into the URL. In this case, your URL would be structured similar to `http://localhost:5444/MyWebService/Customers.asmx?WSDL`.

In the Add Web Reference dialog box, change the reference from the default name to something a little more meaningful. If you are working on a single machine, the Web reference might have the name of `localhost`; if you are actually working with a remote Web service, the name is the inverse of the URL, such as `com.wrox.www`. In either case, renaming it so that the name makes a little more sense and is easy to use within your application is best. In the example here, the Web reference is renamed `WroxCustomers`.

FIGURE 31-8

Clicking the Add Reference button causes Visual Studio to make an actual reference to the Web service from the `web.config` file of your application (shown in Figure 31-8). You might find some additional files under the App_WebReferences folder — such as a copy of the Web service's WSDL file.

Your consuming application's `web.config` file contains the reference to the Web service in its `<appSettings>` section. Listing 31-6 shows the addition.

LISTING 31-6: Changes to the web.config file after making a reference to the Web service

Available for download on Wrox.com

```
<configuration xmlns="http://schemas.microsoft.com/.NetConfiguration/v2.0">
   <appSettings>
      <add key="WroxCustomers.Customers"
       value="http://www.wrox.com/MyWebService/Customers.asmx"/>
   </appSettings>
</configuration>
```

You can see that the `WroxCustomers` reference has been made along with the name of the Web service, providing a key value of `WroxCustomers.Customers`. The `value` attribute takes a value of the location of the Customers Web service, which is found within the `Customers.asmx` page.

Invoking the Web Service from the Client Application

Now that a reference has been made to the XML Web service, you can use it in your ASP.NET application. Create a new Web Form in your project. With this page, you can consume the Customers table from the remote Northwind database directly into your application. The data is placed in a GridView control.

On the design part of the page, place a Button and a GridView control so that your page looks something like the one shown in Figure 31-9.

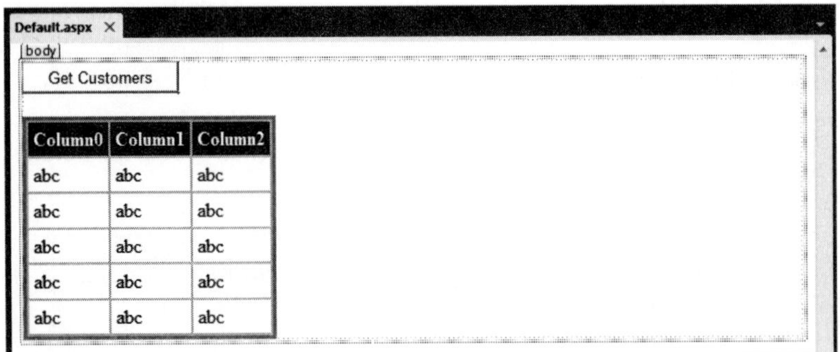

FIGURE 31-9

The idea is that, when the end user clicks the button contained on the form, the application sends a SOAP request to the Customers Web service and gets back a SOAP response containing the Customers table, which is then bound to the GridView control on the page. Listing 31-7 shows the code for this simple application.

LISTING 31-7: Consuming the Customers Web service in an ASP.NET page

Available for download on Wrox.com

```
<%@ Page Language="VB" %>

<script runat="server">
   Protected Sub Button1_Click(ByVal sender As Object, ByVal e As System.EventArgs)
        Dim ws As New WroxCustomers.Customers()
        GridView1.DataSource = ws.GetCustomers()
        GridView1.DataBind()
   End Sub
</script>

<html xmlns="http://www.w3.org/1999/xhtml" >
<head runat="server">
    <title>Web Service Consumer Example</title>
</head>
<body>
    <form id="form1" runat="server">
    <div>
        <asp:Button ID="Button1" Runat="server" Text="Get Customers"
         OnClick="Button1_Click" />
        <br />
        <br />
        <asp:GridView ID="GridView1" Runat="server" BorderWidth="1px"
         BackColor="#DEBA84" CellPadding="3" CellSpacing="2" BorderStyle="None"
         BorderColor="#DEBA84">
            <FooterStyle ForeColor="#8C4510" BackColor="#F7DFB5"></FooterStyle>
            <PagerStyle ForeColor="#8C4510" HorizontalAlign="Center"></PagerStyle>
            <HeaderStyle ForeColor="White" Font-Bold="True"
             BackColor="#A55129"></HeaderStyle>
            <SelectedRowStyle ForeColor="White" Font-Bold="True"
             BackColor="#738A9C"></SelectedRowStyle>
            <RowStyle ForeColor="#8C4510" BackColor="#FFF7E7"></RowStyle>
        </asp:GridView>
    </div>
    </form>
</body>
</html>
```

C#

```
<%@ Page Language="C#" %>

<script runat="server">
    protected void Button1_Click(Object sender, EventArgs e) {
       WroxCustomers.Customers ws = new WroxCustomers.Customers();
        GridView1.DataSource = ws.GetCustomers();
        GridView1.DataBind();
    }
</script>
```

The end user is presented with a simple button. Clicking it causes the ASP.NET application to send a SOAP request to the remote XML Web service. The returned DataSet is bound to the GridView control, and the page is redrawn, as shown in Figure 31-10.

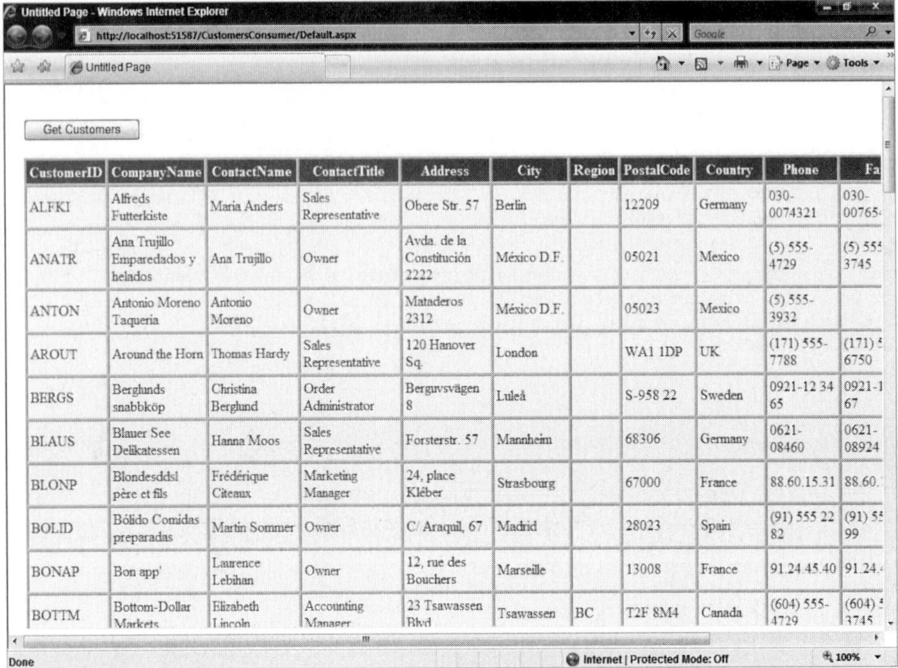

CustomerID	CompanyName	ContactName	ContactTitle	Address	City	Region	PostalCode	Country	Phone	Fa
ALFKI	Alfreds Futterkiste	Maria Anders	Sales Representative	Obere Str. 57	Berlin		12209	Germany	030-0074321	030-00765
ANATR	Ana Trujillo Emparedados y helados	Ana Trujillo	Owner	Avda. de la Constitución 2222	México D.F.		05021	Mexico	(5) 555-4729	(5) 555 3745
ANTON	Antonio Moreno Taqueria	Antonio Moreno	Owner	Mataderos 2312	México D.F.		05023	Mexico	(5) 555-3932	
AROUT	Around the Horn	Thomas Hardy	Sales Representative	120 Hanover Sq.	London		WA1 1DP	UK	(171) 555-7788	(171) 6750
BERGS	Berglunds snabbköp	Christina Berglund	Order Administrator	Berguvsvägen 8	Luleå		S-958 22	Sweden	0921-12 34 65	0921-1 67
BLAUS	Blauer See Delikatessen	Hanna Moos	Sales Representative	Forsterstr. 57	Mannheim		68306	Germany	0621-08460	0621-08924
BLONP	Blondesddsl père et fils	Frédérique Citeaux	Marketing Manager	24, place Kléber	Strasbourg		67000	France	88.60.15.31	88.60.
BOLID	Bólido Comidas preparadas	Martin Sommer	Owner	C/ Araquil, 67	Madrid		28023	Spain	(91) 555 22 82	(91) 55 99
BONAP	Bon app'	Laurence Lebihan	Owner	12, rue des Bouchers	Marseille		13008	France	91.24.45.40	91.24.
BOTTM	Bottom-Dollar Markets	Elizabeth Lincoln	Accounting Manager	23 Tsawassen Blvd	Tsawassen	BC	T2F 8M4	Canada	(604) 555-4729	(604) 3745

FIGURE 31-10

The Customers Web service is invoked by the instantiation of the `WroxCustomers.Customers` proxy object:

```
Dim ws As New WroxCustomers.Customers()
```

Then, you can use the `ws` object like any other object within your project. In the code example from Listing 31-7, the result of the `ws.GetCustomers()` method call is assigned to the `DataSource` property of the GridView control:

```
GridView1.DataSource = ws.GetCustomers()
```

As you develop or consume more Web services within your applications, you will see more of their power and utility.

OVERLOADING WEBMETHODS

In the object-oriented world of .NET, using method overloading in the code you develop is quite possible. A true object-oriented language has support for *polymorphism,* of which method overloading is a part. Method overloading enables you to have multiple methods that use the same name but have different signatures. With method overloading, one method can be called, but the call is routed to the appropriate method based on the full signature of the request. Listing 31-8 shows an example of standard method overloading.

LISTING 31-8: Method overloading in .NET

Available for download on Wrox.com

VB

```
Public Function HelloWorld() As String
   Return "Hello"
End Function

Public Function HelloWorld(ByVal FirstName As String) As String
   Return "Hello " & FirstName
End Function
```

```
public string HelloWorld() {
   return "Hello";
}

public string HelloWorld(string FirstName) {
   return "Hello " + FirstName;
}
```

In this example, both methods have the same name, `HelloWorld`. So, which one is called when you invoke `HelloWorld`? Well, it depends on the signature you pass to the method. For example, you might provide the following:

```
Label1.Text = HelloWorld()
```

This yields a result of just `Hello`. However, you might invoke the `HelloWorld()` method using the following signature:

```
Label1.Text = HelloWorld("Bill Evjen")
```

Then you get back a result of `Hello Bill Evjen`. As you can see, method overloading is a great feature that your ASP.NET applications can effectively utilize — but how do you go about overloading `WebMethods`?

If you have already tried to overload any of your `WebMethods`, you probably got the following error when you pulled up the Web service in the browser:

```
Both System.String HelloWorld(System.String) and System.String HelloWorld() use the
message name 'HelloWorld'. Use the MessageName property of the WebMethod custom
attribute to specify unique message names for the methods.
```

As this error states, the extra step you have to take to overload `WebMethods` is to use the `MessageName` property. Listing 31-9 shows how.

LISTING 31-9: WebMethod overloading in .NET

Available for download on Wrox.com

VB

```
<WebMethod(MessageName:="HelloWorld")> _
Public Function HelloWorld() As String
   Return "Hello"
End Function

<WebMethod(MessageName:="HelloWorldWithFirstName")> _
Public Function HelloWorld(ByVal FirstName As String) As String
   Return "Hello " & FirstName
End Function
```

```
[WebMethod(MessageName="HelloWorld")]
public string HelloWorld() {
   return "Hello";
}

[WebMethod(MessageName="HelloWorldWithFirstName")]
public string HelloWorld(string FirstName) {
   return "Hello " + FirstName;
}
```

In addition to adding the `MessageName` property of the `WebMethod` attribute, you must disable your Web service's adherence to the WS-I Basic Profile specification — which it wouldn't be doing if you performed `WebMethod` overloading with your Web services. You can disable the conformance to the WS-I Basic Profile specification in a couple of ways. One way is to add the `<WebServiceBinding>` attribute to your code, as illustrated in Listing 31-10.

LISTING 31-10: Changing your Web service so it does not conform to the WS-I Basic Profile spec

VB

```
<WebServiceBinding(ConformsTo := WsiProfiles.None)> _
Public Class MyOverloadingExample
   ' Code here
End Class
```

C#

```
[WebServiceBinding(ConformsTo = WsiProfiles.None)]
public class WroxMath : System.Web.Services.WebService
{
   // Code here
}
```

The other option is to turn off the WS-I Basic Profile capability in the `web.config` file, as shown in Listing 31-11.

Available for download on Wrox.com

LISTING 31-11: Turning off conformance using the web.config file

```
<configuration>
  <system.web>
    <webServices>
      <conformanceWarnings>
        <remove name="BasicProfile1_1" />
      </conformanceWarnings>
    </webServices>
  </system.web>
</configuration>
```

After you have enabled your Web service to overload `WebMethods`, you can see both `WebMethods` defined by their `MessageName` value properties when you pull up the Web service's interface test page in the browser (see Figure 31-11).

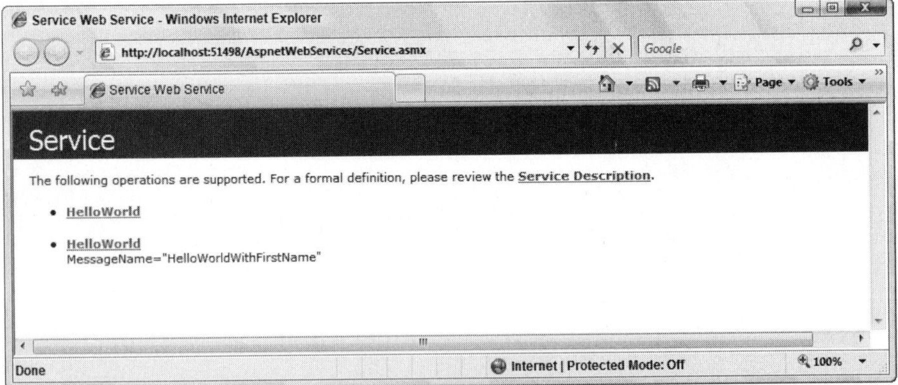

FIGURE 31-11

Although you can see the names of the `WebMethods` are the same, the `MessageName` property shows that they are distinct methods. When the developer consuming the Web service makes a Web reference to your Web service, he will see only a single method name available (in this example, `HelloWorld`). It is shown via the Visual Studio 2010 IntelliSense in the application consuming these methods (see Figure 31-12).

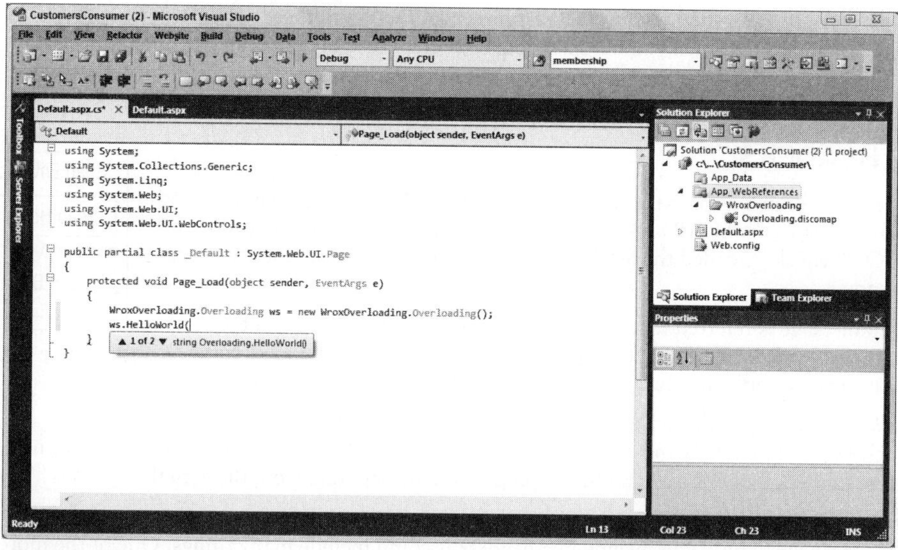

FIGURE 31-12

In the box that pops up to guide developers on the signature structure, you can see two options available — one is an empty signature, and the other requires a single string.

CACHING WEB SERVICE RESPONSES

Caching is an important feature in almost every application that you build with .NET. Chapter 22 covers most of the caching capabilities available to you in ASP.NET, but a certain feature of Web services in .NET enables you to cache the SOAP response sent to any of the service's consumers.

First, by way of review, remember that caching is the capability to maintain an in-memory store where data, objects, and various items are stored for reuse. This feature increases the responsiveness of the applications you build and manage. Sometimes, returning cached results can greatly affect performance.

XML Web services use an attribute to control caching of SOAP responses — the `CacheDuration` property. Listing 31-12 shows its use.

LISTING 31-12: Utilizing the CacheDuration property

Available for download on Wrox.com

VB

```
<WebMethod(CacheDuration:=60)> _
Public Function GetServerTime() As String
   Return DateTime.Now.ToLongTimeString()
End Function
```

C#

```
[WebMethod(CacheDuration=60)]
public string GetServerTime() {
   return DateTime.Now.ToLongTimeString();
}
```

As you can see, `CacheDuration` is used within the `WebMethod` attribute much like the `Description` and `Name` properties. `CacheDuration` takes an `Integer` value that is equal to the number of seconds during which the SOAP response is cached.

When the first request comes in, the SOAP response is cached by the server, and the consumer gets the same timestamp in the SOAP response for the next minute. After that minute is up, the stored cache is discarded, and a new response is generated and stored in the cache again for servicing all other requests for the next minute.

Among the many benefits of caching your SOAP responses, you will find that the performance of your application is greatly improved when you have a response that is basically re-created again and again without any change.

USING SOAP HEADERS

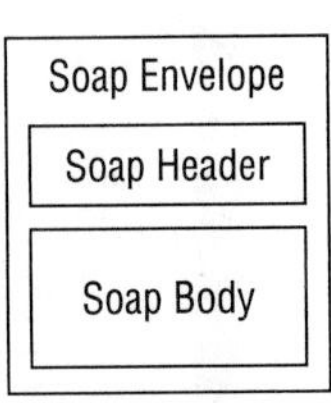

FIGURE 31-13

One of the more common forms of extending the capabilities of SOAP messages is to add metadata of the request to the SOAP message itself. The metadata is usually added to a section of the SOAP envelope called the *SOAP header*. Figure 31-13 shows the structure of a SOAP message.

The entire SOAP message is referred to as a *SOAP envelope*. Contained within the SOAP message is the *SOAP body* — a piece of the SOAP message that you have been working with in every example thus far. It is a required element of the SOAP message.

The one optional component of the SOAP message is the SOAP header. It is the part of the SOAP message in which you can place any metadata about the overall SOAP request instead of incorporating it in the signature of any of your `WebMethods`. Keeping metadata separate from the actual request is important.

What kind of information should you include in a header? It could include many things. One of the more common items placed in the SOAP header is any authentication/authorization functionality required to consume your Web service or to get at specific pieces of logic or data. Placing usernames and passwords inside the SOAP headers of your messages is a good example of what you might include.

Building a Web Service with SOAP Headers

You can build upon the sample `HelloWorld` Web service that is presented in the default `.asmx` page when it is first pulled up in Visual Studio (from Listing 31-4). Name the new `.asmx` file `HelloSoapHeader.asmx`. The initial step is to add a class that is an object representing what is to be placed in the SOAP header by the client, as shown in Listing 31-13.

LISTING 31-13: A class representing the SOAP header

Available for download on Wrox.com

VB

```
Public Class HelloHeader
   Inherits System.Web.Services.Protocols.SoapHeader

   Public Username As String
   Public Password As String
End Class
```

C#

```
public class HelloHeader : System.Web.Services.Protocols.SoapHeader
{
   public string Username;
   public string Password;
}
```

The class, representing a SOAP header object, has to inherit from the `SoapHeader` class from `System.Web.Services.Protocols.SoapHeader`. The `SoapHeader` class serializes the payload of the `<soap:header>` element into XML for you. In the example in Listing 31-13, you can see that this SOAP header requires two elements — simply a username and a password, both of type `String`. The names you create in this class are those used for the subelements of the SOAP header construction, so naming them descriptively is important.

Listing 31-14 shows the Web service class that creates an instance of the `HelloHeader` class.

LISTING 31-14: A Web service class that utilizes a SOAP header

Available for download on Wrox.com

VB

```
<WebService(Namespace:="http://www.wrox.com/helloworld")>
<WebServiceBinding(ConformsTo:=WsiProfiles.BasicProfile1_1,
  EmitConformanceClaims:=True)> _
Public Class HelloSoapHeader
    Inherits System.Web.Services.WebService

    Public myHeader As HelloHeader

    <WebMethod(), SoapHeader("myHeader")>
    Public Function HelloWorld() As String
        If (myHeader Is Nothing) Then
           Return "Hello World"
        Else
           Return "Hello " & myHeader.Username & ". " & _
              "<br>Your password is: " & myHeader.Password
        End If
    End Function

End Class
```

C#

```
[WebService(Namespace = "http://www.wrox.com/helloworld")]
[WebServiceBinding(ConformsTo = WsiProfiles.BasicProfile1_1)]
public class HelloSoapHeader : System.Web.Services.WebService
{

    public HelloHeader myHeader;

    [WebMethod]
    [SoapHeader("myHeader")]
    public string HelloWorld() {
        if (myHeader == null) {
           return "Hello World";
        }
        else {
           return "Hello " + myHeader.Username + ". " +
              "<br>Your password is: " + myHeader.Password;
        }
    }

}
```

The Web service, `HelloSoapHeader`, has a single `WebMethod` — `HelloWorld`. Within the Web service class, but outside of the `WebMethod` itself, you create an instance of the `SoapHeader` class. You can do so with the following line of code:

```
Public myHeader As HelloHeader
```

Now that you have an instance of the `HelloHeader` class that you created earlier called `myHeader`, you can use that instantiation in your `WebMethod`. Because Web services can contain any number of `WebMethods`, it is not a requirement that all `WebMethods` use an instantiated SOAP header. You specify whether a `WebMethod` will use a particular instantiation of a SOAP header class by placing the `SoapHeader` attribute before the WebMethod declaration.

```
<WebMethod(), SoapHeader("myHeader")>
Public Function HelloWorld() As String
   ' Code here
End Function
```

In this example, the `SoapHeader` attribute takes a `string` value of the name of the instantiated `SoapHeader` class — in this case, `myHeader`.

From here, the WebMethod actually makes use of the myHeader object. If the myHeader object is not found (meaning that the client did not send in a SOAP header with his constructed SOAP message), a simple "Hello World" is returned. However, if values are provided in the SOAP header of the SOAP request, those values are used within the returned string value.

Consuming a Web Service Using SOAP Headers

Building an ASP.NET application that makes a SOAP request to a Web service using SOAP headers is not really difficult. Just as with the Web services that do not include SOAP headers, you make a Web Reference to the remote Web service directly in Visual Studio.

For the ASP.NET page, create a simple page with a single Label control. The output of the Web service is placed in the Label control. Listing 31-15 shows the code for the ASP.NET page.

LISTING 31-15: An ASP.NET page working with an XML Web service using SOAP headers

Available for download on Wrox.com

```
<%@ Page Language="VB" %>

<script runat="server">
    Protected Sub Page_Load(ByVal sender As Object, ByVal e As System.EventArgs)
        Dim ws As New localhost.HelloSoapHeader()
        Dim wsHeader As New localhost.HelloHeader()

        wsHeader.Username = "Bill Evjen"
        wsHeader.Password = "Bubbles"
        ws.HelloHeaderValue = wsHeader

        Label1.Text = ws.HelloWorld()
    End Sub
</script>

<html xmlns="http://www.w3.org/1999/xhtml" >
<head runat="server">
    <title>Working with SOAP headers</title>
</head>
<body>
    <form id="form1" runat="server">
    <div>
        <asp:Label ID="Label1" Runat="server"></asp:Label>
    </div>
    </form>
</body>
</html>
```

C#

```
<%@ Page Language="C#" %>

<script runat="server">
    protected void Page_Load(object sender, System.EventArgs e) {
        localhost.HelloSoapHeader ws = new localhost.HelloSoapHeader();
        localhost.HelloHeader wsHeader = new localhost.HelloHeader();

        wsHeader.Username = "Bill Evjen";
        wsHeader.Password = "Bubbles";
        ws.HelloHeaderValue = wsHeader;

        Label1.Text = ws.HelloWorld();
    }
</script>
```

Two objects are instantiated. The first is the actual Web service, HelloSoapHeader. The second, which is instantiated as wsHeader, is the SoapHeader object. After both of these objects are instantiated and before making the SOAP request in the application, you construct the SOAP header. This is as easy as assigning values to the `Username` and `Password` properties of the `wsHeader` object. After these properties are assigned, you associate the `wsHeader` object to the `ws` object through the use of the `HelloHeaderValue` property. After you have made the association between the constructed SOAP header object and the actual `WebMethod` object (`ws`), you can make a SOAP request just as you would normally do:

```
Label1.Text = ws.HelloWorld()
```

Running the page produces the result in the browser shown in Figure 31-14.

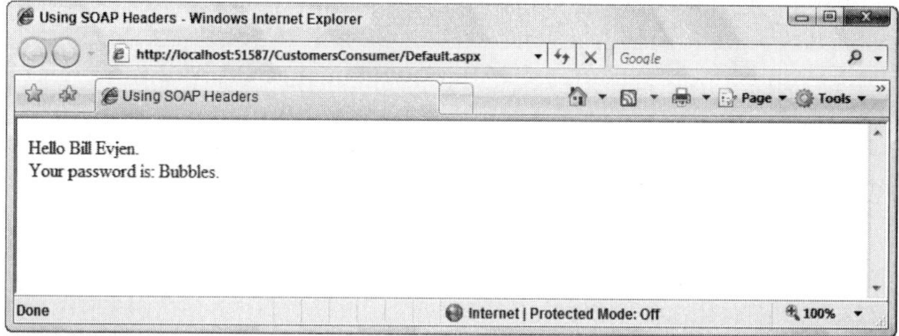

FIGURE 31-14

What is more interesting, however, is that the SOAP request reveals that the SOAP header was indeed constructed into the overall SOAP message, as shown in Listing 31-16.

LISTING 31-16: The SOAP request

```
<?xml version="1.0" encoding="utf-8" ?>
<soap:Envelope xmlns:soap="http://schemas.xmlsoap.org/soap/envelope/"
 xmlns:xsi="http://www.w3.org/2001/XMLSchema-instance"
 xmlns:xsd="http://www.w3.org/2001/XMLSchema">
   <soap:Header>
      <HelloHeader xmlns="http://www.wrox.com/helloworld/">
         <Username>Bill Evjen</Username>
         <Password>Bubbles</Password>
      </HelloHeader>
   </soap:Header>
   <soap:Body>
      <HelloWorld xmlns="http://www.wrox.com/helloworld/" />
   </soap:Body>
</soap:Envelope>
```

This code returns the SOAP response shown in Listing 31-17.

LISTING 31-17: The SOAP response

```
<?xml version="1.0" encoding="utf-8" ?>
<soap:Envelope xmlns:soap="http://schemas.xmlsoap.org/soap/envelope/"
 xmlns:xsi="http://www.w3.org/2001/XMLSchema-instance"
 xmlns:xsd="http://www.w3.org/2001/XMLSchema">
   <soap:Body>
      <HelloWorldResponse xmlns="http://www.wrox.com/helloworld/">
         <HelloWorldResult>Hello Bill Evjen. Your password is:
          Bubbles</HelloWorldResult>
      </HelloWorldResponse>
   </soap:Body>
</soap:Envelope>
```

Requesting Web Services Using SOAP 1.2

Most Web services out there use SOAP version 1.1 for the construction of their messages. With that said, SOAP 1.2 became a W3C recommendation in June 2003 (see `www.w3.org/TR/soap12-part1/`). The nice thing about XML Web services in the .NET Framework platform is that they are capable of communicating in both the 1.1 and 1.2 versions of SOAP.

In an ASP.NET application that is consuming a Web service, you can control whether the SOAP request is constructed as a SOAP 1.1 message or a 1.2 message. Listing 31-18 changes the previous example so that the request uses SOAP 1.2 instead of the default setting of SOAP 1.1.

LISTING 31-18: An ASP.NET application making a SOAP request using SOAP 1.2

Available for download on Wrox.com

VB

```
<%@ Page Language="VB" %>

<script runat="server">
    Protected Sub Page_Load(ByVal sender As Object, ByVal e As System.EventArgs)
        Dim ws As New localhost.HelloSoapHeader()
        Dim wsHeader As New localhost.HelloHeader()

        wsHeader.Username = "Bill Evjen"
        wsHeader.Password = "Bubbles"
        ws.HelloHeaderValue = wsHeader

        ws.SoapVersion = System.Web.Services.Protocols.SoapProtocolVersion.Soap12

        Label1.Text = ws.HelloWorld()
    End Sub
</script>
```

C#

```
<%@ Page Language="C#" %>

<script runat="server">
    protected void Page_Load(object sender, System.EventArgs e) {
        localhost.HelloSoapHeader ws = new localhost.HelloSoapHeader();
        localhost.HelloHeader wsHeader = new localhost.HelloHeader();

        wsHeader.Username = "Bill Evjen";
        wsHeader.Password = "Bubbles";
        ws.HelloHeaderValue = wsHeader;

        ws.SoapVersion = System.Web.Services.Protocols.SoapProtocolVersion.Soap12;

        Label1.Text = ws.HelloWorld();
    }
</script>
```

In this example, you first provide an instantiation of the Web service object and use the `SoapVersion` property. The property takes a value of `System.Web.Services.Protocols.SoapProtocolVersion.Soap12` to work with SOAP 1.2 specifically.

With this bit of code in place, the SOAP request takes the structure shown in Listing 31-19.

LISTING 31-19: The SOAP request using SOAP 1.2

```
<?xml version="1.0" encoding="utf-8"?>
<soap:Envelope xmlns:soap="http://www.w3.org/2003/05/soap-envelope"
 xmlns:xsi="http://www.w3.org/2001/XMLSchema-instance"
 xmlns:xsd="http://www.w3.org/2001/XMLSchema">
   <soap:Header>
      <HelloHeader xmlns="http://www.wrox.com/helloworld/">
```

```
            <Username>Bill Evjen</Username>
            <Password>Bubbles</Password>
         </HelloHeader>
      </soap:Header>
      <soap:Body>
         <HelloWorld xmlns="http://www.wrox.com/helloworld/" />
      </soap:Body>
   </soap:Envelope>
```

One difference between the two examples is the `xmlns:soap` namespace that is used. The difference actually resides in the HTTP header. When you compare the SOAP 1.1 and 1.2 messages, you see a difference in the `Content-Type` attribute. In addition, the SOAP 1.2 HTTP header does not use the `soapaction` attribute because this is now combined with the `Content-Type` attribute.

You can turn off either SOAP 1.1 or 1.2 capabilities with the Web services that you build by making the proper settings in the `web.config` file, as shown in Listing 31-20.

LISTING 31-20: Turning off SOAP 1.1 or 1.2 capabilities

Available for download on Wrox.com

```
<configuration xmlns="http://schemas.microsoft.com/.NetConfiguration/v2.0">
   <system.web>
      <webServices>
         <protocols>
            <remove name="HttpSoap"/> <!-- Removes SOAP 1.1 abilities -->
            <remove name="HttpSoap1.2"/> <!-- Removes SOAP 1.2 abilities -->
         </protocols>
      </webServices>
   </system.web>
</configuration>
```

CONSUMING WEB SERVICES ASYNCHRONOUSLY

All the Web services that you have been working with in this chapter have been done *synchronously*. This means that after a request is sent from the code of an ASP.NET application, the application comes to a complete standstill until a SOAP response is received.

The process of invoking a `WebMethod` and getting back a result can take some time for certain requests. At times, you are not in control of the Web service from which you are requesting data and, therefore, you are not in control of the performance or response times of these services. For these reasons, you should consider consuming Web services *asynchronously*.

An ASP.NET application that makes an asynchronous request can work on other programming tasks while the initial SOAP request is awaiting a response. When the ASP.NET application is done working on the additional items, it can return to get the result from the Web service.

The great news is that to build an XML Web service that allows asynchronous communication, you don't have to perform any additional actions. All `.asmx` Web services have the built-in capability for asynchronous communication with consumers. The Web service in Listing 31-21 is an example.

LISTING 31-21: A slow Web service

Available for download on Wrox.com

VB

```
Imports System.Web
Imports System.Web.Services
Imports System.Web.Services.Protocols

<WebServiceBinding(ConformsTo:=WsiProfiles.BasicProfile1_1,
  EmitConformanceClaims:=True)> _
Public Class Async
```

continues

LISTING 31-21 *(continued)*

```
    Inherits System.Web.Services.WebService

    <WebMethod()> _
    Public Function HelloWorld() As String
        System.Threading.Thread.Sleep(1000)
        Return "Hello World"
    End Function

End Class
```

C#

```
using System;
using System.Web;
using System.Web.Services;
using System.Web.Services.Protocols;

[WebService(Namespace = "http://www.wrox.com/AsyncHelloWorld")]
[WebServiceBinding(ConformsTo = WsiProfiles.BasicProfile1_1)]
public class Async : System.Web.Services.WebService
{

    [WebMethod]
    public string HelloWorld() {
        System.Threading.Thread.Sleep(1000);
        return "Hello World";
    }

}
```

This Web service returns a simple `Hello World` as a string, but before it does, the Web service makes a 1000-millisecond pause. This is done by putting the Web service thread to sleep using the `Sleep` method.

Next, take a look at how an ASP.NET application can consume this slow Web service asynchronously, as shown in Listing 31-22.

LISTING 31-22: An ASP.NET application consuming a Web service asynchronously

Available for download on Wrox.com

VB

```
<%@ Page Language="VB" %>

<script runat="server">
    Protected Sub Page_Load(ByVal sender As Object, ByVal e As System.EventArgs)
        Dim ws As New localhost.Async()
        Dim myIar As IAsyncResult

        myIar = ws.BeginHelloWorld(Nothing, Nothing)

        Dim x As Integer = 0

        Do Until myIar.IsCompleted = True
            x += 1
        Loop

        Label1.Text = "Result from Web service: " & ws.EndHelloWorld(myIar) &
            "<br>Local count while waiting: " & x.ToString()
    End Sub
</script>

<html xmlns="http://www.w3.org/1999/xhtml" >
<head runat="server">
    <title>Async consumption</title>
</head>
```

```
<body>
    <form id="form1" runat="server">
    <div>
        <asp:Label ID="Label1" Runat="server"></asp:Label>
    </div>
    </form>
</body>
</html>
```

C#

```
<%@ Page Language="C#" %>

<script runat="server">
    protected void Page_Load(object sender, System.EventArgs e) {
        localhost.Async ws = new localhost.Async();
        IAsyncResult myIar;

        myIar = ws.BeginHelloWorld(null, null);

        int x = 0;

        while (myIar.IsCompleted == false) {
            x += 1;
        }

        Label1.Text = "Result from Web service: " + ws.EndHelloWorld(myIar) +
           "<br>Local count while waiting: " + x.ToString();
    }
</script>
```

When you make the Web reference to the remote Web service in the consuming ASP.NET application, you not only see the `HelloWorld WebMethod` available to you in IntelliSense, but you also see a `BeginHelloWorld()` and an `EndHelloWorld()`. To work with the Web service asynchronously, you must utilize the `BeginHelloWorld()` and `EndHelloWorld()` methods.

Use the `BeginHelloWorld()` method to send a SOAP request to the Web service, but instead of the ASP.NET application waiting idly for a response, it moves on to accomplish other tasks. In this case, it is not doing anything that important — just counting the amount of time it is taking in a loop.

After the SOAP request is sent from the ASP.NET application, you can use the `IAsyncResult` object to check whether a SOAP response is waiting. You do this by using `myIar.IsCompleted`. If the asynchronous invocation is not complete, the ASP.NET application increases the value of x by one before making the same check again. The ASP.NET application continues to do this until the XML Web service is ready to return a response. The response is retrieved using the `EndHelloWorld()` method call.

The results of running this application are similar to what is shown in Figure 31-15.

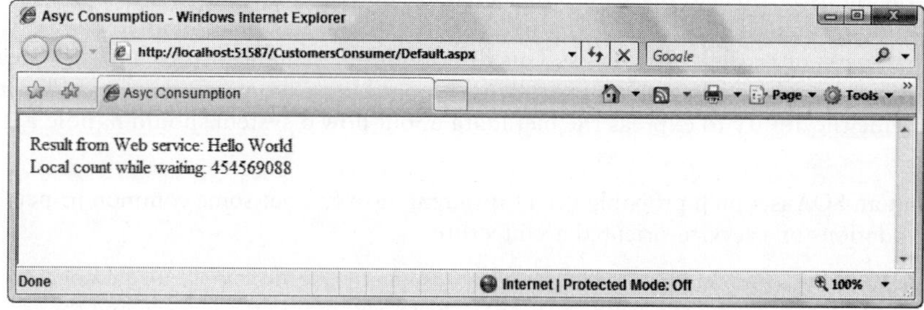

FIGURE 31-15

WINDOWS COMMUNICATION FOUNDATION

Since the introduction of the .NET Framework 3.0, Microsoft has made available a new way to build Web services beyond the ASP.NET-based Web services presented in this chapter.

Until the .NET Framework 3.0 came out, building components that were required to communicate a message from one point to another was not a simple task because Microsoft offered more than one technology that you could use for such an action.

For instance, you could have used ASP.NET Web services (as just discussed), Web Service Enhancements 3.0 (WSE), MSMQ, Enterprise Services, .NET Remoting, and even the `System.Messaging` namespace. Each technology has its own pros and cons. ASP.NET Web Services (also known by some as *ASMX Web Services*) provided the capability to easily build interoperable Web services. The WSE enabled you to easily build services that took advantage of some of the WS-* message protocols. MSMQ enabled the queuing of messages, which made working with solutions that were only intermittently connected easy. Enterprise Services, provided as a successor to COM+, offered an easy means to build distributed applications. .NET Remoting was a fast way to move messages from one .NET application to another. Moreover, these are Microsoft options only. These options do not include all the ones available in other environments, such as the Java world.

With so many options available to a Microsoft developer, deciding which path to take with the applications you are trying to build can be tough. With this in mind, Microsoft has created the Windows Communication Foundation (WCF).

WCF is a relatively new framework for building service-oriented applications. Microsoft wanted to provide its developers with a framework to quickly get a proper service-oriented architecture up and running. Using the WCF, you will be able to take advantage of all the items that make distribution technologies powerful. WCF is the answer and the successor to all these other message distribution technologies.

The Larger Move to SOA

Upon examining WCF, you will find that it is part of a larger movement that organizations are making toward the much-talked-about *service-oriented architecture*, or *SOA*. An SOA is a message-based service architecture that is vendor-agnostic. As a result, you have the capability to distribute messages across a system, and the messages are interoperable with other systems that would otherwise be considered incompatible with the provider system.

Looking back, you can see the gradual progression to the service-oriented architecture model. In the 1980s, the revolution arrived with the concept of everything being an object. When object-oriented programming came on the scene, it was enthusiastically accepted as the proper means to represent entities within a programming model. The 1990s took that idea one step further, and the component-oriented model was born. This model enabled objects to be encapsulated in a tightly coupled manner. It was only recently that the industry turned to a service-oriented architecture because developers and architects needed to take components and have them distributed to other points in an organization, to their partners, or to their customers. This distribution system needed to have the means to transfer messages between machines that were generally incompatible with one another. In addition, the messages had to include the ability to express the metadata about how a system should handle a message.

If you ask 10 people what an SOA is, you'll probably get 11 different answers, but some common principles are considered to be foundations of a service-oriented architecture:

- **Boundaries are explicit:** Any data store, logic, or entity uses an interface to expose its data or capabilities. The interface provides the means to hide the behaviors within the service, and the interface front-end enables you to change this behavior as required without affecting downstream consumers.

- **Services are autonomous:** All the services are updated or versioned independently of one another. Thus, you do not upgrade a system in its entirety; instead, each component of these systems is an individual entity within itself and can move forward without waiting for other components to progress forward. Note that with this type of model, after you publish an interface, that interface must remain unchanged. Interface changes require new interfaces (versioned, of course).
- **Services are based upon contracts, schemas, and policies:** All services developed require a contract regarding what is required to consume items from the interface (usually done through a WSDL document). Along with a contract, schemas are required to define the items passed in as parameters or delivered through the service (using XSD schemas). Finally, policies define any capabilities or requirements of the service.
- **Service compatibility that is based upon policy:** The final principle enables services to define policies (decided at runtime) that are required to consume the service. These policies are usually expressed through WS-Policy.

If your own organization is considering establishing an SOA, the WCF is a framework that works on these principles and makes implementing it relatively simple. The next section looks at what the WCF offers. Then you can dive into building your first WCF service.

WCF Overview

As stated, the Windows Communication Foundation is a means to build distributed applications in a Microsoft environment. Although the distributed application is built upon that environment, this does not mean that consumers are required to be Microsoft clients or to take any Microsoft component or technology to accomplish the task of consumption. On the other hand, building WCF services means you are also building services that abide by the principles set forth in the aforementioned SOA discussion and that these services are vendor-agnostic — thus, they can be consumed by almost anyone.

You can build WCF services using Visual Studio 2010. Note that because this is a .NET Framework 3.0 or greater component, you are actually limited to the operating systems in which you can run a WCF service. Whereas the other Microsoft distribution technologies mentioned in this chapter do not have too many limitations on running on Microsoft operating systems, an application built with WCF can only run on Windows XP SP2, Windows Vista, Windows 7, or Windows Server 2008.

If you are already familiar with WCF, it is interesting to note that some improvements have been made to WCF within the .NET Framework 4 release. A lot of focus was put on increasing the productivity of developers and providing quick options for common tasks such as creating syndicated services, as well as better debugging and serialization options. You will find that the performance for WCF has increased, especially when hosted in IIS7. Other new features include new support for working with the ADO.NET Entity Framework, improvements to the configuration editor, and more.

Building a WCF Service

Building a WCF service is not hard to accomplish. The assumption here is that you have installed the .NET Framework 4 for the purpose of these examples. If you are using Visual Studio 2010, the view of the project from the New Web Site dialog box is as shown in Figure 31-16.

FIGURE 31-16

When you build a WCF project in this manner, the idea is that you build a traditional class library that is compiled down to a DLL that can then be added to another project. The separation of code and project is a powerful division on larger projects. That said, you can, however, just as easily build a WCF service directly in your .NET project, whether that is a console application or a Windows Forms application. The approach taken for the examples in this chapter shows you how to build a WCF service that is hosted in a console application. Keep in mind that for the services you actually build and deploy, building them directly as a WCF Service Library project and using the created DLL in your projects or in IIS itself is usually better.

Before we jump into building a WCF service, first consider what makes up a service built upon the WCF framework.

What Makes a WCF Service

When looking at a WCF service, you should understand that it is made up of three parts: the service, one or more endpoints, and an environment in which to host the service.

A service is a class that is written in one of the .NET-compliant languages. The class can contain one or more methods that are exposed through the WCF service. A service can have one or more endpoints. An endpoint is used to communicate through the service to the client.

Endpoints themselves are also made up of three parts. These parts are usually defined by Microsoft as the ABC of WCF. Each letter of WCF means something in particular in the WCF model, including the following:

- "A" is for address.
- "B" is for binding.
- "C" is for contract.

Basically, you can think of this as follows: "A" is the *where*, "B" is the *how*, and "C" is the *what*. Finally, a hosting environment is where the service is contained. This constitutes an application domain and process. All three of these elements (the service, the endpoints, and the hosting environment) are put together to create a WCF service offering, as depicted in Figure 31-17.

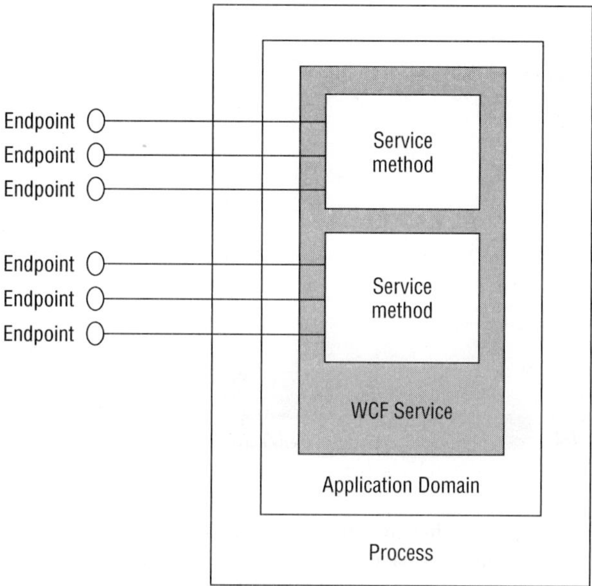

FIGURE 31-17

The next step is to create a basic service using the WCF framework.

Creating Your First WCF Service

To build your service, prior to hosting it, you must perform two main steps. First, you must create a service contract. Second, you must create a data contract. The service contract is really a class with the methods that you want to expose from the WCF service. The data contract is a class that specifies the structure you want to expose from the interface.

After you have a service class in place, you can host it almost anywhere. When running this service from Visual Studio 2010, you will be able to use the same built-in hosting mechanisms that are used by any standard ASP.NET application. To build your first WCF application, choose File ➪ New ➪ Web Site from the Visual Studio 2010 menu and call the project `WCFService1`.

The example this chapter will run through here demonstrates how to build the WCF service by building the interface, followed by the service itself.

Creating the Service Framework

The first step is to create the services framework in the project. To do this, right-click on the project and select Add New Item from the provided menu. From the Add New Item dialog box, select WCF Service, and name the service Calculator.svc, as illustrated in Figure 31-18.

FIGURE 31-18

This step creates a `Calculator.svc` file, a `Calculator.cs` file, and an `ICalculator.cs` file. The `Calculator.svc` file is a simple file that includes only the page directive, whereas the `Calculator.cs` does all the heavy lifting. The `Calculator.cs` file is an implementation of the `ICalculator.cs` interface.

Working with the Interface

To create your service, you need a service contract. The service contract is the interface of the service. This consists of all the methods exposed, as well as the input and output parameters that are required to invoke the methods. To accomplish this task, turn to the `ICalculator.vb` or `ICalculator.cs` (depending on the language you are using). Listing 31-23 presents the interface you need to create.

LISTING 31-23: Creating the interface

```
Imports System
Imports System.ServiceModel

<ServiceContract()> _
Public Interface ICalculator
    <OperationContract()> _
    Function Add(ByVal a As Integer, ByVal b As Integer) As Integer

    <OperationContract()> _
    Function Subtract(ByVal a As Integer, ByVal b As Integer) As Integer

    <OperationContract()> _
    Function Multiply(ByVal a As Integer, ByVal b As Integer) As Integer

    <OperationContract()> _
    Function Divide(ByVal a As Integer, ByVal b As Integer) As Integer
End Interface
```

C#

```
using System.ServiceModel;

[ServiceContract]
public interface ICalculator
{
    [OperationContract]
    int Add(int a, int b);

    [OperationContract]
    int Subtract(int a, int b);

    [OperationContract]
    int Multiply(int a, int b);

    [OperationContract]
    int Divide(int a, int b);
}
```

This is pretty much the normal interface definition you would expect, but with a couple of new attributes included. To gain access to these required attributes, you must make a reference to the `System.ServiceModel` namespace. This gives you access to the `<ServiceContract()>` and `<OperationContract()>` attributes.

You use the `<ServiceContract()>` attribute to define the class or interface as the service class, and it needs to precede the opening declaration of the class or interface. In this case, the example in the preceding code is based upon an interface:

```
<ServiceContract()> _
Public Interface ICalculator

   ' Code removed for clarity

End Interface
```

Within the interface, four methods are defined. Each method is going to be exposed through the WCF service as part of the service contract. For this reason, each method is required to have the `<OperationContract()>` attribute applied.

```
<OperationContract()> _
Function Add(ByVal a As Integer, ByVal b As Integer) As Integer
```

Utilizing the Interface

The next step is to create a class that implements the interface. Not only is the new class implementing the defined interface, but it is also implementing the service contract. For this example, add this class to the same `Calculator.vb` or `.cs` file. The following code, illustrated in Listing 31-24, shows the implementation of this interface.

LISTING 31-24: Implementing the interface

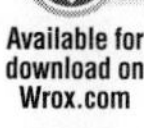

Available for download on Wrox.com

VB

```
Public Class Calculator
    Implements ICalculator

    Public Function Add(ByVal a As Integer, ByVal b As Integer) As Integer
       Implements ICalculator.Add

        Return (a + b)
    End Function

    Public Function Subtract(ByVal a As Integer, ByVal b As Integer) As Integer
```

continues

LISTING 31-24 *(continued)*

```
        Implements ICalculator.Subtract

         Return (a - b)
    End Function

    Public Function Multiply(ByVal a As Integer, ByVal b As Integer) As Integer
        Implements ICalculator.Multiply

         Return (a * b)
    End Function

    Public Function Divide(ByVal a As Integer, ByVal b As Integer) As Integer
        Implements ICalculator.Divide

         Return (a / b)
    End Function
End Class
```

C#

```
public class Calculator : ICalculator
{
    public int Add(int a, int b)
    {
        return (a + b);
    }

    public int Subtract(int a, int b)
    {
        return (a - b);
    }

    public int Multiply(int a, int b)
    {
        return (a * b);
    }

    public int Divide(int a, int b)
    {
        return (a / b);
    }
}
```

From these new additions, you can see that you don't have to do anything different to the `Calculator` class. It is a simple class that implements the `ICalculator` interface and provides implementations of the `Add()`, `Subtract()`, `Multiply()`, and `Divide()` methods.

With the interface and the class available, you now have your WCF service built and ready to go. The next step is to get the service hosted. Note that this is a simple service — it exposes only simple types, rather than a complex type. This enables you to build only a service contract and not have to deal with the construction of a data contract. You learn about the construction of data contracts later in this chapter.

Hosting the WCF Service in a Console Application

The next step is to take the service just developed and host it in some type of application process. Many hosting options are available, including the following:

- Console applications
- Windows Forms applications
- Windows Presentation Foundation (WPF) applications
- Managed Windows Services
- Internet Information Services (IIS) 5.1
- Internet Information Services (IIS) 6.0
- Internet Information Services (IIS) 7.0 and the Windows Activation Service (WAS)

As stated earlier, this example hosts the service in the developer Web server provided by Visual Studio 2010. You can activate hosting a couple of ways — either through the direct coding of the hosting behaviors or through declarative programming (usually done via the configuration file).

Compiling and running this application produces the results illustrated in Figure 31-19.

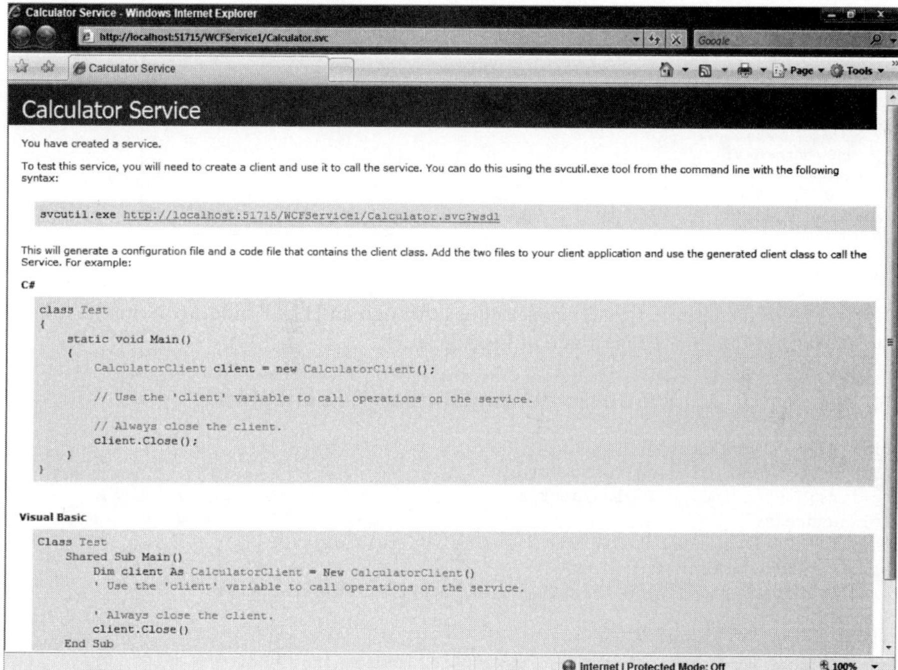

FIGURE 31-19

You will notice that the resulting page is quite similar to how it appears when you build an ASP.NET Web service.

Reviewing the WSDL Document

The page presented in Figure 31-19 is the information page about the service. In the image, notice the link to the WSDL file of the service. As with ASP.NET Web services, a WCF service can also auto-generate the WSDL file. Clicking the WSDL link shows the WSDL in the browser, as illustrated in Figure 31-20.

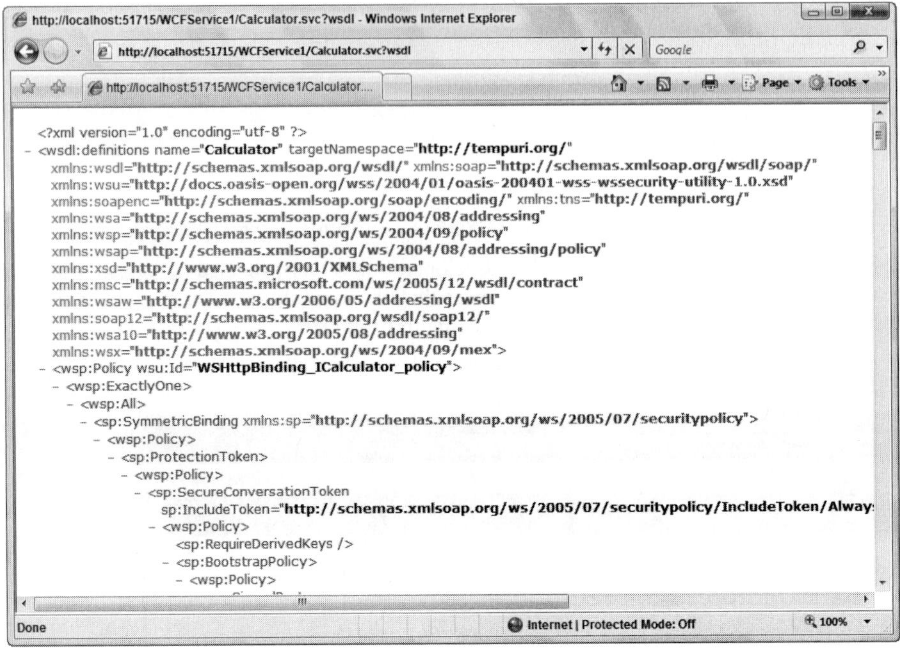

FIGURE 31-20

With this WSDL file, you can consume the service it defines through an HTTP binding. Note the following element at the bottom of the document, as shown in Listing 31-25.

LISTING 31-25: The part of the WSDL file showing the service's endpoint

```
<wsdl:service name="Calculator">
   <wsdl:port name="WSHttpBinding_ICalculator"
    binding="tns:WSHttpBinding_ICalculator">
      <soap12:address
       location="http://localhost:51715/WCFService1/Calculator.svc" />
      <wsa10:EndpointReference>
         <wsa10:Address>http://localhost:51715/WCFService1/Calculator.svc
         </wsa10:Address>
         <Identity
         xmlns="http://schemas.xmlsoap.org/ws/2006/02/addressingidentity">
         <Upn>Lipper-STL-LAP\Bill</Upn>
         </Identity>
      </wsa10:EndpointReference>
   </wsdl:port>
</wsdl:service>
```

This element in the XML document indicates that in order to consume the service, the end user must use SOAP 1.2 over HTTP. This is indicated through the use of the `<soap12:address>` element in the document. The `<wsa10:EndpointReference>` is a WS-Addressing endpoint definition.

Using this simple WSDL document, you can now build a consumer that makes use of this interface.

BUILDING THE WCF CONSUMER

Now that an HTTP service is out there, which you built using the WCF framework, the next step is to build a consumer application in ASP.NET that uses the simple `Calculator` service. The consumer sends its request via HTTP using SOAP. This section describes how to consume this service. Open Visual Studio

2010 and create a new ASP.NET application. Although this example uses an ASP.NET application, you can make this consumer call through any other application type within .NET as well.

Call the new ASP.NET application `WCFConsumer`. This application consumes the `Calculator` service, so it should be laid out with two text boxes and a button to initiate the service call. For this example, you will only use the `Add()` method of the service.

Adding a Service Reference

After you have laid out your ASP.NET page, make a reference to the new WCF service. You do this in a manner quite similar to how you do it with XML Web service references. Right-click on the solution name from the Visual Studio Solution Explorer and select Add Service Reference from the dialog box that appears. This capability to add a service reference is included in Visual Studio 2010 — previously (prior to Visual Studio 2008), you had only the Add Reference and Add Web Reference options.

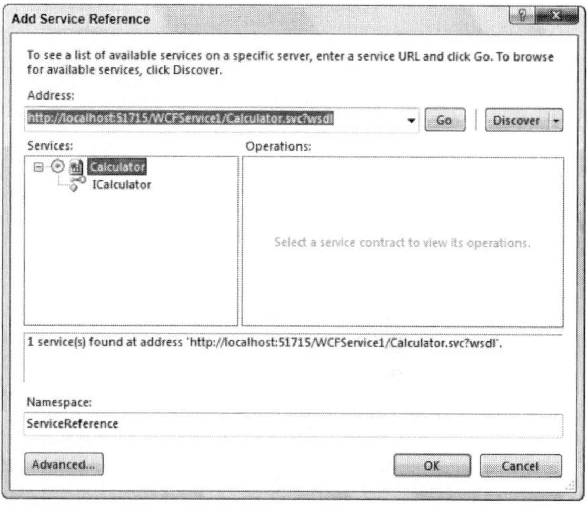

FIGURE 31-21

After you have selected Add Service Reference, the Add Service Reference dialog box, shown in Figure 31-21, appears.

The Add Service Reference dialog box asks you for two things: the Service URI or Address (basically a pointer to the WSDL file) and the name you want to give to the reference. The name you provide the reference is the name that will be used for the instantiated object that enables you to interact with the service.

Referring to Figure 31-21, you can see that the name provided to the Service Address setting is what is used for the running service from earlier in this chapter. Click OK in the Add Service Reference dialog box. This adds to your project a Service Reference folder containing some proxy files, as shown in Figure 31-22.

FIGURE 31-22

Indeed, the Service Reference folder is added and a series of files are contained within this folder. The other important addition to note is the `System.ServiceModel` reference, made for you in the References folder. This reference was not there before you made reference to the service through the Add Service Reference dialog.

Configuration File Changes

Looking at the `web.config` file, you can see that Visual Studio has placed information about the service inside the document, as illustrated in Listing 31-26.

LISTING 31-26: Additions made to the web.config file by Visual Studio

```
<system.serviceModel>
   <bindings>
      <wsHttpBinding>
```

continues

LISTING 31-26 *(continued)*

```
          <binding name="WSHttpBinding_ICalculator" closeTimeout="00:01:00"
           openTimeout="00:01:00" receiveTimeout="00:10:00" sendTimeout="00:01:00"
           bypassProxyOnLocal="false" transactionFlow="false"
           hostNameComparisonMode="StrongWildcard" maxBufferPoolSize="524288"
           maxReceivedMessageSize="65536" messageEncoding="Text"
           textEncoding="utf-8" useDefaultWebProxy="true" allowCookies="false">
             <readerQuotas maxDepth="32" maxStringContentLength="8192"
              maxArrayLength="16384" maxBytesPerRead="4096"
              maxNameTableCharCount="16384"/>
             <reliableSession ordered="true" inactivityTimeout="00:10:00"
              enabled="false"/>
             <security mode="Message">
                <transport clientCredentialType="Windows" proxyCredentialType="None"
                 realm=""/>
                <message clientCredentialType="Windows"
                 negotiateServiceCredential="true" algorithmSuite="Default"
                 establishSecurityContext="true"/>
             </security>
          </binding>
       </wsHttpBinding>
    </bindings>
    <client>
       <endpoint address="http://localhost:51715/WCFService1/Calculator.svc"
        binding="wsHttpBinding" bindingConfiguration="WSHttpBinding_ICalculator"
        contract="ServiceReference.ICalculator" name="WSHttpBinding_ICalculator">
          <identity>
             <userPrincipalName value="Lipper-STL-LAP\Bill"/>
          </identity>
       </endpoint>
    </client>
 </system.serviceModel></ServiceReference>
```

The important part of this configuration document is the `<client>` element. This element contains a child element called `<endpoint>` that defines the *where* and *how* of the service consumption process.

The `<endpoint>` element provides the address of the service — `http://localhost:51715/WCFService1/Calculator.svc` — and it specifies which binding of the available WCF bindings should be used. In this case, the `wsHttpBinding` is the required binding. Even though you are using an established binding from the WCF framework, from the client side, you can customize how this binding behaves. The settings that define the behavior of the binding are specified using the `bindingConfiguration` attribute of the `<endpoint>` element. In this case, the value provided to the `bindingConfiguration` attribute is `WSHttpBinding_ICalculator`, which is a reference to the `<binding>` element contained within the `<wsHttpBinding>` element.

As demonstrated, Visual Studio 2010 makes the consumption of these services fairly trivial. The next step is to code the consumption of the service interface into the GUI that you created as one of the first steps earlier in this chapter.

Writing the Consumption Code

The code to consume the interface is quite minimal. The end user places a number in each of the two text boxes provided and clicks the button to call the service to perform the designated operation on the provided numbers. Listing 31-27 is the code from the button click event.

LISTING 31-27: The button click event to call the service

Available for download on Wrox.com

VB

```
Protected Sub Button1_Click(ByVal sender As Object, ByVal e As System.EventArgs)
  Handles Button1.Click

  Dim ws As New ServiceReference.CalculatorClient()
  Dim result As Integer

   result = ws.Add(TextBox1.Text, TextBox2.Text)
   Response.Write(result.ToString())

   ws.Close()
End Sub
```

C#

```
protected void Button1_Click(object sender, EventArgs e)
{
   ServiceReference.CalculatorClient ws = new ServiceReference.CalculatorClient();

   int result = ws.Add(int.Parse(TextBox1.Text), int.Parse(TextBox2.Text));
   Response.Write(result);

   ws.Close();
}
```

This code is quite similar to what is done when working with Web references from the XML Web services world. First is an instantiation of the proxy class, as shown with the creation of the `svc` object:

```
Dim ws As New ServiceReference.CalculatorClient()
```

Working with the `ws` object now, the IntelliSense options provide you with the appropriate `Add()`, `Subtract()`, `Multiply()`, and `Divide()` methods.

As before, the requests and responses are sent over HTTP as SOAP 1.2. This concludes the short tutorial demonstrating how to build your own WCF service using the HTTP protocol and consume this service directly into an ASP.NET application.

Working with Data Contracts

Thus far, when building the WCF services, the defined data contract has relied upon simple types or primitive datatypes. In the case of the earlier WCF service, a .NET type of `Integer` was exposed, which in turn was mapped to an XSD type of `int`. Although you may not be able to see the input and output types defined in the WSDL document provided via the WCF-generated one, they are there. These types are actually exposed through an imported `.xsd` document (`Calculator.xsd` and `Calculator1.xsd`). Listing 31-28 presents this bit of the WSDL document.

LISTING 31-28: Imported types in the WSDL document

```
<wsdl:types>
   <xsd:schema targetNamespace="http://tempuri.org/Imports">
      <xsd:import
       schemaLocation="http://localhost:51715/WCFService1/Calculator.svc?xsd=xsd0"
       namespace="http://tempuri.org/" />
      <xsd:import
       schemaLocation="http://localhost:51715/WCFService1/Calculator.svc?xsd=xsd1"
       namespace="http://schemas.microsoft.com/2003/10/Serialization/" />
   </xsd:schema>
</wsdl:types>
```

Typing in the XSD location of `http://localhost:51715/WCFService1/Calculator.svc?xsd=xsd0` gives you the input and output parameters of the service. For instance, looking at the definition of the `Add()` method, you will see the following bit of code, as shown in Listing 31-29.

LISTING 31-29: Defining the required types in the XSD

```
<xs:element name="Add">
  <xs:complexType>
    <xs:sequence>
      <xs:element minOccurs="0" name="a" type="xs:int" />
      <xs:element minOccurs="0" name="b" type="xs:int" />
    </xs:sequence>
  </xs:complexType>
</xs:element>
<xs:element name="AddResponse">
  <xs:complexType>
    <xs:sequence>
      <xs:element minOccurs="0" name="AddResult" type="xs:int" />
    </xs:sequence>
  </xs:complexType>
</xs:element>
```

This bit of XML code indicates that two required input parameters (`a` and `b`) are of type `int`; in return, the consumer gets an element called `<AddResult>`, which contains a value of type `int`.

As a builder of this WCF service, you did not have to build the data contract because this service used simple types. When using complex types, you have to create a data contract in addition to your service contract.

Building a Service with a Data Contract

For an example of working with data contracts, create a new WCF service (another WCF service project) called `WCF_WithDataContract`. In this case, you still need an interface that defines your service contract, and then another class that implements that interface. In addition to these items, you also need another class that defines the data contract.

As with the service contract, which makes use of the `<ServiceContract()>` and the `<OperationContract()>` attributes, the data contract uses the `<DataContract()>` and `<DataMember()>` attributes. To gain access to these attributes, you must make a reference to the `System.Runtime.Serialization` namespace in your project and import this namespace into the file.

The custom type in this case is a `Customer` type, as presented in Listing 31-30.

LISTING 31-30: Building the Customer type

Available for download on Wrox.com

VB

```
Imports System
Imports System.ServiceModel
Imports System.Runtime.Serialization

<DataContract()>
Public Class Customer
    <DataMember()>
    Public FirstName As String

    <DataMember()>
    Public LastName As String
End Class

<ServiceContract()>
Public Interface IHelloCustomer
    <OperationContract()>
    Function HelloFirstName(ByVal cust As Customer) As String

    <OperationContract()>
    Function HelloFullName(ByVal cust As Customer) As String
```

```
End Interface
```

```
using System.Runtime.Serialization;
using System.ServiceModel;

[DataContract]
public class Customer
{
    [DataMember]
    public string Firstname;

    [DataMember]
    public string Lastname;
}

[ServiceContract]
public interface IHelloCustomer
{
    [OperationContract]
    string HelloFirstName(Customer cust);

    [OperationContract]
    string HelloFullName(Customer cust);
}
```

Here, you can see that the `System.Runtime.Serialization` namespace is also imported, and the first class in the file is the data contract of the service. This class, the `Customer` class, has two members: `FirstName` and `LastName`. Both of these properties are of type `String`. You specify a class as a data contract through the use of the `<DataContract()>` attribute:

```
<DataContract()>
Public Class Customer

    ' Code removed for clarity

End Class
```

Now, any of the properties contained in the class are also part of the data contract through the use of the `<DataMember()>` attribute:

```
<DataContract()>
Public Class Customer
    <DataMember()>
    Public FirstName As String

    <DataMember()>
    Public LastName As String
End Class
```

Finally, the `Customer` object is used in the interface, as well as the class that implements the `IHelloCustomer` interface, as shown in Listing 31-31.

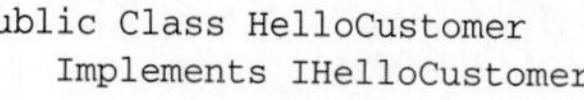

LISTING 31-31: Implementing the interface

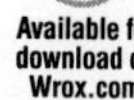

Available for download on Wrox.com

```
Public Class HelloCustomer
    Implements IHelloCustomer

    Public Function HelloFirstName(ByVal cust As Customer) As String
      Implements IHelloCustomer.HelloFirstName
        Return "Hello " & cust.FirstName
    End Function
```

continues

LISTING 31-31 *(continued)*

```
    Public Function HelloFullName(ByVal cust As Customer) As String
      Implements IHelloCustomer.HelloFullName
        Return "Hello " & cust.FirstName & " " & cust.LastName
    End Function
End Class
```

C#

```
public class HelloCustomer: IHelloCustomer
{
    public string HelloFirstName(Customer cust)
    {
        return "Hello " + cust.Firstname;
    }

    public string HelloFullName(Customer cust)
    {
        return "Hello " + cust.Firstname + " " + cust.Lastname;
    }
}
```

Building the Consumer

Now that the service is running and in place, the next step is to build the consumer. To begin, build a new ASP.NET application from Visual Studio 2010 and call the project `HelloWorldConsumer`. Again, right-click on the solution and select Add Service Reference from the options provided in the menu.

From the Add Service Reference dialog box, add the location of the WSDL file for the service and click OK. This adds the changes to the references and the `web.config` file just as before, enabling you to consume the service. The code presented in Listing 31-32 shows what is required to consume the service if you are using a Button control to initiate the call.

LISTING 31-32: Consuming a custom type through a WCF service

Available for download on Wrox.com

VB

```
Protected Sub Button1_Click(ByVal sender As Object, ByVal e As System.EventArgs)
  Handles Button1.Click

    Dim ws As New ServiceReference.HelloCustomerClient()
    Dim myCustomer As New ServiceReference.Customer()

    myCustomer.Firstname = "Bill"
    myCustomer.Lastname = "Evjen"

    Response.Write(ws.HelloFullName(myCustomer))

    ws.Close()
End Sub
```

C#

```
protected void Button1_Click(object sender, EventArgs e)
{
    ServiceReference.HelloCustomerClient ws = new
       ServiceReference.HelloCustomerClient();
    ServiceReference.Customer myCustomer = new ServiceReference.Customer();

    myCustomer.Firstname = "Bill";
    myCustomer.Lastname = "Evjen";

    Response.Write(ws.HelloFullName(myCustomer));

    ws.Close();
}
```

As a consumer, after you make the reference, you will notice that the service reference provides both a `HelloCustomerClient` object and the `Customer` object, which was defined through the service's data contract.

Therefore, the preceding code block just instantiates both of these objects and builds the `Customer` object before it is passed into the `HelloFullName()` method provided by the service.

Looking at WSDL and the Schema for HelloCustomerService

When you make a reference to the `HelloCustomer` service, you will find the following XSD imports in the WSDL:

```
<wsdl:types>
   <xsd:schema targetNamespace="http://tempuri.org/Imports">
    <xsd:import
     schemaLocation="http://localhost:51715/WCFService1/HelloCustomer.svc?xsd=xsd0"
     namespace="http://tempuri.org/" />
    <xsd:import
     schemaLocation="http://localhost:51715/WCFService1/HelloCustomer.svc?xsd=xsd1"
     namespace="http://schemas.microsoft.com/2003/10/Serialization/" />
    <xsd:import
     schemaLocation="http://localhost:51715/WCFService1/HelloCustomer.svc?xsd=xsd2"
     namespace="http://schemas.datacontract.org/2004/07/" />
   </xsd:schema>
</wsdl:types>
```

`http://localhost:51715/WCFService1/HelloCustomer.svc?xsd=xsd2` provides the details on your `Customer` object. Here is the code from this file:

```
<?xml version="1.0" encoding="utf-8" ?>
<xs:schema elementFormDefault="qualified"
 targetNamespace="http://schemas.datacontract.org/2004/07/"
 xmlns:xs="http://www.w3.org/2001/XMLSchema"
 xmlns:tns="http://schemas.datacontract.org/2004/07/">
   <xs:complexType name="Customer">
      <xs:sequence>
         <xs:element minOccurs="0" name="Firstname" nillable="true"
          type="xs:string" />
         <xs:element minOccurs="0" name="Lastname" nillable="true"
          type="xs:string" />
      </xs:sequence>
   </xs:complexType>
   <xs:element name="Customer" nillable="true" type="tns:Customer" />
</xs:schema>
```

This code is an XSD description of the `Customer` object. Making a reference to the WSDL includes the XSD description of the `Customer` object and gives you the ability to create local instances of this object.

Using this model, you can easily build your services with your own defined types.

Defining Namespaces

Note that the services built in the chapter have no defined namespaces. If you looked at the WSDL files that were produced, you would see that the namespace provided is `http://tempuri.org`. Obviously, you do not want to go live with this default namespace. Instead, you must define your own namespace.

To accomplish this task, the interface's `<ServiceContract()>` attribute enables you to set the namespace, as shown here:

```
<ServiceContract(Namespace:="http://www.lipperweb.com/ns/")>
Public Interface IHelloCustomer
    <OperationContract()>
    Function HelloFirstName(ByVal cust As Customer) As String
```

```
        <OperationContract()>
        Function HelloFullName(ByVal cust As Customer) As String
    End Interface
```

Here, the `<ServiceContract()>` attribute uses the `Namespace` property to provide a namespace.

USING WCF DATA SERVICES

Prior to the release of the .NET Framework 4, the release of the .NET Framework 3.5 SP1 provided tremendous focus on the concept of the Entity Data Model (EDM) and what these models bring to your application's reusability. Again, an EDM is an abstract conceptual model of data as you want to represent it in your code. Chapter 29 of this book provides more information on EDMs and how to work with them.

Another outstanding feature found in this release of the .NET Framework is the WCF Data Services framework. This feature enables you to easily create a cloud interface to your client applications that provides everything from simple read capabilities to a full CRUD model (create, read, update, and delete functions). This feature was previously referred to as ADO.NET Data Services.

When you are working with ASP.NET, there is now a lot more focus on putting work down on the client as well as the server. In the past, much of the development focused on performing as much on the server as possible and delivering completed operations and UI back down to the client simply for viewing. With the release of "smart clients" and AJAX-enabled applications, much of the work is now being offloaded to the client. WCF Data Services makes exposing back-end capabilities over the wire to enable more work to be performed on the client even easier than before.

WCF Data Services works to create a services layer to your back-end data source. Doing so yourself, especially if you are working with a full CRUD model, means a lot of work. WCF Data Services allow you to get a service layer that is URI-driven. Figure 31-23 shows the general architecture when you're working with WCF Data Services.

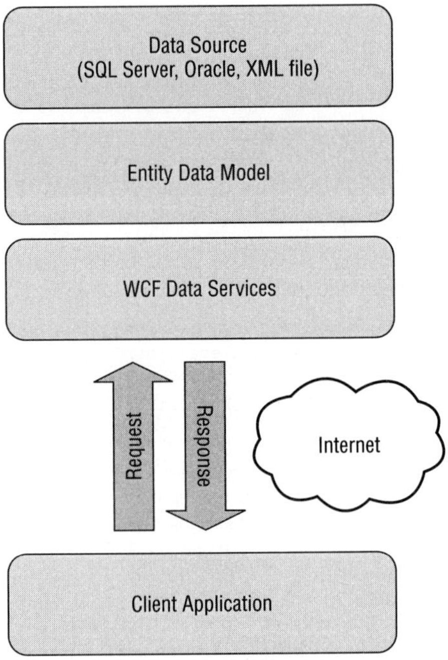

FIGURE 31-23

As you can see from this figure, the WCF Data Services layer is not the layer that interacts with the database. Instead, you are working with an EDM layer that is the mapping layer between the data store and the cloud-based interface. When working with your EDM, you are able to use LINQ to SQL and LINQ to Entities (something that you have been introduced to in the last few chapters of this book).

WCF Data Services allow you to quickly expose interactions with the application's underlying data source as RESTful-based services. The current version of WCF Data Services allows you to work with the datastores using JSON or Atom-based XML. Again, JSON is what ASP.NET AJAX uses for doing out-of-bounds calls to get around doing a complete page refresh.

CREATING YOUR FIRST SERVICE

Figuring out how to build a complete services layer to your database for all create, read, update, and delete functions would take some serious time and thought. However, WCF Data Services makes this task much more feasible, as you will see as you work through this first example.

To build a services layer, first create a standard ASP.NET Web Application called Web_ADONETDS in either Visual Basic or C#. Note, you need to use the .NET Framework 3.5 SP1 along with Visual Studio 2008 SP1 or the .NET Framework 4 with Visual Studio 2010 for this example to work.

This, of course, creates a standard Web application that is not different from normal. Because WCF Data Services works from an underlying database, you will need to add one. For this example, add the `NORTHWND.mdf` database as you previously used in other chapters of this book. Place this database within the App_Data folder of your project.

Adding Your Entity Data Model

After you have the database in place, you next create an Entity Data Model that WCF Data Services will work with. To do this, right-click on your project and select Add ➪ New Item from the list of options in the provided menu.

The Add New Item dialog appears. As illustrated in Figure 31-24, add an ADO.NET Entity Data Model to your project.

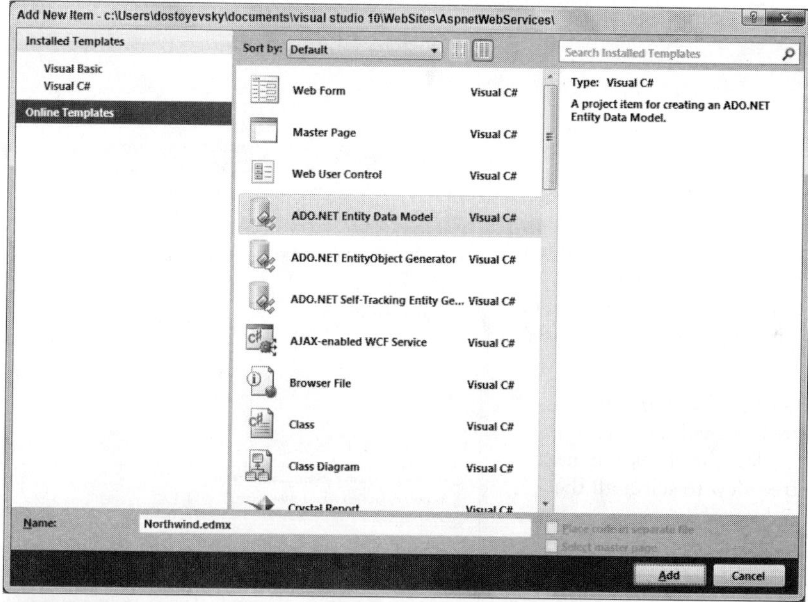

FIGURE 31-24

As shown in the figure, name your ADO.NET Entity Data Model file `Northwind.edmx`. Chapter 29 of this book covers the ADO.NET Entity Framework and its capabilities of building your EDM using Visual Studio. When you create the `Northwind.edmx` file by clicking Add, the Entity Data Model Wizard appears, offering you the option of creating an empty EDM or creating one from a pre-existing database. For this example, choose the option to create one from the pre-existing (Northwind) database. Then click Next in the wizard.

The next screen of the wizard will find your `NORTHWND.mdf` database and pre-define the connection settings and how they will be stored within your application. Figure 31-25 presents this second screen of the wizard.

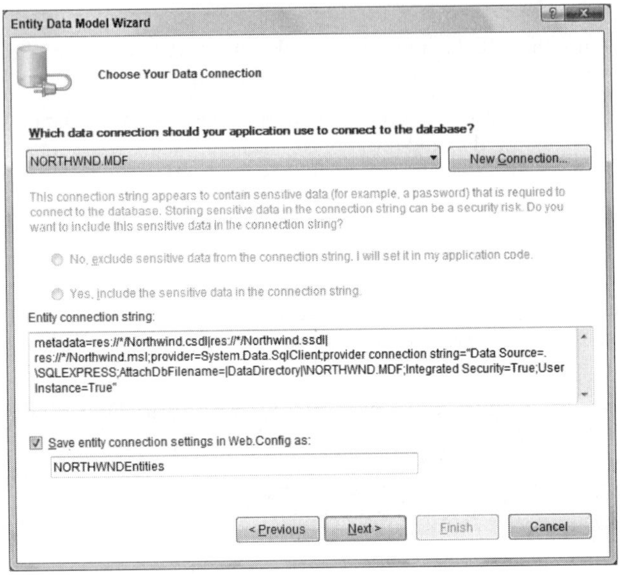

FIGURE 31-25

In the screenshot in Figure 31-25, notice that the connection string and the locations of the mapping details are going to be stored within the `web.config` file. You can also see on this screen that you are naming the instance of the model `NORTHWNDEntities` in the text box at the bottom of the wizard. This name is important to note because you will use it later in this example.

The next screen allows you to select the tables, views, or stored procedures that will be part of the model. For this example, select the check box next to the Table item in the tree view to select all the tables in the database, as shown in Figure 31-26.

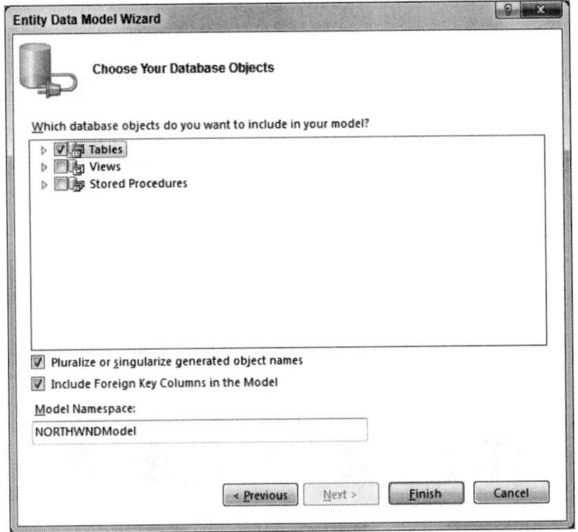

FIGURE 31-26

After selecting the Table check box, click the Finish button to have Visual Studio create the EDM for you. You will notice that Visual Studio will create a visual representation of the model for you in the O/R Designer.

If you look at the `Northwind.designer.vb` or the `Northwind.designer.cs` file in your solution, you will see all the generated code for your EDM in place. This class file is named `NORTHWNDEntities`.

Creating the Service

Now that the EDM is in place along with the database, the next step is to add your WCF Data Service. To accomplish this, right-click on your project within the Visual Studio Solution Explorer and select Add ➪ New Item from the provided menu. The Add New Item dialog appears again; select WCF Data Service from the middle section of the provided dialog (see Figure 31-27).

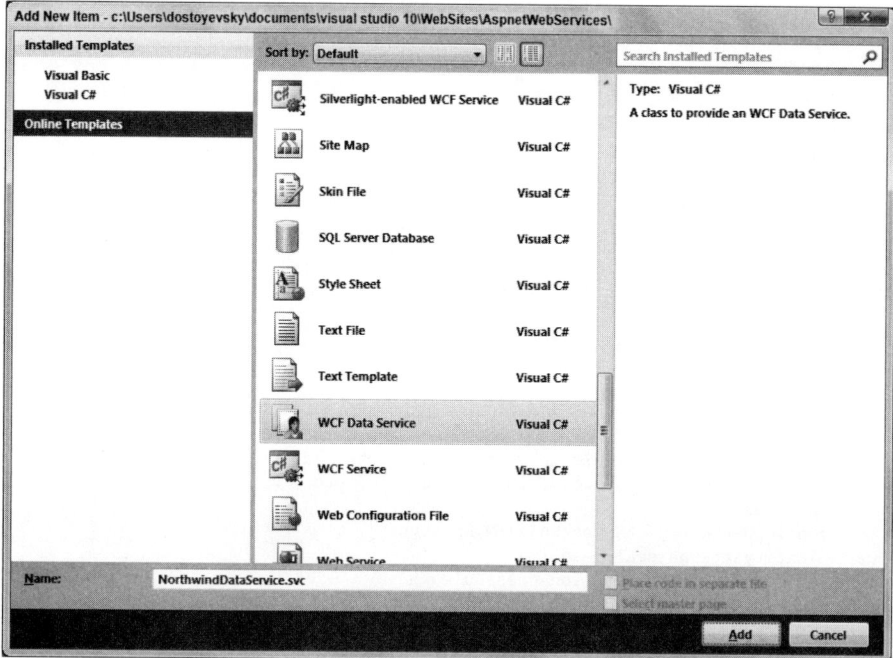

FIGURE 31-27

As shown in the figure, name your WCF Data Service `NorthwindDataService.svc`. When done, click the Add button and Visual Studio will then generate a WCF service for you on your behalf. Listing 31-33 shows the code of the default service file.

LISTING 31-33: The default .svc file for a WCF Data Service

VB

```
Imports System.Data.Services
Imports System.Linq
Imports System.ServiceModel.Web

Public Class NorthwindDataService
    ' TODO: replace [[class name]] with your data class name

        Inherits DataService(Of [[class name]])

    ' This method is called only once to initialize service-wide
        policies.
    Public Shared Sub InitializeService(ByVal config As
      IDataServiceConfiguration)
        ' TODO: set rules to indicate which entity sets and service
            operations are visible, updatable, etc.
        ' Examples:
        ' config.SetEntitySetAccessRule("MyEntityset",
            EntitySetRights.AllRead)
        ' config.SetServiceOperationAccessRule("MyServiceOperation",
            ServiceOperationRights.All)
    End Sub

End Class
```

continues

LISTING 31-33 *(continued)*

C#

```
using System;
using System.Collections.Generic;
using System.Data.Services;
using System.Linq;
using System.ServiceModel.Web;

namespace Web_ADONETDS
{
    public class NorthwindDataService :
      DataService< /* TODO: put your data source class name here */ >
    {
        // This method is called only once to initialize
             service-wide policies.
        public static void
            InitializeService(IDataServiceConfiguration config)
        {
            // TODO: set rules to indicate which entity sets and
                 service operations are visible, updatable, etc.
            // Examples:
            // config.SetEntitySetAccessRule("MyEntityset",
                 EntitySetRights.AllRead);
            // config.SetServiceOperationAccessRule
                 ("MyServiceOperation", ServiceOperationRights.All);
        }
    }
}
```

The code generated here is the base framework for what you are going to expose through WCF Data Services. It will not work, however, until you accomplish the big TODO that the code specifies. The first step is to put in the name of the EDM instance using the code presented in Listing 31-34.

LISTING 31-34: Changing the WCF Data Service to work with your EDM

VB

```
Public Class NorthwindDataService

     Inherits DataService(Of NORTHWNDEntities)

     ' Code removed for clarity

End Class
```

C#

```
public class NorthwindDataService : DataService<NORTHWNDEntities>
{

   // Code removed for clarity

}
```

Now your application is at a state in which the database, the EDM, and the service to work with the EDM are in place. Upon compiling and pulling up the `NorthwindDataService.svc` file in the browser, you are presented with the following bit of XML:

```
<?xml version="1.0" encoding="utf-8" standalone="yes" ?>
<service xml:base="http://localhost:4113/NorthwindDataService.svc/"
 xmlns:atom="http://www.w3.org/2005/Atom"
 xmlns:app="http://www.w3.org/2007/app"
 xmlns="http://www.w3.org/2007/app">
  <workspace>
    <atom:title>Default</atom:title>
  </workspace>
</service>
```

If you don't see this XML, then you need to turn off the feed reading capabilities of your IE browser by selecting Tools ➪ Internet Options. From the provided dialog, select the Content tab and, within the Feeds section, click on the Select button. From there, you will be able to uncheck the "Turn on feed reading" check box.

The result of the earlier XML is supposed to be a list of all the available sets that are present in the model, but by default, WCF Data Services locks everything down. To unlock these sets from the model, go back to the `InitializeService()` function and add the following bolded code, as illustrated in Listing 31-35.

LISTING 31-35: Opening up the service for reading from the available tables

Available for download on Wrox.com

VB

```
Imports System.Data.Services
Imports System.Linq
Imports System.ServiceModel.Web

Public Class NorthwindDataService
    Inherits DataService(Of NORTHWNDEntities)

    Public Shared Sub InitializeService(ByVal config _
      As IDataServiceConfiguration)

        config.SetEntitySetAccessRule("*", EntitySetRights.AllRead)
    End Sub

End Class
```

C#

```
using System;
using System.Collections.Generic;
using System.Data.Services;
using System.Linq;
using System.ServiceModel.Web;
using System.Web;

namespace Web_ADONETDS
{
    public class NorthwindDataService : DataService<NORTHWNDEntities>
    {
        public static void
          InitializeService(IDataServiceConfiguration config)
        {

            config.SetEntitySetAccessRule("*",
              EntitySetRights.AllRead);
        }
    }
}
```

In this case, every table is opened up to access. Everyone who accesses the tables has the ability to read from them but no writing or deleting abilities. All tables are specified through the use of the asterisk (*), and the right to the underlying data is set to read-only through the `EntitySetRights` enum being set to `AllRead`.

Now, when you compile and run this service in the browser, you see the following bit of XML:

```
<?xml version="1.0" encoding="utf-8" standalone="yes"?>
<service xml:base="http://localhost:4113/NorthwindDataService.svc/"
 xmlns:atom="http://www.w3.org/2005/Atom"
 xmlns:app="http://www.w3.org/2007/app"
 xmlns="http://www.w3.org/2007/app">
```

```
  <workspace>
    <atom:title>Default</atom:title>
    <collection href="Categories">
      <atom:title>Categories</atom:title>
    </collection>
    <collection href="CustomerDemographics">
      <atom:title>CustomerDemographics</atom:title>
    </collection>
    <collection href="Customers">
      <atom:title>Customers</atom:title>
    </collection>
    <collection href="Employees">
      <atom:title>Employees</atom:title>
    </collection>
    <collection href="Order_Details">
      <atom:title>Order_Details</atom:title>
    </collection>
    <collection href="Orders">
      <atom:title>Orders</atom:title>
    </collection>
    <collection href="Products">
      <atom:title>Products</atom:title>
    </collection>
    <collection href="Region">
      <atom:title>Region</atom:title>
    </collection>
    <collection href="Shippers">
      <atom:title>Shippers</atom:title>
    </collection>
    <collection href="Suppliers">
      <atom:title>Suppliers</atom:title>
    </collection>
    <collection href="Territories">
      <atom:title>Territories</atom:title>
    </collection>
  </workspace>
</service>
```

The output of this XML is in the AtomPub format, one of the two available formats of XML that are made available from WCF Data Services. The other format is JSON, which is used in the AJAX world. The AtomPub example was retrieved due to the following header being in place:

```
GET /NorthwindDataService.svc/ HTTP/1.1
Accept: application/atom+xml
Accept-Language: en-us
User-Agent: Mozilla/4.0 (compatible; MSIE 7.0; Windows NT 6.1; Trident/4.0; SLCC2;
.NET CLR 2.0.50727; .NET CLR 3.5.30729; .NET CLR 3.0.30729; Media Center PC 6.0;
.NET4.0C; .NET4.0E; .NET CLR 1.1.4322)
UA-CPU: x86
Accept-Encoding: gzip, deflate
Host: localhost.:4113
Connection: Keep-Alive
```

```
GET /NorthwindDataService.svc/ HTTP/1.1
Accept: */*
Accept-Language: en-US,fi-FI;q=0.7,ru-RU;q=0.3
User-Agent: Mozilla/4.0 (compatible; MSIE 7.0; Windows NT 6.1; Trident/4.0;
SLCC2; .NET CLR 2.0.50727; .NET CLR 3.5.30729; .NET CLR 3.0.30729;
Media Center PC 6.0; .NET4.0C; .NET4.0E; .NET CLR 1.1.4322)
UA-CPU: x86
Accept-Encoding: gzip, deflate
Host: localhost:50122
Connection: Keep-Alive
```

```
Cache-Control: no-cache
<?xml version="1.0" encoding="utf-8" standalone="yes"?>
<error
xmlns="http://schemas.microsoft.com/ado/2007/08/dataservices/
   metadata">
  <code></code>
  <message xml:lang="en-US">Unsupported media type requested.</message>
</error>
```

Here, `application/atom+xml` is used, and therefore, the AtomPub format is used. Changing the Accept header to read `application/json` will instead give you the following response:

```
{ "d" : {
"EntitySets": [
"Categories", "CustomerDemographics", "Customers", "Employees",
"Order_Details", "Orders", "Products", "Region", "Shippers",
"Suppliers", "Territories"
]
} }
```

The format of the preceding code is what you would need just for an ASP.NET AJAX page. Next, this chapter explores how to query the interface.

QUERYING THE INTERFACE

You query the interface using three components: the URI, the action of the HTTP header, and the HTTP verb that you are using in the query. One of the more common ways to query the interface is to perform a read operation against the datastore.

Looking back on an example header from earlier in this chapter, you can see something like the code shown in Listing 31-36.

LISTING 31-36: An example request HTTP header

```
GET /NorthwindDataService.svc/Products HTTP/1.1
Accept: application/atom+xml
Accept-Language: en-us
User-Agent: Mozilla/4.0 (compatible; MSIE 7.0; Windows NT 6.1;
Trident/4.0; SLCC2; .NET CLR 2.0.50727; .NET CLR 3.5.30729;
.NET CLR 3.0.30729; Media Center PC 6.0; .NET4.0C; .NET4.0E; .NET CLR 1.1.4322)
UA-CPU: x86
Accept-Encoding: gzip, deflate
Host: localhost.:4113
Connection: Keep-Alive
```

The result that is returned in this case is based on what is returned within the Accept HTTP header. Shown here is the Accept value of `application/atom+xml`. You could have also had the header of `*/*` for a wildcard, and WCF Data Services would simply default to AtomPub in this case. Again, if you wanted the result returned as JSON, then you would have the Accept value of `application/json`.

The method that you are calling is determined by the URI used. In the example in Listing 31-36, the URI is `/NorthwindDataService.svc/Products`, meaning that the Products set from the EDM is called and the results of the Products table from the Northwind database will be returned.

Listing 31-36 is also a read statement because the HTTP verb that is used is a GET statement. Table 31-1 details the list of HTTP verbs and how they map to the data access type.

TABLE 31-1

HTTP VERB	DATA ACCESS TYPE
POST	Create
GET	Read
PUT	Update
DELETE	Delete

The next section looks at different ways to query the underlying interface provided by WCF Data Services for reading content out of the database.

Reading a Table of Data

Reading out an entire table of contents is based on the URI that is passed in. You read the contents by specifying the particular entity set that you are interested in. For example, type the following query into the browser's address bar:

```
http://localhost/NorthwindDataService.svc/Products
```

In this case, you are requesting the entire contents of the Products table by providing only the entity set Products in the URI. Figure 31-28 shows the result of this request.

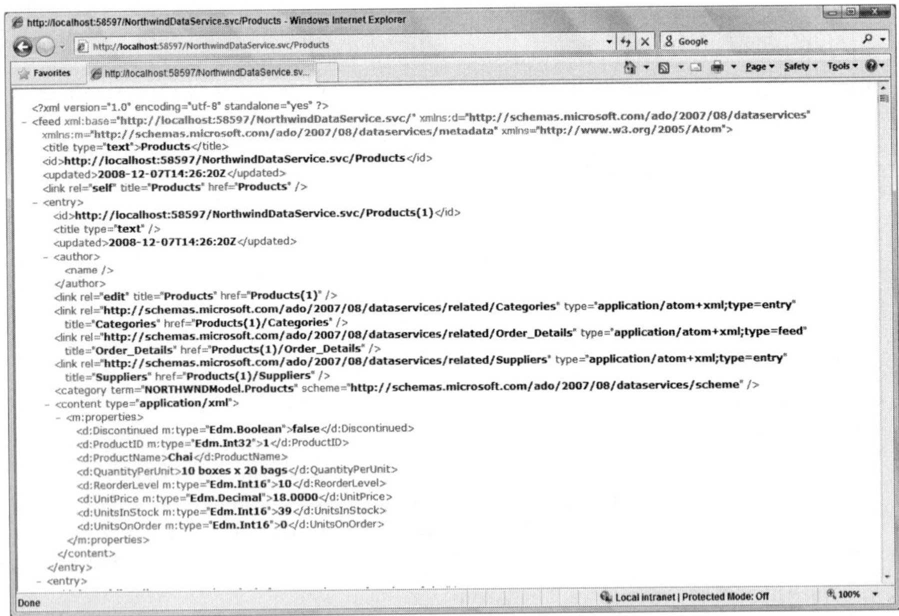

FIGURE 31-28

The following syntax is another example of this type of request:

```
http://localhost/NorthwindDataService.svc/Customers
```

In this case, you will receive a complete list of the customers from the Customers table in the database. If you look at the table-level information that is available from the URI call, you will find the following (as an example):

```
<title type="text">Customers</title>
<id>http://localhost:4113/NorthwindDataService.svc/Customers</id>
<updated>2009-11-30T19:36:24Z</updated>
<link rel="self" title="Customers" href="Customers" />
```

Here, you see that you receive a title (the entity name), as well as the full URI as the <id> element. You also get the timestamp of when the query was run in the <updated> element. Finally, you get a link referencing the item itself (other links also exist to the entity's relationships beyond this one) if you are going to programmatically construct URIs.

Reading a Specific Item from the Table

The previous example showed you how to pull an entire collection from the table or entity set using a URI such as:

```
http://localhost/NorthwindDataService.svc/Products
```

If you look at one of the product items contained within the result collection, you will see something like what's illustrated in Listing 31-37.

LISTING 31-37: Reviewing one of the items from the Products query

```
<entry>
   <id>http://localhost:4113/NorthwindDataService.svc/Products(4)</id>
   <title type="text"></title>
   <updated>2009-11-30T19:36:24Z</updated>
   <author>
     <name />
   </author>
   <link rel="edit" title="Products" href="Products(4)" />
   <link rel="http://schemas.microsoft.com/ado/2007/08/
      dataservices/related/Categories"
    type="application/atom+xml;type=entry" title="Categories"
    href="Products(4)/Categories" />
   <link rel="http://schemas.microsoft.com/ado/2007/08/
      dataservices/related/Order_Details"
    type="application/atom+xml;type=feed" title="Order_Details"
    href="Products(4)/Order_Details" />
   <link rel="http://schemas.microsoft.com/ado/2007/08/
      dataservices/related/Suppliers"
    type="application/atom+xml;type=entry" title="Suppliers"
    href="Products(4)/Suppliers" />
    <category term="NORTHWNDModel.Products"
     scheme="http://schemas.microsoft.com/ado/2007/08/
       dataservices/scheme" />
    <content type="application/xml">
      <m:properties>
        <d:Discontinued m:type="Edm.Boolean">false</d:Discontinued>
        <d:ProductID m:type="Edm.Int32">4</d:ProductID>
        <d:ProductName>Chef Anton's Cajun Seasoning</d:ProductName>
        <d:QuantityPerUnit>48 - 6 oz jars</d:QuantityPerUnit>
        <d:ReorderLevel m:type="Edm.Int16">0</d:ReorderLevel>
        <d:UnitPrice m:type="Edm.Decimal">22.0000</d:UnitPrice>
        <d:UnitsInStock m:type="Edm.Int16">53</d:UnitsInStock>
        <d:UnitsOnOrder m:type="Edm.Int16">0</d:UnitsOnOrder>
      </m:properties>
    </content>
  </entry>
```

If you look at the <id> value of this product, you will find the following:

```
http://localhost:4113/NorthwindDataService.svc/Products(4)
```

You can see that the reference to this particular product is `Products(4)`, which means that you are interested in the fourth item in the Product collection. Typing that URI into the browser's address bar will give you only that particular product.

If you review the XML, you will find that the `<content>` element contains all the data from the specific product that you are looking at. This is constructed as a properties collection.

Although you see a list of properties for this customer, you are also able to get at individual properties themselves through URI declarations such as:

```
http://localhost:4113/NorthwindDataService.svc/Products(4)/ProductName
```

Using a construct like the preceding will return only the `ProductName` property of this product. Here is the result:

```
<?xml version="1.0" encoding="utf-8" standalone="yes"?>
<ProductName
 xmlns="http://schemas.microsoft.com/ado/2007/08/dataservices">
   Chef Anton's Cajun Seasoning
</ProductName>
```

It is important to realize that this number reference from `Products(4)` is not an index reference but the ID reference. For an example, type in the following URI (obviously, your port number will be different from mine, which is set to 4113):

```
http://localhost:4113/NorthwindDataService.svc/Customers(1)
```

You might think that you would get the first customer in the list from the Customers table, but the number one (1) is not an identifier for any customer in the table. If you provided this statement, you wouldn't get anything in return. If you look at the entire list of customers, you will find one of the customers as an example, as shown in Listing 31-38.

LISTING 31-38: Reviewing one of the individual customers

```
<entry>
   <id>http://localhost:4113/NorthwindDataService.svc
     /Customers('ALFKI')</id>
   <title type="text"></title>
   <updated>2009-11-30T20:20:28Z</updated>
   <author>
     <name />
   </author>
   <link rel="edit" title="Customers" href="Customers('ALFKI')" />
   <link rel="http://schemas.microsoft.com/ado/2007/08/
      dataservices/related/Orders"
    type="application/atom+xml;type=feed" title="Orders"
    href="Customers('ALFKI')/Orders" />
    <link rel="http://schemas.microsoft.com/ado/2007/08/
       dataservices/related/CustomerDemographics"
     type="application/atom+xml;type=feed" title="CustomerDemographics"
     href="Customers('ALFKI')/CustomerDemographics" />
    <category term="NORTHWNDModel.Customers"
     scheme="http://schemas.microsoft.com/ado/2007/08/
       dataservices/scheme" />
    <content type="application/xml">
      <m:properties>
        <d:Address>Obere Str. 57</d:Address>
        <d:City>Berlin</d:City>
        <d:CompanyName>Alfreds Futterkiste</d:CompanyName>
        <d:ContactName>Maria Anders</d:ContactName>
        <d:ContactTitle>Sales Representative</d:ContactTitle>
        <d:Country>Germany</d:Country>
        <d:CustomerID>ALFKI</d:CustomerID>
        <d:Fax>030-0076545</d:Fax>
```

```
        <d:Phone>030-0074321</d:Phone>
        <d:PostalCode>12209</d:PostalCode>
        <d:Region m:null="true" />
      </m:properties>
    </content>
  </entry>
```

If you look at the `<id>` element, you will see that the way to pull up a specific customer (such as this one) is not by specifying `Customers(1)`, but instead by using `Customers('ALFKI')`. This means that you would use a URI such as the following:

```
http://localhost:4113/NorthwindDataService.svc/Customers('ALFKI')
```

Using this construct will return the information on only the customer with the ID of `ALFKI`.

Working with Relationships

Working with WCF Data Services obviously makes getting at your database and working with it through a RESTful interface in the cloud easy. One great advantage to working with the ADO.NET Entity Framework and WCF Data Services is that these items make working with object relationships just as easy.

Going back to the Entity Data Model that was designed earlier in this chapter, you will notice that the objects have a built-in relationship that is visually shown in the O/R Designer. Figure 31-29 presents this view.

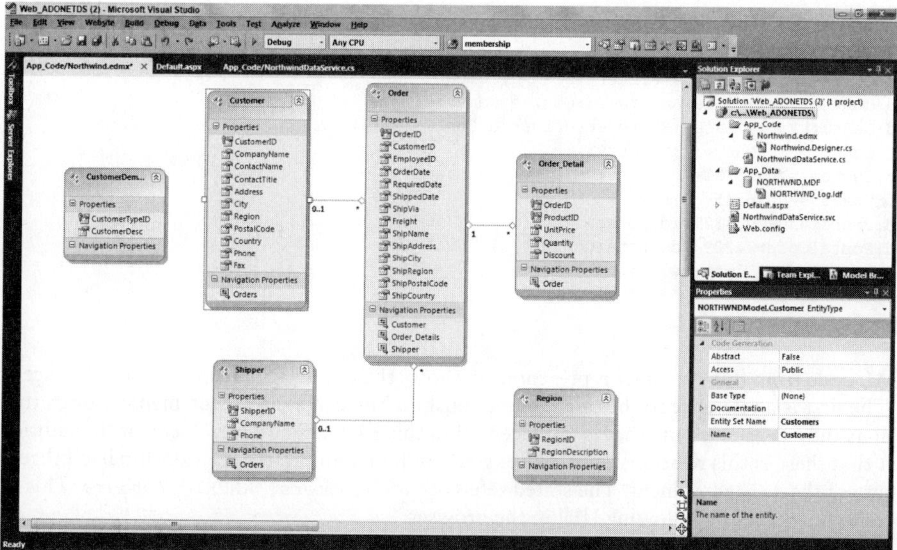

FIGURE 31-29

From this figure, you can see that the `Customers` object has a relationship with the `Orders` object (among others). You can also work down this object chain using WCF Data Services because it is represented in your EDM.

To understand how these relationships are represented, take another look a customer's output from WCF Data Services (shown in Listing 31-39).

LISTING 31-39: Reviewing the customer relationships

```
<entry>
  <id>http://localhost:4113/NorthwindDataService.svc
    /Customers('ALFKI')</id>
  <title type="text"></title>
  <updated>2009-11-30T20:20:28Z</updated>
  <author>
    <name />
  </author>
  <link rel="edit" title="Customers" href="Customers('ALFKI')" />

  <link rel="http://schemas.microsoft.com/ado/2007/08/
     dataservices/related/Orders"
   type="application/atom+xml;type=feed" title="Orders"
   href="Customers('ALFKI')/Orders" />
   <link rel="http://schemas.microsoft.com/ado/2007/08/
     dataservices/related/CustomerDemographics"
    type="application/atom+xml;type=feed" title="CustomerDemographics"
    href="Customers('ALFKI')/CustomerDemographics" />

   <category term="NORTHWNDModel.Customers"
    scheme="http://schemas.microsoft.com/ado/2007/08/
      dataservices/scheme" />
   <content type="application/xml">
     <m:properties>
       <d:Address>Obere Str. 57</d:Address>
       <d:City>Berlin</d:City>
       <d:CompanyName>Alfreds Futterkiste</d:CompanyName>
       <d:ContactName>Maria Anders</d:ContactName>
       <d:ContactTitle>Sales Representative</d:ContactTitle>
       <d:Country>Germany</d:Country>
       <d:CustomerID>ALFKI</d:CustomerID>
       <d:Fax>030-0076545</d:Fax>
       <d:Phone>030-0074321</d:Phone>
       <d:PostalCode>12209</d:PostalCode>
       <d:Region m:null="true" />
     </m:properties>
   </content>
 </entry>
```

The bolded XML code from this customer representation shows the two relationships that are in place for this customer. The first is a reference to the `Orders` relationship. You can see this statement through the `rel` attribute as well as the `title` attribute that is in place within this particular `<link>` element. In addition to just a statement that there is this relationship in place, you will find a link to the relationship itself through the `href` attribute of the `<link>` element. The stated reference is `Customers('ALFKI')/Orders`. This means that you can now type the following URI in the browser:

```
http://localhost:4113/NorthwindDataService.svc/
  Customers('ALFKI')/Orders
```

Typing this URI means that you are interested in drilling down to the customer with the ID of `ALFKI` and his orders in the system. In response, you get what is presented in Figure 31-30.

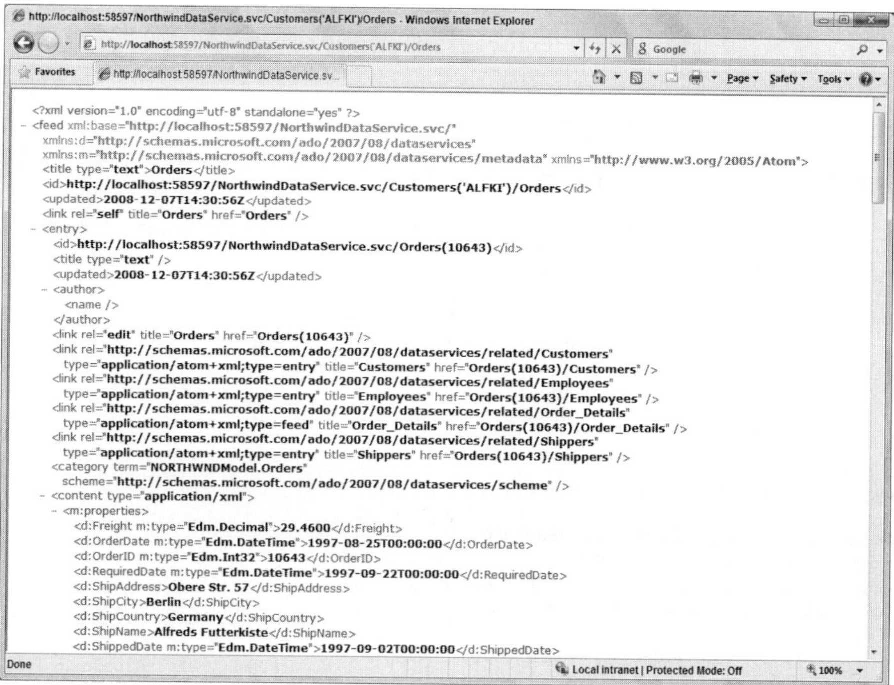

FIGURE 31-30

This figure shows all the orders from the `ALFKI` customer. Another interesting aspect is that you have all the nested relationships even at this level. You really will find all the available relationships at every level. Here are the relationships found for one of the orders of this customer:

```
<link rel="http://schemas.microsoft.com/ado/2007/08/
   dataservices/related/Customers"
 type="application/atom+xml;type=entry" title="Customers"
 href="Orders(10643)/Customers" />
<link rel="http://schemas.microsoft.com/ado/2007/08/
   dataservices/related/Employees"
 type="application/atom+xml;type=entry" title="Employees"
 href="Orders(10643)/Employees" />
<link rel="http://schemas.microsoft.com/ado/2007/08/
   dataservices/related/Order_Details"
 type="application/atom+xml;type=feed" title="Order_Details"
 href="Orders(10643)/Order_Details" />
<link rel="http://schemas.microsoft.com/ado/2007/08/
   dataservices/related/Shippers"
 type="application/atom+xml;type=entry" title="Shippers"
 href="Orders(10643)/Shippers" />
```

The preceding code shows four relationships — one refers back to the customer of the particular order that you are looking at (Order ID 10643); the others are for the `Employee` objects associated with this order, the order details (through the `Order_Details` object), and the connection to the `Shippers` object.

Expanding on Associations

So far, you have seen the entity associations mentioned through these `<link>` elements and the ability to re-query with a new URI to dig into these associated details. You are also able to pull these associations out in the same query if you want.

Getting these associations is possible through the use of the some querystring parameters that have been made available through WCF Data Services. For example, suppose you are making the following query:

```
http://localhost:4113/NorthwindDataService.svc/Products(1)
```

This query gives you the output presented in Listing 31-40.

LISTING 31-40: Calling for a single product

```
<?xml version="1.0" encoding="utf-8" standalone="yes"?>
<entry xml:base="http://localhost:4113/NorthwindDataService.svc/"
 xmlns:d="http://schemas.microsoft.com/ado/2007/08/dataservices"
 xmlns:m="http://schemas.microsoft.com/ado/2007/08/
   dataservices/metadata" xmlns="http://www.w3.org/2005/Atom">
  <id>http://localhost:4113/NorthwindDataService.svc/Products(1)</id>
  <title type="text"></title>
  <updated>2009-11-30T23:22:55Z</updated>
  <author>
    <name />
  </author>
  <link rel="edit" title="Products" href="Products(1)" />

<link rel="http://schemas.microsoft.com/ado/2007/08/
     dataservices/related/Categories"
   type="application/atom+xml;type=entry" title="Categories"
   href="Products(1)/Categories" />

  <link rel="http://schemas.microsoft.com/ado/2007/08/
    dataservices/related/Order_Details"
   type="application/atom+xml;type=feed" title="Order_Details"
   href="Products(1)/Order_Details" />
  <link rel="http://schemas.microsoft.com/ado/2007/08/
    dataservices/related/Suppliers"
   type="application/atom+xml;type=entry" title="Suppliers"
   href="Products(1)/Suppliers" />
  <category term="NORTHWNDModel.Products"
   scheme="http://schemas.microsoft.com/ado/2007/08/
    dataservices/scheme" />
  <content type="application/xml">
    <m:properties>
      <d:Discontinued m:type="Edm.Boolean">false</d:Discontinued>
      <d:ProductID m:type="Edm.Int32">1</d:ProductID>
      <d:ProductName>Chai</d:ProductName>
      <d:QuantityPerUnit>10 boxes x 20 bags</d:QuantityPerUnit>
      <d:ReorderLevel m:type="Edm.Int16">10</d:ReorderLevel>
      <d:UnitPrice m:type="Edm.Decimal">18.0000</d:UnitPrice>
      <d:UnitsInStock m:type="Edm.Int16">39</d:UnitsInStock>
      <d:UnitsOnOrder m:type="Edm.Int16">0</d:UnitsOnOrder>
    </m:properties>
  </content>
</entry>
```

The bolded portion of this code shows the link to the Categories entity set. In this mode, if you want the category of this product, then you must make an additional call to get this item using `http://localhost:4113/NorthwindDataService.svc/Products(1)/Categories`. Using this will give you a completely separate result.

However, if you want to get this related set of data points for the product in a single call, you can use the expand keyword in your URI query:

```
http://localhost:4113/NorthwindDataService.svc/
  Products(1)?$expand=Categories
```

For this query to work, you can use one of the available keywords in your querystring, in this case expand. You simply use a familiar format of ?$expand= followed by the name of the associated entity sets.

This query gives a result set similar to what is presented in Listing 31-41.

LISTING 31-41: Adding additional entity sets

```
<?xml version="1.0" encoding="utf-8" standalone="yes"?>
<entry xml:base="http://localhost:4113/NorthwindDataService.svc/"
 xmlns:d="http://schemas.microsoft.com/ado/2007/08/dataservices"
 xmlns:m="http://schemas.microsoft.com/ado/2007/08/
   dataservices/metadata" xmlns="http://www.w3.org/2005/Atom">
  <id>http://localhost:4113/NorthwindDataService.svc/Products(1)</id>
  <title type="text"></title>
  <updated>2009-12-03T01:04:12Z</updated>
  <author>
    <name />
  </author>
  <link rel="edit" title="Products" href="Products(1)" />
  <link rel="http://schemas.microsoft.com/ado/2007/08/
     dataservices/related/Categories"
   type="application/atom+xml;type=entry" title="Categories"
   href="Products(1)/Categories">

    <m:inline>
      <entry>
        <id>http://localhost:4113/NorthwindDataService.svc/
          Categories(1)</id>
        <title type="text"></title>
        <updated>2009-12-03T01:04:12Z</updated>
        <author>
          <name />
        </author>
        <link rel="edit" title="Categories" href="Categories(1)" />
        <link rel="http://schemas.microsoft.com/ado/2007/08/
           dataservices/related/Products"
         type="application/atom+xml;type=feed" title="Products"
         href="Categories(1)/Products" />
        <category term="NORTHWNDModel.Categories"
         scheme="http://schemas.microsoft.com/ado/2007/08/
          dataservices/scheme" />
        <content type="application/xml">
          <m:properties>
            <d:CategoryID m:type="Edm.Int32">1</d:CategoryID>
            <d:CategoryName>Beverages</d:CategoryName>
            <d:Description>Soft drinks, coffees, teas, beers,
               and ales</d:Description>
            <d:Picture m:type="Edm.Binary">
              FRwvAAIAAAhAPAAADHrQX+</d:Picture> <!-- some removed -->
          </m:properties>
        </content>
      </entry>
    </m:inline>

  </link>
  <link rel="http://schemas.microsoft.com/ado/2007/08/
     dataservices/related/Order_Details"
   type="application/atom+xml;type=feed" title="Order_Details"
   href="Products(1)/Order_Details" />
  <link rel="http://schemas.microsoft.com/ado/2007/08/
     dataservices/related/Suppliers"
   type="application/atom+xml;type=entry" title="Suppliers"
```

continues

LISTING 31-41 *(continued)*

```
    href="Products(1)/Suppliers" />
  <category term="NORTHWNDModel.Products"
    scheme="http://schemas.microsoft.com/ado/2007/08/
      dataservices/scheme" />
  <content type="application/xml">
    <m:properties>
      <d:Discontinued m:type="Edm.Boolean">false</d:Discontinued>
      <d:ProductID m:type="Edm.Int32">1</d:ProductID>
      <d:ProductName>Chai</d:ProductName>
      <d:QuantityPerUnit>10 boxes x 20 bags</d:QuantityPerUnit>
      <d:ReorderLevel m:type="Edm.Int16">10</d:ReorderLevel>
      <d:UnitPrice m:type="Edm.Decimal">18.0000</d:UnitPrice>
      <d:UnitsInStock m:type="Edm.Int16">39</d:UnitsInStock>
      <d:UnitsOnOrder m:type="Edm.Int16">0</d:UnitsOnOrder>
    </m:properties>
  </content>
</entry>
```

From this code, you can see that the `<link>` element that was specific for the category is now expanded to include what was once a separate call inline. In addition to expanding a single associated entity set, you can expand multiple items:

```
http://localhost:4113/NorthwindDataService.svc/
  Products(1)?$expand=Categories,Suppliers
```

In this case, both the Categories and the Suppliers sections are expanded within the Product entity set call.

You can also keep digging into the nested associated entity sets. For example, look at this:

```
http://localhost:4113/NorthwindDataService.svc/
  Products(1)?$expand=Suppliers/Products
```

Using this construct, you are looking at the first product from the product list and expanding the section for the internal suppliers of this product. Then, within the suppliers, the associated products that these suppliers sell are also included in the result set. As you can see, there is a lot of power in the ease with which you can drill down into nested relationships.

Ordering in Result Sets

Another way to manipulate the result set that comes from the URI query is to get the results of the collection placed in a specific order as you define it. You can do so using the `orderby` keyword as a querystring command:

```
http://localhost:4113/NorthwindDataService.svc/
  Products?$orderby=ProductName
```

In this case, you get back a complete list of products that are in alphabetical order according to the entity's `ProductName` field value. You are also able to assign an ascending or descending value to the order provided. By default, an ascending order is assigned. This means that the preceding query is the same as the following:

```
http://localhost:4113/NorthwindDataService.svc/
  Products?$orderby=ProductName asc
```

Notice that there is an actual space between the `ProductName` and `asc` items in the URI. If you want these in the reverse order, or descending order, then use the following construct:

```
http://localhost:4113/NorthwindDataService.svc/
  Products?$orderby=ProductName desc
```

You can also perform nested sorting using WCF Data Services:

```
http://localhost:4113/NorthwindDataService.svc/
  Products?$orderby=Discontinued asc, ProductName asc
```

Moving Around Result Sets

As an end user of this interface, you can probably see that you might be working with fairly large result sets, depending on what is in the database. If you need only a portion of the database table and you are requesting all of your customers (which might be 100,000 or more), what then?

In this case, WCF Data Services provides the capability to grab just smaller subsets of the content as pages and to navigate through the page that you need. This is done through the combination of two querystring commands: `top` and `skip`.

They are also quite powerful in their own right. For instance, with the `top` command, you are able to pull the top *n*-number of items based on the sort that is being used. For example, consider this command:

```
http://localhost:4113/NorthwindDataService.svc/Customers?$top=5
```

Here, the top five entities, in this case based on the `CustomerID` value, are pulled from the database and returned. If you want the top entities based on a different value, then you can use something like the following:

```
http://localhost:4113/NorthwindDataService.svc/
   Products?$orderby=UnitsOnOrder desc&$top=5
```

Using this example, the top five products, according to the number of units that are on order, are returned in the result set.

You are able to use the `skip` command to basically skip the first set of defined items. For instance, you can do something similar to the following:

```
http://localhost:4113/NorthwindDataService.svc/
   Customers?$skip=5
```

In this case, the customers are returned minus the first five that would normally be returned. There is some question as to the value of this command, but its power is evident when used in combination with the `top` keyword.

```
http://localhost:4113/NorthwindDataService.svc/
   Customers?$skip=10&$top=10
```

In this case, you are skipping the first ten entities and then grabbing the following ten entities from that point onward. This means that you are really grabbing page two of sets that consist of ten items each. This would make performing a type of database-pagination process quite easy by using this process to use URI commands to get at the page of data you require.

Filtering Content

The final command is one of the more powerful commands at your disposal. It is a type of screening that allows you to filter the content that you are truly interested in receiving from the database. This is all done through the use of the `filter` command:

```
http://localhost:4113/NorthwindDataService.svc/
   Customers?$filter=Country eq 'Germany'
```

Using the filter command preceded by a dollar sign (`$`), the value of this command is `Country eq 'Germany'`. With this filtering command, you are requesting a list of customers located in the country of `Germany`. The database property in this case is `Country`, and within the URI it is important that you are specifying this property in its proper case. This means that if you used `country` instead of `Country`, you would not get any items in the result set.

The `Germany` value is put in single quotes and the operator is specified as a set of characters, rather than a true equals sign (=). When using the `filter` command, you specify the equal operator with the `eq` string. Table 31-2 lists the logical operators that you are able to use.

TABLE 31-2

OPERATOR	DESCRIPTION	EXAMPLE
`Eq`	Equal	`Country eq 'Germany'`
`Ne`	Not equal	`Country ne 'Germany'`
`Gt`	Greater than	`$filter = UnitsOnOrder gt 20`
`Ge`	Greater than or equal	`$filter = UnitsOnOrder ge 20`
`Lt`	Less than	`$filter = UnitsOnOrder lt 20`
`Le`	Less than or equal	`$filter = UnitsOnOrder le 20`
`And`	Logical and	`$filter = UnitsOnOrder gt 0 and UnitsInStock gt 0`
`Or`	Logical or	`$filter = UnitsOnOrder gt 0 or UnitsOnOrder lt 100`
`Not`	Logical not	`$filter = UnitsOnOrder gt 0 not ProductName eq 'Chang'`

In addition to logical operators, you can use a number of arithmetic operators, as shown in Table 31-3.

TABLE 31-3

OPERATOR	DESCRIPTION	EXAMPLE
`Add`	Add	`$filter = UnitsOnOrder add 5 gt 20`
`Sub`	Subtract	`$filter = UnitsOnOrder sub 5 gt 20`
`Mul`	Multiply	`$filter = UnitsOnOrder mul 5 gt 20`
`Div`	Divide	`$filter = UnitsOnOrder div 5 gt 20`
`Mod`	Modulo	`$filter = UnitsOnOrder mod 100 gt 20`

A long list of string, date, and math functions is also available:

- `substringof`
- `startswith`
- `indexof`
- `remove`
- `substring`
- `toupper`
- `concat`
- `hour`
- `month`
- `year`
- `floor`
- `endswith`
- `length`
- `insert`
- `replace`
- `tolower`
- `trim`
- `day`
- `minute`
- `second`
- `round`
- `ceiling`

You would use these functions like this:

```
http://localhost:4113/NorthwindDataService.svc/
   Products?$filter = endswith(QuantityPerUnit, 'bottles')
```

In this case, you are retrieving all the products from the database that have a property `QuantityPerUnit` that ends with the string `bottles`.

CONSUMING WCF DATA SERVICES IN ASP.NET

Now that you understand how to build a WCF Data Service, the next step is to consume this service in an ASP.NET application. Keep in mind that consuming a WCF Data Service in all types of .NET applications is obviously possible, but this chapter focuses on using this technology within ASP.NET itself.

For an example of consuming a data service, create a standard ASP.NET application within Visual Studio. On the `Default.aspx` page, create a simple page that contains only a styled GridView server control. Listing 31-42 presents an example of this page.

Available for download on Wrox.com

LISTING 31-42: A standard ASP.NET page with a GridView control

```
<%@ Page Language="C#" AutoEventWireup="true"
    CodeFile="Default.aspx.cs" Inherits="_Default" %>

<html xmlns="http://www.w3.org/1999/xhtml">
<head runat="server">
    <title>Working with Data Services</title>
</head>
<body>
    <form id="form1" runat="server">
    <div>
        <asp:GridView ID="GridView1" runat="server" BackColor="White"
            BorderColor="#DEDFDE" BorderStyle="None" BorderWidth="1px"
            CellPadding="4"
            ForeColor="Black" GridLines="Vertical">
            <RowStyle BackColor="#F7F7DE" />
            <FooterStyle BackColor="#CCCC99" />
            <PagerStyle BackColor="#F7F7DE" ForeColor="Black"
             HorizontalAlign="Right" />
            <SelectedRowStyle BackColor="#CE5D5A" Font-Bold="True"
             ForeColor="White" />
            <HeaderStyle BackColor="#6B696B" Font-Bold="True"
             ForeColor="White" />
            <AlternatingRowStyle BackColor="White" />
        </asp:GridView>
    </div>
    </form>
</body>
</html>
```

Now that you have a basic page ready, right-click on your project within the Visual Studio Solution Explorer and select Add Service Reference from the provided menu. The Add Service Reference dialog appears.

Because a WCF Data Service is a standard `.svc` file, you can make reference to your `Northwind.svc` file within the text box provided and click the Go button. Figure 31-31 shows something similar to what appears.

As you can see from the figure, all the underlying objects are represented in the dialog. Within the Namespace text box, you can name the reference `Northwind` and then click OK to accept this configuration.

The next step is to work with this reference from the code-behind page. This work is shown in Listing 31-43.

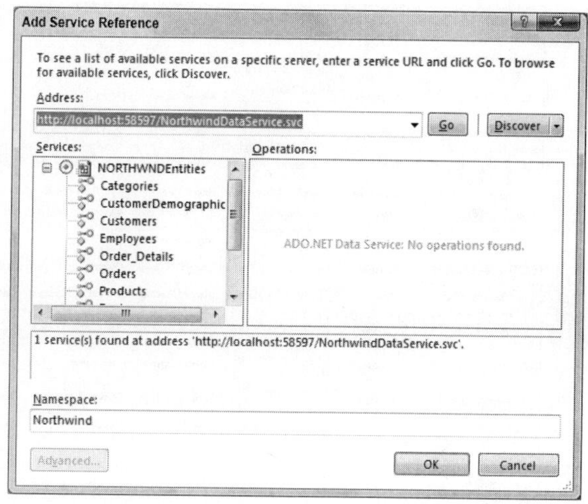

FIGURE 31-31

LISTING 31-43: Working with a WCF Data Service

Available for download on Wrox.com

VB

```
Imports Northwind

Partial Class _Default
    Inherits System.Web.UI.Page

    Protected Sub Page_Load(ByVal sender As Object,
      ByVal e As System.EventArgs) Handles Me.Load

        Dim svc As New NORTHWNDEntities(New _
            Uri("http://localhost:4113/NorthwindDataService.svc").ToString())

        GridView1.DataSource = svc.Customers
        GridView1.DataBind()

    End Sub
End Class
```

C#

```
using System;
using Northwind;

public partial class _Default : System.Web.UI.Page
{
    protected void Page_Load(object sender, EventArgs e)
    {
        NORTHWNDEntities svc = new NORTHWNDEntities(new
          Uri("http://localhost:4113/NorthwindDataService.svc").ToString());

        GridView1.DataSource = svc.Customers;
        GridView1.DataBind();
    }
}
```

In the preceding code, it is simply a matter of making a reference to the Entity Data Model that the service exposes through the URI of the data service. This EDM instantiation will include a list of all the capabilities that interact with the underlying service. In the case of Listing 31-43, the entire Customers table is returned through the use of `svc.Customers`. This result set is then bound to the GridView control. Figure 31-32 shows the results.

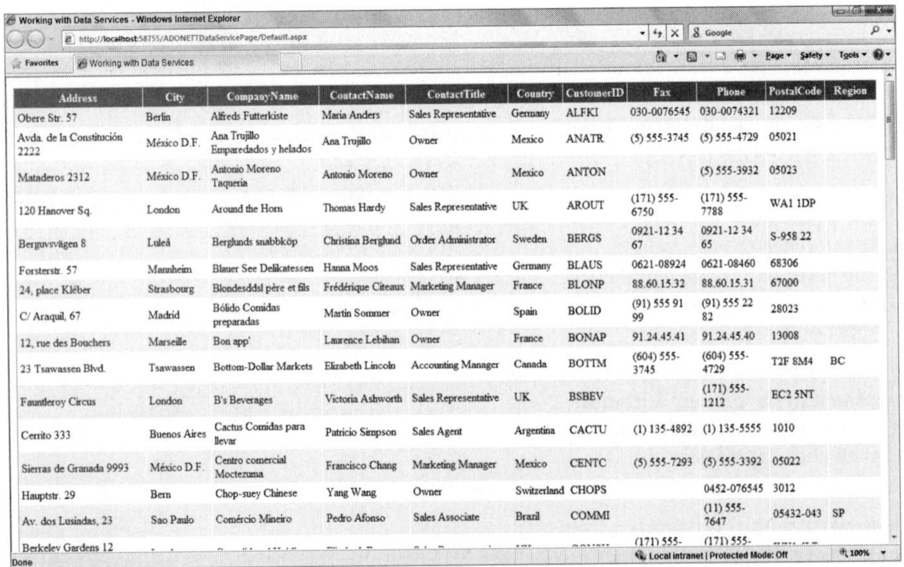

Address	City	CompanyName	ContactName	ContactTitle	Country	CustomerID	Fax	Phone	PostalCode	Region
Obere Str. 57	Berlin	Alfreds Futterkiste	Maria Anders	Sales Representative	Germany	ALFKI	030-0076545	030-0074321	12209	
Avda. de la Constitución 2222	México D.F.	Ana Trujillo Emparedados y helados	Ana Trujillo	Owner	Mexico	ANATR	(5) 555-3745	(5) 555-4729	05021	
Mataderos 2312	México D.F.	Antonio Moreno Taquería	Antonio Moreno	Owner	Mexico	ANTON		(5) 555-3932	05023	
120 Hanover Sq.	London	Around the Horn	Thomas Hardy	Sales Representative	UK	AROUT	(171) 555-6750	(171) 555-7788	WA1 1DP	
Berguvsvägen 8	Luleå	Berglunds snabbköp	Christina Berglund	Order Administrator	Sweden	BERGS	0921-12 34 67	0921-12 34 65	S-958 22	
Forsterstr. 57	Mannheim	Blauer See Delikatessen	Hanna Moos	Sales Representative	Germany	BLAUS	0621-08924	0621-08460	68306	
24, place Kléber	Strasbourg	Blondesddsl père et fils	Frédérique Citeaux	Marketing Manager	France	BLONP	88.60.15.32	88.60.15.31	67000	
C/ Araquil, 67	Madrid	Bólido Comidas preparadas	Martín Sommer	Owner	Spain	BOLID	(91) 555 91 99	(91) 555 22 82	28023	
12, rue des Bouchers	Marseille	Bon app'	Laurence Lebihan	Owner	France	BONAP	91.24.45.41	91.24.45.40	13008	
23 Tsawassen Blvd.	Tsawassen	Bottom-Dollar Markets	Elizabeth Lincoln	Accounting Manager	Canada	BOTTM	(604) 555-3745	(604) 555-4729	T2F 8M4	BC
Fauntleroy Circus	London	B's Beverages	Victoria Ashworth	Sales Representative	UK	BSBEV		(171) 555-1212	EC2 5NT	
Cerrito 333	Buenos Aires	Cactus Comidas para llevar	Patricio Simpson	Sales Agent	Argentina	CACTU	(1) 135-4892	(1) 135-5555	1010	
Sierras de Granada 9993	México D.F.	Centro comercial Moctezuma	Francisco Chang	Marketing Manager	Mexico	CENTC	(5) 555-7293	(5) 555-3392	05022	
Hauptstr. 29	Bern	Chop-suey Chinese	Yang Wang	Owner	Switzerland	CHOPS		0452-076545	3012	
Av. dos Lusíadas, 23	Sao Paulo	Comércio Mineiro	Pedro Afonso	Sales Associate	Brazil	COMMI		(11) 555-7647	05432-043	SP
Berkeley Gardens 12	[illegible]	[illegible]	[illegible]	[illegible]	[illegible]	[illegible]	(171) 555-	(171) 555-	[illegible]	

FIGURE 31-32

In addition to a query as simple as the one in the preceding code, you can also start using some of the command logic presented earlier in this chapter when using LINQ within your code. Listing 31-44 shows a query against the Customer table in which you are interested only in seeing the customers that have a `Country` value of `Germany`.

Available for download on Wrox.com

LISTING 31-44: Using LINQ

```
Dim svc As New NORTHWNDEntities(New _
   Uri("http://localhost:4113/NorthwindDataService.svc").ToString())

Dim query = From c In svc.Customers
            Where c.Country.Contains("Germany")
            Select c

GridView1.DataSource = query
GridView1.DataBind()
```

```
NORTHWNDEntities svc = new NORTHWNDEntities(new
   Uri("http://localhost:4113/NorthwindDataService.svc").ToString());

var query = from c in svc.Customers
            where c.Country.Contains("Germany")
            select c;

GridView1.DataSource = query;
GridView1.DataBind();
```

In this code, a LINQ query is performed and this object is then bound as the `DataSource` value of the GridView control. This will produce another list of items in the grid.

SUMMARY

This chapter was a whirlwind tour of XML Web services in the .NET platform. It is definitely a topic that merits an entire book of its own. The chapter showed you the power of exposing your data and logic as SOAP and also how to consume these SOAP messages directly in the ASP.NET applications you build.

In addition to pointing out the power you have for building and consuming basic Web services, the chapter spent some time helping you understand caching, performance, the use of SOAP headers, and more. A lot of power is built into this model; every day, the Web services model is starting to make stronger inroads into various enterprise organizations. It is becoming more likely that to get at some data or logic you need for your application, you will employ the tactics presented in this chapter.

While not exhaustive, this chapter broadly outlined the basics of the framework. As you start to dig deeper in the technology, you will find capabilities that are strong and extensible.

WCF Data Services is a powerful and new way to expose out your database content. This chapter examined working with commands against the interface to filter out specific content. A number of commands can be used as part of the URI to get at the specific result sets you are interested in.

However, using code, and more specifically LINQ, is also just as possible to get at the results from the interface that you are looking for when working with your ASP.NET pages. If you want to keep these queries hidden from end users and encapsulated within your code, then this is the best approach. Remember that querystrings also have a limit to the number of characters that they can hold, so sometimes working in the code using LINQ might be your only option.

32

Building Global Applications

WHAT'S IN THIS CHAPTER?

- Globalizing your applications
- Defining culture, both server-side and client-side
- Working with local and global resources

Developers usually build Web applications in their native language, and then, as the audience for the application expands, they realize the need to globalize the application. Of course, the ideal is to build the Web application to handle an international audience right from the start — but, in many cases, this may not be possible because of the extra work it requires.

It is good to note that with the ASP.NET Framework, a considerable effort has been made to address the internationalization of Web applications. You quickly realize that changes to the API, the addition of capabilities to the server controls, and even Visual Studio itself equip you to do the extra work required more easily to bring your application to an international audience. This chapter looks at some of the important items to consider when building your Web applications for the world.

CULTURES AND REGIONS

The ASP.NET page that is pulled up in an end user's browser runs under a specific culture and region setting. When building an ASP.NET application or page, the defined culture in which it runs is dependent upon both a culture and region setting coming from the server in which the application is run or from a setting applied by the client (the end user). By default, ASP.NET runs under a culture setting defined by the server.

The world is made up of a multitude of cultures, each of which has a language and a set of defined ways in which it views and consumes numbers, uses currencies, sorts alphabetically, and so on. The .NET Framework defines cultures and regions using the *Request for Comments 1766* standard definition (tags for identification of languages) that specifies a language and region using two-letter codes separated by a dash. Table 32-1 provides examples of some culture definitions.

TABLE 32-1

CULTURE CODE	DESCRIPTION
en-US	English language; United States
en-GB	English language; United Kingdom (Great Britain)
en-AU	English language; Australia
en-CA	English language; Canada

Looking at the examples in this table, you can see that four distinct cultures are defined. These four cultures have some similarities and some differences. All four cultures speak the same language (English). For this reason, the language code of `en` is used in each culture setting. After the language setting comes the region setting. Even though these cultures speak the same language, distinguishing them further by setting their region (such as `US` for the United States, `GB` for the United Kingdom, `AU` for Australia, and `CA` for Canada) is important. As you are probably well aware, the English language in the United States is slightly different from the English language that is used in the United Kingdom, and so forth. Beyond language, differences exist in how dates and numerical values are represented. This is why a culture's language and region are presented together.

The differences do not break down by the country only. Many times, countries contain more than a single language, and each area has its own preference for notation of dates and other items. For example, `en-CA` specifies English speakers in Canada. Because Canada is not only an English-speaking country, it also includes the culture setting of `fr-CA` for French-speaking Canadians.

Understanding Culture Types

The culture definition you have just seen is called a *specific culture* definition. This definition is as detailed as you can possibly get — defining both the language and the region. The other type of culture definition is a *neutral culture* definition. Each specific culture has a specified neutral culture that it is associated with. For example, the English language cultures shown in the previous table are separate, but they also all belong to one neutral culture EN (English). The diagram presented in Figure 32-1 displays how these culture types relate to one another.

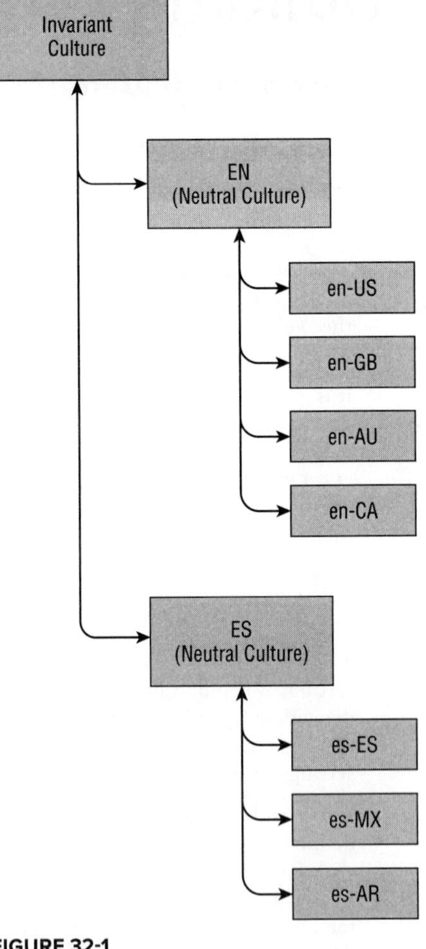

FIGURE 32-1

From this diagram, you can see that many specific cultures belong to a neutral culture. Higher in the hierarchy than the neutral culture is an *invariant culture*, which is an agnostic culture setting that should be utilized when passing items (such as dates and numbers) around a network. When performing these kinds of operations, make your backend data flows devoid of user-specific culture settings. Instead, apply these settings in the business and presentation layers of your applications.

Also, pay attention to the neutral culture when working with your applications. Invariably, you are going to build applications with views that are more dependent on a neutral culture than on a specific culture.

For example, if you have a Spanish version of your application, you probably make this version available to all Spanish speakers regardless of their regions. In many applications, it will not matter if the Spanish speaker is from Spain, Mexico, or Argentina. In a case where it does make a difference, use the specific culture settings.

The ASP.NET Threads

When the end user requests an ASP.NET page, this Web page is executed on a thread from the thread pool. The thread has a culture associated with it. You can get information about the culture of the thread programmatically and then check for particular details about that culture, as shown in Listing 32-1.

LISTING 32-1: Checking the culture of the ASP.NET thread

Available for download on Wrox.com

```
Protected Sub Page_Load(ByVal sender As Object, ByVal e As System.EventArgs) Handles Me.Load
      Dim ci As CultureInfo = System.Threading.Thread.CurrentThread.CurrentCulture
      Response.Write("<b><u>CURRENT CULTURE'S INFO</u></b>")
      Response.Write("<p><b>Culture's Name:</b> " & ci.Name.ToString() & "<br>")
   Response.Write("<b>Culture's Parent Name:</b> " & ci.Parent.Name.ToString() & _
      "<br>")
   Response.Write("<b>Culture's Display Name:</b> " & ci.DisplayName.ToString() & _
      "<br>")
   Response.Write("<b>Culture's English Name:</b> " & ci.EnglishName.ToString() & _
      "<br>")
   Response.Write("<b>Culture's Native Name:</b> " & ci.NativeName.ToString() & _
      "<br>")
   Response.Write("<b>Culture's Three Letter ISO Name:</b> " &
      ci.Parent.ThreeLetterISOLanguageName.ToString() & "<br>")
   Response.Write("<b>Calendar Type:</b> " & ci.Calendar.ToString() & "</p >")
End Sub
```

C#

```
protected void Page_Load(object sender, EventArgs e)
{
   CultureInfo ci = System.Threading.Thread.CurrentThread.CurrentCulture;
   Response.Write("<b><u>CURRENT CULTURE'S INFO</u></b>");
   Response.Write("<p><b>Culture's Name:</b> " + ci.Name.ToString() + "<br>");
   Response.Write("<b>Culture's Parent Name:</b> " + ci.Parent.Name.ToString() +
      "<br>");
   Response.Write("<b>Culture's Display Name:</b> " + ci.DisplayName.ToString() +
      "<br>");
   Response.Write("<b>Culture's English Name:</b> " + ci.EnglishName.ToString() +
      "<br>");
   Response.Write("<b>Culture's Native Name:</b> " + ci.NativeName.ToString() +
      "<br>");
   Response.Write("<b>Culture's Three Letter ISO Name:</b> " +
      ci.Parent.ThreeLetterISOLanguageName.ToString() + "<br>");
   Response.Write("<b>Calendar Type:</b> " + ci.Calendar.ToString() + "</p >");
}
```

This bit of code in the `Page_Load` event checks the `CurrentCulture` property. You can place the result of this value in a `CultureInfo` object. To get at this object, you import the `System.Globalization` namespace into your Web page. The `CultureInfo` object contains a number of properties that provide you with specific culture information. The following items, which are displayed in a series of simple `Response.Write` statements, are only a small sampling of what is actually available. Running this page produces results similar to what is shown in Figure 32-2.

From this figure, you can see that the en-US culture is the default setting in which the ASP.NET thread executes. In addition to this information, you can use the `CultureInfo` object to get at a lot of other descriptive information about the culture.

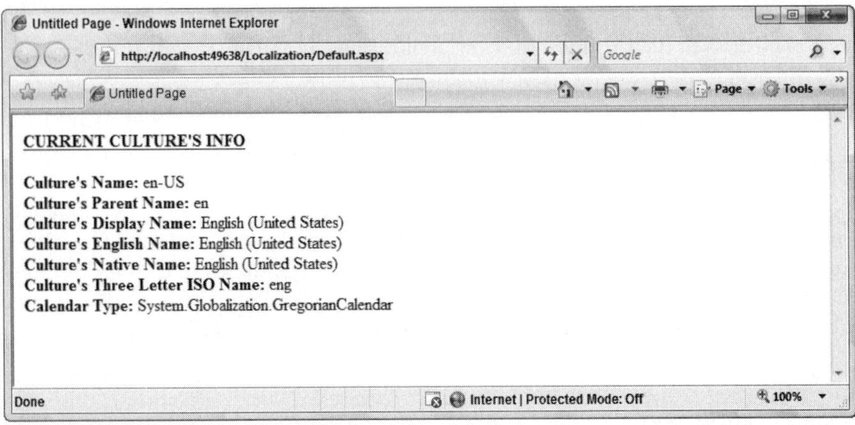

FIGURE 32-2

You can always change a thread's culture on the overloads provided via a new instantiation of the `CultureInfo` object, as presented in Listing 32-2.

LISTING 32-2: Changing the culture of the thread using the CultureInfo object

Available for download on Wrox.com

VB

```
Protected Sub Page_Load(ByVal sender As Object, ByVal e As System.EventArgs) Handles Me.Load

    System.Threading.Thread.CurrentThread.CurrentCulture = New CultureInfo("th-TH")

    Dim ci As CultureInfo = System.Threading.Thread.CurrentThread.CurrentCulture
    Response.Write("<b><u>CURRENT CULTURE'S INFO</u></b>")
    Response.Write("<p><b>Culture's Name:</b> " & ci.Name.ToString() & "<br>")
    Response.Write("<b>Culture's Parent Name:</b> " & ci.Parent.Name.ToString() & _
       "<br>")
    Response.Write("<b>Culture's Display Name:</b> " & ci.DisplayName.ToString() & _
       "<br>")
    Response.Write("<b>Culture's English Name:</b> " & ci.EnglishName.ToString() & _
       "<br>")
    Response.Write("<b>Culture's Native Name:</b> " & ci.NativeName.ToString() & _
       "<br>")
    Response.Write("<b>Culture's Three Letter ISO Name:</b> " & _
       ci.Parent.ThreeLetterISOLanguageName.ToString() & "<br>")
    Response.Write("<b>Calendar Type:</b> " & ci.Calendar.ToString() & "</p >")
End Sub
```

C#

```
protected void Page_Load(object sender, EventArgs e)
{

    System.Threading.Thread.CurrentThread.CurrentCulture = new CultureInfo("th-TH");
    CultureInfo ci = System.Threading.Thread.CurrentThread.CurrentCulture;
    Response.Write("<b><u>CURRENT CULTURE'S INFO</u></b>");
    Response.Write("<p><b>Culture's Name:</b> " + ci.Name.ToString() + "<br>");
    Response.Write("<b>Culture's Parent Name:</b> " + ci.Parent.Name.ToString() +
       "<br>");
    Response.Write("<b>Culture's Display Name:</b> " + ci.DisplayName.ToString() +
       "<br>");
    Response.Write("<b>Culture's English Name:</b> " + ci.EnglishName.ToString() +
       "<br>");
    Response.Write("<b>Culture's Native Name:</b> " + ci.NativeName.ToString() +
       "<br>");
    Response.Write("<b>Culture's Three Letter ISO Name:</b> " +
```

```
        ci.Parent.ThreeLetterISOLanguageName.ToString() + "<br>");
    Response.Write("<b>Calendar Type:</b> " + ci.Calendar.ToString() + "</p>");
}
```

In this example, only a single line of code is added to assign a new instance of the `CultureInfo` object to the `CurrentCulture` property of the thread being executed by ASP.NET. The culture setting enables the `CultureInfo` object to define the culture you want to utilize. In this case, the Thai language of Thailand is assigned, producing the results shown in Figure 32-3.

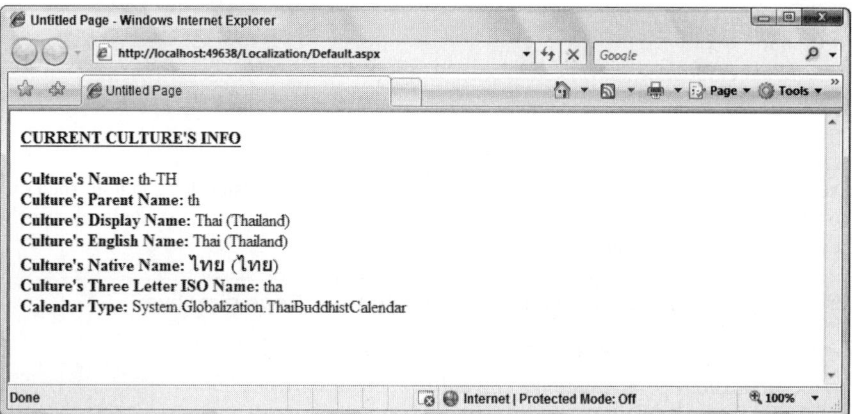

FIGURE 32-3

From this figure, you can see that the .NET Framework goes so far as to provide the native name of the language used even if it is not a Latin-based letter style. In this case, the results are presented for the Thai language in Thailand, as well as some of the properties that are associated with this culture (such as an entirely different calendar from the one used in Western Europe and the United States). Remember that you reference `System.Globalization` to get at the `CultureInfo` object.

Server-Side Culture Declarations

ASP.NET enables you to easily define the culture that is used either by your entire ASP.NET application or by a specific page within your application. You can specify the culture for any of your ASP.NET applications by means of the appropriate configuration files. In the default install of ASP.NET, no culture is specified, as is evident when you look at the global `web.config.comments` file (meant for documentation purposes) found in the ASP.NET 4 CONFIG folder (`C:\WINDOWS\Microsoft.NET\Framework\v4.0.21006\CONFIG`). (If you are using ASP.NET 3.5, remember that ASP.NET 3.5 is built on top of ASP.NET 2.0 and uses the same configuration files.) In the `web.config.comments` file, you find a `<globalization>` section of the configuration document, shown in Listing 32-3.

Available for download on Wrox.com

LISTING 32-3: The <globalization> section in the web.config.comments file

```
<globalization requestEncoding="utf-8" responseEncoding="utf-8" fileEncoding=""
 culture="" uiCulture="" enableClientBasedCulture="false"
 responseHeaderEncoding="utf-8" resourceProviderFactoryType=""
 enableBestFitResponseEncoding="false" />
```

Note the two attributes represented in bold — `culture` and `uiCulture`. The `culture` attribute enables you to define the culture to use for processing incoming requests, whereas the `uiCulture` attribute enables you define the default culture needed to process any resource files in the application. (The use of these attributes is covered later in the chapter.)

As you look at the configuration declaration in Listing 32-3, you can see that nothing is specified for the culture settings. One option you have when specifying a culture on the server is to define this culture in the server version of the `web.config` file found in the CONFIG folder. This causes every ASP.NET 4 application on this server to adopt this particular culture setting. The other option is to specify these settings in the `web.config` file of the application, as shown in Listing 32-4.

LISTING 32-4: Defining the <globalization> section in the web.config file

Available for download on Wrox.com

```
<configuration>
  <system.web>

    <globalization culture="ru-RU" uiCulture="ru-RU" />

  </system.web>
</configuration>
```

In this case, the culture established for just this ASP.NET application is the Russian language in the country of Russia. In addition to setting the culture at either the server-wide or the application-wide level, another option is to set the culture at the page level, as shown in Listing 32-5.

LISTING 32-5: Defining the culture at the page level using the @Page directive

```
<%@ Page Language="VB" UICulture="ru-RU" Culture="ru-RU" %>
```

This example determines that the Russian language and culture settings are used for everything on the page. You can see this in action by using this `@Page` directive and a simple calendar control on the page. Figure 32-4 shows the output.

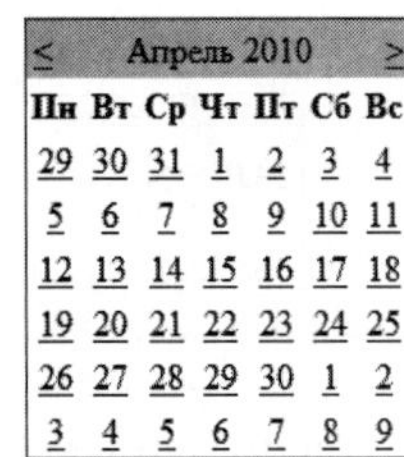

FIGURE 32-4

Client-Side Culture Declarations

In addition to using server-side settings to define the culture for your ASP.NET pages, you also have the option of defining the culture with what the client has set as his preference in a browser instance.

When end users install Microsoft's Internet Explorer and some of the other browsers, they have the option to select their preferred cultures in a particular order (if they have selected more than a single culture preference). To see this in action in IE, select Tools ➪ Internet Options from the IE menu. On the first tab provided (General), you see a Languages button at the bottom of the dialog. Select this button and the Language Preference dialog appears, as shown in Figure 32-5.

In this figure, you can see that two cultures are selected from the list of available cultures. To add any additional cultures to the list, click the Add button in the dialog and select the appropriate culture from the list. After you have selected cultures that are present in the list, you can select the order in which you prefer to use them. In the case of Figure 32-5, the Finnish culture is established as the most preferred culture, whereas the U.S. version of English is selected as the second preference. A user with this setting gets the Finnish language version of the application before anything else; if a Finnish version is not available, a U.S. English version is presented.

Language Preference

Language Preference

Add the languages you use to read websites, listing in order of preference. Only add the ones you need, as some characters can be used to impersonate websites in other languages.

Language:

Finnish (Finland) [fi-FI]
English (United States) [en-US]

Move up
Move down
Remove
Add...

Prefix and suffix options

Do not add 'www' to the beginning of typed web addresses

Specify the suffix (for example .net) that should be added to typed web addresses when you press Ctrl + Shift + Enter.

Suffix:

OK
Cancel

FIGURE 32-5

After the end user selects a culture, you can use the auto feature provided in ASP.NET 4. Instead of specifying a distinct culture in any of the configuration files or from the `@Page` directive, you can also state that ASP.NET should automatically select the culture provided by the end user requesting the page. This is done using the `auto` keyword, as shown in Listing 32-6.

LISTING 32-6: Changing the culture to the end user's selection

```
<%@ Page Language="VB" UICulture="auto" Culture="auto" %>
```

With this construction in your page, the dates, calendars, and numbers now appear in the preferred culture of the requestor. What happens, however, if you have translated resources in resource files (shown later in the chapter) that depend on a culture specification? What if you only have specific translations, and so cannot handle every possible culture that might be returned to your ASP.NET page? In this case, you can specify the auto option with an additional fallback option if ASP.NET cannot find the culture settings of the user (such as culture-specific resource files). Listing 32-7 shows this usage.

LISTING 32-7: Providing a fallback culture from the auto option

```
<%@ Page Language="VB" UICulture="auto:en-US" Culture="auto:en-US" %>
```

In this case, the automatic detection is utilized, but if the culture the end user prefers is not present, then en-US is used.

Translating Values and Behaviors

In the process of globalizing your ASP.NET application, you may notice a number of items that are done differently from building an application that is devoid of globalization, including how dates are represented and currencies are shown. This next section touches upon some of these topics.

Understanding Differences in Dates

Different cultures specify dates and time very differently. For instance, take the following date as an example:

```
08/11/2010
```

What is this date exactly? Is it August 11, 2010 or is it November 8, 2010? I repeat: When storing values such as date/time stamps in a database or other some type of backend system, you should always use the same culture (or invariant culture) for these items so that you avoid any mistakes. Converting these items for use by the end user should be the job of the business logic layer or the presentation layer.

Setting the culture at the server level or in the `@Page` directive (as discussed earlier) enables ASP.NET to make these conversions for you. You can also simply assign a new culture to the thread in which ASP.NET is running. For example, look at the code listing presented in Listing 32-8.

LISTING 32-8: Working with date/time values in different cultures

Available for download on Wrox.com

```
Protected Sub Page_Load(ByVal sender As Object, ByVal e As System.EventArgs) Handles Me.Load
    Dim dt As DateTime = New DateTime(2010, 8, 11, 11, 12, 10, 10)
    System.Threading.Thread.CurrentThread.CurrentCulture = New CultureInfo("en-US")
    Response.Write("<b><u>en-US</u></b><br>")
    Response.Write(dt.ToString() & "<br>")

    System.Threading.Thread.CurrentThread.CurrentCulture = New CultureInfo("ru-RU")
    Response.Write("<b><u>ru-RU</u></b><br>")
    Response.Write(dt.ToString() & "<br>")

    System.Threading.Thread.CurrentThread.CurrentCulture = New CultureInfo("fi-FI")
```

continues

LISTING 32-8 *(continued)*

```
        Response.Write("<b><u>fi-FI</u></b><br>")
        Response.Write(dt.ToString() & "<br>")

        System.Threading.Thread.CurrentThread.CurrentCulture = new CultureInfo("th-TH")
        Response.Write("<b><u>th-TH</u></b><br>")
        Response.Write(dt.ToString())
    End Sub
```

C#

```
    protected void Page_Load(object sender, EventArgs e)
    {
        DateTime dt = new DateTime(2010, 8, 11, 11, 12, 10, 10);
        System.Threading.Thread.CurrentThread.CurrentCulture = new CultureInfo("en-US");
        Response.Write("<b><u>en-US</u></b><br>");
        Response.Write(dt.ToString() + "<br>");

        System.Threading.Thread.CurrentThread.CurrentCulture = new CultureInfo("ru-RU");
        Response.Write("<b><u>ru-RU</u></b><br>");
        Response.Write(dt.ToString() + "<br>");

        System.Threading.Thread.CurrentThread.CurrentCulture = new CultureInfo("fi-FI");
        Response.Write("<b><u>fi-FI</u></b><br>");
        Response.Write(dt.ToString() + "<br>");

        System.Threading.Thread.CurrentThread.CurrentCulture = new CultureInfo("th-TH");
        Response.Write("<b><u>th-TH</u></b><br>");
        Response.Write(dt.ToString());
    }
```

In this case, four different cultures are utilized, and the date/time construction used by each culture is written to the browser screen using a `Response.Write` command. Figure 32-6 shows the result from this code operation.

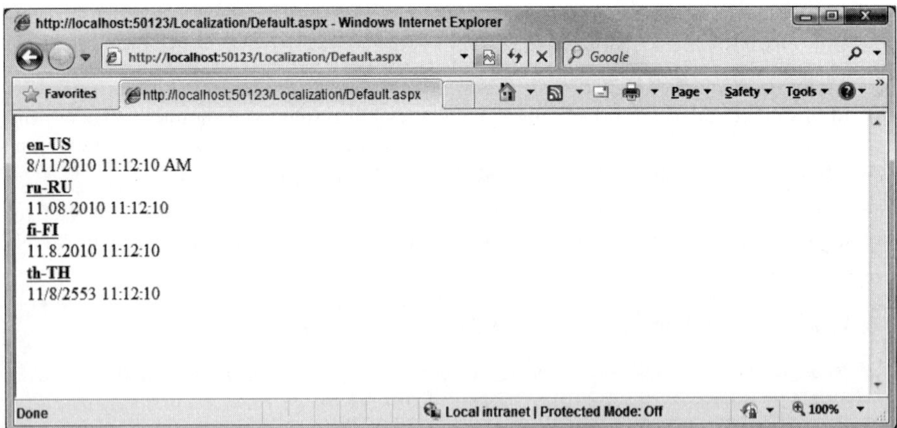

FIGURE 32-6

As you can see, the formats used to represent a date/time value are dramatically different from one another — and one of the cultures, the Thai culture (th-TH), even uses an entirely different calendar that labels this year as 2553.

Understanding Differences in Numbers and Currencies

In addition to date/time values, numbers are constructed quite differently from one culture to the next. How can a number be represented differently in different cultures? Well, it has less to do with the actual number (although certain cultures use different number symbols) and more to do with how the number separators are used for decimals or for showing amounts such as thousands, millions, and more. For example, in the English culture of the United States (en-US), you see numbers represented in the following fashion:

```
5,123,456.00
```

From this example, you can see that the en-US culture uses a comma as a separator for thousands and a period for signifying the start of any decimals that might appear after the number is presented. This number appears quite differently when working with other cultures. Listing 32-9 shows you an example of representing numbers in other cultures.

LISTING 32-9: Working with numbers in different cultures

Available for download on Wrox.com

```
Protected Sub Page_Load(ByVal sender As Object, ByVal e As System.EventArgs) Handles Me.Load
   Dim myNumber As Double = 5123456.00
   System.Threading.Thread.CurrentThread.CurrentCulture = New CultureInfo("en-US")
   Response.Write("<b><u>en-US</u></b><br>")
   Response.Write(myNumber.ToString("n") & "<br>")

   System.Threading.Thread.CurrentThread.CurrentCulture = new CultureInfo("vi-VN")
   Response.Write("<b><u>vi-VN</u></b><br>")
   Response.Write(myNumber.ToString("n") & "<br>")

   System.Threading.Thread.CurrentThread.CurrentCulture = new CultureInfo("fi-FI")
   Response.Write("<b><u>fi-FI</u></b><br>")
   Response.Write(myNumber.ToString("n") & "<br>")

   System.Threading.Thread.CurrentThread.CurrentCulture = new CultureInfo("fr-CH")
   Response.Write("<b><u>fr-CH</u></b><br>")
   Response.Write(myNumber.ToString("n"))
End Sub
```

C#

```
protected void Page_Load(object sender, EventArgs e)
{
   double myNumber = 5123456.00;
   System.Threading.Thread.CurrentThread.CurrentCulture = new CultureInfo("en-US");
   Response.Write("<b><u>en-US</u></b><br>");
   Response.Write(myNumber.ToString("n") + "<br>");

   System.Threading.Thread.CurrentThread.CurrentCulture = new CultureInfo("vi-VN");
   Response.Write("<b><u>vi-VN</u></b><br>");
   Response.Write(myNumber.ToString("n") + "<br>");

   System.Threading.Thread.CurrentThread.CurrentCulture = new CultureInfo("fi-FI");
   Response.Write("<b><u>fi-FI</u></b><br>");
   Response.Write(myNumber.ToString("n") + "<br>");

   System.Threading.Thread.CurrentThread.CurrentCulture = new CultureInfo("fr-CH");
   Response.Write("<b><u>fr-CH</u></b><br>");
   Response.Write(myNumber.ToString("n"));
}
```

Running this short example produces the results presented in Figure 32-7.

FIGURE 32-7

From this example, you can see that the other cultures represented here show numbers in quite a different format than that of the en-US culture. The second culture listed in the figure, vi-VN (Vietnamese in Vietnam), constructs a number exactly the opposite from the way it is constructed in en-US. The Vietnamese culture uses periods for the thousand separators and a comma for signifying decimals. Finnish, on the other hand, uses spaces for the thousand separators and a comma for the decimal separator, whereas the French-speaking Swiss use a high comma for separating thousands and a period for the decimal separator. As you can see, "translating" numbers to the proper construction so that users of your application can properly understand the numbers represented is important.

You also represent numbers when working with currencies. *Converting* currencies so that end users understand the proper value of an item is one thing, but translating the construction of the currency just as you would a basic number is another.

Each culture has a distinct currency symbol used to signify that a number represented is an actual currency value. For example, the en-US culture represents a currency in the following format:

```
$5,123,456.00
```

The en-US culture uses a U.S. Dollar symbol ($), and the location of this symbol is just as important as the symbol itself. For en-US, the $ symbol directly precedes the currency value (with no space in between the symbol and the first character of the number). Other cultures use different symbols to represent a currency and often place those currency symbols in different locations. Change the previous Listing 32-9 so that it now represents the number as a currency. Listing 32-10 presents the necessary changes.

LISTING 32-10: Working with currencies in different cultures

Available for download on Wrox.com

VB

```
Protected Sub Page_Load(ByVal sender As Object, ByVal e As System.EventArgs) Handles Me.Load
    Dim myNumber As Double = 5123456.00
    System.Threading.Thread.CurrentThread.CurrentCulture = New CultureInfo("en-US")
    Response.Write("<b><u>en-US</u></b><br>")

    Response.Write(myNumber.ToString("c") & "<br>")

    System.Threading.Thread.CurrentThread.CurrentCulture = new CultureInfo("vi-VN")
    Response.Write("<b><u>vi-VN</u></b><br>")

    Response.Write(myNumber.ToString("c") & "<br>")

    System.Threading.Thread.CurrentThread.CurrentCulture = new CultureInfo("fi-FI")
    Response.Write("<b><u>fi-FI</u></b><br>")

    Response.Write(myNumber.ToString("c") & "<br>")
```

```
        System.Threading.Thread.CurrentThread.CurrentCulture = new CultureInfo("fr-CH")
        Response.Write("<b><u>fr-CH</u></b><br>")

        Response.Write(myNumber.ToString("c"))

    End Sub
```

C#

```
    protected void Page_Load(object sender, EventArgs e)
    {
        double myNumber = 5123456.00;
        System.Threading.Thread.CurrentThread.CurrentCulture = new CultureInfo("en-US");
        Response.Write("<b><u>en-US</u></b><br>");

        Response.Write(myNumber.ToString("c") + "<br>");

        System.Threading.Thread.CurrentThread.CurrentCulture = new CultureInfo("vi-VN");
        Response.Write("<b><u>vi-VN</u></b><br>");

        Response.Write(myNumber.ToString("c") + "<br>");

        System.Threading.Thread.CurrentThread.CurrentCulture = new CultureInfo("fi-FI");
        Response.Write("<b><u>fi-FI</u></b><br>");

        Response.Write(myNumber.ToString("c") + "<br>");

        System.Threading.Thread.CurrentThread.CurrentCulture = new CultureInfo("fr-CH");
        Response.Write("<b><u>fr-CH</u></b><br>");

        Response.Write(myNumber.ToString("c"));
    }
```

Run this example to see how these cultures represent currency values, as illustrated in Figure 32-8.

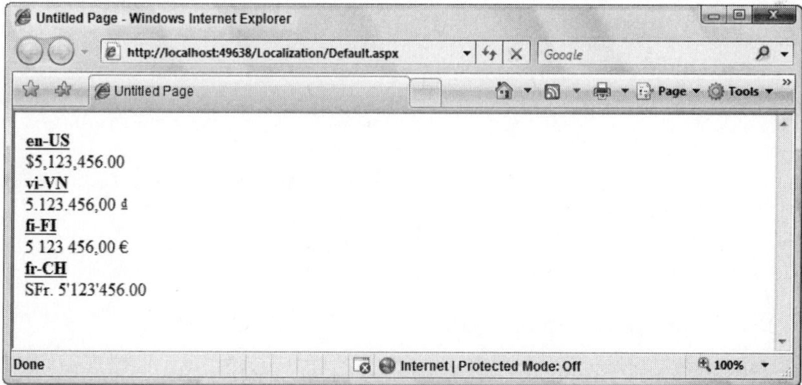

FIGURE 32-8

From this figure, you can see that not only are the numbers constructed quite differently from one another, but the currency symbol and the location of the symbol in regard to the number are quite different as well.

When working with currencies, note that when you are using currencies on an ASP.NET page, you have provided an automatic culture setting for the page as a whole (such as setting the culture in the `@Page` directive). You must specify a specific culture for the currency that is the same in all cases *unless* you are actually doing a currency conversion. For instance, if you are specifying a U.S. Dollar currency value on your ASP.NET page, you do not want to specify that the culture of the currency is something else (for example, the Euro). An exception would be if you actually performed a currency conversion and showed the appropriate Euro value along with the culture specification of the currency. Therefore, if you are using an automatic culture setting on your ASP.NET page and you are *not* converting the currency, you perform something similar to what appears in Listing 32-11 for currency values.

LISTING 32-11: Reverting to a specific culture when displaying currencies

VB

```
Dim myNumber As Double = 5123456.00
Dim usCurr As CultureInfo = New CultureInfo("en-US")
Response.Write(myNumber.ToString("c", usCurr))
```

C#

```
double myNumber = 5123456.00;
CultureInfo usCurr = new CultureInfo("en-US");
Response.Write(myNumber.ToString("c", usCurr));
```

Understanding Differences in Sorting Strings

You have learned to translate textual values and alter the construction of the numbers, date/time values, currencies, and more when you are globalizing an application. You should also take note when applying culture settings to some of the programmatic behaviors that you establish for values in your applications. One operation that can change based upon the culture setting applied is how .NET sorts strings. You might think that all cultures sort strings in the same way (and generally they do), but sometimes differences exist in how sorting occurs. To give you an example, Listing 32-12 shows you a sorting operation occurring in the en-US culture.

LISTING 32-12: Working with sorting in different cultures

Available for download on Wrox.com

VB

```
Protected Sub Page_Load(ByVal sender As Object, ByVal e As System.EventArgs)
   System.Threading.Thread.CurrentThread.CurrentCulture = New CultureInfo("en-US")

   Dim myList As List(Of String) = New List(Of String)

   myList.Add("Washington D.C.")
   myList.Add("Helsinki")
   myList.Add("Moscow")
   myList.Add("Warsaw")
   myList.Add("Vienna")
   myList.Add("Tokyo")

   myList.Sort()

   For Each item As String In myList
      Response.Write(item.ToString() + "<br>")
   Next
End Sub
```

C#

```
protected void Page_Load(object sender, EventArgs e)
{
   System.Threading.Thread.CurrentThread.CurrentCulture = new CultureInfo("en-US");

   List<string> myList = new List<string>();
   myList.Add("Washington D.C.");
   myList.Add("Helsinki");
   myList.Add("Moscow");
   myList.Add("Warsaw");
   myList.Add("Vienna");
   myList.Add("Tokyo");

   myList.Sort();

   foreach (string item in myList)
```

```
        {
            Response.Write(item.ToString() + "<br>");
        }
    }
```

For this example to work, you have to import the `System.Collections` and the `System.Collections.Generic` namespaces, because this example makes use of the `List(Of String)` object.

In this example, a generic list of capitals from various countries of the world is created in random order. Then the `Sort()` method of the generic `List(Of String)` object is invoked. This sorting operation sorts the strings based upon how sorting is done for the defined culture in which the ASP.NET thread is running. Listing 32-12 shows the sorting as it is done for the en-US culture. Figure 32-9 shows the result of this operation.

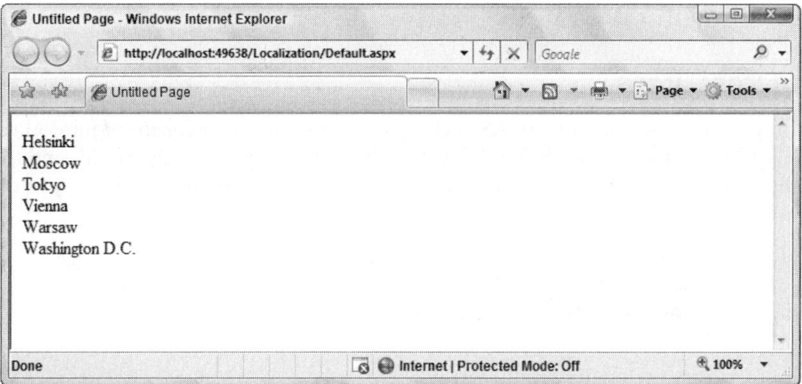

FIGURE 32-9

This result is much what you would expect. Now, however, change the previous example from Listing 32-12 so that the culture is set to Finnish, as shown in Listing 32-13.

LISTING 32-13: Changing the culture to Finnish

VB

```
System.Threading.Thread.CurrentThread.CurrentCulture = New CultureInfo("fi-FI")
```

C#

```
System.Threading.Thread.CurrentThread.CurrentCulture = new CultureInfo("fi-FI");
```

If you run the same bit of code under the Finnish culture setting, you get the results presented in Figure 32-10.

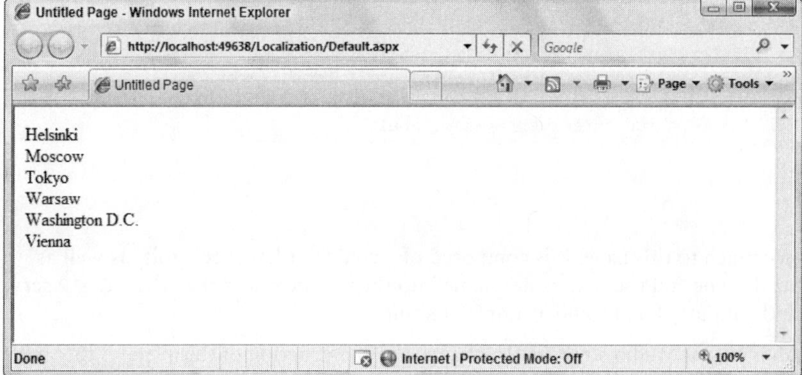

FIGURE 32-10

If you examine the difference between the Finnish culture sorting done in Figure 32-10 and the U.S. English culture sorting done in Figure 32-9, you see that the city of Vienna is in a different place in the Finnish version. This is because, in the Finnish language, no difference exists between the letter *V* and the letter *W*. Because no difference exists, if you are sorting using the Finnish culture setting, then `Vi` comes after `Wa` and, thus, Vienna comes last in the list of strings in the sorting operation.

ASP.NET 4 RESOURCE FILES

When you work with ASP.NET, all resources are handled by a resource file. A resource file is an XML-based file that has a `.resx` extension. You can have Visual Studio 2010 help you construct this file. Resource files provide a set of items that are utilized by a specified culture. In your ASP.NET applications, you store resource files as either local resources or global resources. The following sections look at how to use each type of resource.

Making Use of Local Resources

You would be surprised how easily you can build an ASP.NET page so that it can be *localized* into other languages. Really, the only thing you must do is build the ASP.NET page as you normally would, and then use some built-in capabilities from Visual Studio 2010 to convert the page to a format that allows you to plug in other languages easily.

To see this in action, build a simple ASP.NET page as presented in Listing 32-14.

LISTING 32-14: Building the basic ASP.NET page to localize

Available for download on Wrox.com

```
<%@ Page Language="VB" %>

<script runat="server">
    Protected Sub Button1_Click(ByVal sender As Object, _
      ByVal e As System.EventArgs)
        Label2.Text = TextBox1.Text
    End Sub
</script>

<html xmlns="http://www.w3.org/1999/xhtml">
<head runat="server">
    <title>Sample Page</title>
</head>
<body>
    <form id="form1" runat="server">
    <div>
        <asp:Label ID="Label1" runat="server"
         Text="What is your name?"></asp:Label><br />
        <br />
        <asp:TextBox ID="TextBox1" runat="server"></asp:TextBox>
        <asp:Button ID="Button1" runat="server" Text="Submit Name" /><br />
        <br />
        <asp:Label ID="Label2" runat="server"></asp:Label>
    </div>
    </form>
</body>
</html>
```

As you can see, there is not much to this page. It is composed of a couple of Label controls, as well as TextBox and Button controls. The end user enters her name into the text box, and then the `Label2` server control is populated with the inputted name and a simple greeting.

The next step is what makes Visual Studio so great. To change the construction of this page so that it can be localized easily from resource files, open the page in Visual Studio and select Tools ➪ Generate Local

Resource from the Visual Studio menu. Note that you can select this tool only when you are in the Design view of your page. It will not work in the split view or the code view of the page.

Selecting the Generate Local Resource from the Tool menu option causes Visual Studio to create an App_LocalResources folder in your project if you do not have one already. A `.resx` file based upon this ASP.NET page is then placed in the folder. For instance, if you are working with the `Default.aspx` page, the resource file is named `Default.aspx.resx`. Figure 32-11 shows these changes.

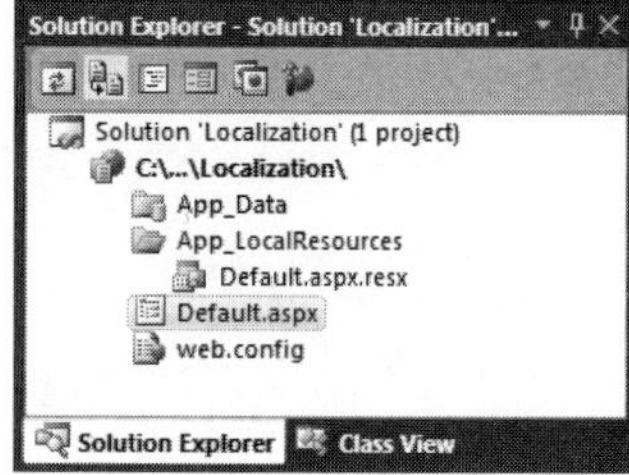

FIGURE 32-11

If you right-click on the `.resx` file and view the code, notice that the `.resx` file is nothing more than an XML file with an associated schema at the beginning of the document. The resource file that is generated for you takes every possible property of every translatable control on the page and gives each item a key value that can be referenced in your ASP.NET page. If you look at the code of the page, notice that all the text values that you placed in the page have been left in the page, but they have also been placed inside the resource file. You can see how Visual Studio changed the code of the `Default.aspx` page in Listing 32-15.

Available for download on Wrox.com

LISTING 32-15: Looking at how Visual Studio altered the page code

```
<%@ Page Language="VB" Culture="auto" meta:resourcekey="PageResource1"
    UICulture="auto" %>

<script runat="server">
    Protected Sub Button1_Click(ByVal sender As Object, _
      ByVal e As System.EventArgs)
        Label2.Text = TextBox1.Text
    End Sub
</script>

<html xmlns="http://www.w3.org/1999/xhtml" >
<head runat="server">
    <title>Sample Page</title>
</head>
<body>
    <form id="form1" runat="server">
    <div>
        <asp:Label ID="Label1" runat="server" Text="What is your name?"
         meta:resourcekey="Label1Resource1"></asp:Label><br />
        <br />
        <asp:TextBox ID="TextBox1" runat="server"
         meta:resourcekey="TextBox1Resource1"></asp:TextBox> 
        <asp:Button ID="Button1"
         runat="server" Text="Submit Name"
         meta:resourcekey="Button1Resource1" /><br />
        <br />
        <asp:Label ID="Label2" runat="server"
         meta:resourcekey="Label2Resource1"></asp:Label>
    </div>
    </form>
</body>
</html>
```

From this bit of code, you can see that the `Culture` and `UICulture` attributes have been added to the `@Page` directive with a value of `auto`, thus enabling this application to be localized. Also, the attribute `meta:resourcekey` has been added to each of the controls along with an associated value. This is the key from the `.resx` file that was created on your behalf. Double-clicking on the `Default.aspx.resx` file opens the resource file in the Resource Editor, which you will find is built into Visual Studio. Figure 32-12 shows this editor.

In the figure, note that a couple of properties from each of the server controls have been defined in the resource file. For instance, the Button server control has its `Text` and `ToolTip` properties exposed in this resource file, and the Visual Studio localization tool has pulled the default `Text` property value from the control based on what you placed there. Looking more closely at the Button server control constructions in this file, you can see that both the `Text` and `ToolTip` properties have a defining `Button1Resource1` value preceding the property name. This key is used in the Button server control you saw earlier:

```
<asp:Button ID="Button1"
 runat="server" Text="Submit Name"
 meta:resourcekey="Button1Resource1" />
```

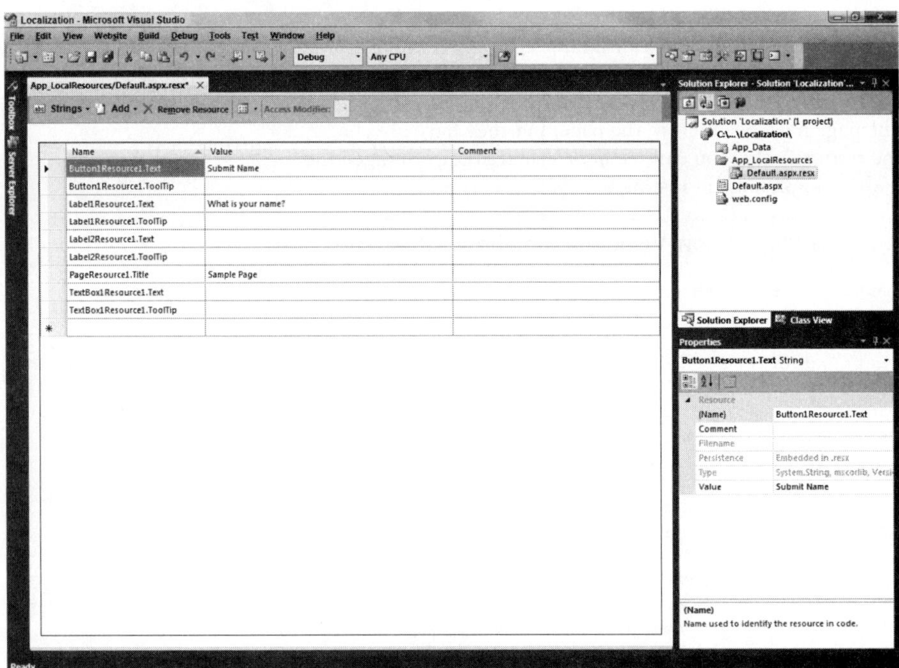

FIGURE 32-12

You can see that a `meta:resourcekey` attribute has been added and, in this case, it references `Button1Resource1`. All the properties using this key in the resource file (for example, the `Text` and `ToolTip` properties) are applied to this Button server control at runtime.

Adding Another Language Resource File

Now that the `Default.aspx.resx` file is in place, this is a file for an invariant culture. No culture is assigned to this resource file. If no culture can be determined, this resource file is then utilized. To add another resource file for the `Default.aspx` page that handles another language altogether, you copy and paste the `Default.aspx.resx` file into the same App_LocalResources folder and rename the newly copied file. If you use `Default.aspx.fi-FI.resx`, you give the following keys the following values to make a Finnish language resource file:

```
Button1Resource1.Text   Lähetä Nimi
Label1Resource1.Text    Mikä sinun nimi on?
PageResource1.Title     Näytesivu
```

You want to create a custom resource in both resource files using the key `Label2Answer`. The `Default.aspx.resx` file should have the following new key:

```
Label2Answer    Hello
```

Now you can add the key `Label2Answer` to the `Default.aspx.fi-FI.resx` file, as shown here:

```
Label2Answer    Hei
```

You now have resources for specific controls and a resource that you can access later programmatically.

Finalizing the Building of the Default.aspx Page

Finalizing the `Default.aspx` page, you want to add a `Button1_Click` event so that when the end user enters a name into the text box and clicks the Submit button, the `Label2` server control provides a greeting to him or her that is pulled from the local resource files. When all is said and done, you should have a `Default.aspx` page that resembles the one in Listing 32-16.

LISTING 32-16: The final Default.aspx page

Available for download on Wrox.com

VB

```
<%@ Page Language="VB" Culture="auto" meta:resourcekey="PageResource1"
    UICulture="auto" %>

<script runat="server">
    Protected Sub Button1_Click(ByVal sender As Object, _
      ByVal e As System.EventArgs)

       Label2.Text = GetLocalResourceObject("Label2Answer").ToString() & _
         " " & TextBox1.Text
    End Sub
</script>

<html xmlns="http://www.w3.org/1999/xhtml" >
<head runat="server">
    <title>Sample Page</title>
</head>
<body>
    <form id="form1" runat="server">
    <div>
        <asp:Label ID="Label1" runat="server" Text="What is your name?"
         meta:resourcekey="Label1Resource1"></asp:Label><br />
        <br />
        <asp:TextBox ID="TextBox1" runat="server"
         meta:resourcekey="TextBox1Resource1"></asp:TextBox> 
        <asp:Button ID="Button1"
         runat="server" Text="Submit Name"
         meta:resourcekey="Button1Resource1" OnClick="Button1_Click" /><br />
        <br />
        <asp:Label ID="Label2" runat="server"
         meta:resourcekey="Label2Resource1"></asp:Label>
    </div>
    </form>

</body>
</html>
```

C#

```
<%@ Page Language="C#" Culture="auto" meta:resourcekey="PageResource1"
    UICulture="auto" %>

<script runat="server">
    protected void Button1_Click(object sender, EventArgs e)
    {
        Label2.Text = GetLocalResourceObject("Label2Answer").ToString() + " " +
           TextBox1.Text;
    }
</script>
```

In addition to pulling local resources using the `meta:resourcekey` attribute in the server controls on the page to get at the exposed attributes, you can also get at any property value contained in the local resource file by using the `GetLocalResourceObject`. When using `GetLocalResourceObject`, you simply use the name of the key as a parameter, as shown here:

```
GetLocalResourceObject("Label2Answer")
```

You could just as easily get at any of the control's property values from the resource file programmatically using the same construct:

```
GetLocalResourceObject("Button1Resource1.Text")
```

With the code from Listing 32-16 in place and the resource files completed, you can run the page, entering a name in the text box and then clicking the button to get a response, as illustrated in Figure 32-13.

FIGURE 32-13

What happened behind the scenes that caused this page to be constructed in this manner? First, only two resource files, `Default.aspx.resx` and `Default.aspx.fi-FI.resx`, are available. The `Default.aspx.resx` resource file is the invariant culture resource file, whereas the `Default.aspx.fi-FI.resx` resource file is for a specific culture (fi-FI). Because I requested the `Default.aspx` page, and my browser is set to en-US as my preferred culture, ASP.NET found the local resources for the `Default.aspx` page. From there, ASP.NET made a check for an en-US–specific version of the `Default.aspx` page. Because there is not a specific page for the en-US culture, ASP.NET made a check for an EN (neutral culture)–specific page. Not finding a page for the EN neutral culture, ASP.NET was then forced to use the invariant culture resource file of `Default.aspx.resx`, producing the page presented in Figure 32-13.

Now, if you set your IE language preference as fi-FI and rerun the `Default.aspx` page, you see a Finnish version of the page, as illustrated in Figure 32-14.

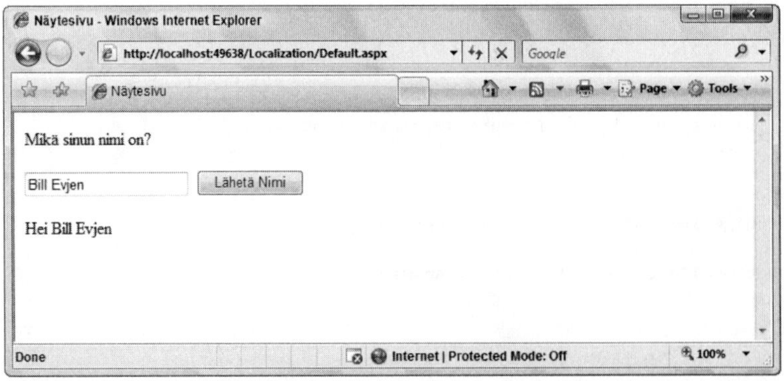

FIGURE 32-14

In this case, setting the IE language preference to fi-FI results in this culture's page instead of the invariant culture page that was presented earlier. ASP.NET found this specific culture through use of the `Default.aspx.fi-FI.resx` resource file.

You can see that all the control properties that were translated and placed within the resource file are utilized automatically by ASP.NET, including the page title presented in the title bar of IE.

Neutral Cultures Are Generally More Preferred

When you are working with the resource files from this example, note that one of the resources is for a *specific culture*. The `Default.aspx.fi-FI.resx` file is for a specific culture — the Finnish language as spoken in Finland. Another option would be to make this file work not for a specific culture but, instead, for a neutral culture. To accomplish this task, you simply name the file `Default.aspx.FI.resx` instead. In this example, having a specific culture declared really does not make that much difference because no other countries speak Finnish. It would make sense for languages such as German, Spanish, or French. These languages are spoken in multiple countries. For instance, if you are going to have a Spanish version of the `Default.aspx` page, you could definitely build it for a specific culture, such as `Default.aspx.es-MX.resx`. This construction is for the Spanish language as spoken in Mexico. With this in place, if someone requests the `Default.aspx` page with the language setting of es-MX, that user is provided with the contents of this resource file. However, what if the requestor has a setting of es-ES? He will not get the `Default.aspx.es-MX.resx` resource file but, instead, the invariant culture resource file of `Default.aspx.resx`. If you are going to make only a single translation into German, Spanish, or another language for your site or any of your pages, you want to construct the resource files to be for neutral cultures rather than for specific cultures.

If you have the resource file `Default.aspx.ES.resx`, then it won't matter if the end user's preferred setting is set to es-MX, es-ES, or even es-AR — the user gets the appropriate ES neutral culture version of the page.

Making Use of Global Resources

Besides using only local resources that specifically deal with a particular page in your ASP.NET application, you also have the option of creating *global* resources that can be used across multiple pages. To create a resource file that can be utilized across the entire application, right-click on the solution in the Solution Explorer of Visual Studio and select Add New Item. From the Add New Item dialog, select Resource file.

Selecting this option provides you with a `Resource.resx` file. Visual Studio places this file in a new folder called App_GlobalResources. Again, this first file is the invariant culture resource file. Add a single string resource giving it the key of `PrivacyStatement` and a value of some kind (a long string).

After you have the invariant culture resource file completed, the next step is to add another resource file, but this time name it `Resource.fi-FI.resx`. Again, for this resource file, give a string key of `PrivacyStatement` and a different value altogether from the one you used in the other resource file.

The idea of a global resource file is that you have access to these resources across your entire application. You can gain access to the values that you place in these files in several ways. One way is to work the value directly into any of your server control declarations. For instance, you can place this privacy statement in a Label server control, as presented in Listing 32-17.

LISTING 32-17: Using a global resource directly in a server control

```
<asp:Label ID="Label1" runat="server"
 Text='<%$ Resources: Resource, PrivacyStatement %>'></asp:Label>
```

With this construction in place, you can now grab the appropriate value of the `PrivacyStatement` global resource, depending upon the language preference of the end user requesting the page. To make this construction work, you use the keyword Resources followed by a colon. Next, you specify the name of the resource file class. In this case, the name of the resource file is `Resource` because this statement goes to the `Resource.resx` and `Resource.fi-FI.resx` files in order to find what it needs. After specifying the particular resource file to use, the next item in the statement is the key — in this case, `PrivacyStatement`.

Another way of achieving the same result is to use some built-in dialogs within Visual Studio. To do so, highlight the server control you want in Visual Studio from Design view so that the control appears within the Properties window. For this example, highlight a Label server control. From the Properties window, you click the button within the Expressions property. This launches the Expressions dialog and enables you to bind the `PrivacyStatement` value to the `Text` property of the control, as illustrated in Figure 32-15.

FIGURE 32-15

To make what you see in the above figure work, highlight the Text property in the Bindable properties list. You then select an expression type from a drop-down list on the right side of the dialog. Your options include AppSettings, ConnectionStrings, and Resources. Select the Resources option and you are then asked for the `ClassKey` and `ResourceKey` property values. The `ClassKey` is the name of the file that should be utilized. In this example, the name of the file is `Resource.resx`. Therefore, use the `Resource` keyword as a value. You are provided with a drop-down list in the `ResourceKey` property section with all the keys available in this file. Because only a single key exists at this point, you find only the `PrivacyStatement` key in this list. Make this selection and click the OK button. The Label server control changes and now appears as it was presented earlier in Listing 32-17.

One nice feature is that the resources provided via global resources are available in a strongly typed manner. For instance, you can programmatically get at a global resource value by using the construction presented in Listing 32-18.

LISTING 32-18: Programmatically getting at global resources

VB

```
Label1.Text = Resources.Resource.PrivacyStatement
```

C#

```
Label1.Text = Resources.Resource.PrivacyStatement;
```

In Figure 32-16, you can see that you have full IntelliSense for these resource values.

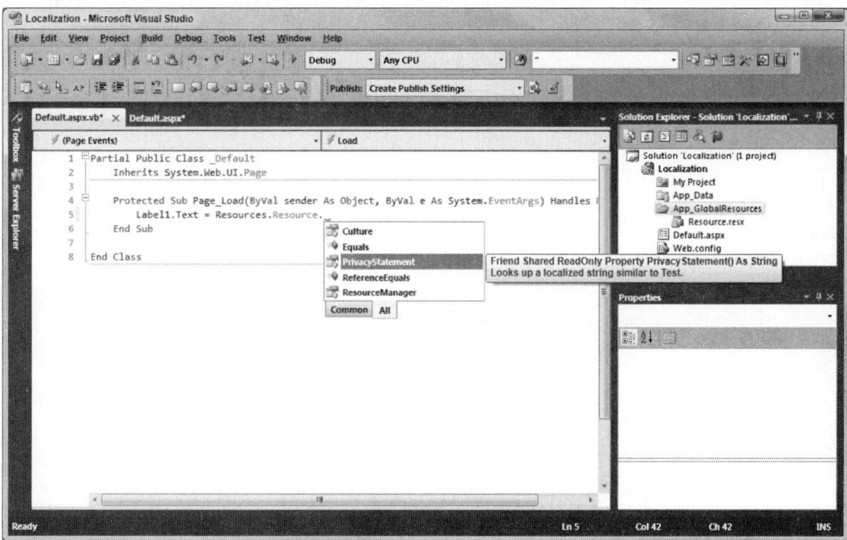

FIGURE 32-16

LOOKING AT THE RESOURCE EDITOR

Visual Studio 2010 provides an editor for working with resource files. You have already seen some of the views available from this editor. Resources are categorized visually by the data type of the resource. So far, this chapter has dealt only with the handling of strings, but other categories exist (such as images, icons, audio files, miscellaneous files, and other items). These options are illustrated in Figure 32-17.

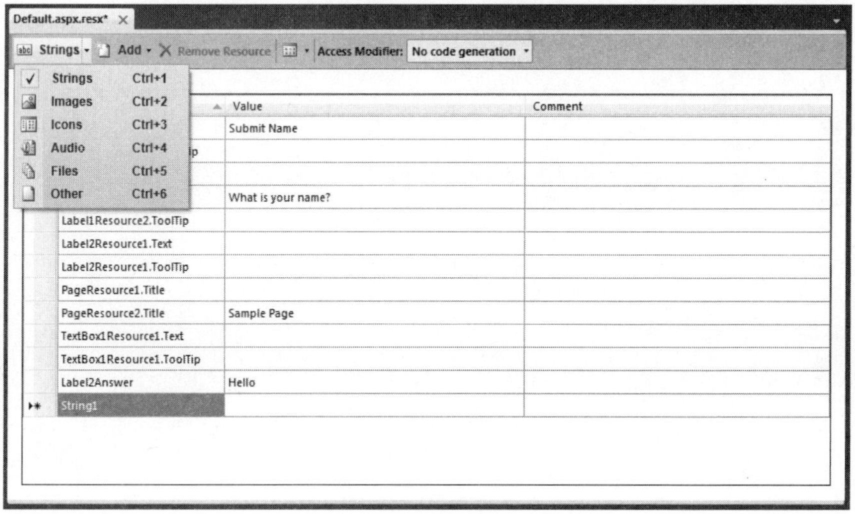

FIGURE 32-17

SUMMARY

We hope you see the value in globalizing your ASP.NET applications so that they can handle multiple cultures. This chapter looked at some of the issues you face when globalizing your applications and some of the built-in tools provided via both Visual Studio and the .NET Framework to make this process easier for you.

Globalizing your applications is really almost as easy as taking ASP.NET pages that have been already created and running the appropriate Visual Studio tool over the files to rebuild the pages to handle translations.

33

Configuration

WHAT'S IN THIS CHAPTER?

- Introduction to the ASP.NET configuration file
- An overview of the ASP.NET configuration settings
- Encrypting portions of your configuration files
- An examination of the ASP.NET configuration APIs
- Storing and retrieving sensitive information

Those of you who remember the "Classic" ASP days know that ASP's configuration information was stored in a binary repository called the Internet Information Services (IIS) metabase. To configure a classic ASP application, you had to modify the metabase, either through script or, more commonly, through the IIS Microsoft Management Console (MMC) snap-in.

Unlike classic ASP, all the available versions of ASP.NET do not require extensive use of the IIS metabase. Instead, ASP.NET uses an XML file-based configuration system that is much more flexible, accessible, and easier to use. When building ASP.NET, the ASP.NET team wanted to improve the manageability of the product. Although the release of ASP.NET 1.0 was a huge leap forward in Web application development, it really targeted the developer. What was missing was the focus on the administrator — the person who takes care of Web applications after they are built and deployed. ASP.NET today makes configuring an ASP.NET application quite easy for you by working either directly with the various configuration files or by using GUI tools that, in turn, interact with configuration files. Before examining the various GUI-based tools in detail in Chapter 36, you first take an in-depth look at how to work directly with the XML configuration files to change the behavior of your ASP.NET applications.

The journey into these configuration enhancements starts with an overview of configuration in ASP.NET.

CONFIGURATION OVERVIEW

ASP.NET configuration is stored in two primary XML-based files in a hierarchal fashion. XML is used to describe the properties and behaviors of various aspects of ASP.NET applications.

The ASP.NET configuration system supports two kinds of configuration files:

- Server or machine-wide configuration files such as the `machine.config` file
- Application configuration files such as the `web.config` file

Because the configuration files are based upon XML, the elements that describe the configuration are, therefore, case-sensitive. Moreover, the ASP.NET configuration system follows camel-casing naming conventions. If you look at the session state configuration example shown in Listing 33-1, for example, you can see that the XML element that deals with session state is presented as `<sessionState>`.

Available for download on Wrox.com

LISTING 33-1: Session state configuration

```
<?xml version="1.0" encoding="UTF-8" ?>
<configuration>
<system.web>
    <sessionState
       mode="InProc"
       stateConnectionString="tcpip=127.0.0.1:42424"
       stateNetworkTimeout="10"
       sqlConnectionString="data source=127.0.0.1; user id=sa; password=P@55worD"
       cookieless="false"
       timeout="20" />
  </system.web>
</configuration>
```

The benefits of having an XML configuration file instead of a binary metabase include the following:

- The configuration information is human-readable and can be modified using a plain text editor such as Notepad, although using Visual Studio 2010 or another XML-aware editor is recommended. Unlike a binary metabase, the XML-based configuration file can be easily copied from one server to another, as with any simple file. This feature is extremely helpful when working in a Web farm scenario.
- When some settings are changed in the configuration file, ASP.NET automatically detects the changes and applies them to the running ASP.NET application. ASP.NET accomplishes this by creating a new instance of the ASP.NET application and directing end users to this new application.
- The configuration changes are applied to the ASP.NET application without the need for the administrator to stop and start the Web server. Changes are completely transparent to the end user.
- The ASP.NET configuration system is extensible.
- Application-specific information can be stored and retrieved very easily.
- The sensitive information stored in the ASP.NET configuration system can optionally be encrypted to keep it from prying eyes.

Server Configuration Files

Every ASP.NET server installation includes a series of configuration files, such as the `machine.config` file. This file is installed as a part of the default .NET Framework installation. You can find `machine.config` and the other server-specific configuration files in `C:\Windows\Microsoft.NET\Framework\v4.0.21006\CONFIG`. They represent the default settings used by all ASP.NET Web applications installed on the server.

Some of the server-wide configuration files include the following:

- `machine.config`
- `machine.config.comments`
- `machine.config.default`
- `web.config`
- `web.config.comments`
- `web.config.default`
- `web_hightrust.config`
- `web_hightrust.config.default`
- `web_lowtrust.config`
- `web_lowtrust.config.default`

- web_mediumtrust.config
- web_mediumtrust.config.default
- web_minimaltrust.config
- web_minimaltrust.config.default

The system-wide configuration file, machine.config, is used to configure common .NET Framework settings for all applications on the machine. As a rule, editing or manipulating the machine.config file is not a good idea unless you know what you are doing. Changes to this file can affect all applications on your computer (Windows, Web, and so on).

Because the .NET Framework supports side-by-side execution mode, you might find more than one installation of the machine.config *file if you have multiple versions of the .NET Framework installed on the server. If you have .NET Framework versions 1.0, 1.1, 2.0, and 4 running on the server, for example, each .NET Framework installation has its own* machine.config *file. This means that you will find four* machine.config *file installations on that particular server. It is interesting to note that the .NET Framework 3.5 is really just a bolt-on to the .NET Framework 2.0. (It includes extra DLLs, which are sometimes referred to as extensions.) Thus, the .NET Framework 3.5 uses the same* machine.config *file as the .NET Framework 2.0. It is important to note that the .NET Framework 4 is a completely new CLR and doesn't have the same 2.0 dependency that the .NET Framework 3.5 does. The .NET 4 version of the framework includes its own* machine.config *file.*

In addition to the machine.config file, the .NET Framework installer also installs two more files called machine.config.default and machine.config.comments. The machine.config.default file acts as a backup for the machine.config file. If you want to revert to the factory setting for machine.config, simply copy the settings from the machine.config.default to the machine.config file.

The machine.config.comments file contains a description for each configuration section and explicit settings for the most commonly used values. machine.config.default and machine.config.comment files are not used by the .NET Framework runtime; they're installed in case you want to revert to default factory settings and default values.

You will also find a root-level web.config file in place within the same CONFIG folder as the machine .config. When making changes to settings on a server-wide basis, you should always attempt to make these changes in the root web.config file rather than in the machine.config file. You will find that files like the machine.config.comments and the machine.config.default files also exist for the web.config files (web.config.comments and web.config.default).

By default, your ASP.NET Web applications run under a *full trust* setting. You can see this setting by looking at the <securityPolicy> and <trust> sections in the root-level web.config file. Listing 33-2 presents these sections.

Available for download on Wrox.com

LISTING 33-2: The root web.config showing the trust level

```
<configuration>

    <location allowOverride="true">
        <system.web>
            <securityPolicy>
                <trustLevel name="Full" policyFile="internal" />
                <trustLevel name="High" policyFile="web_hightrust.config" />
                <trustLevel name="Medium" policyFile="web_mediumtrust.config" />
```

continues

LISTING 33-2 *(continued)*

```
                <trustLevel name="Low"  policyFile="web_lowtrust.config" />
                <trustLevel name="Minimal" policyFile="web_minimaltrust.config" />
            </securityPolicy>
            <trust level="Full" originUrl="" />
        </system.web>
    </location>

</configuration>
```

The other policy files are defined at specific trust levels. These levels determine the code-access security (CAS) allowed for ASP.NET. To change the trust level in which ASP.NET applications can run on the server, you simply change the `<trust>` element within the document or within your application's instance of the `web.config` file. For example, you can change to a medium trust level using the code shown in Listing 33-3.

Available for download on Wrox.com

LISTING 33-3: Changing the trust level to medium trust

```
<configuration>
<location allowOverride="false">
        <system.web>
            <securityPolicy>
                <trustLevel name="Full" policyFile="internal" />
                <trustLevel name="High" policyFile="web_hightrust.config" />
                <trustLevel name="Medium" policyFile="web_mediumtrust.config" />
                <trustLevel name="Low" policyFile="web_lowtrust.config" />
                <trustLevel name="Minimal" policyFile="web_minimaltrust.config" />

            </securityPolicy>
            <trust level="Medium" originUrl="" />
        </system.web>
    </location>

</configuration>
```

In this case, not only does this code mandate use of the `web_mediumtrust.config` file, but also (by setting the `allowOverride` attribute to `false`) it forces this trust level upon every ASP.NET application on the server. Individual application instances are unable to change this setting by overriding it in their local `web.config` files because this setting is in the root-level `web.config` file.

If you look through the various trust level configuration files (such as the `web_mediumtrust.config` file), notice that they define what kinds of actions you can perform through your code operations. For example, the `web_hightrust.config` file allows for open FileIO access to any point on the server as illustrated in Listing 33-4.

Available for download on Wrox.com

LISTING 33-4: The web_hightrust.config file's definition of FileIO CAS

```
<IPermission
   class="FileIOPermission"
   version="1"
   Unrestricted="true"
/>
```

If, however, you look at the medium trust `web.config` file (`web_mediumtrust.config`), you see that this configuration file restricts ASP.NET to *only* those FileIO operations within the application directory. Listing 33-5 presents this definition.

Available for download on Wrox.com

LISTING 33-5: FileIO restrictions in the web_mediumtrust.config file

```
<IPermission
   class="FileIOPermission"
   version="1"
```

```
        Read="\$AppDir\$"
        Write="\$AppDir\$"
        Append="\$AppDir\$"
        PathDiscovery="\$AppDir\$"
    />
```

Seeing in which trust level you can run your ASP.NET applications and changing the `<trust>` section to enable the appropriate level of CAS is always a good idea.

Application Configuration File

Unlike the `machine.config` file, each and every ASP.NET application has its own copy of configuration settings stored in a file called `web.config`. If the Web application spans multiple subfolders, each subfolder can have its own `web.config` file that inherits or overrides the parent's file settings.

To update servers in your farm with these new settings, you simply copy this `web.config` file to the appropriate application directory. ASP.NET takes care of the rest — no server restarts and no local server access is required — and your application continues to function normally, except that it now uses the new settings applied in the configuration file.

Applying Configuration Settings

When the ASP.NET runtime applies configuration settings for a given Web request, `machine.config` (as well as any of the `web.config` files configuration information) is merged into a single unit, and that information is then applied to the given application. Configuration settings are inherited from any parent `web.config` file or `machine.config`, which is the root configuration file or the ultimate parent. Figure 33-1 presents an example of this.

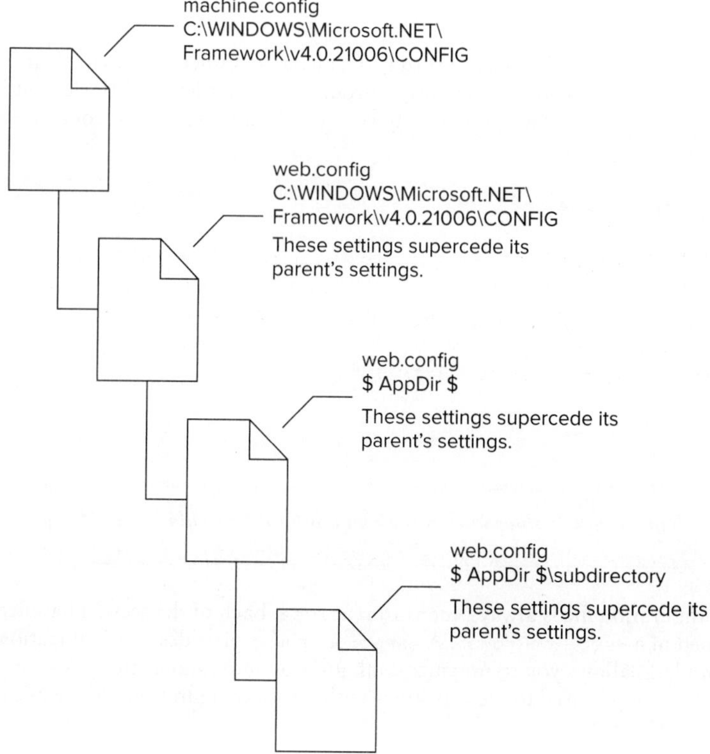

FIGURE 33-1

The configuration for each Web application is unique; however, settings are inherited from the parent. For example, if the `web.config` file in the root of your Web site defines a session timeout of 10 minutes, then that particular setting overrides the default ASP.NET setting inherited from the `machine.config` or the root `web.config` file. The `web.config` files in the subdirectories or subfolders can override these settings or inherit the settings (such as the 10-minute session timeout).

The configuration settings for virtual directories are independent of the physical directory structure. Unless the manner in which the virtual directories are organized is exclusively specified, configuration problems can result.

Note that these inheritance/override rules can be blocked in most cases by using the `allowOverride = "false"` mechanism shown earlier in Listing 33-3.

Detecting Configuration File Changes

ASP.NET automatically detects when configuration files, such as `machine.config` or `web.config`, are changed. This logic is implemented based on listening for file-change notification events provided by the operating system.

When an ASP.NET application is started, the configuration settings are read and stored in the ASP.NET cache. A file dependency is then placed on the entry within the cache in the `machine.config` and/or `web.config` configuration file. When the configuration file update is detected in the `machine.config`, ASP.NET creates a new application domain to service new requests. The old application domain is destroyed as soon as it completes servicing all its outstanding requests.

Configuration File Format

The main difference between `machine.config` and `web.config` is the filename. Other than that, their schemas are the same. Configuration files are divided into multiple groups. The root-level XML element in a configuration file is named `<configuration>`. This pseudo `web.config` file has a section to control ASP.NET, as shown in Listing 33-6.

LISTING 33-6: A pseudo web.config file

Available for download on Wrox.com

```
<?xml version="1.0" encoding="UTF-8"?>
<configuration>
  <configSections>
    <section name="[sectionSettings]" type="[Class]"/>
    <sectionGroup name="[sectionGroup]">
      <section name="[sectionSettings]" type="[Class]"/>
    </sectionGroup>
  </configSections>
</configuration>
```

Values within brackets [ ] have unique values within the real configuration file.

The root element in the XML configuration file is always `<configuration>`. Each of the section handlers and settings are optionally wrapped in a `<sectionGroup>`. A `<sectionGroup>` provides an organizational function within the configuration file. It allows you to organize configuration into unique groups — for instance, the `<system.web>` section group is used to identify areas within the configuration file specific to ASP.NET.

The <configSections> section is the mechanism to group the configuration section handlers associated with each configuration section. When you want to create your own section handlers, you must declare them in the <configSections> section. The <httpModules> section has a configuration handler that is set to System.Web.Caching.HttpModulesSection, and the <sessionState> section has a configuration handler that is set to System.Web.SessionState.SessionStateSection classes, as shown in Listing 33-7.

Available for download on Wrox.com

LISTING 33-7: HTTP module configuration setting from the machine.config file

```
<configSections>
   <sectionGroup>
      <section name="httpModules"
       type="System.Web.Configuration.HttpModulesSection,
          System.Web, Version=4.0.0.0, Culture=neutral,
          PublicKeyToken=b03f5f7f11d50a3a"/>
   </sectionGroup>
</configSections>
```

COMMON CONFIGURATION SETTINGS

The ASP.NET applications depend on a few common configuration settings. These settings are common to both the web.config and machine.config files. In this section, you look at some of these common configuration settings.

Connection Strings

In ASP.NET 1.0 and 1.1, all the connection string information was stored in the <appSettings> section. However, ever since ASP.NET 2.0, a section called <connectionStrings> was included that stores all kinds of connection-string information. Even though storing connection strings in the <appSettings> element works fine, it poses the following challenges:

- When connection strings are stored in appSettings section, it is impossible for a data-aware control such as SqlCacheDependency or MembershipProvider to discover the information.
- Securing connection strings using cryptographic algorithms is a challenge.
- Last, but not least, this feature does not apply to ASP.NET only; rather, it applies to all the .NET application types including Windows Forms, Web Services, and so on.

Because the connection-string information is stored independently of the appSettings section, it can be retrieved using the strongly typed collection method ConnectionStrings. Listing 33-8 gives an example of how to store connection strings.

Available for download on Wrox.com

LISTING 33-8: Storing a connection string

```
<configuration>
  <connectionStrings>
    <add
        name="ExampleConnection"
        connectionString="server=401kServer;database=401kDB;
        uid=WebUser;pwd=P@$$worD9" />
  </connectionStrings>
</configuration>
```

Listing 33-9 shows how to retrieve the connection string (ExampleConnection) in your code.

LISTING 33-9: Retrieving a connection string

VB

```
Public Sub Page_Load (sender As Object, e As EventArgs)
    ...
    Dim dbConnection as New
      SqlConnection(ConfigurationManager.ConnectionStrings("ExampleConnection")
            .ConnectionString)
    ...
End Sub
```

C#

```
public void Page_Load (Object sender, EventArgs e)
{
    ...
    SqlConnection dbConnection = new
      SqlConnection(ConfigurationManager.ConnectionStrings["ExampleConnection"]
            .ConnectionString);
    ...
}
```

This type of construction has a lot of power. Instead of hard-coding your connection strings into each and every page within your ASP.NET application, you can store one instance of the connection string centrally (in the `web.config` file, for example). Now, if you have to make a change to this connection string, you can make this change in only *one* place rather than in multiple places.

Configuring Session State

Because Web-based applications utilize the stateless HTTP protocol, you must store the application-specific state or user-specific state where it can persist. The `Session` object is the common store where user-specific information is persisted. Session store is implemented as a `Hashtable` and stores data based on key/value pair combinations.

ASP.NET 1.0 and 1.1 had the capability to persist the session store data in `InProc`, `StateServer`, and `SqlServer`. Since ASP.NET 2.0, you've been able to add one more capability called `Custom`. The `Custom` setting gives the developer a lot more control regarding how the session state is persisted in a permanent store. For example, out of the box ASP.NET does not support storing session data on non-Microsoft databases such as Oracle, DB2, or Sybase. If you want to store the session data in any of these databases or in a custom store such as an XML file, you can implement that by writing a custom provider class. (See the section "Custom State Store" later in this chapter and Chapter 21 to learn more about the session state features in ASP.NET 4.)

You can configure the session information using the `<sessionState>` element as presented in Listing 33-10.

Available for download on Wrox.com

LISTING 33-10: Configuring session state

```
<sessionState
 mode="StateServer"
 cookieless="false"
 timeout="20"
 stateConnectionString="tcpip=ExampleSessionStore:42424"
 stateNetworkTimeout="60"
 sqlConnectionString=""
/>
```

The following list describes some of the attributes for the `<sessionState>` element shown in the preceding code:

- `mode`: Specifies whether the session information should be persisted. The mode setting supports five options: `Off`, `InProc`, `StateServer`, `SQLServer`, and `Custom`. The default option is `InProc`.
- `cookieless`: Specifies whether HTTP cookieless Session key management is supported.

- `timeout`: Specifies the `Session` lifecycle time. The `timeout` value is a sliding value; at each request, the timeout period is reset to the current time plus the timeout value. For example, if the `timeout` value is 20 minutes and a request is received at 10:10 AM, the timeout occurs at 10:30 AM.
- `stateConnectionString`: When `mode` is set to `StateServer`, this setting is used to identify the TCP/IP address and port to communicate with the Windows Service providing state management.
- `stateNetworkTimeout`: Specifies the timeout value (in seconds) while attempting to store state in an out-of-process session store such as `StateServer`.
- `sqlConnectionString`: When `mode` is set to `SQLServer`, this setting is used to connect to the SQL Server database to store and retrieve session data.

Web Farm Support

Multiple Web servers working as a group are called a *Web farm*. If you would like to scale out your ASP.NET application into multiple servers inside a Web farm, ASP.NET supports this kind of deployment out of the box. However, the session data needs to be persisted in an out-of-process session state such as `StateServer` or `SQLServer`.

State Server

Both `StateServer` and `SQLServer` support the out-of-process session state. However, the `StateServer` stores all the session information in a Windows Service, which stores the session data in memory. Using this option, if the server that hosts the session state service goes down in the Web farm, all the ASP.NET clients that are accessing the Web site fail; there is no way to recover the session data.

You can configure the session state service using the Services dialog available by choosing Start ➪ Settings ➪ Control Panel ➪ Administrative Tools ➪ Computer Management if you are using Windows XP, and Start ➪ Control Panel ➪ System and Security ➪ Administrative Tools ➪ Services if you are using Windows 7 (as shown in Figure 33-2).

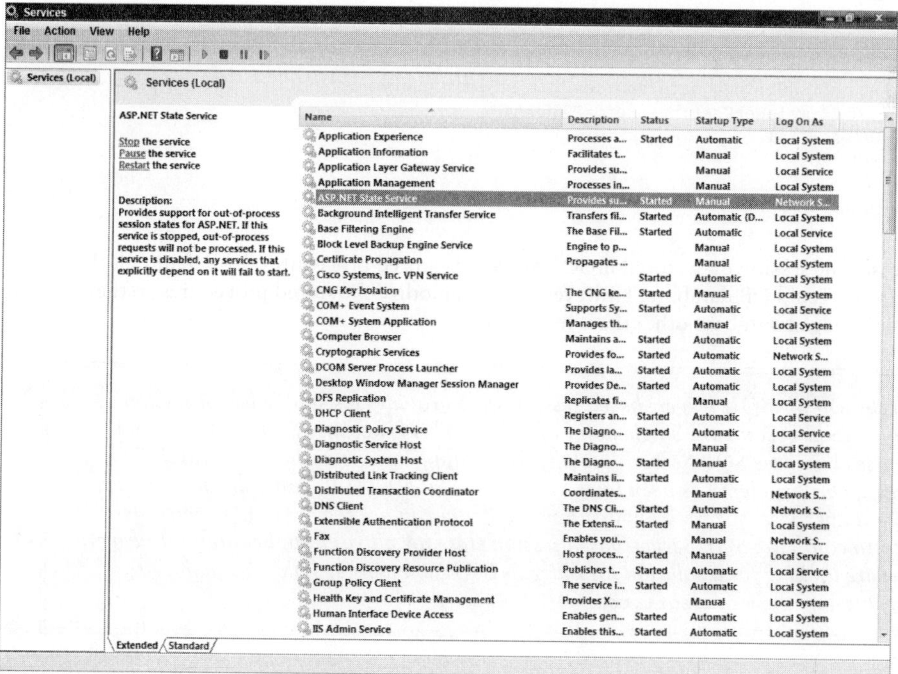

FIGURE 33-2

Alternatively, you can start the session state service by using the command prompt and entering the `net start` command, like this:

```
C:\Windows\Microsoft.NET\Framework\v4.0.21006\> net start aspnet_state

The ASP.NET State Service service is starting.

The ASP.NET State Service service was started successfully.
```

All compatible versions of ASP.NET share a single state service instance, which is the service installed with the highest version of ASP.NET. For example, if you have installed ASP.NET 4 on a server where ASP.NET 2.0 and 1.1 are already running, the ASP.NET 4 installation replaces the ASP.NET 2.0's state server instance. The ASP.NET 4 service is guaranteed to work for all previous compatible versions of ASP.NET.

SQL Server

When you choose the `SQLServer` option, session data is stored in a Microsoft SQL Server database. Even if SQL Server goes down, the built-in SQL Server recovery features enable you to recover all the session data. Configuring ASP.NET to support SQL Server for session state is just as simple as configuring the Windows Service. The only difference is that you run a T-SQL script that ships with ASP.NET, `InstallSqlState.sql`. The T-SQL script that uninstalls ASP.NET SQL Server support, called `UninstallSqlState.sql`, is also included. The install and uninstall scripts are available in the Framework folder. Listing 33-11 shows an example of using the SQL Server option.

Available for download on Wrox.com

LISTING 33-11: Using the SQLServer option for session state

```
<configuration>
  <system.web>
    <sessionState
      mode="SQLServer"
      sqlConnectionString="data source=ExampleSessionServer;
      user id=ExampleWebUser;password=P@55worD"
      cookieless="false"
      timeout="20"
    />
  </system.web>
</configuration>
```

ASP.NET accesses the session data stored in SQL Server via stored procedures. By default, all the session data is stored in the Temp DB database. However, you can modify the stored procedures so they are stored in tables in a full-fledged database other than Temp DB.

Even though the SQL Server–based session state provides a scalable use of session state, it could become the single point of failure. This is because SQL Server session state uses the same SQL Server database for all applications in the same ASP.NET process. This problem has been fixed ever since ASP.NET 2.0, and you can configure different databases for each application. Now you can use the `aspnet_regsql.exe` *utility to configure SQL Server-based session state for all your applications. However, if you are looking for a solution for older .NET Frameworks, a fix is available at* `http://support.microsoft.com/kb/836680`.

Because the connection strings are stored in the strongly typed mode, the connection string information can be referenced in other parts of the configuration file. For example, when configuring session state to be stored in SQL Server, you can specify the connection string in the `<connectionStrings>`section, and then you can specify the name of the connection string in the `<sessionState>` element, as shown in Listing 33-12.

Available for download on Wrox.com

LISTING 33-12: Configuring session state with a connection string

```
<configuration>

  <connectionStrings>
     <add name = "ExampleSqlSessionState"
         connectionString = "data source=ExampleSessionServer;
         user id=ExampleWebUser;password=P@55worD" />
  </connectionStrings>

  <system.web>
    <sessionState
      mode="SQLServer"
      sqlConnectionString="ExampleSqlSessionState"
      cookieless="false"
      timeout="20"
    />
  </system.web>

</configuration>
```

Custom State Store

The session state in ASP.NET 4 is based on a pluggable architecture with different providers that inherit the `SessionStateStoreProviderBase` class. If you want to create your own custom provider or use a third-party provider, you must set the mode to `Custom`.

You specify the custom provider assembly that inherits the `SessionStateStoreProviderBase` class, as shown in Listing 33-13.

Available for download on Wrox.com

LISTING 33-13: Working with your own session state provider

```
<configuration>
   <system.web>

      <sessionState
          mode="Custom"
          customProvider="CustomStateProvider">
        <providers>
          <add name="CustomStateProvider"
           type="CustomStateProviderAssembly,
             CustomStateProviderNamespace.CustomStateProvider"/>
        </providers>
      </sessionState>

   </system.web>
</configuration>
```

In the previous example, you have configured the session state mode as `Custom` because you have specified the provider name as `CustomStateProvider`. From there, you add the provider element and include the type of the provider with namespace and class name.

You can read more about the provider model and custom providers in Chapters 11 and 12.

Compilation Configuration

ASP.NET supports the dynamic compilation of ASP.NET pages, Web services, HttpHandlers, ASP.NET application files (such as the `Global.asax` file), source files, and so on. These files are automatically compiled on demand when they are first required by an ASP.NET application.

Any changes to a dynamically compiled file causes all affected resources to become automatically invalidated and recompiled. This system enables developers to quickly develop applications with a minimum of process overhead because they can just click Save to immediately cause code changes to take effect within their applications.

The ASP.NET 1.0 and 1.1 features are extended in ASP.NET 2.0, 3.5, and 4 to account for other file types, including class files. You can configure the ASP.NET compilation settings using the `<compilation>` section in the `web.config` or `machine.config` files. The ASP.NET engine compiles the page when necessary and saves the generated code in code cache. This cached code is used when executing the ASP.NET pages. Listing 33-14 shows the syntax for the `<compilation>` section.

LISTING 33-14: The <compilation> section

```
<!-- compilation Attributes -->
<compilation
  tempDirectory="" [String]
  debug="false" [true|false]
  strict="false" [true|false]
  explicit="true" [true|false]
  batch="true" [true|false]
  optimizeCompilations="false" [true|false]
  urlLinePragmas="false" [true|false]
  batchTimeout="900" [in Seconds][number]
  maxBatchSize="1000" [number]
  maxBatchGeneratedFileSize="1000" [number]
  numRecompilesBeforeAppRestart="15" [number]
  defaultLanguage="vb" [String]
  targetFramework="" [String]
  assemblyPostProcessorType="" [String]
  >
   <assemblies>
      <add assembly="" [String, Required, Collection Key] />
   </assemblies>
   <buildproviders>
     <add extension="" [String, Required, Collection Key]
       type="" [String, Required] />
   </buildproviders>
   <folderLevelBuildProviders
      <add name="" [String, Required, Collection Key]
       type="" [String, Required] />
   </folderLevelBuildProviders>
   <expressionBuilders
      <add expressionPrefix="" [String, Required, Collection Key]
       type="" [String, Required] />
   </expressionBuilders>
   <codeSubDirectories>
     <add directoryName="" [String, Required, Collection Key] />
   </codeSubDirectories>
</compilation>
```

Now take a more detailed look at these `<compilation>` attributes:

- `batch`: Specifies whether the batch compilation is supported. The default value is `true`.
- `maxBatchSize`: Specifies the maximum number of pages/classes that can be compiled into a single batch. The default value is 1000.
- `maxBatchGeneratedFileSize`: Specifies the maximum output size of a batch assembly compilation. The default value is 1000KB.
- `batchTimeout`: Specifies the amount of time (minutes) granted for batch compilation to occur. If this timeout elapses without compilation being completed, an exception is thrown. The default value is 15 minutes.
- `optimizeCompilations`: Specifies whether dynamic compilation compiles the entire site or only the items that have changed. When set to `False` (the default), the entire site will recompile when top-level files are changed; a setting of `True` will recompile only the changed files.
- `debug`: Specifies whether to compile production assemblies or debug assemblies. The default is `false`.
- `defaultLanguage`: Specifies the default programming language, such as `VB` or `C#`, to use in dynamic compilation files. Language names are defined using the `<compiler>` child element. The default value is `VB`.
- `explicit`: Specifies whether the Microsoft Visual Basic code compile option is explicit. The default is `true`.
- `numRecompilesBeforeAppRestart`: Specifies the number of dynamic recompiles of resources that can occur before the application restarts.
- `strict`: Specifies the setting of the Visual Basic strict compile option.
- `urlLinePragmas`: Instructs the compiler if it should use URLs rather than physical paths (which is the default behavior).
- `tempDirectory`: Specifies the directory to use for temporary file storage during compilation. By default, ASP.NET creates the temp file in the `[WinNT\Windows]\Microsoft.NET\Framework\[version]\Temporary ASP.NET Files` folder.
- `assemblies`: Specifies assemblies that are used during the compilation process.
- `codeSubDirectories`: Specifies an ordered collection of subdirectories containing files compiled at runtime. Adding the `codeSubDirectories` section creates separate assemblies.
- `buildproviders`: Specifies a collection of build providers used to compile custom resource files.
- `folderLevelBuildProviders`: Specifies a collection of build providers used to compile custom resource files in specific folders.
- `expressionBuilders`: Specifies a collection of resource strings to be utilized during the compilation process.

Browser Capabilities

Identifying and using the browser's capabilities is essential for Web applications. The browser capabilities component was designed for the variety of desktop and device browsers, such as Microsoft's Internet Explorer, Google's Chrome, Safari, Netscape, Opera, Blackberry, iPhone, and so on. The `<browserCaps>` element enables you to specify the configuration settings for the browser capabilities component. The `<browserCaps>` element can be declared at the machine, site, application, and subdirectory level.

The `HttpBrowserCapabilities` *class contains all the browser properties. The properties can be set and retrieved in this section. The* `<browserCaps>` *element has been deprecated since ASP.NET 2.0 and now you should instead focus on using* `.browser` *files.*

When a request is received from a browser, the browser capabilities component identifies the browser's capabilities from the request headers.

For each browser, compile a collection of settings relevant to applications. These settings may either be statically configured or gathered from request headers. Allow the application to extend or modify the capabilities settings associated with browsers and to access values through a strongly typed object model. The ASP.NET mobile capabilities depend on the browser capabilities component.

In ASP.NET 4, all the browser capability information is represented in browser definition files. The browser definitions are stored in `*.browser` file types and specified in XML format. A single file may contain one or more browser definitions. The `*.browser` files are stored in the `Config\Browsers` subdirectory of the `Framework` installation directory (for example, `[WinNT\Windows]\Microsoft.NET\Framework\v4.0.21006\CONFIG\Browsers`), as shown in Figure 33-3. Application-specific browser definition files are stored in the `/Browsers` subdirectory of the application.

In ASP.NET 1.0 and 1.1, the browser cap information was stored in the `machine.config` *and* `web.config` *files themselves.*

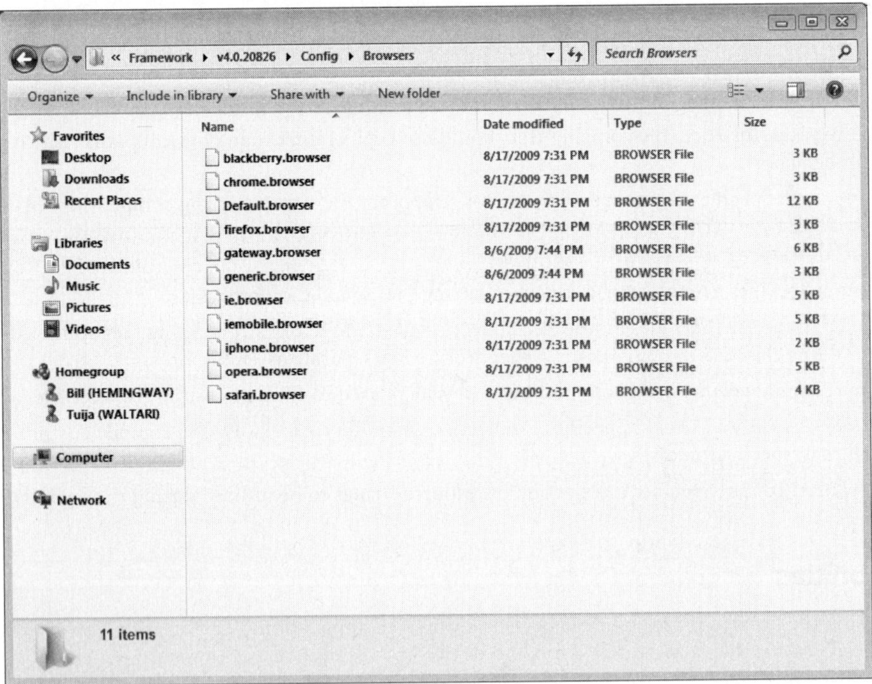

FIGURE 33-3

The browser definition file format defines each browser as an entity, self-contained in a `<browser>` XML element. Each browser has its own ID that describes a class of browser and its parent class. The root node of a browser definition file is the `<browsers>` element and multiple browser entries identified using the `id` attribute of the `<browser>` element.

Listing 33-15 shows a section of the `ie.browser` file.

LISTING 33-15: Content of ie.browser file

```
<browsers>
    <browser id="IE" parentID="Mozilla">
        <identification>
            <userAgent match="MSIE
            (?'version'(?'major'\d+)(\.(?'minor'\d+)?)
            (?'letters'\w*))(?'extra'[^)]*)" />
            <userAgent nonMatch="IEMobile" />
        </identification>

        <capture>
            <userAgent match="Trident/(?'layoutVersion'\d+)" />
        </capture>

        <capabilities>
            <capability name="browser" value="IE" />
            <capability name="layoutEngine" value="Trident" />
            <capability name="layoutEngineVersion value="${layoutVersion}" />
            <capability name="extra" value="${extra}" />
            <capability name="isColor" value="true" />
            <capability name="letters" value="${letters}" />
            <capability name="majorversion" value="${major}" />
            <capability name="minorversion" value="${minor}" />
            <capability name="screenBitDepth" value="8" />
            <capability name="type" value="IE${major}" />
            <capability name="version" value="${version}" />
        </capabilities>
    </browser>
...
```

The `id` attribute of the `<browser>` element uniquely identifies the class of browser. The `parentID` attribute of the `<browser>` element specifies the unique ID of the parent browser class. Both the `id` and the `parentID` are required values.

Before running an ASP.NET application, the framework compiles all the browser definitions into an assembly and installs the compilation in GAC. When the browser definition files at the system level are modified, they do not automatically reflect the change in each and every ASP.NET application. Therefore, updating this information becomes the responsibility of the developer or the installation tool. You can send the updated browser information to all the ASP.NET applications by running the `aspnet_regbrowsers.exe` *utility provided by the framework. When the* `aspnet_regbrowsers.exe` *utility is called, the browser information is recompiled and the new assembly is stored in the GAC; this assembly is reused by all the ASP.NET applications. Nevertheless, browser definitions at the application level are automatically parsed and compiled on demand when the application is started. If any changes are made to the application's* `/Browsers` *directory, the application is automatically recycled.*

Custom Errors

When the ASP.NET application fails, the ASP.NET page can show the default error page with the source code and line number of the error. However, this approach has a few problems:

- The source code and error message might not make any sense to a less-experienced end user.
- If the same source code and the error messages are displayed to a hacker, subsequent damage could result.

Displaying too much error information could provide important implementation details that in most cases you want to keep from the public. Figure 33-4 shows an example.

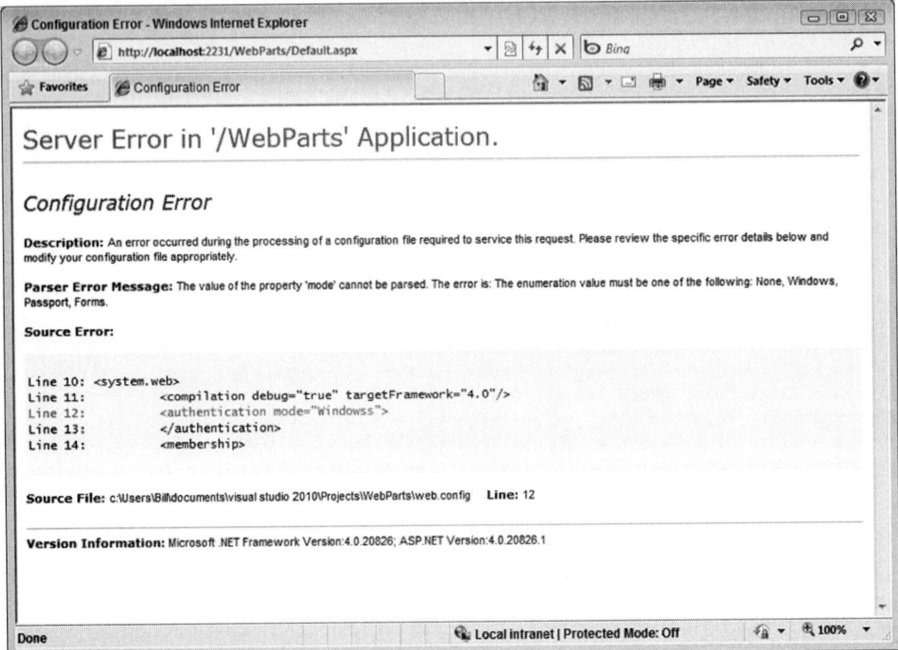

FIGURE 33-4

However, ASP.NET provides excellent infrastructure to prevent this kind of error information. The `<customErrors>` section provides a means for defining custom error messages in an ASP.NET application. The syntax is as follows:

```
<customErrors defaultRedirect="[url]" mode="[on/off/remote]">
   <error statusCode="[statuscode]" redirect="[url]" />
</customErrors>
```

- `defaultRedirect`: Specifies the default URL to which the client browser should be redirected if an error occurs. This setting is optional.
- `mode`: Specifies whether the status of the custom errors is enabled, disabled, or shown only to remote machines. The possible values are `On`, `Off`, and `RemoteOnly`. `On` indicates that the custom errors are enabled. `Off` indicates that the custom errors are disabled. `RemoteOnly` indicates that the custom errors are shown only to remote clients.
- `customErrors`: The `<customErrors>` section supports multiple `<error>` sub-elements that are used to define custom errors. Each `<error>` sub-element can include a `statusCode` attribute and a URL.

Authentication

In Chapter 20, you see the authentication process in detail. In this section, you can review configuration-specific information. Authentication is a process that verifies the identity of the user and establishes the identity between the server and a request. Because HTTP is a stateless protocol, the authentication information is persisted somewhere in the client or the server; ASP.NET supports both of these.

You can store the server-side information in `Session` objects. When it comes to client side, you have many options:

- Cookies
- ViewState
- URL
- Hidden fields

ASP.NET supports following authentication methods out of the box:

- Windows authentication
- Passport authentication
- Forms Authentication

If you want to disable authentication, you can use the setting `mode = "None"`:

```
<authentication mode="None" />
```

Windows Authentication

ASP.NET relies on IIS's infrastructure to implement Windows authentication, and Windows authentication enables you to authenticate requests using Windows Challenge/Response semantics. When the Web server receives a request, it initially denies access to the request (which is a challenge). This triggers the browser to pop up a window to collect the credentials; the request responds with a hashed value of the Windows credentials, which the server can then choose to authenticate.

To implement Windows authentication, you configure the appropriate Web site or virtual directory using IIS. You can then use the `<authentication>` element to mark the Web application or virtual directory with Windows authentication. Listing 33-16 illustrates this process.

LISTING 33-16: Setting authentication to Windows authentication

```
<configuration>
  <system.web>

    <authentication mode="Windows">

  </system.web>
</configuration>
```

You can declare the `<authentication>` *element only at the machine, site, or application level. Any attempt to declare it in a configuration file at the subdirectory or page level results in a parser error message.*

Passport Authentication

ASP.NET relies on the Passport SDK to implement Passport authentication. It is important to note that even though you can apply these settings in ASP.NET, this technology has been deprecated by Microsoft. Passport is a subscription-based authentication mechanism that allows end users to remember a single username/password pair across multiple Web applications that implement Passport authentication.

ASP.NET authenticates users based on the credentials presented by users. The Passport service sends a token back to authenticate. The token is stored in a site-specific cookie after it has been authenticated with `login.passport.com`. Using the `redirectUrl` attribute of the `<passport>` authentication option, you can control how non-authenticated Passport users are directed, as in the following example:

```
<passport redirectUrl="/Passport/SignIn.aspx" />
```

Forms Authentication

Forms authentication is the widely used authentication mechanism. To configure forms authentication you use the `<authentication>` section along with the `<forms>` subsection. Listing 33-17 shows the structure of an `<authentication>` section that deals with forms authentication in the configuration file.

LISTING 33-17: The <authentication> section working with forms authentication

```
<configuration>
   <system.web>

      <authentication mode="Forms">
         <forms
            name=".ASPXAUTH" [String]
            loginUrl="login.aspx" [String]
            protection="All" [All|None|Encryption|Validation]
            timeout="30" [in Minutes][number]
            path="/" [String]
            requireSSL="false" [true|false]
            slidingExpiration="true" [true|false]
            cookieless="UseDeviceProfile"
               [UseUri|UseCookies|AutoDetect|UseDeviceProfile]
            defaultUrl="default.aspx" [String]
            enableCrossAppRedirects="false" [true|false]
            ticketCompatibilityMode="Framework20"
               [Framework20|Framework40]
            domain="" [String]>
            <credentials passwordFormat="SHA1" [Clear|SHA1|MD5]>
              <user name="" [String, Required, CollectionKey]
               password="" [String, Required] />
            </credentials>
         </forms>
      </authentication>

   </system.web>
</configuration>
```

Each attribute is shown in detail in the following list:

- `name`: Specifies the name of the HTTP authentication ticket. The default value is `.ASPXAUTH`.
- `loginUrl`: Specifies the URL to which the request is redirected if the current request doesn't have a valid authentication ticket.
- `protection`: Specifies the method used to protect cookie data. Valid values are `All`, `None`, `Encryption`, and `Validation`.
  - `Encryption`: Specifies that content of the cookie is encrypted using `TripleDES` or `DES` cryptography algorithms in the configuration file. However, the data validation is not done on the cookie.
  - `Validation`: Specifies that content of the cookie is not encrypted, but validates that the cookie data has not been altered in transit.
  - `All`: Specifies that content of the cookie is protected using both data validation and encryption. The configured data validation algorithm is used based on the `<machineKey>` element, and Triple DES is used for encryption. The default value is `All`, and it indicates the highest protection available.
  - `None`: Specifies no protection mechanism is applied on the cookie. Web applications that do not store any sensitive information and potentially use cookies for personalization can look at this option. When `None` is specified, both encryption and validation are disabled.

- `timeout`: Specifies cookie expiration time in terms of minutes. The `timeout` attribute is a sliding value, which expires *n* minutes from the time the last request was received. The default value is 30 minutes.
- `path`: Specifies the path to use for the issued cookie. The default value is / to avoid difficulties with mismatched case in paths because browsers are strictly case-sensitive when returning cookies.
- `requireSSL`: Specifies whether Forms authentication should happen in a secure HTTPS connection.
- `slidingExpiration`: Specifies whether valid cookies should be updated periodically when used. When this option is set to `False`, a ticket is good for only the duration of the period for which it is issued, and a user must re-authenticate even during an active session.
- `cookieless`: Specifies whether cookieless authentication is supported. Supported values are `UseCookies`, `UseUri`, `Auto`, and `UseDeviceProfile`. The default value is `UseDeviceProfile`.
- `defaultUrl`: Specifies the default URL used by the login control to control redirection after authentication.
- `enableCrossAppRedirects`: When set to `true`, this allows for redirection to URLs that are not in the current application.
- `ticketCompatibilityMode`: By default, the `Framework20` setting uses local time for the ticket expiration date, while setting it to `Framework40` will use UTC.
- `domain`: Specifies the domain name string to be attached in the authentication cookie. This attribute is particularly useful when the same authentication cookie is shared among multiple sites across the domain.

Having the `loginUrl` be an SSL URL (`https://`) is strongly recommended to keep secure credentials secure from prying eyes.

Anonymous Identity

Many application types require the capability to work with anonymous users, although this is especially true for e-commerce Web applications. In these cases, your site must support *both* anonymous and authenticated users. When anonymous users are browsing the site and adding items to a shopping cart, the Web application needs a way to uniquely identify these users. For example, if you look at busy e-commerce Web sites such as `Amazon.com` or `BN.com`, they do not have a concept called anonymous users. Rather these sites assign a unique identity to each user.

In ASP.NET 1.0 and 1.1, no out-of-the box feature existed to enable a developer to achieve this identification of users. Most developers used `SessionID` to identify users uniquely. They experienced a few pitfalls inherent in this method. Since the introduction of ASP.NET 2.0, ASP.NET has had anonymous identity support using the `<anonymousIdentification>` section in the configuration file. Listing 33-18 shows the `<anonymousIdentification>` configuration section settings.

LISTING 33-18: Working with anonymous identification in the configuration file

```
<configuration>
  <system.web>

    <anonymousIdentification
                enabled="false" [true|false]
                cookieName=".ASPXANONYMOUS" [String]
                cookieTimeout="100000" [in Minutes][number]
                cookiePath="/" [String]
                cookieRequireSSL="false" [true|false]
```

continues

LISTING 33-18 *(continued)*

```
                    cookieSlidingExpiration = "true" [true|false]
                    cookieProtection = "Validation"
                       [None|Validation|Encryption|All]
                    cookieless="UseCookies"
                       [UseUri|UseCookies|AutoDetect|UseDeviceProfile]
                    domain="" [String] />

    </system.web>
  </configuration>
```

The `enabled` attribute within the `<anonymousIdentification>` section specifies whether the anonymous access capabilities of ASP.NET are enabled. The other attributes are comparable to those in the `<authentication>` section from Listing 33-17. When you are working with anonymous identification, the possibility exists that the end user will have cookies disabled in their environments. When cookies are not enabled by the end user, the identity of the user is then stored in the URL string within the end user's browser.

Authorization

The authorization process verifies whether a user has the privilege to access the resource he is trying to request. ASP.NET supports both file and URL authorization. The authorization process dictated by an application can be controlled by using the `<authorization>` section within the configuration file. The `<authorization>` section, as presented in Listing 33-19, can contain subsections that either allow or deny permission to a user, a group of users contained within a specific role in the system, or a request that is coming to the server in a particular fashion (such as an HTTP GET request). Optionally, you can also use the `<location>` section to grant special authorization permission to only a particular folder or file within the application.

LISTING 33-19: Authorization capabilities from the configuration file

```
 <authorization>
   <allow users="" roles="" verbs="" />
   <deny users="" roles="" verbs="" />
</authorization>
```

URL Authorization

The URL authorization is a service provided by `URLAuthorizationModule` (inherited from `HttpModule`) to control the access to resources such as `.aspx` files. The URL authorization is very useful if you want to allow or deny certain parts of your ASP.NET application to certain people or roles.

For example, you might want to restrict the administration part of your ASP.NET application only to administrators and deny access to others. You can achieve this task very easily with URL authorization. URL Authorization can be configurable based on the user, the role, or HTTP verbs such as HTTP GET request or HTTP POST request.

You can configure URL authorization in the `web.config` file with `<allow>` and `<deny>` attributes. For example, the code in Listing 33-20 shows how you can allow the user `Bubbles` and deny the groups `Sales` and `Marketing` access to the application.

Available for download on Wrox.com

LISTING 33-20: Allowing and denying entities from the <authorization> section

```
<system.web>
   <authorization>
       <allow users="Bubbles" />
```

```
        <deny roles="Sales, Marketing" />
    </authorization>
</system.web>
```

The <allow> and <deny> elements support users, roles, and verbs values. As you can see from the previous code example, you can add multiple users and groups by separating them with commas.

Two special characters, an asterisk (*) and a question mark (?), are supported by URLAuthorizationModule. The asterisk symbol represents all users (anonymous and registered) and the question mark represents only anonymous users. The following code example in Listing 33-21 denies access to all anonymous users and grants access to anyone contained within the Admin role.

LISTING 33-21: Denying anonymous users

Available for download on Wrox.com

```
<system.web>
    <authorization>
        <allow roles="Admin" />
        <deny users="?" />
    </authorization>
</system.web>
```

You can also grant or deny users or groups access to certain HTTP methods. In the example in Listing 33-22, access to the HTTP GET method is denied to the users contained within the Admin role, whereas access to the HTTP POST method is denied to all users.

LISTING 33-22: Denying users and roles by verb

Available for download on Wrox.com

```
<system.web>
    <authorization>
        <deny verbs="GET" roles="Admin" />
        <deny verbs="POST" users="*" />
    </authorization>
</system.web>
```

File Authorization

Constructing the authorization section within the configuration file so that what is specified can be applied to a specific file or directory using the <location> element is possible. For example, suppose you have a root directory called Home within your application and nested within that root directory you have a subdirectory called Documents. Suppose you want to allow access to the Documents subdirectory only to those users contained within the Admin role. Listing 33-23 illustrates this scenario.

LISTING 33-23: Granting access to the Documents subdirectory for the Admin role

Available for download on Wrox.com

```
<configuration>
   <location path="Documents">
      <system.web>
         <authorization>
            <allow roles="Admin" />
            <deny users="*" />
         </authorization>
      </system.web>
</location>
</configuration>
```

The ASP.NET application does not verify the path specified in the path attribute. If the given path is invalid, ASP.NET does not apply the security setting.

You can also set the security for a single file as presented in Listing 33-24.

LISTING 33-24: Granting access to a specific file for the Admin role

Available for download on Wrox.com

```
<configuration>
   <location path="Documents/Default.aspx">
      <system.web>
         <authorization>
            <allow roles="Admin" />
            <deny users="*" />
         </authorization>
      </system.web>
   </location>
</configuration>
```

Locking-Down Configuration Settings

ASP.NET's configuration system is quite flexible in terms of applying configuration information to a specific application or folder. Even though the configuration system is flexible, in some cases you may want to limit the configuration options that a particular application on the server can control. For example, you could decide to change the way in which the ASP.NET session information is stored. This lock-down process can be achieved using the `<location>` attributes `allowOverride` and `allowDefinition`, as well as the `path` attribute.

Listing 33-25 illustrates this approach. A `<location>` section in this `machine.config` file identifies the path `"Default Web Site/ExampleApplication"` and allows any application to override the `<trace>` setting through the use of the `allowOverride` attribute.

LISTING 33-25: Allowing a <trace> section to be overridden in a lower configuration file

Available for download on Wrox.com

```
<configuration>
    <location path="Default Web Site/ExampleApplication" allowOverride="true">
        <trace enabled="false"/>
    </location>
</configuration>
```

The trace attribute can be overridden because the `allowOverride` attribute is set to `true`. You are able to override the tracing setting in the `ExampleApplication`'s `web.config` file and enable the local `<trace>` element, thereby overriding the settings presented in Listing 33-25.

However, if you had written the attribute as `allowOverride = "false"` in the `<location>` section of the `machine.config` file, the `web.config` file for `ExampleApplication` is unable to override that specific setting.

ASP.NET Page Configuration

When an ASP.NET application has been deployed, the `<pages>` section of the configuration file enables you to control some of the default behaviors for each and every ASP.NET page. These behaviors include options such as whether you should buffer the output before sending it or whether session state should be enabled for the entire application. Listing 33-26 shows an example of using the `<pages>` section.

LISTING 33-26: Configuring the <pages> section

Available for download on Wrox.com

```
<configuration>
  <system.web>

    <pages buffer="true" [true|false]
     enableSessionState="true" [false|ReadOnly|false]
```

```
        enableViewState="true" [true|false]
        enableViewStateMac="false" [true|false]
        autoEventWireup="true" [true|false]
        smartNavigation="false" [true|false]
        maintainScrollPositionOnPostBack="false" [true|false]
        masterPageFile="" [String]
        theme="" [String]
        styleSheetTheme="" [String]
        maxPageStateFieldLength="-1" [number]
        pageBaseType="System.Web.UI.Page" [String]
        userControlBaseType="System.Web.UI.UserControl" [String]
        pageParserFilterType="" [String]
        compilationMode="Always" [Auto|Never|Always]
        viewStateEncyptionMode="Auto" [Auto|Always|Never]
        asyncTimeout="45" [in Seconds][number]
        clientIDMode="AutoID" [Inherit|AutoID|Predictable|Static]
        controlRenderingCompatibilityVersion="4.0" [Version]
        validateRequest="true" [true|false] >
           <namespaces
              autoImportVBNamespace="true" [true|false] >
             <add namespace="" [String, Required, Collection Key] />
           </namespaces>
           <controls />
           <tagMapping />
      </pages>

   </system.web>
</configuration>
```

The following list gives you some of the ASP.NET page configuration information elements in detail:

- `buffer`: Specifies whether the requests must be buffered on the server before they are sent to the client.
- `enableSessionState`: Specifies whether the session state for the current ASP.NET application should be enabled. The possible values are `true`, `false`, or `readonly`. The `readonly` value means that the application can read the session values but cannot modify them.
- `enableViewState`: Specifies whether the ViewState is enabled for all the controls. If the application does not use ViewState, you can set the `value` to `false` in the application's `web.config` file.
- `autoEventWireup`: Specifies whether ASP.NET can automatically wire-up common page events such as Load or Error.
- `smartNavigation`: Smart navigation is a feature that takes advantage of IE as a client's browser to prevent the redrawing that occurs when a page is posted back to itself. Using smart navigation, the request is sent through an `IFRAME` on the client, and IE redraws only the sections of the page that have changed. By default, this option is set to `false`. When it is enabled, it is available only to Internet Explorer browsers; all other browsers get the standard behavior.
- `maintainScrollPositionOnPostback`: Specifies whether or not to return the user to the exact same position on the page after the postback occurs. If set to `False` (the default), the user is returned to the top of the page.
- `masterPageFile`: Identifies the master page for the current ASP.NET application. If you want to apply the master page template to only a specific subset of pages (such as pages contained within a specific folder of your application), you can use the `<location>` element within the `web.config` file:

```
<configuration>
        <location path="ExampleApplicationAdmin">
                <system.web>
                        <pages masterPageFile=
                         "~/ExampleApplicationAdminMasterPage.master" />
                </system.web>
        </location>
</configuration>
```

- `theme`: Specifies the name of the theme to use for the page. Themes are covered in Chapter 6.
- `styleSheetTheme`: Defines the theme to use after control declaration.
- `maxPageStateFieldLength`: If set to a positive number, ASP.NET will separate out the ViewState into chucks that are smaller than the defined size. The default value is `-1`, meaning all the ViewState comes down in one piece.
- `pageBaseType`: Specifies the base class for all the ASP.NET pages in the current ASP.NET application. By default, this option is set to `System.Web.UI.Page`. However, if you want all ASP.NET pages to inherit from some other base class, you can change the default via this setting.
- `userControlBaseType`: Specifies the base class for all the ASP.NET user controls in the current ASP.NET application. The default is `System.Web.UI.UserControl`. You can override the default option using this element.
- `validateRequest`: Specifies whether ASP.NET should validate all the incoming requests that are potentially dangerous, such as the cross-site script attack and the script injection attack. This feature provides out-of-the-box protection against cross-site scripting and script injection attacks by automatically checking all parameters in the request, ensuring that their content does not include HTML elements. For more information about this setting, visit `www.asp.net/faq/RequestValidation.aspx`.
- `namespaces`: Optionally, you can import a collection of assemblies that can be included in the precompilation process.
- `compilationMode`: Specifies how ASP.NET should compile the current Web application. Supported values are `Never`, `Always`, and `Auto`. A setting of `compilationMode = "Never"` means that the pages should never be compiled. A part error occurs if the page has constructs that require compilation. Setting `compilationMode = "Always"` means that the pages are always compiled. When you set `compilationMode = "Auto"`, ASP.NET does not compile the pages if that is possible.
- `viewStateEncryptionMode`: Specifies whether or not to encrypt the ViewState.
- `asyncTimeout`: Specifies the number of seconds that the page should wait for an asynchronous handler to finish during an asynchronous operation.
- `clientIDMode`: Specifies the algorithm that should be used to create the `ClientID` values for server controls on your page. The default setting is `AutoID` while the default value for the server controls is `Inherit`.
- `controlRenderingCompatibilityVersion`: Specifies the version of ASP.NET to use when controls render their HTML.

Include Files

Unlike ASP.NET 1.0 and 1.1, ASP.NET 2.0 to 4 support *include* files in both the `machine.config` and the `web.config` files. When configuration content is to be included in multiple places or inside the location elements, an include file is an excellent way to encapsulate the content.

Any section in a configuration file can include content from a different file using the `configSource` attribute in the `<pages>` section. The value of the attribute indicates a virtual relative filename to the include file. Listing 33-27 is an example of such a directive.

LISTING 33-27: Adding additional content to the web.config file

```
<configuration>
    <system.web>
        <pages configSource="SystemWeb.config" />
    </system.web>
</configuration>
```

The configuration include files can contain information that applies to a single section, and a single include file cannot contain more than one configuration section or a portion of a section. If the `configSource` attribute is present, the section element in the source file should not contain any other attribute or any child element.

Nevertheless, the include file is not a full configuration file. It should contain only the include section, as presented in Listing 33-28.

LISTING 33-28: The SystemWeb.config file

```
<pages authentication mode="Forms" />
```

The `configSource` attribute cannot be nested. An include file cannot nest another file inside it using the `configSource` attribute.

When an ASP.NET configuration file is changed, the application is restarted at runtime. When an external include file is used within the configuration file, the configuration reload happens without restarting the application.

Configuring ASP.NET Runtime Settings

The general configuration settings are those that specify how long a given ASP.NET resource, such as a page, is allowed to execute before being considered timed-out. The other settings specify the maximum size of a request (in kilobytes) or whether to use fully qualified URLs in redirects. To specify these settings you use the `<httpRuntime>` section within a configuration file. The `<httpRuntime>` element is applied at the ASP.NET application at the folder level. Listing 33-29 shows the default values used in the `<httpRuntime>` section.

Available for download on Wrox.com

LISTING 33-29: The <httpRuntime> section

```
<configuration>
  <system.web>

    <httpRuntime
      useFullyQualifiedRedirectUrl="false"
      enable="true"
      executionTimeout="90"
      maxRequestLength="4096"
      requestLengthDiskThreshold="512"
      appRequestQueueLimit="5000"
      minFreeThreads="8"
      minLocalRequestFreeThreads="4"
      enableKernelOutputCache="true" />

  </system.web>
</configuration>
```

Enabling and Disabling ASP.NET Applications

The `enable` attribute specifies whether the current ASP.NET application is enabled. When set to `false`, the current ASP.NET application is disabled, and all the clients trying to connect to this site receive the HTTP 404 — File Not Found exception. This value should be set only at the machine or application level. If you set this value in any other level (such as subfolder level), it is ignored. This great feature enables the administrators to bring down the application for whatever reason without starting or stopping IIS. The default value is `true`.

Outside of this setting, you can also take applications offline quickly by simply placing an `App_Offline.htm` file in the root of your application. This `.htm` file does not need to actually contain anything (it will not make any difference). Just having the file in the root directory causes the application domain to come down, and all requests to the application get a Page Not Found error.

Fully Qualified Redirect URLs

The `useFullyQualifiedRedirectUrl` attribute specifies whether the client-side redirects should include the fully qualified URL. When you are programming against the mobile devices, some devices require specifying fully qualified URLs. The default value is `false`.

Request Time-Out

The `executionTimeout` setting specifies the timeout option for an ASP.NET request time-out. The value of this attribute is the amount of time in seconds during which a resource can execute before ASP.NET times out the request. The default setting is 110 seconds. If you have a particular ASP.NET page or Web service that takes longer than 110 seconds to execute, you can extend the time limit in the configuration.

Maximum Request Length

The `maxRequestLength` attribute specifies the maximum file-size upload accepted by ASP.NET runtime. For example, if the ASP.NET application is required to process huge files, then this setting is the one you will want to change. The default is 4096. This number represents kilobytes (KB or around 4MB).

Web applications are prone to attacks these days. The attacks range from a script injection attack to a denial of service (DoS) attack. The DoS is a typical attack that bombards the Web server with requests for large files. This huge number of requests ultimately brings down the Web server. The `maxRequestLength` attribute could save you from a DoS attack by setting a restriction on the size of requests.

Buffer Uploads

In ASP.NET 1.0 or 1.1, when an HTTP post is made (either a normal ASP.NET form post, file upload, or an XMLHTTP client-side post), the entire content is buffered in memory. This works out fine for smaller posts. However, when memory-based recycling is enabled, a large post can cause the ASP.NET worker process to recycle before the upload is completed. To avoid the unnecessary worker process recycling, ASP.NET 4 includes a setting called `requestLengthDiskThreshold`. This setting enables an administrator to configure the file upload buffering behavior without affecting the programming model. Administrators can configure a threshold below which requests will be buffered into memory. After a request exceeds the limit, it is transparently buffered on disk and consumed from there by whatever mechanism is used to consume the data. The valid values for this setting are numbers between `1` and `Int32.MaxSize` in KB.

When file buffering is enabled, the files are uploaded to the codegen folder. The default path for the codegen folder is the following:

```
[WinNT\Windows]\Microsoft.NET\Framework\[version]\Temporary ASP.NET Files\
[ApplicationName]
```

The files are buffered using a random name in a subfolder within the codegen folder called Uploads. The location of the codegen folder can be configured on a per-application basis using the `tempDirectory` attribute of the `<compilation>` section.

This is not a change in ASP.NET; rather it is an internal change. When an ASP.NET 1.0 or 1.1 application is migrated to the .NET Framework 2.0, 3.5, or 4, the ASP.NET application automatically takes advantage of this feature.

Thread Management

ASP.NET runtime uses free threads available in its thread pool to fulfill requests. The `minFreeThreads` attribute indicates the number of threads that ASP.NET guarantees is available within the thread pool. The default number of threads is eight. For complex applications that require additional threads to complete processing, this attribute simply ensures that the threads are available and that the application will not be blocked while waiting for a free thread to schedule more work. The `minLocalRequestFreeThreads` attribute controls the number of free threads dedicated for local request processing; the default is four.

Application Queue Length

The `appRequestQueueLimit` attribute specifies the maximum number of requests that ASP.NET queues for the current ASP.NET application. ASP.NET queues requests when it does not have enough free threads to process them. The `minFreeThreads` attribute specifies the number of free threads the ASP.NET application should maintain, and this setting affects the number of items stored in the queue.

When the number of requests queued exceeds the limit set in the `appRequestQueueLimit` *setting, all the incoming requests are rejected and an* `HTTP 503 - Server Too Busy` *error is thrown back to the browser.*

Output Caching

The `enableKernelOutputCache` specifies whether the output caching is enabled at the IIS kernel level (`Http.sys`). At present, this setting applies only to Web servers IIS6 and higher.

Configuring the ASP.NET Worker Process

When a request for an ASP.NET page is received by IIS, it passes the request to an unmanaged DLL called `aspnet_isapi.dll`. The `aspnet_isapi.dll` further passes the request to a separate worker process, `aspnet_wp.exe` if you are working with IIS5, which runs all the ASP.NET applications. With IIS6 and higher, however, all the ASP.NET applications are run by the `w3wp.exe` process. The ASP.NET worker process can be configured using the `<processModel>` section in the `machine.config` file.

All the configuration sections talked about so far are read by managed code. On the other hand, the `<processModel>` *section is read by the* `aspnet_isapi.dll` *unmanaged DLL. Because the configuration information is read by an unmanaged DLL, the changed process model information is applied to all ASP.NET applications only after an IIS restart.*

The code example in Listing 33-30 shows the default format for the `<processModel>` section.

LISTING 33-30: The structure of the <processModel> element

```
<processModel
    enable="true|false"
    timeout="hrs:mins:secs|Infinite"
    idleTimeout="hrs:mins:secs|Infinite"
    shutdownTimeout="hrs:mins:secs|Infinite"
    requestLimit="num|Infinite"
    requestQueueLimit="num|Infinite"
    restartQueueLimit="num|Infinite"
```

continues

LISTING 33-30 *(continued)*

```
        memoryLimit="percent"
        cpuMask="num"
        webGarden="true|false"
        userName="username"
        password="password"
        logLevel="All|None|Errors"
        clientConnectedCheck="hrs:mins:secs|Infinite"
        responseDeadlockInterval="hrs:mins:secs|Infinite"
        responseRestartDeadlockInterval="hrs:mins:secs|Infinite"
        comAuthenticationLevel="Default|None|Connect|Call|
        Pkt|PktIntegrity|PktPrivacy"
        comImpersonationLevel="Default|Anonymous|Identify|
        Impersonate|Delegate"
        maxWorkerThreads="num"
        maxIoThreads="num"
        autoConfig="true|false"
        minWorkerThreads="num"
        minIoThreads="num"
        serverErrorMessageFile=""
        pingFrequency="hrs:mins:secs|Infinite"
        pingTimeout="hrs:mins:secs|Infinite"
        maxAppDomains="number"
    />
```

The following section looks at each of these attributes in more detail:

- `enable`: Specifies whether the process model is enabled. When set to `false`, the ASP.NET applications run under IIS's process model.

When ASP.NET is running under IIS6 or higher in native mode, the IIS6 or higher process model is used and most of the `<processModel>` *section within the configuration file is simply ignored. The* `autoConfig` *and* `requestQueueLimit` *attributes are still applied in this case.*

- `timeout`: Specifies how long the worker process lives before a new worker process is created to replace the current worker process. This value can be extremely useful if a scenario exists where the application's performance starts to degrade slightly after running for several weeks, as in the case of a memory leak. Rather than your having to manually start and stop the process, ASP.NET can restart automatically. The default value is `Infinite`.
- `idleTimeout`: Specifies how long the worker process should wait before it is shut down. You can shut down the ASP.NET worker process automatically using the `idleTimeout` option. The default value is `Infinite`. You can also set this value to a time using the format, HH:MM:SS:.
- `shutdownTimeout`: Specifies how long the worker process is given to shut itself down gracefully before ASP.NET calls the `Kill` command on the process. `Kill` is a low-level command that forcefully removes the process. The default value is 5 seconds.
- `requestLimit`: Specifies when the ASP.NET worker process should be recycled after a certain number of requests are served. The default value is `Infinite`.
- `requestQueueLimit`: Instructs ASP.NET to recycle the worker process if the limit for queued requests is exceeded. The default setting is 5000.
- `memoryLimit`: Specifies how much physical memory the worker process is allowed to consume before it is considered to be misbehaving or leaking memory. The default value is 60 percent of available physical memory.

- `username` **and** `password`: By default, all ASP.NET applications are executed using the ASPNET identity. If you want an ASP.NET application to run with a different account, you can provide the username and the password pair using these attributes.
- `logLevel`: Specifies how the ASP.NET worker process logs events. The default setting is to log errors only. However, you can also disable logging by specifying `None` or you can log everything using `All`. All the log items are written to the Windows Application Event Log.
- `clientConnectedCheck`: The `clientConnectedCheck` setting enables you to check whether the client is still connected at timed intervals before performing work. The default setting is 5 seconds.
- `responseDeadlockInterval`: Specifies how frequently the deadlock check should occur. A deadlock is considered to exist when requests are queued and no responses have been sent during this interval. After a deadlock, the process is restarted. The default value is 3 minutes.
- `responseRestartDeadlockInterval`: Specifies, when a deadlock is detected by the runtime, how long the runtime should wait before restarting the process. The default value is 9 minutes.
- `comAuthenticationLevel`: Controls the level of authentication for DCOM security. The default is set to `Connect`. Other values are `Default`, `None`, `Call`, `Pkt`, `PktIntegrity`, and `PktPrivacy`.
- `comImpersonationLevel`: Controls the authentication level for COM security. The default is set to `Impersonate`. Other values are `Default`, `Anonymous`, `Identify`, and `Delegate`.
- `webGarden`: Specifies whether Web Garden mode is enabled. The default setting is `false`. A Web Garden lets you host multiple ASP.NET worker processes on a single server, thus providing the application with better hardware scalability. Web Garden mode is supported only on multiprocessor servers.
- `cpuMask`: Specifies which processors should be affinities to ASP.NET worker processes when `webGarden = "true"`. The `cpuMask` is a hexadecimal value. The default value is all processors, shown as `0xFFFFFFFF`.
- `maxWorkerThreads`: Specifies the maximum number of threads that exist within the ASP.NET worker process thread pool. The default is 20.
- `maxIoThreads`: Specifies the maximum number of I/O threads that exist within the ASP.NET worker process. The default is 20.
- `autoConfig`: Specifies whether to configure the ASP.NET application's performance settings.
- `minWorkerThreads`: Specifies the minimum number of threads that exist within the ASP.NET worker process thread pool. The default is `1`.
- `minIoThreads`: Specifies the minimum number of I/O threads that exist within the ASP.NET worker process. The default is 1.
- `serverErrorMessageFile`: Specifies the page to use for content for the error message rather than the default "Server Unavailable" message.
- `pingFrequency`: Specifies the time interval at which the ISAPI extension pings the worker process to determine whether it is running.
- `pingTimeout`: Specifies the time interval at which a worker process is restarted after not responding.
- `maxAppDomains`: Sets the absolute maximum number of application domains for one process.

Running Multiple Web Sites with Multiple Versions of Framework

In the same context as the ASP.NET worker process, multiple Web sites within the given Web server can host multiple Web sites, and each of these sites can be bound to a particular version of a .NET Framework. This is typically done using the `aspnet_regiis.exe` utility. The `aspnet_regiis.exe` utility is shipped with each version of the framework.

This utility has multiple switches. Using the `-s` switch allows you to install the current version of the .NET Framework runtime on a given Web site. Listing 33-31 shows how to install .NET Framework version 1.1 on the ExampleApplication Web site.

LISTING 33-31: Installing .NET Framework version 1.1 on the ExampleApplication Web site

```
C:\WINDOWS\Microsoft.NET\Framework\v1.1.4322>
   aspnet_regiis -s W3SVC/1ROOT/ExampleApplication
```

Storing Application-Specific Settings

Every Web application must store some application-specific information for its runtime use. The `<appSettings>` section of the `web.config` file provides a way to define custom application settings for an ASP.NET application. The section can have multiple <add> sub-elements. Its syntax is as follows:

```
<appSettings>
    <add key="[key]" value="[value]"/>
</appSettings>
```

The <add> sub-element supports two attributes:

- `key`: Specifies the key value in an `appSettings` hash table
- `value`: Specifies the value in an `appSettings` hash table

Listing 33-32 shows how to store an application-specific connection string. The `key` value is set to `ApplicationInstanceID`, and the `value` is set to the ASP.NET application instance and the name of the server on which the application is running.

LISTING 33-32: Application instance information

```
<appSettings>
    <add key="ApplicationInstanceID" value="Instance1onServerOprta"/>
</appSettings>
```

Programming Configuration Files

In ASP.NET 1.0 and 1.1 versions of the Framework provided APIs that enabled you only to read information from the configuration file. You had no way to write information into the configuration file because no out-of-the-box support was available. However, some advanced developers wrote their own APIs to write the information back to the configuration files. Because the `web.config` file is an XML file, developers were able to open configuration file using the `XmlDocument` object, modify the settings, and write it back to the disk. Even though this approach worked fine, the way to access the configuration settings were not strongly typed. Therefore, validating the values was always a challenge.

However, ASP.NET today includes APIs (ASP.NET Management Objects) to manipulate the configuration information settings in `machine.config` and `web.config` files. ASP.NET Management Objects provide a strongly typed programming model that addresses targeted administrative aspects of a .NET Web Application Server. They also govern the creation and maintenance of the ASP.NET Web configuration. Using the ASP.NET Management Objects, you can manipulate the configuration information stored in the configuration files in the local or remote computer. These can be used to script any common administrative tasks or the writing of installation scripts.

All the ASP.NET Management Objects are stored in the `System.Configuration` and `System.Web.Configuration` namespaces. You can access the configuration using the `WebConfigurationManager` class. The `System.Configuration.Configuration` class represents a merged view of the configuration settings from the `machine.config` and hierarchical `web.config` files. The `System.Configuration` and `System.Web.Configuration` namespaces have multiple classes that enable you to access nearly all the settings available in the configuration file. The main difference between `System.Configuration` and `System.Web.Configuration` namespaces is that the `System.Configuration` namespace contains all the classes that apply to all the .NET applications. On the other hand, the `System.Web.Configuration` namespace contains the classes that are applicable only to ASP.NET Web applications. Table 33-1 shows the important classes in `System.Configuration` and their uses.

TABLE 33-1

CLASS NAME	PURPOSE
`Configuration`	Enables you to manipulate the configuration stored in the local computer or a remote one.
`ConfigurationElementCollection`	Enables you to enumerate the child elements stored inside the configuration file.
`AppSettingsSection`	Enables you to manipulate the `<appSettings>` section of the configuration file.
`ConnectionStringsSettings`	Enables you to manipulate the `<connectionStrings>` section of the configuration file.
`ProtectedConfigurationSection`	Enables you to manipulate the `<protectedConfiguration>` section of the configuration file.
`ProtectedDataSection`	Enables you to manipulate the `<protectedData>` section of the configuration file.

Table 33-2 shows some of the classes from the `System.Web.Configuration` and their uses.

TABLE 33-2

CLASS NAME	PURPOSE
`AuthenticationSection`	Enables you to manipulate the `<authentication>` section of the configuration file.
`AuthorizationSection`	Enables you to manipulate the `<authorization>` section of the configuration file.
`CompilationSection`	Enables you to manipulate the `<compilation>` section of the configuration file.
`CustomErrorsSection`	Enables you to manipulate the `<customErrors>` section of the configuration file.
`FormsAuthenticationConfiguration`	Enables you to manipulate the `<forms>` section of the configuration file.
`GlobalizationSection`	Enables you to manipulate the `<globalization>` section of the configuration file.
`HttpHandlersSection`	Enables you to manipulate the `<httpHandlers>` section of the configuration file.
`HttpModulesSection`	Enables you to manipulate the `<httpModules>` section of the configuration file.
`HttpRuntimeSection`	Enables you to manipulate the `<httpRuntime>` section of the configuration file.
`MachineKeySection`	Enables you to manipulate the `<machineKey>` section of the configuration file.
`MembershipSection`	Enables you to manipulate the `<membership>` section of the configuration file.
`PagesSection`	Enables you to manipulate the `<pages>` section of the configuration file.
`ProcessModelSection`	Enables you to manipulate the `<processModel>` section of the configuration file.
`WebPartsSection`	Enables you to manipulate the `<webParts>` section of the configuration file.

All the configuration classes are implemented based on simple object-oriented based architecture that has an entity class that holds all the data and a collection class that has methods to add, remove, enumerate, and so on. Start your configuration file programming with a simple connection string enumeration, as shown in the following section.

Enumerating Connection Strings

In a Web application, you can store multiple connection strings. Some of them are used by the system and the others may be application-specific. You can write a very simple ASP.NET application that enumerates all the connection strings stored in the `web.config` file, as shown in Listing 33-33.

LISTING 33-33: The web.config file

Available for download on Wrox.com

```
<?xml version="1.0" ?>
<configuration>

    <appSettings>
        <add key="symbolServer" value="192.168.1.1" />
    </appSettings>
    <connectionStrings>
        <add name="ExampleApplication"
        connectionString="server=ExampleApplicationServer;
        database=ExampleApplicationDB;uid=WebUser;pwd=P@$$worD9"
        providerName="System.Data.SqlClient"
        />
    </connectionStrings>
    <system.web>
        <compilation debug="false" targetFramework="4.0" />
        <authentication mode="None" />
    </system.web>

</configuration>
```

As shown in Listing 33-33, one application setting points to the symbol server, and one connection string is stored in the `web.config` file. Use the `ConnectionStrings` collection of the `System.Web.Configuration.WebConfigurationManager` class to read the connection strings, as shown in Listing 33-34.

LISTING 33-34: Enum.aspx

Available for download on Wrox.com

VB

```
Protected Sub Page_Load(ByVal sender As Object, ByVal e As System.EventArgs)
    GridView1.DataSource =
        System.Web.Configuration.WebConfigurationManager.ConnectionStrings
    GridView1.DataBind()
End Sub
```

C#

```
protected void Page_Load(object sender, EventArgs e)
{
    GridView1.DataSource =
      System.Web.Configuration.WebConfigurationManager.ConnectionStrings;
    GridView1.DataBind();
}
```

As shown in Listing 33-34, you've bound the `ConnectionStrings` property collection of the `WebConfigurationManager` class into the GridView control. The `WebConfigurationManager` class returns an instance of the `Configuration` class and the `ConnectionStrings` property is a static (shared in Visual Basic) property. Therefore, you are just binding the property collection into the GridView control. Figure 33-5 shows the list of connection strings stored in the ASP.NET application.

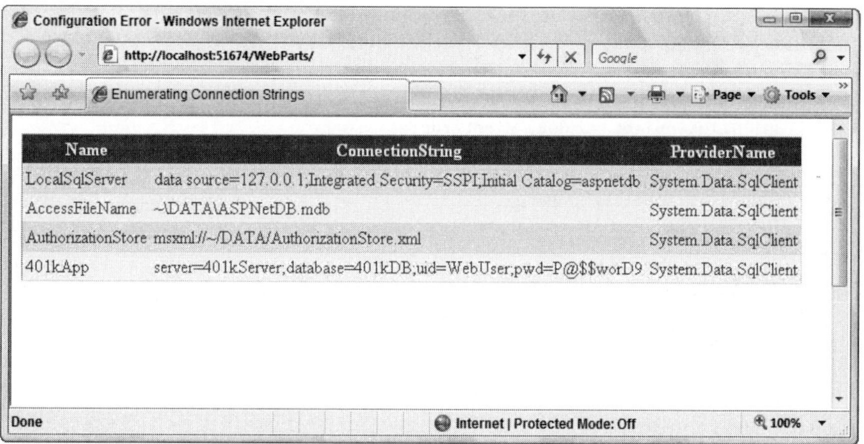

FIGURE 33-5

Adding a connection string at runtime is also a very easy task. If you do it as shown in Listing 33-35, you get an instance of the configuration object. Then you create a new `connectionStringSettings` class. You add the new class to the collection and call the update method. Listing 33-35 shows examples of this in both VB and C#.

LISTING 33-35: Adding a connection string

Available for download on Wrox.com

VB

```
Protected Sub Button1_Click(ByVal sender As Object, ByVal e As System.EventArgs)
    ' Get the file path for the current web request
    Dim webPath As String = Request.ApplicationPath

    Try
        ' Get configuration object of the current web request
        Dim config As Configuration =
          System.Web.Configuration.WebConfigurationManager.OpenWebConfiguration (webPath)

        ' Create new connection setting from text boxes
        Dim newConnSetting As New
        ConnectionStringSettings(txtName.Text, txtValue.Text, txtProvider.Text)

        ' Add the connection string to the collection
        config.ConnectionStrings.ConnectionStrings.Add(newConnSetting)

        ' Save the changes
        config.Save()
    Catch cEx As ConfigurationErrorsException
        lblStatus.Text = "Status: " + cEx.ToString()
    Catch ex As System.UnauthorizedAccessException
        ' The ASP.NET process account must have read/write access to the directory
        lblStatus.Text = "Status: " + "The ASP.NET process account must have
        read/write access to the directory"
    Catch eEx As Exception
        lblStatus.Text = "Status: " + eEx.ToString()
    End Try

    ShowConnectionStrings()
```

continues

LISTING 33-35 *(continued)*

```
 End Sub
```

C#

```
protected void Button1_Click(object sender, EventArgs e)
{
    // Get the file path for the current web request
    string webPath = Request.ApplicationPath;

    // Get configuration object of the current web request
    Configuration config =
    System.Web.Configuration.WebConfigurationManager.OpenWebConfiguration(webPath);

    // Create new connection setting from text boxes
    ConnectionStringSettings newConnSetting = new
    ConnectionStringSettings(txtName.Text, txtValue.Text, txtProvider.Text);

    try
    {
        // Add the connection string to the collection
        config.ConnectionStrings.ConnectionStrings.Add(newConnSetting);

        // Save the changes
        config.Save();
    }
    catch (ConfigurationErrorsException cEx)
    {
        lblStatus.Text = "Status: " + cEx.ToString();
    }
    catch (System.UnauthorizedAccessException uEx)
    {
        // The ASP.NET process account must have read/write access to the directory
        lblStatus.Text = "Status: " + "The ASP.NET process account must have" +
           "read/write access to the directory";
    }
    catch (Exception eEx)
    {
        lblStatus.Text = "Status: " + eEx.ToString();
    }

    // Reload the connection strings in the list box
    ShowConnectionStrings();
}
```

Manipulating a machine.config File

The `OpenMachineConfiguration` method of the `System.Configuration.ConfigurationManager` class provides a way to manipulate the `machine.config` file. The `OpenMachineConfiguration` method is a static method.

Listing 33-36 shows a simple example that enumerates all the section groups stored in the `machine.config` file. As shown in this listing, you're getting an instance of the configuration object using the `OpenMachineConfiguration` method. Then you are binding the `SectionGroups` collection with the GridView control.

LISTING 33-36: Configuration groups from machine.config

Available for download on Wrox.com

VB

```
Protected Sub Button2_Click(ByVal sender As Object, ByVal e As System.EventArgs)
    ' List all the SectionGroups in machine.config file
    Dim configSetting As Configuration =
      System.Configuration.ConfigurationManager.OpenMachineConfiguration()
```

```
    GridView1.DataSource = configSetting.SectionGroups
    GridView1.DataBind()
End Sub
```

C#

```
protected void Button2_Click(object sender, EventArgs e)
{
    // List all the SectionGroups in machine.config file
    Configuration configSetting =
      System.Configuration.ConfigurationManager.OpenMachineConfiguration();
    GridView1.DataSource = configSetting.SectionGroups;
    GridView1.DataBind();
}
```

In the same way, you can list all the configuration sections using the `Sections` collections, as shown in Listing 33-37.

LISTING 33-37: Configuration sections from machine.config

Available for download on Wrox.com

VB

```
Protected Sub Button2_Click(ByVal sender As Object, ByVal e As System.EventArgs)
    ' List all the SectionGroups in machine.config file
    Dim configSetting As Configuration = _
      System.Configuration.ConfigurationManager.OpenMachineConfiguration()
    GridView1.DataSource = configSetting.Sections
    GridView1.DataBind()
End Sub
```

C#

```
protected void Button2_Click(object sender, EventArgs e)
{
    // List all the SectionGroups in machine.config file
    Configuration configSetting =
      System.Configuration.ConfigurationManager.OpenMachineConfiguration();
    GridView1.DataSource = configSetting.Sections;
    GridView1.DataBind();
}
```

Manipulating web.config from Remote Servers

The ASP.NET Management Objects also provide a way to read configuration information from remote servers.

For example, if you want to manipulate the Expense Web application's configuration file located on the imaginary `Optra.Microsoft.com` site, you can do so as shown in Listing 33-38.

LISTING 33-38: Manipulating a remote server's web.config file

Available for download on Wrox.com

VB

```
' Connect to the web application Expense on Optra.Microsoft.com server
Dim configSetting As Configuration =
   System.Web.Configuration.WebConfigurationManager.OpenWebConfiguration _
      ("/Expense", "1", "Optra.Microsoft.com")

Dim section As System.Configuration.ConfigurationSection =
   configSetting.GetSection("appSettings")

Dim element As KeyValueConfigurationElement = _
   CType(configSetting.AppSettings.Settings("keySection"),
     KeyValueConfigurationElement)

If Not element Is Nothing Then
   Dim value As String = "New Value"
```

continues

LISTING 33-38 *(continued)*

```
        element.Value = value

        Try
            config.Save()
        Catch ex As Exception
            Response.Write(ex.Message)
        End Try
    End If
```

C#

```
// Connect to the web application Expense on Optra.Microsoft.com server
Configuration configSetting =
    System.Web.Configuration.WebConfigurationManager.OpenWebConfiguration
    ("/Expense", "1", "Optra.Microsoft.com");

ConfigurationSection section = configSetting.GetSection("appSettings");

KeyValueConfigurationElement element =
    configSetting.AppSettings.Settings["keySection"];

if (element != null)
{
    string value = "New Value";
    element.Value = value;

    try
    {
        configSetting.Save();
    }
        catch (Exception ex)
    {
        Response.Write(ex.Message);
    }
}
```

The code in Listing 33-38 demonstrates how to give the machine address in the constructor method to connect to the remote server. Then you change a particular `appSettings` section to a new value and save the changes.

Protecting Configuration Settings

When ASP.NET 1.0 was introduced, all the configuration information was stored in human-readable, clear-text format. However since ASP.NET 1.1 a new way has been available to store the configuration information inside the registry using the Data Protection API (or DPAPI).

For example, Listing 33-39 shows how you can store a process model section's username and password information inside the registry.

LISTING 33-39: Storing the username and password in the registry and then referencing these settings in the machine.config file

```
<processModel
    userName="registry:HKLM\SOFTWARE\ExampleApp\Identity\ASPNET_SETREG,userName"
    password="registry:HKLM\SOFTWARE\ExampleApp\Identity\ASPNET_SETREG,password"
/>
```

ASP.NET 1.0 also acquired this functionality as a fix. Visit the following URL for more information: `http://support.microsoft.com/kb/329290`.

ASP.NET 4 includes a system for protecting sensitive data stored in the configuration system. It uses industry-standard XML encryption to encrypt specified sections of configuration that contain any sensitive data.

Developers often feel apprehensive about sticking sensitive items such as connection strings, passwords, and more in the `web.config` file. For this reason, ASP.NET makes possible the storing of these items in a format that is not readable by any human or machine process without intimate knowledge of the encryption techniques and keys used in the encryption process.

One of the most encrypted items in the `web.config` file is the `<connectionStrings>` section. Listing 33-40 shows an example of a `web.config` file with an exposed connection string.

Available for download on Wrox.com

LISTING 33-40: A standard connection string exposed in the web.config file

```
<?xml version="1.0"?>

<configuration>

    <appSettings/>

    <connectionStrings>
      <add name="AdventureWorks"
   connectionString="Server=localhost;Integrated Security=True;Database=AdventureWorks"
        providerName="System.Data.SqlClient" />
    </connectionStrings>

    <system.web>

        <compilation debug="false" />

        <authentication mode="Forms">
           <forms name="Wrox" loginUrl="Login.aspx" path="/">
              <credentials passwordFormat="Clear">
                 <user name="BillEvjen" password="Bubbles" />
              </credentials>
           </forms>
        </authentication>

    </system.web>
</configuration>
```

In this case, you might want to encrypt this connection string to the database. To accomplish this, the install of ASP.NET provides a tool called *aspnet_regiis.exe*. You find this tool at `C:\WINDOWS\Microsoft.NET\Framework\v4.0.21006`. To use this tool to encrypt the `<connectionStrings>` section, open a command prompt and navigate to the specified folder using `cd C:\WINDOWS\Microsoft.NET\Framework\v4.0.21006`. Another option is to just open the Visual Studio 2010 Command Prompt. After you are in one of these environments, you use the syntax presented in Listing 33-41 to encrypt the `<connectionStrings>` section.

LISTING 33-41: Encrypting the <connectionString> section

```
aspnet_regiis-pe "connectionString"-app "/EncryptionExample"
```

Running this bit of script produces the results presented in Figure 33-6.

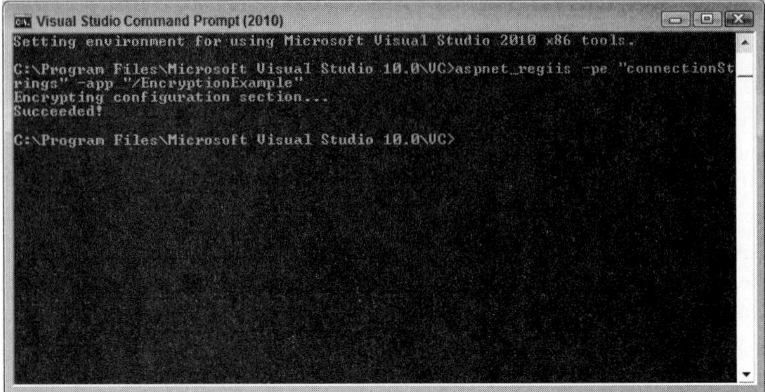

FIGURE 33-6

Looking over the script used in the encryption process, you can see that the `-pe` command specifies the section in the `web.config` file to encrypt, whereas the `-app` command specifies which application to actually work with. If you look back at the `web.config` file and examine the encryption that occurred, you see something similar to the code in Listing 33-42.

LISTING 33-42: The encrypted <connectionStrings> section of the web.config file

```
<?xml version="1.0"?>

<configuration>

    <appSettings/>

    <connectionStrings
     configProtectionProvider="RsaProtectedConfigurationProvider">
        <EncryptedData Type="http://www.w3.org/2001/04/xmlenc#Element"
            xmlns="http://www.w3.org/2001/04/xmlenc#">
            <EncryptionMethod
             Algorithm="http://www.w3.org/2001/04/xmlenc#tripledes-cbc" />
            <KeyInfo xmlns="http://www.w3.org/2000/09/xmldsig#">
                <EncryptedKey xmlns="http://www.w3.org/2001/04/xmlenc#">
                    <EncryptionMethod
                     Algorithm="http://www.w3.org/2001/04/xmlenc#rsa-1_5" />
                    <KeyInfo xmlns="http://www.w3.org/2000/09/xmldsig#">
                        <KeyName>Rsa Key</KeyName>
                    </KeyInfo>
                    <CipherData>
                        <CipherValue>
                         0s99STuGx+CdDXmWaOVc0prBFA65
                         Yub0VxDS7nOSQ79AAYcxKG7Alq1o
                         M2BqZGSmElc7c4w93qgZn0CNN
                         VHGhDLE1OjHPV942HaYhcddK5
                         5XY5j7L3WSEJFj68E2Ng9+EjU
                         o+oAGJVhCAuG8owQBaQ2Bri3+
                         tfUB/Q8LpOW4kP8=
                        </CipherValue>
                    </CipherData>
                </EncryptedKey>
            </KeyInfo>
            <CipherData>
                <CipherValue>
                 03/PtxajkdVD/5TLGddc1/
                 C8cg8RFYl8MiRXh71h4ls=
                </CipherValue>
```

```
            </CipherData>
        </EncryptedData>
    </connectionStrings>

  <system.web>

        <compilation debug="false" />

        <authentication mode="Forms">
           <forms name="Wrox" loginUrl="Login.aspx" path="/">
              <credentials passwordFormat="Clear">
                 <user name="BillEvjen" password="Bubbles" />
              </credentials>
           </forms>
        </authentication>


    </system.web>
</configuration>
```

Now when you work with a connection string in your ASP.NET application, ASP.NET itself automatically decrypts this section to utilize the values stored. Looking at the `web.config` file, you can see a subsection within the `<system.web>` section that exposes a username and password as clear text. This is also something that you might want to encrypt in order to keep it away from prying eyes. Because it is a subsection, you use the script presented in Listing 33-43.

LISTING 33-43: Encrypting the <authentication> section

```
aspnet_regiis-pe "system.web/authentication"-app "/EncryptionExample"
```

This code gives you the partial results presented in Listing 33-44.

LISTING 33-44: The encrypted <authentication> section of the web.config file

```
<authentication configProtectionProvider="RsaProtectedConfigurationProvider">
   <EncryptedData Type="http://www.w3.org/2001/04/xmlenc#Element"
    xmlns="http://www.w3.org/2001/04/xmlenc#">
      <EncryptionMethod
       Algorithm="http://www.w3.org/2001/04/xmlenc#tripledes-cbc" />
         <KeyInfo xmlns="http://www.w3.org/2000/09/xmldsig#">
            <EncryptedKey xmlns="http://www.w3.org/2001/04/xmlenc#">
               <EncryptionMethod
                Algorithm="http://www.w3.org/2001/04/xmlenc#rsa-1_5" />
               <KeyInfo xmlns="http://www.w3.org/2000/09/xmldsig#">
                  <KeyName>Rsa Key</KeyName>
               </KeyInfo>
               <CipherData>
                  <CipherValue>
                   GzTlMc89r3ees9EoMedFQrLo3FI5p3JJ9DMONWe
                   ASIww89UADkihLpmzCUPa3YtiCfKXpodr3Xt3RI
                   4zpveulZs5gIZUoX8aCl48U89dajudJn7eoJqai
                   m6wuXTGI5XrUWTgYdELCcFCloW1c+eGMRBZpNi9
                   cir4xkkh2SsHBDE=
                  </CipherValue>
               </CipherData>
            </EncryptedKey>
         </KeyInfo>
         <CipherData>
            <CipherValue>
             3MpRm+Xs+x5YsndH20lZau8/t+3RuaGv5+nTFoRXaV
             tweKdgrAVeB+PXnTjydq/u4LBXKMKmHzaBtxrqEHRD
             mNZgigLWVtfIRQ6P8cgBwtdIFhFmjm3B4tg/rA8dpJ
```

continues

LISTING 33-44 *(continued)*

```
                ivDav2kDPp+SZ6yZ9LJzhBIe9TdJvwBQ9gJTGNVRft
                QOvdvH8c4KwYfiwZa9WCqys9WOZmw6g1a5jdW3hM//
                jiMizY1MwCECVh+T+y+f/vpP0xCkoKT9GGgHRMMrQd
                PqHUd5s7rUYp1ijQgrh1oPIXr6mx/XtzdXV8bQiEsg
                CLhsqphoVVwxkvmUKEmDQdOzdrB4sqmKgoHR3wCPyB
                npH58g==
               </CipherValue>
             </CipherData>
           </EncryptedData>
         </authentication>
```

After you have sections of your `web.config` file encrypted, you need a process to decrypt these sections to their original unencrypted values. To accomplish this task, you use the `aspnet_regiis` tool illustrated in Listing 33-45.

LISTING 33-45: Decrypting the <connectionStrings> section in the web.config file

```
aspnet_regiis-pd "connectionString"-app "/EncryptionExample"
```

Running this script returns the encrypted values to original values.

Editing Configuration Files

So far in this chapter, you have learned about configuration files and what each configuration entry means. Even though the configuration entries are in an easy, human-readable XML format, editing these entries can be cumbersome. To help with editing, Microsoft ships three tools:

- Visual Studio 2010 IDE
- Web Site Administration Tool
- ASP.NET Snap-In for IIS 6.0 or Windows 7's Internet Information Services (IIS) Manager

One of the nice capabilities of the Visual Studio 2010 IDE is that it supports IntelliSense-based editing for configuration files, as shown in Figure 33-7.

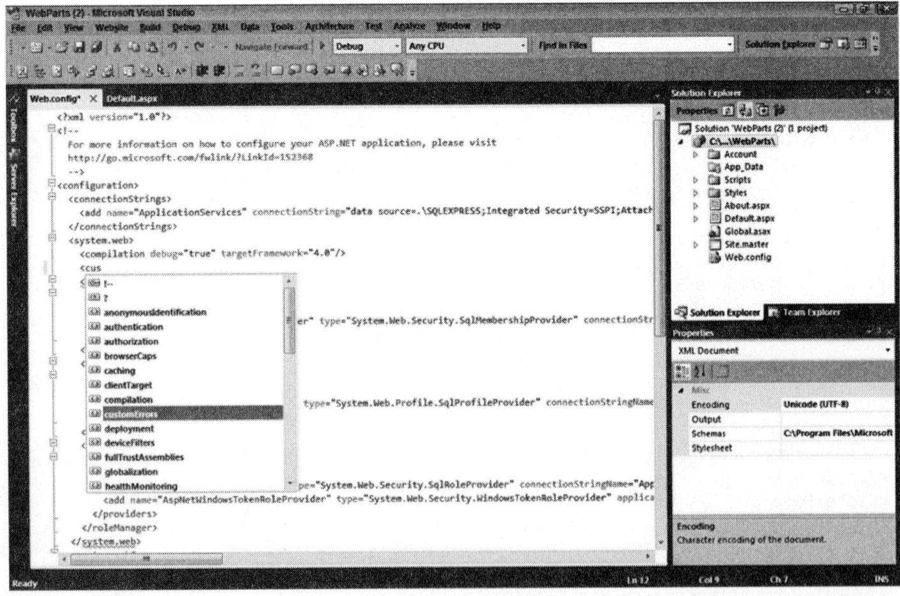

FIGURE 33-7

The Visual Studio 2010 IDE also supports XML element syntax checking, as shown in Figure 33-8.

XML element syntax checking and IntelliSense for XML elements are accomplished using the XSD-based XML validation feature available for all the XML files inside Visual Studio 2010. The configuration XSD file is located at <drive>`:\Program Files\Microsoft Visual Studio 10.0\Xml\Schemas\DotNetConfig.xsd`.

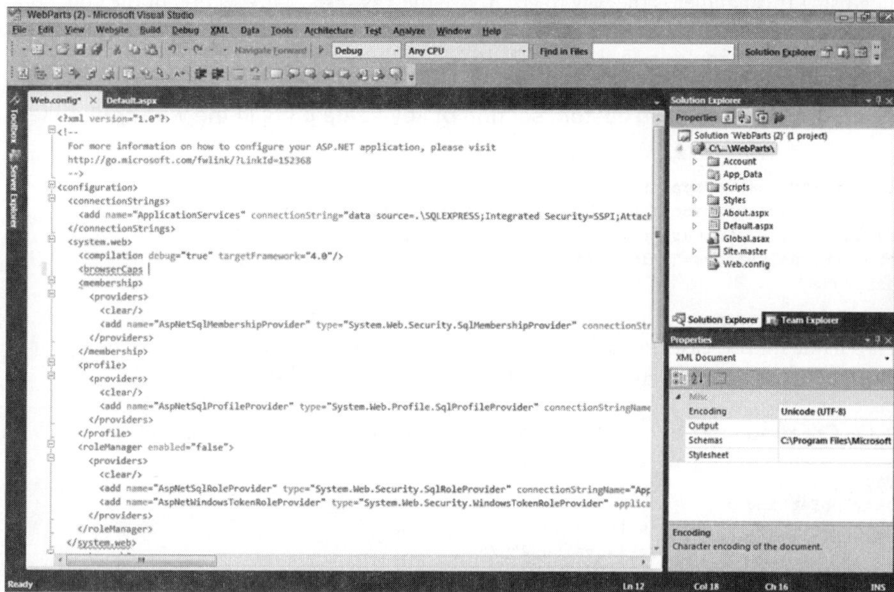

FIGURE 33-8

The Visual Studio 2010 IDE also adds two new useful features via the XML toolbar options that can help you with formatting the configuration settings:

- **Reformat Selection:** This option reformats the current XML notes content.
- **Format the whole document:** This option formats the entire XML document.

The Web Site Administration Tool and the ASP.NET Snap-In for IIS 6.0 or Window 7's IIS Manager allow you to edit the configuration entries without knowing the XML element names and their corresponding values. Chapter 35 covers these tools in more detail.

CREATING CUSTOM SECTIONS

In addition to using the `web.config` file as discussed, you can also extend it and add your own custom sections to the file that you can make use of just as with the other sections.

One way of creating custom sections is to use some built-in handlers that enable you to read key-value pairs from the `.config` file. All three of the following handlers are from the `System.Configuration` namespace:

- `NameValueFileSectionHandler`: This handler works with the current `<appSettings>` section of the `web.config` file. You are able to use this handler to create new sections of the configuration file that behave in the same manner as the `<appSettings>` section.
- `DictionarySectionHandler`: This handler works with a dictionary collection of key-value pairs.

- `SingleTagSectionHandler`: This handler works from a single element in the configuration file and allows you to read key-value pairs that are contained as attributes and values.

Next, this chapter looks at each of these handlers and some programmatic ways to customize the configuration file.

Using the NameValueFileSectionHandler Object

If you are looking to create a custom section that behaves like the `<appSettings>` section of the `web.config` file, then using this handler is the way to go. Above the `<system.web>` section of the `web.config` file, make a reference to the `NameValueFileSectionHandler` object, along with the other default references you will find in an ASP.NET 4 application. Listing 33-46 shows this additional reference.

LISTING 33-46: Creating your own custom section of key-value pairs in the web.config file

Available for download on Wrox.com

```
<configSections>
   <section name="MyCompanyAppSettings"
    type="System.Configuration.NameValueFileSectionHandler, System,
       Version=4.0.0.0, Culture=neutral, PublicKeyToken=b77a5c561934e089"
    restartOnExternalChanges="false" />
</configSections>
```

After you have made this reference to the `System.Configuration.NameValueFileSectionHandler` object and have given it a name (in this case, `MyCompanyAppSettings`), then you can create a section in your `web.config` file that makes use of this reference, as illustrated in Listing 33-47.

LISTING 33-47: Creating your own custom key-value pair section in the web.config

Available for download on Wrox.com

```
<configuration>
   <MyCompanyAppSettings>
      <add key="Key1" value="This is value 1" />
      <add key="Key2" value="This is value 2" />
   </MyCompanyAppSettings>
   <system.web>

      <!-- Removed for clarity -->

   </system.web>

</configuration>
```

After you have this code in place within your `web.config` file, you can then programmatically get access to this section, as illustrated in Listing 33-48.

LISTING 33-48: Getting access to your custom section in the web.config file

Available for download on Wrox.com

VB

```
Dim nvc As NameValueCollection = New NameValueCollection()
nvc = System.Configuration.ConfigurationManager.GetSection("MyCompanyAppSettings")

Response.Write(nvc("Key1") + "<br />")
Response.Write(nvc("Key2"))
```

C#

```
NameValueCollection nvc = new NameValueCollection();
nvc = ConfigurationManager.GetSection("MyCompanyAppSettings") as
   NameValueCollection;

Response.Write(nvc["Key1"] + "<br />");
Response.Write(nvc["Key2"]);
```

For this to work, you must import the `System.Collections.Specialized` namespace into the file, because this is where you will find the `NameValueCollection` object.

Using the DictionarySectionHandler Object

The `DictionarySectionHandler` works nearly the same as the `NameValueFileSectionHandler`. The difference, however, is that the `DictionarySectionHandler` returns a `HashTable` object instead of returning an `Object`.

Listing 33-49 presents this handler.

LISTING 33-49: Making a reference to the DictionarySectionHandler object

Available for download on Wrox.com

```
<configSections>
   <section name="MyCompanyAppSettings"
    type="System.Configuration.DictionarySectionHandler, System,
       Version=4.0.0.0, Culture=neutral, PublicKeyToken=b77a5c561934e089"
    restartOnExternalChanges="false" />
</configSections>
```

With this configuration setting in place, you can then make the same `MyCompanyAppSettings` section in the `web.config` file, as shown in Listing 33-50.

LISTING 33-50: Creating a custom key-value pair section in the web.config file

Available for download on Wrox.com

```
<configuration>
   <MyCompanyAppSettings>
      <add key="Key1" value="This is value 1" />
      <add key="Key2" value="This is value 2" />
   </MyCompanyAppSettings>

   <system.web>

      <!-- Removed for clarity -->

   </system.web>

</configuration>
```

Now that the `web.config` file is ready, you can call the items from code using the `Configuration` API, as illustrated in Listing 33-51.

LISTING 33-51: Getting access to your custom section in the web.config file

Available for download on Wrox.com

VB

```
Dim ht As Hashtable = New Hashtable()
ht = System.Configuration.ConfigurationManager.GetSection("MyCompanyAppSettings")

Response.Write(ht("Key1") + "<br />")
Response.Write(ht("Key2"))
```

C#

```
Hashtable ht = new Hashtable();
ht = ConfigurationManager.GetSection("MyCompanyAppSettings") as
   Hashtable;

Response.Write(ht["Key1"] + "<br />");
Response.Write(ht["Key2"]);
```

Using the SingleTagSectionHandler Object

The `SingleTagSectionHandler` works almost the same as the previous `NameValueFileSectionHandler` and `DictionarySectionHandler`. However, this object looks to work with a single element that contains the key-value pairs as attributes.

Listing 33-52 presents this handler.

LISTING 33-52: Making a reference to the SingleTagSectionHandler object

Available for download on Wrox.com

```
<configSections>
<section name="MyCompanyAppSettings"
    type="System.Configuration.SingleTagSectionHandler, System,
       Version=4.0.0.0, Culture=neutral, PublicKeyToken=b77a5c561934e089"
    restartOnExternalChanges="false" />
</configSections>
```

With this configuration setting in place, you can make a different `MyCompanyAppSettings` section in the `web.config` file, as presented in Listing 33-53.

LISTING 33-53: Creating a custom key-value pair section in the web.config file

Available for download on Wrox.com

```
<configuration>
   <MyCompanyAppSettings Key1="This is value 1" Key2="This is value 2" />
   <system.web>

      <!-- Removed for clarity -->

   </system.web>

</configuration>
```

Now that the `web.config` file is complete, you can call the items from code using the `Configuration` API, as illustrated in Listing 33-54.

LISTING 33-54: Getting access to your custom section in the web.config file

Available for download on Wrox.com

VB

```
Dim ht As Hashtable = New Hashtable()
ht = System.Configuration.ConfigurationManager.GetSection("MyCompanyAppSettings")

Response.Write(ht("Key1") + "<br />")
Response.Write(ht("Key2"))
```

C#

```
Hashtable ht = new Hashtable();
ht = ConfigurationManager.GetSection("MyCompanyAppSettings") as
   Hashtable;

Response.Write(ht["Key1"] + "<br />");
Response.Write(ht["Key2"]);
```

Using Your Own Custom Configuration Handler

You can also create your own custom configuration handler. To do this, you first must create a class that represents your section in the `web.config` file. In your App_Code folder, create a class called `MyCompanySettings`. Listing 33-55 shows this class.

LISTING 33-55: The MyCompanySettings class

Available for download on Wrox.com

VB

```
Public Class MyCompanySettings
    Inherits ConfigurationSection

    <ConfigurationProperty("Key1", DefaultValue:="This is the value of Key 1", _
       IsRequired:=False)> _
    Public ReadOnly Property Key1() As String
        Get
            Return MyBase.Item("Key1").ToString()
```

```
        End Get
    End Property

    <ConfigurationProperty("Key2", IsRequired:=True)> _
    Public ReadOnly Property Key2() As String
        Get
            Return MyBase.Item("Key2").ToString()
        End Get
    End Property

End Class
```

C#

```
using System.Configuration;

public class MyCompanySettings : ConfigurationSection
{
    [ConfigurationProperty("Key1", DefaultValue = "This is the value of Key 1",
     IsRequired = false)]
    public string Key1
    {
        get
        {
            return this["Key1"] as string;
        }
    }

    [ConfigurationProperty("Key2", IsRequired = true)]
    public string Key2
    {
        get
        {
            return this["Key2"] as string;
        }
    }
}
```

You can see that this class inherits from the `ConfigurationSection` and the two properties that are created using the `ConfigurationProperty` attribute. You can use a couple of attributes here, such as the `DefaultValue`, `IsRequired`, `IsKey`, and `IsDefaultCollection`.

After you have this class in place, you can configure your application to use this handler, as illustrated in Listing 33-56.

Available for download on Wrox.com

LISTING 33-56: Making a reference to the MyCompanySettings object

```
<configSections>
   <section name="MyCompanySettings" type="MyCompanySettings" />
</configSections>
```

You can now use this section in your `web.config` file, as illustrated in Listing 33-57.

Available for download on Wrox.com

LISTING 33-57: Creating your own custom key-value pair section in the web.config file

```
<configuration>
   <MyCompanySettings Key2="Here is a value for Key2" />

   <system.web>

      <!-- Removed for clarity -->

   </system.web>

</configuration>
```

Using this configuration you can programmatically access this key-value pair from code, as illustrated in Listing 33-58.

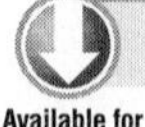

LISTING 33-58: Accessing a custom section in the web.config file

Available for download on Wrox.com

```
Dim cs As MyCompanySettings = New MyCompanySettings()
cs = ConfigurationManager.GetSection("MyCompanySettings")

Response.Write(cs.Key1 + "<br />")
Response.Write(cs.Key2)
```

```
MyCompanySettings cs = ConfigurationManager.GetSection("MyCompanySettings") as
   MyCompanySettings;

Response.Write(cs.Key1 + "<br />");
Response.Write(cs.Key2);
```

SUMMARY

In this chapter, you have seen the ASP.NET configuration system and learned how it does not rely on the IIS metabase. Instead, ASP.NET uses an XML configuration system that is human-readable.

You also looked at the two different ASP.NET XML configuration files:

- `machine.config`
- `web.config`

The `machine.config` file applies default settings to all Web applications on the server. However, if the server has multiple versions of the framework installed, the `machine.config` file applies to a particular framework version. On the other hand, a particular Web application can customize or override its own configuration information using `web.config` files. Using a `web.config` file, you can also configure the applications on an application-by-application or folder-by-folder basis.

Next, you looked at some typical configuration settings that you can apply to an ASP.NET application, such as configuring connection strings, session state, browser capabilities, and so on. Then you looked at an overview of ASP.NET Admin Objects and learned how to program configuration files. Finally, you learned how to protect the configuration section using cryptographic algorithms.

34

Instrumentation

WHAT'S IN THIS CHAPTER?

- Monitoring your applications with the event log and performance counters
- Utilizing health monitoring for your applications

Many ASP.NET developers do more than just build an application and walk away. They definitely think about how the application will behave after it is deployed. *Instrumentation* is the task that developers undertake to measure and monitor their ASP.NET applications. Depending on the situation, some instrumentation operations occur at design time, whereas others are ongoing processes that begin at runtime.

ASP.NET 4 gives you greater capability to apply instrumentation techniques to your applications. You will find that the ASP.NET Framework includes a large series of performance counters, the capability to work with the Windows Event Tracing system, possibilities for application tracing (covered in Chapter 23), and the most exciting part of this discussion — a health monitoring system that allows you to log a number of different events over an application's lifetime.

You can monitor a deployed application in several ways. First, you learn how to work with the Windows event log. Then the chapter moves on to a discussion of performance counters, application tracing, and health monitoring in turn. By the end of the chapter, you will have a better understanding of what is going on within your ASP.NET applications. Instrumentation is key to this task.

WORKING WITH THE EVENT LOG

When working with Visual Studio 2010, you can get to the event log in the Server Explorer of the IDE in a few different ways. You can get to the event log section in the Server Explorer by expanding the view of the server you want to work with (by clicking the plus sign next to the server) until you see the Event Logs section. You also have the option to right-click the Event Logs node and select Launch Event Viewer from the list of available options. This selection displays the same Event Viewer you are familiar with. From the Event Viewer or from the Server Explorer you can work directly with events recorded to your system.

Another option available from the Server Explorer is to expand the Event Logs node of the tree view in the Server Explorer so that you can see the additional nodes, such as Application, Security, and System. If you are on Windows 7, you will see a series of additional event categories. Expanding any of these sub-nodes allows you to see all the events that have been registered in the event log. These events are arranged by type, which makes browsing for specific events rather easy, as illustrated in Figure 34-1.

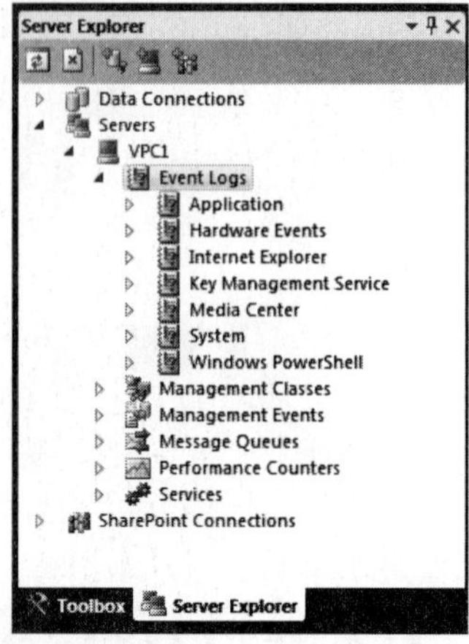

FIGURE 34-1

Reading from the Event Log

Reading and writing events to and from the event log from your .NET application is possible. If you are interested in reading events from the event log, you can do so rather simply by using the `EventLog` object that is provided by .NET in the `System.Diagnostics` namespace.

To see an example of using this object, you can create an ASP.NET page that displays all the entries contained within a specified event log. To create it, you need a DropDownList control, a Button control, and a GridView control. In Visual Studio .NET 2002 and 2003, a Components tab was located within the Toolbox, and you could simply drag and drop the Event Log component onto your design surface in order to start working with it. Since Visual Studio 2005, you won't find this tab within the Toolbox, but finding the objects you need still isn't too hard. Listing 34-1 shows the simple ASP.NET page that enables you to easily display the contents of the event log.

LISTING 34-1: Displaying the contents of the event logs within the browser

Available for download on Wrox.com

VB

```
<%@ Page Language="VB" %>
<%@ Import Namespace="System.Diagnostics" %>

<script runat="server">
    Protected Sub Button1_Click(ByVal sender As Object,
      ByVal e As System.EventArgs)

        Dim el As EventLog = New EventLog()
        el.Source = DropDownList1.SelectedItem.Text

        GridView1.DataSource = el.Entries
        GridView1.DataBind()
    End Sub
</script>

<html xmlns="http://www.w3.org/1999/xhtml" >
<head runat="server">
    <title>Working with Event Logs</title>
</head>
<body>
    <form id="form1" runat="server">
    <div>
        <asp:DropDownList ID="DropDownList1" runat="server">
            <asp:ListItem>Application</asp:ListItem>
            <asp:ListItem>Security</asp:ListItem>
            <asp:ListItem>System</asp:ListItem>
        </asp:DropDownList>
        <asp:Button ID="Button1" runat="server" OnClick="Button1_Click"
         Text="Submit" /><br />
        <br />
        <asp:GridView ID="GridView1" runat="server"
         BackColor="LightGoldenrodYellow" BorderColor="Tan"
            BorderWidth="1px" CellPadding="2" ForeColor="Black" GridLines="None">
            <FooterStyle BackColor="Tan" />
            <SelectedRowStyle BackColor="DarkSlateBlue" ForeColor="GhostWhite" />
            <PagerStyle BackColor="PaleGoldenrod" ForeColor="DarkSlateBlue"
             HorizontalAlign="Center" />
            <HeaderStyle BackColor="Tan" Font-Bold="True" />
```

```
                <AlternatingRowStyle BackColor="PaleGoldenrod" />
                <RowStyle VerticalAlign="Top" />
            </asp:GridView>
        </div>
        </form>
</body>
</html>
```

```
<%@ Page Language="C#" %>
<%@ Import Namespace="System.Diagnostics" %>

<script runat="server">
    protected void Button1_Click(object sender, EventArgs e)
    {
        EventLog el = new EventLog();
        el.Source = DropDownList1.SelectedItem.Text;

        GridView1.DataSource = el.Entries;
        GridView1.DataBind();
    }
</script>
```

Note that you must run this code sample with credentials that have administrative rights for it to work.

For this code to work, you import the `System.Diagnostics` namespace if you are not interested in fully qualifying your declarations. After you do so, you can create an instance of the `EventLog` object to give you access to the `Source` property. In assigning a value to this property, you use the `SelectedItem.Text` property from the DropDownList control on the page. Next, you can provide all the `EventLog` entries as the data source value to the GridView control. Finally, you bind this data source to the GridView. In the end, you get something similar to the results illustrated in Figure 34-2.

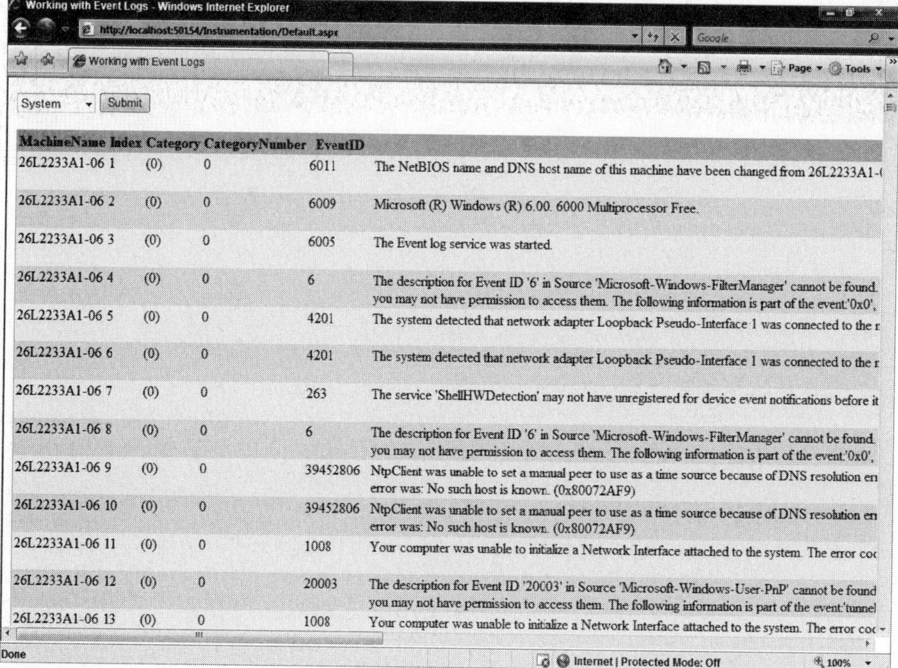

FIGURE 34-2

As you can see, pulling all the events from the event log and writing them to the browser screen is simple. The next section looks at writing values back to the event log.

Writing to the Event Log

Not only can you read from the event logs, but you can write to them as well. This capability can be quite handy if you want to record specific events in an event log. Table 34-1 provides a short description of the main event logs available to you. Windows 7 has other event categories, but these are the main event categories that you will use.

TABLE 34-1

EVENT LOG	DESCRIPTION
Application	Enables you to record application-specific events, including whether a certain event was fired, a page was loaded, or a customer made a specific purchase
Security	Enables you to track security-related issues such as security changes and breaches
System	Enables you to track system-specific items such as issues that arise with components or drivers

From your code, you can write to any of the event logs defined in the preceding table as well as to any custom event logs that you might create. To accomplish this task, create an example ASP.NET page that contains a multiline TextBox control and a Button control. On the `Button1_Click` event, you register the text you want placed in the text box directly into the Application event log. Your ASP.NET page should be similar to what is presented in Listing 34-2.

LISTING 34-2: Writing to the Application event log

Available for download on Wrox.com

VB

```
<%@ Page Language="VB" %>
<%@ Import Namespace="System.Diagnostics" %>

<script runat="server">
    Protected Sub Page_Load(ByVal sender As Object,
      ByVal e As System.EventArgs)

        If Not EventLog.SourceExists("My Application") Then
            EventLog.CreateEventSource("My Application", "Application")
        End If
    End Sub

    Protected Sub Button1_Click(ByVal sender As Object,
      ByVal e As System.EventArgs)

        Dim el As EventLog = New EventLog()
        el.Source = "My Application"
        el.WriteEntry(TextBox1.Text)

        Label1.Text = "ENTERED: " & TextBox1.Text
    End Sub
</script>

<html xmlns="http://www.w3.org/1999/xhtml" >
<head runat="server">
    <title>Working with Event Logs</title>
</head>
<body>
    <form id="form1" runat="server">
    <div>
        <asp:TextBox ID="TextBox1" runat="server" Height="75px"
         TextMode="MultiLine" Width="250px"></asp:TextBox><br />
        <br />
```

```
            <asp:Button ID="Button1" runat="server" OnClick="Button1_Click"
             Text="Submit to custom event log" /><br />
            <br />
            <asp:Label ID="Label1" runat="server"></asp:Label> </div>
        </form>
    </body>
    </html>
```

C#

```
<%@ Page Language="C#" %>
<%@ Import Namespace="System.Diagnostics" %>

<script runat="server">
    protected void Page_Load(object sender, EventArgs e)
    {
        if (!EventLog.SourceExists("My Application"))
        {
            EventLog.CreateEventSource("My Application", "Application");
        }
    }

    protected void Button1_Click(object sender, EventArgs e)
    {
        EventLog el = new EventLog();
        el.Source = "My Application";
        el.WriteEntry(TextBox1.Text);

        Label1.Text = "ENTERED: " + TextBox1.Text;
    }
</script>
```

Again, for this code to work, you must import the `System.Diagnostics` namespace. In the `Page_Load` event of the page, ASP.NET is checking whether the event source exists for `My Application`. If no such source exists in the Application event log, it is created using the `CreateEventSource()` method.

```
el.CreateEventSource("My Application", "Application")
```

The first parameter of the method takes the name of the source that you are creating. The second parameter of this method call takes the name of the event log that you are targeting. After this source has been created, you can start working with the `EventLog` object to place an entry into the system. First, the `EventLog` object is assigned a source. In this case, it is the newly created `My Application`. Using the `WriteEntry()` method, you can write to the specified event log. You can also assign the source and the message within the `WriteEntry()` method in the following manner:

```
el.WriteEntry("My Application", TextBox1.Text);
```

The ASP.NET page produces something similar to what is illustrated in Figure 34-3.

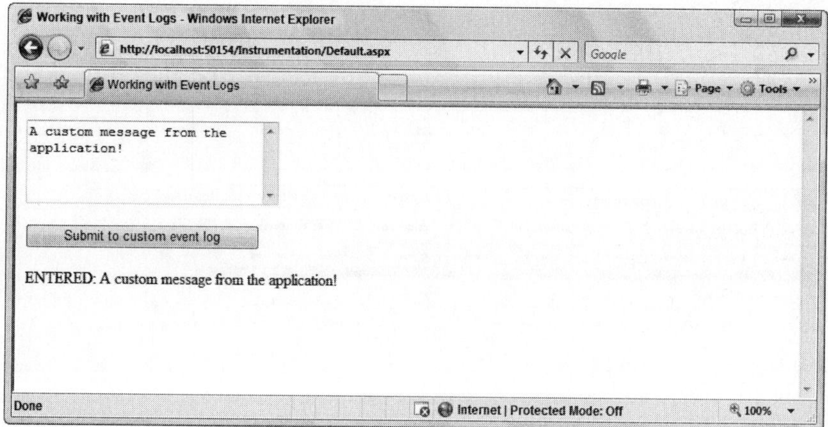

FIGURE 34-3

After you have all this code in place, you can look in the Event Viewer and see your entry listed in the Application event log. Figure 34-4 illustrates what happens when you double-click the entry.

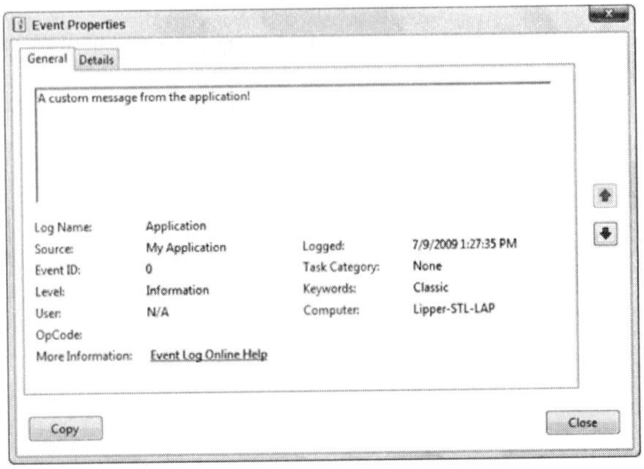

Later in this chapter, you see some of the automatic ways in which ASP.NET can record events for you in the event log and in some other data stores (such as Microsoft's SQL Server). Next, it is time to turn your attention to working with performance counters.

FIGURE 34-4

USING PERFORMANCE COUNTERS

Utilizing performance counters is important if you want to monitor your applications as they run. What exactly is monitored is up to you. A plethora of available performance counters are at your disposal in Windows and you will find that more than 60 counters are specific to ASP.NET.

Viewing Performance Counters Through an Administration Tool

You can see these performance counters by opening the Performance dialog found in the Control Panel and then Administration Tools if you are using Windows XP. If you are using Windows 7, select Control Panel ➪ System and Security ➪ Administrative Tools ➪ Performance Monitor. Figure 34-5 shows the dialog opened in Windows 7.

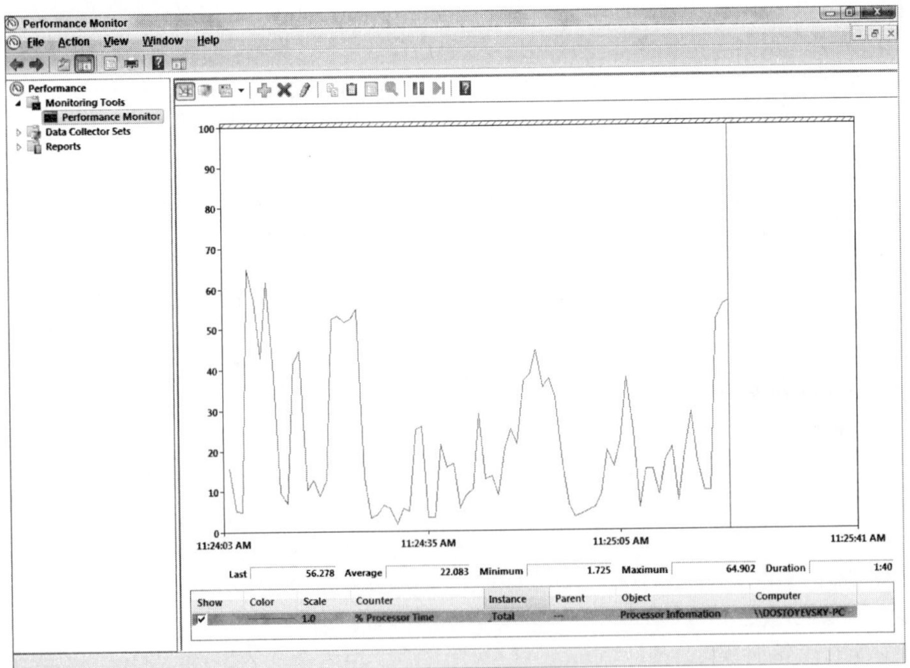

FIGURE 34-5

Clicking the plus sign in the menu enables you to add more performance counters to the list. A number of ASP.NET–specific counters appear in the list shown in Figure 34-6.

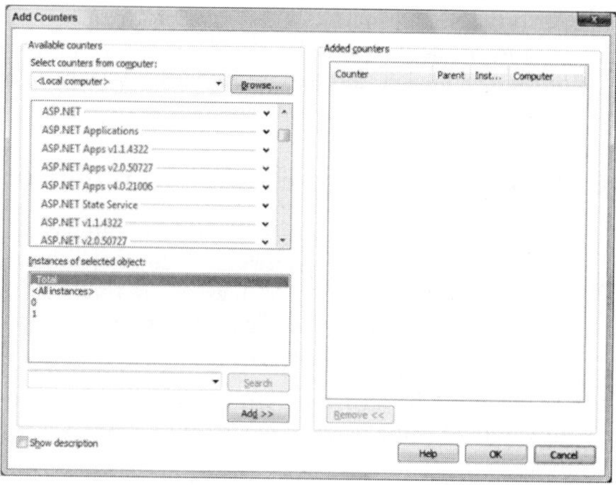

FIGURE 34-6

The following list details some of the ASP.NET–specific performance counters that are at your disposal, along with a definition of the counter (also available by selecting the Show Description check box from within the dialog).

- **Application Restarts.** Number of times the application has been restarted during the Web server's lifetime.
- **Applications Running.** Number of currently running Web applications.
- **Audit Failure Events Raised.** Number of audit failures in the application since it was started.
- **Audit Success Events Raised.** Number of audit successes in the application since it was started.
- **Error Events Raised.** Number of error events raised since the application was started.
- **Infrastructure Error Events Raised.** Number of HTTP error events raised since the application was started.
- **Request Error Events Raised.** Number of runtime error events raised since the application was started.
- **Request Execution Time.** The number of milliseconds it took to execute the most recent request.
- **Request Wait Time.** The number of milliseconds the most recent request was waiting in the queue.
- **Requests Current.** The current number of requests, including those that are queued, currently executing, or waiting to be written to the client. Under the ASP.NET process model, when this counter exceeds the `requestQueueLimit` defined in the `processModel` configuration section, ASP .NET begins rejecting requests.
- **Requests Disconnected.** The number of requests disconnected because of communication errors or user terminations.
- **Requests Queued.** The number of requests waiting to be processed.
- **Requests Rejected.** The number of requests rejected because the request queue was full.
- **State Server Sessions Abandoned.** The number of sessions that have been explicitly abandoned.
- **State Server Sessions Active.** The current number of sessions currently active.
- **State Server Sessions Timed Out.** The number of sessions timed out.
- **State Server Sessions Total.** The number of sessions total.
- **Worker Process Restarts.** The number of times a worker process has restarted on the machine.
- **Worker Processes Running.** The number of worker processes running on the machine.

These are some of the performance counters for just the ASP.NET category. Here you will find categories for other ASP.NET–specific items such as:

- ASP.NET
- ASP.NET Applications
- ASP.NET Apps v4.0.21006
- ASP.NET State Service
- ASP.NET v4.0.21006

Performance counters can give you a rather outstanding view of what is happening in your application. The data retrieved by a specific counter is not a continuous thing because the counter is really taking a snapshot of the specified counter every 400 milliseconds, so be sure to take that into account when analyzing the data produced.

Building a Browser-Based Administrative Tool

In addition to viewing the performance counters available to you through the Performance dialog, you can also get at the performance counter values programmatically. This is possible by working with the `System.Diagnostics` namespace in the .NET Framework. This namespace gives you access to performance counter–specific objects such as the `PerformanceCounterCategory` and `PerformanceCounter` objects.

To show you how to work with these objects, this next example creates an ASP.NET page that enables you to view any value from a performance counter directly in the browser. To accomplish this task, create a basic ASP.NET page that includes three DropDownList controls, a Button control, and a Label control. This gives you the results presented in Figure 34-7.

Listing 34-3 shows the code required for Figure 34-7.

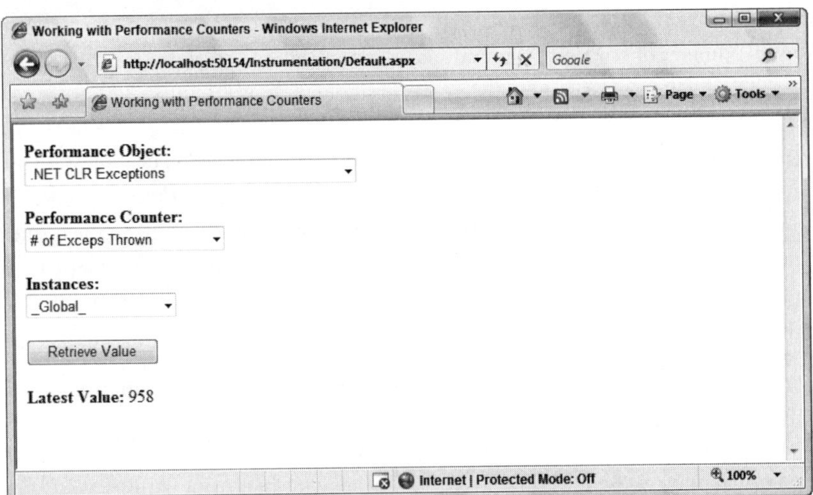

FIGURE 34-7

LISTING 34-3: Working with performance counters in ASP.NET

Available for download on Wrox.com

VB

```
<%@ Page Language="VB" %>
<%@ Import Namespace="System.Diagnostics" %>
<%@ Import Namespace="System.Collections.Generic" %>

<script runat="server">
    Protected Sub Page_Load(ByVal sender As Object, ByVal e As System.EventArgs)
        If Not Page.IsPostBack Then
            Dim pcc As List(Of String) = New List(Of String)

            For Each item As PerformanceCounterCategory In _
              PerformanceCounterCategory.GetCategories()
                pcc.Add(item.CategoryName)
            Next
```

```
            pcc.Sort()
            pcc.Remove(".NET CLR Data")

            DropDownList1.DataSource = pcc
            DropDownList1.DataBind()

            Dim myPcc As PerformanceCounterCategory
            myPcc = New PerformanceCounterCategory(DropDownList1.SelectedItem.Text)

            DisplayCounters(myPcc)
        End If
    End Sub

    Protected Sub DisplayCounters(ByVal pcc As PerformanceCounterCategory)
        DisplayInstances(pcc)

        Dim myPcc As List(Of String) = New List(Of String)

        If DropDownList3.Items.Count > 0 Then
            For Each pc As PerformanceCounter In _
              pcc.GetCounters(DropDownList3.Items(0).Value)
                myPcc.Add(pc.CounterName)
            Next
        Else
            For Each pc As PerformanceCounter In pcc.GetCounters()
                myPcc.Add(pc.CounterName)
            Next
        End If

        myPcc.Sort()

        DropDownList2.DataSource = myPcc
        DropDownList2.DataBind()
    End Sub

    Protected Sub DisplayInstances(ByVal pcc As PerformanceCounterCategory)
        Dim listPcc As List(Of String) = New List(Of String)

        For Each item As String In pcc.GetInstanceNames()
            listPcc.Add(item.ToString())
        Next

        listPcc.Sort()

        DropDownList3.DataSource = listPcc
        DropDownList3.DataBind()
    End Sub

    Protected Sub DropDownList1_SelectedIndexChanged(ByVal sender As Object, _
      ByVal e As System.EventArgs)
        Dim pcc As PerformanceCounterCategory
        pcc = New PerformanceCounterCategory(DropDownList1.SelectedItem.Text)

        DropDownList2.Items.Clear()
        DropDownList3.Items.Clear()

        DisplayCounters(pcc)
    End Sub

    Protected Sub Button1_Click(ByVal sender As Object, _
      ByVal e As System.EventArgs)
```

continues

LISTING 34-3 *(continued)*

```
        Dim pc As PerformanceCounter

        If DropDownList3.Items.Count > 0 Then
            pc = New PerformanceCounter(DropDownList1.SelectedItem.Text, _
              DropDownList2.SelectedItem.Text, DropDownList3.SelectedItem.Text)
        Else
            pc = New PerformanceCounter(DropDownList1.SelectedItem.Text, _
              DropDownList2.SelectedItem.Text)
        End If

        Label1.Text = "<b>Latest Value:</b> " & pc.NextValue().ToString()
    End Sub
</script>

<html xmlns="http://www.w3.org/1999/xhtml">
<head runat="server">
    <title>Working with Performance Counters</title>
</head>
<body>
    <form id="form1" runat="server">
    <div>
        <strong>Performance Object:</strong><br />
        <asp:DropDownList ID="DropDownList1" runat="server" AutoPostBack="True"
         OnSelectedIndexChanged="DropDownList1_SelectedIndexChanged">
        </asp:DropDownList><br />
        <br />
        <strong>Performance Counter:</strong><br />
        <asp:DropDownList ID="DropDownList2" runat="server">
        </asp:DropDownList><br />
        <br />
        <strong>Instances:</strong><br />
        <asp:DropDownList ID="DropDownList3" runat="server">
        </asp:DropDownList><br />
        <br />
        <asp:Button ID="Button1" runat="server" OnClick="Button1_Click"
         Text="Retrieve Value" /><br />
        <br />
        <asp:Label ID="Label1" runat="server"></asp:Label></div>
    </form>
</body>
</html>
```

C#

```
<%@ Page Language="C#" %>
<%@ Import Namespace="System.Diagnostics" %>
<%@ Import Namespace="System.Collections.Generic" %>

<script runat="server">
    protected void Page_Load(object sender, EventArgs e)
    {
        if (!Page.IsPostBack)
        {
            List<string> pcc = new List<string>();

            foreach (PerformanceCounterCategory item in
               PerformanceCounterCategory.GetCategories())
            {
                pcc.Add(item.CategoryName);
            }
```

```
            pcc.Sort();
            pcc.Remove(".NET CLR Data");

            DropDownList1.DataSource = pcc;
            DropDownList1.DataBind();

            PerformanceCounterCategory myPcc;
            myPcc = new
               PerformanceCounterCategory(DropDownList1.SelectedItem.Text);

            DisplayCounters(myPcc);
        }
    }

    void DisplayCounters(PerformanceCounterCategory pcc)
    {
        DisplayInstances(pcc);

        List<string> myPcc = new List<string>();

        if (DropDownList3.Items.Count > 0)
        {
            foreach (PerformanceCounter pc in
               pcc.GetCounters(DropDownList3.Items[0].Value))
            {
                myPcc.Add(pc.CounterName);
            }
        }
        else
        {
            foreach (PerformanceCounter pc in pcc.GetCounters())
            {
                myPcc.Add(pc.CounterName);
            }
        }

        myPcc.Sort();

        DropDownList2.DataSource = myPcc;
        DropDownList2.DataBind();
    }

    void DisplayInstances(PerformanceCounterCategory pcc)
    {
        List<string> listPcc = new List<string>();

        foreach (string item in pcc.GetInstanceNames())
        {
            listPcc.Add(item.ToString());
        }

        listPcc.Sort();

        DropDownList3.DataSource = listPcc;
        DropDownList3.DataBind();
    }

    protected void DropDownList1_SelectedIndexChanged(object sender, EventArgs e)
    {
```

continues

LISTING 34-3 *(continued)*

```
            PerformanceCounterCategory pcc;
            pcc = new PerformanceCounterCategory(DropDownList1.SelectedItem.Text);
            DropDownList2.Items.Clear();
            DropDownList3.Items.Clear();

            DisplayCounters(pcc);
        }
        protected void Button1_Click(object sender, EventArgs e)
        {
            PerformanceCounter pc;
            if (DropDownList3.Items.Count > 0)
            {
                pc = new PerformanceCounter(DropDownList1.SelectedItem.Text,
                  DropDownList2.SelectedItem.Text, DropDownList3.SelectedItem.Text);
            }
            else
            {
                pc = new PerformanceCounter(DropDownList1.SelectedItem.Text,
                  DropDownList2.SelectedItem.Text);
            }

            Label1.Text = "<b>Latest Value:</b> " + pc.NextValue().ToString();
        }
    </script>
```

To make this code work, you have to deal with only a couple of performance-counter objects such as the `PerformanceCounterCategory` and the `PerformanceCounter` objects. The first drop-down list is populated with all the categories available. These values are first placed in a `List (Of String)` object that enables you to call a `Sort()` method and allows you to remove any categories you are not interested in by using the `Remove()` method before binding to the DropDown List control.

The category selected in the first drop-down list drives what appears in the second and third drop-down lists. The second drop-down list displays a list of counters that are available for a particular category. You might tend to think that the third drop-down list of instances is based upon the counter that is selected, but instances are set at the category level.

When the button on the page is clicked, a new instance of the `PerformanceCounter` object is created and, as you can see from the example, it can be instantiated in several ways. The first constructor takes just a category name and a counter name, whereas the second constructor takes these two items plus the instance name utilized. After a `PerformanceCounter` is created, the `NextValue()` method pulls a sample from the specified item, thus producing the results that are illustrated in Figure 34-7.

APPLICATION TRACING

ASP.NET does an excellent job of displaying trace information either directly on the requested pages of your ASP.NET application or in a trace log that you can find at `http://[server]/[application]/trace.axd`. Sample screenshots of both of these scenarios appear in Figure 34-8.

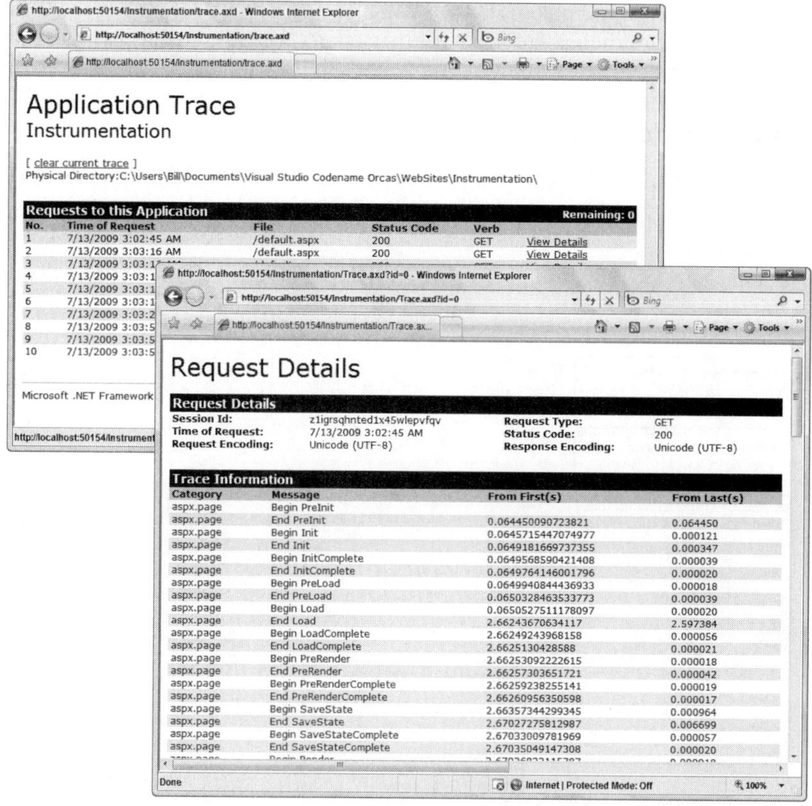

FIGURE 34-8

Chapter 23 provides detailed information on working with tracing for instrumentation.

UNDERSTANDING HEALTH MONITORING

One of the more exciting instrumentation capabilities provided by ASP.NET is the health monitoring system introduced in ASP.NET 2.0. ASP.NET health monitoring is built around various health monitoring events (which are referred to as *Web events*) occurring in your application. Using the health monitoring system enables you to use event logging for Web events such as failed logins, application starts and stops, or any unhandled exceptions. The event logging can occur in more than one place; therefore, you can log to the event log or even back to a database. In addition to this disk-based logging, you can also use the system to e-mail health monitoring information.

By default, the health monitoring system is already enabled. All default errors and failure audits are logged into the event logs on your behalf. For example, throwing an error produces an entry in the event log, as illustrated in Figure 34-9.

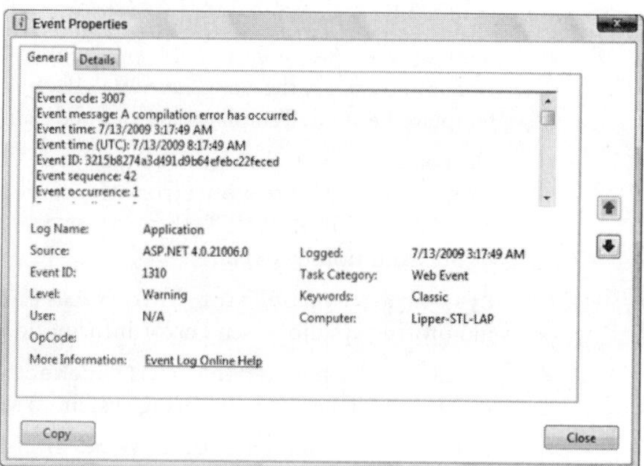

FIGURE 34-9

By default, these errors are registered in the event logs, but you can also record these events in a couple of other places. You define where you record these event messages through the various providers available to the health monitoring system. These providers are briefly covered next.

The Health Monitoring Provider Model

Chapter 11 offers quite a bit of information about what a provider model is and how the health monitoring system works with providers, but a short review of the providers available to the health monitoring system is warranted here, as well.

The health monitoring system has the most built-in providers in ASP.NET. Figure 34-10 contains a diagram of the available providers.

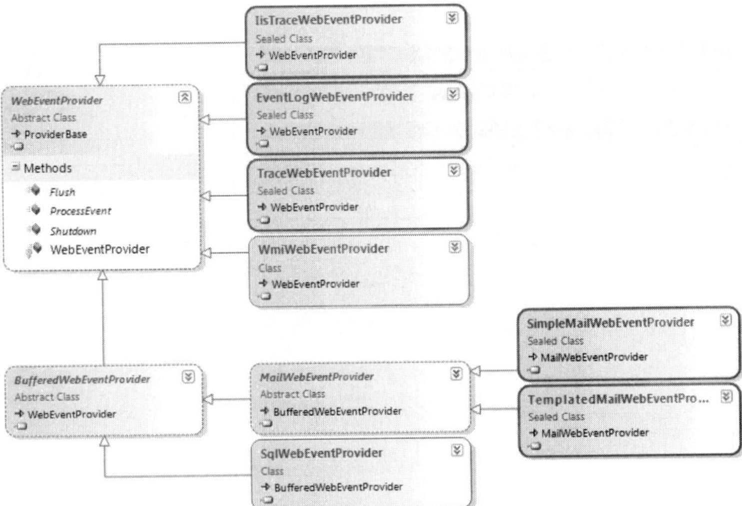

FIGURE 34-10

Seven providers are available to the health monitoring system right out of the box:

- `System.Web.Management.EventLogWebEventProvider`: Enables you to use the ASP.NET health monitoring system to record security operation errors and all other errors into the Windows event log.
- `System.Web.Management.SimpleMailWebEventProvider`: Allows you to use the ASP.NET health monitoring system to send error information in an e-mail.
- `System.Web.Management.TemplatedMailWebEventProvider`: Similar to the `SimpleMailWebEventProvider`, the `TemplatedMailWebEventProvider` class lets you send error information in a templated e-mail. Templates are defined using a standard `.aspx` page.
- `System.Web.Management.SqlWebEventProvider`: Enables you to use the ASP.NET health monitoring system to store error information in SQL Server. Like the other SQL providers for the other systems in ASP.NET, the `SqlWebEventProvider` stores error information in SQL Server Express Edition by default.
- `System.Web.Management.TraceWebEventProvider`: Enables you to use the ASP.NET health monitoring system to send error information to the ASP.NET page tracing system.
- `System.Web.Management.IisTraceWebEventProvider`: Provides you with the capability to use the ASP.NET health monitoring system to send error information to the IIS tracing system.
- `System.Web.Management.WmiWebEventProvider`: Enables you to connect the ASP.NET health monitoring system to the Windows Management Instrumentation (WMI) event provider.

Health Monitoring Configuration

By default, the `EventLogWebEventProvider` object is what is utilized for all errors and failure audits. These rules are defined along with the providers and what Web events to trap in the root `web.config` file found at `C:\WINDOWS\Microsoft.NET\Framework\v4.0.21006\CONFIG`. All the information for the health monitoring section is defined within the `<healthMonitoring>` section of this file. Even though these items are defined in the root `web.config` file, you can also override these settings and define them yourself in your application's `web.config` file.

To define the health monitoring capabilities and behaviors in your `web.config` file, place a `<healthMonitoring>` section within the `<system.web>` section of your configuration file:

```
<configuration>
  <system.web>

    <healthMonitoring enabled="true">

    </healthMonitoring>

  </system.web>
</configuration>
```

The `<healthMonitoring>` section can include a number of subsections, including the following:

- `<bufferModes>`
- `<eventMappings>`
- `<profiles>`
- `<providers>`
- `<rules>`

You will look next at some of the core sections and how you can use these sections to define health monitoring tasks in your application's `web.config` file.

<eventMappings>

The `<eventMappings>` section of the health monitoring system allows you to define friendly names for specific events that can be captured. You can declare a number of events in this section, but doing so doesn't mean that they are utilized automatically. Remember that when placing events in this section, you are just simply defining them in this configuration file for reuse in other sections. Listing 34-4 shows an example of event mapping.

Available for download on Wrox.com

LISTING 34-4: Using the <eventMappings> section

```
<configuration>
  <system.web>

    <healthMonitoring enabled="true">

      <eventMappings>

        <clear />

        <add name="All Events"
         type="System.Web.Management.WebBaseEvent,System.Web,
           Version=4.0.0.0,Culture=neutral,PublicKeyToken=b03f5f7f11d50a3a"
         startEventCode="0" endEventCode="2147483647" />
        <add name="Heartbeats"
         type="System.Web.Management.WebHeartbeatEvent,System.Web,
```

continues

LISTING 34-4 *(continued)*

```
              Version=4.0.0.0,Culture=neutral,PublicKeyToken=b03f5f7f11d50a3a"
            startEventCode="0" endEventCode="2147483647"/>
          <add name="Application Lifetime Events"
            type="System.Web.Management.WebApplicationLifetimeEvent,System.Web,
              Version=4.0.0.0,Culture=neutral,PublicKeyToken=b03f5f7f11d50a3a"
            startEventCode="0" endEventCode="2147483647"/>
          <add name="Request Processing Events"
            type="System.Web.Management.WebRequestEvent,System.Web,
              Version=4.0.0.0,Culture=neutral,PublicKeyToken=b03f5f7f11d50a3a"
            startEventCode="0" endEventCode="2147483647"/>
          <add name="All Errors"
            type="System.Web.Management.WebBaseErrorEvent,System.Web,
              Version=4.0.0.0,Culture=neutral,PublicKeyToken=b03f5f7f11d50a3a"
            startEventCode="0" endEventCode="2147483647"/>
          <add name="Infrastructure Errors"
            type="System.Web.Management.WebErrorEvent,System.Web,
              Version=4.0.0.0,Culture=neutral,PublicKeyToken=b03f5f7f11d50a3a"
            startEventCode="0" endEventCode="2147483647"/>
          <add name="Request Processing Errors"
            type="System.Web.Management.WebRequestErrorEvent,System.Web,
              Version=4.0.0.0,Culture=neutral,PublicKeyToken=b03f5f7f11d50a3a"
            startEventCode="0" endEventCode="2147483647"/>
          <add name="All Audits"
            type="System.Web.Management.WebAuditEvent,System.Web,
              Version=4.0.0.0,Culture=neutral,PublicKeyToken=b03f5f7f11d50a3a"
            startEventCode="0" endEventCode="2147483647"/>
          <add name="Failure Audits"
            type="System.Web.Management.WebFailureAuditEvent,System.Web,
              Version=4.0.0.0,Culture=neutral,PublicKeyToken=b03f5f7f11d50a3a"
            startEventCode="0" endEventCode="2147483647"/>
          <add name="Success Audits"
            type="System.Web.Management.WebSuccessAuditEvent,System.Web,
              Version=4.0.0.0,Culture=neutral,PublicKeyToken=b03f5f7f11d50a3a"
            startEventCode="0" endEventCode="2147483647"/>
        </eventMappings>

      </healthMonitoring>

    </system.web>
  </configuration>
```

From this section, you can see that a number of different event types are defined within this `<eventMappings>` section. Not all these definitions are required, just the ones you are interested in working with. Because these definitions are important, look at how the first one is listed:

```
<add name="All Events"
  type="System.Web.Management.WebBaseEvent,System.Web,
    Version=4.0.0.0,Culture=neutral,PublicKeyToken=b03f5f7f11d50a3a"
  startEventCode="0" endEventCode="2147483647"/>
```

The <add> element takes a number of different attributes. The first, `name`, allows you to give a user-friendly name that can be used later in one of the other sections of the document. In this case, the friendly name provided is `All Events`.

The next attribute is the `type` attribute. This enables you to define the .NET event object with which this event mapping is associated. In this case, it is the base event used by all the other event types as a base class. Although the object definition with the `type` attribute is shown on multiple lines in this book, you should define it on a single line for it to work. All the possible Web events it might associate with are found in the `System.Web.Management` namespace.

Each Web event that is recorded has an identifier (code) associated with it, and you can use the `startEventCode` attribute to define a starting point for this code definition. In the preceding example, the event code starts at `0` and increments from there until it reaches the number defined in the `endEventCode` attribute. In this case, the ending event code is `2147483647`.

Table 34-2 defines each event type you can find in the `System.Web.Management` namespace.

TABLE 34-2

WEB EVENT (SYSTEM.WEB.MANAGEMENT)	DESCRIPTION
`WebBaseEvent`	The `WebBaseEvent` class is the base class for all Web event types. You can, therefore, use this instance within the `<eventMappings>` section in order to create a definition to capture all events.
`WebHeartbeatEvent`	This event defines Web events that are recorded only at specific intervals instead of every time they occur.
`WebApplicationLifetimeEvent`	This event defines Web events that occur on the scale of the application and its lifecycle. These types of events include application starts and stops as well as compilation starts and stops.
`WebRequestEvent`	This event defines Web events that occur during a request cycle and include items such as when a transaction for a request is committed or aborted.
`WebBaseErrorEvent`	The `WebBaseErrorEvent` class is the base class for all Web events that deal with error types. You can, therefore, use this instance within the `<eventMappings>` section to create a definition to capture all error events.
`WebErrorEvent`	This event defines Web events that occur because of configuration errors or any compilation or parsing errors.
`WebRequestErrorEvent`	This event defines Web events that occur because requests are aborted or requests are larger than allowable as defined by the `maxRequestLength` attribute in the configuration file. It also includes any validation errors or any unhandled exceptions.
`WebAuditEvent`	The `WebAuditEvent` class is the base class for all Web events that deal with login attempts. These attempts can either fail or succeed. You can use this instance within the `<eventMappings>` section to write a definition to capture all login attempts.
`WebFailureAuditEvent`	This event defines Web events that occur because of failed login attempts.

Now that all the error definitions are in place within the `<eventMappings>` section, the next step is to further define the structure your health monitoring system will take by detailing the `<providers>` section, which is also found within the `<healthMonitoring>` section.

<providers>

As you saw earlier in Figure 34-10, seven different providers that you can use within the health monitoring system are available to you out of the box. By default, ASP.NET records these events to the event logs using the `EventLogWebEventProvider`, but you can also modify the provider model so that it uses any of the other providers available. You can also build your own custom providers so you can record these Web events to any data store you want.

You can find more information on building custom providers in Chapter 12.

Providers are declared within the `<providers>` section, which is nested within the `<healthMonitoring>` section of the document. Within the root `web.config` file found at

C:\WINDOWS\Microsoft.NET\Framework\v4.0.21006\CONFIG, you find a short list of declared providers. You can also declare other providers in your application's web.config file as presented in Listing 34-5.

Available for download on Wrox.com

LISTING 34-5: Using the <providers> section

```
<configuration>
   <system.web>

      <healthMonitoring enabled="true">

         <eventMappings>
            <!-- Code removed for clarity -->
         </eventMappings>
         <providers>

            <clear />

            <add name="EventLogProvider"
             type="System.Web.Management.EventLogWebEventProvider,System.Web,
               Version=4.0.0.0,Culture=neutral,PublicKeyToken=b03f5f7f11d50a3a" />
            <add name="SqlWebEventProvider"
             connectionStringName="LocalSqlServer"
             maxEventDetailsLength="1073741823"
             buffer="false" bufferMode="Notification"
             type="System.Web.Management.SqlWebEventProvider,System.Web,
               Version=4.0.0.0,Culture=neutral,PublicKeyToken=b03f5f7f11d50a3a" />
            <add name="WmiWebEventProvider"
             type="System.Web.Management.WmiWebEventProvider,System.Web,
             Version=4.0.0.0,Culture=neutral,PublicKeyToken=b03f5f7f11d50a3a" />

         </providers>
      </healthMonitoring>

   </system.web>
</configuration>
```

In this example, you see three separate health monitoring providers declared in the web.config file. A provider is defined for storing Web events in the event logs, another for storing in SQL Server, and finally another for the Windows Management Instrumentation (WMI) system.

By declaring these providers within the <providers> section of the web.config file, you don't ensure that these providers are *actually* utilized. Instead, they are simply defined and ready for you to use. You specify which providers to use within the <rules> section of the <healthMonitoring> section, which is defined shortly.

You can add defined providers by using the <add /> element within the <providers> section. Within the <add /> element, you find a series of available attributes. The first one is the name attribute. This allows you to provide a friendly name to the defined provider instance that you will use later when specifying the provider to actually use. The name can be anything you want. The type attribute allows you to define the class used for the provider. In some cases, this is all you need (for example, for the event log provider). If you are working with a database-linked provider, however, you must further define attributes such as the connectionString attribute, along with the buffer and bufferMode attributes. These are covered in more detail later in this chapter.

After your providers are defined in the <healthMonitoring> section of the document, the next step is to determine which Web events to work with and which provider(s) should be utilized in the monitoring of these events. Both these operations are accomplished from within the <rules> section.

<rules>

The <rules> section allows you to define the Web events to monitor and the providers to tie them to when one of the monitored Web events is actually triggered. When you are using the health monitoring system, you can actually assign multiple providers to watch for the same Web events. This means that you can store the same Web event in both the event logs *and* in SQL Server. That capability is powerful. Listing 34-6 provides an example of using the `<rules>` section within your application's `web.config` file.

Available for download on Wrox.com

LISTING 34-6: Using the <rules> section

```
<configuration>
   <system.web>

      <healthMonitoring enabled="true">

         <eventMappings>
            <!-- Code removed for clarity -->
         </eventMappings>

         <providers>
            <!-- Code removed for clarity -->
         </providers>
         <rules>

            <clear />

            <add name="All Errors Default" eventName="All Errors"
             provider="EventLogProvider"
             profile="Default" minInstances="1" maxLimit="Infinite"
             minInterval="00:01:00" custom="" />
            <add name="Failure Audits Default" eventName="Failure Audits"
             provider="EventLogProvider" profile="Default" minInstances="1"
             maxLimit="Infinite" minInterval="00:01:00" custom="" />

         </rules>
      </healthMonitoring>

   </system.web>
</configuration>
```

In this example, two types of Web events are being recorded. You specify rules (the Web events to monitor) by using the `<add />` element within the `<rules>` section. The `name` attribute allows you to provide a friendly name for the rule definition. The `eventName` is an important attribute because it takes a value of the Web event to monitor. These names are the friendly names that you defined earlier within the `<eventMappings>` section of the `<healthMonitoring>` section. The first `<add />` element provides a definition of monitoring for `All Errors` via the `eventName` attribute. Looking back, you can see that this was, indeed, defined in the `<eventMappings>` section.

```
<eventMappings>
   <add name="All Errors"
    type="System.Web.Management.WebBaseErrorEvent,System.Web,
       Version=4.0.0.0,Culture=neutral,PublicKeyToken=b03f5f7f11d50a3a"
    startEventCode="0" endEventCode="2147483647" />
</eventMappings>
```

After specifying which Web event to work with through the `eventName` attribute, the next step is to define which provider to use for this Web event. You do this using the `provider` attribute. In the case of the first `<add />` element, the `EventLogProvider` is utilized. Again, this is the friendly name that was used for the provider definition in the `<providers>` section, as shown here:

```
<providers>
  <add name="EventLogProvider"
   type="System.Web.Management.EventLogWebEventProvider,System.Web,
     Version=4.0.0.0,Culture=neutral,PublicKeyToken=b03f5f7f11d50a3a" />
</providers>
```

The three attributes discussed so far are required attributes. The rest are considered optional attributes. The `minInstances` attribute defines the minimum number of times this Web event must occur before it is logged. The `maxLimit` attribute defines the maximum number of instances of the defined Web event that can be recorded. If instances are likely to occur because of some continuous loop, you might want to add a value here. The `minInterval` attribute denotes the minimum time allowed between log entries. This means that if the `minInterval` is set to `00:01:00` and two Web events being monitored occur within 15 seconds of each other, the first one is recorded but the second instance is discarded because it falls within the 1-minute setting.

Within the `<rules>` section, you can also see a `profile` attribute defined in the `<add />` elements of the rules defined. The value of this attribute comes from a definition that is supplied from the `<profiles>` section of the `<healthMonitoring>` section. This section is discussed next.

<profiles>

The `<profiles>` section enables you to define some of the behaviors for Web event monitoring. These definitions are utilized by any number of rule definitions within the `<rules>` section. Listing 34-7 presents an example use of the `<profiles>` section.

LISTING 34-7: Using the <profiles> section

Available for download on Wrox.com

```
<configuration>
  <system.web>

    <healthMonitoring enabled="true">

      <eventMappings>
        <!-- Code removed for clarity -->
      </eventMappings>

      <providers>
        <!-- Code removed for clarity -->
      </providers>

      <rules>
        <!-- Code removed for clarity -->
      </rules>
      <profiles>

        <clear />

        <add name="Default" minInstances="1" maxLimit="Infinite"
         minInterval="00:01:00" custom="" />
        <add name="Critical" minInstances="1" maxLimit="Infinite"
         minInterval="00:00:00" custom="" />

      </profiles>
    </healthMonitoring>

  </system.web>
</configuration>
```

As with the other sections, you add a profile definition by using the `<add />` element within the `<profiles>` section. The `name` attribute allows you to provide a friendly name that is then utilized from the definitions placed within the `<rules>` section, as illustrated here:

```
<rules>
  <add name="All Errors Default" eventName="All Errors"
   provider="EventLogProvider"
   profile="Default" minInstances="1" maxLimit="Infinite"
   minInterval="00:01:00" custom="" />
</rules>
```

The definitions in the `<profiles>` section also use the attributes `minInstances`, `maxLimit`, and `minInterval`. These have the same meanings as if they were used directly in the `<rules>` section (see the explanation in the previous section). The idea here, however, is that you can more centrally define these values and use them across multiple rule definitions.

Writing Events via Configuration: Running the Example

Using the sample <healthMonitoring> section (illustrated in the previous listings in this chapter), you can now write all errors as well as audits that fail (failed logins) to the event log automatically.

To test this construction in the <healthMonitoring> section, create a simple ASP.NET page that allows you to divide two numbers and then show the result of the division on the screen. Figure 34-11 shows an example ASP.NET page.

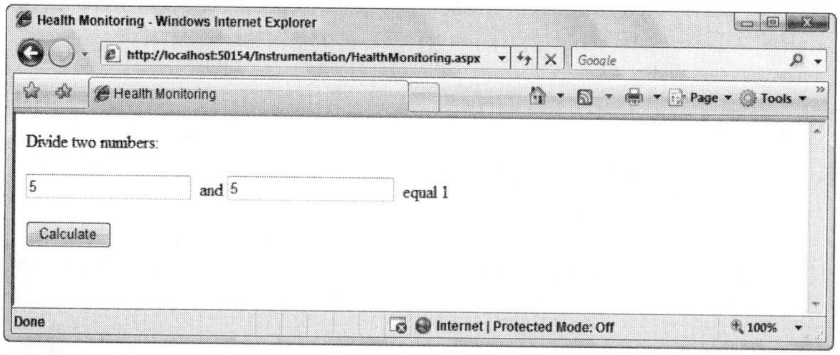

FIGURE 34-11

As you can see from this page, you can enter a single number in the first text box and another in the second text box, and click the Calculate button. This allows the two numbers to be divided. The result appears in a Label control on the page. In this example, the code intentionally does not use any exception handling. Therefore, if the end user tried to divide 5 by 0 (zero), an exception is thrown. This event, in turn, causes the exception to be written to the event log. In fact, if you run a similar example and look in the event log, you find that the error has indeed been written as you have specified it should be within the `web.config` file. Figure 34-12 shows the report from the event log.

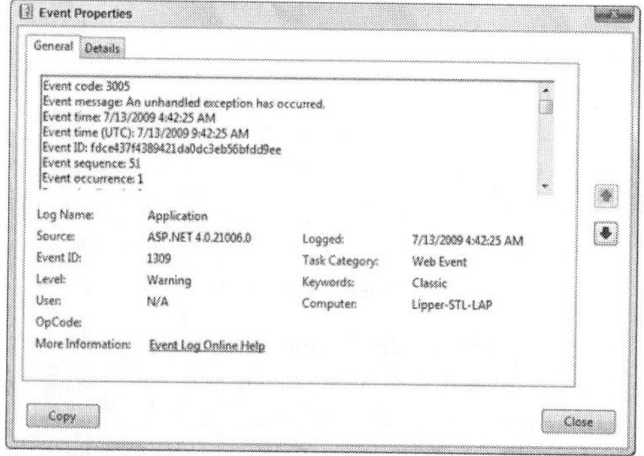

FIGURE 34-12

Routing Events to SQL Server

Pushing Web events to the event log is something most Web applications do and is also something you should consider if you have overridden these built-in (and default) features. Even more powerful than writing them to the event log, however, is being able to write them to a database.

Writing them to a database allows you to actually create a larger history, makes them more secure, and allows you to more easily retrieve the values and use them in any type of administration application that you might create.

This capability was briefly introduced in the introduction of this book and is not that difficult to work with. If you work from the same <healthMonitoring> section created earlier in this chapter, writing the events to SQL Server is as simple as adding some <add /> elements to the various sections.

As shown in the previous <providers> section, a declaration actually exists for recording events into SQL Server. It is presented here again:

```
<providers>

  <clear />

  <add name="EventLogProvider"
```

```
        type="System.Web.Management.EventLogWebEventProvider,System.Web,
          Version=4.0.0.0,Culture=neutral,PublicKeyToken=b03f5f7f11d50a3a" />

       <add name="SqlWebEventProvider"
        connectionStringName="LocalSqlServer"
        maxEventDetailsLength="1073741823"
        buffer="false" bufferMode="Notification"
        type="System.Web.Management.SqlWebEventProvider,System.Web,
          Version=4.0.0.0,Culture=neutral,PublicKeyToken=b03f5f7f11d50a3a" />

        <add name="WmiWebEventProvider"
        type="System.Web.Management.WmiWebEventProvider,System.Web,
          Version=4.0.0.0,Culture=neutral,PublicKeyToken=b03f5f7f11d50a3a" />

    </providers>
```

If you look over this bit of code, you see the definition to record events into SQL Server is presented in the bold section within the `<providers>` section. The section in bold shows a connection to the SQL Server instance that is defined by the `ApplicationServices` connection string name. You can find this connection string in the `machine.config` file, and you see that it points to an auto-generated SQL Server Express file that ASP.NET can work with.

```
<connectionStrings>
   <add name="ApplicationServices"
    connectionString="data source=.\SQLEXPRESS;Integrated
    Security=SSPI;AttachDBFilename=|DataDirectory|aspnetdb.mdf;User Instance=true"
    providerName="System.Data.SqlClient" />
</connectionStrings>
```

To work with Microsoft's SQL Server 2008, you simply create a new connection string within your ASP.NET application's `web.config` *file and reference the friendly name provided to this connection from the* `<add />` *element of the* `<providers>` *section.*

Although this SQL Server instance is declared and defined, it is not utilized by any of the rules that you have established. Looking at the previous sections, you can see that within the `<rules>` section of the health monitoring section of the `web.config` file, only two rules exist: a rule to write all errors to the event log and another rule to write failure audits to the event log. To add a new rule to write errors (all errors again) to SQL Server, you use the construction shown in Listing 34-8.

LISTING 34-8: Creating a rule to write events to SQL Server

Available for download on Wrox.com

```
<configuration>
   <system.web>

      <healthMonitoring enabled="true">

         <eventMappings>
            <!-- Code removed for clarity -->
         </eventMappings>

         <providers>
            <!-- Code removed for clarity -->
         </providers>

         <rules>

            <clear />

            <add name="All Errors Default" eventName="All Errors"
             provider="EventLogProvider"
```

```
                profile="Default" minInstances="1" maxLimit="Infinite"
                minInterval="00:01:00" custom="" />
               <add name="Failure Audits Default" eventName="Failure Audits"
                provider="EventLogProvider" profile="Default" minInstances="1"
                maxLimit="Infinite" minInterval="00:01:00" custom="" />
               <add name="All Errors SQL Server" eventName="All Errors"
                provider="SqlWebEventProvider"
                profile="Default" minInstances="1" maxLimit="Infinite"
                minInterval="00:01:00" custom="" />

          </rules>

        </healthMonitoring>

    </system.web>
  </configuration>
```

To be able to write to SQL Server, you must create a new `<add />` element within the `<rules>` section of the document. The friendly name provided via the `name` attribute must be unique in the list of defined rules or you encounter an error. In this case, the name of the rule is `All Errors SQL Server` and like the `All Errors Default` rule, it points to the event mapping of `All Errors` as shown via the `eventName` attribute. The `provider` attribute then points to the SQL Server definition contained within the `<providers>` section. In this case, it is `SqlWebEventProvider`.

With all this in place, run the ASP.NET page (shown earlier) that allows you to throw an error by dividing by zero. If you run this page a couple of times, you see that ASP.NET has automatically created an `ASPNETDB.MDF` file in your project (if you didn't already have one).

You can then open the SQL Server Express Edition database and expand the Tables node in the Visual Studio Server Explorer. In this list of available tables, you find a new table called `aspnet_WebEvent_Events`. Right-click this table and select Show Table Data from the menu. A dialog similar to what is illustrated in Figure 34-13 appears.

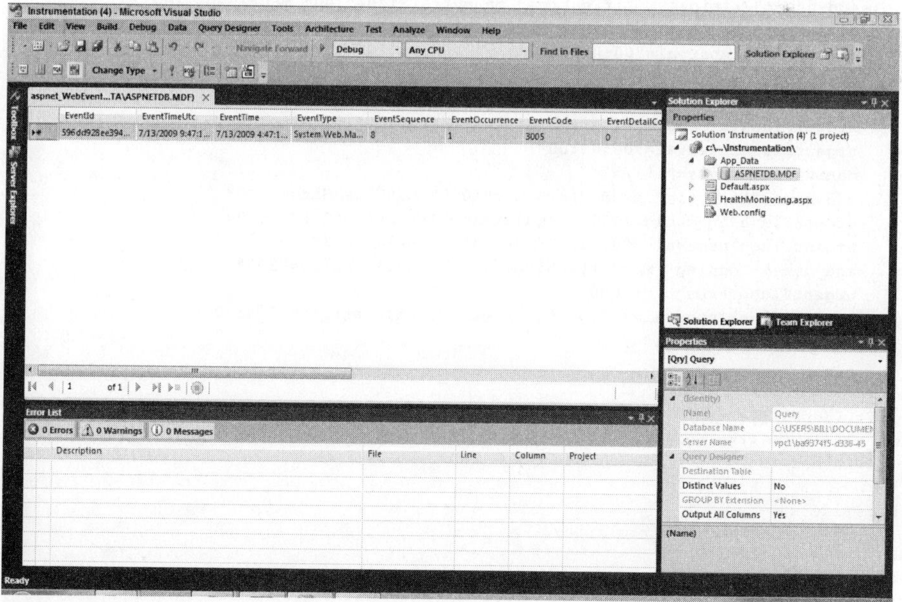

FIGURE 34-13

As you can see from this figure, the entire event is now stored within SQL Server (it is the first and only event at the moment). One of the nice things about this example is that not only is this event recorded to the database, but it is also written to the event log because you can use more than a single provider for each event. You can just as easily use a provider that comes from MailWebEventProvider and send the error out as an e-mail message.

Buffering Web Events

When you start working with Web events that you want to write to a database (such as SQL Server) or send via an e-mail, you soon realize that doing so can lock up your database or result in a huge amount of e-mail (especially if your application is sent into some perpetual loop of errors). For this reason, you can see why these providers inherit from BufferedWebEventProvider.

BufferedWebEventProvider does exactly what it says — it *buffers* (or queues) your collected Web events before performing the specified action upon them. The reason you might want to buffer is to eliminate the possibility of your database being pounded or your e-mail box being flooded.

Definitions of how the buffering should occur are located in the <bufferModes> section within the <healthMonitoring> section of the web.config file. Listing 34-9 presents an example of the <bufferModes> section.

LISTING 34-9: Using the <bufferModes> section

Available for download on Wrox.com

```
<configuration>
   <system.web>

      <healthMonitoring enabled="true">
         <bufferModes>

            <clear />

            <add name="Critical Notification" maxBufferSize="100" maxFlushSize="20"
             urgentFlushThreshold="1" regularFlushInterval="Infinite"
             urgentFlushInterval="00:01:00"
             maxBufferThreads="1" />
            <add name="Notification" maxBufferSize="300" maxFlushSize="20"
             urgentFlushThreshold="1" regularFlushInterval="Infinite"
             urgentFlushInterval="00:01:00"
             maxBufferThreads="1" />
            <add name="Analysis" maxBufferSize="1000" maxFlushSize="100"
             urgentFlushThreshold="100" regularFlushInterval="00:05:00"
             urgentFlushInterval="00:01:00" maxBufferThreads="1" />
            <add name="Logging" maxBufferSize="1000" maxFlushSize="200"
             urgentFlushThreshold="800"
             regularFlushInterval="00:30:00" urgentFlushInterval="00:05:00"
             maxBufferThreads="1" />

         </bufferModes>
         <eventMappings>
            <!-- Code removed for clarity -->
         </eventMappings>

         <providers>
            <!-- Code removed for clarity -->
         </providers>

         <rules>
            <!-- Code removed for clarity -->
         </rules>
```

```
        <profiles>
           <!-- Code removed for clarity -->
        </profiles>

      </healthMonitoring>

   </system.web>
</configuration>
```

In this code, you can see four buffer modes defined. Each mode has a friendly name defined using the `name` attribute. For each mode, a number of different attributes can be applied. To examine these attributes, take a closer look at the `Logging` buffer mode:

```
<add name="Logging"
 maxBufferSize="1000"
 maxFlushSize="200"
 urgentFlushThreshold="800"
 regularFlushInterval="00:30:00"
 urgentFlushInterval="00:05:00"
 maxBufferThreads="1" />
```

This buffer mode is called *Logging* and, based on the values assigned to its attributes, any provider using this buffer mode sends the messages to the database or via e-mail every 30 minutes. This is also referred to as *flushing* the Web events. The time period of 30 minutes is defined using the `regularFlushInterval` attribute. Therefore, every 30 minutes, ASP.NET sends 200 messages to the database (or via e-mail). It will not send more than 200 messages at a time because of what is specified in the `maxFlushSize` attribute. Well, what happens if more than 200 messages are waiting within that 30-minute time period? ASP.NET still sends only 200 messages every 30 minutes and holds additional messages when the number exceeds 200. The maximum number of messages held in the queue cannot exceed 1,000 messages. This number is set through the `maxBufferSize` attribute. However, after the total in the queue hits 800 messages, ASP.NET starts flushing the messages every 5 minutes instead of every 30 minutes. The change in frequency of messages is determined by the `urgentFlushThreshold` attribute, and the time interval used to send messages when the `urgentFlushThreshold` is hit is determined by the `urgentFlushInterval` attribute.

After you have defined the buffering modes you want to use, the next step is to apply them. To analyze the process, look back on how the `SqlWebEventProvider` is declared:

```
<providers>

   <clear />

   <add name="EventLogProvider"
    type="System.Web.Management.EventLogWebEventProvider,System.Web,
      Version=4.0.0.0,Culture=neutral,PublicKeyToken=b03f5f7f11d50a3a" />

   <add name="SqlWebEventProvider"
    connectionStringName="LocalSqlServer"
    maxEventDetailsLength="1073741823"
    buffer="false" bufferMode="Notification"
    type="System.Web.Management.SqlWebEventProvider,System.Web,
      Version=4.0.0.0,Culture=neutral,PublicKeyToken=b03f5f7f11d50a3a" />

   <add name="WmiWebEventProvider"
    type="System.Web.Management.WmiWebEventProvider,System.Web,
      Version=4.0.0.0,Culture=neutral,PublicKeyToken=b03f5f7f11d50a3a" />

</providers>
```

Again, this event is shown in bold. The most important attribute is the `buffer` attribute. By default, buffering of messages is turned off, which you do by setting the `buffer` attribute to `false`. The `bufferMode` attribute allows you to assign one of the defined buffer modes created within the `<bufferModes>` section. In this case, the `Notification` buffer mode is referenced. Changing the buffer attribute to `true` enables the events to be sent only to SQL Server according to the time intervals defined by the `Notification` buffer mode.

E-mailing Web Events

When monitoring a server for Web events, you are not *always* going to be networked into a server or actively monitoring it every second. This doesn't mean that you won't want to know immediately if something is going very wrong with your ASP.NET application. For this reason, you will find the `SimpleMailWebEventProvider` and the `TemplatedMailWebEventProvider` objects quite beneficial.

Using the SimpleMailProvider

The `SimpleMailWebEventProvider` sends Web events as a simple text e-mail, as shown in Figure 34-14.

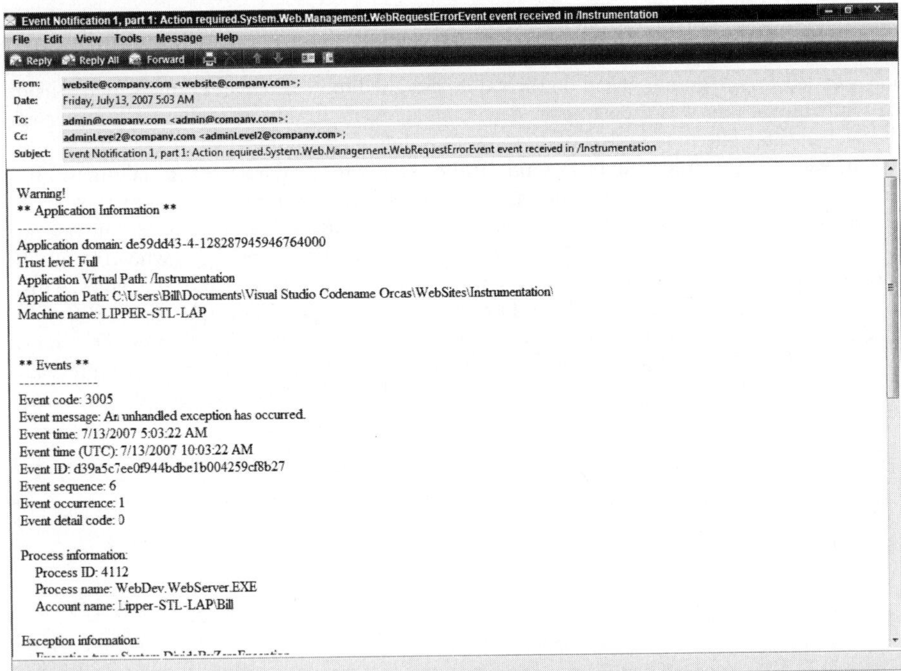

FIGURE 34-14

To set up this provider, you place an additional `<add />` element within the `<providers>` section, as illustrated in Listing 34-10.

LISTING 34-10: Adding a SimpleMailWebEventProvider instance

```
<add name="SimpleMailProvider"
 type="System.Web.Management.SimpleMailWebEventProvider, System.Web,
   Version=4.0.0.0, Culture=neutral, PublicKeyToken=b03f5f7f11d50a3a"
 from="website@company.com"
 to="admin@company.com"
 cc="adminLevel2@company.com"
 bcc="director@company.com"
 bodyHeader="Warning!"
 bodyFooter="Please investigate ASAP."
```

```
    subjectPrefix="Action required."
    buffer="false"
    maxEventLength="4096"
    maxMessagesPerNotification="1" />
```

After the provider is added, you also add a rule that uses this provider in some fashion (as you do with all the other providers). You do this by referencing the `SimpleMailWebEventProvider` name within the provider attribute of the `<add />` element contained in the `<rules>` section.

For this code to work, be sure that you set up the SMTP capabilities correctly in your `web.config` file. Listing 34-11 presents an example.

LISTING 34-11: Setting up SMTP in the web.config file

```
<configuration>

  <system.web>
     <!-- Code removed for clarity -->
  </system.web>

  <system.net>
    <mailSettings>
      <smtp deliveryMethod="Network">
        <network
          host="localhost"
          port="25"
          defaultCredentials="true"
        />
      </smtp>
    </mailSettings>
  </system.net>

</configuration>
```

If you do not have a quick way of setting up SMTP and still want to test this code, you can also have ASP.NET create e-mail messages and store them to disk by setting up the `<smtp>` section as illustrated in Listing 34-12.

LISTING 34-12: Another option for setting up the SMTP section

```
<configuration>

  <system.web>
     <!-- Code removed for clarity -->
  </system.web>

  <system.net>
    <mailSettings>
      <smtp deliveryMethod="SpecifiedPickupDirectory">
        <specifiedPickupDirectory pickupDirectoryLocation ="C:\"/>
      </smtp>
    </mailSettings>
  </system.net>

</configuration>
```

In this scenario, the e-mails will be just placed within the `C:\` root directory.

Using the TemplatedMailWebEventProvider

Another option for e-mailing Web events is to use the `TemplatedMailWebEventProvider` object. This object works basically the same as the `SimpleMailWebEventProvider`, but the `TemplatedMailWebEventProvider` allows you to create more handsome e-mails (they might get noticed more). As with the other providers, you use the `<add />` element within the `<providers>` section to add this provider. Listing 34-13 shows this process.

LISTING 34-13: Adding a TemplatedMailWebEventProvider

```
<add name="TemplatedMailProvider"
 type="System.Web.Management.TemplatedMailWebEventProvider, System.Web,
   Version=4.0.0.0, Culture=neutral, PublicKeyToken=b03f5f7f11d50a3a"
 template="../MailTemplates/ErrorNotification.aspx"
 from="website@company.com"
 to="admin@company.com"
 cc="adminLevel2@company.com"
 bcc="director@company.com"
 subjectPrefix="Action required."
 buffer="false"
 detailedTemplateErrors="true"
 maxMessagesPerNotification="1" />
```

After adding the provider, you also must add a rule that uses this provider in some fashion (as you do with all the other providers). You add it by referencing the `TemplatedMailWebEventProvider` name within the provider attribute of the `<add />` element contained in the `<rules>` section. Be sure to set up the `<smtp>` section, just as you did with the `SimpleMailWebEventProvider`.

After these items are in place, the next step is to create an `ErrorNotification.aspx` page. Listing 34-14 presents this page construction.

LISTING 34-14: Creating the ErrorNotification.aspx page

Available for download on Wrox.com

VB

```
<%@ Page Language="VB" %>
<%@ Import Namespace="System.Web.Management" %>

<script runat="server">
    Protected Sub Page_Load(ByVal sender As Object, ByVal e As System.EventArgs)
        Dim meni As MailEventNotificationInfo = _
          TemplatedMailWebEventProvider.CurrentNotification
        Label1.Text = "Events Discarded By Buffer: " & _
          meni.EventsDiscardedByBuffer.ToString()
        Label2.Text = "Events Discarded Due To Message Limit: " & _
          meni.EventsDiscardedDueToMessageLimit.ToString()
        Label3.Text = "Events In Buffer: " & meni.EventsInBuffer.ToString()
        Label4.Text = "Events In Notification: " & _
          meni.EventsInNotification.ToString()
        Label5.Text = "Events Remaining: " & meni.EventsRemaining.ToString()
        Label6.Text = "Last Notification UTC: " & _
          meni.LastNotificationUtc.ToString()
        Label7.Text = "Number of Messages In Notification: " & _
          meni.MessagesInNotification.ToString()

        DetailsView1.DataSource = meni.Events
        DetailsView1.DataBind()
    End Sub
</script>

<html xmlns="http://www.w3.org/1999/xhtml">
   <head><title>My Page</title></head>
   <body>
      <form id="form1" runat="server">
         <asp:label id="Label1" runat="server"></asp:label><br />
```

```
            <asp:label id="Label2" runat="server"></asp:label><br />
            <asp:label id="Label3" runat="server"></asp:label><br />
            <asp:label id="Label4" runat="server"></asp:label><br />
            <asp:label id="Label5" runat="server"></asp:label><br />
            <asp:label id="Label6" runat="server"></asp:label><br />
            <asp:label id="Label7" runat="server"></asp:label><br />

            <br />

            <asp:DetailsView ID="DetailsView1" runat="server" Height="50px"
             Width="500px" BackColor="White" BorderColor="#E7E7FF" BorderStyle="None"
             BorderWidth="1px" CellPadding="3" GridLines="Horizontal">
               <FooterStyle BackColor="#B5C7DE" ForeColor="#4A3C8C" />
               <EditRowStyle BackColor="#738A9C" Font-Bold="True"
                ForeColor="#F7F7F7" />
               <RowStyle BackColor="#E7E7FF" ForeColor="#4A3C8C" />
               <PagerStyle BackColor="#E7E7FF" ForeColor="#4A3C8C"
                HorizontalAlign="Right" />
               <HeaderStyle BackColor="#4A3C8C" Font-Bold="True"
                ForeColor="#F7F7F7" />
               <AlternatingRowStyle BackColor="#F7F7F7" />
            </asp:DetailsView>
        </form>
    </body>
</html>
```

C#

```
<%@ Page Language="C#" %>
<%@ Import Namespace="System.Web.Management" %>

<script runat="server">
    protected void Page_Load(object sender, EventArgs e)
    {
        MailEventNotificationInfo meni =
          TemplatedMailWebEventProvider.CurrentNotification;
        Label1.Text = "Events Discarded By Buffer: " +
          meni.EventsDiscardedByBuffer.ToString();
        Label2.Text = "Events Discarded Due To Message Limit: " +
          meni.EventsDiscardedDueToMessageLimit.ToString();
        Label3.Text = "Events In Buffer: " + meni.EventsInBuffer.ToString();
        Label4.Text = "Events In Notification: " +
          meni.EventsInNotification.ToString();
        Label5.Text = "Events Remaining: " + meni.EventsRemaining.ToString();
        Label6.Text = "Last Notification UTC: " +
          meni.LastNotificationUtc.ToString();
        Label7.Text = "Number of Messages In Notification: " +
          meni.MessagesInNotification.ToString();

        DetailsView1.DataSource = meni.Events;
        DetailsView1.DataBind();
    }
</script>
```

To work with the `TemplatedMailWebEventProvider`, you first import the `System.Web.Management` namespace. This is done so you can work with the `MailEventNotificationInfo` and `TemplatedMailWebEventProvider` objects. You then create an instance of the `MailEventNotificationInfo` object and assign it a value of the `TemplatedMailWebEventProvider.CurrentNotification` property. Now, you have access to an entire series of values from the Web event that was monitored.

Figure 34-15 shows this e-mail message.

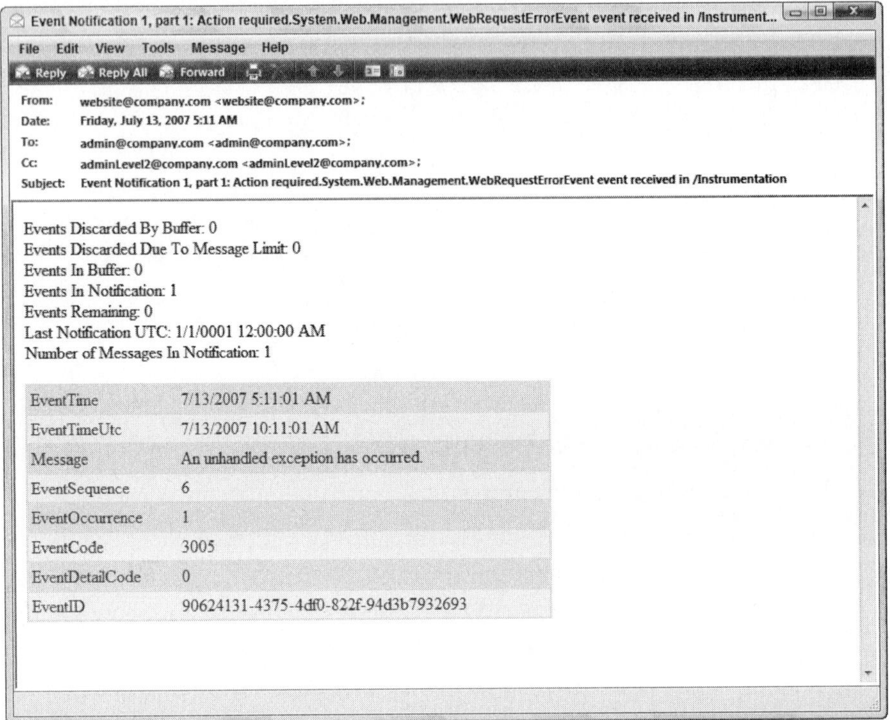

FIGURE 34-15

As you can see in this figure, the e-mail message is more readable in this format.

SUMMARY

Whereas ASP.NET 1.x was really focused on the developer, ASP.NET 2.0 through 4 have made tremendous inroads into making life easier for the administrator of the deployed ASP.NET application. In addition to a number of GUI-based management and administration tools (covered in the next chapter), you can now record and send notifications about the health (good or bad) of your ASP.NET applications using the ASP.NET health monitoring capabilities.

35

Administration and Management

WHAT'S IN THIS CHAPTER?

- Managing applications settings with the ASP.NET Web Site Administration Tool
- Using the IIS Manager to manage ASP.NET applications

You have almost reached the end of this book; you have been introduced to ASP.NET 4 with its wonderful features designed to help you become a better and more efficient programmer. However, with all advancement comes complexity, as is the case in the areas of ASP.NET configuration and management. The good news is that the ASP.NET development team realized this and provided tools and APIs that enable developers to configure and manage ASP.NET–based applications with reliability and comfort.

This chapter covers these tools in great detail in an effort to educate you about some of the options available to you. This chapter explores two powerful configuration tools: the ASP.NET Web Site Administration Tool, a Web-based application, and the IIS Manager, which is used to configure your ASP.NET applications.

THE ASP.NET WEB SITE ADMINISTRATION TOOL

When ASP.NET was first released, it introduced the concept of an XML-based configuration file for its Web applications. This `web.config` file is located in the same directory as the application itself. It is used to store a number of configuration settings, some of which can override configuration settings defined in `machine.config` file or in the root server's `web.config` file. Versions of ASP.NET before ASP.NET 2.0, however, did not provide an administration tool to make it easy to configure the settings. Because of this, a large number of developers around the world ended up creating their own configuration tools to avoid having to work with the XML file manually.

The ASP.NET Web Site Administration Tool enables you to manage Web site configuration through a simple, easy-to-use Web interface. It eliminates the need for manually editing the `web.config` file. If no `web.config` file exists when you use the administration tool for the first time, it creates one. By default, the ASP.NET Web Site Administration Tool also creates the standard `ASPNETDB.MDF` SQL Server Express Edition file in the App_Data folder of your Web site to store application data. The changes made to most settings in the ASP.NET Web Site Administration Tool take effect immediately. You find them reflected in the `web.config` file.

The default settings are automatically inherited from any configuration files that exist in the root folder of a Web server. The ASP.NET Web Site Administration Tool enables you to create or update your own settings for your Web application. You can also override the settings inherited from up-level configuration files, if an override for those settings is allowed. If overriding is not permitted, the setting appears dimmed in the administration tool.

The ASP.NET Web Site Administration Tool is automatically installed during installation of the .NET Framework version 4. To use the administration tool to administer your own Web site, you must be logged in as a registered user of your site and have read and write permissions to the `web.config` file.

You cannot access the ASP.NET Web Site Administration Tool remotely or even locally through IIS. Instead, you access it with Visual Studio 2010, which, in turn, uses its integrated web server (formally named Cassini) to access the administration tool.

To access this tool through Visual Studio 2010, open the Web site and click the ASP.NET Configuration button found in the menu located at the top of the Solution Explorer pane. Another way to launch this tool is to select ASP.NET Configuration from the Website option in the main Visual Studio menu. Figure 35-1 shows the ASP.NET Web Site Administration Tool's welcome page.

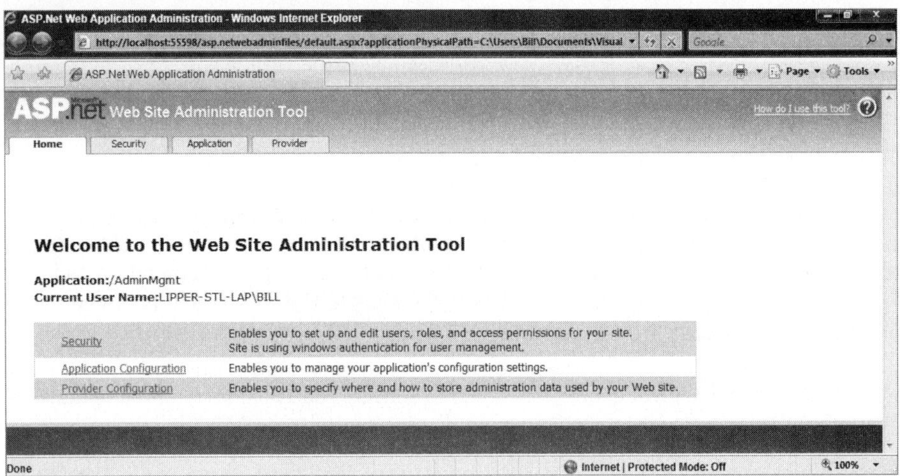

FIGURE 35-1

The ASP.NET Web Site Administration Tool features a tabbed interface that groups related configuration settings. The following sections describe the tabs and the configuration settings that they manage.

The Home Tab

The Home tab (shown previously in Figure 35-1) is a summary that supplies some basic information about the application you are monitoring or modifying. It provides the name of the application and the current user context in which you are accessing the application. In addition, you see links to the other administration tool tabs that provide you with summaries of their settings. To make any changes to your Web application, you simply click the appropriate tab or link.

Remember that most changes to configuration settings made using this administration tool take effect immediately, causing the Web application to be restarted and currently active sessions to be lost if you are using an InProc session. The best practice for administrating ASP.NET is to make configuration changes to a development version of your application and later publish these changes to your production application. That's why this tool can't be used outside of Visual Studio.

Some settings (those in which the administration tool interface has a dedicated Save button) do not save automatically. You can lose the information typed in these windows if you do not click the Save button to propagate the changes you made to the `web.config` file. The ASP.NET Web Site Administration Tool also times out after a period of inactivity. Any settings that do not take effect immediately and are not saved will be lost if this occurs.

As extensive as the ASP.NET Web Site Administration Tool is, it manages only some of the configuration settings that are available for your Web application. All other settings require modification of configuration files manually, by using the Microsoft Management Console (MMC) snap-in for ASP.NET if you are using Windows XP, using the Internet Information Services (IIS) Manager if you are using Windows 7, or by using the `Configuration` API.

The Security Tab

You use the Security tab to manage access permissions to secure sections of your Web application, user accounts, and roles. From this tab, you can select whether your Web application is accessed on an intranet or from the Internet. If you specify the intranet, Windows-based authentication is used; otherwise, forms-based authentication is configured. The latter mechanism relies on you to manage users in a custom datastore, such as SQL Server database tables. The Windows-based authentication employs the user's Windows logon for identification.

User information is stored in a SQL Server Express database by default (`ASPNETDB.MDF`). The database is automatically created in the App_Data folder of the Web application. Storing such sensitive information on a different and more secure database, perhaps located on a separate server, is recommended. Changing the data store might mean that you also need to change the underlying data provider. To accomplish this, you simply use the Provider tab to select a different data provider. The Provider tab is covered later in this chapter.

You can configure security settings on this tab in two ways: select the Setup Wizard, or simply use the links provided for the Users, Roles, and Access Management sections. Figure 35-2 shows the Security tab.

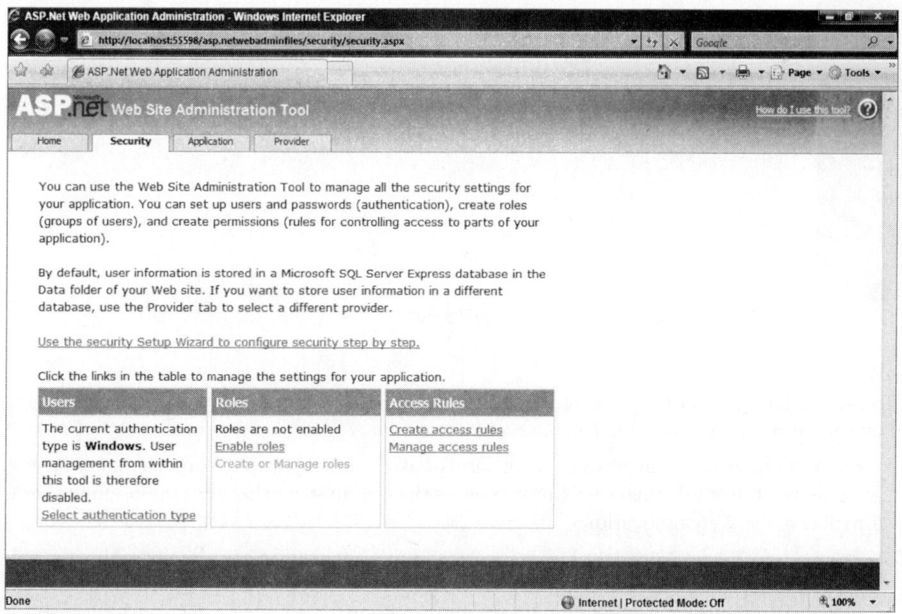

FIGURE 35-2

You can use the wizard to configure initial settings. Later, you will learn other ways to create and modify security settings.

The Security Setup Wizard

The Security Setup Wizard provides a seven-step process ranging from selecting the way the user will be authenticated to selecting a data source for storing user information. This is followed by definitions of roles, users, and access rules.

Be sure to create all folders that need special permissions before you engage the wizard.

Follow these steps to use the Security Setup Wizard:

1. On the Security tab, click the "Use the Security Setup Wizard to configure security step by step" link. The wizard welcome screen (shown in Figure 35-3) appears and is informational only. It educates you on the basics of security management in ASP.NET. When you finish reading the screen, click Next.

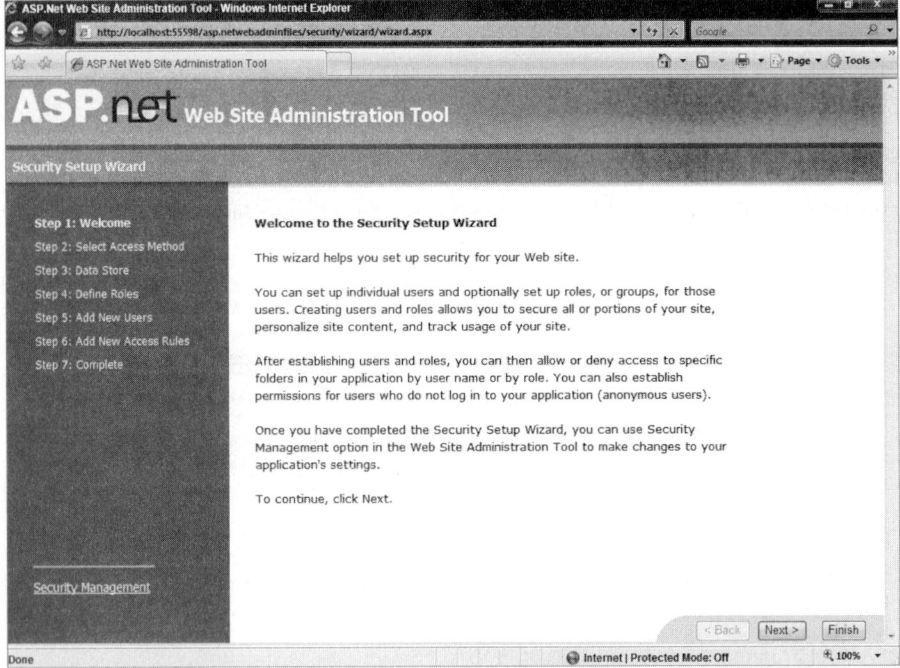

FIGURE 35-3

2. Select Access Method. From the Select Access Method screen, shown in Figure 35-4, select your access method (authentication mechanism). You have two options:

   - **From the Internet:** Indicates you want forms-based authentication. You must use your own database of user information. This option works well in scenarios where non-employees need to access the Web application.
   - **From a Local Area Network:** Indicates users of this application are already authenticated on the domain. You do not have to use your own user information database. Instead, you can use the Windows web server domain user information.

   Select From the Internet, and click the Next button.

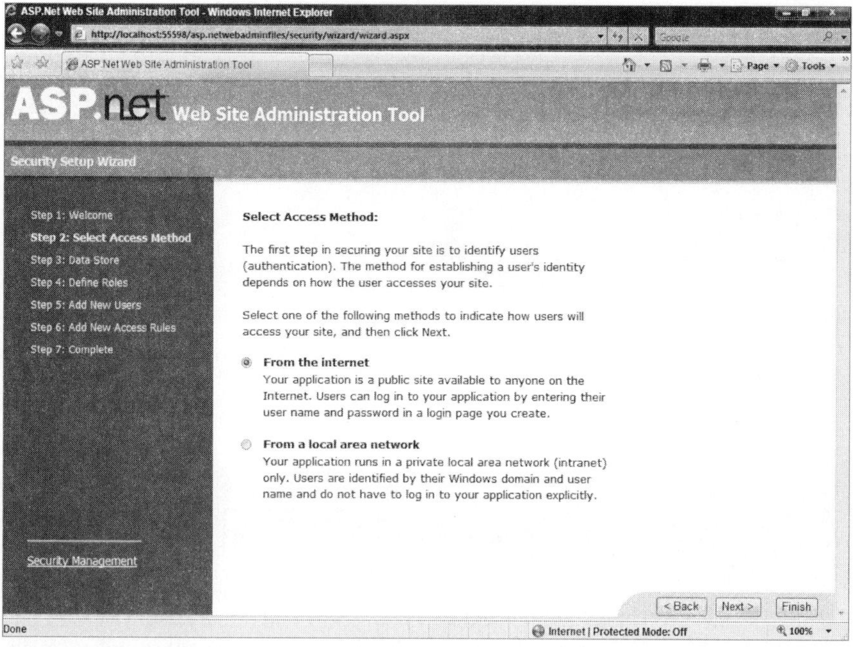

FIGURE 35-4

3. Data Store. As mentioned earlier, the ASP.NET Web Site Administration Tool uses SQL Server Express Edition by default. You can configure additional providers on the Providers tab. In the Step 3 screen shown in Figure 35-5, only an advanced provider is displayed because no other providers have been configured yet. Click Next.

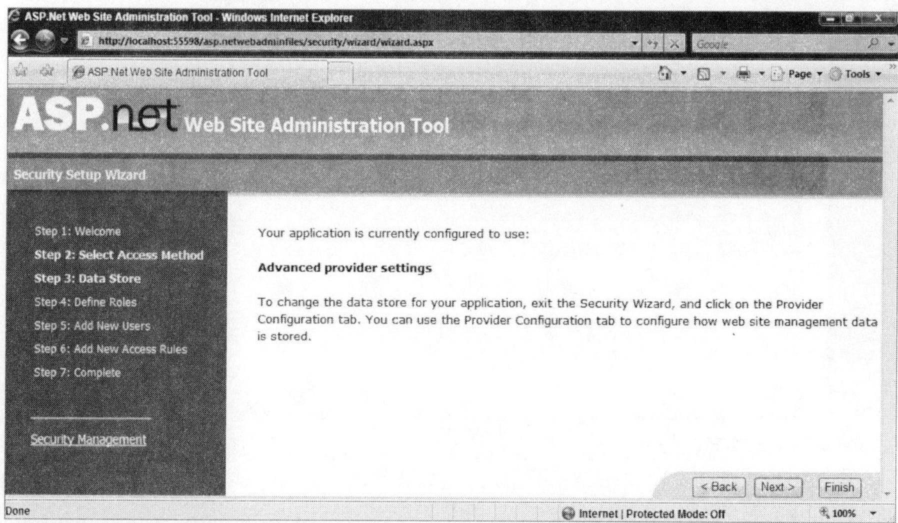

FIGURE 35-5

4. Define Roles. If you are happy with all users having the same access permission, you can simply skip this step by deselecting the Enable Roles for This Web Site check box (see Figure 35-6). If this box is not selected, clicking the Next button takes you directly to the User Management screens. Select this box to see how to define roles using this wizard. When you are ready, click Next.

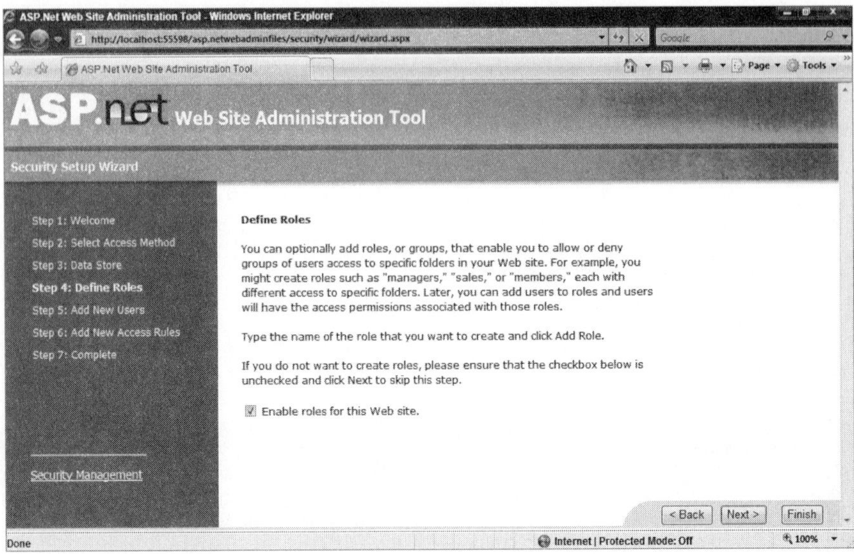

FIGURE 35-6

The next screen (see Figure 35-7) in the wizard enables you to create and delete roles. The roles simply define categories of users. Later, you can provide users and access rules based on these roles. Go ahead and create roles for Administrator, Human Resources, Sales, and Viewer. Click Next.

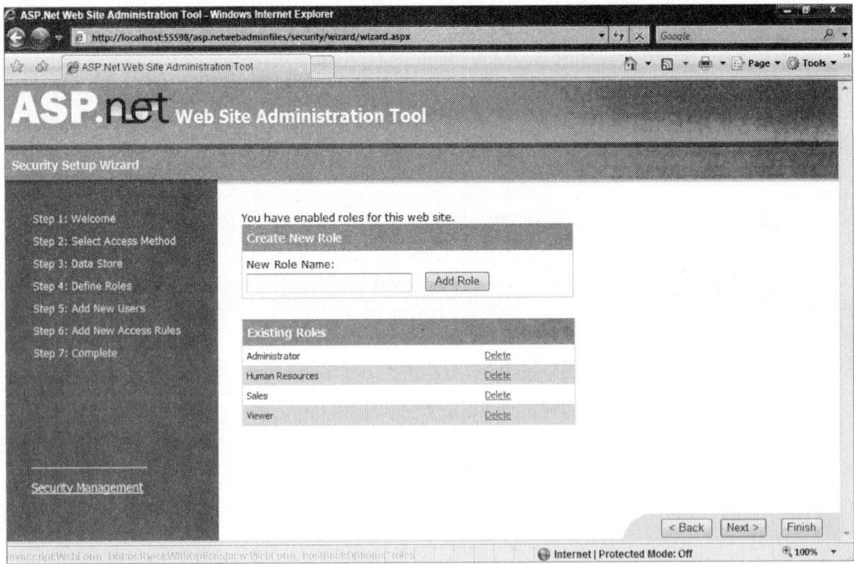

FIGURE 35-7

5. Add New Users. Earlier, you selected the From the Internet option, so the wizard assumes that you want to use forms authentication and provides you with the option of creating and managing users. The From a Local Area Network option, remember, uses Windows-based authentication.

   The Add New Users screen (see Figure 35-8) enables you to enter the username, password, e-mail address, and a security question and answer.

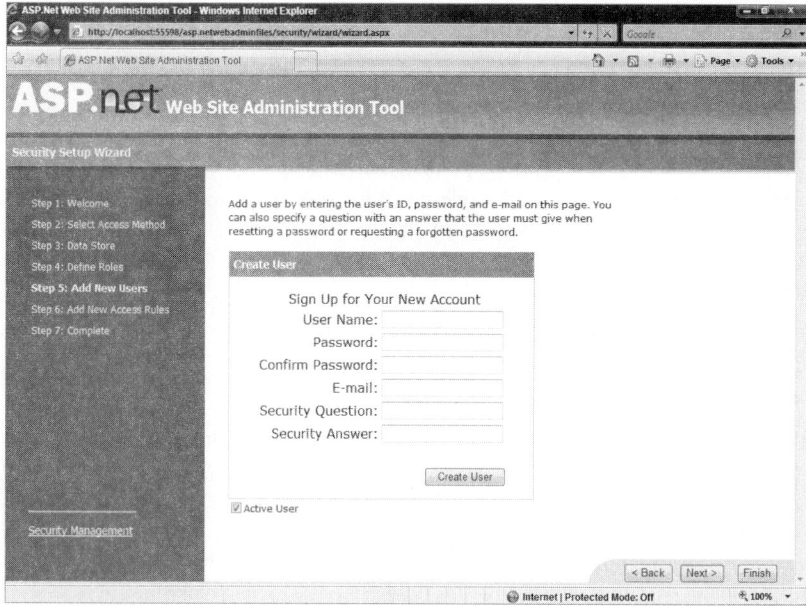

FIGURE 35-8

You can create as many users as you like; but to delete or update information for users, you must leave the wizard and manage the users separately. As mentioned earlier, the wizard is simply for creating the initial configuration for future management. Click Next.

6. Add New Access Rules (see Figure 35-9). First, select the folder in the Web application that needs special security settings. Then choose the role or user(s) to whom the rule will apply. Select the permission (Allow or Deny) and click the Add This Rule button. For example, if you had a folder named Secure you could select it and the Administrator role, and then click the Allow radio button to permit all users in the Administrator role to access the Secure folder.

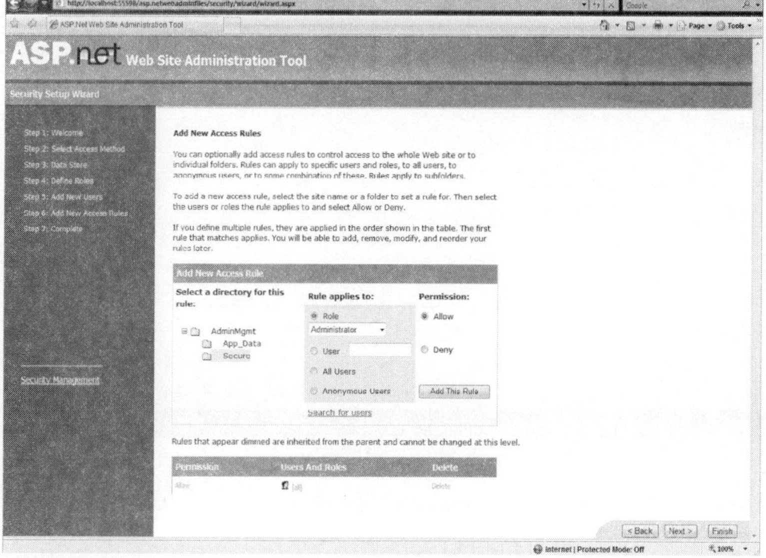

FIGURE 35-9

All folders that need special permissions must be created ahead of time. The information shown in the wizard is cached and is not updated if you decide to create a new folder inside your Web application while you are already on this screen, so remember to create your special security folders before starting the wizard.

The wizard gives you the capability to apply access rules to either roles or specific users. The Search for Users option is handy if you have defined many users for your Web site and want to search for a specific user.

All access rules are shown at the bottom on the screen, and you can delete a specific rule and start again. Rules are shown dimmed if they are inherited from the parent configuration and cannot be changed here.

When you are ready, click Next.

7. The last screen in the Security Setup Wizard is an information page. Click the Finish button to exit the wizard.

Creating New Users

The ASP.NET Web Site Administration Tool's Security tab provides ways to manage users without using the wizard and is very helpful for ongoing maintenance of users, roles, and access permissions.

To create a new user, simply click the Create User link on the main page of the Security tab (shown earlier in Figure 35-2). The Create User screen, shown in Figure 35-10, appears, enabling you to provide username, password, confirmation of password, e-mail, and the security question and answer. You can assign a new user to any number of roles in the Roles list; these are roles currently defined for your Web application. Use this tool to create users named Admin, HRUser, and SalesUser and assign them the corresponding roles.

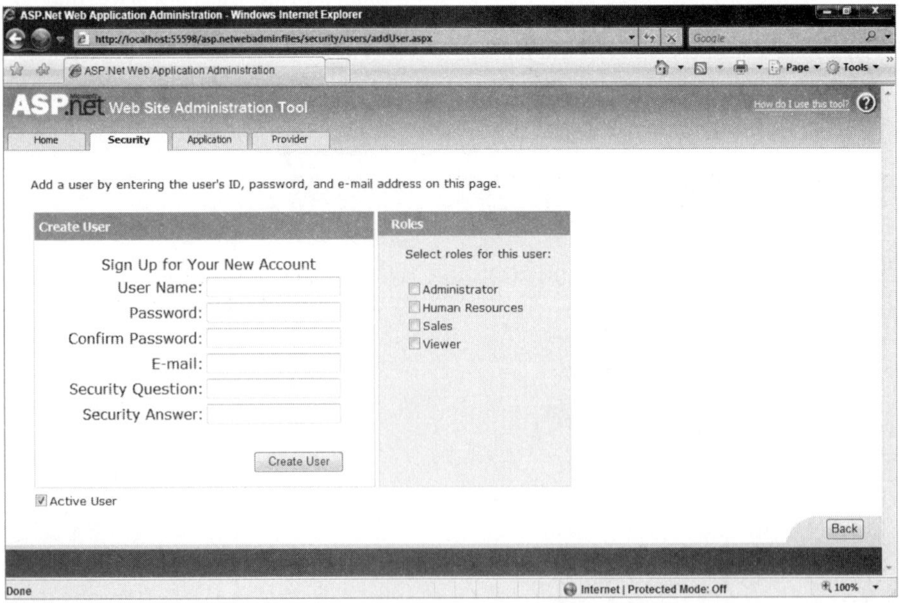

FIGURE 35-10

Managing Users

You can manage existing users by clicking the Manage Users link on the Security tab. A new screen displays a list of all existing users (see Figure 35-11). A search option is available, which makes finding a specific user easier if the list is long.

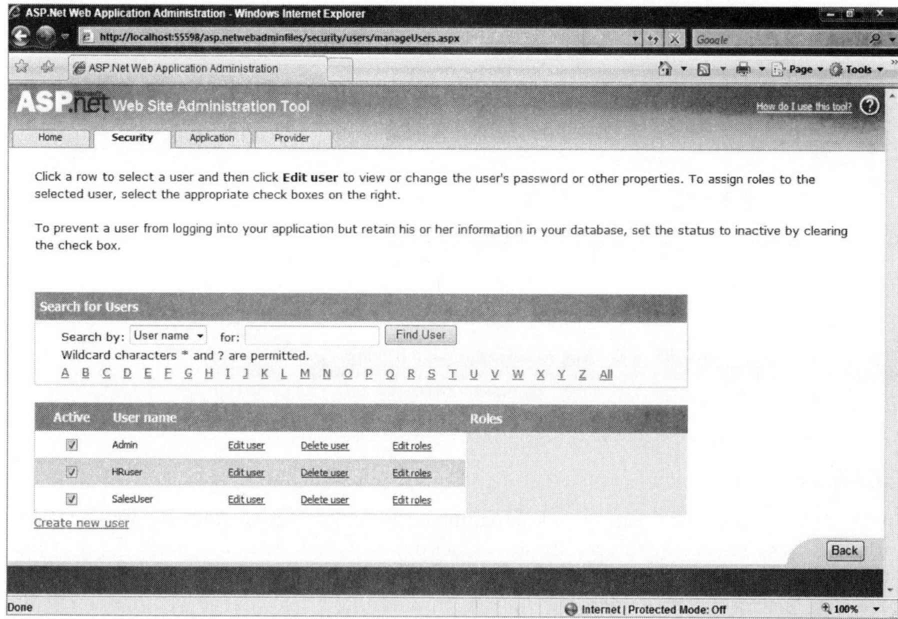

FIGURE 35-11

Find the user you want to manage, and then you can update his information, delete the user, reassign roles, or set the user to active or inactive.

Managing Roles

Two links are provided in the Security tab for managing roles: Disable Roles and Create or Manage Roles. Clicking Disable Roles does just that — disables role management in the Web application; it also dims the other link.

Click the Create or Manage Roles link to start managing roles and assigning users to specific roles. A screen displays all roles you have defined so far. You have options to add new roles, delete existing roles, or manage specific roles.

Click the Manage link next to a specific role, and a screen shows all the users currently assigned to that role (see Figure 35-12). You can find other users by searching for their names, and you can then assign them to or remove them from a selected role.

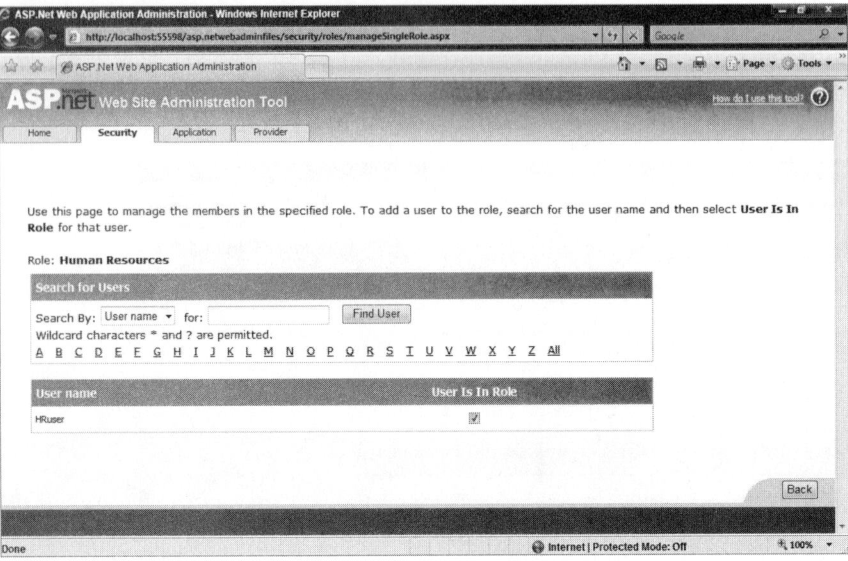

FIGURE 35-12

Managing Access Rules

The Security tab provides options for creating and managing access rules. Access rules are applied either to an entire Web application or to specific folders inside it. Clicking the Create Access Rules link takes you to the Add New Access Rule screen, where you can view a list of the folders inside your Web application (see Figure 35-13). You can select a specific folder, select a role or a user, and then choose whether you want to enable access to the selected folder.

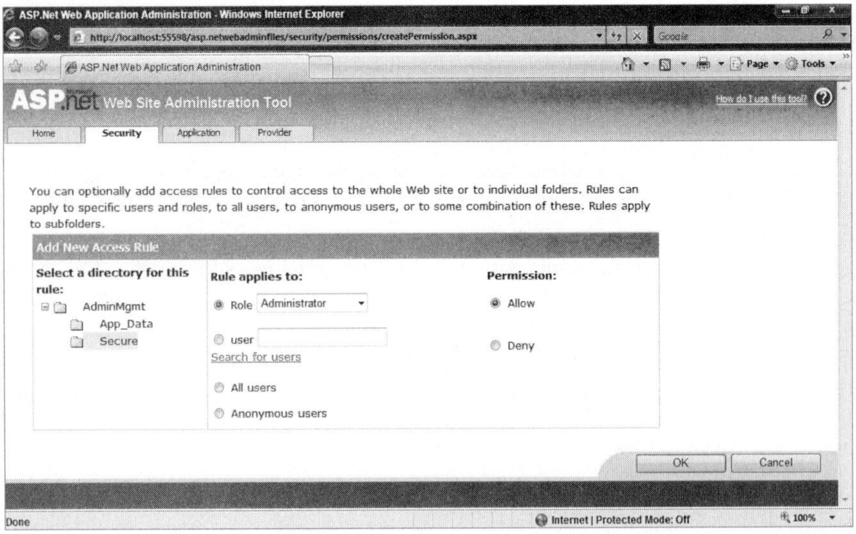

FIGURE 35-13

Clicking Manage Access Rules on the Security tab takes you to the Manage Access Rules screen, which shows all existing access rules (see Figure 35-14).You can remove any of these rules and add new ones. You can also readjust the list of access rules if you want to apply them in a specific order.

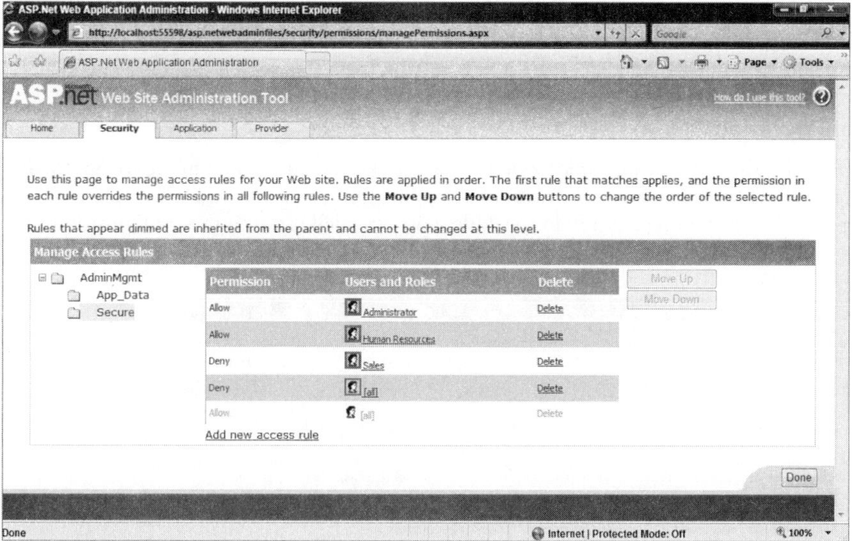

FIGURE 35-14

The Application Tab

The Application tab provides a number of application-specific configurations, including the configuration of appSettings, SMTP mail server settings, debugging and trace settings, and starting/stopping the entire Web application.

Managing Application Settings

The left side of the screen shows links for creating and managing application settings. The settings are stored in the `<appSettings>` section of the `web.config` file. Most ASP.NET programmers are used to manually modifying this tag in previous versions of ASP.NET. Figure 35-15 shows the Application tab.

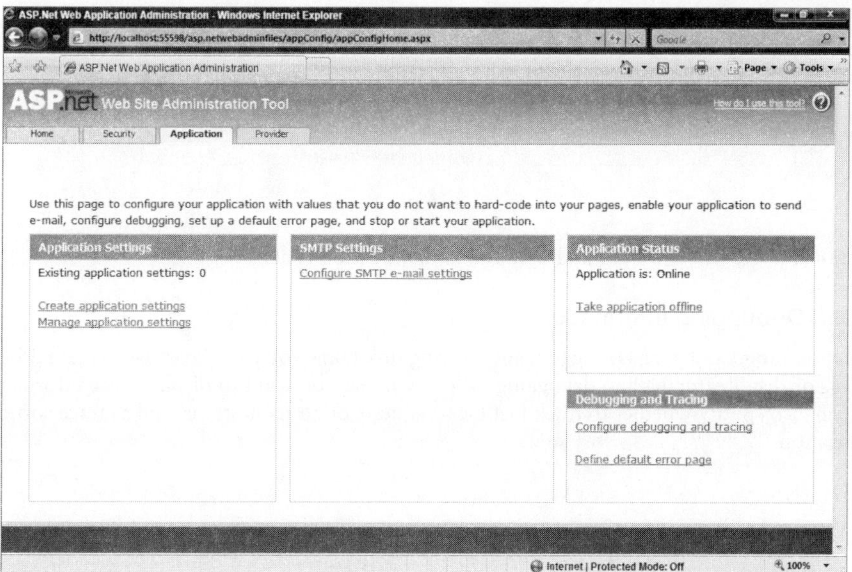

FIGURE 35-15

Clicking the Create Application Settings link takes you to a screen where you can provide the name and the value information. Clicking Manage Application Settings takes you to a screen where you can view existing settings and edit or delete them. You can also create a new setting from this screen.

Managing SMTP Configuration

Click the Configure SMTP E-Mail Settings link to view a screen like the one shown in Figure 35-16. The configure SMTP mail settings feature is useful if your Web application can send auto-generated e-mails. Instead of denoting SMTP server configuration in the code, you can spell it out in the configuration file by entering values here in the administration tool.

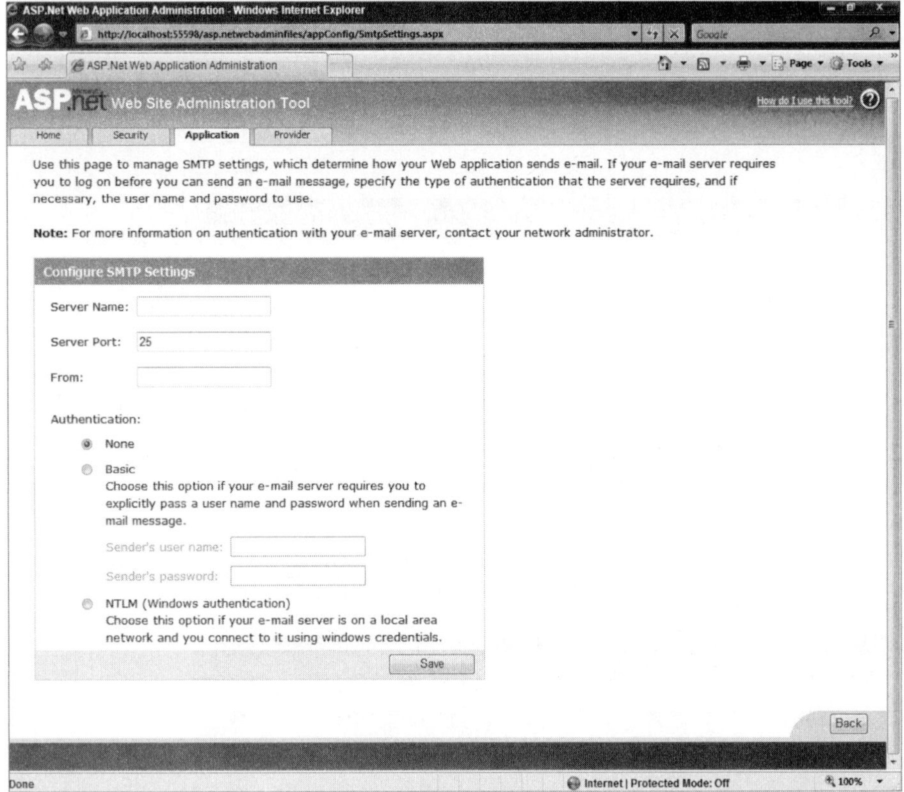

FIGURE 35-16

Specify the server name, port, sender e-mail address, and authentication type.

Managing Tracing and Debugging Information

Clicking the Application tab's Configure Debugging and Tracing link takes you to a screen (see Figure 35-17) where you can enable or disable tracing and debugging. Select whether you want to display trace information on each page. You can also specify whether to track just local requests or all requests, as well as trace sorting and caching configuration.

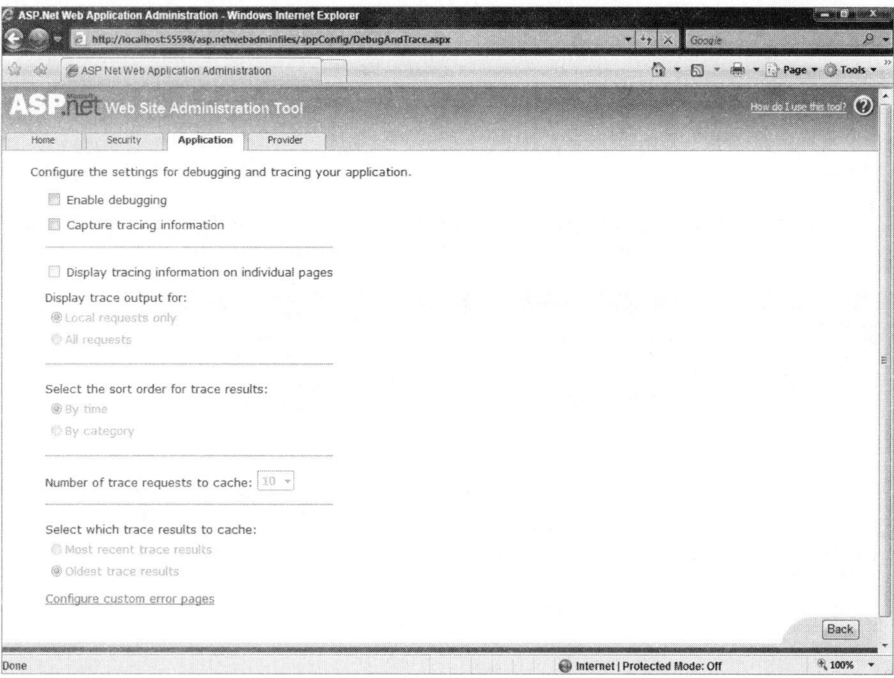

FIGURE 35-17

To configure default error pages, you simply click Define Default Error Page on the screen you saw in Figure 35-15. This takes you to a screen where you can select a URL that is used for redirection in case of an error condition (see Figure 35-18).

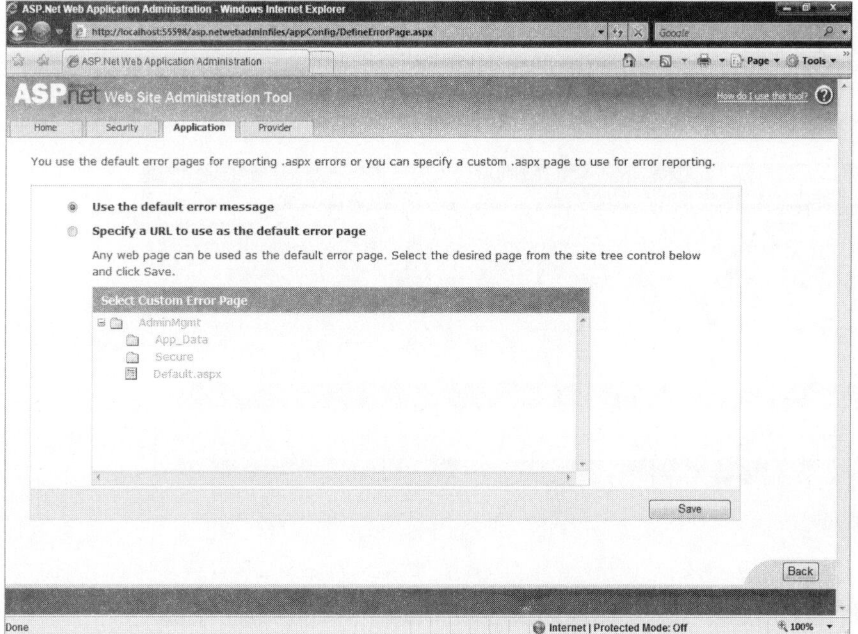

FIGURE 35-18

Taking an Application Offline

You can take your entire Web application offline simply by clicking the Take Application Offline link (again, refer to Figure 35-15). The link stops the app domain for your Web application. This feature is useful if you want to perform a scheduled maintenance for an application.

The Provider Tab

The final tab in the ASP.NET Web Site Administration Tool is Provider, shown in Figure 35-19. You use it to set up additional providers and to determine the providers your application will use.

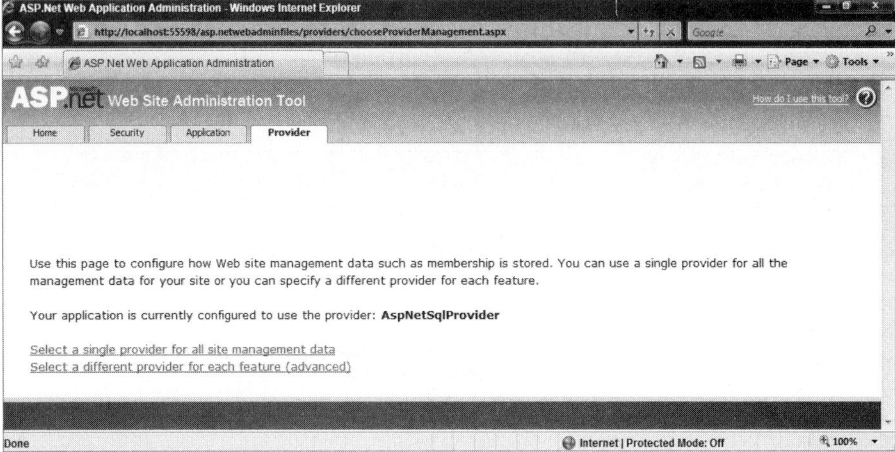

FIGURE 35-19

The Provider page is simple, but it contains an important piece of information: the default data provider with which your application is geared to work. In Figure 35-19, the application is set up to work with the `AspNetSqlProvider` provider, the default data provider.

The two links on this tab let you set up either a single data provider or a specific data provider for each of the features in ASP.NET that requires a data provider. If you click the latter, the screen shown in Figure 35-20 appears. It enables you to pick the available providers separately for Membership and Role management.

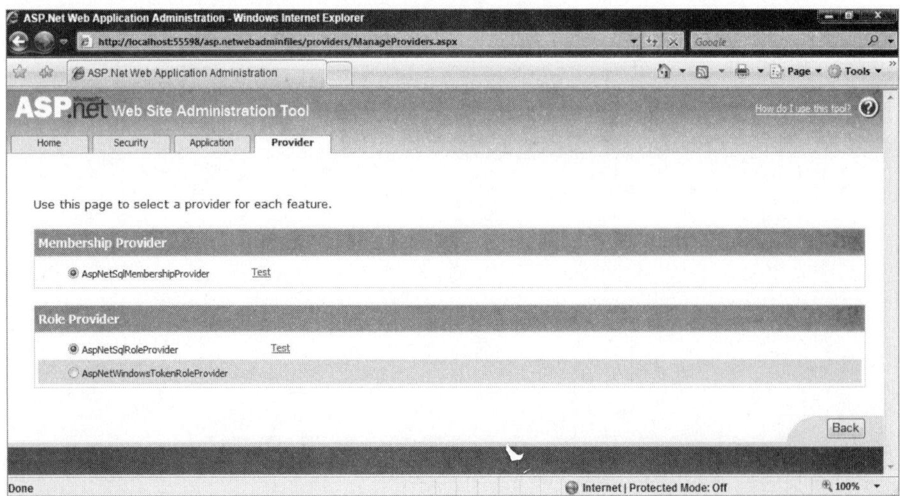

FIGURE 35-20

As you can see from the screenshots and brief explanations provided here, you could now handle a large portion of the necessary configurations through a GUI. You no longer have to figure out which setting must be placed in the `web.config` file. This functionality becomes even more important as the `web.config` file grows. In ASP.NET 1.0/1.1, the `web.config` file was a reasonable size, but with all the features provided by ASP.NET 2.0 or 3.5, the `web.config` file became very large. Again, like ASP.NET 1.0/1.1, the `web.config` file in ASP.NET 4 is now quite small by default. These GUI-based tools are an outstanding way to configure some of the most commonly needed settings. However, many settings cannot be modified with the Web Server Administration Tool, so you will still need to edit the `web.config` file in many cases.

CONFIGURING ASP.NET IN IIS ON WINDOWS 7

If you are using IIS as the basis of your ASP.NET applications, you will find that configuring the ASP.NET application directly through the Internet Information Services (IIS) Manager is quite easy if you are using Windows 7. To access the ASP.NET configurations, open IIS and expand the Sites folder, which contains all the sites configured to work with IIS. Remember that not all your Web sites are configured to work in this manner because it is also possible to create ASP.NET applications that make use of the ASP.NET built-in Web server.

After you have expanded the IIS Sites folder, right-click one of the applications in this folder; the options available to you for configuration will appear in the IIS Manager (see Figure 35-21).

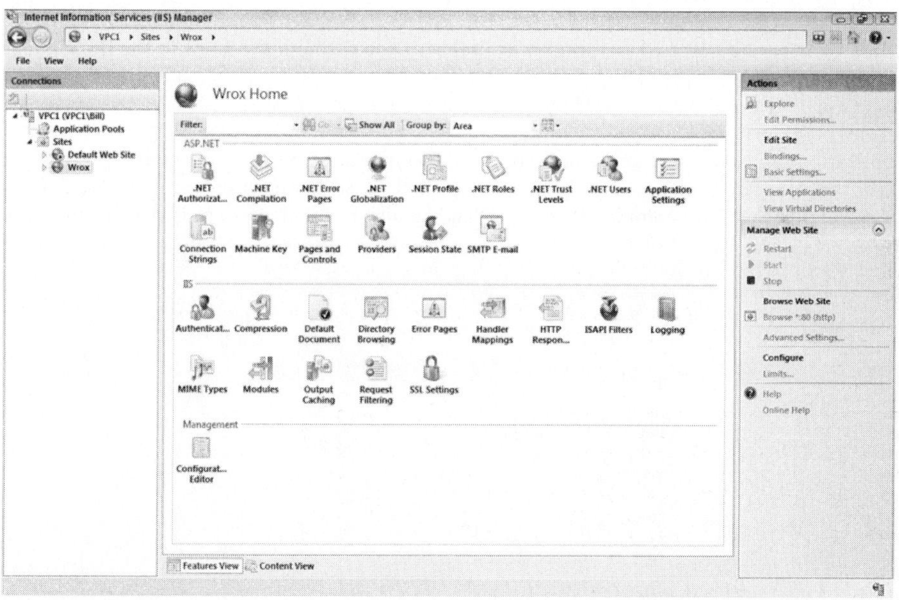

FIGURE 35-21

The options available to you enable you to completely configure ASP.NET or even configure IIS itself. The focus of this chapter is on the ASP.NET section of the options. In addition to the options you can select from one of the available icons, you can also configure some basic settings of the application by clicking the Basic Settings link in the Actions pane on the right side of the IIS Manager. When you click the Basic Settings link, the Edit Web Site dialog box appears, as shown in Figure 35-22.

Changes you are making in the IIS Manager are actually being applied to the `web.config` *file of your application; making changes to the Default Web site (the root node) lets you edit the* `machine.config` *file.*

This dialog box enables you to change the following items:

- **Web site name:** The name of the Web site. In the case of Figure 35-22, naming the Web site "Wrox" means that the URL will be `http://[IP address or domain name]/Wrox`.
- **Application pool:** The application pool you are going to use for the application. You will notice that you have two options by default — DefaultAppPool (which uses the .NET Framework 4 and an integrated pipeline mode) and Classic .NET AppPool (which uses the .NET Framework 4 and a classic pipeline mode).

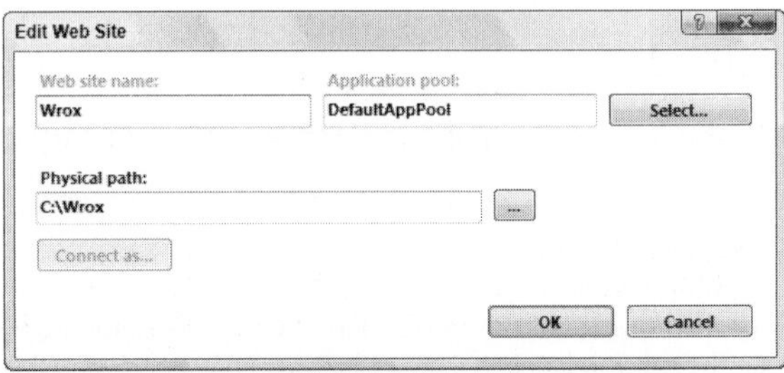

FIGURE 35-22

- **Physical path:** The folder location where the ASP.NET application can be found. In this case, it is `C:\Wrox`.

The sections that follow review some of the options available to you through the icons in the IIS Manager.

.NET Compilation

You use the Application tab to make changes that are more specific to the pages in the context of your application. From the .NET Compilation dialog (accessible via the IIS Manager) shown in Figure 35-23, you can change how your pages are compiled and run. You can also make changes to global settings in your application.

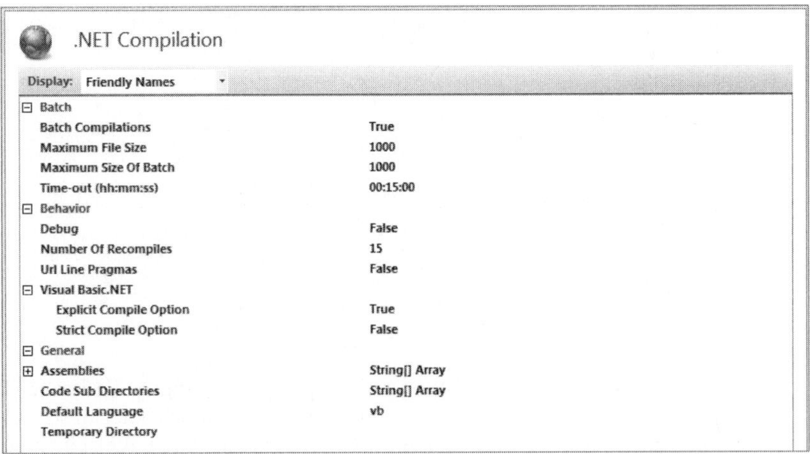

FIGURE 35-23

This section of the IIS Manager deals with compilation of the ASP.NET application and how some of the pages of the application will behave. The Batch section deals with the batch compilation of the application — first, whether or not it is even supported and then, details on batch sizes and the time it takes to incur the compilation.

The Behavior section deals with whether or not the compilation produces a release or debug build; you will also find some Visual Basic–specific compilation instructions on whether Option Explicit or Option Script are enabled across the entire application.

The General section focuses on the assemblies that are referenced as well as your code subdirectories if you are going to break up your App_Code folder into separate compiled instances (required for when you want to incorporate Visual Basic and C# code in the same application). You can also specify the default language that is used in the compilation process — such as `VB` or `C#`.

.NET Globalization

The .NET Globalization option in the IIS Manager enables you to customize how your ASP.NET application deals with culture and the encoding of the requests and responses. Figure 35-24 shows the options available in this dialog.

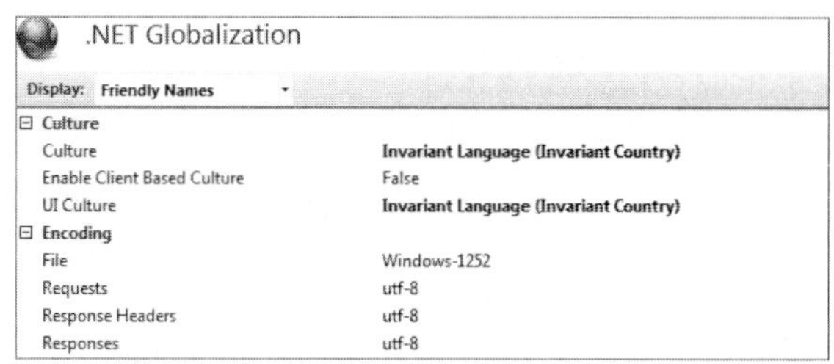

FIGURE 35-24

In addition to picking a specific Culture or UI Culture setting, you can also select Auto Detect, which will pick up the culture of the client if it is available. By default, you can also see that the encoding of the requests and the responses are set to `utf-8`, which will work fine for most Latin-based languages.

.NET Profile

The IIS Manager.NET Profile options enable you to customize how your ASP.NET application deals with the ASP.NET personalization system. This system was discussed earlier in Chapter 14 of this book. Figure 35-25 shows the dialog that is provided when you add a new profile to the personalization system.

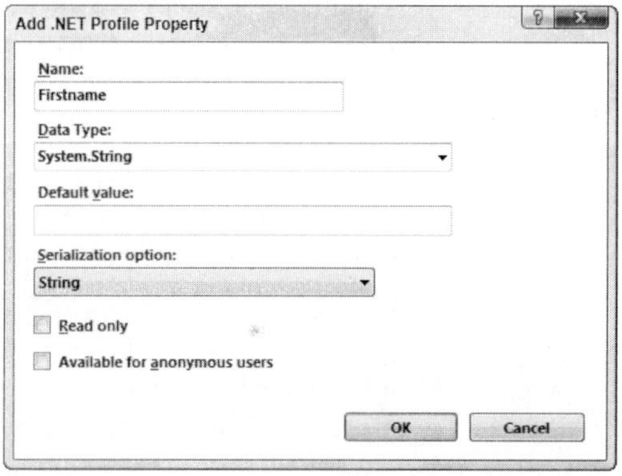

FIGURE 35-25

In this case, as presented in Figure 35-25, you can specify the name of the personalization property, the data type used, its default value, how it is serialized, and whether it is read-only or available for anonymous users. To better understand these settings, it is important to review Chapter 14.

In addition to building properties to use in the personalization system, you can also specify the provider that is used by the system as a whole. By default, it will be using the AspNetSqlProfileProvider, as illustrated in Figure 35-26. You can get to this dialog by selecting the 'Set Default Provider' link from the .NET Profile section.

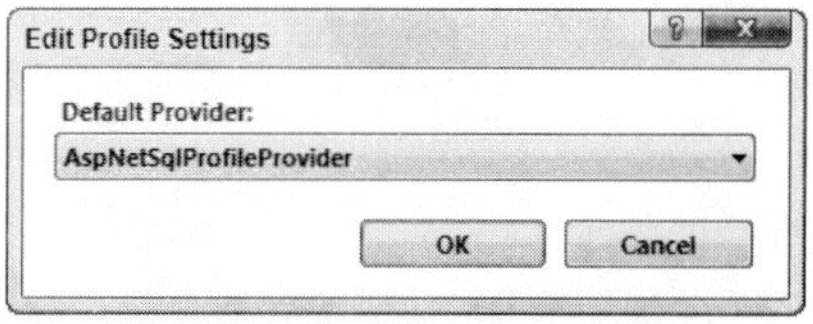

FIGURE 35-26

.NET Roles

You can enable role-based management by adding roles to your application from the .NET Roles section of the IIS Manager. Figure 35-27 shows an example of adding a role called Admin to the application after clicking on the Add link from the Actions section.

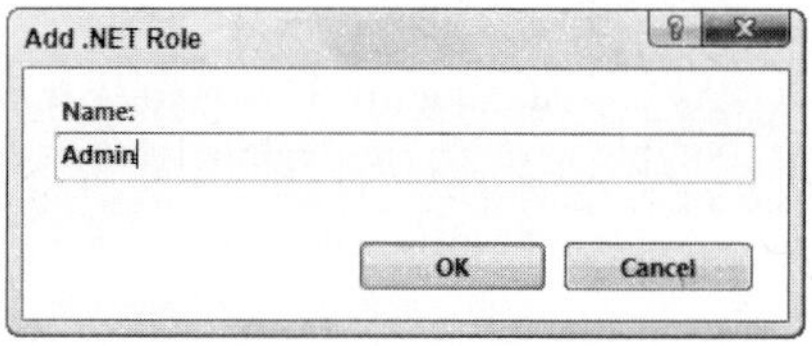

FIGURE 35-27

Clicking OK will add the role to the system and the role will then be shown in a list of roles from the main screen of the section, as illustrated in Figure 35-28.

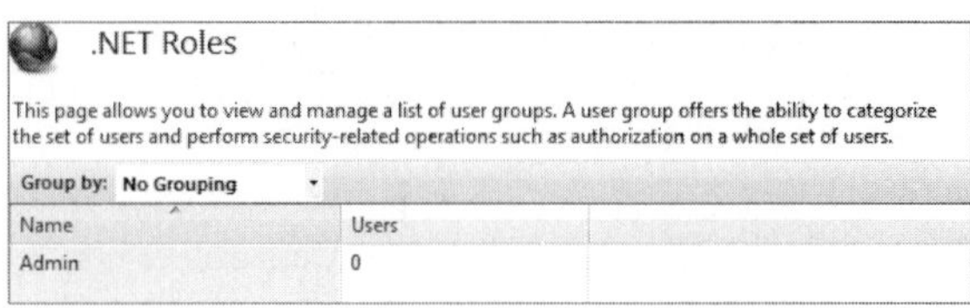

FIGURE 35-28

By default, there will be no users added to the role. You will be able to add users to roles through the .NET Users section, discussed shortly.

.NET Trust Levels

The .NET Trust Levels section of the IIS Manager allows you to specify the level of security to apply to your application through the selection of a specific pre-generated configuration file. This is illustrated in the list of options presented in Figure 35-29.

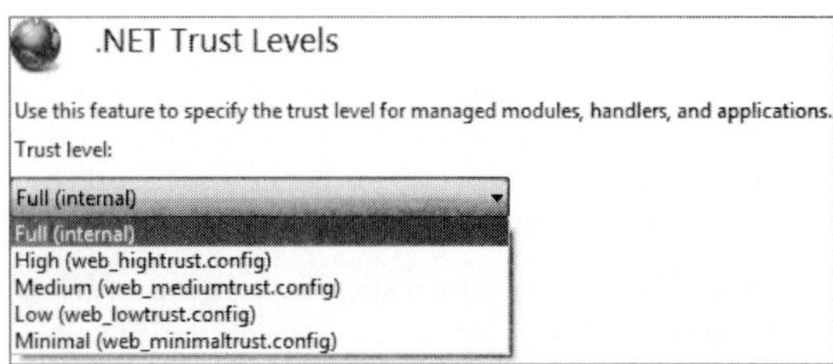

FIGURE 35-29

By default, your application makes use of the `web.config` file, but specifying a different trust level will cause the application to use a different `.config` file. All of these `.config` files are found at `C:\Windows\Microsoft.NET\Framework\v4.0.`*`xxxxx`*`\CONFIG`.

.NET Users

Probably one of the easiest ways to work with the ASP.NET membership system (covered in Chapter 15 of this book) is to create your users in the .NET Users section of the IIS Manager. Adding a user is easy to do through the dialogs provided, as illustrated in Figure 35-30.

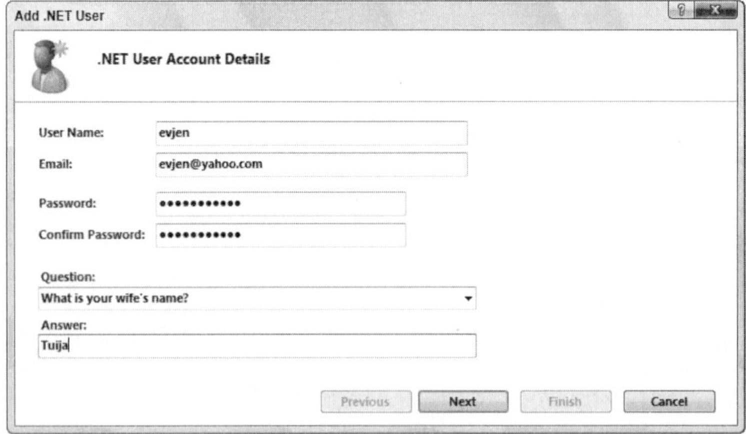

FIGURE 35-30

As shown in Figure 35-30, you can provide the username, password, and security question and answer in a simple wizard. Figure 35-31 shows the second screen of the wizard.

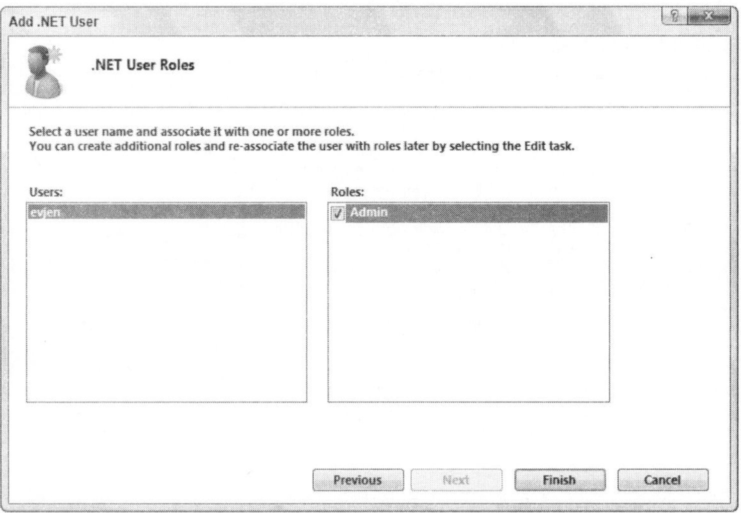

FIGURE 35-31

In this second screen of the wizard, you can assign users to specific roles that are present in the role management system. Because the Admin role was created earlier in this chapter, I am able to assign the user to this particular role as it exists in the system.

After a user is created, you can then see the entire list of users for this particular application from the main .NET Users screen, as illustrated in Figure 35-32.

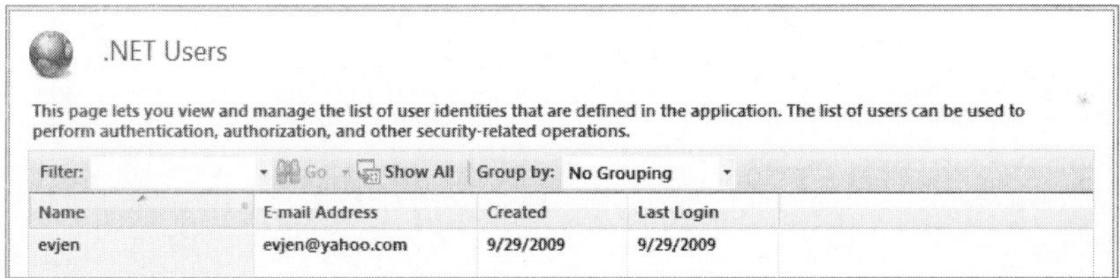

FIGURE 35-32

Application Settings

In the IIS Application Settings section of the IIS Manager you can click the Add or Edit button, and the Edit/Add Application Settings dialog opens (see Figure 35-33).

After you enter a key and value pair, click OK; the settings appear in the list in the main dialog. Then you can edit or delete the settings from the application.

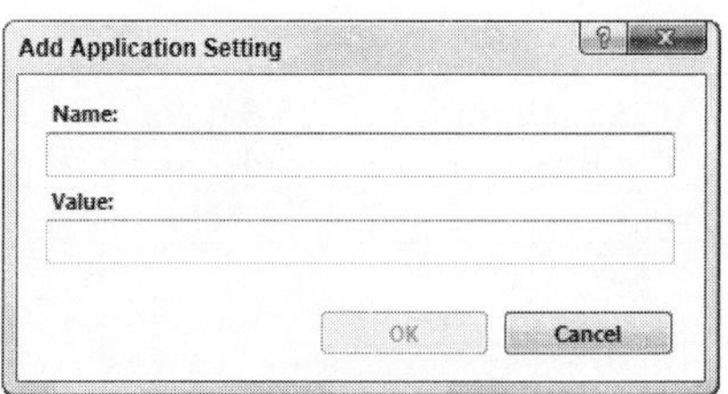

FIGURE 35-33

Connection Strings

In the Connection Strings section of the IIS Manager you can add a connection string to your application by clicking its Add button. You also can edit or remove existing connection strings. Figure 35-34 shows the Edit Connection String dialog for the default connection string — LocalSqlServer.

Figure 35-35 shows that adding a brand-new connection is also rather simple.

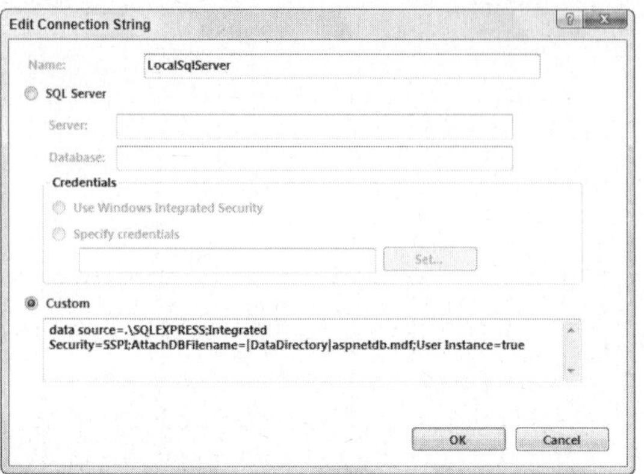

FIGURE 35-34

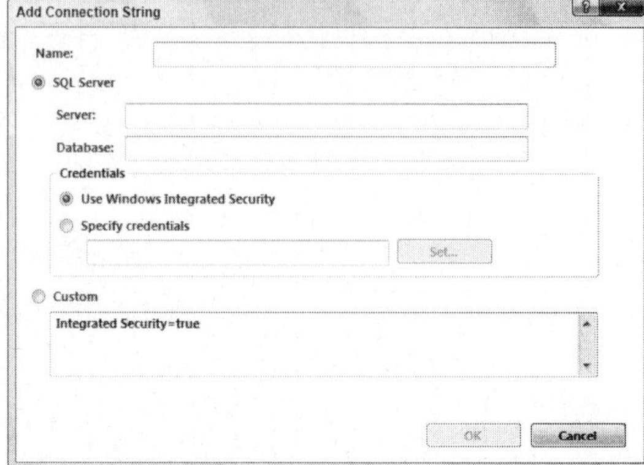

FIGURE 35-35

Pages and Controls

The Pages and Controls section of the IIS Manager deals with a group of settings that control the overall ASP.NET pages (`.aspx`) and user controls in the application (`.ascx`). Figure 35-36 shows the available settings for this section.

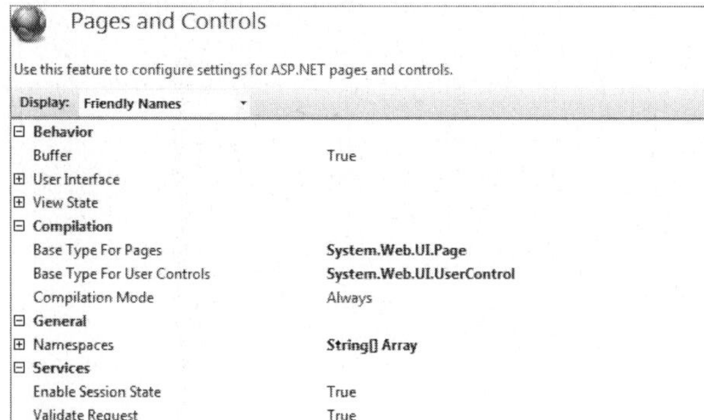

FIGURE 35-36

Providers

The Providers section of IIS deals with all the providers that are defined within the application. From the example in Figure 35-37, you can see that only two providers are defined for the .NET Roles engine — a SQL Server role provider and a Windows Token role provider.

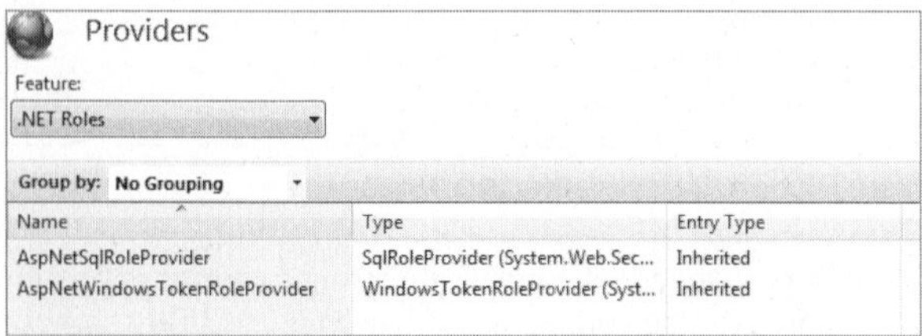

FIGURE 35-37

You can look at all the other engines found in ASP.NET by selecting the option in the drop-down list at the top of the dialog.

Session State

ASP.NET applications, being stateless in nature, are highly dependent on how state is stored. The Session State section of the IIS Manager (see Figure 35-38) enables you to change a number of different settings that determine how state management is administered.

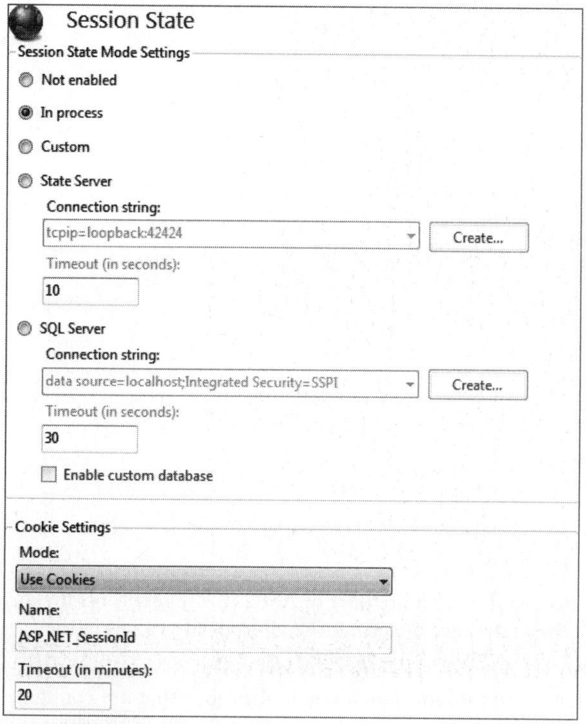

FIGURE 35-38

You can apply state management to your applications in a number of ways, and this dialog allows for a number of different settings — some of which are enabled or disabled based on what is selected. The following list describes the items available in the Session State Settings section:

- **Session state mode:** Determines how the sessions are stored by the ASP.NET application. The default option (shown in Figure 35-38) is InProc. Other options include Off, StateServer, and SQLServer. Running sessions in-process (InProc) means that the sessions are stored in the same process as the ASP.NET worker process. Therefore, if IIS is shut down and then brought up again, all the sessions are destroyed and unavailable to end users. StateServer means that sessions are stored out-of-process by a Windows service called ASPState. SQLServer is by far the most secure way to deal with your sessions; it stores them directly in SQL Server. StateServer is also the least performance-efficient method.
- **Cookieless mode:** Changes how the identifiers for the end user are stored. The default setting uses cookies (UseCookies). Other possible settings include UseUri, AutoDetect, and UseDeviceProfile.
- **Session timeout:** Sessions are stored for only a short period of time before they expire. For years, the default has been 20 minutes. Modifying the value here changes how long the sessions created by your application are valid.

SMTP E-mail

If you need to work with an application that delivers e-mail, then you must specify the settings to do this. You define the required settings for sending e-mail using SMTP through the SMTP E-mail section of the IIS Manager (see Figure 35-39).

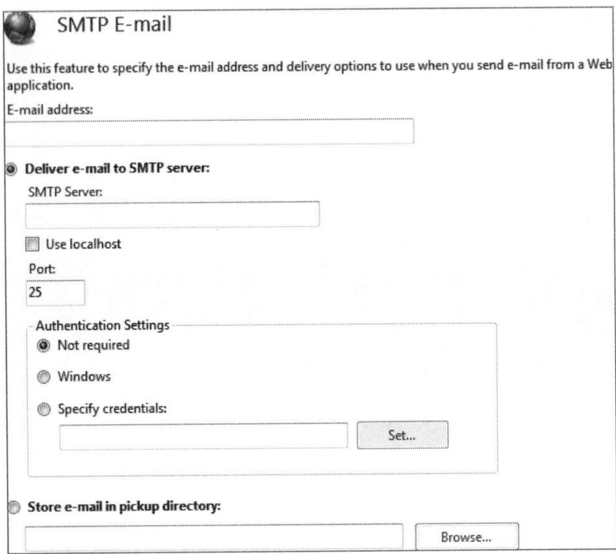

FIGURE 35-39

SUMMARY

This chapter showed you some of the management tools which are part of ASP.NET. These tools make the `web.config` file more manageable because they take care of setting the appropriate values in the application's configuration file.

The IIS Manager console in Windows 7 is a wonderful tool for managing applications that are configured to work with IIS. The ASP.NET Web Site Administration Tool provides even more value to administrators and developers by enabling them to easily manage settings.

36

Packaging and Deploying ASP.NET Applications

WHAT'S IN THIS CHAPTER?

- Understanding packaging and deploying fundamentals
- Selecting a deployment method
- Building ASP.NET Web Packages

Packaging and deploying ASP.NET applications are topics that usually receive little attention. This chapter takes a more in-depth look at how you can package and deploy your ASP.NET applications after they are built. After you have developed your ASP.NET application on a development computer, you will need to deploy the finished product to a quality assurance or staging server, and eventually onto a production server.

An important reason to consider the proper packaging and deploying of your ASP.NET applications is that many applications are built as saleable products, starter kits, or solutions. In this case, you may have to allow complete strangers to download and install these products in their own environments that you have absolutely no control over. If this is the case, giving the consumer a single installer file that ensures proper installation of the application in any environment is ideal.

Nevertheless, regardless of whether you will distribute your web application outside your company you still need a way to deploy it to another server where it can be tested before production deployment. You should never assume that it would be perfect just because it worked on your computer. Most of the time you just develop using the internal Web server in Visual Studio, so you will need a full test using IIS before you assume all is well. Even if you do test with IIS on your computer, deployment-related factors still need to be ironed out and fully tested before the application goes to production.

Before you start choosing your deployment approach you should understand the basics of packaging and deploying ASP.NET applications. In the process of packaging your ASP.NET applications, you are putting your applications into a package and utilizing a process of deployment that is initiated through a deployment procedure, such as using a Windows installer or even the new ASP.NET Web Package that is now available via Visual Studio 2010.

DEPLOYMENT PIECES

So what are you actually deploying? ASP.NET contains a lot of pieces that are all possible parts of the overall application and need to be deployed with the application for it to run properly. The following list details some of the items that are potentially part of your ASP.NET application and need deployment consideration when you are moving your application:

- `.aspx` pages
- The code-behind pages for the `.aspx` pages (`.aspx.vb` or `.aspx.cs` files)
- User controls (`.ascx`)
- Web service files (`.asmx` and `.wsdl` files)
- `.htm` or `.html` files
- Image files such as `.jpg` or `.gif`
- ASP.NET system folders such as App_Code and App_Themes
- JavaScript files (`.js`)
- Cascading Style Sheets (`.css`)
- Configuration files such as the `web.config` file
- .NET components and compiled assemblies
- Data files such as `.mdb` files
- IIS settings
- Registry keys

STEPS TO TAKE BEFORE DEPLOYING

Before deploying your ASP.NET Web applications, you should take some basic steps to ensure that your application is *ready* for deployment. These steps are often forgotten and are mentioned here to remind you of how you can ensure that your deployed application performs at its best.

Before you begin, *turn off* debugging in the `web.config` file. You do this by setting the `debug` attribute in the `<compilation>` element to `false`, as shown in Listing 36-1.

LISTING 36-1: Setting debug to false before application deployment

```
<configuration>
   <system.web>

      <compilation debug="false" targetFramework="4.0" />

   </system.web>
</configuration>
```

By default, most developers set the `debug` attribute to `true` when developing their applications. Doing this inserts debug symbols into the compiled ASP.NET pages. These symbols degrade the performance of any application. After the application is built and ready to be deployed, keeping these debug symbols in place is unnecessary.

For those who have been coding ASP.NET for some time now, it is important to note that the Debug option in the drop-down list in the Visual Studio menu does not accomplish much in changing the configuration file or anything similar (shown in Figure 36-1). In the ASP.NET 1.0 and 1.1 days, Visual Studio .NET (as it was called at that time) actually controlled the compilation of the ASP.NET project to a DLL. Now, and ever since ASP.NET 2.0, it is actually ASP.NET itself that controls the compilation process at runtime.

Therefore, although the drop-down with the Debug designation is present, it really has no meaning in the context of building an ASP.NET project. You completely control the compilation designation through what is set in the `web.config` file, as shown earlier in Listing 36-1.

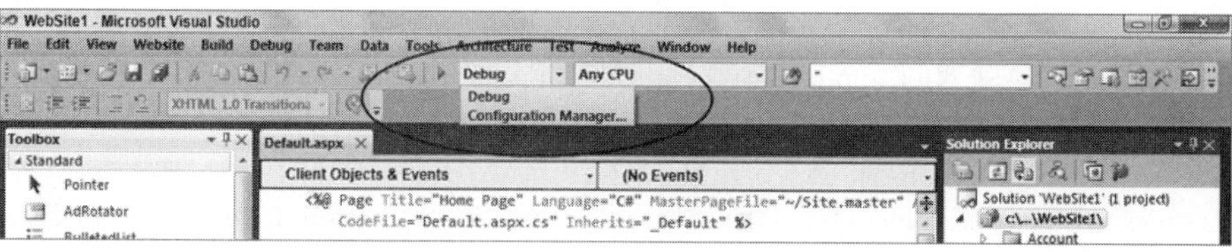

FIGURE 36-1

You will also find that you can provide `Web.Debug.config` and `Web.Release.config` files in your application as well. Using `Web.Debug.config` allows you to put settings in the configuration file that will be utilized when you do a deployment or run of the application while in the debug mode. You can use the same approach with the `Web.Release.config` file when running or deploying the application in the Release mode. This approach with the configuration files allows you to use different database connection strings, change the authentication mode, and more. You will find using these varied configuration files beneficial if you are working with more than one environment (for example, testing, staging, and production).

METHODS OF DEPLOYING WEB APPLICATIONS

Remember that deployment is the last step in a process. The first is setting up the program — packaging the program into a component that is best suited for the deployment that follows. You can actually deploy a Web application in a number of ways. You can use the XCopy capability that simply wows audiences when demonstrated (because of its simplicity). A second method is to use Visual Studio 2010's capability to copy a Web site from one location to another using the Copy Web Site feature, as well as an alternative method that uses Visual Studio to deploy a precompiled Web application. The final method uses Visual Studio to build an installer program that can be launched on another machine. After reviewing each of the available methods, you can decide which is best for what you are trying to achieve. Start by looking at the simplest of the three methods: XCopy.

Using XCopy

Because of the nature of the .NET Framework, deploying .NET applications is considerably easier now than it was to deploy applications constructed using Microsoft's predecessor technology — COM. Applications in .NET compile down to assemblies, and these assemblies contain code that is executed by the Common Language Runtime (CLR). One great thing about assemblies is that they are self-describing. All the details about the assembly are stored within the assembly itself. In the Windows DNA world, COM stored all its self-describing data within the server's registry, so installing (as well as uninstalling) COM components meant shutting down IIS. Because a .NET assembly stores this information within itself, XCOPY deployment is possible and no registry settings are needed. Installing an assembly is as simple as copying it to another server and you do not need to stop or start IIS while this is going on.

XCOPY is mentioned here because it is the command-line way of basically doing a copy-and-paste of the files you want to move. XCOPY, however, provides a bit more functionality than just a copy-and-paste, as you will see shortly. XCOPY enables you to move files, directories, and even entire drives from one point to another.

The default syntax of the XCOPY command is as follows:

```
xcopy [source] [destination] [/w] [/p] [/c] [/v] [/q] [/f] [/l] [/g]
   [/d[:mm-dd-yyyy]] [/u] [/i] [/s [/e]] [/t] [/k] [/r] [/h] [{/a|/m}] [/n] [/o]
   [/x] [/exclude:file1[+[file2]][+file3]] [{/y|/-y}] [/z]
```

To see an example of using the XCOPY feature, suppose you are working from your developer machine (`C:\`) and want to copy your ASP.NET application to a production server (`Y:\`). In its simplest form, the following command would do the job:

```
xcopy c:\Websites\Website1 y:\Websites\ /f /e /k /h
```

This command copies the files and folders from the source drive to the destination drive. Figure 36-2 shows an example of this use on the command line.

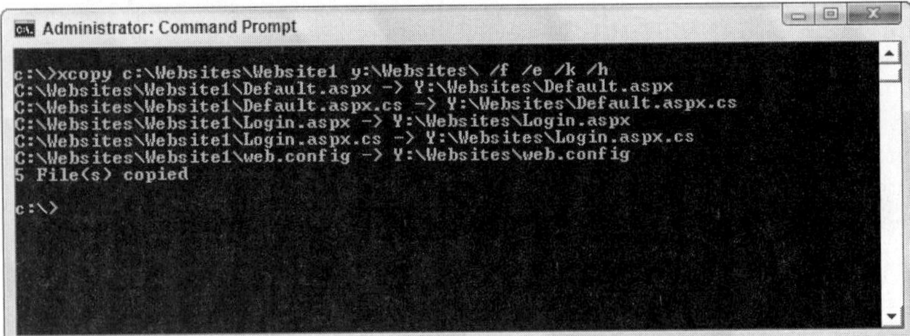

FIGURE 36-2

When you copy files using XCOPY, be aware that this method does not allow for the automatic creation of any virtual directories in IIS. When copying a new Web application, you also need to create a virtual directory in the destination server and associate this virtual directory with the application you are copying. It is a simple process, but you must take these extra steps to finalize the site copy actions.

You can provide a number of parameters to this XCOPY command to get it to behave as you want it to. Table 36-1 details these parameters.

TABLE 36-1

PARAMETER	DESCRIPTION
`/w`	Displays the message: `Press any key to begin copying file(s)`. It waits for your response to start the copying process.
`/p`	Asks for a confirmation on each file being copied. This is done in a file-by-file manner.
`/c`	Ignores errors that might occur in the copying process.
`/v`	Performs a verification on the files being copied to make sure they are identical to the source files.
`/q`	Suppresses any display of the XCOPY messages.
`/f`	Displays the filenames for the source and destination files while the copying process is occurring.
`/l`	Displays a list of the files to be copied to the destination drive.
`/g`	Builds decrypted files for the destination drive.
`/d`	When used as simply `/d`, the only files copied are those newer than the existing files located in the destination location. Another alternative is to use `/d[:mm-dd-yyyy]`, which copies files that have been modified either on or after the specified date.

PARAMETER	DESCRIPTION
/u	Copies only source files that already exist in the destination location.
/i	If what is being copied is a directory or a file that contains wildcards and the same item does not exist in the destination location, a new directory is created. The XCOPY process also copies all the associated files into this directory.
/s	Copies all directories and their subdirectories only if they contain files. All empty directories or subdirectories are not copied in the process.
/e	Copies all subdirectories regardless of whether these directories contain files.
/t	Copies the subdirectories only and not the files they might contain.
/k	By default, the XCOPY process removes any read-only settings that might be contained in the source files. Using `/k` ensures that these read-only settings remain in place during the copying process.
/r	Copies only the read-only files to the destination location.
/h	Specifies that the hidden and system files, which are usually excluded by default, are included.
/a	Copies only files that have their archive file attributes set, and leaves the archive file attributes in place at the XCOPY destination.
/m	Copies only files that have their archive file attributes set, and turns off the archive file attributes.
/n	Copies using the NTFS short file and short directory names.
/o	Copies the discretionary access control list (DACL) in addition to the files.
/x	Copies the audit settings and the system access control list (SACL) in addition to the files.
/exclude	Allows you to exclude specific files. The construction used for this is `exclude:File1.aspx + File2.aspx + File3.aspx`.
/y	Suppresses any prompts from the XCOPY process that ask whether to overwrite the destination file.
/-y	Adds prompts to confirm an overwrite of any existing files in the destination location.
/z	Copies files and directories over a network in restartable mode.
/?	Displays help for the XCOPY command.

Using XCOPY is an easy way to move your applications from one server to another with little work on your part. If you have no problem setting up your own virtual directories, this mode of deployment should work just fine for you.

When the Web application is copied (and if placed in a proper virtual directory), it is ready to be called from a browser.

Using the VS Copy Web Site Option

The next option for copying a Web site is to use a GUI provided by Visual Studio 2010. This Copy Web Site GUI enables you to copy Web sites from your development server to either the same server or a remote server (as you can when you use the XCOPY command).

You can open this Copy Web Site dialog in Visual Studio in two ways. The first way is to click in the Copy Web Site icon in the Visual Studio Solution Explorer. Figure 36-3 shows this icon.

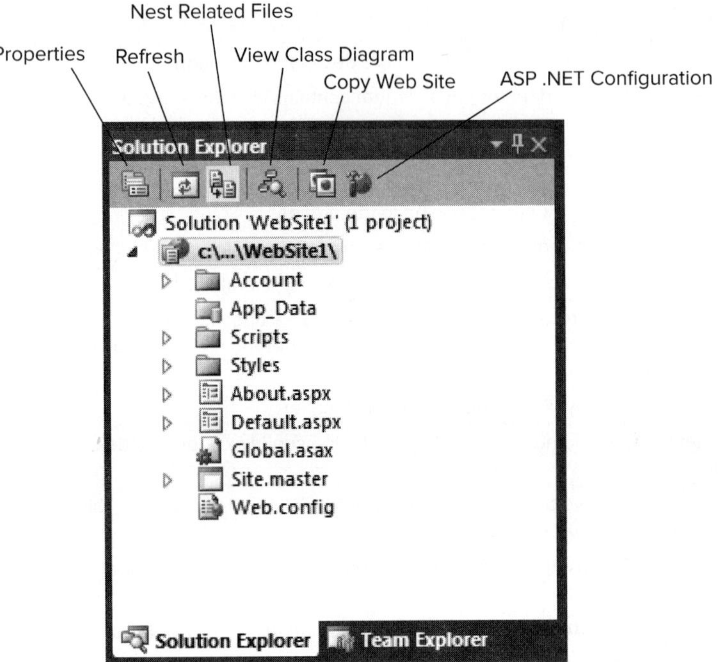

FIGURE 36-3

The other way to open the Copy Web Site GUI is to choose Website ➪ Copy Web Site from the Visual Studio menu. Using either method opens the Copy Web Site GUI in the Document window, as illustrated in Figure 36-4.

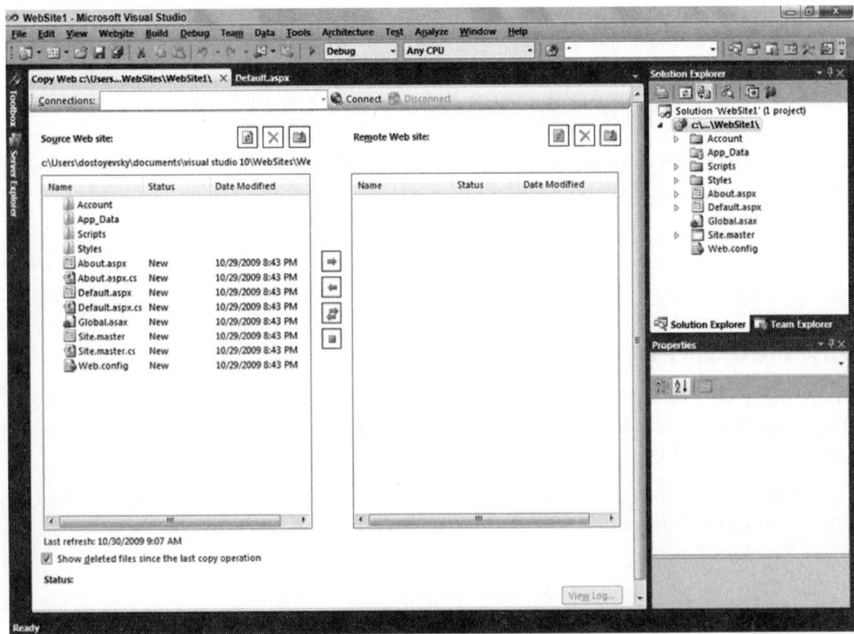

FIGURE 36-4

From this GUI, you can click the Connect To a Remote Server button (next to the Connections text box). This action opens the Open Web Site dialog shown in Figure 36-5.

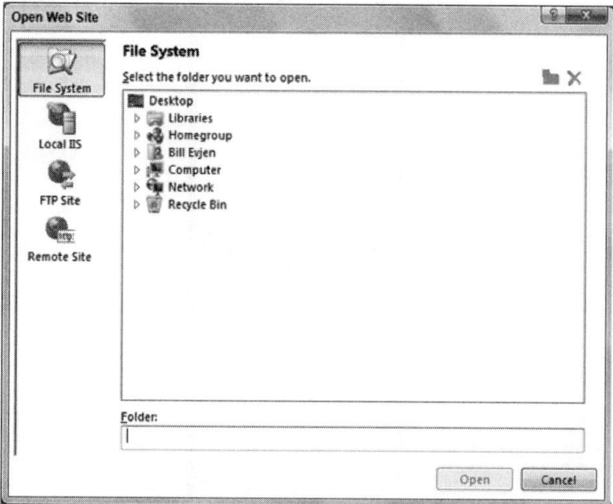

FIGURE 36-5

As you can see from this dialog, you have a couple of options to connect to and copy your Web application. These options include the following:

- **File System:** This option allows you to navigate through a file explorer view of the computer. If you are going to install on a remote server from this view, you must have already mapped a drive to the installation location.
- **Local IIS:** This option enables you to use your local IIS in the installation of your Web application. From this part of the dialog, you can create new applications as well as new virtual directories directly. You can also delete applications and virtual directories from the same dialog. The Local IIS option does not permit you to work with IIS installations on any remote servers.
- **FTP Site:** This option enables you to connect to a remote server using FTP capabilities. From this dialog, you can specify the server that you want to contact using a URL or IP address, the port you are going to use, and the directory on the server that you will work with. From this dialog, you can also specify the username and password that may be required to access the server via FTP. Note that if you access this server with this dialog via FTP and provide a username and password, the items are transmitted in plain text.
- **Remote Site:** This option enables you to connect to a remote site using FrontPage Server Extensions. From this option in the dialog, you can also choose to connect to the remote server using Secure Sockets Layer (SSL).

After being connected to a server, you can copy the contents of your Web application to it by selecting all or some of the files from the Source Web Site text area. After you select these files in the dialog, some of the movement arrows become enabled. Clicking the right-pointing arrow copies the selected files to the destination server. In Figure 36-6 you can see that, indeed, the files have been copied to the remote destination.

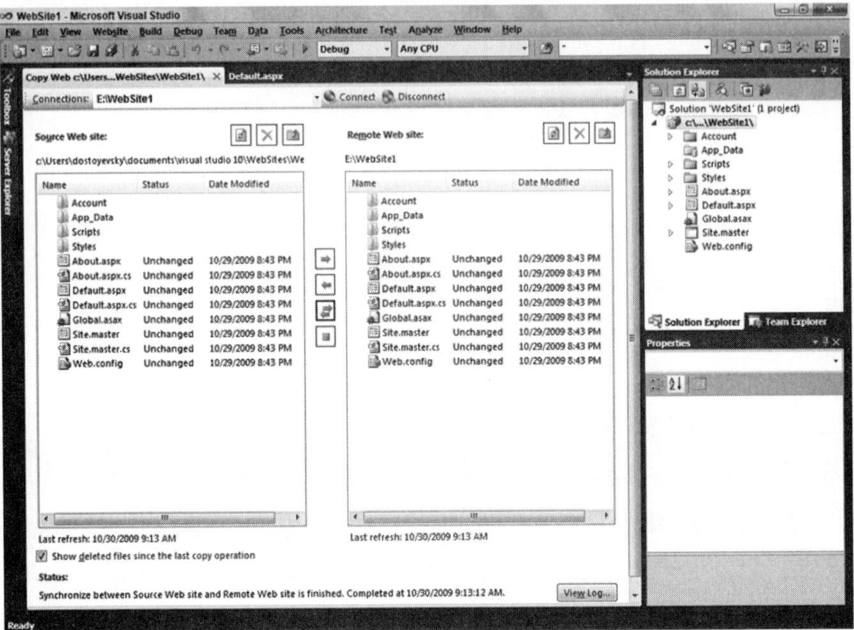

FIGURE 36-6

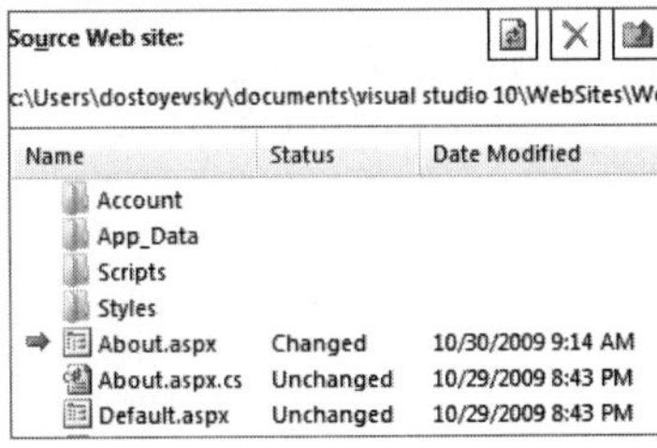

FIGURE 36-7

If you open the same copy dialog later, after working on the files, you see an arrow next to the files that have been changed in the interim and are, therefore, newer than those on the destination server (see Figure 36-7).

These arrows enable you to select only the files that must be copied again and nothing more. All the copying actions are recorded in a log file. You can view the contents of this log file from the Copy Web Site dialog by clicking the View Log button at the bottom of the dialog. This opens the `CopyWebSite.log` text file. From the copy that you made previously, you can see the transaction that was done. Here is an example log entry:

```
Copy from 'C:\Websites\Website1' to 'E:\Website1' started at 10/6/2009 7:52:31 AM.
            Create folder App_Data in the remote Web site.


            Copy file Default.aspx from source to remote Web site.
            Copy file Default.aspx.cs from source to remote Web site.
            Copy file About.aspx from source to remote Web site.
            Copy file About.aspx.cs from source to remote Web site.
            Copy file web.config from source to remote Web site.

Copy from 'C:\Websites\Website1' to 'E:\Website1' is finished. Completed at 10/6/2009 7:52:33 AM.
```

Deploying a Precompiled Web Application

In addition to using Visual Studio to copy a Web application from one location to another, using this IDE to deploy a precompiled application is also possible. The process of precompiling a Web application is explained in Chapter 1. ASP.NET 4 includes a precompilation process that allows for a process referred to as *precompilation for deployment*.

What happens in the precompilation for deployment process is that each page in the Web application is built and compiled into a single application DLL and some placeholder files. These files can then be deployed together to another server and run from there. The nice thing about this precompilation process is that it obfuscates your code by placing all page code (as well as the page's code-behind code) into the DLL, thereby making it more difficult for your code to be stolen or changed if you select this option in the compilation process. This is an ideal situation when you are deploying applications your customers are paying for, or applications that you absolutely do not want changed in any manner after deployment.

Chapter 1 showed you how to use the command-line tool `aspnet_compiler.exe` to accomplish the task of precompilation. Although this method is great for precompiling your Web applications and deploying them to remote servers, you can also use Visual Studio 2010 to accomplish the precompilation and deployment process.

To accomplish this task, open the project you want to deploy and get the application ready for deployment by turning off the debugging capabilities as described earlier in the chapter. Then open the precompilation and deployment dialog by choosing Build ➪ Publish Web Site in the Visual Studio menu. The Publish Web Site dialog shown in Figure 36-8 appears.

Using the Browse (. . .) button in this dialog, you can choose any remote location to which you want to deploy the application. As in earlier examples, your options are a file system location, a place in the local IIS, a location accessed using FTP, or a location accessed via FrontPage Server Extensions.

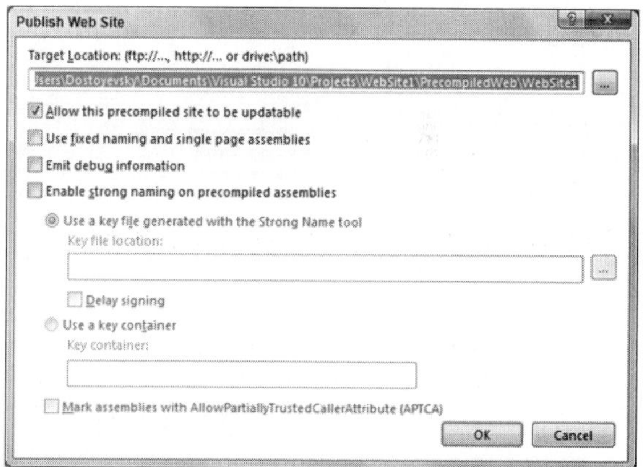

FIGURE 36-8

Other options in this dialog include the "Allow this precompiled site to be updateable" check box. When this option is selected, the site will be compiled and copied without any changes to the `.aspx` pages. This means that after the precompilation process, you can still make minor changes to the underlying pages, and the application will work and function as normal. If this check box is not selected, all the code from the pages is stripped out and placed inside one or more DLLs. In this state, the application is not updateable because updating any of the placeholder files from this compilation process is impossible.

Another option in this dialog is to assign a strong name to the DLL that is created in this process. You can select the appropriate check box and assign a key to use in the signing process. The created DLL from the precompilation will then be a strong assembly — signed with the key of your choice.

When you are ready to deploy, click OK in the dialog and then the open application is built and published. *Published* means that the application is deployed to the specified location. Looking at this location, you can see that a `bin` directory has now been added that contains some precompiled DLLs, which is your Web application. This is illustrated in Figure 36-9.

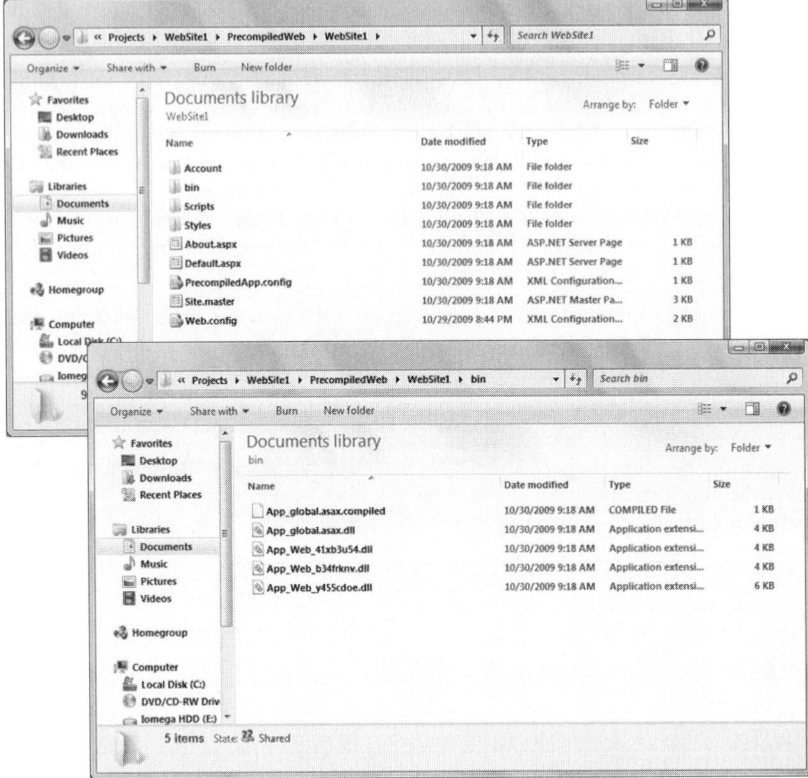

FIGURE 36-9

In this state, the code contained in any of the ASP.NET-specific pages is stripped out and placed inside the DLL. The files that you see are actually just placeholders that the DLL needs for reference.

Building an ASP.NET Web Package

One of the easiest ways to deploy your Web application is to use the new built-in publishing features from Visual Studio 2010. Behind the scenes, this new capability uses Microsoft's Web Deployment Tool, also known as MSDeploy, which means that if you want to deploy this tool to your server this server must have MSDeploy on the machine for the hydration of your application to actually work.

The package that is created and passed around is an actual physical file — a `.zip` file. This `.zip` file contains everything you need to redeploy your Web application with all of its settings into the new environment. In addition to the `.zip` file, it also includes a manifest file and a command file that are used to initiate the installation of the package on the host machine.

The first way in which this application can be deployed is to use the new 1-Click Publishing capability found in Visual Studio 2010. To do this, right-click on the project within the Visual Studio Solution Explorer and select the Publish option from the provided menu. The Publish Web dialog appears, as shown in Figure 36-10.

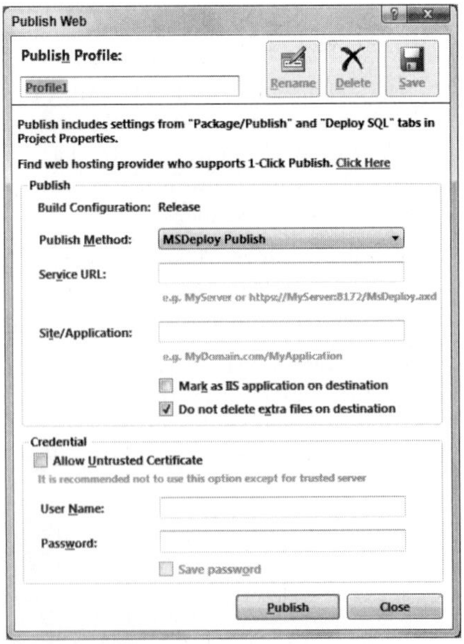

FIGURE 36-10

Because many developers are continually deploying their Web applications to their testing, staging, and production environments, there is a capability to store your deployment options in a profile that you can use again and again. Also notice in the dialog in Figure 36-10 that the build configuration is set to Release for this deployment. This setting comes from what you have set in the toolbar of Visual Studio 2010 before you select the Publish option.

The Publish Web dialog contains the following options as defined in Table 36-2.

TABLE 36-2

SETTING	DESCRIPTION
Profile name	The name of your saved profile. This provides you the ability to reuse your settings as a default for repeated deployments.
Build Configuration	Specifies whether the build compilation will be done in either the Debug or Release mode. You can first establish this setting from the toolbar of Visual Studio.
Publish Method	The method you want to employ for the deployment. The possible options include MSDeploy Publish, FTP, File System, and FPSE.
Service URL	Specifies the location of the MSDeploy on the host server. This URL points to the actual IIS handler that has the MSDeploy capability and will be constructed similar to `http://myhostserver:8172/MsDeploy.axd`.
Site/Application	Specifies the location where your application will be deployed. Here you can specify the site as well as the virtual directory to place the application. An example of this is `MyDomain.com/MyApplication`.
Mark as IIS application on destination	If this option is selected, IIS will treat the endpoint defined in the Site/Application textbox as the application root.
Do not delete extra files on destination	If this option is not selected, the 1-Click Publishing option will first delete everything on the host server location before applying the files and settings.
Allow Untrusted Certificate	If this option is selected, you will trust certificates that are self-published or certificates that don't match the URL of the destination.
User Name	The username used for IIS connections.
Password	The password used for IIS connections.
Save password	Specifies to the Visual Studio publishing feature whether to save the password in the profile.

Besides using the MSDeploy option, you will find that the other options provided through the new Publish Web dialog are even simpler. Figure 36-11 shows you the settings for the other three deployment options provided.

YOU CAN DOWNLOAD THE CODE FOUND IN THIS BOOK. VISIT WROX.COM AND SEARCH FOR ISBN 9780470502204

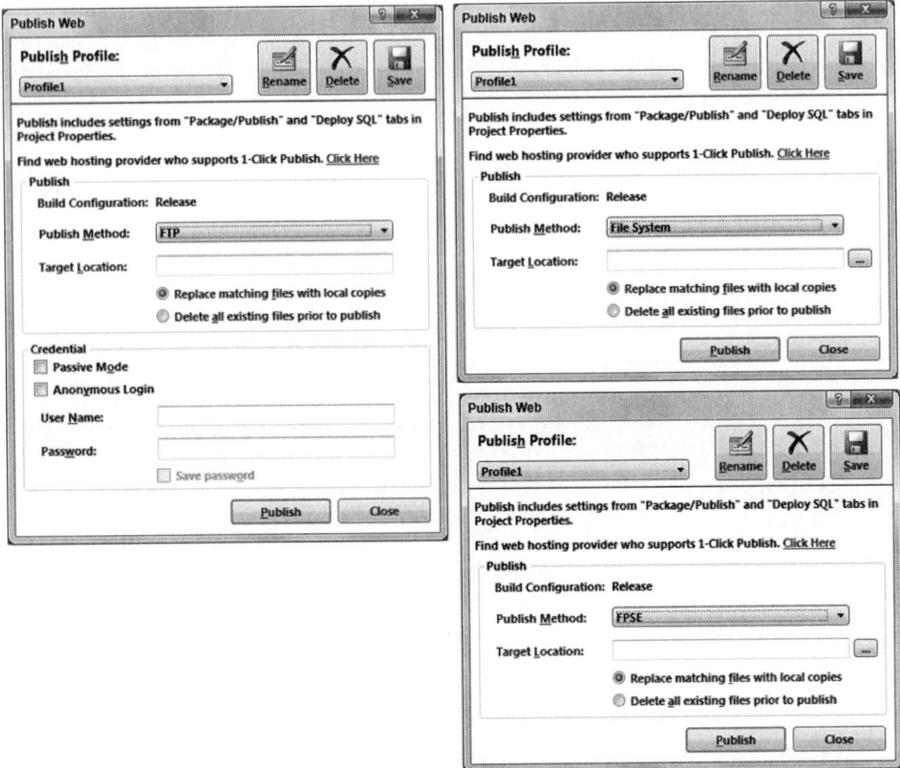

FIGURE 36-11

In this figure you can see some standard settings for doing deployments using FTP, the file system, or FrontPage Server Extensions.

The interesting thing with the MSDeploy capabilities that Visual Studio 2010 now works with is that instead of just connecting to a remote MSDeploy handler and running your deployment real-time, you can also create an MSDeploy package that can be run at any time.

Visual Studio 2010 now includes the ability to create these packages that can then be e-mailed or by other means provided to someone else to run on their systems. To create a Web deployment package, right-click on the project within the Visual Studio Solution Explorer and choose the Create Package option from the provided menu.

When you select the Create Package option, the progress of the package creation appears in the Visual Studio status bar. After you're notified that the Publish succeeded, you can find the entire package in your application's obj folder, such as

```
C:\Users\Evjen\Documents\Visual Studio 10\
 Projects\MyWebApplication\MyWebApplication\obj\Release\Package
```

Within this folder are all the files that constitute the package. Figure 36-12 presents these files.

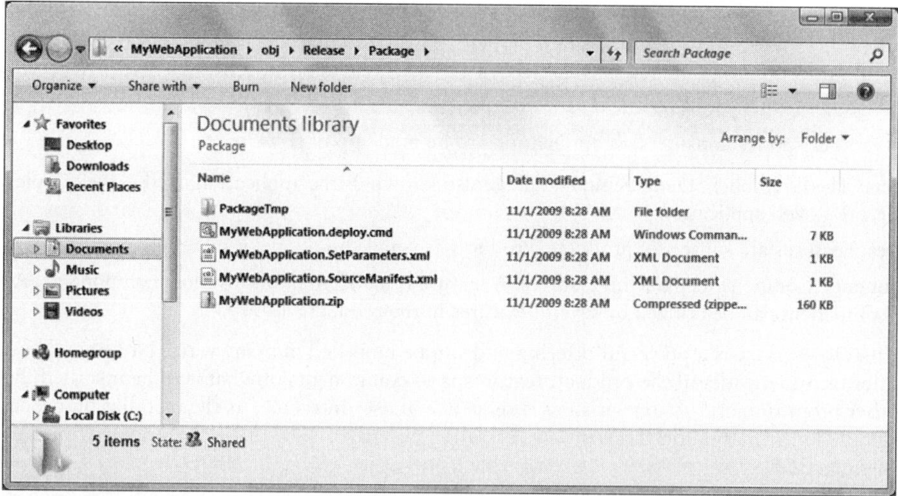

FIGURE 36-12

All of these files constitute the package that you can use in the deployment process.

- The `MyWebApplication.deploy.cmd` file is what your infrastructure team would use to run on the host machine (which has MSDeploy) to install the application and all the settings that are required for the application.
- The other files, `MyWebApplication.SetParameters.xml` and `MyWebApplication.SourceManifest.xml`, are used to define the settings used in the installation process.
- The final file, `MyWebApplication.zip`, contains the contents of the application.

With this package, passing another team the installation required for your application is easy. A nice example of this usage is if you are deploying to a Web farm because multiple deployments need to occur and you want these deployments to all be the same. Running your installations from this single package ensures this similarity.

The other nice advantage to this package system is that it allows you to save your previous deployments, and if you need to go back and verify deployments, you can easily grab hold of a saved package. It also makes rollbacks easy for your deployment process.

Building an Installer Program

The final option you should look at is how to use Visual Studio to build an installation program. After the program is constructed, a consumer can run the installation program on a server where it performs a series of steps to install the Web application.

Packaging your Web application into an installer program works in many situations. For example, if you sell your Web application, one of the simpler ways for the end user to receive the application is as an executable that can be run on the computer and installed — all without much effort on his part.

The Windows Installer

The Windows Installer service was introduced with Windows 2000, although it is also available in Windows Server 2003 and Windows Server 2008. This service was introduced to make the installation process for your Windows-based applications as easy as possible.

You use the Windows Installer technology not only for ASP.NET applications but also for any type of Windows-based application. The Windows Installer service works by creating a set of rules that determine how the application is to be installed. These rules are packaged into a Windows Installer Package File that uses the `.msi` file extension.

The Windows Installer service considers all applications to be made up of three parts:

- **Products:** The large-bucket item being installed, also known as the application itself. An example is the ASP.NET Web application.
- **Features:** Features are subsets of products. Products are made up of one or more features.
- **Components:** Components make up features. A feature is made up of one or more components. A single component can be utilized by several features in the product.

The Windows Installer service is a powerful offering and can be modified in many ways. Not only does the Windows Installer technology detail the product, features, and components of what is to be installed, but it can also take other programmatic actions or show a sequence of user interfaces as the installation process proceeds. For detailed information on the Windows Installer, be sure to view the MSDN documentation on the Windows Installer SDK.

With that said, working with the Windows Installer SDK is complicated at best; that was the reason for the release of the Visual Studio Installer (VSI) as an add-on with Visual Studio 6. This addition made the steps for building an installer much easier to follow. Visual Studio 2010 continues to expand on this capability. You have quite a few options for the deployment projects you can build with Visual Studio 2010. Such projects include the following:

- **Setup Project:** This project type allows you to create a standard Windows Installer setup for a Windows application.
- **Web Setup Project:** This project type is covered in this chapter. It's the type of setup project you use to create an installer for an ASP.NET Web application.
- **Merge Module Project:** This project type creates a merge module similar to a cabinet file. A merge module, such as a cabinet file, allows you to package a group of files for distribution but not for installation. The idea is that you use a merge module file with other setup programs. This project type produces a file type with an extension of `.msm`.
- **Setup Wizard:** This selection actually gives you a wizard to assist you through one of the other defined project types.
- **Cab Project:** This project type creates a cabinet file (`.cab`) that packages a group of files for distribution. It is similar to a merge module file, but the cabinet file is different in that it allows for installation of the files contained in the package.

Although a number of different setup and deployment project types are at your disposal, the Web Setup Project is the only one covered in this chapter because it is the project you use to build an installer for an ASP.NET Web application.

Actions of the Windows Installer

You might already be thinking that using the Windows Installer architecture for your installation program seems a lot more complicated than using the methods shown previously in this chapter. Yes, it is a bit more complicated — mainly because of the number of steps required to get the desired result; but in the end, you get a lot more control over how your applications are installed.

Using an installer program gives you programmatic logic over how your applications are installed. You also gain other advantages, such as:

- The capability to check whether the .NET Framework is installed, as well as which version of the Framework is installed

- The capability to read or write values to the registry
- The capability to collect information from the end user during the installation process
- The capability to run scripts
- The capability to include such features such as dialogs and splash screens during the installation process

Creating a Basic Installation Program

You can apply a tremendous amount of customization to the installation programs you build. Start, however, by looking at how to create a basic installation program for your ASP.NET Web application. To create an installer for your application, open the project for which you want to create a deployment project in Visual Studio and add an installer program to the solution. To do this, you add the setup program as a new project contained within the same solution. Choose File ➪ New ➪ Project from the Visual Studio menu. The New Project dialog launches.

From the New Project dialog, expand Other Project Types from the left pane in the dialog and then select Setup and Deployment. A list of all the available setup and deployment projects in Visual Studio appears. For the purposes of this example, select Web Setup Project (shown in Figure 36-13).

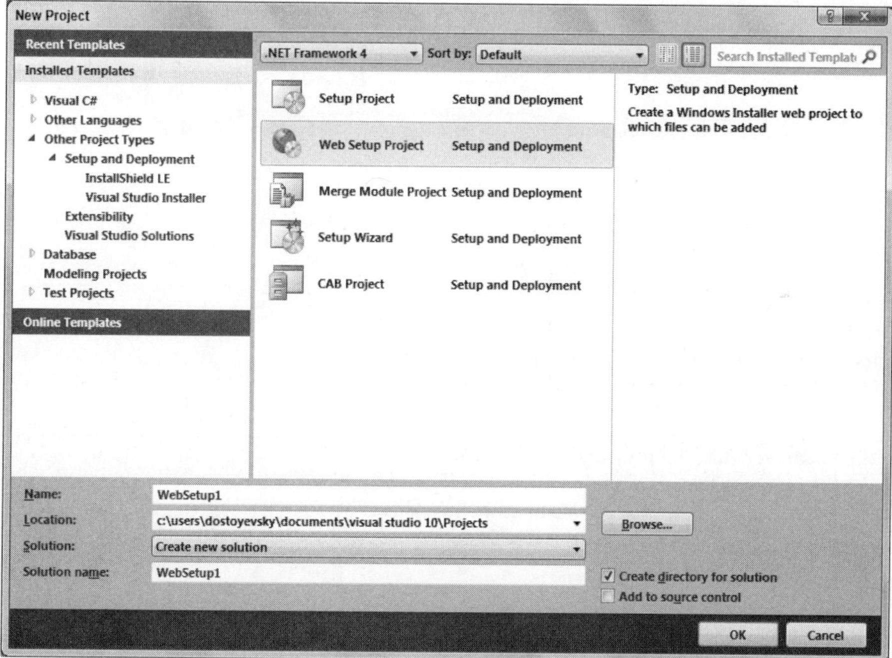

FIGURE 36-13

Clicking OK in this dialog adds the Web Setup Project type to your solution. It uses the default name of `WebSetup1`. Visual Studio also opens the File System Editor in the document window, which is shown in Figure 36-14.

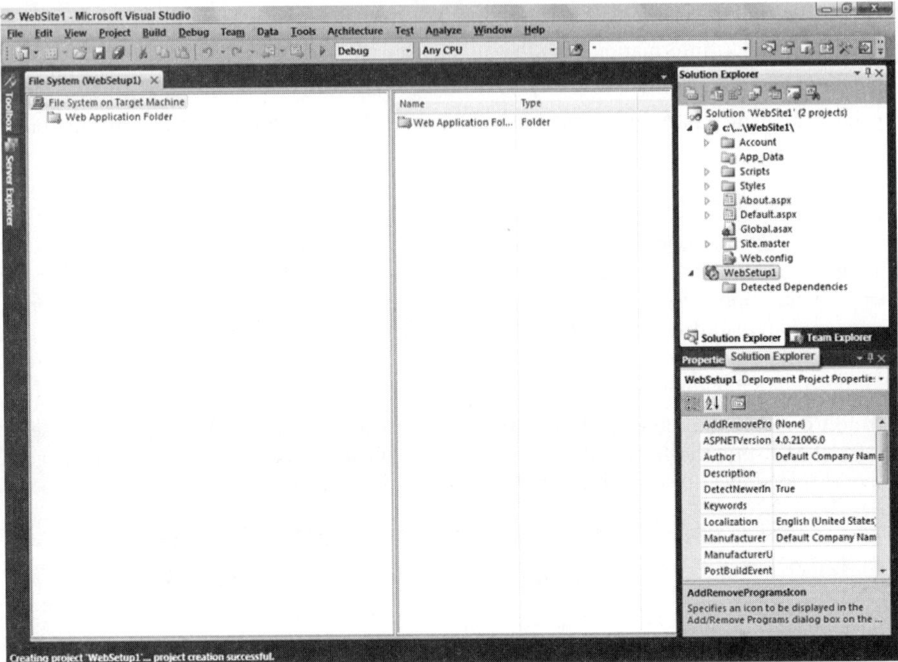

FIGURE 36-14

The File System Editor shows a single folder: the Web Application Folder. This is a representation of what is going to be installed on the target machine. Now add the files from the WebSite1 project to this folder, which you do by choosing Project ➪ Add ➪ Project Output from the Visual Studio menu. The Add Project Output Group dialog opens. This dialog (shown in Figure 36-15) enables you to select the items you want to include in the installer program.

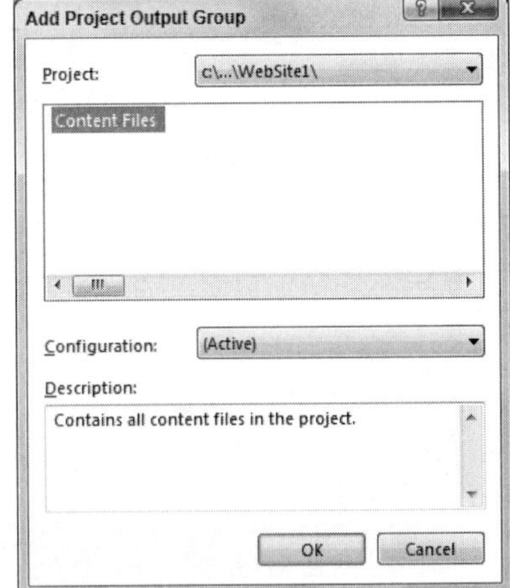

FIGURE 36-15

From this dialog, you can see that the project, Wrox, is already selected. Highlight the Content Files option and click OK. This adds all the files from the Wrox project to the WebSetup1 installer program. This addition is then represented in the File System Editor as well.

After the files are added to the installer program, click the Launch Conditions Editor button in the Solution Explorer (see Figure 36-16) to open the editor. The Launch Conditions Editor also appears in Visual Studio's document window. From this editor, you can see that a couple of conditions are already defined for you. Obviously, for Web applications, it is important that IIS be installed. Logically, one of the defined conditions is that the program must perform a search to see whether IIS is installed before installing the application. You should also stipulate that the installation server must have version 4 of the .NET Framework installed.

To establish this condition, right-click the Requirements On Target Machine node. Then select Add .NET Framework Launch Condition (as shown in Figure 36-17).

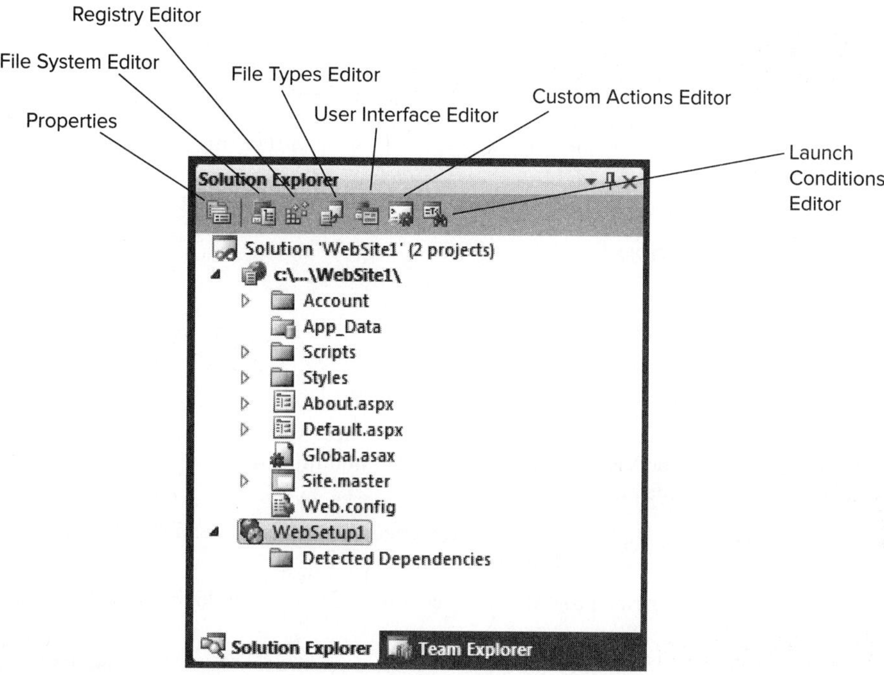

FIGURE 36-16

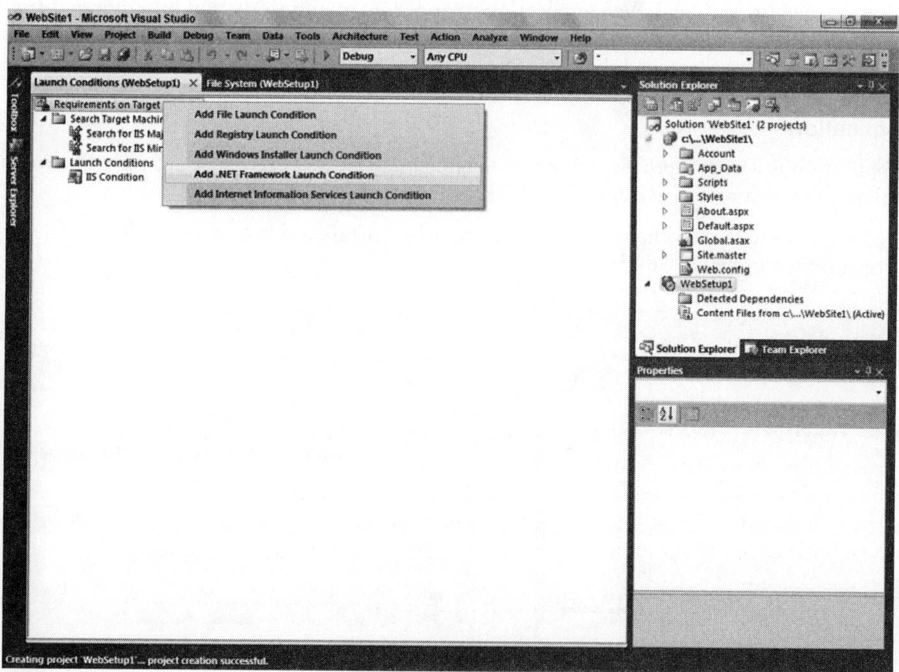

FIGURE 36-17

This adds the .NET Framework requirement to the list of launch conditions required for a successful installation of the Web application.

As a final step, highlight the WebSetup1 program in the Visual Studio Solution Explorer so you can modify some of the properties that appear in the Properties window. For now, just change some of the self-explanatory properties, but you will review these again later in this chapter. For this example, however, just change the following properties:

- `Author`: Wrox
- `Description`: This is a test project.
- `Manufacturer`: Wrox
- `ManufacturerUrl`: `http://www.wrox.com`
- `SupportPhone`: 1-800-555-5555
- `SupportUrl`: `http://www.wrox.com/support/`

Now the installation program is down to its simplest workable instance. Make sure Release is selected as the active solution configuration in the Visual Studio toolbar; then build the installer program by choosing Build ➪ Build WebSetup1 from the menu.

Looking in `C:\Documents and Settings\<username>\My Documents\Visual Studio 2010\Projects\Wrox\WebSetup1\Release`, you find the following files:

- `Setup.exe`: This is the installation program. It is meant for machines that do not have the Windows Installer service installed.
- `WebSetup1.msi`: This is the installation program for those machines that have the Windows Installer service installed.

That's it! You now have your ASP.NET Web application wrapped up in an installation program that can be distributed in any manner you want. It can then be run and installed automatically for the end user. Take a quick look in the following section at what happens when the consumer actually fires it up.

Installing the Application

Installing the application is a simple process (as it should be). Double-click the `WebSetup1.msi` file to launch the installation program. The Welcome screen shown in Figure 36-18 appears.

From this dialog, you can see that the name of the program being installed is `WebSetup1`. Clicking Next gives you the screen shown in Figure 36-19.

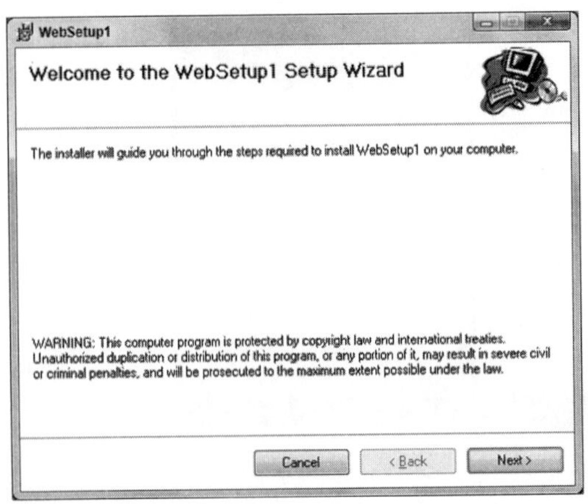

FIGURE 36-18

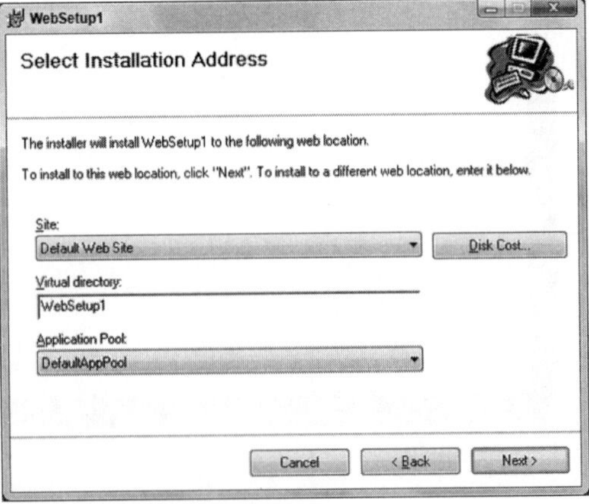

FIGURE 36-19

This screen tells you what you are installing (the Default Web Site) as well as the name of the virtual directory created for the deployed Web application. The consumer can feel free to change the name of the virtual directory in the provided text box. A button in this dialog allows for an estimation of the disk cost (space required) for the installed application. In .NET 4, the installer also allows the end user to choose the application pool he or she is interested in using for the application. The next series of screens install the `WebSetup1` application (shown in Figure 36-20).

After the application is installed, you can find the WebSetup1 folder and application files located in the `C:\Inetpub\wwwroot` folder (within IIS). The application can now be run on the server from this location.

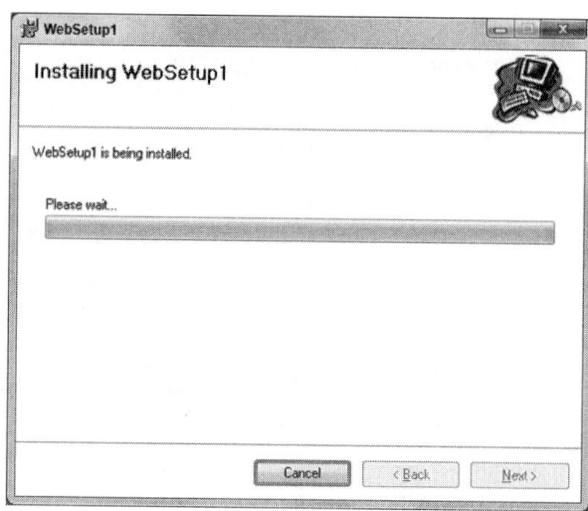

FIGURE 36-20

Uninstalling the Application

To uninstall the application, the consumer has a couple of options. One option is to re-launch the `.msi` file and use the option to either repair the current installation or to remove the installation altogether (as shown in Figure 36-21).

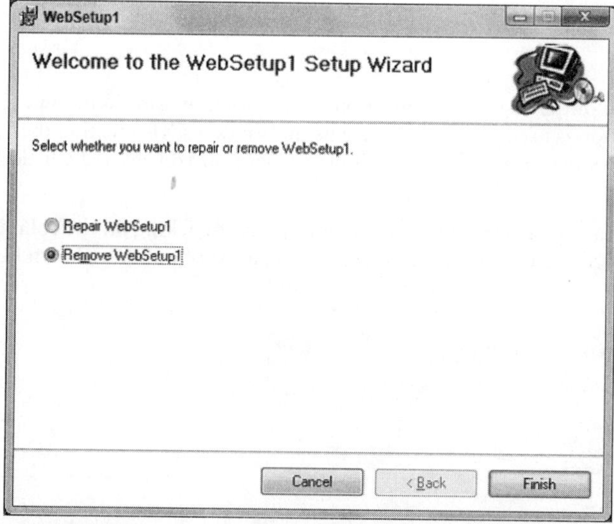

FIGURE 36-21

The other option is to open the Add/Remove Programs dialog from the server's Control Panel. On the Control Panel, you see `WebSetup1` listed (as shown in Figure 36-22).

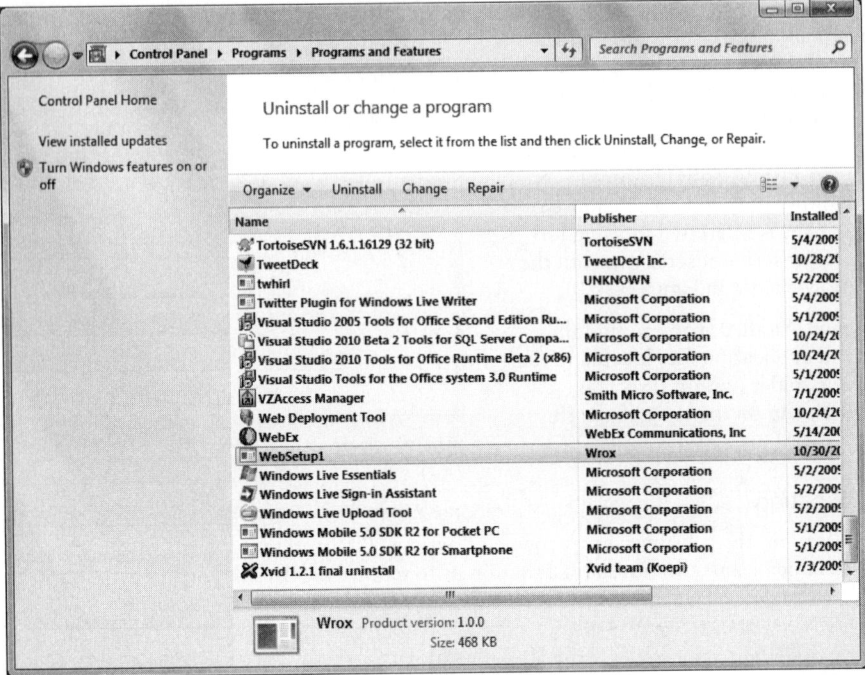

FIGURE 36-22

This dialog holds information about the size of the installed application and, if you are using Windows XP, it will also show you how often the application is used. Also, if you are using Windows XP, clicking the support link opens the Support Info dialog, which shows the project's properties that you entered a little earlier (see Figure 36-23).

However, if you are using Windows 7, you can get at the same information by right-clicking on the column headers and selecting the More option from the provided menu. This gives you a list of options (shown here in Figure 36-24), providing the same information as what you can see in Windows XP.

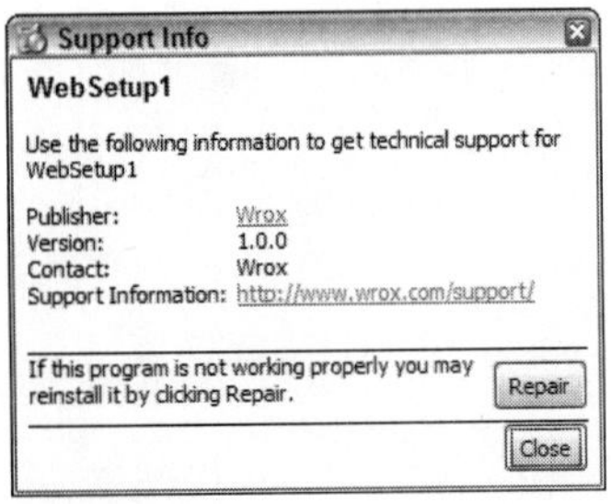

FIGURE 36-23

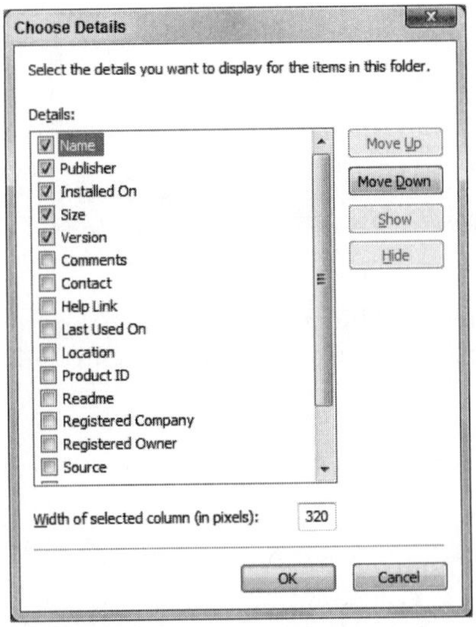

FIGURE 36-24

From the Add/Remove Programs dialog, you can remove the installation by clicking the Remove button of the selected program.

LOOKING MORE CLOSELY AT INSTALLER OPTIONS

The Windows Installer service easily installs a simple ASP.NET Web application. The installer takes care of packaging the files into a nice `.msi` file from which it can then be distributed. Next, the `.msi` file takes care of creating a virtual directory and installing the application files. The installer also makes uninstalling the application from the server just as easy. All these great services are provided with very little work on the user's part.

Even though this approach addresses almost everything needed for an ASP.NET installer program, the setup and deployment project for Web applications provided by Visual Studio really provides much more in the way of options and customizations. This next section looks at the various ways you can work with modifying the installer program.

Working with the Deployment Project Properties

You can work with the project properties of the installer from Visual Studio in several ways. The first way is by right-clicking the installer project from the Solution Explorer of Visual Studio and selecting Properties from the menu. This opens the WebSetup1 Property Pages dialog shown in Figure 36-25.

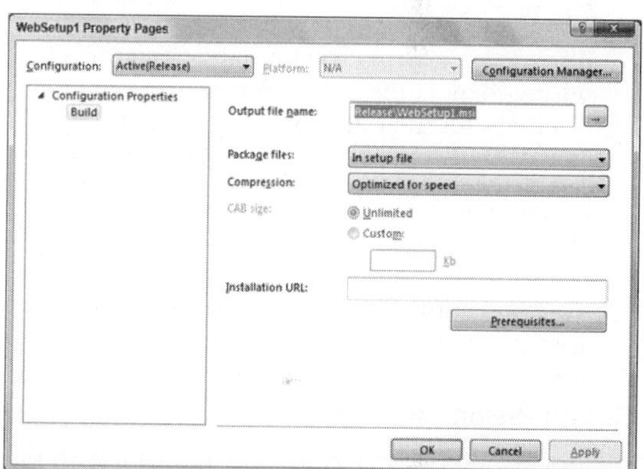

FIGURE 36-25

This dialog has some important settings for your installer application. Notice that, like other typical projects, this setup and deployment project allows for different active build configuration settings. For instance, you can have the active build configuration set to either Release or Debug. You can also click on the Configuration Manager button to get access to configuration settings for all the projects involved. In addition, this dialog enables you to add or remove build configurations from the project.

The Output File Name

The Output File Name setting lets you set the name of the `.msi` file that is generated. By default, it is the name of the project, but you can change this value to anything you want. The properties section also allows you to modify the location where the built `.msi` is placed on the system after the build process occurs.

Package Files

The Package files section of this properties page enables you to specify how the application files are packaged in the `.msi` file. The available options include the following:

- **As loose, uncompressed files:** This option builds the project so that a resulting `.msi` file is created without the required application files. Instead, these application files are kept separate from the `.msi` file but copied to the same location as the `.msi` file. With this type of structure, you must distribute both the `.msi` file and the associated application files.
- **In setup file:** This option (which is the default option) packages the application files inside the `.msi` file. This makes distribution an easy task because only a single file is distributed.

- **In cabinet file(s):** This option packages all the application files into a number of cabinet files. The size of the cabinet files can be controlled through this same dialog (discussed shortly). This type of installation process is ideal to use if you have to spread the installation application over a number of DVDs, CDs, or floppy disks.

Installation URL

Invariably, the ASP.NET applications you build have some component dependencies. In most cases, your application depends on some version of the .NET Framework. The installation of these dependencies, or components, can be made part of the overall installation process. This process is also referred to as *bootstrapping*. Clicking the Prerequisites button next to the Installation URL text box gives you a short list of available components that are built into Visual Studio in order to bootstrap to the installation program you are constructing (see Figure 36-26).

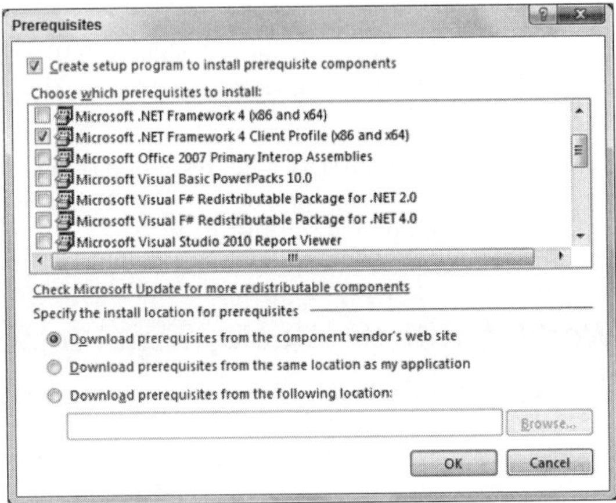

FIGURE 36-26

As you can see from when you first enter this settings dialog, the .NET Framework 4 and the Windows Installer 3.1 options are enabled by default, and you check the other components (thereby enabling them) only if your Web application has some kind of dependency on them.

From this dialog, you can also set how the dependent components are downloaded to the server where the installation is occurring. The options include downloading from Microsoft, from the server where the application originated, or from a defined location (URL) specified in the provided text box.

Compression

The Windows Installer service can work with the compression of the application files included in the build process so that they are optimized for either speed or size. You also have the option to turn off all compression optimizations. The default setting is Optimized for Speed.

CAB Size

The CAB Size section of the properties page is enabled only if you select In Cabinet File(s) from the Package Files drop-down list, as explained earlier. If this is selected, it is enabled with the `Unlimited` radio button selected. As you can see from this section, the two settings are `Unlimited` and `Custom`:

- `Unlimited`: This selection means that only a single cabinet file is created. The size of this file is dependent on the size of the collection of application files in the Web application and the type of compression selected.
- `Custom`: This selection allows you to break up the installation across multiple cabinet files. If the `Custom` radio button is selected, you can enter the maximum size of the cabinet files allowed in the provided text box. The measure of the number you place in the text box is in kilobytes (KB).

Additional Properties

You learned one place where you can apply settings to the installer program; however, at another place in Visual Studio you can find even more properties pertaining to the entire installer program. By selecting the `WebSetup1` installer program in the Solution Explorer, you can work with the installer properties directly from the Properties window of Visual Studio. Table 36-3 lists the properties that appear in the Properties window.

TABLE 36-3

PROPERTY	DESCRIPTION
AddRemoveProgramsIcon	Defines the location of the icon used in the Add/Remove Programs dialog found through the system's Control Panel.
Author	The author of the installer. This could be the name of a company or individual.
Description	Allows for a textual description of the installer program.
DetectNewerInstalledVersion	Instructs the installer to make a check on the installation server if a newer version of the application is present. If one is present, the installation is aborted. The default setting is `True` (meaning that the check will be made).
Keywords	Defines the keywords used when a search is made for an installer.
Localization	Defines the locale for any string resources and the runtime user interface. An example setting is `English (United States)`.
Manufacturer	Defines the name of the company that built or provided the installer program.
ManufacturerUrl	Defines the URL of the company that built or provided the installer program.
PostBuildEvent	Specifies a command line executed after the build ends.
PreBuildEvent	Specifies a command line executed before the build begins.
ProductCode	Defines a string value that is the unique identifier for the application. An example value is `{885D2E86-6247-4624-9DB1-50790E3856B4}`.
ProductName	Defines the name of the program being installed.
RemovePreviousVersions	Specifies as a `Boolean` value whether any previous versions of the application should be uninstalled prior to installing the fresh version. The default setting is `False`.
RestartWWWService	Specifies as a `Boolean` value whether or not IIS should be stopped and restarted for the installation process. The default value is `False`.
RunPostBuildEvent	Defines when to run the post-build event. The default setting is `On successful build`. The other possible value is `Always`.
SearchPath	Defines the path to use to search for any files, assemblies, and merge modules on the development machine.
Subject	Allows you to provide additional descriptions for the application.
SupportPhone	Specifies the support telephone number for the installed program.
SupportUrl	Specifies the URL by which the end user can get support for the installed application.
TargetPlatform	Defines the target platform of the installer. Possible values include `x86`, `x64`, and `Itanium`.
Title	Defines the title of the installer program.
UpgradeCode	Defines a shared identifier that can be used from build to build. An example value is `{A71833C7-3B76-4083-9D34-F074A4FFF544}`.
Version	Specifies the version number of the installer, cabinet file, or merge module. An example value is `1.0.1`.

The following sections look at the various editors provided to help you build and customize the construction of the installer. You can get at these editors by clicking the appropriate icon in the Solution Explorer in Visual Studio or by choosing View ➪ Editor in the Visual Studio menu. These editors are explained next.

The File System Editor

The first editor that appears when you create your installer program is the File System Editor. The File System Editor enables you to add folders and files that are to be installed on the destination server. In addition to installing folders and files, it also facilitates the creation of shortcuts. Figure 36-27 shows this editor.

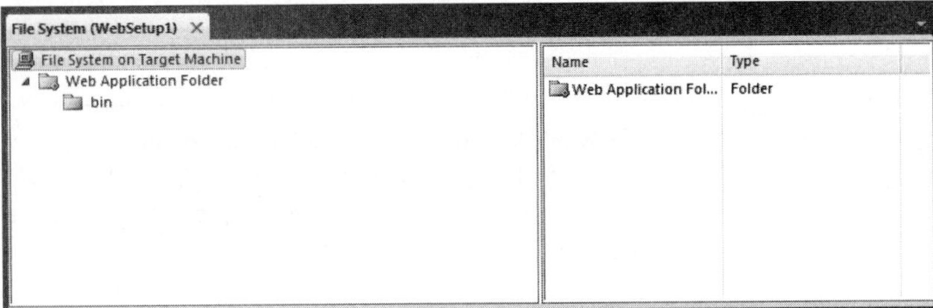

FIGURE 36-27

The File System Editor has two sections. The left section is the list of folders to be installed during the installation process. By default, only the Web Application Folder is shown. Highlighting this folder, or one of the other folders, gives you a list of properties for that folder in the Properties window of Visual Studio. Table 36-4 details some of the properties you might find in the Properties window.

TABLE 36-4

PROPERTY	DESCRIPTION
`AllowDirectoryBrowsing`	Allows browsing of the selected directory in IIS. The default value is `False`.
`AllowReadAccess`	Specifies whether the selected folder should have Read access. The default value is `True`.
`AllowScriptSourceAccess`	Specifies the script source access of the selected folder. The default value is `False`.
`AllowWriteAccess`	Specifies whether the selected folder should have Write access. The default value is `False`.
`ApplicationProtection`	Defines the IIS Application Protection property for the selected folder. Possible values include `vsdapLow`, `vsdapMedium`, and `vsdapHigh`. The default value is `vsdapMedium`.
`AppMappings`	Enables you to define the IIS application mappings for the selected folder.
`DefaultDocument`	Defines the default document of the selected folder. The default value is `Default.aspx`.
`ExecutePermissions`	Defines the IIS Execute Permissions property. Possible values include `vsdepNone`, `vsdepScriptsOnly`, `vsdepScriptsAndExecutables`. The default value is `vsdepScriptsOnly`.
`Index`	Specifies the IIS Index of this resource property for the selected folder. The default value is `True`.

PROPERTY	DESCRIPTION
IsApplication	Specifies whether an IIS application root is created for the installed application. The default value is True.
LogVisits	Specifies the IIS Log Visits property for the selected folder. The default value is True.
VirtualDirectory	Defines the name of the virtual directory created. The default value is the name of the project.

Adding Items to the Output

You can add files, folders, and assemblies to the installer output quite easily. To add some of these items to the output list, right-click the folder and select Add from the menu. You have four choices: Web Folder, Project Output, File, and Assembly.

If you want to add a custom folder to the output (for example, an Images folder), you can select Web Folder and provide the name of the folder. This enables you to create the folder structure you want.

If you want to add system folders, you highlight the File System on Target Machine node and then choose Action ➪ Add Special Folder. A large list of folders that are available for you to add to the installer program appears. You can also get at this list of folders by simply right-clicking a blank portion of the left pane of the File System Editor (see Figure 36-28).

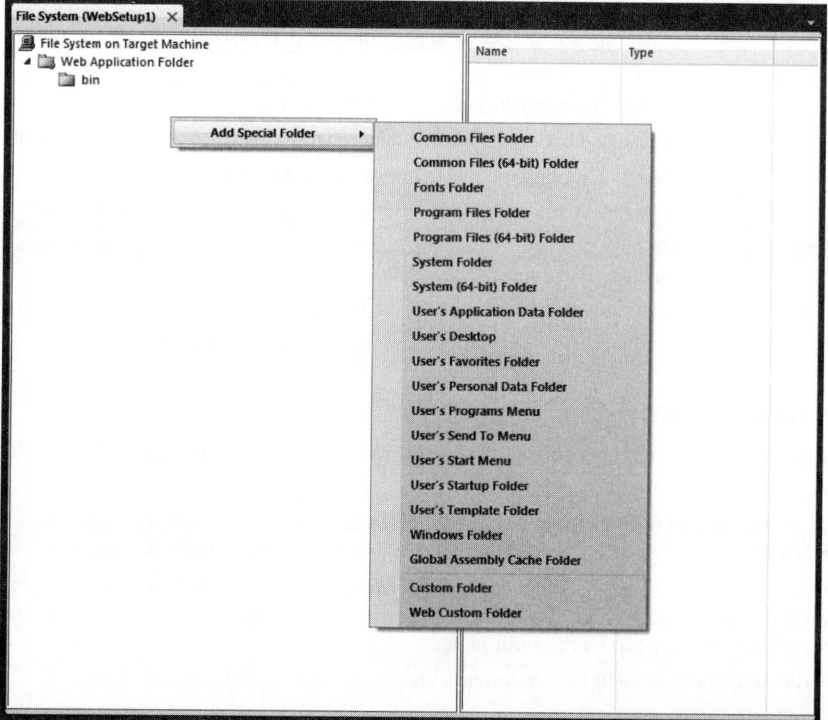

FIGURE 36-28

Table 36-5 defines the possible folders you can add to the installer structure you are building.

TABLE 36-5

FOLDERS AND MENUS	DESCRIPTION
Common Files Folder	Meant for non-system files not shared by multiple applications.
Common Files (64-bit) Folder	Meant for non-system files on a 64-bit machine not shared by multiple applications.
Fonts Folder	Meant for only fonts you want installed on the client's machine.
Program Files Folder	A Windows Forms application would be a heavy user of this folder because most applications are installed here.
Program Files (64-bit) Folder	A Program Files folder meant for 64-bit machines.
System Folder	Meant for storing files considered shared system files.
System (64-bit) Folder	Meant for storing files on 64-bit machines considered shared system files.
User's Application Data Folder	A hidden folder meant for storing data that is application- and user-specific.
User's Desktop	Meant for storing files on a user's desktop (also stores these files in the My Desktop folder).
User's Favorites Folder	Meant for storing files in a user's Favorites folder (browser-specific).
User's Personal Data Folder	Meant for storing personal data specific to a single user. This is also referred to as the My Documents folder.
User's Programs Menu	Meant for storing shortcuts, which then appear in the user's program menu.
User's Send To Menu	Meant for storing files that are presented when a user attempts to send a file or folder to a specific application (by right-clicking the folder or file and selecting Send To).
User's Start Menu	Meant for storing files in the user's Start menu.
User's Startup Folder	Meant for storing files that are initiated whenever a user logs into his machine.
User's Template Folder	Meant for storing templates (applications like Microsoft's Office).
Windows Folder	Meant for storing files in the Windows root folder. These are usually system files.
Global Assembly Cache Folder	Meant for storing assemblies that can then be utilized by all the applications on the server (shared assemblies).
Custom Folder	Another way of creating a unique folder.
Web Custom Folder	Another way of creating a unique folder that also contains a bin folder.

Creating a Desktop Shortcut to the Web Application

For an example of using one of these custom folders, try placing a shortcut to the Web application on the user's desktop:

1. Right-click on a blank portion of the left pane in the File System Editor and choose Add Special Folder ➪ User's Desktop. This adds that folder to the list of folders presented in the left pane.
2. Because you want to create a desktop shortcut to the Web Application Folder and not to the desktop itself, you next right-click the Web Application folder and select Create Shortcut to Web Application Folder. The created shortcut appears in the right pane.
3. Right-click the shortcut and rename it to something a little more meaningful, such as Wrox Application.
4. Because you do not want to keep the shortcut in this folder, drag the shortcut from the Web Application Folder and drop it onto the User's Desktop folder.

With this structure in place, this installer program not only installs the application (as was done previously), but it also installs the application's shortcut on the user's desktop.

The Registry Editor

The next editor is the Registry Editor. This editor enables you to work with the client's registry in an easy and straightforward manner. Using this editor, you can perform operations such as creating new registry keys, providing values for already existing registry keys, and importing registry files. Figure 36-29 shows the Registry Editor.

FIGURE 36-29

From this figure, you can see that the left pane provides the standard registry folders, such as HKEY_CLASSES_ROOT and HKEY_LOCAL_MACHINE, as well as others. You right-click one of these folders to add a new key from the menu selection. This creates a new folder in the left pane where it is enabled for renaming. By right-clicking this folder, you can add items such as those illustrated in Figure 36-30.

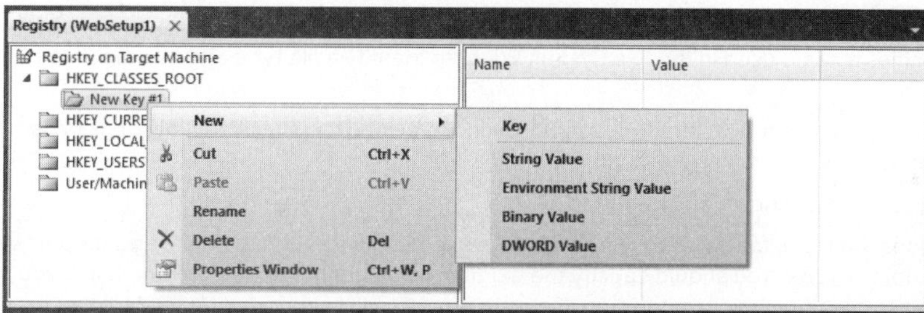

FIGURE 36-30

As you can see in the figure, you can add items such as the following:

- Key
- String Value
- Environment String Value
- Binary Value
- DWORD Value

Selecting String Value allows you to apply your settings for this item in the right pane, as illustrated in Figure 36-31.

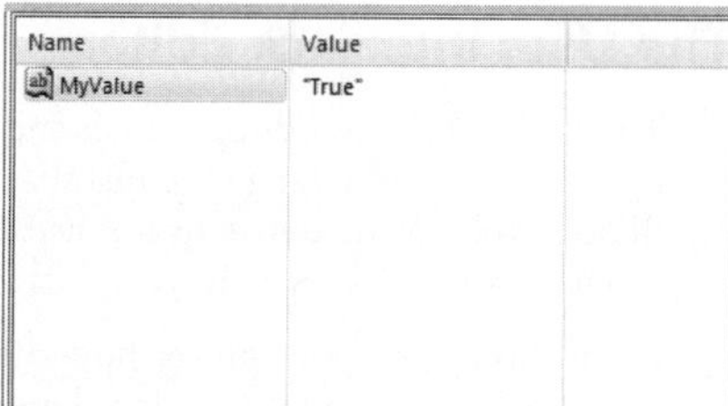

FIGURE 36-31

The other values work in a similar manner.

The File Types Editor

All files on a Windows operating system use file extensions to uniquely identify themselves. A file such as `Default.aspx`, for example, uses the file extension `.aspx`. This file extension is then associated with ASP.NET. Another example is `.xls`. This file extension is associated with Microsoft Excel. When someone attempts to open an `.xls` file, the file is passed to the Excel program because of mappings that have been made on the computer to associate these two entities.

Using the File Types Editor in Visual Studio, you can also make these mappings for the applications you are trying to install. Right-clicking the File Types On Target Machine allows you to add a new file type. From here, you can give your file type a descriptive name and provide a file extension (shown in Figure 36-32).

FIGURE 36-32

Highlighting the defined file type provides some properties that you can set in the Visual Studio Properties window, as shown in Table 36-6.

TABLE 36-6

PROPERTY	DESCRIPTION
`Name`	Specifies a name used in the File System Editor to identify a file type and its associated settings.
`Command`	Specifies the executable file (`.exe`) that is launched when the specified file extension is encountered.
`Description`	Defines a textual description for the file type.
`Extensions`	Defines the file extension associated with the executable through the `Command` property. An example is `wrox`. You should specify the extension without the period in front of it. If you are going to specify multiple extensions, you can provide a list separated by semicolons.
`Icon`	Defines the icon used for this file extension.
`MIME`	Specifies the MIME type associated with this file type. An example is `application/msword`.

The User Interface Editor

The User Interface Editor defines the dialogs used in the installation process. You can change the installation process greatly with the dialogs you decide to use or not use. By default, these dialogs (shown in Figure 36-33) appear in your installer.

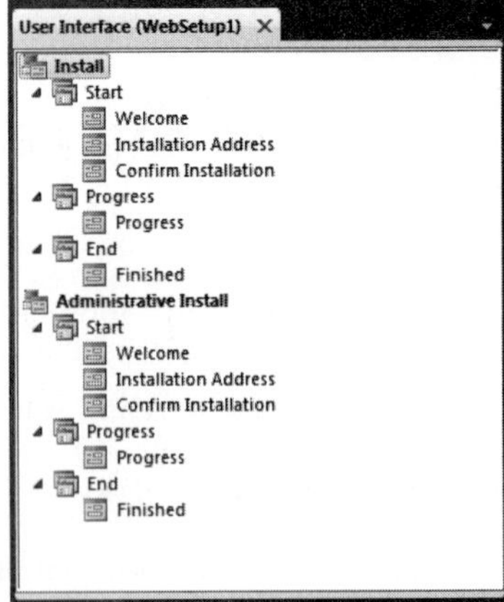

FIGURE 36-33

From this figure, you can see how the dialogs are divided into two main sections. The first section, labeled Install, is the dialog sequence used for a typical install. However, because some applications might require it, a second installation process is defined through the Administrative Install. The Administrative Install process is initiated only if the user is logged onto the machine under the Administrator account. If this is not the case, the Install section is used instead.

By default, the Install and Administrative Install sections are exactly the same. Both the Install and Administrative Install sections are further divided into three subsections: Start, Progress, and End. These sections are defined in the following list:

- **Start:** A sequence of dialogs that appears before the installation occurs. By default, the Start section includes a welcome screen, a definition stating where the application is to be installed, and a dialog asking for an installation confirmation.
- **Progress:** The second stage, the Progress stage, is the stage in which the actual installation occurs. Throughout this stage no interaction occurs between the installer program and the end user. This is the stage where the end user can watch the installation progress through a progress bar.
- **End:** The End stage specifies to the end user whether the installation was successful. Many installer programs use this stage to present the customer with release notes and `ReadMe.txt` files, as well as the capability to launch the installed program directly from the installer program itself.

Adding Dialogs to the Installation Process

Of course, you are not limited to just the dialogs that appear in the User Interface Editor by default. You can add a number of other dialogs to the installation process. For instance, right-click the Start node and select Add Dialog (or highlight the Start node and choose Action ➪ Add Dialog). This opens the Add Dialog dialog, as shown in Figure 36-34.

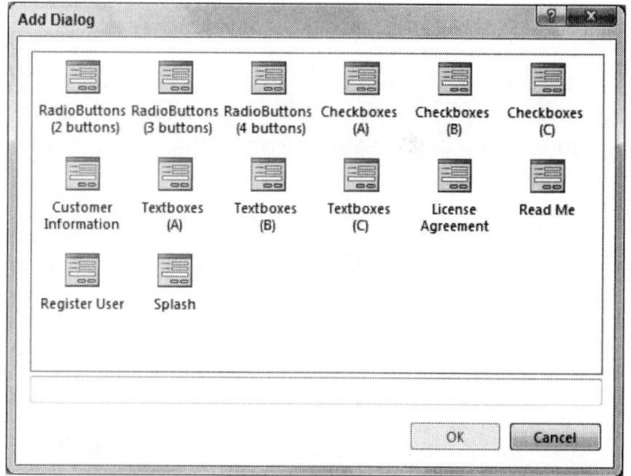

FIGURE 36-34

As you can see from this figure, you can add quite a number of different steps to the installation process, such as license agreements and splash screens. After adding a dialog to the process, you can highlight the dialog to get its properties to appear in the Properties window so that you can assign the items needed. For example, you can assign the image to use for the splash screen or the `.rtf` file to use for the license agreement.

When you add an additional dialog to the installation process (for instance, to the Install section), be sure to also install the same dialog on the Administrative Install (if required). If no difference exists between the two user types in the install process, be sure to add the dialogs in unison to keep them the same.

Changing the Order in Which the Dialogs Appear in the Process

In working with the dialogs in the Start, Process, and End sections of the User Interface Editor, you can always determine the order in which these dialogs appear. Even if you are working with the default dialogs, you can easily change their order by right-clicking the dialog and selecting Move Up or Move Down, as shown in Figure 36-35.

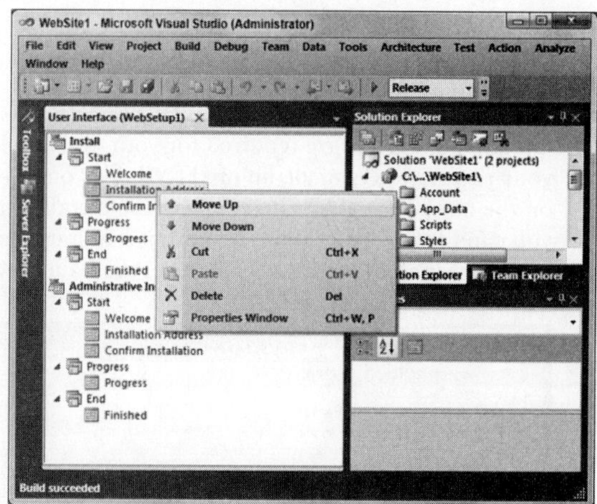

FIGURE 36-35

The Custom Actions Editor

The Custom Actions Editor is a powerful editor that enables you to take the installer one step further and perform custom actions during various events of the installation cycle (but always *after* the installation process is completed) such as Install, Commit, Rollback, and Uninstall. Figure 36-36 presents the Custom Actions Editor.

FIGURE 36-36

The idea is that you can place a reference to a `.dll`, `.exe`, or `.vbs` file from one of the folders presented in the Custom Actions Editor to perform a custom action. For example, you can insert a custom action to install a database into Microsoft's SQL Server in the Commit folder (after the install has actually been committed).

Descriptions of the four available folders are as follows:

- **Install:** This is the point at which the installation of the files for the Web application are finished being installed. Although the files are installed, this point is right before the installation has been committed.
- **Commit:** This is the point at which the actions of the installation have been actually committed (taken) and are considered successful.
- **Rollback:** This is the point at which the installation has failed and the computer must return to the same state that it was in before the installation occurred.
- **Uninstall:** This is the point at which a successfully installed application is uninstalled for a machine.

Using these capabilities, you can take the installation process to the level of complexity you need for a successfully installed application.

The Launch Conditions Editor

Certain conditions are required for your Web application to run on another server automatically. Unless your application is made up of HTML files only, you must make sure that the .NET Framework is installed on the targeted machine to consider the install a success. The Launch Conditions Editor is an editor that you can use to ensure that everything that must be in place on the installation computer for the installation to occur is there. Figure 36-37 shows the Launch Conditions Editor.

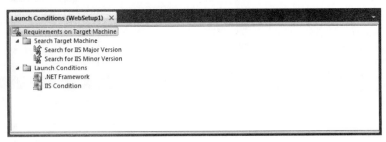

FIGURE 36-37

In this figure, you can see some of the conditions required in this instance. The first folder defines the items that must be in place on the computer where the installation is to occur. A search is done on the computer to see whether IIS is installed. It can also check whether any files or registry keys are present on the computer before the installation occurs.

The second folder is important because certain conditions must be in place before the installation. This folder shows two conditions. One is that the .NET Framework must be installed, and the second is that IIS must be installed. You can add these types of launch conditions by right-clicking the Requirements On Target Machine node in the dialog. A short list of conditions then appears.

After a condition is in place, you can highlight the condition to see the property details of this condition in the Properties window. For instance, highlighting the IIS Condition gives you some basic properties in the Properties window. One of these is the `Condition` property. By default, for an IIS Condition, the value of the `Condition` property is the following:

```
IISVERSION >= "#4"
```

This means that the requirement for this installation is that IIS must be equal to or greater than version 4. If it is not, the installation fails. If the IIS version is 4, 5, or 6, the installation can proceed. You can feel free to change this value to whatever you deem necessary. You can change the value to `IISVERSION >= "#5"`, for example, to ensure it is either IIS 5.0, 6.0, or 7.0 at a minimum.

Another example of fine-tuning these launch conditions is the .NET Framework condition that enables you to set the minimum version of the .NET Framework you want to allow. You do this by setting the `Version` property of the condition.

SUMMARY

As you can see, you have many possibilities for installing your ASP.NET applications — from the simplest mode of just copying the files to a remote server (sort of a save-and-run mode) to building a complex installer program that can run side events, provide dialogs, and even install extra items such as databases and more.

Just remember that when working on the installation procedures for your Web applications, you should be thinking about making the entire process logical and easy for your customers to understand. You do not want to make people's lives too difficult when they are required to programmatically install items on another machine.

Migrating Older ASP.NET Projects

In some cases, you build your ASP.NET 4 applications from scratch — starting everything new. In many instances, however, this is not an option. You need to take an ASP.NET application that was previously built on the 1.0, 1.1, 2.0, or 3.5 versions of the .NET Framework and migrate the application so that it can run on the .NET Framework 4.

This appendix focuses on migrating ASP.NET 1.*x*, 2.0, or 3.5 applications to the 4 Framework.

MIGRATING IS NOT DIFFICULT

Be aware that Microsoft has done a lot of work to ensure that the migration process from ASP.NET 1.*x* is as painless as possible. In most cases, your applications run with no changes needed.

When moving a 1.*x*, 2.0, or 3.5 application to 4, you don't have to put the ASP.NET application on a new server or make any changes to your present server beyond installing the .NET Framework 4.

After you install the .NET Framework 4, you see the framework versions on your server at C:\WINDOWS\Microsoft.NET\Framework, as illustrated in Figure A-1.

In this case, you can see that all the official versions of the .NET Framework installed, including v1.0.3705, v1.1.4322, v2.0.50727, v3.0, v3.5, and v4.0.

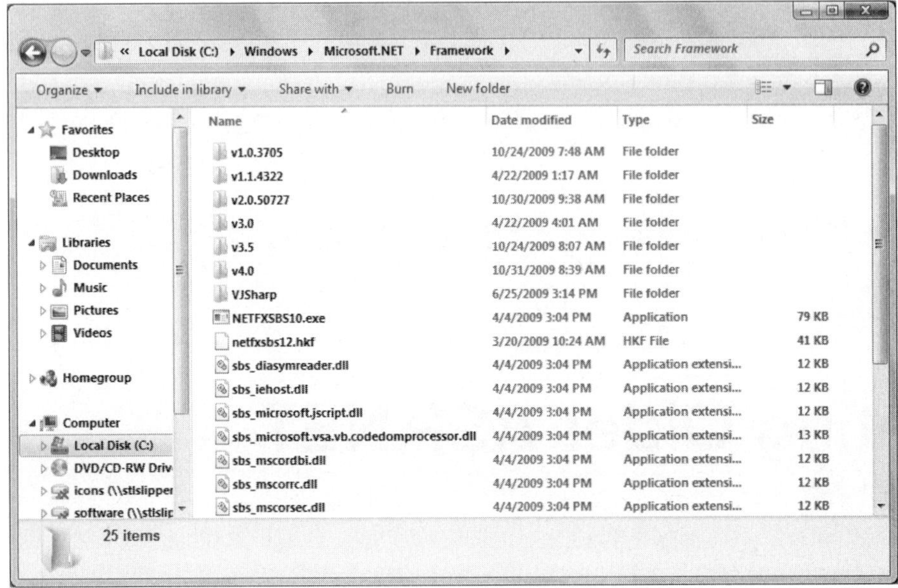

FIGURE A-1

Running Multiple Versions of the Framework Side by Side

From this figure, you can see that running multiple versions of the .NET Framework side by side is possible. ASP.NET 1.0, ASP.NET 1.1, ASP.NET 2.0, ASP.NET 3.5, and ASP.NET 4 applications can all run from the same server. Different versions of ASP.NET applications that are running on the same server run in their own worker processes and are isolated from one another.

Upgrading Your ASP.NET Applications

When you install the .NET Framework 4, it does not remap all your ASP.NET applications so that they now run off of the new framework instance. Instead, you selectively remap applications to run off of the ASP.NET 4 Framework.

To accomplish this task if you are migrating ASP.NET 1.*x* applications to ASP.NET 2.0, you use the ASP.NET MMC Snap-In that is a part of the .NET Framework 2.0 install. You get to this GUI-based administration application by right-clicking and selecting Properties from the provided menu using Windows XP when you are working with your application domain in Microsoft's Internet Information Services (IIS). After selecting the MMC console (the Properties option), select the ASP.NET tab, and something similar to that shown in Figure A-2 appears.

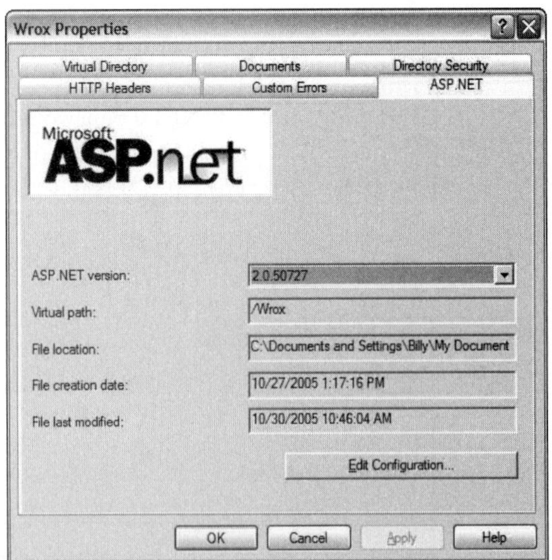

FIGURE A-2

You can see from this figure that an option exists for selecting the application's ASP.NET version (the top-most option). This allows you to select the version of the .NET Framework in which this ASP.NET application should run. In this case, the Wrox application on my machine was retargeted to the 2.0 release of ASP.NET when I selected 2.0.50727 in the drop-down list.

You should always test your older ASP.NET application by first running on the newer version of ASP.NET in a developer or staging environment. Do not change the version to a newer version on a production system without first testing for any failures.

If you are not ready to upgrade your entire application to a newer version of ASP.NET, one option is to create additional virtual directories in the root virtual directory of your application and target the portions of the application to the versions of the .NET Framework that you want them to run on. This enables you to take a stepped approach in your upgrade process.

If you are upgrading from ASP.NET 2.0 or ASP.NET 3.5 to ASP.NET 4, there really is very little that you have to do. Upgrading to version 4 is a bit different than it was when upgrading from version 2.0 to 3.5 because the 3.5 version of the .NET Framework was built upon the .NET Framework 2.0. In this case, the `System.Web` DLL in both versions of the framework was the same. Now, though, the .NET Framework 4 is a complete recompilation of the framework.

The differences are even more evident when working with the IIS Manager on Windows 7. From this management tool, you can see that the DefaultAppPool is running off version 4.0.*xxxxx* of the .NET Framework, as shown in Figure A-3.

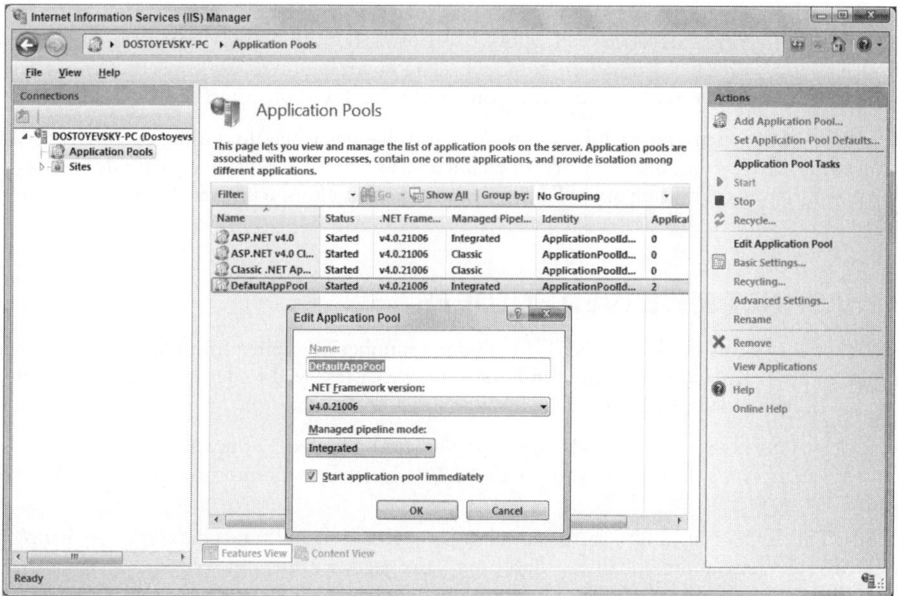

FIGURE A-3

Upgrading your application to ASP.NET 4 using Visual Studio 2010 will cause the IDE to make all the necessary changes to the application's configuration file. This is illustrated later in this appendix.

WHEN MIXING VERSIONS — FORMS AUTHENTICATION

If you have an ASP.NET application that utilizes multiple versions of the .NET Framework then, as was previously mentioned, you must be aware of how forms authentication works in ASP.NET 2.0, 3.5, and 4.

In ASP.NET 1.*x*, the forms authentication process uses Triple DES encryption (3DES) for the encryption and decryption process of the authentication cookies. Ever since ASP.NET 2.0, though, it has now been changed to use the AES (*Advanced Encryption Standard*) encryption technique.

AES is faster and more secure. However, because the two encryption techniques are different, you must change how ASP.NET 4 generates these keys. You do this by changing the `<machineKey>` section of the `web.config` file in your ASP.NET 4 application so that it works with Triple DES encryption instead (as presented in Listing A-1).

LISTING A-1: Changing your ASP.NET 4 application to use Triple DES encryption

```
<configuration>
   <system.web>

      <machineKey validation="3DES" decryption="3DES"
       validationKey="1234567890123456789012345678901234567890"
       decryptionKey="1234567890123456789012345678901234567890" />

   </system.web>
</configuration>
```

By changing the machine key encryption/decryption process to utilize Triple DES, you enable the forms authentication to work across an ASP.NET application that is using both the .NET Framework 1.*x* and 4. Also, this example shows the `validationKey` and `decryptionKey` attributes using a specific set of keys. These keys should be the same as those you utilize in your ASP.NET 1.*x* application.

You should understand that you are not required to make these changes when upgrading an ASP.NET 2.0 or 3.5 application to ASP.NET 4 because they are all enabled to use AES encryption and are not using Triple DES encryption. If you are mixing an ASP.NET 1.*x* application along with ASP.NET 2.0, 3.5, or 4, then you must move everything to use Triple DES encryption, as shown in Listing A-1.

UPGRADING — ASP.NET RESERVED FOLDERS

As described in Chapter 1 of this book, ASP.NET 4 includes a number of application folders that are specific to the ASP.NET Framework. In addition to the Bin folder that was a reserved folder in ASP.NET 1.*x*, the following folders are all reserved in ASP.NET 2.0, 3.5, and 4:

- **Bin:** This folder stores the application DLL and any other DLLs used by the application. This folder was present in both ASP.NET 1.0 and 1.1. It is also present in both ASP.NET 2.0, 3.5, and 4.
- **App_Code:** This folder is meant to store your classes, `.wsdl` files, and typed datasets. Any items stored in this folder are automatically available to all the pages within your solution.
- **App_Data:** This folder holds the data stores utilized by the application. It is a good, central spot to store all the data stores used by your application. The App_Data folder can contain Microsoft SQL Express files (`.mdf` files), Microsoft Access files (`.mdb` files), XML files, and more.
- **App_Themes:** Themes are a way of providing a common look-and-feel to your site across every page. You implement a theme by using a `.skin` file, CSS files, and images used by the server controls of your site. All these elements can make a theme, which is then stored in the App_Themes folder of your solution.

- **App_GlobalResources:** This folder enables you to store resource files that can serve as data dictionaries for your applications if these applications require changes in their content (based on things such as changes in culture). You can add Assembly Resource Files (`.resx`) to the App_GlobalResources folder, and they are dynamically compiled and made part of the solution for use by all the .aspx pages in the application.
- **App_LocalResources:** Quite similar to the App_GlobalResources folder, the App_LocalResources folder is a simple method to incorporate resources that can be used for a specific page in your application.
- **App_WebReferences:** You can use the App_WebReferences folder and have automatic access to the remote Web services referenced from your application.
- **App_Browsers:** This folder holds `.browser` files, which are XML files used to identify the browsers making requests to the application and to elucidate the capabilities these browsers have.

The addition of the `App_` prefix to the folder names ensures that you already do not have a folder with a similar name in your ASP.NET 1.*x* applications. If, by chance, you do have a folder with one of the names you plan to use, you should change the name of your previous folder to something else because these ASP.NET 4 application folder names are unchangeable.

ASP.NET 4 PAGES COME AS XHTML

ASP.NET 4, by default, constructs its pages to be XHTML-compliant. You can see the setting for XHTML 1.0 Transitional in the Visual Studio 2010 IDE, as shown in Figure A-4.

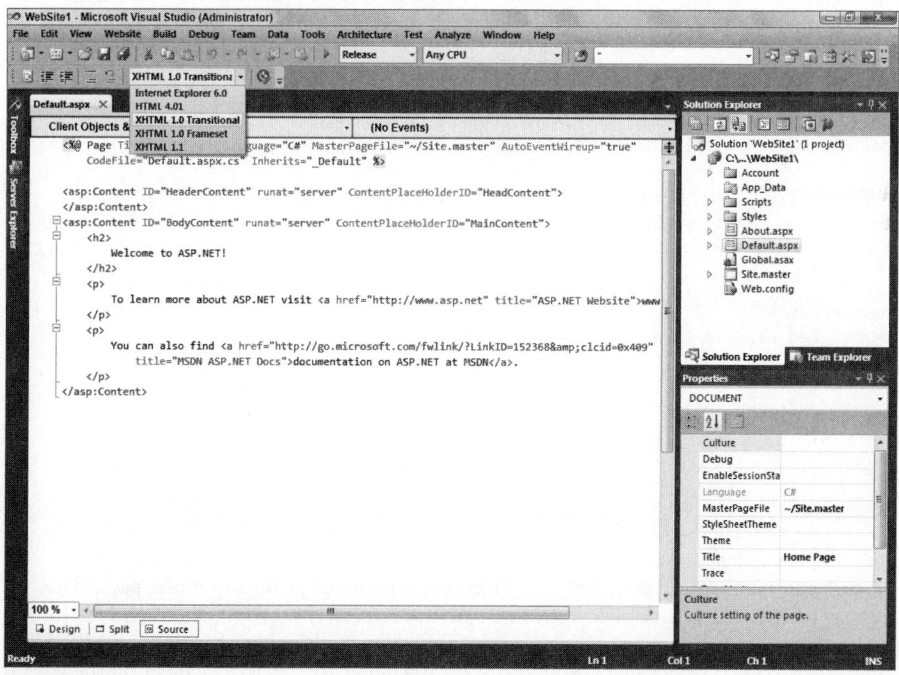

FIGURE A-4

In this case, you can see a list of options for determining how the ASP.NET application outputs the code for the pages. By default, it is set to `XHTML 1.0 Transitional`. You can also make a change to the `web.config` file so that the output is not XHTML-specific (as illustrated in Listing A-2).

LISTING A-2: Reversing the XHTML capabilities of your ASP.NET 4 application

```
<configuration>
   <system.web>

      <xhtmlConformance mode="Legacy" />

   </system.web>
</configuration>
```

Setting the `mode` attribute to `Legacy` ensures that XHTML is not used, but instead, ASP.NET 4 will use what was used in ASP.NET 1.*x*.

Note that using the `Legacy` setting as a value for the `mode` attribute will sometimes cause you problems for your application if you are utilizing AJAX. One of the symptoms that you might experience is that instead of doing a partial page update (as AJAX does), you will get a full-page postback instead. This is because the page is not XHTML compliant. The solution is to set the mode property to `Traditional` or `Strict` and to make your pages XHTML compliant.

If you take this approach, you also have to make some additional changes to any new ASP.NET 4 pages that you create in Visual Studio 2010. Creating a new ASP.NET 4 page in Visual Studio 2010 produces the results illustrated in Listing A-3.

LISTING A-3: A typical ASP.NET 4 page

```
<%@ Page Language="VB" %>

<!DOCTYPE html PUBLIC "-//W3C//DTD XHTML 1.0 Transitional//EN"
 "http://www.w3.org/TR/xhtml1/DTD/xhtml1-transitional.dtd">

<script runat="server">

</script>

<html xmlns="http://www.w3.org/1999/xhtml">
<head runat="server">
    <title>Untitled Page</title>
</head>
<body>
    <form id="form1" runat="server">
    <div>

    </div>
    </form>
</body>
</html>
```

From this listing, you can see that a `<!DOCTYPE ...>` element is included at the top of the page. This element signifies to some browsers (such as Microsoft's Internet Explorer) that the page is XHTML-compliant. If this is not the case, then you want to remove this element altogether from your ASP.NET 4 page. In addition to the `<!DOCTYPE>` element, you also want to change the `<html>` element on the page from

```
<html xmlns="http://www.w3.org/1999/xhtml">
```

to the following:

```
<html>
```

The original also signifies that the page is XHTML-compliant (even if it is not) and must be removed if your pages are not XHTML-compliant.

NO HARD-CODED .JS FILES IN ASP.NET 4

ASP.NET 1.*x* provides some required JavaScript files as hard-coded `.js` files. For instance, in ASP.NET a JavaScript requirement was necessary for the validation server controls and the smart navigation capabilities to work. If you are utilizing either of these features in your ASP.NET 1.*x* applications, ASP.NET could pick up the installed `.js` files and use them directly.

These `.js` files are found at `C:\WINDOWS\Microsoft.NET\Framework\v1.0.3705\ASP.NETClientFiles`. Looking at this folder, you see three `.js` files — two of which deal with the smart navigation feature (`SmartNav.js and SmartNavIE5.js`) and one that deals with the validation server controls (`WebUIValidation.js`). Because they are hard-coded `.js` files, opening them and changing or altering the code in these files to better suit your needs is possible. In some cases, developers have done just that.

If you have altered these JavaScript files in any manner, you must change some code when migrating your ASP.NET application to ASP.NET 2.0, 3.5, or 4. ASP.NET 4 dynamically includes `.js` files from the `System.Web.dll` instead of hard-coding them on the server. In ASP.NET 4, the files are included via a handler — `WebResource.axd`.

CONVERTING ASP.NET 1.*X* APPLICATIONS IN VISUAL STUDIO 2010

As previously mentioned, if you have a pre-existing ASP.NET 1.*x* application, you can run the application on the ASP.NET 4 runtime by simply making the appropriate changes in IIS to the application pool. Using the IIS manager or the MMC Snap-In, you can select the appropriate framework on which to run your application from the provided drop-down list.

ASP.NET 4 applications work with the Visual Studio 2010 IDE. If you still intend to work with ASP.NET 1.0 or 1.1 applications, you should keep Visual Studio .NET 2002 or 2003, respectively, installed on your machine. Installing Visual Studio 2010 gives you a complete, new copy of Visual Studio and does not upgrade the previous Visual Studio .NET 2002 or 2003 IDEs. All copies of Visual Studio can run side by side.

If you want to run ASP.NET 1.*x* applications on the .NET Framework, but you also want to convert the entire ASP.NET project for the application to ASP.NET 4, you can use Visual Studio 2010 to help you with the conversion process. After the project is converted in this manner, you can take advantage of the features that ASP.NET 4 offers.

To convert your ASP.NET 1.*x* application to an ASP.NET 4 application, you simply open the solution in Visual Studio 2010. This starts the conversion process.

When you open the solution in Visual Studio 2010, it warns you that your solution will be upgraded if you continue. It does this by popping up the Visual Studio Conversion Wizard, as presented in Figure A-5.

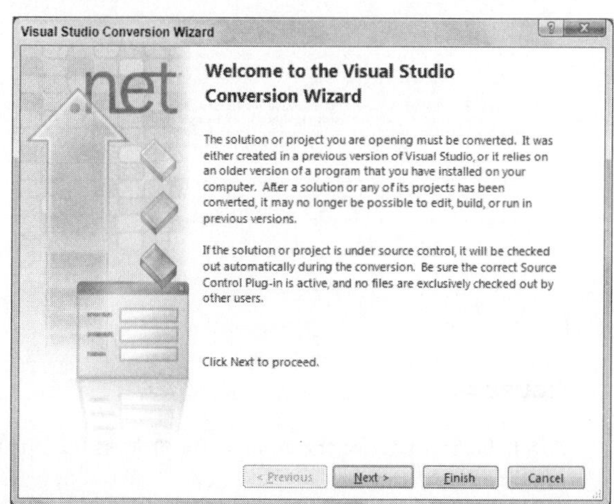

FIGURE A-5

Notice that the upgrade wizard has been dramatically improved from the early days of Visual Studio .NET to this newer one provided by Visual Studio 2010. To start the conversion process of your ASP.NET 1.*x* applications, click the Next button in the wizard. This example uses the open source Issue Tracker Starter Kit — an ASP.NET 1.1 starter kit found on the ASP.NET Web site at `www.asp.net`.

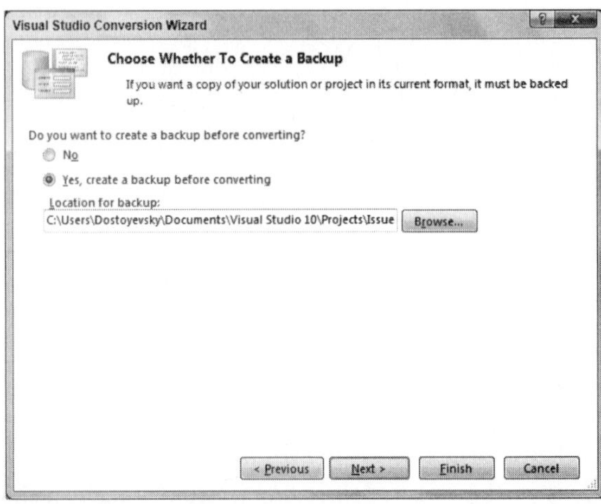

FIGURE A-6

The first step in the process is deciding whether you want the Visual Studio 2010 Conversion Wizard to create a backup of the ASP.NET 1.1 application before it attempts to convert it to an ASP.NET 4 application. Definitely, if this is your only copy of the application, you want to make a backup copy even though this conversion wizard does a good job in the conversion process. The conversion wizard also enables you to specify the location where you want to store the backup copy, as shown in Figure A-6.

The final step is a warning on how to handle the project if it is controlled by a source control system. If it is, you want to ensure that the project or any of its components are checked out by someone. You also want to ensure that the check-in capabilities are enabled. This warning is shown in Figure A-7.

When you are ready to convert the project, click the Finish button. The actual conversion process could take some time, so allow a few minutes for it. When the process is complete, you are offered a completion notification that also enables you to see the conversion log that was generated from the conversion process (see Figure A-8).

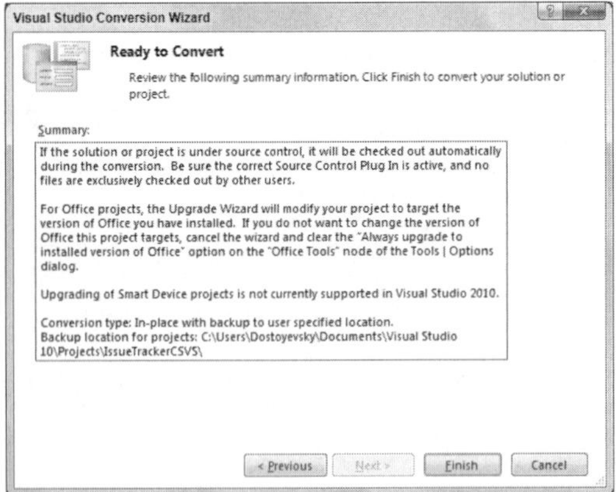

FIGURE A-7

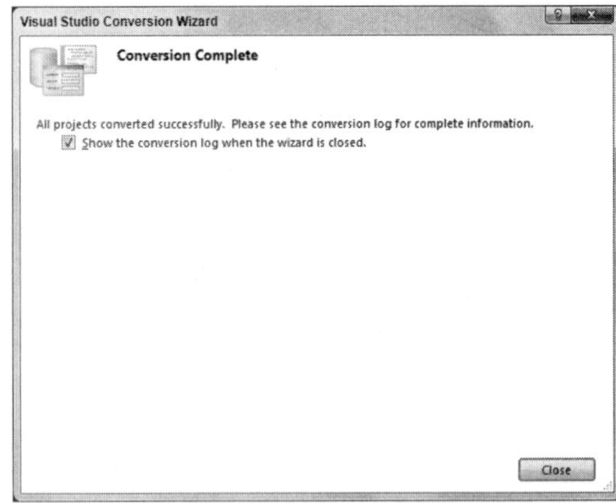

FIGURE A-8

After the first part of the conversion process for this project is done, the conversion log appears, as shown in Figure A-9.

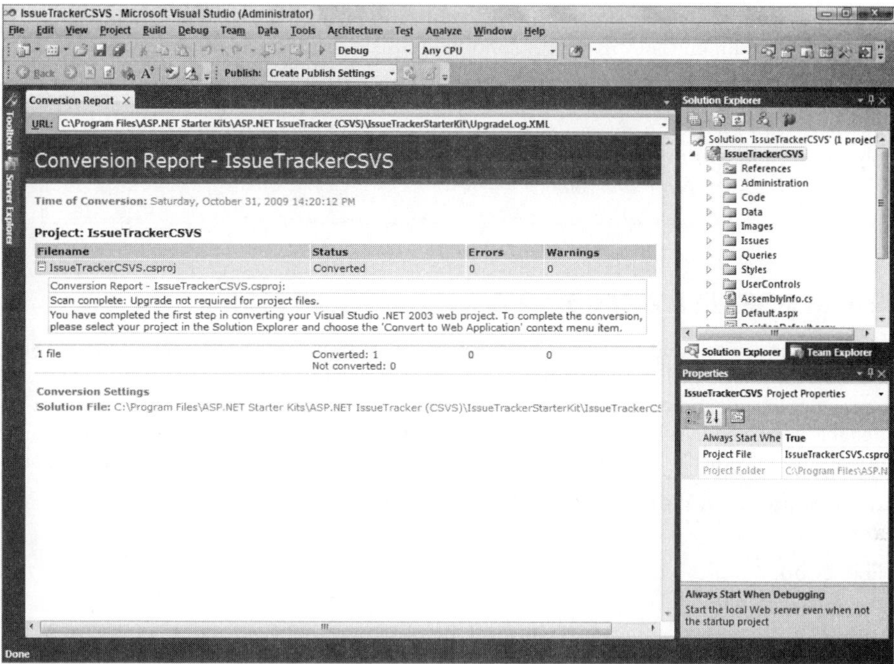

FIGURE A-9

The next step is to convert the project to a Web Application. To do so, right-click on the project within the Visual Studio 2010 Solution Explorer and select Convert to Web Application from the provided menu. The warning shown in Figure A-10 then appears.

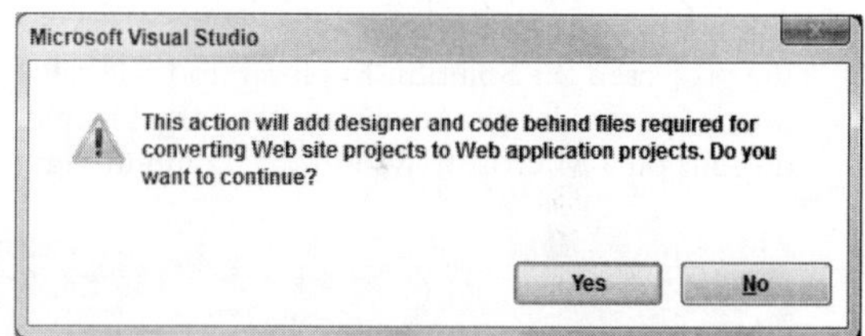

FIGURE A-10

As you look over the project in the Solution Explorer, notice that some major changes have been made to the project. Some of these changes include the following:

- All class files are removed from their folders and placed in the new App_Code folder. The folder from which the class files were removed is left in place, even if the folder is empty after all the class files are removed.
- All the Visual Studio .NET 2002/2003 Web project files are deleted because Visual Studio 2010 does not use these any longer.
- The application's DLL is deleted from the Bin folder.
- The code-behind classes for the `.aspx` pages are converted to partial classes (presented here in C#). This is what the code behind for the `Default.aspx` page looked like before the conversion:

```
public class _Default : System.Web.UI.Page
{
   // Code removed for clarity
}
```

- After the conversion process, the page class appears as shown here:

```
public partial class _Default : System.Web.UI.Page
{
   // Code removed for clarity
}
```

After the project is converted, you can build and run the application from Visual Studio 2010. The application is now built and run on the ASP.NET 4 runtime.

Remember: Do not upgrade production solutions without testing your programs first in a staging environment to ensure that your application is not affected by the changes between versions of the .NET Framework.

MIGRATING FROM ASP.NET 2.0/3.5 TO 4

Visual Studio 2010 enables you to build applications at more than one framework. For instance, Visual Studio .NET 2002 would only let you build 1.0 applications. If you wanted to build .NET Framework 1.1 applications, then you were required to install and use Visual Studio .NET 2003. At the same time, Visual Studio .NET 2003 would not enable you to build .NET Framework 1.0 applications, meaning that if you were dealing with applications that made use of either framework, then you were required to have both IDEs on your computer.

When you create a new project in Visual Studio 2010, you have the option of targeting the project at any of the following frameworks:

- .NET Framework 2.0
- .NET Framework 3.0
- .NET Framework 3.5
- .NET Framework 4

If you open an ASP.NET application that is built upon the .NET Framework 2.0, you can retarget the application to a newer version of the framework quite easily from the IDE. To do this, right-click on the project in the Solution Explorer and select Property Pages from the provided menu. This gives you a form that enables you to change the target framework of the application. In this case, you can see the default options on a Microsoft Windows 7 computer (as shown in Figure A-11).

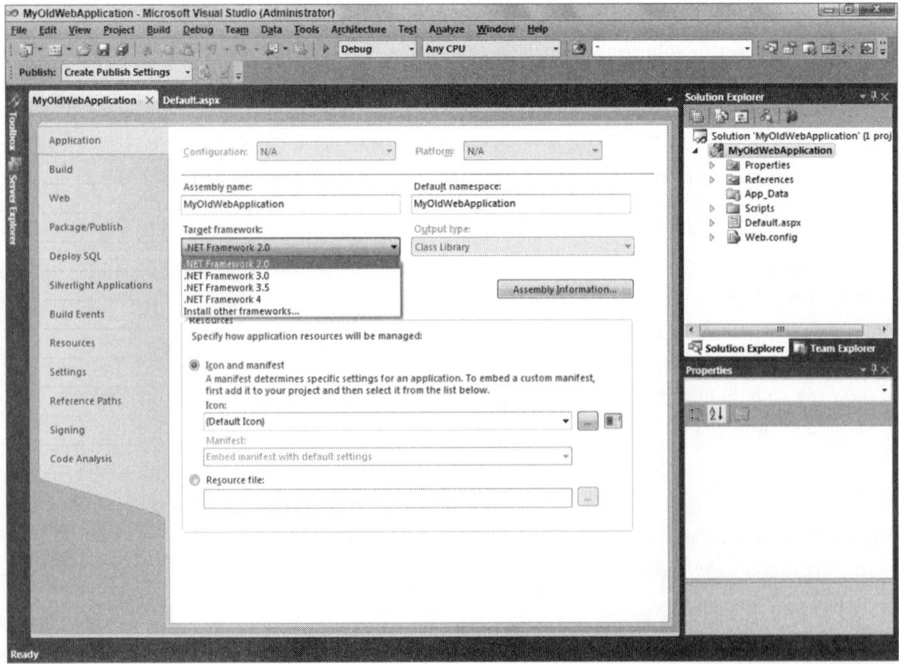

FIGURE A-11

Changing the target framework as is illustrated in Figure A-11, you will notice that Visual Studio 2010 needs to close and reopen your solution. After this is complete, you will see that even the `web.config` file was changed to account for working with the newer version of the framework. You might have to address some issues that deal with any breaking changes that have been presented between the releases of ASP.NET, but you can get a quick list of those problems by building the solution within Visual Studio.

SUMMARY

The nice thing with the Visual Studio 2010 IDE is that you are able to upgrade just your ASP.NET solution and not upgrade the framework version that your solution is targeted to. Though, in upgrading your ASP.NET solution to the .NET Framework 4, you might find that Visual Studio makes this an easy task to achieve.

This appendix took a look at upgrading using the IDE as well as some important changes between the releases that are aimed at making your migration as easy as possible.

B

ASP.NET Ultimate Tools

I've always believed that I'm only as good as my tools. I've spent years combing the Internet for excellent tools to help me be a more effective developer. There are thousands of tools out there to be sure, many overlapping in functionality with others. Some tools do one thing incredibly well and others aim to be a Swiss Army knife with dozens of small conveniences packed into their tiny toolbars. Here is a short, exclusive list of some of the ASP.NET tools that I keep turning back to. These are tools that I find myself using consistently while developing ASP.NET-based Web sites. I recommend that you give them a try if they sound useful. Many are free; some are not. In my opinion, each is worth at least a trial on your part, and many are worth your hard-earned money as they'll save you precious time.

These tools can be easily searched for in your favorite search engine and found in the first page. For those that are harder to find, I've included URLs. I also encourage you to check out my annually updated Ultimate Tools List at `www.hanselman.com/tools`, and you might also enjoy my weekly podcast at `www.hanselminutes.com` as we often discover and share new tools for the developer enthusiast.

Enjoy!

— Scott Hanselman

DEBUGGING MADE EASIER

"There has never been an unexpectedly short debugging period in the history of computers."

— Steven Levy

Firebug

There are so many great things about this application one could write a book about it. Firebug is actually a Firefox plug-in, so you'll need to download and install Firefox to use it.

Figure B-1 shows Firebug analyzing all the network traffic required to download my page. This shows a very detailed graph of when each asset is downloaded and how long it took from first byte to last byte as seen in Figure B-1.

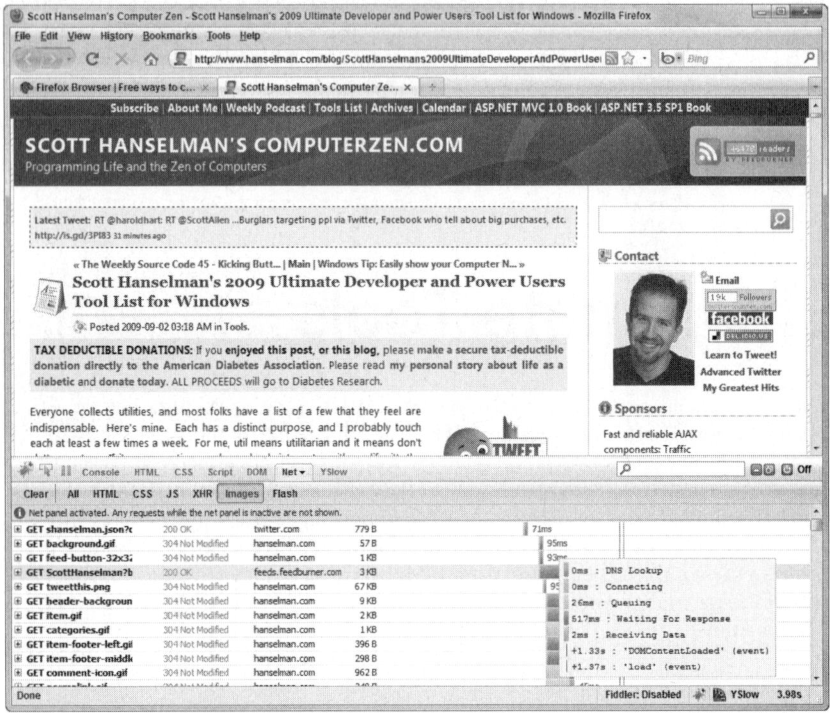

FIGURE B-1

It has a wealth of interesting features that allow you to inspect HTML and deeply analyze your CSS, including visualization of some more complicated CSS techniques such as offsets, margins, borders, and padding. Firebug also includes a powerful JavaScript debugger that will enable you to debug JavaScript within Firefox. Even more interesting is its JavaScript profiler and a very detailed error handler that helps you chase down even the most obscure bugs.

Finally, Firebug includes an interactive console feature like the Visual Studio Immediate window that lets you execute JavaScript on-the-fly, as well as console debugging that enables classic "got here" debugging. Firebug is indispensable for the Web developer and it's highly recommended.

There is also Firebug Lite in the form of a JavaScript file. You can add it to the pages in which you want a console debugger to work in Internet Explorer, Opera, or Safari. This file will enable you to do "got here" debugging using the Firebug JavaScript `console.log` *method.*

YSlow

YSlow is an add-on to an add-on. Brought to you by Yahoo!, YSlow extends Firebug and analyzes your Web pages using Yahoo!'s 13 rules for fast Web sites. In Figure B-2, you can see Yahoo!'s YSlow analyzing my blog.

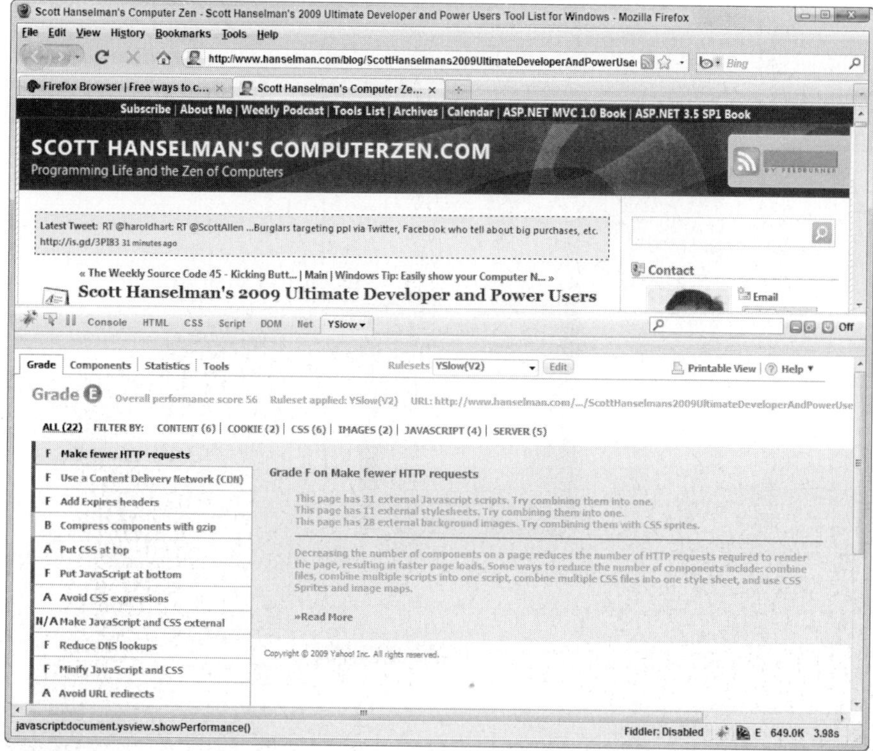

FIGURE B-2

In some instances, I do well, but in others I receive a failing grade. For example, rule number one says to make fewer HTTP requests. My site has too many external assets. Each one of these requires an HTTP request, so I suspect I could speed up my site considerably with some refactoring.

Not every rule will apply to you exactly, but Yahoo! knows what they're doing and it's worth your time to use this tool and consider your grades in each category. At the very least, you'll gain insight into how your application behaves. For example, Figure B-3 shows how many HTTP requests and bytes are transmitted with an empty cache versus a primed one.

HTTP Requests - 181		HTTP Requests - 119	
Total Weight - 649.0K		**Total Weight - 80.3K**	
2 HTML/Text	61.7K	2 HTML/Text	61.7K
32 JavaScript File	149.7K	22 JavaScript File	13.9K
11 Stylesheet File	25.6K	2 Stylesheet File	0.0K
1 Flash Object	4.5K	92 Image	4.6K
28 CSS Image	31.4K	1 Favicon	0.0K
106 Image	372.3K		
1 Favicon	3.6K		

FIGURE B-3

YSlow is free and is an excellent resource to help you get a clear understanding about how hard the client's browser must work in order to view your Web site.

IE8 Developer Tools and Firefox WebDeveloper

Both of these developer toolbars are free and absolutely essential for Web development. The IE8 Developer Tools are from Microsoft and come built-in with IE8. You just activate them by pressing F12. It extends Internet Explorer 8 with features such as DOM inspection, JavaScript profiling, and element outlining. You can even visualize the box-model as seen in Figure B-4.

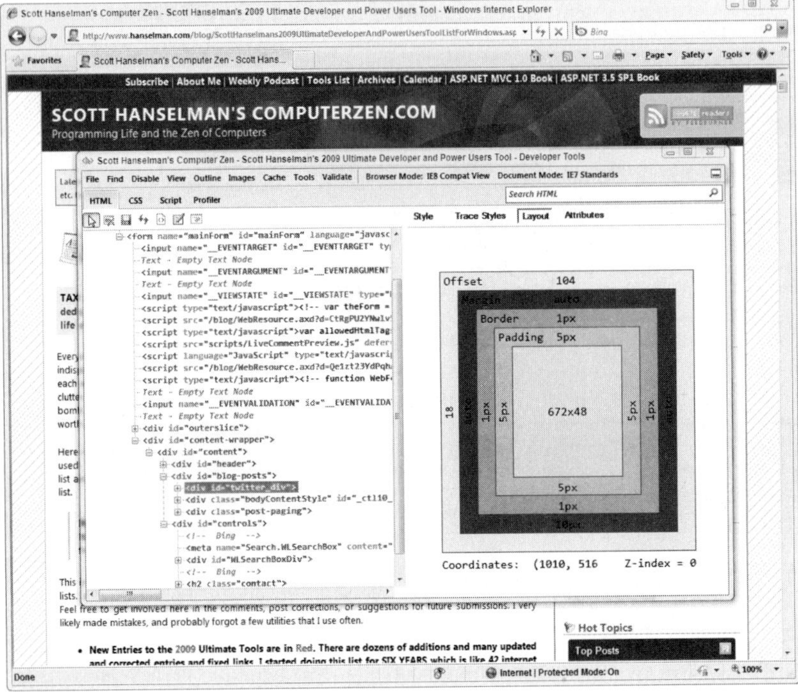

FIGURE B-4

Firefox has a similar but even more powerful Web Developer Toolbar created by Chris Pederick. It takes a slightly different direction for its user interface by including a number of menus, each literally chock full of menu options. You can disable cookies, CSS, images, inspect elements, form inputs, and outline tables, as shown in Figure B-5.

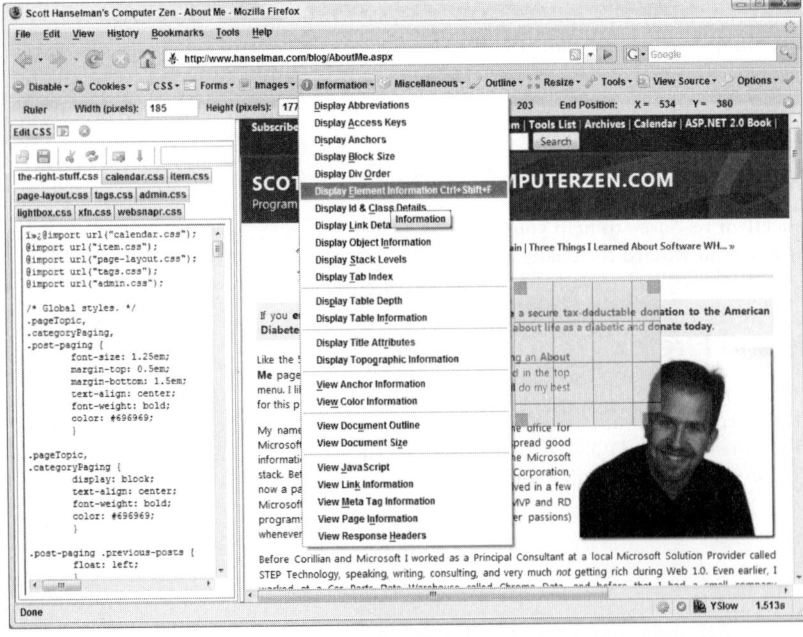

FIGURE B-5

ASP.NET developers today need their sites to look great in both browsers. These two toolbars put a host of usefulness at your fingertips. Highly recommended.

jQuery and jQuery UI

While not explicitly "tools," the JavaScript libraries jQuery and its partner jQuery UI make complex JavaScript tasks a joy. Yes, there were JS libraries before jQuery, but it's hard to overestimate how much jQuery not only changed the Web, but made JavaScript fun again.

JQuery includes a clean selector engine that makes moving around the HTML DOM (Document Object Model) trivial, allowing you to select and filter nodes and easily apply events and animations to them.

JQuery also includes methods for easily making AJAX calls. It's such a great library that the Microsoft ASP.NET MVC team decided to ship jQuery with ASP.NET MVC, making it the first Open Source product to ship with .NET along with full support. The IntelliSense improvements in the Visual Studio 2010 IDE along with the jQuery "vs-doc" files that Microsoft contributed back to the jQuery team mean that using jQuery in ASP.NET 4 is a natural fit.

JQuery UI is an additional library that adds even more animation support on top of jQuery, but more importantly adds a scaffold for themeable high-level widgets like sliders, calendars, and more. Check them out at `http://jquery.com` and `http://jqueryui.com` as shown in Figure B-6.

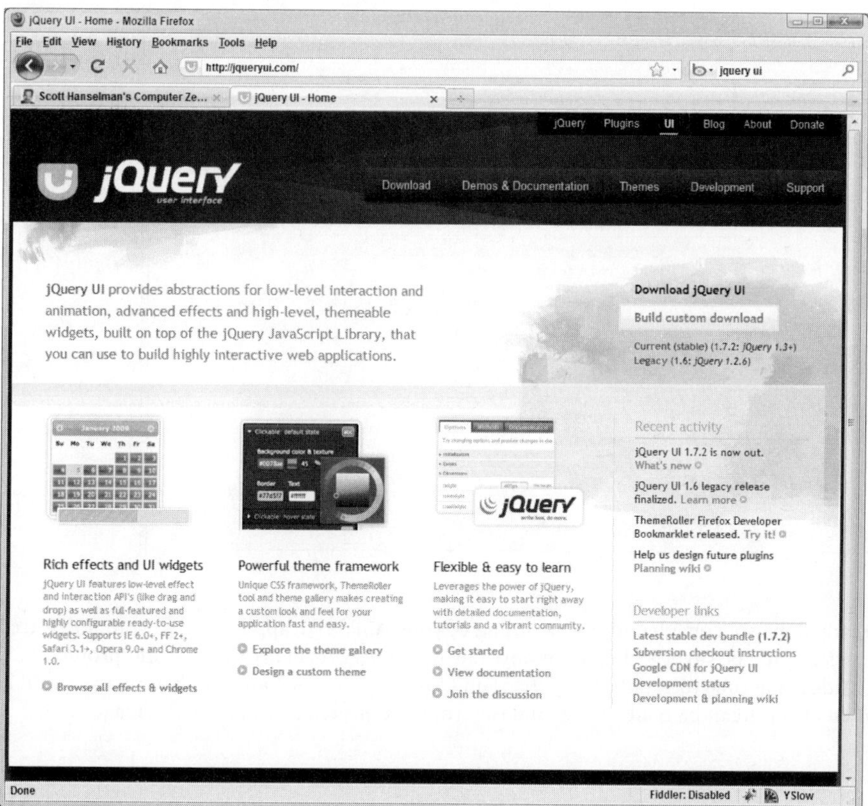

FIGURE B-6

Profilers: dotTrace or ANTS

If you're not measuring your code with a good profiler you really don't realize what you're missing out on. Only a profiler can give you extensive metrics and a clear understanding of what your code is doing.

Some SKUs of Visual Studio 2010 include a Profiler in the top-level Analyze menu. In addition there are excellent third-party profilers such as JetBrains' dotTrace and Red Gate Software's ANTS that are worth your 10-day trial.

.NET profilers instrument a runtime session of your code and measure how many times each line is hit and how much time is spent executing that line, as shown in Figure B-7. They create a hierarchical series of reports that allow you to analyze time spent not only within a method, but within child methods executed through the stack. Reports can be saved and multiple versions can be analyzed as you improve your applications, revision after revision.

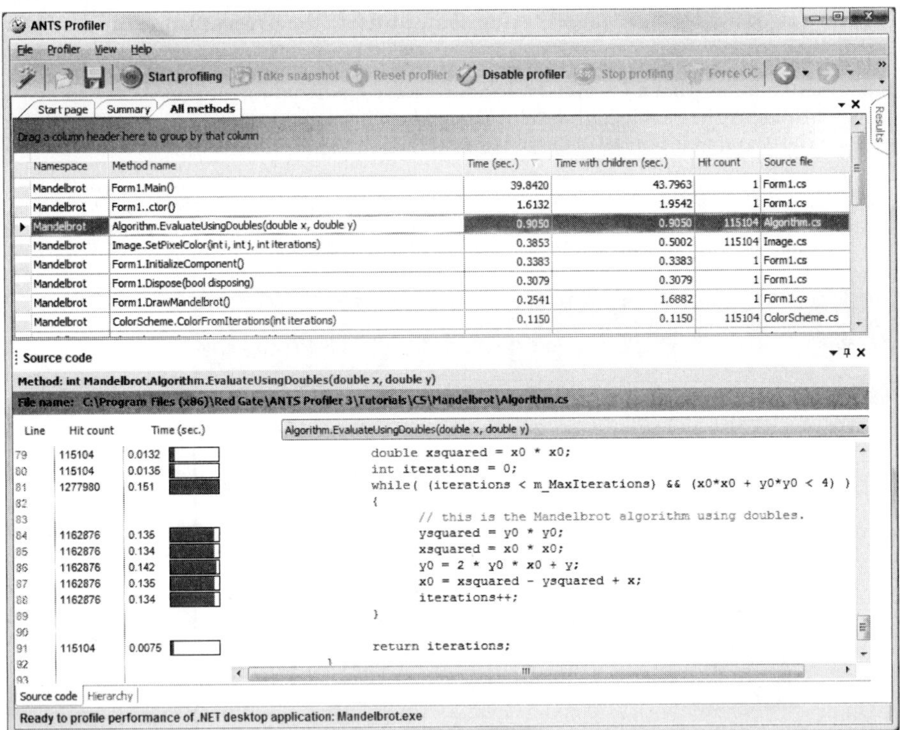

FIGURE B-7

If you haven't already done so, consider adding profiling of your ASP.NET application to your software development lifecycle. You'd be surprised to learn how few developers formally analyze and profile their applications. Set aside some time to profile an application that you've never looked at before and you'll be surprised how much faster it can be made using analysis from a tool such as ANTS or dotTrace.

REFERENCES

"He who lends a book is an idiot. He who returns the book is more of an idiot."

— ANONYMOUS, ARABIC PROVERB

PositionIsEverything.net, QuirksMode.org, and HTMLDog.com

When you're creating Web sites that need to look nice on all browsers, you're bound to bump into bugs, "features," and general differences in the popular browsers. Web pages are composed of a large combination of standards (HTML, CSS, JS). These standards are not only open to interpretation, but their implementations can differ in subtle ways, especially when they interact.

Reference Web sites, such as PositionIsEverything and QuirksMode, collect hundreds of these hacks and workarounds. Then they catalog them for your benefit. Many of these features aren't designed, but rather discovered or stumbled upon.

HTMLDog is a fantastic Web designer's resource for HTML and CSS. It's full of tutorials, articles, and a large reference section specific to XHTML. QuirksMode includes many resources for learning JavaScript and CSS and includes many test and demo pages demonstrating the quirks. PositionIsEverything is hosted by John and Holly Bergevin and showcases some of the most obscure bugs and browser oddities with demo examples for everything.

Visibone

Visibone is known for its amazing reference cards and charts that showcase Color, Fonts, HTML, JavaScript, and CSS. Visibone reference cards and booklets are available online and are very reasonably priced. The best value is the Browser Book available at `www.visibone.com/products/browserbook.html`. I recommend the laminated version. Be sure to put your name on it because your co-workers will make it disappear.

www.asp.net

I work for Microsoft on the team that runs `www.asp.net`. The site is a huge resource for learning about ASP.NET and the various technologies around it. Figure B-8 shows part of the Community page for the site, where you'll link to my Weblog, among others, and links to other community resources. The `www.asp.net/learn/` section includes dozens and dozens of videos about general ASP.NET and how to use it.

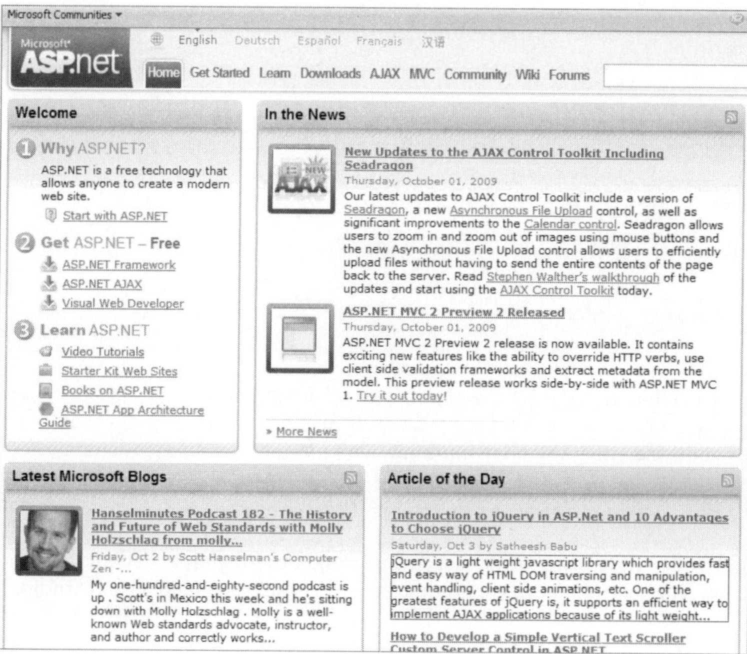

FIGURE B-8

TIDYING UP YOUR CODE

"After every war someone has to tidy up."

— Wislawa Szymborska

Refactor! for ASP.NET from Devexpress

Refactoring support in Visual Studio 2010 continues to get better. The third-party utilities continue to push the envelope, adding value to the IDE. Refactor! for ASP.NET adds refactoring to the ASP.NET source view.

For example, in Figure B-9 while hovering over the Refactor! context menu and selecting the "Extract UserControl" refactoring, a preview of the changes that *would* be made appear within the source view. A new UserControl would be created in a new file `WebUserControl0.ascx`. The currently selected label control would turn into a `WebUserControl0` control. You can then choose a new name for the UserControl immediately after the refactoring.

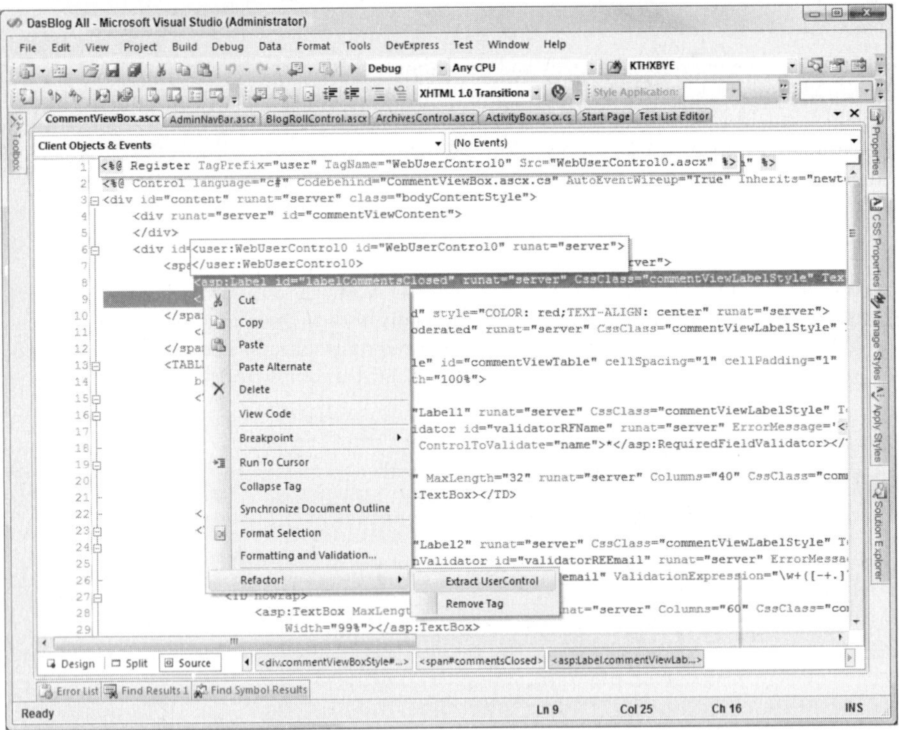

FIGURE B-9

The most amazing thing about Refactor! for ASP.NET is that it's a free download from `www.devexpress.com/Products/NET/IDETools/RefactorASP/`. It includes 28 refactorings that make it easier to simplify your code and your ASP.NET markup.

Code Style Enforcer

Code Style Enforcer from Joel Fjordén does just that. It's a DXCore Plugin that enforces code style rules that you configure. DXCore is the free engine from DevExpress that Refactor! uses to extend Visual Studio.

Every team has a coding standard that they'd like programmers to follow, but it's not only hard to keep track of all the rules, it's tedious. Are methods supposed to be CamelCased or Pascalcased? Are we putting "m_" in front of member fields?

Code Style Enforcer is a lot like Microsoft Word's spelling and grammar checker except for code. As shown in Figure B-10, identifiers that do not meet the code style guidelines are underlined in red, though you can't see the color in the black and white figure here. You can right-click on each error, and Code Style Enforcer will use DxCore to refactor and fix each violation.

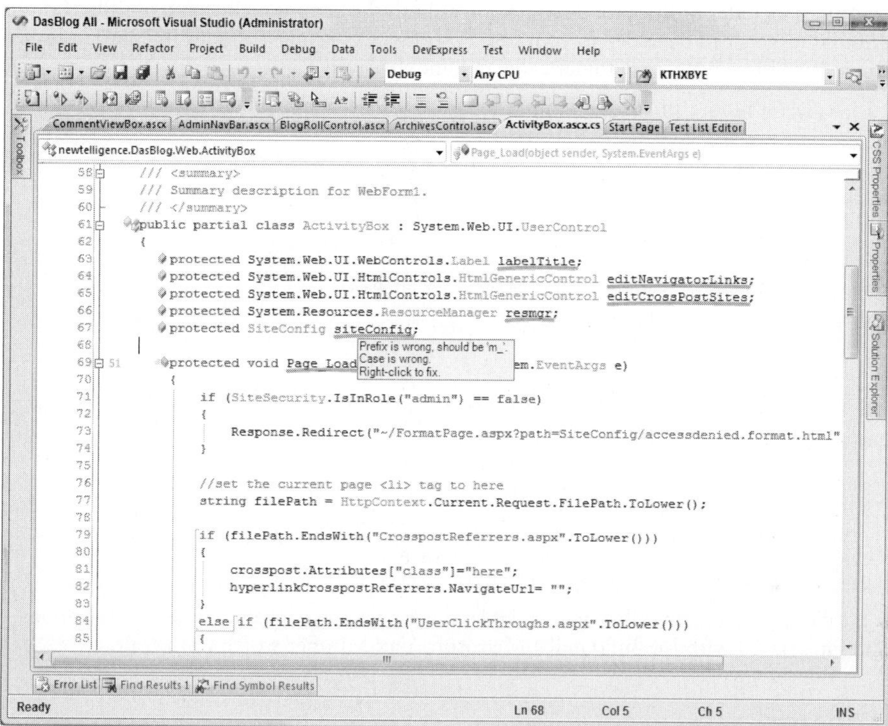

FIGURE B-10

Style guidelines are configurable and the default uses Juval Lowy's excellent C# Code Style Guidelines available from `www.idesign.net`. The latest version will also generate code rule violation reports for a solution using XML and XSLT, providing customizable different templates. Code Style Enforcer is an excellent tool to add to your team's toolbox.

Microsoft Ajax Minifier — JavaScript Minimizer

When creating an ASP.NET Web site, you often find yourself creating custom JavaScript files. During development, you want these files to be commented and easy to read. During production, however, every byte counts and it's nice to reduce the size of your JavaScript files with a JavaScript "minimizer."

Microsoft Ajax Minifier is a C# application that offers compression of JavaScript or simple "minification" by stripping comments and white space. It's been released on CodePlex within the ASP.NET project at `http://aspnet.codeplex.com`.

You'd be surprised how well these techniques work. For example, Steve Kallestad once reported that a copy of the JavaScript library Prototype 1.50 was 70K before JavaScript-specific compression. It became 30K after the process, and then reached only 14K when gzip HTTP compression was applied. From 70K to 14K is a pretty significant savings.

JavaScript-specific compression does things such as renaming variables to single letters, being aware of global variable renaming vs. local variable renaming, as well as stripping unnecessary white space and comments.

Microsoft Ajax Minifier includes utilities for compression at both the command line and within MSBuild projects. The MSBuild targets can be added to your build process. Consequently, your integration server is continuous so you receive these benefits automatically and unobtrusively.

As an example, a JavaScript library might start out looking like this:

```
var Prototype = {
  Version: '1.5.0',
  BrowserFeatures: {
    XPath: !!document.evaluate
  },

  ScriptFragment: '(?:<script.*?>)((\n|\r|.)*?)(?:<\/script>)',
  emptyFunction: function() {},
  K: function(x) { return x }
}
```

Minified, the JavaScript might end up looking like this (as an example). . . but it will still work!

```
 (c(){f 7.2q(/<\\/?[&bepsi;>]+>/5a,"")}),2C:(c(){f 7.2q(P 5d(1m.5s,"9n"),"")}),9j:(c(){k 9m=P
5d(1m.5s,"9n");k 9k=P 5d(1m.5s,"ce");f(7.E(9m)||[]).1F((c(91){f(91.E(9k)||["",""])[1]}))}),
3P:(c(){f7.9j().1F((c(4s){f 6A(4s)}))}),cd:(c(){k 1h=N.4f("1h");k 2V=N.cc(7);1h.63(2V);f
1h.2P}),cb:(c(){k 1h=N.4f("1h");1h.2P=7.9i();f 1h.2O[0]?(1h.2O.o>1?$A(1h.2O).2A("",(c(3Y,1G){f
3Y+1G.4j})):1h.2O[0].4j):""}),6J:(c(9h){k E=7.4d().E(/([&bepsi;?#]*)(#.*)?$/);h(!E){f{}}f E[1].
3m(9h||"&").2A({},(c(2E,Q){h((Q=Q.3m("="))[0]){k v=9g(Q[0]);k 1=Q[1]?9g(Q[1]):1b;h(2E[v]!==1b){
h(2E[v].3k!=1M){2E[v]=[2E[v>}h(1){2E[v].M(1)}}1k{2E[v]=1}}f 2E}))}),2F:(c(){f 7.3m("")})
```

There are many JavaScript minimizing libraries available; this is just one of them. However, its options, completeness, and integration with MSBuild make Microsoft Ajax Minifier worth trying out.

EXTENDING ASP.NET

"Oh man! :-) I have shoot into my foot myself ;-) Sorry!"

— MATZ

ASP.NET AJAX Control Toolkit

The AJAX Control Toolkit is a collaboration between Microsoft and the larger ASP.NET community. Its goal was to provide the largest collection of Web client components available. It includes excellent examples if you want to learn how to write ASP.NET Ajax yourself, and then it gives you the opportunity to give back and have your code shared within the community.

There are literally dozens of controls that build on and extend the ASP.NET Ajax Framework. Some of the controls are simple and provide those nice "little touches" such as drop shadows, rounded corners, watermarks, and animations. Others provide highly functional controls such as calendars, popups, and sliders.

Complete source is available for all the controls so that they can be extended and improved by you. These controls are more than just samples; they are complete and ready to be used in your applications.

There's a complete site showcasing the Toolkit and MSAjax at `http://www.asp.net/ajax/` with examples of each control so you can try each one to see if it meets your needs, as illustrated in Figure B-11, for example. There's even a new Content Distribution Network (CDN) so you can let Microsoft pay the bandwidth for hosting these JavaScript libraries. They'll be faster and closer to the user as well!

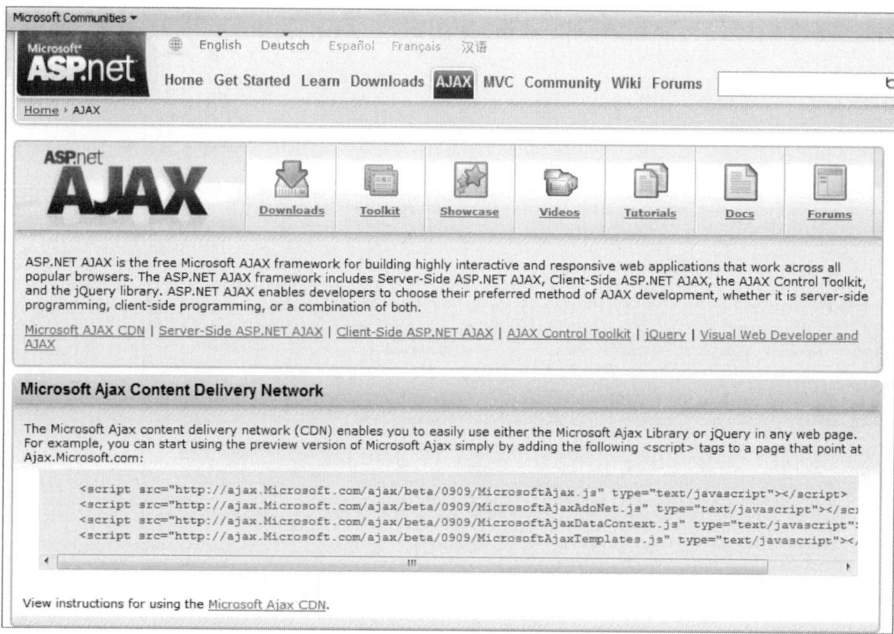

FIGURE B-11

Note also that these JavaScript libraries include "reference tags" for each JavaScript file providing complete JavaScript IntelliSense support within Visual Studio 2008 and above.

Atif Aziz's ELMAH — Error Logging Modules and Handlers

Troubleshooting errors and unhandled exceptions in your applications can be a full-time job. Rather than writing your own custom global exception handlers every time, consider looking at ELMAH (Error Logging Modules And Handlers) from Atif Aziz. It's a very flexible application-wide error logging facility with pluggable extension points to the interfaces at nearly every location. You can even configure it in your application without re-compilation or even redeployment. Simply modify your `web.config` file to include the error logging modules and handlers, and then you'll receive a single Web page to remotely review the entire log of unhandled exceptions.

ELMAH captures so much information about exceptions that it can reconstitute the original "yellow screen of death" that ASP.NET would have generated given an exception, even if customErrors was turned off. It's almost like TiVo for your exceptions! Figure B-12 shows ELMAH, providing a developer's view, including all the details you might need to debug this error.

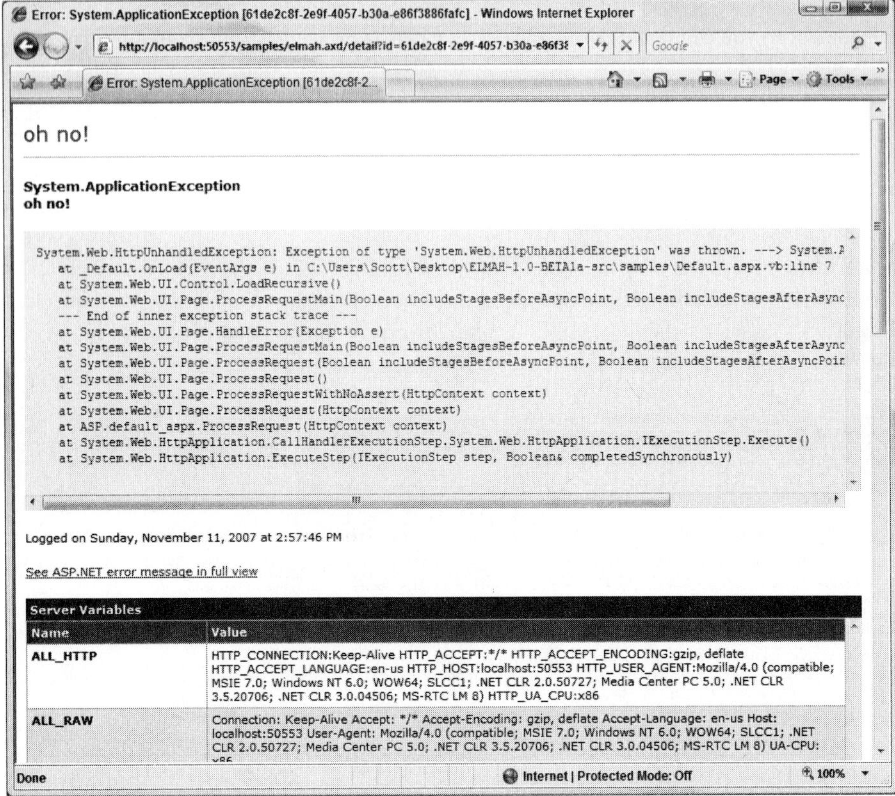

FIGURE B-12

Another clever feature is an RSS feed that shows the last 15 years from your log. This flexible tool is open source and the recent beta includes support for medium trust environments. You can plug in SQL Server or use an XML file to manage your error logs. I highly recommend you take the time to learn about ELMAH.

Helicon's ISAPI_Rewrite and IIS7 URLRewrite

Users of the Apache Web server sing the praises of the power of `mod_rewrite`, their URL rewriting mechanism. IIS6 users have this available to them in the form of the ISAPI_Rewrite module from Helicon. It's incredibly fast because it's written in pure C. It integrates nicely with ASP.NET in the IIS "Classic" Pipeline because URLs are rewritten before ASP.NET realizes anything has happened. IIS7 users can use the new URL Rewriting Module I'll talk about in a moment.

Because it uses regular expressions, ISAPI_Rewrite can initially be very frustrating due to its terse syntax. However, if you are patient, it can be an incredibly powerful tool for your tool belt.

I recently discovered that there were a dozen ways to visit my blog that all lead to the same location. This was confusing Google because it appeared that my blog had multiple addresses. I wanted not only to canonicalize my URL but also send back a 301 HTTP redirect to search indexes, thereby raising my standing within the search by appearing to have only one official URL.

For example, all of these links were valid ways to reach my blog:

- www.hanselman.com/blog/
- www.hanselman.com/blog/default.aspx
- www.hanselman.com/blog
- http://hanselman.com/blog/
- http://hanselman.com/blog/default.aspx
- http://hanselman.com/blog
- www.hanselman.com/blog/Default.aspx
- www.computerzen.com/blog/
- www.computerzen.com
- http://computerzen.com/blog/
- http://computerzen.com/

Notice that there's a difference between a trailing slash and no trailing slash in the eyes of a search engine. Using ISAPI Rewrite, I created this rather terse but very effective configuration file:

```
[ISAPI_Rewrite]
RewriteRule /blog/default\.aspx http\://www.hanselman.com/blog/ [I,RP]
RewriteCond Host: &bepsi;hanselman\.com
RewriteRule (.*) http\://www.hanselman.com$1 [I,RP]
RewriteCond Host: &bepsi;computerzen\.com
RewriteRule (.*) http\://www.hanselman.com$1 [I,RP]
RewriteCond Host: &bepsi;www.computerzen\.com
RewriteRule (.*) http\://www.hanselman.com/blog/ [I,RP]
```

The I and RP at the end of the line indicate that this match is case insensitive and the redirect should be permanent rather than temporary. The rules that include a $1 at the end of line cause the expression to include any path after the domain name. This allows the rule to apply site-wide and provides these benefits to every single page on my site. It's powerful and that's worth your time.

There's also an IIS7-specific URL Rewrite Module available at `http://www.iis.net/extensions/URLRewrite`. It is easier to use than ISAPI Rewrite because it includes a complete UI for managing and creating rewrites and an import tool for bringing your existing Apache-style rewrites into IIS7.

An extra bonus is that the IIS7 rewrite tool runs inside the managed pipeline for an extra performance boost when you're using it on ASP.NET applications.

GENERAL PURPOSE DEVELOPER TOOLS

"If you get the dirty end of the stick, sharpen it and turn it into a useful tool."

— Gen. Colin L. Powell (Ret.)

Telerik's Online Code Converter

Creating samples that should appear in both C# and Visual Basic can be very tedious without the assistance of something like Telerik's CodeChanger.com.

While it's not an officially supported tool, this little application will definitely get you 80 percent of the way when converting between Visual Basic and C#.

It also understands a surprising number of rather obscure syntaxes, as shown in Figure B-13, where I tried to convert an immediate `if` from C#'s `?:` syntax to VB's `IIf` syntax. It's not only useful for the writer, and blog author, but also anyone who's trying to switch projects between the two languages.

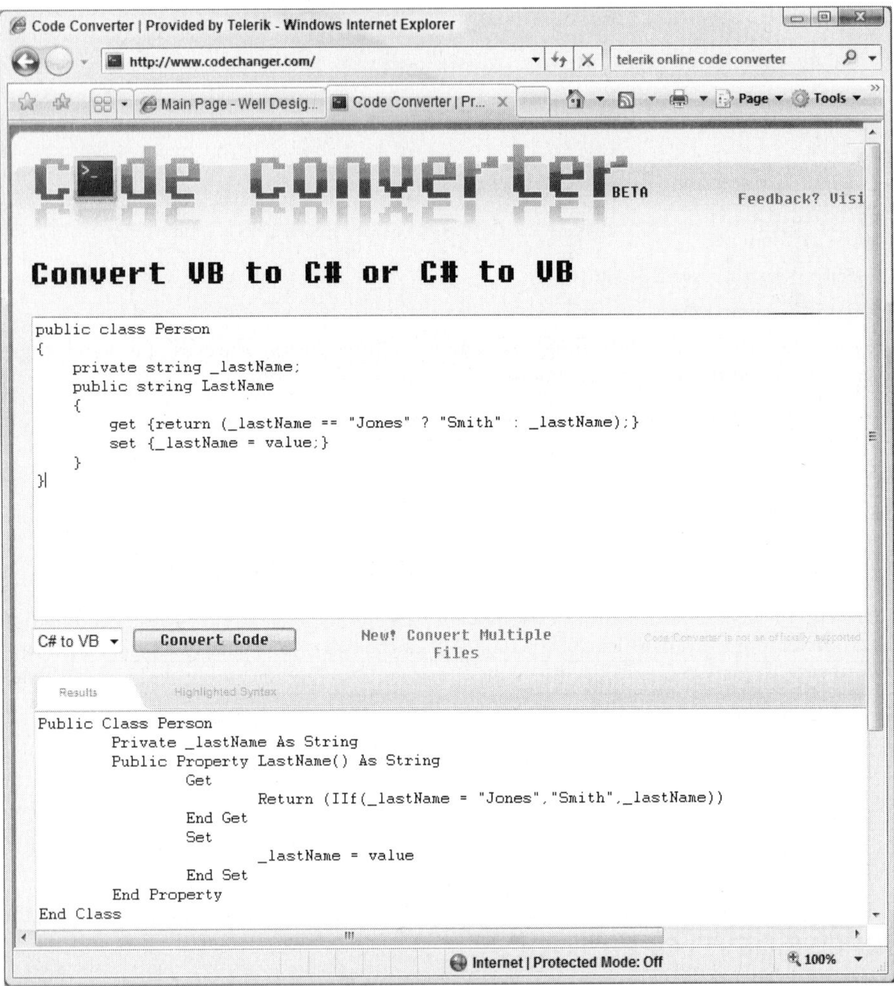

FIGURE B-13

WinMerge and Differencing Tools

Everyone has their favorite merge tool. Whether yours is WinMerge (Figure B-14), or Beyond Compare, or the old standby WinDiff, just make sure that you have one in your list of tools that you're very familiar with. When managing large numbers of changes across large numbers of individuals on software development teams, a good merge tool can help you untangle even the most complicated conflicting checkins.

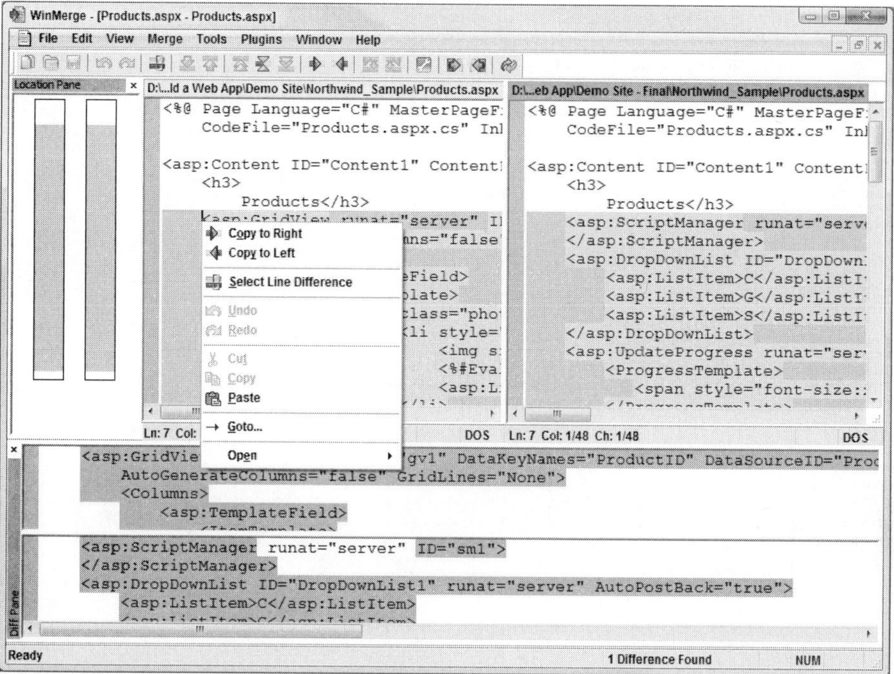

FIGURE B-14

A number of different plug-ins are available for WinMerge that extend its functionality to include comparison of Word and Excel documents and XML files.

Other highly recommended merge tools include Beyond Compare from Scooter Software and DiffMerge from SourceGear. Each of these three tools integrates with Windows Explorer, so comparing files is as easy as a right-click.

Reflector

If you're not using Reflector, your .NET developer experience is lesser for it. Reflector is an object browser, decompiler, help system, powerful plug-in host, and incredible learning tool. This tiny utility, originally from Microsoft developer Lutz Roeder and now maintained by Redgate, is consistently listed as the number one most indispensable tool available to the .NET developer after Visual Studio.

Reflector is amazing because it not only gives you a representation of the programmer's intent by transforming IL back into C# or VB, but it includes analysis tools that help you visualize dependencies between methods in the .NET Base Class Library and within your code or any third-party code. In Figure B-15, you can see not only a C# representation of the code inside System.RolePrincipal, but more importantly the methods that use it within the framework. You can continue on as deep as you want within the theoretical call stack.

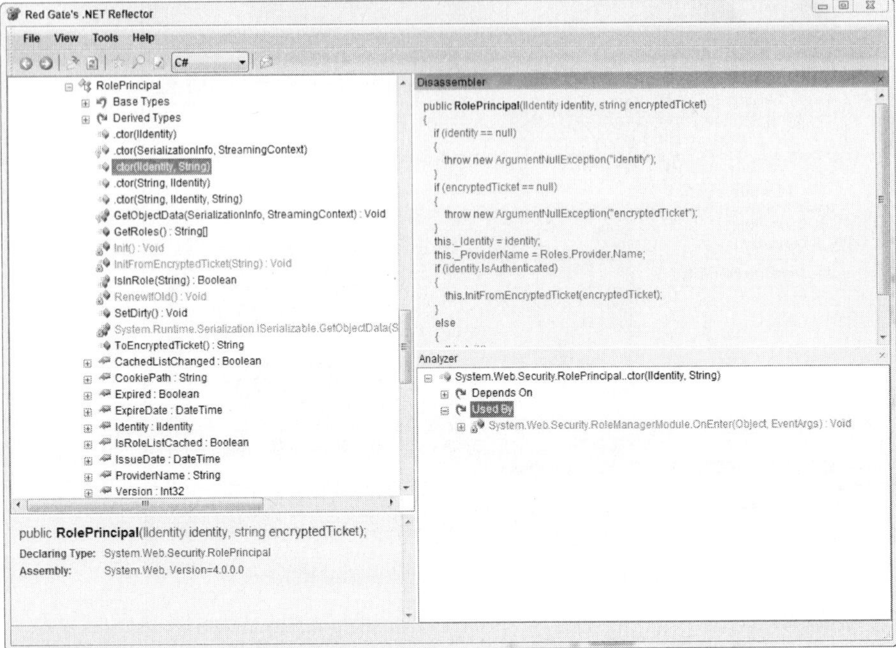

FIGURE B-15

While Reflector's decompilation abilities may become less useful with the release of the Base Class Library source code under the Microsoft Reference License, its abilities as an object browser and its vibrant plug-in community will keep this tool on the top shelf for years to come. After purchasing the software from Lutz, Redgate is taking Reflector even closer to the stuff of legend with a new step-into feature that will allow you to debug into code that you don't have by automatically decompiling it and "fooling" the debugger into thinking you *do* have the source.

Process Explorer

Last, but unquestionably not least, is Process Explorer from Mark Russinovich. To call it "Task Manager on steroids" would not even begin to do it justice. Process Explorer puts Windows itself under a microscope by allowing you to peer inside your active processes, their threads, and the environment to get a clearer understanding about what is actually going on. Advanced and detailed use of this tool, along with the entire SysInternals Suite of Tools, should be required for all developers.

In Figure B-16, I'm looking at the Properties dialog box of an application running under the Visual Studio 2010 Web Server while a debugging session is in process. I can see the process tree, the DLLs loaded into the Web server's process, their versions, and their paths, making this an excellent tool for debugging assembly loading and versioning issues.

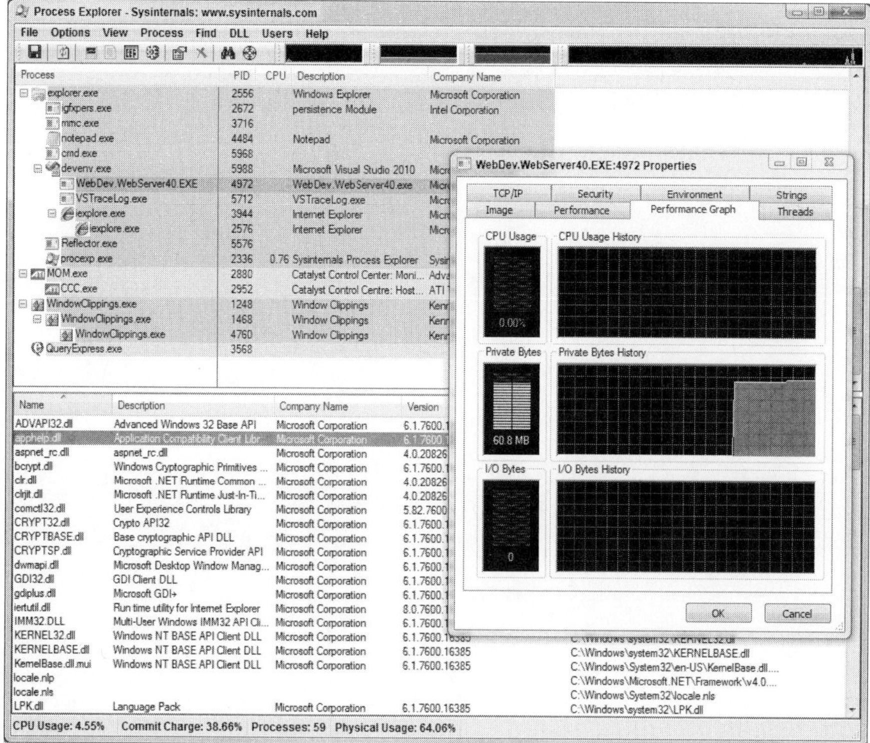

FIGURE B-16

SUMMARY

Having the right tools can mean the difference between a week of time spent with your head against the wall versus five minutes of quick analysis in debugging. The right tool can mean the difference between a tedious and keyboard-heavy code slogging or a refactoring session that is actually pleasant. I encourage you to try each of the tools listed here, as well as to explore the ecosystem of available tools to find those that make your development experience not just more productive but more enjoyable.

Silverlight 3 and ASP.NET

Silverlight is a Web platform from Microsoft that allows you to create and run Rich Internet Applications (RIAs) on all major browsers available on both Mac and Windows. Silverlight applications execute within a browser plug-in installed on the local machine similar to the way Flash animations run. The Silverlight plug-in supports all the wow factors that you would expect from a RIA platform, such as vector-based graphics and animations and full audio and video integration, including high-definition video support.

Beginning with version 2, the platform introduced a cross-browser, cross-platform version of the .NET Framework. This means developers can write Silverlight applications in any .NET language and use the rich Silverlight base class library, networking stack, controls, and XAML-based UI, all without requiring the end user to install the actual .NET Framework.

Although giving more than an introduction to Silverlight 3 is outside the scope of this book, this appendix will focus on the key points that an ASP.NET developer needs to know about integrating a Silverlight application into a new or existing ASP.NET application.

The appendix starts by showing you how to create a new Silverlight application in Visual Studio. Next, it looks at how you can add the Silverlight player to your Web pages using HTML and JavaScript, and the available options for configuring the player's behavior in your application. Finally, the appendix demonstrates how to add interoperability between Silverlight and the browser using JavaScript.

If you are interested in learning more about creating RIA applications with Silverlight 3, then you might want to pick up a copy of Wrox's *Silverlight 3 Programmer's Reference* by J. Ambrose Little, Jason Beres, Grant Hinkson, Devin Rader, and Joe Croney (Wiley, 2009).

GETTING STARTED

To get you started creating Silverlight applications, Visual Studio 2010 offers several Silverlight-specific project templates that allow you to set up both a Silverlight project and a Web site to host it. Figure C-1 shows the project template in Visual Studio's New Project dialog.

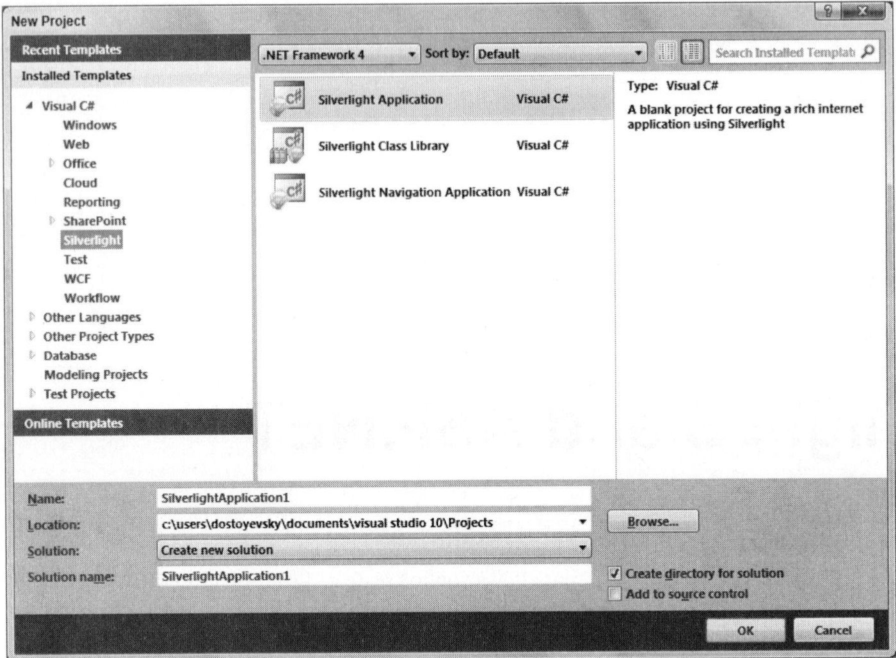

FIGURE C-1

The Silverlight Application project template sets up a new Silverlight application that compiles to the XAP file for deployment to your Web server. An XAP file is the deployment package that Silverlight 3 uses that generally contains all the assemblies and resources used by an application and a manifest file, which tells Silverlight about the contents of the XAP.

An XAP file is simply a ZIP archive. You can change the extension of the XAP file from `.xap` *to* `.zip`*, and then open the archive using your favorite ZIP utility.*

The Silverlight Navigation application also sets up a new Silverlight application, but adds references to the assemblies required to use Silverlight 3's navigation framework and includes a set of default XAML files that set up a basic application that uses the navigation framework.

The Silverlight Class Library project template sets up a basic Silverlight class library. A class library enables you to create assemblies that are compiled against the Silverlight libraries and that you can reference in other Silverlight application projects. When an external assembly is referenced by a Silverlight application, it is, by default, automatically included in the XAP file generated by the Silverlight application.

A Silverlight class library might appear to be very similar to a standard class library project; however, one significant difference exists. The Silverlight class library references libraries that are specific to Silverlight, so even though both projects have references to identically named assemblies (such as System and System.Core), these references actually point to different assemblies. You can see an example by looking at the `Path` *property of the assembly references. This detail is important to remember because you cannot simply reference an existing .NET class library in a Silverlight application. It must be explicitly compiled against the Silverlight 3 framework assemblies.*

As with other Visual Studio project types, you can select the .NET Framework version you want to target from the New Project dialog. When you open the framework version selection drop-down list, however, you will notice that it does not include options for selecting a Silverlight version. Instead, changing the target framework on this dialog determines the framework version the host Web site will be configured for.

Clicking the New Project dialog's OK button loads the New Silverlight Application dialog, shown in Figure C-2, which allows you to configure the Silverlight application. By default, Visual Studio assumes you want to create a new Web application in which to host the Silverlight application, but you can also choose to generate a new Web Site or a new ASP.NET MVC Web Project. Additionally, if you are adding a new Silverlight project to an existing solution, Visual Studio will detect any existing Web sites in that solution and allow you to associate the Silverlight project with the existing site.

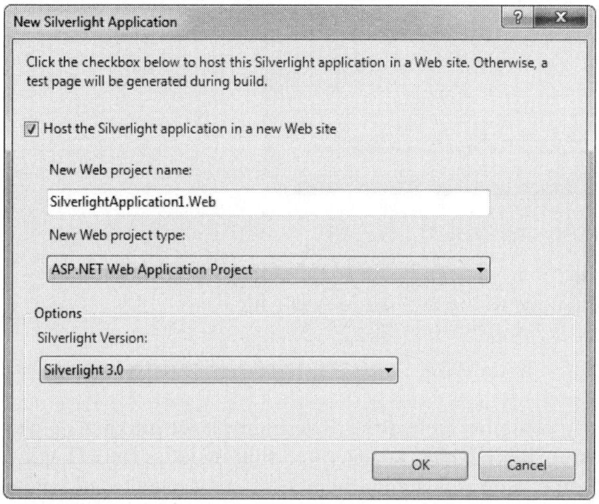

FIGURE C-2

Choosing not to associate the Silverlight application with any Web project means Visual Studio will dynamically generate a host Web page when you run the application.

After you configure the Web application association, you are done configuring the Silverlight application, and it is loaded in Visual Studio. Figure C-3 shows the default solution structure of a newly created Silverlight application. In this case, a new Web site project has also been created and added to the solution.

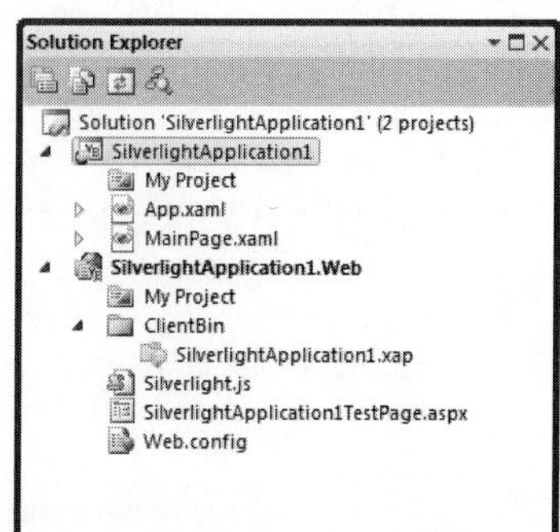

FIGURE C-3

You can see that Visual Studio automatically includes in the Silverlight application default `App.xaml` and `MainPage.xaml` files that contain the application content. The Web application created with the Silverlight application includes HTML and ASP.NET test host pages, as well as the `ClientBin` folder, where the Silverlight application's compiled XAP file is placed.

Should you ever want to change the Silverlight application associated with a Web project, or even add additional Silverlight associations to a Web project, you can do so by accessing the Silverlight Applications section of the Web projects Properties dialog, as shown in Figure C-4.

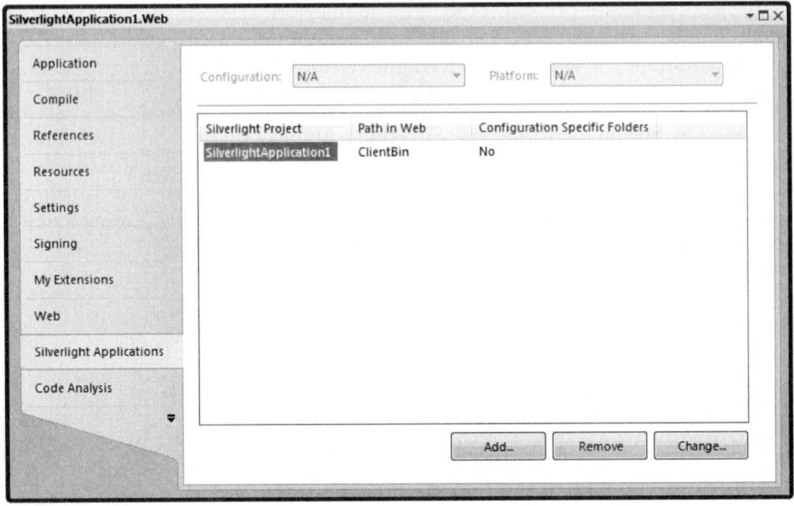

FIGURE C-4

After you have created your new Silverlight application, you can begin to develop your Silverlight application by adding the appropriate XAML and code to the `MainPage.xaml` file.

USING THE SILVERLIGHT PLUG-IN

Because Silverlight is a browser plug-in, eventually you must embed the Silverlight player into a host Web page. When you set up a new host Web site, a test ASP.NET page is generated that includes the HTML and JavaScript needed to embed the player, but you can do this manually in a different page by adding an `<object>` tag to your page, filling in all the appropriate object `<param>` tags, and including the appropriate JavaScript files and code. Listing C-1 shows the contents of the test ASP.NET page.

Available for download on Wrox.com

LISTING C-1: Embedding the Silverlight plug-in into an ASP.NET page

```
<html xmlns="http://www.w3.org/1999/xhtml" >
<head runat="server">
    <title>AppC</title>

    <style type="text/css">
    html, body {
        height: 100%;
        overflow: auto;
    }
    body {
        padding: 0;
        margin: 0;
    }
    #silverlightControlHost {
        height: 100%;
        text-align:center;
    }
    </style>
    <script type="text/javascript" src="Silverlight.js"></script>
    <script type="text/javascript">
        function onSilverlightError(sender, args) {
            var appSource = "";
            if (sender != null && sender != 0) {
              appSource = sender.getHost().Source;
            }
```

```
            var errorType = args.ErrorType;
            var iErrorCode = args.ErrorCode;

            if (errorType == "ImageError" ||
                errorType == "MediaError") {
              return;
            }

            var errMsg =
                "Unhandled Error in Silverlight Application " +
                appSource + "\n" ;

            errMsg += "Code: "+ iErrorCode + "    \n";
            errMsg += "Category: " + errorType + "       \n";
            errMsg += "Message: " + args.ErrorMessage + "     \n";

            if (errorType == "ParserError") {
                errMsg += "File: " + args.xamlFile + "     \n";
                errMsg += "Line: " + args.lineNumber + "     \n";
                errMsg += "Position: " + args.charPosition + "     \n";
            }
            else if (errorType == "RuntimeError") {
                if (args.lineNumber != 0) {
                    errMsg += "Line: " + args.lineNumber + "     \n";
                    errMsg += "Position: " +
                              args.charPosition + "     \n";
                }
                errMsg += "MethodName: " + args.methodName + "     \n";
            }

            throw new Error(errMsg);
        }
    </script>
</head>

<body>
  <form id="form1" runat="server" style="height:100%;">
      <div id="silverlightControlHost">
          <object data="data:application/x-silverlight-2,"
                      type="application/x-silverlight-2"
                      width="100%" height="100%">
                      <param name="source" value="ClientBin/AppC.xap"/>
                      <param name="onerror" value="onSilverlightError" />
                      <param name="background" value="white" />
                      <param name="minRuntimeVersion"
                           value="3.0.40818.0" />
                      <param name="autoUpgrade" value="true" />
                      <a href="http://go.microsoft.com/fwlink/
                             ?LinkID=149156&v=3.0.40818.0"
                             style="text-decoration: none;">
                      <img
                         src="http://go.microsoft.com/fwlink/
                              ?LinkId=108181"
                         alt="Get Microsoft Silverlight"
                         style="border-style: none"/>
                      </a>
          </object><iframe id="_sl_historyFrame"
                              style='visibility:hidden;
                              height:0;width:0;border:0px'>
                   </iframe></div>
  </form>
</body>
</html>
```

This HTML embeds the Silverlight plug-in into your page using an `<object>` tag, and the JavaScript provides functionality such as detecting whether or not the plug-in is installed (and proceeds to install if it is not) and what version is installed.

Exploring the HTML markup a bit, you can see that within the object tag are a number of `<param>` tags, which are used to specify the parameters of the player.

Two of the more important parameters of the Silverlight plug-in are `minRumtimeVersion` and `autoUpgrade`. The `minRunTimeVersion` property allows you to specify the minimum Silverlight version the client must have to run your application. As you can see in Listing C-1, the default templates automatically set it to the current Silverlight 3 version. The `autoUpgrade` property tells the control whether or not it should automatically render the appropriate JavaScript needed to automatically upgrade the client's version of Silverlight if it does not meet the minimum version requirement. Using these properties together makes providing your end users with a positive experience when interacting with your Web site easy.

If the end user has a version of Silverlight installed that is older than the application requires and the Silverlight control is not configured to autoupgrade, then the default template includes content that lets the user know he or she needs to upgrade. You, of course, can customize this content, which is shown in Listing C-2.

Available for download on Wrox.com

LISTING C-2: Providing custom content when the Silverlight plug-in is not installed

```
<object data="data:application/x-silverlight-2,"
    type="application/x-silverlight-2" width="100%" height="100%">
    <param name="source" value="ClientBin/AppC.xap"/>
    <param name="onerror" value="onSilverlightError" />
    <param name="background" value="white" />
    <param name="minRuntimeVersion" value="3.0.40818.0" />
    <param name="autoUpgrade" value="true" />
    <h1>Whoops!</h1>
    <p>Looks like you don't have the right version of
      Silverlight installed.  This means you&#39;re missing out
      on the greatest thing on the Internet!</p>
    <p>I really suggest that you go download the latest
      version of Silverlight as it will greatly enhance
      your life.</p>
</object>
```

This sample shows custom HTML content added to the object tag, which tells end users about the content they could be viewing if they installed the right version of Silverlight.

A handful of other interesting properties are available on the Silverlight control and are discussed in the following sections.

windowless

The `windowless` parameter (which applies only when running on Windows) enables you to configure the Silverlight plug-in to be displayed directly by the browser rather than having its own render window as it normally would. Running the plug-in in windowless mode allows the control's content to overlap and better blend with other surrounding HTML content.

Listing C-3 shows how you can use the `windowless` property to more seamlessly integrate your Silverlight application into its host HTML page. In this case, the Silverlight application has had its root UserControl's background color set to its default transparent color.

Available for download on Wrox.com

LISTING C-3: Setting the windowless property

```
<object data="data:application/x-silverlight-2,"
    type="application/x-silverlight-2" width="400" height="300">
    <param name="source" value="ClientBin/AppC.xap"/>
    <param name="onerror" value="onSilverlightError" />
    <param name="background" value="transparent" />
    <param name="minRuntimeVersion" value="3.0.40818.0" />
    <param name="autoUpgrade" value="true" />
    <param name="windowless" value="true" />
    <a href="http://go.microsoft.com/fwlink/
             ?LinkID=149156&v=3.0.40818.0"
       style="text-decoration: none;">
        <img src="http://go.microsoft.com/fwlink/?LinkId=108181"
            alt="Get Microsoft Silverlight" style="border-style: none"/>
    </a>
</object>
```

You can see in Figure C-5 how enabling and disabling the `windowless` property affects how the plug-in is rendered in the browser.

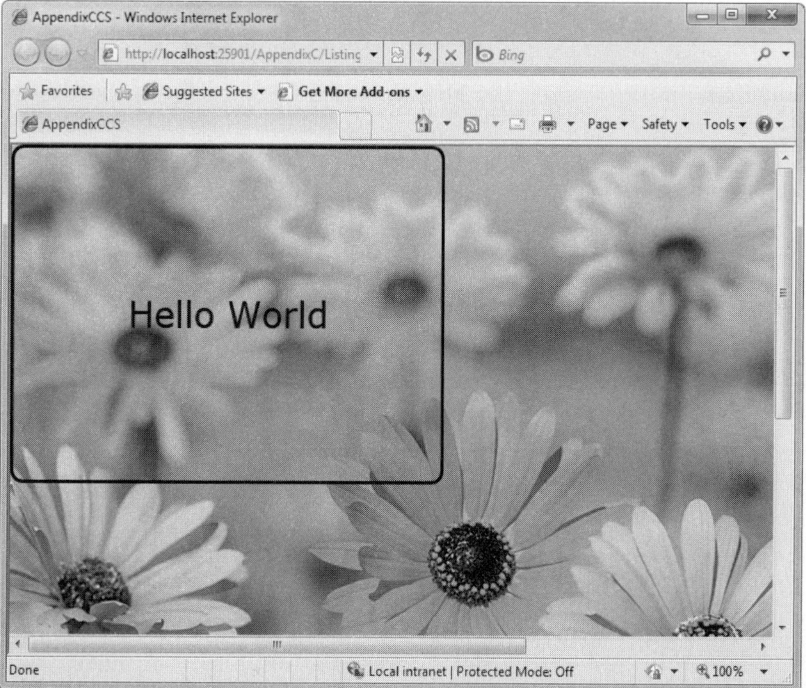

FIGURE C-5

With the `windowless` property set to `true`, the underlying DIV containing the image shows through.

The Silverlight plug-in background is set to White by default. Therefore, to achieve the transparency shown in Figure C-5, you must explicitly set the plug-in's background parameter to Transparent. Also note that the Silverlight User Control template in Visual Studio has its root layout element's background property set to White by default, which you also must change to see the transparency shown in Figure C-5.

Use caution when enabling the `windowless` property as performance can be significantly hindered when using the plug-in in windowless mode. Specifically, complex animations and high-definition video content will not perform as well when running in windowless mode.

splashScreenSource

The `splashScreenSource` parameter enables you to specify the URI of an XAML file that the Silverlight plug-in should use to replace its default "loading" splash screen. The splash screen is the content that Silverlight displays while downloading and loading its application content, which is typically an XAP file. Replacing the default splash screen enables you to provide a highly customized experience to your users; however, you must note a number of restrictions when providing your own splash screen content. First, unlike the `source` parameter, which accepts both XAML and XAP files, the `splashScreenSource` property accepts only a simple XAML file. Second, significant restrictions exist regarding the XAML that is allowed to be run for the splash screen.

Finally, the splash screen XAML URI must come from the same domain as the Silverlight application and the hosting page. As part of this step, you must make sure your Web server is properly configured to serve files with a `.xaml` extension, which may mean adding a new MIME type to your Web server.

To create a new splash screen content XAML file, you can simply add a new Silverlight 1.0 JScript Page to your Web application, as shown in Figure C-6.

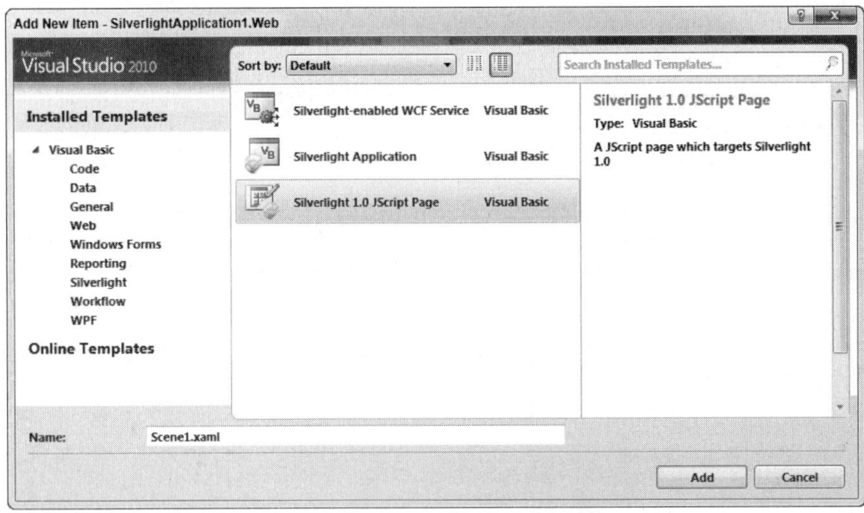

FIGURE C-6

Next, you simply add some content to the default canvas of the XAML file. Listing C-4 shows a simple TextBlock as the content of the XAML file.

LISTING C-4: Simple splash screen XAML content

Available for download on Wrox.com

```
<Canvas xmlns="http://schemas.microsoft.com/client/2007"
        xmlns:x="http://schemas.microsoft.com/winfx/2006/xaml">
  <Canvas x:Name="contentCanvas" Width="240" Height="74" >
    <TextBlock x:Name="textBlock">
      <Run FontSize="48" Text="Loading..."/>
    </TextBlock>
  </Canvas>
</Canvas>
```

Finally, you specify the XAML file as the `splashScreenSource` in the Silverlight control (Listing C-5).

Available for download on Wrox.com

LISTING C-5: Specifying the splash screen source

```
<object data="data:application/x-silverlight-2,"
    type="application/x-silverlight-2" width="100%" height="100%">
  <param name="source" value="ClientBin/AppendixCCS.xap"/>
  <param name="onerror" value="onSilverlightError" />
  <param name="background" value="white" />
  <param name="minRuntimeVersion" value="3.0.40818.0" />
  <param name="autoUpgrade" value="true" />
  <param name="splashScreenSource" value="ListingC-4.xaml" />
  <a href="http://go.microsoft.com/fwlink/
          ?LinkID=149156&v=3.0.40818.0"
     style="text-decoration: none;">
          <img src="http://go.microsoft.com/fwlink/?LinkId=108181"
                  alt="Get Microsoft Silverlight"
                  style="border-style: none"/>
  </a>
</object>
```

When you run your application, you should now see that the default Silverlight splash screen has been replaced by the custom splash screen content.

To test your splash screen, make sure the XAP being downloaded is large enough. Silverlight displays the splash screen only if the content load time exceeds 0.5 seconds. To simulate a longer load time, you can artificially inflate the XAP size by embedding a large resource in your application.

Although the XAML in Listing C-4 is completely static, Silverlight does allow you to provide a better experience to your end users by adding animation to the splash screen XAML, and by using two JavaScript events that the plug-in exposes, which provide information relevant to the plug-in's loading process. The `onSourceDownloadProgressChanged` and `onSourceDownloadCompleted` events provide details about the current state of the source download and notification that the download has completed. Using these events in JavaScript, you can provide your end users with download progress information by using the Silverlight JavaScript API to change the splash screen XAML content. Using the JavaScript API to manipulate XAML is discussed in depth later in this appendix.

Note that although the plug-in will fire the `onSourceDownloadCompleted` event, when this point in the plug-in lifecycle is reached, the plug-in immediately stops displaying the splash screen content and begins to display main application content. You have no opportunity to provide any type of graceful transition from the splash screen to the main player content.

initParams

The `initParams` parameter enables you to pass initialization parameters that you can use inside of your application into the Silverlight player. `initParams` accepts a comma-delimited list of key/value pairs, as shown in Listing C-6.

Available for download on Wrox.com

LISTING C-6: Specifying initParams in the Silverlight control

```
<object data="data:application/x-silverlight-2,"
    type="application/x-silverlight-2" width="100%" height="100%">
  <param name="source" value="ClientBin/AppendixCCS.xap"/>
  <param name="onerror" value="onSilverlightError" />
  <param name="background" value="white" />
  <param name="minRuntimeVersion" value="3.0.40818.0" />
  <param name="autoUpgrade" value="true" />
```

(continues)

LISTING C-6 *(continued)*

```
    <param name="initParams"
           value="DefaultColor=Blue,DefaultStartPoint=Customer" />
    <a href="http://go.microsoft.com/fwlink/
            ?LinkID=149156&v=3.0.40818.0"
       style="text-decoration: none;">
           <img src="http://go.microsoft.com/fwlink/?LinkId=108181"
                     alt="Get Microsoft Silverlight"
                     style="border-style: none"/>
    </a>
</object>
```

The list of initialization parameters is exposed as a property of type `Dictionary<string, string>` off the application's Startup event arguments. Listing C-7 demonstrates how you can use initialization parameters to alter the content loaded by the Silverlight application at startup.

LISTING C-7: Accessing the initParams in the Silverlight application

Available for download on Wrox.com

VB

```
Private Sub Application_Startup(ByVal o As Object,
                                ByVal e As StartupEventArgs) _
                                Handles Me.Startup
        Select e.InitParams("DefaultStartPoint")
            Case "Customer"
                Me.RootVisual = New Customer()
            Case "Order"
                Me.RootVisual = New Order()
            Case Else
                Me.RootVisual = New Home()
        End Select
    End Sub
```

C#

```
private void Application_Startup(object sender, StartupEventArgs e)
{
    this.RootVisual = new Page();
    switch (e.InitParams["DefaultStartPoint"])
    {
        case "Customer":
            this.RootVisual = new Customer();
            break;
        case "Order":
            this.RootVisual = new Order();
            break;
        default:
            this.RootVisual = new Home();
            break;
    }
}
```

In this listing, the application uses the `InitParams` property, which is a member of `StartUpEventArgs`, within the application's `Startup` event. As mentioned earlier, the `InitParams` passed into the plug-in are exposed as a Dictionary, which allows you to access the parameters as key/value pairs, in this case using the value of the DefaultStartPoint key to select a specific XAML UserControl as the application's RootVisual.

enablehtmlaccess

The `enablehtmlaccess` parameter indicates whether the Silverlight player can access the Document Object Model (DOM) of the host page. The default value allows access to elements from the same domains. Specifying a true value broadens access to any domain, whereas a false value blocks all DOM access.

This property is important if you want to allow or deny communication between the Silverlight plug-in and JavaScript running on a browser, which is discussed later in this appendix.

enableAutoZoom

The `enableAutoZoom` parameter allows you to configure whether or not the plug-in should respect the zoom settings from its host. For example, in Internet Explorer 8 you can set a zoom level. By default, Silverlight will respect this level as it is changed. Using this parameter you can opt out of this behavior.

enableGPUAcceleration

The `enableGPUAcceleration` parameter allows you to indicate that you want to leverage the video hardware for rendering in your application. To enable this feature you also must set the `CacheMode` property on the XAML elements in your application that you want to accelerate.

You can also use the `enableGPUAcceleration` parameter in conjunction with several other useful diagnostics parameters, such as the `enableCacheVisualization` parameter, which allows you to see visually which parts of your application are taking advantage of GPU rendering; `enableFramerateCounter`, which adds a display showing the current application frame rate; and the `enableRedrawRegions` parameter, which allows you to see which regions of the plug-in are being redrawn with each frame.

enableNavigation

The `enableNavigation` parameter allows you to control the behavior of the HyperlinkButton controls in the application, configuring that application to allow or disallow navigation to external URIs. The parameter accepts two values: all, which allows HyperlinkButtons to navigate to any URI, and none, which prevents this behavior.

Regardless of the parameter setting, relative URIs for internal navigation are always permitted.

Plug-in API

The Silverlight plug-in also includes a full client-side API that you can use to interact with the control in the browser using JavaScript. You can find a complete description of the plug-in's client-side API at `http://msdn.microsoft.com/en-us/library/cc838259(VS.95).aspx`.

The plug-in's JavaScript API lets you change various property settings such as the plug-in source, splash screen source, and scale mode. Additionally, you can use these APIs to handle events raised by the plug-in, such as the `OnLoad` event.

Table C-1 lists the events exposed by the Silverlight plug-in and a description of the event.

TABLE C-1

PLUG-IN EVENT	DESCRIPTION
`onLoad`	Occurs when the plug-in and its content are successfully loaded
`onError`	Occurs when something prevents the plug-in or content from loading
`onResize`	Occurs when the `ActualWidth` or `ActualHeight` properties of the plug-in change
`onFullScreenChanged`	Occurs when the player enters or leaves Full Screen mode
`onZoom`	Occurs when the plug-in receives a host-generated zoom event
`onSourceDownloadCompleted`	Occurs when the plug-in source has been downloaded
`onSourceDownloadProgressChanged`	Occurs as the download progress of the plug-in changes

The default host page template in Visual Studio automatically configures a JavaScript handler for the plug-in's `onError` event in order to provide a more graceful handling of errors that might happen in the player.

SILVERLIGHT AND JAVASCRIPT

After you have a Silverlight control embedded in a host Web page, you can begin to add interaction between your Silverlight application running in the Silverlight plug-in, and the host Web page running in a browser window. You have two ways to interoperate between the Silverlight plug-in and the browser.

- The first option is to use the plug-in's JavaScript APIs. Introduced in Silverlight 1.0, these APIs allow developers to programmatically reach into the Silverlight plug-in and manipulate the plug-in or XAML content running inside of the plug-in.

Although most of the original Silverlight 1.0 JavaScript APIs exist in newer versions of Silverlight, certain features have been removed in favor of managed code options now available. For example, the original `CreateFromXaml` *method that was available in the Silverlight 1.0 APIs has been removed in favor of using the managed* `XamlReader` *class inside of your Silverlight application.*

- The second option is to use the HTML Bridge, which was introduced with Silverlight 2. The HTML Bridge is a set of managed APIs that allow you to reach out from the Silverlight plug-in and access elements of the browser, like the Document Object Model (DOM) of the host, as well as to expose managed code contained in the plug-in and allow it to be executed from JavaScript running the host page.

JavaScript API

Now, take a look at how you can use the Silverlight plug-in's JavaScript APIs to reach into the plug-in and manipulate content running in a Silverlight application. Listing C-8 shows a sample that uses JavaScript to get a reference to the Silverlight application's root visual element. After the reference is obtained, the JavaScript simply displays an alert showing that object's type.

LISTING C-8: Accessing the root visual element using JavaScript

Available for download on Wrox.com

```
<script type="text/javascript" language="javascript">
    var plugin = document.getElementById("silverlightControl");

    function plugin_onload(sender) {
        var root = plugin.content.Root;
        alert(root);
    }
</script>
```

If you are familiar with JavaScript, then the code in this sample should look fairly simple to you. First, using the `getElementById` function, the sample gets a reference to the Silverlight plug-in and assigns it to the global plug-in variable. Next, the `plugin_onload` function, which uses the plug-in variable to access the Silverlight content property, is defined. The `content` property represents Silverlight's visual tree, which contains a reference to all the visual elements in the Silverlight application. Finally, the code uses the `Root` property to access root visual elements of the application's visual tree.

After the JavaScript code is written, you still need a way to tell the Silverlight plug-in that it should use the `plugin_onload` function to handle its `Loaded` event. To do that, you can provide the function name to the plug-in by specifying it in a `<param>` tag:

```
<param name="onload" value="plugin_onload" />
```

Waiting for the plug-in's `Loaded` event to fire before trying to access elements in the Silverlight application is a good idea because trying to access content prior may cause null reference exceptions. Waiting for the `Loaded` event ensures that Silverlight has completed successfully loading all of its content.

Running the code in Listing C-8, you should see that the JavaScript alert tells you that the Root element in the plug-in is of type UserControl. Knowing this, you can start to walk through the rest of the application's visual tree.

The JavaScript APIs also allow you to access and change element properties. For example, suppose you want to dynamically change the text of a TextBlock element in your Silverlight application. You can do this via the JavaScript API by locating the named TextBlock element, and then setting its `Text` property, as demonstrated in Listing C-9.

LISTING C-9: Accessing XAML elements and properties in JavaScript

Available for download on Wrox.com

```
function plugin_onload(sender) {
    var root = plugin.content.Root;

    var textBlock1 = root.FindName("textBlock1");
    if (textBlock1 != null) {
        textBlock1.Text = "Hello from the Host!";
    }
}
```

This sample shows the use of the plug-in's `FindName` method to locate the named element `textBlock1` in the element tree. After it is located, you simply set its `Text` property.

You can even get and set dependency properties on elements, although to do that, you must use the `getValue` and `setValue` functions provided by the element. Listing C-10 demonstrates setting an attached property on the TextBlock.

LISTING C-10: Setting attached properties in JavaScript

Available for download on Wrox.com

```
function plugin_onload(sender) {
    var root = plugin.content.Root;

    var textBlock1 = root.FindName("textBlock1");
    if (textBlock1 != null) {
        textBlock1.Text = "Hello from the Host!";
    }

    var currentColumn = textBlock1.getValue("Grid.Column");
    if (currentColumn == 0) {
        textBlock1.setValue("Grid.Column", 1);
    }
}
```

Being able to access elements contained in the XAML also allows you to connect event handlers to element events.

It's important to note that although the Silverlight 1.0 JavaScript APIs allowed you to access and manipulate every XAML element available in Silverlight 1.0, the same cannot be said of later Silverlight JavaScript APIs. After Silverlight 1.0, a significant number of new XAML elements were added to the platform. These elements make designing and laying out applications much easier; however, not all of those elements have been exposed through the JavaScript API. You can find the full JavaScript API for Silverlight 3 at `http://msdn.microsoft.com/en-us/library/bb979679(VS.95).aspx`. This documentation lists all the XAML elements that have been exposed to the JavaScript APIs.

Also, with the addition of significant new functionality in Silverlight since version 1.0, many XAML elements gained new properties, methods, and events. However, not all of these properties are useful unless used in conjunction with other features available only in the managed API. You can find a list of objects, types, and members that are not accessible via the JavaScript API, or that somehow otherwise expose only limited functionality via the JavaScript API, at `http://msdn.microsoft.com/en-us/library/cc964287(VS.95).aspx`.

HTML Bridge

Even though the Silverlight JavaScript APIs can be useful, Silverlight contains a powerful set of managed APIs that allow you not only to manipulate XAML elements from JavaScript, but also to access any managed type, method, property, or event included in the Silverlight application from JavaScript. Additionally, the APIs allow you to access the entire browser DOM (including JavaScript code) from within the Silverlight plug-in. Reaching out from the Silverlight plug-in into the browser allows you to add interesting interoperability capabilities to your application, such as accessing properties of the current browser window or leveraging existing JavaScript libraries you may have.

The HTML Bridge managed code APIs are contained in the `System.Windows.Browser` namespace (located in the `System.Windows.Browser.dll` assembly). The primary class in the `System.Windows.Browser` namespace that you will work with is the `HtmlPage` class, whose primary function is to allow you to access and manipulate the browser's DOM. The class exposes a variety of static properties that enable you to access the actual HTML document, the browser window, basic browser information such as the name and version, and even the Silverlight plug-in itself. Additionally, as you'll see in the next section, it includes several static methods that help you expose managed code included in your Silverlight application, via JavaScript APIs.

Exposing Managed Code in JavaScript

Exposing managed code via JavaScript APIs is a powerful tool that can help form a bridge between managed code developers and developers who are skilled in JavaScript. The easiest way to expose managed types to JavaScript is to use the `ScriptableType` attribute on the class you want to expose. Using this attribute exposes any public member of the class to JavaScript, including methods, properties, and events. Listing C-11 shows how you can use the `ScriptableType` attribute on a custom Silverlight class.

LISTING C-11: Exposing a class using the ScriptableType attribute

Available for download on Wrox.com

```
<System.Windows.Browser.ScriptableType()>
Public Class Employee
    Private _status As Boolean = False

    Public Sub New()

    End Sub

    Public Property FirstName() As String
    Public Property LastName() As String
    Public Property Department() As String
    Public Property SSN() As String
    Public Property StartDate() As DateTime

    Public ReadOnly Property Status As Boolean
        Get
            Return _status
        End Get
    End Property

    Public Sub ChangeStatus(ByVal status As Boolean)
        Me._status = status
    End Sub
```

```
    Public Function GetFullName() As String
        Return String.Format("{0} {1}", Me.FirstName, Me.LastName)
    End Function
End Class
```

C#

```
[System.Windows.Browser.ScriptableType()]
public class Employee
{
    private bool _status = false;

    public Employee()
    {
    }

    public string FirstName { get; set; }
    public string LastName { get; set; }
    public string Department { get; set; }
    public string SSN { get; set; }
    public DateTime StartDate { get; set; }
    public bool Status { get { return _status; } }

    public void ChangeStatus(bool status)
    {
        this._status = status;
    }

    public string GetFullName()
    {
        return string.Format("{0} {1}", this.FirstName, this.LastName);
    }
}
```

After you have decorated a type with the `ScriptableType` attribute, you can register instances of that type as scriptable objects. Registering the instances allows them to be accessed from the host Web page using JavaScript. To register an object instance, use the `RegisterScriptableObject` method of the `HtmlPage` class, as shown in Listing C-12.

LISTING C-12: Registering the scriptable type

Available for download on Wrox.com

VB

```
Private Sub Application_Startup(ByVal o As Object,
                                ByVal e As StartupEventArgs) _
                                Handles Me.Startup
    Me.RootVisual = New MainPage()

    Dim employee As Employee = New Employee()
    System.Windows.Browser.HtmlPage.RegisterScriptableObject(
                                    "Employee", employee)
End Sub
```

C#

```
private void Application_Startup(object sender, StartupEventArgs e)
{
    this.RootVisual = new Page();

    Employee employee = new Employee();
    HtmlPage.RegisterScriptableObject("Employee", employee);
}
```

`RegisterScriptableObject` requires two parameters: a `Key`, which represents the name used to register the object, and the actual object instance you want to expose. Although you can call the `RegisterScriptableObject` anywhere in your code, in the preceding sample it is called in the application Startup event, allowing you to access this member in JavaScript as soon as the Silverlight application is loaded.

Listing C-13 shows you how to use the Silverlight plug-in's JavaScript API to access the registered object instance from JavaScript and call its `ChangeStatus` method.

LISTING C-13: Accessing scriptable objects from JavaScript

Available for download on Wrox.com

```
function onLoaded(sender) {
    alert("Current Status: " + plugin.Content.Employee.Status);
    plugin.Content.Employee.ChangeStatus(true);
    alert("Updated Status: " + plugin.Content.Employee.Status);
}
```

Notice that Silverlight exposes the managed type as a property of the plug-in's `Content` object. The property name exposed from the `Content` object is determined by the `Key` parameter provided in the `RegisterScriptableObject`. Therefore, in Listing C-12, had you used "Foo" as the key, you would have accessed the object in JavaScript by using `plugin.Content.Foo.Status`.

As stated earlier, applying the `ScriptableType` attribute exposes all public members of a type to the JavaScript API, but you may not want to do that. Thankfully, Silverlight provides the more granular `ScriptableMember` attribute, which allows you to more specifically control which members of a type are exposed through the JavaScript API. The use of this attribute is shown in Listing C-14. Rather than decorating the entire `Employee` class with the `ScriptableType`, only specific members are exposed by using the `ScriptableMember` attribute.

LISTING C-14: Exposing specific class properties using the ScriptableMember attribute

Available for download on Wrox.com

VB

```
Public Class Employee
    Private _status As Boolean = False

    Public Sub New()

    End Sub

    <System.Windows.Browser.HtmlPage.ScriptableMember()>
    Public Property FirstName() As String
    <System.Windows.Browser.HtmlPage.ScriptableMember()>
    Public Property LastName() As String
    Public Property Department() As String
    Public Property SSN() As String
    <System.Windows.Browser.HtmlPage.ScriptableMember()>
    Public Property StartDate() As DateTime

    <System.Windows.Browser.HtmlPage.ScriptableMember()>
    Public ReadOnly Property Status As Boolean
        Get
            Return _status
        End Get
    End Property

    Public Sub ChangeStatus(ByVal status As Boolean)
        Me._status = status
    End Sub

    Public Function GetFullName() As String
        Return String.Format("{0} {1}", Me.FirstName, Me.LastName)
    End Function
End Class
```

```
public class Employee
{
    private bool _status = false;
```

```
        public Employee()
        {
        }

        [ScriptableMember]
        public string FirstName { get; set; }
        [ScriptableMember]
        public string LastName { get; set; }
        public string Department { get; set; }
        public string SSN { get; set; }
        [ScriptableMember()]
        public DateTime StartDate { get; set; }
        [ScriptableMember()]
        public bool Status { get { return _status; } }

        public void ChangeStatus(bool status)
        {
            this._status = status;
        }

        public string GetFullName()
        {
            return string.Format("{0} {1}", this.FirstName, this.LastName);
        }
    }
```

The `ScriptableMember` attribute also enables you to change the name of the member that is exposed through the JavaScript API by setting an alias on the member being exposed. This is shown in the following code where the `Status` property has been given the alias `CurrentStatus`.

```
[ScriptableMember(ScriptAlias = "CurrentStatus")]
public bool Status { get { return _status; } }
```

In addition to accessing existing type instances, the HTML Bridge allows you to register specific types as Creatable Types. A *Creatable Type* is a type that can be instantiated directly in JavaScript. For example, rather than instantiating an instance of the `Employee` type in managed code and registering that specific instance, Silverlight allows you to register the `Employees` type as `Creatable` and instantiate new instances of it directly in JavaScript.

To register a type as creatable using the JavaScript API, call the `HtmlPage` object's `RegisterCreatableType` method, as shown here:

```
HtmlPage.RegisterCreatableType("Employee", typeof(Employee));
```

This method requires two parameters, a `ScriptAlias` and the type to expose. After it is exposed, you can use JavaScript to instantiate the `Employee` class, as shown in Listing C-15.

Available for download on Wrox.com

LISTING C-15: Creating managed types in JavaScript

```
function onLoaded(sender) {
    var employee = plugin.Content.services.createObject("Employee");
    employee.FirstName = "John";
    employee.LastName = "Doe";
}
```

Notice that to create the type in JavaScript, you use the Silverlight JavaScript API's `createObject` function, passing it the `ScriptAlias` provided to the `RegisterCreatableType` method. After it is created, you can set properties and call functions on the object just as you would any other JavaScript object.

Accessing the DOM Using Managed Code

So far in this section, you have seen how you can expose managed code to JavaScript. However, the HTML Bridge is a two-way street, allowing you to also access the browser. Accessing the browser allows you to access the DOM, reference specific elements in the DOM, execute JavaScript functions contained in the host page, or even access aspects of the browser window that contains the host page.

In this section, you look at some of the APIs included in the HTML Bridge that can help you access information about the browser window and the HTML document, beginning with returning to the familiar `HtmlPage` object, which exposes three important properties, `BrowserInformation`, `Document`, and `Window`.

The `BrowserInformation` property returns a `BrowserInformation` object, which, as the name implies, allows you to access basic information about the browser the application is currently running in such as the browser name, version, and platform.

The `Document` property returns an `HtmlDocument` object, which represents the browser's document object. The managed `HtmlDocument` provides similar functionality to its JavaScript equivalent, allowing you to locate elements in the document using the familiar `GetElementByID` and `GetElementByTagName` methods, as well as create new HTML elements and attach and detach events to HTML elements.

When working with existing HTML elements obtained from the `HtmlDocument`, or when new elements are created, the HTML Bridge uses the `HtmlElement` object, which represents the managed version of basic HTML elements present in the DOM. As with the `HtmlDocument` object, the `HtmlElement` object exposes much of the same functionality as its client-side peer, enabling you to get and set element property and attribute values, and access and manipulate its collection of child elements.

Listing C-16 demonstrates the use of the `HtmlDocument` and `HtmlElement` objects to dynamically manipulate the loaded document structure.

LISTING C-16: Manipulating the HTML document structure

Available for download on Wrox.com

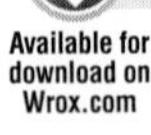
VB

```
Public Sub AddListItem()
    Dim unorderedlist As System.Windows.Browser.HtmlElement =
        System.Windows.Browser.HtmlPage.Document.GetElementById(
                                                    "demoList")

    If unorderedlist IsNot Nothing Then

        Dim listitem As System.Windows.Browser.HtmlElement =
            System.Windows.Browser.HtmlPage.Document.CreateElement(
                                                    "li")
        listitem.SetAttribute("Id", "listitem1")
        listitem.SetAttribute("innerHTML", "Hello World!")
        unorderedlist.AppendChild(listitem)
    End If
End Sub
```

C#

```
public void AddListItem()
{
    System.Windows.Browser.HtmlElement unorderedlist =
        System.Windows.Browser.HtmlPage.Document.GetElementById(
                                                    "demoList");

    if (unorderedlist != null)
    {
        System.Windows.Browser.HtmlElement listitem =
            System.Windows.Browser.HtmlPage.Document.CreateElement(
                                                    "li");
        listitem.SetAttribute("Id", "listitem1");
        listitem.SetAttribute("innerHTML", "Hello World!");
        unorderedlist.AppendChild(listitem);
    }
}
```

In this sample, the HtmlDocument's GetElementById method is used to locate a specific unordered list element in the DOM. If it is found, then a new HtmlElement representing an HTML list item is created and its id and innerHTML attributes set. Then, the new list item element is added as a child of the unordered list element.

Finally, the Window property of the HtmlPage object returns an HtmlWindow, which provides you with a managed representation of the browser's window object. The HtmlWindow allows you to do things such as raise Alert and Prompt dialogs, navigate to new URIs or bookmarks, create instances of JavaScript types, and evaluate strings containing arbitrary JavaScript code.

Listing C-17 demonstrates how to create a managed representation of a JavaScript type.

LISTING C-17: Creating a JavaScript type in managed code

Available for download on Wrox.com

VB

```
Public Sub Calculate()
    Dim calculator =
        System.Windows.Browser.HtmlPage.Window.CreateInstance(
                                                "Calculator")
    Dim sum = Convert.ToInt32(calculator.Invoke("add", 5, 1))
    System.Windows.Browser.HtmlPage.Window.Alert(sum.ToString())
End Sub
```

C#

```
public void Calculate()
{
    var calculator =
        System.Windows.Browser.HtmlPage.Window.CreateInstance(
                                                "Calculator");
    var sum = Convert.ToInt32(calculator.Invoke("add", 5, 1));
    System.Windows.Browser.HtmlPage.Window.Alert(sum.ToString());
}
```

This sample uses the HtmlWindow object's CreateInstance method, which requires two parameters, a string containing the type you want to create, and an object array containing the type's creation parameters. The method returns an instance of a ScriptObject, which you can then use to call methods and properties of the JavaScript type.

Finally, take a look at how you can use the HtmlWindow object to call a JavaScript function located in the host Web page. The following code shows a simple JavaScript function that could be included in the HTML page hosting the Silverlight plug-in:

```
function Add(a, b) {
    return a + b;
}
```

To execute this function, use Silverlight's Invoke method, which is exposed from the HtmlWindow object, shown here:

```
HtmlWindow window = HtmlPage.Window;
object result = window.Invoke("Add", new object[] {1,2});
```

The Invoke method takes two parameters—the name of the function you want to execute and an object array of function parameters—and returns an object type.

SUMMARY

This appendix introduced some of the basic concepts that an ASP.NET developer must know to integrate a Silverlight application into a Web site, and to add interoperability between the Silverlight application and its host Web page. The appendix started by introducing the basics of creating a new Silverlight application and the tools that are available for Visual Studio 2010 developers. It showed you how you can automatically have Visual Studio create a new Web site project to host your Silverlight application or even associate the Silverlight application with an existing Web site.

Next, you looked at the Silverlight plug-in and how to embed it into a Web page. You looked at the configuration parameters exposed by the plug-in that allow you to customize the default Silverlight loading splash screen and pass initialization parameters into the Silverlight plug-in.

Finally, you explored the different options Silverlight provides for interoperating between JavaScript and managed code. You first looked at how to use the Silverlight plug-in's JavaScript API to reach into a Silverlight application and manipulate its XAML content. This appendix also demonstrated how to use the HTML Bridge to expose managed code contained in a Silverlight application out to the browser via a JavaScript API, to directly access browser properties information from within your Silverlight application, to manipulate the browser's DOM, and to run client-side JavaScript code from within a Silverlight application.

Dynamic Types and Languages

When Microsoft originally introduced .NET, many developers, especially those coming from Visual Basic 6 (or earlier), were brought into a new world of statically typed languages. No longer were developers allowed to create variant types, or easily create instances of objects at runtime using late binding. The new .NET-based languages forced them to define all of their objects using a well-known type, and if the compiler did not recognize that type, it would throw errors back at them.

Purists out there will argue that .NET does indeed support late binding, and it is true that VB.NET can accommodate late binding through disabling the Option Strict command, though this is certainly discouraged in most situations. In C# if you want to simulate late binding you have to resort to reflection, which usually means a lot more lines of code and application complexity.

Although statically typed languages have many advantages such as strict type safety and the ability to leverage the compiler to optimize based on well-known type information, you do lose a bit of flexibility that you get from a dynamically typed language. Additionally, the lack of dynamism does make interoperating between .NET and dynamic languages more difficult. You may have experienced this if you have ever had to create applications that require COM interop.

This appendix takes a look at some of the work Microsoft has done to embrace the concepts of dynamic languages and how it continues to make working directly with, as well as interoperating with, dynamic languages easier for developers.

IMPLICIT TYPES

When Microsoft introduced .NET 3.5, one of the new concepts it introduced was the concept of implicit types, which is expressed in C# using the `var` keyword or in VB.NET by declaring a variable without the `As` operator. Implicit types allow you to declare a variable whose type is implicitly inferred from the expression used to initialize the variable. In other words, implicit types allow you to declare variables in a fairly dynamic way in your code, while through a bit of compiler magic retaining the benefits of a statically typed variable at runtime. An example of using implicit types is shown in Listing D-1.

LISTING D-1: Implicit types using the var keyword

Available for download on Wrox.com

VB

```
Protected Sub Page_Load(ByVal sender As Object, ByVal e As System.EventArgs)
    Dim foo = 1
End Sub
```

C#

```
protected void Page_Load(object sender, EventArgs e)
{
    var foo = 1;
}
```

In this sample, a variable `foo` is declared as an implicit type, and immediately assigned a numeric value of "1". Because the variable is assigned a numeric, the compiler will automatically infer that the variable `foo` should actually be of type `Int32`. In fact if you decompile the code to its Intermediate Language (IL), you will see that the code actually output by the compiler emits the variable as the correct type. Trying to assign a different type to this variable as shown in Listing D-2 results in a type mismatch exception.

LISTING D-2: Violating static type rules

Available for download on Wrox.com

VB

```
Protected Sub Page_Load(ByVal sender As Object, ByVal e As System.EventArgs)
    Dim foo = 1
    foo = "abc"
End Sub
```

C#

```
protected void Page_Load(object sender, EventArgs e)
{
    var foo = 1;
    foo = "abc";
}
```

Trying to compile this code results in a compiler error letting you know that a string cannot be assigned to the `foo` variable.

THE DYNAMIC LANGUAGE RUNTIME

To help developers gain back some of that flexibility, as well as bring the general goodness that the .NET Framework offers to a wider audience of developers, in 2007 Microsoft announced it had begun working on a new initiative called the Dynamic Language Runtime, or DLR. The DLR is a dynamic runtime that is built on top of the Common Language Runtime (CLR). It brings to the CLR a dynamic type system, dynamic method dispatch, dynamic code generation, and a hosting API. Currently, a number of languages have been created on the DLR, including ports of the popular languages Python and Ruby.

The IronPython language is the only Dynamic Language implementation officially developed and maintained by Microsoft, and it runs on a release schedule separate from .NET Framework and Visual Studio. Other languages are developed and maintained by third-party developers.

You can find more information on IronPython, the DLR implementation of Python, at `www.codeplex.com/IronPython`.

You can find more information on IronRuby, the DLR implementation of Ruby, at `www.codeplex.com/IronRuby`.

Because the development of DLR-based languages has thus far been separate from the CLR-based languages, support for these languages inside of Visual Studio is generally lacking, with most implementations providing little to no support for common features like project and file templates and code editor support such as code coloring and IntelliSense.

After you've loaded the languages on your system, you can develop standalone applications using them or leverage language libraries from other static languages like C# or VB.NET. Listing D-3 demonstrates using IronPython code from within an ASP.NET application using both C# and VB.NET.

LISTING D-3: Calling IronPython libraries from ASP.NET

Available for download on Wrox.com

```
<%@ Page Language="VB" Strict="false" %>

<script runat="server">
    Dim items() As Integer = Enumerable.Range(1, 5).ToArray()
    Dim subitems() As Integer = Enumerable.Range(1, 7).ToArray()

    Dim random As Object

    Protected Sub Page_Load(ByVal sender As Object,
                            ByVal e As System.EventArgs)
        System.IO.Directory.SetCurrentDirectory(
            Environment.GetFolderPath(
                Environment.SpecialFolder.ProgramFiles) &
                "\IronPython 2.6 CTP for .NET 4.0 Beta 2\Lib")

        Dim py As Microsoft.Scripting.Hosting.ScriptRuntime =
            IronPython.Hosting.Python.CreateRuntime()

        random = py.UseFile("random.py")

        Me.Repeater1.DataSource = items
        Me.Repeater1.DataBind()

    End Sub

    Protected Sub Repeater1_ItemDataBound(ByVal sender As Object,
        ByVal e As System.Web.UI.WebControls.RepeaterItemEventArgs)

        Dim lbl As Label = CType(e.Item.FindControl("Label"), Label)
        lbl.Text = String.Format("List Number: {0}", e.Item.ItemIndex)

        Dim list As BulletedList =
            CType(e.Item.FindControl("BulletedList"), BulletedList)

        random.shuffle(subitems)

        list.DataSource = subitems
        list.DataBind()
    End Sub
</script>

<html xmlns="http://www.w3.org/1999/xhtml">
<head id="Head1" runat="server">
    <title></title>
</head>
<body>
    <form id="form1" runat="server">
    <div>
        <asp:Repeater ID="Repeater1" runat="server" OnItemDataBound="Repeater1_ItemDataBound">
            <ItemTemplate>
                <p>
                    <asp:Label runat="server" ID="Label" />
                    <br />
                    <asp:BulletedList runat="server" ID="BulletedList" />
                </p>
            </ItemTemplate>
        </asp:Repeater>
    </div>
    </form>
</body>
</html>
```

continues

LISTING D-3 *(continued)*

```
<script runat="server">
int[] items = Enumerable.Range(1, 5).ToArray();
int[] subitems = Enumerable.Range(1, 7).ToArray();
dynamic random;

protected void Page_Load(object sender, EventArgs e)
{
    System.IO.Directory.SetCurrentDirectory(
        Environment.GetFolderPath(
            Environment.SpecialFolder.ProgramFiles) +
            @"\IronPython 2.6 CTP for .NET 4.0 Beta 2\Lib");

    Microsoft.Scripting.Hosting.ScriptRuntime py =
        IronPython.Hosting.Python.CreateRuntime();
    random = py.UseFile("random.py");

    this.Repeater1.DataSource = items;
    this.Repeater1.DataBind();
}

protected void Repeater1_ItemDataBound(object sender,
                                       RepeaterItemEventArgs e)
{
    Label lbl = (Label)e.Item.FindControl("Label");
    lbl.Text = string.Format("List Number: {0}",e.Item.ItemIndex);

    BulletedList list = (BulletedList)e.Item.FindControl("BulletedList");
    random.shuffle(subitems);
    list.DataSource = subitems;
    list.DataBind();
}
</script>
```

You can see in this listing that when the page is loaded, the IronPython library `random.py` is loaded using the DLR's hosting API. As each item in the `items` array is bound to the Repeater, its `subitems` are shuffled into a random order using the IronPython library.

DYNAMIC LOOKUP

In C# 4, the language embraces dynamism even more by a new feature called dynamic lookup. Dynamic lookup brings a truly dynamic type declaration mechanism to C#, allowing you to explicitly declare variables as a dynamic type in your code and dynamically invoke methods against that type at runtime. This differs from implicit type in that dynamic types remain truly dynamic even at runtime, whereas implicit types are converted to static types at compile-time. Listing D-4 shows a simple example of using the new dynamic keyword.

Available for download on Wrox.com

LISTING D-4: Creating a dynamic type using the dynamic keyword

```
<script runat="server">
    protected void Page_Load(object sender, EventArgs e)
    {
        dynamic value =
            "Even though assigned a string, the type is still dynamic";
    }
</script>
```

In this sample, the property value is assigned a simple string as a value; however unlike with implicit types, the variable remains typed as a dynamic type even at runtime. You can see this if you are trying to access any member of the variable in Visual Studio. Normally Visual Studio would show you a list of available properties and methods as well as the type of the variable, but because this type is dynamic, none of this information is known until runtime. Visual Studio tells you this using a tooltip, as shown in Figure D-1.

```
<script runat="server">
    protected void Page_Load(object sender, EventArgs e)
    {
        dynamic value = "This is actually a string";

        value.
    }   (dynamic expression)
</script>   This operation will be resolved at runtime.
```

FIGURE D-1

At runtime, the Dynamic Language's dynamic dispatch system uses dynamic invocation to execute methods and properties of the type. This means that you can add and remove members from a type at runtime. .NET provides two mechanisms to do this: the `ExpandoObject` class and the `DynamicObject` class.

The `ExpandoObject` class can be used in relatively simple scenarios where you need to add or remove members dynamically. Listing D-5 demonstrates using the `ExpandoObject`.

LISTING D-5: Using the ExpandoObject to define dynamic object properties

Available for download on Wrox.com

```
dynamic contact = new System.Dynamic.ExpandoObject();
contact.Name = "John Doe";
contact.Phone = "201-555-5555";
contact.Address = new System.Dynamic.ExpandoObject();
contact.Address.Street = "123 Main St";
contact.Address.City = "Anywhere";
contact.Address.State = "WA";
contact.Address.Postal = "12345";
```

In this listing you can see that an `ExpandoObject` is created and several properties added. These properties are added dynamically at runtime and stored internally as an `IDictionary<String,Object>`, which the `ExpandoObject` implements internally to maintain the list of members.

If you need more control over what specific operations can be performed on a dynamic object, or what happens when an operation like a getting and setting properties or method call occurs, you can create objects that derive from `DynamicObject`. An example of deriving from the `DynamicObject` class is shown using the `JsonObject` class in Listing D-6.

LISTING D-6: Creating a custom DynamicObject type

Available for download on Wrox.com

```
namespace DynamicRest {

    public sealed class JsonObject :
                                        DynamicObject,
                                        IDictionary<string, object>,
                                        IDictionary
    {

        private Dictionary<string, object> _members;

        public JsonObject()
        {
            _members = new Dictionary<string, object>();
        }

        public JsonObject(params object[] nameValuePairs) : this() {
            if (nameValuePairs != null) {
                if (nameValuePairs.Length % 2 != 0) {
                    throw new ArgumentException(
                        "Mismatch in name/value pairs.");
                }
```

continues

LISTING D-6 *(continued)*

```
            for (int i = 0; i < nameValuePairs.Length; i += 2) {
                if (!(nameValuePairs[i] is string)) {
                    throw new ArgumentException(
                        "Name parameters must be strings.");
                }

                _members[(string)nameValuePairs[i]] =
                     nameValuePairs[i + 1];
            }
        }
    }

    public override bool TryConvert(ConvertBinder binder,
                                    out object result)
    {
        Type targetType = binder.ReturnType;

        if ((targetType == typeof(IEnumerable)) ||
            (targetType ==
                typeof(IEnumerable<KeyValuePair<string, object>>)) ||
            (targetType == typeof(IDictionary<string, object>)) ||
            (targetType == typeof(IDictionary)))
        {
            result = this;
            return true;
        }

        return base.TryConvert(binder, out result);
    }

    public override bool TryDeleteMember(DeleteMemberBinder binder)
    {
        return _members.Remove(binder.Name);
    }

    public override bool TryGetMember(GetMemberBinder binder,
                                      out object result)
    {
        object value;
        if (_members.TryGetValue(binder.Name, out value))
        {
            result = value;
            return true;
        }

        return base.TryGetMember(binder, out result);
    }

    public override bool TrySetMember(SetMemberBinder binder,
                                      object value)
    {
        _members[binder.Name] = value;
        return true;
    }

    // ++++
    // Non-related interface implementations removed for clarity
  }
}
```

The JsonObject class is part of a larger library based on a sample written by Nikhil Kothari that simplifies retrieving and parsing JSON-formatted data. Normally, to deal with JSON data in .NET, you have to create proxy types that mirror the structure of the JSON and then perform complex parsing operations to parse the JSON data into collections of the custom types. Using the dynamic capabilities of C# 4, you can simplify this by parsing of the JSON data into generic types that expose the data via dynamic properties and methods, which are inferred at runtime.

Listing D-6 shows how you can override methods like TryGetMember and TrySetMember to control how properties on the type are gotten and set. In this case, members are stored in an internal Dictionary object in the JsonObject class.

Teams within Microsoft are also leveraging the new dynamic capabilities of .NET 4 to make COM interop operations easier. The Office Primary Interop Assemblies (PIAs), which provide a managed layer over the Office COM Automation APIs, have been updated to leverage the dynamic capabilities of C#. Listing D-7 demonstrates how to interact with Excel from .NET using the PIAs.

LISTING D-7: Using the new Office PIAs to interact with Excel

Available for download on Wrox.com

VB

```
Dim excelApp As New Microsoft.Office.Interop.Excel.Application()
excelApp.Visible = True
excelApp.Workbooks.Add()

Dim workSheet As Microsoft.Office.Interop.Excel.Worksheet =
    excelApp.ActiveSheet
workSheet.Cells(1, "A") = "ID Number"
workSheet.Cells(1, "B") = "Current Balance"

Dim row = 1

For Each acct In accounts
    row = row + 1
    workSheet.Cells(row, "A") = acct.ID
    workSheet.Cells(row, "B") = acct.Balance
Next

workSheet.Columns(1).AutoFit()
workSheet.Columns(2).AutoFit()
```

C#

```
var excelApp = new Application();
excelApp.Visible = true;
excelApp.Workbooks.Add();

Worksheet workSheet = excelApp.ActiveSheet;
workSheet.Cells[1, "A"] = "ID Number";
workSheet.Cells[1, "B"] = "Current Balance";

var row = 1;
foreach (var acct in accounts)
{
    row++;
    workSheet.Cells[row, "A"] = acct.ID;
    workSheet.Cells[row, "B"] = acct.Balance;
}

workSheet.Columns[1].AutoFit();
workSheet.Columns[2].AutoFit();
```

In prior versions of the PIAs, accessing certain APIs such as the Columns collection shown in the sample would have required you to cast the objects returned to the appropriate type to access that type's properties and methods. The new versions, however, leverage the dynamic keyword to remove this requirement and allow for dynamic lookup of those properties and methods.

SUMMARY

Microsoft continues to expand the functionality of the .NET Framework and its languages by investing in features to bring more dynamism to the languages. These features give you additional programming tools in your toolbelt, allowing you to leverage the features, or even the programming languages that make the most sense for your specific application. From built-in features of C# and VB.NET such as implicit types and dynamic lookup, to entirely new languages such as IronPython and IronRuby, the choices available to you continue to expand.

ASP.NET Online Resources

AUTHOR BLOGS AND TWITTER IDS

Bill Evjen: www.geekswithblogs.net/evjen

@billevjen

Scott Hanselman: www.hanselman.com/blog/

@shanselman

Devin Rader: http://blogs.infragistics.com/blogs/devin_rader/

@devinrader

ASP.NET INFLUENTIAL BLOGS

Scott Guthrie: weblogs.asp.net/scottgu/

Rick Strahl: www.west-wind.com/weblog/

K. Scott Allen: odetocode.com/blogs/scott/

Phil Haack: www.haacked.com/

Steve Smith: www.stevesmithblog.com/

G. Andrew Duthie: blogs.msdn.com/gduthie/

Scott Mitchell: scottonwriting.net/sowBlog/

Nikhil Kothari: www.nikhilk.net/

WEB SITES

123ASPX Directory: www.123aspx.com

4 Guys from Rolla: www.4guysfromrolla.com

ASP 101: www.asp101.com

ASP Alliance: aspalliance.com

ASP Alliance Lists: aspadvice.com

The ASP.NET Developer Portal: msdn.microsoft.com/asp.net

ASP.NET Homepage: `www.asp.net`

ASP.NET Resources: `www.aspnetresources.com`

ASP.NET World: `www.aspnetworld.com`

International .NET Association: `www.ineta.org`

Microsoft's ASP.NET AJAX Site: `www.asp.net/ajax/`

Microsoft's ASP.NET MVC Site: `www.asp.net/mvc/`

Microsoft's Classic ASP Site: `msdn.microsoft.com/en-us/library/aa286483.aspx`

Microsoft Developer Centers: `msdn.microsoft.com/developercenters`

Microsoft Forums: `www.microsoft.com/communities/forums/default.mspx`

Microsoft Newsgroups: `msdn.microsoft.com/newsgroups/`

Microsoft's Open Source Project Community: `www.codeplex.com`

.NET 247: `www.dotnet247.com`

RegExLib: `www.regexlib.com`

The ServerSide .NET: `www.theserverside.net`

XML for ASP.NET: `www.xmlforasp.net`

TWITTER FOLKS WORTH FOLLOWING

`@scottgu`

`@haacked`

`@brada`

`@ambroselittle`

`@sondreb`

`@chrislove`

`@wrox`

`@dseven`

`@randyholloway`

`@migueldeicaza`

`@donxml`

`@moon`

`@kvgros`

`@richcampbell`

`@christoc`

`@csells`

`@keyvan`

`@danwahlin`

`@devhammer`

`@jglozano`

`@shawnwildermuth`

`@julielermanvt`

`@codinghorror`

`@spolsky`

`@elijahmanor`

`@robconery`

`@jeremydmiller`

`@angrycoder`

`@rickstrahl`

INDEX

A

B

D

E

F

G

H

I

J

K

L

P

S

T

U

V

X

Y

Z